THE AMERICAN HISTORICAL ASSOCIATION'S

Guide to Historical Literature

THE AMERICAN HISTORICAL ASSOCIATION'S

Guide to
Historical Literature

THIRD EDITION

General Editor
Mary Beth Norton

Associate Editor
Pamela Gerardi

VOLUME TWO

New York   Oxford
OXFORD UNIVERSITY PRESS
1995

Oxford University Press

Oxford   New York
Athens   Auckland   Bangkok   Bombay
Calcutta   Cape Town   Dar es Salaam   Delhi
Florence   Hong Kong   Istanbul   Karachi
Kuala Lumpur   Madras   Madrid   Melbourne
Mexico City   Nairobi   Paris   Singapore
Taipei   Tokyo   Toronto

and associated companies in
Berlin   Ibadan

Published by Oxford University Press, Inc.,
200 Madison Avenue, New York, NY 10016

Oxford is a registered trademark of Oxford University Press

Library of Congress Cataloging-in-Publication Data

The American Historical Association's guide to historical literature /
general editor, Mary Beth Norton ; associate editor, Pamela Gerardi.
—3rd ed.
p.   cm.
Contains nearly 27,000 annotated citations (primarily to English
language works) divided into forty-eight sections; citations refer
chiefly to works published between 1961 and 1992.
Includes indexes.
1. History—Bibligraphy. 2. Bibliography—Best books—History.
I. Norton, Mary Beth. II. Gerardi, Pamela, 1956– . III. American
Historical Association. IV. Title: Guide to historical literature.
Z6201.A55 1995   [D20]   016.9—dc20 94-36720   CIP

ISBN 0-19-509953-2 (vol. 2)
ISBN 0-19-505727-9 (2-vol. set)

Printing (last digit): 9 8 7 6 5 4 3 2 1
Printed in the United States of America
on acid-free paper

GALE STOKES

Eastern Europe

All of the countries covered in this section came into existence, or had their character greatly changed, as a result of World War I. In Central Europe, Poland reappeared as an independent state, Czechoslovakia came into being as a new multinational creation, and Hungary changed from half of a great empire to a relatively small and weak independent state. In southeastern Europe, Greece and Serbia received most of Macedonia in the Balkan wars (1912–1913). Albania also came into existence in 1912. In 1918, Greece, Bulgaria, and Albania remained only slightly changed, but Serbia entered into the new multinational state of Yugoslavia. At the same time Romania doubled its size with the seizure of Transylvania. These small, weak, and inexperienced new countries soon faced a resurgent Nazi Germany in the west and a revolutionary Soviet Union in the east. Overwhelmed in the late 1930s by the former and late in the following decade by the latter, Eastern Europe temporarily lost its character as a region with a specifically European history and became associated in the minds of English speakers with communism and the Soviet Union.

Many of the people who lived in these countries rejected the appellation "eastern Europe" when it lumped them together with Russia and the Soviet Union. Some East-Central Europeans in particular held that since Russia was part of the Orthodox and not the Catholic world, and since it was heavily influenced by the Mongol presence, its history had an entirely different trajectory from their own, which they saw as part of the European cultural space. Southeast European intellectuals did not object to the term Eastern Europe so much as they did to being considered outside the historical patterns of even Central Europe. Most of southeastern Europe was Eastern Orthodox and was for hundreds of years part of the Ottoman empire, but in the nineteenth century the Balkan countries adopted Western political institutions and cultural norms, so that today educated persons in southeastern Europe feel themselves fully part of Europe. Greece was the only country not affected by these concerns. A British client during the nineteenth century, after World War II Greece became, eventually, part of the European Community and distanced itself from its Balkan allies and competitors.

In the years between the imposition of Stalinism in 1948 and the collapse of communism in 1989, historians in Eastern Europe were forced to pursue their craft in ways consistent with the political aims of their socialist governments. Some did so willingly, others reacted with sly attempts to mitigate the falsity of the obligation under which they worked, and still others pursued topics that had no political significance. Cut off from natural forms of interaction with their colleagues outside the socialist world, the work of East European historians remained relatively traditional, despite a heavily Marxist cast. The structure of scholarship in Eastern Europe also remained traditional: professors retained their prestige and power and academies of science promoted research through institutes. Good historical scholarship, however, has come out of Eastern Europe over the past thirty years, especially in areas in which the ideological stakes were small, such as medieval history, Ottoman studies, and economic history of the pre-Marxist era. East Europeans have contributed significantly to such subjects as feudalism, art history, world-systems analysis (particularly the notion of the second serfdom), revolution, and proto-industrialization. Publication of sources and research guides has also made a lasting contribution. Whereas little of this work has appeared in English, some scholarly work has appeared either in journals or in monograph series in Western languages.

Inevitably, the English-language historiography of Eastern Europe has reflected the history writing, political conditions, and organization of scholarship in the region. In the nineteenth century, the main sources of historical information about Eastern Europe in English came from travelers' accounts, from diplomats who had served in the region, and the occasional journalistic flurries over events and public issues, such as the Greek Revolution of 1821, the Hungarian Revolution of 1848, and the eastern crisis of 1875–1878. Before and during World War I, a handful of British journalists, notably Henry Wickam Steed, R. W. Seton-Watson, and Harold Temperley, became interested in Central and southeastern Europe. They produced a small number of still useful studies as well as a large quantity of popular material. Formation of the journal *New Europe* at the end of the war gave Seton-Watson an opportunity to present semi-scholarly articles about the new countries of Eastern Europe, and in 1922 a group of scholars at the University of London began the *Slavonic and East European Review*, the first English-language journal devoted to scholarship of the region. During the interwar years, studies of Eastern Europe tended to concentrate on issues of political importance, but during those years a modest historiography on central and southeastern Europe arose in English, particularly from the pens of a few English writers such as B. H. Sumner and Alan Palmer. In the United States, interest in Slavic countries was concentrated in a handful of universities and focused primarily on Russia and the Soviet Union rather than on Eastern Europe.

After World War II, Cold War attitudes heavily influenced historical writing, if not always in content, then often in the selection of subjects for study. Political topics were most favored, often those linked in some way with socialism. But if the cold war sometimes limited the imagination of scholars, it proved an enormous boon to the development of the field of East European studies. Even the small number of students who turned their investigations to pre–twentieth-century subjects often trained in area resource centers funded by the United States government for purposes of national defense, and most took advantage of research fellowships, such as the Fulbright program or the International Research and Exchanges Board grants, funded by federal monies. The rapid growth of the English-language histories of Eastern Europe that this funding promoted received a setback in the 1970s and early 1980s when a serious dearth of academic positions discouraged graduate students from entering the field.

The growth of history writing on Eastern Europe was an aspect of a more general growth in Slavic studies. In 1941, when World War II disrupted British scholarship, a group of interested Americans began to publish the *Slavonic Review* in the United States. In 1945 that effort led to the creation of the American *Slavonic and East European Review*, which in 1961 became the *Slavic Review*. Today most historians working on Eastern Europe belong to the membership organization founded to support that journal, the American Association for the Advancement of Slavic Studies. The association supports a wide variety of activities that enhance the study of the region. The *Slavic Review* has not published many articles on Eastern Europe, but the *East European Quarterly*, begun in 1967, and *East European Politics and Societies*, begun in 1986, have filled that gap. Very important has been the East European Monograph series, begun by Stephen Fischer-Galati in 1967. Since that time Professor Fischer-Galati has seen over three hundred titles into print. The works in this series vary greatly in quality and in focus, but the overwhelming majority are historical works. Together they constitute the single most important body of published English-language research in the field. Many examples will be found in this bibliography.

Cold War attitudes were not the only factor that limited historians writing about Eastern Europe. The variety and difficulty of the languages of the region made it time consuming for nonnative speakers to enter the field. In part for this reason, and in part because of natural affinity, a significant proportion of the historians writing about Eastern Europe in English are ethnically connected with the region. Linguistic complexity also made it difficult to conduct cross-cultural or area-wide research. Most historians, both inside and outside Eastern Europe, concentrated on the country of their ethnic group or on the East European language they learned first. One of the few generalizations that can be made about East European history writing is that it tends to focus on single nations or states.

Conditions in the communist states of Eastern Europe hindered research as well. Unlike research in West European countries, which may be conducted by any interested person, in Eastern Europe Westerners were permitted into archives only as "official persons" with approved topics. Even in the most open state, Yugoslavia, research into sensitive issues—and there were many—was not possible. In other countries, with the exception of Greece, not only was access to archives restricted, but the limited availability of Western publications made open and stimulating interchanges with local scholars difficult. History was so politicized by the national leadership in a country like Romania that serious work in many areas became almost impossible.

The field of East European history in the West, therefore, is relatively undeveloped. This is indicated in this bibliography by the presence of many collections of essays and of a number of broad introductory works. English-speaking scholars typically entered the field through diplomatic history, political history of individual countries, biography, or the study of nationalism. This was not only because these are more obvious fields for foreigners, but because these areas are stressed in the East European countries themselves. Some national histories are more developed than others. The English-language historiography of Poland, for example, is richer than that of Romania. But, in general, the great historiographical innovations or controversies of the past twenty years in the West have affected the field very little. Because of the impossibility of independent feminist movements in Eastern Europe until very recently, for example, work on gender issues is only beginning, both there and in the West. Postmodernist philosophy, although known in Eastern Europe, has not yet made its appearance in the field of history. Ordinary social history, when practiced at all, was more likely to be done by anthropologists and sociologists than by historians.

Having read these remarks, users who turn to this bibliography are likely to be pleasantly surprised. Despite all, a great many excellent books have appeared in English, and it seems likely that their number will increase. The revolutions of 1989 have opened up vast new possibilities. East European historians are turning their attention to the blank spots of their national histories, until now out of bounds, and a vastly greater interchange between West and East European historians has begun. The new freedom has stimulated interest among young scholars and produced a cottage industry of articles about the transition from communism to democracy. The passions of nationalism may limit the possibilities for revisionist work, and the sociology of scholarship changes only slowly, but East Europeans are much more concerned today with their interactions with the rest of Europe and the world than they have ever been in the past. It appears likely that the scholarship of the next generation, both inside and outside Eastern Europe, will be considerably more varied than that of the past generation.

Works in this section have been selected on the basis of their relevance to the national histories of the peoples involved, but since every East European people was part of an empire for long periods of its history, useful works may be found as well in the listings for the appropriate empires (Russian, German, Austrian, and Ottoman). In addition, readers may wish to consult the sections on international relations, especially for the great international conflicts, such as the Crimean War, the eastern crisis of 1875–1878, World Wars I and II, and the Cold War.

Entries are arranged under the following headings:

[Contributors: AF = Andrea Feldman, APS = Ann Pottinger Saab, CWI = Charles W. Ingrao, DM = David MacKenzie, DMP = Duncan M. Perry, EB = Elez Biberaj, EM = Ezra Mendelsohn, GS = Gale Stokes, HLA = Hugh L. Agnew, IB = Ivo Banac, JSH = John S. Hill, KAH = Keith A. Hitchins, KP = Kenneth Pennington, MK = Mária M. Kovács, MR = Mieczysław Rozbicki, NR = Norman Rich, NSK = Nancy Shields Kollmann, PWS = Paul W. Schroeder, RC = Richard Clogg, RJC = Richard J. Crampton, RRM = Ralph R. Menning, RS = Reeva S. Simon, SBV = Steven Béla Várdy, SM = Sally Marks, WLB = William Lee Blackwood]

REFERENCE WORKS AND REGIONAL HISTORIES

33.1 Ivo Andrić. *Bridge on the Drina.* 1959 ed. William H. McNeill, Introduction. Lovett F. Edwards, trans. Chicago: University of Chicago Press, 1977. ISBN 0-226-02045-2. ▸ Novel with historical sweep and acute sensibility that makes it perhaps the single best introduction to history of Balkans. [GS]

33.2 Ivo Banac, ed. *Eastern Europe in revolution.* Ithaca, N.Y.: Cornell University Press, 1992. ISBN 0-8014-2711-8 (cl), 0-8014-9997-6 (pbk). ▸ One of best of many edited books appearing in two years following 1989 revolutions; events described with clarity and analyzed with sophistication. [GS]

33.3 Judy Batt. *East Central Europe from reform to transformation.* New York: Council on Foreign Relations for London Royal Institute of International Affairs, 1991. ISBN 0-87609-106-0. ▸ Solid analysis of economic elements in collapse of communist rule. Despite problems, author generally optimistic about "steady maturation of the popular will to 'regain the West.'" [GS]

33.4 Judy Batt. *Economic reform and political change in Eastern Europe: a comparison of the Czechoslovak and Hungarian experiences.* New York: St. Martin's, 1988. ISBN 0-312-01196-2. ▸ Sophisticated study of logic of reform during 1980s. Believes political reform required for successful economic reform, but questions whether political reform once begun could be controlled. Analysis applicable to other East European countries. [GS]

33.5 Iván T. Berend and György Ránki. *East Central Europe in the nineteenth and twentieth centuries.* Eva Palmai, ed. Budapest: Akadémiai Kiadó, 1977. ISBN 963-05-1309-9. ▸ Summary treatment through World War II by two of Hungary's best and most prolific historians. [GS]

33.6 Iván T. Berend and György Ránki. *The European periphery and industrialization, 1780–1914.* Eva Palmai, trans. Cambridge: Cambridge University Press, 1982. ISBN 0-521-24210-X. ▸ World

system theory analysis of "long nineteenth century." Development varied greatly, but one side always had all advantages. Useful statistics. [GS]

33.7 Stephen Borsody. *The tragedy of Central Europe: Nazi and Soviet conquest and aftermath.* Rev. ed. New Haven: Yale Concilium on International and Area Studies, 1980. (Yale Russian and East European publications, 2.) ISBN 0-936586-01-X. ▸ Intelligent discussion of Europe's East-West division in interwar years and first postwar decade from point of view of so-called middle zone. Stresses disastrous effects of nationalism and virtues of federalism. Revised and updated version of *The Triumph of Tyranny* (1960). [GS]

33.8 James F. Brown. *Surge to freedom: the end of communist rule in Eastern Europe.* Durham, N.C.: Duke University Press, 1991. ISBN 0-8223-1126-7 (cl), 0-8223-1145-3 (pbk). ▸ Textbook treatment of events of 1989 by former head of research for Radio Free Europe. Includes chronology of events and historical background. [GS]

33.9 Zbigniew K. Brzezinski. *The grand failure: the birth and death of communism in the twentieth century.* 1989 ed. New York: Collier, 1990. ISBN 0-02-030730-6 (pbk). ▸ Updated version of former national security adviser's analysis of communism's "misguided effort to impose total rationality on social affairs." Value lies in author's dual status as scholar and policy maker. [GS]

33.10 Zbigniew K. Brzezinski. *The Soviet Bloc: unity and conflict.* Rev. ed. Cambridge, Mass.: Harvard University Press, 1967. (Russian Research Center studies, 37.) ▸ Remains standard treatment of Soviet theory and practice of domination over Eastern Europe, 1945–65. [GS]

33.11 Richard V. Burks. *The dynamics of communism in Eastern Europe.* Princeton: Princeton University Press, 1961. ▸ Convincingly argued thesis that in Eastern Europe main source of Communists was numerically weak ethnic groups, except among those with strong antipathy toward Russia. [GS]

33.12 Robert F. Byrnes, ed. *Communal families in the Balkans: the zadruga; essays by Philip E. Mosley and essays in his honor.* Margaret Mead, Introduction. Notre Dame, Ind.: University of Notre Dame Press, 1976. ISBN 0-268-00569-9. ▸ Mosley was pioneer in study of Balkan extended family, traditionally most important premodern Balkan social formation. Some contributors present revisionist view, others, useful historical or social insights. [GS]

33.13 Daniel Chirot, ed. *The origins of backwardness in Eastern Europe: economics and politics from the Middle Ages until the early twentieth century.* Berkeley: University of California Press, 1989. ISBN 0-520-06421-6. ▸ Collection of seven effective articles ranging over several centuries stressing areawide issues of development. [GS]

33.14 David Crowe and John Kolsti, eds. *The gypsies of Eastern Europe.* Ian Hancock, Introduction. Armonk, N.Y.: Sharpe, 1991. ISBN 0-87332-671-7. ▸ Collection of articles, especially on gypsy (Roma) holocaust and postwar situation and on difficulties faced by Eastern Europe's most mistreated ethnic group. [GS]

33.15 Dimitrije Djordjević. *Révolutions nationales des peuples balkaniques, 1804–1914.* Jorjo Tadić, ed. Margita Ristić, trans. Belgrade: Institute of History, 1965. ▸ Presentation of Balkan history as related to European history, not needing European impact to achieve significance. Stresses commonalities of awakening and maturation rather than national intepretations. Balanced for its time. [GS]

33.16 Dimitrije Djordjević and Stephen Fischer-Galati. *The Balkan revolutionary tradition.* New York: Columbia University Press, 1981. ISBN 0-231-05098-4. ▸ Thesis that revolution is a fundamental ingredient of Balkan history not convincingly sustained, but contains valuable typology of Balkan revolutions. [GS]

33.17 Francis Dvornik. *The Slavs in European history and civilization.* New Brunswick, N.J.: Rutgers University Press, 1962. ▸ Comprehensive study of Slav peoples up to 1848; good coverage of early modern Poland-Lithuania, Ukraine, and Belorus. Attention to culture and religion, as well as political chronicle. Antiquated pan-Slavism but informative. [GS/NSK]

33.18 François Fejtő. *A history of the peoples' democracies: Eastern Europe since Stalin.* Daniel Weissbort, trans. New York: Praeger, 1971. ▸ Straightforward, detailed political history, 1953–70. [GS]

33.19 John V. A. Fine, Jr. *The early medieval Balkans: a critical survey from the sixth to the late twelfth century.* Ann Arbor: University of Michigan Press, 1983. ISBN 0-472-10025-4. ▸ Standard treatment (with 33.20) of medieval Balkan history. Detailed, full of informed and sometimes controversial analysis. [GS]

33.20 John V. A. Fine, Jr. *The late medieval Balkans: a critical survey from the late twelfth century to the Ottoman conquest.* Ann Arbor: University of Michigan Press, 1987. ISBN 0-472-10079-3. ▸ Continuation of 33.19. [GS]

33.21 Timothy Garton Ash. *The magic lantern: the revolution of '89 witnessed in Warsaw, Budapest, Berlin, and Prague.* New York: Random House, 1990. ISBN 0-394-58884-3. ▸ Eyewitness accounts, by knowledgeable journalist, of several important moments, particularly in Czechoslovakia, during revolutions of 1989. Well informed and well written; captures excitement and drama of events. [GS/JSH]

33.22 Timothy Garton Ash. *The uses of adversity: essays on the fate of Central Europe.* 1989 ed. New York: Vintage, 1990. ISBN 0-679-73199-7. ▸ Excellent collection of essays by premier journalist covering Eastern Europe in 1980s who spoke languages, knew participants. Extremely well written; useful and interesting analysis. [GS]

33.23 Misha Glenny. *The rebirth of history: Eastern Europe in the age of democracy.* 2d ed. Harmondsworth: Penguin, 1992. ISBN 0-14-014394-7 (pbk). ▸ Vivacious journalistic account of 1980s by well-informed Central European correspondent of BBC's World Service. [GS]

33.24 Thomas Hammond, ed. *Witnesses to the origins of the cold war.* Seattle: University of Washington Press, 1982. (Publications on Russia and Eastern Europe of the School of International Studies, 10.) ISBN 0-295-95892-8. ▸ Fascinating firsthand accounts of immediate postwar situation in Eastern Europe. Good historiographical essay on roots of debate concerning origins of cold war. [GS]

33.25 Paul L. Horecky, ed. *East Central Europe: a guide to basic publications.* Chicago: University of Chicago Press, 1969. ISBN 0-226-35189-0. ▸ Exhaustive annotated bibliography of publications in English through 1960s. Basic resource. [GS]

33.26 Paul L. Horecky, ed. *Southeastern Europe: a guide to basic publications.* Chicago: University of Chicago Press, 1969. ISBN 0-226-35190-4. ▸ Exhaustive annotated bibliography of publications in English through 1960s. Basic resource. [GS]

33.27 Miroslav Hroch. *Social preconditions of national revival in Europe: a comparative analysis of the social composition of patriotic groups among the smaller European nations.* Ben Gowkes, trans. Cambridge: Cambridge University Press, 1985. ISBN 0-521-22891-3. ▸ Updated translation of seminal Czech study; argument positing bourgeoisie as social agent of national consciousness not actually proved, but microstudies and three-phase theory of nationalism's early development very influential. [GS]

33.28 Robert L. Hutchings. *Soviet–East European relations: consolidation and conflict, 1968–1980.* 1983 ed. Madison: University of Wisconsin Press, 1987. ISBN 0-299-09310-7. ▸ Solid monograph arguing that apparently coherent East European alliance system of 1970s actually beset by internal contradictions and held together by force. [GS]

33.29 Barbara Jelavich. *History of the Balkans.* 2 vols. Cambridge: Cambridge University Press, 1983. (Joint Committee on Eastern Europe publication series, 12.) ISBN 0-521-25249-0 (v. 1, cl), 0-521-25448-5 (v. 2, cl), 0-521-27458-3 (v. 1, pbk), 0-521-27459-1 (v. 2, pbk). ▸ Standard history of Balkans. Well organized; good maps and illustrations. Volume 1 covers eighteenth and nineteenth centuries, volume 2, the twentieth. English-language bibliography. [GS]

33.30 Barbara Jelavich and Charles Jelavich. *The establishment of the Balkan national states, 1804–1920.* Seattle: University of Washington Press, 1977. ISBN 0-295-95444-2. ▸ Straightforward, reliable political history. Maintains that positive gain of establishing national states outweighed possible negative judgments of nationalism. Extensive bibliographical essay of works in English. [GS]

33.31 Charles Jelavich, ed. *The Balkans in transition: essays on the development of Balkan life and politics since the eighteenth century.* Berkeley: University of California Press, 1963. ▸ Widely used collection of valuable, if somewhat dated, essays. See especially Roberts, "Politics in a Small State," which suggests issues not always apparent to analysts from large states. [GS]

33.32 Michael C. Kaser, ed. *The economic history of Eastern Europe, 1919–1975.* 3 vols. Oxford: Clarendon, 1985–86. ISBN 0-19-828444-6 (v. 1), 0-19-828445-4 (v. 2), 0-19-828446-2 (v. 3). ▸ Detailed scholarly economic history by first-rate specialists. Volumes 1 and 2 concern interwar period, volume 3 post–World War II. [GS]

33.33 Robert R. King. *Minorities under communism: nationalities as a source of tension among Balkan communist states.* Cambridge, Mass.: Harvard University Press, 1973. ISBN 0-674-57632-2. ▸ Post-1989 resurgence of nationalism makes this thorough study especially useful. [GS]

33.34 Hans Kohn. *Pan-Slavism: its history and ideology.* 2d ed. New York: Vintage, 1960. ▸ Classic study of evolution of nineteenth-century ideal of Slav unity. Chapter 1 on early awakenings of ethnic consciousness particularly germane. [GS]

33.35 Milan Kundera. *The joke: definitive version.* New York: HarperCollins, 1992. ISBN 0-06-019030-2. ▸ A novel conveying style and corruption of Stalinist society in Eastern Europe with great panache. Excellent as introduction to socialist period. [GS]

33.36 John R. Lampe and Marvin R. Jackson. *Balkan economic history, 1550–1950: from imperial borderlands to developing nations.* Bloomington: Indiana University Press, 1982. (Joint Committee on Eastern Europe publication series, 10.) ISBN 0-253-30368-0. ▸ Thorough economic history of Balkans; many tables and charts. Standard work. [GS]

33.37 Paul Lendvai. *Anti-Semitism without Jews: communist Eastern Europe.* Garden City, N.Y.: Doubleday, 1971. ▸ Pioneering discussion of how antisemitism served as deliberate tool for consolidating Soviet power and as intraparty weapon in Poland, despite paucity of Jews. [GS]

33.38 Paul Lendvai. *Eagles in cobwebs: nationalism and communism in the Balkans.* Garden City, N.Y.: Doubleday, 1969. ▸ Engagingly written history of postwar Eastern Europe through 1968. Reliable and very readable. [GS]

33.39 William H. McNeill. *America, Britain, and Russia: their cooperation and conflict, 1941–1946.* 1953 ed. New York: Johnson Reprint, 1970. ▸ Best single introduction (despite date of publication) to creation of international framework within which post–World War II Eastern Europe operated. [GS]

33.40 William H. McNeill. *Europe's steppe frontier, 1500–1800.* Chicago: University of Chicago Press, 1964. ▸ Analysis of closing of Europe's open frontier through consolidation of agrarian bureaucratic empires (Ottoman, Habsburg, Romanov). Rare grasp of macrohistorical processes conveyed without excess theoretical baggage. Original and readable. [GS/NSK]

33.41 David Mitrany. *Marx against the peasant: a study in social dogmatism.* Chapel Hill: University of North Carolina Press, 1951. ▸ Retains value as interpretation of Marxist revolutions as misguided efforts to modernize peasantry rather than proletarian events. Discusses agrarian reforms of interwar period, green parties, and populism. [GS]

33.42 Wilbert E. Moore. *Economic demography of eastern and southern Europe.* 1945 ed. New York: Arno, 1972. ISBN 0-405-04576-X. ▸ Basic source for agricultural and social history of interwar eastern Europe. League of Nations statistics have been questioned, but retain indicative value. [GS]

33.43 Victor Nee and David Stark, eds. *Remaking the economic institutions of socialism: China and Eastern Europe.* Stanford, Calif.: Stanford University Press, 1989. ISBN 0-8047-1494-0 (cl), 0-8047-1495-9 (pbk). ▸ Six excellent analyses of East European economic problems under socialism, particularly in Hungary. [GS]

33.44 Robin Okey. *Eastern Europe, 1740–1980: feudalism to communism.* 2d ed. Minneapolis: University of Minnesota Press, 1986. ISBN 0-8166-1561-6 (pbk). ▸ Brief introductory history of Eastern Europe. Primarily useful for classroom. [GS]

33.45 Hugh Poulton. *The Balkans: minorities and states in conflict.* London: Minority Rights Publications, 1991. ISBN 1-873194-25-0 (cl), 1-873194-05-6 (pbk). ▸ Particularly volatile subject impartially presented. Good summaries of historical events. [GS]

33.46 Pedro Ramet, ed. *Christianity under stress.* Vol. 1: *Eastern Christianity and politics in the twentieth century.* Vol. 2: *Catholicism and politics in communist societies.* Vol. 3: *Protestantism and politics in Eastern Europe and Russia: the communist and post-communist eras.* 3 vols. Durham, N.C.: Duke University Press, 1988–92. ISBN 0-8223-0827-4 (v. 1, cl), 0-8223-1010-4 (v. 2, cl), 0-8223-1047-3 (v. 2, pbk), 0-8223-1241-7 (v. 3, cl). ▸ Series on Christianity in twentieth-century communist states, especially Eastern Europe. Articles of varying quality, but together offer broad-ranging discussion of religion under communism. [GS]

33.47 Sabrina Petra Ramet. *Social currents in Eastern Europe: the sources and meaning of the great transformation.* Durham, N.C.: Duke University Press, 1991. ISBN 0-8223-1129-1 (cl), 0-8223-1148-8 (pbk). ▸ Argues political repluralization of Eastern Europe grew out of broadly conceived repluralization of culture. Not completely successful, but one of few works on social currents. [GS]

33.48 György Ránki. *Economy and foreign policy: the struggle of the great powers for hegemony in the Danube valley, 1919–1939.* Boulder: East European Monographs; distributed by Columbia University Press, 1983. (East European monographs, 141.) ISBN 0-88033-032-5. ▸ Discussion of how European powers sought to fill new post–World War I East European political structures with economic content. Nazi Germany won, but decisively overplayed its hand. Sophisticated Marxist perspective. [GS]

33.49 Joseph Rothschild. *East Central Europe between the two world wars.* 1974 ed. Seattle: University of Washington Press, 1990. ISBN 0-295-95350-0 (cl, 1974), 0-295-95357-8 (pbk). ▸ Solid, detailed, and reliable political history of each country of region. Good election statistics. Widely used in college courses. [GS]

33.50 Joseph Rothschild. *Return to diversity: a political history of East Central Europe since World War II.* New York: Oxford University Press, 1989. ISBN 0-19-504574-2 (pbk). ▸ Despite title, particularly strong in introductory sections about interwar period, World War II, and immediate postwar period; includes Balkans. Excellent paperback textbook. [GS]

33.51 Jacques Rupnik. *The other Europe.* Rev. ed. New York: Pantheon, 1989. ISBN 0-8052-4077-2 (pbk). ▸ Witty, stimulating discussion covering World War II to 1988. Although written to accompany television series, most suitable for knowledgeable readers. [GS]

33.52 Timothy W. Ryback. *Rock around the Bloc: a history of rock music in Eastern Europe and the Soviet Union.* New York: Oxford University Press, 1990. ISBN 0-19-505633-7. ▸ Lennonist "soundtrack of the Gorbachev revolution" with detailed historical background to 1946. Comprehensive and well written. [GS]

33.53 George Schöpflin and Nancy Wood, eds. *In search of Central Europe.* Cambridge: Polity, 1989. ISBN 0-7456-0547-8. ▸ Excellent collection of both contemporary and classic articles debating "What is Central Europe?" Provoked by Milan Kundera's 1984 article claiming that Russia is outside of Europe. [GS]

33.54 Hugh Seton-Watson. *The East European revolution.* 3d ed. New York: Praeger, 1956. ▸ Valuable history of World War II and sovietization. Includes sections on societies, economies, and religious affairs. [GS]

33.55 Hugh Seton-Watson. *Eastern Europe between the wars, 1918–1941.* 1962 3d ed. Boulder: Westview, 1986. ISBN 0-8133-7092-2 (pbk). ▸ Obviously frustrated discussion of ethnic problems from fifty years ago; well worthwhile in light of today's ethnic struggles. [GS]

33.56 Thomas W. Simons, Jr. *Eastern Europe in the postwar world.* New York: St. Martin's, 1991. ISBN 0-312-06169-2 (cl), 0-312-06168-4 (pbk). ▸ Intelligent reading of postwar period by experienced diplomat with scholarly bent. [GS]

33.57 H. Gordon Skilling. *Samizdat and an independent society in Central and Eastern Europe.* Columbus: Ohio State University Press, 1989. ISBN 0-8142-0487-2. ▸ Collection of interrelated articles on independent movements of Eastern Europe in 1970s and 1980s; detailed sources. [GS]

33.58 Leften Stavros Stavrianos. *The Balkans since 1453.* 1958 ed. New York: Rinehart, 1965. ▸ Superb pioneering history of Balkans that retains its value. Well written; extensive bibliography in Western languages. [GS]

33.59 Traian Stoianovich. *A study in Balkan civilization.* New York: Knopf, 1967. ▸ Provocative work incorporating anthropological and sociological approaches to create synthetic interpretation of Balkan history. [GS]

33.60 Gale Stokes, ed. *From Stalinism to pluralism: a documentary history of Eastern Europe since 1945.* New York: Oxford University Press, 1991. ISBN 0-19-506381-3 (cl), 0-19-506382-1 (pbk). ▸ Collection of forty-seven documents with annotations and connecting narrative. Includes such authors as Havel, Djilas, Miłosz, Kundera, Kołakowski, as well as Churchill, Brezhnev, Gorbachev, and Brandt. Widely used on college campuses. [GS]

33.61 Orest Subtelny. *Domination of Eastern Europe: native nobilities and foreign absolutism, 1500–1715.* Kingston, Ont.: McGill-Queen's University Press, 1986. ISBN 0-7735-0438-9. ▸ Failure of nobilities of Poland, Hungary, Lithuania, Ukraine, and Moldavia to resist absolutism successfully constituted "general crisis" more tightly interwoven than contemporary "general crisis" in West. Political chronicle, skillfully isolating historical turning point for Eastern Europe. [GS/NSK]

33.62 Peter F. Sugar. *Native fascism in the successor states.* Santa

Barbara, Calif.: ABC-Clio, 1971. ISBN 0-87436-073-0. ▸ Well-rounded collection of articles on fascism in Eastern Europe during interwar period. [GS]

33.63 Peter F. Sugar. *Southeastern Europe under Ottoman rule, 1354–1804.* Seattle: University of Washington Press, 1977. ISBN 0-295-95443-4. ▸ Best study of impact of House of Osman on Balkans. Reinterprets social decline as ossification and considers millet system (autonomy of Orthodox church) as based on false premises. [GS]

33.64 Peter F. Sugar and Ivo J. Lederer, eds. *Nationalism in Eastern Europe.* 1969 ed. Seattle: University of Washington Press, 1971. (Far Eastern and Russian Institute, Publications on Russia and Eastern Europe, 1.) ISBN 0-295-95008-0 (cl), 0-295-95147-8 (pbk). ▸ Collection of short histories of nationalism in each East European country. Articles are traditional in approach. Stimulating introduction; reliable data. [GS]

33.65 B. H. Sumner. *Russia and the Balkans, 1870–1880.* 1937 ed. Hamden, Conn.: Archon, 1962. ▸ Still the great diplomatic history on this subject. [GS]

33.66 Jenő Szűcs. *Nation und Geschichte: Studien.* Cologne: Böhlau, 1981. ISBN 3-412-03381-2. ▸ Collection of essays thoroughly examining problem of how early forms of ethnic and national consciousness differed from modern nationalism. Created major scholarly controversy at time of publication in Hungarian (1974). [MK/SBV]

33.67 Jenő Szűcs. *Les trois Europes.* Veronique Charaire, Gabon Klahiczay, and Philippe Thoneau-Dangin, trans. Paris: L'Harmattan, 1985. ISBN 2-85802-529-8. ▸ Comprehensive study of historical cleavages among three different regions of Europe, tracing evolution of West, Central, and East European societies from medieval to modern times. [MK]

33.68 Leslie C. Tihany. *A history of middle Europe: from the earliest times to the age of the world wars.* New Brunswick, N.J.: Rutgers University Press, 1976. ISBN 0-8135-0814-2. ▸ Brief, broad-ranging survey arguing East Europeans are historically dependent, inland peoples whose route to twentieth-century independence remains problematic. [GS]

33.69 Nikolai Todorov. *The Balkan city, 1400–1900.* Seattle: University of Washington Press, 1983. (Publications on Russia and Eastern Europe of the School of International Studies, 12.) ISBN 0-295-95897-9. ▸ Pioneering study of urban development in region not usually considered urban. Richly documented with statistical tables. [GS]

33.70 E. Garrison Walters. *The other Europe: eastern Europe to 1945.* Syracuse, N.Y.: Syracuse University Press, 1987. ISBN 0-8156-2412-3 (cl), 0-8156-2440-9 (pbk). ▸ Straightforward text, useful in classroom and for general introduction to history of region. [GS]

33.71 Doreen Warriner. *Revolution in Eastern Europe.* London: Turnstile, 1950. ▸ Sympathetic account of post–World War II changes, especially economic, serving as reminder that in 1950 it was quite possible to be optimistic about socialism's prospects in Eastern Europe. [GS]

33.72 Sharon L. Wolchik and Alfred G. Meyer, eds. *Women, state, and party in Eastern Europe.* Durham, N.C.: Duke University Press, 1985. ISBN 0-8223-0660-3 (cl), 0-8223-0659-X (pbk). ▸ One of few books on subject and therefore starting point for further work. Collection of twenty good articles. [GS]

33.73 Robert L. Wolff. *The Balkans in our time.* Rev. ed. Cambridge, Mass.: Harvard University Press, 1974. ISBN 0-674-06051-2. ▸ History of Balkans, 1939–53, focusing on details of postwar communist takeover, including economic issues. Significant achievement in its day, less useful today. [GS]

SEE ALSO

30.125 Robert A. Kann and Zdeněk V. David. *The peoples of the eastern Habsburg lands, 1526–1918.*

34.189 Barbara Jelavich. *Russia's Balkan entanglements, 1806–1914.*

47.16 Mathew S. Anderson. *The Eastern question, 1774–1923.*

47.355 Andrew Rossos. *Russia and the Balkans.*

48.355 Bennett Kovrig. *Of walls and bridges.*

48.467 Charles Gati. *The bloc that failed.*

ALBANIA

33.74 Julian Amery. *Sons of the Eagle: a study in guerilla war.* London: Macmillan, 1948. ▸ Personal account of British role in helping Albanian resistance during World War II. Frank admission of failure of Western policy in preventing Communists from coming to power in Albania. [EB]

33.75 Elez Biberaj. *Albania: a socialist maverick.* Boulder: Westview, 1990. ISBN 0-8133-0513-6. ▸ Critical examination of communist policies, focusing primarily on period following Enver Hoxha's demise in 1985. Based on Albanian sources. [EB]

33.76 Constantine A. Chekrezi. *Albania, past and present.* 1919 ed. New York: Arno, 1971. ISBN 0-405-02740-0. ▸ Authoritative, detailed survey of Albania's history to World War I including political, social, and economic conditions. Wide-ranging treatment of Albanian diaspora, including in United States. [EB]

33.77 Christo A. Dako. *Albania: the master key to the Near East.* Boston: Grimes, 1919. ▸ Passionate defense of Albania's right to be independent state by leading Albanian-American political activist. Useful review of Albanian question from Balkan wars to end of World War I. [EB]

33.78 *Fjalori Enciklopedik Shqiptar* (The Albanian encyclopedic dictionary). Tirana, Albania: Academy of Sciences of the People's Republic of Albania, 1985. ▸ Wide-ranging reference work, covering history, personalities, government, institutions, armed forces, economy, and society. Highly biased in favor of Albanian Communist party. Flawed by serious omissions of precommunist era. [EB]

33.79 William E. Griffith. *Albania and the Sino-Soviet rift.* Cambridge, Mass.: MIT Press, 1963. ▸ Albania's break with Soviet Union and its alliance with China. Most comprehensive account of critical period in Albania's post–World War II history. Indispensable. [EB]

33.80 Anton Logoreci. *The Albanians: Europe's forgotten survivors.* London: Gollancz, 1977. ISBN 0-575-02229-9. ▸ Synopsis of Albania's history from ancient times to mid-1970s. Highly critical examination of policies of communist regime and resultant chronic ills facing Albanian society. [EB]

33.81 Ramadan Marmullaku. *Albania and the Albanians.* Hamden, Conn.: Archon, 1975. ISBN 0-208-01558-2. ▸ Well-documented history of Albania, focusing primarily on post–World War II period. Sympathetic analysis of communist regime's foreign and domestic policies. Section on Albanians in Yugoslavia very useful. [EB]

33.82 Nicholas C. Pano. *The People's Republic of Albania.* Baltimore: Johns Hopkins University Press, 1968. ▸ Outstanding analysis of developments in Albania under communist rule, 1945–67, based heavily on primary sources. Rich in factual material and interpretation. [EB]

33.83 Stefanaq Pollo and Arben Puto. *The history of Albania: from its origins to the present day.* Carol Wiseman and Ginnie Hole, trans. London: Routledge & Kegan Paul, 1981. ISBN 0-7100-0365-X. ▸ Outline of country's history by communist Albania's leading historians from ancient times to 1970s. Marxist interpretation biased in favor of Albanian Communist party. Treatment of developments since 1930s seriously flawed. [EB]

33.84 Peter R. Prifti. *Socialist Albania since 1944: domestic and foreign developments*. Cambridge, Mass.: MIT Press, 1978. ISBN 0-262-16070-6. ‣ Comprehensive study of Albania under communist rule, 1944–77. Perceptive analysis of politics, society, military, and foreign policy. Authoritative work, indispensable for any student of Albanian affairs. [EB]

33.85 Vandeleur Robinson. *Albania's road to freedom*. London: Allen & Unwin, 1941. ‣ Analysis of Albanian politics, society, and religion during King Zog's rule. Useful information on Zog's style of leadership and corruption that permeated his government. Sympathetic but frankly critical of Zog's policies. [EB]

33.86 Stavro Skendi. *The Albanian national awakening, 1878–1912*. Princeton: Princeton University Press, 1967. ‣ Competent study of national movements leading to proclamation of Albania's independence in 1912. Well researched; fills important void in study of Albania's modern history. Excellent bibliography. [EB]

33.87 Sommerville Story, ed. *The memoirs of Ismail Kemal Bey, 1844–1919*. New York: Dutton, 1920. ‣ Illuminating memoirs of Albanian patriot, who before proclaiming his country's independence in 1912 had risen to senior positions in Ottoman empire. Valuable insights regarding disintegration of empire. [EB]

33.88 Joseph Swire. *Albania: the rise of a kingdom*. 1929 ed. New York: Arno, 1971. ISBN 0-405-02777-X. ‣ Ambitious review of Albania from Congress of Berlin to rise of Ahmet Zog. Most authoritative survey of Albanian history for this period. Invaluable starting point for further research. [EB]

BULGARIA

33.89 James Barros. *The League of Nations and the great powers: the Greek-Bulgarian incident, 1925*. Oxford: Clarendon, 1970. ISBN 0-19-821484-7. ‣ Detailed study of clash contained by League of Nations. Standard work on subject, backed by archival research. [RJC]

33.90 John D. Bell. *The Bulgarian Communist party from Blagoev to Zhivkov*. Stanford, Calif.: Hoover Institution Press, 1986. ISBN 0-8179-8202-7 (pbk). ‣ Excellent survey of party from its origins through seizure of power after World War II and evolution of policies and personalities thereafter. [RJC]

33.91 John D. Bell. *Peasants in power: Alexander Stamboliski and the Bulgarian Agrarian National Union, 1899–1923*. Princeton: Princeton University Press, 1977. ISBN 0-691-07584-0. ‣ Biography of major statesman with valuable background information on society, politics, and agrarian ideology. Essential work. [RJC]

33.92 Cyril Edwin Black. *The establishment of constitutional government in Bulgaria*. 1943 ed. New York: Johnson Reprint, 1970. ‣ Seminal study of construction of Bulgaria's new political system after liberation. Wealth of detail on formation and early evolution of political parties. Includes English text of major constitutional documents. [RJC]

33.93 Michael M. Boll. *The cold war in the Balkans: American foreign policy and the emergence of communist Bulgaria, 1943–1947*. Lexington: University Press of Kentucky, 1984. ISBN 0-8131-1527-2. ‣ Argument that United States had clearer political objectives in Bulgaria for postwar period than did Soviet Union. Full of important detail. [RJC]

33.94 Michael M. Boll, ed. *The American military mission in the Allied Control Commission for Bulgaria, 1944–1947: history and transcripts*. Boulder: East European Monographs; distributed by Columbia University Press, 1985. (East European monographs, 176.) ISBN 0-88033-068-6. ‣ Documents illustrating political situation in Bulgaria and tensions between Western states and Soviet Union. Essential for postwar period and communist takeover. [RJC]

33.95 James F. Brown. *Bulgaria under communist rule*. New York: Praeger, 1970. ‣ Detailed examination of communist rule, 1953–69. Remains essential text for period of communist domination. [RJC]

33.96 Frederick B. Chary. *The Bulgarian Jews and the Final Solution, 1940–44*. Pittsburgh: University of Pittsburgh Press, 1972. ISBN 0-8229-3251-2. ‣ Standard work with excellent analysis of motives, evolution, and results of Bulgarian policy that saved many Jews. Avoids partisanship that generally bedevils study of this issue in Bulgarian historiography. [RJC]

33.97 James F. Clarke. *Bible societies, American missionaries, and the national revival of Bulgaria*. New York: Arno, 1971. ISBN 0-405-02783-4. ‣ Reprint of Harvard thesis that remains one of best English-language sources for Bulgaria during first three-quarters of nineteenth century. [RJC]

33.98 James F. Clarke and Dennis P. Hupchick, eds. *The pen and the sword: studies in Bulgarian history*. Boulder: East European Monographs; distributed by Columbia University Press, 1988. (East European monographs, 252.) ISBN 0-88033-149-6. ‣ Collection of articles by pioneer historian of Bulgaria, mainly concerning historiography, Western religions in Bulgaria, and Bulgarian national revival. [GS]

33.99 Stephen Constant. *Foxy Ferdinand, 1861–1948: tsar of Bulgaria*. 1979 ed. New York: Watts, 1980. ISBN 0-531-09930-X. ‣ Most recent biography of prince who dominated Bulgaria from 1887 to 1918. Useful background material. Elegant and competent summation of previous knowledge. [RJC]

33.100 Richard J. Crampton. *Bulgaria, 1878–1918: a history*. Boulder: East European Monographs; distributed by Columbia University Press, 1983. (East European monographs, 138.) ISBN 0-88033-029-5. ‣ Detailed survey from establishment of new state to 1918; treats social and economic development as well as political evolution. Standard English-language treatment. [GS]

33.101 Richard J. Crampton. "Bulgarian society in the early nineteenth century." In *Balkan society in the age of Greek independence*. Richard Clogg, ed., pp. 157–204. Totowa, N.J.: Barnes & Noble, 1981. ISBN 0-389-20024-7. ‣ Survey of social structure with emphasis on landholding systems, land distribution, and situation of Bulgarians in towns. Rare Western-language study of these questions. [RJC]

33.102 Richard J. Crampton. *A short history of modern Bulgaria*. Cambridge: Cambridge University Press, 1987. ISBN 0-521-25340-3 (cl), 0-521-27323-4 (pbk). ‣ Survey from emergence of national consciousness in nineteenth century to mid-1980s with concentration on post-1918 period. Main focus on political evolution. Standard work. [GS]

33.103 Richard J. Crampton, comp. *Bulgaria*. Santa Barbara, Calif.: ABC-Clio, 1989. ISBN 1-85109-104-1. ‣ Bibliography with special section on history; many other historical works listed under other headings. Includes introductory essay surveying Bulgarian history from arrival of Bulgarians in Balkans. [RJC]

33.104 Karel Durman. *Lost illusions: Russian policies towards Bulgaria in 1877–1887*. Stockholm: Uppsala University; distributed by Almqvist & Wiksell, 1988. (Uppsala studies on the Soviet Union and Eastern Europe, 1.) ISBN 91-554-2153-9 (pbk), ISSN 0284-3080. ‣ Extensive study of love-hate relationship between Bulgarians and Russians in first decade of Bulgarian independence. Wide use of primary sources plus cool judgment. [RJC]

33.105 Wolfgang-Uwe Friedrich. *Bulgarien und die Mächte, 1913–1915: ein Beitrag zur Weltkriegs und Imperialismusgeschichte*. Stuttgart: Steiner, 1985. ISBN 3-515-04050-1. ‣ Exhaustive and most recent Western study of Bulgaria's entry into World War I. Excellent treatment of internal political issues as well as diplomacy. [RJC]

33.106 Khristo Gandev. *The Bulgarian people during the fifteenth century: a demographic and ethnographic study.* Sofia, Bulgaria: Sofia Press, 1987. ▸ Discussion in Section 1 of "de-Bulgarianizing" policies of Ottomans after conquest of Bulgaria in late fourteenth century. Explanation of how Bulgarian culture and consciousness survived in family and village in Section 2. Useful for social history. [RJC]

33.107 Alexander Gerschenkron. "Some aspects of industrialization in Bulgaria, 1879–1939." In *Economic backwardness in historical perspective: a book of essays.* Alexander Gerschenkron, ed., pp. 198–234, 422–35. New York: Praeger, 1965. ▸ Classic treatment of subject arguing that Bulgaria experienced growth without structural change. All subsequent Western examinations of Bulgarian economic history influenced by or highly conscious of this study. [RJC]

33.108 Stephane Groueff. *Crown of thorns: the reign of King Boris III of Bulgaria, 1918–1943.* Lanham, Md.: Madison, 1987. ISBN 0-8191-5778-3. ▸ Use of many previously neglected or unobtainable sources to create fascinating biography. Shows Boris as reluctant but wily ruler, probably murdered by unnamed assailant. [RJC]

33.109 Francesco Guida, Armando Pitassio, and Rita Tolomeo. *Nascita di uno stato balcanico: la Bulgaria di Alessandro di Battenberg nella corrispondenza diplomatica italiana (1879–1886).* Naples, Italy: Scientifiche Italiane, 1988. ISBN 88-7104-5068. ▸ Discussion of state formation in Bulgaria. Includes many previously unpublished documents from French and Italian diplomatic archives. Useful information on social and political developments. [RJC]

33.110 Magarditsch A. Hatschikjan. *Tradition und Neuorientierung in der bulgarischen Aussenpolitik, 1944–1948: die "nationale Aussenpolitik" der Bulgarischen Arbeiterpartei (Kommunisten).* Munich: Oldenbourg, 1988. ISBN 3-486-55001-2. ▸ Reformulation of foreign policy an essential ingredient in communist takeover. Superb analysis of process using wide range of sources. [RJC]

33.111 Hans-Joachim Hoppe. *Bulgarien, Hitlers eigenwilliger Verbündeter: eine Fallstudie zur nationalsozialistischen Südosteuropapolitik.* Stuttgart: Deutsche-Verlags-Anstalt, 1979. (Studien zur Zeitgeschichte, 15.) ISBN 3-421-01904-5. ▸ Excellent for Bulgarian diplomacy under Boris III. Hostile study backed by extensive use of wide range of primary material. Very useful detail on diplomacy and on general political situation. [RJC]

33.112 *Istoriya na Bulgariya* (History of Bulgaria). 7 vols. to date. Sofia, Bulgaria: Bulgarian Academy of Sciences, 1980–. ▸ Most complete and authoritative history of Bulgaria. Another seven volumes planned, but Bulgaria's current economic plight makes this questionable. Early volumes have Marxist tinge. [RJC]

33.113 Mito Isusov et al., ed. *Problems of transition from capitalism to socialism in Bulgaria.* Sofia, Bulgaria: Bulgarian Academy of Sciences, 1975. ▸ Useful as example of Marxist historiography on communist takeover. Thoughtful academic treatment with much valuable detail on social aspects of problem. [RJC]

33.114 Machiel Kiel. *Art and society of Bulgaria in the Turkish period, a sketch of the economic, juridical, and artistic preconditions of Bulgarian post-Byzantine art and its place in the development of the art of the Christian Balkans, 1360/70–1700: a new interpretation.* Maastricht, The Netherlands: von Gorcum, 1985. ISBN 90-232-2061-7. ▸ Using Ottoman sources, shows that despite previous assumptions church architecture and mural painting flourished under Turkish rule, partly because of tolerant nature of Ottoman law. [RJC]

33.115 Joachim V. Königslöw. *Ferdinand von Bulgarien: vom Beginn der Thronkandidatur bis zur Anerkennung durch die Grossmächte, 1886 bis 1896.* Munich: Oldenbourg, 1970. ISBN 3-486-47341-7. ▸ Detailed study of crisis following breach between Bulgaria and Russia. Excellent for policies of Stefan Stambolov and for building of Ferdinand's power base. [RJC]

33.116 Dimitur Kosev et al. *Atlas po bulgarska istoriia* (An atlas of Bulgarian history). Sofia, Bulgaria: Bulgarian Academy of Sciences, 1963. ▸ Maps covering all periods of Bulgarian history from arrival of Slavs in Balkans to post–World War II. Includes economic, cultural, and social information. Useful adjunct to historical studies. [RJC]

33.117 Huey L. Kostanick. *Turkish resettlement of Bulgarian Turks, 1950–1953.* 1957 ed. New York: Johnson Reprint, 1968. ▸ Sound, scholarly examination of policies leading to expulsion of ethnic Turks and relationship of policy to developments such as collectivization. [RJC]

33.118 Vladimir Kostov. *The Bulgarian umbrella: the Soviet direction and operations of the Bulgarian secret service in Europe.* Ben Reynolds, trans. New York: St. Martin's, 1988. ISBN 0-312-02387-1. ▸ Revelations by former secret service official; important source for structure and methods. Emphasizes Soviet domination of communist Bulgaria. [RJC]

33.119 John R. Lampe. *The Bulgarian economy in the twentieth century.* New York: St. Martin's, 1986. ISBN 0-312-10785-4. ▸ Unique Western treatment. Excellent insights into political developments. Revises some interpretations, ascribing more individuality to Bulgarian policy. Information made available after 1989 questions some of statistics used. [RJC]

33.120 George Clenton Logio. *Bulgaria, past and present.* 1936 ed. New York: AMS Press, 1974. ISBN 0-404-56133-0. ▸ Much useful detail especially on Bulgarian financial situation in interwar period. Valuable for contemporary examination of reparations and indebtedness problems. Also sound on political evolution. [RJC]

33.121 Bernard Lory. *Le sort de l'héritage ottoman en Bulgarie: l'exemple des villes bulgares, 1878–1900.* Istanbul, Turkey: Isis, 1985. ▸ Examination of different cultural traditions in Bulgaria after liberation. Shows influence of Ottoman traditions on Bulgarian life. Most original, interesting, and important book on Bulgarian history published this century. [RJC]

33.122 Mercia MacDermott. *The apostle of freedom: a portrait of Vasil Levski against a background of nineteenth-century Bulgaria.* 1967 ed. Sofia, Bulgaria: Sofia Press, 1979. ▸ Portrait of leading martyr of Bulgaria's movement for political independence. Somewhat romanticized but useful for Bulgarian national revival; underestimates importance of religious question. [RJC]

33.123 Mercia MacDermott. *A history of Bulgaria, 1393–1885.* New York: Praeger, 1962. ▸ Relies heavily and uncritically on Bulgarian Marxist sources and concentrates on national revival of nineteenth century. One of few English treatments of national revival. [RJC]

33.124 Clarence A. Manning and Roman Smal-Stocki. *The history of modern Bulgarian literature.* 1960 ed. Westport, Conn.: Greenwood, 1974. ▸ Rare English-language treatment of general development of Bulgarian literature. [RJC]

33.125 Georgi Markov. *The truth that killed.* 1983 ed. Liliana Brisby, trans. Annabel Markov, Introduction. New York: Tichnor & Fields, 1984. ISBN 0-89919-296-3. ▸ Much detail on early years of communist rule, on cultural policies, and on nature of communist hierarchy in Bulgaria by author murdered in London in 1978. [RJC]

33.126 Thomas A. Meininger. *The formation of a nationalist Bul-*

garian intelligentsia, 1835–1878. New York: Garland, 1987. ISBN 0-8240-8028-9. ▸ Detailed analysis of origins, upbringing, education, employment, income, and politics of 191 nationalist intellectuals from national revival period. Unique study with much useful and original data. [GS]

33.127 Thomas A. Meininger. *Ignatiev and the establishment of the Bulgarian exarchate, 1864–1872: a study in personal diplomacy.* Madison: Historical Society of Wisconsin for University of Wisconsin, Department of History, 1970. ▸ Important English-language source for vital process of assertion of Bulgarian separateness in church administration. [RJC]

33.128 Marshall Lee Miller. *Bulgaria during the Second World War.* Stanford, Calif.: Stanford University Press, 1975. ISBN 0-8047-0870-3. ▸ Comprehensive survey concentrating on political and diplomatic affairs. Excellent discussion of death of King Boris. Best Western-language survey of subject. [RJC]

33.129 Dimitur N. Mishev. *The Bulgarians in the past.* 1919 ed. New York: Arno, 1971. ISBN 0-405-02766-4. ▸ Valuable example of precommunist nationalist school of history. Surveys Bulgarian culture and national identity from seventh to nineteenth century. [RJC]

33.130 Charles A. Moser. *Dimitrov of Bulgaria: a political biography of Dr. Georgi M. Dimitrov.* Ottawa, Ill.: Caroline House, 1979. ISBN 0-89803-011-0. ▸ Biography of agrarian leader prominent in interwar years and after war. Includes much useful background and discussion of agrarian ideology. [RJC]

33.131 Tatyana Nestorova. *American missionaries among the Bulgarians (1858–1912).* Boulder: East European Monographs; distributed by Columbia University Press, 1987. (East European monographs, 218.) ISBN 0-88033-114-3. ▸ Nonsentimental account of efforts to convert Bulgarians, based on missionary archives. Contains useful information on Bulgarian life, especially education. [RJC]

33.132 Nissan Oren. *Bulgarian communism: the road to power, 1934–1944.* 1971 ed. Westport, Conn.: Greenwood, 1985. ISBN 0-313-24741-2. ▸ Treatment of internal party tensions, including Left Opposition, and with party's position inside authoritarian Bulgaria. Indispensable for study of Bulgaria in this period. [RJC]

33.133 Nissan Oren. *Revolution administered: agrarianism and communism in Bulgaria.* Baltimore: Johns Hopkins University Press, 1973. ISBN 0-8018-1209-7 (cl), 0-8018-1210-0 (pbk). ▸ Outline of conflict between these two main radical forces and survey of building of communist authority and application of communist policies up to 1970. Valuable, reliable text. [RJC]

33.134 Marin V. Pundeff. *Bulgaria: a bibliographical guide.* 1965 ed. New York: Arno, 1968. ▸ Includes 1,243 entries, many on history, and a bibliographical essay on each subject heading. [RJC]

33.135 Joseph Rothschild. *The Communist party of Bulgaria: origins and development, 1883–1936.* Rev. ed. New York: AMS Press, 1972. ISBN 0-404-07164-3. ▸ Traces ideological, social, and political origins and development of party and its attendant trade unions. Essential text for this period with much additional detail on general political and social conditions. [RJC]

33.136 Steven Runciman. *A history of the first Bulgarian empire.* London: Bell, 1930. ▸ Sketch of early history of Bulgarians in Bulgaria followed by detailed discussion of relations between Bulgaria and Byzantium. Classic study; useful and varied appendixes. [RJC]

33.137 Irwin T. Sanders. *Balkan village.* Lexington: University Press of Kentucky, 1949. ▸ Study of social structure and customs in village near Sofia in 1930s. Classic study, remains fresh and

important. Read in conjunction with author's study of Greece (33.301). [RJC]

33.138 Bilal N. Simsir. *The Turks of Bulgaria, 1878–1985.* London: Rustem Brothers, 1988. ISBN 9963-565-10-7. ▸ Concentrates on education, cultural facilities, institutional representation, and emigration rights as well as religious provision for Turks in Bulgaria. Wealth of information; reasonably dispassionate. [RJC]

33.139 Atanas Slavov. *With the precision of bats.* Washington, D.C.: Occidental, 1986. ISBN 0-911050-59-0. ▸ Extraordinary autobiography by exile, poet, and literary critic. Brilliant evocation of Bulgaria from end of World War II to early 1970s. Incisive, witty, unique. [RJC]

33.140 Zachary Stoyanoff. *Pages from the autobiography of a Bulgarian insurgent.* M. W. Potter, trans. London: Arnold, 1913. ▸ Classic account of Uprising of 1876 by a leading participant. Rare example of source material in English. [RJC]

33.141 Joseph Swire. *Bulgarian conspiracy.* London: Hale, 1939. ▸ Detailed account of interwar political history, concentrating on destabilizing effect of Macedonian factions. Champions perpetrators of 1934 coup, but has valuable insights and firsthand information. [RJC]

33.142 Stefan Troebst. *Die bulgarisch-jugoslawische Kontroverse um Makedonien, 1967–1982.* Munich: Oldenbourg, 1983. ISBN 3-486-51521-7. ▸ Traces development of this longstanding problem with illuminating detail on such issues as rivalries over church affiliation and Macedonian language. [RJC]

SEE ALSO
8.326 Robert Browning. *Byzantium and Bulgaria.*

CZECHOSLOVAKIA

33.143 Edvard Beneš. *Memoirs of Dr. Eduard Beneš: from Munich to new war and new victory.* 1954 ed. Godfrey Lias, trans. Westport, Conn.: Greenwood, 1978. ISBN 0-313-20592-2. ▸ Former Czech president on Munich, exile, and return to Czechoslovakia. Interesting for Czechoslovak-Soviet relations, efforts to get Munich Pact annulled, and decision to expel Sudeten Germans after 1945. [HLA]

33.144 Edvard Beneš. *My war memoirs.* 1928 ed. Paul Selver, trans. Westport, Conn.: Greenwood, 1971. ISBN 0-8371-4763-8. ▸ Account of working with Masaryk and others for Czechoslovak independence during World War I. Insights into reluctance of Western powers to accept breakup of Austria-Hungary. [HLA]

33.145 Reginald R. Betts. *Essays in Czech history.* London: Athlone, 1969. ISBN 0-485-11095-4. ▸ Essays mostly on aspects of religious and cultural history of Czech lands during Middle Ages, often idiosyncratic. Also includes consideration of Masaryk's philosophy of history. [HLA]

33.146 Jon Bloomfield. *Passive revolution: politics and the Czechoslovak working class, 1945–48.* New York: St. Martin's, 1979. ISBN 0-312-59788-6. ▸ Careful study of external and internal factors leading to communist takeover in Czechoslovakia in 1948. Concludes that February events neither supported nor opposed by majority, but only passively accepted. [HLA]

33.147 Karl Bosl, ed. *Handbuch der Geschichte der böhmischen Länder.* 4 vols. Stuttgart: Hiersemann, 1967–74. ISBN 3-7772-6602-7 (set). ▸ Most thorough detailed survey of history of Bohemia and associated lands in any major Western language. Volume 1 covers to beginning of Hussite revolution, volume 2 to the national revival, volume 3 from 1848 to 1919, and volume 4 the era of modern mass democracy and dictatorship. Excellent bibliographies with emphasis on literature in German. [HLA]

33.148 Peter Brock. *The political and social doctrines of the Unity of Czech Brethren in the fifteenth and early sixteenth centuries.* The

Hague: Mouton, 1957. ▸ Unique study of state and society in doctrines of Unity of Czech (Bohemian) Brethren, offshoot of Hussite reform movement. Special interest in teaching on non-violence and nonparticipation in state affairs. [HLA]

33.149 Peter Brock. *The Slovak national awakening: an essay in the intellectual history of East Central Europe.* Toronto: University of Toronto Press, 1976. ISBN 0-8020-5337-8. ▸ Emergence of modern Slovak national ideology, from Antonín Bernolák through Jan Kollár and Pavel Josef Šafařík to L'udovít Štúr and his contemporaries. Elegant essay in intellectual history. Also available on microform from Ann Arbor, Mich.: University Microfilms International, 1991. [HLA]

33.150 Peter Brock and H. Gordon Skilling, eds. *The Czech renascence of the nineteenth century: essays presented to Otakar Odložilík in honour of his seventieth birthday.* Toronto: University of Toronto Press, 1970. ISBN 0-8020-5233-9. ▸ Valuable essays honoring important emigré historian, covering aspects of Czech national revival in roughly chronological order. Includes articles of intellectual, political, and literary nature. [HLA]

33.151 Johann W. Brugel. *Czechoslovakia before Munich: the German minority problem and British appeasement policy.* Cambridge: Cambridge University Press, 1973. ISBN 0-521-08687-6. ▸ Internal dynamic and foreign policy aspects of German-Czech relations, 1918–38. Balanced, well-grounded account; critical of policy in Central Europe in era of appeasement. [HLA]

33.152 F. Gregory Campbell. *Confrontation in Central Europe: Weimar Germany and Czechoslovakia.* 1975 ed. Chicago: University of Chicago Press, 1978. ISBN 0-226-09252-6. ▸ Excellent study in diplomatic history showing that although relations between Czechoslovakia and Weimar Germany were correct, they were also antagonistic. [HLA]

33.153 Gary B. Cohen. *The politics of ethnic survival: Germans in Prague, 1861–1914.* 1975 ed. Princeton: Princeton University Press, 1981. ISBN 0-691-05332-4. ▸ Fascinating social history of German community in Prague as its land and city were affected by Czech national revival. Sheds considerable light on Czech-German relations. [HLA]

33.154 Karen Dawisha. *The Kremlin and the Prague Spring.* Berkeley: University of California Press, 1984. ISBN 0-520-04971-3. ▸ Highly detailed study of Soviet and Czechoslovak decision making during Prague Spring. Uses social science model of crisis behavior to argue that Czech and Slovak leaders did not communicate with Warsaw Pact counterparts. [HLA]

33.155 Kenneth J. Dillon. *King and estates in the Bohemian lands, 1526–1564.* 1976 ed. New York: Lang, 1982. (Studies presented to the International Commission for the History of Representative and Parliamentary Institutions, 57.) ISBN 0-685-06610-X. ▸ Thorough study of Bohemian Estates' relationship with Ferdinand of Habsburg from 1526 to 1564, focusing on Ottoman threat, finance, issues of religion, and balance of power between crown and Estates. [HLA]

33.156 Fred H. Eidlin. *The logic of "normalization": the Soviet intervention in Czechoslovakia of 21 August 1968 and the Czechoslovak response.* Boulder: East European Monographs; distributed by Columbia University Press, 1980. ISBN 0-914710-68-0. ▸ Careful analysis of Soviet aims and tactics in 1968 and Czech and Slovak passive resistance. Stagnant political normality emerged from occupation regime; Czech and Slovak response to it. [HLA]

33.157 Keith Eubank. *Munich.* Norman: University of Oklahoma Press, 1963. ▸ Benchmark study of internal and external politics of Munich Four-Power Agreement and collapse of first Czechoslovak republic. [HLA]

33.158 Robert John Weston Evans. *Rudolf II and his world: a study in intellectual history, 1576–1612.* Rev. ed. New York: Oxford University Press, 1984. ISBN 0-19-821961-X (pbk). ▸ Fascinating discussion of lively court life in Prague under Rudolf II, covering activities of scholars around court and religious problems. [HLA]

33.159 František W. Galan. *Historic structures: the Prague School project, 1928–1946.* Austin: University of Texas Press, 1984. ISBN 0-292-73032-2. ▸ Thorough study of school of historical linguistics begun at Prague in 1920s. Traces growth of one of most influential modern streams of linguistic theory. [HLA]

33.160 Bruce M. Garver. *The Young Czech party, 1874–1901, and the emergence of a multi-party system.* New Haven: Yale University Press, 1978. ISBN 0-300-01781-2. ▸ Excellent on Czech politics in later nineteenth century, focusing on breakup of National party and emergence of Young Czechs. Brief Young Czech success helped emergence of multiparty system based on social interests. [HLA]

33.161 Marketa Goetz-Stankiewicz. *The silenced theatre: Czech playwrights without a stage.* Toronto: University of Toronto Press, 1979. ISBN 0-8020-5426-9. ▸ Czech playwrights include Kohout, Havel, and others. Focus largely on 1970s, some discussion of Stalinism and Prague Spring. Valuable picture of counterculture in "normalized" Czechoslovakia. [HLA]

33.162 Peter Hames. *The Czechoslovak New Wave.* Berkeley: University of California Press, 1985. ISBN 0-520-04859-8. ▸ Standard study of films of New Wave that made Czech and Slovak cinema world renowned. [HLA]

33.163 A. H. Hermann. *A history of the Czechs.* London: Lane, 1975. ISBN 0-7139-0486-0. ▸ Brief survey of Czech history (without Slovaks) highlighting twentieth century; earlier periods also treated. Useful introduction for beginning student. [HLA]

33.164 Frederick G. Heymann. *George of Bohemia, king of heretics.* Princeton: Princeton University Press, 1965. ▸ Classic study of important fifteenth-century Bohemian king. Sees Jiří's reign, dominated by religious and political threats, as example of early modern new monarchy with similarities elsewhere in Europe. [HLA]

33.165 Frederick G. Heymann. *John Žižka and the Hussite revolution.* 1955 ed. Princeton: Princeton University Press, 1969. ▸ Important study of war leader of Hussite movement, now nationalist symbol of militancy. Fits Žižka into context of early fifteenth century, also showing legacy as military tactician. [HLA]

33.166 Frederick G. Heymann. *Poland and Czechoslovakia.* 1966 ed. Westport, Conn.: Greenwood, 1979. ISBN 0-8371-9773-2. ▸ Very useful, brief history of Czechs and Slovaks and their northern neighbor, detailing a relationship often antagonistic, sometimes cooperative. Supplements other survey histories. [HLA]

33.167 Peter Hrubý. *Daydreams and nightmares: Czech communist and ex-communist literature, 1917–1987.* Boulder: East European Monographs; distributed by Columbia University Press, 1990. (East European monographs, 290.) ISBN 0-88033-187-3. ▸ Useful examination of why intellectuals played such important role, through daydreams of better society, in producing nightmare of Czechoslovak socialism. Argues that Communists deliberately subverted intelligentsia. [HLA]

33.168 Peter Hrubý. *Fools and heroes: the changing role of communist intellectuals in Czechoslovakia.* Oxford: Pergamon, 1980. ISBN 0-08-024276-6. ▸ Account of how fools of 1948 became heroes of 1968, focusing on personal experiences of intellectuals. Illuminates intellectual history of postwar Czechoslovakia to Prague Spring. [HLA]

33.169 Kálman Janics. *Czechoslovak policy and the Hungarian minority, 1945–1948.* Gyula Illyés, ed. Stephen Borsody, trans. New York: Social Science Monographs; distributed by Columbia University Press, 1982. (East European monographs, 122.) ISBN

0-914710-99-0. ▸ Adaptation of account by Czechoslovak-Hungarian of policy toward Magyar minority in Czechoslovakia after World War II. Warmly engaged on Hungarian side; substantive, not vituperative, polemic. [HLA]

33.170 Yeshayahu A. Jelinek. *The lust for power: nationalism, Slovakia, and the Communists, 1918–1948.* Boulder: East European Monographs; distributed by Columbia University Press, 1983. (East European monographs, 130.) ISBN 0-88033-019-8. ▸ Valuable analysis of relationship between Slovak nationalism and Slovak Communists. Nationalism always tool of Communists, but communism never subordinated to it. [HLA]

33.171 Yeshayahu A. Jelinek. *The parish republic: Hlinka's Slovak People's party, 1939–1945.* Boulder: East European Quarterly; distributed by Columbia University Press, 1976. (East European monographs, 14.) ISBN 0-914710-07-9. ▸ Standard-setting study of independent Slovak state and its single party, Hlinka Slovak People's party. Shows features of Slovak situation that hampered full development of Nazi-style state. [HLA]

33.172 Owen V. Johnson. *Slovakia, 1918–1938: education and the making of a nation.* Boulder: East European Monographs; distributed by Columbia University Press, 1985. (East European monographs, 180.) ISBN 0-88033-072-4. ▸ Social, cultural, and political development of modern Slovak nation. Includes summary of pre–World War I situation and general national political trends in interwar republic. [HLA]

33.173 Josef Kalvoda. *The genesis of Czechoslovakia.* Boulder: East European Monographs; distributed by Columbia University Press, 1986. (East European monographs, 209.) ISBN 0-88033-106-2. ▸ Thorough, detailed look at activities at home and abroad, leading to emergence of independent Czechoslovakia. Takes revisionist position on influence of Masaryk. [HLA]

33.174 Howard Kaminsky. *A history of the Hussite revolution.* Berkeley: University of California Press, 1967. ▸ Fascinating account of Hussite religious movement in context of late medieval religious and social movements. Considers it both religious reformation and social and religious revolution. [HLA]

33.175 Karel Kaplan. *The short march: the communist takeover in Czechoslovakia.* New York: St. Martin's, 1987. ISBN 0-312-72209-5. ▸ Disillusioned insider's account of politics of communist takeover from 1945 to 1948. Author had access to party archives and uses many otherwise inaccessible documents. [HLA]

33.176 George F. Kennan. *From Prague after Munich: diplomatic papers, 1938–1940.* Princeton: Princeton University Press, 1968. ISBN 0-691-05620-X (cl), 0-691-01063-3 (pbk). ▸ Documents from American diplomat in rump Czechoslovakia who later became architect of containment. Illuminates many aspects of post-Munich situation in Czechoslovakia. [HLA]

33.177 Robert Joseph Kerner. *Bohemia in the eighteenth century: a study in political, economic, and social history with special reference to the reign of Leopold II, 1790–1792.* 2d ed. Joseph F. Zacek, Introduction. Orono, Me.: Academic International, 1969. ISBN 0-87569-007-6. ▸ Unsurpassed on Bohemia during Leopold II's reign by founder of Czech historical studies in United States. Updated with introduction covering developments in literature since its first publication. [HLA/CWI]

33.178 Stanley Buchholz Kimball. *Czech nationalism: a study of the national theater movement, 1845–1883.* Urbana: University of Illinois Press, 1964. ▸ Excellent study of Czech nationalist movement of nineteenth century focusing on language, especially efforts to found national theater as best example of linguistic nationalism in this period. [HLA]

33.179 Stanislav J. Kirschbaum, ed. *Slovak politics: essays on Slovak history in honor of Joseph M. Kirschbaum.* Cleveland, Ohio: Slovak Institute, 1983. ISBN 0-9610908-0-4. ▸ Useful collection of articles on Slovak topics from 1848 to 1948, honoring Slovak autonomist and emigré leader. Focus on leading personalities of Slovak political life, some nationalist overtones. [HLA]

33.180 Stanislav J. Kirschbaum and Anne C. R. Roman, eds. *Reflections on Slovak history.* Toronto: Slovak World Congress, 1987. ISBN 0-921985-00-2. ▸ Mixed collection of conference papers dealing with aspects of Slovak history and politics. [HLA]

33.181 Josef Korbel. *The communist subversion of Czechoslovakia, 1938–1948: the failure of coexistence.* Princeton: Princeton University Press, 1959. ▸ Eyewitness account of Czechoslovak politics during war and reconstruction up to communist takeover of 1948 by diplomat in Beneš government. Sees Communists as bent on monopoly of power throughout period. [HLA]

33.182 Josef Korbel. *Twentieth-century Czechoslovakia: the meanings of its history.* New York: Columbia University Press, 1977. ISBN 0-231-03724-4. ▸ Thoughtful interpretation of his country's modern history by former diplomat of Beneš government. Influence of Masaryk's views on Czech history discussed; focuses on three crisis years of 1938, 1948, and 1968. [HLA]

33.183 Carol Skalnik Leff. *National conflict in Czechoslovakia: the making and remaking of a state, 1918–1987.* Princeton: Princeton University Press, 1988. ISBN 0-691-07768-1. ▸ Czech-Slovak relations, especially question of autonomy versus centralism since foundation of independent Czechoslovakia in 1918. Much of interest cast in social science conceptual framework. [HLA]

33.184 Jozef Lettrich. *History of modern Slovakia.* 1955 ed. Toronto: Slovak Research and Studies Center, 1985. ▸ Most balanced standard survey of Slovak history. Covers developments since 1918 with much on independent Slovak state. Critical of Czech policies, but lacking stridency of some nationalist Slovak accounts. [HLA]

33.185 Radomír Luža. *The transfer of the Sudeten Germans: a study of Czech-German relations, 1933–1962.* New York: New York University Press, 1964. ▸ Fundamental aspects of Czech-German relations as background to Czechoslovak expulsion of Sudeten Germans after World War II. Sets decision in international and temporal context but sympathetic to Czechoslovak view. [HLA]

33.186 Josef Macek. *The Hussite movement in Bohemia.* 1958 ed. New York: AMS Press, 1980. ISBN 0-404-16237-1. ▸ Brief study by Czech historian dismissed after 1968. Classic Marxist account of Hussite movement, stressing social-revolutionary aspects. [HLA]

33.187 Paul R. Magocsi. *The shaping of a national identity: Subcarpathian Rus', 1848–1948.* Cambridge, Mass.: Harvard University Press, 1978. ISBN 0-674-80579-8. ▸ Exhaustive study of how Subcarpathian Rusyns were exposed to and adopted nationalism. Subcarpathian Rus' was easternmost part of Czechoslovakia from 1918 to 1939. Rich and challenging. [GS]

33.188 Victor S. Mamatey and Radomír Luža. *A history of the Czechoslovak Republic, 1918–1948.* Princeton: Princeton University Press, 1973. ISBN 0-691-05205-0. ▸ Multiple authors provide chronologically arranged essays on significant developments in Czechoslovak state from independence to communist takeover. Quickly became English standard for modern Czechoslovak history. [HLA]

33.189 Tomáš G. Masaryk. *The making of a state: memories and observations, 1914–1918.* 1927 ed. Henry Wickham Steed, ed. and trans. New York: Fertig, 1969. ▸ Masaryk's own account of wartime experiences in struggle for Czechoslovak independence. Gives good flavor of Masaryk's unique philosophical politics. [HLA]

33.190 Tomáš G. Masaryk. *The meaning of Czech history.* René

Wellek, ed. Peter Kussi, trans. Chapel Hill: University of North Carolina Press, 1974. ISBN 0-8078-1227-7. ‣ Masaryk's thoughts on Czech history from various sources including his *The Czech Question*. Very valuable for illuminating Masaryk's idiosyncratic interpretation of Czech history and his place in Czech national thought. [HLA]

33.191 Tomáš G. Masaryk. *President Masaryk tells his story.* 1935 ed. Karel Čapek, interviewer. New York: Arno, 1971. ISBN 0-405-02739-3 (cl), 0-405-02739-7 (pbk). ‣ Fascinating interviews with Masaryk on number of contemporary issues. [HLA]

33.192 Vojtěch Mastný. *The Czechs under Nazi rule: the failure of national resistance, 1939–1942.* New York: Columbia University Press, 1971. ISBN 0-231-03303-6. ‣ Painstaking study of Czechs' reaction to political dismemberment and occupation. Domestic resistance crushed by Germans by 1942, not to reappear until closing days of war. [HLA]

33.193 Kevin McDermott. *The Czech Red Unions, 1918–1929: a study of their relations with the Communist party and the Moscow Internationals.* Boulder: East European Monographs; distributed by Columbia University Press, 1988. (East European monographs, 239.) ISBN 0-88033-136-4. ‣ Detailed analysis of impact of Czechoslovak Communist party and Soviet agencies on pro-communist Czechoslovak unions. Concludes unions preserved some autonomy of action until 1929. [HLA]

33.194 Joseph A. Mikus. *Slovakia and the Slovaks.* Washington, D.C.: Three Continents, 1977. ISBN 0-914478-88-5 (cl), 0-914478-89-3 (pbk). ‣ Survey of Slovak history, culture, and politics, directed at countering perceived Hungarian or Czech colonial and atheistic communist distortions. Classic example of history refracted through nationalist prism. [HLA]

33.195 Zdeněk Mlynář. *Nightfrost in Prague: the end of humane socialism.* Paul Wilson, trans. New York: Karz, 1980. ISBN 0-918294-08-8. ‣ Participant's account of Soviet-led intervention in Czechoslovakia in 1968. Focuses on personalities; one of main heroes is Zdeněk Mlynář. [HLA]

33.196 Zdeňka Munzer, ed. *We were and we shall be: the Czechoslovak spirit through the centuries.* Charles Granville and Villa V. Bechyně, trans. Edvard Beneš, Introduction. New York: Ungar, 1941. ‣ Collection of translations published during World War II to represent Czechoslovakia to allied public. Still valuable as collection of sources for Czech history, especially Czech nationalism. [HLA]

33.197 Martin R. Myant. *The Czechoslovak economy, 1945–1988: the battle for economic reform.* Cambridge: Cambridge University Press, 1989. ISBN 0-521-35314-9. ‣ Thorough survey of economic history of Czechoslovakia under socialism. Emphasis on (failed) attempts to reform Stalinist, Soviet-style economic model imposed after 1948. [HLA]

33.198 Martin R. Myant. *Socialism and democracy in Czechoslovakia, 1945–1948.* New York: Cambridge University Press, 1981. ISBN 0-521-23668-1. ‣ Valuable study of crucial postwar years when, according to author, socialist development genuinely popular. Explanation for reasons why Soviet model was imitated, rather than Czechoslovak form of socialism developed. [HLA]

33.199 Arne Novák. *Czech literature.* William E. Harkins, ed. Peter Kussi, trans. Ann Arbor: Michigan Slavic Publications, 1976. (Joint Committee on Eastern Europe, Publication series, 4.) ‣ Translation of classic literary history by twentieth-century Czech scholar. Very useful introduction to subject with few works in English. [HLA]

33.200 Otakar Odložilík. *The Hussite king: Bohemia in European affairs, 1440–1471.* New Brunswick, N.J.: Rutgers University Press, 1965. ‣ Carefully researched work devoting attention to

international setting of Jiří's reign and his precocious efforts to organize union of European states to preserve peace. [HLA]

33.201 Otakar Odložilík. "Modern Czechoslovak historiography." *Slavonic and East European review* 30.2 (1952) 376–93. ISSN 0037-6795. ‣ Still useful as survey of development in Czechoslovak historiography from late nineteenth through mid-twentieth century. [HLA]

33.202 Věra Olivová. *The doomed democracy: Czechoslovakia in a disrupted Europe, 1914–38.* George Theiner, trans. Montreal: McGill-Queen's University Press, 1972. ISBN 0-7735-0152-5. ‣ History of interwar Czechoslovakia (published 1968). Positive attitude to aspects of First Republic; gives good account of Czechoslovak policies during era of appeasement. Marxist approach. [HLA]

33.203 Lawrence D. Orton. *The Prague Slav Congress of 1848.* Boulder: East European Monographs; distributed by Columbia University Press, 1978. (East European monographs, 46.) ISBN 0-914710-39-7. ‣ Only English-language study of major event of 1848 Revolution in Bohemia, not just for Czechs, but for all Slavs. Evaluates both contemporary and subsequent reactions to congress, while detailing its origins and course. [HLA]

33.204 Stanley Z. Pech. *The Czech Revolution of 1848.* Chapel Hill: University of North Carolina Press, 1969. ‣ Wide-ranging, thematic as well as chronological study. Separate chapters analyze role of students, peasantry, and women. Author sympathizes with radicals, not liberal leaders like Palacký or Havlíček. [HLA]

33.205 Theodore Prochánka. *The Second Republic: the disintegration of post-Munich Czechoslovakia, October 1938–March 1939.* Boulder: East European Monographs; distributed by Columbia University Press, 1981. (East European monographs, 90.) ISBN 0-914710-84-2. ‣ Well-balanced study of Czechoslovakia from Munich to Nazi occupation. Follows both diplomatic constellation and domestic events, especially Czech-Slovak political squabbling over autonomy. [HLA]

33.206 Barbara K. Reinfeld. *Karel Havlíček (1821–1856): a national liberation leader of the Czech renascence.* Boulder: East European Monographs; distributed by Columbia University Press, 1982. (East European monographs, 98.) ISBN 0-914710-92-3. ‣ Political and literary biography of second great nationalist leader of mid-nineteenth century, after Palacký. Good discussion of publicist and satirist Havlíček's major role in developing Czech nationalism. [HLA]

33.207 Hans Renner. *A history of Czechoslovakia since 1945.* Evelien Hurst-Buist, trans. London: Routledge, 1989. ISBN 0-415-00363-6. ‣ Useful short survey of Czechoslovak history from end of World War II to eve of Velvet Revolution. No new interpretation, but accessible introduction. [HLA]

33.208 Condoleezza Rice. *The Soviet Union and the Czechoslovak army, 1948–1983: uncertain allegiance.* Princeton: Princeton University Press, 1984. ISBN 0-691-06921-2. ‣ Relationship between Czechoslovak and Soviet armies within framework of Warsaw Pact and post-1968 treaties stationing Soviet troops on Czechoslovak soil. Suggests lingering doubts in Soviet minds about Czechoslovak armed forces. [HLA]

33.209 Hubert Řípka. *Czechoslovakia enslaved: the story of the communist coup d'état.* 1950 ed. Westport, Conn.: Hyperion, 1979. ISBN 0-88355-710-X. ‣ Participant's account of communist takeover in 1948. Generally supportive of Beneš, but not without criticism of his role and that of other politicians, notably Socialists. [HLA]

33.210 Andrew Rossos. "Czech historiography, Part 1." *Canadian Slavonic papers* 24.3 (1982) 245–60. ISSN 0008-5006. ‣ Most up-to-date survey of Czech historical writing; excellent grounding in growth of discipline and orientation among various schools of interpretation. Part 1 covers to end of eighteenth century. See also 33.211. [HLA]

33.211 Andrew Rossos. "Czech historiography, Part 2." *Canadian Slavonic papers* 24.4 (1982) 359–85. ISSN 0008-5006. ▸ Continuation of excellent survey of Czech historiography (33.210), concentrating on nineteenth and twentieth centuries. [HLA]

33.212 Eva Schmidt-Hartmann. *Thomas G. Masaryk's realism: origins of a Czech political concept.* Munich: Oldenbourg, 1984. (Veröffentlichungen des Collegium Carolinum, 52.) ISBN 3-486-51851-8. ▸ Thorough study of development of Masaryk's political philosophy, especially concept of political realism. Contributes to recent reevaluation of Masaryk's role in Czechoslovak history. [HLA]

33.213 R. W. Seton-Watson. *A history of the Czechs and Slovaks.* 1943 ed. Hamden, Conn.: Archon, 1965. ▸ Probably best history of Czechs and Slovaks in English, by founder of historical studies of region in Anglo-American world. Deservedly a classic. [HLA]

33.214 R. W. Seton-Watson, ed. *Slovakia then and now: a political survey by many Slovak authors.* London: Allen & Unwin, 1931. ▸ Essays by twenty-five leading Slovak historians of interwar Czechoslovakia on aspects of contemporary conditions with some contrasts to previous life under Hungary. Lengthy introduction by editor. Available on microtransparency from New Haven: Human Relations Area Files, 1955. [HLA]

33.215 William Shawcross. *Dubček: Dubček and Czechoslovakia, 1968–1990.* Rev. ed. London: Hogarth, 1990. ISBN 0-7012-0899-6. ▸ Vivid, sympathetic biography of leader of Prague Spring by journalist with remarkable knack for being in right place at right time. [HLA]

33.216 Milan Šimečka. *The restoration of order: the normalization of Czechoslovakia, 1969–1976.* A. G. Brain, trans. London: Verso, 1984. ISBN 0-86091-081-4 (cl), 0-86091-786-X (pbk). ▸ Better than any other work of comparable length, gives idea of life under socialism. Addresses issues of individual compromise and resistance under all-pervasive political system. [HLA]

33.217 H. Gordon Skilling. *Charter 77 and human rights in Czechoslovakia.* London: Allen & Unwin, 1981. ISBN 0-04-321026-0. ▸ Pathbreaking study of emergence of Charter 77, detailing origins, personnel, methods, accomplishments, and limitations of intellectual dissident movement. Includes translations of many significant Charter 77 documents. [HLA]

33.218 H. Gordon Skilling. *Czechoslovakia's interrupted revolution.* Princeton: Princeton University Press, 1976. ISBN 0-691-05234-4 (cl), 0-691-10040-3 (pbk). ▸ Wealth of detail makes this the standard reference on 1968. Analyzes participation of social groups and national minorities in effective combination of chronological and thematic approaches. [HLA]

33.219 Josef Škvorecký. *All the bright young men and women: a personal history of the Czech cinema.* Michael Schonberg, trans. Toronto: Martin, 1971. ISBN 0-88778-056-3. ▸ Engaging memoir of Czechoslovak intellectual milieu from which New Wave cinema sprang. Illuminating anecdotes and telling criticism of films, not intended as thorough scholarly discussion. [HLA]

33.220 M. Spinka. *John Hus: a biography.* Princeton: Princeton University Press, 1968. ▸ Biography of Czech reformer. Covers early life, education, theology, and reform ideals; trial and conviction of heresy; and execution by Council of Constance. [KP]

33.221 Eugen Steiner. *The Slovak dilemma.* Cambridge: Cambridge University Press, 1973. ISBN 0-521-20050-4. ▸ Discussion of perplexities of Slovakia's modern history with refreshing degree of detachment from nationalist stereotypes. Author self-described Slovak Jewish twice-disillusioned former Communist. [HLA]

33.222 Norman Stone and Eduard Strouhal, eds. *Czechoslovakia: crossroads and crises, 1918–1988.* New York: St. Martin's, 1989. ISBN 0-312-03201-3. ▸ Useful collection of essays published to commemorate seventieth anniversary of founding of Czechoslovak state. [HLA]

33.223 Zdeněk L. Suda. *Zealots and rebels: a history of the ruling Communist party of Czechoslovakia.* Stanford, Calif.: Hoover Institution Press, 1980. ISBN 0-8179-7342-7. ▸ Survey of development of Communist party of Czechoslovakia from break with Social Democrats through normalization. Excellent starting point for students of postwar Czech and Slovak political history. [HLA]

33.224 Ivan Svítak. *The Czechoslovak experiment, 1968–1969.* New York: Columbia University Press, 1971. ISBN 0-231-03462-8. ▸ Collection of essays, speeches, and articles by author during Prague Spring. Reflects his iconoclastic Marxist philosophy and gives flavor of part of reform movement. Not an analytical study. [HLA]

33.225 Roman Szporluk. *The political thought of Thomas G. Masaryk.* Boulder: East European Monographs; distributed by Columbia University Press, 1981. (East European monographs, 85.) ISBN 0-914710-79-6. ▸ Significant analysis of Masaryk's political ideas, recognizing flaws in his thought and in state it helped shape, but affirming Masaryk's identification with and contribution to his nation and its state. [HLA]

33.226 Edward Taborský. *President Edvard Beneš between East and West, 1938–1948.* Stanford, Calif.: Hoover Institution Press, 1981. (Hoover Press publications, 246.) ISBN 0-8179-7461-X. ▸ Beneš's years in exile and return to his native land, by his personal secretary. Does not shirk difficult issues of Beneš's performance during these critical years, though retains certain sympathy for him. [HLA]

33.227 Alice Teichová. *The Czechoslovak economy, 1918–1980.* London: Routledge, 1988. ISBN 0-415-00376-8. ▸ Most complete survey available in English of development of Czechoslovak economy in twentieth century. [HLA]

33.228 Alice Teichová. *An economic background to Munich: international business and Czechoslovakia, 1918–1938.* London: Cambridge University Press, 1974. ISBN 0-521-20065-2. ▸ Interesting view of economies of interwar era, discussing influence of international economic factors on foreign policy. [HLA]

33.229 Samuel Harrison Thomson. *Czechoslovakia in European history.* 1953 ed. Hamden, Conn.: Archon, 1965. ▸ English-language classic, now dated in many respects, but still useful as starting point for study. [HLA]

33.230 Paul Vyšný. *Neo-Slavism and the Czechs, 1898–1914.* Cambridge: Cambridge University Press, 1977. ISBN 0-521-21230-8. ▸ Excellent account of last gasp of nineteenth-century political pan-Slavism, especially detailing role of Czechs, Karel Kramář among most important. [HLA]

33.231 Bernard Wheaton. *Radical socialism in Czechoslovakia: Bohumír Šmeral, the Czech road to socialism, and the origins of the Czechoslovak Communist party, 1917–1921.* Boulder: East European Monographs; distributed by Columbia University Press, 1986. (East European monographs, 213.) ISBN 0-88033-110-0. ▸ Detailed account of creation of Czechoslovak Communist party through split with old Social Democrats, focusing on Bohumír Šmeral's political position. Suggests that Czechoslovak socialism originated here. [HLA]

33.232 Elizabeth Wiskemann. *Czechs and Germans: a study of the struggle in the historic provinces of Bohemia and Moravia.* 2d ed. London: Macmillan and St. Martin's, 1967. ▸ Classic account of Czech-German relations under Austria and during interwar period. Much detail on politics of Henlein's Sudetendeutsche Partei leading up to Munich crisis and aftermath. [HLA]

33.233 Sharon L. Wolchik. *Czechoslovakia in transition: politics, economics, and society.* London: Pinter, 1991. ISBN 0-86187-408-0 (cl), 0-86187-409-9 (pbk). ▸ Survey of political, economic, and social development of Czechoslovakia, focusing on recent period with some historical introduction. Carries story over into transition from totalitarianism to pluralist democracy. [HLA]

33.234 Joseph F. Zacek. *Palacký: the historian as scholar and nationalist.* The Hague: Mouton, 1970. ▸ Excellent English-language biography of this most important figure of Czech nineteenth-century life. Based on wide range of secondary sources with judicious use of primary documents. [HLA]

33.235 Zbyněk A. B. Zeman. *The Masaryks: the making of Czechoslovakia.* London: Weidenfeld & Nicolson, 1976. ISBN 0-297-77096-9. ▸ Balanced, combined biography of father and son, presents account of their lives and history of country they shaped. Includes their views and those of their opponents. [HLA]

33.236 Paul E. Zinner. *Communist strategy and tactics in Czechoslovakia, 1918–1948.* 1963 ed. Westport, Conn.: Greenwood, 1975. ISBN 0-8371-8550-5. ▸ Painstaking analysis of policies of Communist party of Czechoslovakia from 1918 to takeover of 1948. Emphasizes continuity in communist policy aimed at establishing total monopoly of power. [HLA]

SEE ALSO
30.147 William E. Wright. *Serf, seigneur, and sovereign.*
47.418 Betty M. Unterberger. *The United States, revolutionary Russia, and the rise of Czechoslovakia.*
47.455 D. S. Perman. *The shaping of the Czechoslovak state.*

GREECE

33.237 George M. Alexander. *The prelude to the Truman Doctrine: British policy in Greece, 1944–1947.* Oxford: Clarendon, 1982. ISBN 0-19-822653-5. ▸ Assumption by United States of Britain's traditional role as Greece's principal external patron. Sympathetic to British motives, arguing that London sought to boost moderate center rather than reactionary right. [RC]

33.238 Alexis Alexandris. *The Greek minority of Istanbul and Greco-Turkish relations, 1918–1974.* 2d ed. Athens: Centre for Asia Minor Studies, 1992. ISBN 960-85021-4-4. ▸ Decline of last remnant of the Greek East, communities of Istanbul, Imvros, and Tenedos, which were exempted from 1922 Exchange of Populations. Judicious treatment using Turkish as well as Greek sources. [RC]

33.239 Marc D. Angel. *The Jews of Rhodes: the history of a Sephardic community.* New York: Sepher-Hermon, 1978. ISBN 0-87203-072-5. ▸ Jews of Rhodes never Greek citizens before virtual destruction in World War II. One of few accessible studies of Sefardic community, remnants of which are now scattered worldwide. [RC]

33.240 Helen Angelomatis-Tsougarakis. *The eve of the Greek revival: British travellers' perceptions of early nineteenth-century Greece.* London: Routledge, 1990. ISBN 0-415-03482-5. ▸ Geographic setting, institutions, education, culture, and economy of Greek lands in critical decades before independence. Careful distillation of what may be gleaned from travelers' accounts. [RC]

33.241 Gerasimos Augustinos. *Consciousness and history: nationalist critics of Greek society, 1897–1914.* Boulder: East European Quarterly; distributed by Columbia University Press, 1977. (East European monographs, 32.) ISBN 0-914710-25-7. ▸ Intellectual introspection consequent on defeat in Thirty Day War with Turkey (1897). Stimulating exercise in intellectual history. [RC]

33.242 Antony Beevor. *Crete: the battle and the resistance.* London: Murray, 1991. ISBN 0-7195-4857-8. ▸ German airborne invasion of Crete in May 1941, subsequent occupation, and British-

supported resistance. Up to date, making use of Ultra intelligence material. [RC]

33.243 Martin Blinkhorn and Thanos Veremis, eds. *Modern Greece: nationalism and nationality.* Athens: Sage-Eliamep, 1990. ISBN 960-7061-00-4. ▸ Five contributions representative of best writing by younger generation of Greek scholars on nationalism, brigandage, irredentism, Macedonian question, and recent trends in historiography. [RC]

33.244 John Campbell and Philip Sherrard. *Modern Greece.* New York: Praeger, 1968. ▸ Indispensable introduction to subject distinguished by emphasis on nature of Greek society and its underlying value systems, on role of Orthodox church, and on cultural developments. [RC]

33.245 Mary Jo Clogg and Richard Clogg, comps. *Greece.* Oxford: ABC-Clio, 1980. ISBN 0-903450-30-5. ▸ Annotated listing of 830 titles (almost all in English) relating to most aspects of Greek history and society. Comprehensively indexed. [RC]

33.246 Richard Clogg. *A concise history of Greece.* Cambridge: Cambridge University Press, 1991. ISBN 0-521-37228-3 (cl), 0-521-37830-3 (pbk). ▸ Introductory history of Greece from rise of national movement in eighteenth century to fall of Panellenio Sosialistiko Kinema (PASOK) socialist government in 1989. Numerous illustrations and maps. [RC]

33.247 Richard Clogg. *Parties and elections in Greece: the search for legitimacy.* Durham, N.C.: Duke University Press, 1987. ISBN 0-8223-0794-4 (cl), 0-8223-0823-1 (pbk). ▸ Thorough discussion of politics since World War II. Numerous tables of electoral statistics with examples of key political texts. [RC/GS]

33.248 Richard Clogg. *Politics and the academy: Arnold Toynbee and the Koraes Chair.* London: Cass and King's College, Centre of Contemporary Studies, 1986. ISBN 0-7146-3290-2. ▸ Greek donors forced Toynbee's involuntary resignation from modern Greek studies chair at King's College, London, in 1924. Classic study of dangers to historical scholarship implicit in reliance on funding from interested parties. [RC/GS]

33.249 Richard Clogg. *A short history of modern Greece.* 2d ed. Cambridge: Cambridge University Press, 1986. ISBN 0-521-32837-3 (cl), 0-521-33804-2 (pbk). ▸ Standard short history of Greece since fall of Constantinople. Main focus on twentieth century with emphasis on political history. [RC/GS]

33.250 Richard Clogg, ed. *The struggle for Greek independence: essays to mark the 150th anniversary of the Greek War of Independence.* Hamden, Conn.: Archon, 1973. ISBN 0-208-01303-2. ▸ Scholarly essays covering various aspects of national movement and of 1820s War of Independence. [RC/GS]

33.251 Richard Clogg, ed. and trans. *The movement for Greek independence, 1770–1821: a collection of documents.* London: Macmillan, 1976. ISBN 0-333-19275-3. ▸ Development of movement for Greek independence in crucial decades before 1821 as seen through contemporary documents, many translated from Greek. [RC]

33.252 Dimitri Constas, ed. *The Greek-Turkish conflict in the 1990s: domestic and external influences.* London: Macmillan, 1991. ISBN 0-333-53927-3. ▸ Analysis of critical issue in Greek foreign policy during last quarter of twentieth century: relations with (much larger) neighbor and former ruler, Turkey. Essays cover most aspects of difficult relationship. [RC]

33.253 Theodore A. Couloumbis. *The United States, Greece, and Turkey: the troubled triangle.* New York: Praeger, 1983. ISBN 0-03-052551-9 (cl), 0-03-052546-2 (pbk). ▸ Unhappy course of post–World War II relations with Greece's principal external patron, United States, and largest neighbor, Turkey. Balanced, well-informed introduction to most sensitive dimensions of current foreign policy. [RC]

33.254 Charles W. Crawley. *The question of Greek independence: a study of British policy in the Near East, 1821–1833.* 1930 ed. New York: Fertig, 1973. ‣ Dated but still useful diplomatic history in traditional mode, placing Greek struggle for independence in wider international context and explaining how Britain, Russia, and France came to be protecting powers. [RC]

33.255 Nancy Crawshaw. *The Cyprus revolt: an account of the struggle for union with Greece.* London: Allen & Unwin, 1978. ISBN 0-04-940053-3. ‣ Failure of campaign for *enosis* (union) with Greece and emergence in 1960 of independent state, in negation of principle of self-determination. Well-documented study carries story to aftermath of 1974 Turkish invasion. [RC]

33.256 Douglas Dakin. *The Greek struggle in Macedonia, 1897–1913.* Thessalonike, Greece: Institute for Balkan Studies, 1966. (Hetaireia Makedonikon Spoudon, Hidryma Mleton Chersonesou tou Haimou, Ekdoseis, 89.) ‣ History of Macedonian revolutionary movements from Greek perspective. Chapter on British and French policy. Excellent research; makes good use of Greek sources. Contains small factual errors about Slav-based Macedonian movements. [RC/RS/PWS/DMP]

33.257 Douglas Dakin. *The unification of Greece, 1770–1923.* New York: St. Martin's, 1972. ‣ Greek history seen as story of four wars of independence, hence heavy concentration on foreign factors. Useful tables. [RC]

33.258 Rae Dalven. *The Jews of Ioannina.* Philadelphia: Cadmus, 1990. ISBN 0-930685-03-2. ‣ Before Holocaust, most Greek Jews were Spanish-speaking Sefardim. Those of Ioannina were Romaniot, descended from Byzantine times. Disorganized mine of information; one of few accessible studies of Greek Jewry. [RC]

33.259 *Ellada: istoria kai politismos* (Greece: history and culture). 7 vols. Thessalonike, Greece: Malliaris-Paideia, 1982. ‣ Comprehensive coverage of Greek history from ancient times to present. Deals also with geography, politics, economy, and culture. [RC]

33.260 Charles A. Frazee. *The Orthodox church and independent Greece, 1821–1852.* Cambridge: Cambridge University Press, 1969. ISBN 0-521-07247-6. ‣ Fate of Orthodox church during War of Independence, subsequent ending of its privileged position, and its subordination to state. Scholarly study of church-state relations at critical period. [RC]

33.261 Great Britain, Naval Intelligence Division. *Dodecanese.* 2d ed. London: Admiralty, Naval Intelligence Division, 1943. ‣ History, physical and economic geography of Dodecanese while still under Italian rule. Dated but still useful. [RC]

33.262 Great Britain, Naval Intelligence Division. *Greece.* 3 vols. London: Admiralty, Naval Intelligence Division, 1944–45. ‣ History, physical and economic geography with excellent maps. Inevitably dated but still of primary importance. [RC]

33.263 Peter Hammond. *The waters of Marah: the present state of the Greek church.* New York: Macmillan, 1956. ‣ Church of Greece during difficult years of post–World War II civil war. Rare glimpse of church at grassroots level by sympathetic observer. [RC]

33.264 George P. Henderson. *The revival of Greek thought, 1620–1830.* Edinburgh: Scottish Academic; distributed by Chatto & Windus, 1971. ISBN 0-7011-1767-2. ‣ Study of neo-Hellenic Enlightenment, crucial element in development of national movement in late eighteenth and early nineteenth centuries. Inclined to overstress originality of contribution of Greek illuminati. [RC]

33.265 Michael Herzfeld. *Ours once more: folklore, ideology, and the making of modern Greece.* 1982 ed. New York: Pella, 1986. ISBN 0-918618-32-0. ‣ Development of folklore studies in independent kingdom. Lively analysis of political uses of folklore in constructing national identity. [RC]

33.266 Robin D. S. Higham. *Diary of a disaster: British aid to Greece, 1940–1941.* Lexington: University Press of Kentucky, 1986. ISBN 0-8131-1564-7. ‣ Study of Operation Lustre, British attempt to shore up Greek resistance to Italian and German invasions. Highly critical of campaign imposed by Churchill on his commanders and doomed from outset. [RC]

33.267 George F. Hill. *The Ottoman province: the British colony, 1571–1948.* Vol. 4 of *A history of Cyprus.* 1940–52 ed. Harry Luke, ed. Cambridge: Cambridge University Press, 1972. ISBN 0-521-05262-9. ‣ History of only area of substantial Greek settlement in Near East that remains outside boundaries of Greek state. Dated but still useful. [RC]

33.268 John Louis Hondros. *Occupation and resistance: the Greek agony, 1941–44.* New York: Pella, 1983. ISBN 0-918618-19-3 (pbk). ‣ Analysis of German, Italian, and Bulgarian occupation of Greece during World War II. Balanced; makes good use of German sources. [RC]

33.269 John O. Iatrides. *Revolt in Athens: the Greek communist second round, 1944–1945.* Princeton: Princeton University Press, 1972. ISBN 0-691-05203-4. ‣ Discussion of communist insurgency in Athens in December 1944 and its suppression by British forces. Level-headed account of subject that has aroused much controversy. [RC]

33.270 Romilly J. H. Jenkins. *The Dilessi murders.* London: Longman, 1961. ‣ Study of capture, attempted ransom, and murder of British aristocrats in 1870; ramifications for domestic politics and Anglo-Greek relations. Jaundiced view of nineteenth-century politics with much quoted disquisitions. [RC]

33.271 Howard Jones. *A new kind of war: America's global strategy and the Truman Doctrine in Greece.* New York: Oxford University Press, 1989. ISBN 0-19-504581-5. ‣ Looks at Greece as key battlefield of cold war. Truman Doctrine and massive military and economic assistance to anticommunist forces in 1946–49 civil war as pattern for global containment of communism. [RC]

33.272 Bernard Kayser et al., eds. *Oikonomikos kai koinonikos atlas tes Ellados* (Economic and social atlas of Greece). Athens: National Statistical Service of Greece, 1964. ‣ Expression in map form of valuable statistical data, mainly derived from 1961 census. [RC]

33.273 Alexander Kitroeff. *The Greeks in Egypt, 1919–1937: ethnicity and class.* London: Ithaca Press for Oxford University, St. Antony's College, Middle East Centre, 1989. (St. Antony's Middle East monographs, 20.) ISBN 0-86372-109-5. ‣ Important study of one of most significant of Greek diaspora communities, which, at its peak, numbered over 100,000. Stresses stratified nature of community. [RC]

33.274 Paschalis M. Kitromilides and Marios L. Evriviades, comps. *Cyprus.* Oxford: ABC-Clio, 1982. ISBN 0-903450-40-2. ‣ Annotated listing of 689 titles (almost all in English) relating to most aspects of Cypriot history and society. Comprehensively indexed. [RC]

33.275 Evangelos Kofos. *Greece and the Eastern crisis, 1875–1878.* Thessalonike, Greece: Institute for Balkan Studies, 1975. ‣ Thorough discussion of impact of Balkan crisis of 1870s on Greece, a marginal player not party to 1878 Congress of Berlin. [RC]

33.276 Giannes S. Koliopoulos. *Brigands with a cause: brigandage and irredentism in modern Greece, 1821–1912.* Oxford: Clarendon, 1987. ISBN 0-19-822863-5. ‣ Attempt by Greek state both to tame brigandage and to exploit it in furtherance of irredentism. Fine study arguing value system of brigands had profound impact on wider society. [RC]

33.277 Giannes S. Koliopoulos. *Greece and the British connection, 1935–1941.* Oxford: Clarendon, 1977. ISBN 0-19-822523-7. ▸ Balanced, thoroughly documented discussion of Greek-British relations, political and strategic, at time of restoration of King George II and Metaxas dictatorship. [RC]

33.278 Adamantios Koraes. "Report on the present state of civilization in Greece." In *Nationalism in Asia and Africa.* Elie Kedourie, ed., pp. 153–87. London: Weidenfeld & Nicolson, 1970. ISBN 0-297-00357-7 (cl), 0-297-00358-5 (pbk). ▸ Essay on background to Greek national movement. Contemporary analysis of considerable perspicacity and modernity by leading figure of neo-Hellenic Enlightenment. [RC]

33.279 D. George Kousoulas. *Revolution and defeat: the story of the Greek Communist party.* London: Oxford University Press, 1965. ▸ Discussion of rise of Greek communism from interwar obscurity to wartime predominance and eventual defeat in 1946–49 civil war. Unsympathetic to communist aspirations. [RC]

33.280 Keith R. Legg. *Politics in modern Greece.* Stanford, Calif.: Stanford University Press, 1969. ISBN 0-8047-0705-7. ▸ Description of political system on eve of 1967 military dictatorship with particular emphasis on process of recruitment to political elite and role of patronage. Rare analysis by Western political scientist. [RC]

33.281 George B. Leon. *Greece and the great powers, 1914–1917.* Thessalonike, Greece: Institute for Balkan Studies, 1974. (Institute for Balkan studies, Publications, 143.) ▸ Analysis of interplay of international and domestic politics during World War I as country riven by National Schism, division between supporters of Entente and advocates of neutrality. [RC]

33.282 George B. Leon. *The Greek socialist movement and the First World War: the road to unity.* Boulder: East European Quarterly; distributed by Columbia University Press, 1976. (East European monographs, 18.) ISBN 0-914710-11-7. ▸ Study of impact of World War I on small, fragmented, and hitherto marginal Greek labor movement. In Europe, war led to fragmentation of socialist movement; catalyst for unification in Greece. [RC]

33.283 Michael Llewellyn-Smith. *Ionian vision: Greece in Asia Minor, 1919–1922.* New York: St. Martin's, 1973. ▸ Background to and course of disastrous occupation of western Asia Minor between 1919 and 1922, spelling end of irredentist vision of Great Idea. Authoritative coverage of military, international, and domestic dimensions. [RC]

33.284 John C. Loulis. *The Greek Communist party, 1940–1944.* London: Croom Helm, 1982. ISBN 0-7099-1612-4. ▸ Role of Communist party during critical years of German, Italian, and Bulgarian occupation. Good use of communist Greek sources. [RC]

33.285 Ionnes Makriyannis. *The memoirs of General Makiriannis, 1797–1864.* H. A. Lidderdale, ed. and trans. London: Oxford University Press, 1966. ▸ Vivid account of personal experiences of prominent participant in Greek Revolution. Good accounts of political and social controversies, as well as material on reign of King Othon through 1843. [GS]

33.286 George Th. Mavrogordatos. *Stillborn republic: social coalitions and party strategies in Greece, 1922–1936.* Berkeley: University of California Press, 1983. ISBN 0-520-04358-8. ▸ Groundbreaking attempt to make sense of tumultuous interwar Greek politics. Posits underlying conflict between Venizelist modernizers (identified with Republic) and anti-Venizelist adherents of traditional order (identified with monarchy). [RC]

33.287 Mark Mazower. *Greece and the inter-war economic crisis.* Oxford: Clarendon, 1991. ISBN 0-19-820205-9. ▸ Fine monograph on economic history; impact of Great Depression on Greek economy and its repercussions for political system. Despite relatively rapid recovery, slide to authoritarian dictatorship in 1936 unchecked. [RC]

33.288 William H. McNeill. *The metamorphosis of Greece since World War II.* Chicago: University of Chicago Press, 1978. ISBN 0-226-56156-9. ▸ Stimulating if sometimes speculative study of rapid pace of social and economic change; relative success of urbanization attributed to transference of rural values to cities through internal migration. [RC]

33.289 William Miller. *Greek life in town and country.* London: Newnes, 1905. ▸ Anatomy of Greece at turn of century. One of most informative and perceptive books ever written about country by acute and sympathetic observer. Available on microfilm from New Haven: Micrographic Systems of Connecticut, 1988. [RC]

33.290 Charles C. Moskos. *Greek Americans: struggle and success.* 2d ed. New Brunswick, N.J.: Transaction, 1989. ISBN 0-88738-778-0. ▸ History of Greek-American community as process of becoming middle class. Lively and up-to-date analysis informed by insights of sociologist. [RC]

33.291 Nicos P. Mouzelis. *Modern Greece: facets of underdevelopment.* New York: Holmes & Meier, 1978. ISBN 0-8419-0357-3. ▸ Essays on capitalism, class structure, underdevelopment, and dictatorship. Sophisticated neo-Marxist analysis of distorted evolution of Greek society. [RC]

33.292 S. Victor Papacosma. *The military in Greek politics: the 1909 coup d'état.* Kent, Ohio: Kent State University Press, 1977. ISBN 0-87338-208-0. ▸ Setting pattern for subsequent military interventions, 1909 coup marked major turning point in Greek history. One of few scholarly analyses of role of military in Greek politics. [RC]

33.293 Theodoros H. Papadopoullos. *Studies and documents relating to the history of the Greek church and people under Turkish domination.* 1952 2d ed. Aldershot, England: Variorum, 1990. ISBN 0-86078-278-6. ▸ Text of poem on eighteenth-century controversy about need for non-Orthodox to be baptised on conversion. Prefaced with much valuable information about Greek church. Disorganized but essential reading. [RC]

33.294 Procopis Papastratis. *British policy towards Greece during the Second World War, 1941–1944.* Cambridge: Cambridge University Press, 1984. ISBN 0-521-24342-4. ▸ Detailed analysis of contradictions resulting from Foreign Office's support for unpopular monarch and military's wish to maximize resistance, entailing support for king's enemies. [RC]

33.295 John A. Petropoulos. *Politics and statecraft in the kingdom of Greece, 1833–1843.* Princeton: Princeton University Press, 1968. ▸ Indispensable guide to nature of Greek politics during nonconstitutional period of King Otto's reign when political allegiances tended to revolve around protecting powers Britain, France, and Russia. [RC/SM]

33.296 Charles Price, ed. *Greeks in Australia.* Canberra: Australian National University Press; distributed by International Scholarly Book Services, 1975. ISBN 0-7081-0571-8. ▸ Profile of more than 200,000 Greeks who, since World War II, have migrated to Australia, second largest Greek community outside Greece, after United States. Six papers of varying quality. [RC]

33.297 Heinz A. Richter. *British intervention in Greece: from Varkiza to civil war, February 1945 to August 1946.* Marion Sarafis, trans. London: Merlin, 1985. ISBN 0-85036-301-5 (cl), 0-85036-301-2 (cl). ▸ Background to 1946–49 civil war with particular emphasis on British involvement in Greek affairs. Relentlessly critical of British policy. [RC]

33.298 Heinz A. Richter, comp. *Greece and Cyprus since 1920: bibliography of contemporary history.* Heidelberg: Wissenschaftliche Verlag Nea Hellas, 1984. ISBN 3-924445-00-1. ▸ Listing of more than 11,000 titles in wide variety of languages, including Greek, relating to all aspects of Greek (including Cypriot) history and society during present century. No annotations. [RC]

33.299 Steven Runciman. *The Great Church in captivity: a study of the patriarchate of Constantinople from the eve of the Turkish conquest to the Greek War of Independence.* Cambridge: Cambridge University Press, 1968. ISBN 0-521-07188-7. ▸ Role of Orthodox church under Ottoman rule with heavy emphasis on relations of patriarchate with Western Christendom. Scholarly but underestimates anticlericalism of both elites and masses. [RC]

33.300 Theodore Saloutos. *The Greeks in the United States.* 1964 ed. Cambridge, Mass.: Harvard University Press, 1975. ISBN 0-674-36325-6. ▸ History of largest of many Greek communities outside borders of Greek state. Classic in field of Greek American studies. [RC]

33.301 Irwin T. Sanders. *Rainbow in the rock: the people of rural Greece.* Cambridge, Mass.: Harvard University Press, 1962. ▸ Pioneering anthropological study of rural Balkan life. Read in conjunction with author's Bulgarian study (33.137). [GS]

33.302 Michalis Spourdalakis. *The rise of the Greek Socialist party.* London: Routledge, 1988. ISBN 0-415-00499-3. ▸ The "short march" to power of Andreas Papandreou's pan-Hellenic socialist movement (PASOK). Informative introduction to PASOK phenomenon, attempt to institute socialism in country where workforce mostly self-employed. [RC]

33.303 William St. Clair. *That Greece might still be free: the Philhellenes in the War of Independence.* London: Oxford University Press, 1972. ISBN 0-19-215194-0. ▸ Jaundiced account of activities of do-gooders, cranks, and idealists who flocked to enlist in insurgent cause following outbreak of struggle for independence in 1821. [RC]

33.304 Ian McDougall Guthrie Stewart. *The struggle for Crete, 20 May–1 June 1941: the story of a lost opportunity.* 1966 ed. Oxford: Oxford University Press, 1991. ISBN 0-19-285230-2 (pbk). ▸ Detailed study of Germany's only major airborne assault of World War II and touch-and-go battle for strategically important island. Despite subsequent release of official records, retains its value. [RC]

33.305 Apostolos Vacalopoulos. *The Greek nation, 1453–1669: the cultural and economic background of modern Greek society.* New Brunswick, N.J.: Rutgers University Press, 1976. ISBN 0-8135-0810-X. ▸ Thorough scholarly discussion of Ottoman conquest of Hellenic world that preceded flowering of Hellenism in seventeenth century. Continues 8.203. [GS]

33.306 Timothy Ware. *Eustratios Argenti: a study of the Greek church under Turkish rule.* Oxford: Clarendon, 1964. ▸ Life and times of leading Orthodox theologian-polemicist from eighteenth century. Although Argenti's writings may seem arid, this well-written exegesis throws much incidental light on church under Ottoman rule. [RC]

33.307 Christopher M. Woodhouse. *The battle of Navarino.* Chester Springs, Pa.: Dufour Editions, 1965. ▸ Lively account of defeat in 1827 of Turco-Egyptian fleet by combined British, French, and Russian fleet in last great battle of age of sail; ensured emergence of independent Greece. [RC]

33.308 Christopher M. Woodhouse. *Capodistria: the founder of Greek independence.* London: Oxford University Press, 1973. ISBN 0-19-211196-5. ▸ Scholarly, well-documented study of Count Ioannis Kapodistrias, Corfiot Greek who rose to prominence in Russian service and subsequently became first president of Greece. [RC]

33.309 Christopher M. Woodhouse. *The Greek War of Independence: its historical setting.* 1952 ed. New York: Russell & Russell, 1975. ISBN 0-8462-1782-1. ▸ First successful nationalist uprising in eastern Europe. Succinct introduction to complexities of 1820s. Complements Dakin 47.61. [RC/PWS]

33.310 Christopher M. Woodhouse. *Karamanlis: the restorer of Greek democracy.* Oxford: Clarendon, 1982. ISBN 0-19-822584-9. ▸ Political career of dominant figure in political life during second half of twentieth century. Well-informed, if somewhat uncritical. [RC]

33.311 Christopher M. Woodhouse. *The rise and fall of the Greek colonels.* New York: Watts, 1985. ISBN 0-531-09798-6. ▸ Anatomy of only military dictatorship established in noncommunist Europe since World War II. Judicious appraisal of unsavory episode. [RC]

33.312 Christopher M. Woodhouse. *The struggle for Greece, 1941–1949.* 1976 ed. Brooklyn Heights, N.Y.: Beekman, 1979. ISBN 0-8464-0042-1. ▸ Three rounds in communist bid for power in 1940s, culminating in communist defeat in civil war of 1946–49. Sophisticated analysis by participant in events. [RC]

33.313 Dionysios A. Zakythinos. *The making of modern Greece: from Byzantium to independence.* K. R. Johnstone, trans. and Introduction. Totowa, N.J.: Rowman & Littlefield, 1976. ISBN 0-87471-796-5. ▸ History of Greek lands during Tourkokratia, or period of Ottoman rule. Old-fashioned, unsystematic but useful summation of Greek scholarship. [RC]

SEE ALSO
47.129 Domna N. Dontas. *Greece and the great powers, 1863–1875.*
47.456 N. Petsalis-Diomidis. *Greece at the Paris Peace Conference, 1919.*
48.392 Lawrence S. Wittner. *American intervention in Greece, 1943–1949.*

HUNGARY TO WORLD WAR I

33.314 Albert Apponyi. *The memoirs of Count Apponyi.* New York: Macmillan, 1935. ▸ Very useful memoirs covering six decades (1872–1933) by one of most sophisticated spokesmen of conservative Hungarian nationalism who advocated independence until 1918, then sought revision of Treaty of Trianon. [SBV]

33.315 János M. Bak, György Bónis, and James Ross Sweeney, eds. and trans. *The laws of the medieval kingdom of Hungary, 1000–1301.* Andor Csizmadia, Introduction. Bakersfield, Calif.: Schlacks, 1989. ▸ First of multivolume, bilingual (Latin-English) edition of Hungary's laws since its foundation as Christian kingdom. Work will ultimately consist of six parts (series) and over two dozen volumes. Present volume contains annotated legislation of Árpád period in Hungarian history (1000–1301). [SBV]

33.316 János M. Bak and Béla K. Király, eds. *From Hunyadi to Rákóczi: war and society in late medieval and early modern Hungary.* Boulder and New York: Social Science Monographs and Brooklyn College Press; distributed by Columbia University Press, 1982. (East European monographs, 104.) ISBN 0-930888-13-8. ▸ Mixed collection of twenty-nine essays on medieval and early modern warfare centered on Hungary but also involving Habsburg empire, Ottoman empire, and Russia. [SBV]

33.317 Elemér Bakó, comp. *Guide to Hungarian studies.* 2 vols. Stanford, Calif.: Hoover Institution Press, 1973. (Hoover Institution bibliographical series, 52.) ISBN 0-8179-2521-X. ▸ Most comprehensive guide to Hungarian studies, containing 120-page chronology and 4,426 entries in bibliography, statistics, geography, demography, ethnography, history, legal studies, government, politics, economics, religion, language, literature, fine arts, education, scientific research, press, diaspora, and Hungarians in America as well as serial and name indexes. [SBV]

33.318 Elemér Bakó and William Sólyom-Fekete, comps. *Hungarians in Rumania and Transylvania: a bibliographical list of publications in Hungarian and West European languages compiled from the holdings of the Library of Congress.* Washington, D.C.: United States Government Printing Office, 1969. (Ninety-first Congress, First session, House document no. 91–134.) ▸ Readily available bibliography of over 2,000 works dealing primarily with Hungarian history and with history of Hungarians in Transylvania in thirteen topical categories. [SBV]

33.319 George Barany. *Stephen Széchenyi and the awakening of Hungarian nationalism, 1791–1841.* Princeton: Princeton University Press, 1968. ▸ Detailed, scholarly study on life and times of one of Hungary's most famous political figures during reform period (1825–48). [SBV]

33.320 Antal Bartha. *Hungarian society in the ninth and tenth centuries.* K. Balázs, trans. Budapest: Akadémiai Kiadó, 1975. (Studia historica Academiae Scientiarum Hungaricae, 85.) ISBN 963-05-0308-5. ▸ Scholarly analysis of ninth-century horse-nomadic societies in eastern Europe and their influence on Magyar tribal federation. [SBV]

33.321 Kálmán Benda et al., eds. *Magyarország történeti kronológiája: a kezdetektől 1970-ig* (Hungary's historical chronology from the beginnings to 1970). Vol. 1: *To 1526.* Vol. 2: *1526–1848.* Vol. 3: *1848–1944.* Vol. 4: *1944–1970.* 2d ed. 4 vols. Budapest: Akadémiai Kiadó, 1983. ISBN 963-05-3183-6 (set). ▸ Most complete chronological summary of Hungarian history; often comprehensible even to non-Hungarian speakers because of brevity of entries. Prepared by about thirty scholars from Institute of History of Hungarian Academy of Sciences. Each volume edited by specialist of period. [SBV]

33.322 Iván T. Berend and György Ránki. *Hungary: a century of economic development.* New York: Barnes & Noble, 1974. ISBN 0-06-490371-0. ▸ Survey of Hungary's economic development since mid-nineteenth century by two noted experts. Coverage of socialist economy more positive than warranted by developments since 1960s. [SBV]

33.323 Marianna D. Birnbaum. *Humanists in a shattered world: Croatian and Hungarian Latinity in the sixteenth century.* Columbus, Ohio: Slavica, 1986. ISBN 0-89357-155-5. ▸ Continuation of 33.324. Highly learned analysis of Latin-language creative writings of sixteenth-century humanist poets, writers, and scholars. [SBV]

33.324 Marianna D. Birnbaum. *Janus Pannonius, poet and politician.* Zagreb: Jugoslavenska Akademija Znanosti i Umjetnosti, 1981. (Djela Jugoslavenske Akademije Znanosti i Umjetnosti, Razreda za Filologiju, 56.) ▸ Balanced, sophisticated life and times of Hungarian-Croat humanist poet and scholar, one of king's close advisers until involvement in conspiracy against Matthias Corvinus (1458–90) in 1471. [SBV]

33.325 Paul Bődy. *Joseph Eötvös and the modernization of Hungary, 1840–1870: a study of ideas of individuality and social pluralism in modern politics.* 2d ed. Boulder: East European Monographs; distributed by Columbia University Press, 1985. (East European monographs, 174.) ISBN 0-88033-066-X. ▸ Careful political portrait of one of great liberal statesmen of nineteenth-century Hungary. Emphasis on Eötvös's proposals concerning Hungary's minority problems and position within empire. [SBV]

33.326 Paul Bődy, ed. *Hungarian statesmen of destiny, 1860–1960.* Boulder: Social Science Monographs, 1989. (East European monographs, 262.) ISBN 0-88033-159-3. ▸ Biographical essays on Ferenc Deák, Baron József Eötvös, Count Gyula Andrássy, Count István Tisza, Admiral Miklós Horthy, Count

István Bethlen, Endre Bajcsy-Zsilinszky, and Imre Nagy. Quality ranges from good to excellent. [SBV]

33.327 Csaba Csapodi and Klára Csapodi-Gárdonyi, eds. *Bibliotheca Corviniana: the library of King Matthias Corvinus of Hungary.* 2d ed. Zsuzsanna Horn, trans. Bertha Gaster, translation ed. Budapest: Corvina Kiadó and Magyar Helikon, 1981. ISBN 963-13-1183-X (cl), 963-13-1184-8 (pbk). ▸ Profusely illustrated and annotated scholarly work on Matthias Corvinus's famed library in Buda. Introductory essay describes library's origins, content, and fate after Hungary's demise in 1526. [SBV]

33.328 Lóránt Czigány. *The Oxford history of Hungarian literature from the earliest times to the present.* Oxford: Clarendon, 1984. ISBN 0-19-815781-9. ▸ Scholarly yet popular synthesis of Hungarian literary history from eleventh century to mid-1980s by British-Hungarian scholar. Work geared to needs of Western readers. [SBV]

33.329 George Deák. *The economy and polity in early twentieth-century Hungary: the role of the National Association of Industrialists.* Boulder: East European Monographs; distributed by Columbia University Press, 1990. (East European monographs, 288.) ISBN 0-88033-185-2. ▸ Careful scholarly discussion of conditions surrounding foundation of National Association of Industrialists (GyOSz), and association's role in Hungary's economic and political development up to 1914. [SBV]

33.330 István Deák. *Beyond nationalism: a social and political history of the Habsburg officer corps, 1848–1918.* New York: Oxford University Press, 1990. ISBN 0-19-504505-X. ▸ Award-winning history of imperial and royal officer corps during Austro-Hungarian empire's last seven decades. Officer corps' dynastic loyalty transcended narrow nationalism of empire's ethnic groups. [SBV]

33.331 István Deák. *The lawful revolution: Louis Kossuth and the Hungarians, 1848–1849.* New York: Columbia University Press, 1979. ISBN 0-231-04602-2. ▸ Highly regarded assessment of Kossuth's role in Hungary's struggle against Habsburg absolutism in 1848–49. Argues that Kossuth and Hungarians acted within framework of constitution. [SBV]

33.332 János Decsy. *Prime Minister Gyula Andrássy's influence on Habsburg foreign policy during the Franco-German War of 1870–1871.* Boulder: East European Quarterly; distributed by Columbia University Press, 1979. (East European monographs, 52.) ISBN 0-914710-44-3. ▸ Basic study of Andrássy's efforts to tilt Austria-Hungary's foreign policy toward Germany during Franco-Prussian War. Andrássy motivated by fear of Russia and desire to preserve Austro-Hungarian dualism. [SBV]

33.333 Laszlo Deme. *The radical Left in the Hungarian Revolution of 1848.* Boulder: East European Quarterly; distributed by Columbia University Press, 1976. (East European monographs, 19.) ISBN 0-914710-12-5. ▸ Scholarly discussion of radical Left in 1848, whose members were to left of Kossuth and whose roots reached back to Hungarian Jacobin conspiracy of 1794–95. [SBV]

33.334 Tekla Dömötör. *Hungarian folk beliefs.* Bloomington: Indiana University Press, 1982. ISBN 0-253-32876-4. ▸ Comprehensive history of popular culture and religion in Hungary. [MK]

33.335 Géza Fehér. *Turkish miniatures from the period of Hungary's Turkish occupation.* Lili Halápy and Elisabeth West, trans. Budapest: Corvina Kaidó and Magyar Helikon, 1978. ISBN 963-13-5077-5, 963-207-222-7. ▸ Fifty-one beautifully reproduced and annotated Turkish miniatures from fifteenth through seventeenth centuries that portray historical events and serve as sources for Hungarian history. [SBV]

33.336 Erik Fügedi. *Castle and society in medieval Hungary, 1000–1437.* János M. Bak, trans. Budapest: Akadémiai Kiadó; distributed by Kultura, 1986. (Studia historica Academiae Scientiarum Hungaricae, 187.) ISBN 963-05-3802-4. ▸ Description of castle building in medieval Hungary, especially after Mongol invasion (1241–42). Castle building accompanied by growth of aristocracy and decline of royal power. [SBV]

33.337 Erik Fügedi. *Kings, bishops, nobles, and burghers in medieval Hungary.* János M. Bak, ed. London: Variorum, 1986. ISBN 0-86078-177-1. ▸ Collection of thirteen pathbreaking essays in three languages (English, French, German) by noted Hungarian medievalist on many aspects of medieval and early modern Hungarian history. [SBV]

33.338 Astrik L. Gabriel. *The medieval universities of Pécs and Pozsony: commemoration of the 500th and 600th anniversary of their foundation, 1367–1467–1967.* 1967 ed. Notre Dame, Ind.: University of Notre Dame, Medieval Institute, 1969. ▸ Short but well-documented comparative study of foundation of two of medieval Hungary's three universities (third, Buda in 1395) by expert on medieval universities. [SBV]

33.339 László Gerevich, ed. *Towns in medieval Hungary.* T. Szendrei, trans. P. C. McCulloch, translation ed. Boulder: Social Science Monographs and Atlantic Research & Publications; distributed by Columbia University Press, 1990. (East European monographs, 297.) ISBN 0-88033-194-1. ▸ Survey of development of towns, urban classes, guilds, town life, manufacturing, and fortifications in medieval Hungary, and towns' relationship to crown and feudal society. [SBV]

33.340 Péter Hának, ed. *One thousand years: a concise history of Hungary.* Zsuzsa Béres, trans. Budapest: Corvina Kiadó, 1988. ISBN 963-13-2520-2. ▸ Well-written synthesis of Hungarian history by group of excellent historians still working under constraints of communist system. [SBV]

33.341 Andrew Handler. *An early blueprint for Zionism: Győző Istóczy's political anti-Semitism.* Boulder: East European Monographs; distributed by Columbia University Press, 1989. ISBN 0-88033-158-5. ▸ Critical assessment of life and times of founder of first Hungarian antisemitic party in 1880s. Istóczy was eventually hounded out of political life. [SBV]

33.342 Joseph L. Held. *Hunyadi, legend and reality.* Boulder: East European Monographs; distributed by Columbia University Press, 1985. (East European monographs, 178.) ISBN 0-88033-070-8. ▸ Careful study of origins, life, and times of famous Ottoman opponent János Hunyadi, *vojevod* (governor) of Transylvania, regent of Hungary, and father of King Matthias Corvinus. [SBV]

33.343 Bálint Hóman and Gyula Szekfű. *Magyar történet* (Hungarian history). 8th ed. 5 vols. Ferenc Glatz, Introduction. Budapest: Maecenas Kiadó, 1990. ▸ Five-volume work (originally published 1928–34 in 8 volumes), still best major synthesis of Hungarian history. Written under influence of Geistesgeschichte school; with shortcomings, but still superior to published volumes (1, 3–8) of ongoing ten-volume Marxist synthesis. [SBV]

33.344 Andrew C. Janos. *The politics of backwardness in Hungary, 1825–1945.* Princeton: Princeton University Press, 1982. ISBN 0-691-07633-2 (cl), 0-691-10123-X (pbk). ▸ Original study, arguing that Hungary's dependent relationship toward Europe was important formative factor in its political history in nineteenth and early twentieth century. [GS]

33.345 Thomas Kabdebó, comp. *Hungary.* Oxford: ABC-Clio, 1980. (World bibliographical series, 15.) ISBN 0-903450-28-3. ▸ Comprehensive English-language bibliography on Hungary embracing numerous disciplines and over one thousand years of Hungarian history. [SBV]

33.346 Antal Kampis. *The history of art in Hungary.* 1966 ed. Lili Halápy, trans. London: Wellingborough, Collets, 1967. ▸ Popular but scholarly summary of development of Hungarian art and

architecture from time of Magyar conquest in ninth century to 1960s. Standard work in English. [SBV]

33.347 Patrick J. Kelleher. *The Holy Crown of Hungary.* Rome: American Academy in Rome, 1951. (Papers and monographs of the American Academy in Rome, 13.) ▸ First English-language scholarly study on origins and constitutional significance of Hungary's Holy Crown venerated as that given to King St. Stephen by Pope Sylvester II (1000 CE). Still of value. [SBV]

33.348 Béla K. Király. *Ferenc Deák.* Boston: Twayne, 1975. ISBN 0-8057-3030-3. ▸ Life and times of politically moderate Ferenc Deák, primary architect of Austro-Hungarian compromise of 1867. [SBV]

33.349 Béla K. Király. *Hungary in the late eighteenth century: the decline of enlightened despotism.* New York: Columbia University Press, 1969. ▸ Scholarly description of late eighteenth-century Hungarian feudal society, beginnings of Hungarian nationalism, and Hungarian feudal revolt against Josephinian modernization. Complements Marczali 33.364. [SBV]

33.350 Gábor Klaniczay. *The uses of supernatural power: the transformation of popular religion in medieval and early modern Europe.* Karen Margolis, trans. Princeton: Princeton University Press, 1990. ISBN 0-691-07377-5. ▸ Collection of proven scholarly essays on history of medieval European Christianity, cult of royal saints, and popular magical beliefs with focus on Hungarian developments. [MK]

33.351 Manó Kogutowicz. *Teljes földrajzi és történelmi atlasz* (A complete geographical and historical atlas). 5th ed. Budapest: Magyar Földrajzi Intézet, 1911. ▸ Still best one-volume historical atlas of Hungary. Contains 130 maps and 80 insets, most in color. [SBV]

33.352 John Komlos. *Nutrition and economic development in the eighteenth-century Habsburg monarchy: an anthropometric history.* Princeton: Princeton University Press, 1989. ISBN 0-691-04257-8. ▸ Statistical examination of relationship between availability and quality of food and between physical stature and health of population; relevant to both halves of Habsburg empire. [SBV]

33.353 Domokos G. Kosáry. *Culture and society in eighteenth-century Hungary.* Zsuzsa Béres, trans. Budapest: Corvina Kiadó, 1987. ISBN 963-13-2522-9 (pbk). ▸ Abridged translation of major survey of eighteenth-century Hungary. Discusses Hungarian social, political, religious, educational, and cultural institutions as well as beginnings of national revival. [SBV]

33.354 Domokos G. Kosáry. *A history of Hungary.* 1941 ed. New York: Arno, 1970. ISBN 0-405-02755-9. ▸ Classic one-volume synthesis reflecting traditional views of interwar Hungarian historiography. Also published as *History of the Hungarian Nation* (section "Hungary Since Trianon" added by Steven Béla Várdy). [SBV]

33.355 Domokos G. Kosáry. *The press during the Hungarian Revolution of 1848–1849.* Boulder: Social Science Monographs and Atlantic Research & Publications; distributed by Columbia University Press, 1986. (East European monographs, 198.) ISBN 0-88033-091-0. ▸ Detailed description of influence of Hungarian press during Revolution of 1848–49. First instance in Hungarian history when press influenced political developments. [SBV]

33.356 Zoltán J. Kosztolnyik. *Five eleventh-century Hungarian kings: their policies and their relations with Rome.* Boulder: East European Quarterly; distributed by Columbia University Press, 1981. (East European monographs, 79.) ISBN 0-914710-73-7. ▸ Narrative survey of Hungarian history from Prince Géza (r. 972–997) and King St. Stephen (r. 997/1000–38) to King St. Ladislas (r. 1077–95). Emphasizes spread of Christianity and relationships with papal court. [SBV]

33.357 Zoltán J. Kosztolnyik. *From Coloman the Learned to Béla III, 1095–1196: Hungarian domestic policies and their impact upon foreign affairs.* Boulder: East European Monographs; distributed by Columbia University Press, 1987. (East European monographs, 220.) ISBN 0-88033-116-X. ▸ Pedantic study of twelfth-century Hungary and its relations with Holy Roman Empire, Byzantium, and papacy. Discusses problems of succession, royal administration, and ecclesiastical administration. [SBV]

33.358 John Lukacs. *Budapest, 1900: a historical portrait of a city and its culture.* New York: Weidenfeld & Nicolson, 1988. ISBN 1-55584-060-4 (cl), 0-8021-3250-2 (pbk). ▸ Intellectually challenging portrait of Hungary's capital at height of Austro-Hungarian dualism. Presents vivid picture of city, people, politics, and cultural life. [SBV]

33.359 Lajos Lukács. *The Vatican and Hungary, 1846–1878: reports and correspondence on Hungary of the apostolic nuncios in Vienna.* Zsófia Kormos, trans. Budapest: Akadémiai Kiadó, 1981. ISBN 963-05-2446-5. ▸ Reports by Vienna-based apostolic nuncios on Hungarian Catholic church and Hungarian politics. Documents preceded by two-hundred-page essay on Hungarian-Vatican relations. [SBV]

33.360 C. A. Macartney. *Hungary: a short history.* Chicago: Aldine, 1962. ▸ Short, reliable, and readable survey of Hungarian history by noted British historian who had unique feeling for Hungarian history. [SBV]

33.361 C. A. Macartney. *The Magyars in the ninth century.* 1930 ed. Cambridge: Cambridge University Press, 1968. ISBN 0-521-07391-X. ▸ Useful scholarly work on preconquest Hungarian society by British pioneer of Hungarian studies. Based on Byzantine, Arabic, Slav, and Western chronicles. [SBV]

33.362 C. A. Macartney. *The medieval Hungarian historians: a critical and analytical guide.* Cambridge: Cambridge University Press, 1953. ▸ Interpretive study of nearly thirty medieval Hungarian chronicles and legends including Anonymous, Gesta Hungarorum (twelfth century), Kézai, Gesta Hungarorum (thirteenth century), and Viennese Illuminated Chronicle (fourteenth century). Available as photocopy from Ann Arbor, Mich.: University Microfilms International, 1982. [SBV]

33.363 Elemér Mályusz. *Kaiser Sigismund in Ungarn, 1387–1437.* Anikó Szmodits, trans. Budapest: Akadémiai Kiadó, 1990. ISBN 963-05-4978-6. ▸ Study by Hungary's most distinguished medievalist on rule of Sigismund, the Holy Roman Emperor, as king of Hungary. [MK]

33.364 Henrik Marczali. *Hungary in the eighteenth century.* 1910 ed. Harold W. V. Temperley, Introduction. New York: Arno, 1971. ISBN 0-405-02760-5. ▸ Useful survey on Hungary's eighteenth-century feudal society and institutions by Hungary's greatest historian of positivist school. Still best portrait of Hungary after reconquest. [SBV/CWI]

33.365 William O. McCagg, Jr. *Jewish nobles and geniuses in modern Hungary.* 1972 ed. Boulder: East European Monographs; distributed by Columbia University Press, 1986. (East European monographs, 3.) ISBN 0-88033-092-9. ▸ Pioneering study of unique role of Magyarized Jews (many ennobled) in modern Hungarian history. Emphasizes contributions to culture, learning, economic development, and science. [SBV]

33.366 Ervin Pamlényi, ed. *A history of Hungary.* László Boros et al., trans. Margaret Morris and Richard E. Allen, translation eds. London: Collets, 1975. ISBN 0-569-07700-1. ▸ Single-volume general history by seven of best historians from communist period. Useful for early periods, increasingly ideological and unreliable for modern period. [GS]

33.367 Géza Perjés. *The fall of the medieval kingdom of Hungary: Mohács 1526–Buda 1541.* Mario D. Fenyő, trans. Boulder: Social Science Monographs and Atlantic Research & Publications; distributed by Columbia University Press, 1989. (East European monographs, 255.) ISBN 0-88033-152-6. ▸ History of Hungary from before Battle of Mohács to conquest of Buda. Concludes Hungarians would have fared better had they accepted Süleyman's alleged offer of vassalage. [SBV]

33.368 Julianna Puskás. *From Hungary to the United States, 1880–1914.* Maria Bales, trans. Éva Pálmai, translation ed. Budapest: Akadémiai Kiadó, 1982. (Studia historica Academiae Scientiarum Hungaricae, 184.) ISBN 963-05-3020-1. ▸ Careful survey describing such important push-and-pull factors as Hungary's agricultural overpopulation and United States' need for unskilled or semiskilled industrial workers. [SBV]

33.369 Martyn C. Rady. *Medieval Buda: a study of municipal government and jurisdiction in the kingdom of Hungary.* Boulder: East European Monographs; distributed by Columbia University Press, 1985. (East European monographs, 182.) ISBN 0-88033-074-0. ▸ Urbanization and local self-government in medieval towns of Buda, Óbuda, and Pest, which later merged into Budapest. Good assessment of role of German burghers in medieval Hungarian urban life. [SBV]

33.370 György Ránki and Attila Pók, eds. *Indiana University studies on Hungary.* Vol. 1: *Hungarian history—world history.* Vol. 2: *Bartók and Kodály revisited.* Vol. 3: *Hungary and European civilization.* Budapest: Akadémiai Kiadó, 1984–89. ISBN 963-05-3997-7 (v. 1), 963-05-4510-1 (v. 2), 963-05-5502-6 (v. 3). ▸ First three volumes of ongoing series contain forty diverse but useful essays on many aspects of Hungarian history and culture from Middle Ages to post–World War II period. [SBV]

33.371 Denis Sinor. *History of Hungary.* 1959 ed. Westport, Conn.: Greenwood, 1976. ISBN 0-8371-9024-X. ▸ Popular survey of Hungarian history which, by virtue of author's expertise, is more thorough for medieval and early modern periods than for modern and recent periods. [SBV]

33.372 Stephen Sisa. *The spirit of Hungary: a panorama of Hungarian history and culture.* 2d ed. Morristown, N.J.: Vista, 1990. ISBN 0-9628422-0-6. ▸ Most readable and popular English-language survey of Hungarian history and civilization. [SBV]

33.373 Michael Sozan. *The history of Hungarian ethnography.* Washington, D.C.: University Press of America, 1977. ISBN 0-8191-0361-6. ▸ Excellent one-volume history of Hungarian ethnography, ethnology, folklore, and multidisciplinary field of Hungarology by American-trained cultural anthropologist. Useful cultural history. [SBV]

33.374 Peter F. Sugar et al., eds. *A history of Hungary.* Bloomington: Indiana University Press, 1990. ISBN 0-253-35578-8. ▸ Useful, reliable volume on all periods of Hungarian history authored by nineteen scholars representing divergent views. Strongest for pre-1945 period. [SBV]

33.375 György Szabad. *Hungarian political trends between the revolution and the compromise (1849–1867).* Éva Pálmai, trans. Budapest: Akadémiai Kiadó, 1977. (Studia historica Academiae Scientiarum Hungaricae, 128.) ISBN 963-05-1221-1. ▸ Scholarly survey of developments between Revolution of 1848–49 and Austro-Hungarian compromise of 1867. Compromise was compact between Hungary's leaders and Habsburgs, without taking into consideration non-Germans or non-Magyars. [SBV]

33.376 Bence Szabolcsi and György Kroó. *A concise history of Hungarian music.* 2d ed. Sára Karig and Fred MacNicol, trans. Florence Knepler, translation ed. Budapest: Corvina Kiadó, 1974. ISBN 963-13-6652-9. ▸ Short history of Hungarian music by prominent Hungarian musicologist. [SBV]

33.377 Joseph Széplaki, ed. and comp. *Hungarians in the United States and Canada: a bibliography.* Steven Béla Várdy, Introduction. Minneapolis: University of Minnesota, Immigration History Research Center, 1977. (Immigration History Research Center ethnic bibliography, 2.) ‣ Nearly one thousand titles relating to Hungary, Hungarians, and Hungarian immigrants in North America. Roughly half of entries deal with Hungary, half with Hungarians in North America. [SBV]

33.378 Lajos Tardy. *Beyond the Ottoman empire: fourteenth- to sixteenth-century Hungarian diplomacy in the East.* János Boris, trans. Szeged, Hungary: Universitas Szegediensis de Attila Josef Nominata, 1978. (Studia Uralo-Altaica, 13.) ‣ Description of Hungary's and Transylvania's diplomatic relations with Ottoman empire, Safavid Persia, and Caucasus region between late fourteenth and late sixteenth centuries. [SBV]

33.379 J. Telek, comp. *History of Hungary and the Hungarians, 1848–1971: a selected bibliography.* Rev. ed. 2 vols. Toronto: Hungarian Historical Studies, 1980. (Hungarian historical studies, 1, 3.) ISBN 0-920984-04-5 (v. 1), 0-920984-06-1 (v. 2). ‣ Volume 1 (1848–1971) contains about 4,200 independent works relating to Hungary and Hungarian history based largely on collection of University of Toronto library. Volume 2 (1848–1977) lists nearly 9,400 items on history, politics, society, culture, economy, foreign relations, diaspora, including syntheses, monographs, periodicals, and newspapers. [SBV]

33.380 János Thuróczy. *Chronicle of the Hungarians.* Frank Mantello, trans. Pál Engel, Introduction. Bloomington: Indiana University, Research Institute for Inner Asian Studies, 1991. (Uralic and Altaic series, 155. Medievalia Hungarica, 2.) ISBN 0-933070-27-6. ‣ English translation of János Thuróczy's (ca. 1435–90) chronicle on Hungarian history, 1382–1488. Although published during Renaissance (1488), this important source reflects characteristics of medieval chronicle. [SBV]

33.381 Steven Béla Várdy. *Modern Hungarian historiography.* Boulder: East European Quarterly; distributed by Columbia University Press, 1976. (East European monographs, 16.) ISBN 0-914710-08-7. ‣ Useful synthesis of Hungarian historiography and its impact in two centuries before rise of Marxism. [GS/SBV]

33.382 Steven Béla Várdy, Géza Grosschmid, and L. S. Domonkos, eds. *Louis the Great, king of Hungary and Poland.* Boulder: East European Monographs; distributed by Columbia University Press, 1986. (East European monographs, 194.) ISBN 0-88033-087-2. ‣ Six-hundreth anniversary collection of two dozen scholarly essays by American, Canadian, German, Hungarian, Italian, and Polish scholars on age of Anjous in Hungary and Poland. Fills significant void. [SBV]

33.383 Steven Béla Várdy and Agnes Huszár Várdy. *The Austro-Hungarian mind: at home and abroad.* Boulder: East European Monographs; distributed by Columbia University Press, 1989. (East European monographs, 254.) ISBN 0-88033-151-8. ‣ Collected essays of authors concerning Hungarian romanticism, Baron Joseph Eötvös, Hungarian liberalism and nationalism, Treaty of Trianon and Hungarian national minorities, and Hungarians in America. [GS]

33.384 Domokos Varga. *Hungary in greatness and decline: the fourteenth and the fifteenth centuries.* Martha Szacsvay Lipták, trans. Atlanta: Hungarian Cultural Foundation, 1982. (State University of New York at Buffalo Program in East European and Slavic studies, 13.) ISBN 0-914648-11-X. ‣ Well-written, popular, heavily illustrated synthesis of Hungarian history between 1308 and 1526. Period saw rulers like Louis the Great and Matthias Corvinus, yet ended in tragedy of Mohács (1526). [SBV]

SEE ALSO
8.336 Ferenc Makk. *The Árpáds and the Comneni.*
8.341 Gyula Moravcsik. *Byzantium and the Magyars.*
9.205 István Dienes. *The Hungarians cross the Carpathians.*

9.206 István Fodor. *In search of a new homeland.*
31.85 John Komlos. *The Habsburg monarchy as a customs union.*

HUNGARY SINCE WORLD WAR I

33.385 Tamás Aczél and Tibor Méray. *The revolt of the mind: a case history of intellectual resistance behind the Iron Curtain.* 1959 ed. New York: Praeger, 1960. ‣ Perhaps best insight into psychological changes experienced by Hungarian intellectuals, who after 1953 became disenchanted with communism and worked to undermine it. [SBV]

33.386 William M. Batkay. *Authoritarian politics in a transitional state: István Bethlen and the Unified party in Hungary, 1919–1926.* Boulder: East European Monographs; distributed by Columbia University Press, 1982. (East European monographs, 102.) ISBN 0-914710-96-6. ‣ Detailed study of political leadership of Count István Bethlen, who as prime minister was responsible for consolidation of Hungary following its dismemberment after World War I. [SBV]

33.387 Iván T. Berend. *The Hungarian economic reforms, 1953–1988.* Cambridge: Cambridge University Press, 1990. ISBN 0-521-38037-5. ‣ Detailed, well-informed economic history of varieties of reforms and retrograde steps that helped make Hungary more open to economic change after 1989. [GS]

33.388 István Bibó. *Democracy, revolution, self-determination: selected writings.* Károly Nagy, ed. András Boros-Kazai, trans. Boulder: Social Science Monographs; distributed by Columbia University Press, 1991. (East European monographs, 317.) ISBN 0-88033-214-X. ‣ Penetrating analysis of Hungary's pressing social, political, and psychological problems, including national minority issues and antisemitism, by one of Hungary's most influential social thinkers. [SBV]

33.389 Stephen Borsody, ed. *The Hungarians: a divided nation.* New Haven: Yale Center for International and Area Studies; distributed by Slavica, 1988. ISBN 0-936586-07-9. ‣ Collection of sixteen interpretive scholarly essays and documents on historic Hungary's dismemberment and on condition of Hungarian minorities in successor states, especially since World War II. [SBV]

33.390 Randolph L. Braham, comp. *The Hungarian Jewish catastrophe: a selected and annotated bibliography.* 2d rev. ed. Boulder: Social Sciences Monographs and City University of New York, Institute of Holocaust Studies; distributed by Columbia University Press, 1984. (East European monographs, 162.) ISBN 0-88033-054-6. ‣ Near-complete bibliography in a dozen languages on Holocaust in Hungary prepared by greatest authority on this topic. [SBV]

33.391 John F. Cadzow, Andrew Ludányi, and Louis J. Elteto, eds. *Transylvania: the roots of ethnic conflict.* Kent, Ohio: Kent State University Press, 1983. ISBN 0-87338-283-8. ‣ Scholarly essays exploring past relationships among Transylvania's ethnic groups and post–World War II Romania's oppressive policies toward its minorities, with particular attention to Hungarians. [SBV]

33.392 István Deák. "Hungary." In *The European Right: a historical profile.* Hans Rogger and Eugen Weber, eds., pp. 364–407. Berkeley: University of California Press, 1965. ‣ Skilled discussion of Horthy regime in interwar Hungary, which, despite harboring aristocrats, advocating nationalist Christian policy, and opposing socialism, was not Nazi. Retained loyalty of Hungarians and almost saved Hungary's Jews. [GS]

33.393 Nándor F. Dreisziger. *Hungary's way to World War II.* Astor Park, Fla.: Danubian, 1968. ‣ Thorough summary of Hungary's foreign policy between two world wars; driven by intense belief in legitimacy of revising Treaty of Trianon. [SBV]

33.394 Irene Raab Epstein. *Gyula Szekfü: a study in the political* *basis of Hungarian historiography.* 1974 ed. New York: Garland, 1987. ISBN 0-8240-8024-6 (pbk). ▸ Scholarly treatment of life and times of Hungary's most influential historian. Discusses Szekfű's pervasive influence on Hungarian mind and gradual disenchantment with Hungary's neobaroque society. [SBV]

33.395 François Fejtő. *Behind the rape of Hungary.* Jean-Paul Sartre, Introduction. New York: MacKay, 1957. ▸ Penetrating analysis of Hungary's involvement in World War II and her fate in Soviet Bloc by noted Hungarian emigré intellectual. [SBV]

33.396 Andrew Felkay. *Hungary and the U.S.S.R., 1956–1988: Kádár's political leadership.* Westport, Conn.: Greenwood, 1989. ISBN 0-313-25982-8. ▸ Learned, detailed analysis of interrelationship between Hungary and Soviet Union in three decades following Hungarian Revolution of 1956; emphasizes Kádár's role. [SBV]

33.397 Mario D. Fenyő. *Hitler, Horthy, and Hungary: German-Hungarian relations, 1941–1944.* New Haven: Yale University Press, 1972. ISBN 0-300-01468-6. ▸ Detailed analysis of Hungary's relationship to Nazi Germany during World War II, including Regent Horthy's compliance with some of Germany's demands and his efforts to escape this dangerous alliance. [SBV]

33.398 Charles Gati. *Hungary and the Soviet Bloc.* Durham, N.C.: Duke University Press, 1986. ISBN 0-8223-0684-0 (cl), 0-8223-0747-2 (pbk). ▸ Sophisticated analysis of Hungary's post–World War II development and its relationship to Soviet Union and other members of Soviet Bloc in light of country's economic and political liberalization. [SBV]

33.399 Iván L. Hálasz de Béky. *A bibliography of the Hungarian Revolution, 1956.* Toronto: University of Toronto Press, 1963. ▸ First thorough bibliography of Hungarian Revolution of 1956. Contains over 2,000 entries, including 428 books in over two dozen languages. See Wagner, ed. 33.454 for supplement. [SBV]

33.400 Joseph L. Held, ed. *The modernization of agriculture: rural transformation in Hungary, 1848–1975.* Boulder: East European Monographs; distributed by Columbia University Press, 1980. (East European monographs, 63.) ISBN 0-914710-60-5. ▸ Five scholarly essays on agricultural modernization in Hungary following emancipation of serfs in 1848 and collectivization of lands after World War II. [SBV]

33.401 Jorg K. Hoensch. *A history of modern Hungary, 1867–1986.* Kim Traynor, trans. London: Longman, 1988. ISBN 0-582-01484-0 (cl), 0-582-25109-5 (pbk). ▸ Eminently readable, reliable account of modern Hungarian history covering political, social, and economic developments of last century and a half, but mostly since World War I. [SBV]

33.402 Marida Hollos and Béla C. Maday, eds. *New Hungarian peasants: an East Central European experience with collectivization.* Boulder: Social Science Monographs and Brooklyn College Press; distributed by Columbia University Press, 1983. (East European monographs, 134.) ISBN 0-88033-024-4. ▸ Collection of thirteen scholarly essays on Hungarian peasant life following forced collectivization of countryside. Authors are Hungarian and Western cultural anthropologists and folklorists. [SBV]

33.403 Miklós Nagybányai Horthy. *Confidential papers.* Miklós Szinai and László Szűcs, eds. Budapest: Corvina Kiadó, 1965. ▸ Sixty-five translated documents (letters, memoranda, declarations) from, to, and about Admiral Horthy (1868–1957) for period 1919–44. Selections and introduction reveal editors' strong anti-Horthy bias. [SBV]

33.404 Miklós Nagybányai Horthy. *Memoirs.* 1957 ed. Nicholas Roosevelt, Introduction. Westport, Conn.: Greenwood, 1978. ISBN 0-313-20345-8. ▸ Memoirs of Hungary's ex-regent, written during exile in early 1950s. Useful and pleasant reading, but writ-

ten with aim of justifying Horthy's leadership before and during World War II. [SBV]

33.405 Paul Ignotus. *Hungary.* New York: Praeger, 1972. ▸ Intellectually stimulating summary of Hungary's nineteenth- and twentieth-century development by noted emigré intellectual. Discussion of modern Hungarian intellectual life particularly interesting. [SBV]

33.406 Elemér Illyés. *National minorities in Romania: change in Transylvania.* Boulder: East European Monographs; distributed by Columbia University Press, 1982. (East European monographs, 112.) ISBN 0-88033-005-8. ▸ Detailed account of national minority question and Ceauşescu's oppressive rule in Transylvania; particular attention paid to formerly dominant Hungarians. [SBV]

33.407 Oszkár Jászi. *Revolution and counter-revolution in Hungary.* 1924 ed. E. W. Dickes, trans. R. W. Seton-Watson, Introduction. New York: Fertig, 1969. ▸ Personal account of Hungary's post–World War I revolutions by leading liberal intellectual. Jászi supported Károlyi's liberalism, disagreed with Béla Kun's communism, and was forced to flee Horthy's conservative regime. [SBV]

33.408 Gyula Juhász. *Hungarian foreign policy, 1919–1945.* Sándor Simon, trans. Mária Kovács, translation ed. Budapest: Akadémiai Kiadó, 1979. ISBN 963-05-1882-1. ▸ Scholarly synthesis of Hungarian foreign policy during interwar period and World War II by respected Hungarian authority on modern Hungarian diplomatic history. [SBV]

33.409 Miklós Kállay. *Hungarian premier: a personal account of a nation's struggle in the Second World War.* 1954 ed. Westport, Conn.: Greenwood, 1970. ISBN 0-8371-3965-1. ▸ Kállay's account of his efforts to take Hungary out of alliance with Hitler during his prime ministership in 1942–44. Less self-justifying than most political memoirs. [SBV]

33.410 Michael Károlyi. *Memoirs of Michael Károlyi: faith without illusions.* 1956 ed. Catherine Károlyi, trans. A.J.P. Taylor, Introduction. New York: Dutton, 1957. ▸ Autobiography of head of newly independent Hungarian state in 1918, who attempted to reform Hungary in liberal democratic spirit and to satisfy victorious Entente powers; both efforts unsuccessful. Partisan tone. [GS]

33.411 Nathaniel Katzburg. *Hungary and the Jews: policy and legislation, 1920–1943.* Ramat-Gan, Israel: Bar-Ilan University Press, 1981. ISBN 965-226-020-7. ▸ History of Jews in Hungary during interwar years, with particular attention to quota laws (*numerus clausus*) and application before Holocaust. Reaction of traditionally loyal and acculturated community. Important case study. [SBV/EM]

33.412 Stephen D. Kertész. *Between Russia and the West: Hungary and the illusions of peacemaking, 1945–1947.* Notre Dame, Ind.: University of Notre Dame Press, 1984. ISBN 0-268-01079-x. ▸ Partially autobiographical but still scholarly description of Hungary's fate at Paris Peace Conference of 1947. Paris Treaty confirmed World War I settlement of Trianon with additional minor territorial losses to Hungary. [SBV]

33.413 Stephen D. Kertész. *Diplomacy in a whirlpool: Hungary between Nazi Germany and Soviet Russia.* Notre Dame, Ind.: University of Notre Dame Press, 1953. ▸ Scholarly review of Hungary's revisionist foreign policy and involvement in World War II. Colored by author's personal reminiscences as civil servant and diplomat. Available on microfilm from Cambridge, Mass.: Harvard University Library Microreproduction Service. [SBV]

33.414 Béla K. Király, Barbara Lotze, and Nándor F. Dreisziger, eds. *The first war between socialist states: the Hungarian Rev-*

olution of 1956 and its impact. New York: Social Science Monographs and Brooklyn College Press; distributed by Columbia University Press, 1984. (East European monographs, 152.) ISBN 0-88033-044-9. ▸ Collection of learned articles with coverage of all aspects of Hungarian Revolution of 1956. Explores causes as well as immediate and long-term effects of Revolution. [SBV]

33.415 Béla K. Király, Peter Pastor, and Ivan Sanders, eds. *Essays on World War I: total war and peacemaking, a case study of Trianon*. New York: Social Science Monographs and Brooklyn College Press; distributed by Columbia University Press, 1982. (East European monographs, 105.) ISBN 0-930888-18-9. ▸ Collection of nearly three dozen essays on origins and impact of Treaty of Trianon (1920) on Hungary and Hungarian minorities in successor states. [SBV]

33.416 János Kis. *Politics in Hungary: for a democratic alternative*. Gábor J. Follinus, trans. Timothy Garton Ash, Introduction. New York: Social Science Monographs and Atlantic Research & Publications; distributed by Columbia University Press, 1989. ISBN 0-88033-963-2. ▸ Thoughtful oppositional essays taken from *Beszélő* (Speaker), Hungary's most famous underground journal in 1980s by journal's editor and founding president of Alliance of Free Democrats, important post-1989 party. [GS]

33.417 Sándor Kopácsi. *In the name of the working class: the inside story of the Hungarian Revolution*. Daniel Stoffman and Judy Stoffman, trans. George Jonas, Foreword. New York: Grove Press, 1987. ISBN 0-8021-0010-4. ▸ Useful personal story of Hungarian Revolution of 1956 by former police chief of Budapest who sided with Revolution and was condemned to death, but survived to tell his story. [SBV]

33.418 Bennett Kovrig. *Communism in Hungary: from Kun to Kádár*. Stanford, Calif.: Hoover Institution Press, 1979. (Hoover Institution publication, 211.) ISBN 0-8179-7112-2. ▸ Masterly history of communism and Communist party of Hungary with special attention to Hungarian Soviet Republic of 1919 and post–World War II communist regimes of Rákosi and Kádár. [SBV]

33.419 Bennett Kovrig. *The Hungarian People's Republic*. Baltimore: Johns Hopkins University Press, 1970. ISBN 0-8018-1126-0 (cl), 0-8018-1128-7 (pbk). ▸ Straightforward scholarly portrait of communist Hungary in period between World War II and 1970. [SBV]

33.420 Miklós Lackó. *Arrow-cross men, national socialists, 1935–1944*. Budapest: Akadémiai Kiadó, 1969. (Studia historica Academiae Scientiarum Hungaricae, 61.) ▸ History of Hungarian fascist (Arrow Cross) movement under Ferenc Szálasi and his forerunners between 1935 and 1944 by respected Marxist scholar. Emphasis on movement's heyday, 1938–39. [SBV]

33.421 William Lomax, ed. *Eye-witness in Hungary: the Soviet invasion of 1956*. 1980 ed. Nottingham, England: Spokesman, 1981. ISBN 0-85124-291-X (cl, 1980), 0-85124-327-4 (pbk). ▸ Personal narratives by participants and observers of Hungarian Revolution of 1956. [SBV]

33.422 William Lomax, ed. *Hungarian workers' councils in 1956*. William Lomax and Julian Schöpflin, trans. Boulder: Social Science Monographs; distributed by Columbia University Press, 1991. (East European monographs, 294.) ISBN 0-88033-191-7. ▸ Well-selected compendium of primary sources including proclamations, memoranda, official documents, and personal narratives concerning activities of Hungarian workers' councils during Revolution of 1956. [SBV]

33.423 C. A. Macartney. *Hungary and her successors: the Treaty of Trianon and its consequences, 1919–1937*. 1937 ed. London: Oxford University Press, 1968. ▸ Combined with *October Fifteenth* (33.424), presents best panoramic view of interwar Hungary's development. Classic. [SBV]

33.424 C. A. Macartney. *October fifteenth: a history of modern Hungary, 1929–1945*. 2d ed. 2 vols. Edinburgh: Edinburgh University Press, 1961. ▸ Along with *Hungary and Her Successors* (33.423), constitutes most comprehensive English-language history of interwar Hungary by traditional British historian, who viewed Hungary with much sympathy. Earlier title: *A History of Hungary* (1956–57). [SBV]

33.425 Kati Marton. *Wallenberg*. New York: Random House, 1982. ISBN 0-394-52360-1. ▸ Sensitive portrayal of Swedish diplomat Raoul Wallenberg and his efforts to save Hungarian Jews from deportation and extermination. One of best books on Wallenberg. [SBV]

33.426 József Mindszenty. *Memoirs*. Richard Winston, Clara Winston, and Jan van Heurck, trans. New York: Macmillan, 1974. ISBN 0-02-585050-4. ▸ Reminiscences of head of Hungarian Catholic church on his struggle against communism, imprisonment, role in 1956, and asylum at American embassy in Budapest. Reflects his personal philosophy and conservative views. [SBV]

33.427 István I. Mócsy. *The effects of World War I, the uprooted: Hungarian refugees and their impact on Hungarian domestic politics, 1918–1921*. Boulder and New York: Social Science Monographs and Brooklyn College Press; distributed by Columbia University Press, 1983. (East European monographs, 147.) ISBN 0-88033-039-2. ▸ Basically scholarly monograph on how Hungarian domestic politics were influenced by hundreds of thousands of Hungarian refugees driven out of territories lost by Hungary. [SBV]

33.428 Miklós Molnár. *Budapest, 1956: a history of the Hungarian Revolution*. Jeannetta Ford, trans. London: Allen & Unwin, 1971. ISBN 0-04-947020-5. ▸ Revised translation of highly regarded French-language history of revolution. Author an essayist, literary critic, and participant. [SBV]

33.429 Miklós Molnár. *From Béla Kun to János Kádár: seventy years of Hungarian communism*. Arnold J. Pomerans, trans. New York: Berg; distributed by St. Martin's, 1990. ISBN 0-85496-599-8. ▸ Major synthesis of Hungarian communist movement by French-Hungarian scholar. Welcome counterpart to official histories published in Hungary before collapse of communism. [SBV]

33.430 John Flournoy Montgomery. *Hungary: the unwilling satellite*. New York: Devin-Adair, 1947. ▸ Former United States ambassador's sympathetic account of Hungary between 1933 and 1946. During tenure in Hungary (1933–41), Montgomery came to appreciate country's difficult position between Nazi Germany and Soviet Russia. [SBV]

33.431 Ferenc Nagy. *Struggle behind the Iron Curtain*. Stephen K. Swift, trans. New York: Macmillan, 1948. ▸ Reminiscences of struggle against communist takeover by Hungary's post–World War II prime minister. Narrative colored by his personal involvement. Available on microform from Cambridge, Mass.: Harvard University Library Microreproduction Service. [SBV]

33.432 Zsuzsa L. Nagy. *The liberal opposition in Hungary, 1919–1945*. Pál Felix, trans. Mária Kovács, translation ed. Budapest: Akadémiai Kiadó, 1983. (Studia historica Academiae Scientiarum Hungaricae, 185.) ISBN 963-05-2998-X. ▸ Highly regarded description of activities of liberal opposition in Hungary between two world wars by one of Hungary's gifted liberal historians. [SBV]

33.433 Nicholas M. Nagy-Talavera. *The green shirts and others: a history of fascism in Hungary and Rumania*. Stanford, Calif.: Hoover Institution Press, 1970. (Hoover Press publication, 85.) ISBN 0-8179-1851-5. ▸ Comparative study of Hungarian (Arrow Cross) and Romanian (Iron Guard) movements before and during World War II by one who survived their terror. Scholarly treatment, although influenced by personal experience. [SBV]

33.434 Mária Ormos. *From Padua to the Trianon, 1918–1920.* Miklós Uszkay, trans. Boulder and Highland Lakes, N.J.: Social Science Monographs and Atlantic Research & Publications; distributed by Columbia University Press, 1991. (East European monographs, 298.) ISBN 0-88033-195-X. ▸ Balanced analysis of impact of French foreign policy on fate of Austria-Hungary, particularly Hungary, between armistice and peace treaty. [SBV]

33.435 Peter Pastor, ed. *Revolutions and interventions in Hungary and its neighbor states, 1918–1919.* Boulder and Highland Lakes, N.J.: Social Science Monographs and Atlantic Research & Publications; distributed by Columbia University Press, 1988. (East European monographs, 240.) ISBN 0-88033-137-2. ▸ Collection of scholarly essays analyzing post-World War I turbulence in Hungarian lands. [SBV]

33.436 Ferenc Pölöskei. *Hungary after two revolutions, 1919–1922.* Mária Kovács, ed. E. Csicseri-Rónai, trans. Budapest: Akadémiai Kiadó, 1980. (Studia historica Academiae Scientiarum Hungaricae, 132.) ISBN 963-05-2481-3. ▸ Scholarly summary of establishment of post-World War I counterrevolutionary regime as interpreted by respected Marxist historian. Special attention to role of Admiral Horthy and Count Bethlen. [SBV]

33.437 János Radványi. *Hungary and the superpowers: the 1956 revolution and realpolitik.* Stanford, Calif.: Hoover Institution Press, 1972. (Hoover Press publication, 111.) ISBN 0-8179-1111-1. ▸ Insider's view of case of Hungary at United Nations General Assembly by Hungary's United Nations representative after 1956; colored by author's involvement. Also treats Hungarian-American relations and international diplomacy. [SBV]

33.438 Thomas L. Sakmyster. *Hungary, the great powers, and the Danubian crisis, 1936–1939.* Athens: University of Georgia Press, 1980. ISBN 0-8203-0469-7. ▸ Survey of Hungary's foreign policy after World War I (1918) followed by detailed treatment of country's efforts at revisionism while attempting to find place among rival great powers. [SBV]

33.439 William Shawcross. *Crime and compromise: János Kádár and the politics of Hungary since revolution.* New York: Dutton, 1974. ISBN 0-525-08735-4. ▸ Unflattering biography of Kádár, who was used by Soviets to legitimize suppression of 1956 Revolution, but who also started Hungary on road to liberalization. [SBV]

33.440 Thomas Spira. *German-Hungarian relations and the Swabian problem: from Károlyi to Gömbös, 1919–1936.* Boulder: East European Quarterly; distributed by Columbia University Press, 1977. (East European monographs, 25.) ISBN 0-914710-18-4. ▸ Painstaking study of problem posed by presence of large ethnic German group in Hungary between 1919 and 1936 and Hungarian government's efforts to deal with them. [SBV]

33.441 Thomas Spira. *The German-Hungarian-Swabian triangle, 1936–1939: the road to discord.* Boulder: East European Monographs; distributed by Columbia University Press, 1990. (East European monographs, 285.) ISBN 0-88033-182-8. ▸ Scholarly analysis of growing Nazi influence on Hungary's German minorities, Hitler's attempts to enlist their services, and Hungary's efforts to diffuse this problem. Sequel to 33.440. [SBV]

33.442 István Szent-Miklósy. *With the Hungarian Independence movement, 1943–1947: an eyewitness account.* New York: Praeger, 1988. ISBN 0-275-92574-9. ▸ History of Hungarian Independence movement, an anti-German and anti-Soviet underground organization, by one of its founders and members. [SBV]

33.443 Loránt Tilkovszky. *Pál Teleki (1879–1941): a biographical sketch.* Budapest: Akadémiai Kiadó, 1974. (Studia historica Academiae Scientiarum Hungaricae, 86.) ISBN 963-05-00371-9. ▸ Life and times of interwar Hungary's scholarly prime minister. Presentation colored by negative view of Teleki current in Hungary in 1970s. [SBV]

33.444 Rudolf L. Tőkés. *Béla Kun and the Hungarian Soviet Republic: the origins and role of the Communist party of Hungary in the revolutions of 1918–1919.* New York: Praeger for Hoover Institution on War, Revolution, and Peace, 1967. ▸ Standard study of origins of socialism in Hungary and birth and role of Hungarian Communist party in series of revolutions following collapse of Austria-Hungary. [SBV]

33.445 Raphael Vágó. *The grandchildren of Trianon: Hungary and the Hungarian minority in the communist states.* Boulder: East European Monographs; distributed by Columbia University Press, 1989. (East European monographs, 258.) ISBN 0-88033-155-0. ▸ Sympathetic yet scholarly discussion of fate of Hungarians left on other side of frontiers after Treaty of Trianon; special attention to Transylvania. [SBV]

33.446 Ferenc A. Váli. *Rift and revolt in Hungary: nationalism versus communism.* Cambridge, Mass.: Harvard University Press, 1961. ▸ Probably best scholarly summary of post–World War II developments in Hungary that led to Revolution of 1956. [SBV]

33.447 Ferenc A. Váli. *A scholar's odyssey.* Karl W. Ryavec, ed. Ames: Iowa State University Press, 1990. ISBN 0-8138-1533-9. ▸ High-quality memoirs of Hungarian-American scholar who during World War II played minor role in Hungary's secret efforts to leave war. [SBV]

33.448 Steven Béla Várdy. *Clio's art in Hungary and in Hungarian-America.* Boulder: East European Monographs; distributed by Columbia University Press, 1985. (East European monographs, 179.) ISBN 0-88033-071-6. ▸ Collection of twelve useful scholarly studies on Hungarian historiography, concentrating on main historical schools, subdisciplines, scholarly institutions, and on impact of Treaty of Trianon on Hungarian mind. [SBV/GS]

33.449 Steven Béla Várdy. *The Hungarian-Americans.* Boston: Twayne, 1985. ISBN 0-8057-8425-X. ▸ Only English-language work on history, society, politics, and culture of Hungarian-Americans covering all immigrant waves. Deals with causes of emigration and with constant interaction with mother country. [SBV]

33.450 Gábor Vermes. *István Tisza: the liberal vision and conservative statecraft of a Magyar nationalist.* Boulder: East European Monographs; distributed by Columbia University Press, 1985. (East European monographs, 184.) ISBN 0-88033-077-5. ▸ Award-winning study of most influential conservative nationalist statesman of early twentieth-century Hungary. Tisza died with Austro-Hungarian empire he tried to preserve. [SBV]

33.451 Iván Völgyes. *Hungary: a nation of contradictions.* Boulder: Westview, 1982. ISBN 0-89158-929-5. ▸ Brief but well-written introduction to Hungary, Hungarians, and Hungarian society by prolific political scientist. [SBV]

33.452 Iván Völgyes, ed. *Hungary in revolution, 1918–19: nine essays.* Lincoln: University of Nebraska Press, 1971. ISBN 0-8032-0788-3. ▸ Well-known specialists discuss domestic issues and foreign relations during Károlyi and Kun regimes. [SBV]

33.453 Iván Völgyes and Nancy Völgyes. *The liberated female: life, work, and sex in socialist Hungary.* Boulder: Westview, 1977. ISBN 0-89158-815-9. ▸ Survey of position of women in post–World War II Hungary. Points out increased burden represented by three roles: as employees, as mothers-homemakers, and as social-sexual partners. [SBV]

33.454 Francis S. Wagner, ed. *The Hungarian Revolution in perspective.* Washington, D.C.: F. F. Memorial Foundation, 1967. ▸ Tenth-anniversary compendium of useful observations and assessments on Hungarian Revolution of 1956. Includes Halász de Béky's supplement (1,269 items) to his earlier multilingual bibliography (33.399). [SBV]

33.455 Paul E. Zinner. *Revolution in Hungary.* New York: Columbia University Press, 1962. ▸ One of best treatments of origins, course, and outcome of Hungarian Revolution of 1956 on basis of numerous refugee oral histories. Rich source for specialists. [SBV/JSH]

SEE ALSO
21.283 Randolph L. Braham. *The politics of genocide.*
47.454 Peter Pastor. *Hungary between Wilson and Lenin.*

POLAND TO WORLD WAR I

33.456 *Antemurale 7–8* (1963). ISSN 0066-4642. ▸ Two volumes of this periodical devoted entirely to 1863 January Insurrection. Wealth of information on number of significant issues. [MR]

33.457 Szymon Askenazy. *Le prince Joseph Poniatowski, maréchal de France (1763–1813).* B. Kozakiewicz and Paul Cazin, trans. Paris: Plon-Nourrit, 1921. ▸ Biography of one of most colorful individuals in Napoleonic Poland. Also masterful portrayal of Poland in late eighteenth and early nineteenth century. [MR]

33.458 Lidia Becela et al., eds. *Who's who in Poland.* Warsaw: Interpress, 1982. ISBN 3-921220-56-4. ▸ General guide, most useful for information regarding renowned personalities in politics, arts, and sciences. [MR]

33.459 M. B. Biskupski and James S. Pula, eds. *Polish democratic thought from the Renaissance to the Great Emigration: essays and documents.* Boulder: East European Monographs; distributed by Columbia University Press, 1990. (East European monographs, 289.) ISBN 0-88033-186-6. ▸ Five interpretive essays augmented by excellent selection of most fundamental documents of Polish legal tradition. Indispensable collection. [MR]

33.460 Stanislaus A. Blejwas. *Realism in Polish politics: Warsaw positivism and national survival in nineteenth-century Poland.* New Haven: Yale Concilium on International and Area Studies; distributed by Slavica, 1984. ISBN 0-936586-05-2. ▸ Traces origins of Organic Work (cultural and intellectual endeavors instead of armed insurrection) and examines influence of positivist ideas on Polish political philosophy. Invaluable work for understanding ideological trends in late nineteenth century. [MR]

33.461 Robert Blobaum. *Feliks Dzierżyński and the SDKPiL: a study of the origins of Polish communism.* Boulder: East European Monographs; distributed by Columbia University Press, 1984. (East European monographs, 154.) ISBN 0-88033-046-5. ▸ Valuable inquiry into history of Polish Marxist ideology and its political manifestations. One of few works in English analyzing Dzierżyński's pre-Soviet activities and role in revolutionary party Social Democracy of the Kingdom of Poland and Lithuania. [MR]

33.462 Celina Bobińska and Andrzej Pilch, eds. *Employment-seeking emigrations of the Poles world-wide: nineteenth and twentieth century.* Danuta E. Zukowska, trans. Kraków: Państwowe Wydawnictwo Naukowe, 1975. (Zeszyty Naukowe Uniwersytetu Jagiellońskiego, 417. Prace polonijne, 1.) ▸ Collection of seven essays focusing on economic causes of emigration; no material provided on post-1939 exodus. Analytically and methodologically sound. [MR]

33.463 Peter Brock. *Nationalism and populism in partitioned Poland: selected essays.* London: Orbis, 1973. ISBN 0-901149-09-8. ▸ Several short monographic essays on nationalism, populism, and ethnic minorities in nineteenth century. Augmented by useful bibliography. [MR]

33.464 Władysław Czapliński and Tadeusz Ładógoski, eds. *The*

historical atlas of Poland. Maria Paczynska, trans. Warsaw: Państwowe Przedsiębiorstwo Wydawnictwo Kartograficznych, 1986. ISBN 83-7000-016-9, 83-7000-037-1. ▸ Features color maps of Polish lands from early Stone Age to present, each accompanied by brief commentary. Most reliable collection of historical maps of Poland. [MR]

33.465 Norman Davies. *God's playground: a history of Poland.* Rev. ed. 2 vols. Oxford: Clarendon, 1982. ISBN 0-19-821943-1 (v. 1), 0-19-821944-X (v. 2). ▸ Vivid and colorful narrative, but not always factually accurate. Enjoyable to read yet difficult to use as guide or as reference work. [MR]

33.466 Norman Davies. *Poland past and present: a select bibliography of works in English.* Newtonville, Mass.: Oriental Research Partners, 1977. ISBN 0-89250-010-7 (cl), 0-89250-011-5 (pbk). ▸ One of most useful guides on Poland, especially in area of humanities and social sciences. Somewhat dated but includes good history section. [MR]

33.467 Harry E. Dembkowski. *The Union of Lublin: Polish federalism in the golden age.* Boulder: East European Monographs; distributed by Columbia University Press, 1982. (East European monographs, 116.) ISBN 0-88033-009-0. ▸ Detailed account of negotiations leading to creation of Polish-Lithuanian Commonwealth in 1569, but also intriguing story of Union. Skillful presentation of political ramifications. [MR]

33.468 Jean Fabre. *Stanislas-Auguste Poniatowski et l'Europe des Lumières: étude de cosmopolitisme.* 2d ed. Paris: Ophrys, 1984. (Association des publications près les Univérsites de Strasbourg, 116.) ▸ Comprehensive biography. Recreates Poniatowski's life and skillfully presents his dilemmas in context of sociopolitical conditions of eighteenth-century Europe. [MR]

33.469 J. K. Fedorowicz, Maria Bogucka, and Henry K. Samsonwicz, eds. *A republic of nobles: studies in Polish history to 1864.* J. K. Fedorowicz, trans. Cambridge: Cambridge University Press, 1982. ISBN 0-521-24093-X. ▸ Well-balanced anthology on wide variety of topics from Middle Ages to late nineteenth century. Accurately reflects contemporary Polish scholarship. [MR]

33.470 Samuel Fiszman, ed. *The Polish Renaissance in its European context.* Bloomington: Indiana University Press, 1988. ISBN 0-253-34627-4. ▸ Valuable anthology of interpretive essays on Polish society, law, religion, science, art, and architecture during Renaissance. Separate section devoted to literary tradition of Jan Kochanowski. [MR]

33.471 Alvin Marcus Fountain II. *Roman Dmowski: party, tactics, ideology, 1895–1907.* Boulder: East European Monographs; distributed by Columbia University Press, 1980. (East European monographs, 60.) ISBN 0-914710-53-2. ▸ Early political career of one of Poland's foremost statesmen and leader of influential National Democratic party. Good introduction to Polish nationalism. [MR]

33.472 Aleksander Gieysztor et al. *History of Poland.* 2d ed. Krystyna Cekalska et al., trans. Warsaw: Polish Scientific Publishers, 1979. ISBN 83-01-00392-8. ▸ One of most comprehensive works on Polish history. Six preeminent Polish historians present Polish political, cultural, and economic history from tenth century to 1939. Relatively unmarred by Marxist interpretations. [MR]

33.473 Oskar Halecki and Antony Polonsky. *A history of Poland.* 9th ed. London: Routledge & Kegan Paul, 1983. ISBN 0-7102-0050-1 (pbk). ▸ Popular overview of Polish history from tenth century to end of World War II, highlighting significant events. Good introduction written in undemanding style. [MR]

33.474 Marceli Handelsman. *Napoléon et la Pologne, 1806–1807: d'après les documents des Archives Nationales et les archives du ministère des affaires étrangères.* Paris: Librairies Felix Alcan et Guillaumin Ruenies, 1909. ▸ Valuable brief study centering on Napoleon's role in creation of Duchy of Warsaw and on influence on Polish politics; also Bonaparte's designs for Poland as member of European community. [MR]

33.475 Paweł Jasienica. *Piast Poland.* Alexander T. Jordan, trans. Miami, Fla.: American Institute of Polish Culture, 1985. ISBN 0-87052-134-9. ▸ Narrative history of country during Piast dynasty. If not most exhaustive, certainly best penned book on medieval Poland. Intuitive grasp of central issues. [MR]

33.476 Jacek Jędruch. *Constitutions, elections, and legislatures of Poland, 1493–1977: a guide to their history.* Washington, D.C.: University Press of America, 1982. ISBN 0-8191-2508-3 (cl), 0-8191-2509-1 (pbk). ▸ Overview of Polish constitutional history, including biographical sketches of important legislators. Helpful introduction. [MR]

33.477 August Gerald Kanka. *Poland: an annotated bibliography of books in English.* New York: Garland, 1988. ISBN 0-8240-8492-6. ▸ Useful general guide to publications in variety of fields; sections on history. [MR]

33.478 Herbert H. Kaplan. *The first partition of Poland.* 1962 ed. New York: AMS Press, 1972. ISBN 0-404-03636-8. ▸ Scholarly account of first dismemberment of Polish state by Prussia, Russia, and Austria. One of few works addressing this topic. [MR]

33.479 Stefan Kieniewicz. *The emancipation of the Polish peasantry.* Chicago: University of Chicago Press, 1969. ISBN 0-226-43524-5. ▸ Profound depiction of social and economic conditions within partitioned state and of such related issues as participation in uprisings and role of Russian government. [MR]

33.480 Władysław Konopczyński et al., eds. *Polski Słownik Biograficzny* (Polish biographical dictionary). 32 vols. to date. Kraków: Skład Główny w Księg, Gebethnera i Wolffa, 1935–. ▸ Most comprehensive Polish biographical dictionary available. Still in production (has reached letter R). [MR]

33.481 Stanisław Kot. *Socinianism in Poland: the social and political ideas of the Polish anti-Trinitarians in the sixteenth and seventeenth centuries.* Earl Morse Wilbur, trans. Boston: Starr King, 1957. ▸ First-rate history of one of most active Protestant sects in Poland, stressing sect's relationship with other Protestants, role of Catholic church, and attitude of state toward religious dissenters. [MR]

33.482 Manfred Kridl, Władysław Malinowski, and Józef Wittlin, eds. *For your freedom and ours: Polish progressive spirit from the fourteenth century to the present.* 2d ed. Krystyna M. Olszer, ed. of 2d ed. New York: Ungar, 1981. ISBN 0-8044-1477-7 (cl), 0-8044-6615-7 (pbk). ▸ Whiggish anthology of writings that contributed to development and strengthening of Polish democratic traditions. Broad, representative sample reaching back to sixteenth century. [MR]

33.483 George Krzywicki-Herburt. "Polish philosophy." In vol. 6 of *The encyclopedia of philosophy.* Paul Edwards, ed., pp. 363–70. New York: Macmillan, 1967. ▸ Concise but fact-filled introduction to Polish philosophy. Starting with Scholastics, discusses all significant philosophical trends from Middle Ages to present. [MR]

33.484 Marian Kukiel. *Czartoryski and European unity, 1770–1861.* Princeton: Princeton University Press, 1955. ▸ Despite strong Polish nationalist bias, important for Czartoryski's activities for Polish independence under Alexander, as leader in 1830, and as head of aristocratic emigration. Special attention to Russo-Polish relations within larger European context. [MR/PWS]

33.485 Wacław Lednicki. *Life and culture of Poland as reflected in Polish literature.* New York: Roy, 1944. ▸ Poland's liberal traditions presented through works of Renaissance thinkers and nineteenth-century poets. Valuable commentary on cultural and political developments in Poland in relation to similar trends in western Europe. [MR]

33.486 R. F. Leslie. *Polish politics and the revolution of November 1830.* London: Athlone, 1956. ▸ Focuses primarily on social conditions at time of uprising. Argues unconvincingly that important political and military developments had only limited influence on outcome of crisis. [MR]

33.487 R. F. Leslie. *Reform and insurrection in Russian Poland, 1856–1865.* 1963 ed. Westport, Conn.: Greenwood, 1969. ISBN 0-8371-2415-8. ▸ Examination of sociopolitical conditions at time of January Insurrection. Much attention to peasant-lord relations, but understates impact of broader political issues affecting outcome of uprising. [MR]

33.488 R. F. Leslie, ed. *The history of Poland since 1863.* Rev. ed. Cambridge: Cambridge University Press, 1983. ISBN 0-521-22645-7 (cl), 0-521-27501-6 (pbk). ▸ Focuses primarily on socioeconomic and political issues, tending to ignore significant foreign and domestic policy issues. Useful text but should be read with degree of circumspection. [MR]

33.489 Robert Howard Lord. *The second partition of Poland: a study in diplomatic history.* Cambridge, Mass.: Harvard University Press, 1915. ▸ Explicative and analytic study focusing on political and diplomatic activity in context of European developments. Most complete work on this theme. Available on microform from Dayton, Ohio: Microlection, 1974. [MR]

33.490 Rett R. Ludwikowski. *Continuity and change in Poland: conservatism in Polish political thought.* Washington, D.C.: Catholic University of America Press, 1991. ISBN 0-8132-0743-6. ▸ Depicts representative trends in neglected area of intellectual history, especially nineteenth-century thought; tackles such issues as Alexander Wielopolski's policy and phenomenon of triloyalism. [MR]

33.491 Czesław Miłosz. *The history of Polish literature.* 2d ed. Berkeley: University of California Press, 1983. ISBN 0-520-04465-7 (cl), 0-520-04477-0 (pbk). ▸ Fact-filled survey of literary works from Middle Ages to second half of twentieth century. Nobel laureate does not shy away from sharing opinions with reader. [MR]

33.492 Benjamin P. Murdzek. *Emigration in Polish social-political thought, 1870–1914.* Boulder: East European Quarterly; distributed by Columbia University Press, 1977. (East European monographs, 33.) ISBN 0-914710-26-5. ▸ Well-documented analysis of underlying causes of emigration; Prussian, Russian, and Austrian emigration policies; and Polish attitudes on whole phenomenon of emigration and exile. [MR]

33.493 Norman M. Naimark. *The history of the "proletariat": the emergence of Marxism in the Kingdom of Poland, 1870–1887.* Boulder: East European Quarterly; distributed by Columbia University Press, 1979. (East European monographs, 54.) ISBN 0-914710-50-8. ▸ Penetrating study of first Marxist party in Poland. Skillful presentation in context of sociopolitical ferment in Russian-controlled country. [MR]

33.494 Jan Chryzostom Pasek. *The memoirs of Jan Chryzostom z Gosławic Pasek.* 1971 ed. Maria A. J. Święcicka, ed. and trans. New York: Kosciuszko Foundation, 1978. (Library of Polish studies, 8.) ISBN 0-917004-15-9. ▸ Invaluable memoir of seventeenth-century squire. Captivating travelog written by soldier who shares impressions on customs, culture, and politics of peoples inhabiting lands between Denmark and Muscovy. Unique. [MR]

33.495 Peter J. Potichnyj, ed. *Poland and Ukraine: past and present.* Edmonton: Canadian Institute of Ukrainian Studies, 1980. ISBN 0-920862-05-5 (cl), 0-920862-07-1 (pbk). ▸ Highly readable, representative collection addressing questions of national consciousness, ethnic prejudice, religious life, and sociopolitical conditions of last three hundred years. [MR]

33.496 William F. Reddaway et al., eds. *The Cambridge history of Poland.* 2 vols. Cambridge: Cambridge University Press, 1941–55. ‣ Thorough, scholarly compilation dealing with major currents of Polish history. Somewhat dated but remains one of best in this field. [MR]

33.497 William J. Rose. *The rise of Polish democracy.* London: Bell, 1944. ‣ Dated but solid old-fashioned scholarship. Good as basic introduction to nineteenth-century labor, peasant movement, triloyalism, and socialism. Separate section covers political institutions. [MR]

33.498 Harold B. Segel. *Renaissance culture in Poland: the rise of humanism, 1470–1543.* Ithaca, N.Y.: Cornell University Press, 1989. ISBN 0-8014-2286-8. ‣ Successfully integrates Polish Renaissance, ignored by scholars during cold war, into European Renaissance. [MR]

33.499 Joan S. Skurnowicz. *Romantic nationalism and liberalism: Joachim Lelewel and the Polish national idea.* Boulder: East European Monographs; distributed by Columbia University Press, 1981. (East European monographs, 83.) ISBN 0-914710-77-X. ‣ Biography of nineteenth-century historian and political thinker. Profound examination of Polish political climate. [MR]

33.500 Daniel Stone. *Polish politics and national reform, 1775–1788.* Boulder: East European Quarterly; distributed by Columbia University Press, 1976. (East European monographs, 22.) ISBN 0-914710-15-X. ‣ Well-documented study of Poland's efforts at reform after first partition. Impressive grasp of relevant political issues of era. [MR]

33.501 Bogdan Suchodolski. *A history of Polish culture.* E. J. Czerwiński, trans. Warsaw: Interpress, 1986. ISBN 83-223-2142-2. ‣ Monumental if somewhat monotonous survey of Polish culture. Polish history reinterpreted and restated in culturally significant terms. [MR]

33.502 Bogdan Suchodolski, ed. *Poland, the land of Copernicus.* Bogusław Buczkowski et al., trans. Warsaw: Ossolineum, 1973. ‣ Excellent collection of interpretive essays on art, music, religion, science, and politics beginning with sixteenth century. Assumes rudimentary knowledge of Polish history. Very good anthology. [MR]

33.503 Bogdan Suchodolski et al., eds. *Wielka encyklopedia powszechna* (The great encyclopedia). 13 vols. Warsaw: Państwowe Wydawnictwo Naukowe, 1962–70. ‣ Most complete Polish encyclopedia. All-inclusive reference work with excellent citations on history. Certain topics censored under communist rule. [MR]

33.504 Janusz Tazbir. *A state without stakes: Polish religious toleration in the sixteenth and seventeenth centuries.* 1972 ed. Alexander T. Jordan, trans. New York: Kosciuszko Foundation, 1973. (Library of Polish studies, 3.) ‣ History of religious dissent and its reception by state. Most informative on various Protestant groups. [MR]

33.505 Frank W. Thackeray. *Antecedents of revolution: Alexander I and the Polish kingdom, 1815–1825.* Boulder: East European Monographs; distributed by Columbia University Press, 1980. (East European monographs, 67.) ISBN 0-914710-61-3. ‣ Good comparative work focusing on Russian treatment of Congress Kingdom. Reveals much more of inner workings of Russian diplomatic corps than of policy toward Poland. [MR]

33.506 Lech Trzeciakowski. *The Kulturkampf in Prussian Poland.* Katarzyna Kretkowska, trans. New York: East European Monographs; distributed by Columbia University Press, 1990. (East European monographs, 283.) ISBN 0-88033-180-1. ‣ One of best studies of Bismarck's policy to forcibly germanize Polish population in former Polish provinces. [MR]

33.507 Wenceslas J. Wagner, ed. *Polish law throughout the ages.* Stanford, Calif.: Hoover Institution Press, 1970. (Hoover Press publication, 91.) ISBN 0-8179-1911-2. ‣ Collection of essays on constitutional, civil, criminal, and administrative law. Related fields also discussed. Unique but limited in scope. [MR]

33.508 Andrzej Walicki. *The Enlightenment and the birth of modern nationhood: Polish political thought from noble republicanism to Tadeusz Kosciuszko.* Emma Harris, trans. Notre Dame, Ind.: University of Notre Dame Press, 1989. ISBN 0-268-00618-0. ‣ Excellent study tracing origins of modern concept of nationhood in writings of Poland's eighteenth-century savants. [MR/GS]

33.509 Andrzej Walicki. *Philosophy and romantic nationalism: the case of Poland.* Oxford: Clarendon, 1982. ISBN 0-19-827250-2. ‣ Primary work on Polish philosophy and intellectual tradition of nineteenth century. Penetrating analysis of most influential currents of Polish thought. One of best studies in any language. [MR]

33.510 Andrzej Walicki. *Stanisław Brzozowski and the Polish beginnings of "Western Marxism."* Oxford: Clarendon, 1989. ISBN 0-19-827328-2. ‣ Argumentative but convincing biography of philosopher and literary critic whose contributions to Marxist philosophy went largely unnoticed. Argues that Brzozowski, not Lukács, introduced humanist Marxism as part of European intellectual tradition. [MR]

33.511 Piotr S. Wandycz. *The lands of partitioned Poland, 1795–1918.* Seattle: University of Washington Press, 1974. ISBN 0-295-95351-9. ‣ Most exhaustive study of partitioned Poland in English. Illuminates all key developments in three partition zones. Augmented by invaluable bibliographical essay. [MR]

33.512 Bernard D. Weinryb. *The Jews of Poland: a social and economic history of the Jewish community in Poland from 1100 to 1800.* Philadelphia: Jewish Publication Society of America, 1976. ISBN 0-8276-0016-X. ‣ Excellent presentation of Jewish life in Poland in all of its aspects: social, cultural, economic, political, and legal. [MR]

33.513 Henryk Wereszycki. "Polish insurrections as a controversial problem in Polish historiography." *Canadian Slavonic papers* 9 (1967) 98–121. ISSN 0008-5006. ‣ Excellent polemical article addressing recurring issue in Polish history: to fight or not to fight. Debate continues to fascinate professional historians and Polish public alike. [MR]

33.514 Joseph Wiśniewski. *Who's who in Poland.* Toronto: Professional Translators and Publishers, 1981. ISBN 0-919583-00-8. ‣ Useful alphabetical guide to names followed by section on organs of state, political parties, societies, trade unions, etc. [MR]

33.515 Adam Zamoyski. *The Polish way: a thousand-year history of the Poles and their culture.* 1987 ed. New York: Watts, 1988. ISBN 0-531-15069-0. ‣ Handsomely illustrated, well-written survey of Polish history, focused largely on Poland's cultural traditions. [MR]

33.516 Adam Żółtowski. *Border of Europe: a study of the Polish eastern provinces.* London: Hollis & Carter, 1950. ‣ Nineteenth- and twentieth-century political events in Galicia and eastern Lithuania. Also touches on relevant military affairs and cultural development. Well written. [MR]

SEE ALSO
21.182 Aleksander Hertz. *The Jews in Polish culture.*
34.302 Frank E. Sysyn. *Between Poland and the Ukraine.*

POLAND SINCE WORLD WAR I

33.517 Władysław Anders. *An army in exile: the story of the Second Polish Corps.* Harold Macmillan, Introduction. London:

Macmillan, 1949. ▸ Creation of Polish exile army in Russia and its subsequent history as told by its commander. Key work presenting Polish military effort, 1939–45, and its larger political context. Also available on microform from Cambridge, Mass.: Harvard University Library Microreproduction Service. [WLB]

33.518 Neal Ascherson. *The Polish August: the self-limiting revolution.* New York: Viking, 1982. ISBN 0-670-56305-6. ▸ Captivating history of Polish politics from end of World War II to establishment of Solidarity. Excellent introduction by socialist journalist. [MR]

33.519 Władysław Bartoszewski and Zofia Lewin, eds. *Righteous among nations: how Poles helped the Jews, 1939–1945.* London: Earlscourt, 1969. ▸ Useful collection of personal accounts and documents recording aid to Jews provided by Polish underground and Polish civilians. [WLB]

33.520 Józef Beck. *Final report.* New York: Speller, 1957. ▸ Exposé of Polish interwar foreign policy focusing on period after 1926. Composed by Poland's post-1932 foreign minister while in Romanian detention. Indispensable for understanding sometimes self-defeating Polish actions. [WLB]

33.521 Nicholas William Bethell. *Gomułka: his Poland, his communism.* Rev. ed. Harmondsworth: Penguin, 1972. ISBN 0-14-021470-4. ▸ Convincing analysis of Polish history from perspective of Gomułka's career. Concentrates primarily on prelude and aftermath of October 1956 and inherent shortcomings of communist reform. [WLB]

33.522 Nicholas William Bethell. *The war Hitler won: the fall of Poland, September 1939.* 1972 ed. New York: Holt Rinehart & Winston, 1973. ISBN 0-03-001376-3. ▸ Wide-ranging, well-written narrative discussing months surrounding Germany's conquest of Poland. Entertaining introduction to diplomatic and strategic background and to great power policies vis-à-vis Poland. [WLB]

33.523 Joseph L. Black and John W. Strong, eds. *Sisyphus and Poland: reflections on martial law.* Winnepeg, Canada: Frye, 1986. ISBN 0-919741-46-0. ▸ Collection of essays providing impressive overview of Poland following Solidarity's delegalization. Divided into following categories: historical and social context, East Central Europe, Western perception, and Poland. [WLB]

33.524 Lucjan Blit. *The eastern pretender, Bolesław Piasecki: his life and times.* London: Hutchinson, 1965. ▸ Although author tends to demonize subject, provides valuable insights into Polish extreme Right and Communists' postwar attempts to exploit Catholicism for their own ends. [WLB]

33.525 Tadeusz Bór-Komorowski. *The secret army.* 1950 ed. Nashville: Battery, 1984. ISBN 0-89839-082-6. ▸ Sincere depiction of Polish underground army by its commander and leader of Warsaw uprising. Large portion of book devoted to ill-fated uprising. [WLB]

33.526 Adam Bromke. *The meaning and uses of Polish history.* Boulder: East European Monographs; distributed by Columbia University Press, 1987. (East European monographs, 212.) ISBN 0-88033-109-7. ▸ Useful for translations of texts by twentieth-century Polish political thinkers. Traces evolution of nationalist thought and Catholicism's political role. [WLB]

33.527 Adam Bromke. *Poland's politics: idealism vs. realism.* Cambridge, Mass.: Harvard University Press, 1967. (Russian Research Center studies, 51.) ▸ Based on rather simplistic and not entirely accurate dichotomy in modern Polish political thought, but provides provocative perspective on many issues that lend themselves to discussion. [WLB]

33.528 Abraham Brumberg, ed. *Poland: genesis of a revolution.* New York: Random House, 1983. ISBN 0-394-52323-7 (cl), 0-394-71025-8 (pbk). ▸ Collection of essays discussing Solidari-

ty's context and its components. Augmented by translations of contemporary Polish texts. Convenient, effective book for introducing history of Solidarity. [WLB]

33.529 Bohdan B. Budurowycz. "Poland and the Ukrainian problem, 1921–1939." *Canadian Slavonic papers* 25.4 (1983) 473–500. ISSN 0008-5006. ▸ Well-balanced overview of political history of interwar Poland's largest national minority. Helps reader understand more fully one of interwar state's greatest weaknesses. [WLB]

33.530 Bohdan B. Budurowycz. *Polish-Soviet relations, 1932–1939.* New York: Columbia University Press, 1963. ▸ Scholarly study contributing effectively to understanding of interwar Poland's perilous position between two great powers. Well-balanced diplomatic history. [WLB]

33.531 Michael Checinski. *Poland: communism, nationalism, anti-Semitism.* New York: Karz-Cohl, 1982. ISBN 0-918294-18-5. ▸ Traces history and explains role of official communist antisemitism in postwar Poland. Incisive dissection of communist rule by informed insider. [WLB]

33.532 Jan M. Ciechanowski. *Defeat in victory.* Garden City, N.Y.: Doubleday, 1947. ▸ Description of Polish question during World War II from vantage point of Poland's ambassador to United States. Important source for wartime Polish diplomacy. Available on microform from Cambridge, Mass.: Harvard University Library Microreproduction Service. [WLB]

33.533 Jan M. Ciechanowski. *The Warsaw rising of 1944.* London: Cambridge University Press, 1974. ISBN 0-521-20203-5. ▸ Provocative, controversial, critical examination of political and ideological factors that led to fateful uprising. Significant study of World War II Polish politics and Poland's contemporary place in Europe. [WLB]

33.534 Anna M. Cienciała. *Poland and the Western powers, 1938–1939: a study in the interdependence of Eastern and Western Europe.* London: Routledge & Kegan Paul, 1968. ISBN 0-7100-5021-6. ▸ Trenchant examination of Poland's position within prewar European order. Portrays Polish policies as determined largely by posture of France and Great Britain, which failed to recognize ultimate consequences of interdependence. [WLB]

33.535 Anna M. Cienciała and Titus Komarnicki. *From Versailles to Locarno: keys to Polish foreign policy, 1919–1925.* Lawrence: University Press of Kansas, 1984. ISBN 0-7006-0247-X. ▸ Issue-oriented sequel to Komarnicki's study on birth of Poland (33.562). Identifies major determinants of Second Republic's place in Europe. Excellent introduction to Polish interwar foreign policy. [WLB]

33.536 John Coutouvidis and Jaime Reynolds. *Poland, 1939–1947.* Leicester: Leicester University Press, 1986. ISBN 0-7185-1211-1 (cl), 0-7185-1273-1 (pbk). ▸ Textbook-style study focusing on three arenas of World War II internal Polish political history: London government, underground state, and Moscow-based Communists. Presents Polish perspective on war, liberation, and reconstruction. [WLB]

33.537 Norman Davies. *White eagle, red star: the Polish-Soviet war, 1919–20.* New York: St. Martin's, 1972. ▸ Well-written, very detailed study of war and its significance for both main actors and rest of Europe. Examines diplomatic, military, political, and social aspects of war. [WLB]

33.538 Jan B. De Weydenthal. *The Communists of Poland: an historical outline.* Rev. ed. Stanford, Calif.: Hoover Institution Press, 1986. (Hoover Press publication, 347.) ISBN 0-8179-8472-0. ▸ Broad institutional history concerned primarily with post-1945 events. Five-phase chronological division with political science emphasis. Establishes Polish communism's dependence on Moscow as defining factor in its historical development. [WLB]

33.539 M. K. Dziewanowski. *The Communist party of Poland: an outline of history.* Cambridge, Mass.: Harvard University Press, 1976. ISBN 0-674-15055-4. ‣ Broad narrative, interpretive overview spanning period from origins of socialism in Poland through Gierek's rule. Thematically focused political history providing access to broader historical issues. [WLB]

33.540 M. K. Dziewanowski. *Joseph Piłsudski: a European federalist, 1918–1922.* Stanford, Calif.: Hoover Institution Press, 1969. (Hoover Press publication, 79.) ISBN 0-8179-1791-8. ‣ Well-argued presentation of Piłsudski as twentieth-century propagator of ideals of pre-1795, multinational Polish-Lithuanian Commonwealth. Informative study of events from Polish perspective. [WLB]

33.541 M. K. Dziewanowski. *Poland in the twentieth century.* New York: Columbia University Press, 1977. ISBN 0-231-03577-2. ‣ Competent general overview of Polish history encompassing important pre-twentieth-century antecedents and extending into 1970s. Effective introductory reading. [WLB]

33.542 David J. Engel. *In the shadow of Auschwitz: the Polish government-in-exile and the Jews, 1939–1942.* Chapel Hill: University of North Carolina Press, 1987. ISBN 0-8078-1737-6. ‣ Extremely thorough, refreshingly scholarly study of exiled Polish government's reaction to plight of Jews in occupied Poland in period leading up to systematic mass extermination. [WLB/EM]

33.543 Józef Garliński. *The Enigma war.* 1979 ed. New York: Scribner's, 1980. ISBN 0-684-15866-3. ‣ Popularly written story of how Allies broke and used German Enigma code in World War II. Polish cryptographers supplied initial breakthrough in 1930s. [WLB]

33.544 Józef Garliński. *Poland in the Second World War.* New York: Hippocrene, 1985. ISBN 0-87052-002-4. ‣ Comprehensive overview of Polish wartime history. Covers all major issues and major categories of events. Fine synthetic introductory work also of interest to specialists. [WLB]

33.545 Józef Garliński. *Poland, SOE, and the Allies.* Paul Stevenson, trans. London: Allen & Unwin, 1969. ISBN 0-04-355006-1. ‣ Study of relationship between underground state and British authorities (Special Operations Executive) responsible for aiding resistance movements in occupied Europe. Sheds light on broader political and strategic limits confronting Poland. [WLB]

33.546 Timothy Garton Ash. *The Polish revolution: Solidarity.* Rev. ed. New York: Viking Penguin, 1991. ISBN 0-14-014037-9. ‣ Highly insightful, very readable account of Solidarity's inception and subsequent history up to martial law. Although journalistic, places Solidarity within broader historical context. [WLB]

33.547 Stanisław Gomułka and Antony Polonsky, eds. *Polish paradoxes.* London: Routledge, 1990. ISBN 0-415-04375-1. ‣ Thought-provoking collection of essays devoted to relationship between Polish past and present as it applies to politics and society in 1980s. [WLB]

33.548 Lawrence Goodwyn. *Breaking the barrier: the rise of Solidarity in Poland.* New York: Oxford University Press, 1991. ISBN 0-19-506122-5. ‣ Argumentative, repetitive book holding that Polish workers, particularly those of Szczecin in 1970, invented Solidarity's demands of 1980 independently of intelligentsia, which did not grasp workers' ability for self-activation. [GS]

33.549 Jan Tomasz Gross. *Polish society under German occupation: the Generalgouvernement, 1939–1944.* Princeton: Princeton University Press, 1979. ISBN 0-691-09381-4. ‣ Examination of Polish society's response to German occupation from sociological vantage point. Focuses on process whereby society created alternative organizational structures. Ambitious, successful blending of sociological methods with historical perspective. [WLB]

33.550 Jan Tomasz Gross. *Revolution from abroad: the Soviet conquest of Poland's western Ukraine and western Belorussia.* Princeton: Princeton University Press, 1988. ISBN 0-691-09433-0. ‣ Reconstruction of conditions engendered and exploited by Soviet occupation of eastern Poland. Original study of sovietization as sociological process. Inspires broader conclusions and comparisons concerning totalitarian conquest and rule. [WLB]

33.551 Yisrael Gutman et al., eds. *The Jews of Poland between two world wars.* Hanover, N.H.: University Press of New England for Brandeis University Press, 1989. (Tauber Institute for the Study of European Jewry series, 10.) ISBN 0-87451-446-0. ‣ One of largest collections of essays dealing with this period of Jewish history. Impressive in scope and quality. [MR]

33.552 Celia S. Heller. *On the edge of destruction: Jews of Poland between the two world wars.* New York: Columbia University Press, 1977. ISBN 0-231-03819-4. ‣ Most prominent, albeit controversial, English-language representative of historiography portraying interwar Second Polish Republic as prelude to German-implemented Holocaust. [WLB]

33.553 Jerzy Holzer. *"Solidarität": die Geschichte einer freien Gewerkschaft in Polen.* Hans Henning Hahn, ed. Munich: Beck, 1985. ISBN 3-406-30603-9. ‣ History of Solidarity during its most dynamic and volatile period, 1980–81. Written by activist in movement; offers intriguing firsthand accounts of some critical developments. [MR]

33.554 Stephan M. Horak. *Poland and her national minorities, 1919–39: a case study.* New York: Vantage, 1961. ‣ Although plagued by distortions, remains only comprehensive overview of this thorny subject in English. Adequate introduction to various non-Polish ethnic groups. [WLB]

33.555 Instytut Historyczny Imienia Generała Sikorskiego. *Documents on Polish-Soviet relations, 1939–1945.* 2 vols. London: Heinemann, 1961–67. ‣ Extremely valuable English-language research tool permitting reader to draw conclusions on Polish-Soviet relations and Polish question. Documentation drawn from wide variety of contemporary sources. Usefully augments multivolume Polish-Russian edition on same subject. [WLB]

33.556 Wacław Jędrzejewicz. *Piłsudski: a life for Poland.* Zbigniew K. Brzezinski, Introduction. New York: Hippocrene, 1982. ISBN 0-88254-633-3. ‣ Richly detailed study of figure who decisively influenced pre-1918 Polish struggle for independence and subsequent development of independent Second Republic. Readable, informative political biography. [WLB]

33.557 George V. Kacewicz. *Great Britain, the Soviet Union, and the Polish government in exile (1939–1945).* The Hague: Nijhoff, 1979. ISBN 90-247-2096-6. ‣ Thorough scholarly analysis of London-based Polish government-in-exile and impact of Anglo-Soviet relations on Polish policies, and freedom of maneuver. Also focuses on Soviet-Polish relations. [WLB]

33.558 Jakub Karpiński. *Countdown: the Polish upheavals of 1956, 1968, 1970, 1976, 1980, ...* Olga Amsterdamska and Gene M. Moore, trans. New York: Karz-Cohl, 1982. ISBN 0-918294-14-2 (cl), 0-918294-15-0 (pbk). ‣ Sociologist's accessible chronological survey of sequence of post-1945 events that led to Solidarity. As title suggests, presents Polish society's resistance to communism as self-perpetuating process. [WLB]

33.559 Jan Karski. *The great powers and Poland, 1919–1945: from Versailles to Yalta.* Lanham, Md.: University Press of America, 1985. ISBN 0-8191-4398-7 (cl), 0-8191-4399-5 (pbk). ‣ Broad overview addressing all major issues pertaining to independent Poland's place in world through World War II. Argues that Polish interests always subordinated to those of great powers. [WLB]

33.560 Jan Karski. *Story of a secret state.* Boston: Houghton-Mifflin, 1944. ‣ First English-language account of underground state.

Written by participant who acted as courier between Poland and West. Highly readable description of conditions in Poland. [WLB]

33.561 Michael T. Kaufman. *Mad dreams, saving graces: Poland, a nation in conspiracy.* New York: Random House, 1989. ISBN 0-394-55486-8. ▸ Intensely personal account of Poland in 1980s by *New York Times* correspondent. Good anecdotes that capture feeling of "normalized" Poland. [MR]

33.562 Titus Komarnicki. *Rebirth of the Polish republic: a study in the diplomatic history of Europe, 1914–1920.* London: Heinemann, 1957. ▸ Extensive overview of diplomatic developments surrounding Poland's recovery of independence and subsequent border struggles. Emphasizes Western powers' policies, and significance of eastern borders for Poland's place in Europe. [WLB]

33.563 Josef Korbel. *Poland between East and West: Soviet and German diplomacy toward Poland, 1919–1933.* Princeton: Princeton University Press, 1963. ▸ Broad overview presenting and explaining geopolitical dynamic underlying interwar Poland's precarious position between two great powers. Methods and approach characteristic of traditional diplomatic history; lacks systematic source study. Available on microform from Ann Arbor, Mich.: University Microfilms, 1977. [WLB]

33.564 Andrzej Korboński. *Politics of socialist agriculture in Poland, 1945–1960.* New York: Columbia University Press, 1965. ▸ Addresses Polish Communists' approach to agrarian question in predominantly rural society. Good sociopolitical examination of interplay between politics and agriculture and reasons collectivization failed. [WLB]

33.565 Stefan Korboński. *The Polish underground state: a guide to the underground, 1939–1945.* Marta Erdman, trans. New York: Hippocrene, 1981. (East European monographs, 39.) ISBN 0-914710-32-X. ▸ Written by one of underground state's most senior politicians, combines systematic description of underground institutions and groups with narrative tracing their history in occupied Poland. Good fact-finding tool. [WLB]

33.566 Stefan Korboński. *Warsaw in chains.* Norbert Guterman, trans. New York: Macmillan, 1959. ▸ Intensely personal account of establishment of communist rule in postwar Poland. Author's diary supplemented by commentary on key political developments. [MR]

33.567 Stanisław Kot. *Conversations with the Kremlin and dispatches from Russia.* London: Oxford University Press, 1963. ▸ Polish-Soviet wartime relations portrayed from perspective of reports of Polish exile government's representative in Moscow. Valuable documentary account of Poland's difficult position vis-à-vis erstwhile enemy turned ally. [WLB]

33.568 Roman Laba. *The roots of Solidarity: a political sociology of Poland's working-class democratization.* Princeton: Princeton University Press, 1991. ISBN 0-691-07862-9. ▸ Examination of Baltic strikes of 1970–71, which unsuccessfully advocated independent union and interfactory strike committee ten years before Solidarity. Good discussion of Solidarity's nonnational, peaceful iconography. [GS]

33.569 Leopold Łabędź, ed. *Poland under Jaruzelski: a comprehensive sourcebook on Poland during and after martial law.* New York: Scribner's, 1984. ISBN 0-684-18116-9. ▸ Representative and convincing compilation of contemporary statements and writings dwelling on political life in Poland after Solidarity's delegalization. Opens window on political culture, particularly its underground segment. [WLB]

33.570 Zbigniew Landau and Jerzy Tomaszewski. *The Polish economy in the twentieth century.* Wojciech Roszkowski, trans. London: Croom Helm, 1985. ISBN 0-7099-1607-8. ▸ Highly competent overview of modern Polish economic history by two prominent Polish historians. Straightforward chronological organization and clear presentation of basic topical categories. [WLB]

33.571 Jules Laroche. *La Pologne de Piłsudski: souvenirs d'une ambassade, 1926–1935.* Paris: Flammarion, 1953. ▸ Memoirs of French ambassador to Poland (1935–39), replete with penetrating observations. Valuable for Polish and diplomatic history. Available on microform from Cambridge, Mass.: Harvard University Library Microreproduction Service. [MR]

33.572 Keith John Lepak. *Prelude to Solidarity: Poland and the politics of the Gierek regime.* New York: Columbia University Press, 1988. ISBN 0-231-06608-2. ▸ Overview of Polish politics (foreign and domestic) during ten-year period preceding emergence of Solidarity. Useful if not profound examination of significant developments. [MR]

33.573 Jan Józef Lipski. *Diplomat in Berlin, 1933–1939: papers and memoirs of Józef Lipski, ambassador of Poland.* Wacław Jędrzejewicz, ed. New York: Columbia University Press, 1968. ▸ Annotated collection of papers and memoirs of Poland's ambassador to Nazi Germany. Should be consulted by anyone interested in deeper understanding of Poland's relations with Hitler's Germany. [WLB]

33.574 Jan Józef Lipski. *KOR: a history of the Workers' Defense Committee in Poland, 1976–1981.* Olga Amsterdamska and Gene M. Moore, trans. Berkeley: University of California Press, 1991. ISBN 0-520-05243-9. ▸ Most detailed history of political organization whose activities preceded creation of Solidarity, written by one of KOR's founding members. Classic primary source. [MR]

33.575 Richard C. Lukas. *Bitter legacy: Polish-American relations in the wake of World War II.* Lexington: University Press of Kentucky, 1982. ISBN 0-8131-1460-8. ▸ Continuation of author's study of war years (33.577). Focuses on United States' policies while arguing convincingly that nature of postwar relations resulted directly from decisions and policies of war years. [WLB]

33.576 Richard C. Lukas. *The forgotten holocaust: the Poles under German occupation, 1939–1944.* 1986 ed. New York: Hippocrene, 1990. ISBN 0-8131-1566-3 (cl, 1986), 0-87052-632-4 (pbk). ▸ Depiction of German occupation in relation to Nazi goal of exterminating Polish nation. Convenient overview; significant though polemical contribution to discussion on Polish-Jewish relations. [WLB]

33.577 Richard C. Lukas. *The strange allies: the United States and Poland, 1941–1945.* Knoxville: University of Tennessee Press, 1978. ISBN 0-87049-229-2. ▸ Concentrates on role of Polish question in United States foreign policy and clearly delineates Poland's subordinate position. Helps define United States wartime involvement in eastern Europe and origins of cold war. [WLB]

33.578 Juliusz Łukasiewicz. *Diplomat in Paris, 1936–1939.* Wacław Jędrzejewicz, ed. New York: Columbia University Press, 1970. ISBN 0-231-03308-7. ▸ Annotated collection of papers and memoirs of interwar Poland's last ambassador to France. Extremely valuable source for understanding nature of Poland's relations with its most important ally. [WLB]

33.579 Andrzej Micewski. *Cardinal Wyszyński: a biography.* William R. Brand and Katarzyna Mroczkowska-Brand, trans. San Diego, Calif.: Harcourt Brace Jovanovich, 1984. ISBN 0-15-115785-5. ▸ Full-scale biography of head of Poland's Catholic church during most oppressive period of communist rule. Indispensable for understanding church-state relations. [MR]

33.580 Andrew A. Michta. *Red eagle: the army in Polish politics, 1944–1988.* Stanford, Calif.: Hoover Institution Press, 1990. (Hoover Press publication, 386.) ISBN 0-8179-8861-0 (cl), 0-8179-8862-9 (pbk). ▸ Overview of Polish army's role in post-1945 state, culminating in officer corps' direct intervention in politics in 1980s. Methodologically focused on civil-military relations in communist system. [WLB]

33.581 Stanisław Mikołajczyk. *The rape of Poland: pattern of Soviet aggression.* New York: Whittlesey House, 1948. ▸ Account of 1939–48 period by last premier of exile government who, in 1945, returned to Poland as political leader. Narrative focused on origins of communist rule. Crucial for understanding communist government's treatment of returning emigré politicians. [WLB]

33.582 Ronald C. Monticone. *The Catholic church in communist Poland, 1945–1985: forty years of church-state relations.* Boulder: East European Monographs; distributed by Columbia University Press, 1986. (East European monographs, 205.) ISBN 0-88033-102-X. ▸ Intensely polemical study of uneasy relationship. Highlights development of mutual policy changes from confrontation to accommodation. Argues interests of state and church secured at expense of working class. [MR]

33.583 Léon Noël. *L'agression allemande contre la Pologne.* Paris: Flammarion, 1946. ▸ Memoirs of French ambassador to Poland (1935–39), critical of Ambassador Beck's foreign policy. Indispensable to understanding French policy toward its Polish ally. Available on microform from Cambridge, Mass.: Harvard University Library Microreproduction Service. [MR]

33.584 Jan Nowak. *Courier from Warsaw.* Detroit: Wayne State University Press, 1982. ISBN 0-8143-1725-1. ▸ Gripping firsthand account of underground state and Polish wartime politics. Provides readable, detailed description of key events from perspective of both occupied Poland and London. [WLB]

33.585 David Ost. *Solidarity and the politics of anti-politics: opposition and reform in Poland since 1968.* Philadelphia: Temple University Press, 1990. ISBN 0-87722-655-5. ▸ Stimulating analysis of Solidarity as social movement dedicated to transcending traditional categories of political thought and activity. Particularly useful for examining East European revolution of 1989–90. [WLB]

33.586 Józef Piłsudski. *The memories of a Polish revolutionary and soldier.* 1931 ed. D. R. Gillie, ed. and trans. New York: AMS Press, 1971. ISBN 0-404-05049-2. ▸ Annotated volume containing almost all of Piłsudski's writings up to 1923 with exception of year 1920. Very useful source for understanding Polish struggle for independence and Piłsudski's role. [WLB]

33.587 Józef Piłsudski and Michael Tukhachevski. *Year 1920 and its climax: Battle of Warsaw during the Polish-Soviet war, 1919–1920, with the addition of Soviet Marshal Tukhachevski's march beyond the Vistula.* New York: Piłsudski Institute of America, 1972. ▸ Unique publication offering reader opportunity to juxtapose views of war's two opposing military leaders, Piłsudski and Tukhachevski. Also offers invaluable information on conflict's strategic and political background. [WLB]

33.588 Antony Polonsky. *Politics in independent Poland, 1921–1939: the crisis of constitutional government.* Oxford: Clarendon, 1972. ISBN 0-19-827182-4. ▸ Traces failure of interwar Poland's political system and its shift away from imperfect parliamentary democracy to authoritarian system. Presents interrelationship between politics, society, and economy. Best study in English. [WLB]

33.589 Antony Polonsky, ed. *The great powers and the Polish question, 1941–45: a documentary study in cold war origins.* London: London School of Economics and Political Science, 1976. ISBN 0-85328-046-0. ▸ Primary source collection permitting reader to draw independent conclusions concerning one of most crucial chapters in modern Polish history. Ideal for introducing students to primary documents. [WLB]

33.590 Antony Polonsky, ed. *"My brother's keeper?" Recent Polish debates on the Holocaust.* London: Routledge for Institute for Polish-Jewish Studies, 1990. ISBN 0-415-04232-1. ▸ Collection of essays, first published in Poland, debating Polish-Jewish relations during war. Also transcript of international discussion entitled "Ethical Problems of the Holocaust in Poland." [WLB]

33.591 Antony Polonsky and Bolesław Drukier. *The beginnings of communist rule in Poland.* London: Routledge & Kegan Paul, 1980. ISBN 0-7100-0540-7. ▸ Based on collection of documents removed from Poland in 1972. Supplemented by thorough introductory essay and glossary. Unique English-language source for studying critical phase in communist seizure of power. [WLB]

33.592 Anita Prazmowska. *Britain, Poland, and the Eastern Front, 1939.* Cambridge: Cambridge University Press, 1987. ISBN 0-521-33148-X. ▸ Controversial interpretation of Anglo-Polish relations and hence of realistic ability to withstand Nazi aggression. Depicts Britain as much weaker force than traditional appeasement rubric suggests. [WLB]

33.593 Harry M. Rabinowicz. *The legacy of Polish Jewry: a history of Polish Jews in the inter-war years, 1919–1939.* New York: Yoseloff, 1965. ▸ Study primarily of plight of Jews and impact of antisemitism; also valuable information on cultural and political developments within Jewish community. [WLB]

33.594 Arthur R. Rachwald. *In search of Poland: the superpowers' response to Solidarity, 1980–89.* Stanford, Calif.: Hoover Institution Press, 1990. (Hoover Press publication, 396.) ISBN 0-8179-8961-7 (cl), 0-8179-8962-5 (pbk). ▸ Narrative monograph shedding light on international aspects of Solidarity and its challenge to communism. Useful comparisons may be drawn by juxtaposing this period with World War II. [WLB]

33.595 Edward Raczyński. *In Allied London.* 1962 ed. London: Weidenfeld & Nicolson, 1963. ▸ Diary of Polish ambassador to England during World War II. Gives Polish perspective on diplomatic and political developments directly affecting Poland but often beyond exile government's control. Helpful for understanding London's attitude. [WLB]

33.596 Peter K. Raina. *Poland 1981: towards social renewal.* London: Allen & Unwin, 1985. ISBN 0-04-335052-6. ▸ Year of Solidarity as failed attempt at fundamentally reforming Polish society through compromise rather than revolution. Presents extensive documentation produced by main actors, both official and nonofficial institutions. [WLB]

33.597 Peter K. Raina. *Political opposition in Poland, 1954–1977.* London: Poets & Painters, 1978. ▸ Chronological overview of rise of opposition to communist rule in Poland focusing on role of intellectuals. Useful presentation of society's journey from de-Stalinization to pre-Solidarity period. [WLB]

33.598 Henry Rollet. *La Pologne au vingtième siècle.* Paris: Pedone, 1984. ISBN 2-233-00147-8. ▸ Comprehensive study by former French diplomat sympathetic to Poland and its problems. [MR]

33.599 Hans Roos [Hans-Otto Meissner]. *A history of modern Poland: from the foundation of the state in the First World War to the present day.* J. R. Forster, trans. New York: Knopf, 1966. ▸ Well-written, succinct but substantive overview of five decades of Polish history. Fine introductory work for those seeking to familiarize themselves with main themes and issues of period. [WLB]

33.600 Joseph Rothschild. *Piłsudski's coup d'état.* New York: Columbia University Press, 1966. ▸ 1926 seizure of power presented as manifestation of deep crisis of interwar Polish politics. Explains failure of subsequent attempts to legitimize authoritarian rule. Clear historical narrative and thorough analysis. [WLB]

33.601 Edward J. Rozek. *Allied wartime diplomacy: a pattern in Poland.* 1958 ed. Boulder: Westview, 1989. ISBN 0-8133-7899-0.

‣ Penetrating study of Soviet efforts to outmaneuver Allied powers during World War II. Begins in 1939 and ends with establishment of postwar communist government. [MR]

33.602 Witold Staniewicz. "The agrarian problem in Poland between the two world wars." *Slavonic and East European review* 43.100 (1964) 23–33. ISSN 0037-6795. ‣ Concise, informative presentation of most important problem plaguing interwar Poland's socioeconomic fabric. Introduces both economic and political aspects. [WLB]

33.603 Jadwiga Staniszkis. *Poland's self-limiting revolution.* Princeton: Princeton University Press, 1984. ISBN 0-691-09403-9. ‣ Highly original, thought-provoking analysis of socialist Poland from corporatist perspective. Although focused primarily on Solidarity, illuminates dominant social mechanisms established after 1945 and places them in historical context. [WLB]

33.604 Keith Sword, Norman Davies, and Jan M. Ciechanowski. *The formation of the Polish community in Great Britain, 1939–50.* London: University of London, School of Slavonic and East European Studies, 1989. ISBN 0-903425-17-3. ‣ Scholarly study of Polish presence in Great Britain rooted in war and exile. Contains three sections addressing community's growth, government-in-exile, and postwar resettlement. [WLB]

33.605 Jack Taylor. *The economic development of Poland, 1919–1950.* 1952 ed. Westport, Conn.: Greenwood, 1970. ISBN 0-8371-3379-3. ‣ Although superseded by more recent scholarship, particularly useful for study's main focus on interwar period. [WLB]

33.606 Sarah Meiklejohn Terry. *Poland's place in Europe: General Sikorski and the origin of the Oder-Neisse line, 1939–1943.* Princeton: Princeton University Press, 1983. ISBN 0-691-07643-x (cl), 0-691-10136-1 (pbk). ‣ Controversial analysis of Sikorski's efforts to secure Poland's position in Europe by restructuring Central Europe and redefining relations with Russia. Illuminates Sikorski's policies and Polish wartime dilemma. [WLB]

33.607 Józef Tischner. *Marxism and Christianity: the quarrel and the dialogue in Poland.* Marek B. Zaleski and Benjamin Fiore, trans. Washington, D.C.: Georgetown University Press, 1987. ISBN 0-87840-419-8 (cl), 0-87840-456-2 (pbk). ‣ Serious analysis of philosophical tenets of Marxism and philosophical underpinnings of Christian doctrine presented in context of Polish political climate. Polemical exercise par excellence. [MR]

33.608 Teresa Torańska. *"Them": Stalin's Polish puppets.* Agnieszka Kołakowska, trans. Harry Willets, Introduction. New York: Harper & Row, 1987. ISBN 0-06-015657-0. ‣ Fascinating series of interviews with former top-ranking party officials directly involved in establishing communist system in Poland. Offers unique window into Communists' psychology and reasoning. [WLB]

33.609 Elizabeth K. Valkenier. "The rise and decline of official Marxist historiography in Poland, 1945–1983." *Slavic review* 44.4 (1985) 663–80. ISSN 0037-6779. ‣ Broad synthesis of developments concentrating primarily on post-1959 period. For details on 1945–59 period consult author's two earlier articles (33.610 and 33.611). [WLB]

33.610 Elizabeth K. Valkenier. "Soviet impact on Polish postwar historiography, 1946–1950." *Journal of Central European affairs* 11.4 (1952) 372–96. ISSN 0885-2472. ‣ Survey tracing impact of ideology and politics on historical writing. Unique contribution to generally understudied topic. [WLB]

33.611 Elizabeth K. Valkenier. "Sovietization and liberalization in Polish postwar historiography." *Journal of Central European affairs* 19.2 (1959) 149–73. ISSN 0885-2472. ‣ Continuation of author's chronological survey of Polish historiography (33.610). Further illuminates relationship between ideology and historian's

craft. Addresses how Polish intellectual climate benefitted from weakening ideological absolutism. [WLB]

33.612 Harald von Riekhoff. *German-Polish relations, 1918–1933.* Baltimore: Johns Hopkins University Press, 1971. ISBN 0-8018-1310-7. ‣ Very competent, balanced, scholarly study of relations between Poland and Weimar Republic. Based on both German and Polish sources. Standard study. [WLB]

33.613 Piotr S. Wandycz. *France and her eastern allies, 1919–1925: French-Czechoslovak-Polish relations from the Paris Peace Conference to Locarno.* Minneapolis: University of Minnesota Press, 1962. ‣ Pioneering study of French efforts to construct new alliance system in eastern Europe to shore up Versailles settlement; remains indispensable for understanding interwar Poland's place in Europe. Also helps explain inherent weaknesses of interwar Europe's international system and East Central Europe's crucial place within it. [WLB/JSH]

33.614 Piotr S. Wandycz. *Polish diplomacy, 1914–1945: aims and achievements.* Keith Sword, ed. London: Orbis for School of Slavonic and East European Studies, 1988. ISBN 0-903425-15-7. ‣ Most concise general overview of topic. Bibliographical essay should be consulted by anyone interested in Polish foreign policy during this period. [WLB]

33.615 Piotr S. Wandycz. *Soviet-Polish relations, 1917–1921.* Cambridge, Mass.: Harvard University Press, 1969. (Russian Research Center studies, 59.) ISBN 0-674-82780-5. ‣ Extensively researched examination of Soviet-Polish relations during critical formative phase of interwar period. Explains underlying dynamic of relationship and determinants of Poland's position in Eastern Europe. [WLB/SM]

33.616 Piotr S. Wandycz. *The twilight of French eastern alliances, 1926–1936: French-Czechoslovak-Polish relations from Locarno to the remilitarization of the Rhineland.* Princeton: Princeton University Press, 1988. ISBN 0-691-05528-9. ‣ Sequel to author's first work on same subject (33.615); blames ruin of French alliance system on Locarno agreements and Depression. Superb tool for placing East Central Europe within broad framework of international relations between the wars. [WLB/JSH]

33.617 Piotr S. Wandycz. *The United States and Poland.* Cambridge, Mass.: Harvard University Press, 1980. ISBN 0-674-92685-4. ‣ Broad survey and synthesis of history of relations between two states concentrating on twentieth century. Discusses internal determinants of foreign policy and broad East-West context. [WLB]

33.618 Richard M. Watt. *Bitter glory: Poland and its fate, 1918 to 1939.* 1979 ed. New York: Simon & Schuster, 1982. ISBN 0-671-45379-3 (cl), 0-671-45378-5 (pbk). ‣ Very readable, generally sympathetic narrative history of interwar Poland. Serves well as general introduction. [WLB]

33.619 Jerzy J. Wiatr. *The soldier and the nation: the role of the military in Polish politics, 1918–1985.* Boulder: Westview, 1988. ISBN 0-8133-0358-3. ‣ Broad analysis of army's role in society and its evolution over time. Accessible political sociology with historical emphasis that highlights important continuities and discontinuities. [WLB]

33.620 Richard A. Woytak. *On the border of war and peace: Polish intelligence and diplomacy in 1937–1939 and the origins of the Ultra secret.* Boulder: East European Quarterly; distributed by Columbia University Press, 1979. (East European monographs, 49.) ISBN 0-914710-42-7. ‣ Narrative focusing on role of intelligence gathering in relation to diplomacy. Of interest mainly as background to great Allied Enigma cryptological victory over Germany. [WLB]

33.621 Edward D. Wynot, Jr. "The Polish Germans, 1919–1939: national minority in a multinational state." *Polish review*

17.1 (1972) 23–64. ISSN 0032-2970. ▸ Informative overview focusing primarily on German minority's demographics, organizational structure, and political development. Useful introduction to topic lacking extensive English-language literature. [WLB]

33.622 Edward D. Wynot, Jr. *Polish politics in transition: the Camp of National Unity and the struggle for power, 1935–1939.* Athens: University of Georgia Press, 1974. ISBN 0-8203-0337-2. ▸ Scholarly examination of post-1935 Polish politics and society, focusing on emergence of would-be omnipotent, statist political movement. Contrasts statist political failures with limited socioeconomic successes. [WLB]

33.623 Edward D. Wynot, Jr. *Warsaw between the world wars: profile of the capital city in a developing land, 1918–1939.* Boulder: East European Monographs; distributed by Columbia University Press, 1983. (East European monographs, 129.) ISBN 0-88033-018-X. ▸ Good case study of Warsaw's development in interwar years and overall role within Second Republic. Placed within paradigm of developing country, city's history acquires broader comparative significance. [WLB]

33.624 Steven Zaloga and Victor Madej. *The Polish campaign, 1939.* New York: Hippocrene, 1985. ISBN 0-88254-994-4. ▸ Profile of interwar Polish army designed to dispel common myths surrounding September 1939. Information on military's development, doctrine, equipment, organization, and performance. Useful for narrow military and broader strategic studies. [WLB]

33.625 Adam Zamoyski. *The battle for the marchlands.* Boulder: East European Monographs; distributed by Columbia University Press, 1981. (East European monographs, 88.) ISBN 0-914710-82-6. ▸ Monograph focusing on political and military aspects of Russo-Polish war from Polish perspective. Identifies reasons for Russia's 1920 defeat at gates of Warsaw. Most helpful as study of strategic planning. [WLB]

33.626 J. K. Zawodny. *Death in the forest: the story of the Katyn forest massacre.* 1962 ed. New York: Hippocrene, 1988. ISBN 0-87052-563-8. ▸ Exhaustive analysis of murder of Polish officers by NKVD (Soviet secret police). Convincingly identifies perpetrators and their motives. Sheds important light on Soviet system and Polish-Soviet relations. [WLB]

33.627 J. K. Zawodny. *Nothing but honour: the story of the Warsaw uprising, 1944.* Stanford, Calif.: Hoover Institution Press, 1978. (Hoover Press publication, 183.) ISBN 0-8179-6831-8. ▸ Thorough scholarly study, providing reliable and pertinent information concerning military, political, and diplomatic aspects. [WLB]

33.628 Ferdynand Zweig. *Poland between two wars: a critical study of social and economic changes, 1942.* London: Secker & Warburg, 1944. ▸ Still useful interpretation of interwar Poland's socioeconomic development by contemporary Polish scholar. Analyzes difficulty of post-1918 unification and problems inherent in development. [WLB]

SEE ALSO
21.172 Chimen Abramsky, Maciej Jachimczyk, and Anthony Polonsky, eds. *The Jews in Poland.*
21.288 Lucjan Dobroszycki, ed. *The chronicle of the Łódź ghetto, 1941–1944.*
21.301 Joseph Marcus. *Social and political history of the Jews in Poland, 1919–1939.*
47.449 Kay Lundgreen-Nielsen. *The Polish problem at the Paris Peace Conference.*
48.118 Neal Pease. *Poland, the United States, and the stabilization of Europe, 1919–1933.*

ROMANIA

33.629 Cornelia Bodea. *The Romanians' struggle for unification, 1834–1849.* Lilliana Teodoreanu, trans. Bucharest: Publishing

House of the Academy of the Socialist Republic of Romania, 1970. (Bibliotheca historica Romaniae, Studies, 25.) ▸ Study of efforts by Romanian intellectuals in Moldavia, Wallachia, and Transylvania to achieve national solidarity and promote political self-determination. Marshalls impressive evidence of strong common national consciousness aiming at eventual political unity. [KAH]

33.630 George Călinescu. *History of Romanian literature.* 4th ed. Milan, Italy: UNESCO-Nagard, 1988. ▸ Massive, critical investigation of currents and personalities that shaped literary expression, mainly in nineteenth and twentieth centuries. Erudite, highly personal account; often reads like novel. [KAH]

33.631 Daniel Chirot. *Social change in a peripheral society: the creation of a Balkan colony.* New York: Academic Press, 1976. ISBN 0-12-173150-2. ▸ Stimulating historical sociology. Analyzes development of Wallachia from medieval communal trading society, to protocolony of Ottoman empire, to modern neocolonial grain-exporting society tied to Western capitalism. [GS]

33.632 Andrea Deletant and Dennis Deletant, comps. *Romania.* Oxford: ABC-Clio, 1985. ISBN 1-85109-002-9. ▸ Annotated bibliography of books and articles, majority in English, covering all disciplines. Concerned especially with twentieth century. [KAH]

33.633 Alexandru Duțu. *European intellectual movements and modernization of Romanian culture.* Adriana Ionescu-Pârâu, trans. Bucharest: Publishing House of the Academy of the Socialist Republic of Romania, 1981. (Bibliotheca historica Romaniae, Studies, 64.) ▸ Intellectual and cultural currents among Romanians within Southeast European context from sixteenth to nineteenth century. Illuminating study of how Romanian intellectuals drew from European sources. Revised translation. [KAH]

33.634 Alexandru Duțu. *Romanian humanists and European culture: a contribution to comparative cultural history.* Bucharest: Publishing House of the Academy of the Socialist Republic of Romania, 1977. (Bibliotheca historica Romaniae, Studies, 55.) ▸ Analysis of evolution of humanist thought in Romanian principalities in seventeenth and eighteenth centuries from comparative perspective. Masterful study of mentalities, specifically of how Romanian intellectuals formed their idea of Europe. [KAH]

33.635 W. G. East. *The union of Moldavia and Wallachia, 1859: an episode in diplomatic history.* 1929 ed. New York: Octagon Books, 1973. ISBN 0-374-92450-3. ▸ Napoleon III favored union as case study in nationalism, but was checked by the powers; union came from direct action in principalities. Narrowly diplomatic; based primarily on British documents. [APS]

33.636 Philip Gabriel Eidelberg. *The great Rumanian peasant revolt; origins of a modern jacquerie.* Leiden: Brill, 1974. ISBN 90-04-03781-0. ▸ Analysis of background to massive outbreak of rural violence, rather than of violence itself. Thorough investigation focusing on agricultural contracts, village cooperatives and banks, lessees, agrarian reformers, and populist doctrines. [KAH]

33.637 Mary Ellen Fischer. *Nicolae Ceaușescu: a study in political leadership.* Boulder: Rienner, 1989. ISBN 0-931477-83-2. ▸ Career of Romanian communist dictator with analysis of his domestic and foreign policies. Thorough examination of interweaving of nationalism and Leninism and of personal strengths and weaknesses. [KAH]

33.638 Vlad Georgescu. *Political ideas and the Enlightenment in the Romanian principalities, 1750–1831.* Boulder: East European Quarterly; distributed by Columbia University Press, 1971. (East European monographs, 1.) ISBN 0-231-02842-3. ▸ Detailed analysis of thought of Romanian intellectuals on nature of man in society, theory of state, etc. Shows Romanian principalities intellectually and culturally between western and southeastern Europe. [KAH]

33.639 Vlad Georgescu. *The Romanians: a history.* Matei Cali-nescu, ed. Alexandra Bley-Vroman, trans. Columbus: Ohio State University Press, 1991. ISBN 0-8142-0511-9. ‣ Most recent general survey from origins of Romanian people to end of Ceauşescu regime. Emphasis on nineteenth and twentieth centuries and communist era. [KAH]

33.640 Trond Gilberg. *Modernization in Romania since World War II.* New York: Praeger, 1975. ISBN 0-275-28783-1. ‣ Thorough discussion of economic, social, and political change as organized and directed by Communist party. Case study of processes and agents of multilateral development in previously largely agricultural country. [KAH]

33.641 Trond Gilberg. *Nationalism and communism in Romania: the rise and fall of Ceauşescu's personal dictatorship.* Boulder: Westview, 1990. ISBN 0-8133-7497-9. ‣ Well-written study of transformation of society through application of principles of Leninism and their Romanian variant, Ceauşescuism. Many-sided approach to tension between traditional values and revolution imposed from above. [KAH]

33.642 Constantin C. Giurescu, ed. *Chronological history of Romania.* 2d ed. Bucharest: Editura Enciclopedică Română, 1974. ‣ Selective descriptive listing of important events from prehistory to 1971, focusing on political and economic development. Tables of rulers and bibliography. [KAH]

33.643 Klaus-Detlev Grothusen, ed. *Rumänien.* Göttingen: Vandenhoeck & Ruprecht, 1977. (Südosteuropa-Handbuch, 2.) ISBN 3-525-36201-3. ‣ Comprehensive articles on political, economic, and social structures and on domestic and foreign policies of Romanian Communist party since World War II. Several articles in English. Tables and bibliography. [KAH]

33.644 Armin Heinen. *Die Legion "Erzengel Michael" in Rumänien: soziale Bewegung und politische Organisation; ein Beitrag zum Problem des internationalen Faschismus.* Munich: Oldenbourg, 1986. (Südosteuropäische Arbeiten, 83.) ISBN 3-486-53101-8. ‣ Origins and development of Romanian fascism in interwar period, especially Iron Guard. Shows changes in social structure, ideology, and activities of Guard. Most authoritative account available. Thorough bibliography. [KAH]

33.645 Andreas Hillgruber. *Hitler, König Carol, und Marschall Antonescu: die deutsch-romanischen Bezeihungen, 1938–1944.* 2d ed. Wiesbaden: Steiner, 1965. (Veröffentlichungen des Instituts für Europäische Geschichte, Mainz, 5.) ‣ Most extensive account of Romanian-German relations in late 1930s and during war against Soviet Union. Analyzes bases of cooperation and causes of disagreement using extensive contemporary German sources. [KAH]

33.646 Keith Hitchins. *The idea of nation: the Romanians of Transylvania, 1691–1849.* Bucharest: Editura Ştiinţifică şi Enciclopedică, 1985. ‣ Scholarly examination of origins and development of national consciousness, focusing on Orthodox and Uniate churches and Western-oriented intellectuals. Sees Revolution of 1848 as culmination of early national movement. [KAH/GS]

33.647 Keith Hitchins. *Orthodoxy and nationality: Andreiu Şaguna and the Rumanians of Transylvania, 1846–1873.* Cambridge, Mass.: Harvard University Press, 1977. ISBN 0-674-64491-3. ‣ Excellent discussion of role of Orthodox church, higher clergy, and lay intellectuals in modern national movement. Describes influence of changing social attitudes, especially growth of secularism and lingering attraction of romanticism. [KAH/GS]

33.648 Keith Hitchins. *The Rumanian national movement in Transylvania, 1780–1849.* Cambridge, Mass.: Harvard University Press, 1969. ISBN 0-674-78035-3. ‣ Balanced, clear study of growth of national consciousness, its expression in works of his-tory and language, and role of clerical and lay intellectuals. Focuses on Orthodox and Uniate churches as national institutions. [KAH/GS]

33.649 Keith Hitchins. *Studies on Romanian national consciousness.* Pelham, N.Y.: Nagard, 1983. ‣ Essays by leading authority covering period between eighteenth-century Enlightenment and decades between two world wars. Emphasizes role of intellectuals and bourgeoisie and influence of international relations on national movements. [KAH/GS]

33.650 Ghiţa Ionescu. *Communism in Rumania, 1944–1962.* 1964 ed. Westport, Conn.: Greenwood, 1976. ISBN 0-8371-8168-2. ‣ Focus on political and economic structures of totalitarian state-in-the-making. Dated but still useful in showing decisive influence of Soviet Union on policies and personnel of Romanian Communist party. [KAH]

33.651 Barbara Jelavich. *Russia and the formation of the Romanian national state, 1821–1878.* Cambridge: Cambridge University Press, 1984. (Joint Committee on Eastern Europe publication series, 13.) ISBN 0-521-25318-7. ‣ Thorough investigation of role of great power in movement for self-determination of strategically located small neighbor. Shows how Romanian leaders balanced internal political demands and foreign policy constraints. [KAH]

33.652 Barbara Jelavich. *Russia and the Rumanian national cause, 1858–1859.* 1959 ed. Hamden, Conn.: Archon, 1974. ISBN 0-208-01430-6. ‣ Sound case study of interaction of great power foreign policy aims and small-country domestic political aspirations. Explains Russia's ambiguous role in Romanians' struggle for union of Moldavia and Wallachia. [KAH]

33.653 Kenneth Jowitt. *Revolutionary breakthroughs and national development: the case of Romania, 1944–1965.* Berkeley: University of California Press, 1971. ISBN 0-520-01762-5. ‣ Penetrating analysis of strategies followed by Communist party to transform Romanian society. Comparative study of nation building as general theoretical problem and specific political process in Romania. [KAH]

33.654 Kenneth Jowitt, ed. *Social change in Romania, 1860–1940: a debate on development in a European nation.* Berkeley: University of California, Institute of International Studies, 1978. (Institute of International Studies, Research series, 36.) ISBN 0-87725-136-3. ‣ Original studies of structural transformation of dependent, agricultural country examined from various theoretical perspectives. Emphasizes role of intellectuals as promoters of europeanization and as protectors of indigenous values and institutions. [KAH]

33.655 Frederick Kellogg. *A history of Romanian historical writing.* Bakersfield, Calif.: Schlacks, 1990. ‣ Essentially a lengthy bibliographic article. Not analytical but useful compendium of information and references. [GS]

33.656 Robert R. King. *History of the Romanian Communist party.* Stanford, Calif.: Hoover Institution Press, 1980. (Hoover Press publication, 233.) ISBN 0-8179-7332-X. ‣ Reliable survey of evolution of communism from negligible influence in interwar period to totalitarian system after World War II. Analyzes party elites, relationship between party and society, and persistence of nationalism. [KAH]

33.657 Gail Kligman. *The wedding of the dead: ritual, poetics, and popular culture in Transylvania.* Berkeley: University of California Press, 1988. ISBN 0-520-06001-6. ‣ Social organization and identity in Maramureş, northern Romania, as revealed in traditional family and community rituals. Original study based on extensive fieldwork and deep knowledge of rural society. [KAH]

33.658 Dov B. Lungu. *Romania and the great powers, 1933–1940.* Durham, N.C.: Duke University Press, 1989. ISBN 0-8223-0915-

7. ▸ Up-to-date survey showing how Romanian governments first chose alignment with West and collective security; then balance among West, Germany, and Soviet Union; and finally alignment with Germany; all to no avail. [KAH]

33.659 Lothar Maier. *Rumänien auf dem Weg zur Unabhängigkeitserklärung, 1866–1877: Schein und Wirklichkeit liberaler Verfassung und staatlicher Souveranität.* Munich: Oldenbourg, 1989. (Südosteuropäische Arbeiten, 88.) ISBN 3-486-55171-X. ▸ Analysis of political and economic development between adoption of Western-style constitution and declaration of independence. Focuses on evolution of political parties, railroad construction, and state finances. Best available account. [KAH]

33.660 David Mitrany. *The land and the peasant in Rumania: the war and agrarian reform, 1917–21.* 1930 ed. New York: Greenwood, 1968. ▸ Detailed description of agrarian laws enacted after World War I and evaluation of their economic effectiveness and general social importance within context of century of agricultural development. Wealth of information. [KAH]

33.661 John Michael Montias. *Economic development in communist Rumania.* Cambridge, Mass.: MIT Press, 1967. ▸ Fundamental, comprehensive investigation of main branches of national economy and critical evaluation of government policy. Shows how Romania was integrated into economy of Soviet-dominated Eastern Europe. [KAH]

33.662 Basil Munteanu. *Modern Rumanian literature.* Bucharest: Curentul, 1939. ▸ Survey of main literary currents from late romanticism to modernism and avant-garde between the two world wars. Serves also as general introduction to intellectual life of period. [KAH]

33.663 Mircea Păcurariu. *Istoria Bisericii Ortodoxe Române* (History of the Romanian Orthodox church). 3 vols. Bucharest: Editura Institutului Biblic şi de Misiune al Bisericii Ortodoxe Române, 1980–81. ▸ Romanian Orthodox church from beginnings of Christianity in Romanian lands to 1970s. Most extensive account available of doctrine, institutions, and role of church. Indispensable. [KAH]

33.664 Ştefan Pascu, ed. *Atlas pentru istoria României* (Atlas for the history of Romania). Bucharest: Editura Didactica şi Pedagogică, 1983. ▸ Maps tracing development of lands now inhabited by Romanians from Paleolithic to 1980. Best work of its kind covering settlement, social movements, battles, international relations, and economy. [KAH]

33.665 Ştefan Pascu et al., eds. *Bibliografia istorică a României* (Historical bibliography of Romania). 7 vols. Bucharest: Publishing House of the Academy of the Socialist Republic of Romania, 1970–. ▸ Comprehensive, continuing listing of books and articles published 1944–89 by Romanian and foreign scholars. Two volumes devoted to nineteenth century cover works published before 1944. [KAH]

33.666 Maurice Pearton. *Oil and the Romanian state.* Oxford: Clarendon, 1971. ISBN 0-19-828246-X. ▸ Thorough investigation of oil industry as important contributor to growth of modern Romanian economy. Emphasizes effects of changing international economic and political relations on organization and development of the industry. [KAH]

33.667 David Prodan. *Supplex Libellus Valachorum.* Franz Killyen, trans. Bucharest: Publishing House of the Academy of the Socialist Republic of Romania, 1971. ▸ Evolution of Romanian movement for autonomy and self-determination in Transylvania in eighteenth century. Pioneering study, focusing on relationship of intellectuals to peasant population within context of Austrian Enlightenment. German with French summary. [KAH]

33.668 Paul D. Quinlan. *Clash over Romania: British and American policies toward Romania, 1938–1947.* Oakland, Calif.: American Romanian Academy of Arts and Sciences, 1977. (American Romanian Academy of Arts and Sciences, 2.) ISBN 0-686-23263-1. ▸ Study of efforts of regional power to pursue an independent foreign and domestic policy in midst of acute great power rivalries. Covers negotiations for separate peace in 1943–44 and during Soviet takeover. [KAH]

33.669 Mac Linscott Ricketts. *Mircea Eliade: the Romanian roots, 1907–1945.* 2 vols. Boulder: East European Monographs; distributed by Columbia University Press, 1988. (East European monographs, 248.) ISBN 0-88033-145-3. ▸ Examination of career of historian of religions, seeker of true Romanian spirituality, and avant-garde novelist who epitomized aspirations of an entire generation. Significant introduction to interwar Romanian intellectual life. [KAH]

33.670 Thad W. Riker. *The making of Romania.* 1931 ed. New York: Arno, 1971. ISBN 0-405-02772-9. ▸ Sets achievement of nationhood into context of great powers' often irrelevant interests and quarrels. Pro-Romanian account based on wide array of foreign diplomatic and consular materials plus published Romanian sources. [APS]

33.671 Henry L. Roberts. *Rumania: political problems of an agrarian state.* 1951 ed. Hamden, Conn.: Archon, 1969. ISBN 0-208-00651-6. ▸ Treats political and economic obstacles to development of Western-style parliamentary democracy in interwar period. Penetrating judgments of liberal and National Peasant governments, rightist dictatorships, and initial stages of communist rule. [KAH]

33.672 R. W. Seton-Watson. *A history of the Roumanians from Roman times to the completion of unity.* 1934 ed. Hamden, Conn.: Archon, 1963. ▸ Dated but still useful survey, focusing on political and diplomatic history. Sympathetic to struggles of Romanians to achieve national independence and unification. [KAH]

33.673 Michael Shafir. *Romania, politics, economics, and society: political stagnation and simulated change.* Boulder: Rienner, 1985. ISBN 0-931477-02-6 (cl), 0-931477-03-4 (pbk). ▸ Intelligent book on Ceauşescu's Romania. [GS]

33.674 Henri H. Stahl. *Traditional Romanian village communities: the transition from the communal to the capitalist mode of production in the Danube region.* Daniel Chirot and Holly Coulter Chirot, trans. Cambridge: Cambridge University Press, 1980. ISBN 0-521-22957-X. ▸ Original investigation of social and economic structures in rural society between fifteenth and twentieth centuries. Sociological rather than historical approach to fundamental questions of agrarian relations. [KAH]

33.675 Pompiliu Teodor, ed. *Enlightenment and Romanian society.* Cluj-Napoca: Dacia, 1980. ▸ Comprehensive investigation of political and economic conditions and diverse intellectual currents among Romanians on both sides of Carpathians in eighteenth century. Comparative, European approach. [KAH]

33.676 Kurt W. Treptow, ed. *Dracula: essays on the life and times of Vlad Ţepeş.* Boulder: East European Monographs; distributed by Columbia University Press, 1991. (East European monographs, 698.) ISBN 0-88033-220-4. ▸ One of few serious books in English on sensationalized subject. Presents scholarly articles and translations of source materials, genealogy, chronology, and bibliography. [GS]

33.677 Andreas C. Tsantis and Roy Pepper. *Romania, the industrialization of an agrarian economy under socialist planning: report of a mission sent to Romania by the World Bank.* Washington, D.C.: World Bank, 1979. ISBN 0-8018-2269-6 (cl), 0-8018-2262-9 (pbk). ▸ Analysis of resources, strategies, and management of economic modernization and estimate of future prospects based on abundant statistical data. Thorough, generally favorable report on communist regime's economic activity in 1970s. [KAH]

33.678 David Turnock. *An economic geography of Romania.* London: Bell, 1974. ISBN 0-7135-1628-3. ▸ Detailed description of population, resources, industry, agriculture, and commerce from World War I to 1960s. Compares communist economic policies and accomplishments with those of interwar governments. [KAH]

33.679 David Turnock. *The Romanian economy in the twentieth century.* New York: St. Martin's, 1986. ISBN 0-312-69164-5. ▸ Account of economic policy and development of agriculture, industry, and infrastructure under interwar and communist regimes viewed in international context. Copious detail and extensive bibliographical citations. [KAH]

33.680 Katherine Verdery. *National ideology under socialism: identity and cultural politics in Ceauşescu's Romania.* Berkeley: University of California Press, 1991. ISBN 0-520-07216-2. ▸ Origins of idea of nation and its persistence. Adduces ample evidence of debate within Communist party and among historians, philosophers, and other intellectuals about meaning of nation. [KAH]

33.681 Katherine Verdery. *Transylvanian villagers: three centuries of political, economic, and ethnic change.* Berkeley: University of California Press, 1983. ISBN 0-520-04879-2. ▸ Penetrating critical study of evolution of rural community over three centuries observed from within and from perspective of broad political and social change. History, anthropology, and sociology skillfully combined to illuminate processes of ethnic identification. [KAH]

33.682 Eugen Weber. "Romania." In *The European Right: a historical profile.* Hans Rogger and Eugen Weber, eds., pp. 501–74. Berkeley: University of California Press, 1965. ▸ Most extensive analysis in English of Romanian fascism in interwar period. Focuses on religious content of Iron Guard doctrine and messianic role of its leader, Corneliu Codreanu. [KAH]

SEE ALSO
47.465 Sherman David Spector. *Rumania at the Paris Peace Conference.*

YUGOSLAV LANDS TO 1918

Bosnia and Hercegovina

33.683 Ivo Andrić. *The development of spiritual life in Bosnia under the influence of Turkish rule.* Želimir B. Juričić and John F. Loud, eds. and trans. Durham, N.C.: Duke University Press, 1990. ISBN 0-8223-1063-5. ▸ Marginal as scholarly work by today's standards, Andrić's dissertation retains its interest in light of author's later career as Nobel Prize–winning author who wrote on Bosnian themes. [GS]

33.684 Vladimir Dedijer. *The road to Sarajevo.* New York: Simon & Schuster, 1966. ▸ Treats events surrounding assassination of Austro-Hungarian heir apparent, Archduke Francis Ferdinand, in 1914. Demonstrates responsibility of Young Bosnians, aided by Serbia. Detailed primary sources makes it most comprehensive study. [DMP/DM/SM]

33.685 Robert J. Donia. *Islam under the double eagle: the Muslims of Bosnia and Hercegovina, 1878–1914.* Boulder: East European Quarterly; distributed by Columbia University Press, 1981. (East European monographs, 78.) ISBN 0-914710-72-9. ▸ Sociohistorical study of Muslim political organization under Austro-Hungarian occupation. Examines role of factions in rise of Muslim national organization in Sarajevo, Mostar, and Travnik. Significant insights into Muslim political mobilization. [DMP]

33.686 Arthur J. Evans. *Through Bosnia and the Herzegovina on foot during the insurrection, August and September 1875.* 1877 2d ed. New York: Arno, 1971. ISBN 0-405-02746-X. ▸ Observations regarding political, social, cultural, religious, and military situation. Contains useful insights and data especially concerning culture and geography. Excellent travel account. [DMP]

33.687 John V. A. Fine, Jr. *The Bosnian church: a new interpretation, a study of the Bosnian church and its place in state and society from the thirteenth to the fifteenth centuries.* Boulder: East European Quarterly; distributed by Columbia University Press, 1975. (East European monographs, 10.) ISBN 0-914710-03-6. ▸ Original, scholarly study based on painstaking analysis of limited documentary evidence. [GS]

33.688 Bernadotte E. Schmitt. *Annexation of Bosnia, 1908–1909.* 1937 ed. New York: Fertig, 1970. ▸ Detailed scholarly analysis of events surrounding Austro-Hungarian annexation. Draws on heretofore unpublished documents. Remains most complete picture of events. [DMP]

33.689 Peter F. Sugar. *The industrialization of Bosnia-Hercegovina, 1878–1918.* Seattle: University of Washington Press, 1963. ▸ Modernization under Habsburg monarchy. Comprehensive treatment of process and effects of industrialization on society; shows that feudal structure remained in place. [DMP]

Croatia

33.690 Ivo Banac. *The Croatian language question.* Zagreb: Croatian Writer's Association, 1990. ▸ Detailed overview of history of Croat language. Essential for understanding Croat culture and history. [AF/IB]

33.691 Wolf Dietrich Behschnitt. *Nationalismus bei Serben und Kroaten, 1830–1914: Analyse und Typologie der nationalen Ideologie.* Munich: Oldenbourg, 1980. ISBN 3-486-49831-2. ▸ Comparative view of selected Serb and Croat national movements, leaders, and programs with interesting conclusions on dominant national-ideological trends in both communities. Excellent textual analysis. [AF/IB]

33.692 Catherine Wendy Bracewell. *The uskoks of Senj: piracy, banditry, and holy war in the sixteenth-century Adriatic.* Ithaca, N.Y.: Cornell University Press, 1992. ISBN 0-8014-2674-X. ▸ Well-written and researched study of uskoks (social bandits in Croat region bordering on Ottoman, Habsburg, and Venetian realms) showing complexity of their motivations and sources of their support. [GS]

33.693 Francis W. Carter. *Dubrovnik (Ragusa): a classic city-state.* London: Seminar, 1972. ISBN 0-12-812950-6. ▸ Synthesis of main political, social, and cultural trends from perspective of geographer. Despite weaknesses, best Western-language study of Croatia's most important medieval center. [AF/IB]

33.694 Elinor Murray Despalatović. *Ljudevit Gaj and the Illyrian movement.* Boulder: East European Quarterly; distributed by Columbia University Press, 1975. (East European monographs, 12.) ISBN 0-914710-05-2. ▸ Excellent biography of principal figure of Croat revival that takes into account most important issues connected with revivalist era. Notable for archival sources and bibliographical references. [AF/IB]

33.695 Mirjana Gross. *Povijest pravaške ideologije* (History of ideology of the Croatian Party of (State) Right). Zagreb: Sveučilište u Zagrebu-Institut za Hrvatsku Povijest, 1973. (Institut za Hrvatsku Povijest, Monografije, 4.) ▸ Best appraisal of ideological trends in most influential Croat national party of late nineteenth century. Particularly important as corrective for distortions on this sensitive topic. [AF/IB]

33.696 Stanko Guldescu. *The Croatian-Slavonian kingdom, 1526–1792.* The Hague: Mouton, 1970. ▸ Continuation of author's history of medieval Croatia (33.697), up to age of revolution. Useful survey of neglected part of Habsburg monarchy, despite heavy Croat national bias. [AF/IB/CWI]

33.697 Stanko Guldescu. *History of medieval Croatia.* The Hague: Mouton, 1964. ▸ Unimaginative overview of basic issues in Croat history from period of settlement to beginning of Habsburg period. No new insights, but handy for English-speaking audiences. See also 33.696. [AF/IB]

33.698 Josip Horvat. *Politička povijest Hrvatske* (Political history of Croatia). 1936 ed. 2 vols. Zagreb: Cesarec, 1989. ISBN 86-393-0151-4 (set), 86-393-0152-2 (v. 1), 86-393-0153-0 (v. 2). ▸ Superb narrative history by Croatia's premier political commentator. Covers main trends in Croat affairs from national revival to establishment of Yugoslavia. [AF/IB]

33.699 Wolfgang Kessler. *Politik, Kultur, und Gesellschaft in Kroatien und Slawonien in der ersten Hälfte des neunzehnten Jahrhunderts: Historiographie und Grundlagen.* Munich: Oldenbourg, 1981. ISBN 3-486-49951-3. ▸ Interpretation of Croat national revival using methodology of social history. Excellent insight into structural questions of Croat society and culture, but decidedly weaker on aspects of historical continuity. [AF/IB]

33.700 Nada Klaić. *Povijest Hrvata u ranom srednjem vijeku* (History of the Croats in the early medieval period). Zagreb: Školska Knjiga, 1971. ▸ Controversial history of Croatia under early medieval national dynasty by foremost recent historian of period. Noted for spirited historiographical arguments and bold new interpretations. See also 33.701. [AF/IB]

33.701 Nada Klaić. *Povijest Hrvata u razvijenom srednjem vijeku* (History of the Croats in the high Middle Ages). Zagreb: Školska Knjiga, 1976. ▸ Continuation of author's history of medieval Croatia (33.700) up to end of Anjou dynasty. More spirited discussion of controversial points particularly on matters of documentary authentication. [AF/IB]

33.702 Vjekoslav Klaić. *Povijest Hrvata od najstarijih vremena do svršetka XIX stoljeća* (History of Croats from antiquity to end of nineteenth century). 1972 ed. 5 vols. Zagreb: Nakladni Zavod MH, 1985. ▸ Despite title, this multivolume standard work ends with reigns of first three Habsburgs. Excellent example of older historiography. Array of erudite information, notably on dynastic and diplomatic affairs. [AF/IB]

33.703 Bariša Krekić. *Dubrovnik in the fourteenth and fifteenth centuries: a city between East and West.* Norman: University of Oklahoma Press, 1972. ISBN 0-8061-0999-8. ▸ Excellent overview of Dubrovnik history during golden age. Emphasis on social conditions and economic life with survey of political and diplomatic affairs. [AF/IB]

33.704 Grga Novak. *Prošlost Dalmacije* (Dalmatia's past). 2 vols. Zagreb: Hrvatskog Izdavlačkog Bibliografskog Zavoda, 1944. (Zemije i narodi, 4–5.) ▸ Best synthesis of Croatia's southernmost region by noted archaeologist and historian, prehistory to 1918. [AF/IB]

33.705 Gunter Schödl. *Kroatische Nationalpolitik und "Jugoslavenstvo": Studien zu national Integration und regionaler Politik in Kroatien-Dalmatien am Beginn des zwanzigsten Jahrhunderts.* Munich: Oldenbourg, 1990. (Südosteuropäische Arbeiten, 89.) ISBN 3-486-55301-1. ▸ Important scholarly study of how integrative form of Serbo-Croat alliance centered in Dalmatia proved unable to establish Yugoslavism capable of creating Yugoslav nation. [GS]

33.706 R. W. Seton-Watson. *German, Slav, and Magyar: a study in the origins of the Great War.* 1916 ed. New York: Fertig, 1968. ▸ Harsh wartime assessment of Austro-Hungarian policy toward Croats and other South Slavs. Distillation of author's earlier study on South Slav question (33.707). [AF/IB]

33.707 R. W. Seton-Watson. *The southern Slav question and the Habsburg monarchy.* 1911 ed. New York: Fertig, 1969. ▸ Superb background to national conflicts in Croat lands of dual monarchy by leading British authority. Special emphasis on developments before annexation crisis. Most authoritative Western source on Croatia. [AF/IB]

33.708 Jaroslav Šidak. *Hrvatski narodni preporod: Ilirski pokret* (Croatian national revival: the Illyrian movement). Zagreb: Školska Knjiga and Stvarnost, 1988. ▸ Summary view of Croat revival movement by foremost historian of subject. Political developments with excellent presentation of ideological and social aspects. [AF/IB]

33.709 Jaroslav Šidak et al. *Povijest hrvatskog naroda, 1860–1914* (History of the Croat people, 1860–1914) . Zagreb: Školska Knjiga, 1968. ▸ Superb overview of Croat affairs during period of constitutional rule in Habsburg monarchy. Essential for understanding political, social, and economic trends. Excellent bibliographic guide and graphs. [AF/IB]

33.710 Ferdo Šišić. *Pregled povijesti hrvatskoga naroda* (Review of the history of the Croat nation). 1916 ed. Zagreb: Matica Hrvatska, 1962. ▸ Synthesis of political developments in Croatia from early medieval period to 1918. Outdated in parts and heavy on dynastic and diplomatic affairs, but remains best guide for span of Croat history. [AF/IB]

33.711 Ivo Sivrić. *Bishop J.G. Strossmayer: new light on Vatican I.* Chicago: Franciscan Herald, 1975. ISBN 0-8199-0491-0. ▸ Sympathetic account of most notable Croat ecclesiastical figure of late nineteenth century; emphasizes role at First Vatican Council. Important for understanding key issues of interchurch relations and South Slav reciprocity. [AF/IB]

33.712 Lujo Voinovitch. *Histoire de Dalmatie.* 2d ed. 2 vols. Paris: Hachette, 1934. ▸ History of Croatia's southernmost region by leading diplomatic historian. Strong on international background and historical drama; antiquity to 1918. [AF/IB]

SEE ALSO
    30.136 Gunther E. Rothenberg. *The Austrian military border in Croatia, 1522–1747.*
    30.137 Gunther E. Rothenberg. *The military border in Croatia, 1740–1881.*

Macedonia

33.713 George F. Abbott. *Tale of a tour in Macedonia.* London: Arnold, 1903. ▸ Englishman's account of conditions in Ottoman Macedonia in 1900. Insightful and lively presentation of life and culture of inhabitants. [DMP]

33.714 Fikret Adanir. *Die makedonische Frage, ihre Entstehung und Entwicklung bis 1908.* Wiesbaden: Steiner, 1979. (Frankfurter historische Abhandlungen, 20.) ISBN 3-515-02914-1. ▸ Macedonian question from inception in nineteenth century. Uses documents in several languages to present lucid and balanced interpretation. [DMP/NR]

33.715 Christ Anastasoff. *The tragic peninsula: a history of the Macedonian movement for independence since 1878, with ten maps, thirty-six illustrations, and a research bibliography on the Balkans.* St. Louis: Blackwell Wielandy, 1938. ▸ History of Macedonian liberation struggle. Valuable for treatment of post-1903 developments, especially Ivan Mihailov era. Considers people of Macedonia as Bulgarians. Apologetic tone. [DMP]

33.716 Henry N. Brailsford. *Macedonia: its races and their future.* 1906 ed. New York: Arno, 1971. ISBN 0-405-02738-9. ▸ Conditions at turn of twentieth century. Provides unequaled insight into and detailed information about political, social, economic, ethnic, and religious affairs by observant British journalist. [DMP]

33.717 Stoyan Christowe. *Heroes and assassins.* New York: McBride, 1935. ▸ Popular history of Macedonian liberation movements through 1930 by Macedonian-born American journalist and politician. Contains valuable material on Todor Aleksandrov and Ivan Mihailov. Regards Slavs of Macedonia as Bulgarians. [DMP]

33.718 Tihomir R. Georgevitch [Djordjević]. *Macedonia.* New York: Macmillan, 1918. ‣ Macedonian history from ancient times into twentieth century. Documents Serb effort and rationale for seeking to possess Macedonia. Serb perspective. Available on microfilm from Ann Arbor: University of Michigan, University Library, Preservation Office Microfilming Unit, 1991. [DMP]

33.719 A. Goff and Hugh A. Fawcett. *Macedonia: a plea for the primitive.* London: Lane, 1921. ‣ Post–World War I description of Macedonia, its peoples and cultures. Excellent descriptions of living conditions during period by two Englishmen. [DMP]

33.720 Georgina Mary Muir Mackenzie [Sebright] and Adelina Paulina Irby. *Travels in the Slavonic provinces of Turkey in Europe.* 1866 ed. New York: Arno, 1971. ISBN 0-405-02758-3. ‣ Account of Balkan conditions during 1860s. Valuable observations by two British women on cultures, administration, and affairs of peoples in Bosnia, Kosovo, Macedonia, and elsewhere. One of best travel accounts. [DMP]

33.721 Mercia McDermott. *Freedom or death: the life of Gotse Delchev.* London: Journeyman, 1978. ISBN 0-904526-32-1. ‣ Biography of Macedonian liberation movement leader who died in 1903. Best account of one of most important symbolic figures of period, his life and views. Bulgarian perspective. [DMP]

33.722 Frederick Moore. *The Balkan trail.* 1906 ed. New York: Arno, 1971. ISBN 0-405-02768-0. ‣ Events in Ottoman Macedonia during and after 1903 Ilinden uprising. One of few accounts of Albanians in Macedonia. Lively firsthand information. [DMP]

33.723 Duncan M. Perry. *The politics of terror: the Macedonian revolutionary movements, 1893–1903.* Durham, N.C.: Duke University Press, 1988. ISBN 0-8223-0813-4. ‣ Detailed scholarly history and analysis of Internal Macedonian Revolutionary Organization (IMRO) and Supreme Macedonian Committee. Emphasizes organizational development and demonstrates liberation struggle against Ottomans was popularly based. [DMP/GS]

33.724 *Report of the International Commission to Inquire into the Causes and Conduct of the Balkan Wars.* Washington, D.C.: Carnegie Endowment for International Peace, 1914. (Carnegie Endowment for International Peace, Division of Intercourse and Education, 4.) ‣ Analysis of Balkan politics and military activities chiefly in Macedonia. Balanced investigation by distinguished international panel of statesmen, journalists, and professors. [DMP]

33.725 Laura Beth Sherman. *Fires on the mountain: the Macedonian revolutionary movement and the kidnapping of Ellen Stone.* Boulder: East European Monographs; distributed by Columbia University Press, 1980. (East European monographs, 62.) ISBN 0-914710-55-9. ‣ Account of kidnapping of American missionary Ellen Stone and companion by Internal Macedonian Revolutionary Organization (IMRO) insurgents in 1901. Draws on substantial primary material to detail kidnapping and associated events. [DMP]

33.726 H. R. Wilkinson. *Maps and politics: a review of the ethnographic cartography of Macedonia.* Liverpool, England: Liverpool University Press, 1951. ‣ Superb analysis of ethnographic maps. Shows demography manipulated for political reasons. Underscores impossibility of satisfying all sides regarding ethnic make-up of Macedonia. Most objective and exhaustive study in any language. [DMP]

Serbia and Montenegro

33.727 John Clinton Adams. *Flight in winter.* Princeton: Princeton University Press, 1942. ‣ Stirring account of awful retreat of defeated Serb army through Albanian mountains in winter of 1915, showing, in author's view, that "humanity is still unac-

countably idealistic and dishearteningly irrational." Available as photocopy from Berkeley: University of California, Library Photographic Service, 1984. [GS]

33.728 Zarija Besić et al., eds. *Istorija Crne Gore* (History of Montenegro). 3 vols. Titograd, Montenegro: Red. za Istoriju Crne Gore, 1967–. ‣ Most complete history of Montenegro: volume 1 from ancient times to end of twelfth century; volume 2 to end of fifteenth century; and volume 3 to end of eighteenth century. [DM]

33.729 Thomas Butler. *Monumenta Serbocroatica: a bilingual anthology of Serbian and Croatian texts from the twelfth to the nineteenth century.* Ann Arbor: Michigan Slavic Publications, 1980. (Joint Committee on Eastern Europe publication series, 6.) ISBN 0-930042-32-8. ‣ Judicious selection of religious and secular texts including church, Slav, and legal documents, medieval belles-lettres, eighteenth-century revival materials, documents from nineteenth-century national revolution, and folklore. [DM]

33.730 Vaso Čubrilović. *Istorija političke misli u Srbiji XIX veka* (The history of Serb political thought in the nineteenth century). Belgrade: Prosveta, 1958. ‣ Classic study of development of political ideas in Serbia by participant in assassination of Franz Ferdinand turned professional historian. [GS]

33.731 Milovan Djilas. *Njegoš: poet, prince, bishop.* Michael Boro Petrovich, trans. and Introduction. New York: Harcourt Brace & World, 1966. ‣ Extraordinary biography of prince-bishop of Montenegro and greatest Serb poet. Full treatment of Njegoš as ruler, poet, bishop, and man by famous Montenegrin dissident. [DM]

33.732 Alex N. Dragnich. *Serbia, Nikola Pašić, and Yugoslavia.* New Brunswick, N.J.: Rutgers University Press, 1974. ISBN 0-8135-0773-1. ‣ Brief, favorable account of long political career of Nikola Pašić as outstanding Serb and Yugoslav statesman, based mainly on periodical and secondary literature. [DM]

33.733 Slavko Gavrilović et al., ed. *Istorija srpskog naroda* (History of the Serb nation). 6 vols. to date. Belgrade: Srpska Književna Zadruga, 1981–. ‣ Most complete and comprehensive history of Serb people in Serbia and outside from beginning to 1918. Complete sections on cultural, economic, and political history. Magnificently illustrated. [DM]

33.734 Charles Jelavich. *Tsarist Russia and Balkan nationalism: Russian influence in the internal affairs of Bulgaria and Serbia, 1879–1886.* 1958 ed. Berkeley: University of California Press, 1962. ‣ Detailed treatment of Russo-Bulgarian and Russo-Serb relations after the Berlin Congress. Based on correspondence of Russian foreign minister Giers, and Austrian and British archives. Useful for national histories of Bulgaria and Serbia. [DM/RRM]

33.735 Slobodan Jovanović. *Sabrana dela* (Collected works). Belgrade: Gece Kon, 1932–36. ‣ Detailed history of Serbia, 1838–1903, by one of great historians of twentieth century. Contains essays on state, constitutional theory, and leading Serbs. Still standard. [DM]

33.736 David MacKenzie. *Apis, the congenial conspirator: the life of Colonel Dragutin T. Dimitrijević.* Boulder: East European Monographs; distributed by Columbia University Press, 1989. (East European monographs, 265.) ISBN 0-88033-162-3. ‣ Biography of Colonel Dragutin Dimitrijević, leader of Serb nationalist organization, the Black Hand. Sympathetic description of his pre-World War I effort to unite all Serbs and struggle within officer corps and Serb government. [DM/GS]

33.737 David MacKenzie. *Ilija Garašanin: Balkan Bismarck.* Boulder: East European Monographs; distributed by Columbia University Press, 1985. (East European monographs, 181.) ISBN 0-88033-073-2. ‣ Scholarly biography of Serb statesman and national leader who helped establish bases for independent Serbia as interior minister, foreign minister, and premier (1843–67). [DM]

33.738 David MacKenzie. *The Serbs and Russian pan-Slavism, 1875–1878.* Ithaca, N.Y.: Cornell University Press, 1967. ▸ Detailed monograph describing relations between imperial Russia and Serbs (Serbia, Montenegro, Austrian Serbs) during Balkan crisis (1875–1878), including ties between Russian pan-Slav societies and Serbs. [DM/RRM]

33.739 Woodford McClellan. *Svetozar Marković and the origins of Balkan socialism.* Princeton: Princeton University Press, 1964. ▸ Scholarly study of first Balkan socialist of European stature and founder of Serb Radical-Socialist party. Describes Marković's philosophy, brief career, and impact on subsequent generations. [DM]

33.740 Matija Nenadović. *The memoirs of Prota Matija Nenadović.* Lovett F. Edwards, ed. and trans. Oxford: Clarendon, 1969. ISBN 0-19-821476-6. ▸ Firsthand account by Serb religious figure during first Serb insurrection (1804–13) of dealings with its leader, Karadjordje Petrović. Excellent explanatory introduction; appendix on Nenadović at Congress of Vienna. [DM]

33.741 Dositej Obradović. *The life and adventures of Dimitrije Obradović, who as a monk was given the name Dositej, written and published by himself.* George Rapall Noyes, ed. and trans. Berkeley: University of California Press, 1953. ▸ Autobiography of most important, and perhaps only, Serb rationalist of Enlightenment. Good primary source. [GS]

33.742 Stevan K. Pavlowitch. *Anglo-Russian rivalry in Serbia, 1837–1839: the mission of Colonel Hodges.* Paris: Mouton, 1961. ▸ Thorough monograph describing beginnings of autonomous Serbia's relations with European powers. Based on primary Serb, Austrian, and British sources. [DM]

33.743 Michael Boro Petrovich. *A history of modern Serbia, 1804–1918.* New York: Harcourt Brace Jovanovich, 1976. ISBN 0-15-140950-1. ▸ Most complete history in English describing authoritatively and objectively emergence of Serb society and state from first insurrection to unification of Yugoslavia. Essential for understanding modern Yugoslavia. [DM]

33.744 Leopold von Ranke. *The history of Servia and the Servian Revolution.* 1848 ed. Mrs. Alexander Kerr, trans. New York: Da Capo, 1973. ISBN 0-306-70051-4. ▸ Classic account by great German historian covering era of Ottoman rule, Serb institutions, character, and literature. Traces Serb history to fall of Prince Milos in 1838. Relies on Vuk Karadžić. [DM]

33.745 Gale Stokes. *Legitimacy through liberalism: Vladimir Jovanović and the transformation of Serbian politics.* Seattle: University of Washington Press, 1975. (Publications on Russia and Eastern Europe of the Institute for Comparative and Foreign Area Studies, 5.) ISBN 0-295-95384-5. ▸ Monograph describing emergence of liberalism in Serbia and Vojvodina, 1848–71, through career of its leader, Vladimir Jovanović. Argues liberalism permitted Jovanović to outflank prince. Very complete bibliography. [DM]

33.746 Gale Stokes. *Politics as development: the emergence of political parties in nineteenth-century Serbia.* Durham, N.C.: Duke University Press, 1990. ISBN 0-8223-1016-3. ▸ Thorough, readable monograph on development of political parties in late nineteenth-century Serbia, focusing especially on emergence of Radical party, chief organizer of peasantry. [DM]

33.747 Holm Sundhaussen. *Historische Statistik Serbiens, 1834–1914: mit europäischen Vergleichsdaten.* Munich: Oldenbourg, 1989. (Südosteuropäische Arbeiten, 87.) ISBN 3-486-55011-X. ▸ Impressive, pioneering compilation; voluminous statistical data culled from wide variety of Serb and foreign sources, providing remarkable picture of far-reaching changes in most aspects of public and private life. [DM]

33.748 John D. Treadway. *The falcon and the eagle: Montenegro and Austria-Hungary, 1908–1914.* West Lafayette, Ind.: Purdue University Press, 1983. ISBN 0-911198-65-2. ▸ Well-written, well-researched, and detailed monograph describing Montenegro's role in European power politics in years before World War I with overview of Montenegrin history. [DM/SM]

33.749 Wayne S. Vucinich. *Serbia between East and West: the events of 1903–1908.* 1954 ed. New York: AMS Press, 1968. ▸ Clearly written monograph describing last years of Obrenović dynasty and first years of regime of Peter Karadjordjević; covers predominance of Radical party and Nikola Pašić. [DM]

33.750 Wayne S. Vucinich, ed. *The first Serbian uprising, 1804–1813.* Boulder: Social Science Monographs; distributed by Columbia University Press, 1982. (East European monographs, 107.) ISBN 0-930888-15-4. ▸ Thirteen fine essays on revolt against Ottoman rule and role of its chief leader, Karadjordje Petrović. Deals with major historiographic controversies about insurrection. [DM]

33.751 Duncan Wilson. *The life and times of Vuk Stefanović Karadžić, 1789–1864: literacy, literature, and national independence in Serbia.* 1970 ed. Ann Arbor: Michigan Slavic Publications, 1986. ISBN 0-930042-63-8 (pbk). ▸ Fascinating account of creator of modern Serb alphabet, author of classic Serb dictionary, and greatest collector of folk epics. Rare cultural and intellectual history of early nineteenth-century Balkans. [GS]

Slovenia

33.752 Thomas M. Barker. *Social revolutionaries and secret agents: the Carinthian Slovene partisans and Britain's Special Operations Executive.* Boulder: East European Monographs; distributed by Columbia University Press, 1990. ISBN 0-88033-173-9. ▸ Short narrative with extensive documents of Slovenian Partisan resistance to Nazis; not solely a story of self-sacrifice. [GS]

33.753 Bogo Grafenauer. *Zgodovina slovenskega naroda* (History of the Slovene nation). 2d ed. 3 vols to date (1, 2, 5). Ljubljana, Slovenia: Državna Založba Slovenije, 1964–. ▸ Incomplete but excellent multivolume history of early periods of Slovene history whose value has outlasted communist period. [GS]

33.754 Toussaint Hočevar. *The structure of the Slovenian economy, 1848–1963.* New York: Studia Slovenica, 1965. (Studia Slovenica, 5.) ▸ Solid, detailed, but unimaginative economic history of Slovenia. Many statistics and charts. [GS]

33.755 Janko Prunk. *Pot krščanskih socialistov v Osvobodilno fronto slovenskega naroda* (The path of the Christian Socialists into the Liberation Front of the Slovene people). Ljubljana, Slovenia: Cankarjeva založba, 1977. ▸ Important study of Christian Socialist group (Left Catholics), headed by Edvard Kocbek, leading Slovene intellectual, and process that led to its participation in partisan movement. Key to Slovene sociocultural development. [AF/IB]

33.756 Carole Rogel. *The Slovenes and Yugoslavism, 1890–1914.* Boulder: East European Quarterly; distributed by Columbia University Press, 1977. ISBN 0-914710-17-6. ▸ Excellent brief monograph describing how Slovene ties to Habsburgs loosened in years preceding World War I. Concentrates on nationalist youth. [GS]

YUGOSLAVIA, 1918–1991

33.757 Louis Adamic. *The native's return: an American immigrant visits Yugoslavia and discovers his old country.* New York: Harper, 1934. ▸ Personal account of King Alexander's dictatorship by leftist Slovene expatriate. Most influential interwar document on fragility of Yugoslav state. [AF/IB]

33.758 Stella Alexander. *Church and state in Yugoslavia since 1945*. Cambridge: Cambridge University Press, 1979. ISBN 0-521-21942-6. ▸ Best-informed account of communist policy toward Christian churches. Considers both church-state relations and denominational development. [AF/IB]

33.759 Stella Alexander. *The triple myth: a life of Archbishop Alojzije Stepinac*. Boulder: East European Monographs; distributed by Columbia University Press, 1987. (East European monographs, 226.) ISBN 0-88033-122-4. ▸ Measured biography of Zagreb's controversial archbishop, dominant figure in Croatia's Catholic hierarchy during monarchist, occupational, and communist regimes. Debunks various myths about Stepinac; provides important insights into ecclesiastical history. [AF/IB]

33.760 Phyllis Auty. *Tito*. New York: Ballantine, 1972. ▸ Abridged version of Auty's biography of Tito (33.761). [AF/IB]

33.761 Phyllis Auty. *Tito: a biography*. Rev. ed. Harmondsworth: Penguin, 1974. ISBN 0-14-021800-9. ▸ Conventional and excessively favorable account of Tito's life up to 1970. Based on uncritical Yugoslav sources; must be used with caution. Abridged version available (33.760). [AF/IB]

33.762 Phyllis Auty. *Yugoslavia*. New York: Walker, 1965. ▸ Derivative account of country's twentieth-century history, noted for uncritical view of post-1945 developments. [AF/IB]

33.763 Phyllis Auty and Richard Clogg, eds. *British policy towards wartime resistance in Yugoslavia and Greece*. London: Macmillan, 1975. ISBN 0-333-16634-5. ▸ Proceedings of conference with particularly cogent contributions by Barker and Deakin. [AF/IB]

33.764 Ivan Avakumović. *History of the Communist party of Yugoslavia*. Aberdeen: Aberdeen University Press, 1964. ▸ Early account of Yugoslav communist politics up to 1941. Incomplete in handling of nationality issues; otherwise thorough. [AF/IB]

33.765 Neil Balfour and Sally Mackay. *Paul of Yugoslavia: Britain's maligned friend*. London: Hamilton, 1980. ISBN 0-241-10392-4. ▸ Apologetic biography by subject's former son-in-law who was determined to show distortion of Prince Paul's record and loyal friendship to West in spite of alleged pro-Axis sympathies. [AF/IB]

33.766 Ivo Banac. *The national question in Yugoslavia: origins, history, politics*. Ithaca, N.Y.: Cornell University Press, 1984. ISBN 0-8014-1675-2 (cl), 0-8014-9493-1 (pbk). ▸ Noted study of background to national conflicts in Yugoslavia's formative period. Structural analysis of various South Slav national ideologies. [AF/IB]

33.767 Ivo Banac. *With Stalin against Tito: cominformist splits in Yugoslav communism*. Ithaca, N.Y.: Cornell University Press, 1988. ISBN 0-8014-2186-1. ▸ Detailed study of pro-Soviet sympathizers within Communist party of Yugoslavia in crisis of 1948. Comprehensive history of main issues in Yugoslav communism especially with regard to national question. [AF/IB]

33.768 Elisabeth Barker. *British policy in South-East Europe in the Second World War*. London: Macmillan, 1976. ISBN 0-333-15994-2. ▸ Sophisticated, detailed study of British wartime policy toward Balkan countries with special reference to Yugoslavia. Notable for balanced explanation of support for Tito. [AF/IB]

33.769 Nora Beloff. *Tito's flawed legacy: Yugoslavia and the West since 1939*. Boulder: Westview, 1985. ISBN 0-8133-0322-2. ▸ Anti-Tito polemic made less convincing by author's unfamiliarity with issues and context. [AF/IB]

33.770 Dušan Bilandžić. *Historija Socialističke Federativne*

Republike Jugoslavije: glavni procesi, 1918–1985 (History of the Socialist Federative Republic of Yugoslavia: main tendencies, 1918–1945). 3d ed. Zagreb: Školska Knjiga, 1985. ▸ Best analysis of Yugoslav political developments with emphasis on postwar period by Yugoslavia's leading political historian. Gives accepted communist interpretations, but with suggestive virtuosity that permits alternative interpretations. [AF/IB]

33.771 Dušan Bilandžić. *Jugoslavija poslije Tita, 1980–1985* (Yugoslavia after Tito, 1980–1985). Zagreb: Globus, 1986. ISBN 86-343-0041-2. ▸ Continuation of author's study of postwar Yugoslav developments (33.770) in period immediately after Tito. Background to major conflicts of 1990s. [AF/IB]

33.772 Ljubo Boban. *Maček i politika Hrvatske seljačke stranke, 1928–1941: iz povijesti hrvatskog pitanja* (Maček and the policy of the Croat Peasant party, 1928–1941: from the history of the Croat question). 2 vols. Zagreb: Liber, 1974. ▸ Influential, detailed history of Maček's policies in 1930s. Besides thoroughgoing account of Croat national question, includes best overview of period's politics and diplomacy. [AF/IB]

33.773 Alfredo Breccia. *Jugoslavia, 1939–1941: diplomazia della neutralità*. Milan, Italy: Giuffré, 1978. ▸ Most detailed, balanced analysis of Yugoslavia's diplomatic entanglements on eve of World War II. [AF/IB]

33.774 John C. Campbell. *Tito's separate road: America and Yugoslavia in world politics*. New York: Harper & Row for the Council on Foreign Relations, 1967. ▸ Thoughtful overview of Yugoslavia's foreign policy with special account of engagement with United States. [AF/IB]

33.775 John C. Campbell, ed. *Successful negotiation: Trieste 1954, an appraisal by the five participants*. Princeton: Princeton University Press, 1976. ISBN 0-691-05658-7. ▸ Insightful accounts of Trieste dispute by five diplomats (American, British, Yugoslav, Italian) who participated in 1954 settlement. [AF/IB]

33.776 Stephen Clissold. *Djilas: the progress of a revolutionary*. Hugh Seton-Watson, Introduction. New York: Universe, 1983. ISBN 0-87663-431-5. ▸ Detailed, sympathetic biography of Djilas. Principal weaknesses: lack of context and insufficient attention to cultural history. [AF/IB]

33.777 Stephen Clissold. *Whirlwind: an account of Marshal Tito's rise to power*. New York: Philosophical Library, 1949. ▸ Impressionistic, personal narration of Partisan saga. Notable as pioneering document that promoted Tito's reputation in West. [AF/IB]

33.778 Stephen Clissold, ed. *A short history of Yugoslavia: from early times to 1966*. 1966 ed. Cambridge: Cambridge University Press, 1969. ISBN 0-521-09531-X (pbk). ▸ Relevant sections by Seton-Watson, Laffan, Clissold, and Auty represent handy syntheses by leading British specialists. [AF/IB]

33.779 Ferdo Čulinović. *Jugoslavija izmedju dva rata* (Yugoslavia between two wars). 2 vols. Zagreb: Yugoslav Academy of Sciences and Arts, 1961. (Izdanja historijskog instituta Jugoslavenske akademije znanosti i umjetnosti u Zagrebu, 1–2.) ▸ Standard history of interwar years by legal historian who toed party line. Thorough and predictable, but contains material not covered elsewhere. Strong on politics, weak on social and cultural history. [AF/IB]

33.780 Christopher Cviic. *Remaking the Balkans*. New York: Council on Foreign Relations, 1991. ISBN 0-87609-114-1. ▸ Sophisticated and superior study of crisis leading to war in Yugoslavia (1991) by leading British journalist specializing in Balkans. [AF/IB]

33.781 Frederick William D. Deakin. *The embattled mountain*. New York: Oxford University Press, 1971. ▸ Personal account of

Partisan war in Yugoslavia by leading member of British mission to Tito. Highly favorable to Partisans. [AF/IB]

33.782 Vladimir Dedijer. *The battle Stalin lost: memoirs of Yugoslavia, 1948–1953*. New York: Viking, 1971. ISBN 0-670-14978-0. ▸ Chaotic, disorganized account of Tito-Stalin split as suggested by materials in author's diary. Important as syllabus of official Yugoslav views on split. Particularly unenlightening in its domestic-political discussion. [AF/IB]

33.783 Vladimir Dedijer. *Tito*. 1953 ed. New York: Arno, 1972. ISBN 0-405-04565-4. ▸ Official biography of Tito by his principal information officer. Revealing in its emphases and omissions. Important for its role in shaping Tito's public image and reputation. [AF/IB]

33.784 Bogdan D. Denitch. *The legitimation of a revolution: the Yugoslav case*. New Haven: Yale University Press, 1976. ISBN 0-300-01906-8. ▸ Sympathetic sociological study of sources of postwar regime's legitimacy. Notable for polemics against domestic opposition. [AF/IB]

33.785 Aleksa Djilas. *The contested country: Yugoslav unity and communist revolution, 1919–1953*. Cambridge, Mass.: Harvard University Press, 1991. (Russian Research Center studies, 85. Harvard historical studies, 108.) ISBN 0-674-16698-1. ▸ Schematic study of relationship between Yugoslavism, liberalism, and communism and their alleged tension with Croat and Serb national ideologies. [AF/IB]

33.786 Milovan Djilas. *Conversations with Stalin*. Michael Boro Petrovich, trans. New York: Harcourt Brace & World, 1962. ISBN 0-15-622591-3 (pbk). ▸ Dramatic, enlightening account of Yugoslav-Soviet leadership gatherings by leading Yugoslav participant. Important as source on Stalin's postwar policy. One of few firsthand accounts of Stalin. [AF/IB/GS]

33.787 Milovan Djilas. *Land without justice*. William Jovanovich, Introduction. New York: Harcourt Brace Jovanovich, 1958. ▸ First part of author's autobiography (with 33.788, 33.789, and 33.791). Deals with Djilas's childhood and youth in Montenegro. Rare account of Montenegrin mores in twenties. [AF/IB]

33.788 Milovan Djilas. *Memoir of a revolutionary*. Drenka Willen, trans. New York: Harcourt Brace Jovanovich, 1973. ISBN 0-15-158850-3. ▸ Second volume of autobiography (with 33.787, 33.789, and 33.791) on 1930s including author's student period in Belgrade, introduction to communist movement, his imprisonment, and rise in party hierarchy. Excellent source for communist factionalism and atmosphere among left-wing intellectuals. [AF/IB]

33.789 Milovan Djilas. *Rise and fall*. San Diego, Calif.: Harcourt Brace Jovanovich, 1985. ISBN 0-15-177572-9. ▸ Last volume of Djilas's autobiography (with 33.787, 33.788, and 33.791) bringing account to his removal from leadership in 1954. Valuable information about Yugoslav leadership and its policies in immediate postwar period, notably toward Soviet Union. [AF/IB]

33.790 Milovan Djilas. *Tito: the story from inside*. Vasilije Kojić and Richard Hayes, trans. New York: Harcourt Brace Jovanovich, 1980. ISBN 0-15-190474-X. ▸ Hastily written, uneven account of author's association with Tito. Contains few new insights, but much winding speculation. [AF/IB]

33.791 Milovan Djilas. *Wartime*. New York: Harcourt Brace Jovanovich, 1977. ISBN 0-15-194609-4. ▸ Continuation of author's autobiography (with 33.787, 33.788, and 33.789) on partisan struggle in Yugoslavia. Grand, dark, brooding, and frequently inaccurate, but excellent source on mentality of revolutionaries who reinvented Yugoslavia. [AF/IB]

33.792 Dimitrije Djordjević, ed. *The creation of Yugoslavia, 1914–1918*. Santa Barbara, Calif.: ABC-Clio, 1980. ISBN 0-87436-253-9. ▸ Uneven collection of conference papers on unification of Yugoslavia, Serb war aims in 1914–18, and related issues. [AF/IB]

33.793 Alex N. Dragnich. *The first Yugoslavia: search for a viable political system*. Stanford, Calif.: Hoover Institution Press, 1983. ISBN 0-8179-7841-0. ▸ Schematic history of interwar Yugoslavia aimed at demonstrating nonexistence of Great Serb hegemony. [AF/IB]

33.794 Konstantin Fotitch. *The war we lost: Yugoslavia's tragedy and the failure of the West*. New York: Viking, 1948. ▸ Personal, highly colored account of Tito-Mihailović controversy by former royalist envoy. [AF/IB]

33.795 Stephen Graham. *Alexander of Jugoslavia: strong man of the Balkans*. London: Cassell, 1938. ▸ Superficial biography of Yugoslav king and dictator, but useful for otherwise scarce materials on subject. Journalistic and adulatory. [AF/IB]

33.796 George W. Hoffman and Fred Warner Neal. *Yugoslavia and the new communism*. New York: Twentieth Century Fund, 1962. ▸ Sympathetic account of Yugoslav regime at height of its reputation in West. Contains useful data. [AF/IB]

33.797 J. B. Hoptner. *Yugoslavia in crisis, 1934–41*. 1962 ed. New York: Columbia University Press, 1963. ▸ Successful examination of Yugoslavia's attempts to accommodate itself to prewar diplomatic, political, and economic pressures of great powers. Favorable account of Prince Paul's role. [AF/IB]

33.798 Ladislaus Hory and Martin Broszat. *Der kroatische Ustascha-Staat, 1941–1945* (Croatian Ustaša state, 1941–1945). Stuttgart: Deutsche-Verlags-Anstalt, 1964. ▸ Uneven account of Pavelić regime in Croatia by former German occupation official in partnership with well-known historian. [AF/IB]

33.799 Barbara Jancar-Webster. *Women and revolution in Yugoslavia, 1941–1945*. Denver: Arden, 1990. ISBN 0-912869-09-7 (cl), 0-912869-10-0 (pbk). ▸ Women's role in Yugoslav Partisan movement. Based on research in Yugoslav archives and on interviews with women who fought in war. Notable chapter on "new" feminism in Yugoslavia in 1980s. [AF/IB]

33.800 Charles Jelavich. *South Slav nationalisms—textbooks and Yugoslav union before 1914*. Columbus: Ohio State University Press, 1990. ISBN 0-8142-0500-3. ▸ Detailed scholarly work demonstrating that narrowly oriented readers, histories, and geographies used in Serbia, Croatia, and Slovenia prior to World War I failed to prepare those people for Yugoslavism. [GS]

33.801 A. Ross Johnson. *The transformation of communist ideology: the Yugoslav case, 1945–1953*. Cambridge, Mass.: MIT Press, 1972. ISBN 0-262-10012-6. ▸ Erudite study of changes in Communist party's ideology from Stalinism to native Titoist innovations. [AF/IB]

33.802 Ilija Jukić. *The fall of Yugoslavia*. Dorian Cooke, trans. New York: Harcourt Brace Jovanovich, 1974. ISBN 0-15-130100-X. ▸ Polemical account of Yugoslav events during World War II by minor Yugoslav foreign service officer of Croat nationality but pro-Yugoslav sentiment. Much information on government-in-exile in London. [AF/IB]

33.803 Josef Korbel. *Tito's communism*. Denver: University of Denver Press, 1951. ▸ Early study of Titoism by first postwar Czechoslovak envoy to Yugoslavia who subsequently defected to West. Shrewd personal assessments of Yugoslav leaders and their conflict with Moscow. [AF/IB]

33.804 Bogdan Krizman. *Ante Pavelić i Ustaše* (Ante Pavelić and the Ustašas). Zagreb: Globus, 1978. ▸ First of four-volume study of Ustaša movement written with increased expansiveness and declining interest. Lacking interpretive vigor but extremely strong in documentation. Essential for political history of Pavelić's movement and its record. Subsequent volumes will take story to period of Italo-German condominium in Croatia (1941–43), German predominance (1943–45), and Pavelić's exile (1945–59). [AF/IB]

33.805 Bogdan Krizman. *Vanjska politika jugoslavenske države, 1918–1941: diplomatsko-historijski pregled* (Foreign policy of the Yugoslav state, 1918–1941: diplomatic-historical overview). Zagreb: Školska Knjiga, 1975. ▸ Best survey of interwar diplomatic history by leading historian of Yugoslav foreign relations. Handy and accessible with excellent chronology and bibliographical guide. [AF/IB]

33.806 Stanko Lasić. *Miroslav Krleža i Nezavisna Država Hrvatske (10.4.1941–8.5.1945)* (Miroslav Krleža and the Independent State of Croatia [April 10, 1941–May 8, 1945]). Vol. 3 of *Krležologija ili povijest kritičke misli o Miroslavu Krleži* (History of critical thought about Miroslav Krleža). Zagreb: Globus, 1989. 3 vols. ISBN 86-343-0596-1 (set). ▸ Literary history dealing with Miroslav Krleža, leading Croat writer, and how he fared under Ustaša regime, but actually best study of intellectual and political milieu in occupied Croatia. Essential for understanding Ustaša phenomenon. Final volume of three-volume set on Krleža studies. [AF/IB]

33.807 Stanko Lasić. *Sukob na književnoj ljevici, 1928–1952* (Conflict on the literary Left, 1928–1952). Zagreb: Liber, 1970. ▸ Stark overview of most important clash among Yugoslavia's leftist intellectuals over literary freedom and strategic course of communist movement. Probably single most important volume in postwar literary and intellectual history. [AF/IB]

33.808 Michael Lees. *The rape of Serbia: the British role in Tito's grab for power, 1943–1944.* San Diego, Calif.: Harcourt Brace Jovanovich, 1990. ISBN 0-15-195910-2. ▸ Exaggerated account by British liaison officer with Chetniks of how British policy supposedly aided communist revolution in Yugoslavia. Apology for Chetnik movement of Draža Mihailović, whose collaborationist aspect is whitewashed. [AF/IB]

33.809 Vladko Maček. *In the struggle for freedom.* 1957 ed. Elizabeth Gazi and Stjepan Gazi, trans. University Park: Pennsylvania State University Press, 1968. ▸ Memoirs by principal Croat politician of 1930s and leader of Croat Peasant party. Though annoyingly unrevealing in many key sections, still best source for Croat view of period after 1929. [AF/IB]

33.810 Fitzroy Maclean. *Eastern approaches.* 1949 ed. London: Cape, 1966. ISBN 0-224-61155-0. ▸ Author's memoirs of time spent in prewar Russia, wartime Middle East, and North Africa, and as British military mission commander in Yugoslavia. More personal than his biography of Tito. American edition, *Escape to Adventure*, available on microform from Cambridge, Mass.: Harvard University Library Reproduction Service. [AF/IB]

33.811 Fitzroy Maclean. *The heretic: the life and times of Josip Broz Tito.* New York: Harper & Brothers, 1957. ▸ Standard, sympathetic Western biography by leading British liaison officer to Yugoslav Partisans. Composed without primary research and based largely on personal accounts and conversations with principals. [AF/IB]

33.812 David Martin. *The web of disinformation: Churchill's Yugoslav blunder.* San Diego, Calif.: Harcourt Brace Jovanovich, 1990. ISBN 0-15-180704-3. ▸ Apologia on behalf of Mihailović and Chetniks. Case hinges on allegedly mistaken British policy on behalf of Tito's Partisans supposedly inspired by communist agents in British service. Farfetched. [AF/IB]

33.813 Matteo J. Milazzo. *The Chetnik movement and the Yugoslav resistance.* Baltimore: Johns Hopkins University Press, 1975. ISBN 0-8018-1589-4. ▸ Excellent analysis of Chetniks, regional peculiarities of their movement, collaboration with Italians, and

Mihailović's attempts to control noncommunist armed formations. Particularly notable for discussion of areas under Italian occupation. [AF/IB]

33.814 Albert Mousset. *Le royaume des Serbes, Croates, et Slovenes.* Paris: Bossard, 1921. ▸ Early study of Yugoslav kingdom that includes basic information on its earliest phase. [AF/IB]

33.815 Fred Warner Neal. *Titoism in action: the reforms in Yugoslavia after 1948.* Berkeley: University of California Press, 1958. ▸ Best of early American social-science assessments of Titoism by noted area specialist. Typical of hopes engendered by Yugoslav innovations of 1950s. [AF/IB]

33.816 Bogdan C. Novak. *Trieste, 1941–1954: the ethnic, political, and ideological struggle.* Chicago: University of Chicago Press, 1970. ISBN 0-226-59621-4. ▸ Most detailed account of Trieste question with extensive background on competing Yugoslav and Italian claims to this strategic port city. Notable for its analysis of Italian and Yugoslav communist politics. [AF/IB]

33.817 Viktor Novak. *Antologija jugoslovenske misli i narodnog jedinstva (1390–1930)* (Anthology of Yugoslav thought and national unity). Belgrade: Državna štamparija, 1930. ▸ Collection of documents and readings attempting to bolster ideological strength of rather weak idea of yugoslavism. Useful for graduate students. [GS]

33.818 Stephen E. Palmer, Jr. and Robert R. King. *Yugoslav communism and the Macedonian question.* Hamden, Conn.: Archon, 1971. ISBN 0-208-00821-7. ▸ Most comprehensive history of communist encounter with problems of Macedonia. Well researched, extremely informative, and well argued. Best available source in Western language on overall issues of Macedonia. [AF/IB]

33.819 *Patriot or traitor: the case of General Mihailovich: proceedings and report of the Commission of Inquiry of the Committee for a Fair Trial for Draja Mihailovich.* David Martin, Introduction. Stanford, Calif.: Hoover Institution Press, 1978. (Hoover Press publication, 191.) ISBN 0-8179-6911-X. ▸ Attempt to undermine official Yugoslav case against Chetniks. Transcript of proceedings prefaced by introductory essay. [AF/IB]

33.820 Stevan K. Pavlowitch. *The improbable survivor: Yugoslavia and its problems, 1918–1988.* Columbus: Ohio State University Press, 1988. ISBN 0-8142-0486-4. ▸ Attempt to present history of Yugoslav politics from unification to crisis of 1980s. Insights into Stalinism and Titoism; also current areas of discontent: nationalism, Albanians, and religion. Generally underresearched and opinionated. [AF/IB]

33.821 Stevan K. Pavlowitch. *Yugoslavia.* New York: Praeger, 1971. ▸ Generally successful summary of Yugoslav twentieth-century developments. Covers period from unification to late 1960s. Good analysis of party politics. [AF/IB]

33.822 Branko Petranović. *Revolucija i kontrarevolucija u Jugoslaviji, 1941–1945* (Revolution and counterrevolution in Yugoslavia, 1941–1945). Belgrade: Rad, 1983. ▸ Influential attempt at synthetic view of Yugoslav wartime developments. Noted for substituting category of counterrevolution for what official Yugoslav historiography previously considered Chetnik collaborationism. [AF/IB]

33.823 Svetozar Pribitchevitch. *La dictature du roi Alexandre, contribution à l'étude de la democratie (les problèmes yougoslave et balkanique): documents inédits et révélations.* Paris: Boussuet, 1933. ▸ Extremely valuable account of King Alexander's policies before and after introduction of royal dictatorship by leading Serb politician from Croatia who became king's opponent, victim, and bitter critic. [AF/IB]

33.824 Pedro Ramet. *Nationalism and federalism in Yugoslavia,*

1962–19. 2d ed. Bloomington: Indiana University Press, *1992.* ISBN 0-253-34794-7 (cl), 0-253-20703-7 (pbk). ‣ Best available account of nationality concerns in Tito's federalist phase. Important contribution in favor of proposition that Yugoslav politics resembles states-system. Analytical, but occasionally thin on documentation. [AF/IB]

33.825   Pedro Ramet, ed. *Yugoslavia in the 1980s.* Boulder: Westview, 1985. ISBN 0-8133-7012-4 (pbk). ‣ Collection of uneven contributions on early stages of Yugoslavia's disintegration. Ramet, Rusinow, and Jancar are particularly valuable on political issues and questions of social movements. [AF/IB]

33.826   Dragiša N. Ristić. *Yugoslavia's revolution of 1941.* University Park: Pennsylvania State University Press, 1966. ‣ Firsthand account of coup d'état in Belgrade on 27 March 1941. Discussion of political pressures that led to signing of Tripartite Pact and military takeover. Generally favorable to putschists. [AF/IB]

33.827   Walter R. Roberts. *Tito, Mihailović, and the Allies, 1941–1945.* 1973 ed. Durham, N.C.: Duke University Press, 1987. ISBN 0-8223-0773-1 (pbk). ‣ Interesting diplomatic history of relationship between United States, Britain, and Soviet Union toward resistance forces in Yugoslavia. Serves as corrective to pro-Tito accounts that preceded it. [AF/IB]

33.828   Dennison I. Rusinow. *The Yugoslav experiment, 1948–1974.* 1977 ed. Berkeley: University of California Press for Royal Institute of International Affairs, 1978. (Campus, 215.) ISBN 0-520-03730-8. ‣ Best available overview of Yugoslav politics during Tito's leadership. Carefully crafted, documented, and argued narrative history by veteran observer. [AF/IB]

33.829   Dennison I. Rusinow, ed. *Yugoslavia: a fractured federalism.* Washington, D.C.: Wilson Center Press, 1988. ISBN 0-943875-08-0 (cl), 0-943875-07-2 (pbk). ‣ Uneven collection of papers on nationality issues of 1980s. Covers span of opinions from Yugoslav and American specialists represented at Wilson Center conference. [AF/IB]

33.830   James J. Sadkovich. *Italian support for Croatian separatism, 1927–1937.* New York: Garland, 1987. ISBN 0-8240-8030-0. ‣ Excellent study of Croat oppositional politics. Author utilizes generally underresearched Italian sources to demonstrate nature of Italian interest in Yugoslav affairs and interdependence of Croat factions during early 1930s. [AF/IB]

33.831   Dragovan Šepić. *Vlada Ivana Šubašića* (Government of Ivan Šubašić). Zagreb: Globus, 1983. ‣ Essential study for transition from wartime government-in-exile to communized regime. Šepić, leading Croat diplomatic historian, was Šubašić's secretary and writes with sympathy for his highly controversial former superior. [AF/IB]

33.832   Hugh Seton-Watson et al., eds. *R. W. Seton-Watson and the Yugoslavs: correspondence, 1906–1941.* London and Zagreb: British Academy and Yugoslav Academy, 1976. ‣ Fascinating collection of letters in several languages, including many in English, between main promoter of Yugoslavism in England and concerned politicians inside and outside Yugoslavia. [GS]

33.833   Gerson S. Sher. *Praxis: Marxist criticism and dissent in socialist Yugoslavia.* Bloomington: Indiana University Press, 1977. ISBN 0-253-34592-8. ‣ Detailed and sympathetic study of Praxis group, notable circle of revisionist Marxist philosophers with extensive connections abroad. Fails to place group within context of actual Yugoslav political and cultural problems. [AF/IB]

33.834   Paul Shoup. *Communism and the Yugoslav national question.* New York: Columbia University Press, 1968. ‣ Early study of nationality concerns in Yugoslav communist politics. Studious and comprehensive, but without benefit of numerous subsequently released sources. [AF/IB]

33.835   Frederick B. Singleton. *A short history of the Yugoslav peoples.* Cambridge: Cambridge University Press, 1985. ISBN 0-521-25478-7 (cl), 0-521-27485-0 (pbk). ‣ Derivative of author's earlier study (33.836) of principal twentieth-century Yugoslav themes. Many of earlier problems remain. [AF/IB]

33.836   Frederick B. Singleton. *Twentieth-century Yugoslavia.* New York: Columbia University Press, 1976. ISBN 0-231-04016-4 (cl), 0-231-08341-6 (pbk). ‣ Pedestrian summary of principal Yugoslav themes of this century with special emphasis on social development. Numerous factual and interpretive errors. [AF/IB]

33.837   Slobodan Stankovic. *The end of the Tito era: Yugoslavia's dilemmas.* Stanford, Calif.: Hoover Institution Press, 1981. (Hoover Press publication, 236.) ISBN 0-8179-7362-1 (pbk). ‣ Excellent summary of Yugoslavia's problems at point of Tito's passing. Remarkably prescient in several areas, but nevertheless tame in respect to what followed. [AF/IB]

33.838   Eric R. Terzuolo. *Red Adriatic: the Communist parties of Italy and Yugoslavia.* Boulder: Westview, 1985. ISBN 0-8133-7121-X. ‣ Comparative study of relations between Italian and Yugoslav Communist parties. Careful product of primary research with keen argumentation and insights. [AF/IB]

33.839   Jozo Tomasevich. *The Chetniks.* Vol. 1 of *War and revolution in Yugoslavia, 1941–1945.* Stanford, Calif.: Stanford University Press, 1975. ISBN 0-8047-0857-6. ‣ Best and definitive history of Chetnik decline into active collaboration with Axis powers until total defeat in 1945. Includes historical background on prewar Yugoslavia. [AF/IB]

33.840   Jozo Tomasevich. *Peasants, politics, and economic change in Yugoslavia.* Stanford, Calif.: Stanford University Press, 1955. ‣ Best social history of political, social, and economic development of South Slav nations and lands before and after World War I. Particularly important as study of peasantry and agriculture during interwar period. [AF/IB]

33.841   Ruth Trouton. *Yugoslavia, 1900–1950: a study of a development of Yugoslavia peasant society as affected by education.* London: Routledge & Kegan Paul, 1952. ‣ Sociological study of modernization in Yugoslav traditional society. Sketchy and didactic in places where evidence is lacking. [AF/IB]

33.842   Adam B. Ulam. *Titoism and the Cominform.* 1952 ed. Westport, Conn.: Greenwood, 1971. ISBN 0-8371-3404-8. ‣ Early history of Soviet-Yugoslav dispute. Shrewd and prescient in its analysis of factional background and foreign policy implications. [AF/IB]

33.843   Wayne S. Vucinich, ed. *Contemporary Yugoslavia: twenty years of socialist experiment.* Berkeley: University of California Press, 1969. ‣ Selected papers from conference on Yugoslav history and politics. Note Vucinich's paper on interwar Yugoslavia and especially Tomasevich's article on Yugoslavia during World War II, best single work on topic. [AF/IB]

33.844   Mark C. Wheeler. *Britain and the war for Yugoslavia, 1940–1943.* Boulder: East European Monographs; distributed by Columbia University Press, 1980. (East European monographs, 64.) ISBN 0-914710-57-5. ‣ History of British diplomatic relations with Yugoslav exile government and establishment of relations with Tito and Yugoslav partisans. Reliable though predictable insights into British relations with Mihailović and Chetnik movement. [AF/IB]

33.845   Duncan Wilson. *Tito's Yugoslavia.* Cambridge: Cambridge University Press, 1979. ISBN 0-521-22654-4. ‣ Thorough but unimaginative assessment of Yugoslav politics under Tito up to 1978. Synthesis of conventional Western views on Yugoslavia and Yugoslav socialism. [AF/IB]

SEE ALSO
   47.443 Ivo J. Lederer. *Yugoslavia at the Paris Peace Conference.*

Section 34

DANIEL H. KAISER

Rus', Russia, and the Russian Empire

When the last edition of the *Guide* appeared in 1961, Fritz Epstein, appraising the study of Russian history, observed that "knowledge of the Russian language [is] the privilege of a very limited number of historians outside the Soviet Union," explaining in part the small presence of English-language studies of Russia in the *Guide*. Over the last thirty years, however, the study of Russian history among English speakers has flourished. Not only is Russian taught widely at all levels now, but the growth and support for Russian area centers at leading American universities, the founding and expansion of regular research travel to the former Soviet Union, and the steady increase of library collections in Russian have all contributed to a deeper knowledge of and contact with Russian history and culture.

Increased opportunities for study have brought in their wake a great harvest of English-language studies on Russia's past, so that one can now compile a rather good bibliography with almost no Russian titles, yet make small concession to coverage or quality. It is hardly surprising, then, that bibliographies cataloguing the study of Russia and eastern Europe, and which in the early 1960s were just coming into being, now appear annually, each numbering hundreds of pages. These developments confirm that the study of Russian history in the United States has made great strides over the last three decades.

The effects of the founding of Russian history in the United States continue to linger, however. Surveying the scholarship now available in English on Russian history, one cannot escape the conclusion that the politics of our era have deeply affected the professional agenda. Undeniably the most popular subject of English-speaking historians of Russia has been the state and its influence on society. The recurring backdrop to these studies is the perceived inability of Russia to create a liberal democratic society. This alleged failure has informed studies about reform, the political and legal process, and of course the founding of political parties. These subjects, in turn, led ineluctably to consideration of the origin of the Russian Revolution. Such a preoccupation is fully understandable given the political context. The 1960s witnessed a frenetic contest between Russian communism and American and Western capitalism that encouraged scholars to develop explanations for Russia's seemingly contrary development. At the same time, much of the financial support that in the postwar years sustained the study of Russia and the Soviet Union in the United States came from governmental agencies interested in exactly these questions. The result was an intensive scrutiny of the conditions—intellectual, economic, sociological, and political—that had generated Marxism-Leninism and the Soviet state. Even scholars whose ostensible subject was more remote in time claimed to have found in the study of early modern Russia the seeds of the peculiar political organism that came to full flower late in the twentieth century. To be sure, preoccupation with the state and its authority was hardly a new theme in Russian history. The most prominent historians in late imperial Russia had also focused their gaze upon the state, and Soviet historians too came to turn more and more attention upon the genesis of the revolution that had legitimated Soviet society and, not coincidentally, their own work. Many of these studies were excellent and remain valuable, but concentration on these issues helped guarantee that many other aspects of Russian history remained unstudied.

Over the last decade or so, attention has gradually shifted away from politics, government, diplomacy, and the state to a more comprehensive conception of Russia's past. Economic and social history have made the most visible gains. Of course, some aspects of economic history were popular already in the 1960s, having received their inspiration from modernization theory. Consequently, the first studies of Russian industrialization actually maintained a focus not dissimilar to that dominant in political studies of the time: how had Russia's development deviated from the more successful, more integrated process of industrialization in western Europe and North America? Historians also found much of interest in the system of serfdom and in how this institution had contributed not only to the economic but also to the political impoverishment of Russia. More recently, however, the economic history of Russia has taken on a different tone, devoting more attention to the impact of the economy on individuals and regions. Historians have also begun to appraise the effect of individuals and organizations upon the economy. Much remains to be done in this area, but the first signs are encouraging.

A similar process has characterized the writing of the social history of Russia. For a long time, there was very little social history as such, so dominant was politics in the scholarly consciousness. But in fact it was political history that helped stimulate more study of Russian society. Some of the first books devoted specifically to social history concentrated on Russia's workers and the environments in which they lived, giving some depth to the more narrowly political histories that had preceded them. Russia's peasants, on the other hand, had long had their historians, and it is a tribute to Geroid Tanquary Robinson that his book on rural Russia (34.240), first published in 1932, should remain valuable today. But Robinson's global perspective has gradually yielded to local studies that, though still few in number, reveal a rich mosaic of differences in peasant society, complicating the generalizations that had emerged from the classic studies. Furthermore, recent monographs have gradually attempted to join Russia's experience to those of other societies in Europe rather than emphasize the differences that have so long fascinated historians. More work along this line is in progress and can be expected to better frame the Russian social experience.

Perhaps even more important, in the last decade or two the social history of Russia has come to include classes previously little studied. As a result, one finds in the bibliography below recent monographs on the merchantry, parish clergy, physicians, educators, and other professionals, each work broadening and particularizing our understanding of imperial Russian society. Also new to the bibliography is a small but growing literature on women and gender, now including at least some studies of women of all classes and all periods of Russian history. And the first few community studies have provided extraordinary insight into village dynamics over long stretches of time. These gains are further testimony to the maturation of Russian history over the last several decades.

All the same, the achievements seem modest in comparison with similar work on western Europe and America. When, for example, one considers the extensive bibliography of local studies on France, England, Germany, and Sweden, it is clear that Russian social history has a very long way to go. Of course, there were, in the past, many obstacles to conducting such studies in what used to be the Soviet Union. But bureaucratic obstructions cannot explain all the gaps in the literature. We do not now have, for example, any studies of petty tradesmen or artisans, even for the capital cities, whose records have always been relatively easy to access. But the lack of local history is a far more serious matter. Despite the efforts of historians who in recent years have studied the largest cities in the Russian empire, the history of Russia's provinces remains almost as poorly known today as it was decades ago. It may be that only now, when contemporary political rivalry seems finally to have abated, can historians turn their full attention to more local, specific studies from which new syntheses may be generated in the future.

For reasons already adumbrated above, intellectual history has long occupied a special place in Russian historiography. Graduate students who in the 1960s prepared for their general examinations could hardly bypass a bulky body of literature devoted to the influence of romanticism, rationalism, and nationalism on nineteenth-century Russian intellectuals. These movements, and the individuals most closely associated with them, all drew extensive attention, as the bibliography below will confirm. At least some of the attraction of this subject matter was political: if, as Lenin and others maintained, the Russian revolutionary movement had its genesis in the noblemen of the late eighteenth and early nineteenth centuries, then those interested in understanding the radical intellectuals of the late nineteenth century must consider the dilemmas confronted by their predecessors. The reader of the bibliography below will find, therefore, an ample supply of studies of Herzen, Belinskii, Aksakov, Chernyshevskii, Nechaev, Bakunin, and other nineteenth-century thinkers and the movements they headed or inspired.

One will not find in these works, however, much evidence of the methods that have revolutionized intellectual history elsewhere. There is considerable irony in this fact, inasmuch as Bakhtin and Lotman—whose names are known around the world—made their contributions to intellectual history in Russian. But, except for a very small group of works, Russian intellectual history has yet to exploit the ideas of either of these thinkers; nor has any other recent influence on intellectual history had much impact on Russian intellectual history thus far. Furthermore, the study of Russian culture has yet to connect effectively the discourse between popular and elite culture. The recent spate of works on reading publics is a beginning, but much remains available for study.

Another area of Russian history to show vigorous growth over the last three decades is the study of Russia before Peter the Great. Perhaps as a result of the presentist concerns of the postwar era, few historians who received their degrees before 1960 concentrated on early Russia. Those who did were for the most part Byzantinists or historians of the church. Linguists and scholars of literature also made a contribution. But monographs on Russia before Peter the Great were rare. The growth in the post-1960 era of university faculties in Russian studies did, however, make space available for historians of Rus' and Muscovy. By the late 1960s these historians and their students had begun to make an impact, reassessing the origins of fundamental social and political institutions. Serfdom, slavery, elite society, bureaucratic institutions, the law, and other subjects have received thorough examination. English-speaking scholars have also shown considerable sophistication in dealing with the sometimes difficult and extensive manuscript traditions that surround many of the most essential medieval sources. If Russian archives open wide in the years ahead, this experience may be put to very good use.

All the advances noted above are heartening confirmation of the emergence of Russian history from its postwar adolescence. But further progress will require addressing themes over and above the gaps already observed. So far, almost nothing at all has been published on environmental history, especially the means by which significant geographic and topographic factors have helped shape economic and social organization. Such studies should moderate the preoccupation with political boundaries and draw attention to those enduring features of the landscape that affected human society long before any Rus' and Russian state arose. We also still know very little about the history of climate in Russia and only slightly more about vectors of mortality and morbidity. Both themes present formidable challenges, but examples from other parts of the world point the way to innovative source work by which one may approach these subjects. The history of technology in Russia remains unstudied. And finally, the histories of the non-Russian peoples of the Russian empire also remain largely unexplored in English, particularly for the period before 1917. For too long the discipline has adopted a perspective that reflects Moscow's dominance over the outlying territory. Perhaps in this area, too, political change will speed new directions in the writing of history.

Entries are arranged under the following headings:

Reference Works
  Encyclopedias and Historical Dictionaries
  Bibliographies
  Handbooks
  Surveys
  Photography Albums
  Historiography
  Geography
  Atlases

Politics and Government
  Kievan Rus'
  Muscovy
  Imperial Russia
  Ideologies and Instruments of Power
  Bureaucracies and Political Elites
  Politics and Political Parties
  Rebellion
  Peasant Emancipation of 1861
  Revolution of 1905

Foreign Relations
  Early Influences
  Early Diplomacy: China
  Imperial Diplomacy
  Imperial Wars
  Armies and Armaments

Economy and Society
  General Socioeconomic Studies
  Kievan Rus' and Muscovy
  Imperial Russia
  Society
  Special Social Problems

Ethnic Relations within Rus' and Russia
  Ukrainians, Belorusians, and Other Slavs
  Baltic Germans
  Jews
  Armenians and Georgians
  Siberia and Siberians
  Cossacks
  Volga Germans and Turks

Reading Culture
  Literacy
  Publishing and Readers
  Censorship

Literature and Literary Politics
  Kievan Rus'
  Muscovy
  Imperial Russia

Law and Culture

Education and Schools

Main Currents and Figures of Russian Thought
  General Studies
  Eighteenth Century
  Nineteenth Century
  Westernizers
  Slavophiles
  Marxism and Populist Radicalism

Origins of Revolutionary Intelligentsia

Popular Culture

Arts and Culture

Religion and Culture: Russian Orthodoxy
  General Studies
  Kievan Rus'

Muscovy
Imperial Russia
Schism and Schismatics
Parish Clergy
Theology

Science and Culture
  General Studies
  Science
  Medicine
  Technology

[Contributors: DHK = Daniel H. Kaiser, DTO = Daniel T. Orlovsky, GJM = Gary J. Marker, GS = Gale Stokes, JCB = Joseph C. Bradley, LRG = Loren R. Graham, MR = Mieczysław Rozbicki, NSK = Nancy Shields Kollmann, SCF = Simon C. Franklin, SLH = Steven L. Hoch, US = Uli Schamiloglu]

REFERENCE WORKS

Encyclopedias and Historical Dictionaries

34.1 Ivan Efimovich Andreevskii, Konstantin Konstantinovich Arsen'ev, and Fedor Fomich Petrushevich, eds. *Entsiklopedicheskii slovar'* (Encyclopedic dictionary). 82 vols. St. Petersburg: Efron, 1890–1904. ‣ Extraordinary encyclopedia containing enormous number of detailed articles on Russia prepared by specialists of the day. Two supplementary volumes published 1906–1907. Reprint edition now appearing in Russia. [DHK]

34.2 Archie Brown et al., eds. *The Cambridge encyclopedia of Russia and the Soviet Union.* Cambridge: Cambridge University Press, 1982. ISBN 0-521-23169-8. ‣ Brief essays survey territory of Russia, its arts, religion, politics, sciences, and history. Well illustrated; abundant maps. Competent, concise overviews. [DHK]

34.3 Roger Caratini. *Dictionnaire des nationalités et des minorités de l'ex-URSS.* 2d ed. Paris: Larousse, 1992. ISBN 2-03-720263-6. ‣ Convenient, relatively up-to-date compilation of basic demographic and other descriptive material. [DTO]

34.4 George Jackson, ed. *Dictionary of the Russian Revolution.* Robert Devlin, assistant ed. Westport, Conn.: Greenwood, 1989. ISBN 0-313-21131-0. ‣ Serviceable introductory articles. Covers key personalities, parties, events, etc. [DTO]

34.5 Robin R. Milner-Gulland and Nikolai Dejevsky. *Cultural atlas of Russia and the Soviet Union.* New York: Facts on File, 1989. ISBN 0-8160-2207-0. ‣ About half of book devoted to historical survey of Russia with many maps and color photographs. Special attention to the history of painting and architecture. Time lines and general bibliography. [DHK]

34.6 Aleksandr Mikhailovich Prokhorov, ed. *The great Soviet encyclopedia.* 31 vols. plus index. New York: Macmillan, 1973–83. ‣ Heavy on Marxist-Leninist interpretations but nonetheless useful. Translation of the third Russian edition. [DHK]

34.7 *Russkii biograficheskii slovar'* (Russian biographical dictionary). 1896–1918 ed. 29 vols. New York: Kraus Reprint Corporation and Norman Ross, 1962–91. ISBN 0-88354-350-8 (v. 3A), 0-88354-351-6 (v. 20A). ‣ Publication interrupted by Revolution. Still, extremely helpful; each entry accompanied by bibliography. In 1991 Aspect Press, Moscow, began publishing a reprint edition, and in 1992 Norman Ross published two missing volumes (V, T). [DHK]

34.8 Harold Shukman, ed. *The Blackwell encyclopedia of the Russian Revolution.* London: Blackwell, 1988. ISBN 0-631-15238-5. ‣ Short articles on Russian Revolution by leading specialists. [DTO]

34.9 Paul D. Steeves, ed. *The modern encyclopedia of religions in Russia and the Soviet Union.* 5 vols. to date. Gulf Breeze, Fla.: Academic International Press, 1988–. ISBN 0-87569-106-4 (set).

▸ Individual articles on wide variety of themes, both narrowly religious and more broadly cultural. Quality of essays varies, but each accompanied by bibliography. [DHK]

34.10 Joseph L. Wieczynski, ed. *Modern encyclopedia of Russian and Soviet history.* 55 vols. to date. Gulf Breeze, Fla.: Academic International Press, 1976–. ISBN 0-87569-064-5. ▸ Although not all articles of equal quality, encyclopedia provides important synthesis of knowledge on a vast range of subjects. Supplemental volumes still appearing. [DHK]

34.11 E. M. Zhukov, ed. *Sovetskaia istoricheskaia entsiklopediia* (Soviet historical encyclopedia). 16 vols. Moscow: Sovetskaia Entsiklopediia, 1961–76. ▸ General historical encyclopedia (in Russian only) with many specialized articles on Russia. Heavy overlay of Marxist-Leninist interpretation; omits consideration of some controversial subjects. [DHK]

Bibliographies

34.12 *American bibliography of Slavic and East European studies* (continues *American bibliography of Russian and East European studies*). Columbus, Ohio: American Association for the Advancement of Slavic Studies, 1956–. ISSN 0094-3770. ▸ Annual, comprehensive listing of English-language and selected foreign-language materials published in United States and Canada. Topically organized with full name indexes. [DHK]

34.13 Philip Clendenning and Roger P. Bartlett. *Eighteenth-century Russia: a select bibliography of works published since 1955.* Newtonville, Mass.: Oriental Research Partners, 1981. ISBN 0-89250-110-3 (cl), 0-89250-111-1 (pbk). ▸ Topically organized with special sections on ethnic minorities; introductions to sections. Annotations rare. Part 1 treats English-language, often introductory titles; part 2 lists French, German, and Russian titles. [DHK]

34.14 Anthony G. Cross and Gerald Stanton Smith. *Eighteenth-century Russian literature, culture, and thought: a bibliography of English-language scholarship and translations.* Newtonville, Mass.: Oriental Research Partners, 1984. ISBN 0-89250-334-3. ▸ Very detailed list, with few annotations, of books and articles touching on cultural life. Separate sections devoted to important individuals. [DHK]

34.15 *European bibliography of Soviet, East European, and Slavonic studies.* Birmingham: University of Birmingham, 1975–. ISSN 0140-492X. ▸ European equivalent to *American Bibliography of Slavic and East European Studies* (34.12). English, French, and German titles predominate. Topical organization with name indexes. [DHK]

34.16 Sheila Fitzpatrick and Lynne Viola, eds. *A researcher's guide to sources on Soviet social history in the 1930s.* Armonk, N.Y.: Sharpe, 1990. ISBN 0-87302-497-9. ▸ Excellent bibliographic essays on social and economic history of Stalin era. Written by leading specialists on each topic. Indispensable guide to Russian-language sources. [DTO]

34.17 Stephan M. Horak, comp. *Russia, the USSR, and Eastern Europe: a bibliographic guide to English-language publications, 1964–74.* Rosemary Niesewender, ed. Littleton, Colo.: Libraries Unlimited, 1979. ISBN 0-87287-178-9. ▸ Useful introduction to newer literature supplemented by two successor volumes. Annotations and reference to reviews, normally from *Slavic Review*, *Russian Review*, *Slavonic and East European Review.* Continued in 34.18 and 34.19. [DHK]

34.18 Stephan M. Horak, comp. *Russia, the USSR, and Eastern Europe: a bibliographic guide to English-language publications, 1975–80.* Littleton, Colo.: Libraries Unlimited, 1982. ISBN 0-87287-297-1. ▸ Continues and updates 34.17. Same system of organization and reference to reviews.

34.19 Stephan M. Horak, comp. *Russia, the USSR, and Eastern Europe: a bibliographic guide to English-language publications, 1981–85.* Littleton, Colo.: Libraries Unlimited, 1987. ISBN 0-87287-561-X. ▸ Last volume in series (with 34.17 and 34.18). About two-thirds of entries pertain to Russia and Soviet Union. Annotations and references to scholarly reviews. [DHK]

34.20 Tania Konn, ed. *Soviet studies guide.* London: Bowker-Saur, 1992. ISBN 0-86291-790-5. ▸ Topical listing of reference works and general bibliographies. [DTO]

34.21 Harry W. Nerhood, comp. *To Russia and return: an annotated bibliography of travelers' English-language accounts of Russia from the ninth century to the present.* Columbus: Ohio State University Press, 1968. ▸ Dated but still useful list of published travelers' accounts arranged chronologically; most from twentieth century, but many predate modern era. Helpful annotations. [DHK]

34.22 Bohdan S. Wynar. *Ukraine: a bibliographic guide to English-language publications.* Englewood, Colo.: Ukrainian Academic Press, 1990. ISBN 0-87287-761-2. ▸ Thorough compilation of large body of literature, Ukrainian history, culture, and politics. [DTO]

34.23 Tova Yedlin and Jean Wilman, comps. *Women in Russia and the Soviet Union, December 1984.* Ottawa: Carleton University, 1985. (Institute of Soviet and East European Studies, Bibliography, 3.) ▸ Alphabetic listing (primarily English) on women in Russia and the Soviet Union. Supplement by Janet Hycr published in 1988. Wide-ranging subject matter, popular and scholarly entries, mostly on Soviet era. [DHK]

Handbooks

34.24 Robert Auty and Dimitri Obolensky, eds. *An introduction to Russian history.* New York: Cambridge University Press, 1976. ISBN 0-521-20893-9. ▸ Series of essays, by distinguished historians, organized chronologically and devoted mainly to politics. Good surveys of geography and church history. Bibliographies for each section somewhat dated, but include classics. [DHK]

34.25 *Eastern Europe and the Commonwealth of Independent States.* London: Europa, 1992. ISSN 0962-1040. ▸ One of the better compilations of data on Russia and successor states of Soviet Union, relevant for research on demise of Soviet Union. [DTO]

34.26 Manfred Hellmann, Klaus Zernack, and Gottfried Schramm, eds. *Handbuch der Geschichte Russlands.* 3 vols. Stuttgart: Hiersemann, 1976–86. ISBN 3-7772-7621-9 (set). ▸ Detailed survey of issues with bibliographic addenda to each section. Volume 1 examines geography, ethnogenesis, and history to 1613. Volume 2 follows Romanov dynasty through 1856. Volume 3 treats reform era, industrialization, revolution, and Soviet power through 1945. [DHK]

34.27 Sergei Germanovich Pushkarev, comp. *Dictionary of Russian historical terms from the eleventh century to 1917.* George Vernadsky and Ralph Talcott Fisher, Jr., eds. New Haven: Yale University Press, 1970. ISBN 0-300-01136-9. ▸ Terminology of political, economic, and social history. Entries range from plain definitions to brief interpretive essays. [SCF]

34.28 Knud Rahbek Schmidt. *Soziale Terminologie in russischen Texten des frühen Mittelalters (bis zum Jahre 1240).* Copenhagen: Munksgaard, 1964. ▸ Excellent dictionary of terms organized around major sources of Kievan Rus', especially the Primary Chronicle, Novgorod chronicles, and legal texts. Relatively little attention to literature texts. Index of terms. [DHK]

34.29 Hans-Joachim Torke, ed. *Lexikon der Geschichte Russlands: von den Anfangen bis zur Oktober-Revolution.* Munich: Beck, 1985. ISBN 3-406-30447-8. ▸ Helpful collection of short articles, normally featuring relevant literature, on principal problems and issues of Russian history. Also several maps, tables of most important dates, equivalent names for German and Russian entries. [DHK]

Surveys

34.30 Michael T. Florinsky. *Russia: a history and an interpretation.* 2 vols. New York: Macmillan, 1953. ▸ Introductory survey through 1917. Balanced attention to internal developments, foreign affairs, culture, and arts. Dated but still useful. [DHK]

34.31 Vasilii Osipovich Kliuchevskii. *A history of Russia.* 1911–31 ed. 5 vols. C. J. Hogarth, trans. New York: Russell & Russell, 1960. ▸ Survey from Kievan Rus' to succession of Nicholas I (1825). Special attention to social structure, economics, and domestic administration. Transcribed lectures in antiquated English nevertheless convey author's insight and mastery of sources. Updated translations of seventeenth- and early eighteenth-century portions preferable (see 34.71, 34.89). [NSK/SCF]

34.32 Alexander Kornilov. *Modern Russian history from the age of Catherine the Great to the end of the nineteenth century.* 1943 rev. ed. Alexander S. Kaun, trans. John Shelton Curtiss, bibliographer. New York: Russell & Russell, 1970. ▸ Detailed narrative concentrating on internal politics, often with liberal critique. Little attention to foreign affairs except for major wars of the century. Originally published in Russian in 1912. [DHK]

34.33 Pavel Nikolaevich Miliukov et al. *History of Russia.* 3 vols. Charles Lam Markmann, trans. New York: Funk & Wagnalls, 1968. ▸ Contributions from many leading academics in late imperial Russia make this set a valuable compendium. Treatment of early history sketchy; focus on last years of the empire. Better on cultural and administrative than on social or economic history. Originally published in French in 1932. [DHK]

34.34 Richard Pipes. *Russia under the Old Regime.* New York: Scribner's, 1974. ISBN 0-684-14041-1 (cl), 0-684-14225-2 (pbk). ▸ Controversial, broad-brushed survey of Russian history up to 1880s. Argument that environment and historical events contributed to emergence of patrimonial state which blended rights of sovereignty and ownership. [DHK]

34.35 Nicholas V. Riasanovsky. *A history of Russia.* 4th ed. New York: Oxford University Press, 1984. ISBN 0-19-503365-5, 0-19-503361-2 (college). ▸ Broad coverage of society, culture, economy, and particularly politics from pre-Kievan times to present. Balanced survey; good introduction; helpful maps. [NSK]

34.36 Hugh Seton-Watson. *The Russian empire, 1801–1917.* Oxford: Clarendon, 1967. ▸ Now rather dated but still competent survey; heavy on politics and foreign policy. [DHK]

34.37 Sergei M. Soloviev. *History of Russia from earliest times.* 14 vols. to date. Peter von Wahlde and G. Edward Orchard, eds. Gulf Breeze, Fla.: Academic International Press, 1976–. ISBN 0-87569-027-0 (v. 7 and v. 8), 0-87569-066-1 (v. 9), 0-87569-098-X (v. 14), 0-87569-111-0 (v. 15), 0-87569-124-2 (v. 16), 0-87569-034-3 (v. 24), 0-87569-108-0 (v. 25), 0-87569-042-4 (v. 29), 0-87569-079-3 (v. 34), 0-87569-047-5 (v. 35), 0-87569-117-X (v. 42), 0-87569-091-2 (v. 45), 0-87569-122-6 (v. 48). ▸ English edition of most influential survey of Russian history by dean of nineteenth-century Russian historians. Emphasizes state institutions and their evolution. Volumes appear irregularly and out of sequence. [DHK]

SEE ALSO
9.1 Shirin Akiner. *Islamic peoples of the Soviet Union.*

Photography Albums

34.38 Y. Barchatova et al. *A portrait of tsarist Russia: unknown photographs from the Soviet archives.* Michael Robinson, trans. New York: Pantheon, 1989. ISBN 0-394-58031-1. ▸ Mostly photos

of individuals, including representatives of various trades and crafts as well as workers. Additionally cityscapes and street scenes. Useful introduction to late imperial Russia. [DHK]

34.39 Kyril FitzLyon and Tatiana Browning. *Before the Revolution: a view of Russia under the last tsar.* Woodstock, N.Y.: Overlook, 1978. ISBN 0-87951-079-X (cl), 0-87951-167-2 (pbk). ▸ Poignant photographs document special ceremonies, various ethnic and religious minorities, and the mundane crafts in last days of Russian empire. Introductory essay. [DHK]

34.40 Marvin Lyons. *Russia in original photographs, 1860–1920.* 1977 ed. Andrew Wheatcroft, ed. Boston: Routledge & Kegan Paul, 1983. ISBN 0-7100-9243-1 (pbk). ▸ Individual portraits, mostly of elite, but also excellent images of peasant Russia and emerging urban Russia. Central Asia, imperial army, World War I, and Revolution receive special treatment. [DHK]

34.41 Chloe Obolensky. *The Russian empire: a portrait in photographs.* Max Hayward, Introduction. New York: Random House, 1979. ISBN 0-394-41029-7. ▸ Usual posed photos but many excellent pictures of village, factory, and street life in the late empire; also non-Russian cultures in Central Asia, the Caucasus, and western provinces. [DHK]

34.42 S. M. Prokudin-Gorskii. *Photographs for the tsar: the pioneering color photography of Sergei Mikhailovich Prokudin-Gorskii commissioned by Tsar Nicholas II.* Robert H. Allshouse, ed. New York: Dial, 1980. ISBN 0-8037-6996-2. ▸ Photographer who invented three-part color process that won tsar's support and led to subsidized and authorized excursions around the empire. Images unusual more for their color than for their subjects. [DHK]

34.43 Jonathan Sanders. *Russia, 1917: the unpublished Revolution.* New York: Abbeville, 1989. ISBN 0-89659-775-X. ▸ Previously unpublished photographs arranged in monthly chronicle of Revolution. [DTO]

Historiography

34.44 Anatole G. Mazour. *Modern Russian historiography.* Rev. ed. Westport, Conn.: Greenwood, 1975. ▸ Introductory vignettes on eighteenth- and nineteenth-century historians; now badly dated; for updates see appropriate articles in *Modern Encyclopedia of Russian and Soviet History* (34.10). [DHK]

34.45 George Vernadsky. *Russian historiography: a history.* Sergei Germanovich Pushkarev, ed. Nicholas Lupinin, trans. Belmont, Mass.: Nordland, 1978. ISBN 0-913124-25-7. ▸ Unfinished volume of brief essays on major historians and historical schools of pre-Revolutionary Russia. Not much analysis, but helpful introductions to lives and works of important historians. [DHK]

Geography

34.46 James H. Bater and R. A. French, eds. *Studies in Russian historical geography.* 2 vols. London: Academic Press, 1983. ISBN 0-12-081201-0 (v. 1), 0-12-081202-9 (v. 2). ▸ Seventeen essays covering sixteenth to nineteenth century, examining, among other things, forest usage, soil erosion, introduction of three-field system, southern frontiers, and character of towns. Insightful, detailed surveys. [NSK]

34.47 John C. Dewdney. *A geography of the Soviet Union.* 3d ed. Oxford: Pergamon, 1979. ISBN 0-08-023739-8 (cl), 0-08-023738-X (pbk). ▸ Surveys of topography, climate, vegetation, and historical geography with now outdated discussion of Soviet economy. Heavy on jargon, lots of proper nouns, but good tables and maps. [DHK]

34.48 Judith Pallot and Denis J. B. Shaw. *Landscape and settlement in Romanov Russia, 1613–1917.* New York: Oxford University Press, 1990. ISBN 0-19-823246-2. ▸ Stimulating essays on how society adjusted to natural environment—regional specialization, patterns of landholding, and agriculture. Territorial expansion a key factor in bringing about change. [SLH]

Atlases

34.49 Allen F. Chew. *An atlas of Russian history: eleven centuries of changing borders.* Rev. ed. New Haven: Yale University Press, 1970. ISBN 0-300-01445-7 (pbk). ‣ Thirty-four maps documenting territorial changes from ninth through twentieth century. One-page essay faces each map, describing principal developments. [DHK]

34.50 Martin Gilbert. *Atlas of Russian history.* 1972 ed. New York: Dorset, 1985. ISBN 0-88029-018-8. ‣ Almost 150 maps, treating topics from prehistory through Soviet era; mostly political and economic themes. Information capsules inset in each map. [DHK]

34.51 Paul R. Magocsi. *Ukraine, a historical atlas.* Geoffrey J. Matthews, cartographer. Toronto: University of Toronto Press, 1985. ISBN 0-8020-3428-4 (cl), 0-8020-3429-2 (pbk). ‣ Twenty-five maps, each accompanied by one-page essay highlighting chief events related to period featured. [DHK]

POLITICS AND GOVERNMENT

Kievan Rus'

34.52 Henrik Birnbaum. *Lord Novgorod the Great: essays in the history and culture of a medieval city-state.* Vol. 1: *The historical background.* Columbus, Ohio: Slavica, 1981. ISBN 0-89357-088-5 (v. 1, pbk). ‣ Chapters on Novgorod's origins, history (twelfth to fifteenth century), social structure, and political institutions. Excellent study giving generally favorable evaluation of Novgorodian democracy. [NSK]

34.53 Samuel Hazzard Cross and Olgerd P. Sherbowitz-Wetzor, eds. and trans. *The Russian Primary Chronicle: Laurentian text.* 3d ed. Cambridge, Mass.: Mediaeval Academy of America, 1973. (Mediaeval Academy of America publications, 60.) ‣ Narrative of Russian prehistory and history to the early twelfth century. Essential starting point for study of origins of Rus'. [SCF]

34.54 Martin Dimnik. *Mikhail, prince of Chernigov and grand prince of Kiev, 1224–1246.* Toronto: Pontifical Institute of Mediaeval Studies, 1981. (Pontifical Institute of Mediaeval Studies, Texts and studies, 52.) ISBN 0-88844-052-9. ‣ Innovative approach to regional and dynastic politics during the Mongol invasions. Stresses traditionally underestimated importance of Chernigov. [SCF]

34.55 John L. I. Fennell. *The crisis of medieval Russia, 1200–1304.* London: Longman, 1983. ISBN 0-582-48150-3 (pbk). ‣ End of Kievan Rus' and impact of Mongol invasions. Decline attributed not to economic effects of conquest but to political failure. Best available political history of the period. [SCF]

34.56 Mykhailo Hrushevsky. "The traditional scheme of 'Russian' history and the problem of a rational organization of the history of the East Slavs." In *From Kievan Rus' to modern Ukraine: formation of the Ukrainian nation.* Cambridge, Mass.: Harvard University, Ukrainian Studies Fund, 1984. ISBN 0-9609822-2-1 (pbk). ‣ Kievan Rus' as prehistory of Ukraine, not Russia. Seminal article by major proponent of Ukrainian perspective on early East Slavic history. [SCF]

34.57 George A. Perfecky, trans. *The Galician-Volynian Chronicle, an annotated translation.* Vol. 2 of *The Hypatian Codex.* Munich: Fink, 1973. (Harvard series in Ukrainian studies, 16.2). ‣ Textual and historical commentaries on history of western Rus'. Most detailed narrative source for thirteenth-century Rus'. [SCF]

34.58 Boris Aleksandrovich Rybakov. *Kievan Rus.* Sergei Sos-

sinsky, trans. Moscow: Progress, 1989. ISBN 5-01-001154-9. ‣ Rus' to the mid-thirteenth century; ancient origins and glorious achievements. Lively mixture of Marxism, imagination, and xenophobic nationalism from a senior Soviet academician. [SCF]

34.59 George Vernadsky. *Kievan Russia.* Vol. 2 of *A history of Russia.* 1948 ed. New Haven: Yale University Press, 1973. ISBN 0-300-01647-6 (pbk). ‣ Political, economic, social, and cultural survey. First published 1948, still most comprehensive and judicious general history of pre-Mongol Rus' in English. [SCF]

34.60 George Vernadsky. *The origins of Russia.* 1959 ed. Westport, Conn.: Greenwood, 1975. ‣ Peoples and states of Eurasian steppes from antiquity to formation of Kievan Rus'. Speculative but erudite and coherent. [SCF]

34.61 Serge A. Zenkovsky, ed. *The Nikonian Chronicle.* 5 vols. Serge A. Zenkovsky and Betty Jean Zenkovsky, trans. Princeton: Kingston Press and Darwin Press, 1984–89. ISBN 0-940670-00-3 (v. 1), 0-940670-01-1 (v. 2), 0-940670-02-X (v. 3), 0-940670-03-8 (v. 4), 0-940670-04-6 (v. 5). ‣ Full translation of most voluminous (though not always most reliable) narrative source for medieval Russia; sixteenth-century compilation. [SCF]

Muscovy

34.62 Gustave Alef. *The origins of Muscovite autocracy: the age of Ivan III.* Wiesbaden: Harrassowitz, 1986. ISBN 3-447-02606-5. ‣ Focus on military reforms, court political struggles, new central institutions, and evolution of elite under Ivan III (1462–1505) to trace consolidation of central power. Painstaking prosopography and political chronicle. [NSK]

34.63 Robert O. Crummey. *The formation of Muscovy, 1304–1613.* London: Longman, 1987. ISBN 0-582-49152-5 (cl), 0-582-49153-3 (pbk). ‣ How small principality under Mongol rule became powerful independent state. Chapters on politics, church, arts and culture, and Time of Troubles. Integrates new perspectives and recent literature. [NSK/SCF]

34.64 Robert O. Crummey. "Ivan the Terrible." In *Windows on the Russian past: essays on Soviet historiography since Stalin.* Samuel H. Baron and Nancy Whittier Heer, eds., pp. 57–74. Columbus, Ohio: American Association for the Advancement of Slavic Studies, 1977. ‣ Survey of revisionist interpretations of Ivan IV and Oprichnina during Khrushchev thaw (1960s). Comprehensive, informative; good introduction to problems surrounding controversial ruler. [NSK]

34.65 Robert O. Crummey. "Reform under Ivan IV: gradualism and terror." In *Reform in Russia and the U.S.S.R.: past and prospects.* Robert O. Crummey, ed., pp. 12–27. Urbana: University of Illinois Press, 1989. ISBN 0-252-01612-2. ‣ Best English summary of sixteenth-century reforms of local government and others. Rejects interpretations of Oprichnina as either social engineering or counterreform, seeing its roots in Ivan's troubled personality. Thoughtful, informative. [NSK]

34.66 John L. I. Fennell. *The emergence of Moscow, 1304–1359.* Berkeley: University of California Press, 1968. ‣ Politics among Russian principalities under Mongol rule, focusing on Moscow's struggle with Tver' and relations with Novgorod and Golden Horde. Painstaking political history grounded in comprehensive chronicle analysis. [NSK/SCF]

34.67 John L. I. Fennell. *Ivan the Great of Moscow.* London: Macmillan, 1963. ‣ Rule of "gatherer of Russian lands" (1462–1505) with emphasis on foreign policy and territorial expansion. Detailed political chronicle. [NSK]

34.68 Robert Craig Howes, ed. and trans. *The testaments of the grand princes of Moscow.* Ithaca, N.Y.: Cornell University Press, 1967. ‣ Growth of Muscovy as revealed in testaments of its princes. Substantial introductory analysis and narrative as well as texts and annotated translations. [SCF]

34.69 Lindsey A. J. Hughes. *Sophia, regent of Russia, 1657–1704.* New Haven: Yale University Press, 1990. ISBN 0-300-04790-8. ▸ Sophia in context of social, political, and cultural changes of this transitional era; debunks numerous sensationalist myths. Sensitive and realistic portrayal of Sophia as less westernized than usually held. [NSK]

34.70 John L. H. Keep. "Russia, 1613–45." In *The new Cambridge modern history.* J. P. Cooper, ed., vol. 4, pp. 602–19. Cambridge: Cambridge University Press, 1970. ISBN 0-521- 07618-8. ▸ Discusses election of Mikhail Romanov; repelling Poles and Swedes; Filaret's economic, administrative, and military reforms; foreign war; ecclesiastical reforms; and trade and social development. Excellent brief survey chronicling growth of autocracy. [NSK]

34.71 Vasilii Osipovich Kliuchevskii. *A course in Russian history: the seventeenth century.* Natalie Duddington, trans. Alfred J. Rieber, Introduction. Chicago: Quadrangle, 1968. ▸ From pen of one of greatest of all historians of Russia. Retranslation of volume 3 of Russian edition, much superior to 1913 Hogarth edition. [DHK]

34.72 Nancy Shields Kollmann. *Kinship and politics: the making of the Muscovite political system, 1345–1547.* Stanford, Calif.: Stanford University Press, 1987. ISBN 0-8047-1340-5. ▸ Argues the primacy of kinship ties in attaining boyar status and of marriage connections in court politics; prosopography of elite. Provocative reinterpretation of court political conflicts. [NSK]

34.73 Philip Longworth. *Alexis, tsar of all the Russias.* London: Secker & Warburg, 1984. ISBN 0-436-25688-6. ▸ Political chronicle (1645–76) with attention to foreign wars, court struggle, and conflict with Patriarch Nikon. Broad coverage of domestic and foreign sources. [NSK]

34.74 C. Bickford O'Brien. *Russia under two tsars, 1682–1689: the regency of Sophia Alekseevna.* Berkeley: University of California Press, 1952. ▸ Culture, economy, court political struggles, and especially foreign policy in 1680s. Straightforward political history. [NSK]

34.75 Werner Phillip. "Russia, the beginning of westernization." In *The new Cambridge modern history.* F. L. Carsten, ed., vol. 5, pp. 571–91. Cambridge: Cambridge University Press, 1961. ▸ Expansion into Ukraine and Belorus, military and economic reforms, administration, church reforms, and conflicts with Patriarch Nikon under Aleksei Mikhailovich (r. 1645–76). Excellent introductory survey. [NSK]

34.76 Sergei Fedorovich Platonov. *Boris Godunov, tsar of Russia.* L. Rex Pyles, trans. Gulf Breeze, Fla.: Academic International Press, 1973. ISBN 0-87569-024-6. ▸ Late sixteenth-century social and economic crises and court political struggles. Boris depicted as westernizing liberal. Despite idealizing bent, excellent detail of sources, personalities, and events. [NSK]

34.77 Sergei Fedorovich Platonov. *Ivan the Terrible.* Joseph L. Wieczynski, ed. and trans. Gulf Breeze, Fla.: Academic International Press, 1974. ISBN 0-87569-054-8. ▸ Depicts Oprichnina as rational (a stance seriously challenged) and Ivan as prescient sixteenth-century leader without denying Ivan's irrationality. Still the most nuanced, brief account of Ivan. [NSK]

34.78 Sergei Fedorovich Platonov. *The Time of Troubles: a historical study of the internal crisis and social struggle in sixteenth- and seventeenth-century Muscovy.* John T. Alexander, trans. Lawrence: University Press of Kansas, 1970. ISBN 0-7006-0061-2 (cl), 0-7006-0062-0 (pbk). ▸ Masterfully sets social, geographical, and political setting before analyzing tumults as three-fold crisis:

dynastic, social, and national. First Russian edition appeared in 1924, but remains best analysis. [NSK]

34.79 Alexander Evgen'evich Presniakov. *The formation of the Great Russian state: a study of Russian history in the thirteenth to fifteenth centuries.* A. E. Moorhouse, trans. Alfred J. Rieber, Introduction. Chicago: Quadrangle, 1970. ▸ Rise of Moscow stressing fourteenth-century struggle with Tver'; extends to fifteenth-century conquests. Significance of land-tenure system, inheritance, and succession. First Russian edition in 1918; remains influential. [NSK/SCF]

34.80 Alexander Evgen'evich Presniakov. *The tsardom of Muscovy.* Robert F. Price, ed. and trans. Gulf Breeze, Fla.: Academic International Press, 1978. ISBN 0-87569-052-4 (cl), 0-87569-090-4 (pbk). ▸ Nuanced analysis of social and ideological forces supporting Muscovite autocracy; stress on boyars' interrelations with ruler, church, and lesser servitors. Political chronicle interwoven. Effective patrimonial interpretation. [NSK]

34.81 Ruslan G. Skrynnikov. *Boris Godunov.* Hugh F. Graham, ed. and trans. Gulf Breeze, Fla.: Academic International Press, 1982. ISBN 0-87569-046-7. ▸ Political biography of Boris Godunov (1598–1605) with attention to social and economic policy. Parallels Platonov's idealization of Boris (34.76). [NSK]

34.82 Ruslan G. Skrynnikov. *Ivan the Terrible.* Hugh F. Graham, ed. and trans. Gulf Breeze, Fla.: Academic International Press, 1981. ISBN 0-87569-039-4. ▸ Argues that Oprichnina directed against opposition nobility, but depicts Ivan as nearly irrational. Highly informative survey; interesting example of revisionism after Khrushchev thaw. [NSK]

34.83 Ruslan G. Skrynnikov. *The Time of Troubles: Russia in crisis, 1604–1618.* Hugh F. Graham, ed. and trans. Gulf Breeze, Fla.: Academic International Press, 1988. ISBN 0-87569-097-1. ▸ Detailed chronicle of events, condemning boyars and praising Russian people for mobilizing to end crisis. Lacks adequate introduction and conclusion and perhaps too nationalistic, but offers fascinating detail. [NSK]

34.84 George Vernadsky. *Russia at the dawn of the modern age.* Vol. 4 of *A history of Russia.* 6th rev. ed. New Haven: Yale University Press, 1969. ▸ Reigns of Ivan III and Vasilii III (1462–1533) with excellent study of Ukrainian and Belorusian social structure, rise of Zaporozhian Cossacks, and Union of Brest (1596). Often idiosyncratic but encyclopedic. [NSK]

34.85 George Vernadsky. *The tsardom of Muscovy, 1547–1682.* Vol. 5 of *A history of Russia.* 6th rev. ed. New Haven: Yale University Press, 1969. ▸ Political chronicle with extensive attention to Siberia and Ukraine plus author's theoretical summary of "rhythms" of Russian history. Eurasian focus gives salutary breadth. [NSK]

Imperial Russia

34.86 John T. Alexander. *Catherine the Great: life and legend.* New York: Oxford University Press, 1989. ISBN 0-19-505236-6 (cl), 0-19-5056162-4 (pbk). ▸ Comprehensive, definitive biography of major empress of eighteenth century. Shows her skill in establishing independent power base, generating important reforms, and keeping sexual favoritism sheltered from affairs of state. [GJM]

34.87 Matthew S. Anderson. *Peter the Great.* London: Thames & Hudson, 1978. ISBN 0-500-87008-x. ▸ Traditional biography emphasizing the individual and his foreign policy; lesser attention to domestic reforms and Peter's clash with son Aleksei. Peter as revolutionary transformer. [NSK]

34.88 Isabel De Madariaga. *Russia in the age of Catherine the Great.* New Haven: Yale University Press, 1981. ISBN 0-300-02515-7 (cl), 0-300-02843-1 (pbk). ▸ Magisterial account of how enlightened despot involved state in reforming law and government and in generating secularized cultural life. State-sponsored efforts to improve economic productivity and to soften burdens of serfdom. [GJM]

34.89 Vasilii Osipovich Kliuchevskii. *Peter the Great.* 1958 ed. Liliana Archibald, trans. Boston: Beacon, 1984. ISBN 0-8070-5647-2 (pbk). ▸ Classic account of conflict between modernizing despot and reluctant society. Demonstrates simultaneous achievements and costs of Petrine reforms and assault on Muscovite way of life. On balance, endorses changes. [GJM]

34.90 John P. LeDonne. *Ruling Russia: politics and administration in the age of absolutism, 1762–1796.* Princeton: Princeton University Press, 1984. ISBN 0-691-05425-8. ▸ Attempt to resuscitate language of class to characterize social and political relations in late eighteenth century. Controversial discussion of how state building and noble authority coexisted and complemented one another. [GJM]

34.91 W. Bruce Lincoln. *In war's dark shadow: Russians before the Great War.* 1983 ed. New York: Simon & Schuster, 1986. ISBN 0-671-62821-6. ▸ Survey of three decades before 1917 aimed at general audience, but using primary sources and recent scholarly literature. Chapters on state officials, industrialists, workers, peasants, revolutionaries, artists, and writers. [JCB]

34.92 W. Bruce Lincoln. *Nicholas I, emperor and autocrat of all the Russias.* DeKalb: Northern Illinois University Press, 1989. ISBN 0-87580-548-5. ▸ Valuable biography of tsar, as contemporaries saw him, when Russia was at pinnacle of her power. Society plagued by few self-doubts. Places tsar in more positive light. [SLH]

34.93 Claes Peterson. *Peter the Great's administrative and judicial reforms: Swedish antecedents and the process of reception.* Stockholm: Nord, 1979. (Skrifter utg. av Institutet for Rattshistorisk Forskning, Serien 1: Rattshistoriskt bibliotek, 29.) ISBN 91-85190-11-X (pbk), ISSN 0534-2716. ▸ Extent to which Swedish models influenced reorganization of armed forces, creation of administrative collegia, and secularization of church. Northern War and Swedish prisoners central to building Russian system. [GJM]

34.94 Marc Raeff. "The domestic policies of Peter the Third and his overthrow." *American historical review* 65.5 (1970) 1289–1310. ISSN 0002-8762. ▸ Court politics in 1762. Controversial explanation of alienation between ruler and metropolitan nobility over status, service, and access to throne. Family parties conspired to replace emperor and assassinate him. [GJM]

34.95 Marc Raeff. *Understanding imperial Russia: state and society in the old regime.* Arthur Goldhammer, trans. New York: Columbia University Press, 1984. ISBN 0-231-05842-X (cl), 0-231-05843-8 (pbk). ▸ Stimulating, ambitious review of political life over two centuries. Transplantation and evolution of well-ordered police state based on principles of cameralism. Over time state becomes repressive, impediment to national development. [GJM/NSK/SLH]

34.96 Marc Raeff. *The well-ordered police state: social and institutional change through law in the Germanies and Russia, 1600–1800.* New Haven: Yale University Press, 1983. ISBN 0-300-02869-5. ▸ Classic argument that governmental power grew with rise of central bureaucracies. Cameralism became ideological model of emerging bureaucratic systems in Central and East Europe. Succeeded in Central Europe, failed in East. [GJM]

34.97 Hugh Ragsdale, ed. *Paul I: a reassessment of his life and reign.* Pittsburgh: University Center for International Studies, University of Pittsburgh, 1979. (UCIS series in Russian and Eastern European studies, 2.) ISBN 0-916002-28-4. ▸ Well-researched essays on upbringing and personality of the emperor and on foreign and domestic policies. More than simply reacting against

Catherine, Paul institutionalized separation between emperor and service state. [DHK/GJM]

34.98 Hans Rogger. *Russia in the age of modernisation, 1881–1917.* London: Longman, 1983. ISBN 0-582-48911-3 (cl), 0-582-48912-1 (pbk). ▸ Competent, traditional top-down study, focusing mainly on political and institutional history. Special attention to non-Russian nationalities, foreign relations, 1905 Revolution. Documents crisis of authority, government separated from society. [DHK]

34.99 Eugene Schuyler. *Peter the Great, emperor of Russia: a study of historical biography.* 1884 ed. 2 vols. New York: Russell & Russell, 1967. ▸ Painstakingly traces Peter's life from court politics at his accession (1682) to his death in 1725 with emphasis on his personality and foreign wars. Excellent detail, breadth of source coverage. [NSK]

34.100 B. H. Sumner. *Peter the Great and the emergence of Russia.* 1950 ed. New York: Collier, 1962. ISBN 0-02-037760-6 (pbk). ▸ By developing an army and navy, aggressive, modernizing ruler wins wars against Sweden and Ottoman empire, making Russia major actor in Europe. In the process political institutions undergo major transformation. Classic. [GJM]

34.101 Richard Wortman. "Rule by sentiment: Alexander II's journeys through the Russian empire." *American historical review* 95.3 (1990) 745–71. ISSN 0002-8762. ▸ Novel analysis of royal rites crucial in establishing monarchial authority. Tsar's travel manifested an illusion of love and taken as mandate obviating need for reform. [SLH]

34.102 George L. Yaney. *The systematization of Russian government: social evolution in the domestic administration of imperial Russia, 1711–1905.* Urbana: University of Illinois Press, 1973. ISBN 0-252-00248-2. ▸ Stimulating discussion of two centuries of bureaucratic formalism in vain attempt to impose rational models of political organization over uncongenial society and culture. Shift from colleges to ministries facilitated central control. [GJM/SLH]

Ideologies and Instruments of Power

34.103 Michael Cherniavsky. *Tsar and people: studies in Russian myths.* New Haven: Yale University Press, 1961. ▸ Myth of ruler from Kievan saintly princes and princely saints to sovereign emperor and later myth of holy Russia. Probably exaggerates the social diffusion of this theoretical trend, but stimulating. [NSK]

34.104 S. M. Kashtanov. "The centralised state and feudal immunities in Russia." *Slavonic and East European review* 49.115 (1971) 235–54. ISSN 0037-6795. ▸ Exposes significant deviations from general trend of contracting immunities in sixteenth century as state dispersed grants to cultivate support. Important insight into flexibility of autocratic policy. [NSK]

34.105 Edward L. Keenan, Jr. "Muscovite political folkways." *Russian review* 45.2 (1986) 115–82. ISSN 0036-0341. ▸ Defines Muscovite political culture: conservatism of village, boyars' kinship networks, counterculture of dissent, etc. Traces its endurance to 1970s. Theorizing on grand scale; suggestive on Muscovite period. [NSK]

34.106 David B. Miller. "The *Velikie Minei Cheti* and the *Stepennaia Kniga* of Metropolitan Makarii and the origins of Russian national consciousness." *Historische Veröffentlichungen: Forschungen zur osteuropäischen Geschichte* 26 (1979) 263–382. ISSN 0067-5903. ▸ Two grandiose historical-literary compilations of mid-sixteenth century that exalted ruler as autocrat and placed Moscow at center of Orthodoxy. In-depth study of autocratic trend in political thought. [NSK]

34.107 Jaroslaw Pelenski. "The origins of the official Muscovite claims to the 'Kievan inheritance.'" *Harvard Ukrainian studies* 1.1

(1977) 29–52. ISSN 0363-5570. ▸ Exposition of historical moment (mid-fifteenth century) when Muscovite ideologists formulated theory of continuity of Russian history with Kievan Rus'. Careful analysis of texts. [NSK]

34.108 Nicholas V. Riasanovsky. *Nicholas I and official nationality in Russia, 1825–1855.* 1959 ed. Berkeley: University of California Press, 1969. ▸ Classic exposition of ideology governing Russian domestic and foreign policy for thirty years. Marvel and mistake of autocracy found in its extraordinarily doctrinaire rigidity and consistency. [SLH]

34.109 Daniel Rowland. "The problem of advice in Muscovite tales about the Time of Troubles." *Russian history* 6.2 (1979) 259–83. ISSN 0094-288X. ▸ Argues that political theory was God-dependent, demanding righteous advice-giving by society and piety from ruler. Excellent corrective to constitutional or class-based interpretations of contemporary theory and, implicitly, praxis. [NSK]

34.110 Ihor Ševčenko. "A neglected Byzantine source of Muscovite political ideology." In *Byzantium and the Slavs in letters and culture.* Ihor Ševčenko, ed., pp. 49–91. Cambridge, Mass.: Harvard Ukrainian Research Institute, 1991. ISBN 0-916458-12-1. ▸ Examination of selective use in Rus' writings (especially sixteenth-century Muscovite works) of excerpt from sixth-century theorist, Agapetus, stressing divine nature of sovereign authority. Close textual study. [NSK]

Bureaucracies and Political Elites

34.111 Gustave Alef. *Rulers and nobles in fifteenth-century Muscovy.* London: Variorum, 1983. ISBN 0-86078-120-8. ▸ Reprinted articles on Boyar Duma, Muscovite postal system, Council of Florence (1438–39), and aristocratic politics. Articles on fifteenth-century civil war and symbols of Muscovite autocracy important and influential. [DHK]

34.112 Terence Emmons and Wayne S. Vucinich, eds. *The zemstvo in Russia: an experiment in local self-government.* Cambridge: Cambridge University Press, 1982. ISBN 0-521-23416-6. ▸ Essays for specialists on composition and function of these bodies as framework for study of state and society. Evidence of less political activism than previously believed; peasants were hostile or indifferent. [SLH/JCB]

34.113 Antony N. Grobovsky. *The "Chosen Council" of Ivan IV: a reinterpretation.* Brooklyn, N.Y.: Gaus, 1969. ▸ Argument that this assumed privy council cannot be empirically identified and is figment of historiographical imagination. Undermines established interpretations of Russian political and institutional development. [NSK]

34.114 Uwe Halbach. *Der russische Fürstenhof vor dem sechzehnten Jahrhundert: eine vergleichende Untersuchung zur politischen Lexicologie und Verfassungsgeschichte der alten Rus'.* Stuttgart: Steiner, 1985. (Quellen und Studien zur Geschichte des östlichen Europa, 23.) ISBN 3-515-04151-6. ▸ Important study of development of princely court as physical, institutional, and symbolic focus of authority. From simple organization and practical functions to more elaborate structures in Muscovy. [SCF]

34.115 Lindsey A. J. Hughes. *Russia and the West: the life of a seventeenth-century westernizer, Prince Vasily Vasil'evich Golitsyn (1643–1714).* Newtonville, Mass.: Oriental Research Partners, 1984. ISBN 0-89250-147-2. ▸ Biography of dominant figure in Sophia's regency with emphasis on political struggles and foreign affairs. Straightforward political account with some attention to cultural transformations of era. [NSK]

34.116 Robert E. Jones. *Provincial development in Russia: Catherine II and Jakob Sievers.* New Brunswick, N.J.: Rutgers University Press, 1984. ISBN 0-8135-1026-0. ▸ Reliable discussion of

how empress attracted men of state to become provincial governors. Sievers, serving in Novgorod and Tver', established local institutions and attempted to involve local elites in activities with moderate success. [GJM]

34.117 John P. LeDonne. "Ruling families in the Russian political order, 1689–1825." *Cahiers du monde russe et soviétique* 28.3–4 (1987) 233–322. ISSN 0008-0160. ▸ Prosopographical analysis of continuity in political factions and family networks at court with attention to institutional sources of stability (commitment to autocracy, serfdom, and patronage). Stimulating; detail balanced by interpretation. [NSK]

34.118 Dominic C. B. Lieven. *Russia's rulers under the old regime.* New Haven: Yale University Press, 1989. ISBN 0-300-04371-6 (cl), 0-300-04937-4 (pbk). ▸ Sympathetic collective biography based on service records of men who served on State Council between 1894 and 1914. Efficient civil servants understood Russia's problems and were not stereotypical inept reactionaries. [JCB]

34.119 W. Bruce Lincoln. *In the vanguard of reform: Russia's enlightened bureaucrats, 1825–1861.* DeKalb: Northern Illinois University Press, 1982. ISBN 0-87580-084-X (cl), 0-87580-536-1 (pbk). ▸ Persuasive, comprehensive account of origins of reform legislation. Neither military defeat nor failure of servile economy impelled change. Unusual group of young officials demanded efficient, innovative, aggressive administration. [SLH]

34.120 Brenda Meehan-Waters. *Autocracy and aristocracy: the Russian service elite of 1730.* New Brunswick, N.J.: Rutgers University Press, 1982. ISBN 0-8135-0938-6. ▸ Pioneering prosopographical profile of families of highest rank in 1730, when succession crisis created opportunity for old families to establish oligarchy. Unsuccessful due to opposition of other service families. [GJM/NSK]

34.121 Forrest A. Miller. *Dmitrii Miliutin and the reform era in Russia.* Nashville: Vanderbilt University Press, 1968. ISBN 0-8265-1112-0. ▸ Sympathetic assessment of planning, politics, and implementation of military reforms during reign of Alexander II. Concludes policies served best interests of nation. [SLH]

34.122 Daniel T. Orlovsky. *The limits of reform: the ministry of internal affairs in imperial Russia, 1802–1881.* Cambridge, Mass.: Harvard University Press, 1981. ISBN 0-674-53435-2. ▸ Ministry as paradigm of autocratic government. Creation and evolution of new institutions which failed to harness social change and build consensus. Meticulous institutional history with focus on reign of Alexander II. [SLH/JCB]

34.123 Thomas S. Pearson. *Russian officialdom in crisis: autocracy and local self-government, 1861–1900.* Cambridge: Cambridge University Press, 1989. ISBN 0-521-36127-3. ▸ Excellent account of struggle among state officials and dynamics of central government policy regarding local self-government and land captains. [JCB]

34.124 Walter M. Pintner and Don Karl Rowney, eds. *Russian officialdom: the bureaucratization of Russian society from the seventeenth to the twentieth century.* Chapel Hill: University of North Carolina Press, 1980. ISBN 0-8078-1392-3 (cl), 0-8078-4062-9 (pbk). ▸ Pathbreaking studies of bureaucratic mobility, organizational change in tsarist and Soviet period, and social background of state servitors. Statistical tables help explicate expanding administrative control over social and economic life. [SLH/NSK]

34.125 Marc Raeff. *Michael Speransky, statesman of imperial Russia, 1772–1839.* 1957 ed. Westport, Conn.: Hyperion, 1979. ISBN 0-88355-709-6. ▸ Classic biography of quintessential man of state from background as seminarian to career as loyal professional. Committed to pursuit of *Rechtstaat* (state ordered by law) within autocratic system rather than fundamental reform or constitutionalism. [GJM/SLH]

34.126 David L. Ransel. *The politics of Catherinean Russia: the Panin party.* New Haven: Yale University Press, 1975. ISBN 0-300-01795-2. ▸ Provocative analysis of aristocratic family networks which played significant role in policy, appointments, and defending common interests. Leading foreign policy advisers employed patronage and helped create Northern system in 1760s. [GJM]

34.127 Richard G. Robbins. *Famine in Russia, 1891–92: the imperial government responds to a crisis.* New York: Columbia University Press, 1975. ISBN 0-231-03836-4. ▸ Focus on administration of famine relief. Government-enlisted aid of local self-government raised expectations of new opportunities for cooperation between state and society. [JCB]

34.128 Richard G. Robbins. *The tsar's viceroys: Russian provincial governors in the last years of the empire.* Ithaca, N.Y.: Cornell University Press, 1987. ISBN 0-8014-2046-6. ▸ In the absence of effective institutional mechanism, provincial administration depended on personality and competence of governors. Best available study on subject. [JCB]

34.129 Hartmut Rüss. *Adel und Adelsopposition im Moskauer Staat.* Wiesbaden: Steiner, 1975. (Quellen und Studien zur Geschichte des östlichen Europa, 7.) ISBN 3-515-01903-0. ▸ Examines boyars and their conflicts with rulers from fourteenth century to Vasilii III (1505–33). Argues provocatively that Muscovite elite was European-type nobility. Social-political chronicle. [NSK]

34.130 S. Frederick Starr. *Decentralization and self-government in Russia, 1830–1870.* Princeton: Princeton University Press, 1972. ISBN 0-691-03090-1 (cl), 0-691-10008-X (pbk). ▸ Fine discussion of attempts at reconstituting decrepit system of provincial government and ideologies behind these plans. Legislative solutions integrated into realities of fast-changing nation bound by old habits. [SLH]

34.131 Hans-Joachim Torke. *Die staatsbedingte Gesellschaft im moskauer Reich: zar und zemlja in der altrussischen Herrschaftsverfassung, 1613–1689.* Leiden: Brill, 1974. ISBN 90-04-03979-1. ▸ Examining state institutions (local administration, collective petitions, Councils of Land, urban government), argues that this state-driven society resembled neither European *Standestaat* (corporate state) nor absolutism. Insightful balance of theory and empirical evidence. [NSK]

34.132 Rex A. Wade and Scott J. Seregny, eds. *Politics and society in provincial Russia: Saratov, 1590–1917.* Columbus: Ohio State University Press, 1989. ISBN 0-8142-0494-5. ▸ Essays concentrating on nineteenth century with special attention to emergence of revolutionary movement, worker organization, peasant collective action, and Stolypin reforms. Provincial emphasis helpful corrective to preoccupation with capitals. [DHK]

34.133 Francis William Wcislo. *Reforming rural Russia: state, local society, and national politics, 1855–1914.* Princeton: Princeton University Press, 1990. ISBN 0-691-05574-2. ▸ Detailed synthesis of attempts to accommodate autocracy to more progressive order against backdrop of socioeconomic change. Bureaucratic reform failed to generate civil society mainly because of opposition of autocratic elites. [JCB/DHK]

34.134 Neil B. Weissman. *Reform in tsarist Russia: the state bureaucracy and local government, 1900–1914.* New Brunswick, N.J.: Rutgers University Press, 1981. ISBN 0-8135-0926-2. ▸ Failure to reform inefficient, antiquated local government because neither nobles nor liberal and local self-government leaders could accept continued dominance of state bureaucracy. Specialist study of impasse in late imperial polity. [JCB]

34.135 Petr Andreevich Zaionchkovsky. *The Russian autocracy in crisis, 1878–1882.* Gary M. Hamburg, ed. and trans. Gulf Breeze, Fla.: Academic International Press, 1979. ISBN 0-87569-031-9. ▸ Unjust emancipation settlement plus terror of 1870s resulted in fear and confusion of governing elite. Autocracy considered, then rejected, consultative role of society. From late dean of Soviet historians. [JCB]

34.136 Petr Andreevich Zaionchkovsky. *The Russian autocracy under Alexander III.* David R. Jones, ed. and trans. Gulf Breeze, Fla.: Academic International Press, 1976. ISBN 0-87569-067-X. ▸ Survey of legislative discussion with chapters on Alexander III and his advisers, Ministry of Interior, local self-government, judicial reforms, educational policies, land captains, and counterreforms. Soviet classic. [JCB]

34.137 Larisa G. Zakharova. "Autocracy, bureaucracy, and the reforms of the 1860s in Russia." *Soviet studies in history* 29.3 (1990–91) 6–33. ISSN 0038-5867. ▸ Best available discussion of reform as watershed in evolution of socioeconomic and political relationships. Traditional politics of change overcome and new processes devised, but guarantees that might have safeguarded reforms weak. [SLH]

Politics and Political Parties

34.138 Olga Crisp and Linda H. Edmondson, eds. *Civil rights in imperial Russia.* Oxford: Clarendon, 1989. ISBN 0-19-822867-8. ▸ Specialist articles on 1905, labor, provisional government, freedom of the press and association, religious toleration, ethnicity, and property rights. [JCB]

34.139 Robert O. Crummey. "'Constitutional' reform during the Time of Troubles." In *Reform in Russia and the U.S.S.R.: past and prospects.* Robert O. Crummey, ed., pp. 28–44. Urbana: University of Illinois Press, 1989. ISBN 0-252-01612-2. ▸ Argues that political agreements of 1606, 1610, and 1613 imposed traditional rather than constitutional limits on ruler, which Romanovs proceeded to flout. Thoughtful discussion of Muscovite political culture. [NSK]

34.140 Robert Edelman. *Gentry politics on the eve of the Russian Revolution: the Nationalist party, 1907–1917.* New Brunswick, N.J.: Rutgers University Press, 1980. ISBN 0-8135-0885-1. ▸ Formation of party based in middle gentry of western provinces. Divisions within party after Stolypin's assassination. Marxist approach linking social structure, class identity, political party, and ideology. Pioneering specialist study. [JCB]

34.141 Terence Emmons. *Formation of political parties and the first national elections in Russia.* Cambridge, Mass.: Harvard University Press, 1983. ISBN 0-674-30935-9. ▸ Essential work on origins, leaders, social bases, and programs of Constitutional Democratic and Octobrist parties; electoral campaigns and composition of first two Dumas. [JCB]

34.142 Leopold H. Haimson, ed. *The politics of rural Russia, 1905–1914.* Bloomington: Indiana University Press, 1979. ISBN 0-253-11345-8. ▸ Specialized essays on Octobrist party, Nationalist party, State Council, United Nobility, and peasantry in elections to Fourth Duma. Landed nobility dominated political life and resisted further political reform. [JCB]

34.143 Gary M. Hamburg. *The politics of the Russian nobility, 1881–1905.* New Brunswick, N.J.: Rutgers University Press, 1984. ISBN 0-8135-1009-0. ▸ Important book showing symbiotic relationship between state and nobility disintegrated by 1900. Nobles suffered from agrarian crisis, but still played major role in state administration though no longer as ruling class. [JCB]

34.144 Geoffrey A. Hosking. *The Russian constitutional experiment: government and Duma, 1907–1914.* Cambridge: Cambridge University Press, 1973. ISBN 0-521-20041-5. ▸ Deterioration of relationship between government and moderate public opinion. Traditional pessimistic appraisal of success of constitutionalism within tsarism. [JCB]

34.145 Esther Kingston-Mann. *Lenin and the problem of Marxist peasant revolution.* New York: Oxford University Press, 1983. ISBN 0-19-503278-0 (cl), 0-19-503618-2 (pbk). ‣ Sympathetic study of evolution, after 1902, of Lenin's attitude toward peasantry, away from orthodox Marxism and toward theory to capitalize on growing peasant militance. [JCB]

34.146 John P. LeDonne. *Absolutism and ruling class: the formation of the Russian political order, 1700–1825.* New York: Oxford University Press, 1991. ISBN 0-19-506805-X. ‣ Using laws as evidence of social experience, provocative argument characterizes landed nobility as force dominating government throughout Catherine's reign. Paul's coup intended to regain independence, but only provoked assassination. [GJM]

34.147 Alfred Levin. *The Second Duma: a study of the Social-Democratic party and the Russian constitutional experiment.* 2d ed. Hamden, Conn.: Archon, 1966. ‣ Russian politics between 1905 and 1907. Kadets tried to make Duma, most representative parliament in Russia's history, into instrument of constitutional government, but Social-Democrats not interested in parliamentary government. Best available study on subject. [DHK]

34.148 Alfred Levin. *The Third Duma: election and profile.* Hamden, Conn.: Archon, 1973. ISBN 0-208-01325-3. ‣ Electoral law of 3 June 1907 ensured victory of propertied elements and of Russian nationalism. Detailed empirical analysis of relationships among political parties, voter attitudes, and factions within Duma. [JCB]

34.149 Roberta Thompson Manning. *The crisis of the old order in Russia: gentry and government.* Princeton: Princeton University Press, 1982. ISBN 0-691-05349-9 (cl), 0-691-10133-7 (pbk). ‣ Gentry conservatism and political activism in response to calls for universal suffrage and land expropriation in 1905. Gentry victory in 1907 electoral law responsible for failure of constitutionalism. Controversial interpretation. [JCB]

34.150 Maureen Perrie. *The agrarian policy of the Russian Socialist-Revolutionary party from its origins through the Revolution of 1905–1907.* New York: Cambridge University Press, 1976. ISBN 0-521-21213-8. ‣ Divisions within Socialist-Revolutionaries, especially over issue of seizure of land by peasants themselves and over efficacy of terror. Informative, thorough account of important party at crucial moment. [JCB]

34.151 Christopher Rice. *Russian workers and the Socialist-Revolutionary party through the Revolution of 1905–07.* New York: St. Martin's, 1988. ISBN 0-312-01674-3. ‣ Socialist-Revolutionary party had both urban and rural base. Despite considerable growth, party too weak to maintain both constituencies; after 1907, urban branch disintegrated. Importance of peasant revolutionary. [DHK]

34.152 Jacob Walkin. *The rise of democracy in pre-Revolutionary Russia: political and social institutions under the last three czars.* New York: Praeger, 1962. ‣ Main political and social institutions of late imperial Russia and their interrelationship. Classic presentation of thesis that Russian society making progress, but intransigent government and World War I brought on disaster. [JCB]

Rebellion

34.153 John T. Alexander. *Autocratic politics in a national crisis: the imperial government and Pugachev's revolt.* Bloomington: Indiana University Press for the International Affairs Center, 1969. (Russian and East European studies, 38.) ‣ Detailed, sophisticated examination of how society with weakly developed local

government faced Cossack and peasant revolt at home while military governors fought distant Turkish war. Provincial administrative reform resulted. [GJM]

34.154 Paul Avrich. *Russian rebels, 1600–1800.* 1972 ed. New York: Norton, 1976. ISBN 0-805-23458-6 (cl, 1972), 0-393-00836-3 (pbk). ‣ How Cossack rebels employed pretender myth to foment revolts. Social mix of rebellions varied, but peasants involved in eighteenth century. Role of social resentment and popular myth. Broad, synthetic narrative. [GJM]

34.155 Daniel Field. *Rebels in the name of the tsar.* 1976 ed. Boston: Unwin Hyman, 1989. ISBN 0-04-445190-3 (pbk). ‣ Novel use of case studies examining relationship between folk and educated public, including officialdom. How naïve monarchism endured so long and dissipated so quickly. [SLH]

34.156 Anatole G. Mazour. *The first Russian revolution, 1825: the Decembrist movement, its origins, development, and significance.* 1937 ed. Stanford, Calif.: Stanford University Press, 1961. ‣ Based largely on Soviet accounts, standard narrative of noble officers rebelling against autocracy in pursuit of constitutional regime. Secret circles of disappointed veterans of victory over Napoleon evolve inexorably into opposition. [GJM]

Peasant Emancipation of 1861

34.157 Terence Emmons. *The Russian landed gentry and the peasant emancipation of 1861.* Cambridge: Cambridge University Press, 1968. ISBN 0-521-07340-5. ‣ Involvement of nobility in preparation of reform and in provincial politics. Autocracy had to confront public opinion. Politics of emancipation reveals that bureaucratized autocracy far from a Weberian bureaucratic system. [SLH]

34.158 Daniel Field. *The end of serfdom: nobility and bureaucracy in Russia, 1855–1861.* Cambridge, Mass.: Harvard University Press, 1976. (Russian Research Center studies, 75.) ISBN 0-674-25240-3. ‣ How cautious, traditionalist regime found courage to destroy fundamental institution. Important, detailed discussion of process of reform to comprehend astonishing reversals of course that characterized both nobility and bureaucracy. [SLH]

34.159 W. Bruce Lincoln. *The Great Reforms: autocracy, bureaucracy, and the politics of change in imperial Russia.* DeKalb: Northern Illinois University Press, 1990. ISBN 0-87580-155-2 (cl), 0-87580-549-3 (pbk). ‣ Best available synthesis of recent research, arguing that reforms designed to create civic responsibility, yet government denied political dimensions to individual initiative. Only single-volume study in English. [SLH/JCB]

34.160 David A. J. Macey. *Government and peasant in Russia, 1861–1906: the prehistory of the Stolypin reforms.* DeKalb: Northern Illinois University Press, 1987. ISBN 0-87580-122-6. ‣ Detailed specialist study of formation of policy to break up peasant commune. Groundwork laid before Stolypin by means of perceptual revolution about peasant question. [JCB]

34.161 George L. Yaney. *The urge to mobilize: agrarian reform in Russia, 1861–1930.* Urbana: University of Illinois Press, 1982. ISBN 0-252-00910-X. ‣ Complex and idiosyncratic survey of agrarian reform (primarily Stolypin) and emergence of group of agrarian specialists as key in attempts to transform countryside. [JCB]

34.162 Petr Andreevich Zaionchkovsky. *The abolition of serfdom in Russia.* Susan Wobst, ed. and trans. Terence Emmons, Introduction. Gulf Breeze, Fla.: Academic International Press, 1978. ISBN 0-87569-072-6. ‣ Best Soviet study of drafting, implementation, and reception of emancipation legislation, emphasizing impact of Crimean War as motive. Though bourgeois in character, end of servile status decidedly improved peasants' lot. [JCB/SLH]

34.163 Larisa G. Zakharova. "Autocracy and the abolition of serfdom in Russia, 1856–1861." Gary M. Hamburg, ed. and trans. *Soviet studies in history* 26.2 (1987) 11–115. ISSN 0038-5867. ‣ Government's preparation of 1861 peasant emancipation. Basic discussion emphasizing politics as central element of process that shaped statutes. State an independent actor in policy formulation. [SLH]

Revolution of 1905

34.164 Abraham Ascher. *Russia in disarray.* Vol. 1 of *The Revolution of 1905.* Stanford, Calif.: Stanford University Press, 1988. ISBN 0-8047-1436-3 (v. 1). ‣ Masterly synthesis of recent scholarship combining social and political history. Focus on liberal intelligentsia caught between intransigent state and radicalized workers. Basic work. [JCB]

34.165 Laura Engelstein. *Moscow 1905: working-class organization and political conflict.* Stanford, Calif.: Stanford University Press, 1982. ISBN 0-8047-1118-6. ‣ Important study of grassroots organizations and activities of artisans, factory workers, left-liberal white-collar employees. Increasing polarization in autumn due to government refusal to recognize worker autonomy. [JCB]

34.166 Gerald D. Suhr. *1905 in St. Petersburg: labor, society, and revolution.* Stanford, Calif.: Stanford University Press, 1989. ISBN 0-8047-1499-1. ‣ Nuanced study shows openness of workers to both liberals and socialists, and influence of autonomous labor movement on latter. Government intolerance of public organization turned economic demands into political ones. [JCB]

34.167 Marc Szeftel. *The Russian constitution of April 23, 1906: political institutions of the Duma monarchy.* 1976 ed. New York: Lang, 1982. (Studies presented to the International Commission for the History of Representative and Parliamentary Institutions, 61.) ISBN 0-685-06608-8. ‣ Detailed commentary on 1906 constitution and appraisal of Duma monarchy's attempt to reconcile bureaucratic absolutism and representative government. Constitutional order emerged and government could have avoided revolution. [JCB]

34.168 Andrew M. Verner. *The crisis of Russian autocracy: Nicholas II and the 1905 Revolution.* Princeton: Princeton University Press, 1990. ISBN 0-691-04773-1. ‣ Detailed, informative examination of 1905 through prism of last Romanov, whose upbringing and outlook determined response of government. Emperor could not adapt to emerging alternative ideologies, thereby dooming autocracy. [JCB/DHK]

FOREIGN RELATIONS
Early Influences

34.169 H. R. Ellis Davidson. *The Viking road to Byzantium.* London: Allen & Unwin, 1976. ISBN 0-04-940049-5. ‣ Best available account of Viking expansion in eastern Europe in ninth to twelfth centuries. Their role as traders and mercenaries in emergence of Rus' and in Byzantium. [SCF]

34.170 Boris Dmitrievich Grekov and A. Iu. Iakubovskii. *La Horde d'Or: la domination tatare au treizième et au quatorzième siècle de la mer jaune à la mer noire.* François Thuret, trans. Paris: Payot, 1939. ‣ Iakubovskii analyzes Mongol invasion, Horde's economic, social, and political organization, and cities and "civilization"; Grekov examines conquest of Northeast Rus' and fourteenth-century political relations, summarizing Mongol impact on Russia. [NSK]

34.171 Charles J. Halperin. *Russia and the Golden Horde: the Mongol impact on medieval Russian history.* 1985 ed. London: Tauris, 1987. ISBN 0-85043-057-8 (cl), 0-85043-058-6 (pbk). ‣ Studies effects of Mongol rule on Muscovite institutions across shared cultural frontier despite silence on Mongols in ecclesias-

tically generated sources. Overly complex argument; good survey of Mongol impact on Russia. [NSK/SCF]

34.172 Charles J. Halperin. *The Tatar yoke.* Columbus, Ohio: Slavica, 1986. ISBN 0-89357-161-X (pbk). ‣ Innovative study of Russian attitudes toward Mongols. Bias in sources due to conspiracy of silence leading to basic misunderstanding by modern historians. [SCF]

34.173 John Meyendorff. *Byzantium and the rise of Russia: a study of Byzantino-Russian relations in the fourteenth century.* Crestwood, N.Y.: St. Vladimir's Seminary Press, 1989. ISBN 0-88141-079-9. ‣ Subtle, specialized, yet accessible account of Russo-Byzantine fourteenth-century diplomatic and ecclesiastical relations. Maintained single metropolitancy for East Slavs despite demands for more by Moscow, Lithuania, Tver', Italian Black Sea colonies, and Golden Horde. [SCF/NSK]

34.174 Thomas S. Noonan. "Russia's eastern trade, 1150–1350: the archaeological evidence." *Archivum eurasiae medii aevi* 3 (1983) 201–64. ISSN 0724-8822. ‣ Examination of Oriental glass, pottery, silks, metalware, combs and cowrie shells from sites in Russia and Ukraine. Finds no decline of Eastern trade after tenth century and no cessation of Eastern trade after Mongol conquest. [SCF]

34.175 Dimitri Obolensky. *Byzantium and the Slavs: collected studies.* London: Variorum, 1971. ISBN 0-902089-44-5. ‣ Authoritative and influential articles on Russo-Byzantine political and cultural relations. Byzantium as essential context for understanding of medieval Russian culture. [SCF]

34.176 Jaroslaw Pelenski. *Russia and Kazan: conquest and imperial ideology (1438–1560s).* The Hague: Mouton, 1974. ‣ Authoritative overview of khanate followed by excellent study of legal, historical, and dynastic justifications for Moscow's conquest of Kazan (1552). Kazan in Orthodox anti-Islamic rhetoric. [NSK/US]

34.177 Vilhelm L. P. Thomsen. *The relations between ancient Russia and Scandinavia and the origin of the Russian state: three lectures.* 1877 ed. New York: Franklin, 1964. ‣ Origins of Kievan Rus'. State founded by Scandinavians, not Slavs. Major work presenting the case for Normanist interpretation. [SCF]

34.178 *Varangian problems: report on the first international symposium on the theme "The eastern connections of the Nordic people in the Viking period and early Middle Ages," Moesgaard, University of Aarhus, 7th–11th October 1968.* Copenhagen: Munksgaard, 1970. (Scando-Slavica, supplementum, 1.) ISBN 87-16-00456-6. ‣ Papers and discussions on role of Varangians (Scandinavians) in Rus'. Archaeology, literature, and history by Soviet and non-Soviet contributors giving various perspectives. [SCF]

34.179 George Vernadsky. *The Mongols and Russia.* Vol. 3 of *A history of Russia.* 1943 ed. New Haven: Yale University Press, 1969. ISBN 0-300-1008-7. ‣ Details Mongol conquest, organization of entire Mongol empire, politics of Golden Horde, interrelations of Horde and Northeast Rus' (1360s to 1450s) and Mongol impact on Russia. Informative but idiosyncratic. [NSK/SCF]

SEE ALSO
33.40 William H. McNeill. *Europe's steppe frontier, 1500–1800.*

Early Diplomacy: China

34.180 Mark Mancall. *Russia and China: their diplomatic relations to 1728.* Cambridge, Mass.: Harvard University Press, 1971. ISBN 0-674-78115-5. ‣ Best available study of military and economic relations along Amur. Special attention to Treaties of Nerchinsk (1689) and Kyakhta (1727) that established diplomatic regime in Sino-Russian relations. [DHK]

34.181 Vladimir Stepanovich Miasnikov. *The Ch'ing empire and the Russian state in the seventeenth century.* Vic Schneierson, trans. Moscow: Progress, 1985. ISBN 0-7147-2200-6. ▸ Origins of Sino-Russian diplomatic contacts with special attention to Treaty of Nerchinsk (1689). Culmination of Emperor K'ang-hsi's strategem to seize Russian domains on Amur. Russian perspective. [DHK]

Imperial Diplomacy

34.182 Muriel Atkin. *Russia and Iran, 1780–1828.* Minneapolis: University of Minnesota Press, 1980. ISBN 0-8166-0924-1. ▸ Important narrative of Russian expansion into eastern Caucasus (Georgia), bureaucratic relationship between officials in Petersburg, deteriorating position of Iran, and great power politics. [DHK]

34.183 Glynn Barratt. *Russia in Pacific waters, 1715–1825.* Vancouver: University of British Columbia Press, 1981. ISBN 0-7748-0117-4. ▸ Scientific and mercantile exploration more important to this theater of Russian expansion than military or political considerations. Governmental caution doomed Russian ventures in North Pacific. Useful perspective. [DHK]

34.184 Nikolai Nikolaevich Bolkhovitinov. *The beginnings of Russian-American relations, 1775–1815.* Elena Levin, trans. L. H. Butterfield, Introduction. Cambridge, Mass.: Harvard University Press, 1975. ISBN 0-674-06455-0. ▸ Exhaustive survey of political, economic, and cultural contacts in early years of American republic. Argues that, despite differences between parties, early relationship characterized by peaceful resolution of controversies. [DHK]

34.185 Raymond H. Fisher. *Bering's voyages: whither and why.* Seattle: University of Washington Press, 1977. ISBN 0-295-95562-7. ▸ Study detailing progress of explorations; voyages part of conscious policy to establish Russian outpost in North America. Replete with excellent maps. [DHK]

34.186 Dietrich Geyer. *Russian imperialism: the interaction of domestic and foreign policy, 1860–1914.* Bruce Little, trans. New Haven: Yale University Press, 1987. ISBN 0-300-03796-1. ▸ Synthetic study of Russia's pursuit of aggressive foreign policy despite domestic economic and social weakness. [JCB]

34.187 Patricia K. Grimsted. *The foreign ministers of Alexander I: political attitudes and the conduct of Russian diplomacy, 1801–1825.* Berkeley: University of California Press, 1969. ISBN 0-520-01387-5. ▸ Best available analysis of political attitudes and functions of eight men who formed and implemented foreign policy. Personal predilections often more important than national interests, economics, domestic politics, or social pressures. [SLH]

34.188 Barbara Jelavich. *A century of Russian foreign policy, 1814–1914.* Philadelphia: Lippincott, 1964. ▸ Excellent overview which emphasizes skill and consistency of tsarist diplomacy in century of declining Russian power. Tsars central to process of preserving 1815 boundaries. [DHK]

34.189 Barbara Jelavich. *Russia's Balkan entanglements, 1806–1914.* Cambridge: Cambridge University Press, 1991. ISBN 0-521-40126-7. ▸ Fine discussion of connections that drove Russia into obligations dangerous to its interests with emotional commitments that were difficult to control. Wars' high cost limited resources available for internal development. [SLH/GS]

34.190 Norman E. Saul. *Distant friends: the United States and Russia, 1763–1867.* Lawrence: University Press of Kansas, 1991. ISBN 0-7006-0438-3. ▸ First of proposed three-volume set surveys mutually beneficial relations from first naval contact through Alaska purchase. Commercial interests, mutual Anglophobia, and concerted efforts of individuals united two powers. Comprehensive. [DHK]

34.191 Norman E. Saul. *Russia and the Mediterranean, 1797–1807.* Chicago: University of Chicago Press, 1970. ISBN 0-226-73540-0. ▸ Basic assessment of how events here played major role in formation of Russian diplomatic and military policy. Tsars joined two formidable alliances to reverse tide of French advances. [SLH]

SEE ALSO
　47.85 Harold N. Ingle. *Nesselrode and the Russian rapprochement with Britain, 1836–1844.*
　47.301 George F. Kennan. *The decline of Bismarck's European order.*

Imperial Wars

34.192 Dominic C. B. Lieven. *Russia and the origins of the First World War.* New York: St. Martin's, 1983. ISBN 0-312-69608-6. ▸ Russia's position within great power system. Domestic sources of Russian foreign policy—Nicholas II, Foreign Ministry, army and navy, political parties, press, and public opinion. [JCB]

SEE ALSO
　47.105 John Shelton Curtiss. *Russia's Crimean War.*
　47.115 Norman Rich. *Why the Crimean War? A cautionary tale.*

Armies and Armaments

34.193 John Bushnell. *Mutiny amid repression: Russian soldiers in the Revolution of 1905–1906.* Bloomington: Indiana University Press, 1985. ISBN 0-253-33960-X. ▸ Soldiers' revolution of 1905–1906 was special case of peasant rebellion. Soldiers mutinied after psychological inhibitions to rebellion were removed and ceased their rebellion when they perceived regime's authority as intact. [JCB]

34.194 John Shelton Curtiss. *The Russian army under Nicholas I, 1825–1855.* Durham, N.C.: Duke University Press, 1965. ▸ Organization of military command, training of troops, life of officers and men. Creation of strong anti-intellectual atmosphere made for loyalty to regime. [SLH]

34.195 William C. Fuller, Jr. *Civil-military conflict in imperial Russia, 1881–1914.* Princeton: Princeton University Press, 1985. ISBN 0-691-05452-5. ▸ Growing military professionalism at source of conflict between army and autocracy-bureaucracy. Declining position of and financial stringency in army under tsarism. [JCB]

34.196 John L. H. Keep. *Soldiers of the tsar: army and society in Russia, 1462–1874.* Oxford: Clarendon, 1985. ISBN 0-19-822575-X. ▸ Four centuries of institutional and social evolution of armed forces. Recruitment, military justice, provisioning, military settlements, uprisings, reforms, and relations with civilian society. Daily life in military harsh. [GJM/SLH/NSK]

34.197 Elise K. Wirtschafter. *From serf to Russian soldier.* Princeton: Princeton University Press, 1990. ISBN 0-691-05585-8. ▸ Social conditions of lower ranks. Patterns of control, cohesion, and conflict in military society. Army, despite poor administration, abuses, arbitrariness, and inadequate resources, functioned reasonably well. [SLH/GJM]

ECONOMY AND SOCIETY

General Socioeconomic Studies

34.198 Jerome Blum. *Lord and peasant in Russia from the ninth to the nineteenth century.* 1961 ed. Princeton: Princeton University Press, 1971. ISBN 0-691-00764-0 (pbk). ▸ Broad survey of relations between large private landowners and peasantry against background of political and economic evolution. How few destroyed freedom of millions and how social injustice endured. [SLH/NSK]

34.199 Peter I. Liashchenko. *History of the national economy of*

Russia to the 1917 Revolution. L. M. Herman, trans. New York: Macmillan, 1949. (American Council of Learned Societies, Russian Translation Project series, 4.) ‣ Urban and agrarian economies from Kievan era, in Ukraine and Belorus as well as Russia; one of rare English-language works on pre-Petrine economy. Informative despite rigid Soviet Marxist social analysis. [NSK]

Kievan Rus' and Muscovy

34.200 Alexandre Eck. *Le moyen âge russe.* 2d ed. Marc Szeftel, Introduction, rev. bibliography. The Hague: Mouton, 1968. ‣ Society and economy of fourteenth- and fifteenth-century Northeast Rus'; unparalleled on peasants, princes, servitors, and church. Resembles Pavlov-Sil'vanskii's interpretation which pioneered Russian view of "feudalism" in this era. [NSK]

34.201 Boris Dmitrievich Grekov. *Kiev Rus.* Dennis Ogden, ed. Y. Sdobnikov, trans. Moscow: Foreign Languages Publishing House, 1959. ‣ Pre-Mongol Rus' as feudal society. Classic Soviet Marxist study of economic foundations and social structures. Economy based on agriculture, not commerce. [SCF]

34.202 Janet Martin. *Treasure of the land of darkness: the fur trade and its significance for medieval Russia.* Cambridge: Cambridge University Press, 1986. ISBN 0-521-32019-4. ‣ International fur trade from Northeast Europe, ninth to fifteenth centuries. Using Russian and translated Islamic sources, assesses economic, political significance for Kiev, Novgorod, and Moscow. Broad-ranging interpretation. [NSK/SCF/US]

34.203 Thomas S. Noonan. "The monetary history of Kiev in the pre-Mongol period." *Harvard Ukrainian studies* 11.3–4 (1987) 384–443. ISSN 0363-5570. ‣ Comprehensive survey of Islamic, Byzantine, west European, and native coins in southern Rus'. Links to economic and political history. Full catalogs of finds appended. [SCF]

34.204 Robert E. F. Smith. "Medieval agrarian society in its prime: Russia." In *The Cambridge economic history of Europe.* 2d ed. Michael Moissey Postan, ed., vol. 1, pp. 506–48. Cambridge: Cambridge University Press, 1971. ISBN 0-521-04503-3. ‣ Surveys physical environment, agricultural settlement patterns (villages, estates), farming techniques, social relations, interaction with state, from Kievan Rus' to sixteenth century. Excellent introduction; good bibliography. [NSK]

34.205 Robert E. F. Smith. *Peasant farming in Muscovy.* Cambridge: Cambridge University Press, 1977. ISBN 0-521-20912-9. ‣ Peasant implements, farming techniques, diet, and family structure; case studies of Moscow and Toropets and Kazan regions with some attention to state and landlord exactions, through seventeenth century. Microscopic agrarian history. [NSK]

34.206 Michael W. Thompson. *Novgorod the Great: excavations at the medieval city directed by A. V. Artsikhovsky and B. A. Kolchin.* New York: Praeger, 1967. ‣ Essays on richest archaeological complex of medieval Russia. Fascinating glimpse into material life and literacy (including the birchbark charters) in tenth- to fifteenth-century trading center. Illustrated. [NSK/SCF]

Imperial Russia

34.207 William L. Blackwell. *The beginnings of Russian industrialization, 1800–1860.* Princeton: Princeton University Press, 1968. ISBN 0-691-05104-6. ‣ Basic assessment of backwardness in Russian economic development. Why Russia failed to industrialize rapidly during early nineteenth century. Explores immediate causes and background of industrial growth at end of century. [SLH]

34.208 Ian Blanchard. *Russia's "age of silver": precious metal production and economic growth in the eighteenth century.* London: Routledge, 1989. ISBN 0-415-00831-X. ‣ Integration into world economy led Russia to become world's largest silver producer, supplanting Spanish America. Expansion rivaled British per capita economic growth, but did not lead to industrial boom. Technical narrative. [GJM]

34.209 Olga Crisp. *Studies in the Russian economy before 1914.* New York: Barnes & Noble, 1976. ISBN 0-06-491317-1. ‣ Important essays on pattern of industrial development, preemancipation peasantry, French investment, banking, and monetary policy. Casts doubt on antistatist interpretations that dominated pre-Revolutionary economic history and analyses. [SLH/JCB]

34.210 Peter Gatrell. *The tsarist economy, 1850–1917.* New York: St. Martin's, 1986. ISBN 0-312-82191-3. ‣ Important starting point for examination of economic issues posed by liberal, populist, and Marxist-Leninist traditions. Russia neither uniformly backward nor capitalist. Deemphasizes role of state and peasant commune. [JCB/SLH]

34.211 Gregory Guroff and Fred V. Carstensen, eds. *Entrepreneurship in imperial Russia and the Soviet Union.* Princeton: Princeton University Press, 1983. ISBN 0-691-05376-6 (cl), 0-691-10141-8 (pbk). ‣ Specialized essays on structure of enterprises, state economic policy, and ethnic business elites. Business management skills and innovation, usually associated with free-market economies, also evident in tsarist and Soviet society. [SLH/JCB]

34.212 Steven L. Hoch. "The banking crisis, peasant reform, and economic development in Russia, 1857–1861." *American historical review* 96.3 (1991) 795–820. ISSN 0002-8762. ‣ Impact of liquidity problems in state credit institutions on emancipation of 1861. Harsh terms of emancipation settlement largely a consequence of banking crisis. Innovative perspective on central problem. [SLH]

34.213 Arcadius Kahan. *The plow, the hammer, and the knout: an economic history of eighteenth-century Russia.* Chicago: University of Chicago Press, 1985. ISBN 0-226-42253-4. ‣ Magisterial, encyclopedic analysis of systems of production, trade, and economic life. Despite backward and inefficient agriculture, population participated in market formation and widespread trade and export. [GJM]

34.214 Arcadius Kahan. *Russian economic history: the nineteenth century.* Roger Weiss, ed. Chicago: University of Chicago Press, 1989. ISBN 0-226-42242-9 (cl), 0-226-42243-7 (pbk). ‣ Essays on serfdom, industrialization, literacy, and education. Against received opinion, argues state not guiding force in economy, but often led in wrong direction or stood in way of development. [SLH]

34.215 Tim McDaniel. *Autocracy, capitalism, and revolution in Russia.* Berkeley: University of California Press, 1988. ISBN 0-520-05532-2 (cl), 0-520-06071-7 (pbk). ‣ Stimulating argument that autocracy and capitalism subverted each other, and revolutionary labor movement dealt final blow to both. Paralysis of reform and failure of government labor policy. [JCB]

34.216 John P. McKay. *Pioneers for profit: foreign entrepreneurship and Russian industrialization, 1885–1913.* Chicago: University of Chicago Press, 1970. ISBN 0-226-55990-4. ‣ Positive corrective to Soviet view of role of foreign entrepreneurs and investment and of partnerships with native business. Emphasis on French, Belgian, and German firms. [JCB]

34.217 Thomas C. Owen. *The corporation under Russian law, 1800–1917: a study in tsarist economic policy.* Cambridge: Cambridge University Press, 1991. ISBN 0-521-39126-1. ‣ Sophisticated examination of interplay between tsarist legal system and modern capitalism through study of corporation. Duality of corporate law and bureaucratic practice simultaneously promoted and hampered development of capitalist institutions. [JCB/SLH]

34.218 Walter M. Pintner. *Russian economic policy under Nicholas I*. Ithaca, N.Y.: Cornell University Press, 1967. ▸ Basic analysis of how state mobilized resources. Autocracy had no general theory of development, regarded state intervention as beyond means of nation. Reign marked by unusual passivity toward development of country. [SLH]

34.219 Lewis H. Siegelbaum. *The politics of industrial mobilization in Russia, 1914–1917: a study of the war industries committees.* New York: St. Martin's, 1983. ISBN 0-312-62699-1. ▸ Stimulating specialist study of attempts of industrialists to mobilize war production, reflecting political and social conflicts between state and society and among industrialists themselves. [JCB]

34.220 Mikhail Ivanovich Tugan-Baranovskii. *The Russian factory in the nineteenth century*. Arthur Levin and Claora S. Levin, trans. Homewood, Ill.: Richard D. Irwin for American Economic Association, 1970. ▸ Classic account; first appeared in 1898 when Russia was deep into industrialization. Approvingly surveys preindustrial manufacturing and emergence of capitalist factories in nineteenth century. [DHK]

34.221 Theodore H. Von Laue. *Sergei Witte and the industrialization of Russia*. 1963 ed. New York: Atheneum, 1974. ISBN 0-689-70196-9. ▸ Standard study of Witte system of government-sponsored and government-financed economic growth during 1890s. [JCB]

34.222 Colin M. White. *Russia and America: the roots of economic divergence*. London: Croom Helm, 1987. ISBN 0-7099-5246-5. ▸ Stimulating comparative discussion of systems of production, market formation, and governmental authority at local and regional levels. Despite ecological similarities, different social organizations led to separate paths of development. [GJM]

Society

34.223 Gregory L. Freeze. "The *soslovie* [estate] paradigm and Russian social history." *American historical review* 91.1 (1986) 11–36. ISSN 0002-8762. ▸ Challenges traditional conception. Estate system arose later, more dynamic than previously realized. Mixed system of classes and estates emerged, making it difficult to control or mobilize society. [SLH]

Nobility

34.224 Seymour Becker. *Nobility and privilege in late imperial Russia*. DeKalb: Northern Illinois University Press, 1985. ISBN 0-87580-133-1 (cl), 0-87580-539-6 (pbk). ▸ Provocative revisionist history, arguing that nobility had business acumen and was not in decline, that substantial landed proprietors emerged out of noble estate, and that autocracy, not nobility, was to blame for failure of reform. [JCB]

34.225 Michael Confino. *Domaines et seigneurs en Russie vers la fin du dix-huitième siècle: étude de structures agraires et de mentalités économiques*. Paris: Institut d'Études Slaves, 1963. (Collection historique de l'Institut d'Études Slaves, 18.) ▸ Study of published works of Free Economic Society to discern noble attitudes toward, and structure and operation of, agrarian economy and society. Valuable though rather dated. [DHK]

34.226 Robert O. Crummey. *Aristocrats and servitors: the boyar elite in Russia, 1613–1689*. Princeton: Princeton University Press, 1983. ISBN 0-691-05389-8. ▸ Family ties, political alliances, service careers, economic interests, religious and cultural lives of Moscow's noble officials traced over time. Astute, in-depth analysis of change and continuity in elite. [NSK]

34.227 Robert E. Jones. *The emancipation of the Russian nobility, 1762–1785*. Princeton: Princeton University Press, 1973. ISBN 0-691-05208-5. ▸ Basic account of how state pursued independent bureaucratic presence in provinces. Shocked by Pugachev

revolt, government conceded control of countryside to provincial nobles. [GJM]

34.228 Arcadius Kahan. "The costs of westernization in Russia: the gentry and the economy in eighteenth-century Russia." *Slavic review* 25.1 (1966) 40–66. ISSN 0037-6779. ▸ Classic essay demonstrating prohibitive expenses brought about by process of becoming metropolitan, cosmopolitan nobility. Reveals that only small percentage of elites could bear high economic burden of urban life. [GJM]

Peasantry and Serfdom

34.229 Roger P. Bartlett, ed. *Land commune and peasant community in Russia: communal forms in imperial and early Soviet society*. New York: St. Martin's, 1990. ISBN 0-312-04066-0. ▸ Pioneering collection of articles on institutions of village life, land use, regional differentiation, and interaction between village and larger society. [JCB]

34.230 Michael Confino. *Systèmes agraires et le progrès agricole: l'assolement triennal en Russie aux 18e–19e siècles: étude d'économie et de sociologie rurales*. Paris: Mouton, 1969. (Études sur l'économie et la sociologie des pays slaves, 14.) ▸ Groundbreaking analysis of three-field system, disadvantageous to increased productivity, as pillar of rural life. Russian social structure prohibited absorption of new techniques. [SLH]

34.231 Peter Czap, Jr. "'A large family: the peasant's greatest wealth': serf households in Mishino, Russia, 1814–1858." In *Family forms in historic Europe*. Richard Wall, ed., pp. 105–51, Cambridge: Cambridge University Press, 1983. ISBN 0-521-24547-8. ▸ Pioneering local study of peasant household size, finding prevalence of large, multifamily households adapted to economic requirements of serfdom. [DHK]

34.232 Evsey Domar. "The causes of slavery or serfdom: a hypothesis." *Journal of economic history* 30.1 (1970) 18–32. ISSN 0022-0507. ▸ Roots of East European and Russian sixteenth- and seventeenth-century enserfment in sociopolitical balance of maintaining a privileged elite in conditions of available land and mobile peasantry. Insightful interpretation. [NSK]

34.233 Ben Eklof and Stephen Frank, eds. *The world of the Russian peasant: post-emancipation culture and society*. Boston: Unwin Hyman, 1990. ISBN 0-04-445478-3 (pbk). ▸ Articles on commune, peasant women, contacts with industrial labor and army, education, popular justice, popular religion, and peasant art. Excellent introduction to subject. [JCB]

34.234 August von Haxthausen. *Studies on the interior of Russia*. Abr. ed. S. Frederick Starr, ed. Eleanore M. Schmidt, trans. Chicago: University of Chicago Press, 1972. ISBN 0-226-32022-7 (cl), 0-226-32023-5 (pbk). ▸ Classic, influential travel account of German nobleman in 1843. Peasant commune seen as basis for unity and cohesion lacking in western Europe. Social cohesion founded on hierarchical and patriarchal lines. [SLH]

34.235 Richard Hellie. *Enserfment and military change in Muscovy*. Chicago: University of Chicago Press, 1971. ISBN 0-226-32645-4. ▸ Argues that "middle service class" (provincial cavalrymen) won enserfment as political concession when it was becoming obsolete. Complex argument, but excellent detail on service class, process of enserfment, and military reforms. [NSK]

34.236 Steven L. Hoch. *Serfdom and social control in Russia: Petrovskoe, a village in Tambov*. Chicago: University of Chicago Press, 1986. ISBN 0-226-34583-1 (cl), 0-226-34585-8 (pbk). ▸ Convincing, original sociological analysis of structures of authority, marked by collusion between patriarchs and bailiffs, intergenerational conflict, and system of reward and punishment to maintain serfdom from below. [SLH/GJM]

34.237 Esther Kingston-Mann and Timothy Mixter, eds. *Peas-*

ant economy, culture, and politics of European Russia, 1800–1921. Princeton: Princeton University Press, 1991. ISBN 0-691-05595-5 (cl), 0-691-00849-3 (pbk). ▸ Groundbreaking conference papers examining inner workings of peasant society and issues such as labor markets, gender, and collective action. Based on archival sources and employing comparative perspective. [JCB/SLH]

34.238 Peter Kolchin. *Unfree labor: American slavery and Russian serfdom.* Cambridge, Mass.: Belknap, 1987. ISBN 0-674-92097-X (cl), 0-674-92098-8 (pbk). ▸ Original, wide-ranging comparison emphasizing relative autonomy of serfs, greater frequency of their resistance, and relative lack of moral foundation for serfdom. Both groups nevertheless equally alienated from society. [GJM/SLH]

34.239 Edgar Melton. "Enlightened seigniorialism and its dilemmas in serf Russia, 1750–1830." *Journal of modern history* 62.4 (1990) 675–708. ISSN 0022-2801. ▸ Fine discussion of attempts by liberal serf owners to eliminate arbitrary exercise of authority. Seigniors unable to resolve problems of governing communities in which equality and consensus did not exist. [SLH]

34.240 Geroid T. Robinson. *Rural Russia under the old regime: a history of the landlord-peasant world and a prologue to the peasant revolution of 1917.* Berkeley: University of California Press, 1967. ISBN 0-520-01075-2. ▸ Specific interpretations challenged by recent research, but remains standard institutional history of state-landlord-peasant relationship with emphasis on post-emancipation period. [JCB]

34.241 Teodor Shanin. *The awkward class, political sociology of peasantry in a developing society: Russia, 1910–1925.* Oxford: Clarendon, 1972. ISBN 0-19-821493-6. ▸ Cyclical mobility of peasant household explains absence of permanent differentiation in village and peasant resistance to Bolshevik policy predicated on polarization. Influential work in peasant studies. [JCB]

34.242 Teodor Shanin. *The roots of otherness: Russia's turn of century.* Vol. 1: *Russia as a "developing society."* Vol. 2: *Russia, 1905–07: revolution as a moment of truth.* New Haven: Yale University Press, 1986. ISBN 0-300-03659-0 (v. 1, cl), 0-300-3660-4 (v. 1, pbk), 0-300-03661-2 (v. 2, cl), 0-300-03661-0 (v. 2, pbk). ▸ Provocative essays arguing Russian peasants politically rational, but not in liberal or classical socialist way, and economically rational, though outside capitalist economy. Failure of 1905 Revolution determined political discourse encouraging monarchists and Marxists each to value their own vision of "revolution from above." "Otherness," syndrome of dependent development. [JCB/DHK]

34.243 Wayne S. Vucinich, ed. *The peasant in nineteenth-century Russia.* Stanford, Calif.: Stanford University Press, 1968. ISBN 0-8047-0637-9 (cl), 0-8047-0638-7 (pbk). ▸ Standard collection of articles introduces reader to peasant way of life, emancipation, religion, village commune, and peasant in army and factory. [JCB]

34.244 Christine D. Worobec. *Peasant Russia: family and community in the post-emancipation period.* Princeton: Princeton University Press, 1991. ISBN 0-691-03151-7. ▸ Stimulating portrait of inner world of peasant Russia through study of formal and informal community structures, villagers' interrelationships, families, and rituals. Durability of structures cushioned and impeded modernization. [JCB]

SEE ALSO
  35.214 Dorothy Atkinson. *The end of the Russian land commune, 1905–1930.*

Slavery

34.245 Richard Hellie. "Muscovite slavery in comparative perspective." *Russian history* 6.2 (1979) 133–209. ISSN 0094-288x.

▸ Overview with brief comparisons to all relevant societies and times; typology and law, ethnicity, social origins, prices, owners, slave occupations, manumission, etc. Slavery as safety net in subsistence society. [NSK]

34.246 Richard Hellie. *Slavery in Russia, 1450–1725.* Chicago: University of Chicago Press, 1982. ISBN 0-226-32647-0. ▸ Expands themes of 34.245 with more charts and data. Finds domestic origin of Russian slaves historically unusual. Quantitative and comparative history in overwhelming, occasionally fascinating, detail. [NSK]

Urban Development

34.247 Barbara A. Anderson. *Internal migration during modernization in late nineteenth-century Russia.* Princeton: Princeton University Press, 1980. ISBN 0-691-09386-5. ▸ Important analysis of population migration to industrializing capital cities and provincial backwaters. Prose sometimes off-putting, but argues that migrants' own attitude toward industrialization and modernization affected destination. [DHK]

34.248 James H. Bater. *St. Petersburg: industrialization and change.* Montreal: McGill-Queen's University Press, 1976. ISBN 0-7735-0266-1. ▸ Ambitious study of city's economic and social structure, focusing on 1860s and decade before World War I. Highlights destructive effects of industrialization and urbanization on quality of life of poor. [JCB]

34.249 Joseph Bradley. *Muzhik and Muscovite: urbanization in late imperial Russia.* Berkeley: University of California Press, 1985. ISBN 0-520-05168-8. ▸ Stimulating analysis of urban growth, peasant immigration, and rapid changes in economy and labor force. Efforts to cope with pressure on municipal housing and welfare services resulted in changing priorities of social reform. [JCB]

34.250 Daniel R. Brower. *The Russian city between tradition and modernity, 1850–1900.* Berkeley: University of California Press, 1990. ISBN 0-520-06764-9. ▸ Best available synthesis of recent research maintaining that rapid economic growth and transient populations strained attempts to maintain public order and ameliorate living conditions. [JCB]

34.251 Thomas Stanley Fedor. *Patterns of urban growth in the Russian empire during the nineteenth century.* Chicago: University of Chicago, Department of Geography, 1975. (Department of Geography research papers, 163.) ISBN 0-89065-070-5. ▸ Documents the uneven growth of Russia's cities: little increase until serf emancipation, but greater thereafter. Finds growing internal trade rather than industrialization was central to this change. Specialist study. [DHK]

34.252 David Griffiths and George E. Munro, eds. and trans. *Catherine II's charters of 1785 to the nobility and the towns.* Bakersfield, Calif.: Schlacks, 1991. (Laws of Russia, Series 2: Imperial Russia, 289.) ▸ Russian and English texts of charters intended to create firmer basis for estate system in Russia. Lengthy introduction describing legislative intent and practical limitations of empress' social agenda. Important primary sources. [GJM]

34.253 Michael F. Hamm, ed. *The city in late imperial Russia.* Bloomington: Indiana University Press, 1986. ISBN 0-253-31370-8. ▸ Chapters introduce Moscow, St. Petersburg, Kiev, Warsaw, Riga, Odessa, Tiflis, and Baku, and examine economic and demographic change, ethnicity, quality of urban life, municipal government, and political conflict. [JCB]

34.254 Patricia Herlihy. *Odessa: a history, 1794–1914.* Cambridge, Mass.: Harvard Ukrainian Research Institute, 1986. ISBN 0-916458-08-3 (cl), 0-916458-15-6 (pbk). ▸ Excellent case study of social and cultural accommodation among ethnic communities. Why rapid development early in nineteenth century slowed.

With economy deteriorating, city could not meld citizenry into cohesive unit. [SLH]

34.255 J. Michael Hittle. *The service city: state and townsmen in Russia, 1600–1800.* Cambridge, Mass.: Harvard University Press, 1979. ISBN 0-674-80170-9. ‣ Exceptionalism of Russian urban development against European backdrop. Towns as administrative and military, rather than economic, centers. State domination of urban estates. Standard interpretation. [GJM/NSK]

34.256 Volodymyr I. Mezentsev. "The territorial and demographic development of medieval Kiev and other major cities of Rus': a comparative analysis based on recent archaeological research." *Russian review* 48.2 (1989) 145–70. ISSN 0036-0341. ‣ Size and populations of major towns of Kievan Rus'. Finds no evidence of twelfth-century economic decline of Kiev. Best hypothesis on seemingly inscrutable topic. [SCF]

34.257 Eduard Muhle. *Die städtischen Handelszentren der nordwestlichen Rus': Anfänge und frühe Entwicklung altrussischer Städte bis gegen Ende des zwölften Jahrhunderts.* Stuttgart: Steiner, 1991. ISBN 3-515-05616-5. ‣ Discussion of emergence of urban economic and social structures stressing role of long-distance trade rather than local factors. Major synthesis based on archaeological and written sources. [SCF]

34.258 Gilbert Rozman. *Urban networks in Russia, 1750–1800, and premodern periodization.* Princeton: Princeton University Press, 1976. ISBN 0-691-09364-4. ‣ Technical discussion showing growth of cities more robust than often imagined. Towns connected by market, common economic activities, and administrative responsibilities. Russian pattern comparable to experiences of several non-European countries. [GJM]

34.259 Robert W. Thurston. *Liberal city, conservative state: Moscow and Russia's urban crisis, 1906–1914.* New York: Oxford University Press, 1987. ISBN 0-19-504331-6 (cl), 0-19-504330-8 (pbk). ‣ Useful study of conflict between tutelage of central government and a city government interested in moderate modernization, municipal improvements, and greater local control. [JCB]

34.260 Mikhail Nikolaevich Tikhomirov. *The towns of ancient Rus.* Y. Sdobnikov, trans. Moscow: Foreign Languages Publishing House, 1959. ‣ Economic, demographic, architectural, social, and cultural analysis of emergence of towns in Kievan Rus'. Thorough survey by respected Soviet historian. [SCF]

Merchants and Townsfolk

34.261 Samuel H. Baron. *Explorations in Muscovite history.* Hampshire, England: Variorum, 1991. ISBN 0-86078-302-2. ‣ Authoritative collection of reprinted articles examines entrepreneurship, mercantilism, seafaring and discovery, and early maps of Russia. Important newly published essays reconsider Muscovite merchants and influence of Herberstein. [DHK]

34.262 Samuel H. Baron. *Muscovite Russia: collected essays.* London: Variorum, 1980. ISBN 0-86078-063-5. ‣ Essays on Muscovy's comparatively weak urban and merchant development and on revisions of Soviet Marxist historical paradigms. Each article a gem of empirical research and theoretical significance. [NSK]

34.263 Paul Bushkovitch. *The merchants of Moscow, 1580–1650.* Cambridge: Cambridge University Press, 1980. ISBN 0-521-22589-2. ‣ Chapters on trade routes (Archangel, Baltic, Poland, Ottoman empire, Persia), internal trade, and merchants. Places merchants in East European perspective. Argues, against mainstream, that they were a viable economic group. [NSK]

34.264 Edith W. Clowes, Samuel D. Kassow, and James L. West, eds. *Between tsar and people: educated society and the quest for public identity in late imperial Russia.* Princeton: Princeton University Press, 1991. ISBN 0-691-03153-3 (cl), 0-691-00851-5 (pbk). ‣ Pioneering collection of essays on search for social iden-

tities among groups labeled middle class or bourgeois in the West and on Russian variant of public sphere and civil society. [JCB]

34.265 Richard Hellie. "The stratification of Muscovite society: the townsmen." *Russian history* 5.2 (1978) 119–75. ISSN 0094-288x. ‣ Definitive survey of seventeenth-century town life, urban society, and its divisions. Argues that by midcentury state fastened townsmen permanently to their station, just as serfdom defined peasants. [DHK]

34.266 Thomas C. Owen. *Capitalism and politics in Russia: a social history of the Moscow merchants, 1855–1905.* Cambridge: Cambridge University Press, 1981. ISBN 0-521-23173-6. ‣ In return for state support, merchants loyal to autocracy not to liberalism. Imaginatively traces affinity between great merchants and Slavophile and nationalist ideologies. [JCB]

34.267 Alfred J. Rieber. *Merchants and entrepreneurs in imperial Russia.* Chapel Hill: University of North Carolina Press, 1982. ISBN 0-8078-1481-4 (cl), 0-8078-4305-9 (pbk). ‣ Best available study of Russian commercial and industrial leadership during entire imperial period. No united business class evolved in Russia because merchants and entrepreneurs divided by estate, ethnicity, and region. [SLH/JCB]

34.268 Jo Ann Ruckman. *The Moscow business elite: a social and cultural portrait of two generations, 1840–1905.* DeKalb: Northern Illinois University Press, 1984. ISBN 0-87580-096-3. ‣ Insightful study of children and grandchildren of former serfs who contributed to charity, philanthropy, art patronage, but less to politics. [JCB]

Working Class

34.269 Victoria E. Bonnell. *Roots of rebellion: workers' politics and organizations in St. Petersburg and Moscow, 1900–1914.* Berkeley: University of California Press, 1983. ISBN 0-520-04740-0 (cl), 0-520-05114-9 (pbk). ‣ Exhaustive study of political organizations created by workers themselves. Experiences molded complex mix of craft, class, and revolutionary consciousness. Artisans and skilled workers most significant in trade union and revolutionary movement. [JCB]

34.270 Robert Edelman. *Proletarian peasants: the Revolution of 1905 in Russia's southwest.* Ithaca, N.Y.: Cornell University Press, 1987. ISBN 0-8014-2008-8 (cl), 0-8014-9473-7 (pbk). ‣ Stimulating case study shows that by employing tactics of industrial labor and striking for higher wages in 1905, peasant laborers behaved more as proletarians than as other peasants. [JCB]

34.271 Theodore H. Friedgut. *Life and work in Russia's Donbass, 1869–1924.* Vol. 1 of *Iuzovka and revolution.* Princeton: Princeton University Press, 1989. ISBN 0-691-05554-8. ‣ Mining and metallurgical workers of John Hughes's New Russia Company, emphasizing housing and households, family budgets, health, and working conditions. Grassroots labor history at its best. [JCB]

34.272 Rose L. Glickman. *Russian factory women: workplace and society, 1880–1914.* Berkeley: University of California Press, 1984. ISBN 0-520-04810-5 (cl), 0-520-05736-8 (pbk). ‣ Interface of class and gender and original analysis of reasons why women workers less militant than men. No proletarian solidarity on gender issues. [JCB]

34.273 Robert Eugene Johnson. *Peasant and proletarian: the working class of Moscow in the late nineteenth century.* New Brunswick, N.J.: Rutgers University Press, 1979. ISBN 0-8135-0870-3. ‣ Important study documenting continued peasant mentality of Moscow's working class as reflected in migration and family patterns, common village bonds, and collective action. [JCB]

34.274 Robert B. McKean. *St. Petersburg between the revolutions: workers and revolutionaries, June 1907–February 1917.* New Haven: Yale University Press, 1990. ISBN 0-300-04791-6.

▸ Argues with enormous detail that economic and social structures frustrated labor organization and that subelite of radical parties much more influential than emigré leadership; war therefore central to 1917. [JCB/DHK]

34.275 Henry Reichman. *Railwaymen and revolution: Russia, 1905.* Berkeley: University of California Press, 1987. ISBN 0-520-05716-3. ▸ Broad-based, left-liberal All-Russian Railroad Union versus Bolshevik-led Union of Railroad Employees and issue of general strike. Marxist analysis of class and class conflict. Sympathetic to Bolsheviks. [JCB]

34.276 Jeremiah Schneiderman. *Sergei Zubatov and revolutionary Marxism: the struggle for the working class in tsarist Russia.* Ithaca, N.Y.: Cornell University Press, 1976. ISBN 0-8014-0876-8. ▸ Valuable analysis of origins, implementation, accomplishments, and ultimate failure of "police socialism," the government's attempt to control workers by creating its own unions. [JCB]

34.277 Allan K. Wildman. *The making of a workers' revolution: Russian social democracy, 1891–1903.* Chicago: University of Chicago Press, 1967. ▸ Marxist opinion and policy on labor question. Agitation begun by intellectuals but acquired life of its own among laborers. Influential work in labor history. [JCB]

34.278 Reginald E. Zelnik. *Labor and society in tsarist Russia: the factory workers of St. Petersburg, 1855–1870.* Stanford, Calif.: Stanford University Press, 1971. ISBN 0-8047-0740-5. ▸ How industrialization within an autocratic polity and traditional social structure conditioned development of urban working class. Exploration of labor question that stimulated series of specialist studies. [SLH/JCB]

34.279 Reginald E. Zelnik. "Russian Bebels: an introduction to the memoirs of the Russian workers Semen Kanatchikov and Matvei Fisher." *Russian review* 35.3–4 (1976) 249–89, 417–47. ISSN 0036-0341. ▸ Pioneering examination of formation of social and political identities in late nineteenth and early twentieth centuries. [JCB]

Women

34.280 Barbara Evans Clements, Barbara Alpern Engel, and Christine D. Worobec, eds. *Russia's women: accommodation, resistance, transformation.* Berkeley: University of California Press, 1991. ISBN 0-520-07023-2 (cl), 0-520-07024-0 (pbk). ▸ Pathbreaking collection of articles treating various experiences and roles of women in Russian society, mainly in period before 1917. Childbirth, witchcraft, infant-care cultures, peasant-healers, and other roles examined. [JCB/DHK]

34.281 Linda H. Edmondson. *Feminism in Russia, 1900–1917.* Stanford, Calif.: Stanford University Press, 1984. ISBN 0-8047-1212-3. ▸ Valuable study of struggle for equal political and legal rights, history of women's groups, national meetings, and social issues. Lukewarm support from intelligentsia, internal divisions, and turmoil beginning in 1914 explain failures. [JCB]

34.282 Charles J. Halperin, ed. *Women in medieval Russia.* Tempe: Arizona State University, 1983. (*Russian history*, 10.2.) ISSN 0094-288X. ▸ Eight articles on women and property in Novgorod and Muscovy, women's seclusion, exemplary women, women and slavery, Muscovite convents, etc. Important themes; one of few works on this crucial topic. [NSK]

34.283 Eve Levin. *Sex and society in the world of the Orthodox Slavs, 900–1700.* Ithaca, N.Y.: Cornell University Press, 1989. ISBN 0-8014-2260-4. ▸ Geographically and chronologically wide-ranging study of ecclesiastical image of sexuality, marriage, incest, illicit sex, and rape. Necessary but unfortunate emphasis on law over practice. [NSK/SCF]

34.284 Richard Stites. *The women's liberation movement in Russia: feminism, nihilism, and bolshevism, 1860–1930.* New ed. Princeton: Princeton University Press, 1991. ISBN 0-691-05254-9 (cl), 0-691-10058-6 (pbk). ▸ Pioneering synthesis. Conflict of two models of liberation based on gender and on class. Zestful merger of intellectual, social, and political history. Afterword surveys literature published since 1978 edition. [JCB]

Families

34.285 Beatrice Farnsworth. "The litigious daughter-in-law: family relations in rural Russia in the second half of the nineteenth century." *Slavic review* 45.1 (1986) 49–64. ISSN 0037-6779. ▸ Colorful essay uses court records to document physical abuse and property claims which dominated women's complaints, sustaining popular image of unfortunate daughter-in-law. [DHK]

34.286 David L. Ransel. *Mothers of misery: child abandonment in Russia.* Princeton: Princeton University Press, 1988. ISBN 0-691-05522-X (cl), 0-691-00848-5 (pbk). ▸ Pioneering history of foundling homes, chief symbol of tsarist solicitude for masses, developed in eighteenth and nineteenth centuries. Notwithstanding official concern, system unable to respond to needs or protect children's welfare. [SLH/GJM]

34.287 David L. Ransel, ed. *The family in imperial Russia: new lines of historical research.* Urbana: University of Illinois Press, 1978. ISBN 0-252-00701-8. ▸ Pathbreaking collection of articles on marriage and household patterns, family and labor force, folklore, and family and medical profession. Shift from large coresident groups to conjugal families more extreme than in West. [SLH/JCB]

Special Social Problems

Crime and Social Deviancy

34.288 Barbara Alpern Engel. "St. Petersburg prostitutes in the late nineteenth century: a personal and social profile." *Russian review* 48.1 (1989) 21–44. ISSN 0036-0341. ▸ Important sociological study identifies age, origins, former occupation, and circumstances of first intercourse of Petersburg prostitutes. Often socially marginal, prostitutes came from "incomplete," mostly peasant, families, but were independent and defied regulation. [DHK]

34.289 Cathy Frierson. "Crime and punishment in the Russian village: rural concepts of criminality at the end of the nineteenth century." *Slavic review* 46.1 (1987) 55–69. ISSN 0037-6779. ▸ Innovative discussion of peasants' narrow concepts of crime depending upon intent, degree of harm, and community membership. Harm to property or person might lead to community action independent of courts. [DHK]

34.290 Joan Neuberger. "Stories of the street: hooliganism in the St. Petersburg popular press." *Slavic review* 48.2 (1989) 177–94. ISSN 0037-6779. ▸ Petty criminality from pages of middle-class press. Hooliganism as conflict over power, indicator of deteriorating social consensus, and factor in polarization between labor and liberal elite. Provocative. [DHK]

34.291 Richard Stites. "Prostitute and society in pre-Revolutionary Russia." *Jahrbücher für Geschichte Osteuropas* 31.3 (1983) 348–64. ISSN 0021-4019. ▸ Good introduction to life among prostitutes. Surveys public opinion on prostitution, which entered debate through Chernyshevskii, Dostoevskii, and others. Uses some of same sources as Engel (34.288), but adds material from fiction. [DHK]

Charity and Social Welfare

34.292 Adele Lindenmeyr. "Charity and the problem of unemployment: industrial homes in late imperial Russia." *Russian review* 45.1 (1986) 1–22. ISSN 0036-0341. ▸ Fascinating look at work relief. Industrial homes, first founded in 1880s, successful neither at employing their charges nor improving public morality; peculiar Russian adaptation of European idea. [DHK]

34.293 Adele Lindenmeyr. "Work, charity, and the elderly in late nineteenth-century Russia." In *Old age in preindustrial society.* Peter N. Stearns, ed., pp. 232–47. New York: Holmes & Meier, 1982. ISBN 0-8419-0645-9. ▸ Deprived even of token work, elderly had to turn either to informal peasant care, to rare charitable institutions, or to begging. Pathbreaking. [DHK]

Diet

34.294 David Christian. *Living water: vodka and Russian society on the eve of emancipation.* New York: Oxford University Press, 1990. ISBN 0-19-822286-6. ▸ Novel analysis of vodka as social, economic, and political institution. Aided social and economic elites in breaking down self-sufficiency of traditional communities and helped in redistributing wealth. [SLH]

34.295 Steven L. Hoch. "Serf diet in nineteenth-century Russia." *Agricultural history* 56.2 (1982) 391–414. ISSN 0002-1482. ▸ Uses estate records on household serfs to chart food consumption and estimates field serfs' diet from figures on agricultural production. Finds that nutrition normally adequate. [DHK]

34.296 Robert E. F. Smith and David Christian. *Bread and salt: a social and economic history of food and drink in Russia.* Cambridge: Cambridge University Press, 1984. ISBN 0-521-25812-X. ▸ Stimulating, novel treatment of how diet and climatic conditions influenced systems of food preservation and generated state resources through monopolies in distilling and salt mining. [SLH]

ETHNIC RELATIONS WITHIN RUS' AND RUSSIA

Ukrainians, Belorusians, and Other Slavs

34.297 Oskar Halecki. *Borderlands of Western civilization: a history of East Central Europe.* New York: Ronald Press, 1952. ▸ Slavs from origins to twentieth century. Strong on Poland and Polish-Lithuanian Commonwealth. Informative survey, despite pan-Slavism and Polonophile bias. [NSK]

34.298 John-Paul Himka. *Galician villagers and the Ukrainian national movement in the nineteenth century.* New York: St. Martin's, 1988. ISBN 0-312-01609-3. ▸ Emergence of national consciousness among peasants of western (Austrian) Ukraine. Based on study of newspapers whose rural correspondents demonstrated and provoked awakening among peasants. Useful but unidimensional. [DHK]

34.299 Mykhailo Hrushevsky. *A history of Ukraine.* 1941 ed. O. J. Frederickson, ed. Hamden, Conn.: Archon, 1970. ISBN 0-208-00967-1. ▸ Survey from earliest times to nineteenth century. Classic refutation of Russocentric interpretation of East Slavic history by dean of Ukrainian historical scholarship. [NSK]

34.300 Andrzej Kamiński. "The Cossack experiment in *szlachta* democracy in the Polish–Lithuanian Commonwealth: the Hadiach (Hadziacz) Union." *Harvard Ukrainian studies* 1.2 (1977) 178–97. ISSN 0363-5570. ▸ Details terms of proposed constitutional union of Ukraine with Polish-Lithuanian Commonwealth in 1658. Reveals westernized political culture of some Ukrainian leadership during Khmelnytsky's revolution. Excellent study of key turning point. [NSK]

34.301 Orest Subtelny. *Ukraine, a history.* Toronto: University of Toronto Press, 1988. ISBN 0-8020-5808-6 (cl), 0-8020-6775-1 (pbk). ▸ From Kievan Rus' to twentieth century; excellent coverage of Galicia-Volhynia and Zaporozhian Cossacks. Comprehensive survey (culture, society, economy) and political chronicle; excellent introduction. [NSK]

34.302 Frank E. Sysyn. *Between Poland and Ukraine: the dilemma of Adam Kysil, 1600–1653.* Cambridge, Mass.: Harvard Ukrainian Research Institute, 1985. ISBN 0-916458-08-3. ▸ Biography of chief negotiator between Poland-Lithuania and Cossacks in 1648 becomes vehicle for analyzing cultural world of seventeenth-century Rus' elite. Case study with broad significance. [NSK/MR]

SEE ALSO
33.17 Francis Dvornik. *The Slavs in European history and civilization.*
33.61 Orest Subtelny. *Domination of Eastern Europe.*

Baltic Germans

34.303 Anders Henriksson. *The tsar's loyal Germans, the Riga German community: social change and the nationality question, 1855–1905.* Boulder: East European Monographs; distributed by Columbia University Press, 1983. (East European monographs, 131.) ISBN 0-88033-020-1. ▸ First-class study of interplay between social and national interests of Germans, the preindustrial social elite, as they confronted Russification and Latvian nationalism. Socioeconomic environment more important than national identity. [JCB/DHK]

34.304 Edward C. Thaden. *Russia's western borderlands, 1710–1870.* Princeton: Princeton University Press, 1984. ISBN 0-691-05420-7. ▸ Excellent case study of how local elites defended rights and privileges against imperial integration. Autocracy not consistent in centralization policy and relied on coopted elites to maintain social order. [SLH]

34.305 Edward C. Thaden, ed. *Russification in the Baltic provinces and Finland, 1855–1914.* Princeton: Princeton University Press, 1981. ISBN 0-691-05314-6 (cl), 0-691-10103-5 (pbk). ▸ Impact of policies of last three tsars in Estland, Livland, Courland, and Finland. Russification stepped up in reigns of Alexander III and Nicholas II, provoking increased opposition. Important subject. [DHK]

Jews

34.306 Irwin Michael Aronson. *Troubled waters: the origins of the 1881 anti-Jewish pogroms in Russia.* Pittsburgh: University of Pittsburgh Press, 1990. ISBN 0-8229-3656-9. ▸ Revisionist study blames socioeconomic circumstances rather than official conspiracy. Economic boom differentiated some Jews, who became target of non-Jewish competitors, who in turn egged on victimized urban poor. [DHK]

34.307 John D. Klier. *Russia gathers her Jews: the origins of the "Jewish question" in Russia, 1772–1825.* DeKalb: Northern Illinois University Press, 1986. ISBN 0-87580-117-X. ▸ Partitions of Poland bring large Jewish population into empire. Basic study of government policy seeking to capitalize on economic usefulness of Jews and simultaneously control them in Pale of Settlement. [GJM]

SEE ALSO
21.200 Hans Rogger. *Jewish policies and right-wing politics in imperial Russia.*
21.205 Michael Stanislawski. *Tsar Nicholas I and the Jews.*
21.210 Steven Zipperstein. *The Jews of Odessa.*

Armenians and Georgians

34.308 David Marshall Lang. *Armenia: cradle of civilization.* 3d rev. ed. London: Allen & Unwin, 1980. ISBN 0-04-956009-3. ▸ Survey from earliest civilization on Armenian territory with special attention to Urartu (Armenia's first nation state), christianization, and Russian annexation (1828 and after). Separate chapters on art, literature, and learning. [DHK]

34.309 David Marshall Lang. *The Georgians.* New York: Praeger, 1966. ▸ Grand survey of Georgia and Georgian culture from prehistory through eighteenth century, emphasizing civilization, literature, architecture, and arts. Richly illustrated. [DHK]

34.310 Ronald Grigor Suny. *The making of the Georgian nation.* Bloomington: Indiana University Press and Hoover Institution Press, 1988. ISBN 0-253-33623-6 (cl), 0-253-21277-4 (pbk). ▸ Sympathetic, comprehensive survey of ethnogenesis and early history, experience within Russian empire, and Soviet era. Emergence of self-conscious nationality was result, in part, of imperial intrusion. [JCB/DHK]

34.311 Christopher J. Walker. *Armenia: the survival of a nation.* Rev. 2d ed. New York: St. Martin's, 1990. ISBN 0-312-04230-2. ▸ Nineteenth- and early twentieth-century Armenian history; two chapters follow Russian occupation and annexation, but most of book examines Turkish-Armenian relations, including 1915 extermination. General survey. [DHK]

Siberia and Siberians

34.312 George V. Lantzeff. *Siberia in the seventeenth century: a study of the colonial administration.* 1943 ed. New York: Octagon Books, 1972. ISBN 0-374-94774-0. ▸ Examines central and local institutions, fiscal administration, interaction with natives, secular and ecclesiastical colonization. Extremely valuable in-depth study of Muscovite local administration, showing endemic corruption and Siberia's immense profitability for Moscow. [NSK]

34.313 George V. Lantzeff and Richard A. Pierce. *Eastward to empire: exploration and conquest on the Russian open frontier, to 1750.* Montreal: McGill-Queen's University Press, 1973. ISBN 0-7735-0133-9. ▸ Expansion by Novgorod, Vladimir-Suzdal', and especially Moscow to Urals, Siberia, Far East, and Pacific and Arctic shores; chapters on Siberian Cossacks and Stroganovs. Detailed political chronicle. [NSK]

Cossacks

34.314 Linda Gordon. *Cossack rebellions: social turmoil in the sixteenth-century Ukraine.* Albany, N.Y.: State University of New York Press, 1983. ISBN 0-87395-654-0 (cl), 0-87395-653-2 (pbk). ▸ Social, economic, and political context of uprisings which preceded Khmelnytsky's revolution. Sees Cossacks not as marginal but as social response to fundamental economic and political transformations of eastern Europe. Stimulating. [NSK]

34.315 Philip Longworth. *The Cossacks.* New York: Holt Rinehart & Winston, 1970. ISBN 0-03-081855-9. ▸ Sixteenth to early twentieth centuries; Zaporozhian Cossack revolution; Don Cossacks in seventeenth- and eighteenth-century social uprisings and later tsarist service. More political chronicle than social analysis. [NSK]

34.316 Robert H. McNeal. *Tsar and Cossack, 1855–1914.* New York: St. Martin's, 1987. ISBN 0-312-82188-3. ▸ Informative study of military service, civil administration, and economic situation of (primarily) Don Cossacks. Despite economic cost, government supported Cossacks for political reasons. [JCB]

Volga Germans and Turks

34.317 Roger P. Bartlett. *Human capital: the settlement of foreigners in Russia, 1762–1804.* Cambridge: Cambridge University Press, 1979. ISBN 0-521-22205-2. ▸ To improve economy and populate sparsely settled regions in south and along Volga, Catherine the Great attracted immigrant communities, mostly from southern Germany. Detailed source study of state-immigrant relations. [GJM]

34.318 Andreas Kappeler. *Russlands erste Nationalitäten: das Zarenreich und die Völker der Mittleren Wolga vom sechzehnten bis neunzehnten Jahrhundert.* Cologne: Böhlau, 1982. (Beiträge zur Geschichte Osteuropas, 14.) ISBN 3-412-03481-9. ▸ Careful anal-

ysis of Muscovite conquest of Kazan, rebellions against Muscovite rule, administration, and colonization with attention to native social structure and change. Based on Russian sources, underestimates potential of indigenous sources. [NSK/US]

READING CULTURE

Literacy

34.319 Simon Franklin. "Literacy and learning in early medieval Russia." *Speculum* 60.1 (1985) 1–38. ISSN 0038-7134. ▸ Proliferation, characteristics, and social background of literacy, 1050-1200, considered within context of growth of bureaucratic administration. Comprehensive, persuasive, and important. [SCF]

34.320 Gary Marker. "Literacy and literacy texts in Muscovy: a reconsideration." *Slavic review* 49.1 (1990) 74–89. ISSN 0037-6779. ▸ Documents increasing publication of primers in late seventeenth century; modest increase in publication of materials for higher order literacy. Nevertheless, literacy rate well below 10 percent of population. Innovative methodology. [DHK]

34.321 Max J. Okenfuss. *The discovery of childhood in Russia: the evidence of the Slavic primer.* Newtonville, Mass.: Oriental Research Partners, 1980. ISBN 0-89250-337-8. ▸ How literacy texts provide alternative images of childhood and pedagogy. Different texts teach divergent lessons, leading to separate worldviews across social spectrum. Stimulating view of classroom as significant social threshold. [GJM]

Publishing and Readers

34.322 Jeffrey Brooks. *When Russia learned to read: literacy and popular literature, 1861–1917.* Princeton: Princeton University Press, 1985. ISBN 0-691-05450-9 (cl), 0-691-00821-3 (pbk). ▸ Pioneering study of popular culture and its foes. Peasants dominated production and consumption of chapbooks. Appearance of "Western" themes such as science and success, yet continued antipathy to market economy. [JCB]

34.323 Gary Marker. *Publishing, printing, and the origins of intellectual life in Russia, 1700–1800.* Princeton: Princeton University Press, 1985. ISBN 0-691-05441-X. ▸ Basic, close analysis of how print communication became focus of secular literate culture. State's monopoly gave way to private interests, enabling commercial and intellectual forces to establish position in Russian printing. [GJM]

34.324 Louise McReynolds. *The news under Russia's old regime.* Princeton: Princeton University Press, 1991. ISBN 0-691-03180-0. ▸ Focusing on individual newspapers from mid-nineteenth to early twentieth century, examines first press entrepreneurs, changing reporting styles, and enlarged readerships. Important study documents how newspapers contributed to fashioning civil society. [DHK]

34.325 Charles A. Ruud. *Russian entrepreneur: publisher Ivan Sytin of Moscow, 1851–1934.* Montreal: McGill-Queen's University Press, 1990. ISBN 0-7735-0773-6. ▸ Attempts of publishing magnate to steer between radical intelligentsia and government in efforts to modernize and democratize Russian society. Useful case study. [JCB]

Censorship

34.326 Marianna Tax Choldin. *A fence around the empire: Russian censorship of Western ideas under the tsars.* Durham, N.C.: Duke University Press, 1985. ISBN 0-8223-0625-5. ▸ Specialist study of censorship legislation, important censors, and analysis of censored texts. Foreign censorship a porous barrier, retained despite ineffectiveness. [SLH/JCB]

34.327 Sidney Monas. *The Third Section: police and society in*

Russia under Nicholas I. Cambridge, Mass.: Harvard University Press, 1961. (Russian Research Center studies, 42.) ‣ Imaginative discussion of how political atmosphere influenced individuals, literary culture, and journalistic practices. Censors could not reconcile political role with self-image as intellectuals. [GJM/SLH]

34.328 K. A. Papmehl. *Freedom of expression in eighteenth-century Russia.* The Hague: Nijhoff, 1971. ‣ Enlightened absolutism accommodated advent of secular world of letters. Well-researched account of how regime permitted relative freedom of printed word throughout century, making it golden age for freedom of speech. [GJM]

34.329 Charles A. Ruud. *Fighting words: imperial censorship and the Russian press, 1804–1906.* Toronto: University of Toronto Press, 1982. ISBN 0-8020-5565-6. ‣ Best available treatment of development of institutions related to censorship. Periodical press grew rapidly in second half of nineteenth century despite efforts of imperial censors to slow its progress. [SLH/JCB]

34.330 Peter Stansfield Squire. *The Third Department: the establishment and practices of the political police in the Russia of Nicholas I.* London: Cambridge University Press, 1968. ISBN 0-521-07148-8. ‣ Institutional structure of political controls and censorship during second quarter of nineteenth century. Detailed, reliable account of how state recruited intellectuals and confounded them by appointing military officials as their superiors. [GJM/SLH]

LITERATURE AND LITERARY POLITICS

Kievan Rus'

34.331 Henrik Birnbaum. "Lord Novgorod the Great: its place in medieval culture." *Viator: medieval and Renaissance studies* 8 (1977) 215–54. ISSN 0083-5897, ISBN 0-520-03363-9. ‣ Explores Novgorodian literary culture, art, and architecture with emphasis on South Slavic influence, religious free-thinking, and humanist trends. Excellent survey. [NSK]

34.332 Simon Franklin, trans. and Introduction. *Sermons and rhetoric of Kievan Rus'.* Cambridge, Mass.: Harvard Ukrainian Research Institute, 1991. (Harvard library of early Ukrainian literature, English translations, 5.) ISBN 0-916458-41-5. ‣ Translations of three major ecclesiastical writers. Important introduction to political and literary context of Rus' culture and Byzantium. [SCF]

34.333 Muriel Heppell, trans. *The "Paterik" of the Kievan Caves Monastery.* Cambridge, Mass.: Harvard Ukrainian Research Institute, 1989. (Harvard library of early Ukrainian literature, English translations, 1.) ISBN 0-916458-27-X. ‣ History and legends of most influential monastery of Kievan Rus', eleventh to early thirteenth century. Major source for cultural and social history. [SCF]

34.334 Gail Lenhoff. *The martyred princes Boris and Gleb: a sociocultural study of the cult and the texts.* Columbus, Ohio: Slavica, 1989. ISBN 0-89357-204-7. ‣ Stimulating, innovative study of writings on earliest saints (eleventh and twelfth centuries) linked to political and social context. Critique of notions of generic convention in early Russian literature. [SCF]

34.335 Dmitrii Sergeevich Likhachev. *The great heritage: the classical literature of Old Rus'.* Doris Bradbury, trans. Moscow: Progress, 1981. ‣ Survey of major works of medieval Russian literature by most distinguished modern historian of Russian culture. Humanist approach, emphasizing cultural history. [SCF]

34.336 Francis J. Thomson. "The nature of the reception of Christian Byzantine culture in Russia in the tenth to thirteenth centuries and its implications for Russian culture." *Slavica gandensia* 5 (1978) 107–39. ‣ Scope of early Russian reading. Polemically critical of notion that there was any intellectual breadth or originality in literature of Kievan Rus'. [SCF]

Muscovy

34.337 William Edward Brown. *A history of seventeenth-century Russian literature.* Ann Arbor: Ardis, 1980. ISBN 0-88233-343-7. ‣ Medieval (chronicles, saints' lives) and modern (exemplary and picaresque tales, historical and chivalric romances) prose genres, oral and learned verse as insight into cultural changes of this century. Introductory survey. [NSK]

34.338 Edward L. Keenan, Jr. *The Kurbskii-Groznyi apocrypha: the seventeenth-century genesis of the "Correspondence" attributed to Prince A. M. Kurbskii and Tsar Ivan IV.* Daniel C. Waugh, Appendix. Cambridge, Mass.: Harvard University Press, 1971. (Russian Research Center studies, 66.) ISBN 0-674-50580-8. ‣ Argues from manuscript, textual, and linguistic evidence that these texts were generated as political and/or literary exercises from 1630s to 1680s. Controversy that has stimulated reassessment of Muscovite literary culture. [NSK]

34.339 Edward L. Keenan, Jr. "Putting Kurbskii in his place, or, Observations and suggestions concerning the place of the *History of the Grand Prince of Muscovy* in the history of Muscovite literary culture." In *Beiträge zur dritten Internationalen Konferenz über altrussische Geschichte (Oxford, 1.–4. 9. 1975).* Manfred Hildermeier, ed. Wiesbaden: Harrassowitz, 1978. ISBN 3-447-01873-9. ‣ Presents text, considered late sixteenth-century history, as late seventeenth-century literary work through analysis of manuscripts, convoy, language, genre, sources, and literary context. Suggestive, particularly on seventeenth-century culture. [NSK]

34.340 Edward L. Keenan, Jr. "The trouble with Muscovy: some observations upon problems of the comparative study of form and genre in historical writing." *Medievalia et humanistica: studies in medieval and Renaissance culture,* n.s., 5 (1974) 103–26. ISSN 0076-6127. ‣ Argues that absence of classical works of history left Muscovy with only medieval annals tradition. Demonstrates unwieldiness and opacity of that genre. Suggestive comments on sixteenth-century culture. [NSK]

Imperial Russia

34.341 Marcus C. Levitt. *Russian literary politics and the Pushkin celebration of 1880.* Ithaca, N.Y.: Cornell University Press, 1989. ISBN 0-8014-2250-7. ‣ Pushkin as idea of late nineteenth-century Russian culture, representing secular Russian identity independent of both tsar and church. Key moment in Russian self-consciousness. Innovative interpretation. [JCB/DHK]

34.342 L. R. Lewitter. "Peter the Great, Poland, and the westernization of Russia." *Journal of the history of ideas* 19 (1958) 493–506. ISSN 0022-5037. ‣ Explores seventeenth-century Ukrainian, Jesuit-influenced political theorists (Yavorskii, Prokopovich), and penetration of Latin and Polish political works into early eighteenth-century Russia. Detailed perspective on Petrine culture. [NSK]

34.343 Nicholas V. Riasanovsky. *The image of Peter the Great in Russian history and thought.* New York: Oxford University Press, 1985. ISBN 0-19-503456-2. ‣ Exhaustive account of westernizing ruler represented in literature, journalism, and scholarship over 250 years. Defenders support European focus and modernization; opponents emphasize his violence and hostility to old Russian culture. [GJM]

34.344 William Mills Todd. *Fiction and society in the age of Pushkin: ideology, institutions, and narrative.* Cambridge, Mass.: Harvard University Press, 1986. ISBN 0-674-29945-0. ‣ Technical, sophisticated examination of styles, social institutions, and cultural codes that played prominent role in regulating intellectual life. Power of such codes to control intimate polite society of Russian literary salons. [GJM]

LAW AND CULTURE

34.345   Richard Hellie. "Early modern Russian law: the Ulozhenie of 1649." *Russian history* 15.2–4 (1988) 155–80. ISSN 0094-288X. ▸ Introduces translation (which appeared separately, 1988) of main code of pre-Petrine Russia. Circumstances of compilation, sources, and function of law. Specialized commentary appears in subsequent issues of same journal. Essential background. [DHK]

34.346   Daniel H. Kaiser. *The growth of the law in medieval Russia.* Princeton: Princeton University Press, 1980. ISBN 0-691-05311-1. ▸ Traces endurance of traditional East Slavic dyadic norms, emergence of more complex triadic law in context of changing social relations (twelfth to fifteenth century). Increasing intervention by rulers, growth of administration. Pathbreaking. [NSK/SCF]

34.347   Ann M. Kleimola. *Justice in medieval Russia: Muscovite judgment charters (pravye gramoty) of the fifteenth and sixteenth centuries.* Philadelphia: American Philosophical Society, 1975. (Transactions of the American Philosophical Society, n.s., 65.2.) ISBN 0-87169-656-8, ISSN 0065-9746. ▸ Definitive study of records of land litigation, focusing on court officials, role of testimony and written evidence, "God's Justice," and judicial referral. Argues that, despite sometimes irrational proofs, judicial process rational. [DHK]

34.348   George Vernadsky, trans. *Medieval Russian laws.* 1947 ed. New York: Norton, 1969. ▸ Complete annotated translations of main early Russian codes of law with introductory essay. Essential source. [SCF]

34.349   Richard Wortman. *The development of a Russian legal consciousness.* Chicago: University of Chicago Press, 1976. ISBN 0-226-90776-7. ▸ How pursuit of legal order fits within Enlightenment and romantic view of autocratic state as arbiter of legal and social conflict. Pioneering study of emergence of legal ethos and professionalization of legal experts. [SLH/GJM/JCB]

EDUCATION AND SCHOOLS

34.350   Joseph L. Black. *Citizens for the fatherland: education, educators, and pedagogical ideals in eighteenth-century Russia.* Boulder: East European Quarterly; distributed by Columbia University Press, 1979. (East European monographs, 53.) ISBN 0-914-71046-X. ▸ In pursuit of improved administration and enlightened gentry, absolutist state developed secular secondary education. Although state and society produced numerous projects, few enacted. Careful essay includes translation of *Book on the Duties of Man and Citizen* (1783). [GJM]

34.351   Daniel R. Brower. *Training the nihilists: education and radicalism in tsarist Russia.* Ithaca, N.Y.: Cornell University Press, 1975. ISBN 0-8014-0874-1. ▸ Specialist study of reforms in university and polytechnic institutes in mid-nineteenth century. Numerical analysis of social and economic background of radical youth of 1860s and impact of curricula and student culture. [GJM]

34.352   Ben Eklof. *Russian peasant schools: officialdom, village culture, and popular pedagogy in Russia, 1861–1914.* 1986 ed. Berkeley: University of California Press, 1990. ISBN 0-520-05171-8 (cl, 1986), 0-520-06957-9 (pbk). ▸ Peasants, as rational actors, took initiative in drive for schooling, but strategy was defensive: schooling was protection against educated world. Peasant objectives dovetailed with government's, and peasants remained outsiders. Influential book. [JCB]

34.353   Nicholas Adolph Hans. *History of Russian educational policy (1701–1917).* New York: Russell & Russell, 1964. ▸ Broad sweep of state's promotion of schools over two centuries. Classic account of government as agency of progress in fostering learning and literacy to ever-wider segments of society. Excellent tables. [GJM]

34.354   Christine Johanson. *Women's struggle for higher education in Russia, 1855–1900.* Kingston: McGill-Queen's University Press, 1987. ISBN 0-7735-0565-2. ▸ Specialist institutional study of expansion of educational opportunities for women in context of reforms of 1860s. Special attention to medical education and later restriction of women's access to higher education. [JCB/DHK]

34.355   Samuel D. Kassow. *Students, professors, and the state in tsarist Russia.* Berkeley: University of California Press, 1989. ISBN 0-520-05760-0. ▸ Relationship between universities and state as paradigm for failure to formulate new relationship between state and society. Best available study of subject. [JCB]

34.356   L. R. Lewitter. "Poland, the Ukraine, and Russia in the seventeenth century." *Slavonic and East European review* 27.68, 69 (1948, 1949) 157–71, 414–29. ISSN 0037-6795. ▸ Surveys resurgence of Orthodox theology and culture in seventeenth-century Ukraine and its influence on Muscovite education and literature. Excellent detail on neglected era. [NSK]

34.357   James C. McClelland. *Autocrats and academics: education, culture, and society in tsarist Russia.* Chicago: University of Chicago Press, 1979. ISBN 0-226-55661-1. ▸ Traditional survey of education from 1700 to 1917. Describes contradiction between needs of modernization of entire society and elitist character of educational system. Sketches of representative academics. [JCB]

34.358   Scott J. Seregny. *Russian teachers and peasant revolution: the politics of education in 1905.* Bloomington: Indiana University Press, 1989. ISBN 0-253-35031-X. ▸ Important study of radicalization of rural school teachers. Traces origin of national teachers' professional movement, culminating in union in 1905 and subsequent repression. For the specialist. [JCB]

34.359   Allen Sinel. *The classroom and the chancellery: the state and educational reform in Russia under Count Dmitrii Tolstoi.* Cambridge, Mass.: Harvard University Press, 1973. (Russian Research Center studies, 72.) ISBN 0-674-13481-8. ▸ Traditional institutional history of centralized educational system. Intended to modernize nation yet allowed no autonomy for its beneficiaries; paradigm for dilemma of late imperial Russia. [JCB]

34.360   Alexander Sydorenko. *The Kievan academy in the seventeenth century.* Ottawa: University of Ottawa Press, 1977. ISBN 0-7766-0901-7. ▸ Chronicles curriculum, organization, and achievements of academy that provided not only Ukrainian intellectual leadership but progressive thought to Moscow as well. Useful perspectives for Russian cultural history. [NSK]

34.361   Cynthia H. Whittaker. *The origins of modern Russian education: an intellectual biography of Count Sergei Uvarov, 1786–1855.* DeKalb: Northern Illinois University Press, 1984. ISBN 0-87580-100-5. ▸ Basic biography of defender of Enlightenment who became ideologist of conservative state under Nicholas I. As minister of education, attempted to employ education for needed development without undermining imperial absolutism. [SLH/GJM]

MAIN CURRENTS AND FIGURES OF RUSSIAN THOUGHT

General Studies

34.362   Isaiah Berlin. *Russian thinkers.* Henry Hardy and Aileen Kelly, eds. New York: Viking, 1978. (Isaiah Berlin, Selections, 1.) ISBN 0-670-61371-1 (cl), 0-14-022260-X (pbk). ▸ Provocative, classic essays discussing advent of intelligentsia in nineteenth century. Intellectuals as moral voice for freedom and individual liberty in autocratic society; ideas as political force. [GJM]

34.363 Andrzej Walicki. *A history of Russian thought from the Enlightenment to Marxism.* 1979 ed. Hilda Andrews-Rusiecka, trans. Oxford: Clarendon, 1988. ISBN 0-19-827704-0 (pbk). ▸ Comprehensive, synthetic text covering leading thinkers and ideas from mid-eighteenth to late nineteenth century. Drift away from support of state and toward search for social constituency and basis of freedom. [GJM]

Eighteenth Century

34.364 W. Gareth Jones. *Nikolay Novikov, enlightener of Russia.* Cambridge: Cambridge University Press, 1984. ISBN 0-521-25822-7. ▸ Best available biography of leading publisher, journalist, and intellectual of Catherinian era. Demonstrates absence of political opposition to ruler among intellectuals until repression of late 1780s. [GJM]

34.365 Allen McConnell. *A Russian philosophe: Alexander Radishchev, 1749–1802.* Westport, Conn.: Hyperion, 1981. ISBN 0-8305-0080-4. ▸ Traditional biography traces life of well-born, well-educated, and well-traveled nobleman. How his sense of service to nation and commitment to Enlightenment led to estrangement from authority. [GJM]

34.366 Marc Raeff. *Origins of the Russian intelligentsia: the eighteenth-century nobility.* New York: Harcourt Brace Jovanovich, 1966. ISBN 0-15-670150-2. ▸ Petrine reforms transformed lives, education, and careers of service gentry. Service to society grew from alienation from family, school, and service. Innovative, controversial view of impact of humanistic Enlightenment on aristocracy. [GJM]

34.367 Hans Rogger. *National consciousness in eighteenth-century Russia.* Cambridge, Mass.: Harvard University Press, 1960. (Russian Research Center studies, 38.) ISBN 0-674-60150-5. ▸ Basic analysis of westernized noble intellectuals becoming preoccupied with fatherland's standing in European context. Despite differences of opinion, most saw nation improving and moving toward Enlightenment, becoming part of Europe. [GJM]

34.368 David Saunders. *The Ukrainian impact on Russian culture, 1750–1850.* Edmonton: University of Alberta, Canadian Institute of Ukrainian Studies; distributed by University of Toronto Press, 1985. ISBN 0-920-86232-2 (cl), 0-920-86234-9 (pbk). ▸ Best available discussion on how Ukraine supplied disproportionately large number of state servitors, intellectuals, and prominent political figures who still maintained separate identity, but were not nationalists. Important subject. [GJM/DHK]

Nineteenth Century

34.369 Joseph L. Black. *Nicholas Karamzin and Russian society in the nineteenth century: a study in Russian political and historical thought.* Toronto: University of Toronto Press, 1975. ISBN 0-8020-5335-1. ▸ Careful examination of how leading Russian conservative expressed support for Enlightenment, progress, and faith in reason and individual. Advocate of state as defender of Russian freedom and security. [GJM]

34.370 Edward James Brown. *Stankevich and his Moscow circle, 1830–1840.* Stanford, Calif.: Stanford University Press, 1966. ▸ Helpful study of little-known figure of 1830s who attracted talented, aspiring young poets and thinkers. Study of romanticism and *Naturphilosophie* played formative role in maturation of leading thinkers of midcentury. [GJM]

34.371 Nicholas Mikhailovich Karamzin. *Memoir on ancient and modern Russia: a translation and analysis.* 1959 ed. Richard Pipes, ed. and trans. New York: Atheneum, 1972. ▸ Polemical review of Russian history by leading conservative intellectual of the day.

Urged emperor to maintain existing social and political institutions and oppose flirtation with constitutionalism. Important primary source. [GJM/SLH]

34.372 Evgenii Lampert. *Sons against fathers: studies in Russian radicalism and revolution.* Oxford: Clarendon, 1965. ▸ Classic interpretive essay on split between generations of 1840s and 1860s; fathers as gentlemen moralists, sons as exponents of action. Leading oppositionists pursuing basis for moving from words to deeds. [GJM]

34.373 Martin Edward Malia. *Alexander Herzen and the birth of Russian socialism, 1812–1855.* New York: Grosset & Dunlap, 1971. ▸ Influential if controversial account of Russian radicalism as influenced by German idealism. Socialism as amorphous vision of democracy. Oppositionism resulted from inability to find niche in society and from domestic unhappiness. [GJM]

34.374 Raymond T. McNally. *Chaadayev and his friends: an intellectual history of Peter Chaadayev and his Russian contemporaries.* Tallahassee, Fla.: Diplomatic Press, 1971. ISBN 0-910512-11-6. ▸ Stimulating, intellectual biography of quintessential exponent of Russian Enlightenment. Crisis converted him to romantic antinationalism. Despair over politics led him to pen philosophical letters advocating, momentarily, mass conversion to Catholicism. [GJM]

34.375 Martin A. Miller. *The Russian revolutionary emigrés, 1825–1870.* Baltimore: Johns Hopkins University Press, 1986. ISBN 0-8018-3303-5. ▸ Careful narrative of political exile beginning with Decembrists and evolving into familiar, if bitter, experience for midcentury Socialists and following generations. Life in emigration and development of Russian political communities abroad. [GJM]

34.376 Michael Boro Petrovich. *The emergence of Russian Panslavism, 1856–1870.* 1956 ed. Westport, Conn.: Greenwood, 1985. ISBN 0-313-24742-0. ▸ Classic, synthetic account of intellectual roots of expansionist ideology from Slavophilism and Official Nationality. How Slavic nationalisms stimulated intellectuals to articulate historical worldview based on ascendancy of Slavs, eventually unified. [GJM]

34.377 Nicholas V. Riasanovsky. *A parting of ways: government and the educated public in Russia, 1801–1855.* Oxford: Clarendon, 1976. ISBN 0-19-822533-4. ▸ Best available study of intellectual trends, culminating in rise of intelligentsia and rejection of state as progressive force. Unchanging state and society in face of changing European context and national consciousness. [GJM/SLH]

34.378 Leonard Bertram Schapiro. *Rationalism and nationalism in Russian nineteenth-century political thought.* New Haven: Yale University Press, 1967. ▸ Notwithstanding shifting philosophies and political outlooks, how certain themes and problems defined ideology. Preoccupation with reason, justice, and Russia's standing in Europe filter through and across generations. Stimulating. [GJM]

34.379 Edward C. Thaden. *Conservative nationalism in nineteenth-century Russia.* Seattle: University of Washington Press, 1964. ▸ Ideologies defending autocratic state and Russian uniqueness more significant than often believed. Substantive discussion of how opponents of liberalism maintained uneasy partnership with officialdom and established visibility in periodical press. [GJM]

Westernizers

34.380 Herbert Eugene Bowman. *Vissarion Belinski, 1811–1848: a study in the origins of social criticism in Russia.* 1954 ed. New York: Russell & Russell, 1969. ▸ Outstanding literary and social critic of 1830s and 1840s helped to transform journalism into voice of opposition. Thoughtful essay on intelligentsia circles as institutions of support and resistance to state. [GJM]

34.381 Derek Offord. *Portraits of early Russian liberals: a study of the thought of T. N. Granovsky, V. P. Botkin, P. V. Annenkov, A. V. Druzhinin, and K. D. Kavelin.* Cambridge: Cambridge University Press, 1985. ISBN 0-521-30550-0. ▸ Ideas of individual westernizers of 1840s who did not take radical turn. Impact of Hegelianism on their cast of mind. Activities as journalists and academics carefully assessed. Ambivalence toward Russian state. [GJM]

Slavophiles

34.382 Peter K. Christoff. *An introduction to nineteenth-century Russian Slavophilism: a study in ideas.* 4 vols. The Hague, Princeton, and Boulder: Mouton, Princeton University Press, and Westview, 1961–91. ISBN 90-279-2297-7 (v. 2), 0-691-05334-0 (v. 3), 0-8133-8080-4 (v. 4). ▸ Hypothesis that Slavophilism constituted authentic and original Russian philosophy expressing essential core of Russian nationalism. Separate volumes on A. S. Khomiakov, originator of Christian doctrine of *sobornost*; I. V. Kireevskii, supra-rationalist; K. S. Aksakov, originator of choric principle; and Iurii Samarin, the "practical" Slavophile. Involved, often dense arguments. [GJM/DHK]

34.383 Abbott Gleason. *European and Muscovite: Ivan Kireevsky and the origins of Slavophilism.* Cambridge, Mass.: Harvard University Press, 1972. (Russian Research Center studies, 68.) ISBN 0-674-26924-1. ▸ Cosmopolitan, highly educated nobleman turned from European orientation to advocate of Russian nationalism and conservatism. Stimulating analysis of paradox of Frenchified elite evoking ideology of separatism from Europe. [GJM]

34.384 Nicholas V. Riasanovsky. *Russia and the West in the teaching of the Slavophiles: a study of romantic ideology.* 1952 ed. Gloucester, Mass.: Smith, 1965. ▸ Slavophilism as variety of European conservative nationalism. Standard account of how German idealism came to serve as framework for nativist ideology against Peter the Great, Western influence, and bureaucratic state. [GJM]

34.385 Andrzej Walicki. *The Slavophile controversy: a history of conservative utopia in nineteenth-century Russian thought.* 1975 ed. Hilda Andrews-Rusiecka, trans. Notre Dame, Ind.: University of Notre Dame Press, 1989. ISBN 0-268-01734-4 (pbk). ▸ Complex, controversial study of romantic nationalism of 1830s and 1840s. Idealization of Russian past as variety of European yearning for *Gemeinschaft* (community) as antidote to perceived atomization of modern life. [GJM]

Marxism and Populist Radicalism

34.386 Arthur P. Mendel. *The dilemmas of progress in tsarist Russia: legal Marxism and legal populism.* Cambridge, Mass.: Harvard University Press, 1961. (Russian Research Center studies, 43.) ▸ Classic comparison of theories of Mikhailovskii, Vorontsov, Danielson, Plekhanov, Struve, Berdiaev, and Bulgakov on peasant commune-based socialism versus postcapitalist, industrial-based socialism. [JCB]

34.387 Richard Pipes. *Peter Struve.* Vol. 1: *Liberal on the Left, 1870–1905.* Vol. 2: *Liberal on the Right, 1905–1944.* Cambridge, Mass.: Harvard University Press, 1970–80. ISBN 0-674-84595-1 (v. 1), 0-674-84600-1 (v. 2). ▸ Traditional intellectual and political biography of founder of Russian Social Democratic party who broke with Lenin and with tradition of radical intelligentsia. Volume 1 covers period through apex of Struve's influence. Volume 2 continues biography through split with Lenin, increasing disillusionment, emigration, and years of political decline. [JCB/DHK]

34.388 Alexander Vucinich. *Social thought in tsarist Russia: the quest for a general science of society, 1861–1917.* Chicago: University of Chicago Press, 1976. ISBN 0-226-86624-6. ▸ Views of Russian intellectuals on nature of society, law, justice, knowledge, science, and progress. Good overview. [JCB]

34.389 Andrzej Walicki. *The controversy over capitalism: studies in the social philosophy of the Russian populists.* 1969 ed. Notre Dame, Ind.: University of Notre Dame Press, 1989. ISBN 0-268-00770-5 (pbk). ▸ Standard introduction to thought shaped by experience of backwardness during process of modernization and Marxist-populist controversy. [JCB]

34.390 Andrzej Walicki. *The legal philosophies of Russian liberalism.* New York: Oxford University Press, 1987. ISBN 0-19-824930-6. ▸ Reaction against legal positivism and utopianism. Emphasis on establishment of rule of law and discovery of potential of law to secure liberty at end of nineteenth century. Specialist study. [JCB]

ORIGINS OF REVOLUTIONARY INTELLIGENTSIA

34.391 Barbara Alpern Engel. *Mothers and daughters: women of the intelligentsia in nineteenth-century Russia.* 1983 ed. Cambridge: Cambridge University Press, 1985. ISBN 0-521-25125-7 (cl, 1983), 0-521-31301-5 (pbk). ▸ Stimulating account of how Great Reform changed perspectives and opportunities for educated noblewomen, leading to outer-directed activity among daughters. Recovery of women's voices in intelligentsia generations of 1850s to 1860s. [GJM]

34.392 Abbott Gleason. *Young Russia: the genesis of Russian radicalism in the 1860s.* New York: Viking, 1980. ISBN 0-670-79459-7. ▸ Student movement for autonomy, reform, and emancipation of society as variation of counterculture. How populism emerged from milieu of student-intelligentsia opposition. Provocative comparison to American student politics of 1960s. [GJM]

34.393 Deborah Hardy. *Land and freedom: the origins of Russian terrorism, 1876–1879.* New York: Greenwood, 1987. ISBN 0-313-25596-2. ▸ Nuanced account of origins of terrorism in conspiratorial camaraderie and "mystique of terrorism" rather than in frustrations with village propaganda. [JCB]

34.394 Aileen Kelly. *Mikhail Bakunin: a study in the psychology and politics of utopianism.* 1982 ed. New Haven: Yale University Press, 1987. ISBN 0-300-03874-7 (pbk). ▸ How mental world of major radical and anarchist thinker derived from personal experience and family background. Provocative attempt to sketch personality portrait to explain ideology. [GJM]

34.395 Arthur P. Mendel. *Michael Bakunin: roots of apocalypse.* New York: Praeger, 1981. ISBN 0-03-059218-6. ▸ Education and experiences within Russian and European revolutionary circles. Ambitious analysis of how romantic celebration of individual transformed into idealization of peasantry and then into destructive revolutionary violence. [GJM]

34.396 Norman M. Naimark. *Terrorists and Social Democrats: the Russian revolutionary movement under Alexander III.* Cambridge, Mass.: Harvard University Press, 1983. ISBN 0-674-87464-1. ▸ Underground and revolutionary organizations, 1881–94. Marxists and members of People's Will shared common experiences and views more than Plekhanov's characterizations suggest. Persuasive. [JCB]

34.397 Irina Paperno. *Chernyshevsky and the age of realism: a study in the semiotics of behavior.* Stanford, Calif.: Stanford University Press, 1988. ISBN 0-8047-1453-3 (cl), 0-8047-1454-1 (pbk). ▸ Correspondences between personal experiences and ideological categories of leading Russian realist thinker of 1850s and 1860s. Intellectually ambitious attempt at reading polemics as coded language revealing preoccupation with everyday life. [GJM]

34.398 Philip Pomper. *Peter Lavrov and the Russian revolutionary movement.* Chicago: University of Chicago Press, 1972. ISBN 0-226-67520-3. ▸ Traditional intellectual biography of theoretician of revolutionary populism. [JCB]

34.399 Philip Pomper. *The Russian revolutionary intelligentsia.* 1970 ed. Northbrook, Ill.: Davidson, 1986. ISBN 0-88295-749-X (pbk). ▸ Broad introductory survey of left-wing movements from Decembrists (1825) to 1914. Emphasis on individual thinkers, ideology, and intellectual setting. How left moved from isolation to active political engagement. [GJM]

34.400 Philip Pomper. *Sergei Nechaev.* New Brunswick, N.J.: Rutgers University Press, 1979. ISBN 0-8135-0867-3. ▸ Psychobiography of infamous nineteenth-century conspirator, author of politics of revenge. Best available. [JCB]

34.401 Franco Venturi. *Roots of revolution: a history of the populist and socialist movements in nineteenth-century Russia.* 1960 ed. Francis Haskell, trans. Isaiah Berlin, Introduction. Chicago: University of Chicago Press, 1983. ISBN 0-226-8570-9 (pbk). ▸ Encyclopedic review of Russian radical ideologies and groups (1820s to 1880s). Discussion of how opposition movement gained force and momentum, leading to ever greater activity until assassination of Alexander II. [GJM/JCB]

34.402 William F. Woehrlin. *Chernyshevskii: the man and the journalist.* Cambridge, Mass.: Harvard University Press, 1971. (Russian Research Center studies, 67.) ISBN 0-674-11385-3. ▸ Detailed introduction to central figure in mid-nineteenth-century Russian radicalism. Background as seminarian and university student gives depth and systematic quality to his writings. Realism as call to action. [GJM]

34.403 Richard Wortman. *The crisis of Russian populism.* London: Cambridge University Press, 1967. ▸ Stimulating study of way peasants filled psychological void for generation of intellectuals whose idealized images clashed with realities of peasant life. [JCB]

POPULAR CULTURE

34.404 Catriona Kelly. *Petrushka: the Russian carnival puppet theatre.* Cambridge: Cambridge University Press, 1990. ISBN 0-521-37520-7. ▸ Fairgrounds entertainment for lower classes in late imperial Russian towns. Puppet theater provided setting for humor, carnality, reinforcing and reversing social norms; sanitized and destroyed in 1930s. Stimulating, well-researched study. [GJM]

34.405 Alexander D. Nakhimovsky and Alice Stone Nakhimovsky, eds. *The semiotics of Russian cultural history: essays by Iurii M. Lotman, Lidiia Ia. Ginsburg, Boris A. Uspenskii.* Boris Gasparov, Introduction. Ithaca, N.Y.: Cornell University Press, 1985. ISBN 0-8014-1183-1 (cl), 0-8014-9294-7 (pbk). ▸ In groundbreaking, complex essays, leading semioticians of history and literature propose that Russian culture functioned according to dual model of opposites that precluded neutral zones. Textualizes popular and elite culture. [GJM]

34.406 Russell Zguta. *Russian minstrels: a history of the skomorokhi.* Philadelphia: University of Pennsylvania Press, 1978. ISBN 0-8122-7753-8. ▸ Considers minstrels single phenomenon from Kiev Rus' to Muscovy. For Muscovite era, explores minstrels' culture, interaction with state, and contributions to later Russian music, dance, and theater. Fascinating insights into popular culture. [NSK]

ARTS AND CULTURE

34.407 William C. Brumfield. *The origins of modernism in Russian architecture.* Berkeley: University of California Press, 1991. ISBN 0-520-06929-3. ▸ Mixture of tradition and innovation in style moderne, reflecting cultural disjuncture and search for identity in late nineteenth to early twentieth century. Skillfully integrates history of architecture with engineering, professions, and urban development. [JCB]

34.408 James Cracraft. *The Petrine revolution in Russian architecture.* Chicago: University of Chicago Press, 1988. ISBN 0-226-11664-6 (cl), 0-226-11663-8 (pbk). ▸ Stimulating essay showing how emperor revolutionized Muscovite building, disorderly and unconnected to Western architectural patterns. Imported trained architects, employed blueprints, and adopted building and city plans reflecting Western classicism and formalism. [GJM/NSK]

34.409 George Heard Hamilton. *The art and architecture of Russia.* 3d ed. New York: Penguin, 1983. ISBN 0-14-056006-8 (cl), 0-14-056106-4 (pbk). ▸ From Kiev Rus' to early twentieth century; excellent attention to icon-painting and wooden and stone architecture in Muscovy. Comprehensive, helpfully illustrated, good introduction to Rus' and Muscovite culture. [NSK]

34.410 Viktor Nikitich Lazarev. *Old Russian murals and mosaics from the eleventh to the sixteenth century.* London: Phaidon, 1966. ▸ Origins and development of monumental art. Copious illustrations, substantial narrative, annotations on individual churches. [SCF]

34.411 William Richardson. *Zolotoe Runo and Russian modernism, 1905–1910.* Ann Arbor: Ardis, 1986. ISBN 0-88233-795-5. ▸ Art and literature of silver age examined by focusing on prominent journal, *Zolotoe Runo* (Golden Fleece). Specialist study. [JCB]

34.412 Theofanis G. Stavrou, ed. *Art and culture in nineteenth-century Russia.* Bloomington: Indiana University Press, 1983. ISBN 0-253-31051-2. ▸ Useful articles on Russian intelligentsia, Moscow and Petersburg as cultural symbols, national consciousness in music, emergence of nineteenth-century art and architecture, sculpture, caricature, and folk art. [JCB]

34.413 Elizabeth K. Valkenier. *Ilya Repin and the world of Russian art.* New York: Columbia University Press, 1990. ISBN 0-231-06964-2. ▸ Peculiarities of Russian artistic culture and changing fortunes of Russian realism carefully examined through life and career of best known nineteenth-century painter. [JCB]

34.414 Elizabeth K. Valkenier. *Russian realist art, the state and society: the Peredvizhniki and their tradition.* 1977 ed. New York: Columbia University Press, 1989. ISBN 0-231-06970-7. ▸ Revisionist account of painters of the Society of Traveling Exhibitions. More bourgeois, nationalistic, and less revolutionary than Soviet popularizers have shown. [JCB]

SEE ALSO
35.392 Robert C. Williams. *Artists in revolution.*

RELIGION AND CULTURE: RUSSIAN ORTHODOXY

General Studies

34.415 *Christianity and Russia.* Moscow: Social Sciences Today, 1988. (Religious studies in the USSR, 3.) ISBN 5-02-022353-0. ▸ Reprints in English of standard Soviet analyses of christianization, the church in feudal era, seventeenth-century schism, Petrine reforms, and function of state church in late empire. [DHK]

34.416 Pavel Nikolaevich Miliukov. *Outlines of Russian culture.* Vol. 1: *Religion and the church.* 1942 ed. Michael Karpovich, ed. Valentine Ughet and Eleanor Davis, trans. New York: Barnes, 1960. ▸ From beginnings of Russian Christianity through nineteenth century; survey of sixteenth-century church institutions and ideology and of seventeenth-century schism and community that perpetuated it. Good introduction. [NSK]

34.417 Robert L. Nichols and Theofanis G. Stavrou, eds. *Rus-

sian Orthodoxy under the old regime. Minneapolis: University of Minnesota Press, 1978. ISBN 0-8166-0846-6 (cl), 0-8166-0847-4 (pbk). ▸ Essays concentrating mainly on church-state relationship in imperial period. Concludes with useful bibliography of works on church in Western European languages. [DHK]

34.418 Igor Smolitsch. *Geschichte der russischen Kirche, 1700–1917.* 1964 ed. Wiesbaden: Harrassowitz, 1991. ISBN 3-447-03059-3. ▸ Massive, mostly institutional history of Orthodox church in synodal (imperial) period. Special attention to Petrine reforms, church-state relations, church schools, and diocesan administration. [DHK]

Kievan Rus'

34.419 Ludolf Müller. *Die Taufe Russlands: die Frühgeschichte des russischen Christentums bis zum Jahre 988.* Munich: Wewel, 1987. (Quellen und Studien zur russischen Geistesgeschichte, 6.) ISBN 3-87904-104-0. ▸ Spread of Christianity in Rus' before official conversion. Compact survey of evidence and opinions. [SCF]

34.420 Gerhardt Podskalsky. *Christentum und theologische Literatur in der Kiever Rus' (988–1237).* Munich: Beck, 1982. ISBN 3-406-08296-3. ▸ Range and characteristics of written culture in pre-Mongol Rus'. Succinct descriptions, extensive bibliographies. Most thorough, judicious guide to subject. [SCF]

34.421 Andrzej Poppe. *The rise of Christian Russia.* London: Variorum, 1982. ISBN 0-86078-105-4. ▸ Collected articles on conversion of Rus' to Christianity and church organization in tenth to twelfth centuries. [SCF]

34.422 Alexis P. Vlasto. *The entry of the Slavs into Christendom: an introduction to the medieval history of the Slavs.* Cambridge: Cambridge University Press, 1970. ISBN 0-521-07459-2. ▸ Comprehensive study of conversions of Slavic peoples, ninth to eleventh century. Could be called entry of Slavs into Middle Ages. Background to religious geography of Eastern Europe. [SCF]

34.423 Vladimir Vodoff. *Naissance de la chrétienté russe: la conversion du prince Vladimir de Kiev (988) et ses conséquences (11e–13e siècles).* Paris: Fayard, 1988. ISBN 2-213-02109-0. ▸ Christian institutions and culture in Kievan Rus'. Generally judicious synthesis of recent research. Useful tables, maps, and bibliography. [SCF]

Muscovy

34.424 Paul Bushkovitch. *Religion and society in Russia: the sixteenth and seventeenth centuries.* New York: Oxford University Press, 1992. ISBN 0-19-506946-3. ▸ Argues transition from public to private religiosity, paving way for Petrine reforms. Fascinating discussions of monastic authority, elite spirituality, canonization, miracle cults, Ukrainian influence, and rise of sermon. Groundbreaking. [NSK]

34.425 Iosif Volotskii. *The monastic rule of Iosif Volotsky.* David M. Goldfrank, ed. and trans. Kalamazoo: Cistercian, 1983. ISBN 0-87907-836-7 (pbk). ▸ Detailed introduction to and translation of rule of one of most influential monasteries in late medieval Russia (until destroyed by Poles early in seventeenth century). [DHK]

Imperial Russia

34.426 James Cracraft. *The church reform of Peter the Great.* Stanford, Calif.: Stanford University Press, 1971. ISBN 0-8047-0747-2. ▸ Detailed political analysis of transition from patriarchal to synodal church. Secularization and state building forced Orthodoxy to accept subservient status. Theological defenders of autocratic power, so-called Protestants of Russian Orthodoxy. [GJM]

Schism and Schismatics

34.427 Michael Cherniavsky. "The Old Believers and the new religion." In *The structure of Russian history: interpretive essays.* Michael Cherniavsky, ed., pp. 140–88. New York: Random House, 1970. ISBN 0-9876543-2-1. ▸ Assessment of seventeenth-century church schism's political theology as apocalyptic, culminating in depiction of Peter I as Antichrist. Intriguing interpretation of schism as response to secular absolutism. Striking illustrations. [NSK]

34.428 Robert O. Crummey. *The Old Believers and the world of Antichrist: the Vyg community and the Russian state, 1694–1855.* Madison: University of Wisconsin Press, 1970. ISBN 0-299-05560-4. ▸ Excellent case study traces seventeenth-century origin of Old Believer community, its economic efflorescence, and persecution. Network of sectarian communities on periphery adapted to tension with state and official church. [NSK/GJM]

34.429 William Palmer, comp. and trans. *The patriarch and the tsar.* 6 vols. London: Trübner, 1871–76. ▸ Compendium of contemporary sources (translated) on seventeenth-century church schism (by Patriarch Nikon, Paul of Aleppo, Paisius Ligarides) and nineteenth-century study of seventeenth- to early eighteenth-century church relations with further quotations from sources. Fascinating, rare detail. Available on microfiche from Chicago: American Theological Library Association. 0-8370-7495-9 (v. 1), 0-8370-7574-2 (v. 2), 0-8370-7562-9 (v. 3), 0-8370-7656-0 (v. 4–6). [NSK]

34.430 Pierre Pascal. *Avvakum et les débuts du raskol: la crise religieuse au dix-septième siècle en Russie.* Paris: Centre d'Études Russe, "Istina," 1938. ▸ Places this founder of Russian Old Belief in context of seventeenth-century religious thought and reform; traces his life, writings, and thought. Definitive account; good introduction to background of schism. Also available in photocopy from Paris: Mouton, 1969. [NSK]

Parish Clergy

34.431 Ioann Stefanovich Belliustin. *Description of the clergy in rural Russia: the memoirs of a nineteenth-century parish priest.* Gregory L. Freeze, trans. Ithaca, N.Y.: Cornell University Press, 1985. ISBN 0-8014-1796-1 (cl), 0-8014-9335-8 (pbk). ▸ Analysis and condemnation of monastic and episcopal system of Orthodox church. Attacked monks, poverty of parish clergy, ritualism, even dogma. A protestantism of Eastern rite. Key primary source. [SLH]

34.432 Gregory L. Freeze. *The parish clergy in nineteenth-century Russia: crisis, reform, counter-reform.* Princeton: Princeton University Press, 1983. ISBN 0-691-05381-2. ▸ Best available study of reform in church administration, economics of parish service, seminary life, and changing political and social attitudes of parish clergy. Attempts at professionalization of clergy by clerical liberals. [JCB/SLH]

34.433 Gregory L. Freeze. *The Russian levites: parish clergy in the eighteenth century.* Cambridge, Mass.: Harvard University Press, 1977. (Russian Research Center studies, 78.) ISBN 0-674-78175-9. ▸ Under pressure from state and ecclesiastic authorities, and resented by peasant communities, local priests became *de facto* closed caste. Seminary education created cultural division between priests and laity. Careful, specialist study. [GJM]

34.434 Jack E. Kollman, Jr. "The Stoglav council and parish priests." *Russian history* 7.1–2 (1980) 65–91. ISSN 0094-288X. ▸ Reform proposals on priests' education, marital status, ordination, appointment, income, duties, and supervision. Rare glimpse into clergy, parishes, and state of mid-sixteenth-century church. [NSK]

Theology

34.435 George P. Fedotov. *The Russian religious mind.* Vol. 1: *Kievan Christianity, the tenth to the thirteenth centuries.* Vol. 2: *The Middle Ages, the thirteenth to the fifteenth centuries.* Vol. 1, 1946 ed.; vol. 2, 1966 ed. John Meyendorff, ed. Belmont, Mass.: Nordland, 1975. ISBN 0-913124-18-4 (v. 1), 0-913124-12-2 (v. 2). ▸ Volume 1 discusses early Russian religious consciousness and ethics; Kievan Rus' as golden age of Russian spirituality. Volume 2, official and popular religion in Muscovy. Seen as spiritual decline due to growth of autocracy. Special treatment for Saints Sergei, Stephen of Perm, Nil Sorskii, and others. Ambitious, influential interpretation. [SCF]

34.436 Georges Florovsky. *Ways of Russian theology.* 1972 ed. Vaduz: Europa Buchervertriebanstalt; distributed by Notable & Academic Books, 1987. (Collected works of Georges Florovsky, 5.) ISBN 3-905238-01-2. ▸ Classic essays on place of religious doctrine within Russian culture through mid-nineteenth century. Why Russian church silent on many central theological issues of Eastern Christianity; profound impact of Byzantine tradition. [GJM/NSK]

SCIENCE AND CULTURE
General Studies

34.437 Alexander Vucinich. *Science in Russian culture.* Vol. 1: *A history to 1860..* Vol. 2: *1861–1917.* Stanford, Calif.: Stanford University Press, 1963–70. ISBN 0-8047-0738-3 (v. 2). ▸ Peter the Great employed mostly Europeans to found Imperial Academy of Science. Conflicts between native interests and foreign specialists generated long-term struggle. Volume 2 treats science in Russian thought, education, scientific societies, as well as developments in mathematics and life, physical, and earth sciences. Best available survey. [GJM]

Science

34.438 Valentin Boss. *Newton and Russia: the early influence, 1698–1796.* Cambridge, Mass.: Harvard University Press, 1972. (Russian Research Center studies, 69.) ISBN 0-674-62275-8. ▸ Overview of personal and institutional contacts with British scientists and Royal Academy which lead to awareness of Newtonianism in St. Petersburg. Vignettes trace contacts between English and Russian science and mathematics. [GJM]

34.439 Bonifatii Mikhailovich Kedrov. *Den' odnogo velikogo otkrytiia* (The day of a great discovery). Moscow: Izdatel'stvo Sotsial'no-Ekonomicheskoi Literatury, 1958. ▸ Hour-by-hour account of creation of periodic table of chemical elements by Russian chemist Dmitrii Mendeleev. Influence of external and internal factors. Deserves English translation. [LRG]

34.440 Ann Hibner Koblitz. *A convergence of lives, Sophia Kovalevskaia: scientist, writer, revolutionary.* Boston: Birkhauser, 1983. ISBN 0-8176-3162-3. ▸ Biography of mathematician and study of female scientific intelligentsia in nineteenth century. Useful insights into history of science and gender. [JCB]

34.441 Galina Eugen'evna Pavlova and Aleksandr Sergeevich Fedorov. *Mikhail Vasilievich Lomonosov: his life and work.* Rev. ed. Richard Hainsworth, ed. of translation. Arthur Aksenov, trans. Moscow: Mir, 1984. ▸ Best available (though not definitive) biography of Lomonosov, sometimes called Russia's Benjamin Franklin. Discusses his work in chemistry, metallurgy, ceramics, natural philosophy, and poetry and his relations with state authorities. [LRG]

34.442 Daniel P. Todes. *Darwin without Malthus: the "struggle

for existence" in Russian evolutionary thought. Oxford: Oxford University Press, 1989. ISBN 0-19-505830-5. ▸ Discerning, careful analysis of Russian reception of Darwinism, particularly resistance to Darwin's concept of struggle for existence. Influence of external factors on scientific thought. [LRG]

34.443 Alexander Vucinich. *Darwin in Russian thought.* Berkeley: University of California Press, 1988. ISBN 0-520-06283-3. ▸ Influence and controversy generated by Darwin and politicization of Darwin from 1860s to 1909. Informative summaries of scientific works and schools amidst changing intellectual climate. Somewhat broader perspective than Todes 34.442. [JCB]

Medicine

34.444 John T. Alexander. *Bubonic plague in early modern Russia: public health and urban disaster.* Baltimore: Johns Hopkins University Press, 1980. ISBN 0-8018-2322-6. ▸ Groundbreaking discussion of how absolutist state tried to mobilize modern medicine and counteract superstition to deal with epidemics. Public suspicion of doctors, organizational confusion, and inappropriate training impeded effort. [GJM]

34.445 Laura Engelstein. "Morality and the wooden spoon: Russian doctors view syphilis, social class, and sexual behavior." *Representations* 14 (1986) 169–208. ISSN 0734-6018. ▸ Russian physicians identified syphilis either as sexual in origin, associating it with urban Westernization, or nonsexual, defining it by social and gender roles instead of clinical epidemiology. Innovative essay. [DHK]

34.446 Nancy M. Frieden. *Russian physicians in an era of reform and revolution.* Princeton: Princeton University Press, 1981. ISBN 0-691-05335-9. ▸ Groundbreaking book constructs model of Russian professionalization characterized by power of association and service ethos but also dependence on state and lack of self-regulation and autonomy. [JCB]

34.447 John F. Hutchinson. *Politics and public health in revolutionary Russia, 1890–1913.* Baltimore: Johns Hopkins University Press, 1990. ISBN 0-8018-3957-2. ▸ Revisionist social history of medical profession divided between champions of community medicine and new specialists who favored centralization. Bolshevik health policy result of tsarist tradition, growing technical expertise, and wartime experience. [JCB]

34.448 Roderick E. McGrew. *Russia and the cholera, 1823–1832.* Madison: University of Wisconsin Press, 1965. ISBN 0-299-03710-X. ▸ Best available discussion of response of society to calamity of cholera. During epidemic, medical profession, though small, performed well. Civil and military administration failed miserably. [SLH]

34.449 Susan Gross Solomon and John F. Hutchinson. *Health and society in revolutionary Russia.* Bloomington: Indiana University Press, 1990. ISBN 0-253-35332-7. ▸ Groundbreaking articles analyzing public health in late nineteenth- and early twentieth-century Russia, including both scientific and political developments, particularly emergence of scientific medicine. Governmental policies toward health and disease. [LRG]

Technology

34.450 Joseph Bradley. *Guns for the tsar: American technology and the small-arms industry in nineteenth-century Russia.* DeKalb: Northern Illinois University Press, 1990. ISBN 0-87580-154-4. ▸ Technological change and modernization in small arms industry as original case study of relationship between government, military, and industry. Explores attitude toward private entrepreneurship, labor-management relations, and diffusion of innovation in developing country. [JCB]

34.451 Richard M. Haywood. *The beginnings of railway development in Russia in the reign of Nicholas I, 1835–1842*. Durham, N.C.: Duke University Press, 1969. ▸ Introductory account of advent of railroads in Russia. Attitude of tsarist government and public and private interests in railway development. Technology transfer from West. [LRG]

34.452 Edward V. Williams. *The bells of Russia: history and technology*. Princeton: Princeton University Press, 1985. ISBN 0-691-09131-5. ▸ Significance of bells in history of Russian technology and metallurgy. Description of specific characteristics of Russian bells and links between technology and religion. [LRG]

DANIEL T. ORLOVSKY

Soviet Union

The history of the Russian Revolution and of the Soviet Union (1917–1991) has been written, rewritten, and now will be written again in the light of the watershed (one can call it revolutionary) demise of Soviet power, the Communist party and state, and the Soviet Union as an empire. Despite the boom in Russian studies in the decades after World War II, the field of Soviet history had long been something of an intellectual outpost, a fringe enterprise furthered by a small number of pioneers (E. H. Carr, M. Lewin, S. Fitzpatrick, R. Pipes, R. Tucker, A. Dallin, and S. Cohen, for example) whose major contributions set the foundations for serious historical study of the Soviet era. During the 1980s, a recognizable and distinct field of Soviet history emerged, and the historiography of the Soviet period reached new levels of competence and creativity just when *perestroika* (the chain of revolutionary events and processes long simmering in the conjunctures of domestic politics and society and in the changed international structure, but unleashed by General Secretary Mikhail Gorbachev) was reaching full stride. Historians of the Soviet period had assimilated methods and approaches used by historians of other cultures and nations, and were especially influenced by social history and the new cultural history. These historians immersed themselves in previously unused, newly available published and archival sources and wrote much that is reflected in this bibliography. Still, the field of Soviet history has come under attack by historians and publicists in the wake of the demise of communism. These critics see the field as either apologetic for the Soviet regime or too open to nonteleological interpretation, especially of the first decades of Soviet power; that is, interpretations that avoid black-and-white moral judgments and that see possibilities, alternatives, and especially the capacity of social forces to shape the regime. It remains important to recognize this stream of criticism. According to this view, the Soviet Union was a totalitarian party-state that was unreformable, illegitimate, and immoral, and historians have committed major "sins" in attempting to apply methods of Western social science to the unique Soviet experience, in accepting Soviet self-proclaimed visions of the past as well as Soviet sources uncritically, and in failing to grasp the totalitarian nature of the party and state. Moreover, such critics argue, historians wanted to believe in the possibility of reform or democratic socialism emerging out of the Soviet present and saw Gorbachev as its midwife, and so they let this dominate and distort their work. But, according to Martin Malia (35.9), for example, the reforms did not produce a democratic socialism. Instead, they killed the Soviet Union, an inevitable outcome because the system itself—the immoral, totalitarian, uniquely Russian system—was a total system, dominated by politics, that could not be changed in piecemeal fashion. To study it at all, to attempt to have any sort of empathy, as would be normal in most relationships between historian and subject, amounted to moral abnegation. To see any sort of autonomous social sphere, any pattern of unintended consequences, to study social and cultural processes, to ask the questions, why and how this totalitarian or administrative-command system came about, how it operated and mobilized social participation and even enthusiasm, as well as opposition, is proclaimed a severe form of historical malpractice. Recognizing this historiographical vision is one thing, but it remains just as important not to be swept away in a blanket condemnation of the field.

Prior to the late 1970s and 1980s, Soviet history was a small field for two reasons: first, graduate advisors discouraged students from embarking on research on the Soviet period because of lack of access to archival sources, because of the highly politicized nature of historiography in the Soviet Union itself, because of the absence of a reliable scholarly community, and because of their distaste for the subject matter; and, second, there was an established tendency to view the Soviet period as the scholarly domain of political scientists and others working in the social sciences who had a more presentist or policy orientation. The opening up of opportunities to live and work in Russia by the International Research and Exchanges Board (IREX) and a rising interest in significant and exciting research projects on the history of imperial Russia, however, brought established scholars, who had published significant works on the imperial era, and a new generation of graduate students into the arena of Soviet history. These scholars began to build on the growing historiography of the late imperial Russia and of the revolutions of 1917 to illuminate the historical processes that shaped the Soviet experience. This new historiography was influenced by the various themes and methods (social and cultural history, questions of class, gender, language, etc.) that had become prominent in the larger professional community. But of course, the development of the Soviet field did not run parallel to the growth of other historiographies. There remained the very large task of primary discovery to be accomplished, and the field had to come to terms with the moral implications of the world's first attempt to construct a socialist state in an empire that covered one-sixth of the earth's surface.

During the 1970s and early 1980s, a new generation of historians, who had the advantage of extended research time in the USSR, first made important breakthroughs in the study of the revolutions of 1917, both the February Revolution, which destroyed the Old Regime and the Romanov dynasty and was followed by a short seven-month attempt to build democracy in the maelstrom of war and social upheaval, and the bolshevik-led October Revolution, which brought Lenin's party to power and was the world's first large-scale attempt to overcome the market and build socialism. Later in the 1980s, they were joined by a younger group of "new Soviet historians" who produced dissertations and their first published works on the post-1917 period. They pushed research into the Civil War era (1918–1920) and on into the period of the New Economic Policy (NEP) in the 1920s, and then into the period of cultural revolution, collectivization, and industrialization according to the five-year plans, the purges, and the adumbration of the full blown Stalin cult (1929–1941). Works on 1917 largely focused on labor history and the Bolshevik party, although there were important works written on the army, navy, regional history of the Revolution (Baku and Saratov, for example), and the major political parties (the Mensheviks, Socialist-Revolutionaries, Kadets, etc.). The contributions of social history were especially important here, though it must be said that the new historiography resulted in many more books about workers than about peasants and all too little emphasis on such topics as the non-bolshevik Left, professional and lower-middle-class groups, and the nationality questions. And indeed, although major challenging studies have appeared recently (R. Pipes 35.81), the revolutions of 1917 still await their synthesis in the form of a major study comparable in narrative skill, objectivity, and analytic power to W. H. Chamberlin's classic (35.19, 35.58), first published in 1935.

The goal of the new Soviet history was to illuminate the Soviet experience, viewed as the product of a revolutionary process with roots stretching back into the last decades of the Old Regime and 1917 itself. Here too the major emphasis has been on social and institutional history and the new cultural history with important works on labor and industrialization, bureaucracy and state building, history of the Communist party, the peasantry and collectivization, gender and the family, the Red Army, the role of intermediary institutions (such as the Komsomol), trade unions, science and ecology, the Soviet novel, art and architecture, popular culture, the fate of the nationalities, and the recrudescence of the empire. The new Soviet history has produced new under-standings of such major themes as War Communism, the New Economic Policy, and socialist realism and also stimulated serious debate about the sources of bolshevik authoritarianism (ideology versus the exigencies of revolution and civil war), the nature of War Communism (whether planned or haphazard reactions; whether Lenin was for it or against it), the possibilities of NEP as an alternative path of development, and the connections of Stalinism to NEP and to Lenin himself. The new Soviet history, how-ever, has not played down the role of high politics and leaders, above all Lenin and Stalin; rather the effort has been to link the world of the social and cultural to politics, and those few scholars who have attempted to fold Stalin's personal role in the tragedies (or triumphs) of Soviet history into bland impersonal bureaucratic structures and pro-cesses have received their fair share of criticism directly from practitioners of the new historiography themselves.

Although the new Soviet history may claim rightfully to have made major contri-butions, a vast terrain remains unexplored as does the special problem of closure—the fact that the formal aspect of Soviet power, of the Soviet experience, ended in 1991 (some would say via a revolution as profound as that of October 1917). What is the overall significance of the Soviet experiment—for Russia, for its neighbors, for the world? The end of the USSR requires us to refocus our questions. Students of the French Revolution are after all still debating whether that Revolution truly transformed France, and, if so, how. They still debate Tocqueville's vision of a revolution that served continuity by providing an outlet for changes already launched under the Old Regime. They also continue to debate the morality of that Revolution—and of revolution in general. The pendulum of interpretation swings back and forth, and we can probably expect similar shifts in interpretation of the Russian Revolution. Historical study of the years 1939–1991 is still in its infancy, for example. And there are still conceptual and methodological problems that must be faced if the enormous opportunities for schol-arship opened by *perestroika* and the collapse of the Soviet Union are to be exploited fully. First and foremost the new sources that are available—archival, published (and indeed recorded or filmed or photographed), and oral—must be accurately cataloged and mapped. Second, the special interpretative challenges attached to the decoding of Soviet sources must be recognized. Language and categories must be read for the special meanings that underlay the social and cultural foundations of the Soviet expe-rience. Third, we must hope that a new generation of scholars emerges in Russia and the successor states, a group that can come to terms with the Soviet past and will work to establish a dialogue with scholars abroad. Fourth, new historical attention must be paid to non-Russians of the former Soviet empire and the entire subject of national identity and nationalism. Fifth, there should be a renewed focus on demography and social and occupational mapping. Finally, historians must recognize that there is a tremendous amount of basic research to be done before major generalizations can emerge about the Soviet period, and further they must understand that mere entrance into the party, Central Committee, or even KGB archives is not a substitute for well-formulated research projects and erudition, a sense of the Soviet past built upon the *longue durée* of Russian history and culture and indeed the history and cultures of the non-Russian peoples of the former empire. The archives will not necessarily provide the answers to all questions, but new sources combined with hypotheses involving unintended consequences of central government policies, the interpenetration of state and society, and the open-endedness of revolution (and indeed of much of Soviet history as expressed by the idea of alternatives) will throw into sharper relief the tragedies of the Soviet experience and the accountabilities of Soviet leaders and rank-and-file alike.

Entries are arranged under the following headings:

General Studies

Political History

Nationalities and National Identities

Economic History

Social and Institutional History

Cultural History

Religion

Science and Technology

[Contributors: AD = Alexander Dallin, DJR = Donald J. Raleigh, DKR = Don K. Rowney, DTO = Daniel T. Orlovsky, GF = Gregory Freeze, HK = Hiroaki Kuromiya, JCB = Joseph C. Bradley, LRG = Loren R. Graham, LS = Lewis Siegelbaum, LV = Lynne Viola, MVH = Mark von Hagen, RGS = Ronald Grigor Suny, RS = Richard Stites, WGR = William G. Rosenberg]

GENERAL STUDIES

35.1 M. K. Dziewanowski. *A history of Soviet Russia.* 3d ed. Englewood Cliffs, N.J.: Prentice-Hall, 1989. ISBN 0-13-392275-8. ▸ Standard history. Includes coverage of last decade of Old Regime. [DTO]

35.2 Merle Fainsod. *How Russia is ruled.* 1963 rev. ed. Cambridge, Mass.: Harvard University Press, 1967. (Russian Research Center studies, 11.) ISBN 0-674-41000-9. ▸ Classic study of government, party and certain social institutions in Soviet Russia. Based on totalitarian model, but remarkably subtle and sophisticated. [DTO]

35.3 Mikhail Heller and Aleksandr Nekrich. *Utopia in power: the history of the Soviet Union from 1917 to the present.* 1986 ed. Phyllis B. Carlos, trans. New York: Simon & Schuster, 1992. ISBN 0-671-64535-8. ▸ Passionate, trenchantly anti-Soviet survey of Soviet history by two eminent Russian intellectuals. Detailed and especially strong on cultural matters, foreign policy, and domestic developments often not covered in works by Western scholars. [DTO]

35.4 Geoffrey A. Hosking. *The first socialist society: a history of the Soviet Union from within.* Rev. ed. Cambridge, Mass.: Harvard University Press, 1990. ISBN 0-674-30442-X. ▸ Lucid, balanced survey of domestic, social, and political developments. Strong

chapters on nationality question and experience of World War II. No material on foreign policy. [DTO]

35.5 Jerry F. Hough and Merle Fainsod. *How the Soviet Union is governed.* Cambridge, Mass.: Harvard University Press, 1979. ISBN 0-674-41030-0. ▸ Highly controversial rewrite of Fainsod's classic study of Russian government (35.2), notable for its in-depth treatment of Soviet institutions. Heavy emphasis on comparative government frameworks and notion that Soviet Union was participatory system. [DTO]

35.6 Mary McAuley. *Soviet politics, 1917–1991.* Oxford: Oxford University Press, 1992. ISBN 0-19-878066-4 (cl), 0-19-878067-2 (pbk). ▸ Revision of standard survey of Soviet political institutions, notable for its clarity. Earlier title: *Politics and the Soviet Union.* [DTO]

35.7 David MacKenzie and Michael W. Curran. *A history of the Soviet Union.* 2d ed. Belmont, Calif.: Wadsworth, 1991. ISBN 0-534-14910-3. ▸ Balanced survey. Includes historiographic discussion of key problems. [DTO]

35.8 Woodford McClellan. *Russia: a history of the Soviet period.* 2d ed. Englewood Cliffs, N.J.: Prentice-Hall, 1990. ISBN 0-13-784505-7. ▸ Short survey of Soviet history. Balanced coverage of social, political, and cultural topics. [DTO]

35.9 Martin Edward Malia. *The Soviet tragedy: a history of socialism in Russia, 1917–1991.* New York: Free Press, 1994. ISBN 0-02-919795-3. ▸ Spirited critique of failure of Soviet project and of Western Sovietology that places blame squarely on ideology as opposed to any innate nondemocratic attributes of Russia. [DTO]

35.10 Georg von Rauch. *A history of Soviet Russia.* 6th ed. Peter Jacobsohn and Annette Jacobsohn, trans. New York: Praeger, 1972. ▸ Standard German text revealing great sensitivity to geopolitical factors in central and Eastern Europe. [DTO]

35.11 Donald W. Treadgold. *Twentieth-century Russia.* 7th ed. Boulder: Westview, 1990. ISBN 0-8133-1010-5 (cl), 0-8133-1011-3 (pbk). ▸ Detailed, thorough text connecting last decades of imperial Russia to Revolution and Soviet period. [DTO]

35.12 Adam B. Ulam. *A history of Soviet Russia.* New York: Praeger, 1976. ISBN 0-275-89260-3. ▸ Short, readable account drawing on author's immense knowledge of Lenin, Stalin, and Soviet foreign policy. Notable for its literary qualities. [DTO]

POLITICAL HISTORY

February and October Revolutions of 1917

35.13 Edward Acton. *Rethinking the Russian Revolution.* London: Arnold; distributed by Routledge, Chapman & Hall, 1990. ISBN 0-7131-6609-6 (cl), 0-7131-6530-8 (pbk). ▸ Review of historiographical controversies about 1917 situated within narrative of principal events. Contrasts recent revisionist interpretations sympathetically with orthodox Soviet, liberal, and libertarian leftist viewpoints, giving full picture of current understanding. [WGR]

35.14 Robert Paul Browder and Alexander Kerensky, eds. and comps. *The Russian provisional government, 1917: documents.* 3 vols. Stanford, Calif.: Stanford University Press, 1961. ISBN 0-8047-0023-0. ▸ Selected documents in translation on all aspects of Revolution pertaining to provisional government, edited by one of its principal figures. Invaluable for English-language readers, but occasional distortions in translation; scholars should check originals. [WGR]

35.15 James Bunyan and Harold H. Fisher. *The Bolshevik Revolution, 1917–1918: documents and materials.* 1934 ed. Stanford, Calif.: Stanford University Press, 1965. (Hoover War Library publications, 3.) ▸ Study of bolshevik seizure of power and party policies and views during period from October through Treaty of Brest-Litovsk to general crisis of late winter 1918. [WGR]

35.16 Jane Burbank. *Intelligentsia and revolution: Russian views of bolshevism, 1917–1922.* 1986 ed. New York: Oxford University Press, 1989. ISBN 0-19-504061-9 (cl, 1986), 0-19-504573-4 (pbk). ‣ Empathetic analysis of populist, menshevik, liberal, and other perspectives on meaning of bolshevism and implications of bolshevik rule. Argues intelligentsia in 1922 changed little in its outlook. Careful treatment of P. B. Axelrod, Iulii Martov, W. S. Vishniak, Chernov, P. N. Miliukov, Petr Borngardavich Struve, Nikolai Berdiaev, and monarchist Ol'denberg, among others. Good bibliography. [WGR/DJR]

35.17 E. N. Burdzhalov. *Russia's second revolution: the February 1917 uprising in Petrograd.* Donald J. Raleigh, ed. and trans. Bloomington: Indiana University Press, 1987. ISBN 0-253-20440-2 (cl), 0-253-35037-9 (pbk). ‣ Analysis of collapse of tsarist Russian institutions in early 1917 by leading Russian historian. First serious Soviet study of February events in Petrograd suggesting Bolsheviks' own confusion. Russian edition published 1967. [WGR]

35.18 E. H. Carr. *The Bolshevik Revolution, 1917–1923.* 1950–53 ed. 3 vols. London: Macmillan, 1985. (A history of Soviet Russia, 1–3.) ISBN 0-393-30195-8 (v. 1, pbk), 0-393-30197-4 (v. 2, pbk), 0-393-30199-0 (v. 3, pbk). ‣ Seminal, comprehensive history focusing on bolshevik power (volume 1), its socioeconomic impact (volume 2), and its consequences internationally (volume 3). Unfairly criticized for emphasizing contextual circumstances contributing to bolshevik dictatorship and ignoring Lenin's "lust for power." [WGR]

35.19 William Henry Chamberlin. *The Russian Revolution, 1917–1921.* Vol. 1: *1917–1918: from the overthrow of the czar to the assumption of power by the Bolsheviks.* 1935 ed. Princeton: Princeton University Press, 1987. ISBN 0-691-05492-4 (v. 1, cl), 0-691-00814-0 (v. 1, pbk). ‣ Classic, richly detailed account by Moscow correspondent of *The Christian Science Monitor.* Sets social and economic conditions of 1917 in comprehensive political narrative. New bibliography by Diane Koenker. [WGR]

35.20 Victor M. Chernov. *The great Russian Revolution.* 1936 ed. Philip E. Mosely, ed. and trans. New York: Russell & Russell, 1966. ‣ Memoir history by leading populist and controversial minister of agriculture in 1917. Highly critical of gentry and political Right, as well as Kerensky, his liberal allies, and bolshevik Left; sympathetic to peasantry. [WGR]

35.21 Barbara Evans Clements. "Baba and Bolshevik: Russian women and revolutionary change." *Soviet Union/Union Sovietique* 12.2 (1985) 161–84. ISSN 0163-6057. ‣ Excellent introduction to complex problems of gendered politics and perceptions in revolutionary Russia by leading historian of Russian and Soviet women. [WGR]

35.22 Barbara Evans Clements. "Working-class and peasant women in the Russian Revolution, 1917–23." *Signs* 8 (1982) 215–35. ISSN 0097-9740. ‣ Sympathetic, insightful treatment of Revolution and social upheaval and effects on lives and social positions. [WGR]

35.23 Beatrice Farnsworth. *Alexandra Kollontai: socialism, feminism, and the Bolshevik Revolution.* Stanford, Calif.: Stanford University Press, 1980. ISBN 0-8047-1073-2. ‣ One of several good biographies of leading communist feminist, but containing best discussion of uneasy relationship between feminist movements and Bolsheviks' coming to power. Good introduction to "woman question" in Russian Revolution. Bibliography. [WGR]

35.24 Marc Ferro. *October 1917: a social history of the Russian Revolution.* Norman Stone, trans. London: Routledge & Kegan Paul, 1980. ISBN 0-7100-0534-2. ‣ Analysis of disintegration of

February system and foundations of new society by leading French historian, with attention to popular opinions and mentalities. [WGR]

35.25 Edith Rogovin Frankel, Jonathan Frankel, and Baruch Knei-Paz, eds. *Revolution in Russia: reassessments of 1917.* Cambridge: Cambridge University Press, 1992. ISBN 0-521-40523-8 (cl), 0-521-40585-8 (pbk). ‣ Essays on political power, mass action, peasants, workers, bourgeoisie, nationalities, and Bolsheviks by leading historians of 1917. Lacks bibliography. [WGR]

35.26 Ziva Galili. *The menshevik leaders in the Russian Revolution: social realities and political strategies.* Princeton: Princeton University Press, 1989. ISBN 0-691-05567-X. ‣ Superb analysis of menshevik dilemma in 1917, focusing on dual power problem, labor relations, and crisis of coalition politics. Especially strong on formation of coalition government in spring 1917. [WGR]

35.27 Graeme Gill. *Peasants and government in the Russian Revolution.* New York: Barnes & Noble, 1979. ISBN 0-06-492406-8. ‣ Examination of provisional government's policies toward countryside and peasant response. Sees land hunger, crop failure, and impatience with provisional government as main causes of rural unrest. Admirable effort at comprehensiveness based on minimal source base. [WGR/LV]

35.28 Iurii Vladimirovich Got'e. *Time of troubles: the diary of Iurii Vladimirovich Got'e, Moscow, July 8, 1917 to July 23, 1922.* Terence Emmons, ed. and trans. Princeton: Princeton University Press, 1988. ISBN 0-691-05520-3. ‣ Critical observations of one of Moscow's most prominent professors. Description of personal experience, transformation of Moscow University, and dissolution of prerevolutionary intellectual and professional life. Richly annotated by Emmons. [WGR/DJR]

35.29 Tsuyoshi Hasegawa. *The February Revolution: Petrograd, 1917.* Seattle: University of Washington Press, 1981. (Publications on Russia and Eastern Europe by the School of International Studies, 9.) ISBN 0-295-95765-4. ‣ Detailed narrative of tsarist Russia's political fall, abdication of tsar, and establishment of provisional government in Petrograd. Concludes high politics responsive to mass pressures. [WGR]

35.30 Daniel H. Kaiser, ed. *The workers' revolution in Russia, 1917: the view from below.* Cambridge: Cambridge University Press, 1987. ISBN 0-521-34166-3 (cl), 0-521-34971-0 (pbk). ‣ Essays on urban environments in Petrograd and Moscow and social dimensions of protest. Revisionist work emphasizing revolution from below; arguments not always successful. Critical review of literature. [WGR]

35.31 John L. H. Keep. *The Russian Revolution: a study in mass mobilization.* New York: Norton, 1976. ISBN 0-393-05616-3. ‣ Broad study based on published materials of bolshevik efforts to mobilize and, in author's view, manipulate workers and peasants in support of October Revolution. [WGR]

35.32 Alexander Kerensky. *Russia and history's turning point.* New York: Duell, Sloan & Pearce, 1965. ‣ Updated version of self-serving 1927 memoir history, *The Catastrophe,* by leading figure of provisional regime. Revealing psychological self-portrait. [WGR]

35.33 Diane P. Koenker. *Moscow workers and the 1917 Revolution.* Princeton: Princeton University Press, 1981. ISBN 0-691-05323-5 (cl), 0-691-10188-4 (pbk). ‣ First-rate study from below of workers and revolution in Moscow. Good bibliography. [WGR]

35.34 Diane P. Koenker and William G. Rosenberg. *Strikes and revolution in Russia, 1917.* Princeton: Princeton University Press, 1989. ISBN 0-691-05578-5. ‣ Detailed analysis of strikes and labor protest in 1917, exploring mobilization of labor and management, factory relations, perceptions and representations of protest, social identities, and relationship between labor protest and politics. [WGR]

35.35 Martin McCauley, ed. *The Russian Revolution and the Soviet state, 1917–1921: documents.* 1975 ed. London: Macmillan, 1988. ISBN 0-333-16609-4 (cl), 0-333-25798-7 (pbk). ► Documents on February events, policies of regime in 1917, Civil War and intervention, and bolshevik social, political, economic, and cultural policies to 1921. Some materials on everyday life. [WGR]

35.36 Roger Pethybridge. *The spread of the Russian Revolution: essays on 1917.* London and New York: Macmillan and St. Martin's, 1972. ISBN 0-333-13244-0. ► Study of railroads, post and telegraph, press, and propaganda. Admirable early effort at history from below based on published sources. [WGR]

35.37 Richard Pipes. *The Russian Revolution.* 1990 ed. New York: Vintage, 1991. ISBN 0-679-73660-3 (pbk). ► Comprehensive, controversial synthesis emphasizing destructive role of radical intelligentsia, weakness of tsarist and nonbolshevik political figures, and evils of bolshevism. [WGR]

35.38 Alexander Rabinowitch. *The Bolsheviks come to power: the Revolution in Petrograd.* New York: Norton, 1976. ISBN 0-393-05586-8 (cl), 0-393-00893-2 (pbk). ► Best study of October Revolution in Petrograd. Argues against simplistic explanations of October as *coup d'état* by monolithic party by showing extensive diversity and disorganization within party and by linking bolshevik actions with popular outlooks. [WGR]

35.39 Alexander Rabinowitch. *Prelude to Revolution: the Petrograd Bolsheviks and the July 1917 uprising.* 1968 ed. Bloomington: Indiana University Press, 1991. ISBN 0-253-34768-8 (cl), 0-253-20661-8 (pbk). ► Detailed analysis of July mutiny against provisional government that deemphasizes Bolshevik party's leadership role. [WGR]

35.40 Oliver H. Radkey. *The agrarian foes of bolshevism: promise and default of the Russian socialist revolutionaries, February to October, 1917.* New York: Columbia University Press, 1958. ► Comprehensive, critical study of agrarian populists suggesting political ineptitude betrayed popular interests. [WGR]

35.41 Oliver H. Radkey. *Russia goes to the polls: the election to the All-Russian Constituent Assembly, 1917.* Rev. ed. Ithaca, N.Y.: Cornell University Press, 1989. ISBN 0-8014-2360-0. ► Results of only fully democratic national election in Russian history before 1991. New bibliography. Earlier title: *The Election to the Russian Constituent Assembly of 1917.* [WGR]

35.42 Donald J. Raleigh. *Revolution on the Volga: 1917 in Saratov.* Ithaca, N.Y.: Cornell University Press, 1986. ISBN 0-8014-1790-2. ► Excellent, comprehensive study of impact of Revolution in provincial city once governed by Petr Arkadevich Stolypin, presented as paradigm of 1917 in provinces. Based on extensive archival research. [WGR]

35.43 John Reed. *Ten days that shook the world.* 1935 ed. New York: Lightyear, 1992. ISBN 0-89968-271-5 (cl). ► Classic memoir history of October events by observant, sympathetic, American of somewhat confused political views. First published 1919. Reprint of 1935 edition with foreword by V. I. Lenin. [WGR]

35.44 William G. Rosenberg. *Liberals in the Russian Revolution: the Constitutional Democratic party, 1917–1921.* Princeton: Princeton University Press, 1974. ISBN 0-691-05221-2 (cl), 0-691-10023-3 (pbk). ► Comprehensive study of Constitutional Democratic party, its liberal ideologies, and leadership during 1917, Civil War, and early emigration. Focuses on role in government, ideological divisions, and political tactics. [WGR]

35.45 Norman E. Saul. *Sailors in revolt: the Russian Baltic fleet in 1917.* Lawrence: Regents Press of Kansas, 1978. ISBN 0-7006-0166-x. ► Limited to descriptive analysis of Baltic fleet, but only

scholarly English-language work focusing on Russian sailors in 1917. [WGR]

35.46 S. A. Smith. *Red Petrograd: revolution in the factories, 1917–1918.* 1983 ed. Cambridge: Cambridge University Press, 1985. ISBN 0-521-24759-4 (cl, 1983), 0-521-31618-9 (pbk). ► Analysis of labor activism in capital by sensitive, skillful historian. Particularly good discussion of labor-management relations. Good bibliography. [WGR]

35.47 N. N. Sukhanov. *The Russian Revolution, 1917: a personal record.* 1955 ed. Joel Carmichael, ed. and trans. Princeton: Princeton University Press, 1984. ISBN 0-691-05406-1 (cl), 0-691-00799-3 (pbk). ► Sensitive, very informative reporter's account from menshevik internationalist point of view. Abridged from *Zapiski o revoliutsii, 1922–23.* [WGR]

35.48 Leon Trotsky. *The history of the Russian Revolution.* 1932 ed. 3 vols. in 1. Max Eastman, trans. New York: Monad; distributed by Pathfinder, 1980. ISBN 0-913460-83-4 (pbk). ► Detailed memoir history of events from February 1917 through October and aftermath by one of Revolution's most prominent figures. [WGR]

35.49 P. V. Volobueva, ed. *Oktiabr' 1917: velichaishee sobytie veka ili sotsial'naia katastrofa* (October 1917: the greatest event of the century or social catastrophe). Moscow: Politicheskoi Literatury, 1991. ISBN 5-250-01722-3. ► Sixteen essays by leading Soviet historians of 1917, analyzing and critiquing literature and their own previous conceptualizations. Excellent introduction to intellectual turmoil provoked by old system's collapse. [WGR]

35.50 Rex A. Wade. *Red guards and workers' militias in the Russian Revolution.* Stanford, Calif.: Stanford University Press, 1984. ISBN 0-8047-1167-4. ► Exploration of how Revolution was armed in streets and factories. Important corrective to analyses limited to high politics and bolshevik conspiracies. [WGR]

35.51 Allan K. Wildman. *The end of the Russian Imperial Army.* 2 vols. Princeton: Princeton University Press, 1980–87. ISBN 0-691-05287-5 (v. 1), 0-691-05504-1 (v. 2). ► Comprehensive analysis, superbly researched, of old army's disintegration, soldiers' revolt, and army's role in struggle for Soviet power and peace. [WGR]

SEE ALSO
47.420 Rex A. Wade. *The Russian search for peace, February–October 1917.*

Civil War and War Communism, 1918–1921

35.52 David Arans, comp. *How we lost the Civil War: bibliography of Russian émigré memoirs on the Russian Revolution, 1917–1921.* Newtonville, Mass.: Oriental Research Partners, 1988. ISBN 0-89250-34-3. ► Complete references to 559 Russian-language memoirs, organized topically, representing spectrum of political views. Titles of all entries translated into English and each entry annotated; indexed. [DJR]

35.53 Paul Avrich. *Kronstadt, 1921.* 1970 ed. Princeton: Princeton University Press, 1991. ISBN 0-691-00868-X. ► Full-scale, authoritative, judicious, and colorfully written account of background, course, and savage suppression of insurrection. Sees rebellion as prototype of later searches by disillusioned radicals for original ideals of Revolution. [DJR]

35.54 Alexis Vasil'evich Babine. *A Russian Civil War diary: Alexis Babine in Saratov, 1917–1922.* Donald J. Raleigh, ed. Durham, N.C.: Duke University Press, 1988. ISBN 0-8223-0835-5. ► Visceral, antibolshevik, personal account of Revolution and Civil War in important provincial town bringing to life terrible daily struggle to survive. Rare local perspective. [DJR]

35.55 J.F.N. Bradley. *Civil War in Russia, 1917–1920.* New

York: St. Martin's, 1975. ▸ Brief survey focusing on military campaigns and foreign policy. Draws on declassified Western archives, Smolensk and Trotsky archives. Traditional emphasis on superior organization, ruthless determination, and propaganda efforts of Bolsheviks. [DJR]

35.56 Vladimir N. Brovkin. *The Mensheviks after October: socialist opposition and the rise of the bolshevik dictatorship.* Ithaca, N.Y.: Cornell University Press, 1987. ISBN 0-8014-1858-5 (cl), 0-8014-9976-3 (pbk). ▸ Fullest account to date of Menshevik party during first year of Soviet rule. Sees antidemocratic nature of bolshevism as reason for transformation of Soviet government into dictatorship. [DJR]

35.57 Vladimir N. Brovkin, ed. and trans. *Dear comrades: menshevik reports on the Bolshevik Revolution and the Civil War.* Stanford, Calif.: Hoover Institution Press, 1991. (Hoover archival documentaries, Hoover Press publications, 389.) ISBN 0-8179-8981-1 (cl), 0-8179-8982-x (pbk). ▸ Forty-two documents throwing valuable light on conditions in urban industrial centers, especially on workers' politics and protest actions. [DJR]

35.59 William Henry Chamberlin. *The Russian Revolution, 1917–1921.* Vol. 2: *1918–1921: from the Civil War to the consolidation of power.* 1935 ed. Princeton: Princeton University Press, 1987. ISBN 0-691-05493-2 (v. 2, cl), 0-691-00815-9 (v. 2, pbk). ▸ Panoramic account, first published 1935, still valuable today. Role of tsarist system and war in causing Revolution, and impact of psychological, political, economic, and geographical factors in explaining Red victory in Civil War. Clear exposition of War Communism as complex of related domestic, social, economic, and cultural policies meant to create socialism rapidly. [DJR]

35.59 Victor M. Fic. *The Bolsheviks and the Czechoslovak legion: the origin of their armed conflict, March–May 1918.* New Delhi: Abhinav, 1978. ▸ Detailed account of important episode often seen as opening salvo of Civil War. Challenge to official Soviet interpretation that France and Britain instigated legion into uprising. [DJR]

35.60 Orlando Figes. *Peasant Russia, Civil War: the Volga countryside in revolution, 1917–1921.* Oxford: Clarendon, 1989. ISBN 0-19-822898-8. ▸ Explanation of conditional peasant support for Bolsheviks in terms of political and social developments in villages. Examination of long-term impact of conflict on future peasant-state relations. Excellent social and regional history based on original archival research. [DJR/LV]

35.61 Sheila Fitzpatrick. "The Civil War as a formative experience." In *Bolshevik culture: experiment and order in the Russian Revolution.* Abbott Gleason, Peter Kenez, and Richard Stites, eds., pp. 57–76. Bloomington: Indiana University Press, 1985. (Special study of the Kennan Institute for Advanced Russian Studies, the Wilson Center, 5.) ISBN 0-253-31206-x. ▸ Study of Civil War as formative experience welcomed by Lenin. Suggests possible generational impact of 1917–21 period. Portrays Stalin as good Leninist. Provocative essay centering on Soviet future ideology. [DJR/DKR]

35.62 Sheila Fitzpatrick. *The commissariat of the enlightenment: Soviet organization of education and the arts under Lunacharsky, October 1917–1921.* Cambridge: Cambridge University Press, 1970. ISBN 0-521-07919-5. ▸ Discussion of institutional aspects of commissariat, its formulation of policy, workings, key personnel, and activities. Loyalty of Anatoly Vasilievich Lunacharsky to personal convictions. Thorough, valuable study of Soviet cultural policy. [DJR]

35.63 Peter Fleming. *The fate of Admiral Kolchak.* New York: Harcourt, Brace & World, 1963. ▸ Moving, tragic story of White leader presiding over not very creditable enterprise. Discusses failure to rally popular support, maintain discipline, and curb corruption. Well-written traditional, popular history. [DJR]

35.64 David Footman. *Civil War in Russia.* 1961 ed. Westport, Conn.: Greenwood, 1975. ISBN 0-8371-8306-5. ▸ General survey treating major military campaigns. Emphasis on Communist party's corporate spirit and discipline as chief considerations in tipping scales in favor of Reds. Traditional political history. [DJR]

35.65 Israel Getzler. *Kronstadt, 1917–1921: the fate of a Soviet democracy.* Cambridge: Cambridge University Press, 1983. ISBN 0-521-24479-x. ▸ Sympathetic account of golden age of Soviet democracy in Russia's famous naval base, focusing on 1917–18. Examines meaning of demise of Kronstadt's Soviet democracy and failure of desperate attempt to restore it in March 1921. [DJR]

35.66 William Husband. *Revolution in the factory: the birth of the Soviet textile industry, 1917–1920.* New York: Oxford University Press, 1990. ISBN 0-19-506435-6. ▸ Account of dynamics of revolutionary politics, trade unions, and economic considerations in central industrial region. Brief but significant study of how textile workers supported Revolution as they perceived it. [DJR]

35.67 Frederick I. Kaplan. *Bolshevik ideology and the ethics of Soviet labor, 1917–1920: the formative years.* New York: Philosophical Library, 1968. ▸ Discusses correspondence between bolshevik ideology and labor policy, and how ideology occasions cast of mind. Nontraditional, epistemological, and psychological study. [DJR]

35.68 Peter Kenez. *Civil War in South Russia, 1918: the first year of the Volunteer Army.* Berkeley: University of California Press, 1971. ISBN 0-520-01709-9. ▸ Narrowly focused but judicious study based largely on unpublished materials in Western archives. Discusses how inability of apolitical White generals to develop appealing program and their Russian nationalism doomed movement to failure. [DJR]

35.69 Peter Kenez. *Civil War in South Russia, 1919–1920: the defeat of the Whites.* Berkeley: University of California Press for Hoover Institution on War, Revolution, and Peace, 1977. ISBN 0-520-03346-9. ▸ Social and political history analyzing programs and propaganda of both Bolsheviks and their major rivals. Sees White failure in inability to build appropriate, effective institutions. [DJR]

35.70 S. S. Khromov et al. *Grazhdanskaia voina i voennaia interventsiia v SSSR: entsiklopediia* (The Civil War and military intervention in the USSR: encyclopedia). 1983 ed. Moscow: Sovetskaia Entsiklopediia, 1987. ▸ Most comprehensive Soviet reference work on subject, but dated entries are testimony to status quo historical scholarship before Gorbachev reforms. [DJR]

35.71 Diane P. Koenker, William G. Rosenberg, and Ronald Grigor Suny, eds. *Party, state, and society in the Russian Civil War: explorations in social history.* Bloomington: Indiana University Press, 1989. ISBN 0-253-33262-1 (cl), 0-253-20541-7 (pbk). ▸ Nineteen essays exploring administration and state building, intelligentsia and workers, and social and demographic impact and legacy of conflict. Volume assesses reasons for erosion of democratic practices by looking at circumstances and ideology. [DJR]

35.72 Lars T. Lih. *Bread and authority in Russia, 1914–1921.* Berkeley: University of California Press, 1990. ISBN 0-520-06584-0. ▸ Valuable, broadly researched study of food supply crisis in Russia during war, Revolution, and Civil War and attempted solutions of successive governments. Attempts to show how crisis affected future development of Soviet Union. [DJR/LV]

35.73 W. Bruce Lincoln. *Red victory: a history of the Russian Civil War.* New York: Simon & Schuster, 1989. ISBN 0-671-63166-7 (cl), 0-671-73286-2 (pbk). ▸ Part three of trilogy on war and revolution in Russia (see also 34.91). Richly anecdotal, vividly written popular/scholarly traditional history. [DJR]

35.74 Richard Luckett. *The White generals: an account of the*

White movement and the Russian Civil War. New York: Viking, 1971. ISBN 0-670-76265-2. ‣ First full-scale study in English of White movement's military campaigns and leaders. Explains failure in terms of personal qualities of generals and inability to challenge Bolsheviks with sound political program. [DJR]

35.75 Michael Malet. *Nestor Makhno in the Russian Civil War.* London: Macmillan for London School of Economics and Political Science, 1982. ISBN 0-333-25969-6. ‣ Sympathetic attempt to place activities of this important Ukrainian anarchist within context of Civil War. Emphasis on conflict of ideas rather than on military events. [DJR]

35.76 Silvana Malle. *The economic organization of War Communism, 1918–1921.* Cambridge: Cambridge University Press, 1985. ISBN 0-521-30292-7. ‣ Study of all facets of economic life with emphasis on food procurement and transition to New Economic Policy. Most exhaustive Western study of subject, with excellent historiographical introduction. [DJR]

35.77 Lynn Mally. *Culture of the future: the Proletkult movement in revolutionary Russia.* Berkeley: University of California Press, 1990. ISBN 0-520-06577-8. ‣ Social and institutional history of Bolsheviks' bold Revolutionary cultural experiment, with emphasis on contentiousness of efforts to found new cultural order. Discusses popularity of movement, splits within party and among other Soviet institutions on cultural policy, and meaning of Proletkult's ultimate failure. [DJR/RS]

35.78 Evan Mawdsley. *The Russian Civil War.* Boston: Allen & Unwin, 1987. ISBN 0-04-947024-8 (cl), 0-04-947025-6 (pbk). ‣ Authoritative, up-to-date general survey emphasizing military, political, and diplomatic developments. Argues Civil War and Stalinism were likely consequences of bolshevik seizure of power in October 1917. [DJR]

35.79 Mary McAuley. *Bread and justice: state and society in Petrograd, 1917–1922.* Oxford: Clarendon, 1991. ISBN 0-19-821982-2. ‣ Detailed study of first five years of Soviet administration in Petrograd. Focuses on food supply, but casts net much wider with extended treatment of party and state institutions at all levels, unions, cultural institutions and the like. Concludes Bolshevik party turned authoritarian in part because of ideology of transformation and equality and frustration with grassroots democracy. [DTO]

35.80 Richard Pipes. *The formation of the Soviet Union: communism and nationalism, 1917–1923.* Rev. ed. Cambridge, Mass.: Harvard University Press, 1964. (Russian Research Center studies, 13.) ISBN 0-674-30950-2. ‣ Survey of growth of Russian empire, its disintegration in 1917, and short-lived independence of borderlands. Emphasis on how Communists exploited new nationalisms to seize power and expand. [DJR]

35.81 Richard Pipes. *Russia under the Bolshevik regime.* New York: Knopf; distributed by Random House, 1994. ISBN 0-394-50242-6. ‣ Final volume of trilogy on Russian Revolution, its antecedents and aftermath. Strong arguments blaming Revolution and its failures on intelligentsia and authoritarian nature of Russian political and social institutions. Downplays ideology and social factors. Sees major influence of bolshevik practice upon Italian and German fascism. [DTO]

35.82 Oliver H. Radkey. *The unknown civil war in Soviet Russia: a study of the green movement in the Tambov region, 1920–1921.* Stanford, Calif.: Hoover Institution Press, 1976. (Hoover Institution publications, 155.) ISBN 0-8179-6551-3. ‣ Detailed, sympathetic study of spontaneous antibolshevik, anti-outsider peasant movement led by A. S. Antonov that endangered Soviet state. Based on intelligent interrogation of jaundiced sources. Examines how Communist party overcame threat and lasting repercussions on system. [DJR/LV]

35.83 Christopher Read. *Culture and power in revolutionary Russia: the intelligentsia and the transition from tsarism to communism.* New York: St. Martin's, 1990. ISBN 0-312-03681-7. ‣ Close study of Soviet government's policies toward culture and intelligentsia during Civil War. Revisionist work sees New Economic Policy as step in direction of greater cultural intervention by authorities. [DJR]

35.84 Thomas F. Remington. *Building socialism in bolshevik Russia: ideology and industrial organization, 1917–1921.* Pittsburgh: University of Pittsburgh Press, 1984. ISBN 0-8229-3809-X. ‣ Valuable case studies examining bolshevik attempt to create socialist society through social mobilization. Suggests mobilization itself inherently defeated socialist objectives of Revolution. [DJR]

35.85 Richard Sakwa. *Soviet Communists in power: a study of Moscow during the Civil War, 1918–21.* New York: St. Martin's, 1988. ISBN 0-312-01582-8. ‣ Study of internal organizational and administrative developments of government and importance of bolshevik ideology in determining the course of events and early bolshevik authoritarianism. Well-documented but narrowly focused examination of politics in Russian capital. [DJR]

35.86 Leonard Bertram Schapiro. *The origin of the communist autocracy: political opposition in the Soviet state, first phase, 1917–1921.* 2d ed. Cambridge, Mass.: Harvard University Press, 1977. ISBN 0-674-64451-4 (cl), 0-674-64452-2 (pbk). ‣ Chronicle of confused idealism of Mensheviks and arbitrary illegality inherent in regime created by Lenin. Classic attempt to demonstrate continuity between Lenin and Stalin; originally published 1955. [DJR/DKR]

35.87 Peter Scheibert. *Lenin an der Macht: das russische Volk in der Revolution, 1918–1922.* Weinheim, Germany: Acta Humaniora, 1984. ISBN 3-527-17503-2. ‣ Comprehensive study of enormous social costs of Civil War in Petrograd, Moscow, and provinces. Based on contemporary sources with emphasis on role of Lenin and ideology. [DJR]

35.88 Robert Service. *The Bolshevik party in revolution: a study in organisational change, 1917–1923.* New York: Barnes & Noble, 1979. ISBN 0-06-496180-X. ‣ Study of bureaucratization of Bolshevik party during Civil War. Transformation of mass party with democratic features into rigidly authoritarian one explained by designs of hardline leaders and Civil War circumstances. [DJR]

35.89 Canfield F. Smith. *Vladivostok under Red and White rule: revolution and counterrevolution in the Russian Far East, 1920–1922.* Seattle: University of Washington Press, 1975. (Publications on Russia and Eastern Europe by the Institute for Comparative and Foreign Area Studies, 6.) ISBN 0-295-95383-7. ‣ Examination of unraveling of political, diplomatic, and military efforts for control over eastern Siberia. Stress on failure of Whites, superior organization and discipline of Bolsheviks, and Japanese presence in explaining communist victory. [DJR]

SEE ALSO
47.428 George A. Brinkley. *The volunteer army and Allied intervention in South Russia.*

The 1920s and the New Economic Policy

35.90 Alan M. Ball. *Russia's last capitalists: the nepmen, 1921–1929.* Berkeley: University of California Press, 1987. ISBN 0-520-05717-1. ‣ Study of zigzag policy of Soviet government toward private entrepreneurs during era of New Economic Policy. Argues that NEP-men made significant contribution to recovery and functioning of economy, despite restrictions, petty and large. [LS]

35.91 G. A. Bordiugov and V. A. Kozlov. "The turning point of 1929 and the Bukharin alternative." *Soviet studies in history*

28.4 (1990) 15–33. ISSN 0038-5867. ▸ Analysis of failure of faction, led by Nikolai Bukharin, to take advantage of relative stability in mid-1920s to maintain investment priorities. [LS]

35.92 E. H. Carr. *Socialism in one country, 1924–1926.* 1958–64 ed. Harmondsworth: Penguin, 1970–72. (A history of Soviet Russia, 5–7.) ▸ Political history from state-centered perspective. Emphasizes institutions and unresolved conflicts within party and its instrumentalities. [LS]

35.93 Stephen F. Cohen. "Bolshevism and Stalinism." In *Stalinism: essays in historical interpretation.* Robert C. Tucker, ed., pp. 3–29. New York: Norton, 1977. ISBN 0-393-05608-2. ▸ Revisionist account arguing against continuity thesis with respect to bolshevism and Stalinism. Latter identified with excess, extraordinary extremism. [LS]

35.94 Stephen F. Cohen. *Bukharin and the Bolshevik Revolution: a political biography, 1888–1938.* 1973 ed. Oxford: Oxford University Press, 1980. ISBN 0-19-502697-7 (pbk). ▸ Exposition and celebration of Bukharin's creative thinking about socialism. Emphasizes importance of Bukharin alternative to turn toward Stalinism after death of Lenin. [LS]

35.95 Richard B. Day. *Leon Trotsky and the politics of economic isolation.* Cambridge: Cambridge University Press, 1973. ISBN 0-521-20089-X. ▸ Reinterpretation of divisions within party on basis of internationalist versus isolationist strategies for economic development, with Trotsky leading exponent of former. [LS/HK]

35.96 Michael S. Farbman. *Bolshevism in retreat.* London: Collins, 1923. ▸ Study of introduction of New Economic Policy signifying defeat of system of "frenzied centralization" and transformation of peasant from object to subject. [LS]

35.97 Sheila Fitzpatrick, Alexander Rabinowitch, and Richard Stites, eds. *Russia in the era of NEP: explorations in Soviet society and culture.* Bloomington: Indiana University Press, 1991. ISBN 0-253-32224-3 (cl), 0-253-20657-X (pbk). ▸ Eighteen scholarly essays on transformation of urban and rural society and culture in Russia during era of New Economic Policy (1921–29). [LS]

35.98 Lars T. Lih. "Political testament of Lenin and Bukharin and the meaning of NEP." *Slavic review* 50.2 (1991) 241–52. ISSN 0037-6779. ▸ Analysis of consistency of Lenin's and Bukharin's thinking about state and social policy across divide of 1921. Sees New Economic Policy as continuation of Civil War policies by new means. [LS]

35.99 Michal Mirski. *The mixed economy: NEP and its lot.* Roger A. Clarke, trans. Copenhagen: Rosenkilde & Bagger, 1984. (Kobenhavns Universitete, Slaviske Institut, Studier, 10.) ISBN 87-423-0431-8. ▸ Critique of leftist thinking which led to sabotage of Leninist strategy for economic recovery and prosperity. Vindicates Bukharinist perspective. [LS]

35.100 Roger Pethybridge. *The social prelude to Stalinism.* New York: St. Martin's, 1974. ▸ Study of large-scale utopian thinking of Bolsheviks imposed on small-scale social reality. Examines impact of war, cultural backwardness, and Marxist ideology on social policy. [LS]

35.101 Donald J. Raleigh, ed. "The Soviet Union in the 1920s: a roundtable." *Soviet studies in history* 28.2 (1989). ISSN 0038-5867. ▸ Discussion among leading Soviet historians of New Economic Policy period originally published in *Voprosy Istorii* 9 (1988) 3–58. Emphasizes idea of alternatives to Stalin's violent revolution from above.[LS]

35.102 Michal Reiman. *The birth of Stalinism: the USSR on the eve of the "second revolution."* George Saunders, trans. Bloomington: Indiana University Press, 1987. ISBN 0-253-31196-9. ▸ Study of intraparty struggles from 1926 based on documents in German Foreign Ministry archive. [LS]

35.103 Lewis H. Siegelbaum. *Soviet state and society between revolutions, 1918–1929.* Cambridge: Cambridge University Press, 1992. ISBN 0-521-36215-6 (cl), 0-521-36987-8 (pbk). ▸ Synthesis and historiographical commentary on social and political history of Soviet Russia and Soviet Union between 1917 Revolution and Stalin Revolution. [LS]

The 1930s and the Purges

35.104 Robert Conquest. *The Great Terror: a reassessment.* New York: Oxford University Press, 1990. ISBN 0-19-505580-2. ▸ Most detailed account of Stalin's terror in 1930s, focusing on Stalin as executioner. Sources and statistics still questioned by scholars. Revision of 1968 edition: *The Great Terror: Stalin's Purge of the Thirties.* [HK/AD]

35.105 Robert V. Daniels. *The conscience of the Revolution: communist opposition in Soviet Russia.* 1960 ed. New York: Simon & Schuster, 1969. ▸ Detailed account of intraparty struggle in 1920s and 1930s. Analyzes leaders, ideologies, and power structures of party. [HK]

35.106 Isaac Deutscher. *The prophet outcast: Trotsky, 1929–1940.* 1963 ed. New York: Viking, 1965. ▸ Explicitly Trotskyite defense of Leon Trotsky as major opponent of Stalin. Describes Trotsky's defense of October Revolution as betrayed by Stalin and Trotsky's prophetic warnings as justified by history. [HK]

35.107 Merle Fainsod. *Smolensk under Soviet rule.* 1958 ed. Boston: Unwin Hyman, 1989. ISBN 0-04-445389-2. ▸ Best regional history of Soviet region under Soviet rule. Based on party archives of Smolensk captured during World War II. Classic, influential depiction of Soviet history according to totalitarian model; includes much fascinating material. [HK/LV]

35.108 J. Arch Getty. *The origins of the great purges: the Soviet Communist party reconsidered, 1933–1938.* Cambridge: Cambridge University Press, 1985. ISBN 0-521-25921-5. ▸ Sharp critique of totalitarian interpretation of Stalin's terror; its prosaic analysis of terror variously judged. Focuses on inefficiencies of party control and center-periphery conflict. [HK]

35.109 J. Arch Getty and Roberta T. Manning, eds. *Stalinist Terror: new perspectives.* Cambridge: Cambridge University Press, 1993. ISBN 0-521-44125-0 (cl), 0-521-44670-8 (pbk). ▸ Collection of essays, some republished, by leading revisionists. Breaks no new conceptual ground and offers no new explanations, but brings to public domain fresh statistical materials on Terror. Emphasizes social and multilayered political factors in the Terror. [DTO]

35.110 Graeme Gill. *The origins of the Stalinist political system.* Cambridge: Cambridge University Press, 1990. ISBN 0-521-38266-1. ▸ Analysis of formation of Stalin's personal dictatorship, emphasizing Stalin's personality, political environment, and center-periphery relations. Rejects continuity between Leninist and Stalinist rule. [HK]

35.111 O. V. Khlevniuk. *1937-i: Stalin, NKVD, i sovetskoe obshchestvo* (1937: Stalin, NKVD, and Soviet society). Moscow: Respublika, 1992. ISBN 5-250-01537-9. ▸ Best account in Russian of Stalin's Great Terror. Analyzes Stalin's quest for absolute power, but also examines interaction between state terror and people and reasons for conformity and resistance. [HK]

35.112 Hryhory Kostiuk. *Stalinist rule in the Ukraine: a study of the decade of mass terror, 1929–1939.* Munich: Institute for the Study of the USSR, 1960. (Institute for the Study of the USSR, Publications: series 1, 47.) ▸ Most detailed account of Stalinist terror in Ukraine in 1930s. Analyzes national aspirations of Ukraine and suspicions of Moscow as reasons for extraordinarily extensive terror in Ukraine. [HK]

35.113 Roy Medvedev. *All Stalin's men.* 1983 ed. Harold Shukman, trans. Garden City, N.Y.: Anchor/Doubleday, 1984. ISBN 0-385-18388-7 (cl), 0-385-19038-7 (jacket). ▸ Brief political biographies of Stalin's henchmen: Kliment Efremovich Voroshilov, I. A. Mikoyan, Mikail Andreevich Suslov, Viaceslav Molotov, L. M. Kaganovich, and Georgi Malenkov, emphasizing their unswerving loyalty. Includes little-known material. [HK]

35.114 Roy Medvedev. *Let history judge: the origins and consequences of Stalinism.* Rev. ed. George Shriver, ed. and trans. New York: Columbia University Press, 1989. ISBN 0-231-06350-4 (cl), 0-231-06351-2 (pbk). ▸ Detailed chronicle of repression, harshly criticizing Stalinism from democratic-socialist point of view. Includes *glasnost* revelations. [HK]

35.115 Gabor Tamas Rittersporn. *Stalinist simplifications and Soviet complications: social tensions and political conflicts in the USSR, 1933–1953.* Chur, Switzerland: Harwood Academic, 1991. ISBN 3-7186-5107-6 (cl), 3-7186-5105-X (pbk). ▸ Revisionist study challenging totalitarian interpretation of Stalinist terror. Presents terror as expression of fruitless attempts to subordinate society to party-state. Translation of *Simplifications staliniennes et complications sovietique: tensions sociales et conflits politiques en URSS, 1933–1953* (1988). [HK]

35.116 Aleksandr I. Solzhenitsyn. *The Gulag Archipelago, 1918–1956: an experiment in literary investigation.* Thomas P. Whitney and H. Willetts, trans. New York: Harper & Row, 1974–78. ISBN 0-06-013914-5 (v. 1, cl), 0-06-013911-0 (v. 2, cl), 0-06-013912-9 (v. 3, cl), 0-06-080332-0 (v. 1, pbk), 0-06-080345-2 (v. 2, pbk), 0-06-080396-7 (v. 3, pbk). ▸ Detailed analysis of Soviet labor-camp system by dissident Soviet writer and Nobel prize winner. Employs literary method of analysis and polyphonic description. Contends Gulag system originated with Lenin, not with Stalin. Translation of *Arkhipelag Gulag, 1918–1956: opyt khudozhestvennogo issledovaniia* (1973–75). [HK]

35.117 B. Starkov. "Narkom Ezhov (People's Commissar Ezhov)." *Dialog* 4.1749 (1990) 19–26. ISSN 0234-0631. ▸ First biography of chief of Stalin's secret police. Concludes Ezhov was undistinguished party functionary of low moral and political character rewarded by Stalin with power for his personal devotion. [HK]

35.118 Robert C. Tucker. *Stalin as revolutionary, 1879–1929: a study in history and personality.* New York: Norton, 1973. ISBN 0-393-05487-X (cl), 0-393-00738-3 (pbk). ▸ Psychological study emphasizing linkage between Stalin's dictatorial personality and "social milieu and political situation." Depicts Stalin as revolutionary who wants to become a second Lenin. [HK]

35.119 Robert C. Tucker. *Stalin in power: the revolution from above, 1929–1941.* New York: Norton, 1990. ISBN 0-393-02881-X. ▸ Sequel to 35.118. Presents Stalin as twentieth-century Peter the Great and Ivan the Terrible. His revolution from above revived Russian tradition of state-sponsored revolutionary change. [HK]

35.120 Adam B. Ulam. *Stalin: the man and his era.* Rev. ed. Boston: Beacon, 1989. ISBN 0-8070-7005-X. ▸ Sparsely documented, but one of best among many biographies of Stalin. Explains cult of Stalin by his appeal within framework of socialism to "religious-existentialist craving in human nature." New introduction. [HK]

35.121 Dmitri Volkogonov. *Stalin: triumph and tragedy.* Harold Shukman, ed. and trans. New York: Grove Weidenfeld, 1991. ISBN 0-8021-1165-3. ▸ First Soviet biography of Stalin published after his death. Contrasts Stalin's achievements (triumph of socialism) and terror (tragedy). Based on much new archival material. Translation of Russian original *Triumf i tragediia* (1989). [HK]

World War II and the Cold War

35.122 Catherine Andreyev. *Vlasov and the Russian liberation movement: Soviet reality and émigré theories.* Cambridge: Cambridge University Press, 1987. ISBN 0-521-30545-4. ▸ Study of Russian Army of Liberation, headed by Andrei Vlasov, former Red Army general turned German collaborator. Emphasizes conscious anti-Stalin stance, not opportunism, and suggests broad base of anti-Soviet sentiments in occupied territory. [HK]

35.123 John A. Armstrong. *Ukrainian nationalism.* 3d ed. Englewood, Colo.: Ukrainian Academic Press, 1990. ISBN 0-87287-755-8. ▸ Study focusing on Ukrainian nationalist movement during World War II. Analyzes its ideologies and geographical specificities; emphasizes wide gulf between intellectual elite and population. [HK]

35.124 John Barber. "Popular reactions in Moscow to the German invasion of June 22, 1941." *Soviet Union/Union Sovietique* 18.1–3 (1991) 5–18. ISSN 0094-2863. ▸ Discussion of popular responses to German invasion based on new archival data. Emphasizes spontaneity of varied reactions—patriotic, defeatist, and anti-Soviet—under Stalin's regime. [HK]

35.125 John Barber and Mark Harrison. *The Soviet home front, 1941–1945: a social and economic history of the USSR in World War II.* London: Longman, 1991. ISBN 0-582-00964-2 (cased), 0-582-00965-0 (pbk). ▸ Pioneering effort by two British specialists to describe how Soviet system stood up to German invasion and burdens of war. [AD]

35.126 Seweryn Bialer, ed. *Stalin and his generals: Soviet military memoirs of World War II.* 1969 ed. Boulder: Westview, 1984. ISBN 0-86531-610-4. ▸ Probably best selection of Soviet memoirs, edited and annotated, on war years, including material on Stalin's role as leader. [AD/MVH]

35.127 G. A. Bordiugov. "Velikaia Otechestvennaia: podvig i obmanutye nadezhdy (The Great Fatherland War: the great deeds and dashed hopes)." In *Istoriia otechestva: liudi, idei, resheniia, ocherki istorii Sovetskogo gosudarstva* (A history of the fatherland: people, ideas, decisions, essays on the history of the Soviet state). V. A. Kozlov, comp., pp. 257–83. Moscow: Politizdat, 1991. ISBN 5-250-01799-1. ▸ Very good analysis of popular mood during war, based on recently declassified archival material. Discusses both anti- and pro-Soviet sentiments, but emphasizes inability and unwillingness of state to meet popular needs. [HK]

35.128 Yury Boshyk, ed. *Ukraine during World War II, history and its aftermath: a symposium.* Edmonton: University of Alberta, Canadian Institute of Ukrainian Studies; distributed by University of Toronto Press, 1986. ISBN 0-920862-37-3 (cl), 0-920862-36-5 (pbk). ▸ Collection of articles dealing with German occupation of Ukraine, Ukrainian nationalism, collaborationism, Ukrainian-Jewish relations, and investigations of war criminals in North America. Includes many documents. [HK]

35.129 Timothy Dunmore. *Soviet politics, 1945–1953.* New York: St. Martin's, 1984. ISBN 0-312-74869-8. ▸ Overview emphasizing postwar Soviet politics as bureaucratic rather than totalitarian or pluralist. Sees origins of Khrushchevian reforms in postwar years. [HK]

35.130 Timothy Dunmore. *The Stalinist command economy: the Soviet state apparatus and economic policy, 1945–53.* New York: St. Martin's, 1980. ISBN 0-312-75516-3. ▸ Good account of postwar Soviet economic administration and policy making. Refutes totalitarian school of Soviet politics and emphasizes bureaucratic infighting in decision making. [HK]

35.131 John Erickson. *The road to Stalingrad.* Vol. 1 of *Stalin's war with Germany.* New York: Harper & Row, 1975. ISBN 0-06-011141-0. ▸ Best account of war up to battle for Stalingrad. Holds

Stalin responsible for both initial military fiasco and subsequent rally. [HK]

35.132 Harvey Fireside. *Icon and swastika: the Russian Orthodox church under Nazi and Soviet control.* Cambridge, Mass.: Harvard University Press, 1971. (Russian Research Center studies, 62.) ISBN 0-674-44160-5. ▸ Views those churches under German occupation as "experimental group" and those under Soviet rule as "control group." Documents religious revival under German occupation. Attributes the 1943 "concordat" between state and church to the latter's patriotism. [HK]

35.133 Werner G. Hahn. *Postwar Soviet politics: the fall of Zhdanov and the defeat of moderation, 1946–53.* Ithaca, N.Y.: Cornell University Press, 1982. ISBN 0-8014-1410-5. ▸ Revision of traditional views of postwar Soviet politics by emphasizing A. Zhdanov not as hardliner but as moderate in context of period. Analyzes conflict between Zhdanov and Georgi Malenkov. [HK]

35.134 Ivan V. Karasev. "The reconstruction of agriculture in Pskov Oblast', 1945–1953." *Soviet studies* 43.2 (1991) 301–09. ISSN 0038-5859. ▸ Analysis of fall and reconstruction of collective farm system. Emphasizes destructive impact of postwar Soviet policy on agriculture. [HK]

35.135 Susan J. Linz, ed. *The impact of World War II on the Soviet Union.* Totowa, N.J.: Rowman & Allanheld, 1985. ISBN 0-8476-7378-2 (cl), 0-8476-7379-0 (pbk). ▸ Collection of essays dealing with war's impact on Soviet politics, economy, society, and culture. Finds costs of war corresponded roughly to prewar economic achievements. Explores question of how and why regime survived. [HK]

35.136 William O. McCagg, Jr. *Stalin embattled, 1943–1948.* Detroit: Wayne State University Press, 1978. ISBN 0-8143-1591-7. ▸ Analysis of war's impact on Soviet domestic and foreign policy. Emphasizes emergence of various contending groups within country. Stalin described as wishing to maintain peace and wartime Grand Alliance in postwar years. [HK]

35.137 Aleksandr Nekrich. *"22 June 1941": Soviet historians and the German invasion.* Vladimir Petrov, comp. Columbia: University of South Carolina Press, 1968. ISBN 0-87249-134-X. ▸ Account by Soviet historian challenging official version of initial stage of war. Blames Stalin for terror against military high command and for failure in military preparations. [HK]

35.138 Mark Von Hagen. "Soviet soldiers and officers on the eve of the German invasion: towards a description of social psychology and political attitudes." *Soviet Union/Union Sovietique* 18.1–3 (1991) 79–101. ISSN 0094-2863. ▸ Psychological analysis of Soviet military forces' combat readiness based on new archival data. Reveals many negative attitudes but emphasizes patriotism of soldiers. [HK]

35.139 V. N. Zemskov. "Massovoe osvobozhdenie spetsposelentsev i ssyl'nykh (1954–1960 gg.) (The mass release of special deportees and exiles [1954–1960])." *Sotsiologicheskie issledovaniia* (Sociological studies) 18.1 (1991) 5–26. ISSN 0132-1625. ▸ Valuable statistical analysis of deportees and exiles according to ethnic, political, and other criteria. Based on secret police documents still inaccessible to foreign historians. [HK]

35.140 E. Zubkova. "Obshchestvennaia atmosfera posle voiny (1945–1946) (The social atmosphere after the war [1945–1946])." *Svobodnaia mysl'* (Free thought) 2.6 (1992) 4–14. ISSN 0131-1212. ▸ Study emphasizing strong antiregime moods within context of extremely harsh material conditions. Examination of reasons why they failed to lead to reform. [HK]

SEE ALSO
48.248 Alexander Dallin. *German rule in Russia, 1941–1945.*

Stalin's Last Years and Beyond

35.141 George W. Breslauer. *Khrushchev and Brezhnev as leaders: building authority in Soviet politics.* London: Allen & Unwin, 1982. ISBN 0-04-329040-X (cl), 0-04-329041-8 (pbk). ▸ Sophisticated analysis and comparison of two Soviet leaders, their styles and self-images, political priorities, and handling of political elite. [AD/DKR]

35.142 Communist Party of the Soviet Union, Central Committee, ed. *History of the Communist party of the Soviet Union (Bolsheviks): a short course.* 1939 ed. Westport, Conn.: Greenwood, 1975. ISBN 0-8371-8018-X. ▸ Famous (or infamous) "Short Course," whose authorship was later (falsely) claimed by Joseph Stalin. Hardly reliable historical account, but rather guide to what Stalin wanted world to believe. [AD]

35.143 Robert Conquest. *Power and policy in the U.S.S.R.: the study of Soviet dynastics.* 1961 ed. New York: St. Martin's, 1962. ▸ Ambitious, successful reconstruction of Soviet elite politics in post-Stalin years, based on close, careful reading of open sources. [AD]

35.144 Ralph Carter Elwood et al., eds. *Resolutions and decisions of the Communist party of the Soviet Union.* 5 vols. to date. Toronto: University of Toronto Press, 1974–. ISBN 0-8020-2157-3 (set). ▸ Most extensive English-language collection of Communist party documents. Careful and authoritative. [AD]

35.145 Nancy Whittier Heer. *Politics and history in the Soviet Union.* Cambridge, Mass.: MIT Press, 1971. ISBN 0-262-08045-1. ▸ Discussion, in some detail, of political function of history and history writing in Soviet Union and abuses and costs of censorship, intimidation, and self-regulation. [AD]

35.146 Ronald J. Hill and Peter Frank. *The Soviet Communist party.* 3d ed. Boston: Allen & Unwin, 1986. ISBN 0-04-497024-2 (pbk). ▸ Study tracing changes in functions and performance, structure, membership, and personnel, with extensive use of Soviet arguments and examples. [AD]

35.147 Jerry F. Hough. *The Soviet prefects: the local party organs in industrial decision-making.* Cambridge, Mass.: Harvard University Press, 1969. (Russian Research Center studies, 58.) ▸ Able analysis of day-to-day role of Communist party at local and regional levels and place in economy and administration. [AD]

35.148 Chalmers A. Johnson, ed. *Change in communist systems.* Stanford, Calif.: Stanford University Press, 1970. ISBN 0-8047-0723-5. ▸ Includes, along with other stimulating pieces, Lowenthal's essay "Development vs. Utopia in Communist policy" as emblematic of ongoing tension in Soviet system and, over time, victory of development perspective over utopian vision. [AD]

35.149 Nikita Khrushchev. *Khrushchev remembers. Khrushchev remembers: the last testament. Khrushchev remembers: the glasnost tapes.* 3 vols. Strobe Talbott and Jerrold L. Schecter, eds. and trans. Boston: Little, Brown, 1970–90. ISBN 0-316-47297-2 (1990). ▸ Edited version of thoughts and recollections of Nikita Khrushchev, taped after ouster from office in 1964 and transmitted abroad without official sanction. Some important insights. [AD]

35.150 Carl A. Linden. *Khrushchev and the Soviet leadership, with an epilogue on Gorbachev.* Rev. ed. Baltimore: Johns Hopkins University Press, 1990. ISBN 0-8018-4008-2 (cl), 0-8018-4009-0 (pbk). ▸ Careful study showing presence of contending strains within Soviet leadership after Stalin, ultimately leading to Nikita Khrushchev's ouster. [AD]

35.151 Leonard Bertram Schapiro. *The Communist party of the Soviet Union.* 1970 2d ed. New York: Random House, 1971. ISBN 0-394-70745-1. ▸ Standard Western account of history of Russian Communist party for generations of students. Based on superb knowledge of sources but also, in retrospect, excessive belief in party's homogeneity and effectiveness. [AD]

35.152 Michel Tatu. *Power in the Kremlin: from Khrushchev to Kosygin.* 1968 ed. Helen Katel, trans. New York: Viking, 1970. ISBN 0-670-57028-1 (cl), 0-670-00282-8 (pbk). ‣ Study of dynamics of Soviet politics in post-Stalin period as observed and analyzed by Moscow correspondent of *Le Monde.* May be best "Kremlinological" analysis. [AD]

35.153 Robert C. Tucker, ed. *Stalinism: essays in historical interpretation.* New York: Norton, 1977. ISBN 0-393-05608-2. ‣ Collection of sophisticated essays by prominent experts, seeking to define Stalinism and place it in appropriate historical context, be it Russian or Leninist. [AD]

Gorbachev and the End of Soviet Power

35.154 John B. Dunlop. *The rise of Russia and the fall of the Soviet empire.* Princeton: Princeton University Press, 1993. ISBN 0-691-07875-0. ‣ Detailed study of Russian nationalism and question of Russian national identity as they developed and intersected with Gorbachev's reforms and subsequent demise of Soviet Union. Superb analysis of parties and groups. Argues that re-creation of Russia was instrumental in politics leading to Gorbachev's fall and rise of Yeltsin. [DTO]

35.155 Ed A. Hewett. *Reforming the Soviet economy: equality versus efficiency.* Washington, D.C.: Brookings Institution, 1988. ISBN 0-8157-3604-5 (cl), 0-8157-3603-7 (pbk). ‣ Excellent structural analysis of Soviet economy and of various reform efforts of 1950s through major reforms under Gorbachev. Especially insightful in its weighing of formal aspects against actual operations of economy and reforms themselves. [DTO]

35.156 Geoffrey A. Hosking. *The awakening of the Soviet Union.* Rev. ed. Cambridge, Mass.: Harvard University Press, 1991. ISBN 0-674-05551-9 (pbk). ‣ Well-balanced survey of Gorbachev years flavored by optimism of early reforms under *perestroika.* Organized thematically. [DTO]

35.157 Stephen Kotkin. *Steeltown, USSR: Soviet society in the Gorbachev era.* Berkeley: University of California Press, 1992. ISBN 0-520-07354-1 (pbk). ‣ Masterly account of impact and actual workings of *perestroika* on society and politics of famous steel-producing complex and city built by Stalin from scratch at beginning of his industrialization drive. Based on extensive interviews and observations. Important corrective to overly idealistic or abstract portrayals of Gorbachev's reforms. [DTO]

35.158 David Remnick. *Lenin's tomb: the last days of the Soviet empire.* New York: Random House, 1993. ISBN 0-679-42376-1. ‣ Pulitzer prize–winning reportage of background and events surrounding August 1991 coup and breakup of Soviet Union. Emphasizes rediscovery of history as motor force in events leading to coup. Rich in personal testimony from across political and cultural landscape. [DTO]

35.159 Richard Sakwa. *Gorbachev and his reforms, 1985–1990.* New York: Prentice-Hall, 1991. ISBN 0-13-362427-7. ‣ Detailed study of Gorbachev years emphasizing role of leadership in reform process. Positive vision of Gorbachev as "revolutionary" who set Soviet Union on path of "normal," that is, non-messianic, development. [DTO]

Foreign Policy

35.160 Max Beloff. *The foreign policy of Soviet Russia, 1929–1941.* 2 vols. London: Oxford University Press, 1947–49. ‣ Thorough, careful, inevitably without access to archival sources. Early British study; fine sequel to Fischer volumes (35.168). [AD]

35.161 Seweryn Bialer, ed. *The domestic context of Soviet foreign policy.* Boulder: Westview, 1981. ISBN 0-89158-783-7. ‣ Essays by leading specialists analyzing different dimensions of linkages between domestic and foreign conduct, including role of ideology, perceptions, and economic constraints. [AD]

35.162 George W. Breslauer and Philip E. Tetlock, eds. *Learning in U.S. and Soviet foreign policy.* Boulder: Westview, 1991. ISBN 0-8133-8264-5 (cl), 0-8133-8265-3 (pbk). ‣ Includes series of case studies of Soviet foreign policy since World War II in addition to theoretical and comparative discussions. [AD]

35.163 Feliks Chuev. *Sto sorok besed s Molotovym: iz dnevnika F. Chueva* (One hundred forty conversations with Molotov: from the diary of F. Chuev). Moscow: Terra, 1991. ISBN 5-85255-042-6. ‣ Reproduction of credible conversations with former Soviet foreign minister and Politburo member during his years of retirement by poet-author. Some valuable nuggets along with doctrinaire nonsense. [AD]

35.164 Alexander Dallin. "Stalin and the German invasion." *Soviet Union/Union Sovietique* 18.1–3 (1991) 19–37. ISSN 0094-2863. ‣ Updated analysis of Soviet diplomacy in immediate pre–World War II years based partly on new revelations by Moscow. Emphasizes Stalin's role in 1939 and 1941. [HK]

35.165 Karen Dawisha. *Eastern Europe, Gorbachev, and reform: the great challenge.* 2d ed. Cambridge: Cambridge University Press, 1990. ISBN 0-521-38498-2 (cl), 0-521-38652-7 (pbk). ‣ Reexamination of Eastern Europe in terms of continuities and changes in Soviet role and interests in region. [AD]

35.166 Jane Degras, ed. *The Communist International, 1919–1943: documents.* 1956–65 ed. 3 vols. London: Cass, 1971. ISBN 0-7146-1554-4 (v. 1), 0-7146-1555-2 (v. 2), 0-7146-1556-0 (v. 3). ‣ Authoritative collection, sponsored by Royal Institute of International Affairs, covering activities and meetings of Comintern, including links with Russian party and government. [AD]

35.167 Jane Degras, ed. *Soviet documents on foreign policy, 1917–41.* 1951–53 ed. 3 vols. New York: Octagon Books, 1978. ISBN 0-374-92096-6 (set). ‣ Valuable compendium including diplomatic notes, official statements, speeches, and press interviews. Far more complete (though still selective) Soviet series entitled: *Dokumenty vneshnei politiki SSSR* (1957–77), 21 volumes covering 1917–38. [AD]

35.168 Louis Fischer. *The Soviets in world affairs: a history of the relations between the Soviet Union and the rest of the world, 1917–1929.* 2d ed. 2 vols. Princeton: Princeton University Press, 1951. ‣ Early but still valuable account by journalist-researcher with good access to Soviet leaders, including Foreign Minister George Chicherin. [AD]

35.169 John Lewis Gaddis. *Russia, the Soviet Union, and the United States: an interpretive history.* 2d ed. New York: McGraw-Hill, 1990. ISBN 0-07-557258-3. ‣ Compact, well-written synthesis of Soviet-American relations, stressing interplay of interests and ideologies. Based on solid research. [AD]

35.170 Alexander L. George. *Managing U.S.–Soviet rivalry: problems of crisis prevention.* Boulder: Westview, 1983. ISBN 0-86531-500-0 (cl), 0-86531-501-9 (pbk). ‣ Important framework and solid case studies, including rise and fall of detente, arms control negotiations, and regional conflicts. [AD]

35.171 Galia Golan. *The Soviet Union and national liberation movements in the Third World.* Boston: Unwin Hyman, 1988. ISBN 0-04-445111-3. ‣ Insightful study of Soviet theoretical disputes and patterns of behavior by prominent specialist. See also her *Soviet Policies in the Middle East: From World War II to Gorbachev* (1990). [AD]

35.172 Andrei Gromyko. *Memoirs.* Harold Shukman, trans. New York: Doubleday, 1989. ISBN 0-385-41288-6. ‣ Memoirs of long-term foreign minister. Revealing, useful, yet overall disappointing and marked by lack of candor. [AD]

35.173 Andrei Gromyko and B. N. Ponomarev, eds. *Soviet foreign policy, 1917–1980.* 4th rev. ed. 2 vols. Moscow: Progress, 1981. ▸ Detailed official Soviet history of Soviet foreign policy with no effort at balance. More valuable for public presentation than for motives of Soviet behavior. [AD]

35.174 Jonathan Haslam. "Soviet foreign policy, 1939–1941: isolation and expansion." *Soviet Union/Union Sovietique* 18.1–3 (1991) 103–21. ISSN 0094-2863. ▸ Traditional diplomatic history, incorporating new revelations by Moscow. Emphasizes Stalin's personality and ideology. [HK]

35.175 Robbin F. Laird and Erik P. Hoffman, eds. *Soviet foreign policy in a changing world.* Hawthorne, N.Y.: Aldine, 1986. ISBN 0-202-24166-1 (cl), 0-202-24167-X (pbk). ▸ Comprehensive collection of essays exploring evolution of many facets of Soviet foreign policy in Eastern and Western Europe and Third World, as well as arms control. [AD]

35.176 Ivo J. Lederer. *Russian foreign policy: essays in historical perspective.* New Haven: Yale University Press, 1962. ▸ Essays by specialists comparing Russian foreign policy in tsarist and Soviet periods. Stimulating, informative, but at times debatable. [AD]

35.177 Margot Light. *The Soviet theory of international relations.* New York: St. Martin's, 1988. ISBN 0-312-01889-4 (cl), 0-312-01891-6 (pbk). ▸ Analysis of theoretical framework and its evolution governing public presentation of Soviet view of world affairs and at least some internal debates over it. [AD]

35.178 Richard Lowenthal. *World communism: the disintegration of a secular faith.* New York: Oxford University Press, 1964. ▸ Expert examination of conflicts in international movement and their impact on communist beliefs and conduct; includes Stalin-Tito split, East European crises, and Sino-Soviet rift. [AD]

35.179 Michael J. Sodaro. *Moscow, Germany, and the West from Khrushchev to Gorbachev.* Ithaca, N.Y.: Cornell University Press, 1990. ISBN 0-8014-2529-8 (cl), 0-8014-9762-0 (pbk). ▸ Sophisticated reconstruction of Soviet policy toward Germany based on prodigious research and some good guesses. [AD]

35.180 Thomas Wolfe. *The SALT experience.* Cambridge, Mass.. Ballinger, 1979. ISBN 0-88410-079-0. ▸ Balanced, informed analysis of SALT I and II diplomacy, examining conflicting objectives and technical capabilities. [AD]

35.181 Donald S. Zagoria. *The Sino-Soviet conflict, 1956–1961.* 1962 ed. New York: Atheneum, 1964. ▸ Early, painstaking effort to find course of Sino-Soviet relationship and disputed issues in public print, broadcasts, and official statements. Stands up well, though incomplete in light of later sources. [AD]

35.182 William Zimmerman. *Soviet perspectives on international relations, 1956–1967.* Princeton: Princeton University Press, 1969. ▸ Astute examination of assumptions underlying Soviet foreign policy analysis and behavior and changes in post-Stalin era. [AD]

SEE ALSO

NATIONALITIES AND NATIONAL IDENTITIES

35.183 Alexandre A. Bennigsen and S. Enders Wimbush. *Muslim national communism in the Soviet Union: a revolutionary strategy for the colonial world.* 1979 ed. Chicago: Chicago University Press, 1980. (Publications of the Center for Middle Eastern Studies, 11.) ISBN 0-226-04235-9 (cl, 1979), 0-226-04236-7 (pbk). ▸ Study of national communism among Soviet Muslims in 1920s focusing on life and work of Volga Tatar, Mir-Said Sultan Galiev. Attempts to understand attraction of Marxism to Muslims. [RGS]

35.184 Hélène Carrère d'Encausse. *The great challenge: nationalities and the bolshevik state, 1917–1930.* Nancy Festinger, trans. Richard Pipes, Foreword. New York: Holmes & Meier, 1992. ISBN 0-8419-1285-8. ▸ Discussion of application of Marxist-Leninist theory of nationalities in 1920s. Detailed treatment of national communisms and cultural revolution. Largely political, rather than social or ethnographic study. [RGS]

35.185 Walker Connor. *The national question in Marxist-Leninist theory and strategy.* Princeton: Princeton University Press, 1984. ISBN 0-691-07655-3 (cl), 0-691-10163-9 (pbk). ▸ Comprehensive investigation of Marxism's applications in field of ethnic relations in Soviet Union, Yugoslavia, Vietnam, and China. Explains effects of policy of regional cultural autonomy. [RGS]

35.186 Robert Conquest, ed. *Soviet nationalities policy in practice.* New York: Praeger, 1967. ▸ Brief account of theory and practice of Soviet nationalities policies. Very unsympathetic to Soviet practices. [RGS]

35.187 Zvi Y. Gitelman. *Jewish nationality and Soviet politics: the Jewish sections of the CPSU, 1917–1930.* Princeton: Princeton University Press, 1972. ISBN 0-691-07542-5. ▸ Detailed monographic study of Jews in period of Revolution and New Economic Policy. Discusses effects of contradictory policies of integration into Soviet system and cultural revival. Important study of first decade of Soviet nationality policies. [RGS]

35.188 Steven Guthier. "The popular base of Ukrainian nationalism in 1917." *Slavic review* 38.1 (1979) 30–47. ISSN 0037-6779. ▸ Argues voting for Ukrainian parties demonstrated widespread sense of nationality among Ukrainians in 1917. [RGS]

35.189 Lubomyr Hajda and Mark Beissinger, eds. *The nationalities factor in Soviet politics and society.* Boulder: Westview, 1990. ISBN 0-8133-7689-0 (cl), 0-8133-1067-9 (pbk). ▸ Collection of essays by historians, political scientists, and economists on peoples of Soviet Union in Gorbachev period. Analytic, interpretive chapters treat various regions and problems. [RGS]

35.190 Richard G. Hovannisian. *The Republic of Armenia.* 2 vols. to date. Berkeley: University of California Press, 1971. ISBN 0-520-01805-2 (v. 1), 0-520-04186-0 (v. 2). ▸ Encyclopedic treatment of short-lived Armenian republic, 1918–20. Definitive discussion of politics and foreign policy of independent Armenia. [RGS]

35.191 Caroline Humphrey. *Karl Marx collective: economy, society, and religion in a Siberian collective farm.* Cambridge and Paris: Cambridge University Press and Éditions de la Maison des Sciences de l'Homme, 1983. ISBN 0-521-24456-0 (cl), 0-521-27401-X (pbk). ▸ Ethnographic study of Buryats of Siberia, based on field work on collective farms. Explores social relations, religious mentalities, and necessary adjustments to Soviet reality. [RGS]

35.192 Rasma Karklins. *Ethnic relations in the USSR: the perspective from below.* Boston: Allen & Unwin, 1986. ISBN 0-04-323028-8. ▸ Explores self-consciousness of non-Russians in late Soviet period, using Soviet ethnosociological studies. Excellent analysis of popular attitudes toward ethnicity and environment shaping those attitudes. [RGS]

35.193 Firuz Kazemzadeh. *The struggle for Transcaucasia, 1917–*

1921. Michael Karpovich, Introduction. New York: Philosophical Library, 1951. ‣ Classic account of Revolution in Transcaucasia. Balanced and detailed, model of political history. [RGS]

35.194 Bohdan Krawchenko. *Social change and national consciousness in twentieth-century Ukraine.* New York: St. Martin's, 1985. ISBN 0-312-73160-4. ‣ Study of national formation of Ukraine in Russian empire and Soviet Union. Social historical investigation of consolidation of Ukrainian nationality and counterpressures of empire. [RGS]

35.195 W. Bruce Lincoln. *The conquest of a continent: Siberia and the Russians.* New York: Random House, 1994. ISBN 0-679-41214-X. ‣ Broad pioneering survey of vast geographical, cultural, and symbolic space known as Siberia in history of Russia. Raises issue of regionalism and its fate in Russian Revolution and under Soviet regime. [DTO]

35.196 Irina Livezeanu. "Moldavia, 1917–1990: nationalism and internationalism then and now." *Armenian review* 43.2–3/170–71 (1990) 153–93. ISSN 0004-2366. ‣ Discussion of formation of Moldavian nationality in twentieth century, under both Romanian and Soviet rule. Nuanced treatment of variety of orientations to be found in current Moldovan debates. [RGS]

35.197 Michael Lowy. "Marxists and the national question." *New Left review* 96 (March–April 1976) 81–100. ISSN 0028-6060. ‣ Perceptive article on early Marxist writings on nationality. Critical review of Stalin's contribution to Soviet formulation of national question. [RGS]

35.198 Nancy Lubin. *Labour and nationality in Soviet Central Asia: an uneasy compromise.* Princeton: Princeton University Press, 1984. ISBN 0-691-07674-X. ‣ Discussion of demographic problems, labor shortages, and ethnic tensions in Soviet Central Asia. Cool, perceptive treatment of major sources of conflict and discontent; based on fieldwork in region. [RGS]

35.199 James E. Mace. *Communism and the dilemmas of national liberation: national communism in Soviet Ukraine, 1918–1933.* Cambridge, Mass.: Harvard Ukrainian Research Institute and Ukrainian Academy of Arts and Sciences in the United States; distributed by Harvard University Press, 1983. ISBN 0-674-14875-4, 0-916458-09-1. ‣ Monographic study of rise and fall of national communism in Ukraine in 1920s. Shows literary and political influences on consolidation of Ukrainian national consciousness under Soviets. [RGS]

35.200 Michael Mandelbaum, ed. *The rise of nations in the Soviet Union: American foreign policy and the disintegration of the USSR.* New York: Council on Foreign Relations, 1991. ISBN 0-87609-100-1. ‣ Essays on collapse of central Soviet authority and its impact on non-Russian peoples. Recommendations for American foreign policy at end of Gorbachev period. [RGS]

35.201 Mary Kilbourne Matossian. *The impact of Soviet policies in Armenia.* 1962 ed. Westport, Conn.: Hyperion, 1981. ISBN 0-8305-0081-2. ‣ Historical study of Soviet Armenia in its first forty years. Treats political elite, demographic and economic changes, cultural life, and effects of Soviet imperial control. Clear, effective survey. [RGS]

35.202 Alexander J. Motyl. *Sovietology, rationality, nationality: coming to grips with nationalism in the USSR.* New York: Columbia University Press, 1990. ISBN 0-231-07326-7. ‣ Discussion of political science theory, its uses and abuses in Sovietology, and crisis of Soviet state. Highly original analysis, with special expertise on Ukraine. [RGS]

35.203 Aleksandr Nekrich. *The punished peoples: the deportation and fate of Soviet minorities at the end of the Second World War.* George Saunders, trans. New York: Norton, 1978. ISBN 0-393-05646-5. ‣ Story of nationalities deported as collaborators by Stalin from their historic homelands to Central Asia. Examination of nationality practices of Stalin by Soviet scholar in West. [RGS/HK]

35.204 Richard Pipes. *The formation of the Soviet Union: communism and nationalism, 1917–1923.* 1964 rev. ed. Cambridge, Mass.: Harvard University Press, 1980. (Russian Research Center studies, 13.) ISBN 0-674-30950-2. ‣ Classic study of non-Russian peoples in period of Revolution and Civil War. Thorough treatment of political conflicts between nationalists and Bolsheviks. Sympathetic to nationalists and antagonistic to Communists. [RGS]

35.205 Toivo U. Raun. *Estonia and the Estonians.* Stanford, Calif.: Hoover Institution Press, 1987. (Hoover Press publication, 351.) ISBN 0-8179-8511-5 (cl), 0-8179-8512-3 (pbk). ‣ Comprehensive history of Estonians from prehistoric times to 1980s, with emphasis on last 200 years. Careful, dispassionate treatment of problems of small ethnicities within Soviet Union. [RGS]

35.206 Roman Serbyn and Bohdan Krawchenko, eds. *Famine in Ukraine, 1932–1933.* Edmonton: University of Alberta, Canadian Institute of Ukrainian Studies; distributed by University of Toronto Press, 1986. ISBN 0-920862-43-8. ‣ Collection of articles defending controversial thesis that man-made famine in Ukraine, 1932–33, was engineered by Stalin against Ukrainian nationalists. Compares with 1921–23 famine. [RGS]

35.207 Gerhard Simon. *Nationalism and policy toward the nationalities in the Soviet Union: from totalitarian dictatorship to post-Stalinist society.* Karen Forster and Oswald Forster, trans. Boulder: Westview, 1991. ISBN 0-8133-7494-4. ‣ Comprehensive, authoritative treatment of Soviet policy toward non-Russian peoples from Stalin period to mid-1980s. [RGS/AD]

35.208 Ronald Grigor Suny. *The Baku commune, 1917–1918: class and nationality in the Russian Revolution.* Princeton: Princeton University Press, 1972. ISBN 0-691-05193-3. ‣ Microstudy of Revolution in oil-producing center of Russian empire where relatively moderate Bolsheviks controlled soviets. Examination of overlapping conflicts of class and ethnicity. [RGS]

35.209 Ronald Grigor Suny. *Looking toward Ararat: the Armenians in modern history.* Bloomington: Indiana University Press, 1993. ISBN 0-253-35583-4 (cl), 0-253-20773-8 (pbk). ‣ Collection of essays on formation of modern Armenian national consciousness. Explores how traditions were invented, passed down, and modified in making of nations. [RGS]

35.210 Ronald Grigor Suny. *The revenge of the past: nationalism, revolution, and the collapse of the Soviet Union.* Stanford, Calif.: Stanford University Press, 1993. ISBN 0-8047-2134-3 (cl), 0-8047-2247-1 (pbk). ‣ Theoretically informed essays on class and nationality, nationality question in 1917 Revolution, Soviet experience, and Gorbachev's dilemmas. [DTO]

35.211 Ronald Grigor Suny, ed. *Transcaucasia, nationalism, and social change: essays in the history of Armenia, Azerbaijan, and Georgia.* Ann Arbor: University of Michigan Press, 1983. ‣ Essays by specialists on history, demography, economics, and politics of Transcaucasia. First volume dedicated to region as a whole. [RGS]

35.212 Nicholas P. Vakar. *Belorussia: the making of a nation, a case study.* Cambridge, Mass.: Harvard University Press, 1956. (Russian Research Center studies, 21.) ‣ Historical treatment of formation of Belorussian ethnic distinction and evolution of Belorusian republic within Soviet Union. Fullest study to date of Belorusian Soviet Socialist Republic. [RGS]

SEE ALSO

ECONOMIC HISTORY

Peasantry and the Agrarian Question

35.213 Helmut Altrichter. *Die Bauern von Tver: vom Leben auf dem russischen Dorfe zwischen Revolution und Kollektivierung.* Munich: Oldenbourg, 1984. ISBN 3-486-52071-7. ▸ Regional social history of society, economy, and politics of Tver countryside, emphasizing endurance of peasant culture and traditions. Discusses destruction of peasant agriculture in collectivization. [LV]

35.214 Dorothy Atkinson. *The end of the Russian land commune, 1905–1930.* Stanford, Calif.: Stanford University Press, 1983. ISBN 0-8047-1148-8. ▸ Traditional institutional summary of agrarian reforms and role and function of commune in peasant society and economy. Discusses minimal impact of Stolypin reforms, resurgence of commune after 1917, and its destruction with collectivization. Stresses endurance of peasant culture and institutions in face of state efforts at modernization and change. [LV/JCB]

35.215 Fedor Belov. *The history of a Soviet collective farm.* New York: Praeger for Research Program on the U.S.S.R., 1955. (Studies of the Research Program on the U.S.S.R., 13.) ▸ Memoir of post–World War II collective farming by collective farm chair who later defected from Soviet Union. Picture of official neglect and farm administration wheeling and dealing to survive. Highlights failure of communist ideology and triumph of bureaucratic ingenuity. [LV]

35.216 A. V. Chayanov. *The theory of peasant economy.* Daniel Thorner, Basile Kerblay, and R.E.F. Smith, eds. Madison: University of Wisconsin Press, 1986. ISBN 0-299-10570-9. ▸ Study of peasant household as basic unit of village economy, emphasizing multidirectional and cyclical socioeconomic mobility of peasant family within precapitalist rural order. Major challenger to 1920s Marxist studies of rural class polarization. [LV]

35.217 Robert Conquest. *The harvest of sorrow: Soviet collectivization and the terror-famine.* New York: Oxford University Press, 1986. ISBN 0-19-504054-6. ▸ Conservative study of Ukrainian famine of 1932–33, representing Ukrainian nationalist viewpoint. Sees deliberate policy of genocide aimed against recalcitrant Ukrainian peasantry and Ukrainian nationalism. [LV]

35.218 Terry Cox. *Peasants, class, and capitalism: the rural research of L. N. Kritsman and his school.* Oxford: Clarendon, 1986. ISBN 0-19-878014-1. ▸ Survey of 1920s Marxist research on Russian peasantry. Portrays Kritsman school as dynamic researchers, rather than dogmatists of anti-Marxist literature. Research based on class analysis of village suggesting gradual social polarization. [LV]

35.219 Terry Cox and Gary Littlejohn, eds. *Kritsman and the agrarian Marxists.* London: Cass, 1984. ISBN 0-7146-3237-6. ▸ Essays on research of L. N. Kritsman's Marxist approach to rural sociology in 1920s, with scholarly commentary. Analysis of socioeconomic relations among peasant households as basis of understanding class dynamics of village. [LV]

35.220 V. P. Danilov. *Rural Russia under the new regime.* Orlando Figes, trans. Bloomington and London: Indiana University Press and Hutchinson, 1988. ISBN 0-253-35075-1. ▸ Social history of Russian peasantry in 1920s, discussing population, social stratification, land use, and economy. Sees family as basis of peasant economy in precapitalist countryside. Concludes that despite optimal conditions for peasant agriculture in 1920s, potential limited; collectivization premature. [LV]

35.221 R. W. Davies. *The socialist offensive: the collectivisation of Soviet agriculture 1929–1930.* Vol. 1 of *The industrialisation of Soviet Russia.* Cambridge, Mass.: Harvard University Press, 1980. ISBN 0-674-81480-0. ▸ Examination of background, policy, and implementation of collectivization. Sees collectivization as result of interplay of central, regional, and local Communist party initiatives and actions. Challenges traditional top-down view of Stalinist politics. [LV]

35.222 R. W. Davies. *The Soviet collective farm, 1929–1930.* Vol. 2 of *The industrialisation of Soviet Russia.* Cambridge, Mass.: Harvard University Press, 1980. ISBN 0-674-82600-0. ▸ Study of development and organization of collective farm economy, with attention to structure of farms, machine-tractor stations, and socialization of property, labor, and income. Emphasizes improvisational nature of policy implementation in early years of collectivization. [LV]

35.223 Beatrice Farnsworth. "Village women experience the Revolution." In *Bolshevik culture: experiment and order in the Russian Revolution.* Abbott Gleason, Peter Kenez, and Richard Stites, eds., pp. 238–60. Bloomington: Indiana University Press, 1985. ISBN 0-253-31206-X. ▸ Study of Russian peasant women in 1920s, focusing on failure of communist emancipatory goals for village women. Finds persistence of female privatism in form of women's economic role in domestic economy and vested interest in private property. [LV]

35.224 Harold H. Fisher. *The famine in Soviet Russia, 1919–1923: the operations of the American Relief Administration.* 1927 ed. Freeport, N.Y.: Books for Libraries, 1971. ISBN 0-8369-5650-8. ▸ Firsthand account of American relief efforts in Russian post–Civil War famine. Discusses impact of Revolution and Civil War on peasantry. [LV]

35.225 Sigrid Grosskopf. *L'alliance ouvrière et paysanne en U.R.S.S., 1921–1928: le problème du blé.* Paris: Maspero, 1976. ISBN 2-7071-0838-3. ▸ Analysis of agrarian policy in 1920s, focusing on party politics and grain procurement crisis. Sees New Economic Policy as failed alternative. [LV]

35.226 Werner G. Hahn. *The politics of Soviet agriculture, 1960–1970.* Baltimore: Johns Hopkins University Press, 1972. ISBN 0-8018-1359-X. ▸ Examination of formation of agricultural policy under Nikita Khrushchev and during early Brezhnev period. Discusses conflicts among leaders and between center and periphery over development of agricultural policies. Conflict theory approach. [LV]

35.227 Maurice Hindus. *Red bread: collectivization in a Russian village.* 1931 ed. Bloomington: Indiana University Press, 1988. ISBN 0-253-34953-2 (cl), 0-253-20485-2 (pbk). ▸ Firsthand account of collectivization in author's native village. Dispassionate description of peasants' reactions to communist policies of First Five-Year Plan era. [LV]

35.228 James Hughes. *Stalin, Siberia, and the crisis of the New Economic Policy.* Cambridge: Cambridge University Press, 1991. ISBN 0-521-38039-1. ▸ Regional, revisionist study of Siberian agriculture and politics in 1920s. Notes large *kulak* (wealthy peasants) stratum in Siberia and moderate rural Communist party favoring New Economic Policy. Concludes Stalin generalized on basis of Siberian conditions in decision to collectivize. [LV]

35.229 Naum Jasny. *The socialized agriculture of the USSR: plans and performance.* 1949 ed. Stanford, Calif.: Stanford University Press, 1967. (Grain economic series of the Food Research Institute of Stanford University, 5.) ▸ Survey of agricultural development and policy, examining central role of Communist party and failure of collectivized agriculture. Traditional account, statistically oriented. [LV]

35.230 Esther Kingston-Mann. *Lenin and the problem of Marxist peasant revolution.* New York: Oxford University Press, 1983. ISBN 0-19-503278-0. ▸ Revisionist examination of Lenin's adaptation of Marxist theory to agrarian Russia and peasant revolt. Theoretical reworking allows Lenin flexibility in tactics and program to seize initiative in 1917. Relevant to Third World studies. [LV]

35.231 P. I. Kushner, ed. *The village of Viriatino: an ethnographic study of a Russian village from before the Revolution to the present.* Sula Benet, ed. and trans. Garden City, N.Y.: Anchor, 1970. ▸ Soviet ethnographic account spanning Revolution. Examines impact of urban ways on village. Finds endurance of key features of peasant culture. [LV]

35.232 Moshe Lewin. *The making of the Soviet system: essays in the social history of interwar Russia.* New York: Pantheon, 1985. ISBN 0-394-54302-5 (cl), 0-394-72900-5 (pbk). ▸ Collection of revisionist' essays on topics in Soviet social history, 1917–41. Emphasis on peasantry and rural policies. New Economic Policy as alternative to Stalinism; postrevolutionary disintegration of classes as social context for emergence of Stalinist leviathan state. [LV]

35.233 Moshe Lewin. *Russian peasants and Soviet power: a study of collectivization.* 1968 ed. Irene Nove, trans. New York: Norton, 1975. ISBN 0-393-00752-9. ▸ Revisionist analysis of social structure, economics, and politics of precollectivization peasantry and Communist party rural policies, seeing New Economic Policy as alternative to Stalinism. Finds ideological inability to adapt to New Economic Policy in countryside. [LV]

35.234 D. J. Male. *Russian peasant organisation before collectivisation: a study of commune and gathering, 1925–1930.* Cambridge: Cambridge University Press, 1971. ISBN 0-521-07884-9. ▸ Study of state-peasant relations under New Economic Policy. Finds minimal impact of Revolution on peasant institutions and culture; commune dominated village politics and acted as obstacle to party's economic and ideological goals. [LV/DKR]

35.235 Roberta Thompson Manning. *Government in the Soviet countryside in the Stalinist thirties: the case of Belyi Raion in 1937.* Pittsburgh: University of Pittsburgh, Russian and East European Studies Program, 1984. (Carl Beck papers in Russian and East European studies, 301.) ▸ Case study of local administration in rural district based on Smolensk archives, revealing undergovernment, ineffective Communist party and government controls, and backwardness. Revisionist account challenging totalitarian model of Soviet politics. [LV]

35.236 Zhores A. Medvedev. *Soviet agriculture.* New York: Norton, 1987. ISBN 0-393-02472-5. ▸ Survey of history of Soviet agriculture to present. Examines centrality of agriculture to economics and politics, and failure of socialized agriculture, lost alternatives, and potential of privatization. Traditional, but balanced account. [LV]

35.237 Stephan Merl. *Der Agrarmarkt und die Neue Ökonomische Politik: die Anfänge staatlicher Lenkung der Landwirtschaft in der Sowjetunion, 1925–1928.* Munich: Oldenbourg, 1981. ISBN 3-486-50021-X. ▸ Revisionist work on rural policy under New Economic Policy. Discusses political and economic development of rural policy in 1920s; documents government's failure to pursue Lenin's cooperative plan seriously and chronic underfunding of agriculture. [LV]

35.238 Stephan Merl. *Die Anfänge der Kollektivierung in der Sowjetunion: der Übergang zur staatlichen Reglementierung der Produktions- und Marktbeziehungen im Dorf (1928–1930).* Wiesbaden: Harrassowitz, 1985. (Veröffentlichungen des Osteuropa-

Institutes München, Reihe: Geschichte, 52.) ISBN 3-447-02507-7. ▸ Examination of state policies and actions in grain procurement crisis and first phase of collectivization. Concludes funding problems, shortages of farm machinery, and mismanagement of early collectives made failure of collectivization inevitable. Stresses alternatives to collectivization. [LV]

35.239 James R. Millar and Alec Nove. "A debate on collectivization: was Stalin really necessary?" *Problems of communism* 25 (July–August 1976) 49–62. ISSN 0032-941. ▸ Study of relation of collectivization to industrialization, 1928–32. Examines traditional view of collectivization as capital accumulation process versus revisionist view of failure of collectivization to free up capital for industrialization. [LV]

35.240 Robert F. Miller. *One hundred thousand tractors: the MTS and the development of controls in Soviet agriculture.* Cambridge, Mass.: Harvard University Press, 1970. (Russian Research Center studies, 60.) ISBN 0-674-63875-1. ▸ Study of establishment of machine tractor stations and their relation to local rural administration in 1930s, examining interaction of economic, political, and ideological factors in policy making and implementation. Stresses situational factors and, to lesser extent, conflict model. [LV/DKR]

35.241 William Moskoff. *The bread of affliction: the food supply in the USSR during World War II.* Cambridge: Cambridge University Press, 1990. (Soviet and East European studies, 76.) ISBN 0-521-37499-5. ▸ Study of agriculture and food supply during war. Concludes decentralization of production and distribution and rise of private initiative replaced centralized agricultural economy. Sees morale and patriotism as motivating factor that spurred food production and supply. [LV/HK]

35.242 Olga A. Narkiewicz. *The making of the Soviet state apparatus.* Manchester: Manchester University Press, 1970. ISBN 0-7190-0401-2. ▸ Study of policy and administration in countryside in 1920s. Analyzes basic conflict of town versus countryside and urban Communist party in agrarian nation and dilemmas of New Economic Policy. Sees collectivization as emergency response to peasant resistance brought about by grain requisitions. [LV]

35.243 Sidney I. Ploss. *Conflict and decision-making in Soviet Russia: a case study of agricultural policy, 1953–1963.* Princeton: Princeton University Press, 1965. ▸ Analysis of agricultural policy and reform in Khrushchev period. Examines factions in Communist party leadership (neo-Stalinists and moderates) and their impact on decision making. Conflict model approach. [LV]

35.244 Teodor Shanin. *The awkward class: political sociology of peasantry in a developing society, Russia, 1910–1925.* Oxford: Clarendon, 1972. ISBN 0-19-821493-6. ▸ Social and political analysis of Russian peasantry based on theories of A. V. Chayanov (35.216). Multidirectional mobility of peasant households due to changing size of families and family partitions prevents sociopolitical polarization. Challenges Marxist paradigm. [LV]

35.245 Susan Gross Solomon. *The Soviet agrarian debate: a controversy in social science, 1923–1929.* Boulder: Westview, 1977. ISBN 0-89158-339-4. ▸ Revisionist assessment of rural sociology in 1920s, focusing on debate between schools of L. N. Kritsman (see Cox and Littlejohn, eds. 35.219) and of A. V. Chayanov (35.216). Finds cultural pluralism during New Economic Policy permitted development of alternative approaches to rural sociology. [LV]

35.246 Yuzuru Taniuchi. *The village gathering in Russia in the mid-1920s.* R.E.F. Smith, ed. Birmingham: University of Birmingham, 1968. (Soviet and East European monographs, 1.) ▸ Peasant commune during New Economic Policy. Discusses failure of rural soviets, endurance of traditional communal administration. Finds minimal communist impact in countryside despite regime's attempt to begin collectivization from below using traditional peasant institutions and conflict of Marxist class scheme with rural realities. [LV]

35.247 Daniel Thorniley. *The rise and fall of the Soviet rural Communist party, 1927–39.* New York: St. Martin's, 1988. ISBN 0-312-01360-4. ‣ Analysis of structure, composition, and activities of rural Communist party. Finds chaotic organization, ineffective central control, and undergovernment of countryside. Challenges traditional view of monolithic rural party under Moscow's complete control. [LV]

35.248 Lynne Viola. *"Bab'i bunty* and peasant women's protest during collectivization." *Russian review* 45.1 (1986) 23–42. ISSN 0036-0341. ‣ Analysis of women's resistance to Communist party's rural policies. Sees women's actions as rational, conscious political acts carried out under guise of party's image of women as irrational and apolitical. Designed as stratagem of peasant protest. [LV]

35.249 Lynne Viola. *The best sons of the fatherland: workers in the vanguard of Soviet collectivization.* New York: Oxford University Press, 1987. ISBN 0-19-504134-8. ‣ Revisionist assessment of sociopolitical dynamics of collectivization focusing on industrial workers and collectivization. Examines mobilization of social support for First Five-Year Plan and interplay of central, regional, and local initiatives in implementation of collectivization. Revisionist assessment of sociopolitical dynamics of collectivization. [LV]

35.250 Nicolas Werth. *La vie quotidienne des paysans Russes de la Revolution à la collectivisation, 1917–1939.* Paris: Hachette, 1984. ISBN 2-01-008678-3. ‣ Bottom-up history of politics, society, and culture of peasantry. Finds coexistence of old and new after revolution and sees collectivization as end of traditional peasant culture. [LV]

SEE ALSO
34.161 George Yaney. *The urge to mobilize.*

Labor

35.251 Vladimir Andrle. *Workers in Stalin's Russia: industrialization and social change in a planned economy.* Hemel Hempstead, England, and New York: Harvester Wheatsheaf and St. Martin's, 1988. ISBN 0-312-02390-1. ‣ Treatment of interactions between social processes of industrial work, mobilization politics, and managerial bureaucracies in historical sociological terms. Analyzes workers' adaptive behaviors. [LS]

35.252 John Barber. "The standard of living of Soviet industrial workers, 1928-1941." In *L'industrialisation de l'URSS dans les années trente: actes de la table ronde organisée par le Centre d'Études des Modes d'Industrialisation de l'École des Hautes Études en Sciences Sociales (10 et 11 décembre 1981).* Charles Bettelheim, ed., pp. 109–22. Paris: École des Hautes Études en Sciences Sociales, 1982. (Recherches d'histoire et de sciences sociales, 5.) ISBN 2-7132-0812-2. ‣ Examination of fluctuations in standard of living based on time-budget studies of working-class families in Moscow and Leningrad. Emphasizes sexual division of labor within working-class household. [LS]

35.253 James Bunyan, ed. *The origin of forced labor in the Soviet state, 1917–1921: documents and materials.* Baltimore and Stanford, Calif.: Johns Hopkins University Press and Hoover Institution on War, Revolution, and Peace, 1967. ‣ Collection of documents on militarization of labor, establishment of forced labor camps, and other restrictive regimes during Civil War period. Editorialized in language of cold war. [LS]

35.254 William J. Chase. *Workers, society, and the Soviet state: labor and life in Moscow, 1918–1929.* 1987 ed. Urbana: University of Illinois Press, 1990. ISBN 0-252-06129-2. ‣ Examination of wid-

ening gap between party's and workers' agendas and how centrifugal and centripetal forces shaped and were shaped by party strategies for labor mobilization. [LS]

35.255 William J. Chase and Lewis H. Siegelbaum. "Worktime and industrialization in the U.S.S.R., 1917–1941." In *Worktime and industrialization: an international history.* Gary S. Cross, ed., pp. 183–216. Philadelphia: Temple University Press, 1988. ISBN 0-87722-582-6. ‣ Study of struggles over definition and content of work- and leisure-time. Argues experimentation during First Five-Year Plan failed to achieve state control over worktime. [LS]

35.256 David J. Dallin and Boris I. Nicolaevsky. *Forced labor in Soviet Russia.* 1947 ed. New York: Octagon Books, 1974. ISBN 0-374-92040-0. ‣ Pioneering study of institutionalized prison work forces. First serious attempt to outline role of forced labor in Soviet economic development. [DKR]

35.257 Donald Filtzer. *Soviet workers and Stalinist industrialization: the formation of modern Soviet production relations, 1928–1941.* Armonk, N.Y.: Sharpe, 1986. ISBN 0-87332-374-2. ‣ Examination of how state policy of breaking overt resistance of workers through their atomization led to covert bargaining between individual workers and managers, wreaking havoc on planned economy. [LS]

35.258 Sheila Fitzpatrick. *Education and social mobility in the Soviet Union, 1921–1934.* Cambridge: Cambridge University Press, 1979. ISBN 0-521-22325-3. ‣ Study of making of "Brezhnev generation." Discusses party policy of promoting workers from bench to managerial and technical positions via technical training. [LS]

35.259 John Hatch. "The "Lenin levy" and the social origins of Stalinism: workers and the Communist party in Moscow, 1921–1928." *Slavic review* 48.4 (1989) 558–77. ISSN 0037-6779. ‣ Study of how recruitment of factory workers into party led to unanticipated articulation of workers' grievances within party cells. Leninists emerge as supporters of Stalin. [LS]

35.260 Susan M. Kingsbury and Mildred Fairchild. *Factory, family, and woman in the Soviet Union.* New York: Putnam, 1935. ‣ Heavily statistical analysis of women in Soviet work force and state's provision of social services. [LS]

35.261 Diane P. Koenker. "Class and consciousness in a socialist society: workers in the printing trades during NEP." In *Russia in the era of NEP: explorations in Soviet society and culture.* Sheila Fitzpatrick, Alexander Rabinowitch, and Richard Stites, eds., pp. 34–57. Bloomington: Indiana University Press, 1991. ISBN 0-253-32224-3 (cl), 0-253-20657-X (pbk). ‣ Study of ambiguities of working-class identity where traditional associations with class no longer seem to apply. [LS]

35.262 Hiroaki Kuromiya. *Stalin's industrial revolution: politics and workers, 1928–1932.* Cambridge: Cambridge University Press, 1988. ISBN 0-521-35157-X. ‣ Examination of institutional shake-ups and social transformations accompanying industrialization of First Five-Year Plan. Looks at how Stalin pushed through industrialization via class-war strategy. [LS]

35.263 Hiroaki Kuromiya. "Workers' *artels* and Soviet production relations." In *Russia in the era of NEP: explorations in Soviet society and culture.* Sheila Fitzpatrick, Alexander Rabinowitch, and Richard Stites, eds., pp. 72–88. Bloomington: Indiana University Press, 1991. ISBN 0-253-32224-3 (cl), 0-253-20657-X (pbk). ‣ Analysis of how and why "traditional" labor institution known as *artel*—derived from and analogous in its functions to village commune—survived throughout 1920s and was (formally) suppressed during First Five-Year Plan. [LS]

35.264 David Mandel. *The Petrograd workers and the Soviet seizure of power: from the July days, 1917, to July 1918.* New York: St. Martin's, 1984. ISBN 0-312-60395-9. ‣ Study of redistribution of power and authority in Petrograd's factories, July 1917 to July 1918, based on Marxist categories. [LS]

35.265 Solomon Schwarz. *Labor in the Soviet Union.* 1951 ed. New York: Praeger, 1952. ▸ Comprehensive survey of Soviet labor policy from October Revolution through 1951. Argues state progressively tightened its grip over workers. Available on microform from Ann Arbor: University Microfilms International. [LS]

35.266 John Scott. *Behind the Urals: an American worker in Russia's city of steel.* 1942 ed. Bloomington: Indiana University Press, 1989. ISBN 0-253-35125-1 (cl), 0-253-20536-0 (pbk). ▸ Classic firsthand account of Magnitogorsk's early years by American who worked as welder and foreman. Chronicles tragedies and triumphs of construction and operation of plant and city. [LS]

35.267 Lewis H. Siegelbaum. "Production collectives and communes and the 'imperatives' of Soviet industrialization, 1929–1931." *Slavic review* 45.1 (1986) 65–84. ISSN 0037-6779. ▸ Study of formation of egalitarian work units as defense mechanisms against wage insecurity. Finds party ambivalence toward spontaneous collectivism among workers. [LS]

35.268 Lewis H. Siegelbaum. *Stakhanovism and the politics of productivity in the USSR, 1935–1941.* Cambridge: Cambridge University Press, 1988. ISBN 0-521-34548-0. ▸ Discussion of how campaign to intensify industrial production was handled by workers, managers, and party functionaries. [LS]

35.269 Carmen Sirianni. *Workers control and socialist democracy: the Soviet experience.* London: Verso and NLB, 1982. ISBN 0-86091-054-7 (cl), 0-86091-754-1 (pbk). ▸ Neo-Marxist study of struggles and failures of popular democracy in revolutionary Russia attributed to bolshevik authoritarianism. Comparative perspective on workers control and council democracy. [LS]

35.270 Chris Ward. *Russia's cotton workers and the New Economic Policy: shop-floor culture and state policy, 1921–1929.* Cambridge: Cambridge University Press, 1990. ISBN 0-521-34580-4. ▸ Discussion of workers' strategies that confounded attempts by state to rationalize production of cotton goods and otherwise increase labor productivity. [LS]

Industrialization

35.271 Ronald Amann and Julian Cooper, eds. *Industrial innovation in the Soviet Union.* New Haven: Yale University Press, 1982. ISBN 0-300-02772-9. ▸ Collection of case studies of Soviet industrialization and research and development (machine tool, chemical, defense). Focuses on 1960s and 1970s, but includes historical background as well. [HK]

35.272 A. A. Barsov. *Balans stoimostnykh obmenov mezhdu gorodom i derevnei* (Balance of value exchanges between city and countryside). Moscow: Nauka, 1969. ▸ Careful analysis of origins of resources for industrialization, emphasizing suffering of both city and countryside. Both theoretical and statistical. [HK]

35.273 Abram Bergson and Herbert S. Levine, eds. *The Soviet economy: toward the year 2000.* London: Allen & Unwin, 1983. ISBN 0-04-335045-3 (cl), 0-04-335053-4 (pbk). ▸ Examines long-term trends in various sectors of economy and how Soviet defense policies affected economy. Forecasts now outdated but data useful. [HK]

35.274 Manfred von Boetticher. *Industrialisierungspolitik und Verteidigungskonzeption der UdSSR, 1926–1930: Herausbildung des Stalinismus und "äußere Bedrohung."* Düsseldorf: Droste, 1979. ISBN 3-7700-0526-0. ▸ Discussion of relations between military security and Soviet industrialization. Controversial thesis that threat of war deployed by Stalin to mobilize public opinion not major factor. Emphasizes destabilization of internal security as cause for industrialization of military. [HK]

35.275 R. W. Davies. "The socialist market: a debate in Soviet industry, 1932–33." *Slavic review* 42.2 (1984) 201–23. ISSN 0037-6779. ▸ Study of how problems with central planning led Soviet experts (particularly M. Birbraer) to explore "market socialism" and how and why this exploration failed. [HK]

35.276 R. W. Davies. *The Soviet economy in turmoil, 1929–1930.* Vol. 3 of *The industrialization of Soviet Russia.* Cambridge, Mass.: Harvard University Press, 1989. ISBN 0-674-82655-8. ▸ Study of how implementation of central planning led to breakdown of economy in critical years 1929–30. Examines both ideological foundations and pragmatic response. [HK]

35.277 R. W. Davies, ed. *From tsarism to the New Economic Policy: continuity and change in the economy of the USSR.* Ithaca, N.Y.: Cornell University Press, 1991. ISBN 0-8014-2621-9 (cl), 0-8014-9919-4 (pbk). ▸ Statistical and theoretical study of continuities and discontinuities in Russian and Soviet economies. Discusses long-term trends and foundations of Soviet industrialization under Stalin. [HK]

35.278 R. W. Davies, Julian Cooper, and M. J. Ilic. *Soviet official statistics on industrial production, capital stock, and capital investment, 1928–41.* Birmingham: University of Birmingham, Center for Russian and East European Studies, 1991. (SIPS occasional paper, 1.) ISBN 0-7044-1147-4 (pbk). ▸ Thorough treatment of statistical data on industrial expansion. Supplements and corrects official data with rival estimates. [HK]

35.279 R. W. Davies, Mark Harrison, and S. G. Wheatcroft, eds. *The economic transformation of the Soviet Union, 1913–1945.* Cambridge: Cambridge University Press, 1994. ISBN 0-521-45152-3 (cl), 0-521-45770-X (pbk). ▸ Team-produced survey of key factors in late imperial and Soviet economic development. Dry presentation; most notable for rich statistical material. [DTO]

35.280 Michael R. Dohan. "The economic origins of Soviet autarky, 1927/28–1934." *Slavic review* 35.4 (1976) 603–35. ISSN 0037-6779. ▸ Examination of how foreign trade and industrialization affected each other in formative years of Soviet planned economy. Describes autarky as unintended consequence caused by unforeseen factors. [HK]

35.281 Alexander Erlich. *The Soviet industrialization debate, 1924–1928.* 1960 ed. Cambridge, Mass.: Harvard University Press, 1967. (Russian Research Center studies, 41.) ▸ Study of debates by Soviet politicians and economists about where to find resources for industrialization and how to extract them. Comparison of policies of Eugenii Preobrazhenskii and Nikolai Bukharin. Shows Stalin's political solution. [HK]

35.282 David Granick. *Soviet metal-fabricating and economic development: practice versus policy.* Madison: University of Wisconsin Press, 1967. ▸ Case study of investment and return. Refutes customary explanations of rapid industrialization and emphasizes labor-intensive, rather than capital-intensive, nature of Soviet industry. [HK]

35.283 Mark Harrison. *Soviet planning in peace and war, 1938–1945.* Cambridge: Cambridge University Press, 1985. ISBN 0-521-30371-0. ▸ Examination of how Stalin's industrialization coped with demands of total war. Emphasizes lessons learned that led to post-Stalin economic reform. Good statistical data and comparison with other countries at war. [HK]

35.284 Holland Hunter. "The overambitious First Five-Year Plan." *Slavic review* 32.2 (1973) 237–57. ISSN 0037-6779. ▸ Famous essay that caused constructive controversy. Emphasizes overambitiousness of Stalin's industrialization, stressing plan's lack of internal cohesion. [HK]

35.285 Holland Hunter. *Soviet transportation policy.* Cambridge, Mass.: Harvard University Press, 1957. (Russian Research Center studies, 28.) ▸ Examination of role played by railroad building in Soviet industrialization drive. Despite government's lack of attention, it avoided becoming an Achilles' heel of industrial expansion. [HK]

35.286   Naum Jasny. *Soviet industrialization, 1928–1952*. Chicago: University of Chicago Press, 1961. ▸ Menshevik analysis emphasizing increase in rate of exploitation as source of rapid industrial growth. Sees it as financial, economic, and social revolution. [HK]

35.287   I. S. Koropeckyj. *Location problem in Soviet industry before World War II: the case of the Ukraine*. Chapel Hill: University of North Carolina Press, 1971. ISBN 0-8078-1149-1. ▸ Study of Soviet industrialization in non-Russian areas. Discusses clashes of regional interests in struggle for resources, role of central authorities in decision making, and impact of industrialization on Ukraine. [HK]

35.288   Richard Lewis. *Science and industrialization in the USSR*. New York: Holmes & Meier, 1979. ISBN 0-8419-0494-4. ▸ Discussion of how industrialization developed scientific network. Emphasizes substantial investment in research and development, but concludes domestic research and development was hampered by reliance on foreign technology. [HK]

35.289   A. N. Malafeev. *Istoriia tsenoobrazovaniia v SSSR (1917–1963 gg.)* (A history of price formation in the Soviet Union [1917–1963]). Moscow: Mysl', 1964. ▸ Examination of how prices were formed under centrally planned economy. Discusses role of money in industrialization and planned economy. Soviet Marxist analysis, yet critical of many official policies. [HK]

35.290   Alec Nove. *An economic history of the USSR, 1917–1991: new and final edition*. 3d ed. Harmondsworth: Penguin, 1992. ISBN 0-14-015774-3 (pbk). ▸ Concise but excellent treatment of Soviet economic history. Analyzes consequences of rapid industrialization. Full of useful syntheses and suggestions for alternatives. [HK]

35.291   William G. Rosenberg and Lewis H. Siegelbaum, eds. *Social dimensions of Soviet industrialization*. Bloomington: Indiana University Press, 1993. ISBN 0-253-34993-1 (cl), 0-253-20772-X (pbk). ▸ Fresh research on social and cultural dimensions of Stalin's industrialization drive of early 1930s. Highlights unintended consequences of planned economy. [DTO]

35.292   Lewis H. Siegelbaum. "Guide to document series on industrialization." In *A researcher's guide to sources on Soviet social history in the 1930s*. Sheila Fitzpatrick and Lynne Viola, eds., pp. 132–45. Armonk, N.Y.: Sharpe, 1990. ISBN 0-87332-497-8. ▸ Very useful guide to numerous Soviet publications of documents on industrialization: what they contain and how to use them. Covers various republics and regions. [HK]

35.293   S. G. Wheatcroft, R. W. Davies, and Julian Cooper. "Soviet industrialization reconsidered: some preliminary conclusions about economic development between 1926 and 1941." *Economic history review*, Second series, 39.2 (1986) 264–94. ISSN 0013-0117. ▸ Meticulous analysis of Stalin's rapid industrialization drive before World War II. Careful statistical analysis, synthetic views, and suggestions for alternatives. [HK]

35.294   World Congress for Soviet and East European Studies. *Soviet investment for planned industrialisation, 1929–1937: policy and practice, selected papers from the Second World Congress for Soviet and East European Studies* (1980). R. W. Davies, ed. Berkeley: Berkeley Slavic Specialties, 1984. ISBN 0-933884-32-X. ▸ Collection of essays on Soviet investment choices and investment in practice. Includes debates on whether Stalinist path proved more effective than alternative Bukharinist policy. [HK]

35.295   Eugene Zaleski. *Planning for economic growth in the Soviet Union, 1918–1932*. Marie-Christine MacAndrew and G. Warren Nutter, eds. and trans. Chapel Hill: University of North Carolina

Press, 1971. ISBN 0-8078-1160-2. ▸ Comprehensive treatment of Soviet strategies for industrialization. Critical analysis of formative years of central planning. Argues economically responsible planning gave way to coercive irrational forms. Good critique of economic data. Translation of *Planification de la croissance et fluctuations économiques en U.R.S.S., 1918–1932* (1962). [HK/DKR]

35.296   Eugene Zaleski. *Stalinist planning for economic growth, 1933–1952*. Marie-Christine MacAndrew and John H. Moore, eds. and trans. Chapel Hill: University of North Carolina Press, 1980. ISBN 0-8078-1370-2. ▸ Comprehensive treatment of consequences of centrally planned industrialization through war and postwar years. Critical appreciation of Soviet strategies. Good critique of statistical data. Translation of *La planification stalinienne: croissance et fluctuations économiques en U.R.S.S., 1933–1952* (1984). [HK]

SOCIAL AND INSTITUTIONAL HISTORY

Women, Gender, and the Family

35.297   Dorothy Atkinson, Alexander Dallin, and Gail Warshofsky Lapidus, eds. *Women in Russia*. Stanford, Calif.: Stanford University Press, 1977. ISBN 0-8047-0910-6 (cl), 0-8047-0920-3 (pbk). ▸ Scholarly anthology dealing with issues of demography, law, economics, child socialization, political participation, and gender politics mainly in Soviet period. [RS]

35.298   Susan Bridger. *Women in the Soviet countryside: women's roles in rural development in the Soviet Union*. Cambridge: Cambridge University Press, 1988. ISBN 0-521-32862-4. ▸ Rare glimpse at reality of Soviet countryside through prism of women's work and family roles on Soviet collective and state farms. [RS]

35.299   Genia K. Browning. *Women and politics in the USSR: consciousness raising and Soviet women's groups*. Brighton, England, and New York: Wheatsheaf and St. Martin's, 1987. ISBN 0-312-00953-4. ▸ Specialized study of Soviet institution reinvigorated in 1980s that later played modest role in post-Soviet surge of women's gender consciousness. [RS]

35.300   Mary Buckley. *Women and ideology in the Soviet Union*. Ann Arbor: University of Michigan Press, 1989. ISBN 0-472-09410-6 (cl), 0-472-06410-X (pbk). ▸ Intelligent analysis of political theory and practice vis-à-vis status of women in Gorbachev era, with background on history of Soviet gender politics. [RS]

35.301   Mary Buckley, ed. *Perestroika and Soviet women*. Cambridge: Cambridge University Press, 1992. ISBN 0-521-41443-1 (cl), 0-521-42738-X (pbk). ▸ Anthology of studies including Russian women writers and commentators as well as British, Australian, and American scholars on issues as diverse as youth subculture, workforce, fiction, and new women's organizations. [RS]

35.302   Barbara Evans Clements. *Bolshevik feminist: the life of Alexandra Kollontai*. Bloomington: Indiana University Press, 1979. ISBN 0-253-31209-4. ▸ Political biography of central figure in history of women's liberation in revolutionary era, notable especially for efforts to mold socialist women's movement during 1905 Revolution, her work in Zhenotdel, and her sexual doctrine. [RS]

35.303   Norton T. Dodge. *Women in the Soviet economy: their role in economic, scientific, and technical development*. Baltimore: Johns Hopkins University Press, 1966. ▸ First serious work on Soviet women in economic system, including not only rural and urban labor, but white-collar employees and women's higher and specialized technical education. [RS]

35.304   Beatrice Farnsworth. *Aleksandra Kollontai: socialism, feminism, and the Bolshevik Revolution*. Stanford, Calif.: Stanford University Press, 1980. ISBN 0-8047-1073-2. ▸ Political biography of central figure in history of women's liberation in revolutionary era. More detailed on subject's political activity in Soviet period than Clements 35.302. [RS]

35.305 Beatrice Farnsworth and Lynne Viola, eds. *Russian peasant women.* New York: Oxford University Press, 1992. ISBN 0-19-506693-6 (cl), 0-19-506694-4 (pbk). ▸ Family, kinship, customary law, childbirth, work, and other aspects of rural women's life covered in anthology of scholarly articles, half dealing with Soviet period. No index or bibliography. [RS]

35.306 Wendy Z. Goldman. *Women, the state, and revolution: Soviet family policy and social life, 1917–1936.* Cambridge: Cambridge University Press, 1993. ISBN 0-521-37404-9. ▸ Rich account of evolution of state policy toward family that chronicles capacity of working-class women during 1920s to turn back radical social policies that worked against their economic interests. Documents convergence of grassroots ambivalence and party and state conservatism to produce far less liberationist social and family policies of 1930s. [DTO]

35.307 Carola Hansson and Karin Liden. *Moscow women: thirteen interviews.* Gerry Bothmer, George Blecher, and Lone Blecher, trans. Gail Warshofsky Lapidus, Introduction. New York: Pantheon, 1983. ISBN 0-394-52332-6 (cl), 0-394-71491-1 (pbk). ▸ Less than satisfactory English-language translation of 35.308, but useful nonetheless. [RS]

35.308 Carola Hansson and Karin Liden. *Samtal med kvinnor i Moskva* (Conversations with women in Moscow). Stockholm: AWE/Geber, 1980. ISBN 91-20-05928-0. ▸ Conversations with thirteen Moscow women in 1970s about life, love, children, and career by Swedish journalist and scholar. [RS]

35.309 Barbara Holland, ed. *Soviet sisterhood.* Bloomington: Indiana University Press, 1985. ISBN 0-253-35420-X (cl), 0-253-28790-1 (pbk). ▸ Anthology providing excellent summaries of women's dilemmas on eve of *perestroika* in realms of ideology, psychology, media, maternity, work, and public life. [RS]

35.310 Gail Warshofsky Lapidus. *Women in Soviet society: equality, development, and social change.* Berkeley: University of California Press, 1979. ISBN 0-520-02868-6. ▸ Sophisticated political and sociological analysis of role of women in state and society, particularly political origins of women's dual obligations and conflicting images in Soviet life. [RS]

35.311 Gail Warshofsky Lapidus, ed. *Women, work, and family in the Soviet Union.* Vladimir Talmy, trans. Armonk, N.Y.: Sharpe, 1982. ISBN 0-87332-181-2 (cl), 0-87332-255-X (pbk). ▸ Collection of articles by Soviet scholars on various aspects of female rural and urban labor force, education, and the family. [RS]

35.312 Tatyana Mamonova, ed. *Women and Russia: feminist writings from the Soviet Union.* Rebecca Park and Catherine A. Fitzpatrick, trans. Boston: Beacon, 1984. ISBN 0-8070-6708-3 (cl), 0-8070-6709-1 (pbk). ▸ One of several editions of dissident feminist works from 1970s exhibiting wide range of opinions on career, propaganda, gender repression, childbirth, artistic expression, prison experience, and religion. [RS]

35.313 Robert H. McNeal. *Bride of the revolution: Krupskaya and Lenin.* Ann Arbor: University of Michigan Press, 1972. ISBN 0-472-61600-5. ▸ First serious political biography of Lenin's wife throwing much light on succession problem in 1920s and also on fate of woman question in Revolution. [RS]

35.314 V. S. Murmantseva. *Sovetskie zhenshchiny v Velikoi Otechestvennoi Voine* (Soviet women in the Great Fatherland War). 2d ed. Moscow: Mysl', 1979. ▸ Pioneering though far from definitive work on role of women in World War II. Discusses recruitment, numbers, ranks, modes of combat, integration with males, casualties, and tensions of war. [RS]

35.315 L. P. Ovchinnikova. *Zhenshchiny v soldatskikh shineliakh* (Women in soldier great coats). Volgograd, Russia: Nizhne-Volzhskoe, 1987. ▸ Popular accounts of women snipers, infantry women, tankers, and pilots in World War II. [RS]

SEE ALSO
34.280 Barbara Evans Clements, Barbara Alpern Engel, and Christine D. Worobec, eds. *Russia's women.*
34.284 Richard Stites. *The women's liberation movement in Russia.*

Komsomol

35.316 Ann Todd Baum. *Komsomol participation in the Soviet First Five-Year Plan.* New York: St. Martin's, 1987. ISBN 0-312-00786-8. ▸ Role of Soviet youth organization in education, industrialization campaigns, and economic life, 1928–1932. Brief prehistory of First Five-Year Plan participation. Based on published sources. [MVH]

35.317 Ralph Talcott Fisher, Jr. *Pattern for Soviet youth: a study of the congresses of the Komsomol, 1918–1954.* New York: Columbia University Press, 1959. ▸ Origins and evolution of Komsomol through proceedings of periodic national congresses. [MVH]

35.318 Nikolai K. Novak-Deker, ed. *Soviet youth: twelve Komsomol histories.* Oliver J. Frederiksen, trans. Munich: Institut zur Erforschung der UdSSR, 1959. (Issledovaniia i materialy, Seriia 1, 51.) ▸ Autobiographical narratives of twelve postwar defectors from Soviet Union focusing on their experience in communist youth organization. [MVH]

35.319 Jim Riordan. "The Komsomol." In *Soviet youth culture.* Jim Riordan, ed., pp. 16–44. Bloomington: Indiana University Press, 1989. ISBN 0-253-35423-4 (cl), 0-253-28795-2 (pbk). ▸ Brief history, organizational structure, membership, and role of Komsomol in Soviet politics and society. Based on published Soviet sources and youth movement press. [MVH]

35.320 Isabel A. Tirado. *Young Guard! The Communist Youth League, Petrograd, 1917–1920.* New York: Greenwood, 1988. ISBN 0-313-25922-4. ▸ Study of origins of Komsomol in Revolution and Civil War and its transformation into bureaucratic institution. Discusses changing social composition, educational activities, economic work, and relationship to Communist party. [MVH/DJR]

Education

35.321 Larry E. Holmes. *The Kremlin and the schoolhouse: reforming education in Soviet Russia, 1917–1931.* Bloomington: Indiana University Press, 1991. ISBN 0-253-32847-0. ▸ Highly original study of bolshevik attempts to transform primary and secondary education during years of War Communism and New Economic Policy. Based on previously untapped archival sources, argues radical reforms of educational establishment were opposed and modified by social pressure from below and from rival bureaucracies and institutions. [DTO]

Trade Unions

35.322 Emily Clark Brown. *Soviet trade unions and labor relations.* Cambridge, Mass.: Harvard University Press, 1966. ▸ Survey of early post-Stalin developments in trade union politics, labor market, trade union centers, regional trade union councils, and labor-management relations. Based on extensive reading in Soviet published sources. [MVH]

35.323 Isaac Deutscher. *Soviet trade unions: their place in Soviet labor policy.* 1950 ed. Westport, Conn.: Hyperion, 1973. ISBN 0-88355-033-4. ▸ Brief history of trade unions in interwar period including account of political battles at trade union congresses, relations of Communist party and trade unions, and role of trade unions in planned economy. Critical account of Soviet labor policy by Trotskyist. [MVH/LS]

35.324 Woldemar Koch. *Die bol'sevistischen Gewerkschaften: eine herrschaftssoziologische Studie.* Rudolfstadt, Germany: Hofbuchdrückerei F. Mitzlaff, 1926. ▸ Important early work on prerevolutionary origins and post-1917 evolution of Russian and Soviet trade unions. Good coverage of administrative structure, membership statistics, and relevant decrees and legislation. [MVH]

35.325 Blair A. Ruble. *Soviet trade unions: their development in the 1970s.* Cambridge: Cambridge University Press, 1981. ISBN 0-521-23704-1. ▸ Brief organizational history of trade unions; legal and social rights of workers; relations between unions, management, and party; and international activities of Soviet trade unions. Based on extensive reading of published Soviet materials. [MVH]

35.326 Jay B. Sorenson. *The life and death of Soviet trade unionism, 1917–1928.* New York: Atherton, 1969. ▸ History of Communist party domination of trade union organizations and destruction of Soviet trade unionism. Focus on dilemma of labor and political dictatorship. Posits rebirth of trade unions in 1960s. [MVH]

State and Bureaucracy

35.327 Oskar Anweiler. *The Soviets: the Russian workers, peasants, and soldiers councils, 1905–1921.* 1974 ed. Ruth Hein, trans. New York: Pantheon, 1975. ISBN 0-394-47105-9. ▸ Outline of transformation of popular assemblies into instruments of state power. Comprehensive description of extension of bolshevik power over grassroots movements in Russian revolutionary era. [DKR]

35.328 John A. Armstrong. *The European administrative elite.* Princeton: Princeton University Press, 1973. ISBN 0-691-07551-4. ▸ Comprehensive study of preparation, selection, advancement of highest career administrators of Russia, France, Britain, and Germany, 1800–1960s. Detailed comparative analysis based on career and other collective biographical data. [DKR]

35.329 John A. Armstrong. "Tsarist and Soviet elite administrators." *Slavic review* 31.1 (1972) 1–28. ISSN 0037-6779. ▸ Pioneering comparative study of pre- and postrevolutionary Russian senior bureaucrats. Points to importance of ideological and technological differences and some fundamental continuities across revolutionary era. [DKR]

35.330 Kendall E. Bailes. "The politics of technology: Stalin and technocratic thinking among Soviet engineers." *American historical review* 79.2 (1974) 445–69. ISSN 0002-8762. ▸ Study of political conflict produced by rise of technical specialists in administration during Soviet industrialization. Excellent synthesis of cross-currents of politics and industrial development under Stalin. [DKR]

35.331 Robert V. Daniels. "The Secretariat and the local organizations in the Russian Communist party, 1921–1923." *American Slavic and East European review* 16.1 (1957) 32–49. ISSN 0037-6779. ▸ Examination of political administration within Communist party of Soviet Union. Pioneering study of institutional development and professionalization by acknowledged Western authority. [DKR]

35.332 R. W. Davies. *Development of the Soviet budgetary system.* 1958 ed. Westport, Conn.: Greenwood, 1979. ISBN 0-313-21191-4. ▸ Narrative of creation and modification of fiscal and accounting systems for planned economy. One of few detailed descriptions of economic institutions under early Stalinism. [DKR]

35.333 John J. Dziak. *Chekisty: a history of the KGB.* Lexington, Mass.: Lexington, 1988. ISBN 0-669-10258-X. ▸ Narrative history

of Soviet security/intelligence administration. Reasonably balanced study in field dominated by sensational works. [DKR]

35.334 George M. Enteen. *The Soviet scholar-bureaucrat: M. N. Pokrovskii and the Society of Marxist Historians.* University Park: Pennsylvania State University Press, 1978. ISBN 0-271-00548-3. ▸ Study of integration of intellectuals into Soviet system through institutionalization. Focus on best known Soviet historian contributes to understanding of his academic work and political role in Soviet era. [DKR]

35.335 J. Arch Getty. "Party and purge in Smolensk, 1933–1937." *Slavic review* 42.1 (1983) 60–79. ISSN 0037-6779. ▸ Important contribution to debate over extent and source of "cleansing" of political and administrative institutions in Stalin era. Based on limited archival research. [DKR]

35.336 John N. Hazard and Isaac Shapiro. *The Soviet legal system: post-Stalin documentation and historical commentary.* Dobbs Ferry, N.Y.: Oceana for Columbia University, Parker School of Foreign and Comparative Law, 1962. ▸ One of very few Western summaries of data both on sources and historical perspective. Balanced synthesis. [DKR]

35.337 Cynthia S. Kaplan. *The party and agricultural crisis management in the USSR.* Ithaca, N.Y.: Cornell University Press, 1987. ISBN 0-8014-2021-0. ▸ Role of local and regional communist organizations in managing and developing agricultural sector after World War II. Excellent synthesis showing conflicts among party organs and between party and local agriculture. [DKR]

35.338 Amy W. Knight. *The KGB: police and politics in the Soviet Union.* Rev. ed. Boston: Unwin Hyman, 1990. ISBN 0-04-445718-9. ▸ Detailed survey of structure and operations of Committee on State Security (KGB) during final decades of Soviet power. Emphasizes complex and often subtle role of KGB in high Soviet politics, combination of accomodation, influence, and raw power. [DTO]

35.339 T. P. Korzhikhina. *Istoriia gosudarstvennykh uchrezhdenii SSSR* (History of the state administrations of the USSR). Moscow: Vysshaia Shkola, 1986. ▸ Single best general history of creation of Soviet state apparatus. Well-integrated basic synthesis using legislation and Communist party documents. [DKR]

35.340 George Leggett. *The Cheka: Lenin's political police, the All-Russian Commission for Combating Counter-Revolution and Sabotage, December 1917 to February 1922.* 1981 ed. Oxford: Clarendon, 1986. ISBN 0-19-822862-7 (pbk). ▸ Full-length study of first Soviet political police, origins and impact on later Soviet history. Balanced study of events and personalities frequently sensationalized. [DKR]

35.341 William E. Odom. *The Soviet volunteers: modernization and bureaucracy in a public mass organization.* 1973 ed. Princeton: Princeton University Press, 1974. ISBN 0-691-08718-0. ▸ Study of mobilization and interaction between public and state institutions. Unique description of institution formation under Stalinism. [DKR]

35.342 Thomas F. Remington. "Institution building in bolshevik Russia: the case of 'state *kontrol'.*" *Slavic review* 41.1 (1982) 91–103. ISSN 0037-6779. ▸ Description of effort to institutionalize revolutionary goals within state administrative apparatus. Focused description of institutionalization of radical workers' movement under early bolshevik government. [DKR]

35.343 T. Harry Rigby. *Lenin's government: SOVNARKOM, 1917–1922.* Cambridge: Cambridge University Press, 1979. ISBN 0-521-22281-8. ▸ Narrative study of formation of early Soviet government and administrative institutions. Best Western survey of early postrevolutionary state. [DKR/DJR]

35.344 Philip G. Roeder. *Red sunset: the failure of Soviet politics.*

Princeton: Princeton University Press, 1993. ISBN 0-691-03306-4 (cl), 0-691-01942-8 (pbk). ▸ Sophisticated new institutional account of creation, development, and failure of Soviet "constitution." Defines constitution as "reciprocal bureaucratic accountability" between political leaders and bureaucratic constituencies. [DTO]

35.345 Don K. Rowney. *Transition to technocracy: the structural origins of the Soviet administrative state.* Ithaca, N.Y.: Cornell University Press, 1989. ISBN 0-8014-2183-7. ▸ Study of growth and impact of technocratic administration in pre- and postrevolutionary Russia. Based on comparison of careers and other biographical data on administrative groups before and after communist revolution. [DKR]

Red Army

35.346 S. F. Akhromeev et al., eds. *Voennyi entsiklopedicheskii slovar'* (Military encyclopedic dictionary). 2d ed. Moscow: Voennoe, 1986. ▸ Important reference work for Red and Soviet Army, including biographies, maps, and organizational histories. Some important shortcomings reflect pre-Gorbachev historiogaphical consensus (e.g., omission of Trotsky and other "disgraced" political leaders), but generally reliable. [MVH]

35.347 Yosef Avidar. *The party and the army in the Soviet Union.* 1983 ed. Dafna Allon, trans. University Park: Pennsylvania State University Press, 1985. ISBN 0-271-00393-6. ▸ Analysis of civil-military relations from death of Stalin to early 1960s, treating debates over doctrine, military education, and tradition. Adheres to totalitarian model of Soviet politics with constant army-party conflict. [MVH]

35.348 Gerda Beitter. *Die Rote Armee im Zweiten Weltkrieg: eine Bibliographie ihrer Truppengeschichten im Zweiten Weltkrieg.* Koblenz, Germany: Bernard & Graefe, 1984. ▸ Extensive bibliographical guide for Red Army military units in World War II. [MVH]

35.349 Francesco Benvenuti. *The Bolsheviks and the Red Army, 1918–1922.* Christopher Woodall, trans. Cambridge: Cambridge University Press, 1988. ISBN 0-521-25771-9. ▸ Examination of origins of Red Army and early political struggles during Civil War. Challenges dualist model of totalitarian approach with analysis of debates within political and military elites. [MVH/DJR]

35.350 Timothy J. Colton. *Commissars, commanders, and civilian authority: the structure of Soviet military politics.* Cambridge, Mass.: Harvard University Press, 1979. (Russian Research Center studies, 79.) ISBN 0-674-14535-6. ▸ Case studies in evolution of relations between Soviet army and Communist party, including Great Purge, World War II, and Zhukov affair. Discusses civil-military relations and role of army in Soviet politics. Challenges totalitarian model of Soviet system with analysis of intra-party and intra-army conflict and cross-institutional alliances. [MVH/AD]

35.351 Timothy J. Colton and Thane Gustafson, eds. *Soldiers and the Soviet state: civil-military relations from Brezhnev to Gorbachev.* Princeton: Princeton University Press, 1990. ISBN 0-691-07863-7 (cl), 0-691-02328-x (pbk). ▸ Essays on transformation of role of army in Soviet politics, society, and economy since Khrushchev. Treats KGB, defense industry and resource allocation, social conflict, response to technological challenge, and context of changes under Gorbachev. [MVH]

35.352 Albert Z. Conner and Robert G. Poirier. *Red Army order of battle in the Great Patriotic War: including data from 1919 to the present.* Novato, Calif.: Presidio, 1985. ISBN 0-89141-237-9. ▸ Detailed presentation of battle formations and histories of armies, corps, and divisions of Red Army in World War II. Reference work includes battle record, composition, and origins and subordination of units. [MVH]

35.353 Alvin D. Coox. *Nomonhan: Japan against Russia, 1939.* 2 vols. Stanford, Calif.: Stanford University Press, 1985. ISBN 0-8047-1160-7 (set). ▸ Best history of battle of Halkaiin [Khalkhin] Gol between Kwantung and Red Armies. Account based largely on Japanese and American archives and Soviet published materials. [MVH]

35.354 Herbert S. Dinerstein. *War and the Soviet Union: nuclear weapons and the revolution in Soviet military and political thinking.* 1962 rev. ed. Westport, Conn.: Greenwood, 1976. ISBN 0-8371-8658-7. ▸ Study of evolution of Soviet military doctrine and civil-military relations since World War II. Special focus on published debates about nuclear warfare, Marxist-Leninist ideology, and domestic politics. [MVH]

35.355 John Erickson. *The road to Berlin: continuing the history of Stalin's war with Germany.* Boulder: Westview, 1983. ISBN 0-89158-795-0. ▸ Most comprehensive English-language account of military campaigns in Soviet-German war from Stalingrad to Berlin. Focuses on performance of Soviet army with detailed analysis of strategies, tactics, and weapons as well as Stalin's relationship to High Command. Includes maps and extensive bibliography. [MVH/HK]

35.356 John Erickson. *The road to Stalingrad: Stalin's war with Germany.* 1975 ed. Boulder: Westview, 1984. ISBN 0-86531-744-5. ▸ Most comprehensive English-language battle account of Soviet-German war from outbreak in spring 1941 through battle of Stalingrad. Focus on Soviet army performance. Maps. [MVH]

35.357 John Erickson. *The Soviet High Command: a military-political history, 1918–1941.* 1962 ed. Boulder: Westview, 1984. ISBN 0-86531-743-7 (pbk). ▸ Most comprehensive organizational and political history of interwar Red Army. Focuses on relations between party and military High Command; pays attention to developments in international relations. [MVH]

35.358 Michel Garder. *A history of the Soviet Army.* New York: Praeger, 1966. ▸ Study of Soviet army from origins in Russian Imperial Army to 1964. Stresses imperial roots of Red Army in organization, personnel, and doctrine. [MVH]

35.359 Raymond L. Garthoff. *Soviet military doctrine.* Glencoe, Ill.: Free Press, 1953. ▸ Examination of origins and evolution of Soviet military doctrine over broad range of topics. Focuses on postwar period and impact of nuclear weapons on military thinking. Includes extensive bibliography. [MVH]

35.360 Dale R. Herspring. *The Soviet High Command, 1967–1989: personalities and politics.* Princeton: Princeton University Press, 1990. ISBN 0-691-07844-0 (cl), 0-691-02318-2 (pbk). ▸ Discussion of civil-military relations during Brezhnev and early Gorbachev periods, treating struggles within Communist party and military over doctrine and national security. Challenges totalitarian model of Soviet politics with view of relations between military and political leadership as more symbiotic than conflictual. [MVH]

35.361 Ellen Jones. *Red Army and society: a sociology of the Soviet military.* Boston: Allen & Unwin, 1985. ISBN 0-04-322011-8. ▸ Study of Soviet armed forces as social institution. Focuses on military manpower including conscription policy, political socialization, and ethnic minorities. Extensive historical background in all chapters. [MVH]

35.362 A. G. Kavtaradze. *Voennye spetsialisty na sluzhbe Respubliki Sovetov, 1917–1920 gg.* (Military specialists in service to the Republic of Soviets, 1917–1920). Vladimir Petrov, ed. Moscow: Nauka, 1988. ISBN 5-02-008451-4. ▸ Crucial role of officers and non-commissioned officers of Russian Imperial Army in early years of Red Army. Based on archival sources; unusually (for Soviet historical accounts) sympathetic treatment of former tsarist officers. [MVH]

35.363 S. M. Kliatskin. *Na zashchite Oktiabria: organizatsiia reguliarnoi armii i militsionnoe stroitel'stvo v Sovetskoi respublike* (In defense of October: the organization of a regular army and militia in the Soviet Republic). Moscow: Nauka, 1965. ▸ Organizational and political history of early years of Red Army, 1917–1920. One of few Soviet accounts based on extensive use of archives. [MVH]

35.364 Roman Kolkowicz. *The Soviet military and the Communist party.* Princeton: Princeton University Press, 1967. ▸ Analysis of origins and evolution of relations between Communist party and Soviet Army. Focus on party control of armed forces. Adheres to classical totalitarian model of Soviet politics with constant army-party conflict. [MVH]

35.365 Ivan Alekseevich Korotkov. *Istoriia sovetskoi voennoi mysli: kratkii ocherk, 1917–iiun' 1941* (The history of Soviet military thought: a short survey, 1917–June 1941). Moscow: Nauka, 1980. ▸ Summary of major controversies in military doctrine of Soviet Army. Despite typical omissions of pre-Gorbachev Soviet historiography, based on extensive and reliable reading of contempory military writings. [MVH]

35.366 B. H. Liddell Hart, ed. *The Red Army: the Red Army, 1918–1945; the Soviet Army, 1946 to the present.* 1956 ed. Gloucester, Mass.: Smith, 1968. ▸ Examination of aspects of history of Red Army from origins through postwar Stalin years (1955). Authors of individual chapters include Soviet and foreign military officers and analysts and reflect wide range of assessment of Red Army strength and reliability. [MVH]

35.367 Richard Luckett. *The White generals: an account of the White movement and the Russian Civil War.* 1971 ed. London: Routledge & Kegan Paul, 1987. ISBN 0-7102-1298-4. ▸ History of major military campaigns of antibolshevik forces in Civil War, 1917–20. Based on extensive reading of memoir literature and published sources. [MVH]

35.368 Michael Parrish. *The U.S.S.R. in World War II: an annotated bibliography of books published in the Soviet Union, 1945–1975, with an addenda for the years 1975–1980.* 2 vols. John Erickson, Introduction. New York: Garland, 1981. ISBN 0-8240-9485-9 (set). ▸ Extensive bibliographical guide to Soviet books treating major military campaigns, armed forces, and geographic areas of World War II. [MVH]

35.369 Albert Seaton. *The Russo-German war, 1941–1945.* 1971 ed. Novato, Calif.: Presidio, 1990. ISBN 0-89141-392-8. ▸ Political, military, and diplomatic history of Soviet-German war, including domestic front. Relies more on German sources than Erickson volumes (35.356, 35.357); greater focus on German than Soviet side in war. [MVH]

35.370 Albert Seaton and Joan Seaton. *The Soviet army: 1918 to the present.* 1986 ed. New York: New American Library, 1987. ISBN 0-453-00551-9 (pbk). ▸ Organizational and political history of Soviet army from origins to 1980s. Views postwar Soviet army as historical successor to Nazi *Wehrmacht*. [MVH]

35.371 Mark Von Hagen. *Soldiers in the proletarian dictatorship: the Red Army and the Soviet socialist state, 1917–1930.* Ithaca, N.Y.: Cornell University Press, 1990. ISBN 0-8014-2420-8. ▸ Examination of civil-military relations from origins of Red Army to collectivization drive. Treats role of Bolshevik party in military affairs and army as institution of political socialization for peasant soldiers. Challenges totalitarian model of Soviet politics with analysis of intra-party and intra-army conflict and cross-institutional alliances. [MVH]

35.372 D. Fedotoff White. *The growth of the Red Army.* 1944 ed. Westport, Conn.: Hyperion, 1980. ▸ Organizational and political history of interwar Red Army. First synthetic history of interwar period based on extensive reading in mostly published sources. [MVH]

35.373 Erich Wollenberg. *The Red Army: a study of the growth of Soviet imperialism.* 1940 ed. Claud W. Sykes, trans. Westport, Conn.: Hyperion, 1973. ISBN 0-88355-056-3. ▸ Organizational and political history of interwar Red Army by former Soviet officer and Trotskyist. [MVH]

SEE ALSO
33.550 Jan Tomaz Gross. *Revolution from abroad.*

CULTURAL HISTORY

General Studies

35.374 Frederick C. Barghoorn. *The Soviet cultural offensive: the role of cultural diplomacy in Soviet foreign policy.* 1960 ed. Westport, Conn.: Greenwood, 1976. ISBN 0-8371-8334-0. ▸ Study of performing artists concertizing abroad and role of officially sponsored culture in international images and relations. [RS]

35.375 John E. Bowlt, ed. and trans. *Russian art of the avant-garde: theory and criticism, 1902–1934.* Rev. ed. New York: Thames & Hudson, 1988. ISBN 0-500-61011-8. ▸ Superb collection of artistic documents on style, politics, and aesthetics of best known of all Russian art movements. Includes writings of Wassily Kandinsky, Kasimir Malevich, Nathalie Goncharova, and others. [RS]

35.376 Sheila Fitzpatrick. *The cultural front: power and culture in revolutionary Russia.* Ithaca, N.Y.: Cornell University Press, 1992. ISBN 0-8014-2196-9 (cl), 0-8014-9516-6 (pbk). ▸ Collected essays, several previously unpublished, of leading historian of Soviet experience. Emphasizes social and institutional facets of cultural revolution. [DTO]

35.377 Sheila Fitzpatrick, ed. *Cultural revolution in Russia, 1928–1931.* Bloomington: Indiana University Press, 1978. ISBN 0-253-31591-3. ▸ Articles on iconoclastic cultural upheaval during First Five-Year Plan, discussing culture wars, education, science, architecture, literature, and other matters. [RS]

35.378 Abbott Gleason, Peter Kenez, and Richard Stites, eds. *Bolshevik culture: experiment and order in the Russian Revolution.* Bloomington: Indiana University Press, 1985. (Special study of the Kennan Institute for Advanced Russian Studies, Wilson Center, 5.) ISBN 0-253-31206-x (cl), 0-253-20513-1 (pbk). ▸ Scholarly studies in ritual, apparel, criminal behavior, education, press, publishing, and cultic movements through early 1920s. [RS/LS]

35.379 Boris Groys. *The total art of Stalinism: avant-garde, aesthetic dictatorship, and beyond.* Charles Rougle, trans. Princeton: Princeton University Press, 1992. ISBN 0-691-05596-3. ▸ Original philosophical interpretation of Stalinism as unified cultural system and its relation to avant-garde. [RS]

35.380 Hans Gunther, ed. *The culture of the Stalin period.* New York: St. Martin's, 1990. ISBN 0-312-03993-x. ▸ Studies on art, architecture, reading, cinema, roots of socialist realism, political holidays, and working-class culture in 1930s. [RS]

35.381 Priscilla Johnson and Leopold Łabędź, eds. *Khrushchev and the arts: the politics of Soviet culture, 1962–1964.* Cambridge, Mass.: MIT Press, 1967. ▸ Discussion of mostly political aspects of literature and other branches of culture such as literary dissidence. [RS]

35.382 Peter Kenez. *The birth of the propaganda state: Soviet methods of mass mobilization, 1917–1929.* Cambridge: Cambridge University Press, 1985. ISBN 0-521-30636-1 (cl), 0-521-31398-8 (pbk). ▸ Historical treatment of tensions between art, politics, and popular taste in 1920s in realm of graphic art, press, oral agitation, book publishing, and mass education. [RS/DKR]

35.383 *Kulturnaya zhizn v SSSR* (Cultural life and the USSR).

Moscow, 1975–. ‣ Documentary, almost daily chronicle of cultural events, creations, and performances. [RS]

35.384 Kurt London. *The seven Soviet arts.* 1937 ed. Eric S. Bensinger, trans. Westport, Conn.: Greenwood, 1970. ISBN 0-8371-4263-6. ‣ Incisive essays on art, music, theater, cinema, literature, architecture, and other arts seen firsthand by keen critic. [RS]

35.385 Nils Ake Nilsson, ed. *Art, society, revolution: Russia, 1917–1921.* Stockholm: Almqvist & Wiksell, 1979. ISBN 91-22-00376-2 (pbk). ‣ Articles on intelligentsia, futurism, Scythianism, theater, and cinema in formative years of Soviet culture. [RS]

35.386 William G. Rosenberg, ed. *Bolshevik visions: first phase of the cultural revolution in Soviet Russia.* 1984 2d ed. 2 vols. Ann Arbor: University of Michigan Press, 1990. ISBN 0-472-09424-6 (v. 1, cl), 0-472-09425-4 (v. 2, cl), 0-472-06424-X (v. 1, pbk), 0-472-06425-8 (v. 2, pbk). ‣ Collection of Soviet documents on moral ideals, sex roles, religion, language, schooling, and arts. [RS]

35.387 Zenovia A. Sochor. *Revolution and culture: the Bogdanov-Lenin controversy.* Ithaca, N.Y.: Cornell University Press, 1988. ISBN 0-8014-2088-1. ‣ Brilliant evocation of rival Marxist visions of culture as they arose out of revolutionary era in Russia, Leninist as control oriented and based on class conflict as source of cultural transformation, Bogdanovite as organic, as necessary prior foundation for building of socialism. Excellent material on *Proletkult.* [DTO]

35.388 Richard Stites. *Revolutionary dreams: utopian vision and experimental life in the Russian Revolution.* 1989 ed. New York: Oxford University Press, 1991. ISBN 0-19-505537-3 (pbk). ‣ Interpretive exploration of festivals, rituals, science fiction, machine music, and other experimental and utopian cultural forms. [RS]

35.389 Nicholas Timasheff. *The great retreat: the growth and decline of communism in Russia.* 1946 ed. New York: Arno, 1972. ISBN 0-405-04595-6. ‣ Classic interpretation of Stalinist era as cultural throwback in realms of science, art, ideas, education, and values. [RS]

35.390 Nina Tumarkin. *Lenin lives! The Lenin cult in Soviet Russia.* Cambridge, Mass.: Harvard University Press, 1983. ISBN 0-674-52430-6. ‣ Study of deification of leader and its long-term impact on arts, communist mythology, and national psychology. [RS]

35.391 Robert C. Williams. *Artists in revolution: portraits of the Russian avant-garde, 1905–1925.* Bloomington: Indiana University Press, 1977. ISBN 0-253-31077-6. ‣ Examination of intellectual, ideological, and stylistic roots and outcome of bolshevik art revolution. Treats proletarian culture, poster, theater, painting, poetry, and film. [RS]

Literature

35.392 Carol Avins. *Border crossings: the West and Russian identity in Soviet literature, 1917–1934.* Berkeley: University of California Press, 1983. ISBN 0-520-04233-6. ‣ Discussion of mutual influences and migrating cultural currents between revolutionary Russia and West. [RS]

35.393 Edward James Brown. *Mayakovsky: a poet in the Revolution.* Princeton: Princeton University Press, 1973. ISBN 0-691-06255-2. ‣ One of best interpretive literary biographies, capturing both revolutionary energy and ambivalence of dominant bolshevik poet. [RS]

35.394 Katerina Clark. *The Soviet novel: history as ritual.* Chicago: University of Chicago Press, 1985. ISBN 0-226-10766-3 (pbk). ‣ Imaginative interpretation of Stalinist cultural system and mythologies, heroes, and master plots of socialist realism. [RS]

35.395 Vera S. Dunham. *In Stalin's time: middle-class values in Soviet fiction.* Rev. ed. Richard Sheldon, Introduction. Durham, N.C.: Duke University Press, 1990. ISBN 0-8223-1085-6. ‣ Innovative readings of literature of socialist realism and middle-class values in general in postwar decade. Emphasizes Big Deal, compromise struck during war between regime and middle class. [RS/HK]

35.396 Max Eastman. *Artists in uniform: a study of literature and bureaucratism.* 1934 ed. New York: Octagon Books, 1972. ISBN 0-374-92453-8. ‣ Dated but still useful study of philosophical background of thought control. [RS]

35.397 Maurice Friedberg. *A decade of euphoria: Western literature in post-Stalin Russia, 1954–64.* Bloomington: Indiana University Press, 1977. ISBN 0-253-31675-8. ‣ Analysis of neglected side of cultural thaw in Khrushchev era; partial revival of imported foreign fiction and its impact. [RS]

35.398 Maurice Friedberg. *Russian classics in Soviet jackets.* New York: Columbia University Press, 1962. ‣ Useful historical survey of Soviet ideological treatment of literary past and changing fate of Pushkin, Tolstoy, and other masters. [RS]

35.399 John Garrard and Carol Garrard. *Inside the Soviet Writer's Union.* New York and London: Free Press and Collier Macmillan, 1990. ISBN 0-02-911320-2. ‣ Study of structure and politics of Soviet literary profession and organization that made and broke careers (and lives) for half century. [RS]

35.400 Geoffrey A. Hosking. *Beyond socialist realism: Soviet fiction since Ivan Denisovich.* New York: Holmes & Meier, 1980. ISBN 0-8419-0484-7. ‣ Examination of deepening of traditional values in Soviet life and art in post-Stalin period as reflected in village prose. [RS]

35.401 Robert A. Maguire. *Red virgin soil: Soviet literature in the 1920s.* 1968 ed. Ithaca, N.Y.: Cornell University Press, 1987. ISBN 0-8014-9447-8 (pbk). ‣ Truly enduring study of Soviet thought and culture in 1920s. Examines major "thick journal" and its literary embroilments. [RS]

Art and Architecture

35.402 *Art into production: Soviet textiles, fashion, and ceramics, 1917–1935.* Oxford: Museum of Modern Art, Oxford, and Crafts Council of England and Wales, 1984. ISBN 0-905836-47-2. ‣ Beautifully designed catalogue of so-called minor arts of first revolutionary decade. [RS]

35.403 Mikhail Guerman, comp. *Art of the October Revolution.* W. Freeman, David Saunders, and C. Binns, trans. Alexander Kokovin, layout. New York: Abrams, 1979. ISBN 0-8109-0675-9. ‣ Numerous photos, posters, paintings, and other graphics, including pictures of rituals and festivals, with brief commentary. [RS]

35.404 Christina Lodder. *Russian constructivism.* 1983 ed. New Haven: Yale University Press, 1985. ISBN 0-300-03406-7 (pbk). ‣ Detailed, illustrated history of major artistic current of 1920s in graphics, stage design, furniture, and other realms of creative expression. [RS]

35.405 S. Frederick Starr. *Melnikov: solo architect in a mass society.* Princeton: Princeton University Press, 1978. ISBN 0-691-03931-3. ‣ Most valuable book available on Soviet architecture as it intersects with ideology, politics, and everyday life. Brilliant analysis and numerous illustrations. [RS]

35.406 V. V. Vanslov. *Chto takoe sotsialisticheskii realizm* (What is socialist realism?). Moscow: Izobrazital'noe Iskusstvo, 1988. ISBN 5-85200-080-9. ▸ Recent, traditionally argued Soviet statement about virtues of socialist realism in painting, poster, and sculpture. Illustrated. [RS]

35.407 L. Vostretsova et al. *Soviet art, 1920's–1930's: Russian Museum, Leningrad.* Vladimir Leniashin, ed. Sharon McKee, trans. New York: Abrams, 1988. ISBN 0-8109-2399-8 (pbk). ▸ Superb full-color reproductions of great avant-garde masters, socialist realist artists, and various minor schools. [RS]

35.408 Stephen White. *The bolshevik poster.* New Haven: Yale University Press, 1988. ISBN 0-300-04339-2. ▸ Expert commentary and political analysis of major poster genres and artists, lavishly illustrated. [RS]

Theater and Opera

35.409 Nikolai A. Gorchakov. *The theater in Soviet Russia.* 1957 ed. Edgar Lehrman, trans. Freeport, N.Y.: Books for Libraries, 1972. ISBN 0-8369-6869-7. ▸ Detailed account of theater. Outdated but still not superseded. [RS]

35.410 Harold B. Segel. *Twentieth-century Russian drama: from Gorky to the present.* New York: Columbia University Press, 1979. ISBN 0-231-04576-X (cl), 0-231-04577-8 (pbk). ▸ Wide-ranging critical and comparative discussion of Soviet plays of every genre. [RS]

35.411 Peter Yershov. *Comedy in the Soviet theater.* 1956 ed. New York: Praeger for Research Program on the U.S.S.R., 1957. (East European Fund: research monographs of the Research Program on the U.S.S.R., 2.) ▸ Informative commentary on little-known subject and its relationship to other forms of comedy. [RS]

Music

35.412 *Istoriya musyki narodov SSSR* (History of the music of the peoples of the USSR). 2 vols. Moscow, 1970. ▸ Informative, if unimaginative, survey of folk and classical music of republics to 1941. [RS]

35.413 Jury Jelagin. *Taming of the arts.* Nicholas Wreden, trans. New York: Dutton, 1951. ▸ Invaluable insider's view of musical and theater life in Stalin era from backstage and orchestra pit. [RS]

35.414 Harlow Robinson. *Sergei Prokofiev: a biography.* New York: Viking, 1987. ISBN 0-670-80419-3. ▸ First serious English-language biography in decades of composer whom many critics rank highest in Soviet musical history. [RS]

35.415 Boris Schwartz. *Music and musical life in Soviet Russia.* Rev. ed. Bloomington: Indiana University Press, 1983. ISBN 0-253-33956-1. ▸ Study of mainstream classical music—opera, ballet, symphony, chamber—and its performance, organizational infrastructure, and political context. [RS]

35.416 Dmitrii Shostakovich. *Testimony: the memoirs of Dmitri Shostakovich.* Solomon Volkov, ed. Antonina W. Bouis, trans. New York: Harper & Row, 1979. ISBN 0-06-014476-9. ▸ Controversial publication of conversations with composer by his pupil and admirer on matters musical and political. [RS]

35.417 Tamara Stepanovna Tkachenko. *Narodnyi tanets: dopushcheno v kachestve ucheb. posobiia dlia khoreograficheskikh otd-nii teatral'nykh in-tov i khoreograficheskikh uchilishch* (The folk dance: issued as a textbook for choreography sections of theater institutes and choreography training schools). Moscow: Iskusstvo, 1954. ▸ Definitive prescription for folk dancing ensembles by noted dancer and choreographer. [RS]

35.418 Alexander Werth. *Musical uproar in Moscow.* 1949 ed. Westport, Conn.: Greenwood, 1973. ISBN 0-8371-6864-3. ▸ Doc-uments and discussion of musical purges of Andrei Zhdanov in late 1940s. [RS]

Cinema

35.419 Andrew Horton and Michael Brashinsky. *The zero hour: glasnost and Soviet cinema in transition.* Princeton: Princeton University Press, 1992. ISBN 0-691-06937-9 (cl), 0-691-01920-7 (pbk). ▸ Skillful, informed analysis of cinematic treatment of history, youth values, women, crime, and other social problems with detailed exegeses of key films. [RS]

35.420 Peter Kenez. *Cinema and Soviet society, 1917–1953.* Cambridge: Cambridge University Press, 1992. ISBN 0-521-41671-X (cl), 0-521-42863-7 (pbk). ▸ Fresh interpretation of film industry, film, and political context with incisive moral and aesthetic judgments and insights. [RS]

35.421 Anna Lawton. *Kinoglasnost: Soviet cinema in our time.* New York: Cambridge University Press, 1992. ISBN 0-521-38117-7 (cl), 0-521-38814-7 (pbk). ▸ Richly informed account, much of it from inside films, industry, cinema public of late Brezhnev and Gorbachev eras, and concludes with great reforms of *glasnost* and *perestroika*. [RS]

35.422 Anna Lawton, ed. *The Red screen: politics, society, and art in Soviet cinema.* London: Routledge, 1992. ISBN 0-415-07818-0 (cl), 0-415-07819-9 (pbk). ▸ Expert studies of cinema history, treating gender and ethnicity as well as more familiar aesthetic categories, from Revolution to recent past. [RS]

35.423 Jay Leyda. *Kino: a history of the Russian and Soviet film.* 3d ed. Princeton: Princeton University Press, 1983. ISBN 0-691-04007-9 (cl), 0-691-00346-7 (pbk). ▸ Classic, indispensable history, enriched by personal memories of working with Sergei Eisenstein in Moscow in 1930s. Focus mainly on art films. Of little use for period after 1945. [RS]

35.424 *Sovetskie khudozhestvennye fil'my: annotirovannyi katalog* (Soviet art films: annotated catalog). 5 vols. to date. Moscow: Iskusstvo, 1961–. ▸ Indispensable guide to production data, personnel, and (not always fully accurate) story lines of virtually all Soviet films produced up to time of publication. [RS]

35.425 Richard Taylor and Ian Christie, eds. *The film factory: Russian and Soviet cinema in documents.* Richard Taylor, trans. Cambridge, Mass.: Harvard University Press, 1988. ISBN 0-674-30125-0. ▸ Useful articles on aspects of cinema history and film art, little-known as well as established masterpieces. [RS]

35.426 Richard Taylor and Ian Christie, eds. *Inside the film factory: new approaches to Russian and Soviet cinema.* London: Routledge, 1991. ISBN 0-415-04951-2. ▸ Useful articles on aspects of cinema history and film art, little-known as well as established masterpieces. [RS]

35.427 Denise J. Youngblood. *Movies for the masses: popular cinema and Soviet society in the 1920s.* Cambridge: Cambridge University Press, 1992. ISBN 0-521-37470-7. ▸ Reviews debates over mass and high culture and artistic creativity in Soviet film industry of 1920s. Excellent analyses of individual films and viewer and critical responses. [DTO]

35.428 Denise J. Youngblood. *Soviet cinema in the silent era, 1917–1935.* Ann Arbor: University of Michigan Research Press, 1985. ISBN 0-8357-1659-7. ▸ Informative treatment of virtually all popular films of 1920s and their critical reception. [RS]

Popular Culture

35.429 Faubion Bowers. *Entertainment in Russia: ballet, theatre, and entertainment in Russia today.* Edinburgh: Nelson, 1959. ▸ Eyewitness observations on circus, comedy, and other popular performance arts in Khrushchev period by keen critic. [RS]

35.430 John Bushnell. *Moscow graffiti: language and subculture.* Boston: Unwin Hyman, 1990. ISBN 0-04-44518-7 (cl), 0-04-445169-5 (pbk). ▸ Examination of youth gangs, sports fans, and street life through their symbols and language. Excellent chapters on history of urban subculture. [RS]

35.431 Kristian Feigelson. *L'U.R.S.S. et sa télévision.* Marc Ferro, Preface. Paris and Seyssel, France: Institut National de l'Audiovisuel and Champ Vallon, 1990. ISBN 2-87673-107-X. ▸ Up-to-date, analytical study of news shows, organization of television, and variety of informational programs, rooted in history of media. [RS]

35.432 Leo Feigin, ed. *Russian jazz: new identity.* London: Quartet Books, 1985. ISBN 0-7043-2506-3. ▸ Anthology of articles on most recent trends in Soviet jazz—new jazz or free jazz—some learned, some apologetic. [RS]

35.433 Julian Graffy and Geoffrey A. Hosking, eds. *Culture and the media in the USSR today.* New York: St. Martin's, 1989. ISBN 0-312-03457-1. ▸ Data on television, press, cinema, theater, and music during first years of *perestroika*. Rich in information and references. [RS]

35.434 P. S. Gurevich and V. N. Ruzhnikov. *Sovetskoe radioveshchanie: Stranitsy istorii* (Soviet radio broadcasting: pages of history). Moscow: Iskusstvo, 1976. ▸ Technical and programing history of Soviet radio. Informative but conventional history of radio services. [RS]

35.435 Kukryniksy. *Po vragam mira!* (At the enemies of peace!). Moscow: Plakat, 1982. ▸ Pictorial anthology of work of three most famous graphic propagandists—Mikhail Kupriyanov, Porfirii Krylov, and Nikolai Sokolov—whose collective pen name was Kukryniksy. Mostly antifascist and anti-NATO. [RS]

35.436 Christel Lane. *Rites of rulers: ritual in industrial society—the Soviet case.* Cambridge: Cambridge University Press, 1981. ISBN 0-521-22608-2 (cl), 0-521-28347-7 (pbk). ▸ Analysis of origins and function of new ritual movement of 1960s—weddings, initiation rites, and patriotic occasions—celebratory counterpart to Khrushchev's antireligious campaign. [RS]

35.437 Klaus Mehnert. *Russians and their favorite books.* Stanford, Calif.: Hoover Institution Press, 1983. (Hoover Press publication, 282.) ISBN 0-8179-7821-6. ▸ Well-informed, impressionistic picture of reading tastes in Khrushchev and Brezhnev eras, particularly war novels, village prose, mystery, and science fiction. [RS]

35.438 Ellen Mickiewicz. *Split signals: television and politics in the Soviet Union.* New York: Oxford University Press, 1988. ISBN 0-19-505463-6. ▸ Close-up view of Soviet "blue screen," television industry, and news management in early years of *glasnost.* [RS]

35.439 Frank J. Miller. *Folklore for Stalin: Russian folklore and pseudofolklore of the Stalin era.* Armonk, N.Y.: Sharpe, 1990. ISBN 0-87332-668-7. ▸ Charts rebirth and politicization of folklore by Stalin culture managers in 1930s. [RS]

35.440 Jack Miller, ed. *Jews in Soviet culture.* New Brunswick, N.J.: Transaction, 1984. ISBN 0-87855-495-5. ▸ Survey of realms of popular culture where Jews have played significant roles including movies, popular music, radio, stage, and television comedy. [RS]

35.441 Jim Riordan, ed. *Soviet youth culture.* Bloomington: Indiana University Press, 1989. ISBN 0-253-35423-4 (cl), 0-253-28795-2 (pbk). ▸ Essays by European scholars on Komsomol, rock subculture, veterans, gangs, schooling, and public policies. [RS]

35.442 Regine Robin. *Socialist realism: an impossible aesthetic.* Catherine Porter, trans. Stanford, Calif.: Stanford University Press, 1991. ISBN 0-8047-1655-2. ▸ Groundbreaking, deep analysis of origin and components of mass literature. Translation of 1986 edition, *Le réalisme socialiste, une esthétique impossible.* [RS]

35.443 Boris Shumyatskii. *Kinematografiya millionov* (Cinematography for the millions). Moscow, 1935. ▸ Founding document of "mass movie" by chief cinema magnate of early Stalin period. [RS]

35.444 Gerald Stanton Smith. *Songs to seven strings: Russian guitar poetry and Soviet "mass song."* Bloomington: Indiana University Press, 1984. ISBN 0-253-35391-2. ▸ Ranges from prerevolutionary song genres (gypsy, cruel song), through official music and Stalinist-style mass song, to Bulat Okudzhava, Alexandr Galich, and Vladimir Vysotsky. [RS]

35.445 S. Frederick Starr. *Red and hot: the fate of jazz in the Soviet Union, 1917–1980.* 1983 ed. New York: Limelight, 1985. ISBN 0-87910-026-5 (pbk). ▸ Striking tapestry of popular culture as a whole, backgrounding vicissitudes of jazz and jazz players from prerevolutionary days to 1980s. [RS]

35.446 Richard Stites. *Russian popular culture: entertainment and society since 1900.* Cambridge: Cambridge University Press, 1992. ISBN 0-521-36214-8 (cl), 0-521-36986-X (pbk). ▸ Unified, interpretive survey of popular song, story, picture, show, movie, radio, television, and leisure time and their relationship to society and politics. [RS]

35.447 Richard Taylor. *Film propaganda: Soviet Russia and Nazi Germany.* New York and London: Barnes & Noble and Croom Helm, 1979. ISBN 0-06-496778-6. ▸ Study of comparative use of propaganda, entertainment, and information in controlled regimes. [RS]

35.448 Richard Taylor. *The politics of the Soviet cinema, 1917–1929.* Cambridge: Cambridge University Press, 1979. ISBN 0-521-22290-7. ▸ Analysis of cinematic masters of 1920s, demystifying conventional view of popularity. [RS]

35.449 Artemy Troitsky. *Back in the USSR: the true story of rock in Russia.* 1987 ed. Boston: Faber & Faber, 1988. ISBN 0-571-12997-8. ▸ Chatty but informative inside look at people and politics of biggest genre of popular culture. [RS]

35.450 Elena Uvarova, ed. *Russkaya sovetskaya estrada* (Russian and Soviet variety stage). 3 vols. Moscow, 1976–81. ▸ Thorough, informative articles on stage comedy, circus, musical comedy, puppet theater, and other popular stage arts, 1917–77, in politically tinged style of Brezhnev period. [RS]

35.451 Mark Yankovskii. *Iskusstvo operetty* (The arts operetta). Moscow: Sovetskii Kompozitor, 1982. ▸ Detailed history of Soviet operetta in context of Viennese and prerevolutionary models. [RS]

SEE ALSO
33.52 Timothy W. Ryback. *Rock around the Bloc.*

RELIGION

35.452 Johannes Chrysostomus. *Kirchengeschichte Russlands der neuesten Zeit.* 3 vols. Munich: Pustet, 1965–68. ▸ Detailed analysis, factually reliable, based on substantial corpus of printed sources. Written from Catholic perspective. [GF]

35.453 John Shelton Curtiss. *The Russian church and the Soviet state, 1917–1950.* 1953 ed. Gloucester, Mass.: Smith, 1965. ▸ Balanced, although based on limited set of printed sources; overview of church-state relations from 1917 Revolution to postwar years. [GF]

35.454 Dimitry Pospielovsky. *The Russian church under the*

Soviet regime, 1917–1982. 2 vols. Crestwood, N.Y.: St. Vladimir's Seminary Press, 1984. ISBN 0-88141-033-0 (set), 0-88141-015-2 (v. 1), 0-88141-016-0 (v. 2). ▸ Written from impassioned Orthodox perspective, draws on broad base of printed sources and contains much factual information. [GF]

35.455 R. Rossler. *Kirche und Revolution in Russland: Patriarch Tichon und der Sowjetstaat*. Cologne: Böhlau, 1969. ▸ Meticulous analysis of church history in early years of Soviet regime, with particular attention to issues raised at Church Council of 1917–18 and ecclesiastical politics in early 1920s. Based solely on printed sources. [GF]

SCIENCE AND TECHNOLOGY

35.456 Mark B. Adams. "The founding of population genetics: contributions of the Chetverikov school, 1923–1945." *Journal of the history of biology* 1.1 (1968) 23–39. ISSN 0022-5010. ▸ Demonstration of importance of Russian geneticists in 1910s and 1920s in creating field of population genetics and importance of school of Sergei Chetverikov. [LRG]

35.457 Mark B. Adams. "From gene fund to gene pool: on the evolution of evolutionary language." *Studies in the history of biology* 3 (1979) 241–85. ▸ Establishment of term "gene pool" in modern genetics as based on earlier Russian term "gene fund." Discussion of role of Russian-American biologist Theodosius Dobzhansky. [LRG]

35.458 Kendall E. Bailes. *Science and Russian culture in an age of revolutions: V. I. Vernadsky and his scientific school, 1863–1945*. Bloomington: Indiana University Press, 1990. ISBN 0-253-31123-3. ▸ Study of life and work of Ukrainian-Soviet geologist, Vladimir Vernadsky, his views on ecology, biogeochemistry, and innovative concepts such as biosphere. Also discusses relationship of early Soviet government with scientists. [LRG]

35.459 Jonathan Coopersmith. *The electrification of Russia, 1880–1926*. Ithaca, N.Y.: Cornell University Press, 1992. ISBN 0-8014-2723-1. ▸ Superb case study of role of engineering profession in electrification and economic development of Russia, both before and after 1917 revolutions. Comparative analysis inspired by models from history of science and technology; based on wide range of published and archival sources. [DTO]

35.460 Murray Feshbach and Alfred Friendly, Jr. *Ecocide in the USSR: health and nature under seige*. New York: Basic Books, 1992. ISBN 0-456-01664-2. ▸ Detailed examination of public health and demographic and ecological disasters under Soviet regime. [LRG]

35.461 Loren R. Graham. *The ghost of the executed engineer: technology and the fall of the Soviet Union*. Cambridge, Mass.: Harvard University Press, 1993. ISBN 0-674-35436-2. ▸ Brief biography based on new archival material of eminent Russian engineer, Petr I. Pal'chinskii, who played major role in Provisional Government of 1917. Tragic story of his later work for the Soviet regime and execution as member of "Industrial party." Life emblematic of role of technology in Soviet experiment and of destructive choices made by regime in its name. [DTO]

35.462 Loren R. Graham. "Science and values: the eugenics movement in Germany and Russia in the 1920's." *American historical review* 82.5 (1977) 1133–64. ISSN 0002-8762. ▸ Comparison of attitudes toward eugenics in 1920s in both Germany and Russia, demonstrating eugenics originally supported by people with diverse political beliefs, including Marxists, Communists, and Social Democrats. [LRG]

35.463 Loren R. Graham. *Science, philosophy, and human behavior in the Soviet Union*. New York: Columbia University Press, 1987. ISBN 0-231-06442-X. ▸ Analysis of role of Marxism in scientific thought in Soviet Union, 1917–85, showing both positive

and negative impacts. Also discusses dialectical materialism's place in Soviet science and in political life. [LRG]

35.464 Loren R. Graham. *The Soviet Academy of Sciences and the Communist party, 1927–1932*. Princeton: Princeton University Press, 1967. ▸ Examination of purge and reorganization of Russia's premier scientific institution, Academy of Sciences, and its transformation into Soviet organization. [LRG]

35.465 David Joravsky. *The Lysenko affair*. Cambridge, Mass.: Harvard University Press, 1970. (Russian Research Center studies, 61.) ISBN 0-674-53985-0. ▸ Story of rise and fall of Trofim Denisovich Lysenko, poorly educated agronomist who seized control of Soviet biological establishment and propagated view of genetics contradicting world science. Soviet Marxism and science. [LRG]

35.466 David Joravsky. *Russian psychology: a critical history*. Oxford: Blackwell, 1989. ISBN 0-631-16337-9. ▸ Interpretive examination of growth of Russian psychology from late nineteenth century through Soviet period. Relationship between psychology and politics. [LRG]

35.467 David Joravsky. *Soviet Marxism and natural science, 1917–1932*. New York: Columbia University Press, 1961. ▸ Examination of disputes among early Soviet Marxists and scientists over relevance and meaning of Marxism for natural science and development of Soviet dialectical materialism. [LRG]

35.468 Paul R. Josephson. *Physics and politics in revolutionary Russia*. Berkeley: University of California Press, 1991. ISBN 0-520-07482-3. ▸ Study of early growth of physics in Soviet Russia, especially at Leningrad Physico-Technical Institute (often called cradle of Soviet physics), and life and work of physicist A. F. Ioffe. [LRG]

35.469 Robert McCutcheon. "The 1936–1937 purge of Soviet astronomers." *Slavic review* 5.1 (1991) 100–17. ISSN 0037-6779. ▸ Unique examination of devastating purge of Soviet astronomers, and its effects on such prominent institutions as Pulkovo Observatory. [LRG]

35.470 Bruce Parrott. *Politics and technology in the Soviet Union*. Cambridge, Mass.: MIT Press, 1983. ISBN 0-262-16092-7. ▸ Examination of Soviet regime's attitudes toward technology throughout its history. Illuminates tensions between goals of Soviet leadership and inertia in bureaucracy. [LRG]

35.471 Esther R. Phillips. "Nicolai Nicolaevich Luzin and the Moscow school of functions." *Historia mathematica* 5 (1978) 275–305. ISSN 0315-0860. ▸ Description of formation of Moscow School of Mathematics, leading force in modern mathematics, and activities of founder N. N. Luzin. [LRG]

35.472 Andrei Sakharov. *Memoirs*. Richard Lourie, trans. New York: Knopf, 1990. ISBN 0-394-53740-8. ▸ Reminiscences of most famous Soviet physicist of century, Andrei Sakharov, major leader in Soviet hydrogen bomb project and later most famous dissident in Soviet history. [LRG]

35.473 Susan Gross Solomon. "Reflections on Western studies of Soviet science." In *The social context of Soviet science*. Linda L. Lubrano and Susan Gross Solomon, eds., pp. 173–204. Boulder: Westview, 1980. ISBN 0-89158-450-1. ▸ Analysis of changes over time in predominant views and interests of Western scholars studying Soviet science. Illustration of importance of social factors in study of science. [LRG]

35.474 Susan Gross Solomon and John F. Hutchinson, eds. *Health and society in revolutionary Russia*. Bloomington: Indiana University Press, 1990. ISBN 0-253-35332-7. ▸ Collection of original essays on public health and its institutions in years of Soviet power. Emphasizes both prerevolutionary roots of public medicine and role of ideology in early Soviet era. [DTO]

35.475 Otto Struve. "The Poulkovo Observatory (1839–1941)." *Sky and telescope* 1.4 (1941) 3–19. ISSN 0037-6604. ▸ Rare description of one of most famous astronomical observatories in world, written by descendant of founder. [LRG]

35.476 Alexander Vucinich. *Empire of knowledge: the Academy of Sciences of the USSR (1917–1970)*. Berkeley: University of California Press, 1984. ISBN 0-520-04871-7. ▸ History of major institution in fundamental science in Soviet Union. Discusses relationship between science and politics. [LRG]

SEE ALSO

4.252 Douglas Weiner. *Models of nature.*

4.401 Kendall E. Bailes. *Technology and society under Lenin and Stalin.*

44.652 Walter A. McDougall. . . . *the heavens and the earth.*

48.298 David Holloway. *The Soviet Union and the arms race.*

FREDERICK E. HOXIE

Native Peoples of the Americas

Until recently, a guide to historical literature on America's native peoples would have been a contradiction in terms. For the vast majority of the time that people have occupied the hemisphere's two continents, communities did not employ written records to keep track of their histories. With the exception of some Mesoamerican societies, knowledge was entrusted to particular individuals who stored it in their memories, shared it in their oratory and songs, and celebrated it in public ceremonies and rituals. Nearly everyone used painting, picture writing, or other modes of visual representation to record elements of their cultural life, but these were generally considered tools to assist those charged with the task of remembering and passing on the community's heritage. Thus, when sustained contact between the Americas and the rest of the world began at the end of the fifteenth century, Europeans found little in the New World that they could recognize as historical writing.

Aside from the Mesoamerican chronicles and the pictographic records mentioned above, written histories of America's native peoples began with the recorded words of outsiders. Indeed, even societies that had a tradition of written record keeping (e.g., the Aztecs) were overwhelmed by Europeans who quickly replaced indigenous histories with their own narratives. Historical writing about the native peoples of the hemisphere was thus grafted onto cultures whose traditions were primarily oral and were rooted in tragedy and misunderstanding. Europeans constructed versions of Indian culture that, no matter how well intentioned, filtered American life through a European lens. In the atmosphere of conquest, native peoples were routinely judged inferior to a Christian standard, and Europeans saw little reason to doubt their judgment that America's native societies were simple, uncivilized, and doomed. Early writers wrote confidently of the peoples they encountered, despite the fact that few spoke indigenous languages or spent significant time studying their subject's social arrangements, religious values, or political systems.

The existence of a native oral tradition, together with the destructive impact of the European invasion, created significant barriers to the establishment of a historical literature on America's indigenous peoples. The conquest obscured native traditions while it elevated the pretensions of early historical writers. Newcomers with an investment in imperial expansion had little interest in understanding the peoples they encountered. Columbus, for example, ignored Caribbean tales of trade and long-distance diplomacy, believing instead that he had encountered a series of isolated and naive primitives who had no political system other than a series of vicious chiefs. John Smith looked past the complex diplomatic world of coastal Algonquin Indians and wrote instead that the native people of the Virginia tidewater were hopelessly warlike and unreliable. Conquistadors testified that the natives of Mexico worshipped the devil, while other soldiers and explorers argued that Indian communities were remnants of the lost tribes of Israel, or people so dedicated to the hunt that they could live without clothing and capture deer by running them down, or warriors so devoted to battle that they would simply die if their societies were forced to live in peace.

The distortions and dislocations of the past cast a continuing shadow over historical writing about native people in the Americas. Chronicles of early contact between Europeans and Indians often provided unparalleled information about ancient native traditions, while they simultaneously ignored or distorted basic elements of tribal life. Later accounts frequently built on such early distortions, and scholars have rarely been able to approach the subject with disinterest. In North America, for example, the epic but fanciful writing of Francis Parkman and the cramped theories of Frederick Jackson Turner continued to shape scholarly perceptions of native peoples for decades following the writers' deaths. It is only in the past half-century that the rise of anthropology as a scholarly discipline, the emergence of revisionist national histories in many American countries, and the beginnings of public sympathy for the rights of native peoples have supported the creation of a new, more balanced historical literature. Examples of that literature are only now beginning to appear in significant numbers.

Native traditions and academic hostility have also discouraged Indian people themselves from embarking on careers as historians. Preference for oral records brings written accounts into doubt. In addition, indigenous communities have had limited access to university educations. And those who ventured into the academy have generally found its customs and expectations off-putting. Extraordinary individuals such as Felipe Guaman Poma de Ayala (R. Adorno 36.387, 36.388), who wrote in seventeenth century Peru, sometimes have emerged to offer written native versions of events, but there were no professionally trained American Indian historians until well into the twentieth century. Following World War II, American Indian historians began to emerge from graduate programs, forming the basis for a community of Indian academic scholars. Encouraging younger students, and eager to connect traditional Indian communities to the wider world, these historians promise to play a crucial role in this field in the decades to come.

Modern historical writing about Indians draws much of its intellectual energy from the discipline of anthropology. Joining most social scientists in rejecting evolutionary or racist hierarchies and agreeing with cultural anthropologists that human communities differ because they adhere to differing traditions and values, modern scholars have learned to describe Aztecs and Utes, or Spaniards and Italians, in their own terms rather than with reference to their contrasting skin color (if any), their degree of Christian faith, or their mastery of military technology. Such an approach has not only encouraged authors to look past the chauvinistic and racist assumptions of the past, but it has also suggested that they explore native literatures and languages in an effort to seek out the native perspective on events. Scholarship inspired by the insights of anthropology has thus sought to correct the distortions of the past and to reconstruct an indigenous tradition of thought and conduct. At its best, this new scholarship has produced writing that broadens dramatically the circle of people whom scholars might include as historical subjects. Those long thought to have "no history" now appear in three dimensions, acting to reconcile conflicting values, to balance competing political interests, and to defend their technological and artistic achievements. And traditions many assumed were entirely too obscure to be recovered have been reconstructed in their own rich complexity and within a distinct historical context. It is this new writing that forms the centerpiece of the citations listed below.

The historical literature on native peoples of course does not follow national boundaries neatly, but the nature of the literature (and the scholarly community) has suggested that this section should be divided along broad national and regional lines. This
section is divided into seven major subsections. They address the indigenous peoples
of modern Canada; the United States (including Alaska but excluding Hawaii); Mexico, Central America and the Caribbean (including the Venzuelan lowlands); highland
South America (from Colombia to Chile); the Amazon; and the southern cone of South
America (Argentina, Chile, and Paraguay). The allocation of entries among these sections roughly reflects the level of scholarly activity in each area and the impact of the
new scholarly trends sketched above. Thus, Canada and highland South America loom
larger than Central America, and the literature on the United States makes up the
largest section. No doubt the section editor's U.S. citizenship has also played a part in
this architecture.

Each of the seven subsections of the list is further subdivided into five parts. This
organization is somewhat artificial, but it should allow readers to focus quickly on topics
that interest them. It also makes clear the areas where the historical literature is relatively
thin and topics have gone unaddressed. Part one is devoted to works on the precontact
era. Rooted in archaelogy and folklore, these studies rise above the technical and narrowly focused literature of those fields and describe indigenous peoples as human actors
in a historical moment. They range from masterly studies of a single culture (e.g. Bruce
Trigger, *The Children of Aataentsic*, 36.2) to regional overviews, to collections of outstanding essays on particular topics in a region's prehistory. Also included are the few
reference works in this area—most prominently Michael Coe's *Atlas of Ancient America*
(36.74)—and introductions to the substantial literature on the Aztec and Inca empires.
These last items include studies of Nahuatl and Quechua poetry and literature, works
that will introduce readers to the conceptual and aesthetic world of precontact America.
Each list of precontact books has been arranged to be multidisciplinary and, even when
the authors are not historians, to emphasize the historical sources of the region's indigenous cultures.

Part two in each subsection is devoted to works that describe the period of European
contact and colonial rule. The length of this period differs from region to region. Europeans arrived in the Caribbean in the fifteenth century, but they did not reach parts
of the Great Basin of Utah and Nevada until the nineteenth. Similarly, colonial rule
ended in the United States in 1783, nearly a half-century before the Spanish left South
America. The titles in part two focus on the differing perceptions that informed first
contacts between Europeans and Americans, the various strategies employed to assert
domination over native people, and the consequences of that domination for indigenous cultures. They include major documentary sources in the form of edited and
annotated chronicles by early European travelers, military officers, priests, and bureaucrats. Notable among these are Bernardino de Sahagún's thirteen volume *Floretine
Codex* (36.303), a priest's compilation of information on Aztec culture, drawn from
native informants and written originally in Nahuatl. The editions of such works listed
here generally include a scholarly apparatus that allows readers to understand the prejudices of the original authors. Also included are a series of works that describe the
demographic consequences of first contact. Books such as Noble David Cook's *Demographic Collapse: Indian Peru* (36.391) make precise the grand theories of precontact
population and the impact of European diseases on native communities.

Parts three and four are often the shortest divisions of the list's subsections. They
contain titles on the experience of native peoples during the nineteenth and twentieth
centuries. Works on the nineteenth century, when nation-states were taking form in
each area and the industrial revolution was altering their economies and social structures, address aspects of culture change among native peoples and describe the impact

of emerging national governments on indigenous traditions. Several works in the United States subsection describe federal policies and their meaning, while Canadian authors describe the effects of the fur trade on Indian societies, and scholars of Central and South America describe religious change, racial intermixture, and technological innovation. Notable here also are recent works on shifting community identities and social structures (e.g. Kristine Jones's essay "Calfucura and Namuncura: Nation Builders of the Pampas," 36.487) and discussions of particularly violent confrontations between native peoples and national states (e.g., F. L. Barron and J. B. Waldram, eds. 36.16 on the Canadian *métis* rebellion).

The twentieth century is generally the most overlooked period of native history—the era when American nation-states found themselves in the company of native communities they had hoped (or assumed) would disappear. Because so many scholars have assumed that indigenous people were Stone Age creatures, locked into the past, it has been difficult for them to treat twentieth-century topics seriously. Nevertheless, each subsection contains several works on the twentieth century, many of them recent. The most diverse of these listings is the United States section on the twentieth century, containing biographies, community studies, and autobiographies. It is interesting to note as well that scholars of Canada and the United States appear to have been most active in this area, perhaps because native peoples south of the Rio Grande are more difficult to isolate as separate elements of national populations. While there is considerable overlap between parts three and four, titles have been selected for each that discuss indigenous communities in these sharply contrasting historical contexts. Finally, each subsection concludes with a list of general and theoretical works that includes synthetic histories, texts, reference books, bibliographies, and conceptual discussions of Indian history. This fifth part of every subsection includes books that do not fit neatly into a single chronological division, as well as titles that introduce readers to the ideas that have fueled the most recent generation of historical scholarship. Among the most important reference works cited are the Smithsonian Institution's *Handbook of North American Indians* (36.214, 36.215, 36.227, 36.228, 36.249, 36.250, 36.259, 36.263, 36.266), the *Handbook of Middle American Indians* (36.317) and the *Handbook of South American Indians* (36.503). While produced largely by anthropologists with a limited interest in historical change, these volumes are invaluable sources for basic information about native groups and the scholarship on them.

Readers are urged to browse the parts of the lists that interest them and to compare the literatures from different parts of the hemisphere. This practice will illuminate the different approaches that sometimes dominate national literatures, and will alert researchers to relevant titles that might contain useful insights on their own topic. Because historical scholarship on native peoples does not fit neatly into any chronological or geographical scheme, it is useful to check all bordering lists before proceeding to other reference works. The same caution applies to the index. Cross-references should enable readers to trace works on native peoples into this list as well as those on the hemisphere's national histories.

Taken together, the titles in this section should help readers peer past the distortions and misinformation that has been so much a part of popular and scholarly writing about native peoples to view traditions that existed for centuries in the Americas—building great cities, extensive trade networks, and compelling networks of kinship, loyalty, and affection. With this clarity of vision, readers should then be able to recognize modern versions of surviving indigenous communities and to see themselves more clearly, not as heirs of an imperial rule, but as people living among others.

[Contributors: DJL = Debra J. Lindsay, DGS = David G. Sweet, EH-D = Evelyn Hu-DeHart, FEH = Frederick E. Hoxie, HM = Harvey Markowitz, KLJ = Kristine L. Jones, MAB = Mark A. Burkholder, MFB = Marguerite F. Beeby, MWH = Mary W. Helms, NDC = Noble David Cook, NMK = Nicholas M. Kliment, RF = Renée Fossett, RLM = Richard L. Millett, SS = Susan Schroeder, WFD = William F. Deverell]

CANADA

Precontact

36.1　John W. Ives. *A theory of Northern Athapaskan prehistory.* Boulder: Westview, 1990. ISBN 0-8133-7517-7. ▸ Interdisciplinary monograph offering distinctive synthesis of Athapaskan prehistory. Argues kinship plays crucial role in shaping economic relationships and strategies. [RF]

36.2　Bruce G. Trigger. *The children of Aataentsic: a history of the Huron people to 1660.* 1976 ed. Kingston, Ont.: McGill-Queen's University Press, 1987. ISBN 0-7735-0626-8 (cl), 0-7735-0627-6 (pbk). ▸ Ethnohistory of Huron confederacy, its wars with Iroquois, and collapse. Model study combining archaeology, ethnography, linguistics, and geography. [RF]

36.3　Bruce G. Trigger. *The Huron: farmers of the North.* 2d ed.

Fort Worth: Holt, Rinehart & Winston, 1990. ISBN 0-03-031689-8. ▸ New edition of 1969 classic by archaeologist with somewhat less emphasis on psychocultural analysis. Coherent picture of society as functioning whole using evidence from many sources and disciplines. [RF]

Colonial Period

36.4　Karen L. Anderson. *Chain her by one foot: the subjugation of women in seventeenth-century New France.* New York: Routledge, 1991. ISBN 0-415-04758-7. ▸ Interesting analysis of relations of subjugation and dominance, arguing they were introduced into egalitarian tribal societies following destruction of their cultural systems. Focus on Huron and Montagnais societies, 1600–50. [RF]

36.5　Lucien Campeau, S.J. *Fondation de la mission huronne, 1635–1637.* Vol. 3 of *Monumenta novae franciae.* Quebec and Rome: Les Presses de l'Université Laval and Monumenta Historica Société Jésu, 1987. (Monumenta historica Societatis Iesu, 130). ISBN 88-7041-130-8. ▸ Edition of correspondence and other documents related to first Jesuit mission to Hurons, 1635–37. Scholarly introduction, bibliography, and extensive notes. Important source for accounts of first contact in New France. [RF]

36.6　Olive P. Dickason. *The myth of the savage and the beginnings of French colonialism in the Americas.* Edmonton: University of Alberta Press, 1984. ISBN 0-88864-036-6. ▸ Examination of European stereotypes of American Indians and their origin. Traces development of concept of "les hommes sauvages." Especially good for description of French perceptions. [RF]

36.7　Daniel Francis and Toby Morantz. *Partners in furs: a history of the fur trade in eastern James Bay, 1600–1870.* Kingston, Ont.: McGill-Queen's University Press, 1983. ISBN 0-7735-0385-4 (cl), 0-7735-0386-2 (pbk). ▸ Investigation of effects of fur trade on social patterns of Algonquian peoples in eastern James Bay region. Central focus on hunting and land-tenure systems and on tribal leadership. Excellent use of ethnographic and historical sources. [RF]

36.8　L. C. Green and Olive P. Dickason. *The law of nations and the New World.* Edmonton: University of Alberta Press, 1989. ISBN 0-88864-129-X. ▸ Exploration of differing concepts of sovereignty, rights of discovery, and effective occupation held by American Indians and Europeans, and how conflicting philosophies created quandary over aboriginal "rights." Best general survey available. [RF]

36.9　Conrad Heidenreich. *Huronia: a history and geography of the Huron Indians, 1600–1650.* Toronto: McClelland & Stewart, 1971. ISBN 0-7710-4076-8. ▸ Geographer's overview of Huron homeland in modern Ontario. Focuses on late precontact period and first years of French contact. Describes Huron social organization, subsistence, and trade. Includes excellent discussion of sources. [RF]

36.10　George T. Hunt. *The wars of the Iroquois: a study of intertribal trade relations.* 1940 ed. Madison: University of Wisconsin Press, 1972. ISBN 0-299-00164-4 (pbk). ▸ Classic monograph arguing relationship between Europeans and Indians structured by preexisting aboriginal alliances; alliances shaped competition during fur trade era. [RF]

36.11　Cornelius J. Jaenen. *Friend and foe: aspects of French-Amerindian cultural contact in the sixteenth and seventeenth centuries.* New York: Columbia University Press, 1976. ISBN 0-231-04088-1. ▸ Chronicle of early relations between French and aboriginal groups, describing them as considerably less friendly and cooperative than most Canadian historians have recognized. Good overview; views encounter from perspective of each group. [RF]

36.12 Dale R. Russell. *The eighteenth-century Western Cree and their neighbours.* Hull, Que.: Canadian Museum of Civilization, 1991. ISBN 0-660-12915-9 (pbk). ▸ History of Cree and Assiniboin, 1690–1781. Discusses historiographical debates on location and migrations of Western Cree and origins of Plains Cree. Best available overview of these widely dispersed groups. [RF]

36.13 Paul C. Thistle. *Indian-European trade relations in the lower Saskatchewan river region to 1840.* Winnipeg: University of Manitoba Press, 1986. ISBN 0-88755-105-X. ▸ Examination of Cree responses to fur trade. Shows Plains aboriginal peoples retained independence from European dominance until mid-nineteenth century. Sophisticated treatment of each group's motivations. [RF]

36.14 Bruce G. Trigger. *Natives and newcomers: Canada's "heroic age" reconsidered.* Kingston, Ont.: McGill-Queen's University Press, 1985. ISBN 0-7735-0594-6 (cl), 0-7735-0595-4 (pbk). ▸ Discredits standard interpretations of Canadian history. Argues native peoples played significant role in the nation's early history. Excellent historical overview of period. [RF]

36.15 J. Colin Yerbury. "The post-contact Chipewyan: trade rivalries and changing territorial boundaries." *Ethnohistory* 23.3 (1976) 237–63. ISSN 0014-1801. ▸ Superb overview of Chipweyan hunting territories in immediate precontact period, together with discussion of European impact on tribal behavior. Challenges many ethnographic assumptions about subarctic life. [RF]

SEE ALSO
45.82 Arthur J. Ray and Donald B. Freeman. *"Give us good measure."*

Nineteenth Century

36.16 F. Laurie Barron and James B. Waldram, eds. *1885 and after: native society in transition.* Regina, Sask.: University of Regina, Canadian Plains Research Center, 1986. ISBN 0-88977-042-5. ▸ Papers of 1985 conference of Native Studies department, University of Saskatchewan, exploring both Indian and *métis* aspects of rebellion and its consequences. Wide array of contemporary scholarship by both natives and nonnatives. [RF]

36.17 Peter Carstens. *The queen's people: a study of hegemony, coercion, and accommodation among the Okanagan of Canada.* Toronto: University of Toronto Press, 1991. ISBN 0-8020-5893-0 (cl), 0-8020-6827-8 (pbk). ▸ Study of origins of Indian reserves using experience of Okanagan Indians as major example. Contains brief history of Indian-white relations in British Columbia and close study of British Columbia reserves. One of few such case studies. [RF]

36.18 Helen Codere. *Fighting with property: a study of Kwakiutl potlatching and warfare, 1792–1830.* 1950 ed. New York: AMS Press, 1988. (American Ethnological Society monographs, 18.) ISBN 0-404-62917-2. ▸ Examination of Northwest Coast institution of potlatch, lavish ceremonial in which food and property are given away to certify individual's claim to hereditary status. Argues that, over time, potlatching superseded warfare and head-hunting as means of social advancement. By one of first anthropologists to make extensive use of historical records. [RF]

36.19 Hugh A. Dempsey. *Crowfoot, chief of the Blackfeet.* 1972 ed. Norman: University of Oklahoma Press, 1989. ISBN 0-8061-1596-3 (pbk). ▸ Uses oral and documentary material to recreate life story of important leader. Places Crowfoot in context of Blackfeet history and in history of Indian-white relations on Canadian prairies of nineteenth century. Excellent focus on one life in complex period. [RF]

36.20 Peter Douglas Elias. *The Dakota of the Canadian Northwest: lessons for survival.* Winnipeg: University of Manitoba Press, 1988. ISBN 0-88755-142-4. ▸ Examination of different economic strategies adopted by Dakota bands that emigrated to Canada after 1862. Identifies Dakota practices aimed at cultural survival. Based on tribal histories and documentary sources. Best available overview of topic. [RF]

36.21 Robin Fisher. *Contact and conflict: Indian-European relations in British Columbia, 1774–1890.* 2d ed. Vancouver: University of British Columbia Press, 1992. ISBN 0-7748-0400-9 (pbk). ▸ Traces history of Indian-white relations in British Columbia from beginnings of maritime trade in eighteenth century to period of widespread European settlement in late nineteenth century. Excellent overview focusing on native persistence and tenacity of small communities. [RF]

36.22 Thomas Flanagan. *Louis "David" Riel: prophet of the New World.* Toronto: University of Toronto Press, 1979. ISBN 0-8020-5430-7 (cl), 0-88780-118-8 (pbk). ▸ Biography of *métis* leader focusing on his personal and emotional life. Interprets Riel's religious views as integral aspect of his political ambition to secure safety and salvation of *métis* people. [RF]

36.23 Thomas Flanagan. *Riel and the rebellion: 1885 reconsidered.* Saskatoon, Sask.: Western Producer Prairie Books, 1983. ISBN 0-88833-108-8 (cl), 0-88833-110-X (pbk). ▸ Controversial examination of Northwest Riel Rebellion challenging view of *métis* leader Riel as popular hero and victim of oppressive Canadian government. [RF]

36.24 Shepard Krech III, ed. *The subarctic fur trade: native social and economic adaptations.* Vancouver: University of British Columbia Press, 1984. ISBN 0-7748-0186-7. ▸ Six papers treating aboriginal economic history in late nineteenth and early twentieth centuries. Emphasis on economic and social adaptations of indigenous peoples to European-American economy. Methodologically sophisticated, focused treatment. [RF]

36.25 D. Peter MacLeod. "The Anishinabeg point of view: the history of the Great Lakes region to 1800 in nineteenth-century Mississauga, Odawa, and Ojibwa historiography." *Canadian historical review* 73.2 (1992) 192–210. ISSN 0008-3755. ▸ Discussion of nineteenth-century histories of aboriginal societies written by native historians Francis Assikinack (1858), Andrew J. Blackbird (1887), George Copway (1850), Peter Jones (1861), and William Whipple Warren (1885). All five accounts concentrate on aboriginal wars, migrations, and territorial expansion of period offering corrective to European-American histories with strong ethnocentric biases. [RF]

36.26 Don G. McLean. *1885: métis rebellion or government conspiracy?* Winnipeg, Man.: Pemmican, 1985. ISBN 0-919143-17-2 (pbk). ▸ Controversial study maintaining Premier John A. Macdonald deliberately encouraged 1885 Riel Rebellion in order to popularize and implement his National Policy. Read with other sources. [RF]

36.27 John S. Milloy. *The Plains Cree: trade, diplomacy, and war, 1790–1870.* Winnipeg: University of Manitoba Press, 1988. ISBN 0-88755-141-6. ▸ Pathbreaking account of Plains Cree diplomatic relations and alliances with other plains tribes. Analyzes Plains Cree political developments, while emphasizing warfare, motives for war, and military alliance. [RF]

36.28 George Nelson. *"The orders of the dreamed": George Nelson on Cree and Northern Ojibwa religion and myth, 1823.* Jennifer S. H. Brown and Robert Brightman, eds. St. Paul: Minnesota Historical Society Press, 1988. ISBN 0-87351-224-3. ▸ Letter-diaries (1823) of fur trader, George Nelson, with his observations on Cree and Ojibwa religious belief and practice. Editors present cultural background for material, including list of spirit personages and discussion of ethics of their project. Thoroughly annotated text, useful source. [RF]

36.29 David A. Nock. *A Victorian missionary and Canadian*

Indian policy: cultural synthesis vs. cultural replacement. Waterloo, Ont.: Wilfrid Laurier University Press for Canadian Corporation for Studies in Religion, 1988. ISBN 0-88920-153-6. ▶ Biography of missionary Edward Francis Wilson (b. 1844) and his influence on making of Canadian Indian policy. Explores Victorian mindset and attitudes toward "heathen" and culture change. [RF]

36.30 Jacqueline Peterson and Jennifer S. H. Brown, eds. *The new peoples: being and becoming métis in North America.* Lincoln: University of Nebraska Press, 1985. ISBN 0-8032-3673-5. ▶ Twelve essays by distinguished scholars exploring origins, historical roles, and societies of Canadian *métis.* Contributions include perspectives of history, anthropology, geography, and economics. [RF]

36.31 Arthur J. Ray. *Indians in the fur trade: their role as trappers, hunters, and middlemen in the lands southwest of Hudson Bay, 1660–1870.* Toronto: University of Toronto Press, 1974. ISBN 0-8020-2118-2 (cl), 0-8020-6226-1 (pbk). ▶ Methodologically sophisticated study of aboriginal peoples in northern Ontario, Manitoba, and Saskatchewan during preconfederation period. Focuses on roles of Indians in fur trade emphasizing aboriginal responses to changing environmental and economic conditions. [RF]

36.32 D. N. Sprague. *Canada and the métis, 1869–1885.* Waterloo, Ont.: Wilfrid Laurier University Press, 1988. ISBN 0-88920-958-8 (cl), 0-88920-964-2 (pbk). ▶ Inquiry into circumstances of *métis* declaration of self-government in Red River in 1869 and ensuing struggle with government of Canada. Particular attention to policies of Premier John A. Macdonald and events culminating in Northwest Riel Rebellion of 1885. Exhaustive overview. [RF]

36.33 D. N. Sprague and R. P. Fryef. *The genealogy of the first métis nation: the development and dispersal of the Red River settlement, 1820–1900.* Winnipeg, Man.: Pemmican, 1983. ISBN 0-919143-34-2. ▶ Nominal lists of *métis* families from 1820 based on census data. Basic research tool in reconstructing *métis* family history. [RF]

36.34 J. Colin Yerbury. *The subarctic Indians and the fur trade, 1680–1860.* Vancouver: University of British Columbia Press, 1986. ISBN 0-7748-0241-3. ▶ Interpretation of Athapaskan history stressing adaptation of aboriginal peoples and societies to physical environment. Demonstrates interdependence of land, aboriginal peoples, and Europeans in formation of Athapaskan cultures. Multidisciplinary overview. [RF]

SEE ALSO
45.163 Jennifer S. H. Brown. *Strangers in blood.*
45.171 Sylvia Van Kirk. *"Many tender ties."*

Twentieth Century

36.35 Neils W. Braroe. *Indian and white: self-image and interaction in a Canadian plains community.* Stanford, Calif.: Stanford University Press, 1975. ISBN 0-8047-0877-0 (cl), 0-8047-1028-7 (pbk). ▶ Sociological study of Cree community on Canadian plains, focusing on maintenance of positive self-image in context of racial antagonism and discrimination. Discusses theoretical implications of his field investigations. Narrow study, widely cited. [RF]

36.36 Robert E. Cail. *Land, man, and the law: the disposal of crown lands in British Columbia, 1871–1913.* Vancouver: University of British Columbia Press, 1974. ISBN 0-7748-0029-1. ▶ Tightly focused description of land policy in British Columbia during period of rapid non-Indian settlement and industrial expansion. Separate chapters describe provincial efforts to extend jurisdiction over mining, timber, water, and rail expansion, as well as to secure government title to tribal lands. [RF]

36.37 Sarah Carter. *Lost harvests: Prairie Indian reserve farmers*

and government policy. Montreal: McGill-Queen's University Press, 1990. ISBN 0-7735-0755-8. ▶ History of Treaty 4 area of Prairie West revising standard interpretations that Canadian government was negligent in abiding by treaties with aboriginal peoples. Concludes neglect part of deliberate policy to undermine Indian independence. Model of newer scholarship stressing policy implementation rather than intentions. [RF]

36.38 Kenneth S. Coates. *Best left as Indians: native-white relations in the Yukon Territory, 1840–1973.* Montreal: McGill-Queens University Press, 1991. ISBN 0-7735-0780-9. ▶ Monographic study of Yukon Indians from fur-trade era to present. Chapters address impact of gold rush, missionization, and recent economic changes. Impact of national policy forms backdrop to entire discussion. Ends with description of modern land claims. Best available focused, historical study of area. [RF]

36.39 Douglas Cole. *Captured heritage: the scramble for Northwest Coast artifacts.* Seattle: University of Washington Press, 1985. ISBN 0-295-96215-1. ▶ History of collectors in British Columbia addressing questions of morality of removing antiquities and artifacts from control of their original societies. Unique approach to sociology of collecting; raises serious ethical and historical issues. [RF/DJL]

36.40 James Frideres. *Native people in Canada: contemporary conflicts.* 3d ed. Englewood Cliffs, N.J.: Prentice-Hall, 1988. ISBN 0-13-609876-2 (pbk). ▶ Historical overview of aboriginal history leading into study of modern era. Discusses treaties and historical development of administration of Department of Indian Affairs. Basic text. [RF]

36.41 Rene Fumoleau. *As long as this land shall last: a history of Treaty 8 and Treaty 11, 1870–1939.* Toronto: McClelland & Stewart, 1973. ISBN 0-7710-3188-2 (pbk). ▶ Specialized, rare discussion of ownership of land and resources in context of aboriginal land claims and treaty promises. [RF]

36.42 Basil H. Johnston. *Indian school days.* Norman: University of Oklahoma Press, 1988. ISBN 0-8061-2226-9. ▶ Delightful memoir of life at Indian boarding school in Ontario by distinguished Canadian anthropologist. Recounts author's own experiences and offers unique window onto treatment of native students, resiliency, and suffering. No footnotes or bibliography but fascinating appendix describing present situation of many former students. [RF]

36.43 J. Anthony Long and Menno Boldt, eds. *Governments in conflict? Provinces and Indian nations in Canada.* Toronto: University of Toronto Press, 1988. ISBN 0-8020-5779-9 (cl), 0-8020-6690-9 (pbk). ▶ Collection of essays by native and nonnative legal scholars, political activists, and government officials addressing complex relationship of Indian communities and local (provincial) governments. Topics range from Quebec to Northwest Territories, but primarily focus on contemporary affairs. Rare work on this aspect of Indian legal affairs. [RF]

36.44 Arthur J. Ray. *The Canadian fur trade in the industrial age.* Toronto: University of Toronto Press, 1990. ISBN 0-8020-2699-0 (cl), 0-8020-6743-3 (pbk). ▶ Monographic examination of twentieth-century fur trade incorporating both aboriginal and European Canadian histories. Concludes end of Hudson's Bay Company monopoly left aboriginal people without support systems during bad times. Sequel to 36.31. [RF]

36.45 Boyce Richardson, ed. *Drumbeat: anger and renewal in Indian country.* Toronto: Summerhill Press for Assembly of First Nations, 1989. ISBN 0-929091-03-5. ▶ Popular overview of conditions facing contemporary Canadian Indians written by several native political leaders and their supporters. Each of eight chapters focuses on different community and its concerns. Introduction and conclusion by national chief of Assembly of First Nations. Stirring introduction to modern politics. [RF]

36.46 Mary Lee Stearns. *Haida culture in custody: the Masset band.* Seattle: University of Washington Press, 1981. ISBN 0-295-95763-8. ▸ History of Pacific coast community over last century focusing on impact of commercial fishing and Europeans on community life. Exemplary monograph that provoked intense reaction from book's subjects because of emphasis on family violence. [RF]

General and Theoretical Works

36.47 Bernard Assiniwi. *Histoire des Indiens du haut et du bas Canada.* Vol. 1: *Mœurs et coutumes des Algonkins et des Iroquois.* Vol. 2: *Deux siècles de civilisation blanche, 1497–1685.* Vol. 3: *De l'épopée à l'integration, 1685 à nos jours.* Montreal: Lemeac, 1974. ▸ Three-volume French text by Canadian Indian providing impressionistic, sympathetic portrait of native peoples in Canada. [RF]

36.48 Jean Barman, Yvonne Herbert, and Don McCaskill, eds. *Indian education in Canada.* Vol. 1: *The legacy.* Vol. 2: *The challenge.* Vancouver: University of British Columbia Press, 1986. ISBN 0-7748-0243-X. ▸ Collection of papers on history of Indian education and on issues facing Canadian Indian educators today. Authors include native and nonnative scholars from history, anthropology, and education. Volume 1 contains essays on Indian schooling from seventeenth to twentieth centuries; volume 2 profiles several approaches to contemporary education. Comprehensive collection offering best available study of native education in Canada. [RF]

36.49 Charles A. Bishop. *The Northern Ojibwa and the fur trade: an historical and ecological study.* Toronto: Holt, Rinehart & Winston of Canada, 1974. ISBN 0-03-928054-3. ▸ Study of shifts in institutional relationships between white and Indian traders and impact of these on environment. Also discusses missionaries, government agents, and relations with other Indian groups. Model ethnohistorical overview. [RF]

36.50 Bruce A. Clark. *Native liberty, crown sovereignty: the existing aboriginal right of self-government in Canada.* Montreal: McGill-Queen's University Press, 1991. ISBN 0-7735-0767-1. ▸ Practicing attorney's manifesto that finds recognition of native sovereignty in Proclamation of 1763. Argues tribal groups enjoy common-law claim to self-government that new Canadian constitution should recognize. Exhaustive discussion of Canadian Indian law. Partisan but forcefully argued study. [RF]

36.51 Kenneth S. Coates. *Canada's colonies.* Toronto: Lorimer, 1985. ISBN 0-88862-932-X (cl), 0-88862-931-1 (pbk). ▸ Useful survey of Northwest Territories and Yukon, from precontact Inuit and Dene to self-government controversies of 1980s. [RF]

36.52 Bruce Cox, ed. *Native people, native lands: Canadian Indians, Inuit and métis.* Ottawa, Ont.: Carleton University Press, 1987. ISBN 0-88629-062-7. ▸ Twenty essays analyzing aboriginal societies and histories. Topics include Iroquois wars, epidemics as factor in warfare, emergence of hunting territories, ethnoecology, band structure, Indian reserves, and *métis.* [RF]

36.53 Olive P. Dickason. *Canada's first nations: a history of founding peoples from earliest times.* Norman: University of Oklahoma Press, 1992. ISBN 0-8061-2438-5 (cl), 0-8061-2439-3 (pbk). ▸ Broad, general, interdisciplinary history of Canada's aboriginal peoples around general theme of erosion of American Indian rights over time. Most recent single-volume overview. [RF]

36.54 Wilson Duff. *The Indian history of British Columbia.* Vol. 1: *The impact of the white man.* 2d ed. Victoria, B.C.: Provincial Museum of Natural History and Anthropology, 1965. (The Indian history of British Columbia, 1. Anthropology in British Columbia, Memoir, 5.) ▸ Spare but useful description of Indian life in British Columbia after arrival of European traders in eighteenth century. Discussion of demography, fur trade, establish-

ment of colonial authority, and consequences of confederation. Includes statistical tables. [RF]

36.55 Ian A. L. Getty and Antoine S. Lussier, eds. *As long as the sun shines and water flows: a reader in Canadian native studies.* Vancouver: University of British Columbia Press, 1983. ISBN 0-7748-0181-6 (cl), 0-7748-0184-0 (pbk). ▸ Papers of native studies colloquium on colonial Indian policy, constitutional developments, Indian treaties and policy, and native responses. Basic introduction to study of administrative and legislative policies affecting Canada's native peoples. [RF]

36.56 John Webster Grant. *Moon of wintertime: missionaries and the Indians of Canada in encounter since 1534.* Toronto: University of Toronto Press, 1984. ISBN 0-8020-5643-1 (cl), 0-8020-6541-4 (pbk). ▸ Summary of 400 years of contact history between aboriginal peoples and European missionaries. Suggests Indian resistance not to Christianity but to cultural domination. Excellent overview. [RF]

36.57 Shepard Krech III. *Native Canadian anthropology and history: a selected bibliography.* Winnipeg, Man.: University of Winnipeg, Rupert's Land Research Centre, 1986. ▸ Classified bibliography in three parts: bibliographies, reference works, general and comparative works, and published primary sources; works relating to specific groups; and thematic works. [RF]

36.58 Catharine McClellan et al. *Part of the land, part of the water: history of the Yukon Indians.* Vancouver, B.C.: Douglas & McIntyre, 1987. ISBN 0-88894-553-1. ▸ History exploring how traditional cultures have adapted to changing conditions based on oral sources. Religion, language, subsistence economies, and political activities changed in response to European presence. Model study based on innovative range of sources. [RF]

36.59 David R. Miller et al. *The first ones: readings in Indian/native studies.* Piapot Reserve #75: Saskatchewan Indian Federated College, 1992. ISBN 1-89580-316-0. ▸ Innovative text in Indian history combining essays on historiography with native testimony, mythology, and reprints of scholarly articles. Concludes with commentaries on contemporary affairs. [RF]

36.60 J. R. Miller. *Skyscrapers hide the heavens: a history of Indian-white relations in Canada.* Toronto: University of Toronto Press, 1991. ISBN 0-8020-6869-3. ▸ Comprehensive account of Indian-white relations in Canada, 1534–1990. Includes maps, useful index. [RF]

36.61 J. R. Miller, ed. *Sweet promises: a reader in Indian-white relations in Canada.* Toronto: University of Toronto Press, 1991. ISBN 0-8020-5945-7 (cl), 0-8020-6818-9 (pbk). ▸ Collection of previously published articles on military alliances, fur-trade relations, government policy, treaties, and struggle for aboriginal rights, covering entire period of European presence in Canada. [RF]

36.62 R. Bruce Morrison and C. Roderick Wilson. *Native peoples: the Canadian experience.* Toronto: McClelland & Stewart, 1986. ISBN 0-7710-6510-8 (pbk). ▸ Overviews of origins, historic life styles, and contemporary features of major aboriginal cultural groups in Canada by eighteen contributors. Suitable for senior high school readers. [RF]

36.63 Donald Purich. *The métis.* Toronto: Lorimer, 1988. ISBN 1-55028-052-X (cl), 1-55028-050-3 (pbk). ▸ Popular introduction to *métis* people and their history. In addition to describing contemporary affairs, presents description of *métis* settlement in nineteenth century and history of group's relations with Alberta, Manitoba, and Canadian government. [RF]

36.64 Peter S. Schmalz. *The Ojibwa of southern Ontario.* Toronto: University of Toronto Press, 1991. ISBN 0-8020-2736-9 (cl), 0-8020-6778-6 (pbk). ▸ Revisionist overview of relations between Ojibwa and Europeans, first contact to mid-twentieth century. Uses aboriginal sources such as oral traditions and band records to include Ojibwa points of view, as well as usual documentary materials. [RF]

36.65 D. N. Sprague. *Canada's treaties with aboriginal people.* Winnipeg: University of Manitoba, Faculty of Law, Canadian Legal History Project, 1991. ▸ Brief history of treaties between Great Britain and Canadian aboriginal peoples and of changing attitudes and policies of imperial and, later, dominion governments toward these agreements. Analyzes effects of Constitution Act (1982) and role of courts in native lands claims cases. [RF]

36.66 Wayne Suttles. *Coast Salish essays.* Seattle: University of Washington Press, 1987. ISBN 0-295-96580-0 (cl), 0-295-96581-9 (pbk). ▸ Sixteen essays spanning three decades of author's work on Coast Salish social systems, belief, art, and survival through European incursion and takeover. Specialized perspectives from distinguished anthropologist. [RF]

36.67 Paul Tennant. *Aboriginal peoples and politics: the Indian land question in British Columbia, 1849–1989.* Vancouver: University of British Columbia Press, 1990. ISBN 0-7748-0347-9 (cl), 0-7748-0369-X (pbk). ▸ Important overview of one of thorniest problems in Canadian Indian policy and law: land claims of native people in British Columbia. Ranges over ethnography, legal history, and Indian policy to portray struggle from onset of European settlement to 1980s. Also contains outstanding history of Indian political activism in province. [RF]

36.68 Wilson D. Wallis and Ruth S. Wallis. *The Micmac Indians of eastern Canada.* Minneapolis: University of Minnesota Press, 1955. ▸ Exhaustive ethnography based on field notes prepared by William C. Orchard (1911, 1912) and elaborated upon by Wallis and Wallis in early 1950s. Includes series of traditional stories and historical narratives. [RF]

36.69 Ruth Holmes Whitehead. *The old man told us: excerpts from Micmac history, 1500–1950.* Halifax, N.S.: Nimbus, 1991. ISBN 0-921054-83-1. ▸ Documentary history of Micmac since first encounter with Europeans, compiled from printed sources and collections of Nova Scotia Museum. Together materials present multifaceted record of Micmac culture as it met and was surrounded by Europeans and their offspring. [RF]

36.70 H. Christoph Wolfart. *Essays in Algonquian bibliography in honour of V. M. Dechene.* Winnipeg: University of Manitoba Press, 1984. ▸ Sophisticated essays on advent of Cree literacy and role of Cree in relations with Europeans in nineteenth-century Manitoba. Describes early Cree hymns, mission versions of Cree, and production of Cree texts. [RF]

UNITED STATES

Precontact

36.71 Douglas B. Bamforth. *Ecology and human organization on the Great Plains.* New York: Plenum, 1988. ISBN 0-306-42956-X. ▸ Thorough investigation of organizational strategies prehistoric hunters and gatherers used to exploit resources of America's central grasslands. Archaeological literature made accessible for nonspecialists. [FEH/HM]

36.72 Alfred W. Bowers. *Mandan social and ceremonial organization.* 1950 ed. Moscow: University of Idaho Press, 1991. ISBN 0-89301-149-5. ▸ Classic ethnography placing central rituals of Mandan religion, including *okipa* ceremony, vision quest, and corn ceremonies in social and cultural context. Incorporates Mandan oral literature into presentation of Mandan history. [FEH/HM]

36.73 David S. Brose et al. *Ancient art of the American Woodland Indians.* New York: Abrams with Detroit Institute of Arts, 1985. ISBN 0-8109-1827-7 (cl), 0-89558-105-1 (pbk). ▸ Profusely illustrated collection of essays exploring origins and patterns of nearly

five thousand years of prehistoric Eastern Woodlands art. [FEH/HM]

36.74 Michael D. Coe et al. *Atlas of ancient America.* New York: Facts on File, 1986. ISBN 0-8160-1199-0. ▸ Fifty-six highly detailed maps of important environmental features, historical events, and cultural achievements for selected geographical areas in North, Central, and South America. Text offers archaeological reconstructions for specified groups and culture areas. [FEH/HM]

36.75 Linda S. Cordell. *Prehistory of the Southwest.* Orlando, Fla.: Academic Press, 1984. ISBN 0-12-188220-9 (cl), 0-12-188222-5 (pbk). ▸ Best recent summary of southwestern archaeology, 9000 BCE–1540 CE. Synthesizes large body of recent scientific data and presents historic overview of region in prehistoric period. [FEH/HM]

36.76 Don E. Dumond. *The Eskimos and Aleuts.* Boulder: Westview, 1977. ISBN 0-89158-638-5. ▸ Comprehensive overview of Eskimo and Aleut physical, cultural, and linguistic evolution, ca. 23,000 BCE–1500 CE. Written in nontechnical language, provides useful introduction to prehistoric Arctic. [FEH/HM]

36.77 Brian Fagan. *The great journey: the peopling of ancient America.* New York: Thames & Hudson, 1987. ISBN 0-500-05045-7. ▸ Summary and evaluation of competing theories of origins and lifeways of prehistoric American Indians. Written for popular audience; synthesizes most recent scholarship on migration of human communities from Asia to America. [FEH/HM]

36.78 George Frison et al. *Prehistoric hunters of the high plains.* 2d ed. San Diego, Calif.: Academic Press, 1991. ISBN 0-12-268561-X. ▸ Comprehensive, nontechnical discussion of archaeological sites and subsistence patterns on prehistoric northwestern plains by region's most prominent archaeologist. Particularly interesting is author's discussion of pre-horse migrations onto plains. [FEH/HM]

36.79 Alvin M. Josephy, Jr., ed. *America in 1492: the world of the Indian peoples before the arrival of Columbus.* 2d ed. New York: Vintage, 1993. ISBN 0-679-74337-5 (pbk). ▸ Series of essays for general reader by distinguished experts on North and South American cultures. Part 1, "We the People," presents seven regional overviews; Part 2, "American Civilization," contains six thematic discussions of art, trade, language, religion, technology, and social systems. Project of Newberry Library's McNickle Center. Includes annotated list of suggested readings. [FEH/HM]

36.80 Malcom Margolin. *The Ohlone way: Indian life in the San Francisco and Monterey areas.* Berkeley: Heyday, 1978. ISBN 0-930588-01-0. ▸ Brief cultural history of Ohlone or Costanoan confederacy whose forty loosely associated tribelets occupied lands between Big Sur and San Francisco Bay. Provides information on modes of subsistence, social life, political organization, and religion. [FEH/HM]

36.81 Ronald J. Mason. *Great Lakes archaeology.* New York: Academic Press, 1981. ISBN 0-12-477850-X. ▸ Introduction to Great Lakes archaeology examining representative cultures, assemblages, and sites to trace evolution of area's Indian peoples from 9500 BCE to first contact with whites. Useful survey text; best available on subject. [FEH/HM]

36.82 Jerald T. Milanich, ed. *The early prehistoric Southeast: a source book.* New York: Garland, 1985. ISBN 0-8240-5880-1. ▸ Nineteen essays primarily concerned with formative period in southeastern prehistory that began ca. 2000 BCE and is characterized by invention of pottery, nascent village life, and expanding trade and population. Cross section of best recent archaeological scholarship. [FEH/HM]

36.83 William N. Morgan. *Prehistoric architecture in the eastern United States.* Cambridge, Mass.: MIT Press, 1980. ISBN 0-262-13160-9. ▸ Heavily illustrated guide providing interpretive reconstructions of eighty-two sites. Traces evolution of architecture in eastern United States, 2200 BCE–1500 CE. [FEH/HM]

36.84 George I. Quimby. *Indian life in the upper Great Lakes, 11,000 B.C. to A.D. 1800.* Chicago: University of Chicago Press, 1960. ▸ Valuable synthesis, primarily descriptions of prehistoric Indians' adaption to environmental change for nontechnical audience. Also discusses shifts in cultural life in wake of European contact. [FEH/HM]

36.85 Dean R. Snow. *The American Indians: their archaeology and prehistory.* New York: Thames & Hudson, 1976. ISBN 0-500-05022-8. ▸ Handsome introduction to precontact North America. Offers series of reconstructions of regional lifeways based on scholarly sources. Clearly written, richly illustrated. [FEH/HM]

36.86 Stuart Struever and Felicia A. Holton. *Koster: Americans in search of their prehistoric past.* Garden City, N.Y.: Anchor/Doubleday, 1979. ISBN 0-385-00406-0. ▸ Report bringing one of most famous archaeological sites in North America alive for nonspecialists. Occupied from 7500 BCE to 1200 CE, this Illinois location allows scholars to trace shift to sedentary agriculture that occurred long before arrival of whites. [FEH/HM]

36.87 William S. Webb and Charles E. Snow. *The Adena people.* 1945 ed. Knoxville: University of Tennessee Press, 1974. ISBN 0-87049-159-8. ▸ Sophisticated but accessible analysis of skeletal and cultural remains from Adena earth mounds in Kentucky. Stresses inventiveness of Adena peoples and ties to Ohio's Hopewell societies. [FEH/HM]

36.88 Waldo R. Wedel. *Prehistoric man on the Great Plains.* Norman: University of Oklahoma Press, 1961. ISBN 0-8061-0501-1. ▸ Classic summary of Great Plains archaeology. Intended for specialist and layperson alike; eschews technical jargon. Creates chronology of sites and phases. [FEH/HM]

36.89 George F. Will and George E. Hyde. *Corn among the Indians of the upper Missouri.* 1917 ed. Lincoln: University of Nebraska Press, 1964. ISBN 0-8032-0892-8. ▸ Examination of significance of corn in indigenous cultures and economies of upper Missouri Indian tribes. Includes list of varieties of corn cultivated by these groups as well as by Chippewas, Winnebagos, Iroquois, and peoples of Southwest. [FEH/HM]

36.90 Gordon R. Willey and Jeremy A. Sabloff. *A history of American archaeology.* 2d ed. New York: Freeman, 1980. ISBN 0-7167-1122-2 (cl), 0-7167-1123-0 (pbk). ▸ Indispensible overview of North American archaeology. Provides history of field and description of continuities in archaeological methods over time. Tightly focused but accessible monograph. [FEH/HM]

Colonial Period

36.91 William Brandon. *New worlds for old: reports from the New World and their effects on the development of social thought in Europe, 1500–1800.* Athens: Ohio University Press, 1986. ISBN 0-8214-0818-6 (cl), 0-8214-0819-4 (pbk). ▸ Intriguing analysis of how accounts of New World peoples influenced European social and political thought. Argues Indian attitudes toward property marked chief difference between them and Europeans. [FEH/HM]

36.92 William Cronon. *Changes in the land: Indians, colonists, and the ecology of New England.* New York: Hill & Wang, 1983. ISBN 0-8090-3405-0 (cl), 0-8090-0158-6 (pbk). ▸ Documents how transition from American Indian to European sovereignty in colonial New England affected area's plant and animal life. Contrasts precolonial and nineteenth-century ecosystems as well as relationships of Indians and whites to land. Excellent overview integrating colonial and native experiences. [FEH/HM]

36.93 Henry F. Dobyns. *Their number become thinned: native American population dynamics in eastern North America.* William R. Swagerty, ed. Knoxville: University of Tennessee Press for Newberry Library, Center for the History of the American

Indian, 1983. ISBN 0-87049-400-7 (cl), 0-87049-401-5 (pbk). ▸ Seven essays documenting devastating effects of Old World diseases on native populations in eastern North America, particularly in Florida. Argues continent was home to as many as eighteen million Indians prior to arrival of Europeans; controversial. [FEH/HM]

36.94 Gregory Evans Dowd. *A spirited resistance: the North American Indian struggle for unity, 1745–1815.* Baltimore: Johns Hopkins University Press, 1992. ISBN 0-8018-4236-0. ▸ History of American Indian efforts to unite in opposition to European expansion. Argues, through profiles of tribal communities in Pennsylvania, Ohio, and Tennessee, Indians came to believe they had more in common with each other than with any whites and shows that warriors of nineteenth century were bearers of this idea. [FEH/HM]

36.95 R. David Edmunds. *The Potawatomi: keepers of the fire.* Norman: University of Oklahoma Press, 1978. ISBN 0-8061-1478-9 (cl), 0-8061-2069-X (pbk). ▸ Award-winning tribal history, begins with Potawatomi's first contact with French in mid-seventeenth century and ends with removal from Indiana to Kansas in 1840s. Examines official relations between Potawatomi and Europeans and consequences of cross-cultural trade, intermarriage, and religious change. [FEH/HM]

36.96 John C. Ewers. *The horse in Blackfoot Indian culture with comparative material from other western tribes.* 1955 ed. Washington, D.C.: Smithsonian Institution Press, 1980. ISBN 0-87474-419-9. ▸ Authoritative study of impact of horse on Blackfeet culture from eighteenth through mid-nineteenth centuries. No comparable study on other American Indian groups. Discussion ranges from material culture to religion. [FEH/HM]

36.97 Jack D. Forbes. *Warriors of the Colorado: the Yumas of the Quechan nation and their neighbors.* Norman: University of Oklahoma Press, 1965. ▸ Anthropologist's history of Indians of lower Colorado River. Excellent overview of region highlighting Yumas' struggle against Spanish, Mexican, and American invaders, sixteenth through mid-nineteenth centuries. [FEH/HM]

36.98 Charles Gibson and Howard Henry Peckham, eds. *Attitutes of colonial powers toward the American Indian.* Salt Lake City: University of Utah Press, 1969. ISBN 0-87480-027-7. ▸ Basic introduction to colonial era. Slim volume of six essays examining colonial Indian policies of Spain, Portugal, Holland, France, and England. Discussion spare but comprehensive. [FEH/HM]

36.99 Gary C. Goodwin. *Cherokees in transition: a study of changing culture and environment prior to 1775.* Chicago: University of Chicago, Department of Geography, 1977. (University of Chicago, Department of Geography, Research paper, 181.) ISBN 0-89065-088-8. ▸ Ecologically centered history of pre- and postcontact Cherokee society and culture. Describes plant and animal life, land use, and settlement patterns before and after arrival of Europeans. Best available overview of Cherokee cultural history. [FEH/HM]

36.100 Barbara Graymont. *The Iroquois in the American Revolution.* Syracuse, N.Y.: Syracuse University Press, 1972. ISBN 0-8156-016-6 (cl), 0-8156-0083-6 (pbk). ▸ Examination of stress colonial conflicts placed on Iroquois culture, economy, and politics and how Iroquois attempted (and failed) to maintain amicable diplomatic relations with both British and Americans. Only major study of Indian group in Revolution. [FEH/HM]

36.101 Erna Gunther. *Indian life on the Northwest Coast of North America, as seen by the early explorers and fur traders during the last decades of the eighteenth century.* Chicago: University of Chicago Press, 1972. ISBN 0-226-31088-4. ▸ Ethnohistory of Nootka, Chinook, Haida, and other Northwest Coast peoples based on documents left by late eighteenth-century Spanish, British, and Russian explorers and traders. Wide-ranging, informative starting point for history of region. [FEH/HM]

36.102 Ramón A. Gutierrez. *When Jesus came, the corn mothers went away: marriage, sexuality, and power in New Mexico, 1500–1846.* Stanford, Calif.: Stanford University Press, 1991. ISBN 0-8047-1816-4 (cl), 0-8047-1832-6 (pbk). ▸ History of Spanish conquest of New Mexico emphasizing its cultural meaning for American Indians, Hispanic colonists who migrated into area, and mixed-race population that emerged there. Focus on sexuality and power offers strikingly original perspective. [FEH/HM]

36.103 Lewis Hanke. *Aristotle and the American Indians: a study in race prejudice in the modern world.* 1959 ed. Bloomington: Indiana University Press, 1970. ISBN 0-253-20132-2. ▸ Account of confrontation in 1550 at Valladolid when scholars debated whether or not American Indians were innately inferior to Europeans. Holy Roman Emperor Charles V and his council witnessed discussion and used arguments presented there to shape imperial policy. [FEH/HM]

36.104 Preston Holder. *The hoe and the horse on the plains: a study of cultural development among North American Indians.* 1970 ed. Lincoln: University of Nebraska Press, 1991. ISBN 0-8032-0730-1. ▸ Uses relationship between Caddoan-speaking farmers and western Sioux hunters to explore relationship of agriculture to nomadism on Great Plains during eighteenth and nineteenth centuries. Based on archaeological data and written for general audience. [FEH/HM]

36.105 Wilbur R. Jacobs. *Dispossessing the American Indian: Indians and whites on the colonial frontier.* 1972 ed. Norman: University of Oklahoma Press, 1985. ISBN 0-8061-1935-7. ▸ Eleven interpretive essays treating various aspects of Indian-white relations in eighteenth-century Eastern Woodlands. Topics include trade and diplomacy, conflict, and British Indian policy. [FEH/HM]

36.106 Francis Jennings. *The ambiguous Iroquois empire: the Covenant Chain confederation of Indian tribes with English colonies from its beginnings to the Lancaster Treaty of 1744.* New York: Norton, 1984. ISBN 0-393-01719-2. ▸ Stirring history of Covenant Chain, confederation of English colonies, Iroquois, and other tribes that British used to dominate frontier diplomacy in eighteenth-century North America. [FEH/HM]

36.107 Francis Jennings. *Empire of fortune: crowns, colonies, and tribes in the Seven Years' War in America.* New York: Norton, 1988. ISBN 0-393-02537-3. ▸ History of what Americans call French and Indian War stressing complex diplomacy among and between Indians and colonists. Argues end of war greatly limited diplomatic autonomy of native people. Penetrating analysis of politics of war. [FEH/HM]

36.108 Francis Jennings. *The invasion of America: Indians, colonialism, and the cant of conquest.* Chapel Hill: University of North Carolina Press for Institute of Early American History and Culture, 1975. ISBN 0-8078-1245-5. ▸ Series of historiographic essays and brief historical studies unmasking Puritan rationalizations for seizure of Indian territories. Demonstrates how both colonials and their scholarly defenders created cant of conquest that still shapes attitudes toward native peoples and influences treatment in historical literature. Useful provocative introduction. [FEH/HM]

36.109 Karen O. Kupperman. *Settling with the Indians: the meeting of English and Indian cultures in America, 1580–1640.* Totowa, N.J.: Rowman & Littlefield, 1980. ISBN 0-8476-6210-1. ▸ Comparison of Indian and English forms of government, technologies, and worldviews during first sixty years of Britain's colonization along east coast of North America. Introductory monograph attempts to understand each group's perception of other. [FEH/HM]

36.110 Michael N. McConnell. *A country between: the Upper Ohio Valley and its peoples, 1724–1774.* Lincoln: University of Nebraska Press, 1992. ISBN 0-8032-3142-3. ▸ History of Indians who migrated to western Pennsylvania and Ohio in eighteenth century and then became enmeshed in frontier conflicts involving French, British, and various groups of colonials. Excellent, detailed descriptions of native communities that Europeans viewed as obstacles to expansion. [FEH/HM]

36.111 James H. Merrell. *The Indians' new world: Catawbas and their neighbors from European contact through the era of removal.* Chapel Hill: University of North Carolina Press for Institute of Early American History and Culture, 1989. ISBN 0-8078-1832-1. ▸ Representative of new Indian history; tribal study containing both topical and chronological chapters. Central theme—tribes blended old and new ways to survive European expansion—carries significant consequences for early American history. [FEH/HM]

36.112 Kenneth M. Morrison. *The embattled Northeast: the elusive ideal of alliance in Abnaki-Euramerican relations.* Berkeley: University of California Press, 1984. ISBN 0-520-05126-2. ▸ Interpretation of Abnaki relations with French and British in colonial Northeast based on documentary, ethnographic, and oral sources. Focused monograph stressing continuing role of traditional beliefs in Abnaki culture and politics. [FEH/HM]

36.113 Gary B. Nash. *Red, white, and black: the peoples of early North America.* 3d ed. Englewood Cliffs, N.J.: Prentice-Hall, 1992. ISBN 0-13-769878-X. ▸ Very general overview of colonial history tracing interactions of Indians, Africans, and Europeans. One of few available synthetic works on entire society at time. [FEH/HM]

36.114 John R. Reid. *A better kind of hatchet: law, trade, and diplomacy in the Cherokee nation during the early years of European contact.* University Park: Pennsylvania State University Press, 1975. ISBN 0-271-01197-1. ▸ Methodologically significant monograph on evolution of Cherokee legal, commercial, and diplomatic assumptions and institutions up to mid-eighteenth century. Demonstrates tribe's ability to create legal responses to new conditions. [FEH/HM]

36.115 Daniel K. Richter. *The ordeal of the longhouse: the peoples of the Iroquois League in the era of European colonization.* Chapel Hill: University of North Carolina Press for Institute of Early American History and Culture, 1992. ISBN 0-8078-2060-1 (cl), 0-8078-4394-6 (pbk). ▸ Masterly history of one of largest native groups of northeastern North America. Presents both Iroquois and European understandings of events and synthesizes wealth of anthropological and historical literature. [FEH/HM]

36.116 Neal Salisbury. *Manitou and providence: Indians, Europeans, and the making of New England, 1500–1643.* New York: Oxford University Press, 1982. ISBN 0-19-503025-7 (cl), 0-19-503454-6 (pbk). ▸ First history of early New England presenting both American Indian and European perspectives on intertribal and Indian-white relations. Useful treatments of Squanto and first contact, conversion, and role of Indians in creation of European identity in America. [FEH/HM]

36.117 Carl O. Sauer. *Sixteenth-century North America: the land and the people as seen by the Europeans.* Berkeley: University of California Press, 1971. ISBN 0-520-01854-0 (cl), 0-520-02777-9 (pbk). ▸ Chronicle of earliest European expeditions to New World. Stresses explorers' impressions of America's landscapes and Indian peoples. Based on obscure documents but presented in highly readable and nontechnical style. [FEH/HM]

36.118 Marvin T. Smith. *Archaeology of aboriginal culture change in the interior Southeast: depopulation during the early historic period.* Gainesville: University Presses of Florida, Florida State Museum, 1987. (Ripley P. Bullen monographs in anthropology and history, 6.) ISBN 0-8130-0846-8. ▸ Scholarly study giving fuller documentation to population collapse that followed European contact. Also demonstrates how archaeological techniques can be used to trace disintegration of indigenous communities. [FEH/HM]

36.119 Margaret C. Szasz. *Indian education in the American colonies, 1607–1783*. Albuquerque: University of New Mexico Press, 1988. ISBN 0-8263-1103-2 (cl), 0-8263-1104-0 (pbk). ▸ Overview of schools and educational enterprises of colonial era. Examines pedagogical assumptions of missionaries and educators from New England to Georgia. Unique treatment of subject. [FEH/HM]

36.120 Daniel H. Usner, Jr. *Indians, settlers, and slaves in a frontier exchange economy: the lower Mississippi Valley before 1783*. Chapel Hill: University of North Carolina Press for Institute of Early American History and Culture, 1992. ISBN 0-8078-2014-8 (cl), 0-8078-4358-x (pbk). ▸ Pathbreaking history of region where three colonial empires overlapped. Traces movement of Europeans and Indians in area and exchange economy that emerged there. Stresses cultural resiliency and mutual accommodation. [FEH/HM]

36.121 Richard White. *The middle ground: Indians, empires, and republics in the Great Lakes region, 1650–1815*. New York: Cambridge University Press, 1991. ISBN 0-521-37104-x. ▸ Innovative history of Great Lakes region, area where Indians and whites met as relative equals in colonial era. Traces behavior of Europeans and range of Indian communities in this "middle ground." [FEH/HM]

36.122 J. Leitch Wright, Jr. *The only land they knew: the tragic story of the American Indians in the Old South*. New York: Free Press, 1981. ISBN 0-02-935790-x. ▸ History of Indian peoples of Southeast to 1800. Examines such topics as historical demography, use of Indians as slaves, and racial and cultural relationships formed in region between Indians and African Americans. Best available regional history of native peoples in colonial era. [FEH/HM]

SEE ALSO

39.539 James Axtell. *The invasion within*.

Nineteenth Century

36.123 Robert F. Berkhofer, Jr. *Salvation and the savage: an analysis of Protestant missions and American Indian response, 1787–1862*. 1965 ed. New York: Atheneum, 1972. ISBN 0-689-70290-6 (pbk). ▸ Pathbreaking history of Protestant Indian missions from late eighteenth to mid-nineteenth centuries avoiding language of conversion, proposing instead to examine goals, doctrines, and methods of both American Indians and Christian adversaries. Reoriented mission studies to examine native religious ideas. [FEH/HM]

36.124 Donald J. Berthrong. *The Southern Cheyennes*. Norman: University of Oklahoma Press, 1963. ISBN 0-8061-1199-2. ▸ Chronicle of Southern Cheyenne history from precontact to final war with federal troops in 1874–75. Model of ethnohistory drawing on ethnographic literature to create historical narrative. [FEH/HM]

36.125 Black Hawk. *An autobiography*. 1833 ed. Donald Jackson, ed. Urbana: University of Illinois Press, 1990. ISBN 0-252-72325-2 (pbk). ▸ Classic autobiography of great Sauk leader, Ma-ka-tai-me-she-kia-kiak. Discusses political intrigues and controversies leading up to Black Hawk War (1832), experiences as federal prisoner, and subsequent tours through United States. [FEH/HM]

36.126 Helen H. Blish. *A pictographic history of the Oglala Sioux: drawings by Amos Bad Heart Bull*. Lincoln: University of Nebraska Press, 1968. ISBN 0-8032-0002-1. ▸ Ethnographic analysis of more than four hundred ledger-book drawings by Oglala Sioux artist Amos Bad Heart Bull. Important for insider's perspective on late nineteenth- and early twentieth-century Sioux history and culture. [FEH/HM]

36.127 Colin G. Calloway. *Crown and calumet: British-Indian relations, 1783–1815*. Norman: University of Oklahoma Press, 1987. ISBN 0-8061-2033-9. ▸ Examination of British-Indian relations from Treaty of Paris (1783) to Peace of Ghent (1815) providing continental overview. Argues two sides viewed one another in practical military and diplomatic terms. Emphasizes significant, though declining, Indian power during period. [FEH/HM]

36.128 Angie Debo. *The rise and fall of the Choctaw republic*. 2d ed. Norman: University of Oklahoma Press, 1975. ISBN 0-8061-1247-6 (pbk). ▸ Study of political evolution of Choctaw people from period prior to removal to Indian Territory (present-day Oklahoma) through termination of Choctaw republic in 1907 when Oklahoma became state. Excellent use of one tribe's experience to understand history of southeastern Indians under United States domination. [FEH/HM]

36.129 Thomas W. Dunlay. *Wolves for the blue soldiers: Indian scouts and auxiliaries with the United States Army, 1860–1890*. Lincoln: University of Nebraska Press, 1982. ISBN 0-8032-1658-0 (cl), 0-8032-6573-5 (pbk). ▸ Description of American Indians allied with United States Army as scouts during Plains Indian wars. Discusses each group's perception of other and experiences of particular tribes, such as Pawnees and Apaches, who frequently joined American units. Good overview, unavailable in other sources. [FEH/HM]

36.130 Charles Eastman. *From deep woods to civilization: chapters in the autobiography of an Indian*. 1916 ed. Lincoln: University of Nebraska Press, 1977. ISBN 0-8032-0936-3 (cl), 0-8032-5873-9 (pbk). ▸ Accounts of major events in life of Santee Sioux who graduated from Dartmouth College and Boston University Medical School from tribal boyhood to adult career as physician and reform advocate. Includes eloquent critique of federal Indian policy and industrial America. [FEH/HM]

36.131 R. David Edmunds. *The Shawnee prophet*. Lincoln: University of Nebraska Press, 1983. ISBN 0-8032-1850-8, 0-8032-6711-8. ▸ Highly readable scholarly biography of Chief Tecumseh's brother. Persuasively argues prophet Tenskwatawa's movement of religious and cultural revitalization helped consolidate opposition to white expansion into Old Northwest during early nineteenth century and was crucial to Indian alliance with British in War of 1812. [FEH/DGS]

36.132 John R. Finger. *The eastern band of Cherokee, 1819–1900*. Knoxville: University of Tennessee Press, 1984. ISBN 0-87049-409-0 (cl), 0-87049-410-4 (pbk). ▸ Description of how Cherokees who avoided removal to Indian Territory in 1830s managed to maintain identity and portion of their homeland. Draws on ethnographic descriptions as well as historical documents. Best available monograph on this "remnant" group. [FEH/HM]

36.133 Grant Foreman. *Indian removal: the emigration of the Five Civilized Tribes of Indians*. 1932 ed. Norman: University of Oklahoma Press, 1986. ISBN 0-8061-0019-2 (cl), 0-8061-1172-0 (pbk). ▸ Benchmark study of United States Indian policy tracing removal of Choctaws, Creeks, Chickasaws, Cherokees, and Seminoles from homelands in southeastern United States to Indian Territory. Now more than half-century old, remains classic overview of entire removal process. [FEH/HM]

36.134 Michael D. Green. *The politics of Indian removal: Creek government and society in crisis*. Lincoln: University of Nebraska Press, 1982. ISBN 0-8032-2109-6 (cl), 0-8032-7015-1 (pbk). ▸ Description of strategies Creeks employed to forestall white encroachment onto their lands during early nineteenth century and how strategies effected major changes in Creek society and culture. Analysis of internal politics unmatched in other monographs. [FEH/HM]

36.135 William T. Hagan. *The Indian Rights Association: the Herbert Welsh years, 1882–1904*. Tucson: University of Arizona

Press, 1985. ISBN 0-8165-0879-8. ‣ Study of federal efforts to assimilate Indians focusing on largest humanitarian reform organization of nineteenth century. Thorough description including assumptions and platforms of early leaders. [FEH/HM]

36.136 Reginald Horsman. *Expansion and American Indian policy, 1783–1812.* 1967 ed. Norman: University of Oklahoma Press, 1992. ISBN 0-8061-2422-9 (pbk). ‣ Monographic study examining early attempts by United States government to develop national Indian policy that balanced territorial expansion with respect for natural rights of American Indians. First modern survey of tumultuous era. [FEH/HM]

36.137 Albert L. Hurtado. *Indian survival on the California frontier.* New Haven: Yale University Press, 1988. ISBN 0-300-04147-0. ‣ Innovative analysis exploring dynamics of clashing cultures from political, economic, social, and sexual perspectives. Topics include role of Indians in Mexican era, impact of gold rush, and native strategies for survival. [FEH/HM/WFD]

36.138 George E. Hyde. *Red Cloud's folk: a history of the Oglala Sioux Indians.* 1937 ed. Norman: University of Oklahoma Press, 1979. ISBN 0-8061-1520-3 (pbk). ‣ Tribal history of Oglala division of Teton Dakota, mid-seventeenth to late nineteenth century. Based in part on oral interviews, narrative includes excellent descriptions of Battle of the Little Bighorn, seizure of Black Hills, and establishment of Pine Ridge Reservation. [FEH/HM]

36.139 George E. Hyde. *Spotted Tail's folk: a history of the Brulé Sioux.* 1961 ed. Norman: University of Oklahoma Press, 1976. ISBN 0-8061-1380-4 (pbk). ‣ Classic narrative history of Brulé division of Teton Dakota, seventeenth through late nineteenth centuries. Argues Spotted Tail central in shaping Brulé responses to reservation life. [FEH/HM]

36.140 Steven L. Johnson. *Guide to American Indian documents in the Congressional Series set, 1817–1899: a project of the Institute for the Development of Indian Law.* New York: Clearwater, 1977. ISBN 0-88354-107-6. ‣ Chronological listing of more than 10,000 reports and documents on Indians generated by governmental agencies. Excellent index providing access to massive body of material on nineteenth-century American Indians. [FEH/HM]

36.141 Alvin M. Josephy, Jr. *The Nez Perce Indians and the opening of the Northwest.* New Haven: Yale University Press, 1965. ‣ Highly readable history of Nez Perce people begins with overview of their traditional lifeways and then examines relationship with whites through 1877 Nez Perce War. [FEH/HM]

36.142 Sergei Kan. *Symbolic immortality: the Tlingit potlatch of the nineteenth century.* Washington, D.C.: Smithsonian Institution Press, 1989. ISBN 0-87474-686-8. ‣ Sophisticated analysis of mortuary cycle of Northwest Coast's Tlingit Indians discussing role of public rituals in era of change and exploring their political, religious, and emotional significance. [FEH/HM]

36.143 William G. McLoughlin. *Cherokees and missionaries, 1789–1839.* New Haven: Yale University Press, 1984. ISBN 0-300-03075-4. ‣ Detailed but highly readable analysis of eighteenth- and nineteenth-century Protestant missions among Cherokees. Identifies sociocultural factors in Cherokee society that influenced tribe's response to Christianity. [FEH/HM]

36.144 H. Craig Miner. *The corporation and the Indian: tribal sovereignty and industrial civilization in Indian Territory, 1865–1907.* 1976 ed. Norman: University of Oklahoma Press, 1989. ISBN 0-8061-2205-6. ‣ Exposes role of railroad, coal, and oil companies in undermining Indian Territory's Cherokee, Osage, and Choctaw peoples. Emphasizes collaboration of tribal leaders in this process. Focused analysis unavailable in other works. [FEH/HM]

36.145 James Mooney. *The Ghost Dance religion and the Sioux outbreak of 1890.* 1896 ed. Raymond J. DeMallie, ed. Lincoln: University of Nebraska Press, 1991. ISBN 0-8032-3155-5 (cl), 0-8032-8177-3 (pbk). ‣ Classic study of Wounded Knee massacre written shortly after conflict. Based on first-person research by pioneering ethnographer. Compares movement with earlier episodes of Indian religious and cultural revitalization. [FEH/HM]

36.146 Theda Perdue. *Nations remembered: an oral history of the Five Civilized Tribes, 1865–1907.* Westport, Conn.: Greenwood, 1980. ISBN 0-313-22097-2. ‣ Documents collective experience of Indian Territory's southeastern Indians from Civil War to Oklahoma statehood. Based on interviews conducted in 1930s by Writers' Project of Work Projects Administration. Unique window on Indian perceptions of events. [FEH/HM]

36.147 Theda Perdue. *Slavery and the evolution of Cherokee society, 1540–1866.* Knoxville: University of Tennessee Press, 1979. ISBN 0-87049-259-4 (cl), 0-87049-530-5 (pbk). ‣ Unique monograph demonstrating how institution of slavery became agent of cultural change within Cherokee society. In particular, modern slavery transformed number of traditional social practices and produced new group of tribal leaders. [FEH/HM]

36.148 Karen D. Peterson. *Plains Indian art from Fort Marion.* Norman: University of Oklahoma Press, 1971. ISBN 0-8061-0888-6. ‣ Album and analysis of drawings by twenty-six Plains Indian prisoners of war held at Fort Marion, Florida, in 1870s. Story of these artists opens window on American Indian perceptions of assimilation era. [FEH/HM]

36.149 George H. Phillips. *Chiefs and challengers: Indian resistance and cooperation in Southern California.* Berkeley: University of California Press, 1975. ISBN 0-520-02719-1. ‣ Historian's account of strategies of resistance and accommodation devised by Luiseno, Cupeno, and Cahuilla Indians in face of Hispanic and Anglo-American colonization in eighteenth- and nineteenth-century California. Emphasis on public politics and intergroup conflict providing one of few modern overviews on era of California history. [FEH/HM]

36.150 Peter J. Powell. *People of the Sacred Mountain: a history of the Northern Cheyenne chiefs and warrior societies, 1830–1879.* 2 vols. New York: Harper & Row, Native American Publishing Program, 1981. ISBN 0-06-451550-8. ‣ Reverential description of role of council chiefs and warrior societies in Northern Cheyenne history by Anglican priest. Draws heavily on Cheyenne oral tradition and documentary research. [FEH/HM]

36.151 Ronald N. Satz. *American Indian policy in the Jacksonian era.* Lincoln: University of Nebraska Press, 1975. ISBN 0-8032-0823-5. ‣ Useful overview of early nineteenth-century federal Indian policy focusing on conditions that produced removal of Five Civilized Tribes from southeastern United States. Also describes conditions tribes faced on reaching Indian Territory. [FEH/HM]

36.152 Bernard W. Sheehan. *Seeds of extinction: Jeffersonian philanthropy and the American Indian.* Chapel Hill: University of North Carolina Press for Institute of Early American History and Culture, 1973. ISBN 0-8078-1203-x. ‣ Investigates assumptions informing Jefferson's "philanthropic" Indian policy and reasons why it failed. Emphasizes humanitarian intent of Jefferson and offers judicious view of period. [FEH/HM]

36.153 Florence C. Shipek. *The autobiography of Delfina Cuero: a Diegueno Indian.* Los Angeles: Dawson's Book Shop, 1968. ‣ Unique autobiography containing recollections of Diegueno Indian woman from southernmost California. Demonstrates how some families coped with destructive consequences of Anglo-American conquest of California. [FEH/HM]

36.154 Robert A. Trennert, Jr. *Alternative to extinction: federal Indian policy and the beginnings of the reservation system, 1846–51.* Philadelphia: Temple University Press, 1975. ISBN 0-87722-030-1. ‣ Locates philosophical roots of modern reservation system in

1850s when federal authorities sought to facilitate expansion while guarding American Indians from extinction. Unique study of pre–Civil War years. [FEH/HM]

36.155 William E. Unrau. *The Kansas Indians: a history of the wind people, 1673–1873.* 1971 ed. Norman: University of Oklahoma Press, 1986. ISBN 0-8061-1965-9 (pbk). ▸ Standard but well-executed tribal history tracing Kansas Indians from ancestral times to 1873 removal from reservation in upper Neosho Valley of Kansas to Indian Territory. [FEH/HM]

36.156 Robert M. Utley. *The Indian frontier of the American West, 1846–1890.* Albuquerque: University of New Mexico Press, 1984. ISBN 0-8263-0715-9 (cl), 0-8263-0716-7 (pbk). ▸ Well-written synopsis of Indian-white conflict in trans-Mississippi West. Includes discussions of foundations of reservation policy and military encounters from Civil War to Wounded Knee. [FEH/HM]

36.157 Deward E. Walker, Jr. *Conflict and schism in Nez Perce acculturation: a study of religion and politics.* 1968 ed. Moscow: University of Idaho Press, 1991. ISBN 0-89301-105-3. ▸ Anthropologist's account of introduction of Christianity among Nez Perce beginning with missionaries of early nineteenth century and ending with modern period. Technical but interesting discussion of impact of religious change. [FEH/HM]

36.158 Anthony F. C. Wallace. *The death and rebirth of the Seneca.* 1969 ed. New York: Vintage, 1972. ISBN 0-394-71699-X. ▸ Classic, psychocultural history of Iroquois revitalization in early nineteenth century. Explores how preaching of Seneca chief Handsome Lake reshaped tribal traditions to fit new conditions. Beautifully written monograph. [FEH/HM]

36.159 Mary E. Young. *Redskins, ruffleshirts, and rednecks: Indian allotments in Alabama and Mississippi, 1830–1860.* 1958 ed. Norman: University of Oklahoma Press, 1961. ▸ Hair-raising chronicle of methods employed by settlers, speculators, and corporations to acquire lands of Choctaws, Chickasaws, and Creeks removed to Indian Territory, as well as allotments of tribal members who chose to stay behind. [FEH/HM]

SEE ALSO
4.264 Curtis M. Hinsley, Jr. *Savages and scientists.*
37.142 Alfred W. Crosby, Jr. *The Columbian exchange.*
37.571 Sherburne F. Cook. *The conflict between the California Indian and white civilization.*
37.583 Elizabeth A. H. John. *Storms brewed in other men's worlds.*

Twentieth Century

36.160 Margaret Archuleta. *Shared visions: Native American painters and sculptors of the twentieth century.* Phoenix: Heard Museum, 1991. ISBN 0-934351-21-X (pbk). ▸ Outstanding overview prepared for historic show presented at Heard Museum and other venues, 1991–93. Essays by various specialists. Historical treatment ranging from turn-of-century amateurs to contemporary performance artists. [FEH]

36.161 Janet Catherine Berlo, ed. *The early years of Native American art history: the politics of scholarship and collecting.* Seattle: University of Washington Press, 1992. ISBN 0-295-97202-5. ▸ Collection of specialized essays examining how museums and collectors have shaped definition of American Indian art. Essays discuss role of early anthropologists, curators, and dealers in emphasizing "primitive" work over contemporary or European-influenced materials. Opens broad issue of definition and meaning of native art. [FEH/HM]

36.162 Karen I. Blu. *The Lumbee problem: the making of an American Indian people.* Cambridge: Cambridge University Press, 1980. ISBN 0-521-22525-6 (cl), 0-521-29542-4 (pbk). ▸ Analysis of how Lumbee Indians of North Carolina achieved public recognition despite having no records of treaties, no reservation, no Indian language, or distinctly Indian customs on which to base their claim. Significant discussion of concept of ethnic identity as well as Lumbee history. [FEH/HM]

36.163 Leonard A. Carlson. *Indians, bureaucrats, and land: the Dawes Act and the decline of Indian farming.* Westport, Conn: Greenwood, 1981. ISBN 0-313-22533-8. ▸ Analysis of Dawes or General Allotment Act of 1887 utilizing methods of new economic history. Argues political interests overrode humanitarian ones in decision to divide reservation lands among tribal members. Straightforward thesis argued clearly, despite sophisticated quantitative manipulations. [FEH/HM]

36.164 Stephen Cornell. *The return of the native: American Indian political resurgence.* New York: Oxford University Press, 1988. ISBN 0-19-503772-3 (cl), 0-19-506575-1 (pbk). ▸ Historical overview by sociologist of political strategies of contemporary American Indians to regain control over lives, future, and place in American society. Attempts to explain relationship between recent cultural revivals and Indian politics. [FEH/HM]

36.165 Vine Deloria, Jr. *Custer died for your sins: an Indian manifesto.* 1969 ed. Norman: University of Oklahoma Press, 1988. ISBN 0-8061-2129-7 (pbk). ▸ Landmark statement by contemporary Indian intellectual that became manifesto of political resurgence of 1970s and 1980s. Chapters on images of Indians, laws and treaties, anthropologists, missionaries, reservations, Indian humor, Indian leadership, and Bureau of Indian Affairs. [FEH/HM]

36.166 Vine Deloria, Jr., and Clifford M. Lytle. *The nations within: the past and future of American Indian sovereignty.* New York: Pantheon, 1984. ISBN 0-394-72566-2 (pbk). ▸ Highly readable overview of Indian policy reforms of 1930s and efforts of Indian advocate John Collier to humanize American treatment of tribes. Emphasizes Collier's defeats, but recognizes positive consequences of New Deal reforms in post–World War II period. [FEH/HM]

36.167 Raymond J. DeMallie, ed. *The sixth grandfather: Black Elk's teaching given to John G. Neihardt.* Lincoln: University of Nebraska Press, 1984. ISBN 0-8032-1664-5 (cl), 0-8032-6564-6 (pbk). ▸ Poet John Neihardt's 1931 and 1944 interviews with Lakota spiritual leader Nicholas Black Elk. Exceedingly useful for light it sheds on Neihardt's role as Black Elk's amanuensis as well as on Sioux spiritual leader's biography and religious perspectives. [FEH/HM]

36.168 George Devereux. *Mohave ethnopsychiatry and suicide: the psychiatric knowledge and the psychic disturbances of an Indian tribe.* 1961 ed. St. Clair Shores, Mich.: Scholarly Press, 1976. (Smithsonian Institute of American Ethnology, 175.) ISBN 0-403-03420-5 (cl), 0-403-03650-X (pbk). ▸ Detailed study of Mojave theories and treatments for mental disorders; classic of ethnopsychiatry. Unique perspective on culture and worldview of this desert-dwelling community. [FEH/HM]

36.169 Dorothy Dunn. *American Indian painting of the Southwest and Plains areas.* Albuquerque: University of New Mexico Press, 1968. ▸ Definitive scholarly treatment of region's native painters offering descriptions of indigenous painting traditions and ways in which those traditions entered modern art market in first decades of twentieth century. More than thirty color plates and a hundred illustrations. [FEH]

36.170 Donald L. Fixico. *Termination and relocation: federal Indian policy, 1945–1966.* Albuquerque: University of New Mexico Press, 1986. ISBN 0-8263-1191-1. ▸ Workmanlike overview of Indian policies of Truman and Eisenhower administrations. Focuses on how these presidents sought to terminate United States government's trust relationship with Indian tribes and to relocate their members to urban areas. [FEH/HM]

36.171 Morris W. Foster. *Being Comanche: a social history of an American Indian community.* Tucson: University of Arizona Press, 1991. ISBN 0-8165-1246-9. ▸ Overview of Comanche community life by anthropologist. Traces role of face-to-face relationships in maintaining tribal identity and regulating community behavior. Good example of anthropological monograph drawing on historical sources. [FEH/HM]

36.172 Loretta Fowler. *Arapahoe politics: symbols in crisis of authority, 1851–1978.* Lincoln: University of Nebraska Press, 1982. ISBN 0-8032-1956-3 (cl), 0-8032-6862-9 (pbk). ▸ Fascinating study of creation and manipulation of political symbols among Arapahoe. Focuses on twentieth century and elements of cultural continuity in modern Arapahoe life. [FEH/HM]

36.173 Loretta Fowler. *Shared symbols, contested meanings: Gros Ventre culture and history, 1778–1984.* Ithaca, N.Y.: Cornell University Press, 1987. ISBN 0-8014-1878-X (cl), 0-8014-9450-8 (pbk). ▸ Anthropologist's treatment of Gros Ventre's concept of identity from first encounters with Europeans to recent past. Extended essay on meaning of tribal identity summarizing Gros Ventre history; describes community's ongoing struggles over cultural symbols of identity and community solidarity. [FEH/HM]

36.174 Robert Fleming Heizer and Theodora Kroeber, eds. *Ishi, the last Yahi: a documentary history.* Berkeley: University of California Press, 1979. ISBN 0-520-04366-9 (cl), 0-520-03296-9 (pbk). ▸ Anthology of documents primarily concerned with life of Ishi, last of California's Yahi Indians, before and after his "discovery" by whites in early twentieth century. [FEH/HM]

36.175 Hazel W. Hertzberg. *The search for an American Indian identity: modern pan-Indian movements.* Syracuse, N.Y.: Syracuse University Press, 1971. ISBN 0-8156-0076-3 (cl), 0-8156-2245-7 (pbk). ▸ One of few studies of early twentieth century. Examines nationwide organizations (such as Society of American Indians) that have stressed common Indian interests in maintaining Indian identity within dominant society. [FEH/HM]

36.176 Frederick E. Hoxie. *A final promise: the campaign to assimilate the Indians, 1880–1920.* 1984 ed. Cambridge: Cambridge University Press, 1989. ISBN 0-521-37987-3. ▸ Detailed analysis of changing principles and goals characterizing late nineteenth- and early twentieth-century campaign to assimilate American Indians. Emphasizes role of national politics and shifts in conceptions of race and citizenship in policy formulation. [FEH/HM]

36.177 Peter Iverson. *Carlos Montezuma and the changing world of American Indians.* Albuquerque: University of New Mexico Press, 1982. ISBN 0-8263-0641-1. ▸ Biography of influential Southern Yavapai spokesman of late nineteenth and early twentieth centuries. Traces his opposition to Bureau of Indian Affairs and his gradual disenchantment with assimilation. [FEH/HM]

36.178 Joseph G. Jorgensen. *The Sun Dance religion: power for the powerless.* 1972 ed. Chicago: University of Chicago Press, 1974. ISBN 0-226-41085-4 (cl, 1972), 0-226-41086-2 (pbk). ▸ Comparative analysis of modern Shoshone and Ute Sun Dance religions attempting to explain both origin and persistence. Narrowly focused anthropological account based on both archival research and field interviews. [FEH/HM]

36.179 Alvin M. Josephy, Jr. *Now that the buffalo's gone: a study of today's American Indians.* New York: Knopf, 1982. ISBN 0-394-46672-1. ▸ Broad history of recent Indian history clarifying viewpoints and aspirations of contemporary political activists. Uses case studies of recent confrontations to highlight particular themes in history of Indian-white relations. For general reader. [FEH/HM]

36.180 Harry A. Kersey, Jr. *The Florida Seminoles and the New Deal, 1933–1942.* Boca Raton: Florida Atlantic University Press, 1989. ISBN 0-8130-0928-6. ▸ Description of mixed reception and results of Indian commissioner John Collier's attempt to revitalize Seminole culture and economy through Franklin Roosevelt's so-called Indian New Deal. Unique focus on Florida gives monograph particular value. [FEH/HM]

36.181 Ruth Kirk. *Tradition and change on the Northwest Coast: the Makah, Nuu-Chah-Nulth, Southern Kwakiutl, and Nuxalk.* Seattle: University of Washington Press, 1986. ISBN 0-295-96628-9 (cl), 0-295-96396-4 (pbk). ▸ Examination of enduring elements in worldviews and lifeways of selected tribes living in central British Columbia and northwestern Washington state. Includes views of contemporary tribal elders and descriptions of shifts in social organization resulting from contact with outsiders. Best available overview of these themes in region. [FEH/HM]

36.182 Martha Knack and Omer C. Stewart. *As long as the river shall run: an ethnohistory of Pyramid Lake Indian Reservation.* Berkeley: University of California Press, 1984. ISBN 0-520-04868-7. ▸ Exhaustive history of conflict between Northern Paiutes and white miners, ranchers, and farmers over one of largest sources of water in Great Basin. Demonstrates power of non-Indian economic interests in shaping reservation life. [FEH/HM]

36.183 Dorothea Leighton and John Adair. *People of the middle place: a study of the Zuni Indians.* New Haven: Human Relations Area Files Press, 1966. ISBN 0-87536-320-2. ▸ Representative of early phase of psychological anthropology, examines development of Zuni personality in sociocultural, geographical, and historical context. Offers excellent insights into persistence of cultural beliefs in twentieth century. [FEH/HM]

36.184 Margot Liberty, ed. *American Indian intellectuals.* St. Paul: West, 1978. (Proceedings of the American Ethnological Society, 1976.) ISBN 0-8299-0223-6. ▸ Invaluable profiles of American Indians, most who lived in twentieth century. Unique study of people who struggled to interpret and defend tribal traditions in industrial era. [FEH/HM]

36.185 James J. Lopach et al. *Tribal government today: politics on Montana Indian reservations.* Boulder: Westview, 1990. ISBN 0-8133-7868-0. ▸ Plodding but useful examination of contemporary Montana tribes. Separate chapters on Crow, Blackfeet, Northern Cheyenne, Fort Peck, Fort Belknap, Rocky Boy, and Flathead reservations discuss governmental structure, tribal law, and local politics. [FEH/HM]

36.186 Gordon Macgregor. *Warriors without weapons: a study of the society and personality development of the Pine Ridge Sioux.* Chicago: University of Chicago Press, 1946. ▸ Pioneering culture and personality study. Describes sociocultural, geographical, and historical determinants of personality development on South Dakota's Pine Ridge Sioux Reservation. [FEH/HM]

36.187 Lewis Meriam. *The problem of Indian administration.* 1928 ed. New York: Johnson Reprint, 1971. (Brookings Institution studies in administration, 17.) ▸ Survey of social conditions generally credited with establishing need for new approach to federal Indian policy and setting agenda for Indian New Deal of 1930s. Study, directed by Meriam, drafted by team of social scientists including American Indians. [FEH/HM]

36.188 L. G. Moses and Raymond Wilson, eds. *Indian lives: essays on nineteenth- and twentieth-century native American leaders.* Albuquerque: University of New Mexico Press, 1985. ISBN 0-8263-0814-7 (cl), 0-8263-0815-5 (pbk). ▸ Eight biographical sketches of American Indians who struggled to maintain Indian identity in face of pressures to conform to European American mainstream. Brief but readable portraits buttressed with descriptions of sources. [FEH/HM]

36.189 Mountain Wolf Woman. *Mountain Wolf Woman, sister of Crashing Thunder: the autobiography of a Winnebago Indian.*

Nancy O. Lurie, ed. Ann Arbor: University of Michigan Press, 1961. ISBN 0-472-09109-3 (cl), 0-472-06109-7(pbk). ‣ Reminiscences of Winnebago woman (b. 1884), rich in information on traditions and changing culture of her people. Mountain Wolf Woman recounts tribal childhood, adult dislocations, and decision to follow teachings of Native American church. [FEH/HM]

36.190 Mourning Dove. *Mourning Dove: a Salishan autobiography.* Jay Miller, ed. Lincoln: University of Nebraska Press, 1990. ISBN 0-8032-3119-9. ‣ Description of Salish Indian culture on Colville Reservation in late nineteenth and early twentieth century by first American Indian woman to publish a novel. Masterly editing and annotations make this excellent source for recent history of plateau region. [FEH/HM]

36.191 J. Anthony Paredes, ed. *Indians of the southeastern United States in the late twentieth century.* Tuscaloosa: University of Alabama Press, 1992. ISBN 0-8173-0534-3. ‣ Collection of essays, each on different American Indian group in contemporary Southeast. Offers diverse portraits and reveals diverse tribal strategies for cultural survival in industrial age. [FEH/HM]

36.192 Dorothy R. Parker. *Singing an Indian song: a biography of D'Arcy McNickle.* Lincoln: University of Nebraska Press, 1992. ISBN 0-8032-3687-5. ‣ Only full-length biography tracing course of D'Arcy McNickle's life from his reservation childhood in Montana through career in American Indian political and cultural affairs. Examines life and Indian identity of modern leader. [FEH/HM]

36.193 Donald L. Parman. *The Navajos and the New Deal.* New Haven: Yale University Press, 1976. ISBN 0-300-01832-0. ‣ Detailed history of Indian New Deal among Navajo Indians. Describes both reform efforts of 1930s and mixed success within tribe. Excellent descriptions of tribal political leaders. [FEH/HM]

36.194 Nicholas C. Peroff. *Menominee drums: tribal termination and restoration, 1954–1974.* Norman: University of Oklahoma Press, 1982. ISBN 0-8061-1703-6. ‣ Account of Menominee's successful overthrow of congressionally mandated termination. Focuses on role of DRUMS (Determination of Rights and Unity for Menominee Shareholders) in restoration movement. [FEH/HM]

36.195 Paul Radin. *The autobiography of a Winnebago Indian.* 1920 ed. New York: Dover, 1963. ISBN 0-486-20096-5. ‣ Recollections of S. B., a Winnebago man born in mid-nineteenth century, containing much valuable information on responses of one individual to stresses generated by industrial life and expansion of non-Indian settlement. Compliments Mountain Wolf Woman 36.189. [FEH/HM]

36.196 Dorothy Jean Ray. *Aleut and Eskimo art: tradition and innovation in South Alaska.* 1981 ed. Seattle: University of Washington Press, 1987. ISBN 0-295-96410-3 (pbk). ‣ Richly illustrated analysis tracing evolution of Aleut, Yupik, and Pacific Eskimo art into modern period. Emphasizes contemporary strategies for preserving traditional ideas. [FEH/HM]

36.197 Luther Standing Bear. *My people, the Sioux.* 1928 ed. E. A. Brininstool, ed. Lincoln: University of Nebraska Press, 1975. ISBN 0-8032-5793-7 (pbk). ‣ Autobiography providing insider's perspective on adjustments of Teton Sioux to early reservation life and plea for white understanding of Indian cultures. Articulate native voice from period usually described by non-Indians alone. [FEH/HM]

36.198 John Stands in Timber and Margot Liberty. *Cheyenne memories.* 1967 ed. Lincoln: University of Nebraska Press, 1972. ISBN 0-8032-5751-1 (pbk). ‣ History of Northern Cheyennes as recalled and interpreted by members of that tribe. Based on records and testimony of co-author Stands in Timber, one of the

last Cheyenne to hear the tribal story from those who lived it. [FEH/HM]

36.199 Stan Steiner. *The new Indians.* New York: Harper & Row, 1968. ‣ Portraits of contemporary reservation life disclosing growing use of political organizing and protest by American Indians in 1960s. Vividly written by journalist eager to point out continuing injustices suffered by Indian people. [FEH/HM]

36.200 Omer C. Stewart. *Peyote religion: a history.* Norman: University of Oklahoma Press, 1987. ISBN 0-8061-2068-1. ‣ Definitive history of modern Peyote movement. Extensive field and archival research undergird overview of origin and diffusion of Peyote faith from late nineteenth century to present. [FEH/HM]

36.201 Imre Sutton et al. *Irredeemable America: the Indian's estate and land claims.* Albuquerque: University of New Mexico Press with Institute for Native American Studies, 1985. (History series, 1.) ISBN 0-8263-0806-6. ‣ Collection of fifteen articles on different aspects of United States Claims Commission, established 1946 to adjudicate claims filed by tribes for lands illegally taken by United States government. Contributions from geographers, anthropologists, and historians. [FEH/HM]

36.202 Margaret C. Szasz. *Education and the American Indian: the road to self-determination, 1928–1973.* 2d ed. Albuquerque: University of New Mexico Press, 1977. ISBN 0-8263-0468-0. ‣ Examination of transformation of Indian schooling from program for assimilation to vehicle for tribal self-determination rooted primarily in printed sources. Places education in broad, historical framework. [FEH/HM]

36.203 Graham D. Taylor. *The New Deal and American Indian tribalism: the administration of the Indian Reorganization Act, 1934–1945.* Lincoln: University of Nebraska Press, 1980. ISBN 0-8032-4403-7. ‣ Important general study examining why John Collier's Indian Reorganization Act of 1934 failed to achieve central goals of revitalizing tribal political and economic systems. Stresses national policies rather than local conditions. [FEH/HM]

36.204 James W. Vanstone. *Point Hope: an Eskimo village in transition.* 1962 ed. New York: AMS Press, 1988. (American Ethnological Society monographs, 35.) ISBN 0-404-62934-2. ‣ Classic ethnography documenting effects of acculturation on cultural institutions and identity of Eskimos of Point Hope, village on northern coast of Kotzebue Sound. [FEH/HM]

36.205 Fred W. Voget. *The Shoshoni-Crow Sun Dance.* Norman: University of Oklahoma Press, 1984. ISBN 0-8061-1886-5. ‣ Modern anthropologist's description of Crow ceremony adopted from Wind River Shoshones in 1941. Includes descriptions of ritual, symbolism of event, and its status in contemporary Crow ritual life. [FEH/HM]

36.206 Charles F. Wilkinson. *American Indians, time, and law: native societies in a modern constitutional democracy.* New Haven: Yale University Press, 1987. ISBN 0-300-03589-6 (cl), 0-300-04136-5 (pbk). ‣ Description of recent (post-1959) developments in American Indian legal status before Supreme Court. Emphasizes legal viability of tribal governments and defends wisdom of their persistence. [FEH/HM]

SEE ALSO
44.380 Marjane Ambler. *Breaking the iron bonds.*
44.387 Kenneth R. Philp. *John Collier's crusade for Indian reform, 1920–1954.*

General and Theoretical Works

36.207 Patricia Albers and Beatrice Medicine. *The hidden half: studies in Plains Indian women.* Washington, D.C.: University Press of America, 1983. ISBN 0-8191-2956-9 (cl), 0-8191-2957-7 (pbk). ‣ Pioneering reassessment of women's roles in American Indian societies. Essays organized under following headings:

images of women, women's work, status of women, and female identity. [FEH/HM]

36.208 Russell L. Barsh and James Y. Henderson. *The road: Indian tribes and political freedom.* Berkeley: University of California Press, 1980. ISBN 0-520-04636-6. ▸ Sobering history of erosion of American Indian political freedom and sovereignty by two legal scholars, one a member of Micmac tribe. Offers critique of extent to which Western democracies can accommodate Indian peoples. [FEH/HM]

36.209 H. David Brumble III. *An annotated bibliography of American Indian and Eskimo autobiographies.* Lincoln: University of Nebraska Press, 1981. ISBN 0-8032-1175-9. ▸ Most comprehensive listing of published, first-person narratives by American Indians and Eskimos. Also contains entries for autobiographical materials in manuscript and on tape. [FEH/HM]

36.210 Colin G. Calloway, ed. *New directions in American Indian history.* Norman: University of Oklahoma Press, 1988. (D'Arcy McNickle Center bibliographies in American Indian history, 1.) ISBN 0-8061-2147-5. ▸ Nine critical reviews of contemporary scholarship in American Indian history. Includes chapters on use of quantitative methods, feminism, *métis* history, history of Southern Plains, Indians and the law, linguistics, economics, and religion. Useful bibliographies. [FEH/HM/NMK]

36.211 James A. Clifton, ed. *Being and becoming Indian: biographical studies of North American frontiers.* Belmont, Calif.: Wadsworth, 1989. ISBN 0-534-10999-3 (cl), 0-534-10998-5 (pbk). ▸ Fourteen papers examining how Indians living in both white and Indian worlds organized their identities and lives. Excellent treatments, prefaced by polemical theoretical introduction. [FEH/HM]

36.212 Felix Cohen. *Felix Cohen's "Handbook of Federal Indian Law."* Charlottesville, Va.: Michie and Bobbs-Merrill, 1982. ISBN 0-87215-413-0. ▸ Modern revision of Cohen's landmark synthesis of federal Indian law published originally in 1940. Legal treatise that has been used heavily by modern courts; includes chapters on basis of Indian law; history of Indian policy; source and scope of federal authority in Indian affairs; nature of state authority in Indian affairs; and jurisdiction. [FEH/HM]

36.213 Elizabeth Colson. *The Makah Indians: a study of an Indian tribe in modern American society.* 1953 ed. Westport, Conn.: Greenwood, 1974. ISBN 0-8371-7153-9. ▸ Detailed presentation of life on Makah reservation at Neah Bay, Washington, in early 1940s. Ethnography recognizing distinctiveness of community while emphasizing Makah assimilation and tribe's relationship with whites living on and around reservation. [FEH/HM]

36.214 David Damas, ed. *The handbook of North American Indians.* Vol. 5: *The Arctic.* Washington, D.C.: Smithsonian Institution Press, 1984. ISBN 0-87474-191-2 (set). ▸ Comprehensive reference work; most recent available on the subject. Collection of scholarly essays on Arctic prehistory, history of all of region's major cultural groups. [FEH/HM]

36.215 Warren L. D'Azevedo, ed. *The handbook of North American Indians.* Vol. 11: *The Great Basin.* Washington, D.C.: Smithsonian Institution and United States General Printing Office, 1986. ISBN 0-87474-191-2 (v. 11), 0-16-004581-9 (v. 11). ▸ Comprehensive reference work; most recent available. Forty-five state-of-the-art essays on environment, cultural history, and indigenous peoples of North America's Great Basin. [FEH/HM]

36.216 Angie Debo. *A history of the Indians of the United States.* 1970 ed. Norman: University of Oklahoma Press, 1984. ISBN 0-8061-1888-1. ▸ Sensitive retelling of history of United States–Indian relations; good introduction. Particularly valuable for treatment of Oklahoma Indians written by pioneer in field at end of her career. [FEH/HM]

36.217 Brian W. Dippie. *The vanishing American: white attitudes and U.S. Indian policy.* 1982 ed. Lawrence: University Press of Kansas, 1991. ISBN 0-7006-0507-X. ▸ Overview of Indian-white relations. Argues myth of vanishing Indian has governed both popular conceptions of American Indians and policies adopted by United States government. Originally written as dissertation in American Studies. [FEH/HM]

36.218 Edward P. Dozier. *The Pueblo Indians of North America.* 1970 ed. New York: Waveland, 1983. ISBN 0-88133-059-0 (pbk). ▸ Excellent summary of Pueblo history and culture focusing on Pueblo adjustments to changing environmental, socioeconomic, and political conditions. Cultural overview by one of first American Indians to pursue career in anthropology. [FEH/HM]

36.219 Philip Drucker. *Indians of the Northwest Coast.* 1955 ed. Garden City, N.Y.: National History Press for the American Museum of Natural History, 1963. ▸ Unsurpassed survey of Indian peoples and cultures of Northwest Coast treating area-wide patterns as well as regional specializations. Good introduction to area's native cultures. [FEH/HM]

36.220 Fred Eggan. *Social organization of the western Pueblos.* 1950 ed. Chicago: University of Chicago Press, 1973. ISBN 0-226-19076-5 (pbk). ▸ Classic analysis of Pueblo social organization based on integration of historical and anthropological methods. Offers introduction to field of social anthropology as well as to internal structure of Hopi and Zuni communities. [FEH/HM]

36.221 John C. Ewers. *The Blackfeet: raiders on the northwestern plains.* Norman: University of Oklahoma Press, 1958. ISBN 0-8061-1836-9. ▸ Outstanding history of confederacy of Piegan (Pikuni), Blood (Kainah), and Blackfeet (Siksika) tribes of Montana, prehistory to 1950, by anthropologist. Focuses particularly on changes in material cultures of community. [FEH/HM]

36.222 Christian F. Feest. *Indians of northeastern North America.* Leiden: Brill, 1986. ISBN 90-04-07833-9. ▸ Panoramic treatment of history and cultures of native peoples of North America's Northeast. Includes sections on religious, political, and economic institutions. [FEH/HM]

36.223 William W. Fitzhugh and Susan A. Kaplan. *Inua: spirit world of the Bering Sea Eskimo.* Washington, D.C.: Smithsonian Institution Press for National Museum of Natural History, 1982. ISBN 0-87474-430-X (cl), 0-87474-429-6 (pbk). ▸ Visually stunning presentation of traditional Bering Sea Eskimo lifeways, based on collected artifacts, photographs, and notes of Edward Nelson, who conducted ethnological and natural history research for Smithsonian, 1877–81. [FEH/HM]

36.224 James M. Goodman. *The Navajo atlas: environment, resources, people, and history of the Dine Bikeyah.* Norman: University of Oklahoma Press, 1982. ISBN 0-8061-1621-8 (cl), 0-8061-2032-0 (pbk). ▸ Forty-eight maps profiling selected aspects of Navajo environment, history, population, livelihood, resources, and services. Atlas needs to be used in conjunction with other sources on Navajo. [FEH/HM]

36.225 Rayna Green. *Native American women: a contextual bibliography.* Bloomington: Indiana University Press, 1983. ISBN 0-253-33976-6. ▸ Cites and evaluates 672 books, articles, films, government reports, and dissertations by or about American Indian women. Finds most treatments of Indian women selective, stereotyped, and damaging. [FEH/HM]

36.226 Howard L. Harrod. *Renewing the world: Plains Indian religion and morality.* Tucson: University of Arizona Press, 1987. ISBN 0-8165-0958-1. ▸ Synthetic overview presenting central categories of Plains Indian morality and religion. Describes how cultural values are encoded in oral traditions and rituals. [FEH/HM]

36.227 Robert Fleming Heizer, ed. *Handbook of North American Indians.* Vol. 8: *California.* Washington, D.C.: Smithsonian Institution Press, 1978. ISBN 0-87474-191-2 (set). ▸ Basic reference work; seventy-one scholarly essays providing detailed profiles of prehistory, history, and cultures of more than sixty California groups. [FEH/HM]

36.228 June Helm, ed. *Handbook of North American Indians.* Vol. 6: *Subarctic.* Washington, D.C.: Smithsonian Institution Press, 1981. ISBN 0-87474-191-2 (set). ▸ Basic reference work; sixty-six essays on ecology, history, languages, and cultures of Subarctic native peoples. [FEH/HM]

36.229 Edward E. Hill. *Guide to the records of the National Archives of the United States relating to American Indians.* Washington, D.C.: National Archives and Records Service, 1981. ISBN 0-911333-13-4. ▸ Indispensable guide to vast storehouse of materials on Indian peoples and Indian-white relations contained within various branches and divisions of United States National Archives. [FEH/HM]

36.230 Frederick E. Hoxie, ed. *Indians in American History: an introduction.* Arlington Heights, Ill.: Harlan Davidson, 1988. ISBN 0-88295-855-0 (pbk). ▸ Introductory text; thirteen chronologically arranged essays presenting Indian side of chapters in American history not usually provided by textbooks. Includes annotated bibliographies. [FEH/HM]

36.231 Charles M. Hudson. *The southeastern Indians.* Knoxville: University of Tennessee Press, 1976. ISBN 0-87049-187-3 (cl), 0-87049-248-9 (pbk). ▸ Panoramic introduction, useful to beginner and specialist alike, on history, cultures, and social institutions of Indians of southeastern United States. By anthropologist sensitive to role of historical events. [FEH/HM]

36.232 R. Douglas Hurt. *Indian agriculture in America: prehistory to the present.* Lawrence: University Press of Kansas, 1987. ISBN 0-7006-0337-9. ▸ Synthesis of contemporary archaeological, historical, botanical, and anthropological information on American Indian agricultural methods and cultigens. Avoids sweeping narrative; chapters arranged chronologically and contain subdivisions for region and topic. [FEH/HM]

36.233 Charles J. Kappler, ed. *Indian affairs: laws and treaties.* 1904–41 2d ed. 5 vols. Washington, D.C.: United States Government Printing Office, 1975–79. ▸ Compendium of treaties, laws, and executive orders concerning relations between American Indian tribes and United States. Basic reference tool compiled early in twentieth century and subsequently revised. [FEH/HM]

36.234 Felix M. Keesing. *The Menomini Indians of Wisconsin.* 1939 ed. Madison: University of Wisconsin Press, 1987. ISBN 0-229-10970-4 (cl), 0-299-10974-7 (pbk). ▸ Ambitious tribal history focusing on changes in Menominee society and culture resulting from three centuries of white contact. Three themes dominate: modification of indigenous tribal lifeways, economic dependency, and social disorganization. [FEH/HM]

36.235 Alice B. Kehoe. *North American Indians: a comprehensive account.* 2d ed. Englewood Cliffs, N.J.: Prentice-Hall, 1992. ISBN 0-13-624362-2. ▸ Written as textbook, provides introductory tribal histories and regional overviews for Indian peoples located in eight North American culture areas. [FEH/HM]

36.236 Kate Peck Kent. *Navajo weaving: three centuries of change.* Santa Fe, N.M.: School of American Research Press; distributed by University of Washington Press, 1985. ISBN 0-933452-12-8 (cl), 0-933452-13-6 (pbk). ▸ Image-filled history identifying continuities and changes in techniques and aesthetics of Navajo weaving from mid-seventeenth century to present. Stresses innovative quality of tribal weavers. [FEH/HM]

36.237 Ruth Landes. *Ojibwa religion and the Mdewiwin.* Madison: University of Wisconsin Press, 1968. ▸ Sophisticated analysis by anthropologist of Ojibwa spirituality and ritual as they relate

to curing society known as Mdewiwin. Stresses impact of historical change on religious belief. [FEH/HM]

36.238 Eleanor Burke Leacock and Nancy O. Lurie. *North American Indians in historical perspective.* 1971 ed. Prospect Heights, Ill.: Waveland, 1988. ISBN 0-88133-377-8. ▸ Unique collection of fourteen essays examining how Indian peoples from nine culture areas responded to contact with Europeans and European Americans. Introduction, by American Indian anthropologist D'Arcy McNickle, presents excellent overview of Indian-white relations. [FEH/HM]

36.239 Robert H. Lowie. *Indians of the plains.* 1954 ed. Lincoln: University of Nebraska Press, 1982. ISBN 0-8032-7907-8 (cl), 0-8032-2858-9 (pbk). ▸ Incomparable introduction to Plains Indian peoples offering chapters on material culture, social organization, religion, prehistory, history, and acculturation. Indispensable preface by Raymond J. DeMallie. [FEH/HM]

36.240 John J. Mathews. *The Osages: children of the middle waters.* 1961 ed. Norman: University of Oklahoma Press, 1981. ISBN 0-8061-1770-2 (pbk). ▸ Classic tribal history, among first by tribal member. Author, Osage novelist and historian, describes tribal lifeways before and after contact with whites; impressionistic, evocative treatment. [FEH/HM]

36.241 D'Arcy McNickle. *They came here first: the epic of the American Indian.* Rev. ed. New York: Octagon Books, 1975. ISBN 0-374-95550-6. ▸ First general history written by American Indian. Popular work describing Indian cultures from pre-Columbian times through various phases of European and European American domination. Sympathetic, moving interpretation. [FEH/HM]

36.242 George Peter Murdock and Timothy J. O'Leary. *Ethnographic bibliography of North America.* Vol. 1: *General North America.* 4th ed. New Haven: Human Relations Area Files Press, 1975. ISBN 0-87536-205-2. ▸ Basic reference tool. Somewhat dated but indispensable compendium of bibliographies for hundreds of American Indian tribes living north of Mexico. [FEH/HM]

36.243 Peter Nabokov, ed. *Native American testimony: a chronicle of Indian-white relations from prophecy to the present, 1492–1992.* New York: Viking, 1991. ISBN 0-670-83704-0. ▸ Anthology of documents, speeches, and other statements, organized by topic (e.g., trade, missionaries, first encounters). Designed to present American Indian perspectives on Indian-white relations. [FEH/HM]

36.244 Peter Nabokov and Robert Easton. *Native American architecture.* New York: Oxford University Press, 1989. ISBN 0-19-503781-2. ▸ Lavishly illustrated volume providing unique overview of American Indian built environment. Organized by nine broad culture areas and sensitive to impact of history on design and construction. Good antidote to soft descriptions of ideas and rituals. [FEH/HM]

36.245 Byron Nelson, Jr., et al. *Our home forever: a Hupa Indian of Northern California.* 1978 ed. Laura Bayer, ed. Salt Lake City: Howe, 1988. ISBN 0-935704-47-7 (pbk). ▸ Model of recent efforts by tribes to present their own histories. Based on oral and written history, describes Hupa's struggle to survive in face of ethnocidal ambitions of whites. [FEH/HM]

36.246 William W. Newcomb, Jr. *The Indians of Texas: from prehistoric to modern times.* Austin: University of Texas Press, 1961. ISBN 0-292-73271-6 (cl), 0-292-78425-2 (pbk). ▸ Dated overview offering nontechnical summary of prehistory, indigenous cultures, and decimation of original inhabitants of area now comprising Texas. [FEH/HM]

36.247 Vynola Beaver Newkumet and Howard L. Meridith. *Hasinai: a traditional history of the Caddo confederacy.* College Station: Texas A&M University Press, 1988. ISBN 0-89096-342-8. ▸ Imaginative summary of Caddo cultural history structured around sequence of traditional ceremonial dances integrating tribe's collective memory. Tribal history that begins to present elusive native point of view. [FEH/HM]

36.248 Roger L. Nichols, ed. *The American Indian, past and present.* 4th ed. New York: McGraw-Hill, 1992. ISBN 0-07-046499-5. ▸ Collection of twenty-four chronologically arranged essays exploring such issues as changing status of Indians in American history, competition between Indians and whites over land and resources, federal Indian policies, and Indian sovereignty and self-determination. [FEH/HM]

36.249 Alfonso Ortiz, ed. *Handbook of North American Indians.* Vol. 9: *Southwest.* Washington, D.C.: Smithsonian Institution Press and United States Government Printing Office, 1979. ISBN 0-87474-189-0 (v. 9), 0-16-004577-0 (v. 9). ▸ Basic reference work containing fifty-nine scholarly essays on archaeology, languages, cultures, and postcontact histories of Pueblo peoples of Southwest. Includes extensive bibliography. [FEH/HM]

36.250 Alfonso Ortiz, ed. *Handbook of North American Indians.* Vol. 10: *Southwest.* Washington, D.C.: Smithsonian Institution Press and Unites States Government Printing Office, 1983. ISBN 0-87474-190-4 (v. 10), 0-16-004579-7 (v. 10). ▸ Basic reference work; complements volume 9 of *Handbook of North American Indians* (36.249). Fifty-six articles on non-Puebloan Indians of Southwest covering prehistory, linguistics, ethnography, and history. [FEH/HM]

36.251 Marla N. Powers. *Oglala women: myth, ritual, and reality.* Chicago: University of Chicago Press, 1986. ISBN 0-226-67748-6 (cl), 0-226-67749-4 (pbk). ▸ Investigation of relationship between traditional concepts of gender and contemporary women's roles among Oglala Lakota of South Dakota by modern anthropologist. Representative of small literature on Indian women's experience. [FEH/HM]

36.252 Francis Paul Prucha. *A bibliographical guide to the history of Indian-white relations in the United States.* Chicago: University of Chicago Press, 1977. ISBN 0-226-68477-6 (cl), 0-226-68476-8 (pbk). ▸ Essential bibliographical reference in study of Indian-white relations. Contains approximately 9,700 citations for sources ranging from government documents, to academic literature, to popular press. See also 35.254. [FEH/HM]

36.253 Francis Paul Prucha. *The Great Father: the United States government and the American Indians.* 2 vols. Lincoln: University of Nebraska Press, 1984. ISBN 0-8032-3668-9 (set). ▸ Monumental, two-volume treatment of United States Indian policy incorporating and surpassing many of author's previous monographic studies. Policy history in exhaustive detail with meticulous accuracy. Analysis often sympathizes with humanitarian motives of policy makers. [FEH/HM]

36.254 Francis Paul Prucha. *Indian-white relations in the United States: a bibliography of works published, 1975–1980.* Lincoln: University of Nebraska Press, 1982. ISBN 0-8032-3665-4 (cl) 0-8032-8705-4 (pbk). ▸ Update of author's *Bibliographical Guide to the History of Indian-White Relations in the United States* (36.252), with 3,400 additional citations; shares original's outline and approach. [FEH/HM]

36.255 Robert H. Ruby and John A. Brown. *Indians of the Pacific Northwest: a history.* Norman: University of Oklahoma Press, 1981. ISBN 0-8061-1731-1, 0-8061-2113-0. ▸ Popular history of Indian inhabitants of Washington, Oregon, Idaho, and western Montana from mid-eighteenth to early twentieth centuries. Useful introduction; well illustrated, clearly organized. [FEH/HM]

36.256 Florence C. Shipek. *Pushed into the rocks: Southern California Indian land tenure, 1769–1986.* Lincoln: University of

Nebraska Press, 1988. ISBN 0-8032-4178-X. ▸ Examination of continuities and changes in patterns of land tenure and use among Indian tribes of southern California from precontact through various phases of European and American domination. Unique chronicle of dispossession. Spare style. [FEH/HM]

36.257 William S. Simmons. *Spirit of the New England tribes: Indian history and folklore, 1620–1984.* Hanover, N.H.: University Press of New England, 1986. ISBN 0-87451-370-7 (cl), 0-87451-372-3 (pbk). ▸ Overview of region's folklore exploring both persistence and change in key symbols and motifs. Particularly sensitive to sources of innovation and how folklore responds to historical events. [FEH/HM]

36.258 Paul Stuart. *Nations within a nation: historical statistics of American Indians.* Westport, Conn.: Greenwood, 1987. ISBN 0-313-23813-8. ▸ Wealth of statistical information on American Indians culled from such federal agencies as Bureau of Census, Bureau of Indian Affairs, and Indian Health Service. Figures reflect both strengths and weaknesses of those sources. [FEH/HM]

36.259 Wayne Suttles, ed. *Handbook of North American Indians.* Vol. 7: *Northwest Coast.* Washington, D.C.: Smithsonian Institution Press and United States Government Printing Office, 1990. ISBN 0-16-020390-2. ▸ Basic reference work; fifty-six essays examining various aspects of Northwest Coast archaeological, linguistic, ethnographic, and historical research. Extensive illustrations and several original maps. [FEH/HM]

36.260 William R. Swagerty, ed. *Scholars and the Indian experience: critical reviews of recent writings in the social sciences.* Bloomington: Indiana University Press for D'Arcy McNickle Center for the History of the American Indian, 1984. ISBN 0-253-35095-6 (cl), 0-253-35096-4 (pbk). ▸ Eleven review essays on variety of subfields of American Indian history including prehistory, demography, Indian relations in colonial North America, fur trade, United States Indian policy, Indians and environment, and contemporary American Indians. [FEH/HM]

36.261 Helen Hornbeck Tanner et al., eds. *Atlas of Great Lakes Indian history.* Norman: University of Oklahoma Press, 1987. ISBN 0-8061-1515-7 (cl), 0-8061-2056-8 (pbk). ▸ Superb retelling, in maps and accompanying texts, of Indian-white relations in upper Great Lakes from mid-seventeenth through late nineteenth centuries. Covers village locations, subsistence patterns, and major conflicts with Europeans. Valuable to professional and amateur historians. [FEH/HM]

36.262 Russell Thornton. *American Indian holocaust and survival: a population history since 1492.* Norman: University of Oklahoma Press, 1987. ISBN 0-8061-2074-6 (cl), 0-8061-2220-X (pbk). ▸ General treatment of historical demography of American Indians. Offers guide through various estimates of North America's precontact population and reasons for its decline during centuries following white contact. [FEH/HM]

36.263 Bruce G. Trigger, ed. *Handbook of North American Indians.* Vol. 15: *Northeast.* Washington, D.C.: Smithsonian Institution Press and United States Government Printing Office, 1978. ISBN 0-87474-195-5 (v. 15), 0-16-004575-4 (v. 15). ▸ Basic reference work; seventy-three synoptic articles on histories, cultures, and contemporary situations of Indian peoples of northeastern United States and southeastern Canada. [FEH/HM]

36.264 Christopher Vecsey, ed. *Religion in native North America.* Moscow: University of Idaho Press, 1990. ISBN 0-89301-136-3 (cl), 0-89301-135-5(pbk). ▸ Eleven essays by students of religion on selected aspects of contemporary American Indian religions and non-Indian participation in Indian beliefs and practices. Useful overview of recent scholarship in field. [FEH/HM]

36.265 Wilcomb E. Washburn. *The Indian in America.* New York: Harper & Row, 1975. ISBN 0-06-014534-X (cl), 0-06-

131855-8 (pbk). ▸ General history of Indian-white relations describing precontact indigenous cultures and tracing changes wrought by white contact. Widely available, highly readable. [FEH/HM]

36.266 Wilcomb E. Washburn, ed. *Handbook of North American Indians*. Vol. 4: *History of Indian-white relations*. Washington, D.C.: Smithsonian Institution and United States Government Printing Office, 1988. ISBN 0-87474-184-X (v. 4), 0-16-004583-5 (v. 4). ▸ Fifty-seven essays providing scholarly syntheses of major areas in history of Indian-white relations including various phases of colonial and United States Indian policy; military, political, economic, and religious relations; and images of Indians in non-Indian society. [FEH/HM]

36.267 Richard White. *The roots of dependency: subsistence, environment, and social change among the Choctaws, Pawnees, and Navajos*. Lincoln: University of Nebraska Press, 1983. ISBN 0-8032-4722-2 (cl), 0-8032-9724-6 (pbk). ▸ History of Indian land use through three case studies. Attributes collapse of Choctaw, Pawnee, and Navajo subsistence systems to consequences of bringing Indian resources into orbit of market economy. [FEH/HM]

36.268 Walter L. Williams. *The spirit and the flesh: sexual diversity in American Indian culture*. 1986 ed. Boston: Beacon, 1992. ISBN 0-8070-4615-9. ▸ Historical and ethnological study of *berdache*: American Indian male whose cross-sexual dress and behavior set him apart from other males in society. Unique introduction to subject. [FEH/HM]

36.269 W. Raymond Wood and Margot Liberty, eds. *Anthropology on the Great Plains*. Lincoln: University of Nebraska Press, 1980. ISBN 0-8032-4708-7. ▸ Collection of twenty-two essays that together provide remarkable overview of important trends in scholarship and findings of scholars in archaeology, ethnology, and cultural history. [FEH/HM]

SEE ALSO
40.399 Robert F. Berkhofer, Jr. *The white man's Indian*.

MEXICO

Precontact

36.270 Patricia Rieff Anawalt. *Indian clothing before Cortés: Mesoamerican costumes from the codices*. Norman: University of Oklahoma Press, 1981. ISBN 0-8061-1650-1 (cl), 0-8061-2288-9 (pbk). ▸ Comprehensive inventory of traditional attire and adornment, based on representations from pictorial manuscripts. [SS]

36.271 Inga Clendinnen. *Aztecs: an interpretation*. Cambridge: Cambridge University Press, 1991. ISBN 0-521-40093-7. ▸ Creative, provocative study of ritual behavior and human sacrifice as expression of all-pervasive and obsessive preoccupation with religion. [SS]

36.272 Nigel Davies. *The Toltecs, until the fall of Tula*. 1977 ed. Norman: University of Oklahoma Press, 1987. ISBN 0-8061-1394-4 (cl, 1977), 0-8061-2071-1 (pbk). ▸ Commendable effort to connect and evaluate all that is known of people and state of Toltecs. Overview of group believed pivotal to development of preconquest Mesoamerica. [SS]

36.273 Diego Duran. *"Book of the Gods and Rites" and the ancient calendar*. Fernando Horcasitas and Doris Heyden, eds. and trans. Norman: University of Oklahoma Press, 1971. ISBN 0-8061-1201-8. ▸ Important translation of invaluable accounts of sixteenth-century Nahua culture and society with particular emphasis on religion—gods, feasts, ceremonies, and rituals. Includes information on markets, ball game, and Nahua calendar. [SS]

36.274 Ross Hassig. *Aztec warfare: imperial expansion and political control*. Norman: University of Oklahoma Press, 1988. ISBN 0-8061-2121-1. ▸ Detailed study of Nahua ideology of empire.

Treats warfare, subjugation, tribute obligations, and impact of military leaders on local communities. Includes biographical sketches of key individuals. [SS]

36.275 Alfredo López Austin. *The human body and ideology: concepts of the ancient Nahuas*. 2 vols. Thelma Ortíz de Montellano and Bernard Ortíz de Montellano, trans. Salt Lake City: University of Utah Press, 1988. ISBN 0-87480-260-1 (set). ▸ Nahua (Aztec) ideology of human body and its relation to society, as understood at time of arrival of Spaniards. Discusses worldview, medicine, and death through analysis of indigenous texts. [SS]

36.276 Jerome A. Offner. *Law and politics in Aztec Texcoco*. Cambridge: Cambridge University Press, 1983. ISBN 0-521-23475-1. ▸ Sociopolitical history of indigenous Texcoco in central Mexico and analysis of its legal system. Treats political hierarchy and jurisprudence, stressing persistence of indigenous law. [SS]

36.277 Mary Elizabeth Smith. *Picture writing from ancient southern Mexico: Mixtec place signs and maps*. Norman: University of Oklahoma Press, 1973. ISBN 0-8061-1029-5. ▸ Detailed analysis of Mixtec histories as portrayed in pictorial place signs and maps presents preconquest culture through postconquest records. Offers historical, genealogical, and cartographic information through iconographic analysis. [SS]

Colonial Period

36.278 Arthur J. O. Anderson, Frances Berdan, and James Lockhart, eds. and trans. *Beyond the codices: the Nahua view of colonial Mexico with linguistic essays by Ronald W. Langacker*. Berkeley: University of California Press, 1976. ISBN 0-520-02974-7. ▸ Primary Nahuatl documents in English with commentary; basic source prepared by leading scholars. Discussion of types of Nahuatl-language documents, their significance, and potential uses. Starting point for appreciating exciting sources. [SS/MAB]

36.279 John Bierhorst, comp. and trans. *Cantares Mexicanos: songs of the Aztecs* and *A Nahuatl-English dictionary and concordance to the Cantares Mexicanos, with an analytical transcription and grammatical notes*. Stanford, Calif.: Stanford University Press, 1985. ISBN 0-8047-1182-8 (cl), 0-8047-1183-6 (cl). ▸ Rich corpus of Nahuatl songs and verse for ritual use in English translation. [SS]

36.280 Woodrow Borah. *Justice by insurance: the General Indian Court of colonial Mexico and the legal aides of the half-real*. Berkeley: University of California Press, 1983. ISBN 0-520-04845-8. ▸ History of establishment and development of court for Indians in viceroyalty of central Mexico. Important, groundbreaking study of institution that limited exploitation of native population. [SS/MAB]

36.281 Louise M. Burkhart. *The slippery earth: Nahua-Christian moral dialogue in sixteenth-century Mexico*. Tucson: University of Arizona Press, 1989. ISBN 0-8165-1088-1. ▸ Nahua understanding of Christian moral dialogue as reflected in Nahuatl terminology employed by Franciscans in their religious texts for Indians. Fascinating view of religious interaction. [SS]

36.282 Inga Clendinnen. *Ambivalent conquests: Maya and Spaniard in Yucatán, 1517–1570*. Cambridge: Cambridge University Press, 1987. ISBN 0-521-33397-0 (cl), 0-521-37981-4, (pbk). ▸ Spanish *entradas* (expeditions into native territories) and Maya responses on Yucatán peninsula during early conquest period. Sensitive narrative discussing motivations and actions on both sides of cultural divide. Stimulating multidisciplinary perspective. [SS/MAB]

36.283 S. L. Cline. *Colonial Culhuacán, 1580–1600: a social history of an Aztec town*. Albuquerque: University of New Mexico Press, 1986. ISBN 0-8263-0884-8. ▸ Important regional study of Nahua society in sixteenth-century Mexico through translation and analysis of Nahuatl testaments. Striking portrait of native life in early years of Spanish rule. [SS/MAB]

36.284 George A. Collier, Renato I. Rosaldo, and John D. Wirth, eds. *The Inca and Aztec states, 1400–1800: anthropology and history.* New York: Academic Press, 1982. ISBN 0-12-181180-8. ‣ Important collection of essays presenting recent research on indigenous peoples and states in two major regions of complex civilization both before and after Spanish conquest. [SS/MAB]

36.285 Hernán Cortés. *Letters from Mexico.* Anthony Pagden, ed. and trans. New Haven: Yale University Press, 1986. ISBN 0-300-03724-4 (cl), 0-300-03799-6 (pbk). ‣ Skillful edition of five detailed reports of Spanish conquistador Hernán Cortés describing earliest exploits in eastern and central Mexico and Honduras. [SS]

36.286 Nancy M. Farriss. *Maya society under colonial rule: the collective enterprise of survival.* Princeton: Princeton University Press, 1984. ISBN 0-691-07668-5 (cl), 0-691-10158-2 (pbk). ‣ Landmark work combining insights from variety of disciplines. Focuses on impact of Spanish colonial rule on Mayan social organization. [SS/MAB]

36.287 Charles Gibson. *The Aztecs under Spanish rule: a history of the Indians of the valley of Mexico, 1519–1810.* Stanford, Calif.: Stanford University Press, 1964. ISBN 0-8047-0196-2 (cl), 0-8047-0912-2 (pbk). ‣ Monumental, definitive study of native peoples in valley of Mexico, conquest to independence. Unsurpassed, reliable introduction. [SS/MAB]

36.288 William B. Griffen. *Culture change and shifting populations in central northern Mexico.* Tucson: University of Arizona Press, 1969. ISBN 0-8165-0140-8 (pbk). ‣ Groundbreaking monograph focusing on generalized indigenous responses to Spanish intrusions into northern regions of New Spain. Describes demographic and cultural innovations caused by trade, missions, and introduction of horse. [SS]

36.289 Serge Gruzinski. *Man-gods in the Mexican highlands: Indian power and colonial society, 1520–1800.* Eileen Corrigan, trans. Stanford, Calif.: Stanford University Press, 1989. ISBN 0-8047-1513-0. ‣ Study of nonelite indigenous societies, particularly religious systems, acculturation patterns, and social dynamics. Exposition of four case studies of Indians who opposed Spanish rule. Based on actual testimonies offered by ordinary people in ecclesiastical proceedings. [SS/MAB]

36.290 H. R. Harvey, ed. *Land and politics in the valley of Mexico: a two-thousand-year perspective.* Albuquerque: University of New Mexico Press, 1991. ISBN 0-8263-1255-1. ‣ Key essays on indigenous society, government, economics, and land use relating to specific polities in valley of Mexico. Combines important sampling of interdisciplinary archaeological data, native codices, and early colonial documents. [SS]

36.291 Robert Stephen Haskett. *Indigenous rulers: an ethnohistory of town government in colonial Cuernavaca.* Albuquerque: University of New Mexico Press, 1991. ISBN 0-8263-1286-1 (cl), 0-8263-1287-X (pbk). ‣ Detailed study of continuity and change in indigenous society and government in Cuernavaca during colonial period. Includes economic ventures and material culture; relies on native-language sources. [SS/MAB]

36.292 Grant D. Jones. *Maya resistance to Spanish rule: time and history on a colonial frontier.* Albuquerque: University of New Mexico Press, 1989. ISBN 0-8263-1161-X (cl), 0-8263-1258-6 (pbk). ‣ Essential study of native resistance to Spanish rule on Belize-Yucatán frontier. Traces persistence of Tipu sociopolitical structures through analysis of calendric religious rituals, aggression, and withdrawal. [SS/MWH]

36.293 Frances Karttunen and James Lockhart. *The art of Nahuatl speech: the Bancroft Dialogues.* Los Angeles: UCLA Latin

American Center Publications, 1987. (UCLA Latin American studies, 65.) ISBN 0-87903-065-8. ‣ English translation and philological and historical analysis of Bancroft (Library) Dialogues, the "Huehuetlatolli-Discursos en Mexicano," elegant masterpieces of Nahuatl speech. Intended as introduction to Nahua culture for Jesuit priests. [SS]

36.294 J. Jorge Klor de Alva, H. B. Nicholson, and Eloise Quinones Keber, eds. *The work of Bernardino de Sahagun: pioneer ethnographer of sixteenth-century Aztec Mexico.* New York: State University of New York at Albany, 1988. (Institute for Mesoamerican Studies on Culture and Society, 2.) ISBN 0-942041-11-9 (pbk). ‣ Valuable, wide-ranging collection of essays analyzing both character and scholarship of Mesoamerica's greatest sixteenth-century ethnohistorian. Discussions of Nahuatl linguistics, religion, record keeping, calendrics, and social organization as well as Franciscan scholar's revisionist writings. [SS]

36.295 Miguel León-Portilla, ed. *The Aztec image of self and society: an introduction to Nahua culture.* Salt Lake City: University of Utah Press, 1992. ISBN 0-87480-360-8. ‣ Reassessment of last thirty years of Nahua scholarship; for scholarly audience. Revision and first English edition of author's classic *Los Antiguos Mexicanos a Través de sus "Crónicas y Cantares"* (1961). [SS]

36.296 Miguel León-Portilla, ed. *The broken spears: the Aztec account of the conquest of Mexico.* Rev. ed. Lysander Kemp, trans. Boston: Beacon, 1992. ISBN 0-8070-5501-8. ‣ Collection of excerpts from indigenous accounts about conquest. Unique text containing primary Nahuatl materials in English translation. [SS/MAB]

36.297 James Lockhart. *Nahuas and Spaniards: postconquest central Mexican history and philology.* Stanford, Calif.: Stanford University Press and UCLA Latin American Center, 1991. (UCLA Latin American studies, 76.) ISBN 0-8047-1953-5 (cl), 0-8047-1954-3 (pbk). ‣ Thirteen authoritative essays (five previously unpublished) treating postconquest Nahuas and Spanish-Nahua interaction through colonial period. Contains interdisciplinary analyses of Nahua culture and language. [SS]

36.298 James Lockhart, Frances Berdan, and Arthur J. O. Anderson. *The Tlaxcalan Actas: a compendium of the records of the Cabildo of Tlaxcala (1545–1627).* Salt Lake City: University of Utah Press, 1986. ISBN 0-87480-253-9. ‣ Early colonial Nahuatl city council records in English translation, revealing sociopolitical organization and inner workings of Nahua town. Traces attempts to preserve autonomy through social organization, religious exchange, and economy. [SS]

36.299 Francisco López de Gómara. *Cortés: the life of the conqueror by his secretary.* 1964 ed. Lesley Byrd Simpson, ed. and trans. Berkeley: University of California Press, 1966. ISBN 0-520-00493-0 (pbk). ‣ Activities of Hernán Cortés in Mexico, as recorded by sixteenth-century Spanish cleric. Vivid account of encounter with native peoples in central Mexico and subsequent conquest. [SS]

36.300 Daniel T. Reff. *Disease, depopulation, and culture change in northwestern New Spain, 1518–1764.* Salt Lake City: University of Utah Press, 1991. ISBN 0-87480-355-1. ‣ Demographic and cultural consequences of European diseases among native populations of northwest New Spain. Focuses on Jesuit missions and indigenous response to Christianity. [SS]

36.301 Ralph L. Roys. *Ritual of the Bacabs.* Norman: University of Oklahoma Press, 1965. ‣ English translations of Yucatec Maya incantations for healing. Contains *curanderos*' rituals, sacred almanacs, and ethnopharmacopoeia. [SS]

36.302 Hernando Ruiz de Alarcón. *Treatise on the heathen superstitions and customs that today live among the Indians native to this New Spain, 1629.* J. Richard Andrews and Ross Hassig, eds. and trans. Norman: University of Oklahoma Press, 1983. ISBN 0-8061-1832-6. ▸ English translation and detailed study of early seventeenth-century Nahuatl- and Spanish-language accounts of indigenous religious worship in west-central Mexico. Intended as exposé of "heathen" practice, offers trove of information on traditional Nahua beliefs. [SS]

36.303 Bernardino de Sahagún. *Florentine codex: "General History of the Things of New Spain."* 2d ed. 13 vols. Arthur J. O. Anderson and Charles E. Dibble, eds. and trans. Santa Fe, N.M., and Salt Lake City: School of American Research and University of Utah, 1950–1982. (Monographs of the School of American Research, 14.) ISBN 0-87480-082-X (set). ▸ English translation from Nahuatl of most comprehensive sixteenth-century ethnohistory of peoples of Central Mexico. Author used native informants to assemble encyclopedic account of preconquest and early colonial Nahua culture. [SS]

36.304 Bernardino de Sahagún. *Introductions and indices: introductions, Sahagún's "Prologues and Interpolations," general bibliography, general indices.* Arthur J. O. Anderson and Charles E. Dibble, eds. Charles E. León-Portilla and Miguel León-Portilla, trans. Santa Fe, N.M., and Salt Lake City: School of American Research and University of Utah, 1982. ISBN 0-87480-082-X (set), 0-87480-165-6. ▸ Introduction to Sahagún and his *Historia General* (36.303). English translation of Sahagún's *Prologues and Interpolations* and indexes to twelve volumes of the *Historia*. [SS]

36.305 Susan Schroeder. *Chimalpahin and the kingdoms of Chalco.* Tucson: University of Arizona Press, 1991. ISBN 0-8165-1182-9. ▸ Social and philological study of Nahuatl accounts of Chimalpahin, Nahuatl-language annalist of Indian Mexico to 1620, to reconstruct indigenous confederation of kingdoms during pre-Hispanic and early colonial periods. Detailed history of Indian kingdoms of Amaquemecan, Chalco. [SS/MAB]

36.306 Ronald Spores. *The Mixtecs in ancient and colonial times.* Norman: University of Oklahoma Press, 1984. ISBN 0-8061-1884-9. ▸ Detailed study of origins and development of Mixtec polities in Oaxaca, precontact period to independence. Examines political leadership, especially impact of Spanish rule. [SS/MAB]

36.307 William B. Taylor. *Drinking, homicide, and rebellion in colonial Mexican villages.* Stanford, Calif.: Stanford University Press, 1979. ISBN 0-8047-0997-1. ▸ Monograph describing social life in Indian towns following Spanish conquest. Argues drinking, rebellion, and murder often expression of resistance to Europeans. Analysis attempts to connect individual and collective behavior. Superb blending of archival research and social science literature. [SS/MAB]

36.308 Robert Wasserstrom. *Class and society in central Chiapas.* Berkeley: University of California Press, 1983. ISBN 0-520-04670-6. ▸ Excellent, extensive study of change and continuity in Chiapaneca society, contact through 1970s, using indigenous sources to reconstruct native perspective. Traces migrations begun in response to Spanish (and Mexican) rule. Also describes religious and economic impact of European presence. [SS/EH-D]

36.309 Alonso de Zorita. *Life and labor in ancient Mexico: the brief and summary relation of the lords of New Spain.* Benjamin Keen, trans. New Brunswick, N.J.: Rutgers University Press, 1963. ▸ English translation of primary account of Nahua sociopolitical organization in Mexico Tenochtitlan, Tlacopan, and Texcoco during early colonial period. Original text written by Spanish judge and includes descriptions of officeholding as well as tribute, labor, and demography. Excellent introduction. [SS]

SEE ALSO
37.10 Peter Gerhard. *A guide to the historical geography of New Spain.*
37.130 J. Benedict Warren. *The conquest of Michoacán.*
37.264 Ross Hassig. *Trade, tribute, and transportation.*

37.292 William B. Taylor. *Landlord and peasant in colonial Oaxaca.*
37.342 John K. Chance. *Race and class in colonial Oaxaca.*
37.600 David Hurst Thomas, ed. *Columbian consequences.* Vol. 1.

Nineteenth Century

36.310 Paul Friedrich. *Agrarian revolt in a Mexican village.* Chicago: University of Chicago Press, 1977. ISBN 0-226-26481-5 (pbk). ▸ Important monograph describing ramifications of prolonged political upheaval on economic and social systems in Tarascan village. Role of native leaders of particular significance. [SS]

36.311 Nelson Reed. *The caste war of Yucatán.* Stanford, Calif.: Stanford University Press, 1964. ISBN 0-8047-0164-4 (cl), 0-8047-0165-2 (pbk). ▸ Outstanding analysis of native rebellion against creole, ladino, and national government in nineteenth century. Includes discussion of role of Talking Cross millenarian movement and emergence of guerrilla warfare. Good discussion of social and economic systems of Yucatán. [SS/EH-D]

Twentieth Century

36.312 Victoria Reifler Bricker. *The Indian Christ, the Indian king: the historical substrate of Maya myth and ritual.* Austin: University of Texas Press, 1981. ISBN 0-292-73824-2. ▸ Provocative study of ethnic conflict and resistance as revealed in myth, folklore, and numerous other ritual activities. Undermines notion of placid and timeless Maya culture. [SS]

36.313 James B. Greenberg. *Blood ties: life and violence in rural Mexico.* Tucson: University of Arizona Press, 1989. ISBN 0-8165-1091-1. ▸ Important study of historical context for provocation and persistance of conflict, violence, and inter-ethnic rivalry in south-central Mexico. [SS]

36.314 Fernando Horcasitas, ed. and trans. *Life and death in Milpa Alta: a Nahuatl chronicle of Díaz and Zapata, from the Nahuatl recollections of Doña Luz Jiménez.* Norman: University of Oklahoma Press, 1972. ISBN 0-8061-1001-5. ▸ Society and tradition in rural Mexico at turn of century. Personal recollections of Nahuatl speaker who lived at time of Mexican Revolution. [SS]

36.315 Frank J. Lipp. *The Mixe of Oaxaca: religion, ritual, and healing.* Austin: University of Texas Press, 1991. ISBN 0-292-76517-7. ▸ Important study of little known Mixe populations in contemporary Oaxaca. Focuses on religious beliefs, ritual behavior, medical practice, and calendrics—all of which have origins in pre-Hispanic times. [SS]

36.316 Edward H. Spicer. *The Yaquis: a cultural history.* Tucson: University of Arizona Press, 1980. ISBN 0-8165-0589-6 (cl), 0-8165-0588-8 (pbk). ▸ Comprehensive treatment of Yaqui Indians from earliest contact through first half of twentieth century. Major themes include relations with Jesuits and Yaqui cultural persistence through migrations and partial dispersion into the United States. [SS]

General and Theoretical Works

36.317 Howard Francis Cline, ed. *Guide to ethnohistorical sources.* 4 vols. Austin: University of Texas Press, 1972–75. (Handbook of Middle American Indians, 12–15.) ISBN 0-292-70152-7 (v. 12), 0-292-70153-5 (v. 13), 0-292-70153-3 (v. 14), 0-292-70154-3 (v. 15). ▸ Comprehensive, invaluable reference collection of known ethnohistorical materials relating to Mesoamerican Indians. [SS]

36.318 Murdo J. MacLeod and Robert Wasserstrom, eds. *Spaniards and Indians in southeastern Mesoamerica: essays on the history of ethnic relations.* Lincoln: University of Nebraska Press, 1983. ISBN 0-8032-3082-6. ▸ Essays on Maya Indian culture in Yucatán,

Chiapas, and Guatemala from colonial to modern period. Focuses on religious and economic interactions, stressing differences between Mayas and Nahuas. [SS/MWH]

36.319 Edward H. Spicer. *Cycles of conquest: the impact of Spain, Mexico, and the United States on the Indians of the Southwest, 1533–1960.* Tucson: University of Arizona Press, 1962. ISBN 0-8165-0021-5 (pbk). ‣ Synthetic treatment of borderlands' natives and their cultures over four centuries. Covers indigenous life, Spanish mission influence, and subsequent political incorporation into United States. Extraordinarily rich volume. [SS/MAB]

36.320 J. Eric S. Thompson. *Maya history and religion.* Norman: University of Oklahoma Press, 1970. ‣ Classic overview of Maya history and religion from preconquest times to present. Based on colonial documents, archaeological materials, and current accounts from twentieth-century native informants. [SS]

36.321 Joseph W. Whitecotton. *The Zapotecs: princes, priests, and peasants.* Norman: University of Oklahoma Press, 1977. ISBN 0-8061-1374-X (cl), 0-8061-1914-4 (pbk). ‣ General study of Zapotec populations in Oaxaca. Includes ancient native social structure and religious life, impact of Spanish rule, and Zapotecs in modern age. Considers difference between Spanish and Mexican regimes. [SS]

SEE ALSO
37.87 Benjamin Keen. *The Aztec image in Western thought.*
37.206 Sherburne F. Cook and Woodrow Borah. *Essays in population history.*

CENTRAL AMERICA AND THE CARIBBEAN

Precontact

36.322 William M. Denevan, ed. *The native population of the Americas in 1492.* 2d ed. Madison: University of Wisconsin Press, 1992. ISBN 0-299-13430-X (cl), 0-299-13434-2 (pbk). ‣ Valuable collection of essays presenting recent European scholarship on size of native population of the Americas on eve of contact. Includes information on slave trade in Central America and Caribbean. Highlights disagreement over population size. [MWH/MAB]

36.323 William R. Fowler, Jr. *The cultural evolution of ancient Nahua civilizations: the Pipil-Nicarao of Central America.* Norman: University of Oklahoma Press, 1989. ISBN 0-8061-2197-1. ‣ Historical ethnography, using archival sources, of Pipil and Nicarao of Southwest Mesoamerica and Northwest Central America in sixteenth century and before. Detailed reconstruction of indigenous ecology, social and political life, and ideology. [MWH]

36.324 John W. Fox. *Quiché conquest: centralism and regionalism in highland Guatemalan state development.* Albuquerque: University of New Mexico Press, 1978. ISBN 0-8263-0461-3. ‣ Cultural impact of conquest of Guatemalan highlands by Quiché people in three centuries prior to European conquest. Good introduction to indigenous polities of Guatemala. [MWH]

36.325 Mary W. Helms. *Ancient Panama: chiefs in search of power.* Austin: University of Texas Press, 1979. ISBN 0-292-73817-X. ‣ Reconstruction, from early Spanish accounts, of locations, customs, and traditions of indigenous chiefdoms of Panamanian isthmus at time of Spanish contact. Pioneering study with emphasis on politics, trade, and symbolism. [MWH]

36.326 Mary W. Helms. "The Indians of the Caribbean and circum-Caribbean at the end of the fifteenth century." In *The Cambridge history of Latin America.* Leslie Bethell, ed., vol. 1, pp. 37–58. Cambridge: Cambridge University Press, 1984. ISBN 0-521-23223-6 (v. 1). ‣ Life styles and cultural traditions of native inhabitants of the Greater and Lesser Antilles, northern South America, and Central America on eve of European contact. General introduction for serious, general reader. [MWH]

36.327 Eugenia Ibarra Rojas. *Las sociedades cacicales de Costa Rica (siglo xvi).* San Jose: Editorial de la Universidad de Costa Rica, 1990. ISBN 9977-67-143-5 (pbk). ‣ Reconstruction, from archival materials, of location; economic, kinship, and political systems; and cosmology of indigenous chiefdoms of Costa Rica on eve of European conquest. Important study, unavailable in English. [MWH]

36.328 Frederick W. Lange and Doris Stone, eds. *The archaeology of lower Central America.* Albuquerque: University of New Mexico Press, 1984. ISBN 0-8263-0717-5. ‣ Symposium papers detailing archaeological investigations from Honduras and El Salvador to northwestern Colombia. Papers focus on details of particular sites, nature of excavations, artifacts recovered, and floral and faunal remains identified. Technical overview. [MWH]

36.329 Doris Stone. *Pre-Columbian man finds Central America: the archaeological bridge.* Cambridge, Mass.: Peabody Museum Press, 1972. ISBN 0-87365-776-4 (pbk). ‣ Overview of prehistory of region from Guatemala through Panama from earliest times to European conquest. Focuses on ceramic typologies and regional developments to reconstruct prehistoric lifeways. [MWH]

Colonial Period

36.330 Bartolomé de Las Casas and Arthur Helps. *"Tears of the Indians" and "The Life of Las Casas."* Lewis Hanke, Introduction. Williamstown, Mass.: John Lilburne, 1970. ‣ Republication of 1896 edition of biography of Las Casas and English translation of his most widely known tract denouncing cruelty to Indians. Basic source on priest and his campaign for humanitarian treatment of native people. [MWH]

36.331 Troy S. Floyd. *The Anglo-Spanish struggle for Mosquitia.* Albuquerque: University of New Mexico Press, 1967. ‣ Detailed colonial history of Caribbean coast of Central America emphasizing British-Spanish relations and alliance between the British and Miskito Indians. [MWH]

36.332 Mary W. Helms. "Miskito slaving and culture contact." *Journal of anthropological research* 39.2 (1983) 179–97. ISSN 0091-7710. ‣ Analysis of conditions underlying notorious slave raids by Miskito Indians against weaker Indian populations of eastern Central America in early eighteenth century. Anthropologist interprets cultural behavior with historical documents. [MWH]

36.333 Mary W. Helms. "Negro or Indian? The changing identity of a frontier population." In *Old roots in new lands.* Ann M. Pescatello, ed., pp. 157–72. Westport, Conn.: Greenwood, 1977. ISBN 0-8371-9476-8. ‣ Only interpretive essay using documentary sources to trace changing ethnic identity accorded by colonial and postcolonial agents to mixed indigenous-African population of eastern Nicaragua and Honduras, now known as Miskito Indians but formerly termed Zambos. [MWH]

36.334 Robert M. Hill II. *Colonial Cakchiquels: highland Maya adaptations to Spanish rule, 1600–1700.* Fort Worth: Holt, Reinhart & Winston, 1992. ISBN 0-03-073444-4 (pbk). ‣ Scholarly reconstruction, using Spanish documentary sources, of Cakchiquel Maya culture. Basic introduction with emphasis on social organization, land tenure, and strategies of native resistance. [MWH]

36.335 W. George Lovell. *Conquest and survival in colonial Guatemala: a historical geography of the Cuchumatán highlands, 1500–1821.* Rev. ed. Montreal: McGill-Queen's University Press, 1992. ISBN 0-7735-0903-8. ‣ Colonial experience of Maya Indians and Spanish conquerors in western Guatemala. Emphasis on demographic adjustments, colonial administration, and land use under Spanish rule. [MWH]

36.336 Linda A. Newson. *Indian survival in colonial Nicaragua.*

Norman: University of Oklahoma Press, 1987. ISBN 0-8061-2008-8. ‣ Study of factors responsible for severe decline yet limited survival of indigenous populations of Nicaragua during Spanish colonial era. Particularly useful for discussion of western and central Nicaragua. [MWH]

36.337 Irving Rouse. *The Tainos: rise and decline of the people who greeted Columbus.* New Haven: Yale University Press, 1992. ISBN 0-300-05181-6. ‣ General overview of development of Tainos of Greater Antilles through prehistory, Spanish contact, and effect of European contact. Attempts to evaluate Taino contribution to Western culture. [MWH]

36.338 Carl O. Sauer. *The early Spanish Main.* 1966 ed. Berkeley: University of California Press, 1992. ISBN 0-520-01125-2 (cl), 0-520-01415-4 (pbk). ‣ Interpretive account of indigenous inhabitants and physical and cultural environment of Greater Antilles and Panamanian isthmus based on accounts written by first generation of Spanish conquerors. Master stylist and distinguished geographer reconstructs indigenous cultures and dynamics of early contact. [MWH/MAB]

36.339 William L. Sherman. *Forced native labor in sixteenth-century Central America.* Lincoln: University of Nebraska Press, 1979. ISBN 0-8032-4100-3. ‣ Exhaustive archival study of Indian forced labor. Traces impact of forced labor on native cultural traditions and evolution of colonial policies toward indigenous populations. [MWH/MAB]

36.340 Samuel M. Wilson. *Hispaniola: Caribbean chiefdoms in the age of Columbus.* Tuscaloosa: University of Alabama Press, 1990. ISBN 0-8173-0462-2. ‣ Cultural reconstruction of indigenous Taino Indian culture. Traces effects of European contact on natives in late fifteenth and early sixteenth centuries. Based primarily on documents from early contact period. [MWH]

SEE ALSO

37.276 Murdo J. MacLeod. *Spanish Central America.*

37.565 Miles L. Wortman. *Government and society in Central America, 1680–1840.*

37.600 David Hurst Thomas, ed. *Columbian consequences.* Vol. 3.

Nineteenth Century

36.341 Luis A. Ferrero. "Ethnohistory and ethnography in the Central Highlands—Atlantic Watershed and Diquis." In *Between continents/between seas.* Elizabeth P. Benson, ed. and Michael J. Snarskis, trans., pp. 93–103. New York: Abrams with Detroit Institute of Arts, 1981. ISBN 0-8109-0729-1 (cl), 0-89558-088-8 (pbk). ‣ Reconstruction of traditional lifeways and customs of surviving indigenous population of southern and eastern Costa Rica, including Atlantic plains and Talamancan area, using colonial records and nineteenth-century travelers' accounts. [MWH]

36.342 Eleonore von Oertzen, Lioba Rossbach, and Volker Wünderich, eds. *The Nicaraguan Mosquitia in historical documents 1844–1927: the dynamics of ethnic and regional history.* Berlin: Reimer, 1990. ISBN 3-496-00476-2. ‣ Collection of archival documents, in English and German, pertaining to indigenous populations, ethnic relations, and colonial conditions of Miskito Coast. Provides illuminating backdrop for understanding of twentieth-century ethnic relations in Nicaragua. [MWH]

SEE ALSO

38.325 Craig L. Dozier. *Nicaragua's mosquito shore.*

Twentieth Century

36.343 Ignacio Bizarro Ujpán. *Campesino: the diary of a Guatemalan Indian.* James D. Sexton, ed. and trans. Tucson: University of Arizona Press, 1985. ISBN 0-8165-0814-3. ‣ Personal account by Maya Indian of daily life in rural highland Guatemala, 1977–

83. Topics include poverty, family ties, and impact of nation's political turmoil. [MWH]

36.344 John D. Early. *The demographic structure and evolution of a peasant system: the Guatemalan population.* Boca Raton: University Presses of Florida, 1982. ISBN 0-8130-0734-8. ‣ Examination of demographic structure and demographic change in Guatemala between 1950 and 1977. Focuses on rural Maya population and its integration into national population structure. Influential discussion of problem of cultural bias in census enumerations. [MWH]

36.345 Mary W. Helms. *Asang: adaptations to culture contact in a Miskito community.* Gainesville: University Presses of Florida, 1971. ISBN 0-8130-0298-2. ‣ Reconstruction of colonial history and description of conditions in Miskito Indian community in eastern Nicaragua before Sandinista revolution. Groundbreaking monograph emphasizing how groups can be involved in economic aspects of colonialism while remaining politically autonomous. [MWH]

36.346 Mary W. Helms. "Coastal adaptations as contact phenomena among the Miskito and Cuna Indians of lower Central America." In *Prehistoric coastal adaptations: the economy and ecology of maritime Middle America.* Barbara L. Stark and Barbara Voorhies, eds., pp. 121–49. New York: Academic Press, 1978. ISBN 0-12-663250-2. ‣ Detailed comparison of gradual move to Caribbean coastal settlement as result of European contact by Miskito of eastern Nicaragua and Cuna of northeastern Panama. Interpretive essay with examples ranging from sixteenth to twentieth centuries. Specialized study best read with Helms 36.345. [MWH]

36.347 Beatriz Manz. *Refugees of a hidden war: the aftermath of counterinsurgency in Guatemala.* Albany: State University of New York Press, 1988. ISBN 0-88706-765-5 (cl), 0-88706-767-3 (pbk). ‣ Basic study of dramatic impact of 1980s Guatemalan political violence and military repression on highland Guatemalan Maya Indians and countryside. Also describes flight of population across Guatemalan border and subsequent emergence of refugee problem in Mexico. [MWH]

36.348 Klaudine Ohland and Robin Schneider, eds. *National revolution and indigenous identity: the conflict between Sandinists and Miskito Indians on Nicaragua's Atlantic Coast.* Copenhagen: International Work Group for Indigenous Affairs, 1983. (International Work Group for Indigenous Affairs, 47.) ISSN 0105-4503. ‣ Collection of documents intended to illuminate conditions that produced armed conflict between Sandinista revolutionaries and Miskito Indians in eastern Nicargua in early 1980s. Discusses failure of Sandinist policies designed to produce integration. [MWH]

36.349 David Stephen and Phillip Wearne. *Central America's Indians.* London: Minority Rights Group, 1984. (Minority Rights Group report, 62.) ISSN 0305-6252. ‣ Overview of current distribution of native populations from Guatemala through Panama. Extensive discussion of Guatemalan native populations and human rights issues in region during twentieth century. Good introduction to subject for general reader. [MWH]

36.350 Carlos M. Vilas. *State, class, and ethnicity in Nicaragua: capitalist modernization and revolutionary change on the Atlantic coast.* Susan Norwood, trans. Boulder: Rienner, 1989. ISBN 1-55587-163-1. ‣ Basic monograph analyzing reactions of eastern Nicaraguan ethnic groups to Sandinista revolution. Comprehensive study focusing particularly on social, economic, and cultural elements that complicated national plans for integration of Atlantic Nicaragua into rest of country. [MWH]

36.351 Philip D. Young. *Ngawbe: tradition and change among the Western Guaymi of Panama.* Urbana: University of Illinois Press, 1971. ISBN 0-252-00143-5. ‣ Reaction and adaptation to European contact by Guaymi Indians of west-central Panama. Cultural overview describing community's indigenous customs and tracing change, seventeenth century to present. [MWH]

General and Theoretical Works

36.352 Jack D. Forbes. *Black Africans and native Americans: color, race, and caste in the evolution of red-black peoples.* New York: Blackwell, 1988. ISBN 0-631-15665-8. ▸ Classic, stimulating discussion of evolution of racial classification systems since 1500 and impact on both African Americans and American Indians. Focus on both Caribbean and mainland of the Americas. Argues many American Indians included in colonial classifications of color associated with African Americans. [MWH]

36.353 Nancie L. Gonzalez. *Sojourners of the Caribbean: ethnogenesis and ethnohistory of the Garifuna.* Urbana: University of Illinois Press, 1988. ISBN 0-252-01453-7. ▸ Specialized study of colonial history and cultural adaptation of Black Carib or Garifuna of Atlantic coast of Central America (Belize, eastern Guatemala, northern Honduras). Traces evolution of Black Carib ethnicity from eighteenth century to present. [MWH]

36.354 Peter Hulme. *Colonial encounters: Europe and the native Caribbean, 1492–1797.* 1986 ed. New York: Routledge, 1992. ISBN 0-415-01146-9. ▸ Broad critical analysis of Spanish encounter with Antillean natives and comparisons with English colony of Virginia. Important overview of colonization process comparing various European stereotypes of native peoples. [MWH]

36.355 Grant D. Jones, ed. *Anthropology and history in Yucatán.* Austin: University of Texas Press, 1977. ISBN 0-292-70314-7. ▸ Collection of essays detailing survival and adaptation of lowland Maya cultures of Belize, Peten (Guatemala), and Yucatán from conquest to present day. Emphasis on combining historical and anthropological approaches to study of culture change. [MWH]

36.356 Norman B. Schwartz. *Forest society: a social history of Peten, Guatemala.* Philadelphia: University of Pennsylvania Press, 1990. ISBN 0-8122-8248-5 (cl), 0-8122-1316-5 (pbk). ▸ Definitive study of conquest, colonization, social development, economic patterns, and native-Spanish relations, 1697 to present, in department of Peten, modern lowland Guatemala. [MWH/RLM]

36.357 Carol A. Smith, ed. *Guatemalan Indians and the state, 1540–1988.* Austin: University of Texas Press, 1990. ISBN 0-292-72744-5. ▸ Series of provocative essays examining relationship between Indian culture and Guatemalan national political life. Controversial argument about significance of Indian presence in Guatemalan life and centrality of Indian-government relations in country's political and economic history. [MWH/RLM]

HIGHLAND SOUTH AMERICA

Precontact

36.358 Marcia Ascher and Robert Ascher. *Code of the Quipu: a study of media, mathematics, and culture.* Ann Arbor: University of Michigan Press, 1981. ISBN 0-472-09325-8 (cl), 0-472-08018-1 (pbk). ▸ Description of Andean knotted-string mnemonic device. How they were made and used; *quipu* maker specialist; hierarchy and pattern; format; and category and summation. One of few studies of fascinating device. [NDC]

36.359 David L. Browman. "Pastoral nomadism in the Andes." *Current anthropology* 15.4 (1974) 188–96. ISSN 0094-4920. ▸ Best available introduction to study of camelid herding in central Peruvian Andes. Attempts to establish carrying capacity and discuss effectiveness of unusual example of indigenous pastoralism. [NDC]

36.360 Geoffrey W. Conrad and Arthur A. Demarest. *Religion and empire: the dynamics of Aztec and Inca expansionism.* Cam-

bridge: Cambridge University Press, 1984. ISBN 0-521-24357-2 (cl), 0-521-31896-3 (pbk). ▸ Provocative explanation of rapid Aztec and Inca expansion as consequence of split inheritance and cult of *panacas* (lineage of the ruler). Argues need for economic and human resources to support cult of the ancestors led inevitably to military expansion. [NDC]

36.361 Terence D'Altroy. "Transitions in power: centralization of Wanka political organization under Inka rule." *Ethnohistory* 34.1 (1987) 78–102. ISSN 0014-1801. ▸ Examination of integration of powerful ethnic entity into administrative structure in Peru's central highlands. Pierces stereotype of uniform Inca empire and carries important implications for other regions. [NDC]

36.362 Arthur A. Demarest. *Viracocha: the nature and antiquity of the Andean high god.* Cambridge, Mass.: Peabody Museum of Archaeology and Ethnology, 1981. (Peabody Museum monographs, 6.) ISBN 0-87365-906-6. ▸ Excellent introductory history of Inca upper religious pantheon, including Illapa/Thunupa complex so important to indigenous social organization. Traces concept of "high" god as far back as Tiahuanaco period. [NDC]

36.363 Pierre Duviols. "La dinastía de los Incas: ¿monarquía o diarquía? Argumentos heuristicos a favor de una tésis estructuralista." *Journal de la Société des Américanistes* 66 (1979) 67–73. ▸ Interpretation of nature of Inca political system, based on pervasive concept of duality. Important theoretical overview of indigenous Andean empire. [NDC]

36.364 Waldemar Espinosa Soriano. *La destrucción del imperio de los Incas: la rivalidad política y señorial de los curacazgos andinos.* Lima: Realbo de Papal, 1974. ▸ Monograph pointing out weakness of short-lived Inca state and fissures based on rivalries between local ethnic entities and their political lords. Primary focus on Chincha. [NDC]

36.365 Regina Harrison. *Signs, songs, and memory in the Andes: translating Quechua language and culture.* Austin: University of Texas Press, 1989. ISBN 0-292-77627-6 (cl), 0-292-77628-4 (pbk). ▸ Valuable, unique reconstruction of Quechua life and thought draws on fields of anthropology, linguistics, and literary criticism. Spatial concentration on Ecuador. [NDC]

36.366 John Hyslop. *Inka settlement planning.* Austin: University of Texas Press, 1990. ISBN 0-292-73852-8. ▸ Systematic study of architecture and settlement planning exploring relationship between mythic concept and physical place in Andean world. Excellent introduction to Inca cultural and political achievement. [NDC]

36.367 Catherine J. Julien. *Hatunqolla: a view of Inca rule from the Lake Titicaca region.* Berkeley: University of California Press, 1983. ISBN 0-520-09682-7. ▸ Perceptive, important study of Hatunqolla of northern edge of Lake Titicaca under Inca rule and in early Spanish era. [NDC]

36.368 Paul Kosok. *Life, land, and water in ancient Peru.* New York: Long Island University Press, 1965. ISBN 0-913252-00-X. ▸ Beautifully illustrated introduction to relation of water to people in Peru, especially along desert coast. Describes irrigation systems and evolution of region's agricultural technology. [NDC]

36.369 Edward P. Lanning. *Peru before the Incas.* Englewood Cliffs, N.J.: Prentice-Hall, 1967. ▸ Dated but still useful introduction to preconquest era of Andean America. Provides brief summary of indigenous peoples prior to establishment of Inca empire. [NDC]

36.370 Craig Morris and Donald E. Thompson. *Huánuco Pampa: an Inca city and its hinterland.* London: Thames & Hudson, 1985. ISBN 0-500-39020-7. ▸ Account of provincial Inca capital in Peru's north-central highlands. Exhaustive overview covering architecture and ceramics; economy, ritual, and politics;

subsistence and storage; roads, bridges, and way stations; and ethnic entities in Huánuco region. [NDC]

36.371 John V. Murra. *The economic organization of the Inka state.* Greenwich, Conn.: JAI Press, 1979. ISBN 0-89232-118-0. ‣ Basic source for understanding of complexities of Inca economy, at local and state levels. Focuses especially on role of redistribution. Publication of 1955 University of Chicago thesis. [NDC]

36.372 John V. Murra. *Formaciones económicas y políticas del mundo andino.* Lima: Instituto de Estudios Peruanos, 1975. (Historia andina, 3.) ‣ Collection of author's most important contributions to Andean ethnohistory, including seminal work on vertical control of natural resources; corn, potatoes, and agricultural ritual; importance of cloth; *yana* (servants); *quipu* (knotted-string records); and exchange of *mullu* shells (used widely in rituals). [NDC]

36.373 John V. Murra, Nathan Wachtel, and Jacques Revel, eds. *Anthropological history of Andean polities.* New York: Cambridge University Press, 1986. ISBN 0-521-24667-9. ‣ Fundamental series of specialized articles centering on themes of ecology and society, ethnic group and state systems of classification, symbolic representations and practices, and shift from ethnic polities to communities. [NDC]

36.374 Franklin Pease G.Y. *Del Tawantinsuyu a la historia del Perú.* 2d ed. Lima: Pontificia Universidad Católica del Perú, 1989. (Historia andina, 5.) ‣ Interpretation of Tawantinsuyu by leading Peruvian ethnohistorian. Concentrates on sources of Inca power, empire's redistributive economy, verticality in Peruvian geography, Lupaqa kingdom, and Collaguas. First edition won Howard Francis Cline Memorial Prize (1979). [NDC]

36.375 Franklin Pease G.Y. *El dios creador andino.* Lima: Mosca Azul, 1973. ‣ Brilliant, lasting analysis of nature and meaning of myths of Wiraqocha and Inkarrí in the Andes. [NDC]

36.376 Robert Randall. "Qoyllur Rit'i: an Inca fiesta of the Pleiades." *Bulletin de l'Institut Français d'Études Andines* 11 (1982) 37–81. ‣ Anthropological analysis of Andean crop rituals linking fiestas to astronomical observations and events. Original approach to indigenous agriculture. [NDC]

36.377 Maria Rostworowski de Diez Canseco. *Etnía y sociedad: costa peruana prehispánica.* Lima: Instituto de Estudios Peruanos, 1977. (Historia andina, 4.) ‣ Valuable description of ethnic groups in Chillón valley before Spanish conquest. Includes discussion of "merchants" of Chincha valley, central coastal fishermen, and coca-leaf producers near Pacific coast. [NDC]

36.378 Maria Rostworowski de Diez Canseco. *Historia del Tahuantinsuyu.* Lima: Instituto de Estudios Peruanos, 1988. (Historia andina, 13.) ‣ New interpretive analysis of Inca state. Examines expansion, social composition (*curacas* [chieftains], *yana* [servants], "merchants," artisans, *mitmaq* [special migrants], *mamacona* [virgins dedicated to state religion]), natural resources, and economic redistribution. [NDC]

36.379 John H. Rowe. "An account of the shrines of ancient Cuzco." *Ñawpa Pacha* 17 (1979) 2–80. ISSN 0077-6297. ‣ Overall survey of Cuzco shrines by leading American scholar. Descriptions based on accounts of early chroniclers as well as modern field study. [NDC]

36.380 Frank Salomon. *Native lords of Quito in the age of the Incas: the political economy of North-Andean chiefdoms.* New York: Cambridge University Press, 1986. ISBN 0-521-30299-4. ‣ Prizewinning ethnohistoric study of socioeconomic modifications taking place on northern edge of Tawantinsuyu in fifteenth and sixteenth centuries. Includes analysis of ecological variation, subsistence activities, merchants and centralized exchange, and nature of Inca power. [NDC]

36.381 Frank Salomon and George L. Urioste, trans. *The Huarochirí Manuscript: a testament of ancient and colonial Andean religion.* Austin: University of Texas Press, 1991. ISBN 0-292-73052-7 (cl), 0-292-73053-5 (pbk). ‣ English translation and Quechua transcription of report (housed in Biblioteca Nacional of Madrid) made during campaigns against idolatry by Spanish clerics in late sixteenth to early seventeenth century. Insight into Huarochirí religious beliefs and relationship to social and economic life. [NDC]

36.382 Henrique Urbano. *Wiracocha y Ayar: heroes y funciones en las sociedades andinas.* Cuzco: Centro de Estudios Rurales Andinos "Bartolomé de Las Casas," 1981. (Biblioteca de la tradición oral andian, 3.) ‣ Peruvian scholar's provocative evaluation of role and significance of concept of Wiraqocha in indigenous Andean cultures. Provides original insight into native religious ideas. [NDC]

36.383 Gary Urton. *At the crossroads of the earth and sky: an Andean cosmology.* Austin: University of Texas Press, 1981. ISBN 0-292-70349-X. ‣ Synthesis of Andean astronomical lore based on early colonial chroniclers and oral reports. Elucidates close link between celestial phenomena and daily activities in Quechua society. [NDC]

36.384 Gary Urton. *The history of a myth: Pacariqtambo and the origin of the Inkas.* Austin: University of Texas Press, 1990. ISBN 0-292-73051-9 (cl), 0-292-73057-8 (pbk). ‣ Study of intersection of family past, based on legal records in private archive and history, and official Inca history, as used by elite of village of Pacariqtambo. Important perspectives on relation of Inca origin myth and rituals associated with local political structures. [NDC]

36.385 R. Tom Zuidema. *The ceque system of Cuzco.* Leiden: Brill, 1964. ‣ Provocative, intellectually challenging examination of mythic-spatial structure of Inca capital of Cuzco. Argues city organized around series of lines radiating outward (*ceques*), linking shrines and providing structural foundation for Cuzco society. [NDC]

36.386 R. Tom Zuidema. *Inca civilization in Cuzco.* Jean-Jacques Decoster, trans. Austin: University of Texas Press, 1990. ISBN 0-292-73850-1 (cl), 0-292-73851-X (pbk). ‣ Overview of Inca culture in its capital city by leading Inca specialist. Treats origin myths, kinship, marriage, duality, *ayllu* (basic social unit), and *ceque* system (spatial plan for religious sites). [NDC]

SEE ALSO

Colonial Period

36.387 Rolena Adorno. *Cronista y principe: la obra de don Felipe Guaman Poma de Ayala.* Lima: Pontificia Universidad Católica del Perú, 1989. ‣ Detailed, powerful presentation of career and thought of most important Andean American author, who spoke out for native rights and imperial reform in seventeenth century. [NDC]

36.388 Rolena Adorno. *Guaman Poma: writing and resistance in colonial Peru.* Austin: University of Texas Press, 1986. ISBN 0-292-72452-7. ‣ Study of Guaman Poma's "Nuera Crónica y Buen Gobierno" (1615) as form of literature in which the colonized explain conquest and subjugation. Emphasizes he favored native rule, opposed colonialism, was anti-Inca but pro-Andean, anticlerical but pro-Catholic. Fascinating analysis of theory and practice of cross-cultural communication. [NDC/MAB]

36.389 Josep M. Barnadas. *Charcas: orígenes históricos de una* *sociedad colonial, 1535–1565.* La Paz: Centro de Investigación y Promoción del Campesinado, 1973. ▸ Massive survey of early colonial society in *Audiencia* (High Court) of Charcas in modern Bolivia. Stresses Indian ethnic groups distributed in *encomiendas* (Indian grants), as well as evolution and impact of highland mining economy. [NDC]

36.390 Germán Colmenares. *La provincia de Tunja en el Nuevo Reino de Granada: ensayo de historia social, 1539–1800.* 1970 ed. Tunja, Colombia: Academia Boyacense de Historia, 1984. (Biblioteca de la Academia Boyacense de Historia, Serie obras fundamentales, 1.) ▸ Excellent analysis of socioeconomic history of Chibcha under Spanish rule. Focuses particularly on indigenous systems of agriculture, colonial tribute system, and demographic impact of imperial rule. [NDC]

36.391 Noble David Cook. *Demographic collapse: Indian Peru, 1520–1620.* New York: Cambridge University Press, 1981. ISBN 0-521-23995-8. ▸ Careful estimate of preconquest aboriginal population; method based on evaluations of several models, including disease mortality, census projections, depopulation ratios, and carrying capacity. Last section treats regional variations of depopulation following European contact. [NDC/MAB]

36.392 Pierre Duviols. *Cultura andina y represión: procesos y visitas de idolatrías y hechicerías, Cajatambo, siglo 17.* Cuzco: Centro de Estudios Rurales Andinos "Bartolomé de Las Casas," 1986. (Archivos de historia andina, 5.) ▸ History of campaign against Indian idolatries by Spanish clerics in early seventeenth century with geographical focus on Cajatambo in highlands north of Lima and Huaylas. Lengthy introductory essay followed by published documents of findings. [NDC]

36.393 Sabine MacCormack. *Religion in the Andes: vision and imagination in early colonial Peru.* Princeton: Princeton University Press, 1991. ISBN 0-691-09468-3. ▸ Although Christianity was victorious in Andes by 1660, below the surface, ancient beliefs and rites continued to express social and cosmic order. Important monograph describing new religious order from viewpoint of both native and outsider. [NDC]

36.394 Alejandro Malaga Medina. "Las reducciónes en el Perú, 1532–1600." *Historia y cultura* 8 (1974) 141–72. ▸ Survey of nature and impact of Viceroy Francisco de Toledo's Indian settlement policies undertaken in 1570s. Includes important background on evolution of similar settlement activities in Mesoamerica. [NDC]

36.395 Norman Meiklejohn. *La iglesia y los Lupaqas de Chucuito durante la colonia.* Puno, Peru: Instituto de Estudios Aymaras, 1988. (Archivos de historia andina, 7.) ▸ Unique, basic study of spiritual conquest (Christian) of Aymara-speaking peoples of Lake Titicaca district, first by Dominicans, then by Jesuits. [NDC]

36.396 Luis Millones. *Historia y poder en los Andes centrales (desde los orígenes al siglo XVII).* Madrid: Alianza Editorial, 1987. ISBN 84-206-4214-2. ▸ Ethnohistorical interpretation by leading Peruvian anthropologist. Examines role of religion in creation and maintenance of state from local ethnic deities to large superstructure of Inca and Spanish religious systems. Reviews Taki Onqoy reaction to Spanish rule. [NDC]

36.397 Udo Oberem. *Notas y documentos sobre miembros de la familia del Inca Atahualpa en el siglo XVI.* Guayaquil, Ecuador: Casa de Cultura Ecuatoriana, 1976. (Estudios etnohistoricos del Ecuador, 1.) ▸ Collection of documents with interpretive essay on Inca ruler Atahualpa and his descendants through seventeenth century. Compiled by leading ethnohistorian of Ecuador. [NDC]

36.398 Juan M. Ossio, ed. *Ideología messiánica del mundo Andino.* Lima: Ignacio Prado Pastor, 1973. ▸ Excellent collection of articles providing systematic study of strong messianic movements operating just below surface of Andean life in colonial era. Specialists examine Christianity, religious syncretism, and rebellion. [NDC]

36.399 Raul Porras Barrenechea. *Los cronistas del Perú (1528–1650) y otros ensayos.* Rev. ed. Lima: Banco de Crédito del Perú, 1986. (Biblioteca clasicos del Peru, 2.) ▸ Basic reference work on early colonial historians of Peru. Contains extensive editorial comments by leading Peruvian scholar, Franklin Pease. [NDC]

36.400 Maria Rostworowski de Diez Canseco. *Recursos naturales renovables y pesca, siglos XVI y XVII.* Lima: Instituto de Estudios Peruanos, 1981. (Historia andina, 8.) ▸ Groundbreaking description and history of resources of Peruvian coast, especially fish. Includes narrative of extractive strategies of foodstuffs from late Inca times to early eighteenth century. Analyzes various means of exploitation as well as various ways products exchanged internally. [NDC]

36.401 Nicolás Sánchez-Albornoz. *Indios y tributos en el Alto Perú.* Lima: Instituto de Estudios Peruanos, 1978. (Historia andina, 6.) ▸ Basic examination of nature and function of Indian tribute in upper Peru (Bolivia). Notes link between tributary categories (*forasteros* and *originarios*) for Potosí draft labor (*mita*) and demographic and economic stability of Indian community. [NDC]

36.402 Irene Silverblatt. *Moon, sun, and witches: gender ideologies and class in Inca and colonial Peru.* Princeton: Princeton University Press, 1987. ISBN 0-691-07726-6 (cl), 0-691-02258-5 (pbk). ▸ Discussion of role of gender in Inca culture. Stresses concepts of Andean duality and *ayllu*, role of myth, and "chosen" women. Traces deteriorating position of women in colonial peasant society and postcontact effort to link female witchcraft and the devil. [NDC/MFB]

36.403 Karen Spalding. *Huarochirí: an Andean society under Inca and Spanish rule.* Stanford, Calif.: Stanford University Press, 1984. ISBN 0-8047-1123-2. ▸ Balanced ethnohistorical account of peoples of Huarochirí, important district in Peruvian highlands near Lima. Stresses modifications as result of conquest, role of native chiefs in process, and relationship with colonial administrative center of Lima. [NDC/MAB]

36.404 Steve J. Stern. *Peru's Indian peoples and the challenge of Spanish conquest: Huamanga to 1640.* Madison: University of Wisconsin Press, 1982. ISBN 0-299-08900-2. ▸ Significant monograph tracing role of *caciques* (chiefs) in central highland district of Huamanga (Ayacucho) in transformation from Inca rule to colonial Spanish rule. Views *caciques* largely as successful brokers in process of change. Marxist analysis focusing heavily on political economy of colonialism. [NDC/MAB]

36.405 Nathan Wachtel. *The vision of the vanquished: the Spanish conquest of Peru through Indian eyes, 1530–1570.* Ben Reynolds and Siân Reynolds, trans. New York: Barnes & Noble, 1977. ISBN 0-06-497260-7. ▸ Now classic discussion of disintegration of Inca polity and shock of conquest with European arrival. Describes attempted rebellion and transformations permitting effective Spanish domination of Andean America. [NDC/MAB]

36.406 Ann M. Wightman. *Indigenous migration and social change: the forasteros of Cuzco, 1570–1720.* Durham, N.C.: Duke University Press, 1990. ISBN 0-8223-1000-7. ▸ Migrations in Cuzco district from time of forced-settlement policy (*reducciones*) of Viceroy Toledo in sixteenth century. *Forasteros* were Indians who migrated to new communities, giving up access to community (*ayllu*) lands and freeing themselves from obligations associated with forced-labor draft (*mita*). Finest study of *forasteros* to date. [NDC/MAB]

36.407 Margarita Zamora. *Language, authority, and indigenous history in the "Comentarios Reales de los Incas."* New York: Cambridge University Press, 1988. ISBN 0-521-35087-5. ▸ Uses modern discourse analysis to separate historical reality from fiction in early accounts of Inca empire. Evaluation of influences on and impact of writings of Garcilaso de la Vega, mestizo chronicler of Incas. [NDC]

Nineteenth and Twentieth Centuries

36.408 Richard N. Adams. *A community in the Andes: problems and progress in Muquiyauyo.* Seattle: University of Washington Press, 1959. (American Ethnological Society monographs, 31.) ISBN 0-295-73747-6. ▸ Pioneering community study; geographical and ethnohistorical introduction followed by daily life (agriculture, labor, household activities, life cycle, community) and cultural change. [NDC]

36.409 Joseph William Bastien. *Healers of the Andes: Kallawaya herbalists and their medicinal plants.* Salt Lake City: University of Utah Press, 1987. ISBN 0-87480-278-4. ▸ Comprehensive study of Andean group specializing in healing. Examines pre-Columbian practice; presents three modern practitioners of traditional medicine and discusses Andean versus European concepts of disease. Includes compendium of medicinal plants. [NDC]

36.410 Susan C. Bourque and K. Barbara Warren. *Women of the Andes: patriarchy and social change in two Peruvian towns.* Ann Arbor: University of Michigan Press, 1981. ISBN 0-472-09330-4 (cl), 0-472-06330-8 (pbk). ▸ Comparative depiction of female subordination in two small highland communities, Mayobamba and Chiuchin. Themes include childbirth, marriage, and family politics; sexual division of economy; women and agrarian class system; and role of women in social change and development. [NDC]

36.411 Stephen B. Brush. *Mountain, field, and family: the economy and human ecology of an Andean valley.* Philadelphia: University of Pennsylvania Press, 1977. ISBN 0-8122-7728-7. ▸ Ethnological account of peoples of Uchumarca. Brilliant, yet brief, ethnohistorical introduction followed by chapters on community structure, subsistence patterns, reciprocity, role of kinship, and peasant integration into modern world. [NDC]

36.412 Paul L. Doughty. *Huaylas: an Andean district in search of progress.* Ithaca, N.Y.: Cornell University Press, 1968. ▸ Overview of people of Huaylas with ethnohistorical introduction followed by chapters on social structure and mobility, subsistence activities, community organization, education, and religion. Concludes community can be, as here, force for progressive change. [NDC]

36.413 Jorge A. Flores-ochoa. *Pastoralists of the Andes: the Alpaca herders of Paratia.* Ralph Bolton, trans. Philadelphia: Institute for the Study of Human Issues, 1979. ISBN 0-915980-89-4. ▸ Important monograph examining pastoral economy. Focus on community in Peruvian department of Puno. Topics discussed include ecosystem, man, culture and society, herders, weavers and traders, and nature of pastoralism. [NDC]

36.414 Billie Jean Isbell. *To defend ourselves: ecology and ritual in an Andean village.* 1978 ed. Prospect Heights, Ill.: Waveland, 1985. ISBN 0-88133-173-2. ▸ Excellent, focused ethnography of village of Chuschi in central Peruvian highlands. Examines social classes, duality and *ayllu* (basic social unit), political structures, kinship and marriage, community ritual, concept of reciprocity, and urban migration. [NDC]

36.415 Julia Meyerson. *'Tambo: life in an Andean village.* Austin: University of Texas Press, 1990. ISBN 0-292-78077-X (cl), 0-292-78078-8 (pbk). ▸ Modern ethnography of annual life cycle in small Andean village not far from Cuzco. Cultural overview of persistent native community. [NDC]

SEE ALSO
37.353 Brooke Larson. *Colonialism and agrarian transformation in Bolivia.*

38.451 Thomas M. Davies, Jr. *Indian integration in Peru.*
38.460 Florencia E. Mallon. *The defense of community in Peru's central highlands.*

General and Theoretical Works

36.416 Ralph Bolton and Enrique Mayer, eds. *Andean kinship and marriage.* Washington, D.C.: American Anthropological Association, 1977. (Special publication of the American Anthropological Association, 7.) ▸ Important series of articles on marriage rules in Andes. Unique, multidimensional perspective on indigenous social life of region. [NDC]

36.417 Hans C. Buechler and Judith-Maria Buechler. *The Bolivian Aymara.* New York: Holt, Rinehart & Winston, 1971. ISBN 0-03-081380-8. ▸ Balanced, readable community study of Compi on shores of Lake Titicaca. Cultural overview; chapters on economic organization, childhood, family, community, and festivals and religion. [NDC]

36.418 Noble David Cook. *The people of the Colca valley: a population study.* Boulder: Westview, 1982. ISBN 0-86531-390-3. ▸ Analysis of global population change in valley, 1500–1972. Topics include marriage, birth and death rates, migration (*forasteros* and *originarios*), duality and *ayllu* (community) organization. Primary focus on colonial era. [NDC/MAB]

36.419 Louis C. Faron. *From conquest to agrarian reform: ethnicity, ecology, and economy in the Chancay Valley, Peru, 1533 to 1964.* Pittsburgh: University of Pittsburgh, Department of Anthropology, 1985. (Ethnology monographs, 8.) ▸ Sweeping attempt to outline changing patterns of ethnicity, ecology, and economy in one valley over long period. Focuses on social mobility in Chancay or nearby Lima. [NDC]

36.420 Louis C. Faron. *The Mapuche Indians of Chile.* 1968 ed. New York: Waveland, 1986. ISBN 0-88133-247-X. ▸ Short survey describing Mapuche culture and tracing their cultural survival through time. Topics covered include warfare and peacemaking, agriculture, descent, residence patterns, status of women, marriage, domestic life, politics, religion, shamanism, and death and burial rites. [NDC]

36.421 Daniel R. Gross, ed. *Peoples and cultures of native South America: an anthropological reader.* Garden City, N.Y.: Natural History Press for American Museum of Natural History, 1973. ISBN 0-385-05725-3 (cl), 0-385-05728-8 (pbk). ▸ Useful introductory reader on indigenous South Americans. Important series of articles on Andean region by Menzel, Rowe, Murra, Salomon, Zuidema, and Quispe. [NDC]

36.422 Carlos Monge. *Acclimatization in the Andes: historical confirmations of "climatic aggression" in the development of Andean man.* Baltimore: Johns Hopkins University Press, 1948. ▸ Classic statement of biological adaptations of homo sapiens for survival at high elevations. Presents technical and biological information in accessible format. [NDC]

36.423 John V. Murra. "Current research and prospects in Andean ethnohistory." *Latin American research review* 5 (1970) 3–36. ISSN 0023-8791. ▸ Important historiographical article by leading scholar in Andean studies. Outlines accomplishments and details research needs. [NDC]

36.424 Udo Oberem. *Los Quijos: historia de la transculturación de un grupo indigena en el oriente Ecuatoriano, 1538–1956.* 1971 ed. 2 vols. Otavalo, Ecuador: Instituto Otavaleño de Antropologia, 1980. (Colección Pendoneros, 16.) ▸ Basic, comprehensive ethnohistory of important upper Amazon basin group living in modern-day Ecuador. Explores mechanisms for survival in face of pressure from missions and *hacienda* (plantation) system. [NDC/DGS]

36.425 Juan M. Ossio. "Aspectos simbólicos de las comidas andinas." *America indigena* 48 (1988) 549–70. ISSN 0185-1179. ▸ Symbolic analysis of Andean cuisine that finds complementary oppositions in many basic foodstuffs: male and female, upper and lower, hot and cold. Interesting theoretical introduction. [NDC]

36.426 Franklin Pease G.Y. "Etnohistoria andina: un estado de la cuestión." *Historia y cultura* 10 (1976–77) 207–28. ▸ Sweeping review of scholarship on history of indigenous peoples in the Andes. Critical commentary, useful bibliography. [NDC]

36.427 Roger Neil Rasnake. *Domination and cultural resistance: authority and power among an Andean people.* Durham, N.C.: Duke University Press, 1988. ISBN 0-8223-0809-6. ▸ Useful study of political power in Yura. Description of indigenous organization of society, *Saya-ayllu,* as well as discussions of colonial administration and subsequent changes under various regimes. [NDC/MAB]

36.428 John H. Rowe. "A interview with John V. Murra." *Hispanic American historical review* 84 (64) 633–53. ISSN 0018-2168. ▸ Profile of leading Andean scholar in United States. Provides important biographical insights into career and scholarship. [NDC]

36.429 Julian H. Steward and Louis C. Faron. *Native peoples of South America.* New York: McGraw-Hill, 1959. ▸ Condensation of multivolume *Handbook of South American Indians* (36.503); remains useful, short introduction to subject. Numerous encyclopedic descriptions of peoples and cultural traditions. [NDC]

AMAZON BASIN

Precontact

36.430 William M. Denevan. *An aboriginal cultural geography of the Llanos de Mojos de Bolivia.* Berkeley: University of California Press, 1966. ▸ Historical geographer's contribution to social history of savanna chiefdoms of Bolivian Amazon. Focuses on ancient ridged-field farming system, subsistence strategies, population history, and role of colonial missions in social change. [DGS]

36.431 Donald W. Lathrap. *The upper Amazon.* New York: Praeger, 1970. ▸ Survey of prehistory of Arawakan, Tupian, and Panoan peoples of Peruvian Amazon, in light of archaeology (particularly ceramic remains) and contemporary ethnography. Contradicts Meggers 36.463 on origins of Amazon culture. [DGS]

36.432 Anna C. Roosevelt. *Parmana: prehistoric maize and manioc subsistence along the Amazon and Orinoco.* New York: Academic Press, 1980. ISBN 0-12-595350-X. ▸ Persuasive argument using archaeology and early documents, that prehistoric maize cultivation combined with rich sources of animal protein to allow dense settlement and chiefdoms in alluvial lowlands of Amazon and Orinoco rivers. [DGS]

SEE ALSO
2.106 Anna C. Roosevelt. *Moundbuilders of the Amazon.*

Colonial Period

36.433 Michael F. Brown. "Beyond resistance: a comparative study of utopian renewal in Amazonia." *Ethnohistory* 38.4 (1991) 388–413. ISSN 0014-1801. ▸ Revisionist view of Amazon Indian millenarianism. Utopian renewal as response to internal political processes and contradictions, some predating encounter with Europeans. Points to limits of resistance as way of viewing Indian self-definition. [DGS]

36.434 João Daniel, S.J. *Tesouro Descoberto no Rio Amazonas.* 1975 ed. 2 vols. Rio de Janeiro: Divisão de Publiçãoes e Divulgaco, 1976. (Anais da Biblioteca Nacional, 95.) ▸ First full publication of richest colonial Portuguese source on Amazon Indian culture. Monumental treatise on all aspects of Amazonian life in mid-eighteenth century, written by exiled Jesuit missionary working without notes in Lisbon prison. [DGS]

36.435 Alexandre Rodrigues Ferreira. *Viagem filosófica pelas capitanias do Grão Pará, Rio Negro, Mato Grosso, e Cuiabá: memórias, antropologia.* Rio de Janeiro: Conselho Federal de Cultura, 1974. ▸ Twenty essays on Amazonian Indian societies and artifacts by great scientific traveler of 1780s, published here for first time in accessible form. Basic source for colonial Indian history. [DGS]

36.436 Waltraud Grohs. *Los Indios del Alto Amazonas del siglo xvi al xviii: populaciónes y migracións en la antigua provincia de Maynas.* Jan Castro y Velazquez, trans. Bonn: Universität Oberem, 1974. (Bonner Amerikanistische Studien, 2.) ▸ Meticulous demographic history of Indian peoples of old Jesuit mission territory of Maynas, in Peruvian Amazon. Discusses process of social transformation within mission system. German summary. [DGS]

36.437 John Hemming. *Red gold: the conquest of the Brazilian Indians.* Cambridge, Mass.: Harvard University Press, 1978. ISBN 0-674-75107-8 (cl), 0-674-01725-0 (pbk). ▸ Brazilian Indian encounters with Portuguese missionaries, Indian slave traders, settlers, and forest product collectors in eastern South America and Amazon Valley, 1500–1750. Excellent, well-written introduction. [DGS/MAB]

36.438 Jonathan D. Hill, ed. *Rethinking history and myth: indigenous South American perspectives on the past.* Urbana: University of Illinois Press, 1988. ISBN 0-252-01543-6 (cl), 0-252-06028-8 (pbk). ▸ Ten essays by anthropologists exploring ways of understanding past interactions with colonialist outsiders which may be found in rituals and narratives of Amazonian and other native South American societies. [DGS]

36.439 Jean-Marcel Hurault. *Français et Indiens en Guyana: 1604–1972.* 1972 ed. Cayenne, French Guiana: Guyane Presse Diffusion, 1989. ▸ Ethnographer's detailed history of Indian peoples of French Guiana. Traces changing relationship of native peoples to French settlers and colonial government. [DGS]

36.440 Mathias C. Kiemen. *The Indian policy of the Portuguese in the Amazon region.* 1954 ed. New York: Octagon Books, 1973. ISBN 0-374-94578-0. ▸ Basic text for mission history, shifting legal arrangements, and evolving relationship between church and state with regard to administration of Amazon Indian population of Portuguese Maranhão and Grão Pará in seventeenth century. [DGS]

36.441 Colin M. Maclachlan. "The Indian labor structure in the Portuguese Amazon region." In *Colonial roots of modern Brazil: papers of the Newberry Library Conference.* Dauril Alden, ed., pp. 199–230. Berkeley: University of California Press, 1973. ISBN 0-520-02140-1. ▸ Brief review of history of Indian slavery and mission system, later replaced by government-operated Directorate of Indian Labor in eighteenth-century Grão Pará and Maranhão. [DGS]

36.442 Alfred Metraux. "The revolution of the ax." *Diogenes* 29 (1959) 28–40. ISSN 0392-1921. ▸ Classic formulation of mechanism by which tropical forest Indians became dependent upon early missionaries as suppliers of iron tools which, once experienced, quickly became indispensable for traditional tropical forest work. [DGS]

36.443 Robert V. Morey. "A joyful harvest of souls: disease and the destruction of the Llanos Indians." *Antropológica* 52 (1979) 77–108. ISSN 0003-6110. ▸ Study of demographic and social impact of epidemics spreading from Jesuit mission stations to Guahibo and Achagua peoples of Venezuelan llanos. Focuses primarily on eighteenth century. [DGS]

36.444 Moreira Neto and Carlos de Araujo. *Indios da Amazônia,*

de maioria a minoria (1750–1850). Petrópolis, Brazil: Vozes, 1988.
▸ Interpretive social history of decline and assimilation of more accessible indigenous communities of Brazilian Amazonia in postmission late colonial and early national periods. Extensive documentary appendixes. [DGS]

36.445 Curt Nimuendajú. *The Tapajó*. John H. Rowe, ed and trans. Berkeley: Kroeber Anthropological Society, 1952. ▸ Unique reconstruction from archaeological material and early colonial documents of riverine Amazonian culture which became extinct in early eighteenth century. [DGS]

36.446 David G. Sweet. "Native resistance in eighteenth-century Amazonia: the 'abominable Muras' in war and peace." *Radical history review* 53 (1992) 49–80. ISSN 0163-6545. ▸ Overview of experiences of Muras of central Amazonia from initial isolation, through decades of all-out war against Portuguese missionaries and settlers, to process of peaceful accommodation. Emphasizes role of captives and women in cultural transition. [DGS]

36.447 Neil L. Whitehead. "Carib ethnic soldiering in Venezuela, the Guianas, and the Antilles, 1492–1820." *Ethnohistory* 37.4 (1990) 357–85. ISSN 0014-1801. ▸ Highly original essay locating formulation of Carib ethnicity in history of group's military cooperation with Dutch and French. [DGS]

36.448 Neil L. Whitehead. *Lords of the tiger spirit: a history of the Caribs in colonial Venezuela and Guyana, 1498–1820*. Providence: Foris, 1988. ISBN 90-6765-240-7. ▸ Brilliant revisionist ethnohistory of principal native protagonists in colonial history of lower Orinoco basin. Topics include demography and culture, military conquests, and alliances with Dutch versus Spaniards. Concludes with reexamination of Caribs' image as warlike cannibals. [DGS]

Nineteenth Century

36.449 Mary Noel R.S.M. Menezes. *British policy towards the Amerindians in British Guiana, 1803–1873*. Oxford: Clarendon, 1977. ISBN 0-19-821567-3. ▸ Best available study of government Indian policy in any part of lowland tropical America; to be read with author's separately published collection of edited primary documents. Latter, a rich source for Indian history of Guyana. [DGS]

36.450 Robin M. Wright and Jonathan D. Hill. "History, ritual, and myth: nineteenth-century millenarian movements in the Northwest Amazon." *Ethnohistory* 33.1 (1986) 31–54. ISSN 0014-1801. ▸ Description of millenarian movement on upper Rio Negro in 1850s. Draws on both oral tradition and documentary record to argue movement created ritual space free from oppressive neocolonial system of debt bondage. [DGS]

SEE ALSO
37.460 John Hemming. *Amazon frontier*.

Twentieth Century

36.451 Victor Daniel Bonilla. *Servants of god or masters of men? The story of a Capuchin mission in Amazonia*. Rosemary Sheed, trans. Harmondsworth: Penguin, 1972. ISBN 0-14-021436-4. ▸ Critical history of repressive government-sponsored twentieth-century Catholic mission to Indians of upper Putumayo valley in southern Colombia. Presented as paradigm for entire history of Indian-white relations in the Americas. [DGS]

36.452 Michael F. Brown and Eduardo Fernández. *War of shadows: the struggle for utopia in the Peruvian Amazon*. Berkeley: University of California Press, 1991. ISBN 0-520-07435-1. ▸ Description of resistance to missionaries and settlers among Ashaninka Indians of Peruvian montana. Group, which worked against outsiders since seventeenth century, joined forces with Marxist-Len-inist guerrillas in 1965 and were crushed in subsequent government repression. [DGS]

36.453 Ferrira de Castro. *O instinto supremo*. Rio de Janeiro: Civilização Brasileira, 1968. ▸ Documentary novel about implementation of General Candido Rondon's enlightened policy for Indian pacification. Accessible work showing extraordinary humane policies carried out on Rio Madeira by Brazilian Indian Protection Service team under famed anthropologist Curt Nimuendajú during 1920s. [DGS]

36.454 Gunter Kroemer. *Cuxiuara, o Purús dos indígenas: ensaio etno-histórico e etnográfico sobre os Indios do Medio Purús*. São Paulo: Edições Loyola, 1985. (Coleção Missao aberta, 10.) ▸ Regional history of Indian resistance and accommodation to missionaries, rubber gatherers, and government Indian Service agents from eighteenth century to present. Includes ethnographic notes on four surviving tribes. [DGS]

36.455 Blanca Muratorio. *The life and times of grandfather Alonso: culture and history in the upper Amazon*. New Brunswick, N.J.: Rutgers University Press, 1991. ISBN 0-8135-1684-6 (cl), 0-8135-1685-4 (pbk). ▸ Pathbreaking, rich social history of cultural resistance among neo-Indian lowland Quechua of eastern Ecuador. Narrative constructed from archival research and told around eloquent testimony of Quechua elder. [DGS]

36.456 Yolanda Murphy and Robert F. Murphy. *Women of the forest*. 2d ed. New York: Columbia University Press, 1985. ISBN 0-231-06088-2 (cl), 0-231-06089-0 (pbk). ▸ Study of changing gender relations among Mundurucu, once feared as warriors, but now among few surviving peoples of Central Amazonia today. Challenges myth of "archaic female dominance." [DGS]

36.457 G. Reichel-Dolmatoff. *The shaman and the jaguar: a study of narcotic drugs among the Indians of Colombia*. Philadelphia: Temple University Press, 1975. ISBN 0-87722-038-7. ▸ Historical and ethnographic study of use of narcotic snuffs essential to ritual practices and recreation of Indians of upper Rio Negro valley in Northwest Amazonia. [DGS]

36.458 Karl Schwerin. *Oil and steel: processes of Karinya culture change in response to industrial development*. Los Angeles: University of California Press, Latin American Center, 1966. (Latin American studies, 4.) ▸ Comparative study of social and economic changes in two plains Carib communities of eastern Venezuelan llanos, as influenced by development of oilfield near one and steel mill near other during 1950s and 1960s. [DGS]

36.459 Michael Taussig. *Shamanism, colonialism, and the wild man: a study in terror and healing*. Chicago: University of Chicago Press, 1987. ISBN 0-226-79012-6. ▸ Detailed, illuminating, but disjointed and ahistorical reflection on Indian experience with rubber barons, missionaries, and magic in twentieth-century Putumayo. Brilliant dissection of image making engendered and provoked by colonialism. [DGS]

36.460 Norman E. Whitten, Jr. *Sacha Runa: ethnicity and adaptation of Ecuadorian jungle Quichua*. Urbana: University of Illinios Press, 1976. ISBN 0-252-00553-8. ▸ Ethnography and social history of Canelos Quechua Indians of Ecuadorian Amazon. Best available monograph focusing on cultural continuities and strategies Quechuas employed to survive and expand in face of ethnocidal pressures. [DGS]

General and Theoretical Works

36.461 Jean Pierre Chaumeil. *Historia y migraciones de los Yagua de finales del siglo XVII hasta nuestros dias*. Maria del Carmen Urbano, trans. Lima: Centro Amazónico de Antropología y Aplicación Práctica, 1981. (Serie antropologica, 3.) ▸ Detailed ethnohistory of Yagua of Peru-Colombia border region. Includes descriptions of encounters with missionaries, rubber gatherers, and development officials since seventeenth century. Special attention to causes of group's frequent migrations. [DGS]

36.462 Juan Friede. *Los Andakí, 1538–1947: historia de la aculturación de una tribu selvática.* Mexico: Fondo de Cultura Económica, 1953. ▸ Pioneering ethnohistory of people forced out of upper Magdalena River valley by Spaniards in sixteenth century. Following this, Andakí reconstructed their society on Caquetá River in Amazonia and survived four centuries of traumatic change. [DGS]

36.463 Betty Jane Meggers. *Amazonia: man and culture in a counterfeit paradise.* Chicago and New York: Aldine and Atherton, 1971. ISBN 0-202-01016-3 (cl), 0-202-01044-9 (pbk). ▸ Basic introduction to cultural ecology of Amazonia, contrasting *varzea* and *terra firme* as environments for Indian social development from prehistoric times to present. Useful tool despite some now controversial interpretations. [DGS]

36.464 Nancy Morey and Robert V. Morey. "Foragers and farmers: differential consequences of Spanish contact." *Ethnohistory* 20.3 (1973) 229–246. ISSN 0014-1801. ▸ Comparison of Spanish and national influences on horticultural Achagua and hunter-gatherer Guahibo of Venezuelan llanos. Traces events from sixteenth century onward to explain why Guahibo persist but Achagua have disappeared. [DGS]

36.465 Anthony W. Stocks. *Los nativos invisibles: notas sobre la historia y realidad actual de los Cocamilla del Río Huallaga, Peru.* Annette Rosenvinge de Uriarte and Armando Valdés Palacios, trans. Lima: Centro Amazónico de Antropología y Aplicación Práctica, 1981. (Serie antropologica, 4.) ▸ Ethnohistory of Cocamilla of Peruvian Amazon who maintained limited autonomy for 300 years by providing essential services to settlers. Also discusses problem of modern-day egalitarian society confronting hierarchical frontier society and stratified national state. [DGS]

36.466 Stefano Varese. *La sal de los cerros: una aproximación as mundo Campa.* 2d ed. Lima: Retalbo de Papel Ediciónes, 1973. (Serie reencuentro, 11.) ▸ Classic ethnohistory of Campa of Peruvian Amazon, centered on encounters with Spanish missions in seventeenth century, open rebellion in eighteenth century, and survival within national society's tightening circle during nineteenth and twentieth centuries. [DGS]

SOUTHERN CONE

Precontact

36.467 J. Roberto Bárcenas, ed. *Culturas indígenas de la Patagonia.* Spain: Sociedad Estatal Quinto Centenario, Producción Turner Libros, 1992. ISBN 84-7506-328-4. ▸ Important collection of essays based on recent archaeological, ethnological, and ethnohistorical research in Patagonia and Tierra del Fuego. [KLJ]

36.468 Tom D. Dillehay. *Araucanía: presente y pasado.* Santiago: Bello, 1990. ISBN 956-13-0747-1. ▸ Collection of author's essays (in Spanish) analyzing pre-Hispanic (archaeological) record of Araucanía as well as ethnographic interpretation of ceremonial space based on Mapuche cosmology and concepts of ethnicity. [KLJ]

36.469 Jorge L. Hidalgo et al., ed. *Culturas de Chile: prehistoria, desde sus orígenes hasta los albores de la conquista.* Santiago: Bello, 1989. ▸ Up-to-date overview of prehistoric societies living in northern regions of Chile up to time of Spanish conquest. Good introduction to ethnohistory of southern Andean regions. [KLJ]

Colonial Period

36.470 Pedro de Angelis, ed. *Colección de viages y expediciones a los campos de Buenos Aires y a las costas de Patagonia.* 1836 ed. Buenos Aires: Plus Ultra, 1969. ▸ Best-known, accessible collection of archival sources documenting Spanish exploration and

reconnaissance of Argentina, including Chaco, Northwest, Buenos Aires and environs, Patagonia, and Tierra del Fuego. Includes accounts of Spanish reconnaisance efforts (sixteenth and seventeenth centuries) and military records recording first encounters with native inhabitants of interior (eighteenth and early nineteenth centuries). [KLJ]

36.471 Jean-Pierre Blancpain. *Les Araucans et la frontière dans l'histoire du Chili des origines au dix-neuvième siècle: une épopée américaine.* Frankfurt: Vervuert, 1990. (Lateinamerika-Studien, 26.) ISBN 3-89354-726-6. ▸ Concise summary of frontier relations between Araucanía (Mapuche) and Europeans in Chile, sixteenth to seventeenth century. Important discussion of early contact period and strong analysis of transformation in frontier relations in century following Chilean independence. [KLJ]

36.472 Rodolfo M. Casamiquela. *Un nuevo panorama etnologico del area pan-pampeana y patagonica adyacente: Pruebas etnohistoricas de la filiacion Tehuelche septentrional de los Querandies.* Santiago: Museo Nacional de Historia Naturales, 1969. ▸ Ethnohistorical treatise detailing evidence of Tehuelche penetration of Araucanian (Mapuche) society. Detailed, difficult, but significant. [KLJ]

36.473 Martin Dobrizhoffer. *An account of the Abipones: an equestrian people of Paraguay.* 1822 ed. New York: Johnson Reprint, 1970. ▸ Translation of eighteenth-century Jesuit chronicle of attempts to missionize Guaycuruan Indians of Gran Chaco. [KLJ]

36.474 Thomas Falkner. *A description of Patagonia and the adjoining parts of South America, London, 1744.* 1935 ed. New York: AMS Press, 1976. ISBN 0-404-14747-X. ▸ Jesuit account of failed missionizing efforts in pampas south of Buenos Aires; descriptive commentary reveals araucanization of indigenous groups in pampas. [KLJ]

36.475 Alvaro Jara. *Guerra y sociedad en Chile: y otras temas afines.* 3d ed. Santiago: Editorial Universitaria, 1984. ▸ Classic study of war and society in Chile describing development and justification of slavery in sixteenth century. Central argument is that forms of warfare with native peoples were linked and contributed to development of social forms in Chile. [KLJ]

36.476 Leonardo León Solis. *Maloqueros y conchavadores en Araucanía y las pampas, 1700–1800.* Temuco, Chile: Ediciones Universidad de la Frontera, 1990. (Serie Quinto centenario, 7.) ISBN 956-236-029-5. ▸ Careful, well-documented history of Mapuche (Araucanía) relations with Spanish in Chile and Argentina. [KLJ]

36.477 Raul Mandrini. *Argentina indigena: los aborígenes a la llegada de los Españoles.* Buenos Aires: Centro Editor de America Latina, 1983. (Historia testimonial Argentina, 1.) ISBN 950-250-121-7. ▸ Assessment of indigenous peoples and their first encounters with Spanish by contemporary ethnohistorian. Valuable survey containing new perspectives and interpretations. [KLJ]

36.478 Robert C. Padden. "Cultural change and military resistance in Araucanian Chile, 1550–1730." In *Native South Americans: ethnology of the least known continent.* Patricia J. Lyon, ed., pp. 327–42. Boston: Little, Brown, 1974. ▸ Overview of Mapuche adaptation to Spanish incursions raising theoretical questions, including varying ways Mapuche political and military organization affected both cultural persistence and native adaptation to Spanish presence. [KLJ]

36.479 Miguel Angel Palermo. "Reflexiones sobre el llamado complejo ecuestre en la Argentina." *Runa* 16 (1986) 157–77. ISSN 0325-1217. ▸ Critique and analysis of development of so-called horse complex that emerged in Argentine pampas following Spanish introduction of horse in sixteenth century. [KLJ]

36.480 Jorge Pinto Rodriguez et al. *Misioneros en la Araucanía, 1600–1900: un capitulo de historia fronteriza en Chile.* 1988 ed.

Bogotá: Consejo Episcopal Latinoamericano, 1990. (Colección V centenario, 38.) ISBN 958-625-020-2. ▸ Collection of essays based on recent research assessing successes and failures of missionizing attempts within (Chilean) Araucanía. [KLJ]

36.481 James Schofield Saeger. "Eighteenth-century Guaycuruan missions in Paraguay." In *Indian-religious relations in colonial Spanish America.* Susan E. Ramirez, ed., pp. 55–86. Syracuse, N.Y.: Syracuse University, Maxwell School of Citizenship & Public Affairs, 1989. (Foreign and comparative studies, 9.) ISBN 0-915984-32-6. ▸ Discussion of first encounters, missionization, and conflicts between Guaycuruan and Spaniards in Gran Chaco region, 1550–1750. Reflects newer sensitivity to cross-cultural interactions in early contact era. [KLJ]

36.482 Richard W. Slatta. "'Civilization,' battles, 'barbarism': Argentine frontier strategies, 1516–1880." *Inter-American review of bibliography* 39.2 (1989) 177–194. ISSN 0020-4994. ▸ Excellent summary chronology of government military actions against Indians in expansion of southern Argentine frontier, 1516–1880. Reinterpretation of groundbreaking work of Walther (36.505). [KLJ]

36.483 Susan Migden Socolow. "Spanish captives in Indian societies: cultural contact along the Argentine frontier, 1600–1835." *Hispanic American historical review* 72.1 (1992) 73–99. ISSN 0018-2168. ▸ Study of creole experience as captives in Indian societies, as recorded in Spanish and Argentine records. Demonstrates complexity of captive experience. [KLJ]

36.484 Sergio Villalobos R. et al. *Relaciones fronterizas en la Araucanía.* Santiago: Ediciones Universidad Católica de Chile, 1982. ▸ Collection of essays by leading Chilean scholars describing frontier relations between Araucanians (Mapuche) and Chileans; focus on late colonial and nineteenth-century relations. Contains political chronologies, ethnological overviews, and previously unedited archival sources. [KLJ]

SEE ALSO
37.546 James Schofield Saeger. "Another view of the mission as a frontier institution."

Nineteenth Century

36.485 Pascal Cona. *Vida y costumbres de los indígenas araucanos en la segunda midtad del siglo XIX.* 3d ed. Santiago: Pehuen, 1984. ▸ One of few Mapuche autobiographies in print, published in Mapuche language with Spanish translation. Contains important ethnographic descriptions of late nineteenth-century frontier relations in both Chile and Argentina. [KLJ]

36.486 Auguste Guinnard. *Three years' slavery among the Patagonians: an account of his captivity, from the third French edition, by Charles S. Cheltnam.* London: Bentley, 1871. ▸ Captivity narrative of member of geographical society of France; transcends tropes of genre to provide important descriptive detail of interethnic relations in Argentine pampas and Patagonia, particularly breakdown of alliance networks in immediate post-Rosas era. [KLJ]

36.487 Kristine L. Jones. "Calfucura and Namuncura: nation builders of the pampas." In *The human tradition in Latin America: the nineteenth century.* Judith Ewell and William H. Beezley, eds., pp. 175–86. Wilmington, Del.: Scholarly Resources, 1989. ISBN 0-8420-2331-3 (cl), 0-8420-2332-1 (pbk). ▸ Interpretive history of migration of Chilean Araucanía (Mapuche) into Argentine pampas and subsequent social and cultural expansion. [KLJ]

36.488 Kristine L. Jones. "Nineteenth-century travel accounts of Argentina." *Ethnohistory* 33.2 (1986) 195–211. ISSN 0014-1801. ▸ Textual analysis of nineteenth-century British travel accounts and descriptions of Indian-white frontier relations. [KLJ]

36.489 Alcide Dessalines d'Orbigny. *El hombre Americano, con-*

siderado en sus "Aspectos Fisiologicos y Morales." 2d ed. Buenos Aires: Editorial Futuro, 1944. ▸ French naturalist's scientific report of expedition carried out 1826–33. Ethnographic account of Indian movements describes moment of permanent Araucanian expansion into Argentina; also contains detailed commentary on Bolivian Indians. [KLJ]

36.490 E. Glyn Williams. "An ecological perspective of socioterritorial organization among the Tehuelche in the nineteenth century." In *Peasants, primitives, and proletariats: the struggle for identity in South America.* David L. Browman and Ronald A. Schwarz, eds., pp. 75–105. The Hague: Mouton, 1979. ISBN 90-279-7880-8. ▸ Ecological approach to historical reinvestigation of socioterritorial organization of Tehuelche in southern Argentina. [KLJ]

Twentieth Century

36.491 Bernardo Berdichewsky. *The Araucanian Indian in Chile.* Copenhagen: International Work Group for Indigenous Affairs, 1975. (International Work Group for Indigenous Affairs, 20.) ▸ Summary of government relations with Araucanians in Chile under President Augusto Pinochet following overthrow of Salvador Allende. [KLJ]

36.492 Anne Chapman. *Drama and power in a hunting society: the Selk-Nam of Tierra del Fuego.* New York: Cambridge University Press, 1982. ISBN 0-521-23884-6. ▸ Ethnographic monograph documenting ritual and symbolic worldview of Selk-Nam (Ona) in Tierra del Fuego. Study based on archival research and ethnographic fieldwork carried out in 1960s and 1970s among few remaining Selk-Nam. Contains brief overview of history and environment. [KLJ]

36.493 Rolf Foerster and Sonia Montecino Aguierre. *Organizaciones, lideres, y contiendas Mapuches (1900–1970).* Santiago: Centro de Estudios de la Mujer, 1988. ▸ Important documentary source describing and analyzing Mapuche organizations, political and otherwise. Based on oral history as well as published materials; work reveals dynamism of Mapuche confronting political process of subordination. [KLJ]

36.494 M. Inez Hilger. *Araucanian child life and its cultural background.* Washington, D.C.: Smithsonian Institution Press, 1957. (Smithsonian miscellaneous collections, 33.) ▸ Ethnological study of Araucanian (Mapuche) child life conducted in 1950s. Describes life cycle and larger social and political considerations for Araucanía in Chile and Argentina; particularly valuable to historians for indications of postconquest change. [KLJ]

36.495 M. Inez Hilger. *Huenun Namku: an Araucanian Indian of the Andes remembers the past.* Norman: University of Oklahoma Press, 1966. ▸ Transcriptions of field notes taken by anthropologist in 1946 from lessons delivered in formal oratory fashion by Huenun Namku, Mapuche (Araucanian) elder in Chile. Offers unique insight into contemporary social life. [KLJ]

36.496 Milan Stuchlik. *Life on a half share: mechanisms of social recruitment among the Mapuche of southern Chile.* New York: St. Martin's, 1976. ISBN 0-903983-37-0. ▸ Study of three Mapuche communities in Chile by social anthropologist from Naprstek Museum in Prague. Useful to historians for detailed study of local-level politics and social mechanisms for exchange and redistribution. [KLJ]

36.497 Mischa Titiev. *Araucanian culture in transition.* Ann Arbor: University of Michigan Press, 1951. ▸ Classic synchronic ethnography of Mapuche society in Chile in 1948 with attention to changing patterns of culture. [KLJ]

General and Theoretical Works

36.498 Jose Bengoa. *Historia del Pueblo Mapuche, siglo XIX y XX.* 2d ed. Santiago: Ediciones Sur, 1987. ▸ History of Mapuche

(Araucanian) people in southern Andes. Strongly influenced by sociological training of author, favors structural interpretations in overview of relations between Mapuche and Chilean government in nineteenth and twentieth centuries. [KLJ]

36.499 Bernardo Berdichewsky. "Abipon," "Ashluslay," "Araucanians." Entries in *Encyclopedia of Indians of the Americas.* Keith Irvine, ed. St. Clair Shores, Mich.: Scholarly Press, 1974. ISBN 0-403-01795-5. ‣ Useful synthesis in English of cultural history of Araucanian (Mapuche) and other native peoples in Chile. [KLJ]

36.500 Louis C. Faron. *The Mapuche Indians of Chile.* New York: Holt, Rinehart & Winston, 1968. ‣ Case study in cultural anthropology providing important understanding of social structure and underlying worldviews of Mapuche society. [KLJ]

36.501 Samuel K. Lothrop. "Indians of the Parana Delta, Argentina." *Annals of the New York Academy of Sciences* 33 (1932) 72–232. ISSN 0077-8923. ‣ Summary of archaeological and historical evidence of native peoples in littoral region of Argentina and Uruguay. Basic ethnographic overview; still best introduction to area. [KLJ]

36.502 Samuel K. Lothrop. *The Indians of Tierra del Fuego.* 1928 ed. New York: AMS Press, 1978. (Museum of the American Indian, Heye Foundation, 10.) ISBN 0-404-15868-4. ‣ Survey of archaeological, ethnological, and historical evidence of Indians in Tierra del Fuego. [KLJ]

36.503 Julian H. Steward, ed. *Handbook of South American Indians.* Vol. 1: *The marginal tribes.* Vol. 2: *The Andean civilizations.* Vol. 3: *The tropical forest tribes.* Vol. 4: *The Circum-Caribbean tribes.* Vol. 5: *The comparative ethnology of South American Indians.* Vol. 6: *Physical anthropology, linguistics, and cultural geography of South American Indians.* Vol. 7: *Index.* 1944–49 ed. 7 vols. New York: Cooper Square, 1963. ‣ Somewhat dated but still primary reference work summarizing archaeological and historical research on Indians of South America. For southern cone see especially, Metraux, Bird, and Cooper in volume 1, and Bird, Lothrop, and Cooper in volume 2. [KLJ]

36.504 Sergio Villalobos R. *Los Pehuenches en la vida fronteriza: investigaciones.* Santiago: Ediciones Universidad Católica de Chile, 1989. ISBN 956-14-0228-8. ‣ History of Chilean relations with Pehuenche (ethnic subgroup in Araucanía) in eighteenth and nineteenth centuries. [KLJ]

36.505 Juan Carlos Walther. *La conquista del Desierto: Lucha de fronteras con el Indio.* 1948 ed. Buenos Aires: Editorial Universitaria de Buenos Aires, 1970. ‣ Historical overview of principal encounters and military operations against Indians in Argentine pampas and Patagonia, 1527–1885. Classic study of frontier expansion in Argentina. [KLJ]

36.506 Thomas I. Welch, comp. *The Indians of South America: a bibliography.* Washington, D.C.: Organization of American States, Columbus Memorial Library, 1987. (Hipolito Unanue bibliographic series, 2.) ‣ Useful bibliographic reference; topics organized according to country (not tribe); contains mostly ethnographic references. [KLJ]

MARK A. BURKHOLDER

Latin America to 1800

The mid-1960s marked a watershed for colonial Latin American history; the publication of three important syntheses—C. Gibson, *Spain in America* (37.82); J. H. Parry, *The Spanish Seaborne Empire* (37.96); and J. Lynch, *Spain Under the Habsburgs* (now published in a revised edition under different titles, 29.19, 29.20)—symbolically ended the postwar era of scholarship. These synthetic works incorporated the latest findings and implications of demographic studies, especially those of L. B. Simpson, W. Borah, and S. F. Cook—the Berkeley school—and ethnohistorical research, notably that of Gibson (36.287).

Since the mid-1960s, colonialists have approached familiar topics in a fresh way and introduced new areas of research. Aided by the insights, theory, and methodology of the social sciences, research in social, economic, demographic, and ethnohistory has supplanted the study of administrative and ecclesiastical institutions, the Black Legend in its multiple forms, and exploration and conquest (except for recent interest associated with the Quincentenary). Substantial scholarly interchange between historians from the United States, Latin American countries, and Europe has greatly enriched the field. Widespread use of computers, moreover, has facilitated major advances in prosopographical, demographic, and economic history.

Numerous scholars have explored the composition and background of colonial elites and laid to rest much previously accepted wisdom about creole exclusion from high office and conflict between creoles and peninsulars. A thorough examination of slavery has clarified the institution, its participants, and its conditions. Studies of the history of women have elucidated their various social and economic roles and considered marriage and sexuality. Prosopographical analyses of miners and merchants have given new social and economic dimensions to the time-worn topics of mining and trade. Secular and religious administrative history has expanded through prosopographical research. Although still in its infancy, price history has made some progress. Detailed examination of treasury records is clarifying royal income and expenditure and suggesting broad economic trends. Reexamination of labor systems has called into question the economic significance of debt peonage.

Increasingly historians have delved into new types of primary sources. In the late 1960s J. Lockhart turned colonialists' attention to notarial records as an important source for social history. More recently Lockhart and a number of his students have used Nahuatl-language documents in an effort to better understand the native societies of New Spain under Spanish rule. Historians have also studied legal cases that illuminate social and economic topics and have examined in detail late colonial censuses.

The most striking characteristic of research since the mid-1960s is its focus on regional studies. Regional and local history have nearly supplanted broader studies and shifted the focus to places such as Oaxaca, Guadalajara, Morelos, Lambayeque, Caracas, and the Bahia. This approach offers the advantages of probing an area in greater depth and of finishing the research in a reasonable period of time. The disadvantage is that until a number of similar studies have been completed for a variety of different locales, generalizations derived from a local or regional examination are at best only suggestive. Regional studies may also question, challenge, or affirm previously accepted generalizations. They have transformed, for example, the once stereotypical view of the *hacienda* (landed estate) in New Spain.

A tremendous surge in the number of colonialists, beginning in the 1960s, has led to greater exploitation of archival materials and an unprecedented volume of published research. It is surprising, however, that this research has not yet resulted in the kind of reappraisal of colonial history that occurred with the earlier demographic findings of the Berkeley school. By charting the disastrous and immediate decline of the native population in New Spain, its implications for colonial society, the economy, and labor institutions, and the subsequent stagnation and renewed growth of the population, these demographers established a periodization for the colony's history that continues to influence numerous historians. Although research of the past quarter-century has not made such a breakthrough, it has so enriched colonial historiography that one can now lecture easily on topics whose consideration was earlier impossible. The remainder of this essay will focus on topics that have dominated the literature in recent years.

Gibson's magisterial *The Aztecs Under Spanish Rule* (36.287) stimulated exciting research on American Indians in New Spain and other regions. William B. Taylor (37.292), J. K. Chance (37.341, 37.342), N. M. Farriss (36.286), K. Spalding (36.403), and B. Larson (37.353) have blended history and anthropology in outstanding examinations that, like Gibson's, follow a people's fate throughout the colonial era. Ann M. Wightman's detailed study (36.406) examines the causes and implications of natives abandoning their home villages. Together, these studies and others included in this bibliography have fleshed out a picture of indigenous life under Spanish rule in multiple locations that clarifies both the nature and extent of colonial exploitation and the ways in which the natives responded.

Much work in recent years has focused on the "seventeenth-century crisis"—its existence, duration, and causes—and what it meant for the relationship between Spain and the colonies. Particular attention has been paid to changes in silver production, its exportation, and government revenues. The issue is clouded, however, by the fact that figures for silver production are for registered, and hence taxed, silver. While the existence of contraband bullion is well known, its extent has yet to be determined, although suggestive figures are now available.

What is presently termed "seventeenth-century crisis" was initially defined as a depression and focused on New Spain. In his brilliant monograph *New Spain's Century of Depression* (37.243), W. Borah used demographic data to argue that New Spain's economy contracted after 1576. Subsequent research challenged both the alleged cause (labor shortage) and the duration (for more than a century) of this depression. Central to the discussion has been silver production, the motor of New Spain's external trade. Peter J. Bakewell (37.241) demonstrated that a shortage of mercury rather than labor was responsible for a decline in silver production that, in any case, began later, in the 1630s. Jonathan I. Israel (37.267) asserted in a provocative article that Mexico suffered from a prolonged depression from 1620 to the 1660s, thus reinforcing the concept of crisis although refining its duration. Taking a longer view, J. J. TePaske and H. S. Klein

(37.295) countered on the basis of fiscal records that New Spain's registered (not total) silver production was greater at the end of the seventeenth century than at the beginning, and that the economy, while it went through cyclical advances and declines, overall was probably stagnant rather than depressed during the seventeenth century. Richard L. Garner's long-term registered silver production figures (37.260) confirmed the absence of a prolonged depression and the upward trend of silver production. Louisa S. Hoberman (37.312) rejected the use of the term "depression" and contended that the economy's "contraction" lasted only from the 1640s to the 1660s or 1670s. Richard Boyer (37.338) argued against the existence of a depression, contending that New Spain underwent a transition to capitalism, economic diversification, and vibrant regional economies. The last word has yet to be written concerning New Spain's "depression," "transition," or "contraction" in the seventeenth century. All that seems clear now is that until there is a better appreciation of actual bullion production, in contrast to the smaller figures for registered production, the debate will continue.

In contrast to the case for New Spain, the existence of seventeenth-century crises in Central America and Peru seems clear. Murdo J. MacLeod (37.276) has argued convincingly for a lengthy depression in Central America from the 1630s to 1690, and in some ways beyond, based on a labor shortage and the lack of a cash crop. For Peru, P. J. Bakewell's (37.239) figures for registered (not total) production at Potosí show declining silver production from the early 1590s until the 1730s. Employing fiscal records for Peru, K. J. Andrien (37.152) has supported the existence of a fiscal crisis there, with roots in declining mining production evident in the 1620s. It developed into a major crisis by the 1660s and continued into the eighteenth century.

Although the decline of mining production in seventeenth-century Peru has long been established, the magnitude of the gap between registered and actual bullion production remains debatable and ignorance precludes rendering a final judgment on the extent of the seventeenth-century crisis. Figures based primarily on reports in Dutch gazettes, published by M. Morineau (37.314), indicate that amounts of American bullion (and thus trade) reaching Europe in the late seventeenth century were substantially higher than production estimates based on registered bullion. Building on his earlier examination of Spain under the Habsburgs that stressed the growing economic independence of the colonies during the seventeenth century, J. Lynch (29.19) employed Morineau's figures in his revised work and further strengthened his argument. Lynch's conclusion that Spain suffered a depression in the seventeenth century but that the colonies did not remains provocative but disputable. Additional regional economic studies and a better understanding of total bullion production and exportation will help to resolve this question.

The explosion of publications since the mid-1960s is most pronounced for eighteenth-century topics, particularly those addressing Bourbon reforms during the rule of Charles III. Substantial attention, too, has been paid to social and economic history after mid-century. The result is a better appreciation of both the continuities between Habsburg and Bourbon rule and the limited and regionally varied consequences of the reforms. Much work remains to be done on the early decades of Bourbon rule, however, although a few studies, for example, M. A. Burkholder and D. S. Chandler (37.155), have analyzed specific aspects of the first half of the eighteenth century within the context of broader examinations.

Bourbon efforts to reassert control over the colonies accelerated after the British capture of Havana. Subsequent attempts to increase government revenue, reform administration, and improve defense have attracted the attention of numerous historians since the mid-1960s. Brian R. Hamnett, D. A. Brading, L. Arnold, and D. S. Chandler, among others, have studied attempts at administrative reform in Mexico. Brading's argument (37.482) that the reforms constituted a "revolution in government" has been widely, but not universally, accepted. Similar studies for Peru include books by J. R. Fisher (37.499) and K. W. Brown (37.483). Susan M. Socolow (37.554) examined the creation of a viceregal bureaucracy in Buenos Aires. Jacques A. Barbier (37.476) demonstrated the persistence of a pre-reform political culture in Chile and thus challenged the wholesale applicability of Brading's "revolution in government."

Prior to the 1970s only L. N. McAlister (37.530) had examined military reform after the loss of Havana. Since then the creation of standing armies and expansion of militias has been thoroughly documented in books by C. I. Archer (37.474) for Mexico; L. G. Campbell (37.490) for Peru; and A. J. Kuethe (37.520, 37.519) for New Granada and Cuba.

Knowledge of merchants, commerce, and mining has been greatly improved as a result of studies by Brading (37.482), Socolow (37.554), J. E. Kicza (37.515), and Fisher (37.500, 29.174). Nils Jacobsen and H. J. Puhle (37.512) have edited a rich set of essays comparing the economies of Peru and New Spain, 1760–1810.

The idea of an eighteenth-century *pax hispanica*, broken rarely by rebellions and riots, has been seriously shaken in works by S. J. Stern (37.558), F. Katz (38.239), W. B. Taylor (36.307), J. R. Fisher et al. (37.501), and K. J. Andrien (37.473).

Taken together, eighteenth-century studies have dispelled the pre-1960s notion that the change of dynasties in 1700 inaugurated a new era for Spanish America. They have, moreover, underscored the divergent courses of reform in different regions of the empire and emphasized regional social and economic diversity. For New Spain, where the viceroyalty has attracted the most attention, there is now an appreciation that economic conditions for the majority of the population began deteriorating in the latter part of the century, despite an ever increasing silver production. Thus the once rosy view of the outcome of the Bourbon reforms is fading.

Compared to the outpouring of literature on colonial Spanish America, the attention given to colonial Brazil has been slight. Outstanding books that deserve notice, however, include those by D. Alden (37.457); A.J.R. Russell-Wood (37.393); K. R. Maxwell (37.465); and S. B. Schwartz (37.172, 37.284).

Special mention should be made of important contributions by Latin American and European historians that are now being translated into English. For example, M. Góngora's collection of essays (37.83) and work by E. Tandeter (37.268) are now available. Unfortunately, E. Florescano's seminal study (37.503) in price history has not yet been translated into English, but its influence on subsequent work in English has been substantial. The French *mentalité* approach is exemplified in studies by J. Lafaye (37.413) and N. Wachtel (36.405), and in a forthcoming book by S. Gruzinski.

Sorely lacking, until recently, have been broad synthetic histories of the colonial period that incorporated the literature written since the mid-1960s. Cambridge University Press recently devoted two volumes of the multivolume *Cambridge History of Latin America* (37.71) to the colonial period. Syntheses are now available for Mexico (C. M. MacLachlan and J. E. Rodríguez O 37.91), for Latin America to 1700 (L. N. McAlister 37.92), for the whole of the colonial world, (M. A. Burkholder and L. L. Johnson 37.73; J. Lockhart and S. B. Schwartz 37.89), and for the Borderlands or Spanish frontier in North America (D. J. Weber 37.601). Recent publications about both Spain and her empire by J. Lynch (29.18, 29.19, 29.20) also deserve special notice.

While the publications of the last quarter century opened new paths and clarified some old topics, large gaps still need to be filled. Chronologically, the seventeenth and early eighteenth centuries remain only lightly touched, although the situation has improved considerably with publications by P. J. Bakewell (37.241), J. I. Israel (37.350), and K. Andrien (37.152). Compared to New Spain, all other regions of the Spanish empire as well as Brazil remain understudied. Despite gains made in the study about colonial women, no major monograph focusing on them has yet appeared. Study of the consequences of ecological change resulting from the introduction of European animals remains in its infancy despite the well-known work by A. Crosby (37.142) on the Columbian exchange. Far too little is known about popular culture. It is clear that opportunities still abound for original, creative research on colonial Latin America.

The bibliography that follows focuses primarily on readily available English-language materials. The availability and utility of the Griffin and Warren *Guide* (37.35) allows this bibliography to focus principally on publications since the mid-1960s. The user should note that a number of publications included in section 36, "Native Peoples of the Americas" and section 38, "Latin America since 1800" also contain material of use to colonialists.

Entries are arranged under the following headings:

Reference Works
  Guides, Encyclopedias, and Atlases
  Bibliographic Aids

General Studies

Exploration and Early Settlement of the Caribbean

Conquest and Early Settlement of Mexico and Central America

Conquest and Early Settlement of South America

Intellectual Problems Raised by Conquest and the Columbian Exchange

Imperial Organization and Administration

Church and Inquisition

Changes in the Colonial Population

African Slavery and the Slave Trade

Economy

Commerce

Defense

Colonial Society

Cities and the Urban Environment

Cultural Life and Institutions

Spanish America, 1680s–1760s

Brazil in the Age of Expansion

Reform and Expansion in Spanish America, 1760s–1800

Spanish Borderlands

[Contributors: DGS=David G. Sweet, DJW = David J. Weber, EH-D = Evelyn Hu-DeHart, FEH = Frederick E. Hoxie, HM = Harvey Markowitz, JML = Jennifer M. Lloyd, JPG = Jack P. Greene, KLJ = Kristine L. Jones, MAB = Mark A. Burkholder, MFB = Marguerite F. Beeby, MWH = Mary W. Helms, NDC = Noble David Cook, RJW = Richard J. Walter, SHB=Suzanne H. Burkholder, SLE = Stanley L. Engerman, SS = Susan Schroeder, TC = Thomas Cohen]

REFERENCE WORKS

Guides, Encyclopedias, and Atlases

37.1 Thomas C. Barnes, Thomas H. Naylor, and Charles W. Polzer. *Northern New Spain: a research guide.* Tucson: University of Arizona Press, 1981. ISBN 0-8165-0709-0 (pbk). ‣ Introduction to types of colonial documentation, location of documentary collections, structure of government, types of colonial officials, money and currency, and weights and measures. Useful to all colonialists. [MAB]

37.2 Silvio A. Bedini, ed. *The Christopher Columbus encyclopedia.* 2 vols. New York: Simon & Schuster, 1992. ISBN 0-13-142662-1 (set), 0-13-142670-2 (v. 1), 0-13-142688-5 (v. 2). ‣ Entries by numerous scholars on European and American subjects that figure prominently in European expansion abroad to about 1620 with heavy emphasis on Columbus. One of most useful reference works available for age of exploration and early settlement. [MAB]

37.3 Harold Blakemore and Clifford T. Smith, eds. *Latin America: geographical perspectives.* 2d ed. London: Methuen, 1983. ISBN 0-416-32830-X (pbk). ‣ Eleven chapters with country or multi-country focus by seven authors. Very useful geographical introduction to Latin America with some attention to precolonial and colonial eras. [MAB]

37.4 Moshe Brawer. *Atlas of South America.* New York: Simon & Schuster, 1991. ISBN 0-13-050642-7. ‣ Most recent atlas available. Sections on major geographical features, flora and fauna, mineral resources, population, and history. Also sections on each country. Excellent maps and illustrations. [MAB]

37.5 Mark A. Burkholder. *Biographical dictionary of councilors of the Indies, 1717–1808.* Westport, Conn.: Greenwood, 1986. ISBN 0-313-24024-8. ‣ Biographical entries for 172 men who were named to or served on Council of Indies from 1717 to 1808. Provides information on careers and some genealogical material. [MAB]

37.6 Mark A. Burkholder and D. S. Chandler. *Biographical dictionary of Audiencia ministers in the Americas, 1687–1821.* Westport, Conn.: Greenwood, 1982. ISBN 0-313-22038-7. ‣ Biographical entries for 697 men named to serve on Spain's colonial Audiencias from 1687 to 1821. Provides information on careers and some genealogical material. [MAB]

37.7 Gilbert J. Butland. *Latin America: a regional geography.* 3d ed. New York: Wiley, 1972. ISBN 0-470-12658-2. ‣ Basic geography including overview of physical and economic endowments. Surveys geographical characteristics either by country or region. [MAB]

37.8 Simon Collier, Thomas E. Skidmore, and Harold Blakemore, eds. *The Cambridge encyclopedia of Latin America and the Caribbean.* 2d ed. Cambridge: Cambridge University Press, 1992. ISBN 0-521-41322-2. ‣ General reference work with sections on physical environments, economy, peoples, history, politics and society, and dimensions of culture. Numerous excellent maps and tables. [MAB]

37.9 Helen Delpar, ed. *Encyclopedia of Latin America.* New York: McGraw-Hill, 1974. ISBN 0-07-055645-8. ‣ Provides information on history, economy, politics, arts, and other aspects of Latin America. Includes entries on individuals, events, institutions, organizations, and terminology. Finest single-volume reference work on Latin America. [MAB]

37.10 Peter Gerhard. *A guide to the historical geography of New Spain.* New York: Cambridge University Press, 1972. ISBN 0-521-08073-8. ‣ Maps and historical narrative for each of 129 *alcaldías mayores* (administrative districts) in central and southern Mexico from 1519 to 1821. Extraordinarily valuable reference work. [MAB/SS]

37.11 Peter Gerhard. *The north frontier of New Spain.* Princeton: Princeton University Press, 1982. ISBN 0-691-09394-6. ‣ Maps and historical narrative for each *alcaldía mayor* (administrative district) of Nueva Galicia, Nueva Vizcaya, Sinaloa, Sonora, and other regions of northern Mexico from 1519 to 1821. Extraordinarily valuable reference work. [MAB]

37.12 Peter Gerhard. *The southeast frontier of New Spain.* Princeton: Princeton University Press, 1979. ISBN 0-691-05273-5. ‣ Maps and historical narrative for each provincial administrative unit of Yucatán, Laguna de Términos, Chiapas, and Soconusco from 1517 to 1821. Extraordinarily valuable reference work. [MAB]

37.13 Richard E. Greenleaf and Michael C. Meyer, eds. and comps. *Research in Mexican history: topics, methodology, sources, and a practical guide to field research.* Lincoln: University of Nebraska Press, 1973. ISBN 0-8032-5773-2. ‣ Excellent introduction for beginning scholar. Includes review of major documentary collections, suggested research topics, and bibliographic aids. Essays contributed by numerous authors. [MAB]

37.14 Kenneth J. Grieb et al., eds. *Research guide to Central America and the Caribbean.* Madison: University of Wisconsin Press, 1985. ISBN 0-299-10050-2. ‣ Guide to archival repositories or research centers, their holdings, and conditions of access. Includes essays identifying future directions for research. Eighty-three chapters by different authors. Essential introduction to research. [MAB]

37.15 Lewis Hanke and Celso Rodríguez, comps. *Guía de las fuentes en el Archivo General de Indias para el estudio de la administración española en México y en el Perú, 1535–1700.* 3 vols. Cologne: Böhlau, 1977. ISBN 3-412-05176-4. ▸ Discussion of viceregal administration, providing brief biographies and bibliographies of viceroys and presenting catalog of correspondence and documents of viceroys located in General Archives of the Indies. Fundamental starting point for research on many topics using materials in this archive. [MAB]

37.16 David P. Henige. *Colonial governors from the fifteenth century to the present: a comprehensive list.* Madison: University of Wisconsin Press, 1970. ISBN 0-299-05440-3. ▸ Comprehensive compilation for thirteen colonizing countries. Includes listings of viceroys, presidents, captains-general, and governors as relevant for Spanish America and Brazil. Valuable reference tool. [MAB]

37.17 Cathryn L. Lombardi, John V. Lombardi, and K. Lynn Stoner. *Latin American history: a teaching atlas.* Madison: University of Wisconsin Press for the Conference on Latin American History, 1983. ISBN 0-299-09710-2 (cl), 0-299-09714-5 (pbk). ▸ One hundred and four maps on environment, Iberian background, Indian background, discovery and conquest, administrative districts, trade, resources, competition, independence, modern boundaries, international relations, population, economies, and society. Very useful. [MAB]

37.18 Sara de Mundo Lo. *Index to Spanish American collective biography.* 4 vols. Boston: Hall, 1981–85. ISBN 0-8161-8181-0 (v. 1), 0-8161-8529-8 (v. 2), 0-8161-8636-7 (v. 3), 0-8161-8650-2 (v. 4). ▸ Useful selective bibliography designed to provide access to information about lives of individuals associated with Latin American history, culture, and institutions: 922 entries for Mexico; 1,060 for Andean countries. [MAB]

37.19 Clara Louisa Penney. *Printed books, 1468–1700, in the Hispanic Society of America: a listing.* New York: Hispanic Society of America, 1965. ▸ Very useful catalog of extensive rare book collection, including numerous publications by Spanish American as well as Spanish authors. Presented in alphabetical order by author with useful cross-references. [MAB]

37.20 John Jay TePaske et al. *Research guide to Andean history: Bolivia, Chile, Ecuador, and Peru.* Durham, N.C.: Duke University Press, 1981. ISBN 0-8223-0450-3. ▸ Valuable introduction, by numerous experienced contributors, to research materials and archives for both colonial and national periods. Includes suggestions for further research. [MAB]

37.21 David P. Werlich. *Research tools for Latin American historians: a select, annotated bibliography.* New York: Garland, 1980. ISBN 0-8240-9762-9. ▸ More than one thousand entries by source type and by individual countries. Entries to materials in English, Spanish, Portuguese, French, and German. More useful to historians of modern Latin America than colonialists. [MAB]

Bibliographic Aids

37.22 "The Americas: a cumulative index, volumes 21–47, July, 1964 through April, 1991." *The Americas* 48.1 (1991) 9–128. ISSN 0003-1615. ▸ Companion piece to index published in 1967 for volumes 1–20. Entries by author, title, and subject. Very helpful bibliographic tool. [MAB]

37.23 Jacques A. Barbier and Mark A. Burkholder. "Colonial Spanish America: the Bourbon period." *History teacher* 20.2 (1987) 221–50. ISSN 0018-2745. ▸ Two hundred thirty-nine entries to material useful in preparing lectures, assigning essay topics, and orienting graduate students. Divided into introductory overview, selected topics, and major regions. [MAB]

37.24 Joseph D. Bernard and Randall Rasmussen. "A bibliography of bibliographies for the history of Mexico." *Latin American research review* 13.2 (1978) 229–35. ISSN 0023-8791. ▸ Lists

159 bibliographies, both well known and obscurely located, to facilitate access to aspects of Mexican history from preconquest to 1970s. Valuable compilation. [MAB]

37.25 *Bibliographic guide to Latin American studies.* Boston: Hall, 1978–. ISSN 0162-5314. ▸ Annual guide containing items cataloged at University of Texas at Austin and additional items from Library of Congress with full catalog information. [MAB]

37.26 Woodrow Borah. "Trends in recent studies of colonial Latin American cities." *Hispanic American historical review* 64.3 (1984) 535–54. ISSN 0018-2168. ▸ Focuses on studies published in 1970s and early 1980s. Concludes state of literature precludes many well-founded generalizations. Careful, wide-ranging review. [MAB]

37.27 Rubens Borba de Moraes. *Bibliographia Brasiliana: rare books about Brazil published from 1504 to 1900 and works by Brazilian authors of the colonial period.* Rev. ed. 2 vols. Los Angeles: University of California Press at Los Angeles, Latin American Center Publications, 1983. (Reference series, 10.) ISBN 0-87903-109-3 (set). ▸ Revised edition of 1958 work completed in 1979. Annotated entries; full index. Very valuable compilation. [MAB]

37.28 Frederick P. Bowser. "The African in colonial Spanish America: reflections on research achievements and priorities." *Latin American research review* 7.1 (1972) 77–94. ISSN 0023-8791. ▸ Important review of earlier research, analysis of research problems, and suggestions for future research by preeminent scholar of topic. [MAB]

37.29 Fred Bronner. "Urban society in colonial Spanish America: research trends." *Latin American research review* 21.1 (1986) 7–72. ISSN 0023-8791. ▸ Excellent analysis of broadly defined literature relating to urban society. Updates earlier reviews by Lockhart (37.44) and Mörner (37.48). [MAB]

37.30 Leon G. Campbell. "Recent research on Andean peasant revolts, 1750–1820." *Latin American research review* 14.1 (1979) 3–49. ISSN 0023-8791. ▸ Useful review of availability of primary sources, secondary works, unpublished materials, general histories of Andean peasant revolts, and relationship between Bourbon reforms, economy, cultural nationalism, and peasant rebellions. [MAB]

37.31 Marcello Carmagnani. "The inertia of Clio: the social history of colonial Mexico." *Latin American research review* 20.1 (1985) 149–66. ISSN 0023-8791. ▸ Keen analysis of literature published primarily in 1970s, emphasizing shift from institutional to social and economic perspectives. Suggests new periodization with focus on 1640s to 1730s. Debate follows in *Latin American Research Review* 20.1 (1985) 176–83. [MAB]

37.32 Daniel Raposo Cordeiro et al. *A bibliography of Latin American bibliographies: social sciences and humanities.* Vol. 1. Metuchen, N.J.: Scarecrow, 1979. ISBN 0-8108-1170-7. ▸ Supplements original works by Arthur E. Gropp. Most imprints listed are 1969–74 for monographs and 1966–74 for periodical articles. Continuation of important bibliographic aid (37.36, 37.37). [MAB]

37.33 Francis A. Dutra. *A guide to the history of Brazil, 1500–1822: the literature in English.* Santa Barbara, Calif.: ABC-Clio, 1980. ISBN 0-87436-263-6 (cl), 0-87436-292-X (pbk). ▸ Extraordinary annotated bibliography of 939 items including books, chapters, essays, articles, documents, and dissertations. Index of authors, editors, translators, and illustrators. [MAB]

37.34 Charles Gibson. "Writings on colonial Mexico." *Hispanic American historical review* 55.2 (1975) 287–323. ISSN 0018-2168. ▸ Masterful review of historiography of preceding thirty years with sections on age of conquest, postconquest sixteenth century, seventeenth century, eighteenth century, and topics and trends. [MAB]

37.35 Charles C. Griffin and J. Benedict Warren, eds. *Latin America: a guide to the historical literature.* Austin: University of Texas Press for the Conference on Latin American History, 1971. (Conference on Latin American History publications, 4.) ISBN 0-292-70089-X. ▸ Fundamental annotated bibliography with six sections: reference, general background, colonial Latin America, independence, and postindependence. Entries (7,087) primarily to works in Spanish and English. [MAB]

37.36 Arthur E. Gropp, ed. *A bibliography of Latin American bibliographies published in periodicals.* 2 vols. Metuchen, N.J.: Scarecrow, 1976. ISBN 0-8108-0838-2. ▸ Companion work to 37.37. List of bibliographic work in periodicals through 1965 on virtually all topics; 9,715 entries. Author-subject index. Important resource. [MAB]

37.37 Arthur E. Gropp et al., eds. *A bibliography of Latin American bibliographies* with *Supplements.* 5 vols. Metuchen, N.J.: Scarecrow, 1968-87. ISBN 0-8108-1170-7 (2d suppl.), 0-8108-1524-9 (3d suppl.), 0-8108-1941-4 (4th suppl.) ▸ Updates 1942 work of same title by C. K. Jones. Three supplements have been published. Organized by nearly seventy subjects. Encyclopedic coverage; starting point for many topics. [MAB]

37.38 *Hispanic American periodicals index.* Los Angeles: UCLA Latin American Center Publications, 1975–. ISSN 0270-8558. ▸ Annual guide to articles in major Western languages of interest to Latin Americanists and, since 1977, to materials about Hispanic population in United States. Important bibliographic tool. [MAB]

37.39 "Index to *Hispanic American Historical Review,* 1976–1985." *Hispanic American historical review* 66.1 (1986) 1–225. ISSN 0018-2168. ▸ Author-title index, topical index, tables of contents, obituaries, editors of *Hispanic American Historical Review,* officers of Conference on Latin American History, and editorial and advisory board members. [MAB]

37.40 Benjamin Keen. "Main currents in United States writings on colonial Spanish America, 1884–1984." *Hispanic American historical review* 65.4 (1985) 657–82. ISSN 0018-2168. ▸ Important review of historiographic trends rather than detailed bibliography. Points out political, social, economic, and cultural factors influencing historians. [MFB]

37.41 John E. Kicza. "The social and ethnic historiography of colonial Latin America: the last twenty years." *William and Mary quarterly,* Third series, 45 (1988) 453–88. ISSN 0043-5597. ▸ Fine historiographical review including references to unpublished dissertations as well as published secondary sources. [MAB]

37.42 Herbert S. Klein and Jacques A. Barbier. "Recent trends in the study of Spanish American colonial public finance." *Latin American research review* 23.1 (1988) 35–62. ISSN 0023-8791. ▸ Valuable introduction to rapidly expanding literature. Discusses benefits and difficulties in using annual statements of colonial treasuries and implications of early studies for seventeenth-century crisis and eighteenth-century imperialism. [MAB]

37.43 Meri Knaster. *Women in Spanish America: an annotated bibliography from pre-conquest to contemporary times.* Boston: Hall, 1977. ISBN 0-8161-7865-8. ▸ Multidisciplinary bibliography of 2,534 entries divided topically, with 101 entries for conquest and colonial era. Includes unpublished dissertations and Master's theses. Author and subject indexes. Pioneering compilation. [MAB]

37.44 James Lockhart. "The social history of colonial Spanish America: evolution and potential." *Latin American research review* 7.1 (1972) 6–45. ISSN 0023-8791. ▸ Essential review of variety of sources available for writing social history as well as historical literature that has employed them. [MAB]

37.45 John V. Lombardi et al. *Venezuelan history: a comprehen-*

sive working bibliography. Boston: Hall, 1977. ISBN 0-8161-7876-3. ▸ Extremely helpful compilation of 4,647 entries, about 350 of which specifically treat history of colonial era. Variety of other sections including church, civilization, education, geography, and population. Author index. [MAB]

37.46 Sidney David Markman, comp. *Colonial Central America: a bibliography.* Tempe: Arizona State University, Center for Latin American Studies, 1977. ISBN 0-87918-023-4. ▸ Annotated bibliography of 1,446 titles divided into colonial and modern period, art and architectural history (general), art and architecture (colonial Guatemala), bibliography, documentary sources, maps and plans. Catalog of 704 documents. [MAB]

37.47 Frédéric Mauro. "Recent works on the political economy of Brazil in the Portuguese empire." *Latin American research review* 19.1 (1984) 87–105. ISSN 0023-8791. ▸ Reviews historiographical developments since 1970, emphasizing recent advances in knowledge. Good summary. [MAB]

37.48 Magnus Mörner. "The Spanish American *hacienda*: a survey of recent research and debate." *Hispanic American historical review* 53.2 (1973) 183–216. ISSN 0018-2168. ▸ Excellent review of historiography. Emphasizes absurdity of investigations stopping in 1810 and suggests directions for further research. [MAB]

37.49 Walter Bernard Redmond. *Bibliography of the philosophy in the Iberian colonies of America.* The Hague: Nijhoff, 1972. ISBN 90-247-1190-8. ▸ Catalog of colonial philosophical writings, both in manuscript and printed form (1,154 entries) and related secondary literature (275 entries). Indispensable guide for intellectual historians. [MAB]

37.50 Stanley R. Ross et al., eds. *Guide to the Hispanic American historical review, 1956–1975.* Durham, N.C.: Duke University Press, 1980. ISBN 0-8223-0429-5. ▸ Very useful, succinct summaries of articles, notes, and comments. Principal sections on colonial history, organized by region; wars of independence; and national period, organized by region or country. Includes book reviews. [MAB]

37.51 A.J.R. Russell-Wood. "United States scholarly contributions to the historiography of colonial Brazil." *Hispanic American historical review* 65.4 (1985) 683–723. ISSN 0018-2168. ▸ Important survey, including list of doctoral dissertations on colonial Brazil, 1892–1984. Laments waning interest in colonial Brazil and paucity of debates on historical issues. [MAB]

37.52 William F. Sater, ed. *The history teacher: special issue on teaching Latin American history.* Long Beach: California State University for the Society for History Education, 1981. (*History Teacher,* 14.3.) ISSN 0018-2745. ▸ Nine essays outlining basic bibliography for teaching Argentine, Chilean, and Peruvian history. Covers women, family, colonial military, and military-civilian relations since independence. Good initial bibliographies. [MAB]

37.53 Stuart B. Schwartz. "Brazil: the colonial period." In *Latin American scholarship since World War II: trends in history, political science, literature, geography, and economics.* Roberto Esquenazi-Mayo and Michael C. Meyer, eds., pp. 23–49. Lincoln: University of Nebraska Press, 1971. ISBN 0-8032-0783-2. ▸ Valuable introduction to literature for period covered. Emphasizes changes and increased professionalization in colonial Brazilian historiography during preceding twenty-five years. [MAB]

37.54 Stuart B. Schwartz. "State and society in colonial Spanish America: an opportunity for prosopography." In *New approaches to Latin American history.* Richard Graham and Peter H. Smith, eds., pp. 3–35. Austin: University of Texas Press, 1974. ISBN 0-292-75506-6. ▸ Important essay underscoring potential of prosopography to reveal social and economic ties of bureaucrats to local societies and thus to clarify bases for decisions they made. [MAB]

37.55 Susan Migden Socolow. "Recent historiography of the Río de la Plata: colonial and early national periods." *Hispanic American historical review* 64.1 (1984) 105–20. ISSN 0018-2168. ‣ Review of literature of preceding decade, emphasizing exciting work in economic and social history and suggesting topics for further research. Thoughtful analysis. [MAB]

37.56 Karen Spalding. "The colonial Indian: past and future research and perspectives." *Latin American research review* 7.1 (1972) 47–76. ISSN 0023-8791. ‣ Still impressive review focused on Peru and on productive interplay between history and anthropology. Emphasizes benefits from reexamining traditional sources from new perspectives. [MAB]

37.57 K. Lynn Stoner. "Directions in Latin American women's history, 1977–1985." *Latin American research review* 21.1 (1986) 202–09. ISSN 0023-8791. ‣ Wide-ranging review of historical writing, emphasizing increased integration of female experience with major historical themes. Examines works for both colonial and national periods. [MAB]

37.58 John Jay TePaske. "Quantification in Latin American colonial history." In *The dimensions of the past: materials, problems, and opportunities for quantitative work in history.* Val R. Lorwin and Jacob M. Price, eds., pp. 431–76. New Haven: Yale University Press, 1972. ISBN 0-300-01439-2. ‣ Fine introduction to topic. Examines previous use of quantification and availability of data. Provides suggestions for further investigation and extensive bibliography of secondary sources. [MAB]

37.59 John Jay TePaske. "Recent trends in quantitative history: colonial Latin America." *Latin American research review* 10.1 (1975) 51–62. ISSN 0023-8791. ‣ Valuable survey of work published since 1970. Complements earlier work on quantification in Latin American colonial history (37.58). Emphasizes extensive quantifiable archival sources available and laments gulf between quantifiers and nonquantifiers. [MAB]

37.60 John Jay TePaske. "Spanish America: the colonial period." In *Latin American scholarship since World War II: trends in history, political science, literature, geography, and economics.* Roberto Esquenazi-Mayo and Michael C. Meyer, eds., pp. 5–22. Lincoln: University of Nebraska Press, 1971. ISBN 0-8032-0783-2. ‣ Examination of research trends of preceding twenty-five years, noting shifts from prior emphases, new approaches, and major contributions. Very useful statement for period covered; good introduction to earlier historical studies. [MAB]

37.61 Jack Ray Thomas. *Biographical dictionary of Latin American historians and historiography.* Westport, Conn.: Greenwood, 1984. ISBN 0-313-23004-8. ‣ Biographical sketches of early Spanish chroniclers of Latin America and Latin American historians to mid-twentieth century. Valuable introduction to their lives and works. [MAB]

37.62 University of Texas at Austin. *Catalog of the Latin American Collection* and *Supplements.* 31 vols.; 19 suppl. vols. Boston: Hall, 1969–77. ISSN 0098-8804 (supplements). ‣ Complete listing of largest Latin American collection in United States through reproduction of card catalog. Four supplements totaling nineteen volumes published through 1977. Invaluable bibliographic aid. [MAB]

37.63 Eric Van Young. "Mexican rural history since Chevalier: the historiography of the colonial *hacienda.*" *Latin American research review* 18.3 (1983) 5–61. ISSN 0023-8791. ‣ Excellent review of literature of Mexican rural history written since early 1950s. Notes new works, new methodologies, and new sources employed. Suggestions for future research. [MAB]

37.64 Eric Van Young. "Recent Anglophone scholarship on Mexico and Central America in the age of revolution (1750–1850)." *Hispanic American historical review* 65.4 (1985) 725–43.

ISSN 0018-2168. ‣ Outstanding analysis of published works and areas needing further research. [MAB]

37.65 Henry R. Wagner. *The Spanish Southwest, 1542–1794: an annotated bibliography.* 1937 ed. 2 vols. New York: Arno, 1968. (Quivira Society publications, 7.1–2.) ISBN 0-405-00079-0 (set). ‣ Spanish imprints and their subsequent editions and translations meticulously described in chronological order. Based on first-hand examination of rare imprints in numerous collections. Remains indispensable. [DJW]

37.66 Peter Walne, ed. *A guide to manuscript sources for the history of Latin America and the Caribbean in the British Isles.* London: Oxford University Press for University of London, Institute of Latin American Studies, 1973. ISBN 0-19-818152-3. ‣ Repositories and materials are listed in alphabetical order of English counties, then Scotland, Wales, Northern Ireland, and Republic of Ireland. Lists some remarkable documents. [MAB]

37.67 Christopher Ward. "Historical writing on colonial Panama." *Hispanic American historical review* 69.4 (1989) 691–713. ISSN 0018-2168. ‣ Valuable overview of little-known literature, suggesting topics for further research. [MAB]

37.68 Elizabeth Wilder Weismann. "The history of art in Latin America, 1500–1800: some trends and challenges in the last decade." *Latin American research review* 10.1 (1975) 7–50. ISSN 0023-8791. ‣ Bibliography of serious research published since 1963. Emphasizes need for publication of documents, fieldwork, and photographic catalogs of colonial art. Valuable listing and commentary. [MAB]

37.69 Richard D. Woods. *Reference materials on Latin America in English: the humanities.* Metuchen, N.J.: Scarecrow, 1980. ISBN 0-8108-1294-0. ‣ Listing of 1,252 annotated reference works on virtually every conceivable topic listed in alphabetical order by author. Includes some works rarely encountered elsewhere. Author, title, and subject indexes. [MAB]

GENERAL STUDIES

37.70 Dauril Alden, ed. *Colonial roots of modern Brazil: papers of the Newberry Library Conference.* Berkeley: University of California Press, 1973. ISBN 0-520-02140-1. ‣ Seven papers on political and socioeconomic aspects of colonial Brazil by excellent historians. Includes historiographical essay by Charles Boxer, preeminent historian of Portuguese empire. Valuable collection. [MAB]

37.71 Leslie Bethell, ed. *Colonial Latin America.* Vols. 1–2 of *The Cambridge history of Latin America.* Cambridge: Cambridge University Press, 1984. ISBN 0-521-23223-6 (v. 1), 0-521-24516-8 (v. 2). ‣ Thirty-four chapters examining major topics of Spanish American and Brazilian history from preconquest to 1808. Most comprehensive history of colonial Latin America available in English. Invaluable work. [MAB]

37.72 D. A. Brading. *The first America: the Spanish monarchy, creole patriots, and the liberal state, 1492–1867.* Cambridge: Cambridge University Press, 1991. ISBN 0-521-39130-X. ‣ Detailed, highly original work examining efforts of Spanish Americans to define distinctive identity. Successfully integrates intellectual, social, economic, and political history. Primarily colonial history. [MAB]

37.73 Mark A. Burkholder and Lyman L. Johnson. *Colonial Latin America.* New York: Oxford University Press, 1990. ISBN 0-19-504542-4 (cl), 0-19-506110-1 (pbk). ‣ Synthetic work surveying Latin America from preconquest to independence. Special attention to social and economic topics and unusually full treatment to eighteenth century. [MAB]

37.74 Guillermo Céspedes del Castillo. *América hispánica (1492–1898).* Barcelona: Editorial Labor, S.A., 1983. ISBN 84-335-9437-

0 (cl), 84-335-9426-5 (pbk). ▸ Fine synthesis of colonial Spanish America that, unlike most overviews, includes discussion of territorial losses Spain suffered in Spanish-American War. [MAB]

37.75 Pierre Chaunu. *Sevilla y América: siglos 16 y 17*. Rafael Sánchez Mantero, trans. Sevilla: Universidad de Sevilla, 1983. (Anales de la Universidad Hispalense: Serie filosofia y letras, 65.) ISBN 84-7405-255-6. ▸ Brief authoritative survey extracted from author's voluminous studies of trade. Particularly valuable for numerous graphic summaries on trade. [MAB]

37.76 John H. Coatsworth. "Patterns of rural rebellion in Latin America: Mexico in comparative perspective." In *Riot, rebellion, and revolution: rural social conflict in Mexico*. Friedrich Katz, ed., pp. 21–62. Princeton: Princeton University Press, 1988. ISBN 0-691-07739-8 (cl), 0-691-02265-8 (pbk). ▸ Examination of types, frequency, location, and causes of rural rebellions from 1700 to 1899. Impressive analysis, concluding significance of rural rebellions remains underestimated. [MAB]

37.77 Bailey W. Diffie. *A history of colonial Brazil, 1500–1792*. Edwin J. Perkins, comp. Malabar, Fla.: Krieger, 1987. ISBN 0-89874-685-x (cl), 0-89464-214-6 (pbk). ▸ Detailed and informative survey of colonial Brazil from 1500 to 1792; posthumously completed. Particularly valuable discussion of Brazil's territorial expansion. [MAB]

37.78 Henry F. Dobyns and Paul L. Doughty. *Peru: a cultural history*. New York: Oxford University Press, 1976. ISBN 0-19-5-02089-8. ▸ Synthetic examination of Peruvian history, pre-Incas to 1975. Five chapters carry story to eve of independence. Fine introduction. [MAB]

37.79 John H. Elliott. *Imperial Spain, 1469–1716*. 1963 ed. New York: New American Library, 1977. ISBN 0-452-00465-9. ▸ Fundamental survey and indispensable background reading for all students of colonial Spanish America. Particularly helpful on international relations and political history. [MAB]

37.80 John H. Elliott. *The Old World and the New, 1492–1650*. 1970 ed. Cambridge: Cambridge University Press, 1992. ISBN 0-521-42709-6 (pbk). ▸ Four stimulating essays on impact of New World on sixteenth- and early seventeenth-century Europe. Valuable contribution particularly for intellectual history. [MAB]

37.81 Richard L. Garner and William B. Taylor, eds. and comps. *Iberian colonies, New World societies: essays in memory of Charles Gibson*. 1985 ed. University Park, Pa.: Garner, 1986. ▸ Eleven varied essays on topics ranging from immediate postconquest transitions to revolutionary language and breakup of empire. [MAB]

37.82 Charles Gibson. *Spain in America*. New York: Harper & Row, 1966. ISBN 0-06-133077-9 (pbk). ▸ General survey of Spain's colonies in New World. Remains superb introduction to field although treatment of eighteenth century in particular is dated. [MAB]

37.83 Mario Góngora. *Studies in the colonial history of Spanish America*. Richard Southern, trans. Cambridge: Cambridge University Press, 1975. ISBN 0-521-20686-3. ▸ Seven essays focused on conquest, Spain's right to rule, administration, forms of labor, Enlightenment, periodization, and New World in eschatological and utopian writings. Shows a master's touch. [MAB]

37.84 Clarence H. Haring. *The Spanish empire in America*. 1947 ed. San Diego, Calif.: Harcourt Brace Jovanovich, 1985. ISBN 0-15-684701-9 (pbk). ▸ Detailed history of Spanish empire in America with particular emphasis on its institutions. Still best institutional history available and valuable reference work. [MAB]

37.85 Alistair Hennessy. *The frontier in Latin American history*. Albuquerque: University of New Mexico Press, 1978. ISBN 0-8263-0466-4 (cl), 0-8263-0467-2 (pbk). ▸ Stimulating examination of application of Turner frontier thesis (40.120) to Latin America, discussing conquistadors, crown, and church; types of frontier; frontier society and culture; and contracting frontier. Compares frontier experiences of United States, Canada, Australia, and South Africa. [MAB]

37.86 Henry Kamen. *Spain, 1469–1714: a society of conflict*. 2d ed. London: Longman, 1991. ISBN 0-582-06723-5 (pbk). ▸ Survey of Spanish history with strong emphasis on social and economic matters. Good complement to Elliott's synthesis (37.79). Excellent background reading for colonialists. [MAB]

37.87 Benjamin Keen. *The Aztec image in Western thought*. 1971 ed. New Brunswick, N.J.: Rutgers University Press, 1990. ISBN 0-8135-1572-6 (pbk). ▸ Unique, detailed examination of changing views of Aztecs from conquest of Mexico to 1969 and their relationship to socioeconomic, political, and ideological patterns of their time. [MAB/SS]

37.88 James Lang. *Portuguese Brazil: the king's plantation*. New York: Academic Press, 1979. ISBN 0-12-436480-2. ▸ Good survey of colonial Brazil from Portuguese settlement to independence by historical sociologist. Concludes with comparative examination of imperial reorganization after 1750 in Spanish America, English America, and Brazil. [MAB]

37.89 James Lockhart and Stuart B. Schwartz. *Early Latin America: a history of colonial Spanish America and Brazil*. New York: Cambridge University Press, 1983. ISBN 0-521-23344-5 (cl), 0-521-29929-2 (pbk). ▸ Bold synthesis of Spanish American and Brazilian history from preconquest to independence, treating early Latin America as single unit. Emphasizes social and economic history. Notable sections on Brazil. [MAB]

37.90 Colin M. MacLachlan. *Spain's empire in the New World: the role of ideas in institutional and social change*. Berkeley: University of California Press, 1988. ISBN 0-520-05697-3. ▸ Analyzes philosophical matrix that enabled Habsburg monarchs to maintain flexible, stable governing system in America and Bourbon monarchs' unsuccessful efforts to overturn it. Stimulating, provocative essay. [MAB]

37.91 Colin M. MacLachlan and Jaime E. Rodríguez O. *The forging of the cosmic race: a reinterpretation of colonial Mexico*. Berkeley: University of California Press, 1980. ISBN 0-520-03890-8. ▸ Revisionist synthesis emphasizing emergence of mestizo society and development of balanced and integrated economy ended by destruction of silver mines at independence. Remains best survey of colonial Mexico. [MAB]

37.92 Lyle N. McAlister. *Spain and Portugal in the New World, 1492–1700*. Minneapolis: University of Minnesota Press, 1984. ISBN 0-8166-1216-1 (cl), 0-8166-1218-8 (pbk). ▸ Clear, detailed, general survey of Spanish and Portuguese empires in the Americas up to about 1700. Especially notable for emphasis on importance of Iberian background. [MAB]

37.93 Michael C. Meyer and William L. Sherman Sherman. *The course of Mexican history*. 4th ed. New York: Oxford University Press, 1991. ISBN 0-19-506599-9 (cl), 0-19-506600-6 (pbk). ▸ Synthesis of Mexican history from pre-Columbian times to date of publication. Substantial portion devoted to colonial Mexico. Leading work since original publication in 1979. [MAB]

37.94 Magnus Mörner. *The Andean past: land, societies, and conflicts*. New York: Columbia University Press, 1985. ISBN 0-231-04726-6. ▸ General survey from preconquest to early 1980s; over one-third devoted to colonial era. Valuable overview and introduction to subject. [MAB]

37.95 Luis Navarro García. *Hispanoamérica en el siglo 18*. Sevilla: Universidad de Sevilla, 1975. ISBN 84-600-6802-1. ▸ General survey of Spanish America and Brazil, emphasizing administration, economy and trade, defense, and international affairs.

Useful overview, giving more than usual attention to period before 1763. [MAB]

37.96 J. H. Parry. *The Spanish seaborne empire.* 1966 ed. Berkeley: University of California Press, 1990. ISBN 0-520-07140-9. ‣ Excellent detailed survey of Spanish empire in America from origins to independence. Particularly valuable for inclusion of Spanish historical context. [MAB]

37.97 J. H. Parry. *Trade and dominion: the European overseas empires in the eighteenth century.* 1971 ed. London: Sphere, 1974. ISBN 0-351-17742-6. ‣ Synthetic account, highlighting conflicts among empires around the world. Includes technical descriptions of ships and navigation. Provides comparative perspective for Latin America. [MAB]

37.98 J. H. Parry, Robert G. Keith, and Michael Francis Jimenez, eds. *New Iberian world: a documentary history of the discovery and settlement of Latin America to the early seventeenth century.* 5 vols. New York: Times Books, 1984. ISBN 0-8129-1070-2 (set). ‣ Translated documents on native societies; Iberian precedents; formal structure of empire; discovery; settlement of West Indies and discovery and conquest of Mexico, Central America, Andean regions, and other parts of South America. Monumental compilation of mostly traditional forms of documentation. [MAB]

37.99 Caio Prado Junior. *The colonial background of modern Brazil.* Suzette Macedo, trans. Berkeley: University of California Press, 1967. ‣ Long-popular examination of population and settlement, diverse aspects of material life, and social and political life. Remains informative introduction. [MAB]

37.100 Stanley J. Stein and Barbara H. Stein. *The colonial heritage of Latin America: essays on economic dependence in perspective.* New York: Oxford University Press, 1970. ‣ Six essays, four on colonial period, focusing on economy and society and emphasizing structures of dependence. Stimulating, provocative formulation. [MAB]

37.101 Ralph Lee Woodward, Jr. *Central America: a nation divided.* 2d ed. New York: Oxford University Press, 1985. ISBN 0-19-503592-5 (cl), 0-29-503593-3 (pbk). ‣ Synthetic examination from pre-Hispanic civilizations to 1975. Four chapters carry story through independence. Best survey available. [MAB]

SEE ALSO

EXPLORATION AND EARLY SETTLEMENT OF THE CARIBBEAN

37.102 Ferdinand Colón. *The life of the admiral Christopher Columbus by his son Ferdinand.* 1959 ed. Benjamin Keen, trans. and annotator. New Brunswick, N.J.: Rutgers University Press, 1992. ISBN 0-8135-1801-6. ‣ Sympathetic biography of famous explorer as recounted by his son. Based on Spanish and Italian versions. Valuable although biased source. New introduction added in 1992. [MAB]

37.103 Christopher Columbus. *The Diario of Christopher Columbus's first voyage to America, 1492–1493: abstracted by Fray Bar-* *tolomé de Las Casas.* Oliver Dunn and James E. Kelley, Jr., trans. Norman: University of Oklahoma Press, 1989. ISBN 0-8061-2101-7. ‣ Best translation and transcription of Columbus's logbook of first voyage as abstracted by Las Casas. Includes introduction on procedure and concordance. See Henige 37.106 for caveats on this source. [MAB]

37.104 Felipe Fernández-Armesto. *Columbus.* 1991 ed. New York: Oxford University Press, 1992. ISBN 0-19-215898-8 (cl, 1991), 0-19-285260-4 (pbk). ‣ Fine up-to-date biography delving into character of explorer as well as recounting his efforts at court, four voyages to New World, and his final days. [MAB]

37.105 Troy S. Floyd. *The Columbus dynasty in the Caribbean, 1492–1526.* Albuquerque: University of New Mexico Press, 1973. ISBN 0-8263-0283-1. ‣ Useful account of early colonization. Examines establishment of Spanish rule in four major Caribbean islands from 1492 to death of Diego Colón in 1526. [MAB]

37.106 David P. Henige. *In search of Columbus: the sources for the first voyage.* Tucson: University of Arizona Press, 1991. ISBN 0-8165-1090-3. ‣ Critical analysis of documentation of Columbus's first voyage, its use and misuse by historians, and historiographical debate over exactly where Columbus landed. Penetrating evaluations. [MAB]

37.107 Samuel Eliot Morison. *The European discovery of America: the southern voyages, A.D. 1492–1616.* New York: Oxford University Press, 1974. ‣ Ambitious, synthetic, monumental narrative of exploration, voyage by voyage, from Columbus to discovery of Cape Horn. Traditional Eurocentric perspective by reknowned authority. [MAB]

37.108 J. H. Parry. *The discovery of South America.* New York: Taplinger, 1979. ISBN 0-8008-2233-1. ‣ Broader than title suggests, includes European discovery of lands from Rio Grande to Cape Horn. Extensive quotations of contemporary narratives; 120 illustrations. Excellent, readable introduction. [MAB]

37.109 William D. Phillips, Jr., and Carla Rahn Phillips. *The worlds of Christopher Columbus.* Cambridge: Cambridge University Press, 1992. ISBN 0-521-35097-2. ‣ Life and activities of Christopher Columbus in broad perspective, analyzing both antecedents and results of voyages as they related to Europe, Asia, and Africa. Fine scholarly synthesis. [MAB]

37.110 Ruth Pike. *Enterprise and adventure: the Genoese in Seville and the opening of the New World.* Ithaca, N.Y.: Cornell University Press, 1966. ‣ Important examination of Genoese entrepreneurs in Seville and Caribbean and their participation in early colonial trade. Emphasizes importance of colonial trade for their growing economic predominance in Spain. [MAB]

37.111 Kirkpatrick Sale. *The conquest of paradise: Christopher Columbus and the Columbian legacy.* 1990 ed. New York: Plume, 1991. ISBN 0-452-26669-6 (pbk). ‣ Revisionist, critical examination of Columbus and of Spanish and English colonization and its impact on native populations and ecological environments. Written for popular audience and certain to irritate specialists. [MAB]

37.112 Paolo Emilio Taviani. *Christopher Columbus: the grand design.* John Gilbert, ed. William Weaver, trans. London: Orbis, 1985. ISBN 0-85613-922-X. ‣ Extraordinarily detailed biography, dealing with multitude of questions and interpretations surrounding famous mariner. Essential work; effectively stops in 1492. Translation of revised Italian edition. [MAB]

37.113 Charles Verlinden and Florentino Pérez-Embid. *Cristóbal Colón y el descubrimiento de América.* Madrid: Ediciones Rialp, S.A., 1967. ‣ Excellent synthesis of famed explorer's life and times by two leading authorities. [MAB]

37.114 Louis-André Vigneras. *The discovery of South America* *and the Andalusian voyages.* Chicago: University of Chicago Press for the Newberry Library, 1976. ISBN 0-226-85609-7. ▸ Examination of early voyages that paved way for conquest and colonization of Venezuela and Colombia and discovery of the Pacific. Presents fascinating details of business of discovery. For specialists. [MAB]

SEE ALSO

22.98 J. H. Parry. *The age of reconnaissance.*
36.338 Carl O. Sauer. *The early Spanish Main.*

CONQUEST AND EARLY SETTLEMENT OF MEXICO AND CENTRAL AMERICA

37.115　Ida Altman. "Spanish society in Mexico City after the conquest." *Hispanic American historical review* 71.3 (1991) 413–45. ISSN 0018-2168. ▸ Valuable examination of early colonial society. During first thirty years after conquest, enduring socioeconomic and institutional structures of New Spain, centered principally on Mexico City, emerged and crystallized. [MAB]

37.116　Donald E. Chipman. *Nuño de Guzmán and the province of Pánuco in New Spain, 1518–1533.* 1966 ed. Glendale, Calif.: Clark, 1967. ▸ Detailed study of Spanish conquest, settlement, and exploitation of Pánuco, led by infamous Guzmán. Examines political, military, social, religious, and economic affairs. Remains valuable. [MAB]

37.117　Hernán Cortés. *Letters from Mexico.* Anthony Pagden, ed. and trans. John H. Elliott, Introduction. New York: Grossman, 1971. ▸ Fine translation and introduction mark classic, albeit sometimes fanciful, contemporary account of conquest of Mexico by its conquerer and leader. [MAB]

37.118　Bernal Díaz del Castillo. *The discovery and conquest of Mexico, 1517–1521.* Irving A. Leonard, Introduction. A. P. Maudslay, trans. New York: Farrar, Straus, & Cudahy, 1956. ▸ Translation of primary account of discovery of New Spain by footsoldier who accompanied Fernando Cortés. Rich, detailed masterpiece, presenting common soldier's view. [MAB]

37.119　C. Harvey Gardiner. *The constant captain: Gonzalo de Sandoval.* Carbondale: Southern Illinois University Press, 1961. ▸ Still valuable study of one of Fernando Cortés's key lieutenants and his participation in conquest and early settlement of New Spain. [MAB]

37.120　C. Harvey Gardiner. *Naval power in the conquest of Mexico.* 1956 ed. New York: Greenwood, 1969. ISBN 0-8371-2457-3. ▸ Well-written, fascinating account of construction of ships and key role of naval power in Fernando Cortés's successful siege of Tenochtitlán. [MAB]

37.121　Charles Gibson. "Conquest, capitulation, and Indian treaties." *American historical review* 83.1 (1978) 1–15. ISSN 0002-8762. ▸ Outstanding essay, exploring use of treaties and capitulations in Spanish reconquest and almost total absence in conquest of Americas. Pursues more general problem of historical inquiry. [MAB]

37.122　Robert Himmerich y Valencia. *The encomenderos of New Spain, 1521–1555.* Austin: University of Texas Press, 1991. ISBN 0-292-72068-8. ▸ Model prosopographical examination of 506 *encomenderos* (recipients of grants of Indian labor and tribute) accompanied by biographical sketches of each. Informative analysis; complements Lockhart 37.136. [MAB]

37.123　Peggy K. Liss. *Mexico under Spain, 1521–1556: society and the origins of nationality.* Chicago: University of Chicago Press, 1975. ISBN 0-226-48495-5. ▸ Overview of emergence of Mexican identity during first decades after Spanish conquest. Stimulating synthesis. [MAB]

37.124　Francisco López de Gómara. *Cortés: the life of the con-*

queror by his secretary. 1964 ed. Lesley Byrd Simpson, ed. and trans. Berkeley: University of California Press, 1966. ISBN 0-520-00493-0 (pbk). ▸ Translation of important source for conquest of Mexico. [MAB]

37.125　R. C. Padden. *The hummingbird and the hawk: conquest and sovereignty in the Valley of Mexico, 1503–1541.* 1967 ed. New York: Harper & Row, 1970. ▸ Beautifully written account; begins with survey of Aztec history and concludes with Bishop Juan de Zumárraga's efforts to extirpate apostasy. Heavy emphasis on interrelation of religion and sovereignty. [MAB]

37.126　Philip Wayne Powell. *Mexico's Miguel Caldera: the taming of America's first frontier, 1548–1597.* Tucson: University of Arizona Press, 1977. ISBN 0-8165-0569-1. ▸ Examines life, times, and actions of mestizo frontiersman who won fame as soldier fighting Chichimecas and then helped shape peace on frontier. Complements 37.331. [MAB]

37.127　William H. Prescott. *History of the conquest of Mexico and history of the conquest of Peru.* New York: Random House, 1966. ▸ Convenient edition of classic histories of conquest first published in 1843 and 1847. Wonderfully written romantic accounts but must be supplemented by subsequent treatments. [MAB]

37.128　G. Michael Riley. *Fernando Cortés and the marquesado in Morelos, 1522–1547: a case study in the socioeconomic development of sixteenth-century Mexico.* Albuquerque: University of New Mexico Press, 1973. ISBN 0-8263-0263-7. ▸ Fine case study of important early estate. Examines *encomiendas* (grants of Indian labor and tribute), tribute, labor, land, production, and revenues on Fernando Cortés's estate in Morelos. [MAB]

37.129　John Grier Varner and Jeannette Johnson Varner. *Dogs of the conquest.* Norman: University of Oklahoma Press, 1983. ISBN 0-8061-1793-1. ▸ Examination of introduction of dogs and their uses by Spaniards in major expeditions of conquest throughout the Americas. Uniquely highlights often-mentioned but little-studied dimension of conquest. [MAB]

37.130　J. Benedict Warren. *The conquest of Michoacán: the Spanish domination of the Tarascan kingdom in western Mexico, 1521–1530.* Norman: University of Oklahoma Press, 1985. ISBN 0-8061-1858-X. ▸ Detailed examination of process of Spanish domination over Tarascans culminating in execution of last native king, Cazonci. Discusses role of indigenous institutions in resistance and impact of Christianity. Valuable history of conquest, Spanish-Tarascan relations, and *encomienda* (system of forced Indian labor and tribute). [MAB/SS]

SEE ALSO

36.282 Inga Clendinnen. *Ambivalent conquests.*
36.296 Miguel León-Portilla, ed. *The broken spears.*

CONQUEST AND EARLY SETTLEMENT OF SOUTH AMERICA

37.131　Kenneth J. Andrien and Rolena Adorno. *Transatlantic encounters: Europeans and Andeans in the sixteenth century.* Berkeley: University of California Press, 1991. ISBN 0-520-07228-6. ▸ Eight essays on Old World heritage to encounter period, European and Andean resources in encounter period, and cultural and artistic encounters. Unusually distinguished group of authors. Very informative. [MAB]

37.132　José Ignacio Avellaneda. "The men of Nikolaus Federmann: conquerors of the New Kingdom of Granada." *The Americas* 43.4 (1987) 385–94. ISSN 0003-1615. ▸ Prosopographical examination of conquerors giving information on age, place of birth, prior Indies' experience, literacy, social rank, and subsequent influence in New Granada. Useful albeit brief and incomplete data. [MAB]

37.133　John Hemming. *The conquest of the Incas.* 1970 ed. New

York: Harcourt Brace Jovanovich, 1973. ISBN 0-15-122560-5 (cl), 0-15-622300-7 (pbk). ▸ Relates conquest of Peru from Pizarro's victories to execution of Túpac Amaru in 1572. Masterful, detailed narrative of Spanish victory and its implications. [MAB]

37.134 John Hemming. *The search for El Dorado.* 1978 ed. New York: Dutton, 1979. ISBN 0-87690-323-5. ▸ Well-written, well-illustrated introduction to conquest of New Granada and pursuit of its riches. More than coffee table book it appears to be at first glance. [MAB]

37.135 F. A. Kirkpatrick. *The Spanish conquistadores.* 1946 2d ed. New York: Barnes & Noble, 1967. ▸ Dated (first edition, 1934) but still useful, brief, general introduction to exploration and conquest throughout Indies. [MAB]

37.136 James Lockhart. *The men of Cajamarca: a social and biographical study of the first conquerors of Peru.* Austin: University of Texas Press for the Institute of Latin American Studies, 1972. (Latin American monographs, 27.) ISBN 0-292-75001-3. ▸ Prosopographical examination of 168 men who captured Inca emperor Atahuallpa in 1532. Includes biographical sketches of participants. Valuable clarification of conquistadors' backgrounds and subsequent careers. [MAB]

37.137 James Lockhart. *Spanish Peru, 1532–1560: a colonial society.* Madison: University of Wisconsin Press, 1968. ISBN 0-299-04660-5 (cl), 0-299-04664-8 (pbk). ▸ Examination of social and economic groups that formed a complete colonial society in Peru by 1560. Extraordinarily influential demonstration of value of notarial records for social history. [MAB]

37.138 José de Oviedo y Baños. *The conquest and settlement of Venezuela.* Jeannette Johnson Varner, trans. Berkeley: University of California Press, 1987. ISBN 0-520-05851-8. ▸ Conquest and settlement of Venezuela and consequences for native population to 1600. Translation of classic history by eighteenth-century author. [MAB]

37.139 Susan E. Ramírez. "The 'dueño de Indios': thoughts on the consequences of the shifting bases of power of the 'curaca de los viejos antiguos' under the Spanish in sixteenth-century Peru." *Hispanic American historical review* 67.4 (1987) 575–610. ISSN 0018-2168. ▸ Within forty years of conquest, *curacas* (native chieftains) on north coast of Peru focused on siphoning off surplus for Spaniards rather than providing good government by traditional means. Very important article. [MAB]

37.140 Rafael Varón Gabai and Auke Pieter Jacobs. "Peruvian wealth and Spanish investments: the Pizarro family during the sixteenth century." *Hispanic American historical review* 67.4 (1987) 657–95. ISSN 0018-2168. ▸ Informative case study of Pizarros, engaged in business activities from initial stages of conquest of Peru. Investments in Peru and especially in Spain provided long-term economic security. [MAB]

SEE ALSO
36.405 Nathan Wachtel. *The vision of the vanquished.*
36.437 John Hemming. *Red gold.*

INTELLECTUAL PROBLEMS RAISED BY CONQUEST AND THE COLUMBIAN EXCHANGE

37.141 Nicholas P. Canny and Anthony Pagden, eds. *Colonial identity in the Atlantic world, 1500–1800.* Princeton: Princeton University Press, 1987. ISBN 0-691-05372-3. ▸ Eight essays, three related to development of colonial identity in Atlantic world, Brazil, and Spanish America. Valuable studies; see also Brading 37.72. [MAB/JPG]

37.142 Alfred W. Crosby, Jr. *The Columbian exchange: biological and cultural consequences of 1492.* 1972 ed. Westport, Conn.: Greenwood, 1973. ISBN 0-8371-5821-4 (cl), 0-8371-7228-4 (pbk). ▸ Brilliant examination of results of introduction of Old

World diseases, plants, and animals into New World and vice versa. [MAB]

37.143 Lewis Hanke. *All mankind is one: a study of the disputation between Bartolomé de Las Casas and Juan Ginés de Sepúlveda in 1550 on the intellectual and religious capacity of the American Indians.* De Kalb: Northern Illinois University Press, 1974. ISBN 0-87580-043-2. ▸ Examination of nature of Indians according to Spaniards giving background to 1550 disputation, Las Casas's treatise, and aftermath of conflict. Valuable introduction to *In Defense of the Indians* (37.147). [MAB]

37.144 Lewis Hanke. *The Spanish struggle for justice in the conquest of America.* 1949 ed. Boston: Little, Brown, 1965. ▸ Examines Spanish struggle to institute just laws and to act justly in New World in sixteenth century. Includes synthesis of Hanke's earlier related publications. [MAB]

37.145 Lee Eldridge Huddleston. *Origins of the American Indians: European concepts, 1492–1729.* Austin: University of Texas Press for the Institute of Latin American Studies, 1967. (Latin American monographs, 11.) ISBN 0-292-73693-2. ▸ Informative review of ideas of major writers who dealt with question of origins of American Indians. Emphasizes development of two intellectual traditions following Jesuit historian José de Acosta and theorist Gregorio García. [MAB]

37.146 Benjamin Keen. "The Black Legend revisited: assumptions and realities." *Hispanic American historical review* 49.4 (1969) 703–19. ISSN 0018-2168. ▸ Concludes Black Legend of Spanish abuse and cruelty toward native population not legend; all major corollaries of concept are open to serious questioning and concept confuses and distorts subject of Spanish-Indian relations. Stimulating. Debate follows in *Hispanic American Historical Review* 51.1 (1971) 112–27 and 51.2 (1971) 336–55. [MAB]

37.147 Bartolomé de Las Casas. *In defense of the Indians: the defense of the most reverend lord, Don Fray Bartolomé de Las Casas, of the Order of Preachers, late bishop of Chiapa, against the persecutors and slanderers of the peoples of the New World discovered across the seas.* 1974 ed. Stafford Poole, ed. and trans. De Kalb: Northern Illinois University Press, 1992. ISBN 0-87580-556-6. ▸ First publication of work Las Casas wrote late in career (d. 1566). Vigorous defense of native peoples against colonial policies and practices. Elaborates on position taken in Valladolid debate, 1550–51. Important text. See above, Hanke 37.143. [MAB]

37.148 William H. McNeill. *Plagues and peoples.* 1976 ed. New York: Anchor, 1989. ISBN 0-385-12122-9 (pbk). ▸ Chapter on transoceanic exchanges, 1500–1700, includes substantial material on adverse effects of Old World diseases on native populations in Americas. [MAB]

37.149 Edmundo O'Gorman. *The invention of America: an inquiry into the historical nature of the New World and the meaning of its history.* 1961 ed. Westport, Conn.: Greenwood, 1972. ISBN 0-8371-6470-2. ▸ Stimulating philosophical discourse criticizing idea that America was discovered, arguing it was invented through complex process that gave newly found lands proper meaning of their own. [MAB/JML]

37.150 Anthony Pagden. *The fall of natural man: the American Indian and the origins of comparative ethnology.* Cambridge: Cambridge University Press, 1982. ISBN 0-521-22202-8. ▸ Outstanding intellectual history, focusing on changing Spanish perceptions of natural man. Includes discussion of logist Juan Ginés de Sepúlveda, defender of Indians Bartolomé de Las Casas, and Jesuit historian José de Acosta. [MAB]

37.151 John C. Super. *Food, conquest, and colonization in sixteenth-century Spanish America.* Albuquerque: University of New Mexico Press, 1988. ISBN 0-8263-1049-4 (cl), 0-8263-1061-3 (pbk). ▸ Argues convincingly that, in general, both native population and conquistadors and their descendants had adequate food supplies and diet superior to that in Europe. Thoughtful and provocative. [MAB]

IMPERIAL ORGANIZATION AND ADMINISTRATION

37.152   Kenneth J. Andrien. *Crisis and decline: the viceroyalty of Peru in the seventeenth century.* Albuquerque: University of New Mexico Press, 1985. ISBN 0-8263-0791-4. ▸ Fine examination of economy and finance, treasury system and fiscal bureaucracy, efforts at reform and resulting resistance, and imperial decline in seventeenth-century Peru. [MAB]

37.153   Gildas Bernard. *Le secrétariat d'état et le conseil espagñol des Indes (1700–1808).* Geneva: Droz, 1972. ▸ Useful institutional examination of Council of the Indies and especially of secretary of state for the Indies. Includes list of council members and tables of officials. [MAB]

37.154   Peter T. Bradley. *Society, economy, and defence in seventeenth-century Peru: the administration of the Count of Alba de Liste (1655–1661).* Liverpool: University of Liverpool, Centre for Latin American Studies, 1992. (Monograph series, 15.) ISBN 0-902806-21-1. ▸ Informative monographic examination of viceregal administration. Considers management of crown revenue, silver trade, Indian affairs, war in Chile and defence of Peru, church and university, and supervision of personnel. [MAB]

37.155   Mark A. Burkholder and D. S. Chandler. *From impotence to authority: the Spanish crown and the American Audiencias, 1687–1808.* Columbia: University of Missouri Press, 1977. ISBN 0-8262-0219-5. ▸ Prosopographical examination of nearly 700 Audiencia ministers named from 1687 to 1821. Clarifies extent of creole service on courts and Crown's discrimination against creoles. [MAB]

37.156   Margaret E. Crahan. "Spanish and American counterpoint: problems and possibilities in Spanish colonial administrative history." In *New approaches to Latin American history.* Richard Graham and Peter H. Smith, eds., pp. 36–70. Austin: University of Texas Press, 1974. ISBN 0-292-75506-6. ▸ Thoughtful analysis of colonial administrative history, arguing for reexamination of comparable and related processes in Spain and America. Suggests directions for further research. [MAB]

37.157   Della M. Flusche. "Chilean councilmen and export policies, 1600–1699." *The Americas* 36.4 (1980) 479–97. ISSN 0003-1615. ▸ Brief but informative examination of price fixing and monopoly export contracts, commercial taxes, and port and wheat regulations. Demonstrates importance of city council in financial and economic matters. [MAB]

37.158   Lewis Hanke and Celso Rodríguez, eds. *Los virreyes españoles en América durante el gobierno de la casa de Austria: México.* 5 vols. Madrid: Atlas, 1976–78. ISBN 84-363-0-490 (v. 1), 84-363-0492-6 (v. 2), 84-363-0493-4 (v. 3), 84-363-0494-2 (v. 4), 84-363-0496-9 (v. 5). ▸ Extraordinarily valuable compilation, providing access to royal instructions and judicial reviews of viceroys of Mexico from 1535 to 1700. Includes bibliography, summary of documents published, selected documents, and some lists of other related documents for each viceroy. [MAB]

37.159   Lewis Hanke and Celso Rodríguez, eds. *Los virreyes españoles en América durante el gobierno de la casa de Austria: Perú.* 7 vols. Madrid: Atlas, 1976–80. ISBN 84-363-0498-5 (v. 1), 84-363-500-0 (v. 2), 84-363-0505-1 (v. 3), 84-363-0507-8 (v. 4), 84-363-0515-9 (v. 5), 84-363-0516-7 (v. 6), 84-363-0531-0 (v. 7). ▸ Extraordinarily valuable compilation, providing access to royal instructions and judicial reviews of viceroys of Peru from 1544 to 1700. Includes bibliography, summary of documents published, selected documents, and some lists of other related documents for each viceroy. [MAB]

37.160   Robert Stephen Haskett. "Indian town government in colonial Cuernavaca: persistence, adaptation, and change." *Hispanic American historical review* 67.2 (1987) 203–31. ISSN 0018-2168. ▸ Region's town governments and native ruling group retained both vigor and substantial local autonomy until independence. Pre-Hispanic tradition remained significant. Important revisionist article. [MAB]

37.161   Guillermo Lohmann Villena. *Los ministros de la Audiencia de Lima en el reinado de los Borbones (1700–1821): esquema de un estudio sobre un núcleo dirigente.* Sevilla: Escuela de Estudios Hispano-Americanos de Sevilla, 1974. (Publicaciones de la Escuela de Estudios Hispano-Americanos de Sevilla, 222.) ISBN 84-00-03994-7. ▸ Prosopographical examination of members of Lima's High Court, identifying family and geographical origins, marriages, and career patterns. Includes biographical sketch of each minister. Rich, informative study. [MAB]

37.162   Guillermo Lohmann Villena. *Los regidores perpetuos del cabildo de Lima (1535–1821): crónica y estudio de un grup de gestión.* 2 vols. Sevilla: Diputación Provincial de Sevilla, 1983. (Publicaciones de la Excelentísima, Diputación Provincial de Sevilla, Sección: historia, Serie: 5 centenario del descubrimiento de América, 1.) ISBN 84-500-8598-5 (set), 84-500-8599-3 (v. 1), 84-500-8600-0 (v. 2). ▸ Extraordinarily rich prosopographical study examining Lima's city council with particular attention to social, economic, regional, and family backgrounds of its members. Includes biographical sketch of each councilman. [MAB]

37.163   João Lopes Sierra. *A governor and his image in baroque Brazil: the funereal eulogy of Afonso Furtado de Castro do Rio de Mendonça.* Stuart B. Schwartz, ed. Ruth E. Jones, trans. Minneapolis: University of Minnesota Press, 1979. ISBN 0-8166-0879-2. ▸ Unique publication, dealing with actions, life, and death of seventeenth-century governor (1671–75). Valuable for observations on military campaigns, religious life in Salvador, and elite's concerns in little-studied period. [MAB]

37.164   Peter Marzahl. *Town in the empire: government, politics, and society in seventeenth-century Popayán.* Austin: University of Texas Press for Institute of Latin American Studies, 1978. (Latin American monographs, 45.) ISBN 0-292-78028-1 (cl), 0-292-78029-X (pbk). ▸ Impressive study of economy, society, and local and provincial government in modest town and region in present-day Colombia. Argues creoles' possession of social and economic power but not political authority was appropriate. [MAB]

37.165   John Preston Moore. *The cabildo in Peru under the Hapsburgs.* Durham, N.C.: Duke University Press, 1954. ▸ Dated but still valuable institutional study of creation, responsibilities, and operation of city councils in Peru. Emphasizes decadence of councils in seventeenth century. [MAB]

37.166   Fernando Muro Romero. *Las presidencias–gobernaciones en Indias (siglo 16).* Sevilla: Escuela de Estudios Hispano-Americanos de Sevilla, 1975. (Publicaciones de la Escuela de Estudios Hispano-Americanos de Sevilla, 229.) ISBN 84-00-04233-6. ▸ Examination of military and administrative organization of different provinces, alternative forms of organization, and relations between presidency-governorships and viceroys of New Spain and Peru. Informative study of early administration. [MAB]

37.167   J. H. Parry. *The Audiencia of New Galicia in the sixteenth century: a study in Spanish colonial government.* 1948 ed. Westport, Conn.: Greenwood, 1985. ISBN 0-313-24957-1. ▸ Detailed examination of Audiencia (High Court) of New Galicia from its foundation in 1548 to 1600. Classic administrative history of tribunal and its relations with Indians, conquistadors, and church. [MAB]

37.168   J. H. Parry. *The sale of public office in the Spanish Indies under the Hapsburgs.* Berkeley: University of California Press, 1953. ▸ Examination of sale of notarial offices, miscellaneous fee-earning offices, municipal dignities, and salaried offices. Emphasizes sales increased corruption and multiplication of offices. [MAB]

37.169 John Leddy Phelan. *The kingdom of Quito in the seventeenth century: bureaucratic politics in the Spanish empire.* Madison: University of Wisconsin Press, 1967. ▸ Examination of Quito, its Audiencia (High Court), and general *visita* (inspection). Important examination of workings of colonial bureaucracy, emphasizing adverse consequences of inadequate salaries. [MAB]

37.170 A.J.R. Russell-Wood. "Local government in Portuguese America: a study in cultural divergence." *Comparative studies in society and history* 16.2 (1974) 187–231. ISSN 0010-4175. ▸ Case study of mining town of Vila Rica, emphasizing additional roles council members assumed and bureaucratic infrastructure created as town grew. Employs theory of converging structures analysis. Valuable. [MAB]

37.171 Ernesto Schäfer. *El consejo real y supremo de las Indias: su historia, organización y labor administrativa hasta la terminación de la casa de Austria.* 1930–47 ed. 2 vols. Nendeln, Liechtenstein: Kraus Reprint, 1975. ▸ Examines council and House of Trade, colonial organization, legislation, commerce, navigation, and science. Includes lists of council members, members of House of Trade, viceroys, governors, archbishops, and bishops. Unsurpassed. [MAB]

37.172 Stuart B. Schwartz. *Sovereignty and society in colonial Brazil: the High Court of Bahia and its judges, 1609–1751.* Berkeley: University of California Press, 1973. ISBN 0-520-02195-9. ▸ Pioneering, detailed examination of High Court of Bahia from its founding to 1751. Superb prosopographical analysis of members of court, emphasizing ties to local society. [MAB]

37.173 Francisco Tomás y Valiente. *La venta de oficios en Indias (1492–1606).* Madrid: Instituto de Estudios Administrativos, 1972. ▸ Examination of private sale of positions in Castile and Indies to 1558 and of crown's subsequent direct involvement in sales and systematization of sales, renunciation, and inheritance of office. Revises Parry 37.168. [MAB]

SEE ALSO
29.119 Helen Nader. *Liberty in absolutist Spain.*
36.280 Woodrow Borah. *Justice by insurance.*
36.291 Robert Stephen Haskett. *Indigenous rulers.*

CHURCH AND INQUISITION

37.174 Father Pablo Joseph de Arriaga. *The extirpation of idolatry in Peru.* L. Clark Keating, ed. and trans. Lexington: University Press of Kentucky, 1968. ▸ Publication (in Lima, 1621) of results of Arriaga's investigations of idolatry among Peruvian natives. Important source of information about religion and customs of natives. [MAB]

37.175 Martin A. Cohen. *The martyr: the story of a secret Jew and the Mexican Inquisition in the sixteenth century.* Philadelphia: Jewish Publication Society of America, 1973. ISBN 0-8276-0011-9. ▸ Study of Luis de Carvajal the Younger's capture in 1589, trial, and death in 1596 by order of Inquisition as unrepentant judaizer. Detailed case study, including substantial background material. [MAB]

37.176 Victoria Hennessey Cummins. "The church and business practices in late sixteenth-century Mexico." *The Americas* 44.4 (1988) 421–40. ISSN 0003-1615. ▸ Demonstrates common use of shady business practices with intermittent and inconsistent efforts to enforce regulations; buyer had to beware. Active credit market circumvented church's strictures on usury. Very informative. [MAB]

37.177 Victoria Hennessey Cummins. "Imperial policy and church income: the sixteenth-century Mexican church." *The Americas* 43.1 (1986) 87–104. ISSN 0003-1615. ▸ Concludes

church was relatively weak, dependent institution, supported by king and with power only to carry out its function and serve as counterpoint to religious orders. Useful analysis. [MAB]

37.178 Donald L. Gibbs. "The economic activities of nuns, friars, and their *conventos* in mid-colonial Cuzco." *The Americas* 45.3 (1989) 343–62. ISSN 0003-1615. ▸ Useful survey of understudied group, focusing on years 1680 to 1710. Life styles and financial activities of Cuzco's orders similar to those elsewhere in Peru and Mexico at same time. [MAB]

37.179 Richard E. Greenleaf. "The great *visitas* of the Mexican Holy Office, 1645–1669." *The Americas* 44.4 (1988) 399–420. ISSN 0003-1615. ▸ Highly informative study of inquisitorial abuses against Portuguese judaizers which led to full-scale investigation of Holy Office and numerous indictments. Confiscation of judaizers' wealth solidified Inquisition's budget for remainder of century. [MAB]

37.180 Richard E. Greenleaf. "The Inquisition brotherhood: Cofradia de San Pedro Martir of colonial Mexico." *The Americas* 40.2 (1983) 171–207. ISSN 0003-1615. ▸ Informative survey examining membership, privileges, administration, activities, finances, and inner conflicts of brotherhood from 1656 to 1837. [MAB]

37.181 Richard E. Greenleaf. *The Mexican Inquisition of the sixteenth century.* Albuquerque: University of New Mexico Press, 1969. ISBN 8263-0130-4. ▸ Examination of first Inquisitors, episcopal Inquisition, tribunal of the Holy Office, and Inquisition and Calvinists in Mexico. Demythologizes Inquisitorial activities. [MAB]

37.182 Richard E. Greenleaf. *Zumárraga and the Mexican Inquisition, 1536–1543.* 1961 ed. Washington, D.C.: Academy of American Franciscan History, 1962. (Monograph series, 4.) ▸ Detailed examination of Inquisitorial activities of first bishop and archbishop of Mexico. Illuminates Inquisitorial activities before establishment of Inquisition tribunal. [MAB]

37.183 Richard E. Greenleaf, ed. *The Roman Catholic church in colonial Latin America.* 1971 ed. Tempe: Arizona State University, Center for Latin American Studies, 1977. ISBN 0-87918-034-X. ▸ Anthology with twenty-three selections; well balanced chronologically. Includes section on arts and letters. Good introduction to topic. [MAB]

37.184 Stanley M. Hordes. "The Inquisition as economic and political agent: the campaign of the Mexican Holy Office against the crypto-Jews in the mid-seventeenth century." *The Americas* 39.1 (1982) 23–38. ISSN 0003-1615. ▸ Informative study, showing how Inquisition, motivated by economic and political goals, disrupted commercial activities of *conversos* and gained control over their estates through confiscation. [MAB]

37.185 Eugene H. Korth. *Spanish policy in colonial Chile: the struggle for social justice, 1535–1700.* Stanford, Calif.: Stanford University Press, 1968. ▸ Detailed examination of problems associated with efforts by Spanish crown and especially Jesuits to protect Araucanians from exploitation. Particularly useful discussion of Indian slavery. [MAB]

37.186 Henry Charles Lea. *The Inquisition in the Spanish dependencies: Sicily-Naples-Sardinia-Milan-the Canaries-Mexico-Peru-New Granada.* New York: Macmillan, 1908. ▸ Includes lengthy chapters on Inquisition in Mexico, Philippines, Peru, and New Granada. Informative pioneering work still worth consulting. [MAB]

37.187 Francisco Morales, O.F.M. *Ethnic and social background of the Franciscan friars in seventeenth-century Mexico.* Washington, D.C.: Academy of American Franciscan History, 1973. (Monograph series, 10.) ▸ Highly informative prosopographical study, examining selection of candidates, admission of a few Indians and mestizos, and geographic, social, and occupational backgrounds of other candidates and their families. [MAB]

37.188 Magnus Mörner. *The political and economic activities of the Jesuits in the La Plata region: the Hapsburg era.* 1953 ed. Albert Read, trans. Stockholm: Victor Pettersons for Library and Institute of Ibero-American Studies, Stockholm, 1977. ▸ Classic, still authoritative study examining activities of Jesuits in La Plata to 1700 within broad context of social, political, and economic conditions. Also available as photocopy from Ann Arbor: University Microfilms International. [MAB]

37.189 Mary Elizabeth Perry and Anne J. Cruz, eds. *Cultural encounters: the impact of the Inquisition in Spain and the New World.* Berkeley: University of California Press, 1991. (Publications of the University of California at Los Angeles Center for Medieval and Renaissance Studies, 24.) ISBN 0-520-07098-4. ▸ Uneven collection of essays, five dealing with Inquisition in Mexico. Particularly valuable is Greenleaf's review of historiography of Inquisition in Mexico. [MAB]

37.190 John Leddy Phelan. *The millennial kingdom of the Franciscans in the New World.* 2d ed. Berkeley: University of California Press, 1970. ISBN 0-520-01404-9. ▸ Classic study (first published 1956) of writings of Franciscan Gerónimo de Mendieta (1525–1604). Sets golden age of Indian church at 1524–64 and Babylonian captivity at 1564–96. [MAB]

37.191 Stafford Poole. "Church law on the ordination of Indians and *castas* in New Spain." *Hispanic American historical review* 61.4 (1981) 637–50. ISSN 0018-2168. ▸ Important clarification of eligibility for ordination. From 1591 onward, Indians in New Spain not formally excluded from clergy; mestizos and other *castas* could be ordained. [MAB]

37.192 Stafford Poole. "The last years of Archbishop Pedro Moya de Contreras, 1586–1591." *The Americas* 47.1 (1990) 1–38. ISSN 0003-1615. ▸ Completes previously published study of Moya de Contreras (37.193) on basis of newly discovered documentation. Moya served as unofficial adviser on Indies' affairs and represented *letrado* ideal. [MAB]

37.193 Stafford Poole. *Pedro Moya de Contreras: Catholic reform and royal power in New Spain, 1571–1591.* Berkeley: University of California Press, 1987. ISBN 0-520-05551-9. ▸ Examination of Moya's career as Inquisitor of New Spain, archbishop of Mexico, and viceroy of Mexico with special attention to Third Mexican Provincial Council (1585). Excellent study of important figure. [MAB]

37.194 Robert Ricard. *The spiritual conquest of Mexico: an essay on the apostolate and the evangelizing methods of the mendicant orders in New Spain, 1523–1572.* 1966 ed. Lesley Byrd Simpson, trans. Berkeley: University of California Press, 1974. ISBN 0-520-02760-4. ▸ Analysis of evangelization activities of Franciscans, Dominicans, and Augustinians in Mexico from 1523 to 1572. Still best study of early efforts to christianize native population. [MAB]

37.195 James D. Riley. "The wealth of the Jesuits in Mexico, 1670–1767." *The Americas* 33.2 (1976) 226–66. ISSN 0003-1615. ▸ Excellent detailed examination, revising Chevalier's view (37.248) that Jesuits were excellent managers. Demonstrates their blunders and conservatism in management. Their distinctiveness came from watching expenses and responding when profits declined. [MAB]

37.196 John Frederick Schwaller. *Church and clergy in sixteenth-century Mexico.* Albuquerque: University of New Mexico Press, 1987. ISBN 0-8263-0973-9. ▸ Discussion of positions held by secular clerics, focuses especially on social origins and career patterns of clerics themselves. Clearly demonstrates importance of creoles in clergy. [MAB]

37.197 John Frederick Schwaller. *Origins of church wealth in*

Mexico: ecclesiastical revenues and church finances, 1523–1600. Albuquerque: University of New Mexico Press, 1985. ISBN 0-8263-0813-9. ▸ Examines tithe collection and distribution, parish revenues, pious works, and alms. Considers period 1575–85 watershed for church. Valuable study of important topic. [MAB]

37.198 Susan A. Soeiro. "The social and economic role of the convent: women and nuns in colonial Bahia, 1677–1800." *Hispanic American historical review* 54.2 (1974) 209–32. ISSN 0018-2168. ▸ Pioneering study of Destêrro convent, which catered to Bahia's elite, receiving substantial dowries when daughters were admitted. Finds nuns could exercise individual initiative, independence, and self-fulfillment in nonreligious spheres. [MAB]

37.199 Antonine Tibesar. *Franciscan beginnings in colonial Peru.* Washington, D.C.: Academy of American Franciscan History, 1953. (Monograph series, 1.) ▸ Chronicles arrival of Franciscans in Peru in 1531 and their labors among native population until 1590. Study of important chapter in history of church in Peru. [MAB]

37.200 Adriaan C. Van Oss. *Catholic colonialism: a parish history of Guatemala, 1524–1821.* Cambridge: Cambridge University Press, 1986. ISBN 0-521-32072-0. ▸ Important examination of Catholic church in understudied region. Examines geography of spiritual conquest, parish structure, parish finance, internal operation, secularization of regular clergy, and characteristics of clergy. [MAB]

CHANGES IN THE COLONIAL POPULATION

37.201 Suzanne Austin Alchon. *Native society and disease in colonial Ecuador.* Cambridge: Cambridge University Press, 1991. ISBN 0-521-40186-0. ▸ Informative, stimulating discussion, emphasizing relationship between biological and social responses and political conditions to disease in north-central highlands of Ecuador from pre-Spanish conquest to eighteenth century. [MAB]

37.202 Woodrow Borah and Sherburne F. Cook. *The aboriginal population of Central Mexico on the eve of the Spanish conquest.* Berkeley: University of California Press, 1963. ▸ Influential, controversial effort to determine preconquest population using preconquest fiscal material. Examines tribute system of Triple Alliance. Estimates population between 20 and 28 million. See also Borah and Cook 37.203. [MAB]

37.203 Woodrow Borah and Sherburne F. Cook. *The population of Central Mexico in 1548: an analysis of the "Suma de Visitas de Pueblos."* Berkeley: University of California Press, 1960. ▸ Estimates 1548 population to be 7.8 million on basis of compilation of descriptions of roughly half of principal towns. Important demographic research (with Borah and Cook 37.202). [MAB]

37.204 Peter Boyd-Bowman. "Patterns of Spanish emigration to the Indies until 1600." *Hispanic American historical review* 56.4 (1976) 580–604. ISSN 0018-2168. ▸ Landmark study, examining peninsular regional origins and New World destinations for nearly 55,000 emigrants. Emphasizes centrality of Seville in emigration and that over half of women emigrants from Andalusia. [MAB]

37.205 Noble David Cook and W. George Lovell, eds. *"Secret judgments of God": Old World disease in colonial Spanish America.* Woodrow Borah, Introduction. Norman: University of Oklahoma Press, 1991. ISBN 0-8061-2372-9. ▸ Fine collection of eight essays by nine authors and conclusion by editors, focusing on Central Mexico, Guatemala, Ecuador, Sabana de Bogotá, Upper Peru, Quito, and southern Chile. [MAB]

37.206 Sherburne F. Cook and Woodrow Borah. *Essays in population history.* 3 vols. Berkeley: University of California Press, 1971–79. ISBN 0-520-02272-6 (set), 0-520-01764-1 (v. 1), 0-520-

02272-6 (v. 2), 0-520-03560-7 (v. 3). ‣ Eighteen essays on diverse topics in population history in Mexico, Caribbean, and California, many focusing on colonial era. Valuable compilation by pathbreaking scholars of historical demography. [MAB/SS]

37.207 Sherburne F. Cook and Woodrow Borah. *The Indian population of Central Mexico, 1531–1610*. Berkeley: University of California Press, 1960. ‣ Extremely influential monograph. Postulates far higher initial population and greater and more rapid decrease. Revision of 1948 study by Sherburne F. Cook and Lesley Byrd Simpson. [MAB]

37.208 Sherburne F. Cook and Woodrow Borah. *The population of the Mixteca Alta, 1520–1960*. Berkeley: University of California Press, 1968. ‣ Examination of long-term changes in population for relatively small region. Estimated population fell from 700,000 in 1520 to 30,000 in 1670 before trend reversed. Influential monograph. [MAB]

37.209 David P. Henige. "On the contact population of Hispaniola: history as higher mathematics." *Hispanic American historical review* 58.2 (1978) 217–37. ISSN 0018-2168. ‣ Examination of population figures given in Borah and Cook 37.203. Concludes available sources preclude estimating size or measuring rate of decline. Debate follows in *Hispanic American Historical Review* 58.4 (1978) 700–12. [MAB]

37.210 Linda A. Newson. *The cost of conquest: Indian decline in Honduras under Spanish rule*. Boulder: Westview, 1986. ISBN 0-8133-7273-9 (pbk). ‣ Examines Indian cultures and environments on eve of conquest, conquest and its consequences, economy and cultural changes, and changes in population size. Valuable historical demography. [MAB]

37.211 Linda A. Newson. "Indian population patterns in colonial Latin America." *Latin American research review* 20.3 (1985) 41–74. ISSN 0023-8791. ‣ Review of regional variations, impact of disease, nature of Indian societies, quality of economic resources, labor systems, and missions and their consequences for native populations. Thoughtful analysis. [MAB]

37.212 Arij Ouweneel. "Growth, stagnation, and migration: an explorative analysis of the *tributario* series of Anáhuac (1720–1800)." *Hispanic American historical review* 71.3 (1991) 531–77. ISSN 0018-2168. ‣ Population of Anáhuac grew in 1720s and from 1780s onward. Between these peaks, number of tributaries stagnated or fell. Substantial migration occurred within highland itself. Stimulating hypotheses. [MAB]

37.213 David J. Robinson, ed. *Migration in colonial Spanish America*. Cambridge: Cambridge University Press, 1990. ISBN 0-521-36281-4. ‣ Fifteen chapters by sixteen authors examining migration of varied groups in different regions and for different times. Demonstrates extensive spatial mobility. Valuable collection; important topic. [MAB]

37.214 David J. Robinson, ed. *Studies in Spanish American population history*. Boulder: Westview, 1981. ISBN 0-86531-268-0. ‣ Ten essays on population history in diverse locations of colonial Spanish America. Useful collection; important topic. [MAB]

37.215 Angel Rosenblat. *La población de América en 1492: viejos y nuevos cálculos*. Mexico: El Colegio de México, 1967. (Publicaciones del Centro de Estudios Históricos, 1.) ‣ Critical analysis of demographic figures of Borah and Cook (37.203), reaffirming author's earlier much smaller estimates. Part of important continuing debate. [MAB]

37.216 Nicolás Sánchez-Albornoz. *The population of Latin America: a history*. W.A.R. Richardson, trans. Berkeley: University of California, 1974. ISBN 0-520-01766-8. ‣ Valuable synthetic examination of demographic history of Latin America from pre-Columbian era to year 2000. Colonialists will find chapters 2–4 particularly useful. [MAB]

37.217 Rudolph A. Zambardino. "Mexico's population in the sixteenth century: demographic anomaly or mathematical illusion?" *Journal of interdisciplinary history* 11.1 (1980) 1–27. ISSN 0022-1953. ‣ Mathematician's examination of population estimates, especially those by Borah and Cook (37.203). Criticizes mathematical assumptions employed. Concludes population perhaps 5–10 million in 1518. Valuable analysis. [MAB]

SEE ALSO
36.322 William M. Denevan, ed. *The native population of the Americas in 1492*.
36.391 Noble David Cook. *Demographic collapse*.
36.406 Ann M. Wightman. *Indigenous migration and social change*.
36.418 Noble David Cook. *The people of the Colca valley*.

AFRICAN SLAVERY AND THE SLAVE TRADE

37.218 Frederick P. Bowser. *The African slave in colonial Peru, 1524–1650*. Stanford, Calif.: Stanford University Press, 1974. ISBN 0-8047-0840-1. ‣ Detailed examination of slave trade to Peru and especially slaves and free persons of color in Peru. Outstanding contribution to literature on slavery in colonial Spanish America. [MAB]

37.219 Patrick J. Carroll. *Blacks in colonial Veracruz: race, ethnicity, and regional development*. Austin: University of Texas Press, 1991. ISBN 0-292-70780-0. ‣ Careful examination relating slave trade and slavery in Veracruz region to regional production, market, and capital development from 1519 to 1830. Excellent regional study. [MAB]

37.220 David L. Chandler. "Family bonds and the bondsman: the slave family in colonial Colombia." *Latin American research review* 16.2 (1981) 107–31. ISSN 0023-8791. ‣ Demographic analysis of data from 1650 to 1826. Finds two-thirds of all adult slaves lived in family units. Church, crown, and colonists encouraged family bonds. Fascinating regional study. [MAB]

37.221 Lyman L. Johnson. "Manumission in colonial Buenos Aires, 1776–1810." *Hispanic American historical review* 59.2 (1979) 258–79. ISSN 0018-2168. ‣ Valuable local study. Majority of manumitted slaves purchased their freedom. Few were progeny of owners or freed for old age or infirmity. Most were born in Buenos Aires's jurisdiction. [MAB]

37.222 Herbert S. Klein. *African slavery in Latin America and the Caribbean*. New York: Oxford University Press, 1986. ISBN 0-19-503837-1. ‣ General comparative survey of experience of African slaves in Portuguese-, Spanish-, and French-speaking regions of America from sixteenth to nineteenth century. Excellent synthesis. [MAB/RJW]

37.223 Herbert S. Klein. *The Middle Passage: comparative studies in the Atlantic slave trade*. Princeton: Princeton University Press, 1978. ISBN 0-691-03119-3 (cl), 0-691-10064-0 (pbk). ‣ Examination of American demand for slaves, various country's slave trades, and slave mortality rates during transatlantic crossing from 1700 to mid-nineteenth century. Thorough, thoughtful study. [MAB/SLE]

37.224 Paul E. Lovejoy, ed. *Africans in bondage: studies in slavery and the slave trade*. Madison: University of Wisconsin, Madison African Studies Program, 1986. ISBN 0-299-97020-5. ‣ Collection of essays. Of interest to colonialists are numerical distribution of slaves to Spanish America (1703–39), slave prices in Portuguese southern Atlantic (1600–1830), and arrival of smallpox in America. [MAB]

37.225 Patricia A. Mulvey. "Slave confraternities in Brazil: their role in colonial society." *The Americas* 39.1 (1982) 39–68. ISSN 0003-1615. ‣ Examination of religious, social, and economic functions of urban slave confraternities. Emphasizes proliferation of these brotherhoods in urban areas in eighteenth and early nineteenth centuries. Useful study of important institution. [MAB]

37.226 Colin A. Palmer. *Human cargoes: the British slave trade to Spanish America, 1700–1739.* Urbana: University of Illinois Press, 1981. ISBN 0-252-00846-4. ▸ Examination of British slave trade to Spanish America with particular emphasis on asiento trade. Concludes South Sea Company made good profits from it. Valuable analysis. [MAB]

37.227 Colin A. Palmer. *Slaves of the white god: blacks in Mexico, 1570–1650.* Cambridge, Mass.: Harvard University Press, 1976. ISBN 0-674-81085-6. ▸ Examination of African slave trade and slavery in Mexico. Demonstrates importance of slavery for economy and highlights slaves' efforts to preserve African traditions. [MAB]

37.228 Donald Ramos. "Community, control, and acculturation: a case study of slavery in eighteenth-century Brazil." *The Americas* 42.4 (1986) 419–51. ISSN 0003-1615. ▸ Focuses on slavery in Vila Rica do Ouro Preto, center of gold-mining district, from 1695 to 1823. Emphasizes role of church in process of integrating slaves into society. Useful regional study. [MAB]

37.229 Donald Ramos. "Slavery in Brazil: a case study of Diamantina, Minas Gerais." *The Americas* 45.1 (1988) 47–59. ISSN 0003-1615. ▸ Revisionist analysis of mortality, morbidity, hospitalization, and flight of slaves employed (1750s) in diamond-mining district of Brazil. Concludes diamond contractors sought to prolong slaves' lives. [MAB]

37.230 Leslie B. Rout, Jr. *The African experience in Spanish America, 1502 to the present day.* Cambridge: Cambridge University Press, 1976. ISBN 0-521-20805-X (cl), 0-521-29010-4 (pbk). ▸ Survey of African experience in Spanish America. Part 1 covers slave trade, slavery, and related topics useful for colonialists. [MAB]

37.231 A.J.R. Russell-Wood. *The black man in slavery and freedom in colonial Brazil.* New York: St. Martin's, 1982. ISBN 0-312-08326-2. ▸ Ten essays illuminating domestic and collective behavior and opportunities of slaves, free blacks, and mulattoes in Brazil's society, economy, and culture. Important contribution. [MAB]

37.232 A.J.R. Russell-Wood. "Iberian expansion and the issue of black slavery: changing Portuguese ideas, 1440–1770." *American historical review* 83.1 (1978) 16–42. ISSN 0002-8762. ▸ Extremely informative, valuable study, concluding Portuguese attitudes justifying black slavery survived in colonial and independent Brazil long after being disavowed in Portugal. [MAB]

37.233 William Frederick Sharp. *Slavery on the Spanish frontier: the Colombian Chocó, 1680–1810.* Norman: University of Oklahoma Press, 1976. ISBN 0-8061-1375-8. ▸ Important examination of African slavery in gold-producing region of Chocó. Concludes slavery and mining profitable for most owners. Valuable economic history. [MAB]

37.234 Robert Brent Toplin, ed. *Slavery and race relations in Latin America.* Westport, Conn.: Greenwood, 1974. ISBN 0-8371-7374-4. ▸ Five of fourteen useful essays on Chile, New Granada, and Amazonia in colonial period. [MAB]

37.235 Dennis N. Valdés. "The decline of slavery in Mexico." *The Americas* 44.2 (1987) 167–94. ISSN 0003-1615. ▸ Informative overview concluding slavery by 1820s long dead. Eighteenth century was era of mulatto slave and period of decline of institution. [MAB]

37.236 Julio Pinto Vallejos. "Slave control and slave resistance in colonial Minas Gerais, 1700–1750." *Journal of Latin American studies* 17.1 (1985) 1–34. ISSN 0022-216X. ▸ Useful examination of problem of slave control; how royal officials and municipal councils addressed it and patterns of slave resistance. Emphasizes instability and insecurity of society. [MAB]

SEE ALSO
22.243 Philip D. Curtin. *The Atlantic slave trade.*
38.566 Katia M. de Queirós Mattoso. *To be a slave in Brazil, 1550–1888.*

ECONOMY

37.237 Ida Altman and James Lockhart, eds. *Provinces of early Mexico: variants of Spanish-American regional evolution.* Los Angeles: University of California Press at Los Angeles Latin American Center Publications, 1976. (University of California at Los Angeles Latin American studies, 36.) ISBN 0-87903-036-4. ▸ Ten essays exploring different regions of Mexico at different times and from different perspectives between 1519 and 1810. Valuable contribution to social and economic history of New Spain. [MAB]

37.238 Peter J. Bakewell. *Miners of the red mountain: Indian labor in Potosí, 1545–1650.* Albuquerque: University of New Mexico Press, 1984. ISBN 0-8263-0769-8. ▸ Examines mining in Potosí, types of Indian labor employed, work performed, and working conditions. Valuable to read with Cole 37.250. [MAB]

37.239 Peter J. Bakewell. "Registered silver production in the Potosí district, 1550–1735." *Jahrbuch für Geschichte von Staat, Wirtschaft, und Gesellschaft Lateinamerikas* 12 (1975) 67–103. ISSN 0075-2673. ▸ Examination of annual production of silver in colonial Peru's main mining district on basis of mining taxes collected. Important contribution revealing production trends. [MAB]

37.240 Peter J. Bakewell. *Silver and entrepreneurship in seventeenth-century Potosi: the life and times of Antonio López de Quiroga.* Albuquerque: University of New Mexico Press, 1988. ISBN 0-8263-1097-4 (cl), 0-8263-1098-2 (pbk). ▸ Portrait of life and times of most remarkable miner and businessman in seventeenth-century Potosí. Adds humanistic dimension to author's many important contributions to mining history. [MAB]

37.241 Peter J. Bakewell. *Silver mining and society in colonial Mexico: Zacatecas, 1546–1700.* New York: Cambridge University Press, 1971. ISBN 0-521-08227-7. ▸ Detailed examination of silver mining and society in Mexico. Presents substantial data on silver production and its relationship to availability of mercury. Extremely important contribution. [MAB]

37.242 Ward Barrett. "World bullion flows, 1450-1800." In *The rise of merchant empires: long-distance trade in the early modern world, 1350-1750.* James D. Tracy, ed., pp. 224–54. New York: Cambridge University Press, 1990. ISBN 0-521-38210-6. ▸ Review of estimates of bullion production, most from the Americas, and where bullion went. Estimates include those by Alexander von Humboldt, Michael Morineau, and B. H. Slicher van Bath. Important evaluation. [MAB]

37.243 Woodrow Borah. *New Spain's century of depression.* 1951 ed. Norwood, Pa.: Norwood Editions, 1976. ▸ Important argument based on demographic data; from 1576 until more than century later New Spain's economy was contracting. Extremely influential monograph; hypothesis revised by later research, including Bakewell 37.241. [MAB]

37.244 Woodrow Borah and Sherburne F. Cook. *Price trends of some basic commodities in Central Mexico, 1531–1570.* Berkeley: University of California Press, 1958. ▸ Pioneering effort in understudied dimension of economic history. Examines price trends of maize, wheat, clothing, cloth, some lesser commodities, and labor. [MAB]

37.245 Peter Boyd-Bowman. "Two country stores in seventeenth-century Mexico." *The Americas* 228.3 (1972) 237–51. ISSN

0003-1615. ▸ Fascinating inventories revealing kinds of merchandise stocked, where it was from, and its value. Extremely informative for understanding daily life. [MAB]

37.246 D. A. Brading. *Haciendas and ranchos in the Mexican Bajío: León, 1700–1860.* New York: Cambridge University Press, 1978. ISBN 0-521-22200-1. ▸ Regional study useful to economic and social historians and demographers. Focuses on emergence of medium-sized cereal-growing properties, demographic change, and society. [MAB/EH-D]

37.247 D. A. Brading and Harry E. Cross. "Colonial silver mining: Mexico and Peru." *Hispanic American historical review* 52.4 (1972) 545–79. ISSN 0018-2168. ▸ Examination of mining techniques, refining, labor, royal policy, capital structure, and production. Estimates total bullion production on basis of mercury consumed in amalgamation process of silver production and estimated silver smelted and gold produced. [MAB]

37.248 François Chevalier. *Land and society in colonial Mexico: the great hacienda.* 1963 ed. Alvin Eustis, trans. Lesley Byrd Simpson, ed. Berkeley: University of California Press, 1970. ISBN 0-520-00229-6 (cl), 0-520-01665-3 (pbk). ▸ Examination of formation and evolution of secular and ecclesiastical landed estates in Mexico. Although many conclusions challenged, remains starting point for *hacienda* (landed estate) studies. [MAB]

37.249 Lawrence A. Clayton. *Caulkers and carpenters in a New World: the shipyards of colonial Guayaquil.* Athens: Ohio University, Center for International Studies, 1980. (Papers in international studies, Latin American series, 8.) ISBN 0-89680-103-9. ▸ Useful, unique examination of organization, economics, government regulation, and production of shipbuilding industry in Guayaquil in sixteenth and seventeenth centuries. [MAB]

37.250 Jeffrey A. Cole. *The Potosí mita, 1573–1700: compulsory Indian labor.* Stanford, Calif.: Stanford University Press, 1985. ISBN 0-8047-1256-5. ▸ Examination of establishment, use, and administration of forced-labor draft for silver mining at Potosi. Complements Bakewell 37.238. [MAB]

37.251 Harry E. Cross. "South American bullion production and export, 1550–1750." In *Precious metals in the later medieval and early modern worlds.* John F. Richards, ed. Durham, N.C.: Carolina Academic Press, 1983. ISBN 0-89089-224-5. ▸ Important effort to estimate bullion production for whole of South America by applying several approaches to registered output that increase it to more reasonable levels. [MAB]

37.252 Nicholas P. Cushner. *Farm and factory: the Jesuits and development of agrarian capitalism in colonial Quito, 1600–1767.* Albany: State University of New York Press, 1982. ISBN 0-87395-570-6 (cl), 0-87395-571-4 (pbk). ▸ Valuable economic history focusing on relationship between textile mill and farms and ranches in colonial Quito. Emphasizes Jesuits' investments, rational use of profits, and reinvestment. Part of valuable trilogy (with 37.253 and 37.254). [MAB]

37.253 Nicholas P. Cushner. *Jesuit ranches and the agrarian development of colonial Argentina, 1650–1767.* Albany: State University of New York Press, 1983. ISBN 0-87395-707-5 (cl), 0-87395-708-3 (pbk). ▸ Part of valuable trilogy (with 37.252 and 37.254) examining farmsteads and ranches, mule trade, functioning farm, labor force, finance, credit, money, and colonial trade. Emphasizes preeminence of Jesuit rural properties and effect on agricultural production. [MAB]

37.254 Nicholas P. Cushner. *Lords of the land: sugar, wine, and Jesuit estates of coastal Peru, 1600–1767.* Albany: State University of New York Press, 1980. ISBN 0-87395-438-6 (cl), 0-87395-447-5 (pbk). ▸ Examination of Jesuit estates of coastal Peru, their productivity, use of labor, profitability, finances, and trade. Valuable

regional study emphasizing that estates were meant to be profitable. Part of valuable trilogy (with 37.252 and 37.253). [MAB]

37.255 Keith A. Davies. *Landowners in colonial Peru.* Austin: University of Texas Press, 1984. ISBN 0-292-74639-3. ▸ Detailed examination of rural property, landowners, and wine economy of Arequipa from mid-sixteenth to late seventeenth century. Emphasizes landowners' capitalism and efforts to retain properties. Important regional study. [MAB]

37.256 Susan M. Deeds. "Rural work in Nueva Vizcaya: forms of labor coercion on the periphery." *Hispanic American historical review* 69.3 (1989) 425–49. ISSN 0018-2168. ▸ Fine regional examination of agricultural labor. Slavery and *encomienda* (system of forced native labor) flourished in seventeenth century and *repartimiento* (required rotational labor) survived until late eighteenth century. [MAB]

37.257 William H. Dusenberry. *The Mexican mesta: the administration of ranching in colonial Mexico.* Urbana: University of Illinois Press, 1963. ▸ Examination of stock raising in New Spain and stockmen's association created to regulate it (1537–1812). Remains useful study of important institution. [MAB]

37.258 Elizabeth Fonseca. *Costa Rica colonial: la tierra y el hombre.* Ciudad Universitaria Rodrigo Facio, Costa Rica: Editorial Universitaria Centroamericana, 1983. ISBN 9-9773002-9-1. ▸ Study of evolution of small properties in Costa Rica's Central Valley. Significant contribution to colonial agrarian history. [MFB]

37.259 J. H. Galloway. *The sugar cane industry: an historical geography from its origins to 1914.* Cambridge: Cambridge University Press, 1989. ISBN 0-521-24853-1. ▸ General study containing substantial chapters on Atlantic sugar industry, ca. 1450–1680, and American sugar industry in eighteenth century. Valuable examination of important topic. [MAB]

37.260 Richard L. Garner. "Long-term silver-mining trends in Spanish America: a comparative analysis of Peru and Mexico." *American historical review* 93.4 (1988) 898–935. ISSN 0002-8762. ▸ Sophisticated analysis of Spanish American silver production. Finds overall production rising, 1559–1627, then declining, 1628–97, and then rising to record levels, 1698–1810. Notes significantly different trends for each region. [MAB]

37.261 Lolita Gutiérrez Brockington. *The leverage of labor: managing the Cortés haciendas in Tehuantepec, 1588–1688.* Durham, N.C.: Duke University Press, 1989. ▸ Informative socioeconomic examination of development of *haciendas* (landed estates) and livestock raising prior to 1588; treats administration and slave and nonslave labor. Demonstrates profit-oriented enterprise. [MAB]

37.262 Charles H. Harris III. *A Mexican family empire: the latifundio of the Sánchez Navarros, 1765–1867.* Austin: University of Texas Press, 1975. ISBN 0-292-75020-X. ▸ Valuable case study tracing evolution of enormous Sánchez Navarro estates in Coahuila with attention to family, land, ranching, labor, production, commerce, and politics. Part 1 covers 1765–1821. [MAB]

37.263 Robert Stephen Haskett. "'Our suffering with the Taxco tribute': involuntary mine labor and indigenous society in Central New Spain." *Hispanic American historical review* 71.3 (1991) 447–75. ISSN 0018-2168. ▸ Silver-mine owners in Taxco region used various forms of involuntary tribute labor that profoundly and adversely affected native communities forced to provide workers. Important contribution. [MAB]

37.264 Ross Hassig. *Trade, tribute, and transportation: the sixteenth-century political economy of the valley of Mexico.* Norman: University of Oklahoma Press, 1985. ISBN 0-8061-1911-X. ▸ Informative examination of pre- and postconquest economy of Valley of Mexico with emphasis on changes resulting from shift to mule and wagon transportation after conquest. Analysis of entire

Nahua system of agriculture, transportation, and consumption. [MAB/SS]

37.265 Julia Hirschberg. "An alternative to *encomienda*: Puebla's *indios de servicio*, 1531–45." *Journal of Latin American studies* 11.2 (1979) 241–64. ISSN 0022-216X. ▸ Informative examination of labor system that served as bridge between preconquest and early colonial labor draft and *repartimiento* (rotational) labor. System provided limited, officially supervised, and broadly distributed access to labor. [MAB]

37.266 Evelyn Hu-DeHart. *Missionaries, miners, and Indians: Spanish contact with the Yaqui nation of northwestern New Spain, 1533–1820.* Tucson: University of Arizona Press, 1981. ISBN 0-8165-0740-6 (cl), 0-8165-0755-4 (pbk). ▸ Discussion of contact and eventual conflict between Jesuits, miners, and *hacendados* (estate owners) and Yaquis. Emphasizes survival of Yaqui culture. [MAB]

37.267 Jonathan I. Israel. "Mexico and the 'general crisis' of the seventeenth century." *Past and present* 63 (1974) 33–57. ISSN 0031-2746. ▸ Provocative study arguing Mexico suffered from prolonged depression, 1620 to 1660s, experiencing economic crisis, fiscal pressure, campaign to restrain official corruption, and political instability. [MAB]

37.268 Lyman L. Johnson and Enrique Tandeter, eds. *Essays on the price history of eighteenth-century Latin America.* Albuquerque: University of New Mexico Press, 1990. ISBN 0-8263-1163-6 (cl), 0-8263-1164-4 (pbk). ▸ Pioneering work in important, underdeveloped area of economic history. Twelve chapters, most with regional focus, by fourteen authors. [MAB]

37.269 Robert G. Keith. *Conquest and agrarian change: the emergence of the hacienda system on the Peruvian coast.* Cambridge, Mass.: Harvard University Press, 1976. ISBN 0-674-16293-5. ▸ Important regional study examining emergence of *hacienda* (landed estate) system in seven major valleys of coastal Peru and its consolidation in early seventeenth century. [MAB]

37.270 Robert G. Keith. "*Encomienda, hacienda,* and *corregimiento* in Spanish America: a structural analysis." *Hispanic American historical review* 51.3 (1971) 431–46. ISSN 0018-2168. ▸ Perceptive, important contribution, focusing on discontinuities between essentially precapitalistic *encomienda* (system of forced labor and tribute) and basically capitalistic *hacienda* (landed estate), and continuities between *encomienda* and *corregimiento de indios* (Spanish institution for administering native population). [MAB]

37.271 Jay Kinsbruner. *Petty capitalism in Spanish America: the pulperos of Puebla, Mexico City, Caracas, and Buenos Aires.* Boulder: Westview, 1987. ISBN 0-8133-7272-0 (pbk). ▸ Informative, unique study presenting cross-cultural profile of small retail grocers, ca. 1750–1850. Considers capitalization and profitability, grocers as entrepreneurs, and problems of grocery-store ownership. [MAB]

37.272 Herman W. Konrad. *A Jesuit hacienda in colonial Mexico: Santa Lucía, 1576–1767.* Stanford, Calif.: Stanford University Press, 1980. ISBN 0-8047-1050-3. ▸ Detailed examination of origin, expansion, administration and management, and life of one of colonial Mexico's most prosperous estates over nearly two centuries. Extraordinarily rich study. [MAB]

37.273 M. F. Lang. "New Spain's mining depression and the supply of quicksilver from Peru, 1600–1700." *Hispanic American historical review* 48.4 (1968) 632–41. ISSN 0018-2168. ▸ Informative note outlining crown policy toward and shipment of mercury from Huancavelica to Mexico. [MAB]

37.274 Richard B. Lindley. *Haciendas and economic development: Guadalajara, Mexico at independence.* Austin: University of Texas Press, 1983. (University of Texas at Austin, Institute of Latin

American Studies, Latin American monographs, 58.) ISBN 0-292-72042-4. ▸ Despite title, substantial attention to late colonial economy and society in Guadalajara. Emphasizes importance of kinship ties in securing financial credit essential for economic survival. Valuable local study. [MAB]

37.275 James Lockhart. "*Encomienda* and *hacienda*: the evolution of the great estate in the Spanish Indies." *Hispanic American historical review* 49.3 (1969) 411–29. ISSN 0018-2168. ▸ Groundbreaking article examining relationship between two important institutions, stressing functions and connections. Notes replacement of *encomienda* (system of forced labor) by *hacienda* (landed estate system) represented a shift in emphasis, not distinctly new institution. [MAB]

37.276 Murdo J. MacLeod. *Spanish Central America: a socioeconomic history, 1520–1720.* Berkeley: University of California Press, 1973. ISBN 0-520-02137-1. ▸ Detailed socioeconomic history. Emphasis on economic booms and busts tracing Indian and Spanish adaptation. Major contribution to colonial economic history and debate over seventeenth-century depression. [MAB/MWH]

37.277 Cheryl English Martin. *Rural society in colonial Morelos.* Albuquerque: University of New Mexico Press, 1985. ISBN 0-8263-0797-3. ▸ Examines Morelos, Mexico from 1521 to 1810, particularly focusing on its sugar industry, population changes, land use, commercial agriculture, and life and labor. Valuable regional study. [MAB]

37.278 Elinor G. K. Melville. "Environmental and social change in the Valle del Metzquital, Mexico, 1521–1600." *Comparative studies in society and history* 32.1 (1990) 24–53. ISSN 0010-4175. ▸ Very important revisionist work demonstrating changes in land use, overgrazing, and ecological change resulted in decline of region's productive potential and influenced development of large estates. [MAB]

37.279 Michael E. Murphy. *Irrigation in the Bajío region of colonial Mexico.* Boulder: Westview, 1986. ISBN 0-8133-7271-2 (pbk). ▸ Historical reconstruction of irrigation and urban supply systems in Celaya, Salvatierra, Salamanca, and Querétaro. Discusses irrigated agriculture, water law, and technology of water works. Contribution to understudied topic. [MAB]

37.280 Wayne S. Osborn. "Indian land retention in colonial Metztitlán." *Hispanic American historical review* 53.2 (1973) 217–38. ISSN 0018-2168. ▸ Valuable regional study, demonstrating that Indian villages of Metztitlán retained lands more effectively than did villages in northern Mexico. [MAB]

37.281 Susan E. Ramírez. *Provincial patriarchs: land tenure and the economics of power in colonial Peru.* Albuquerque: University of New Mexico Press, 1986. ISBN 0-8263-0818-X. ▸ Examination of landholding elite in Lambayeque, Peru, during colonial period. Argues landed elite's power rested on wealth not simply on land. Important contribution to *hacienda* (landed estate) literature. [MFB]

37.282 David R. Ringrose. "Carting in the Hispanic world: an example of divergent development." *Hispanic American historical review* 50.1 (1970) 30–50. ISSN 0018-2168. ▸ Perceptive, informative, comparative examination of carting in Spain, Mexico, and Argentina. Emphasizes reliance on land transportation not limitation on economic growth as often claimed. [MAB]

37.283 Richard J. Salvucci. *Textiles and capitalism in Mexico: an economic history of the obrajes, 1539–1840.* Princeton: Princeton University Press, 1987. ISBN 0-691-07749-5. ▸ Detailed examination of woolen-textile manufactories, their owners, laborers, markets, and failure to survive integration into world market after 1790. Sophisticated economic analysis. [MAB]

37.284 Stuart B. Schwartz. *Sugar plantations in the formation of*

Brazilian society: Bahia, 1550–1835. New York: Cambridge University Press, 1985. ISBN 0-521-30934-4 (cl), 0-521-31399-6 (pbk). ▸ Examination of origins, operation, society, profitability, and persistence of sugar plantations. Outstanding contribution that also illuminates sugar trade and slavery in Bahia over extended period. [MAB]

37.285 William L. Sherman. *Forced native labor in sixteenth-century Central America.* Lincoln: University of Nebraska Press, 1979. ISBN 0-8032-4100-3. ▸ Detailed examination of each type of forced labor in Central America and progression from one form to another. [MAB]

37.286 Lesley Byrd Simpson. *The encomienda in New Spain: the beginning of Spanish Mexico.* Rev. ed. Berkeley: University of California Press, 1982. ISBN 0-520-04629-3 (cl), 0-520-04630-7 (pbk). ▸ Detailed examination of development of dominant labor system employed in Caribbean and New Spain during initial decades after conquest. Still useful. [MAB]

37.287 Lesley Byrd Simpson, ed. and trans. *The laws of Burgos of 1512–1535: royal ordinances for the good government and treatment of the Indians.* 1960 ed. Westport, Conn.: Greenwood, 1978. ISBN 0-313-21019-5. ▸ Translation of first codified legislation related to living and working conditions of native population and responsibilities of *encomenderos* (recipients of native labor and tribute) toward Indians assigned to them. Important source. [MAB]

37.288 Karen Spalding, ed. *Essays in the political, economic, and social history of colonial Latin America.* Newark: University of Delaware, Latin American Studies Program, 1982. (University of Delaware, Latin American Studies Program, Occasional papers and monographs, 3.) ▸ Excellent, varied essays by expert scholars. [MAB]

37.289 John C. Super. "Querétaro *obrajes*: industry and society in provincial Mexico, 1600–1810." *Hispanic American historical review* 56.2 (1976) 197–216. ISSN 0018-2168. ▸ Thoughtful, informative examination of social and economic characteristics of *obraje* (textile workshop) ownership; capital, supply, distribution, and labor; and number of looms operating in eighteenth century. [MAB]

37.290 William B. Taylor. "Land and water rights in the viceroyalty of New Spain." *New Mexico historical review* 50.3 (1975) 189–212. ISSN 0028-6206. ▸ Excellent introduction to and valuable discussion of water grants and adjudication of water rights. Land ownership carried implied right to available water. Indian communities normally entitled to irrigation water. [MAB]

37.291 William B. Taylor. "Landed society in New Spain: a view from the south." *Hispanic American historical review* 54.3 (1974) 387–415. ISSN 0018-2168. ▸ Thoughtful, persuasive discussion of Indian and Spanish landholding from Oaxaca to Guatemala. Very different from that in central and northern Mexico; Indians retained substantial holdings and Spanish landholding unstable. [MAB]

37.292 William B. Taylor. *Landlord and peasant in colonial Oaxaca.* Stanford, Calif.: Stanford University Press, 1972. ISBN 0-8047-0796-0. ▸ Detailed study of landholding by Spaniards, church, and Indians in colonial Oaxaca. Argues colonial *hacienda* (landed estate) and labor and tribute systems enabled traditional forms of leadership and practice to persist. Outstanding regional study. Includes comparison with *haciendas* of northern Mexico. [MAB]

37.293 John Jay TePaske. "New World silver: Castile and the Philippines, 1590–1800." In *Precious metals in the later medieval and early modern worlds.* John F. Richards, ed., pp. 425–45. Durham, N.C.: Carolina Academic Press, 1983. ISBN 0-89089-224-5. ▸ Important examination of flow of American silver to Castile and

Philippines. Emphasizes 1660 as turning point in royal policies and when Mexico displaced Peru as leading provider of funds to Spain. [MAB]

37.294 John Jay TePaske and Alvaro Jara, comps. *Eighteenth-century Ecuador.* Vol. 4 of *The royal treasuries of the Spanish empire in America.* Durham, N.C.: Duke University Press, 1990. ISBN 0-8223-0486-4 (set), 0-8223-1042-2 (v. 4, cl), 0-8223-0814-2 (v. 4, pbk). ▸ Compilation of income and expenditure for royal treasuries of Ecuador for most of eighteenth century and part of nineteenth. Fundamental source for fiscal and economic history. [MAB]

37.295 John Jay TePaske and Herbert S. Klein. "The seventeenth-century crisis in New Spain: myth or reality?" *Past and present* 90 (1981) 116–35. ISSN 0031-2746. ▸ Use of treasury accounts of income and expenditure for New Spain to argue silver production rose in seventeenth century and economy was stagnant. Controversy follows in *Past and Present* 97 (1982) 145–61. [MAB]

37.296 John Jay TePaske and Herbert S. Klein, comps. *Ingresos y egresos de la real hacienda de Nueva España.* 2 vols. Mexico City: Instituto Nacional de Antropología e Historia, 1986–88. ISBN 968-6038-31-0 (set), 968-6038-32-9 (v. 1), 968-6038-33-7 (v. 2). ▸ Presentation of income and expenditures for treasury offices of Acapulco, Arispe, Bolaños, Campeche, Chihuahua, Durango, Guadalajara, Guanajuato, and Mérida. Part of fundamental fiscal series. [MAB]

37.297 John Jay TePaske and Herbert S. Klein, comps. *The royal treasuries of the Spanish empire in America.* 4 vols. Durham, N.C.: Duke University Press, 1982–90. ISBN 0-8223-0486-4 (set), 0-8223-0530-5 (v. 1), 0-8223-0531-3 (v. 2), 0-8223-0532-1 (v. 3), 0-8223-1042-2 (v. 4). ▸ Compilation of royal treasury account summaries for Peru, Upper Peru (Bolivia), Chile, and Río de la Plata. Introduction describes treasury system and sources. Fundamental source for fiscal and economic history. [MAB]

37.298 John Jay TePaske, José Hernández Paloma, and Mari Luz Hernández Paloma, comps. *La real hacienda de Nueva España: la real caja de México (1576–1816).* Mexico: Instituto Nacional de Antropología e Historia, SEP, Departamento de Investigaciones Históricas, Seminario de Historia Económica, 1976. (Colección científica: fuentes [Historia económica de México], 41.) ▸ Reconstruction of income and expenditures of royal treasury in Mexico City. Fundamental source for economic history of colonial Mexico. [MAB]

37.299 Ann Twinam. *Miners, merchants, and farmers in colonial Colombia.* Austin: University of Texas Press, 1982. (University of Texas at Austin, Institute of Latin American Studies, Latin American monographs, 57.) ISBN 0-292-72034-3. ▸ Examines gold mining, commerce, agriculture, and Medellín elite primarily for period 1770–1810. Emphasizes presence of pragmatic entrepreneurs. Fine social, economic, and political history of region. [MAB]

37.300 Eric Van Young. *Hacienda and market in eighteenth-century Mexico: the rural economy of the Guadalajara region, 1675–1820.* Berkeley: University of California Press, 1981. ISBN 0-520-04161-5. ▸ Excellent economic analysis of Guadalajara region with particular attention to Guadalajara as market, late *hacienda* (landed estate) system, growing population, and conflicts over land. Sophisticated study. [MAB]

37.301 Juan A. Villamarín and Judith E. Villamarín. *Indian labor in mainland Spanish America.* Newark: University of Delaware, Latin American Studies Program, 1975. (University of Delaware Latin American Studies Program, Occasional papers and monographs, 1.) ▸ Review of slavery, *yanaconaje* (form of servile labor), *encomienda* (system of forced labor), *repartimiento* (rotational labor system), and free labor and examination of differential development. Includes case studies from different regions. Valuable overview of labor systems. [MAB]

37.302 Ann Zulawski. "Wages, ore sharing, and peasant agriculture: labor in Oruro's silver mines, 1607–1720." *Hispanic American historical review* 67.3 (1987) 405–30. ISSN 0018-2168. ▸ Discussion of accessibility of agricultural communities and difficulties of enforcing labor system based on wages alone; importance of preserving system with both wages and semi-legal ore sharing. Very informative. [MAB]

COMMERCE

37.303 Woodrow Borah. *Early colonial trade and navigation between Mexico and Peru.* Berkeley: University of California Press, 1954. ▸ Examination of nature and extent of trade, including link with Philippines and efforts to regulate and tax from 1530s to official suppression of trade in 1631. Older but still important study. [MAB]

37.304 Huguette Chaunu and Pierre Chaunu. *Séville et l'Atlantique (1504–1650).* 8 vols. in 11. Paris: Colin, 1955–59. (École Pratique des Hautes Études, Section 6. Centre de Recherches Historique: ports-routes-trafics, 6.) ▸ Monumental examination of structure, nature, and extent of trade between Spain and her American colonies with wealth of quantitative data, charts, and graphs. Among most important and influential works ever published on Spanish and colonial Spanish American economic history. [MAB]

37.305 Pierre Chaunu. *Les Philippines et le Pacifique des Ibériques (seizième, dix-septième, dix-huitième siècles).* 2 vols. Paris: Service d'Édition et de Vente des Publications de l'Education, 1960–66. (École Pratique des Hautes Études, Section 6. Centre de Recherches Historique: ports-routes-trafics, 11–11 bis.) ▸ Supplement to monumental Chaunu and Chaunu study (37.304), providing trade, economic, and fiscal information and analysis of Manila trade from late sixteenth to late eighteenth century. Extremely valuable. [MAB]

37.306 Lawrence A. Clayton. "Trade and navigation in the seventeenth-century viceroyalty of Peru." *Journal of Latin American studies* 7.1 (1975) 1–21. ISSN 0022-216x. ▸ Instructive, useful outline of major aspects of trade and navigation, including contraband. Argues economy was robust and expansive. Concludes Peru maturing, growing, and becoming more self-sufficient. [MAB]

37.307 Harry E. Cross. "Commerce and orthodoxy: a Spanish response to Portuguese commercial penetration of the viceroyalty of Peru, 1580–1640." *The Americas* 35.2 (1978) 151–67. ISSN 0003-1615. ▸ Very informative examination of rise to prominence of Portuguese merchants in Peru and successful efforts of Spanish merchant monopolists working in conjunction with Inquisition to oust them. [MAB]

37.308 Antonio García-Baquero González. *Cádiz y el Atlántico, 1717–1778: el comercio colonial español bajo el monopolio gaditano.* 2 vols. Sevilla: Escuela de Estudios Hispano-Americanos, Consejo Superior de Investigaciones Científicas: Excelentísima Diputación Provincial de Cádiz, 1976. (Publicaciones de la Escuela de Estudios Hispano-Americanos de Sevilla, 237.) ISBN 84-00-03581-X. ▸ Major study of structure, regulation, and magnitude of trade. Examines merchants, capital, imports and exports. Sees slow growth from 1717 to 1747 and more rapid growth from 1748 to 1778. Massive database comprises volume two. [MAB]

37.309 Lutgardo García Fuentes. *El comercio español con América, 1650–1700.* Sevilla: Escuela de Estudios Hispano-Americanos, Consejo Superior de Investigaciones Científicas, 1980. (Publicaciones de la Excelentísima: Diputación Provincial de Sevilla, Sección historia, ser. 1a, 16. Publicaciones de la Escuela de Estudios Hispano-Americanos de Sevilla, 265.) ISBN 84-00-04674-9. ▸ Examination of organization and evolution of trade, crown's efforts to benefit from it, sailings, exports and imports of various products, and importation of bullion. Helps fill major gap. [MAB]

37.310 Lutgardo García Fuentes. "En torno a la reactivación del comercio indiano en tiempos de Carlos II." *Anuario de estudios americanos* 36 (1979) 251–86. ISSN 0210-5810. ▸ Very important examination of growth in volume and value of trade between Spain and colonies from 1660s to 1700. [MAB]

37.311 Clarence H. Haring. *Trade and navigation between Spain and the Indies in the time of the Hapsburgs.* 1918 ed. Gloucester, Mass.: Smith, 1964. ▸ Superseded by Chaunus' monumental study (37.304), but remains useful introduction to institutions associated with trading system. [MAB]

37.312 Louisa Schell Hoberman. *Mexico's merchant elite, 1590–1660: silver, state, and society.* Durham, N.C.: Duke University Press, 1991. ISBN 0-8223-1134-8. ▸ Examination of Mexico's wholesale merchants and their varied roles in Mexican economy. Illuminates important chapter of Mexico's still neglected century. [MAB]

37.313 Frédéric Mauro. *Le Portugal, le Brésil et l'Atlantique au dix-septième siècle (1570–1670): étude économique.* 2d ed. Paris: Fondation Calouste Gulbenkian, Centre Culturel Portugais, 1983. ▸ Central study of seventeenth-century Brazilian history integrating Brazil's economic history with that of Portugal, Atlantic Islands, and West Africa. Fundamental work. [MAB]

37.314 Michel Morineau. *Incroyables gazettes et fabuleux métaux: les retours des trésors américains d'après les gazettes hollandaises (XVIe–XVIIIe siècles).* London and Paris: Cambridge University Press and Édition de la Maison des Sciences de l'Homme, 1985. ISBN 0-521-25384-5 (cl), 2-7351-0013-8 (cl), 2-7351-0112-6 (pbk). ▸ Brings together five previously published studies related to importation of American bullion. Many figures for imported silver substantially exceed estimates by students of silver production. Revolutionary implications. [MAB]

37.315 Zacarías Moutoukias. "Power, corruption, and commerce: the making of the local administrative structure in seventeenth-century Buenos Aires." *Hispanic American historical review* 68.4 (1988) 771–801. ISSN 0018-2168. ▸ Through corruption, local military and civilian representatives of central authority integrated themselves into local elite, thus associating it with imperial functions. New information and fine analysis. [MAB]

37.316 Javier Ortiz de la Tabla Ducasse. *Comercio exterior de Veracruz, 1778–1821: crisis de dependencia.* Sevilla: Escuela de Estudios Hispano-Americanos, 1978. (Publicaciones de la Escuela de Estudios Hispano-Americanos de Sevilla, 243.) ISBN 84-00-03765. ▸ Informative examination of controversy over free trade within empire, merchant guild of Veracruz, provincial and external trade, and neutral trade. Emphasizes disruption for Mexico resulting from free trade. [MAB]

37.317 Carla Rahn Phillips. "The growth and composition of trade in the Iberian empires, 1450–1750." In *The rise of merchant empires: long-distance trade in the early modern world, 1350–1750.* James D. Tracy, ed. New York: Cambridge University Press, 1990. ISBN 0-521-38210-6. ▸ Excellent overview based on thorough examination of relevant secondary literature. [MAB]

37.318 G. Earl Sanders. "Counter-contraband in Spanish America: handicaps of the governors in the Indies." *The Americas* 34.1 (1977) 59–80. ISSN 0003-1615. ▸ Informative examination of many difficulties governors had in stopping contraband, focusing on region of Cartagena de Indias in early eighteenth century. Emphasizes complexity of counter-contraband. [MAB]

37.319 William Lytle Schurz. *The Manila galleon.* 1939 ed. Manila: Historical Conservation Society, 1985. (Historical Conservation Society, 40.) ▸ Account of trade between Philippines and Mexico carried by Manila galleon. Remains most complete narrative in English. [MAB]

37.320 John C. Super. "Partnership and profit in the early Andean trade: the experiences of Quito merchants, 1580–1610." *Journal of Latin American studies* 11.2 (1979) 265–81. ISSN 0022-216X. ▸ Important pioneering study of conditions influencing commercial success: organization of merchant enterprises, profits earned from trade, and use of profits. Most annual profits ranged from 10 to 30 percent. [MAB]

37.321 Sergio Villalobos R. *Comercio y contrabando en el Río de la Plata y Chile, 1700–1811.* 1965 ed. Buenos Aires: Editorial Universitaria de Buenos Aires, 1986. ISBN 950-23-0246-X. ▸ Valuable overview of trade emphasizing extent to which it took place outside theoretically monopolistic system. Free trade decreed in early nineteenth century only legitimized existing situation. [MAB]

DEFENSE

37.322 Kenneth R. Andrews. *The Spanish Caribbean: trade and plunder, 1530–1630.* New Haven: Yale University Press, 1978. ISBN 0-300-02197-6. ▸ Impressive overview; considers Caribbean distinct historical unit between conquest and establishment of non-Hispanic colonies. Analyzes Spanish settlement, society, government, trade, foreign traders and pirates, contraband, and foreign settlement. [MAB]

37.323 C. R. Boxer. *The Dutch in Brazil, 1624–1654.* 1957 ed. Hamden, Conn.: Archon, 1973. ISBN 0-208-01338-5. ▸ Detailed, readable examination of Dutch assault on Brazil, Dutch colonial settlement and policies, and ultimate Dutch defeat and withdrawal. Standard account. [MAB]

37.324 Peter T. Bradley. *The lure of Peru: maritime intrusion into the South Sea, 1598–1701.* New York: St. Martin's, 1989. ISBN 0-312-04061-X. ▸ Narrative of interlopers in Pacific from Dutch arrival in 1598 to arrival of French traders in 1701 and repercussions of their actions on Peru. Valuable complement to Gerhard 37.329. [MAB]

37.325 Peter T. Bradley. "Maritime defence of the viceroyalty of Peru (1600–1700)." *The Americas* 36.2 (1979) 155–74. ISSN 0003-1615. ▸ Informative analysis of size and condition of fleets used to defend Peru. Consisted of maximum of six ships with three or four normal. Penury limited number and size of ships, maintenance, and crews. [MAB]

37.326 Lawrence A. Clayton. "Local initiative and finance in defense of the viceroyalty of Peru: the development of self-reliance." *Hispanic American historical review* 54.2 (1974) 284–304. ISSN 0018-2168. ▸ Local resources and private initiative of merchants in particular central to providing defense for coastal Peru in seventeenth century. Self-reliance marked further maturation of colony. Valuable contribution. [MAB]

37.327 Peter Earle. *The sack of Panamá: Sir Henry Morgan's adventures on the Spanish Main.* New York: Viking, 1982. ISBN 0-670-61425-4. ▸ Exciting narrative examining four campaigns by Jamaican privateers beginning in 1666 and concluding with sack of city of Panama in 1671 and one successful counterattack by Spaniards. [MAB]

37.328 A. O. Exquemelin. *The buccaneers of America.* Jack Beeching, Introduction. Alexis Brown, trans. Baltimore: Penguin, 1969. ▸ Vivid contemporary account of French and English piracy in Caribbean region in late seventeenth century. [MAB]

37.329 Peter Gerhard. *Pirates on the west coast of New Spain, 1575–1742.* Glendale, Calif.: Clark, 1960. ▸ Useful discussion of Elizabethan pirates, Dutch pirates, buccaneers, and English privateers and smugglers. Concludes somewhat arbitrarily with

British admiral George Anson's capture of Manila galleon in early 1740s. [MAB]

37.330 Paul E. Hoffman. *The Spanish crown and the defense of the Caribbean, 1535–1585: precedent, patrimonialism, and royal parsimony.* Baton Rouge: Louisiana State University Press, 1980. ISBN 0-8071-0583-X. ▸ Important, detailed examination of defense in Caribbean employing quantitative analysis as well as narrative sources. Concludes Spain's evolving defensive policy generally adequate and sensible. [MAB]

37.331 Philip Wayne Powell. *Soldiers, Indians, and silver: the northward advance of New Spain, 1550–1600.* Berkeley: University of California Press, 1952. ▸ Description of frontier conflict and Spanish military resources and strategy following discovery of silver at Zacatecas. Fascinating narrative; still authoritative. [MAB]

37.332 David Tengwall. "A study in military leadership: Portuguese South Atlantic empire." *The Americas* 40.1 (1983) 73–94. ISSN 0003-1615. ▸ Informative discussion of several types of *sargento mor,* the coordinator of military operations within his captaincy, in Brazil from 1640 to 1706 with special attention to appointment process. [MAB]

SEE ALSO
29.131 Carla Rahn Phillips. *Six galleons for the king of Spain.*

COLONIAL SOCIETY

37.333 Bartolomé Arzáns de Orsúa y Vela. *Historia de la villa imperial de Potosí.* 3 vols. Lewis Hanke and Gunnar Mendoza, eds. Providence: Brown University Press, 1965. ▸ Astonishing, richly detailed history of greatest mining center in New World from its discovery in 1545 to 1737. Invaluable source. [MAB]

37.334 Bartolomé Arzáns de Orsúa y Vela. *Tales of Potosí.* R. C. Padden, ed. Frances A. López Morillas, trans. Providence: Brown University Press, 1975. ISBN 0-87057-144-3. ▸ Delightful, translated collection of anecdotes drawn from Arzáns's monumental work with helpful introduction. Anecdotes span period 1598 to 1716. Vividly captures flavor of times. [MAB]

37.335 Stephanie Blank. "Patrons, clients, and kin in seventeenth-century Caracas: a methodological essay in colonial Spanish American social history." *Hispanic American historical review* 54.2 (1974) 260–83. ISSN 0018-2168. ▸ Methodologically sophisticated, computerized analysis of Caracas elite, 1595–1627, emphasizing importance of kinship as key tie defining elite and connecting it to clients. [MAB]

37.336 C. R. Boxer. *Women in Iberian expansion overseas, 1415–1815: some facts, fancies, and personalities.* New York: Oxford University Press, 1975. ISBN 0-19-5-19817-4. ▸ Valuable cross-cultural exploration of women's role in Portuguese colonies of Africa, Asia, and America. Discusses misogyny and development of Mary cult. [MFB]

37.337 Richard Boyer. "Juan Vásquez, muleteer of seventeenth-century Mexico." *The Americas* 37.4 (1981) 421–43. ISSN 0003-1615. ▸ Delightful account of cuckolded muleteer who remarried and ran afoul of Inquisition for bigamy. Provides insight into lower-class society. [MAB]

37.338 Richard Boyer. "Mexico in the seventeenth century: transition of a colonial society." *Hispanic American historical review* 57.3 (1977) 455–78. ISSN 0018-2168. ▸ Mexico City replaced Seville as metropole as New Spain underwent transition to capitalism, economic diversification, and vigorous regional economies. Rejects idea that seventeenth century was century of depression. Important article. [MAB]

37.339 Fred Bronner. "Peruvian *encomenderos* in 1630: elite circulation and consolidation." *Hispanic American historical review*

57.4 (1977) 633–59. ISSN 0018-2168. ▸ Outstanding analysis of formation of new effective elite based on office, land, and trade and focused in Lima. By 1630 descent from conquistadors and early settlers insufficient for elite status. [MAB]

37.340 Elinor C. Burkett. "In dubious sisterhood: class and sex in Spanish colonial South America." *Latin American perspectives* 4.12–13 (1977) 1926. ISSN 0094-582X. ▸ Examination of urban female experience in early colonial Peru. Concludes class and race, not gender, were central in defining female relationships. Thoughtful analysis. [MAB]

37.341 John K. Chance. *Conquest of the sierra: Spaniards and Indians in colonial Oaxaca*. Norman: University of Oklahoma Press, 1989. ISBN 0-8061-2222-6. ▸ Valuable ethnohistorical examination. Demonstrates resilience of sierra Zapotecs' communal structures and assesses impact of Spanish trading practices, based on force, on communities' social organization. [MAB]

37.342 John K. Chance. *Race and class in colonial Oaxaca*. Stanford, Calif.: Stanford University Press, 1978. ISBN 0-8047-0937-8. ▸ Examination of economy and society in urban Antequera Oaxaca, preconquest to 1812, by historical anthropologist. Concludes property, race, and political power were primary determinants of rank. Stimulating and provocative. [MAB/SS]

37.343 Paul Charney. "The implications of godparental ties between Indians and Spaniards in early colonial Lima." *The Americas* 47.3 (1991) 295–313. ISSN 0003-1615. ▸ Useful examination of ties that enabled native nobility to enter social network with Spaniards and gain benefits, including protection from other Spaniards. Spaniards, too, benefited in gaining access to land and labor. [MAB]

37.344 Alexandra Parma Cook and Noble David Cook. *Good faith and truthful ignorance: a case of transatlantic bigamy*. Durham, N.C.: Duke University Press, 1991. ISBN 0-822-31086-4. ▸ Stimulating historical reconstruction of trials and tribulations of sixteenth-century Spanish bigamist. Valuable for understanding complex relationships between religious, social, and legal systems. [MFB]

37.345 Robert J. Ferry. *The colonial elite of early Caracas: formation and crisis, 1567–1767*. Berkeley: University of California Press, 1989. ISBN 0-520-06399-6. ▸ Fine social and economic history of elite formation and maintenance with emphasis on importance of cacao. Shows many reforms associated with King Charles III (r. 1759–88) were introduced earlier (1750s). [MAB]

37.346 Rae Flory and David Grant Smith. "Bahian merchants and planters in the seventeenth and early eighteenth centuries." *Hispanic American historical review* 58.4 (1978) 571–94. ISSN 0018-2168. ▸ Argues usual merchant-planter dichotomy overstates division between two groups. Merchant gains in early eighteenth century marked integration into established elite that had incorporated successful merchants since early seventeenth century. Important revisionist article. [MAB]

37.347 Della M. Flusche. *Two families in colonial Chile*. Lewiston: Mellen, 1989. ISBN 0-8894-6491-X. ▸ Detailed chronicle of establishment and development of Irrazával-Zárate and Toro Mazote families from sixteenth through eighteenth centuries. Valuable insight into Chilean colonial life. [MFB]

37.348 Della M. Flusche and Eugene H. Korth. "A dowry office in seventeenth-century Chile." *The historian* 49.2 (1987) 204–22. ISSN 0018-2370. ▸ Useful case study of use of office on Santiago municipal council as dowry. Demonstrates how paternal wealth and dowry office could compensate for illegitimacy. [MAB]

37.349 Lewis Hanke. *Bartolomé Arzáns de Orsúa y Vela's "History of Potosí."* Providence: Brown University Press, 1965. (Colver lectures in Brown University, 1965.) ▸ Places Arzáns's history (37.333, 37.334) in perspective of other Spanish writings on New World, discusses Arzáns as historian, and indicates value of his work. Very helpful introduction to the *History*. [MAB]

37.350 Jonathan I. Israel. *Race, class, and politics in colonial Mexico, 1610–1670*. New York: Oxford University Press, 1975. ISBN 0-19-821860-5. ▸ Examines major groups of Mexican society in seventeenth century and effect of social tensions on Mexican politics. Important contribution to still understudied period. [MAB]

37.351 Richard Konetzke, ed. *Colección de documentos para la historia de la formación social de Hispanoamérica, 1493–1810*. 3 vols. in 5. Madrid: Consejo Superior de Investigaciones Científicas, 1953–62. ▸ Extraordinarily rich collection of documents related to colonial society. Fundamental resource. [MAB]

37.352 Eugene H. Korth and Della M. Flusche. "Dowry and inheritance in colonial Spanish America: peninsular law and Chilean practice." *The Americas* 43.4 (1987) 395–410. ISSN 0003-1615. ▸ Valuable examination of Castilian laws regarding dowries with specific Chilean examples to illustrate their workings. [MAB]

37.353 Brooke Larson. *Colonialism and agrarian transformation in Bolivia: Cochabamba, 1550–1900*. Princeton: Princeton University Press, 1988. ISBN 0-691-07738-X (cl), 0-691-10241-4 (pbk). ▸ Excellent long-term economic and ethnohistorical study of Bolivia's major agricultural region. Emphasizes local adaptation to colonial domination. Well grounded in social theory as well as archival sources. [MAB/NDC]

37.354 Asunción Lavrin. "Women in convents: their economic and social role in colonial Mexico." In *Liberating women's history: theoretical and critical essays*. Berenice A. Carroll, ed., pp. 250–71. Urbana: University of Illinois Press, 1976. ISBN 0-252-00441-8 (cl), 0-252-00569-4 (pbk). ▸ Masterly survey emphasizing nunneries' success in protecting unmarried elite females and important economic role as landowners and providers of credit in colonial cities. [MAB]

37.355 Asunción Lavrin, ed. *Latin American women: historical perspectives*. Westport, Conn.: Greenwood, 1978. ISBN 0-313-20309-1. ▸ Twelve essays from colonial period to twentieth century. Revises traditional image of women by illustrating that women of all classes had important influence in society. Good introduction and overview with suggestions for future research. [MFB/RJW]

37.356 Asunción Lavrin, ed. *Sexuality and marriage in colonial Latin America*. Lincoln: University of Nebraska Press, 1989. ISBN 0-8032-2885-6. ▸ Stimulating, well-written essays by nine social historians on personal lives of colonial Latin Americans. Authors discuss sexuality, marriage, divorce, illegitimacy, sexual witchcraft, and confession. [MFB]

37.357 Asunción Lavrin and Edith B. Couturier. "Dowries and wills: a view of women's socioeconomic role in colonial Guadalajara and Puebla, 1640–1790." *Hispanic American historical review* 59.2 (1979) 280–304. ISSN 0018-2168. ▸ Pioneering investigation of dowries and wills giving insight into women's status in colonial Mexican society. Suggests women's power greater than previously thought; role reinterpretation needed. [MFB]

37.358 Seymour B. Liebman. *The Jews in New Spain: faith, flame, and the Inquisition*. Coral Gables, Fla.: University of Miami Press, 1970. ISBN 0-87024-129-X. ▸ Informative examination of Jewish experience in New Spain with emphasis on Inquisition's treatment of Jews. Primary focus on experience before 1650. Rich in examples. [MAB]

37.359 Seymour B. Liebman. *New World Jewry, 1493–1825: requiem for the forgotten*. New York: KTAV, 1982. ISBN 0-87068-277-6. ▸ Overview of history of Jews in Latin America with ample reference to actions of Inquisitions. Informative introduction to topic. [MAB]

37.360 James Lockhart and Enrique Otte, eds. and trans. *Letters and people of the Spanish Indies: sixteenth century.* New York: Cambridge University Press, 1976. ISBN 0-521-20883-1 (cl), 0-521-09990-0 (pbk). ‣ Collection of translated documents relating diverse perspectives toward conquest, variety of life in colonies, and view of officials, clerics, and laymen. Unique compilation that humanizes conquest and colonization. [MAB]

37.361 Edgar F. Love. "Marriage patterns of persons of African descent in a colonial Mexico City parish." *Hispanic American historical review* 51.1 (1971) 79–91. ISSN 0018-2168. ‣ Examination of 1,662 marriages, 1646–1746, in which one or both parties were of African descent. Eight hundred forty-seven persons of non-African ancestry married persons of color. [MAB]

37.362 W. George Lovell. *Conquest and survival in colonial Guatemala: a historical geography of the Cuchumatán highlands, 1500–1821.* Rev. ed. Montreal: McGill-Queen's University Press, 1992. ISBN 0-7735-0903-8. ‣ Examination of physical and human geography, preconquest culture, population size at contact, conquest, postconquest organization, economic demands, ethnic relations, landholding patterns, and demographic changes. Excellent historical geography. [MAB/MWH]

37.363 Luis Martin. *Daughters of the conquistadores: women of the viceroyalty of Peru.* 1983 ed. Dallas: Southern Methodist University Press, 1989. ISBN 0-87074-297-3. ‣ Entertaining anecdotal history of women in colonial Peru. Substantial contribution with four very informative chapters on religious life. [MFB]

37.364 Lyle N. McAlister. "Social structure and social change in New Spain." *Hispanic American historical review* 43.3 (1963) 349–70. ISSN 0018-2168. ‣ Classic analysis arguing social structure based on estates eroding in late colonial period while class structure was emerging, but shift too slow to accommodate social tensions. Remains fundamental article. [MAB]

37.365 Robert McCaa. "*Calidad, clase,* and marriage in colonial Mexico: the case of Parral, 1788–90." *Hispanic American historical review* 64.3 (1984) 477–501. ISSN 0018-2168. ‣ Fine analysis, combining parish records with census data. *Calidad* (racial and social status) and *clase* (occupation and economic standing) sharply constrained chances of marrying, its timing, and mate selection. *Calidad* as important as *clase* in marital pairings. [MAB]

37.366 Amos Megged. "Accommodation and resistance of elites in transition: the case of Chiapa in early colonial Mesoamerica." *Hispanic American historical review* 71.3 (1991) 477–500. ISSN 0018-2168. ‣ Examination of high degree of cooperation between native elites and Spanish patrons and role of hispanicized Indian elites in protecting interests of colonial government in their communities. Challenges Zeitlin 37.384. [MAB]

37.367 Magnus Mörner. "Economic factors and stratification in colonial Spanish America with special regard to elites." *Hispanic American historical review* 63.2 (1983) 335–69. ISSN 0018-2168. ‣ Predominant pattern of social stratification characterized by impact of commercial capital and symbiosis of hierarchical system of medieval Spanish derivation and colonial order of authority-subordination. Important synthetic article. [MAB]

37.368 Magnus Mörner. *Perfil de la sociedad rural del Cuzco a fines de la colonia.* Lima: Universidad del Pacífico, Departamento Académico de Ciencias Sociales y Políticas, 1978. (Monografías-Instituto de Estudios Latino-Americanos de Estocolmo, 3.) ‣ Examination of rural Cuzco, 1689–1786, with special attention to social change and conflict. Valuable analysis by masterful historian. [MAB]

37.369 Magnus Mörner. *Race mixture in the history of Latin America.* Boston: Little, Brown, 1967. ‣ Examination of biological blending of Indians, Iberians, and Africans in New World from conquest to twentieth century. Best introduction to topic. [MAB]

37.370 Josephe Mugaburu and Francisco Mugaburu. *Chronicle of colonial Lima: the diary of Josephe and Francisco Mugaburu, 1640–1697.* Robert Ryal Miller, ed. and trans. Norman: University of Oklahoma Press, 1975. ISBN 0-8061-1134-8. ‣ Translation of diary providing fascinating glimpse into social life of seventeenth-century Lima. Unusual source. [MAB]

37.371 Muriel Nazzari. *Disappearance of the dowry: women, families, and social change in São Paulo, Brazil (1600–1900).* Stanford, Calif.: Stanford University Press, 1991. ISBN 0-8047-1928-4. ‣ Examination of changes in practice of dowry and reversal of attitude toward dowry that led to its disappearance. Based on judical processes of settlement of estates. Rich social history. [MAB]

37.372 Sandra L. Orellana. *The Tzutujil Mayas: continuity and change, 1250–1630.* Norman: University of Oklahoma Press, 1984. ISBN 0-8061-1739-7. ‣ Ethnohistorical examination of regional culture before Spanish conquest and changes resulting from conquest. Focus on acculturation. Useful regional study. [MAB]

37.373 José F. de la Peña. *Oligarquía y propiedad en la Nueva España (1550–1624).* Mexico: Fondo de Cultura Económica, 1983. ISBN 968-16-0412-1. ‣ Detailed examination of New Spain's economy in first quarter of seventeenth century and economic and political bases of powerful oligarchy. Informative, stimulating study. [MAB]

37.374 Dwight E. Petersen. "Sweet success: some notes on the founding of a Brazilian sugar dynasty, the Pais Barreto family of Pernambuco." *The Americas* 40.3 (1984) 325–48. ISSN 0003-1615. ‣ Informative examination of rise of prominent family in late sixteenth and early seventeenth centuries through military service, favorable marriage, purchase of land, investment in sugar production, and government service. [MAB]

37.375 David J. Robinson, ed. *Social fabric and spatial structure in colonial Latin America.* Ann Arbor: University Microfilms International for Syracuse University, Department of Geography, 1979. ISBN 0-8357-0419-x. ‣ Eleven chapters by thirteen authors on varied topics on New Granada, Ecuador, Mexico, Brazil, Bolivia, Buenos Aires, and Trujillo, Peru. Valuable collection. [MAB]

37.376 A.J.R. Russell-Wood. "Black and mulatto brotherhoods in colonial Brazil: a study in collective behavior." *Hispanic American historical review* 54.4 (1974) 567–602. ISSN 0018-2168. ‣ Important social history of brotherhoods, officially sanctioned corporate entities that cushioned blacks and mulattoes against white-dominated society and furthered social integration. By eighteenth century, they existed in virtually every town. [MAB]

37.377 A.J.R. Russell-Wood. "Prestige, power, and piety in colonial Brazil: the third orders of Salvador." *Hispanic American historical review* 69.1 (1989) 61–89. ISSN 0018-2168. ‣ Pioneering study of third orders of St. Francis, the Carmelites, and St. Dominic. Emphasizes members' network as self-perpetuating nucleus of power and prestige in colonial Bahia. [MAB]

37.378 A.J.R. Russell-Wood. "Women and society in colonial Brazil." *Journal of Latin American studies* 9.1 (1977) 1–34. ISSN 0022-216x. ‣ Examination of ideologies, values, attitudes, and legal position of women, social role of white women, women as head of household, and white women and society. Informative elucidation of understudied topic. [MAB]

37.379 Eduardo R. Saguier. "The social impact of a middleman minority in a divided host society: the case of the Portuguese in early seventeenth-century Buenos Aires." *Hispanic American historical review* 65.3 (1985) 467–91. ISSN 0018-2168. ‣ Portuguese immigrants assimilated rapidly—learned Spanish, invested in land, married local creole women, and became involved in local politics—shifting from middleman to dominant position. Valuable. [MAB]

37.380 Patricia Seed. *To love, honor, and obey in colonial Mexico: conflicts over marriage choice, 1574–1821.* Stanford, Calif.: Stanford University Press, 1988. ISBN 0-8047-1457-6. ▸ Informative, thoughtful, and stimulating discussion of marriage practices as revealed by conflicts between parents and children over marriage choices. Broadens knowledge of marriage and family in colonial Mexico. [MFB]

37.381 David Grant Smith. "Old Christian merchants and the foundation of the Brazil Company, 1649." *Hispanic American historical review* 54.2 (1974) 233–59. ISSN 0018-2168. ▸ Persuasive revisionist challenge to long-held view that New Christian capital financed company. Several Old Christian merchant-bankers, some of whom were familiars of Inquisition, were among major investors. [MAB]

37.382 Karen Spalding. "*Kurakas* and commerce: a chapter in the evolution of Andean society." *Hispanic American historical review* 53.4 (1973) 581–99. ISSN 0018-2168. ▸ Provincial native leaders (*kurakas*) enjoyed special privileges and adapted European patterns of economic activity at cost of alienation from native social patterns. Important contribution. [MAB]

37.383 Karen Spalding. "Social climbers: changing patterns of mobility among the Indians of colonial Peru." *Hispanic American historical review* 50.4 (1970) 645–64. ISSN 0018-2168. ▸ Spanish conquest opened opportunities that substantially altered internal structure of Indian society. Many natives who allied early with Spaniards used connection to improve position. Seminal article. [MAB]

37.384 Judith Francis Zeitlin. "Ranchers and Indians on the southern isthmus of Tehuantepec: economic change and indigenous survival in colonial Mexico." *Hispanic American historical review* 69.1 (1989) 23–60. ISSN 0018-2168. ▸ Valuable regional study examining different responses by Zoque, Zapotec, and Huave populations to ranching boom of 1580 to 1620. Analyzes how they survived. [MAB]

37.385 Ann Zulawski. "Social differentiation, gender, and ethnicity: urban Indian women in colonial Bolivia, 1640–1725." *Latin American research review* 25.2 (1990) 93–113. ISSN 0023-8791. ▸ Important study of range of Indian women's market participation and how gender, class, and ethnicity interacted to foster diversity in their activities but limit economic possibilities. [MAB]

SEE ALSO

CITIES AND THE URBAN ENVIRONMENT

37.386 Michael L. Conniff. "Guayaquil through independence: urban development in a colonial system." *The Americas* 33.3 (1977) 385–410. ISSN 0003-1615. ▸ Informative sketch of early development of the city examining in some detail system of labor and production during eighteenth and early nineteenth centuries. Argues Guayaquil was humane case of urban development. [MAB]

37.387 Joseph B. Fichandler and Thomas F. O'Brien, Jr. "Santiago Chile, 1541–1581: a case study of urban stagnation." *The Americas* 33.2 (1976) 205–25. ISSN 0003-1615. ▸ Demonstrates landed interests dominated Santiago and sought to exploit its resources rather than abandoning it for countryside estates. Emphasizes centrality of city council in promoting interests of *encomenderos* (recipients of grants of Indian labor and tribute). [MAB]

37.388 Valerie Fraser. *The architecture of conquest: building in the viceroyalty of Peru, 1535–1635.* Cambridge: Cambridge University Press, 1990. ISBN 0-521-34316-X. ▸ Examination of architecture in Peru and its conscious use as instrument of subjugation. Emphasizes importance of architecture in construction and consolidation of Spanish empire. [MAB]

37.389 Mario Góngora. "Urban social stratification in colonial Chile." *Hispanic American historical review* 55.3 (1975) 421–48. ISSN 0018-2168. ▸ Valuable overview of aristocracy, merchants, lawyers and professionals, Spanish artisans, poor Spaniards, Indians, and urban castes, principally for Santiago and La Serena. All groups accepted values of aristocracy. [MAB]

37.390 Julia Hirschberg. "Social experiment in New Spain: a prosopographical study of the early settlement at Puebla de los Angeles, 1531–1534." *Hispanic American historical review* 59.1 (1979) 1–33. ISSN 0018-2168. ▸ Diverse goals in founding Puebla not met as conquistadors, *encomenderos* (recipients of grants of native labor and tribute), and residents of Mexico City settled there. Convincing revisionist view that town's planned innovations were successful. [MAB]

37.391 Louisa Schell Hoberman. "Bureaucracy and disaster: Mexico City and the flood of 1629." *Journal of Latin American studies* 6.2 (1974) 211–30. ISSN 0022-216X. ▸ Comprehensive, informative study of bureaucratic response to devastating flood and efforts at relief, emergency repairs, and prevention of recurrence, involving restoration and enlargement of drainage canal. [MAB]

37.392 Louisa Schell Hoberman and Susan Migden Socolow, eds. *Cities and society in colonial Latin America.* Albuquerque: University of New Mexico Press, 1986. ISBN 0-8263-0844-9 (cl), 0-8263-0845-7 (pbk). ▸ Informative chapters on large landowners, merchants, bureaucrats, churchmen, female religious, military, artisans, suppliers, sellers, servants, slaves, and underclass by nine authors. Fine introduction and conclusion by editors. [MAB]

37.393 A.J.R. Russell-Wood. *Fidalgos and philanthropists: the Santa Casa da Misericórdia of Bahia, 1550–1755.* Berkeley: University of California Press, 1968. ▸ Important institutional, social, and economic study examining lay brotherhood of Santa Casa de Misericórdia of Bahia from 1549 to 1763. Also illuminates society and economy of Bahia. [MAB]

37.394 Richard P. Schaedel, Jorge E. Hardoy, and Nora Scott Kinzer, eds. *Urbanization in the Americas from its beginnings to the present.* The Hague: Mouton; distributed by Aldine de Gruyter, 1978. ISBN 0-202-90054-1. ▸ Anthology including ten papers on urbanizaton in colonial Latin America. [MAB]

37.395 Susan Migden Socolow. "Women and crime: Buenos Aires, 1757–97." *Journal of Latin American studies* 12.1 (1980) 39–54. ISSN 0022-216X. ▸ Informative, useful examination of seventy criminal court cases involving women. After 1777 more women involved in crime as plaintiff or defendant. Most crimes against women either domestic disturbances or sexual offenses. [MAB]

37.396 Guy P. C. Thomson. *Puebla de los Angeles: industry and society in a Mexican city, 1700–1850.* Boulder: Westview, 1989.

ISBN 0-8133-7781-1. ▸ Valuable regional study examining economy, social structure, political economy of Mexico's second city and major center of manufacturing, 1700–1830, and its economy and politics in subsequent era of protectionism. [MAB]

37.397 Kathy Waldron. "Public land policy and use in colonial Caracas." *Hispanic American historical review* 61.2 (1981) 258–77. ISSN 0018-2168. ▸ Underscores stability of central city, 1700–1770, despite more than tripling of population. Analyzes change in city council policy and 900 land grants from 1770 to 1809. Much new information. [MAB]

37.398 Stephen Webre. "Water and society in a Spanish American city: Santiago de Guatemala, 1555–1773." *Hispanic American historical review* 70.1 (1990) 57–84. ISSN 0018-2168. ▸ Examination of sources of water, administration and finance of municipal water system, and inequitable access to water. Elite households enjoyed best access. Informative introduction to understudied topic. [MAB]

CULTURAL LIFE AND INSTITUTIONS

37.399 Dauril Alden and Joseph C. Miller. "Out of Africa: the slave trade and the transmission of smallpox to Brazil, 1560–1831." *Journal of interdisciplinary history* 18.2 (1987) 195–224. ISSN 0022-1953. ▸ Argues that, for most of period, primary source of smallpox contagion in Brazil was tropical Africa. Smallpox probably did not become endemic in Brazil until nineteenth century. [MAB]

37.400 Ricardo Archila. *Historia de la medicina en Venezuela: época colonial.* Caracas: Tip. Vargas, S.A., 1961. ▸ Classification and synthesis of facts about doctors, surgeons, hospitals, pharmacists, epidemics and hygiene in colonial Venezuela. Thorough history emphasizing seventeenth and eighteenth centuries. [MFB]

37.401 Carmen Castañeda. *La educación en Guadalajara durante la colonia, 1552–1821.* Mexico City: El Colegio de México for El Colegio de Jalisco, 1984. ISBN 9-681-20288-0. ▸ Institutional history of primary- to university-level education in Guadalajara with prosopographical outline of students and faculty. Important contribution to history of education. [MFB]

37.402 Leopoldo Castedo. *A history of Latin American art and architecture from pre-Columbian times to the present.* Phyllis Freeman, ed. and trans. New York: Praeger, 1969. ▸ Valuable introduction, over one-third devoted to colonial period. Numerous, excellent illustrations. [MAB]

37.403 Donald B. Cooper. *Epidemic disease in Mexico City, 1761–1813: an administrative, social, and medical study.* Austin: University of Texas Press for Institute of Latin American Studies, 1965. (University of Texas at Austin, Institute of Latin American Studies, Latin American monographs, 3.) ▸ Detailed study documenting five epidemics and measures taken to combat them. Important contribution to medical history. [MFB]

37.404 Munro S. Edmonson, ed. *Sixteenth-century Mexico: the work of Sahagún.* Albuquerque: University of New Mexico Press, 1974. ISBN 0-8263-0335-8. ▸ Chapters by eleven authors focusing on methodology and continued utility of *General History of the Things of New Spain* by Franciscan friar Bernardino de Sahagún. Instructive discussions. [MAB]

37.405 Iris H. W. Engstrand. *Spanish scientists in the New World: the eighteenth-century expeditions.* Seattle: University of Washington Press, 1981. ISBN 0-295-95764-6. ▸ Analysis of Spain's scientific enlightenment as revealed in botanical surveys and scientific expeditions in 1780s and 1790s. Valuable contribution to understanding nature of Enlightenment in Spain and Spanish America. [MAB]

37.406 Antonello Gerbi. *The dispute of the New World: the history of a polemic, 1750–1900.* Rev. ed. Jeremy Moyle, trans. Pitts-

burgh: University of Pittsburgh Press, 1973. ISBN 0-8229-3250-4. ▸ Fascinating account of European views, starting with French naturalist Buffon and Prussian encyclopedist Cornelius de Pauw, that America was inferior continent. Major contribution to study of Enlightenment in Europe and in Spanish America. [MAB]

37.407 Pilar Gonzalbo Aizpuru. *Historia de la educación en la época colonial: el mundo indígena.* Mexico City: El Colegio de México, Centro de Estudios Históricos, 1990. ISBN 9-681-20441-7. ▸ Extensive summary of indigenous education in colonial Mexico. Primary emphasis on sixteenth century. Invaluable reference for types of schools and intent of founding religious orders. [MFB]

37.408 Pilar Gonzalbo Aizpuru. *Historia de la educación en la época colonial: la educación de los criollos y la vida urbana.* Mexico City: El Colegio de México, Centro de Estudios Historicós, 1990. ISBN 9-681-20449-2. ▸ Comprehensive survey of all levels of creole education in Mexico. Primary emphasis on sixteenth century. Invaluable insight into characteristics and guiding principles of specific schools. [MFB]

37.409 Felipe Guaman Poma de Ayala. *El primer nueva corónica y buen gobierno.* 3 vols. John V. Murra and Rolena Adorno, eds. Jorge L. Urioste, trans. Mexico City: Siglo Veintiuno, 1980. ISBN 968-23-0972-7 (set). ▸ Critical edition and translation of extraordinary text completed in 1615 by Peruvian Indian chronicler. Valuable source on Incas before, during, and after conquest by author opposed to colonialism. Four hundred illustrations. [MAB]

37.410 David A. Howard. *The Royal Indian Hospital of Mexico City.* Tempe: Arizona State University, Center for Latin American studies, 1980. (Arizona State University Center for Latin American Studies, Special study, 20.) ISBN 0-87918-045-5. ▸ Primarily institutional study of Royal Indian Hospital in Mexico City during eighteenth century. Brief but informative examination of little-known institution. [MAB]

37.411 Pál Kelemen. *Baroque and rococo in Latin America.* 2d ed. New York: Dover, 1967. ISBN 0-486-21698-5. ▸ Detailed history of art; includes 192 plates. Classic introduction. [MAB]

37.412 George Kubler and Martin Soria. *Art and architecture in Spain and Portugal and their American dominions, 1500–1800.* 1959 ed. Baltimore: Penguin, 1969. ▸ Still authoritative, detailed survey of architecture, sculpture, and painting. Devotes significantly more attention to developments in Spain than in the Americas. One hundred ninety-two pages of illustrations. [MAB]

37.413 Jacques Lafaye. *Quetzalcóatl and Guadalupe: the formation of Mexican national consciousness, 1531–1813.* Benjamin Keen, trans. Chicago: University of Chicago Press, 1976. ISBN 0-226-46794-5. ▸ Examination of syncretism of Indian and Spanish myths that formed basis for Mexican national consciousness symbolized by Virgin of Guadalupe. Important contribution to intellectual history of Mexico. [MAB]

37.414 John Tate Lanning. *Academic culture in the Spanish colonies.* 1940 ed. Port Washington, N.Y.: Kennikat, 1971. ISBN 0-8046-1380-X. ▸ Pioneering essays on universities, introduction of enlightened ideas, medicine, and public health in Spanish colonies. Still useful introduction, despite author's later, more detailed works (37.415, 37.417, 37.418). [MAB]

37.415 John Tate Lanning. *The eighteenth-century Enlightenment in the University of San Carlos de Guatemala.* Ithaca, N.Y.: Cornell University Press, 1956. ▸ Examination of introduction of enlightened ideas into colonial university. Demonstrates that by 1770 university neither intellectually isolated nor was Spanish crown obscurantist. Important contribution. [MAB]

37.416 John Tate Lanning. *Pedro de la Torre: doctor to conquerors.* Baton Rouge: Louisiana State University Press, 1974. ISBN 0-8071-0064-1. ▸ Examines adventures of sixteenth-century practitioner and reveals state of medical practice after conquest of New Spain. Fascinating slice of medical and social history. [MAB]

37.417   John Tate Lanning. *The Royal Protomedicato: the regulation of the medical professions in the Spanish empire.* John Jay TePaske, ed. Durham, N.C.: Duke University Press, 1985. ISBN 0-8223-0651-4. ‣ Study of institution responsible for licensing physicians and other medical practitioners. Monumental work, illuminating efforts to regulate medicine as well as actual practice and practitioners. [MAB]

37.418   John Tate Lanning. *The university in the kingdom of Guatemala.* Ithaca, N.Y.: Cornell University Press, 1955. ‣ Examines formation, academic organization and life, and financial struggles of University of San Carlos. Meticulous study of higher education in colonial world. [MAB]

37.419   Irving A. Leonard. *Baroque times in old Mexico: seventeenth-century persons, places, and practices.* 1959 ed. Westport, Conn.: Greenwood, 1981. ISBN 0-313-22826-4. ‣ Brilliant tapestry of intellectual life and times in seventeenth-century Mexico. Unique contribution and required reading for colonialists. [MAB]

37.420   Irving A. Leonard. *Books of the brave: being an account of books and of men in the Spanish conquest and settlement of the sixteenth-century New World.* 1949 ed. Rolena Adorno, Introduction. Berkeley: University of California Press, 1992. ISBN 0-520-07990-6 (cl), 0-520-07816-0 (pbk). ‣ Examination of extensive literature brought to New World by conquistadors and their successors to 1600. Still important contribution to intellectual history of colonial Spanish America. [MAB]

37.421   Sidney David Markman. *Architecture and urbanization in colonial Chiapas, Mexico.* Philadelphia: American Philosophical Society, 1984. (Memoirs of the American Philosophical Society, 153.) ISBN 0-87169-153-1. ‣ Valuable study of determinants of architecture and urbanization: settlement patterns, urbanization, town planning, and urban history, materials and methods of construction and style, and architectural monuments. [MAB]

37.422   Sidney David Markman. *Colonial architecture of Antigua, Guatemala.* Philadelphia: American Philosophical Society, 1966. (Memoirs of the American Philosophical Society, 64.) ‣ Impressive examination of history of Antigua, elements of its architectual style, and monuments divided into four periods: seventeenth century to 1680, 1680–1717, 1717–51, and 1751–73. Illustrated. [MAB]

37.423   Luis Martin. *The intellectual conquest of Peru: the Jesuit College of San Pablo, 1568–1767.* New York: Fordham University Press, 1968. ‣ Institutional study of founding, activities, and demise of Jesuit College of San Pablo in Lima. Useful introduction to nature and conditions of pre-university education. [MAB]

37.424   Robert James Mullen. *Dominican architecture in sixteenth-century Oaxaca.* Tempe: Arizona State University, Center for Latin American Studies, 1975. ISBN 0-87918-016-1. ‣ Informative regional art history. Identifies Dominican residences, analyzes and categorizes architectural styles, dates churches and residences, and traces distinctive architectural features. Illustrated. [MAB]

37.425   Ronald L. Numbers, ed. *Medicine in the New World: New Spain, New France, and New England.* Knoxville: University of Tennessee Press, 1987. ISBN 0-87049-517-8. ‣ Collection of papers presented at 1980 International Congress of History of Medicine. Compares and analyzes medical methods and techniques used in Spanish, French, and English colonies. [MFB]

37.426   Sandra L. Orellana. *Indian medicine in highland Guatemala: the pre-Hispanic and colonial periods.* Albuquerque: University of New Mexico Press, 1987. ISBN 0-826-30931-3. ‣ Synthetic, ethnohistorical study of pre- and postconquest medicine. Useful information on healing practices, Spanish influence on native practices, and medicinal plants. [MFB]

37.427   Anthony Pagden. *Spanish imperialism and the political imagination: studies in European and Spanish–American social and political theory, 1513–1830.* New Haven: Yale University Press, 1990. ISBN 0-300-04676-6. ‣ Six original essays examining influence of Spanish empire on European intellectual history and development of divergent ideologies of independence in Spanish America. [MAB]

37.428   Gabrielle G. Palmer. *Sculpture in the kingdom of Quito.* Albuquerque: University of New Mexico Press, 1987. ISBN 0-8263-0930-5. ‣ After lengthy introduction to Spanish sculpture, focuses on sculpture in Quito in eighteenth century. Emphasizes distinctive style of Quito school of polychrome wood sculpture. Twenty-nine superb color plates. [MAB]

37.429   Octavio Paz. *Sor Juana, or, the traps of faith.* Margaret Sayers Peden, trans. Cambridge, Mass.: Belknap, 1988. ISBN 0-674-82105-X. ‣ Detailed examination of life, times, and writings of colonial Mexico's reknowned "tenth muse." Major contribution to Sor Juana studies and cultural history. [MAB]

37.430   Mariano Picón-Salas. *A cultural history of Spanish America: from conquest to independence.* 1962 ed. Irving A. Leonard, trans. Berkeley: University of California Press, 1966. ‣ Translation of classic introduction to topic first published in 1944. Remains readable, useful survey. [MAB]

37.431   Marilyn Ekdahl Ravicz. *Early colonial religious drama in Mexico: from Tzompantli to Golgotha.* Washington, D.C.: Catholic University of America Press, 1970. ISBN 0-8132-0495-X. ‣ Unique study examining use of religious drama as didactic device to acculturate Indians of Mexico. Includes translations of several dramas. [MAB]

37.432   Paul M. Roca. *Spanish Jesuit churches in Mexico's Tarahumara.* Tucson: University of Arizona Press, 1979. ISBN 0-8165-0651-5 (cl), 0-8165-0572-1 (pbk). ‣ Review of region's background and informative examination of head and subordinate churches built by Jesuits between 1611 and 1767. Includes biographical directory of Jesuit and other key individuals. [MAB]

37.433   Charles E. Ronan, S.J. *Francisco Javier Clavijero, S.J. (1731–1787): figure of the Mexican Enlightenment, his life and works.* Rome and Chicago: Institutum Historicum S.I. and Loyola University Press, 1978. (Bibliotheca Instituti Historici S.I., 40.) ISBN 0-685-03108-X (pbk). ‣ Valuable, revisionist examination of life and writings of pioneer in introducing modern philosophy into Mexico. Writing in exile, Mexican Jesuit linked Mexican creole civilization with Aztec world. [MAB]

37.434   Michael M. Smith. *The "Real Expedición Marítima de la Vacuna" in New Spain and Guatemala.* Philadelphia: American Philosophical Society, 1974. (Transactions of the American Philosophical Society, n.s., 64, Part 1.) ISBN 0-87169-641-X. ‣ Monographic examination of Balmis Expedition to introduce vaccination for smallpox in New World, 1803–1806. Useful study. [MAB]

37.435   Colin Steele. *English interpreters of the Iberian New World from Purchas to Stevens: a bibliographical study, 1603–1726.* Oxford: Dolphin Book, 1975. ISBN 84-399-2778-9. ‣ Unique examination of English translations of Spanish and Portuguese books in context of prevailing political situation to determine their impact and vice versa. Includes bibliography of translations. [MAB]

37.436   Robert Stevenson. *Music in Aztec and Inca territory.* 1968 ed. Berkeley: University of California Press, 1976. ISBN 0-520-03169-5. ‣ Examination of music between conquest and 1800 in relation to events which directly expressed or affected native musical life. First study to juxtapose music of these two cultures. Unique work. [MAB]

37.437 Robert Stevenson. *The music of Peru: aboriginal and vice-regal epochs.* Washington, D.C.: Pan American Union, 1960. ▸ Survey of history of Peruvian indigenous and colonial music. Important work in underdeveloped field. [MFB]

37.438 Robert Stevenson, ed. *Christmas music from baroque Mexico.* Berkeley: University of California Press, 1974. ISBN 0-520-02036-7. ▸ Synthesis and study of Mexican music focusing primarily on seventeenth century. Divided between text and music with seventeen transcripts of works by twelve composers. [MFB]

37.439 Manuel Toussaint. *Colonial art in Mexico.* Elizabeth Wilder Weismann, ed. and trans. Austin: University of Texas Press, 1967. ▸ Classic work of art history. First published in 1949 but still valuable. Examines architecture, painting, sculpture, and minor arts. Liberally illustrated. [MAB]

37.440 John Grier Varner. *El Inca: the life and times of Garcilaso de la Vega.* Austin: University of Texas Press, 1968. ISBN 0-292-78375-2. ▸ Biographical study of famous sixteenth-century mestizo author Gómez Suárez de Figueroa, known as Inca Garcilaso de la Vega, from early years in Peru to death in Spain. Fine, well-written study. [MAB]

37.441 Garcilaso de la Vega. *Royal commentaries of the Incas and general history of Peru.* 2 vols. H. V. Livermore, trans. Austin: University of Texas Press, 1966. ▸ Fine translation of one of first books about America by sixteenth-century American. Generally accepted as major literary work. Classic. [MAB]

37.442 Elizabeth Wilder Weismann. *Art and time in Mexico from the conquest to the revolution.* Judith Handcock Sandoval, photographer. New York: Harper & Row, 1985. ISBN 0-06-438506-X (cl), 0-06-430143-5 (pbk). ▸ Survey of fortifications, cities, missions, cathedrals, popular art, civic architecture, houses, and *haciendas.* Fine introduction to Mexican art; well illustrated. [MAB]

37.443 John E. Woodham. "The influence of Hipólito Unanue on Peruvian medical science, 1789–1830: a reappraisal." *Hispanic American historical review* 50.4 (1970) 693–714. ISSN 0018-2168. ▸ Peruvian physicians' acceptance of renowned fellow physician Unanue's belief that climate influenced disease served to undo much of his progress in freeing Peruvian medicine from dependence on authority. New dogma replaced old. Careful analysis. [MAB]

SEE ALSO
29.160 A. Owen Aldridge, ed. *The Ibero-American Enlightenment.*
36.388 Rolena Adorno. *Guaman Poma.*

SPANISH AMERICA, 1680s–1760s

37.444 Roland Dennis Hussey. *The Caracas Company, 1728–1784: a study in the history of Spanish monopolistic trade.* 1934 ed. New York: Arno, 1977. ISBN 0-405-09768-9. ▸ Study of most successful colonial trading company from its formation to its termination. Although dated, notably by Ferry 37.345, it retains utility. [MAB]

37.445 Jorge Juan and Antonio de Ulloa. *Discourse and political reflections on the kingdoms of Peru.* John Jay TePaske, ed. and trans. Besse Alberta Clement, trans. Norman: University of Oklahoma Press, 1978. ISBN 0-8061-1482-7. ▸ Fine translation of 1749 secret report by two Spaniards sent to South America by the crown. Outlines in detail exploitation of native population, corruption, and creole-peninsular hostility. Valuable source. [MAB]

37.446 Peggy K. Liss. *Atlantic empires: the network of trade and revolution, 1713–1826.* Baltimore: Johns Hopkins University Press, 1983. ISBN 0-8018-2742-6. ▸ Examination of network of trade, revolution, and ideology that bound Spain, Portugal, and Britain to their American colonies. Penetrating analysis and synthesis of period. [MAB]

37.447 Adalberto López. *The revolt of the comuñeros* [sic], *1721–1735: a study in the colonial history of Paraguay.* Cambridge, Mass.: Schenkman, 1976. ISBN 0-87073-124-6. ▸ Useful summary of background to and nature of Comunero Revolt in Paraguay. [MAB]

37.448 Colin M. MacLachlan. *Criminal justice in eighteenth-century Mexico: a study of the Tribunal of the Acordada.* Berkeley: University of California Press, 1974. ISBN 0-520-02416-8. ▸ Examination of need for, foundation, structure, activities of, and opposition to most important law enforcement agency in eighteenth-century Mexico. Sound monograph emphasizing institution's Mexican origin. [MAB]

37.449 John Robert McNeill. *Atlantic empires of France and Spain: Louisbourg and Havana, 1700–1763.* Chapel Hill: University of North Carolina Press, 1985. ISBN 0-8078-1669-8. ▸ Comparative economic and military study. Valuable elucidation of Spanish royal policy and Cuban economic and social realities for overly neglected period. [MFB]

37.450 John Preston Moore. *The cabildo in Peru under the Bourbons: a study in the decline and resurgence of local government in the Audiencia of Lima, 1700–1824.* Durham, N.C.: Duke University Press, 1966. ▸ Examination of city councils of Peru, their responsibilities and activities, and effects of establishment of intendant system. Approach dated but contains some useful information. [MAB]

37.451 Charles F. Nunn. *Foreign immigrants in early Bourbon Mexico, 1700–1760.* Cambridge: Cambridge University Press, 1979. ISBN 0-521-22051-3. ▸ Examination of origins and occupations of voluntary foreign immigrants to New Spain, perhaps 1,500 in number, between 1700 and 1760. Economic and social implications of their presence were modest. [MAB]

37.452 J.C.M. Ogelsby. "Spain's Havana squadron and the preservation of the balance of power in the Caribbean, 1740–1748." *Hispanic American historical review* 49.3 (1969) 473–88. ISSN 0018-2168. ▸ Useful examination emphasizing good service of Admiral Rodrigo de Torres and utility of squadron after 1742 as it helped to maintain balance of power and to preserve Spain's position in Caribbean. [MAB]

37.453 James Schofield Saeger. "Institutional rivalries, jurisdictional disputes, and vested interests in the viceroyalty of Peru: José de Antequera and the rebellion of Paraguay." *The Americas* 32.1 (1975) 99–116. ISSN 0003-1615. ▸ Solid analysis of famous rebellion of Paraguay (1721–35). Emphasizes institutional paralysis as Paraguayans and Jesuits recognized conflicting authorities. [MAB]

37.454 James Schofield Saeger. "Origins of the rebellion of Paraguay." *Hispanic American historical review* 52.2 (1972) 215–29. ISSN 0018-2168. ▸ Solid examination placing rebellion in historical perspective. Argues rebellion (1721–35) primarily local movement fostered by imperial neglect, economic grievances, and jealousy of prosperous Jesuit missions. [MAB]

37.455 Robert Wasserstrom. "Ethnic violence and indigenous protest: the Tzeltal (Maya) rebellion of 1712." *Journal of Latin American studies* 12.1 (1980) 1–19. ISSN 0022-216X. ▸ Anthropologist's examination of causes and legacy of major revolt in Chiapas. [MAB]

SEE ALSO
29.200 Geoffrey J. Walker. *Spanish politics and imperial trade, 1700–1789.*

BRAZIL IN THE AGE OF EXPANSION

37.456 Dauril Alden. "The population of Brazil in the late eighteenth century: a preliminary survey." *Hispanic American historical review* 43.2 (1963) 173–205. ISSN 0018-2168. ▸ Careful examination of censuses and what they show about regional distribution of population and racial composition of population. Demonstrates substantial population growth. [MAB]

37.457 Dauril Alden. *Royal government in colonial Brazil: with special reference to the administration of the marquis of Lavradio, viceroy, 1769–1779.* Berkeley: University of California Press, 1968. ▸ Detailed examination of administration of viceroy marquis of Lavradio, illuminating both background and politics, economy, and international conflicts of Brazil. Extraordinarily rich volume. [MAB]

37.458 Rudy Bauss. "Rio Grande do Sul in the Portuguese empire: the formative years, 1777–1808." *The Americas* 39.4 (1983) 519–35. ISSN 0003-1615. ▸ Brief but informative examination of economic production and commercial ties of major producer of dried meat, hides, and wheat. Notes importance as contraband center and emphasizes region's significance in integrating Brazil economically. [MAB]

37.459 C. R. Boxer. *The golden age of Brazil, 1695–1750: growing pains of a colonial society.* Berkeley: University of California Press in cooperation with the Sociedade de Estudos Históricos Dom Pedro Segundo, Rio de Janeiro, 1962. ▸ Rich survey of early eighteenth-century Brazil by outstanding scholar. Particularly valuable for social and economic analysis. [MAB]

37.460 John Hemming. *Amazon frontier: the defeat of the Brazilian Indians.* Cambridge, Mass.: Harvard University Press, 1987. ISBN 0-674-01725-0. ▸ Informative description and analysis of policy toward native population (mostly Amazonian) and its consequences from second half of eighteenth century to 1910. Particular attention to directorate system (1757–98). Also discusses work of Catholic missionaries and pioneer anthropologists, expanding frontier, and rubber boom. [MAB/DGS]

37.461 John Norman Kennedy. "Bahian elites, 1750–1822." *Hispanic American historical review* 53.3 (1973) 415–39. ISSN 0018-2168. ▸ Excellent regional study examining coalescence of elite, comprised of wealthy rural landowners and merchants, high-ranking bureaucrats, and high-ranking military officers. Finds place of birth not important. [MAB]

37.462 Elizabeth Anne Kuznesof. *Household economy and urban development: São Paulo, 1765 to 1836.* Boulder: Westview, 1986. ISBN 0-8133-7181-3 (pbk). ▸ Important, detailed demographic examination of process and impact of economic change and expansion of city of São Paulo on household and family. [MAB]

37.463 Elizabeth Anne Kuznesof. "The role of the merchants in the economic development of São Paulo, 1765–1850." *Hispanic American historical review* 60.4 (1980) 571–92. ISSN 0018-2168. ▸ Important examination of structural reasons why cooperation between merchants and traditional elite was important to both, not only to acquire social status but also to achieve finite economic and political ends. [MAB]

37.464 Colin M. MacLachlan. "Slavery, ideology, and institutional change: the impact of the Enlightenment on slavery in late eighteenth-century Maranhão." *Journal of Latin American studies* 11.1 (1979) 1–17. ISSN 0022-216X. ▸ Valuable background and perspective for eventual abolition of slavery. Argues intellectual changes brought about by Enlightenment modified social support for slavery and ultimately slavery itself. [MAB]

37.465 Kenneth Maxwell. *Conflicts and conspiracies: Brazil and Portugal, 1750–1808.* New York: Cambridge University Press, 1973. ISBN 0-521-20053-9. ▸ Examination of far-reaching changes in Portuguese imperial system and its effect on Brazil with reinterpretation of Minas conspiracy (1788–89). One of finest studies in any language on policies of Marquis de Pombal and his successors. [MAB/TC]

37.466 Alida C. Metcalf. "Fathers and sons: the politics of inheritance in a colonial Brazilian township." *Hispanic American historical review* 66.3 (1986) 455–84. ISSN 0018-2168. ▸ Fascinating analysis of favoring sons-in-law over sons in São Paulo in attempts by family to preserve property and to prevent its fragmentation from generation to generation. [MAB/TC]

37.467 Alida C. Metcalf. "Women and means: women and family property in colonial Brazil." *Journal of social history* 24.2 (1990) 277–98. ISSN 0022-4529. ▸ Informative examination of women of propertied class of Santana de Paraíba in 1775. Shows only widows could independently control property they legally owned but did not enjoy same rights as men. [MAB]

37.468 F.W.O. Morton. "The royal timber in late colonial Bahia." *Hispanic American historical review* 58.1 (1978) 41–61. ISSN 0018-2168. ▸ Royal efforts (1796–1800) to conserve Bahian forests in interests of crown failed as local elites employed classical liberal economic doctrines to justify self interest. Insightful discussion of politics. [MAB]

37.469 Donald Ramos. "Marriage and the family in colonial Vila Rica." *Hispanic American historical review* 55.2 (1975) 200–25. ISSN 0018-2168. ▸ Wide range of family types present; few of patriarchal, extended type. Minority of heads of family household married. Marriage a symbol often associated with high social status. Revisionist argument. [MAB]

37.470 A.J.R. Russell-Wood. "Manuel Nunes Viana: paragon or parasite of empire?" *The Americas* 37.4 (1981) 479–98. ISSN 0003-1615. ▸ Fascinating portrait of charismatic backlands leader of captaincies of Bahia, Minas Gerais, and Pernambuco in early eighteenth century who led Emboabas in 1708–1709. [MAB]

37.471 Robert Allan White. "Fiscal policy and royal sovereignty in Minas Gerais: the capitation tax of 1735." *The Americas* 34.2 (1977) 207–29. ISSN 0003-1615. ▸ Informative examination of reasons for and implementation of capitation tax. Considered culmination of gradual effort to bring royal authority to region. [MAB]

REFORM AND EXPANSION IN SPANISH AMERICA, 1760s–1800

37.472 Samuel Amaral. "Public expenditure financing in the colonial treasury: an analysis of the Real Caja de Buenos Aires accounts, 1789–91." *Hispanic American historical review* 64.2 (1984) 287–95. ISSN 0018-2168. ▸ Highlights how entries and outlays of government accounts included transfers to and from other accounts and thus inflated totals. Commentary follows in *Hispanic American Historical Review* 64.2 (1984) 297–322. [MAB]

37.473 Kenneth J. Andrien. "Economic crisis, taxes, and the Quito Insurrection of 1765." *Past and present* 129 (1990) 104–31. ISSN 0031-2746. ▸ Important socioeconomic examination of little-studied revolt. Argues steady erosion of economy from late seventeenth century provided essential context for insurrection. Emphasis applicable to other insurrections. [MAB]

37.474 Christon I. Archer. *The army in Bourbon Mexico, 1760–1810.* Albuquerque: University of New Mexico Press, 1977. ISBN 0-8263-0442-7. ▸ Detailed examination of military in Mexico, 1760–1810. Outstanding social and institutional history, playing down significance of *fuero militar* (legal privileges enjoyed by military) emphasized by McAlister 37.530. [MAB]

37.475 Christon I. Archer. "Bourbon finances and military policy in New Spain, 1759–1812." *The Americas* 37.3 (1981) 315–50. ISSN 0003-1615. ▸ Impressive examination emphasizing expense of Mexican army and influence costs had on military policy. After 1796 problem of financing defense increased. Hidalgo Revolt (1810) brought increased army autonomy. [MAB]

37.476 Jacques A. Barbier. *Reform and politics in Bourbon Chile, 1755–1796.* Ottawa: University of Ottawa Press, 1980. ISBN 2-7603-5010-X (pbk). ‣ Detailed examination of politics, local elites, and ultimately unsuccessful royal efforts at reform in Chile. Outstanding political history placing political conflict in social and economic context. [MAB]

37.477 Jacques A. Barbier. "Venezuelan 'libranzas,' 1788–1807: from economic nostrum to fiscal imperative." *The Americas* 37.4 (1981) 457–78. ISSN 0003-1615. ‣ Demonstrates use of bills of exchange to sustain exportation of tropical products to Spain (1788–97) and subsequent use as way to channel funds to government (1802–1807). Detailed, convincing argument. [MAB]

37.478 Jacques A. Barbier and Allan J. Kuethe, eds. *The North American role in the Spanish imperial economy, 1760–1819.* Manchester: Manchester University Press, 1984. ISBN 0-7190-0964-2. ‣ High-quality contributions by ten historians growing out of Forty-Fourth International Congress of Americanists, 1982. [MAB]

37.479 Bernard E. Bobb. *The viceregency of Antonio María Bucareli in New Spain, 1771–1779.* Austin: University of Texas Press, 1962. ‣ Still one of few detailed examinations of a viceroy's activities. Examines Bucareli and his actions regarding church, defense, interior provinces, California colonization, mining, and financial administration. [MAB]

37.480 Jackie R. Booker. "The Veracruz merchant community in late Bourbon Mexico: a preliminary portrait, 1770–1810." *The Americas* 45.2 (1988) 187–99. ISSN 0003-1615. ‣ Informative, brief survey revealing most merchants were Spanish bachelor immigrants who joined relatives in trade and subsequently married. Complements Brading 37.482 and Socolow 37.554. [MAB]

37.481 D. A. Brading. "Government and elite in late colonial Mexico." *Hispanic American historical review* 53.3 (1973) 389–414. ISSN 0018-2168. ‣ Valuable overview and analysis examining composition of elite, creole participation in bureaucracy, political benefits obtained by different parts of elite, and changes resulting from independence. [MAB]

37.482 D. A. Brading. *Miners and merchants in Bourbon Mexico, 1763–1810.* Cambridge: Cambridge University Press, 1971. ISBN 0-521-07874-1. ‣ Three lengthy essays on administrative change, miners and merchants, and Guanajuato. Highly influential work that in many ways initiated broad reconsideration of late eighteenth century. [MAB]

37.483 Kendall W. Brown. *Bourbons and brandy: imperial reform in eighteenth-century Arequipa.* Albuquerque: University of New Mexico Press, 1986. ISBN 0-8263-0829-5. ‣ Detailed examination of economic, social, and political conditions and Bourbon efforts at reform in Arequipa. Concludes with rebellion of 1780. Model regional study. [MAB]

37.484 Kendall W. Brown. "Jesuit wealth and economic activity within the Peruvian economy: the case of colonial southern Peru." *The Americas* 44.1 (1987) 23–43. ISSN 0003-1615. ‣ Useful case study challenging common exaggerations of Jesuit wealth. Examines economic holdings and activities of Jesuit colleges of Arequipa and Moquegua. Finds negligible impact on regional economy. [MAB]

37.485 Rose Marie Buechler. *The mining society of Potosí, 1776–1810.* Ann Arbor: University Microfilms International for the Department of Geography, Syracuse University, 1981. (Dellplain Latin American studies, 7.) ISBN 0-8357-0591-9. ‣ Useful study of Bourbon reforms, Nordenflicht Expedition, Caroline code and *mita nueva* (new labor draft), church versus state over Indian labor, mining society, and mercury-shortage crisis. [MAB]

37.486 Mark A. Burkholder. "The Council of the Indies in the late eighteenth century: a new perspective." *Hispanic American historical review* 56.3 (1976) 404–23. ISSN 0018-2168. ‣ Revisionist study based on examination of councilors' prior knowledge of New World. Argues Council of the Indies' importance increased after 1773 declaration of equality with Council of Castile. [MAB]

37.487 Mark A. Burkholder. "From creole to peninsular: the transformation of the Audiencia of Lima." *Hispanic American historical review* 52.3 (1972) 395–415. ISSN 0018-2168. ‣ Examination of reversal of creole majority on Audiencia of Lima as result of peninsular appointments of 1775 through 1779. Henceforth peninsulars were majority of court. [MAB]

37.488 Mark A. Burkholder. *Politics of a colonial career: José Baquijano and the Audiencia of Lima.* 2d ed. Wilmington, Del.: S.R. Books, 1990. ISBN 0-8420-2353-4 (cl), 0-8420-2352-6 (pbk). ‣ Examination of ultimately successful efforts of Peruvian creole to secure appointment to Audiencia of Lima. Views Baquijano's career from empire-wide perspective. [MAB]

37.489 Leon G. Campbell. "A colonial establishment: creole domination of the Audiencia of Lima during the late eighteenth century." *Hispanic American historical review* 52.1 (1972) 1–25. ISSN 0018-2168. ‣ Demonstrates creole participation on Lima's High Court and judges' extensive local ties. Should be read in conjunction with Burkholder 37.487. [MAB]

37.490 Leon G. Campbell. *The military and society in colonial Peru, 1750–1810.* Philadelphia: American Philosophical Society, 1978. ISBN 0-87169-123-X. ‣ Examination of military in Peru with particular attention to Túpac Amaru Revolt and its aftermath. Useful study of important institution. [MAB]

37.491 Leon G. Campbell. "Women and the great rebellion in Peru, 1780–1783." *The Americas* 42.2 (1985) 163–95. ISSN 0003-1615. ‣ Focuses on roles played by Micaela Bastidas, Thomasa Titu Condemaita, and other women, family members of rebels, from rural southern highlands. Useful analysis of broader issues. [MAB]

37.492 John K. Chance and William B. Taylor. "Estate and class in a colonial city: Oaxaca in 1792." *Comparative studies in society and history* 19.4 (1977) 454–87. ISSN 0010-4175. ‣ Analysis of census and parochial data to clarify relationship between race, occupation, and social rank in late colonial Oaxaca. Finds economic occupation more important than race. Debate follows in *Comparative Studies in Society and History* 21 (1979) 421–35, 25 (1983) 703–24. [MAB]

37.493 D. S. Chandler. *Social assistance and bureaucratic politics: the montepíos of colonial Mexico, 1767–1821.* Albuquerque: University of New Mexico Press, 1991. ISBN 0-8263-1306-X. ‣ Tightly focused study of organization, financing, and operation of royal pension agencies in New Spain. Valuable for insights into social as well as administrative history. [MAB]

37.494 Concolorcorvo [pseud. Carrió de la Vandera (Bandera)]. *El Lazarillo: a guide for inexperienced travelers between Buenos Aires and Lima, 1773.* Walter D. Kline, ed. and trans. Bloomington: Indiana University Press, 1965. ‣ Translation of travelog from Montevideo to Potosí to Lima. Entertaining and informative. Few works of this genre exist for colonial Latin America. [MAB]

37.495 Edith B. Couturier. "The philanthropic activities of Pedro Romero de Terreros, first count of Ricla." *The Americas* 32.1 (1975) 13–30. ISSN 0003-1615. ‣ Valuable study examining and analyzing philanthropies of wealthy miner, merchant, and landowner. Emphasizes blending of private interests and public benefits and Romero's view that recipients were indebted to him. [MAB]

37.496 Javier Cuenca Esteban. "Statistics of Spain's colonial trade, 1792–1820: consular duties, cargo inventories, and balances of trade." *Hispanic American historical review* 61.3 (1981) 381–428. ISSN 0018-2168. ‣ Trade figures confirm collapse of Spain's colonial trade during two wars with England. Turning point in trade came in 1808–09. Valuable statistics. [MAB]

37.497 Nancy M. Farriss. *Crown and clergy in colonial Mexico, 1759–1821: the crisis of ecclesiastical privilege.* London: Athlone, 1968. ISBN 0-485-13121-8. ‣ Study of relations between church and state, underscoring royal efforts to increase authority over church and resulting alienation of numerous clerics. Major contribution to understanding Bourbon reforms. [MAB]

37.498 John R. Fisher. *Commercial relations between Spain and Spanish America in the era of free trade, 1778–1796.* Liverpool: University of Liverpool, Centre of Latin-American Studies, 1985. (Monograph series, 13.) ISBN 0-902806-11-2 (cl), 0-902806-12-2 (pbk). ‣ Review of Spanish trade policy, 1700–89, and examination of exports to and and imports from Spanish America. Trade expanded substantially, 1782–96, with Spanish America benefiting more than Spain. Meticulous, informative monograph. [MAB]

37.499 John R. Fisher. *Government and society in colonial Peru: the intendant system, 1784–1814.* London: University of London and Athlone, 1970. ISBN 0-485-13129-3. ‣ Detailed study of introduction of intendant system in Peru and intendants' financial, economic, and administrative activities. Fundamental work for history of late colonial Peru. [MAB]

37.500 John R. Fisher. *Silver mines and silver miners in colonial Peru, 1776–1824.* Liverpool: University of Liverpool, Centre for Latin American Studies, 1977. (University of Liverpool, Centre for Latin-American Studies monograph series, 7.) ISBN 0-902806-06-8. ‣ Examination of components of silver-mining industry in Peru. Demonstrates previously unexpected vigor to 1811. Valuable description, analysis, and presentation of production data. [MAB]

37.501 John R. Fisher, Allan J. Kuethe, and Anthony McFarlane, eds. *Reform and insurrection in Bourbon New Granada and Peru.* Baton Rouge: Louisiana State University Press, 1990. ISBN 0-8071-1569-x. ‣ Chapters discussing political, economic, and commercial reform and resistance and rebellion in Quito, Arequipa, and regions of Colombia. Uneven but valuable overall. [MAB]

37.502 Lillian Estelle Fisher. *The last Inca revolt, 1780–1783.* Norman: University of Oklahoma Press, 1966. ‣ Narrative account of most threatening rebellion in colonial era. Dated; does not provide detailed social and economic context. [MAB]

37.503 Enrique Florescano. *Precios del maíz y crisis agrícolas en México (1708–1810): ensayo sobre el movimiento de los precios y sus consecuencias económicas y sociales.* Rev. ed. Mexico City: Ediciones Era, 1986. ISBN 968-411-153-3. ‣ Extremely influential study of corn prices and effects of agricultural crises on producers, consumers, employment, migration to city, epidemics, and banditry. Fundamental contribution. [MAB]

37.504 Juan Carlos Garavaglia. "Economic growth and regional differentiations: the River Plate region at the end of the eighteenth century." Diane Meléndez, trans. *Hispanic American historical review* 65.1 (1985) 51–89. ISSN 0018-2168. ‣ Valuable comparative analysis. Concludes Bourbon reforms accentuated changes already underway. Important differences between Buenos Aires, Montevideo, Santa Fe, Corrientes, Tucumán, Catamarca, La Rioja, Misiones, and Cuyo. [MAB]

37.505 Juan Carlos Garavaglia and Juan Carlos Grosso. "Mexican elites of a provincial town: the landowners of Tepeaca (1700–1870)." *Hispanic American historical review* 70.2 (1990) 255–93. ISSN 0018-2168. ‣ Description of elite formation and maintenance with four family case studies. Emphasizes *hacen-*

dados' (estate owners) "rationality" and their expenditures to safeguard fundamental values: prominent position in their social milieu and religious piety. [MAB]

37.506 Richard L. Garner. "Price trends in eighteenth-century Mexico." *Hispanic American historical review* 65.2 (1985) 279–325. ISSN 0018-2168. ‣ Sophisticated analysis based on prices of maize, wheat, and beans and on tithe revenues. Trends generally upward. [MAB]

37.507 Scarlett O'Phelan Godoy. *Rebellions and revolts in eighteenth-century Peru and Upper Peru.* Cologne: Böhlau, 1985. ISBN 3-412-01085-5. ‣ Overview of production and fiscality followed by review of rebellions from 1730 to 1780s. Emphasizes dynamic nature of social struggle and three periods of rebellion. Best study of topic. [MAB]

37.508 Linda Greenow. *Credit and socioeconomic change in colonial Mexico: loans and mortgages in Guadalajara, 1720–1820.* Boulder: Westview, 1983. ISBN 0-86531-467-5. ‣ Examines significance of credit, various institutional dimensions of and participation in Nueva Galicia's credit market, fluctuations in credit, and flow of credit. Fine contribution to economic and social history. [MAB]

37.509 Michael T. Hamerly. *Historia social y económica de la antigua provincia de Guayaquil, 1763–1842.* Walter R. Spurrier, trans. Guayaquil, Ecuador: Archivo Histórico del Guayas, 1973. (Archivo Histórico del Guayas: colección monográfica, 3.) ‣ Detailed social, economic, and demographic history providing much new information about region, its peoples, and their lifestyles. Includes lengthy discussion of sources. Essential contribution. [MAB]

37.510 Brian R. Hamnett. *Politics and trade in southern Mexico, 1750–1821.* Cambridge: Cambridge University Press, 1971. ISBN 0-521-07860-1. ‣ Fine examination of *repartimiento* (forced sale of goods and acceptance of cash advances), trade, finance, efforts at reform, and coming of independence in Oaxaca. Emphasizes emergence and strengthening of regionalism in late colonial Mexico. [MAB]

37.511 Alexander von Humboldt. *Political essay on the kingdom of New Spain.* Mary Maples Dunn, ed. John Black, trans. New York: Knopf, 1972. ISBN 0-394-47556-9 (cl), 0-394-31510-3 (pbk). ‣ Abridged translation of extraordinarily perceptive description and analysis of New Spain at end of colonial era. Fundamental document. Originally published 1811. [MAB]

37.512 Nils Jacobsen and Hans-Jürgen Puhle, eds. *The economies of Mexico and Peru during the late colonial period, 1760–1810.* Berlin: Colloquium, 1986. ISBN 3-76780-666-5 (pbk). ‣ Fifteen chapters on mining sector, agriculture and livestock raising, artisanal and manufacturing sectors, commerce, and public sector with introduction by editor and several commentaries. Outstanding collection. [MAB]

37.513 Lyman L. Johnson. "The entrepreneurial reorganization of an artisan trade: the bakers of Buenos Aires, 1770–1820." *The Americas* 37.2 (1980) 139–60. ISSN 0003-1615. ‣ Examination of success of bakers, immigrant dominated craft, in overthrowing artisanal structures and moving toward factory production. Fascinating glimpse into little-studied realm of society. [MAB]

37.514 Lyman L. Johnson. "The silversmiths of Buenos Aires: a case study in the failure of corporate social organization." *Journal of Latin American studies* 8.2 (1976) 181–213. ISSN 0022-216x. ‣ Examination of artisan group most successful in creating and sustaining an officially endorsed, self-regulating, corporate structure but unable to establish guild. Enriches knowledge of artisans, relatively little-studied group. [MAB]

37.515 John E. Kicza. *Colonial entrepreneurs: families and business in Bourbon Mexico City.* 1 vol. to date. Albuquerque: University of New Mexico Press, 1983–. ISBN 0-8263-0655-1 (v. 1). ▸ Fascinating view of some of most exciting and dynamic groups in late colonial society. Examines composition of elite, different branches of commerce, and manufacturing in Bourbon Mexico City. [MAB]

37.516 John E. Kicza. "The *pulque* trade of late colonial Mexico City." *The Americas* 37.2 (1980) 193–222. ISSN 0003-1615. ▸ Very informative description of construction and operation of *pulquerías*, amount of *pulque* (fermented drink) consumed, tax revenue resulting, and ownership and management of production and distribution of *pulque*. Stresses elite involvement. [MAB]

37.517 Herbert S. Klein. "Structure and profitability of royal finance in the viceroyalty of the Río de la Plata in 1790." *Hispanic American historical review* 53.3 (1973) 440–69. ISSN 0018-2168. ▸ Careful, detailed examination of revenue and expenditures. Forty percent of expenditures devoted to civil, military, juridical, and clerical bureaucracy. Viceroyalty paid its own way but sent little revenue to Spain. [MAB]

37.518 Herbert S. Klein. "The structure of the *hacendado* class in late eighteenth-century Alto Peru: the Intendencia de La Paz." *Hispanic American historical review* 60.2 (1980) 191–212. ISSN 0018-2168. ▸ Estimates size, distribution, relative wealth, and composition of landed elite. Notes important role of women in *hacendado* (estate owner) class and limited land ownership by church. Fine regional examination. [MAB]

37.519 Allan J. Kuethe. *Cuba, 1753–1815: crown, military, and society.* Knoxville: University of Tennessee Press, 1986. ISBN 0-87049-487-2. ▸ Discussion of military reform in Cuba in imperial political context and consideration of its social implications. Excellent study almost unique in its appreciation of relationship between court politics and reform. [MAB]

37.520 Allan J. Kuethe. *Military reform and society in New Granada, 1773–1808.* Gainesville: University Presses of Florida, 1978. ISBN 0-8130-0570-1. ▸ Sophisticated, substantial study demonstrating varied impact of military reform on diverse regions of New Granada. [MAB]

37.521 Allan J. Kuethe and Lowell Blaisdell. "French influence and the origins of the Bourbon colonial reorganization." *Hispanic American historical review* 71.3 (1991) 579–607. ISSN 0018-2168. ▸ Revisionist article stressing limited French influence on Spanish colonial policy; Spain unwilling to sacrifice economic or diplomatic interests. Important reexamination emphasizing antecedents to reforms of Charles III. [MAB]

37.522 Allan J. Kuethe and G. Douglas Inglis. "Absolutism and enlightened reform: Charles III, the establishment of the *alcabala*, and commercial reorganization in Cuba." *Past and present* 109 (1985) 118–43. ISSN 0031-2746. ▸ Excellent examination of politics of reform from imperial perspective. Emphasizes consultation and compromise in addressing issues. [MAB]

37.523 Doris M. Ladd. *The making of a strike: Mexican silver workers' struggles in Real del Monte, 1766–1775.* Lincoln: University of Nebraska Press, 1988. ISBN 0-8032-2876-7. ▸ Pioneering work in Mexican labor history. Examines first strike in history of Mexican labor emphasizing workers and work conditions, protests, and growing solidarity. Explains how workers organized and won. [MAB]

37.524 Asunción Lavrin. "The role of the nunneries in the economy of New Spain in the eighteenth century." *Hispanic American historical review* 46.4 (1966) 371–93. ISSN 0018-2168. ▸ Excellent introduction to economic role of convents. Discusses both lending activities and internal management of resources. Concludes convents were important urban property holders. [MAB]

37.525 Sonya Lipsett-Rivera. "Puebla's eighteenth-century agrarian decline: a new perspective." *Hispanic American historical review* 70.3 (1990) 463–81. ISSN 0018-2168. ▸ Thoughtful, informative analysis enriching discussion of Puebla's decline. Focuses on conflicts over water rights and specifically over access to irrigation as cause of economic decline. [MAB]

37.526 John V. Lombardi. *People and places in colonial Venezuela.* Bloomington: Indiana University Press, 1976. ISBN 0-253-34330-5. ▸ Introduction to population of Bishopric of Caracas in late colonial period and presentation of extensive census data from 1771 to 1838. Indispensable for historical demographers. [MAB]

37.527 Jane M. Loy. "Forgotten *comuneros*: the 1781 revolt in the *llanos* of Casanare." *Hispanic American historical review* 61.2 (1981) 235–57. ISSN 0018-2168. ▸ Sales tax imposed on cotton in 1780 provoked Indians to attack tax collectors and led to creoles and Indians maintaining political autonomy for four months. Valuable addition to *comunero* ("rebel") literature. [MAB]

37.528 John Lynch. *Spanish colonial administration, 1782–1810: the intendant system in the viceroyalty of the Río de la Plata.* 1958 ed. New York: Greenwood, 1969. ▸ Detailed study of introduction of intendant system and intendants' financial, economic, and administrative activities. Fundamental work for late colonial Río de la Plata. [MFB]

37.529 Juan Marchena Fernández. *Oficiales y soldados en el ejército de América.* Sevilla: Escuela de Estudios Hispano-Americanos, 1983. (Publicaciones de la Escuela de Estudios Hispano-Americanos de Sevilla, 286.) ISBN 84-00-05379-6. ▸ Extremely informative study of officers and soldiers, based on their service records. Considers geographical and social backgrounds, age, length of service, and marital status. Imperial perspective. [MAB]

37.530 Lyle N. McAlister. *The "fuero militar" in New Spain, 1764–1800.* 1957 ed. Westport, Conn.: Greenwood, 1974. ISBN 0-8371-7554-2. ▸ Pioneering examination of military reform in New Spain. Argues expansion of military's legal privileges undermined royal authority and contributed to development of praetorian tradition. Cf. Archer 37.474. [MAB]

37.531 P. Michael McKinley. *Pre-revolutionary Caracas: politics, economy, and society, 1777–1811.* Cambridge: Cambridge University Press, 1985. ISBN 0-521-30450-4. ▸ Revisionist study portraying Caracas as extraordinarily well-balanced and harmonious society marked by economic growth, political stability, and social calm. Provocative thesis buttressed by impressive research. [MAB]

37.532 Gary M. Miller. "Bourbon social engineering: women and conditions of marriage in eighteenth-century Venezuela." *The Americas* 46.3 (1990) 261–90. ISSN 0003-1615. ▸ Part of prosopographical study of Spanish regular army officers. Demonstrates substantial crown involvement in determining officers' marriages. Officers' wives enjoyed better marriage conditions than most women. Very informative. [MAB]

37.533 Gary M. Miller. "Status and loyalty of regular army officers in late colonial Venezuela." *Hispanic American historical review* 66.4 (1986) 667–96. ISSN 0018-2168. ▸ Examines officer population, social origins and promotion, political power, wealth and economic status, and loyalty during First Republic. Valuable addition to studies of colonial military. [MAB]

37.534 Alfredo Moreno Cebrián. *El corregidor de indios y la economía peruana del siglo 18 (los repartos forzosos de mercancías).* Madrid: Consejo Superior de Investigaciones Científicas; Instituto G. Fernández de Oviedo, 1977. ISBN 84-00-03694-8. ▸ Rich, monumental examination of provincial administration. Considers sale of appointments, salaries, use of forced sale of merchandise, exploitation of natives, and efforts to reform system by establishing intendancies. [MAB]

37.535 Claude Morin. *Michoacán en la Nueva España del siglo 18: crecimiento y desigualdad en una economía colonial.* Roberto Gómez Ciriza, trans. Mexico: Fondo de Cultura Económica, 1979. ISBN 968-16-0348-6. ▸ Detailed, extraordinarily rich

37.536 Pedro Alonso O'Crouley. *A description of the kingdom of New Spain.* Seán Galvin, ed. and trans. San Francisco: Howell, 1972. ▸ Traveler's account of places visited, flora, fauna, and various curiosities. Useful as one of few such accounts available, but far inferior to Humboldt 37.511. [MAB]

37.537 Arij Ouweneel and Catrien C.J.H. Bijleveld. "The economic cycle in Bourbon Central Mexico: a critique of the *recaudación del diezmo líquido en pesos.*" *Hispanic American historical review* 69.3 (1989) 479–530. ISSN 0018-2168. ▸ Questions usefulness of tithe data of colonial Mexican bishoprics as index of agrarian production. Examines seventeen indicators of economic development. Commentary follows in *Hispanic American Historical Review* 69.3 (1989) 531–57. [MAB]

37.538 Robert W. Patch. "Agrarian change in eighteenth-century Yucatán." *Hispanic American historical review* 65.1 (1985) 21–49. ISSN 0018-2168. ▸ Rising Indian population after 1750 led to colonization of new settlements in eastern Yucatán but increased tenancy in western Yucatán with rise of *hacienda* (landed estate) in late eighteenth century. [MAB]

37.539 John Leddy Phelan. *The people and the king: the comunero revolution in Colombia, 1781.* Madison: University of Wisconsin Press, 1978. ISBN 0-299-07290-8. ▸ Thorough examination of Comunero Revolt. Argues Bourbon reforms sundered unwritten constitution and hence political stability in region. Thoughtful, provocative contribution. [MAB]

37.540 Ruth Pike. "Penal servitude in the Spanish empire: *presidio* labor in the eighteenth century." *Hispanic American historical review* 58.1 (1978) 21–40. ISSN 0018-2168. ▸ Judges commonly sentenced criminals, whether military men or civilians, to labor at military garrisons. In late eighteenth century such labor was considered rehabilitative. Informative article written from imperial perspective. [MAB]

37.541 Eugenio Piñeiro. "The cacao economy of the eighteenth-century province of Caracas and the Spanish cacao market." *Hispanic American historical review* 68.1 (1988) 75–100. ISSN 0018-2168. ▸ Caracas Company profited in cacao trade in part through fraud and contraband and its presence encouraged greater production. Finds weak forward and fiscal linkages. Revisionist interpretation. [MAB]

37.542 Herbert Ingram Priestley. *José de Gálvez, visitor-general of New Spain (1765–1771).* 1916 ed. Philadelphia: Porcupine, 1980. ISBN 0-87991-605-2. ▸ Detailed examination of celebrated *visita* (general inspection) of New Spain conducted by Gálvez. Also remains valuable for understanding subsequent reforms implemented by Gálvez as minister of the Indies. [MAB]

37.543 Jane M. Rausch. *A tropical plains frontier: the llanos of Colombia, 1531–1831.* Albuquerque: University of New Mexico Press, 1984. ISBN 0-8263-0761-2. ▸ Valuable regional study examining frontier region, missionary activities, rebellions, social and economic setting, wars of independence, and transformation of frontier to political and economic dependency. [MAB]

37.544 James D. Riley. "Crown law and rural labor in New Spain: the status of *gañanes* during the eighteenth century." *Hispanic American historical review* 64.2 (1984) 259–85. ISSN 0018-2168. ▸ Fine discussion of labor law of 1785 which abolished practice of tying workers to estates on basis of birth and modified treatment of workers' debts. Reflected emergence of increasingly mobile Indian population. [MAB]

37.545 David J. Robinson and Teresa Thomas. "New towns in eighteenth-century Northwest Argentina." *Journal of Latin American studies* 6.1 (1974) 1–33. ISSN 0022-216x. ▸ Informative, pioneering study of establishment of eighteen new towns, all but two in province of Cuyo, to improve administrative control, defense, and education. Represents significant innovation in spatial organization. [MAB]

37.546 James Schofield Saeger. "Another view of the mission as a frontier institution: the Guaycuruan reductions of Santa Fe, 1743–1810." *Hispanic American historical review* 65.3 (1985) 493–517. ISSN 0018-2168. ▸ Analysis of Jesuit missionization of Abipones and Macobies in eastern Chico region. Missions served as buffer zones that aided development of Santa Fe. Places Guaycuruan missions in comparative perspective. New approach to Boltonian view of missions as agents of European influence (37.568). [MAB/KLJ]

37.547 James Schofield Saeger. "Survival and abolition: the eighteenth-century Paraguayan *encomienda.*" *The Americas* 38.1 (1981) 59–85. ISSN 0003-1615. ▸ *Encomienda* (system of forced labor) still important when crown decided to abolish it in 1770s. Decision was major blow to upper-class Paraguayans and ultimately disastrous for crown. Thorough study. [MAB]

37.548 James Schofield Saeger, ed. *Essays on eighteenth-century race relations in the Americas.* Bethlehem, Pa.: Lawrence Henry Gipson Institute, 1987. ISBN 0-944828-00-0. ▸ Six essays, including Mörner on slavery, race relations, and Bourbon reorganization in eighteenth-century Spanish America and Gibson on Mexican *ejido* (Indian village lands) in the eighteenth century. Useful. [MAB]

37.549 Ricardo Salvatore and Jonathan C. Brown. "Trade and proletarianization in late colonial Banda Oriental: evidence from the Estancia de las Vacas, 1791–1805." *Hispanic American historical review* 67.3 (1987) 431–59. ISSN 0018-2168. ▸ Case study of Uruguayan state. Gauchos resisted proletarianization and preserved cultural traditions of illegality and freedom, resulting in high turnover in *estancia*'s (large estates) labor force. Debate follows in *Hispanic American Historical Review* 69.4 (1989) 715–45. [MAB]

37.550 Michael C. Scardaville. "Alcohol abuse and tavern reform in late colonial Mexico City." *Hispanic American historical review* 60.4 (1980) 643–71. ISSN 0018-2168. ▸ Growing alcohol consumption among poor at 1,600 taverns led to expanded police forces and efforts at reform that accomplished little. Fascinating contribution to social history. [MAB]

37.551 Patricia Seed. "Social dimensions of race: Mexico City, 1753." *Hispanic American historical review* 62.4 (1982) 569–606. ISSN 0018-2168. ▸ Important analysis of relationship between race and division of labor founded on essentially different economic roles of Indians, blacks, and peninsulars. Intermediate racial groups reflected social origin of parent groups. [MAB]

37.552 Robert Jones Shafer. *The economic societies in the Spanish world, 1763–1821.* Syracuse, N.Y.: Syracuse University Press, 1958. ▸ Examination of origins and activities of economic societies in Spain and particularly in Spanish America. Remains important contribution to understanding crown-encouraged diffusion of enlightened ideas. [MAB/SHB]

37.553 Susan Migden Socolow. *The bureaucrats of Buenos Aires, 1769–1810: amor al real servicio.* Durham, N.C.: Duke University Press, 1987. ISBN 0-8223-0753-7. ▸ Detailed study of rapidly expanded royal bureaucracy in Buenos Aires. Fine social and administrative history examining bureaucrats, their career patterns, remuneration, local ties, and corruption. [MAB]

37.554 Susan Migden Socolow. *The merchants of Buenos Aires, 1778–1810: family and commerce.* New York: Cambridge University Press, 1978. ISBN 0-521-21812-8. ▸ Study of merchants of Buenos Aires and their social ties, investments, life style, religious participation, and political and social awareness. Important study of dynamic and influential group. [MAB]

37.555 Ward Stavig. "Ethnic conflict, moral economy, and population in rural Cuzco on the eve of the Thupa Amaro II rebellion." *Hispanic American historical review* 68.4 (1988) 737–70. ISSN 0018-2168. ▸ Concludes by 1780 long-term structural changes and conflicts, economic tensions, population fluctuations, and local problems combined to create conjuncture ripe for rebellion. Leaders' personal influence determined who supported it. Thoughtful analysis. [MAB]

37.556   Arthur Robert Steele. *Flowers for the king: the expedition of Ruiz and Pavón and the flora of Peru.* Durham, N.C.: Duke University Press, 1964. ▸ Beautifully written study of botanical expedition to Peru (1778–88). Examines participants, their findings, and milieu within which they labored. Underscores practical nature of Enlightenment. [MAB]

37.557   Stanley J. Stein. "Bureaucracy and business in the Spanish empire, 1759–1804: failure of a Bourbon reform in Mexico and Peru." *Hispanic American historical review* 61.1 (1981) 2–28. ISSN 0018-2168. ▸ Failure to pay local administrators adequately, persistence of *repartimiento de mercancias* (forced sale of goods), and division among high-ranking officials undermined intendant system and prevented its reform. Debate follows in *Hispanic American Historical Review* 62.3 (1982) 460–77. [MAB]

37.558   Steve J. Stern, ed. *Resistance, rebellion, and consciousness in the Andean peasant world, eighteenth to twentieth centuries.* Madison: University of Wisconsin Press, 1987. ISBN 0-299-11350-7 (cl), 0-299-11354-X (pbk). ▸ Seven of twelve chapters focus on colonial period. Stern's reappraisal of insurrection, 1742–82, especially impressive. [MAB]

37.559   Michael M. Swann. *Tierra adentro: settlement and society in colonial Durango.* Boulder: Westview, 1982. ISBN 0-86531-399-7. ▸ Overview of regional settlement and growth, but primary focus on population analysis for 1765–1810. Includes analysis of city of Durango. Valuable demographic examination. [MAB]

37.560   William B. Taylor. "Banditry and insurrection: rural unrest in central Jalisco, 1790–1816." In *Riot, rebellion, and revolution: rural social conflict in Mexico.* Friedrich Katz, ed., pp. 205–46. Princeton: Princeton University Press, 1988. ISBN 0-691-07739-8 (cl), 0-691-02265-8 (pbk). ▸ Keen analysis of main forms of rural unrest in terms of social values and changing economy, polity, and village society. Unrest increased first as banditry and then as insurrection. [MAB]

37.561   Antonine Tibesar. "The Lima pastors, 1750–1820: their origins and studies as taken from their autobiographies." *The Americas* 28.1 (1971) 39–56. ISSN 0003-1615. ▸ Valuable prosopographical examination that reveals most priests were creoles and many were from Lima with family ties to civil or military bureaucracy. Priests served obligations adequately. [MAB]

37.562   John Tutino. "Power, class, and family: men and women in the Mexican elite, 1750–1810." *The Americas* 39.3 (1983) 359–81. ISSN 0003-1615. ▸ Examination of families atop Mexico's landed elite. Demonstrates patriarchs normally dominated elite clans, most family resources, and internal family social relations. Useful clarification of elite women's position. [MAB]

37.563   Sergio Villalobos R. *El comercio y la crisis colonial.* 2d ed. Santiago, Chile: Editorial Universitaria, 1990. ▸ Excellent study of trade with particular attention to trade between Chile and Peru and Buenos Aires and to contraband trade, early eighteenth century to 1810. [MAB]

37.564   Arthur P. Whitaker, ed. *Latin America and the Enlightenment: essays.* 1961 2d ed. Frederico de Onis, Introduction. Ithaca, N.Y.: Cornell University Press, 1967. ▸ Reprint of five essays published in 1942 and one new essay. Primary focus on Spanish America. Readable, informative introduction to topic by group of eminent historians. [MAB]

37.565   Miles L. Wortman. *Government and society in Central America, 1680–1840.* New York: Columbia University Press, 1982. ISBN 0-231-05212-X. ▸ Social, economic, and political study of establishment of colonial rule in Guatemala and fragmentation of imperial regime; parts 1 and 2 carry story to 1821. Significant contribution to understudied area. Includes information on Indian community and livelihood. [MAB/MWH]

37.566   Celia Wu. "The population of the city of Querétaro in 1791." *Journal of Latin American studies* 16.2 (1984) 277–307. ISSN 0022-216X. ▸ Demographic examination of elite and structure of employment and correlation of occupation and ethnic status. Concludes society organized more by caste than class lines. Contribution to debate begun by Chance and Taylor 37.492. [MAB]

SEE ALSO
   29.161 Jacques A. Barbier. *The culmination of the Bourbon reforms, 1787–1792.*
   29.162 Jacques A. Barbier. *Peninsular finance and colonial trade.*
   36.307 William B. Taylor. *Drinking, homicide, and rebellion in colonial Mexican villages.*
   38.191 Linda Arnold. *Bureaucracy and bureaucrats in Mexico City, 1742–1835.*
   38.192 Silvia Marina Arrom. *The women of Mexico City, 1790–1857.*
   38.231 Brian R. Hamnett. *Roots of insurgency.*
   38.243 Doris M. Ladd. *The Mexican nobility at independence, 1780–1826.*
   38.270 John Tutino. *From insurrection to revolution in Mexico.*
   38.599 Jonathan C. Brown. *A socioeconomic history of Argentina, 1776–1860.*

SPANISH BORDERLANDS

37.567   John Francis Bannon. *The Spanish borderlands frontier, 1513–1821.* 1970 ed. Albuquerque: University of New Mexico Press, 1976. ISBN 0-8263-0309-9 (pbk). ▸ Ambitious summary and first synthesis since Herbert Eugene Bolton's in 1921. Comparison of Hispanic and Anglo-American frontier institutions and society. Offers scant insight into Hispanic society or Hispanic impact on Indian societies. [DJW]

37.568   John Francis Bannon, ed. *Bolton and the Spanish borderlands.* Norman: University of Oklahoma Press, 1964. ▸ Seventeen essays by Herbert Eugene Bolton (1870–1952), who defined field of borderlands history, trained generation of key historians, and wrote prolifically. Uncritical but best introduction to his career and works. [DJW]

37.569   Amy Bushnell. *The king's coffer: proprietors of the Spanish Florida treasury, 1565–1702.* Gainesville: University Presses of Florida, 1981. ISBN 0-8130-0690-2. ▸ Goes beyond institutional and administrative history to provide fresh insights into social and cultural life in Spanish St. Augustine. Treasury officials, who formed local elite, perpetuated themselves in office and put own interests above crown's. [DJW]

37.570   William S. Coker and Thomas D. Watson. *Indian traders of the southeastern Spanish borderlands: Panton, Leslie & Company and John Forbes & Company, 1783–1847.* Gainesville and Pensacola: University Presses of Florida and University of West Florida Press, 1986. ISBN 0-8130-0801-8. ▸ Under unique arrangement, firm of Scotsmen monopolized Indian trade in Spanish territory with British trade goods. As political fortunes changed, so did firm's loyalties. Comprehensive study with attention to rapidly changing political context. [DJW]

37.571   Sherburne F. Cook. *The conflict between the California Indian and white civilization.* 1940–43 ed. 4 vols. in 1. Berkeley: University of California Press, 1976. ISBN 0-520-03142-3 (cl), 0-520-03143-1 (pbk). ▸ Quantitative, strikingly revisionist study examining physical, demographic, and behavioral responses of California Indians to competition for material resources. Argues

Spanish impact, especially in Franciscan missions, was largely negative—disease, malnutrition, demoralization, and high mortality. Still influential. [DJW/FEH/HM]

37.572 Warren L. Cook. *Flood tide of empire: Spain and the Pacific Northwest, 1543–1819.* New Haven: Yale University Press, 1973. ISBN 0-300-01577-1. ▸ Broadly conceived analysis of Spanish activity and international repercussions. Includes Spain's interest in reaching northwest coast from Mississippi valley and fresh evidence of Spain's efforts to block American overland expansion. [DJW]

37.573 Gilbert R. Cruz. *Let there be towns: Spanish municipal origins in the American Southwest, 1610–1810.* College Station: Texas A&M University Press, 1988. ISBN 0-89096-314-2. ▸ Case study of six municipalities: El Paso, Laredo, Los Angeles, San Antonio, Santa Fe, and San Jose. Romantic, uncritical, and outdated but notable as only monograph on towns in Spanish borderlands. [DJW]

37.574 Light Townsend Cummins. *Spanish observers and the American Revolution, 1775–1783.* Baton Rouge: Louisiana State University Press, 1991. ISBN 0-8071-1690-4. ▸ Discussion of overt and covert roles of Spanish agents in Anglo-American colonies who influenced Spanish policy toward American Revolution and American rebel leadership itself; seen as Spanish diplomatic success. Key work on previously neglected subject. [DJW]

37.575 Janet R. Fireman. *The Spanish Royal Corps of Engineers in the western borderlands: instrument of Bourbon reform, 1764 to 1815.* Glendale, Calif.: Clark, 1977. ISBN 0-87062-116-5. ▸ Pioneering study of specially trained military unit founded in 1711. Engineers sent to northern New Spain, planned defenses, drew maps, surveyed roads, and gathered economic and demographic data. [DJW]

37.576 Jack D. Forbes. *Apache, Navaho, and Spaniard.* 1960 ed. Westport, Conn.: Greenwood, 1980. ISBN 0-313-22021-2. ▸ Pioneering ethnohistorical reconstruction of southern Athapascan peoples, their relationships with Spaniards and with other Indians, from early sixteenth century until great rebellions of 1680s. Reflects Indian viewpoints. [DJW]

37.577 Robert L. Gold. *Borderland empires in transition: the triple nation transfer of Florida.* Carbondale: Southern Illinois University Press, 1969. ISBN 0-8093-2539-X. ▸ When England acquired Florida in 1763, Spain hastily relocated all of its subjects to Cuba; half of French inhabitants of western Florida remained. Model evaluation of effect of imperial geopolitics on locales. [DJW]

37.578 Ramón A. Gutiérrez. *When Jesus came, the corn mothers went away: marriage, sexuality, and power in New Mexico, 1500–1846.* Stanford, Calif.: Stanford University Press, 1991. ISBN 0-8047-1816-4 (cl), 0-8047-1832-6 (pbk). ▸ Analysis of Pueblo-Franciscan interaction in seventeenth century and Hispanic society subsequently. Focus on how church, state, and oligarchy used marriage to enforce social order. Highly imaginative and theoretically sophisticated. [DJW]

37.579 Thomas D. Hall. *Social change in the Southwest, 1350–1880.* Lawrence: University Press of Kansas, 1989. ISBN 0-7006-0374-3. ▸ Sociological analysis of interactions of Indians, Hispanics, and Anglo-Americans to explain accompanying changes in social structure. Case study of Southwest to test and refine world-systems theory. [DJW]

37.580 John H. Hann. *Apalachee: the land between the rivers.* Gainesville: University Presses of Florida and Florida State Museum, 1988. (Ripley P. Bullen monographs in anthropology and history, 7.) ISBN 0-8130-0854-9. ▸ Re-creation of Apalachee Indian society (present-day Tallahassee) from archaeological and ethnohistorical sources, pre-Spanish era to collapse in early eigh-

teenth century. Encyclopedic, multidisciplinary, rich in documents. [DJW]

37.581 Paul E. Hoffman. *A new Andalucia and a way to the Orient: the American Southeast during the sixteenth century.* Baton Rouge: Louisiana State University Press, 1990. ISBN 0-8071-1552-5. ▸ Spanish, French, and English exploration from Chesapeake Bay to Florida and Gulf of Mexico. Argues European exploration shaped by two imaginary places—Chicora (a new Andalucia) and passage isthmus to Asia. [DJW]

37.582 Jack Jackson. *Los mesteños: Spanish ranching in Texas, 1721–1821.* College Station: Texas A&M University Press, 1986. ISBN 0-89096-230-8. ▸ Development of range cattle industry, markets, and government regulations. Identifies key ranching families. Highly detailed; enters debate on cradle of western ranching techniques on side of Texas not Anglo-American South. [DJW]

37.583 Elizabeth A. H. John. *Storms brewed in other men's worlds: the confrontation of Indians, Spanish, and French in the Southwest, 1540–1795.* 1975 ed. Lincoln: University of Nebraska Press, 1981. ISBN 0-8032-7554-4 (pbk). ▸ Detailed, skillful narrative of Spanish-French-Indian relations from western Louisiana through New Mexico. Incorporates Indian perspectives and experiences; describes their cultures and motivations through careful use of ethnologies and European documents. Lacks significant engagement with literature of anthropology. [DJW]

37.584 Oakah L. Jones, Jr. *Los paisanos: Spanish settlers on the northern frontier of New Spain.* Norman: University of Oklahoma Press, 1979. ISBN 0-8061-1432-0. ▸ Civilian society, culture, and institutions. Argues civilians more numerous, influential, and culturally distinctive than earlier supposed. Encyclopedic province-by-province overview. [DJW]

37.585 Oakah L. Jones, Jr. *Pueblo warriors and Spanish conquest.* Norman: University of Oklahoma Press, 1966. ▸ Explains Spanish use of armed, mounted Pueblo Indians as allies in campaigns against neighboring tribes in eighteenth-century New Mexico. Pueblos willing participants. Balanced assessment of policy's effectiveness for Spain. [DJW]

37.586 John L. Kessell. *Friars, soldiers, and reformers: Hispanic Arizona and the Sonora mission frontier, 1767–1856.* Tucson: University of Arizona Press, 1976. ISBN 0-8165-0547-0 (cl), 0-8165-0487-3 (pbk). ▸ Successor to 37.588, sharing same qualities. Examines establishment and survival of Franciscan Piman missions in hostile political environment of late Bourbon Spain and missions' ultimate secularization under Mexico. [DJW]

37.587 John L. Kessell. *Kiva, cross, and crown: the Pecos Indians and New Mexico, 1540–1840.* 1979 ed. Albuquerque: University of New Mexico Press, 1987. ISBN 0-8263-0968-2 (pbk). ▸ Pueblo-Spanish-Plains Indian relations and intermural pueblo affairs, seen in key eastern pueblo of Pecos. Judiciously interpreted, vividly written. Best in-depth introduction to Spanish colonial New Mexico. [DJW]

37.588 John L. Kessell. *Mission of Sorrows: Jesuit Guevavi and the Pimas, 1691–1767.* Ernest J. Burrus, Foreword. Tucson: University of Arizona Press, 1970. ISBN 0-8165-0192-0. ▸ Spanish Arizona from beginnings to expulsion of Jesuits as seen from single mission. Meticulous research, engaging writing, most satisfying in-depth introduction to early Arizona. See also Kessell 37.586. [DJW]

37.589 Noel M. Loomis and Abraham P. Nasatir. *Pedro Vial and the roads to Santa Fe.* Norman: University of Oklahoma Press, 1967. ▸ Study of Spanish exploration of southern plains (1786–1812), opening routes from Santa Fe to San Antonio, Natchez, and St. Louis. Much fresh information regarding long-forgotten Spanish precursors of well-known Anglo Americans. [DJW]

37.590 Eugene Lyon. *The enterprise of Florida: Pedro Menéndez* *de Avilés and the Spanish conquest of Florida, 1565–1568*. 1976 ed. Gainesville: University Presses of Florida, 1983. ISBN 0-8130-0533-7 (cl), 0-8130-0777-1 (pbk). ▸ Revisionist study of Spanish settlement on Atlantic coast culminated decades of effort, not simple response to French intrusion. High-ranking officer (*adelantado*) Pedro Menéndez de Avilés and his extended family presented as ambitious, multifaceted entrepreneurs. Originally published as *The Adelantamiento of Florida, 1565–1568*. [DJW]

37.591 Michael C. Meyer. *Water in the Hispanic Southwest: a social and legal history, 1550–1850*. Tucson: University of Arizona Press, 1984. ISBN 0-8165-0825-9. ▸ Examination of relationships between water and Hispanic society. Most land contained no implied right to water for irrigation. Under Spain and Mexico equity and need took precedence over absolute rights to water. [DJW]

37.592 John Preston Moore. *Revolt in Louisiana: the Spanish occupation, 1766–1770*. Baton Rouge: Louisiana State University Press, 1976. ISBN 0-8071-0180-X. ▸ Argues French resistance to Spanish authority stemmed from local merchant elite that feared economic reforms, not from ineptitude of conciliatory Spanish governor Ulloa. Key revisionist study of pivotal moment. [DJW]

37.593 Max L. Moorhead. *The Apache frontier: Jacobo Ugarte and Spanish Indian relations in northern New Spain, 1769–1791*. Norman: University of Oklahoma Press, 1968. ▸ Spanish Indian policy from vantage point of head of Interior Provinces, 1786–1790. Ugarte battled bureaucracy as well as Apaches; argues Ugarte's implementation primarily responsible for policy's success. [DJW]

37.594 Max L. Moorhead. *The presidio: bastion of the Spanish borderlands*. 1975 ed. David J. Weber, Foreword. Norman: University of Oklahoma Press, 1991. ISBN 0-8061-1239-5 (cl, 1975), 0-8061-2317-6 (pbk). ▸ First synthesis and still standard work on military garrisons established on northern edge of New Spain, excepting Californias. Includes evolution of military policy. Analyzes structures, troops, supplies, and relationships to civilians. [DJW]

37.595 Abraham P. Nasatir. *Borderland in retreat: from Spanish Louisiana to the far Southwest*. Ann Arbor: University Microfilms International: Books on Demand, 1976. ISBN 0-8357-7351-5 (pbk). ▸ Study of Spain's retreat presented as losing struggle with France, England, and/or United States in six subregions. Synthesis of author's prodigious life's work. Difficult and confusing prose style limits use to specialists. [DJW]

37.596 Gerald E. Poyo and Gilberto Hinojosa, eds. *Tejano origins in eighteenth-century San Antonio*. Austin: University of Texas Press for the University of Texas, Institute of Texan Cultures at San Antonio, 1991. ISBN 0-292-71138-7. ▸ Seven essays examining ethnic groups and processes of adaptation and compromise that produced distinctive community identity. Revisionist view emphasizing social dynamics over institutions and asserting Hispanic roots of present-day Texas. [DJW]

37.597 Marc Simmons. *Spanish government in New Mexico*. 2d ed. Albuquerque: University of New Mexico Press, 1990. ISBN 0-8263-1199-7 (pbk). ▸ Pioneering study of provincial, district, and municipal administration, financial affairs, and military or-

ganization, 1776–1821, based on archival sources. Suggests New Mexico wealthier and more complex than previously supposed. [DJW]

37.598 Engel Sluiter. *The Florida situado: quantifying the first eighty years, 1571–1651*. Gainesville: University of Florida Libraries, 1985. (Research publications of the P. K. Yonge Library of Florida History, University of Florida, 1.) ▸ First systematic study of subsidy paid to Spanish Florida. Based on research in Veracruz and Mexico treasuries. Concludes subsidy paid more regularly than Florida officials claimed or historians believed. [DJW]

37.599 John Jay TePaske. *The governorship of Spanish Florida, 1700–1763*. Durham, N.C.: Duke University Press, 1964. ISBN 0-317-26867-8 (pbk). ▸ Administration, justice, finances, religion, defense, and Indian policy as addressed by key administrative officer, who often improved local solutions demanded by frontier exigencies. Starting point for further research. [DJW]

37.600 David Hurst Thomas, ed. *Columbian consequences*. 3 vols. Washington, D.C.: Smithsonian Institution Press, 1989–91. ISBN 0-87474-908-5 (v. 1), 0-87474-390-7 (v. 2), 0-87474-388-5 (v. 3). ▸ Ninety-four articles on Spanish borderlands by anthropologists, archaeologists, and historians treating wide variety of discrete subjects. Revisionist; best guide to increasingly interdisciplinary borderlands historiography. [DJW/SS]

37.601 David J. Weber. *The Spanish frontier in North America*. New Haven: Yale University Press, 1992. ISBN 0-300-05198-0. ▸ Synthesis of Spanish activity in present United States from California to Florida; first since Bannon 37.567. Argues for broadening scope of early American history to explore frontiers as places of contention and transformation. [DJW]

37.602 David J. Weber, ed. *The idea of Spanish borderlands*. New York: Garland, 1991. ISBN 0-8240-0780-8. ▸ Key essays on significance and historiography of borderlands school. Includes founder Herbert E. Bolton, who promoted idea that Spain's empire in North America was integral to United States history. Other essays by or about Bolton's predecessors, followers, and critics. [DJW]

37.603 Robert S. Weddle. *The French thorn: rival explorers in the Spanish sea, 1682–1762*. College Station: Texas A&M University Press, 1991. ISBN 0-89096-480-7. ▸ Sequel to 36.646 treating Spanish-French exploration and expansion on northern coast of Gulf of Mexico. Major theme: ongoing geographical ignorance. Based on archival research; lively writing. [DJW]

37.604 Robert S. Weddle. *Spanish sea: the Gulf of Mexico in North American discovery, 1500–1685*. College Station: Texas A&M University Press, 1985. ISBN 0-89096-211-1. ▸ European exploration and settlement of Gulf, especially its north coast, to La Salle. Sees Gulf, scene of earliest exploration of North American interior, as more appropriate than Atlantic coast as starting point for United States history. Clarifies many details. Best overview. [DJW]

37.605 J. Leitch Wright, Jr. *Anglo-Spanish rivalry in North America*. Athens: University of Georgia Press, 1971. ISBN 0-8203-0305-4. ▸ Concise overview of Spanish responses to English intrusions into northern fringes of its empire, sixteenth century to 1820, and Spain's steady loss of ground. Based on published and unpublished sources. [DJW]

RICHARD J. WALTER

Latin America since 1800

As with most fields of historical study, there has been an enormous expansion of scholarly works on Latin America in recent decades, perhaps more than in most fields. This scholarly boom on Latin America since 1800, however, is related, directly and indirectly, to a particular historical event: the Cuban Revolution of 1959. That Revolution, in its infancy when the last *Guide* appeared, stimulated first a notable outpouring of materials on the event itself and on the previously little-studied (by non-Cuban historians) Cuba. While scholars and policymakers struggled to understand the background, significance, and consequences of the Revolution, the challenge posed by a communist Cuba allied with the Soviet Union led the United States government and major foundations to direct unprecedented attention and resources to Latin American studies in general. Generous grants were provided to bolster and expand graduate programs and Latin American institutes at leading universities with longstanding academic strengths in the area and helped create centers of study in other institutions that previously had shown little concern for the nations south of the border. As a result, the 1960s became something of a golden age for Latin American studies, and while support and attention have ebbed and flowed since then, much of that momentum has carried through to the early 1990s.

This generous support produced a bumper crop of graduate students and future historians, most of whom received extensive training in languages, were exposed to advanced techniques in the social sciences, and had the opportunity to spend long periods in Latin American countries to conduct their field research. There, they were joined by scholars of earlier generations, who also benefited from this new surge of interest. As the decade ended and into the following years, a number of former Peace Corps volunteers entered the ranks of Latin American historians, bringing to their work the special perspective gained from several years of living and working at the grassroots level in the region. Moreover, as Latin America became an area of increasing national and international interest, talented journalists added their experiences and insights to the growing historiography of the area. A number of the new historians were women, and their ranks swelled substantially in the 1970s and 1980s.

Generally, the new scholars of the post-1959 generation took a more critical view of Latin American history than had their predecessors. Influenced by the events in Cuba and later the Vietnam War, they were particularly skeptical of and often opposed to U.S. policy in the region. While this critical view is seen most clearly in the study of diplomatic history and inter-American affairs, it is also visible in examinations of Latin

American societies themselves. Moving away from an emphasis on individuals and events, historians of Latin America increasingly focused on the social classes and forces, economic structures, and political institutions that perpetuated and reinforced authoritarian governments and blocked progressive change. In the process, they reversed the tendency noted by H. Cline in his introduction to the 1961 *Guide* "to eschew narrative or analysis of the recent past." As the material listed below amply shows, the post–World War II history of Latin America has received and continues to receive considerable scholarly emphasis.

Another important result of the U.S. boom in Latin American studies was the creation in 1965 of a national and international organization, the Latin American Studies Association. Historians played a leading role in the creation of the association and made up a large part of its constituency. Nonetheless, it drew members from a wide variety of fields, reflecting the growing interdisciplinary nature of the study of the region. One of the first major activities of the association was the production of a new journal, the *Latin American Research Review*, which contained essays on the state of research in various areas and provided practical advice on such matters as access to holdings of archives and documentary collections in the United States and abroad, the development of new research methodologies, the status of ongoing studies, and suggestions for future work.

The 1960s also saw a considerable expansion in publication opportunities for research in the field. University and commercial presses developed special series for Latin American studies and generally expanded their lists of Latin American titles. Finally, in addition to the *Latin American Research Review*, new journals such as the *Journal of Interamerican Studies and World Affairs*, *Latin American Perspectives*, and the *Journal of Latin American Studies* established themselves as important outlets for scholarly publication.

Since the 1960s, scholarly interests in Latin America frequently paralleled U.S. policy interests. There was a dramatic increase, for example, in studies on countries such as Brazil and Chile, that, like Cuba, experienced in the 1960s and 1970s important political changes with major implications for and involvement with U.S. foreign policies. A similar trend occurred for Central American countries in the 1980s. Two important countries with somewhat lower policy profiles, Argentina and Mexico, continued to draw consistent scholarly attention. Work on the Andean republics (Venezuela, Colombia, Ecuador, Peru, and Bolivia) and Paraguay and Uruguay grew, but overall these nations received less attention than others.

As in most fields of historical research, Latin Americanists adopted diverse and changing approaches to their material and subject matter. In the late 1960s and early 1970s, many fell under the sway of dependency theory and focused on the relationship between individual Latin American nations or the region as a whole and the capitalist world system centered in the United States and western Europe. In the 1970s and 1980s, other scholars took issue with the dependency theory, often producing lively intellectual exchanges. Latin Americanists, clearly influenced by larger scholarly trends in the United States and Europe, adopted many of the techniques and approaches of the social sciences to their own efforts. They concentrated more on social and economic groups and forces than had previously been the case and emphasized the historical role of those left out of many prior accounts—black slaves, Indian peasants, immigrant and migrant workers, and women. Increasingly, historians drew on sources such as census manuscripts, local legal records, government economic reports, and election results and applied sophisticated quantitative methods to determine or to speculate on the historical trends and consequences they represented. Family history, labor history, women's history, and history of popular culture, among other topics, became important subspecialties.

For the most part, throughout the period since the 1960s, the majority of Latin American historians of the postindependence years have continued to focus their efforts and develop their special expertise on individual countries. In some instances, they sought to narrow the focus even more to particular cities, regions, provinces, or states. This trend has been most notable in work on Brazil and Mexico, where research on state histories has produced important results and provided building blocks for more synthetic national histories. Others have developed a larger regional perspective on issues related to institutions, such as the military, or particular groups, such as workers, women, students, and peasants. A number of scholars have used a regional comparative approach to highlight similarities and differences between and among the various Latin American countries or to compare the Latin American historical experience with that of nations outside the region. Perhaps the best example of such efforts has been the impressive and growing literature on black slavery in Latin America, often compared with the development of that institution in the United States.

As historical specialties and expertise have grown, attempts to bring diverse perspectives to bear on a common theme or issue have been facilitated by frequent scholarly conferences, a rare occurrence before the 1960s. These conferences, most often held in the United States or in Latin America and frequently attended by scholars from around the world, in turn often have resulted in valuable collaborative publications, a practice that seems likely to continue.

The titles below, which underscore these trends, were chosen and organized according to criteria developed for the present *Guide*. First, this section is selective, representing only a relatively small proportion of the thousands of titles that have appeared on Latin America over the past three decades. (In any given year, the leading journal in the field, the *Hispanic American Historical Review*, receives between 300 and 400 books to list or review.) Second, it aims to provide breadth rather than depth of coverage, seeking to show the broad diversity of subjects and approaches that have characterized the field since the early 1960s. Third, it generally includes the most recent works on particular topics. This has meant that only a relatively few items from the 1961 *Guide* have been listed. This, of course, is not intended as a reflection on the quality of the works published before 1960 but is simply a response to the demands of this project. Fourth, given the space limitation, most of the items below are monographs and collections of essays, interspersed with some major articles. The majority are written by historians, but a substantial number are the work of social scientists—anthropologists, economists, political scientists, sociologists—and others who include historical material and perspective in their work. Fifth, the great bulk of the items are in English and are by North American and British authors. A few items are in Spanish, and an attempt has been made to include a number of English translations of major works by Latin American scholars. A significant number of the listed works are by Latin Americans who have found employment in academic institutions in the United States and Great Britain and have published in English.

The material has been organized alphabetically by author's last name and by country. The two largest countries, Brazil and Mexico, are in separate categories, while the others are listed in larger geographical groupings. Items in the "General" category deal with the region as a whole or with a number of countries. The same holds true for the material under the rubric Inter-American Affairs, while the individual country sections include works that treat the specific relationship between the country and the United States. Reference works, historiographical material, and journals relate primarily to items that focus on the period since 1800. It should be noted, however, that several important works covering the entire scope of Latin American history have been included in the preceding section on colonial Latin American history. Of particular importance are the *Handbook of Latin American Studies*, the *Hispanic American Historical*

Review, the *Journal of Latin American Studies*, the *Latin American Research Review*, and C. C. Griffin, ed., *Latin America: A guide to the Historical Literature*.

ACKNOWLEDGMENTS   *I would like to thank my collaborators on this project and also professors Henry Berger, Department of History, Washington University in St. Louis; Charles Bergquist, Department of History, University of Washington in Seattle; Judith Ewell, Department of History, College of William and Mary; and William Sater, Department of History, California State University, Long Beach, for their advice and assistance. We also want to recognize Gina Homes, Tony Johnston, Bette Marbs, and Scott C. Sessions for their valuable work on this project.*

[Contributors: AS = Adrian Shubert, DCJ = Donald C. Jackson, EDL = Erick D. Langer, EH-D = Evelyn Hu-DeHart, MAB = Mark A. Burkholder, MWH = Mary W. Helms, NDC = Noble David Cook, RJW = Richard J. Walter, RLM = Richard L. Millett, RML = Robert M. Levine]

REFERENCE WORKS

38.1 ABC-Clio Information Services. *Latin American politics: a historical bibliography.* Santa Barbara, Calif.: ABC-Clio, 1984. ISBN 0-87436-377-2. ▸ Over 3,000 annotated entries of books and articles on politics of region and particular countries. Extensive subject-author index. [RJW]

38.2 Russell H. Bartley and Stuart L. Wagner, comps. *Latin America in basic historical collections: a working guide.* Stanford, Calif.: Hoover Institution Press, 1972. ISBN 0-8179-2511-2. ▸ Description of collections of historical materials on Latin America in principal archives, libraries, and special collections in United States, Europe, and Latin America. Useful for graduate students and scholars. [RJW]

38.3 Jean-Pierre Bernard et al., eds. *Guide to the political parties of South America.* Michael Perl, trans. Harmondsworth: Penguin, 1973. ISBN 0-14-021625-1. ▸ Dated but useful compilation of basic information by various contributors on major and minor parties in 1960s. Translation of 1969 French edition. [RJW]

38.4 John F. Bratzel, ed. *Latin American history.* 2d ed. New York: Weiner, 1988. ISBN 0-910129-97-5 (pbk). ▸ Reproduction of course syllabi on Latin America from sixty-two American college and university courses offered by twenty-five instructors in 1980s. Useful information on how various teachers approach problems of course organization and presentation. [RJW]

38.5 Robert S. Byars and Joseph L. Love, eds. *Quantitative social science research on Latin America.* Urbana: University of Illinois Press, 1973. (Center for Latin American and Caribbean Studies, 1.) ISBN 0-252-00335-7. ▸ Essays describing state of research based on quantitative methods by historian, sociologist, political scientist, geographer, and archaeologist. Useful for fields covered; failed to include economist. [RJW]

38.6 Howard Francis Cline, ed. and comp. *Latin American history: essays on its study and teaching, 1898–1965.* 2 vols. Austin: University of Texas Press for the Conference on Latin American History, 1968. (Conference on Latin American history publications, 1.) ISBN 0-292-08210-5. ▸ Valuable collection of articles tracing development of teaching of Latin American history in United States. Organized chronologically with information on professional associations, research guides and agendas, and teaching materials. [RJW]

38.7 John P. Cole. *Latin America: an economic and social geography.* 2d ed. Totowa, N.J.: Rowman & Littlefield, 1975. ISBN 0-87471-703-5. ▸ Useful compilation of basic demographic, economic, and social data focusing on themes of development and perceptions. Based on information from secondary sources. [RJW]

38.8 Bettina Corke, ed. *Who is who in government and politics in Latin America.* New York: Decade Media, 1984. ISBN 0-910365-02-4. ▸ Brief biographical sketches of major political and intellectual figures in each country. [RJW]

38.9 Roberto Cortés Conde and Stanley J. Stein, eds. *Latin America: a guide to economic history, 1830–1930.* Berkeley: University of California Press, 1977. ISBN 0-520-02956-9. ▸ Annotated guide to 4,552 English-, Portuguese-, and Spanish-language items on economic history of Argentina, Brazil, Chile, Mexico, Colombia, and Peru with introductory historiographical essays. Well-organized, collaborative effort. [RJW]

38.10 Robert L. Delorme, comp. *Latin America, 1983–1987: a social science bibliography.* New York: Greenwood, 1988. ISBN 0-313-26406-6, ISSN 0742-6895. ▸ Unannotated listing of 3,942 books and articles, updating previous volumes for 1967–79 and 1979–83. Information on bibliographies and reference sources, organized by region and by individual country. Well-designed, useful source for period covered. [RJW]

38.11 Roberto Esquenazi-Mayo and Michael C. Meyer, eds. *Latin American scholarship since World War II: trends in history, political science, literature, geography, and economics.* Lincoln: University of Nebraska Press, 1971. ISBN 0-8032-0783-2. ▸ Essays by nineteen scholars; seven by historians, on postwar scholarship, showing state of field and suggesting areas for future research. Pioneering effort, but coverage of economics and geography limited. [RJW]

38.12 John J. Finan and John Child. *Latin America, international relations: a guide to information sources.* Detroit: Gale Research, 1981. (International relations information guide series, 11.) ISBN 0-8103-1325-1. ▸ Mostly annotated listings of 1,416 items, including bibliographies, aids, books, and articles on general topics and individual countries. Good, basic guide with author and subject indexes. [RJW]

38.13 Gerald Michael Greenfield and Sheldon L. Maram, eds. *Latin American labor organizations.* New York: Greenwood, 1987. ISBN 0-313-22834-5. ▸ Coverage of twenty-six Latin American countries and cases, outlining development of national labor movements with bibliographies and biographies of major organizations. Uneven but with considerable information on individual organizations. [RJW]

38.14 Phil Gunson, Andrew Thompson, and Greg Chamberlain. *The dictionary of contemporary politics of South America.* New York: Macmillan, 1989. ISBN 0-02-913145-6. ‣ Alphabetically organized listing and brief description of major political leaders, parties, movements, and terms with frequent cross-references and list of entries by country. [RJW]

38.15 Preston E. James and C. W. Mintel. *Latin America.* 5th ed. New York: Wiley, 1986. ‣ Well-written, clearly presented geographic survey. Dated but useful. [RJW]

38.16 Michael C. Meyer, ed. and comp. *Supplement to a bibliography of United States–Latin American relations since 1810.* Lincoln: University of Nebraska Press, 1979. ISBN 0-8032-3051-6. ‣ Updates and adds to material presented in Trask, Meyer, and Trask 38.21. [RJW]

38.17 Benjamín Núñez. *Dictionary of Afro–Latin American civilization.* Westport, Conn.: Greenwood, 1980. ISBN 0-313-21138-8. ‣ Painstaking compilation of over 4,500 entries, organized alphabetically with useful and extensive subject index. Emphasizes Caribbean. [RJW]

38.18 W. Dirk Raat. *The Mexican Revolution: an annotated guide to recent scholarship.* Boston: Hall, 1982. ISBN 0-8161-8352-X. ‣ Useful annotated bibliographic guide to historical literature on Mexican Revolution published up until 1980. Includes books and articles by scholars from Mexico, United States, Great Britain, and other European countries. [RJW]

38.19 Martin H. Sable. *Latin American urbanization: a guide to literature, organizations, and personnel.* 1971 ed. Metuchen, N.J.: Scarecrow, 1985. ISBN 0-8108-0354-2. ‣ Massive one-man effort with almost 7,000 entries under categories of bibliography, urban organizations, and urban specialists with geographic and thematic subcategories. Dated; indexing incomplete. [RJW]

38.20 Frederick E. Snyder, comp. *Latin American society and legal culture: a bibliography.* Westport, Conn.: Greenwood, 1985. ISBN 0-313-24858-3. ‣ Interdisciplinary listing of about 2,200 entries organized around themes of legal history and relationship between law and socioeconomic development. Unannotated and lacks subject index. [RJW]

38.21 David F. Trask, Michael C. Meyer, and Roger R. Trask, eds. and comps. *A bibliography of United States–Latin American relations since 1810: a selected list of eleven thousand published references.* Lincoln: University of Nebraska Press, 1968. ‣ Massive compilation of reference works, books, and articles, organized chronologically and by country with author index. Invaluable source. [RJW]

38.22 Richard W. Wilkie, ed. *Latin American population and urbanization analysis: maps and statistics, 1950–1982.* Los Angeles: University of California, UCLA Latin American Center Publications, 1985. (Statistical abstract of Latin America, Supplement series, 8.) ISBN 0-87903-242-1. ‣ Basic reference source for period when Latin America's population more than doubled. Graphs, tables, and photographs for twenty countries. [RJW]

HISTORIOGRAPHY

38.23 Charles W. Arnade. "The historiography of colonial and modern Bolivia." *Hispanic American historical review* 42.3 (1962) 333–84. ISSN 0018-2168. ‣ Useful introduction to historiography of generally neglected country. Stresses small number of Bolivian historians and lack of archival research in their work. [RJW]

38.24 David C. Bailey. "Revisionism and recent historiography of the Mexican Revolution." *Hispanic American historical review* 58.1 (1978) 62–79. ISSN 0018-2168. ‣ Informative review of literature, since mid-1960s, on revolution. Underscores diverse views and use of new methodologies and material. [RJW]

38.25 Joseph R. Barager. "The historiography of the Río de la Plata area since 1830." *Hispanic American historical review* 39.4 (1959) 588–642. ISSN 0018-2168. ‣ Useful overview emphasizing competing schools of historical analysis. Points to gaps in literature and need for regional focus. [RJW]

38.26 Charles W. Bergquist. "Recent United States studies in Latin American history: trends since 1965." *Latin American research review* 9.1 (1974) 3–35. ISSN 0023-8791. ‣ Critical review of boom in Latin American historical studies following Cuban Revolution. Focuses on impact of social science methodology and emphasis on social and economic developments. [RJW]

38.27 Jonathan C. Brown. "The bondage of old habits in nineteenth-century Argentina." *Latin American research review* 21.2 (1986) 3–31. ISSN 0023-8791. ‣ Review of literature published since 1970s with suggestions for future research. Underscores social and political continuities within context of dramatic economic growth. [RJW]

38.28 David Bushnell. "South America." *Hispanic American historical review* 65.4 (1985) 767–87. ISSN 0018-2168. ‣ Broad overview of United States historians' work on South American history over twentieth century with focus on period since 1960. Emphasizes main trends and suggests topics and countries for future emphasis. [RJW]

38.29 Simon Collier. "The historiography of the 'Portalian' period (1830–1891) in Chile." *Hispanic American historical review* 57.4 (1977) 670–90. ISSN 0018-2168. ‣ Insightful review of literature on nineteenth-century golden age of Chilean history, underscoring revisionist views based on socioeconomic analysis. Mostly focuses on Spanish-language works by Chilean authors. [RJW]

38.30 Arthur F. Corwin. "Mexican emigration history, 1900–1970: literature and research." *Latin American research review* 8.2 (1973) 3–24. ISSN 0023-8791. ‣ Review of scant literature on important topic, analyzing Mexican view and opportunities for research. Emphasizes influence of liberal Carey McWilliams on United States views of phenomenon. [RJW]

38.31 Jorge I. Domínguez. "Consensus and divergence: the state of the literature on inter-American relations in the 1970s." *Latin American research review* 13.1 (1978) 87–126. ISSN 0023-8791. ‣ Selective critical review of recent works on United States–Latin American relations since 1970. Suggests eight categories of analysis; discusses areas of scholarly agreement and, more commonly, disagreement. [RJW]

38.32 Richard Graham and Peter H. Smith, eds. *New approaches to Latin American history.* Austin: University of Texas Press, 1974. ISBN 0-292-75506-6. ‣ Nine suggestive essays on state of research on politics, slavery, regionalism, immigration, and psychohistory. Reviews literature; proposes directions for future scholarly work. [RJW]

38.33 William Griffith. "The historiography of Central America since 1830." *Hispanic American historical review* 40.4 (1950) 548–69. ISSN 0018-2168. ‣ Presentation of generally passionate and polemical nature of historical writing on region. [RJW]

38.34 John J. Johnson. "One hundred years of historical writing on modern Latin America by United States historians." *Hispanic American historical review* 65.4 (1985) 745–65. ISSN 0018-2168. ‣ Broad selective overview of field, divided into focus on particular periods: 1885–1920, 1920–40, 1940–60, and 1960–84. Argues for broader, synthetic works. [RJW]

38.35 William Paul McGreevey. "Recent research on the economic history of Latin America." *Latin American research review* 3.2 (1968) 89–117. ISSN 0023-8791. ‣ Treatment of period from end of colonial period to 1960s, emphasizing shift in interest to contemporary problems. Good basic bibliography and statistical analysis of scholarly trends. [RJW]

38.36 Robert A. Potash. "The historiography of Mexico since 1821." *Hispanic American historical review* 40.3 (1960) 383–424. ISSN 0018-2168. ‣ Good overview, emphasizing work of Mexican historians and influence of reforms and intervention of nineteenth century and Revolution of 1910 as main areas of study. Discusses specific periods and suggests future research. [RJW]

38.37 William F. Sater. "A survey of recent Chilean historiography." *Latin American research review* 14.2 (1979) 55–88. ISSN 0023-8791. ‣ Comprehensive survey of productive period of historical scholarship, examining works in Spanish and English. Extensive citations. [RJW]

38.38 Thomas E. Skidmore. "The historiography of Brazil, 1889–1964, Part 1." *Hispanic American historical review* 55.4 (1975) 716–48. ISSN 0018-2168. ‣ Detailed survey of historical scholarship on Brazil over previous fifteen years with main emphasis on political and economic studies. Extensive, well-organized review of literature. [RJW]

38.39 Thomas E. Skidmore. "The historiography of Brazil, 1889–1964, Part 2." *Hispanic American historical review* 56.1 (1976) 81–109. ISSN 0018-2168. ‣ Detailed survey of historical scholarship on Brazil over previous fifteen years with main emphasis on political and economic studies. Extensive, well-organized review of literature. [RJW]

38.40 Robert Freeman Smith. "Twentieth-century Cuban historiography." *Hispanic American historical review* 44.1 (1964) 44–73. ISSN 0018-2168. ‣ Review of work of Cuban historians operating out of strong historiographical tradition. Interesting report on state of literature prior to revolution. [RJW]

38.41 Adam Szaszdi. "The historiography of the republic of Ecuador." *Hispanic American historical review* 44.4 (1964) 503–50. ISSN 0018-2168. ‣ Overview of mostly Spanish-language works with focus primarily on colonial period. Notes lack of support for historical profession in Ecuador. [RJW]

38.42 Ralph Lee Woodward, Jr. "The historiography of modern Central America since 1960." *Hispanic American historical review* 64.5 (1987) 461–96. ISSN 0018-2168. ‣ Extensive review of material published since 1960, emphasizing growing professionalization of literature. Notes predominance of national studies and urges regional approach. [RJW]

INTER-AMERICAN AFFAIRS

38.43 Samuel L. Baily. *The United States and the development of South America, 1945–1975.* New York: New Viewpoints, 1976. ISBN 0-531-05387-3 (cl), 0-531-05594-9 (pbk). ‣ Well-researched, clearly written analysis of attempts by United States to maintain dominance in South America, underscoring struggle between liberals and conservatives in policy-making apparatus. [RJW]

38.44 M. Margaret Ball. *The OAS in transition.* Durham, N.C.: Duke University Press, 1969. ‣ Well-documented reference work, tracing history, structure, and function of Organization of American States, principal institutional forum for inter-American relations. [RJW]

38.45 Gordon Connell-Smith. *The United States and Latin America: an historical analysis of inter-American relations.* New York: Wiley, 1974. ISBN 0-470-16856-0. ‣ British scholar's critical synthesis, emphasizing practical as opposed to idealistic concerns of policy makers. Main focus on twentieth century. [RJW]

38.46 Julio Cotler and Richard R. Fagen, eds. *Latin America and the United States: the changing political realities.* Stanford, Calif.: Stanford University Press, 1974. ISBN 0-8047-0860-6 (cl), 0-8047-0861-4 (pbk). ‣ Conference papers and commentaries by United States and Latin American scholars covering differing perspectives, Brazilian and Mexican relations with United States, military, and multinational corporations. Good picture of major issues and state of research in early 1970s. [RJW]

38.47 Richard R. Fagen, ed. *Capitalism and the state in U.S.–Latin American relations.* Stanford, Calif.: Stanford University Press, 1979. ISBN 0-8047-1020-1 (cl), 0-8047-1040-6 (pbk). ‣ Conference essays on various aspects of nature of contemporary capitalism and state as it affects United States policy toward Latin America. Diverse case studies. [RJW]

38.48 Michael J. Francis. *The limits of hegemony: United States relations with Argentina and Chile during World War II.* Notre Dame, Ind.: University of Notre Dame Press, 1977. ISBN 0-268-01260-1. ‣ Clearly presented study of decision making in United States and interaction with domestic conditions and politics in Argentina and Chile with some interesting comparisons. [RJW]

38.49 Mary A. Gardner. *The Inter-American Press Association: its fight for freedom of the press, 1926–1960.* Austin: University of Texas Press for Institute of Latin American Studies, 1967. (Latin American monographs, 6.) ‣ Well-written review of principal institution to defend freedom of press in Americas. Balanced narrative, discounting ties between Association and United States government. [RJW]

38.50 Mark T. Gilderhus. *Pan-American visions: Woodrow Wilson in the Western Hemisphere, 1913–1921.* Tucson: University of Arizona Press, 1986. ISBN 0-8165-0936-0. ‣ Concise analysis of Wilson's attempts to create pan-American order as precursor to League of Nations. Focuses on Mexico and major countries of South America as well as Wilson's principal advisers on Latin American affairs. [RJW]

38.51 Herbert Goldhamer. *The foreign powers in Latin America.* Princeton: Princeton University Press, 1972. ISBN 0-691-05646-3. ‣ Analysis of role of European, Japanese, and United States policies toward Latin America in post–World War II era. Focus on 1960s. Perceptive and precise, with amusing anecdotes. [RJW]

38.52 David Green. *The containment of Latin America: a history of the myths and realities of the Good Neighbor policy.* Chicago: Quadrangle Books, 1971. ISBN 0-8129-0160-6. ‣ Revisionist view, arguing President Franklin D. Roosevelt's policy part of larger, continuous strategy to maintain United States dominance in Latin America. Provocative argument. Should be read with Wood 38.77. [RJW]

38.53 Kenneth J. Grieb. *The Latin American policy of Warren G. Harding.* 1976 ed. Fort Worth: Texas Christian University Press, 1977. ‣ Nine case studies arguing President Harding initiated more conciliatory approach toward Latin America than predecessors. Revisionist view. New preface and maps. [RJW]

38.54 David G. Haglund. *Latin America and the transformation of U.S. strategic thought, 1936–1940.* Albuquerque: University of New Mexico Press, 1984. ISBN 0-8263-0747-7. ‣ Emphasizes role of developments in Latin America in effecting changes in United States policy toward Europe and outbreak of World War II. Argues effectively for centrality of Latin America in this process. [RJW]

38.55 Margaret Daly Hayes. *Latin America and the U.S. national interest: a basis for U.S. foreign policy.* Boulder: Westview, 1984. ISBN 0-86531-462-4 (cl), 0-86531-547-7 (pbk). ‣ Argues Latin America's importance to United States shifted from military to economic and political concerns. Good information on economic changes. [RJW]

38.56 R. A. Humphreys. *Latin America and the Second World War.* Vol. 1: *1939–1942.* Vol. 2: *1942–1945.* 2 vols. London: Athlone for Institute of Latin American Studies, 1981–82. (University of London, Institute of Latin American Studies monographs,

10–11.) ISBN 0-485-11710-2 (v. 1), 0-485-17711-0 (v. 2). ▸ Volume 1 is well-documented, concise overview of how each Latin American republic responded to early stages of war; strong on British role. Volume 2 places considerable emphasis on British and United States relations with Argentina; focus on bilateral relations. [RJW]

38.57 John J. Johnson. *A hemisphere apart: the foundations of United States policy toward Latin America.* Baltimore: Johns Hopkins University Press, 1990. ISBN 0-8018-3953-x. ▸ Effective outline of development of attitudes among early policy makers toward Latin America. Shift from United States support for insurgency to limited interest based on changing domestic conditions. Should be read with Whitaker 38.74. [RJW]

38.58 John J. Johnson, ed. *Latin America in caricature.* Austin: University of Texas Press, 1980. ISBN 0-292-74626-1. ▸ Analysis of development of United States attitudes toward Latin America through examination and presentation of editorial cartoons. Innovative work, accessible to students. Complements Reid 38.68. [RJW]

38.59 Michael L. Krenn. *U.S. policy toward economic nationalism in Latin America, 1917–1929.* Wilmington, Del.: Scholarly Resources, 1990. ISBN 0-8420-2346-1. ▸ Case studies on Colombia, Venezuela, and Brazil showing Latin American resistance to United States efforts to exert economic influence. Argues patterns set in this period persist. Read with Tulchin 38.73. [RJW]

38.60 Michael J. Kryzanek. *U.S.–Latin American relations.* 2d ed. New York: Praeger, 1990. ISBN 0-275-93206-0 (cl), 0-275-93207-9 (pbk). ▸ Balanced, accessible overview, early nineteenth century to 1980s, with focus on details of policy making. [RJW]

38.61 Lester D. Langley. *America and the Americas: the United States in the Western Hemisphere.* Athens: University of Georgia Press, 1989. ISBN 0-8203-1103-0 (cl), 0-8203-1104-9 (pbk). ▸ General overview, colonial period to Reagan administration. Underscores major cultural differences between United States and Latin America. [RJW]

38.62 Abraham F. Lowenthal. *Partners in conflict: the United States and Latin America in the 1990s.* Rev. ed. Baltimore: Johns Hopkins University Press, 1990. ISBN 0-8018-4061-9 (cl), 0-8018-4059-7 (pbk). ▸ Well-written critical overview of United States policy toward Latin America since 1960s. Separate chapters on Mexico, Brazil, and Caribbean Basin. [RJW]

38.63 Abraham F. Lowenthal, ed. *Exporting democracy: the United States and Latin America.* Baltimore: Johns Hopkins University Press, 1991. ISBN 0-8018-4131-3. ▸ Essays reviewing twentieth-century relations in general with case studies of Argentina, Chile, Dominican Republic, Mexico, Nicaragua, role of United States business and labor, and economic forces. Thoughtful analyses of recent developments. [RJW]

38.64 Donald J. Mabry, ed. *The Latin American narcotics trade and U.S. national security.* Westport, Conn.: Greenwood, 1989. ISBN 0-313-26786-3. ▸ Essays focusing primarily on contemporary problems, with policy suggestions. Sketchy historical framework. [RJW]

38.65 John D. Martz, ed. *United States policy in Latin America: a quarter century of crisis and challenge, 1961–1986.* Lincoln: University of Nebraska Press, 1988. ISBN 0-8032-3097-4. ▸ Wide-ranging essays by well-known scholars. Good for classroom use. [RJW]

38.66 John D. Martz and Lars Schoultz, eds. *Latin America, the United States, and the inter-American system.* Boulder: Westview, 1980. ISBN 0-89158-874-4. ▸ Useful essays by social scientists focusing on theoretical questions, conflicting values and perceptions, and human rights. [RJW]

38.67 Dexter Perkins. *Hands off: a history of the Monroe Doctrine.* 1941 ed. Boston: Little, Brown, 1952. ▸ Dated, traditional, but still informative review of doctrine and its effects from early nineteenth century to onset of World War II. [RJW]

38.68 John T. Reid. *Spanish-American images of the United States, 1790–1960.* Gainesville: University Presses of Florida, 1977. ISBN 0-8130-0547-7. ▸ Views of well-known writers and visitors to United States, often seeing northern republic as model. Traces changes over time. Complements Johnson 38.58. [RJW]

38.69 L. Ronald Scheman, ed. *The Alliance for Progress: a retrospective.* New York: Praeger, 1988. ISBN 0-275-92763-6. ▸ Informative overview of major United States aid program for Latin America with contributions by academics and policy makers. Provides generally positive view of Alliance's efforts and results. [RJW]

38.70 Lars Schoultz. *National security and United States policy toward Latin America.* Princeton: Princeton University Press, 1987. ISBN 0-691-07741-x (cl), 0-691-02267-4 (pbk). ▸ Analysis of divisions and disputes among policy makers over meaning of stability and how to promote it in Latin America. Useful insights based on interviews and published documents; well researched and clearly presented. [RJW]

38.71 Joseph Smith. *Illusions of conflict: Anglo-American diplomacy toward Latin America, 1865–1896.* Pittsburgh: University of Pittsburgh Press, 1979. ISBN 0-8229-3387-x. ▸ Well-researched diplomatic history, underscoring commonality of interests between Great Britain and United States in Latin America with former recognizing paramount political interests of latter in hemisphere. [RJW]

38.72 Barbara Stallings. *Banker to the Third World: U.S. portfolio investment in Latin America, 1900–1986.* Berkeley: University of California Press, 1987. ISBN 0-520-05726-0 (cl), 0-520-06164 (pbk). ▸ Analysis of stages of United States investment in Latin America, noting characteristics and long-term trends with case study of Peru. Useful for understanding debt crisis of 1980s. [RJW]

38.73 Joseph S. Tulchin. *The aftermath of war: World War I and U.S. policy toward Latin America.* New York: New York University Press, 1971. ISBN 0-8147-8152-7. ▸ Well-researched if occasionally limited study of decision making. Focuses on 1914–25 period, arguing policy makers aimed for nonintervention militarily while promoting United States investment in region. See also Krenn 38.59. [RJW]

38.74 Arthur Preston Whitaker. *The United States and the independence of Latin America, 1800–1830.* 1941 ed. New York: Norton, 1964. ▸ Detailed, straightforward treatment of formative period of United States policy toward Latin America. [RJW]

38.75 Howard J. Wiarda, ed. *The Iberian–Latin American connection: implications for U.S. foreign policy.* Boulder and Washington, D.C.: Westview and American Enterprise Institute, 1986. ISBN 0-8133-0424-5 (pbk). ▸ Essays on various aspects of post-Franco Spain's changing relationships with Latin America, set in historical context. Useful collection on generally neglected topic. [RJW]

38.76 Bryce Wood. *The dismantling of the Good Neighbor policy.* Austin: University of Texas Press, 1985. ISBN 0-292-71547-1. ▸ Review of changes in United States policy from mid–World War II to 1950s with focus on Argentina, Bolivia, and Guatemala. Balanced successor volume to 38.77. [RJW]

38.77 Bryce Wood. *The making of the Good Neighbor policy.* 1961 ed. New York: Norton, 1967. ▸ Detailed examination of how policy was conceived, implemented, and received. Well-documented, standard account. [RJW]

LATIN AMERICA

General Studies

38.78 Bill Albert. *South America and the First World War: the impact of the war on Brazil, Argentina, Peru, and Chile.* New York: Cambridge University Press, 1988. ISBN 0-521-34650-9. ▸ Comparative study arguing war did not produce significant industrial development and reinforced patterns of export-oriented growth. Somewhat repetitive from case to case. [RJW]

38.79 Robert Jackson Alexander. *Communism in Latin America.* New Brunswick, N.J.: Rutgers University Press, 1957. ▸ Detailed critical overview. Dated but informative, expecially on communism and labor. [RJW]

38.80 Robert Jackson Alexander. *Organized labor in Latin America.* New York: Free Press, 1965. ▸ Survey of labor organization, emphasizing politicized nature of these movements. No discussion of working classes outside of organized movements. [RJW]

38.81 Robert Jackson Alexander. *Prophets of the revolution: profiles of Latin American leaders.* New York: Macmillan, 1962. ▸ Biographical sketches of twelve major political figures of twentieth-century Latin America, some based on personal interviews. Good source for basic information, although author has favorites. [RJW]

38.82 Marvin Alisky. *Latin American media: guidance and censorship.* Ames: Iowa State University Press, 1981. ISBN 0-8138-1525-8. ▸ Focuses on nations which at time of publication had policies of censorship, guidance, and freedom. Strong on Mexico, but overall somewhat dated. [RJW]

38.83 Joseph L. Arbena, ed. *Sport and society in Latin America: diffusion, dependency, and the rise of mass culture.* New York: Greenwood, 1988. ISBN 0-313-24774-9. ▸ Well-written essays on neglected subject, focusing on baseball in Mexico and Caribbean and soccer in South America. Underscores role of sports in larger society and as part of popular culture. [RJW]

38.84 Eric N. Baklanoff. *Expropriation of U.S. investments in Cuba, Mexico, and Chile.* New York: Praeger, 1975. ISBN 0-275-09780-3. ▸ Study of economic and political factors involved in expropriations. Concludes takeovers often based on false assumptions and proved to be ultimately unprofitable. Counters conventional wisdom. [RJW]

38.85 Diana Balmori, Stuart F. Voss, and Miles Wortman. *Notable family networks in Latin America.* Chicago: University of Chicago Press, 1984. ISBN 0-226-03639-1. ▸ Focuses on nineteenth-century families, their activities and power. Contains useful historiographical essay. [RJW]

38.86 Gerard Behague. *Music in Latin America: an introduction.* Englewood Cliffs, N.J.: Prentice-Hall, 1979. ISBN 0-13-608919-4 (cl), 0-13-608901-1 (pbk). ▸ Well-constructed overview of neglected topic. Comprehensive, balanced, and informative. [RJW]

38.87 Victor Andrés Belaunde. *Bolívar and the political thought of the Spanish American revolution.* 1938 ed. New York: Octagon Books, 1967. ▸ Broader than title suggests; provides good overview of course of wars of independence and shifting ideas of principal figure, Simón Bolívar, as circumstances changed. Dated but still insightful. [RJW]

38.88 Charles W. Bergquist. *Labor in Latin America: comparative essays on Chile, Argentina, Venezuela, and Colombia.* Stanford, Calif.: Stanford University Press, 1986. ISBN 0-8047-1253-0 (cl), 0-8047-1311-1 (pbk). ▸ Connects strengths and weaknesses of twentieth-century labor movements to nature of export structures. Stimulating argument, highlighted by evocative descriptions of working conditions. [RJW]

38.89 Leslie Bethell, ed. *The Cambridge history of Latin America.* Vol. 3: *From independence to c. 1870.* Vols. 4–5: *C. 1870–1930.* Vol. 7: *Latin America since 1930: Mexico, Central America, and the Caribbean.* Vol. 8: *Latin America since 1930: Spanish South America.* Cambridge: Cambridge University Press, 1984–91. ISBN 0-521-23224-4 (v. 3), 0-521-23225-2 (v. 4), 0-521-24517-6 (v. 5), 0-521-24518-4 (v. 7), 0-521-26652-1 (v. 8). ▸ Five volumes in multivolume series of essays on Latin American history by leading scholars. Volume 3 contains useful bibliographic essays and state-of-art analyses of wars of independence in Spanish America, Brazil, and Caribbean. Volumes 4–5 focus on politics, international economy, diplomatic relations with United States and Europe, population growth, urbanization, plantation economies and culture, labor relations, art, literature, music, and Catholic church. Volumes 7–8 contain essays examining countries of Central and South America and Caribbean since 1930. [RJW]

38.90 Leslie Bethell and Ian Roxborough, eds. *Latin America between the Second World War and the cold war, 1944–1948.* Cambridge: Cambridge University Press, 1992. ISBN 0-521-43032-1. ▸ Interesting series of essays by country experts on important transitional period in eleven Latin American nations (Brazil, Chile, Argentina, Bolivia, Venezuela, Peru, Mexico, Cuba, Nicaragua, Costa Rica, Guatemala). Concluding chapter analyzes general trends. [RJW]

38.91 Cole Blasier. *The giant's rival: the USSR and Latin America.* Rev. ed. Pittsburgh: University of Pittsburgh Press, 1987. ISBN 0-8229-3576-7 (cl), 0-8229-5400-1 (pbk). ▸ Review of Soviet policies in Latin America within cold war context. Questionable assumptions; useful information. [RJW]

38.92 John S. Brushwood. *The Spanish-American novel: a twentieth-century survey.* Austin: University of Texas Press, 1975. ISBN 0-292-77515-6. ▸ Comprehensive catalog of authors and works. Useful as overview and reference but lacking in analysis and comparisons. [RJW]

38.93 Victor Bulmer-Thomas, ed. *Britain and Latin America: a changing relationship.* Cambridge: Cambridge University Press with Royal Institute of International Affairs, 1989. ISBN 0-521-37205-4. ▸ Various experts' observations on sharply declining role of Great Britain in postwar Latin America. Useful information on economic resources but little analysis. [RJW]

38.94 E. Bradford Burns. *Latin America: a concise interpretive history.* 5th ed. Englewood Cliffs, N.J.: Prentice-Hall, 1990. ISBN 0-13-526782-X. ▸ Overview, arranged thematically and chronologically. Emphasizes forces for change. Good for classroom use. [RJW]

38.95 E. Bradford Burns. *The poverty of progress: Latin America in the nineteenth century.* 1980 ed. Berkeley: University of California Press, 1983. ISBN 0-520-05078-9 (pbk). ▸ Essay on nineteenth-century development of Latin America, focusing on modernizers and modernization. Provocative, critical view questioning benefits of models of growth. [RJW]

38.96 David Bushnell and Neill Macaulay. *The emergence of Latin America in the nineteenth century.* New York: Oxford University Press, 1988. ISBN 0-19-504463-0 (cl), 0-19-504464-9 (pbk). ▸ Synthetic overview of nineteenth century to 1880 with comparative points well made. Rejects dependency theory and class analysis. Good for classroom, using humor and connections to twentieth-century issues. [RJW]

38.97 Douglas S. Butterworth and John K. Chance. *Latin American urbanization.* New York: Cambridge University Press, 1981. ISBN 0-521-23713-0 (cl), 0-521-28175-X (pbk). ▸ Somewhat disjointed effort, focusing on internal migration and urban anthropology. Considerable information on state of research. [RJW]

38.98 Manuel Caballero. *Latin America and the Comintern, 1919–1943.* New York: Cambridge University Press, 1986. ISBN 0-521-32581-1. ▸ Concise analysis by Venezuelan historian, emphasizing parties established and role of intellectuals in promoting Marxism-Leninism and theories of revolution. [RJW]

38.99 Fernando Henrique Cardoso and Enzo Faletto. *Dependency and development in Latin America.* Marjory Mattingly Urquidi, trans. Berkeley: University of California Press, 1978. ISBN 0-520-03193-8 (cl), 0-520-03527-5 (pbk.). ▸ Classic treatment of dependency theory by two Latin American scholars, arguing for transition from capitalism to socialism. Somewhat dated but essential for understanding argument. [RJW]

38.100 Elsa M. Chaney. *Supermadre: women in politics in Latin America.* Austin: University of Texas Press for Institute of Latin American Studies, 1979. (Latin American monographs, 50.) ISBN 0-292-77554-7. ▸ Examination of exclusion of women from politics until suffrage and democratic system opened up to them, using Chile and Peru as examples. Pioneering study, suggesting further areas of research. [RJW]

38.101 Ronald H. Chilcote and Joel C. Edelstein, eds. *Latin America: the struggle with dependency and beyond.* 1974 ed. Cambridge, Mass.: Schenckman; distributed by Halsted, 1983. ISBN 0-470-15555-8 (cl), 0-470-15556-6 (pbk). ▸ Collection of essays examining modern history of Guatemala, Mexico, Argentina, Brazil, Chile, and Cuba from perspective of dependency theory. Dogmatic but detailed and provocative. [RJW]

38.102 Robert H. Claxton. *Investigating natural hazards in Latin American history.* Carrollton: West Georgia College, 1986. ISSN 0081-8682. ▸ Essays on impact of disease, earthquakes, and weather-related catastrophes on various Latin American countries. Good introduction to important but neglected topic. [RJW]

38.103 David Collier, ed. *The new authoritarianism in Latin America.* Princeton: Princeton University Press, 1979. ISBN 0-691-07616-2 (cl), 0-691-02194-5 (pbk). ▸ Important collection of essays by North and Latin American social scientists on development of bureaucratic-authoritarian states in 1960s and 1970s, focusing on Argentina, Brazil, Chile, and Uruguay. Challenging theoretical discussions. [RJW]

38.104 Ruth Berins Collier and David Collier. *Shaping the political arena: critical junctures, the labor movement, and regime dynamics in Latin America.* Princeton: Princeton University Press, 1991. ISBN 0-691-07830-0 (cl), 0-691-02313-1 (pbk). ▸ Massive comparative study of incorporation of labor movement into political structures of Argentina, Brazil, Chile, Colombia, Mexico, Peru, Uruguay, and Venezuela. Well-researched framework for study of twentieth-century politics. [RJW]

38.105 Michael L. Conniff, ed. *Latin American populism in comparative perspective.* Albuquerque: University of New Mexico Press, 1982. ISBN 0-8263-0580-6 (cl), 0-8263-0581-4 (pbk). ▸ Essays on Argentina, Brazil, Mexico, Peru, and Venezuela with comparative case studies on United States and Russia, examining

important Latin American political phenomenon of twentieth century. Basic anthology. [RJW]

38.106 Wayne A. Cornelius and Robert V. Kemper, eds. *Metropolitan Latin America: the challenge and the response.* Beverly Hills, Calif.: Sage, 1978. ISBN 0-8039-0661-7 (cl), 0-8039-0662-5 (pbk). ▸ Case studies, within common organizational framework, of Guadalajara, Mexico City, Bogotá, Medellín, Port-au-Prince, Guayaquil, Lima, Caracas, and Rio de Janiero by social scientists, urban planners, architects, and geographer. Lacks historical depth but has useful bibliography. [RJW]

38.107 Roberto Cortés Conde and Shane J. Hunt, eds. *The Latin American economies: growth and the export sector, 1880–1930.* New York: Holmes & Meier, 1985. ISBN 0-8419-0771-4. ▸ Case studies of export growth in Argentina, Brazil, Chile, Colombia, and Peru, emphasizing vulnerability to foreign market conditions as well as contributions to national development. Good comparative study, raising questions for further analysis. [RJW]

38.108 William Rex Crawford. *A century of Latin American thought.* Rev. ed. Cambridge, Mass.: Harvard University Press, 1961. ▸ Clear introduction to and overview of lives and thoughts of Latin America's principal intellectuals, arranged in chronological order. Dated but useful. [RJW]

38.109 Glen Caudill Dealy. *The public man: an interpretation of Latin American and other Catholic countries.* Amherst: University of Massachusetts Press, 1977. ISBN 0-87023-239-8. ▸ Essays on religion and *caudillaje* (dictatorship), based on scholarly sources and observations on common daily behavior and attitudes. Concise and thought provoking. [RJW]

38.110 Carmen Diana Deere and Magdalena León. *Rural women and state policy: feminist perspectives on Latin American agricultural development.* Boulder: Westview, 1987. ISBN 0-8133-7391-3 (cl), 0-8133-7390-5 (pbk). ▸ Essays on various countries, supplemented by comparative chapters on migration and agrarian reform in postwar era. Well-written analyses. [RJW]

38.111 Torcuato S. Di Tella. *Latin American politics: a theoretical framework.* Austin: University of Texas Press, 1990. ISBN 0-292-74661-X (cl), 0-292-74664-4 (pbk). ▸ Argentine political sociologist's view, focusing on relationship between classes and institutions. Complex theorizing based on solid historical foundation. [RJW]

38.112 Peter Dorner. *Latin American land reforms in theory and practice: a retrospective analysis.* Madison: University of Wisconsin Press, 1992. ISBN 0-299-13160-2 (cl), 0-299-13164-5 (pbk). ▸ Overview of land reform in Latin America in twentieth century; set within comparative framework with policy suggestions. Concise, balanced, but occasionally jargon ridden. [RJW]

38.113 Paul W. Drake. *The money doctor in the Andes: the Kemmerer missions, 1923–1933.* Durham, N.C.: Duke University Press, 1989. ISBN 0-8223-0880-0. ▸ Lively, well-researched account of impact of Princeton economics professor Edwin Walter Kemmerer and his advice to governments of Colombia, Chile, Ecuador, Bolivia, and Peru. [RJW]

38.114 Paul W. Drake and Eduardo Silva, eds. *Elections and democratization in Latin America, 1980–85.* San Diego: University of California, Center for Iberian and Latin American Studies, 1986. ▸ Collection of papers covering democratic developments of early 1980s throughout Latin America. Original, informative essays providing good overview. [RJW]

38.115 Kenneth Duncan and Ian Rutledge, eds. *Land and labour in Latin America: essays on the development of agrarian capitalism in the nineteenth and twentieth centuries.* New York: Cambridge University Press, 1977. ISBN 0-521-21206-5. ▸ Detailed, informative essays on landowning patterns and rural labor, focusing mostly on nineteenth century. Introductory essay lays out main themes. [RJW]

38.116 Judith Laikin Elkin. *Jews of the Latin American republics.* Chapel Hill: University of North Carolina Press, 1980. ISBN 0-8078-1408-3. ▸ Ambitious if occasionally uneven narrative synthesis of material on important group in Latin America, focusing on Argentina, Brazil, and Mexico. Compares Jewish experience in North and South America. [RJW]

38.117 Judith Ewell and William H. Beezley, eds. *The human tradition in Latin America: the nineteenth century.* Wilmington, Del.: Scholarly Resources, 1989. ISBN 0-8420-2331-3 (cl), 0-8420-2332-1 (pbk). ▸ Useful collection of biographical sketches of famous and not so famous in Latin American history. Accessible, lively, and good for classroom use. [RJW]

38.118 Judith Ewell and William H. Beezley, eds. *The human tradition in Latin America: the twentieth century.* Wilmington, Del.: Scholarly Resources, 1989. ISBN 0-8420-2331-3 (cl), 0-8420-2332-1 (pbk). ▸ Companion to 38.117. [RJW]

38.119 Mark Falcoff and Fredrick B. Pike, eds. *The Spanish Civil War, 1936–39: American hemispheric perspectives.* Lincoln: University of Nebraska Press, 1982. ISBN 0-8032-1961-X. ▸ Well-crafted, original essays on impact of Spanish conflict on domestic politics and foreign policies of United States, Argentina, Colombia, Chile, Cuba, Mexico, and Peru. Latin Americans responded to issues familiar to them (land reform, church-state relations, and role of military), not fascism versus democracy. [RJW/AS]

38.120 Ernest Feder. *The rape of the peasantry: Latin America's landholding system.* Garden City, N.Y.: Anchor, 1971. ▸ Good analysis of development of land concentration in few hands (*latifundio*) and efforts at reform in 1960s. Focus on Andean republics. [RJW]

38.121 Cesar Fernández Moreno and Julio Ortega, eds. *Latin America in its literature.* Ivan A. Schulman, ed. Mary G. Berg, trans. New York: Holmes & Meier, 1980. ISBN 0-8419-0530-4. ▸ Fourteen critical essays by well-known Latin American intellectuals, underscoring rich literary developments of postwar era. Emphasizes diversity. [RJW]

38.122 Jean Franco. *The modern culture of Latin America.* Rev. ed. Harmondsworth: Penguin, 1970. ISBN 0-14-021153-5. ▸ Innovative, insightful view of role of writers and artists within larger social and political context of twentieth-century Latin America. Emphasizes intellectuals as social conscience of nation. [RJW]

38.123 André Gunder Frank. *Capitalism and underdevelopment in Latin America: historical studies of Chile and Brazil.* Rev. ed. New York: Monthly Review Press, 1969. ▸ Early statement of dependency school, emphasizing Latin America's position within world capitalist system. Questionable use of historical material. Should be read with Cardoso and Faletto 38.99. [RJW]

38.124 Celso Furtado. *Economic development of Latin America: a survey from colonial times to the Cuban Revolution.* Suzette Macedo, trans. New York: Cambridge University Press, 1970. ISBN 0-521-07828-8. ▸ Useful if limited overview. Focus on twentieth-century economies of major Latin American countries, emphasizing structural and institutional factors. [RJW]

38.125 Eduardo Galeano. *Open veins of Latin America: five centuries of the pillage of a continent.* Cedric Belfrage, trans. New York: Monthly Review Press, 1973. ISBN 0-85345-279-2. ▸ Impassioned Marxist interpretation of Latin American history by Uruguayan author, emphasizing continuous foreign exploitation of region. Dogmatic but powerful presentation. [RJW]

38.126 William P. Glade. *The Latin American economies: a study of their institutional evolution.* New York: American Book, 1969. ▸ Fact-filled overview, emphasizing tension between external

modernizing forces and internal traditional institutions dating to Spanish colonial period. Informative but not always convincing. [RJW]

38.127 Richard Graham. *Independence in Latin America: a comparative approach.* New York: Knopf, 1972. ISBN 0-394-31641-X. ▸ Concise interpretive essay, focusing on background to wars of independence (1808–25) and impact of European-based ideas of modernization. Scant material on wars themselves, but useful comparative insights. Complements Lynch 38.150 and Robertson 47.64. [RJW]

38.128 Richard Graham, ed. *The idea of race in Latin America, 1870–1940.* Austin: University of Texas Press, 1990. ISBN 0-292-73856-0 (cl), 0-292-73857-9 (pbk). ▸ Essays on racial thinking in Brazil, Argentina, Cuba, and Mexico; focuses on elite. Concise introduction. See also Harris 38.131. [RJW]

38.129 Tulio Halperín-Donghi. *The aftermath of revolution in Latin America.* Josephine de Bunsen, trans. New York: Harper & Row, 1973. ISBN 0-06-136097-X (cl), 0-06-131711-X (pbk). ▸ Analysis of internal developments and role of British economic interests in period following wars of independence (1825–50). Slim volume, useful for instructors but difficult for students. [RJW]

38.130 Jorge E. Hardoy, ed. *Urbanization in Latin America: approaches and issues.* Garden City, N.Y.: Anchor, 1975. ISBN 0-385-08240-1. ▸ Collection of twelve essays focusing on historical background, city in transition, future prospects, and case studies of Argentina, Brazil, and Mexico. Uneven and repetitive but useful overview. [RJW]

38.131 Marvin Harris. *Patterns of race in the Americas.* 1964 ed. New York: Norton, 1974. ISBN 0-393-00727-8. ▸ Pioneering look at Indians in highlands, blacks in tropical lowlands, and Europeans in temperate zones, comparing race relations in Latin America and United States. Should be read with Graham, ed. 38.128. [RJW]

38.132 Alfred Hasbrouck. *Foreign Legionaires in the liberation of Spanish South America.* 1928 ed. New York: Octagon Books, 1969. ▸ Dated but still basic account of important contributions of foreign mercenary soldiers to the Spanish American wars of independence. [RJW]

38.133 Jane S. Jaquette, ed. *The women's movement in Latin America: feminism and the transition to democracy.* Boston: Unwin Hyman, 1989. ISBN 0-04-445186-5 (cl), 0-04-445185-7 (pbk). ▸ Essays on role of women in movements from authoritarian to democratic rule in Brazil, Argentina, Chile, Uruguay, and Peru in 1980s. Raises questions about role of women's organizations as political context changes. [RJW]

38.134 John J. Johnson. *The military and society in Latin America.* Stanford, Calif.: Stanford University Press, 1964. ▸ Comprehensive interpretation of role of military in Latin America from wars of independence to 1960s. Well researched and clearly presented. [RJW]

38.135 John J. Johnson. *Political change in Latin America: the emergence of the middle sectors.* Stanford, Calif.: Stanford University Press, 1958. ▸ Landmark comparative study of role of middle classes in promoting political change in Argentina, Brazil, Chile, Mexico, and Uruguay. [RJW]

38.136 Lyman L. Johnson, ed. *The problem of order in changing societies: essays on crime and policing in Argentina and Uruguay.* Albuquerque: University of New Mexico Press, 1990. ISBN 0-8263-1184-4. ▸ Six essays on generally neglected subject. Somewhat uneven in quality but accessible to students. [RJW]

38.137 Kenneth L. Karst and Keith S. Rosenn. *Law and development in Latin America: a case book.* Berkeley: University of California Press, 1975. ISBN 0-520-02955-0. ‣ Essays and documents on law and social change. Intended for law schools, but with useful information on historical development of legal institutions in Latin America. [RJW]

38.138 Benjamin Keen and Mark Wasserman. *A short history of Latin America.* 2d ed. Boston: Houghton-Mifflin, 1984. ISBN 0-395-34362-3 (pbk). ‣ Concise interpretive history, focusing on major countries of Latin America from viewpoint of dependency theory. Well-written and accessible. [RJW]

38.139 Robert G. Keith, ed. *Haciendas and plantations in Latin American history.* New York: Holmes & Meier, 1977. ISBN 0-8419-0319-0. ‣ Comprehensive overview for general reader, focusing on development of agrarian systems with theoretical discussion of plantation-hacienda typology. [RJW]

38.140 John King. *Magical reels: a history of cinema in Latin America.* London: Verso, 1990. ISBN 0-86091-295-7 (cl), 0-86091-513-1 (pbk). ‣ History of Latin American film industry from silent era to 1980s with emphasis on state policies and their impact. Informative overview. [RJW]

38.141 Davis Lehman. *Democracy and development in Latin America: economics, politics, and religion in the postwar period.* Philadelphia: Temple University Press, 1990. ISBN 0-87722-723-3. ‣ Analysis of popular religion-based struggles for social and economic justice and political democracy with focus on Argentina, Brazil, and Chile. Good review of subject, highlighting major proponents and movements. [RJW]

38.142 Daniel H. Levine, ed. *Religion and political conflict in Latin America.* Chapel Hill: University of North Carolina Press, 1986. ISBN 0-8078-1689-2 (cl), 0-8078-4150-1 (pbk). ‣ Essays on relationship between religion and society with case studies of El Salvador, Nicaragua, Brazil, Chile, Colombia, and Bolivia. Focuses on development between Catholic church and popular religious movements. [RJW]

38.143 Robert M. Levine. *Images of history: nineteenth- and early twentieth-century Latin American photographs as documents.* Durham, N.C.: Duke University Press, 1989. ISBN 0-8223-0883-5 (cl), 0-8223-0894-0 (pbk). ‣ Pioneering study of relationship between photography and Latin American society and use of photographs as historical evidence. Innovative, well illustrated, and effectively presented. [RJW]

38.144 Edwin Lieuwen. *Arms and politics in Latin America.* Rev. ed. New York: Praeger for Council on Foreign Relations, 1961. ‣ Dated but interesting overview of role of military in Latin America with comments on United States policy in postwar era. Should be read with Johnson 38.134. [RJW]

38.145 Juan J. Linz and Alfred Stepan, eds. *The breakdown of democratic regimes: Latin America.* Baltimore: Johns Hopkins University Press, 1978. ISBN 0-8018-2023-5 (pbk). ‣ Excellent analysis by historians and social scientists to explain democratic successes and failures, primarily in postwar era. Part of larger project including European examples; six important essays focusing on Argentina, Colombia, Venezuela, Brazil, and Peru. [RJW]

38.146 Sheldon B. Liss. *Marxist thought in Latin America.* Berkeley: University of California Press, 1984. ISBN 0-520-05021-5 (cl), 0-520-05022-3 (pbk). ‣ Focuses on leading radical figures of twentieth century, using Marxism as broad category. Lacks historical context and ignores some important figures and forces. [RJW]

38.147 Joseph L. Love and Nils Jacobsen, eds. *Guiding the invisible hand: economic liberalism and the state in Latin American history.* New York: Praeger, 1988. ISBN 0-275-92945-0. ‣ Essays on acceptance of economic liberalism in nineteenth-century Latin America, showing variations over time and region. Questions dependency theory. [RJW]

38.148 Brian Loveman and Thomas M. Davies, Jr., eds. *The politics of anti-politics: the military in Latin America.* Lincoln: University of Nebraska Press, 1978. ISBN 0-8032-0954-1 (cl), 0-8032-7900-0 (pbk). ‣ Anthology of readings on role of military in Argentina, Bolivia, Chile, Brazil, and Peru, emphasizing military rejection of partisan politics. Good for classroom use. [RJW]

38.149 Abraham F. Lowenthal and John Samuel Fitch, eds. *Armies and politics in Latin America.* Rev. ed. New York: Holmes & Meier, 1976. ISBN 0-8419-0913-X (cl), 0-8419-0916-4 (pbk). ‣ Essays providing comprehensive synthesis, by North and Latin American scholars. Updates Lieuwen 38.144. [RJW]

38.150 John Lynch. *The Spanish American revolutions, 1808–1826.* 2d ed. New York: Norton, 1986. ISBN 0-393-02349-4 (cl), 0-393-95537-0 (pbk). ‣ Excellent synthesis, emphasizing social and economic forces affecting elites. Little attention to military and diplomatic issues. [RJW]

38.151 Joseph Maier and Richard W. Weatherhead, eds. *The Latin American university.* Albuquerque: University of New Mexico Press, 1979. ISBN 0-8263-0487-7. ‣ Essays focusing on political role of foreign influences on evolution of Latin American university. Informative introduction and overview. [RJW]

38.152 James M. Malloy, ed. *Authoritarianism and corporatism in Latin America.* Pittsburgh: University of Pittsburgh Press, 1977. ISBN 0-8229-3328-4 (cl), 0-8229-5275-0 (pbk). ‣ Eighteen essays focusing on corporatist tradition and its consequences for Latin American society and politics. Comprehensive treatment with emphasis on theory. [RJW]

38.153 Carlos Marichal. *A century of debt crises in Latin America: from independence to the Great Depression, 1820–1930.* Princeton: Princeton University Press, 1989. ISBN 0-691-07792-4 (cl), 0-691-02299-2 (pbk). ‣ Judicious synthesis of Latin America's foreign loan and debt experience, providing background to crisis of 1980s. Raises interesting questions. [RJW]

38.154 Gerhard Masur. *Simón Bolívar.* Albuquerque: University of New Mexico Press, 1948. (School of Inter-American Affairs, Inter-American studies, 4.) ‣ Clearly sympathetic and still most detailed biography in English of main figure of Spanish American struggle for independence from Spain. [RJW]

38.155 J. Lloyd Mecham. *Church and state in Latin America: a history of politico-ecclesiastical relations.* Rev. ed. Chapel Hill: University of North Carolina Press, 1966. ‣ Detailed, well-researched account. Dated but still basic source on subject up to 1960s. [RJW]

38.156 Magnus Mörner. *Adventurers and proletarians: the story of migrants in Latin America.* Pittsburgh: University of Pittsburgh Press, 1985. ISBN 0-8229-3505-8. ‣ Clear, concise overview of main features of immigration into Latin America in nineteenth and twentieth centuries. Useful if limited introduction. [RJW]

38.157 June Nash and Helen Icken Safa, eds. *Sex and class in Latin America: women's perspectives on politics, economics, and the family in the Third World.* 1976 ed. Brooklyn: Bergin, 1980. ISBN 0-89789-004-3 (cl), 0-89789-003-5 (pbk). ‣ Sixteen wide-ranging essays, emphasizing theoretical and methodological issues. Important collection on state of research. [RJW]

38.158 Frederick M. Nunn. *Yesterday's soldiers: European military professionalism in South America, 1890–1940.* Lincoln: University of Nebraska Press, 1983. ISBN 0-8032-3305-1. ‣ Study of German and French influences on militaries of Argentina, Brazil, Chile, and Peru, emphasizing impact of ideas on civilian-military relations. Important analysis with implications for post–World War II era. [RJW]

38.159 George Philip. *Oil and politics in Latin America: nationalist movements and state companies.* Cambridge: Cambridge University Press, 1982. ISBN 0-521-23865-X. ▸ Detailed synthesis of how Latin American states developed national oil companies, primarily in post–World War II era. Emphasizes political rather than economic aspects of issue. [RJW]

38.160 Fredrick B. Pike. *Hispanismo, 1898–1936: Spanish conservatives and liberals and their relations with Spanish America.* Notre Dame, Ind.: University of Notre Dame Press, 1971. ISBN 0-268-00449-8. ▸ Analysis of various Spanish intellectuals and institutions and their attitudes toward Spanish America. One of few studies to discuss relations between Spain and Spanish America in twentieth century. [RJW]

38.161 Fredrick B. Pike. *Spanish America, 1900–1970: tradition and social innovation.* New York: Norton, 1973. ISBN 0-393-05488-8 (cl), 0-393-09340-9 (pbk). ▸ Concise, well-written overview of continuity and adaptability of basic institutions of Latin America with specific case studies covering most of region. [RJW]

38.162 D.C.M. Platt. *Latin America and British trade, 1806–1914.* 1972 ed. New York: Barnes & Noble, 1973. ISBN 0-06-495605-9. ▸ Sophisticated overview of British economic role in Latin America, focusing on competition with Germany and United States and placing relative decline of British investment at turn of century into larger context. Basic work on subject. [RJW]

38.163 Rollie E. Poppino. *International communism in Latin America: a history of the movement, 1917–1963.* New York: Free Press, 1964. ▸ Dated but useful overview, emphasizing strengths and weaknesses of communism's appeal. Based primarily on printed sources. [RJW]

38.164 Joseph Ramos. *Neoconservative economics in the southern cone of Latin America, 1973–1983.* Baltimore: Johns Hopkins University Press, 1986. ISBN 0-8018-3040-0. ▸ Examination of economic policies of military regimes in Chile, Argentina, and Uruguay in 1970s and 1980s, underscoring their failures. Neglects external factors. [RJW]

38.165 William Spence Robertson. *The life of Miranda.* 1929 ed. New York: Cooper Square, 1969. ▸ Extensive, colorful biography of main precursor of Spanish American independence, Francisco de Miranda of Venezuela. [RJW]

38.166 William Spence Robertson. *Rise of the Spanish American republics as told in the lives of the liberators.* 1918 ed. New York: Free Press, 1965. ▸ Pioneering study of wars of independence through biographical sketches of main leaders. Dated but still engaging and informative. [RJW]

38.167 Alain Rouquié. *The military and the state in Latin America.* Paul E. Sigmund, trans. Berkeley: University of California Press, 1987. ISBN 0-520-05559-4 (cl), 0-520-06664-2 (pbk). ▸ Uneven overview of role of military and military-civilian relations in nineteenth and twentieth centuries. Focus mainly on officer corps of army. Readable synthesis. [RJW]

38.168 William Rowe and Vivian Schelling. *Memory and modernity: popular culture in Latin America.* London: Verso, 1991. ISBN 0-86091-322-6 (cl), 0-86091-541-7 (pbk). ▸ Useful introduction and overview of development and role of popular culture as expressed in music, dance, ceremonies, and through mass media. Accessible and suited to classroom use. [RJW]

38.169 Roberto Segre, ed. *Latin America in its architecture.* Fernando Kusnetzoff, ed. Edith Grossman, trans. New York: Holmes & Meier, 1981. ISBN 0-8419-0532-0. ▸ Eight essays by Latin American architects with critical view of elite control of design. Dogmatic, but useful historical information and perspective. [RJW]

38.170 John Sheahan. *Patterns of development in Latin America: poverty, repression, and economic strategy.* Princeton: Princeton University Press, 1987. ISBN 0-691-07735-5 (cl), 0-691-02264-X (pbk). ▸ Review of economic policies and performances of past twenty-five years analyzing why growth has not produced more equity. Informative for various regimes but lacks historical perspective. [RJW]

38.171 Paul E. Sigmund. *Multinationals in Latin America: the politics of nationalization.* Madison: University of Wisconsin Press, 1980. ISBN 0-299-08260-1 (cl), 0-299-08264-4 (pbk). ▸ General overview with case studies of Mexico, Cuba, Chile, Peru, and Venezuela. Good synthesis with firm grasp of political, economic, and historical factors. [RJW]

38.172 Thomas E. Skidmore and Peter H. Smith. *Modern Latin America.* 3d ed. New York: Oxford University Press, 1992. ISBN 0-19-507648-6 (cl), 0-19-507649-4 (pbk). ▸ Well-written and up-to-date text focusing on twentieth century. Emphasizes major countries, leaving out Colombia, Venezuela, and others. [RJW]

38.173 Richard W. Slatta. *Cowboys of the Americas.* New Haven: Yale University Press, 1990. ISBN 0-300-04529-8. ▸ Broad comparative view, emphasizing Spanish influences. Well written and well illustrated; somewhat repetitive. [RJW]

38.174 Richard W. Slatta, ed. *Bandidos: the varieties of Latin American banditry.* Westport, Conn.: Greenwood, 1987. ISBN 0-313-25301-3. ▸ Essays on bandits in Mexico, Venezuela, Argentina, Brazil, Bolivia, Cuba, and Colombia. Useful for regional comparisons. Takes issue with Hobsbawm's analysis (28.315) of social banditry and bandit myth. [RJW]

38.175 Doris Sommer. *Foundational fictions: the national romances of Latin America.* Berkeley: University of California Press, 1991. ISBN 0-520-07110-7. ▸ Sprightly, pathbreaking analysis of major romantic novels of nineteenth-century Latin America and their relationship to state building. Sophisticated, imaginative blending of literature and history. [RJW]

38.176 Hobart A. Spalding, Jr. *Organized labor in Latin America: historical case studies of workers in dependent societies.* New York: New York University Press, 1977. ISBN 0-8147-7787-2. ▸ Concise, well-written overview of development of organized labor in twentieth century, emphasizing common patterns within international context. Complements Bergquist 38.88. [RJW]

38.177 Nancy Leys Stepan. *"The Hour of Eugenics": race, gender, and nation in Latin America.* Ithaca, N.Y.: Cornell University Press, 1991. ISBN 0-8014-2569-7 (cl), 0-8014-9795-7 (pbk). ▸ Significant addition to literature on eugenics movement and its adaptation in Latin America. Main focus on major figures in Brazil, Argentina, and Mexico. [RJW]

38.178 Mark D. Szuchman, ed. *The middle period in Latin America: values and attitudes in the seventeenth–nineteenth centuries.* Boulder: Rienner, 1989. ISBN 1-55587-138-0. ▸ Thought-provoking, original essays, applying concept of mentalities to Latin America. [RJW]

38.179 Richard S. Tedlow, ed. "Business in Latin America." *Business history review* 59.4 (1985) 543–679. ISSN 0007-6805. ▸ Essays on various countries describing domestic business activities as well as foreign-owned companies. Questions applicability of sweeping theories. [RJW]

38.180 Claudio Véliz. *The centralist tradition of Latin America.* Princeton: Princeton University Press, 1980. ISBN 0-691-05280-8 (cl), 0-691-10085-3 (pbk). ▸ Comprehensive essay ranging over entire sweep of Latin American history to explain tendency toward strong central authority and government. Well written, emphasizing unique features of Latin American experience. [RJW]

38.181 Frederick Stirton Weaver. *Class, state, and industrial structure: the historical process of South American industrial growth.*

Westport, Conn.: Greenwood, 1980. ISBN 0-313-22114-6. ▸ Concise synthesis, emphasizing stages of industrial growth and rejecting liberal and dependency theories in favor of staple theory. Accessible overview with some gaps. [RJW]

38.182 Arthur Preston Whitaker and David C. Jordan. *Nationalism in contemporary Latin America.* New York: Free Press, 1966. ▸ Well-written introduction to and overview of important and complex subject. Includes case studies. [RJW]

38.183 Howard J. Wiarda. *Corporatism and national development in Latin America.* Boulder: Westview, 1981. ISBN 0-86531-031-0. ▸ Essays on current political developments within historical framework. Emphasizes eclectic and personal view. [RJW]

38.184 Howard J. Wiarda. *Politics and social change in Latin America: still a distinct tradition?* 3d ed. Boulder: Westview, 1992. ISBN 0-8133-1057-1 (cl), 0-8133-1058-X (pbk). ▸ Revised, expanded version of 38.185, with new essays added to reinforce theme of continuity. Useful, provocative collection. [RJW]

38.185 Howard J. Wiarda, ed. *Politics and social change in Latin America: the distinct tradition.* 2d rev. ed. Amherst: University of Massachusetts Press, 1982. ISBN 0-87023-333-5 (pbk). ▸ Essays by historians and social scientists emphasizing continuities in face of change, using culturalist, political, and structural modes of analysis. General rather than specific; lacks case studies. [RJW]

38.186 John D. Wirth, ed. *Latin American oil companies and the politics of energy.* Lincoln: University of Nebraska Press, 1985. ISBN 0-8032-4728-1. ▸ Well-written survey of energy policy with essays on Argentina, Brazil, Mexico, Venezuela, Standard Oil of New Jersey, and state companies. [RJW]

38.187 Gary W. Wynia. *The politics of Latin American development.* 3d ed. New York: Cambridge University Press, 1990. ISBN 0-521-38027-8 (cl), 0-521-38924-0 (pbk). ▸ Imaginative introduction to Latin American politics in postwar era; general themes buttressed with case studies. Examines economic and external factors. Accessible and well written. [RJW]

38.188 Leopoldo Zea. *The Latin American mind.* James H. Abbott and Lowell Dunham, trans. Norman: University of Oklahoma Press, 1963. ▸ Overview of social and political thought in nineteenth and twentieth centuries, focusing on major countries, thinkers, and philosophical currents. Useful analysis by important Latin American scholar. [RJW]

SEE ALSO
29.217 Michael P. Costeloe. *Response to revolution.*
37.85 Alistair Hennessy. *The frontier in Latin American history.*
37.216 Nicolás Sánchez-Albornoz. *The population of Latin America: a history.*
37.222 Herbert S. Klein. *African slavery in Latin America and the Caribbean.*
37.355 Asuncíon Lavrin, ed. *Latin American women.*
37.369 Magnus Mörner. *Race mixture in the history of Latin America.*
47.55 Russell H. Bartley. *Imperial Russia and the struggle for Latin American independence, 1808–1828.*
48.488 Jack Child. *Geopolitics and conflict in South America.*

Mexico

38.189 Rodney D. Anderson. *Outcasts in their own land: Mexican industrial workers, 1906–1922.* DeKalb: Northern Illinois University Press, 1976. ISBN 0-87580-054-8. ▸ Important study of impact of labor strikes just before Mexican Revolution (1910–20). Discusses Porfirian policies toward labor and industry, industrial working conditions, and role of workers in Francisco Madero's struggle against president-dictator Porfirio Díaz (1876–1911). [EH-D]

38.190 Timothy E. Anna. *The fall of the royal government in Mex-* *ico City.* Lincoln: University of Nebraska Press, 1978. ISBN 0-8032-0957-6. ▸ Detailed examination of events leading up to independence, from perspective of elites (Spanish as well as creole) in Mexico City. [EH-D]

38.191 Linda Arnold. *Bureaucracy and bureaucrats in Mexico City, 1742–1835.* Tucson: University of Arizona Press, 1988. ISBN 0-8165-1068-7. ▸ Uses unusual periodization to analyze continuities and changes of bureaucracy in Mexico City from late colonial era to early republic. Based on analysis of careers of 2,733 bureaucrats; includes copious and valuable biographical and statistical data. [EH-D/MAB]

38.192 Silvia Marina Arrom. *The women of Mexico City, 1790–1857.* Stanford, Calif.: Stanford University Press, 1985. ISBN 0-8047-1233-6. ▸ Examination of changes in legal status and demographic and employment patterns of women of Mexico City with attention to age, marital status, and class factors. Includes interesting analysis of *marianismo* (cult of female spiritual superiority). Fine example of feminist scholarship. [EH-D]

38.193 David C. Bailey. *¡Viva Cristo Rey! The Cristero Rebellion and the church-state conflict in Mexico.* Austin: University of Texas Press, 1974. ISBN 0-292-78700-6. ▸ Church-state conflict during Calles-Obregón period (1920s), particularly warfare between Catholic peasants (*Cristeros*) and peasants loyal to revolutionary regime. Good though not comprehensive treatment. [EH-D]

38.194 William H. Beezley. *Insurgent governor: Abraham González and the Mexican Revolution in Chihuahua.* Lincoln: University of Nebraska Press, 1973. ISBN 0-8032-0821-9. ▸ Most comprehensive study of important but lesser known early revolutionary figure in Madero movement who served as first revolutionary governor of Chihuahua. [EH-D]

38.195 Thomas Benjamin. *A rich land, a poor people: politics and society in modern Chiapas.* Albuquerque: University of New Mexico Press, 1989. ISBN 0-8263-1132-6. ▸ Good general history of southern state of Chiapas, from independence to end of 1980s. Emphasis on landed elite's control and exploitation of poor Indian masses. [EH-D]

38.196 Thomas Benjamin and William McNellie, eds. *Other Mexicos: essays on regional Mexican history, 1876–1911.* Albuquerque: University of New Mexico Press, 1984. ISBN 0-8263-0754-x (cl), 0-8263-0755-8 (pbk). ▸ Original essays based mostly on archival research, covering various regions during Porfirio Díaz's regime with attention to causes that led to revolution (or to nonparticipation in some cases). [EH-D]

38.197 Thomas Benjamin and Mark Wasserman, eds. *Provinces of the revolution: essays on regional Mexican history 1910–1925.* Albuquerque: University of New Mexico Press, 1990. ISBN 0-8263-1205-5. ▸ Original essays based mostly on archival research, covering different regions of Mexico during revolution and early 1920s. Sequel to 38.196, although regions covered not necessarily the same. [EH-D]

38.198 D. A. Brading, ed. *Caudillo and peasant in the Mexican Revolution.* New York: Cambridge University Press, 1980. ISBN 0-521-22997-9. ▸ Original studies of specific regional armed revolutionary leaders (*caudillos*) and their respective relationship to land and local peasantry. Most studies eventually published as monographs. [EH-D]

38.199 Anita Brenner. *The wind that swept Mexico: the history of the Mexican Revolution, 1910–1942.* 1943 2d ed. George R. Leighton, photo. comp. Austin: University of Texas Press, 1984. ISBN 0-292-70106-3. ▸ Classic study of revolution from outbreak to end of Cárdenas era, using historical photographs arranged in chronological order with running commentaries. [EH-D]

38.200 R. Buve, ed. *Haciendas in Central Mexico from late colonial times to the revolution: labour conditions, hacienda management,* *and its relation to the state.* Amsterdam: Centre for Latin American Research and Documentation, 1984. ▸ Six important essays by Mexican and European scholars of Mexican haciendas, centering around questions of production, labor, political, economic, and institutional changes. Published in Europe, not readily accessible in United States. [EH-D]

38.201 Frances Erskine Inglis Calderón de la Barca. *Life in Mexico: Frances Calderón de la Barca.* 1832 ed. Berkeley: University of California Press, 1982. ISBN 0-520-04661-7 (cl), 0-520-04662-5 (pbk). ▸ Amusing, insightful, pointed observations and commentary on Mexican culture, politics, and everyday life of rich and poor in mid-nineteenth-century Mexico, by Scottish wife of Spanish ambassador. [EH-D]

38.202 Roderic Ai Camp. *Entrepreneurs and politics in twentieth-century Mexico.* New York: Oxford University Press, 1978. ISBN 0-19-505719-8. ▸ Interesting analysis based on author's copious collection of political biographical data on Mexico's leading capitalists, entrepreneurs, and politicians. Biographical portions provide useful reference work. [EH-D]

38.203 Roderic Ai Camp. *Mexico's leaders: their education and recruitment.* Tucson: University of Arizona Press, 1980. ISBN 0-8165-0701-5 (cl), 0-8165-0660-4 (pbk). ▸ Thorough, systematic examination of relationship between education and political recruitment from 1922 to 1950s. Based on author's copious collection of political biographies, 1935–75 (38.202). [EH-D]

38.204 Lawrence A. Cardoso. *Mexican emigration to the United States, 1897–1931: socio-economic patterns.* Tucson: University of Arizona Press, 1980. ISBN 0-8165-0678-7 (cl), 0-8165-0659-0 (pbk). ▸ Examination of both Mexican and American policies and attitudes, covering early history of Mexican immigration to United States from late nineteenth century to Great Depression. Important topic sometimes ignored by Mexicanists. [EH-D]

38.205 Barry Carr. *Marxism and communism in twentieth-century Mexico.* Lincoln: University of Nebraska Press, 1992. ISBN 0-8032-1458-8. ▸ Comprehensive study of Mexican Left, from Mexican Communist party to other leftist groups. Shows Left's reaction to revolution and efforts to organize Mexican workers. [EH-D]

38.206 Jean Charlot. *The Mexican mural renaissance: 1920–1925.* 1963 ed. New York: Hacker, 1979. ISBN 0-87817-251-3. ▸ Still best examination of Mexican mural movement and revolutionary art style, by observer-participant. Good treatments of life and works of Dr. Atl (Gerardo Murillo, pseudonym), Diego Rivera, José Clemente Orozco, David Siqueiros, and Fernando Leal. [EH-D]

38.207 Howard Francis Cline. *The United States and Mexico.* Rev. ed. Cambridge, Mass.: Harvard University Press, 1969. ▸ Survey and synthesis of United States–Mexican relations from colonial era to 1950s with attention to periods of Mexican Revolution, General and President Lázaro Cárdenas (1934–40), and President Miguel Alemán (1946–52). Dated but still useful. [EH-D]

38.208 John H. Coatsworth. *Growth against development: the economic impact of railroads in Porfirian Mexico.* DeKalb: Northern Illinois University Press, 1981. ISBN 0-87580-075-0. ▸ Innovative economic analysis of Porfiriato (1876–1911), focusing on impact of foreign-built railroads on national economic growth and land distribution. [EH-D]

38.209 James D. Cockcroft. *Intellectual precursors of the Mexican Revolution, 1900–1913.* 1968 ed. Austin: University of Texas Press for Institute of Latin American Studies, 1976. (Latin American monographs, 14.) ISBN 0-292-78379-5 (cl, 1968), 0-292-73808-0 (pbk). ▸ Studies of middle- and upper-class revolutionary intellectuals in north who laid ideological and political groundwork for successful overthrow of President Porfirio Díaz (1876–1911). Dated but still useful. [EH-D]

38.210 James D. Cockcroft. *Mexico: class formation, capital accumulation, and the state.* 1983 ed. New York: Monthly Review Press, 1990. ISBN 0-85345-560-0 (cl), 0-85345-561-9 (pbk). ▸ Good Marxist analysis of Mexican history from colonial era to 1980s with emphasis on formation of social classes and their relationship to each other and to state. [EH-D]

38.211 Wayne A. Cornelius. *Politics and the migrant poor in Mexico City.* Stanford, Calif.: Stanford University Press, 1975. ISBN 0-8047-0880-0. ▸ One of few studies of Mexico's urban poor, result of massive internal migration after World War II. Examines process of this population's political mobilization. [EH-D]

38.212 Wayne A. Cornelius, Judith Gentleman, and Peter H. Smith, eds. *Mexico's alternative political futures.* San Diego: University of California, San Diego, Center for U.S.–Mexican Studies, 1989. (Monograph series, 30.) ISBN 0-935391-84-3 (cl), 0-935391-83-5 (pbk). ▸ Interesting essays focusing on limits and opportunities for future political change in Mexico. Examines presidential and congressional elections of 1988. Useful for understanding 1980s. [EH-D]

38.213 Daniel Cosío Villegas, ed. *El historia moderna de México.* Vol. 1: *La república restaurada: la vida política.* Vol. 2: *La república restaurada: la vida económica.* Vol. 3: *La república restaurada: la vida social.* Vol. 4: *El Porfiriato: la vida social.* Vols. 5–6: *El Porfiriato: la vida política exterior.* Vol. 7: *El Porfiriato: la vida económica.* Vols. 8–9: *El Porfiriato: la vida política.* Vol. 10: *La vida política exterior.* Edition varies. 10 vols. Mexico: Editorial Hermes, 1984–91. ▸ Important reference work by leading Mexican scholars. Volumes 1–3 treat political, economic, and social history of restored republic (1867–76), including reestablishment of constitutional government, agricultural and economic development, railroads, education, and arts. Volumes 4–10 treat Porfiriato (1876–1911) with volume 4 focusing on society, education, working conditions, and labor migration. Volumes 5–6 examine exterior political relationships with United States and Europe. Volume 7 looks at Porfirian industry, mining, agriculture, and railroads. Volumes 8–10 discuss internal politics in Porfirian Mexico. [EH-D]

38.214 Ann L. Craig. *The first agraristas: an oral history of a Mexican agrarian reform movement.* Berkeley: University of California Press, 1983. ISBN 0-520-04708-7. ▸ Human story behind agrarian reform through voices of participants and leaders in Jalisco village, 1924-1940. [EH-D]

38.215 Charles Curtis Cumberland. *Mexican Revolution: genesis under Madero.* 1952 ed. Austin: University of Texas Press, 1974. ISBN 0-292-75018-8 (cl), 0-292-75017-X (pbk). ▸ Study of initial phase of Mexican Revolution as led by landowner (*hacendado*) Francisco Madero. Dated but still best political study of Madero, person and movement. [EH-D]

38.216 Charles Curtis Cumberland. *Mexican Revolution: the constitutionalist years.* David C. Bailey, Introduction. Austin: University of Texas Press, 1972. ISBN 0-292-75000-5 (cl), 0-292-75016-1 (pbk). ▸ Traces violent civil war years (1913–17) after Francisco Madero's assassination, as Constitutionalists (Venustiano Carranza, Alvaro Obregón, and Francisco [Pancho] Villa) fought Victoriano Huerta, Emiliano Zapata, and each other for power and final control. Best one-volume study of this period. [EH-D]

38.217 Marilyn P. Davis. *Mexican voices/American dreams: an oral history of Mexican immigration to the United States.* New York: Holt, 1990. ISBN 0-8050-1216-8. ▸ Moving re-creation of human and personal side of Mexican immigration story, weaving diverse voices of more than ninety migrants, their families, and employers. [EH-D]

38.218   John W. F. Dulles. *Yesterday in Mexico: a chronicle of the revolution, 1919–1936.* Austin: University of Texas Press, 1961. ▸ Detailed compilation of political events and developments under presidents Alvaro Obregón and Plutarco Elías Calles (1920s). Weak analysis but one of few books on period, contains useful information. [EH-D]

38.219   Romeo R. Flores Caballero. *Counterrevolution: the role of the Spaniards in the independence of Mexico, 1804–38.* Jaime E. Rodríguez O., trans. Lincoln: University of Nebraska Press, 1974. ISBN 0-8032-0805-7. ▸ Exploration of important question of whether expulsion of Spaniards after independence was primarily responsible for Mexico's economic contraction in early national period. [EH-D]

38.220   Carlos Fuentes. *The death of Artemio Cruz.* 1964 ed. Sam Hileman, trans. New York: Farrar, Straus & Giroux, 1991. ISBN 0-374-13559-2 (cl), 0-374-52283-9 (pbk). ▸ Explores meaning of Mexican Revolution through life of fictional character who became member of Mexico's postrevolutionary elite. Translation of, arguably, Fuentes's best novel. [EH-D]

38.221   Mario T. García. *Desert immigrants: the Mexicans of El Paso, 1880–1920.* New Haven: Yale University Press, 1981. ISBN 0-300-02520-3 (cl), 0-300-02883-0 (pbk). ▸ Innovative study by Mexican American scholar of El Paso's Mexican immigrant community, focusing on impact of race and class on employment, housing, education, politics, and culture. [EH-D]

38.222   Luis J. González. *San José de Gracia: Mexican village in transition.* 1974 ed. John Upton, trans. Austin: University of Texas Press, 1983. ISBN 0-292-77507-5 (cl, 1974), 0-292-77571-7 (pbk). ▸ Innovative examination of modern Mexican history (mid-nineteenth to mid-twentieth century) from perspective of author's home village. Prototype of new historical genre of microhistory. [EH-D]

38.223   Richard Griswold del Castillo. *The treaty of Guadalupe Hidalgo: a legacy of conflict.* Norman: University of Oklahoma Press, 1990. ISBN 0-8061-2240-4. ▸ Only in-depth study of drafting and diplomacy behind monumental but often ignored treaty that created United States Southwest out of Mexican territory. [EH-D]

38.224   Stephen H. Haber. *Industry and underdevelopment: the industrialization of Mexico, 1890–1940.* Stanford, Calif.: Stanford University Press, 1989. ISBN 0-8047-1487-8. ▸ Important contribution to Mexican economic and business history. Focus on individual companies and entrepreneurs (mostly foreigners) of Porfiriato (1876–1911) who survived revolution and thrived afterwards. [EH-D]

38.225   Charles A. Hale. *Mexican liberalism in the age of Mora, 1821–1853.* New Haven: Yale University Press, 1968. ▸ Important intellectual history of first decades after Mexican independence. Examines earliest liberal thinkers of Mexico within context of liberalism in Atlantic world, but modified by local conditions. Also available from Ann Arbor: University Microfilms International. [RJW]

38.226   Charles A. Hale. *The transformation of liberalism in late nineteenth-century Mexico.* Princeton: Princeton University Press, 1989. ISBN 0-691-07814-9. ▸ Intellectual history of late nineteenth century, focusing on impact of positivism on Porfirian thought and politics. Serious study of difficult topic. Complements Zea 38.283. [EH-D]

38.227   Linda B. Hall. *Alvaro Obregón: power and revolution in Mexico, 1911–1920.* College Station: Texas A&M University Press, 1981. ISBN 0-89096-113-1. ▸ Significant study of early career of key revolutionary leader. Ends before Obregón became president in 1920. [EH-D]

38.228   Hugh M. Hamill, Jr. *The Hildago revolt: prelude to Mexican independence.* 1966 ed. Westport, Conn.: Greenwood, 1981. ISBN 0-313-22848-5. ▸ Still best political biography of key independence leader and his mass-based movement. Attention to social, economic, intellectual, and political background. [EH-D]

38.229   Nora Hamilton. *The limits of state autonomy: post-revolutionary Mexico.* Princeton: Princeton University Press, 1982. ISBN 0-691-07641-3 (cl), 0-691-02211-9 (pbk). ▸ Examination of postrevolutionary Mexico from early concerns with social welfare and nationalism to dependence (1934–40). Strong on theory. [EH-D]

38.230   Nora Hamilton and Timothy F. Harding, eds. *Modern Mexico: state economy and social conflict.* Beverly Hills, Calif.: Sage, 1986. ISBN 0-8039-2577-8 (cl), 0-8039-2552-2 (pbk). ▸ Provocative, important essays on topics such as state, economy, working class and popular mobilization, rural sector, agrarian reform, and peasantry. [EH-D]

38.231   Brian R. Hamnett. *Roots of insurgency: Mexican regions, 1750–1824.* Cambridge: Cambridge University Press, 1986. ISBN 0-521-32148-4. ▸ Innovative study of regional characteristics of overlapping insurgencies during independence period and connections between social tensions of late colonial period with disruptions of early national period. Important regional perspective. [EH-D/MAB]

38.232   Roger D. Hansen. *The politics of Mexican development.* 1971 ed. Baltimore: Johns Hopkins University Press, 1974. ISBN 0-8018-1193-7 (cl, 1971), 0-8018-1651-3 (pbk). ▸ Mexico's political economy in postrevolutionary period with focus on economic miracle of 1950s and on state and official party (PRI). Dated but still useful. [EH-D]

38.233   Charles H. Harris III. *A Mexican family empire: the latifundio of the Sánchez Navarros, 1765–1867.* Austin: University of Texas Press, 1975. ISBN 0-292-75020-X. ▸ Early history of leading entrepreneurial family, based largely on family papers. Attention to commercial and agricultural activities, labor recruitment, and working conditions. [EH-D]

38.234   John Mason Hart. *Anarchism and the Mexican working class, 1860–1931.* 1978 ed. Austin: University of Texas Press, 1987. ISBN 0-292-70400-3. ▸ Important comprehensive study of Mexican anarchism from origins to demise. Attention to anarcho-syndicalists (PLM) during revolution. [EH-D]

38.235   John Mason Hart. *Revolutionary Mexico: the coming and process of the Mexican Revolution.* 1987 ed. Berkeley: University of California Press, 1988. ISBN 0-520-05995-6 (pbk). ▸ Significant interpretation of revolution, focusing on social classes and impact of United States investment. Well researched and densely packed with new information. [EH-D]

38.236   Judith Adler Hellman. *Mexico in crisis.* 2d ed. New York: Holmes & Meier, 1983. ISBN 0-8419-0840-0 (cl), 0-8419-0895-8 (pbk). ▸ Account of human costs and political consequences of Mexico's post-1940 economic miracle with focus on political crises from 1968 through 1980s. Good analysis and accessible to nonspecialist. [EH-D]

38.237   Evelyn Hu-DeHart. *Yaqui resistance and survival: the struggle for land and autonomy, 1821–1910.* Madison: University of Wisconsin Press, 1984. ISBN 0-299-09660-2. ▸ Narrative history of Yaqui nation of northern Mexico from independence to revolution as example of how indigenous peoples resist forced integration, assimilation, and loss of land and identity. [EH-D]

38.238   Gilbert M. Joseph. *Rediscovering the past at Mexico's periphery: essays on the history of modern Yucatán.* Tuscaloosa: University of Alabama Press, 1986. ISBN 0-8173-0268-9. ▸ Yucatán's social and political history from henequen monocrop in late nineteenth century to socialism in 1920s. Fine example of good regional history. [EH-D]

38.239 Friedrich Katz. *The secret war in Mexico: Europe, the United States, and the Mexican Revolution.* Loren Goldner, trans. Chicago: University of Chicago Press, 1981. ISBN 0-226-42588-6. ▸ Best study on relationships between key figures of revolution (Venustiano Carranza, Pancho Villa, and Alvaro Obregón) and foreign powers (United States, Great Britain, and Germany), based on United States, Mexican, and little-known European sources. [EH-D]

38.240 Friedrich Katz, ed. *Riot, rebellion, and revolution: rural social conflict in Mexico.* Princeton: Princeton University Press, 1988. ISBN 0-691-07739-8 (cl), 0-691-02265-8 (pbk). ▸ Essays on various kinds of rural movements from pre-Hispanic period through 1940, with focus on nineteenth century and Mexican Revolution. Important contributions to Mexican agrarian history. [EH-D]

38.241 Alan Knight. *The Mexican Revolution.* Vol. 1: *Porfirians, liberals, and peasants.* Vol. 2: *Counter-revolution and reconstruction.* 1986 ed. 2 vols. Lincoln: University of Nebraska Press, 1990. ISBN 0-8032-7772-5 (set), 0-8032-7770-9 (v. 1), 0-8032-7771-7 (v. 2). ▸ Significant and comprehensive study of Revolution. Volume 1 documents and analyzes populist uprising of peasants, peons, and workers against Porfirio Díaz and later against Francisco Madero himself, as well as Madero's attempts at liberal reform. Volume 2 continues interpretive history with focus on Huertismo and constitutionalist movement, concluding with examination of new political order that Pancho Villa, Emiliano Zapata, Venustiano Carranza, and Alvaro Obregón attempted to establish. Reasserts thesis that revolution was indeed major popular uprising and mass social movement. [EH-D]

38.242 Robert J. Knowlton. *Church property and the Mexican reform, 1856–1910.* DeKalb: Northern Illinois University Press, 1976. ISBN 0-87580-055-6. ▸ Detailed study of liberal land reforms from Benito Juárez to Porfirio Díaz, specifically disamortization and nationalization of church-held or -controlled land. Serious effort on difficult topic. [EH-D]

38.243 Doris M. Ladd. *The Mexican nobility at independence, 1780–1826.* Austin: University of Texas Press for Institute of Latin American Studies, 1976. (Latin American monographs, 40.) ISBN 0-292-75026-9 (cl), 0-292-75027-7 (pbk). ▸ Detailed examination of elite from late colonial period to end of independence. Emphasis on economic interests in land, agriculture, finance, and commerce. Includes valuable biographical and financial data. [EH-D/MAB]

38.244 Edwin Lieuwen. *Mexican militarism: the political rise and fall of the revolutionary army.* 1968 ed. Westport, Conn.: Greenwood, 1981. ISBN 0-313-22911-2. ▸ Transformation of revolutionary armies into single professional army controlled by state. Dated but still useful; one of few studies on important topic. [EH-D]

38.245 Donald J. Mabry. *The Mexican university and the state: student conflicts, 1910–1971.* College Station: Texas A&M University Press, 1982. ISBN 0-89096-128-X. ▸ Study of politics in Mexico centering around semi-autonomous national university. Explores relationship between university and state. One of few studies of its kind. [EH-D]

38.246 Anna Macías. *Against all odds: the feminist movement in Mexico to 1940.* Westport, Conn.: Greenwood, 1982. ISBN 0-313-23028-5. ▸ Important study of development of Mexican feminism and feminist movement with particular attention to revolution and reformist Cárdenas regime. [EH-D]

38.247 Oscar J. Martínez. *Troublesome border.* Tucson: University of Arizona Press, 1988. ISBN 0-8165-1033-4. ▸ Important study of border from perspective of Mexico, United States, and border people themselves. Also discusses problems arising from environmental degradation and immigration. [EH-D]

38.248 Jean A. Meyer. *The Cristero rebellion: The Mexican people between church and state, 1926–1929.* Richard Southern, trans. Cambridge: Cambridge University Press, 1976. ISBN 0-521-21031-3. ▸ Examination of sociological, geographic, military, and economic characteristics of Catholic guerrillas (*Cristeros*). Translation of three-volume Spanish-language work. Complements Bailey 38.193. [EH-D]

38.249 Lorenzo Meyer. *Mexico and the United States in the oil controversy, 1917–1942.* Muriel Vasconcellos, trans. Austin: University of Texas Press, 1977. ISBN 0-292-75032-3. ▸ Exploration of diplomatic relationship between United States and Mexico from revolution through Lázaro Cárdenas's presidency with emphasis on nationalization of foreign-owned oil industry. Important Mexican perspective on controversy. [EH-D]

38.250 Michael C. Meyer. *Huerta: a political portrait.* Lincoln: University of Nebraska Press, 1972. ISBN 0-8032-0802-2. ▸ Still most complete political biography of arch counterrevolutionary Victoriano Huerta, who seized power from President Madero but failed to win support from other revolutionary leaders and United States president Woodrow Wilson. [EH-D]

38.251 Carl J. Mora. *Mexican cinema: reflections of a society, 1896–1980.* Rev. ed. Berkeley: University of California Press, 1982. ISBN 0-520-04304-9. ▸ Detailed study of Mexican film industry, film criticism, and films themselves. Shows how films reflect themes in Mexican culture, identity, society, and politics. [EH-D]

38.252 Octavio Paz. *The labyrinth of solitude, The other Mexico, Return to the labyrinth of solitude, Mexico and the United States, and The philanthropic ogre.* 1985 rev. ed. Lysander Kemp, Yara Milor, and Rachel Phillips Belash, trans. Harmondsworth: Penguin, 1990. ISBN 0-14-015426-4. ▸ Mexico's premier poet and Nobel laureate explores Mexican character, culture, personality, and self-identity in series of illuminating essays that have become literary classics. [EH-D]

38.253 T. G. Powell. *Mexico and the Spanish Civil War.* Albuquerque: University of New Mexico Press, 1981. ISBN 0-8263-0546-6. ▸ Mexico's policies toward Spain during Spanish Civil War, with attention to President Lázaro Cárdenas and Mexican Communist party. Important contribution to Mexican foreign relations and diplomatic history. [EH-D]

38.254 Robert E. Quirk. *The Mexican Revolution and the Catholic church, 1910–1929.* Bloomington: Indiana University Press, 1973. ISBN 0-253-33800-X. ▸ Critical study of church-state relations from revolution through *Cristero* rebellion. Includes analysis of Vatican's and United States clergy's attitudes toward revolution. [EH-D]

38.255 W. Dirk Raat, ed. *Mexico: from independence to revolution, 1810–1910.* Lincoln: University of Nebraska Press, 1982. ISBN 0-8032-3858-4 (cl), 0-8032-8904-9 (pbk). ▸ Twenty-six essays and original documents with commentary by editor, covering entire nineteenth century from independence to outbreak of revolution. Good as supplementary text. [EH-D]

38.256 W. Dirk Raat and William H. Beezley, eds. *Twentieth-century Mexico.* Lincoln: University of Nebraska Press, 1986. ISBN 0-8032-3868-1 (cl), 0-8032-8914-6 (pbk). ▸ Sequel to nineteenth-century collection (38.255). Contains twenty-six critical essays, mostly by North American scholars, on revolution and twentieth century. Designed as classroom text. [EH-D]

38.257 Douglas W. Richmond. *Venustiano Carranza's nationalist struggle, 1893–1920.* Lincoln: University of Nebraska Press, 1983. ISBN 0-8032-3863-0. ▸ One of few political biographies of constitutionalist chief. Focuses on Carranza's nationalism and relationship with United States president Wilson. [EH-D]

38.258 Jaime E. Rodríguez O, ed. *The independence of Mexico and* *the creation of the new nation.* Los Angeles: University of California, UCLA Latin American Center Publications, 1989. (UCLA Latin American studies, 69.) ISBN 0-87903-070-4. ▸ Bilingual text of important essays by foreign and Mexican scholars on political, ideological, economic, and fiscal issues of new nation. [EH-D]

38.259 Ramón Eduardo Ruiz. *The great rebellion: Mexico 1905–1924.* New York: Norton, 1980. ISBN 0-393-01323-5 (cl), 0-393-95129-4 (pbk). ▸ Sometimes controversial interpretation of revolution, arguing that insufficient attention to social justice for workers and peasants qualifies struggle as only rebellion. [EH-D]

38.260 Ramón Eduardo Ruiz. *Triumphs and tragedy: a history of the Mexican people.* New York: Norton, 1992. ISBN 0-393-03023-7. ▸ Long interpretive essay on Mexican history, by prolific senior historian who has written extensively on modern Mexico. Central theme is Mexico's dependency on United States. [EH-D]

38.261 Heather Fowler Salamini. *Agrarian radicalism in Veracruz, 1920–38.* Lincoln: University of Nebraska Press, 1978. ISBN 0-8032-0952-5. ▸ Notable example of good regional history, focusing on violent, immediate postrevolutionary Veracruz, then dominated by regional *caudillos* (revolutionary leaders) committed to radical agrarian and other reforms. [EH-D]

38.262 Steven E. Sanderson. *Agrarian populism and the Mexican state: the struggle for land in Sonora.* Berkeley: University of California Press, 1981. ISBN 0-520-04056-2. ▸ Important case study of Mexican populism, agrarian politics, and land struggle in rich commercial agricultural state of Sonora during Lázaro Cárdenas and Luis Echeverría regimes. [EH-D]

38.263 Alex M. Saragoza. *The Monterrey elite and the Mexican state, 1880–1940.* Austin: University of Texas Press, 1988. ISBN 0-292-71113-1. ▸ Important study tracing origins and history of Mexico's leading modern industrial elite. Focuses on its confrontations with state, particularly with President Cárdenas. [EH-D]

38.264 Henry C. Schmidt. *The roots of lo mexicano: self and society in Mexican thought, 1900–1934.* College Station: Texas A&M University Press, 1978. ISBN 0-89096-048-8. ▸ Intellectual and cultural history of early twentieth century with attention to writers Samuel Ramos, José Vasconcelos, Antonio Caso, Alfonso Reyes, and Daniel Cosío Villegas, all of whom struggled with issues of Mexican identity. [EH-D]

38.265 Frans J. Schryer. *The rancheros of Pisaflores: the history of a peasant bourgeoisie in twentieth-century Mexico.* Toronto: University of Toronto Press, 1980. ISBN 0-8020-5466-8. ▸ Agrarian study that broke new ground by focusing on middle peasants as key group in understanding revolutionary politics, rural class structure, and land-tenure patterns. [EH-D]

38.266 Richard N. Sinkin. *The Mexican reform, 1855–1876: a study in liberal nation-building.* Austin: University of Texas Press for Institute of Latin American Studies, 1979. (Latin American monographs, 49.) ISBN 0-292-75044-7 (cl), 0-292-75045-7 (pbk). ▸ Applies modernization theory to study of nation building by nineteenth-century liberals, their struggle for power and legitimacy, and relationship with rebellious peasants and with United States. [EH-D]

38.267 Donald Fithian Stevens. *Origins of instability in early republican Mexico.* Durham, N.C.: Duke University Press, 1991. ISBN 0-8223-1136-4. ▸ One of few studies to focus on political development of early republic. Analyzes contradiction between liberalism and entrenched colonial policies. [EH-D]

38.268 Barbara A. Tenenbaum. *The politics of penury: debts and taxes in Mexico, 1821–1856.* Albuquerque: University of New Mexico Press, 1986. ISBN 0-8263-0890-2. ▸ In-depth analysis of public debt and taxes during early republic and connection between debt and political instability. Also discusses role of private moneylenders in rescuing bankrupt central government. Serious effort on difficult topic. [EH-D]

38.269 John Kenneth Turner. *Barbarous Mexico.* 1911 ed. Sinclair Snow, Introduction. Austin: University of Texas Press, 1969. ISBN 0-292-78418-X (cl), 0-292-70737-1 (pbk). ▸ Classic exposé of Porfirian labor practices by muckraking United States socialist journalist. Helped to discredit Porfirio Díaz in United States popular opinion. [EH-D]

38.270 John Tutino. *From insurrection to revolution in Mexico: social bases of agrarian violence, 1750–1940.* Princeton: Princeton University Press, 1986. ISBN 0-691-07721-5 (cl), 0-691-02294-1 (pbk). ▸ Innovative study taking long view of Mexican agrarian history from late colonial period to President Cárdenas's reforms. Identifies peasant perceptions of security and autonomy as key to understanding behavior and actions. [EH-D]

38.271 Paul J. Vanderwood. *Disorder and progress: bandits, police, and Mexican development.* Rev. ed. Wilmington, Del.: Scholarly Resources, 1992. ISBN 0-8420-2438-7 (cl), 0-8420-2439-5 (pbk). ▸ Ambitious study of social banditry and formation of President Porfirio Díaz's despised and controversial rural police force, his key instrument for establishing peace and order through use of force and terror. [EH-D]

38.272 Mary Kay Vaughn. *The state, education, and social class in Mexico, 1880–1928.* DeKalb: Northern Illinois University Press, 1982. ISBN 0-87580-079-3. ▸ Important study on federal educational policies from presidents Porfirio Díaz to Plutarco Elías Calles and Alvaro Obregón. Critical inquiry into whether schooling advanced social justice after revolution. [EH-D]

38.273 Josefina Zoraida Vázquez and Lorenzo Meyer. *The United States and Mexico.* Chicago: University of Chicago Press, 1985. ISBN 0-226-85023-4. ▸ Critical study of United States foreign policy vis-à-vis Mexico by two of Mexico's leading scholars. Valuable Mexican perspective on United States–Mexican relations. [EH-D]

38.274 Stuart F. Voss. *On the periphery of nineteenth-century Mexico: Sonora and Sinaloa, 1810–1877.* Tucson: University of Arizona Press, 1982. ISBN 0-8165-0768-6 (cl), 0-8165-0693-0 (pbk). ▸ Political history of urban elites in Mexico's northwest from independence to election of Porfirio Díaz. Examines chaotic period insufficiently studied by scholars. [EH-D]

38.275 Arturo Warman. *"We come to object": the peasants of Morelos and the national state.* Stephen K. Ault, trans. Baltimore: Johns Hopkins University Press, 1980. ISBN 0-8018-2170-3. ▸ Examination of how Zapatista peasants in Morelos maintained economic base and way of life, relationship with *hacendados*, and state and capitalist markets. Complements Womack 38.282. [EH-D]

38.276 Mark Wasserman. *Capitalists, caciques, and revolution: the native elite and foreign enterprise in Chihuahua, Mexico, 1854–1911.* Chapel Hill: University of North Carolina Press, 1984. ISBN 0-8078-1580-2. ▸ Good example of regional and elite history. Traces rise of Terrazas-Creel clan, its economic enterprises, connection to United States investments, and political monopoly. [EH-D]

38.277 David J. Weber. *The Mexican frontier, 1821–1846: the American Southwest under Mexico.* Albuquerque: University of New Mexico Press, 1982. ISBN 0-8263-0602-0 (cl), 0-8263-0603-9 (pbk). ▸ Thoroughly researched, original analysis of how California, Arizona, New Mexico, and Texas made transition from Spanish and Mexican frontier to United States capitalist system. Examined from Mexican and Anglo-American perspectives. [EH-D]

38.278 Allen Wells. *Yucatán's gilded age: haciendas, henequen, and International Harvester, 1860–1915.* Albuquerque: University of New Mexico Press, 1985. ISBN 0-8263-0781-7. ▸ Important, readable regional study of how Yucatán integrated into international economy through cash crop (henequen) and International Harvester Company. Also discusses relationship between semi-slave workers and henequen planters. [EH-D]

38.279 James W. Wilkie. *The Mexican Revolution: federal expenditure and social change since 1910.* Berkeley: University of California Press, 1967. ISBN 0-520-01568-1. ▸ Uses federal yearly budgetary projections and actual expenditures to assess degree of positive social change from 1910 to 1970s. Innovative but ultimately questionable methodology. [EH-D]

38.280 Eric R. Wolf. *Sons of the shaking earth.* 1959 ed. Chicago: University of Chicago Press, 1974. ISBN 0-226-90500-4 (pbk). ▸ Broad interpretive synthesis of sweep of Mexican history from earliest human appearance to twentieth century. Good book to begin study of Mexico. Classic. [EH-D]

38.281 George Wolfskill and Douglas W. Richmond, eds. *Essays on the Mexican Revolution: revisionist views of the leaders.* Michael C. Meyer, Introduction. Austin: University of Texas Press, 1979. ISBN 0-292-72026-2. ▸ Original, revisionist essays on five of six most important leaders: Francisco Madero, Francisco (Pancho) Villa, Venustiano Carranza, Alvaro Obregón, and Lázaro Cárdenas. Inexplicably, Emiliano Zapata is omitted. [EH-D]

38.282 John Womack, Jr. *Zapata and the Mexican Revolution.* 1969 ed. New York: Vintage, 1970. ISBN 0-394-70853-9 (pbk). ▸ Definitive study of revolutionary and peasant movement he led from origins in late Porfiriato to 1920, just after his assassination. Explores relationship with other leaders, especially Francisco (Pancho) Villa. Narrative and epic. [EH-D]

38.283 Leopoldo Zea. *Positivism in Mexico.* Josephine H. Schulte, trans. Austin: University of Texas Press, 1974. ISBN 0-292-76413-8. ▸ Intellectual history of modern Mexico, by country's leading philosopher. Focuses on antecedents and origins of positivism and its impact on politics and society, especially during Porfiriato (1876–1911). [EH-D]

SEE ALSO
36.308 Robert Wasserstrom. *Class and society in central Chiapas.*
36.311 Nelson Reed. *The caste war of Yucatán.*
37.93 Michael C. Meyer and William L. Sherman. *The course of Mexican history.*
37.246 D. A. Brading. *Haciendas and ranchos in the Mexican Bajío, León, 1700–1860.*
40.360 Carey McWilliams. *North from Mexico.*
44.394 James D. Cockcroft. *Outlaws in the promised land.*

CENTRAL AMERICA

General Studies

38.284 Charles D. Ameringer. *The democratic Left in exile: the antidictatorial struggle in the Caribbean, 1945–1959.* Coral Gables, Fla.: University of Miami Press, 1974. ISBN 0-87024-238-5. ▸ Landmark study of efforts of democratic Left to overthrow entrenched dictators in Nicaragua, Dominican Republic, and other nations. Gives special attention to role of leftist leader José Figueres of Costa Rica. [RLM]

38.285 Thomas P. Anderson. *Politics in Central America: Guatemala, El Salvador, Honduras, and Nicaragua.* Rev. ed. New York: Praeger, 1988. ISBN 0-275-92805-5 (cl), 0-275-92883-7 (pbk). ▸ Capable, well-written account of post-1960 history of these four nations with heavy emphasis on political developments and United States policies. [RLM]

38.286 Thomas P. Anderson. *The war of the dispossessed: Honduras and El Salvador, 1969.* Lincoln: University of Nebraska Press, 1981. ISBN 0-8032-1009-4. ▸ Adequate summary of 1969 conflict between El Salvador and Honduras, emphasizing rising conflicts during 1960s and course and impact of war itself. [RLM]

38.287 Louis E. Baumgartner. *José del Valle of Central America.* Durham, N.C.: Duke University Press, 1963. ▸ Biography of intellectual and political leader of Central America's independence movement. Best available account in English of region's formative years. [RLM]

38.288 Victor Bulmer-Thomas. *The political economy of Central America since 1920.* Cambridge: Cambridge University Press, 1987. ISBN 0-521-34284-8 (cl), 0-521-34839-0 (pbk). ▸ Groundbreaking study of links between economic developments and political change in Central America with special emphasis on role of production for export. Basic to understanding recent Central American history. [RLM]

38.289 James Dunkerley. *Power in the Isthmus: a political history of modern Central America.* London: Verso, 1988. ISBN 0-86091-196-9 (cl), 0-86091-912-9 (pbk). ▸ Lengthy study, stressing class conflicts and United States policy as prime determinants of regional developments. Primary emphasis on 1980s, but devotes considerable space to history, 1910–80. [RLM]

38.290 John E. Findling. *Close neighbors, distant friends: United States–Central American relations.* New York: Greenwood, 1987. ISBN 0-313-23679-8. ▸ Somewhat pedestrian account of United States dealings with Central America, 1800-1980, based largely on United States sources. Most complete study of topic available. [RLM]

38.291 Thomas L. Karnes. *The failure of union: Central America, 1824–1960.* Rev. ed. Tempe: Arizona State University, Center for Latin American Studies, 1976. ISBN 0-87918-028-5. ▸ Valuable study of Central America's repeatedly frustrated efforts to form political union. Includes useful material on British and United States policies in region. [RLM]

38.292 Thomas L. Karnes. *Tropical enterprise: the Standard Fruit and Steamship Company in Latin America.* Baton Rouge: Louisiana State University Press, 1978. ISBN 0-8071-0395-0. ▸ Best available history of American banana company in Central America and Caribbean during first half of twentieth century. Contains useful material on Honduras, Nicaragua, and Haiti. [RLM]

38.293 Thomas M. Leonard. *The United States and Central America, 1944–1949: perceptions of political dynamics.* University: University of Alabama Press, 1984. ISBN 0-8173-0190-9. ▸ Groundbreaking study of United States policies toward Central America in era of major political upheavals. Based exclusively on United States sources. [RLM]

38.294 Dario Moreno. *U.S. policy in Central America: the endless debate.* Miami: Florida International University Press, 1990. ISBN 0-8130-1005-5 (cl), 0-8130-1020-9 (pbk). ▸ Despite occasional errors and organizational problems, useful survey of United States relations with Central America under Carter, Reagan, and early Bush administrations. [RLM]

38.295 Mario Rodríguez. *A Palmerstonian diplomat in Central America: Frederick Chatfield, Esq.* Tucson: University of Arizona Press, 1964. ▸ Traditional study of British–United States rivalries in Central America from independence through 1850s. Also provides useful information on Central America's internal politics in this neglected period. [RLM]

38.296 Richard V. Salisbury. *Anti-imperialism and international competition in Central America, 1920–1929.* Wilmington, Del.: Scholarly Resources, 1989. ISBN 0-8420-2304-6. ▸ Scholarly study of opposition to United States policies toward Central America in general and Nicaragua in particular. Gives special emphasis to roles of Mexico, Costa Rica, and Spain. [RLM]

38.297 Thomas D. Schoonover. *The United States in Central*

America, 1860–1911: episodes of social imperialism and imperial rivalry in the world system. Durham, N.C.: Duke University Press, 1991. ISBN 0-8223-1160-7. ‣ Pioneering study of development of United States hegemony in Central America, relating events to rivalries with European powers. Extensive use of European as well as United States and Central American sources. [RLM]

38.298 Ralph Lee Woodward, Jr., ed. *Central America: historical perspectives on the contemporary crisis.* New York: Greenwood, 1988. ISBN 0-313-25938-0. ‣ Mixed collection of articles on wide variety of topics, including Belize, Mexico, and Central America, Catholic church in Honduras, and culture in revolutionary Nicaragua. Introductory essay especially valuable. [RLM]

SEE ALSO
37.101 Ralph Lee Woodward, Jr. *Central America.*
48.492 Walter LaFeber. *Inevitable revolutions.*

Belize

38.299 O. Nigel Bolland. *Belize: a new nation in Central America.* Boulder: Westview, 1986. ISBN 0-8133-0005-3. ‣ Best available introduction to Belize, heavy on social and political conditions, but contains sound summary of nation's history from colonization to independence. [RLM]

38.300 Cedric H. Grant. *The making of modern Belize: politics, society, and British colonialism in Central America.* Cambridge: Cambridge University Press, 1976. ISBN 0-521-20731-2. ‣ Now somewhat dated but still best available history of post-1930 Belize. Especially useful for understanding social and economic developments. [RLM]

Costa Rica

38.301 Charles D. Ameringer. *Don Pepe: a political biography of José Figueres of Costa Rica.* Albuquerque: University of New Mexico Press, 1978. ISBN 0-8263-0480-X. ‣ Examination of career of dominant figure in post–World War II Costa Rica, shedding valuable light on relations among Central American states, 1948–75 period. [RLM]

38.302 John Patrick Bell. *Crisis in Costa Rica: the Revolution of 1948.* Austin: University of Texas Press for Institute of Latin American Studies, 1971. (Latin American monographs, 24.) ISBN 0-292-70147-0. ‣ Best available history, in English, of pivotal events of 1948 which transformed Costa Rica and had significant effect on many other parts of Central America and Hispanic Caribbean. [RLM]

38.303 Lowell Gudmundson. *Costa Rica before coffee: society and economy on the eve of the export boom.* Baton Rouge: Louisiana State University Press, 1986. ISBN 0-8071-1274-7. ‣ Revisionist study of nineteenth-century Costa Rica, attacking traditional view of society founded on rural egalitarianism. Useful and thought provoking, despite some questionable political assertions. [RLM]

38.304 Mario Samper. *Generations of settlers: rural households and markets on the Costa Rican frontier, 1850–1935.* Boulder: Westview, 1990. ISBN 0-8133-8021-9. ‣ Valuable study of expansion of small-scale coffee farming in Costa Rica. Emphasizes labor shortages as important factor in nation's economic, social, and political development. [RLM]

38.305 Mitchell A. Seligson. *Peasants of Costa Rica and the development of agrarian capitalism.* Madison: University of Wisconsin Press, 1980. ISBN 0-299-07760-8. ‣ Scholarly account of economic and social development of twentieth-century Costa Rica. Debunks myth of rural equality in Costa Rica. [RLM]

38.306 Watt Stewart. *Keith and Costa Rica: a biographical study of Minor Cooper Keith.* Albuquerque: University of New Mexico Press, 1964. ‣ Well-researched, sympathetic biography of founder of United Fruit Company, emphasizing activities in Costa Rica, 1871–1900. [RLM]

El Salvador

38.307 Thomas P. Anderson. *Matanza: El Salvador's communist revolt of 1932.* Lincoln: University of Nebraska Press, 1971. ISBN 0-8032-0794-8. ‣ Pioneering study of peasant uprising and subsequent army massacre in 1932 which influenced pattern of nation's politics for next six decades. [RLM]

38.308 Enrique A. Baloyra. *El Salvador in transition.* Chapel Hill: University of North Carolina Press, 1982. ISBN 0-8078-1532-2 (cl), 0-8078-4093-9 (pbk). ‣ Well-written, liberal view of roots of El Salvador's conflicts in 1980s. Includes account of development of extreme Right in El Salvador and United States responses to political violence there. [RLM]

38.309 James R. Brockman. *The word remains: a life of Oscar Romero.* Maryknoll, N.Y.: Orbis, 1982. ISBN 0-88344-364-3 (pbk). ‣ Uncritical but informative study of life of archbishop of El Salvador. Important for understanding role of church in Central America and causes of violent conflicts in 1980s. [RLM]

38.310 Héctor Lindo-Fuentes. *Weak foundations: the economy of El Salvador in the nineteenth century, 1821–1898.* Berkeley: University of California Press, 1991. ISBN 0-520-06927-7. ‣ Scholarly account of development of Salvadoran economy, stressing impact of coffee production, development of landless peasantry, and creation of powerful, semifeudal elite. [RLM]

38.311 Max G. Manwaring and Court Prisk, eds. *El Salvador at war: an oral history of conflict from the 1979 insurrection to the present.* Washington, D.C.: National Defense University Press, 1988. ISBN 0-16-001693-2. ‣ Large collection of documents, excerpts from publications, interviews, and other sources, including all sides to El Salvador's civil conflict. Emphasizes military and political aspects, neglecting social and economic factors. [RLM]

38.312 Patricia Parkman. *Nonviolent insurrection in El Salvador: the fall of Maximiliano Hernández Martínez.* Tucson: University of Arizona Press, 1988. ISBN 0-8165-1062-8. ‣ Carefully researched, scholarly account of 1944 uprising which toppled military dictator and launched regional movement against military dictatorships. Fills major gap in literature. [RLM]

38.313 Stephen Webre. *José Napoleon Duarte and the Christian Democratic party in Salvadoran politics, 1960–1972.* Baton Rouge: Louisiana State University Press, 1979. ISBN 0-8071-0462-0. ‣ Scholarly study of formative years of El Salvador's Christian Democratic party and early career of party leader and key figure in Salvadoran politics. [RLM]

Guatemala

38.314 Piero Gleijeses. *Shattered hope: the Guatemalan Revolution and the United States, 1944–1954.* Princeton: Princeton University Press, 1991. ISBN 0-691-07817-3. ‣ Detailed, well-researched account of Guatemalan history and United States policies toward that nation. Critical of United States policies, but argues President Jacobo Arbenz (1950–54) actually was a communist. [RLM]

38.315 Kenneth J. Grieb. *Guatemalan caudillo: the regime of Jorge Ubico, Guatemala, 1931–1944.* Athens: Ohio University Press, 1971. ISBN 0-8214-0379-6. ‣ Well-researched study of president-dictator and pivotal figure in twentieth-century Guatemalan history. Contains important material on dispute with Belize and on relations with Mexico and United States. [RLM]

38.316 Jim Handy. *Gift of the devil: a history of Guatemala.* Boston: South End Press, 1984. ISBN 0-89608-248-2 (cl), 0-89608-247-4 (pbk). ‣ Provocative, highly critical history of Guatemala, emphasizing period since 1945. Stresses economic factors and blames United States for many problems in nation's development. [RLM]

38.317 Richard H. Immerman. *The CIA in Guatemala: the foreign policy of intervention.* 1982 ed. Austin: University of Texas Press, 1985. ISBN 0-292-78045-1 (cl), 0292-71083-6 (pbk). ‣ Well-researched, balanced account of United States–Guatemalan relations, 1945–1954, focusing on United States role in overthrowing government of President Jacobo Arbenz. [RLM]

38.318 Ralph Lee Woodward, Jr. *Class privilege and economic development: the Consulado de Comercio of Guatemala, 1793–1871.* Chapel Hill: University of North Carolina Press, 1966. ‣ Detailed, somewhat technical study which sheds considerable light on economic and social conditions in nineteenth-century Guatemala. [RLM]

SEE ALSO
36.356 Norman B. Schwartz. *Forest society.*
36.357 Carol A. Smith, ed. *Guatemalan Indians and the state, 1540–1988.*

Honduras

38.319 Robert MacCameron. *Bananas, labor, and politics in Honduras, 1954–1963.* Syracuse, N.Y.: Syracuse University, Maxwell School of Citizenship and Public Affairs, 1983. (Foreign and comparative studies, Latin American series, 5.) ISBN 0-915984-96-2 (pbk). ‣ Valuable study of critical decade in Honduran history. Focus on efforts to organize banana workers and on responses of both banana companies and Honduran government. [RLM]

38.320 James A. Morris. *Honduras, caudillo politics, and military rulers.* Boulder: Westview, 1984. ISBN 0-86531-178-1. ‣ Broadest available monograph in English on twentieth-century Honduras. Focus on political history and on relations with United States. [RLM]

38.321 Nancy Peckenham and Annie Street, eds. *Honduras: portrait of a captive nation.* New York: Praeger, 1985. ISBN 0-03-01819-6 (cl), 0-03-01822-6 (pbk). ‣ Compilation of documents and excerpts from other publications, many translated from Spanish; covers Honduran history from Spanish conquest to late 1980s. Clear left-wing bias but still very useful. [RLM]

38.322 Mario Posas and Rafael del Cid. *La construcción del sector público y del Estado nacional de Honduras, 1876–1979.* 2d ed. San José, Costa Rica: Editorial Universitaria Centroamericana, 1983. ISBN 9977-03-0000-3. ‣ Groundbreaking effort to explore economic and social basis of emergence of Honduran national state. Marxist-influenced analysis; well documented and highly informative. [RLM]

Nicaragua

38.323 Alejandro Bolaños-Geyer. *William Walker: the gray-eyed man of destiny.* Vols. 3 and 4. Lake St. Louis, Mo.: Privately printed, 1990. ISBN 0-9620858-9-8 (v. 3), 1-877926-00-0 (v. 4). ‣ Last two volumes of massive four-volume work covering American filibuster's activities in Central America. Somewhat pedestrian but most complete account available in English of Walker's career. [RLM]

38.324 John A. Booth. *The end and the beginning: the Nicaraguan Revolution.* 2d rev. ed. Boulder: Westview, 1985. ISBN 0-8133-0108-4 (cl), 0-8133-0109-2 (pbk). ‣ Early account of Sandinista overthrow of Somoza dynasty in Nicaragua. Somewhat dated and colored by its sympathy for Sandinistas, but still useful summary of events in late 1970s. [RLM]

38.325 Craig L. Dozier. *Nicaragua's Mosquito shore: the years of British and American presence.* University: University of Alabama Press, 1985. ISBN 0-8173-0226-3. ‣ Important contribution to

understanding of neglected region of Central America. Includes material on United States–British rivalry, ethnic relations in Central America, and Nicaraguan politics in nineteenth and early twentieth centuries. Some information on Miskito Indians. [RLM/MWH]

38.326 David I. Folkman, Jr. *The Nicaragua route.* Salt Late City: University of Utah Press, 1972. ISBN 0-87480-032-3. ‣ Fascinating study of efforts to develop travel across Nicaraguan isthmus in nineteenth century. Useful for understanding United States and British policies, activities of William Walker, and nineteenth-century regional history. [RLM]

38.327 Donald C. Hodges. *Intellectual foundations of the Nicaraguan Revolution.* Austin: University of Texas Press, 1986. ISBN 0-292-73838-2 (cl), 0-292-73843-9 (pbk). ‣ Well-researched study of thought of General Sandino and its relationship to ideology of Nicaragua's Sandinistas. Useful for understanding recent Nicaraguan history, but underestimates Leninist influences on Sandinistas. [RLM]

38.328 Willian Kamman. *A search for stability: United States diplomacy towards Nicaragua, 1925–1933.* Notre Dame, Ind.: University of Notre Dame Press, 1968. ISBN 0-268-00249-5. ‣ Cautious, somewhat dated, but still useful account of United States policy in Nicaragua during second intervention (1925–33). Emphasizes United States policy formulation, neglecting Nicaraguan internal factors. [RLM]

38.329 Stephen Kinzer. *Blood of brothers: life and war in Nicaragua.* New York: Putnam, 1991. ISBN 0-399-13594-4 (pbk). ‣ Controversial, well-written account of political and military conflict in Nicaragua during 1980s by *New York Times* correspondent in that nation. [RLM]

38.330 Neill Macaulay. *The Sandino affair.* 1967 ed. Durham, N.C.: Duke University Press, 1985. ISBN 0-8223-0696-4 (pbk). ‣ Stimulating study of General Augusto C. Sandino's resistance to United States intervention in Nicaragua in 1920s and 1930s. Special attention to military campaigns. [RLM]

38.331 Richard L. Millett. *Guardians of the dynasty.* Maryknoll, N.Y.: Orbis, 1977. ISBN 0-88344-169-1. ‣ Detailed, important history of Nicaraguan military and Somoza family dynasty it helped produce and maintain. Considerable emphasis on United States policies. [RLM]

38.332 Gregorio Selser. *Sandino.* Cedric Belfrage, trans. New York: Monthly Review Press, 1981. ISBN 0-85345-558-9 (cl), 0-85345-559-7 (pbk). ‣ Sympathetic biography of Nicaragua guerrilla leader, highly critical of United States. Valuable if at times uncritical of Sandino. Condensed version of two-volume 1959 study. [RLM]

SEE ALSO
44.855 Roy Gutman. *Banana diplomacy.*
44.857 Robert A. Pastor. *Condemned to repetition.*

Panama

38.333 Michael L. Conniff. *Black labor on a white canal: Panama, 1904–1981.* Pittsburgh: University of Pittsburgh Press, 1985. ISBN 0-8229-3509-0. ‣ Pioneering history of West Indian population in Panama, most of whom came to build canal. Provides vital insights into social and ethnic divisions that have helped shape Panamanian history. [RLM]

38.334 Michael L. Conniff. *Panama and the United States: the forced alliance.* Athens: University of Georgia Press, 1992. ISBN 0-8203-1359-9 (cl), 0-8203-1360-2 (pbk). ‣ Ambitious history of United States–Panamanian relations, stressing unequal nature of relationship. Critical of most United States policies. Complements LaFeber 48.493. [RLM]

38.335 David G. McCullough. *The path between the seas: the creation of the Panama Canal, 1870–1914.* New York: Simon & Schuster, 1977. ISBN 0-671-22563-4. ▸ Detailed study of French-financed failure and successful American effort to construct canal through Panama. Well written but based largely on United States sources. Diplomatic, social, and engineering history. [RLM/DCJ]

38.336 Larry LaRae Pippin. *The Remón era: an analysis of a decade of events in Panama, 1947–1957.* Stanford, Calif.: Stanford University, Institute of Hispanic American and Luso-Brazilian Studies, 1964. ▸ Contains numerous gaps and limited analysis, but only available in-depth study of critical era which saw emergence of military as Panama's dominant political force. [RLM]

38.337 Steve C. Ropp. *Panamanian politics: from guarded nation to national guard.* New York and Stanford, Calif.: Praeger and Hoover Institution Press, 1982. ISBN 0-03-060622-5. ▸ Balanced account of development of Panama as nation and process by which national guard came to dominate its politics. Especially useful for its analysis of Torrijos era (1968–81). [RLM]

38.338 Margaret E. Scranton. *The Noriega years: U.S.–Panamanian relations, 1981–1990.* Boulder: Rienner, 1991. ISBN 1-55587-204-2. ▸ First scholarly effort to analyze United States–Panamanian relations leading up to 1989 intervention. Not as entertaining as numerous journalistic accounts but more reliable and analytical. [RLM]

SEE ALSO
48.438 Walter LaFeber. *The Panama Canal.*

CARIBBEAN

General Studies

38.339 Franklin W. Knight. *The Caribbean: the genesis of a fragmented nationalism.* 2d ed. New York: Oxford University Press, 1990. ISBN 0-19-505440-7 (cl), 0-19-505441-5 (pbk). ▸ Expanded version of 1978 work that broke new ground by combining history of Latin and Commonwealth Caribbean and emphasizing common problems in efforts to become viable independent societies. [RLM]

38.340 Lester D. Langley. *The banana wars: an inner history of American empires, 1900–1934.* Lexington: University Press of Kentucky, 1983. ISBN 0-8131-1496-9. ▸ Scholarly account of United States interventions in Caribbean, Central America, and Mexico. Based on extensive research in military and diplomatic records. [RLM]

38.341 Lester D. Langley. *Struggle for the American Mediterranean: United States–European rivalry in the Gulf-Caribbean, 1776–1904.* Athens: University of Georgia Press, 1976. ISBN 0-8203-0364-X. ▸ Detailed examination of competition between United States and European powers, notably Great Britain, France, and Spain, for trade and influence in nineteenth-century Central America and Caribbean. [RLM]

38.342 Gordon K. Lewis. *The growth of the modern West Indies.* New York: Monthly Review Press, 1968. ▸ Detailed examination of evolution of society and politics in Commonwealth Caribbean, including Belize and Guyana, from 1918 through 1966. Highly critical of both British and American influences. [RLM]

38.343 Gordon K. Lewis. *Main currents in Caribbean thought: the historical evolution of Caribbean society in its ideological aspects, 1492–1900.* Baltimore: Johns Hopkins University Press, 1983. ISBN 0-8018-2589-X (cl), 0-8018-3492-9 (pbk). ▸ Sweeping survey of Caribbean thought from sixteenth through nineteenth centuries. Emphasis on pro- and antislavery ideologies and growth of nationalist ideas. Basic for understanding region's intellectual roots. [RLM]

38.344 John Bartlow Martin. *U.S. policy in the Caribbean.* Boulder: Westview, 1978. ISBN 0-89158-061-1. ▸ Somewhat dated but useful survey of United States relations with greater Caribbean, focusing on 1953–77 period. Includes material on Puerto Rico, black power movement in Caribbean, and Central America. [RLM]

38.345 Manuel Moreno Fraginals, Frank Moya Pons, and Stanley L. Engerman, eds. *Between slavery and free labor: the Spanish-speaking Caribbean in the nineteenth century.* Baltimore: Johns Hopkins University Press, 1985. ISBN 0-8018-3224-1. ▸ Despite problems of coherence and overlap, valuable effort to study slavery and postslave societies. Focus on Cuba and Dominican Republic with limited attention to Puerto Rico and Haiti. [RLM]

38.346 Dana Gardner Munro. *Intervention and dollar diplomacy in the Caribbean, 1900–1921.* 1964 ed. Westport, Conn.: Greenwood, 1980. ISBN 0-313-22510-9. ▸ Excellent study of Central America and Latin Caribbean combining extensive research with author's experiences as United States diplomat. Argues security rather than economic interests determined United States policy. [RLM]

38.347 Dana Gardner Munro. *The United States and the Caribbean republics, 1921–1933.* Princeton: Princeton University Press, 1974. ISBN 0-691-04623-9. ▸ Useful survey of United States policy toward Central America and Caribbean by historian who held key diplomatic posts in region during period. [RLM]

38.348 J. H. Parry, P. M. Sherlock, and A. P. Maingot. *A short history of the West Indies.* 4th ed. New York: St. Martin's, 1987. ISBN 0-312-00442-7 (cl), 0-312-00443-5 (pbk). ▸ Standard history of region, strongest on Commonwealth Caribbean. Coverage of twentieth century and treatment of modern society greatly strengthened by addition of Anthony Maingot as third co-author. Still best introduction to region's history. [RLM/MAB]

38.349 Eric Williams. *From Columbus to Castro: the history of the Caribbean.* 1970 ed. New York: Vintage, 1984. ISBN 0-394-71502-0 (pbk). ▸ Pioneering regional history by first prime minister of Trinidad and Tobago, emphasizing heritage of slavery and foreign exploitation of region. [RLM]

SEE ALSO
48.494 Lester D. Langley. *The United States and the Caribbean in the twentieth century.*

Cuba

38.350 Jules Robert Benjamin. *The United States and Cuba: hegemony and dependent development, 1880–1934.* Pittsburgh: University of Pittsburgh Press, 1977. ISBN 0-8229-3347-0. ▸ Provocative study of United States domination of Cuban elites through 1930s. Stresses intellectual, psychological, and economic factors. Primary focus on ouster of dictator Gerardo Machado and rise of dictator Fulgencio Batista. [RLM]

38.351 Jules Robert Benjamin. *The United States and the origins of the Cuban Revolution: an empire of liberty in an age of national liberation.* Princeton: Princeton University Press, 1990. ISBN 0-691-07836-X. ▸ History of Cuban-American relations. Focus on social, economic, and cultural ties, emphasizing how such relations helped shape Cuba's history. Important addition to traditional policy-oriented studies. [RLM]

38.352 Ramón L. Bonachea and Marta San Martín. *The Cuban insurrection, 1952–1959.* New Brunswick, N.J.: Transaction, 1974. ISBN 0-87855-074-7 (cl), 0-87855-576-5 (pbk). ▸ Provocative survey of movements involved in overthrow of Cuban dictator Fulgencio Batista. Emphasizes importance of groups and forces other than those directly controlled by Fidel Castro. [RLM]

38.353 Jorge I. Domínguez. *To make a world safe for revolution: Cuba's foreign policy.* Cambridge, Mass.: Harvard University Press, 1989. ISBN 0-674-89325-5. ▸ Workmanlike survey of

Cuba's foreign policy under Castro; balanced, dispassionate account. Organized geographically. [RLM]

38.354 Richard R. Fagen. *The transformation of political culture in Cuba.* Stanford, Calif.: Stanford University Press, 1969. ISBN 0-8047-0702-2. ‣ In-depth, systematic analysis of mass mobilization programs of Cuban revolutionary regime. Focuses on campaign to eliminate illiteracy. Balanced, well written, informative. [RJW]

38.355 John M. Kirk. *José Martí: mentor of the Cuban nation.* Tampa: University Presses of Florida, 1983. ISBN 0-8130-0736-4 (cl), 0-8130-0812-3 (pbk). ‣ More than simple narrative of life of Cuban revolutionary and intellectual leader, focuses on sources, nature, and impact of Martí's ideas. Includes valuable chronology and good survey of previous studies. [RLM]

38.356 Franklin W. Knight. *Slave society in Cuba during the nineteenth century.* Madison: University of Wisconsin Press, 1970. ISBN 0-299-05790-9 (cl), 0-299-05794-1 (pbk). ‣ Classic study of slavery in late colonial Cuba and pressures leading to emancipation. Basic reading for understanding Cuban social history. [RLM]

38.357 Louis A. Pérez, Jr. *Army politics in Cuba, 1898–1958.* Pittsburgh: University of Pittsburgh Press, 1976. ISBN 0-8229-3303-9. ‣ Groundbreaking study of development and ultimate destruction of Cuban army. Emphasizes military's involvement in and corruption by Cuban politics and negative effects of United States involvement. [RLM]

38.358 Louis A. Pérez, Jr. *Cuba between empires: 1878–1902.* Pittsburgh: University of Pittsburgh Press, 1983. ISBN 0-8229-3472-8. ‣ Excellent, well-researched study of vital period in Cuban history, emphasizing prolonged struggle for independence and impact of transition from Spanish rule to independence under American domination. [RLM]

38.359 Louis A. Pérez, Jr. *Cuba: between reform and revolution.* New York: Oxford University Press, 1988. ISBN 0-19-504587-4 (cl), 0-19-504586-6 (pbk). ‣ Ambitious synthesis of Cuban history, focusing on how faulty political structures and external domination hampered efforts to develop national identity and resolve internal conflicts. Excellent bibliography. [RLM]

38.360 Louis A. Pérez, Jr. *Cuba under the Platt amendment, 1902–1934.* Pittsburgh: University of Pittsburgh Press, 1986. ISBN 0-8229-3533-3. ‣ Critical study of formative years of Cuban nationhood, stressing growing domination of United States and persistent corruption and instability in internal politics. [RLM]

38.361 Rosalie Schwartz. *Lawless liberators: political banditry and Cuban independence.* Durham, N.C.: Duke University Press, 1989. ISBN 0-8223-0882-7. ‣ Provocative study of internal conflicts preceding independence. Insights into historical roots of rural violence in Cuba. [RLM]

38.362 Rebecca J. Scott. *Slave emancipation in Cuba: the transition to free labor, 1860–1899.* Princeton: Princeton University Press, 1985. ISBN 0-691-07667-7 (cl), 0-691-10157-4 (pbk). ‣ Revisionist study of emancipation in Cuba, stressing regional differences and economic factors. Relates frustrations of postemancipation period to subsequent African-Cuban support for independence. [RLM]

38.363 Jaime Suchlicki. *Cuba, from Columbus to Castro.* 3d ed. Washington, D.C.: Brassey's, 1990. ISBN 0-08-037450-6. ‣ General history of Cuba, emphasizing period since independence. Critical of both United States policies and government of Fidel Castro. [RLM]

38.364 Tad Szulc. *Fidel: a critical portrait.* New York: Morrow, 1986. ISBN 0-688-04645-2. ‣ Lengthy, critical, but sympathetic biography of Cuban leader by veteran *New York Times* reporter

who covered Cuba for decades. Based on extensive interviews with Castro and those who knew him. [RLM]

38.365 Hugh Thomas. *Cuba: the pursuit of freedom.* New York: Harper & Row, 1971. ISBN 0-06-014259-6. ‣ Massive history of Cuba, emphasizing twentieth century; critical both of Castro's revolution and United States involvements with that nation. [RLM]

38.366 Maurice Zeitlin. *Revolutionary politics and the Cuban working class.* 1967 ed. New York: Harper & Row, 1970. ‣ Good sociological study of effects of Castro revolution on Cuba's industrial workers, based on interviews and survey data. Presents favorable view of regime. [RJW]

Dominican Republic

38.367 G. Pope Atkins. *Arms and politics in the Dominican Republic.* Boulder: Westview, 1981. ISBN 0-86531-112-9. ‣ Critical account of Dominican Republic's armed forces and their ties to United States, focusing on post-1965 period. Characterizes military as "collection of personal fiefdoms," rather than cohesive institution. [RLM]

38.368 G. Pope Atkins and Larman C. Wilson. *The United States and the Trujillo regime.* New Brunswick, N.J.: Rutgers University Press, 1972. ISBN 0-8135-0714-6. ‣ Heavily documented account of United States relations with longtime dictator of Dominican Republic. At times tedious but still best available account of this prolonged, tangled relationship. [RLM]

38.369 Bruce J. Calder. *The impact of intervention: the Dominican Republic during the U.S. occupation of 1916–1924.* Austin: University of Texas Press, 1984. ISBN 0-292-73830-7. ‣ Best available scholarly study of United States occupation of Dominican Republic. Emphasizes resistance to military government and failure of United States efforts to transform Dominican society and politics. [RLM]

38.370 Robert D. Crassweller. *Trujillo: the life and times of a Caribbean dictator.* New York: Macmillan, 1966. ‣ Highly readable biography of Dominican Republic's long-time dictator. Flawed and somewhat dated but still best overall account of Trujillo's bloody career. [RLM]

38.371 Piero Gleijeses. *The Dominican crisis: the 1965 constitutionalist revolt and American intervention.* Lawrence Lipson, trans. Baltimore: Johns Hopkins University Press, 1978. ISBN 0-8018-2025-1. ‣ Inconsistent but generally successful effort to put events of 1965 into historical perspective. Based on extensive research and numerous interviews. Best available overall account. [RLM]

38.372 H. Hoetink. *The Dominican people, 1850–1900: notes for a historical sociology.* Stephen K. Ault, trans. Baltimore: Johns Hopkins University Press, 1982. ISBN 0-8018-2223-8. ‣ Indispensable guide to understanding formation of modern Dominican social institutions by leading Dutch scholar. [RLM]

38.373 Michael J. Kryzanek and Howard J. Wiarda. *The politics of external influence in the Dominican Republic.* New York: Praeger, 1988. ISBN 0-275-92992-2. ‣ Emphasis on foreign influences, but contains much of value on internal Dominican history, especially during 1970s and 1980s. Sound data; sometimes questionable analysis. [RJW]

English-Speaking Caribbean

38.374 Hilary McD. Beckles. *A history of Barbados: from Amerindian settlement to nation state.* New York: Cambridge University Press, 1990. ISBN 0-521-35374-2 (cl), 0-521-35879-5 (pbk). ‣ Recent survey of history of Barbados. Helps explain relative prosperity and long-standing democratic traditions of island republic. [RLM]

38.375 Ken I. Boodhoo. *Eric Williams: the man and the leader.* Lanham, Md.: University Press of America, 1986. ISBN 0-8191-5103-3 (cl), 0-8191-5104-1 (pbk). ▸ Pioneering biography of politician and scholar who dominated Trinidad and Tobago from 1956 until his death in 1981. Efforts at probing Williams's psyche sometimes questionable, but book still quite useful. [RLM]

38.376 Bridget Brereton. *A history of modern Trinidad, 1783–1962.* Exeter, N.H.: Heinemann, 1981. ISBN 0-435-98116-1 (pbk). ▸ Best available history of Trinidad and Tobago under British rule. Especially useful for World War II period and movement for independence. [RLM]

38.377 Samuel J. Hurwitz and Edith F. Hurwitz. *Jamaica: a historical portrait.* New York: Praeger, 1971. ▸ Increasingly dated but still best available general history of Jamaica. [RLM]

38.378 Darrell E. Levi. *Michael Manley: the making of a leader.* 1989 ed. Athens: University of Georgia Press, 1990. ISBN 0-8203-1221-5. ▸ Examination of career of dominant individual in recent Jamaican history and course of politics since independence. Study often controversial like its subject. [RLM]

Haiti

38.379 Patrick Bellegarde-Smith. *Haiti: the breached citadel.* Boulder: Westview, 1990. ISBN 0-8133-7172-4. ▸ Historical summary by distinguished Haitian scholar. Includes sections on women and society, vodun cosmology, and Haitian social thought and literature. Excellent introduction to Haiti's tragic history. [RLM]

38.380 C.L.R. James. *The black Jacobins: Toussaint L'Ouverture and the San Domingo Revolution.* 1963 2d ed. New York: Vintage, 1989. ISBN 0-679-72467-2 (pbk). ▸ Brilliant, emotional account of Haitian struggle for independence, emphasizing economic factors and role of Toussaint L'Ouverture. First edition, 1938. [RLM]

38.381 David Nicholls. *From Dessalines to Duvalier: race, colour, and national independence in Haiti.* Cambridge: Cambridge University Press, 1979. ISBN 0-521-22177-3. ▸ Sweeping general history of Haiti emphasizing roles of race and class. Somewhat dated but still very useful. [RLM]

38.382 Brenda Gayle Plummer. *Haiti and the great powers, 1902–1915.* Baton Rouge: Louisiana State University Press, 1988. ISBN 0-8071-1409-X. ▸ Controversial study of international rivalry over Haiti, leading up to 1915 United States occupation. Stresses how Haitian elite tried to influence foreign powers to their own advantage. [RLM]

38.383 Hans Schmidt. *The United States occupation of Haiti, 1915–1934.* New Brunswick, N.J.: Rutgers University Press, 1971. ISBN 0-8135-24-0690-5. ▸ Best available account of prolonged United States occupation of Haiti. Based largely on United States sources and highly critical of American policies. [RLM]

38.384 Michel-Rolph Trouillot. *Haiti: state against nation, the origins and legacy of Duvalierism.* New York: Monthly Review Press, 1990. ISBN 0-85345-755-7 (cl), 0-85345-756-5 (pbk). ▸ Marxist-oriented effort to place Duvalier dictatorship in context of Haitian history, emphasizing class conflict and foreign exploitation. [RLM]

Puerto Rico

38.385 Raymond Carr. *Puerto Rico: a colonial experiment.* New York: New York University Press and Vintage, 1984. ISBN 0-8147-1389-0 (cl), 0-394-72431-3 (pbk). ▸ Best available history of American rule in Puerto Rico, written by leading British scholar. Critical of many practices and consequences of United States policies. [RLM]

38.386 Gordon K. Lewis. *Puerto Rico: freedom and power in the Caribbean.* New York: Monthly Review Press, 1963. ▸ Classic study of Puerto Rican history and society under United States control. Advocates independence and socialism as remedies for island's problems. Biased and somewhat dated but still insightful, informative, and frequently provocative. [RLM]

38.387 Arturo Morales Carrión, ed. *Puerto Rico: a political and cultural history.* New York and Nashville: Norton and American Association for State & Local History, 1983. ISBN 0-393-01740-0. ▸ Best general history of Puerto Rico from Spanish settlement to 1980. Experiences as former deputy assistant secretary of state influence analysis, but bias limited and book very valuable. [RLM]

ANDEAN REPUBLICS

Bolivia

38.388 James Dunkerley. *Rebellion in the veins: political struggle in Bolivia, 1952–82.* London: Verso, 1984. ISBN 0-86091-089-X (cl), 0-86091-794-0 (pbk). ▸ Chronological and narrative approach to Bolivian Revolution and its political and social ramifications. Well written and accessible. [EDL]

38.389 J. Valerie Fifer. *Bolivia: land, location, and politics since 1825.* Cambridge: Cambridge University Press, 1973. ISBN 0-521-07829-6. ▸ Detailed examination of problems of integrating Bolivia since independence. Especially good on border disputes; how country lost half its territory since independence. [EDL]

38.390 Luis J. González and Gustavo A. Sánchez Salazar. *The great rebel: Che Guevara in Bolivia.* Helen R. Lane, trans. New York: Grove, 1969. ▸ Objective journalistic account of Che Guevara's attempt at guerrilla warfare in Bolivia, based on extensive interviews of participants on both sides. [EDL]

38.391 Erwin P. Grieshaber. "Survival of Indian communities in nineteenth-century Bolivia: a regional comparison." *Journal of Latin American studies* 12.2 (1980) 223–69. ISSN 0022-216X. ▸ Discussion of persistence of Indian communities in Bolivia; exhaustive use of tribute records. Shows regional differences important, with northern communities faring better than southern. [EDL]

38.392 Herbert S. Klein. *Bolivia: the evolution of a multi-ethnic society.* 2d ed. New York: Oxford University Press, 1992. ISBN 0-19-505734-1 (cl), 0-19-505735-X (pbk). ▸ Best history of Bolivia, prehistory to 1990. Incorporates social and economic history in largely political narrative. Excellent bibliographic essay. [EDL]

38.393 Herbert S. Klein. *Parties and political change in Bolivia, 1880–1952.* 1969 ed. Cambridge: Cambridge University Press, 1971. ISBN 0-521-07614-5. ▸ Best political narrative of seventy years before outbreak of 1952 Revolution. Shows how Chaco War (1932–35) brought middle sectors and other lower-class groups into Bolivian politics. [EDL]

38.394 Erick D. Langer. *Economic change and rural resistance in southern Bolivia, 1880–1930.* Stanford, Calif.: Stanford University Press, 1989. ISBN 0-8047-1491-6. ▸ Important, pioneering discussion of consolidation of land by elite and worsening of labor conditions in Chuquisaca province as result of decline of silver mining. Analysis of resulting Indian rebellions, rural labor strikes, banditry, and their migration to Argentina. [EDL]

38.395 William Lee Lofstrom. "The promise and problems of reform: attempted social and economic change in the first years of Bolivian independence." Ph.D. dissertation. Ithaca, N.Y.: Cornell University Press, 1972. ▸ Careful study showing how Antonio José Sucre's administration (1825–27) dramatically changed Bolivia's institutions, bringing Catholic church under state control and reforming tribute and educational systems. Also available on microfilm from Ann Arbor: University Microfilms International. [EDL]

38.396 Guillermo Lora. *A history of the Bolivian labour movement, 1848–1971.* Laurence Whitehead, ed. Christine Whitehead, trans. Cambridge: Cambridge University Press, 1977. ISBN 0-521-21400-9. ▸ Most complete history of labor movement in Bolivia from Trotskyist viewpoint. [EDL]

38.397 James M. Malloy. *Bolivia: the uncompleted revolution.* Pittsburgh: University of Pittsburgh Press, 1970. ISBN 0-8229-3203-2. ▸ Best political narrative in English of Bolivian Revolution of 1952 and its aftermath to 1960. [EDL]

38.398 James M. Malloy and Richard S. Thorn, eds. *Beyond the revolution: Bolivia since 1952.* Pittsburgh: University of Pittsburgh Press, 1971. ISBN 0-87223-220-2. ▸ Series of essays examining effects of Bolivian Revolution of 1952 in public finance, agrarian reform, labor, and mining. Good introduction to effects of revolution. [EDL]

38.399 George McCutchen McBride. *The agrarian Indian communities of highland Bolivia.* New York: Oxford University Press, 1921. (American Geographical Society research series, 5.) ▸ Classic analysis of survival of Indian communities in Bolivia, based on Indian tribute records. Shows communities diminished by two-thirds by early twentieth century. Available on microfilm from Sunnyvale, Calif.: Bay Microfilm, 1992. [EDL]

38.400 Thomas Millington. *Debt politics after independence: the funding conflict in Bolivia.* Gainesville: University Presses of Florida, 1992. ISBN 0-8130-1140-X. ▸ Traces origins of Bolivian foreign debt since independence to lack of funding of country's internal debt, producing deficits that required foreign loans. Concise treatment adding to growing historiography on important subject. [EDL]

38.401 Christopher Mitchell. *The legacy of populism in Bolivia: from the MNR to military rule.* New York: Praeger, 1977. ISBN 0-03-039671-9. ▸ Critical account of Bolivian Revolution of 1952, showing how middle-class leadership of national revolutionary movement (MNR) was ineffective. Traces failure of true social revolution to multiclass nature of movement. [EDL]

38.402 Antonio Mitre. *Los patriarcas de la plata: estructura socioeconómica de la minería boliviana en el siglo XIX.* Lima: Instituto de Estudios Peruanos, 1981. ▸ Only historical analysis of silver-mining industry in Bolivia during nineteenth century, based largely on records of Huanchaca Company. [EDL]

38.403 Tristan Platt. *Estado boliviano y ayllu andino: tierra y tributo en el norte de Potosí.* Lima: Instituto de Estudios Peruanos, 1982. (Historia andina, 9.) ▸ Seminal work showing how relations between Indian communities and Bolivian state rested on implicit pact of reciprocity. Shows parallels between late nineteenth-century efforts and policies of 1952 Revolution. [EDL]

38.404 James W. Wilkie. *The Bolivian Revolution and U.S. aid since 1952: financial background and context of political decisions.* Los Angeles: University of California, UCLA Latin American Center Publications, 1969. (Latin American studies, 13.) ▸ Superb, imaginative use of social and economic statistics to show how United States aid distorted Bolivian Revolution of 1952, leading to revival of military and militarism. [EDL]

38.405 David H. Zook, Jr. *The conduct of the Chaco War.* New York: Bookman, 1961. ▸ Best diplomatic and military account of Chaco War in English from both Bolivian and Paraguayan perspectives. [EDL]

Colombia

38.406 Charles W. Bergquist. *Coffee and conflict in Colombia, 1886–1910.* Durham, N.C.: Duke University Press, 1978. ISBN 0-8223-0418-X. ▸ Provocative, important reinterpretation of causes of War of a Thousand Days (1899–1902) as manifestation of struggle between export-import interests and traditional agriculturalists. [EDL]

38.407 Charles W. Bergquist, Ricardo Peñaranda, and Gonzalo Sánchez, eds. *Violence in Colombia: the contemporary crisis in historical perspective.* Wilmington, Del.: Scholarly Resources, 1992. ISBN 0-8420-2369-0 (cl), 0-8420-2376-3 (pbk). ▸ Excellent collection on roots of violence in Colombia, which go back to political and social conflicts of nineteenth century. [EDL]

38.408 Herbert Braun. *The assassination of Gaitán: public life and urban violence in Colombia.* Madison: University of Wisconsin Press, 1985. ISBN 0-299-10360-9. ▸ Excellent study; uses death of prominent politician Gaitán to show how elite consensus in Colombia between 1930 and 1950 broke down, leading to civil war called La Violencia. [EDL]

38.409 David Bushnell. *The Santander regime in Gran Columbia.* 1954 ed. Westport, Conn.: Greenwood, 1970. ISBN 0-8371-2981-8. ▸ Careful, detailed description of Francisco de Paula Santander's (1821–27) attempts to establish liberal government following independence from Spain. Underscores difficulties of state building in this period. [EDL]

38.410 Malcolm Deas. "The fiscal problems of nineteenth-century Colombia." *Journal of Latin American studies* 14.2 (1982) 287–328. ISSN 0022-216X. ▸ Seminal article exploring political economy of poverty as way to understand Colombian society. [EDL]

38.411 Helen Delpar. *Red against blue: the Liberal party in Colombian politics, 1863–1899.* University: University of Alabama Press, 1981. ISBN 0-8173-0030-9. ▸ Best study in English on Liberal party. Traces party's rise from 1820s to dominant phase (1863–85) and role as opposition party (1886–99). [EDL]

38.412 Robert H. Dix. *Colombia: the political dimensions of change.* New Haven: Yale University Press, 1967. ▸ Good account of political history of Colombia within modernization paradigm. Sees reformism of Liberals in 1934 as modernizing. [EDL]

38.413 James D. Henderson. *Conservative thought in twentieth-century Latin America: the ideas of Laureano Gómez.* Athens: Ohio University, Center for International Studies, Center for Latin American Studies, 1988. ISBN 0-89680-148-9. ▸ Discussion of ideas of Laureano Gómez, president of Colombia (1950–53), and how he rationalized his corporative and elitist government to himself. [EDL]

38.414 James D. Henderson. *When Colombia bled: a history of the Violencia in Tolima.* University: University of Alabama Press, 1985. ISBN 0-8173-0212-3. ▸ Detailed analysis of La Violencia (civil war) in key department of Colombia. One of best studies on armed conflict between liberal and conservative forces (1948–65). [EDL]

38.415 Michael Francis Jiménez. "Traveling far in grandfather's car: the life cycle of central Colombian coffee estates: the case of Viotá, Cundinamarca (1900–30)." *Hispanic American historical review* 69.2 (1989) 185–219. ISSN 0018-2168. ▸ Important study showing modern capitalist features of coffee plantations in Colombia despite what might appear to be traditional feudal characteristics. [EDL]

38.416 Catherine LeGrand. *Frontier expansion and peasant protest in Colombia, 1850–1936.* Albuquerque: University of New Mexico Press, 1986. ISBN 0-8263-0851-1. ▸ Examination of process of frontier expansion in Colombia with special emphasis on squatters. Contrasts written law on state lands with consolidation of these lands by large landowners. [EDL]

38.417 William Paul McGreevey. *An economic history of Colombia, 1845–1930.* Cambridge: Cambridge University Press, 1971. ISBN 0-521-07909-8. ▸ Provocative economic history of Colombia. Contrasts tobacco cultivation on large estates to Antioqueño coffee smallholders, whose prosperity created industrialization through demand for nonluxury goods. [EDL]

38.418 Kenneth N. Medhurst. *The church and labour in Colombia.* Manchester: Manchester University Press, 1984. ISBN 0-7190-0969-3. ▸ Concentrates on Unión de Trabajadores Colombianos, Jesuit-founded labor federation, from mid-1940s to 1970s. Shows Catholic church's potential for change and its limitations. [EDL]

38.419 Paul Oquist. *Violence, conflict, and politics in Colombia.* New York: Academic Press, 1980. ISBN 0-12-527750-4. ▸ Basic for understanding twentieth-century Colombia. Traces causes of La Violencia (1948–65) to breakdown in state. [EDL]

38.420 Marco Palacios. *Coffee in Colombia, 1850–1970: an economic, social, and political history.* Cambridge: Cambridge University Press, 1980. ISBN 0-521-22204-4. ▸ Excellent study, showing on what terms Colombia entered world coffee economy. Dispels myth of egalitarian frontier. [EDL]

38.421 James William Park. *Rafael Núñez and the politics of Colombian regionalism, 1863–1886.* Baton Rouge: Louisiana State University Press, 1985. ISBN 0-8071-1235-6. ▸ Well-researched discussion of rise and disintegration of Liberal party in nineteenth century, using career of Núñez, Colombia's president (1880–94). [EDL]

38.422 James J. Parsons. *Antioquia's corridor to the sea: an historical geography of the settlement of Uraba.* Berkeley: University of California Press, 1967. ▸ Important exercise in historical geography showing how pioneer region of Colombia was settled through spontaneous migration. [EDL]

38.423 Stephen J. Randall. *Colombia and the United States: hegemony and interdependence.* Athens: University of Georgia Press, 1992. ISBN 0-8203-1402-1 (cl) 0-8203-1401-3 (pbk). ▸ Most recent contribution to Colombian–United States relations, including effect of drug wars. [EDL]

38.424 Frank Safford. *The ideal of the practical: Colombia's struggle to form a technical elite.* Austin: University of Texas Press for Institute of Latin American Studies, 1976. (Latin American monographs, 39.) ISBN 0-292-73803-X. ▸ Seminal study, showing how economic and political conditions not conducive to development of technical elite. Politics much more lucrative endeavor; scientifically inclined found energies absorbed in politics. [EDL]

38.425 Frank Safford. "Social aspects of politics in nineteenth-century Spanish America: New Granada, 1825–1850." *Journal of social history* 5.3 (1972) 344–70. ISSN 0022-4529. ▸ Argues regional divisions, family origins, and experiences such as education and war affected party alignments. Brings new understanding to nineteenth-century Spanish American politics. [EDL]

38.426 Richard E. Sharpless. *Gaitán of Colombia: a political biography.* Pittsburgh: University of Pittsburgh Press, 1978. ISBN 0-8229-3354-3. ▸ One of best biographies on maverick liberal politician whose assassination in 1948 sparked civil war (La Violencia). Gaitán used dislocations of modernization to mobilize urban proletariat. [EDL]

38.427 T. Lynn Smith. *Colombia: social structure and the process of development.* Gainesville: University Presses of Florida, 1967. ▸ Useful compendium and analysis on changes in land tenure and rural society in Colombia, especially for twentieth century. [EDL]

38.428 David Sowell. *The early Colombian labor movement: artisans and politics in Bogotá, Colombia, 1832–1919.* Philadelphia: Temple University Press, 1992. ISBN 0-87722-965-1. ▸ Examination of artisan political behavior for long nineteenth century, showing how they played off different partisan interests to protect

own interests. Well-researched treatment of previously neglected subject. [EDL]

38.429 Miguel Urrutia. *The development of the Colombian labor movement.* New Haven: Yale University Press, 1969. ▸ Good overview of Colombian labor movement since independence. Shows how movement gained force with accession of Liberals to power in 1930s. [EDL]

38.430 Leon Zamosc. *The agrarian question and the peasant movement in Colombia: struggles of the National Peasant Association, 1967–1981.* Cambridge and Geneva: Cambridge University Press and United Nations Research Institute for Social Development, 1986. ISBN 0-521-32010-0. ▸ Stimulating analysis, within Marxist framework, of rise of National Association of Peasant Users from state-controlled to revolutionary organization. Explains regional basis for organization and its quick demise in 1970s. [EDL]

Ecuador

38.431 Catherine M. Conaghan. *Restructuring domination: industrialists and the state in Ecuador.* Pittsburgh: University of Pittsburgh Press, 1988. ISBN 0-8229-3826-X. ▸ Excellent study of conditions contributing to reformist policies in Ecuador during 1970s and 1980s. Focus on participation of industrialist class. [EDL]

38.432 John Samuel Fitch. *The military coup d'état as a political process: Ecuador, 1948–1966.* Baltimore: Johns Hopkins University Press, 1977. ISBN 0-8018-1915-6. ▸ Analysis of civil-military relations in context of successful and abortive coups. Uses extensive interviews with former military officers. [EDL]

38.433 Osvaldo Hurtado. *Political power in Ecuador.* 1980 ed. Nick D. Mills, Jr., ed. and trans. Boulder: Westview, 1985. ISBN 0-8133-0264-1 (pbk). ▸ Study of oligarchy and *hacienda* (plantation system) as predominant forces shaping Ecuador domestically and internationally. Excellent for nonspecialists. [EDL]

38.434 John D. Martz. *The military in Ecuador: policies and politics of authoritarian rule.* Albuquerque: University of New Mexico, Latin American Institute, 1988. (Occasional paper series, 3.) ▸ Insightful political study of military government, 1972–88. [EDL]

38.435 John D. Martz. *Politics and petroleum in Ecuador.* New Brunswick, N.J.: Transaction, 1987. ISBN 0-88738-132-4. ▸ Fine analysis of events of petroleum era, both boom and bust. [EDL]

38.436 Enrique Ayala Mora, ed. *Nueva historia del Ecuador.* 11 vols. Quito: Corporación Editora Nacional and Editorial Grijalbo Ecuatoriana, 1988–91. ISBN 9978-84-001-X (set), 9978-84-002-8 (v. 1), 9978-84-004-4 (v. 2), 9978-84-005-2 (v. 3), 9978-84-006-0 (v. 4), 9978-84-007-9 (v. 5), 9978-84-008-7 (v. 6), 9978-84-009-5 (v. 7), 9978-84-010-9 (v. 8), 9978-84-003-6 (v. 9), 9978-84-011-7 (v. 10), 9978-84-012-5 (v. 11). ▸ Collection of essays of varying quality, concentrating on politics. Valuable history of Ecuador. [EDL]

38.437 Fredrick B. Pike. *The United States and the Andean republics: Peru, Bolivia, and Ecuador.* Cambridge, Mass.: Harvard University Press, 1977. ISBN 0-674-92300-6. ▸ Excellent study of both foreign relations and internal histories of Andean republics. [EDL]

38.438 M. R. Redclift. *Agrarian reform and peasant organisation on the Ecuadorian coast.* London: Athlone, 1978. (University of London, Institute of Latin American Studies monographs, 8.) ISBN 0-485-17708-0, ISSN 0076-0486. ▸ Sound case study providing valuable overview of agrarian development in Ecuador. [EDL]

38.439 Linda Alexander Rodríguez. *The search for public policy: regional politics and government finances in Ecuador, 1830–1940.*

Berkeley: University of California Press, 1985. ISBN 0-520-05150-5. ▸ Seminal study of public policy toward government finances in Ecuador during first 110 years of nationhood. [EDL]

38.440 David W. Schodt. *Ecuador: an Andean enigma.* Boulder: Westview, 1987. ISBN 0-8133-0230-7. ▸ Good synthetic treatment of Ecuador. Up to date and competent. [EDL]

38.441 Frank MacDonald Spindler. *Nineteenth-century Ecuador: a historical introduction.* Fairfax, Va.: University Publishing Associates for George Mason University Press, 1987. ISBN 0-8026-0015-8. ▸ Detailed political history supported by primary and secondary sources. Somewhat narrowly conceived. [EDL]

38.442 Mark J. Van Aken. *King of the night: Juan José Flores and Ecuador, 1824–1864.* Berkeley: University of California Press, 1989. ISBN 0-520-06277-9 (pbk). ▸ Carefully researched and well-written biography addressing issue of Latin American monarchism, using wide variety of sources. [EDL]

38.443 Jacques M. P. Wilson. *The development of education in Ecuador.* Coral Gables, Fla.: University of Miami Press, 1970. ISBN 0-87024-164-8. ▸ Case study of Ecuadorian education system as model of educational problems and issues in underdevelopment. [EDL]

38.444 David H. Zook, Jr. *Zarumilla-Marañon: the Ecuador-Peru dispute.* New York: Bookman, 1964. ▸ Details of history of most important border dispute in Ecuadorian history. Confined by lack of access to governmental archives. [EDL]

Peru

38.445 Carlos A. Astiz. *Pressure groups and power elites in Peruvian politics.* Ithaca, N.Y.: Cornell University Press, 1969. ISBN 0-8014-0538-6. ▸ Astute historical appraisal of why contemporary Peruvian political system has remained essentially the same despite attempts at reform. [EDL]

38.446 Peter Blanchard. *The origins of the Peruvian labor movement, 1883–1919.* Pittsburgh: Pittsburgh University Press, 1982. ISBN 0-8229-3455-8. ▸ Narrative overview of Peruvian working class, divided into four groups: mutual aid societies, anarchists, workers participating in direct action, and rural workers. Finds Peru developed strong worker movement before populism. [EDL]

38.447 Peter Blanchard. *Slavery and abolition in early republican Peru.* Wilmington, Del.: Scholarly Resources, 1992. ISBN 0-8420-2400-X (cl) 0-8420-2429-8 (pbk). ▸ Discussion of social and economic factors that supported slavery in nineteenth-century Peru. Useful follow-up to Bowser 37.218. [EDL]

38.448 François Bourricaud. *Power and society in contemporary Peru.* Paul Stevenson, trans. New York: Praeger, 1970. ▸ Classic analysis of Peruvian political behavior, particularly good on appeal of Alianza Popular Revolucionaria Americana to Peruvian masses. [EDL]

38.449 Manuel Burga and Alberto Flores Galindo. *Apogeo y crisis de la república aristocrática: oligarquia, aprismo y comunismo en el Peru, 1895–1932.* 3d rev. ed. Lima: Ediciones Rikchay Peru, 1984. ▸ Discussion of how oligarchy was unable to formulate national project. Mass-based movements, such as Communists and Apristas, also unable to offer acceptable solutions. [EDL]

38.450 Jesús Chavarría. *José Carlos Mariátegui and the rise of modern Peru, 1890–1930.* Albuquerque: University of New Mexico Press, 1979. ISBN 0-8263-0507-5. ▸ Excellent intellectual history of Peru's most important thinker, placing him within political and intellectual context. [EDL]

38.451 Thomas M. Davies, Jr. *Indian integration in Peru: a half century of experience, 1900–1948.* 1970 ed. Lincoln: University of Nebraska Press, 1974. ISBN 0-8032-0834-0. ▸ Comprehensive survey of legislation on Indians in Peru; especially good on legislative effects of indigenism. [EDL]

38.452 Elizabeth Dore. *The Peruvian mining industry: growth, stagnation, and crisis.* Boulder: Westview, 1988. ISBN 0-8133-7061-2. ▸ Extensive quantitative analysis attacking notion that international prices determined mining production since 1900. Instead, domestic inputs more important in determining output. [EDL]

38.453 C. Harvey Gardiner. *The Japanese and Peru, 1873–1973.* Albuquerque: University of New Mexico Press, 1975. ISBN 0-8263-0391-9. ▸ Good overview of Japanese-Peruvian relations and fate of Japanese laborers who worked on Peruvian coast. [EDL]

38.454 Dennis L. Gilbert. *The oligarchy and the old regime in Peru.* Ithaca, N.Y.: Cornell University Press, 1977. (Cornell University, Latin American Studies Program, dissertation series, 69.) ▸ Focus on three elite Peruvian families to show how Peru moved from oligarchic control at turn of century to indirect rule until 1968. [EDL]

38.455 Michael J. Gonzales. *Plantation agriculture and social control in northern Peru, 1875–1933.* Austin: University of Texas Press for Institute of Latin American Studies, 1985. (Latin American monographs, 62.) ISBN 0-292-76491-X. ▸ Superb analysis of sugar plantation complex on northern Peruvian coast and varying forms of labor employed. [EDL]

38.456 Paul Gootenberg. *Between silver and guano: commercial policy and the state in postindependence Peru.* Princeton: Princeton University Press, 1989. ISBN 0-691-07810-6 (cl), 0-691-02342-5 (pbk). ▸ Argues that most powerful groups within Peruvian elites were mainly protectionist until 1840s. *Caudillo* (authoritarian) form of government promoted protectionism during this period. [EDL]

38.457 Howard Handelman. *Struggle in the Andes: peasant political mobilization in Peru.* Austin: University of Texas Press for Institute of Latin American Studies, 1974. (Latin American monographs, 35.) ISBN 0-292-77513-X. ▸ Best analysis of peasant land invasions in Peru in 1960s. Shows how government coopted politically active Central Highlands but repressed illiterate peasants in South. [EDL]

38.458 Jeffrey L. Klaiber. *Religion and revolution in Peru, 1824–1976.* Notre Dame, Ind.: University of Notre Dame Press, 1977. ISBN 0-268-01599-6. ▸ Effectively argues republican era Catholic church never monolith wedded to conservative policies. Instead, able to channel reformism through popular religiosity throughout its history. [EDL]

38.459 Peter F. Klarén. *Modernization, dislocation, and Aprismo: origins of the Peruvian Aprista Party.* Austin: University of Texas Press for Institute of Latin American Studies, 1973. (Latin American monographs, 32.) ISBN 0-292-76001-9. ▸ Seminal book, locating origins of Aprista party in northern Peruvian valleys, where modernization created proletariat open to revolutionary rhetoric of Victor Raúl Haya de la Torre, founder of APRA. [EDL]

38.460 Florencia E. Mallon. *The defense of community in Peru's central highlands: peasant struggle and capitalist transition, 1860–1940.* Princeton: Princeton University Press, 1983. ISBN 0-691-07647-2 (cl), 0-691-10140-x (pbk). ▸ Examination of Peruvian Central Highlands in Marxist framework. Shows how interaction of highland peasant community and outside world and penetration of foreign capital by 1940s created rural proletariat. [EDL/NDC]

38.461 Rory Miller, ed. *Region and class in modern Peruvian history.* Liverpool: University of Liverpool, Institute of Latin American Studies, 1987. (University of Liverpool, Institute of Latin

American Studies series, 14.) ISBN 0-902806-20-3. ‣ Sampling of some of best British work on Peru, from late colonial period to rise of Sendero Luminoso (Shining Path) guerrilla movement. [EDL]

38.462 David Scott Palmer. *Peru: the authoritarian tradition.* New York: Praeger, 1980. ISBN 0-03-046116-2 (cl), 0-03-046111-1 (pbk). ‣ Political scientist shows how corporatism and authoritarianism relate to Spanish heritage. Good comparisons with other Latin American countries and sensitivity to relations with outside powers. [EDL]

38.463 Fredrick B. Pike. *The modern history of Peru.* New York: Praeger, 1967. ‣ Still one of best syntheses of Peruvian history in English. Especially strong on intellectual and political history. [EDL]

38.464 Fredrick B. Pike. *The politics of the miraculous in Peru: Haya de la Torre and the spiritualist tradition.* Lincoln: University of Nebraska Press, 1986. ISBN 0-8032-3672-7. ‣ Controversial intellectual biography, arguing Haya de la Torre, founder of APRA party, influenced by spiritualism in revolt against Western reason and made movement quasi-religious. [EDL]

38.465 Michael J. Sallnow. *Pilgrims of the Andes: regional cults in Cusco.* Washington, D.C.: Smithsonian Institution Press, 1987. ISBN 0-87474-826-7. ‣ Masterful history of cults in Cusco region, essential for anyone working on folk religious history in Andes. [EDL]

38.466 Steve Stein. *Populism in Peru: the emergence of the masses and the politics of social control.* Madison: University of Wisconsin Press, 1980. ISBN 0-299-07990-2. ‣ Concentrates on 1931 electoral conflict between military officers Luis M. Sánchez Cerro of the Revolutionary Union and APRA's Víctor Raúl Haya de la Torre to show how populism did not promote meaningful social change. [EDL]

38.467 Watt Stewart. *Chinese bondage in Peru: a history of the Chinese coolie in Peru, 1849–1874.* 1951 ed. Westport, Conn.: Greenwood, 1970. ISBN 0-8371-2977-X. ‣ Superb history of Chinese forced laborers in Peru, who worked in Guano islands off coast of Peru and in northern coastal plantations. [EDL]

38.468 Lewis Taylor. *Bandits and politics in Peru: landlord and peasant violence in Hualgayoc, 1900–30.* Cambridge: University of Cambridge, Centre of Latin American Studies, 1987. (Cambridge Latin American miniatures, 2.) ISBN 0-904927-29-6 (pbk), ISSN 0266-7541. ‣ Stimulating and provocative, if brief, analysis of endemic banditry in Cajamarca (northern Peru), taking into account social and political forces that made banditry possible. [EDL]

38.469 Rosemary Thorp and Geoffrey Bertram. *Peru, 1890–1977: growth and policy in an open economy.* New York: Columbia University Press, 1978. ISBN 0-231-03433-4. ‣ Discussion of how Peru's foreign-financed and export-led growth impoverished country over long run, despite sporadic efforts by governments to become economically independent. [EDL]

Venezuela

38.470 Robert Jackson Alexander. *The Communist party of Venezuela.* Stanford, Calif.: Hoover Institution Press, 1969. ‣ History of Communist party of Venezuela through its structure and organization, local political environment, and relations with other communist parties. Important addition to literature, but lacks analysis of recent political events. [EDL]

38.471 Robert Jackson Alexander. *Rómulo Betancourt and the transformation of Venezuela.* New Brunswick, N.J.: Transaction, 1982. ISBN 0-87855-450-5. ‣ Biography of most important democratic reformer in twentieth-century Venezuela. Detailed narrative history of Venezuelan politics. [EDL]

38.472 Robert D. Bond, ed. *Contemporary Venezuela and its role in international affairs.* New York: New York University Press, 1977. ISBN 0-8147-0991-5 (cl), 0-8147-0992-3 (pbk). ‣ Essays of uneven quality by six specialists on Venezuela's domestic political development, economic and social future, and role in world politics. [EDL]

38.473 Winfield J. Burggraaff. *The Venezuelan armed forces in politics, 1935–1959.* Columbia: University of Missouri Press, 1972. ISBN 0-8262-0121-0. ‣ Survey of Venezuelan military's role. Focuses on professionalism and downplays military's role in politics. [EDL]

38.474 George Edmund Carl. *First among equals: Great Britain and Venezuela, 1810–1910.* Ann Arbor: University Microfilms International for Syracuse University, Department of Geography, 1980. ISBN 0-8357-0574-9 (pbk). ‣ Detailed discussion of Britain's commercial relations with Venezuela during nineteenth century. Shows inequality of relationship but argues Venezuela had few other choices. [EDL]

38.475 Gustavo Coronel. *The nationalization of the Venezuelan oil industry: from technocratic success to political failure.* Lexington, Mass: Lexington Books, 1983. ISBN 0-669-06763-6. ‣ Detailed examination of political intervention in PETROVEN by national government. Personal perspective of detrimental government intervention. [EDL]

38.476 Raymond E. Crist and Edward P. Leahy. *Venezuela: search for a middle ground.* New York: Van Nostrand Reinhold, 1969. ‣ Detailed, expert study of economic, political, and social development. Valuable as introductory text, sometimes overly simplistic. [EDL]

38.477 Steve Ellner. *Venezuela's Movimiento al Socialismo: from guerilla defeat to innovative politics.* Durham, N.C.: Duke University Press, 1988. ISBN 0-8223-0808-8. ‣ Well-researched case study of Venzuela's Movimiento al Socialismo. Useful as study of political parties. [EDL]

38.478 Judith Ewell. *The indictment of a dictator: the extradition and trial of Marcos Pérez Jiménez.* College Station: Texas A&M University Press, 1981. ISBN 0-89096-109-3. ‣ Amply documented account of prolonged trial of former dictator Marcos Pérez Jiménez and the role of President Rómulo Betancourt (1958–63) as upholder of democracy. Well researched and useful. [EDL]

38.479 Judith Ewell. *Venezuela: a century of change.* Stanford, Calif.: Stanford University Press, 1984. ISBN 0-8047-1213-1. ‣ Careful analysis of Venezuela's political, economic, social, and cultural changes from late nineteenth through late twentieth century. Excellent treatment of Venezuela's development. [EDL]

38.480 Robert L. Gilmore. *Caudillism and militarism in Venezuela, 1810–1920.* Athens: Ohio University Press, 1964. ‣ Overview of period of dictatorial rule. Uneven analysis. [EDL]

38.481 Daniel C. Hellinger. *Venezuela: tarnished democracy.* Boulder: Westview, 1991. ISBN 0-8133-0700-7. ‣ Well-written critique of Venezuela's fragile democracy, arguing increased centralization of power. [EDL]

38.482 Donald L. Herman. *Christian democracy in Venezuela.* Chapel Hill: University of North Carolina Press, 1980. ISBN 0-8078-1425-3. ‣ Analysis of Christian Democratic party, its ideology, structure, and performance. Useful political analysis. [EDL]

38.483 Donald L. Herman, ed. *Democracy in Latin America: Colombia and Venezuela.* New York: Praeger, 1988. ISBN 0-275-92478-5. ‣ Useful anthology comparing and contrasting elite accommodation and integration in two political systems. Underscores danger to democratic continuity. [EDL]

38.484 Holger H. Herwig. *Germany's vision of empire in Venezuela, 1871–1914.* Princeton: Princeton University Press, 1986. ISBN 0-691-05483-5. ▸ Excellent case study of European imperialism and its motivations. Extensive use of German archives. [EDL]

38.485 Daniel H. Levine. *Conflict and political change in Venezuela.* Princeton: Princeton University Press, 1973. ISBN 0-691-07547-6. ▸ Interesting explanation of Venezuelan politics in terms of conflict resolution using interviews with party officials. [EDL]

38.486 John V. Lombardi. *The decline and abolition of Negro slavery in Venezuela, 1820–1854.* Westport, Conn.: Greenwood, 1971. ISBN 0-8371-3303-3. ▸ Well-documented history of abolition of slavery in Venezuela. [EDL]

38.487 John V. Lombardi. *Venezuela: the search for order, the dream of progress.* New York: Oxford University Press, 1982. ISBN 0-19-503013-3 (cl), 0-19-503014-1 (pbk). ▸ Readable, general overview of main trends in evolution of Venezuela, using many supporting materials. Selective bibliographic essay. Well-balanced account; best survey available. [EDL/MAB]

38.488 John D. Martz. *Acción Democrática: evolution of a modern political party in Venezuela.* Princeton: Princeton University Press, 1966. ▸ Penetrating study of major political party; but no central argument. [EDL]

38.489 Robert Paul Matthews. *Violencia rural en Venezuela, 1840–1858: antecedentes socioeconómicos de la guerra federal.* Marie Françoise de Petzoldt, trans. Caracas: Monte Avila Editores, 1977. ▸ Valuable work on antecedents of Venezuelan Federal War pitting Federalists against Centralists. [EDL]

38.490 B. S. McBeth. *Juan Vicente Gómez and the oil companies in Venezuela, 1908–1935.* New York: Cambridge University Press, 1983. ISBN 0-521-24717-9. ▸ Survey of oil companies in Venezuela containing best available information on financial relations between companies and Venezuelan government. Excellent treatment of impact of oil industry on Venezuelan economy and society. [EDL]

38.491 John Duncan Powell. *Political mobilization of the Venezuelan peasant.* Cambridge, Mass.: Harvard University Press, 1971. ISBN 0-674-68626-8. ▸ Descriptive, analytical history of peasants in contemporary politics using modernization paradigm. [EDL]

38.492 Stephen G. Rabe. *The road to OPEC: United States relations with Venezuela, 1919–1976.* Austin: University of Texas Press, 1982. ISBN 0-292-76020-5. ▸ Well-written work on historical conditions after World War I that led United States oil interests to Venezuela. [EDL]

38.493 William Roseberry. *Coffee and capitalism in the Venezuelan Andes.* Austin: University of Texas Press for Institute of Latin American Studies, 1983. (Latin American monographs, 59.) ISBN 0-292-71535-8. ▸ Historical-anthropological approach dealing with structures affecting Venezuelan peasant life. Marxist theory stronger than analysis. [EDL]

38.494 Philip B. Taylor, Jr. *The Venezuelan golpe de estado of 1958: the fall of Marco Pérez Jiménez.* Washington, D.C.: Institute for the Comparative Study of Political Systems, 1968. ▸ Descriptive narrative of unconstitutional military seizure of power. Little conceptual framework. [EDL]

38.495 Franklin Tugwell. *The politics of oil in Venezuela.* Stanford, Calif.: Stanford University Press, 1975. ISBN 0-8047-0881-9. ▸ Application of dependency theory to Venezuelan petroleum industry. Argues that as revenues rose, profits slowly shifted to host government. [EDL]

38.496 Winthrop R. Wright. *Café con leche: race, class, and national image in Venezuela.* Austin: University of Texas Press, 1990. ISBN 0-292-71128-x (pbk). ▸ Well-written study of race relations in one of Latin America's most racially mixed countries. [EDL]

Brazil

38.497 Sonia E. Alvárez. *Engendering democracy in Brazil: women's movements in transition politics.* Princeton: Princeton University Press, 1990. ISBN 0-691-07856-4 (cl), 0-691-02325-5 (pbk). ▸ Best available study of women's movements, 1975–85, under military hegemony. Regime's indifference to feminist issues helped movement grow, although partisan conflict fragmented mass-based women's coalitions. [RML]

38.498 George Reid Andrews. *Blacks and whites in São Paulo, Brazil, 1888–1988.* Madison: University of Wisconsin Press, 1991. ISBN 0-299-13100-9 (cl), 0-299-13104 (pbk). ▸ Major, well-documented study of race relations in Brazilian city with more immigrants than any other. Complements Degler 38.523 and Morse 38.568. [RML]

38.499 David P. Appleby. *The music of Brazil.* Austin: University of Texas Press, 1983. ISBN 0-292-75068-4. ▸ Flawed but useful account of Brazil's major composers, ignoring popular vein. [RML]

38.500 Roderick J. Barman. *Brazil: the forging of a nation, 1789–1852.* Stanford, Calif.: Stanford University Press, 1988. ISBN 0-8047-1437-1. ▸ Credits external factors, including American and French revolutions, with making transfer of Portuguese monarchy to Brazil and subsequent independence possible. Admirably detailed. [RML]

38.501 Roger Bastide. *The African religions of Brazil: toward a sociology of the interpenetration of civilizations.* Helen Sebba, trans. Baltimore: Johns Hopkins University Press, 1978. ISBN 0-8018-2056-1 (cl), 0-8018-2130-4 (pbk). ▸ Traces transmission of spiritism from Africa to Brazil via importation of slaves and examines Afro-Brazilian religion as form of resistance. Comprehensive, extensively documented, and well written. [RML]

38.502 José Maria Bello. *A history of modern Brazil, 1889–1964.* James L. Taylor, trans. Rollie E. Poppino, new and concluding chapter. Stanford, Calif.: Stanford University Press, 1966. ▸ Traditional, conservative, narrative history examining political history of Brazil according to periodization of presidential administrations. [RML]

38.503 Leslie Bethell. *The abolition of the Brazilian slave trade: Britain, Brazil, and the slave trade question, 1807–1869.* Cambridge: Cambridge University Press, 1970. ISBN 0-521-07583-1. ▸ Seminal study of slave trade in its broadest context, using extensive documentation found in Britain and Brazil. [RML]

38.504 Dain Borges. *The family in Bahia, Brazil, 1870–1945.* Stanford, Calif.: Stanford University Press, 1992. ISBN 0-8047-1921-7. ▸ Cogent, extremely well-documented study of basic institution in Brazilian society, showing change from patriarchal model to one more conjugal and nuclear. [RML]

38.505 E. Bradford Burns. *Nationalism in Brazil: a historical survey.* New York: Praeger, 1968. ▸ Classic study of Brazilian nationalist ideas, dating from late 1850s and early 1860s, and men who espoused them. [RML]

38.506 E. Bradford Burns. *The unwritten alliance: Rio-Branco and Brazilian-American relations.* New York: Columbia University Press, 1966. ▸ Basic narration of story of Brazil's diplomatic prowess in late nineteenth and early twentieth centuries under leadership of foreign minister, the Baron of Rio-Branco. [RML]

38.507 E. Bradford Burns, ed. *Perspectives on Brazilian history.* New York: Columbia University Press, 1967. ▸ Nine provocative essays translated from works of leading Brazilian historians with excellent bibliographical essay placing their writings in perspective. [RML]

38.508 Catholic Church. Archdiocese of São Paulo. *Torture in Brazil: a report.* Joan Dassin, ed. Jaime Wright, trans. New York: Vintage, 1986. ISBN 0-394-74456-X. ‣ Invaluable translations of documents gathered by lawyers working with Brazilian Catholic church concerning more than 7,000 military trials. Shows torture and brutality routine. [RML]

38.509 Billy Jaynes Chandler. *The bandit king: Lampião of Brazil.* College Station: Texas A&M University Press, 1978. ISBN 0-89096-050-X. ‣ In-depth study rejecting notion that northeastern bandit leader Antonio Silvino Lampião was social bandit; rather, he was outlaw. [RML]

38.510 Ronald H. Chilcote. *The Brazilian Communist party: conflict and integration, 1922–1971.* New York: Oxford University Press, 1974. ISBN 0-19-501707-2. ‣ Clearly presented, straightforward account chronicling party's history and its failure to win mass support. [RML]

38.511 Ronald H. Chilcote. *Power and the ruling classes in Northeast Brazil: Juaeiro and Petrolina in transition.* New York: Cambridge University Press, 1990. ISBN 0-521-37384-0. ‣ Case study based on interviews during two distinct research trips evaluating patterns of power and influence among elites in Juazeiro (Bahia) and Petrolina (Pernambuco), adjacent cities on São Francisco River. Sophisticated analysis. [RML]

38.512 Michael L. Conniff. *Urban politics in Brazil: the rise of populism, 1925–1945.* Pittsburgh: University of Pittsburgh Press, 1981. ISBN 0-8229-3438-8. ‣ Unique case study of mayor of Rio de Janiero, Pedro Ernesto, emphasizing how populist politics mobilized mass support during mid-1930s. Book narrower than title implies. [RML]

38.513 Michael L. Conniff and Frank D. McCann, eds. *Modern Brazil: elites and masses in historical perspective.* Lincoln: University of Nebraska Press, 1989. ISBN 0-8032-3131-8. ‣ Twelve original essays on twentieth-century political and economic elites and their relations with rest of population. Good information on Brazil under military government and emerging democratization. [RML]

38.514 Robert Edgar Conrad. *Children of God's fire: a documentary history of black slavery in Brazil.* Princeton: Princeton University Press, 1983. ISBN 0-691-07658-8 (cl), 0-691-10153-1 (pbk). ‣ Unique selection of documents in translation emphasizing cruelty of system. [RML]

38.515 Robert Edgar Conrad. *The destruction of Brazilian slavery, 1850–1888.* Berkeley: University of California Press, 1973. ISBN 0-520-02139-8 (cl), 0-520-02371-4 (pbk). ‣ Major study claiming merchants and industrialists were not sympathetic to abolition but northeastern planters were. [RML]

38.516 Robert Edgar Conrad. *World of sorrow: the African slave trade to Brazil.* Baton Rouge: Louisiana State University Press, 1986. ISBN 0-8071-1245-3. ‣ Attacks slave trade as inhuman and ruthless. Important, insightful, well-documented study; complements Bethell 38.503. [RML]

38.517 Emilia Viotti da Costa. *The Brazilian empire, myths and histories.* 1985 ed. Chicago: Dorsey, 1988. ISBN 0-256-06239-0 (pbk). ‣ Previously published essays, all revised, discussing key themes ranging from myth of racial democracy to lack of real change after overthrow of monarchy. Revisionist view. [RML]

38.518 João Cruz Costa. *A history of ideas in Brazil.* Suzette Macedo, trans. Berkeley: University of California Press, 1964. ‣ Brief but classic study better titled "A history of elite ideas." Illustrates derivative nature of most Brazilian intellectual movements. [RML]

38.519 Euclydes da Cunha. *Rebellion in the backlands.* 1944 ed. Samuel Putnam, trans. Chicago: University of Chicago Press, 1970. ‣ Masterful translation of classic positivist polemic agonizing over Brazil's mixed-race heritage. See also Levine 38.557. [RML]

38.520 Warren Dean. *Brazil and the struggle for rubber: a study in environmental history.* New York: Cambridge University Press, 1987. ISBN 0-521-33477-2. ‣ Pioneering study offering new and convincing reasons for failure of Amazon rubber boom to last or bring prosperity to region. [RML]

38.521 Warren Dean. *The industrialization of São Paulo, 1880–1945.* Austin: University of Texas Press for Institute of Latin American Studies, 1969. (Latin American monographs, 17.) ISBN 0-292-70004-0. ‣ Well-argued study of how coffee-based agricultural prosperity eventually provided impetus for São Paulo's rapid growth and industrialization. [RML]

38.522 Warren Dean. *Rio Claro: a Brazilian plantation system, 1820–1920.* Stanford, Calif.: Stanford University Press, 1976. ISBN 0-8047-0902-5. ‣ Pioneering study of São Paulo's coffee region, dealing with planter-worker relations, land use, and operation of export system in international economy. [RML]

38.523 Carl N. Degler. *Neither black nor white: slavery and race relations in Brazil and the United States.* 1971 ed. Madison: University of Wisconsin Press, 1986. ISBN 0-299-10914-3 (pbk). ‣ Pulitzer Prize–winning study, comparing slavery in Brazil and United States. Finds that while blacks did not fare as well in Brazil as myth holds, in more recent times mulattos, persons of intermediate coloration, came to hold higher status than blacks. [RML]

38.524 Ralph Della Cava. *Miracle at Joaseiro.* New York: Columbia University Press, 1970. ISBN 0-231-03293-5. ‣ First study using archival materials of popular messianic movement headed by Padre Cícero Romão Baptista. Deftly shows how Cícero thrived by cooperating with and eventually dominating local and state politics. [RML]

38.525 Todd A. Diacon. *Millenarian vision, capitalist reality: Brazil's Contestado Rebellion, 1912–1916.* Durham, N.C.: Duke University Press, 1991. ISBN 0-8223-1157-7 (cl), 0-8223-1167-4 (pbk). ‣ Short study combining material analysis with examination of millenarian ideology to show causes of Contestado. Blames foreign capital, state power, and local bosses for sparking rebellion. [RML]

38.526 John W. F. Dulles. *Anarchists and Communists in Brazil, 1900–1935.* Austin: University of Texas Press, 1973. ISBN 0-292-70302-2. ‣ Detailed narrative study documenting shifting leadership in two movements. Shows how frequently government suppressed them. [RML]

38.527 John W. F. Dulles. *Brazilian communism, 1935–1945: repression during world upheaval.* Austin: University of Texas Press, 1983. ISBN 0-292-70741-X. ‣ Chronicle of brief rise and fall of Brazil's tiny communist movement, that was crushed after failed uprising in November 1935. Seamless narrative based largely on interviews, newspapers, and secondary sources. [RML]

38.528 Marshall C. Eakin. *British enterprise in Brazil: the St. John d'el Rey Mining Company and the Morro Velho Gold Mine, 1830–1930.* Durham, N.C.: Duke University Press, 1989. ISBN 0-8223-0914-9. ‣ Important case study of British enterprise in Brazil. Reveals economic success did not necessarily translate into political influence, although company did act as powerful agent for local social change. [RML]

38.529 Peter L. Eisenberg. *The sugar industry of Pernambuco: modernization without change, 1840–1910.* Berkeley: University of California Press, 1974. ISBN 0-520-01731-5. ‣ Pioneering study arguing free labor was so cheap by 1870s that sugar producers could go along with abolition yet maintain traditional forms of exploitation and social control of work force. [RML]

38.530 Gilberto Ferrez. *Photography in Brazil, 1840–1900*. Stella de Sa Rego, trans. Albuquerque: University of New Mexico Press, 1990. ISBN 0-8263-1211-X. ▸ Handsomely produced photographs by nineteenth-century photographers offering insight into ways photographers and their clients wanted Brazil to appear. [RML]

38.531 Thomas Flory. *Judge and jury in imperial Brazil, 1808–1871: social control and political stability in the new state*. Austin: University of Texas Press for Institute of Latin American Studies, 1981. (Latin American monographs, 53.) ISBN 0-292-74015-8. ▸ Expanded dissertation, showing how appointive judges exerted moderate independence despite being products of elite culture. [RML]

38.532 Peter Flynn. *Brazil: a political analysis*. Boulder: Westview, 1978. ISBN 0-89158-747-0. ▸ Important overview of Brazilian history through military dictatorship of 1970s, emphasizing political, diplomatic, and economic aspects. [RML]

38.533 Maurício A. Font. *Coffee, contention, and change in the making of modern Brazil*. Oxford: Blackwell, 1990. ISBN 1-57786-042-4. ▸ Challenges monistic view of industrialization as misleading. Underlying processes of class differentiation and action prevented planters from gaining tight hold on state institutions. Based on original research into social organization in São Paulo coffee sector. [RML]

38.534 Joe Foweraker. *The struggle for land: a political economy of the pioneer frontier in Brazil from 1930 to the present day*. New York: Cambridge University Press, 1981. ISBN 0-521-23555-3. ▸ Examination of frontier as dependent element in world capitalist order; therefore finds instability and violence to be predictable result of process of accumulation. Marxist analysis with policy implications. [RML]

38.535 John D. French. *The Brazilian workers' ABC: class conflict and alliances in modern São Paulo*. Chapel Hill: University of North Carolina Press, 1992. ISBN 0-8078-2029-6 (cl), 0-8078-4368-7 (pbk). ▸ Revisionist grassroots study of emergence of Brazilian system of politics and labor relations, 1900–53, in industrialized region on outskirts of São Paulo. Challenges prevailing view that has portrayed Brazilian populism as demobilizing experience. [RML]

38.536 Gilberto Freyre. *Order and progress: Brazil from monarchy to republic*. 1970 ed. Rod W. Horton, ed. and trans. Ludwig Lauerhaus, Introduction. Berkeley: University of California Press, 1986. ISBN 0-520-5682-5 (pbk). ▸ Abridged English-language translation of classic and controversial study of abolition and its aftermath. Kinder to landholders and Brazil's landowning elite than most subsequent studies. [RML]

38.537 Winston Fritsch. *External constraints on economic policy in Brazil, 1889–1930*. Pittsburgh: University of Pittsburgh Press, 1988. ISBN 0-8229-1147-7. ▸ Detailed study, contending outside political and economic constraints more influential than any other forces in influencing republican era economic policy. Read with Topik 38.590. [RML]

38.538 Richard Graham. *Britain and the onset of modernization in Brazil, 1850–1914*. 1968 ed. London: Cambridge University Press, 1972. ISBN 0-521-07078-3 (cl), 0-521-09681-2 (pbk). ▸ Pioneering study arguing British investment contributed to spread of coffee culture and therefore to major changes in economy. Provided infrastructure investment, but its hegemony also hindered development. [RML]

38.539 Richard Graham. *Patronage and politics in nineteenth-century Brazil*. Stanford, Calif.: Stanford University Press, 1990. ISBN 0-8047-1593-9. ▸ Richly documented study of patronage at

local and national levels, providing comprehensive overview of how imperial political system worked. [RML]

38.540 Sandra Lauderdale Graham. *House and street: the domestic world of servants and masters in nineteenth-century Rio de Janeiro*. New York: Cambridge University Press, 1988. ISBN 0-521-35484-6. ▸ Valuable study showing how female domestics strove to maintain dignity and independence despite arduous working conditions. [RML]

38.541 David T. Haberly. *Three sad races: racial identity and national consciousness in Brazilian literature*. New York: Cambridge University Press, 1983. ISBN 0-521-24722-5. ▸ Examines six writers from nineteenth and early twentieth century, including mulattos Lima Barreto and Machado de Assis, in light of their views and prejudices on race. Important for cultural history. [RML]

38.542 June E. Hahner. *Civilian-military relations in Brazil, 1889–1898*. Columbia: University of South Carolina Press, 1969. ISBN 0-87249-146-3. ▸ Detailed political analysis of first decade following overthrow of monarchy. [RML]

38.543 June E. Hahner. *Poverty and politics: the urban poor in Brazil, 1870–1920*. Albuquerque: University of New Mexico Press, 1986. ISBN 0-8263-0878-3. ▸ Useful account of hardships suffered by urban poor, diverse in their origins but marginalized by economic and political system. [RML]

38.544 L. Hallewell. *Books in Brazil: a history of the publishing trade*. Metuchen, N.J.: Scarecrow, 1982. ISBN 0-8108-1591-5. ▸ Unusual, valuable intellectual history of Brazilian letters focusing on leading figures in history of publishing. [RML]

38.545 Clarence H. Haring. *Empire in Brazil*. 1958 ed. New York: Norton, 1968. ▸ Dated, too narrowly concerned with political events, but still best single-volume study of monarchy. [RML]

38.546 Marvin Harris. *Town and country in Brazil*. 1956 ed. New York: Norton, 1971. ▸ Penetrating study of small town, Minas Velhas, in Minas Gerais, examining social mobility, economic conditions, and relations with outside world. [RML]

38.547 Stanley E. Hilton. *Brazil and the great powers, 1930–1939: the politics of trade rivalry*. Austin: University of Texas Press for Institute of Latin American Studies, 1975. (Latin American monographs, 38.) ISBN 0-292-70713-4. ▸ Description of tug-of-war between Allies and Axis over Brazilian trade and, ultimately, participation in war. Uses extensive documentation in Brazil, Europe, and United States. [RML]

38.548 Thomas H. Holloway. *Immigrants on the land: coffee and society in São Paulo, 1886–1934*. Chapel Hill: University of North Carolina Press, 1980. ISBN 0-8078-1430-X. ▸ Original study correcting "oppressive planter" myth. Planters neither despotic nor progressive; they simply did not understand factors of production. [RML]

38.549 Martha Knisely Huggins. *From slavery to vagrancy in Brazil: crime and social control in the Third World*. New Brunswick, N.J.: Rutgers University Press, 1985. ISBN 0-8135-1044-9. ▸ Stimulating monograph on how elites refined vagrancy to permit them to treat marginal people as criminals during and after transition to free labor in northeast. [RML]

38.550 Carolina Maria de Jesus. *Beyond all pity*. David St. Clair, trans. London: Earthscan, 1990. ISBN 1-85383-071-2 (pbk). ▸ English translation of *Quarto de Despejo*, all-time Brazilian best-selling diary of black woman from slums of São Paulo. Peevish but very insightful. [RML]

38.551 Mary C. Karasch. *Slave life in Rio de Janeiro, 1808–1850*. Princeton: Princeton University Press, 1987. ISBN 0-691-07708-8. ▸ Masterful study of urban slave life in Rio de Janeiro; extensively illustrated. Complements work of Freyre 38.536 and Conrad 38.514. [RML]

38.552 Elizabeth Anne Kuznesof. *Household composition and economy in an urbanizing community: São Paulo, 1765 to 1836.* Boulder: Westview, 1965. ISBN 0-8133-7181-3. ▸ Pioneering, comprehensive study, based on census reports, tracing changes in family patterns in context of urban development. [RML]

38.553 Nathaniel H. Leff. *Economic structure and change, 1822–1947.* Vol. 1 of *Underdevelopment and development in Brazil.* London: Allen & Unwin, 1982. ISBN 0-04-330324-2. ▸ Analytical, statistically based study of why Brazil failed to develop economically in manner similar to United States. [RML]

38.554 Nathaniel H. Leff. *Reassessing the obstacles to economic development.* Vol. 2 of *Underdevelopment and development in Brazil.* London: Allen & Unwin, 1983. ISBN 0-04-330325-0. ▸ Focus on Brazil's impoverished northeast. Holds that agricultural backwardness, inadequate transportation, inelastic land-tenure systems, and too small tax base all led to stagnation. [RML]

38.555 Darrell E. Levi. *The Prados of São Paulo, Brazil: an elite family and social change, 1840–1930.* Athens: University of Georgia Press, 1987. ISBN 0-8203-0944-3. ▸ Interesting examination of role of Prado family, planter clan influential in abolition, journalism, and politics of early republican era. See also Lewin 38.559. [RML]

38.556 Robert M. Levine. *Pernambuco in the Brazilian Federation, 1889–1937.* Stanford, Calif.: Stanford University Press, 1978. ISBN 0-8047-0944-0. ▸ Part of original, integrated analysis of regionalism. Analyzes agrarian-dominated society directed by elite whose feet were planted firmly in past and determined to protect privileged position by resisting change except on their terms. See also Love 38.561 and Wirth 38.595. [RML]

38.557 Robert M. Levine. *Vale of tears: revisiting the Canudos massacre in northeastern Brazil, 1893–1897.* Berkeley: University of California Press, 1992. ISBN 0-520-07524-2. ▸ Reinterpretation and assessment of causes for phenomenal attraction of backlands millenarian Canudos and reasons for its destruction. Canudos a massacre, not rebellion. [RML]

38.558 Robert M. Levine. *The Vargas regime: the critical years, 1934–1938.* New York: Columbia University Press, 1970. ISBN 0-231-03370-2. ▸ Basic study, characterizing President Getúlio Vargas (1930–45) as cynical, nonideological figure who manipulated both Left and Right to preserve centralizing, undemocratic apparatus which he jettisoned in 1938 for mild version of fascism. [RML]

38.559 Linda Lewin. *Politics and Parentela in Paraiba: a case study of family-based oligarchy in Brazil.* Princeton: Princeton University Press, 1987. ISBN 0-691-07719-3. ▸ Sophisticated study of Epitácio Pessôa clan as case study of oligarch-based behavior in republican Brazil and relations between local, provincial, and national elites. [RML]

38.560 Joseph L. Love. *Rio Grande do Sul and Brazilian regionalism, 1882–1930.* Stanford, Calif.: Stanford University Press, 1971. ISBN 0-8047-0759-6. ▸ Important study of tumultuous history of Brazil's southernmost state in context of regional economic development, social structure, and political fortune. Complements Wirth 38.595, Levine 38.556, and Love 38.561. [RML]

38.561 Joseph L. Love. *São Paulo in the Brazilian Federation, 1889–1937.* Stanford, Calif.: Stanford University Press, 1980. ISBN 0-8047-0991-2. ▸ Third volume in original trilogy on regionalism with Levine 38.556 and Wirth 38.595. Succinct demonstration of burdens of São Paulo's political and economic leadership and state's fate after centralizing 1930 Revolution. [RML]

38.562 Neill Macaulay. *Dom Pedro: the struggle for liberty in Bra-*

zil and Portugal, 1798–1834. Durham, N.C.: Duke University Press, 1986. ISBN 0-8223-0681-6. ▸ Lively, engaging biography of Pedro I. Argues that Pedro's adherence to Portuguese liberalism facilitated transition from royal absolutism to constitutional monarchy in Brazil and Portugal. [RML]

38.563 Neill Macaulay. *The Prestes column: revolution in Brazil.* New York: New Viewpoints, 1974. ISBN 0-531-05356-3 (cl), 0-531-05563-9 (pbk). ▸ Adventurous narrative of march through backlands by dissident military cadets who attempted to carry *tenente* (lieutenant) ideology to rural population and led to 1930 Revolution. Lively and accessible. [RML]

38.564 Anyda Marchant. *Viscount Mauá and the empire of Brazil: a biography of Irineu Evangelista de Sousa, 1813–1889.* Berkeley: University of California Press, 1965. ▸ Traditional biography of self-made entrepreneur whose rise and fall mirrored, in many ways, fate of empire. [RML]

38.565 Roberto da Matta. *Carnivals, rogues, and heroes: an interpretation of the Brazilian dilemma.* John Drury, trans. Notre Dame, Ind.: University of Notre Dame Press, 1991. ISBN 0-268-00780-2. ▸ Fresh, provocative interpretation of dilemma between authoritarian, hierarchical aspects of society and tendencies to invert order and permit poor to fight back, if only symbolically. [RML]

38.566 Katia M. de Queirós Mattoso. *To be a slave in Brazil, 1550–1888.* Arthur Goldhammer, trans. New Brunswick, N.J.: Rutgers University Press, 1986. ISBN 0-8135-1154-2 (cl), 0-8135-1155-0 (pbk). ▸ Unique comparison of slave life in different parts of Brazil and within different parts of slave population. Considers manumitted slaves intermediaries between bondsmen and freemen willing to reject African world. Fine synthesis and overview. See also Karasch 38.551. [RML/MAB]

38.567 Samuel A. Morley. *Labor markets and inequitable growth: the case of authoritarian capitalism in Brazil.* Cambridge: Cambridge University Press, 1982. ISBN 0-521-24439-0. ▸ Argues that under military government (1964–85), poor benefited more than most economists have maintained. Growing inequality in income distribution seen as result of skill-intensive growth in labor-surplus economy, not of inequitable government policy. [RML]

38.568 Richard M. Morse. *From community to metropolis: biography of São Paulo, Brazil.* New York: Octagon Books, 1974. ISBN 0-374-95914-5. ▸ Lucid portrait of industrializing city, emphasizing cultural and social themes. [RML]

38.569 Richard M. Morse. *New World soundings: culture and ideology in the Americas.* Baltimore: Johns Hopkins University Press, 1989. ISBN 0-8018-3376-0. ▸ Erudite compilation of essays on subjects ranging from speech and poetry to mythic adventures of "Marechal McLuhanaíma," world's first Brazilianist. [RML]

38.570 Joaquim Nabuco. *Abolitionism: the Brazilian antislavery struggle.* Robert Edgar Conrad, ed. and trans. Urbana: University of Illinois Press, 1977. ISBN 0-252-00601-1. ▸ Classical statement by Brazil's leading proponent for abolition of slavery in late nineteenth century. [RML]

38.571 Jeffrey D. Needell. *A tropical belle epoque: elite culture and society in turn-of-the-century Rio de Janeiro.* New York: Cambridge University Press, 1987. ISBN 0-521-33374-1. ▸ Unique monograph demonstrating how Brazil's cultural leaders strained to Europeanize Brazilian behavior, turning their backs, in turn, on Brazil's African and indigenous legacy. [RML]

38.572 Victor Nunes Leal. *Coronelismo: the municipality and representative government in Brazil.* June Henfrey, trans. New York: Cambridge University Press, 1977. ISBN 0-521-21488-2. ▸ Classic study of structure of institutionalized political domination under republic at local and state level. [RML]

38.573 Eul-Soo Pang. *Bahia in the first Brazilian republic: coronelismo and oligarchies, 1889–1934.* Gainesville: University Presses of Florida, 1979. ISBN 0-8130-0604-X. ‣ Broad-based monograph, documenting tenacious hold of political bosses (*coronéis*) and oligarchic rule in republican era Bahia. Complements Levine 38.556, Love 38.560, and Wirth 38.595 on regionalism. [RML]

38.574 Jose Pastore. *Inequality and social mobility in Brazil.* Robert M. Oxley, trans. Madison: University of Wisconsin Press, 1982. ISBN 0-299-08830-8. ‣ Controversial view that despite obstacles, many Brazilians have profited from so-called economic miracle and achieved upward mobility. [RML]

38.575 Luiz Bresser Pereira. *Development and crisis in Brazil, 1930–1983.* Marcia Van Dyke, trans. Boulder: Westview, 1984. ISBN 0-86531-559-0. ‣ Analysis by leading economist of Brazil's economic successes and failures during Vargas period and after. Underestimates degree of industrialization and state intervention practiced before 1930. [RML]

38.576 Janice E. Perlman. *The myth of marginality: urban poverty and politics in Rio de Janeiro.* Berkeley: University of California Press, 1976. ISBN 0-520-02596-2. ‣ Controversial study, arguing that rather than lazy, docile, and pessimistic, Rio's poor are hardworking, hopeful, and highly motivated to achieve upward mobility. [RML]

38.577 José Honório Rodríques. *The Brazilians: their character and aspirations.* Ralph Edward Dimmick, trans. Austin: University of Texas Press, 1967. ‣ Romanticized but influential essay, claiming conciliation and compromise shaped Brazilian national character. Overlooks contradictory examples. [RML]

38.578 Ronald M. Schneider. *Order and progress: a political history of Brazil.* Boulder: Westview, 1991. ISBN 0-8133-1077-6. ‣ Brief overview, stressing military's role. Contrast with more critical studies by Skidmore (38.583, 38.584), Stepan, ed. (38.587), and Flynn (38.532). [RML]

38.579 Simon Schwartzman. *A space for science: the development of the scientific community in Brazil.* University Park: Pennsylvania State University Press, 1991. ISBN 0-271-00740-0. ‣ Translation of important 1979 work detailing efforts by Brazilian scientists to overcome governmental inefficiency to establish stable, scientific community. [RML]

38.580 Ron Seckinger. *The Brazilian monarchy and the South American republics, 1822–1831: diplomacy and state building.* Baton Rouge: Louisiana State University Press, 1984. ISBN 0-8071-1156-2. ‣ Extensively documented, pioneering effort. Examines origins of international relations between Brazil and its neighbors. Aspirations for cooperation overshadowed by Brazil's ambitions for continental leadership. [RML]

38.581 Robert W. Shirley. *The end of a tradition: culture change and devlopment in the municipio of Cunha, São Paulo, Brazil.* New York: Columbia University Press, 1971. ISBN 0-231-03193-9. ‣ Major study of cultural change and development in São Paulo municipality of Cunha. Finds progress rapidly eradicating surviving practices carried over from colonial period. Complements Harris 38.546 and Morse 38.568. [RML]

38.582 Thomas E. Skidmore. *Black into white: race and nationality in Brazilian thought.* New York: Oxford University Press, 1974. ISBN 0-19-501776-5. ‣ Interpretive work lamenting failure of elites to cast off racial myths. Discusses survival of theory favoring whitening as racial solution. Complements Freyre 38.536 and Degler 38.523. [RML]

38.583 Thomas E. Skidmore. *Politics in Brazil, 1930–1964: an experiment in democracy.* New York: Oxford University Press, 1967. ‣ Finds reasons for 1964 military coup rooted in watershed era of Dr. Getúlio Vargas (1930–45), when nationalistic military men and civilians overthrew old republic (1889–1930). [RML]

38.584 Thomas E. Skidmore. *The politics of military rule in Brazil, 1964–1985.* New York: Oxford University Press, 1988. ISBN 0-19-503898-3. ‣ Best available overview of military dictatorship period and slow return to civilian government. [RML]

38.585 Stanley J. Stein. *The Brazilian cotton manufacture: textile enterprise in an underdeveloped area, 1850–1950.* Cambridge, Mass.: Harvard University Press, 1957. ‣ Pioneering study of Brazil's first industrial enterprise, textile manufacturing, analyzing role of government intervention. See also Topik 38.590. [RML]

38.586 Stanley J. Stein. *Vassouras, a Brazilian coffee county, 1850–1900: the roles of planter and slave in a plantation society.* 1957 ed. Princeton: Princeton University Press, 1985. ‣ Landmark study of decline of slavery in rural town in province of Rio de Janeiro. [RML]

38.587 Alfred Stepan, ed. *Democratizing Brazil: problems of transition and consolidation.* New York: Oxford University Press, 1989. ISBN 0-19-505151-3 (cl), 0-19-505152-1 (pbk). ‣ Collection of incisive analyses of Brazil's emergence from military rule and its prospects for political and social progress by leading experts from Brazil and outside. [RML]

38.588 Nancy Leys Stepan. *Beginnings of Brazilian science: Oswaldo Cruz, medical research, and policy, 1890–1920.* New York: Science History, 1976. ISBN 0-88202-032-3. ‣ Important study of development of Brazilian science. Traces career of pioneer epidemiologist and creation of research institute in Rio de Janeiro named for him. [RML]

38.589 Verena Stolcke. *Coffee planters, workers, and wives: class conflict and gender relations on São Paulo coffee plantations, 1850–1980.* New York: St. Martin's, 1988. ISBN 0-312-01693-X. ‣ Apt sociological investigation of role of family in São Paulo work force during declining period of coffee prosperity from 1870 through late twentieth century. See also Dean 38.521 and Stein 38.586. [RML]

38.590 Steven Topik. *The political economy of the Brazilian state, 1889–1930.* Austin: University of Texas Press for Institute of Latin American Studies, 1987. (Latin American monographs, 71.) ISBN 0-292-76500-2. ‣ Convincing argument that state played much more assertive, even interventionist, role in setting economic policy than previously assumed. [RML]

38.591 Robert Brent Toplin. *The abolition of slavery in Brazil.* 1972 ed. August Meier, ed. New York: Atheneum, 1975. ISBN 0-689-70526-3 (pbk). ‣ Major English-language study of process of abolition in Brazil. See also Nabuco 38.570. [RML]

38.592 William G. Tyler. *The Brazilian industrial economy.* Lexington, Mass.: Heath, 1981. ISBN 0-669-03448-7. ‣ Important economic analysis, crediting import substitution and policies favoring industrialization with permitting Brazil to survive oil crisis of 1970s and to build for further growth in future decades. [RML]

38.593 Fernando Uricoechea. *The patrominial foundations of the Brazilian bureaucratic state.* Berkeley: University of California Press, 1980. ISBN 0-520-03853-3. ‣ Important study of national guard, which replaced colonial militia as vehicle for imposing stability and order. See also Pang 38.573. [RML]

38.594 Barbara Weinstein. *The Amazon rubber boom, 1850–1920.* Stanford, Calif.: Stanford University Press, 1983. ISBN 0-8047-1168-2. ‣ Study of impact of political decentralization and regionalism in Amazonian economy in light of rubber economy's eventual collapse, from perspective of dependency theory. See also Dean 38.520. [RML]

38.595 John D. Wirth. *Minas Gerais in the Brazilian Federation,*

1889–1937. Stanford, Calif.: Stanford University Press, 1977. ISBN 0-8047-0932-7. ▸ One of trilogy of pioneering independent volumes examining in depth how Brazil's federal system functioned from vantage point of leading region. See also Love 38.561 and Levine 38.556. [RML]

38.596 John D. Wirth. *The politics of Brazilian development, 1930–1954.* Stanford, Calif.: Stanford University Press, 1970. ISBN 0-8047-0710-3. ▸ Important study of trade imbalance of 1930s, struggle to build modern steel mill at Volta Redonda, and organization of government's petroleum monopoly in 1950s. Explores President Vargas's role as populist economic nationalist. [RML]

SEE ALSO
    48.161 Frank D. McCann, Jr. *The Brazilian-American alliance, 1937–1945.*

SOUTHERN CONE

Argentina

38.597 George Reid Andrews. *The Afro-Argentines of Buenos Aires, 1800–1900.* Madison: University of Wisconsin Press, 1980. ISBN 0-299-08290-3. ▸ Examination of history of black community in Buenos Aires, emphasizing role in and contributions to larger society. Rebuts myth concerning blacks' "disappearance" over course of century. [RJW]

38.598 Samuel L. Baily. *Labor, nationalism, and politics in Argentina.* New Brunswick, N.J.: Rutgers University Press, 1967. ▸ Good synthetic overview history of Argentine labor from late nineteenth century to 1950s, emphasizing Juan D. Perón's (1946–55) appeal to new migrant workers. [RJW]

38.599 Jonathan C. Brown. *A socioeconomic history of Argentina, 1776–1860.* Cambridge: Cambridge University Press, 1979. ISBN 0-521-22219-2. ▸ Highly informative examination of economic and social changes, markets and production as Argentina moved from traditional to modern technology. Focuses on international markets for Argentina's products and influence of native technology on production and transport. Challenges dependency theory. Two chapters on colonial period. [RJW/MAB]

38.600 Allison W. Bunkely. *The life of Sarmiento.* 1952 ed. New York: Greenwood, 1969. ISBN 0-8371-2392-5. ▸ Sympathetic, informative biography of one of Argentina's most important thinkers and statesmen. Dated but still useful, especially on Sarmiento's literary contributions. [RJW]

38.601 Miron Burgin. *The economic aspects of Argentine federalism, 1820–1852.* 1946 ed. New York: Russell & Russell, 1971. ▸ Pioneering study, examining relationships among political, economic, and regional forces. Important analysis of economic policies of dictator Juan Manuel de Rosas. [RJW]

38.602 David Bushnell. *Reform and reaction in the Platine provinces, 1810–1852.* Gainesville: University Presses of Florida, 1983. ISBN 0-8130-0757-7 (pbk). ▸ Examination of process of liberal reforms in postindependence Argentina and Uruguay. Draws on archival material to show continuity of policies and their consequences. [RJW]

38.603 Susan Calvert and Peter Calvert. *Argentina: political culture and instability.* Pittsburgh: University of Pittsburgh Press, 1989. ISBN 0-8229-1156-6. ▸ Study of Argentine failure to develop politically. Finds answer in clash between conservative Hispanic and liberal European cultural traditions. Some oversimplification but insightful look at country's history of instability. [RJW]

38.604 Alberto Ciria. *Parties and power in modern Argentina, 1930–1946.* Carlos A. Astiz, trans. Albany: State University of New York Press, 1974. ISBN 0-87395-0079-8 (cl), 0-87395-179-4 (microfiche). ▸ Pioneering work by Argentine political scientist

on pre-Perón period. Lacks coherence but contains useful information on parties and power groups from Argentine perspective. Translation of 1964 Spanish-language edition. [RJW]

38.605 Simon Collier. *The life, music, and times of Carlos Gardel.* Pittsburgh: University of Pittsburgh Press, 1986. ISBN 0-8229-3535-X. ▸ Engaging biography of one of Argentina's and Latin America's most popular entertainers. Examines larger impact of Gardel on Argentine society. [RJW]

38.606 Robert D. Crassweller. *Perón and the enigmas of Argentina.* New York: Norton, 1987. ISBN 0-393-02381-8. ▸ Lively, readable biography of Argentina's best-known leader. Overlaps with Page 38.635, but more analysis and larger historical framework. [RJW]

38.607 Carlos F. Díaz Alejandro. *Essays on the economic history of the Argentine republic.* New Haven: Yale University Press, 1970. ISBN 0-300-01193-8. ▸ Review of major features of Argentina's twentieth-century economic history, emphasizing importance of exports in explaining growth and decline. Contains considerable statistical information and challenges many commonly held assumptions. [RJW]

38.608 Mark Falcoff and Ronald H. Dolkart, eds. *Prologue to Perón: Argentina in depression and war, 1930–1943.* Berkeley: University of California Press, 1975. ISBN 0-520-02874-0. ▸ Essays on politics, economic development, foreign policy, intellectual currents, popular culture, and regional events in decade before Perón. Good complement to Ciria 38.604. [RJW]

38.609 H. S. Ferns. *Britain and Argentina in the nineteenth century.* Oxford: Clarendon, 1960. ▸ Extensive, well-documented review of relations between Argentina and its most important investor and trading partner before World War II. Generally sympathetic treatment of British role in Argentina. [RJW]

38.610 Aldo Ferrer. *The Argentine economy.* Marjory Mattingly Urquidi, trans. Berkeley: University of California Press, 1967. ▸ Description of different stages of Argentine economic development with focus on post-1930 period. Valuable synthesis and overview, clearly written and accessible. Author later cabinet minister. [RJW]

38.611 Darrell F. Fineup, Russell H. Brannon, and Frank A. Fender. *The agricultural development of Argentina: a policy and development perspective.* New York: Praeger, 1969. ▸ Review of Argentine agricultural history, arguing neglect has led to many contemporary problems. Contains considerable statistical information and policy recommendations. [RJW]

38.612 Nicholas Fraser and Marysa Navarro. *Eva Perón.* New York: Norton, 1981. ISBN 0-393-01457-6. ▸ Scholarly biography of Argentina's best-known female political figure. Generally objective, separating myth from reality. [RJW]

38.613 Ezequiel Gallo. *Farmers in revolt: the revolutions of 1893 in the province of Santa Fe, Argentina.* London: Athlone for University of London, Institute of Latin American Studies, 1976. (University of London, Institute of Latin American Studies monographs, 7.) ISBN 0-485-17707-2. ▸ Examination of role of small farmers and immigrants in provincial politics and formation of Radical party. Well researched with broader implications. [RJW]

38.614 Richard Gillespie. *Soldiers of Perón: Argentina's Montoneros.* New York: Oxford University Press, 1983. ISBN 0-19-821131-7. ▸ Account of Argentina's best-known revolutionary organization of 1970s. Generally well documented; not always objective. [RJW]

38.615 Roger Gravil. *The Anglo-Argentine connection, 1900–1939.* Boulder: Westview, 1985. ISBN 0-8133-0113-0 (pbk). ▸ Analysis of British role in Argentina, complementing Ferns

38.599. Well-written and extensively documented revisionist account, questioning British dominance. [RJW]

38.616 Donna J. Guy. *Argentine sugar politics: Tucumán and the Generation of Eighty.* Tempe: Arizona State University, Center for Latin American Studies, 1980. ISBN 0-87918-043-9. ‣ Analysis of economic development and elite politics in Argentine interior during late nineteenth century. Underscores importance of Tucumán to national considerations. Useful provincial study. [RJW]

38.617 Donna J. Guy. *Sex and danger in Buenos Aires: prostitution, family, and nation in Argentina.* Lincoln: University of Nebraska Press, 1991. ISBN 0-8032-2139-8. ‣ Pioneering study of prostitution, relating it to larger themes of national identity and social control. Excellent information on popular culture and attitudes. [RJW]

38.618 Tulio Halperín-Donghi. *Politics, economics, and society in Argentina in the revolutionary period.* Richard Southern, trans. Cambridge: Cambridge University Press, 1975. ISBN 0-521-20493-3. ‣ Important study of social, economic, and political change throughout Argentina during and after wars of independence, which author argues were revolutionary. Informative, revisionist, demanding. Translation of 1972 Spanish-language edition. [RJW]

38.619 Donald C. Hodges. *Argentina, 1943–1987: the national revolution and resistance.* Rev. ed. Albuquerque: University of New Mexico Press, 1988. ISBN 0-8263-1055-9 (cl), 0-8263-1056-7 (pbk). ‣ Outline of postwar Argentine political history, focusing on Perónism and leftist revolutionary organizations. Interesting information on guerrilla groups, buttressed by interviews, but often opinionated and subjective. [RJW]

38.620 Joel Horowitz. *Argentine unions, the state, and the rise of Perón, 1930–1945.* Berkeley: University of California, Institute of International Studies, 1990. (Research series, 76.) ISBN 0-87725-176-2, ISSN 0068-6093. ‣ Detailed account of five major unions in pre-Perón period. Argues continuity in development of labor movement. Complements Falcoff and Dolkart, eds. 38.608 and Tamarin 38.663. [RJW]

38.621 José Luis de Imaz. *Los que mandan (Those who rule).* Carlos A. Astiz, trans. and Introduction. Albany: State University of New York Press, 1970. ISBN 0-87395-044-5. ‣ Pioneering study by Argentine sociologist of major elite groups, including armed forces, government officials, landed property owners, business interests, church, and labor leaders. Somewhat dated but useful for immediate postwar period. Translation of 1964 Spanish-language edition. [RJW]

38.622 Daniel James. *Resistance and integration: Peronism and the Argentine working class, 1946–1976.* Cambridge: Cambridge University Press, 1988. ISBN 0-521-34635-5. ‣ Excellent analysis of labor and state in postwar Argentina. Uses wide range of documentation, including oral interviews, to provide in-depth, personal picture of workers and their organizations. [RJW]

38.623 William Jeffrey. *Mitre and Argentina.* New York: Library Publishers, 1952. ‣ Informative biography of Argentine statesman Bartolomé Mitre (1821–1906). Laudatory but only study available in English. [RJW]

38.624 V. W. Leonard. *Politicians, pupils, and priests: Argentine education since 1943.* New York: Lang, 1989. ISBN 0-8204-0748-8. ‣ Examination of role of Catholic church in educational history of postwar Argentina. Focuses on struggle to include religious education in public schools and establish private Catholic universities. Balanced, well researched, informative. [RJW]

38.625 Colin M. Lewis. *British railways in Argentina, 1857–1914: a case study of foreign investment.* London: Athlone for University of London, Institute of Latin American Studies; distributed by Humanities Press, 1983. (Institute of Latin American Studies monographs, 12.) ISBN 0-391-02772-7, ISSN 0776-0846. ‣ Detailed account stressing positive contributions of British railroads to Argentine development. Questions nationalist critique of British capital. Complements Wright 38.673. [RJW]

38.626 Paul H. Lewis. *The crisis of Argentine capitalism.* 1990 ed. Chapel Hill: University of North Carolina Press, 1992. ISBN 0-8078-1862-3 (cl, 1990), 0-8078-4356-3 (pbk). ‣ Political scientist's analysis of turbulent history of Argentina after World War II, emphasizing role of business and industrial sectors. Well-written, provocative analysis. [RJW]

38.627 John Lynch. *Argentine dictator: Juan Manuel de Rosas, 1829–1852.* New York: Oxford University Press, 1981. ISBN 0-19-821129-5. ‣ Well-documented, well-written, balanced biography of Argentina's best-known nineteenth-century *caudillo* (dictator). Should be read with Halperín-Donghi 38.618 and Sarmiento 38.646. [RJW]

38.628 Ezequiel Martínez Estrada. *X-ray of the pampa.* Alain Swietlicki, trans. Thomas Francis McGann, Introduction. Austin: University of Texas Press, 1971. ISBN 0-292-70140-3. ‣ Classic essay on Argentine history and national character. Insightful personal view, emphasizing isolation and alienation. Translation of 1933 Spanish-language edition. [RJW]

38.629 Thomas Francis McGann. *Argentina, the United States, and the inter-American system, 1880–1914.* Cambridge, Mass.: Harvard University Press, 1957. ‣ Well-written analysis of Argentina's elite Generation of Eighty and its attempts to establish position of hemispheric leadership. [RJW]

38.630 Sandra McGee Deutsch. *Counterrevolution in Argentina, 1900–1932: the Argentine Patriotic League.* Lincoln: University of Nebraska Press, 1986. ISBN 0-8032-1669-6. ‣ Probing analysis of Argentina's major right-wing organization of early twentieth century. Well written, objective, informative. [RJW]

38.631 Ronaldo Munck. *Argentina, from anarchism to Peronism: workers, unions, and politics, 1855–1985.* London: Zed, 1987. ISBN 0-86232-570-6 (cl), 0-86232-571-4 (pbk). ‣ Comprehensive synthetic overview of Argentine labor history; some useful statistical information. Informed by larger context of European and North American labor history, but occasionally uneven in quality. [RJW]

38.632 Ronald C. Newton. *German Buenos Aires, 1900–1933: social change and cultural crisis.* Austin: University of Texas Press, 1977. ISBN 0-292-72714-3. ‣ Interesting study of relatively small but influential immigrant community. Well-researched in German-language sources. Raises question of Nazism's diffusion in Argentina. [RJW]

38.633 Ronald C. Newton. *The "Nazi menace" in Argentina, 1931–1947.* Stanford, Calif.: Stanford University Press, 1992. ISBN 0-8047-1929-2. ‣ Detailed account of relations among Argentina, Germany, Great Britain, and United States before, during, and after World War II. Well-researched account; explores and explodes various misconceptions. [RJW]

38.634 Guillermo A. O'Donnell. *Modernization and bureaucratic-authoritarianism: studies in South American politics.* Berkeley: University of California, Institute of International Studies, 1973. (Politics of modernization series, 9.) ISBN 0-87725-209-2. ‣ Sophisticated view of Argentine civilian and military governments of 1960s and 1970s by Argentine social scientist. Landmark study of bureaucratic-authoritarian regimes; demands close attention. [RJW]

38.635 Joseph A. Page. *Perón: a biography.* New York: Random House, 1983. ISBN 0-394-52297-4. ‣ Thorough, readable biography of Juan Perón with good information on exile experience. Often anecdotal. [RJW]

38.636 Robert A. Potash. *The army and politics in Argentina: 1928–1945, Yrigoyen to Perón.* Stanford, Calif.: Stanford University Press, 1969. ‣ Well-researched, clearly presented, balanced view of role of Argentina's principal political force in twentieth century. Essential source, well-received in Argentina. [RJW]

38.637 Robert A. Potash. *The army and politics in Argentina: 1945–1962, Perón to Frondizi.* Stanford, Calif.: Stanford University Press, 1980. ISBN 0-8047-1056-2. ‣ Successor volume to 38.636. Suggests civilian weaknesses led to propensity for military intervention. [RJW]

38.638 Laura Randall. *An economic history of Argentina in the twentieth century.* New York: Columbia University Press, 1978. ISBN 0-231-03358-3. ‣ Focuses on various sectors of Argentine economy, emphasizing monetary policy. Considerable statistical information. Counters dependency theory, not always successfully. [RJW]

38.639 Vera Blinn Reber. *British mercantile houses in Buenos Aires, 1810–1880.* Cambridge, Mass.: Harvard University Press, 1979. ISBN 0-674-08245-1. ‣ Interesting if narrow view of British merchant houses' role in promoting economic growth and development in Argentina. Good information on British community. Should be read with Ferns 38.609. [RJW]

38.640 Karen L. Remmer. *Party competition in Argentina and Chile: political recruitment and public policy, 1890–1930.* Lincoln: University of Nebraska Press, 1984. ISBN 0-8032-3871-1. ‣ Interesting comparative view of political developments in Argentina and Chile, focusing on parties, leadership, and policies. Political science methodology within well-constructed historical context. [RJW]

38.641 Ysabel F. Rennie. *The Argentine republic.* 1945 ed. Westport, Conn.: Greenwood, 1975. ISBN 0-8371-7739-1. ‣ Dated but still lively introduction to Argentina's nineteenth- and early twentieth-century history. Especially strong on development of economic nationalism from 1930 to 1943. [RJW]

38.642 David Rock. *Argentina, 1516–1987: from Spanish colonization to Alfonsín.* Rev. ed. Berkeley: University of California Press, 1987. ISBN 0-520-06178-0. ‣ Comprehensive historical review, based mostly on secondary sources. Argues dependent economy determined course of Argentine development. Controversial and stimulating. [RJW]

38.643 David Rock. *Politics in Argentina, 1890–1930: the rise and fall of radicalism.* Cambridge: Cambridge University Press, 1975. ISBN 0-521-20663-4. ‣ Focuses on presidencies of Hipólito Yrigoyen (1916–22, 1928–30) and Marcelo T. de Alvear (1922–28), underscoring limits of populist and clientelistic policies of Radical party. Basic source for politics of period. [RJW]

38.644 José Luis Romero. *A history of Argentine political thought.* Thomas Francis McGann, trans. and Introduction. Stanford, Calif.: Stanford University Press, 1963. ‣ Overview of Argentine political history from Spanish colonial period to Perón by distinguished Argentine historian. Informed, insightful, written from liberal viewpoint. [RJW]

38.645 Stanley R. Ross and Thomas Francis McGann, eds. *Buenos Aires: 400 years.* Austin: University of Texas Press, 1982. ISBN 0-292-70738-X. ‣ Wide-ranging essays on history of Argentine capital city, showing socioeconomic growth, larger national role, and culture. [RJW]

38.646 Domingo F. Sarmiento. *Life in the Argentine republic in the days of the tyrants; or, civilization and barbarism.* 1868 ed. New York: Hafner, 1974. ‣ Classic nineteenth-century Argentine history, analyzing roots of dictatorship and underdevelopment. Partisan, passionate, insightful. [RJW]

38.647 Lars Schoultz. *The populist challenge: Argentine electoral behavior in the postwar era.* Chapel Hill: University of North Carolina Press, 1983. ISBN 0-8078-5059-4. ‣ Peronism and its consequences through statistical analysis of election results. Methodologically demanding; clearly presented. [RJW]

38.648 James R. Scobie. *Argentina: a city and a nation.* 2d ed. New York: Oxford University Press, 1971. ISBN 0-19-501480-4. ‣ Dated but well-written overview, stressing socioeconomic factors and role of Buenos Aires in nation's development. [RJW]

38.649 James R. Scobie. *Buenos Aires: plaza to suburb, 1870–1910.* New York: Oxford University Press, 1974. ISBN 0-19-501821-4. ‣ Well-researched analysis of capital city's development, emphasizing commercial-bureaucratic nature. [RJW]

38.650 James R. Scobie. *Revolution on the pampas: a social history of Argentine wheat, 1860–1919.* Austin: University of Texas Press for Institute of Latin American Studies, 1964. (Latin American monographs, 1.) ‣ Broader than title suggests, covering various aspects of nation's agricultural development. Should be read with Fineup, Brannon, and Fender 38.611, Solberg 38.660, and Taylor 38.664. [RJW]

38.651 James R. Scobie. *Secondary cities of Argentina: the social history of Corrientes, Salta, and Mendoza, 1850–1910.* Samuel L. Baily, ed. Stanford, Calif.: Stanford University Press, 1988. ISBN 0-8047-1419-3. ‣ Innovative comparative history of three provincial capitals, focusing on demography, local factors, residential patterns, work, leisure time, and class structure. [RJW]

38.652 Nicolas Shumway. *The invention of Argentina.* Berkeley: University of California Press, 1991. ISBN 0-520-06906-4. ‣ Imaginative literary analysis of main thinkers and statesmen of nineteenth century. Argues that polarized attitudes persist into contemporary period. [RJW]

38.653 Richard W. Slatta. *Gauchos and the vanishing frontier.* Lincoln: University of Nebraska Press, 1983. ISBN 0-8032-4134-8. ‣ Well-researched history of Argentine cowboy, focusing on social conditions and pressures leading to exploitation and eventual revival in literature. Concise, informative. [RJW]

38.654 Peter H. Smith. *Argentina and the failure of democracy: conflict among political elites, 1904–1955.* Madison: University of Wisconsin Press, 1974. ISBN 0-299-06600-2. ‣ Pioneering statistical study of political divisions through close analysis of congressional composition and roll calls. [RJW]

38.655 Peter H. Smith. *Politics and beef in Argentina: patterns of conflict and change.* New York: Columbia University Press, 1969. ‣ Examination of role of beef industry as major interest group in Argentine politics. Early example of social science methodology employed to examine Argentine history. [RJW]

38.656 William C. Smith. *Authoritarianism and the crisis of the Argentine political economy.* Stanford, Calif.: Stanford University Press, 1989. ISBN 0-8047-1672-2. ‣ Political scientist's view of Argentine history from 1960s to 1980s, focusing on economic policy and political instability. Sophisticated, informative. [RJW]

38.657 Eugene F. Sofer. *From pale to pampa: a social history of the Jews of Buenos Aires.* New York: Holmes & Meier, 1982. ISBN 0-8419-0428-6. ‣ Well-researched analysis of important Jewish community in Buenos Aires. Should be read with Weisbrot 38.671. [RJW]

38.658 Carl E. Solberg. *Immigration and nationalism: Argentina and Chile, 1890–1914.* Austin: University of Texas Press for Institute of Latin American Studies, 1970. (Latin American monographs, 18.) ISBN 0-292-70020-2. ‣ Comparative study of impact of immigration and nationalist reaction to it. Well-researched and clearly presented. [RJW]

38.659 Carl E. Solberg. *Oil and nationalism in Argentina: a history.* Stanford, Calif.: Stanford University Press, 1979. ISBN

0-8047-0985-8. ▸ Focuses on politics of oil, mainly from 1907 to 1930. Places Argentine example into larger Latin American context. [RJW]

38.660 Carl E. Solberg. *The prairies and the pampas: agrarian policy in Canada and Argentina, 1880–1930*. Stanford, Calif.: Stanford University Press, 1987. ISBN 0-8047-1346-4. ▸ Imaginative comparative study, focusing on state policies, agriculture, and land tenure patterns. Challenges dependency analysis. [RJW]

38.661 Mark D. Szuchman. *Mobility and integration in urban Argentina: Córdoba in the liberal era*. Austin: University of Texas Press for Institute of Latin American Studies, 1980. (Latin American monographs, 52.) ISBN 0-292-75057-9. ▸ Examination of social class and mobility in major interior capital city during nineteenth century. Argues despite immigration little change occurred in social structure. Mixes quantitative methods with other sources. [RJW]

38.662 Mark D. Szuchman. *Order, family, and community in Buenos Aires, 1810–1860*. Stanford, Calif.: Stanford University Press, 1988. ISBN 0-8047-1461-4. ▸ Drawing on extensive use of census manuscripts, traces family history during formative period of Argentine nation. Effectively underscores continuity and desire for political order. [RJW]

38.663 David Tamarin. *The Argentine labor movement, 1930–1945: a study in the origins of Peronism*. Albuquerque: University of New Mexico Press, 1985. ISBN 0-8263-0779-5. ▸ Well-documented overview of labor prior to Perón. Underscores developing divisions of period which allowed for Perón to take over movement. [RJW]

38.664 Carl C. Taylor. *Rural life in Argentina*. Baton Rouge: Louisiana State University Press, 1948. ▸ Detailed analysis of Argentine agriculture and rural society by rural sociologist. Dated but still full of valuable information. [RJW]

38.665 J. M. Taylor. *Eva Perón: the myths of a woman*. Chicago: University of Chicago Press, 1979. ISBN 0-226-79143-2. ▸ Anthropologist's view of Eva Perón, focusing on how different social classes perceived Argentina's most famous and influential female politician. Concise and clear. Should be read with Fraser and Navarro 38.612. [RJW]

38.666 Joseph S. Tulchin. *Argentina and the United States: a conflicted relationship*. Boston: Twayne, 1990. ISBN 0-8057-7900-0 (cl), 0-8057-9204-X (pbk). ▸ Well-written, balanced overview, showing sensitivity to domestic developments in both nations which affected their international relationship. Comprehensive, up-to-date treatment. [RJW]

38.667 Carlos H. Waisman. *Reversal of development in Argentina: postwar counterrevolutionary policies and their structural consequences*. Princeton: Princeton University Press, 1987. ISBN 0-691-07740-1 (cl), 0-691-02266-6 (pbk). ▸ Argentine political sociologist's view of why country declined in postwar era, tracing roots to counterrevolutionary policies of 1930s and 1940s. Stimulating, insightful, if occasionally difficult to follow. [RJW]

38.668 Richard J. Walter. *The province of Buenos Aires and Argentine politics, 1912–1943*. Cambridge: Cambridge University Press, 1985. ISBN 0-521-30337-0. ▸ Well-researched, clear examination of role of Argentina's largest province in national political developments. Looks particularly at struggle between Conservative and Radical parties. [RJW]

38.669 Richard J. Walter. *The Socialist party of Argentina, 1890–1930*. Austin: University of Texas Press for Institute of Latin American Studies, 1977. (Latin American monographs, 42.) ISBN 0-292-77539-3 (cl), 0-292-77540-7 (pbk). ▸ Detailed study of growth of what was then Latin America's most important and successful socialist party. Focuses on elections and congressional activity. [RJW]

38.670 Richard J. Walter. *Student politics in Argentina: the university reform and its effects, 1918–1964*. New York: Basic Books, 1968. ▸ Discussion of major changes in university students' role in both university and national politics. [RJW]

38.671 Robert Weisbrot. *The Jews of Argentina: from the Inquisition to Perón*. Philadelphia: Jewish Publication Society of America, 1979. ISBN 0-8276-0114-X. ▸ Overview of Jewish community, informed by comparisons with United States. Good on Perón and Jews. [RJW]

38.672 Randall Bennett Woods. *The Roosevelt foreign policy establishment and the "good neighbor": the United States and Argentina, 1941–1945*. Lawrence: Regents Press of Kansas, 1979. ISBN 0-7006-0188-0. ▸ Uses model of bureaucratic politics to examine United States policy toward Argentina during World War II. Informative on United States; less useful for Argentine view. [RJW]

38.673 Winthrop R. Wright. *British-owned railways in Argentina: their effect on economic nationalism, 1854–1948*. Austin: University of Texas Press for Institute of Latin American Studies, 1974. (Latin American monographs, 34.) ISBN 0-292-70710-X. ▸ Detailed treatment of major British investment in Argentina, particularly strong on nationalist reaction in 1930s. Some gaps but best overview of subject. [RJW]

38.674 Gary W. Wynia. *Argentina in the postwar era: politics and economic policy making in a divided society*. Albuquerque: University of New Mexico Press, 1978. ISBN 0-8263-0481-8 (cl), 0-8263-0482-6 (pbk). ▸ Political scientist's attempt to unravel mystery of Argentina's postwar decline, focusing on policy making under different kinds of regimes. Complements Lewis 38.626, Smith 38.656, and Waisman 38.667. [RJW]

Chile

38.675 Robert Jackson Alexander. *Arturo Alesandri: a biography*. 2 vols. Ann Arbor: University Microfilms International for Rutgers University, Latin American Institute, 1977. ISBN 0-8357-0288-X. ▸ Detailed biography of one of Chile's dominant twentieth-century politicians, twice president (1920–25, 1932–38) of country. Laudatory but comprehensive. [RJW]

38.676 Alan Angell. *Politics and the labour movement in Chile*. London: Oxford University Press for Royal Institute of International Affairs, 1972. ISBN 0-19-214991-1. ▸ History of major labor unions and their relations to principal political parties. Thorough, readable, well documented, objective. [RJW]

38.677 Genaro Arriagada. *Pinochet: the politics of power*. Nancy Morris, trans. Boston: Allen & Unwin, 1988. ISBN 0-04-497061-7 (cl), 0-04-497062-5 (pbk). ▸ Concise, informative examination of role of armed forces and domination of country by President Augusto Pinochet (1973–90) as well as role of opposition. [RJW]

38.678 Arnold J. Bauer. *Chilean rural society from the Spanish conquest to 1930*. New York: Cambridge University Press, 1975. ISBN 0-521-20727-4. ▸ Well-researched, balanced treatment of impact of insertion into world market economy on relations between rural landowners and laborers and on government neglect of rural sector. [RJW]

38.679 Jere R. Behrman. *Foreign trade regimes and economic development: Chile*. New York: National Bureau of Economic Research; distributed by Columbia University Press, 1976. (National Bureau of Economic Research: a special conference series on foreign trade regimes and economic development, 8.) ISBN 0-87014-500-2. ▸ Application of comparative model to relations between Chile's international sector and certain internal macroeconomic objectives. Underscores failures of policy and suggests alternatives. Basic work on subject. [RJW]

38.680 Harold Blakemore. *British nitrates and Chilean politics,*

1886–1896: Balmaceda and North. London: Athlone for Institute of Latin American Studies, 1974. ISBN 0-485-17704-8. ▸ Careful examination of relationship between foreign interests and internal political developments in Chile, including civil war of 1891. Challenges Marxist analysis. Complements Frank 38.123. [RJW]

38.681 Frank Bonilla and Myron Glazer. *Student politics in Chile*. New York: Basic Books, 1970. ISBN 0-465-08258-0. ▸ Sociologists' view of student activism, focusing on University of Chile in Santiago. Depends heavily on survey research. [RJW]

38.682 Ben G. Burnett. *Political groups in Chile: the dialogue between order and change*. Austin: University of Texas Press for Institute of Latin American Studies, 1970. (Latin American monographs, 21.) ISBN 0-292-70084-9. ▸ Description of major political institutions and interest groups prior to presidency of Salvador Allende (1970–73). Basic overview and introduction. [RJW]

38.683 Robert N. Burr. *By reason or force: Chile and the balancing of power in South America, 1830–1905*. 1965 ed. Berkeley: University of California Press, 1974. ISBN 0-520-02644-6. ▸ Basic analysis of Chile's foreign policy, underscoring nation's sophistication in promoting and protecting its interests. Should be read with Pike 38.708. [RJW]

38.684 Cesar Caviedes. *The politics of Chile: a sociographical assessment*. Boulder: Westview, 1979. ISBN 0-89158-365-3. ▸ Basic information on geography, social classes, elite families, and election results, 1932–73, emphasizing regionalization of democratic politics. Thorough, balanced. [RJW]

38.685 Peter S. Cleaves. *Bureaucratic politics and administration in Chile*. Berkeley: University of California Press, 1974. ISBN 0-520-02448-6. ▸ Detailed analysis of policy making during administration of Eduardo Frei (1964–70). Focus on comparative administration with little attention to ideological or historical context. [RJW]

38.686 Stephen Clissold. *Bernardo O'Higgins and the independence of Chile*. New York: Praeger, 1969. ▸ Straightforward account of leading figure of Chile's movement for independence from Spain. Emphasizes O'Higgins's liberal reforms. Complements Collier 38.687. [RJW]

38.687 Simon Collier. *Ideas and politics of Chilean independence, 1808–1833*. New York: Cambridge University Press, 1967. ▸ Essential source, emphasizing impact of ideas and development of revolutionary mystique. Clear picture of major revolutionary figures and their programs. [RJW]

38.688 Pamela Constable and Arturo Valenzuela. *A nation of enemies: Chile under Pinochet*. New York: Norton, 1991. ISBN 0-393-03011-3 (cl), 0-393-30985-1 (pbk). ▸ Riveting, generally balanced, comprehensive account of Chilean society during rule of president-dictator Augusto Pinochet (1973–90). Somewhat journalistic but very readable. [RJW]

38.689 Peter DeShazo. *Urban workers and labor unions in Chile, 1902–1927*. Madison: University of Wisconsin Press, 1983. ISBN 0-229-09220-8. ▸ Well-researched analysis of urban workers' movements, underscoring anarchist and anarcho-syndicalist role. Challenges assertion that migrant workers spearheaded labor movement. [RJW]

38.690 Paul W. Drake. *Socialism and populism in Chile, 1932–1952*. Chicago: University of Illinois Press, 1978. ISBN 0-252-00657-7. ▸ Essential study of history of Socialist party to describe political developments over twenty-year period and implications for Allende experience. Comprehensive, well written, and balanced. [RJW]

38.691 Mark Falcoff. *Modern Chile, 1970–1989: a critical history*. New Brunswick, N.J.: Transaction, 1989. ISBN 0-88738-257-6.

▸ Main focus on Allende period, emphasizing political flaws and failures. Downplays United States role. [RJW]

38.692 Julio Faúndez. *Marxism and democracy in Chile: from 1932 to the fall of Allende*. New Haven: Yale University Press, 1988. ISBN 0-300-04024-5. ▸ Overview of Chilean politics, focusing on Socialist and Communist parties. Informative for nonspecialist. [RJW]

38.693 Federico G. Gil. *The political system of Chile*. Boston: Houghton-Mifflin, 1966. ▸ Comprehensive study of Chilean politics and political history. Dated but still solid and informative. [RJW]

38.694 Federico G. Gil, Ricardo E. Lagos, and Henry A. Landsberger, eds. *Chile at the turning point: lessons of the socialist years, 1970–1973*. John S. Gitlitz, trans. Philadelphia: Institute for the Study of Human Issues, 1979. ISBN 0-915980-88-6. ▸ Conference papers and commentary from scholars and government officials, providing comprehensive and thoughtful analysis. [RJW]

38.695 Ivan Jaksic. *Academic rebels in Chile: the role of philosophy in higher education and politics*. Albany: State University of New York Press, 1989. ISBN 0-88706-878-2 (cl), 0-88706-879-0 (pbk). ▸ Best available study examining influence of Chilean philosophers, covering period from independence to Pinochet dictatorship. [RJW]

38.696 Robert R. Kaufman. *The politics of land reform in Chile, 1950–1970: public policy, political institutions, and social change*. Cambridge, Mass.: Harvard University Press, 1972. ISBN 0-674-68920-8. ▸ Focuses on efforts at agrarian reform under presidents Jorge Alessandri (1958–64) and Eduardo Frei (1964–70), emphasizing urban-rural cleavages as important constraints. Good research on early period. [RJW]

38.697 Jay Kinsbruner. *Diego Portales: interpretative essays on the man and times*. The Hague: Nijhoff, 1967. ▸ Revisionist look at political leader generally considered principal creator of postindependence Chile. Downplays Portales's impact and influence, although not a comprehensive study. [RJW]

38.698 Henry W. Kirsch. *Industrial development in a traditional society: the conflict of entrepreneurship and modernization in Chile*. Gainesville: University Presses of Florida, 1977. ISBN 0-8130-0563-9. ▸ Detailed description of industrial growth in Chile, especially before 1930. Focuses on role of ruling oligarchy in directing industrial development. Provocative analysis. [RJW]

38.699 Brian Loveman. *Chile: the legacy of Hispanic capitalism*. 2d rev. ed. New York: Oxford University Press, 1988. ISBN 0-19-505218-8 (cl), 0-19-505219-6 (pbk). ▸ Overview of Chilean history with emphasis on nineteenth and twentieth centuries. Well written, comprehensive, and accessible for nonspecialists and students. [RJW]

38.700 Brian Loveman. *Struggle in the countryside: politics and rural labor in Chile, 1919–1973*. Bloomington: Indiana University Press, 1976. (International Development Research Center: studies in development, 10.) ISBN 0-253-35565-6. ▸ Examination of agrarian reform and reconstruction of role of peasantry in process. Innovative research shapes complex argument. [RJW]

38.701 Markos J. Mamalakis. *The growth and structure of the Chilean economy: from independence to Allende*. New Haven: Yale University Press, 1976. ISBN 0-300-01860-6. ▸ Thorough overview stressing successes and failures of governmental economic policy. Clearly written and well documented. [RJW]

38.702 George McCutchen McBride. *Chile: land and society*. 1936 ed. New York: Octagon Books, 1971. (American Geographical Society research series, 19.) ISBN 0-374-95429-1. ▸ Dated but valuable study of agrarian problems and rural institutions, emphasizing sharp contrast between landowners and peasants. Comprehensive and well written. Available on microfiche from NCR/Microcard Editions. [RJW]

38.703 Michael Monteon. *Chile in the nitrate era: the evolution of economic dependence, 1880–1930.* Madison: University of Wisconsin Press, 1982. ISBN 0-299-08820-0. ▸ Analysis of links between government policy and nitrate industry, emphasizing British role. Presents information from viewpoint of dependency theory. [RJW]

38.704 Theodore H. Moran. *Multinational corporations and the politics of dependence: copper in Chile.* 1974 ed. Princeton: Princeton University Press, 1977. ISBN 0-691-04204-7 (cl), 0-691-00359-9 (pbk). ▸ Case study of foreign ownership of Chile's main resource and export from end of World War II to overthrow of Allende in 1973. Considerable theory mixed with basic information on crucial component of Chilean economy. [RJW]

38.705 Frederick M. Nunn. *Chilean politics, 1920–1931: the honorable mission of the armed forces.* Albuquerque: University of New Mexico Press, 1970. ▸ Detailed view of military intervention in Chilean politics in mid-1920s highlighting role of Carlos Ibáñez, president from 1927 to 1931. Clearly presented, balanced view. [RJW]

38.706 Thomas F. O'Brien. *The nitrate industry and Chile's crucial transition: 1870–1891.* New York: New York University Press, 1982. ISBN 0-8147-6159-3. ▸ Examination of role of nitrates in development of Chilean economy, focusing on elite investment patterns. Challenges dependency analysis. Should be read with Blakemore 38.680 and Monteon 38.703. [RJW]

38.707 James F. Petras. *Politics and social forces in Chilean development.* 1969 ed. Berkeley: University of California Press, 1970. ISBN 0-520-01799-4. ▸ Sociologist's view of relation between social classes and politics in twentieth-century Chile. Provocative Marxist analysis. [RJW]

38.708 Fredrick B. Pike. *Chile and the United States, 1880–1962: the emergence of Chile's social crisis and the challenge to United States diplomacy.* Notre Dame, Ind.: University of Notre Dame Press, 1963. ▸ Broader than title suggests, providing comprehensive overview of Chilean historical development, focusing on social issues. Dated but extensively researched and informative. [RJW]

38.709 Ian Roxborough, Philip O'Brien, and Jackie Roddick. *Chile: the state and revolution.* New York: Holmes & Meier, 1977. ISBN 0-8419-0234-8. ▸ View of Allende regime from perspective of British labor Left with emphasis on foreign intervention and divisions within governing coalition. Dogmatic but useful. [RJW]

38.710 William F. Sater. *Chile and the United States: empires in conflict.* Athens: University of Georgia Press, 1990. ISBN 0-8203-1249-5 (cl), 0-8203-1250-9 (pbk). ▸ Comprehensive overview. Should be read with Pike 38.708. [RJW]

38.711 William F. Sater. *Chile and the war of the Pacific.* Lincoln: University of Nebraska Press, 1986. ISBN 0-8032-4155-0. ▸ Detailed treatment of Chile's conflict with Peru and Bolivia (1879–83) over control of northern nitrate region. Extensively researched, basic source on subject. [RJW]

38.712 William F. Sater. *The heroic image in Chile: Arturo Prat, secular saint.* Berkeley: University of California Press, 1973. ISBN 0-520-02235-1. ▸ Examination of impact of popular hero of Pacific War on Chilean society and exploitation of his image by various groups. Well grounded in larger historical context and broader than title suggests. [RJW]

38.713 Paul E. Sigmund. *The overthrow of Allende and the politics of Chile, 1964–1976.* Pittsburgh: University of Pittsburgh Press, 1977. ISBN 0-8229-3355-1 (cl), 0-8229-5287-4 (pbk). ▸ Careful analysis of problems faced by presidential administrations of Christian Democrat Eduardo Frei (1964–70) and Socialist Salvador Allende (1970–73). Downplays role of United States in overthrow of Allende. [RJW]

38.714 Brian H. Smith. *The church and politics in Chile: challenges to modern Catholicism.* Princeton: Princeton University Press, 1982. ISBN 0-691-07629-4 (cl), 0-691-10119-1 (pbk). ▸ Focusing on internal divisions within church, examines role and relationship with various administrations since 1930s. Extensively researched and placed within context of larger church-state issues. [RJW]

38.715 Barbara Stallings. *Class conflict and economic development in Chile, 1958–1973.* Stanford, Calif.: Stanford University Press, 1978. ISBN 0-8047-0978-5. ▸ Analysis of economic policy and political changes under presidents Jorge Allesandri (1958–64), Eduardo Frei (1964–70), and Salvador Allende (1970–73). Stimulating comparative analysis based on extensive statistical information. [RJW]

38.716 Arturo Valenzuela. *Political brokers in Chile: local government in a centralized polity.* Durham, N.C.: Duke University Press, 1977. ISBN 0-8223-0380-9. ▸ View of relationship between local and national politics and government. Good insights into political history, especially for nineteenth century. [RJW]

38.717 J. Samuel Valenzuela and Arturo Valenzuela, eds. *Military rule in Chile: dictatorship and oppositions.* Baltimore: Johns Hopkins University Press, 1986. ISBN 0-8018-3154-7. ▸ Important series of essays by various contributors focusing on regime of Augusto Pinochet (1973–90). Set within larger context of military rule throughout Latin America. [RJW]

38.718 Peter Winn. *Weavers of revolution: the Yarur workers and Chile's road to socialism.* New York: Oxford University Press, 1986. ISBN 0-19-503960-2. ▸ Gripping account of takeover of textile factory in Santiago during Allende period. Bottom-up history, based on oral interviews. [RJW]

38.719 Allen Woll. *A functional past: the uses of history in nineteenth-century Chile.* Baton Rouge: Louisiana State University Press, 1982. ISBN 0-8071-0977-0. ▸ Informative discussion of Chile's rich historiographical tradition and its uses in developing national identity. [RJW]

38.720 Thomas C. Wright. *Landowners and reform in Chile: the Sociedad Nacional de Agricultura, 1919–40.* Champaign: University of Illinois Press, 1982. ISBN 0-252-00853-7. ▸ Detailed account of efforts of principal landowners' organization and lobbying group to stymie agrarian reform. Should be read with Bauer 38.678 and Loveman 38.700. [RJW]

38.721 George F. W. Young. *The Germans in Chile: immigration and colonization, 1849–1914.* Staten Island, N.Y.: Center for Migration Studies, 1974. ISBN 0-913256-14-5. ▸ Study of small but influential German community, located mostly in southern Chile. Should be read with McBride 38.702 and Solberg 38.658. [RJW]

38.722 Maurice Zeitlin and Richard Earl Ratcliff. *Landlords and capitalists: the dominant class of Chile.* Princeton: Princeton University Press, 1988. ISBN 0-691-07757-6 (cl), 0-691-02276-3 (pbk). ▸ Sociologists' view of Chilean elite in mid-1960s, underscoring links between finance and landowning capital. Difficult reading but informative. [RJW]

Paraguay

38.723 Michael Grow. *The Good Neighbor policy and authoritarianism in Paraguay: United States economic expansion and great power rivalry in Latin America during World War II.* Lawrence: Regents Press of Kansas, 1981. ISBN 0-7006-0213-5. ▸ Analysis of Roosevelt administration's successful effort to lure Paraguay away from Nazi influence. Good information on domestic politics in 1930s and 1940s. [RJW]

38.724 Charles J. Kolinski. *Independence or death! The story of the Paraguayan War*. Gainesville: University of Florida Press, 1965. ▸ Comprehensive history of war between Paraguay and combined forces of Argentina and Brazil (1865–70) with disastrous consequences for Paraguay. Balanced view based on secondary sources. [RJW]

38.725 Paul H. Lewis. *Paraguay under Stroessner*. Chapel Hill: University of North Carolina Press, 1980. ISBN 0-8078-1437-7. ▸ Essential source for understanding most important leader of twentieth-century Paraguay, president-dictator Alfredo Stroessner (1954–89). Good analysis of leader's control of Colorado party, main source of support. [RJW]

38.726 Paul H. Lewis. *The politics of exile: Paraguay's Febrerista party*. Chapel Hill: University of North Carolina Press, 1968. ▸ Detailed examination of major opposition party from 1930s to 1960s. Political scientist's view, drawing on oral interviews with party leaders. [RJW]

38.727 Paul H. Lewis. *Socialism, liberalism, and dictatorship in Paraguay*. New York and Stanford, Calif.: Praeger and Hoover Institution Press, 1982. ISBN 0-03-061563-1. ▸ Concise overview of Paraguayan history, emphasizing Stroessner period (1954–89). Stresses unique features of Paraguayan development. [RJW]

38.728 Carlos R. Miranda. *The Stroessner era: authoritarian rule in Paraguay*. Boulder: Westview, 1990. ISBN 0-8133-0995-6. ▸ Review of history of Paraguay under thirty-five-year rule of Stroessner, emphasizing authoritarian culture and explanation for dictatorship. Updates Lewis 38.725 in clear, concise study. [RJW]

38.729 Joseph Pincus. *The economy of Paraguay*. New York: Praeger, 1968. ▸ One of few studies of subject. Somewhat dated and overly optimistic in predictions, but useful information and statistics. [RJW]

38.730 Riordan Roett and Richard Scott Sacks. *Paraguay: the personalist legacy*. Boulder: Westview, 1991. ISBN 0-86531-272-9. ▸ Concise overview, focusing on economics, politics, and international relations after 1945. Brings story up to and through fall of Stroessner. [RJW]

38.731 Harris Gaylord Warren. *Paraguay: an informal history*. 1949 ed. Westport, Conn.: Greenwood, 1982. ISBN 0-313-23651-8. ▸ General synthesis, based on secondary materials. [RJW]

38.732 Harris Gaylord Warren. *Paraguay and the Triple Alliance; the post-war decade, 1869–1878*. Austin: University of Texas Press for Institute of Latin American Studies, 1978. (Latin American monographs, 44.) ISBN 0-292-76445-6 (cl), 0-292-76444-8 (pbk). ▸ Examination of important and neglected period in Paraguayan history in judicious and objective manner, emphasizing failure of political leadership to aid country's recovery. Well researched, based on archival sources. [RJW]

38.733 Harris Gaylord Warren. *Rebirth of the Paraguayan Republic: the first Colorado era, 1878–1904*. Pittsburgh: University of Pittsburgh Press, 1985. ISBN 0-8229-3507-4. ▸ Continues study begun in 38.731, focusing on rivalry between Liberal and Colorado parties and efforts made to rebuild nation following War of the Triple Alliance (1865–70). Essential work for period. [RJW]

38.734 Thomas Whigham. *The politics of river trade: tradition and development in the Upper Plata, 1780–1870*. Albuquerque: University of New Mexico Press, 1991. ISBN 0-8263-1312-4. ▸ Innovative regional analysis of political and economic developments in Paraguay and Argentine province of Corrientes. Questions assumption that Paraguay's autonomy and isolation fostered economic development. [RJW]

38.735 Richard Alan White. *Paraguay's autonomous revolution, 1810–1840*. Albuquerque: University of New Mexico Press, 1978. ISBN 0-8263-0486-9. ▸ Revisionist view of dictatorship of José Gaspar de Francia (1811–40), arguing for emergence of intense nationalism based on popular revolution. Provocative if not always convincing. [RJW]

38.736 John Hoyt Williams. *The rise and fall of the Paraguayan republic, 1800–1870*. Austin: University of Texas Press for Institute of Latin American Studies, 1979. (Latin American monographs, 48.) ISBN 0-292-77016-2 (cl), 0-292-77017-0 (pbk). ▸ Useful for basic understanding of country which had opportunity for autonomous development. Well-written overview with some questionable assertions. [RJW]

Uruguay

38.737 M.H.J. Finch. *A political economy of Uruguay since 1870*. New York: St. Martin's, 1982. ISBN 0-312-62244-9. ▸ Useful overview of political conflicts and economic policy, focusing on state autonomy and rural stagnation. [RJW]

38.738 Russell H. Fitzgibbon. *Uruguay: portrait of a democracy*. 1954 ed. New York: Russell & Russell, 1966. ▸ Sympathetic view of Uruguay's development from perspective of political scientist. Dated but informative. [RJW]

38.739 Charles Guy Gillespie. *Negotiating democracy: politicians and generals in Uruguay*. Cambridge: Cambridge University Press, 1991. ISBN 0-521-40152-6. ▸ Analysis of transition from authoritarian to democratic rule in Uruguay in 1980s, focusing on role of political parties. Important study, based on numerous interviews with major figures and survey data. [RJW]

38.740 Edy Kaufman. *Uruguay in transition: from civilian to military rule*. New Brunswick, N.J.: Transaction, 1979. ISBN 0-87855-242-1. ▸ Analysis of breakdown of one of Latin America's most enduring democracies in 1960s and 1970s, focusing on economic decline, rise of Tupamaro guerrilla group, and military intervention. Concise review of period. [RJW]

38.741 Göran G. Lindahl. *Uruguay's new path: a study in politics during the first Colegiado, 1919–33*. Albert Read, trans. Stockholm: Library & Institute of Ibero-American Studies, 1962. ▸ Detailed, well-researched study of Uruguay's pioneering experiment with government by committee. Basic source. [RJW]

38.742 John Street. *Artigas and the emancipation of Uruguay*. Cambridge: Cambridge University Press, 1959. ▸ Balanced, informative biography of major figure in Uruguay's early nineteenth-century struggle for independence. [RJW]

38.743 Milton I. Vanger. *José Batlle y Ordóñez of Uruguay: the creator of his times, 1902–1907*. Cambridge, Mass.: Harvard University Press, 1963. ▸ Favorable view of president of Uruguay (1903–1907, 1911–15) who instituted major social, economic, and political changes. Detailed, well-researched, informative source on Batlle and period. [RJW]

38.744 Milton I. Vanger. *The model country: José Batlle y Ordóñez of Uruguay, 1907–1915*. Hanover, N.H.: University Press of New England for Brandeis University, 1980. ISBN 0-87451-184-4. ▸ Companion to 38.743; emphasizes leadership skills and party performance as opposed to class-based support as keys to Batlle's success. Well written, clearly presented. [RJW]

38.745 Martin Weinstein. *Uruguay: the politics of failure*. Westport, Conn.: Greenwood, 1975. ISBN 0-8371-7845-2. ▸ Concise overview of Uruguayan political history, focusing on period from turn of century to 1960s with brief attention to democratic breakdown of 1970s. Useful introduction. [RJW]

38.746 Lawrence Weschler. *A miracle, a universe: settling accounts with torturers*. New York: Pantheon, 1990. ISBN 0-394-58207-1. ▸ Powerful journalistic account of repression, human rights abuses, and transitions to democracy in Brazil and Uruguay in 1970s and 1980s. [RJW]

JACK P. GREENE

Colonial North America

During the nineteenth century and the first quarter of the twentieth, historians of the area that became the United States devoted enormous energy to the study of the colonial era. Led by Herbert Levi Osgood and Charles M. Andrews, the first generation of professional historians, like students of other eras and places among their contemporaries, concentrated on political history. They mainly studied the seventeenth century and stressed the process of colony founding, the development of provincial and local political institutions, and relations between the colonies and the parent state. Few paid much attention to developments in economic, social, or cultural history. Although many of them insisted that the proper frame of reference for colonial British American history included all the British colonies in America, they largely focused on the thirteen that revolted in 1776.

The next fifty years witnessed two dramatic reversals in this well-established pattern. Between 1925 and 1950, historical interest in the colonial period declined palpably. Relatively few scholars chose to do research in the field, and those who did found themselves protesting the prevailing view that colonial history had all been written. Beginning in the early 1950s, however, the study of what one scholar correctly characterized as the "neglected first half of American history" underwent an astonishing renaissance that, almost a half century later, shows no signs of abating.

Until the late 1960s, a large proportion of this renewed interest in early America centered on the American Revolution, on such traditional questions as why the Revolution occurred, what kind of phenomenon it was, and how it related to the Constitution of 1787–1788, another focus of investigation. Scholars of the earlier period similarly concentrated on conventional institutional and political subjects within established interpretive frameworks.

As the number of scholars working in early American history proliferated through the 1960s, however, more and more turned to the one hundred and fifty years before the Revolution. The subtle and brilliant works of Perry Miller on New England Puritanism as a moral and explanatory system that changed with social and economic circumstances inspired intensive study in intellectual history, as numerous historians sought to elaborate and modify Miller's portrait of Puritan religious and intellectual development, to analyze the history of political and social thought, and to show how inherited notions about themselves and other peoples conditioned the European's attitudes toward the non-Europeans they encountered in America.

This new respect for ideas and values as important components of historical situations, a respect that was greatly enhanced by studies on the political ideology of the late colonial and Revolutionary years, was soon accompanied by a new interest in the economic, demographic, and social history of the colonies, areas that had previously been only vaguely charted. The impetus for this development came from two principal sources. Perhaps the most significant of these came from related social science disciplines, which in the decades immediately after World War II acquired, especially in the United States, a new respectability and a new sophistication. Social science influences intruded upon colonial history in two ways. A few social scientists—primarily econometric historians, historical geographers, historical sociologists, and cultural anthropologists—made important contributions to the field.

But the impact of the social sciences upon British American colonial historical studies was far too pervasive to be explained solely by the examples of a few people. As the social sciences penetrated the undergraduate curricula of universities and colleges in the United States and acquired a popular readership, historians themselves increasingly began to take over and employ, if usually only implicitly, the language, concepts, methods, and concerns of the social sciences, especially sociology, psychology, economics, and anthropology. In time, this development encouraged a demonstrable interest, unusual in historians of earlier generations, in the explicit use of theory and methods, including statistics and quantification, drawn largely from the social sciences.

The new interest among colonial historians in social, economic, demographic, and other areas of history was further reinforced by the example of new schools of methodology and historical inquiry on the other side of the Atlantic. The French Annales school had for a generation been striving for an *histoire totale* that would subordinate the history of public life to a more expanded concern for the recovery of all aspects of a population's experience, from the environmental and material to the social and intellectual, from the macro- to the micro-level, and from the most prominent inhabitants to the most marginal. An important concomitant of this development was a renewed emphasis upon local history.

By the early 1960s the orientation of this group had been taken up by those involved in the study of early modern England, where a powerful intensification of interest in Tudor and Stuart history was already in progress. Scholars concerned with the social sources of the English Revolution of the mid-seventeenth century; with the relationship between social structure, culture, and belief systems, especially as it was manifested by the recently formed Cambridge Group for the History of Population and Social Structure; and with the interaction between population history and economic, social, and political change, provided students of colonial British America with new models of how the new interest in the concerns of social science could translate into an illumination of a particular era of the past.

At the same time, the findings of these historians provided colonial historians with an expanded context for their work. They made it clearer than ever before that colonial British America was part of a larger British American world, a world to which it was in every phase of its existence intimately connected. This new perspective in turn fostered an understanding of the extent to which between 1607 and 1763 colonial British America, stretching from Barbados north to Newfoundland, was a broad socioeconomic, cultural, and political unit, only some portions of which seceded between 1776 and 1783. This broader orientation directed attention to those many island and mainland colonies that did not become part of the United States.

Initially, the interest in local history focused on New England, the intellectual and religious history of which had become so prominent in the 1960s and early 1970s. But researchers quickly began to study localities and societies farther south. For much of the first two decades of their investigations, they concentrated on the dominant male settler populations of the colonies, and their many discoveries had three important results. First was the recognition that colonial British America was divisible not just into separate colonial political entities but also into six broad regions according to differences in methods of land use, settlement patterns, socioeconomic organization, and cultural orientation: the Chesapeake, comprising Virginia, Maryland, northern North Carolina, and perhaps southern Delaware; the Atlantic islands, including the nonstaple-producing colonies of Bermuda and the Bahamas; New England, composed of Massachusetts and its offshoot colonies, Connecticut, Rhode Island, New Hampshire, and Nova Scotia; the West Indies, including until 1763 Barbados, Jamaica, and the Leeward Island colonies of Antigua, Montserrat, Nevis, and St. Christopher; the Middle Colonies, comprising New York, New Jersey, Pennsylvania, and northern Delaware; and the Lower South, containing South Carolina, southern North Carolina, and Georgia.

Second was the recognition that the experience of New England, with its powerful religious orientation and relatively spare physical environment, deviated considerably from the experiences of other regions and could not therefore be used as a model for the understanding of the rest of colonial British America. The result of this recognition was to undermine the credibility, as explanatory devices, of the modernization and *Gemeinschaft-Gesellschaft* models, with their views of Western historical development as a process of "declension" from an organic, communal subsistence, religious, and personal society to a more individualistic, market-oriented, secular, and impersonal one. Such models had been attractive because they seemed to fit reasonably well the New England experience as it was limned by Miller and several younger historians of New England communities. But they fundamentally distorted the experiences of all other regions. Colonial historians are now experimenting with the development of alternative models that stress the development of colonial regional societies from simple to complex, European-style societies.

Heightened interest in the settler societies of colonial British America perforce called attention not just to regional variations among them but to divisions within those societies. An early interest in differences among white settlers in wealth, material conditions of life, and opportunities soon yielded a concern for recovering the experiences of the large black populations imported almost entirely as slaves by settlers. Beginning in the late 1960s, this concern led to considerable work on the size, origins, role, and cultures of the slave populations—a major share of the people living in the plantation colonies from Maryland south to Barbados and a significant part of those residing in the farm colonies from Pennsylvania north. By the late 1970s other scholars were producing similar investigations of the many American Indians who, though gradually being displaced by the settlers, throughout the colonial era constituted a powerful presence within and adjacent to settler societies. The appropriation and development of anthropological techniques of ethnology and ethnography, and a growing interest in the field of historical archaeology from anthropology, aided the study of both African Americans and American Indians and produced a deeper appreciation of the multiracial, fundamentally exploitative character of colonial societies.

Investigations of the role of women, stimulated by the women's movement, have led to another major expansion of knowledge about the societies of colonial British America. Not only have those studies uncovered much new information about the domestic and public lives of both free and enslaved women but, by analyzing the many ways in which those societies were gendered, they have also deepened our understanding of the dynamics and imperatives of the male culture that sought to master them. Studies of patterns of land and resource use, the product of a growing contemporary concern with the environment, have, like studies of blacks, American Indians, and women, further enhanced our appreciation of the drive for mastery in the construction of the socioeconomic worlds of colonial British America.

Studies of the use of resources, of non-dominant groups, of social development, and of intellectual and material life have inevitably implied a concern for cultural formation in colonial British America, and since the mid-1980s this concern has been manifest in much work in the field. A growing number of scholars have begun to explore ways in which individuals, groups, and larger entities represented and identified themselves, and the processes by which the identities they constructed shaped the broader imperatives and meanings of the societies in which they lived as well as patterns of interaction within those societies.

This efflorescence of scholarship, which during the last decade has begun to lead some historians back to classic questions in political and constitutional history, has made colonial British America a field of great excitement. As its practitioners seek to find still newer approaches to their investigations, they will no doubt continue to surprise themselves with the directions and implications of their work.

In the entries that follow, the term "metropolitan" refers to the parent state or society of England or, after 1707, of Great Britain. The term "imperial" refers to those developments that pertained to the entire extended English-speaking world. The term "British North America" refers to all the continental colonies, including those provinces that would remain attached to Britain after the American Revolution and would much later become part of Canada. Because this volume contains no section for the British West Indies after 1763, this section includes entries for works on the West Indies into the early nineteenth century.

Entries are arranged under the following headings:

[Contributors: CMJ = Christopher M. Joyce, CRP = Carla Rahn Phillips, DMS = Darren M. Staloff, EVW = Edward V. Woodward, JPG = Jack P. Greene, LAN = Lynn A. Nelson, SSG = Stephen S. Gosch, WDP = William D. Phillips, Jr.]

EUROPEAN DISCOVERY AND EXPLORATION

39.1 David B. Quinn. *Set fair for Roanoke: voyages and colonies, 1584–1606.* Chapel Hill: University of North Carolina Press for America's Four Hundredth Anniversary Committee, 1985. ISBN 0-8078-1606-X (cl), 0-8078-4123-4 (pbk). ▸ Detailed recounting of effort to establish colony on Roanoke Island, 1584–90. Effectively uses that experience to explore general problems encountered by early English colonizers. [JPG]

39.2 Carl Ortwin Sauer. *Sixteenth-century North America: the land and the people as seen by the Europeans.* Berkeley: University of California Press, 1971. ISBN 0-520-01854-0 (cl), 0-520-02777-9 (pbk). ▸ Brief survey of reactions of European explorers to lands and peoples of North America during sixteenth century. [JPG]

SEE ALSO
3.180 G. V. Scammell. *The world encompassed.*

GENERAL AND REGIONAL STUDIES

39.3 Charles M. Andrews. *The colonial period of American history.* 1934–38 ed. 4 vols. New Haven: Yale University Press, 1977.

▸ Classic but uncompleted study of settlement and early institutional development of English colonies in North America, Atlantic, and West Indies during seventeenth century. Volume 4 surveys metropolitan commercial and political policy throughout colonial period. [JPG]

39.4 Ray Allen Billington, ed. *The reinterpretation of early American history: essays in honor of John Edwin Pomfret.* San Marino, Calif.: Huntington Library, 1966. ▸ Influential collection of ten essays summarizing much of existing literature, to date of publication, on colonial history. [JPG]

39.5 Daniel J. Boorstin. *The Americans: the colonial experience.* 1958 ed. New York: Vintage, 1964. ▸ Broad experiential interpretation of emergence of American cultures during colonial era. Particularly useful treatment of professions. [JPG]

39.6 T. H. Breen. *Puritans and adventurers: change and persistence in early America.* New York: Oxford University Press, 1980. ISBN 0-19-502728-0. ▸ Collection of nine essays dealing with aspects of histories of seventeenth-century New England and Virginia. [JPG]

39.7 Richard D. Brown. *Modernization: the transfomation of American life, 1600–1865.* 1976 ed. Prospect Heights, Ill.: Waveland, 1988. ISBN 0-88133-362-X. ▸ Early, suggestive, and still useful effort to build general synthesis of early American history around theme and concept of modernization. [JPG]

39.8 Wesley Frank Craven. *The colonies in transition, 1660–1713.* New York: Harper & Row, 1968. ▸ Excellent survey of history of English colonies in America between Restoration of Charles II and Treaty of Utrecht. [JPG]

39.9 Lawrence Henry Gipson. *The British empire before the American Revolution.* Rev. ed. 15 vols. New York: Knopf, 1958–70. ▸ Panoramic portrait of larger British world during third quarter of eighteenth century. Volume 14, bibliography; volume 15, guide to manuscripts. [JPG]

39.10 Jack P. Greene and J. R. Pole, eds. *Colonial British America: essays in the new history of the early modern era.* Baltimore: Johns Hopkins University Press, 1984. ISBN 0-8018-3054-0 (cl), 0-8018-3055-9 (pbk). ▸ Collection of fifteen essays surveying state of knowledge about colonial British America as of early 1980s. [JPG]

39.11 David D. Hall, John M. Murrin, and Thad W. Tate, eds. *Saints and revolutionaries: essays on early American history.* New York: Norton, 1984. ISBN 0-393-01751-6 (cl), 0-393-95522-2 (pbk). ▸ Collection of eleven significant essays, seven on colonial period, by students of Edmund S. Morgan. [JPG]

39.12 Kenneth A. Lockridge. *Settlement and unsettlement in early America: the crisis of political legitimacy before the Revolution.* Cambridge: Cambridge University Press, 1981. ISBN 0-521-23707-6. ▸ Brief, synthetic comparison of societies established in early seventeenth-century New England and Virginia. [JPG]

39.13 Herman Merivale. *Lectures on colonization and colonies.* 1861 ed. New York: Kelley, 1967. ▸ Classic, still useful work on socioeconomic processes involved in colonization. [JPG]

39.14 Gary B. Nash. *Race, class, and politics: essays on American colonial and revolutionary society.* Urbana: University of Illinois Press, 1986. ISBN 0-252-01211-9. ▸ Important collection of twelve previously published essays dealing with politics and race and class relations. [JPG]

39.15 Gary B. Nash. *Red, white, and black: the peoples of early North America.* 3d ed. Englewood Cliffs, N.J.: Prentice-Hall, 1992. ISBN 0-13-769878-X (pbk). ▸ Early, very general effort to produce multicultural history of colonial North America by incorporating American Indians and African Americans into narrative. [JPG]

39.16 Herbert Levi Osgood. *The American colonies in the eighteenth century.* 1924–25 ed. 4 vols. Gloucester, Mass.: Smith, 1958. ▸ Still fullest narrative history of British North American colonies from 1700 to end of Seven Years' War (1763). Especially valuable for its detailed narrative of political history of particular colonies during still neglected period before 1750. [JPG]

39.17 Herbert Levi Osgood. *The American colonies in the seventeenth century.* 1904 ed. 3 vols. Gloucester, Mass.: Smith, 1957. ▸ Still best comprehensive political history of British North American colonies before Glorious Revolution of 1688–89. [JPG]

39.18 David B. Quinn, ed. *Early Maryland in a wider world.* Detroit: Wayne State University Press, 1982. ISBN 0-8143-1689-1. ▸ Useful collection of ten essays on background to English colonization with special focus on Maryland. [JPG]

39.19 James Morton Smith, ed. *Seventeenth-century America: essays in colonial history.* 1959 ed. Westport, Conn.: Greenwood, 1980. ISBN 0-313-22075-1. ▸ Contains eleven excellent essays exploring aspects of history of English continental colonies during seventeenth century. [JPG]

39.20 David G. Sweet and Gary B. Nash, eds. *Struggle and survival in colonial America.* Berkeley: University of California Press, 1981. ISBN 0-520-04110-0. ▸ Series of articles on history of ordinary participants in creation of early modern American colonial worlds. Six of twenty-one essays deal with people in colonial British America. [JPG]

39.21 Alden T. Vaughan and George Athan Billias, eds. *Perspectives on early American history: essays in honor of Richard B. Morris.* New York: Harper & Row, 1973. ISBN 0-06-014504-8. ▸ Collection of twelve essays, six on colonial period and three on major colonial historians, with bibliography of writings of Richard B. Morris. [JPG]

39.22 Silvio Zavala. *Program of the history of the New World.* Vol. 2: *The colonial period in the history of the New World.* Abridged ed. Max Savelle, ed. and trans. Mexico City: Instituto Panamericano de Geografía e Historia, 1962. (Instituto Panamericano de Geografía e Historia, Comisión de Historia: Publicación, 102–3, 108.) ▸ General comparative survey of early modern American colonization to end of European American empires. [JPG]

SEE ALSO
37.141 Nicholas P. Canny and Anthony Pagden, eds. *Colonial identity in the Atlantic world, 1500–1800.*

Atlantic Context

39.23 Angus Calder. *Revolutionary empire: the rise of the English-speaking empires from the fifteenth century to the 1780s.* New York: Dutton, 1981. ISBN 0-525-19080-5. ▸ Best one-volume survey of history of early modern British world to 1780s. Successfully endeavors to make history of colonies, Ireland, and Scotland part of British history. [JPG]

39.24 K. G. Davies. *The North Atlantic world in the seventeenth century.* Minneapolis: University of Minnesota Press, 1974. ISBN 0-8166-0716-3. ▸ General history of British, French, and Dutch activities in North America, Caribbean, and West Africa. Makes useful distinction between two types of colonizing activities: commercial outposts intended to gather products for distribution, and colonies of European settlement established to produce commodities such as tobacco and sugar. [JPG]

39.25 Ralph Davis. *The rise of the Atlantic economies.* Ithaca, N.Y.: Cornell University Press, 1973. ISBN 0-8014-0801-6. ▸ Authoritative account of economic development of European Atlantic empires from Portuguese expansion in fifteenth century to American Revolution. [JPG]

39.26 Michael Kraus. *The Atlantic civilization: eighteenth-century origins.* 1949 ed. Ithaca, N.Y.: Cornell University Press, 1966. ▸ Early treatment of cohering North Atlantic world, with chapters on commercial and intellectual relations between British colonies and England. [JPG]

39.27 James Lang. *Conquest and commerce: Spain and England in the Americas.* New York: Academic Press, 1975. ISBN 0-12-436450-0. ▸ Brief but suggestive comparative study of Spanish and English colonization in America to late eighteenth century. [JPG]

39.28 Max Savelle. *Empires to nations: expansion in America, 1713–1824.* Vol. 5. Minneapolis: University of Minnesota Press, 1974. ISBN 0-8166-0709-5. ▸ Broad study of process of European colonization in Americas during eighteenth and early nineteenth centuries emphasizing plural character of societies that emerged. [JPG]

39.29 Thomas M. Truxes. *Irish-American trade, 1660–1783.* Cambridge: Cambridge University Press, 1988. ISBN 0-521-35373-4. ▸ Detailed exploration of substantial and growing trade between Ireland and colonial British America. Fills important gap. [JPG]

SEE ALSO
3.210 J. H. Parry. *Trade and dominion.*
23.129 Ian K. Steele. *The English Atlantic, 1675–1740.*

British Politics and Administration

39.30 Charles M. Andrews. *The colonial background of the American Revolution: four essays in American colonial history.* 1931 rev. ed. New Haven: Yale University Press, 1971. ISBN 0-300-00004-9 (pbk). ▸ Classic overview of key aspects in metropolitan-colonial relationship during century before Revolution. [JPG]

39.31 Thomas C. Barrow. *Trade and empire: the British Customs Service in colonial America, 1660–1775.* Cambridge, Mass.: Harvard University Press, 1967. ▸ Rather general study of operation of British Customs Service in North American colonies between Restoration of Charles II and Declaration of Independence. [JPG]

39.32 Arthur H. Basye. *The Lord Commissioners of Trade and Plantations commonly known as the Board of Trade, 1748–1782.* New Haven: Yale University Press, 1925. ▸ Succinct account of last thirty-four years of Board of Trade in British colonial administration. [JPG]

39.33 Arthur C. Bining. *British regulation of the colonial iron industry.* 1933 ed. Clifton, N.J.: Kelley, 1973. ISBN 0-678-00924-4. ▸ Still best analysis of British efforts to restrict colonial manufacturing. [JPG]

39.34 Robert M. Bliss. *Revolution and empire: English politics and the American colonies in the seventeenth century.* Manchester: Manchester University Press; distributed by St. Martin's, 1990. ISBN 0-7190-2383-1. ▸ Most successful attempt yet to relate North American colonization to seventeenth-century English politics. [JPG]

39.35 Beverley W. Bond, Jr. *The quitrent system in the American colonies.* 1919 ed. Charles M. Andrews, Introduction. Gloucester, Mass.: Smith, 1965. ▸ Classic study of metropolitan efforts to collect rents from royal land grants and difficulties encountered. [JPG]

39.36 Carl Bridenbaugh. *Mitre and sceptre: transatlantic faiths, ideas, personalities, and politics, 1689–1775.* New York: Oxford University Press, 1962. ▸ Examination of religious dimensions of metropolitan-colonial relations. [JPG]

39.37 James J. Burns. *The colonial agents of New England.* 1935 ed. Philadelphia: Porcupine, 1975. ISBN 0-87991-350-9. ▸ Early account of colonial agency and people who held those posts for New England colonies. [JPG]

39.38 Dora Mae Clark. *The rise of the British treasury: colonial administration in the eighteenth century.* 1960 ed. Hamden, Conn.: Archon, 1969. ISBN 0-208-00788-1. ‣ Careful study of role of treasury in colonial administration. [JPG]

39.39 Evarts B. Greene. *The provincial governor in the English colonies of North America.* 1898 ed. New York: Russell & Russell, 1966. ‣ Pioneering but still useful study of institution of governorship in English colonies. [JPG]

39.40 G. H. Guttridge. *The colonial policy of William III in America and the West Indies.* 1922 ed. Hamden, Conn.: Archon, 1966. ‣ Older study of important, defining era in metropolitan-colonial relations. [JPG]

39.41 Michael G. Hall. *Edward Randolph and the American colonies, 1676–1703.* Chapel Hill: University of North Carolina Press for Institute of Early American History and Culture, 1960. ‣ Good, short account of early British efforts to bring colonies under closer supervision and of difficulties Randolph encountered as agent of imperial change. [JPG]

39.42 Lawrence A. Harper. *The English navigation laws: a seventeenth-century experiment in social engineering.* 1939 ed. New York: Octagon Books, 1973. ISBN 0-374-93667-6. ‣ Older study that remains most thorough exploration of law and practice of English navigation system. [JPG]

39.43 James A. Henretta. *"Salutary neglect": colonial administration under the duke of Newcastle.* Princeton: Princeton University Press, 1972. ISBN 0-691-05196-8. ‣ Detailed study of use of patronage in colonial sphere and its effect on British colonial administration during what historian Edmund Burke called era of salutary neglect. [JPG]

39.44 Joseph E. Illick. *William Penn the politician: his relations with the English government.* Ithaca, N.Y.: Cornell University Press, 1965. ‣ Best analysis of relationship of key proprietary figure with metropolitan government. [JPG]

39.45 Gertrude A. Jacobsen. *William Blathwayt: a late seventeenth-century English administrator.* New Haven and London: Yale University Press and Oxford University Press, 1933. ‣ Only full-length study of member of metropolitan bureaucracy that formed colonial policy. [JPG]

39.46 Richard R. Johnson. *Adjustment to empire: the New England colonies, 1675–1715.* New Brunswick, N.J.: Rutgers University Press, 1981. ISBN 0-8135-0907-6. ‣ Excellent analysis of conflicts stimulated by metropolitan efforts to restrict autonomy of New England colonies during late seventeenth century and of their gradual integration into emerging imperial system. [JPG]

39.47 Richard R. Johnson. *John Nelson, merchant adventurer: a life between empires.* New York: Oxford University Press, 1991. ISBN 0-19-506505-0. ‣ Case study of man whose trading activities across boundaries between French settlements in Acadia and Canada gave him expertise that made him valuable consultant for English policy makers. [JPG]

39.48 Michael Kammen. *Empire and interest: the American colonies and the politics of mercantilism.* Philadelphia: Lippincott, 1970. ‣ Much too cursory effort to show how various interests affected governance and operation of empire. [JPG]

39.49 A. Berriedale Keith. *Constitutional history of the first British empire.* Oxford: Clarendon, 1930. ‣ Comprehensive analysis of constitutional development of early modern British empire. [JPG]

39.50 Alice M. Keys. *Cadwallader Colden: a representative eighteenth-century official.* 1906 ed. New York: AMS Press, 1967. ‣ Old but still useful study of long-term metropolitan bureaucrat in colonies. [JPG]

39.51 Walter A. Knittle. *Early eighteenth-century Palatine emigration: a British government redemptioner project to manufacture naval stores.* 1937 ed. Baltimore: Genealogical Publishing, 1965. ‣ Still valuable account of early metropolitan effort to turn colonial economy to serve metropolitan needs. [JPG]

39.52 Klaus E. Knorr. *British colonial theories, 1570–1850.* 1944 ed. London: Cass, 1964. ‣ Still most comprehensive study of changing ideas of colonization among English and British people during first three centuries of British overseas empire. [JPG]

39.53 Richard Koebner. *Empire.* Cambridge: Cambridge University Press, 1961. ‣ Imaginative linguistic exploration of changing meaning of term empire, according special attention to its use in early modern British empire. [JPG]

39.54 Leonard W. Labaree. *Royal government in America: a study of the British colonial system before 1783.* 1930 ed. New York: Ungar, 1958. ‣ Classic study of organization and operation of royal government in Britain's American colonies during early modern era. [JPG]

39.55 Edward P. Lily. *The colonial agents of New York and New Jersey.* Washington, D.C.: Catholic University of America Press, 1936. ‣ Study of colonial agency and people who filled it for colonies of New York and New Jersey. [JPG]

39.56 Ella Lonn. *The colonial agents of the southern colonies.* 1945 ed. Gloucester, Mass.: Smith, 1965. ‣ Probably best study of functioning of colonial agents within British imperial system. [JPG]

39.57 David S. Lovejoy. *The Glorious Revolution in America.* 1972 ed. Middletown, Conn.: Wesleyan University Press; distributed by Harper & Row, 1987. ISBN 0-8195-6177-0 (pbk). ‣ Effective analysis of relations between England and its American colonies in decades surrounding Glorious Revolution (1689). [JPG]

39.58 Joseph J. Malone. *Pine trees and politics: the naval stores and forest policy in colonial New England, 1691–1775.* 1964 ed. New York: Arno, 1979. ISBN 0-405-11380-3. ‣ Case study of metropolitan attempts to steer New England economy into production of naval stores and masts. [JPG]

39.59 Helen Hill Miller. *Colonel Parke of Virginia: "the greatest hector in the town," a biography.* Chapel Hill, N.C.: Algonquin, 1989. ISBN 0-912697-87-3. ‣ Compelling biography of Virginia-born creole American who cut significant figure in metropolitan England through his military exploits and colonial governorship in Leeward Islands. Only prerevolutionary British colonial governor murdered by colonists. [JPG]

39.60 Alison Gilbert Olson. *Anglo-American politics, 1660–1775: the relationship between parties in England and colonial America.* New York: Oxford University Press, 1973. ‣ Broad effort to interpret colonial politics as reflection of contemporary British politics. Not sufficiently sensitive to local roots of colonial political behavior. [JPG]

39.61 Alison Gilbert Olson. *Making the empire work: London and American interest groups, 1690–1790.* Cambridge, Mass.: Harvard University Press, 1992. ISBN 0-674-54318-1. ‣ Short study of operation of interest groups in metropolitan-colonial relations during century following Glorious Revolution (1689). [JPG]

39.62 Alison Gilbert Olson and Richard Maxwell Brown, eds. *Anglo-American political relations, 1675–1775.* New Brunswick, N.J.: Rutgers University Press, 1970. ISBN 0-8135-0624-7. ‣ Valuable collection of eleven essays touching on many aspects of metropolitan-colonial relations during century after 1675. Essays by Lovejoy, Dunn, Katz, and Shy especially notable. [JPG]

39.63 Lillian M. Penson. *The colonial agents of the British West Indies: a study in colonial administration, mainly in the eighteenth century.* 1924 ed. London: Cass, 1971. ISBN 0-7146-1944-2.

▸ Analysis of office of colonial agent and men who occupied it for West Indian colonies. [JPG]

39.64 J. G. A. Pocock, ed. *Three British revolutions: 1641, 1688, 1776*. Princeton: Princeton University Press, 1980. ISBN 0-691-05293-X (cl), 0-691-10087-X (pbk). ▸ Essays by eleven scholars touching on aspects of relationship between American Revolution and seventeenth-century English revolutions. [JPG]

39.65 J. R. Pole. *Political representation in England and the origins of the American republic*. 1966 ed. Berkeley: University of California Press, 1971. ISBN 0-520-01903-2. ▸ Classic study of development of ideas and practices of representation in seventeenth- and eighteenth-century Britain and British America. [JPG]

39.66 Trevor Richard Reese. *Colonial Georgia: a study in British imperial policy in the eighteenth century*. Athens: University of Georgia Press, 1963. ▸ Valuable study of metropolitan goals in establishing colony of Georgia and meaning of that effort for changing structure of British imperial designs. [JPG]

39.67 John A. Schutz. *Thomas Pownall, British defender of American liberty: a study of Anglo-American relations in the eighteenth century*. Glendale, Calif.: Clark, 1951. ▸ Extensive biographical account of man who figured prominently in metropolitan-colonial affairs of mid-eighteenth century and was governor of Massachusetts. [JPG]

39.68 J. M. Sosin. *English America and imperial inconstancy: the rise of provincial autonomy, 1696–1715*. Lincoln: University of Nebraska Press, 1985. ISBN 0-8032-4154-2. ▸ Study of metropolitan-colonial relations from 1690s to 1715 that cites parsimony and neglect to account for failure of British officials to bring continental colonies under closer supervision. [JPG]

39.69 J. M. Sosin. *English America and the Restoration monarchy of Charles II: transatlantic politics, commerce, and kinship*. Lincoln: University of Nebraska Press, 1980. ISBN 0-8032-4118-6. ▸ Detailed study of metropolitan efforts under Charles II to establish effective governance over continental colonies. [JPG]

39.70 J. M. Sosin. *English America and the revolution of 1688: royal administration and the structure of provincial government*. Lincoln: University of Nebraska Press, 1982. ISBN 0-8032-4131-3. ▸ Detailed exploration of metropolitan-colonial relations for continental colonies from accession of James II to mid-1690s. [JPG]

39.71 Ian K. Steele. *Politics of colonial policy: the Board of Trade in colonial administration, 1696–1720*. Oxford: Clarendon, 1968. ISBN 0-19-821375-1. ▸ Careful study of workings of Board of Trade during first quarter century of its existence. [JPG]

39.72 George Macgregor Waller. *Samuel Vetch: colonial enterpriser*. Chapel Hill: University of North Carolina Press for Institute of Early American History and Culture, 1960. ▸ Engrossing case study of key actor in competition among empires during late seventeenth and early eighteenth century. [JPG]

39.73 Stephen Saunders Webb. *The governors-general: the English army and the definition of the empire, 1569–1681*. Chapel Hill: University of North Carolina Press for Institute of Early American History and Culture, 1979. ISBN 0-8078-1331-1. ▸ Study emphasizing militaristic and autocratic tendencies within English colonizing activities before 1680s. [JPG]

39.74 Stephen Saunders Webb. *1676: the end of American independence*. New York: Knopf, 1984. ISBN 0-394-41414-4. ▸ Study of process by which English government sought to bring colonies under much tighter metropolitan controls during Restoration (1660–84). [JPG]

39.75 Mabel Pauline Wolff. *The colonial agency of Pennsylvania, 1712–1757*. Philadelphia: Wolff, 1933. ▸ Consideration of role of Pennsylvania agents to London during eighteenth century. Also

available on microfilm from University Park: Pennsylvania State University, 1993. [JPG]

SEE ALSO
23.130 A. P. Thornton. *West-India policy under the Restoration*.
41.63 Jack P. Greene and William G. McLoughlin. *Preachers and politicians*.

New England

39.76 James Truslow Adams. *The founding of New England*. 1921 ed. Boston: Little, Brown, 1949. ▸ General narrative history of New England colonies to fall of Dominion of New England (1689). [JPG]

39.77 James Truslow Adams. *Revolutionary New England, 1691–1776*. Boston: Atlantic Monthly, 1923. ▸ Comprehensive history of New England colonies from Glorious Revolution to American Revolution. [JPG]

39.78 Roy H. Akagi. *The town proprietors of the New England colonies: a study of their development, organization, activities, and controversies, 1620–1770*. 1924 ed. Gloucester, Mass.: Smith, 1963. ▸ Classic study of chief movers in expansion of New England during colonial era. [JPG]

39.79 David Grayson Allen. *In English ways: the movement of societies and the transferal of English local law and custom to Massachusetts Bay in the seventeenth century*. 1981 ed. New York: Norton, 1982. ISBN 0-393-95238-X (pbk). ▸ Uses experiences of five New England towns to show extent to which early Massachusetts settlers succeeded in transferring local British cultures to their new homes. [JPG]

39.80 Virginia De John Anderson. *New England's generation: the Great Migration and the formation of society and culture in the seventeenth century*. Cambridge: Cambridge University Press, 1991. ISBN 0-521-40506-8. ▸ Reconsideration of meaning New England settlers attached to Great Migration. Persuasively emphasizes importance of religion in construction of New England society (1629–30). [JPG]

39.81 Robert C. Black III. *The younger John Winthrop*. New York: Columbia University Press, 1966. ▸ Uses life of Winthrop to illuminate expansion process and political life in early New England and to assess Winthrop's achievements as scientific observer. [JPG]

39.82 Francis J. Bremer. *Puritan crisis: New England and the English civil wars, 1630–1670*. New York: Garland, 1989. ISBN 0-8240-6173-X. ▸ Expansion of Miller's argument (39.103, 39.603, 39.604, 39.605, 39.606, 39.607, 39.699) that leaders of New England colonies intended colonies as model for reformation of old England. Explains how that idea shaped their behavior to early 1660s and why it gradually lost force. [JPG]

39.83 Carl Bridenbaugh. *Fat mutton and liberty of conscience: society in Rhode Island, 1636–1690*. Providence: Brown University Press, 1974. ISBN 0-87057-143-5. ▸ Largely descriptive but insightful study of development of Rhode Island society during seventeenth century. [JPG]

39.84 John L. Brooke. *The heart of the commonwealth: society and political culture in Worcester County, Massachusetts, 1713–1861*. Cambridge: Cambridge University Press, 1989. ISBN 0-521-37029-9. ▸ First part of book provides excellent portrait of social and political life of large Massachusetts county, 1713–63. [JPG]

39.85 Richard L. Bushman. *From Puritan to Yankee: character and the social order in Connecticut, 1690–1765*. 1967 ed. Cambridge, Mass.: Harvard University Press, 1980. ISBN 0-674-32551-6. ▸ Marvellous, highly influential book on social and political history of Connecticut between Glorious Revolution and

Stamp Act crisis. No better study of politics of expansion for any colony. [JPG]

39.86 Charles E. Clark. *The eastern frontier: the settlement of northern New England, 1610–1763.* 1970 ed. Hanover, N.H.: University Press of New England, 1983. ISBN 0-87451-252-2 (pbk). ▸ Sweeping social history of New England frontier throughout colonial period. Particularly valuable for its discussion of expansionist tendencies, 1713–63. [JPG]

39.87 Hermann Frederick Clarke and Henry Wilder Foote. *Jeremiah Dummer: colonial craftsman and merchant, 1645–1718.* 1935 ed. New York: Da Capo, 1970. ISBN 0-306-71394-2. ▸ Biography of important merchant and public figure of colonial New England. [JPG]

39.88 Edward M. Cook, Jr. *The fathers of the towns: leadership and community structure in eighteenth-century New England.* Baltimore: Johns Hopkins University Press, 1976. ISBN 0-8018-1741-2. ▸ Imaginative, well-designed macrostudy using extensive prosopographical analysis of political leaders in large number of New England towns to establish persuasive typology among them. [JPG]

39.89 Jere R. Daniell. *Colonial New Hampshire: a history.* Millwood, N.Y.: KTO, 1981. ISBN 0-527-18715-1. ▸ Highly schematic, selective narrative history of colonial New Hampshire. [JPG]

39.90 Bruce C. Daniels. *The fragmentation of New England: comparative perspectives on economic, political, and social divisions in the eighteenth century.* Westport, Conn.: Greenwood, 1988. ISBN 0-313-26358-2. ▸ Valuable collection of previously published essays on many aspects of New England social development. [JPG]

39.91 Richard S. Dunn. *Puritans and yankees: the Winthrop dynasty of New England, 1630–1717.* 1962 ed. New York: Norton, 1971. ISBN 0-393-00597-6. ▸ Effectively traces history of many aspects of first century of New England experience through lives of three generations of prominent Massachusetts and Connecticut family. Emphasizes growing secularization of New England and New England struggle against metropolitan centralization. [JPG]

39.92 Philip S. Haffenden. *New England in the English nation, 1689–1713.* Oxford: Clarendon, 1974. ISBN 0-19-821124-4. ▸ History of failure of metropolitan government to provide military support to New England during first two intercolonial wars. [JPG]

39.93 David D. Hall and David Grayson Allen, eds. *Seventeenth-century New England.* Boston: Colonial Society of Massachusetts; distributed by University Press of Virginia, 1984. (Publications of the Colonial Society of Massachusetts, 63.) ISBN 0-8139-1048-X. ▸ Superb collection of ten authoritative essays touching on many important aspects of seventeenth-century New England history. [JPG]

39.94 Sydney V. James. *Colonial Rhode Island: a history.* New York: Scribner's, 1975. ISBN 0-684-14359-3. ▸ Superb general narrative of history of colonial Rhode Island. [JPG]

39.95 Mary Jeanne Anderson Jones. *Congregational commonwealth: Connecticut, 1636–1662.* Middletown, Conn.: Wesleyan University Press, 1968. ▸ Excellent narrative history of first twenty-five years of Connecticut colony with special attention to formation of Connecticut polity. [JPG]

39.96 Benjamin W. Labaree. *Colonial Massachusetts: a history.* Millwood, N.Y.: KTO, 1979. ISBN 0-527-18714-3. ▸ Good, if rather general, survey of long history of colonial Massachusetts. [JPG]

39.97 George D. Langdon, Jr. *Pilgrim colony: a history of New Plymouth, 1620–1691.* New Haven: Yale University Press, 1966.

▸ Carefully researched, comprehensive history of public life of Plymouth colony. [JPG]

39.98 Douglas Edward Leach. *The northern colonial frontier, 1607–1763.* New York: Holt, Rinehart & Winston, 1966. ▸ Broad, general history of northern frontier of British colonies. [JPG]

39.99 Paul R. Lucas. *Valley of discord: church and society along the Connecticut River, 1636–1725.* Hanover, N.H.: University Press of New England, 1976. ISBN 0-87451-121-6. ▸ Exploration of social and religious conflict in New England during first nine decades of settlement using history of towns established along Connecticut River. [JPG]

39.100 Jackson Turner Main. *Society and economy in colonial Connecticut.* Princeton: Princeton University Press, 1985. ISBN 0-691-04726-X. ▸ Excellent economic and social history of colonial Connecticut, particularly important for its finding that few free males failed to acquire enough property to provide them economic competence as they advanced in age and established themselves. [JPG]

39.101 John Frederick Martin. *Profits in the wilderness: entrepreneurship and the founding of New England towns in the seventeenth century.* Chapel Hill: University of North Carolina Press for Institute of Early American History and Culture, 1991. ISBN 0-8078-2001-6 (cl), 0-8078-4346-6 (pbk). ▸ Impressive exploration of early histories of around sixty New England towns showing importance of profit motive among entrepreneurs who dominated process of town founding. [JPG]

39.102 Lois K. Mathews. *The expansion of New England: the spread of New England settlement and institutions to the Mississippi River, 1620–1865.* 1909 ed. New York: Russell & Russell, 1962. ▸ Early study that remains fullest and best account of spread of New Englanders across northern tier of area that became United States. [JPG]

39.103 Perry Miller. *Orthodoxy in Massachusetts, 1630–1650: a genetic study.* 1933 ed. Gloucester, Mass.: Smith, 1965. ▸ Pioneering work that launched massive effort to recover intellectual and religious world of Puritan settlers of New England. Explores religious dimensions of Massachusetts Bay Colony from Great Migration to 1650. [JPG]

39.104 Edmund S. Morgan. *The Puritan dilemma: the story of John Winthrop.* Oscar Handlin, ed. Boston: Little, Brown, 1958. ▸ Lucid interpretation of Puritan experiment in New England through career of its principal lay leader, John Winthrop. [JPG]

39.105 Frank Shuffelton. *Thomas Hooker, 1586–1647.* Princeton: Princeton University Press, 1977. ISBN 0-691-05249-2. ▸ Lucid biography of leading founder of New England. Assesses Hooker's contribution to Puritanism and to establishment of New England. [JPG]

39.106 Robert J. Taylor. *Colonial Connecticut: a history.* Millwood, N.Y.: KTO, 1979. ISBN 0-527-18710-0. ▸ Strong, if much too brief, general narrative history of colonial Connecticut. [JPG]

39.107 David E. Van Deventer. *The emergence of provincial New Hampshire, 1623–1741.* Baltimore: Johns Hopkins University Press, 1976. ISBN 0-8018-1730-7. ▸ Best social and economic history available for any colony. Covers long period from beginnings of New Hampshire to 1741. [JPG]

39.108 Avihu Zakai. *Theocracy in Massachusetts: reformation and separation in early Puritan New England.* San Francisco: Mellen Research University Press, 1993. ISBN 0-7734-9970-9. ▸ One of first studies to emphasize role of millennial thought in formation of Massachusetts Bay colony and in colony's continuing conception of itself in relation to England. [JPG]

39.109 Michael Zuckerman. *Peaceable kingdoms: New England towns in the eighteenth century.* 1970 ed. New York: Norton, 1978.

ISBN 0-393-00895-9. ▸ Provocative study of operation of New England communities stressing vitality of community and role of consensus in public life. [JPG]

Middle Colonies

39.110 Edwin B. Bronner. *William Penn's "holy experiment": the founding of Pennsylvania, 1681–1701.* 1962 ed. New York: Temple University Press; distributed by Columbia University Press, 1963. ▸ Standard account of first two decades of Pennsylvania colony. [JPG]

39.111 Thomas E. Burke, Jr. *Mohawk frontier: the Dutch community of Schenectady, New York, 1661–1710.* Ithaca, N.Y.: Cornell University Press, 1991. ISBN 0-8014-2541-7. ▸ Useful community study of Schenectady stressing continuing Dutch influences and continuing presence of American Indians and other outsiders in area that remained on frontier of New York throughout colonial era. [JPG]

39.112 Thomas J. Condon. *New York beginnings: the commercial origins of New Netherland.* New York: New York University Press, 1968. ▸ Examination of commercial dimensions of New Netherlands under the Dutch. Suffers from failure to utilize Dutch sources. [JPG]

39.113 Wesley Frank Craven. *New Jersey and the English colonization of North America.* Princeton: Van Nostrand, 1964. ▸ Impressive short analysis of place of New Jersey in colonizing process after Restoration (1660). [JPG]

39.114 Hubertis Cummings. *Richard Peters: provincial secretary and cleric, 1704–1776.* Philadelphia: University of Pennsylvania Press, 1944. ▸ Biography of significant actor in Pennsylvania public life. [JPG]

39.115 Richard S. Dunn and Mary Maples Dunn, eds. *The world of William Penn.* Philadelphia: University of Pennsylvania Press, 1986. ISBN 0-8122-8020-2. ▸ Collection of twenty essays relating to William Penn and his world in both England and America. Nine essays treat colonial Pennsylvania. [JPG]

39.116 Dixon Ryan Fox. *Caleb Heathcote, gentleman colonist: the story of a career in the province of New York, 1692–1721.* 1926 ed. New York: Cooper Square, 1971. ISBN 0-8154-0392-5. ▸ Biography of metropolitan officeholder in New York. [JPG]

39.117 Ruth L. Higgins. *Expansion in New York, with especial reference to the eighteenth century.* 1931 ed. Philadelphia: Porcupine, 1976. ISBN 0-87991-354-1. ▸ Older work; still best account of this important subject. [JPG]

39.118 Joseph E. Illick. *Colonial Pennsylvania: a history.* New York: Scribner's, 1976. ISBN 0-684-14565-0. ▸ Excellent general survey of history of colonial Pennsylvania. [JPG]

39.119 Michael Kammen. *Colonial New York: a history.* New York: Scribner's, 1975. ISBN 0-684-14325-9. ▸ Excellent one-volume history. [JPG]

39.120 Ralph L. Ketcham. *Benjamin Franklin.* New York: Washington Square, 1965. ▸ Clear, concise biography of important Philadelphian. [JPG]

39.121 Sung Bok Kim. *Landlord and tenant in colonial New York: manorial society, 1664–1775.* Chapel Hill: University of North Carolina Press for Institute of Early American History and Culture, 1978. ISBN 0-8078-1290-0. ▸ Excellent book on landlord system that developed in colonial New York and fundamentally altered understanding of tenant motivation and mobility and of nature of agrarian conflict in late colonial era. [JPG]

39.122 Ned C. Landsman. *Scotland and its first American colony, 1683–1765.* Princeton: Princeton University Press, 1985. ISBN 0-691-04724-3. ▸ Important analysis of development of Scottish settlements in New Jersey beginning in late seventeenth century. Notable for its emphasis on Scottish background of those settlements and successful recreation of lowland Scottish culture in New Jersey. [JPG]

39.123 Adrian C. Leiby. *The early Dutch and Swedish settlers of New Jersey.* Princeton: Van Nostrand, 1964. ▸ Brief but authoritative account of Dutch and Swedish activities in area that subsequently became colony of New Jersey. [JPG]

39.124 Peter C. Mancall. *Valley of opportunity: economic culture along the upper Susquehanna, 1700–1800.* Ithaca, N.Y.: Cornell University Press, 1991. ISBN 0-8014-2503-4. ▸ Analysis of cultural transformation of upper Susquehanna Valley from American Indian to European American. Especially notable for its demonstration of powerful influence of land developers in defining new settlements. [JPG]

39.125 Donna Merwick. *Possessing Albany, 1630–1710: the Dutch and English experiences.* Cambridge: Cambridge University Press, 1990. ISBN 0-521-37386-7. ▸ Exploration of largely unsuccessful efforts of Dutch to retain their Dutch culture in decades after English conquest. Focuses on Albany. Marred by author's unabashedly pro-Dutch stance. [JPG]

39.126 John A. Munroe. *Colonial Delaware: a history.* Millwood, N.Y.: KTO, 1978. ISBN 0-527-18711-9. ▸ Only general history of colonial Delaware. Suffers from dearth of secondary literature about colony. [JPG]

39.127 S. G. Nissenson. *The patroon's domain.* 1937 ed. New York: Octagon Books, 1973. ISBN 0-374-96109-3. ▸ Older study; still best account of largely failed efforts of Dutch to people New Netherlands with Europeans by shifting burden of attracting settlers to large landed proprietors. [JPG]

39.128 John E. Pomfret. *Colonial New Jersey: a history.* New York: Scribner's, 1973. ISBN 0-684-13371-7. ▸ Still best narrative treatment of subject although now out of date. [JPG]

39.129 John E. Pomfret. *The province of East New Jersey, 1609–1702: the rebellious proprietary.* Princeton: Princeton University Press, 1962. ▸ Detailed narrative history of colony of East Jersey before it was incorporated into New Jersey in 1702. [JPG]

39.130 John E. Pomfret. *The province of West New Jersey, 1609–1702: a history of the origins of an American colony.* 1956 ed. New York: Octagon Books, 1976. ISBN 0-374-96516-1. ▸ Detailed narrative history of colony of West Jersey before it was incorporated into New Jersey in 1702. [JPG]

39.131 Ellis Lawrence Raesly. *Portrait of New Netherland.* 1945 ed. Port Washington, N.Y.: Friedman, 1965. ▸ Still valuable general history of everyday life in New Netherlands. [JPG]

39.132 Oliver A. Rink. *Holland on the Hudson: an economic and social history of Dutch New York.* Ithaca, N.Y.: Cornell University Press, 1986. ISBN 0-8014-1866-6. ▸ Very useful general analysis of economic and social history of New Netherlands under the Dutch. [JPG]

39.133 Sally Schwartz. *"A mixed multitude": the struggle for toleration in colonial Pennsylvania.* New York: New York University Press, 1987. ISBN 0-8147-7873-9. ▸ Coherent recounting of how heterogeneous settlers of Pennsylvania during colonial era achieved William Penn's ideal of plural society with religious toleration. [JPG/LAN]

39.134 George L. Smith. *Religion and trade in New Netherland: Dutch origins and American development.* Ithaca, N.Y.: Cornell University Press, 1973. ISBN 0-8014-0790-7. ▸ Exploration of materials relating to developments on both sides of Atlantic. Persuasively shows how commercial and secular motives predominated over religious concerns in history of New Netherlands.

Attributes secular character of colony primarily to this factor. [JPG]

39.135 Carl Van Doren. *Benjamin Franklin.* 1938 ed. New York: Bramhall House; distributed by Crown, 1987. ISBN 0-517-62532-6. ▸ Perhaps best written biography of Pennsylvania's most prominent colonial inhabitant. [JPG]

39.136 C. A. Weslager. *The English on the Delaware: 1610–1682.* New Brunswick, N.J.: Rutgers University Press, 1967. ▸ Narrative history of English interest and activities in Delaware River valley before founding of Pennsylvania. [JPG]

39.137 Esmond Wright. *Franklin of Philadelphia.* Cambridge, Mass.: Belknap, 1986. ISBN 0-674-31809-9. ▸ Readable, most recent effort at comprehensive biography of Benjamin Franklin. [JPG]

39.138 Michael Zuckerman, ed. *Friends and neighbors: group life in America's first plural society.* Philadelphia: Temple University Press, 1982. ISBN 0-87722-253-3. ▸ Valuable collection of eight essays on variety of aspects of social history of middle colonies with important historiographical introduction by editor. [JPG]

SEE ALSO
41.554 Don R. Gerlach. *Philip Schuyler and the American Revolution in New York, 1733–1777.*

Chesapeake

39.139 John R. Alden. *George Washington: a biography.* Baton Rouge: Louisiana State University Press, 1984. ISBN 0-8071-1153-8. ▸ Best short biography of Washington. [JPG]

39.140 Kenneth P. Bailey. *The Ohio Company of Virginia and the westward movement, 1748–1792: a chapter in the history of the colonial frontier.* Glendale, Calif.: Clark, 1939. ▸ Still best study of activities of Virginia land developers in trans-Appalachian area. [JPG]

39.141 Philip L. Barbour. *The three worlds of Captain John Smith.* New York: Houghton-Mifflin, 1964. ▸ Important, pioneering study of life of Captain John Smith. Throws much light on his exploits before he came to Virginia colony. [JPG]

39.142 Warren M. Billings, John E. Selby, and Thad W. Tate. *Colonial Virginia: a history.* White Plains, N.Y.: KTO, 1986. ISBN 0-527-18722-4. ▸ Most authoritative, up-to-date, narrative history of colonial Virginia. [JPG]

39.143 Robert E. Brown and B. Katherine Brown. *Virginia, 1705–1786: democracy or aristocracy?* East Lansing: Michigan State University Press, 1964. ▸ Pioneering work in social, economic, and political history of eighteenth-century Virginia. Presents much interesting social and economic data. [JPG]

39.144 Lois Green Carr, Russell R. Menard, and Lorena S. Walsh. *Robert Cole's world: agriculture and society in early Maryland.* Chapel Hill: University of North Carolina Press for Institute of Early American History and Culture, 1991. ISBN 0-8078-1985-9 (cl), 0-8078-4341-5 (pbk). ▸ Superb study of social and economic life of middling planter in seventeenth-century Chesapeake; some supporting documents. [JPG]

39.145 Lois Green Carr, Philip D. Morgan, and Jean B. Russo, eds. *Colonial Chesapeake society.* Chapel Hill: University of North Carolina Press for Institute of Early American History and Culture, 1988. ▸ Includes eleven significant essays on aspects of social history of Chesapeake colonies during eighteenth century. [JPG]

39.146 Wesley Frank Craven. *The southern colonies in the seventeenth century, 1607–1689.* 1949 ed. Baton Rouge: Louisiana State University Press, 1970. ▸ Well-done narrative history of first century of settlement of colonies from Maryland to South Carolina. [JPG]

39.147 Wesley Frank Craven. *White, red, and black: the seventeenth-century Virginian.* 1971 ed. New York: Norton, 1977. ISBN 0-393-00857-6. ▸ Early, yet significant effort to emphasize diversities of cultures in seventeenth-century Virginia. [JPG]

39.148 Douglas Southall Freeman. *George Washington: a biography.* 1948–57 ed. 7 vols. Clifton, N.J.: Kelley, 1975. ISBN 0-678-02828-1 (v. 2), 0-678-02829-x (v. 3), 0-678-02830-3 (v. 4), 0-678-02831-1 (v. 5), 0-678-02833-8 (v. 7). ▸ Still most detailed biography of most famous colonial Virginian. [JPG]

39.149 Rhys Isaac. *The transformation of Virginia, 1740–1790.* 1982 ed. New York: Norton, 1988. ISBN 0-393-95693-8 (pbk). ▸ Imaginative re-creation of cultures of colonial Virginia through examination of cultural conflict. Significant, but somewhat exaggerates coherence of gentry culture and inflates importance of Baptists who challenged it. [JPG]

39.150 Allan Kulikoff. *Tobacco and slaves: the development of southern cultures in the Chesapeake, 1680–1800.* Chapel Hill: University of North Carolina Press for Institute of Early American History and Culture, 1986. ISBN 0-8078-1671-x. ▸ Sprawling interpretation of transformation of Chesapeake society. Particularly valuable for its detailed research on Prince George's County, Maryland, and for paying significant attention to African American population. [JPG]

39.151 Aubrey C. Land. *Colonial Maryland: a history.* Millwood, N.Y.: KTO, 1981. ISBN 0-527-18713-5. ▸ Competent narrative of history of colonial Maryland. [JPG]

39.152 Aubrey C. Land, Lois Green Carr, and Edward C. Papenfuse, eds. *Law, society, and politics in early Maryland: proceedings of the First Conference on Maryland History, June 14–15, 1974.* Baltimore: Johns Hopkins University Press, 1977. ▸ Nine of fifteen essays in volume make important contributions to understanding of social history of colonial Maryland. [JPG]

39.153 J. A. Leo Lemay. *The American dream of Captain John Smith.* Charlottesville: University Press of Virginia, 1991. ISBN 0-8139-1321-7. ▸ Certainly best book-length study of most visible participant in founding of Virginia. [JPG]

39.154 Gloria L. Main. *Tobacco colony: life in early Maryland, 1650–1720.* Princeton: Princeton University Press, 1982. ISBN 0-691-04693-x. ▸ Splendid account of everyday life in Maryland over seven decades. Particularly notable for its depiction of material culture. [JPG]

39.155 Edmund S. Morgan. *American slavery, American freedom: the ordeal of colonial Virginia.* New York: Norton, 1975. ISBN 0-393-05554-x. ▸ Pioneering social history of England's first American colony. Based on detailed research, portions on seventeenth century especially valuable. Treatment of eighteenth century more casual and far less important. [JPG]

39.156 W. Stitt Robinson. *The southern colonial frontier, 1607–1763.* Albuquerque: University of New Mexico Press, 1979. ISBN 0-8263-0502-4 (cl), 0-8263-0503-2 (pbk). ▸ Very general history of frontiers of southern colonies. [JPG]

39.157 Parke Rouse, Jr. *James Blair of Virginia.* Chapel Hill: University of North Carolina Press, 1971. ISBN 0-8078-1175-0. ▸ Competent biography of important figure in religious and political history of early eighteenth-century Virginia. [JPG]

39.158 Charles G. Steffen. *From gentlemen to townsmen: the gentry of Baltimore County, 1660–1776.* Lexington: University Press of Kentucky, 1993. ISBN 0-8131-1829-8. ▸ Careful study of emergence of local county elite during colonial period. [JPG]

39.159 Thad W. Tate and David L. Ammerman, eds. *The Chesapeake in the seventeenth century: essays on Anglo-American society.* Chapel Hill: University of North Carolina Press for Institute of Early American History and Culture, 1979. ISBN 0-8078-1360-5.

▸ Nine important essays on social and political history of Virginia and Maryland. [JPG]

39.160 Alden T. Vaughan. *American genesis: Captain John Smith and the founding of Virginia.* Oscar Handlin, ed. Boston: Little, Brown, 1975. ▸ Brief, readable account of early years of Virginia through role of Smith. [JPG]

SEE ALSO
41.547 James Thomas Flexner. *George Washington.*

Lower South

39.161 John R. Alden. *John Stuart and the southern colonial frontier: a study of Indian relations, war, trade, and land problems in the southern wilderness, 1754–1775.* 1944 ed. New York: Gordian, 1966. ISBN 0-87752-001-1. ▸ Excellent study of southern frontier during mid-eighteenth century and attempts of metropolitan government to regulate relations between settlers and American Indians. Photocopy available from Ann Arbor: University Microfilms International, 1979. [JPG]

39.162 Kenneth Coleman. *Colonial Georgia: a history.* New York: Scribner's, 1976. ISBN 0-684-14556-1 (cl), 0-684-14555-3 (pbk). ▸ Overview of Georgia's brief colonial history. [JPG]

39.163 Verner W. Crane. *The southern frontier, 1670–1732.* 1928 ed. New York: Norton, 1981. ISBN 0-393-00948-3 (pbk). ▸ Excellent early work focusing on intra-European rivalries and Indian-white relations during first half century after English settlement in lower South. [JPG]

39.164 Harvey H. Jackson and Phinizy Spalding, eds. *Forty years of diversity: essays on colonial Georgia.* Athens: University of Georgia Press, 1984. ISBN 0-8203-0705-X. ▸ Fourteen essays providing fresh look at many aspects of history of colonial Georgia. [JPG]

39.165 Hugh T. Lefler and William S. Powell. *Colonial North Carolina: a history.* New York: Scribner's, 1973. ISBN 0-684-13536-1. ▸ Written in older tradition, best narrative history of subject. Needs updating to incorporate recent research. [JPG]

39.166 Robert L. Meriwether. *The expansion of South Carolina, 1729–1765.* 1940 ed. Philadelphia: Porcupine, 1974. ISBN 0-87991-345-2. ▸ Early study that remains best examination of initial stages of territorial expansion of South Carolina beyond low country. [JPG]

39.167 Phinizy Spalding. *Oglethorpe in America.* Chicago: University of Chicago Press, 1977. ISBN 0-226-76846-5. ▸ Persuasive, unusually deft discussion of Oglethorpe's role in founding of Georgia and in other activities in lower southern colonies. Useful for specialist; entertaining for general reader. [JPG/DMS]

39.168 Paul S. Taylor. *Georgia plan: 1732–1752.* Berkeley: University of California Press for Institute of Business and Economic Research, 1972. ▸ Important analysis of Georgia founders' objectives and fate of their plan. [JPG]

39.169 Clarence L. Ver Steeg. *Origins of a southern mosaic: studies of early Carolina and Georgia.* Athens: University of Georgia Press, 1975. (Mercer University Lamar memorial lectures, 17.) ISBN 0-8203-0365-8. ▸ Valuable analysis of selected aspects in formation of early society and economy of South Carolina. [JPG]

39.170 Robert M. Weir. *Colonial South Carolina: a history.* Millwood, N.Y.: KTO, 1983. ISBN 0-527-18721-6. ▸ Excellent general history of colonial South Carolina that effectively builds on new research. [JPG]

39.171 Peter H. Wood. *Black majority: Negroes in colonial South Carolina from 1670 through the Stono Rebellion.* 1974 ed. New York: Norton, 1975. ISBN 0-393-00777-4. ▸ Excellent social history of first seventy years of colony of South Carolina giving primary attention to colony's majority African American population. [JPG]

SEE ALSO
41.314 Alan Gallay. *The formation of a planter elite.*

British Islands

39.172 Edward Brathwaite. *The development of creole society in Jamaica, 1770–1820.* 1971 ed. Oxford: Clarendon, 1978. ISBN 0-19-823195-4. ▸ Comprehensive study of cultural world of late eighteenth-century Jamaica. Creative consideration of complementary roles of whites and blacks in creation of that world. [JPG]

39.173 Carl Bridenbaugh and Roberta Bridenbaugh. *No peace beyond the line: the English in the Caribbean, 1624–1690.* New York: Oxford University Press, 1972. ▸ General narrative history of English settlement in Caribbean before 1690. [JPG]

39.174 Michael Craton and Gail Saunders. *Islanders in the stream: a history of the Bahamian people.* 1 vol. to date. Athens: University of Georgia Press, 1992–. ISBN 0-8203-1382-3 (v. 1). ▸ Modern, comprehensive history of Bahamas colony. Carries story to abolition of slavery in 1834. [JPG]

39.175 Richard S. Dunn. *Sugar and slaves: the rise of the planter class in the English West Indies, 1624–1713.* 1972 ed. New York: Norton, 1973. ISBN 0-393-00692-1. ▸ Best general social history of seventeenth-century English West Indian colonies. [JPG]

39.176 Douglas Hall. *In miserable slavery: Thomas Thistlewood in Jamaica, 1750–86.* London: Macmillan, 1989. ISBN 0-333-48030-9 (pbk). ▸ Re-creation of life on Jamaican plantations through extensive diaries of estate manager. [JPG]

39.177 Vincent T. Harlow. *A history of Barbados, 1625–1685.* 1926 ed. New York: Negro Universities Press, 1969. ▸ Good narrative history of public life of Barbados during its first six decades. [JPG]

39.178 C.S.S. Higham. *The development of the Leeward Islands under the Restoration, 1660–1688: a study of the foundations of the old colonial system.* Cambridge: Cambridge University Press, 1921. ▸ Narrative of three crucial decades in early years of history of Leeward Island colonies. Also available on microfilm from Ann Arbor: University Microfilms International, 1980. [JPG]

39.179 Arthur Percival Newton. *The European nations in the West Indies, 1493–1688.* London: Black, 1933. ▸ Sweeping narrative of European activities in West Indies in two centuries following Columbus's initial encounter with area. [JPG]

39.180 Richard Pares. *Merchants and planters.* Cambridge: Cambridge University Press, 1960. (*Economic history review*, Supplements, 4.) ▸ Excellent, brief volume on establishment of English colonies in West Indies and their early social and economic development. [JPG]

39.181 Frank Wesley Pitman. *The development of the British West Indies, 1700–1763.* 1917 ed. Hamden, Conn.: Archon, 1967. ▸ Still valuable study of socioeconomic development of Britain's West Indian colonies during early eighteenth century. [JPG]

39.182 John Prebble. *The Darien disaster.* 1968 ed. Edinburgh: Mainstream; distributed by Douglas & McIntyre, 1978. ISBN 0-906391-02-4 (pbk). ▸ Well-written study of most significant Scottish effort at colonization before union with England; lacks references. [JPG]

39.183 Gary A. Puckrein. *Little England: plantation society and Anglo-Barbadian politics, 1627–1700.* New York: New York University Press, 1984. ISBN 0-8147-6587-4. ▸ Narrative history of seventeenth-century Barbados drawing heavily on secondary accounts. Primarily valuable for appendix showing relative health of Barbados during eighteenth century. [JPG]

39.184 Karl Watson. *The civilised island, Barbados: a social history, 1750–1816.* Barbados: Watson, 1979. ▸ Rather general study of selected aspects of social history of Barbados. [JPG]

39.185 Henry C. Wilkinson. *The adventurers of Bermuda: a history of the island from its discovery until the dissolution of the Somers Island Company in 1684.* 2d ed. London: Oxford University Press, 1958. ▸ Best available history of colonial Bermuda during its formative years. Based on solid archival research. [JPG]

39.186 Henry C. Wilkinson. *Bermuda in the old empire: a history of the island from the dissolution of the Somers Island Company until the end of the American Revolutionary War, 1684–1784.* London: Oxford University Press, 1950. ▸ Excellent if somewhat dated narrative of history of colonial Bermuda in century before end of American Revolution. [JPG]

French and British Canada

39.187 W. J. Eccles. *The Canadian frontier, 1534–1760.* Rev. ed. Albuquerque: University of New Mexico Press, 1983. ISBN 0-8263-0705-1 (cl), 0-8263-0706-X (pbk). ▸ Excellent general history of Canadian frontier during French era. [JPG]

39.188 W. J. Eccles. *Essays on New France.* Toronto: Oxford University Press, 1987. ISBN 0-19-540580-3. ▸ Twelve previously published essays by leading historian of New France. [JPG]

39.189 W. J. Eccles. *Frontenac: the courtier governor.* 1959 ed. Toronto: McClelland & Stewart, 1965. ▸ Careful biographical study of leading figure in establishment of New France as royal colony. [JPG]

39.190 A.J.B. Johnston. *Religion in life at Louisbourg, 1713–1758.* Kingston, Ont.: McGill-Queen's University Press, 1984. ISBN 0-7735-0427-3. ▸ Brief but detailed study of religious and moral life in colony of Louisbourg. [JPG]

39.191 George A. Rawlyk. *Nova Scotia's Massachusetts: a study of Massachusetts-Nova Scotia relations, 1630–1784.* Montreal: McGill-Queen's University Press, 1973. ISBN 0-7735-0142-8. ▸ Recounts relations between New England and Nova Scotia from early seventeenth century through American Revolution. [JPG]

SEE ALSO
45.66 Naomi E. S. Griffiths. *The contexts of Acadian history, 1686–1784.*

French and Dutch North American Colonies

39.192 Carl A. Brasseaux. *The founding of New Acadia: the beginnings of Acadian life in Louisiana, 1765–1803.* Baton Rouge: Louisiana State University Press, 1987. ISBN 0-8071-1296-8. ▸ Concise social history of emergence of Acadian society in late colonial Louisiana. [JPG]

39.193 Marcel Giraud. *A history of French Louisiana.* Vol. 1: *The reign of Louis XIV, 1698–1715.* Joseph C. Lambert, trans. Baton Rouge: Louisiana State University Press, 1974. ISBN 0-8071-0058-7. ▸ First of five-volume narrative history of French activities in Louisiana. Only first and fifth volumes translated into English. [JPG]

39.194 Marcel Giraud. *A history of French Louisiana.* Vol. 5: *The company of the Indies, 1723–1731.* Brian Pearce, trans. Baton Rouge: Louisiana State University Press, 1987. ▸ Last of five-volume narrative history of French activity in Louisiana. Volumes 2–4 not translated. [JPG]

39.195 Cornelis Ch. Goslinga. *The Dutch in the Caribbean and in the Guianas, 1680–1791.* Maria J. L. van Yperen, ed. Assen: Van Gorcum, 1985. ISBN 90-232-2049-8. ▸ Continuation of author's narrative history of Dutch activities in Caribbean and in Surinam, 1680–1791 (39.196). [JPG]

39.196 Cornelis Ch. Goslinga. *The Dutch in the Caribbean and on the wild coast, 1580–1680.* Assen: Van Gorcum, 1971. ▸ Extended narrative history of first century of Dutch activities in Caribbean and in Surinam. [JPG]

THE PUBLIC REALM
Politics and Society

39.197 W. W. Abbot. *The royal governors of Georgia, 1754–1775.* Chapel Hill: University of North Carolina Press for Institute of Early American History and Culture, 1959. ▸ Insightful look at Georgia politics during its brief history as royal colony through examination of performance of its three royal governors. [JPG]

39.198 John R. Alden. *Robert Dinwiddie: servant of the crown.* Williamsburg, Va.: Colonial Williamsburg Foundation; distributed by University Press of Virginia, 1973. ISBN 0-87935-002-4. ▸ Succinct portrait of imperial official who was unsuccessful governor of Virginia. [JPG]

39.199 Raymond C. Bailey. *Popular influence upon public policy: petitioning in eighteenth-century Virginia.* Westport, Conn.: Greenwood, 1979. ISBN 0-313-20892-1. ▸ Important discussion of petitioning process as form of popular expression of opinion in colonial Virginia. Shows seriousness with which legislature considered such petitions. [JPG]

39.200 Bernard Bailyn. *The origins of American politics.* New York: Knopf, 1968. ▸ Broad, compelling interpretation of colonial politics during last four or five decades of colonial era. Considerably exaggerates instability of colonial public life. [JPG]

39.201 Michael C. Batinski. *The New Jersey assembly, 1738–1775: the making of a legislative community.* Lanham, Md.: University Press of America, 1987. ISBN 0-8191-6089-X. ▸ Study focusing on history of New Jersey legislature and men who served in it during last thirty-seven years of colonial period. Useful for its exploration of relationship between legislators and their constituents and its discussion of changing basis of legislative divisions based on roll-call analysis. [JPG]

39.202 Warren M. Billings. *Virginia's viceroy: Their Majesties' Governor General Francis Howard, baron Howard of Effingham.* Fairfax, Va.: George Mason University Press; distributed by University Publishing, 1991. ISBN 0-913969-28-1. ▸ Succinct but useful study of career of important late seventeenth-century governor of Virginia. [JPG]

39.203 Patricia U. Bonomi. *A factious people: politics and society in colonial New York.* New York: Columbia University Press, 1971. ISBN 0-231-03509-8. ▸ Excellent general study of New York politics over entire colonial era, from Glorious Revolution (1689) to American Revolution. Emphasizes role of competing interest groups which led to early development of partisan political system. Contrast with Bailyn and others who emphasize ideology (41.52). [JPG/CMJ]

39.204 T. H. Breen. *The character of the good ruler: a study of Puritan political ideas in New England, 1630–1730.* 1970 ed. New York: Norton, 1974. ISBN 0-393-00747-2. ▸ Excellent study of changing patterns of politics during first century of Massachusetts Bay Colony. Most sophisticated, comprehensive analysis of Puritan political thought. [JPG]

39.205 Robert E. Brown. *Middle-class democracy and the revolution in Massachusetts, 1691–1780.* 1955 ed. New York: Harper & Row, 1969. ▸ Original study notable for providing first detailed demonstration that male suffrage was far more extensive in America than in England. Forced fundamental reconception of colonial political life. [JPG]

39.206 Kinloch Bull, Jr. *The oligarchs in colonial and revolutionary Charleston: Lieutenant Governor William Bull II and his family.*

Columbia: University of South Carolina Press, 1991. ISBN 0-87249-715-1. ▸ Largely political biography of elite colonial figure who often administered South Carolina through middle decades of eighteenth century. [JPG]

39.207 John F. Burns. *Controversies between royal governors and their assemblies in the northern American colonies.* 1923 ed. New York: Russell & Russell, 1969. ▸ Early study of legislative opposition to British policy in New Jersey, New York, Massachusetts, and New Hampshire. [JPG]

39.208 Richard L. Bushman. *King and people in provincial Massachusetts.* Chapel Hill: University of North Carolina Press for Institute of Early American History and Culture, 1985. ISBN 0-8078-1624-8. ▸ Trenchant consideration of function of monarchy in political culture of one of American colonies least enamored of monarchy. [JPG]

39.209 Lois Green Carr and David W. Jordan. *Maryland's revolution of government, 1689–1692.* Ithaca, N.Y.: Cornell University Press, 1974. (St. Mary's City Commission, 1.) ISBN 0-8014-0793-1. ▸ Detailed account of Maryland rebellion that followed in wake of Glorious Revolution. Provides compelling analysis of rebellion's causes and results. [JPG]

39.210 Desmond Clarke. *Arthur Dobbs, esquire, 1689–1765: surveyor-general of Ireland, prospector and governor of North Carolina.* Chapel Hill: University of North Carolina Press, 1957. ▸ One of better biographies of colonial governor and his transatlantic activities. [JPG]

39.211 Mary Patterson Clarke. *Parliamentary privilege in the American colonies.* 1943 ed. New York: Da Capo, 1971. ISBN 0-306-70237-1. ▸ Careful study of important aspect of efforts by colonial legislatures to mimic metropolitan House of Commons. [JPG]

39.212 Paul W. Conner. *Poor Richard's politicks: Benjamin Franklin and his new American order.* New York: Oxford University Press, 1965. ▸ Notable consideration of operating political assumptions of Benjamin Franklin. [JPG]

39.213 Jere R. Daniell. *Experiment in republicanism: New Hampshire politics and the American Revolution, 1741–1794.* Cambridge, Mass.: Harvard University Press, 1970. ISBN 0-674-27806-2. ▸ Schematic account of New Hampshire politics under domination of Wentworth family. [JPG]

39.214 Bruce C. Daniels, ed. *Power and status: officeholding in colonial America.* Middletown, Conn.: Wesleyan University Press; distributed by Harper & Row, 1986. ISBN 0-8195-5118-X. ▸ Eleven valuable essays on social backgrounds of men who held political office at various levels and in several colonies. Essay by Wendell on speakers of colonial legislatures especially notable. [JPG]

39.215 Bruce C. Daniels, ed. *Town and country: essays on the structure of local government in the American colonies.* Middletown, Conn.: Wesleyan University Press, 1978. ISBN 0-8195-5020-5. ▸ Collection of nine strong essays that together provide best introduction to nature and functioning of local government in colonial British America. [JPG]

39.216 Robert J. Dinkin. *Voting in provincial America: a study of elections in the thirteen colonies, 1689–1776.* Westport, Conn.: Greenwood, 1977. ISBN 0-8371-9543-8. ▸ Extremely useful study of voting laws and practices and participation in elections in British continental colonies founded before 1763, except Nova Scotia. Comparative study. [JPG]

39.217 A. Roger Ekirch. *"Poor Carolina": politics and society in colonial North Carolina, 1729–1776.* Chapel Hill: University of North Carolina Press, 1981. ISBN 0-8078-1475-X. ▸ Excellent study of political life of colonial North Carolina during royal period after 1729. Well informed by awareness of extent to which politics were influenced by social conditions. [JPG]

39.218 George Edward Frakes. *Laboratory for liberty: the South Carolina legislative committee system 1719–1776.* Lexington: University Press of Kentucky, 1970. ISBN 0-8131-1219-2. ▸ Only detailed examination of functioning of committee system in colonial legislature. [JPG]

39.219 Jack P. Greene. *Negotiated authorities: essays in colonial political and constitutional history.* Charlottesville: University Press of Virginia, 1994. ISBN 0-8139-1516-3. ▸ Sixteen essays, fourteen previously published, on wide variety of aspects of colonial constitutional and political history. [JPG]

39.220 Jack P. Greene. *Peripheries and center: constitutional development in the extended polities of the British empire and the United States, 1607–1788.* Athens: University of Georgia Press, 1986. ▸ General examination of emergence of informal imperial constitutional system within early modern British empire. Emphasizes local or colonial roots of constitutional development and how commitment of colonial leaders to that emerging system shaped their responses to revolutionary crises of 1760s and 1770s and creation of American polity after 1776. [JPG]

39.221 Jack P. Greene. *Political life in eighteenth-century Virginia.* Williamsburg, Va.: Colonial Williamsburg Foundation, 1986. ISBN 0-87935-116-0 (pbk). ▸ Succinct description and analysis of operation of Virginia political system during generation preceeding American Revolution. [JPG]

39.222 Jack P. Greene. *The quest for power: the lower houses of assembly in the southern royal colonies, 1689–1776.* 1963 ed. New York: Norton, 1972. ISBN 0-393-00591-7. ▸ Detailed constitutional study of growth of legislative authority in colonies of Virginia, North Carolina, South Carolina, and Georgia. [JPG]

39.223 Lucille Griffith. *The Virginia House of Burgesses, 1750–1774.* Rev. ed. Tuscaloosa: University of Alabama Press, 1970. ISBN 0-8173-5104-3. ▸ Useful analysis of operation and membership of Virginia House of Burgesses during last century of colonial period. Contains prosopographies of members from selected counties. [JPG]

39.224 William S. Hanna. *Benjamin Franklin and Pennsylvania politics.* Stanford, Calif.: Stanford University Press, 1964. ▸ Close analysis of role of Franklin in spearheading opposition to proprietors during 1750s. [JPG]

39.225 Vincent T. Harlow. *Christopher Codrington, 1668–1710.* 1928 ed. London and New York: Hurst and St. Martin's, 1990. ISBN 1-85065-089-6, 0-312-04814-6. ▸ Biography of early West Indian governor. [JPG]

39.226 James H. Hutson. *Pennsylvania politics, 1746–1770: the movement for royal government and its consequences.* Princeton: Princeton University Press, 1972. ISBN 0-691-04611-5. ▸ Cogent study of ongoing conflict between proprietors and Pennsylvania legislature in mid-eighteenth century and abortive movement to convert Pennsylvania into royal colony generated by that conflict. [JPG]

39.227 David W. Jordan. *Foundations of representative government in Maryland, 1632–1715.* Cambridge: Cambridge University Press, 1987. ISBN 0-521-32941-8. ▸ Thorough, insightful prosopographical and institutional study of emergence of representative government in Maryland before 1715. [JPG]

39.228 Michael Kammen. *Deputyes & libertys: the origins of representative government in colonial America.* New York: Knopf, 1969. ▸ Despite its brevity, introduction to this collection of documents contains many useful insights about origins of representative government in colonial British America. [JPG]

39.229 Stanley Nider Katz. *Newcastle's New York: Anglo-Amer-*

ican politics, *1732–1753*. Cambridge, Mass.: Belknap, 1968. ▸ Detailed consideration of New York provincial politics for two decades; especially notable for its consideration of effects of participation in metropolitan patronage system on colony's public life. [JPG]

39.230 Milton M. Klein. *Politics of diversity: essays in the history of colonial New York*. Port Washington, N.Y.: Kennikat, 1974. ISBN 0-8046-9081-2. ▸ Includes nine important essays on political history of colonial New York. [JPG]

39.231 Jon Kukla. *Political institutions in Virginia, 1619–1660*. New York: Garland, 1989. ISBN 0-8240-6188-8. ▸ Study of political development of colonial Virginia to Restoration of Charles II. Argues Virginia political institutions and social order to which they were attached achieved relatively higher level of coherence and considerably greater sophistication than most historians have suggested. [JPG]

39.232 Lawrence H. Leder. *Robert Livingston, 1654–1728, and the politics of colonial New York*. Chapel Hill: University of North Carolina Press for Institute of Early American History and Culture, 1961. ▸ Important account of key participant in conflicted politics of New York during its formative years as English proprietary and royal colony. [JPG]

39.233 Roy N. Lokken. *David Lloyd: colonial lawmaker*. Seattle: University of Washington Press, 1959. ▸ Biographical study of important early Pennsylvania political leader illuminating first four decades of Pennsylvania politics. [JPG]

39.234 Mary Lou Lustig. *Robert Hunter, 1666–1734: New York's Augustan statesman*. Syracuse, N.Y.: Syracuse University Press, 1983. ISBN 0-8156-2296-1. ▸ Impressive study of public career of one of more successful colonial governors who served in four colonies. [JPG]

39.235 David John Mays. *Edmund Pendleton, 1721–1803: a biography*. 1952 ed. 2 vols. Richmond: Virginia State Library, 1984. ISBN 0-88490-119-X (cl), 0-88490-120-3 (pbk). ▸ Outstanding biography of one of most important Virginia political leaders of second half of eighteenth century. [JPG/DMS]

39.236 George Metcalf. *Royal government and political conflict in Jamaica, 1729–1783*. London: Longmans for Royal Commonwealth Society, 1965. (Royal Commonwealth Society, Imperial studies, 27.) ▸ Excellent study of provincial politics of Jamaica over fifty-year period revealing remarkable vigor of colony's political institutions. [JPG]

39.237 Gary B. Nash. *Quakers and politics: Pennsylvania, 1681–1726*. Princeton: Princeton University Press, 1968. ▸ Best available study of political life of early decades of Pennsylvania, especially important for its identification of social and religious roots of political contention. [JPG]

39.238 Donnell MacClure Owings. *His lordship's patronage: offices of profit in colonial Maryland*. Baltimore: Maryland Historical Society, 1953. (Studies in Maryland history, 1.) ▸ Excellent study of proprietary bureaucracy in colonial Maryland. [JPG]

39.239 William Pencak. *War, politics, and revolution in provincial Massachusetts*. Boston: Northeastern University Press, 1981. ISBN 0-930350-10-3. ▸ Comprehensive history of patterns of factional conflict in Massachusetts during royal period. [JPG]

39.240 J. R. Pole. *The gift of government: political responsibility from the English Restoration to American independence*. Athens: University of Georgia Press, 1983. ISBN 0-8203-0652-5. ▸ Brief but penetrating exploration of emergence of idea of political responsibility in England and America. [JPG]

39.241 Thomas L. Purvis. *Proprietors, patronage, and paper money: legislative politics in New Jersey, 1703–1776*. New Brunswick, N.J.: Rutgers University Press, 1986. ISBN 0-8135-1161-5.

▸ Excellent, broad-gauged analysis of legislative politics throughout royal era in colonial New Jersey. [JPG]

39.242 Martin H. Quitt. *Virginia House of Burgesses, 1660–1706: the social, educational, and economic bonds of political power*. New York: Garland, 1989. ISBN 0-8240-6194-2. ▸ Useful prosopographical analysis of membership of Virginia House of Burgesses during important formative period. [JPG]

39.243 Robert C. Ritchie. *The duke's province: a study of New York politics and society, 1664–1691*. Chapel Hill: University of North Carolina Press, 1977. ISBN 0-8078-1292-7. ▸ Persuasive investigation of political life in English-controlled New York through events of Glorious Revolution (1689). [JPG]

39.244 Dietmar Rothermund. *The layman's progress: religious and political experience in colonial Pennsylvania, 1740–1770*. 1961 ed. Philadelphia: University of Pennsylvania Press, 1962. ▸ Early analysis of role of Germans in mid-eighteenth-century Pennsylvania politics. [JPG]

39.245 John A. Schutz. *William Shirley: king's governor of Massachusetts*. Chapel Hill: University of North Carolina Press for Institute of Early American History and Culture, 1961. ▸ Excellent biography of major colonial governor. [JPG]

39.246 Eugene R. Sheridan. *Lewis Morris, 1671–1746: a study in early American politics*. Syracuse, N.Y.: Syracuse University Press, 1981. ISBN 0-8156-2243-0. ▸ Impressive study of enhancement of colonial legislative power and unsuccessful attempts on part of metropolitan officials to curtail it, told through career of central actor in politics of New York and New Jersey. [JPG]

39.247 Richard P. Sherman. *Robert Johnson: proprietary and royal governor of South Carolina*. Columbia: University of South Carolina Press, 1966. ▸ Competent public biography of man who served as governor of South Carolina under both proprietary and royal regimes. [JPG]

39.248 Richard C. Simmons. *Studies in the Massachusetts franchise, 1631–1691*. New York: Garland, 1989. ISBN 0-8240-6178-0. ▸ Useful study of changing nature of franchise requirements in Massachusetts during seventeenth century. [JPG]

39.249 M. Eugene Sirmans. *Colonial South Carolina: a political history, 1663–1763*. Chapel Hill: University of North Carolina Press for Institute of Early American History and Culture, 1966. ▸ Excellent history of South Carolina politics for entire colonial period. [JPG]

39.250 F. G. Spurdle. *Early West Indian government: showing the progress of government in Barbados, Jamaica, and the Leeward Islands, 1660–1783*. Palmerston North, New Zealand: Spurdle, 1963. ▸ Only comprehensive study of West Indian political history. Focuses on tensions between colonial institutions and metropolitan authorities. [JPG]

39.251 Charles S. Sydnor. *Gentlemen freeholders: political practices in Washington's Virginia*. 1952 ed. Westport, Conn.: Greenwood, 1984. ISBN 0-313-24385-9. ▸ Standard study of dynamics of eighteenth-century political culture emphasizing political preparation of leadership. [JPG]

39.252 Theodore Thayer. *Pennsylvania politics and the growth of democracy, 1740–1776*. Harrisburg: Pennsylvania Historical and Museum Commission, 1953. ▸ Written in older tradition; still most comprehensive narrative of Pennsylvania political life in four decades before Revolution. [JPG]

39.253 Albert H. Tillson, Jr. *Gentry and common folk: political culture on a Virginia frontier, 1740–1789*. Lexington: University Press of Kentucky, 1991. ISBN 0-8131-1749-6. ▸ Study of political culture of upper valley of Virginia, finding much less deference in political society than historians have customarily claimed for colonial Virginia. [JPG]

39.254 Alan Tully. *William Penn's legacy: politics and social structure in provincial Pennsylvania, 1726–1755*. Baltimore: Johns Hopkins University Press, 1977. ISBN 0-8018-1932-6. ▸ Excellent study of character of Pennsylvania politics during mid-eighteenth century. Remarkable for its focus on political life of rural counties rather than Philadelphia. [JPG]

39.255 Robert Emmet Wall, Jr. *Massachusetts Bay: the crucial decade, 1640–1650*. New Haven: Yale University Press, 1972. ▸ Detailed analysis of factional struggles in Massachusetts during 1640s. [JPG]

39.256 Richard Waterhouse. *A new world gentry: the making of a merchant and planter class in South Carolina, 1670–1770*. New York: Garland, 1989. ISBN 0-8240-6295-7. ▸ Significant analysis of emergence of gentry class in South Carolina that emphasizes its openness and continuing mercantile ties. Gives major attention to elite's political role. [JPG]

39.257 Agnes M. Whitson. *The constitutional development of Jamaica, 1660 to 1729*. Manchester: Manchester University Press, 1929. ▸ Important early study of constitutional development of West Indian colony. [JPG]

39.258 Robert Zemsky. *Merchants, farmers, and river gods: an essay on eighteenth-century American politics*. Boston: Gambit, 1971. ▸ Sophisticated analysis of nature, function, and operation of political life in mid-eighteenth-century Massachusetts. One of best books available on politics of any early modern British colony. [JPG]

Diplomatic and Military Studies

39.259 Fred Anderson. *A people's army: Massachusetts soldiers and society in the Seven Years' War*. Chapel Hill: University of North Carolina Press, 1984. ▸ Excellent study contrasting Massachusetts soldiers with British regulars during Seven Years' War. Analyzes social bases of those differences and explores war's impact on Massachusetts. [JPG]

39.260 Russell Bourne. *The red king's rebellion: racial politics in New England, 1675–1678*. 1990 ed. New York: Oxford University Press, 1991. ISBN 0-19-506976-5 (pbk). ▸ Study of King Philip's War from American Indian point of view. [JPG]

39.261 John E. Ferling. *A wilderness of miseries: war and warriors in early America*. Westport, Conn.: Greenwood, 1980. ISBN 0-313-22093-X. ▸ General study tracing development of peculiarly American way of war from early colonial era through American Revolution. About half of volume deals with colonial period. [JPG]

39.262 C. H. Haring. *The buccaneers in the West Indies in the seventeenth century*. 1910 ed. Hamden, Conn.: Archon, 1966. ▸ Still useful account of interloping and intercolonial conflict in Caribbean during century of initial English penetration into region. [JPG]

39.263 Dorothy V. Jones. *License for empire: colonialism by treaty in early America*. Chicago: University of Chicago Press, 1982. ISBN 0-226-40707-1. ▸ Fullest discussion of treaty-making process as vehicle for land expropriation in early America. [JPG]

39.264 John Tate Lanning. *The diplomatic history of Georgia: a study of the epoch of Jenkins' Ear*. Chapel Hill: University of North Carolina Press, 1936. ▸ Analysis of struggle between Spain and Britain for control over southeastern North America. [JPG]

39.265 Douglas Edward Leach. *Arms for empire: a military history of the British colonies in North America, 1607–1763*. New York: Macmillan, 1973. ▸ Best general military history of continental colonies. [JPG]

39.266 Douglas Edward Leach. *Flintlock and tomahawk: New England in King Philip's War*. 1958 ed. New York: Norton, 1966.

ISBN 0-393-00340-4. ▸ Authoritative narrative history of King Philip's War (1675–76). [JPG]

39.267 Douglas Edward Leach. *Roots of conflict: British armed forces and colonial Americans, 1677–1763*. Chapel Hill: University of North Carolina Press, 1986. ISBN 0-8078-1688-4. ▸ Short but persuasive consideration of how experiences with metropolitan troops during colonial era helped shape colonial fears of standing armies. [JPG]

39.268 James G. Lydon. *Pirates, privateers, and profits*. Richard B. Morris, Introduction. Upper Saddle River, N.J.: Gregg, 1970. ISBN 0-8398-1176-4. ▸ Brief study of privateers and people who financed them. Focuses on experience of New York in colonial era. [JPG]

39.269 Patrick M. Malone. *The skulking way of war: technology and tactics among the New England Indians*. Lanham, Md.: Madison; distributed by National Book Network, 1991. ISBN 0-8191-8067-X. ▸ Examination of patterns of warfare among seventeenth-century New England American Indians, emphasizing their ingenuity in combining traditional modes of fighting with new European technologies. [JPG]

39.270 Richard Pares. *War and trade in the West Indies, 1739–1763*. 1936 ed. London: Cass, 1963. ▸ Detailed recounting of conflicts among Spanish, English, and French over West Indies during last two intercolonial wars. [JPG]

39.271 Howard H. Peckham. *The colonial wars, 1689–1762*. Chicago: University of Chicago Press, 1964. ▸ Brisk overview of intercolonial wars. [JPG]

39.272 Michael J. Puglisi. *Puritans besieged: the legacies of King Philip's War in the Massachusetts Bay Colony*. Lanham, Md.: University Press of America, 1991. ISBN 0-8191-8278-8 (cl), 0-8191-8291-5 (pbk). ▸ Useful analysis of lingering impact of King Philip's War on Massachusetts during final decades of seventeenth century. [JPG]

39.273 Robert C. Ritchie. *Captain Kidd and the war against the pirates*. Cambridge, Mass.: Harvard University Press, 1986. ISBN 0-674-09501-4. ▸ Sprightly study of famous English pirate. Illuminates forces leading to abandonment of piracy as instrument of state policy and to assault on it during early decades of eighteenth century. [JPG]

39.274 Max Savelle. *The origins of American diplomacy: the international history of Anglo-America, 1492–1763*. New York: Macmillan, 1967. ▸ General narrative of diplomatic history of North America during first three centuries of European activities in North America. Also discusses impact of New World on evolution of international law and European balance of power. [JPG/EVW]

39.275 Harold E. Selesky. *War and society in colonial Connecticut*. New Haven: Yale University Press, 1990. ISBN 0-300-04552-2. ▸ Effectively traces evolution of military system in Connecticut and locates it within political and social life of colony. Covers Indian raids to Louisbourg campaign to Seven Years' War. Profiles common soldiers-officers. [JPG/DMS]

39.276 William L. Shea. *The Virginia militia in the seventeenth century*. Baton Rouge: Louisiana State University Press, 1983. ISBN 0-8071-1106-6. ▸ Brief study of function and effectiveness of militia in both defense and internal affairs of Virginia, 1607–1700. [JPG]

39.277 Ian K. Steele. *Betrayals: Fort William Henry and the massacre*. New York: Oxford University Press, 1990. ISBN 0-19-505893-3. ▸ Impressive analysis of important incident in American Indian–white relations during Seven Years' War. [JPG]

39.278 Carl E. Swanson. *Predators and prizes: American privateering and imperial warfare, 1739–1748*. Columbia: University of

South Carolina Press, 1991. ISBN 0-87249-720-8. ▸ Authoritative study of role of privateering in intercolonial wars, 1739–48, showing its extent and importance in British military effort and large number of colonial ships and merchants involved. [JPG]

39.279 James Titus. *The Old Dominion at war: society, politics, and warfare in late colonial Virginia.* Columbia: University of South Carolina Press, 1991. ISBN 0-87249-724-0. ▸ Careful study of Virginia's participation in Seven Years' War. Emphasizes colony's difficulties in mobilizing military force and explores social and political implications of those difficulties. [JPG/DMS]

39.280 Nicholas B. Wainwright. *George Croghan: wilderness diplomat.* Chapel Hill: University of North Carolina Press for Institute of Early American History and Culture, 1959. ▸ Excellent study of colonial frontiersman and American Indian trader and negotiator. [JPG]

39.281 Paul A. W. Wallace. *Conrad Weiser, 1696–1750: friend of colonist and Mohawk.* 1945 ed. New York: Russell & Russell, 1971. ▸ Account of life and role of prominent cultural broker on northern frontier. [JPG]

39.282 Wilcomb E. Washburn. *The governor and the rebel: a history of Bacon's Rebellion in Virginia.* 1957 ed. New York: Norton, 1972. ISBN 0-393-00645-X. ▸ Most detailed history of Bacon's Rebellion (1676). Marred by author's partisanship for forces that quelled uprising. [JPG]

SEE ALSO
36.108 Francis Jennings. *Empire of fortune.*

Law, Jurisprudence, and Deviance

39.283 Linda Briggs Biemer. *Women and property in colonial New York: the transition from Dutch to English law, 1643–1727.* Ann Arbor: University Microfilms International, 1983. ISBN 0-8357-1392-X. ▸ Useful study showing how English conventions gradually restricted control women exercised over property in Dutch New York. [JPG]

39.284 George Athan Billias, ed. *Law and authority in colonial America: selected essays.* 1965 ed. New York: Dover, 1970. ISBN 0-486-22167-9. ▸ Ten essays on themes of law and authority in colonial America; all but three relate to Massachusetts. [JPG]

39.285 Stephen Botein. *Early American law and society.* New York: Knopf; distributed by Random House, 1983. ISBN 0-394-33252-0 (pbk). ▸ Very brief but suggestive overview of some of central themes in relationship between law and society in colonial America. [JPG]

39.286 Hoyt P. Canady. *Gentlemen of the bar: lawyers in colonial South Carolina.* New York: Garland, 1987. ISBN 0-8240-8254-0. ▸ Useful analysis of development of legal profession in colonial South Carolina, showing varied educational backgrounds and multiple economic activities of lawyers. [JPG/DMS]

39.287 Jonathan M. Chu. *Neighbors, friends, or madmen: the Puritan adjustment to Quakerism in seventeenth-century Massachusetts Bay.* Westport, Conn.: Greenwood, 1985. ISBN 0-313-24809-5. ▸ Analysis of legal response of Massachusetts authorities to Quakerism, 1656–81. Sheds considerable light on Puritan approach to heresy and character and on eventual abandonment of Quaker persecutions. [JPG]

39.288 Daniel R. Coquillette, ed. *Law in colonial Massachusetts, 1630–1800: a conference held 6 and 7 November 1981.* Boston: Colonial Society of Massachusetts; distributed by University Press of Virginia, 1984. (Publications of the Colonial Society of Massachusetts, 62.) ISBN 0-8139-1052-8. ▸ Important volume containing nineteen monographic essays covering many aspects of legal history of colonial Massachusetts. [JPG]

39.289 George Dargo. *Roots of the republic: a new perspective on early American constitutionalism.* New York: Praeger, 1974. ▸ Excellent brief overview of colonial constitutional development. [JPG]

39.290 Alan F. Day. *A social study of lawyers in Maryland, 1660–1775.* New York: Garland, 1989. ISBN 0-8240-6177-2. ▸ Excellent analysis using prosopography to chart emergence of legal profession in colonial Maryland. [JPG]

39.291 Kai T. Erikson. *Wayward Puritans: a study in the sociology of deviance.* New York: Wiley, 1966. ▸ Successfully employs concept of deviance to illuminate patterns and rationale of social control in late seventeenth-century New England. [JPG]

39.292 David H. Flaherty. *Privacy in colonial New England.* Charlottesville: University Press of Virginia, 1972. ISBN 0-8139-0339-4. ▸ Pioneering work on concepts of privacy and private space in colonial America using New England as case study. [JPG]

39.293 David H. Flaherty, ed. *Essays in the history of early American law.* Chapel Hill: University of North Carolina Press for Institute of Early American History and Culture, 1969. ▸ Collection of eighteen previously published essays in colonial legal history. [JPG]

39.294 Julius Goebel, Jr., and T. Raymond Naughton. *Law enforcement in colonial New York: a study in criminal procedure.* 1944 ed. Montclair, N.J.: Patterson Smith, 1970. ISBN 0-87585-122-3. ▸ Pioneering study of functioning of judicial system of important colony. [JPG]

39.295 Douglas Greenberg. *Crime and law enforcement in the colony of New York, 1691–1776.* Ithaca, N.Y.: Cornell University Press, 1976. ISBN 0-8014-1020-7. ▸ Best available study on patterns of crime and law enforcement for any American colony. Explores social foundations of crime, crime rates, and effectiveness of court system. [JPG]

39.296 Hendrik Hartog. *Public property and private power: the corporation of the city of New York in American law, 1730–1870.* 1983 ed. Ithaca, N.Y.: Cornell University Press, 1989. ISBN 0-8014-9560-1 (pbk). ▸ Superb study of changing character of municipal government in New York City; just over quarter deals with colonial era. Emphasizes relative autonomy of town corporation during period. [JPG]

39.297 George Lee Haskins. *Law and authority in early Massachusetts: a study in tradition and design.* 1960 ed. Hamden, Conn.: Archon, 1968. ISBN 0-208-00685-0. ▸ Classic study of Puritan efforts to devise legal system in early Massachusetts. [JPG]

39.298 Peter C. Hoffer. *Law and people in colonial America.* Baltimore: Johns Hopkins University Press, 1992. ISBN 0-8018-4306-5 (cl), 0-8018-4307-3 (pbk). ▸ Broad overview of process by which colonial Americans adapted English law to their own special circumstances and of importance they attached to law. [JPG]

39.299 Peter C. Hoffer and N.E.H. Hull. *Impeachment in America, 1635–1805.* New Haven: Yale University Press, 1984. ISBN 0-300-03053-3. ▸ Fullest consideration of origins of idea of impeachment in area that became United States. Argues American practice was more important than English inheritance in shaping later American conceptions. Less than quarter of work deals with colonial period. [JPG]

39.300 Peter C. Hoffer and N.E.H. Hull. *Murdering mothers: infanticide in England and New England, 1558–1803.* 1981 ed. New York: New York University Press, 1984. (New York University, School of Law series in legal history, 2.) ▸ Comparative study of child murder in England and New England and its relationship to social control of sexual behavior. [JPG]

39.301 N.E.H. Hull. *Female felons: women and serious crime in colonial Massachusetts.* Urbana: University of Illinois Press, 1987. ISBN 0-252-01315-8. ▸ Detailed examination of treatment of women felons in colonial Massachusetts Superior Court. Notable for its finding that women and men received roughly equal treatment. [JPG]

39.302 Mary Ann Jimenez. *Changing faces of madness: early American attitudes and treatment of the insane.* Hanover, N.H.: University Press of New England for Brandeis University Press, 1987. ▸ General treatment of madness in Massachusetts. Covers colonial period but chiefly revolutionary and early national eras. [JPG]

39.303 Yasuhide Kawashima. *Puritan justice and the Indian: white man's law in Massachusetts, 1630–1763.* Middletown, Conn.: Wesleyan University Press; distributed by Harper & Row, 1986. ISBN 0-8195-5068-X. ▸ Useful look at changing system of law developed in colonial Massachusetts to deal with American Indians. [JPG]

39.304 James H. Kettner. *The development of American citizenship, 1608–1870.* Chapel Hill: University of North Carolina Press for Institute of Early American History and Culture, 1978. ISBN 0-8078-1326-5. ▸ Excellent exploration of naturalization practices and emergence of idea of United States citizenship as act of volition and consent. About forty percent of volume covers colonial roots. [JPG]

39.305 David Thomas Konig. *Law and society in Puritan Massachusetts: Essex County, 1629–1692.* Chapel Hill: University of North Carolina Press, 1979. ISBN 0-8078-1336-2. ▸ Model study of function of litigation in colonial society showing importance of courts in dispute settlement in seventeenth-century New England. [JPG]

39.306 Leonard W. Levy. *The emergence of a free press.* Rev. ed. New York: Oxford University Press, 1985. ISBN 0-19-503506-2 (cl), 0-19-504240-9 (pbk). ▸ Exploration of origins of ideal of free press in colonial British America and United States. Contrasts discrepancy between restrictive law and liberal practice among newspaper printers during colonial era. Earlier title: *Legacy of Suppression* (1960). [JPG]

39.307 Bruce H. Mann. *Neighbors and strangers: law and community in early Connecticut.* Chapel Hill: University of North Carolina Press, 1987. ISBN 0-8078-1756-2. ▸ Excellent social history of law in colonial Connecticut tracing changing patterns of litigation and showing growing rationalization and specialization of legal system in response to rising pressures of commercialization. [JPG]

39.308 Edgar J. McManus. *Law and liberty in early New England: criminal justice and due process, 1620–1692.* Amherst: University of Massachusetts Press, 1993. ISBN 0-87023-824-8. ▸ Recent study of operation of criminal justice system in seventeenth-century New England. [JPG]

39.309 Richard B. Morris. *Studies in the history of American law, with special reference to the seventeenth and eighteenth centuries.* 1958 2d ed. New York: Octagon Books, 1974. ISBN 0-374-95909-9. ▸ Older work containing several essays on aspects of early American legal history. [JPG]

39.310 William E. Nelson. *Dispute and conflict resolution in Plymouth County, Massachusetts, 1725–1825.* Chapel Hill: University of North Carolina Press, 1981. ISBN 0-8078-1454-7. ▸ Careful examination of process of dispute resolution through town meetings, church, and courts. Shows how courts gradually acquired prominence. [JPG]

39.311 A. G. Roeber. *Faithful magistrates and republican lawyers: creators of Virginia legal culture, 1680–1810.* Chapel Hill: University of North Carolina Press, 1981. ISBN 0-8078-1461-X. ▸ Outline of emergence and regularization of legal profession in colonial Virginia. [JPG]

39.312 Philip J. Schwarz. *The jarring interests: New York's boundary makers, 1664–1776.* Albany: State University of New York Press, 1979. ISBN 0-87395-377-0. ▸ Perhaps best study of intercolonial disputes over provincial boundaries and their broader effects. [JPG]

39.313 Philip J. Schwarz. *Twice condemned: slaves and the criminal laws of Virginia, 1705–1865.* Baton Rouge: Louisiana State University Press, 1988. ISBN 0-8071-1401-4. ▸ Single best study of relationship between slaves and criminal justice system for any area of colonial America. Focuses on slave trials; considers slave motives and white fears. [JPG/DMS]

39.314 Donna J. Spindell. *Crime and society in North Carolina, 1663–1776.* Baton Rouge: Louisiana State University Press, 1989. ISBN 0-8071-1467-7. ▸ Brief study of criminal justice system of colonial North Carolina, showing who committed crimes and nature of punishment. [JPG]

39.315 Alan Watson. *Slave law in the Americas.* Athens: University of Georgia Press, 1989. ISBN 0-8203-1179-0. ▸ Comprehensive but very general survey of written slave codes of early modern America. Shows extent to which those codes were rooted in metropolitan legal traditions. Chapter 4 deals with English America. [JPG]

Ideology and Political Culture

39.316 George A. Cook. *John Wise: early American democrat.* 1952 ed. New York: Octagon Books, 1966. ▸ Most thorough study of colonial New England's principal political theorist. [JPG]

39.317 Mary Maples Dunn. *William Penn: politics and conscience.* Princeton: Princeton University Press, 1967. ▸ Cogent, comprehensive exploration of political and religious thought of founder of Pennsylvania. [JPG]

39.318 Lawrence H. Leder. *Liberty and authority: early American political ideology, 1689–1763.* 1968 ed. New York: Norton, 1976. ISBN 0-393-00800-2. ▸ Cursory, superficial attempt to look at colonial British American political thought. But despite importance of topic, remains only serious effort at comprehensive treatment. [JPG]

39.319 Edmund S. Morgan. *Roger Williams: the church and the state.* New York: Harcourt, Brace & World, 1967. ▸ Excellent study of religious and political ideas of one of principal founders of Rhode Island. [JPG]

39.320 Jon Pahl. *Paradox lost: free will and political liberty in American culture, 1630–1760.* Baltimore: Johns Hopkins University Press, 1992. ISBN 0-8018-4334-0. ▸ Examination of how emerging doctrine of free will guided by Providence shaped early American political attitudes toward extremists and non-Europeans. [JPG]

39.321 Caroline Robbins. *The eighteenth-century commonwealthman: studies in the transmission, development, and circumstance of English liberal thought from the Restoration of Charles II until the war with the thirteen colonies.* 1959 ed. New York: Atheneum, 1968. ▸ Early study of commonwealth tradition of political thought with some attention to its effects on some colonial British American thinkers. [JPG]

39.322 Clinton Lawrence Rossiter. *Seedtime of the republic: the origin of the American tradition of political liberty.* New York: Harcourt, Brace, 1953. ▸ Still fullest analysis of prominent colonial British American political thinkers. [JPG]

SEE ALSO
41.40 Edmund S. Morgan. *Inventing the people.*

SOCIAL AND ECONOMIC HISTORY
General Studies

39.323 Bernard Bailyn. *The peopling of British North America: an introduction.* 1986 ed. New York: Vintage, 1988. ISBN 0-394-75779-3 (pbk). ▸ Lucid, if very brief, effort to sketch interpretative framework based on concept of "peopling." [JPG]

39.324 Bernard Bailyn and Philip D. Morgan. *Strangers within the realm: cultural margins of the first British empire.* Chapel Hill: University of North Carolina Press for Institute of Early American History and Culture, 1991. ISBN 0-8078-1952-2 (cl), 0-8078-4311-3 (pbk). ▸ Nine essays on theme of marginal people within early modern British empire. [JPG]

39.325 Carl Bridenbaugh. *Myths and realities: societies of the colonial South.* 1952 ed. Westport, Conn.: Greenwood, 1981. ISBN 0-313-22770-5. ▸ Old-fashioned but extremely useful portrait of three societies—Chesapeake, South Carolina low country, and back country—that subsequently merged to form South. [JPG]

39.326 Jack P. Greene. *Pursuits of happiness: the social development of early modern British colonies and the formation of American culture.* Chapel Hill: University of North Carolina Press, 1988. ISBN 0-8078-1804-0 (cl), 0-8078-4227-3 (pbk). ▸ Comprehensive social history of early modern British colonial world, including Ireland and West Indies, including effort to suggest appropriate interpretive framework. [JPG]

39.327 James A. Henretta. *The origins of American capitalism: collected essays.* Boston: Northeastern University Press, 1991. ISBN 1-55553-109-1. ▸ Collection of seven previously published essays on early American social and economic development. [JPG]

39.328 James A. Henretta and Gregory H. Nobles. *Evolution and revolution: American society, 1600–1820.* Lexington, Mass.: Heath, 1987. ISBN 0-669-08304-6 (pbk). ▸ Brief, very general overview of early American social development to 1820. [JPG]

39.329 Richard Hofstadter. *America at 1750: a social portrait.* 1971 ed. New York: Vintage, 1973. ISBN 0-394-71795-3. ▸ Still valuable, well-written portrait of society of continental colonies around 1750. [JPG]

39.330 Michael Kammen. *People of paradox: an inquiry concerning the origins of American civilization.* 1972 ed. Ithaca, N.Y.: Cornell University Press, 1990. ISBN 0-8014-9755-8 (pbk). ▸ Sweeping, much too general effort to provide framework for interpreting history of early America in terms of countervailing tendencies. Most of volume deals with colonial era. [JPG]

39.331 William S. Sachs and Ari Hoogenboom. *The enterprising colonials: society on the eve of the Revolution.* Chicago: Argonaut, 1965. ▸ One of few efforts to explore dimensions of entrepreneurial impulse among colonial British Americans. [JPG]

SEE ALSO
3.374 Louis Hartz, ed. *The founding of new societies.*

Environment and Settlement

39.332 Andrew Hill Clark. *Acadia: the geography of early Nova Scotia to 1760.* Madison: University of Wisconsin Press, 1968. ISBN 0-299-05080-7. ▸ Excellent study of geographical change in old French colony of Acadia and English colony of Nova Scotia. Focuses on changing population and land use. [JPG]

39.333 Carville V. Earle. *The evolution of a tidewater settlement system: All Hallow's Parish, Maryland, 1650–1783.* Chicago: University of Chicago, Department of Geography, 1975. (Research papers, 170.) ISBN 0-89065-077-2. ▸ Careful study of changing settlement and socioeconomic patterns in colonial Maryland parish from geographical perspective. [JPG]

39.334 Carville V. Earle. *Geographical inquiry and American historical problems.* Stanford, Calif.: Stanford University Press, 1992. ISBN 0-8047-1575-0. ▸ Outstanding collection of essays, about one third of which touch on important problems in colonial era. [JPG]

39.335 James R. Gibson, ed. *European settlement and development in North America: essays on geographical change in honour and memory of Andrew Hill Clark.* Toronto: University of Toronto Press, 1978. ISBN 0-8020-5415-3 (cl), 0-8020-3357-1 (pbk). ▸ Contains eight substantive essays on historical geography of North American places. Essays by Mitchell, Hilliard, and Lemon on colonial British America. [JPG]

39.336 James T. Lemon. *The best poor man's country: a geographical study of early southeastern Pennsylvania.* 1972 ed. New York: Norton, 1976. ISBN 0-393-00804-5. ▸ Excellent study of changing patterns of land use and social dynamics in rapidly developing portion of British colonial world. [JPG]

39.337 David M. Ludlum. *Early American hurricanes, 1492–1870.* Boston: American Meteorological Society, 1963. (History of American weather, 1.) ▸ Sketchy but only serious book-length study of this important subject. [JPG]

39.338 Douglas R. McManis. *Colonial New England: a historical geography.* New York: Oxford University Press, 1975. ISBN 0-19-501907-5. ▸ Short overview of geographical change in colonial New England. [JPG]

39.339 Donald William Meinig. *The shaping of America: a geographical perspective on five hundred years of history.* Vol. 1: *Atlantic America, 1492–1800.* New Haven: Yale University Press, 1986. ISBN 0-300-03548-9 (cl), 0-300-03882-8 (pbk). ▸ Broad, suggestive study of emergence of distinctive cultural regions during first three centuries of European occupation from perspective of historical geography. [JPG]

39.340 Carolyn Merchant. *Ecological revolutions: nature, gender, and science in New England.* Chapel Hill: University of North Carolina Press, 1989. ISBN 0-8078-1858-5 (cl), 0-8078-4254-0 (pbk). ▸ Insightful exploration of ecological transformation of New England under domination of Europeans, with theories about science, society, and gender that underlay that transformation. [JPG]

39.341 Harry Roy Merrens. *Colonial North Carolina in the eighteenth century: a study in historical geography.* Chapel Hill: University of North Carolina Press, 1964. ▸ Excellent historical geography of colonial North Carolina focusing on patterns of land use and economic activity. [JPG]

39.342 Robert D. Mitchell. *Commercialism and frontier: perspectives on the early Shenandoah Valley.* Charlottesville: University Press of Virginia, 1977. ISBN 0-8139-0661-X. ▸ Cogent consideration of changing population, land reorganization, and settlement patterns in first early American West. [JPG]

39.343 Robert D. Mitchell and Paul A. Groves, eds. *North America: the historical geography of a changing continent.* 1987 ed. Savage, Md.: Rowman & Littlefield, 1990. ISBN 0-8476-7549-1 (pbk). ▸ Informed general work; first six chapters deal with colonial North America. [JPG]

39.344 Timothy Silver. *A new face on the countryside: Indians, colonists, and slaves in South Atlantic forests, 1500–1800.* Cambridge: Cambridge University Press, 1990. ISBN 0-521-34374-7 (cl), 0-521-38739-6 (pbk). ▸ Broad consideration of transformation of landscape wrought by Europeans in southern colonies before 1800. [JPG]

39.345 Peter O. Wacker. *Land and people, a cultural geography of preindustrial New Jersey: origins and settlement patterns.* New Brunswick, N.J.: Rutgers University Press, 1975. ▸ Detailed consideration of use of space in colonial New Jersey during colonial era. [JPG]

39.346 Peter O. Wacker. *The Musconetcong Valley of New Jersey: a historical geography.* New Brunswick, N.J.: Rutgers University Press, 1968. ‣ Local study of geographical change through eighteenth century giving special attention to settlement patterns. [JPG]

39.347 David Watts. *The West Indies: patterns of development, culture, and environmental change since 1492.* Cambridge: Cambridge University Press, 1987. ISBN 0-521-24555-9. ‣ Comprehensive study by historical geographer of social development and environmental change with particular attention to Barbados, Jamaica, and Leeward Islands. [JPG]

SEE ALSO
36.92 William Cronon. *Changes in the land.*
40.116 Michael Williams. *Americans and their forests.*

Migration and Population

39.348 Ida Altman and James Horn, eds. *"To make America": European emigration in the early modern period.* Berkeley: University of California Press, 1991. ISBN 0-520-07233-2. ‣ Collection of seven essays on European migration. Essays by Horn and Wokeck deal with emigration to colonial British America. [JPG]

39.349 R. J. Dickson. *Ulster emigration to colonial America, 1718–1775.* London: Routledge & Kegan Paul, 1966. ‣ Best study of eighteenth-century emigration from Ulster to colonial British America. [JPG]

39.350 David Dobson. *Scottish emigration to colonial America, 1607–1785.* Athens: University of Georgia Press, 1994. ISBN 0-8203-1492-7. ‣ Most recent, up-to-date analysis of Scottish migration to America during colonial and revolutionary eras. [JPG]

39.351 Larry Dale Gragg. *Migration in early America: the Virginia Quaker experience.* Ann Arbor: University Microfilms International, 1980. ISBN 0-8357-1095-5. ‣ Uses Quaker removal certificates to measure rates and extent of migration among Quakers from southeastern Pennsylvania to Virginia, North Carolina, and Ohio, 1711–1800. [JPG]

39.352 Ian C. C. Graham. *Colonists from Scotland: emigration to North America, 1707–1783.* Ithaca, N.Y.: Cornell University Press, 1956. ‣ Early but useful analysis of Scottish migration. [JPG]

39.353 Evarts B. Greene and Virginia D. Harrington. *American population before the federal census of 1790.* 1932 ed. Gloucester, Mass.: Smith, 1966. ‣ Basic study of population history of continental colonies in British America. [JPG]

39.354 Douglas Lamar Jones. *Village and seaport: migration and society in eighteenth-century Massachusetts.* Hanover, N.H.: University Press of New England for Tufts University, 1981. ISBN 0-87451-200-X. ‣ Only serious book-length study of important subject of internal migration for any area of colonial British America. [JPG]

39.355 Susan E. Klepp. *Philadelphia in transition: a demographic history of the city and its occupational groups, 1720–1830.* New York: Garland, 1989. ISBN 0-8240-4164-X. ‣ Case study in urban demography for largest colonial city. Details childbearing, marriage, family, size, etc. Finds occupation critical in determining demographic behavior. [JPG]

39.356 Audrey Lockhart. *Some aspects of emigration from Ireland to the North American colonies between 1660 and 1775.* New York: Arno, 1976. ISBN 0-405-09345-4. ‣ Useful consideration of process, timing, and scope of Irish emigration to America in colonial period. [JPG]

39.357 Robert V. Wells. *The population of the British colonies in America before 1776: a survey of census data.* Princeton: Princeton University Press, 1975. ISBN 0-691-04616-6. ‣ Broad consideration of available population data for all Britain's New World colonies, including those in Caribbean and Atlantic. [JPG]

SEE ALSO
3.209 Sidney W. Mintz. *Sweetness and power.*
23.233 David Cressy. *Coming over.*

Local and Urban History

39.358 Thomas J. Archdeacon. *New York City, 1664–1710: conquest and change.* Ithaca, N.Y.: Cornell University Press, 1976. ISBN 0-8014-0944-6. ‣ Social study of New York City during first half century of English governance emphasizing ethnic basis of social organization and residential patterns. [JPG]

39.359 Richard R. Beeman. *The evolution of the southern backcountry: a case study of Lunenburg County, Virginia, 1746–1832.* Philadelphia: University of Pennsylvania Press, 1984. ISBN 0-8122-7926-3. ‣ Excellent study of economic, social, and political development of new county in Virginia piedmont during its first nine decades. [JPG]

39.360 Paul Boyer and Stephen Nissenbaum. *Salem possessed: the social origins of witchcraft.* Cambridge, Mass.: Harvard University Press, 1974. ISBN 0-674-78525-8 (cl), 0-674-78526-6 (pbk). ‣ Influential analysis of social basis of New England witchcraft through microexamination of Salem village at time of outbreak of witch trials in 1692. [JPG]

39.361 Carl Bridenbaugh. *Cities in revolt: urban life in America, 1743–1776.* 1955 ed. New York: Oxford University Press, 1971. ISBN 0-19-501362-X (pbk). ‣ Older work containing much information about social and cultural life of five largest colonial cities. Remains fullest study of colonial urban life in decades just before Revolution. [JPG]

39.362 Carl Bridenbaugh. *Cities in the wilderness: the first century of urban life in America, 1625–1742.* 1938 ed. New York: Oxford University Press, 1971. ISBN 0-19-501361-1. ‣ Superb analysis of origins and character of five largest colonial cities in English continental America before 1740. [JPG]

39.363 Carl Bridenbaugh and Jessica Bridenbaugh. *Rebels and gentlemen: Philadelphia in the age of Franklin.* 1942 ed. Westport, Conn.: Greenwood, 1970. ISBN 0-313-20300-8. ‣ Portrait of Philadelphia social life on eve of American Revolution. [JPG]

39.364 Edward Byers. *The nation of Nantucket: society and politics in an early American commercial center, 1660–1820.* Boston: Northeastern University Press, 1986. ‣ Intelligent community study of economic, social, and political development of important commercial island town of Nantucket. [JPG]

39.365 Robert E. Cray, Jr. *Paupers and poor relief in New York City and its rural environs, 1700–1830.* Philadelphia: Temple University Press, 1988. ISBN 0-87722-542-7. ‣ Best available study of emergence of system of poor relief. Compares practices in New York City with those in three rural counties. [JPG]

39.366 Bruce C. Daniels. *The Connecticut town: growth and development, 1635–1790.* Middletown, Conn.: Wesleyan University Press; distributed by Columbia University Press, 1979. ISBN 0-8195-5036-1. ‣ Broad study of growth of Connecticut towns emphasizing institutional elaboration and social differentiation. [JPG]

39.367 Bruce C. Daniels. *Dissent and conformity on Narragansett Bay: the colonial Rhode Island town.* Middletown, Conn.: Wesleyan University Press; distributed by Harper & Row, 1983. ISBN 0-8195-5083-3. ‣ Brief but valuable study of demographic and institutional development of towns in religiously heterogeneous colony of Rhode Island. [JPG]

39.368 Walter J. Fraser, Jr. *Charleston! Charleston! The history of* *a southern city*. Columbia: University of South Carolina Press, 1989. ISBN 0-87249-643-0. ‣ Inclusive history of Charleston, one third deals with colonial era. [JPG]

39.369 Richard P. Gildrie. *Salem, Massachusetts, 1626–1683: a covenant community*. Charlottesville: University Press of Virginia, 1975. ISBN 0-8139-0532-X. ‣ Careful, comprehensive study of development of maritime community of Salem during its first half century. [JPG]

39.370 Gillian Lindt Gollin. *Moravians in two worlds: a study in changing communities*. New York: Columbia University Press, 1967. ISBN 0-231-03033-9. ‣ Comparative study of community and social development of Moravian communities in Herrnhut, Germany, and Bethlehem, Pennsylvania. Focuses on secularization. [JPG/DMS]

39.371 Charles S. Grant. *Democracy in the Connecticut frontier town of Kent*. 1961 ed. Kenneth A. Lockridge, Introduction. New York: Norton, 1972. ISBN 0-393-00639-5. ‣ Early community study emphasizing relation between land supply and social mobility. [JPG]

39.372 Philip J. Greven. *Four generations: population, land, and family in colonial Andover, Massachusetts*. Ithaca, N.Y.: Cornell University Press, 1970. ISBN 0-8014-0539-4. ‣ Most detailed of early local town studies. Emphasizes relationship between control of land and patriarchal authority in Puritan Massachusetts. [JPG]

39.373 Christine Leigh Heyrman. *Commerce and culture: the maritime communities of colonial Massachusetts, 1690–1750*. New York: Norton, 1984. ISBN 0-393-01781-8. ‣ Imaginative study of growing coherence in two Massachusetts port towns, Marblehead and Gloucester, during first half of eighteenth century. [JPG]

39.374 Jessica Kross. *The evolution of an American town: Newtown, New York, 1642–1775*. Philadelphia: Temple University Press, 1983. ISBN 0-87722-277-0. ‣ Careful local study of changing social, economic, and political character of Long Island town over whole of colonial era. [JPG]

39.375 Enoch Lawrence Lee. *The lower Cape Fear in colonial days*. Chapel Hill: University of North Carolina Press, 1965. ‣ Useful regional study of important area of North Carolina. [JPG]

39.376 Kenneth A. Lockridge. *A New England town, the first hundred years: Dedham, Massachusetts, 1636–1736*. Rev. ed. New York: Norton, 1985. ISBN 0-393-95459-5 (pbk). ‣ One of earliest town studies emphasizing disintegration of social, religious, and political community. [JPG]

39.377 Richard I. Melvoin. *New England outpost: war and society in colonial Deerfield*. New York: Norton, 1989. ISBN 0-393-02600-0. ‣ Excellent study of New England frontier community in seventeenth century. Emphasizes significance of American Indians and war in shaping town life. [JPG]

39.378 Gwenda Morgan. *The hegemony of the law: Richmond County, Virginia, 1692–1776*. New York: Garland, 1989. ISBN 0-8240-6192-6. ‣ Local study of emergence of stable social, political, and legal order in tidewater Virginia county. [JPG]

39.379 Gary B. Nash. *The urban crucible: social change, political consciousness, and the origins of the American Revolution*. Cambridge, Mass.: Harvard University Press, 1979. ISBN 0-674-93056-8. ‣ Systematic discussion of social stratification in Philadelphia, Boston, and New York. Discussion of political factionalism less valuable. [JPG]

39.380 Gregory H. Nobles. *Divisions throughout the whole: politics and society in Hampshire County, Massachusetts, 1740–1775*. Cambridge: Cambridge University Press, 1983. ISBN 0-521-24419-6. ‣ Excellent analysis of shifting social and political structure of western Massachusetts county during generation

before American Revolution. Finds division and discord following Great Awakening; sees gradual erosion of elite. [JPG/DMS]

39.381 James O'Mara. *An historical geography of urban system development: tidewater Virginia in the eighteenth century*. Downsview, England: York University, Department of Geography, Atkinson College, 1983. (Geographical monographs, 13.) ISBN 0-919762-12-3. ‣ Highly quantitative study of process of town formation in colonial Virginia. [JPG]

39.382 James R. Perry. *The formation of a society on Virginia's eastern shore, 1615–1655*. Chapel Hill: University of North Carolina Press for Institute of Early American History and Culture, 1990. ISBN 0-8078-1927-1. ‣ Excellent case study of formation of local society in early Virginia. Persuasive challenge to views of Chesapeake colonies as lacking community. [JPG]

39.383 Sumner Chilton Powell. *Puritan village: the formation of a New England town*. 1963 ed. Middletown, Conn.: Wesleyan University Press, 1970. ISBN 0-8195-6014-6. ‣ Early local study of social formation of New England town. Stresses importance of cultural transfer from Old World. [JPG]

39.384 Robert W. Ramsey. *Carolina cradle: settlement of the Northwest Carolina frontier, 1747–1762*. Chapel Hill: University of North Carolina Press, 1964. ‣ Good local study of dynamic areas of central North Carolina during period of rapid settlement. [JPG]

39.385 John W. Reps. *Tidewater towns: city planning in colonial Virginia and Maryland*. Williamsburg, Va.: Colonial Williamsburg Foundation; distributed by the University Press of Virginia, 1972. ISBN 0-910412-87-1, 0-8139-0332-7. ‣ Best study of metropolitan context and process of town planning in colonial Chesapeake. Valuble sections on Williamsburg and Annapolis. [JPG]

39.386 John W. Reps. *Town planning in frontier America*. 1969 ed. Columbia: University of Missouri Press, 1980. ISBN 0-8262-0316-7 (pbk). ‣ Analysis of city plans in North America, approximately half deals with colonial era. [JPG]

39.387 George C. Rogers, Jr. *Charleston in the age of the Pinckneys*. 1969 ed. Columbia: University of South Carolina Press, 1980. ISBN 0-87249-297-4 (pbk). ‣ Good, concise narrative history of colonial and early national Charleston. [JPG]

39.388 Darrett B. Rutman. *Winthrop's Boston: portrait of a Puritan town, 1630–1649*. 1965 ed. New York: Norton, 1972. ISBN 0-393-00627-1. ‣ Comprehensive study of Boston's first two decades, stressing primacy of economic concerns and religious heterogeneity of inhabitants. [JPG]

39.389 Darrett B. Rutman and Anita H. Rutman. *A place in time: Middlesex County, Virginia, 1650–1750. A place in time: explicatus*. 2 vols. New York: Norton, 1984. ISBN 0-393-01801-6 (v. 1), 0-393-01820-2 (v. 2). ‣ Excellent comprehensive local study of changing social character of Virginia county during colonial period. [JPG]

39.390 Beverly Prior Smaby. *The transformation of Moravian Bethlehem: from communal mission to family economy*. Philadelphia: University of Pennsylvania Press, 1988. ISBN 0-8122-8130-6. ‣ Systematic, valuable examination of social, demographic, and religious effects of reorganization of Bethlehem Moravian community into nuclear households. [JPG/DMS]

39.391 Daniel P. Thorp. *The Moravian community in colonial North Carolina: pluralism on the southern frontier*. Knoxville: University of Tennessee Press, 1989. ISBN 0-87049-605-0. ‣ Valuable examination of first generation of Moravian settlements in western North Carolina showing contrast between this communally oriented religious group and societies around them. [JPG]

39.392 Patricia J. Tracy. *Jonathan Edwards, pastor: religion and society in eighteenth-century Northampton*. New York: Hill &

Wang, 1980. ISBN 0-8090-6195-3 (cl), 0-8090-0149-7 (pbk). ▸ Local study of social development of Northampton, Massachusetts, exploring social roots of town's religious life. [JPG]

39.393 G. B. Warden. *Boston, 1689–1776.* Boston: Little, Brown, 1970. ▸ Political and social history of Boston relating demographic and social change to shifting economic conditions. [JPG]

39.394 Walter Muir Whitehill. *Boston: a topographical history.* 2d rev. ed. Cambridge, Mass.: Belknap, 1968. ▸ Study of changing layout of Boston. [JPG]

39.395 Lynne Withey. *Urban growth in colonial Rhode Island: Newport and Providence in the eighteenth century.* Albany: State University of New York Press, 1984. ISBN 0-87395-751-2 (cl), 0-87395-752-0 (pbk). ▸ Useful, short comparative study of development of Newport and Providence as urban and commercial centers. [JPG]

39.396 Stephanie Grauman Wolf. *Urban village: population, community, and family structure in Germantown, Pennsylvania, 1683–1800.* Princeton: Princeton University Press, 1976. ISBN 0-691-04632-8. ▸ Excellent social study of earliest German community in colonial British America. [JPG]

39.397 Jerome H. Wood, Jr. *Conestoga crossroads: Lancaster, Pennsylvania, 1730–1790.* Harrisburg: Pennsylvania Historical and Museum Commission, 1979. ISBN 0-911124-98-5. ▸ Valuable study of all aspects of social, economic, and political life of ethnically diverse urban community and largest inland town in colonial British America. [JPG]

SEE ALSO
40.290 Sam Bass Warner. *The private city.*

Economy

39.398 Terry Lee Anderson. *The economic growth of seventeenth-century New England: a measurement of regional income.* 1972 ed. New York: Arno, 1975. ISBN 0-405-07255-4. ▸ Suffers from absence of sufficient data to support its economic analysis, but contains some useful hypotheses about important subject. [JPG]

39.399 Van Cleaf Bachman. *Peltries or plantations: the economic policies of the Dutch West India Company in New Netherland, 1623–1639.* Baltimore: Johns Hopkins University Press, 1970. ISBN 0-8018-1064-7. ▸ Best available study of economic objectives of Dutch West India Company in New Netherlands during colony's earliest years and of company's strategies to achieve those objectives. [JPG]

39.400 Bernard Bailyn. *The New England merchants in the seventeenth century.* 1955 ed. Cambridge, Mass.: Harvard University Press, 1964. ▸ Excellent examination of economic, social, and political role of emerging mercantile group of colonial Massachusetts. [JPG]

39.401 William T. Baxter. *The house of Hancock: business in Boston, 1724–1775.* 1945 ed. New York: Russell & Russell, 1965. ▸ Excellent study of successful family business in late colonial Boston. [JPG]

39.402 Percy Wells Bidwell and John I. Falconer. *History of agriculture in the northern United States, 1620–1860.* 1925 ed. Clifton, N.J.: Kelley, 1973. ISBN 0-678-00956-2. ▸ Still best general study of agricultural economy of northern colonies. [JPG]

39.403 Leslie V. Brock. *The currency of the American colonies, 1700–1764: a study in colonial finance and imperial relations.* New York: Arno, 1975. ISBN 0-405-07257-0. ▸ Comprehensive general study of paper currency systems of Britain's continental American colonies during eighteenth century. [JPG]

39.404 Stuart Bruchey. *The roots of American economic growth, 1607–1861: an essay in social causation.* 1965 ed. New York: Harper & Row, 1968. ▸ Overview of emergence of American economy before Civil War. Devotes significant space to colonial era. [JPG]

39.405 Charles F. Carroll. *The timber economy of Puritan New England.* 1973 ed. Providence: Brown University Press, 1974. ISBN 0-8705-7142-7. ▸ Introductory study of how colonial New Englanders used forests to sustain themselves. [JPG]

39.406 Joyce E. Chaplin. *An anxious pursuit: agricultural innovation and modernity in the lower South, 1730–1815.* Chapel Hill: University of North Carolina Press for Institute of Early American History and Culture, 1993. ISBN 0-8078-2084-9. ▸ Impressive analysis of economic culture of lower southern colonies after 1730, focusing on continuing dynamism and involvement in agricultural innovation. [JPG]

39.407 Stanley F. Cheyt. *Lopez of Newport: colonial American merchant prince.* Detroit: Wayne State University Press, 1970. ISBN 0-8143-1407-4. ▸ Excellent biographical and economic study of one of principal merchants of late colonial New England. [JPG]

39.408 Paul G. E. Clemens. *The Atlantic economy and colonial Maryland's Eastern Shore: from tobacco to grain.* Ithaca, N.Y.: Cornell University Press, 1980. ISBN 0-8014-1251-X. ▸ Model study of changing economy of Eastern Shore of Maryland during colonial era. [JPG]

39.409 Converse D. Clowse. *Economic beginnings in colonial South Carolina, 1670–1730.* Columbia: University of South Carolina Press for South Carolina Tricentennial Commission, 1971. (Tricentennial studies, 3.) ISBN 0-87249-186-2. ▸ Useful analysis of slow establishment of secure economic base in colonial South Carolina. [JPG]

39.410 Peter A. Coclanis. *The shadow of a dream: economic life and death in the South Carolina low country, 1670–1920.* New York: Oxford University Press, 1989. ISBN 0-19-504420-7. ▸ Superb economic history of South Carolina low country; substantial portion covers colonial period. [JPG]

39.411 David Steven Cohen. *The Dutch-American farm.* New York: New York University Press, 1992. ISBN 0-8147-1454-4. ▸ Imaginative analysis emphasizing heterogeneity of Dutch settlers and varied cultural heritages they brought to creation of their farms. [JPG]

39.412 Jay Coughtry. *The notorious triangle: Rhode Island and the African slave trade, 1700–1807.* Philadelphia: Temple University Press, 1981. ISBN 0-87722-218-5. ▸ Cogent examination of Rhode Island's extensive participation in slave trade to Africa during eighteenth century. [JPG]

39.413 Byron Fairchild. *Messrs. Pepperrell, merchants at Piscataqua.* Ithaca, N.Y.: Cornell University Press for American Historical Association, 1954. ▸ Valuable case study of colonial mercantile activities in northern New England. [JPG]

39.414 S. W. Fletcher, Jr. *Pennsylvania agriculture and country life, 1640–1840.* 2 vols. Harrisburg: Pennsylvania Historical and Museum Commission, 1950–55. ▸ Useful study of farming practices in colonial and early national Pennsylvania. [JPG]

39.415 Stephen Alexander Fortune. *Merchants and Jews: the struggle for British West Indian commerce, 1650–1750.* Gainesville: University Presses of Florida, 1984. ISBN 0-8130-0735-6. ▸ Study of selected aspects of British West Indian commerce with particular emphasis on Barbados and Jamaica. [JPG]

39.416 Daniel M. Friedenberg. *Life, liberty, and the pursuit of land: the plunder of early America.* Buffalo: Prometheus, 1992. ISBN 0-87975-722-1. ▸ Important volume containing most comprehensive discussion of land development's importance in early American life. Part 1 deals with colonial era. [JPG]

39.417 David W. Galenson. *Traders, planters, and slaves: market behavior in early English America.* Cambridge: Cambridge University Press, 1986. ISBN 0-521-30845-3. ▸ Systematic examination of operation of slave trade to English West Indies before 1723 with some attention to social impact of slavery on West Indian colonies. [JPG]

39.418 Joseph A. Goldenberg. *Shipbuilding in colonial America.* Charlottesville: University Press of Virginia for Mariners Museum, 1976. (Museum publication: Mariners Museum, 33.) ISBN 0-8139-0588-5. ▸ Best available study of one of more important colonial industries. [JPG]

39.419 Lewis Cecil Gray. *History of agriculture in the southern United States to 1860.* 1933 ed. 2 vols. Gloucester, Mass.: Smith, 1958. ▸ Excellent history of agricultural system and practices of southern colonies. [JPG]

39.420 James B. Hedges. *The Browns of Providence plantations.* 2 vols. Providence: Brown University Press, 1952–68. ▸ Fine study of development of mercantile family in colonial Rhode Island. [JPG]

39.421 John M. Hemphill II. *Virginia and the English commercial system, 1689–1733: a study in the development and fluctuations of a colonial economy under imperial control.* New York: Garland, 1985. ISBN 0-8240-6669-3. ▸ Careful analysis of fluctuating economic fortunes of Virginia during four decades following Glorious Revolution and of efforts at political manipulation of economy by both Virginians and metropolitans. [JPG]

39.422 J.R.T. Hughes. *Social control in the colonial economy.* Charlottesville: University Press of Virginia, 1976. ISBN 0-8139-0623-7. ▸ Useful examination of legal and governmental controls over colonial economic life. [JPG]

39.423 Sarah S. Hughes. *Surveyors and statesmen: land measuring in colonial Virginia.* Richmond: Virginia Surveyors Foundation and Virginia Association of Surveyors, 1979. ▸ Most sophisticated study of actual process of land surveying for any area of colonial British America. [JPG]

39.424 Arthur L. Jensen. *The maritime commerce of colonial Philadelphia.* 1963 ed. Madison: State Historical Society of Wisconsin for University of Wisconsin, Department of History, 1966. ▸ Good case study of developing trade of chief colonial port. [JPG]

39.425 James H. Levitt. *For want of trade: shipping and the New Jersey ports, 1680–1783.* Newark: New Jersey Historical Society, 1981. (Thomas Alva Edison studies in New Jersey economic history, Collections of the New Jersey Historical Society, 17.) ISBN 0-911020-03-9. ▸ Useful discussion of overseas and intercoastal trade of colonial New Jersey ports. [JPG]

39.426 Ralph Greenlee Lounsbury. *The British fishery at Newfoundland, 1634–1763.* 1934 ed. Hamden, Conn.: Archon, 1969. ISBN 0-208-00795-4. ▸ Older but still useful study of British activities in Newfoundland fishing center before 1763. [JPG]

39.427 John J. McCusker. *Money and exchange in Europe and America, 1600–1775: a handbook.* Chapel Hill: University of North Carolina Press for Institute of Early American History and Culture, 1978. ▸ Basic tool for ascertaining value of money and rates of exchange for complex Atlantic trading world during seventeenth and eighteenth centuries. [JPG]

39.428 John J. McCusker and Russell R. Menard. *The economy of British America, 1607–1789, with supplementary bibliography.* Rev. ed. Chapel Hill: University of North Carolina Press for Institute of Early American History and Culture, 1991. ISBN 0-8078-4351-2 (pbk). ▸ Extremely valuable, extensive discussion of economic development of colonial British America. [JPG]

39.429 Arthur Pierce Middleton. *Tobacco coast: a maritime history of Chesapeake Bay in the colonial era.* 1953 ed. Baltimore:

Johns Hopkins University Press and Maryland State Archives, 1984. ISBN 0-8018-2534-2 (pbk). ▸ Traditional descriptive study of trade and shipping of Chesapeake. [JPG]

39.430 Louis Morton. *Robert Carter of Nomini Hall: a Virginia tobacco planter of the eighteenth century.* 1945 2d ed. Charlottesville, Va.: Dominion, 1964. ▸ Best single study of operation of eighteenth-century Chesapeake plantation. [JPG]

39.431 Curtis P. Nettels. *The money supply of the American colonies before 1720.* 1934 ed. New York: Kelley, 1964. ▸ Older study of early stages of chronic problem of liquid money supply in English continental colonies. [JPG]

39.432 Thomas Elliot Norton. *The fur trade in colonial New York, 1686–1776.* Madison: University of Wisconsin Press, 1974. ISBN 0-299-06420-4. ▸ Very useful study of a principal trade of colonial New York. [JPG]

39.433 Richard Pares. *A West India fortune.* 1950 ed. Hamden, Conn.: Archon, 1968. ▸ Illuminating analysis of building of West Indian family fortune during eighteenth century. [JPG]

39.434 Richard Pares. *Yankees and creoles: the trade between North America and the West Indies before the American Revolution.* 1956 ed. Hamden, Conn.: Archon, 1968. ▸ Best study of trade between continental and island colonies. [JPG]

39.435 Paul F. Paskoff. *Industrial evolution: organization, structure, and growth of the Pennsylvania iron industry, 1750–1860.* Baltimore: Johns Hopkins University Press, 1983. ISBN 0-8018-2904-6. ▸ Best modern study of early organization of iron industry in colonial and early national Pennsylvania. [JPG]

39.436 Edwin J. Perkins. *The economy of colonial America.* 2d ed. New York: Columbia University Press, 1988. ISBN 0-231-06338-5 (cl), 0-231-06339-3 (pbk). ▸ Best short overview of subject. [JPG]

39.437 Jacob M. Price. *Capital and credit in British overseas trade: the view from the Chesapeake, 1700–1776.* Cambridge, Mass.: Harvard University Press, 1980. ISBN 0-674-09480-8. ▸ Excellent analysis of mobilization of British capital and operation of credit in Chesapeake tobacco trade. [JPG]

39.438 Jacob M. Price. *France and the Chesapeake: a history of the French tobacco monopoly, 1674–1791, and of its relationship to the British and American tobacco trades.* 2 vols. Ann Arbor: University of Michigan Press, 1973. ISBN 0-472-08738-X. ▸ Detailed study of relationship of French tobacco purchases and tobacco economy of Chesapeake. [JPG]

39.439 Jacob M. Price. *Perry of London: a family and a firm on the seaborne frontier, 1615–1753.* Cambridge, Mass.: Harvard University Press, 1992. ISBN 0-674-66306-3. ▸ Valuable discussion of origins and operation of London family firm, which by late colonial era had become most important company trading to Chesapeake. [JPG]

39.440 John C. Rainbolt. *From prescription to persuasion: manipulation of eighteenth-century Virginia economy.* Port Washington, N.Y.: Kennikat, 1974. ISBN 0-8046-9057-X. ▸ Able study of early efforts to redirect economy and social organization of Virginia through diversification and urbanization. [JPG]

39.441 Winifred Barr Rothenberg. *From marketplaces to a market economy: the transformation of rural Massachusetts, 1750–1850.* Chicago: University of Chicago Press, 1992. ISBN 0-226-72953-2. ▸ Study of household economies of rural Massachusetts and of their changing involvement in markets. [JPG]

39.442 Howard S. Russell. *A long, deep furrow: three centuries of farming in New England.* Hanover, N.H.: University Press of New England, 1976. ISBN 0-87451-093-7. ▸ Essential study for understanding New England agricultural practices during colonial and later eras. [JPG]

39.443 Darrett B. Rutman. *Husbandmen of Plymouth: farms and villages in the old colony, 1620–1692.* Boston: Beacon for Plimoth Plantation, 1967. ▸ Useful analysis of agricultural practices in seventeenth-century Plymouth. Abridged version available from University Press of New England, 1982. [JPG]

39.444 Mary M. Schweitzer. *Custom and contract: household, government, and the economy in colonial Pennsylvania.* New York: Columbia University Press, 1987. ISBN 0-231-06288-5. ▸ Original study, best available for any area of colonial British America, of participation of households in commercial markets and how households used government to shape economic policy. [JPG]

39.445 Carole Shammas. *The preindustrial consumer in England and America.* Oxford: Clarendon, 1990. ISBN 0-19-828302-4. ▸ Systematic, comprehensive, and persuasive study of changing character of consumption and distribution of consumer goods in early modern England and colonial America. [JPG]

39.446 James F. Shepherd and Gary M. Walton. *Shipping, maritime trade, and the economic development of colonial North America.* 1973 ed. Cambridge: Cambridge University Press, 1974. ISBN 0-521-08409-1. ▸ Quantitative analysis of patterns of shipping and maritime trade in late colonial period. [JPG]

39.447 Richard B. Sheridan. *Sugar and slavery: an economic history of the British West Indies, 1623–1775.* 1973 ed. Baltimore: Johns Hopkins University Press, 1974. ISBN 0-8018-1580-0. ▸ Excellent economic history of British sugar colonies containing best portraits of social structures of white population during eighteenth century. [JPG]

39.448 James H. Soltow. *The economic role of Williamsburg.* Williamsburg, Va.: Colonial Williamsburg; distributed by University Press of Virginia, 1965. ▸ Interesting case study of economic life of political and administrative town. [JPG]

39.449 Gary M. Walton and James F. Shepherd. *The economic rise of early America.* New York: Cambridge University Press, 1979. ISBN 0-521-22282-6 (cl), 0-521-29433-9 (pbk). ▸ Brief survey of major developments in colonial economy. [JPG]

39.450 Glenn Weaver. *Jonathan Trumbull, Connecticut's merchant magistrate, 1710–1785.* Hartford: Connecticut Historical Society, 1956. ▸ Biography of important political and commercial figure in late colonial and revolutionary New England. [JPG]

39.451 William B. Weeden. *Economic and social history of New England, 1620–1789.* 1890 ed. 2 vols. Williamstown, Mass.: Corner House, 1978. ▸ Older work essential for understanding of economic life of colonial New England. [JPG]

39.452 Philip L. White. *The Beekmans of New York in politics and commerce, 1647–1877.* New York: New York Historical Society, 1956. ▸ One of best studies of colonial mercantile family. [JPG]

SEE ALSO
41.432 Alice Hanson Jones. *Wealth of a nation to be.*

Labor

39.453 Hilary McD. Beckles. *White servitude and black slavery in Barbados, 1627–1715.* Knoxville: University of Tennessee Press, 1989. ISBN 0-87049-601-8. ▸ One of best studies of coerced labor conditions for any seventeenth-century British colony. Shows close connections between servitude and slavery. [JPG]

39.454 A. Roger Ekirch. *Bound for America: the transportation of British convicts to the colonies, 1718–1775.* Oxford: Clarendon, 1987. ISBN 0-19-820092-7. ▸ Excellent social analysis of convict trade to America during eighteenth century showing who was transported and where. [JPG]

39.455 David W. Galenson. *White servitude in colonial America: an economic analysis.* Cambridge: Cambridge University Press, 1981. ISBN 0-521-23686-X. ▸ Econometric analysis of institution of indentured servitude. [JPG]

39.456 Graham Russell Hodges. *New York City cartmen, 1667–1850.* New York: New York University Press, 1986. ▸ Careful study of one group of urban laborers as conditions and character of their work changed over two and a half centuries. [JPG]

39.457 Stephen Innes. *Labor in a new land: economy and society in seventeenth-century Springfield.* Princeton: Princeton University Press, 1983. ISBN 0-691-04698-0 (cl), 0-691-00595-8 (pbk). ▸ Local study emphasizing extensive employment of tenants to develop rich farm lands of Connecticut River valley. [JPG]

39.458 Stephen Innes, ed. *Work and labor in early America.* Chapel Hill: University of North Carolina Press for Institute of Early American History and Culture, 1988. ISBN 0-8078-1798-8 (cl), 0-8078-4236-2 (pbk). ▸ Volume of seven excellent essays on conditions of work and labor in colonial British America. [JPG]

39.459 Marcus Wilson Jernegan. *Laboring and dependent classes in colonial America, 1607–1783.* 1931 ed. Westport, Conn.: Greenwood, 1980. ISBN 0-313-22399-8. ▸ Older work on colonial labor; concentrates on free labor. [JPG]

39.460 Almon Wheeler Lauber. *Indian slavery in colonial times within the present limits of the United States.* 1913 ed. New York: AMS Press, 1969. ▸ Only study of neglected subject. [JPG]

39.461 Irving Mark. *Agrarian conflicts in colonial New York, 1711–1775.* 2d ed. Port Washington, N.Y.: Friedman, 1965. ▸ Interpretation of landlord-tenant conflict as class conflict. [JPG]

39.462 Richard B. Morris. *Government and labor in early America.* 1946 ed. New York: Octagon Books, 1975. ISBN 0-374-95890-4. ▸ Older book providing valuable detail about government regulation of labor. [JPG]

39.463 Marcus Rediker. *Between the devil and and the deep blue sea: merchant seamen, pirates, and the Anglo-American maritime world, 1700–1750.* Cambridge: Cambridge University Press, 1987. ISBN 0-521-30342-7 (cl), 0-521-37983-0 (pbk). ▸ Provocative study of working conditions among sailors in eighteenth-century British Atlantic; romanticizes shipboard community. [JPG]

39.464 Jean B. Russo. *Free workers in a plantation economy: Talbot County, Maryland, 1690–1759.* New York: Garland, 1989. ISBN 0-8240-6195-0. ▸ Important analysis of extensive and varied use of free labor in plantation society with large population of slaves. [JPG]

39.465 Sharon V. Salinger. *"To serve well and faithfully": labor and indentured servants in Pennsylvania, 1682–1800.* Cambridge: Cambridge University Press, 1987. ISBN 0-521-33442-X. ▸ Competent study of institution of indentured servitude as it operated in colonial and early national Pennsylvania. [JPG]

39.466 Abbot Emerson Smith. *Colonists in bondage: white servitude and convict labor in America, 1607–1776.* 1947 ed. New York: Norton, 1971. ISBN 0-393-00592-5. ▸ Classic study of system of free bound labor in colonial British America. [JPG]

39.467 Warren B. Smith. *White servitude in colonial South Carolina.* Columbia: University of South Carolina Press, 1961. ▸ Institutional analysis of indentured labor in this slave society. [JPG]

39.468 Gregory A. Stiverson. *Poverty in a land of plenty: tenancy in eighteenth-century Maryland.* Baltimore: Johns Hopkins University Press, 1977. ISBN 0-8018-1966-0. ▸ Exploration of character of tenancy on proprietary manors of colonial Maryland. Emphasizes generational persistence of tenant families. [JPG]

Family

39.469 Michael Craton and James Walvin. *A Jamaican plantation: the history of Worthy Park, 1670–1970.* London: Allen, 1970. ISBN 0-491-00245-9. ‣ Early chapters provide valuable study of Price family and its rise to prominence during eighteenth century and beyond by examining plantation they developed. [JPG]

39.470 John Demos. *A little commonwealth: family life in Plymouth colony.* 1970 ed. London: Oxford University Press, 1977. ISBN 0-19-501355-7. ‣ Analysis of demographic patterns and material conditions of life among families in seventeenth-century Plymouth. [JPG]

39.471 John Demos. *Past, present, and personal: the family and the life course in American history.* New York: Oxford University Press, 1986. ISBN 0-19-503777-4. ‣ Volume of eight essays, half previously published, many dealing with role of family in colonial New England. [JPG]

39.472 Toby L. Ditz. *Property and kinship: inheritance in early Connecticut, 1750–1820.* Princeton: Princeton University Press, 1986. ISBN 0-691-04735-9. ‣ Excellent close study of inheritance practices in four Connecticut towns during seventy years beginning ca. 1750. [JPG/LAN]

39.473 Firth Haring Fabend. *A Dutch family in the middle colonies, 1660–1800.* New Brunswick, N.J.: Rutgers University Press, 1991. ISBN 0-8135-1627-7. ‣ Excellent family history of five generations of Haring family, yeoman farmers, in colonial New York and New Jersey. [JPG]

39.474 J. William Frost. *The Quaker family in colonial America: a portrait of the Society of Friends.* New York: St. Martin's, 1973. ‣ Analysis of notions of family and operation of family life among colonial Quakers. [JPG]

39.475 Philip J. Greven. *The Protestant temperament: patterns of childrearing, religious experience, and the self in early America.* New York: Knopf, 1977. ISBN 0-394-40423-8. ‣ Imaginative exploration of contrasting child-rearing practices among genteel and evangelical families. [JPG]

39.476 Christopher M. Jedrey. *The world of John Cleaveland: family and community in eighteenth-century New England.* New York: Norton, 1979. ISBN 0-393-01270-0. ‣ Exploration of family and community life in late colonial Massachusetts through family papers of Reverend John Cleaveland. [JPG]

39.477 Alice P. Kenney. *The Gansevoorts of Albany: Dutch patricians in the upper Hudson Valley.* Syracuse, N.Y.: Syracuse University Press, 1969. ‣ Study of three centuries of wealthy Dutch American family in Albany. [JPG]

39.478 Cynthia A. Kierner. *Traders and gentlefolk: the Livingstons of New York, 1675–1790.* Ithaca, N.Y.: Cornell University Press, 1992. ISBN 0-8014-2638-3. ‣ Excellent account of manifold activities of prominent New York family through era of American Revolution. [JPG]

39.479 Randolph Shipley Klein. *Portrait of an early American family: the Shippens of Pennsylvania across five generations.* Philadelphia: University of Pennsylvania Press, 1975. ISBN 0-8122-7700-7. ‣ Analysis of five generations of one of most prominent Quaker families in colonial and revolutionary Pennsylvania. [JPG]

39.480 Aubrey C. Land. *The Dulanys of Maryland: a biographical study of Daniel Dulany, the elder (1685–1753), and Daniel Dulany, the younger (1722–1797).* 1955 ed. Baltimore: Johns Hopkins University Press, 1968. ‣ Excellent study of emergence of prominent immigrant family during early eighteenth century. Also insightful on Maryland politics. [JPG]

39.481 Barry Levy. *Quakers and the American family: British settlement in the Delaware Valley.* New York: Oxford University Press, 1988. ISBN 0-19-504975-6. ‣ Important study of changing dynamics of family life among Quakers in Delaware Valley. [JPG]

39.482 Jan Lewis. *The pursuit of happiness: family and values in Jefferson's Virginia.* Cambridge: Cambridge University Press, 1983. ISBN 0-521-25306-3. ‣ Intellectual history of changing family values among elite Virginians beginning in late colonial and early national periods. [JPG/LAN]

39.483 Kenneth A. Lockridge. *On the sources of patriarchal rage: the commonplace books of William Byrd and Thomas Jefferson and the gendering of power in the eighteenth century.* New York: New York University Press, 1992. ISBN 0-8147-5069-9. ‣ Original look at male Virginia elite attitudes toward women through personal records of Byrd and Jefferson. [JPG]

39.484 Gerald F. Moran and Maris A. Vinovskis. *Religion, family, and the life course: explorations in the social history of early America.* Ann Arbor: University of Michigan Press, 1992. ISBN 0-472-10312-1. ‣ Contains seven previously published essays on aspects of family life in colonial New England. [JPG]

39.485 Edmund S. Morgan. *The Puritan family: religion and domestic relations in seventeenth-century New England.* 1966 ed. Westport, Conn.: Greenwood, 1980. ISBN 0-313-22703-9. ‣ Pioneering study of idea and social dynamics of family in early colonial New England. [JPG]

39.486 Edmund S. Morgan. *Virginians at home: family life in the eighteenth century.* 1952 ed. Williamsburg, Va.: Colonial Williamsburg Foundation, 1987. (Williamsburg in America series, 2.) ‣ Delightfully written introduction to history of family in colonial Virginia. [JPG]

39.487 David E. Narrett. *Inheritance and family life in colonial New York City.* Ithaca, N.Y. and Cooperstown, N.Y.: Cornell University Press and New York State Historical Association, 1992. ISBN 0-8014-2517-4. ‣ Valuable examination of inheritance practices in New York City during colonial era. [JPG]

39.488 Catherine M. Scholten. *Childbearing in American society: 1650–1850.* New York: New York University Press, 1985. ISBN 0-8147-7848-8. ‣ Discussion of changing nature of childbirth and motherhood with emphasis on colonial period. [JPG]

39.489 Carole Shammas, Marylynn Salmon, and Michel Dahlin. *Inheritance in America: from colonial times to the present.* New Brunswick, N.J.: Rutgers University Press, 1987. ISBN 0-8135-1214-X (cl), 0-8135-1266-2 (pbk). ‣ General study of changing inheritance patterns. About one third covers colonial era. [JPG]

39.490 Daniel Blake Smith. *Inside the great house: planter family life in eighteenth-century Chesapeake society.* Ithaca, N.Y.: Cornell University Press, 1980. ‣ Study of nature of family among great Virginia planter families. [JPG]

39.491 Roger Thompson. *Sex in Middlesex: popular mores in a Massachusetts county, 1649–1699.* Amherst: University of Massachusetts Press, 1986. ISBN 0-8702-3516-8. ‣ Valuable community study focusing on sexual mores and domestic relations. [JPG]

39.492 Helena M. Wall. *Fierce communion: family and community in early America.* Cambridge, Mass.: Harvard University Press, 1990. ISBN 0-674-29958-2. ‣ General study of division of authority between family and community emphasizing influence of community. [JPG]

39.493 Paul A. W. Wallace. *The Muhlenbergs of Pennsylvania.* Philadelphia: University of Pennsylvania Press, 1950. ‣ Study of first generations of prominent German Lutheran immigrant family. [JPG]

39.494 John J. Waters, Jr. *The Otis family in provincial and revolutionary Massachusetts.* Chapel Hill: University of North Carolina Press for Institute of Early American History and Culture,

1968. ‣ Excellent case study of rise of elite colonial family. Traces history of five generations of Otis family of Massachusetts, giving particular emphasis to family's participation in public life. [JPG]

Women and Gender

39.495 Hilary McD. Beckles. *Natural rebels: a social history of enslaved black women in Barbados.* New Brunswick, N.J.: Rutgers University Press, 1989. ISBN 0-8135-1510-6 (cl), 0-8135-1511-4 (pbk). ‣ One of best studies to date on conditions of life and labor and role of women slaves of early modern colonial era. [JPG]

39.496 Mary Sumner Benson. *Women in eighteenth-century America: a study of opinion and social usage.* 1935 ed. New York: AMS, 1976. ISBN 0-404-151405-7. ‣ Still valuable study of social attitudes toward women in late colonial era. [JPG]

39.497 Carol F. Karlsen. *The Devil in the shape of a woman: witchcraft in colonial New England.* 1987 ed. New York: Vintage, 1989. ISBN 0-679-72184-3 (pbk). ‣ Suggestive use of witchcraft to study nature of everyday relationships between women and men and gendering of power in early colonial New England. [JPG]

39.498 Lyle Koehler. *A search for power: the "weaker sex" in seventeenth-century New England.* Urbana: University of Illinois Press, 1980. ISBN 0-252-00808-1. ‣ Most comprehensive study of conditions of life for women settlers of seventeenth-century New England. [JPG]

39.499 Marylynn Salmon. *Women and the law of property in early America.* Chapel Hill: University of North Carolina Press, 1986. ISBN 0-8078-1687-6. ‣ Excellent study of property rights of women beginning in late colonial era. [JPG]

39.500 Julia Cherry Spruill. *Women's life and work in the southern colonies.* 1938 ed. Anne Firor Scott, Introduction. New York: Norton, 1972. ISBN 0-393-00662-x. ‣ Classic early study providing much useful information about lives of women in southern colonies. [JPG]

39.501 Roger Thompson. *Women in Stuart England and America: a comparative study.* Boston: Routledge & Kegan Paul, 1974. ISBN 0-7100-7822-6. ‣ General comparative study. [JPG]

39.502 Laurel Thatcher Ulrich. *Good wives: image and reality in the lives of women in northern New England, 1650–1750.* 1982 ed. New York: Oxford University Press, 1983. ISBN 0-19-503360-4 (pbk). ‣ Excellent study of domestic lives of married women. Emphasizes significance of women in household economy of colonial New England. [JPG]

African Americans and Slavery

39.503 Hilary McD. Beckles. *Black rebellion in Barbados: the struggle against slavery, 1627–1838.* 1984 ed. Bridgetown, Barbados: Carib Research & Publications, 1987. ISBN 976-8051-03-5. ‣ Examination of changing patterns of resistance among slaves in important sugar colony of Barbados. [JPG]

39.504 J. Harry Bennett, Jr. *Bondsmen and bishops: slavery and apprenticeship on the Codrington plantations of Barbados, 1710–1838.* Berkeley: University of California Press, 1958. ‣ Careful study of slave system on set of plantations owned by Anglican church. [JPG]

39.505 Ira Berlin and Philip D. Morgan. *Cultivation and culture: labor and the shaping of slave life in the Americas.* Charlottesville: University Press of Virginia, 1993. ‣ Collection of essays on work regimes and household economies of slaves in plantation world of colonial British America and the United States. [JPG]

39.506 T. H. Breen and Stephen Innes. *"Myne owne ground": race and freedom on Virginia's eastern shore, 1640–1676.* New York: Oxford University Press, 1980. ISBN 0-19-502727-2. ‣ Brief study of small population of free African Americans who lived on Virginia's eastern shore during early days of slavery. [JPG]

39.507 Edward L. Cox. *Free coloreds in the slave societies of St. Kitts and Grenada, 1763–1833.* Knoxville: University of Tennessee Press, 1984. ISBN 0-87049-414-7. ‣ Comparative analysis of role of free people of color in two British West Indian colonies. [JPG]

39.508 Michael Craton. *Searching for the invisible man: slaves and plantation life in Jamaica.* Cambridge, Mass.: Harvard University Press, 1978. ISBN 0-674-79629-2. ‣ Effort to recover culture of slave population on large Jamaican plantation. [JPG]

39.509 Michael Craton. *Testing the chains: resistance to slavery in the British West Indies.* Ithaca, N.Y.: Cornell University Press, 1982. ISBN 0-8014-1252-8. ‣ Very useful analysis of character of slave revolts and other forms of resistance in British West Indian colonies. [JPG]

39.510 Thomas J. Davis. *A rumor of revolt: the "great Negro plot" in colonial New York.* New York: Free Press, 1985. ISBN 0-02-907740-0. ‣ Full-scale study of alleged revolt of New York City slaves in 1741, using documentation surrounding revolt to explore conditions of life among enslaved and free African Americans. [JPG]

39.511 Robert Dirks. *The black saturnalia: conflict and ritual expression on British West Indian slave plantations.* Gainesville: University Presses of Florida, 1987. ISBN 0-8130-0843-3. ‣ Useful exploration of many aspects of slave culture in British West Indies. [JPG]

39.512 David Barry Gaspar. *Bondmen and rebels: a study of master-slave relations in Antigua, with implications for colonial British America.* Baltimore: Johns Hopkins University Press, 1985. ISBN 0-8018-2422-2. ‣ Excellent close study of slave society of Antigua during early eighteenth century and of aborted slave revolt of 1736. [JPG]

39.513 Elsa V. Goveia. *Slave society in the British Leeward Islands at the end of the eighteenth century.* 1965 ed. Westport, Conn.: Greenwood, 1980. ISBN 0-313-22156-1. ‣ Pioneering study of functioning of British West Indian slave societies. [JPG]

39.514 Lorenzo J. Greene. *The Negro in colonial New England, 1620–1776.* 1942 ed. Port Washington, N.Y.: Kennikat, 1966. ‣ Useful early study of the not inconsiderable African American population of colonial New England. [JPG]

39.515 Gwendolyn Midlo Hall. *Africans in colonial Louisiana: the development of Afro-creole culture in the eighteenth century.* Baton Rouge: Louisiana State University Press, 1992. ISBN 0-8071-1686-6. ‣ Excellent, comprehensive study of emergence of African creole culture in French Louisiana during colonial era. [JPG]

39.516 Jerome S. Handler. *The unappropriated people: freedmen in the slave society of Barbados.* Baltimore: Johns Hopkins University Press, 1974. ISBN 0-8018-1565-7. ‣ One of best studies of free population for any West Indian colony before emancipation. [JPG]

39.517 Jerome S. Handler and Frederick W. Lange. *Plantation slavery in Barbados: an archaeological and historical investigation.* Cambridge, Mass.: Harvard University Press, 1978. ISBN 0-674-67275-5. ‣ Study of material life of Barbadian slaves, based on analysis of archaeological remains, especially slave burials. [JPG]

39.518 A. Leon Higginbotham, Jr. *In the matter of color: race and the American legal process.* Vol. 1: *The colonial period.* New York: Oxford University Press, 1978. ISBN 0-19-502387-0 (cl), 0-19-502745-0 (pbk). ‣ Largely descriptive study of how courts and legislatures enforced racial distinctions supporting slave systems in Virginia, South Carolina, Georgia, Pennsylvania, New York, and Massachusetts. [JPG]

39.519 Herbert S. Klein. *Slavery in the Americas: a comparative study of Virginia and Cuba.* 1967 ed. Chicago: Elephant Paperbacks, 1989. ISBN 0-929587-04-9. ▸ Study adversely comparing slavery in Protestant Virginia with that in Catholic Cuba. [JPG]

39.520 Peter Kolchin. *American slavery, 1619–1877.* New York: Hill & Wang, 1993. ▸ General synthetic treatment giving considerable attention to development of slave systems during colonial era. [JPG]

39.521 Ronald L. Lewis. *Coal, iron, and slaves: industrial slavery in Maryland and Virginia, 1715–1865.* Westport, Conn.: Greenwood, 1979. ISBN 0-313-20522-1. ▸ Useful study of extensive use of slaves in coal and iron industries of Chesapeake area. [JPG]

39.522 Daniel C. Littlefield. *Rice and slaves: ethnicity and the slave trade in colonial South Carolina.* 1981 ed. Urbana: University of Illinois Press, 1991. ISBN 0-252-06214-0. ▸ Imaginative attack on problems of contributions of Africans to rice culture in Carolina low country and preference among planters for slaves. [JPG]

39.523 Roderick A. McDonald. *The economy and material culture of slaves: goods and chattels on the sugar plantations of Jamaica and Louisiana.* Baton Rouge: Louisiana State University Press, 1993. ISBN 0-8071-1794-3. ▸ Careful comparative study of household economies and material culture of slaves in two sugar colonies. [JPG]

39.524 Edgar J. McManus. *Black bondage in the North.* Syracuse, N.Y.: Syracuse University Press, 1973. ISBN 0-8156-0091-7. ▸ General study of institution of slavery in northern colonies. [JPG]

39.525 Edgar J. McManus. *A history of Negro slavery in New York.* Richard B. Morris, Foreword. Syracuse, N.Y.: Syracuse University Press, 1966. ▸ Descriptive study of operation of institution of slavery in farm colony with large numbers of slaves. [JPG]

39.526 Sidney W. Mintz and Richard Price. *The birth of African-American culture: an anthropological perspective.* 1976 ed. Boston: Beacon, 1992. ISBN 0-8070-0916-4 (cl), 0-8070-0917-2 (pbk). ▸ Superb analysis bringing anthropological perspective to identification and discussion of various historical problems relating to creation of African American cultures in New World. Earlier title: *An Anthropological Approach to the Afro-American Past: A Caribbean Perspective.* [JPG]

39.527 Gerald W. Mullin. *Flight and rebellion: slave resistance in eighteenth-century Virginia.* New York: Oxford University Press, 1972. ISBN 0-19-501514-2. ▸ Suggestive study of functioning of institution of slavery in eighteenth-century Virginia. [JPG]

39.528 Michael Mullin. *Africa in America: slave acculturation and resistance in the American South and the British Caribbean, 1736–1831.* Urbana: University of Illinois Press, 1992. ISBN 0-252-01889-3. ▸ Comparative study of slave family life, household economies, and religion in relation to patterns of resistance and acculturation in West Indies, South Carolina, and Virginia. [JPG]

39.529 Orlando Patterson. *The sociology of slavery: an analysis of the origins, development, and structure of Negro slave society in Jamaica.* 1967 ed. Rutherford, N.J.: Fairleigh Dickinson University Press, 1975. ISBN 0-8386-7469-0. ▸ Impressionistic and highly Eurocentric study of development of slave society in Jamaica. [JPG]

39.530 William D. Piersen. *Black yankees: the development of an Afro-American subculture in eighteenth-century New England.* Amherst: University of Massachusetts Press, 1988. ISBN 0-87023-586-9 (cl), 0-87023-587-7 (pbk). ▸ Suggestive analysis of emergence of African American culture in New England colonies. [JPG]

39.531 Jean R. Soderlund. *Quakers and slavery: a divided spirit.* Princeton: Princeton University Press, 1985. ISBN 0-691-04732-4. ▸ Excellent short study of patterns of slaveholding and emergence of antislavery sentiment among Quakers in Pennsylvania and New Jersey. [JPG]

39.532 Thad W. Tate. *The Negro in eighteenth-century Williamsburg.* 1965 ed. Williamsburg, Va,: Colonial Williamsburg Foundation; distributed by University Press of Virginia, 1985. ISBN 0-91041-229-4. ▸ Good, short study of role and extent of slave population in Virginia's colonial capital. [JPG]

39.533 Thad W. Tate et al. *Race and family in the colonial South: essays.* Winthrop D. Jordan and Sheila L. Skemp, eds. Jackson: University Press of Mississippi, 1987. ISBN 0-87805-333-6 (cl), 0-87805-334-4 (pbk). ▸ Collection of seven essays, most dealing with race rather than family as principal organizing category in southern colonies. [JPG]

39.534 Betty Wood. *Slavery in colonial Georgia, 1730–1775.* Athens: University of Georgia Press, 1984. ISBN 0-8203-0687-8. ▸ Close study of effort to exclude slavery from Georgia and its subsequent role in economic life of colony. Focuses on white owners rather than African Americans. [JPG/DMS]

SEE ALSO
19.915 Suzanne Miers and Igor Kopytoff, eds. *Slavery in Africa.*
41.481 Ira Berlin and Philip D. Morgan, eds. *The slave's economy.*
42.328 Margaret Washington Creel. *A peculiar people.*

American Indians

39.535 Richard Aquila. *The Iroquois restoration: Iroquois diplomacy on the colonial frontier, 1701–1754.* Detroit: Wayne State University Press, 1983. ISBN 0-8143-1717-0. ▸ Study of Iroquois efforts at survival during half century before Seven Years' War. [JPG]

39.536 James Axtell. *After Columbus: essays in the ethnohistory of colonial North America.* New York: Oxford University Press, 1988. ISBN 0-19-505375-3. ▸ Collection of eleven previously published essays on various themes relating to American Indians and their relations with European American settler populations. Good introduction to work of important ethnohistorian. [JPG/WDP/CRP]

39.537 James Axtell. *Beyond 1492: encounters in colonial North America.* New York: Oxford University Press, 1992. ISBN 0-19-506838-6. ▸ Eleven essays, five newly published, on many aspects of American Indian–white interactions in North America during colonial era. [JPG]

39.538 James Axtell. *The European and the Indian: essays in the ethnohistory of colonial North America.* New York: Oxford University Press, 1981. ISBN 0-19-502903-8. ▸ Collection of ten previously published essays on American Indian–white relations. [JPG]

39.539 James Axtell. *The invasion within: the contest of cultures in colonial North America.* New York: Oxford University Press, 1985. ISBN 0-19-503596-8. ▸ Study of contrasting French and English approaches to dealing with American Indians in long, three-way cultural struggle for supremacy over North American continent into eighteenth century. [JPG]

39.540 Philip P. Boucher. *Cannibal encounters: European and island Caribs, 1492–1763.* Baltimore: Johns Hopkins University Press, 1992. ISBN 0-8018-4365-0. ▸ Analysis of relations between Europeans and island Indians during first three centuries of colonization. [JPG]

39.541 Kathryn Holland Braund. *Deerskins and duffels: Creek Indian trade with Anglo-America, 1685–1815.* Lincoln: University of Nebraska Press, 1993. ▸ Analysis of extensive and shifting patterns of trade between Creeks and southern mainland colonies. [JPG]

39.542 David H. Corkran. *The Cherokee frontier: conflict and survival, 1740–62.* 1962 ed. Norman: University of Oklahoma Press, 1966. ▸ Examination of conflicts on southern colonial frontier during last two intercolonial wars from Cherokee point of view. Photocopy available from Ann Arbor: University Microfilms International, 1982. [JPG]

39.543 David H. Corkran. *The Creek frontier, 1540–1783.* Norman: University of Oklahoma Press, 1967. ▸ Detailed effort to construct history of Creeks during three centuries following their encounter with Europeans. [JPG]

39.544 Mathew Dennis. *Cultivating a land of peace: Iroquois-European encounters in seventeenth-century America.* Ithaca and Cooperstown, N.Y.: Cornell University Press and State Historical Association, 1993. ISBN 0-8014-2171-3. ▸ Study of first century of intensive contacts between the Iroquois and Europeans. [JPG]

39.545 William W. Fitzhugh, ed. *Cultures in contact: the impact of European contacts on Native American cultural institutions, A.D. 1000–1800.* Washington, D.C.: Smithsonian Institution Press, 1985. ISBN 0-87474-438-5. ▸ Collection of nine essays on Indian response to European cultural penetration. Five essays deal with colonial British America. [JPG]

39.546 Patrick Frazier. *The Mohicans of Stockbridge.* Lincoln: University of Nebraska Press, 1992. ISBN 0-8032-1986-5. ▸ Careful case study of one of most assimilated groups of American Indians in colonial British North America. [JPG]

39.547 M. Thomas Hatley. *The dividing paths: Cherokees and South Carolinians through the era of Revolution.* New York: Oxford University Press, 1993. ISBN 0-19-506989-7. ▸ Exploration of relations between Cherokees and South Carolina whites through colonial era. [JPG]

39.548 W. R. Jacobs. *Diplomacy and Indian gifts: Anglo-French rivalry along the Ohio and Northwest frontiers, 1748–1763.* Stanford, Calif.: Stanford University Press, 1950. ▸ Early study of American Indian–white relations during era of Seven Years' War. [JPG]

39.549 Shepard Krech III, ed. *Indians, animals, and the fur trade: a critique of "Keepers of the Game."* Athens: University of Georgia Press, 1981. ISBN 0-8203-0563-4. ▸ Includes six essays by anthropologists evaluating Martin thesis (39.550) about cultural change among American Indians, with reply by Martin. [JPG]

39.550 Calvin Martin. *Keepers of the game: Indian-animal relationships and the fur trade.* Berkeley: University of California Press, 1978. ISBN 0-520-03519-4. ▸ Controversial work interpreting changing American Indian attitudes toward animals as reponse to devastation brought on by European diseases. See Krech, ed. 39.549. [JPG/SSG]

39.551 H. C. Porter. *The inconstant savage: England and the North American Indian, 1500–1660.* London: Duckworth; distributed by Southwest Book Services, 1979. ISBN 0-7156-0968-8. ▸ Extended analysis of sixteenth-and seventeenth-century English attitudes toward American Indians. [JPG]

39.552 Daniel K. Richter and James H. Merrell, eds. *Beyond the covenant chain: the Iroquois and their neighbors in Indian North America, 1600–1800.* Syracuse, N.Y.: Syracuse University Press, 1987. ISBN 0-8156-2416-6. ▸ Contains nine essays exploring Iroquois and their relations with other groups of American Indians. [JPG]

39.553 Helen C. Rountree. *The Powhatan Indians of Virginia: their traditional culture.* Norman: University of Oklahoma Press,

1989. ISBN 0-8061-2156-4. ▸ Comprehensive look at American Indian culture confronted and then supplanted by Virginia settlers. [JPG]

39.554 Howard S. Russell. *Indian New England before the Mayflower.* Hanover, N.H.: University Press of New England, 1980. ISBN 0-87451-162-3. ▸ Comprehensive treatment of American Indian culture in area that became New England. [JPG]

39.555 Allen W. Trelease. *Indian affairs in colonial New York: the seventeenth century.* 1960 ed. Port Washington, N.Y.: Kennikat, 1971. ISBN 0-8046-8096-5. ▸ Excellent, short book on New York–American Indian relations during earliest years of New York colony. [JPG]

39.556 Daniel H. Usner, Jr. *Indians, settlers, and slaves in a frontier exchange economy: the lower Mississippi Valley before 1783.* Chapel Hill: University of North Carolina Press for Institute of Early American History and Culture, 1992. ISBN 0-8078-2014-8 (cl), 0-8078-4358-x (pbk). ▸ Excellent multiethnic history of new colonial world created in lower Mississippi Valley during eighteenth century. [JPG]

39.557 Alden T. Vaughan. *The New England frontier: Puritans and Indians, 1620–1675.* Rev. ed. New York: Norton, 1979. ISBN 0-393-00950-5. ▸ Lucid study of Puritan policy toward their American Indian neighbors and rationale behind it. [JPG]

39.558 Anthony F. C. Wallace. *King of the Delawares: Teedyuscung, 1700–1763.* 1949 ed. Freeport, N.Y.: Books for Libraries, 1970. ISBN 0-8369-5588-9. ▸ Excellent effort to reconstruct life of important American Indian leader. [JPG]

39.559 Peter H. Wood, Gregory A. Waselkov, and M. Thomas Hatley, eds. *Powhatan's mantle: Indians in the colonial Southeast.* Lincoln: University of Nebraska Press, 1989. ISBN 0-8032-4745-1. ▸ Excellent collection of twelve essays on American Indian population of southeastern North America and their relations among themselves and with Europeans. [JPG]

SEE ALSO
36.11 Cornelius J. Jaenen. *Friend and foe.*
36.110 Michael N. McConnell. *A country between.*
36.111 James H. Merrell. *The Indians' new world.*
36.115 Daniel K. Richter. *The ordeal of the longhouse.*
36.121 Richard White. *The middle ground.*

Ethnicity

39.560 William R. Brock. *Scotus Americanus: a survey of the sources for links between Scotland and America in the eighteenth century.* Edinburgh: Edinburgh University Press, 1982. ISBN 0-85224-420-7. ▸ Suggestive general assessment of Scottish contribution to societies and cultures of colonial British America. [JPG]

39.561 Jon Butler. *The Huguenots in America: a refugee people in New World society.* Cambridge, Mass.: Harvard University Press, 1983. ISBN 0-674-41320-2. ▸ Well-written, if somewhat general, modern study of French Protestants who settled in colonial British North America. [JPG]

39.562 Wayland F. Dunaway. *The Scotch-Irish of colonial Pennsylvania.* 1944 ed. Baltimore: Genealogical, 1985. ISBN 0-8063-0850-8. ▸ Still valuable study of Ulster Scots in colony to which they migrated in largest numbers. [JPG]

39.563 Joyce D. Goodfriend. *Before the melting pot: society and culture in colonial New York City, 1664–1730.* Princeton: Princeton University Press, 1992. ISBN 0-691-04794-4. ▸ Well-designed analysis of social dynamics in most ethnically diverse city in colonial British America. Emphasizes persistence of ethnic traditions through early decades of eighteenth century. [JPG]

39.564 Albert H. Hirsch. *The Huguenots of colonial South Caro-*

lina. 1928 ed. Hamden, Conn.: Archon, 1962. ▸ Analysis of adjustment and assimilation of significant group of French Protestants in lower South. [JPG]

39.565 Amandus Johnson. *The Swedish settlements on the Delaware: their history and relation to the Indians, Dutch, and English, 1638–1664, with an account of the South, the New Sweden, and the American companies, and the efforts of Sweden to regain the colony.* 1911 ed. 2 vols. New York: Franklin, 1970. ▸ Still valuable detailed history of New Sweden. [JPG]

39.566 Alan L. Karras. *Sojourners in the sun: Scottish migrants in Jamaica and the Chesapeake, 1740–1800.* Ithaca, N.Y.: Cornell University Press, 1992. ISBN 0-8014-2691-X. ▸ Analysis of contrasting fortunes of Scottish migrants to Virginia and Jamaica during last half of eighteenth century. [JPG]

39.567 Alice P. Kenney. *Stubborn for liberty: the Dutch in New York.* Syracuse, N.Y.: Syracuse University Press for New York State American Bicentennial Commission, 1975. ISBN 0-8156-0113-1. ▸ Analysis of nature and persistence of Dutch heritage in colonial New York and later United States; one half deals with colonial era. [JPG]

39.568 James Graham Leyburn. *The Scotch-Irish: a social history.* Chapel Hill: University of North Carolina Press, 1962. ▸ Broad social portrait of Ulster Scottish population of early America. [JPG]

39.569 Duane Meyer. *The Highland Scots of North Carolina, 1732–1776.* 1961 ed. Chapel Hill: University of North Carolina Press, 1966. ▸ Interesting social, economic, and political study of most extensive settlement of Highland Scots in colonial British North America. [JPG]

39.570 A. G. Roeber. *Palatines, liberty, and property: German Lutherans in colonial British America.* Baltimore: Johns Hopkins University Press, 1993. ISBN 0-8018-4459-2. ▸ Sophisticated study of transfer of German culture to colonial British America that suggestively explores German dimensions of their political cultures. [JPG]

SEE ALSO
21.269 Jacob Rader Marcus. *The colonial American Jew, 1492–1776.*

CULTURAL HISTORY

General Studies

39.571 Urs Bitterli. *Cultures in conflict: encounters between European and non-European cultures, 1492–1800.* Ritchie Robertson, trans. Stanford, Calif.: Stanford University Press, 1989. ISBN 0-8047-1737-0. ▸ Valuable general interpretation of cultural encounters between various imperial Old World cultures and peoples with whom they came in contact during early modern era. [JPG]

39.572 Bernadette Bucher. *Icon and conquest: a structural analysis of the illustrations of de Bry's "Great Voyages."* Basia Miller Gulati, trans. Chicago: University of Chicago Press, 1981. ISBN 0-226-07832-9 (pbk). ▸ Penetrating analysis by structural anthropologist of iconography of most prolific illustrator of early European contacts with New World. [JPG]

39.573 Harold E. Davis. *The fledgling province: social and cultural life in colonial Georgia, 1733–1776.* Chapel Hill: University of North Carolina Press for Institute of Early American History and Culture, 1976. ISBN 0-8078-1267-6. ▸ Older style social and cultural history of first four decades of Georgia colony. [JPG]

39.574 David Hackett Fischer. *Albion's seed: four British folkways in America.* New York: Oxford University Press, 1989. ISBN 0-19-503794-4. ▸ Uses cultural trait analysis to argue that four distinct societies in colonial British America derived their cultures from one region in Britain. [JPG]

39.575 Stephen Greenblatt. *Marvelous possessions: the wonder of the New World.* 1991 ed. Chicago: University of Chicago Press, 1992. ISBN 0-226-30651-8 (cl, 1991), 0-226-30652-6 (pbk). ▸ Close analysis of several prominent literary texts as basis for explaining how English encountered New World. [JPG]

39.576 Jack P. Greene. *Imperatives, behaviors, and identities: essays in early American cultural history.* Charlottesville: University Press of Virginia, 1992. ISBN 0-8139-1406-X (cl), 0-8139-1408-6 (pbk). ▸ Collection of sixteen essays, all but one previously published, on many aspects of cultural history of colonial and early national periods. [JPG]

39.577 Terry G. Jordan and Matti Kaups. *The American backwoods frontier: an ethnic and ecological interpretation.* Baltimore: Johns Hopkins University Press, 1989. ISBN 0-8018-3686-7. ▸ Provocative study tracing many aspects of early American backwoods culture in Delaware Valley to forest cultures of Finnish and Swedish immigrants. [JPG]

39.578 Michal J. Rozbicki. *Transformation of the English cultural ethos in colonial America: Maryland, 1634–1720.* Lanham, Md.: University Press of America, 1988. ISBN 0-8191-7048-8. ▸ Useful case study of emergence of distinctive culture among dominant settler cultures of early Maryland and its relationship to American Indians and African Americans. [JPG]

39.579 John Seelye. *Prophetic waters: the river in early American life and literature.* New York: Oxford University Press, 1977. ISBN 0-19-502047-2. ▸ Suggestive examination of importance of river as theme in early American cultural productions. [JPG]

39.580 Frederick B. Tolles. *James Logan and the culture of provincial America.* Boston: Little, Brown, 1957. ▸ Engaging exploration of central dimensions of emerging American culture through life of one leader in cultural formation. [JPG]

39.581 Frederick B. Tolles. *Quakers and the Atlantic culture.* 1960 ed. New York: Octagon Books, 1980. ISBN 0-374-97949-9. ▸ Portrait of transatlantic culture of Quaker leaders in America and England. [JPG]

39.582 Louis B. Wright. *The cultural life of the American colonies, 1607–1763.* 1957 ed. New York: Harper, 1962. ▸ Most comprehensive account of forms of cultural life in colonial British North America. [JPG]

SEE ALSO
3.279 Mary B. Campbell. *The witness and the other world.*

Intellectual History

39.583 Loren Baritz. *City on a hill: a history of ideas and myths in America.* 1964 ed. Westport, Conn.: Greenwood, 1980. ISBN 0-313-22268-1. ▸ Analysis of American intellectual history through study of six major figures, including John Winthrop, governor of Massachusetts Bay Colony, and Jonathan Edwards, Great Awakening preacher. [JPG]

39.584 Peter N. Carroll. *Puritanism and the wilderness: the intellectual significance of the New England frontier, 1629–1700.* New York: Columbia University Press, 1969. ▸ Useful inquiry into role of idea of wilderness in thought of New England settlers during seventeenth century. [JPG]

39.585 Richard Crowder. *No featherbed to heaven: a biography of Michael Wigglesworth, 1631–1705.* East Lansing: Michigan State University Press, 1962. ▸ Satisfactory biography of important Puritan intellectual and literary figure. [JPG]

39.586 James West Davidson. *The logic of millennial thought: eighteenth-century New England.* New Haven: Yale University

Press, 1977. ISBN 0-300-01947-5. ▸ Sophisticated examination of extent and employment of millennial thought in eighteenth-century New England. [JPG]

39.587 Richard Beale Davis. *Intellectual life in the colonial South, 1585–1763.* 3 vols. Knoxville: University of Tennessee Press, 1978. ISBN 0-87049-210-1. ▸ Long, comprehensive discussion of full range of intellectual productions in colonies from Georgia to Maryland. [JPG]

39.588 Joseph J. Ellis. *The New England mind in transition: Samuel Johnson of Connecticut, 1696–1772.* New Haven: Yale University Press, 1973. ISBN 0-300-01615-8. ▸ Uses career of Yale professor Samuel Johnson to discuss changing intellectual world of eighteenth-century New England. [JPG]

39.589 Norman Fiering. *Jonathan Edwards's moral thought and its British context.* Chapel Hill: University of North Carolina Press for Institute of Early American History and Culture, 1981. ISBN 0-8078-1473-3. ▸ Detailed, learned examination of eighteenth-century moral philosophy in Edwards's thought. [JPG]

39.590 Norman Fiering. *Moral philosophy at seventeenth-century Harvard: a discipline in transition.* Chapel Hill: University of North Carolina Press for Institute of Early American History and Culture, 1981. ISBN 0-8078-1459-8. ▸ Extensive investigation of ethical thought among seventeenth-century New England Puritans. [JPG]

39.591 Wayne Franklin. *Discoverers, explorers, settlers: the diligent writers of early America.* Chicago: University of Chicago Press, 1979. ISBN 0-226-26071-2. ▸ Suggestive reexamination of literature of encounter during colonial era. Shows how inherited languages shaped European American perceptions of processes of discovery, exploration, and settlement. [JPG]

39.592 Peter Gay. *A loss of mastery: Puritan historians in colonial America.* Berkeley: University of California Press, 1966. ▸ Intelligent discussion of use of past by Puritan New England historians from William Bradford to Jonathan Edwards. [JPG]

39.593 Richard M. Gummere. *The American colonial mind and the classical tradition: essays in comparative culture.* Cambridge, Mass.: Harvard University Press, 1963. ▸ Collection of discrete essays exploring various examples of use of classics by colonial intellectual figures. [JPG]

39.594 James Holstun. *A rational millennium: Puritan utopias of seventeenth-century England and America.* New York: Oxford University Press, 1987. ISBN 0-19-504141-0. ▸ Analysis of early modern utopian tradition and its impact on radical Puritan thought in England and America. [JPG]

39.595 Leonard W. Labaree. *Conservatism in early American history.* 1948 ed. Ithaca, N.Y.: Cornell University Press, 1965. ISBN 0-8014-9008-1. ▸ Exploration of some conditions and many central ideas that sustained intellectual emphasis on order and hierarchy in colonial and republic periods. [JPG]

39.596 Lawrence H. Leder, ed. *The colonial legacy.* Vol. 1: *Loyalist historians.* Vol. 2: *Some eighteenth-century commentators.* Vol. 3: *Historians of nature and man's nature.* Vol. 4: *Early nationalist historians.* 4 vols. in 3. New York: Harper & Row, 1971–73. ISBN 0-06-136052-X (v. 1), 0-06-136053-8 (v. 2), 0-06-136104-6 (v. 3–4). ▸ Thirty essays by modern scholars on lives and works of many prominent eighteenth-century historians and other commentators. [JPG]

39.597 David Levin. *Cotton Mather: the young life of the Lord's remembrancer, 1663–1703.* Cambridge, Mass.: Harvard University Press, 1978. ISBN 0-674-17507-7. ▸ Excellent biography of first forty years of principal New England intellectual. [JPG]

39.598 Gordon K. Lewis. *Main currents in Caribbean thought: the historical evolution of Caribbean society in its ideological aspects,* 1492–1900. Baltimore: Johns Hopkins University Press, 1987. ISBN 0-8018-3492-9. ▸ Comprehensive discussion of rich intellectual productions of people living in British West Indian colonies. [JPG]

39.599 Ernest Benson Lowrie. *The shape of the Puritan mind: the thought of Samuel Willard.* New Haven: Yale University Press, 1974. ISBN 0-300-01714-6. ▸ Examination of thought of cleric Samuel Willard, who produced most systematic early eighteenth-century exposition of Puritan theology. [JPG]

39.600 Henry Farnham May. *The Enlightenment in America.* New York: Oxford University Press, 1976. ISBN 0-19-502018-9 (cl), 0-19-502367-6 (pbk). ▸ Broad examination of movement of ideas from Europe to America, exploring tensions between those ideas and Protestant Christianity. [JPG/LAN]

39.601 Donald H. Meyer. *The democratic Enlightenment.* New York: Putnam, 1976. ISBN 0-399-11686-9. ▸ Effort to provide comprehensive treatment of Enlightenment in America through emphasis on experimentalism of American intellectual life. [JPG/LAN]

39.602 Robert Middlekauff. *The Mathers: three generations of Puritan intellectuals, 1596–1728.* New York: Oxford University Press, 1971. ISBN 0-19-501305-0. ▸ Uses remarkable Mather family to reconstruct intellectual history of Puritanism in New England to early eighteenth century. [JPG]

39.603 Perry Miller. *Errand into the wilderness.* 1956 ed. Cambridge, Mass.: Belknap, 1984. ISBN 0-674-26155-0 (pbk). ▸ Ten essays analyzing various strands of intellectual life, primarily in New England. [JPG]

39.604 Perry Miller. *Jonathan Edwards.* 1949 ed. Amherst: University of Massachusetts Press, 1981. ISBN 0-87023-328-9. ▸ Powerful intellectual discussion of central ideas of colonial British America's leading theologian. [JPG]

39.605 Perry Miller. *Nature's nation.* Cambridge, Mass.: Belknap, 1967. ▸ Collection of fifteen essays, five relating to colonial era, exploring various aspects of New England intellectual life. [JPG]

39.606 Perry Miller. *The New England mind: from colony to province.* 1953 ed. Cambridge, Mass.: Belknap, 1983. ISBN 0-674-61301-5 (pbk). ▸ Brilliant study of transformation of Puritan mind, 1670–1730. [JPG]

39.607 Perry Miller. *The New England mind: the seventeenth century.* 1939 ed. Cambridge, Mass.: Harvard University Press, 1982. ISBN 0-674-61306-6 (pbk). ▸ Starting place for serious work on complex intellectual world of New England founders. [JPG]

39.608 Edmund S. Morgan. *The gentle Puritan: a life of Ezra Stiles, 1727–1795.* 1962 ed. New York: Norton, 1983. ISBN 0-393-30126-5 (pbk). ▸ First-rate biography of significant intellectual figure in eighteenth-century New England. [JPG]

39.609 Samuel Eliot Morison. *The intellectual life of colonial New England.* 4th ed. New York: New York University Press, 1970. ▸ Early effort to present comprehensive portrait of intellectual world of colonial New England, during its first century. [JPG]

39.610 Max Savelle. *Seeds of liberty: the genesis of the American mind.* 1948 ed. Seattle: University of Washington Press, 1965. ▸ Broad discussion of productions of colonial British Americans in all areas of intellectual life. [JPG]

39.611 Herbert Wallace Schneider. *The Puritan mind.* 1930 ed. Ann Arbor: University of Michigan Press, 1966. ▸ Discussion of key ingredients in Puritan thought by philosopher. [JPG]

39.612 Robert A. Williams, Jr. *The American Indian in western legal thought: the discourses of conquest.* New York: Oxford University Press, 1990. ISBN 0-19-505022-3. ▸ Traces origins and operation of ideas formulated by Europeans to justify their conquests and subjugation of natives of New World. [JPG]

39.613   Ola Elizabeth Winslow. *Jonathan Edwards, 1703–1758: a biography.* 1940 ed. New York: Octagon Books, 1973. ‣ Brisk, highly readable biography. [JPG]

39.614   Larzer Ziff. *Puritanism in America: new culture in a new world.* New York: Viking, 1973. ISBN 0-670-58310-3. ‣ Broad interpretive account examining Puritanism as culture shaping all aspects of New England life during colonial era. [JPG]

Mentality and Popular Culture

39.615   Jean-Christophe Agnew. *Worlds apart: the market and the theatre in Anglo-American thought, 1550–1750.* Cambridge: Cambridge University Press, 1986. ISBN 0-521-24322-X. ‣ Imaginative effort to recover history of meanings and feelings through study of expressive practices involved in cultural interplay between commerciality and theatricality in Anglo-American world. [JPG]

39.616   John F. Berens. *Providence and patriotism in early America, 1640–1815.* Charlottesville: University Press of Virginia, 1978. ISBN 0-8139-0779-9. ‣ Cogent analysis of role of providential thought in shaping civic consciousness in colonial and early national periods. [JPG]

39.617   David Bertelson. *The lazy South.* New York: Oxford University Press, 1967. ‣ General look at emergence of distinctive cultural ethos in early South. [JPG]

39.618   T. H. Breen. *Tobacco culture: the mentality of the great tidewater planters on the eve of the Revolution.* Princeton: Princeton University Press, 1985. ISBN 0-691-04729-4. ‣ Imaginative attempt to recover mentality of Virginia tobacco planters during third quarter of eighteenth century and to assess its bearing on their support of revolutionary movement. [JPG]

39.619   Mitchell Robert Breitwieser. *Cotton Mather and Benjamin Franklin: the price of representative personality.* Cambridge: Cambridge University Press, 1984. ISBN 0-521-26768-4. ‣ Imaginative exploration of contrasting self-representations of Mather and Franklin, illuminating interrelationships between them. [JPG]

39.620   Richard L. Bushman. *The refinement of America: persons, houses, cities.* New York: Knopf, 1992. ISBN 0-394-55010-2. ‣ Superb analysis of spread and changing character of idea of gentility and its principal forms of expression in colonial and early national periods. [JPG]

39.621   John Canup. *Out of the wilderness: the emergence of an American identity in colonial New England.* Middletown, Conn.: Wesleyan University Press, 1990. ISBN 0-8195-5226-7. ‣ Suggestive analysis of role of wilderness in construction of corporate identity of New England through first three decades of eighteenth century. [JPG]

39.622   Jane Carson. *Colonial Virginians at play.* 1965 ed. Williamsburg, Va.: Colonial Williamsburg Foundation, 1989. ISBN 0-87935-122-5. ‣ Descriptive account of leisure activities of colonial Virginians. [JPG]

39.623   James H. Cassedy. *Demography in early America: beginnings of the statistical mind, 1600–1800.* Cambridge, Mass.: Harvard University Press, 1969. ISBN 0-674-19775-5. ‣ Pioneering study of many ways colonial British Americans employed statistics to make sense of their world. [JPG]

39.624   Eric Cheyfitz. *The poetics of imperialism: translation and colonization from "The Tempest" to Tarzan.* New York: Oxford University Press, 1991. ISBN 0-19-505095-9. ‣ Through concept of translation, examines relationship between modern American imperialism and cultural superiority implicit in linguistic hierarchies established during earliest encounters between Europeans and American Indians. [JPG]

39.625   Patricia Cline Cohen. *A calculating people: the spread of numeracy in early America.* Chicago: University of Chicago Press, 1982. ISBN 0-226-11283-7. ‣ Useful study of expansion of numeracy from colonial through early national period. [JPG]

39.626   J. E. Crowley. *This Sheba, self: the conceptualization of economic life in eighteenth-century America.* Baltimore: Johns Hopkins University Press, 1974. ISBN 0-8018-1579-7. ‣ Imaginative exploration of relationship between ideas of self, work, and economic life in late colonial and revolutionary periods. [JPG]

39.627   Stephen Foster. *Their solitary way: the Puritan social ethic in the first century of settlement in New England.* New Haven: Yale University Press, 1971. ISBN 0-300-01408-2. ‣ Meticulous, highly valuable analysis of Puritan social thought on order, love, government, wealth, and poverty. [JPG]

39.628   Sylvia Doughty Fries. *The urban idea in colonial America.* Philadelphia: Temple University Press, 1977. ISBN 0-87722-103-0. ‣ Only study of conception of town for colonial America, with several case studies. [JPG]

39.629   Jack P. Greene. *The intellectual construction of America: exceptionalism and identity from 1492 to 1800.* Chapel Hill: University of North Carolina Press, 1993. ISBN 0-8078-2097-0. ‣ Analysis of changing conceptions of America and growing identification of colonial British America and new United States as exceptional group of societies. [JPG]

39.630   Jack P. Greene. *Landon Carter: an inquiry into the personal values and social imperatives of the eighteenth-century Virginia gentry.* 1965 ed. Charlottesville, Va.: Dominion, 1967. ‣ Case study of relationship among personality, values, domestic life, and larger developments in mid-eighteenth-century Virginia. [JPG]

39.631   David D. Hall. *Worlds of wonder, days of judgment: popular religious beliefs in early New England.* New York: Knopf, 1989. ISBN 0-394-50108-X. ‣ Outstanding study of religious dimensions of popular culture of early colonial New England. Treats literacy, wonders, function of church, and rituals. [JPG]

39.632   Peter Hulme. *Colonial encounters: Europe and the native Caribbean, 1492–1797.* 1986 ed. New York: Routledge, 1992. ISBN 0-415-01146-9. ‣ Suggestive examination of encounter between Europeans and American Indians in greater Caribbean from Brazil to Virginia during first three centuries of European colonization. [JPG]

39.633   Howard Mumford Jones. *O strange New World: American culture, the formative years.* 1964 ed. Westport, Conn.: Greenwood, 1982. ISBN 0-313-23494-9. ‣ Bold, comprehensive examination of interplay between Old World culture and conditions in New World to Jacksonian era. [JPG]

39.634   Winthrop D. Jordan. *White over black: American attitudes toward the Negro, 1550–1812.* 1968 ed. New York: Norton, 1977. ISBN 0-393-00841-X. ‣ Profound analysis of white attitudes toward blacks and way those attitudes shaped social, cultural, and mental structures of American slave worlds established under aegis of Britain during early modern era. [JPG]

39.635   Kenneth A. Lockridge. *The diary and life of William Byrd II of Virginia, 1674–1744.* Chapel Hill: University of North Carolina Press for Institute of Early American History and Culture, 1987. ‣ Uses Byrd to depict penetrating portrait of self-fashioning of Virginia gentleman and of his gradual accommodation to Virginia. [JPG]

39.636   O. Mannoni. *Prospero and Caliban: the psychology of colonization.* 1964 2d ed. Pamela Rowesland, trans. Ann Arbor: University of Michigan Press, 1990. ISBN 0-472-09430-0 (cl), 0-472-06430-4 (pbk). ‣ Classic study of psychology of colonization with special attention to colonizers and tension between their feelings of dependence and independence. [JPG]

39.637 Pierre Marambaud. *William Byrd of Westover, 1674–1744*. Charlottesville: University Press of Virginia, 1971. ‣ Lucid study of Byrd's life and world, with special focus on his literary accomplishments. [JPG]

39.638 Leo Marx. *The machine in the garden: technology and the pastoral ideal in America*. 1964 ed. New York: Oxford University Press, 1967. ‣ Pioneering exploration of several important cultural themes in early American life. [JPG]

39.639 Richard L. Merritt. *Symbols of American community, 1735–1775*. 1966 ed. Westport, Conn.: Greenwood, 1976. ISBN 0-8371-9012-6. ‣ Examination of newspapers as index to national identities of continental colonial Americans during generation before Revolution. [JPG]

39.640 Roy Harvey Pearce. *The savages of America: a study of the Indian and the idea of civilization*. Rev. ed. Baltimore: Johns Hopkins University Press, 1965. ‣ Early study of white attitudes toward American Indians. Explores function of idea of savage in early stages of formation of American culture. [JPG]

39.641 Kym S. Rice. *Early American taverns: for the entertainment of friends and strangers*. Chicago: Regnery Gateway with Fraunces Tavern Museum, 1983. ISBN 0-89526-620-2 (cl), 0-89526-842-6 (pbk). ‣ Analysis of social function of taverns as social institutions in early America. [JPG]

39.642 William L. Sachse. *The colonial American in Britain*. 1956 ed. Westport, Conn.: Greenwood, 1978. ISBN 0-313-20474-8. ‣ Analysis of range, types, and experiences of colonials who visited, studied, worked, or migrated to Britain during colonial era. [JPG]

39.643 Bernard W. Sheehan. *Savagism and civility: Indians and Englishmen in colonial Virginia*. Cambridge: Cambridge University Press, 1980. ISBN 0-521-22927-8 (cl), 0-521-29723-0 (pbk). ‣ Excellent examination of English attitudes toward savagism and effect of application of those attitudes to Chesapeake Indians during early years of Virginia colony. [JPG]

39.644 David S. Shields. *Oracles of empire: poetry, politics, and commerce in British America, 1690–1750*. Chicago: University of Chicago Press, 1990. ISBN 0-226-75298-4. ‣ Examination of colonial poetry to explore some of main themes of colonial British American culture during first half of eighteenth century. [JPG]

39.645 Mechal Sobel. *The world they made together: black and white values in eighteenth-century Virginia*. Princeton: Princeton University Press, 1987. ISBN 0-691-04747-2. ‣ Suggestive exploration of some of principal contributions of African Americans to culture of eighteenth-century Virginia. [JPG]

39.646 David E. Stannard. *The Puritan way of death: a study in religion, culture, and social change*. 1977 ed. New York: Oxford University Press, 1979. ISBN 0-19-502521-0. ‣ Analysis of rituals, emotions, and social context associated with death in colonial New England. [JPG]

39.647 Frederick B. Tolles. *Meeting house and counting house: the Quaker merchants of colonial Philadelphia, 1682–1763*. 1948 ed. New York: Norton, 1963. ‣ Excellent analysis of ethos of Quaker merchants in colonial Philadelphia. [JPG]

39.648 Kerry A. Trask. *In the pursuit of shadows: Massachusetts millennialism and the Seven Years' War*. New York: Garland, 1989. ISBN 0-8240-6198-5. ‣ Exploration of socioeconomic roots of ministerial discontent and nature of civil millennialism in mid-eighteenth-century Massachusetts. [JPG]

39.649 Alden T. Vaughan and Virginia Mason Vaughan. *Shakespeare's Caliban: a cultural history*. Cambridge: Cambridge University Press, 1991. ISBN 0-521-40305-7. ‣ Cautious examination of function of character of Caliban in *The Tempest* with consideration of appropriateness of modern scholarly efforts to treat Caliban as emblematic of colonial condition. [JPG]

39.650 Ola Elizabeth Winslow. *Meetinghouse hill, 1630–1783*. 1952 ed. New York: Norton, 1972. ISBN 0-393-00632-8. ‣ Engaging portrait of role of meetinghouse in seventeenth-century New England culture. [JPG]

39.651 Louis B. Wright. *The dream of prosperity in colonial America*. New York: New York University Press, 1965. ‣ Consideration of material appeals that drew colonists to colonial British America. [JPG]

39.652 Louis B. Wright. *The first gentlemen of Virginia: intellectual qualities of the early colonial ruling class*. 1940 ed. Charlottesville: University Press of Virginia, 1964. ‣ Classic study of cultural orientation and achievements of first generation of elite figures in colonial Virginia. [JPG]

39.653 Eviatar Zerubavel. *Terra cognita: the mental discovery of America*. New Brunswick, N.J.: Rutgers University Press, 1992. ISBN 0-8135-1897-0 (cl), 0-8135-1898-9 (pbk). ‣ Brief history of gradual cartographical construction of Americas during sixteenth century. [JPG]

SEE ALSO
36.6 Olive P. Dickason. *The myth of the savage and the beginnings of French colonialism in the Americas*.

Religion and Magic

39.654 Charles W. Akers. *Called unto liberty: a life of Jonathan Mayhew, 1720–1766*. Cambridge, Mass.: Harvard University Press, 1964. ‣ Excellent biography of one of leading liberal Congregational clergymen in mid-eighteenth-century Massachusetts. [JPG]

39.655 Randall H. Balmer. *A perfect babel of confusion: Dutch religion and English culture in the middle colonies*. New York: Oxford University Press, 1989. ISBN 0-19-505873-9. ‣ Suggestive exploration of conflicted relationship between Dutch Calvinism and English culture. Also studies eventual anglicization of Dutch urban population and its separation from pietistic Dutch communities in rural New York and New Jersey. [JPG]

39.656 Emery Battis. *Saints and sectaries: Anne Hutchinson and the antinomian controversy in Massachusetts Bay Colony*. Chapel Hill: University of North Carolina Press for Institute of Early American History and Culture, 1962. ‣ Valuable social analysis of antinomian controversy. [JPG]

39.657 S. Charles Bolton. *Southern Anglicanism: the church of England in colonial South Carolina*. Westport, Conn.: Greenwood, 1982. ISBN 0-313-23090-0. ‣ Comprehensive history of establishment and role of Anglican church in colonial South Carolina. [JPG]

39.658 Patricia U. Bonomi. *Under the cope of heaven: religion, society, and politics in colonial America*. New York: Oxford University Press, 1986. ISBN 0-19-504118-6. ‣ Major reexamination of role of religion in shaping of early American life. Stresses increasing vitality of religion and increase in church attendance over period from Restoration (1660) to American Revolution. [JPG]

39.659 Theodore Dwight Bozeman. *To live ancient lives: the primitivist dimension in Protestantism*. Chapel Hill: University of North Carolina Press for Institute of Early American History and Culture, 1988. ISBN 0-8078-1785-6. ‣ Suggestive reinterpretation of New England Puritanism emphasizing its backward-looking character. [JPG]

39.660 Francis J. Bremer. *The Puritan experiment: New England society from Bradford to Edwards*. Alden T. Vaughan, Introduction. New York: St. Martin's, 1976. ‣ Impressive general survey of role of Puritanism in shaping of New England society down through early decades of eighteenth century. [JPG]

39.661 B. R. Burg. *Richard Mather of Dorchester*. Lexington:

University Press of Kentucky, 1976. ISBN 0-8131-1343-1. ‣ Uses Mather's life to illuminate aspects of religious development during first generation of Puritan settlement in Massachusetts. [JPG]

39.662 Jon Butler. *Power, authority, and the origins of American denominational order: the English churches in the Delaware Valley, 1680–1730.* Philadelphia: American Philosophical Society, 1978. (Transactions of the American Philosophical Society, 68.2.) ISBN 0-87169-682-7. ‣ Study stressing role of clerical elites in forming denominational order that emerged in Pennsylvania and New Jersey during early decades of colonization. [JPG]

39.663 Charles Lloyd Cohen. *God's caress: the psychology of Puritan religious experience.* New York: Oxford University Press, 1986. ISBN 0-19-503973-4. ‣ Learned, nuanced examination of doctrine of conversion and meaning of conversion experience in seventeenth-century New England. [JPG]

39.664 John Corrigan. *The hidden balance: religion and the social theories of Charles Chauncy and Jonathan Mayhew.* Cambridge: Cambridge University Press, 1987. ISBN 0-521-32777-6. ‣ Exploration of religious and social ideas of two prominent and influential Congregational clergymen in mid-eighteenth-century Massachusetts. Good insightful study; argumentative rather than innovative. [JPG/DMS]

39.665 Michael J. Crawford. *Seasons of grace: colonial New England's revival tradition in its British context.* New York: Oxford University Press, 1991. ISBN 0-19-506393-7. ‣ Discussion of how concept of religious revival developed in British American world during eighteenth century with specific focus on its New England variant. [JPG]

39.666 Andrew Delbanco. *The Puritan ordeal.* Cambridge, Mass.: Harvard University Press, 1989. ISBN 0-674-74055-6. ‣ Literary analysis emphasizing push factors in migration to New England and travails of early settlers as part of paradigmatic experience of americanization. [JPG]

39.667 John Demos. *Entertaining Satan: witchcraft and the culture of early New England.* New York: Oxford University Press, 1982. ISBN 0-19-503131-8. ‣ Intensive study of psychological and social dimensions of witchcraft in colonial New England and of historical explanations and meanings contemporaries gave to their culture's experiences with witchcraft. [JPG]

39.668 Emory Elliott. *Power and the pulpit in Puritan New England.* Princeton: Princeton University Press, 1975. ISBN 0-691-07206-X. ‣ Interpretation of how Puritan ministers revised their sermons to respond to changing needs of their congregations during second and third generations of settlement. [JPG]

39.669 John Tracy Ellis. *Catholics in colonial America.* Baltimore: Helicon, 1965. ‣ Standard history of Catholics and Catholicism in English continental colonies. [JPG]

39.670 Melvin B. Endy, Jr. *William Penn and early Quakerism.* Princeton: Princeton University Press, 1973. ISBN 0-691-07190-X. ‣ Careful study of Penn's Quakerism. [JPG]

39.671 Stephen Foster. *The long argument: English Puritanism and the shaping of New England culture, 1570–1700.* Chapel Hill: University of North Carolina Press for Institute of Early American History and Culture, 1991. ISBN 0-8078-1951-4. ‣ Learned, sophisticated analysis of English background of New England Puritan culture and of ongoing relationship between England and New England throughout seventeenth century. [JPG]

39.672 J. William Frost. *A perfect freedom: religious liberty in Pennsylvania.* Cambridge: Cambridge University Press, 1990. ISBN 0-521-38545-8. ‣ Clear account of emergence of idea and practice of religious liberty in Pennsylvania. First half covers colonial era. [JPG]

39.673 Edwin S. Gaustad. *The Great Awakening in New England.* 1957 ed. Chicago: Quadrangle, 1968. ‣ Classic study of origins,

course, and impact of Great Awakening in New England colonies. [JPG]

39.674 Edwin S. Gaustad. *Liberty of conscience: Roger Williams in America.* Grand Rapids, Mich.: Eerdmans, 1991. ISBN 0-8028-0153-6. ‣ Most recent biography of controversial religious dissenter, emphasizing his contribution to individual religious liberty. [JPG]

39.675 Wesley M. Gewehr. *The Great Awakening in Virginia, 1740–1790.* 1930 ed. Gloucester, Mass.: Smith, 1965. ‣ Still most comprehensive account of emergence of evangelical religion in eighteenth-century Virginia. [JPG]

39.676 W. Clark Gilpin. *The millenarian piety of Roger Williams.* Chicago: University of Chicago Press, 1979. ISBN 0-226-29397-1. ‣ Examination of nature and evolution of religious dissenter's piety. [JPG]

39.677 Richard Godbeer. *The Devil's dominion: magic and religion in early New England.* Cambridge: Cambridge University Press, 1992. ISBN 0-521-40329-4. ‣ Exploration of importance of magic and its affinities with religion in early colonial New England. [JPG]

39.678 C. C. Goen. *Revivalism and separatism in New England, 1740–1800: strict Congregationalists and separate Baptists in the Great Awakening.* 1962 ed. Middletown, Conn.: Wesleyan University Press; distributed by Harper & Row, 1987. ISBN 0-8195-5186-4 (cl), 0-8195-6133-9 (pbk). ‣ Examination of religious splintering in Connecticut between Great Awakening and close of eighteenth century. [JPG]

39.679 Edward M. Griffin. *Old brick: Charles Chauncy of Boston, 1705–1787.* Minneapolis: University of Minnesota Press, 1980. ISBN 0-8166-0907-1. ‣ Good biography of leading mid-eighteenth-century Massachusetts Congregational minister. [JPG]

39.680 Philip F. Gura. *A glimpse of Zion's glory: Puritan radicalism in New England, 1620–1660.* Middletown, Conn.: Wesleyan University Press, 1984. ISBN 0-8195-5095-7. ‣ Excellent account of significant role of radical Puritan sects, including antinomians, millenarians, and Socinians, in early New England religious life. [JPG]

39.681 David D. Hall. *The faithful shepherd: a history of the New England ministry in the seventeenth century.* Chapel Hill: University of North Carolina Press for Institute of Early American History and Culture, 1972. ISBN 0-8078-1193-9. ‣ Best study of ministry as calling or profession for any part of colonial America. [JPG]

39.682 Michael G. Hall. *The last American Puritan: the life of Increase Mather.* Middletown, Conn.: Wesleyan University Press; distributed by Harper & Row, 1988. ISBN 0-8195-5128-7. ‣ Superb modern account of life of Mather using his career as window on social, cultural, and political change in late seventeenth- and early eighteenth-century Massachusetts. [JPG]

39.683 Charles E. Hambrick-Stowe. *The practice of piety: Puritan devotional disciplines in seventeenth-century New England.* Chapel Hill: University of North Carolina Press for Institute of Early American History and Culture, 1982. ISBN 0-8078-1518-7. ‣ Impressive, detailed examination of devotional ideas and practices among seventeenth-century New England Puritans. [JPG]

39.684 Chadwick Hansen. *Witchcraft at Salem.* 1969 ed. New York: New American Library, 1970. ISBN 0-451-61947-1. ‣ Interpretation of Salem witchcraft episodes emphasizing extensiveness and success of witchcraft practiced there. [JPG]

39.685 Joseph Haroutunian. *Piety versus moralism: the passing of the New England theology.* 1932 ed. New York: Harper & Row, 1970. ‣ Early analysis of emerging theological conflict between religious liberalism and piety in New England following Great Awakening. [JPG]

39.686 Alan Heimert. *Religion and the American mind from the Great Awakening to the Revolution.* Cambridge, Mass.: Harvard University Press, 1966. ▸ Analysis of emerging religious divisions among mid-eighteenth-century ministers, mostly in New England, and some suggestions about relationship of those divisions to American Revolution. (JPG)

39.687 E. Brooks Holifield. *The covenant sealed: the development of Puritan sacramental theology in old and New England, 1570–1720.* New Haven: Yale University Press, 1974. ISBN 0-300-01733-2. ▸ Important examination of Puritan uses of sacramentalism in both Old and New Worlds to early eighteenth century. (JPG)

39.688 Cornelius J. Jaenen. *The role of the church in New France.* 1976 ed. Ottawa: Canadian Historical Association, 1985. (Historical booklet, 40.) ISBN 0-88798-107-0. ▸ Excellent, brief study of function of church in society of New France. (JPG)

39.689 Sydney V. James. *A people among peoples: Quaker benevolence in eighteenth-century America.* Cambridge, Mass.: Harvard University Press, 1963. ▸ Intelligent analysis of changing nature and emphases of Quakerism in eighteenth-century colonial British America. (JPG)

39.690 James W. Jones. *The shattered synthesis: New England Puritanism before the Great Awakening.* New Haven: Yale University Press, 1973. ISBN 0-300-01619-0. ▸ Exploration of century of changes in New England Puritanism that provided preconditions of religious awakenings of 1730s and 1740s. (JPG)

39.691 William Kellaway. *The New England Company, 1649–1776: missionary society to the American Indians.* 1961 ed. New York: Barnes & Noble, 1962. ▸ Studies rather desultory New England missionary activities among American Indians of region. (JPG)

39.692 J. A. Leo Lemay, ed. *Deism, masonry, and the Enlightenment: essays honoring Alfred Owen Aldridge.* Newark and London: University of Delaware Press and Associated University Presses, 1987. ISBN 0-87413-317-3. ▸ Seven of nine essays deal with aspects of expressions of deistic thought and freemasonry in England and America during colonial era. (JPG)

39.693 David S. Lovejoy. *Religious enthusiasm in the New World: heresy to revolution.* Cambridge, Mass.: Harvard University Press, 1985. ISBN 0-674-75864-1. ▸ Well-constructed general study of history of religious extremism in colonial era. (JPG)

39.694 Richard F. Lovelace. *The American pietism of Cotton Mather: origins of American evangelicalism.* Grand Rapids, Mich.: Christian University Press; distributed by Eerdmans, 1979. ISBN 0-8028-1750-5. ▸ Effort to reinterpret Mather's theology and practice of Christianity, stressing his relationship to pietism as well as Puritanism. (JPG)

39.695 Mason I. Lowance, Jr. *Increase Mather.* New York: Twayne, 1974. ISBN 0-8057-0477-9. ▸ Short modern study of leading seventeenth-century Puritan religious figure. (JPG)

39.696 Jack D. Marietta. *The reformation of American Quakerism, 1748–1783.* Philadelphia: University of Pennsylvania Press, 1984. ISBN 0-8122-7922-0. ▸ Excellent history of reorientation and revitalization of Quaker movement in mid-eighteenth-century colonial and revolutionary periods. Analyzes disciplinary cases in Pennsylvania meetings. Quakers undertook purge to counter perceived growing moral laxness. (JPG/LAN)

39.697 William G. McLoughlin. *Isaac Backus and the American pietistic tradition.* Oscar Handlin, ed. Boston: Little, Brown, 1967. ▸ Excellent analysis of prominent Baptist minister, placing him in emerging pietistic tradition in late colonial and revolutionary periods. Study of pietism and religious controversy rather than full biography. (JPG/DMS)

39.698 William G. McLoughlin. *Soul liberty: the Baptists' struggle in New England, 1630–1833.* Providence and Hanover, N.H.: Brown University Press and University Press of New England, 1991. ISBN 0-87451-532-7. ▸ Valuable collection of fifteen essays mostly on Baptist challenge to Congregational religious establishment in New England. (JPG)

39.699 Perry Miller. *Roger Williams: his contribution to the American tradition.* 1953 ed. New York: Atheneum, 1974. ▸ Analysis of religious and political thought of religious dissenter. (JPG)

39.700 Frederick V. Mills, Sr. *Bishops by ballot: an eighteenth-century ecclesiastical revolution.* New York: Oxford University Press, 1978. ISBN 0-19-502411-7. ▸ Significant examination of colonial Anglican church, extent to which it became an issue in quarrels of 1760s, and its transformation following American Revolution. (JPG)

39.701 Herbert M. Morais. *Deism in eighteenth-century America.* 1934 ed. New York: Russell & Russell, 1960. ▸ Standard study of subject. (JPG)

39.702 Edmund S. Morgan. *Visible saints: the history of a Puritan idea.* New York: New York University Press, 1963. ▸ Engaging, penetrating look at quest for church of the elect among seventeenth-century Puritans. (JPG)

39.703 Kenneth B. Murdock. *Increase Mather: the foremost American Puritan.* 1953 ed. New York: Russell & Russell, 1966. ▸ Useful biography of Mather. (JPG)

39.704 Claude M. Newlin. *Philosophy and religion in colonial America.* 1962 ed. New York: Greenwood, 1968. ▸ Cursory exploration of mid-eighteenth-century religious thought in New England. (JPG)

39.705 Emil Oberholzer, Jr. *Delinquent saints: disciplinary action in the early Congregational churches of Massachusetts.* 1956 ed. New York: AMS, 1968. ▸ Best study of church discipline in seventeenth-century New England churches. (JPG)

39.706 Charles Edward O'Neill. *Church and state in French colonial Louisiana: policy and politics to 1732.* New Haven: Yale University Press, 1966. ▸ Examination of interconnections between government and church in Louisiana under French regime. (JPG)

39.707 Carla Gardina Pestana. *Quakers and Baptists in colonial Massachusetts.* Cambridge: Cambridge University Press, 1991. ISBN 0-521-41111-4. ▸ Examination of histories of first two dissenting sects in colonial Massachusetts, Salem Quakers and Boston Baptists, from their first appearance through end of colonial era. (JPG)

39.708 Norman Pettit. *The heart prepared: grace and conversion in Puritan spiritual life.* 2d ed. Middletown, Conn.: Wesleyan University Press, 1989. ISBN 0-8195-6224-6. ▸ Intelligent inquiry into emotional dimensions of early New England religious life. Studies process by which people prepared themselves for conversion. (JPG)

39.709 Richard W. Pointer. *Protestant pluralism and the New York experience: a study of eighteenth-century religious diversity.* Bloomington: Indiana University Press, 1988. ISBN 0-253-34643-6. ▸ Careful examination of effects of religious diversity on religious life of colonial and revolutionary New York. (JPG/LAN)

39.710 Robert G. Pope. *The half-way covenant: church membership in Puritan New England.* Princeton: Princeton University Press, 1969. ISBN 0-691-07156-X. ▸ Careful examination of changing patterns of church membership in seventeenth-century New England. (JPG)

39.711 Darrett B. Rutman. *American Puritanism: faith and practice.* Philadelphia: Lippincott, 1970. ▸ Brief portrait of seventeenth-century New England Puritans focusing on interaction between religious belief and social behavior. Also examines anti-slavery sentiments. [JPG/LAN]

39.712 Lester B. Scherer. *Slavery and the churches in early America, 1619–1819.* Grand Rapids, Mich.: Eerdmans, 1975. ISBN 0-8028-1580-4. ‣ Brief survey of attitude of churches toward slavery, emphasizing how little any of them did to christianize slaves. [JPG]

39.713 Leigh Eric Schmidt. *Holy fairs: Scottish communions and American revivals in the early modern period.* Princeton: Princeton University Press, 1989. ISBN 0-691-04760-X. ‣ Examination of development and changing function of communion season, a Scottish religious festival, its transfer to colonial America, and its relationship to spread of evangelical religion. Revises previous views of evangelical Protestantism. [JPG/DMS]

39.714 George Selement. *Keepers of the vineyard: the Puritan ministry and collective culture in colonial New England.* Lanham, Md.: University Press of America, 1984. ISBN 0-8191-3876-2 (cl), 0-8191-3877-0 (pbk). ‣ Brief but suggestive account of role of ministers in creating collective culture in New England during first three generations of settlement. [JPG]

39.715 Daniel B. Shea, Jr. *Spiritual autobiography in early America.* 1968 ed. Madison: University of Wisconsin Press, 1988. ISBN 0-299-11650-6 (cl), 0-299-11654-9 (pbk). ‣ Careful literary analysis of genre of spiritual autobiography in colonial New England with concluding chapter on Benjamin Franklin's and other later writers' relationship to earlier forms and conventions. [JPG]

39.716 Kenneth Silverman. *The life and times of Cotton Mather.* 1984 ed. New York: Columbia University Press, 1985. ISBN 0-231-06125-0 (pbk). ‣ Excellent biography of New England's most prolific religious writer during late seventeenth and early eighteenth century. [JPG]

39.717 Alan Simpson. *Puritanism in old and New England.* 1955 ed. Chicago: University of Chicago Press, 1967. ‣ Early series of reflections on development of Puritanism in England and its transfer to New World. [JPG]

39.718 Winton U. Solberg. *Redeem the time: the Puritan sabbath in early America.* Cambridge, Mass.: Harvard University Press, 1977. ISBN 0-674-75130-2. ‣ Excellent analysis of practice of sabbath observance in seventeenth-century English colonial America, primarily in New England but also in New York and Restoration colonies. [JPG]

39.719 Marion L. Starkey. *The Devil in Massachusetts: a modern enquiry into the Salem witch trials.* 1949 ed. Garden City, N.Y.: Doubleday, 1969. ‣ Highly readable narrative of best-known witch trials in early America, largely superseded by later works. [JPG]

39.720 Keith W. F. Stavely. *Puritan legacies: "Paradise Lost" and the New England tradition, 1630–1890.* New York: Cornell University Press, 1987. ISBN 0-8014-2016-4. ‣ Study showing *Paradise Lost* provided structure of feeling, helping to shape religious culture of early New England. [JPG]

39.721 F. Ernest Stoeffler, ed. *Continental pietism and early American Christianity.* Grand Rapids, Mich.: Eerdmans, 1976. ISBN 0-8028-1641-X. ‣ Contains seven essays considering various manifestations of influence of European pietism in early American religious culture. [JPG]

39.722 William K. B. Stoever. *"A faire and easie way to heaven": covenant theology and antinomianism in early Massachusetts.* Middletown, Conn.: Wesleyan University Press, 1978. ISBN 0-8195-5024-8. ‣ Concise, persuasive examination of antinomian controversy of 1636–38 in Massachusetts. [JPG]

39.723 Harry S. Stout. *The New England soul: preaching and religious culture in colonial New England.* New York: Oxford University Press, 1986. ISBN 0-19-503958-0. ‣ Uses sermons to examine important role and significance of preaching in New England religious culture over entire colonial era. [JPG]

39.724 James Tanis. *Dutch Calvinistic pietism in the middle colonies: a study in the life and theology of Theodorus Jacobus Frelinghuysen.* 1967 ed. The Hague: Nijhoff, 1968. ‣ Study of changing character of Dutch Calvinism through career of Great Awakening leader who played key role in setting agenda for Awakening among other ethnic groups and denominations. [JPG/LAN]

39.725 Leonard J. Trinterud. *The forming of an American tradition: a re-examination of colonial Presbyterianism.* 1949 ed. Freeport, N.Y.: Books for Libraries, 1970. ISBN 0-8369-5450-5. ‣ Full and authoritative exploration of theology and spread of early American Presbyterianism. [JPG]

39.726 Seymour Van Dyken. *Samuel Willard, 1640–1707: preacher of orthodoxy in an era of change.* Grand Rapids, Mich.: Eerdmans, 1972. ISBN 0-8028-3408-6. ‣ Competent study of theology of second generation clergyman in colonial Massachusetts. [JPG]

39.727 Richard Weisman. *Witchcraft, magic, and religion in seventeenth-century Massachusetts.* Amherst: University of Massachusetts Press, 1984. ISBN 0-87023-415-3. ‣ Recent examination of forms of witchcraft practiced in seventeenth-century Massachusetts. Views witches as victims of social conflict. [JPG]

39.728 Marilyn J. Westerkamp. *Triumph of the laity: Scots-Irish piety and the Great Awakening, 1625–1760.* New York: Oxford University Press, 1988. ISBN 0-19-504401-0. ‣ Reinterpretation of Great Awakening, stressing its roots in Scots-Irish Presbyterian revivalism dating back to early seventeenth century and finding its immediate cause in spiritual dissatisfaction of laity. [JPG]

39.729 Selma R. Williams. *Divine rebel: the life of Anne Marbury Hutchinson.* New York: Holt, Rinehart & Winston, 1981. ISBN 0-03-055846-8. ‣ Biographical study of early New England's most vociferous religious rebel. [JPG]

39.730 Robert J. Wilson III. *The benevolent deity: Ebenezer Gay and the rise of rational religion in New England, 1696–1787.* Philadelphia: University of Pennsylvania Press, 1984. ISBN 0-8122-7891-7. ‣ Exploration of emergence of liberal religion in eighteenth-century New England through career of one of its leading practitioners. [JPG]

39.731 Ola Elizabeth Winslow. *John Eliot: apostle to the Indians.* Boston: Houghton-Mifflin, 1968. ‣ Sprightly biography of most prominent missionary to American Indians in seventeenth-century New England. [JPG]

39.732 John Frederick Woolverton. *Colonial Anglicanism in North America.* Detroit: Wayne State University Press, 1984. ISBN 0-8143-1755-3. ‣ Authoritative, comprehensive study of role, significance, and theology of Anglican church among continental colonies. [JPG]

39.733 Arthur J. Worrall. *Quakers in the colonial Northeast.* Hanover, N.H.: University Press of New England, 1980. ISBN 0-87451-174-7. ‣ Traces Quaker experience in New England and New York during seventeenth and eighteenth centuries. [JPG]

39.734 Conrad Wright. *The beginnings of Unitarianism in America.* 1955 ed. Hamden, Conn.: Archon, 1976. ISBN 0-208-01612-0. Succinct, well-written account of growth of Arminianism and other forms of liberal theology in New England in seventeenth and eighteenth centuries. [JPG]

39.735 J. William T. Youngs, Jr. *God's messengers: religious leadership in colonial New England, 1700–1750.* Baltimore: Johns Hopkins University Press, 1976. ISBN 0-8018-1799-4. ‣ Well-crafted, comprehensive examination of calling of ministers in eighteenth-century New England. [JPG]

39.736 Avihu Zakai. *Exile and kingdom: history and apocalypse in the Puritan migration to America.* Cambridge: Cambridge University Press, 1992. ISBN 0-521-40381-2. ► Traces millennial traditions that formed important part of Puritan theology in England and helped to shape nature of Puritan enterprise in New England. [JPG]

39.737 Larzer Ziff. *The career of John Cotton: Puritanism and the American experience.* Princeton: Princeton University Press, 1962. ► Examination of Puritan religious experiment through life of leading Puritan cleric in early New England. [JPG]

SEE ALSO
40.723 Jon Butler. *Awash in a sea of faith.*

Education

39.738 James Axtell. *The school upon a hill: education and society in colonial New England.* New Haven: Yale University Press, 1974. ISBN 0-300-01723-5. ► Lucid examination of processes by which children were socialized into New England culture and philosophies that underlay them. [JPG]

39.739 Bernard Bailyn. *Education in the forming of American society: needs and opportunities for study.* 1960 ed. New York: Norton, 1972. ISBN 0-393-00643-3. ► Broad interpretive essay on nature and operation of educative processes in early America, with many suggestions for further research. [JPG]

39.740 Richard D. Brown. *Knowledge is power: the diffusion of information in early America, 1700–1865.* New York: Oxford University Press, 1989. ISBN 0-19-504417-7 (cl), 0-19-057265-0 (pbk). ► Imaginative discussion of sources, production, flows, and agencies of dissemination of information in early America. [JPG]

39.741 John Calam. *Parsons and pedagogues: the S.P.G. adventure in American education.* New York: Columbia University Press, 1971. ISBN 0-231-03371-0. ► Study of goals and operation of Society for the Propagation of the Gospel's efforts at school founding in Britain's continental colonies. [JPG]

39.742 Lawrence A. Cremin. *American education: the colonial experience, 1607–1783.* New York: Harper & Row, 1970. ► Rich, comprehensive history of ideas informing early American education and institutions through which colonials transmitted those ideas to the young. [JPG]

39.743 Edwin S. Gaustad. *George Berkeley in America.* New Haven: Yale University Press, 1979. ISBN 0-300-02394-4. ► Examination of brief American career of English philosopher George Berkeley, including his efforts to establish college for American Indians in Bermuda. [JPG]

39.744 Albert Frank Gegenheimer. *William Smith: educator and clergyman, 1727–1803.* Philadelphia: University of Pennsylvania Press, 1943. ► Biography of important figure in founding of colleges in eighteenth century. [JPG]

39.745 Jurgen Herbst. *From crisis to crisis: American college government, 1636–1819.* Cambridge, Mass.: Harvard University Press, 1982. ISBN 0-674-32345-9. ► Interpretation of institutional development of early American colleges. Concentrates on patterns of governance and emphasizes their civic status. [JPG]

39.746 Kenneth A. Lockridge. *Literacy in colonial New England: an enquiry into the social context of literacy in the early modern West.* New York: Norton, 1974. ISBN 0-393-05522-1 (cl), 0-393-09263-1 (pbk). ► Most extensive study of extent of literacy for any area of colonial British America, based on counting signatures on wills. Despite growing male literacy, New England society remained parochial. Population density and Protestant intensity led to better schooling. [JPG/LAN]

39.747 Robert Middlekauff. *Ancients and axioms: secondary edu-cation in eighteenth-century New England.* New Haven: Yale University Press, 1963. ► Best available examination of forms and content of secondary education in eighteenth-century New England. [JPG]

39.748 Howard Miller. *The revolutionary college: American Presbyterian higher education, 1707–1837.* New York: New York University Press, 1976. ISBN 0-8147-5407-6. ► First third of volume deals with early Presbyterian settlements in colonies, development of demand for creation of Presbyterian institutions of higher learning, and founding of Princeton in middle of eighteenth century. [JPG]

39.749 Samuel Eliot Morison. *The founding of Harvard College.* 1935 ed. Cambridge, Mass.: Harvard University Press, 1968. ► Detailed examination of establishment and early years of first institution of higher learning in British America. [JPG]

39.750 Samuel Eliot Morison. *Harvard College in the seventeenth century.* 2 vols. Cambridge, Mass.: Harvard University Press, 1936. ► Detailed, comprehensive history. [JPG]

39.751 Douglas Sloan. *The Scottish enlightenment and the American college ideal.* New York: Columbia University, Teachers College Press, 1971. ► Loose collection of essays examining selected aspects of impact of Scottish enlightenment ideas on early American higher education. [JPG]

39.752 Louis Leonard Tucker. *Puritan protagonist: President Thomas Clap of Yale College.* Chapel Hill: University of North Carolina Press for Institute of Early American History and Culture, 1962. ► Excellent biography of mid-eighteenth-century president of Yale with analysis of his educational role. [JPG]

39.753 Richard Warch. *School of the prophets: Yale College, 1701–1740.* New Haven: Yale University Press, 1973. ISBN 0-300-01605-0. ► Careful, comprehensive study of first four decades of Yale College. [JPG]

SEE ALSO
36.119 Margaret C. Szasz. *Indian education in the American colonies, 1607–1783.*

Literature

39.754 Sacvan Bercovitch. *The Puritan origins of the American self.* New Haven: Yale University Press, 1975. ISBN 0-300-01754-5. ► Probing examination of origins of idea of chosenness as central ingredient in cultural identification of New England and its later incorporation into American myth and its expression in nineteenth-century American writing. [JPG]

39.755 Ursula Brumm. *American thought and religious typology.* John Hooglund, trans. New Brunswick, N.J.: Rutgers University Press, 1970. ISBN 0-8135-0621-2. ► Examination of Puritan fascination with typology and influence of phenomenon on subsequent development of New England literature. [JPG]

39.756 Patricia Caldwell. *The Puritan conversion narrative: the beginnings of American expression.* 1983 ed. Cambridge: Cambridge University Press, 1985. ISBN 0-521-31147-0 (pbk). ► Exploration of testimonies of spiritual experience as Puritan literary expressions during early years of New England. [JPG]

39.757 Robert Daly. *God's altar: the world and the flesh in Puritan poetry.* Berkeley: University of California Press, 1978. ISBN 0-520-03480-5. ► Study of doctrine of accommodation and symbolic thinking in seventeenth-century Puritan poetry. [JPG]

39.758 Richard Beale Davis. *Literature and society in early Virginia, 1608–1840.* Baton Rouge: Louisiana State University Press, 1973. ISBN 0-8071-0215-6. ► Collection of fifteen previously published essays on aspects of literature of colonial and early national Virginia. First nine chapters treat colonial period. [JPG]

39.759 Norman S. Grabo. *Edward Taylor*. Boston: Twayne, 1988. ISBN 0-8057-7521-8. ▸ Excellent interpretation of life as well as poetic and devotional works of most important seventeenth-century English American poet. [JPG]

39.760 Howard Mumford Jones. *The literature of Virginia in the seventeenth century*. 2d ed. Charlottesville: University Press of Virginia, 1968. ▸ Older effort to describe and analyze literature produced in and about seventeenth-century Virginia. [JPG]

39.761 Karl Keller. *The example of Edward Taylor*. Amherst: University of Massachusetts Press, 1975. ISBN 0-87023-174-X. ▸ Exploration of development of Puritan aesthetic through prose and poetry of Taylor. [JPG]

39.762 J. A. Leo Lemay. *Men of letters in colonial Maryland*. Knoxville: University of Tennessee Press, 1972. ▸ Full, cogent analysis of principal writers of surprisingly rich literary culture of colonial Maryland. [JPG]

39.763 J. A. Leo Lemay, ed. *Essays in early Virginia literature honoring Richard Beale Davis*. New York: Franklin, 1977. ISBN 0-89102-067-5. ▸ Includes thirteen essays on aspects of early Virginia literature, several on colonial era. [JPG]

39.764 David Leverenz. *The language of Puritan feeling: an exploration in literature, psychology, and social history*. New Brunswick, N.J.: Rutgers University Press, 1980. ISBN 0-8135-0882-7. ▸ Account of Puritan emotional life that interprets effort to establish intimacy with God as search for coherence and authority in world bereft of both. [JPG]

39.765 Mason I. Lowance, Jr. *The language of Canaan: metaphor and symbol in New England from the Puritans to the transcendentalists*. Cambridge, Mass.: Harvard University Press, 1980. ISBN 0-674-50949-8. ▸ Valuable for its close study of changing interpretations of typology in seventeenth-century New England and its discussion of persistence of millennial expectations among later generations of writers in New England tradition. [JPG]

39.766 Robert Micklus. *The comic genius of Dr. Alexander Hamilton*. Knoxville: University of Tennessee Press, 1990. ISBN 0-87049-633-6. ▸ Analysis of life and writings of Maryland lawyer Alexander Hamilton, placing him in broad colonial American cultural framework. [JPG/DMS]

39.767 Kenneth B. Murdock. *Literature and theology in colonial New England*. 1949 ed. Westport, Conn.: Greenwood, 1970. ISBN 0-8371-3990-2. ▸ Pioneering effort to explore Puritan contributions to literature and theology in colonial New England. [JPG]

39.768 Karen E. Rowe. *Saint and singer: Edward Taylor's typology and the poetics of meditation*. New York: Cambridge University Press, 1986. ISBN 0-521-30865-8. ▸ Detailed exploration of beginnings of American typological poetics focusing on parallels between Taylor's sermons and his poetry. [JPG]

39.769 William J. Scheick. *The will and the word: the poetry of Edward Taylor*. Athens: University of Georgia Press, 1974. ISBN 0-8203-0314-3. ▸ Study of aesthetic qualities in Taylor's poetry. [JPG]

39.770 Ann Stanford. *Anne Bradstreet: the worldly Puritan, an introduction to her poetry*. 1974 ed. New York: Franklin, 1975. ISBN 0-89102-030-6. ▸ Analysis of Bradstreet's poetics against background of early modern English poetic practice. [JPG]

39.771 Cecelia Tichi. *New World, new earth: environmental reform in American literature from the Puritans through Whitman*. New Haven: Yale University Press, 1979. ISBN 0-300-02287-5. ▸ Examination of theme of environmental mastery in American literature, first third covers colonial period. [JPG]

39.772 Elizabeth Wade White. *Anne Bradstreet: "the tenth muse."*

New York: Oxford University Press, 1971. ISBN 0-19-501440-5. ▸ Examination of life and poetry of Bradstreet. [JPG]

SEE ALSO
40.530 Sacvan Bercovitch. *The American jeremiad.*

Fine Arts

39.773 Frederick S. Allis, Jr. *Music in colonial Massachusetts, 1630–1820: a conference held by the Colonial Society of Massachusetts, May 17 and 18, 1973*. 1980 ed. 2 vols. Boston: Colonial Society of Massachusetts; distributed by University Press of Virginia, 1985. (Publications of the Colonial Society of Massachusetts, 53–54.) ▸ Eleven articles touching on many aspects of both religious and secular music performed in homes, churches, and public places in colonial Massachusetts. [JPG]

39.774 Waldron Phoenix Belknap, Jr. *American colonial painting: materials for a history*. Cambridge, Mass.: Belknap, 1959. ▸ Collection of author's articles and notes on early American portraiture, published posthumously. Emphasizes English mezzotint sources for colonial paintings. [JPG]

39.775 Wayne Craven. *Colonial American portraiture: the economic, religious, social, cultural, philosophical, scientific, and aesthetic foundations*. Cambridge: Cambridge University Press, 1986. ISBN 0-521-32044-5. ▸ Excellent comprehensive study of colonial American portraiture. Attempts to set both artists and subjects in their broadest social context. [JPG]

39.776 Jonathan L. Fairbanks and Robert F. Trent. *New England begins: the seventeenth century*. 3 vols. Boston: Museum of Fine Arts, 1982. ISBN 0-87846-210-4 (set, pbk). ▸ Three-volume catalog of graphic representations and material objects on seventeenth-century New England in exhibit at Boston Museum of Fine Arts. [JPG]

39.777 Graham Hood. *Charles Bridges and William Dering: two Virginia painters, 1735–1750*. Williamsburg, Va.: Colonial Williamsburg Foundation; distributed by University Press of Virginia, 1978. ISBN 0-87935-047-4. ▸ Study of paintings of two of most prolific portrait painters in colonial Virginia. [JPG]

39.778 Irving Lowens. *Music and musicians in early America*. New York: Norton, 1964. ▸ Contains three chapters on colonial music, focusing on *Bay Psalmbook* and first music textbook. [JPG]

39.779 Jessie J. Poesch. *The art of the Old South: painting, sculpture, architecture, and the products of craftsmen, 1560–1860*. 1983 ed. New York: Harrison House; distributed by Crown, 1989. ISBN 0-517-68053-X. ▸ Comprehensive discussion of artistic expression in South, devoting considerable space to colonial era. [JPG]

39.780 Ian M. G. Quimby, ed. *American painting to 1776: a reappraisal*. Charlottesville: University Press of Virginia for Henry Francis du Pont Winterthur Museum, 1971. (Winterthur Conference report, 1971.) ▸ Important early collection of essays. [JPG]

39.781 Ian M. G. Quimby, ed. *Arts of the Anglo-American community in the seventeenth century*. Charlottesville: University Press of Virginia for Henry Francis du Pont Winterthur Museum, 1975. (Winterthur Conference report, 1974.) ISBN 0-8139-0612-1. ▸ Contains nine essays on aspects of material culture and metal and textile crafts in seventeenth-century colonial English America. [JPG]

39.782 Hugh F. Rankin. *The theatre in colonial America*. Chapel Hill: University of North Carolina Press, 1965. ▸ Introductory study of repertories of many companies performing dramatic works in theaters before Revolution. [JPG]

39.783 E. P. Richardson. *Painting in America, from 1502 to the present*. New York: Crowell, 1965. ▸ Comprehensive survey; early portions trace work of painters and transplantation of drawing and painting skills from Old World to America. [JPG]

39.784 Richard H. Saunders and Ellen G. Miles. *American colonial portraits, 1700–1776.* Washington, D.C.: Smithsonian Institution Press for National Portrait Gallery, 1987. ISBN 0-87474-694-9 (cl), 0-87474-695-7 (pbk). ▸ Catalog of exhibition at National Portrait Gallery that included paintings from all eighteenth-century British American colonies and portraits of colonials done in Old World. Study of participation of colonists in art. [JPG]

39.785 O. G. Sonneck. *Early concert life in America.* 1907 ed. New York: Da Capo, 1978. ISBN 0-306-77591-3. ▸ Only study of this dimension of early American cultural life. [JPG]

39.786 John Barry Talley. *Secular music in colonial Annapolis: the Tuesday Club, 1745–56.* Urbana: University of Illinois Press, 1988. ISBN 0-252-01402-2. ▸ Fullest study of secular music in colonial British America. [JPG]

39.787 Walter Muir Whitehill. *The arts in early American history: an essay by Walter Muir Whitehill.* Chapel Hill: University of North Carolina Press for Institute of Early American History and Culture, 1965. ▸ Discussion of function of various arts in early America, existing literature at time on those subjects, and areas requiring further work. [JPG]

39.788 Louis B. Wright et al. *The arts in America: the colonial period.* New York: Scribner's, 1966. ▸ Broad survey of visual and material arts in continental colonial British America. [JPG]

Science, Technology, and Medicine

39.789 Otho T. Beall, Jr., and Richard H. Shryock. *Cotton Mather: first significant figure in American medicine.* 1954 ed. Baltimore: Johns Hopkins University Press, 1968. (Publications of the Institute of the History of Medicine, First series: monographs, 5.) ▸ Careful study of Mather's significant medical practice. [JPG]

39.790 Silvio A. Bedini. *Thinkers and tinkers: the early American men of science.* New York: Scribner's, 1975. ISBN 0-684-14268-6. ▸ Useful discussion of collective contributions of practioners of applied science in areas such as navigation, surveying, and instrument making and of those who disseminated scientific information. [JPG]

39.791 Whitfield J. Bell, Jr. *The colonial physician and other essays.* New York: Science History, 1975. ISBN 0-88202-024-2. ▸ Collection of previously published essays on various physicians and their work in colonial Philadelphia. [JPG]

39.792 Whitfield J. Bell, Jr. *Early American science.* Chapel Hill: University of North Carolina Press for Institute of Early American History and Culture, 1955. ▸ Survey of existing work in field with suggestions for further research. [JPG]

39.793 Edmund Berkeley and Dorothy Smith Berkeley. *Dr. Alexander Garden of Charles Town.* Chapel Hill: University of North Carolina Press, 1969. ▸ Careful look at varied medical and scientific work of Charleston doctor. [JPG]

39.794 Edmund Berkeley and Dorothy Smith Berkeley. *Dr. John Mitchell: the man who made the map of North America.* Chapel Hill: University of North Carolina Press, 1974. ISBN 0-8078-1221-8. ▸ Excellent biography of colonial Virginia botanist and cartographer. [JPG]

39.795 Edmund Berkeley and Dorothy Smith Berkeley. *John Clayton: pioneer of American botany.* Chapel Hill: University of North Carolina Press, 1963. ▸ Lucid analysis of life and scientific contributions of colonial Virginia botanist. [JPG]

39.796 Edmund Berkeley and Dorothy Smith Berkeley. *The life and travels of John Bartram: from Lake Ontario to the River St. John.* Tallahassee: University Presses of Florida, 1982. ISBN 0-8130-0700-3. ▸ Careful study of scientific career and travels of naturalist. [JPG]

39.797 Larry L. Burkhart. *The good fight: medicine in colonial Pennsylvania.* New York: Garland, 1989. ISBN 0-8240-3395-7. ▸ Impressive examination of disease environment, physicians, and medical practice in colonial Pennsylvania. Finds Pennsylvania most medically advanced area in North America. [JPG/DMS]

39.798 St. Julien Ravenel Childs. *Malaria and colonization in the Carolina low country, 1526–1696.* Baltimore: Johns Hopkins University Press, 1940. ▸ Early analysis of disease environment of southeastern low country. [JPG]

39.799 I. Bernard Cohen. *Franklin and Newton: an inquiry into speculative Newtonian experimental science and Franklin's work in electricity as an example thereof.* 1956 ed. Cambridge, Mass.: Harvard University Press for American Philosophical Society, 1966. (Memoirs of the American Philosophical Society, 43.) ▸ Detailed exploration of Benjamin Franklin's celebrated electrical experiments as study in practice of Newtonian science. [JPG]

39.800 John Duffy. *Epidemics in colonial America.* 1953 ed. Baton Rouge: Louisiana State University Press, 1971. ISBN 0-8046-1664-7. ▸ Comprehensive survey of range and types of epidemics that often raged in colonial British America. [JPG]

39.801 Joseph Ewan and Nesta Ewan. *John Banister and his natural history of Virginia 1678–1692.* Urbana: University of Illinois Press, 1970. ISBN 0-252-00075-7. ▸ Close study of scientific work of colonial English America's first resident naturalist. [JPG]

39.802 George Frederick Frick and Raymond Phineas Stearns. *Mark Catesby: the colonial Audubon.* Urbana: University of Illinois Press, 1961. ▸ Thorough analysis of life and scientific and artistic accomplishments of important naturalist artist of colonial lower South. [JPG]

39.803 Brooke Hindle. *Technology in early America: needs and opportunities for study, with a directory of artifact collections by Lucius F. Ellsworth.* Chapel Hill: University of North Carolina Press for Institute of Early American History and Culture, 1966. ▸ Useful survey of diffuse literature on early American technology with suggestions for further research. [JPG]

39.804 Kenneth F. Kiple. *The Caribbean slave: a biological history.* Cambridge: Cambridge University Press, 1984. ISBN 0-521-26874-5. ▸ Study of mortality, disease, diet, demography, and health among slave populations of British West Indies. [JPG]

39.805 *Medicine in colonial Massachusetts, 1620–1820: a conference held 25 and 26 May 1978.* Boston: Colonial Society of Massachusetts; distributed by University Press of Virginia, 1980. (Publications of the Colonial Society of Massachusetts, 57.) ▸ Twelve essays on practices and practioners of medicine in colonial Massachusetts. [JPG]

39.806 Richard B. Sheridan. *Doctors and slaves: a medical and demographic history of slavery in the British West Indies, 1680–1834.* Cambridge: Cambridge University Press, 1985. ISBN 0-521-25965-7. ▸ Thorough study of medical treatment of slaves in West Indian colonies. [JPG]

39.807 Richard Harrison Shryock. *Medicine and society in America, 1660–1860.* 1960 ed. Ithaca, N.Y.: Cornell University Press, 1977. ISBN 0-8014-9093-6. ▸ Short survey of social history of early American medicine with chapters on medical profession, practice, thought, disease, and health conditions. [JPG]

39.808 Raymond Phineas Stearns. *Science in the British colonies of America.* Urbana: University of Illinois Press, 1970. ISBN 0-252-00120-6. ▸ Detailed, comprehensive survey of scientific activities throughout colonial British America. [JPG]

39.809 Joseph I. Waring. *A history of medicine in South Carolina, 1670–1825.* Charleston: South Carolina Medical Association, 1964. ▸ Study of medical practice and disease environment in Britain's most sickly continental colony. [JPG]

39.810 Patricia A. Watson. *Angelical conjunction: the preacher-physicians of colonial New England.* Knoxville: University of Tennessee Press, 1991. ISBN 0-87049-696-4. ▸ Intelligent analysis of important medical role of Puritan clerics and economic significance of their medical practices. [JPG]

39.811 Ola Elizabeth Winslow. *A destroying angel: the conquest of smallpox in colonial Boston.* Boston: Houghton-Mifflin, 1974. ISBN 0-395-18453-3. ▸ Traces history of smallpox devastations in Boston through successful adoption of vaccination campaign at end of eighteenth century. [JPG]

SEE ALSO
41.469 Brooke Hindle. *The pursuit of science in revolutionary America, 1735–1789.*

Material Culture

39.812 Douglas V. Armstrong. *The old village and the great house: an archaeological and historical examination of Drax Hall plantation, St. Ann's Bay, Jamaica.* Urbana: University of Illinois Press, 1990. ISBN 0-252-01617-3. ▸ Sophisticated archaeological and historical examination of Drax Hall sugar plantation in Jamaica. [JPG]

39.813 Rosamund R. Beirne and John H. Scarff. *William Buckland, 1734–1774: architect of Virginia and Maryland.* Baltimore: Maryland Historical Society, 1958. (Maryland Historical Society, Studies in Maryland history, 4.) ▸ Study of life and architecture of most prominent colonial Chesapeake builder. [JPG]

39.814 Peter Benes. *The masks of orthodoxy: folk gravestone carving in Plymouth County, Massachusetts, 1689–1805.* Amherst: University of Massachusetts Press, 1977. ISBN 0-87023-237-1. ▸ Detailed local study of gravestone art of distinctive county in colonial Massachusetts. [JPG]

39.815 Carl Bridenbaugh. *The colonial craftsman.* 1950 ed. Chicago: University of Chicago Press, 1961. ▸ Detailed survey of handicraft and artisanal productions in colonial urban centers. [JPG]

39.816 Carl Bridenbaugh. *Peter Harrison: first American architect.* Chapel Hill: University of North Carolina Press, 1949. ▸ Biographical study thoroughly analyzing all of Harrison's architectural work. [JPG]

39.817 Diana Williams Combs. *Early gravestone art in Georgia and South Carolina.* Athens: University of Georgia Press, 1986. ISBN 0-8203-0788-2. ▸ Looks at gravestones of eighteenth-century South Carolina and Georgia in artistic and social context. [JPG]

39.818 Abbott Lowell Cummings. *The framed houses of Massachusetts Bay, 1625–1725.* Cambridge, Mass.: Belknap, 1979. ISBN 0-674-31680-0. ▸ Superb, detailed study of transfer of English timber houses and building practices to early Massachusetts. [JPG]

39.819 James Deetz. *In small things forgotten: the archaeology of early American life.* Garden City, N.Y.: Anchor, 1977. ISBN 0-385-08031-X. ▸ Short, general study suggestively using archaeological findings to trace material lives of whites and African Americans in colonial America. [JPG]

39.820 Marian Card Donnelly. *The New England meeting houses of the seventeenth century.* Middletown, Conn.: Wesleyan University Press, 1968. ▸ Detailed account of architecture of New England churches during seventeenth century. [JPG]

39.821 Antoinette F. Downing and Vincent J. Scully, Jr. *The architectural heritage of Newport, Rhode Island, 1640–1915.* 1967 2d rev. ed. New York: American Legacy; distributed by Crown, 1982. ISBN 0-517-09719-2. ▸ Survey of rich colonial architecture of Newport. [JPG]

39.822 Martha Gandy Fales. *Joseph Richardson and family, Philadelphia silversmiths.* Middletown, Conn.: Wesleyan University Press for Historical Society of Pennsylvania, 1974. ISBN 0-8195-4076-5. ▸ Exhaustive case study of business and products of three generations of family of Philadelphia silversmiths who started their business in second quarter of eighteenth century. [JPG]

39.823 Henry Chandlee Forman. *The architecture of the Old South: the medieval style, 1585–1850.* 1948 ed. New York: Russell & Russell, 1967. ▸ Study emphasizing persistence of medieval construction modes and architectural styles in southern building during colonial and early national eras. [JPG]

39.824 Anthony Garvan. *Architecture and town planning in colonial Connecticut.* New Haven: Yale University Press, 1951. ▸ Study of village design and buildings in colonial Connecticut. Emphasizes variety of architectural styles. [JPG]

39.825 Henry Glassie. *Folk housing in middle Virginia: a structural analysis of historic artifacts.* Knoxville: University of Tennessee Press, 1975. ISBN 0-87049-173-3. ▸ Imaginative look at vernacular housing as index to cultural aspirations of middle-level people who built them. [JPG]

39.826 Bernard L. Herman. *Architecture and rural life in central Delaware, 1700–1900.* Knoxville: University of Tennessee Press, 1987. ISBN 0-87049-519-4. ▸ Survey of rural Delaware architecture covering eighteenth and nineteenth centuries. [JPG]

39.827 Graham Hood. *The governor's palace in Williamsburg: a cultural study.* Williamsburg, Va.: Colonial Williamsburg Foundation; distributed by University of North Carolina Press, 1991. ISBN 0-87935-082-2. ▸ Commendable examination of cultural intent and social functions of one of colonial Virginia's most important public buildings. [JPG]

39.828 William N. Hosley, Jr. *Great river: art and society of the Connecticut Valley, 1635–1820.* Hartford, Conn.: Wadsworth Atheneum, 1985. ISBN 0-918333-03-2. ▸ Catalog of exhibition at Wadsworth Atheneum focusing on cultural dimensions of 370 material objects from Connecticut River region. [JPG]

39.829 Ivor Noël Hume. *Martin's Hundred.* New York: Knopf, 1982. ISBN 0-394-50728-2. ▸ Interpretation of manifold findings of archaeological excavations of early Virginia settlement. [JPG]

39.830 William M. Kelso. *Kingsmill plantations, 1619–1800: archaeology of country life in colonial Virginia.* Orlando, Fla.: Academic Press, 1984. ISBN 0-12-403480-2. ▸ Detailed study of archaeology of daily life on lower James River plantation during colonial era. [JPG]

39.831 Fiske Kimball. *Domestic architecture of the American colonies and of the early republic.* 1922 ed. New York: Dover, 1966. ▸ Dated survey, remains useful because of its comprehensiveness. [JPG]

39.832 John T. Kirk. *American chairs: Queen Anne and Chippendale.* New York: Knopf, 1972. ISBN 0-394-47328-0. ▸ Exploration of styles and cultural origins of 150 eighteenth-century American chairs. [JPG]

39.833 Ann Leighton. *American gardens in the eighteenth century: "for use or for delight."* 1976 ed. Amherst: University of Massachusetts Press, 1986. ISBN 0-87023-531-1 (pbk). ▸ Survey of American gardening practices and plants cultivated in them during eighteenth century. [JPG]

39.834   Ann Leighton. *Early American gardens: "for meate or medicine."* 1970 ed. Amherst: University of Massachusetts Press, 1986. ISBN 0-87023-530-3 (pbk). ▸ Study of function and character of seventeenth-century English American gardens. [JPG]

39.835   Allan I. Ludwig. *Graven images: New England stonecarving and its symbols, 1650–1815.* 1966 ed. Middletown, Conn.: Wesleyan University Press, 1975. ISBN 0-8195-6040-5. ▸ Examination of religious symbolism of gravestone iconography in early New England. [JPG]

39.836   Robert P. Maccubin and Peter Martin, eds. *British and American gardens in the eighteenth century: eighteen illustrated essays on garden history.* Williamsburg, Va.: Colonial Williamsburg Foundation, 1984. ISBN 0-87935-105-5. ▸ Valuable collection of articles on seventeenth- and eighteenth-century Anglo-American gardening and landscape design. [JPG]

39.837   Brooks McNamara. *The American playhouse in the eighteenth century.* Cambridge, Mass.: Harvard University Press, 1969. ▸ Architectural history of more than seventy playhouses built in colonial and early national America. [JPG]

39.838   Hugh Morrison. *Early American architecture: from the first colonial settlements to the national period.* 1952 ed. New York: Dover, 1987. ISBN 0-486-25492-5 (pbk). ▸ Comprehensive one-volume treatment of early American buildings. [JPG]

39.839   James A. Mulholland. *A history of metals in colonial America.* University: University of Alabama Press, 1981. ISBN 0-8173-0052-X (cl), 0-8173-0053-8 (pbk). ▸ General study by metallurgist of metal production, especially copper and iron, and metalworking in colonial British America. [JPG]

39.840   William J. Murtaugh. *Moravian architecture and town planning: Bethlehem, Pennsylvania, and other eighteenth-century American settlements.* Chapel Hill: University of North Carolina Press, 1967. ▸ Useful study of use of German architectural traditions in buildings of Bethlehem, Pennsylvania, and Salem, North Carolina. [JPG]

39.841   William H. Pierson, Jr. *American buildings and their architects.* Vol. 1: *The colonial and neoclassical styles.* 1970 ed. New York: Oxford University Press, 1986. ISBN 0-19-504216-6 (v. 1, pbk). ▸ Detailed architectural analysis and evaluation of selected colonial American buildings. [JPG]

39.842   Daniel D. Reiff. *Small Georgian houses in England and Virginia: origins and development through the 1750s.* Newark: University of Delaware Press, 1986. ISBN 0-87413-254-1. ▸ Excellent comparative study of styles and building practices in English and Virginia Georgian houses. [JPG]

39.843   Dell Upton. *Holy things and profane: Anglican parish churches in colonial Virginia.* Cambridge, Mass.: MIT Press, 1986. ISBN 0-262-21008-8. ▸ Superb study of Virginia parish church architecture as expression not only of religious but also of social and political aspirations and values of people responsible for building them. [JPG]

39.844   Thomas Tileston Waterman. *The dwellings of colonial America.* Chapel Hill: University of North Carolina Press, 1950. ▸ General study of most expensive houses built in colonial America. [JPG]

39.845   Thomas Tileston Waterman. *The mansions of Virginia, 1706–1776.* 1945 ed. Chapel Hill: University of North Carolina Press, 1946. ▸ Comprehensive survey of genteel domestic architecture. [JPG]

39.846   David H. Watters. *"With bodilie eyes": eschatological themes in Puritan literature and gravestone art.* Ann Arbor: University Microfilms International, 1981. ISBN 0-8357-1249-4.

▸ Analysis of evolution of New England gravestone iconography to early nineteenth century. [JPG]

39.847   Marcus Whiffen. *The eighteenth-century houses of Williamsburg: a study of architecture and building in the colonial capital of Virginia.* 2d rev. ed. Williamsburg, Va.: Colonial Williamsburg Foundation; distributed by University Press of Virginia, 1987. ISBN 0-87935-123-3. ▸ Close study of building practices in surviving houses. [JPG]

39.848   Marcus Whiffen. *The public buildings of Williamsburg, colonial capital of Virginia: an architectural history.* Williamsburg, Va.: Colonial Williamsburg, 1958. ▸ Outstanding analysis of architectural history of Williamsburg's public buildings. [JPG]

39.849   Walter Muir Whitehill, ed. *Boston furniture of the eighteenth century: a conference held by the Colonial Society of Massachusetts, 11 and 12 May 1972.* Boston: Colonial Society of Massachusetts, distributed by University Press of Virginia, 1974. (Publications of the Colonial Society of Massachusetts, 48.) ▸ Eight essays on Boston furniture industry, including its makers and styles. [JPG]

SEE ALSO
   40.587 Robert Blair St. George, ed. *Material life in America, 1600–1860.*

Books, Journalism, and Printing

39.850   Charles E. Clark. *The public prints: the newspaper in Anglo-American culture, 1665–1740.* New York: Oxford University Press, 1994. ▸ Comprehensive study of role of newspapers in colonial culture to 1740. [JPG]

39.851   Hennig Cohen. *The South Carolina Gazette, 1732–1775.* Columbia: University of South Carolina Press, 1953. ▸ Best detailed analysis of contents of specific colonial newspaper. [JPG]

39.852   Richard Beale Davis. *A colonial southern bookshelf: reading in the eighteenth century.* Athens: University of Georgia Press, 1979. (Mercer University Lamar memorial lectures, 21.) ISBN 0-8203-0450-6. ▸ Comprehensive survey of book holdings in colonial southern libraries. [JPG]

39.853   William L. Joyce et al., eds. *Printing and society in early America.* Worcester, Mass.: American Antiquarian Society, 1983. ISBN 0-912296-55-0. ▸ Ten essays on aspects of book trade, printing, and literacy. [JPG]

39.854   Charles T. Laugher. *Thomas Bray's grand design: libraries of the Church of England in America, 1695–1785.* Chicago: American Library Association, 1973. ISBN 0-8389-0151-4. ▸ Brief look at Anglican movement to establish libraries throughout British North America and what happened to them. [JPG]

39.855   Douglas C. McMurtrie. *A history of printing in the United States: the story of the introduction of the press and of its history and influence during the pioneer period in each state in the Union.* Vol. 2: *Middle and South Atlantic states.* 1936 ed. New York: Franklin, 1969. ▸ Classic comprehensive history of American printing, devoting much space to colonial era. [JPG]

39.856   Jeffrey A. Smith. *Printers and press freedom: the ideology of early American journalism.* New York: Oxford University Press, 1988. ISBN 0-19-505144-0. ▸ Examination of ideology and practice of eighteenth-century American journalism. Stresses limited effects of laws against seditious libel and aggressiveness of colonial publishers in establishment of practical tradition of freedom of press. Also available in photocopy from Ann Arbor: University Microfilms International, 1989. [JPG]

39.857   Isaiah Thomas. *The history of printing in America, with a* *biography of printers and an account of newspapers.* 1874 2d ed. 2 vols. Marcus A. McCorison, ed. New York: Weathervane; distributed by Crown, 1970. ISBN 0-517-17202-X. ▸ First and still very valuable history of early American printing by founder of American Antiquarian Society. [JPG]

39.858 Edwin Wolf II. *The library of James Logan of Philadelphia, 1674–1751.* Philadelphia: Library Company of Philadel-

phia, 1974. ISBN 0-914076-51-5. ▸ Analytic, bibliographical study of one of largest personal libraries accumulated in colonial British America. [JPG]

39.859 Lawrence C. Wroth. *The colonial printer.* 1938 2d ed. Charlottesville, Va.: Dominion, 1964. ▸ Remains most authoritative account of work and craft of colonial newspaper, magazine, and book publishers. [JPG]

L E W I S   P E R R Y

United States, General

When interpreting American history in its entirety, the question of whether America has some essential meaning almost invariably arises. For a century and a half, a succession of patriotic writers sought to trace the essential strengths of the American character to the landing of the pilgrims at Plymouth Rock. For almost as long, critics of the gloomy, repressive aspects of American society traced the roots of these aspects to America's Puritanical origins. In recent times, writers whose motives are neither patriotic exaltation nor critical debunking have continued to pursue the origins of American traits in seventeenth-century New England. Not only was the United States created through great transoceanic migrations, but the nation was also founded at the outset of the age of democratic revolutions. It was easy to place it in the vanguard of the liberation of humankind from past enthrallment. At the very least, it was possible to see America's history as a great test of the capacity of democratic institutions to elevate the human mind.

The books and articles listed below are the work of scholars who report conclusions based on their own research or, especially if their work covers several centuries, synthesize information drawn from the research of others. Some deny the relevance of Puritan or colonial origins to subsequent historical developments; not all of them take democracy as their theme. But in turning scholarly methods to the task of interpreting all of American history, they cannot escape, even if they wish to, the challenge of identifying the fundamental patterns of American politics, society, and character. Even when they critique popular misconceptions or show that the past was more complex than the public commonly recognizes, they are still drawn to longstanding debates over the meaning of America.

Although great nineteenth-century writers like George Bancroft and Henry Adams launched such debates, modern scholarship refers more directly to works by F. J. Turner, C. A. Beard, M. R. Beard, V. L. Parrington, and their colleagues and students, known collectively as the "progressive" historians, who enlivened historical discussion in the first half of this century. Turner's essay "The Significance of the Frontier in American History" (1893), is probably the most influential work ever written about the American past. It epitomized the wish, shared by many progressives, of repudiating scholarship that treated American history as an outgrowth of European (or Teutonic) roots. At the Atlantic shore, at the Cumberland Gap, at the Great Plains, the frontier recurrently stripped away the accumulated habits of the Old World and sent forth the American in ever-renewed distinctiveness. The Turnerian image of a shifting frontier promoting individualism and community reached many classrooms through texts like F. Merk's *History of the Westward Movement* (40.124) and R. A. Billington and M. Ridge's *Westward Expansion* (40.120). The influence of the frontier on American society and character remains a key topic of historical investigation and debate.

The progressive historians were committed not only to rejecting the old idea of European genesis of American institutions, but also to promoting a view of American development in which the clash of sections and economic interests received greater attention. Sometimes they analyzed key events, as in Beard's work on the Constitution; but, in general, the progressives' commitments led them to favor strong works on the entire span of American history. Their interpretive audacity and tenacity, in fact, ensured that when subsequent historians generalized about the American past, they did so in terms laid down by the progressives. This has been notably true of Turner's frontier thesis, which generations of scholars have sought to confirm or disprove, to modify or reassert, but seldom to ignore. It is also true of works such as the Beards' exciting *The Rise of American Civilization* (40.15), which was used as a text in high schools and colleges to the 1960s. In this view, more fundamental conflicts between economic groups could be found beneath the superficial contests of politics; even the Civil War was only "by the accidents of climate, soil, and geography . . . a sectional struggle." If the "planting interest" had been scattered throughout the union, conflict with those who promoted a new industrial order would still have been unavoidable. Later historians, such as Arthur Schlesinger, Jr., modified and gave more subtle versions of American history as a succession of conflicts involving business, finance, labor, and agriculture. The endurance of the progressive interpretation remains impressive.

Still another example of progressives setting the terms for subsequent discourse is V. L. Parrington's *Main Currents of American Thought* (1927), which arrayed two centuries of American writers in a dialogue: on the one hand, conservatives and autocrats resisted democratic progress, while on the other hand, more laudable figures sought to advance reform and uplift the populace and promote individualism. Parrington's understanding of economic and political conflict was never as acute as the Beards', but his portraits of generations of intellectuals in conflict made *Main Currents* one of the most widely read works on the history of the United States for several generations. The author of a recent survey of intellectual history, P. Carter, recalls that he found a copy of Parrington's opus "lying on a table in a tin quonset-hut library on a muddy Navy base in Gulfport, Mississippi; opened it"; and was soon "hooked" (40.485, p. 268). Just as Merk and Billington extended Turner's influence and Schlesinger was responsible for a modern interpretation that improved on the Beards', something of Parrington's progressive temperament carried through in M. E. Curti's *The Growth of American Thought* (40.487), first published in 1943 and still widely used by students and teachers.

Scholarly reaction rose up against the progressives in the decade or so after World War II—a reaction so intense that a student of changing historical interpretations characterizes the works of that era as counterprogressivism (G. Wise, *American Historical Explanations* [40.32]). One element in this reaction was an emphasis on myths and symbols that have persisted throughout American history; another was a renewed appreciation of religious conviction, ethnic loyalty, and cultural factors in the American experience. The counterprogressives frequently stressed the absence of deep-seated conflict in the American past. In reversing many of the progressives' interpretations, however, they were no less committed to writing book-length interpretive essays on enduring patterns in the American experience. Louis Hartz's *The Liberal Tradition in America* (40.88), D. J. Boorstin's *The Genius of American Politics* (40.722), and R. Hofstadter's *The American Political Tradition* (40.89) are good examples of influential works that convinced many readers that the differences between American parties have never been extreme. As C. L. Rossiter explained in *The American Quest* (1971), "most Americans . . . were dedicated in common to the beauties of personal liberty, the security of constitutionalism, the rightness of democracy, the wrongness of class distinctions, the virtue of private property, the moral necessity of hard work, the certainty of progress, and above all the uniqueness, superiority, and high destiny of the United States of America."

By the 1960s such "consensus school" works were themselves under attack by scholars who stressed, once again, the importance of persistent conflict in history. Controversy often focused on long-term trends, no less in W. A. Williams's *The Contours of American History* (40.733) or in various works on the underclasses and underside of American history than in previous works like those of Hartz and Boorstin. Nevertheless, perhaps as a consequence of the waves of reexamination and reappraisal that challenged progressivism and its successors and competitors, more and more historians came to prefer projects dealing with carefully defined topics. And as new methods, inspired by social science, new sources, and new subjects attracted a rising generation of scholars, historical scholarship on the United States came to focus ever more intensely on narrowly drawn problems pursued with relentless rigor in scholarly subcommunities whose work seemed to resist synthesis. Some scholars expressed doubt about any kind of overarching interpretation. Textbooks like the Beards', written in a unified voice, gave way to multiauthored works to which specialists contributed, in different voices, chapters on those fragments of the past they had mastered. To many historians of the United States, truth resided in the details of relatively brief episodes; anything more was suspect.

Any list of "general" works is bound to be affected by a retreat from faith in the possibility of general knowledge. Readers of the lists below may find a dearth of recent works on some subjects. Yet it may also be noted that prominent historians have repeatedly and consistently deplored excessive specialization and fragmentation. (See, for example, H. G. Gutman's widely quoted "The Missing Synthesis: Whatever Happened to History?" in *The Nation* [21 November 1981].) Some called for a return to narrative as an escape from disconnected, problem-oriented historiography. Others, like Gutman, hoped that an integration of work in the "new" histories of recent decades with some enduring themes in the American past might lead to worthy successors to the *Rise of American Civilization*. In such a spirit, E. Foner in *The New American History* (40.22) has suggested that "the fragmentation of historical study may have been overstated. . . . American history at its best remains . . . an ongoing mode of collective self-discovery about the nature of our society."

In quest of a new synthesis, scholars in recent decades have looked in several directions. Some have turned to the concept of modernization and have sought to trace the transition from traditional attitudes and behavior to those that are more typical of industrialized and even postindustrial societies. Others have stressed "organizational" themes in both public and private sectors as large institutions extended their reach over a national society. There is rising interest in the consequences for the environment of past behavior and traditional outlooks. Interest in some older themes—such as sectional conflict, the persistence of ethnocultural factors in political life, and the shaping of an "exceptional" society and culture—has never died out, as the listings below will show.

At the present time, however, the most pressing challenge faced by those who write about United States history as a whole may be to unify what we have learned about once neglected groups into a coherent account of the American past. This is a challenge created by the recent excellent scholarship on women, African Americans, American Indians, Hispanics and Latinos, immigrants, workers, farmers, gays and lesbians, and many others. The challenge also derives from the conflicts in a society that expects its history to be multicultural, to reflect the astonishing diversity of American life and yet also to take the form of a coherent narrative. Yet the point of origin for such a narrative now seems contested. Ramón Gutíerrez, whose *When Jesus Came, the Corn Mothers Went Away: Marriage, Sexuality, and Power in New Mexico, 1500–1846* (37.578) is such an important exemplar of recent scholarship that contributors proposed it for at least four different parts of this section and for two other sections, has been quoted as saying, "I wanted to show American historians that there was a vibrant center of social, cultural, and economic activity in the Rio Grande valley. Most of the time, Plymouth is where it all starts off" (*Chronicle of Higher Education*, 2 December 1992).

It is no longer possible to speak of a single origin or typical experience for all groups of Americans, and it may be that, for some time to come, impressive general works on American history will be unable to broaden their focus beyond the separate experiences of women, African Americans, and other groups. Success will not come easily. Patricia Nelson Limerick (40.27, p.1023) has reflected on disappointment with her own efforts to link these separate histories: "Resolving to write a version of American history that incorporates the perspectives and experiences of various cultures and classes ranks as one of the world's easiest intellectual acts. Acting on the resolution, however, ranks among the toughest."

It is a great challenge to merge disparate histories into some account of the public sphere where they come together. Thomas Bender (40.16, p. 132) has argued: "The present task is to begin establishing the relationship over time of the interclass, multiethnic, and multicultural center, what I call public culture, and the smaller, more homogeneous . . . groups of the periphery. . . . A focus on public culture and its changing connections with cultures smaller than the whole offers an image of society capacious enough to sustain a synthetic narrative." Some might dissent from the specific terms that Bender chooses, and there remain some historians who dislike all sweeping generalization and attempts at synthesis. It seems likely, nevertheless, that historians will be engaged for some time to come in trying to understand the interaction between the many separate histories of Americans and the common past of the United States.

In using the lists in this section, please note that some key reference works appear at the outset, but others are listed in the appropriate subsections below. Thus *Notable American Women* appears with other scholarship in women's history, the *Encyclopedia of American Political History* under politics, and the *Harvard Encyclopedia of American Ethnic Groups* under ethnicity.

Readers should be aware that nearly all publishers have at least one general textbook, and sometimes several, most of them multiauthored and revised and updated every four or five years. Some of these books are derivative and pedestrian, but some of the best thinking and writing about the American past are presented in this form. The difficulties of constructing a multicultural synthesis are familiar to textbook writers, who sometimes face them with remarkable creativity. Useful textbooks on special topics, such as the South, the West, cities, or women, appear in the subsections devoted to those topics. Some of these works, like *We Who Built America* (40.396), retell American history from a new perspective and revitalize the search for a democratic meaning in the nation's past.

Entries are arranged under the following headings:

Reference Works

General Studies and Textbooks

Political History
National Government
Parties and Party Politics
The Constitution and the Law
Political Ideologies
Persistent Issues
State Government and Politics

Sectional and Regional History
Geography and the Environment
The Frontier
Sections and Regions
The South
The Northeast
The Midwest
The Great Plains and Borderlands
The West

Economic History
Agriculture
Finance, Banking, and Commerce
Patterns, Trends, and Cycles
Manufacturing
Labor

Social History
Rural and Local Society
Urban history
Class
Family, Generations, and Child Rearing

Race, Ethnicity, and Minorities
Overviews
African Americans
Colonized Minorities
Immigrant Minorities
Race and Ethnicity
Racism, Nativism, and Prejudice

Gender and Sexuality
Women
Men
Homosexuality
Sexuality
Gender

Intellectual Life and Culture
Intellectual Life
Religion and Theology
Literature
Fine Arts
Social Sciences
Education
Popular Culture
Material Culture
Folklore

Foreign Relations
Overviews
Public Officials and Policy Making
Relations With Other Regions and Nations
Foreign Trade
War and Peace
Goals and Sources

Psyche and Character
National Character
Psychohistory

Exceptionalism
Proponents
Critiques of Exceptionalism
Comparative Studies

[Contributors: ARLC = Andrew R. L. Cayton, BBY = Bernard B. Yamron, CAM = Clyde A. Milner, II, CJG = Carl J. Guarneri, DLC = David L. Carlton, DMS = Darren M. Staloff, DRG = Donna R. Gabaccia, DSS = Daniel Scott Smith, EH-D = Evelyn Hu-Dehart, FEH = Frederick E. Hoxie, GJK = Gary J. Kornblith, HIK = Howard I. Kushner, HM = Harvey Markowitz, JB = Jon Butler, JGC = Jonathan G. Cedarbaum, JSH = John S. Hill, JTL = John T. Landry, KWK = Kenneth W. Keller, LCP = Lewis Perry, LGB = Lucy G. Barber, MW = Margaret Washington, NF = Nora Faires, NMK = Nicholas M. Kliment, PEM = Pamela E. Mack, PFF = Phyllis F. Field, PLH = Peter L. Hahn, RWS = Robert W. Smith, Jr., SGM = Sally G. McMillen, TAM = Teresa A. Murphy, TDH = Thomas D. Hamm, VBB = Victoria Bissell Brown, WFD = William F. Deverell, WMD = William M. Doyle, WWR = William W. Register, Jr.]

REFERENCE WORKS

40.1 Eric H. Boehm et al., eds. *America: history and life.* 30 vols. to date. Santa Barbara, Calif.: ABC-Clio, 1972–. ISSN 0002-7065. ▸ Ongoing series providing invaluable annual bibliographies of annotated articles, books, book reviews, and dissertations. Available at many libraries on CD-ROM disc. Excellent place to start. [LCP]

40.2 Mary Kupiec Cayton, Elliott J. Gorn, and Peter W. Williams, eds. *Encyclopedia of American social history.* 3 vols. New York: Scribner's, 1992. ISBN 0-684-19246-2 (set). ▸ Extended essays providing broad coverage based on current research. Examines chronological periods, approaches and methods, ethnicity, religion, regions, cities, countryside, class, gender, social movements, and popular culture. [LCP]

40.3 Eric Foner and John Arthur Garraty, eds. *The reader's companion to American history.* Boston: Houghton-Mifflin, 1991. ISBN 0-395-51372-3. ▸ Brief, readable essays presenting up-to-date interpretations on wide range of topics: biographies, court cases, movements, events, and issues such as abortion. Alphabetically organized, useful maps and tables. [LCP]

40.4 Frank B. Freidel. *Harvard guide to American history.* Rev. ed. 2 vols. Cambridge, Mass.: Belknap, 1974. ISBN 0-674-37560-2 (cl), 0-674-37555-6 (pbk). ▸ One of most useful aids to historical inquiry ever published. Combines chapters of useful advice with well-organized bibliographies. Now out-of-date; supplement with *America: History and Life* (40.1). [LCP]

40.5 Wilbur E. Garrett, ed. *Historical atlas of the United States.* Centennial ed. Washington, D.C.: National Geographic Society, 1988. ISBN 0-87044-747-5. ▸ Lavish, oversized set of maps, accompanied by timelines and much compressed information for each era. Detail sometimes overwhelming but historical processes colorfully presented and illustrated. [LCP]

40.6 Kenneth T. Jackson, ed. *Atlas of American history.* 2d rev. ed. New York: Scribner's, 1984. ISBN 0-684-18411-7. ▸ Chronological series of black-and-white maps depicting everything from explorations and wars to missile complexes and hazardous waste sites. May surprise some readers how much information these convey. [LCP]

40.7 Allen Johnson et al. *Dictionary of American biography.* 29 vols. New York: Scribner's, 1928–90. ISBN 0-684-13199-4 (suppl. 3), 0-684-14126-4 (suppl. 4), 0-684-15054-9 (suppl. 5), 0-684-16226-1 (suppl. 6), 0-684-16794-8 (suppl. 7), 0-684-18618-7 (suppl. 8), 0-684-19114-8 (Index). ▸ Long-standard biographical source. Some brilliant, authoritative essays, but uneven and out-of-date, even with eight supplements. New project, headed by John Garraty, now under way. [LCP]

40.8 James R. Masterson, ed. *Writings on American history, 1962–73: a subject bibliography of books and monographs.* 10 vols.

Washington, D.C., and White Plains: American Historical Association and Kraus Reprint, 1985. ISBN 0-527-98268-7 (set). ▸ Lists of books. For more information on articles and other sources, see subsequent annual volumes and preceding ones to 1906. Good description of these bibliographies in Prucha, ed. 40.10. [LCP]

40.9 Charles O. Paullin. *Atlas of the historical geography of the United States.* John K. Wright, ed. Washington, D.C. and New York: Carnegie Institution of Washington and American Geographical Society of New York, 1932. (Carnegie Institution of Washington publications, 401.) ▸ Extensive set of highly informative maps with statistics and interpretive commentary. Covers explorations, climate, transportation, cities and towns, public-land surveys, government grants, voting, ethnicity, religion, and much else. [LCP]

40.10 Francis Paul Prucha, ed. *Handbook for research in American history: a guide to bibliographies and other reference works.* Lincoln: University of Nebraska Press, 1987. ISBN 0-8032-3682-4 (cl), 0-8032-8719-4 (pbk). ▸ Clearly written, well-organized guide containing sensible advice accompanied by adequate information on selected reference works. Addressed to graduate students, but will serve many other readers. Good starting point. [LCP]

40.11 Jack Salzman, ed. *American studies: an annotated bibliography* and *1984–1988* supplement. 3 vols. Cambridge: Cambridge University Press, 1986–90. ISBN 0-521-32555-2 (set), 0-521-36559-7 (suppl.) ▸ Includes only books, but with unusually helpful annotations. Stronger on culture, popular culture, literature, and intellectual life than many other bibliographies. [LCP]

40.12 Donald F. Tingley, ed. *Social history of the United States: a guide to information sources.* Detroit: Gale Research, 1979. (American government and history information guide series, 3.) ISBN 0-8103-1366-9. ▸ Series of hardcover bibliographies on American history and culture. Brief annotation stating authors' contentions and purposes. Must be supplemented by *America: History and Life* (40.1). [LCP]

40.13 United States. Department of Commerce, Bureau of the Census. *Historical statistics of the United States: colonial times to 1970.* 1975 bicentennial ed. 2 vols. White Plains, N.Y.: Kraus Reprint, 1989. ISBN 0-527-91756-7 (set). ▸ Tables presenting data on population, economy, health, climate, philanthropy, and many other topics. Indispensable. [LCP]

GENERAL STUDIES AND TEXTBOOKS

40.14 Bernard Bailyn et al. *The great republic: a history of the American people.* 4th ed. 2 vols. Lexington, Mass.: Heath, 1992. ISBN 0-669-20986-4 (v. 1), 0-669-20987-2 (v. 2). ▸ Brilliant and sophisticated essays brought together in one account of American past. Well illustrated. [LCP]

40.15 Charles A. Beard and Mary Ritter Beard. *The rise of American civilization.* 1929 ed. New York: Macmillan, 1930. ▸ Masterpiece of United States history textbooks, with extraordinarily long-lasting influence. Emphasis on agrarian-industrial conflict, cultural history of coming of machine age. Standard for all historiographical movements. [LCP]

40.16 Thomas Bender. "Wholes and parts: the need for synthesis in American history." *Journal of American history* 73.1 (1986) 120–36. ISSN 0021-8723. ▸ Current "new" history only most recent in series of approaches fragmenting understanding. Absence of successor to the Beards' great synthesis (40.15). Promise held by renewed focus on "public culture." [LCP]

40.17 Kent Blaser. "*The Rise of American Civilization* and the contemporary crisis." *The history teacher* 26.1 (1992) 71–90. ISSN 0018-2745. ▸ Recurrent criticism of historians for failing to match Beards' great textbook (40.15). Importance of interdisciplinary

study of civilization. Beards' success flowed from being intellectually challenging. [LCP]

40.18 Paul S. Boyer et al. *The enduring vision: a history of the American people.* 2d ed. Lexington, Mass.: Heath, 1993. ISBN 0-669-28114-X. ▸ Excellent multiauthored textbook, making thoughtful effort to integrate findings of new social history in political narrative. [LCP]

40.19 Dorothy Sue Cobble and Alice Kessler-Harris. "The new labor history in American history textbooks." *Journal of American history* 79.4 (1993) 1534–45. ISSN 0021-8723. ▸ Careful analysis of seven widely used college textbooks to see whether findings of new scholarship are incorporated. Concludes issues of social class and occupational transformation too often overlooked. [LCP]

40.20 James West Davidson et al. *Nation of nations: a narrative history of the American republic.* New York: McGraw-Hill, 1990. ISBN 0-07-557213-3. ▸ One of many good multiauthored textbooks. Unusually thorough and detailed, with extensive appendixes and maps. Good place to look up facts of political history, with strong multicultural emphasis. [LCP]

40.21 Carl N. Degler. *Out of our past: the forces that shaped modern America.* 3d ed. New York: Harper & Row, 1984. ISBN 0-06-131985-6 (pbk). ▸ Presentist perspective on uses of the past for understanding thought and society today. Well-written, thoughtful introduction. [LCP]

40.22 Eric Foner, ed. *The new American history.* Philadelphia: Temple University Press for American Historical Association, 1990. ISBN 0-87722-698-9 (cl), 0-87722-699-7 (pbk). ▸ Thoughtful essays on achievements of new historiographical movements attacking earlier consensus approach. Examines how research on women, minorities, and working classes altered historical knowledge. Suggests new scholarly agenda. [LCP]

40.23 Thomas R. Frazier, ed. *The underside of American history.* 5th ed. 2 vols. San Diego: Harcourt Brace Jovanovich, 1987. ISBN 0-15-592852-X (v. 1, pbk), 0-15-592853-8 (v. 2, pbk). ▸ Essays, many excerpted from well-known works, on oppression, conflict, and protest. Artifact of New Left historical interests shaped by 1960s. May seem unsubtle in contrast with more recent scholarship. [LCP]

40.24 James A. Henretta et al. *America's history.* 2 vols. Chicago: Dorsey, 1987. ISBN 0-256-03545-8 (v. 1, pbk), 0-256-03547-4 (v. 2, pbk). ▸ Widely used college textbook that makes sustained effort to integrate findings of new social history into conventional political narrative. Stronger presentation of national developments than in multicultural textbooks. [LCP]

40.25 Richard Hofstadter. *The progressive historians: Turner, Beard, Parrington.* 1968 ed. Chicago: University of Chicago Press, 1979. ISBN 0-226-34818-0. ▸ Reflections on three influential historians by leading scholar in generation that challenged their work. Interpretations of frontier, Constitution, and perennial issues in United States history. Elegantly written. [LCP]

40.26 Stanley I. Kutler and Stanley N. Katz, eds. *The promise of American history: progress and prospects.* Baltimore: Johns Hopkins University Press, 1982. ISBN 0-8018-3032-X (cl), 0-8018-3031-1 (pbk). ▸ Valuable historiographical essays on unusually diverse subjects. Also printed as volume 10.4 of *Reviews in American History.* Some overlap with authors in Foner, ed. 40.22. [LCP]

40.27 Patricia Nelson Limerick. "Disorientation and reorientation: the American landscape discovered from the West." *Journal of American history* 79.3 (1992) 1021–49. ISSN 0021-8723. ▸ Reflections on prevailing Eurocentric perspectives and difficulty of multicultural narration in United States history. How West appeared to those who discovered it from East, especially Chinese and Japanese immigrants. See Turner 40.125. [LCP]

40.28 Leon F. Litwack and Winthrop D. Jordan. *The United States.* Vol. 1: *Conquering a continent.* Vol. 2: *Becoming a world power.* 7th ed. Englewood Cliffs, N.J.: Prentice-Hall, 1991. ISBN 0-13-933514-5 (v. 1), 0-13-933490-4 (v. 2). ▸ Based on earlier distinguished textbook by Richard Hofstadter, William Miller, and Daniel Aaron. Strong emphasis on social themes, labor and the working classes, and race. Unusually engaged and compelling. [LCP]

40.29 Marvin Meyers, John G. Cawelti and Alexander Kern, eds. *Sources of the American republic: a documentary history of politics, society, and thought.* Rev. ed. 2 vols. Glenview, Ill.: Scott-Foresman, 1967. ▸ One of many collections of source materials illustrating and interpreting American past. Unusually comprehensive with elegant and informative introductions to each document. [LCP]

40.30 Mary Beth Norton et al. *A people and a nation: a history of the United States.* 3d ed. 2 vols. Boston: Houghton-Mifflin, 1990. ISBN 0-395-43308-8 (v. 1), 0-395-43309-6 (v. 2). ▸ One of many good multiauthored textbooks, with helpful illustrations and maps. Emphasis on social history and private life, with material often absent from older textbooks. Readable but not condescending. Frequently revised. [LCP]

40.31 George Brown Tindall and David E. Shi. *America: a narrative history.* 3d ed. 2 vols. New York: Norton, 1992. ISBN 0-393-96149-4 (v. 1, pbk), 0-393-96151-6 (v. 2, pbk). ▸ Highly readable textbook with considerable attention to biography. Compact, with fewer illustrations than some others. Previous editions authored only by Tindall. [LCP]

40.32 Gene Wise. *American historical explanations: a strategy for grounded inquiry.* 2d ed. Minneapolis: University of Minnesota Press, 1980. ISBN 0-8166-0954-3 (cl), 0-8166-0957-8 (pbk). ▸ Incisive, though idiosyncratic, study of changing schools of historical interpretation in twentieth century. Strongest on Perry Miller, consensus school, and American studies movement. [LCP]

POLITICAL HISTORY

National Government

40.33 Henry J. Abraham. *Justices and presidents: a political history of appointments to the Supreme Court.* 3d ed. New York: Oxford University Press, 1992. ISBN 0-19-506557-3. ▸ Examination of presidents' reasons for judicial appointments and evaluation of subsequent performance of judges on bench. More descriptive than analytic. [PFF]

40.34 Richard A. Baker. *The Senate of the United States: a bicentennial history.* Malabar, Fla.: Krieger, 1988. ISBN 0-89874-865-X (cl), 0-89874-865-8 (pbk). ▸ Brief institutional history supplemented with primary source material. [PFF]

40.35 Wilfred E. Binkley. *The man in the White House: his powers and duties.* 1958 ed. Westport, Conn.: Greenwood, 1978. ISBN 0-313-20536-1. ▸ Classic study of role of president within political system. Develops nature of presidency through use of historical examples emphasizing most important presidents. [PFF]

40.36 William R. Brock. *The evolution of American democracy.* New York: Dial, 1970. ▸ Democracy in America constantly redefined by challenge of socioeconomic and cultural changes. Continuity in democracy despite these changes is distinctive American characteristic. Accessible interpretation. [PFF]

40.37 Ralph Clark Chandler, ed. *A centennial history of the American administrative state.* New York: Macmillan, 1987. ISBN 0-02-905301-3 (cl), 0-02-320660-8 (pbk). ▸ Overview of current scholarship on administrative bureaucracy. Historically informed essays on how national government has been organized over time. [PFF]

40.38 Edward Samuel Corwin. *The president, office and powers, 1787–1984: history and analysis of practice and opinion.* 5th rev. ed. New York: New York University Press, 1984. ISBN 0-8147-1390-4 (cl), 0-8147-1391-2 (pbk). ▸ Classic view of president's office and powers as they developed through constitutional and political influences. Comprehensive exposition of constitutional approach. [PFF]

40.39 Thomas E. Cronin, ed. *Inventing the American presidency.* Lawrence: University Press of Kansas, 1989. ISBN 0-7006-0405-7 (cl), 0-7006-0406-5 (pbk). ▸ Informative essays on historical development of presidential office and its powers. Early precedents seen as shaping office. [PFF]

40.40 William A. Degregorio. *The complete book of U.S. presidents.* 3d ed. New York: Barricade, 1991. ISBN 0-942637-37-2 (cl), 0-942637-38-0 (pbk). ▸ Comparable, detailed biographical information on all presidents and their administrations. Includes scholarly rankings of presidents. [PFF]

40.41 George B. Galloway. *History of the House of Representatives.* 2d rev. ed. Sidney Wise, Revisions. New York: Crowell, 1976. ISBN 0-690-01101-6. ▸ Historical development of House institutions and House's role within national government. Focuses on consequences rather than causes of changes. [PFF]

40.42 Henry F. Graff, ed. *The presidents: a reference history.* New York: Scribner's, 1984. ISBN 0-684-17607-6. ▸ Lengthy original essays evaluating accomplishments and impacts of presidential administrations through Jimmy Carter. Overview of current scholarship. [PFF]

40.43 Jack P. Greene, ed. *Encyclopedia of American political history.* 3 vols. New York: Scribner's, 1984. ISBN 0-684-17003-5 (set). ▸ Ninety lengthy essays on political issues, themes, institutions, processes, and developments. Comprehensive overview of current scholarly trends. [PFF]

40.44 William Lasser. *The limits of judicial power: the Supreme Court in American politics.* Chapel Hill: University of North Carolina Press, 1988. ISBN 0-8078-1810-0 (cl), 0-8078-4233-8 (pbk). ▸ Defense of judicial activism by showing Court's ability to withstand criticism and retain political effectiveness, 1850s to Burger court. Useful interpretation emphasizing continuities in American political experience. [PFF]

40.45 Sidney M. Milkis and Michael Nelson. *The American presidency: origins and development, 1776–1990.* Washington, D.C.: Congressional Quarterly Press, 1990. ISBN 0-87187-542-X. ▸ Chronological study of presidency. Early presidents most significant shapers of institution. [PFF]

40.46 Bradley D. Nash et al. *Organizing and staffing the presidency.* New York: Center for the Study of the Presidency, 1980. (Proceedings series, 3.) ISBN 0-938204-01-7 (cl), 0-938204-02-5 (pbk). ▸ Comprehensive, informative discussion of development of reforms in executive branch since George Washington. [PFF]

40.47 William H. Nelson, ed. *Theory and practice in American politics.* Chicago: University of Chicago Press for William Marsh Rice University, 1964. ▸ Analysis of Constitution, Supreme Court, civil-military relations, and more by prominent historians. Demonstrates continuity of American political forms and character. [PFF]

40.48 Neal R. Peirce and Lawrence D. Longley. *The people's president: the electoral college in American history and the direct vote alternative.* Rev. ed. New Haven: Yale University Press, 1981. ISBN 0-300-02612-9 (cl), 0-300-02704-4 (pbk). ▸ Examination of origins of electoral college, its effect on election results, and historic efforts to change it. Prescriptive work; looks toward reform. [PFF]

40.49 Ronald M. Peters, Jr. *The American speakership: the office* *in historical perspective.* Baltimore: Johns Hopkins University Press, 1990. ISBN 0-8018-3955-6. ‣ Examination of how policy and partisan needs, House traditions, and nature of presidential leadership shaped Speaker as leader of House. Rich contextualist analysis. [PFF]

40.50 Arthur M. Schlesinger, Jr., ed. *History of American presidential elections, 1789–1968,* with supplement, *1972–1984.* 10 vols. New York: Chelsea House, 1986. ISBN 0-87754-491-3 (set), 0-87754-492-1 (suppl). ‣ Collection of lengthy scholarly essays on each presidential election with platforms and other primary sources appended. Uneven in quality, but generally reflective of latest scholarship. [PFF]

40.51 Joel H. Silbey. "Delegates fresh from the people: American congressional and legislative behavior." *Journal of interdisciplinary history* 13.4 (1983) 603–27. ISSN 0022-1953. ‣ View of how new quantitative studies of representative bodies have reshaped understanding of political history. Synthetic work; suggests agenda for further research. [PFF]

40.52 Gil Troy. *See how they ran: the changing role of the presidential candidate.* New York: Free Press, 1991. ISBN 0-02-933035-1. ‣ Chronologically arranged analysis of campaign activities of presidential candidates. Sees political culture as dictator of changing candidate roles. Regardless of roles, candidates' positions obscured. [PFF]

Parties and Party Politics

40.53 Richard C. Bain and Judith H. Parris. *Convention decisions and voting records.* 2d ed. Washington, D.C.: Brookings Institution, 1973. ISBN 0-8157-0768-1. ‣ Survey of major party national conventions describes organization, platforms, and nominations and analyzes major votes. Historically informed descriptions. [PFF]

40.54 Paula Baker. "The domestication of politics: women and American political society, 1780–1920." *American historical review* 89.3 (1984) 620–47. ISSN 0002-8762. ‣ Reconceptualization of politics to incorporate how women's lives were shaped by government in pre-suffrage era and role played in defining politics. [PFF]

40.55 William Nisbet Chambers and Walter Dean Burnham, eds. *The American party systems: stages of political development.* 2d ed. New York: Oxford University Press, 1975. ISBN 0-19-501916-4 (cl), 0-19-501917-2 (pbk). ‣ Interdisciplinary essays developing role and function of party systems across time. Classic work in new political history. [PFF]

40.56 Jerome M. Clubb, William H. Flanigan, and Nancy H. Zingale. *Partisan realignment: voters, parties, and government in American history.* 1980 ed. Boulder: Westview, 1990. ISBN 0-8133-1031-8 (pbk). ‣ Examination of how electoral shifts in times of party realignment translate into policy shifts. Social scientific, theoretically based analysis. [PFF]

40.57 Sara M. Evans and Harry C. Boyte. *Free spaces: the sources of democratic change in America, with a new introduction.* 1986 ed. Chicago: University of Chicago Press, 1992. ISBN 0-226-22257-8 (pbk). ‣ Analysis of places where ordinary people have become empowered to seek political change: Knights of Labor, African American churches, Populist party, women's groups. New Left demonstration of authentic American radical tradition. [PFF]

40.58 Samuel P. Huntington. *American politics: the promise of disharmony.* Cambridge, Mass.: Belknap, 1981. ISBN 0-674-03020-6 (cl), 0-674-03021-4 (pbk). ‣ Examination of how reform movements from Revolution to 1960s have dealt with gap between ideals and performance of democratic government. Exceptionalist interpretation of American democracy legitimating internal conflict as price of democracy. [PFF]

40.59 Bernard K. Johnpoll and Lillian Johnpoll. *The impossible dream: the rise and demise of the American Left.* Westport, Conn.: Greenwood, 1981. ISBN 0-313-22488-9. ‣ Synthesis emphasizing impact of Left on politics. Covers leftist leaders, movements, and ideologies from seventeenth-century to New Left. Excellent introduction to subject. [PFF]

40.60 Robert Lloyd Kelley. *The cultural pattern in American politics: the first century.* New York: Knopf, 1979. ISBN 0-394-50279-5 (cl), 0-394-31954-0 (pbk). ‣ Sees ethnocultural, religious, and subcultural origins of voters as principal determinants of political divisions through Reconstruction. Aggressively stated, controversial interpretation. [PFF]

40.61 Paul Kleppner. *Who voted? The dynamics of electoral turnout, 1870–1980.* New York: Praeger, 1982. ISBN 0-03-058933-9. ‣ Uses longitudinal voting patterns to identify who voted and why. Modern decreases in turnout linked more to population characteristics than procedural changes. Contribution to debate on motivation of American voters. [PFF]

40.62 Paul Kleppner et al. *The evolution of American electoral systems.* Westport, Conn.: Greenwood, 1981. ISBN 0-313-21379-8 (cl), 0-313-23608-9 (pbk). ‣ Cooperative scholarly effort to define character of successive party systems in United States. Social scientific approach articulating new agenda for political historians. [PFF]

40.63 George H. Mayer. *The Republican party, 1854–1966.* 2d ed. New York: Oxford University Press, 1967. ‣ Analysis of party's impact through activities of national leadership and party's efforts to adapt to changing America. Sees partisanship over ideology in motivation of actions. Good basic overview. [PFF]

40.64 Keith Ian Polakoff. *Political parties in American history.* New York: Wiley, 1981. ISBN 0-471-07747-X (pbk). ‣ Examination of role of political parties in shaping responses to national growth and development. Narrative synthesis emphasizing continuities in parties over time. [PFF]

40.65 Austin Ranney. *Curing the mischiefs of faction: party reform in America.* Berkeley: University of California Press, 1975. ISBN 0-520-02650-0 (cl), 0-520-03215-2 (pbk). ‣ Uses evidence of past reform efforts to construct theory explaining internal and external party reform. Social scientific approach. [PFF]

40.66 Steven J. Rosenstone, Roy L. Behr, and Edward H. Lazarus. *Third parties in America: citizen response to major party failure.* Princeton: Princeton University Press, 1984. ISBN 0-691-07673-1 (cl), 0-691-02225-9 (pbk). ‣ Uses third-party voting and behavior in presidential elections, 1840–1980, to create theory of party-system deterioration and revitalization. Sees third parties as producers of greater representation and party responsiveness. Methodologically rigorous. [PFF]

40.67 Robert Allen Rutland. *The Democrats: from Jefferson to Carter.* Baton Rouge: Louisiana State University Press, 1979. ISBN 0-8071-0574-0. ‣ Overview of Democrats' ideology and impact of their party leaders on American history. Demonstrates continuity of party's values despite changing uses made of government. [PFF]

40.68 Arthur M. Schlesinger, Jr., ed. *History of U.S. political parties.* 1973 ed. 4 vols. New York: Chelsea House, 1981. ISBN 0-8352-0594-0 (cl, set), 0-87754-134-5 (pbk, set). ‣ Lengthy analytical essays by leading scholars on major parties and third parties subdivided by time periods. Extensive primary source supplements. Broad overview of current research. [PFF]

40.69 Joel H. Silbey. "Beyond realignment and realignment theory: American political eras, 1789–1989." In *The end of realignment? Interpreting American electoral eras.* Byron E. Shafer, ed., pp. 3–23. Madison: University of Wisconsin Press, 1991. ISBN 0-299-12970-5 (cl), 0-299-12974-8 (pbk). ‣ Critique of realignment theory as way to generalize about historic voting patterns. Shifts in mass political behavior better define distinct political eras. [PFF]

40.70 James L. Sundquist. *Dynamics of the party system: alignment and realignment of political parties in the United States.* Rev. ed. Washington, D.C.: Brookings Institution, 1983. ISBN 0-8157-8226-8 (cl), 0-8157-8225-X (pbk). ▸ Analysis of voting shifts of 1850s, 1890s, and 1930s to create theory explaining circumstances and forms of partisan change. Social scientific placement of historical events in context of broader political patterns. [PFF]

SEE ALSO
44.706 David Shannon. *The Socialist party of America.*

The Constitution and the Law

40.71 Irving Brant. *The Bill of Rights: its origin and meaning.* 1965 ed. New York: New American Library, 1967. ▸ Identification of sixty-three pledges of freedom in Constitution and its amendments, their origins, and how courts have interpreted them. Libertarian critique of government as defender of personal freedom. [PFF]

40.72 Lawrence M. Friedman. *A history of American law.* 2d ed. New York: Simon & Schuster, 1985. ISBN 0-671-81591-1 (cl), 0-671-52807-6 (pbk). ▸ Chronological study of trends in federal and state laws as well as legal profession from colonial period through nineteenth century. New legal history emphasizing law as reflective of society. [PFF]

40.73 Kermit L. Hall. *The magic mirror: law in American history.* New York: Oxford University Press, 1989. ISBN 0-19-504459-2 (cl), 0-19-504460-6 (pbk). ▸ Evolution of American law and legal institutions and major ideas that define judicial system from colonial period to present. Historic role of law in America. Synthesis of current research. [PFF]

40.74 Morton J. Horwitz. *The transformation of American law, 1780–1860.* Cambridge, Mass.: Harvard University Press, 1977. ISBN 0-674-90370-6 (cl), 0-674-90371-4 (pbk). ▸ Examination of how common law rather than constitutional law affected and was affected by social change as America moved toward corporate capitalism. Convincing argument that judicial interpretation forwarded needs of political economy. Law as tool of powerful groups. [PFF]

40.75 James Willard Hurst. *The growth of American law: the law makers.* Boston: Little, Brown, 1950. ▸ Pioneering, progressive interpretation of legal institutions showing development of law influenced by technology and social reality rather than great judges and key cases. [PFF]

40.76 Robert J. Janosik, ed. *Encyclopedia of the American judicial system: studies of the principal institutions and processes of law.* 3 vols. New York: Scribner's, 1987. ISBN 0-684-18858-9 (v. 1), 0-684-18859-7 (v. 2), 0-684-18860-0 (v. 3), 0-684-17807-9 (set). ▸ Eighty-eight lengthy analytical essays by scholars on substance, processes, and institutions of American law and law enforcement. Comprehensive overview of current research. [PFF]

40.77 Michael G. Kammen. *A machine that would go of itself: the Constitution in American culture.* New York: Knopf; distributed by Random House, 1986. ISBN 0-394-52905-7. ▸ Intellectual history emphasizing primarily elite perspectives. Shows how constitution has been viewed in American culture since its origin. Wide-ranging cultural analysis; important work. [PFF/RWS]

40.78 Alfred H. Kelly, Winfred A. Harbison, and Herman Belz. *The American Constitution: its origins and development.* 7th ed. 2 vols. New York: Norton, 1991. ISBN 0-393-96056-0 (v. 1, pbk), 0-393-96119-2 (v. 2, pbk). ▸ Chronological history of Constitution from origins through interpretation by Supreme Court. Survey updated frequently to include new research. [PFF]

40.79 Gary L. McDowell. *Curbing the courts: the Constitution and the limits of judicial power.* Baton Rouge: Louisiana State University Press, 1988. ISBN 0-8071-1339-5. ▸ Useful interpretation tracing judicial activism chronologically from proscriptive to prescriptive eras. Conservative argument for procedural reforms rather than constitutional amendments to limit judicial activism. [PFF]

40.80 Broadus Mitchell and Louise Pearson Mitchell. *A biography of the constitution of the United States: its origins, adoption, interpretation.* 2d ed. New York: Oxford University Press, 1975. ISBN 0-19-501932-6. ▸ Links Constitution's development to social experiences of country. Examines Constitutional Convention, ratification, amendments, laws, and major court decisions to demonstrate Constitution's durability. Basic introduction. [PFF]

40.81 John V. Orth. *The judicial power of the United States: the Eleventh Amendment in American history.* New York: Oxford University Press, 1987. ISBN 0-19-504099-6. ▸ Analysis of historical application of only constitutional amendment to limit Supreme Court's jurisdiction. Sees market factors and resultant political pressures as shapers of judicial outcomes. Thought-provoking interpretation. [PFF]

40.82 Harry N. Scheiber. "American constitutional history and the new legal history: complementary themes in two modes." *Journal of American history* 68.2 (1981) 337–50. ISSN 0021-8723. ▸ Study of American law as product of socioeconomic factors; constitution and courts are complementary, mutually necessary activities, not alternative historical approaches. Important integration of new legal and constitutional history. [PFF]

40.83 John R. Schmidhauser. *The Supreme Court as final arbiter in federal-state relations, 1789–1957.* 1958 ed. Westport, Conn.: Greenwood, 1973. ISBN 0-8371-6945-3. ▸ Examination of historic cases to show how judges and ideologies affected Supreme Court as umpire between states and national government. Classic nationalistic interpretation of Court's role. [PFF]

40.84 G. Edward White. *The American judicial tradition: profiles of leading American judges.* Rev. ed. New York: Oxford University Press, 1988. ISBN 0-19-505726-0 (cl), 0-19-505685-X (pbk). ▸ Analysis of leading jurists at state and national levels who influenced development of judicial system as they responded to changing America. Overview of judicial tradition as it influenced political institutions. [PFF]

40.85 William M. Wiecek. *Liberty under law: the Supreme Court in American life.* Baltimore: Johns Hopkins University Press, 1988. ISBN 0-8018-3595-X (cl), 0-8018-3596-8 (pbk). ▸ Chronological analysis of role of Supreme Court as interpreter or definer of fundamental law. Careful development of constraints curbing oligarchic tendencies inherent in judicial review. Important interpretation. [PFF]

Political Ideologies

40.86 Joyce Oldham Appleby. *Liberalism and republicanism in the historical imagination.* Cambridge, Mass.: Harvard University Press, 1992. ISBN 0-674-53012-8 (cl), 0-674-53013-6 (pbk). ▸ Critique of republicanism as organizing principle in American politics. Sees ideological roots of American politics in liberalism rather than "republican synthesis." [PFF]

40.87 David H. Bennett. *The party of fear: from nativist movements to the New Right in American history.* Chapel Hill: University of North Carolina Press, 1988. ISBN 0-8078-1772-4. ▸ Balanced survey of antiforeign movements since 1790s. Sees transferral of un-American label to native eastern elites beginning in 1930s. [PFF]

40.88 Louis Hartz. *The liberal tradition in America: an interpretation of American political thought since the Revolution.* 1955 ed.

Tom Wicker, Introduction. San Diego: Harcourt Brace Jovanovich, 1991. ISBN 0-15-651269-6 (pbk). ▸ Classic consensus interpretation of American politics as liberal. Emphasis on mainstream elites as typifying American thought and tradition. Reprint with new introduction. [PFF]

40.89 Richard Hofstadter. *The American political tradition and the men who made it.* 1948 ed. New York: Vintage, 1974. ISBN 0-394-70009-0. ▸ Classic study of American political thinkers stressing continuities and essential agreements despite different locations along political spectrum. Consensus, exceptionalist history at its best. [PFF]

40.90 Robert Lloyd Kelley. "Ideology and political culture from Jefferson to Nixon." *American historical review* 82.3 (1977) 531–62. ISSN 0002-8762. ▸ Bicentennial-inspired overview of American public life since Revolution as centered in political parties. Emphasis on continuity and persistence of both cultural and class cleavages. [PFF]

40.91 Staughton Lynd. *Intellectual origins of American radicalism.* 1968 ed. Cambridge, Mass.: Harvard University Press, 1982. ISBN 0-674-45780-3. ▸ Development of ideas of radical elites from 1750 to Civil War. New Left challenge to definition of American thought as always respecting private power and state. [PFF]

40.92 J. R. Pole. *The pursuit of equality in American history.* Berkeley: University of California Press, 1978. ISBN 0-520-03286-1 (cl), 0-520-03947-5 (pbk). ▸ Uniformity of rights as public policy issue since colonial times. Philosophical work linking historic difficulties in defining equality to mixed outcomes. Questions equality as basic political ideal. [PFF]

40.93 Daniel T. Rodgers. *Contested truths: keywords in American politics since independence.* New York: Basic Books, 1987. ISBN 0-465-01415-1 (cl), 0-465-01416-X (pbk). ▸ Examination of historical use of such concepts as natural rights, the people, and freedom by American political thinkers. Concludes politicians rejected expedient rationales for actions but expediently defined high principles. Perceptive analysis. [PFF]

40.94 Clinton L. Rossiter. *Conservatism in America: the thankless persuasion.* 1962 2d rev. ed. Cambridge, Mass.: Harvard University Press, 1982. ISBN 0-674-16510-1 (pbk). ▸ Survey of conservative thought of elites, tracing it to its ideological origins and explaining its development in context of historical events. Strongest for antebellum period. [PFF]

40.95 Max J. Skidmore. *American political thought.* New York: St. Martin's, 1978. ISBN 0-312-02894-6 (cl), 0-312-02895-4 (pbk). ▸ Chronological exposition of political ideas stressing underlying assumptions and impact on political actions. Discusses role of ideas of political elites in shaping policy outcomes. Basic introduction. [PFF]

Persistent Issues

40.96 Henry J. Abraham. *Freedom and the court: civil rights and liberties in the United States.* 5th ed. New York: Oxford University Press, 1988. ISBN 0-19-505516-0. ▸ Important interpretation of evolution of Court's role in choosing between individual and societal rights. Finds commitment to rights as constitutionally, rather than socially, determined. [PFF]

40.97 Murray R. Benedict. *Farm policies of the United States, 1790–1950: a study of their origins and development.* 1953 ed. New York: Octagon Books, 1966. ▸ Broad survey of development of government policies on land, conservation, tenancy, tariffs, price supports, money, trusts, and transportation as they affected farmers. More descriptive than analytic or prescriptive. [PFF]

40.98 John M. Dobson. *Two centuries of tariffs: the background and emergence of the U.S. International Trade Commission.* Washington, D.C.: International Trade Commission, United States Government Printing Office, 1976. ▸ Comprehensive, interpretive survey of tariff policy of United States placing policy in context of development and role of International Trade Commission. [PFF]

40.99 John Hope Franklin. *Racial equality in America.* Chicago: University of Chicago Press, 1976. ISBN 0-226-26073-9. ▸ Traces disparity between ideal of equality and reality of discrimination through political events and ideas of political leaders from seventeenth century to present. Defense of equality as essential but still unachieved. Basic starting point. [PFF]

40.100 James Willard Hurst. *The legitimacy of the business corporation in the law of the United States, 1780–1970.* Charlottesville: University Press of Virginia, 1970. ISBN 0-8139-0294-6. ▸ Historical overview of social and legal position of business corporation. Sees corporate law as function of needs of affected groups and of previous experience. Nonconspiratorial interpretation stressing unplanned and poorly conceived nature of regulation. Also available from Ann Arbor: University Microfilms International. [PFF]

40.101 Edward P. Hutchinson. *Legislative history of American immigration policy, 1798–1965.* Philadelphia: University of Pennsylvania Press for Balch Institute for Ethnic Studies, 1981. ISBN 0-8122-7796-1. ▸ Survey of immigration laws at state and national levels. Relates laws to concerns of past eras and predicts future trends. Authoritative, descriptive, analytic. [PFF]

40.102 Michael B. Katz. *In the shadow of the poorhouse: a social history of welfare in America.* New York: Basic Books, 1986. ISBN 0-465-03226-5 (cl), 0-465-03225-7 (pbk). ▸ Links government welfare practices to uncertain, contradictory goals and political needs. Critique of benevolent state. [PFF]

40.103 Thomas K. McCraw. "Regulation in America: a review article." *Business history review* 49.2 (1975) 159–83. ISSN 0007-6805. ▸ Overview and critique of scholarly attempts to explain and assess impact of legislation regulating business. Identification of points of agreement and deft explanation of reasons for differing perspectives. [PFF]

40.104 John Opie. *The law of the land: two hundred years of American farmland policy.* Lincoln: University of Nebraska Press, 1987. ISBN 0-8032-3553-4. ▸ Valuable overview of assumptions behind federal government's land policies. Shows destructive consequences of treating land as merely market commodity rather than natural resource. [PFF]

40.105 Harry N. Scheiber. "Property law, expropriation, and resource allocation by government: the United States, 1789–1910." *Journal of economic history* 33.1 (1973) 232–51. ISSN 0022-0507. ▸ Perceptive analysis of willingness of government to seize private property for state or corporation, commonplace before 1910. Examines similarity of United States to other developing nations in this respect. [PFF]

40.106 Walter I. Trattner. *From poor law to welfare state: a history of social welfare in America.* 4th ed. New York and London: Free Press and Collier Macmillan, 1989. ISBN 0-02-932711-3 (cl), 0-02-932712-1 (pbk). ▸ Survey of major trends in welfare since colonial times, examining both public and private efforts. Progressive interpretation sympathetic to governmental efforts. [PFF]

SEE ALSO
44.675 Margaret Weir, Ann Shola Orloff, and Theda Skocpol, eds. *The politics of social policy in the United States.*

State Government and Politics

40.107 Daniel Elazar. *The American partnership: intergovernmental cooperation in the nineteenth-century United States.* Chicago: University of Chicago Press, 1962. ▸ Study of selected states to show cooperation with national government in areas of land, canals, education, railroads, and banking in states-rights nineteenth century. Finds pragmatic, nonideological policy formation and continuity in operation of federal system. [PFF]

40.108 James W. Fesler, ed. *The fifty states and their local governments.* New York: Knopf, 1967. ▸ Examination of role and functioning of state and local government through time; how larger regional political patterns developed. Analyzes significance of political differences among states. Basic overview. [PFF]

40.109 W. Brooke Graves, ed. *Intergovernmental relations in the United States.* 1940 ed. New York: Arno, 1978. ▸ Classic analysis of relations between federal and state governments, between states, and among local governments. Traces larger pattern of state decline. Earlier title: *American intergovernmental relations: their origins, historical development, and current status.* [PFF]

40.110 Russel Blaine Nye. *Midwestern progressive politics: a historical study of its origins and development, 1870–1958.* Rev. ed. East Lansing: Michigan State University Press, 1959. ▸ Definition of regional political tradition as outgrowth of progressive thought going back to Granger movement. Synthesis integrating discrete state histories. [PFF]

40.111 William H. Riker. *The development of American federalism.* Boston: Kluwer Academic, 1987. ISBN 0-89838-225-4. ▸ Collection of essays, written over career, developing origins and historical consequences of federal system. Reflects growing disenchantment with wisdom of central state. Specialized and philosophical. [PFF]

SECTIONAL AND REGIONAL HISTORY

Geography and the Environment

40.112 D. W. Meinig. *Atlantic America, 1492–1800.* Vol. 1 of *The shaping of America: a geographical perspective on five hundred years of history.* New Haven: Yale University Press, 1986. ISBN 0-300-03548-9 (cl), 0-300-03882-8 (pbk). ▸ Geographer's approach to conquest and colonization of North America. Stresses dynamism of relationships between people and places while avoiding geographic determinism. [ARLC]

40.113 Carolyn Merchant. *Ecological revolutions: nature, gender, and science in New England.* Chapel Hill: University of North Carolina Press, 1989. ISBN 0-8078-1858-5 (cl), 0-8078-4254-0 (pbk). ▸ Study of nature and significance of ecological transformations in greater New England, 1600–1850. Notable example of possibilities of combining environmental history and feminist theory. [ARLC]

40.114 Roderick Nash. "The exporting and importing of nature: nature-appreciation as a commodity, 1850–1980." *Perspectives in American history* 12 (1979) 517–60. ISSN 0079-0990. ▸ Interpretation of European Americans: from transformers of landscapes to tourists. Growth of international capitalism first destroys natural environments, then creates demand for them. Only technological, urban, crowded societies appreciate wilderness. [ARLC]

40.115 John R. Stilgoe. *Common landscape of America, 1580 to 1845.* New Haven: Yale University Press, 1982. ISBN 0-300-02699-4. ▸ Readable analysis of making of colonial landscape within consensual model of American history. Sees North American environment product of common sense, emulation, and expediency, rather than specific designs or theory. [ARLC]

40.116 Michael Williams. *Americans and their forests: a historical geography.* Cambridge: Cambridge University Press, 1989. ISBN 0-521-332478. ▸ Synthetic treatment of evolving relationship between forests and humans from sixteenth through twentieth centuries. Discusses economic and cultural significance of clearing and replanting of North American forests. [ARLC]

40.117 Donald Worster et al. "A round table: environmental history." *Journal of American history* 76 (1990) 1087–1147. ISSN 0021-8723. ▸ Brief essays by some leading practitioners of new environmental history. Effectively argues for centrality of field, located at intersection of nature and culture. [ARLC]

40.118 Wilbur Zelinsky. *The cultural geography of the United States.* Rev. ed. Englewood Cliffs, N.J.: Prentice-Hall, 1992. ISBN 0-13-194424-X. ▸ Description of North American spatial configurations as way to understand nature of American identity. Particularly useful for relationship between regions and nation as whole. [ARLC]

SEE ALSO
4.249 Roderick Nash. *Wilderness and the American mind.*
4.599 Donald Worster. *Rivers of empire.*

The Frontier

40.119 James D. Bennett. *Frederick Jackson Turner.* Boston: Twayne, 1975. ISBN 0-8075-7150-6. ▸ Brief, sound analysis and summary of Turner's major writings and arguments of his critics. [ARLC]

40.120 Ray Allen Billington and Martin Ridge. *Westward expansion: a history of the American frontier.* 5th ed. New York: Macmillan, 1982. ISBN 0-02-309860-0. ▸ Chronological survey of impact of frontier on American political, economic, and social development. Classic, extended statement of Turner thesis (40.125), celebratory of European American achievements. [ARLC]

40.121 Stanley Elkins and Eric L. McKitrick. "A meaning for Turner's frontier." *Political science quarterly* 69 (1954) 321–353, 565–602. ISSN 0032-3195. ▸ Significant effort to subsume Turner thesis (40.125) within consensual model of American history. Sees essence of frontier democracy in community building, although differences exist between northern and southern experiences. [ARLC]

40.122 Richard Hofstadter and Seymour Martin Lipset, eds. *Turner and the sociology of the frontier.* New York: Basic Books, 1968. ▸ Essays combining historical and sociological approaches to American social development west of Appalachians. Balanced, insightful writings analyzing Turner thesis (40.125). [ARLC]

40.123 Vernon E. Mattson and William E. Marion. *Frederick Jackson Turner: a reference guide.* Boston: Hall, 1985. ISBN 0-8161-7997-2. ▸ Extensive list of annotations of both Turner's writings and writings about Turner, 1895–1962. [ARLC]

40.124 Frederick Merk. *History of the westward movement.* New York: Knopf, 1978. ISBN 0-394-41175-7. ▸ Narrative, analytical, chronological, and geographical survey of expansion of European America from colonial era through second quarter of twentieth century. Argues frontier persists in environmental and development issues. Detailed maps and illustrations. [ARLC/CAM]

40.125 Frederick Jackson Turner. *The frontier in American history.* 1920 ed. Tucson: University of Arizona Press, 1986. ISBN 0-8165-0946-8 (pbk). ▸ One of most influential books ever written by an American historian. Sees significance of settlement of free western land in determining character of American society. [ARLC]

40.126 Richard White. *"It's your misfortune and none of my own": a new history of the American West.* Norman: University of Oklahoma Press, 1992. ISBN 0-8061-2366-4. ▸ Conceives of West as region created by European conquest rather than as embodiment of vanishing frontier. Detailed, subtle synthesis of recent scholarship. [ARLC]

Sections and Regions

40.127 Barbara Allen and Thomas J. Schlereth, eds. *Sense of place: American regional cultures.* Lexington: University Press of

Kentucky, 1990. ISBN 0-8131-1730-5. ▸ Folklore and material culture studies of wide variety of regions or subregions. Interesting data and methodology, but lacks overall interpretive coherence. [ARLC]

40.128 Michael Bradshaw. *Regions and regionalism in the United States.* Jackson: University Press of Mississippi, 1988. ISBN 0-87805-339-5. ▸ Geographer's analysis of concept of North American regionalism and expressions of regionalism in late twentieth century. Effort to unite academic study with government policy and corporate interests. [ARLC]

40.129 Merrill Jensen, ed. *Regionalism in America.* 1951 ed. Westport, Conn.: Greenwood, 1975. ISBN 0-8371-8340-5. ▸ Classic essays tracing and evaluating origins and significance of regionalism in variety of categories, including literature, architecture, painting, folklore, and sociology. [ARLC]

40.130 Howard W. Odum and Harry Estill Moore. *American regionalism: a cultural-historical approach to national integration.* 1938 ed. Gloucester, Mass.: Peter Smith, 1966. ▸ Sociological analysis of different regions and meaning of regionalism for different academic disciplines. Classic statement of regionalism as theory sympathetic to social change rather than quaint provincialism. [ARLC]

40.131 Michael Steiner and Clarence Mondale. *Region and regionalism in the United States: a source book for the humanities and social sciences.* New York: Garland, 1988. ISBN 0-8240-9048-9. ▸ Exhaustive annotated bibliography of books and articles dealing with concept of regionalism by scholars in wide variety of disciplines. [ARLC]

40.132 Frederick Jackson Turner. *The significance of sections in American history.* 1932 ed. Gloucester, Mass.: Peter Smith, 1959. ▸ Details characteristics—mostly political and economic—and importance of sections, primarily in first half of nineteenth century. Classic study of regional interests and interaction. [ARLC]

SEE ALSO
  44.102 Michael O'Brien. *The idea of the American South, 1920–1941.*

The South

40.133 John B. Boles. *Black southerners, 1619–1869.* Lexington: University Press of Kentucky, 1983. ISBN 0-8131- 0303-7 (cl), 0-8131-0161-1 (pbk). ▸ Judicious synthetic history of black southerners from earliest slave importations to aftermath of emancipation. Focuses on diversity and historical change in slavery and cultural and social creativity of slaves. [DLC]

40.134 John B. Boles and Evelyn Thomas Nolen, eds. *Interpreting southern history: historiographical essays in honor of Sanford W. Higginbotham.* Baton Rouge: Louisiana State University Press, 1987. ISBN 0-8071-1318-2 (cl), 0-8071-1361-1 (pbk). ▸ Successor volume to Link and Patrick, eds. 40.145. Essays discuss historical literature of American South written since mid-1960s. [DLC]

40.135 W. J. Cash. *The mind of the South.* 1941 ed. New York: Vintage, 1991. ISBN 0-679-73647-6 (pbk). ▸ Classic, colorful synthesis by tormented journalist. Finds profound unity and continuity, stemming from persistent frontier and dominant personality type, the rough but romantic "man at the center." [DLC]

40.136 James C. Cobb. *Industrialization and southern society, 1877–1984.* Lexington: University Press of Kentucky. ISBN 0-8131-0304-5. ▸ Synthetic account of southern industrialization, focusing on post–World War II era. Regards southern industry as shaped by traditional character of southern society, especially its oligarchy and conservatism. [DLC]

40.137 William J. Cooper, Jr., and Tom E. Terrill. *The American South: a history.* 1990 ed. 2 vols. New York: McGraw-Hill, 1991.

ISBN 0-07-063743-1 (1 vol. ed.), 0-07-063741-5 (v. 1), 0-07-063743-2 (v. 2). ▸ Most recent general textbook survey of subject. [DLC]

40.138 Carl N. Degler. *Place over time: the continuity of southern distinctiveness.* Baton Rouge: Louisiana State University Press, 1977. ISBN 0-8071-0299-7 (cl), 0-8071-1031-0 (pbk). ▸ Series of lectures arguing American South retains distinctive identity within larger American society, traceable ultimately to legacy of plantation slavery. [DLC]

40.139 Elizabeth Fox-Genovese and Eugene D. Genovese. *Fruits of merchant capital: slavery and bourgeois property in the rise and expansion of capitalism.* New York: Oxford University Press, 1983. ISBN 0-19-503157-1 (cl), 0-19-503158-X (pbk). ▸ Essays by two distinguished, provocative former Marxists treating Revolutionary France and New World slavery. Stresses conservatism of early modern merchant capitalism and its support of precapitalist forms in peripheral regions. [DLC]

40.140 David R. Goldfield. *Cotton fields and skyscrapers: southern city and region, 1607–1980.* Baton Rouge: Louisiana State University Press, 1982. ISBN 0-8071-1029-9. ▸ In contrast to Goldfield and Brownell, eds. 40.141, stresses influence of regional characteristics such as rural dominance, biracialism, and economic colonialism on character of southern cities. [DLC]

40.141 David R. Goldfield and Blaine A. Brownell, eds. *The city in southern history: the growth of urban civilization in the South.* Port Washington, N.Y.: Kennikat, 1977. ISBN 0-8046-9078-2. ▸ Five essays providing synthetic overview of southern urban history from colonial times to present. For most part, stresses internally generated city characteristics. Sees cities as exceptions to southern stereotypes. [DLC]

40.142 Dewey W. Grantham. *The life and death of the solid South: a political history.* Lexington: University Press of Kentucky, 1988. ISBN 0-8131-0308-8 (cl), 0-8131-0813-6 (pbk). ▸ Most recent, fullest synthesis of southern political history from Reconstruction to recent times, centering on creation and dissolution of one-party, restricted suffrage regime of 1890s to 1960s. [DLC]

40.143 Fred C. Hobson. *Tell about the South: the southern rage to explain.* Baton Rouge: Louisiana State University Press, 1983. ISBN 0-8071-1112-0 (cl), 0-8071-1131-7 (pbk). ▸ Study of southern intellectuals' attempts to explain their region and/or themselves, ranging from antebellum period through World War II. Literary study, consisting of closely linked essays on major figures. [DLC]

40.144 Jay B. Hubbell. *The South in American literature, 1607–1900.* 1954 ed. Durham, N.C.: Duke University Press, 1973. ISBN 0-8223-0091-5. ▸ Encyclopedic survey of subject in 1954; foundation work for southern literary studies. Should be supplemented with Rubin et al., eds. 40.151. Also available from Ann Arbor: University Microfilms International. [DLC]

40.145 Arthur S. Link and Rembert W. Patrick, eds. *Writing southern history: essays in historiography in honor of Fletcher M. Green.* 1965 ed. Westport, Conn.: Greenwood, 1981. ISBN 0-313-22782-9. ▸ Essays on historical literature written before mid-1960s. With Boles and Nolen, eds. 40.134, starting point for identifying most significant work in field. [DLC]

40.146 F. Ray Marshall. *Labor in the South.* Cambridge, Mass.: Harvard University Press, 1967. ISBN 0-674-50700-2. ▸ Encyclopedic survey of history of southern labor relations, focusing on institutional development. Written by eminent labor economist, later Secretary of Labor under Carter. [DLC]

40.147 Michael O'Brien. *Rethinking the South: essays in intellectual history.* Baltimore: Johns Hopkins University Press, 1988. ISBN 0-8018-3617-4. ▸ Witty essays by British-born scholar of southern intellectual life. Offers transatlantic perspective. Focus on problematic nature of southern intellectual as category of analysis. [DLC]

40.148 Ulrich B. Phillips. "The central theme of southern history." *American historical review* 34.1 (1928) 30–43. ISSN 0002-8762. ‣ Focus on causes of American Civil War. Theme, that South should remain white-man's country, is one that students of region must confront. [DLC]

40.149 David M. Potter. "The enigma of the South." *Yale Review* 51.1 (1961) 142–51. ISSN 0044-0124. ‣ Classic effort to define essential character of southern history, more comprehensive than racism or agrarianism. Stresses persistence of folk culture in South despite industrialization and urbanization elsewhere. [DLC]

40.150 David C. Roller and Robert W. Twyman, eds. *The encyclopedia of southern history.* Baton Rouge: Louisiana State University Press, 1979. ISBN 0-8071-0575-9. ‣ Basic reference work for southern history, with some 2,900 articles covering most standard topics. [DLC]

40.151 Louis D. Rubin, Jr., et al., eds. *The history of southern literature.* 1985 ed. Baton Rouge: Louisiana State University Press, 1990. ISBN 0-8071-1251-8 (cl, 1985), 0-8071-1643-2 (pbk). ‣ Encyclopedic survey of southern literature from roots in European expansion to recent times, succeeds Hubbell 40.144. Inevitably uneven, but full. [DLC]

40.152 Charles Grier Sellers, Jr., ed. *The southerner as American.* 1960 ed. New York: Dutton, 1966. ‣ Civil-rights era effort of southern liberals to define regional identity that was not dependent on Jim Crow. Stresses, by South's historical diversity, indeterminancy and participation in United States liberal heritage. [DLC]

40.153 Charles Reagan Wilson and William Ferris, eds. *Encyclopedia of southern culture.* Chapel Hill: University of North Carolina Press, 1989. ISBN 0-8078-1823-2. ‣ Basic reference work, but far more interdisciplinary than Roller and Twyman, eds. 40.150, with stress on popular culture. Selection and organization often eccentric, but brings together much unique information. [DLC]

40.154 C. Vann Woodward. *The burden of southern history.* 1968 rev. ed. Baton Rouge: Louisiana State University Press, 1977. ISBN 0-8071-0837-5 (cl, 1970), 0-8071-0133-8 (pbk). ‣ Essays by most distinguished historian of American South. Especially valuable discussions of historical experience as basis of southern identity and region's role as corrective to American exceptionalism. [DLC]

40.155 C. Vann Woodward. *The strange career of Jim Crow.* 3d rev. ed. New York: Oxford University Press, 1974. ISBN 0-19-501805-2 (pbk). ‣ Partly superseded, but still place to start in history of southern race relations. Argument that segregation was mutable helped give intellectual underpinning to civil-rights movement. [DLC]

40.156 Bertram Wyatt-Brown. *Southern honor: ethics and behavior in the Old South.* New York: Oxford University Press, 1982. ISBN 0-19-503119-9 (cl), 0-19-503310-8 (pbk). ‣ Sweeping interpretation of fabric of southern life, not limited to antebellum period. Stresses role of honor in shaping white male behavior, particularly in recourse to personal violence and community justice. [DLC/MW]

SEE ALSO
44.254 Gavin Wright. *Old South, New South.*

The Northeast

40.157 Richard D. Brown. *Massachusetts: a bicentennial history.* New York: Norton, 1978. ISBN 0-393-05666-X (cl). ‣ Brief synthesis interpreting history of core New England state in terms of clash between tradition and modernity. Sees Massachusetts both as harbinger of modernity and as its exporter to rest of nation. [DLC]

40.158 Thomas C. Cochran. *Pennsylvania: a bicentennial history.* New York: Norton, 1978. ISBN 0-393-05635-X. ‣ Readable examination of Pennsylvania's role as incubator of American industrial, urban, and business revolution. Focuses on economic and business history; less strong on rural life and social history. [DLC]

40.159 David Maldwyn Ellis. *New York: state and city.* Ithaca, N.Y.: Cornell University Press, 1979. ISBN 0-8014-1180-7. ‣ Brief synthetic account of pivotal state, stressing continuous traditions of ethnic pluralism, political corruption and reform, and economic empire building. [DLC]

40.160 Oscar Handlin. "Yankees." In *Harvard encyclopedia of American ethnic groups.* Stephan Thernstrom, ed., pp. 1028–30. Cambridge, Mass.: Belknap, 1980. ISBN 0-674-37512-2. ‣ Treats descendants of New England Puritans as regional group analogous to white southerners, but shows history to be one of outmigration, increasing internal division, and declining importance in home region. [DLC]

40.161 Stewart H. Holbrook. *Yankee exodus: an account of migration from New England.* 1950 ed. Seattle: University of Washington Press, 1968. ‣ Anecdotal and ethnocentric, but much information on New England influence on nation and its transmission through migration. Supplements Rosenberry 40.163. [DLC]

40.162 George W. Pierson. "The obstinate concept of New England: a study in denudation." *New England quarterly* 28.1 (1955) 3–7. ISSN 0028-4866. ‣ Learned reflections on New England's loss of regional coherence through urbanization, industrialization, and immigration. Nonetheless, insists on continuing relevance of region. [DLC]

40.163 Lois Kimball Mathews Rosenberry. *The expansion of New England: the spread of New England settlement and institutions to the Mississippi River, 1620–1865.* 1909 ed. New York: Russell & Russell, 1962. ‣ Old classic, arguing for distinctive New England frontier and New England region stretching across upper Midwest. Stresses transmission of institutions to western lands and their alteration by frontier. [DLC]

40.164 Richard Harrison Shryock. "The Middle Atlantic area in American history." *Proceedings of the American Philosophical Society* 108.2 (1964) 147–55. ISSN 0003-049X. ‣ Meditation on lack of regional historiography; suggests region's diversity and its location at core of original United States deprived it of self-consciousness and sense of grievance at root of regional identity. [DLC]

40.165 Donald Garrison Brinton Thompson. *Gateway to a nation: the Middle Atlantic states and their influence on the development of the nation.* Rindge, N.H.: Richard R. Smith, 1956. ‣ Rare treatment of Middle Atlantic states as region, developing Turnerian notion of region as seedbed of American society and gateway for people and ideas from outside. Boosterish tone. [DLC]

SEE ALSO
42.144 Hal S. Barron. *Those who stayed behind.*

The Midwest

40.166 Andrew R. L. Cayton and Peter S. Onuf. *The Midwest and the nation: rethinking the history of an American region.* Bloomington: Indiana University Press, 1990. ISBN 0-253-31525-5. ‣ Attempt to weave scholarship of a generation into synthetic whole. Sketches formation of distinctive regional culture ironically predicated on denial of uniqueness. [ARLC]

40.167 David C. Klingaman and Richard K. Vedder, eds. *Essays* *in nineteenth century economic history: the Old Northwest*. Athens: Ohio University Press, 1975. ISBN 8214-0170-fl. ▸ Analyzes agricultural, demographic, and transportation origins of region. Valuable for efforts, mostly implicit, to develop sense of Old Northwest as distinctive place. [ARLC]

40.168 David C. Klingaman and Richard K. Vedder, eds. *Essays on the economy of the Old Northwest*. Athens: Ohio University Press, 1987. ISBN 0-8214-0875-5. ▸ Provides wealth of detail and interesting methodological approaches to region's history. Informative on labor systems, demographic changes, literacy rates, banking systems, transportation networks, and industrialization. [ARLC]

40.169 Frank Kramer. *Voices in the valley: mythmaking and folk belief in the shaping of the Middle West*. Madison: University of Wisconsin Press, 1964. ▸ Outlines folk cultures among settlers, including American Indians, amid development from community of essence, to agricultural millennium, then to naked reality of industrial organization. [ARLC]

40.170 James H. Madison, ed. *Heartland: comparative histories of the midwestern states*. Bloomington: Indiana University Press, 1988. ISBN 0-253-31423-2 (cl), 0-253-20576-x (pbk). ▸ Overview of twelve states of Old Northwest and Great Plains. Conventional, nontheoretical, but valuable for comparisons of states' evolution within regional framework. [ARLC]

40.171 Thomas T. McAvoy et al. *The Midwest: myth or reality? A symposium*. Notre Dame, Ind.: University of Notre Dame Press, 1961. ▸ Essays on social protest, industry, agriculture, cultural isolation, and intellectual life. Assesses nature of Middle West and its future from mid-twentieth-century perspective. [ARLC]

40.172 Richard Lyle Power. *Planting Corn Belt culture: the impress of upland southerner and Yankee in the Old Northwest*. 1953 ed. Westport, Conn.: Greenwood, 1983. ISBN 0-313-24060-4. ▸ Study of daily life, arguing Middle Western culture emerged out of dialectic between North and South. Limited in methodology and time frame, but influential. [ARLC]

40.173 James R. Shortridge. *The Middle West: its meaning in American culture*. Lawrence: University Press of Kansas, 1989. ISBN 0-7006-0388-3. ▸ Pastoralism at heart of Middle Western regional identity. Significant interpretation of origins of region's reputation as most American of all regions of United States. [ARLC]

SEE ALSO
42.186 William Cronon. *Nature's metropolis*.

The Great Plains and Borderlands

40.174 Ray August. "Cowboys vs. rancheros: the origins of western American livestock law." *Southwestern historical quarterly* 96.4 (1993) 457–88. ISSN 0038-478X. ▸ Traces legal traditions governing livestock to Middle Ages. Concludes Walter Prescott Webb, Frederick Jackson Turner, and others wrong; environment did not overturn cultural continuity. Parallels claimed for water and community-property laws. [LCP]

40.175 Walter L. Buenger and Robert A. Calvert, eds. *Texas through time: evolving interpretations*. College Station: Texas A&M University Press, 1991. ISBN 0-89096-490-4 (cl), 0-89096-468-8 (pbk). ▸ Good sampling of current research on women, Mexicans, African Americans, American Indians, and modernization. Less biting than some recent revisionist work on frontier and West. Rejects romantic strain in Texas historiography. [LCP]

40.176 Merlin P. Lawson and Maurice E. Baker, eds. *The Great Plains: perspectives and prospects*. Lincoln: Center for Great Plains Studies; distributed by University of Nebraska Press, 1981. ISBN 0-938932-00-4. ▸ Conference essays, many on future prospects

for water, urban problems, and other issues. Includes good historical perspectives on droughts, natural resources, even ideology of rugged individualism. [LCP]

40.177 Fred Shannon. *An appraisal of Walter Prescott Webb's The Great Plains: a study in institutions and environment*. 1940 ed. Westport, Conn.: Greenwood, 1940. ISBN 0-313-21211-2. ▸ Commissioned critique of work considered most influential since World War I. Overwhelming assault on Webb's evidence, which some dismiss as nitpicking. Includes comments of prominent social scientists. [LCP]

40.178 Walter Prescott Webb. *The Great Plains*. 1931 ed. Lincoln: University of Nebraska Press, 1981. ISBN 0-8032-9702-5 (pbk). ▸ Classic examination of topic, prehistory to cattle kingdom. Sometimes poetic, sometimes technical, on subjects like barbed wire, water law, and land use. Concludes unique, vast environment destroyed old formulas of living. [LCP]

40.179 David J. Weber, ed. *New Spain's far northern frontier*. Albuquerque: University of New Mexico Press, 1979. ISBN 0-8263-0498-2 (cl), 0-8263-0499-0 (pbk). ▸ Anthology of brief, readable essays on borderlands with emphasis on region from Texas to California. Some classics, but mostly recent. [LCP]

The West

40.180 Anne M. Butler. *Daughters of joy, sisters of misery: prostitutes in the American West, 1865–1900*. 1985 ed. Urbana: University of Illinois Press, 1987. ISBN 0-252-01139-2 (cl, 1985) 0-252-01466-9 (pbk). ▸ Important social-historical work on western American prostitution in nineteenth century. Discusses class, racial, and ethnic dimensions of regional prostitution. [WFD]

40.181 Sucheng Chan. *This bittersweet soil: the Chinese in California agriculture, 1860–1910*. Berkeley: University of California Press, 1986. ISBN 0-520-05376-1. ▸ Rich social historical portrait of Chinese role in California agriculture during nineteenth century. Best single volume exploring importance of understudied group of agricultural laborers. [WFD]

40.182 William Cronon, George A. Miles, and Jay Gitlin, eds. *Under an open sky: rethinking America's western past*. New York: Norton, 1992. ISBN 0-393-02993-X. ▸ Collection of essays devoted to assessing latest work in western American history. Important volume for understanding field's growth and direction over past generation. Excellent introduction. [WFD/CAM]

40.183 Mike Davis. *City of quartz: excavating the future in Los Angeles*. 1990 ed. New York: Vintage, 1992. ISBN 0-679-73806-1 (pbk). ▸ Edgy, often brilliant, and freewheeling investigation of modern Los Angeles. History and social criticism smartly melded. [WFD]

40.184 G. Thomas Edwards and Carlos A. Schwantes, eds. *Experiences in a promised land: essays in Pacific Northwest history*. Seattle: University of Washington Press, 1986. ISBN 0-295-96328-X (cl), 0-295-96329-8 (pbk). ▸ Collected essays providing good overview of region's culture and history. Particularly strong on regional labor and politics. [WFD]

40.185 Stephen Fox. *John Muir and his legacy: the American conservation movement*. 1981 ed. Madison: University of Wisconsin Press, 1985. ISBN 0-299-10634-9 (pbk). ▸ Both an important biography of critical figure in western and national environmentalism and good contextual overview of growth of early conservation. [WFD]

40.186 Robert V. Hine. *Community on the American frontier: separate but not alone*. Norman: University of Oklahoma Press, 1980. ISBN 0-8061-1678-1. ▸ Good overview of western communitarian ethic. Examines struggle for individual freedom and community loyalty for survival on frontier. Important rejoinder to individualism theme of regional history. Covers many utopian colonies and rationales within important national context. [WFD/CAM]

40.187 Norris Hundley, Jr. *The great thirst: Californians and water, 1770s–1990s.* Berkeley: University of California Press, 1992. ISBN 0-520-07786-5. ▸ California water history across two centuries. Grand synthesis of effects of western aridity on settlement, growth, social conditions, politics, and law. Contrasts Indian, Spanish, and Mexican community-minded approaches with competitive, self-interested, and increasingly complex policies of majority culture. [WFD/CAM/JTL]

40.188 William Issel and Robert W. Cherny. *San Francisco, 1865–1932: politics, power, and urban development.* Berkeley: University of California Press, 1986. ISBN 0-520-05263-3 (cl), 0-520-06033-4 (pbk). ▸ Examination of post–Gold Rush urban growth in northern California. Explores political dynamics, labor organization, and boss rule in rich detail. [WFD]

40.189 David Alan Johnson. *Founding the Far West: California, Oregon, and Nevada, 1840–1890.* Berkeley: University of California Press, 1992. ISBN 0-520-07348-7. ▸ Study of political cultures of three western states and their absorption into Union. Rich comparative analysis within context of rapid industrialization and development. [WFD]

40.190 William L. Kahrl. *Water and power: the conflict over Los Angeles' water supply in the Owens Valley.* Berkeley: University of California Press, 1982. ISBN 0-520-04431-2 (cl), 0-520-05068-1 (pbk). ▸ Rich narrative discussion of city's search for water supply hundreds of miles away in Sierra foothills. Focus on urban growth, politics, and aridity at outset of twentieth century. [WFD]

40.191 Howard Roberts Lamar. *The far Southwest, 1846–1912: a territorial history.* 1966 ed. New York: Norton, 1970. ISBN 0-393-00522-4. ▸ Study of development of state and territorial governments in Southwest. Still best single-volume examination of political transitions in new territories and states of Southwest. [WFD/CAM]

40.192 Howard Roberts Lamar, ed. *The reader's encyclopedia of the American West.* 1977 ed. New York: Harper & Row, 1987. ISBN 0-06-015726-7. ▸ Extremely useful desk reference on western issues, events, and people. [WFD]

40.193 Patricia Nelson Limerick. *The legacy of conquest: the unbroken past of the American West.* New York: Norton, 1987. ISBN 0-393-02390-7 (cl), 0-393-30497-3 (pbk). ▸ Thematic essays from "new" western historian. Important revisionist text arguing for western American continuity across artificial divides of frontier lines or transitions to new centuries. Lively writing, excellent bibliography. [WFD/CAM]

40.194 Arthur F. McEvoy. *The fisherman's problem: ecology and law in the California fisheries, 1850–1980.* Cambridge: Cambridge University Press, 1986. ISBN 0-521-32427-0 (cl), 0-521-38586-5 (pbk). ▸ Exploration of immensely complex world of American Indian fishery rights on West Coast. Innovative; melds environmental and legal history. [WFD]

40.195 Carey McWilliams. *Factories in the field: the story of migratory farm labor in California.* 1939 ed. Santa Barbara, Calif.: Peregrine, 1971. ISBN 0-87905-005-5. ▸ Arguably still best portrait of California farm laborers and history of state's bonanza agribusiness. [WFD]

40.196 Peggy Pascoe. *Relations of rescue: the search for female moral authority in the American West, 1874–1939.* New York: Oxford University Press, 1990. ISBN 0-19-506008-3. ▸ Gripping study of activities of Protestant missionary women among Chinese prostitutes, Mormon women in polygamous marriages, unmarried mothers, and American Indians. Superb analysis of class, religion, gender, and social dynamics from post–Civil War period through Great Depression. [WFD/CAM]

40.197 Donald J. Pisani. *From the family farm to agribusiness: the irrigation crusade in California and the West, 1850–1931.* Berkeley: University of California Press, 1984. ISBN 0-520-05127-0. ▸ Deeply researched social, cultural, and legal discussion of western water and irrigation issues, rise of massive irrigation projects, and changing farming patterns. Richest on California within larger context. [WFD]

40.198 Leonard Pitt. *The decline of the Californios: a social history of the Spanish-speaking Californians, 1846–1890.* 1966 ed. Berkeley: University of California Press, 1971. ISBN 0-520-01019-1 (cl), 0-520-01637-8 (pbk). ▸ Examination of early California, as United States began exerting political, economic, and military authority. Displacement of former Californio elite result of overwhelming influx of anglophone migrants. [WFD]

40.199 Earl Spencer Pomeroy. *The Pacific slope: a history of California, Oregon, Washington, Idaho, Utah, and Nevada.* 1966 ed. Lincoln: University of Nebraska Press, 1991. ISBN 0-8032-8729-1. ▸ Classic synthetic work from pioneer era through time of western tourism. Treats urban growth, impact of railroad, regional character, and place in the nation. Still important introduction to states of Far West. [WFD/CAM]

40.200 Marc Reisner. *Cadillac desert: the American West and its disappearing water.* 1986 ed. New York: Penguin, 1987. ISBN 0-14-010432-1 (pbk). ▸ Wide-ranging, informative account of past century. Rich narrative bringing personalities to life in midst of dramatic western struggles over water. [WFD]

40.201 Michael L. Smith. *Pacific visions: California scientists and the environment, 1850–1915.* New Haven: Yale University Press, 1987. ISBN 0-300-03264-1. ▸ Ranges across scientific disciplines and cultures. Good introduction to how Far West was brought into nation not only politically, but also as scientific laboratory. [WFD]

40.202 John Walton. *Western times and water wars: state, culture, and rebellion in California.* Berkeley: University of California Press, 1992. ISBN 0-520-07245-6. ▸ Thoughtful anthropological investigation of human interaction with Owens River Valley. Ranges across American Indian environmental contact and various stages of development of "Anglo" civilization. [WFD]

40.203 Donald Worster. *Under Western skies: nature and history in the American West.* New York: Oxford University Press, 1992. ISBN 0-19-505820-8. ▸ Collected essays wandering thematically across western landscape. Good introduction to environmental history by one of its most thoughtful practitioners. [WFD]

40.204 Mark Wyman. *Hard-rock epic: western miners and the industrial revolution, 1860–1910.* Berkeley: University of California Press, 1979. ISBN 0-520-03678-6. ▸ Sound account of western mining districts during period of intense conflict and violence. Good introduction to the region's rich labor history. [WFD]

SEE ALSO

36.137 Albert Hurtado. *Indian survival on the California frontier.*

42.275 Alexander Plaisted Saxton. *The indispensable enemy.*

42.399 Elliot West. *Growing up with the country.*

42.405 Lawrence H. Larsen. *The urban West at the end of the frontier.*

42.432 Rodman Wilson Paul. *Mining frontiers of the far West, 1848–1880.*

42.437 Oscar Osburn Winther. *The transportation frontier.*

42.462 John Mack Faragher. *Women and men on the overland trail.*

43.135 Cletus E. Daniel. *Bitter harvest.*

44.248 Michael P. Malone and Richard W. Etulain. *The American West.*

ECONOMIC HISTORY

Agriculture

40.205 Alan I. Marcus and Richard Lowitt, eds. "The United States Department of Agriculture in historical perspective." *Agricultural history* 64.2 (1990) 1–331. ISSN 0002-1482. ▸ Symposium on wide range of topics: science, experiment stations, conservation, labor supply, nutrition, insects, regulation, art, individuals, the two Henry Wallaces. [LCP]

40.206 Edward L. Schapsmeier and Frederick H. Schapsmeier, eds. *Encyclopedia of American agricultural history*. Westport, Conn.: Greenwood, 1975. ISBN 0-8371-7958-0. ▸ Hundreds of brief entries, many only sentence or two. Broad coverage of cultural, political topics as well as obvious agricultural ones. Extremely helpful indexes. [LCP]

40.207 John T. Schlebecker. *Whereby we thrive: a history of American farming, 1607–1972*. Ames: Iowa State University Press, 1975. ISBN 0-8138-0090-0. ▸ Focus on commercial farming, land use, and markets. Less coverage of policy, ideology, education, farmers' movements, slavery, or American Indians. Basic survey, valuable within self-determined limits. [LCP]

40.208 John L. Shover. *First majority, last minority: the transforming of rural life in America*. DeKalb: Northern Illinois University Press, 1976. ISBN 0-87580-056-4 (cl), 0-87580-522-1 (pbk). ▸ Discussion of changes caused by technology, agribusiness, and disappearance of farm communities. Includes local studies on Ohio, Pennsylvania, and Michigan. Provides historical perspective for doubts about benefits of modernization. [LCP]

40.209 Robert P. Swierenga. "Theoretical perspectives on the new rural history: from environmentalism to modernization." *Agricultural history* 56.3 (1982) 495–502. ISSN 0002-1482. ▸ Commentary on recent proposals for more systematic study of rural life. Studies how to broaden knowledge of agriculture beyond limits of economic history. Not for beginners. [LCP]

Finance, Banking, and Commerce

40.210 Michael Baskin. "The development of corporate financial markets in Britain and the United States, 1600–1914: overcoming asymmetric information." *Business history review* 62 (1988) 199–237. ISSN 0007-6805. ▸ Analysis of effect of adverse selection problem on development of new financial instruments and financial practices. Excellent, concise overview of financial development in private sector. [WMD]

40.211 Vincent P. Carosso. *Investment banking in America*. Cambridge, Mass.: Harvard University Press, 1970. ISBN 0-674-46574-1. ▸ Comprehensive study emphasizing evolution of investment banking in twentieth century. Definitive; excellent balance between historical detail and analysis. [WMD]

40.212 Lester V. Chandler. *Benjamin Strong: central banker*. Washington, D.C.: Brookings Institution, 1958. ▸ Superbly written account of role of one of most influential figures in American central banking. Indispensable for understanding changing role of Federal Reserve in America's monetary system. [WMD]

40.213 Lance Edwin Davis. "The capital markets and industrial concentration: the U.S. and U.K., a comparative study." *Economic history review* 19 (1966) 255–72. ISSN 0013-0117. ▸ Comparative analysis of relationship between industrial concentration, banking, and capital market development. One of most respected accounts of financial determinants in emergence of big business. [WMD]

40.214 Lance Edwin Davis. "The investment market, 1870–1914: the evolution of a national market." *Journal of economic history* 25 (1965) 355–400. ISSN 0022-0507. ▸ Indispensable analysis of factors enabling capital market integration in United States. New types of financial intermediaries emerged in response to interregional interest-rate differentials. Excellent statistical appendix. [WMD]

40.215 George W. Edwards. *The evolution of finance capitalism*. 1938 ed. New York: Kelley, 1967. ▸ Analysis of measures taken to secure financial strength and protect asset values in industries weakened by ineffective management and competition. Excellent overview of causes and consequences of frequently misunderstood phenomenon. [WMD]

40.216 Milton Friedman and Anna Jacobson Schwartz. *A monetary history of the United States, 1867–1960*. Princeton: National Bureau of Economic Research Studies; distributed by Princeton University Press, 1963. (Business cycles, 12.) ISBN 0-691-00354-8 (pbk). ▸ Indispensable description of monetary trends, analysis of monetary policy and evolution of United States monetary system. Sophisticated, detailed, controversial; makes considerable use of economic and financial theory. [WMD]

40.217 Raymond W. Goldsmith. *Financial structure and development*. New Haven: Yale University Press, 1969. ▸ Advanced, highly theoretical analysis of financial evolution. New financial instruments and institutions emerged to accommodate changes in composition of industry and demand for capital, with effects on subsequent economic development. [WMD]

40.218 R. B. Hawtrey. *The gold standard in theory and practice*. 5th ed. Westport, Conn.: Greenwood, 1980. ISBN 0-313-22104-9. ▸ Examination of development of self-adjusting international payments mechanism, gold-standard orthodoxy, and how governments circumvent this mechanism. Readers should be acquainted with international finance and monetary economics. [WMD]

40.219 John A. James. *Money and capital markets in postbellum America*. Princeton: Princeton University Press, 1978. ISBN 0-691-04218-7. ▸ Study of evolution of banking system and interregional fund-transfer mechanisms, in context of movement toward financial market integration. Concise, important; useful for specialists but accessible to beginners. [WMD]

40.220 Herman E. Krooss and Paul Studenski. *Financial history of the United States: fiscal, monetary, banking, and tariff, including financial administration and state and local finances*. 2d ed. New York: McGraw-Hill, 1963. ▸ Primarily descriptive treatment of state and federal government finance and federal government involvement in evolution of United States monetary system. Accessible, good reference source. [WMD]

40.221 Simon Kuznets. *Capital in the American economy: its formation and financing*. Princeton: Princeton Unversity Press for National Bureau of Economic Research, 1961. (National Bureau of Economic Research studies in capital formation and financing, 9.) ▸ Trends in real-capital accumulation and evolution of financial structures during nineteenth and twentieth centuries. Sophisticated, highly abstract synthesis of economic theory and descriptive statistics. [WMD]

40.222 Margaret Myers. *The New York money market*. Vol. 1: *origins and development*. New York: Columbia University Press, 1931. ▸ Description of confluence of forces that caused New York to emerge as America's leading financial center. Comprehensive treatment of both stock exchanges and lesser-known financial institutions. [WMD]

40.223 Thomas V. Navin and Marian V. Sears. "The rise of a market for industrial securities, 1877–1902." *Business history review* 29 (1955) 255–72. ISSN 0007-6805. ▸ Changes in business organization, consolidations, mergers that induced innovation of new financial practices, intermediaries, and a centralized, formal industrial-securities market. Readable, concise, much historical detail. [WMD]

40.224 Fritz Redlich. *The molding of American banking, men and ideas.* 1947 ed. 2 vols. in 1. New York: Johnson Reprint, 1968. ▸ Unbelievably detailed account of individuals and ideas that shaped United States banking system. Emphasizes individual bankers, particular institutions, and historical detail rather than theoretical analysis. Earlier title: *History of American Business Leaders: A Series of Studies*, vol. 2. [WMD]

40.225 Robert Sobel. *The big board: a history of the New York stock market.* New York: Free Press, 1965. ▸ Richly detailed account of evolution of stock exchange from small, informal market to center of America's financial activity. Accessible, emphasizes actual workings of market and ancillary institutions. [WMD]

40.226 Mary Elizabeth Sushka and Barrett W. Brown. "Banking structure and the national capital market, 1869–1914." *Journal of economic history* 44 (1984) 463–78. ISSN 0022-0507. ▸ Financial market integration occurred earlier than previously thought, and monopoly power of banks declined as financial practices became more sophisticated. Valuable supplement to similar works by Sylla (40.227) and Davis (40.213, 40.214). [WMD]

40.227 Richard Sylla. "Federal policy, banking market structure, and capital mobilization in the United States, 1863–1913." *Journal of economic history* 29 (1969) 657–86. ISSN 0022-0507. ▸ Study of National Banking Act, its effects on banking market concentration and consequences for capital mobility and industrial finance. Useful, concise overview of banking history. [WMD]

40.228 Paul Trescott. *Financing American enterprises: the story of commercial banking.* New York: Harper & Row, 1963. ▸ Good, basic account of evolution of commercial banking system, lending practices, and relationship to industrial development. Very accessible, more suitable for beginners than specialists. [WMD]

Patterns, Trends, and Cycles

40.229 Adolph A. Berle, Jr., and Gardiner C. Means. *The modern corporation and private property.* 1968 rev. ed. New Brunswick, N.J.: Transaction, 1991. ISBN 0-88738-887-6. ▸ Reasons for rise of corporation, its legal consequences, and its effects on concepts of assets and capital. Indispensable for students of business history and institutional change. [WMD]

40.230 Stuart Bruchey, Alfred D. Chandler, Jr., and Louis Galambos, eds. *The changing economic order: readings in American business and economic history.* New York: Harcourt Brace & World, 1968. ISBN 0-15-506110-0. ▸ Excellent compilation using case studies to analyze role of particular individuals and institutions in American economic development. Emphasis on business history, but good treatment of labor, agriculture, and government as well. [WMD]

40.231 Lance Edwin Davis, Richard A. Easterlin, and William N. Parker. *American economic growth: an economist's history of the United States.* New York: Harper & Row, 1972. ISBN 0-06-041557-6. ▸ Excellent, comprehensive analysis of many important themes in American economic history. Makes considerable use of basic economic theory but not too difficult for beginners. [WMD]

40.232 Lance Edwin Davis and Douglass Cecil North. *Institutional change and American economic growth.* Cambridge: Cambridge University Press, 1971. ISBN 0-521-08111-4. ▸ Provocative analysis of causes and consequences of institutional evolution in American economy. Somewhat controversial use of economic theory and assumption of optimizing behavior to interpret institutional change. [WMD]

40.233 Robert R. Fogel and Stanley L. Engerman. *A reinterpretation of American economic history.* New York: Harper & Row, 1971. ISBN 0-06-042109-6. ▸ Statistics and economic theory used to reexamine some familiar themes. Accessible to those with backgrounds in basic economic theory. Excellent example of new economic history. [WMD]

40.234 Peter George. *The emergence of industrial America: strategic factors in American economic growth since 1870.* Albany: State University of New York Press, 1982. ISBN 0-87395-578-1 (cl), 0-87395-579-X (pbk). ▸ Concise analysis of major themes in American economic development with emphasis on political and social consequences of technological and organizational change. Excellent overview of basic issues in economic history. [WMD]

40.235 Jonathan R. T. Hughes. *The governmental habit redux: economic controls from colonial times to the present.* Rev. ed. Princeton: Princeton University Press, 1991. ISBN 0-691-04272-1. ▸ Lively, provocative examination of ubiquity of government regulation, mostly at state and local levels throughout America's history and expanding economic role of federal government during recent times. [WMD/PFF]

40.236 Jonathan R. T. Hughes. *The vital few: the entrepreneur and American economic progress.* Rev. ed. New York: Oxford University Press, 1986. ISBN 0-19-504038-4 (pbk). ▸ Study of entrepreneurial spirit, individual entrepreneurs as indispensable stimulus to economic development. Deemphasizes importance of abstract, aggregate phenomena such as technology and demographics in economic change. [WMD]

40.237 Susan Previant Lee and Peter Passell. *A new economic view of American history.* New York: Norton, 1979. ISBN 0-393-95067-0. ▸ Analysis of American economic development using economic theory and statistics. Analytical rather than descriptive. Excellent, accessible example of new economic history. [WMD]

40.238 Ralph L. Nelson. *Merger movements in American industry, 1895–1956.* Princeton: Princeton University Press, 1959. (National Bureau of Economic Research, General series, 66.) ▸ Highly detailed analysis of major periods of horizontal merger activity. Still one of best available sources of information on this important phenomenon. Relates merger waves to business and capital-market cycles. [WMD/DLC]

40.239 Douglass Cecil North. *Growth and welfare in the American past: a new economic history.* 3d ed. Englewood Cliffs, N.J.: Prentice-Hall, 1983. ISBN 0-13-366161-X. ▸ Analysis of economic trends and their impact on individual and aggregate well being. Excellent synthesis of new economic history with social, political, and other traditional forms of historical inquiry. [WMD]

40.240 Glenn Porter, ed. *Encyclopedia of American economic history: studies of the principal movements and ideas.* 3 vols. New York: Scribner's, 1980. ISBN 0-684-16271-7 (set). ▸ Contributors include many noted economic and business historians writing in their primary areas of specialization. Comprehensive and general; organized by topic. [WMD]

40.241 C. Joseph Pusateri. *A history of American business.* 2d ed. Arlington Heights, Ill.: Harlan Davidson, 1988. ISBN 0-88295-844-5 (cl), 0-88295-859-3 (pbk). ▸ Accessible synthesis of individual company histories and general business history. Considerable emphasis on role of individual business leaders. [WMD]

40.242 Jeffrey G. Williamson, ed. *Late nineteenth-century American development: a general equilibrium history.* Cambridge: Cambridge University Press, 1974. ISBN 0-521-20469-0. ▸ Uses microeconomic theory to shed new light on familiar themes. One of more rigorous examples of new economic history. Advanced work in the field. Also available from Ann Arbor: University Microfilms International. [WMD]

SEE ALSO
44.177 Alfred D. Chandler, Jr. *Strategy and structure.*

Manufacturing

40.243 Victor S. Clark. *History of manufactures in the United States*. 3 vols. New York: McGraw-Hill for Carnegie Institution, 1929. ‣ Old, but classic, encyclopedic introduction to subject up to date of publication. [DLC]

40.244 Louis Galambos. "What have CEOs been doing?" *Journal of economic history* 48.2 (1988) 243–58. ISSN 0022-0507. ‣ Sketches modern development of American business history, focusing on quest of corporate leadership for control of environment, operational efficiency, and innovation. [DLC]

40.245 David A. Hounshell. *From the American system to mass production, 1800–1932: the development of manufacturing technology in the United States*. Baltimore: Johns Hopkins University Press, 1984. ISBN 0-8018-2975-5 (cl), 0-8018-3158-x (pbk). ‣ Survey of development of mass production from earliest uses of interchangeable parts to Henry Ford's assembly line. Stresses persistent economic problems with mass production and its ultimate failure to deliver on promise. [DLC]

40.246 Glenn Porter and Harold C. Livesay. *Merchants and manufacturers: studies in the changing structure of nineteenth-century marketing*. Baltimore: Johns Hopkins University Press, 1971. ISBN 0-8018-1251-8. ‣ Series of industry case studies illustrating subordinate position of manufacturers in early nineteenth-century commercial economy and centrality of market control to rise of large-scale industry after Civil War. [DLC]

40.247 Peter Temin. "Manufacturing." In *American economic growth: an economist's history of the United States*. Lance Edwin Davis et al., eds., pp. 418–67. New York: Harper & Row, 1972. ISBN 0-06-041557-6. ‣ General survey, 1810–1960, from economist's viewpoint. Focuses on cotton textiles and iron and steel with other industries treated in aggregate. Stresses general trends in prices, output, and productivity; addresses major economic issues in pattern of growth. [DLC]

40.248 Rolla Milton Tryon. *Household manufactures in the United States, 1640–1860: a study in industrial history*. 1917 ed. New York: Johnson Reprint, 1966. ‣ Classic study of importance of household in colonial and early national manufacturing. Outline of steps and timing of transition to factory system in early nineteenth century. [DLC]

40.249 Paul Uselding. "Manufacturing." In *Encyclopedia of American economic history: studies of the principal movements and ideas*. 3 vols. Glenn Porter, ed., vol. 1, pp. 397–412. New York: Scribner's, 1980. ISBN 0-684-16271-7 (set), 0-684-16510-4 (v. 1). ‣ Brief synthesis of United States manufacturing development to early twentieth century, stressing transition to factory system, political-legal environment, and role of labor. [DLC]

SEE ALSO

4.404 Alfred D. Chandler, Jr. *The visible hand*.

44.199 Louis Galambos and Joseph Pratt. *The rise of the corporate commonwealth*.

Labor

40.250 Harry Braverman. *Labor and monopoly capital: the degradation of work in the twentieth century*. New York: Monthly Review Press, 1975. ISBN 0-85345-340-3. ‣ Classic study by Marxist worker-intellectual. Reasserts centrality of capitalist expropriation of knowledge, and thus of worker skills and control in workplace, to modern history of labor and technology. [DLC]

40.251 John R. Commons et al. *History of labour in the United States*. 1918–35 ed. 4 vols. New York: Kelley, 1966. ISBN 0-678-00142-1 (set), 0-678-04036-2 (v. 1), 0-678-04037-0 (v. 2), 0-678-04038-9 (v. 3), 0-678-04039-7 (v. 4). ‣ Classic institutionalist synthesis, stressing distinctive experience of American workers, resulting narrow job consciousness of American unions, and lack

of broad political agenda. Often refuted, but still influential. [DLC]

40.252 Foster Rhea Dulles and Melvyn Dubofsky. *Labor in America: a history*. 4th ed. Arlington Heights, Ill.: Harlan Davidson, 1984. ISBN 0-88295-824-0 (cl), 0-88295-825-9 (pbk). ‣ Standard single-volume survey, organized around history of American labor movements from early nineteenth century to recent times. [DLC]

40.253 Philip Sheldon Foner. *History of the labor movement in the United States*. Vol. 1, 1947 ed.; vols 2–10, 2d ed. 10 vols. to date. New York: International Publishers, 1947–92. ISBN 0-7178-0091-1 (v. 1, cl), 0-7178-0092-x (v. 2, cl), 0-7178-0093-8 (v. 3, cl), 0-7178-0094-6 (v. 4, cl), 0-7178-0570-0 (v. 5, cl), 0-7178-0602-2 (v. 6, cl), 0-7178-0638-3 (v. 7, cl), 0-7178-0653-7 (v. 8, cl), 0-7178-0673-1 (v. 9, cl), 0-7178-0690-1 (v. 10, cl), 0-7178-0376-7 (v. 1, pbk), 0-7178-0388-0 (v. 2, pbk), 0-7178-0389-9 (v. 3, pbk), 0-7178-0396-1 (v. 4, pbk), 0-7178-0562-x (v. 5, pbk), 0-7178-0595-6 (v. 6, pbk), 0-7178-0627-8 (v. 7, pbk), 0-7178-0652-9 (v. 8, pbk), 0-7178-0674-x (v. 9, pbk), 0-7178-0691-x (v. 10, pbk). ‣ Great, multivolume, Marxist synthesis. Stresses role of working people in pressing for social and economic progress; places sympathies with industrial and unskilled workers as opposed to narrow crafts unionists. [DLC]

40.254 David M. Gordon, Richard Edwards, and Michael Reich. *Segmented work, divided workers: the historical transformation of labor in the United States*. Cambridge: Cambridge University Press, 1982. ISBN 0-521-23721-1 (cl), 0-521-28921-1 (pbk). ‣ Proposed conceptual framework for American labor history, integrating it with hypothetical "long swings" that have characterized modern economic development. Disputed but provocative. [DLC]

40.255 James R. Green. *The world of the worker: labor in twentieth-century America*. Eric Foner, ed. New York: Hill & Wang, 1980. ISBN 0-8090-9830-x (cl), 0-8090-0132-2 (pbk). ‣ Early synthesis of new radical labor history from late nineteenth century to 1970s. Stresses militant struggles of ordinary workers for control of working and personal lives, despite betrayal by leaders. [DLC]

40.256 Herbert G. Gutman. "Work, culture, and society in industrializing America, 1820–1920." *American historical review* 78.3 (1973) 531–87. ISSN 0002-8762. ‣ Classic essay proposing new framework for United States labor history during industrialization. Shifts focus from labor movement to sociocultural experience of workers as they became industrial proletariat. [DLC]

40.257 Stanley Lebergott. *Manpower in economic growth: the American record since 1800*. New York: McGraw-Hill, 1964. ‣ Pioneering statistical study, presenting and analyzing data on composition, utilization, and welfare of American work force. Outlines long-term shifts. Standard reference for historical labor statistics and starting point for most later work. [DLC/GJK]

40.258 Bruce Levine et al. *Who built America? Working people and the nation's economy, politics, culture, and society*. 2 vols. New York: Pantheon, 1989–92. ISBN 0-394-54663-6 (v. 1, cl), 0-394-58650-6 (v. 2, cl), 0-679-72699-3 (v. 1, pbk), 0-679-73022-2 (v. 2, pbk). ‣ Last work of Herbert Gutman's American Social History Project; massive textbook synthesis of new labor history, reinterpreting all United States history as that of work and workers. Stresses tradition of contention for all levels of American society. [DLC]

40.259 David Montgomery. *Workers' control in America: studies in the history of work, technology, and labor struggles*. 1979 ed. Cambridge: Cambridge University Press, 1980. ISBN 0-521-22580-9 (cl, 1979), 0-521-28006-0 (pbk). ‣ Seminal essays focusing on labor relations on shop floor. Stresses tradition of workers' control of productive process and their sometimes successful efforts to preserve it. [DLC]

40.260 Maurice F. Neufeld, Daniel J. Leab, and Dorothy Swanson, eds. *American working-class history: a representative bibliography.* New York: Bowker, 1983. ISBN 0-8352-1752-3. ‣ Over 7,000 entries, organized by chronological period, by trades and industries, by state and region. Sections on women, minorities, leaders, radical movements, and other topics. Not annotated. [LCP]

40.261 Selig Perlman. *A theory of the labor movement.* 1928 ed. Philadelphia: Porcupine Press, 1979. ISBN 0-87991-818-7 (pbk). ‣ Single-volume exposition of explanatory framework underlying Commons et. al. 40.251. Anti-utopian, stresses role of bread-and-butter unions in adjusting workers to industrial America. [DLC]

40.262 Daniel T. Rodgers. "Tradition, modernity, and the American industrial worker: reflections and critique." *Journal of interdisciplinary history* 7.4 (1977) 655–81. ISSN 0022-1953. ‣ Critique of labor history—notably Gutman 40.256—influenced by modernization theory. Contends worker response to industrial labor, past and present, cannot easily be understood in terms of tradition and modernity. [DLC]

SEE ALSO

44.216 David Brody. *Workers in industrial America.*
44.231 Christopher L. Tomlins. *The state and the unions.*

SOCIAL HISTORY

Rural and Local Society

40.263 Thomas Bender. *Community and social change in America.* 1978 ed. Baltimore: Johns Hopkins University Press, 1982. ISBN 0-8018-2924-0 (pbk). ‣ Argues modernization and mobility did not destroy nineteenth-century sense of community: Americans moved from one community to another. Provocative blend of historical research and social theory. [KWK]

40.264 Ray Allen Billington. *Local history is alive and well.* Ann Arbor, Mich.: Bentley Historical Library, 1974. (Michigan historical collections, 23.) ‣ Brief but wise commentary on recent revival of local history, its causes, methods, and contributions. Defines role for libraries and depositories in preserving and promoting local sense of identity. [KWK]

40.265 Michael G. Kammen. "Challenges and opportunities in writing state and local history." In *Selvages and biases: the fabric of history in American culture,* pp. 154–73. Ithaca, N.Y.: Cornell University Press, 1987. ISBN 0-8014-1924-7. ‣ Call to end isolation of local history with citation of numerous articles, praise of best work in field, and suggestions for further research. [KWK]

40.266 Richard Lingeman. *Small town America: a narrative history, 1620 to the present.* 1980 ed. Boston: Houghton-Mifflin, 1981. ISBN 0-395-31540-9 (pbk). ‣ Non-quantitative social history of rural communities from colonies to 1970s. Discusses Western towns, manufacturing, architecture, literary images, holidays, government, social class, and Nonconformists. For general reader. [KWK]

40.267 James C. Olson. *The role of local history.* Nashville: American Association for State and Local History, 1965. ‣ Pamphlet defining local history in relation to recreation, tourism, patriotism, and understanding of national history. Growing academic interest in subject. Points out benefits of sense of local identity. [KWK]

40.268 David J. Russo. *Families and communities: a new view of American history.* Nashville: American Association for State and Local History Press, 1974. ISBN 0-910050-11-2. ‣ Plea for new kinship-oriented approach to local history examining levels of communities from local, to national, to world. Basic work on subject. [KWK]

40.269 David J. Russo. *Keepers of our past: local historical writing in the United States, 1820s–1930s.* Westport, Conn.: Greenwood, 1988. ISBN 0-313-26236-5. ‣ Covers antiquarians, to formulaic local historians, to academic authors. Spirited reminders of amateur local history's popular appeal. [KWK]

40.270 Page Smith. *As a city on a hill: the town in American history.* New York: Knopf, 1966. ‣ Discussion of small towns in East and Midwest, their establishment, religion, economy, politics, social structure, and ideology. Focuses on town as basic social institution. Introductory work with good bibliography, though not up to date. [KWK]

40.271 Thomas H. Smith. "The renascence of local history." *The historian* 35.1 (1972) 1–17. ISSN 0018-2370. ‣ Renewal of interest in local history since mid-1950s as shown by monographs and dissertations. Treats African Americans, cities, protest movements, education, local government, and labor organizations. Focuses on subject matter more than method. [KWK]

40.272 George R. Stewart. *Names on the land: a historical account of place-naming in the United States.* 4th ed. San Francisco: Lexikos, 1982. ISBN 0-938530-02-X (pbk). ‣ Classic study of American Indian, Spanish, French, and English names with regional variations. Refutes inaccurate tales about names. Discusses patriotic influences and modern approaches to topic. Useful maps revealing migration patterns. [KWK]

40.273 Robert P. Swierenga. "Agriculture and rural life: the new rural history." In *Ordinary people and everyday life: perspectives on the new social history.* James B. Gardner and George Rollie Adams, eds., pp. 91–113. Nashville: American Association for State and Local History Press, 1983. ISBN 0-910050-66-X. ‣ Review of landmark scholarly studies applying behavioral science and statistical methods to countryside culture. Brief but effective introduction to topic. [KWK]

Urban history

40.274 Alexander B. Callow, ed. *American urban history: an interpretive reader with commentaries.* 3d ed. New York: Oxford University Press, 1982. ISBN 0-19-502981-X. ‣ Examination of growth of cities from interdisciplinary perspective for entire span of American history. Essays by major authorities in field with useful commentary and historiographical analysis. [KWK]

40.275 Michael H. Ebner. "Urban history: retrospect and prospect." *Journal of American history* 68 (1981) 69–84. ISSN 0021-8723. ‣ Assessment of development of field, especially methodological changes. Calls for more cooperation between specialists and general historians. Suggestions for future research. [KWK]

40.276 Charles Glaab and A. Theodore Brown. *A history of urban America.* 2d ed. New York: Macmillan, 1976. ISBN 0-02-344110-0. ‣ Comprehensive survey of cities as dynamic forces in American culture from colonies to mid-twentieth century. Useful synthesis of research, organized by theme. Landmark in its field. [KWK]

40.277 Constance McLaughlin Green. *American cities in the growth of the nation.* 1957 ed. New York: Harper & Row, 1965. ‣ Well-written sketches of development of seaboard, river, manufacturing, railroad, Great Plains, Northwest, and capital cities. Capsule histories emphasizing each city's unique character with discussion of common economic and social problems. [KWK]

40.278 Tamara K. Hareven and Randolph Langenbach. *Amoskeag: life and work in an American factory city.* New York: Pantheon, 1978. ISBN 0-394-48841-7 (cl), 0-394-73855-1 (pbk). ‣ Study of Amoskeag Mills of Manchester, New Hampshire. Interviews with forty workers about family life, labor organization, and ethnic conflict. Model oral history with photographs. [KWK]

40.279 Kenneth T. Jackson. *Crabgrass frontier: the suburbanization of the United States.* 1985 ed. New York: Oxford University Press, 1987. ISBN 0-19-503610-7 (cl, 1985), 0-19-504983-7 (pbk). ‣ Development of American suburbs from late eighteenth century to 1985, through phases of growth of transportation, New Deal, baby boom, and drive-in. Detailed survey criticizing loss of community. [KWK]

40.280 Kenneth T. Jackson and Stanley K. Schultz, eds. *Cities in American history.* New York: Knopf, 1972. ISBN 0-394-47558-5, 0-394-31147-7 (text ed.) ‣ Essays interpreting urban history themes of poverty, mass transit, vice, race, government, and city planning. Urban history at its most confident. [KWK]

40.281 Diana Klebanow, Franklin L. Jonas, and Ira M. Leonard. *Urban legacy: the story of America's cities.* New York: New American Library, 1977. ISBN 0-451-61586-7. ‣ Popular, comprehensive survey, colonial era to 1970s. Covers particular cities as well as general trends such as immigration, industrialization, and city design. Maps, statistical tables, illustrations, and bibliography. [KWK]

40.282 Margaret Marsh. *Suburban lives.* New Brunswick, N.J.: Rutgers University Press, 1990. ISBN 0-8135-1483-5 (cl), 0-8135-1484-3 (pbk). ‣ Analysis of meaning of life styles from Victorian era to 1950s. Treats domesticity, child rearing, work and leisure patterns, and family relationships. Widely researched; shows suburban ideals as male-defined. [KWK]

40.283 Raymond A. Mohl. *The new city: urban America in the industrial age, 1860–1920.* Arlington Heights, Ill.: Harlan Davidson, 1985. ISBN 0-88295-830-5 (pbk). ‣ Survey covering demography, migration, immigration, transportation, building, housing, industrialization, planning, government, reform, modernization, environment. Concise, useful introduction to main issues in field. [KWK]

40.284 Raymond A. Mohl, ed. *The making of urban America.* Wilmington, Del.: Scholarly Resources, 1988. ISBN 0-8420-2270-8 (cl), 0-8420-2271-6 (pbk). ‣ Essays reflecting current research on wide range of topics, colonial era to 1980s. Challenges established views about decline of community, importance of political machines, and beneficial results of New Deal. [KWK]

40.285 Raymond A. Mohl and Neil Betten, eds. *Urban America in historical perspective.* New York: Weybright & Talley, 1970. ‣ Essays written with view toward recent city problems. Distinguishes pre-industrial from industrial cities and both from modern metropolis. Basic introduction to research in ethnicity and race. [KWK]

40.286 Eric H. Monkkonen. *America becomes urban: the development of U.S. cities and towns, 1780–1980.* Berkeley: University of California Press, 1988. ISBN 0-520-06191-8 (cl), 0-520-06972-2 (pbk). ‣ Study of American cities as new forms with distinct phases of development. Revisionist examination of finance, transportation, housing, crime, planning, and mobility. Synthetic but much primary-source research. [KWK]

40.287 John W. Reps. *The making of urban America: a history of city planning in the United States.* 1965 ed. Princeton: Princeton University Press, 1991. ISBN 0-691-04525-9 (cl), 0-691-00618-0 (pbk). ‣ Landmark study of American town planning, colonial era to early twentieth century. Emphasizes variety of urban designs and regional patterns. Numerous illustrations and maps, thorough bibliography. [KWK]

40.288 Stanley K. Schultz. *Constructing urban culture: American cities and city planning, 1800–1920.* Philadelphia: Temple University Press, 1989. ISBN 0-87722-587-7. ‣ Well-documented synthesis showing modern city planning originated before 1890s.

Includes early schemes from novelists, architects, lawyers, judges, and engineers. Discusses influences of technology and conflicts between municipal regulation and private property. [KWK]

40.289 John R. Stilgoe. *Borderland: origins of the American suburb, 1820–1939.* New Haven: Yale University Press, 1988. ISBN 0-300-04257-4. ‣ Examination of why commuters chose to live in countryside. Covers residential architecture, popular literary images, and suburban political and economic power. Well illustrated, extensive use of material objects; little attention to connections with broader trends. [KWK]

40.290 Sam Bass Warner. *The private city: Philadelphia at three periods of its growth.* 2d ed. Philadelphia: University of Pennsylvania Press, 1968. ISBN 0-8122-8061-X (cl), 0-8122-1243-6 (pbk). ‣ Influential study of colonial, antebellum, and Great Depression city. Analysis of urban failure and relation to decline of community. Early application of quantitative methods. [KWK]

40.291 Sam Bass Warner. *Urban wilderness: a history of the American city.* New York: Harper & Row, 1972. ISBN 0-06-014531-5. ‣ Critical survey of land use, construction of types of cities, neighborhoods, reform, housing, and health care. Important review of historical background of contemporary urban problems. [KWK]

SEE ALSO
42.190 Theodore Hershberg, ed. *Philadelphia.*

Class

40.292 E. Digby Baltzell. *Philadelphia gentlemen: the making of a national upper class.* 1958 ed. New Brunswick, N.J.: Transaction, 1989. ISBN 0-88738-789-6. ‣ Emergence of business elite with implications for other Eastern cities, seventeenth through twentieth centuries. Ethnic, religious, and cultural as well as economic origins. Sociological study with sound historical basis. [KWK]

40.293 Loren Baritz. *The good life: the meaning of success for the American middle class.* 1989 ed. New York: Perennial Library, 1990. ISBN 0-06-097275-0 (pbk). ‣ Biting critique of twentieth-century bourgeois outlook shown in advertising, communications, fashion, marriage, work, and child rearing. Panoramic view of topic, free of jargon. [KWK]

40.294 Rowland Berthoff. *An unsettled people: social order and disorder in American history.* New York: Harper & Row, 1971. ‣ Influential survey of colonial, atomized Jacksonian, and industrial societies. Class structure and institutions challenged by individualism, although nation required social order. Nonquantitative social history offering broad generalizations. [KWK]

40.295 Michael H. Frisch and Daniel J. Walkowitz, eds. *Working-class America: essays on labor, community, and American society.* Urbana: University of Illinois Press, 1983. ISBN 0-252-00953-3 (cl), 0-252-00954-1 (pbk). ‣ Study of impact of industrialization on culture, women's roles, political power, organization, and ethnicity. Essays reflect interdisciplinary methods and new trends in research on social classes. [KWK]

40.296 Herbert G. Gutman. *Work, culture, and society in industrializing America: essays in American working-class and social history.* 1976 ed. New York: Vintage, 1977. ISBN 0-394-72251-5. ‣ Essays offering convincing new interpretations of class behavior. Analyzes relations of class to race, religion, ethnicity, and ideology of labor movement. Discusses impact of Protestantism, industrialism, and radicalism. Sweeping title essay and case studies by pioneer of new labor history. [KWK/GJK]

40.297 Tamara K. Hareven, ed. *Anonymous Americans: explorations in nineteenth-century social history.* Englewood Cliffs, N.J.: Prentice-Hall, 1971. ISBN 0-13-038398-8. ‣ Essays on overlooked but not inarticulate groups. Cautions against narrow definition of social class and includes both middle and working classes.

Quantitative social history oriented to contemporary issues. [KWK]

40.298 P.M.G. Harris. "The social origins of American leaders: the demographic foundations." *Perspectives in American history* 3 (1969) 159–344. ISSN 0266-1322. ‣ Analysis of changes in composition of elites occurring in twenty-two-and-one-half-year cycles, colonial era to 1960s. Extensive review of relevant scholarly literature. Conclusions in need of statistical testing; elites hard to define. [KWK]

40.299 Irving Krauss. *Stratification, class, and conflict.* New York: Free Press, 1976. ISBN 0-02-917690-5. ‣ Sociological introduction surveying relationship of class to life cycle from infancy to old age. Discusses industrialization, connections with American history, and recent trends. Theoretical with extensive use of historical materials. [KWK]

40.300 Stow Persons. *The decline of American gentility.* New York: Columbia University Press, 1973. ISBN 0-231-03015-0. ‣ Study of why old genteel mores disappeared from late-eighteenth and nineteenth-century America. After Revolution new gentry elite replaced colonial elites. Influential examination of culture as intellectuals saw it. [KWK]

40.301 Stow Persons. "The origins of the gentry." In *Essays on history and literature.* Robert Hamlett Bremner, ed., pp. 83–119. Columbus: Ohio State University Press, 1966. ISBN 0-8142-0029-X. ‣ Nonquantitative, impressionistic interpretation of rise of American elite, distinguished from industrial plutocracy and eighteenth-century upper class. [KWK]

40.302 Edward Pessen. *The log cabin myth.* 1984 ed. New Haven: Yale University Press, 1986. ISBN 0-300-03166-1 (cl, 1984), 0-300-03754-6 (pbk). ‣ Skeptical essay testing democratic claims of presidents. Compares social and economic background of presidents' families with those of ordinary people. Concludes presidents chosen because they support basic American socioeconomic patterns. [KWK]

40.303 Edward Pessen, ed. *Three centuries of social mobility in America.* Lexington, Mass.: Heath, 1974. ISBN 0-669-89391-9. ‣ Essays exploring theme in colonial, revolutionary, Jacksonian, and early industrial eras and twentieth century. Contrasts historical and sociological views, but organizing concept not sharply defined. Statistical tables, maps, bibliography. [KWK]

40.304 Daniel Scott Smith. "Cyclical, secular, and structural change in American elite composition." *Perspectives in American history* 4 (1970) 351–374. ISSN 0266-1322. ‣ Tests assertion that upper class is closed from colonial era to late nineteenth century. Urges use of new data and methods to study structural changes and social values. Challenges Harris 40.298; methodologically advanced. [KWK]

40.305 Charles Stephenson and Robert Asher, eds. *Life and labor: dimensions of American working-class history.* Albany: State University of New York Press, 1986. ISBN 0-88706-173-7 (cl), 0-88706-172-9 (pbk). ‣ Provocative introduction to trends in recent research detailing effects of industrialization and technology on mobility, leisure, women, and unions. New approaches to subject, including quantitative analysis. [KWK]

SEE ALSO
44.240 Stephan Thernstrom. *The other Bostonians.*

Family, Generations, and Child Rearing

40.306 W. Andrew Achenbaum. *Old age in the new land: the American experience since 1790.* Baltimore: Johns Hopkins University Press, 1979. ISBN 0-8018-2107-X. ‣ Examination of changing status and perceptions of aged, growth of elderly population, and problems of aging. Based on statistical data. Argues against other scholarship; suggests topics for further research. [KWK]

40.307 Margo J. Anderson. *The American census: a social history.* New Haven: Yale University Press, 1988. ISBN 0-300-04014-8. ‣ Broad synthesis of recent interpretations of social implications and administrative and political history of census. Discusses use in welfare policy, apportionment, relation to immigration, race, unemployment, and industrialization. Illustrated with tables. [KWK/DSS]

40.308 Lee L. Bean, Geraldine P. Mineau, and Douglas L. Anderton. *Fertility change on the American frontier: adaptation and innovation.* Berkeley: University of California Press, 1990. ISBN 0-520-06633-2. ‣ Groundbreaking study of 185,000 family genealogies in Mormon collection. Argues western life promoted population growth, which declined when society adapted to modernization and capitalist market. Huge data base. [KWK]

40.309 Robert Hamlett Bremner, ed. *Children and youth in America: a documentary history.* 3 vols. in 5. Cambridge, Mass.: Harvard University Press, 1970. ISBN 0-674-11610-0 (v. 1). ‣ Chronologically arranged collection of documents concerning public policy toward children, colonial to present, including activities of voluntary agencies and family life. Covers education, dependency, labor, health, and minorities. Basic source. [KWK]

40.310 Arthur W. Calhoun. *A social history of the American family from colonial times to the present.* 1917–19 Ed. 3 vols. New York: Arno, 1973. ISBN 0-405-03886-0. ‣ Classic, early account based on extensive research in printed sources. Progressive Era assumptions about social improvement and race. Dated. [KWK]

40.311 Howard P. Chudacoff. *How old are you? Age consciousness in American culture.* Princeton: Princeton University Press, 1989. ISBN 0-691-04768-5. ‣ Useful historical overview of youth, maturity, and old age. Argues awareness of age is dominant characteristic of American society, especially after 1850. [KWK]

40.312 Stephanie Coontz. *The social origins of private life: a history of American families, 1600–1900.* London: Verso, 1988. ISBN 0-86091-191-8 (cl), 0-86091-907-2 (pbk). ‣ Examination of family as production unit combining private choice and economic function. Forecasts future of family structure. Synthesis of other works from radical perspective. Advanced analysis. [KWK]

40.313 David Hackett Fischer. *Growing old in America.* Rev. ed. Oxford: Oxford University Press, 1978. ISBN 0-19-502366-8. ‣ Unique survey of aging, colonial era to 1970. Sees antebellum shift to individualism as deep change transforming relations with old people; further transformation of status of aged underway in modern period. [KWK]

40.314 Michael Gordon, ed. *The American family in social-historical perspective.* 3d ed. New York: St. Martin's, 1983. ISBN 0-312-02314-6 (cl), 0-312-02313-8 (pbk). ‣ Collected essays showing new approaches to such topics as household, marriage, women, life stages, ethnicity, sex, and demography. Best compendium of research by leading scholars. [KWK]

40.315 William Graebner. *A history of retirement: the meaning and function of an American institution, 1885–1978.* 1980 ed. New Haven: Yale University Press, 1984. ISBN 0-300-02356-1 (cl, 1980), 0-300-03300-1 (pbk). ‣ Discussion of how corporate capitalism, unemployment, liberalism, and welfare laws affected retirement. Raises policy questions concerning social security. Groundbreaking study using new primary sources. [KWK]

40.316 Carole Haber. *Beyond sixty-five: the dilemma of old age in America's past.* Cambridge: Cambridge University Press, 1985. ISBN 0-521-25096-X (cl), 0-521-31507-7 (pbk). ‣ Discussion of medical theories, scientific classifications, institutionalization, pensions, geriatrics, and how aging affected bureaucracy. Weak on early America, stresses nineteenth century. [KWK]

40.317 Tamara K. Hareven. *Family time and industrial time: the relationship between the family and work in a New England indus-*

trial community. Cambridge: Cambridge University Press, 1982. ISBN 0-521-23094-2 (cl), 0-521-28914-9 (pbk). ▸ Innovative use of oral history and social science methods to examine family and industrialization in single company over time. Discusses roles of factory, labor migration, households, and labor organization. [KWK/DSS]

40.318 Tamara K. Hareven and Maris A. Vinovskis, eds. *Family and population in nineteenth-century America.* Princeton: Princeton University Press, 1978. ISBN 0-691-04655-7 (cl), 0-691-10069-1 (pbk). ▸ Advanced essays by historical demographers on fertility, family and household structure, and migration. Sees industrialization as less destructive than generally claimed. Sampling illustrative of new approaches to family history. [KWK]

40.319 Joseph M. Hawes and Elizabeth I. Nybakken, eds. *American families: a research guide and historical handbook.* Westport, Conn.: Greenwood, 1991. ISBN 0-313-26233-0. ▸ Changing interpretations of preindustrial, nineteenth century, Depression, World War II, and postwar eras. Chapters on women, African Americans, American Indians, and immigrants. Wide-ranging essays with generous bibliography; fine introduction. [KWK]

40.320 N. Ray Hiner and Joseph M. Hawes, eds. *Growing up in America.* Urbana: University of Illinois Press, 1985. ISBN 0-252-01209-7 (cl), 0-252-01218-6 (pbk). ▸ Essays on colonial child rearing, and African American, American Indian, and nineteenth- and twentieth-century families. Influenced by psychological and sociological concepts in recent historical work on childhood. [KWK]

40.321 Jean E. Hunter and Paul T. Mason, eds. *The American family: historical perspectives.* Pittsburgh: Duquesne University Press, 1991. ISBN 0-8207-0219-6. ▸ Study of connections between family and class, production, politics, inheritance, race, and ethnicity. Reflects recent scholarly trends; not recommended as introduction to field. [KWK]

40.322 Susan M. Juster and Maris A. Vinovskis. "Changing perspectives on the American family in the past." *Annual review of sociology* 13 (1987) 193–216. ISSN 0360-0572, ISBN 0-8243-2213-4. ▸ Study of household composition, generations, family cycle, and stages of life from infancy to old age. Discusses childbearing, early child development, adolescence, and aging. Extensive bibliography. [KWK]

40.323 Allan J. Lichtman and Joan R. Challinor, eds. *Kin and communities: families in America.* Washington, D.C.: Smithsonian Institution Press, 1979. ISBN 0-87474-608-6 (cl), 0-87474-609-4 (pbk). ▸ Accessible surveys of prehistory, polygyny, Bering Strait migrations. Essays on specific topics: the Adamses, Great Depression, farms, and African Americans. Discussions of use of photographs and oral history. [KWK]

40.324 Steven Mintz and Susan Kellogg. *Domestic revolutions: a social history of American family life.* 1988 ed. New York: Free Press, 1989. ISBN 0-02-921290-1 (cl, 1988), 0-02-921291-X (pbk). ▸ Introductory text based on recent research with emphasis on period since 1900. Stresses events that brought change, especially rise of individualism. Balanced, nontechnical synthesis for general reader. [KWK]

40.325 Donald M. Scott and Bernard Wishy, eds. *America's families: a documentary history.* New York: Harper & Row, 1982. ISBN 0-06-014048-8 (cl), 0-06-090903-X (pbk). ▸ Comprehensive, chronologically arranged document collection. Covers courtship, marriage, child rearing, Westward expansion, industrialization, motherhood, African Americans, utopians, contraception, abortion, and women's movement. Subject index and bibliography. [KWK]

40.326 Rudy Ray Seward. *The American family: a demographic history.* Beverly Hills, Calif.: Sage, 1978. ISBN 0-8039-1112-2 (cl),

0-8039-1113-0 (pbk). ▸ Examination of impact of urbanization, industrialization, and postindustrial trends on family structure. Stresses family stability and deemphasizes industrial change. Good introductory synthesis with original research on later periods. [KWK]

40.327 David Van Tassel and Peter N. Stearns. *Old age in a bureaucratic society: the elderly, the experts, and the state in American history.* New York: Greenwood, 1986. ISBN 0-313-25000-6. ▸ Lively essays reflecting new scholarship on history of aging, attitudes toward aging, and public policy. Includes demographic analysis, historiographical summary, and suggested research topics. Contributors disagree over social-policy implications. [KWK]

RACE, ETHNICITY, AND MINORITIES

Overviews

40.328 Thomas J. Archdeacon. *Becoming American: an ethnic history.* New York: Free Press, 1983. ISBN 0-02-900830-1 (cl), 0-02-900980-4 (pbk). ▸ Overview, colonial times to present, with attention to both immigrant and colonized minorities, immigration restriction, and American identity. [DRG]

40.329 Roger Daniels. *Coming to America: a history of immigration and ethnicity in American life.* New York: HarperCollins, 1990. ISBN 0-06-016098-5. ▸ Encyclopedic survey of Africans, Europeans, and Asians focusing on entrance into United States. Attention to racism, nativism, and immigration policy. [DRG]

40.330 Leonard Dinnerstein, Roger L. Nichols, and David L. Reimers. *Natives and strangers: blacks, Indians, and immigrants in America.* 2d ed. New York: Oxford University Press, 1990. ISBN 0-19-505722-8. ▸ Brief, readable overview of immigrant and racial minorities, colonial times to present. Attention to racism, nativism, and campaigns for equality. [DRG]

40.331 Joshua A. Fishman et al. *Language loyalty in the United States.* 1966 ed. New York: Arno, 1978. ISBN 0-405-11078-2. ▸ Examination of non English-language usage, bilingualism, and foreign-language press, 1910–60. Information on ethnic associations' efforts to preserve mother tongues. Linguistic and sociological approaches. [DRG]

40.332 Lawrence H. Fuchs. *The American kaleidoscope.* Hanover, N.H.: University Press of New England, 1990. ISBN 0-8195-5122-8. ▸ Important overview of American identity, racial and ethnic exclusion and inclusion, since colonial times. Optimistic but recognizes limits, particularly challenge of integrating underclass into social fabric. [DRG/NMK]

40.333 Thomas Sowell. *Ethnic America: a history.* New York: Basic Books, 1981. ISBN 0-465-02074-7 (cl), 0-465-02075-5 (pbk). ▸ Controversial comparison of immigrants, European Americans, Asian Americans, Latin Americans, and African Americans. Emphasizes economic context and human capital over culture, but finds considerable progress for all groups. [DRG]

40.334 Stephan Thernstrom, ed. *Harvard encyclopedia of American ethnic groups.* Cambridge, Mass.: Harvard University Press, 1980. ISBN 0-674-37512-2. ▸ Broad coverage of ethnic, racial, and religious groups. Thematic essays on key topics. Essential reference work. [DRG]

African Americans

40.335 Mary Frances Berry and John W. Blassingame. *Long memory: the black experience in America.* New York: Oxford University Press, 1982. ISBN 0-19-502909-7 (cl), 0-19-502910-0 (pbk). ▸ Essential study covering from settlement and slavery to black nationalism of 1960s. Emphasizes legacy of oppression into present and continuities in African American experiences. [DRG]

40.336 John H. Bracey, August Meier, and Elliott M. Rudwick. *Black nationalism in America.* Indianapolis: Bobbs-Merrill, 1970. ISBN 0-672-60150-8. ‣ Important collection of documents covering colonial black church to Black Panther party. Valuable introduction; emphasizes recurring tensions between integration and nationalist strategies for change. [DRG]

40.337 Harold X. Connolly. *A ghetto grows in Brooklyn.* New York: New York University Press, 1977. ISBN 0-8147-1371-8. ‣ Covers first African American colonial settlement to postwar boom, all in context of changing New York. Focuses on intensifying ghetto. Good blend of ethnic and urban history. [DRG]

40.338 Philip Sheldon Foner. *Organized labor and the black worker, 1619–1982.* 2d ed. New York: International Publishers, 1982. ISBN 0-7178-0601-4 (cl), 0-7178-0594-8 (pbk). ‣ Overview from emancipation to 1970s. Emphasizes exclusionary labor practices; attention to efforts of African American workers to build alliances within major American labor unions. [DRG]

40.339 Jimmie Lewis Franklin. *Journey toward hope: a history of blacks in Oklahoma.* Norman: University of Oklahoma Press, 1982. ISBN 0-8061-1810-5. ‣ Good example of regional approach in African American history, viewing state as crossroads between South and West. Overview from territorial times to present. [DRG]

40.340 John Hope Franklin and Alfred A. Moss, Jr. *From slavery to freedom: a history of Negro Americans.* 6th ed. New York: Knopf, 1988. ISBN 0-394-56362-X (cl), 0-394-37013-9 (pbk). ‣ Pioneering survey, first published in 1947 and significantly updated in recent editions. African origins and slave trade through Reagan years. Emphasis on change in postwar period. [DRG]

40.341 Paula Giddings. *When and where I enter: the impact of black women on race and sex in America.* New York: Morrow, 1984. ISBN 0-688-01943-9. ‣ Overview of African American women's resistance to racism from slavery to 1965 Moynihan report on *Negro Family.* Attention to feminist and women's organizations. Integrates approaches from ethnic and women's studies. [DRG]

40.342 Herbert G. Gutman. *The black family in slavery and freedom, 1750–1925.* 1976 ed. New York: Vintage, 1977. ISBN 0-394-47116-4 (cl, 1976), 0-394-72451-8 (pbk). ‣ Historical survey; shows kin and family ties surviving slavery and emancipation and stresses accompanying urbanization. Important critique of Moynihan's thesis on origins of black family disorganization. [DRG]

40.343 William H. Harris. *The harder we run: black workers since the Civil War.* New York: Oxford University Press, 1982. ISBN 0-19-502940-2 (cl), 0-19-502941-0 (pbk). ‣ Readable survey emphasizing difficulties of African Americans in finding any employment for much of period. Discusses relations between black and white workers in labor unions. [DRG]

40.344 Darlene Clark Hine, ed. *Black women in America: an historical encyclopedia.* 2 vols. Brooklyn: Carlson, 1993. ISBN 0-926019-61-9. ‣ Major accomplishment, opening up undeveloped field. Much biographical information to be found nowhere else. Valuable chronology of black women's historical experience and list of repositories. [LCP]

40.345 Darlene Clark Hine, ed. *The state of Afro-American history: past, present, and future.* Baton Rouge: Louisiana State University Press, 1986. ISBN 0-8071-1254-2. ‣ Important themes in contemporary historiography, including historical study of slavery, emancipation, urbanization, and teaching of black history. [DRG]

40.346 Lawrence W. Levine. *Black culture and black consciousness: Afro-American folk thought from slavery to freedom.* 1977 ed. Oxford: Oxford University Press, 1978. ISBN 0-19-502088-X (cl, 1977), 0-19-502374-9 (pbk). ‣ Pathbreaking application of folklore, anthropological and ethnomusicological approaches.

Includes tales, religion, song, humor, and heroes in nineteenth and twentieth centuries. [DRG]

40.347 Ronald L. Lewis. *Black coal miners in America: race, class, and community conflict, 1780–1980.* Lexington: University Press of Kentucky, 1987. ISBN 0-8131-1610-4. ‣ Useful case study of African Americans in United Mine Workers. Two centuries of racial conflict and efforts at working-class solidarity. [DRG]

40.348 Jay R. Mandle. *Not slave, not free: the African American economic experience since the Civil War.* Durham, N.C.: Duke University Press, 1992. ISBN 0-8223-1172-0 (cl), 0-8223-1220-4 (pbk). ‣ Brief, readable survey. Traces poverty of contemporary African Americans to plantation economy of South and its demise as regional economy. [DRG]

40.349 August Meier, Jr., and Elliott M. Rudwick. *From plantation to ghetto.* 3d ed. New York: Hill & Wang, 1976. ISBN 0-8090-4792-6 (cl), 0-8090-0122-5 (pbk). ‣ Short, readable survey from West Africa to postwar campaign for equality. Remains useful after thirty years. [DRG]

40.350 Donald G. Nieman. *Promises to keep: African-Americans and the constitutional order, 1776 to the present.* New York: Oxford University Press, 1991. (Organization of American Historians bicentennial essays on the Bill of Rights.) ISBN 0-19-505560-8 (cl), 0-19-505561-6 (pbk). ‣ Survey of influence of race on legal thinking since independence. Demonstrates malleability of Constitution but shows how law most frequently functions as tool of white supremacy. Brief, readable. [DRG]

40.351 Benjamin Quarles. *The Negro in the making of America.* 2d rev. ed. New York: Collier, 1987. ISBN 0-02-036140-8 (pbk). ‣ Measures progress from African origins to 1970s through African American leaders and activists. Early, readable synthesis. [DRG]

40.352 W. Sherman Savage. *Blacks in the West.* Westport, Conn.: Greenwood, 1976. ISBN 0-8371-8775-3. ‣ Study of pioneering African Americans in frontier areas from slavery to civil rights movement. Special attention to blacks in military, industries, and professions. Example of regional approach. [DRG]

40.353 Herbert Shapiro. *White violence and black response: from Reconstruction to Montgomery.* Amherst: University of Massachusetts Press, 1988. ISBN 0-87023-577-X (cl), 0-87023-578-8 (pbk). ‣ Survey of physical brutality as continuous and important dimension of social control of minorities. Focus on African American resistance. Readable synthesis. [DRG]

40.354 Sterling Stuckey. *Slave culture: nationalist theory and the foundations of black America.* New York: Oxford University Press, 1987. ISBN 0-19-504265-4 (cl), 0-19-505664-7 (pbk). ‣ Intellectual survey emphasizing autonomous value system originating in Africa, perpetuated under slavery, and influencing all subsequent African American life. [DRG]

Colonized Minorities

40.355 Rodolfo Acuña. *Occupied America: a history of Chicanos.* 3d ed. New York: Harper & Row, 1988. ISBN 0-06-040163-X (pbk). ‣ Pioneering and originally controversial survey of Southwest as place of conflict between Mexico and United States in nineteenth and twentieth centuries. [DRG]

40.356 Albert Camarillo. *Chicanos in a changing society: from Mexican pueblos to American barrios in Santa Barbara and Southern California, 1848–1930.* Cambridge, Mass.: Harvard University Press, 1979. ISBN 0-674-11395-0 (cl), 0-674-11396-9 (pbk). ‣ Social history of urban Mexicans emphasizes influence of nineteenth-century events, especially war with Mexico and United States acquisition of Southwest on American-Chicano relations in twentieth century. Particularly good example of case-study approach. [DRG/WMD]

40.357 Joseph P. Fitzpatrick. *Puerto Rican Americans: the meaning of migration to the mainland.* 2d ed. Englewood Cliffs, N.J.: Prentice-Hall, 1987. ISBN 0-13-740135-3 (pbk). ▸ Sociological survey of backgrounds, jobs, families, community, and racial concepts of colonized minority. Attention to history of territory and migration to New York. [DRG]

40.358 Richard Allan Griswold del Castillo. *La familia: Chicano families in the urban Southwest, 1848 to the present.* Notre Dame, Ind.: University of Notre Dame Press, 1984. ISBN 0-268-01272-5 (cl), 0-268-01273-3 (pbk). ▸ Survey of life from Mexican era, and American colonization, to present. Emphasizes conflicts between familism and demands of capitalist production. [DRG]

40.359 Ramón A. Gutiérrez. *When Jesus came, the corn mothers went away: marriage, sexuality, and power in New Mexico, 1500–1846.* Stanford, Calif.: Stanford University Press, 1991. ISBN 0-8047-1816-4 (cl), 0-8047-1832-6 (pbk). ▸ Study of Spanish conquest and impact on Pueblo Indians. Pioneering application of gender and anthropological approaches to southwestern history. [DRG]

40.360 Carey McWilliams. *North from Mexico: the Spanish-speaking people of the United States.* Rev. ed. New York: Greenwood and Praeger, 1990. ISBN 0-313-26631-X (cl), 0-275-93224-9 (pbk), (ISSN 0084-9219). ▸ Classic, dated, but still good starting place. Covers from colonization and conquest to recent past. Information on both Chicanos and Mexican immigrants. [DRG/EH-D]

40.361 Alfredo Mirandé and Evangelina Enríquez. *La Chicana: the Mexican-American woman.* Chicago: University of Chicago Press, 1979. ISBN 0-226-53159-7. ▸ Interdisciplinary survey of cultural heritage, work, family, and feminism. Sociological and literary approaches. [DRG]

40.362 David Montejano. *Anglos and Mexicans in the making of Texas, 1836–1986.* Austin: University of Texas Press, 1987. ISBN 0-292-77566-0 (cl), 0-292-77596-2 (pbk). ▸ Excellent case study, from acquisition by United States and development of commercial agriculture to segregation and postwar integration. Focus on ethnicity, nation building, and economic development. Sociological and historical approaches. [DRG]

40.363 Clara E. Rodríguez. *Puerto Ricans: born in the U.S.A.* Boston: Unwin Hyman, 1989. ISBN 0-04-497041-2 (cl), 0-04-497042-0 (pbk). ▸ Study of minority resulting from United States colonial expansion. Valuable attention to racial attitudes. Sociological approach provides background for understanding education, demographics, and residence in mainland. [DRG]

Immigrant Minorities

40.364 John Bodnar. *The transplanted: a history of immigrants in urban America.* Bloomington: Indiana University Press, 1985. ISBN 0-253-31347-3 (cl), 0-253-20416-X (pbk). ▸ Overview of migration, immigrant family's confrontation with capitalism, work and radicalism, and community life after 1830. Broad, influential synthesis of scholarly research stressing European immigrants. Revision of Handlin's view of immigrant alienation (40.372). [DRG/NF]

40.365 John J. Bukowczyk. *And my children did not know me: a history of the Polish Americans.* Bloomington: Indiana University Press, 1987. ISBN 0-253-30701-5 (cl), 0-253-20391-0 (pbk). ▸ Good synthesis of recent research on backgrounds, work, family, community, and generational change. Discusses meaning of ethnic politics in contemporary America. [DRG]

40.366 Roger Daniels. *Asian America: Chinese and Japanese in the United States since 1850.* Seattle: University of Washington Press, 1988. ISBN 0-295-96669-6. ▸ Important study of two largest Asian immigrant groups and their adaptation to United States

life. Sees persistent discrimination, not culture, as main differentiator from European immigrants. [DRG]

40.367 Charlotte Erickson. *Invisible immigrants: the adaptation of English and Scottish immigrants in nineteenth-century America.* Coral Gables, Fla.: University of Miami Press, 1972. ISBN 0-87024-213-X. ▸ Examines adaptation of farmers, artisans, and professionals to American life. Uses letters as sources. [DRG]

40.368 Donna Rae Gabaccia, comp. *Immigrant women in the United States: a selectively annotated multidisciplinary bibliography.* New York: Greenwood, 1989. ISBN 0-313-26452-X. ▸ Interdisciplinary introduction to large, expanding, and little-known literature. Covers past and present migrations. [DRG]

40.369 Manuel Gamio. *Mexican immigration to the United States: a study of human migration and adjustment.* 1930 ed. New York: Dover, 1971. ISBN 0-486-22721-9. ▸ Early overview of migration, jobs, race relations, community life, and culture, beginning in late nineteenth century. Influential in introducing ethnographic methodologies. [DRG]

40.370 Evelyn Nakano Glenn. *Issei, nisei, war bride: three generations of Japanese American women in domestic service.* Philadelphia: Temple University Press, 1986. ISBN 0-87722-412-9. ▸ Best work on group of Asian immigrant women. Sociological approach. [DRG]

40.371 Victor R. Greene. *American immigrant leaders, 1800–1910: marginality and identity.* Baltimore: Johns Hopkins University Press, 1987. ISBN 0-8018-3355-8. ▸ Case studies of Irish, German, Norwegian, Swedish, Jewish, Polish, and Italian leaders as mediators between ethnic group and broader society. Abandons filiopietism to develop typology of leadership. Not hagiographic. [DRG]

40.372 Oscar Handlin. *The uprooted: the epic story of the great migrations that made the American people.* 1973 2d ed. Boston: Little, Brown, 1990. ISBN 0-316-34313-7. ▸ Classic interpretation of immigration experience. Metaphor of alienation revised by research of 1970s, but still important point of departure. [DRG]

40.373 Marcus Lee Hansen. *The Atlantic migration, 1607–1860: a history of the continuing settlement of the United States.* 1940 ed. Arthur M. Schlesinger, ed. New York: Harper, 1961. ▸ Pathbreaking study of European immigration into United States focusing on continuities over time. Early classic in immigration history. [DRG/NF]

40.374 Arthur Hertzberg. *The Jews in America: four centuries of an uneasy encounter, a history.* New York: Simon & Schuster, 1989. ISBN 0-671-62709-0. ▸ Encyclopedic study from first settlement in New Amsterdam to 1970s. Focuses on changing ethnic and religious identities and central role of immigration in shaping Jewish self-understanding. [DRG]

40.375 Maldwyn Allen Jones. *American immigration.* 2d ed. Chicago: The University of Chicago Press, 1992. ISBN 0-226-40634-2 (cl), 0-226-40633-4 (pbk). ▸ Overview of migration, immigrant adjustment, and nativism, colonial times to present. [DRG]

40.376 Michael C. LeMay. *From open door to Dutch door: an analysis of U.S. immigration policy since 1820.* New York: Praeger, 1987. ISBN 0-275-92492-0 (cl), 0-275-92628-1 (pbk). ▸ Traces increasing ethnic restrictions after 1870s and subsequent elimination of racial and ethnic discrimination since World War II. Attention to refugees and naturalization. Only available overview. [DRG]

40.377 Frederick C. Luebke. *Germans in the new world: essays in the history of immigration.* Urbana: University of Illinois Press, 1990. ISBN 0-252-01680-7. ▸ Examination of religion, language, and politics in United States and Brazil. Important example of comparative methodology for study of American ethnic groups. [DRG]

40.378 Jacob Rader Marcus. *United States Jewry, 1776–1985.* 4 vols. Detroit: Wayne State University Press, 1989–93. ISBN 0-8143-2186-0 (v. 1), 0-8143-2188-7 (v. 3). ▸ First two volumes cover early settlements and arrival of Jews from Germany. Emphasizes dual worlds of Jewish Americans. Comprehensive rather than interpretive. [DRG]

40.379 H. Brett Melendy. *Asians in America: Filipinos, Koreans, and East Indians.* 1977 ed. New York: Hippocrene, 1981. ISBN 0-88254-513-2. ▸ Overview of development of three rapidly growing immigrant groups. Section on Filipinos best historical introduction to citizenship, labor, and cultural issues. [DRG]

40.380 Kerby A. Miller. *Emigrants and exiles: Ireland and the Irish exodus to North America.* New York: Oxford University Press, 1985. ISBN 0-19-503594-1. ▸ Provocative synthesis covering seventeenth through early twentieth centuries. Challenges view of America as promised land; stresses migrants' unwillingness to emigrate. Links Irish American nationalism to homeland politics. [DRG/NF]

40.381 James Stuart Olson. *Catholic immigrants in America.* Chicago: Nelson-Hall, 1987. ISBN 0-8304-1037-6. ▸ Religious life of German, East European, Mediterranean, and Hispanic immigrants. Explores issues related to religion, language, and acculturation. [DRG]

40.382 Michael J. Piore. *Birds of passage: migrant labor and industrial societies.* 1979 ed. Cambridge: Cambridge University Press, 1980. ISBN 0-521-22452-7 (cl, 1979), 0-521-28058-3 (pbk). ▸ United States immigration in comparative and global perspective. World-systems approach focusing on links between United States and immigrant homelands. [DRG]

40.383 George E. Pozzetta. "Immigrants and ethnics: the state of Italian-American historiography." *Journal of American ethnic History* 9.1 (1989) 67–95. ISSN 0278-5927. ▸ Good introduction to important immigrant group for which no adequate overview currently exists. [DRG]

40.384 George E. Pozzetta, ed. *American immigration and ethnicity: a twenty-volume series of distinguished essays.* 20 vols. New York: Garland, 1991. ISBN 0-8240-7401-7 (v. 1), 0-8240-7402-5 (v. 2), 0-8240-7403-3 (v. 3), 0-8240-7404-1 (v. 4), 0-8240-7405-X (v. 5), 0-8240-7406-8 (v. 6), 0-8240-7407-6 (v. 7), 0-8240-7408-4 (v. 8), 0-8240-7409-2 (v. 9), 0-8240-7410-6 (v. 10), 0-8240-7411-4 (v. 11), 0-8240-7412-2 (v. 12), 0-8240-7413-0 (v. 13), 0-8240-7414-9 (v. 14), 0-8240-7415-7 (v. 15), 0-8240-7416-5 (v. 16), 0-8240-7417-3 (v. 17), 0-8240-7418-1 (v. 18). 0-8240-7419-X (v. 19), 0-8240-7420-3 (v. 20). ▸ Collection of interdisciplinary scholarly articles. Best introduction to breadth and range of historical research, 1970s to 1980s. [DRG]

40.385 LaVern Rippley. *The German-Americans.* Boston: Twayne, 1976. ISBN 0-8057-8405-5. ▸ Historical overview of migration, work, religion, schooling, arts, and press among arguably largest American ethnic group. [DRG]

40.386 Harald Runblom and Hans Norman, eds. *From Sweden to America: a history of the migration; a collective work of the Uppsala Migration Research Project.* Minneapolis: University of Minnesota Press, 1976. (Studia historica Upsaliensia, 74.) ISBN 0-8166-0776-1. ▸ Collected essays on emigration and adaptation in United States. Important application of geographical and historical demography approaches, exploiting exemplary Swedish sources. [DRG]

40.387 Theodore Saloutos. *The Greeks in the United States.* Cambridge, Mass.: Harvard University Press, 1964. ▸ Pioneering study of southern European immigrant group. Covers religion, business, nationalism, community, and politics from first settlements to 1950s. Focus on generational change. [DRG]

40.388 Theron F. Schlabach. *Peace, faith, nation: Mennonites and Amish in nineteenth-century America.* Scottsdale, Pa.: Herald, 1988. ISBN 0-8361-3102-9. ▸ Readable examination of beliefs, pacifism, schisms, and farming communities of little-studied ethno-religious group, 1790–1900. Information on arrival of immigrants from Russia. [DRG]

40.389 Maxine Schwartz Seller, ed. *Immigrant women.* Philadelphia: Temple University Press, 1981. ISBN 0-87722-190-1 (cl), 0-87722-191-X (pbk). ▸ Selections from scholarly essays, autobiographies, and biographies. Focuses on foreign-born women of nineteenth and twentieth centuries. Emphasizes women's agency and successful adaptation. [DRG]

40.390 Ingrid Semmingsen. *Norway to America: a history of the migration.* Einar Haugen, trans. Minneapolis: University of Minnesota Press, 1978. ISBN 0-8166-0842-3. ▸ Survey of Norwegian immigrants from pioneers of 1825 to Americanization of later generations in twentieth century. Focus on settlement, land, contacts with Americas, and ethnic organizations. [DRG]

40.391 Dale R. Steiner. *Of thee we sing: immigrants and American history.* San Diego: Harcourt Brace Jovanovich, 1987. ISBN 0-15-567385-8 (pbk). ▸ Study of individual lives, colonial times to present, in context of general patterns of immigration. Biographical approach. Useful for beginners. [DRG]

40.392 Ronald Takaki. *Strangers from a different shore: a history of Asian Americans.* 1989 ed. New York: Penguin, 1990. ISBN 0-14-013885-4. ▸ Survey of migration, exclusion, and adaptation to American life of Chinese, Japanese, Koreans, Indians, and Filipinos. Most comprehensive survey on topic. [DRG]

40.393 Shi-shan Henry Tsai. *The Chinese experience in America.* Bloomington: Indiana University Press, 1986. ISBN 0-253-31359-7 (cl), 0-253-20387-2 (pbk). ▸ Covers from early sojourners to most recent immigrations. Focuses on exclusion, community life, and ethnic institutions. Descriptive but comprehensive. [DRG]

40.394 Rudolph J. Vecoli. "Contadini in Chicago: a critique of *The Uprooted.*" *Journal of American history* 51.3 (1964) 404–17. ISSN 0021-8723. ▸ First revision of Handlin's views of immigrant alienation (40.372). New perspectives on Italian peasant origins, cultural diversity, and persistence of group customs. [DRG]

40.395 Rudolph J. Vecoli and Suzanne M. Sinke, eds. *A century of European migrations, 1830–1930.* Urbana: University of Illinois Press, 1991. ISBN 0-252-01796-X. ▸ Collection of scholarly articles on largest groups of nineteenth-century migrants. Useful introduction to recent historical research. [DRG]

40.396 Carl Wittke. *We who built America.* 1964 rev. ed. Cleveland: Case Western Reserve University Press, 1967. ▸ Survey of immigrant groups, colonial times through old and new migrations of nineteenth century. Attention to nativism and immigrant contributions. Classic in immigration history. [DRG]

40.397 Virginia Yans-McLaughlin, ed. *Immigration reconsidered: history, sociology, and politics.* New York: Oxford University Press, 1990. ISBN 0-19-505510-1 (cl), 0-19-505511-X (pbk). ▸ Collection of historiographical and interdisciplinary essays. International approach to migration studies. Essential. [DRG]

SEE ALSO
    21.268 Jacob Rader Marcus. *The American Jewish woman, 1654–1980.*
    42.249 Hasia Diner. *Erin's daughters in America.*

Race and Ethnicity

40.398 Mario Barrera. *Race and class in the Southwest: a theory of racial inequality.* Notre Dame, Ind.: University of Notre Dame Press, 1979. ISBN 0-268-01600-3 (cl), 0-268-01601-1 (pbk). ▸ Pioneering work in Chicano studies. Covers from conquest and colonization by United States to impact of Depression and United States racial and labor policies. [DRG]

40.399   Robert F. Berkhofer, Jr. *The white man's Indian: images of the American Indian from Columbus to the present.* 1978 ed. New York: Vintage, 1979. ISBN 0-394-48485-1 (cl, 1978), 0-394-72794-0 (pbk). ▸ Best general overview recounting evolution of popular, scientific, and artistic representations of American Indians in English-speaking North America and their influence on United States Indian policy. [DRG/FEH/HM/CAM]

40.400   Milton M. Gordon. *Assimilation in American life: the role of race, religion, and national origins.* 1964 ed. New York: Oxford University Press, 1971. ISBN 0-19-500896-0. ▸ Important sociological study of key concept in study of immigration. Influencial in historical studies of 1970s and 1980s. [DRG]

40.401   Thomas F. Gossett. *Race: the history of an idea in America.* 1963 ed. New York: Random House, 1989. ISBN 0-8052-0106-8 (pbk). ▸ Survey of changing racial attitudes from Europeans' first encounter with American Indians to postwar era. Emphasis on anthropology and imperialism as sources of popular ideas. [DRG]

40.402   Stuart Creighton Miller. *The unwelcome immigrant: the American image of the Chinese, 1785–1882.* 1969 ed. Berkeley: University of California Press, 1974. ISBN 0-520-01380-8 (cl, 1969), 0-520-02620-9 (pbk). ▸ Study of images of Chinese among traders and Protestant missionaries in eighteenth and early nineteenth century and their influence on restriction of immigration beginning in 1870s. Demonstrates deep-seated national prejudice against Chinese immigrants. [DRG/NF]

40.403   Gunnar Myrdal. *An American dilemma: the Negro problem and modern democracy.* 1944 ed. 2 vols. New York: Pantheon, 1975. ISBN 0-394-73042-9 (v. 1, pbk), 0-394-73043-7 (v. 2, pbk). ▸ Classic study of American race relations and moral issues of racial discrimination at midcentury. Covers economics, politics, class, and protest in African American history. [DRG]

40.404   Werner Sollors. *Beyond ethnicity: consent and descent in American culture.* New York: Oxford University Press, 1986. ISBN 0-19-503694-8. ▸ Study of changing historical understandings of ethnic group and ethnic identity, emphasizing construction of both. Attention to African American, American Indian, and immigrant groups. Interpretations based on literary sources. Interdisciplinary and essential. [DRG]

40.405   Stephen Steinberg. *The ethnic myth: race, ethnicity, and class in America.* Rev. ed. Boston: Beacon, 1989. ISBN 0-8070-4151-3. ▸ Emphasizes economic structures as determinants of ethnic and racial patterns in employment and education. Uses sociological methods and models. [DRG]

40.406   Ronald Takaki. *Iron cages: race and culture in nineteenth-century America.* 1979 ed. New York: Oxford University Press, 1990. ISBN 0-19-506385-6. ▸ Comparative analysis of racial domination of Mexicans, African Americans, American Indians, and Asians. Emphasis on class as element of American racism. Interprets writings of selected white men through Gramscian concept of cultural hegemony. [DRG/NF]

40.407   Joel Williamson. *The crucible of race: black-white relations in the American South since emancipation.* New York: Oxford University Press, 1984. ISBN 0-19-503382-5. ▸ Essential examination of relations between African Americans and white southerners, changing from inclusion during slavery through exclusion of racial discrimination. Emphasizes mingling of white and black in making of American culture. [DRG]

Racism, Nativism, and Prejudice

40.408   Herbert Aptheker. *Anti-racism in U.S. history: the first two hundred years.* New York: Greenwood, 1992. ISBN 0-313-28199-8, ISSN 0084-9219. ▸ Marxist perspectives on race and ethnicity from colonial times through emancipation. Attention to whites and Europeans who fought slavery and racial prejudice. Unique summary. [DRG]

40.409   Mary Frances Berry. *Black resistance, white law: a history of constitutional racism in America.* New York: Appleton-Century-Crofts, 1971. ISBN 0-390-08840-4. ▸ Focus on constitutionally sanctioned violence against blacks, viewed as disquieting presence in American life, and on suppression of continuous black resistance. Essential. [DRG]

40.410   Arnoldo De León. *They called them greasers: Anglo attitudes toward Mexicans in Texas, 1821–1900.* Austin: University of Texas Press, 1983. ISBN 0-292-70363-5 (cl), 0-292-78054-0 (pbk). ▸ Study of evolving racial attitudes and their institutionalization, Texas republic to early twentieth century. Finds racial attitudes more important than ethnocentrism for understanding "Anglo"-Mexican relations. [DRG]

40.411   David A. Gerber, ed. *Anti-Semitism in American history.* Urbana: University of Illinois Press, 1986. ISBN 0-252-01214-3. ▸ Collection of scholarly articles exploring varied ideological forms and exclusionary practices in nineteenth and twentieth centuries. Offers definition of antisemitism. Basic reading. [DRG]

40.412   John Higham. *Strangers in the land: patterns of American nativism, 1860–1925.* 2d ed. New Brunswick, N.J.: Rutgers University Press, 1988. ISBN 0-8135-1317-0 (cl), 0-8135-1308-1 (pbk). ▸ Examination of sources of xenophobia and historical origins of immigration restriction. Not significantly revised from 1955 original edition. [DRG]

40.413   Gary Y. Okihiro. *Cane fires: the anti-Japanese movement in Hawaii, 1865–1945.* Philadelphia: Temple University Press, 1991. ISBN 0-87722-799-3. ▸ Discrimination against migrant plantation laborers as backdrop for understanding attitudes of military and ordinary Americans during World War II. Revises popular views of Hawaii as successful interracial melting pot. Valuable case study. [DRG]

40.414   Philip Perlmutter. *Divided we fall: a history of ethnic, religious, and racial prejudice in America.* Ames: Iowa State University Press, 1992. ISBN 0-8138-0644-5 (cl), 0-8138-0592-9 (pbk). ▸ Uneven but ambitious effort to treat forms of prejudice usually examined separately. Emphasizes plurality of prejudice and repeated efforts to transcend bigotry in all groups. [DRG]

40.415   Alexander Plaisted Saxton. *The rise and fall of the white republic: class politics and mass culture in nineteenth-century America.* London: Verso, 1990. ISBN 0-86091-271-X (cl), 0-86091-986-2 (pbk). ▸ Outline of relationships between republicanism and racial inequality. Examines evolution through press, theater, and Western heroes. Notable for intellectual and cultural approach and sources. [DRG]

40.416   C. Vann Woodward. *American counterpoint: slavery and racism in the North-South dialogue.* 1971 ed. Oxford: Oxford University Press, 1983. ISBN 0-19-503269-1 (pbk). ▸ Exploration of lineages of racism and regionalism in American thought. Views southerners and African Americans as oldest and largest ethnic minorities in United States. [DRG]

GENDER AND SEXUALITY

Women

40.417   Adele Logan Alexander. *Ambiguous lives: free women of color in rural Georgia, 1789–1979.* Fayetteville: University of Arkansas, 1991. ISBN 1-55728-214-5 (cl), 0-55728-215-3 (pbk). ▸ Uncovers complexities of nineteenth-century free black women: ambiguities of color bar and extent of miscegenous relationships in rural South. Focus on author's family; fascinating account. [SGM]

40.418   Margaret Hope Bacon. *Mothers of feminism: the story of Quaker women in America.* San Francisco: Harper & Row, 1986.

ISBN 0-06-250043-0 (cl), 0-06-250046-5 (pbk). ‣ Standard work on Quaker women as leaders in reform, colonial period to present. Advocated modern ideas of feminism, abolition, reform, and women's equality. Nineteenth-century emphasis. [SGM]

40.419 Mirra Bank, comp. *Anonymous was a woman.* New York: St. Martin's, 1979. ISBN 0-312-04185-3 (cl), 0-312-04186-1 (pbk). ‣ Basic, illustrated study, developed in connection with a film. Presents women's traditional approach to folk art during eighteenth and nineteenth centuries. Includes needlework and painting with relevant writings. [SGM]

40.420 Lois W. Banner. *American beauty.* New York: Knopf; distributed by Random House, 1983. ISBN 0-394-51923-X. ‣ Social history of women's fashion and appearance, early nineteenth century to present. Shows changing perceptions of beauty, rise of beauty industry, conflict between feminism and fashion, and beauty as power and oppression. [SGM]

40.421 G. J. Barker-Benfield and Catherine Clinton, eds. *Portraits of American women: from settlement to the present.* New York: St. Martin's, 1991. ISBN 0-312-03687-6 (pbk). ‣ Twenty-five readable essays by different scholars about women who contributed to public realm. Includes Pocahontas, Mercy Otis Warren, Phillis Wheatley, Alice Paul, and Georgia O'Keefe. Shows variety of female experience. [SGM]

40.422 Rosalyn Baxandall, Linda Gordon, and Susan Reverby, eds. *America's working women: a documentary history, 1600 to the present.* New York: Vintage, 1976. ISBN 0-394-49150-5 (cl), 0-394-72208-6 (pbk). ‣ Wealth of primary documents on songs, protests, memoirs, and union records. Focuses on women's experiences as paid workers. Useful, inclusive approach to class, race, and period. [SGM]

40.423 Mary Ritter Beard, ed. *America through women's eyes.* 1933 ed. Westport, Conn.: Greenwood, 1969. ISBN 0-8371-0301-0. ‣ Illustration of women's roles, colonial period to 1930s, through telling primary sources and editor's commentary. Classic study influential in launching United States women's history. [SGM]

40.424 Betty Boyd Caroli. *First ladies.* New York: Oxford University Press, 1987. ISBN 0-19-503768-5 (cl), 0-19-505654-X (pbk). ‣ Brief profiles of presidents' wives from Martha Washington to Nancy Reagan. How they defined position, relationships with media, and public perceptions. Scant biographical information. [SGM]

40.425 William H. Chafe. *Women and equality: changing patterns in American culture.* 1977 ed. Oxford: Oxford University Press, 1978. ISBN 0-19-502158-4 (cl, 1977), 0-19-502365-X (pbk). ‣ Six provocative essays on modern women's movement with comparisons to civil rights. Shows gender determining place in society. Uses social theory to explain subordination of African Americans and women. [SGM]

40.426 Ruth Schwartz Cowan. *More work for mother: the ironies of household technology from the open hearth to the microwave.* New York: Basic Books, 1984. ISBN 0-465-04731-9 (cl), 0-465-04732-7 (pbk). ‣ Study of impact of changing technology on women's lives over three centuries. Provocative argument that labor-saving inventions increased women's duties and housework became more exclusively female. [SGM]

40.427 Carl N. Degler. *At odds: women and the family in America from the Revolution to the present.* New York: Oxford University Press, 1980. ISBN 0-19-502657-8 (cl), 0-19-502934-8 (pbk). ‣ Interpretive overview with nineteenth-century emphasis. Presents family stability as dependent on women's subordination to husband and children and thus at odds with women's desire for equality. [SGM]

40.428 Mabel Deutrich and Virginia C. Purdy, eds. *Clio was a woman: studies in the history of American women.* Washington, D.C.: Howard University Press, 1980. (National Archives Conferences, 16.) ISBN 0-88258-077-9. ‣ Sixteen essays presented at 1976 conference. Somewhat outdated but broad-ranging scholarship by leading historians in field. [SGM]

40.429 Ann Douglas. *The feminization of American culture.* 1977 ed. New York: Doubleday, 1978. ISBN 0-385-24241-7 (pbk). ‣ Important study of rise of mass culture among nineteenth-century middle-class women, ministers, and male authors. Argues sentimental fiction and anti-intellectualism overcame genuine art and culture. [SGM]

40.430 Sara M. Evans. *Born for liberty: a history of women in America.* New York: Free Press, 1989. ISBN 0-02-902990-2. ‣ Well-written introduction to changing roles and diverse experiences of women. Sees women as central to nation's social, economic, and political upheavals. [SGM]

40.431 Eleanor Flexner. *Century of struggle: the women's rights movement in the United States.* Rev. ed. Cambridge, Mass.: Belknap, 1975. ISBN 0-674-10651-2. ‣ Classic if somewhat outdated chronicle, early nineteenth century to 1920. Argues for importance of women's suffrage movement as it reemerged and triumphed, but also shows internal conflict and opposition to its goals. [SGM]

40.432 Jean E. Friedman. *The enclosed garden: women and community in the evangelical South, 1830–1900.* Chapel Hill: University of North Carolina Press, 1985. ISBN 0-8078-1644-2. ‣ Interesting study of church, kin, and community to explain Southern women's failure to engage in reform. Sees male control of family and community as impeding female bonding and autonomy. [SGM]

40.433 Jean E. Friedman, William G. Shade, and Mary Jane Capozzoli, eds. *Our American sisters: women in American life and thought.* 4th ed. Lexington, Mass.: Heath, 1987. ISBN 0-669-11020-5 (pbk). ‣ Twenty-five well-selected essays by prominent historians, covering women's varied experiences from colonial period to present. Useful textbook with emphasis on nineteenth century. [SGM]

40.434 Carol Groneman and Mary Beth Norton, eds. *"To toil the livelong day": America's women at work, 1780–1980.* Ithaca, N.Y.: Cornell University Press, 1987. ISBN 0-8014-1847-X (cl), 0-8014-9452-4 (pbk). ‣ Seventeen essays showing variety of and change in women's labor. Demonstrates direction of new research including domestic, factory, and farm labor. Examines relationship of employer and employee, union involvement, class, and racial tensions. [SGM]

40.435 Barbara J. Harris. *Beyond her sphere: women and the professions in American history.* 1978 ed. Westport, Conn.: Greenwood, 1980. ISBN 0-313-20415-2 (cl, 1978), 0-313-22734-9 (pbk), ISSN 0147-104X. ‣ Introductory view, 1800 to present, focusing on professional white women, their education, economic roles, family concerns, and how they overcame ideas of female inferiority and domesticity. [SGM]

40.436 Dolores Hayden. *The grand domestic revolution: a history of feminist designs for American homes, neighborhoods, and cities.* 1981 ed. Cambridge, Mass.: MIT Press, 1983. ISBN 0-262-08108-3 (cl, 1981), 0-262-58055-1 (pbk). ‣ Interesting study examining experimental, collectivist visions of housekeeping, 1800 to present. Material feminism after Civil War outlined spatial arrangements and elevated domesticity to foster equality. [SGM]

40.437 Helen Lefkowitz Horowitz. *Alma mater: design and experience in the women's colleges from their nineteenth-century beginnings to the 1930s.* New York: Knopf; distributed by Random House, 1984. ISBN 0-394-53439-5. ‣ Focus on seven sisters (Bryn Mawr, Smith, Radcliffe, Barnard, Mount Holyoke, Vassar,

Wellesley) and three other colleges. Addresses how physical environment and architecture affected student experience and how cultural values defined women's roles. [SGM]

40.438 Edward T. James, Janet Wilson James, and Paul S. Boyer, eds. *Notable American women, 1607–1950: a biographical dictionary.* 3 vols. Cambridge, Mass.: Belknap, 1971. ISBN 0-674-62731-8 (set, cl), 0-674-62734-2 (set, pbk). ‣ Three invaluable volumes with well-written biographies of more than 1,300 significant American women, 1607–1950. Balanced coverage of race, region, ethnicity, and profession. [SGM]

40.439 Janet Wilson James, ed. *Women in American religion.* 1978 ed. Philadelphia: University of Pennsylvania Press, 1980. ISBN 0-8122-7780-5 (cl), 0-8122-1104-9 (pbk). ‣ Essays by thirteen scholars on overlooked topic. Treats colonial, evangelical, and Jewish women and women as ministers, missionaries, and Catholic sisters. Religion seen as both confining and liberating. [SGM]

40.440 Joan M. Jensen. *Loosening the bonds: mid-Atlantic farm women, 1750–1850.* New Haven: Yale University Press, 1986. ISBN 0-300-03366-4 (cl), 0-300-04265-5 (pbk). ‣ Original, groundbreaking study of women's role in economy. Refreshing focus on rural women of Pennsylvania and Delaware. Discusses household work, domestic production, and how women challenged patriarchy by creating important economic roles on farm. [SGM/DMS/VBB]

40.441 Jacqueline Jones. *Labor of love, labor of sorrow: black women, work, and the family from slavery to the present.* 1985 ed. New York: Vintage, 1986. ISBN 0-394-74536-1 (pbk). ‣ Well-researched study emphasizing poor, rural, southern black women. Explores how they redefined paid work to fit family needs central to their lives. Finds double burden of color and gender ever present. Excellent integration of labor and family history. [SGM/LGB]

40.442 Susan Estabrook Kennedy. *If all we did was to weep at home: a history of white working-class women in America.* Bloomington: Indiana University Press, 1979. ISBN 0-253-19154-8 (cl), 0-253-20267-1 (pbk). ‣ Ambitious synthesis, 1600 to 1970s, with chief focus on twentieth century. Despite industrialization's impact, working-class women's aspirations offset by strong interest in home. [SGM]

40.443 Linda K. Kerber and Jane Sherron De Hart, eds. *Women's America: refocusing the past.* 3d ed. New York: Oxford University Press, 1991. ISBN 0-19-506261-2 (cl), 0-19-506262-0 (pbk). ‣ Panoramic in scope, colonial period to present, includes important documents, essays, and excerpts from significant monographs by prominent historians. [SGM]

40.444 Alice Kessler-Harris. *Out to work: a history of wage-earning women in the United States.* New York: Oxford University Press, 1982. ISBN 0-19-503024-9 (cl), 0-19-503353-1 (pbk). ‣ Comprehensive study of transformation of female wage laborers, colonial period to 1970s, with emphasis on twentieth century. Sees women as victims of market segmentation, limited skills, and confining social ideology. [SGM]

40.445 Gerda Lerner, ed. *Black women in white America: a documentary history.* 1972 ed. New York: Vintage, 1992. ISBN 0-679-74314-6. ‣ Influential collection of primary sources, many previously unpublished, slavery era to 1970s. Demonstrates, in women's own words, degree of oppression and will and strength to survive. [SGM]

40.446 Gerda Lerner, ed. *The female experience: an American documentary.* 1977 ed. New York: Oxford University Press, 1992. ISBN 0-19-507258-8. ‣ Carefully selected primary documents, many published for first time, reflecting diversity of women's lives and gradual effort to free themselves from male-dominated world. [SGM]

40.447 Julie A. Matthei. *An economic history of women in America: women's work, the sexual division of labor, and the development of capitalism.* New York: Schocken, 1982. ISBN 0-8052-3804-2 (cl), 0-8052-0744-9 (pbk). ‣ Study of women's engagement in paid labor, colonial period to present. Detailed exploration of changes in women's lives and relationship between capitalism and sexual division of labor. [SGM]

40.448 Glenna Matthews. *"Just a housewife": the rise and fall of domesticity in America.* New York: Oxford University Press, 1987. ISBN 0-19-503859-2. ‣ Useful examination of changing attitudes toward housework, colonial period to 1960s. How domesticity lost aura of reverence with rise of consumerism in early twentieth century. [SGM]

40.449 Sandra L. Myres. *Westering women and the frontier experience, 1800–1915.* Albuquerque: University of New Mexico Press, 1982. ISBN 0-8263-0625-x (cl), 0-8263-0626-8 (pbk). ‣ How women's responses to frontier life modified gender roles. Adept analysis of debate over myth and reality. Though lonely and confined to home, frontier women found new opportunities for work, reform, and public involvement. [SGM/CAM]

40.450 Mary Beth Norton, ed. *Major problems in American women's history: documents and essays.* Lexington, Mass.: Heath, 1989. ISBN 0-669-14490-8. ‣ Collection of primary sources representative of varied issues and periods, accompanied by well-written essays presenting current debates and contrasting historiographical interpretations. [SGM]

40.451 Margaret W. Rossiter. *Women scientists in America: struggles and strategies to 1940.* Baltimore: Johns Hopkins University Press, 1982. ISBN 0-8018-2443-5 (cl), 0-8018-2509-1 (pbk). ‣ Recounts careers of women who chose science as profession, 1800s to 1940. Discusses educational achievements and hurdles overcome. Pathbreaking overview and analysis; best starting place for any exploration of women in science. [SGM/JGC/PEM]

40.452 Sheila M. Rothman. *Woman's proper place: a history of changing ideals and practices, 1870 to the present.* New York: Basic Books, 1978. ISBN 0-465-09203-9 (cl), 0-465-09204-7 (pbk). ‣ Definitions of womanhood and woman's social aims during one-hundred-year period. Differentiates four ideals and explains changing attitudes. Well-written synthesis; focus on middle class. [SGM]

40.453 Rosemary Radford Ruether and Rosemary Skinner Keller, eds. *Women and religion in America.* 3 vols. New York: Harper & Row, 1981–86. ISBN 0-06-066829-6 (v. 1, cl), 0-06-066832-6 (v. 2, cl) 0-06-066833-4 (v. 3, cl), 0-06-064303-x (v. 2, pbk). ‣ Interpretive essays on varied religious experiences of Jewish, Catholic, and Protestant women with relevant documents. Best source for topic that deserves more study. [SGM]

40.454 Anne Firor Scott. *Natural allies: women's associations in American history.* Urbana: University of Illinois Press, 1991. ISBN 0-252-01846-x. ‣ First broad effort to explore women's work in voluntary associations from antebellum period into twentieth century. Sees women forming natural alliances across class and race in effort to do good. [SGM]

40.455 Anne Firor Scott. *The Southern lady: from pedestal to politics, 1830–1930.* Chicago: University of Chicago Press, 1970. ISBN 0-226-74346-2 (cl), 0-226-74347-0 (pbk). ‣ Groundbreaking study. Reveals dichotomy between ideal and real in elite antebellum Southern women's lives. Civil War a watershed in giving women confidence to engage actively in reform, but always as ladies. [SGM]

40.456 Kathryn Kish Sklar and Thomas Dublin, eds. *Women and power in American history: a reader.* 2 vols. Englewood Cliffs, N.J.: Prentice-Hall, 1991. ISBN 0-13-962218-7 (v. 1), 0-13-962234-9 (v. 2). ‣ Essays with emphasis on new research in women's history over past twenty years. Shows variety of female experience and women's acquisition of power from work, family, and community. [SGM]

40.457 Carroll Smith-Rosenberg. *Disorderly conduct: visions of gender in Victorian America.* New York: Knopf; distributed by Random House, 1985. ISBN 0-394-53545-6 (cl), 0-19-504039-2 (pbk). ▸ Interesting, innovative essays on medical and sexual issues and women's culture. Includes influential study of nineteenth-century female friendship and bonding. [SGM]

40.458 Barbara Miller Solomon. *In the company of educated women: a history of women and higher education in America.* New Haven: Yale University Press, 1985. ISBN 0-300-03314-1. ▸ Best available study, colonial era to present, of women's educational opportunities, access to institutions, college experiences, and feminism in education. Argues female education brought uneven advances. [SGM]

40.459 Susan Strasser. *Never done: a history of American housework.* New York: Pantheon, 1982. ISBN 0-394-51024-0 (cl), 0-394-70841-5 (pbk). ▸ Basic study of women's domestic duties and technologies transforming work in home. Covers nineteenth and twentieth centuries. [SGM]

40.460 Susan Burroughs Swan. *Plain and fancy: American women and their needlework, 1700–1850.* New York: Holt, Rinehart & Winston, 1977. ISBN 0-03-015121-X. ▸ Illustrated study showing importance of needlework to women, eighteenth and nineteenth centuries. Describes instruction, varied skills, and how needlework reflected changes in women's lives. Well written and unique. [SGM]

40.461 Mary Roth Walsh. *"Doctors wanted, no women need apply": sexual barriers in the medical profession, 1835–1975.* New Haven: Yale University Press, 1977. ISBN 0-300-02024-4 (pbk), 0-300-02414-2 (pbk). ▸ Examination of women's arduous efforts to become physicians. Some success by late nineteenth century, followed by male backlash in twentieth with quotas at medical schools until 1960s. Focus on Boston area. [SGM]

40.462 Lynn Y. Weiner. *From working girl to working mother: the female labor force in the United States, 1820–1980.* Chapel Hill: University of North Carolina Press, 1985. ISBN 0-8078-1612-4 (cl), 0-8078-4159-5 (pbk). ▸ Overview of women in labor force, changing behavior of female workers, and shifting attitudes of society. Public policies upheld middle-class ideas, although lower-class women were majority of female workers. [SGM]

40.463 Nancy Woloch. *Women and the American experience.* New York: Knopf; distributed by Random House, 1984. ISBN 0-394-53515-4 (cl), 0-394-32319-X (pbk). ▸ Ten narrative episodes placed in historical context. Introduces issues featured in scholarship of last two decades: family life, women's domestic and paid work, and public involvement. [SGM]

SEE ALSO
1.479 Gerda Lerner. *The majority finds its past.*
4.758 Darlene Clark Hine. *Black women in white.*
4.760 Susan Reverby. *Ordered to care.*
4.813 Regina Markell Morantz-Sanchez. *Sympathy and science.*
42.460 Susan Armitage and Elizabeth Jameson, eds. *The women's West.*
42.467 Glenda Riley. *The female frontier.*
42.539 Barbara Leslie Epstein. *The politics of domesticity.*
44.269 Barbara Sicherman and Carol Hurd Green, eds. *Notable American women.*
44.310 Claudia D. Goldin. *Understanding the gender gap.*

Men

40.464 Mark C. Carnes. *Secret ritual and manhood in Victorian America.* New Haven: Yale University Press, 1989. ISBN 0-300-

04424-0 (cl), 0-300-05146-8 (pbk). ▸ Study of nineteenth-century secret fraternal lodges, including Freemasons and Odd Fellows. Finds men rejected feminized religion; used fraternal rituals to reaffirm conception of manhood. [SGM]

40.465 Mark C. Carnes and Clyde Griffen, eds. *Meanings for manhood: constructions of masculinity in Victorian America.* Chicago: University of Chicago Press, 1990. ISBN 0-226-09364-6 (cl), 0-226-09365-4 (pbk). ▸ Collection of essays exploring boyhood, friendship, marriage, and work as experienced by males and interpreted by moralists in century of shifting definitions of gender roles. Good sampling of current research. [LCP]

40.466 Mary Ann Clawson. *Constructing brotherhood: class, gender, and fraternalism.* Princeton: Princeton University Press, 1989. ISBN 0-691-09447-0. ▸ Social theory used to study fraternal orders over past two centuries. Male lodges gained following by fostering kinship bonds; declined as service clubs emerged early in twentieth century. [SGM]

40.467 John Demos. "The changing faces of fatherhood." In *Past, present, and personal: the family and the life course in American history.* 1986 ed, pp. 41–67. New York: Oxford University Press, 1988. ISBN 0-19-503777-4 (cl), 0-19-504766-4 (pbk). ▸ Focuses on father and changing role in family. Effort to rethink family and parental roles generally. [SGM]

40.468 Joe L. Dubbert. *A man's place: masculinity in transition.* Englewood Cliffs, N.J.: Prentice-Hall, 1979. ISBN 0-13-552059-2 (cl), 0-13-552042-8 (pbk). ▸ Provocative argument that masculinity enjoyed golden age on frontier when strength and courage important but declined as frontier closed. Middle-class men created new images through war and sports. [SGM]

40.469 Elizabeth H. Pleck and Joseph H. Pleck, comps. *The American man.* Englewood Cliffs, N.J.: Prentice-Hall, 1980. ISBN 0-13-028159-X (cl), 0-13-028142-5 (pbk). ▸ Anthology of essays, most previously published, on American men from seventeenth century to 1970s. Useful for wide range of topics, but appeared too early to reflect current theory and research. [LCP]

40.470 E. Anthony Rotundo. *American manhood: transformations in masculinity from the Revolution to the modern era.* New York: Basic Books, 1993. ISBN 0-465-01409-7. ▸ Readable analysis of generations, love, and work complementing recent scholarship on women. Turn of nineteenth century crucial era of transformation. Qualities associated with manhood not essential, but socially constructed. [LCP]

Homosexuality

40.471 Lillian Faderman. *Odd girls and twilight lovers: a history of lesbian life in twentieth-century America.* New York: Columbia University Press, 1991. ISBN 0-231-07488-3. ▸ Sweeping, well-researched account of lesbian life, showing diversity of experiences, changes in identity and status, and gradual destigmatization of life style. Uses oral history, memoirs, and correspondence. [SGM]

40.472 Jonathan Ned Katz. *Gay American history: lesbians and gay men in the U.S.A., a documentary history.* Rev. ed. New York: Meridian, 1992. ISBN 0-452-01092-6. ▸ Important collection of documents tracing homosexuality and homophobia for past 350 years. Includes useful commentary. Well researched. [SGM]

Sexuality

40.473 John D'Emilio and Estelle B. Freedman. *Intimate matters: a history of sexuality in America.* 1988 ed. New York: Harper & Row, 1989. ISBN 0-06-015855-7 (cl), 0-06-091550-1 (pbk). ▸ Study of how sexuality, its meaning, and efforts to regulate sexual behavior have been transformed in American life from colonial period to present. Comprehensive, groundbreaking work. [SGM]

40.474 Linda Gordon. *Woman's body, woman's right: a social history of birth control in America.* New York: Penguin, 1990. ISBN 0-14-004683-6 (cl), 0-14-013127-2 (pbk). ▸ Strongly argued approach to birth control efforts and reproductive freedom, late nineteenth century to present. Marxist-feminist interpretation stressing social class and capitalism. [SGM]

40.475 Judith Walzer Leavitt. *Brought to bed: child-bearing in America, 1750–1950.* 1986 ed. New York: Oxford University Press, 1988. ISBN 0-19-503843-6 (cl), 0-19-505690-6 (pbk). ▸ Stimulating study of changing ideas and practices. Woman-centered, domestic activity became hospital, male-controlled event. Females exerted some power in desire for safer births until twentieth century. [SGM]

40.476 James C. Mohr. *Abortion in America: the origins and evolution of national policy, 1800–1900.* 1978 ed. Oxford: Oxford University Press, 1979. ISBN 0-19-502249-1 (cl, 1978), 0-19-502616-0 (pbk). ▸ Clear chronicle of transformation of public policy from acceptance of abortion in 1800 to virtual illegality by 1900. Physicians and medical associations prime movers struggling to gain monopoly. Underestimates importance of gender ideology in shaping outcome. [SGM/VBB]

40.477 Kathy Pciss, Christina Simmons, and Robert A. Padgug, eds. *Passion and power: sexuality in history.* Philadelphia: Temple University Press, 1989. ISBN 0-87722-596-6 (cl), 0-87722-637-7 (pbk). ▸ Interesting essays on sex and sexuality from leftist perspective. Varied topics include pornography, homosexuality, violence, venereal disease, African Americans, and birth control. Topics shown as central to history. [SGM]

40.478 James Reed. *The birth control movement and American society: from private vice to public virtue.* 1978 ed. Princeton: Princeton University Press, 1984. ISBN 0-691-09404-7 (cl), 0-691-02830-3 (pbk). ▸ Well-researched examination focusing on significant individuals responsible for social change. Best overall history of topic. [SGM]

40.479 Richard W. Wertz and Dorothy C. Wertz. *Lying-in: a history of childbirth in America.* New York: Free Press, 1977. ISBN 0-02-934510-3. ▸ Study of shifting theories and attitudes, which affected techniques, setting, and procedures over 350 years. Pioneering history of childbirth. [SGM]

SEE ALSO
   4.812 Judith Walzer Leavitt. *Women and health in America.*

Gender

40.480 Sarah Deutsch. *No separate refuge: culture, class, and gender on an Anglo-Hispanic frontier in the American Southwest, 1880–1940.* 1987 ed. New York: Oxford University Press, 1989. ISBN 0-19-50441-5 (cl, 1987), 0-19-506073-3 (pbk). ▸ Important argument for central role women played in processes of conquest, economic and cultural subordination, and assimilation among Hispanics in Southwest. [SGM]

40.481 Ellen K. Rothman. *Hands and hearts: a history of courtship in America.* New York: Basic Books, 1984. ISBN 0-465-02880-2. ▸ Examination of middle-class courting behavior, 1770–1920. Shows ambiguities of gender roles and, like Lystra 42.631, challenges concept of passionless Victorians. [SGM/DSS]

40.482 E. Anthony Rotundo. "Learning about manhood: gender ideals and the middle-class family in nineteenth-century America." In *Manliness and morality: middle-class masculinity in Britain and America, 1800–1940.* J. A. Mangan and James Walvin, eds., pp. 35–51. New York: St. Martin's, 1987. ISBN 0-312-00797-3. ▸ Overview by pioneering scholar on how manhood was con-

structed in crucial century of transition. Brief, readable example of current theory and approaches to gender in history. [LCP]

SEE ALSO
42.631 Karen Lystra. *Searching the heart.*
44.335 Peter G. Filene. *Him/her self.*

INTELLECTUAL LIFE AND CULTURE

Intellectual Life

40.483 Charles Albro Barker. *American convictions: cycles of public thought, 1600–1850.* Philadelphia: Lippincott, 1970. ▸ Useful survey of main ideas in public-community life. Explores tensions between freedom and organizational imperatives in development of democracy. Links intellectual life to social and political history. [LCP]

40.484 Thomas Bender. *New York intellect: a history of intellectual life in New York City, from 1750 to the beginnings of our own time.* 1987 ed. Baltimore: Johns Hopkins University Press, 1988. ISBN 0-8018-3639-5 (pbk). ▸ Searching exploration of changing structures of intellectual life—civic, literary, and academic—as exemplified by leading figures and institutions in metropolis. Meanings of democratic culture. [TDH]

40.485 Paul A. Carter. *Revolt against destiny: an intellectual history of the United States.* New York: Columbia University Press, 1989. ISBN 0-231-06616-3. ▸ Broad interpretive history, focusing especially on long cultural-political shadows of ancient Israel and ancient Rome. Readable, provocative, personal. [TDH]

40.486 Paul Keith Conkin. *Puritans and pragmatists: eight eminent American thinkers.* 1968 ed. Bloomington: Indiana University Press, 1976. ISBN 0-253-34720-3 (cl), 0-253-20197-7 (pbk). ▸ Careful explications of philosophies of Jonathan Edwards, Benjamin Franklin, John Adams, Ralph Waldo Emerson, Charles Peirce, William James, Thomas Dewey, and George Santayana. Argues for roots of pragmatism in Puritanism and the continuing legacies of both. [TDH]

40.487 Merle Eugene Curti. *The growth of American thought.* 1964 3d ed. New Brunswick, N.J.: Transaction, 1982. ISBN 0-87855-434-3 (cl), 0-87855-849-9 (pbk). ▸ Crowning work of the progressive school of American intellectual history. Readable, extremely influential, good source on many institutions and developments. Somewhat dated. [TDH]

40.488 Elizabeth Flower and Murray G. Murphey. *A history of philosophy in America.* 2 vols. New York: Capricorn, 1977. ISBN 0-399-11650-8 (v. 1), 0-399-11743-1 (v. 2). ▸ Authoritative work on philosophy of mind and ethics, institutions, and thinkers. Central role of philosophy in America as mediator between or synthesizer of science and religion. [LCP]

40.489 Thomas L. Haskell, ed. *The authority of experts: studies in history and theory.* Bloomington: Indiana University Press, 1984. ISBN 0-253-31079-2. ▸ Key collection of essays on major issue of recognition of intellectuals as professionals with authoritative knowledge. Historians exploring philosophical and public policy issues in dialogue with other scholars. [LCP]

40.490 John Higham and Paul Keith Conkin, eds. *New directions in American intellectual history.* Baltimore: Johns Hopkins University Press, 1979. ISBN 0-8018-2183-5. ▸ Conference essays honoring Merle Curti on theory and practice of intellectual history and links with other disciplines. Covers Puritan legacy, religious and republican traditions, professions, popular culture, and personality. [LCP]

40.491 Richard Hofstadter. *Anti-intellectualism in American life.* 1963 ed. New York: Knopf, 1970. ISBN 0-394-70317-0. ▸ Examination of persistent strain of hostility to life of the mind and to people concerned with ideas, particularly in religious and political life. Elegant and influential essay. [TDH]

40.492 David A. Hollinger. *In the American province: studies in the history and historiography of ideas.* 1985 ed. Baltimore: Johns Hopkins University Press, 1989. ISBN 0-8018-3826-6 (pbk). ▸ Probing essays on intellectuals' specialized knowledge and cosmopolitan ideals. Discusses significance of works by Walter Lippmann, William James, Perry Miller, and others. Touches on historical practice and theoretical currents in other disciplines. [LCP]

40.493 David A. Hollinger and Charles Capper, eds. *The American intellectual tradition.* 2 vols. New York: Oxford University Press, 1989. ISBN 0-19-505774-0 (set), 0-19-504461-4 (v. 1, pbk), 0-19-504462-2 (v. 2, pbk). ▸ Excerpts from writings of leading figures in United States intellectual culture. Emphasis on intellectuals and their concerns: religion, science, art, economics, and politics. Good, basic collection. [TDH]

40.494 Bruce Kuklick. *Churchmen and philosophers from Jonathan Edwards to John Dewey.* New Haven: Yale University Press, 1985. ISBN 0-300-03269-2. ▸ Examination of scientific philosophical tradition as outgrowth of Trinitarian Congregationalism. Embraces most important trends in philosophy, theology, and education from eighteenth to twentieth centuries. [TDH]

40.495 Alexandra Oleson and John Voss, eds. *The organization of knowledge in modern America, 1860–1920.* Baltimore: Johns Hopkins University Press, 1979. ISBN 0-8018-2108-8. ▸ Conference essays exploring major issue of institutional patterns in modern intellectual endeavors. Covers many fields from mathematics to agricultural sciences. Important insights into rise of universities and development of professions. [LCP]

40.496 Lewis Perry. *Intellectual life in America: a history.* 1984 ed. Chicago: University of Chicago Press, 1989. ISBN 0-226-66101-6. ▸ Readable survey of both ideas and communities of discourse in which they were discussed and expounded. Focuses on position of intellectuals and conceptions of intellect in American society. [TDH]

40.497 Stow Persons. *American minds: a history of ideas.* 1958 ed. New York: Holt, Rinehart & Winston, 1960. ▸ Polished accounts of colonial religion, Enlightenment, romantic democracy, naturalistic mind, and twentieth-century neodemocratic thought. Leading characteristics of each period. Highly selective, informative, often penetrating. [LCP]

40.498 David Shi. *The simple life: plain living and high thinking in American culture.* New York: Oxford University Press, 1986. ISBN 0-19-503475-9. ▸ Survey of ideal of voluntary simplicity as expressed and attempted from Puritans and Quakers to 1960s counterculture. Though rarely attained and sometimes unpopular, calls to simplicity served as necessary jeremiads against selfish materialism. Parallels earlier studies of agrarian myth and Adamic identity. [CJG]

40.499 Robert Allen Skotheim. *American intellectual histories and historians.* 1966 ed. Westport, Conn.: Greenwood, 1978. ISBN 0-313-20120-X. ▸ Thoughtful analysis of leading practitioners in field through 1940s. Not very theoretical, but judicious accounts of history of ideas and American studies as departures from progressive historiography. [LCP]

40.500 Morton White. *Science and sentiment in America: philosophical thought from Jonathan Edwards to John Dewey.* New York: Oxford University Press, 1972. ISBN 0-19-501519-3. ▸ Essays on most distinguished philosophers in American canon and how these men responded to challenge of science. Discusses dangers of anti-intellectual appeals to intuition. [LCP]

SEE ALSO
4.531 Daniel J. Czitrom. *Media and the American mind.*

Religion and Theology

40.501 Sydney E. Ahlstrom. *A religious history of the American people.* New Haven: Yale University Press, 1972. ISBN 0-300-01475-9 (cl), 0-300-01762-6 (pbk). ▸ Sweeping, magisterial, chronological survey of American religion, focusing on mainline Protestant denominations. Masterpiece of liberal-progressive school of church history. [TDH]

40.502 Sydney E. Ahlstrom, ed. *Theology in America: the major Protestant voices from Puritanism to neo-orthodoxy.* Indianapolis: Bobbs-Merrill, 1967. ▸ Good selection of sermons, essays, and addresses by thirteen mainstream religious leaders. [LCP]

40.503 Catherine L. Albanese. *America: religions and religion.* 2d ed. Belmont, Calif.: Wadsworth, 1992. ISBN 0-534-16488-9. ▸ Survey of diverse topics ranging from traditional denominationalism to occult. Posits division between ordinary religion, which is cultural, and extraordinary religion, which is transcendent. [TDH]

40.504 Catherine L. Albanese. *Nature religion in America from the Algonkian Indians to the new age.* Chicago: University of Chicago Press, 1990. ISBN 0-226-01145-3. ▸ Survey of religious responses to nature, colonial times to present. Argues for American ambivalence between harmony with and mastery over nature. [TDH]

40.505 Robert Mapes Anderson. *Vision of the disinherited: the making of American Pentecostalism.* New York: Oxford University Press, 1979. ISBN 0-19-502502-4. ▸ Examination of Pentecostalism as religious movement growing out of holiness movement, appealing especially to poor and marginalized. Blends intellectual and social history of religion. [TDH]

40.506 Leonard J. Arrington and Davis Bitton. *The Mormon experience: a history of the Latter-Day Saints.* New York: Random House, 1979. ISBN 0-394-74102-1. ▸ Readable, narrative history also addresses intellectual and social questions of interest to historians. Sympathetic but not uncritical. [TDH]

40.507 Hugh Barbour and J. William Frost. *The Quakers.* Westport, Conn.: Greenwood, 1988. ISBN 0-313-22816-7. ▸ History of Society of Friends in United States with attention to British roots. Balanced, objective, and inclusive of all types of Quakers. [TDH]

40.508 Joseph L. Blau. *Judaism in America: from curiosity to third faith.* Chicago: University of Chicago Press, 1976. ISBN 0-226-05727-5. ▸ Interpretive survey organized around four central themes in American Jewish history: voluntarism, Protestantism, pluralism, and moralism. Special emphasis on how American culture has affected Jewish faith. [TDH]

40.509 William H. Brackney, ed. *Baptist life and thought, 1600–1980: a source book.* Valley Forge, Pa.: Judson Press with American Baptist Historical Society, 1983. ISBN 0-8170-0959-0. ▸ Authoritative collection of basic source documents and materials for Baptist history, supplemented by extensive bibliography. [TDH]

40.510 Emory Stevens Bucke, ed. *History of American Methodism.* New York: Abingdon Press, 1964. ▸ Massive, detailed history of various Methodist groups in United States. Heavily weighted toward intellectual, theological, and institutional history. [TDH]

40.511 Jay P. Dolan. *The American Catholic experience: a history from colonial times to the present.* Garden City, N.Y.: Doubleday, 1985. ISBN 0-385-15206-X (cl), 0-385-15207-8 (pbk). ▸ Social history of Roman Catholics in United States, focusing on experiences of people rather than church as institution. Readable survey. [TDH]

40.512 Nathan O. Hatch and Mark A. Noll, eds. *The Bible in America: essays in cultural history.* New York: Oxford University Press, 1982. ISBN 0-19-503099-0 (cl), 0-19-503100-8 (pbk).

▸ Essays on centrality of Bible in American culture. Evangelical in focus, but with sound scholarship. [TDH]

40.513 James J. Hennesey. *American Catholics: a history of the Roman Catholic community in the United States.* New York: Oxford University Press, 1981. ISBN 0-19-502946-1. ▸ Survey, covering period from Spanish exploration to present, with special emphasis on ethnicity. Particularly good integration with social and political history. [TDH]

40.514 William R. Hutchison. *The modernist impulse in American Protestantism.* 1976 ed. Durham, N.C.: Duke University Press, 1992. ISBN 0-8223-1237-98 (cl), 0-8223-1248-4 (pbk). ▸ Intellectual portrait of liberal Protestant thought from antebellum period to 1930s. Sympathetic but not uncritical. Based on extensive collective biography; standard presentation of movement. [TDH]

40.515 C. Eric Lincoln and Laurence H. Mamiya. *The black church in the African-American experience.* Durham, N.C.: Duke University Press, 1990. ISBN 0-8223-1057-0 (cl), 0-8223-1073-2 (pbk). ▸ Sociology and history of seven largest African-American denominations. Although as much sociology as history, best work available on subject in its entirety. [TDH]

40.516 Charles H. Lippy and Peter W. Williams, eds. *Encyclopedia of the American religious experience: studies of traditions and movements.* 3 vols. New York: Scribner's, 1987. ISBN 0-684-18062-6 (set). ▸ Widely inclusive work reflecting state of scholarship of American religious history. Best available reference work. [TDH]

40.517 George M. Marsden. *Fundamentalism and American culture: the shaping of twentieth-century evangelicalism, 1870–1925.* 1980 ed. New York: Oxford University Press, 1982. ISBN 0-19-502758-2 (cl, 1980), 0-19-503083-4 (pbk). ▸ Traces roots of fundamentalism to nineteenth-century Evangelicalism. Emphasis on fundamentalism's intellectual integrity and ambivalence toward denominationalism. Nuanced, critical, sympathetic, incisive. [TDH]

40.518 George M. Marsden. *Religion and American culture.* San Diego: Harcourt Brace Jovanovich, 1990. ISBN 0-15-576583-3. ▸ Brief survey addressing unusually probing questions about contradictions between prevailing religiosity and secularism. Discusses repositioning of faith as society modernized. Good on fundamentalism, its concerns, its critics. [LCP]

40.519 Martin E. Marty. *Pilgrims in their own land: five hundred years of religion in America.* Boston: Little, Brown, 1984. ISBN 0-316-54867-7. ▸ Biographical approach to American religious history. No overarching interpretive scheme, but vivid portrayals of leaders and movements. [TDH]

40.520 William G. McLoughlin. *Modern revivalism: Charles Grandison Finney to Billy Graham.* New York: Ronald Press, 1959. ▸ One of first works to take revivalism seriously and to attempt to integrate its full sweep into United States history. Somewhat dated now, but still compelling for period covered. [TDH]

40.521 William G. McLoughlin. *Revivals, awakenings, and reform: an essay on religion and social change in America, 1607–1977.* Chicago: University of Chicago Press, 1978. ISBN 0-226-56091-0. ▸ Exploration of sources of religious awakenings in periods of social stress through five examples, Puritans to 1960s. Elegant melding of intellectual and social history. [TDH/TAM]

40.522 R. Laurence Moore. *Religious outsiders and the making of Americans.* New York: Oxford University Press, 1986. ISBN 0-19-503663-8 (cl), 0-19-505188-2 (pbk). ▸ Challenge to traditional understandings of mainline and marginal religious groups. Argues outsider status often made for vibrant participation in and contributions to American religion. [TDH]

40.523 E. Clifford Nelson. *The Lutherans in North America.* Philadelphia: Fortress, 1975. ISBN 0-8006-0409-1. ▸ Readable, detailed, dispassionate history of various Lutheran groups in United States and Canada. [TDH]

40.524 Mark A. Noll. *A history of Christianity in the United States and Canada.* Grand Rapids, Mich.: Eerdmans, 1992. ISBN 0-8028-3703-4 (cl), 0-8028-0651-1 (pbk). ▸ Important recent textbook focusing on rise and decline of Protestant dominance in American religion. Sympathetic to Evangelicals; includes attention to gender, race, and class. [TDH]

40.525 Frederick A. Norwood. *The story of American Methodism: a history of the United Methodists and their relations.* Nashville, Tenn.: Abingdon, 1974. ISBN 0-687-39640-9 (cl), 0-687-39641-7 (pbk). ▸ Survey of Methodist groups in United States, firmly grounded in social history. Better for period before 1844, but overall one of best denominational histories available. [TDH]

40.526 David Robinson. *The Unitarians and the Universalists.* Westport, Conn.: Greenwood, 1985. ISBN 0-313-20946-4. ▸ Narrative history focusing on intellectual and theological developments, but sketchy on social and political aspects. Still best and most up-to-date work available. [TDH]

40.527 Howard M. Sachar. *A history of the Jews in America.* New York: Knopf, 1992. ISBN 0-394-57353-6. ▸ Monumental study; well written, informative, and convincing. Despite extended discussions of Americanization, accommodation, and Zionism, leaves no doubt of survival and great influence of Judaism in America. [LCP]

40.528 Jan Shipps. *Mormonism: the story of a new religious tradition.* Urbana: University of Illinois Press, 1985. ISBN 0-252-01159-7. ▸ Argues Mormonism must be understood not simply as bizarre or unusual sect, but as new religion. Excellent at integrating questions of Mormon faith with intellectual and social history. [TDH]

40.529 Cushing Strout. *The new heavens and new earth: political religion in America.* 1973 ed. New York: Harper & Row, 1975. ISBN 0-06-014171-9 (1973), 0-06-131895-7. ▸ Uses Tocqueville's observations (40.732) on centrality of religion as theme, or set of themes, to examine religious issues from Puritanism to neo-orthodoxy. Discusses political conflict over slavery, women's suffrage, and civil rights. [LCP/JB]

SEE ALSO
21.251 Nathan Glazer. *American Judaism.*

Literature

40.530 Sacvan Bercovitch. *The American jeremiad.* Madison: University of Wisconsin Press, 1978. ISBN 0-299-07350-5 (cl), 0-299-07354-8 (pbk). ▸ Influential work based on Puritan political sermons and subsequent political and literary texts. Argues for middle-class consensus unmatched in any other modern culture. Interdisciplinary American studies perspective. [LCP]

40.531 Malcolm Bradbury and Howard Temperley, eds. *Introduction to American studies.* 2d ed. London: Longman, 1989. ISBN 0-582-01526-X. ▸ Thirteen essays by British scholars on themes and periods of United States culture. Strong focus on literature. Good introduction to backgrounds in art, popular culture, social and political history. [LCP]

40.532 Emory Elliott, ed. *Columbia literary history of the United States.* New York: Columbia University Press, 1988. ISBN 0-231-05812-8. ▸ Most comprehensive, up-to-date, general work available. Inclusive in treatment of both major figures and also of previously neglected topics. Valuable long essays on periods and themes. [TDH]

40.533 Alfred Kazin. *An American procession.* 1984 ed. New York: Random House, 1985. ISBN 0-394-50378-3 (cl, 1984), 0-394-72923-4 (pbk). ▸ Canonical American authors, 1830–1930, interpreted by writer who has commented on America's literary scene for a half-century. From Ralph Waldo Emerson on truth to moderns on truth's disappearance. [LCP]

40.534 Paul Lauter et al., eds. *The Heath anthology of American literature.* 2 vols. Lexington, Mass.: Heath, 1990. ISBN 0-669-12064-2 (v. 1), 0-669-12065-0 (v. 2). ▸ Extremely successful result of collaborative project to broaden and diversify what constitutes American literature. Rich, huge, multicultural canon that should alter scholarship as well as classroom. [LCP]

40.535 Robert E. Spiller et al. *Literary history of the United States.* 4th ed. New York: Macmillan, 1974. ISBN 0-02-613160-9. ▸ Chronological treatment emphasizing European origins and influences. Organized around periods and standard authors with traditional themes: sectionalism, expansionism, realism, progress, and mobility. [TDH]

40.536 Cushing Strout. *Making American tradition: visions and revisions from Ben Franklin to Alice Walker.* New Brunswick, N.J.: Rutgers University Press, 1990. ISBN 0-8135-1516-5. ▸ Interpretation of American literature as responses of American authors to their predecessors. Emphasis on major writers, biographical in focus. [TDH]

Fine Arts

40.537 Matthew Baigell. *A history of American painting.* New York: Praeger, 1974. ▸ Biographical approach, focused on leading painters in various periods. Particular emphasis on physical, cultural, and intellectual impact of American environment. [TDH]

40.538 Milton W. Brown. *American art to 1900: painting, sculpture, architecture.* New York: Abrams, 1977. ISBN 0-8109-0207-9. ▸ Narrative account of leading movements and artists, balanced between amateur and professional. Lavishly illustrated, but not focused on cultural or intellectual analysis. [TDH]

40.539 Gilbert Chase. *America's music from the Pilgrims to the present.* Rev. 3d ed. Urbana: University of Illinois Press, 1987. ISBN 0-252-00454-X. ▸ Pioneering work breaking away from conception of American music as European concert forms. Encyclopedic in treatment, including everything from anthems to Gospel to Charles Ives to Elvis Presley. [TDH]

40.540 Ronald L. Davis. *A history of music in American life.* 1980–82 ed. 3 vols. Malabar, Fla.: Krieger, 1982. ISBN 0-89874-625-6 (set, cl), 0-89874-080-0 (set, pbk). ▸ Encyclopedic treatment of all forms of music. Emphasis on popular music and on twentieth century. Readable but lacks notes or credits. [TDH]

40.541 Charles Hamm. *Music in the New World.* New York: Norton, 1983. ISBN 0-393-95193-6. ▸ Basic, readable narrative history of music in United States, beginning with American Indian forms. Special attention to popular music, from slave songs, to shape-note singing, to jazz, to rock and roll. [TDH]

40.542 H. Wiley Hitchcock. *Music in the United States: a historical introduction.* 3d ed. Englewood Cliffs, N.J.: Prentice-Hall, 1988. ISBN 0-13-608407-9. ▸ Divides American music into cultivated and vernacular traditions, both resulting from interplay of European and American influences. Emphasis on stylistic trends and major artists. Good introduction. [TDH]

40.543 George McCue, ed. *Music in American society, 1776–1976: from Puritan hymn to synthesizer.* New Brunswick, N.J.: Transaction, 1977. ISBN 0-87855-209-X (cl), 0-87855-634-7 (pbk). ▸ Collection of essays emphasizing popular and cultural aspects of American music. Wide-ranging topics, but uneven in quality. [TDH]

40.544 Daniel M. Mendelowitz. *A history of American art.* 2d ed. New York: Holt, Rinehart & Winston, 1973. ISBN 0-03-089475-1 (pbk). ▸ Survey of art, architecture, painting, sculpture, and graphic and decorative arts. Emphasis on high rather than popular arts. [TDH]

40.545 Charlotte Streifer Rubinstein. *American women artists from early Indian times to the present.* Boston: Hall, 1982. ISBN 0-8161-8535-2 (pbk). ▸ Survey of broad range of women as artists, with emphasis on twentieth century. Central purpose to restore women as actors in American art. [TDH]

40.546 Irving L. Sablosky. *American music.* Chicago: University of Chicago Press, 1969. ISBN 0-226-73324-6. ▸ Narrative treatment of broad themes in development of different types of American music. Emphasizes uniquely American features, while acknowledging diverse sources and influences. [TDH]

40.547 John Wilmerding. *American art.* Harmondsworth: Penguin, 1976. ISBN 0-14-0560-40-8. ▸ Art as reflection of social and cultural currents of periods. Gives special attention to intellectual context and background of artists and their works. Good basic introduction. [TDH]

Social Sciences

40.548 William J. Barber, ed. *Breaking the academic mould: economists and American higher learning in the nineteenth century.* Middletown, Conn.: Wesleyan University Press, 1988. ISBN 0-8195-5165-7. ▸ Critical, incisive discussion of development of discipline of economics, focusing on themes of professionalization. Study of leading colleges and universities rather than individuals. [TDH]

40.549 Robert Bierstedt. *American sociological theory: a critical history.* New York: Academic Press, 1981. ISBN 0-12-097480-0 (cl), 0-12-097482-7 (pbk). ▸ Study of leading American sociologists from William Graham Sumner to Robert K. Merton. Literate, critical, and controversial in inclusion and exclusion of subjects. [TDH]

40.550 JoAnne Brown and David K. Van Keuren, eds. *The estate of social knowledge.* Baltimore: Johns Hopkins University Press, 1991. ISBN 0-8018-4060-0. ▸ Eleven essays on various aspects of history of social sciences in United States. Focus on impact of culture on disciplines and their rise or decline in influence. Excellent survey of complex subject. [TDH]

40.551 Bernard Crick. *The American science of politics: its origins and conditions.* 1959 ed. Berkeley: University of California Press, 1967. ▸ History of idea in United States that politics is something to be studied scientifically; not a history of political science. Influential and still very useful. [TDH]

40.552 Joseph Dorfman. *The economic mind in American civilization.* 1946–59 ed. 5 vols. New York: Kelley, 1966–69. ▸ Magisterial survey of economic thought and thinkers, colonial times to 1933. Heavily weighted toward academics and social history. Now somewhat dated. [TDH]

40.553 Raymond Seidelman and Edward J. Harpham. *Disenchanted realists: political science and the American crisis, 1884–1984.* Albany: State University of New York Press, 1985. ISBN 0-87395-994-9 (cl), 0-87395-995-7 (pbk). ▸ Discussion of interaction of political scientists with reform politics. Although political scientists usually disenchanted with government and politics, interest in reform has steadily declined. Excellent treatment. [TDH]

40.554 George W. Stocking, Jr. *Race, culture, and evolution: essays in the history of anthropology.* 1968 ed. Chicago: University of Chicago Press, 1982. ISBN 0-226-77494-5 (pbk). ▸ Most influential, highly regarded work available on history of American anthropology. Addresses concerns both of anthropologists and intellectual historians. [TDH]

SEE ALSO

4.191 Carl N. Degler. *In search of human nature.*

Education

40.555 Richard Hofstadter and Walter P. Metzger. *The development of academic freedom in the United States.* 1955 ed. New York: Columbia University Press, 1969. ‣ Development of rights to inquiry and expression with decline of religious and political control of colleges and universities. Emphasis on period since 1865. Dated but still best study available. [TDH]

40.556 Helen Lefkowitz Horowitz. *Campus life: undergraduate cultures from the end of the eighteenth century to the present.* 1987 ed. Chicago: University of Chicago Press, 1988. ISBN 0-226-35373-7 (pbk). ‣ Higher education experienced from student point of view, with special emphasis on centrality of extracurricular. Sensitive to impact of larger culture and gender, race, and class. [TDH]

40.557 Michael B. Katz. *Reconstructing American education.* Cambridge, Mass.: Harvard University Press, 1987. ISBN 0-674-75092-6 (cl). ‣ Radical historian's view of public schooling in nineteenth century, emphasizing ties of education and market. Education in service of developing capitalism. [TDH]

40.558 David Nasaw. *Schooled to order: a social history of public schooling in the United States.* New York: Oxford University Press, 1979. ISBN 0-19-502529-6. ‣ Public education as social control of masses to preserve existing order. Emphasis on how education served economic needs of capitalist elite and preserved their hegemony. [TDH]

40.559 S. Alexander Rippa. *Education in a free society: an American history.* 7th ed. New York: Longman, 1992. ISBN 0-8013-0606-X. ‣ Narrative history, integrating American social and intellectual history with history of education. Often updated; standard text, balanced and thoughtful. [TDH]

40.560 Frederick Rudolph. *The American college and university: a history.* 1962 ed. Athens: University of Georgia Press, 1990. ISBN 0-8203-1285-1 (cl), 8-8203-1284-3 (pbk). ‣ Institutional history of higher education, colonial times to mid-twentieth century. Particular focus on student experiences and impact of intellectual trends in American society. [TDH]

40.561 Frederick Rudolph. *Curriculum: a history of the American undergraduate course of study since 1636.* San Francisco: Jossey-Bass, 1977. ISBN 0-87589-358-9. ‣ Examination of what undergraduates have studied. Descriptive, meticulously researched work of both social and educational history. [TDH]

40.562 Joel H. Spring. *The American school, 1642–1983: varieties of historical interpretation of the foundations and development of American education.* Rev. 2d ed. New York: Longman, 1990. ISBN 0-8013-0468-7. ‣ Summary both of major developments and how historians have interpreted them. Special attention to interaction of social, political, and intellectual influences. [TDH]

40.563 Rush Welter. *Popular education and democratic thought in America.* New York: Columbia University Press, 1962. ‣ Education as central issue for democratic thought and politics. Searching, wide-ranging intellectual history with focus on institutions, ending in 1930s. [LCP]

Popular Culture

40.564 Kenneth Cmiel. *Democratic eloquence: the fight over popular speech in nineteenth-century America.* 1990 ed. Berkeley: University of California Press, 1991. ISBN 0-520-07485-8. ‣ Subtle analysis of conflict between advocates of refined standards and champions of middling rhetoric and vernacular. Responses to rise of assertive, democratic public. Sees dictionaries and biblical translation as cultural battlegrounds. [LCP]

40.565 Richard Wightman Fox and T. J. Jackson Lears, eds. *The power of culture: critical essays in American history.* Chicago: University of Chicago Press, 1993. ISBN 0-226-25954-4 (cl), 0-226-25955-2 (pbk). ‣ Case studies, from colonial murder narratives to conflicting artistic taste in 1990s, demonstrating vitality of cultural history today. Topics include family values, consumerism, technology, and mass culture. [LCP]

40.566 Christopher D. Geist and Jack Nachbar, eds. *The popular culture reader.* 3d ed. Bowling Green, Ohio: Bowling Green University Popular Press, 1983. ISBN 0-87972-095-6 (cl), 0-87972-094-8 (pbk). ‣ Rich selection of articles showing diverse approaches in currently lively field. Few essays on nineteenth-century culture; many on Barbie dolls, prize fighters, monster movies, and Harlequin romances. [LCP]

40.567 Lawrence W. Levine. *Highbrow/lowbrow: the emergence of cultural hierarchy in America.* Cambridge, Mass.: Harvard University Press, 1988. ISBN 0-674-39076-8 (cl), 0-674-39077-6 (pbk). ‣ Attack on prejudices elevating high culture above popular culture. Examines Shakespearean drama as instance of nineteenth-century democracy's rich shared public culture. Sees sacralized and aesthetic categories as hierarchical distortions and impositions. [LCP]

40.568 Russell Lynes. *The lively audience: a social history of the visual and performing arts in America, 1890–1950.* New York: Harper & Row, 1985. ISBN 0-06-015434-9 (cl), 0-06-091254-5 (pbk). ‣ Examination of culture industry from architecture, to museums, to jazz, to theatre. Emphasis on diverse expectations of democratic patrons. Takes no side in disputes over what is high art, what is popular. [LCP]

40.569 Maxine Schwartz Seller, ed. *Ethnic theatre in the United States.* Westport, Conn.: Greenwood, 1983. ISBN 0-313-21230-9. ‣ Twenty essays, plus appendixes, on theatre among African Americans, American Indians, Armenians, Byelorussians, Mexicans, Puerto Ricans, Ukrainians, Jews, Finns, Slovaks, Poles, Lithuanians, Latvians, and several other European immigrant groups in America. [LCP]

40.570 Robert C. Toll. *On with the show! The first century of show business in America.* New York: Oxford University Press, 1976. ISBN 0-19-502057-X. ‣ Coffee-table book, profusely illustrated, with essays based on sound scholarship. From P.T. Barnum to Flo Ziegfeld: circuses, minstrel shows, melodramas, Wild West shows, musical comedy, burlesque, and vaudeville. Good starting point. [LCP]

40.571 Alan Trachtenberg. *Reading American photographs: images as history, Mathew Brady to Walker Evans.* New York: Hill & Wang, 1989. ISBN 0-8090-8037-0. ‣ Photographic interpretations of society from depression of 1837 to depression of 1930s. Five great photographers: Mathew Brady, Timothy O'Sullivan, Lewis Hine, Alfred Stieglitz, and Walker Evans. Model of recent cultural studies scholarship extending beyond written texts. [LCP/WWR]

40.572 Don B. Wilmeth, ed. *American and English popular entertainment: a guide to information sources.* Brooks McNamara, foreward. Detroit: Gale Research, 1980. (Performing arts information guide series, 7.) ISBN 0-8103-1454-1. ‣ Books, articles, and dissertations on circus, wild west, fairs, museums, amusement parks, puppets, minstrelsy, burlesque, and theatre. Almost 2,500 annotated entries. Well organized, indexed. [LCP]

40.573 Garff B. Wilson. *Three hundred years of American drama and theatre: from "Ye Bare" and "Ye Cubb to Hair."* Englewood Cliffs, N.J.: Prentice-Hall, 1973. ISBN 0-13-920314-1. ‣ Best textbook survey of theatre history. Especially strong on changes in acting styles and production practice. Includes imaginary visits to theatre in 1770, 1850, 1902, and 1960s. [LCP]

SEE ALSO
44.46 Richard Wightman Fox and T. J. Jackson Lears, eds. *The culture of consumption.*

Material Culture

40.574 "Bibliography issue 1983." *American quarterly* 35.3 (1983). ISSN 0003-0678. ▸ Entire issue devoted to material culture. Articles by leading scholars on cultural landscapes, vernacular architecture, household furnishings, technology, and folkloristics. Reports on state of art. [KWK]

40.575 Simon J. Bronner. *Grasping things: folk material culture and mass society in America.* Lexington: University Press of Kentucky, 1986. ISBN 0-8131-1572-8. ▸ Advanced behavioral analysis with theoretical emphasis of material objects and communities in Pennsylvania, Indiana, Mississippi, Michigan, and New York. Examines housing styles, handwork, impact of mass culture and consumption. [KWK]

40.576 Simon J. Bronner, ed. *American material culture and folklife: a prologue and a dialogue.* 1985 ed. Logan: Utah State University Press, 1992. ISBN 0-87421-156-5. ▸ Essays on folk culture, customs, and community studies. Methodological discussion, analyses of musical instruments, furniture, tombstones, housing, museums, historical societies, and cities. Diverse approaches, includes editor's interpretive notes. [KWK]

40.577 Henry Glassie. *Pattern in the material folk culture of the eastern United States.* 1968 ed. Philadelphia: University of Pennsylvania Press, 1971. ISBN 0-8122-7569-1 (cl), 0-8122-1013-1 (pbk). ▸ Breakthrough examination of neglected subject. Preindustrial buildings, cooking, and tools of eastern United States reveal both regional and non-regional patterns of distribution. [KWK]

40.578 Brooke Hindle, ed. *America's wooden age: aspects of its early technology.* Tarrytown, N.Y.: Sleepy Hollow Press, 1985. ISBN 0-912882-15-8 (cl), 0-912882-60-3 (pbk). ▸ Essays by leading authorities concerning eighteenth- and nineteenth-century woodworking, lumbering, mathematical instruments, water mills, and water power. Well-illustrated introduction to various approaches to material culture. [KWK]

40.579 Brooke Hindle, ed. *Material culture of the wooden age.* Tarrytown, N.Y.: Sleepy Hollow Press, 1981. ISBN 0-912882-45-X. ▸ Essays on wood construction at home, on farm, and in transportation and production. Also discusses potash, naval stores, and charcoal iron making. Covers colonial era to nineteenth century. Well illustrated. [KWK]

40.580 Richard E. Meyer, ed. *Cemeteries and gravemarkers: voices of American culture.* Ann Arbor: University Microfilms International Research Press, 1989. ISBN 0-8357-1903-0. ▸ Provocative essays on Victorian children's graves, regional variations, cemetery business, epitaphs, tourist and leisure uses of burial grounds, and burial among American Indians, African Americans, Hispanics, and Mormons. Illustrated. [KWK]

40.581 Ivor Noel-Hume. *Historical archaeology.* 1969 ed. New York: Norton, 1975. ISBN 0-393-00783-9. ▸ Introductory handbook on methods for conducting historical excavation, recording finds, and caring for artifacts. Illustrated survey, with comprehensive bibliography, by Williamsburg's chief archaeologist. [KWK]

40.582 Ian M. G. Quimby, ed. *Material culture and the study of American life.* New York: Norton for Winterthur Museum, 1978. ISBN 0-393-05661-9 (cl), 0-393-05665-1 (pbk). ▸ Interdisciplinary essays on role of European Americans and Native Americans by museum professional, archaeologist, and historians. Use of artifacts to understand American history. [KWK]

40.583 Thomas J. Schlereth. *Cultural history and material culture:*

everyday life, landscapes, museums. Ann Arbor, Mich.: University Microfilms International Research Press, 1990. ISBN 0-8357-1899-9. ▸ Novel analysis using material evidence, including flora, mail order catalogues, toys, office work, world's fairs, landscapes of cities and midwestern towns, and museums, as artifacts. Provocative interpretations. [KWK]

40.584 Thomas J. Schlereth, ed. *Material culture: a research guide.* Lawrence: University Press of Kansas, 1985. ISBN 0-7006-0274-7 (cl), 0-7006-0275-5 (pbk). ▸ Essays from several disciplines on landscape images, vernacular architecture, home furnishings, and decorative arts. Emphasis on interdisciplinary need to develop methodology and analysis. [KWK]

40.585 Thomas J. Schlereth, ed. and comp. *Material culture studies in America.* Nashville: American Association for State and Local History, 1982. ISBN 0-910050-61-9 (cl), 0-910050-67-8 (pbk). ▸ Essays on history, theory, method, practice, and status of field. Introduction to various approaches from several regions of nation. [KWK]

40.586 David Charles Sloane. *The last great necessity: cemeteries in American history.* Baltimore: Johns Hopkins University Press, 1991. ISBN 0-8018-4068-6. ▸ Broad survey, colonial era to present, demonstrating increased separation from and removal of reminders of death. Well illustrated, based on new primary sources, with bibliographical essay. Best available. [KWK]

40.587 Robert Blair St. George, ed. *Material life in America, 1600–1860.* Boston: Northeastern University Press, 1988. ISBN 1-55553-019-2 (cl), 1-55553-020-6 (pbk). ▸ Provocative essays on methods, American Indians, African Americans, colonies, women, landscapes, and buildings. Techniques from folklore, anthropology, and decorative arts research applied to understanding community organization and politics. [KWK]

Folklore

40.588 Simon J. Bronner. *American folklore studies: an intellectual history.* Lawrence: University Press of Kansas, 1986. ISBN 0-7006-0306-9 (cl), 0-7006-0313-1 (pbk). ▸ Discusses early scholarly applications of theories of evolution, professionalization of field, development of ethnography. Provocative discussion of folklore as reaction to industrialization, impact of feminism, and other topics. [KWK]

40.589 Jan Harold Brunvand. *The study of American folklore: an introduction.* 3d ed. New York: Norton, 1986. ISBN 0-393-95495-1 (cl), 0-393-95580-X (pbk). ▸ Guide to basic folklore types in America. Discusses history as source of ballads, riddles, and proverbs; role of local historical legends; and historical methods of tracing tales' origins. Succinct, accessible, authoritative. [KWK]

40.590 Tristram Potter Coffin, ed. *Our living traditions: an introduction to American folklore.* Lanham, Md.: University Press of America, 1986. ISBN 0-8191-5355-9. ▸ Essays by leading scholars from interdisciplinary perspective. Definitions of folklore and folklife, historical origins of songs, dances, folktales, games, riddles, superstitions, and speech. Lively, nontechnical introduction. [KWK]

40.591 Tristram Potter Coffin and Hennig Cohen, eds. *Folklore in America: tales, songs, superstitions, proverbs, riddles, games, folk drama, and folk festivals with seventeen folk melodies.* 1966 ed. Lanham, Md.: University Press of America, 1986. ISBN 0-8191-5355-9 (pbk). ▸ Examination of Old World origins of folklore, its transit to and modification in America. Selections taken from *Journal of American Folklore.* Introduction to field through wide variety of examples. [KWK]

40.592 Richard M. Dorson. *American folklore.* Rev. ed. Chicago: University of Chicago Press, 1977. ISBN 0-226-15859-4. ▸ Introduction to basic aspects of American folklore including humor, regionalism, immigrants, African Americans, and heroes. Succinct summary with table of folk motifs, bibliography, and chronology by leading scholar. [KWK]

40.593 Richard M. Dorson. *American folklore and the historian.* Chicago: University of Chicago Press, 1971. ISBN 0-226-15868-3. ‣ Examination of theory and research techniques of folklore from perspective of academic historian. Relates folklore to nationalism, oral tradition, local and cultural history, and American studies. Best available. [KWK]

40.594 Richard M. Dorson, ed. *Handbook of American folklore.* W. Edson Richmond, Introduction. Bloomington: Indiana University Press, 1983. ISBN 0-253-32706-7 (cl), 0-253-20373-2 (pbk). ‣ Sweeping introduction to academic study of folklore: research topics and methods, theory, historical, ethnographical, and sociological interpretation, and presentation. Discusses historical origins, geographic settings, myths. [KWK]

40.595 Duncan Emrich. *Folklore on the land.* 1972 ed. Boston: Little, Brown, 1988. ISBN 0-316-23721-3. ‣ Survey includes history, name giving, children's tales, street cries, songs, epitaphs, and superstitions. Musical notation, good bibliography of sources and scholarship provided. Earlier title: *Folklore on the American Land.* [KWK]

FOREIGN RELATIONS

Overviews

40.596 Thomas Andrew Bailey. *A diplomatic history of the American people.* 10th ed. Englewood Cliffs, N.J.: Prentice-Hall, 1980. ISBN 0-13-214726-2. ‣ Long popular, engaging text, emphasizing role of public opinion and press on foreign policy. [PLH]

40.597 Samuel Flagg Bemis. *A diplomatic history of the United States.* 5th ed. New York: Holt, Reinhart & Winston, 1965. ‣ Topically and chronologically balanced survey, strongest on nineteenth century, and generally sympathetic to United States. [PLH]

40.598 Wayne S. Cole. *An interpretive history of American foreign relations.* Rev. ed. Homewood, Ill.: Dorsey, 1974. ISBN 0-256-01413-2. ‣ Brief, balanced examination of indigenous and foreign influences on American policy. Emphasizes expansionism. [PLH]

40.599 Jerald A. Combs. *American diplomatic history: two centuries of changing interpretations.* Berkeley: University of California Press, 1983. ISBN 0-520-04590-4. ‣ Penetrating survey of diplomatic historiography. Identifies schools of thought within six ages defined by crises in United States history. [PLH]

40.600 Alexander DeConde. *A history of American foreign policy.* 3d ed. 2 vols. New York: Scribner's; distributed by Macmillan, 1978. ISBN 0-02-327970-2 (v. 1, pbk), 0-02-327980-X (v. 2, pbk). ‣ Survey of diplomacy in context of major domestic and international developments. [PLH]

40.601 Robert H. Ferrell. *American diplomacy: the twentieth century.* 4th ed. New York: Norton, 1988. ISBN 0-393-95609-1. ‣ Foreign policy since 1898 categorized in eras of change as opposed to presidential administrations. Abridgment of author's earlier comprehensive survey. More sympathetic to United States officials than Schulzinger 40.607. [PLH]

40.602 Gerald K. Haines and J. Samuel Walker, eds. *American foreign relations: a historiographical review.* Westport, Conn.: Greenwood, 1981. ISBN 0-313-21061-6. ‣ Sixteen essays by younger scholars examining schools of interpretation in literature on United States diplomacy in various eras and regions. Less coherent than Combs 40.599. [PLH]

40.603 Michael J. Hogan and Thomas G. Paterson, eds. *Explaining the history of American foreign relations.* Cambridge: Cambridge University Press, 1991. ISBN 0-521-40383-9 (cl), 0-521-40736-2 (pbk). ‣ Historiographical overview of trends, research methods, directions of inquiry, and conceptual models for analyzing foreign relations. Penetrating essays by leading diplomatic historians. [PLH]

40.604 Paul M. Kennedy. *The rise and fall of the great powers: economic change and military conflict from 1500 to 2000.* New York: Random House, 1987. ISBN 0-394-54674-1. ‣ Explanation of rise and fall of several empires over half-millennium. Argues United States faces imminent decline because of imperial overstretch. Concludes power derives from but undermines economic productivity. [PLH]

40.605 Walter LaFeber. *The American age: United States foreign policy at home and abroad since 1750.* New York: Norton, 1989. ISBN 0-393-02629-9 (cl), 0-393-95611-3 (pbk). ‣ Examination of social and commercial underpinnings of foreign policy, centralization of policymaking, and decline of American power since 1950s. Broad, informed, insightful, and rich in detail. [PLH]

40.606 Thomas G. Paterson, J. Garry Clifford, and Kenneth J. Hagan. *American foreign policy: a history.* 1988 3d ed. 2 vols. Lexington, Mass.: Heath, 1991. ISBN 0-669-12664-0 (v. 1, pbk), 0-669-12665-9 (v. 2, pbk). ‣ Detailed overview generally critical of United States expansionism. [PLH]

40.607 Robert D. Schulzinger. *American diplomacy in the twentieth century.* 2d ed. New York: Oxford University Press, 1990. ISBN 0-19-505843-7 (cl), 0-19-505844-5 (pbk). ‣ Highly readable survey; grounds foreign relations in domestic political and social developments. Addresses historiographical controversies. More critical of United States officials than Ferrell 40.601. [PLH]

40.608 Paul A. Varg. *America, from client state to world power: six major transitions in United States foreign relations.* Norman: University of Oklahoma Press, 1990. ISBN 0-8061-2251-X. ‣ Synthetic survey emphasizing periods in America's rise as great power and watersheds dividing them. [PLH]

SEE ALSO
48.7 Richard Dean Burns, ed. *Guide to American foreign relations since 1700.*

Public Officials and Policy Making

40.609 Edward P. Crapol, ed. *Women and American foreign policy: lobbyists, critics, and insiders.* 2d ed. Wilmington, Del.: Scholarly Resources, 1992. ISBN 0-8420-2431-X (cl), 0-8420-2430-1 (pbk). ‣ Groundbreaking survey of women influential in diplomacy. Suggests women collectively behaved no differently than men. [PLH]

40.610 Thomas H. Etzold. *The conduct of American foreign relations: the other side of diplomacy.* New York: New Viewpoints, 1977. ISBN 0-531-05390-3 (cl), 0-531-05597-3 (pbk). ‣ Introductory examination of duties and missions of diplomats, functioning and organization of State Department, and bureaucratic rivalries between State and other departments. [PLH]

40.611 Norman A. Graebner, ed. *An uncertain tradition: American secretaries of state in the twentieth century.* New York: McGraw-Hill, 1961. ‣ Survey of personal backgrounds and style; relationships with presidents, legislators, and press; and achievements and failures of fourteen secretaries of state. [PLH]

Relations With Other Regions and Nations

40.612 Harry C. Allen. *Great Britain and the United States: a history of Anglo-American relations (1783–1952).* 1954 ed. Hamden, Conn.: Archon, 1969. ‣ Synthetic survey stressing importance of Anglo-American cooperation and coordination of foreign policy. Influenced by cold war. [PLH]

40.613 Thomas Andrew Bailey. *America faces Russia: Russian-*

American relations from early times to our own day. 1950 ed. Gloucester, Mass.: Peter Smith, 1964. ▸ Concludes provocatively that political relations between Moscow and Washington experienced recurrent conflicts long before Soviet revolution. Compare Williams 40.647 and Gaddis 40.625. [PLH]

40.614 Samuel Flagg Bemis. *The Latin American policy of the United States: an historical interpretation.* 1943 ed. New York: Norton, 1971. ▸ Lively survey of developments from nineteenth century to 1940s. Defensive of United States. [PLH]

40.615 Thomas A. Bryson. *American diplomatic relations with the Middle East, 1784–1975: a survey.* Metuchen, N.J.: Scarecrow, 1977. ISBN 0-8108-0988-5. ▸ Survey of increasing United States government involvement in region. Advocates national interests, especially access to oil, should prevail over domestic political concerns and welfare of oil corporations. [PLH]

40.616 Charles S. Campbell. *From revolution to rapprochement: the United States and Great Britain, 1783–1900.* New York: Wiley, 1974. ISBN 0-471-13341-8 (cl), 0-471-13342-6 (pbk). ▸ Persuasive argument that special relationship of cooperation and collaboration emerged from legacy of hostility and suspicion. Compare Allen 40.612. [PLH]

40.617 Edward W. Chester. *Clash of titans: Africa and U.S. foreign policy.* Maryknoll, N.Y.: Orbis, 1974. ISBN 0-88344-065-2. ▸ Basic overview of United States policy toward continent from slave trade to 1970s. Suggests similarities between emerging African nationalism and African American political experiences. [PLH]

40.618 James W. Cortada. *Two nations over time: Spain and the United States, 1776–1977.* Westport, Conn.: Greenwood, 1978. ISBN 0-313-20319-9. ▸ Balanced examination of political and cultural interaction, emphasizing Spain's resistance to growing American empire through 1898. [PLH]

40.619 Gerald M. Craig. *The United States and Canada.* Cambridge, Mass.: Harvard University Press, 1968. ▸ Detailed, lively survey, analyzing and exploring both discord and more familiar accord. [PLH]

40.620 David Dimbleby and David Reynolds. *An ocean apart: the relationship between Britain and America in the twentieth century.* 1988 ed. New York: Vintage, 1989. ISBN 0-679-72190-8 (pbk). ▸ Lively, penetrating analysis of cultural, political, and economic interaction. Modifies notion that relationship was consistently friendly and warm. [PLH]

40.621 Arthur Power Dudden. *The American Pacific: from the old China trade to the present.* New York: Oxford University Press, 1992. ISBN 0-19-505821-6. ▸ Synthetic survey of United States political, military, economic, and cultural affairs in entire Pacific basin since 1784. [PLH]

40.622 Peter Duignan and Lewis H. Gann. *The United States and Africa: a history.* Cambridge: Cambridge University Press, 1984. ISBN 0-521-26202-X (cl), 0-521-33571-X (pbk). ▸ Thoughtful survey of United States policy in sub-Saharan Africa. Discusses role of black African nationalism in United States thinking. [PLH]

40.623 James A. Field, Jr. *From Gibraltar to the Middle East: America and the Mediterranean world, 1776–1882.* Rev. ed. Chicago: Imprint, 1991. ISBN 1-879176-05-X. ▸ Groundbreaking exploration of experiences of American diplomats, businessmen, missionaries, and intellectuals in Mediterranean basin. Earlier title: *America and the Mediterranean world, 1776–1882.* [PLH]

40.624 J. Valerie Fifer. *United States perceptions of Latin America, 1850–1930: a "new west" south of Capricorn?* Manchester: Manchester University Press; distributed by St. Martin's, 1991. ISBN 0-7190-2845-0. ▸ United States public officials and private devel-

opers eyed southern cone as stage to recreate business expansionism of United States western frontier, but success limited by indigenous political problems. Stimulating survey. [PLH]

40.625 John Lewis Gaddis. *Russia, the Soviet Union, and the United States: an interpretive history.* 2d ed. New York: McGraw-Hill, 1990. ISBN 0-07-557258-3. ▸ Sweeping overview concludes relations sour when two sides pursued universal interests; friendlier when each strove for national interests with willingness to accommodate other. Compare Bailey 40.613 and Williams 40.647. [PLH]

40.626 Hans W. Gatzke. *Germany and the United States: a "special relationship"?* Cambridge, Mass.: Harvard University Press, 1980. ISBN 0-674-35326-9. ▸ Stimulating assessment of political relations and mutual, popular perceptions. Stresses continuity between pre- and post-Nazi Germany in United States thinking. [PLH]

40.627 Leland James Gordon. *American relations with Turkey, 1830–1930: an economic interpretation.* Philadelphia: University of Pennsylvania Press, 1932. ▸ Dated but useful survey. Covers trade, including European states' competing interests, missionary work, and immigration. [PLH]

40.628 Norman Harper. *A great and powerful friend: a study of Australian-American relations between 1900–1975.* 1986 ed. St. Lucia: University of Queensland Press, 1987. ISBN 0-7022-1755-7 (pbk). ▸ Exhaustively detailed survey arguing mutually beneficial political and strategic ties emerged during twentieth century. [PLH]

40.629 Harry N. Howard. *Turkey, the straits, and U.S. policy.* Baltimore: Johns Hopkins University Press, 1974. ISBN 0-8018-1590-8. ▸ Pioneering examination of United States economic and strategic interest in Turkish straits since nineteenth century with emphasis on early cold war era. [PLH]

40.630 Michael H. Hunt. *The making of a special relationship: the United States and China to 1914.* New York: Columbia University Press, 1983. ISBN 0-231-05516-1. ▸ Ambitious, stimulating, convincing study of United States–Chinese interaction in political, economic, and cultural spheres from perspectives of both countries. Shows limits to myth of special relationship. [PLH]

40.631 Akira Iriye. *Across the Pacific: an inner history of American–East Asian relations.* Rev. ed. Chicago: Imprint, 1992. ISBN 1-879176-08-4 (cl), 1-879176-07-6 (pbk). ▸ Insightful assessment of United States, Chinese, and Japanese popular and intellectual conceptions and misconceptions of one another, especially in times of conflict, 1780s to 1960s. [PLH]

40.632 Arnold X. Jiang. *The United States and China.* Chicago: University of Chicago Press, 1988. ISBN 0-226-39947-8. ▸ Chinese resistance to United States imperialism from 1840s to 1940s. Narrow, propagandistic Chinese communist interpretation. Compare Vorontsov 40.644. [PLH]

40.633 Lester D. Langley. *America and the Americas: the United States in the western hemisphere.* 1989 ed. Athens: University of Georgia Press, 1990. ISBN 0-8203-1103-0 (cl), 0-8203-1104-9 (pbk). ▸ Reasoned examination of clash of liberal ideology and national self-interest in formulation of United States policy. Latin American states resisted North American hegemony. [PLH]

40.634 Ernest R. May and James C. Thomson, Jr., eds. *American–East Asian relations: a survey.* Cambridge, Mass.: Harvard University Press, 1972. ISBN 0-674-02285-8. ▸ Collection of essays spanning range of topics and states; pronounced biregional perspective. Rich in sources. [PLH]

40.635 J. Lloyd Mecham. *A survey of United States–Latin American relations.* Boston: Houghton-Mifflin, 1965. ▸ Justifies United

States interventionism on grounds of national security. Traditional conservative alternative to LaFeber 48.492. [PLH]

40.636 Charles E. Neu. *The troubled encounter: the United States and Japan.* 1975 ed. Malabar, Fla.: Krieger, 1987. ISBN 0-88275-951-5 (pbk). ▸ Probing overview. Locates source of World War II hostility in previous political clashes, popular cultural misperceptions, and apathy among leaders. [PLH]

40.637 Michael A. Palmer. *Guardians of the gulf: a history of America's expanding role in the Persian Gulf, 1833–1992.* New York: Free Press, 1992. ISBN 0-02-923843-9. ▸ Extensive account of Persian Gulf War of 1990–91. Examination of growing United States interest in economic and strategic attractions of Persian Gulf, despite strong reluctance to accept commitments for regional security. [PLH]

40.638 Louis A. Perez, Jr. *Cuba and the United States: ties of singular intimacy.* Athens: University of Georgia Press, 1990. ISBN 0-8203-1207-X (cl), 0-8203-1208-8 (pbk). ▸ Critical discussion of cultural, economic, and political interactions in nineteenth and early twentieth centuries that sparked Cuban nationalism that led to revolution. [PLH]

40.639 Edwin O. Reischauer. *The United States and Japan.* 3d ed. Cambridge, Mass.: Harvard University Press, 1965. ▸ Sweeping overview of bilateral relationship in context of society and culture of Japan since sixteenth century. [PLH]

40.640 Karl M. Schmitt. *Mexico and the United States, 1821–1973: conflict and coexistence.* New York: Wiley, 1974. ISBN 0-471-76198-2 (cl), 0-471-76199-0 (pbk). ▸ Empathetic examination of Mexican perceptions of United States and efforts to resist United States territorial and economic encroachments. [PLH]

40.641 Robert W. Stookey. *America and the Arab states: an uneasy encounter.* New York: Wiley, 1975. ISBN 0-471-82975-7 (cl), 0-471-82976-5 (pbk). ▸ Pre–World War I private and cultural contacts produced Arab good will toward United States that was undermined by United States pro-Israel policy after World War II. Examines importance of Arab nationalism and inter-Arab relations to United States policy. [PLH]

40.642 Graham H. Stuart and James L. Tigner. *Latin America and the United States.* 6th ed. Englewood Cliffs, N.J.: Prentice-Hall, 1975. ISBN 0-13-524652-0. ▸ Balanced, careful narrative survey of United States–Latin American relations. Enduring classic. [PLH]

40.643 Frank Trommler and Joseph McVeigh, eds. *America and the Germans: an assessment of a three-hundred-year history.* 2 vols. Philadelphia: University of Pennsylvania Press, 1985. ISBN 0-8122-7996-4 (set), 0-8122-7979-4 (v. 1, cl), 0-8122-7980-8 (v. 2, cl). ▸ Forty-eight essays carefully examining cultural, political, economic, and intellectual interactions between two peoples over three centuries. [PLH]

40.644 Vladilen Vorontsov. *From the missionary days to Reagan: U.S. China policy.* David Skvirsky, trans. Moscow: Progress, 1987. ▸ Pre-*glasnost*, traditional Soviet interpretation critical of both United States imperialism in China and communist Chinese digression from Soviet model. Compare to Jiang 40.632. [PLH]

40.645 Arthur P. Whitaker. *The United States and South America: the northern republics.* 1948 ed. Westport, Conn.: Greenwood, 1974. ISBN 0-8371-6411-7. ▸ Political and diplomatic history of Bolivia, Ecuador, Peru, Colombia, and Venezuela and their relationship with United States, especially in twentieth century. Probing and influential. [PLH]

40.646 Arthur P. Whitaker, ed. *The United States and the southern cone: Argentina, Chile, and Uruguay.* Cambridge, Mass.: Harvard University Press, 1976. ISBN 0-674-92841-5. ▸ Provocative examination of political and economic developments in southern cone

states and United States influence on regional and national developments. Concludes United States interventionism bred anti-Yankee nationalism. [PLH]

40.647 William Appleman Williams. *American-Russian relations, 1781–1947.* 1952 ed. New York: Octagon Books, 1971. ISBN 0-374-98581-2. ▸ United States leaders missed opportunities to improve relations with Russian and Soviet leaders. Early hint of author's well-known radical revisionism. More radical than Bailey 40.613 and Gaddis 40.625. [PLH]

40.648 L. C. Wright. *United States policy toward Egypt, 1830–1914.* New York: Exposition, 1969. ▸ Through political, economic, and cultural ties, United States built goodwill among Egyptians, but also refused to endorse local struggle for independence from British imperialism. Sweeping and informative. [PLH]

40.649 Marvin R. Zahniser. *Uncertain friendship: American-French relations through the cold war.* New York: Wiley, 1975. ISBN 0-471-98106-0 (cl), 0-471-98107-9 (pbk). ▸ Vacillation between accord when confronting common perils and discord in absence of danger. Stimulating analysis; compare Blumenthal 47.19. [PLH]

SEE ALSO

11.40 John K. Fairbank. *The United States and China.*
28.381 H. Stuart Hughes. *The United States and Italy.*
34.190 Norman E. Saul. *Distant friends.*
38.45 Gordon Connell-Smith. *The United States and Latin America.*
38.341 Lester D. Langley. *Struggle for the American Mediterranean.*
38.351 Jules Robert Benjamin. *The United States and the origins of the Cuban revolution.*
38.437 Frederick B. Pike. *The United States and the Andean republics.*
38.666 Joseph S. Tulchin. *Argentina and the United States.*
47.19 Henry Blumenthal. *France and the United States.*
47.20 Kenneth Bourne. *Britain and the balance of power in North America, 1815–1908.*
47.207 Phillip Darby. *Three faces of imperialism.*
48.50 Warren I. Cohen. *America's response to China.*
48.492 Walter LaFeber. *Inevitable revolutions.*
48.494 Lester D. Langley. *The United States and the Caribbean in the twentieth century.*

Foreign Trade

40.650 William H. Becker and Samuel F. Wells, Jr., eds. *Economics and world power: an assessment of American diplomacy since 1789.* New York: Columbia University Press, 1984. ISBN 0-231-04370-8 (cl), 0-231-04371-6 (pbk). ▸ Collection of essays arguing economic motives only occasionally determined United States foreign policy. Response to New Left economic determinism. Compare Williams 40.685. [PLH]

40.651 George E. Brooks. *Yankee traders, old coasters, and African middlemen: a history of American legitimate trade with West Africa in the nineteenth century.* Brookline, Mass.: Boston University Press, 1970. ISBN 0-87270-016-X. ▸ Ambitious examination of origins and growth of United States legitimate (nonslave) trade with West Africa, except Liberia. Analyzes European-American relations and conflicts. [PLH]

40.652 John G. Clark. *The political economy of world energy: a twentieth-century perspective.* 1990 ed. Chapel Hill: University of North Carolina Press, 1991. ISBN 0-8078-1944-1 (cl), 0-8078-4306-7 (pbk). ▸ Thoughtful study of political and economic importance of oil in international realm since 1900. Stresses government-corporate collaboration. [PLH]

40.653 Peter Duignan and Clarence C. Clendenen. *The United*

States and the African slave trade, 1619–1862. Westport, Conn.: Greenwood, 1978. (Hoover Institution studies.) ISBN 0-313-20009-2. ▸ Brief, synthetic overview of importance of slave trade on United States economic and cultural development and on Anglo-American relations. [PLH]

40.654 John G. B. Hutchins. *The American maritime industries and public policy, 1789–1914: an economic history.* Cambridge, Mass.: Harvard University Press, 1941. ▸ Standard, exhaustively detailed survey of United States shipbuilding and shipping industries. Economic and organizational emphasis. [PLH]

40.655 Daniel Yergin. *The prize: the epic quest for oil, money, and power.* New York: Simon & Schuster, 1991. ISBN 0-671-50248-4. ▸ Prize-winning survey of oil as an economic, strategic, and diplomatic factor since the nineteenth century. Sweeping, panoramic, lively, anecdotal. [PLH/BBY]

SEE ALSO
11.256 Ernest R. May and John K. Fairbank, eds. *America's China trade in historical perspective.*
38.72 Barbara Stallings. *Banker to the Third World.*
43.659 Mira Wilkins. *The emergence of multinational enterprise.*
44.190 Mira Wilkins. *The maturing of multinational enterprise.*

War and Peace

40.656 Edward L. Beach. *The United States Navy: two hundred years.* New York: Holt, Rinehart & Winston, 1986. ISBN 0-03-044711-9. ▸ Broad, critical examination of operations and administration during navy's rise to world's most powerful fleet by 1945. [PLH]

40.657 Edward M. Coffman. *The old army: a portrait of the American army in peacetime, 1784–1898.* New York: Oxford University Press, 1986. ISBN 0-19-503750-2. ▸ Pioneering study of United States Army from perspective of new social history. Focuses on officers, enlisted personnel, and dependent family members to examine issues of race, class, professionalism, careerism, gender, religion, social life, and officer-enlisted relations. [PLH]

40.658 Merle Eugene Curti. *Peace or war: the American struggle, 1636–1936.* 1936 ed. New York: Garland, 1972. ISBN 0-8240-0231-8. ▸ Classic survey of peace movements framed as struggle between advocates of war and advocates of order through education. [PLH]

40.659 Charles DeBenedetti. *The peace reform in American history.* Bloomington: Indiana University Press, 1980. ISBN 0-253-13095-6. ▸ Sympathetic survey of efforts of peace advocates to reform American society and deter war. [PLH]

40.660 Charles DeBenedetti, ed. *Peace heroes in twentieth-century America.* Bloomington: Indiana University Press, 1986. ISBN 0-253-34307-0. ▸ Detailed, probing, sympathetic portraits of nine peace advocates. [PLH]

40.661 Kenneth J. Hagan. *This people's navy: the making of American sea power.* New York: Free Press, 1991. ISBN 0-02-913470-6. ▸ Broad, sweeping survey of United States Navy from American Revolution to eve of Persian Gulf War. Emphasizes personalities over battles. [PLH]

40.662 Stephen Howarth. *To shining sea: a history of the United States Navy, 1775–1991.* New York: Random House, 1991. ISBN 0-394-57662-4. ▸ Lively narrative of battles, operations, and other developments involving navy. [PLH]

40.663 Robert Erwin Johnson. *Guardians of the sea: history of the United States Coast Guard, 1915 to the present.* Annapolis: Naval Institute Press, 1987. ISBN 0-87021-720-8. ▸ Groundbreaking study of pre-1915 origins, roles, missions, administration, relationship to military services, and ethnosocial composition of Coast Guard. [PLH]

40.664 Maurice Matloff, ed. *American military history.* Rev. ed. Washington, D.C.: Office of the Chief of Military History, 1973. ▸ Textbook used for instruction in army's officer-training program. Covers army tactics, operations, strategy, and weapons in wars and conflicts since colonial era. [PLH]

40.665 Allan R. Millett. *Semper fidelis: the history of the United States Marine Corps.* Rev. ed. New York: Free Press, 1991. ISBN 0-02-921595-1 (cl), 0-02-921596-X (pbk). ▸ Discussion of how Marine Corps survived as independent unit by adapting itself to new missions and roles including naval police, protectors of empire, amphibious assaulters, and ground combat troops. Steeped in organizational behavior theory. [PLH]

40.666 Allan R. Millett and Peter Maslowski. *For the common defense: a military history of the United States of America.* New York: Free Press, 1984. ISBN 0-02-921580-3. ▸ Military history probing relevant diplomatic, economic, social, and domestic political factors. Masterly, informative survey. [PLH]

40.667 Melvin Small. *Was war necessary? National security and U.S. entry into war.* Beverly Hills, Calif.: Sage, 1980. ISBN 0-8039-1486-5 (cl), 0-8039-1487-3 (pbk). ▸ Study of six wars, 1812–1950, concluding United States national security never threatened at time of United States entry. Interpretation shaped by opposition to war in Vietnam. [PLH]

40.668 Russell F. Weigley. *History of the United States Army.* Rev. ed. Bloomington: Indiana University Press, 1984. ISBN 0-253-20323-6 (pbk). ▸ Comprehensive study of organization, administration, and deployment of both regular and militia (National Guard) components of United States Army, colonial era to 1960s. Discusses civil-military relations and political rivalries. [PLH]

40.669 Ronald A. Wells, ed. *The wars of America: Christian views.* 1981 ed. Macon, Ga.: Mercer, 1991. ISBN 0-86554-334-8 (cl), 0-86554-394-1 (pbk). ▸ Christian historians assess moral and religious dimensions of United States involvement in wars. Probing overview. [PLH]

SEE ALSO
44.786 Michael S. Sherry. *The rise of American air power.*

Goals and Sources

40.670 Richard J. Barnet. *Roots of war: the men and institutions behind U.S. foreign policy.* 1972 ed. Harmondsworth: Penguin, 1981. ▸ Study attributing United States involvement in twentieth-century wars and covert operations to unrestrained bureaucrats, expansive multinational corporations, and neglect of foreign affairs in political discourse. Representative of Vietnam-era revisionism. [PLH]

40.671 Cecil V. Crabb, Jr. *American diplomacy and the pragmatic tradition.* Baton Rouge: Louisiana State University Press, 1989. ISBN 0-8071-1460-X. ▸ Provocative study of pragmatism as consistent intellectual root of American foreign policy through cold war era. [PLH]

40.672 Norman A. Graebner. *America as a world power: a realist appraisal from Wilson to Reagan.* Wilmington, Del.: Scholarly Resources, 1984. ISBN 0-8420-2230-9 (cl), 0-8420-2232-5 (pbk). ▸ Perceptive essays studying tension between idealism and realism in twentieth-century diplomacy. [PLH]

40.673 Reginald Horsman. *Race and manifest destiny: the origins of American racial Anglo-Saxonism.* Cambridge, Mass: Harvard University Press, 1981. ISBN 0-674-74572-8. ▸ Stimulating study of how culture and pseudo-science of nineteenth century influenced white Americans to abandon liberty, exploit ethnic minorities, and establish empire defined by racial hierarchy. [PLH]

40.674 Michael H. Hunt. *Ideology and U.S. foreign policy.* New

Haven: Yale University Press, 1987. ISBN 0-300-03717-1. ▸ Provocative effort to deal with underlying nativism of national behavior. Finds policy rooted in racism, counterrevolution, and quest for greatness and world expansion. Criticizes Kennan 40.676 for dismissing ideology and Williams, ed. 40.686 for neglecting it. [PLH/BBY/JSH]

40.675 Akira Iriye. *From nationalism to internationalism: U.S. foreign policy to 1914.* London: Routledge & Kegan Paul, 1977. ISBN 0-7100-8444-7. ▸ Study of power politics, internationalism, national security, and popular culture as determinants of foreign policy. [PLH]

40.676 George Frost Kennan. *American diplomacy.* Rev. ed. Chicago: University of Chicago Press, 1984. ISBN 0-226-43146-0 (cl), 0-226-43147-9 (pbk). ▸ Classic text of realist school. Celebrates elites who safeguarded vital interests by exercising power shrewdly; decries idealism in policy making. Downplays cultural and economic influences on United States foreign policy. Compare Hunt 40.674. [PLH]

40.677 Tennant S. McWilliams. *The New South faces the world: foreign affairs and the southern sense of self, 1877–1950.* Baton Rouge: Louisiana State University Press, 1988. ISBN 0-8071-1402-2. ▸ Introductory examination of Civil War experiences, economic needs, racialist culture, and democratic idealism of white southern leaders as determinants of southern perceptions of United States foreign policy. [PLH]

40.678 Frederick Merk. *Manifest destiny and mission in American history: a reinterpretation.* 1963 ed. Westport, Conn.: Greenwood, 1983. ISBN 0-313-23844-8. ▸ Identifies sense of mission behind territorial expansionism of early nineteenth century and abandonment of same in later expansionism. Controversial response to Weinberg 40.683. [PLH]

40.679 Robert E. Osgood. *Ideals and self-interest in America's foreign relations: the great transformation of the twentieth century.* Chicago: University of Chicago Press, 1953. ▸ Analysis of arguments Americans made regarding foreign policy as United States became world power. Classic, realist interpretation. Compare Kennan 40.676. [PLH]

40.680 Dexter Perkins. *A history of the Monroe Doctrine.* 1955 rev. ed. Boston: Little, Brown, 1963. ▸ Classic survey of origins, implementation, and modifications of Monroe Doctrine in United States diplomacy from 1820s to 1960s. Earlier title: *Hands off: A History of the Monroe Doctrine.* [PLH]

40.681 Emily S. Rosenberg. *Spreading the American dream: American economic and cultural expansion, 1890–1945.* New York: Hill & Wang, 1982. ISBN 0-8090-8798-7 (cl), 0-8090-0146-2 (pbk). ▸ Pioneering, influential examination of United States quest to Americanize world under rhetoric of modernization. Analyzes tenets of liberal developmentalism—free trade, unrestricted exchange of culture and information, and government involvement. [PLH]

40.682 Richard W. Van Alstyne. *The rising American empire.* 1960 ed. New York: Norton, 1974. ISBN 0-393-00750-2. ▸ Sweeping overview of how foreign rather than domestic incentives and factors stimulated United States growth to world-power status. [PLH]

40.683 Albert K. Weinberg. *Manifest destiny: a study of nationalist expansionism in American history.* 1935 ed. New York: AMS Press, 1979. ISBN 0-404-14706-2. ▸ Study of wide variety of popular ideas and attitudes toward United States territorial expansionism from revolutionary era to 1930s. Compare to Merk 40.678. [PLH]

40.684 William Appleman Williams. *The roots of the modern American empire: a study of the growth and shaping of social consciousness in a marketplace society.* 1969 ed. New York: Vintage, 1970. ▸ Classic, influential analysis of how farmers advocated acquisition of overseas markets during late nineteenth century, well before eastern Republicans became imperialists. Open Door interpretation. [PLH]

40.685 William Appleman Williams. *The tragedy of American diplomacy.* 1972 rev. 2d ed. New York: Norton, 1988. ISBN 0-393-30493-0 (pbk). ▸ Access to raw materials and markets overriding United States concern. Pathbreaking emphasis on self-interest, economic determinants of policy, and government support of business enterprise. Classic, inspiring work of Open Door school. [PLH]

40.686 William Appleman Williams, ed. *From colony to empire: essays in the history of American foreign relations.* 1969 ed. New York: Vintage, 1970. ISBN 0-471-94685-0. ▸ Revisionist essays with common theme that primary goal in United States expansionism was acquisition of resources and markets. Representative of Open Door school of interpretation. Compare Hunt 40.674. [PLH]

SEE ALSO
44.801 Robert A. Dallek. *The American style of foreign policy.*
47.442 Warren F. Kuehl. *Seeking world order.*

PSYCHE AND CHARACTER

National Character

40.687 Jean Baudrillard. *America.* 1988 ed. Chris Turner, trans. London: Verso, 1989. ISBN 0-86091-220-5. ▸ Study of American character based on continuous (re)construction of idea of America. Highly theoretical. [HIK]

40.688 Daniel Joseph Boorstin. *The Americans: the national experience.* New York: Random House, 1965. ▸ Classic statement of how American character was built by entrepreneurial spirit. [HIK]

40.689 Mitchell Robert Breitwieser. *Cotton Mather and Benjamin Franklin: the price of representative personality.* Cambridge: Cambridge University Press, 1984. ISBN 0-521-26768-4. ▸ Looks for origin of American character in contrasting personalities of Mather and Franklin as symbolic metaphors. For advanced readers. [HIK]

40.690 Geoffrey Gorer. *The American people: a study in national character.* Rev. ed. New York: Norton, 1964. ▸ Reductionist psychological-anthropological study of American character based on psychological uniqueness of Americans. [HIK]

40.691 John A. Hague. *American character and culture in a changing world: some twentieth-century perspectives.* Westport, Conn.: Greenwood, 1979. ISBN 0-313-20735-6. ▸ Collection of essays on national character. Wide range of viewpoints. Influential work in American Studies. Readable. [HIK]

40.692 Michael P. Hamilton, ed. *The American character and foreign policy.* Grand Rapids, Mich.: Eerdmans, 1986. ISBN 0-8028-0231-1. ▸ Collection of essays that attempt to link foreign policy with cultural history and national character. Topics include the effects of religion, ethnicity, race, and American character on United States foreign policy. Readable. [HIK]

40.693 Myra Jehlen. *American incarnation: the individual, the nation, and the continent.* Cambridge, Mass.: Harvard University Press, 1986. ISBN 0-674-02426-5. ▸ American character based on essentialist myth of America. Frontier thesis reborn in identification of ideals with landscape. Emphasizes political and cultural individualism. For advanced readers. [HIK]

40.694 Michael G. Kammen. *Mystic chords of memory: the transformation of tradition in American culture.* New York: Knopf, 1991. ISBN 0-394-57769-8. ▸ Deconstruction of American consciousness, collective memory, traditions, and their conflict with idea of progress. Argues for continual democratization of tradition and its meaningful relation to individual. Key work. [HIK]

40.695 Michael G. Kammen. *People of paradox: an inquiry concerning the origins of American civilization.* 1972 ed. New York: Oxford University Press, 1980. ISBN 0-19-502803-1. ‣ Excellent, important study of how American character is informed by ambiguity and contradictions rooted in European origins. Complexity and pluralism define American character. [HIK]

40.696 Arthur Mann. *The one and the many: reflections on the American identity.* Chicago: University of Chicago Press, 1979. ISBN 0-226-50337-2. ‣ Accessible examination of ethnicity and pluralism as American characteristics. American revolutionary experience makes it unique. Sees tension between ideals of democracy and challenges of pluralism. [HIK]

40.697 Perry Miller. "American character." *New England quarterly* 28 (1955) 435–55. ISSN 0028-4866. ‣ American character based on series of past decisions and constantly evolving. Rejects idea of fixed American character or personality. Essential reading. [HIK]

40.698 George W. Pierson. "A restless temper." *American historical review* 69.4 (1964) 969–89. ISSN 0002-8762. ‣ Advanced analysis of mobility as basis for national character. Explores restless change and fluidity as continuous theme of American experience. [HIK]

40.699 David M. Potter. *People of plenty: economic abundance and the American character.* 1954 ed. Chicago: University of Chicago Press, 1968. ‣ Classic interpretation of American character as unique, forged from affluence and material abundance. [HIK]

40.700 David Riesman. *The lonely crowd: a study of the changing American character.* 1961 abr. ed. New Haven: Yale University Press, 1976. ISBN 0-300-01767-7. ‣ Correlates formation of national character with demographic and technological changes. Sees social behavior as cause and effect of character types. Work of great influence on generation of academic writing. Full edition published 1950. [HIK]

40.701 Michael Paul Rogin. *Ronald Reagan, the movie, and other episodes in political demonology.* Berkeley: University of California Press, 1987. ISBN 0-520-05937-9. ‣ Emblematic status of figures like Ronald Reagan, Richard Nixon, and Andrew Jackson related to their self-definition as symbols of American myths. National character defined by fictionalized portrayals. Also discusses D. W. Griffith and McCarthyism. Readable. [HIK]

40.702 Henry Nash Smith. *Virgin land: the American West as symbol and myth.* 1950 ed. Cambridge, Mass.: Harvard University Press, 1978. ISBN 0-674-93952-2 (cl), 0-674-93955-7 (pbk). ‣ Lauded work on how the West shaped American character. Collective myths of Manifest Destiny, Wild West hero, and West as Garden of Eden. Influential in its day. [HIK]

40.703 Ernest Lee Tuveson. *Redeemer nation: the idea of America's millennial role.* Chicago: University of Chicago Press, 1968. ISBN 0-226-81921-3 (pbk). ‣ Study of theological origins of American divine mission. Concludes biblical literalism led to idea of Manifest Destiny. Discussions of Jonathan Edwards, Samuel Hopkins, Robert Owen, Harriet Beecher Stowe, Julia Ward Howe, and Woodrow Wilson. [HIK]

40.704 Rupert Wilkinson. *The pursuit of American character.* New York: Harper & Row, 1988. ISBN 0-06-438876-X (cl), 0-06-430180-X (pbk). ‣ Articulates tension between individualism and affiliation within context of symbolic matrix of four fears: dependence, anarchy, loss of energy, and loss of virtue. Good starting point. Accessible. [HIK]

40.705 Irvin G. Wyllie. *The self-made man in America: the myth of rags to riches.* 1954 ed. New York: Free Press, 1966. ‣ Discus-

sion of nineteenth-century American business leaders' gospels of prosperity and self-made man. Concludes influence of Bible greater than Darwin's. Challenges a persistent myth. [HIK]

Psychohistory

40.706 Robert J. Brugger, ed. *Our selves/our past: psychological approaches to American history.* Baltimore: Johns Hopkins University Press, 1981. ISBN 0-8018-2312-9 (cl), 0-8018-2382-X (pbk). ‣ Representative collection of eighteen essays on various psychological approaches to American history from colonial period to Vietnam War. Topics include leadership in Great Awakening, slavery, sex roles, and role conflict. [HIK]

40.707 Glenn Davis. *Childhood and history in America.* New York: Psychohistory Press with Institute for Psychohistory, 1976. ISBN 0-914434-04-7. ‣ Uses psychogenic theory of L. deMause. Argues American childhood had four progressive submodes, 1840 to 1965, which led to such movements as progessivism. Overly reductionist and ahistorical. [HIK]

40.708 John Demos. "Underlying themes in the witchcraft of seventeenth-century New England." *American historical review* 75.5 (1970) 1311–26. ISSN 0002-8762. ‣ Model use of psychoanalytic theory of hysteria to solve historical issue. Concludes accusations of witchcraft in seventeenth-century Salem informed by underlying hysterical condition of accusers—adolescent girls—brought on by generational conflict. [HIK]

40.709 Erik H. Erikson. *Dimensions of a new identity.* New York: Norton, 1974. ISBN 0-393-05515-9. ‣ Study of Thomas Jefferson's role as emblem of newness and potential for diversity of American character. Concludes this promise remains unfulfilled and that future of United States depends on redemption of Jefferson's model. Important methodological approach. [HIK]

40.710 Don E. Fehrenbacher. "In quest of the psychohistorical Lincoln." *Reviews in American history* 11 (1983) 12–19. ISSN 0048-7511. ‣ Representative critique of psychohistorical writings, using examples of psychobiographies of Lincoln. Concludes evidence weak, too much elaborate theory, mostly unauthenticated, highly controversial, and unscientific. Important viewpoint. [HIK]

40.711 Richard Hofstadter. *The paranoid style in American politics and other essays.* 1965 ed. Chicago: University of Chicago Press, 1979. ISBN 0-226-34817-2. ‣ Collection of essays linking American political fringe movements—anti-Masons, abolitionists, greenbackers, populists, and twentieth-century extreme Right—to paranoia. This view, now widely challenged, shaped generation of scholarship. [HIK]

40.712 Michael G. Kenny. *The passion of Ansel Bourne: multiple personality in American culture.* Washington, D.C.: Smithsonian Institution Press, 1986. ISBN 0-87474-572-1 (cl), 0-87474-569-1 (pbk). ‣ Case studies, nineteenth century to present, concluding multiple personality a culturally specific metaphor not universal mental disorder. Unique interdisciplinary approach connecting cultural anthropology, history, and psychology. [HIK]

40.713 Joel Kovel. *White racism: a psychohistory.* 1970 ed. London: Free Association Books, 1988. ISBN 0-946960-40-2 (pbk). ‣ Uses psychoanalytic projection to uncover origins of United States racism. Concludes ambiguous attitude toward dirt in bourgeois society reflects ambivalence of capitalism. This ambivalence exhibited in unconscious racist representations. [HIK]

40.714 Howard I. Kushner. *American suicide: a psychocultural exploration.* 1989 ed. New Brunswick, N. J.: Rutgers University Press, 1991. ISBN 0-8135-1610-2 (pbk). ‣ Accessible examination of attitudes toward suicide, seventeenth century to present. Concludes structure of professional disciplines prevented adequate theorizing about suicide's etiology. Interdisciplinary alternative using historical case studies to integrate neurobiology, psychoanalysis, and sociology. Earlier title: *Self-Destruction in the Promised Land: A Psychocultural Biology of American Suicide.* [HIK]

40.715   Howard I. Kushner. "Biochemistry, suicide, and history: problems and possibilities." *Journal of interdisciplinary history* 16 (1985) 69–86. ISSN 0022-1953. ▸ Example of how biochemistry can account for ethnic and sex-specific variations among American suicides. Argues psychologically based historical interpretations must not neglect neurobiology and biochemistry. [HIK]

40.716   Christopher Lasch. *The culture of narcissism: American life in an age of diminishing expectations.* 1978 ed. New York: Warner, 1980. ISBN 0-446-97495-1. ▸ Uses concept of narcissism to criticize both modern American capitalism and its critics on the Left. Influential study that (re)introduced concept of narcissism into historical vocabulary. [HIK]

40.717   Michael Paul Rogin. *Fathers and children: Andrew Jackson and the subjugation of the American Indian.* 1975 ed. New York: Vintage, 1976. ISBN 0-394-71881-X. ▸ Integrates Marxist interpretations of nineteenth-century United States with psychoanalytic theory. President Jackson's American Indian policy emblem for later transformation from localized republic to bourgeois democracy. [HIK]

40.718   Dorothy Ross. "Woodrow Wilson and the case for psychohistory." *Journal of American history* 69 (1982) 659–68. ISSN 0021-8723. ▸ Important defense of psychohistory, using example of President Wilson. Psychoanalytic ego psychology provides nonreductionist method for viewing constructive as well as self-destructive behaviors. [HIK]

40.719   Carol Z. Stearns and Peter N. Stearns. *Anger: the struggle for emotional control in America's history.* Chicago: University of Chicago Press, 1986. ISBN 0-226-77151-2. ▸ Innovative analysis of repressed anger as consequence of triumph of romance and affection in modern domestic relations. Offers new term, emotionology, to explore *mentalité* of emotions. [HIK]

40.720   Carol Z. Stearns and Peter N. Stearns, eds. *Emotion and social change: toward a new psychohistory.* New York: Holmes & Meier, 1988. ISBN 0-8419-1048-0. ▸ Collection of essays on history of emotions—love, anger, and jealousy. Emphasis on editors' own work on emotionology. Other essays by Sommers, Demos, Gillis, and Modell use more traditional psychoanalytic categories. [HIK]

40.721   Peter N. Stearns and Carol Z. Stearns. "Emotionology: clarifying the history of emotions and emotional standards." *American historical review* 90 (1985) 813–36. ISSN 0002-8762. ▸ Proposes new term, emotionology, to distinguish between collective emotional standards of a society and emotional experience of individuals and groups. Focuses on social elements that determine manner in which emotions are expressed. Good overview of new approach. [HIK]

SEE ALSO

1.330 Cushing Strout. *The veracious imagination.*
39.667 John Demos. *Entertaining Satan.*

EXCEPTIONALISM

Proponents

40.722   Daniel Joseph Boorstin. *The genius of American politics.* 1953 ed. Chicago: University of Chicago Press, 1973. ISBN 0-226-06490-5 (cl), 0-226-06491-3 (pbk). ▸ Study of consequences of pragmatic history that makes United States suspicious of abstractions. Tendency of American political theory to make theory superfluous. Readable. [HIK]

40.723   Jon Butler. *Awash in a sea of faith: christianizing the American people.* Cambridge, Mass.: Harvard University Press, 1990. ISBN 0-674-05600-0. ▸ Broad study tracing course of American

religion from English European origins to Civil War. Excellent chapter on black Christianity. Important cultural perspective arguing exceptionalism due to unique development of American Protestantism. [HIK/DSS]

40.724   Leon D. Epstein. *Political parties in the American mold.* Madison: University of Wisconsin Press, 1986. ISBN 0-299-10700-0. ▸ Study of American exceptionalism as tied to development of political parties, which were less organized and less effective than European parliamentary parties. [HIK]

40.725   D. H. Lawrence. *Studies in classic American literature.* 1923 ed. Harmondsworth: Penguin, 1977. ISBN 0-14-004437-X (cl), 0-14-003300-9 (pbk). ▸ Development and criticism of literary basis for American exceptionalism. Influential cultural and literary perspective. [HIK]

40.726   Gary Marks. *Unions in politics: Britain, Germany, and the United States in the nineteenth and early twentieth centuries.* Princeton: Princeton University Press, 1989. ISBN 0-691-07801-7 (cl), 0-691-02304-2 (pbk). ▸ Valuable, comprehensive discussion through case studies linking American exceptionalism with development of organized labor. Argues structural dynamics of American politics prevented rise of labor party. [HIK]

40.727   John Harmon McElroy. *Finding freedom: America's distinctive cultural formation.* Carbondale, Ill.: Southern Illinois University Press, 1989. ISBN 0-8093-1515-7. ▸ Exceptionalism based on unique demographic and geographic characteristics. Discusses geography, climate, population density, migration, religion, and psychology to show patriotic distortion of history and culture. Useful perspective. [HIK]

40.728   Michael E. McGerr. "The price of the "new transnational history."" *American historical review* 96 (1991) 1056–1067. ISSN 0002-8762. ▸ Reexamination of work of David Potter, Daniel Boorstin, Louis Hartz and other proponents of exceptionalism. Argues close reading of these texts calls entire typology into question. Finds pure exceptionalism rare. [HIK]

40.729   Reinhold Niebuhr. *The irony of American history.* 1952 ed. New York: Scribner's, 1962. ▸ Classic text by theologian concerned with foreign policy. May reinforce exceptionalism or expose it as false consciousness informed by arrogance and denial of history. [HIK]

40.730   Byron E. Shafer, ed. *Is America different? A new look at American exceptionalism.* Oxford: Clarendon, 1991. ISBN 0-19-827734-2. ▸ Essays reaffirming principles of American exceptionalism. Useful for views of staunchest advocates. [HIK]

40.731   Richard Slotkin. *Regeneration through violence: the mythology of the American frontier, 1600–1860.* Middletown, Conn.: Wesleyan University Press, 1973. ISBN 0-8195-4055-2. ▸ Examination of national character as based on violent myth of regeneration. Symbolic conflict of hunter-hero against nature and Indians. Definitive. [HIK]

40.732   Alexis de Tocqueville. *Democracy in America.* 2 vols. J. P. Mayer and Max Lerner, eds. George Lawrence, trans. Garden City, N.Y.: Doubleday, 1966. ISBN 0-385-08170-7. ▸ Classic text on effects of democratic institutions. Concludes America's position exceptional and unlikely to be duplicated again. [HIK]

40.733   William Appleman Williams. *The contours of American history.* 1961 ed. New York: Norton, 1988. ISBN 0-393-30561-9. ▸ American history defined in three periods: mercantilism, 1740–1828; *laissez nous faire*, 1819–96; and corporation capitalism, 1882–1960s. Sees economic structures as key to American exceptionalism. Bold, erudite. [HIK]

40.734   David M. Wrobel. *The end of American exceptionalism: frontier anxiety from the old West to the New Deal.* Lawrence: University Press of Kansas, 1993. ISBN 0-7006-0561-4. ▸ Argument that worries about fading frontier and decline of essential American qualities preceded Frederick Jackson Turner work. Sees frontier anxiety as persistent theme in political debates. Discusses intellectuals and policy makers on individualism and community. [LCP]

SEE ALSO

4.268 Dorothy Ross. *The origins of American social science.*

Critiques of Exceptionalism

40.735 John A. Agnew. *The United States in the world economy: a regional geography.* Cambridge: Cambridge University Press, 1987. ISBN 0-521-30410-5 (cl), 0-521-31684-7 (pbk). ▸ Useful, critical summary of ideology of exceptionalism as central to construction of American history. Yet American differences shaped in context of world economy. [HIK]

40.736 Nina Baym. "Melodramas of beset manhood: how theories of American fiction exclude women authors." *American quarterly* 33.2 (1981) 123–39. ISSN 0003-0678. ▸ Trenchant critique of exceptionalism's literary canon. Examines omission of female authors who chose global or local themes; concludes misrepresentation of women characters incongruous with myth. [LCP]

40.737 Alexander E. Campbell. "The American past as destiny: the Anglo-American connection." In *American history—British historians: a cross-cultural approach to the American experience.* David H. Burton, ed., pp. 51–72. Chicago: Nelson-Hall, 1976. ISBN 0-88229-280-3. ▸ Useful examination of how Americans' increasing awareness of global interdependence undermines notions of exceptionalism. End of American innocence. [HIK]

40.738 Alan Dawley. "Farewell to American exceptionalism." In *Why is there no socialism in the United States?* Jean Heffer and Jeanine Rovet, eds., pp. 311–15. Paris: Éditions de l'École des Hautes Études en Sciences Sociales, 1988. ISBN 2-7132-0887-4. ▸ Theoretical study presenting United States as different but not exceptional. Articulates methodological issues; focuses on variations and similarities in national developments of capitalism. [HIK]

40.739 Carl N. Degler. "In pursuit of an American history." *American historical review* 92.1 (1987) 1–12. ISSN 0002-8762. ▸ Argues national difference ought to replace notions of national uniqueness or exceptionalism as interpretive assumption of American history. Accessible. [HIK]

40.740 John Patrick Diggins. "Consciousness and ideology in American history: the burden of Daniel J. Boorstin." *American historical review* 76.1 (1971) 99–118. ISSN 0002-8762. ▸ Trenchant critique of reasoning in works on consensus, practicality, and uniqueness. Discusses Boorstin's borrowings from Jefferson and paradoxical closeness to Marx. Irony of resorting to ideology to disown ideology as un-American. [LCP]

40.741 Eric Foner. "Why is there no socialism in the United States?" In *Why is there no socialism in the United States?* Jean Heffer and Jeanine Rovet, eds., pp. 61–64. Paris: Éditions de l'École des Hautes Études en Sciences Sociales, 1988. ISBN 2-7132-0887-4. ▸ Important revisionist statement, rejecting simplistic notions of exceptionalism, but acknowledges differences among industrializing nations especially in organized labor. Important revisionist statement. [HIK]

40.742 Carlton J. H. Hayes. "The American frontier—frontier of what?" In *The Turner thesis concerning the role of the frontier in American history.* Rev. ed. George Rogers Taylor, ed., pp. 66–75. Boston: Heath, 1956. ▸ Identifies vogue of exceptionalist Turner thesis with intellectual isolationism and sees it as false view of indigenous, superior American way of life. Europeanist's eloquent dissent in years after World War II. [LCP]

40.743 Akira Iriye. "Exceptionalism revisited." *Reviews in American history* 16 (1988) 291–97. ISSN 0048-7511. ▸ Concludes that by pursuing self-consciously exceptionalist policies, America may have become dialectically less exceptionalist. [HIK]

40.744 Michael G. Kammen. "The problem of American exceptionalism: a reconsideration." *American quarterly* 45.1 (1993) 1–43. ISSN 0003-0678. ▸ Extremely valuable critique and overview of how transnational industrial similarities undercut claims to American uniqueness or superiority. Nevertheless, differences must not be neglected. [HIK]

40.745 Geir Lundestad. "Moralism, presentism, exceptionalism, provincialism, and other extravagances in American writings on the early cold war years." *Diplomatic history* 13.4 (1989) 527–45. ISSN 0145-2096. ▸ Argument for more comparative approach to diplomatic history. Emphasizes international interconnectedness and integrating non–United States viewpoints into scholarship. For advanced readers. [HIK]

40.746 David W. Noble. *The end of American history: democracy, capitalism, and the metaphor of two worlds in Anglo-American historical writing, 1880–1980.* 1985 ed. Minneapolis: University of Minnesota Press, 1986. ISBN 0-8166-1415-6 (cl), 0-8166-1416-4 (pbk). ▸ Concludes Depression and wars belie American image as exceptional because they expose transnational similarities. Readable. [HIK]

40.747 David W. Noble. *Historians against history: the frontier thesis and the national covenant in American historical writing since 1830.* Minneapolis: University of Minnesota Press, 1965. ▸ Discussion of traditions of historical thought that disconnect America from past and world, George Bancroft to Daniel Boorstin. Sees these theses as imprisoning ideology that prevents creative thought about social problems. [LCP]

40.748 Dorothy Ross. "Historical consciousness in nineteenth-century America." *American historical review* 89 (1984) 909–28. ISSN 0002-8762. ▸ Examination of scholarly resistance to historicism's implied contingency. Influence of assumptions of United States history informed by progress, republicanism, and national mission. Complex analysis. [HIK]

40.749 William C. Spengemann. *A mirror for Americanists: reflections on the idea of American literature.* Hanover, N.H.: University Press of New England for Dartmouth College, 1989. ISBN 0-87451-478-9 (cl), 0-87451-483-5 (pbk). ▸ Finds American literature not unique; construction of idea of exceptionalism ironically emphasized European similarities. Literary emphasis. [HIK]

40.750 Ian Tyrrell. "American exceptionalism in an age of international history." *American historical review* 96 (1991) 1031–55. ISSN 0002-8762. ▸ Important recent critique, leading readers to key literature on exceptionalism and comparative studies. With comments by Michael McGerr and author's response. [HIK]

40.751 Laurence Veysey. "The autonomy of American history reconsidered." *American quarterly* 31 (1979) 455–77. ISSN 0003-0678. ▸ Important examination of trend in United States history toward loss of distinctiveness, most apparent in recent social history revealing United States as part of both larger world system and smaller subsystems. Important work. [HIK]

40.752 Sean Wilentz. "Against exceptionalism: class consciousness and the American labor movement, 1790–1920." *International labor and working class history* 26 (1984) 1–24. ISSN 0147-5479. ▸ Argues against exceptionalism as neglecting history of class consciousness in United States. Points to historiographical gaps. Controversial and theoretical. [HIK]

Comparative Studies

40.753 Miriam Cohen and Michael Hanagan. "The politics of gender and the making of the welfare state." *Journal of social* *history* 24.3 (1991) 469–85. ISSN 0022-4529. ▸ Study of effectiveness of social feminist alliances with welfare reformers to focus on women's needs in United States, France, and Great Britain. In United States feminist ties to Democratic party, with less class emphasis, resulted in some success. For advanced readers. [HIK]

40.754 M. J. Daunton. *Housing the workers, 1850–1914: a comparative perspective.* London: Leicester University Press, 1990. ISBN 0-7185-1315-0. ▸ Study of historical patterns of ownership, financing, legal relations, public policy, and architecture. Sees housing as metaphor for human condition, moral discourse, and private versus public space. Compares northern and southern England, Paris, Vienna, and New York. For advanced readers. [HIK]

40.755 Richard J. Evans. *The feminists: women's emancipation movements in Europe, America, and Australasia, 1820–1920.* Rev. ed. New York: Barnes & Noble, 1979. ISBN 0-06-492044-5. ▸ Study of origins, development, and collapse of feminist movements. Analyzes relationship of feminism to bourgeois liberalism and socialism. Ties course of mainstream feminism to liberalism. Theoretical but accessible. [HIK]

40.756 George M. Fredrickson. *White supremacy: a comparative study in American and South African history.* New York: Oxford University Press, 1981. ISBN 0-19-502759-0. ▸ Insightful comparison of American and South African experiences. Concludes American race relations constructed by geographic conditions, different normative assumptions, and failure to integrate indigenes into labor force. [HIK]

40.757 Raymond Grew. "The comparative weakness of American history." *Journal of interdisciplinary history* 16 (1985) 87–101. ISSN 0022-1953. ▸ Advanced analysis of American historians' resistance to comparative studies. Explanation rests, in part, on assumptions about American exceptionalism. [HIK]

40.758 Stephen H. Haber. "Industrial concentration and the capital markets: a comparative study of Brazil, Mexico, and the United States, 1830–1930." *Journal of economic history* 51.3 (1991) 559–81. ISSN 0022-0507. ▸ Exploration of relationship between structures of industry and development of capitalist markets in initial stages of industrialization. Comparative methodology. For advanced readers. [HIK]

40.759 Steven Hahn. "Class and state in postemancipation societies: southern planters in comparative perspective." *American historical review* 95.1 (1990) 75–99. ISSN 0002-8762. ▸ Compares nineteenth-century Prussian Junkers, Brazilian Fazendeiros, United States southern planters. Concludes United States planters failed to unite industry with agriculture, resulting in loss of political power. Readable. [HIK]

40.760 Patrice Higonnet. *Sister republics: the origins of French and American republicanism.* Cambridge, Mass.: Harvard University Press, 1988. ISBN 0-674-80982-3. ▸ Compares French corporatism with American individualism to explain differences in forms of republicanism. [HIK]

40.761 Seymour Martin Lipset. *Continental divide: the values and institutions of the United States and Canada.* New York: Routledge, 1990. ISBN 0-415-90309-2. ▸ Attributes cultural differences to different foundings. United States revolution emphasized life, liberty, and pursuit of happiness, while Canadian confederation emphasized peace, order, and good government. United States values individualism, Canada collectivism. Readable. [HIK]

40.762 Seymour Martin Lipset. *The first new nation: the United States in historical and comparative perspective.* 1963 ed. New York: Norton, 1979. ISBN 0-393-00911-4. ▸ Examination of conflicting values of equality and achievement in American society, compared with other English-speaking nations. Reveals effects of social institutions in creating conditions for democratic values to take root. Useful sociological view; for advanced readers. [HIK]

40.763 Norbert MacDonald. *Distant neighbors: a comparative history of Seattle and Vancouver.* Lincoln: University of Nebraska Press, 1987. ISBN 0-8032-3111-3. ▸ Useful comparative study tying differences between two cities to different governmental policies regarding development. [HIK]

40.764 Donald B. Meyer. *Sex and power: the rise of women in America, Russia, Sweden, and Italy.* 2d ed. Middletown, Conn.: Wesleyan University Press, 1989. ISBN 0-8195-5153-8 (cl), 0-8195-6214-9 (pbk). ▸ Study of impact of political and economic forces on women's lives. Treats political changes, feminism, and anti-feminism. Problematic editing, often derivative, but still unique approach to subject. [HIK]

40.765 Jane Rendall. *The origins of modern feminism: women in Britain, France, and the United States, 1780–1860.* 1984 ed. Chicago: Lyceum, 1990. ISBN 0-925065-39-0. ▸ Attributes character of national movements to particular patterns of class and political conflict. In United States higher education and economic status plus application of discourse of revolutionary republicanism led to some success. For advanced readers. [HIK]

40.766 Michele Saint Marc. "Monetary history in the long run: how are monetarization and monetarism implicated in France, in the U.K., and in U.S.?" *Journal of European economic history* 18.3 (1989) 551–73. ISSN 0391-5115. ▸ Highly theoretical discussion of evolution of monetary structures in relation to institutions and human behavior. Combines economic history with economic theory. Compares United States, United Kingdom, and France. [HIK]

40.767 C. Vann Woodward, ed. *The comparative approach to American history.* New York: Basic Books, 1968. ISBN 0-465-01339-2 (pbk). ▸ Program for dismissing narrow perspectives. Collected essays on perennial topics such as frontier, slavery, wars, and politics, many arguing for America's uniqueness, others repudiating this as myth. Some essays dated. [LCP]

SEE ALSO
4.403 Alfred D. Chandler, Jr. *Scale and scope.*
34.238 Peter Kolchin. *Unfree labor.*

DAVID L. AMMERMAN

American Revolution and Early Republic, 1754–1815

The direction of early American history has shifted significantly in recent decades. Except for the continuing popularity of biography, narrative history seems in danger of disappearing: new categories of social, gender, and labor history are growing rapidly, and local and regional studies now rank among the most extensive lists.

Despite the changes, however, a historian from the 1940s would find the more recent publications listed here both enlightening and familiar. The emphasis is different, but the discipline is the same. This continuity may be less evident in the decades to come, and the differences between more traditional studies and newly emerging trends may become more difficult to bridge.

The most notable change over the entire period has been the move away from the purely economic focus of progressive history. Prior to World War II much of the work on the American Revolution was influenced by C. Beard's *An Economic Interpretation of the Constitution* (41.185) and focused on underlying economic motivations in the apparently inevitable class struggle. Earlier C. Becker (41.374) had led the way by insisting that the Revolution was not simply for home rule but to determine who would rule at home. Arthur M. Schlesinger, Jr., further explicated this theme in *The Colonial Merchants and the American Revolution, 1763–1776* (41.83). Nearly half a century later the work of Merrill Jensen and his students evidenced the continuing importance of this interpretation. The influence of Marx led historians to dismiss the rhetoric and reveal the underlying motivations that were the real cause of events.

The most significant change began with a renewed interest in intellectual, particularly ideological, history initiated by two historians influenced, not surprisingly, by Perry Miller. During the 1950s and 1960s, E. S. Morgan and B. Bailyn pointed the way toward a new interpretation of the period often referred to as "neo-whig." These scholars downplayed the selfish economic motivations for revolution and, in essence, advanced a more sophisticated version of the pro-American interpretation of the conflict put forth by the Whig historians of the nineteenth century. In *The Stamp Act Crisis* (41.77), Morgan reviewed the documents and found the colonists both more consistent and more ideological in their resistance than had previous historians. In *The Ideological Origins of the American Revolution* (41.52) and *The Origins of American Politics* (39.200), Bailyn similarly proposed that scholars pay more attention to the intellectual framework through which the colonists viewed the world. Together, Morgan and Bailyn turned attention away from the alleged underlying motives of the discourse to the intellectual underpinnings of the discourse itself.

This fascination with the mindset of the colonists on the eve of Revolution has produced a wealth of information on how Americans perceived the world, how that perception changed, and how it differed among the players according to wealth and social position. Rather than delineate various aspects of specific events, historians such as P. Maier and G. S. Wood (41.73, 41.221) concentrated on patterns of thinking. The implicit and sometimes explicit theme of this work has been that the intellectual framework through which any particular event is viewed affects, perhaps determines, the response.

This shift from economic to intellectual determinism has run parallel, oddly enough, with the emergence of a new social history that has concentrated on reconstructing the everyday lives of men and women, previously outside the range of historical studies. Beginning with scholars working primarily in the seventeenth century, this new approach would have an impact on all aspects of early American history. Scholars such as S. C. Powell, D. Rutman, K. Lockridge, M. Zuckerman, R. Gross, and P. J. Greven, Jr., focused on local and social history as the means, not only of understanding broader trends, but of coming to grips with the reality of colonial life.

Although not necessarily at odds with intellectual history, these studies certainly focused on a different kind of evidence. Rather than peruse sermons, essays, pamphlets, and newspapers, the new social historians sifted through wills, inventories, deeds, and local records. They looked at settlement patterns, life expectancy, births, marriages, and death. This approach rapidly spread, producing studies in localities from New England to the Chesapeake and has been further augmented by investigation of labor and poverty in more urban areas. Nearly one-sixth of this bibliography is categorized as regional, social, economic, or urban studies.

Along with and encouraged by this new-found interest in local and social history has been the attention paid to groups once characterized as inarticulate. African Americans, American Indians, women, laborers, and the poor have not only been given more attention, they have been recognized as playing important roles. Although the movement may have begun as a recognition that marginalized groups in present-day society were demanding attention, historians have increasingly recognized that to ignore these groups is to misunderstand the historical record. Early American history is no longer simply an account of the great white men.

The study of African Americans and slavery has been perhaps the most productive topic in this attempt to study previously ignored groups. The strength of the field is suggested by the large number of studies published in the past five years, nearly one-third of the studies cited here. It is also notable that whereas earlier studies explored either slavery or the activities of African Americans in a white world (e.g., D. B. Davis 41.483; B. Quarles 41.496), more recent studies explore the development of an African American community and subculture (e.g., G. B. Nash 41.493; W. D. Pierson 41.494).

The rapid increase of interest in the field of gender history has also begun to produce significant monograph publication. Only a dozen books appear in that section in this bibliography, but nine of these were published in the past decade. Beginning with N. F. Cott's *The Bonds of Womanhood* (41.509) through L. T. Ulrich's *A Midwife's Tale* (41.519), the focus has been, as in the newer work on African Americans, on the lives, community, and mindset of women themselves, rather than on how they fit into the dominant society.

The shifts in emphasis noted above have brought with them significant alterations in the approach to other specific topics and areas of specialization. Military history, for example, bears little resemblance to the old descriptions of battles and strategies. John Shy (41.85, 41.114) has studied the armed struggle in terms of its impact on and interrelationship with the population at large. The very title of C. Royster's *A Revolutionary*

People at War: The Continental Army and American Character, 1775–1783 (41.113) evidences the broader constructs of the new military historians.

Equally remarkable is the increased and altered interest in the study of loyalists over the past thirty years. Since 1960 nearly two dozen monographs have been published in this area, ranging from Bailyn's *The Ordeal of Thomas Hutchinson* (41.118) to E. G. Wilson's *The Loyal Blacks* (41.503) to M. B. Norton's *The British Americans: The Loyalist Exiles in England, 1774–1789* (41.132) and N. MacKinnon's *This Unfriendly Soil: The Loyalist Experience in Nova Scotia, 1783–1791* (45.141). Here, again, the focus has shifted from the dominant society to the culture of those previously viewed as little more than a sideshow to the main event.

Changes are also apparent in the study of popular and material culture over the past three decades. Two-thirds of these studies have appeared in the past ten years, a majority in the past five. Even more striking is the proliferation of monographs clearly influenced by the poststructuralists and the emerging interest in discourse, rhetoric, and the public sphere. Notable among the latter are L. C. Olson's *Emblems of American community in the Revolutionary Era* (41.180), M. Warner's *The Letters of the Republic* (41.461), and L. Ziff's *Writing in the New Nation* (41.463).

Even in legal and constitutional history, the focus has shifted, to some extent, from theory and politics to the social context. Among the most important and interesting monographs in this field are M. J. Horwitz's *The Transformation of American Law, 1780–1860* (40.74) and W. E. Nelson's *Americanization of the Common Law* (41.402), both of which explain changes in the legal system by exploring changes in the social structure. On the other hand, the voluminous work of J. P. Reid continues its focus on a detailed and specific consideration of constitutional rights as critical to understanding the coming of the Revolution.

The interest in local history, observed above, led historians to view the American Revolution from the perspective of towns, urban areas, and individual colonies, or later, states. Much of this recent work has tested existing generalizations about the Revolution and its aftermath, and a substantial body of the literature has suggested that social change began prior to the Revolution. Such studies have also downplayed the significance of the political changes brought about by the war itself.

Although some good political histories appeared in the 1960s and 1970s—B. W. Labaree (41.70) and H. B. Zobel (41.93) are good examples—narrative political history has been in decline. More typical publications include R. A. Ryerson's *The Revolution is Now Begun* (41.81), E. Countryman's *A People in Revolution* (41.379) and G. B. Nash's *The Urban Crucible* (41.401).

Studies of the early republic seem essentially intellectual, even idealist, but with an interesting twist. One group of historians emphasizes the long shadow cast by the continuing prevalence of classical republican ideas; dissenting scholars insist that the liberal and capitalistic thrusts of seveneeth-century England were equally if not more important. The battle has raged furiously and, interestingly enough, both sides have attempted to enlist the findings of the social and demographic historians in support of their respective positions. Here, the studies of the intellectual historians merge with those of their more prosaic brethren in an attempt to delineate the whole of society.

If all of this seems confusing, the incursion of the poststructuralists into the field of history threatens to rend the profession in ways previously familiar only to students of literature. The deconstruction of language, introduced perhaps by the studies of Pocock and Bailyn, continues to attract the interest of newer scholars, particularly in American studies and American literature, and promises to reach proportions almost certainly unintended by those who set it in motion. Some scholars have characterized poststructuralism as essentially ahistorical or even the last gasp of idealism, while others believe that its implications for the profession need to be further explored. Whether or not this debate will escalate remains to be seen.

Clearly the field of early American history offers unlimited opportunities for scholars. Compared to the state of the profession in 1960, there is more diversity, both in subject matter and in disciplinary approach. Demography, historical geography, cultural anthropology, and the study of language have all opened new vistas for the historian.

The field is exciting and provocative but there is, perhaps, one danger. American history, like American literature, has always been an attractive field for the general reader and for undergraduates. It has offered an opportunity for the specialist to communicate with the nonspecialist and to influence the thinking of the entire community. In these days of specialization and sometimes esoteric debate, it ill behooves the historian to forget that the field does, after all, provide a bully pulpit.

Entries are arranged under the following headings:

General Studies
  Overviews
  Topical Surveys

Origins of the Revolution, 1754–1774

Revolutionary War and the Confederation, 1775–1788
  Military History
  Loyalists
  The States and the Nation
  Foreign Relations
  Topical Studies

The Constitution and the Bill of Rights

The New Republic, 1789–1801
  National Government and Politics
  State Government and Politics
  Foreign Relations

The New Republic, 1801–1815
  National Government and Politics
  State Government and Politics
  Foreign Relations and the War of 1812

The Frontier and Indian Relations

Religion

Regional Studies

States and Cities

Society and Economy

Printing, Literature, and the Arts

Science and Education

African Americans

Women and the Family

Biography

[Contributors: CMJ = Christopher M. Joyce, DAR = David A. Rawson, DLA = David L. Ammerman, DMS = Darren M. Staloff, EVW = Edward V. Woodward, LAN = Lynn A. Nelson, RWS = Robert W. Smith, Jr.]

GENERAL STUDIES

Overviews

41.1   John R. Alden. *A history of the American Revolution.* 1969 ed. New York: Da Capo, 1989. ISBN 0-306-80366-6 (pbk). ▸ Political narrative for general audience, with consensus view of Revolution. Discounts internal conflicts between colonies, depicting growing anger and unity against arbitrary British rule as cause of Revolution. Focus on military activities. [DAR]

41.2   Charles McLean Andrews. *The colonial background of the American Revolution: four essays in American colonial history.* 1931 rev. ed. New Haven: Yale University Press, 1971. ISBN 0-300-00004-9 (pbk). ▸ Four essays arguing Revolution cannot be understood only in American context. British colonial policies, especially mercantilism, central to development of crisis. Classic work that defines imperial school. [DAR]

41.3   Ian R. Christie. *Wars and revolutions: Britain, 1760–1815.* Cambridge, Mass.: Harvard University Press, 1982. ISBN 0-674-94760-6. ▸ Chronological examination of government ministries and policies, with passing references to social and economic contexts of political strife. Textbook political history lacking sustained treatment of major radical political movements and groups. [DAR]

41.4   Edward Countryman. *The American Revolution.* New York: Hill & Wang, 1985. ISBN 0-8090-2563-9 (cl), 0-8090-0162-4 (pbk). ▸ Idiosyncratic look into lives of everyday people and how Revolution affected and transformed character of American life and culture. Well-written synthesis of recent scholarship. [EVW]

41.5   Jack P. Greene, ed. *The American Revolution: its character and limits.* New York: New York University Press, 1987. ISBN 0-8147-3012-4. ▸ Twenty-two essays and commentaries treating issues facing Americans in years after Revolution. Diverse, although somewhat elitist, collection of arguments and topics. [EVW]

41.6   Jack P. Greene and J. R. Pole, eds. *The Blackwell encyclopedia of the American Revolution.* Cambridge, Mass.: Blackwell Reference, 1991. ISBN 1-55786-224-3. ▸ Seventy-five articles by outstanding scholars treating events, effects, and themes. Traditional and innovative, informative and provocative. Excellent reference. [DMS]

41.7   James A. Henretta, Michael G. Kammen, and Stanley N. Katz, eds. *The transformation of early American history: society, authority, and ideology.* New York: Knopf; distributed by Random House, 1991. ISBN 0-394-58147-4. ▸ Eleven new, insightful essays in honor of Bernard Bailyn's career. Impressive, diverse essays ranging from common law in early Virginia to late eighteenth-century transition to market capitalism in United States. [DMS]

41.8   J. Franklin Jameson. *The American Revolution considered as a social movement.* 1926 ed. Princeton: Princeton University Press, 1967. ISBN 0-691-00550-8 (pbk). ▸ Social implications and consequences of Revolution. Thematic introduction to social aspects of conflict. [EVW]

41.9   Stephen G. Kurtz and James H. Hutson, eds. *Essays on the American Revolution.* Chapel Hill and New York: University of North Carolina Press and Norton for Institute of Early American History and Culture, 1973. ISBN 0-8078-1204-8 (cl), 0-393-09419-7 (pbk). ▸ Eight original essays raising new questions on political and social evolution of late eighteenth-century American society, meaning and significance of Revolution, and long-term underlying causes of war. [EVW]

41.10   Library of Congress Symposium on the American Revolution, comp. *Fundamental testaments of the American Revolution: papers presented at the second symposium, May 10 and 11, 1973.* Washington, D.C.: Library of Congress, 1973. ISBN 0-8444-0111-0. ▸ Essays explicating social and political contexts of Declaration of Independence, *Common Sense*, Articles of Confederation, and Treaty of Paris. Each provides standard view of context, but from differing interpretive viewpoints. [DAR]

41.11   Library of Congress Symposium on the American Revolution, comp. *Leadership in the American Revolution: papers presented at the third symposium, May 9 and 10, 1974.* Washington, D.C.: Library of Congress, 1974. ISBN 0-8444-0149-8. ▸ Essays from symposium revealing that leadership not useful focus for understanding Revolution. Leadership fragile and incomplete during Revolution; need study of ordinary people. [RWS]

41.12   James Kirby Martin. *In the course of human events: an interpretive exploration of the American Revolution.* Arlington Heights, Ill.: Harlan Davidson, 1979. ISBN 0-88295-794-5 (cl), 0-88295-795-3 (pbk). ▸ Synthetic essay focusing on socioeconomic values, attitudes, and interests that influenced events of era and their resolution. Based on mainline scholarship (new social history) of preceding thirty years. [DAR]

41.13   Robert Middlekauff. *The glorious cause: the American Revolution, 1763–1789.* New York: Oxford University Press, 1982. ISBN 0-19-502921-6 (cl), 0-19-503575-5 (pbk). ▸ Readable, clear, neo-whig synthetic narrative. Sees colonists' religious values and English radical whig thought as driving force behind Revolution. Heavy emphasis on battles and campaigns and their effects on citizens and soldiers. [EVW]

41.14 Edmund S. Morgan. *The birth of the republic, 1763–89.* 1977 ed. Chicago: University of Chicago Press, 1992. ISBN 0-226-53756-0 (cl), 0-226-53757-9 (pbk). ‣ Brief, readable account of revolutionary period. Excellent introduction for general reader. Factually reliable, judicious interpretation. [DMS]

41.15 Edmund S. Morgan. *The challenge of the American Revolution.* New York: Norton, 1976. ISBN 0-393-05603-1 (cl), 0-393-00876-2 (pbk). ‣ Useful essay collection tracing development of author's scholarship, 1948–75. Finds essentially consensus view of revolutionary era. Builds on and clarifies earlier work. [DAR]

41.16 R. R. Palmer. *The age of the democratic revolution: a political history of Europe and America, 1760–1800. Vol. 1: The challenge.* 1959–64 ed. Princeton: Princeton University Press, 1969–70. ISBN 0-691-00569-9 (v. 1, pbk). ‣ Analysis of emergence of democratic revolutions throughout Europe and colonial North America, 1760–91, as challenge of democratic ideas to government by privilege. Impressive attempt to correlate various revolutions. [EVW]

41.17 R. R. Palmer. *The age of the democratic revolution: a political history of Europe and America, 1760–1800. Vol. 2: The struggle.* 1959–64 ed. Princeton: Princeton University Press, 1969–70. ISBN 0-691-00570-2 (v. 2, pbk). ‣ Analysis of revolutionary and counterrevolutionary forces, 1791–1800, to examine and compare American and French revolutions on their own terms within their eighteenth-century contexts. Unconventional comparative history. [EVW]

41.18 John Parker and Carol Urness, eds. *The American Revolution: a heritage of change, the James Ford Bell Library bicentennial conference, University of Minnesota.* Minneapolis: Associates of the James Ford Bell Library, 1975. ‣ Uneven collection of essays, many summarizing familiar themes and views. Best is Greene, offering developmental model of American politics that contrasts with static model of neo-whig interpretations. [DAR]

41.19 Robert E. Shalhope. *The roots of democracy: American thought and culture, 1760–1800.* Boston: Twayne, 1990. ISBN 0-8057-9051-9 (cl), 0-8057-9076-X (pbk). ‣ Synthesis of recent scholarship on late eighteenth-century culture, with emphasis on localist impulses and divergent social and economic views. Hierarchy and order competed with egalitarian individualism and fragmentation of society. Good guide to recent historiography. [DMS]

41.20 Gordon S. Wood. *The radicalism of the American Revolution.* New York: Knopf, 1992. ISBN 0-679-40493-7. ‣ Broad, provocative, and grandiose in scope. Argues Revolution accelerated rejection of hierarchy and patriarchal community, outgrowing both aristocracy and republicanism; appeal to self-interest bound new nation. Will shape debate on period. [DMS]

41.21 Alfred F. Young, ed. *The American Revolution: explorations in the history of American radicalism.* De Kalb: Northern Illinois University Press, 1976. ISBN 0-87580-057-2 (cl), 0-87580-519-1 (pbk). ‣ Provocative collection of essays stressing class conflict as central feature of Revolution. Neoprogressive interpretation of successful lower-class movement. [EVW]

Topical Surveys

41.22 Douglass Adair. *Fame and the Founding Fathers: essays.* H. Trevor Colbourn, ed. New York: Norton for Institute of Early American History and Culture, 1974. ISBN 0-393-05499-3. ‣ Focuses on desire for fame as important motivating factor for founders of republic. Cogent explanation that success resulted from gifted men operating in own self-interest. [CMJ]

41.23 Yehoshua Arieli. *Individualism and nationalism in American ideology.* 1964 ed. Baltimore: Penguin, 1966. ‣ Intellectual history providing good review of late eighteenth-century French,

English, and American social and political thought. American nationalism based on ideological consensus evincing belief in individualism and democracy. Useful synthesis. [DAR]

41.24 Nina N. Bashkina et al., eds. *The United States and Russia: the beginning of relations, 1765–1815.* 1980 ed. Buffalo: Hein, 1982. ISBN 0-89941-229-7. ‣ Important collection of 560 translated and edited documents on wide range of subjects concerning American relations with Russia. Extensive notes, good index, lengthy bibliography, and list of manuscript sources. [EVW]

41.25 Lawrence Delbert Cress. *Citizens in arms: the army and the militia in American society to the War of 1812.* Chapel Hill: University of North Carolina Press, 1982. ISBN 0-8078-1508-X. ‣ Explores ideology behind standing army controversy. Opens interesting questions about colonial attitudes and carefully documents postrevolutionary debate. Ambitious book, shedding light on complex problem. [DMS]

41.26 Peter C. Hoffer. *Revolution and regeneration: life cycle and the historical vision of the generation of 1776.* Athens: University of Georgia Press, 1983. ISBN 0-8203-0667-3 (cl), 0-8203-0679-7 (pbk). ‣ Interesting combination of intellectual and psychohistory. Applies Eriksonian model of psychological development to leaders of era, finding that changes in their thinking correspond to Erikson's four-stage schema of adulthood. [DAR]

41.27 Reginald Horsman. *The diplomacy of the new republic, 1776–1815.* Arlington Heights, Ill.: Harlan Davidson, 1985. ISBN 0-88295-829-1 (pbk). ‣ Brief textbook-style overview of early American foreign relations, recounting major events and influential persons. Useful as introduction to issues of period and major historiographical interpretations of era. [DAR]

41.28 Michael G. Kammen. *A season of youth: the American Revolution and the historical imagination.* New York: Knopf, 1978. ISBN 0-394-49651-5. ‣ Interesting, readable, Pulitzer Prize–winning study. Popular culture transformed radical implications of Revolution into rite-of-passage metaphor—America grows up—serving conservative ends by preserving social hierarchy. Intellectual history methodology using popular culture sources. [DAR]

41.29 Lawrence S. Kaplan. *Colonies into nation: American diplomacy, 1763–1801.* New York: Macmillan, 1972. ‣ Provocative, informed survey of American diplomacy from end of Seven Years' War to ratification of Convention of Mortefontaine. Synthesis of controversial historical interpretations. [EVW]

41.30 Ralph L. Ketcham. *From colony to country: the Revolution in American thought, 1750–1820.* New York: Macmillan, 1975. ISBN 0-02-562930-1. ‣ Competent, well-written discussion of political philosophy and conceptualization of national character. Emphasizes importance of Jeffersonian-Hamiltonian split. Reaffirms earlier work on concepts of revolution, virtue, and republicanism. [LAN]

41.31 Michael P. Kramer. *Imagining language in America from the Revolution to the Civil War.* Princeton: Princeton University Press, 1992. ISBN 0-691-06882-8. ‣ Well-written, readable interpretive study of Daniel Webster, Henry Wadsworth Longfellow, Walt Whitman, James Madison, Horace Bushnell, and Nathaniel Hawthorne, exploring linguistic nationalism. Does not significantly revise standard interpretations. [DMS]

41.32 Adrienne Koch. *Power, morals, and the Founding Fathers: essays in the interpretation of the American Enlightenment.* 1961 ed. Ithaca, N.Y.: Cornell University Press, 1984. ISBN 0-8014-9019-7 (pbk). ‣ Intellectual personality sketches of Thomas Jefferson, Benjamin Franklin, Alexander Hamilton, John Adams, and James Madison. Concludes Madison in particular balanced moral concerns of Jefferson with practical power politics of Hamilton. Insightful, influential interpretation. [LAN]

41.33 Jack Larkin. *The reshaping of everyday life, 1790–1840.*

1988 ed. New York: Harper & Row, 1989. ISBN 0-06-015905-7 (cl, 1988), 0-06-091606-0, (pbk). ▸ Easy to read, eclectic discussion of changes in everyday life styles. Explores furniture, funerals, hygiene, etc. Written for general audience. [DMS]

41.34 Ralph Lerner. *The thinking revolutionary: principle and practice in the new republic.* Ithaca, N.Y.: Cornell University Press, 1987. ISBN 0-8014-2007-5 (cl), 0-8014-9532-6 (pbk). ▸ Seven essays surveying thought, culture, and seminal thinkers: John Adams, Thomas Jefferson, and Benjamin Franklin. Treats attitudes toward African Americans and American Indians. Not well integrated or synthesized but provides food for thought. [DMS]

41.35 James Kirby Martin. *Men in rebellion: higher government leaders and the coming of the American Revolution.* New Brunswick, N.J.: Rutgers University Press, 1973. ISBN 0-8135-0750-2. ▸ Group biography arguing Revolution result of political conspiracy and paranoia among colonial elite, who saw London threatening their liberties. Builds on Bailyn's whig conspiracy theory (41.52), quantifying extent of paranoia among elite. [DAR]

41.36 Louis P. Masur. *Rites of execution: capital punishment and the transformation of American culture, 1776–1865.* 1989 ed. New York: Oxford University Press, 1991. ISBN 0-19-504899-7 (cl, 1989), 0-19-506663-4 (pbk). ▸ Slim, useful reminder of early American opposition to death penalty. Readable contribution to history of penal reform. Focus on 1780s to 1790s and 1830s to 1840s. [DMS]

41.37 Henry F. May. *The Enlightenment in America.* New York: Oxford University Press, 1976. ISBN 0-19-502018-9, 0-19-502367-6. ▸ Standard, comprehensive discussion of reception of European Enlightenment in America. Typology includes English rational religion, skepticism, eighteenth-century revolutionary thought, and reconciliation of orthodoxy with Scottish realism. [LAN]

41.38 Charles Howard McIlwain. *The American Revolution: a constitutional interpretation.* 1923 ed. New York: Da Capo, 1973. ISBN 0-306-70249-5. ▸ Comparison of America and Ireland; finds Irish constitutional precedents supported patriots' contentions that colonial assemblies not subordinate to Parliament. Classic work placing America in context of English legal history. [DAR]

41.39 Donald H. Meyer. *The democratic Enlightenment.* New York: Putnam, 1976. ISBN 0-399-11686-9. ▸ Traditional view of Enlightenment as philosophical incorporation of scientific revolution. Americans made practical application of experimentalism to religion, morals, and politics. [LAN]

41.40 Edmund S. Morgan. *Inventing the people: the rise of popular sovereignty in England and America.* New York: Norton, 1988. ISBN 0-393-02505-5 (cl), 0-393-30623-2 (pbk). ▸ Argues that American belief in ideal of popular sovereignty distinguished Americans from British and played key role in shaping imperial conflict. Valuable analysis of British and American political thought. [CMJ]

41.41 Curtis P. Nettels. *The emergence of a national economy, 1775–1815.* 1962 ed. Armonk, N.Y.: Sharpe, 1989. ISBN 0-87332-096-4 (pbk). ▸ Political and topical survey of revolutionary and early national economy. Forces seeking integrated economy and native economic institutions successfully battled parochial interests. Outstanding study, careful and detailed. [LAN]

41.42 John Phillip Reid. *The authority of rights.* Vol. 1 of *Constitutional history of the American Revolution.* Madison: University of Wisconsin Press, 1986. ISBN 0-299-10870-8. ▸ Revolution as constitutional conflict between customary rights and arbitrary power; Americans saw rights as property guaranteed by custom and royal charter and Parliament as usurping those rights. Monocausal view with neo-whig overtones. [DAR]

41.43 John Phillip Reid. *The authority to tax.* Vol. 2 of *Consti-*

tutional history of the American Revolution. Madison: University of Wisconsin Press, 1987. ISBN 0-299-11290-X. ▸ Focus on taxation by consent; legalistic distinctions (internal versus external taxes) important to participants, although Americans saw all parliamentary taxes as intrusions on customary rights. Monocausal view with neo-whig overtones. [DAR]

41.44 W. J. Rorabaugh. *The alcoholic republic: an American tradition.* New York: Oxford University Press, 1979. ISBN 0-19-502584-9 (cl), 0-19-50189-0 (pbk). ▸ Portrait of early national America on a binge; cheap whiskey, diversified diet, and eased anxiety over social change. Consolidation of national commercial economy by 1830 ended all three causes. Entertaining, stimulating reading. [LAN]

41.45 Barbara Clark Smith. *After the Revolution: the Smithsonian history of everyday life in the eighteenth century.* New York: Pantheon, 1985. ISBN 0-394-54381-5. ▸ Portrays lives of those who made and used material culture. Complement to Smithsonian exhibit. Excellent illustrations and photographs. [DMS]

41.46 Paul Merrill Spurlin. *The French Enlightenment in America: essays on the times of the Founding Fathers.* Athens: University of Georgia Press, 1984. ISBN 0-8203-0721-1 (pbk). ▸ Eleven essays exploring impact of major French thinkers on American leaders. Balanced, frequently elegant style, good overview of subject. [DMS]

41.47 Paul A. Varg. *Foreign policies of the Founding Fathers.* 1963 ed. East Lansing: Michigan State University Press, 1964. ▸ Synoptic presentation of American diplomatic history, 1774–1812. Discusses interplay of economics and diplomacy with foreign and domestic policy, emphasizing uneven symbiotic relationship between American economy and Europe. [EVW]

41.48 Morton White. *The philosophy of the American Revolution.* New York: Oxford University Press, 1978. ISBN 0-19-502381-1. ▸ Examination of Declaration of Independence terminology. Argues influence of Jean-Jacques Burlamaqui, suggesting conservative motivations for and elitist foundations of Declaration. Traces origins of terms used in contemporary philosophic discourse. Important, influential work. [DAR]

ORIGINS OF THE REVOLUTION, 1754–1774

41.49 W. W. Abbot. *The royal governors of Georgia, 1754–1775.* Chapel Hill: University of North Carolina Press for Institute of Early American History and Culture, 1959. ▸ Good, insightful political history reviewing gubernatorial careers of John Reynolds, Henry Ellis, and James Wright. Clear, well-written, solid scholarship; still worth reading. [DMS]

41.50 David L. Ammerman. *In the common cause: American response to the Coercive Acts of 1774.* Charlottesville: University Press of Virginia, 1974. ISBN 0-8139-0525-7. ▸ Concise summary of actions of First Continental Congress and colonies. Readable, insightful study of often overlooked era. [EVW]

41.51 Fred Anderson. *A people's army: Massachusetts soldiers and society in the Seven Years' War.* 1984 ed. New York: Norton, 1985. ISBN 0-393-95520-6. ▸ Combines social, intellectual, and military history to analyze composition of Massachusetts militia. Presents soldiers as representative of society itself. Emphasizes persistence of old contract ideals in military setting. Excellent example of new military history. [CMJ]

41.52 Bernard Bailyn. *The ideological origins of the American Revolution.* Rev. ed. Cambridge, Mass.: Belknap, 1992. ISBN 0-674-44302-0. ▸ Crucial work that helped define debate on Revolution. Demonstrates link between colonial American political theory and opposition thought of English whig philosophers. Emphasis on Revolution as political and ideological conflict rather than as social movement. Genesis of neo-whig interpretation. [CMJ]

41.53 Colin Bonwick. *English radicals and the American Revolution.* Chapel Hill: University of North Carolina Press, 1977. ISBN 0-8078-1277-3. ‣ Examination of impact of revolutionary crisis on radical thought. Argues English Whigs cognizant of similar threats to their liberty but had little effect on crisis resolution. Complement to neo-whig histories. [DAR]

41.54 James E. Bradley. *Popular politics and the American Revolution in England: petitions, the crown, and public opinion.* Macon, Ga.: Mercer University Press, 1986. ISBN 0-8655-4181-7. ‣ Widespread middle-class opposition prompted government suppression of reports of protest petitions; opponents felt isolated, powerless, and were quieted. Petition analysis challenges Namierian view of compliant British public during revolutionary crisis (24.28). [DAR]

41.55 T. H. Breen. *Tobacco culture: the mentality of the great tidewater planters on the eve of the Revolution.* Princeton: Princeton University Press, 1985. ISBN 0-691-04729-4. ‣ Another ideo-cultural explanation for Virginia revolution. Indebtedness and dependence on international markets undermined gentry confidence in economy and culture; country ideology offered rebirth. Challenging, controversial thesis. [LAN]

41.56 Richard D. Brown. *Revolutionary politics in Massachusetts: the Boston Committee of Correspondence and the towns, 1772–1774.* Cambridge, Mass.: Harvard University Press, 1970. ISBN 0-674-76781-0. ‣ Neo-whig interpretation countering view of Boston committee under Samuel Adams as prime mover. Rural towns politically aware, sophisticated, not controlled by Boston committee; consensus created by Boston's moderating influence. [DAR]

41.57 Ian R. Christie and Benjamin W. Labaree. *Empire or independence, 1760–1776: a British-American dialogue on the coming of the American Revolution.* New York: Norton, 1976. ISBN 0-393-05556-6. ‣ Interesting, valuable juxtaposition of colonial and British developments and perceptions prior to Revolution. Reveals fundamental conflicts between two. Readable, clearly written; for both scholars and general reader. [DMS]

41.58 H. Trevor Colbourn. *The lamp of experience: whig history and the intellectual origins of the American Revolution.* 1965 ed. New York: Norton for Institute of Early American History and Culture, 1974. ISBN 0-393-00714-6. ‣ Demonstrates importance of whig interpretation of English history to American political thought. Colonial leaders shown to view imperial crisis from whig perspective. Important early work in neo-whig school. [CMJ]

41.59 H. T. Dickinson. *Liberty and property: political ideology in eighteenth-century Britain.* New York: Holmes & Meier, 1977. ISBN 0-8419-0351-4. ‣ Survey of work of eighteenth-century philosophers and pamphleteers on relationship between liberty and property. Emphasizes apparent conflict between two. Intellectual history along lines of Bailyn (41.52). [CMJ]

41.60 Marc Egnal. *A mighty empire: the origins of the American Revolution.* Ithaca, N.Y.: Cornell University Press, 1988. ISBN 0-8014-1932-8 (cl), 0-8014-9581-4 (pbk). ‣ Colonial elite divided between expansionists and nonexpansionists; expansionists gained control of colonial assemblies, confronted limits of imperial policy, and caused Revolution. Interpretation rejects shared ideology or social conflict as causative factors. [DAR]

41.61 Joseph Albert Ernst. *Money and politics in America, 1755–1775: a study in the Currency Act of 1764 and the political economy of the Revolution.* Chapel Hill: University of North Carolina Press for Insititute of Early American History and Culture, 1973. ISBN 0-8078-1217-X. ‣ Economic and political study of paper-money question. Finds Parliament regulated colonial currencies to protect British commercial elites; resulting American resentment helped fuel revolutionary crisis. Solid study of relationship between economics and politics. [LAN]

41.62 Jay Fliegelman. *Prodigals and pilgrims: the American Revolution against patriarchal authority, 1750–1800.* 1982 ed. Cambridge: Cambridge University Press, 1984. ISBN 0-521-23719-X (cl, 1982), 0-521-31726-6 (pbk). ‣ Provocative, useful work. Concludes revolt against patriarchalism, in England and America, framed all disputes over authority and obedience, including Revolution. Wide range of sources touches variety of topics. [DMS]

41.63 Jack P. Greene and William G. McLoughlin. *Preachers and politicians: two essays on the origins of the American Revolution.* Worcester, Mass.: American Antiquarian Society, 1977. ISBN 0-912296-14-3. ‣ Two differing, though complementary, views of era. Greene sees changes in British government's colonial policy as central to Revolution; McLoughlin sees Great Awakening unleashing sense of American regeneration and independence. [DAR]

41.64 Nathan O. Hatch. *The sacred cause of liberty: republican thought and the millennium in revolutionary New England.* New Haven: Yale University Press, 1977. ISBN 0-300-02092-9. ‣ Motive for Revolution in New England unique blend of political ideas and religious framework: concludes New England clergy created civil millennialism by integrating real whig politics and Puritan historical thought. In Puritan eyes, oppressive British government replaced papist French as source of satanic conspiracy. Impressive, reliable, important work. [LAN]

41.65 Dirk Hoerder. *Crowd action in revolutionary Massachusetts, 1765–1780.* New York: Academic Press, 1977. ISBN 0-12-351650-1. ‣ Mob action institutionalized as political leaders first used, then lost control of crowd. Seen as means to assert communal values over individual interests. New Left, class-conflict interpretation. [DAR]

41.66 Richard M. Jellison, ed. *Society, freedom, and conscience: the American Revolution in Virginia, Massachusetts, and New York.* New York: Norton, 1976. ISBN 0-393-05582-5 (cl), 0-393-09160-0 (pbk). ‣ Three lectures on distinctive aspects of era. Greene sees status anxiety in Virginia elite; Bushman sees quasi-feudal Massachusetts farmers fearful of losing freedoms; and Kammen sees crisis of conscience in New York. [DAR]

41.67 Merrill Jensen. *The founding of a nation: a history of the American Revolution.* New York: Oxford University Press, 1968. ‣ Standard political history emphasizing deeds, not ideas, motivations, or personalities. Rejects intellectual interpretations of America as commonwealth in tightly detailed chronology of events. [DAR]

41.68 Michael G. Kammen. *A rope of sand: the colonial agents, British politics, and the American Revolution.* 1968 ed. New York: Vintage, 1974. ISBN 0-394-71996-4. ‣ Sees agents as coherent group whose influence declined as interest-group politics overtook British government. Effectiveness ended when London refused to hear agents' petitions favoring American interests. Neo-imperial interpretation. [DAR]

41.69 Bernhard Knollenberg. *Origins of the American Revolution.* 1961 rev. ed. New York: Free Press, 1965. ‣ Argues parliamentary acts, starting 1759, laid foundation for Stamp Act crisis, seeing event as catalyst, not cause, of American discontent. Both challenges and refines imperial school interpretation. [DAR]

41.70 Benjamin W. Labaree. *The Boston Tea Party.* 1964 ed. Boston: Northeastern University Press, 1979. ISBN 0-930350-16-2 (cl), 0-930350-05-7 (pbk). ‣ Authoritative recounting of events surrounding Tea Party. Sees British government fomenting rebellion by ignoring colonial complaints and constitutional concerns. Consensus history influenced by imperial school. [DAR]

41.71 Philip Lawson. *The imperial challenge: Quebec and Britain in the age of the American Revolution.* Montreal: McGill-Queens University Press, 1989. ISBN 0-7735-0698-5. ‣ Revisionist study, tightly focused on British politics. Explores British debate over Quebec after 1763. Persuasively argues that retaining some French law, supporting Catholic church, and not establishing elected assembly were essential to integrating province into British empire. [DMS]

41.72 Library of Congress Symposium on the American Revolution, comp. *The development of a revolutionary mentality: papers presented at the first symposium, May 5 and 6, 1972.* Washington, D.C.: Library of Congress, 1972. ISBN 0-8444-0045-9. ▸ Five essays with commentary on republicanism: Commager on Enlightenment influences, Robbins on concept of rule of law, Maier on commonwealth traditions, Norton on loyalist dissents, and Bushman on abuse of power. Foremost scholars contribute some excellent essays. [DAR]

41.73 Pauline Maier. *From resistance to revolution: colonial radicals and the development of American opposition to Britain, 1765–1776.* 1972 ed. New York: Norton, 1992. ISBN 0-393-30825-1 (pbk). ▸ Highly regarded study of colonial attitudes toward Britain leading to Revolution and independence. Good on mob violence and hardening attitudes. Readable for specialists and general interest. [DMS]

41.74 Pauline Maier. *The old revolutionaries: political lives in the age of Samuel Adams.* New York: Norton, 1990. ISBN 0-393-30663-1. ▸ Biographical essays focusing on motivations for involvement of five revolutionary leaders. Argues personal considerations combined with accepted whig traditions to shape their responses. Presents differing views of generation's diverse experiences. [DAR]

41.75 John J. McCusker. *Rum and the American Revolution: the rum trade and the balance of payments of the thirteen continental colonies.* 2 vols. New York: Garland, 1989. ISBN 0-8240-6191-8. ▸ Thorough, detailed discussion of all aspects of sugar-molasses-rum trade, with comparative estimates of consumption, production, imports-exports, etc. Lengthy appendixes, annotation, quantitative data, and tables fill second volume. [DMS]

41.76 Edmund S. Morgan, ed. *Prologue to revolution: sources and documents on the Stamp Act crisis.* 1959 ed. New York: Norton, 1973. ISBN 0-393-09424-3 (pbk). ▸ Primary source reader suitable for classroom or research use. Presents sixty-five documents from Parliament and Privy Council to colonial assemblies and committees of correspondence, with commentary. [DAR]

41.77 Edmund S. Morgan and Helen M. Morgan. *The Stamp Act crisis: prologue to revolution.* 1962 rev. ed. New York: Collier, 1963. ▸ Examination of motives of determined minority and what prompted citizens to follow them in their often violent reaction to what Parliament deemed fair taxes. Brilliant, though somewhat patriotic, contribution. [EVW]

41.78 John Phillip Reid. *In a defiant stance: the conditions of law in Massachusetts Bay, the Irish comparison, and the coming of the American Revolution.* University Park: Pennsylvania State University Press, 1977. ISBN 0-271-01240-4. ▸ Comparative study of American Revolution and 1798 Irish Uprising. Finds unicentric control of government allowed repression in Ireland while multicentric control in America precluded repression; condition of law controlling factor in both. [DAR]

41.79 John Phillip Reid. *In a rebellious spirit: the argument of facts, the liberty riot, and the coming of the American Revolution.* University Park: Pennsylvania State University Press, 1979. ISBN 0-271-00202-6. ▸ Following earlier work (41.78), argues condition of law in Boston created environment where facts presented in court were perceived differently by mob, thus riots resulted from decision to seize smuggled goods. Specialized study. [DAR]

41.80 John Phillip Reid. *In defiance of the law: the standing-army controversy, the two constitutions, and the coming of the American*

Revolution. Chapel Hill: University of North Carolina Press, 1981. ISBN 0-8078-1449-0. ▸ Following earlier work (41.79), argues unprecedented assignment of standing army to America violated customary rights and thus English Constitution. Explores legal constructs and ideas behind neo-whig interpretation. Specialized, legalistic study. [DAR]

41.81 Richard Alan Ryerson. *The revolution is now begun: the radical committees of Philadelphia, 1765–1776.* Philadelphia: University of Pennsylvania Press, 1978. ISBN 0-8122-7734-1. ▸ Extra-legal revolutionary committees drove Pennsylvanians to challenge British policies, then, with rise of politically active rural and middle class, to reform local political order. Well-written synthesis. [EVW]

41.82 John Sainsbury. *Disaffected patriots: London supporters of revolutionary America, 1769–1782.* Kingston, Ont.: McGill-Queen's University Press, 1987. ISBN 0-7735-0556-3. ▸ Sees London tradesmen as primary supporters of Revolution. Embraced constitutional arguments of American leaders and feared similar threats to own liberties, but lacked influence as great merchants to control government policy. Adjunct to neo-whig interpretations. [DAR]

41.83 Arthur M. Schlesinger. *The colonial merchants and the American Revolution, 1763–1776.* 1918 ed. New York: Ungar, 1957. ▸ Merchants initially supported rebels but loyalties divided as colonists took more radical actions. Classic economic interpretation. [EVW]

41.84 Peter Shaw. *American patriots and the rituals of revolution.* Cambridge, Mass.: Harvard University Press, 1981. ISBN 0-674-02644-6 (cl), 0-674-17776-2 (pbk). ▸ Study of ritual language in Massachusetts. Leaders imagined symbolic independence before deciding for separation, crowds incorporated extant ritual into political protest; together they created revolutionary environment. Flawed application of anthropological method. [DAR]

41.85 John Shy. *Toward Lexington: the role of the British army in the coming of the American Revolution.* Princeton: Princeton University Press, 1965. ▸ Discussion of British politics and policies and activities of British officers and soldiers throughout North America. Significant contribution to background of Revolution, focusing on often neglected prewar British army. Also available on photocopy from Ann Arbor: University Microfilms International, 1981. [EVW]

41.86 Peter D. G. Thomas. *British politics and the Stamp Act crisis: the first phase of the American Revolution, 1763–1773.* Oxford: Oxford University Press, 1975. ISBN 0-19-822431-1. ▸ Good, solid, careful study. Emphasis on British policy as it was shaped in response to American conditions. First of three-volume study (with 41.87 and 41.88). [DLA]

41.87 Peter D. G. Thomas. *Tea Party to independence: the third phase of the American Revolution.* Oxford: Clarendon, 1991. ISBN 0-19-820142-7. ▸ Thorough, detailed, provocative effort to counter prevailing historiography. Emphasis on British policy. Proclaims Lord North's policies conciliatory, American, unyielding. Final study in three-volume work (with 41.86 and 41.88). [DMS]

41.88 Peter D. G. Thomas. *The Townshend Duties crisis: the second phase of the American Revolution, 1767–1773.* Oxford: Oxford University Press, 1987. ISBN 0-19-922967-4. ▸ Explores British politics and policies regarding American colonies as empire moved toward Revolution. Careful, detailed, thorough study generally favorable toward mother country. Second of three-volume study (with 41.86 and 41.87). [DLA]

41.89 Robert E. Toohey. *Liberty and empire: British radical solutions to the American problem, 1774–1776.* Lexington: University Press of Kentucky, 1978. ISBN 0-8131-1375-X. ▸ Explores problem of individual liberty versus parliamentary authority. Radicals proposed possible American accommodations and parliamentary reforms, which were rejected because of mercantilist mindset about Parliament and government. Neo-whig interpretation from British perspective. [DAR]

41.90 Robert W. Tucker and David C. Henderson. *The fall of the first British empire: origins of the war of American independence.* Baltimore: Johns Hopkins University Press, 1982. ISBN 0-8018-2780-9. ▸ Challenges aspects of many interpretations. Sees origins in America, not Britain; conflicting notions of customary rights led to American belief that British violated them; government unwilling to suppress dissent and lost control. [DAR]

41.91 John W. Tyler. *Smugglers and patriots: Boston merchants and the advent of the American Revolution.* Boston: Northeastern University Press, 1986. ISBN 0-930350-76-6. ▸ Study of smugglers as leaders of Revolution. Political divisions determined by business specialty and combination of ideology and self-interest. Updated progressive interpretation after Schlesinger 41.83. [RWS]

41.92 Carl Ubbelohde. *The vice-admiralty courts and the American Revolution.* Chapel Hill: University of North Carolina Press for Institute of Early American History and Culture, 1960. ▸ Courts established to try cases under Navigation Acts, creating tension in colonies; not proximate cause of Revolution but ever-present irritant in British-colonial relations. Remains useful description of courts' role and operation. [DAR]

41.93 Hiller B. Zobel. *The Boston Massacre.* New York: Norton, 1970. ISBN 0-393-05376-8. ▸ Definitive account of event. Over preceding five years, order had eroded in streets, making conflict with troops inevitable. Sees proximate cause as inability of local officials to react to developing riot. [DAR]

SEE ALSO
39.200 Bernard Bailyn. *The origins of American politics.*
39.216 Robert J. Dinkin. *Voting in provincial America.*
39.220 Jack P. Greene. *Peripheries and center.*
39.222 Jack P. Greene. *The quest for power.*
39.274 Max Savelle. *The origins of American diplomacy.*

REVOLUTIONARY WAR AND THE CONFEDERATION, 1775–1788

Military History

41.94 R. Arthur Bowler. *Logistics and the failure of the British army in America, 1775–1783.* Princeton: Princeton University Press, 1975. ISBN 0-691-04630-1. ▸ Study of strategy and problems of execution. British army tied to seaports; failure to keep supply lines open a factor in defeat. Balanced study, important for problems of British supply. [RWS]

41.95 Raoul F. Camus. *Military music of the American Revolution.* Chapel Hill: University of North Carolina Press, 1976. ISBN 0-8078-1263-3. ▸ Thorough but highly specialized study of history of American music. Emphasis on field music and its military function. [DMS]

41.96 E. Wayne Carp. *To starve the army at pleasure: Continental Army administration and American political culture.* Chapel Hill: University of North Carolina Press, 1984. ISBN 0-8078-1587-X (cl), 0-8078-4269-9 (pbk). ▸ Analysis of interaction of politics and military on national scale. Sees fear of military centralization as greater than fear of defeat, creating ideological opposition to needed national military administration. Solid, well-documented, sometimes plodding account. [RWS]

41.97 Jonathan R. Dull. *The French navy and American independence: a study of arms and diplomacy.* Princeton: Princeton University Press, 1975. ISBN 0-691-06920-4. ▸ Realist account focusing on calculation of French self-interest. Concludes policy shift from aid to alliance determined by French naval preparedness, not American actions. [RWS]

41.98 John E. Ferling, ed. *The world turned upside down: the American victory in the War of Independence.* Westport, Conn.: Greenwood, 1988. ISBN 0-313-25527-X. ▸ Eleven scholars discuss various aspects of Revolution. Focus on social-political-diplomatic aspects; both useful and illustrative of rich opportunities in new approach to military history. [DMS]

41.99 William M. Fowler, Jr. *Rebels under sail: the American navy during the Revolution.* New York: Scribner's, 1976. ISBN 0-684-14583-9. ▸ Topical approach to naval history focusing on administration and campaigns. Synthesis aimed at nonspecialists; no new interpretations. [RWS]

41.100 Sylvia R. Frey. *The British soldier in America: a social history of military life in the colonial period.* Austin: University of Texas Press, 1981. ISBN 0-292-78040-0. ▸ Study of life in British army during Revolution, focusing on common soldiers. Emphasizes adversity faced by British soldiers and sustaining quality of bonds formed within regiments. [CMJ]

41.101 Robert A. Gross. *The minutemen and their world.* New York: Hill & Wang, 1976. ISBN 0-8090-6933-4 (cl), 0-8090-0120-9 (pbk). ▸ Study of second-generation New England town reaffirming earlier demographic analyses (Greven 39.372, Lockridge 39.746). Concordians had localized focus and little concern for larger revolutionary issues. Presents Revolution as conservative movement to maintain local status quo. Extremely readable and important study illustrative of new social history. [LAN]

41.102 Ira D. Gruber. *The Howe brothers and the American Revolution.* 1972 ed. New York: Norton, 1975. ISBN 0-393-00756-1. ▸ Discussion of conflict between William and Richard Howe and ministry, emphasizing impact of personal conflict on policy. Concludes British chance for victory lost by Howe brothers' attempt to negotiate peace. Extremely well-written, interesting, and influential study. [RWS]

41.103 Don Higginbotham. *George Washington and the American military tradition.* Athens: University of Georgia Press, 1985. ISBN 0-8203-0786-6. ▸ Attributes Washington's success in Revolutionary War to ability to recognize and manage relations between civilian and military interests. Sees American military traditions as outgrowth of Washington's experiences. [CMJ]

41.104 Don Higginbotham. *War and society in revolutionary America: the wider dimensions of conflict.* Columbia: University of South Carolina Press, 1988. ISBN 0-87249-585-X. ▸ Twelve articles covering various aspects of Revolutionary War, from historiography through militia to parallels with Vietnam War. Informative and readable; by mature historian versed in primary and secondary sources. [DMS]

41.105 Don Higginbotham. *The war of American independence: military attitudes, policies, and practice, 1763–1789.* 1971 ed. Boston: Northeastern University Press, 1983. ISBN 0-930350-43-X (cl), 0-930350-44-8 (pbk). ▸ Combination of military and political history. Concludes war main impetus toward nationalist feeling and political consolidation; army and military policy reflections of society. Readable synthesis. [RWS]

41.106 Don Higginbotham, ed. *Reconsiderations on the Revolutionary War: selected essays.* Westport, Conn.: Greenwood, 1978. ISBN 0-8371-9846-1. ▸ Survey and reassessment of literature. Focus on differing American and British strategic traditions. Effort to compare American Revolution to other revolutions. [RWS]

41.107 Ronald Hoffman and Peter J. Albert, eds. *Arms and independence: the military character of the American Revolution.* Charlottesville: University Press of Virginia for United States Capitol Historical Society, 1984. ISBN 0-8139-1007-2. ▸ Selection of essays focusing on revolutionary experience as vehicle for protest and nationalism. Assesses Revolution within context of eighteenth-century warfare. Calls for integration of political, social, and military history. [RWS]

41.108   Piers Mackesy. *The war for America, 1775–1783.* 1964 ed. Lincoln: University of Nebraska Press, 1992. ISBN 0-8032-8192-7 (pbk). ▸ Imperial history of American Revolution on grand scale; sympathetic to Lord George Germain and critical of Sir Henry Clinton. Overstretch after 1778 caused British defeat. [RWS]

41.109   James Kirby Martin and Mark Edward Lender. *A respectable army: the military origins of the republic, 1763–1789.* Arlington Heights, Ill.: Harlan Davidson, 1982. ISBN 0-88295-812-7 (pbk). ▸ Favorable picture of Continental Army placing Continentals at heart of military effort during Revolution. Creation of republican government owed much to Continental Army. Important corrective to myth of citizen-soldier. [CMJ]

41.110   Max M. Mintz. *The generals of Saratoga: John Burgoyne and Horatio Gates.* New Haven: Yale University Press, 1990. ISBN 0-300-04778-9. ▸ Readable discussion of opposing generals in 1777 campaign. Insightful evaluations of their youth, military careers, and politics. Also summarizes post-Saratoga careers. [DMS]

41.111   Howard Henry Peckham, ed. *The toll of independence: engagements and battle casualties of the American Revolution.* Chicago: University of Chicago Press, 1974. ISBN 0-226-65318-8. ▸ Reference work on battle statistics. Traditional focus on major battles and campaigns. Intended as raw data to be used in future quantitative studies. [RWS]

41.112   Hugh F. Rankin. *The North Carolina Continentals.* Chapel Hill: University of North Carolina Press, 1971. ISBN 0-8078-1154-8. ▸ Study of influence of war on homefront and role of state policy in conducting war. Broad conception of military history, similiar to Higginbotham 41.105. First modern study of one state's continental line. [RWS]

41.113   Charles Royster. *A revolutionary people at war: the Continental Army and American character, 1775–1783.* 1979 ed. New York: Norton, 1981. ISBN 0-393-95173-1 (pbk). ▸ Examination of role of military experience in shaping national character. Republican virtue of 1775 became ethic of professionalism after Valley Forge. Combination of social, cultural, political, and military history. [RWS]

41.114   John Shy. *A people numerous and armed: reflections on the military struggle for American independence.* Rev. ed. Ann Arbor: University of Michigan Press, 1990. ISBN 0-472-09431-9 (cl), 0-472-06431-2 (pbk). ▸ Influential collection of essays placing military aspects of Revolution in political perspective. Emphasizes role of force as motivational device for colonists choosing sides in revolutionary crisis. [CMJ]

41.115   Marshall Smelser. *The winning of independence.* 1972 ed. New York: New Viewpoints, 1973. ISBN 0-531-06490-5. ▸ Synthesis of existing literature, intended for general reader. Concludes Continental Army held together long enough for France to enter and win war. [RWS]

41.116   Willard M. Wallace. *Appeal to arms: a military history of the American Revolution.* 1951 ed. Chicago: Quadrangle, 1964. ▸ General account focusing on northern campaign and problems of Continental Army organization. Traditional military history. [RWS]

41.117   Christopher Ward. *The war of the revolution.* 2 vols. John R. Alden, ed. New York: Macmillan, 1952. ▸ Standard campaign history focusing on land battles, with most attention to northern campaigns. Descriptive rather than analytic; useful mainly as reference work. [RWS]

SEE ALSO
   39.275 Harold E. Selesky. *War and society in colonial Connecticut.*

Loyalists

41.118   Bernard Bailyn. *The ordeal of Thomas Hutchinson.* Cambridge, Mass.: Harvard University Press, 1974. ISBN 0-674-64160-4 (cl), 0-674-64161-2 (pbk). ▸ Sympathetic portrayal of Governor Thomas Hutchinson as man trapped in situation he did not understand. Sees American Revolution as tragedy from loyalist perspective. Foremost work of loyalist biography. [RWS]

41.119   Carol Ruth Berkin. *Jonathan Sewall: odyssey of an American loyalist.* New York: Columbia University Press, 1974. ISBN 0-231-03851-8. ▸ Portrait of Sewall as representative of loyalist love-hate relationship with America: criticism of British war policy, and view of Revolution as demagoguery. Unsympathetic; argues Sewall's view did not fit American future. [RWS]

41.120   Wallace Brown. *The good Americans: the loyalists in the American Revolution.* New York: Morrow, 1969. ▸ Survey of loyalists in political context. Based on author's earlier statistical work on compensation claims. Traditional view of loyalists as representing elites. [RWS]

41.121   Wallace Brown. *The king's friends: the composition and motives of the American loyalist claimants.* Providence: Brown University Press, 1965. ISBN 0-87057-092-7. ▸ Study of loyalists who sought compensation from British government, 1777–90. Claimants seen as representative of loyalism. Quantitative study intended as reference. [RWS]

41.122   Kinloch Bull, Jr. *The oligarchs in colonial and revolutionary Charleston: Lieutenant Governor William Bull II and his family.* Columbia: University of South Carolina Press, 1991. ISBN 0-87249-715-1. ▸ Thorough, solid biography. Focus on Bull's influential political role from 1740s to Revolution. Less effective in delineating socioeconomic role and personal beliefs. [DMS]

41.123   Robert M. Calhoon. *The loyalists in revolutionary America, 1760–1781.* New York: Harcourt Brace Jovanovich, 1973. ISBN 0-15-154745-9. ▸ Group biography of loyalists, but with few generalizations. Sees Revolution as civil war for independence. Most comprehensive work of loyalist historiographical revival. [RWS]

41.124   Robert M. Calhoon et al. *The loyalist perception and other essays.* Columbia: University of South Carolina Press, 1989. ISBN 0-87249-615-5. ▸ Eleven articles treating various aspects of loyalist thinking by most thorough scholar in field today. Includes loyalist press, criticisms of revolutionary movement, postwar reintegration into society, treatment by whigs, etc. [DMS]

41.125   Edward J. Cashin. *The King's Ranger: Thomas Brown and the American Revolution on the southern frontier.* Athens: University of Georgia Press, 1989. ISBN 0-8203-1093-X. ▸ Thoroughly researched biography of recently arrived loyalist on southern frontier. Brown's career as commander of King's Rangers explores chaotic conditions of revolutionary South and Native American relations in Georgia and Florida. [DMS]

41.126   Cynthia Dubin Edelberg. *Jonathan Odell: loyalist poet of the American Revolution.* Durham, N.C.: Duke University Press, 1987. ISBN 0-8223-0716-2. ▸ Thoughtful study of poet attached to and influenced by his own time. Reflects variety of personal experiences and typical loyalist attachment to Britain. Enlightening and insightful. [DMS]

41.127   Malcolm Freiberg. *Prelude to purgatory: Thomas Hutchinson in provincial Massachusetts politics, 1760–1770.* New York: Garland, 1990. ISBN 0-8240-6180-2. ▸ Older, unrevised dissertation, long seen as excellent and significant work on revolutionary

Massachusetts. Dated but insightful, good on political thought, well written. [DMS]

41.128 Leonard W. Labaree. *Conservatism in early American history.* 1948 ed. Ithaca, N.Y.: Cornell University Press, 1972. ISBN 0-8014-9008-1. ▸ Colonial elites defended their status through traditional institutions such as established church, sound money, hierarchical politics, and classical education. Loyalists in particular looked to British to defend old order. Originally delivered as lectures. Good, brief analysis of conservative forces. [LAN]

41.129 Robert Stansbury Lambert. *South Carolina loyalists in the American Revolution.* Columbia: University of South Carolina Press, 1987. ISBN 0-87249-506-X. ▸ Extensive research shows list of 6,000 (22 percent of population) who favored British. Narrates experience of loyalists and their postwar dispersal. Detailed, thorough, comprehensive. [DMS]

41.130 Duane Meyer. *The highland Scots of North Carolina, 1732–1776.* Chapel Hill: University of North Carolina Press, 1961. ISBN 0-8078-4199-4 (pbk). ▸ Questions reasons for eighteenth-century highland emigration and group's loyalism during American Revolution; not an exodus of oppressed poor, not forced out. Finds assimilation and fear of reprisal fueled loyalism. [LAN]

41.131 William H. Nelson. *The American tory.* 1961 ed. Boston: Northeastern University Press, 1992. ISBN 1-55553-148-2 (pbk). ▸ Readable, pathbreaking study, but somewhat dated. Absence of conservative tradition in America result of tory emigration; tories dispersed and leaderless. Distinguishes between tories and neutrals throughout revolutionary era. [RWS]

41.132 Mary Beth Norton. *The British-Americans: the loyalist exiles in England, 1774–1789.* Boston: Little, Brown, 1972. ISBN 0-316-61250-2. ▸ Standard work on rich émigrés, contains little on nonelites. Loyalist exiles generally idealistic and badly handled by British government. [RWS]

41.133 Anne M. Ousterhout. *A state divided: opposition in Pennsylvania to the American Revolution.* Westport, Conn.: Greenwood, 1987. ISBN 0-313-25728-0. ▸ Concludes division over independence caused by internal issues. Discusses question of who should rule at home from perspective of disaffected loyalists and neutralists. Well researched, contains useful material. [RWS]

41.134 Janice Potter. *The liberty we seek: loyalist ideology in colonial New York and Massachusetts.* Cambridge, Mass.: Harvard University Press, 1983. ISBN 0-674-53026-8. ▸ General study of loyalism. Loyalists committed to Anglo-American way of life; shared whig ideology, but emphasized fear of democratic tyranny and license. [RWS]

41.135 Philip Ranlet. *The New York loyalists.* Knoxville: University of Tennessee Press, 1986. ISBN 0-87049-503-8. ▸ Argues loyalism in New York weaker than previously believed; proportion of loyalists same as in other states. Posits loyalism as function of British presence. Fresh, provocative analysis with some new evidence. [RWS]

41.136 Paul Hubert Smith. *Loyalists and redcoats: a study in British revolutionary policy.* 1964 ed. New York: Norton, 1972. ISBN 0-393-00626-X. ▸ Standard, influential, readable work. British belief in southern loyalism an excuse to continue war after 1778, but failed to use loyalists effectively. Concludes British failed to grasp problem. [RWS]

41.137 Earle Thomas. *Greener pastures: the loyalist experience of Benjamin Ingraham.* Belleville, Ont.: Mika, 1983. ISBN 0-919303-76-5. ▸ Experience of common man as loyalist and exile on New Brunswick frontier; personal rather than general account. Recreated thought and conversation casts doubt on accuracy. [RWS]

41.138 Esther Clark Wright. *The loyalists of New Brunswick.*

1955 ed. Wolfville, N.S.: E.C. Wright, 1981. ▸ Emigration of 14,000 loyalists of all classes from New York, Connecticut, and New Jersey. Sympathetic account, intended for general public and most useful for genealogists. [RWS]

41.139 Anne Y. Zimmer. *Jonathan Boucher: loyalist in exile.* Detroit: Wayne State University Press, 1978. ISBN 0-8143-1592-5. ▸ Study of Boucher as former whig, socially forward-looking, accomplished lexicographer. Focuses on Boucher's third career in England. Sympathetic study of America's most noted tory. [RWS]

SEE ALSO
45.84 Wallace Brown and Hereward Senior. *Victorious in defeat.*

The States and the Nation

41.140 Willi Paul Adams. *The first American constitutions: republican ideology and the making of the state constitutions in the revolutionary era.* Rita Kimber and Robert Kimber, trans. Chapel Hill: University of North Carolina Press for Institute of Early American History and Culture, 1980. ISBN 0-8078-1388-5. ▸ Reassessment of origins of American republicanism stressing pragmatic and nondoctrinaire qualities of American thinking. Modern European perspective on early republic's constitution-making process. [EVW]

41.141 A. Owen Aldridge. *Thomas Paine's American ideology.* Newark: University of Delaware Press, 1984. ISBN 0-87413-260-6. ▸ Comprehensive analysis of Paine's political writings, 1775–84, emphasizing continuity in Paine's thought. Connects Paine with John Locke, Jean-Jacques Rousseau, and other "moderate" political philosophers. Little new ground broken. [CMJ]

41.142 William G. Anderson. *The price of liberty: the public debt of the American Revolution.* Charlottesville: University Press of Virginia, 1983. ISBN 0-8139-0975-9. ▸ Short study of war bonds and promissory notes. Public finance key issue in creating first American party system. Edition includes Smythe collection of revolutionary debt certificates. [LAN]

41.143 Douglas M. Arnold. *A republican revolution: ideology and politics in Pennsylvania, 1776–1790.* New York: Garland, 1989. ISBN 0-8240-6171-3. ▸ Unrevised doctoral dissertation reviewing conflict over 1776 constitution adopted by Pennsylvania radicals. Challenges traditional interpretation of new state constitutions in 1790 as defeat for principles of American Revolution. [DMS]

41.144 Carl L. Becker. *The Declaration of Independence: a study in the history of political ideas.* 1922 ed. New York: Vintage, 1970. ISBN 0-394-70060-0 (pbk). ▸ Examination of political philosophy of document, with particular attention to British antecedents of natural rights philosophy. Assesses its reception, importance. Classic intellectual history of Declaration. [CMJ]

41.145 Robert A. Becker. *Revolution, reform, and the politics of American taxation, 1763–1783.* Baton Rouge: Louisiana State University Press, 1980. ISBN 0-8071-0654-2. ▸ Tightly focused study of provincial and state tax laws. Costs of Revolution drove attempts to reform standing taxation practices. Useful reference for scholars using revolutionary era tax records. [DAR]

41.146 Henry J. Bourguignon. *The first federal court: the federal appellate prize court of the American Revolution, 1775–1787.* Philadelphia: American Philosophical Society, 1977. (American Philosophical Society, Memoirs, 122.) ISBN 0-87169-122-1, ISSN 0065-9738. ▸ Significant account of often overlooked forerunner of national court system. Examines creation of national judiciary in response to growing need for adjudication in matters of prize law during Revolution. Traces development from concepts of English admiralty law. [CMJ]

41.147 Robert L. Brunhouse. *The counter-revolution in Pennsyl-*

vania, 1776–1790. 1942 ed. New York: Octagon Books, 1971. ISBN 0-374-91050-2. ▸ Progressive interpretation of state politics focusing on constitution of 1776 as high point of radical democracy. Failure to resolve financial problems allowed rise of conservatives. Useful for detail and for defining issues addressed in more recent studies. [RWS]

41.148   Richard Buel, Jr. *Dear liberty: Connecticut's mobilization for the Revolutionary War*. Middletown, Conn.: Wesleyan University Press; distributed by Columbia University Press, 1980. ISBN 0-8195-5047-7. ▸ Integrates social, economic, and military history to explore effect of war on society. Finds war an increasing drain on economy and morale; enthusiasm gone by 1780 and society traumatized for a generation. [RWS]

41.149   Joseph L. Davis. *Sectionalism in American politics, 1774–1787*. Madison: University of Wisconsin Press, 1977. ISBN 0-299-07020-4. ▸ Description of confrontation between nationalists and Federalists over issue of centralization of political power in new nation. South considered center of postrevolutionary nationalism. Sectionalism traced to roots in 1780s. Important work on period; discussion of sectionalisim perhaps overstated. [CMJ]

41.150   Elisha P. Douglass. *Rebels and democrats: the struggle for equal political rights and majority rule during the Revolution*. 1955 ed. Chicago: Dee, 1989. ISBN 0-929587-12-X. ▸ Influential, somewhat dated study finds roots of American democracy in contests over state constitutions. Although democratic elements generally unsuccessful, process legitimated popular ratification and party politics. Late progressive interpretation. [DAR]

41.151   E. James Ferguson. *The power of the purse: a history of American public finance, 1776–1790*. Chapel Hill: University of North Carolina Press for Institute of Early American History and Culture, 1961. ▸ Narrative of public money policies from Revolutionary War through adoption of Alexander Hamilton's funding program. Restates progressive argument that powerful financial speculators had economic interest in redemption of public debt. [LAN]

41.152   Van Beck Hall. *Politics without parties: Massachusetts, 1780–1791*. Pittsburgh: University of Pittsburgh Press, 1972. ISBN 0-8229-3234-2. ▸ Argues that disputes over commerce, not ideology, dominated state politics. Emphasizes continuity rather than change. Based on quantitative analysis; neo-Beardian framework. [RWS]

41.153   H. James Henderson. *Party politics in the Continental Congress*. 1974 ed. Lanham, Md.: University Press of America, 1987. ISBN 0-8191-6525-5 (pbk). ▸ Persuasive, revisionist approach to origins of political parties. Congressional partisan politics based on sectionalism and often intertwined with socioeconomic and ideological characteristics led to first American party system. [EVW]

41.154   Merrill Jensen. *The American Revolution within America*. New York: New York University Press, 1974. ISBN 0-8147-4145-1. ▸ Lucid, scholarly amplification of author's insistence that Revolution unleashed democratic forces later opposed by nation's leadership. Neoprogressivism at its best; provocative, informed, well-reasoned account that has withstood assault of consensus school. [DMS]

41.155   Merrill Jensen. *The Articles of Confederation: an interpretation of the social-constitutional history of the American Revolution, 1774–1781*. 1940 ed. Madison: University of Wisconsin Press, 1970. ISBN 0-299-00204-7. ▸ Examination of Articles in own context, not in context of subsequent events (Constitution). Argues importance of property issues to writers and ratifiers. Progressive history stressing self-interested motives of individuals involved. [DAR]

41.156   Merrill Jensen. *The new nation: a history of the United*

States during the Confederation, 1781–1789. 1950 ed. Boston: Northeastern University Press, 1981. ISBN 0-930350-15-4 (cl), 0-930350-14-6 (pbk). ▸ Synthesis of literature with progressive interpretation seeing Constitution as counterrevolution. Argues for success of Confederation, continuity of political parties. [RWS]

41.157   Donald S. Lutz. *Popular consent and popular control: whig political theory in the early state constitutions*. Baton Rouge: Louisiana State University Press, 1980. ISBN 0-8071-0596-1. ▸ Good study by political scientist building on neo-whig scholarship. Finds early American political thinking well advanced with issues of consent and control central concerns. Federalists broke with whig tradition, reducing direct popular control of government in constitutions. [DAR]

41.158   Jackson Turner Main. *Political parties before the Constitution*. Chapel Hill: University of North Carolina Press for Institute of Early American History and Culture, 1973. ISBN 0-8078-1194-7. ▸ Progressive interpretation of political parties with quantitative analysis of roll-call votes. Finds state political parties formed by proximity to markets. Restatement of author's earlier work (41.160), applied to states. [RWS]

41.159   Jackson Turner Main. *The sovereign states, 1775–1783*. New York: New Viewpoints, 1973. ISBN 0-531-06355-0 (cl), 0-531-06481-6 (pbk). ▸ Democratic impulse released by Revolution tempered by whig ideology, promoting compromise and moderation; social and economic changes reflected trends already at work. Survey for general readers presenting neither radical nor conservative interpretation. [DAR]

41.160   Jackson Turner Main. *The upper house in revolutionary America: 1763–1788*. Madison: University of Wisconsin Press, 1967. ▸ Quantitative analysis of class structure of legislative bodies. Provincial councils became state Senates; elites fought losing battles to retain political prominence in face of democratization embodied in new state constitutions. Solid, thorough, specialized study. [DAR]

41.161   Jerrilyn Greene Marston. *King and Congress: the transfer of political legitimacy, 1774–1776*. Princeton: Princeton University Press, 1987. ISBN 0-691-04745-6. ▸ Asserts Continental Congress was not legislative, but rather executive body that took on crown's role in colonial government without disrupting system. Legal, political history with distinctive viewpoint. [DAR]

41.162   Richard B. Morris. *The forging of the Union, 1781–1789*. New York: Harper & Row, 1987. ISBN 0-06-015733-X (cl), 0-06-091424-6 (pbk). ▸ Discussion of Confederation as period of experimentation, with British trade practices main threat to union. Generally celebratory and nationalistic account, arguing union preceded the states. [RWS]

41.163   Allan Nevins. *The American states during and after the Revolution, 1775–1789*. 1924 ed. New York: Kelley, 1969. ISBN 0-678-00510-9. ▸ Pathbreaking study of era which incorporated internal economic and social divisions into preceding nationalistic political histories. Emphasizes East-West, conservative-radical tensions. Classic work of revisionist, progressive school. Also available on microfiche from Microlection. [DAR]

41.164   Roy F. Nichols. *The invention of the American political parties*. 1967 ed. New York: Free Press, 1972. ▸ Excellent synthesis of scholarship delineating development of political machinery on both national and state levels. Somewhat dated but still outstanding achievement. [DMS]

41.165   Peter S. Onuf. *The origins of the federal republic: jurisdictional controversies in the United States, 1775–1787*. Philadelphia: University of Pennsylvania Press, 1983. ISBN 0-8122-7889-5 (cl), 0-8122-1167-7 (pbk). ▸ Original, important contribution to political history. Argues conflicts between states exposed fundamental weaknesses in their authority; strong national government required to rectify situation and preserve state sovereignty. [CMJ]

41.166 Peter S. Onuf. *Statehood and union: a history of the Northwest Ordinance.* Bloomington: Indiana University Press, 1987. ISBN 0-253-35482-X. ▸ Critical of Northwest Ordinance as practical document, inefficient as guide to settling political disputes in territory. Sees value of document as mainly symbolic, representation of higher law. Best and most recent account of subject. [CMJ]

41.167 Jack N. Rakove. *The beginnings of national politics: an interpretive history of the Continental Congress.* 1979 ed. Baltimore: Johns Hopkins University Press, 1982. ISBN 0-8018-2864-3 (pbk). ▸ Consensus, neo-whig view of revolutionary era. Factionalism not as influential as many believe; Congress sought consensus, coalesced behind independence as response to British intransigence, submerging internal conflicts in process. [DAR]

41.168 John E. Selby. *The Revolution in Virginia, 1775–1783.* Williamsburg: Colonial Williamsburg Foundation; distributed by University Press of Virginia, 1988. ISBN 0-87935-075-X. ▸ Standard study; Virginia leadership able to contain reformist spirit in Virginia, but dragged into revolution. Focus on role of planters, downplays radicalism. [RWS]

41.169 Garry Wills. *Inventing America: Jefferson's Declaration of Independence.* Garden City, N.Y.: Doubleday, 1978. ISBN 0-385-08976-7. ▸ Insightful, provocative, readable study. Argues Declaration was product of Jefferson's philosophy, drawn from ideas of Scottish Enlightenment. Declaration reflects moral sense present in thought of Francis Hutcheson and David Hume rather than John Locke's ideas. [CMJ]

41.170 J. Leitch Wright, Jr. *Florida in the American Revolution.* Gainesville: University Presses of Florida, 1975. ISBN 0-8130-0524-8. ▸ Standard political and military narrative. Sees Florida as imperial pawn and events determined by outside forces. British failed to exploit Florida's strategic position. [RWS]

Foreign Relations

41.171 Jonathan R. Dull. *A diplomatic history of the American Revolution.* New Haven: Yale University Press, 1985. ISBN 0-300-03419-9 (cl), 0-300-03886-0 (pbk). ▸ Revisionist account with international history and world-systems approach. Finds French and British policy toward America determined by European concerns; American actions relatively unimportant. [RWS]

41.172 Ronald Hoffman and Peter J. Albert, eds. *Diplomacy and revolution: the Franco-American alliance of 1778.* Charlottesville: University Press of Virginia for United States Capitol Historical Society, 1981. ISBN 0-8139-0864-7. ▸ Essays and historiographical review with theme of search for power. Realistic accounts focusing on French and American interests rather than idealism. [RWS]

41.173 Ronald Hoffman and Peter J. Albert, eds. *Peace and the peacemakers: the treaty of 1783.* Charlottesville: University Press of Virginia for United States Capitol Historical Society, 1986. ISBN 0-8139-1071-4. ▸ Study of American Revolution within context of European balance of power. Detailed examination of contribution made by Americans in forcing final peace (Treaty of Paris). Revisionist argument that Americans succeeded in spite of themselves. [RWS]

41.174 James H. Hutson. *John Adams and the diplomacy of the American Revolution.* Lexington: University Press of Kentucky, 1980. ISBN 0-8131-1404-7. ▸ Realist account refuting Wharton (41.243) and Gilbert (41.257) view of revolutionary diplomacy. Sees Americans as traditional balance-of-power diplomats. Ideology added dimension of paranoia that made Adams fail as diplomat. [RWS]

41.175 Richard B. Morris. *The peacemakers: the great powers and*

American independence. 1965 ed. Boston: Northeastern University Press, 1983. ISBN 0-930350-35-9 (cl), 0-930350-36-7 (pbk). ▸ Idealistic account, now largely outdated, focusing on American actions. American diplomats as innocents abroad who quickly learned secrets of Old World diplomacy. [RWS]

41.176 Jan Willem Schulte Nordholt. *The Dutch republic and American independence.* Herbert H. Rowen, trans. Chapel Hill: University of North Carolina Press, 1982. ISBN 0-8078-1530-6. ▸ Discussion of origins of Dutch-American relations. Examines political upheaval in Netherlands brought on by contact with American Revolution and Dutch failure to replicate American model. [RWS]

41.177 William C. Stinchcombe. *The American Revolution and the French alliance.* Syracuse, N.Y.: Syracuse University Press, 1969. ISBN 0-8156-2134-5. ▸ Standard study of Franco-American military treaty (1778) from American perspective, with discussion of role of French ministers in American politics. Despite initial enthusiasm, alliance seen as dead after 1783. Important, reliable study. [RWS]

SEE ALSO

23.128 H. M. Scott. *British foreign policy in the age of the American Revolution.*

Topical Studies

41.178 Catherine L. Albanese. *Sons of the fathers: the civil religion of the American Revolution.* Philadelphia: Temple University Press, 1976. ISBN 0-87722-073-5. ▸ Daring approach to study of rhetoric and reality in American culture. Unearths American culture's collective consciousness and underlying structures of American mind at time of Revolution. [EVW]

41.179 Bernard Bailyn and John B. Hench, eds. *The press and the American Revolution.* 1980 ed. Boston: Northeastern University Press, 1981. ISBN 0-930350-32-4 (cl), 0-930350-30-8 (pbk). ▸ Eight essays by various authors on role and importance of press. Questions nature and existence of free press; explores its popularity and expansion. Good for historians of Revolution and printing. [DMS]

41.180 Lester C. Olson. *Emblems of American community in the revolutionary era: a study in rhetorical iconology.* Washington, D.C.: Smithsonian Institution Press, 1991. ISBN 1-56098-066-4. ▸ Study of rhetoric and visual images depicting America, 1765–83. Important analysis of communication available to illiterate and semi-literate. Offers means of probing attitudes and political views. Illustrated. [DMS]

41.181 Kenneth Silverman. *A cultural history of the American Revolution: painting, music, literature, and the theater in the colonies and the United States from the Treaty of Paris to the inauguration of George Washington, 1763–1789.* New York: Crowell, 1976. ISBN 0-690-01079-6. ▸ Extensive survey of "firsts." American high culture not self-conscious creation of antebellum era. Sentimentalism of resistance years gave way to postwar romanticism and nationalism. Impressive, wide-ranging, important study. [LAN]

41.182 Donald Weber. *Rhetoric and history in revolutionary New England.* New York: Oxford University Press, 1988. ISBN 0-19-505104-1. ▸ Textual analysis of revolutionary era sermons in five case studies. Dislocation of Revolution disrupted traditional narrative sermon style, and privileged providential history and politics and evangelical rhetorical style. Good example of recent focus on rhetoric and communication. [LAN]

41.183 David A. Wilson. *Paine and Cobbett: the transatlantic connection.* Kingston, Ont.: McGill-Queen's University Press, 1988. ISBN 0-7735-1013-3. ▸ Explores both relationship between ideas of two radicals and influence of America on each. Clear, well-written, significant contribution. [DMS]

THE CONSTITUTION AND THE BILL OF RIGHTS

41.184   John K. Alexander. *The selling of the Constitutional Convention: a history of news coverage.* Madison, Wisc.: Madison House, 1990. ISBN 0-945612-15-X. ▸ Thoroughly researched study of how newspapers managed news to encourage adoption of whatever Convention proposed. Specialized but useful. [DMS]

41.185   Charles A. Beard. *An economic interpretation of the Constitution of the United States.* 1913 ed. New York: Free Press, 1986. ISBN 0-02-902470-6 (cl), 0-02-902480-3 (pbk). ▸ Classic, if now outdated, progressive statement on Constitution. Sees Convention as battleground between personalty and realty and Constitution as victory of federal security holders over landowners. [RWS]

41.186   Richard R. Beeman, Stephen Botein, and Edward C. Carter, II, eds. *Beyond confederation: origins of the Constitution and American national identity.* Chapel Hill: University of North Carolina Press for Institute of Early American History and Culture, 1987. ISBN 0-8078-1719-8 (cl), 0-8078-4172-2 (pbk). ▸ Attempt to integrate political, ideological, intellectual, and institutional history around theme of incompleteness of revision. Discusses relationship of political reality to constitutional tradition. One of the best such collections. [RWS]

41.187   Catherine Drinker Bowen. *Miracle at Philadelphia: the story of the Constitutional Convention, May to September, 1787.* 1966 ed. Boston: Little, Brown, 1986. ISBN 0-316-10378-0 (cl), 0-316-10398-5 (pbk). ▸ Descriptive, narrative account of Convention, with heroic view of framers. Sacrifices analysis for picturesqueness, adds no new insights; aimed at general reader. [RWS]

41.188   Steven R. Boyd. *The politics of opposition: the Antifederalists and the acceptance of the Constitution.* Millwood, N.Y.: KTO Press, 1979. ISBN 0-527-10465-5. ▸ Challenges traditional idea of Antifederalists as unorganized. Sees organization, ability to channel disaffection, and willingness to work within Constitution as paving way for acceptance. Supplement to other studies. [RWS]

41.189   Robert E. Brown. *Charles Beard and the Constitution: a critical analysis of "An Economic Interpretation of the Constitution."* 1956 ed. Westport, Conn.: Greenwood, 1979. ISBN 0-313-21048-9. ▸ General attack on Beard's methods and conclusions (41.185). First antiprogressive, revisionist work on Constitution. Sees Constitution as victory for middle-class democracy. [RWS]

41.190   Patrick T. Conley and John P. Kaminski, eds. *The Constitution and the states: the role of the original thirteen in the framing and adoption of the federal Constitution.* Madison, Wisc.: Madison House, sponsored by United States Constitution Council of the Thirteen Original States and Center for the Study of the American Constitution, 1988. ISBN 0-945612-02-8. ▸ Thirteen articles summarizing current scholarship on ratification in several states. Comprehensive; more useful for general reader than for scholar. [DMS]

41.191   William Winslow Crosskey and William Jeffrey, Jr. *The political background of the federal convention.* Vol. 3 of *Politics and the Constitution in the history of the United States.* Chicago: University of Chicago Press, 1980. ISBN 0-226-12138-0 (v. 3). ▸ Lexicographical analysis of Constitution with tendency to discard contrary evidence. Concludes framers intended to create national government with few restrictions; goal shared by people. [RWS]

41.192   Thomas J. Curry. *The first freedoms: church and state in America to the passage of the First Amendment.* New York: Oxford University Press, 1986. ISBN 0-19-503661-1. ▸ Survey of ideas and practices of church-state relations in colonial America. Searches for intent of religion clause of First Amendment, finding no support for state organization or regulation of religion. [LAN]

41.193   George Dargo. *Roots of the republic: a new perspective on early American constitutionalism.* New York: Praeger, 1974. ▸ Brief, well-written, general overview. American constitutionalism defined as procedural justice, limitations on government, consent of people, spiritual freedom, free expression, and open process. Focus on American aptitude for change. [RWS]

41.194   Linda Grant De Pauw. *The eleventh pillar: New York state and the federal Constitution.* Ithaca, N.Y.: Cornell University Press, 1966. ▸ Politics dominated by nonideological, personal factions. Compromise of interests secured ratification. First consensus history of New York politics. [RWS]

41.195   Max Farrand. *The framing of the Constitution of the United States.* 1913 ed. New Haven: Yale University Press, 1962. ISBN 0-300-00445-1 (cl), 0-300-00079-0 (pbk). ▸ Convention dominated by conflict between large and small states. Constitution succeeded because it appealed directly to people. Emphasis on common sense of framers rather than political thought. Now dated; was once standard work. [RWS]

41.196   Michael Allen Gillespie and Michael Lienesch, eds. *Ratifying the Constitution.* Lawrence: University Press of Kansas, 1989. ISBN 0-7006-0402-2. ▸ Scholarly articles for each state focusing on local interests affecting ratification. Lengthy introduction sometimes successful in providing interpretive framework. Useful. [DMS]

41.197   Calvin C. Jillson. *Constitution making: conflict and consensus in the federal convention of 1787.* New York: Agathon, 1988. ISBN 0-87586-081-8 (cl), 0-87586-082-6 (pbk). ▸ Technical analysis of voting-bloc alignments, stressing interplay of political principles and economic interests. Solid and persuasive; confirms old interpretations, offers new. [DMS]

41.198   Charles R. Kesler, ed. *Saving the Revolution: "The Federalist Papers" and the American founding.* New York: Free Press, 1987. ISBN 0-02-919730-9. ▸ Textual analyses, mostly from political science perspective. Conservative attempt to demonstrate timeless principles of framers. Sees Federalist Papers as key to understanding Constitution. [RWS]

41.199   Michael J. Lacey and Knud Haakonssen. *A culture of rights: the Bill of Rights in philosophy, politics, and law, 1791 and 1991.* Washington, D.C., and New York: Woodrow Wilson International Center for Scholars and Cambridge University Press, 1991. ISBN 0-521-41637-X. ▸ Excellent essays by various scholars probing interdisciplinary aspects of original formulation and present-day debates. Enlightening, often ground breaking. For scholars and students of constitutional development. [DMS]

41.200   Leonard W. Levy. *The emergence of a free press.* Rev. ed. New York: Oxford University Press, 1987. ISBN 0-19-503506-2 (cl), 0-19-504240-9 (pbk). ▸ Revision of influential earlier work. Includes new material revealing wide freedom of press after 1776, which existed despite lack of solid foundation in law or in theory. Earlier title: *Legacy of Suppression* (1960). [CMJ]

41.201   Leonard W. Levy. *Original intent and the framers' Constitution.* New York: Macmillan, 1988. ISBN 0-02-918791-5. ▸ Highly regarded constitutional historian finds framers on side of Warren Court; original intent was to accept interpretive change. Sometimes polemical attack on conservative, contemporary constitutionalism. [DMS]

41.202   Leonard W. Levy. *Origins of the Fifth Amendment: the right against self-incrimination.* 1968 ed. New York: Macmillan, 1986. ISBN 0-02-919570-5 (cl), 0-02-919580-2 (pbk). ▸ Traces constitutional protection against self-incrimination to roots in English law, where it was upheld in face of attacks by courts during sixteenth and seventeenth centuries. Strong libertarian interpretation. [CMJ]

41.203   Jackson Turner Main. *The Antifederalists: critics of the Constitution, 1781–1788.* 1961 ed. New York: Norton, 1974. ISBN 0-393-00760-X (pbk). ▸ Study of Antifederalists as coherent party and heirs to opposition tradition. Concludes socioeconomic divisions based on geographic proximity to markets. Progressive, conflict-oriented interpretation. [RWS]

41.204 Frederick W. Marks III. *Independence on trial: foreign affairs and the making of the Constitution.* 1973 ed. Wilmington, Del.: Scholarly Resources, 1986. ISBN 0-8420-2272-4 (cl), 0-8420-2272-4 (pbk). ▸ Corrective to accounts emphasizing domestic issues in making of Constitution. Discusses honor and fear of Europe and need for central government to protect carrying trade and promote national security as motivation for reforming government. [RWS]

41.205 Forrest McDonald. *E pluribus unum: the formation of the American republic, 1776–1790.* 2d ed. Indianapolis: Liberty Press, 1979. ISBN 0-913966-58-4 (cl), 0-913966-59-2 (pbk). ▸ Well-written conservative view. As states assumed war debts, bond of union decayed and nation's political future became uncertain. To raise needed taxes, congressional authority became stronger and more centralized, culminating in ratification of Constitution. [EVW]

41.206 Forrest McDonald. *Novus ordo seclorum: the intellectual origins of the Constitution.* Lawrence: University Press of Kansas, 1985. ISBN 0-7006-0284-4 (cl), 0-7006-0311-5 (pbk). ▸ Constitution shaped by conflicting republican ideologies, checked by political experience and practical leaders. Focus on American system of political economy and role of Scottish Enlightenment. Challenges Bailyn 39.200. Often insightful, always provocative. [RWS]

41.207 Forrest McDonald. *We the people: the economic origins of the Constitution.* 1958 ed. New Brunswick, N.J.: Transaction, 1992. ISBN 1-56000-574-2 (pbk). ▸ Concludes almost all possible economic and geographic interests represented at Convention. No one interest could have dominated. Shows that economic data did not fit Beard's model (41.185). [RWS]

41.208 Forrest McDonald and Ellen Shapiro McDonald. *Requiem: variations on eighteenth-century themes.* Lawrence: University Press of Kansas, 1988. ISBN 0-7006-0370-0. ▸ Collection of essays focusing on decline from achievements of Constitution framers. Democracy and central government seen encroaching on and destroying constitutional role of states. Provocative, often polemical. [DMS]

41.209 Andrew Cunningham McLaughlin. *The confederation and the Constitution, 1783–1789.* 1905 ed. New York: Harper & Row, 1968. ▸ Older but still valuable political study. Treats nation making, federalism, colonial system, liberty, and order. Constitution solved problem of imperial organization. [RWS]

41.210 Robert J. Morgan. *James Madison on the Constitution and the Bill of Rights.* Westport, Conn.: Greenwood, 1988. ISBN 0-313-26394-9. ▸ Important attempt to reconstruct Madison's ideas on Constitution, political parties, republicanism, etc. Good insight on framer's concept of constitutional interpretation, little on slavery. [DMS]

41.211 Richard B. Morris. *John Jay, the nation, and the Court.* Boston: Boston University Press, 1967. ISBN 0-8419-8713-0. ▸ Brief, interpretive overview of Jay's views on Constitution. Emphasizes impact of foreign affairs experience on legal outlook. Defensive, somewhat slanted. [DMS]

41.212 Ellen Frankel Paul and Howard Dickman, eds. *Liberty, property, and the foundations of the American Constitution.* Albany: State University of New York Press, 1989. ISBN 0-88706-914-2 (cl), 0-88706-915-0 (pbk). ▸ Readable, remarkably thematic series of articles on Founding Fathers' concept of relationship between property, liberty, and government. Constitution designed to protect rights and quality of American society. [DMS]

41.213 Robert Allen Rutland. *The birth of the Bill of Rights, 1776–1791.* 1983 ed. Boston: Northeastern University Press, 1991. ISBN 1-55553-111-3 (cl), 1-55553-112-1 (pbk). ▸ Descriptive account

of making of Bill of Rights. Bill of Rights based on belief in social compact, limited government, and natural rights. Little systematic attention to English precedents and state bills. [RWS]

41.214 Robert Allen Rutland. *The ordeal of the Constitution: the Antifederalists and the ratification struggle, 1787–1788.* 1966 ed. Boston: Northeastern University Press, 1983. ISBN 0-930350-51-0 (cl), 0-930350-50-2 (pbk). ▸ Comprehensive account of ratification from Antifederalist perspective. Fearful of shift in power from locality to center, Antifederalists credited with forcing addition of Bill of Rights to Constitution. [RWS]

41.215 Stephen L. Schecter, ed. *The reluctant pillar: New York and the adoption of the federal Constitution.* Troy, N.Y.: Russell Sage College, 1985. ISBN 0-930309-00-6 (pbk). ▸ Concludes ratification delayed by political maneuvering for advantage on both sides. Discusses New York governor George Clinton as central figure in New York politics. Intended as reference work for specialist and general reader. [RWS]

41.216 Bernard Schwartz. *The great rights of mankind: history of the American Bill of Rights.* Rev. ed. Madison, Wisc.: Madison House, 1992. ISBN 0-945612-27-3 (cl), 0-945612-28-1 (pbk). ▸ Focusing on American innovations and not English precedents, finds James Madison's amendments were distillation of rights enumerated in state constitutions, extending emerging idea of written guarantee of basic rights. Five-volume documentary collection with brief commentaries. [DAR]

41.217 Richard C. Sinopoli. *The foundations of American citizenship: liberalism, the Constitution, and civic virtue.* New York: Oxford University Press, 1992. ISBN 0-19-507067-4. ▸ Significant study probing argument over liberal versus republican outlook of founders. Both Federalists and Antifederalists sought civic virtue, differences small. Complicated perspective, important for specialists. [DMS]

41.218 David P. Thelen, ed. *The Constitution and American life.* Ithaca, N.Y.: Cornell University Press, 1988. ISBN 0-8014-2185-3 (cl), 0-8014-9512-1 (pbk). ▸ Important collection of essays highlighting modern issues. Focuses on how Constitution shaped political struggles. Attempt at social history of Constitution organized around theme of chasm between president and Congress. [RWS]

41.219 William M. Wiecek. *The guarantee clause of the U.S. Constitution.* Ithaca, N.Y.: Cornell University Press, 1972. ISBN 0-8014-0671-4. ▸ Clause guaranteeing republican government to all states first applied in Rhode Island suffrage cases, but generally underused since evoked in Reconstruction and Progressive eras. Discusses possible use in future cases. Good legal history. [RWS]

41.220 Garry Wills. *Explaining America: The Federalist.* Garden City, N.Y.: Doubleday, 1981. ISBN 0-385-14689-2. ▸ Connects arguments of Federalist Papers to thought of philosopher David Hume, emphasizing public virtue. Opposes traditional interpretation which establishes *The Federalist* as product of John Locke's brand of liberalism. [CMJ]

41.221 Gordon S. Wood. *The creation of the American republic, 1776–1787.* 1969 ed. New York: Norton, 1972. ISBN 0-393-00644-1 (pbk). ▸ Argues for importance of American whig political thought in development of state and national constitutions. United States Constitution combined aristocratic and democratic elements in new form. Landmark study in neo-whig school. [CMJ]

SEE ALSO
40.74 Morton J. Horwitz. *The transformation of American law, 1780–1860.*
40.77 Michael G. Kammen. *A machine that would go of itself.*

THE NEW REPUBLIC, 1789–1801

National Government and Politics

41.222 Joyce Oldham Appleby. *Capitalism and a new social order: the republican vision of the 1790s.* New York: New York University Press, 1984. ISBN 0-8147-0581-2 (pbk). ▸ Synthesized view of intellectual influences at work at founding of American republic. Unsurpassed analysis of various currents of thought in early national period. [EVW]

41.223 Rudolph M. Bell. *Party and faction in American politics: the House of Representatives, 1789–1801.* Westport, Conn.: Greenwood, 1974. ISBN 0-8371-6356-0. ▸ Quantitative analysis of voting behavior in early House of Representatives. Traces movement from value-oriented, factional voting to partisan behavior during 1790s. Solid, reliable, but not for casual reader. [CMJ]

41.224 Kenneth R. Bowling. *The creation of Washington D.C.: the idea and location of the American capital.* Fairfax, Va.: George Mason University Press; distributed by University Publishing Associates, 1991. ISBN 0-913969-29-X. ▸ Careful, broad-ranging, thorough description of political battle to locate capital. Sees debate as dominant in first Congress, development of political and sectional alignments. [DMS]

41.225 Ralph Adams Brown. *The presidency of John Adams.* Lawrence: University Press of Kansas, 1975. ISBN 0-7006-0134-1. ▸ Examines Adams's dedicated leadership in foreign affairs and his success at avoiding war with France, even at risk of disintegration of his party. Best for foreign policy, less full on other aspects of Adams's presidency. [EVW]

41.226 Richard Buel, Jr. *Securing the revolution: ideology in American politics, 1789–1815.* Ithaca, N.Y.: Cornell University Press, 1972. ISBN 0-8014-0705-2. ▸ Insightful, provocative, influential study arguing party conflicts of 1790s ideological in nature, not result of desire for political power. Challenges Beard's emphasis on economic factors as key to early national politics (41.185, 41.266). [CMJ]

41.227 William Nisbet Chambers. *Political parties in a new nation: the American experience, 1776–1809.* 1963 ed. New York: Oxford University Press, 1966. ▸ Synthetic study of early republican politics, emphasizing transition from factionalism to partisanship during 1790s. Generally follows narrative approach. [CMJ]

41.228 Joseph Charles. *The origins of the American party system: three essays.* 1956 ed. New York: Harper & Row, 1961. ▸ Provocative study of presidents Washington, Jefferson, and Madison and their relationships with early political parties. Thoughtful, probing, critical approach to study of national parties in 1790s. [EVW]

41.229 Manning J. Dauer. *The Adams Federalists.* 1968 ed. Westport, Conn.: Greenwood, 1984. ISBN 0-313-22663-6. ▸ Groundbreaking revisionist study. Not so much popularity of Jeffersonian democratic ideals which accounts for fall of federalism as unpopularity of measures adopted by Hamiltonians. [EVW]

41.230 Martin Deamond. *As far as republican principles will admit: essays by Martin Deamond.* William Schambra, ed. Washington, D.C.: American Enterprise Institute for Public Research, 1992. (American Enterprise Institute studies, 527.) ISBN 0-8447-3784-4. ▸ Somewhat dated but often useful defense of Federalists as genuine democrats seeking stable governmental structure. Attacks Progressive school as misreading vocabulary and beliefs. Aimed at scholars and specialists. [DMS]

41.231 David F. Epstein. *The political theory of "The Federalist."* Chicago: University of Chicago Press, 1984. ISBN 0-226-21299-8. ▸ Examines Federalists as heirs to thought of John Locke and Baron Montesquieu. Papers present theory of government designed to preserve both private rights and public good. Difficult book, but important in debate on revolutionary political thought. [CMJ]

41.232 John F. Hoadley. *Origins of American political parties, 1789–1803.* Lexington: University Press of Kentucky, 1986. ISBN 0-8131-1562-0. ▸ Detailed analysis of emergence of factions in Congress, first from region and section, then over foreign policy (1793–97), and finally fairly well-developed legislative parties. [EVW]

41.233 Richard Hofstadter. *The idea of a party system: the rise of legitimate opposition in the United States, 1740–1840.* Berkeley: University of California Press, 1969. ISBN 0-520-01389-1 (cl), 0-520-01754-4 (pbk). ▸ Traces slow acceptance of partisan competition by American political culture, from antiparty attitudes of eighteenth century to full acceptance in Jacksonian period. Places New York in vanguard of process. Influential, well-written, synthetic essay. [CMJ]

41.234 Cecelia Kenyon, ed. *The Antifederalists.* 1966 ed. Boston: Northeastern University Press, 1985. ISBN 0-930350-75-8 (cl), 0-930350-74-X (pbk). ▸ Good selection of Antifederalist writings. Introduction argues Antifederalists were men of little faith who feared national consolidation. Sees Federalists as creators of democracy. Important, influential interpretation. [RWS]

41.235 Ralph L. Ketcham. *Presidents above party: the first American presidency, 1789–1829.* Chapel Hill: University of North Carolina Press for Institute of Early American History and Culture, 1984. ISBN 0-8078-1582-9. ▸ Interesting, insightful overview. Despite divisive issues and partisan struggles, first six presidents shared set of historical values and assumptions, leading each to exalted nonpartisan view of presidency and disdain for political parties. [EVW]

41.236 Adrienne Koch. *Jefferson and Madison, the great collaboration.* 1950 ed. Lanham, Md.: University Press of America, 1986. ISBN 0-8191-5875-5 (cl), 0-8191-5876-3 (pbk). ▸ Well-crafted analysis of republican philosophy. Sees bases of Jeffersonian political philosophy as combination of ideas stemming from collaboration of both Thomas Jefferson and James Madison. [EVW]

41.237 Richard H. Kohn. *Eagle and sword: the Federalists and the creation of the military establishment in America, 1783–1802.* New York: Free Press, 1975. ISBN 0-02-917551-8. ▸ Survey of postrevolutionary political and administrative American military policy through Jefferson's election, demonstrating emergence of peace establishment and illuminating many military episodes in early history of United States. [EVW]

41.238 Stephen G. Kurtz. *The presidency of John Adams: the collapse of federalism, 1795–1800.* 1957 ed. New York: Barnes, 1961. ▸ Excellent, readable, reliable study illuminates personality and career of second president. Focus on presidency portrays Adams as man of principle, sacrificing career to avoid war with France. [DMS]

41.239 Forrest McDonald. *The presidency of George Washington.* 1974 ed. New York: Norton, 1975. ISBN 0-393-00773-1 (pbk). ▸ George Washington as presidential figurehead and not master of affairs. Original research into creation of federal judiciary, panic of 1792, western land speculation, and early transformation of national politics. Readable. [DMS]

41.240 John C. Miller. *The Federalist era, 1789–1801.* 1960 ed. New York: Harper & Row, 1963. ISBN 0-06-133027-2 (pbk). ▸ Careful, detailed, textbook account of period. More summary of existing scholarship than innovative study. Somewhat heavy reading. Good coverage, excellent reference. [DMS]

41.241 James Morton Smith. *Freedom's fetters: the Alien and Sedition laws and the American civil liberties.* 1966 rev. ed. Ithaca, N.Y.:

Cornell University Press, 1989. ▸ Concludes Sedition Act was unconstitutional and its vigorous enforcement by Federalist judges nearly destroyed liberty of political criticism. Important contribution to American constitutional history. [EVW]

41.242 Donald H. Stewart. *The opposition press of the Federalist period.* Albany: State University of New York Press, 1969. ISBN 0-87395-042-9. ▸ Discussion of Democratic-Republican press efforts in shaping political opinion and reflecting public mind as it worked toward Jefferson victory in 1800. Prodigious research revealing intense emotionalism of Federalist-Republican confrontations. [EVW]

41.243 Leslie Wharton. *Polity and the public good: conflicting theories of republican government in the new nation.* Ann Arbor: University Microfilms International Research Press, 1980. ISBN 0-8357-1155-2. ▸ Conventional treatment emphasizing differences between regional varieties of republicanism in early republic. John Taylor of Caroline, John Adams, and Alexander Hamilton offered as regional archetypes. [CMJ]

41.244 Leonard D. White. *The Federalists: a study in administrative history.* 1948 ed. Westport, Conn.: Greenwood, 1978. ISBN 0-313-20101-3. ▸ Comprehensive history of administrations of George Washington and John Adams and struggle between Thomas Jefferson and Alexander Hamilton within this setting. Wealth of information on administrative practices and difficulties; first of this genre. [EVW]

41.245 John Zvesper. *Political philosophy and rhetoric: a study of the origins of American party politics.* New York: Cambridge University Press, 1977. ISBN 0-521-21323-1. ▸ Realistic Federalists better understood human nature than idealistic Republicans. Extensively researched, complex study seems to find consistency of political thought through selected use of evidence. Provocative, sophisticated return to earlier interpretation. [DMS]

State Government and Politics

41.246 Richard R. Beeman. *The Old Dominion and the new nation, 1788–1801.* Lexington: University Press of Kentucky, 1972. ISBN 0-8131-1269-9. ▸ Lucid narrative detailing regional party evolution. Virginia's Federalists and Republicans were members of same planter-slaveowner class, thus political divisions shaped by national and not state issues. [EVW]

41.247 Paul Goodman. *The Democratic-Republicans of Massachusetts: politics in a young republic.* Cambridge, Mass.: Harvard University Press, 1964. ▸ Fresh and significant insights into political parties of the 1790s which differed sharply from colonial and revolutionary era factions. Finds social structures of parties more complex and less homogeneous than previously thought. [EVW]

41.248 Ronald Hoffman and Peter J. Albert, eds. *Sovereign states in an age of uncertainty.* Charlottesville: University Press of Virginia for United States Capitol Historical Society, 1981. ISBN 0-8139-0926-0. ▸ Essays on such topics as state contribution to politics and beginnings of national parties. Discusses growth of sectional rivalries and state strengths and diversities. Uneven, specialized, disparate essays. [RWS]

41.249 Lisle A. Rose. *Prologue to democracy: the Federalists in the South, 1789–1800.* Lexington: University Press of Kentucky, 1968. ▸ Concludes southern Federalists pioneered modern party system by founding partisan interest groups through appointment policies, new techniques of mass appeal, first comprehensive, partisan legislative program. Detailed study of small elite and mechanics of party organization, less attention to broader socioeconomic factors. [EVW]

41.250 Alfred F. Young. *The Democratic Republicans of New York: the origins, 1763–1797.* Chapel Hill: University of North Carolina Press for Institute of Early American History and Cul-

ture, 1967. ▸ Jeffersonians organized independently of national issues; state issues most important for party formation. Modified Beardian analysis (cf. 41.185, 41.266). [RWS]

Foreign Relations

41.251 Harry Ammon. *The Genêt mission.* New York: Norton, 1973. ISBN 0-393-05475-6 (cl), 0-393-09420-0 (pbk). ▸ Well-written narrative of colorful episode. French envoy Edmond Genêt's visit to United States unwittingly led to democratization of political process and polarization of political factions. [EVW]

41.252 Albert H. Bowman. *The struggle for neutrality: Franco-American diplomacy during the Federalist era.* Knoxville: University of Tennessee Press, 1974. ISBN 0-87049-152-0. ▸ Detailed, insightful diplomatic history tracing policies of both countries from Proclamation of Neutrality in 1793 to Convention of 1800. Well-written narrative. [EVW]

41.253 Julian P. Boyd. *Number 7: Alexander Hamilton's secret attempts to control American foreign policy with supporting documents.* Princeton: Princeton University Press, 1964. ▸ Persuasive, fascinating study. Concludes that after 1793 Neutrality Proclamation, Hamilton, in contact with British agent, passed information that compromised American neutrality, forcing rapproachment with British. Originally extended documentary footnote from *Papers of Thomas Jefferson*, volume 17. [DAR]

41.254 Jerald A. Combs. *The Jay Treaty: political battleground of the Founding Fathers.* Berkeley: University of California Press, 1970. ISBN 0-520-01573-8. ▸ Extended treatment of early political parties opposing domestic and foreign goals. Federalists and Republicans genuinely sought to protect country's interests but differed over conceptions of American power. [EVW]

41.255 Alexander DeConde. *Entangling alliance: politics and diplomacy under George Washington.* 1958 ed. Westport, Conn.: Greenwood, 1974. ISBN 0-8371-7232-2. ▸ Provocative, original discussion of Americans divided in support for France or England; Federalists for Great Britain, Republicans for France. Finds early American statesmen resorted to name calling, false accusations, lies, deception, and hysteria in attempt to influence policy. [EVW]

41.256 Alexander DeConde. *The quasi-war: the politics and diplomacy of the undeclared war with France, 1797–1801.* New York: Scribner's, 1966. ▸ America's hostile attitude convinced French foreign minister Talleyrand that France could accomplish its ends without bloodshed and that negotiation was more promising means of isolating England. Balanced use of French sources. [EVW]

41.257 Felix Gilbert. *To the Farewell Address: ideas of early American foreign policy.* 1961 ed. Princeton: Princeton University Press, 1970. ISBN 0-691-00574-5 (pbk). ▸ Evolution of early American foreign policy makers from denouncing traditional diplomacy and balance-of-power system to Alexander Hamilton's aloof *realpolitik* and national interest–based policies. Perceptive analysis of early foreign policy leaders. [EVW]

41.258 Peter P. Hill. *French perceptions of the early American republic, 1783–1793.* Philadelphia: American Philosophical Society, 1988. (American Philosophical Society, Memoirs, 180.) ISBN 0-87169-180-9. ▸ New insights on often neglected period, using consular records. Reveals deterioration of French influence in new nation. Solid, useful study. [DMS]

41.259 Daniel George Lang. *Foreign policy in the early republic: the law of nations and the balance of power.* Baton Rouge: Louisiana State University Press, 1985. ISBN 0-8071-1255-0. ▸ Convincing thesis that writings of men such as Hugo Grotius, Samuel Pufendorf, and most notably, Emmerich de Vattel influenced early

American politicians such as Alexander Hamilton and Thomas Jefferson in 1790s. [EVW]

41.260 Bradford Perkins. *The first rapprochement: England and the United States, 1795–1805.* 1955 ed. Berkeley: University of California Press, 1967. ISBN 0-520-00998-3. ‣ After Jay's Treaty (1795), real reconciliation between United States and Great Britain based on mutual respect and joint recognition of importance of stability. Intensive analysis of British policy. [EVW]

41.261 Charles R. Ritcheson. *Aftermath of revolution: British policy toward the United States, 1783–1795.* 1969 ed. New York: Norton, 1971. ISBN 0-393-00553-4 (pbk). ‣ Detailed account from British side. United States and Great Britain shared equal responsibility for their problematic postwar relations; rapidly expanding commercial connection offered best hope for future accommodations. [EVW]

41.262 William C. Stinchcombe. *The XYZ Affair.* Westport, Conn.: Greenwood, 1980. ISBN 0-313-22234-7. ‣ New information on breakdown of Franco-American relations. Although coming closer to negotiations than previously thought, XYZ Affair (1798) solidified America's determination to separate itself and its fate from Europe. Best study of important diplomatic event. [EVW]

41.263 Paul A. Varg. *New England and foreign relations, 1789–1850.* Hanover, N.H.: University Press of New England, 1983. ISBN 0-87451-224-7. ‣ Study of diplomacy of New England statesmen and reactions of region to national events and trends. Survey of early American diplomacy emphasizing New England's contributions and responses. [EVW]

THE NEW REPUBLIC, 1801–1815

National Government and Politics

41.264 Henry Adams. *History of the United States of America.* Vol. 1: *During the administrations of James Madison*, Vol. 2: *During the administrations of Thomas Jefferson.* 5 vols. Earl N. Harbert, ed. New York: Library of America; distributed by Viking, 1986. ISBN 0-940450-34-8 (v. 1), 0-940450-35-6 (v. 2). ‣ Dated, somewhat biased account of Jeffersonian period by descendant of John Adams. Beautifully written, remains outstanding example of historian's craft published 1889–91. [DMS]

41.265 Lance Banning. *The Jeffersonian persuasion: evolution of a party ideology.* Ithaca, N.Y.: Cornell University Press, 1978. ISBN 0-8014-1151-3. ‣ Establishes Jeffersonians as intellectual heirs of English country politicians. Jeffersonian response to Federalist corruption similar to English opposition thought of Walpole era. Carries neo-whig interpretation into early republican period. [CMJ]

41.266 Charles A. Beard. *Economic origins of Jeffersonian democracy.* 1915 ed. New York: Free Press, 1965. ‣ Classic study of economic conflict. Sees party divisions in early nineteenth century reflecting split over adoption of Constitution. Fascinating, readable, dated. [DMS]

41.267 Daniel J. Boorstin. *The lost world of Thomas Jefferson.* 1948 ed. Chicago: University of Chicago Press, 1981. ISBN 0-226-06496-4 (pbk). ‣ Interesting, informative intellectual survey suggesting coherent Jeffersonian thought. Jeffersonian circle reconciled active and contemplative lives by emphasizing reasoned action for common good and increase of human power over nature. [LAN]

41.268 Roger H. Brown. *The republic in peril: 1812.* 1964 ed. New York: Norton, 1971. ISBN 0-393-00578-X (pbk). ‣ Declaration of war part of bitter American party fight; war necessary if experiment of republican form of government was to succeed. Extensive research into attitudes of members of Twelfth Congress. [EVW]

41.269 Robert Lowry Clinton. *Marbury v. Madison and judicial review.* Lawrence: University Press of Kansas, 1989. ISBN 0-7006-0411-1 (cl), 0-7006-0517-7 (pbk). ‣ Sees in case that established doctrine of judicial review intention to overrule only laws that unconstitutionally enhanced judicial power. Views Blackstone, common law, and limitation on court power as determining the decision. Clever, witty, provocative, controversial. [DMS]

41.270 Theodore J. Crackel. *Mr. Jefferson's army: political and social reform of the military establishment, 1801–1809.* New York: New York University Press, 1987. ISBN 0-8147-1407-2. ‣ Persuasive interpretation and analysis. Jefferson determined to make military instrument of service for new democratic order. West Point founded to train good republican youth for military leadership. [EVW]

41.271 Noble E. Cunningham, Jr. *The Jeffersonian Republicans in power: party operations, 1801–1809.* Chapel Hill: University of North Carolina Press for Institute of Early American History, 1963. ISBN 0-8078-0893-8. ‣ Succeeds author's earlier work on Jeffersonians, focusing on behavior while controlling White House and Congress. Thorough examination of Republican patronage policies and party organization, as well as splits within party. [CMJ]

41.272 Noble E. Cunningham, Jr. *The process of government under Jefferson.* Princeton: Princeton University Press, 1978. ISBN 0-691-04651-4. ‣ Original examination of machinery through which executive and legislative branches of Jefferson's administration operated, focusing on lower-echelon bureaucrats who carried on burdens of day-to-day governmental operations. [EVW]

41.273 George Dargo. *Jefferson's Louisiana: politics and the clash of legal traditions.* Cambridge, Mass.: Harvard University Press, 1975. ISBN 0-674-47370-1. ‣ Well-written, well-researched study of Jefferson administration's attempts to supplant civil law with common law throughout Louisiana territory and preconceived problems with native French-speaking residents. [EVW]

41.274 Richard E. Ellis. *The Jeffersonian crisis: courts and politics in the young republic.* 1971 ed. New York: Norton, 1974. ISBN 0-393-00729-4 (pbk). ‣ Important revisionist analysis finding ideological division within Jefferson camp between radicals and moderates was driving force behind transformation of judiciary at both state and national levels after 1801. [EVW]

41.275 Robert Kenneth Faulkner. *The jurisprudence of John Marshall.* 1968 ed. Westport, Conn.: Greenwood, 1980. ISBN 0-313-22508-7 (pbk). ‣ Comprehensive study of Supreme Court Justice Marshall's political theory, placing jurist within philosophical framework of other Founding Fathers. Emphasizes Marshall's constitutional theory. Standard work on topic. [CMJ]

41.276 David Hackett Fischer. *The revolution of American conservatism: the Federalist party in the era of Jeffersonian democracy.* 1965 ed. Chicago: University of Chicago Press, 1975. ISBN 0-226-25135-7. ‣ Analysis of change in tactics and policy of younger post-Constitution Federalists as they came to terms with existence of mass electorate and set about competing for their vote. Thoroughly researched. [EVW]

41.277 Harold Hellenbrand. *The unfinished revolution: education and politics in the thought of Thomas Jefferson.* Newark: University of Delaware Press, 1990. ISBN 0-87413-370-X. ‣ Jefferson's experiences dictated views on educating citizenry in new nation. Psychoanalytical approach to study motivation and colonial rejection of parental authority. Illuminates aspects of Jefferson's personal views on education. [DMS]

41.278 Daniel Walker Howe. *The political culture of the American Whigs.* Chicago: University of Chicago Press, 1979. ISBN 0-226-35478-4 (cl), 0-226-35479-2 (pbk). ‣ Examination of American whig politics of postrevolutionary era. Whigs adopted elitist political and social philosophy in support of new industrial order. Discovers Marxism as well as moral dimension in whig ideology. Important reinterpretation of Whigs. [CMJ]

41.279 Robert M. Johnstone, Jr. *Jefferson and the presidency: leadership in the young republic.* Ithaca, N.Y.: Cornell University Press, 1978. ISBN 0-8014-11150-5. ► Readable, straightforward insight into Jefferson and presidency. Jefferson's administration as model, developed extraconstitutional sources of power enabling presidents to go beyond institutional restraints imposed by Constitution. [EVW]

41.280 Linda K. Kerber. *Federalists in dissent: imagery and ideology in Jeffersonian America.* 1970 ed. Ithaca, N.Y.: Cornell University Press, 1980. ISBN 0-8014-0560-2 (cl, 1970), 0- 8014-9212-2 (pbk). ► First thorough analysis of federalist ideology as presented in published writings. Federalists blamed Jeffersonians for loss of intellectual vigor. Argues partisan differences were cultural as well as political. [CMJ]

41.281 C. Peter Magrath. *Yazoo: law and politics in the new republic, the case of Fletcher vs. Peck.* 1966 ed. New York: Norton, 1967. ISBN 0-393-00418-X. ► Interesting, generally readable exploration of legal and political interactions on both state and national scene. Explores increasing dominance of Republican party, with perceptive observations on sectional divisions. [DMS]

41.282 Drew R. McCoy. *The elusive republic: political economy in Jeffersonian America.* 1980 ed. New York: Norton, 1982. ISBN 0-393-95239-8 (pbk). ► Complex, original argument that revolutionaries shared beliefs and attitudes about nature, source, and purpose of government and requirements of virtuous and fulfilling society which constituted their republican ideology. [EVW]

41.283 Forrest McDonald. *The presidency of Thomas Jefferson.* Lawrence: University Press of Kansas, 1976. ISBN 0-7006-0147-3. ► Interpretive synthesis of presidential administration. Finds Jeffersonian ideological origins lay with earlier English whig thought. [EVW]

41.284 Charles A. Miller. *Jefferson and nature: an interpretation.* Baltimore: Johns Hopkins University Press, 1988. ISBN 0-8018-3593-3. ► History of ideas reviews central importance of nature to Jefferson's thinking about human nature, morals, political science, etc. Compliments Boorstin 41.267. Insightful, persuasive, important to understanding Jefferson's thought. [DMS]

41.285 Jennifer Nedelsky. *Private property and the limits of American constitutionalism: the Madison framework and its legacy.* Chicago: University of Chicago Press, 1990. ISBN 0-226-56970-5. ► Thoughtful, penetrating study. President Madison's ideology defined constitution, justified protection of inequalities resulting from unequal faculties. Property protection more important to republic than equality, then and today. [DMS]

41.286 Stephen B. Presser. *The original misunderstanding: the English, the Americans, and the dialectic of Federalist jurisprudence.* Durham, N.C.: Carolina Academic Press, 1991. ISBN 0-89089-425-6. ► Sees Justice Samuel Chase constructing constitutional interpretation based on conservative, republican tradition ignored by Justice John Marshall. Aimed at legal historians rather than general reader. Poorly organized, unevenly written. [DMS]

41.287 Robert Allen Rutland. *The presidency of James Madison.* Lawrence: University Press of Kansas, 1990. ISBN 0- 7006-0456-0. ► Readable, generally favorable, balanced account. Useful as brief survey by mature scholar familiar with sources. Competent, informed synthesis rather than innovative. [DMS]

41.288 Thomas C. Shevory. *John Marshall's achievement: law, politics, and constitutional interpretation.* New York: Greenwood, 1989. ISBN 0-313-26477-5, ISSN 0147-1074. ► Conference essays disparate, uneven, but illuminating on aspects of Marshall's deci-

sions, political theory, and view of Court's interpretive function. [DMS]

41.289 Marshall Smelser. *The democratic republic, 1801–1815.* 1968 ed. Prospect Heights, Ill.: Waveland, 1992. ISBN 0-88133-668-8 (pbk). ► Synthesis of recent research leading to thoughtful interpretation. Jefferson was practical politician, not strapped to ideology of Jeffersonian democracy formulated by later generations; James Madison rated on par with Abraham Lincoln. [EVW]

41.290 Jack M. Sosin. *The aristocracy of the long robe: the origins of judicial review in America.* Westport, Conn.: Greenwood, 1989. ISBN 0-313-26733-2. ► Review of inherent tension between judicial review and democracy. Traces rise of legal profession, finding doctrine unprecedented in English and colonial law. Readable, mildly controversial. [DMS]

41.291 Richard J. Twomey. *Jacobins and Jeffersonians: Anglo-American radicalism in the United States.* New York: Garland, 1989. ISBN 0-8240-6199-3. ► Excellent but unrevised 1974 dissertation on transatlantic connection between Anglo-American radicalism and Jeffersonian Republicans. Delineates connection between thought and politics. Includes capsule biographies of leading English exiles in America. [DMS]

41.292 Steven Watts. *The republic reborn: war and the making of liberal America, 1790–1820.* Baltimore: Johns Hopkins University Press, 1987. ISBN 0-8018-3420-1. ► Americans, concerned about apparent contradictions between republicanism and reality of their personal lives, fought War of 1812 as means of forming national character. Provocative cultural history. [EVW]

41.293 Leonard D. White. *The Jeffersonians: a study in administrative history, 1801–1829.* 1951 ed. New York: Free Press, 1965. ► Provocative administrative history focusing on Jeffersonian administrations of Thomas Jefferson, James Madison, James Monroe, and John Quincy Adams. Instead of initiating change, continued to run Federalist administrative machine substantially unaltered. [EVW]

State Government and Politics

41.294 James M. Banner, Jr. *To the Hartford Convention: the Federalists and the origins of party politics in Massachusetts, 1789–1815.* 1969 ed. New York: Knopf, 1970. ► Ideology divided men into hostile camps threatening Massachusetts' stability and revolutionizing Federalist political behavior. Intelligently edited and well-written work helps clear up confusing historical puzzle. [EVW]

41.295 Norman K. Risjord. *The old Republicans: southern conservatism in the age of Jefferson.* New York: Columbia University Press, 1965. ► Traces southern dissent within Jeffersonian movement. Useful survey of old republican positions on national issues. [EVW]

Foreign Relations and the War of 1812

41.296 Harry L. Coles. *The War of 1812.* 1965 ed. Chicago: University of Chicago Press, 1966. ISBN 0-226-11349-3 (cl), 0-226-11350-7 (pbk). ► Outstanding one-volume account of often neglected "second American revolution." Studies military aspects to examine broad themes in early republic's civilization. [EVW]

41.297 Alexander DeConde. *This affair of Louisiana.* New York: Scribner's, 1976. ISBN 0-684-14687-8. ► Standard, reliable study by leading diplomatic historian. Concludes that after military pressure, threats of war, skillful diplomacy, and popular demand, Louisiana Purchase was end result of nationalistic and expansionist ideology of America's political leaders. [EVW]

41.298 Clifford L. Egan. *Neither peace nor war: Franco-American relations, 1803–1812.* Baton Rouge: Louisiana State University

Press, 1983. ISBN 0-8071-1076-0. ‣ Chronological narrative of Franco-American relations from Louisiana Purchase to death of American minister to France, Joel Barlow, in 1812. Modern interpretation of important, often neglected period. [EVW]

41.299 Ronald L. Hatzenbuehler and Robert L. Ivie. *Congress declares war: rhetoric, leadership, and partisanship in the early republic.* Kent, Ohio: Kent State University Press, 1983. ISBN 0-87338-292-7. ‣ Effective rhetoric, group-oriented leadership by James Madison, and republican partisanship combined to induce House of Representatives to declare war against Great Britain in 1812. Innovative analysis. [EVW]

41.300 Donald R. Hickey. *The War of 1812: a forgotten conflict.* Urbana: University of Illinois Press, 1989. ISBN 0-252-01613-0 (cl), 0-252-06059-8 (pbk). ‣ Thorough, well-documented attempt to restore importance of 1812 war. Delineates internal political conflict, military campaigns, and international affairs. Useful to both scholar and general reader. [DMS]

41.301 Reginald Horsman. *The causes of the War of 1812.* 1961 ed. New York: Octagon Books, 1972. ISBN 0-374-93960-8. ‣ Judicious, readable synthesis of many causes of War of 1812. Sees Anglo-French conflict and England's tendency to underestimate pride and intense nationalism of young United States as direct causes of war. [EVW]

41.302 Reginald Horsman. *The War of 1812.* New York: Knopf, 1969. ‣ Balanced narrative of primarily military and naval engagements from invasion of Canada in 1812 to brief analysis of negotiations at Ghent. Grounded in British as well as American primary sources. [EVW]

41.303 Burton Spivak. *Jefferson's English crisis: commerce, embargo, and the republican revolution.* Charlottesville: University Press of Virginia, 1978. ISBN 0-8139-0805-1. ‣ Argues Thomas Jefferson was threatened from without by English maritime power and ambition, and from within by unwanted commercial-urban growth encouraged by English political, social, and economic ideology. Impressive study. [EVW]

41.304 J.C.A. Stagg. *Mr. Madison's war: politics, diplomacy, and warfare in the early American republic, 1783–1830.* Princeton: Princeton University Press, 1983. ISBN 0-691-04702-2 (cl), 0-691-10150-7 (pbk). ‣ Comprehensive combination of synthesis and original research on War of 1812. Discusses domestic politics and localism, war finance, logistics and recruitment, Madison's war management, and campaigning. [EVW]

41.305 Patrick C. T. White. *A nation on trial: America and the War of 1812.* New York: Wiley, 1965. ‣ Interpretive survey of foreign policy, 1803–15, stressing maritime issues of neutral rights and impressment. Concludes War of 1812 ensured economic independence from Europe. Evenhanded account. [EVW]

SEE ALSO
47.51 Bradford Perkins. *Castlereagh and Adams.*

THE FRONTIER AND INDIAN RELATIONS

41.306 Thomas Perkins Abernethy. *Three Virginia frontiers.* Baton Rouge: Louisiana State University Press, 1940. ‣ Standard, rather dated, political and economic study. Still useful distillation of neglected aspect of colonial history. [DMS]

41.307 John R. Alden. *John Stuart and the southern colonial frontier: a study of Indian relations, war, trade, and land problems in the southern wilderness, 1754–1775.* 1944 ed. New York: Gordian, 1966. ISBN 0-87752-001-1. ‣ Older, standard biography of British India superintendant. Excellent narrative of difficult subject. Thorough, influential, somewhat dated, but still useful and readable. [DMS]

41.308 Michael Allen. *Western rivermen, 1763–1861: Ohio and*

Mississippi boatmen and the myth of the alligator horse. Baton Rouge: Louisiana State University Press, 1990. ISBN 0-8071-1561-4. ‣ Investigation of social life among flatboatmen and importance of river myth in Jacksonian America, based on extensive sources. Provides detailed information; more descriptive than analytical. [DMS]

41.309 Steven R. Boyd, ed. *The Whiskey Rebellion: past and present perspectives.* Westport, Conn.: Greenwood, 1985. ISBN 0-313-24536-3, ISSN 0084-9219. ‣ Nine interpretive essays emphasizing formerly obscure areas and people and events. Illustrates depth and complexity of motives and actions on both sides of issue. Important contribution to constitutional history. [EVW]

41.310 Andrew R. L. Cayton. *The frontier republic: ideology and politics in the Ohio country, 1780–1825.* Kent, Ohio: Kent State University Press, 1986. ISBN 0-87338-332-X. ‣ Interpretation and evaluation of ideological origins and ramifications of territorial and state politics and development. Analyzes Ohio Company leaders' and Federalists' vision of Northwest frontier. Well-researched, thorough study of political ideology. [EVW]

41.311 R. David Edmunds. *Tecumseh and the quest for Indian leadership.* Boston and Glenview, Ill.: Little, Brown and Scott, Foresman, 1984. ISBN 0-316-21169-9 (pbk), 0-673-39336-4 (pbk). ‣ Well-researched, well-written account of leader of western Indian uprising. Revisionist in crediting Tenskwatawa (Prophet) with more important role. Good study of Shawnee nation; balanced, important addition to American Indian literature. [DMS]

41.312 Robin F. A. Fabel. *The economy of British West Florida, 1763–1783.* Tuscaloosa: University of Alabama Press, 1988. ISBN 0-8173-0312-X. ‣ Anecdotal study of planter-entrepreneur careers. Concludes British gulf-coast settlement an economic failure; lack of capital and high start-up costs retarded settlement and Indian and Caribbean trade unreliable. Narrow, specialized study. [LAN]

41.313 George W. Franz. *Paxton: a study of community structure and mobility in the colonial Pennsylvania backcountry.* New York: Garland, 1989. ISBN 0-8240-6179-9. ‣ Claims institutions' failure to provide sense of community critical to understanding Paxton boys' 1763 march on Philadelphia. Somewhat dated historiographically. Extensive and useful data from tax and land office records. [DMS]

41.314 Alan Gallay. *The formation of a planter elite: Jonathan Bryan and the southern colonial frontier.* Athens: University of Georgia Press, 1989. ISBN 0-8203-1143-X. ‣ Narrative of prominent planter's role in moving Georgia to Revolution. Effective overview of Georgia's upper class and revolutionary movement, evangelicalism, proslavery rationalizations, frontier and backcountry, and intellectual development. [DMS]

41.315 Reginald Horsman. *The frontier in the formative years, 1783–1815.* New York: Holt, Rinehart & Winston, 1970. ISBN 0-03-083035-4. ‣ Progressive movement of frontier in Old Northwest and Old Southwest, set within broader context of United States national policy of aggressive frontier settlement. Judicious summary and sound interpretation of historiography. [EVW]

41.316 Charles A. Jellison. *Ethan Allen: frontier rebel.* 1969 ed. Syracuse, N.Y.: Syracuse University Press, 1983. ISBN 0-8156-0189-1. ‣ Best available biography. Carefully researched, judicious, skillful narrative style. Good description of political and economic maneuvering during revolutionary period. [DMS]

41.317 Terry G. Jordan and Matti Kaups. *The American backwoods frontier: an ethnic and ecological interpretation.* Baltimore: Johns Hopkins University Press, 1989. ISBN 0-8018-3686-7. ‣ Significant, controversial, cultural geography with emphasis on influence of Finnish settlements as models. Frontier traits rooted in northern Europe. Lively, opens new vistas. [DMS]

41.318 Isabel Thompson Kelsay. *Joseph Brant, 1743–1807: man of two worlds.* 1984 ed. Syracuse, N.Y.: Syracuse University Press, 1986. ISBN 0-8156-0182-4 (cl, 1984), 0-8156-0208-1 (pbk). ‣ Lengthy, detailed, reliable, thoroughly researched biography of Mohawk chief. Well-written, important addition to American Indian studies. [DMS]

41.319 Earl P. Olmstead. *Blackcoats among the Delaware: David Zeisberger on the Ohio frontier.* Kent, Ohio: Kent State University Press, 1991. ISBN 0-87338-422-9 (cl), 0-87338-434-2 (pbk). ‣ Narrative account of establishment and work of Moravian missions among Delaware Indians in eastern Ohio. Emphasis on Zeisberger and Moravian acceptance of native culture. Good insights on cultural conflict; breaks new ground. [DMS]

41.320 Frank Lawrence Owsley, Jr. *Struggle for the gulf borderlands: the Creek War and the Battle of New Orleans, 1812–1815.* Gainesville: University Presses of Florida, 1981. ISBN 0-8130-0662-7. ‣ Examination of very significant southern theater of War of 1812 began as war against Spain-backed Creeks, then war against British resulting in annexation of Florida. First-rate military history. [EVW]

41.321 Francis Paul Prucha. *The sword of the republic: the United States Army on the frontier, 1783–1846.* 1969 ed. Lincoln: University of Nebraska Press, 1987. ISBN 0-8032-3676-X (cl), 0-8032-8713-5 (pbk). ‣ Review of military activities from Revolution to Mexican War, including conflicts with American Indians in Old Northwest, Black Hawk War, and Seminole War. Narrative of disparate events. Detailed, valuable, but short on generalizations. [DMS]

41.322 Malcolm J. Rohrbough. *The trans-Appalachian frontier: people, societies, and institutions, 1775–1850.* New York: Oxford University Press, 1978. ISBN 0-19-502209-2. ‣ Examines migrations and progress of settlement societies as Anglo-American institutions such as law, religion, education, and farming installed in new wilderness. Insightful reassessment of New West. [EVW]

41.323 Thomas P. Slaughter. *The Whiskey Rebellion: frontier epilogue to the American Revolution.* New York: Oxford University Press, 1986. ISBN 0-19-503899-1. ‣ Frontier settlers' desire for autonomy and Federalists' demand for authority stemmed from fundamentally different views of meaning of Revolution. Comprehensive, balanced treatment. [EVW]

41.324 Jack M. Sosin. *The revolutionary frontier, 1763–1783.* 1967 ed. Albuquerque: University of New Mexico Press, 1974. ISBN 0-8263-0331-5. ‣ Analysis intended for general reader. Disputes traditional view of democratizing influence of frontier drawing on work of Frederick Jackson Turner (40.125). Sees little innovation in frontier settlements, whose political establishments were modeled after East. Readable, insightful, provocative study. [RWS]

41.325 Wiley Sword. *President Washington's Indian war: the struggle for the Old Northwest, 1790–1795.* Norman: University of Oklahoma Press, 1985. ISBN 0-8061-1864-4. ‣ Detailed comprehensive account of fate of American Indians, sealed with British evacuation of mid-American forts in 1795, removing last barrier to western expansion. [EVW]

41.326 Mary K. Bonsteel Tachau. *Federal courts in the early republic: Kentucky, 1789–1816.* Princeton: Princeton University Press, 1978. ISBN 0-691-04661-1. ‣ Examination of early Kentucky courts focusing on pivotal figure of district judge Harry Innes. Argues for large role for federal courts in Kentucky. Informative study; reviews technical aspects as well as place of law in ordinary life. [CMJ]

41.327 Alan Taylor. *Liberty men and great proprietors: the revo-*
lutionary settlement on the Maine frontier, 1760–1820. Chapel Hill: University of North Carolina Press for Institute of Early American History and Culture, 1990. ISBN 0-8078-1909-3 (cl), 0-8078-4282-6 (pbk). ‣ Explores settlement of Maine as conflict between wealthy speculators and militant settlers over distribution of land and political power. Results defined meaning of Revolution in rural America. Solid study. [DMS]

41.328 Daniel B. Thorp. *The Moravian community in colonial North Carolina: pluralism on the southern frontier.* Knoxville: University of Tennessee Press, 1989. ISBN 0-87049-605-0. ‣ Illustration of successful frontier pluralism using small, frontier community and based on previously unpublished sources. Provides new insights on economy, women, church, and community. Useful, modern study. [DMS]

41.329 James Titus. *The Old Dominion at war: society, politics, and warfare in late colonial Virginia.* Columbia: University of South Carolina Press, 1991. ISBN 0-87249-724-0. ‣ Explores effects of military policies during Seven Years' War on Virginia's future. Move from conscripted to volunteer army reflected elites' efforts to promote stability. Provocative and persuasive. [DMS]

41.330 Anthony F. C. Wallace. *King of the Delawares: Teedyuscung, 1700–1763.* 1949 ed. Syracuse, N.Y.: Syracuse University Press, 1990. ISBN 0-8156-2498-0. ‣ Pioneering study incorporates tools of anthropology to explore life of important American Indian leader. Clear, convincing, pathbreaking work. Useful to anyone interested in subject. [DMS]

41.331 Jerome H. Wood, Jr. *Conestoga crossroads: Lancaster, Pennsylvania, 1730–1790.* Harrisburg: Pennsylvania Historical and Museum Commission, 1979. ISBN 0-911124-98-5. ‣ Extensive, sometimes overly detailed, discussion of people and events in social, educational, cultural, economic, and physical setting. Important study aimed at both professional and general audience. [DMS]

41.332 J. Leitch Wright, Jr. *Britain and the American frontier, 1783–1815.* Athens: University of Georgia Press, 1975. ISBN 0-8203-0349-6. ‣ Study of frontier as arena where nations vied for power, traced from Peace of Ghent through 1812. Demonstrates global attention that United States frontier generated. [EVW]

41.333 William Wyckoff. *The developer's frontier: the making of the western New York landscape.* New Haven: Yale University Press, 1988. ISBN 0-300-04154-3. ‣ Historical geography concerned with culture and ecology. Rejects Turner's view of frontier (40.125), focusing on wealthy developers as shaping landscape. Thoroughly based on records favorable to developers. [DMS]

SEE ALSO
36.131 R. David Edmunds. *Shawnee prophet.*
45.136 John Bartlet Brebner. *The neutral Yankees of Nova Scotia.*

RELIGION

41.334 Thomas Perkins Abernethy. *The South in the new nation, 1789–1819.* Baton Rouge: Louisiana State University Press, 1961. ‣ Comprehensive treatment of international and interracial contest to settle southern frontier and region's role in national politics during years 1789–1819. Slavery was product not cause of sectional feelings. [EVW]

41.335 Charles W. Akers. *The divine politician: Samuel Cooper and the American Revolution in Boston.* Boston: Northeastern University Press, 1982. ISBN 0-930350-19-7. ‣ Thorough, well-written study of revolutionary Boston's most important clergyman. Insightful on local social history. Readable, definitive biography. [DMS]

41.336 Frank Baker. *From Wesley to Asbury: studies in early American Methodism.* Durham, N.C.: Duke University Press, 1976. ISBN 0-8223-0359-0. ▸ Collection of essays on American sect, dominated by British-born, Wesley-trained lay leaders and circuit preachers; not distinctly indigenous denomination. Mostly personality studies. Conveys good understanding of appeal of early Methodism. [LAN]

41.337 Ruth H. Bloch. *Visionary republic: millennial themes in American thought, 1756–1800.* 1985 ed. Cambridge: Cambridge University Press, 1988. ISBN 0-521-6811-7 (cl, 1985), 0-521-35764-0 (pbk). ▸ Intelligent, careful, perceptive study of late eighteenth-century intellectual history. Focus on millennial expectancy as means to see American history as transitional step in utopian prophecy, culmination of man's progress in return to primitive natural order. [DMS]

41.338 James H. Broussard. *The southern Federalists, 1800–1816.* Baton Rouge: Louisiana State University Press, 1979. ISBN 0-8071-0288-1. ▸ Detailed examination of southern Federalists organization and activities in state and national politics, use of press, and attitudes on issues of democracy, slavery, education, and economic development. [EVW]

41.339 Thomas E. Buckley. *Church and state in revolutionary Virginia, 1776–1787.* Charlottesville: University Press of Virginia, 1977. ISBN 0-8139-0692-X. ▸ Portrait of dissenters as forward looking and integral to religious freedom; understood official establishment as barrier to religious freedom. Sees dissenters as key to disestablishment of church and establishment of republican virtue. Solid if somewhat pedestrian contribution. [RWS]

41.340 Robert M. Calhoon. *Evangelicals and conservatives in the early South, 1740–1861.* Columbia: University of South Carolina Press, 1988. ISBN 0-87249-577-9. ▸ Discussion of process by which Evangelicals moved from opposing southern institutions to accommodation. Solid synthesis by mature scholar firmly grounded in secondary literature. [DMS]

41.341 John Corrigan. *The hidden balance: religion and the social theories of Charles Chauncy and Jonathan Mayhew.* Cambridge: Cambridge University Press, 1987. ISBN 0-521-32777-6. ▸ Explores efforts of two divines to reconcile tensions of post-Awakening society with religious vision. Good, insightful study. Augmentative rather than innovative. [DMS]

41.342 James West Davidson. *The logic of millennial thought: eighteenth-century New England.* New Haven: Yale University Press, 1977. ISBN 0-300-01947-5. ▸ Survey of revolutionary millennialism. Prevalence closely linked to imperial and international political situation, yet had little direct impact on American Revolution. [LAN]

41.343 Edwin S. Gaustad. *Faith of our fathers: religion and the new nation.* San Francisco: Harper & Row, 1987. ISBN 0-06-250347-2. ▸ Well-written, clear discussion of religious attitudes of founders George Washington, John Adams, Benjamin Franklin, Thomas Jefferson, and James Madison. Accurate, interesting. Good for general readers. [DMS]

41.344 Wesley M. Gewehr. *The Great Awakening in Virginia, 1740–1790.* 1930 ed. Gloucester, Mass.: Smith, 1965. ▸ Detailed survey of growth of evangelical Protestantism in Old Dominion and conflict with established Anglican church and political hierarchy. Focuses on Baptists and individual leaders. [LAN]

41.345 C. C. Goen. *Revivalism and separatism in New England, 1740–1800: strict Congregationalists and separate Baptists in the Great Awakening.* 1962 ed. Middletown, Conn.: Wesleyan University Press; distributed by Harper & Row, 1987. ISBN 0-8195-5186-4 (cl), 0-8195-6133-9 (pbk). ▸ Traces assimilation of "awakening" separatist congregations into Baptist denomination. Separatism arose from theological disputes within decadent Puri-

tan establishment. Celebratory history of Baptist Americanism. [LAN]

41.346 Gillian Lindt Gollin. *Moravians in two worlds: a study in changing communities.* New York: Columbia University Press, 1967. ISBN 0-231-03033-9. ▸ Comparison of Herrnhut, Germany to Bethlehem, Pennsylvania, with reference to religious, social, and economic developments. Focus on secularization of two settlements sponsored by Count Zinzendorf. Important for specialists. [DMS]

41.347 Edward M. Griffin. *Old brick: Charles Chauncy of Boston, 1705–1787.* Minneapolis: University of Minnesota Press, 1980. ISBN 0-8166-0907-1. ▸ Places Chauncey firmly in first rank of New England intellectuals. Also explores his political importance. Well-written, readable, definitive biography. [DMS]

41.348 Joseph Haroutunian. *Piety versus moralism: the passing of the New England theology.* 1932 ed. New York: Harper & Row, 1970. ▸ Both Catholicism and Puritan Calvinism reflected medieval influences. Modernization and bourgeois individualism transformed American Calvinism, but its new rational, humanitarian theology failed to fulfill original community religious purpose of settlement. [LAN]

41.349 Nathan O. Hatch. *The democratization of American Christianity.* New Haven: Yale University Press, 1989. ISBN 0-300-04470-4. ▸ Sees religious mass movements after Revolution as democratizing, thus christianizing, United States. Overrode elitism to make American Christianity a populist movement. Insightful, provocative, thoroughly researched. [DMS]

41.350 Alan Heimert. *Religion and the American mind from the Great Awakening to the Revolution.* Cambridge, Mass.: Harvard University Press, 1966. ▸ Exhaustive study of religious controversy in eighteenth century. American clergy in two camps: Evangelicals supported Revolution and popular government; liberal theologians favored hierarchical government and imperial union. [LAN]

41.351 Stephen A. Marini. *Radical sects of revolutionary New England.* Cambridge: Harvard University Press, 1982. ISBN 0-674-74625-2. ▸ Clear, reliable, insightful study of small groups, featuring Freewill Baptists, Shakers, Universalists. Sees abandonment of Calvinism on rural frontier as result of failure of Congregationalism. [DMS]

41.352 William G. McLoughlin. *Isaac Backus and the American pietistic tradition.* Oscar Handlin, ed. Boston: Little, Brown, 1967. ▸ Explores life and thought of premier eighteenth-century Baptist leader. Accurate, readable, skillful; not full biography, rather study of pietism and religious controversy. [DMS]

41.353 Sidney E. Mead. *The lively experiment: the shaping of Christianity in America.* 1963 ed. New York: Harper & Row, 1976. ISBN 0-06-065545-6. ▸ Lecture series arguing vitality of American churches result of competition engendered by religious freedom. Concludes interaction of numerous denominations in democratic environment created American Christianity marked by fundamentalist impulse. [DAR]

41.354 Sidney E. Mead. *The old religion in the brave new world: reflections on the relation between Christendom and the republic.* Berkeley: University of California Press, 1977. ISBN 0-520-03322-1. ▸ Engaging, interesting, somewhat revisionist account. Points to tensions between religion of sects and denominations and Enlightenment religion of republic as enshrined in national rhetoric and institutions. [DMS]

41.355 Frederick V. Mills, Sr. *Bishops by ballot: an eighteenth-century ecclesiastical revolution.* New York: Oxford University Press, 1978. ISBN 0-19-502411-7. ▸ Concludes lack of central authority in America weakened Anglican church during revolutionary era. Episcopal church saved through creation of federation of existing parishes, which created native hierarchy. Specialized, reliable, sometimes tedious reading. [LAN]

41.356 Edmund S. Morgan. *The gentle Puritan: a life of Ezra Stiles, 1727–1795.* 1962 ed. New York: Norton, 1984. ISBN 0-393-30126-5 (pbk). ▸ Exceptionally well-written account of Rhode Island clergyman and Yale president. Explores human side of Puritanism, illuminates eighteenth-century life. Model biography. [DMS]

41.357 Charles B. Sanford. *The religious life of Thomas Jefferson.* Charlottesville: University Press of Virginia, 1984. ISBN 0-8139-0996-1. ▸ Analysis of intellectual manifestations of Jefferson's religious thought. Jefferson heavily influenced by Bible and teachings of Jesus and not pure deist. Intellectual rather than personal biography. [LAN]

41.358 Leigh Eric Schmidt. *Holy fairs: Scottish communions and American revivals in the early modern period.* Princeton: Princeton University Press, 1989. ISBN 0-691-04760-X. ▸ Insightful, well-written account illuminating connection between evangelical revivals and Catholic tradition. Follows decline of holy fairs under attacks of bourgeois decorum. Revises previous views of evangelical Protestantism. [DMS]

41.359 Donald M. Scott. *From office to profession: the New England ministry, 1750–1850.* Philadelphia: University of Pennsylvania Press, 1978. ISBN 0-8122-7737-6. ▸ Eighteenth-century clergymen a moral and political force within region and locality but after 1800 became national class of peripatetic professionals. Argues transformation result of public demand for limited religious services rather than for comprehensive local leadership. Neglects theological developments but clearly explains other changes in clergy. [LAN]

41.360 Beverly Prior Smaby. *The transformation of Moravian Bethlehem: from communal mission to family economy.* Philadelphia: University of Pennsylvania Press, 1988. ISBN 0-8122-8130-6. ▸ Quantitative analysis applied to religious experience. Good use of primary materials to delineate changes in communal structure and religious values. Surprising failure to utilize secondary sources. [DMS]

41.361 James Tanis. *Dutch Calvinistic pietism in the middle colonies: a study in the life and theology of Theodorus Jacobus Frelinghuysen.* The Hague: Nijhoff, 1967. ▸ Intellectual biography of Great Awakening leader. Pietism emphasized new birth and strict morals over rigid theology. Played key role setting agenda for Awakening among other ethnic groups and denominations. [LAN]

41.362 Frederick B. Tolles. *Quakers and the Atlantic culture.* 1960 ed. New York: Octagon Books, 1980. ISBN 0-374-97979-9. ▸ Essay collection briefly summarizing Friends' culture. Quakers created coherent international community based on personal networks and common aesthetic. Quaker worldview dominated by tension between commitment and contamination. [LAN]

41.363 Leonard J. Trinterud. *The forming of an American tradition: a re-examination of colonial Presbyterianism.* 1949 ed. Freeport, N.Y.: Books for Libraries, 1970. ISBN 0-8369-5450-5. ▸ American Presbyterianism synthesized from New England and Ulster traditions. Church committed to colonial liberties and toleration. Revolutionary period saw formalization of church structure in General Assembly. Laudatory history. [LAN]

41.364 Conrad Wright. *The beginnings of Unitarianism in America.* 1955 ed. Hamden, Conn.: Archon, 1976. ISBN 0-208-01612-0. ▸ Still useful study tracing Arminian wing of Puritanism as it moved through antitrinitarianism to unitarianism. Good explication of group's economic, social, and cultural ties. [DMS]

SEE ALSO
39.133 Sally Schwartz. *"A mixed multitude."*
39.696 Jack D. Marietta. *The reformation of American Quakerism, 1748–1783.*
39.709 Richard W. Pointer. *Protestant pluralism and the New York experience.*
39.714 George Selement. *Keepers of the vineyard.*
40.723 Jon Butler. *Awash in a sea of faith.*

REGIONAL STUDIES

41.365 John R. Alden. *The South in the Revolution, 1763–1789.* 1957 ed. Baton Rouge: Louisiana State University Press, 1976. ISBN 0-8071-0003-X (cl), 0-8071-0013-7 (pbk). ▸ Thorough, traditional study by leading scholar. Emphasis on growing southern prosperity and importance of South to nation. Concludes Revolution created southern sectional identity and created sectional divisions that lasted until Civil War. [RWS]

41.366 Jeffrey J. Crow and Larry E. Tise, eds. *The southern experience in the American Revolution.* Chapel Hill: University of North Carolina Press, 1978. ISBN 0-8078-1313-3. ▸ Essays on various topics, most important of which affirm North Carolina Regulator movement as class struggle, exploring internal and external challenges to Virginia leadership. [RWS]

41.367 Bruce C. Daniels. *The fragmentation of New England: comparative perspectives on economic, political, and social divisions in the eighteenth century.* Westport, Conn.: Greenwood, 1988. ISBN 0-313-26358-2. ▸ Nine previously published articles focus on social history and Connecticut. Emphasis on heterogeneity, economic development, social trends, and historiography. Useful on New England and trends in social history. [DMS]

41.368 Ronald Hoffman, Thad W. Tate, and Peter J. Albert, eds. *An uncivil war: the southern backcountry during the American Revolution.* Charlottesville: University Press of Virginia, 1985. ISBN 0-8139-1051-X. ▸ Important collection of essays exploring fractious nature of southern backcountries during American Revolution. Challenge to traditional view of backcountry. [RWS]

41.369 John A. Neuenschwander. *The middle colonies and the coming of the American Revolution.* Port Washington, N.Y.: Kennikat, 1974. ISBN 0-8046-9054-5. ▸ Account of role of moderate and conservative whigs in coming of independence. Finds regional consciousness, based on commercialism and ethnic diversity, fully emerged after independence. Good treatment of whig moderates, less successful on regional consciousness. [RWS]

41.370 Norman K. Risjord. *Chesapeake politics, 1781–1800.* New York: Columbia University Press, 1978. ISBN 0-231-04328-7. ▸ Massive study of Maryland, Virginia, and North Carolina's geographic characteristics, major political leaders, and political divisions focusing on major issues that produced political conflict. Rich quantitative reference material. [EVW]

41.371 Max George Schumacher. *The northern farmer and his markets during the late colonial period.* New York: Arno, 1975. ISBN 0-405-07216-3. ▸ Dissertation (1948) focusing on increasing commercial production of wheat, meat, and flaxseed in North. Argues trade profitable, but production handicaps, especially labor, limited farmers' ability to exploit market. [DAR]

SEE ALSO
45.141 Neil MacKinnon. *This unfriendly soil.*

STATES AND CITIES

41.372 John K. Alexander. *Render them submissive: responses to poverty in Philadelphia, 1760–1800.* Amherst: University of Massachusetts Press, 1980. ISBN 0-87023-289-4. ▸ Critique of middle-class democracy seeing class division as central. Elites moved to limit radical egalitarian implications of Revolution, attempting to reform poor, and demanding deference from them. [LAN]

41.373 Charles Albro Barker. *The background of the Revolution in Maryland.* 1940 ed. Hamden, Conn.: Archon, 1967. ▸ Maryland mature, stable, and economically diversified society by Revolution. Argues proprietary tyranny motivation for Revolution. Downplays class conflict; whiggish and proto-consensus study. [RWS]

41.374 Carl L. Becker. *The history of political parties in the province of New York, 1760–1776.* 1909 ed. Madison: University of Wisconsin Press, 1968. ISBN 0-299-02024-X. ▸ Interprets Revolution as struggle over home rule as well as who should rule at home. Describes politicization of masses. Portrayal of dual nature of Revolution gave birth to progressive school. [CMJ]

41.375 Edward Byers. *The "nation of Nantucket": society and politics in an early American commercial center, 1660–1820.* Boston: Northeastern University Press, 1987. ISBN 0-930350-92-8. ▸ Sees Nantucket, founded by refugees fleeing Puritan restrictiveness, illustrative of New England previously ignored. Traces religious, economic, and political developments through decline during Revolution. Important study. [DMS]

41.376 Christopher Clark. *The roots of rural capitalism: western Massachusetts, 1780–1860.* Ithaca, N.Y.: Cornell University Press, 1990. ISBN 0-8014-2422-4. ▸ Traces economic development in agriculture from simple household production to more complex capitalistic system. Sees major change after 1820 enhancing role of merchants and outsiders. Solid study, cognizant of historiographical precedents. [DMS]

41.377 Charles E. Clark, James S. Leamon, and Karen Bowden, eds. *Maine in the early republic: from revolution to statehood.* Hanover, N.H.: University Press of New England for Maine Historical Society, Maine Humanities Council, 1989. ISBN 0-87451-506-8 (cl), 0-87451-424-X (pbk). ▸ Twelve essays by various authors probing all aspects of political, social, and religious history prior to statehood, 1783–1820. Useful exploration of regional history and emerging national culture. [DMS]

41.378 Peter A. Coclanis. *The shadow of a dream: economic life and death in the South Carolina low country, 1670–1920.* 1989 ed. New York: Oxford University Press, 1991. ISBN 0-19-504420-7 (cl, 1989), 0-19-507267-7 (pbk). ▸ Beautifully written regional economic history delineating spectacular rise and fall of important section. Combines history, economics, and geography to produce outstanding, though occasionally compressed, account. [DMS]

41.379 Edward Countryman. *A people in revolution: the American Revolution and political society in New York, 1760–1790.* Baltimore: Johns Hopkins University Press, 1981. ISBN 0-8018-2625-X. ▸ Study of Revolution as democratic movement that reordered New York politics and society. Direct comparison to French and Russian revolutions. Neoprogressive study after Becker (41.374) and Jensen (41.154). [RWS]

41.380 Elaine Forman Crane. *A dependent people: Newport, Rhode Island in the revolutionary era.* New York: Fordham University Press, 1985. ISBN 0-8232-1111-8. ▸ Study of economically interdependent, diverse population. Revolution caused loss of men and British trade that ended prosperity. Useful study in local social and economic history. [RWS]

41.381 Philip A. Crowl. *Maryland during and after the Revolution: a political and economic study.* New York: AMS Press, 1943. ISBN 0-404-61296-2. ▸ Progressive study with emphasis on who should rule at home. Finds Revolution did not bring equality; politics dominated by upper-class gentry, with local economic interest as main issue. Classic, older study. [RWS]

41.382 Alan Dawley. *Class and community: the industrial revolution in Lynn.* Cambridge, Mass.: Harvard University Press, 1976. ISBN 0-674-13390-0 (cl), 0-674-13395-1 (pbk). ▸ Interesting Marxist analysis of shoe industry. Finds workers resisted capitalist oppression. Moving, often valuable; provocative, sometimes combative. [DMS]

41.383 Thomas M. Doerflinger. *A vigorous spirit of enterprise: merchants and economic development in revolutionary Philadelphia.* Chapel Hill: University of North Carolina Press for Institute of Early American History and Culture, 1986. ISBN 0-8078-1653-1. ▸ Well-written, insightful synthesis of economic, cultural, and social history. Philadelphia's unstable economy created atmosphere of competition and risk taking. Merchant entrepreneurship and vision created industrial revolution and constitutional system. [LAN]

41.384 Paul G. Faler. *Mechanics and manufacturers in the early industrial revolution: Lynn, Massachusetts, 1760–1860.* Albany: State University of New York Press, 1981. ISBN 0-87395-504-8 (cl), 0-87395-505-6 (pbk). ▸ Examines emergence of class consciousness among shoe-factory workers. Traces origins to breakdown of traditional apprenticeship system after 1830. Lacks clarity of Dawley's comparable study (41.382). [DAR]

41.385 Ronald P. Formisano. *The transformation of political culture: Massachusetts parties, 1790s–1840s.* 1983 ed. New York: Oxford University Press, 1984. ISBN 0-19-503124-5 (cl, 1983) 0-19-503509-7 (pbk). ▸ Development of postindependence politics in Massachusetts from its unsophisticated, immature nonsystem origins to established two-party system. Rich thematic style embodying much of recent historiography of American political parties. [EVW]

41.386 Robert L. Ganyard. *The emergence of North Carolina's revolutionary state government.* Raleigh: North Carolina Department of Cultural Resources, Division of Archives and History, 1978. (North Carolina bicentennial pamphlet series, 14.) ISBN 0-86526-122-9 (pbk). ▸ Argues that antagonism to local court system and eastern domination created support for revolutionary cause. Internal struggle merged with larger revolutionary effort. Brief, reliable account. [RWS]

41.387 Larry R. Gerlach. *Prologue to independence: New Jersey in the coming of the American Revolution.* New Brunswick, N.J.: Rutgers University Press, 1975. ISBN 0-8135-0801-0. ▸ Little synthesis among diverse population, politics riven by factions. Move toward independence to keep up with larger neighbors. Little on conflict between assembly and governor. [RWS]

41.388 Paul A. Gilje. *The road to mobocracy: popular disorder in New York City, 1763–1834.* Chapel Hill: University of North Carolina Press for Institute of Early American History and Culture, 1987. ISBN 0-8078-1743-0 (cl), 0-8078-4198-6 (pbk). ▸ Insightful, highly regarded study. Concludes community continued its decline. Colonial mob violence contained within true whig political culture. Market economy and ethnic diversity led to explosion of violence in antebellum New York. [LAN]

41.389 Eugene R. Harper. *The transformation of western Pennsylvania, 1770–1800.* Pittsburgh: University of Pittsburgh Press, 1991. ISBN 0-8229-3678-X. ▸ Uses tax records to demonstrate rapid development and resulting class structure, inequality, economic diversity. Dry, narrow study, aimed primarily at scholars. [DMS]

41.390 Ronald Hoffman. *A spirit of dissension: economics, politics, and the Revolution in Maryland.* Baltimore: Johns Hopkins University Press, 1973. ISBN 0-8018-1521-5. ▸ Perspective on Revolution combining economics, stratification of society, and opportunistic politics. Emphasizes that popular support for Revolution cemented by elite's economic concessions to lower orders while still maintaining their dominance through conservative governing institutions. Significant, thorough work. [RWS]

41.391 Daniel P. Jordan. *Political leadership in Jefferson's Virginia.* Charlottesville: University Press of Virginia, 1983. ISBN 0-8139-0967-8. ▸ Interesting analysis of ninety-eight political leaders. Finds state declined rapidly in prestige and power as Virginia's political leaders failed to address problems of dynamic new era. [EVW]

41.392 Rachel N. Klein. *Unification of a slave state: the rise of the planter class in the South Carolina backcountry, 1760–1808.* Chapel Hill: University of North Carolina Press for Institute of Early American History and Culture, 1990. ISBN 0-8078-1899-2. ▸ Explores complex issues within South Carolina backcountry which brought unity among variety of social classes. Discusses settlement, Revolution, republicanism, political unification, and evangelicalism. Important, sophisticated study by young scholar. [DMS]

41.393 Susan E. Klepp. *Philadelphia in transition: a demographic history of the city and its occupational groups, 1720–1830.* New York: Garland, 1989. ISBN 0-8240-4164-X. ▸ Careful, thorough, somewhat speculative study finding occupation critical in determining demographic behavior. Reconstitutes 744 families to detail childbearing, marriage, family size, etc., of urban population. [DMS]

41.394 Benjamin W. Labaree. *Patriots and partisans: the merchants of Newburyport, 1764–1815.* 1962 ed. New York: Norton, 1975. ISBN 0-393-00786-3 (pbk). ▸ Groundbreaking study of local institutions, influential in refocusing attention. Delineates two generations of merchants; dissects interests and politics. Excellent study demonstrating importance of local history. [DMS]

41.395 George R. Lamplugh. *Politics on the periphery: factions and parties in Georgia, 1783–1806.* Newark: University of Delaware Press, 1986. ISBN 0-87413-288-6. ▸ Concludes as region's western lands brought formerly neglected state more importance in defining its own role in new nation, factions in Georgia centered around personalities, not parties or issues. Balanced, well written. [EVW]

41.396 David S. Lovejoy. *Rhode Island politics and the American Revolution, 1760–1776.* 1958 ed. Providence: Brown University Press, 1969. ISBN 0-87057-053-6. ▸ Informative, traditional study of battle for power within elite, threatened by British policy. Namierian view of local and personal nature of factions (cf. 24.28). [RWS]

41.397 Richard Patrick McCormick. *Experiment in independence: New Jersey in the critical period, 1781–1789.* New Brunswick, N.J.: Rutgers University Press, 1950. ▸ Authoritative study based on deep research and careful analysis focusing on economics. Constitution supported to free New Jersey from New York and Philadelphia imposts. Counterrevolution of conservative Quakers after 1789. [RWS]

41.398 James R. Morrill. *The practice and politics of fiat finance: North Carolina in the confederation, 1783–1789.* Chapel Hill: University of North Carolina Press, 1969. ▸ Careful study of confederation era, but does not pursue its subject into constitutional debate. Finds underdeveloped economy put state at disadvantage; currency emissions and antifederalism justified by state interests. Beardian analysis of economic basis of politics. [RWS]

41.399 John A. Munroe. *Federalist Delaware, 1775–1815.* New Brunswick, N.J.: Rutgers University Press, 1954. ▸ Study of political terrain of Delaware; concludes geographic split between New Castle and two lower counties. Finds continued control by gentry and Federalists. No internal revolution. Deeply informed study of unusual state political culture. [RWS]

41.400 Jerome J. Nadelhaft. *The disorders of war: the Revolution in South Carolina.* Orono: University of Maine Press, 1981. ISBN 0-89101-049-1. ▸ Competent, reliable, local study. Local aristocracy unable to contain forces unleashed by Revolution. Sees Constitution of 1790 as victory for backcountry, interpreting Revolution as question of who should rule at home. [RWS]

41.401 Gary B. Nash. *The urban crucible: social change, political consciousness, and the origins of the American Revolution.* 1979 ed. Cambridge, Mass.: Harvard University Press, 1986. ISBN 0-674-93058-4 (cl), 0-674-93059-2 (pbk). ▸ Quantitative urban history of eighteenth-century Boston, Philadelphia, and New York. Finds declining opportunity caused breakdown of community, resulting in class struggle and proletarian radicalism that drove American Revolution. [LAN]

41.402 William Edward Nelson. *Americanization of the common law: the impact of legal change on Massachusetts society, 1760–1830.* Cambridge, Mass.: Harvard University Press, 1975. ISBN 0-674-02970-4 (cl), 0-674-02972-0 (pbk). ▸ Examination of change in Massachusetts law from consensual system before Revolution to system dominated by competing interest groups in early republic. Weaves legal transformation into fabric of wider social change. [CMJ]

41.403 Gregory H. Nobles. *Divisions throughout the whole: politics and society in Hampshire County, Massachusetts, 1740–1775.* Cambridge: Cambridge University Press, 1983. ISBN 0-521-24419-6. ▸ Careful, important study by leading scholar of backcountry of local records and private papers revealing division and discord following Great Awakening. Sees gradual erosion of elite authority culminating in 1774 Coercive Acts. Emphasizes local events, not influence of Boston. [DMS]

41.404 Edward C. Papenfuse. *In pursuit of profit: the Annapolis merchants in the era of the American Revolution, 1763–1805.* Baltimore: Johns Hopkins University Press, 1975. ISBN 0-8018-1573-8. ▸ Careful, thorough business history focused on firm accounts. Concludes Annapolis merchants remained active in international trade during revolutionary era. British reentry into tobacco trade, however, confirmed Baltimore's supremacy; Annapolis receded as commercial center. [LAN]

41.405 Stephen E. Patterson. *Political parties in revolutionary Massachusetts.* Madison: University of Wisconsin Press, 1973. ISBN 0-299-06260-0. ▸ Quantitative, neoprogressive account influenced by Jensen (cf. 41.154). Finds partisan politics based on divisions between East and West and commercial and subsistence interests. Sees growth of democracy in state. Competent, reliable. [RWS]

41.406 Ronald M. Peters, Jr. *The Massachusetts constitution of 1780: a social compact.* Amherst: University of Massachusetts Press, 1978. ISBN 0-87023-143-X. ▸ Microstudy of text concluding compact based on procedural justice, protection of society over individual, and majority rule. Study of ideas independent of context; methods of political philosophy rather than history. [RWS]

41.407 Carl E. Prince. *New Jersey's Jeffersonian Republicans: the genesis of an early party machine, 1789–1817.* Chapel Hill: University of North Carolina Press for Institute of Early American History and Culture, 1967. ▸ Development of party organization in New Jersey, with detailed description of Republican faction. Rich body of data on formation of early party machinery. Also available from Ann Arbor: University Microfilms International. [EVW]

41.408 Whitman H. Ridgway. *Community leadership in Maryland, 1790–1840: a comparative analysis of power in society.* Chapel Hill: University of North Carolina Press, 1979. ISBN 0-8078-1355-9. ▸ Analysis of political leaders and their decision-making patterns in four diverse areas of Maryland during 1790s and 1830s. Applies theoretical model of community power development used by contemporary social scientists. Specialized, somewhat pedestrian. [EVW]

41.409 Howard B. Rock. *Artisans of the new republic: the tradesmen of New York City in the age of Jefferson.* New York: New York University Press, 1979. ISBN 0-8147-7379-6. ▸ Concludes craftworkers embraced Jeffersonian republicanism as promoting political self-esteem and demanded economic freedom against government regulation and volume competition. First stages of industrialization caused tension, organization, and strikes. Competent, sound, if somewhat dated study. [LAN]

41.410 Steven Rosswurm. *Arms, country, and class: the Philadelphia militia and the "lower sort" during the American Revolution.* New Brunswick, N.J.: Rutgers University Press, 1987. ISBN 0-8135-1248-4. ▸ Description of militia as lower-class political vehicle that failed to produce social revolution. Emphasis on class conflict and repression of poor. Marxist historical materialist study. [RWS]

41.411 Billy G. Smith. *The "lower sort": Philadelphia's laboring people, 1750–1800.* Ithaca, N.Y.: Cornell University Press, 1990. ISBN 0-8014-2242-6. ▸ Thoroughly researched, meticulous study of working poor in Philadelphia, before, during, and after Revolution. Documents difficult, economically unstable life of substantial proportion of city's population. [DMS]

41.412 Charles G. Steffen. *The mechanics of Baltimore: workers and politics in the age of revolution, 1763–1812.* Urbana: University of Illinois Press, 1984. ISBN 0-252-01088-4. ▸ New labor history studying creation of mechanic republicanism from craft producers, and citizenship consciousness among artisan class. Political action and class consciousness necessary for successful labor organization. [LAN]

41.413 Charles S. Sydnor. *Gentlemen freeholders: political practices in Washington's Virginia.* 1952 ed. Westport, Conn.: Greenwood, 1984. ISBN 0-313-24385-9. ▸ Praises colonial Virginia political system, in which voters selected first-rate leaders who protected common interests of rich and poor citizens. Describes process in which future revolutionary leaders cut political teeth. Also published as *American Revolutionaries in the Making.* [CMJ]

41.414 David Szatmary. *Shays' Rebellion: the making of an agrarian insurrection.* Amherst: University of Massachusetts Press, 1980. ISBN 0-87023-295-9. ▸ Portrays rebels as radical traditionalists who intended to overthrow government in order to protect traditional society from commercial encroachment. Focus on economic conflict and fundamental social differences of major antagonists. Good early study somewhat superseded by more recent work. [RWS]

41.415 Robert J. Taylor. *Western Massachusetts in the Revolution.* 1954 ed. Millwood, N.Y.: Kraus Reprint, 1974. ISBN 0-527-89075-8. ▸ Politics from Land Bank to Shays' Rebellion, examining conflict between established agrarian interests and emerging commercial class. Sees conflict as harbinger of Jacksonian spirit. Good local study, somewhat dated. Also available on microfilm from Ann Arbor: University Microfilms International. [RWS]

41.416 Tamara Plakins Thornton. *Cultivating gentlemen: the meaning of country life among the Boston elite.* New Haven: Yale University Press, 1989. ISBN 0-300-04256-6. ▸ Explores Boston's business elite's fascination with rural pursuits and development of rustic suburbs. Good analysis of both public and private ventures and broad historical implications. [DMS]

41.417 Lynn Warren Turner. *The ninth state: New Hampshire's formative years.* Chapel Hill: University of North Carolina Press, 1983. ISBN 0-8078-1541-1. ▸ Study of war in Europe and personal leadership as keys to party formation. Shifting political allegiances of seacoast and frontier. Standard political history for 1776–1815. Also available from Ann Arbor: University Microfilms International. [RWS]

41.418 Richard Walsh. *Charleston's sons of liberty: a study of the artisans, 1763–1789.* Columbia: University of South Carolina Press, 1959. ▸ Brief political and economic study of South Carolina's mechanics. Faced English competition and lack of political power. Independently entered revolutionary movement to promote home manufactures and gain political representation. [LAN]

41.419 Conrad Edick Wright. *The transformation of charity in postrevolutionary New England.* Boston: Northeastern University Press, 1992. ISBN 1-55553-1123-7. ▸ Detailed explanation of shift from individual to collective, institutionalized charity. Downplays social control aspects. Thorough appendix lists organizations. For specialists and scholars. [DMS]

SEE ALSO

39.149 Rhys Isaac. *The transformation of Virginia, 1740–1790.*
39.203 Patricia U. Bonomi. *A factious people.*
39.226 James H. Hutson. *Pennsylvania politics, 1746–1770.*
39.361 Carl Bridenbaugh. *Cities in revolt.*
39.363 Carl Bridenbaugh and Jessica Bridenbaugh. *Rebels and gentlemen.*
39.387 George C. Rogers, Jr. *Charleston in the age of the Pinckneys.*

SOCIETY AND ECONOMY

41.420 Bernard Bailyn. *Voyagers to the West: a passage in the peopling of America on the eve of the Revolution.* New York: Knopf; distributed by Random House, 1986. ISBN 0-394-51569-2. ▸ Comprehensive, well-written statistical analysis of brief emigrant registers. Two streams of British settlers: families from Scotland, servants from London. Families settled frontier, servants fed expanding labor market. [LAN]

41.421 Richard D. Brown. *Knowledge is power: the diffusion of information in early America, 1700–1865.* New York: Oxford University Press, 1989. ISBN 0-19-504417-7 (cl), 0-19-507265-0 (pbk). ▸ Explores connection between power and access to, or control over, sources of information, with insightful case studies of ten individuals. By nineteenth century, increased access to information generated diversity, pluralism, and democratization. Good analysis grounded in thoughtful research. [DMS]

41.422 John M. Bumsted. *The people's clearance: highland emigration to British North America, 1770–1815.* 1967 ed. Edinburgh: Edinburgh University Press, 1982. ISBN 0-85224-419-3. ▸ Well-researched, intelligently formulated, readable study of who emigrated from Scotland and why. Combines understanding of individual lives with analysis of broader issues. [DMS]

41.423 Hoyt P. Canady. *Gentlemen of the bar: lawyers in colonial South Carolina.* New York: Garland, 1987. ISBN 0-8240-8254-0. ▸ Unrevised dissertation detailing growth of bar, legal education, and impact of attorneys on business, society, and politics. Readable, useful, specialized study. [DMS]

41.424 Joyce E. Chaplin. *An anxious pursuit: agricultural innovation and modernity in the lower South, 1730–1815.* Chapel Hill: University of North Carolina Press for Institute of Early American History and Culture, 1993. ISBN 0-8078-2084-9. ▸ Explores interaction between white inhabitants and natural environment. Combines intellectual history with agricultural developments and work patterns to explain contradictory tendencies of modernization. Well-written, important, influential work. [DLA]

41.425 Philip Sheldon Foner. *Labor and the American Revolution.* Westport, Conn.: Greenwood, 1976. ISBN 0-8371-9003-7. ▸ Commemorates workers who created American Revolution. Artisans provided backbone of patriotic societies and organized separately. Imperial crisis and war increased distance between employer and employed, leading to working-class consciousness. [LAN]

41.426 Dall W. Forsythe. *Taxation and political change in the young nation, 1781–1833*. New York: Columbia University Press, 1977. ISBN 0-231-04192-6. ▸ Correlates relationship between political change and political development and creates method for classifying and measuring political change. Concise narrative outline of early American tax and revenue policies. [EVW]

41.427 Gerard W. Gawalt. *The promise of power: the emergence of the legal profession in Massachusetts, 1760–1840*. Westport, Conn.: Greenwood, 1979. ISBN 0-313-20612-0, ISSN 0147-1074. ▸ Prosopography of Massachusetts lawyers reveals profession gained status and influence after Revolution despite loss of formal privilege. Emphasizes lawyers' key roles in business and politics and presence in social elite. Useful and detailed, important reassessment of subject. [CMJ]

41.428 Ronald Hoffman et al., eds. *The economy of early America: the revolutionary period, 1763–1790*. Charlottesville: University Press of Virginia for United States Capitol Historical Society, 1988. ISBN 0-8139-1139-7. ▸ Nine papers on diverse aspects of topic. Several authors summarize significant historiographical trends. Good overview of most recent research with suggestions for future work. Aimed at specialists. [DMS]

41.429 Graham Hood. *Bonnin and Morris of Philadelphia: the first American porcelain factory, 1770–1772*. Chapel Hill: University of North Carolina Press for Institute of Early American History and Culture, 1972. ISBN 0-8078-1200-5. ▸ Combines archaeological evidence, understanding of technology, and research in sources and museums to document porcelain production in pre-revolutionary Philadelphia. For specialized audience. [DMS]

41.430 Stephen Innes, ed. *Work and labor in early America*. Chapel Hill: University of North Carolina Press for Institute of Early American History and Culture, 1988. ISBN 0-8078-1798-8 (cl), 0-8078-4236-2 (pbk). ▸ Product of new interest in labor. Seven historians probe both traditional and nontraditional aspects of neglected group. Good, solid collection reflecting best in social history. [DMS]

41.431 David J. Jeremy. *Transatlantic industrial revolution: the diffusion of textile technologies between Britain and America, 1790–1830s*. Cambridge, Mass.: MIT Press for Merrimack Valley Textile Museum, 1981. ISBN 0-262-10022-3. ▸ Excellent study based on painstaking research. Concerned primarily with mechanism of technological diffusion and origins of American factory system. Important for anyone interested in subject. [DMS]

41.432 Alice Hanson Jones. *Wealth of a nation to be: the American colonies on the eve of the Revolution*. New York: Columbia University Press, 1980. ISBN 0-231-03659-0. ▸ Detailed survey of wealth categories and stratification in 1774: South wealthiest, New England poorest. General trend of economic growth gives standard of living equal or superior to Europe. [LAN]

41.433 Darwin P. Kelsey, ed. *Farming in the new nation: interpreting American agriculture, 1790–1840*. Washington, D.C.: Agricultural History Society, 1972. ▸ Collection of conference papers. Topics include historiography, science and technology, agricultural change, and agricultural history museums. Opens new questions but does not supersede classic surveys. [LAN]

41.434 Jackson Turner Main. *The social structure of revolutionary America*. 1965 ed. Princeton: Princeton University Press, 1969. ISBN 0-691-00562-1. ▸ Argues social and economic stratification less rigid than Europe and varied by region, with significant mobility between lower and middle classes. Quantitative study verifying standing assumptions about era's social structure. Photocopy also available from Ann Arbor: University Microfilms International. [DAR]

41.435 Cathy D. Matson and Peter S. Onuf. *A union of interests: political and economic thought in revolutionary America*. Lawrence: University Press of Kansas, 1990. ISBN 0-7006-0417-0. ▸ Stresses importance of local, conflicting, economic interests in development of federal system. Reverses Beard 41.185 by portraying founders as expanding economic opportunities in order to reconcile regional differences. Wide-ranging, original work; somewhat abstract in style. [DMS]

41.436 Douglass Cecil North. *The economic growth of the United States, 1790–1860*. 1961 ed. New York: Norton, 1966. ISBN 0-393-00346-9 (pbk). ▸ Focus on exports and carrying trade as determinants of economic growth. More essay than history; provides most comprehensive economic analysis of period. [DMS]

41.437 Malcolm J. Rohrbough. *The land office business: the settlement and administration of American public lands, 1789–1837*. 1968 ed. Belmont, Calif.: Wadsworth, 1990. ISBN 0-534-12324-4 (pbk). ▸ Thorough, reliable study of survey and sale procedures through official records and public sources. Finds both federal and state offices understaffed and corruptible and legal systems ill-constructed. Standard work on subject. [LAN]

41.438 W. J. Rorabaugh. *The craft apprentice: from Franklin to the machine age in America*. New York: Oxford University Press, 1986. ISBN 0-19-503647-6. ▸ Good, readable history of decline of an economic institution. Collapse of apprenticeship in antebellum America result of democratization of craft knowledge that undermined hierarchy and industrialization. Machines created labor glut, social dislocation, and industrial anomie. Only study of subject. [LAN]

41.439 Lee Soltow. *Distribution of wealth and income in the United States in 1798*. Pittsburgh: University of Pittsburgh Press, 1989. ISBN 0-8229-3620-8. ▸ Important book measuring distribution of wealth among classes. Supports recent studies showing significant inequality in property distribution. Sophisticated statistical analysis beyond most readers. Significant contribution. [DMS]

41.440 Thomas M. Truxes. *Irish-American trade, 1660–1783*. Cambridge: Cambridge University Press, 1989. ISBN 0-521-35373-4. ▸ Demonstrates importance of Irish-American trade, previously given little attention. Systematic, detailed discussion of each aspect and period. Extensive research, fills important gap. [DMS]

41.441 Barbara M. Tucker. *Samuel Slater and the origins of the American textile industry, 1790–1860*. Ithaca, N.Y.: Cornell University Press, 1984. ISBN 0-8014-1594-2. ▸ Case study of Slater's mill system. Argues industrialization did not destroy colonial social institutions; rather they molded Slater's labor and production system, helping reinforce extant gender roles and religious authority. Revisionist study; rejects class consciousness. [DAR]

SEE ALSO
39.290 Alan F. Day. *A social study of lawyers in Maryland, 1660–1775.*

PRINTING, LITERATURE, AND THE ARTS

41.442 Hennig Cohen. *The South Carolina Gazette, 1732–1775*. Columbia: University of South Carolina Press, 1953. ▸ Account of paper and its editors. Argues close connection with European cultural influences, replications of which are evidenced in *Gazette*. Revolutionary War disrupted system, breaking English ties, and as result culture declined. Careful, reliable, specialized. [DAR]

41.443 Kathryn Zabelle Derounian-Stodola, ed. *Early American literature and culture: essays honoring Harrison T. Meserole*. Newark: University of Delaware Press, 1992. ISBN 0-87413-423-4. ▸ Careful, interesting, diverse articles ranging in focus from promotional tracts to autobiography to poetry, by fourteen scholars. Enlightening on many topics; something for everyone. [DMS]

41.444 Helmut von Effra and Allen Staley. *The paintings of Ben-*

jamin West. New Haven: Yale University Press, 1986. ISBN 0-300-03355-9. ▸ First systematic catalog and analysis of West's work, documenting 739 pieces. Outstanding work, beautifully illustrated, model of art historical scholarship. Urbane, informative text tracing West's career over seventy years. Includes paintings and important drawings. [DAR/DMS]

41.445 Joseph J. Ellis. *After the Revolution: profiles of early American culture*. New York: Norton, 1979. ISBN 0-393-01253-0. ▸ Examination of postrevolutionary artistic community. Finds it afflicted with divided loyalties and imperatives: public virtue versus entrepreneurial motives, aesthetic judgments versus popular tastes. Resulted in inability to produce large group of cultural leaders. Important contribution, well written and readable. [DAR]

41.446 Norman S. Grabo. *The coincidental art of Charles Brockden Brown*. Chapel Hill: University of North Carolina Press, 1981. ISBN 0-8078-1474-1. ▸ Literary analysis of Brown's major works, ca. 1797–1801. Employs analytic concept of doubleness to Brown's narrative structures to make argument that flaws of coincidence evince patterns of self-discovery. Well-written study of minor figure. [DAR]

41.447 Bruce Granger. *American essay serials from Franklin to Irving*. Knoxville: University of Tennessee Press, 1978. ISBN 0-87049-221-7. ▸ Explores popularity and social criticism of essay serials beginning with Benjamin Franklin's "Silence Dogood." Careful, thorough, sensitive study. Elegant prose makes fascinating reading. [DMS]

41.448 Neil Harris. *The artist in American society: the formative years, 1790–1860*. 1966 ed. Chicago: Chicago University Press, 1982. ISBN 0-226-31754-4 (pbk). ▸ Probes role of artist during early years of republic. Ambitious, widely researched, and fresh, if somewhat uneven, approach. Extensive collection of ideas and information; not always readable. [DMS]

41.449 Daniel F. Havens. *The Columbian muse of comedy: the development of a native tradition in early American social comedy, 1787–1845*. Carbondale: Southern Illinois University Press, 1973. ISBN 0-8093-0609-3. ▸ Primarily theatrical history of questionable validity. Some criticism useful but small choice of plays unexplained. No discussion of European context. [DMS]

41.450 Irma B. Jaffe. *John Trumbull: patriot-artist of the American Revolution*. Boston: New York Graphic Society, 1975. ISBN 0-8212-0459-9. ▸ Insightful, balanced study of both art and life of painter who looms large in cultural history of United States. [DMS]

41.451 Richard Klayman. *America abandoned: John Singleton Copley's American years, 1738–1774; an interpretative history*. Lanham, Md.: University Press of America, 1983. ISBN 0-8191-3338-8 (cl), 0-8191-3339-6 (pbk). ▸ Social history attempts to place Copley's career as artist in context of prerevolutionary Boston. Important new direction falls short of mark. [DMS]

41.452 Peter Martin. *The pleasure gardens of Virginia: from Jamestown to Jefferson*. Princeton: Princeton University Press, 1991. ISBN 0-691-04786-3. ▸ Readable, interesting survey of neglected aspect of art history. Competent, thorough description of town gardens and rural plantations. Recommended for students of American material culture and garden historians. [DMS]

41.453 John P. McWilliams, Jr. *The American epic: transforming a genre, 1770–1860*. New York: Cambridge University Press, 1989. ISBN 0-521-37322-0. ▸ Perceptive, provocative study opening new perspectives on connection between literature and politics. Traces evolution of heroic epic from Revolution to Civil War; sees culture influencing writers. [DMS]

41.454 Lillian B. Miller. *Patrons and patriotism: the encouragement of fine arts in the United States, 1790–1860*. Chicago: University of Chicago Press, 1966. ▸ Discussion of public and private

support for arts; surveys and describes important organizations and individuals. Specialists will find directions to more detailed sources. [DMS]

41.455 Barbara Obrerg and Harry S. Stout. *Benjamin Franklin, Jonathan Edwards, and the representation of American culture*. New York: Oxford University Press, 1993. ISBN 0-19-507775-X. ▸ Twelve papers by contemporary scholars examine mind, culture, and language of two archetypal figures. Excellent essays explore subtleties and undermine concept of two antagonistic worldviews. Useful, interesting, provocative volume. [DLA]

41.456 Susan L. Porter. *With an air debonair: musical theatre in America, 1785–1815*. Washington, D.C.: Smithsonian Institution Press, 1991. ISBN 1-56098-063-X. ▸ Detailed, thoroughly researched study highlighting role of musical theater in early America. Describes history and role, but major portion will appeal primarily to music and theater scholars. [DMS]

41.457 Frank Luther Mott. *A history of American magazines*. Vol. 1: *1741–1850*. 1930 ed. Cambridge, Mass.: Harvard University Press, 1970. ISBN 0-674-39550-6. ▸ Seminal compendium tracing development of magazines examining 600 titles. Focuses on editing, management, distribution, and content. Argues for impact of content in forming reading public, especially through democratic ideology. [DAR]

41.458 Jules David Prown. *John Singleton Copley*. 2 vols. Cambridge, Mass.: Harvard University Press for National Gallery of Art, 1966. ▸ Prodigious effort brings together gold mine of information, exhaustive list of artist's work, extensive reproductions. More catalog than analysis; still major contribution. [DMS]

41.459 Edgar P. Richardson, Brooke Hindle, and Lillian B. Miller. *Charles Wilson Peale and his world*. New York: Abrams, 1983. ISBN 0-8109-1478-6. ▸ Exhibition catalog with excellent essays by three specialists. Beautifully illustrated, useful for anyone interested in American art, culture, or science. [DMS]

41.460 Charles Coleman Sellers. *Charles Willson Peale*. New York: Scribner's, 1969. ▸ Minutely detailed study of artist, loaded with facts, primarily useful as reference work. Good index. [DMS]

41.461 Michael Warner. *The letters of the republic: publications and the public sphere in eighteenth-century America*. Cambridge, Mass.: Harvard University Press, 1990. ISBN 0-674-52785-2. ▸ Interesting, persuasive account of transformation wrought by printed word in mid-eighteenth century of discourse, from traditional, status-based authority to modern, impersonal public sphere. Illuminates study of republicanism. [DMS]

41.462 Edwin Wolf II. *The book culture of a colonial American city: Philadelphia books, bookmen, and booksellers*. Oxford: Clarendon, 1988. ISBN 0-19-818406-9. ▸ Thorough, detailed study of books Philadelphians read, when they read them, and where they got them. Avowedly noninterpretive but gold mine of specific information. [DMS]

41.463 Larzer Ziff. *Writing in the new nation: prose, print, and politics in the early United States*. New Haven: Yale University Press, 1991. ISBN 0-300-05040-2. ▸ Provocative study focusing on Jonathan Edwards and Benjamin Franklin to illustrate move from oral to written culture and its effects. Important for serious students of American culture. [DMS]

SCIENCE AND EDUCATION

41.464 Larry L. Burkhart. *The good fight: medicine in colonial Pennsylvania*. New York: Garland, 1989. ISBN 0-8240-3395-7. ▸ Detailed examination of role of ministers, apothecaries, surgeons, and physicians, citing importance of European practitioner immigrants. Finds Pennsylvania most medically advanced area in North America. [DMS]

41.465 Lawrence Arthur Cremin. *American education: the national experience, 1783–1876.* 1980 ed. New York: Harper & Row, 1982. ISBN 0-06-090921-8. ‣ Comprehensive, richly detailed, important for anyone interested in period. Explores household, church, school, and newspapers as well as museums, libraries, and fairs. Outstanding study. [DMS]

41.466 J. Worth Estes. *Hall Jackson and the purple foxglove: medical practice and research in revolutionary America, 1760–1820.* Hanover, N.H.: University Press of New England, 1979. ISBN 0-87451-173-9. ‣ Traces career of prominent New Hampshire physician, illustrating medical practice (particularly in military hospitals, ca. 1781–82) and research into new treatments, especially Jackson's introduction of digitalis to America. Meticulous study by knowledgeable author. [DAR]

41.467 John C. Greene. *American science in the age of Jefferson.* Ames: Iowa State University Press, 1984. ISBN 0-8138-0101-X (cl), 0-8138-0102-8 (pbk). ‣ Excellent study of intellectual attitudes toward science in early national period by historian with impressive knowledge and understanding. Comprehensive, analytical, encyclopedic. Important contribution. [DMS]

41.468 Brooke Hindle. *David Rittenhouse.* 1964 ed. New York: Arno, 1980. ISBN 0-405-12569-0. ‣ Definitive, full-length biography of outstanding Pennsylvania scientist and president of American Philosophical Society. Well-documented, reliable, significant contribution. [DMS]

41.469 Brooke Hindle. *The pursuit of science in revolutionary America, 1735–1789.* Chapel Hill: University of North Carolina Press for Institute of Early American History and Culture, 1956. ‣ Outstanding, sound discussion of various scientific fields; documents impact of Revolution on scientific independence and maturity. Important to both science and intellectual history. [DMS]

41.470 Carl F. Kaestle. *The evolution of an urban school system: New York City, 1750–1850.* Cambridge: Harvard University Press, 1973. ISBN 0-674-27175-0. ‣ Solid, informative study following development from informal, private operation to full-fledged, modern public school system. Focus on efforts of Free School Society to further cultural assimilation. [DMS]

41.471 Herbert Leventhal. *In the shadow of the Enlightenment: occultism and Renaissance science in eighteenth-century America.* New York: New York University Press, 1976. ISBN 0-8147-4965-8. ‣ Interesting, reliable attempt to show continuing importance of non-Enlightenment beliefs and attitudes. Slight modifications do not alter conventional interpretation. [DMS]

41.472 Mark A. Noll. *Princeton and the republic, 1768–1822: the search for a Christian enlightenment in the era of Samuel Stanhope Smith.* Princeton: Princeton University Press, 1989. ISBN 0-691-04764-2. ‣ Detailed consideration of Princetonian education and intellectual climate relating to politics, religion, philosophy, etc. Focus on reduced religious interest and rise of science under university president Smith and attempted reversal under successor, Ashbel Green. [DMS]

41.473 Steven J. Novak. *The rights of youth: American colleges and student revolt, 1798–1815.* Cambridge, Mass.: Harvard University Press, 1977. ISBN 0-674-77016-1. ‣ Brief, graceful, insightful study delineating student unrest and conservative reaction during early nineteenth century. Conclusions sometimes overreach evidence. Well worth reading. [DMS]

41.474 David W. Robson. *Educating republicans: the college in the era of the American Revolution, 1750–1800.* Westport, Conn.: Greenwood, 1985. ISBN 0-313-24606-8. ‣ Review of politicization and transformation of colonial colleges into republican institutions. Downplays conservative, religious, and anti-Jeffersonian

remnants. Provocative reminder of ties between education and politics. [DMS]

41.475 John S. Whitehead. *The separation of college and state: Columbia, Dartmouth, Harvard, and Yale, 1776–1876.* New Haven: Yale University Press, 1973. ISBN 0-300-01606-9. ‣ Insightful, controversial discussion of public versus private status of four colonial colleges in century after independence. Downplays public-private distinction during nineteenth century. [DMS]

41.476 William H. Williams. *America's first hospital: the Pennsylvania Hospital, 1751–1841.* Wayne, Pa.: Haverford House, 1976. ISBN 0-910702-02-0. ‣ Concise, well-organized, imaginative work based on extensive documents. Puts hospital into broader context of changing medical patterns. [DMS]

41.477 Neil Longley York. *Mechanical metamorphosis.* Westport, Conn.: Greenwood, 1985. ISBN 0-313-24475-8. ‣ Excellent introduction discussing major inventors and inventions. Thorough research complements knowledge of technology. Sees Revolution, in part, as quest for technological independence. Interesting. [DMS]

SEE ALSO
4.359 Brooke Hindle. *Technology in early America.*
39.746 Kenneth A. Lockridge. *Literacy in colonial New England.*

AFRICAN AMERICANS

41.478 Ira Berlin. *Slaves without masters: the free Negro in the antebellum South.* 1974 ed. New York: Oxford University Press, 1981. ISBN 0-19-502905-4 (pbk). ‣ Broad-based study of fifteen states, focused on culture and organization of black community. Finds changing conditions and regional differences. Significant social history. [DMS]

41.479 Ira Berlin and Ronald Hoffman, eds. *Slavery and freedom in the age of the American Revolution.* 1983 ed. Urbana: University of Illinois Press for United States Capitol Historical Society, 1986. ISBN 0-252-01363-8 (pbk). ‣ Essay collection surveying African American life and society. Topics include demography, regional differentiation, free black life, and African American culture, religion, and families. [LAN]

41.480 Ira Berlin and Philip D. Morgan, eds. *Cultivation and culture: labor and the shaping of slave life in the Americas.* Charlottesville: University Press of Virginia for Carter G. Woodson Institute in Black Studies, 1993. ISBN 0-8139-1421-3 (cl), 0-8139-1424-8 (pbk). ‣ Eleven essays explore aspects of labor and slavery. Emphasis on ability of slaves to establish control of their lives despite obstacles. Excellent collaborative work by contemporary scholars. [DLA]

41.481 Ira Berlin and Philip D. Morgan, eds. *The slave's economy: independent production by slaves in the Americas.* London: Cass, 1991. ISBN 0-7146-3435-0 (cl), 0-7146-3436-0 (pbk). ‣ Eight essays focusing on how slaves worked for themselves within both Caribbean and mainland North American slave system. Successfully demonstrates gaps in not-so-monolithic institution. Aimed at students and scholars. [DMS]

41.482 Margaret Washington Creel. *A peculiar people: slave religion and community culture among the Gullahs.* 1987 ed. New York: New York University Press, 1989. ISBN 0-8147-1404-8 (cl, 1987), 0-8147-1422-6 (pbk). ‣ Finds African beliefs shaped religion of slaves in Georgia and South Carolina sea islands. Whites not eager to instruct blacks on Christianity; slaves used religion to develop culture of resistance. Interesting, not always persuasive. [DMS]

41.483 David Brion Davis. *The problem of slavery in the age of revolution, 1770–1823.* Ithaca, N.Y.: Cornell University Press, 1975. ISBN 0-8014-0888-1. ‣ Important, influential study discovering ideological underpinnings of Atlantic abolitionist movement. Movement served to morally justify free-labor ideology and exploitation of emerging capitalist order. Cultural Marxist analysis by outstanding scholar. [LAN]

41.484 Olaudah Equiano. *The life of Olaudah Equiano, or, Gustavus Vassa, the African.* 1837 ed. Paul Edwards, ed. New York: Negro Universities Press, 1969. ISBN 0-8371-1839-5. ▸ Classic autobiography by African, enslaved and brought to North America where he traveled extensively and recorded nearly forty years of experiences. Insightful, fascinating account, useful to both scholar and general reader. [DMS]

41.485 James D. Essig. *Bonds of wickedness: American evangelicals against slavery, 1770–1808.* Philadelphia: Temple University Press, 1982. ISBN 0-87722-282-7. ▸ Biographical study of four who linked evangelical Christianity with abolition. Evangelicalism accommodated slavery during early national period, but antislavery preachers, not Quakers or deistic Republicans, laid foundations of abolition. Good study, both interesting and readable. [LAN]

41.486 Leland Ferguson. *Uncommon ground: archaeology and early African America, 1650–1800.* Washington, D.C.: Smithsonian Institution Press, 1992. ISBN 1-56098-058-3 (cl), 1-56098-059-1 (pbk). ▸ Readable, interesting study of African American archaeology exploring material culture, especially colono ware ceramics. Shows African impact and social and ideological implications. Focus on people, not artifacts. [DMS]

41.487 Paul Finkelman. *An imperfect Union: slavery, federalism, and comity.* Chapel Hill: University of North Carolina Press, 1981. ISBN 0-8078-1438-5 (cl), 0-8078-4066-1 (pbk). ▸ Study of legal conflict that arose over slave transit in northern states and territories, 1787–1860. Solidly researched constitutional controversy. [EVW]

41.488 Sylvia R. Frey. *Water from the rock: black resistance in a revolutionary age.* Princeton: Princeton University Press, 1991. ISBN 0-691-04784-7 (cl), 0-691-00626-1 (pbk). ▸ Sees military revolutionary struggle as triangular, involving not just white Americans and British but also slaves. Argues black liberation movement was central to Revolution. Provocative, readable, revisionist work. [DLA]

41.489 James Hugo Johnston. *Race relations in Virginia and miscegenation in the South, 1776–1860.* Amherst: University of Massachusetts Press, 1970. ISBN 0-87023-050-6. ▸ Dissertation (1937) challenging facile images of African Americans then prevalent. Argues interracial relations, especially sexual, were more complex and varied (often ambiguous) than believed. Anticipates 1960s scholarship on slavery. [DAR]

41.490 Staughton Lynd. *Class conflict, slavery, and the United States Constitution: ten essays.* 1968 ed. Westport, Conn.: Greenwood, 1980. ISBN 0-313-22672-5. ▸ Good example of nontraditional approach seeing economic factors as key to historical change and development of southern sectionalism. Interprets Civil War as second revolution. New Left approach attacking stale dichotomy between capitalism and agriculture. [RWS]

41.491 Duncan J. Macleod. *Slavery, race, and the American Revolution.* London: Cambridge University Press, 1974. ISBN 0-521-20502-6 (cl), 0-521-09877-7 (pbk). ▸ Significant, challenging study of relationship between revolutionary creed of freedom and equality and institution of race slavery. Inconsistency of doctrine and practice led to tensions over race relations, free blacks, and emancipation. [LAN]

41.492 Robert McColley. *Slavery and Jeffersonian Virginia.* 2d ed. Urbana: University of Illinois Press, 1973. ISBN 0-252-00346-2 (cl), 0-252-00347-0 (pbk). ▸ Debunks myths that slavery was profitable, expanding institution and that there was little desire for abolition among slaveholding classes. Some anecdotal statistics added to legal-political study. [LAN]

41.493 Gary B. Nash. *Forging freedom: the formation of Philadelphia's black community, 1720–1840.* 1988 ed. Cambridge, Mass.: Harvard University Press, 1991. ISBN 0-674-30934-0 (cl, 1988), 0-674-30933-2 (pbk). ▸ Thoroughly researched study of black urban society, compelling both as narrative and analysis. Good discussion of developing black community. First-rate work, important subject. [DMS]

41.494 William D. Piersen. *Black yankees: the development of an Afro-American subculture in eighteenth-century New England.* Amherst: University of Massachusetts Press, 1988. ISBN 0-87023-586-9 (cl), 0-87023-587-7 (pbk). ▸ Combines history and folklore to illuminate development of unique culture and refusal of blacks to fully assimilate. Combines scanty sources with understanding of oral tradition and custom. Good, new dimension. [DMS]

41.495 Benjamin Quarles. *Black mosaic; essays in Afro-American history and historiography.* Amherst: University of Massachusetts Press, 1988. ISBN 0-87023-604-0 (cl), 0-87023-605-9 (pbk). ▸ Twelve articles by dean of African American historians treating Civil War, Revolution, and abolitionist movement. Documents long career of groundbreaking historian's legacy. [DMS]

41.496 Benjamin Quarles. *The Negro in the American Revolution.* 1961 ed. New York: Norton, 1973. ISBN 0-393-00674-3. ▸ Standard, pioneering survey of role of black soldiers in contending armies. When manpower ran low, blacks performed many military functions. Many sought freedom through army service. [LAN]

41.497 Donald L. Robinson. *Slavery in the structure of American politics, 1765–1820.* 1970 ed. New York: Norton, 1979. ISBN 0-393-00913-0. ▸ Challenges view that Founders believed slavery disappearing. Argues issue was central to American political development, left unresolved because of its divisiveness. Builds on Davis 41.483. [DAR]

41.498 Lester B. Scherer. *Slavery and the churches in early America, 1619–1819.* Grand Rapids, Mich.: Eerdmans, 1975. ISBN 0-8028-1580-4. ▸ Brief synthesis of secondary work finding antislavery sentiment not widespread. Argues abolitionist thought often reflected racist attitudes. Little missionary activity undertaken among slaves, who retained African observances. [LAN]

41.499 Philip J. Schwarz. *Twice condemned: slaves and the criminal laws of Virginia, 1705–1865.* Baton Rouge: Louisiana State University Press, 1988. ISBN 0-8071-1401-4. ▸ Focus on slave trials spotlights conflict between slaves and dominant whites. Considers slave motives, white fears. Valuable study expanding understanding of slave system and changes over time. [DMS]

41.500 James W. St. G. Walker. *The black loyalists: the search for a promised land in Nova Scotia and Sierra Leone, 1783–1870.* 1976 ed. Toronto: University of Toronto Press, 1992. ISBN 0-8020-7402-2. ▸ Explores creolized culture of black loyalists in Nova Scotia. Culture that emerged in Sierra Leone similar to free American blacks in same time period. Best study of subject. [RWS]

41.501 Shane White. *Somewhat more independent: the end of slavery in New York City, 1770–1810.* Athens: University of Georgia Press, 1991. ISBN 0-8203-1245-2. ▸ Important account of transformation both for African Americans and New York City. Illuminates role of blacks and whites in emancipation; powerfully explores emerging free black society. [DMS]

41.502 William M. Wiecek. *The sources of antislavery constitutionalism in America, 1760–1848.* Ithaca, N.Y.: Cornell University Press, 1977. ISBN 0-8014-1089-4. ▸ Good overview of constitutional positions taken by various groups vis-à-vis federal government's role in question of slavery. Masterly, comprehensive constitutional and intellectual history. [DMS]

41.503 Ellen Gibson Wilson. *The loyal blacks.* New York: Putnam, 1976. ISBN 0-399-11683-4. ‣ Social history attempting to recreate sense of black lives; focus on individuals. When Nova Scotia failed to fulfill expectations, black loyalists emigrated to Sierra Leone. For general reader. [RWS]

41.504 Betty Wood. *Slavery in colonial Georgia, 1730–1775.* Athens: University of Georgia Press, 1984. ISBN 0-8203-0687-8. ‣ Explores debate over introduction of slavery into Georgia. Focus on white owners rather than African Americans. Clear, thoroughly informed study. [DMS]

41.505 Arthur Zilversmit. *The first emancipation: the abolition of slavery in the North.* Chicago: University of Chicago Press, 1967. ISBN 0-226-98332-3 (pbk). ‣ Traditional survey, somewhat dated, of role of key individuals in creating legislative and ideological abolition of northern slavery. Concludes ideology took precedence over economic considerations. [LAN]

WOMEN AND THE FAMILY

41.506 Charles W. Akers. *Abigail Adams: an American woman.* Boston: Library of American Biography; distributed by Scott, Foresman, 1980. ISBN 0-673-39318-6 (pbk). ‣ Good introduction with focus on Adams as participant in husband's political life. Interesting view of early Federalist period. [DMS]

41.507 Jeanne Boydston. *Home and work: housework, wages, and the ideology of labor in the early republic.* New York: Oxford University Press, 1990. ISBN 0-19-506009-1. ‣ Women in early republic found unpaid labor denigrated by liberal capitalism. With only wage labor seen as work, role of women actually declined after Revolution. Well researched and written, interesting and scholarly. [DMS]

41.508 Joy Day Buel and Richard Buel, Jr. *The way of duty: a woman and her family in revolutionary America.* New York: Norton, 1984. ISBN 0-393-01767-2 (cl), 0-393-30225-3 (pbk). ‣ Biography of Mary Fish of Connecticut, mother of Benjamin Silliman. Concludes eighteenth-century women took advantage of commercialization to expand cultural horizons. Fish remained child of Puritanism rather than Revolution. Readable, interesting, insightful study. [LAN]

41.509 Nancy F. Cott. *The bonds of womanhood: "women's sphere" in New England, 1780–1835.* New Haven: Yale University Press, 1977. ISBN 0-300-02023-6 (cl), 0-300-02289-1 (pbk). ‣ Sees gender segregation leading to women's bonding together for identity and support. Thoroughly researched, well documented, informative, provocative. Superior gender history. [DMS]

41.510 Toby L. Ditz. *Property and kinship: inheritance in early Connecticut, 1750–1820.* Princeton: Princeton University Press, 1986. ISBN 0-691-04735-9. ‣ Quantitative analysis of probate records and land deeds showing favored preferential partibility with use rights and legacies to other heirs. Commercialization led to equal treatment of heirs based on state market value. Reliable, specialized, sometimes difficult to read. [LAN]

41.511 Bernard Farber. *Guardians of virtue: Salem families in 1800.* New York: Basic Books, 1972. ISBN 0-465-02784-9. ‣ Theoretical study of New England family structure. Carries issues of extended families, biblical models of patriarchal governance, and economic relationships though era of commercialization and class stratification. [LAN]

41.512 Ronald Hoffman and Peter J. Albert, eds. *Women in the age of the American Revolution.* Charlottesville: University Press of Virginia for United States Capitol Historical Society, 1989. ISBN 0-8139-1216-4 (cl), 0-8139-1240-7 (pbk). ‣ Twelve essays on varied aspects of roles and status of women in eighteenth cen-

tury, emphasis on American Revolution. Discussions of race, religion, and class. Diverse and well written, they illuminate trends and point to further studies. [DMS]

41.513 Janet Wilson James. *Changing ideas about women in the United States, 1776–1825.* New York: Garland, 1981. ISBN 0-8240-4858-X. ‣ Thorough survey of prescriptive literature for period. More summary than synthesis; lacks clear thesis. Publication of 1954 dissertation. [LAN]

41.514 Linda K. Kerber. *Women of the republic: intellect and ideology in revolutionary America.* Chapel Hill: University of North Carolina Press for Institute of Early American History and Culture, 1980. ISBN 0-8078-1440-7 (cl), 0-8078-4065-3 (pbk). ‣ Study of women, excluded from active role in new republic, who created new role, republican mother; authors' term and paradigm. Stimulated debate and subsequent literature on women's status in early republic. [LAN]

41.515 Suzanne Lebsock. *The free women of Petersburg: status and culture in a southern town, 1784–1860.* 1984 ed. New York: Norton, 1985. ISBN 0-393-01738-9 (cl, 1984), 0-393-95264-9 (pbk). ‣ Illuminates broad picture by careful, precise study of particulars in single community. Finds women's views of property, family, slavery, death, etc., different from those of men. Readable, with wide audience appeal. Introduced concept of particular women's culture; now much debated. [DMS]

41.516 Jan Lewis. *The pursuit of happiness: family and values in Jefferson's Virginia.* Cambridge: Cambridge University Press, 1983. ISBN 0-521-25306-3. ‣ Study of emotional world of gentry. Eighteenth-century Virginians sought independence in public sphere. Commercialization made public realm dangerous and postrevolution generation sought fulfillment in family and home. Readable, important work throwing new light on old topics. [LAN]

41.517 Mary Beth Norton. *Liberty's daughters: the revolutionary experience of American women, 1750–1800.* 1980 ed. Glenview, Ill.: Scott, Foresman, 1988. ISBN 0-673-39348-8 (pbk). ‣ Survey of women's roles in eighteenth-century America. Female sphere was domestic and limiting. Finds republicanism politicized domesticity and gave women more freedom. [LAN]

41.518 Merril D. Smith. *Breaking the bonds: marital discord in Pennsylvania, 1730–1830.* New York: New York University Press, 1991. ISBN 0-8147-7934-4. ‣ Explores causes of and solutions to disharmony, with focus on both traditional concepts and newly emerging marital expectations, gender roles. Readable, richly detailed synthesis from diverse sources. [DMS]

41.519 Laurel Thatcher Ulrich. *A midwife's tale: the life of Martha Ballard, based on her diary, 1785–1812.* 1990 ed. New York: Vintage, 1991. ISBN 0-679-73376-0 (pbk). ‣ Perceptive, readable analysis of rare diary touching on personal, business, and community life of representative woman. Thoughtful reconstruction of diary illuminates life in post-revolutionary New England community. [DMS]

41.520 Lynn Withey. *Dearest friend: a life of Abigail Adams.* New York: Free Press, 1981. ISBN 0-02-934760-2. ‣ Written for popular audience. Views subject from twentieth-century perspective, follows Adams in relation to her husband. [DMS]

SEE ALSO
    40.440 Joan M. Jensen. *Loosening the bonds.*
    42.609 Christine Stansell. *City of women.*

BIOGRAPHY

41.521 Robert Alberts. *Benjamin West: a biography.* Boston: Houghton-Mifflin, 1978. ISBN 0-395-26289-5. ‣ Thoroughly researched, lengthy, sometimes too-detailed study of artist focusing on role in community. Not for general reader. [DMS]

41.522 John R. Alden. *General Charles Lee: traitor or patriot.* Baton Rouge: Louisiana State University Press, 1951. ‣ Full biography emphasizing debate over allegations of treason; biased toward Lee. Heavily detailed but readable. Valuable to anyone interested in period and military history. [DMS]

41.523 John R. Alden. *George Washington: a biography.* 1984 ed. New York: Dell, 1987. ISBN 0-440-32836-5 (pbk). ‣ Brief, sprightly overview. Well balanced, carefully crafted. Highly recommended one-volume biography. [DMS]

41.524 John R. Alden. *Stephen Sayer: American revolutionary adventurer.* Baton Rouge: Louisiana State University Press, 1983. ISBN 0-8071-1067-1. ‣ Only biography of ambitious American engaged in international adventures, from Russia to Prussia to Edmond Genêt's mission. Good reading, adds to understanding of revolutionary era. [DMS]

41.525 Harry Ammon. *James Monroe: the quest for national identity.* 1971 ed. Charlottesville: University Press of Virginia, 1990. ISBN 0-8139-1266-0 (pbk). ‣ Solid, well-written, carefully researched, standard biography. Combines original work with contributions of others. [DMS]

41.526 A. J. Ayer. *Thomas Paine.* 1988 ed. Chicago: University of Chicago Press, 1990. ISBN 0-226-03339-2. ‣ Analyzes Paine's thought, political philosophy, and religious outlook. Ahistorical approach ignores secondary literature, sometimes inaccurate. Good critical examination of philosophy. [DMS]

41.527 Leonard Baker. *John Marshall: a life in law.* New York: Macmillan, 1974. ISBN 0-02-506360-X. ‣ Extensive, detailed, full-scale biography. Fails to illuminate full importance of Supreme Court justice due to restricted scope. Significant work. [DMS]

41.528 Alexander Balinky. *Albert Gallatin: fiscal theories and politics.* New Brunswick, N.J.: Rutgers University Press, 1958. ‣ Focus on policies as Jefferson's secretary of treasury. Useful addition to literature on important, often neglected founder of American fiscal policy. Aimed at scholars and specialists. Also available from Ann Arbor: University Microfilms International. [DMS]

41.529 W. T. Baxter. *The house of Hancock: business in Boston, 1724–1775.* 1945 ed. New York: Russell & Russell, 1965. ‣ Fascinating narrative of Hancock family; good discussion of business and trade in colonial Boston. Illuminates complicated system of exchange. Dated but useful. [DMS]

41.530 Richard R. Beeman. *Patrick Henry: a biography.* New York: McGraw-Hill, 1974. ISBN 0-07-004280-2. ‣ Brief, readable, interpretive work. Attempts to explain Patrick Henry's enormous political influence in Virginia. Highlights local interests, downplays ideology. [DMS]

41.531 Charles E. Bennett and Donald R. Lennon. *A quest for glory: Major General Robert Howe and the American Revolution.* Chapel Hill: University of North Carolina Press, 1991. ISBN 0-8078-1982-4. ‣ Only biography of senior officer previously unnoticed. Illuminates brief role as senior commander in South, and later at West Point. Useful information on civil-military conflicts in daily routine. [DMS]

41.532 George Athan Billias. *Elbridge Gerry: Founding Father and republican statesman.* New York: McGraw-Hill, 1976. ISBN 0-07-005269-7. ‣ Highly favorable attempt to explain Gerry in context of time and place. Credible effort, hampered by lack of personal papers and documents. [DMS]

41.533 Irving Brant. *James Madison.* 6 vols. Indianapolis: Bobbs-Merrill, 1941–61. ‣ Most detailed, scholarly, authoritative, multivolume study. Thoroughly researched, infinitely detailed, and reliable. Not for casual reader. [DMS]

41.534 Fawn M. Brodie. *Thomas Jefferson: an intimate history.* 1974 ed. New York: Bantam, 1975. ISBN 0-553-25443-X. ‣ Generally favorable biography. Provocative and controversial in arguing that Jefferson had passionate sexual liaison with mulatto slave Sally Hemings. [DLA]

41.535 Chandos Michael Brown. *Benjamin Silliman: a life in the young republic.* Princeton: Princeton University Press, 1989. ISBN 0-691-08533-1. ‣ Well-written, thorough, cultural biography. Illuminates society through detailed, integrated study of representative early American intellectual interested in scientific institutions. [DMS]

41.536 Gerard H. Clarfield. *Timothy Pickering and American diplomacy, 1795–1800.* Columbia: University of Missouri Press, 1969. ISBN 0-8262-8414-0. ‣ Traditional narrative focusing on personal role of overbearing and independent Timothy Pickering in foreign policy events of 1795–1800. Judicious and convincing interpretation of Adams administration's secretary of state. [EVW]

41.537 Paul S. Clarkson and R. Samuel Jett. *Luther Martin of Maryland.* Baltimore: Johns Hopkins University Press, 1970. ISBN 0-8018-1067-1. ‣ Useful study of secondary figure for whom life sources are limited. Primary focus on Constitutional Convention. Traditional approach, breaks little new ground. [DMS]

41.538 John M. Coleman. *Thomas McKean: forgotten leader of the Revolution.* Rockaway, N.J.: American Faculty Press, 1975. ISBN 0-912834-07-2. ‣ Detailed, reliable study of public career. Stops short in 1780. Good study hampered by absence of surviving papers. [DMS]

41.539 Jacob E. Cooke. *Alexander Hamilton.* New York: Scribner's, 1982. ISBN 0-684-17344-1. ‣ Brief, reliable, well-balanced single-volume biography with focus on early national period by foremost student of Hamilton. Easy to read, good for scholars and general reader. [DMS]

41.540 Jacob E. Cooke. *Tench Coxe and the early republic.* Chapel Hill: University of North Carolina for Institute of Early American History and Culture, 1978. ISBN 0-8078-1308-7. ‣ Scholarly, thoroughly researched, detailed account of second-rank governmental official. Reliable, informative; doubtful appeal to general reader. [DMS]

41.541 Noble E. Cunningham, Jr. *In pursuit of reason: the life of Thomas Jefferson.* 1987 ed. New York: Ballantine, 1988. ISBN 0-345-35380-3 (pbk). ‣ Political biography focusing on public career. Valuable introduction with brief survey of nonpolitical life. [DMS]

41.542 Robert Dawidoff. *The education of John Randolph.* New York: Norton, 1979. ISBN 0-393-01242-5. ‣ Thoughtful, perceptive analysis of enigmatic, paradoxical, and brooding figure who eludes historian. Not full biography; mature study touches on various aspects. [DMS]

41.543 Donald J. D'Elia. *Benjamin Rush: philosopher of the American Revolution.* Philadelphia: American Philosophical Society, 1974. (American Philosophical Society transactions, n.s., 64.5.) ISBN 0-87169-645-2, ISSN 0065-9746. ‣ Brief, thoroughly documented attempt to explain physician as coherent, original thinker. Not always successful. [DMS]

41.544 Joseph J. Ellis. *Passionate sage: the character and legacy of John Adams.* New York: Norton, 1993. ISBN 0-393-03479-8. ‣ Perceptive analysis of career after leaving presidency. Focus on breadth and sophistication of mature thought reveals contemporary relevancy rather than usual emphasis on conservatism. Excellent, rewarding study. [DLA]

41.545 Robert Ernst. *Rufus King: American Federalist.* Chapel Hill: University of North Carolina Press for Institute of Early American History and Culture, 1968. ‣ Careful, thorough, detailed narrative of New England Federalist leader and minister to England. Better on detail than analysis. [DMS]

41.546 John E. Ferling. *The first of men: a life of George Washington.* Knoxville: University of Tennessee Press, 1988. ISBN 0-87049-562-3 (cl), 0-87049-628-x (pbk). ▸ Revisionist, speculative biography focuses on military career and psychological insecurity resulting from family experience. Provocative, grounded more in supposition than evidence. [DMS]

41.547 James Thomas Flexner. *George Washington.* Vol. 1: *George Washington: the forge of experience, 1732–1775.* Vol. 2: *George Washington in the American Revolution, 1775–1783.* Vol. 3: *George Washington and the new nation, 1783–1793.* Vol. 4: *George Washington: anguish and farewell, 1793–1799.* 4 vols. Boston: Little, Brown, 1965–72. ISBN 0-316-28597-8 (v. 1), 0-316-28595-1 (v. 2), 0-316-28600-1 (v. 3), 0-316-28602-8 (v. 4). ▸ Well-grounded, carefully researched, sometimes controversial, multivolume study. Readable, entertaining, scholarly. Useful for both specialists and general reader. [DMS]

41.548 James Thomas Flexner. *Washington: the indispensable man.* 1974 ed. New York: New American Library, 1984. ISBN 0-452-25542-2 (pbk). ▸ Distillation of four-volume study; good single-volume introduction. Well written, lively, provocative. Occasionally controversial but well regarded. [DMS]

41.549 Milton E. Flower. *John Dickinson: conservative revolutionary.* Charlottesville: University Press of Virginia for Friends of John Dickinson Mansion, 1983. ISBN 0-8139-0966-x. ▸ Most complete study to date. Solid, thorough, useful, but not definitive. Somewhat stilted style. [DMS]

41.550 Eric Foner. *Tom Paine and revolutionary America.* 1976 ed. New York: Oxford University Press, 1977. ISBN 0-19-501986-5 (cl,1976), 0-19-502182-7 (pbk). ▸ Readable, insightful study of thought and social context and working-class culture. Nontraditional approach. [DMS]

41.551 William M. Fowler, Jr. *The baron of Beacon Hill: a biography of John Hancock.* 1979 ed. Boston: Houghton-Mifflin, 1980. ISBN 0-395-27619-5. ▸ Only available treatment of important revolutionary leader. Traditional, sometimes superficial work; lacks analysis and insight into complexities of Massachusetts politics. [DMS]

41.552 Benjamin Franklin. *The autobiography of Benjamin Franklin.* Leonard W. Labaree et al., ed. New Haven: Yale University Press, 1964. ISBN 0-300-00648-9 (cl), 0-300-00147-9 (pbk). ▸ Superb edition of classic work. Fashioned for scholars and general reader. Highly recommended edition. [DMS]

41.553 Douglas Southall Freeman. *George Washington: a biography.* 1948–57 ed. 7 vols. Clifton, N.J.: Kelley, 1975. ISBN 0-678-02828-1 (v. 2). 0-678-02829-x (v. 3), 0-678-02830-3 (v. 4), 0-678-02831-1 (v. 5), 0-678-02833-8 (v. 7). ▸ Most detailed, voluminous, multivolume study. Traditional approach by foremost scholar. Authoritative reference work; not for casual reader. [DMS]

41.554 Don R. Gerlach. *Philip Schuyler and the American Revolution in New York, 1733–1777.* Lincoln: University of Nebraska Press, 1964. ▸ Sound, extensively researched, traditional narrative biography, focusing on events rather than motivation, challenges Becker thesis of class conflict (41.374); highly favorable toward Schuyler. Good for specialist or general reader with serious interest. [DMS]

41.555 E. Stanley Godbold, Jr., and Robert H. Woody. *Christopher Gadsden and the American Revolution.* Knoxville: University of Tennessee Press, 1983. ISBN 0-87049-362-0 (cl), 0-87049-363-9 (pbk). ▸ Carefully researched, imaginative, useful reconstruction of role of South Carolina's leading radical. Limited by paucity of personal papers. [DMS]

41.556 Constance McLaughlin Green. *Eli Whitney and the birth of American technology.* Glenview, Ill.: Scott, Foresman and Little, Brown Education, 1965. ISBN 0-673-39338-0 (pbk). ▸ Clearly written exploration of social and economic trends. Treats impact of cotton gin and mass production; problems of government bureaucracy strike familiar modern note. Interesting, reliable work. [DMS]

41.557 John Denis Haeger. *John Jacob Astor: business and finance in the early republic.* Detroit: Wayne State University Press, 1991. ISBN 0-8143-1876-2. ▸ Balanced study of Astor's business efforts, ties to government, and mistreatment by historians. Clear, brief, generally favorable biography; excellent review and critique of distortions by other scholars. [DMS]

41.558 David Freeman Hawke. *Benjamin Rush: revolutionary gadfly.* New York: Irvington, 1971. ISBN 0-672-51599-7. ▸ Best biography of Philadelphia physician, ends abruptly in 1790. Sometimes overwhelming in detail, always skillfully written and carefully organized. [DMS]

41.559 David Freeman Hawke. *Paine.* 1974 ed. New York: Norton, 1992. ISBN 0-393-30919-3. ▸ Thoroughly researched, well-written, full biography spans career of influential writer who was neither original nor radical. Sees Paine as reflection of his time. Good bibliography, no footnotes. [DMS]

41.560 John R. Howe, Jr. *The changing political thought of John Adams.* Princeton: Princeton University Press, 1966. ISBN 0-691-04512-7 (cl), 0-691-00566-4 (pbk). ▸ Sound, traditional study, both readable and informative. Concludes Adams's experiences as ambassador dulled his revolutionary ardor. Adams perceived loss of virtue in America which called for revived institutions and national discipline. [LAN]

41.561 Gordon E. Kershaw. *James Bowdoin II: patriot and man of the Enlightenment.* Lanham, Md.: University Press of America, 1991. ISBN 0-8191-8046-7. ▸ Traditional biography recounts Bowdoin's role in Revolution, as governor who defeated Shays, supporter of Constitution, and man of letters. Generally unsuccessful attempt to place Bowdoin among Founding Father elite. [DMS]

41.562 Don R. Gerlach. *Proud patriot: Philip Schuyler and the War of Independence, 1775–1783.* Syracuse, N.Y.: Syracuse University Press, 1987. ISBN 0-8156-2373-9. ▸ Highly favorable and sometimes overly detailed discussion of military career and service in Continental Congress and New York state government. Descriptive narrative, thoroughly researched. Most useful for specialists of Revolution and New York politics. [DMS]

41.563 Ralph L. Ketcham. *Benjamin Franklin.* New York: Washington Square, 1965. ▸ Brief, readable, provocative study. Illuminates Franklin's place in American intellectual history. Recommended for historians and general reader. [DMS]

41.564 Ralph L. Ketcham. *James Madison: a biography.* 1971 ed. Charlottesville: University Press of Virginia, 1990. ISBN 0-8139-1265-2 (pbk). ▸ Careful, thorough, reliable study. Best recent single-volume biography. Generally well-written. Useful for specialist and general reader. [DMS]

41.565 Aubrey C. Land. *The Dulaneys of Maryland: a biographical study of Daniel Dulaney, the Elder (1685–1753) and Daniel Dulaney, the Younger (1722–1797).* 1955 ed. Baltimore: Johns Hopkins University Press, 1968. ▸ Clearly written, entertaining history of important colonial family. Familiarity of author with Maryland history results in interesting and reliable perspective on major events of prerevolutionary period and insights into daily life. [DMS]

41.566 Leonard W. Levy. *Jefferson and civil liberties: the darker side.* 1963 ed. Chicago: Dee, 1989. ISBN 0-929587-11-1 (pbk). ▸ Argues that, contrary to traditional thinking, Jefferson was unlibertarian, possibly antilibertarian in thought and behavior. Provocative and well-documented interpretation. [EVW]

41.567 Milton Lomask. *Aaron Burr*. Vol. 1: *The years from Princeton to vice president, 1756–1805*. New York: Farrar, Straus & Giroux, 1979. ISBN 0-374-10016-0 (v. 1). ▸ Careful, balanced, insightful study dispels many misconceptions. Occasionally hyperbolic, generally sensible. Best available biography. [DMS]

41.568 Paul K. Longmore. *The invention of George Washington*. Berkeley: University of California Press, 1988. ISBN 0-520-06272-8. ▸ Highly favorable, thoroughly researched study of period prior to Revolution focusing on motivation. Depicts Washington as deliberately creating himself as public-spirited patriot. Readable, judiciously based on sources. [DMS]

41.569 Dumas Malone. *Jefferson and his time*. 1948–81 ed. 6 vols. Boston: Little, Brown, 1967–82. ISBN 0-316-54474-4 (v. 1, cl), 0-316-54473-6 (v. 2, cl), 0-316-54475-2 (v. 3, cl), 0-316-54467-1 (v. 4, cl), 0-316-54465-5 (v. 5, cl), 0-316-54463-9 (v. 6, cl), 0-316-54472-8 (v. 1, pbk), 0-316-54470-1 (v. 2, pbk), 0-316-54469-8 (v. 3, pbk), 0-316-54466-3 (v. 4, pbk), 0-316-54464-7 (v. 5, pbk), 0-316-54478-7 (v. 6, pbk). ▸ Reliable, multivolume biography by foremost authority. Clearly written, detailed and thorough. Probes all aspects of subject in traditional account. [DMS]

41.570 Richard K. Matthews. *The radical politics of Thomas Jefferson: a revisionist view*. Lawrence: University Press of Kansas, 1984. ISBN 0-7006-0256-9 (cl), 0-7006-0293-3 (pbk). ▸ Revisionist, even polemical, attempt to make Jefferson's thought an alternative to present-day liberal capitalism. Lucid, provocative, controversial. [DMS]

41.571 David John Mays. *Edmund Pendleton, 1721–1803: a biography*. 1952 ed. 2 vols. Richmond: Virginia State Library, 1984. ISBN 0-88490-119-X (cl), 0-88490-120-3 (pbk). ▸ Thoroughly researched, detailed, scholarly, and well written. Product of twenty-eight year study, illuminates role of Virginia leader generally eclipsed by more famous contemporaries. [DMS]

41.572 Elizabeth P. McCaughey. *From loyalist to Founding Father: the political odyssey of William Samuel Johnson*. New York: Columbia University Press, 1980. ISBN 0-231-04506-9. ▸ Study of Johnson as colonial agent, member of Stamp Act Congress and Constitutional Convention, and United States senator, focusing on image as conciliator and compromiser. Last word on dull figure. [RWS]

41.573 Drew R. McCoy. *The last of the fathers: James Madison and the republican legacy*. Cambridge: Cambridge University Press, 1989. ISBN 0-521-36407-8 (cl), 0-521-40772-9 (pbk). ▸ Approaches Madison as personification of Jeffersonian America. Emphasis on balance and restraint, notes shift from agrarian to commercial aspects. Eloquent, generally sympathetic, except on slavery attitudes. [DMS]

41.574 Forrest McDonald. *Alexander Hamilton: a biography*. 1979 ed. New York: Norton, 1982. ISBN 0-393-01218-2 (cl, 1979), 0-393-30048-X (pbk). ▸ Often insightful, sometimes brilliant, always lively and readable. Strongly biased toward Hamilton; sees Jeffersonian inroads as ultimately destructive of America. [DMS]

41.575 John C. Meleney. *The public life of Aedanus Burke: revolutionary republican in post-revolutionary South Carolina*. Columbia: University of South Carolina Press, 1989. ISBN 0-87249-610-4. ▸ Good study of second-rank revolutionary figure representative of classical republican ideology. Limited comment on South Carolina society, suggests benign aristocratic rule. [DMS]

41.576 Robert Micklus. *The comic genius of Dr. Alexander Hamilton*. Knoxville: University of Tennessee Press, 1990. ISBN 0-87049-633-6. ▸ Solid, readable study of comic author of *The History of the Tuesday Club*. Rescues Hamilton from oblivion.

Reveals greater breadth of early American literature more akin to H. L. Mencken. [DMS]

41.577 Helen Hill Miller. *George Mason: gentleman revolutionary*. Chapel Hill: University of North Carolina Press, 1975. ISBN 0-8078-1250-1. ▸ Good, lively account of revolutionary period; conventional approach, easy to read. Useful account of important Virginian, influential thinker. [DMS]

41.578 John C. Miller. *Sam Adams: pioneer in propaganda*. 1936 ed. Stanford, Calif.: Stanford University Press, 1967. ISBN 0-8047-0024-9 (cl), 0-8047-0025-7 (pbk). ▸ Traditional, somewhat dated. Only scholarly biography on subject. Careful, detailed, useful, readable. [DMS]

41.579 Max M. Mintz. *Gouverneur Morris and the American Revolution*. Norman: University of Oklahoma Press, 1970. ISBN 0-8061-0900-9. ▸ Scholarly, solid, traditional treatment of conservative New Yorker involved in important events of Revolution, early republic prior to 1789. [DMS]

41.580 Jeannette Mirsky and Allan Nevins. *The world of Eli Whitney*. New York: Macmillan, 1952. ▸ Somewhat dated but useful study focusing on cotton gin and development of mass-production techniques. Thoroughly researched and readable. Limited sources restrict explication of personal life. [DMS]

41.581 Paul C. Nagel. *Descent from glory: four generations of the John Adams family*. 1983 ed. New York: Oxford University Press, 1984. ISBN 0-19-503172-5 (cl, 1983), 0-19-503445-7 (pbk). ▸ Fascinating, readable account exploring personal and professional aspects. Thorough, accurate, insightful; for scholars and general reader. [DMS]

41.582 Paul David Nelson. *Anthony Wayne: soldier of the early republic*. Bloomington: Indiana University Press, 1985. ISBN 0-253-30751-1. ▸ Best biography; probing study of both career and personality. Balanced, well crafted, judicious. [DMS]

41.583 Paul David Nelson. *General Horatio Gates: a biography*. Baton Rouge: Louisiana State University Press, 1976. ISBN 0-8071-0159-1. ▸ Careful, thorough, well-written study of enigmatic Revolutionary War general caught up in controversy with Washington. New insights, standard study. [DMS]

41.584 Paul David Nelson. *William Alexander, Lord Stirling*. University: University of Alabama Press, 1987. ISBN 0-8173-0283-2. ▸ Traditional military history stands as best-grounded, gracefully written, standard biography. Details career of self-proclaimed nobleman who rose to prominence in revolutionary army. [DMS]

41.585 R. Kent Newmyer. *Supreme Court Justice Joseph Story: statesman of the old republic*. 1985 ed. Chapel Hill: University of North Carolina Press, 1986. ISBN 0-8078-1626-4 (cl, 1985), 0-8078-4164-1 (pbk). ▸ Fascinating, insightful study of significant jurist. Thorough research underlies balanced, readable, provocative narrative. Model biography. [DMS]

41.586 Merrill D. Peterson. *Thomas Jefferson and the new nation: a biography*. 1970 ed. New York: Oxford University Press, 1986. ISBN 0-19-501909-1 (pbk). ▸ Most detailed single- volume biography. Thoroughly researched, authoritative, judiciously written. Readable. General appeal. [DMS]

41.587 Louis W. Potts. *Arthur Lee: a virtuous revolutionary*. Baton Rouge: Louisiana State University Press, 1981. ISBN 0-8071-0785-9. ▸ Sympathetic study attempting to enhance Lee's importance as American observer in prerevolutionary London. Not entirely successful. [DMS]

41.588 G. S. Rowe. *Thomas McKean: the shaping of an American republicanism*. Boulder: Colorado Associated University Press, 1978. ISBN 0-87081-100-2. ▸ Important contribution to understanding of conservative republicanism and establishment of

American legal system. Well-written, readable, but not full-scale biography. [DMS]

41.589 Charles Royster. *Light-Horse Harry Lee and the legacy of the American Revolution.* New York: Knopf; distributed by Random House, 1981. ISBN 0-394-51337-1. ▸ Insightful, provocative, lively account of colorful figure. Good example of best in military history. Enjoyable. [DMS]

41.590 Boyd Stanley Schlenther. *Charles Thomson: a patriot's pursuit.* Newark: University of Delaware Press, 1990. ISBN 0-87413-368-8. ▸ Most recent study of secretary of Continental Congress. Thorough and readable, explores character as well as career. Informative on Pennsylvanian and national politics. [DMS]

41.591 Ormond Seavey. *Becoming Benjamin Franklin.* University Park: Pennsylvania State University Press, 1988. ISBN 0-271-00627-7. ▸ Portrays *Autobiography* as carefully controlled presentation, exploring specific aspects of self Franklin wanted to exhibit. Finds determined, consistent effort to achieve acceptance. Clear, insightful, and enhances understanding. [DMS]

41.592 Arthur H. Shaffer. *To be an American: David Ramsay and the making of the American consciousness.* Columbia: University of South Carolina Press, 1991. ISBN 0-87249-718-6. ▸ Good intellectual biography of significant figure in development of American identity. Explores social, political, and economic milieu, with emphasis on impact of Ramsay's historical writing in defining American nationalism. [DMS]

41.593 Peter Shaw. *The character of John Adams.* 1976 ed. New York: Norton, 1977. ISBN 0-393-00856-8. ▸ Penetrating personality study combining thorough research with attractive literary style. Brief, excellent study of entire man. [DMS]

41.594 Sheila L. Skemp. *William Franklin: son of a patriot, servant of a king.* New York: Oxford University Press, 1990. ISBN 0-19-505745-7. ▸ Careful, convincing biography of New Jersey loyalist governor, son of famous patriot. Important contribution illuminating middle colony politics as well as career and personality of Franklin and attitudes of loyalists. Good combination of narration and analysis. [DLA]

41.595 Charles Page Smith. *James Wilson, Founding Father, 1742–1798.* 1956 ed. Westport, Conn.: Greenwood, 1973. ISBN 0-8371-6908-9. ▸ Excellent biography of much neglected and abused Founding Father. Generally balanced, sometimes too sympathetic. Emphasis on Wilson as original political thinker. Interesting and perceptive. [DMS]

41.596 Jeffrey Alan Smith. *Franklin and Bache: envisioning the enlightened republic.* New York: Oxford University Press, 1990. ISBN 0-19-505676-0. ▸ Interesting, provocative study. Sees Benjamin Bache as connection between his grandfather, Franklin, and Jeffersonian Republicans. Both portrayed as radical democrats rooted in equality based on educated masses, and preservation of virtue. [DMS]

41.597 Page Smith. *John Adams.* 2 vols. Garden City, N.Y.: Doubleday, 1962. ▸ Exceptionally detailed, careful study. Scholarly, generally well written; good for general reader with serious interest. [DMS]

41.598 Phinizy Spalding. *Oglethorpe in America.* 1977 ed. Athens: University of Georgia Press, 1984. ISBN 0-8203-0734-3 (pbk). ▸ Lively, well-balanced biography of Georgia founder; accents both achievements and failures. Useful for specialist, entertaining to general reader. [DMS]

41.599 Phinizy Spalding and Harvey H. Jackson, eds. *Oglethorpe in perspective: Georgia's founder after two hundred years.* Tuscaloosa: University of Alabama Press, 1989. ISBN 0-8173-0386-3. ▸ Nine articles by various authors probe aspects of Oglethorpe's

long career. Solid, adds new perspectives. Attempt at more personal view limited by paucity of sources. [DMS]

41.600 Gerald Stourzh. *Alexander Hamilton and the idea of republican government.* Stanford, Calif.: Stanford University Press, 1970. ISBN 0-8047-0724-3. ▸ Emphasizes and glorifies Hamilton's role in founding an empire. Interesting challenge to accepted interpretation. Provocative, not always judicious. Also available, Ann Arbor: University Microfilms International. [DMS]

41.601 Gerald Stourzh. *Benjamin Franklin and American foreign policy.* 2d ed. Chicago: University of Chicago Press, 1969. ▸ Portrait of Franklin as systematic thinker committed to agrarian democracy, American expansion, and amelioration of Old World diplomacy. Combination of intellectual and diplomatic history. [RWS]

41.602 Vernon O. Stumpf. *Josiah Martin: the last royal governor of North Carolina.* Durham, N.C.: Carolina Academic Press for Kellenberger Historical Foundation, 1986. ISBN 0-89089-305-5 (cl), 0-89089-304-7 (pbk). ▸ Posthumously published study lacks some coherence, focus on prerevolutionary struggle and machinations of radicals. Favorable treatment of Martin, generally persuasive. [DMS]

41.603 Theodore George Thayer. *Nathanael Greene: strategist of the American Revolution.* New York: Twayne, 1960. ▸ Thoroughly researched, valuable contribution to understanding one of America's best revolutionary generals. Balanced, well organized, clearly written, even compelling. Recommended for anyone interested in period. [DMS]

41.604 Mack Thompson. *Moses Brown: reluctant reformer.* Chapel Hill: University of North Carolina Press for Institute of Early American History and Culture, 1962. ISBN 0-8078-0859-8. ▸ Best biography of Rhode Island Baptist turned Quaker involved in wide-ranging reform movements. Highly readable; luminates life and times. [DMS]

41.605 Carl Van Doren. *Benjamin Franklin.* 1938 ed. New York: Viking Penguin, 1991. ISBN 0-14-015260-1. ▸ Thorough, reliable, traditional, but somewhat dated account. Most complete biography available. Beautifully written, good for general reader. [DMS]

41.606 Clarence L. Ver Steeg. *Robert Morris: revolutionary financier with an analysis of his early career.* 1954 ed. New York: Octagon Books, 1972. ISBN 0-374-98078-0. ▸ Prodigiously researched, detailed account of financier of Revolution. More suitable for scholars and specialists than for general reader. [DMS]

41.607 Carl J. Vipperman. *The rise of Rawlins Lowndes, 1721–1800.* Columbia: University of South Carolina Press, 1978. ISBN 0-87249-259-1. ▸ Portrays rags-to-riches career of moderately important South Carolinian. Author knowledgeable of period, adds to understanding of legal history. Not compelling prose. [DMS]

41.608 Carl J. Vipperman. *William Lowndes and the transition of southern politics, 1782–1822.* Chapel Hill: University of North Carolina Press, 1989. ISBN 0-8078-1826-7. ▸ Careful, reliable account of public life, suffers from lack of personal papers. Sees Lowndes's move to sectionalism resulting from his commitment to traditional republicanism. Useful to students of period. [DMS]

41.609 Willard M. Wallace. *Traitorous hero: the life and fortunes of Benedict Arnold.* 1954 ed. Freeport, N.Y.: Books for Libraries Press, 1990. ISBN 0-8369-5349-5. ▸ Well-written, authoritative, full biography. Attempt at balance despite pro-Arnold bias. Often exciting narrative, useful to scholars and general readers. [DMS]

41.610 Harry M. Ward. *Major General Adam Stephen and the cause of American liberty.* Charlottesville: University Press of Virginia, 1989. ISBN 0-8139-1227-X. ▸ Readable, thoroughly researched biography of ranking Revolutionary War general, court martialed and cashiered from army. Paucity of sources explains limited consideration of private life. [DMS]

41.611 John J. Waters, Jr. *The Otis family in provincial and revolutionary Massachusetts.* 1968 ed. New York: Norton, 1975. ISBN 0-393-00757-X. ▸ Narrates 160 years of family using tools of social history. Extensive research, good narrative style. Useful, stimulating. [DMS]

41.612 Franklin Wickwire and Mary Wickwire. *Cornwallis: the American adventure.* Boston: Houghton-Mifflin, 1970. ▸ Well-written, readable, thoroughly grounded treatment. Sees Cornwallis as capable, competent, not responsible for Yorktown fiasco. Good for general reader and historian. [DMS]

41.613 William B. Wilcox. *Portrait of a general: Sir Henry Clinton in the War of Independence.* New York: Knopf; distributed by Random House, 1964. ▸ Combines good biography with explanation of British military strategy. Recommended for anyone interested in American Revolution. [DMS]

41.614 Esmond Wright. *Franklin of Philadelphia.* 1986 ed. Cambridge, Mass.: Harvard University Press, 1988. ISBN 0-674-31809 (cl, 1986), 0-674-31810-2 (pbk). ▸ Probably best, reliable, up-to-date, single-volume biography of Frankin. Graceful, beautifully written. Delightful reading. [DMS]

THOMAS DUBLIN

United States, 1815–1877

Even a cursory comparison of titles listed in this section on the United States, 1815–1877, with listings in the 1961 *Guide* reveals the dramatic transformation in the nature of historical writing about the United States in the past three decades. Three developments in particular stand out: biography and the narrative of political events no longer dominate historical writing; more focused, analytic writing has dramatically expanded the range of topics historians view as significant; and social science methods increasingly influence historical research and writing.

The changing place of biography within historical writing is reflected in two ways, number and conception. The 1961 *Guide* included a separate listing of biographies that accounted for 15 percent of titles in the United States History section while the percentage of biographies included in this section is decidedly lower. Equally important, recent biographies are conceived in different terms and are more fully integrated within contemporary historiographical debates than was the case before 1960. Today there is no longer the clear-cut divide between history and biography; biography has become a tool of the professional historian, a way to approach issues of causation and social change more generally.

This development reflects a shift in interest in the past thirty years, from the values and behavior of elites toward the values and behavior of ordinary Americans. This trend has led to a refocusing of such traditional fields as political, diplomatic, and intellectual history and a mushrooming of new scholarship in the area of social history. Substantial topical fields in the current edition had virtually no counterparts thirty years ago. Women's history, immigration and ethnic history, and demography and family history, for instance, account for about a fourth of the listings in this section. In contrast, in 1961, works focusing on these topics amounted to only 3 percent of titles listed. Only three of 111 biographies listed in the earlier edition treated women; none treated an African American, Hispanic American, or American Indian. Equally revealing in the field of immigration history is the expansion beyond an earlier Eurocentric focus. Whereas British, German, and Scandinavian immigrants received the lion's share of coverage in the 1961 *Guide,* scholars in recent years have written important treatments of Mexican, Chinese, eastern European Jewish, and Canadian immigrants. Moreover, there has been an increased interest in comparisons of the immigrant and the African American experience. What is striking in reflecting on the titles listed in this section is how much of the terrain of historical scholarship today was beyond the bounds of historical writing a generation earlier.

The transformation of historical writing is also apparent in new ways of studying traditional topics. In the field of intellectual and cultural history, for instance, the study of popular thought and culture has emerged as a particularly vital area of scholarship. Works by D. Grimsted and N. Harris explore two important forms of nineteenth-century popular entertainment, the theater and the circus.

A similar repositioning of focus has been evident in recent scholarship on American slavery. Before 1960, historians emphasized the contribution of slavery to sectional conflict and the outbreak of the Civil War. The few works that explored the institution of slavery in its own right, did so basically from the point of view of and offered apologies for southern slaveowners. In the 1970s and 1980s scholars increasingly examined slave community and culture in their own right. Responding to the interpretation put forth by S. Elkins in his synthesis, *Slavery* (42.279), historians argued against his one-sided treatment of the influence of masters in shaping slave life and slave personality. The works of J. W. Blassingame, H. G. Gutman, and E. D. Genovese, for instance, all speak to the ways that slaves constructed a culture of resistance from a subordinate position within plantation slavery. There is also interest in the cultural interaction of masters and slaves and a debate over the relative influence of paternalism, but that debate is now situated within a context that acknowledges the existence of a slave culture. Disagreement focuses on the character of that culture and the relative importance of contradictory influences.

The flourishing of social movements in the United States in recent decades has led to a dramatic revaluing of the significance of social movements in the past. To the nineteenth-century reform movements emphasized before 1960—nativism, abolitionism, and populism—may now be added labor reform, women's rights, temperance, and utopian communities. The earlier emphasis on consensus in American politics has given way to an assertion of difference and a growing appreciation of the contribution of organized protest groups to the broader American polity.

The historiography of the Civil War and Reconstruction has been similarly transformed in recent years. Earlier works tended to offer a sympathetic view of the plight of the occupied South and to favor President Johnson over the Radical Republicans in the treatment of Reconstruction debates. W.E.B. Du Bois's classic study, *Black Reconstruction* (42.829), was notably absent from the 1961 *Guide*. While interest continues in the political, military, and diplomatic histories of the war, the transition from slavery to freedom and the nature of postemancipation southern society have become major focuses of new research. Recent studies that might be highlighted in this regard include monographs by E. Foner and L. F. Litwack and documents edited by I. Berlin and his colleagues that explore conflicting views of freedom in the aftermath of emancipation and the struggle through which freedpersons contributed to the definition of their new status in a postslavery southern society and economy.

The renewed interest in African Americans as actors in the Civil War era has been mirrored by a sharpened focus on intraregional conflicts among white citizens as well. Works by V. E. Bynum, S. Hahn, and J. M. Wiener explore conflicts among southern whites in this period, while I. Bernstein, D. Montgomery, and G. Palladino explore sources of conflict among northerners during and immediately after the war. Any sense of a solid South or a monolithic North has given way to more complex analyses of divisions within these broad regions.

There has been a similar change in how American labor history has been written over the past thirty years. Antebellum labor history had traditionally been treated as an aspect of political history. Thus, there were studies that treated organized labor and workingmen's parties in the context of Jacksonian democracy, but very few on working-class life. The 1970s and 1980s saw a proliferation of focused industrial and community studies that have deepened understanding of the nature of industrialization in the United States and its social and economic consequences. Where politics has been reintegrated into the broader picture, studies by A. Dawley and S. Wilentz have done so with a clear sense of the social and economic changes at the local level and of how those changes were reflected in the political arena.

Religion is another area that has undergone significant change in the past thirty years. Previously explored as either denominational history or as an aspect of American intellectual or cultural history, religious history has been increasingly integrated into broader themes of American history. The connections between American churches and reform movements have been explored in the works of W. R. Cross, P. E. Johnson, and N. Hewitt, among others. The place of religion in race relations has been an important theme for Genovese and A. J. Raboteau, for instance. Before 1960, historians focused on religion as particularly important in understanding American colonial history; in recent years, equally substantial research and engaging debates have concerned the influence of religion in the nineteenth century.

Treatment of the American West was notably sparse in the 1961 *Guide*, and the titles listed dealt with governmental policy, economic development, westward expansion, and the West in American politics. By comparison, the breadth of western history today is particularly striking. Recent collections of essays have offered useful overviews of broad developments. Interest in environmental issues, the displacement of American Indians, the place of women and immigrants in the West, race relations, and the relationship between law and economic development make western history one of the most dynamic fields in nineteenth-century American history.

In the past three decades historians have increasingly borrowed methods and approaches from the social sciences. This trend is apparent across the entire range of topical fields in this section. The systematic application of neoclassical economic assumptions and methods in historical research has led to the coining of the term "cliometrics," referring to the work of the new economic historians. Led by R. W. Fogel and S. L. Engerman, a new generation of quantitatively inclined scholars, often trained in economics departments, has rewritten the scholarship on American railroads, northern agriculture, and the economics of slavery. In social history, the pioneering work of M. E. Curti, S. Thernstrom, M. B. Katz, and others has applied statistical techniques to the study of geographical and social mobility. In political history, works by L. Benson, R. P. Formisano, M. F. Holt, and J. H. Silbey have subjected electoral politics and legislative voting patterns to sophisticated statistical analysis. Quantitative methods have also been applied in labor history, women's history, and in family and demographic history more generally. It is a rare debate in nineteenth-century historiography that has not been touched by the rapidly increasing use of statistical methods by historians. Finally, social and cultural historians such as Blassingame, Gutman, and B. Wyatt-Brown have borrowed extensively from the work of anthropologists, psychologists, and sociologists as they have examined the character and interaction of black and white cultures in the antebellum South. History has not become a social science in the past three decades, but its character is becoming more complex, and it is no longer viewed by all of its practitioners as residing exclusively in the humanities camp.

The transformation of historical writing about the United States in the nineteenth century has flowed from dramatic changes in American society in recent decades. As the surface prosperity and apparent ideological consensus of the 1950s gave way to a period of intense social conflict and change, and as the composition of the historical profession grew increasingly diverse, historians' views of the past underwent profound change. Although many historians complain of the lack of synthesis of these diverse points of view, none can question how much richer and more complex contemporary interpretations of this nation's past are in comparison to perspectives that held sway as recently as thirty years ago. What we cannot know with any certainty is how historians a generation from now will look back on the transformation in scholarship evident in recent years. The new perspectives they will bring to the study of American history will emerge only slowly with the passage of time. And as new ways of examining historical change supplant those of the current generation, there will be yet more food for thought for future intellectual and cultural historians seeking a usable past.

[Contributors: ARLC = Andrew R. L. Cayton, CAM = Clyde A. Milner II, CJG = Carl J. Guarneri, DAR = David A. Rawson, DF = Daniel Feller, DLC = David L. Carlton, DMS = Darren M. Staloff, DRG = Donna R. Gabaccia, DSS = Daniel Scott Smith, EVW = Edward V. Woodward, FEH = Frederick E. Hoxie, GJK = Gary J. Kornblith, HIK = Howard I. Kushner, HM = Harvey Markowitz, JB = Jon Butler, KWK = Kenneth W. Keller, LAN = Lynn A. Nelson, MW = Margaret Washington, NF = Nora Faires, RJW = Richard J. Walter, SGM = Sally G. McMillen, SHH = Steven H. Hahn, TAM = Teresa A. Murphy, TD = Thomas Dublin, TDH = Thomas D. Hamm, TJMcD = Terrence J. McDonald, VBB = Victoria B. Brown, WFD = William F. Deverell]

POLITICAL HISTORY

Political Culture and Ideology

42.1 John Ashworth. *"Agrarians" and "aristocrats": party political ideology in the United States, 1837–1846.* 1983 ed. Cambridge: Cambridge University Press, 1987. ISBN 0-521-33567-1 (pbk). ▸ Analysis of partisan thought. Argues strident rhetoric reflected fundamental ideological cleavages between egalitarian, agrarian Democrats and socially conservative, commercial Whigs. Democracy and capitalism developed antagonistically, not symbiotically. [DF]

42.2 Jean H. Baker. *Affairs of party: the political culture of northern Democrats in the mid-nineteenth century.* Ithaca, N.Y.: Cornell University Press, 1983. ISBN 0-8014-1513-6 (cl), 0-8014-9883-x (pbk). ▸ Examination of partisan education, values, beliefs, nationalism, racism, and public ceremonies. Argues Civil War era northern parties fostered citizen participation in uniquely inclusive and responsive civic culture. [DF]

42.3 Amy Bridges. *A city in the republic: antebellum New York and the origins of machine politics.* 1984 ed. Ithaca, N.Y.: Cornell University Press, 1987. ISBN 0-8014-9392-7 (pbk). ▸ Traces evolution from patrician to careerist leadership and from communitarian to partisan class- or ethnic-divided polity. Sees bossism as response to changing economic electoral environment, not expression of urban subcultures. [DF]

42.4 William R. Brock. *Parties and political conscience: American dilemmas, 1840–1850.* Millwood, N.Y.: KTO, 1979. ISBN 0-527-11800-1. ▸ Narrative of national politics stressing ideological context. Argues that ineffectuality and loss of moral mission destroyed public faith in national parties in 1840s, portending disunion. [DF]

42.5 Thomas Brown. *Politics and statesmanship: essays on the American Whig party.* New York: Columbia University Press, 1985. ISBN 0-231-05602-8. ▸ Discussion of policies, principles, and leaders. Sees party bond not in constituencies or interests but in common values derived from republicanism: moderation, self-restraint, rationalism, social welfare, disinterested public service, consensus, and compromise. [DF]

42.6 George Dangerfield. *The era of good feelings.* 1952 ed. New York: Harcourt Brace & World, 1963. ▸ Study of national politics and diplomacy, 1811–28, as transition from Jeffersonian to Jacksonian democracy. Stresses economic transformation, nationalism-sectionalism, and foreign (especially Anglo-American) relations. Evocative, elegant style; vivid personality sketches. [DF]

42.7 Eric Foner. *Free soil, free labor, free men: the ideology of the Republican party before the Civil War.* New York: Oxford University Press, 1970. ISBN 0-19-501352-2 (pbk). ▸ Study of thought and policy, showing influence of abolitionist, whig, and democratic legacies. Argues antislavery and antinativism reflected core middle-class beliefs in social mobility, progress, dignity of work, and democracy. [DF]

42.8 Ronald P. Formisano. *The birth of mass political parties: Michigan, 1827–1861*. Princeton: Princeton University Press, 1971. ISBN 0-691-04605-0. ▸ Revisionist analysis of parties' group constituencies. Downplays class divisions, economics, and antislavery; emphasizes ethnic-religious-cultural split between whig/republican evangelicals and democratic anti-evangelicals over nativism, temperance, and church and state. [DF]

42.9 Ronald P. Formisano. *The transformation of political culture: Massachusetts parties, 1790s–1840s*. 1983 ed. New York: Oxford University Press, 1984. ISBN 0-19-503124-5 (cl, 1983), 0-19-503509-7 (pbk). ▸ Study of evolution from deferential antipartisan to egalitarian partisan politics. Ethos and methods changed, while parties reflected continuing economic, cultural, and social rivalry between federalist-whig center and Jeffersonian-Jacksonian periphery. Rich thematic style embodying much recent historiography of American political parties. [DF/EVW]

42.10 William E. Gienapp. *The origins of the Republican party, 1852–1856*. New York: Oxford University Press, 1986. ISBN 0-19-504100-3. ▸ Exhaustive narrative of elections and politicians' power-seeking strategies. Finds ethnocultural issues (nativism, temperance), not sectionalism, disrupting Whigs and Democrats; Republicans outlived Know-Nothings by merging anti-Catholicism with antisouthernism. [DF/NF]

42.11 Robert Gray Gunderson. *The log-cabin campaign*. 1957 ed. Westport, Conn.: Greenwood, 1977. ISBN 0-8371-9395-8. ▸ Colorful, partisan narrative of tumultuous 1840 presidential contest. Censures Whigs for cynical, mindless demagoguery and stunts, obscuring issues to disguise intraparty divisions and aristocratic contempt for democracy. [DF]

42.12 Michael F. Holt. *Forging a majority: the formation of the Republican party in Pittsburgh, 1848–1860*. 1969 ed. Pittsburgh: University of Pittsburgh Press, 1990. ISBN 0-8229-3632-1. ▸ Attributes whig collapse and republican rise primarily to ethnocultural factors (nativism, anti-Catholicism, antisouthernism), not tariff or slavery issues. Stresses Know-Nothing influence in republican coalition. [DF/NF]

42.13 Daniel Walker Howe. *The political culture of the American Whigs*. Chicago: University of Chicago Press, 1979. ISBN 0-226-35478-4 (cl), 0-226-35479-2 (pbk). ▸ Study of party ideology through multiple intellectual biography. Whig worldview, rooted in Protestant moralism, championed econowmic development and social order. Despite political defeats, whig ideas shaped emerging bourgeois ethos. [DF]

42.14 Thomas E. Jeffrey. *State parties and national politics: North Carolina, 1815–1861*. Athens: University of Georgia Press, 1989. ISBN 0-8203-1090-5. ▸ Revisionist study questioning parties' programmatic differences; traditional ethnocultural rivalries, not economic interests, shaped constituencies. Partisans electioneered vigorously, governed ineffectually, and touted national issues to obscure internal differences over state concerns. [DF]

42.15 Paul Kleppner. *The cross of culture: a social analysis of midwestern politics, 1850–1890*. 2d ed. New York: Free Press, 1970. ▸ Provocative, influential, behavioralist interpretation relies on thorough quantitative analysis of voting data and rhetoric. Argues ethnocultural allegiances, more than class interests, explain voting behavior. Ignores broader issues of political power. [NF]

42.16 Marc W. Kruman. *Parties and politics in North Carolina, 1836–1865*. Baton Rouge: Louisiana State University Press, 1983. ISBN 0-8071-1041-8 (cl), 0-8071-1061-2 (pbk). ▸ Sees defining democratic-whig disagreements on political economy and suffrage reform yielding to consensus in 1850s. Still, party competition endured in North Carolina, undercutting secessionism and support for Confederacy. [DF]

42.17 Shaw Livermore, Jr. *The twilight of federalism: the disinte-* gration of the Federalist party, 1815–1830. 1962 ed. New York: Gordian, 1972. ISBN 0-87752-137-9. ▸ Political narrative stressing continued prominence of partisanship and activity of party leaders in northern states after War of 1812. [DF]

42.18 Richard P. McCormick. *The presidential game: the origins of American presidential politics*. New York: Oxford University Press, 1982. ISBN 0-19-503015-X. ▸ Outline of changing nature of presidential elections up to 1844 (epilogue to 1980) showing how popular democracy and political parties reshaped Founding Fathers' concept of presidency and selection process. [DF]

42.19 William G. Shade. *Banks or no banks: the money issue in western politics, 1832–1865*. Detroit: Wayne State University Press, 1972. ISBN 0-8143-1485-9. ▸ Five-state study of response to national Jacksonian bank war. Whigs and Republicans promoted commercialization, Democrats resisted. Voter partisanship reflected ethnocultural divisions, not class lines. [DF]

42.20 Robert E. Shalhope. *John Taylor of Caroline: pastoral republican*. Columbia: University of South Carolina Press, 1980. ISBN 0-87249-390-3. ▸ Virginia agriculturalist and political theorist clung to country-party republicanism in opposition to federal innovations in generation after 1787. Fine contribution to republicanism historiography. [CJG]

42.21 Joel H. Silbey. *The American political nation, 1838–1893*. Stanford, Calif.: Stanford University Press, 1991. ISBN 0-8047-1878-4. ▸ Overview of party organization, tactics, policies, constituencies, and rituals. Sees era as distinguished by dominance of mass, inclusive, aggressively competitive parties. Synthesizes socioeconomic, ideological, and ethnocultural explanations of partisan vitality. [DF]

42.22 Joel H. Silbey. *The partisan imperative: the dynamics of American politics before the Civil War*. New York: Oxford University Press, 1985. ISBN 0-19-503551-8. ▸ Collected essays on antebellum political culture, voting, and Civil War causes. Claims parties reflected mainly local, ethnocultural voter concerns, not national economic or slavery issues. [DF]

42.23 Joel H. Silbey. *The shrine of party: congressional voting behavior, 1841–1852*. Pittsburgh: University of Pittsburgh Press, 1967. ▸ Analysis of roll-call votes. Concludes whig-democratic partisanship, not sectionalism, governed policy alignments. [DF/TJMcD]

42.24 Chilton Williamson. *American suffrage from property to democracy, 1760–1860*. Princeton: Princeton University Press, 1960. ▸ Outline of expansion of voting rights in states in response to egalitarian circumstances, revolutionary ideology, and political expediency. Concludes movement toward white manhood suffrage embraced all sections and parties. [DF]

42.25 Ralph A. Wooster. *Politicians, planters, and plain folk: courthouse and statehouse in the upper South, 1850–1860*. Knoxville: University of Tennessee Press, 1975. ISBN 0-87049-166-0. ▸ Seven-state comparison of state and county government structure and personnel. Finds democratizing trend (especially in West), strong legislative branches, no wealthy slaveholder domination or partisan socioeconomic difference among officeholders. [DF]

Political Biography

42.26 Harry Ammon. *James Monroe: the quest for national identity*. 1971 ed. Charlottesville: University Press of Virginia, 1990. ISBN 0-8139-1266-0 (pbk). ▸ Well-written, carefully researched, standard political biography of Monroe. As president, astutely guided foreign policy and pursued high-minded but ultimately unsuccessful goal of partisan conciliation and political harmony. [DF/DMS]

42.27 Irving H. Bartlett. *Daniel Webster*. New York: Norton,

1978. ISBN 0-393-07524-9. ▸ Biographical character portrait. Probes sources of contradictions in Webster's personality and public image as heroic orator-statesman and grasping, corrupt libertine. [DF]

42.28 Maurice G. Baxter. *One and inseparable: Daniel Webster and the Union.* Cambridge, Mass.: Belknap, 1984. ISBN 0-674-63821-2. ▸ Standard biography presenting Webster as politician, orator, lawyer, and diplomat stressing contribution to nationalism; emphasis on public context. Sympathetic and restrained judgment of his controversial character. [DF]

42.29 Samuel Flagg Bemis. *John Quincy Adams.* Vol. 1: *John Quincy Adams and the foundations of American foreign policy.* Vol. 2: *John Quincy Adams and the Union.* 1949–56 ed. Westport, Conn.: Greenwood, 1980–81. ISBN 0-313-22636-9 (v. 1), 0-313-22637-7 (v. 2). ▸ Standard biography. Views Adams as preeminent American diplomat, responsible for successful national expansion and establishment of enduring diplomatic principle, and as practical crusader against slavery, anticipating Lincoln. [DF]

42.30 Donald B. Cole. *Martin Van Buren and the American political system.* Princeton: Princeton University Press, 1984. ISBN 0-691-04715-4. ▸ Scholarly biography. Sees Van Buren as quintessential party man—innovative, adaptable party builder, adjusting Jeffersonian principle to modernizing society—but inflexible and ineffectual president. [DF]

42.31 David Donald. *Charles Sumner and the coming of the Civil War.* 1960 ed. New York: Fawcett, 1989. ISBN 0-449-90350-8 (pbk). ▸ Standard biography balancing treatment of private life and character with career as orator-statesman. Depicts Sumner as doctrinaire, egotistical, unreflective, stubborn, sensitive, unconsciously ambitious, and happiest in controversy. See author's continuation at 42.828. [DF]

42.32 Drew Gilpin Faust. *James Henry Hammond and the old South: a design for mastery.* Baton Rouge: Louisiana State University Press, 1982. ISBN 0-8071-1048-5. ▸ Biography of South Carolina planter-politician. Hammond's contradictory drive for dominion, insatiable ambition, and craving for intimacy shaped his frustrations as plantation patriarch, southern-rights statesman, and husband and father. [DF]

42.33 Don E. Fehrenbacher. *Prelude to greatness: Lincoln in the 1850s.* 1962 ed. Stanford, Calif.: Stanford University Press, 1964. ISBN 0-8047-0119-9 (cl), 0-8047-0120-2 (pbk). ▸ Reexamination of events catapulting Lincoln to presidency. Suggests Lincoln's character and principles formed early and that republican success after whig failure in Illinois explains his sudden national prominence. [DF]

42.34 Don E. Fehrenbacher, ed. *Abraham Lincoln: speeches and writings.* 2 vols. New York: Library of America; distributed by Viking, 1989. ISBN 0-940450-43-7 (v. 1), 0-940450-63-1 (v. 2). ▸ Two-volume collection of letters, speeches, presidential messages, memoranda, and complete Lincoln-Douglas debates, selected from Roy P. Basler's *Collected Works of Abraham Lincoln.* [DF]

42.35 Larry Gara. *The presidency of Franklin Pierce.* Lawrence: University Press of Kansas, 1991. ISBN 0-7006-0494-4. ▸ Survey of politics, administration, and diplomacy. Confirms conventional view of Pierce as well-meaning but weak, inept, inflexible, overwhelmed, unhappy, pro-southern, and ultimately disastrous executive. [DF]

42.36 LeRoy P. Graf and Ralph W. Haskins, eds. *The papers of Andrew Johnson.* 10 vols. Knoxville: University of Tennessee Press, 1967–92. ISBN 0-87049-079-6 (v. 1), 0-87049-098-2 (v. 2), 0-87049-141-5 (v. 3), 0-87049-183-0 (v. 4), 0-87049-273-X (v. 5), 0-87049-488-0 (v. 7), 0-87049-764-2 (v. 10). ▸ Comprehensive

twelve-volume edition of Johnson's correspondence and other papers. Completed through volume 10 (1866). [DF]

42.37 Mary W. M. Hargreaves. *The presidency of John Quincy Adams.* Lawrence: University Press of Kansas, 1985. ISBN 0-7006-0272-0. ▸ Discussion of politics, administration, and diplomacy. Views Adams as striving for national development, economic integration, sectional harmony, and hemispheric leadership, but thwarted by political ineptitude and Jacksonian particularism. [DF]

42.38 James F. Hopkins et al., eds. *The papers of Henry Clay.* 11 vols. Lexington: University Press of Kentucky, 1959–92. ISBN 0-8131-0051-8 (v. 1), 0-8131-0053-4 (v. 3), 0-8131-0054-2 (v. 4), 0-8131-0055-0 (v. 5), 0-8131-0056-9 (v. 6), 0-8131-0057-7 (v. 7), 0-8131-0058-5 (v. 8), 0-8131-0059-3 (v. 9), 0-8131-0061-5 (v. 11). ▸ Comprehensive edition of Clay's correspondence and other papers, complete in 11 volumes. [DF]

42.39 Robert W. Johannsen. *Stephen A. Douglas.* New York: Oxford University Press, 1973. ISBN 0-19-501620-3. ▸ Standard biography viewing Douglas as exemplary Jacksonian: patriotic, democratic, chauvinistic, ambitious, unreflective, expediently unscrupulous but not unprincipled, and tragically unable to adjust to meet growing slavery controversy. [DF]

42.40 Drew R. McCoy. *The last of the fathers: James Madison and the republican legacy.* Cambridge: Cambridge University Press, 1989. ISBN 0-521-36407-8 (cl), 0-521-40772-9 (pbk). ▸ Intellectual biography of post-presidential years exploring Madison's thought and influence on republicanism, constitutional interpretation, nullification, political economy, and slavery. Sees him as conservative in principle, optimist in temperament. [DF]

42.41 Robert L. Meriwether, ed. *The papers of John C. Calhoun.* 20 vols. to date. Columbia: University of South Carolina Press for South Carolina Society, 1959–. ISBN 0-87249-070-X (v. 1), 0-87249-150-1 (v. 4), 0-87249-210-9 (v. 5), 0-87249-247-8 (v. 6), 0-87249-288-5 (v. 7), 0-87249-337-7 (v. 9), 0-87249-349-0 (v. 10), 0-87249-363-6 (v. 11), 0-87249-382-2 (v. 12), 0-87249-392-X (v. 13), 0-87249-409-8 (v. 14), 0-87249-418-7 (v. 15), 0-87249-436-5 (v. 16), 0-87249-769-0 (v. 20). ▸ Comprehensive twenty-five-volume edition of letters, speeches, and other writings by and to Calhoun. Completed through volume 20 (1844). [DF]

42.42 Haskell M. Monroe, Jr., and James T. McIntosh, eds. *The papers of Jefferson Davis.* Edition varies. 7 vols. to date. Baton Rouge: Louisiana State University Press, 1971–91. ISBN 0-8071-0943-6 (v. 1), 0-8071-0082-X (v. 2), 0-8071-0786-7 (v. 3), 0-8071-1037-X (v. 4), 0-8071-1240-2 (v. 5), 0-8071-1502-9 (v. 6), 0-8071-1726-9 (v. 7). ▸ Selective fourteen-volume edition of Davis papers. Completed through volume 7 (1861). Some earlier volumes now revised. [DF]

42.43 Beverly Wilson Palmer, ed. *The selected letters of Charles Sumner.* 2 vols. Boston: Northeastern University Press, 1990. ISBN 1-55553-078-8. ▸ Two-volume collection of Sumner's most important letters to leading American and British statesmen, reformers, and intellectuals. [DF]

42.44 James Parton. *Life of Andrew Jackson.* 1860 ed. New York: Johnson Reprint, 1967. ▸ Classic, still unrivaled, three-volume biography. Admiring but critical; combines penetrating analysis with thorough research (many eyewitness accounts) and literary grace. Source of enduring characterizations and anecdotes. Available on microfilm from Ann Arbor: University Microfilms International. [DF]

42.45 Merrill D. Peterson. *The great triumvirate: Webster, Clay, and Calhoun.* New York: Oxford University Press, 1987. ISBN 0-19-503877-0. ▸ Three-sided political biography emphasizing contrasting characters, intertwining careers, mutual ambition, and conservatism. Sees them as exemplifying political generation. [DF]

42.46 Norma Lois Peterson. *The presidencies of William Henry Harrison and John Tyler*. Lawrence: University Press of Kansas, 1989. ISBN 0-7006-0400-6. ▸ Discussion of politics, administration, and diplomacy. Emphasizes Harrison-Tyler continuity, diplomatic successes, legislative-executive conflict, Henry Clay's imperiousness, and Tyler's undeserved low repute. [DF]

42.47 Robert V. Remini. *Andrew Jackson*. Vol. 1: *Andrew Jackson and the course of American empire, 1767–1821*. Vol. 2: *Andrew Jackson and the course of American freedom, 1822–1832*. Vol. 3: *Andrew Jackson and the course of American democracy, 1833–1845*. New York: Harper & Row, 1977–84. ISBN 0-06-013574-3 (v. 1), 0-06-014844-6 (v. 2), 0-06-015279-6 (v. 3). ▸ Laudatory biography presenting Jackson as dominant figure of his era, shaper of national expansion, crusader against political corruption, restorer of republican principle, champion of democracy, and tribune of the people. [DF]

42.48 Robert V. Remini. *Henry Clay: statesman for the Union*. New York: Norton, 1991. ISBN 0-393-03004-0. ▸ Massive biography in popular style. Views Clay as devoted unionist of unequaled talents, undercut by insatiable ambition, egotism, recklessness, and poor political judgment. [DF]

42.49 Leonard L. Richards. *The life and times of congressman John Quincy Adams*. New York: Oxford University Press, 1986. ISBN 0-19-504026-0. ▸ Critical study of Adams's post-presidential career. Attributes his actions more to personal motives—ambition, vanity, combativeness, revenge—and antimasonic-whig partisanship than to reputed superior wisdom and virtue. [DF]

42.50 Robert Seager II. *And Tyler, too: a biography of John and Julia Gardner Tyler*. New York: McGraw-Hill, 1963. ▸ Sympathetic but critical treatment of Tyler's politics, especially pre- and post-presidential. Viewed as principled but thin-skinned and devoted to slavery. Emphasis on private life, Tyler family, and Washington society. [DF]

42.51 Charles Grier Sellers, Jr. *James K. Polk*. Vol. 1: *Jacksonian, 1795–1843*. Vol. 2: *Continentalist, 1843–1846*. 1957–66 ed. Norwalk, Conn.: Easton, 1987. ▸ Unfinished epic biography portraying Polk as old republican ideologue; stalwart partisan; indefatigable, manipulative, innovator in executive leadership; and visionary expansionist; but narrowminded and morally insensitive to slavery issue. Rich detail on Tennessee and national politics. [DF]

42.52 Richard H. Sewell. *John P. Hale and the politics of abolition*. Cambridge, Mass.: Harvard University Press, 1965. ▸ Biography of New Hampshire Democrat turned congressional antislavery pioneer, Free-Soil presidential candidate, and Republican, whose career illustrates evolving northern political alignments before Civil War. [DF]

42.53 John Y. Simon, ed. *The papers of Ulysses S. Grant*. 18 vols. to date. Carbondale: Southern Illinois University Press, 1967–. ISBN 0-8093-0248-9 (v. 1), 0-8093-0366-3 (v. 2), 0-8093-0471-6 (v. 3), 0-8093-0507-0 (v. 4), 0-8093-0636-0 (v. 5), 0-8093-0694-8 (v. 6), 0-8093-0880-0 (v. 7), 0-8093-0884-3 (v. 8), 0-8093-0979-3 (v. 9), 0-8093-0980-7 (v. 10), 0-8093-1117-8 (v. 11), 0-8093-1118-6 (v. 12), 0-8093-1197-6 (v. 13), 0-8093-1198-4 (v. 14), 0-8093-1466-5 (v. 15), 0-8093-1467-3 (v. 16), 0-8093-1693-5 (v. 18). ▸ Comprehensive twenty-five-volume edition of Grant correspondence. Volumes 2–14 cover Civil War; completed through volume 18 (1868). [DF]

42.54 Elbert B. Smith. *The presidencies of Zachary Taylor and Millard Fillmore*. Lawrence: University Press of Kansas, 1988. ISBN 0-7006-0362-X. ▸ Analysis of politics, administration, and diplomacy. Defends both men as realistic and effective leaders,

underappreciated by historians; emphasizes continuity and success of their approach to crucial slavery issue. [DF]

42.55 Elbert B. Smith. *The presidency of James Buchanan*. 1975 ed. Lawrence: University Press of Kansas, 1980. ISBN 0-7006-0132-5. ▸ Survey of politics, slavery controversy, and secession crisis. Finds Buchanan neither weak nor indecisive but blindly pro-southern and uncomprehending of northern antislavery; obtusely furthered sectional confrontation by encouraging southern intransigence. [DF]

42.56 Glyndon G. Van Deusen. *William Henry Seward*. New York: Oxford University Press, 1967. ▸ Standard biography of New York whig-republican governor, senator, and President Lincoln's secretary of state. Views him as accomplished, ambitious, wily, visionary, sometimes rash, and most successful at diplomacy. [DF]

42.57 Herbert Weaver, ed. *Correspondence of James K. Polk*. 7 vols. to date. Nashville: Vanderbilt University Press, 1969–. ISBN 0-8265-1146-5 (v. 1), 0-8265-1176-7 (v. 2), 0-8265-1201-1 (v. 3), 0-8265-1206-2 (v. 4), 0-8265-1208-9 (v. 5), 0-8265-1211-9 (v. 6), 0-8265-1225-9 (v. 7). ▸ Comprehensive eleven-volume edition of letters to and from Polk. Completed through volume 7 (1844). [DF]

42.58 Charles M. Wiltse. *John C. Calhoun*. Vol. 1: *Nationalist, 1782–1828*. Vol. 2: *Nullifier, 1829–1839*. Vol. 3: *Sectionalist, 1840–1850*. 1944–51 ed. New York: Russell & Russell, 1968. ▸ Epic biography portraying Calhoun as unionist, champion of states' rights and minority interests, and prescient critic of industrial society and majoritarian tyranny; acquits him of overweening ambition, proslavery monomania, political inconsistency. Admiring, defensive portrait, especially critical of Jacksonians and abolitionists. [DF]

42.59 Charles M. Wiltse, eds. *The papers of Daniel Webster*. 15 vols. Hanover, N.H.: University Press of New England for Dartmouth College, 1974–89. ▸ Selective fifteen-volume edition of Webster's papers in four series: correspondence, legal papers, diplomatic papers, and speeches and formal writings. [DF]

Law and Judicial Doctrine

42.60 Maurice G. Baxter. *Daniel Webster and the Supreme Court*. Amherst: University of Massachusetts Press, 1966. ▸ Topically organized survey of Webster's important cases. Presents him as America's foremost constitutional lawyer, whose weighty influence helped shape judicial doctrine toward aggrandizement of national power. [DF]

42.61 Maxwell Bloomfield. *American lawyers in a changing society, 1776–1876*. Cambridge, Mass.: Harvard University Press, 1976. ISBN 0-674-02910-0. ▸ Multibiographical study of lawyers adapting to conflicting perceptions of their proper community role. Concludes that eventually elitism, professionalism, and private profit prevailed over democratization, public interest, and social service. [DF]

42.62 Don E. Fehrenbacher. *The Dred Scott case: its significance in American law and politics*. New York: Oxford University Press, 1978. ISBN 0-19-502403-6. ▸ Monumental, definitive account. Traces background to progressive constitutionalization of slavery-expansion issue and examines political consequences. Finds Chief Justice Taney's decision an illogical, emotional proslavery diatribe. Abridged as *Slavery, Law, and Politics* (1981). [DF]

42.63 Harold M. Hyman and William W. Wiecek. *Equal justice under law: constitutional development, 1835–1875*. New York: Harper & Row, 1982. ISBN 0-06-014937-X (cl), 0-06-132059-5 (pbk). ▸ Comprehensive narrative. Emphasizes political context of Supreme Court jurisprudence, disruptive impact of slavery,

Reconstruction issues and amendments, and rise of federal power and of civil rights over states' rights. [DF]

42.64 Stanley I. Kutler. *Privilege and creative destruction: the Charles River bridge case.* 1971 ed. Baltimore: Johns Hopkins University Press, 1990. ISBN 0-8018-3983-1. ▸ Argues this famous Supreme Court case (1837) cleared path for railroad development; decision reflected then-prevailing conception of government as agent of economic development and technological innovation. [DF]

42.65 Leonard W. Levy. *The law of the Commonwealth and Chief Justice Shaw.* 1957 ed. New York: Oxford University Press, 1987. ISBN 0-19-504865-2 (cl), 0-19-504866-0 (pbk). ▸ Judicial biography showing how Massachusetts Supreme Court under Shaw used law to promote industrial development while guarding civil liberties and asserting preeminence of public interest over corporate privilege. [DF]

42.66 R. Kent Newmyer. *Supreme Court Justice Joseph Story: statesman of the old republic.* Chapel Hill: University of North Carolina Press, 1985. ISBN 0-8078-1626-4. ▸ Biography of Story as judge, teacher, and scholar. Concludes republican principles, New England social conservatism, and faith in law's morality and rationality shaped his systematizing scholarship, nationalist jurisprudence, and judicial statesmanship. [DF]

42.67 Mark V. Tushnet. *The American law of slavery, 1810–1860: considerations of humanity and interest.* Princeton: Princeton University Press, 1981. ISBN 0-691-04681-6 (cl), 0-691-10104-3 (pbk). ▸ Marxian analysis of southern state codes and judicial decisions. Argues for racial interdependency and white humanity while stressing legal tensions resulting from contradictions between patriarchal and commercial aspects of slavery. [DF/MW]

42.68 G. Edward White. *The Marshall court and cultural change, 1815–1835.* Abr. ed. New York: Oxford University Press, 1991. ISBN 0-19-507058-5 (cl), 0-19-507059-3 (pbk). ▸ Massive examination of Supreme Court's structure, personnel, internal workings, ideological premises, and constitutional jurisprudence. Concludes court reflected its unique milieu, fashioning legal principles to preserve revolutionary republicanism amid pervasive change. [DF]

Public Policy and Foreign Policy

42.69 John S. D. Eisenhower. *So far from God.* New York: Random House, 1989. ISBN 0-394-56051-5. ▸ Comprehensive, detailed, and orderly look at Mexican War from English-language sources. Considers battles, diplomacy, and politics of each event and effects on belligerents. Captivating. [CAM]

42.70 L. Ray Gunn. *The decline of authority: public economic policy and political development in New York, 1800–1860.* Ithaca, N.Y.: Cornell University Press, 1988. ISBN 0-8014-2101-2. ▸ Outline of simultaneous decentralization and democratization of politics and diminution of governmental responsibilities and effectiveness that created disjuncture between powerless public sphere and privatized economy removed from popular control. [DF]

42.71 Ernest R. May. *The making of the Monroe Doctrine.* 1975 ed. Cambridge, Mass.: Harvard University Press, 1992. ISBN 0-674-54340-8 (cl, 1975), 0-674-54341-6 (pbk). ▸ Revisionist account assessing influence of international situation, diplomatic personalities, and domestic politics on policy making. Concludes presidential ambition primarily shaped actions of American principals. See also Perkins 38.67 and Whitaker 38.74. [DF/RJW]

42.72 Malcolm J. Rohrbough. *The land office business: the settlement and administration of American public lands, 1789–1837.* 1968 ed. Belmont, Calif.: Wadsworth, 1990. ISBN 0-534-12324-4 (pbk). ▸ Outline of growth in federal land-sale system, showing how

political pressures, public disfavor, administrative incapacity, party patronage, and official venality undermined effective operation of General Land Office by 1830s. [DF]

42.73 Harry N. Scheiber. *Ohio canal era: a case study of government and the economy, 1820–1861.* 1969 ed. Athens: Ohio University Press, 1987. ISBN 0-8214-0048-7 (cl), 0-8214-0866-6 (pbk). ▸ Political, financial, and administrative history of Ohio canal system, showing importance of state-owned, public enterprise to economic development until undermined by localism which eroded popular confidence and competition from private railoads. [DF]

42.74 John H. Schroeder. *Mr. Polk's war: American opposition and dissent, 1846–1848.* Madison: University of Wisconsin Press, 1973. ISBN 0-299-06160-4. ▸ Survey of Mexican War criticism. Shows how military success, Polk's resoluteness, and conflicting goals and tactics among whig, Calhounite, pacifist, and abolitionist opponents undercut effective resistance. [DF]

42.75 Mark W. Summers. *The plundering generation: corruption and the crisis of the Union, 1849–1861.* New York: Oxford University Press, 1987. ISBN 0-19-505057-6. ▸ Survey of widespread antebellum public malfeasance. Suggests politicians' dishonesty undermined faith in government, discredited parties, and aggravated sectional animosities. [DF]

SEE ALSO
47.51 Bradford Perkins. *Castlereagh and Adams.*

Jacksonian Era

42.76 John M. Belohlavek. *"Let the eagle soar!" The foreign policy of Andrew Jackson.* Lincoln: University of Nebraska Press, 1985. ISBN 0-8032-1187-2. ▸ Comprehensive study, including diplomatic bureaucracy and personnel; emphasis on European relations. Sees Jackson as vigorous but flexible, successfully pursuing traditional aim of expanding overseas trade. [DF]

42.77 Lee Benson. *The concept of Jacksonian democracy: New York as a test case.* 1961 ed. Princeton: Princeton University Press, 1964. ISBN 0-691-04513-5 (cl), 0-691-00572-9 (pbk). ▸ Influential revisionist study of party politics and voting behavior. Decries historians' economic determinism and Jacksonian bias. Denies parties' socioeconomic differences, emphasizing ethnocultural sources of partisanship. Renames era Age of Egalitarianism. [DF]

42.78 Donald B. Cole. *Jacksonian democracy in New Hampshire, 1800–1851.* Cambridge, Mass.: Harvard University Press, 1970. ISBN 0-674-46990-9. ▸ Narrative with voting analysis. Finds party continuity from Thomas Jefferson to Andrew Jackson and significant whig/democratic differences in economic policies and class and regional constituencies. Defends progressive Turner (40.125, 42.131) and Schlesinger (42.90) views of politics. [DF]

42.79 Richard E. Ellis. *The Union at risk: Jacksonian democracy, states' rights, and the nullification crisis.* 1987 ed. New York: Oxford University Press, 1989. ISBN 0-19-503785-5 (cl, 1987), 0-19-506187-X (pbk). ▸ Examination of constitutional, ideological, and political context and ramifications of nullification crisis. Sees outcome as South Carolina victory and presidential defeat, furthering ascendancy of proslavery over Jackson's democratic version of states' rights. [DF]

42.80 Daniel Feller. *The public lands in Jacksonian politics.* Madison: University of Wisconsin Press, 1984. ISBN 0-299-09850-8. ▸ Analysis of national controversies over disposition of western public domain, 1815–37. Stresses transition in congressional voting from East-West sectionalism to whig-democratic partisanship. [DF]

42.81 Walter Hugins. *Jacksonian democracy and the working class: a study of the New York workingmen's movement, 1829–1837.* Stanford, Calif.: Stanford University Press, 1960. ▸ Analysis of leaders and program of New York City Workingmen's party. Argues diverse membership and equal rights philosophy reflected entrepreneurial aspirations to democratize capitalism rather than working-class consciousness. [DF]

42.82 Lawrence Frederick Kohl. *The politics of individualism: parties and the American character in the Jacksonian era.* New York: Oxford University Press, 1989. ISBN 0-19-505374-5 (cl), 0-19-506781-9 (pbk). ▸ Study of partisan thought and rhetoric. Attributes party conflict to temperamental distinction between inner-directed Whigs welcoming impersonal commercializing society and tradition-directed Democrats fearing it. [DF]

42.83 Richard B. Latner. *The presidency of Andrew Jackson: White House politics, 1829–1837.* Athens: University of Georgia Press, 1979. ISBN 0-8203-0457-3. ▸ Analysis with focus on policy making and personnel. Emphasizes Jackson's control of his administration and predominant influence of westerners, not southerners or Van Burenites. [DF]

42.84 Richard Patrick McCormick. *The second American party system: party formation in the Jacksonian era.* Chapel Hill: University of North Carolina Press, 1966. ▸ State-by-state account of whig and democratic organizations as response to regional preferences in successive presidential campaigns. Concludes parties were electoral machines, not policy vehicles. [DF]

42.85 Marvin Meyers. *The Jacksonian persuasion: politics and belief.* 1957 ed. Stanford, Calif.: Stanford University Press, 1976. ISBN 0-8047-0505-4 (cl), 0-8047-0506-2 (pbk). ▸ Study of party ideology and temperament. Sees Democrats as apprehensive and backward-looking, torn between eagerness for material progress and fear of consequent moral dislocation. [DF]

42.86 Edward Pessen. *Jacksonian America: society, personality, and politics.* 1978 rev. ed. Urbana: University of Illinois Press, 1985. ISBN 0-252-01237-2 (pbk). ▸ Sweeping, iconoclastic portrait. Americans were energetic, materialistic, and crude. Unprincipled parties, especially Democrats, cynically served politicians' ambitions, evaded issues, and offered sham democracy to disguise growing inegalitarianism, class rule, and social injustice. [DF]

42.87 Robert V. Remini. *Andrew Jackson and the bank war: a study in the growth of presidential power.* New York: Norton, 1967. ▸ Quick, balanced treatment of central Jacksonian controversy as mainly personal-political power struggle between Jackson and Whigs. Jackson's victory permanently enhanced executive authority. [DF]

42.88 Robert V. Remini. *The election of Andrew Jackson.* 1963 ed. Westport, Conn.: Greenwood, 1980. ISBN 0-313-22396-3. ▸ Standard account of tumultuous 1828 campaign. Describes Jacksonian innovations in party organization and propaganda. [DF]

42.89 Michael Paul Rogin. *Fathers and children: Andrew Jackson and the subjugation of the American Indian.* 1975 ed. New York: Vintage, 1976. ISBN 0-394-71881-X. ▸ Marxian, psychoanalytic interpretation of American character, westward movement, banking controversy, and Jackson's personality. Argues Indian destruction defined Jacksonianism and decisively shaped national identity. [DF/HIK]

42.90 Arthur M. Schlesinger, Jr. *The age of Jackson.* 1945 ed. Boston: Little, Brown, 1953. ▸ Monumental account, starting point for subsequent Jacksonian scholarship. Sees Andrew Jackson as popular tribune in recurring class conflict against business dominance. Relates politics to contemporary literature, religion, and reform. Vivid, exciting narrative. [DF]

42.91 Charles Grier Sellers, Jr. *The market revolution: Jacksonian America, 1815–1846.* New York: Oxford University Press, 1991. ISBN 0-19-503889-4. ▸ Comprehensive history. Sees era's society,

culture, and religion reshaped by pervasive commercial transformation. Jacksonian bank war was agrarian majority's last great stand against bourgeois hegemony: democracy resisting capitalism. [DF]

42.92 James Roger Sharp. *The Jacksonians versus the banks: politics in the states after the panic of 1837.* New York: Columbia University Press, 1970. ISBN 0-231-03260-9. ▸ Focuses on Mississippi, Ohio, Virginia, Pennsylvania, and New York. Sees hard-money, antibanking Democrats as espousing core of party's anti-commercial, anti-entrepreneurial ethos. [DF]

42.93 Sam B. Smith and Harriet Chappell Owsley, eds. *The papers of Andrew Jackson.* 4 vols. to date. Knoxville: University of Tennessee Press, 1980–. ISBN 0-87049-219-5 (v. 1), 0-87049-441-4 (v. 2), 0-87049-650-6 (v. 3), 0-87049-778-2 (v. 4). ▸ Projected, selective, seventeen-volume edition of Jackson's correspondence and other papers. Completed through volume 4 (1820). Available on microfilm from Wilmington, Del.: Scholarly Resources. [DF]

42.94 Peter Temin. *The Jacksonian economy.* New York: Norton, 1969. ISBN 0-393-09841-9 (pbk). ▸ Discussion of economic turmoil of Jacksonian era caused by extrinsic international developments rather than bank war. Cliometric challenge to traditional historiography. [GJK]

42.95 Glyndon G. Van Deusen. *The Jacksonian era, 1828–1848.* 1959 ed. New York: Harper & Row, 1966. ▸ Standard, authoritative narrative of national politics, diplomacy, and war. Traces rise of party competition and its corrosion by intruding sectionalism over slavery. Whigs were conservative and pro-business; Democrats, liberal egalitarians. [DF]

42.96 Harry L. Watson. *Jacksonian politics and community conflict: the emergence of the second American party system in Cumberland County, North Carolina.* Baton Rouge: Louisiana State University Press, 1981. ISBN 0-8071-0857-X. ▸ Local study of whig and democratic origins. Stresses economic basis for parties, which organized around commercial issues (transportation, banking) while adapting traditional republican ideology to mobilize voters. [DF]

42.97 Harry L. Watson. *Liberty and power: the politics of Jacksonian America.* New York: Hill & Wang, 1990. ISBN 0-8090-6546-0. ▸ Synthetic overview of recent scholarship. Emphasizes rise of mass parties and their disagreements over political ideology and economy in era of market revolution. Whigs championed commercialization; Democrats, egalitarianism. [DF]

42.98 Leonard D. White. *The Jacksonians: a study in administrative history, 1829–1861.* New York: Macmillan, 1954. ▸ Standard encyclopedic account of workings of federal government. Structure and functions changed little over time, but politicization and democratization of public service impaired competence and efficiency. [DF]

Sectional Politics

42.99 Thomas B. Alexander. *Sectional stress and party strength: a study of roll-call voting patterns in the United States House of Representatives, 1836–1860.* Nashville: Vanderbilt University Press, 1967. ▸ Statistical analysis finding economic sectionalism overcame partisanship after 1850. Argues for immutable polarization over slavery throughout era, suggesting inevitability of Civil War. [DF]

42.100 Dale Baum. *The Civil War party system: the case of Massachusetts, 1848–1876.* Chapel Hill: University of North Carolina Press, 1984. ISBN 0-8078-1588-8. ▸ Electoral analysis focusing on rise and fall of radical antislavery Republicans. Denies republican-nativist connection; stresses economic over ethnoreligious influences on voting; see Benson 42.77 and Kleppner 42.15. Challenges conventional political periodization. [DF]

42.101 Eugene H. Berwanger. *The frontier against slavery: western anti-Negro prejudice and the slavery extension controversy.* Urbana: University of Illinois Press, 1967. ▸ History of racial discriminatory and exclusionary measures from Ohio to Oregon, 1787–1860. Argues Negrophobia, not moral abolitionism, primarily underlay opposition to slavery's spread. Available on microfilm from Ann Arbor: University Microfilms International. [DF/CAM]

42.102 Frederick J. Blue. *The Free Soilers: third-party politics, 1848–54.* Urbana: University of Illinois Press, 1973. ISBN 0-252-00308-X. ▸ Narrative focusing on party leaders. Emphasizes personal ambition, political opportunism, and racism they shared with Whigs and Democrats. [DF]

42.103 William J. Cooper, Jr. *The South and the politics of slavery, 1828–1856.* Baton Rouge: Louisiana State University Press, 1978. ISBN 0-8071-0385-3 (cl), 0-8071-0775-1 (pbk). ▸ Narrative account. Finds defense of slavery in national arena, not economic or local issues, dominating both whig and democratic appeals throughout era. Partisan zealotry promoted proslavery unity, blunting class divisions. [DF]

42.104 Avery Craven. *The growth of southern nationalism, 1848–1861.* Baton Rouge: Louisiana State University Press, 1953. ▸ Political narrative. Sees slavery as symbolic vehicle for northern industrial domination, not fundamental source of southern nationalism. Attributes secession and Civil War to emotionalism and breakdown of democratic process. Forceful statement of once-prevalent view. [DF]

42.105 Don E. Fehrenbacher. *Lincoln in text and context: collected essays.* Stanford, Calif.: Stanford University Press, 1987. ISBN 0-8047-1329-4. ▸ Reflections on Lincoln, historiography, controversy, and myth. Includes discussion of Civil War causes, Lincoln's record on race and civil liberties, his assassination, and fictional and psychoanalytic readings of his character. [DF]

42.106 Don E. Fehrenbacher. *The South and three sectional crises.* Baton Rouge: Louisiana State University Press, 1980. ISBN 0-8071-0671-2. ▸ Brief exploration of southern congressional posture in Missouri, 1850, and Kansas controversies for causes of secession. Concludes intransigent defense of permanent slavery made sectional conflict inevitable. [DF]

42.107 Paul Finkelman. *An imperfect Union: slavery, federalism, and comity.* Chapel Hill: University of North Carolina Press, 1981. ISBN 0-8078-1438-5 (cl), 0-8078-4066-1 (pbk). ▸ Well-researched history of judicial treatment of interstate slavery issues involving fugitives, transients, and sojourners. Argues antebellum collapse of North-South state reciprocity and federal proslavery tilt ruptured legal nationhood, portending disunion. [DF/EVW]

42.108 Lacy K. Ford, Jr. *Origins of southern radicalism: the South Carolina upcountry, 1800–1860.* New York: Oxford University Press, 1988. ISBN 0-19-504422-3. ▸ Narrative of political, economic, and cultural antecedents of secession. Local politics were boisterously democratic, not aristocratic; yeomen supported secession to defend republican liberty and economic independence against encroaching external threats. [DF]

42.109 George B. Forgie. *Patricide in the house divided: a psychological interpretation of Lincoln and his age.* New York: Norton, 1979. ISBN 0-393-05695-3. ▸ Analysis of antebellum literature and political rhetoric. Suggests politicians' oedipal feelings toward idealized heroic revolutionary fathers shaped their ideas on nationhood and slavery, producing fratricidal Civil War. [DF]

42.110 Alison Goodyear Freehling. *Drift toward dissolution: the Virginia slavery debate of 1831–1832.* Baton Rouge: Louisiana State University Press, 1982. ISBN 0-8071-1035-3. ▸ Analysis centering on state constitutional and legislative proceedings. Sees no abrupt turn from Jeffersonian antislavery to Calhounite proslavery, but continuing paralysis from failure to reconcile conflicting principles, sectional interests, and racism. [DF]

42.111 William W. Freehling. *Prelude to Civil War: the nullification controversy in South Carolina, 1816–1836.* 1966 ed. New York: Oxford University Press, 1992. ISBN 0-19-507681-8 (pbk). ▸ Standard narrative, set in broad context. Argues Carolinians' growing obsession with defending slavery, along with economic distress, underlay strident opposition to federal tariff laws. [DF]

42.112 William W. Freehling. *The road to disunion.* Vol. 1: *Secessionists at bay, 1776–1854.* New York: Oxford University Press, 1990. ISBN 0-19-505814-3. ▸ Revisionist account of slavery controversies in national politics. Emphasizes disunity; upper South looked to terminate slavery, lower South to perpetuate it. Extremists manipulated moderate majority by raising sectional loyalty issues. [DF]

42.113 Kenneth S. Greenberg. *Masters and statesmen: the political culture of American slavery.* Baltimore: Johns Hopkins University Press, 1985. ISBN 0-8018-2762-0 (cl), 0-8018-3744-8 (pbk). ▸ Focus on South Carolina. Argues slaveowning shaped southerners' distinctive conceptions of honor and republican leadership and promoted internal consensus, antipartyism, anglophobia, inflexibility, and secession. [DF]

42.114 Holman Hamilton. *Prologue to conflict: the crisis and compromise of 1850.* 1964 ed. New York: Norton, 1966. ▸ Intensive legislative analysis. Sees Douglas Democrats—not Clay-Webster Whigs—as crucial proponents, compromise as dubious achievement, and Civil War as needless tragedy furthered by ignorance and political shortsightedness. [DF]

42.115 Michael F. Holt. *The political crisis of the 1850s.* 1978 ed. New York: Norton, 1983. ISBN 0-393-95370-X (pbk). ▸ Revisionist narrative attributing cause of Civil War to national party breakdown, not slavery. Parties thrived on competition; growing consensus on issues blurred party identities, producing voter disaffection, fanned politicians into nativism and sectionalism. [DF]

42.116 James L. Huston. *The panic of 1857 and the coming of the Civil War.* Baton Rouge: Louisiana State University Press, 1987. ISBN 0-8071-1368-9. ▸ Narrative of financial crisis and political aftermath. Argues sectional responses to depression exacerbated fundamental conflict of free and slave labor systems. Tariff protectionism strengthened Republicans in crucial Pennsylvania. [DF]

42.117 Harry V. Jaffa. *Crisis of the house divided: an interpretation of the issues in the Lincoln-Douglas debates.* 1959 ed. Seattle: University of Washington Press, 1973. ISBN 0-295-95263-6. ▸ Exploration of both men's political principles, finding fundamental meaning of democracy, freedom, and natural rights was at stake in debates. Condemns southern apologist proponents of "needless war" thesis for obscuring this. [DF]

42.118 Robert W. Johannsen. *Frontier politics and the sectional conflict: the Pacific Northwest on the eve of the Civil War.* Seattle: University of Washington Press, 1955. ▸ History of national issues in Oregon from statehood through secession. Finds state parties reflecting national concerns through conservative unionist lens, with Douglas's democratic popular sovereignty doctrines predominant. [DF]

42.119 Robert W. Johannsen. *The frontier, the Union, and Stephen A. Douglas.* Urbana: University of Illinois Press, 1989. ISBN 0-252-01577-0. ▸ Essays on Douglas, Abraham Lincoln, national expansion, slavery in territories, popular sovereignty, and approach of Civil War. Sees Douglas as representing Americans' romantic faith in western destiny. [DF]

42.120 Stephen E. Maizlish. *The triumph of sectionalism: the* *transformation of Ohio politics, 1844–1856.* Kent, Ohio: Kent State University Press, 1983. ISBN 0-87338-293-5. ▸ Argues antislavery sectionalism usurped traditional economic issues (banking) even before 1850, portending whig-democratic breakup and republican emergence. Nativism was temporary byproduct, not cause, of party disruption. [DF]

42.121   Robert E. May. *The southern dream of a Caribbean empire, 1854–1861.* 1973 ed. Athens: University of Georgia Press, 1989. ISBN 0-8203-1136-7. ▸ Recounts sectionalization of Manifest Destiny, filibusters, and presidential annexationism. Slavery issue quelled northern expansionism and intensified southern thirst for Cuba, Nicaragua, and Mexico, in turn exacerbating sectional tensions. [DF]

42.122   Glover Moore. *The Missouri controversy, 1819–1821.* 1937 ed. Gloucester, Mass.: P. Smith, 1967. ▸ Political, legislative analysis set in socioeconomic context. Questions depth of public concern over Missouri slavery, arguing propagandists fanned controversy for self-interested sectional, partisan, and factional reasons. [DF]

42.123   Allan Nevins. *Ordeal of the Union.* 1947–71 ed. 4 vols. James McPherson, Introduction. New York: Maxwell Macmillan, 1992. ISBN 0-02-035441-X (v. 1), 0-02-035442-8 (v. 2), 0-02-035443-6 (v. 3), 0-02-035445-2 (v. 4). ▸ Epic narrative of oncoming sectional crisis in grand nineteenth-century multivolume tradition. Sees crucial questions of slavery and race at heart of conflict, compounded by political failures of vision and leadership on both sides. Earlier title: Vol. 2, *The Emergence of Lincoln*; Vols. 3–4, *The War for the Union.* [DF]

42.124   David M. Potter. *The impending crisis, 1848–1861.* New York: Harper & Row, 1976. ISBN 0-06-0134034-8 (cl), 0-06-131929-5 (pbk). ▸ Authoritative narrative of political road to Civil War. Places fundamental disagreements over slavery at heart of conflict, exacerbated by southern political shortsightedness. Trenchant, judicious, scholarly synthesis. [DF]

42.125   Joseph G. Rayback. *Free soil: the election of 1848.* Lexington: University Press of Kentucky, 1970. ISBN 0-8131-1222-2. ▸ Campaign narrative focusing on battle for nominations. Sees slavery as dominant issue and widespread northern support for Wilmot Proviso as portending dissolution of Whig and Democratic parties. [DF]

42.126   Richard H. Sewell. *Ballots for freedom: antislavery politics in the United States, 1837–1860.* 1976 ed. New York: Norton, 1980. ISBN 0-393-00966-1 (pbk). ▸ Comprehensive narrative emphasizing continuities between abolitionists, Liberty men, Free-Soilers, and Republicans, all opposed to slavery on moral, egalitarian grounds and willing to employ political means to destroy it. [DF]

42.127   Kenneth M. Stampp. *America in 1857: a nation on the brink.* New York: Oxford University Press, 1990. ISBN 0-19-503902-5. ▸ Portrait of a single year focusing on growing sectional conflict over slavery. Sees President Buchanan's folly in backing Kansas slavery as democratic disaster marking "political point of no return" on road to Civil War. [DF]

42.128   Kenneth M. Stampp. *The imperiled union: essays on the background of the Civil War.* New York: Oxford University Press, 1980. ISBN 0-19-502681-0 (cl), 0-19-502991-7 (pbk). ▸ Reflections on American nationhood, slavery historiography, Republican party, Abraham Lincoln, secession crisis, and Civil War causation. Places slavery at heart of irrepressible sectional conflict and moral antislavery at heart of republicanism. [DF]

42.129   Charles S. Sydnor. *The development of southern sectionalism, 1819–1848.* 1948 ed. Baton Rouge: Louisiana State University Press and the Littlefield Fund for Southern History of the University of Texas, 1968. ▸ Survey of economics, government,

politics, and white culture and society. Emphasizes deterioration from confident nationalism to defensive, emotional, and sectional self-consciousness. Dated by inattention to slave life but still lucid and judicious. [DF]

42.130   J. Mills Thornton, Jr. *Politics and power in a slave society: Alabama, 1800–1860.* Baton Rouge: Louisiana State University Press, 1978. ISBN 0-8071-0259-8 (cl), 0-8071-0891-X (pbk). ▸ Influential state study. Views secession as ultimate product of egalitarian, demagogic, Jacksonian culture focused on defending individual autonomy against economic-political domination by aristocrats, banks, urbanites, government, professional politicians, and northerners. [DF]

42.131   Frederick Jackson Turner. *Rise of the new West, 1819–1829.* 1906 ed. New York: Harper & Row, 1968. ▸ Classic general account (author's only completed book) emphasizing growth of sectionalism and democracy and western influence on national society and politics. [DF]

ECONOMIC AND SOCIAL HISTORY
General Studies

42.132   Ralph L. Andreano, ed. *Economic impact of the American Civil War.* 2d ed. Cambridge, Mass.: Schenkman, 1967. ▸ Collection of reprinted essays on whether Civil War sped or slowed process of American economic growth and development. Introduction to longstanding scholarly debate. [GJK]

42.133   Thomas C. Cochran. *Frontiers of change: early industrialism in America.* 1981 ed. New York: Oxford University Press, 1983. ISBN 0-19-502875-9 (cl, 1981), 0-19-503284-5 (pbk). ▸ Concise, provocative overview of developments to 1850s. Geography and culture—including business system but not market forces per se—explain why American Northeast industrialized early and rapidly. [GJK]

42.134   Conference on Research in Income and Wealth. *Trends in the American economy in the nineteenth century: a report of the National Bureau of Economic Research, New York.* 1960 ed. New York: Arno, 1975. ISBN 0-405-07588-X. ▸ Pioneering papers in new economic history. Estimates of output, income, factor payments, investment, balance of payments based on application of modern economic theory to nineteenth-century quantitative data. [GJK]

42.135   Claudia D. Goldin and Hugh Rockoff, eds. *Strategic factors in nineteenth-century American economic history: a volume to honor Robert W. Fogel.* Chicago: University of Chicago Press, 1992. ISBN 0-226-30112-5. ▸ Cliometric case studies by Fogel's students. Impact of market expansion and integration on different regions and segments of population. Rise in standard of living but not in life expectancy. Pioneering papers in new economic history. [GJK/DSS]

42.136   Morton J. Horwitz. *The transformation of American law, 1780–1860.* 1977 ed. New York: Oxford University Press, 1992. ISBN 0-19-507829-2. ▸ Concludes reinterpretation of property, contract, and commercial law served entrepreneurial interests. Emphasis on social conflict challenges consensus view of Handlin and Handlin 42.156, Hartz 42.157, and Hurst 42.137. [GJK]

42.137   James Willard Hurst. *Law and the conditions of freedom in the nineteenth-century United States.* 1956 ed. Madison: University of Wisconsin Press, 1971. ISBN 0-299-01363-4 (pbk). ▸ Classic analysis of law's positive social function. Concludes nineteenth-century policy makers viewed law as instrument for release of individual creative energy and promotion of economic productivity. [GJK]

42.138   Diane Lindstrom. *Economic development in the Philadelphia region, 1810–1850.* New York: Columbia University Press, 1978. ISBN 0-231-04272-8. ▸ Study finding impetus for Philadelphia's industrial development lay in city-hinterland dynamics of intraregional (not foreign or intersectional) trade. Eastern-demand model challenges North 42.139 and others. [GJK]

42.139 Douglass Cecil North. *The economic growth of the United States, 1790–1860.* 1961 ed. New York: Norton, 1966. ISBN 0-393-00346-9 (pbk). ▸ Discussion of cotton export trade as key to growth, 1815–39, and also spur to Northeast's industrialization. After 1840, domestic market flow more significant. Classic work of new economic history. [GJK/DMS]

42.140 William N. Parker. *America and the wider world.* Vol. 2 of *Europe, America, and the wider world: essays on the economic history of western capitalism.* Cambridge: Cambridge University Press, 1991. ISBN 0-521-25466-3 (cl), 0-521-22749-7 (pbk). ▸ Analysis of southern agriculture, northern agriculture, and northern industry as distinctive manifestations of market capitalism. Synthetic essays focusing on long-term social and economic determinants of development. [GJK]

42.141 Peter Temin. *Causal factors in American economic growth in the nineteenth century.* London: Macmillan, 1975. ISBN 0-333-17087-3. ▸ Account of why United States economy grew intensively beginning in early nineteenth century. Critical review of cliometric literature on growth rates, westward expansion, technological change, railroads, banking, and slavery. [GJK]

42.142 Robert H. Wiebe. *The opening of American society: from the adoption of the Constitution to the eve of disunion.* New York: Knopf, 1984. ISBN 0-394-53583-9. ▸ Contrary to revolutionary gentry's expectations, American society democratized as it grew spatially and commercially. Still, at mid-century, it was divided along class lines. Neo-Turnerian synthesis (see 42.131). [GJK]

Agriculture

42.143 Jeremy Atack and Fred Bateman. *To their own soil: agriculture in the antebellum North.* Ames: Iowa State University Press, 1987. ISBN 0-8138-0086-2. ▸ Northern farmers were economically rational and increasingly profit-oriented yet still tied to Jeffersonian ideal, which was nearly (albeit only temporarily) realized. Cliometric analysis. [GJK]

42.144 Hal S. Barron. *Those who stayed behind: rural society in nineteenth-century New England.* New York: Cambridge University Press, 1984. ISBN 0-521-25784-0. ▸ Case study of mature, rural town of Chelsea, Vermont, stressing experience of those who chose not to migrate to West or cities. Argues outmigration created ethnically homogeneous, socially consensual, and demographically stable community. [DSS/DLC]

42.145 Frederick A. Bode and Donald E. Ginter. *Farm tenancy and the census in antebellum Georgia.* Athens: University of Georgia Press, 1986. ISBN 0-8203-0834-X. ▸ Study of extent of tenancy in Georgia examined through federal census for 1860. Number of landless farmers considered much larger than previously known. Challenges older conceptions of southern political economy. [MW]

42.146 Clarence H. Danhof. *Change in agriculture: the northern United States, 1820–1870.* Cambridge, Mass.: Harvard University Press, 1969. ISBN 0-674-10770-5. ▸ Concludes northern farmers' increasing market orientation stimulated agricultural productivity and promoted both economic and technological development. Entrepreneurial interpretation based mainly on qualitative evidence. [GJK]

42.147 Paul Wallace Gates. *The farmer's age: agriculture, 1815–1860.* 1960 ed. Armonk, N.Y.: Sharpe, 1989. ISBN 0-87332-100-6 (pbk). ▸ Comprehensive survey of agricultural conditions and farmers' concerns organized by region and crop with attention to government, technology, and education. Masterly old economic history. [GJK]

42.148 Harold D. Woodman. *King cotton and his retainers: financing and marketing the cotton crop of the South, 1800–1925.* 1968 ed. Columbia: University of South Carolina Press, 1990. ISBN 0-87249-728-3 (pbk). ▸ Study of antebellum factorage system and postbellum furnishing merchant system which served needs of cotton agriculture, but reinforced South's dependence on outside sources for capital. Qualitative economic history. [GJK]

42.149 Gavin Wright. *The political economy of the cotton South: households, markets, and wealth in the nineteenth century.* New York: Norton, 1978. ISBN 0-393-05686-4 (cl), 0-393-09038-8 (pbk). ▸ Concludes slave plantations produced proportionately more for market than did family farms because of elasticity in labor supply. Consequently South had less incentive to industrialize than North. Cliometric analysis. [GJK]

Industrialization and Capitalist Transformation

42.150 Robert Greenhalgh Albion. *The rise of New York port (1815–1860).* 1939 ed. Boston: Northeastern University Press, 1984. ISBN 0-930350-58-8 (cl), 0-930350-59-6 (pbk). ▸ Narrative and topical history of New York City's emergence as nation's premier entrepot. Classic work written in grand style. [GJK]

42.151 Fred Bateman and Thomas Joseph Weiss. *A deplorable scarcity: the failure of industrialization in the slave economy.* Chapel Hill: University of North Carolina Press, 1981. ISBN 0-8078-1447-4. ▸ Argues antebellum South industrialized less quickly than it might have because planters, though capitalist, shied away from high-risk investments and subordinated profit maximization to other goals. Cliometric analysis. [GJK]

42.152 Alfred D. Chandler, Jr. *The visible hand: the managerial revolution in American business.* Cambridge, Mass.: Belknap, 1977. ISBN 0-674-94051-2 (cl), 0-674-94052-0 (pbk). ▸ Beginning with railroads, managerial bureaucracy replaced market mechanisms in coordinating production and distribution. American economic ascendancy epitomized by organization man, not robber baron. Magisterial business history. [GJK]

42.153 Christopher Clark. *The roots of rural capitalism: western Massachusetts, 1780–1860.* Ithaca, N.Y.: Cornell University Press, 1990. ISBN 0-8014-2422-4. ▸ Study of transition in Connecticut Valley from household production and local exchange to capitalist production for distant markets. Case study framed by scholarly debate over character of preindustrial America. [GJK/DMS]

42.154 Peter J. Coleman. *The transformation of Rhode Island, 1790–1860.* 1963 ed. Westport, Conn.: Greenwood, 1985. ISBN 0-313-24796-X. ▸ Study of how Rhode Island became nation's most industrialized state. Analytical narrative covering demographic, social, and political dimensions of economic development. [GJK]

42.155 Felicia Johnson Deyrup. *Arms makers of the Connecticut Valley: a regional study of the economic development of the small arms industry, 1798–1870.* 1948 ed. York, Pa.: Shumway, 1970. (Smith College studies in history, 33.) ISBN 0-87387-023-9. ▸ History of Springfield Armory and private arms makers that pioneered interchangeability, precision measurement, and specialized machine tools. Enduring study of origins of American system of manufactures. [GJK]

42.156 Oscar Handlin and Mary Flug Handlin. *Commonwealth, a study of the role of government in the American economy: Massachusetts, 1774–1861.* Rev. ed. Cambridge, Mass.: Belknap, 1969. ▸ Concludes Massachusetts public policy and legal doctrine promoted economic development for common good. Evolution from mercantilism to liberal humanitarianism, not laissez-faire. For parallel study, see Hartz 42.157. [GJK]

42.157 Louis Hartz. *Economic policy and democratic thought: Pennsylvania, 1776–1860.* 1948 ed. Gloucester, Mass.: P. Smith, 1970. ▸ Finds that, contrary to laissez-faire, state of Pennsylvania actively sought to promote and regulate economic development. For parallel study, see Handlin and Handlin 42.156. [GJK]

42.158 Clarence D. Long. *Wages and earnings in the United States, 1860–1890.* 1960 ed. New York: Arno, 1975. (National Bureau of Economic Research, General Series, 67.) ISBN 0-405-07603-7. ▸ Statistical analysis of contemporary government reports. Manufacturing workers' real wages and annual earnings rose 50 percent, 1860–90. Varied by industry, occupation, sex, age, region, and establishment. [GJK]

42.159 Albro Martin. *James J. Hill and the opening of the Northwest.* New York: Oxford University Press, 1976. ISBN 0-19-502070-7. ▸ Well-written and researched biography of true rags-to-riches story. Canadian-born Hill only American entrepreneur to build transcontinental railroad without public subsidies. [CAM]

42.160 Otto Mayr and Robert C. Post, eds. *Yankee enterprise: the rise of the American system of manufactures; a symposium.* Washington, D.C.: Smithsonian Institution Press, 1981. ISBN 0-87474-634-5 (cl), 0-87474-631-0 (pbk). ▸ Essays by leading historians of technology, business, labor, and culture exploring definitions, origins, and social dynamics of American system of manufactures. [GJK]

42.161 Glenn Porter and Harold C. Livesay. *Merchants and manufacturers: studies in the changing structure of nineteenth-century marketing.* 1971 ed. Chicago: Dee, 1989. ISBN 0-929587-10-3 (pbk). ▸ Examination of transformation of distribution system for manufactured goods. Control shifted from all-purpose merchants to specialized wholesalers to modern manufacturing corporations. Analytical business history. [GJK]

42.162 Philip Scranton. *Proprietary capitalism: the textile manufacture at Philadelphia, 1800–1885.* 1983 ed. Philadelphia: Temple University Press, 1987. ISBN 0-87722-461-7 (pbk). ▸ Detailed case study of textile industrialization in Philadelphia. Hallmark of industry was proliferation of small, specialized, family-owned firms. Explores advantages in comparison to large-scale corporate firms in New England. [GJK]

42.163 Merritt Roe Smith. *Harpers Ferry armory and the new technology: the challenge of change.* Ithaca, N.Y.: Cornell University Press, 1977. ISBN 0-8014-0984-5 (cl), 0-8014-9181-9 (pbk). ▸ Finds artisans and townspeople, imbued with preindustrial values, resisted mechanization and standardization at Harpers Ferry armory. Disputes view of American culture as highly receptive to technological innovation. [GJK]

42.164 Barbara M. Tucker. *Samuel Slater and the origins of the American textile industry, 1790–1860.* Ithaca, N.Y.: Cornell University Press, 1984. ISBN 0-8014-1594-2. ▸ Case study of Slater's mill system. Concludes traditional culture persisted in Slater's textile factories and communities despite mechanization. Early industrialization characterized by social stability, not class conflict. Contrast to Prude 42.194. [GJK/DAR]

42.165 Caroline F. Ware. *The early New England cotton manufacture: a study in industrial beginnings.* 1931 ed. New York: Russell & Russell, 1966. ▸ Pioneering study of growth of cotton textile industry in New England to 1860. Narrative and topical presentation focuses on capital, marketing, labor supply, working conditions, and reform efforts. [GJK]

SEE ALSO
4.462 Peter Temin. *Iron and steel in nineteenth-century America.*
40.257 Stanley Lebergott. *Manpower in economic growth.*

Working-Class Culture and Labor Protest

42.166 Wayne G. Broehl, Jr. *The Molly Maguires.* 1964 ed. Cambridge, Mass.: Harvard University Press, 1965. ▸ Narrative of events culminating in notorious trials and executions of Irish miners, 1876–77, for murdering bosses in Pennsylvania coalfields. Close attention to ethnic and economic context and role of Pinkerton spy. [GJK]

42.167 Robert V. Bruce. *1877: year of violence.* 1959 ed. Chicago: Dee, 1989. ISBN 0-929587-05-7 (pbk). ▸ Panoramic study of Great Railroad Strike of 1877 and its impact across the United States. Vivid, comprehensive, narrative account. [GJK]

42.168 Milton Cantor, ed. *American working-class culture: explorations in American labor and social history.* Westport, Conn.: Greenwood, 1979. ISBN 0-313-20611-2. ▸ Case studies (many reprinted) exploring how tradition, religion, ethnicity, and gender affected class development. Exemplifies emergence of new labor history focused more on culture than on formal organization. [GJK]

42.169 Alan Dawley. *Class and community: the industrial revolution in Lynn.* Cambridge, Mass.: Harvard University Press, 1976. ISBN 0-674-13390-0 (cl), 0-674-13395-1 (pbk). ▸ Provocative, sometimes combative, vigorously written, radical analysis of struggles of Lynn shoemakers against capitalist exploitation throughout nineteenth century. Political democracy served as safety valve deterring socialist consciousness. [GJK]

42.170 Paul G. Faler. *Mechanics and manufacturers in the early industrial revolution: Lynn, Massachusetts, 1760–1860.* Albany: State University of New York Press, 1981. ISBN 0-87395-504-8 (cl), 0-87395-505-6 (pbk). ▸ Study of gradual emergence of class consciousness among Lynn shoemakers, culminating in Great Strike of 1860. Emphasis on persistence of preindustrial values and cultural dimensions of class formation. [GJK]

42.171 Herbert G. Gutman. *Power and culture: essays on the American working class.* 1976 ed. Ira Berlin, ed. New York: Pantheon, 1987. ISBN 0-394-56026-4. ▸ Studies in cultural diversity and creativity of nineteenth-century workers. Posthumously published collection includes interview with author and assessment of his scholarly contribution by Berlin. [GJK]

42.172 Herbert G. Gutman. *Work, culture, and society in industrializing America: essays in American working-class and social history.* 1976 ed. New York: Vintage, 1977. ISBN 0-394-72251-5 (pbk). ▸ Workers resisted cultural as well as economic depredations of industrial capitalism, scoring noteworthy victories at the local level. Sweeping title essay and case studies by pioneer of the "new" labor history. [GJK]

42.173 Susan E. Hirsch. *Roots of the American working class: the industrialization of crafts in Newark, 1800–1860.* Philadelphia: University of Pennsylvania Press, 1978. ISBN 0-8122-7747-3. ▸ Threatened by specialization, mechanization, and immigration, Newark journeymen retreated into family life, fought back through unions, and divided politically along ethnic lines. Includes quantitative analysis. [GJK]

42.174 Bruce Laurie. *Artisans into workers: labor in nineteenth-century America.* New York: Hill & Wang, 1989. ISBN 0-8090-2752-6 (cl), 0-374-52153-0 (pbk). ▸ Wide-ranging yet compact synthesis of new and old labor history. As industrialization progressed, workers alternately embraced free laborism, radicalism, and prudential unionism, but not socialism. [GJK]

42.175 Bruce Laurie. *Working people of Philadelphia, 1800–1850.* Philadelphia: Temple University Press, 1980. ISBN 0-87722-168-5 (cl), 0-87722-292-4 (pbk). ▸ Case study in new labor history. Concludes Philadelphia's uneven industrialization led to cultural fragmentation among workers. Revivalists, traditionalists, radicals united in 1830s but divided at midcentury. [GJK]

42.176 Walter Licht. *Working for the railroad: the organization of work in the nineteenth century.* Princeton: Princeton University Press, 1983. ISBN 0-691-04700-6 (cl), 0-691-10221-X (pbk). ▸ Concludes early railwaymen enjoyed good pay and upward mobility, but endured hazardous conditions and arbitrary discipline. Pressure for bureaucratization came from below as well as above. [GJK]

42.177 Edward Pessen. *Most uncommon Jacksonians: the radical leaders of the early labor movement.* 1967 ed. Albany: State University of New York Press, 1970. ISBN 0-87395-066-6 (pbk). ▸ Like European socialists, leaders of Working Men's parties and trade unions in 1830s called for fundamental transformation of capitalist society. Disputes consensus view of Jacksonian era. [GJK]

42.178 W. J. Rorabaugh. *The craft apprentice: from Franklin to the machine age in America.* New York: Oxford University Press, 1986. ISBN 0-19-503647-6 (cl), 0-19-50189-0 (pbk). ▸ Evocative social history finding republican ideology and capitalist development initially empowered apprentices, but industrialization reduced them to unskilled machine tenders lacking upward mobility. [GJK/LAN]

42.179 Steven J. Ross. *Workers on the edge: work, leisure, and politics in industrializing Cincinnati, 1788–1890.* New York: Columbia University Press, 1985. ISBN 0-231-05520-X (cl), 0-231-05521-8 (pbk). ▸ Cincinnati wage earners' experiences grew more similar and oppressive, promoting class consciousness, but cultural divisions and republican ideology constrained radicalization. New labor history. [GJK]

42.180 Cynthia J. Shelton. *The mills of Manayunk: industrialization and social conflict in the Philadelphia region, 1787–1837.* Baltimore: Johns Hopkins University Press, 1986. ISBN 0-8018-3208-X. ▸ Case study from Marxist perspective. In contrast to native-born workers elsewhere, immigrant textile workers drew on radical British precedents forcefully resisting industrialization at Manayunk. [GJK]

42.181 Norman Ware. *The industrial worker, 1840–1860: the reaction of American industrial society to the advance of the Industrial Revolution.* 1924 ed. Chicago: Dee, 1990. ISBN 0-929587-25-1 (pbk). ▸ Discussion of workers' response to capitalist degradation; organized defensively in 1840s and aggressively in 1850s, increasingly drawing away from middle-class reformers. Classic analysis, pessimistic perspective. [GJK]

42.182 Sean Wilentz. *Chants democratic: New York City and the rise of the American working class, 1788–1850.* 1984 ed. New York: Oxford University Press, 1986. ISBN 0-19-503342-6 (cl, 1984), 0-19-504012-0 (pbk). ▸ Study of metropolitan industrialization-generated class conflict. Drawing on common republican heritage, master artisans promoted and journeymen resisted bastardization of craft. Magisterial neo-Marxist analysis. [GJK]

42.183 David A. Zonderman. *Aspirations and anxieties: New England workers and the mechanized factory system, 1815–1850.* New York: Oxford University Press, 1992. ISBN 0-19-505747-3. ▸ Topically organized intellectual analysis of reaction of New England workers to early factory system, which ranged from enthusiasm to alienation and protest. Differences rooted in debate over value of work. [GJK]

Urbanization and Community Studies

42.184 Elizabeth Blackmar. *Manhattan for rent, 1785–1850.* Ithaca, N.Y.: Cornell University Press, 1989. ISBN 0-8014-2024-5. ▸ Sophisticated radical analysis of capitalist transformation of housing in New York City. Emergence of tenancy and class-specific spatial organization reflected changing property and power relations. [GJK]

42.185 Stuart M. Blumin. *The emergence of the middle class: social experience in the American city, 1760–1900.* Cambridge: Cambridge University Press, 1989. ISBN 0-521-25075-7 (cl), 0-521-37612-2 (pbk). ▸ Analysis of transition from amorphous "middling sorts" to more cohesive middle class in major cities. Middle-class identity rooted in white-collar work, domesticity, and distinctive patterns of consumption and association. [GJK]

42.186 William Cronon. *Nature's metropolis: Chicago and the Great West.* New York: Norton, 1991. ISBN 0-393-02921-2. ▸ Sophisticated study of Chicago's emergence as metropolis and gateway to West analyzed in terms of commodity flows linking city and hinterland. Emphasis on ecological dimension of capitalist development. [GJK/ARLC]

42.187 John Mack Faragher. *Sugar creek: life on the Illinois prairie.* New Haven: Yale University Press, 1986. ISBN 0-300-03545-4 (cl), 0-300-04263-9 (pbk). ▸ Social history of rural area from dispossession of American Indians through consolidation of stable Euro-American community by midcentury. Broad coverage of land, natives, demography, agriculture, education, religion, and family. [GJK/CAM]

42.188 Clyde Griffen and Sally Griffen. *Natives and newcomers: the ordering of opportunity in mid-nineteenth-century Poughkeepsie.* Cambridge, Mass.: Harvard University Press, 1978. ISBN 0-674-60325-7. ▸ Sophisticated social mobility study emphasizing different experiences of immigrants and native born. As industrialization progressed, self-employment declined, distinction between manual and nonmanual occupations increased, and workers' experiences grew more similar. [GJK/NF]

42.189 Steven Hahn and Jonathan Prude, eds. *The countryside in the age of capitalist transformation: essays in the social history of rural America.* Chapel Hill: University of North Carolina Press, 1985. ISBN 0-8078-1666-3 (cl), 0-8078-4139-0 (pbk). ▸ Case studies in commercialization and industrialization of different rural areas in Northeast, South, and West. Emphasis on social and cultural costs and benefits of development. [GJK]

42.190 Theodore Hershberg, ed. *Philadelphia: work, space, family, and group experience in the nineteenth century; essays toward an interdisciplinary history of the city.* New York: Oxford University Press, 1981. ISBN 0-19-502752-3 (cl), 0-19-502753-1 (pbk). ▸ Analysis of how urbanization and industrialization transformed Philadelphia and its inhabitants' behavior, emphasizing interrelationships of class, race, demography, and location. Collaborative studies utilizing computerized 1850–80 census database, social science models, and quantitative methods. [GJK/DSS/KWK]

42.191 William Henry Pease and Jane H. Pease. *The web of progress: private values and public styles in Boston and Charleston, 1828–1843.* New York: Oxford University Press, 1985. ISBN 0-19-503467-8 (cl), 0-19-505105-X (pbk). ▸ Urban comparison of capitalist North and slave South. Boston diversified and modernized while Charleston did not, largely because of sectional differences in business and work ethics. [GJK]

42.192 Allan R. Pred. *Urban growth and city-systems in the United States, 1840–1860.* Cambridge, Mass.: Harvard University Press, 1980. ISBN 0-674-93091-6. ▸ Conceptual and empirical historical geography. Develops "probabilistic feedback model" to account for growing interdependency of major cities in Northeast and Midwest. [GJK]

42.193 Allan R. Pred. *Urban growth and the circulation of information: the United States system of cities, 1790–1840.* Cambridge, Mass.: Harvard University Press, 1973. ISBN 0-674-93090-8.

▸ Analysis of growth of mercantile cities and emergence of stable urban system explained in terms of evolving information and commodity flows. Emphasis on theoretical implications of evidence from pretelegraphic era. [GJK]

42.194 Jonathan Prude. *The coming of industrial order: town and factory life in rural Massachusetts, 1810–1860.* 1983 ed. Cambridge: Cambridge University Press, 1985. ISBN 0-521-24824-8 (cl, 1983), 0-521-31396-1 (pbk). ▸ Detailed case study emphasizing disruptive impact of textile mills on rural culture. Although devoid of major strikes, industrialization in two Massachusetts towns involved class and community conflicts. [GJK]

42.195 Richard B. Stott. *Workers in the metropolis: class, ethnicity, and youth in antebellum New York City.* Ithaca, N.Y.: Cornell University Press, 1990. ISBN 0-8014-2067-9. ▸ Study of remaking of New York City's working class during 1840s and 1850s as young immigrant workers supplanted native-born artisans. Community study focusing on workers' daily experience. [GJK]

42.196 Stephan Thernstrom. *Poverty and progress: social mobility in a nineteenth-century city.* 1964 ed. Cambridge, Mass.: Harvard University Press, 1974. ISBN 0-674-09500-3 (cl), 0-674-69501-1 (pbk). ▸ Study of unskilled laborers and their sons in Newburyport, Massachusetts, who rarely attained middle-class occupational status but often acquired property—lending credence to mobility ideology. Classic work that generated genre of social mobility studies. [GJK]

42.197 Stephan Thernstrom and Richard Sennett, eds. *Nineteenth-century cities: essays in the new urban history.* New Haven: Yale University Press, 1969. ISBN 0-300-01150-4 (cl), 0-300-01151-2 (pbk). ▸ Case studies of social mobility, residential patterns, political control, and family dynamics in various urban contexts. Pathbreaking analyses employing quantitative methods and sociological theory. Available on microfilm from Ann Arbor: University Microfilms International. [GJK]

42.198 Joseph E. Walker. *Hopewell Village: a social and economic history of an iron-making community.* 1966 ed. Philadelphia: University of Pennsylvania Press, 1974. ISBN 0-8122-7474-1 (cl), 0-8122-1072-7 (pbk). ▸ Detailed study of work and social relations. Prosperity and harmony characterized Hopewell Furnace—including its managers, workers, and environs in southeastern Pennsylvania. [GJK]

42.199 Daniel J. Walkowitz. *Worker city, company town: iron and cotton-worker protest in Troy and Cohoes, New York, 1855–84.* 1978 ed. Urbana: University of Illinois Press, 1981. ISBN 0-252-00667-4 (cl), 0-252-00915-0 (pbk). ▸ Comparative new labor history. Iron workers in Troy more militant than cotton workers in Cohoes because of differences in community context, industrial development, and work force composition. [GJK]

42.200 Anthony F. Wallace. *Rockdale: the growth of an American village in the early industrial revolution.* New York: Knopf, 1978. ISBN 0-394-421205 (cl), 0-393-00991-2 (pbk). ▸ Discussion of how evangelical Christian capitalism defeated freethinking utopian socialism in cultural struggle generated by industrialization in rural Pennsylvania community. Elaborate historical anthropology. [GJK]

42.201 Anthony F. Wallace. *St. Clair: a nineteenth-century coal town's experience with a disaster-prone industry.* 1987 ed. Ithaca, N.Y.: Cornell University Press, 1988. ISBN 0-8014-9900-3 (pbk). ▸ Study of rise, decline, and social dynamics of anthracite coal mining in eastern Pennsylvania. Contrasts operators' optimistic illusions with workers' grim realities. Microcosmic analysis in grand style. [GJK]

42.202 David Ward. *Cities and immigrants: a geography of change in nineteenth-century America.* New York: Oxford University Press, 1971. ▸ Terse overview of spatial effects of urbanization

with special attention to intracity movement of foreign born. Emphasis on housing, transportation, suburbanization, and regional distribution; connects themes to economic change. [NF]

Transportation and Technology

42.203 Monte A. Calvert. *The mechanical engineer in America, 1830–1910: professional cultures in conflict.* Baltimore: Johns Hopkins University Press, 1967. ▸ Discussion of struggle between adherents of traditional shop culture and advocates of formal education over professionalization of mechanical engineering. Sees professionalism as sociohistorical construct. [GJK]

42.204 Thomas C. Cochran. *Railroad leaders, 1845–1890: the business mind in action.* 1953 ed. New York: Russell & Russell, 1966. ▸ Topically organized study of railroad executives' views on business strategy, innovation, labor, and government among other subjects. Enduring example of entrepreneurial approach to business and economic history. [GJK]

42.205 Carl W. Condit. *American building art: the nineteenth century.* New York: Oxford University Press, 1960. ▸ Analytical survey of advances in wood, iron, and concrete construction. Innovations in building techniques reflected technical considerations and relations between technology and utilitarian demands. [GJK]

42.206 Paul A. David. *Technical choice, innovation, and economic growth: essays on American and British experience in the nineteenth century.* London: Cambridge University Press, 1975. ISBN 0-521-20518-2, 0-521-09875-0. ▸ Explains technological progress by choices at microeconomic level rather than by macroeconomic dynamics. Cliometric studies address arguments of Fishlow (42.207), Fogel (42.208), Habbakuk (24.115), and others. Available on microfilm from Ann Arbor: University Microfilms International. [GJK]

42.207 Albert Fishlow. *American railroads and the transformation of the antebellum economy.* Cambridge, Mass.: Harvard University Press, 1965. ISBN 0-674-04263-9 (pbk). ▸ Concludes railroads made important (though not indispensable) contribution to antebellum economic growth. Cliometric analysis often compared to Fogel's more controversial study (42.208). [GJK]

42.208 Robert William Fogel. *Railroads and American economic growth: essays in econometric history.* 1964 ed. Baltimore: Johns Hopkins University Press, 1970. ISBN 0-8018-0201-6 (cl), 0-8018-1148-1 (pbk). ▸ Provocative cliometric study renowned for counterfactual methodology and bold conclusions. Railroads played neither indispensable nor even especially important role in American economic growth. [GJK]

42.209 Carter Goodrich. *Government promotion of American canals and railroads, 1800–1890.* 1960 ed. Westport, Conn.: Greenwood, 1974. ISBN 0-8371-7773-1. ▸ Exemplifies how federal, state, and local governments collaborated with private interests in creating transportation infrastructure for economic development. Extensive survey of older economic history. [GJK]

42.210 Louis C. Hunter. *A history of industrial power in the United States, 1780–1930.* Vol. 1: *Waterpower in the century of the steam engine.* Vol. 2: *Steam power.* Vol. 3: *The transmission of power.* 3 vols. Charlottesville: University Press of Virginia for the Eleutherian Mills-Hagley Foundation, 1979–91. ISBN 0-8139-0782-9 (v. 1), 0-8139-1044-7 (v. 2), 0-262-08198-9 (v. 3). ▸ Study of development of stationary power supplies to drive machinery in mills and factories. Comprehensive survey of technological innovation and application within evolving economic context. [GJK]

42.211 Louis C. Hunter. *Steamboats on the western rivers: an economic and technological history.* 1949 ed. New York: Octagon Books, 1969. ▸ Study of steamboat as critical factor in economic development of Mississippi Valley until displaced by railroad.

Classic analysis of mechanical and business aspects of river transportation. [GJK]

42.212 David J. Jeremy. *Transatlantic industrial revolution: the diffusion of textile technologies between Britain and America, 1790–1830s.* Cambridge, Mass.: MIT Press for Merrimach Valley Textile Museum, 1981. ISBN 0-262-10022-3. ‣ Transmission from Britain and adaptation in U.S. of technologies for cotton and woolen manufacture; also reverse transfer. Multi-stage model with emphasis on early importance of immigrant artisans. [GJK]

42.213 Nathan Rosenberg. *Perspectives on technology.* Cambridge: Cambridge University Press, 1976. ISBN 0-521-20957-9 (cl), 0-521-29011-2 (pbk). ‣ Historical and theoretical essays including pathbreaking study of United States machine tool industry. Technological change essential to long-term economic growth yet defies explanation by neoclassical economics. [GJK]

42.214 Theodore Steinberg. *Nature incorporated: industrialization and the waters of New England.* Cambridge: Cambridge University Press, 1991. ISBN 0-521-39215-2. ‣ Environmental, legal, and social history of impact of industrialization on Merrimack and Charles river valleys. Initial struggle for control of waters yielded to later efforts to reclaim rivers for public. [TD]

42.215 George Rogers Taylor. *The transportation revolution, 1815–1860.* 1951 ed. Armonk, N.Y.: Sharpe, 1977. ISBN 0-87332-101-4 (pbk). ‣ Comprehensive survey and classic synthesis concluding improvements in transportation prompted growth of domestic trade, development of national economy, and early industrialization. [GJK]

SEE ALSO
4.407 Brooke Hindle and Steven Lubar. *Engines of change.*
4.408 David A. Hounshell. *From the American system to mass production, 1800–1932.*
4.422 Bruce Sinclair. *Philadelphia's philosopher mechanics.*
4.603 Daniel Hovey Calhoun. *The American civil engineer.*
24.115 H. J. Habakkuk. *American and British technology in the nineteenth century.*

Wealth and Finance

42.216 Robert F. Dalzell, Jr. *Enterprising elite: the Boston Associates and the world they made.* Cambridge, Mass.: Harvard University Press, 1987. ISBN 0-674-25765-0. ‣ Collective biography of culturally conservative industrial innovators who developed Waltham-Lowell textile system. Argues they cared less about profits than financial security and social stability. [GJK]

42.217 Bray Hammond. *Banks and politics in America, from the Revolution to the Civil War.* 1957 ed. Princeton: Princeton University Press, 1991. ISBN 0-691-04507-0 (cl), 0-691-00553-2 (pbk). ‣ Classic portrait of Jacksonian opponents of Second National Bank as ambitious entrepreneurs, not poor farmers or workers. Concludes expansion of banking reflected business enterprise's ascendancy over agrarianism. [GJK]

42.218 Arthur M. Johnson and Barry E. Supple. *Boston capitalists and western railroads: a study in the nineteenth-century railroad investment process.* Cambridge, Mass.: Harvard University Press, 1967. ‣ Entrepreneurial analysis of capital mobilization before investment banking. Finds Boston capitalists invested in western railroads for both short-term opportunistic and long-term developmental reasons. [GJK]

42.219 Edwin J. Perkins. *Financing Anglo-American trade: the House of Brown, 1800–1880.* Cambridge, Mass.: Harvard University Press, 1975. ISBN 0-674-30145-5. ‣ Study of emergence of House of Brown as preeminent international banking enterprise in United States. Emphasizes firm's financial functions in evolving transatlantic commercial context. [GJK]

42.220 Edward Pessen. *Riches, class, and power before the Civil War.* 1973 ed. New Brunswick, N.J.: Transaction, 1990. ISBN 0-88738-806-x. ‣ Study of elites in major northeastern cities. Contrary to de Tocqueville's classic portrait, Jacksonian America was marked by great economic inequality and little social mobility; the hereditary rich ruled. [GJK]

42.221 Larry Shweikart. *Banking in the American South from the age of Jackson to Reconstruction.* Baton Rouge: Louisiana State University Press, 1987. ISBN 0-8071-1403-0. ‣ Quantitative and qualitative analysis from laissez-faire perspective. Banks contributed more to economic growth in southern states without centralized regulation than in those with it. [GJK]

42.222 Lee Soltow. *Men and wealth in the United States, 1850–1870.* New Haven: Yale University Press, 1975. ISBN 0-300-01814-2. ‣ Cliometric analysis finding samples of federal census data reveal high and stable level of wealth inequality mitigated by pattern of individual gains with age. [GJK]

IMMIGRATION, ETHNICITY, AND RACE

Migration and Settlement

42.223 William F. Adams. *Ireland and Irish emigration to the New World from 1815 to the famine.* 1932 ed. New York: Russell & Russell, 1967. ‣ Early study connecting agricultural and industrial revolutions to mass migration, while analyzing political context in homeland. Overpopulation, absentee landlords, and rural impoverishment encouraged farmers, tenants, weavers, and servants to emigrate. [NF]

42.224 Theodore C. Blegen. *Norwegian migration to America: the American transition.* Vol. 2 of *Norwegian migration to America.* 1931 ed. New York: Haskell, 1969. ISBN 0-8383-0325-0 (set). ‣ Early panorama of emigration: passage, settlement, and organizational life of migrant group, stressing interplay of homeland background and American environment in forging group's identity. Strongest on religion, folkways, and institutions. [NF]

42.225 Donald Fleming and Bernard Bailyn, eds. *Dislocation and emigration: the social background of American immigration.* Cambridge, Mass.: Harvard University, Charles Warren Center for Studies in American History, 1974. (Perspectives in American History, 7.) ‣ Eight pioneering essays tracing homeland patterns that prompted nineteenth- and early twentieth-century migrations. Considers emigrants from Great Britain, Scotland, Wales, Austria, German states, Switzerland, Greece, and Mexico. [NF]

42.226 Jon Gjerde. *From peasants to farmers: the migration from Balestrand, Norway, to the upper Middle West.* Cambridge: Cambridge University Press, 1985. ISBN 0-521-26068-x. ‣ Study of Norwegian agricultural workers who left increasingly stratified society seeking to preserve way of life in rural America. Fine-grained study of chain migrants revealing both cultural persistence and transformation. Focus on kinship, fertility, and land use. [NF/DSS]

42.227 Kristian Hvidt. *Flight to America: the social background of 300,000 Danish emigrants.* New York: Academic Press, 1975. ISBN 0-12-785348-0. ‣ Thoughtful overview of data from handwritten registers on post-1868 immigrants linked to Denmark's police registers. Treats topics ranging from demography, occupations, and motives of migrants to internal and return migration. [NF]

42.228 Walter D. Kamphoefner, Wolfgang Helbich, and Ulrike Sommer, eds. *News from the land of freedom: German immigrants write home.* Susan Carter Vogel, trans. Ithaca, N.Y.: Cornell University Press, 1991. ISBN 0-8014-2523-9. ‣ Correspondence from members of twenty families who left nineteenth-century German states and became farmers, workers, and domestic servants. Fine introductions integrate well-chosen selections into historiography. [NF]

42.229 Royden Loewen. "New themes in an old story: transplanted Mennonites as group settlers in North America, 1874–1879." *Journal of American ethnic history* 11.2 (1992) 3–26. ISSN 0278-5927. ▸ German Pietist communitarians, transplanted to Russia, settled on United States and Canadian plains. Deft comparative study links religious society's experiences to process of global industrialization and concerns of women's and rural history. [NF]

42.230 Robert P. Swierenga. "Religion and immigration patterns: a comparative analysis of Dutch Protestants and Catholics, 1835–1880." *Journal of American ethnic history* 5.3 (1986) 23–45. ISSN 0278-5927. ▸ Demonstrates salience of religious affiliation in migration process, including propensity to emigrate, site of settlement, and adjustment experience. Fine contribution to little-researched topic of diversity within immigrant groups. Links Netherlands and United States records. [NF]

42.231 Frank Thistlethwaite. "Migration from Europe overseas in the nineteenth and twentieth centuries." In *Rapports* (Onzième congrès international des sciences historiques). International Congress of Historical Sciences, ed., vol. 5, pp. 32–60. Stockholm: Almqvist & Wiksell, 1960. ▸ Dramatic call for raising of "salt-water curtain," broadening study of American immigration to include investigation of European origins, intra-European movements, and repatriation. Overarching analysis with great impact on field. [NF]

42.232 Brinley Thomas. *Migration and economic growth: a study of Great Britain and the Atlantic economy.* 2d ed. Cambridge: Cambridge University Press, 1973. ISBN 0-521-08566-7. ▸ Important early demonstration of transatlantic economy. Immigration from England to North America closely followed pattern of long swings in areas' industrial and agricultural fortunes. Neglects local contexts of migration. [NF]

SEE ALSO
40.364 John Bodnar. *The transplanted.*
40.372 Oscar Handlin. *The uprooted.*
40.373 Marcus Lee Hansen. *The Atlantic migration, 1607–1860.*
40.380 Kerby A. Miller. *Emigrants and exiles.*

Community Formation

42.233 Kathleen Neils Conzen. *Immigrant Milwaukee, 1836–1860: accommodation and community in a frontier city.* Cambridge, Mass.: Harvard University Press, 1976. ISBN 0-674-44436-1. ▸ Influential study arguing that dense ethnic enclave encouraged easy adjustment but postponed assimilation. Contends internal diversity promoted institutional life and fostered group identity. Skillfully charts development of German majority in midwestern city. [NF]

42.234 Kathleen Neils Conzen. "Immigrants, immigrant neighborhoods, and ethnic identity: historical issues." *Journal of American history* 66 (1979) 603–16. ISSN 0021-8723. ▸ Brief, insightful review of literature on residential clustering and community formation. Uses nineteenth-century German American examples to argue for multifaceted approach to understanding relationships among geographical concentration, assimilation, and cultural maintenance. [NF]

42.235 Merle Eugene Curti. *The making of an American community: a case study of democracy in a frontier county.* 1959 ed. Stanford, Calif.: Stanford University Press, 1969. ISBN 0-8047-0534-8. ▸ Pioneering effort combining quantitative and qualitative methods, using manuscript censuses and examining entire society. Turnerian argument (42.131) that frontier society promoted democracy and afforded mobility, especially for immigrants. [NF/GJK]

42.236 Robert Ernst. *Immigrant life in New York City, 1825–1863.* 1949 ed. New York: Octagon Books, 1979. ISBN 0-374-92624-7. ▸ Significant early contribution, building on work of

Hansen and Brebner (42.251) and Wittke (42.256). Generally assimilationist treatment, pioneering in urban focus; attention to issues of class and unionism. Concentrates on Germans and Irish. [NF]

42.237 Dean R. Esslinger. *Immigrants and the city: ethnicity and mobility in a nineteenth-century midwestern community.* Port Washington, N.Y.: Kennikat, 1975. ISBN 0-8046-9108-8. ▸ Restless and largely successful foreign and native-born settlers spurred industrial growth of South Bend, Indiana. Concise, quantitative treatment of array of groups, from Canadians to Poles, reflecting limits of genre. [NF]

42.238 David A. Gerber. *The making of an American pluralism: Buffalo, New York, 1825–60.* Urbana: University of Illinois Press, 1989. ISBN 0-252-01595-9. ▸ Rich, dense amalgam of social, political, economic, and religious history. Eventual joining of native-born elites and German and Irish immigrant groups into common, if stratified, society. [NF]

42.239 Laurence A. Glasco. "The life cycles and household structures of American ethnic groups: Irish, German, and native-born whites in Buffalo, New York, 1855." *Journal of urban history* 1 (1975) 339–64. ISSN 0096-1442. ▸ Comparative life-cycle analysis of men and women demonstrating distinctive ethnic patterns. Useful quantitative study of census data; uncovers differences in apprenticeship, employment, wealth, and fertility, while raising questions regarding acculturation. [NF]

42.240 Richard Allan Griswold del Castillo. *The Los Angeles barrio, 1850–1890: a social history.* Berkeley: University of California Press, 1979. ISBN 0-520-03816-9. ▸ Thematic social historical study focusing on formation of Mexican American enclave. Increasing geographic segregation accompanied economic exclusion and encouraged ethnic consciousness. Combines quantitative and qualitative sources for structural analysis of group's experience. [NF]

42.241 Oscar Handlin. *Boston's immigrants: a study in acculturation.* Rev. ed. Cambridge, Mass.: Belknap, 1979. ISBN 0-674-07980-9 (cl), 0-674-07985-X (pbk). ▸ Classic early examination adopting assimilationist framework and dominant-society perspective while focusing on Irish distinctiveness. Irish migrants encountered resistance, hardship, and coalescing Brahmin elite; post–Civil War era bred tolerance. [NF]

42.242 Theodore Hershberg. "Free blacks in antebellum Philadelphia: a study of ex-slaves, freeborn, and socioeconomic decline." *Journal of social history* 5 (1971–72) 183–209. ISSN 0022-4529. ▸ Racial discrimination and structural inequality rendered life increasingly hard for African Americans in second largest United States city. Argues that destructive experience in urban North, along with legacy of slavery, undermined African Americans' progress. [NF]

42.243 Gordon W. Kirk, Jr. *The promise of American life: social mobility in a nineteenth-century immigrant community, Holland, Michigan, 1847–1894.* Philadelphia: American Philosophical Society, 1978. ISBN 0-87169-124-8. ▸ Quantitative study of occupations, wealth, and outmigration. Argues frontier development, more than urbanization or industrialization, fostered immigrant mobility; ethnically homogeneous settlement afforded substantial opportunity for Dutch majority. [NF]

42.244 Leon F. Litwack and August Meier, eds. *Black leaders of the nineteenth century.* Urbana: University of Illinois Press, 1988. ISBN 0-252-01506-1. ▸ Much-needed volume introduces lives of some twenty prominent African Americans. Sixteen short essays in readable style with brief bibliography provided for each essay. [NF]

42.245 Brian C. Mitchell. *The paddy camps: the Irish of Lowell, 1821–61.* Urbana: University of Illinois Press, 1988. ISBN 0-252-

01371-9. ▸ Lively community study showcasing how textile center's immigrants transformed labor force and formed own community. Famine emigration bred hostility among Yankees prompting growing ethnic separation, which in turn fostered immigrant institution building. See Dublin 42.601. [NF]

42.246 Stanley Nadel. *Little Germany: ethnicity, religion, and class in New York City, 1845–80.* Urbana: University of Illinois Press, 1990. ISBN 0-252-01677-7. ▸ Well-researched study making connections with political history and engaging debate on nature of community. Argues massive immigrant settlement forged solidarity based on internal regional and class divisions and differences from native-born society. [NF]

42.247 Robert Clifford Ostergren. *A community transplanted: the trans-Atlantic experience of a Swedish immigrant settlement in the upper Middle West, 1835–1915.* Madison: University of Wisconsin Press, 1988. ISBN 0-299-11320-5 (cl), 0-299-11324-8 (pbk). ▸ Rich, carefully researched study of migrants who left peasant society in Sweden and settled in frontier Minnesota and South Dakota. Sees migrants as links between sending and receiving societies, both changing. Emphasizes cultural persistence. [NF]

SEE ALSO
40.356 Albert Camarillo. *Chicanos in a changing society.*

Acculturation

42.248 Rowland Tappan Berthoff. *British immigrants in industrial America, 1790–1850.* 1953 ed. New York: Russell & Russell, 1968. ▸ Influential survey of groups still neglected in historiography. Most English, Scottish, and Welsh newcomers suffered little discrimination and entered highly skilled jobs in America, yet retained cultural identity. [NF]

42.249 Hasia Diner. *Erin's daughters in America: Irish immigrant women in the nineteenth-century.* Baltimore: Johns Hopkins University Press, 1983. ISBN 0-8018-2871-6 (cl), 0-8018-2872-4 (pbk). ▸ Important study of causes and results of preponderance of females among Irish immigrants. Quantitative and qualitative data reveal Irish women's agency in economic activities, marital choices, social mobility, and ambivalence to feminism. [VBB/DRG]

42.250 Charlotte Erickson. *Invisible immigrants: the adaptation of English and Scottish immigrants in nineteenth-century America.* 1972 ed. Coral Gables, Fla.: University of Miami Press, 1992. ISBN 0-87024-213-X. ▸ Well-edited, introduced, and selected volume of letters from wide range of British settlers in United States agriculture, industry, and professions. Draws on letter-writers' backgrounds to stress their accommodation, not assimilation. [NF]

42.251 Marcus Lee Hansen and John Bartlet Brebner. *The mingling of the Canadian and American peoples. Vol. 1: Historical.* 1940 ed. New York: Arno, 1970. ISBN 0-405-00553-9. ▸ Traces vast migration between Canada and United States, 1600-1940, stressing similarity of national cultures, permeability of border, and easy assimilation of migrants. Completed by John Bartlet Brebner; remains best study of overlooked topic. [NF]

42.252 Terry G. Jordan. *German seed in Texas soil: immigrant farmers in nineteenth-century Texas.* 1966 ed. Austin: University of Texas Press, 1975. ISBN 0-292-73629-0 (cl), 0-292-72707-0 (pbk). ▸ Historical, geographical examination debunking view that Germans were superior farmers; demonstrates distinctive immigrant farming practices and sustained cultural identity. Comparative framework bolsters analysis of dynamics of agricultural assimilation. [NF]

42.253 Walter D. Kamphoefner. *The Westfalians: from Germany to Missouri.* Princeton: Princeton University Press, 1987. ISBN 0-691-04746-4. ▸ Careful transatlantic reconstruction of villagers' lives arguing against assimilationist paradigm; endorses view of transplanted (versus uprooted) immigrants. Chain migrants from protoindustrializing area acculturated slowly in rural America. [NF]

42.254 Dale T. Knobel. "To be an American: ethnicity, fraternity, and the Improved Order of Red Men." *Journal of American ethnic history* 4.1 (1984) 62–87. ISSN 0278-5927. ▸ Intriguing exploration of midcentury culture and ideology. Many German Americans left multiethnic, ultrapatriotic secret society over issues of language maintenance and temperance. Examines divergent meanings of americanization and assimilation and politicization of associationalism. [NF]

42.255 Jonathan D. Sarna. "The 'mythical Jew' and the 'Jew next door' in nineteenth-century America." In *Anti-Semitism in American history.* David A. Gerber, ed., pp. 57–78. Urbana: University of Illinois Press, 1986. ISBN 0-252-01214-3. ▸ Discussion of selected Americans' struggles to reconcile biblical image of Jews with day-to-day experiences with Jewish immigrants. Social-psychological overview arguing immigrant group's response to situation revealed ambivalence to own past and assimilation. [NF]

42.256 Carl Wittke. *Refugees of revolution: the German Forty-Eighters in America.* 1952 ed. Westport, Conn.: Greenwood, 1970. ISBN 0-8371-2988-5. ▸ Standard account of exiles from liberal movements and failed revolutions of 1848–49. Relies mostly on immigrant press to draw collective portrait of diverse, consequential group. Stresses emigrants' contributions and assimilation. [NF]

SEE ALSO
43.245 Victor Greene. *For God and country.*

Labor Relations

42.257 Ira Berlin and Herbert G. Gutman. "Natives and immigrants, free men and slaves: urban workingmen in the antebellum American South." *American historical review* 88 (1983) 1175–1200. ISSN 0002-8762. ▸ Influx of foreign-born men in five southern cities altered economy and society, further eroding standing of blacks (slave and free). Intriguing thesis unites immigration history with pre–Civil War politics and African American history. [NF]

42.258 Mary H. Blewett. "Manhood and the market: the politics of gender and class among the textile workers of Fall River, Massachusetts, 1870–1880." In *Work engendered: toward a new history of American labor.* Ava Baron, ed., pp. 92–113. Ithaca, N.Y.: Cornell University Press, 1991. ISBN 0-8014-2256-6 (cl), 0-8014-9543-1 (pbk). ▸ Examination of how Lancashire weavers and spinners drew on and transformed homeland traditions of work life and protest. Focus on contested meaning of masculinity sharpens understanding of late nineteenth-century working class. [NF]

42.259 Edna Bonacich. "Asian labor in the development of California and Hawaii." In *Labor immigration under capitalism: Asian workers in the United States before World War II.* Lucie Cheng and Edna Bonacich, eds., pp. 130–85. Berkeley: University of California Press, 1984. ISBN 0-520-04829-6. ▸ Places immigration from Asia at center of states' economic transformation. Using global migration framework and Marxist perspective, highlights connections between experiences of Asians, African Americans, and colonialized workers. Pointed, useful survey. [NF]

42.260 Edna Bonacich. "United States capitalist development: a background to Asian immigration." In *Labor immigration under capitalism: Asian workers in the United States before World War II.* Lucie Cheng and Edna Bonacich, eds., pp. 79–129. Berkeley: University of California Press, 1984. ISBN 0-520-04829-6. ▸ Broad Marxist synthesis of nineteenth-century American economic and political history as backdrop for understanding reception of immigrants from Asia. Focuses on rise of monopoly capitalism, complexities in class relations, and racial hostility. [NF]

42.261 Charlotte Erickson. *American industry and the European immigrant, 1860–1885.* 1957 ed. New York: Russell & Russell, 1967. ▸ Provocative, influential examination of mass migration, labor competition, and politics. Finds American industry did not sponsor vast contract labor immigration, 1864–85. Ignores overarching capitalist promotion of cheap labor. [NF]

42.262 Dirk Hoerder. "An introduction to labor migration in the Atlantic economies, 1815–1914." In *Labor migration in the Atlantic economies: the European and North American working classes during the period of industrialization.* Dirk Hoerder, ed., pp. 3–31. Westport, Conn.: Greenwood, 1985. ISBN 0-313-24637-8. ▸ Sweeping reexamination of nineteenth-century European migrations of workers. Sketches complex mosaic of intra-European, transatlantic labor markets and labor pools, including return migrations. Synthesizes broad literature, reviews historiography, and compares acculturation processes. [NF]

42.263 Hartmut Keil and John B. Jentz, eds. *German workers in industrial Chicago, 1850–1910: a comparative perspective.* De Kalb: Northern Illinois University Press, 1983. ISBN 0-87580-089-0. ▸ Fourteen essays examining group's urban experience, focus on German American segment of working class. Analyses of immigrant occupations, union activism, political culture, and neighborhood life contribute to broader understanding of ethnic integration. [NF]

42.264 Howard Roberts Lamar. "From bondage to contract: ethnic labor in the American West." In *The countryside in the age of capitalist transformation: essays in the social history of rural America.* Steven Hahn and Jonathan Prude, eds., pp. 293–324. Chapel Hill: University of North Carolina Press, 1985. ISBN 0-8078-1666-3 (cl), 0-8078-4139-0 (pbk). ▸ Succinct survey stressing importance of bonded, contract labor systems to economy and ethnic group relations in trans-Mississippi United States. Illuminates patterns of Western racism; provides comparisons to United States South and other frontiers. [NF]

42.265 Bruce Laurie, Theodore Hershberg, and George Alter. "Immigrants in industry: the Philadelphia experience, 1850–1880." *Journal of social history* 9 (1975) 219–42. ISSN 0022-4529. ▸ Careful analysis of manufacturing census data to illuminate process of industrialization and foreign-born occupational patterns. Demonstrates limited mechanization in consumer industries, skill levels of Germans higher than Irish workers, and dilution of crafts. [NF]

42.266 Bruce Levine. *The spirit of 1848: German immigrants, labor conflict, and the coming of the Civil War.* Urbana: University of Illinois Press, 1992. ISBN 0-252-01873-7. ▸ Discussion of how cultural, economic, and political influences shaped experience of German American craftworkers. Unites examination of homeland background, industrialization, and making of ethnic working class with analysis of political crisis over slavery. Challenging, ambitious interpretation. [NF]

42.267 June Mei. "Socioeconomic origins of emigration: Guandong to California, 1850–1882." In *Labor immigration under capitalism: Asian workers in the United States before World War II.* Lucie Cheng and Edna Bonacich, eds., pp. 402–34. Berkeley: University of California Press, 1984. ISBN 0-520-04829-6. ▸ Traces class formation within ethnic enclave in group's leading center, revealing dynamics of Chinatown. Outlines distinctive attitudes of capitalists, petite bourgeoisie, and wage workers to homeland politics and adaptation to America. [NF]

Nativism, Racism, and Antisemitism

42.268 David A. Gerber. "Cutting out Shylock: toward a reconceptualization of the origins of anti-Semitism." *Journal of Amer-* *ican history* 69 (1982) 615–37. ISSN 0021-8723. ▸ Thoughtful case study of Buffalo, New York, connecting economic history and social relations. Expansion of commercial capitalism altered Jewish-Gentile relations. Powerful native white Protestant men increasingly denied credit to Jewish entrepreneurs. [NF]

42.269 Elliott J. Gorn. "'Good-bye, boys, I die a true American': homicide, nativism, and working-class culture in antebellum New York City." *Journal of American history* 74 (1987) 388–410. ISSN 0021-8723. ▸ Study of incident of murder of butcher-saloonkeeper to probe nativist sentiment and nature of workingmen's social life. Nuanced analysis of interplay of ethnic, class, and gender politics contributes to reassessment of know-nothingism. [NF]

42.270 Dale T. Knobel. *Paddy and the republic: ethnicity and nationality in antebellum America.* Middletown, Conn.: Wesleyan University Press; distributed by Harper & Row, 1986. ISBN 0-8195-5117-1. ▸ Thought-provoking study of evolving popular image of Irish during pre–Civil War era. Social psychological perspective on prejudice and ethnic stereotypes. Content analysis of various printed sources illuminates period's emerging nationalism and concomitant nativism. [NF]

42.271 Leon F. Litwack. *North of slavery: the Negro in the free states, 1790–1860.* Chicago: University of Chicago Press, 1961. ▸ Traces denial of equal rights for African Americans and support for white supremacy in northern states during nineteenth century. Early study; significant in documenting distinct pattern of racism in North. [NF]

42.272 David Montgomery. "The shuttle and the cross: weavers and artisans in the Kensington riots of 1844." *Journal of social history* 5 (1972) 411–47. ISSN 0022-4529. ▸ Astute exploration of class, ethnic, and religious conflict and antebellum politics. Virulent nativism arose from ashes of urban radicalism in Philadelphia working-class manufacturing suburb. Political demands of evangelical Protestantism fractured class solidarity. [NF]

42.273 George Anthony Peffer. "Forbidden families: emigration experiences of Chinese women under the Page Law, 1875–1882." *Journal of American ethnic history* 6.1 (1986) 28–46. ISSN 0278-5927. ▸ Argues ban on prostitutes from China, passed before Chinese Exclusion Acts (1882 and after), effectively curtailed female immigration, limiting family formation. Exercise in legal history demonstrates ties between views of gender and race. [NF]

42.274 David R. Roediger. *The wages of whiteness: race and the making of the American working class.* London: Verso, 1991. ISBN 0-86091-334-1 (cl), 0-86091-550-6 (pbk). ▸ Neo-Marxist analysis of racism from bottom up. Explores race in forging of class consciousness among white workers; special attention to Irish Americans. [NF/GJK]

42.275 Alexander Plaisted Saxton. *The indispensable enemy: labor and the anti-Chinese movement in California.* Berkeley: University of California Press, 1971. ISBN 0-520-01721-8 (cl), 0-520-02905-4 (pbk). ▸ Absorbing analysis of economic and ideological origins and consequences of attitudes and actions against Chinese immigrants in post–Civil War period. Political leaders, white craft unionists gained by asserting racial definition of nationality. [NF/WFD]

SEE ALSO
40.402 Stuart Creighton Miller. *The unwelcome immigrant.*
40.406 Ronald T. Takaki. *Iron cages.*

THE SLAVE SOUTH

Institution of Slavery and the Slave Trade

42.276 Randolph B. Campbell. *An empire for slavery: the peculiar institution in Texas, 1821–1865.* Baton Rouge: Louisiana State

University Press, 1989. ISBN 0-8071-1505-3. ‣ First comprehensive narrative on numerous facets of Texas servitude—early development, legal structure, economics, and slave life. Excellent, broad-based research; no new interpretations but significant contribution to southern historiography. [MW]

42.277 Stanley W. Campbell. *The slave catchers: enforcement of the fugitive slave law, 1850–1860.* 1970 ed. New York: Norton, 1972. ISBN 0-393-00626-3. ‣ Argues enforcement of 1850 fugitive slave law was effective, contrary to general belief. Important subject, significant data revealed, yet historical treatment and presentation lack vitality. [MW]

42.278 Merton L. Dillon. *Slavery attacked: southern slaves and their allies, 1619–1865.* Baton Rouge: Louisiana State University Press, 1990. ISBN 0-8071-1614-9. ‣ Analysis of internal and external issues leading to emancipation. Slaves' agency and subversive behavior, together with northern antislavery pressure, brought downfall of ruthless, coercive bondage. Old arguments; new, comprehensive, probing synthesis. [MW]

42.279 Stanley Elkins. *Slavery: a problem in American institutional and intellectual life.* 3d ed. Chicago: University of Chicago Press, 1976. ISBN 0-226-20476-6 (cl), 0-226-20477-4 (pbk). ‣ Controversial thesis, original interpretations. Rigid, coercive plantation authority regime created childlike Sambo personality-type among North American slaves, unlike Latin America's more flexible system. See Lane, ed. 42.287. [MW]

42.280 George M. Fredrickson. *The arrogance of race: historical perspectives on slavery, racism, and social inequality.* Middletown, Conn.: Wesleyan University Press, 1988. ISBN 0-8195-5177-5. ‣ Intellectual, comparative, historiographical focus on slavery, racism, and cultural matrixes of white supremacy, citing specific historical actors and historians. New and old essays challenging paternalist perspective and neo-Marxist historians. [MW]

42.281 Eugene D. Genovese. *The slaveholders' dilemma: freedom and progress in southern conservative thought, 1820–1860.* Columbia: University of South Carolina Press, 1992. ISBN 0-87249-783-6. ‣ Proslavery intellectuals admired technological and cultural progress but condemned free-labor capitalism that brought it. Acute, expert analysis by similarly ambivalent Marxist historian. [CJG]

42.282 Eugene D. Genovese. *The world the slaveholders made: two essays in interpretation.* 1969 ed. Middletown, Conn.: Wesleyan University Press; distributed by Harper & Row, 1988. ISBN 0-8195-5198-8 (cl), 0-8195-6204-1 (pbk). ‣ Part 1 compares United States and Latin American slavery as class structures; part 2 interprets George Fitzhugh's proslavery, anticapitalist writings as ideology of a pre- and antibourgeois society. Provocative Marxist viewpoint. [CJG]

42.283 Claudia D. Goldin. *Urban slavery in the American South, 1820–1860: a quantitative history.* Chicago: University of Chicago Press, 1976. ISBN 0-226-30104-4. ‣ Examination of differences in urban and rural slavery and uneven development of institution in cities. Argues against incompatability of slavery with urban life, citing availability of white labor as reason for fluctuations; refutes Wade 42.351. [MW]

42.284 Richard Hofstadter. "U. B. Phillips and the plantation legend." *Journal of Negro history* 29 (1944) 109–24. ISSN 0022-2992. ‣ First major scholar to call for critical interdisciplinary approach to slavery. Discusses limitations of Phillips's paternalism, narrowness of his sources, and unconvincing portrayal of African American slaves as docile and content. [MW]

42.285 Nathan Irvin Huggins. *Black odyssey: the Afro-American ordeal in slavery.* 1977 ed. New York: Vintage, 1979. ISBN 0-394-72687-1 (pbk). ‣ Intricate description of slavery as journey from Africa to America focusing on plantation life as triumph of

human courage and will over unmitigated force. Impressionistic narrative aimed at capturing essence and vitality of slave life. [MW]

42.286 John C. Inscoe. *Mountain masters: slavery and the sectional crisis in western North Carolina.* Knoxville: University of Tennessee Press, 1989. ISBN 0-87049-597-6. ‣ Study of North Carolina yeoman counties and culture, emphasizing thriving agriculture, small but entrenched slave system, and sectional loyalty. Rejects nineteenth-century perspective of Yankee traveler, Frederick Law Olmsted. [MW]

42.287 Ann J. Lane, ed. *The debate over slavery: Stanley Elkins and his critics.* Urbana: University of Illinois Press, 1971. ISBN 0-252-00157-5 (pbk). ‣ Anthology of interdisciplinary articles written in response to Elkins's thesis (42.279), including his rejoinder. Focus on methodology, comparative approach, and Elkins's logic. Useful presentation of major issues in slave studies. [MW]

42.288 James Oakes. *Slavery and freedom: an interpretation of the Old South.* New York: Knopf, 1990. ISBN 0-394-53677-0. ‣ Explores contradiction of slavery's existence in dynamic, liberal economy that took freedom as given. Excellent synthesis of how all Old South social relationships were affected by contradiction. [MW]

42.289 Ulrich Bonnell Phillips. *American Negro slavery: a survey of the supply, employment, and control of Negro labor as determined by the plantation regime.* 1918 ed. Baton Rouge: Louisiana State University Press, 1966. ‣ Classic, early account of slavery in the Americas with focus on slavery in antebellum South. Analysis makes extensive use of plantation records. Marred by assumptions of biological and cultural inferiority of African Americans. [TD]

42.290 Julia Floyd Smith. *Slavery and plantation growth in antebellum Florida, 1821–1860.* Gainesville: University Presses of Florida, 1973. ISBN 0-8130-0323-7. ‣ Extensive examination of plantation records, slave narratives, and census and tax records to support absence of paternalism in Florida slavery. Argues for slavery's profitability, widespread family separation, and cruelty of system. [MW]

42.291 Kenneth M. Stampp. *The peculiar institution: slavery in the ante-bellum South.* 1956 ed. New York: Vintage, 1989. ISBN 0-679-72307-2. ‣ Presents slavery as profitable, exploitive system based on labor coercion which slaves resisted while remaining culturally and communally isolated. Pathbreaking revision of Phillips 42.289; weak on slave life and culture. [MW]

42.292 Michael Tadman. *Speculators and slaves: masters, traders, and slaves in the Old South.* Madison: University of Wisconsin Press, 1989. ISBN 0-299-11850-9. ‣ Critique of paternalist interpretations. Argues for extensive interregional antebellum slave trade, revising previous estimates by using census data and slave traders' records. Views masters as racist, insensitive, profit-oriented. [MW]

42.293 Allen Weinstein, Frank O. Gatell, and David Sarasohn, eds. *American Negro slavery: a modern reader.* 3d ed. New York: Oxford University Press, 1979. ISBN 0-19-502470-2. ‣ Essays focusing on comparative slavery, master-slave relations, origins of bondage, labor, and resistance. Good introduction and contemporary historiographical discussion, but Aptheker's work (see 42.324) conspicuously missing. [MW]

42.294 Theodore Branter Wilson. *The black codes of the South.* Tuscaloosa: University of Alabama Press, 1965. ‣ Examination of southern legislation and court action to control personal, political, social, and economic life of newly freed African Americans which led to Radical Reconstruction. Important work on brief period. [MW]

SEE ALSO
34.238 Peter Kolchin. *Unfree labor.*

Economics of Slavery

42.295 Alfred H. Conrad and John R. Meyer. *The economics of slavery and other studies in econometric history.* Chicago: Aldine, 1964. ▸ Early cliometric analysis reframing debate over slavery's efficiency as economic institution; found that by modern standards, American slavery was profitable. Also essays on methodology, economic growth. [GJK]

42.296 Paul A. David et al. *Reckoning with slavery: a critical study in the quantitative history of American Negro slavery.* New York: Oxford University Press, 1976. ISBN 0-19-502033-2. ▸ Collaborative essays by economic and social historians. Sharp critique of Fogel and Engerman 42.298 for empirical, methodological, and theoretical errors. [GJK]

42.297 Robert William Fogel. *Without consent or contract: the rise and fall of American slavery.* New York: Norton, 1989. ISBN 0-393-01887-3. ▸ Expansion of argument in *Time on the Cross.* American slavery was economically efficient, making triumph of antislavery campaign morally necessary if not historically inevitable. Synthesis of cliometric and conventional approaches. [GJK]

42.298 Robert William Fogel and Stanley L. Engerman. *Time on the cross: the economics of American Negro slavery.* 1974 ed. New York: Norton, 1989. ISBN 0-393-30620-8 (pbk). ▸ Highly controversial cliometric interpretation that efficiency of American slavery materially benefited both profit-minded slaveholders and hard-working slaves. Supplementary volume supplies evidence and calculations. For critique, see David et al. 42.296. [GJK]

42.299 Eugene D. Genovese. *The political economy of slavery: studies in the economy and society of the slave South.* 2d ed. Middletown, Conn.: Wesleyan University Press, 1989. ISBN 0-8195-6208-4 (pbk). ▸ Influential Marxist interpretation of Old South as slave society ruled by precapitalist planter class. Inefficiency and ideology drove planters to seek slavery's expansion, precipitating Civil War. [GJK]

42.300 Richard G. Lowe and Randolph B. Campbell. *Planters and plain folk: agriculture in antebellum Texas.* Dallas: Southern Methodist University Press, 1987. ISBN 0-87074-212-4. ▸ Challenge to thesis that farming economy declined in antebellum era. Argues slave planters' profits not as high as previously believed and farmers created vital economy, sharing in Texas prosperity. [MW]

42.301 William M. Mathew. *Edmund Ruffin and the crisis of slavery in the Old South: the failure of agricultural reform.* Athens: University of Georgia Press, 1988. ISBN 0-8203-1011-5. ▸ Qualitative analysis of problems in southern society, focusing on slavery and southern economics through eyes of Virginia planter and agricultural reformer. [MW]

42.302 John Hebron Moore. *The emergence of the cotton kingdom in the old Southwest: Mississippi, 1770–1860.* Baton Rouge: Louisiana State University Press, 1988. ISBN 0-8071-1382-4 (cl), 0-8071-1404-9 (pbk). ▸ Comprehensive, but somewhat dated socioeconomic perspective on complexities of change, development of new resources, and mechanics of cotton production in Mississippi. [MW]

42.303 William K. Scarborough. *The overseer: plantation management in the Old South.* 1966 ed. Athens: University of Georgia Press, 1984. ISBN 0-8203-0732-7 (cl), 0-8203-0733-5 (pbk). ▸ Sympathetic treatment of overseer concludes friction between planter and overseer stemmed from ill-defined areas of jurisdiction, planter mistrust, and manager's stressful supervisory position. [MW]

42.304 Julia Floyd Smith. *Slavery and rice culture in low country Georgia, 1750–1860.* Knoxville: University of Tennessee Press, 1985. ISBN 0-87049-462-7. ▸ Argues tidewater rice cultivation produced wealth, and planters encouraged slave autonomy through task system, contributing to higher living standard for slaves than elsewhere. Unconvincing paternalist argument; thin evidence. [MW]

SEE ALSO
39.410 Peter A. Coclanis. *The shadow of a dream.*

Southern Society and Culture

42.305 Dickson D. Bruce, Jr. *Violence and culture in the antebellum South.* Austin: University of Texas Press, 1979. ISBN 0-292-77018-9. ▸ Explores cultural context of meaning, sources, and implications of southern violence. Southern beliefs about passion, pessimistic world view, and historical events impelled sense of resignation toward necessity of violence. [MW]

42.306 Orville Vernon Burton. *In my father's house are many mansions: family and community in Edgefield, South Carolina.* 1985 ed. Chapel Hill: University of North Carolina Press, 1987. ISBN 0-8078-1619-1 (cl, 1985), 0-8078-4183-8 (pbk). ▸ Comparison of black and white families in Piedmont county before and after slavery. Emphasizes pervasive influences of evangelical Protestantism, patriarchal values, and racism. [DSS]

42.307 Victoria E. Bynum. *Unruly women: the politics of social and sexual control in the Old South.* Chapel Hill: University of North Carolina Press, 1992. ISBN 0-8078-2016-4 (cl), 0-8078-4361-x (pbk). ▸ Three Piedmont counties provide evidence of female autonomy and resistance within patriarchal constraints. Concludes unmarried, free black women, poor white women, and white yeomen wives defied private and public authority. [VBB]

42.308 Joan E. Cashin. *A family venture: men and women on the southern frontier.* New York: Oxford University Press, 1991. ISBN 0-19-505344-3. ▸ Experiences of slaveholding families' trek to Southwest, focusing on gender, race relations, isolation, sexuality, and how increasing wealth fostered rejection of slaves' humanity. Rich prose, compelling interpretations. [MW]

42.309 Jane Turner Censer. *North Carolina planters and their children, 1800–1860.* 1984 ed. Baton Rouge: Louisiana State University Press, 1990. ISBN 0-8071-1135-x (cl, 1984), 0-8071-1634-3 (pbk). ▸ Comparison of planter society with elites elsewhere. Portrayed as attractive, self-controlled, industrious, and egalitarian—except in slave relations, where cruelty prevailed. Rejects paternalistic approach. [MW/DSS]

42.310 Catherine Clinton. *The plantation mistress: woman's world in the Old South.* New York: Pantheon, 1982. ISBN 0-394-51686-9. ▸ Rich data from 500 manuscript collections, emphasizing female victimization under patriarchal slaveocracy. Analysis minimizes white privilege, female agency, solace in kinship, religion, and motherhood. Focus on elite white women, 1780–1835. [VBB]

42.311 Liliane Crete. *Daily life in Louisiana, 1815–1830.* Patrick Gregory, trans. Baton Rouge: Louisiana State University Press, 1981. ISBN 0-8071-0887-1. ▸ Focuses on New Orleans life during early statehood including creole family, racial variety, religion, leisure, slaves, common folk, and food. Limited by neglect of major sources. Uncritical; lacks originality. [MW]

42.312 Carl N. Degler. *The other South: southern dissenters in the nineteenth century.* 1974 ed. Boston: Northeastern University Press, 1982. ISBN 0-930350-33-2 (cl), 0-930350-34-0 (pbk). ▸ Antislaveryites, unionists, and Populists bore witness to southern diversity but remained minority largely because class and economic views were subordinated to race. Upholds continuity of southern distinctiveness. [CJG]

42.313 Elizabeth Fox-Genovese. *Within the plantation household:*

black and white women of the Old South. Chapel Hill: University of North Carolina Press, 1988. ISBN 0-8078-1808-9 (cl), 0-8078-4232-X (pbk). ‣ Important, controversial work. Study of black and white women as members of elite plantation family. Subordinates racial antagonism, sexuality, and religion in effort to depict distinctly southern household as locus of economy. [VBB]

42.314 John Hope Franklin. *The militant South, 1800–1861.* 1956 ed. Cambridge, Mass.: Belknap, 1970. ‣ Analysis and explanation of southern military and historical penchant for violence. Views rural ambiance, fear of slave insurrection, and self-satisfied arrogance as major factors. Fresh, important perspective on mind of white South. [MW]

42.315 J. William Harris. *Plain folk and gentry in a slave society: white liberty and black slavery in Augusta's hinterlands.* Middletown, Conn.: Wesleyan University Press; distributed by Harper & Row, 1985. ISBN 0-8195-5125-2. ‣ Local community study addressing why nonslaveholders supported Civil War. Examines white ideology, culture, economy, and political independence to explore old argument of fundamental white antipathy toward blacks. [MW]

42.316 Frances Anne Kemble. *Journal of a residence on a Georgia plantation in 1838–1839.* 1961 ed. John A. Scott, ed. Athens: University of Georgia Press, 1984. ISBN 0-8203-0707-6. ‣ English actress's assessment of slavery while married to slaveowner. Accounts reflect British, New England antislavery sentiments alongside racism. Interesting data; useful introduction on Kemble's life by Scott. [VBB]

42.317 Louis D. Rubin, Jr. *The edge of the swamp: a study in the literature and society of the Old South.* Baton Rouge: Louisiana State University Press, 1989. ISBN 0-8071-1495-2. ‣ Analysis of southern literary figures focusing on limited creativity due to defensiveness about slavery, isolation, illiteracy, weak intelligentsia, and planter aspirations. Challenges antibourgeois, paternalistic interpretation of master class. [MW]

42.318 Todd L. Savitt. *Medicine and slavery: the diseases and health care of blacks in antebellum Virginia.* Urbana: University of Illinois Press, 1978. ISBN 0-252-00653-4. ‣ Exhaustive research and analyses. Concludes slave work routine impaired by poor health due to disease, lactose deficiency, sickle cell anemia, poor clothing, and diet. Offers new methods of challenging paternalist thesis. [MW]

42.319 Todd L. Savitt and Ronald L. Numbers, eds. *Science and medicine in the Old South.* Baton Rouge: Louisiana State University Press, 1989. ISBN 0-8071-1464-2. ‣ Examines growth of science in Old South including impact on plantation economy, scientific societies, theology, and southern thought. Medicine section explores health practices, slave folk beliefs, insanity, and domestic medicine. [MW]

42.320 Theresa A. Singleton, ed. *The archaeology of slavery and plantation life.* Orlando, Fla.: Academic Press, 1985. ISBN 0-12-646480-4. ‣ Discussion of adaptability and behavior patterns of owners, managers, and laborers on plantations. Examines artifacts, food, and skeletal remains. Interdisciplinary fusion of history, anthropology, and archaeology. [MW]

42.321 Steven M. Stowe. *Intimacy and power in the Old South: ritual in the lives of the planters.* Baltimore: Johns Hopkins University Press, 1987. ISBN 0-8018-3388-4. ‣ Study of planter rituals as manifestations of collective power, and denial of race or class perspectives. Duels, courtships, and friendships important within internal dynamics of elitist, hierarchial planter culture and family relationships. [MW]

42.322 Earl E. Thorpe. *The Old South: a psychohistory.* 1972 ed. Westport, Conn.: Greenwood, 1979. ISBN 0-313-21113-2. ‣ Psychoanalytical approach examining psychosexual nature of ante-

bellum white racial attitudes, how southern apologists treat slavery, and need to study repressed unconscious in African American history. [MW]

SEE ALSO

Slave Culture, Community, and Resistance

42.323 Roger D. Abrahams. *Singing the master: the emergence of African American culture in the plantation South.* New York: Pantheon, 1992. ISBN 0-394-55591-0. ‣ Study of English harvest celebration that bound master and slave, each with different agenda, reinforcing slave accommodation through minstrelsy. Paternalistic, hegemonic theme imbedded in interesting analysis of slave subversive interplay and performance. [MW]

42.324 Herbert Aptheker. *American Negro slave revolts.* 1943 ed. New York: International Publishers, 1987. ISBN 0-7178-0605-7 (pbk). ‣ Significant, long-ignored work revealing extent and levels of slave resistance and rebellion. Counterbalances perspective that slaves did not resist. Excellent primary documentation. [MW]

42.325 John W. Blassingame. *The slave community: plantation life in the antebellum South.* Rev. ed. New York: Oxford University Press, 1979. ISBN 0-19-502562-8 (cl), 0-19-502563-6 (pbk). ‣ Pioneering, internal examination of life in slave quarters through slave's voice using fugitive narratives, autobiographies, and sociological perspectives. Illustration of plantation personality types challenges Elkins's thesis (42.279). [MW]

42.326 John H. Bracey, August Meier, and Elliott M. Rudwick, eds. *American slavery: the question of resistance.* Belmont, Calif.: Wadsworth, 1971. ISBN 0-534-00017-7. ‣ Collection of essays discussing historical spectrum of slave resistance. Ranges from conservative paternalist argument to daily resistance, acculturation, white repression, slave personality, and New Left approaches. [MW]

42.327 Janet Duitsman Cornelius. *"When I can read my title clear": literacy, slavery, and religion in the antebellum South.* Columbia: University of South Carolina Press, 1991. ISBN 0-87249-737-2. ‣ Analysis of literacy as integral component of slave religious and communal experience despite slaveholders' efforts to prevent its attainment. Links slave literacy to spiritual conciousness, self-esteem, resistance, and freedom. [MW]

42.328 Margaret Washington Creel. *A peculiar people: slave religion and community-culture among the Gullahs.* New York: New York University Press, 1988. ISBN 0-8147-1404-8. ‣ Interpretive, analytical history of Sea Island slave culture emphasizing African heritage, resistance, community consciousness, and social cohesion. Challenges thesis of planter paternalism and slave accommodation. [MW]

42.329 Angela Davis. "Reflections on the black woman's role in the community of slaves." *The black scholar* 3.4 (1971) 2–15. ISSN 0006-4246. ‣ Revolutionary argument for centrality of slave woman's role in slave resistance. Child-rearing and domesticity recast with ironic political meaning. Major source for much subsequent research and debate on gender and slavery. [VBB]

42.330 Paul D. Escott. *Slavery remembered: a record of twentieth-century slave narratives.* Chapel Hill: University of North Carolina Press, 1979. ISBN 0-8078-1340-0 (cl), 0-8078-1343-5 (pbk). ‣ Uses computer analysis to examine information in slave narratives in Federal Writers Project as window into black consciousness. Data reveal levels of slave resistance, endurance, cultural creativity, and adaptability. [MW]

42.331 Christie Farnham. "Sapphire? The issue of dominance in the slave family, 1830–1865." In *To toil the livelong day: America's women at work, 1780–1980.* Carol Groneman and Mary Beth Norton, eds., pp. 68–83. Ithaca, N.Y.: Cornell University Press, 1987. ISBN 0-8014-1847-X (cl), 0-8014-9452-4 (pbk). ▸ Female-headed slave families, women's double work duty in two-parent families, serial marriages do not represent sexual equality. Views African-influenced adaptations to exigencies of slavery as evidence of female self-reliance. [VBB]

42.332 Barbara J. Fields. *Slavery and freedom on the middle ground: Maryland during the nineteenth century.* New Haven: Yale University Press, 1985. ISBN 0-300-02340-5. ▸ Examination of slavery and black-white post–Civil War transition, focusing on black oppression, economic conditions, politics, and social problems. Places emancipation process in national and international perspective. [MW/SHH]

42.333 Eugene D. Genovese. *In red and black: Marxian explorations in southern and Afro-American history.* 1971 ed. Knoxville: University of Tennessee Press, 1984. ISBN 0-8704-9428-7 (cl), 0-87049-429-5 (pbk). ▸ Polemical essays linking black nationalist political concerns of 1960s with African American southern slave heritage. Views existing black struggle as rooted in limitations of past and lacking Marxist vision. [MW]

42.334 Eugene D. Genovese. *Roll, Jordan, roll: the world the slaves made.* 1974 ed. New York: Vintage, 1976. ISBN 0-394-71652-3. ▸ Trendsetting interpretation of paternalism as model for understanding masters and slaves through application of Gramsci's theory of hegemony. Slaves accepted white rule thereby compromising revolutionary potential and accommodating own oppression. [MW]

42.335 Vincent Harding. *There is a river: the black struggle for freedom in America.* 1981 ed. New York: Vintage, 1983. ISBN 0-394-71148-3 (pbk). ▸ Black resistance viewed in terms of continual antislavery theme prominent in intellectual and social thought of black leadership. Affirming, celebratory approach to freedom struggle as vision of hope transcending bondage. [MW]

42.336 Harriet A. Jacobs. *Incidents in the life of a slave girl: written by herself.* Jean Fagan Yellin, ed. Cambridge, Mass.: Harvard University Press, 1987. ISBN 0-674-44745-X (cl), 0-674-44746-8 (pbk). ▸ Definitive edition of female slave narrative comparable in detail and analysis to that of Frederick Douglass. Thorough introduction and annotation enriches valuable source on sexual exploitation, morals, motherhood, escape, abolitionists, and conditional freedom. [VBB]

42.337 Jacqueline Jones. "My mother was much of a woman: black women, work, and the family under slavery." *Feminist studies* 8 (1982) 235–69. ISSN 0046-3663. ▸ Slave women's lives an extreme reflection of all women's lives within patriarchal capitalism: duality of production and reproduction. Extends Davis's thesis (42.329) regarding ironic assertion of African patriarchy as resistance. Slightly revised version of this article appears as chapter 1 of 40.456. [VBB]

42.338 Norrece T. Jones. *Born a child of freedom, yet a slave: mechanisms of control and strategies of resistance in antebellum South Carolina.* Middletown, Conn.: Wesleyan University Press; distributed by Harper & Row, 1990. ISBN 0-8195-5213-5. ▸ Explores conflict between masters and slaves, examining mechanisms and success of white control, slave reaction including counterstrategies, and efforts to undermine white dominance. Challenges paternalism thesis. [MW]

42.339 Charles Joyner. *Down by the riverside: a South Carolina slave community.* Urbana: University of Illinois Press, 1984. ISBN 0-252-01058-2. ▸ Reconstruction of All Saints Parish's Gullah heritage through folklore, ethnography, oral history, and plantation records, highlighting daily life, labor, and culture. Rich,

sensitive narrative fusing African and American culture in paternalistic context. [MW]

42.340 John Lofton. *Denmark Vesey's revolt: the slave plot that lit a fuse to Fort Sumter.* Rev. ed. Kent, Ohio: Kent State University Press, 1983. ISBN 0-87338-296-X (pbk). ▸ Narrative and analysis of most extensive urban slave conspiracy in South Carolina (1822), focusing on social, economic, and political forces shaping African American resistance. Revealing revision of Richard Wade's interpretation. Earlier title: *Insurrection in South Carolina: The Turbulent World of Denmark Vesey.* [MW]

42.341 Ann Patton Malone. *Sweet chariot: slave family and household structure in nineteenth-century Louisiana.* Chapel Hill: University of North Carolina Press, 1992. ISBN 0-8078-2026-1. ▸ Discussion of slave family life in Louisiana emphasizing tendency toward stability, importance of family ties, and community cohesion, despite extreme vulnerability. Excellent research and analysis of household composition in slave quarters. [MW]

42.342 Melton Alonza McLaurin. *Celia, a slave.* Athens: University of Georgia Press, 1991. ISBN 0-8203-1352-1. ▸ Account of trial of slave woman who murdered owner for sexual violation and events surrounding crime. Compelling, yet undeveloped themes on antebellum violence against black women. [MW]

42.343 Stephen B. Oates. *The fires of jubilee: Nat Turner's fierce rebellion.* 1975 ed. New York: Harper & Row, 1990. ISBN 0-06-013228-0 (cl, 1975), 0-06-091670-2 (pbk). ▸ Dramatic study of most chilling American slave uprising through reconstruction of mindset of mystical leader and analysis of racial climate of South. Compelling narrative and documentation; dispels previous fictional account. [MW]

42.344 Gary Y. Okihiro, ed. *In resistance: studies in African, Caribbean, and Afro-American history.* Amherst: University of Massachusetts Press, 1986. ISBN 0-87023-519-2 (cl), 0-87023-520-6 (pbk). ▸ Commemorative papers, focusing on slave resistance, celebrating work of scholar-activist Herbert Aptheker. Reviews studies of resistance in African diaspora, noting their distance from Marxist scholarship. [MW]

42.345 Leslie Howard Owens. *This species of property: slave life and culture in the old South.* 1976 ed. New York: Oxford University Press, 1977. ISBN 0-19-501958-X (1976, cl), 0-19-502245-9 (pbk). ▸ Internal examination of slaves' lifestyle, including culture, personalities, behavior, and living conditions. Uses impressive array of plantation records, narratives, and autobiographies; challenges Elkins's Sambo thesis (42.279). [MW]

42.346 George Rawick. *From sundown to sun up: the making of the black community.* Vol. 1 of *The American slave: a composite autobiography.* Westport, Conn.: Greenwood, 1972. ISBN 0-8371-6299-8. ▸ Pioneering, original interpretation of previously unexamined Works Progress Administration slave narratives, demonstrating social structure in slave quarters, importance of African heritage, resistance, and nature of racism. Counterbalances Elkins's thesis (42.279). [MW]

42.347 Mechal Sobel. *Trabelin' on: the slave journey to an Afro-Baptist faith.* 1979 ed. Princeton: Princeton University Press, 1988. ISBN 0-691-00603-2 (pbk). ▸ Innovative study of antebellum African American values, culture, and institutional development within religious framework. Argues for African heritage and consciousness within African American Christian beliefs, particularly those of Baptist faith. [MW]

42.348 Robert S. Starobin, comp. *Denmark Vesey: the slave conspiracy of 1822.* Englewood Cliffs, N.J.: Prentice-Hall, 1970. ISBN 0-13-198440-3. ▸ Argues for existence of conspiracy and contributes to historiographical debate over propensity of urban slaves to rebel. Uses unexamined manuscript sources. [MW]

42.349 Sterling Stuckey. "Through the prism of folklore: the black ethos in slavery." *Massachusetts review* 9 (1968) 417–37. ISSN 0025-4878. ▸ Exploratory treatise, emphasizing value of slaves' folklore as historical documents for interpreting African American thought, consciousness, and resistance. Significant analysis, pathbreaking implications for slave historiography. [MW]

42.350 William L. Van Deburg. *The slave drivers: black agricultural labor supervisors in the antebellum South.* 1979 ed. New York: Oxford University Press, 1988. ISBN 0-19-505698-1. ▸ First work devoted to black slave supervisors emphasizes complexity of their position. Drivers not tools of masters—alienated from community, from families—nor crushed by their unenviable positions. [MW]

42.351 Richard C. Wade. *Slavery in the cities, the South, 1820–1860.* 1964 ed. New York: Oxford University Press, 1967. ISBN 0-19-500755-7. ▸ Original discussion comparing urban slavery in ten cities. Maintains that complex urban structures, presence of free people of color, and inability to keep races separate contributed to demise of urban slavery. Thesis refuted by Goldin 42.283. [MW]

42.352 Thomas L. Webber. *Deep like the rivers: education in the slave-quarter community, 1831–1865.* New York: Norton, 1978. ISBN 0-393-05685-6. ▸ Reconstructs slave communal life and value system using oral history, emphasizing socialization of young to distrust any white instruction in favor of folk-learning and black ethos. Portrait of slave autonomy. [MW]

42.353 Deborah Gray White. *Ar'n't I a woman? Female slaves in the plantation South.* 1985 ed. New York: Norton, 1987. ISBN 0-393-02217-X (cl, 1985), 0-393-30406-X. ▸ First full-length treatment of female slave experience finds separate female experience privileged motherhood over relations with men or escape. Deconstructs Mammy and Jezebel images. Author's claims to slave sexual equality weaken under contradictory evidence. [VBB]

SEE ALSO

39.313 Philip J. Schwarz. *Twice condemned.*
40.354 Sterling Stuckey. *Slave culture.*

Free People of Color

42.354 Ira Berlin. *Slaves without masters: the free Negro in the antebellum South.* 1974 ed. New York: Oxford University Press, 1981. ISBN 0-19-502905-4 (pbk). ▸ Analysis of growth and development of southern free black communities from early national period through 1875. Meticulous research and comprehensive portrait of caste structure, institutions, black identity, and white domination. [MW/DMS]

42.355 Letitia W. Brown. *Free Negroes in the District of Columbia, 1790–1846.* New York: Oxford University Press, 1972. ISBN 0-19-501552-5. ▸ Examination of growth and development of Washington's African American population focusing on routes to freedom, race relations, and traditions of servitude in Virginia and Maryland. Detailed discussion of individual lives of free people of color. [MW]

42.356 William F. Cheek and Aimee Lee Cheek. *John Mercer Langston and the fight for black freedom, 1829–1865.* Urbana: University of Illinois Press, 1989. ISBN 0-252-01550-9. ▸ First biography of brilliant, privileged African American leader. Social history of period exploring critical issues for free blacks and story of Langston's remarkable career in pre–Civil War America. [MW]

42.357 Leonard P. Curry. *The free black in urban America, 1800–1850: the shadow of the dream.* Chicago: University of Chicago Press, 1981. ISBN 0-226-13124-6. ▸ Case studies of antebellum free communities in largest cities, comparing data, focusing on internal relations, stressing optimism, efforts, sacrifice, and communal pressures in search of American dream. Innovative, original, comparative study. [MW]

42.358 John Hope Franklin. *The free Negro in North Carolina, 1790–1860.* 1943 ed. New York: Norton, 1971. ISBN 0-393-00579-

8. ▸ Exploration of antebellum life of free people of color, tracing internal social structure, legal restraints, racism, and economic factors impeding their progress. Original perspective using previously unexamined sources. [MW]

42.359 Willis Augustus Hodges. *Free man of color: the autobiography of Willis Augustus Hodges.* Willard B. Gatewood, Jr., ed. Knoxville: University of Tennessee Press, 1982. ISBN 0-87049-353-1. ▸ Descended from Virginia blacks free since eighteenth century, Hodges was cofounder of *Ram's Horn.* First publication of 1849 autobiography intended as brief on behalf of southern free people of color. [MW]

42.360 Luther P. Jackson. *Free Negro labor and property holding in Virginia, 1830–1860.* 1942 ed. New York: Russell & Russell, 1971. ▸ Account of free people of color, demonstrating farmers' and tradesmen's important economic and commercial contributions to Virginia life. Impressive research dispelling previously held notions of free black economic liability in Virginia. [MW]

42.361 Michael P. Johnson and James L. Roark. *Black masters: a free family of color in the Old South.* New York: Norton, 1984. ISBN 0-393-01906-3. ▸ History of William Ellison, free African American, wealthy slaveholder, and craftsman. Exceptional individual's life reveals collective experience of free blacks and thin line between slavery and freedom. [MW]

42.362 Larry Koger. *Black slaveowners: free black slave masters in South Carolina, 1790–1860.* Jefferson, N.C.: McFarland, 1985. ISBN 0-89950-160-5. ▸ Portrait of African American slaveholders as either upwardly mobile mulattoes firmly committed to slavery or as purchasers of family members. Overwhelming detail, tedious reading, although impressive on black resourcefulness. [MW]

42.363 Gary B. Mills. *The forgotten people: Cane River's creoles of color.* Baton Rouge: Louisiana State University Press, 1977. ISBN 0-8071-0279-2 (cl), 0-8071-0287-3 (pbk). ▸ History and genealogy of Cane River, Louisiana, people; prosperous, self-contained, antebellum community. Revealing descriptions of inter- and intraracial relationships, placing creoles in broader history of antebellum South. [MW]

42.364 Herbert Sterkx. *The free Negro in ante-bellum Louisiana.* Rutherford, N.J.: Fairleigh Dickinson University Press, 1972. ISBN 0-8386-7837-8. ▸ Study of origins, development, and plight of free people of color, recounting socioeconomic life, legal proscriptions, and economic success. Descriptive narrative ignores complex relations among free blacks and between slaves and free blacks. [MW]

42.365 David O. Whitten. *Andrew Durnford: a black sugar planter in antebellum Louisiana.* Natchitoches, La.: Northwestern State University Press, 1981. ISBN 0-917898-06-0. ▸ Portrait of antebellum life through primary sources left by affluent African American planter and physician. Revealing illustration of Durnford's emulation of whites, including keeping slave mistress and owning seventy-five slaves. [MW]

42.366 Marina Wikramanayake. *A world in shadow: the free black in antebellum South Carolina.* Columbia: University of South Carolina Press, 1973. ISBN 0-87249-242-7. ▸ Challenges southern myth of black indolence. Economically productive free black community marginal to white society; built racial identity with slaves through religion and charity, but fostered class stratification as well. [MW]

THE WEST

General Studies

42.367 Ray Allen Billington and Martin Ridge. *Westward expansion: a history of the American frontier.* 5th ed. New York: Macmillan, 1982. ISBN 0-02-309860-0. ▸ Grandly Turnerian survey of West; covers 1492 to 1896, European colonial society to Populist party, Virginia to California. Excellent analysis of Turner 42.131, helpful maps, and exhaustive bibliography. [CAM]

42.368 William H. Goetzmann. *Exploration and empire: the explorer and the scientist in the winning of the American West.* 1966 ed. New York: Norton, 1978. ISBN 0-393-00881-9 (cl), 0-393-00881-0 (pbk). ▸ Pulitzer Prize–winning study of westward European American expansion, 1805–1900. Examines contributions of mountainmen, trappers, army, and surveyors such as Powell, King, and Hayden. [CAM]

42.369 William H. Goetzmann. *New lands, new men: America and the second great age of discovery.* New York: Viking, 1986. ISBN 0-670-81068-1. ▸ Exploration of age of Enlightenment, seventeenth to nineteenth century, with consideration of ideals of science, progress, and romanticism. [CAM]

42.370 Donald Jackson. *Thomas Jefferson and the Stony Mountains: exploring the West from Monticello.* Urbana: University of Illinois Press, 1981. ISBN 0-252-00823-5. ▸ Important but much overlooked aspect of founder from Virginia. Role in exploration of North American interior made him most towering westerner of them all. [CAM]

42.371 Howard Roberts Lamar, ed. *The reader's encyclopedia of the American West.* New York: Crowell, 1977. ISBN 0-690-00008-1. ▸ Standard reference for trans-Mississippi scholars, despite some unavoidable omissions. One-volume guide to frontier American history, culture, and literature. Treats both nineteenth- and twentieth-century western topics. [CAM]

42.372 Patricia Nelson Limerick, Clyde A. Milner II, and Charles E. Rankin, eds. *Trails: toward a new western history.* Lawrence: University Press of Kansas, 1991. ISBN 0-7006-0500-2 (cl), 0-7006-0501-0 (pbk). ▸ Assessment of new and old historiography. Limerick presents working definition of new regionalism. Several authors critique frontier thesis. Stresses cultural diversity, environmental challenges, global connections, and other new paradigms. [CAM]

42.373 Thomas J. Lyon et al., eds. *A literary history of the American West.* Fort Worth: Texas Christian University Press, 1987. ISBN 0-87565-021-X. ▸ Monumental bibliographic and critical guide to three centuries of western American expression. Categories include "Encountering the West," "Settled In: Many Wests," and "Rediscovering the West." Standard reference. [CAM]

42.374 Michael P. Malone, ed. *Historians and the American West.* Lincoln: University of Nebraska Press, 1983. ISBN 0-8032-3071-0. ▸ Bibliographic and historiographic chapters by prominent western historians. Subjects include American Indians, Spanish Borderlands, Manifest Destiny, mining, exploration, farming, politics, violence, natural resources, transportation, and ethnic and cultural groups. [CAM]

42.375 Gary E. Moulton, ed. *The journals of the Lewis and Clark expedition, Vols. 2–7, Aug. 30, 1803–June 9, 1806.* 7 vols. Lincoln: University of Nebraska Press, 1986–91. ISBN 0-8032-2869-4 (v. 2), 0-8032-2875-9 (v. 3), 0-8032-2877-5 (v. 4), 0-8032-2883-X (v. 5), 0-8032-2893-7 (v. 6), 0-8032-2898-8 (v. 7). ▸ Prize-winning editor Moulton includes detailed indexes, reference lists, introductions, and new scholarship on plants, animals, geography, history, and Indian languages with these diaries. Definitive works on expedition; covers journey to Fort Clatsop, and return with explorers as far as Clearwater Valley. [CAM]

42.376 Roger L. Nichols, ed. *American frontier and western issues: a historiographical review.* Westport, Conn.: Greenwood, 1986. ISBN 0-313-24356-5. ▸ Compilation of essays on wide-ranging issues in American western history. Bibliographic, analytic, and sound. [CAM]

42.377 Morgan B. Sherwood. *Exploration of Alaska, 1865–1900.*

New Haven: Yale University Press, 1965. ▸ Systematic, thorough account revealing that federal government devoted more attention and funds than previously acknowledged. Scientific rather than economic motives spurred most expeditions; Smithsonian Institution an active participant. [CAM]

42.378 Mary Lee Spence and Donald Jackson, eds. *The expeditions of John Charles Fremont.* 3 vols. Urbana: University of Illinois Press, 1970–84. ISBN 0-252-00086-2 (v. 1), 0-252-00249-0 (v. 2), 0-252-00416-7 (v. 3), 0-252-01504-5 (ser.) ▸ Careful reproduction of important letters and excerpts of reports and memoirs, including documents written by interested associates. Each volume encompasses significant time periods, proceeds chronologically, is prefaced with introductory overview, and contains interpretive notes. Illustrated with portraits, maps, fossil and plant plates. Volume 2 supplement reprints court martial proceedings. [CAM]

42.379 Dan L. Thrapp, ed. *Encyclopedia of frontier biography.* 1988 ed. 3 vols. Lincoln: University of Nebraska Press, 1991. ISBN 0-8032-9417-4 (set, pbk), 0-8032-9418-2 (v. 1, pbk), 0-8032-9419-0 (v. 2, pbk), 0-8032-9420-2 (v. 3, pbk). ▸ Impressive collection of approximately 4,500 profiles, representing all races and most occupations, including artists, naturalists, writers, outlaws, lawmen, Indians, missionaries, and travelers; miners intentionally omitted and women somewhat neglected. Bibliographic notes and index cross-references events and names which do not have entries. Excellent reference and research tool. [CAM]

42.380 John D. Unruh. *The plains across: the overland emigrants and the trans–Mississippi West, 1840–1860.* Urbana: University of Illinois Press, 1979. ISBN 0-252-00698-4. ▸ Extensive presentation and analysis of overland migration; underscores aid of American Indians, federal government, and settler communities. Examines forms of communication and causes of mortality. Exhaustively researched, authoritative work. [CAM]

42.381 Richard White. *It's your misfortune and none of my own: a new history of the American West.* Norman: University of Oklahoma Press, 1991. ISBN 0-8061-2366-4. ▸ Masterfully culminates several decades of scholarly reassessment with fresh insights, lucid style, thorough survey of four centuries. Develops numerous themes, destroying popular images and establishing region's identity. [CAM]

SEE ALSO

Western Myth and the National Character

42.382 Ray Allen Billington. *America's frontier heritage.* 1966 ed. Albuquerque: University of New Mexico Press, 1974. ISBN 0-8263-0310-2. ▸ Argues uniqueness of West played important role in shaping national character and attitudes. Defines distinctive traits, applying studies in economics, sociology, psychology, and demographics. Eloquent defense of Turner thesis (42.131). [CAM]

42.383 Ray Allen Billington. *Land of savagery, land of promise: the European image of the American frontier in the nineteenth century.* 1981 ed. Norman: University of Oklahoma Press, 1985. ISBN 0-8061-1929-2 (pbk). ▸ Influence of popular-culture writings on perceptions of America's border regions. Pioneering study utilizing thousands of European novels, letters, travelogues, and promotionals. [CAM]

42.384 John G. Cawelti. *The six-gun mystique.* 1971 ed. Bowling Green, Ohio: Bowling Green State University Popular Press, 1984. ISBN 0-87972-313-0 (cl), 0-87972-314-9 (pbk). ▸ Thorough analysis of the Western; treats adventure novels and films in consideration of myth, symbol, and American frontier. [CAM]

42.385 Brian W. Dippie. *Catlin and his contemporaries: the politics of patronage.* Lincoln: University of Nebraska Press, 1990. ISBN 0-8032-1683-1. ▸ Premier painters of western American Indians and frontier life scrambled for money and still created works of enduring importance. Untangles complex web of relationships with politicians, businessmen, royalty, and others. [CAM]

42.386 William H. Goetzmann and William N. Goetzmann. *The West of the imagination.* New York: Norton, 1986. ISBN 0-393-02370-2. ▸ Beautifully illustrated, substantial complement to PBS television series of same name. Discussion of role of art and popular culture in formation of perceptions of West since 1820. [CAM]

42.387 Anne Farrar Hyde. *An American vision: far western landscape and national culture, 1820–1920.* New York: New York University Press, 1990. ISBN 0-8147-3466-9. ▸ Discussion of growth of American self-perception through development of western imagery, emphasizing literary and visual media used by travelers to describe West. [CAM]

42.388 Robert W. Johannsen. *To the halls of the Montezumas: the Mexican War in the American imagination.* New York: Oxford University Press, 1985. ISBN 0-19-503518-6. ▸ Study of nation's first declared foreign war. Scholarly assessment of nationwide reaction to war stressing debate over purposes of republicanism and idealism about independence. [CAM]

42.389 Patricia Nelson Limerick. *Desert passages: encounters with the American deserts.* 1985 ed. Niwot: University Press of Colorado, 1989. ISBN 0-870811-75-4. ▸ Graceful, profound excursion into ideas. Symbols and impressions expressed by eight authors fall into three categories that sometimes overlap and intertwine: hostile wasteland; potential garden; and redeeming, aesthetic personal refuge. [CAM]

42.390 Bill O'Neal. *Encyclopedia of western gunfighters.* 1979 ed. Norman: University of Oklahoma Press, 1991. ISBN 0-8061-1508-4 (cl, 1979), 0-8061-2335-4 (pbk). ▸ Compilation of all gunfighters—generally viewed as those outside law—in the American West. Over 200 entries including short biography and descriptive listing of gunfights. [CAM]

42.391 Don Russell. *The lives and legends of Buffalo Bill.* 1960 ed. Norman: University of Oklahoma Press, 1979. ISBN 0-8061-1537-8 (pbk). ▸ Definitive study of William Frederick Cody, including both his military and entertainment career. Excellent resource on popular culture and late nineteenth-century West. [CAM]

42.392 Susan Prendergast Schoelwer. *Alamo images: changing perceptions of a Texas experience.* Dallas: DeGolyer Library and Southern Methodist University Press, 1985. (DeGolyer Library publications, 3.) ISBN 0-87074-217-5 (cl), 0-87074-213-2 (pbk). ▸ Richly illustrated text exploring history, folklore, psychology, architecture, and race relations, leading to assessment of Alamo myth and its impact on Texan and American identities. [CAM]

42.393 Richard Slotkin. *The fatal environment: the myth of the frontier in the age of industrialization, 1800–1890.* Middletown, Conn.: Wesleyan University Press; distributed by Harper & Row, 1986. ISBN 0-8195-6183-5 (pbk). ▸ Interpretation of metropolis and frontier as theaters of industrial and border savagery, respectively, with nineteenth-century frontiersman (exemplified by George A. Custer) playing role in both. Fascinating argument. [CAM]

42.394 Kevin Starr. *Americans and the California dream, 1850–1915.* 1973 ed. New York: Oxford University Press, 1986. ISBN 0-19-501644-0 (cl, 1973), 0-19-504233-6 (pbk). ▸ Series of biographical and cultural studies exploring popular images of

Golden State and subsequent expectations of its inhabitants. Thoughtful and stimulating. [CAM]

42.395 Wallace Stegner. *The American West as living space.* Ann Arbor: University of Michigan Press, 1987. ISBN 0-472-09375-4 (cl), 0-472-06375-8 (pbk). ▸ Collected lectures from author's 1986 appearances at University of Michigan Law School. Emphasis on western water, land, and frontier character reinforces author's position as eloquent western spokesman. [CAM]

42.396 Robert M. Utley. *Billy the Kid: a short and violent life.* Lincoln: University of Nebraska Press, 1989. ISBN 0-8032-4553-x. ▸ Common outlaw and murderer, product of chaotic environment, yet enjoyed popular support and achieved fame before he died. Thorough research includes Lincoln County War and protagonists. [CAM]

42.397 Robert M. Utley. *Cavalier in buckskin: George Armstrong Custer and the western military frontier.* Norman: University of Oklahoma Press, 1988. ISBN 0-8061-2150-5. ▸ Counters extremist views of cavalry officer's leadership abilities and political ambition; calls attention to unscrupulous business dealings, dishonesty, and enigmatic personality. Objective analysis of fact and myth. [CAM]

42.398 David J. Weber. *Myth and the history of the Hispanic Southwest: essays.* Albuquerque: University of New Mexico Press, 1988. ISBN 0-8263-1094-x. ▸ Important interpretation of Spanish Borderlands history, emphasizing myth, Protestant-Catholic conflict, European-Indian relations, and need to reconsider Herbert Eugene Bolton's pioneering 1921 work (cf. 37.567). [CAM]

42.399 Elliott West. *Growing up with the country: childhood on the far western frontier.* Albuquerque: University of New Mexico Press, 1989. ISBN 0-8263-1154-7 (cl), 0-8263-1155-5 (pbk). ▸ Rich, compelling social history highlights child's conflict between eastern parental values and new western identity. Landmark study combining histories of three specific frontier settings with individual childhood portraits. [CAM/WFD]

SEE ALSO
40.731 Richard Slotkin. *Regeneration through violence.*

Migration and Settlement

42.400 Leonard J. Arrington. *Brigham Young: American Moses.* New York: Knopf; distributed by Random House, 1985. ISBN 0-394-51022-4. ▸ Expansive biography of Church of Jesus Christ of Latter-day Saints' leader. Functioned as church president, political figure, businessman, colonizer, and persuasive speaker, advocating polygamy and utopianism. [CAM]

42.401 Gordon Morris Bakken. *The development of law on the Rocky Mountain frontier: civil law and society, 1850–1912.* Westport, Conn.: Greenwood, 1983. ISBN 0-313-23285-7. ▸ Exhaustive review of contract, corporate, labor, and water laws; excludes criminal codes. Concludes eastern precedents and English common law inadequate for American West because of aridity, changing markets, and entrepreneurship. [CAM]

42.402 William A. Bowen. *The Willamette Valley: migration and settlement on the Oregon frontier.* Seattle: University of Washington Press, 1978. ISBN 0-295-95590-2. ▸ Detailed geographic study of 1840s western Oregon using computer enhanced maps and charts. Excellent examination of interconnected frontier landscape and settlement process. [CAM]

42.403 David Alan Johnson. *Founding the Far West: California, Oregon, and Nevada, 1840–1890.* Berkeley: University of California Press, 1992. ISBN 0-520-07348-7. ▸ Comparative presentation of early decades of statehood. Complex analysis of political cultures emphasizing contrast between republican and liberal ideologies in nineteenth century. Thorough research providing fresh approach to regional topics. [CAM/WFD]

42.404 Howard Roberts Lamar. *Texas crossings: the Lone Star state and the American Far West, 1836–1986.* Austin: University of Texas Press, 1991. ISBN 0-292-78115-6. ‣ Three essays examine significance of mobility and diverse range of travelers. Considers development of trails and markets and state's connections with California and West. Engaging topic. [CAM]

42.405 Lawrence H. Larsen. *The urban West at the end of the frontier.* Lawrence: Regents Press of Kansas, 1978. ISBN 0-7006-0168-6. ‣ Brief introduction to problems and promises of western urban life in periods following great overland rushes. Examines urban demography, economics, environment, sanitation, services (health, fire, and police), and land technology. Western cities, like eastern cities, reflected values of Gilded Age, shaped by technology and transportation. [CAM]

42.406 Larry M. Logue. *A sermon in the desert: belief and behavior in early St. George, Utah.* Urbana: University of Illinois Press, 1988. ISBN 0-252-01474-X. ‣ Analysis of demographic patterns in frontier Mormon community showing influence of both frontier and Mormonism; 1860s and 1870s. Polygamy common. [DSS]

42.407 Frederick C. Luebke, ed. *Ethnicity on the Great Plains.* Lincoln: University of Nebraska Press for the Center for Great Plains Studies, 1980. ISBN 0-8032-2855-4. ‣ Exploration of development of ethnic communities on Great Plains, especially Prussians, Russian Germans, and Swedes. Insightful analysis of positive and negative effects of isolation on cultural persistence. [CAM]

42.408 Ralph Mann. *After the gold rush: society in Grass Valley and Nevada City, California, 1849–1870.* Stanford, Calif.: Stanford University Press, 1982. ISBN 0-8047-1136-4. ‣ Voluminous data support analyses of social structure and values of two differing mining towns. Clear style and consideration of numerous cultural variables strengthen excellent study. [CAM]

42.409 D. W. Meinig. *The great Columbia Plain: a historical geography, 1805–1910.* Seattle: University of Washington Press, 1968. ‣ Interdependent study of human reaction to and organization of environment. Little-known Columbia Plain includes sand, sage, coulees, canyons, hills, and irrigated valleys. Impressive, scientific, and dense. Excellent maps. [CAM]

42.410 D. W. Meinig. *Southwest: three peoples in geographical change, 1600–1700 [i.e. 1600–1970].* New York: Oxford University Press, 1971. ISBN 0-19-501289-5. ‣ Well-illustrated, controversial study of cultural homogeneity in Arizona and New Mexico. Emphasizes failure of melting pot process in region and urges ethnic pluralism. [CAM]

42.411 H. Craig Miner. *West of Wichita: settling the high plains of Kansas, 1865–1890.* Lawrence: University Press of Kansas, 1986. ISBN 0-7006-0286-0. ‣ Detailed narrative and analysis of settlement stresses individual responses to land and environmental changes not always for good. Examines many groups from Danish socialists to Jews to Exodusters. [CAM]

42.412 John Phillip Reid. *Law for the elephant: property and social behavior on the overland trail.* San Marino, Calif.: Huntington Library, 1980. ISBN 0-87328-104-7. ‣ Pathbreaking book examines legal history of overland trail experience. Contends immigrants respected property rights, informal contracts, and credit obligations. Argument strengthened by rich details from diaries, memoirs, and letters. [CAM]

42.413 John W. Reps. *The forgotten frontier: urban planning in the American West before 1890.* Columbia: University of Missouri Press, 1981. ISBN 0-8262-0351-5 (cl), 0-8262-0352-3 (pbk). ‣ Condensed version of *Cities of the American West.* Examines town planning in variety of western settings. Argues urban residents, not farmers and ranchers, dominated western culture. Includes 100 illustrations. [CAM]

42.414 Moses Rischin and John Livingston, eds. *Jews of the American West.* Detroit: Wayne State University Press, 1991. ISBN 0-8143-2170-4. ‣ Collection of nine essays exploring Jewish culture, social life, and religion in nineteenth-century West. Reveals variety of Jewish experiences within isolated societies and among diverse communities. Broad in scope. [CAM]

42.415 Lillian Schlissel, Byrd Gibbens, and Elizabeth Hampsten. *Far from home: families of the westward journey.* New York: Schocken, 1989. ISBN 0-8052-4052-7. ‣ Poignant examination of personal struggles and daily lives of three families based on letters and diaries. Addresses important questions regarding relationships and burden of migration. [CAM]

42.416 Richard White. *Land use, environment, and social change: the shaping of Island County, Washington.* Seattle: University of Washington Press, 1980. ISBN 0-295-95691-7. ‣ Model study of changes wrought in natural surroundings by American Indian and white occupation and of consequences of these changes for people who made them. Relationship between humans and earth in local context. [CAM]

SEE ALSO

36.267 Richard White. *The roots of dependency.*
40.124 Frederick Merk. *History of the westward movement.*
40.186 Robert V. Hine. *Community on the American frontier.*

Frontier Economy and Environment

42.417 Richard M. Clokey. *William H. Ashley: enterprise and politics in the trans-Mississippi West.* Norman: University of Oklahoma Press, 1980. ISBN 0-8061-1525-4 (cl), 0-521-29542-4 (pbk). ‣ Details Ashley's many roles in entrepreneurship, especially reorganization of fur trade which facilitated exploration and expansion. Politically active as representative of western interests and promoter of Jacksonian nation-building. [CAM]

42.418 Thomas R. Cox. *Mills and markets: a history of the Pacific coast lumber industry to 1900.* Seattle: University of Washington Press, 1974. ISBN 0-295-95349-7. ‣ Important export grew to maturity in age of enterprise, yet remained fragmented and competitive. Explains industry's structure and reaction to external influences. Well-organized, vivid writing. [CAM]

42.419 David Dary. *Cowboy culture: a saga of five centuries.* 1981 ed. Lawrence: University Press of Kansas, 1989. ISBN 0-7006-0390-5. ‣ Follows cowboys and evolution of cowboy culture from Spanish roots to end of open range. Detailed presentation of patterns of daily life and evolution of equipment. [CAM]

42.420 David Dary. *Entrepreneurs of the Old West.* New York: Knopf; distributed by Random House, 1986. ISBN 0-394-52405-5. ‣ Boom-and-bust story of silent army: business people and their towns, banks, stores, and railroads. Describes constant struggle to overcome isolation and battle against regional aridness. [CAM]

42.421 William E. DeBuys. *Enchantment and exploration: the life and hard times of a New Mexico mountain range.* Albuquerque: University of New Mexico Press, 1985. ISBN 0-8263-0819-8 (cl), 0-8263-0820-1 (pbk). ‣ Detailed history of Sangre de Cristo mountain range from American Indian to National Forest Service. Well-crafted discussion integrating geologic, ethnographic, and ecological differences. Punctuated with individual portraits. [CAM]

42.422 James H. Ducker. *Men of the steel rails: workers on the Atchison, Topeka, and Sante Fe railroad, 1869–1900.* Lincoln: University of Nebraska Press, 1983. ISBN 0-8032-1662-9. ‣ Modification of old-school conclusions about labor-management relations. Assesses social function of unions and investigates community, class, and race relations. Skillfully combines individual stories with quantitative analysis. [CAM]

42.423 Robert A. Dykstra. *The cattle towns.* 1968 ed. Lincoln: University of Nebraska Press, 1983. ISBN 0-8032-6561-1 (pbk). ▸ Case studies of Wichita, Abilene, Ellsworth, and Dodge City (all in Kansas) focusing on town building and operation of frontier democracy. Examines business and development of law as response to violence. Exciting narrative. [CAM]

42.424 Robert W. Frazer. *Forts and supplies: the role of the army in the economy of the Southwest, 1846–1861.* Albuquerque: University of New Mexico Press, 1983. ISBN 0-8263-0630-6. ▸ Study of military encouragement and contribution to settlement, agriculture, mining, and ranching in New Mexico Territory up to outbreak of Civil War. Period of unprecedented growth. [CAM]

42.425 Paul Wallace Gates. *Landlords and tenants on the prairie frontier: studies in American land policy.* Ithaca, N.Y.: Cornell University Press, 1973. ISBN 0-8014-0763-X. ▸ Intensive examination of landownership of Upper Mississipi Valley. Cattle kings and bonanza farmers versus smaller landowners until United States government's establishment of Homestead Act (1862). Thorough study of frontier enterprise. [CAM]

42.426 LeRoy R. Hafen, ed. *The mountain men and the fur trade of the Far West: biographical sketches of the participants by scholars of the subject and with introductions by the editor.* 10 vols. Glendale, Calif.: Clark, 1965–72. ▸ Includes over 300 articles by highly regarded contributors, ranging in length from one to twenty-five pages. Editor's lengthy essay in volume 1 provides useful background. Volume 10 includes index and rich bibliography, with archival material, books, articles, newspapers, and dissertations. Illustrated with prints and paintings. [CAM]

42.427 J. S. Holliday. *The world rushed in: the California gold rush experience.* 1981 ed. New York: Simon & Schuster, 1983. ISBN 0-671-25537-1 (cl), 0-671-25538-X (pbk). ▸ Uses argonaut William Swain's well-written, thorough journal and letters to reconstruct typical odyssey from start to finish. Narrative draws on many other sources for interpretation and context. [CAM]

42.428 Howard Roberts Lamar. *The trader on the American frontier: myth's victim.* College Station: Texas A&M University Press, 1977. ISBN 0-89096-033-X. ▸ Reviews importance of trade to natives and whites, maintaining that native cultures often benefited. Suggests new approaches regarding motivations and tactics of those involved in western trade. [CAM]

42.429 James C. Malin. *History and ecology: studies of the grassland.* Robert P. Swierenga, ed. Lincoln: University of Nebraska Press, 1984. ISBN 0-8032-8125-0 (cl), 0-8032-4144-5 (pbk). ▸ Swierenga's profile of Malin's research on Kansas and Great Plains. Introductory essay on Malin's career followed by selections from his work. Emphasizes Malin's research technique and critical analysis. [CAM]

42.430 Michael P. Malone. *Battle for Butte: mining and politics on the northern frontier, 1864–1906.* Seattle: University of Washington Press, 1981. ISBN 0-295-95837-5. ▸ Engaging, analytical study of ascension of Montana mining community to leading role in western metal mining. Examines struggle for control of city as well as of industry. [CAM]

42.431 Rodman Wilson Paul. *The Far West and the Great Plains in transition, 1859–1900.* New York: Harper & Row, 1988. ISBN 0-06-015836-0 (cl), 0-06-091448-3 (pbk). ▸ Mining, agricultural, environmental, and settlement history of elites and common folk of European background. Sees time as one of conflicts in demographics, land use, economics, and race relations. [CAM]

42.432 Rodman Wilson Paul. *Mining frontiers of the Far West, 1848–1880.* Albuquerque: University of New Mexico Press, 1974. ISBN 0-8263-0315-3. ▸ Still important overview of the role of mining from settlement of West to development of industrial mining on grand scale. Emphasizes common traits of communities and technical problems of extractive industry. Clear presentation of technologies. [CAM/WFD]

42.433 Richard H. Peterson. *The bonanza kings: the social origins and business behavior of western mining entrepreneurs, 1870–1900.* 1971 ed. Lincoln: University of Nebraska Press, 1977. ISBN 0-8032-0916-9. ▸ Biographical study of fifty accomplished, wealthy businessmen and their behavior. Historical and economic assessment of their impact in mineral industry with statistical tables and supplementary data. [CAM]

42.434 James P. Ronda. *Astoria and empire.* Lincoln: University of Nebraska Press, 1990. ISBN 0-8032-3896-7. ▸ Story of John Jacob Astor's Pacific Fur Company, set in context of imperialism and struggle for national supremacy in Northwest. Revises older accounts. [CAM]

42.435 Duane A. Smith. *Rocky Mountain mining camps: the urban frontier.* 1967 ed. Niwot: University Press of Colorado, 1992. ISBN 0-87081-266-1. ▸ Study of placer and hard-rock extraction in intermountain West and mining's influence on city and social growth. Focus on limited region and period (1859–90) structures and tightens work. [CAM]

42.436 James Whiteside. *Regulating danger: the struggle for mine safety in the Rocky Mountain coal industry.* Lincoln: University of Nebraska Press, 1990. ISBN 0-8032-4752-4. ▸ Analysis of risks taken by workers and evolution of laws governing workplace conditions, considering economic, technical, institutional, social, and political environments. Distinctive legal study. [CAM]

42.437 Oscar Osburn Winther. *The transportation frontier: trans–Mississippi West, 1865–1890.* 1964 ed. Albuquerque: University of New Mexico Press, 1974. ISBN 0-8263-0317-X. ▸ Factual, descriptive survey of methods, functions, obstacles, needs, and improvements associated with travel, from steamboats to bicycles. Well-chosen maps and illustrations complement informative, sometimes anecdotal text. [CAM/WFD]

42.438 David J. Wishart. *The fur trade of the American West, 1807–1840: a geographical synthesis.* Lincoln: University of Nebraska Press, 1979. ISBN 0-8032-4705-2. ▸ Analysis of strategy, operation, impact, and decline in two production systems, each based on different resources. Exploitive methods stimulated regional economic growth, but led to destruction of environment and native culture. [CAM]

42.439 Otis E. Young, Jr. *Black powder and hand steel: miners and machines on the old western frontier.* Norman: University of Oklahoma Press, 1976. ISBN 0-8061-1269-7. ▸ Engaging narrative and descriptive illustrations explain tools, technology, and procedures in manner accessible to casual reader. Portrays living, working, social conditions, and methods of prospecting. Engaging social history. [CAM]

Indian Wars and Relations

42.440 Gary Clayton Anderson. *Kinsmen of another kind: Dakota-white relations in the Upper Mississippi Valley, 1650–1862.* Lincoln: University of Nebraska Press, 1984. ISBN 0-8032-1018-3. ▸ Important ethnohistorical case study of contact between eastern Dakotas (or Santee Sioux) and European Americans. Peaceful trade and strong bonds gave way to bloody warfare in 1862. [CAM]

42.441 Robert F. Berkhofer, Jr. "The political context of a new Indian history." *Pacific historical review* 40 (1971) 357–81. ISSN 0030-8684. ▸ Scholarly critique advocating use of anthropology in study of American Indians, their lives, and their relationship with whites. Calls for new research methods using factionalism and tribal political system. [CAM]

42.442 Robert F. Berkhofer, Jr. *Salvation and the savage: an analysis of Protestant missions and American Indian response, 1787–*

1862. 1965 ed. Westport, Conn.: Greenwood, 1977. ISBN 0-8371-9745-7. ▸ Anthropological reconstruction of sequences of acculturation by native peoples to Christian mission activity. Role of factions, especially Christian versus pagan, most debated aspect of study. Benchmark of new Indian history. [CAM]

42.443 Robert Ignatius Burns. *The Jesuits and the Indian wars of the Northwest.* New Haven: Yale University Press, 1966. ▸ Three episodes in sharp detail: 1855 treaty troubles, combat in 1855–59, and Nez Perce War of 1877. Portraits of tribal and religious leaders, frontier interactions, and Jesuit peace efforts on grand scale. [CAM]

42.444 Evan S. Connell. *Son of the morning star.* San Francisco, Calif.: North Point, 1984. ISBN 0-86547-160-6. ▸ Evenhanded account of controversial cavalry leader George Armstrong Custer. Novelist Connell brings fresh perspective and compelling narrative to oft-told story. Leading source on Custeriana. [CAM]

42.445 Carol Devens. *Countering colonization: Native American women and Great Lakes missions, 1630–1900.* Berkeley: University of California Press, 1992. ISBN 0-520-07557-9. ▸ Behavioral evidence from missionary accounts testifying to native women's resistance to missionary efforts and native men's accommodation. Theoretical focus on female agency. [VBB]

42.446 Brian W. Dippie. *The vanishing American: white attitudes and U.S. Indian policy.* 1982 ed. Lawrence: University Press of Kansas, 1991. ISBN 0-7006-0507-X. ▸ Insightful study of popular views of American Indians and formulation of federal policy from late eighteenth century to middle of twentieth century. Cultural myth and racial history. [CAM/FEH/HM]

42.447 R. David Edmunds, ed. *American Indian leaders: studies in diversity.* Lincoln: University of Nebraska Press, 1980. ISBN 0-8032-1800-1 (cl), 0-8032-6705-3 (pbk). ▸ Broad collection of articles on prominent American Indians, from Old Briton to Peter MacDonald. Includes contributions by leading specialists. [CAM]

42.448 William T. Hagan. *United States–Comanche relations: the reservation years.* 1976 ed. Norman: University of Oklahoma Press, 1990. ISBN 0-8061-2275-7. ▸ Study of failure of assimilationist policies to turn hunters and raiders into farmers and stock raisers. Profile of Quanah Parker as cultural intermediary. Balanced assessment of governmental actions and native resistance. [CAM]

42.449 Paul L. Hedren, ed. *The great Sioux war, 1876–77: the best from "Montana," the magazine of western history.* Helena: Montana Historical Society Press; distributed by University of Nebraska Press, 1991. ISBN 0-917298-23-3 (cl), 0-917298-24-1 (pbk). ▸ Anthology of articles offering in-depth analysis of causes, successes, and tragedies. Important examinations of territorial politics, George Armstrong Custer, and combat. [CAM]

42.450 Paul Andrew Hutton. *Phil Sheridan and his army.* Lincoln: University of Nebraska Press, 1985. ISBN 0-8032-2329-3 (pbk), 0-8032-7227-8 (pbk). ▸ Thorough account of general's frontier campaigns after 1865, as agent for national expansion and Indian policy. Examines military establishment and politics of command. Energetic writing. [CAM]

42.451 Paul Andrew Hutton, ed. *The Custer reader.* Lincoln: University of Nebraska Press, 1992. ISBN 0-8032-2351-X. ▸ Well-chosen collection of articles and photo essays on famous cavalry leader. Authors assay his role in Civil War, Indian wars, Battle of Little Bighorn, and American myth. [CAM]

42.452 Richard E. Jensen, R. Eli Paul, and John E. Carter. *Eyewitness at Wounded Knee.* Lincoln: University of Nebraska Press, 1991. ISBN 0-8032-1409-X. ▸ Reproduction of all surviving photographs from battlefield and military expedition. Informative captions and careful attribution of photographers. Three schol-

arly essays examine ethnographic, military, and photographic history. [CAM]

42.453 David Lavender. *Let me be free: the Nez Perce tragedy.* New York: HarperCollins, 1992. ISBN 0-06-016707-6. ▸ Reappraisal of Chief Joseph and war of 1877. Tribe remained independent, yet adaptable, until inevitable confrontation with advancing white society. Emphasis on native traditions and culture. [CAM]

42.454 Clyde A. Milner II and Floyd A. O'Neil, eds. *Churchmen and the western Indians, 1820–1920.* Norman: University of Oklahoma Press, 1985. ISBN 0-8061-1950-0. ▸ Essays focus on six diverse churchmen who worked among western American Indians. Biographical format discusses varying missionary efforts to alter or assimilate Indians but native peoples retained some cultural self-determination. [CAM]

42.455 Francis Paul Prucha. *The Great Father: the United States government and the American Indians.* 2 vols. Lincoln: University of Nebraska Press, 1984. ISBN 0-8032-3668-9 (set). ▸ History of federal government's interaction with American Indians. Focus on government policies and impact of policies on Indian history from Jeffersonian emphasis on assimilation to 1980s. Extensive, comprehensive, reference work. [CAM/FEH/HM]

42.456 James P. Ronda. *Lewis and Clark among the Indians.* Lincoln: University of Nebraska Press, 1984. ISBN 0-8032-3870-3. ▸ Full-scale study of contact between explorers and American Indians, from high policy to personal liaisons, from ethnographic data to sharing of food and songs around blazing fires. Fascinating cultural interactions. [CAM]

42.457 Lewis O. Saum. *The fur trader and the Indian.* Seattle: University of Washington Press, 1965. ▸ Survey of observations and opinions of Indians by those whites in early and intimate contact. Reflects wide range of attitudes expressed by nineteenth-century Americans. [CAM]

42.458 Robert M. Utley. *Frontier regulars: the United States Army and the Indian, 1866–1891.* 1973 ed. Lincoln: University of Nebraska Press, 1984. ISBN 0-8032-9551-0 (pbk). ▸ Story of final wars against native peoples on Great Plains with several chapters on military life. Corrects stereotypical conceptions of military heroism. Balanced, standard-setting work. [CAM]

42.459 Robert M. Utley. *The Indian frontier of the American West, 1846–1890.* Albuquerque: University of New Mexico Press, 1984. ISBN 0-8263-0715-9 (cl), 0-8263-0716-7 (pbk). ▸ Well-written synopsis of Indian-white conflict in trans–Mississippi West. Emphasis on military actions, government policies, reservations, and native-white relations. Examines concept of mutually unintelligible thoughtworlds. Solid synthesis; critical of reformers. [CAM/FEH/HM]

SEE ALSO

Women and the Frontier

42.460 Susan Armitage and Elizabeth Jameson, eds. *The women's West.* Norman: University of Oklahoma Press, 1987. ISBN 0-8061-2043-6 (cl), 0-8061-2067-3 (pbk). ▸ Published proceedings of 1983 Women's West Conference demonstrating that imaginative researchers can reveal diversity and contributions of women who settled West. Topics include Mexican Americans, American Indians, homesteaders, methodology, and gender roles. [CAM/SGM]

42.461 Anne M. Butler. *Daughters of joy, sisters of misery: prostitutes in the American West, 1865–90.* Urbana: University of Illinois Press, 1985. ISBN 0-252-01139-2. ▸ Profound historical examination of female prostitutes' personal and professional lives. Explains reasons for women choosing this occupation, its drawbacks for women, and benefits for frontier society. [CAM]

42.462 John Mack Faragher. *Women and men on the overland trail.* New Haven: Yale University Press, 1979. ISBN 0-300-02267-0. ▸ Early but still important investigation of gender roles and relations on overland migrations. Anecdotal challenge to theory of gender equality on frontier. Diary evidence a valuable reminder of women's and men's investment in eastern gender roles. Dated by heavy-handed insistence on female victimization. [VBB/WFD]

42.463 Julie Roy Jeffrey. *Converting the West: a biography of Narcissa Whitman.* Norman: University of Oklahoma Press, 1991. ISBN 0-8061-2359-1. ▸ Biography of pioneer missionary to the Cayuse Indians in Oregon Territory. Explores her gender attitudes, evangelical ambitions, white assumptions, and reception by tribal members. [VBB]

42.464 Julie Roy Jeffrey. *Frontier women: the trans–Mississippi West, 1840–1880.* New York: Hill & Wang, 1979. ISBN 0-8090-4803-5 (cl), 0-8090-0141-1 (pbk). ▸ Sound, well-written argument. Women settled West with crusading desire to domesticate. Persistence of eastern gender ideology did not preclude female agency. Women asserted separate female authority over morals and culture. [VBB]

42.465 Annette Kolodny. *The land before her: fantasy and experience of the American frontiers, 1630–1860.* Chapel Hill: University of North Carolina Press, 1984. ISBN 0-8078-1571-3 (cl), 0-8078-4111-0 (pbk). ▸ Traditional literary study examining impact of women's sensibility on fantasy. Provocative insights suggest further historical research on women's western experience. Western intellectual history with twist of female culture. [VBB]

42.466 Cathy Luchetti. *Women of the West.* 1982 ed. New York: Orion, 1992. ISBN 0-517-59162-6. ▸ Richly illustrated volume revealing everyday lives of western women through diaries, letters, and photographs. Emphasis on women of varying economic, racial, and religious backgrounds makes work particularly effective. [CAM]

42.467 Glenda Riley. *The female frontier: a comparative view of women on the prairies and the plains.* Lawrence: University Press of Kansas, 1988. ISBN 0-7006-0354-9 (cl), 0-7006-0424-3 (pbk). ▸ Provocative, controversial study, arguing that women's common domestic duties on prairie and plains overrode regional variations. Debate persists but even critics concede value of rich data. [CAM/VBB/SGM]

42.468 Glenda Riley. *Women and Indians on the frontier, 1825–1915.* Albuquerque: University of New Mexico Press, 1984. ISBN 0-8263-0778-7 (cl), 0-8263-0780-9 (pbk). ▸ Documents white female settlers' changing attitudes toward Indians following contact. Evidence on white-native female relations more useful than claims about white women's gender ideology. [VBB]

42.469 Lillian Schlissel, ed. *Women's diaries of the westward journey.* New York: Schocken, 1982. ISBN 0-8052-3774-7. ▸ Analysis of 103 women's overland trail accounts plus four entire women's diaries; documents support previous interpretations. Women burdened by work, worry, pregnancy, and childcare; subordinate decision makers in family effort. [VBB]

42.470 Lillian Schlissel, Vicki L. Ruiz, and Janice Monk, eds.

Western women: their land, their lives. Albuquerque: University of New Mexico Press, 1988. ISBN 0-8263-1089-3 (cl), 0-8263-1090-7 (pbk). ▸ Nine essays and critiques well represent current scholarship. Editors demonstrate balance, consistency, and thoughtfulness in collecting samples of most insightful contemporary research. [CAM]

SEE ALSO
40.196 Peggy Pascoe. *Relations of rescue.*
40.449 Sandra L. Myres. *Westering women and the frontier experience, 1800–1915.*
43.401 Ruth Barnes Moynihan. *Rebel for rights.*

RELIGION

42.471 William L. Andrews, ed. *Sisters of the spirit: three black women's autobiographies of the nineteenth century.* Bloomington: Indiana University Press, 1986. ISBN 0-253-35260-6 (cl), 0-253-28704-9 (pbk). ▸ Well-annotated spiritual autobiographies of Jarena Lee, Zilpha Elaw, and Julia Foote. Introduction situates these black female preachers of African Methodism, 1815–50. As revealing of race and gender relations as Christianity. [VBB]

42.472 Ray Allen Billington. *The Protestant crusade, 1800–1860: a study of the origins of American nativism.* 1938 ed. Chicago: Quadrangle, 1964. ▸ Pioneering study of origins of nineteenth-century American anti-Catholicism and ethnic bigotry. Fairly uncritical assimilationist perspective, but rich material on movement's roots, literature, and ultimate failure. [JB/NF]

42.473 John R. Bodo. *The Protestant clergy and public issues, 1812–1848.* 1954 ed. Philadelphia: Porcupine, 1980. ISBN 0-87991-854-3. ▸ Concludes Protestant clergy promoted theocratic ideal of national organization that was politically, socially, and religiously conservative. [TAM]

42.474 Anne M. Boylan. *Sunday school: the formation of an American institution, 1790–1880.* New Haven: Yale University Press, 1988. ISBN 0-300-04019-9. ▸ Examination of development of nineteenth-century America's most extensive Christian instructional system and voluntary educational institution. [JB]

42.475 Theodore D. Bozeman. *Protestants in an age of science: the Baconian ideal and antebellum American religious thought.* Chapel Hill: University of North Carolina Press, 1977. ISBN 0-8078-1299-4. ▸ Study of religious origins of science in nineteenth-century America; stresses complexities in interrelationship, not war between science and religion. [JB]

42.476 Ann Braude. *Radical spirits: spiritualism and women's rights in nineteenth-century America.* Boston: Beacon, 1989. ISBN 0-8070-7500-0. ▸ Exploration of women's spiritual and organizational leadership within nineteenth-century spiritualism and its connections to women's rights movement; illuminates limitations faced by women in other religious traditions. [JB/VBB]

42.477 Charles D. Cashdollar. *The transformation of theology, 1830–1890: positivism and Protestant thought in Britain and America.* Princeton: Princeton University Press, 1989. ISBN 0-691-05555-6. ▸ Discussion of evolution of nineteenth-century American Protestant theology and its connections to European theology and intellectual life. [JB]

42.478 Marie Caskey. *Chariot of fire: religion and the Beecher family.* New Haven: Yale University Press, 1978. ISBN 0-300-02007-4. ▸ Intellectual biography of preeminent evangelical family. Explores differences in theological beliefs, as well as their relationship to major cultural trends, particularly domesticity and secularization of religious beliefs. [TAM]

42.479 Whitney R. Cross. *The burned-over district: the social and intellectual history of enthusiastic religion in western New York, 1800–1850.* 1950 ed. Ithaca, N.Y.: Cornell University Press, 1982. ISBN 0-8014-9232-7. ▸ Classic history of most religiously creative region in antebellum America; discusses relationship of evangelicalism, Mormonism, millennialism, and secular perfectionism to economic and social discontent. [JB]

42.480 Jay P. Dolan. *The immigrant church: New York's Irish and German Catholics, 1815–1865.* 1975 ed. Notre Dame, Ind.: University of Notre Dame Press, 1983. ISBN 0-268-01151-6 (pbk). ▸ Model study of immigrant religion and ethnicity among antebellum New York City Catholics. [JB]

42.481 Katharine L. Dvorak. *An African American exodus: the segregation of the southern churches.* Brooklyn, N.Y.: Carlson, 1991. ISBN 0-926019-25-2. ▸ Discussion of reshaping of African American religious life by freed slaves during and after Civil War. [JB]

42.482 Lawrence Foster. *Religion and sexuality: the Shakers, the Mormons, and the Oneida community.* Urbana: University of Illinois Press, 1984. ISBN 0-252-01119-8 (pbk). ▸ Study of religion's role in reshaping family life and sexual expression in three important antebellum religious and utopian groups. [JB]

42.483 Carl J. Guarneri and David Alvarez, eds. *Religion and society in the American West: historical essays.* Lanham, Md.: University Press of America, 1987. ISBN 0-8191-6431-3 (cl), 0-8191-6432-1 (pbk). ▸ Collection of conference essays exploring interrelationship between religion and western social life and public policy. Treats diverse themes—Mormons, ethnic groups, minor denominations—over extensive geographic territory. [CAM]

42.484 Daniel Walker Howe. *The Unitarian conscience: Harvard moral philosophy, 1805–1861.* 1970 ed. Middletown, Conn.: Wesleyan University Press; distributed by Harper & Row, 1988. ISBN 0-8195-5191-0 (cl), 0-8195-6201-7 (pbk). ▸ Study of ethical and moral thought among New England's most influential religious intellectuals. [JB]

42.485 William R. Hutchison. *The modernist impulse in American Protestantism.* 1976 ed. Durham, N.C.: Duke University Press, 1992. ISBN 0-8223-1237-9 (cl), 0-8223-1248-4 (pbk). ▸ Survey of successes and tribulations of nineteenth-century American liberal Protestantism. Standard presentation of movement; sympathetic but not uncritical. [JB/TDH]

42.486 Paul E. Johnson. *A shopkeeper's millennium: society and revivals in Rochester, New York, 1815–1837.* New York: Hill & Wang, 1978. ISBN 0-8090-8654-9 (cl), 0-8090-0136-5 (pbk). ▸ Model community study of interaction among religion, economic activity, and social reform. [JB]

42.487 Donald G. Mathews. *Religion in the Old South.* Chicago: University of Chicago Press, 1977. ISBN 0-226-51001-8. ▸ Study of religion's vital, sometimes anomalous importance among whites and African Americans in antebellum South. [JB]

42.488 Colleen McDannell. *The Christian home in Victorian America, 1840–1900.* Bloomington: Indiana University Press, 1986. ISBN 0-253-31376-7. ▸ Comparison of evangelical Protestant maternal with Catholic paternal style of worship. Former placed greater emphasis on domestic worship which Catholics later adopted. [DSS/JB]

42.489 Perry Miller, ed. *The transcendentalists: an anthology.* 1950 ed. Cambridge, Mass.: Harvard University Press, 1971. ISBN 0-674-90333-1. ▸ Comprehensive anthology of classic transcendentalist texts with equally classic introduction by America's greatest intellectual historian. [JB]

42.490 T. Scott Miyakawa. *Protestants and pioneers: individualism and conformity on the American frontier.* Chicago: University of Chicago Press, 1964. ▸ Intriguing, rigorous, and still unique comparative history of religious and secular life among Baptists and Presbyterians on Old Northwest frontier. [JB]

42.491 Ronald L. Numbers. *Prophetess of health: Ellen G. White and the origins of Seventh-Day Adventist health reform.* Rev. ed.

Knoxville: University of Tennessee Press, 1992. ISBN 0-87049-712-X (cl), 0-87049-713-8 (pbk). ▸ Biography of one of nineteenth-century America's most controversial religious figures; important discussion of relationship among religion, vernacular medicine, and health. [JB]

42.492 Robert Peel. *Mary Baker Eddy: the years of discovery.* 1966 ed. Boston: Christian Science Publishing Society, 1973. ▸ Professional, sometimes apologetic, biography of nineteenth-century America's most influential woman prophet. First volume of three-volume biography. [JB]

42.493 Albert J. Raboteau. *Slave religion: the "invisible institution" in the antebellum South.* 1978 ed. New York: Oxford University Press, 1980. ISBN 0-19-502438-9 (cl, 1978), 0-19-502705-1 (pbk). ▸ Expansive history of slave Christianity. [JB]

42.494 David S. Reynolds. *Faith in fiction: the emergence of religious literature in America.* Cambridge, Mass.: Harvard University Press, 1981. ISBN 0-674-29172-7. ▸ Discussion of religion's vigorous, sometimes surprising role in nineteenth-century American literature. [JB]

42.495 Sandra Sizer. *Gospel hymns and social religion: the rhetoric of nineteenth-century revivalism.* Philadelphia: Temple University Press, 1978. ISBN 0-87722-142-1. ▸ Study of evolution of nineteenth-century American evangelicalism and importance of hymnology to its growth and change. [JB]

42.496 Timothy L. Smith. *Revivalism and social reform: American Protestantism on the eve of the Civil War.* 1957 ed. Baltimore: Johns Hopkins University Press, 1980. ISBN 0-8018-2477-X (pbk). ▸ Original and influential account of antebellum reform and its origins in urban evangelical Protestantism. [JB]

42.497 Stephen Stein. *The Shaker experience in America: a history of the United Society of Believers.* New Haven: Yale University Press, 1992. ISBN 0-300-05139-5. ▸ Comprehensive revisionist history of nineteenth-century America's most fascinating sect. [JB]

42.498 Ferenc M. Szasz. *The Protestant clergy in the Great Plains and mountain West, 1865–1915.* Albuquerque: University of New Mexico Press, 1988. ISBN 0-8263-1093-1. ▸ Exploration of fate and problems of Protestantism in American West through comparisons of Mormons with mainline denominations—Baptist, Congregational, Episcopal, Methodist, and Presbyterian. [JB/CAM]

42.499 James Turner. *Without god, without creed: the origins of unbelief in America.* Baltimore: Johns Hopkins University Press, 1985. ISBN 0-8018-2494-X. ▸ Origins of nineteenth-century American spiritual doubt. [JB]

SEE ALSO
21.260 Leon A. Jick. *The americanization of the synagogue.*
40.521 William G. McLoughlin. *Revivals, awakenings, and reform.*
40.522 R. Laurence Moore. *Religious outsiders and the making of Americans.*
40.528 Jan Shipps. *Mormonism.*
40.703 Ernest Lee Tuveson. *Redeemer nation.*
41.349 Nathan O. Hatch. *The democratization of American Christianity.*

ANTEBELLUM REFORM
General Studies

42.500 Kenneth Cmiel. *Democratic eloquence: the fight over popular speech in nineteenth-century America.* New York: Morrow, 1990. ISBN 0-688-08352-8. ▸ Study of nineteenth-century debate on styles of public speaking appropriate for democratic society.

Sees movement from language of cultivated gentleman to expert professional. [TAM]

42.501 Merle Eugene Curti. *The American peace crusade, 1815–1860.* 1929 ed. New York: Octagon Books, 1965. ▸ Narrative describing achievements of early peace movements. [TAM]

42.502 John Dunn Davies. *Phrenology: fad and science, a nineteenth-century American crusade.* Hamden, Conn.: Archon, 1971. ISBN 0-208-00952-3. ▸ Discussion of phrenology as way-station on road to secular view of life, consistent with other reform philosophies. Disappears after generation as most important tenets absorbed into mainstream thought. [TAM]

42.503 Paul Goodman. *Towards a Christian republic: antimasonry and the great transition in New England, 1826–1836.* New York: Oxford University Press, 1988. ISBN 0-19-504864-4. ▸ Cultural and political study of antimasonry. Freemasonry attacked because associated with new currents reshaping American society: cosmopolitanism, secularized religion, spreading market, and new middle class. [TAM]

42.504 Jama Lazerow. "Religion and labor reform in antebellum America: the world of William Field Young." *American quarterly* 38 (1986) 265–86. ISSN 0003-0678. ▸ Exploration of New England labor organization in 1840s and 1850s, showing how religion provided inspiration for labor critique, but also limited nature of labor reformers' activism. [TAM]

42.505 Teresa A. Murphy. *Ten-hours labor: religion, reform, and gender in early New England.* Ithaca, N.Y.: Cornell University Press, 1992. ISBN 0-8014-2683-9. ▸ Popular religion and Washingtonian temperance movement important resources in labor activism. Popular religion and social reform contested movements as arenas of struggle rather than social control. Explores problems of female participation in labor movement. [TAM]

42.506 Lewis Perry. *Childhood, marriage, and reform: Henry Clarke Wright, 1797–1870.* Chicago: University of Chicago Press, 1980. ISBN 0-226-61849-8. ▸ Discussion of relationship between family and aggression in life and ideology of radical reformer active in antislavery and nonresistance movements as well as in family reform. [TAM]

42.507 Edwin Rozwenc. *Cooperatives come to America: the history of the protective union store movement, 1845–1867.* 1941 ed. Philadelphia: Porcupine, 1975. ▸ Workingmen and farmers of Northeast, inspired by cooperative experiments in Europe and America, sought partial escape from oppression of industrialism and country merchants in store ownership. [TAM]

42.508 Alice Felt Tyler. *Freedom's ferment: phases of American social history to 1860.* 1944 ed. Freeport, N.Y.: Books for Libraries Press, 1970. ISBN 0-8369-1898-3. ▸ Overview of antebellum reform movements rooted in evangelical religion and frontier democracy. Also important are beliefs in progress and human perfectability. Overview. [TAM]

42.509 Robert H. Walker. *Reform in America: the continuing frontier.* Lexington: University Press of Kentucky, 1985. ISBN 0-8131-1549-3. ▸ Attempt to lay out broad stages through which all reform movements move. [TAM]

42.510 Ronald G. Walters. *American reformers, 1815–1860.* New York: Hill & Wang, 1978. ISBN 0-8090-2557-4 (cl), 0-8090-0130-6 (pbk). ▸ Readable overview of antebellum reform movements. Stresses roots of reform in social and economic transformation of society. [TAM]

SEE ALSO
43.174 Paul S. Boyer. *Urban masses and moral order in America, 1820–1920.*

Abolition

42.511 Robert H. Abzug. *Passionate liberator: Theodore Dwight Weld and the dilemma of reform.* New York: Oxford University Press, 1980. ISBN 0-19-502771-X. ▸ Penetrating biography of radical abolitionist; stresses interrelationships of family life and reform activities. Examines Weld's relationship to authority and move from social activism to personal piety. [TAM]

42.512 Gilbert Hobbs Barnes. *The antislavery impulse, 1830–1844.* 1933 ed. Gloucester, Mass.: P. Smith, 1973. ISBN 0-8446-4020-4. ▸ Stresses importance of western revivalism. Champions Charles G. Finney and Theodore Dwight Weld, castigates William Lloyd Garrison as fanatic, and views Civil War as rooted in moral impulse of antislavery movement, not sectional economic differences. [TAM]

42.513 Larry Ceplair, ed. *The public years of Sarah and Angelina Grimké: selected writings, 1835–1839.* New York: Columbia University Press, 1989. ISBN 0-231-06800-X (cl), 0-231-06801-8 (pbk). ▸ Abridged collection of letters from four-year period, designed to focus solely on abolitionist-feminists' political thinking and activity. Brief introductory material plus annotations. Useful, if incomplete, resource. [VBB]

42.514 David Brion Davis. "The emergence of immediatism in British and American antislavery thought." *Mississippi valley historical review* 49 (1962) 209–30. ISSN 0161-391X. ▸ Argues radical abolitionists viewed slavery as sin rather than social institution. Commitment to immediate emancipation signaled personal transformation of reformer. Emphasizes Atlantic community of reform. [TAM]

42.515 David Brion Davis. *The slave power conspiracy and the paranoid style.* 1969 ed. Baton Rouge: Louisiana State University Press, 1970. ISBN 0-8071-0922-3. ▸ Rapid mobility in antebellum period resulted in self-consciousness about role playing and fear of duplicity which informed idea of slave power conspiracy. Addresses status-anxiety arguments. [TAM]

42.516 Frederick Douglass. *Narrative of the life of Frederick Douglass, an American slave.* Ed. Houston A. Baker, ed. New York: Penguin, 1982. ISBN 0-14-039012-X. ▸ Powerful antislavery tract and classic American autobiography describing life as slave and escape from bondage. [TAM]

42.517 Martin Duberman, ed. *The antislavery vanguard: new essays on the abolitionists.* Princeton: Princeton University Press, 1965. ▸ Important collection of essays providing more sympathetic appraisal of antislavery activists than had earlier existed. [TAM]

42.518 Louis Filler. *The crusade against slavery: friends, foes, and reforms, 1820–1860.* Rev. ed. Algonac, Mich.: Reference Publications, 1986. ISBN 0-917256-29-8 (cl), 0-917256-30-1 (pbk). ▸ Overview finding antislavery movement responded to changing economic and social conditions. Conservative and radical wings of antislavery movement complemented one another. Political antislavery did not eliminate moral reform strategy. [TAM]

42.519 Lawrence J. Friedman. *Gregarious saints: self and community in American abolitionism, 1830–1870.* New York: Cambridge University Press, 1982. ISBN 0-521-24429-3 (cl), 0-521-27015-4 (pbk). ▸ Discussion of social psychology of immediatism, emphasizing social and emotional relationships of abolitionists. [TAM]

42.520 Aileen S. Kraditor. *Means and ends in American abolitionism: Garrison and his critics on strategy and tactics, 1834–1850.* 1969 ed. Chicago: Dee, 1989. ISBN 0-929587-16-2 (pbk). ▸ Sympathetic study of radical abolitionist, William Lloyd Garrison, finding his activities reasonable, not irrational. Concludes split in antislavery movement between reformers and radicals due to mutually exclusive attitudes toward society and tactics rather than personality clashes. [TAM]

42.521 Gerda Lerner. "The political activities of antislavery women." In *The majority finds its past: placing women in history,* pp. 112–28. New York: Oxford University Press, 1979. ISBN 0-19-502597-0 (cl), 0-19-502899-6 (pbk). ▸ Documents female dominance of pre-1850 antislavery petition campaigns which emerged out of work of local female antislavery societies. Trained women to organize and petition for themselves. [VBB]

42.522 William S. McFeely. *Frederick Douglass.* New York: Norton, 1991. ISBN 0-393-02823-2. ▸ Vivid portrayal of important abolitionist, his personal feelings, public activities, and world in which he lived. [TAM]

42.523 John R. McKivigan. *The war against proslavery religion: abolitionism and the northern churches, 1830–1865.* Ithaca, N.Y.: Cornell University Press, 1984. ISBN 0-8014-1589-6. ▸ Concludes northern churches slower to adopt antislavery principles than previously thought. Abolitionists gave important direction to emerging antislavery positions of churches. [TAM]

42.524 Stephen B. Oates. *To purge this land with blood: a biography of John Brown.* 1970 ed. Amherst: University of Massachusetts Press, 1984. ISBN 0-87023-457-9 (cl), 0-87023-458-7 (pbk). ▸ Attempt to understand actions of violent abolitionist by placing him in historical context and exploring impact of his religious upbringing and financial troubles. [TAM]

42.525 William Henry Pease and Jane H. Pease. *They who would be free: blacks' search for freedom, 1830–1861.* 1974 ed. Urbana: University of Illinois Press, 1990. ISBN 0-252-06143-8. ▸ Concludes black abolitionists differed from white abolitionists in perceptions of slavery and freedom and in goals for antislavery movement—placed more practical emphasis on economic opportunity, voting, civil rights, and black identity. [TAM]

42.526 Lewis Perry. *Radical abolitionism: anarchy and the government of God in antislavery thought.* Ithaca, N.Y.: Cornell University Press, 1973. ISBN 0-8014-0754-0. ▸ Discussion of abolitionists' antislavery arguments. Sought to liberate themselves as well as slaves from imposed human authority, looking to divine authority. Emphasizes importance of millennial desire and internal contradictions in logic. [TAM]

42.527 Lewis Perry and Michael Fellman, eds. *Antislavery reconsidered: new perspectives on the abolitionists.* Baton Rouge: Louisiana State University Press, 1979. ISBN 0-8071-0479-5. ▸ Collection of essays placing abolitionism in historical context, including relationships to religion, gender, and economic change. [TAM]

42.528 Benjamin Quarles. *Black abolitionists.* 1969 ed. New York: Da Capo, 1991. ISBN 0-306-80425-5. ▸ African Americans not passive spectators in abolitionist cause, rather they participated actively as leaders and followers within own local and national movements. Pushed radical abolitionist Garrison to criticize colonization. [TAM]

42.529 Leonard L. Richards. *Gentlemen of property and standing: anti-abolition mobs in Jacksonian America.* 1968 ed. New York: Oxford University Press, 1971. ISBN 0-19-501351-4 (pbk). ▸ Concludes mobs not spontaneous, but planned and directed by elite men who felt wealth and standing in community threatened by mass-media techniques, systematic agitation, and centralized control of abolitionists. [TAM]

42.530 C. Peter Ripley, ed. *The black abolitionist papers.* Vol. 1: *Britain.* Vol. 2: *Canada.* Vols. 3–5: *United States of America.* Chapel Hill: University of North Carolina Press, 1985–92. ISBN 0-8078-1625-6 (v. 1), 0-8078-1926-3 (v. 3), 0-8078-1974-3 (v. 4), 0-8078-2007-5 (v. 5). ▸ Selected documents from black participants in antislavery movement, 1830–65. Available on microfilm from Sanford, N.C.: Microfilming Corporation of America. [DF]

42.531 James Brewer Stewart. *Holy warriors: the abolitionists and American slavery.* 1976 ed. New York: Hill & Wang, 1977. ISBN 0-8090-5519-8 (cl), 0-8090-0123-3 (pbk). ▸ Narrative of evolution of antislavery movement from moral persuasion to political and military conflict. Emphasis on how experience and events shaped outlook of activists. [TAM]

42.532 James Brewer Stewart. *Wendell Phillips, liberty's hero.* Baton Rouge: Louisiana State University Press, 1986. ISBN 0-8071-1257-7. ▸ Biography tying important abolitionist to republican tradition. Examines Phillips's broader social and economic criticism as well as family relationships. [TAM]

42.533 John L. Thomas. *The liberator, William Lloyd Garrison: a biography.* Boston: Little, Brown, 1963. ▸ Classic, sympathetic biography examining contradictions of both man and radical antislavery movement he propelled. Important discussion of evangelical and enlightenment roots of reform. [TAM]

42.534 Ronald G. Walters. *The antislavery appeal: American abolitionism after 1830.* 1978 ed. New York: Norton, 1984. ISBN 0-393-95444-7 (pbk). ▸ Abolitionist movement shaped by social context. Addresses abolitionists' concerns about moral impulse of religion, family cohesion, economic change, and sexual control. Emphasizes ideas of movement rather than psychology of participants. [TAM]

42.535 Bertram Wyatt-Brown. *Lewis Tappan and the evangelical war against slavery.* Cleveland, Ohio: Case Western Reserve University Press, 1969. ISBN 0-8295-0146-0. ▸ Seeks to understand and explain actions of leader of conservative wing of antislavery movement, emphasizing religious roots of antislavery activities and relation to business activities. [TAM]

42.536 Bertram Wyatt-Brown. *Yankee saints and southern sinners.* 1985 ed. Baton Rouge: Louisiana State University Press, 1990. ISBN 0-8071-1244-5 (cl, 1985), 0-8071-1607-6 (pbk). ▸ Examination of different cultural values in North and South, especially importance of southern honor. Northern antislavery aimed at creation of new republic based on universal principles, proved destabilizing. [TAM]

42.537 Jean Fagan Yellin. *Women and sisters: the antislavery feminists in American culture.* New Haven: Yale University Press, 1989. ISBN 0-300-04515-8. ▸ Examination of multiple meanings of abolition symbolism for white feminist-abolitionists, black feminist-abolitionists, and antifeminist men using tools of modern literary criticism. Imaginative approach revealing different standpoints. [VBB]

Temperance and Moral Reform

42.538 Jed Dannenbaum. *Drink and disorder: temperance reform in Cincinnati from the Washingtonian Revival to the WCTU.* Urbana: University of Illinois Press, 1984. ISBN 0-252-01055-8. ▸ Temperance more popular than other reforms because it signified order in changing society. Elites saw temperance as way to control others; workers and women saw it as way of controlling own destinies. [TAM]

42.539 Barbara Leslie Epstein. *The politics of domesticity: women, evangelism, and temperance in nineteenth-century America.* Middletown, Conn.: Wesleyan University Press; distributed by Columbia University Press, 1981. ISBN 0-8195-5050-7. ▸ Study of New England culture shaped by gender conflict in evangelical and temperance movements. Traces causes and effects of separate female culture. Identifies female anger at and challenges to male authority in religion and temperance movement. Argues against historians' claims of empowerment through separate culture. [VBB/SGM]

42.540 Lori D. Ginzberg. *Women and the work of benevolence: morality, politics, and class in the nineteenth-century United States.*

New Haven: Yale University Press, 1990. ISBN 0-300-04704-5.
▸ Argues gender ideology obscured reformers' class interests before 1850. Post-1850 women undercut own moral authority espousing male business values in charitable work. Intriguing thesis overlooks contradictory evidence. [VBB]

42.541 Clifford Stephen Griffin. *Their brothers' keepers: moral stewardship in the United States, 1800–1865.* 1960 ed. Westport, Conn.: Greenwood, 1983. ISBN 0-313-24059-0. ▸ Study of leaders of benevolent groups, wealthy or upwardly mobile men who saw religion and reform as means to establish order in rapidly changing society. [TAM]

42.542 Joseph R. Gusfield. *Symbolic crusade: status politics and the American temperance movement.* 2d ed. Urbana: University of Illinois Press, 1986. ISBN 0-252-01321-2 (cl), 0-252-01312-3 (pbk). ▸ Concludes temperance reform reflected fears of social change; type of reform, assimilative or coercive, dependent on status anxiety of dominant group. [TAM]

42.543 Stephen Nissenbaum. *Sex, diet, and debility in Jacksonian America: Sylvester Graham and health reform.* 1980 ed. Belmont, Calif.: Wadsworth, 1988. ISBN 0-534-10915-2. ▸ Discussion of social reformer who formulated ideas about controlling human body, not to adopt values of capitalist marketplace but to deny their power. His self-control plans unintentionally helped form bourgeois character. [TAM]

42.544 John L. Thomas. "Romantic reform in America, 1815–1865." *American quarterly* 17 (1965) 656–81. ISSN 0003-0678. ▸ Belief in individual perfectability and personal moral accountability transformed conservative reform movement aimed at social stability into radical movement committed to social change. [TAM]

42.545 Ian R. Tyrrell. *Sobering up: from temperance to prohibition in antebellum America, 1800–1860.* Westport, Conn.: Greenwood, 1979. ISBN 0-313-20822-0. ▸ Temperance reformers not status-conscious conservatives or anti-institutional outgroup, but upwardly mobile entrepreneurs and professionals using logical, if shortsighted, analysis to solve social problems through institutional means. [TAM]

42.546 Ronald G. Walters. *Primers for prudery: sexual advice to Victorian America.* Englewood Cliffs, N.J.: Prentice-Hall, 1974. ISBN 0-13-700922-4 (cl), 0-13-700914-3 (pbk). ▸ Excerpts from primary documents with commentary tying sexual advice to social and cultural change. Concludes sexual morality, attitudes, and behavior permeated nineteenth-century American culture. [TAM]

SEE ALSO
   41.44 W. J. Rorabaugh. *The alcoholic republic.*

Utopianism

42.547 Arthur Eugene Bestor. *Backwoods utopias: the sectarian origins and the Owenite phase of communitarian socialism in America, 1663–1829.* 2d ed. Philadelphia: University of Pennsylvania Press, 1970. ▸ Attempt to understand communitarian experiments from participants' point of view and relationship of these reforms to American political tradition. [TAM]

42.548 Michael Fellman. *The unbounded frame: freedom and community in nineteenth-century American utopianism.* Westport, Conn.: Greenwood, 1973. ISBN 0-8371-6369-2. ▸ Utopian thought changed in nineteenth century as reform impulse abandoned belief in human perfectability and settled for more limited goals of social improvement. Utopian models seemed less applicable to late nineteenth-century society. [TAM]

42.549 Carl J. Guarneri. *The utopian alternative: Fourierism in nineteenth-century America.* Ithaca, N.Y.: Cornell University Press, 1991. ISBN 0-8014-2467-4. ▸ Broadly conceived study reha-

bilitating Charles Fourier's utopian socialism as flawed but influential third voice in sectional debate over capitalism and slavery. Situates rise and fall of communitarianism in changing contexts of antebellum and Gilded Age culture. [CJG]

42.550 J.F.C. Harrison. *Quest for the new moral world: Robert Owen and the Owenites in Britain and America.* New York: Scribner's, 1969. ▸ Insightful, comparative study of why and how this communitarian movement caught on in two different countries as well as relationship of Owenism to religion and economic change. [TAM]

42.551 Carol A. Kolmerten. *Women in utopia: the ideology of gender in the American Owenite communities.* Bloomington: Indiana University Press, 1990. ISBN 0-253-33192-7. ▸ Examination of gap between promise and reality of gender equality in Owenite communities. Concludes women's confinement to domestic work perpetuated subordination. More satisfying on Owenism and Fanny Wright than class or race. [VBB]

42.552 Raymond Lee Muncy. *Sex and marriage in utopian communities: nineteenth-century America.* 1973 ed. Baltimore: Penguin, 1974. ISBN 0-14-021860-2. ▸ Study of why utopian communities failed. Concludes utopian communities that abolish private property or nuclear family structure survive longer than those that do not because selfish interests challenge communal needs. [TAM]

42.553 John Humphrey Noyes. *History of American socialisms.* 1870 ed. New York: Dover, 1966. ▸ Classic account of utopian communities written (in part) by leader of Oneida community with hope that Christian communitarianism would emerge. [TAM]

42.554 William Henry Pease and Jane H. Pease. *Black utopia: Negro communal experiments in America.* Madison: State Historical Society of Wisconsin, 1963. ▸ Study of planned communities for African Americans in Canada and United States during nineteenth century. Concludes failure result of segregation, white paternalism, and poor planning. [TAM]

Institutional Reform

42.555 Lawrence Arthur Cremin. *American education: the national experience, 1783–1876.* New York: Harper & Row, 1980. ISBN 0-06-010912-2. ▸ Broad survey of educational ideas and institutions, their relationship to nationalism, expansion, immigration, industrialization, and urban development. [TAM]

42.556 Gerald N. Grob. *Mental institutions in America: social policy to 1875.* 1972 ed. New York: Free Press, 1973. ▸ Analysis of institutional changes envisioned by reformers and psychiatrists to help mentally ill. Finds these changes compromised by legislative process and limited funding. Mental hospitals not form of social control. [TAM]

42.557 Michael B. Katz. *The irony of early school reform: educational innovation in mid-nineteenth-century Massachusetts.* 1968 ed. Boston: Beacon, 1972. ISBN 0-8070-3187-9 (cl), 0-8070-3187-9 (pbk). ▸ Argues popular educational reform result of fear of urban poverty and moral decay in industrializing society not outgrowth of humanitarian concern. Reforms foisted on unwilling working class by wealthy and middle-class reformers. [TAM]

42.558 Roger Lane. *Policing the city: Boston, 1822–1885.* Brookfield, Vt.: Gower, 1975. ISBN 0-566-00277-9. ▸ Discussion of growth of professional police force as mandated by growth of cities and replacing personal mechanisms of control. Finds little resentment because police did not change authority structure of state and officers remained close to citizens. [TAM]

42.559 Louis P. Masur. *Rites of execution: capital punishment and the transformation of American culture, 1776–1865.* New York: Oxford University Press, 1989. ISBN 0-19-504899-7. ▸ Analysis of growing importance of private over public punishment as part of larger cultural struggle about public order. [TAM]

42.560   David J. Rothman. *The discovery of the asylum: social order and disorder in the new republic.* 1971 ed. Boston: Little, Brown, 1990. ISBN 0-316-75745-4 (pbk), 0-316-75744-6 (cl). ▸ As old mechanisms of social cohesion disintegrated, new forms of organization needed. Penitentiaries, insane asylums, and poorhouses provided models for new social organization. Challenges Foucault and arguments of work-discipline. [TAM]

42.561   Stanley K. Schultz. *The culture factory: Boston public schools, 1789–1860.* New York: Oxford University Press, 1973. ▸ Exploration of contradictions in reformers' visions with respect to centralization, attendance, and social and ethnic interaction in public schools. Concludes schools modeled on factory system in response to problems posed by immigration, mobility, and urban density. [TAM]

42.562   Allen Steinberg. *The transformation of criminal justice: Philadelphia, 1800–1880.* Chapel Hill: University of North Carolina Press, 1989. ISBN 0-8078-1844-5. ▸ Study of shift from predominantly private prosecution to professional public prosecutors. Despite cost, private prosecution gave poor better access to criminal justice system. [TAM]

WOMEN'S AND GENDER HISTORY

Changing Ideals of Womanhood

42.563   Jeanne Boydston, Mary Kelley, and Anne Margolis, eds. *The limits of sisterhood: the Beecher sisters on women's rights and woman's sphere.* Chapel Hill: University of North Carolina Press, 1988. ISBN 0-8078-1768-6 (cl), 0-8078-4207-9 (pbk). ▸ Exploration of contrasts and similarities in gender ideology of Catherine Beecher, Harriet Beecher Stowe, and Isabella Beecher Hooker demonstrated in editors' commentaries and selections from each woman's writings on female power. [VBB]

42.564   Catherine Clinton. *The other civil war: American women in the nineteenth century.* New York: Hill & Wang, 1984. ISBN 0-8090-7460-5 (cl), 0-8090-0156-X (pbk). ▸ Brief overview of secondary literature attending to southern and western experiences, public and private spaces, typical and atypical women. Concise summary of field but lacks unified conceptual framework. [VBB]

42.565   Frances B. Cogan. *All-American girl: the ideal of real womanhood in mid-nineteenth-century America.* Athens: University of Georgia Press, 1989. ISBN 0-8203-1062-X (cl), 0-8203-1063-8 (pbk). ▸ Late entry in revision of woman-as-victim image. Depends on prescriptive literature to argue middle-class culture of era sustained more than one ideal of womanhood. Claims to originality undermine credibility. [VBB]

42.566   Nancy F. Cott. *The bonds of womanhood: "woman's sphere" in New England, 1780–1835.* New Haven: Yale University Press, 1977. ISBN 0-300-02023-6 (cl), 0-300-02289-1 (pbk). ▸ Landmark study of material and cultural realities creating paradoxical bonds oppressing and uniting women. Chapters on work, domesticity, education, religion, and sisterhood showcase rich evidence of women's confinement to and celebration of separate sphere. [VBB]

42.567   Ann Douglas. *The feminization of American culture.* New York: Knopf, 1977. ISBN 0-394-40532-3. ▸ Early, overstated argument connecting disestablishment of clergy, displacement of female home production, and sentimentalizing of culture. Provocative linkage of gender power with popular culture later improved by class analysis. [VBB]

42.568   Jean E. Friedman. *The enclosed garden: women and community in the evangelical South, 1830–1900.* Chapel Hill: University of North Carolina Press, 1985. ISBN 0-8078-1644-2. ▸ Unique focus on evangelical Christianity and kinship connections to explain retardation of female culture and female reform in South. Patterns persist across race and beyond Civil War. Emphasis provocative and debatable. [VBB/SGM]

42.569   Rayna Green. "The Pochahontas perplex: the image of Indian women in American culture." *The Massachusetts review* 16 (1975) 698–714. ISSN 0025-4878. ▸ Examination of stereotypes burdening American Indian women. Classic virgin-whore paradox complicated by myths of savior princess and drunken squaw. Suggestive links to white and black stereotypes. [VBB]

42.570   Suzanne Lebsock. *The free women of Petersburg: status and culture in a southern town, 1784–1860.* New York: Norton, 1984. ISBN 0-393-01738-9. ▸ Sensitively crafted study of wills, contracts, slave sales, real estate holdings, employment patterns, associational activities, and race and gender relations. Increases in female autonomy more practical than political. [VBB]

42.571   Gerda Lerner. "The lady and the mill girl: changes in the status of women in the age of Jackson." *Midcontinent American studies journal* 10.1 (1969) 5–15. ISSN 0544-0335. ▸ Early call for class analysis in women's history. Concludes industrialization brought new class stratification among women. Female idleness a status symbol, while women's work devalued and working women disempowered. [VBB]

42.572   Mary P. Ryan. *The empire of the mother: American writing about domesticity, 1830–1860.* New York: Institute for Research in History and Haworth, 1982. ISBN 0-86656-133-1. ▸ Examination of domestic popular literature—prescriptive, fictional, reformist—to argue for increase in female authority within family. Situates women in heterosexual, two-generational, domestic networks. [VBB]

42.573   Anne Firor Scott. "What, then, is the American: this new woman?" *Journal of American history* 65 (1978) 679–703. ISSN 0021-8723. ▸ Study of Emma Willard's life and career to complement and complicate image of victimized nineteenth-century woman. Admires Willard's methods for negotiating power and building female bonds and institutions within male-dominated society. [VBB]

42.574   Kathryn Kish Sklar. *Catharine Beecher: a study in American domesticity.* 1973 ed. New York: Norton, 1976. ISBN 0-393-00812-6 (pbk). ▸ Thorough life-and-times account of intellectual, emotional, and political development of formidable reformer-educator. Compelling study of Beecher's creation of self and career within multiple contradictions of antebellum female code. [VBB]

42.575   Carroll Smith-Rosenberg. "The female world of love and ritual." *Signs* 1 (1975) 1–29. ISSN 0097-9740. ▸ Important contribution to literature on cultural construction of sexuality. Limited sample of elite women's letters used to argue for primacy of women's same-sex ties and historical mutability of sexual and social relations. Also reprinted in 40.457. [VBB]

42.576   Barbara Welter. "The cult of true womanhood, 1820–1860." *American quarterly* 18 (1966) 151–75. ISSN 0003-0678. ▸ Classic delineation of female code in prescriptive literature, identifying piety, purity, domesticity, and submissiveness as ideal female traits. Set terms for all subsequent research on gender prescriptions versus female realities. [VBB]

42.577   Barbara Welter. *Dimity convictions: the American woman in the nineteenth century.* Athens: Ohio University Press, 1976. ISBN 0-8214-0352-4 (cl), 0-8214-0358-3 (pbk). ▸ Collection of nine articles describing influence of cult of true womanhood on intellectual, religious, and literary life. Stimulating, early explorations into ramifications of nineteenth-century gender ideology. [VBB]

Feminism and Suffrage

42.578 Bettina Aptheker. "Abolitionism, woman's rights, and the battle over the Fifteenth Amendment." In *Woman's legacy: essays on race, sex, and class in American history*, pp. 9–52. Amherst: University of Massachusetts Press, 1982. ISBN 0-87023-364-5 (cl), 0-87023-365-3 (pbk). ‣ Outline of 1869 split within feminist-abolitionist ranks over Fifteenth Amendment. Sees long-term, racist consequences for suffrage movement; both Elizabeth Cady Stanton and Susan B. Anthony failed to grasp political link between blacks and white women. [VBB]

42.579 Kathleen Barry. *Susan B. Anthony: a biography of a singular feminist*. New York: New York University Press, 1988. ISBN 0-8147-1105-7 (cl). ‣ Life story of leading figure in first United States women's rights movement. Valuable data on childhood, temperance and abolition activism, and relations within female network. Analysis occasionally hindered by adulation. [VBB]

42.580 Barbara J. Berg. *The remembered gate: origins of American feminism, the woman and the city, 1800–1860*. New York: Oxford University Press, 1978. ISBN 0-19-502280-7 (cl), 0-19-502704-3 (pbk). ‣ Early claim for feminist roots in women's antebellum, urban, and benevolent associations; focus on New York City. Illuminating quotes from contemporary sources. Subsequent works by DuBois (42.585) and Ryan (42.635) on urban reform and female religion make argument more complex. [VBB]

42.581 Alice Stone Blackwell. *Growing up in Boston's Gilded Age: the journal of Alice Stone Blackwell, 1872–74*. Marlene Deahl Merrill, ed. New Haven: Yale University Press, 1990. ISBN 0-300-04777-0. ‣ Daughter of Lucy Stone and Henry Blackwell offers unique insight into parents' domestic and social lives, adolescent activities, and concerns of middle-class urban female. Rich data on friendships, religion, and education. [VBB]

42.582 Paula Blanchard. *Margaret Fuller: from transcendentalism to revolution*. 1978 ed. Reading, Mass.: Addison-Wesley, 1987. ISBN 0-201-10458-X (pbk). ‣ Corrective to "Margaret Myth." Presents Fuller as fully human, serious, and intellectual, no more arrogant or neurotic than male counterparts. Situated within gendered and literary context. [VBB]

42.583 Elizabeth Cazden. *Antoinette Brown Blackwell: a biography*. Old Westbury, N.Y.: Feminist Press, 1983. ISBN 0-935312-00-5 (cl), 0-935312-04-8 (pbk). ‣ First full-length biography of Lucy Stone's best friend and political partner. Useful chronology, extensive quotes from Blackwell correspondence. Sheds light on lonely religious struggles, attempts to balance career and family. [VBB]

42.584 Bell Gale Chevigny, comp. *The woman and the myth: Margaret Fuller's life and writings*. Old Westbury, N.Y.: Feminist Press, 1976. ISBN 0-912670-43-6. ‣ Collection of Fuller's writings and contemporaries' writings about Fuller. Texts and thorough introductions trace intellectual evolution and restless ambitions. Useful collection and introductory comments marred by failure to use original texts. [VBB]

42.585 Ellen Carol DuBois. *Feminism and suffrage: the emergence of an independent women's movement in America, 1848–1869*. Ithaca, N.Y.: Cornell University Press, 1978. ISBN 0-8014-1043-6. ‣ Critical analysis of complex interaction between abolition, women's rights, labor movement, and post–Civil War black rights. Key advocate for centrality of suffrage in women's liberation from privatization and dependence. [VBB]

42.586 Celia Morris Eckhardt. *Fanny Wright: rebel in America*. Cambridge, Mass.: Harvard University Press, 1984. ISBN 0-674-29435-1. ‣ Definitive biography of radical abolitionist-utopian-feminist. Blends personal-psychological with public-political. Both critical and celebratory; avoids some, but not all, hard questions. [VBB]

42.587 Elisabeth Griffith. *In her own right: the life of Elizabeth Cady Stanton*. New York: Oxford University Press, 1984. ISBN 0-19-503440-6. ‣ Admiring but critical biography of leading philosopher of first woman's rights movement. Informed by social learning theory. Blends personal and political life through extensive use of Stanton papers, public documents, and secondary literature. [VBB]

42.588 Sarah Grimké. *Letters on the equality of the sexes and other essays*. Elizabeth Ann Bartlett, ed. New Haven: Yale University Press, 1988. ISBN 0-300-04113-6. ‣ Only complete collection of Grimké's feminist writings. Includes previously unpublished essays on education, condition, and legal status of women. Substantive introduction places documents in intellectual, political, and biographical context. [VBB]

42.589 Blanche G. Hersh. *The slavery of sex: feminist-abolitionists in America*. Urbana: University of Illinois Press, 1978. ISBN 0-252-00695-X. ‣ Collective biography of fifty-one feminist-abolitionists. Data suggest importance of education, liberal religion, and supportive parents and husbands in female activism. Evidence more compelling than analysis. [VBB]

42.590 Nancy Hewitt. *Women's activism and social change: Rochester, New York, 1822–1872*. Ithaca, N.Y.: Cornell University Press, 1984. ISBN 0-8014-1616-7. ‣ Useful distinctions between social and economic situation of elite benevolent women, bourgeois evangelicals, and marginal radicals. Traces interactions among female activists in booming center of commerce, religion, and reform. [VBB]

42.591 Carol Lasser and Marlene Deahl Merrill, eds. *Friends and sisters: letters between Lucy Stone and Antoinette Brown Blackwell, 1846–93*. Urbana: University of Illinois Press, 1987. ISBN 0-252-01396-4. ‣ Brief introductions and notes provide background for letters between two important women's rights advocates. Letters reveal deep bond despite distance and differing arenas for reform. Valuable collection. [VBB]

42.592 William Leach. *True love and perfect union: the feminist reform of sex and society*. 2d ed. Middletown, Conn.: Wesleyan University Press, 1989. ISBN 0-8195-6227-0. ‣ Examination of struggle to harmonize individual rights with cooperative communitarianism using traditional humanitarianism and newer social science. Focus on 1850–80 era, using writings of both famous and obscure feminists. [VBB]

42.593 Gerda Lerner. *The Grimké sisters from South Carolina: pioneers for woman's rights and abolition*. 1967 ed. New York: Schocken, 1971. ISBN 0-8052-0321-4 (pbk). ‣ Pathbreaking study of feminist-abolitionists. Maps their journey, political and spiritual terrain, struggles within abolitionism, and women's rights movement. Early feminist interpretation and integration of personal and political. [VBB]

42.594 Anne Firor Scott. "The ever-widening circle: the diffusion of feminist values from the Troy Female Seminary, 1822–1872." *History of education quarterly* 19 (1979) 3–25. ISSN 0018-2680. ‣ Examination of Emma Willard's policy innovations regarding women, education, and state. Integration of traditional female values with feminist impulses explains successes creating female networks, professionalized teaching force, and empowered female descendents. [VBB]

42.595 Elizabeth Cady Stanton. *Eighty years and more: reminiscences of Elizabeth Cady Stanton, 1815–1897*. 1898 ed. New York: Schocken, 1971. ISBN 0-8052-0324-9 (pbk). ‣ Autobiography of leading feminist philosopher-activist of nineteenth century. More light on women's rights movement, female networks, and theories on female condition than on inner process or personal life. Memorable anecdotes. [VBB]

42.596 Elizabeth Cady Stanton and Susan B. Anthony. *The*

Elizabeth Cady Stanton–Susan B. Anthony reader: correspondence, writings, speeches. Rev. ed. Ellen Carol DuBois, ed. Boston: Northeastern University Press, 1992. ISBN 1-555-53149-0 (cl), 1-555-53143-1 (pbk). ▸ Carefully edited collection of documents by both members of legendary political partnership. Introductions to each section and each document trace ideological trajectories and diverging foci. Stanton's philosophical importance well demonstrated. [VBB]

SEE ALSO
40.431 Eleanor Flexner. *Century of struggle.*

Women's Work

42.597 Richard M. Bernard and Maris A. Vinovskis. "The female schoolteacher in antebellum Massachusetts." *Journal of social history* 10 (1977) 332–45. ISSN 0022-4529. ▸ Valuable data on Massachusetts women who feminized teaching force, 1830–60. Twenty percent of white women taught at some time; poor training, low pay, and male domination contributed to high attrition rate. [VBB]

42.598 Mary H. Blewett. *Men, women, and work: class, gender, and protest in the New England shoe industry, 1780–1910.* 1988 ed. Urbana: University of Illinois Press, 1990. ISBN 0-252-01484-7 (cl, 1988), 0-252-06142-X (pbk). ▸ Study of relationship between men and women in shoe industry of Essex County, Massachusetts. Divisions between sexes and between factory labor and outworkers illuminate gender's role in patterns of labor protest. [VBB]

42.599 Mary H. Blewett. *We will rise in our might: workingwomen's voices from nineteenth-century New England.* Ithaca, N.Y.: Cornell University Press, 1991. ISBN 0-8014-2246-9 (cl), 0-8014-9537-7 (pbk). ▸ Primary documents from female workers in shoe industry bound by author's introductions and interlacings. Traces work experience and labor protest into twentieth century. [VBB]

42.600 Jeanne Boydston. *Home and work: housework, wages, and the ideology of labor in the early republic.* New York: Oxford University Press, 1990. ISBN 0-19-506009-1. ▸ History of women's unpaid domestic labor as integral part of industrialization and new labor relations in northeastern United States. Skillfully integrates gender ideology with industrial development to explain devaluation of housework. [VBB]

42.601 Thomas Dublin. *Women at work: the transformation of work and community in Lowell, Massachusetts, 1826–1860.* New York: Columbia University Press, 1979. ISBN 0-231-04166-7 (cl), 0-231-04167-5 (pbk). ▸ Quantitative and qualitative data profile first generation of female industrial workers. Sophisticated analysis weaves demographics, economic development, and gender roles with history of labor movement in early nineteenth century. [VBB]

42.602 Thomas Dublin, ed. *Farm to factory: women's letters, 1830–1860.* 2d ed. New York: Columbia University Press, 1993. ISBN 0-231-08156-1 (cl), 0-231-08157-X (pbk). ▸ Five extensive sets of letters illuminate social networks of female mill workers. Rich introduction and annotation; each set reveals that traditional concerns with health and family ties overshadowed attention to industrialization. [VBB]

42.603 Faye E. Dudden. *Serving women: household service in nineteenth-century America.* Middletown, Conn.: Wesleyan University Press; distributed by Harper & Row, 1983. ISBN 0-8195-5072-8. ▸ Discussion of emergence of distinction between "hired girl" and "domestic servant" with urbanization. Status considerations shaped servants' experience and relations with employers. Descriptive material in lieu of statistical support. [VBB]

42.604 Philip Sheldon Foner, ed. *The factory girls: a collection of writings on life and struggles in the New England factories of the 1840s, by the factory girls themselves, and the story, in their own words, of the first trade unions of women workers in the United States.* Urbana: University of Illinois Press, 1977. ISBN 0-252-00422-1. ▸ Primary documents from New England textile-mill workers' publications. Emphasis on militant view of factory life and efforts at labor organizing and political action. Introductions useful but dated. [VBB]

42.605 Carol Groneman. "'She earns as a child; she pays as a man': women workers in a mid-nineteenth-century New York City community." In *Immigrants in industrial America, 1850–1920: proceedings of a conference sponsored by the Balch Institute and the Eleutherian Mills-Hagley Foundation, November 1–3, 1973.* Richard Ehrlich, ed., pp. 33–46. Charlottesville: University Press of Virginia, 1977. ISBN 0-8139-0678-4. ▸ Early argument for effectiveness of women's paid work in keeping family intact. Data on Irish and Germans in New York's Sixth Ward demonstrate women's economic contribution consistent with traditional family values. [VBB/NF]

42.606 Polly Welts Kaufman. *Women teachers on the frontier.* New Haven: Yale University Press, 1984. ISBN 0-300-03043-6. ▸ Both collective biography of 600 single women sent west to teach by National Board of Popular Education, 1846–56, and reprinting of teachers' letters and one woman's diary. Documents usefully contextualized. [VBB]

42.607 Carol Lasser. "The domestic balance of power: relations between mistress and maid in nineteenth-century New England." *Labor history* 28 (1987) 5–22. ISSN 0023-656X. ▸ Examination of changed nature of employer-servant relations from servants' standpoint. Impersonality of market imperatives allowed servants freedom from personal control of employers; new economic values offered working women some leverage. [VBB]

42.608 Nancy Grey Osterud. *Bonds of community: the lives of farm women in nineteenth-century New York.* Ithaca, N.Y.: Cornell University Press, 1991. ISBN 0-8014-2510-7 (cl), 0-8014-9798-1 (pbk). ▸ Rural women of Nanticoke Valley, New York, used centrality to production and kinship system to mediate subordination to men. Fostered mutuality in work and social life as strategy of empowerment. [VBB]

42.609 Christine Stansell. *City of women: sex and class in New York, 1789–1860.* 1986 ed. Urbana: University of Illinois Press, 1987. ISBN 0-252-01481-2 (pbk). ▸ Innovative study highlighting increasing poverty and dependence of women. Unromantic portrait of female agency and exploitation. Concludes working-class women densely embedded in relations with each other, children, working-class men, reform-minded ladies, and capitalists; survived more by wits than ideology. [VBB/DMS]

42.610 Daniel E. Sutherland. *Americans and their servants: domestic service in the United States from 1800 to 1920.* Baton Rouge: Louisiana State University Press, 1981. ISBN 0-8071-0860-X. ▸ General survey of most common occupation for women in nineteenth century. Service not desirable occupation; few native-white females would become servants, posing problem for employers. [DSS]

42.611 Carole Turbin. "And we are nothing but women: Irish working women in Troy." In *Women of America: a history.* Carol Ruth Berkin and Mary Beth Norton, eds., pp. 203–22. Boston: Houghton-Mifflin, 1979. ISBN 0-395-27067-7. ▸ Study of Collar Laundry Union, Troy, New York, defies stereotype of weak, marginalized female unionists. Explains successful organizing in alliance with men, 1864–69, by particular historical factors, notably Troy women's class consciousness. [VBB]

SEE ALSO
4.415 Judith A. McGaw. *Most wonderful machine.*
40.440 Joan M. Jensen. *Loosening the bonds.*

Health and Medicine

42.612 Susan Cayleff. *Wash and be healed: the water-cure movement and women's health.* Philadelphia: Temple University Press, 1987. ISBN 0-87722-462-5 (cl). ▸ Study of antebellum water-cure movement as both reform of female health care and avenue of female empowerment. Relates appeal of autonomy and communal healing to popularity with middle-class women. [VBB]

42.613 Jane Donegan. *Hydropathic highway to health: women and water-cure in antebellum America.* New York: Greenwood, 1986. ISBN 0-313-23816-2. ▸ Focus on New York state and hydropathic approach to pregnancy and childbirth reveals appeal of water cure to women. Self-reliance encouraged in home nurses, female patients, and female physicians. [VBB]

42.614 Jane Donegan. *Women and men midwives: medicine, morality, and misogyny in early America.* Westport, Conn.: Greenwood, 1978. ISBN 0-8371-9868-2. ▸ Discussion of transition from female-controlled midwifery to male-controlled obstetrics. Integrates developments in medical technology, changes in medical institutions with gender ideology, and rise of women's rights. [VBB]

42.615 John S. Haller and Robin M. Haller. *The physician and sexuality in Victorian America.* Urbana: University of Illinois Press, 1974. ISBN 0-252-00207-5. ▸ Study of medical advice about sexuality (1830–1900) and science behind it. Argues sexual restraint conserved men for public achievement and reflected middle-class search for order, but also opened way to feminism. [CJG]

42.616 Sylvia Hoffert. *Private matters: American attitudes toward childbearing and infant nurture in the urban north, 1800–1860.* Urbana: University of Illinois Press, 1988. ISBN 0-252-01547-9. ▸ Combines maternal letters, diaries, and memoirs with prescriptive literature to describe tension between public and private interpretations of female social duty. Contributes to literature on female agency within patriarchal constraints. [VBB]

42.617 Regina Morantz. "The lady and her physician." In *Clio's consciousness raised: new perspectives on the history of women.* 1974 ed. Mary S. Hartman and Lois W. Banner, eds., pp. 38–53. New York: Octagon Books, 1976. ISBN 0-374-93712-5. ▸ Study of Victorian women's medical care in historical context. Physicians' scientific ignorance more demonstrable than psychological motives; female physicians shared men's assumptions. Strong argument mounted for historical rigor in feminist research. [VBB]

42.618 Regina Morantz. "Making women modern: middle-class women and health reform in nineteenth-century America." *Journal of social history* 10 (1976–77) 490–507. ISSN 0022-4529. ▸ Health reformers' emphasis on educated motherhood and scientific domesticity helped modernize middle-class, urban women. Assertion of rational links between nature's laws and females' moral self-control, empowered without liberating. [VBB]

42.619 Charles E. Rosenberg. "Sexuality, class, and role in nineteenth-century America." *American quarterly* 25 (1973) 131–53. ISSN 0003-0678. ▸ Medical writers, 1830–1900, increasingly associated male continence with economic success, female continence with moral superiority. Contradictory, antirepression masculine tradition offset by powerful female virtue. Anticipated later theories on heterosexual dynamic. [VBB]

42.620 Carroll Smith-Rosenberg. "Puberty to menopause: the cycle of femininity in nineteenth-century America." In *Clio's consciousness raised.* 1974 ed. Mary S. Hartman and Lois W. Banner, eds., pp. 23–37. New York: Octagon Books, 1976. ISBN 0-374-93712-5. ▸ Examination of physicians' attitudes toward female physiology revealing ambivalence about sexuality, desire to rationalize women's subordination, and contradictory images of female as spiritual and animal. Valuable data and descriptions;

theory more psychological than historical. Also reprinted in 40.457. [VBB]

42.621 Carroll Smith-Rosenberg and Charles E. Rosenberg. "The female animal: medical and biological views of woman and her role in nineteenth-century America." *Journal of American history* 60 (1973) 332–56. ISSN 0021-8723. ▸ Analysis of medical literature documenting biological-determinist view of gender. Classic argument that determinist theories not traditional, but reactionary attempt to stem social and gender changes. [VBB]

SEE ALSO
  4.811 Judith Walzer Leavitt. *Brought to bed.*
  40.476 James C. Mohr. *Abortion in America.*

Gender and Sexuality

42.622 David F. Allmendinger, Jr. "Mount Holyoke students encounter the need for life-planning, 1837–1850." *History of education quarterly* 19 (1979) 27–46. ISSN 0018-2680. ▸ Profile of women attending Mount Holyoke. Concludes changed social and economic conditions required preparing daughters for premarital employment. School and teaching altered women's later lives. Strong data allows for interesting argument. [VBB]

42.623 Norma Basch. *In the eyes of the law: women, marriage, and property in nineteenth-century New York.* Ithaca, N.Y.: Cornell University Press, 1982. ISBN 0-8014-1466-0. ▸ Uses New York Married Women's Property Act of 1848 and Married Women's Earnings Act of 1860 to examine women's legal status. Sophisticated handling of legal details and political ironies. [VBB]

42.624 Lee Virginia Chambers-Schiller. *Liberty, a better husband: single women in America, the generations of 1780–1840.* New Haven: Yale University Press, 1984. ISBN 0-300-03164-5 (cl), 0-300-03922-0 (pbk). ▸ Based on writings of 113 elite, northeastern spinsters. Argues for conscious choice against marriage made in particular cultural context. Traces blessings and burdens attendant on choice for this unique group. [VBB]

42.625 Nancy F. Cott. "Passionlessness: an interpretation of Victorian sexual ideology, 1790–1850." *Signs* 4 (1978) 219–36. ISSN 0097-9740. ▸ Exploration of sexual ideology and its contradictory consequences: empowering women with moral superiority aided self-esteem and defensive capacities; obfuscating alternative sources of power and encouraging prudery hindered progress. [VBB]

42.626 Michael Grossberg. *Governing the hearth: law and the family in nineteenth-century America.* Chapel Hill: University of North Carolina Press, 1985. ISBN 0-8078-1646-9 (cl), 0-8078-1647-7 (pbk). ▸ Examination of regulations for marriage, reproduction, illegitimacy, and child custody reveal shifting power over family government. Republican approach to family law resulted in judicial patriarchy. Close argument occasionally obscures broader context. [VBB]

42.627 James Oliver Horton. "Freedom's yoke: gender conventions among antebellum free blacks." *Feminist studies* 12 (1986) 51–76. ISSN 0046-3663. ▸ Northern black newspapers reveal patriarchal gender prescriptions for free blacks: males as providers, females as helpmates. Assertions of male dominance unaltered or intensified by women's economic contribution. [VBB]

42.628 Mary Kelley. *Private woman, public stage: literary domesticity in nineteenth-century America.* New York: Oxford University Press, 1984. ISBN 0-19-503351-5. ▸ Study of twelve authors' struggles to reconcile influence and success with female identity. Focus on psychic paradox implicit in public literary lives rooted in private domestic world. Based on diaries and letters. [VBB]

42.629 Louis J. Kern. *An ordered love: sex roles and sexuality in Victorian utopias; the Shakers, the Mormons, and the Oneida community.* Chapel Hill: University of North Carolina Press, 1981.

ISBN 0-8078-1443-1 (cl), 0-8078-4074-2 (pbk). ▸ Iconoclastic use of Freudian theory to argue against sexual equality or liberation in utopian communities. Views communities as offering cultural alternative to mainstream society. Provocative assumptions. [VBB/TAM]

42.630 Carol Lasser. "'Let us be sisters forever': the sororal model of nineteenth-century female friendship." *Signs* 14 (1988) 158–81. ISSN 0097-9740. ▸ Expands models for interpreting nineteenth-century female friendship without denying erotic possibilities. Suggests elective sisterhood provided fictive kin in mobile, urban society, valuing traditional domestic ties while allowing autonomy and choice. [VBB]

42.631 Karen Lystra. *Searching the heart: women, men, and romantic love in nineteenth-century America.* New York: Oxford University Press, 1989. ISBN 0-19-505817-8. ▸ Provocative, well-written examination of letters between middle-class courting couples and spouses. Infused with romantic sentiment and revealing sexual passion, undermined inequalities of separate spheres and patriarchal legacy. In American studies tradition. [DSS/SGM]

42.632 Jane H. Pease and William Henry Pease. *Ladies, women, and wenches: choice and constraint in antebellum Charleston and Boston.* Chapel Hill: University of North Carolina Press, 1990. ISBN 0-8078-1924-7 (cl), 0-8078-4289-3 (pbk). ▸ Comparison of black and white women's circumstances in two urban settings. Argues slavery shaped constraints under which both races lived. [VBB]

42.633 Ellen K. Rothman. "Sex and self-control: middle-class courtship in America, 1770–1870." *Journal of social history* 15 (1982) 409–25. ISSN 0022-4529. ▸ Challenges theories of increasing emotional and sexual alienation between sexes and tightening code of social separation. Argues, instead, for increasingly accepted assumption of natural female inclination and obligation to regulate sexual behavior. See also book by same author (40.493). [VBB]

42.634 Mary P. Ryan. *Cradle of the middle class: the family in Oneida County, New York, 1790–1865.* New York: Cambridge University Press, 1981. ISBN 0-521-23200-7. ▸ Changes in family relations both effect and cause of economic transformations. Women's public associational activity redefined parental power. Mothers gained private leverage, not public authority. Anticipates Lebsock's southern study (42.570). [VBB]

42.635 Mary P. Ryan. *Women in public: between banners and ballots, 1825–1880.* Baltimore: Johns Hopkins University Press, 1990. ISBN 0-8018-3908-4. ▸ Ambitious set of essays theorizing about representations of gender and women's participation in public life in New York, New Orleans, and San Francisco. Sees women shaping American public and political life. [VBB]

42.636 Kathryn Kish Sklar. "The founding of Mount Holyoke College." In *Women of America: a history.* Carol Ruth Berkin and Mary Beth Norton, eds., pp. 177–201. Boston: Houghton-Mifflin, 1979. ISBN 0-395-27067-7. ▸ Mt. Holyoke represented advancement in education's funding, curriculum, and accessibility for middle-class women. Grassroots support in female Christian community suggests religion's importance in sponsoring female aspirations to educate youth. [VBB]

42.637 Daniel Scott Smith. "Family limitation, sexual control, and domestic feminism in Victorian America." *Feminist studies* 1 (1973) 40–57. ISSN 0046-3663. ▸ Speculative reasoning from declining fertility rates to domestic feminism. Sees exaggerated shift in sexual power from husbands to wives; insightful anticipation of later demonstrations of female autonomy within marriages, households, and communities. [VBB]

42.638 Carroll Smith-Rosenberg. "Beauty, the beast, and the militant woman: a case study in sex roles and social stress in Jacksonian America." *American quarterly* 23 (1971) 562–84. ISSN 0003-0678. ▸ Early interpretation of female moral reform as nascent feminism. Moral reformers used exposure, ostracism, lobbying, and education in claiming righteous female duty to regulate male behavior. Also reprinted in 40.457. [VBB]

42.639 Carroll Smith-Rosenberg. "The hysterical woman: sex roles and role conflict in nineteenth-century America." *Social research* 39 (1972) 652–78. ISSN 0037-783X. ▸ Postulates large numbers of women chose hysteria to express unhappiness over contradictions in and limitations of female role. Overestimates pervasiveness but provocative on psychosocial connections. Reflects early focus on female victimization. Also reprinted in 40.457. [VBB]

42.640 Dorothy Sterling, ed. *We are your sisters: black women in the nineteenth century.* New York: Norton, 1984. ISBN 0-393-01728-1 (cl), 0-393-30252-0 (pbk). ▸ Collection of over 600 documents portraying black women's interior world. Letters, memoirs, interviews, and writings of activist women, and four complete diaries. Editor emphasizes personal and political resistance. [VBB]

SEE ALSO
40.473 John D'Emilio and Estelle B. Freedman. *Intimate matters.*
40.481 Ellen K. Rothman. *Hands and hearts.*

FAMILY HISTORY AND HISTORICAL DEMOGRAPHY

Family Patterns and Structures

42.641 Clifford Edward Clark, Jr. *The American family home, 1800–1960.* Chapel Hill: University of North Carolina Press, 1986. ISBN 0-8078-1675-2 (cl), 0-8078-4151-X (pbk). ▸ Relates American domestic architecture to middle-class ideal of single-family home ownership. Changing interior designs mirrored changes in family. Amply illustrated with photographs and architectural plans. [DSS]

42.642 Robert L. Griswold. *Family and divorce in California, 1850–1890: Victorian illusions and everyday realities.* Albany: State University of New York Press, 1982. ISBN 0-87395-633-8 (cl), 0-87395-634-6 (pbk). ▸ Analysis of evidence in 401 divorce cases in Santa Clara and San Mateo counties. Testimony reveals pervasive influence of Victorian notions of romantic love and companionate marriage on expectations and behavior. [DSS]

42.643 Herbert G. Gutman. *The black family in slavery and freedom, 1750–1925.* 1976 ed. New York: Vintage, 1977. ISBN 0-394-47116-4 (cl, 1976), 0-394-72451-8 (pbk). ▸ Argues against thesis that slavery destroyed two-parent families, emphasizing instead deleterious impact of Northern urban experience. Incidence of single- and two-parent families same for both blacks and whites. [DSS]

42.644 Viviana A. Rotman Zelizer. *Morals and markets: the development of life insurance in the United States.* 1979 ed. New Brunswick, N.J.: Transaction, 1983. ISBN 0-87855-929-9 (pbk). ▸ Sociological study of one economic consequence of rejection of Calvinist fatalism toward death. Now able to bet against death, Americans after the 1840s turned to life insurance as family strategy. [DSS]

Fertility

42.645 Lee L. Bean, Geraldine P. Mineau, and Douglas L. Anderton. *Fertility change on the American frontier: adaptation and innovation.* Berkeley: University of California Press, 1990. ISBN 0-520-06633-2. ▸ Sophisticated analysis of large sample of genealogies of Mormon women born in nineteenth century; focus on transition from frontier era to onset of fertility limitation within marriage. [DSS/KWK]

42.646 Paul A. David and Warren C. Sanderson. "Rudimentary contraceptive methods and the American transition to marital fertility control, 1855–1915." In *Long-term factors in American economic growth*. Stanley L. Engerman and Robert E. Gallman, eds., pp. 307–90. Chicago: University of Chicago Press, 1986. (Conference on Income and Wealth. National Bureau of Economic Research Studies in Income and Wealth, 51.) ISBN 0-226-20928-8. ▸ Concludes northeastern urban white women in vanguard of fertility transition. Important argument claiming other historians have exaggerated incidence of marital intercourse and thus abortion and coitus interruptus. [DSS]

42.647 Richard A. Easterlin. "Population change and farm settlement in the northern United States." *Journal of economic history* 36 (1976) 45–75. ISSN 0022-0507. ▸ Correlates availability of land positively to fertility; broad data base. Economist author invokes bequest motive, desire of parents to provide adequate start in life for children, as explanation for family limitation. [DSS]

42.648 Douglas C. Ewbank. "The marital fertility of American whites before 1920." *Historical methods* 24 (1991) 141–70. ISSN 0161-5440. ▸ Comprehensive review and reanalysis of geographic and temporal variations in several indices of marital fertility. Argues decline in fertility began in New England before Civil War, spread in southwesterly direction. [DSS]

42.649 Michael Haines. *Fertility and occupation: population patterns in industrialization*. New York: Academic Press, 1979. ISBN 0-12-315550-9. ▸ Comparative study of United States, England and Wales, and Prussia, relating fertility to occupational structure, especially age pattern of earnings. Fertility high among miners everywhere. [DSS]

42.650 Steven Ruggles. *Prolonged connections: the rise of the extended family in nineteenth-century England and America*. Madison: University of Wisconsin Press, 1987. ISBN 0-299-11030-3 (cl), 0-299-11034-6 (pbk). ▸ Uses computer microsimulation methods to assess effects of demographic changes in kinship and extended household formation. Surveys and comments on social science literature on family demography and modernization. Readable account of technical topic. [DSS]

42.651 Daniel Scott Smith. "The long cycle in American illegitimacy and prenuptial pregnancy." In *Bastardy and its comparative history: studies in the history of illegitimacy and marital nonconformism in Britain, France, Germany, Sweden, North America, Jamaica, and Japan*. Peter Laslett, Karla Costerveen and Richard M. Smith, eds., pp. 362–78. Cambridge, Mass.: Harvard University Press, 1980. ISBN 0-674-06338-4. ▸ Out-of-wedlock conceptions in United States were low in seventeenth and nineteenth centuries, high in eighteenth century and in present. Higher black-white rates of out-of-wedlock conceptions and decline in those rates in early nineteenth century distinctive American features. [DSS]

42.652 Richard H. Steckel. *The economics of U.S. slave and southern white fertility*. New York: Garland, 1985. ISBN 0-8240-6662-6. ▸ Well-designed study by economist using plantation, probate, and census samples to measure sources of high fertility rates of southern whites and slaves. Finds very high infant mortality rate for slaves. [DSS]

42.653 Maris A. Vinovskis. *Fertility in Massachusetts from the Revolution to the Civil War*. New York: Academic Press, 1981. ISBN 0-12-722040-2. ▸ Case study using technique of multiple regression on town data. Disputes land availability interpretation (Easterlin 42.647). Instead emphasizes role of social and cultural modernization in accounting for reduction in fertility. [DSS]

42.654 Yasukichi Yasuba. *Birth rates of the white population in*

the United States, 1800–1860: an economic study. Baltimore: Johns Hopkins University Press, 1962. ▸ Classic analysis of variation among American states in census ratios of children to women. Argues decreased land availability most important for decline in fertility, particularly before 1840. [DSS]

SEE ALSO
40.318 Tamara K. Harevan and Maris A. Vinovskis, eds. *Family and population in nineteenth-century America*.

Historical Demography

42.655 W. Andrew Achenbaum. *Old age in the new land: the American experience since 1790*. Baltimore: Johns Hopkins University Press, 1978. ISBN 0-8018-2107-X (cl), 0-8018-2355-2 (pbk). ▸ Covers demographic, familial, and occupational characteristics of aged. Stresses role of medical writers in creating negative attitude toward old age after Civil War. [DSS]

42.656 Margo J. Anderson. *The American census: a social history*. New Haven: Yale University Press, 1988. ISBN 0-300-04014-8. ▸ Institutional survey emphasizing controversies and political context of taking and publishing results of census. Critical perspective but balanced treatment. [DSS]

42.657 A. Gordon Darroch. "Migrants in the nineteenth century: fugitives or families in motion?" *Journal of family history* 6 (1981) 257–77. ISSN 0363-1990. ▸ Review of earlier studies to argue that mobility in nineteenth-century communities not particularly disruptive. Family and kinship structured migration process. [DSS]

42.658 Robert William Fogel. "Nutrition and the decline in mortality since 1700: some preliminary findings." In *Long-term factors in American economic growth*. Stanley L. Engerman and Robert E. Gallman, eds., pp. 439–555. Chicago: University of Chicago Press, 1986. (Conference on Income and Wealth. National Bureau of Economic Research Studies in Income and Wealth, 51.) ISBN 0-226-20928-8. ▸ Exploration, based on published family genealogies and Mormon family records, suggesting surprisingly large decrease in male life expectancy in first half of nineteenth century that correlates with shorter average height, suggesting poor nutrition. [DSS]

42.659 Peter D. McClelland and Richard J. Zeckhauser. *Demographic dimensions of the new republic: American interregional migration, vital statistics, and manumissions, 1800–1860*. New York: Cambridge University Press, 1982. ISBN 0-521-24309-2. ▸ Examination of census figures and demographic methods to produce indirect estimates of components of population growth for whites and blacks. [DSS]

42.660 Walter T. K. Nugent. *Structures of American social history*. Bloomington: Indiana University Press, 1981. ISBN 0-253-10356-8. ▸ Three-period Braudellian periodization of American population history; 1870–1920 conjuncture provides transition between frontier-rural and metropolitan modes. Relates demography to social history. [DSS]

42.661 Donald H. Parkerson. "How mobile were nineteenth-century Americans?" *Historical methods* 15 (1982) 99–109. ISSN 0161-5440. ▸ Revisionist study of duration-of-residence question in New York state census of 1855. Persistence studies based on linkage of census records shown to exaggerate considerably extent of mobility. [DSS]

42.662 Stephan Thernstrom and Peter R. Knights. "Men in motion: some data and speculations about urban population mobility in nineteenth-century America." *Journal of interdisciplinary history* 1 (1970) 17–47. ISSN 0022-1953. ▸ Speculates on implications of high rates of population turnover apparent in record-linkage studies. Explores consequences of population flux. [DSS]

42.663 Robert V. Wells. *Revolutions in Americans' lives: a demographic perspective on the history of Americans, their families, and their society.* Westport, Conn.: Greenwood, 1982. ISBN 0-313-23019-6. ▸ Overview, colonial period to present, of shift from high to low vital rates. Interpretation organized around concepts of modernization and demographic transition. [DSS]

42.664 Carroll Wright and William C. Hunt. *History and growth of the United States census, prepared for the Senate Committee on the Census.* 1900 ed. New York: Johnson Reprint, 1966. ▸ Basic reference work; covers first eleven censuses. Includes much source material as well as overall description of each enumeration. [DSS]

INTELLECTUAL AND CULTURAL HISTORY

General Studies

42.665 Daniel Joseph Boorstin. *America and the image of Europe: reflections on American thought.* 1960 ed. Gloucester, Mass.: Smith, 1976. ISBN 0-8446-1703-2. ▸ Collected essays of influential consensus historian find naive stereotypes of Europe in debate over national identity, but otherwise celebrate populist, pragmatic cast of American culture. [CJG]

42.666 Robert V. Bruce. *The launching of modern American science, 1846–1876.* 1987 ed. Ithaca, N.Y.: Cornell University Press, 1988. ISBN 0-8014-9496-6 (pbk). ▸ Prize-winning synthesis of science from arrival of Louis Agassiz to founding of Johns Hopkins University. Stresses role of institution builders: Joseph Henry of Smithsonian Institution, Benjamin Peirce of Harvard, and Alexander D. Bache of Coast Survey. [CJG]

42.667 Daniel Hovey Calhoun. *The intelligence of a people.* Princeton: Princeton University Press, 1973. ISBN 0-691-04619-0. ▸ Innovative, speculative analysis of changing American mental aptitudes from Revolution to Civil War. Chapters on child rearing, preaching, shipbuilding, and bridge building highlight increasing method, standardization, and specialization. [CJG]

42.668 William Charvat. *The origins of American critical thought, 1810–1835.* 1936 ed. New York: Russell & Russell, 1968. ▸ Survey of literary criticism in American magazines stressing influence of Scottish philosophy, egalitarian bias, and moralistic standards; slights South and West. Pioneering study. [CJG]

42.669 Thomas R. Cole. *The journey of life: a cultural history of aging in America.* Cambridge: Cambridge University Press, 1992. ISBN 0-521-41020-7. ▸ Broadly conceived study of ideas of life course. Views of aging in northern middle-class culture evolved from Puritan religious to Victorian social to modern scientific framework. Alternative to Fischer 40.313 and Achenbaum 42.655. [CJG]

42.670 Paul Keith Conkin. *Prophets of prosperity: America's first political economists.* Bloomington: Indiana University Press, 1980. ISBN 0-253-30843-7. ▸ Summary of ideas of economists writing between 1815 and Civil War, including John Taylor, Thomas Skidmore, Calvin Colton, and Henry C. Carey. Thorough, if somewhat labored, supplement to Dorfman 40.552. [CJG]

42.671 David Brion Davis. *The problem of slavery in Western culture.* 1966 ed. New York: Oxford University Press, 1988. ISBN 0-19-505639-6 (pbk). ▸ Learned, sweeping history-of-ideas contribution to debates over slavery and rise of humanitarianism. Ancient in origin, broadly unchanged in features, legitimated by religion and philosophy, slavery nevertheless became morally suspect in 1700s. American colonization, Enlightenment, and evangelical Protestantism played complex roles. [CJG]

42.672 Ruth Elson. *Guardians of tradition: American schoolbooks of the nineteenth century.* Lincoln: University of Nebraska Press, 1964. ISBN 0-8357-3798-5. ▸ Useful compendium of (mostly reassuring) ideas and attitudes relating to God, humanity, nature, and society found in widely used textbooks, 1776–1900. Available on microfilm from Ann Arbor: University Microfilms International. [CJG]

42.673 George M. Fredrickson. *The black image in the white mind: the debate on Afro-American character and destiny, 1817–1914.* 1971 ed. Middletown, Conn.: Wesleyan University Press; distributed by Harper & Row, 1987. ISBN 0-8195-6188-6 (pbk). ▸ Discussion of racial theory and ideology applied to "problem" of black presence in United States and underlying such causes as colonization, proslavery, free soil, Reconstruction, social Darwinism, and progressivism. Stresses pervasiveness of racist assumptions. [CJG]

42.674 John Higham. *From boundlessness to consolidation: the transformation of American culture, 1848–1860.* Ann Arbor: William L. Clements Library, 1969. ▸ Elegant, seminal essay locating origins of shift from antebellum perfectionism to Gilded Age pragmatism in midcentury developments, including moderate antislavery movement, response to European revolutions of 1848, and rise of technical expertise in corporations. [CJG]

42.675 Robert Lloyd Kelley. *The transatlantic persuasion: the liberal-democratic mind in the age of Gladstone.* 1969 ed. New Brunswick, N.J.: Transaction, 1990. ISBN 0-88738-635-0. ▸ Innovative study in transatlantic political and intellectual history. Finds common threads in thought of Anglo-American liberals and democrats in second half of nineteenth century. Chapters on William Gladstone in Britain, George Brown and Alexander Mackenzie in Canada, and Samuel Tilden and Grover Cleveland in United States. [CJG]

42.676 Perry Miller. *The life of the mind in America: from the Revolution to the Civil War.* 1965 ed. New York: Harcourt, Brace, Jovanovich, 1970. ISBN 0-15-651990-9. ▸ Book 1 charts connections between religious and cultural rhetoric in Protestant revivalism; book 2 narrates heroic efforts of jurists to legitimize law in democratic, antilegal culture; book 3 a fragment on science. Books 1–2 and part of book 3 of planned nine-book work; never completed, but important work by premier United States intellectual historian. [CJG]

42.677 Anne Norton. *Alternative Americas: a reading of antebellum political culture.* Chicago: University of Chicago Press, 1986. ISBN 0-226-59510-2. ▸ Civil War grew from conflict of cultural paradigms: pilgrim North reflecting masculinity, repression, and industrialism overcame cavalier South of femininity, leisure, and agrarianism. Provocative, single-minded, semiotic rereading of key texts. [CJG]

42.678 Russel Blaine Nye. *Society and culture in America, 1830–1860.* New York: Harper & Row, 1974. ISBN 0-06-131826-4. ▸ Wide-ranging survey of antebellum literature, art, architecture, education, religion, and science emphasizing pervasive nationalism, romanticism, and belief in progress. Reliable introductory text with good but increasingly dated notes and bibliography. [CJG]

42.679 Charles E. Rosenberg. *The cholera years: the United States in 1832, 1849, and 1866; with a new afterword.* 1962 ed. Chicago: University of Chicago Press, 1987. ISBN 0-226-72679-7 (cl), 0-226-72677-0 (pbk). ▸ Traces shift in response to disease from predominantly moral to social. Treats reactions of both medical and general public opinion. Good example of social history of disease. [DSS]

42.680 Cushing Strout. *The American image of the Old World.* New York: Harper & Row, 1963. ▸ Useful survey of literary and political thought. Rise, development, and decline of tradition portraying alien Old World (whether condemned or admired) as antithesis of New World. Precursor to current debate over American exceptionalism. [CJG]

42.681 Rush Welter. *The mind of America, 1820–1860*. New York: Columbia University Press, 1975. ISBN 0-231-02963-2. ▸ Careful, authoritative analysis of political, social, and economic themes in magazine and pamphlet literature. Finds emerging consensus around individualism, missionary nationalism, minimal government, and free institutions; leaves position of South ambiguous. [CJG]

42.682 Major L. Wilson. *Space, time, and freedom: the quest for nationality and the irrepressible conflict, 1815–1861*. Westport, Conn.: Greenwood, 1974. ISBN 0-8371-7373-6. ▸ Thematic reading of political ideologies differentiating parties as proponents of future-oriented corporate freedom (Whigs), expansionistic federative freedom (Democrats), and synthetic national freedom (Republicans). Rhetorical perspective complements Welter 42.681. [CJG]

42.683 Bernard Wishy. *The child and the republic: the dawn of modern American child nurture*. 1967 ed. Philadelphia: University of Pennsylvania Press, 1972. ISBN 0-8122-7543-8 (cl), 0-8122-1026-3 (pbk). ▸ Study of prescriptive literature about child rearing and its importance to national development. [TAM]

Intellectual Movements and Theory

42.684 Susan P. Conrad. *Perish the thought: intellectual women in romantic America, 1830–1860*. New York: Oxford University Press, 1976. ISBN 0-19-501995-4. ▸ Romantic intuitionism and exaltation of self-opened doors to women's intellectual endeavors, but only activities defined as separate from everyday roles. Treats lives and ideas of Margaret Fuller, Lydia Maria Child, Elizabeth Cady Stanton, others. [CJG]

42.685 Donald Fleming. *John William Draper and the religion of science*. 1950 ed. New York: Octagon Books, 1972. ISBN 0-374-92750-2. ▸ Pioneering study of New York University chemist and physicist who popularized science by constructing cosmology reconciling Protestant theology and evolution, individual agency, and special role for scientific elite. [CJG]

42.686 Jonathan Glickstein. *Concepts of free labor in antebellum America*. New Haven: Yale University Press, 1991. ISBN 0-300-01789-4. ▸ Evangelical culture, liberal ideology, and sectional allegiances shaped middle-class opinion on manual labor, but most writers found mental work intrinsically superior. Difficult but rewarding microanalysis. [CJG]

42.687 Edward H. Madden. *Chauncey Wright and the foundations of pragmatism*. Seattle: University of Washington Press, 1963. ▸ Intellectual biography of neglected figure. Harvard-educated amateur became ablest American defender of evolution as consistent with morality and intelligence; influenced William James and C. S. Pierce. [CJG]

42.688 Waldo Martin, Jr. *The mind of Frederick Douglass*. Chapel Hill: University of North Carolina Press, 1984. ISBN 0-8078-1616-7. ▸ Topical analysis of thought of preeminent black reformer, journalist, and statesman in light of tension between African American and European American cultures. Best on religious and self-made-man themes. Complements McFeeley 42.522. [CJG]

42.689 David S. Reynolds. *Beneath the American renaissance: the subversive imagination in the age of Emerson and Melville*. 1988 ed. Cambridge, Mass.: Harvard University Press, 1989. ISBN 0-674-06545-4. ▸ Important contextual study suggesting highbrow-lowbrow cultural ties. Major writers heavily influenced by forms and content of popular culture: religious tracts, sensational pulp novels, sentimental literature on women, and comic anthologies. [CJG]

42.690 Anne C. Rose. *Transcendentalism as a social movement, 1830–1850*. New Haven: Yale University Press, 1981. ISBN 0-300-

02587-4. ▸ Discussion of how ideas, activities, and lives of transcendentalists were interrelated, particularly with respect to religion, economics, and family life. [TAM]

42.691 Wilson Smith. *Professors and public ethics: studies of northern moral philosophers before the Civil War*. Ithaca, N.Y.: Cornell University Press, 1956. ▸ Collection of biographical essays describing circle of major moral philosophers in first half of nineteenth century, including Francis Lieber and Francis Wayland. Documents involvement beyond classroom in politics and reform. [CJG]

42.692 Roger B. Stein. *John Ruskin and aesthetic thought in America, 1840–1900*. Cambridge, Mass.: Harvard University Press, 1967. ▸ Balanced, wide-ranging monograph exploring how Ruskin's view that foundation of not only aesthetics but all of life was morality struck responsive chords in American literature, science, theology, and economics as well as art and architecture. [CJG]

42.693 Louise Stevenson. *Scholarly means to evangelical ends: the New Haven scholars and the transformation of higher learning in America, 1830–1890*. Baltimore: Johns Hopkins University Press, 1986. ISBN 0-8018-2695-0. ▸ Elite group of scholars created romantic understanding of religion, emphasizing education as basis of culture in response to perception that social cohesion was declining. [TAM]

Nationalism and the American Character

42.694 Yehoshua Arieli. *Individualism and nationalism in American ideology*. 1964 ed. Baltimore: Penguin, 1966. ▸ Ambitious synthesis with transatlantic viewpoint. Pieces together national ideology through histories of key concepts, most important, individualism, which Americans transformed from Tocquevillean critique of new order to utopian affirmation of national character. [CJG]

42.695 John G. Cawelti. *The apostles of the self-made man*. 1965 ed. Chicago: University of Chicago Press, 1988. ISBN 0-226-09870-2. ▸ Categorizes recurrent notions of success from Benjamin Franklin to John Dewey into three traditions: Protestant respectability, economic mobility, and individual or social fulfillment. Clear, engaging readings of popular authors. [CJG]

42.696 Cathy N. Davidson. *Revolution and the word: the rise of the novel in America*. New York: Oxford University Press, 1986. ISBN 0-19-504108-9. ▸ Rise of fiction in early republic represented call for higher standards of education as well as insurgency of female readers against genteel patriarchy of cultural arbiters. Trend-setting blend of literary, intellectual, and social history. [CJG]

42.697 Drew Gilpin Faust. *A sacred circle: the dilemma of the intellectual in the Old South, 1840–1860*. 1977 ed. Philadelphia: University of Pennsylvania Press, 1986. ISBN 0-8122-1229-0 (pbk). ▸ Careful revisionist study moving beyond historians' concentration on George Fitzhugh. Proslavery writers addressed southern rather than northern audience, called for reform of South's economic and intellectual life. [CJG]

42.698 Peter Dobkin Hall. *The organization of American culture, 1700–1900: private institutions, elites, and the origins of American nationality*. 1982 ed. New York: New York University Press, 1984. ISBN 0-8147-3415-4 (cl), 0-8147-3425-1 (pbk). ▸ Provocative trend-setter in institutional history of culture. Finds elite-dominated national business and cultural institutions, through corporations, universities, and professional organizations, replaced earlier local focus of economy and culture. [CJG]

42.699 Donald Harvey Meyer. *The instructed conscience: the shaping of the American national ethic*. Philadelphia: University of Pennsylvania Press, 1972. ISBN 0-8122-7651-5. ▸ Moral philosophy as taught by such educators as Francis Wayland, Mark Hopkins, and Francis Bowen sought to harmonize Protestant traditions with scientific inquiry. Result was secularized Victorian moralism which pervaded official midcentury culture. [CJG]

42.700   Paul C. Nagel. *One nation indivisible: the Union in American thought, 1776–1861.* 1964 ed. Westport, Conn.: Greenwood, 1980. ISBN 0-313-22656-3. ▸ Survey of politicians' sentiments. Within eighty years of independence, idea of union evolved from hopeful experiment to timeless absolute, became repository of ideas on national character and destiny. [CJG]

42.701   Paul C. Nagel. *This sacred trust: American nationality, 1798–1898.* 1971 ed. Westport, Conn.: Greenwood, 1980. ISBN 0-313-22657-1. ▸ Extension and reconsideration of earlier study, *One Nation Indivisible* (42.700), analyzes nationalism as broader concept than unionism and stresses controversy over its meaning for domestic and foreign relations. [CJG]

42.702   Roy H. Pearce. *Savagism and civilization: a study of the Indian and the American mind.* Rev. ed. Berkeley: University of California Press, 1988. ISBN 0-520-06227-2 (pbk). ▸ Explores images of American Indians in religion, literature, and politics, 1600–1850, revealing what Herman Melville called "metaphysics of Indian-hating." By subduing "savage," white Americans proclaimed themselves "civilized" agents of progress. Groundbreaking, morally charged foundation for later studies, e.g., Berkhofer 40.399. Original title: *The Savages of America.* [CJG]

42.703   Merrill D. Peterson. *The Jefferson image in the American mind.* 1960 ed. New York: Oxford University Press, 1985. ISBN 0-19-500698-4 (pbk). ▸ Unique study tracing appropriation of Jefferson's life and ideas from his death (1826) to his bicentennial (1943). Protean founding father became defining reference for Jacksonians and Whigs, abolitionists and proslaveryites, imperialists and anti-imperialists, Progressives, and New Dealers. [CJG]

42.704   Constance Rourke. *American humor: a study of the national character.* 1931 ed. Tallahassee: University Presses of Florida, 1986. ISBN 0-8130-0837-9. ▸ Lively pioneering survey. Yankee, backwoodsman, and blackface humor reflected varied regional traditions and contributed to developing national consciousness; spilled over into serious literature. [CJG]

42.705   Henry Nash Smith. *Virgin land: the American West as symbol and myth.* 1950 ed. Cambridge, Mass.: Harvard University Press, 1978. ISBN 0-674-93952-2 (cl), 0-674-93955-7 (pbk). ▸ Images of westward expansion, frontier hero, and agrarian utopia influenced literature, politics, and historiography from Thomas Jefferson to Frederick Jackson Turner, but offer little insight into realities of urban-industrialism. Founding text of myth-and-symbol American studies approach. [CJG]

42.706   Fred Somkin. *Unquiet eagle: memory and desire in the idea of American freedom, 1815–1860.* Ithaca, N.Y.: Cornell University Press, 1967. ▸ Beneath ebullient Jacksonian era speeches and sermons was undercurrent of nostalgia for republican communal past and anxiety over materialistic, individualistic present. Fine chapter on Lafayette's tour of United States in 1824. Sensitive, prophetically revisionist treatment. [CJG]

42.707   William R. Taylor. *Cavalier and Yankee: the Old South and American national character.* 1961 ed. Cambridge, Mass.: Harvard University Press, 1979. ISBN 0-674-10440-4. ▸ Literary figures of cavalier and yankee expressed sectional stereotypes but also anxieties about increasing mobility and materialism. Northern writers (Cooper, Hale, Paulding) attracted to southern gentility and stability; southerners developed plantation legend as stay against progress. [CJG]

42.708   John William Ward. *Andrew Jackson: symbol for an age.* 1955 ed. New York: Oxford University Press, 1966. ▸ Episodes in Jackson's career transformed into nationalist myths supporting cult of nature, ideal of individualism, and Manifest Destiny.

Innovative use of popular sources, but assumes cultural consensus. [CJG]

Urban America and Middle-Class Culture

42.709   Gunther Barth. *City people: the rise of modern city culture in nineteenth-century America.* New York: Oxford University Press, 1980. ISBN 0-19-502755-8 (cl), 0-19-502753-1 (pbk). ▸ Colorful subject, impressionistic interpretation. Apartment houses, department stores, metropolitan newspapers, baseball parks, and vaudeville theaters forged common urban culture by accommodating diverse individual, class, and ethnic needs. [CJG]

42.710   Thomas Bender. *Toward an urban vision: ideas and institutions in nineteenth-century America.* Lexington: University Press of Kentucky, 1975. ISBN 0-8131-1326-1. ▸ Departing from Jeffersonian tradition, midcentury reformer-intellectuals such as Charles Loring Brace and Frederick Law Olmsted developed contrapuntal approach, juxtaposing art and nature, cityscape and landscape. Response to White and White 43.180. [CJG]

42.711   Burton J. Bledstein. *The culture of professionalism: the middle class and the development of higher education in America.* New York: Norton, 1976. ISBN 0-393-05574-4. ▸ Formation of middle-class consciousness entailed new phenomenon of structuring men's lives according to vertical trajectory of careers exemplifying character, expertise, and success. Modern university developed and spread new culture. [CJG]

42.712   Karen Halttunen. *Confidence men and painted women: a study of middle-class culture in America, 1830–1870.* New Haven: Yale University Press, 1982. ISBN 0-300-02835-0. ▸ Lively data for entertaining thesis. Prescriptive literature on etiquette and morals exposes potential for hypocrisy in antebellum social life. Urban mobility demanded those very rules most easily manipulated by insincere. [VBB]

42.713   Neil Harris. *Humbug: the art of P. T. Barnum.* 1973 ed. Chicago: University of Chicago Press, 1981. ISBN 0-226-31752-8. ▸ Study of Barnum as emblem of democratized antebellum culture, trickster and self-made millionaire whose life and shows blended moral uplift, titillation, and profit. Thoughtful biographical essay as cultural history. [CJG]

42.714   Daniel Walker Howe, ed. *Victorian America.* Philadelphia: University of Pennsylvania Press, 1976. ISBN 0-8122-7713-9. ▸ Essays from *American Quarterly* present Victorianism as Anglo-American middle-class value system congruent with modernization and achieving temporary cultural hegemony in midcentury decades. Useful extension of British perspective to United States. [CJG]

42.715   Milton Rugoff. *The Beechers: an American family in the nineteenth century.* New York: Harper & Row, 1981. ISBN 0-06-014859-4. ▸ Richly documented group biography of influential New England family of ministers, novelists, educators, and reformers whose careers spanned nearly a century of democratization, secularization, and urbanization. [CJG]

SEE ALSO
40.567 Lawrence W. Levine. *Highbrow/lowbrow.*

Art, Music, and Literature

42.716   Daniel Aaron. *The unwritten war: American writers and the Civil War.* 1973 ed. Madison: University of Wisconsin Press, 1987. ISBN 0-299-11390-6 (cl), 0-299-11394-9 (pbk). ▸ Civil War produced no epic poem or great novel but extensive literature of national redemption and celebration that drowned out sensitive writers' dark musings and private regrets. Comprehensive study. [CJG]

42.717   Sacvan Bercovitch. *The office of "The Scarlet Letter."* Baltimore: Johns Hopkins University Press, 1991. ISBN 0-8018-4203-

4. ▸ Rhetorical, ideological analysis of Hawthorne exploring conundrums of liberal dissent in antebellum culture and America generally. *Tour de force* of radical criticism. [CJG]

42.718 Hazel Dicken-Garcia. *Journalistic standards in nineteenth-century America.* Madison: University of Wisconsin Press, 1989. ISBN 0-299-12170-4 (cl), 0-299-12174-7 (pbk). ▸ Analysis of press criticism and standards documenting evolution from information to entertainment, business service to social force. Workmanlike example of new journalism history moving beyond editor and newspaper biographies. [CJG]

42.719 Sarah Elbert. *A hunger for home: Louisa May Alcott and "Little Women."* Philadelphia: Temple University Press, 1984. ISBN 0-87722-317-3. ▸ Neither full-scale biography nor exhaustive literary exegesis. Uses Alcott and her fiction to illustrate liberal feminist's definition of true womanhood. Situates Alcott's writing on political continuum as popularizer of liberal feminism. [VBB]

42.720 David Grimsted. *Melodrama unveiled: American theater and culture, 1800–1850.* 1968 ed. Berkeley: University of California Press, 1987. ISBN 0-520-05996-4. ▸ Melodrama attained huge popularity by praising natural goodness of common people, upholding ideals of domesticity, female purity, and social progress under benevolent providence. Thorough study of plays, actors, and audiences. [CJG]

42.721 Neil Harris. *The artist in American society: the formative years, 1790–1860.* 1966 ed. Chicago: University of Chicago Press, 1982. ISBN 0-226-31754-4 (pbk). ▸ Examination of social attitudes toward visual arts and ideals, careers, and achievements of artists. Long, slow process of legitimizing artistic endeavors hinged on moral approval as well as private patronage and institutional support. Ambitious, widely researched if somewhat uneven approach. [CJG/DMS]

42.722 Elizabeth Johns. *American genre painting: the politics of everyday life.* New Haven: Yale University Press, 1991. ISBN 0-300-05019-4. ▸ Theoretically informed social history of art. Antebellum genre painting reflected middle-class typing of others by class, region, race, and gender; simultaneously encouraged belief in harmony of interests between unequals. [CJG]

42.723 David Leverenz. *Manhood and the American renaissance.* Ithaca, N.Y.: Cornell University Press, 1989. ISBN 0-8014-2281-7. ▸ Caught in shift from comfortable patrician and artisan norms toward rugged individualism, male and female writers wrestled with new code of entrepreneurial manhood. Provocative rereading from gender viewpoint. [CJG]

42.724 Anne Scott MacLeod. *A moral tale: children's fiction and American culture, 1820–1860.* 1975 ed. Hamden, Conn.: Archon, 1990. ISBN 0-208-01552-3 (cl, 1975), 0-208-02292-9 (pbk). ▸ Belief in reality of good and evil was foundation of juvenile literature, whose morality plays preached Protestant pieties. Lively survey. [CJG]

42.725 Leo Marx. *The machine in the garden: technology and the pastoral ideal in America.* 1964 ed. New York: Oxford University Press, 1967. ▸ Classic, influential American studies text eliciting cultural commentary from literature. Major artists and writers evolved complex pastoralism seeking elusive middle landscape that reconciled technology and nature. [CJG]

42.726 F. O. Matthiessen. *American renaissance: art and expression in the age of Emerson and Whitman.* 1941 ed. New York: Oxford University Press, 1968. ISBN 0-19-500759-X. ▸ Classic presentation of achievements of Ralph Waldo Emerson, Henry David Thoreau, Nathaniel Hawthorne, Herman Melville, and Walt Whitman. Centers on writers' merger of aesthetic form and function, but offers reflections on nineteenth-century literature and culture. [CJG]

42.727 Barbara Novak. *Nature and culture: American landscape*

and painting, 1825–1875. New York: Oxford University Press, 1980. ISBN 0-19-502606-3. ▸ Thematic approach relates American landscape tradition to transcendentalism, science, spiritualism, and photography, but especially to concept of nature as God. Interesting comparisons with European art. [CJG]

42.728 Raymond Jackson Wilson. *Figures of speech: American writers and the literary marketplace from Benjamin Franklin to Emily Dickinson.* 1987 ed. Baltimore: Johns Hopkins University Press, 1990. ISBN 0-8018-4003-1. ▸ Accessible study of Benjamin Franklin, Washington Irving, William Lloyd Garrison, Ralph Waldo Emerson, and Emily Dickinson arguing that writers devised idea of purified literary calling in opposition to rise of literature as commodity. [CJG]

42.729 Larzer Ziff. *Literary democracy: the declaration of cultural independence in America.* New York: Penguin, 1982. ISBN 0-14-006199-1 (pbk). ▸ Midcentury writers established American literary independence by transforming antebellum social and cultural concerns into imaginative works. Lucid, context-oriented alternative to Matthiessen 42.726. [CJG]

CIVIL WAR AND RECONSTRUCTION

General Studies

42.730 Richard F. Bensel. *Yankee leviathan: the origins of central state authority in America, 1859–1877.* New York: Cambridge University Press, 1990. ISBN 0-521-39136-9 (cl), 0-521-39817-7 (pbk). ▸ Sweeping analysis of Civil War's centrality to formation of modern nation-state in America. Offers southern separatism as alternative to class conflict and consensus interpretations of political development. [SHH]

42.731 Richard E. Beringer et al. *Why the South lost the Civil War.* Athens: University of Georgia Press, 1986. ISBN 0-8203-0815-3. ▸ Argues against interpretations stressing northern economic and military might or southern states' rights. Claims confederate nationalism weak and southerners lost will to fight. [SHH]

42.732 David Paul Crook. *The North, the South, and the powers, 1861–1865.* New York: Wiley, 1974. ISBN 0-471-18855-7. ▸ Study of Civil War diplomacy focusing on United States relations with England and France. Argues war marked turning point in Atlantic history. [SHH]

42.733 Drew Gilpin Faust. *The creation of Confederate nationalism: ideology and identity in the Civil War South.* Baton Rouge: Louisiana State University Press, 1988. ISBN 0-8071-1509-6. ▸ Essays exploring culture and ideology of Confederacy with special attention to religion, identity, and slavery reform. [SHH]

42.734 George M. Fredrickson. *The inner Civil War: northern intellectuals and the crisis of the Union.* 1965 ed. New York: Harper & Row, 1968. ▸ Study of both intellectual response to collective trauma of war and how war began to reshape intellectual life. [SHH]

42.735 Thavolia Glymph and John J. Kushma, eds. *Essays on the postbellum southern economy.* College Station: Texas A&M University Press; for University of Texas at Arlington, 1985. ISBN 0-89096-227-8. ▸ Essays by four historians on emergence of free labor during Civil War, development of postwar plantation agriculture, and postbellum South in international perspective. [SHH]

42.736 Harold M. Hyman. *A more perfect Union: the impact of the Civil War and Reconstruction on the Constitution.* 1973 ed. Boston: Houghton-Mifflin, 1975. ISBN 0-395-20537-9. ▸ Examination of role of war and Reconstruction in process of advancing centralization of power and authority in United States. [SHH]

42.737 Robert Kaczorowski. *The politics of judicial interpretation: the federal courts, Department of Justice, and civil rights, 1866–1876.*

New York: Oceana Publications, 1985. ISBN 0-379-20818-0. ‣ Study of revolutionary impact of Civil War and Reconstruction on American constitutionalism. Looks at constitutional amendments, civil rights statutes, and role of federal judges and attorneys in South. [SHH]

42.738 J. Morgan Kousser and James M. McPherson, eds. *Region, race, and Reconstruction: essays in honor of C. Vann Woodward.* New York: Oxford University Press, 1982. ISBN 0-19-503075-3. ‣ Collection of essays by students of honoree. Focus on social, economic, and political history of South in middle period. [SHH]

42.739 James M. McPherson. *Battle cry of freedom: the Civil War era.* New York: Oxford University Press, 1988. ISBN 0-19-503863-0. ‣ Most recent and compelling one-volume history of Civil War. Includes treatment of sectional conflict and social and political history with focus on military aspects of war. [SHH]

42.740 Allan Nevins. *The war for the Union.* 4 vols. New York: Scribner's, 1959–71. ISBN 0-684-10429-6. ‣ Classic multivolume political, institutional, and military history of Civil War with broad-ranging insights and assessments. [SHH]

42.741 Stephen B. Oates. *With malice toward none: the life of Abraham Lincoln.* 1977 ed. New York: New American Library, 1978. ISBN 0-451-62314-2 (pbk). ‣ Most recent, controversial one-volume biography. Emphasis on political and military history. [SHH]

42.742 Frank Lawrence Owsley. *King cotton diplomacy: foreign relations of the Confederate States of America.* 2d ed. Chicago: University of Chicago Press, 1966. ‣ Discussion of Confederate efforts to gain diplomatic recognition and intervention from England and France. Emphasizes role of cotton supply. [SHH]

42.743 Joseph H. Parks. *Joseph E. Brown of Georgia.* Baton Rouge: Louisiana State University Press, 1977. ISBN 0-8071-0189-3. ‣ Biography of important, enigmatic secessionist Civil War governor, turned Reconstruction Republican, turned United States senator, and member of Georgia's Bourbon triumvirate. [SHH]

42.744 James L. Roark. *Masters without slaves: southern planters in the Civil War and Reconstruction.* New York: Norton, 1977. ISBN 0-393-05562-0. ‣ Study of revolution planters made to defend their slave society and destruction of that world during Civil War and Reconstruction. [SHH]

42.745 Joel H. Silbey. *A respectable minority: the Democratic party in the Civil War era, 1860–1868.* New York: Norton, 1977. ISBN 0-393-05648-1 (cl), 0-393-09087-6 (pbk). ‣ Analysis of struggle of northern Democrats to survive electoral defeats, challenge policies of Lincoln administration, and contest for state and national power. [SHH]

42.746 Emory Thomas. *The Confederate nation, 1861–1865.* New York: Harper & Row, 1979. ISBN 0-06-014252-9. ‣ Interpretation of Confederate experience arguing secession and war transformed society and politics of Old South. [SHH]

Secession Crisis

42.747 Richard H. Abbott. *The Republican party and the South, 1855–1877: the first southern strategy.* Chapel Hill: University of North Carolina Press, 1986. ISBN 0-8078-1680-9. ‣ Study of Republican party policy and practice regarding building party in southern states. Emphasis on limited resources and attention devoted to task. [SHH]

42.748 Steven A. Channing. *Crisis of fear: secession in South Carolina.* 1970 ed. New York: Norton, 1974. ISBN 0-393-00730-8. ‣ Political and intellectual history of last phase of secession

crisis in vanguard southern state. Sees fear of racial unrest as unifying force of secessionism. [SHH]

42.749 Paul D. Escott. *After secession: Jefferson Davis and the failure of Confederate nationalism.* Baton Rouge: Louisiana State University Press, 1978. ISBN 0-8071-0369-1. ‣ Blames defeat of Confederacy chiefly on alienation of southern white common folk from policies of Davis administration and southern cause. [SHH]

42.750 Michael P. Johnson. *Toward a patriarchal republic: the secession of Georgia.* Baton Rouge: Louisiana State University Press, 1977. ISBN 0-8071-0270-9. ‣ Argues secession was double revolution, struggle both for home rule and over who would rule at home. Inspired by fear of northern Republicans and southern nonslaveholders. [SHH]

42.751 David M. Potter. *Lincoln and his party in the secession crisis.* 1942 ed. New York: AMS Press, 1979. ISBN 0-404-14809-3. ‣ Efforts of Abraham Lincoln and other leading Republicans to find peaceful solution to secession crisis. Refreshingly avoids trap of inevitability of outcome. [SHH]

42.752 Kenneth M. Stampp. *And the war came: the North and the secession crisis, 1860–1861.* 1950 ed. Westport, Conn.: Greenwood, 1980. ISBN 0-313-22566-4. ‣ Study of northern reaction to secession of southern states. Seeks to explain why northerners unwilling to accept disunion. [SHH]

Military History

42.753 Michael C. C. Adams. *Our masters the rebels: a speculation on Union military failure in the East, 1861–1865.* Cambridge, Mass.: Harvard University Press, 1978. ISBN 0-674-64643-6. ‣ Cultural and psychological assessment of Union military defeats. Northerners assumed martial superiority of southerners and doubted ability to defeat them. [SHH]

42.754 Ira Berlin, Joseph P. Reidy, and Leslie S. Rowland, eds. *The black military experience.* New York: Cambridge University Press, 1982. (Freedom: a documentary history of emancipation, 1861–1867, 2.) ISBN 0-521-22984-7. ‣ Documents from National Archives and interpretive essays by editors, covering mobilization and experiences of black troops during Civil War and their role in winning war, ending slavery, and beginning Reconstruction. [SHH]

42.755 Bruce Catton. *Grant takes command.* Boston: Little, Brown, 1969. ‣ Survey of military experience of Ulysses S. Grant and his army from victory at Vicksburg until Confederate surrender at Appomattox. [SHH]

42.756 Dudley T. Cornish. *The sable arm: Negro troops in the Union army, 1861–1865.* 1956 ed. New York: Norton, 1966. ‣ Study of process by which African Americans mobilized by Union army during Civil War. Emphasis on obstacles to be overcome and on contributions to war effort. [SHH]

42.757 Michael Fellman. *Inside war: the guerrilla conflict in Missouri during the American Civil War.* New York: Oxford University Press, 1989. ISBN 0-19-505198-X (cl), 0-19-506471-2 (pbk). ‣ Study of ways in which social changes of 1850s together with sectional conflict provoked most intense and destructive guerrilla war during Civil War. [SHH]

42.758 Douglas Southall Freeman. *R. E. Lee: a biography.* 1934–35 ed. 4 vols. New York: Scribner's, 1961. ‣ Preeminent, full-scale biography of Confederate general. Concentrates overwhelmingly on Civil War years. [SHH]

42.759 Joseph T. Glatthaar. *Forged in battle: the Civil War alliance of black soldiers and white officers.* New York: Free Press, 1990. ISBN 0-02-911815-8. ‣ Exploration of experiences, attitudes, aspirations, and contributions of white Union army officers and black troops they commanded during Civil War. [SHH]

42.760 Herman Hattaway and Archer Jones. *How the North won: a military history of the Civil War.* Urbana: University of Illinois Press, 1983. ISBN 0-252-00918-5. ‣ Military history of Civil War from point of view of high commanders. Emphasizes decisive role of strategy and logistics to outcome. [SHH]

42.761 Alvin M. Josephy, Jr. *The Civil War in the American West.* New York: Knopf; distributed by Random House, 1991. ISBN 0-394-56482-0. ‣ Narrative history of Civil War in trans-Mississippi West, from skirmishes in western Texas and New Mexico to Indian wars in northern Plains. [SHH]

42.762 Ella Lonn. *Desertion during the Civil War.* 1928 ed. Gloucester, Mass.: P. Smith, 1966. ‣ Study of causes and patterns of desertion in Union and Confederate armies. Argues that northern desertions had greater impact on course of war. [SHH]

42.763 William S. McFeely. *Grant: a biography.* 1981 ed. New York: Norton, 1982. ISBN 0-393-01372-3 (cl, 1981), 0-393-30046-3 (pbk). ‣ Most recent and important full-scale biography of Union general and later president of United States. [SHH]

42.764 Grady McWhiney and Perry D. Jamieson. *Attack and die: Civil War military tactics and the southern heritage.* 1982 ed. Tuscaloosa: University of Alabama Press, 1984. ISBN 0-8173-0073-2 (cl, 1982), 0-8173-0229-8 (pbk). ‣ Links causes of Confederate defeat to Celtic-inspired military tactics. Many costly and unnecessary attacks resulted in very high casualties. [SHH]

42.765 Reid Mitchell. *Civil War soldiers.* New York: Viking, 1988. ISBN 0-670-81742-2. ‣ Fresh account of motives and experiences of ordinary soldiers in Union and Confederate armies. [SHH]

42.766 Phillip S. Paludan. *Victims: a true story of the Civil War.* Knoxville: University of Tennessee Press, 1981. ISBN 0-87049-316-7. ‣ Psychological, anthropological, and historical analysis of murder of Union guerrillas by Confederate soldiers in western North Carolina. Looks at impact of war on traditional society. [SHH]

42.767 Benjamin Quarles. *The Negro in the Civil War.* 1953 ed. New York: Da Capo, 1989. ISBN 0-306-80350-X (pbk). ‣ Important early revisionist study of contributions of African Americans, North and South, to winning of Civil War and abolition of slavery. [SHH]

42.768 Charles Royster. *The destructive war: William Tecumseh Sherman, Stonewall Jackson, and the Americans.* New York: Knopf; distributed by Random House, 1991. ISBN 0-394-52485-3. ‣ Examination of activities of two important officers to explore level of destruction to which participants in Civil War committed themselves. [SHH]

42.769 Bell I. Wiley. *The life of Billy Yank: the common soldier of the Union.* 1952 ed. Baton Rouge: Louisiana State University Press, 1978. ISBN 0-8071-0477-9 (cl), 0-8071-0476-0 (pbk). ‣ Lively history of experiences of common soldiers in Union army, in battle, on campaign, and in camp. [SHH]

42.770 Bell I. Wiley. *The life of Johnny Reb: the common soldier of the Confederacy.* 1943 ed. Baton Rouge: Louisiana State University Press, 1978. ISBN 0-8071-0477-9 (cl), 0-8071-0475-2 (pbk). ‣ Lively social history of Confederate army's common soldiers in battle, on campaign, and in camp. [SHH]

42.771 T. Harry Williams. *Lincoln and his generals.* 1952 ed. Westport, Conn.: Greenwood, 1981. ISBN 0-313-22842-6. ‣ Lincoln in his role as commander-in-chief and war director whose greatness as strategist did more than any general to win war. [SHH]

42.772 Ann Douglas Wood. "The war within a war: women nurses in the Union Army." *Civil War history* 18 (1972) 197–212. ISSN 0009-8078. ‣ Nurses in Civil War used maternal status in bid for professional status in medicine. Women waged power struggle, challenging male medical authorities and defying bureaucracy in name of womanly care. [VBB]

The Home Front

42.773 Iver Bernstein. *The New York City draft riots: their significance in American society and politics in the age of the Civil War.* New York: Oxford University Press, 1990. ISBN 0-19-505006-1. ‣ Relation of draft riots to patterns of social and political development in antebellum New York. Role of riots in reshaping political economy of city. [SHH]

42.774 Mary Chesnut. *Mary Chesnut's Civil War.* C. Vann Woodward, ed. New Haven: Yale University Press, 1981. ISBN 0-300-02459-2. ‣ First publishing of classic journal of upper-class Confederate woman. Insightful female view of slavery, southern patriarchy, and Civil War. Definitive edition incorporates previously unpublished material and includes informative introductory essays. [VBB]

42.775 Daniel W. Crofts. *Reluctant Confederates: upper South unionists in the secession crisis.* Chapel Hill: University of North Carolina Press, 1989. ISBN 0-8078-1809-7. ‣ Examination of secession crisis in states of Virginia, North Carolina, and Tennessee. Suggests differences with lower South owing to patterns of slaveholding and strength of whiggery. [SHH]

42.776 Sarah Morgan Dawson. *The Civil War diary of Sarah Morgan.* Charles East, ed. Athens: University of Georgia Press, 1991. ISBN 0-8203-1357-2. ‣ One Confederate female's critical view of life before and during federal occupation of Baton Rouge and New Orleans. Similar to Mary Chesnut's more famous journal (42.774). Complete version of biting personal record. [VBB]

42.777 Drew Gilpin Faust. "Altars of sacrifice: Confederate women and the narratives of war." *Journal of American History* 76 (1990) 1200–1228. ‣ Suggestive exploration of construction of gendered ideology of sacrifice for Confederacy and its growing rejection by white women, rich and poor, as Civil War dragged on. Intriguing perspective on "why South lost Civil War." [TD]

42.778 Frank L. Klement. *The copperheads in the Middle West.* 1960 ed. Gloucester, Mass.: P. Smith, 1972. ‣ Discussion of movement based in Democratic party that contested policies of Lincoln administration. Focus on antiabolitionism and opposition to centralization of state authority. [SHH]

42.779 Grace Palladino. *Another civil war: labor, capital, and the state in the anthracite region of Pennsylvania, 1840–1868.* Urbana: University of Illinois Press, 1990. ISBN 0-252-01671-8. ‣ Study of relation between wartime labor unrest in coal fields and process of political centralization under Republican auspices. [SHH]

42.780 Phillip S. Paludan. *A people's contest: the Union and Civil War, 1861–1865.* 1988 ed. New York: Harper & Row, 1989. ISBN 0-06-015903-0. ‣ Broad-ranging exploration of how North redefined itself through war and great social changes that accompanied it. Links new social history with more traditional political and military history. [SHH]

42.781 George C. Rable. *Civil wars: women and the crisis of southern nationalism.* Urbana: University of Illinois Press, 1989. ISBN 0-252-01597-5. ‣ Exploration of role of white women in both political struggle against North and cultural contest within South. [SHH]

Emancipation and Southern Society

42.782 Stephen V. Ash. *Middle Tennessee society transformed, 1860–1870: war and peace in the upper South.* Baton Rouge: Louisiana State University Press, 1987. ISBN 0-8071-1400-6. ‣ Study of transition from slavery to freedom in upper South. Argues for experience of "third South" and evolution of dual societies divided by race. [SHH]

42.783 Ira Berlin et al., eds. *The destruction of slavery.* New York: Cambridge University Press, 1985. (Freedom: a documentary history of emancipation, 1861–1867, I.) ISBN 0-521-22979-0. ▸ Documents from National Archives and interpretive essays by editors, covering process by which slavery was abolished during Civil War. Attentive to role of blacks and to patterns in different parts of South. [SHH]

42.784 Ira Berlin et al., eds. *The wartime genesis of free labor: the lower South.* New York: Cambridge University Press, 1990. (Freedom: a documentrary history of emancipation, 1861–1867, 3.) ISBN 0-521-39493-7. ▸ Documents from National Archives and interpretive essays by editors, covering rise of new labor arrangements as slavery destroyed during Civil War. Looks at areas under federal and Confederate control. [SHH]

42.785 LaWanda Cox. *Lincoln and black freedom: a study in presidential leadership.* 1981 ed. Urbana: University of Illinois Press, 1985. ISBN 0-252-01173-2 (pbk). ▸ Sympathetic treatment of Lincoln's role in helping to advance cause of black freedom as quickly as circumstances would allow. [SHH]

42.786 Eric Foner. *Nothing but freedom: emancipation and its legacy.* Baton Rouge: Louisiana State University Press, 1983. ISBN 0-8071-1118-X. ▸ Collection of essays on emancipation and its aftermath. Places southern experience in comparative perspective and argues for centrality of struggles over meaning of free labor. [SHH]

42.787 Celine Fremaux Garcia. *Celine: remembering Louisiana, 1850–1871.* Patrick J. Geary, ed. Athens: University of Georgia Press, 1987. ISBN 0-8203-0964-8. ▸ Reminiscence of growing up in middle-class creole family in Civil War era. More revealing of psychological than political dynamics. Chronicles divided loyalties of immigrant French mother. [VBB]

42.788 Gerald David Jaynes. *Branches without roots: genesis of the black working class in the American South, 1862–1882.* 1986 ed. New York: Oxford University Press, 1989. ISBN 0-19-503619-0 (cl, 1986), 0-19-505575-6 (pbk). ▸ Economic history of development of sharecropping. Emphasis on failure of ex-slaves to receive land and ex-masters to receive federal financial assistance. [SHH]

42.789 Leon F. Litwack. *Been in the storm so long.* 1979 ed. New York: Vintage, 1980. ISBN 0-394-74398-9. ▸ Sweeping account of black struggle for freedom during Civil War and early phases of Reconstruction. Discusses making of postwar black community and postwar black oppression. [SHH]

42.790 Edward Magdol. *A right to the land: essays on the freedmen's community.* Westport, Conn.: Greenwood, 1977. ISBN 0-8371-9409-1. ▸ Essays on struggle of various black communities for land and social justice in immediate aftermath of slavery. [SHH]

42.791 James M. McPherson. *The struggle for equality: abolitionists and the Negro in the Civil War and Reconstruction.* Princeton: Princeton University Press, 1964. ▸ Sympathetic examination of role of abolitionists in advancing cause of black civil and political rights during Civil War and Reconstruction. [SHH]

42.792 Roger L. Ransom and Richard Sutch. *One kind of freedom: the economic consequences of emancipation.* Cambridge: Cambridge University Press, 1977. ISBN 0-521-21450-5 (cl), 0-521-29203-4 (pbk). ▸ Analysis of making of black poverty and economic underdevelopment in post–Civil War South. Emphasizes role of extra-market factors such as racism and merchants' territorial monopolies. [SHH]

42.793 C. Peter Ripley. *Slaves and freedmen in Civil War Loui-*

siana. Baton Rouge: Louisiana State University Press, 1976. ISBN 0-8071-0187-7. ▸ Distinctive early experience of Louisiana under military rule anticipated broader failure of Reconstruction to advance black prospects and rights. [SHH]

42.794 Clarence E. Walker. *A rock in a weary land: the African Methodist Episcopal Church during the Civil War and Reconstruction.* Baton Rouge: Louisiana State University Press, 1982. ISBN 0-8071-0883-9. ▸ Study of missionary activities in South of northern-born black church. Discusses political and social as well as religious role highlighting contradictions that African Americans faced. [SHH]

42.795 Michael Wayne. *The reshaping of plantation society: the Natchez district, 1860–1880.* Urbana: University of Illinois Press, 1990. ISBN 0-252-06127-6. ▸ Social history of transition from slavery to freedom in plantation district of Mississippi. Shows persisting landed elite amidst changing labor relations inspired by black struggles. [SHH]

42.796 Vernon L. Wharton. *The Negro in Mississippi, 1865–1890.* 1947 ed. Westport, Conn.: Greenwood, 1984. ISBN 0-313-24568-1. ▸ Study of black experience in Mississippi from end of slavery to advent of segregation and disfranchisement. Especially good treatments of economic and political life. [SHH]

42.797 Joel Williamson. *After slavery: the Negro in South Carolina during Reconstruction, 1861–1877.* 1965 ed. Hanover, N.H.: University Press of New England for Wesleyan University Press, 1990. ISBN 0-8195-6236-X. ▸ Impressive study of black struggle to adapt to changes occasioned by abolition of slavery. Highlights creative black role in economic, political, and community life as well as early rise of segregation. [SHH]

State and Local Studies

42.798 Randolph B. Campbell. *A southern community in crisis: Harrison County, Texas, 1850–1880.* Austin: Texas State Historical Association, 1983. ISBN 0-87611-061-8. ▸ Study of major Texas slaveholding county through trials of secession, war, and Republican Reconstruction. Emphasis on persisting wealth and power of antebellum elite despite political turmoil. [SHH]

42.799 Russell Duncan. *Freedom's shore: Tunis Campbell and the Georgia freedmen.* Athens: University of Georgia Press, 1986. ISBN 0-8203-0876-5. ▸ Study of role of northern-born African American in building black political power in coastal Georgia that outlasted his demise. [SHH]

42.800 William McKee Evans. *Ballots and fence rails: Reconstruction on the lower Cape Fear.* 1967 ed. New York: Norton, 1974. ISBN 0-393-00711-1. ▸ Important local history of Reconstruction. Draws attention to significant political role of African Americans. [SHH]

42.801 Steven Hahn. *The roots of southern populism: yeoman farmers and the transformation of the Georgia upcountry, 1850–1890.* New York: Oxford University Press, 1983. ISBN 0-19-503249-7. ▸ Study of commercialization of nonplantation region, occasioned by Civil War and Reconstruction. Focus on white family farmers and social origins of populist revolt. [SHH]

42.802 William C. Harris. *The day of the carpetbagger: Republican Reconstruction in Mississippi.* Baton Rouge: Louisiana State University Press, 1979. ISBN 0-8071-0366-7. ▸ Lengthy narrative history that sees missed opportunities for equal rights, political tolerance, and material rehabilitation in Mississippi. [SHH]

42.803 Janet S. Hermann. *The pursuit of a dream.* 1981 ed. New York: Vintage, 1983. ISBN 0-394-71375-3. ▸ Fascinating story of community built and rebuilt by Joseph Davis and his slaves at Davis Bend and Mound Bayou, Mississippi. [SHH]

42.804 Thomas Holt. *Black over white: Negro political leadership* *in South Carolina during Reconstruction.* Urbana: University of Illinois Press, 1977. ISBN 0-252-00555-6. ▸ Study of black politics arguing for importance of class divisions within African American community to course and outcome of Reconstruction. [SHH]

42.805 Peter Kolchin. *First freedom: the responses of Alabama's blacks to emancipation and Reconstruction.* Westport, Conn.: Greenwood, 1972. ISBN 0-8371-6385-4. ▸ Examination of black labor, migration, family, education, and political consciousness in early Reconstruction Alabama. [SHH]

42.806 Richard G. Lowe. *Republicans and Reconstruction in Virginia, 1856–1870.* Charlottesville: University Press of Virginia, 1991. ISBN 0-8139-1306-3. ▸ Sympathetic treatment of Virginia Republicans as active reformers who sought to take state from slaveholding past to new age of late nineteenth century. [SHH]

42.807 Jack P. Maddex, Jr. *The Virginia conservatives, 1867–1879: a study in Reconstruction politics.* Chapel Hill: University of North Carolina Press, 1970. ISBN 0-8078-1140-8. ▸ Study of Virginia politics arguing that conservative leaders were new elite who hoped to integrate state into world that northerners were making. [SHH]

42.808 Clarence L. Mohr. *On the threshold of freedom: masters and slaves in Civil War Georgia.* Athens: University of Georgia Press, 1986. ISBN 0-8203-0793-9. ▸ Study showing how social crisis of Civil War laid bare meaning of slavery for whites and blacks, while undermining institution from within as well as from without. [SHH]

42.809 Carl H. Moneyhon. *Republicanism in Reconstruction Texas.* Austin: University of Texas Press, 1980. ISBN 0-292-77553-9. ▸ Rise and fall of republican power owing to party factionalism, democratic violence, and contention between different sections of large state. [SHH]

42.810 Elizabeth Studley Nathans. *Losing the peace: Georgia Republicans and Reconstruction, 1865–1871.* 1968 ed. Baton Rouge: Louisiana State University Press, 1969. ▸ Exploration of failure of Republicans to build broad coalition capable of retaining power. Blames radicals for relying too heavily on federal support. [SHH]

42.811 Horace W. Raper. *William W. Holden: North Carolina's political enigma.* Chapel Hill: University of North Carolina Press, 1985. ISBN 0-8078-5060-8. ▸ Biography of perhaps most prominent figure in North Carolina's political experience of Civil War and Reconstruction. [SHH]

42.812 Joe M. Richardson. *The Negro in the Reconstruction of Florida, 1865–1877.* 1965 ed. Tampa, Fla.: Trend House, 1973. (Florida State University studies, 46.) ISBN 0-88251-038-X. ▸ Study of adjustment of ex-slaves to emancipation and role they played in Florida politics. Critical of Dunning 42.830. [SHH]

42.813 Willie Lee Rose. *Rehearsal for Reconstruction: the Port Royal experiment.* 1964 ed. New York: Oxford University Press, 1976. ▸ Important revisionist study of Reconstruction focusing on experience of South Carolina Sea Islands under wartime federal occupation. [SHH]

42.814 Loren C. Schweninger. *James T. Rapier and Reconstruction.* Chicago: University of Chicago Press, 1978. ISBN 0-226-74240-7. ▸ Biography of freeborn, black political leader of Reconstruction Alabama. [SHH]

42.815 Alrutheus A. Taylor. *The Negro in the Reconstruction of Virginia.* 1926 ed. New York: Russell & Russell, 1969. ▸ Pioneering account of roles of African Americans in Reconstruction of southern state. Examines social and economic changes, community development, and political activity. [SHH]

42.816 Joe Gray Taylor. *Louisiana reconstructed, 1863–1877.* Baton Rouge: Louisiana State University Press, 1974. ISBN 0-8071-0084-6. ▸ Wide-ranging account of Louisiana's complex experience of Reconstruction with political narrative at center. Suggests limited changes in society, economy, and politics. [SHH]

42.817 Ted Tunnell. *Crucible of Reconstruction: war, radicalism, and race in Louisiana, 1862–1877.* Baton Rouge: Louisiana State University Press, 1984. ISBN 0-8071-1181-3. ▸ Brief but interesting examination of rise and fall of republican rule in Louisiana. Sees ability of white militants to gain control of countryside through vigilante violence as key. [SHH]

42.818 Charles Vincent. *Black legislators in Louisiana during Reconstruction.* Baton Rouge: Louisiana State University Press, 1976. ISBN 0-8071-0089-7. ▸ Challenges Dunningite stereotypes (42.830) with close account of African American leaders at local and, especially, state level. Argues direct power limited, but leaders often had education, economic independence, and experience. [SHH]

42.819 Jonathan M. Wiener. *Social origins of the New South: Alabama, 1860–1885.* Baton Rouge: Louisiana State University Press, 1978. ISBN 0-8071-0397-7. ▸ Important study arguing Alabama planters survived Civil War and emancipation, continued to preside over repressive labor system, and stymied industrial development. [SHH]

Reconstruction

42.820 Roberta Sue Alexander. *North Carolina faces the freedmen: race relations during presidential Reconstruction, 1865–1867.* Durham, N.C.: Duke University Press, 1985. ISBN 0-8223-0628-X. ▸ Discussion of black resistance to white-imposed economic and civil dependency immediately after Civil War. Also treats community building among blacks before advent of radical Reconstruction. [SHH]

42.821 Michael Les Benedict. *A compromise of principle: congressional Republicans and Reconstruction, 1863–1869.* New York: Norton, 1974. ISBN 0-393-05524-8. ▸ Roll-call analysis of congressional policy making. Argues for predominant influence of moderate and conservative Republicans. [SHH]

42.822 Eugene H. Berwanger. *The West and Reconstruction.* Urbana: University of Illinois Press, 1981. ISBN 0-252-00868-5. ▸ Focusing on racial thought, study shows westerners more easily supported equal rights for blacks in South than in West. Also shows that western political liberalism waned after 1867. [SHH]

42.823 Claude G. Bowers. *The tragic era: the revolution after Lincoln.* 1929 ed. New York: Blue Ribbon, 1940. ▸ Influential early history of Reconstruction which took very critical view of radical Republicans. [SHH]

42.824 William R. Brock. *An American crisis: Congress and Reconstruction, 1865–1867.* 1963 ed. New York: Harper & Row, 1966. ▸ Analysis of process by which radical republican program was fashioned and enacted in Congress. Highlights tangles created by Constitution and radical failure to dominate ideological and cultural ground. [SHH]

42.825 Fawn M. Brodie. *Thaddeus Stevens: scourge of the South.* 1959 ed. New York: Norton, 1966. ▸ Biography of controversial Republican party congressional leader. Attempts to link public and personal life with psychological perspective. [SHH]

42.826 Dan T. Carter. *When the war was over: the failure of self-reconstruction in the South, 1865–1867.* Baton Rouge: Louisiana State University Press, 1985. ISBN 0-8071-1192-9. ▸ Discussion of ideas and behavior of emerging southern white leadership during presidential Reconstruction. Challenges notion of monolithic or wholly reactionary elite. [SHH]

42.827 Richard N. Current. *Those terrible carpetbaggers.* New York: Oxford University Press, 1988. ISBN 0-19-504872-5.

▸ Focus on ten northerners who played prominent roles in southern Reconstruction. Challenges negative stereotype of carpetbaggers, sketching more complex and generally favorable picture. [SHH]

42.828 David Donald. *Charles Sumner and the rights of man.* New York: Knopf, 1970. ▸ Biographical study of statesman and founder of Free Soil party during period of Civil War and Reconstruction. Looks at role in extending civil and political rights to blacks and in shaping American diplomacy. See author's work on earlier years of Sumner's life (42.31). [SHH]

42.829 W.E.B. Du Bois. *Black Reconstruction in America.* 1935 ed. New York: Atheneum, 1992. ISBN 0-689-70820-3. ▸ Sweeping, pioneering study of Reconstruction as struggle for economic and political democracy. Combines class analysis with attention to direct role of African Americans. Challenges prevailing interpretations (see Dunning 42.830). [SHH]

42.830 William A. Dunning. *Reconstruction, political and economic, 1865–1877.* 1907 ed. New York: Harper & Row, 1968. ▸ Early and extremely influential interpretation, sympathetic to defeated white southerners and to President Johnson. Highly critical of radical Republicans and order they tried to establish. [SHH]

42.831 Michael W. Fitzgerald. *The Union League movement in the deep South: politics and agricultural change during Reconstruction.* Baton Rouge: Louisiana State University Press, 1989. ISBN 0-8071-1526-6. ▸ Study of early political mobilization among freedpersons. Argues for central Union League role in transition from gang labor to sharecropping. [SHH]

42.832 Eric Foner. *Reconstruction: America's unfinished revolution, 1863–1877.* New York: Harper & Row, 1988. ISBN 0-06-015851-4 (cl), 0-06-091453-X (pbk). ▸ Most recent and significant one-volume history of Reconstruction. Special emphasis on transition from slavery to freedom and on African American roles. [SHH]

42.833 Jacqueline Jones. *Soldiers of light and love: northern teachers and Georgia blacks, 1865–1873.* 1980 ed. Athens: University of Georgia Press, 1992. ISBN 0-8203-1442-0 (pbk). ▸ Examination of promise and limits of neoabolitionism and liberal reform seen through experience of white northern teachers among Georgia freedpersons. [SHH]

42.834 William S. McFeely. *Yankee stepfather: General O. O. Howard and the freedmen.* New Haven: Yale University Press, 1968. ▸ Study of northern antislavery reformer and Union general who became commissioner of Freedmen's Bureau. Revisionist account of promise and limits of federal policy toward freedpersons. [SHH]

42.835 Eric L. McKitrick. *Andrew Johnson and Reconstruction.* 1960 ed. New York: Oxford University Press, 1988. ISBN 0-19-505707-4 (pbk). ▸ Important revisionist study casting Andrew Johnson and his policies in critical light. [SHH]

42.836 David Montgomery. *Beyond equality: labor and the radical Republicans, 1862–1872; with a bibliographical afterword.* 1967 ed. Urbana: University of Illinois Press, 1981. ISBN 0-252-00869-3 (pbk). ▸ Pioneering reinterpretation of meaning and limits of Reconstruction. Shows how northern labor struggles provoked crisis for radicals over definition of freedom and equality. [SHH]

42.837 Donald G. Nieman. *To set the law in motion: the Freedmen's Bureau and the legal rights of blacks, 1865–1868.* Millwood, N.Y.: KTO, 1979. ISBN 0-527-67235-1. ▸ Examination of bureau's efforts to provide freedpersons with legal protection and numerous reasons for failure to do so successfully. [SHH]

42.838 Otto H. Olsen. *Carpetbagger's crusade: the life of Albion Winegar Tourgee.* Baltimore: Johns Hopkins University Press,

1965. ▸ Biography of Union officer who settled in North Carolina, helped organize Union League, defended black rights against Klan violence while serving as Superior Court judge, and wrote novel *A Fool's Errand.* [SHH]

42.839 Claude F. Oubre. *Forty acres and a mule: the Freedmen's Bureau and black landownership.* Baton Rouge: Louisiana State University Press, 1978. ISBN 0-8071-0298-9. ▸ Study of federal policy regarding land confiscation and redistribution in South. Discusses role of Freedmen's Bureau in supervising and implementing policy. [SHH]

42.840 Michael Perman. *Reunion without compromise: the South and Reconstruction, 1865–1868.* Cambridge: Cambridge University Press, 1973. ISBN 0-521-20044-X (cl), 0-521-09779-7 (pbk). ▸ Political history of presidential Reconstruction. Argues Andrew Johnson's leniency encouraged southern defiance. [SHH]

42.841 Michael Perman. *The road to redemption: southern politics, 1869–1879.* Chapel Hill: University of North Carolina Press, 1984. ISBN 0-8078-1526-8. ▸ Political history seeing internal divisions in both political parties as central to how southern Democrats redeemed states from political, Reconstruction control. [SHH]

42.842 Lawrence N. Powell. *New masters: northern planters during the Civil War and Reconstruction.* New Haven: Yale University Press, 1980. ISBN 0-300-02217-4. ▸ Important account of northerners who bought or leased plantations in South. New perspective on limits of federal reforms on behalf of freedpersons. [SHH]

42.843 Howard N. Rabinowitz, ed. *Southern black leaders of the Reconstruction era.* Urbana: University of Illinois Press, 1982. ISBN 0-252-00929-0 (cl), 0-252-00972-X (pbk). ▸ Collection of essays on national, state, and grassroots African American leaders. [SHH]

42.844 Terry L. Seip. *The South returns to Congress: men, economic measures, and intersectional relationships, 1868–1879.* Baton Rouge: Louisiana State University Press, 1983. ISBN 0-8071-1052-3. ▸ Examination of careers of southern congressional representatives during Reconstruction. Points to stronger regional than partisan alignments on economic questions. [SHH]

42.845 Robert P. Sharkey. *Money, class, and party: an economic study of the Civil War and Reconstruction.* 1959 ed. Baltimore: Johns Hopkins University Press, 1967. ▸ Revisionist study of political economy of Reconstruction. Challenges idea of united business-republican front. Shows important divisions among Republicans over economic policy. [SHH]

42.846 Kenneth M. Stampp. *The era of Reconstruction, 1865–1877.* 1965 ed. New York: Vintage, 1967. ▸ Important revisionist study challenging Dunning school (42.830) by placing Reconstruction reforms and radical Republicans in favorable light. Emphasizes gains in civil and political rights. [SHH]

42.847 Mark W. Summers. *Railroads, Reconstruction, and the gospel of prosperity: aid under the radical Republicans, 1865–1877.* Princeton: Princeton University Press, 1984. ISBN 0-691-04695-6. ▸ Study of failed effort to build both new South and republican majority in region through means of railroad aid. [SHH]

42.848 Allen W. Trelease. *White terror: the Ku Klux Klan conspiracy and southern Reconstruction.* Westport, Conn.: Greenwood, 1979. ISBN 0-313-21168-X. ▸ Rich account of Klan's role as terrorist arm of Democratic party. Effort to reestablish white supremacy in face of republican mobilization of blacks and white unionists. [SHH]

42.849 Victor Ullman. *Martin R. Delany: the beginnings of black nationalism.* Boston: Beacon, 1971. ISBN 0-8070-5440-2. ▸ Biography of northern-born, African American leader and early advocate of emigration who also played important role during Civil War and Reconstruction. [SHH]

42.850 Okon E. Uya. *From slavery to public service: Robert Smalls, 1839–1915.* New York: Oxford University Press, 1971. ▸ Biography of South Carolina slave who became important political leader during Reconstruction. [SHH]

42.851 C. Vann Woodward. *Reunion and reaction: the compromise of 1877 and the end of Reconstruction.* 1951 ed. New York: Oxford University Press, 1991. ISBN 0-19-506423-2. ▸ Classic account of contested presidential election of 1876 and resulting compromise that ended Reconstruction. Attempt to forge alliance between northern Republicans and whiggish southerners. [SHH]

JOE W. TROTTER

United States, 1877–1920

Over the past three decades, scholars of American history have emphasized neglected dimensions of the American experience. Workers, immigrants, African Americans, and women have gained increasing attention. As emphasis on ordinary people and everyday life gained increasing sway in the field, conventional economic, political, cultural, and intellectual history also underwent change and reinterpretation. These changes reflected not only the growing impact of new methodologies and theoretical perspectives within the discipline, but also the ferment of the civil rights, New Left, antiwar, and women's movements during the 1960s and early 1970s. By the mid-1970s, however, the end of the Vietnam War, the decline of urban industries, the fall of the New Deal social order, and the rapid spread of urban poverty all ushered in a new set of social forces that would challenge the new social history. Since much of the new social history emphasized the primacy of socioeconomic and demographic factors in shaping the American experience, by the late 1980s and early 1990s a new generation of historians pushed culture to the forefront of historical analysis and explanation. Building upon the theoretical insights of anthropologists, literary theorists, and philosophers, such studies broadened the intellectual terrain for the study of class, ethnicity, race, and particularly gender. The bibliography in this section highlights these transformations in historical scholarship on American society from the fall of Reconstruction to the end of World War I.

Between 1877 and 1920, America largely completed its transition from a predominantly agrarian nation to a predominantly urban industrial society. Urban growth, immigration, and the expansion of industrial capitalism proceeded apace. The nation faced the increasing decline of the agricultural sector, the rise of a progressive movement (to redress the most glaring abuses of industrialism), and the intensification of racism at home and abroad. It was during this period that America completed its geographical expansion from the Atlantic to the Pacific and took its place as a new empire with dominion over peoples of color in Hawaii, Puerto Rico, and Guam. Responding to the unequal social impact of industrialism, American-born white workers, immigrants, farmers, women, American Indians, African Americans, and Latino and Asian Americans all embarked upon a series of sociopolitical and economic activities designed to counteract the impact of class, gender, ethnic, and racial discrimination on their lives. Understandably, then, the impact of and response to industrialism has been a major theme in historical research.

The first influential generation of historical scholarship on the subject emerged during the early twentieth century. Drawing upon the critique of American society offered by the progressive reformers, these scholars emphasized the destructive impact of industrialism, the suffering of workers, and the greed of industrialists. In his study *The Robber Barons* (43.20), an outstanding example of this scholarship, Matthew Josephson concluded that: "The members of this new ruling class were generally, and quite aptly, called barons, kings, empire-builders, or even emperors. They were aggressive men, as were the first feudal barons; sometimes they were lawless; in important crises, nearly all of them tended to act without those established moral principles which fixed more or less the conduct of the common people of the community."

In the post–World War II years, scholars launched a growing offensive against the progressive paradigm. According to the new consensus perspective, the quest for material progress possessed all Americans. Evidence of postwar prosperity as well as the imperatives of Cold War, anticommunism, and the nation's growing claims as leader of the free world, all reinforced this viewpoint. In his influential study, *The Response to Industrialism, 1885–1914* (43.500), Samuel Hays concluded that the people of industrial America "sought to do much more than simply control corporations: they sought to cope with industrial change in all its ramifications." Thus, according to Hays, business leaders were symbols of change "rather than the essence of change itself." A decade later Robert Wiebe offered a sweeping synthesis of the period, *The Search for Order, 1877–1920* (43.16). Building upon insights first suggested by Hays, Wiebe stressed the transformation of the nation from a society of intimate face-to-face relations to one of bureaucratic structures, rules, and impersonal sanctions. In Wiebe's view, this was America's "initial experiment in bureaucratic order, an experiment that was still in progress as the nation passed through the First World War." Hays and Wiebe helped to establish the "organizational synthesis" in research on the period. Such scholarship gained its apogee in Alfred Chandler's *Visible Hand: The Managerial Revolution in American Business* (4.404). According to Chandler, "Because the large enterprise administered by salaried managers replaced the small traditional family firm as the primary instrument for managing production and distribution . . . it became the most powerful institution in the American economy and its managers the most influential group of economic decision makers."

Despite fascination with the organizational synthesis, a variety of developments exposed its weaknesses and established the foundations for new interpretations of the period. Under the growing impact of new social movements (particularly the civil rights and women's movements), increasing interest in history "from the bottom up," and the emergence of social history as a field, scholarship on workers, immigrants, women, and racial and ethnic groups proliferated. Led by such scholars as David Brody, David Montgomery, and the late Herbert Gutman, labor historians moved from a primary focus on labor unions to a fuller study of the working class. The new labor history carefully linked the workers' experiences at work to their experiences at home, in neighborhoods, and in the larger community. Leisure time as well as work time; agency as well as exploitation; and fraternal orders, social clubs, and churches as well as labor unions all gained increasing treatment. The new labor history not only transcended the organizational synthesis, but built upon and then supplanted the scholarship of earlier scholars such as John R. Commons and Selig Perlman, pioneers in the establishment of the Wisconsin school of labor history.

Closely intertwined with the development of American labor history, immigration history also underwent dramatic change. Like labor historians, immigration historians responded to blindspots in an earlier interpretive framework. In his epic study, *The Uprooted* (43.246), Oscar Handlin emphasized the disruption of Old World familial and cultural traditions, alienation from the values of mainstream modern America, and segregation within the urban environment. From the mid-1960s through the mid-

1980s, a new immigration historiography emerged. Largely the work of children and grandchildren of European immigrants, a plethora of studies documented the families, friends, and institutional networks that immigrants brought to America, and how these cultural "traditions" served them remarkably well in the new land. In his study of south Italian immigrants, immigration historian Rudolph Vecoli concluded that Handlin overstated the disorganizing effects of emigration and underestimated "the tenacity with which the south Italian peasants at least clung to their traditional social forms and values."

African American, urban, and women's historians also responded to deficiencies in earlier studies. In his seminal study *The Strange Career of Jim Crow* (40.155), historian C. Vann Woodward helped to frame scholarship on the question of race and race relations during the period. Emphasizing the proliferation of segregationist state laws during the late nineteenth and early twentieth centuries, C. Vann Woodward argued that the segregationist system was the product of changes following the fall of Reconstruction rather than an enduring artifact of slavery. But Woodward paid little attention to the role of blacks in shaping their own experience during this period, described by historian Rayford Logan as the "nadir" in African American history. By the mid-1960s, however, a variety of studies placed African Americans, elites, and then workers at the center of the story and helped to transform the debate over the nature, causes, and consequences of Jim Crow (A. Meier 43.301; N. I. Painter 43.305; H. N. Rabinowitz 43.306). From Gilbert Osofsky's study of African American life in Harlem (1963) through Earl Lewis's study of blacks in Norfolk, Virginia (1991), scholarship on black urban history also dramatically expanded, with increasing emphasis on the role of African Americans in shaping their own urban experience.

No less than African American, immigrant, and labor history, women's history was transformed during the 1960s and 1970s. Mary Beard's provocative study *Women as a Force in History* had anticipated emphases on women's influence as well as sexual subordination, but only during the feminist revival of the late 1960s and early 1970s did scholarship on women offer a careful balance between women's "oppression and women's power." Compared to earlier women's history, the new women's history focused on women from a variety of class, racial, and ethnic backgrounds; analyzed friendship, birth control, prostitution, housework, and other topics previously neglected as inconsequential; and, most important, emphasized gender as opposed to merely sexual differences between men and women. The new scholarship challenged the notion that differences between women and men were natural and "immutable." In her study of female social scientists during the Victorian era, for example, Rosalind Rosenberg documented the ways that women of the period rejected prevailing male definitions of "women's nature."

A preponderance of the new social history focused on the city and stimulated changes in the field of urban history. During the early 1960s, historian Eric Lampard urged historians to develop a systematic theoretical framework—one that would analyze the societal forces that helped to create the city itself, differentiate what was peculiar and what was not peculiar to the city, and broaden our understanding of social history by focusing on the urban community. Following Lampard's lead, historian Stephan Thernstrom adopted sophisticated quantitative techniques in his book *Poverty and Progress* (43.202), focused on the lives of the so-called inarticulate residents of Newburyport, and helped to transform prevailing understandings of industrial America as a land of opportunity for ordinary people. According to Thernstrom, few of Newburyport, men and their children "rose very far on the social scale; most of the upward occupational shifts they made left them manual workmen still, and their property mobility, though strikingly widespread, rarely involved the accumulation of anything approaching real wealth." Thernstrom's study stimulated the rapid outpouring of mobility studies. Yet, by the early 1970s, such studies pursued an increasingly narrow quantitative agenda and neglected traditional literary sources of various types, including newspapers, sermons, and manuscript collections. Critics increasingly urged the new urban historians to overcome such limitations by seeking ways to reconcile quantitative and qualitative sources in research on the urban experience.

American political and diplomatic history also underwent significant change during the 1960s and early 1970s. The new political historians (especially Richard Jensen and Paul Kleppner) emphasized the role of ethnicity, race, and religion in the political alignments of Americans. The consensus scholars had smoothed over such cleavages in their efforts to combat the earlier progressive emphasis on class and sectional interests. At the same time, historians revamped our understanding of such political and social movements as populism and progressivism. Whereas Richard Hofstader, in *Age of Reform* (43.555), treated the populists as preoccupied with a mythic "golden age," Lawrence Goodwyn established the outlines of a new paradigm in *The Populist Moment*. Emphasizing the development of what he called a "movement culture" among the farmers, Goodwyn treated their ideas and activities as serious challenges to growing corporate control of the political economy. The concept of progressivism also underwent substantial change. Scholars pinpointed its ambiguous legacy; that is, strenuous efforts to meliorate destructive industrial conditions on the one hand, yet advocacy of immigration restriction and racial disfranchisement of African Americans on the other.

Events of the 1960s and 1970s undermined and then transformed the field of diplomatic history. During the 1950s scholars of American foreign relations, like others of the consensus school, accepted the notion that "national" rather than class or special interests dictated American foreign policy. Such views were counteracted most pointedly in the work of William Appleman Williams, who revived and then revised the progressive emphasis on economic and class determinants of American foreign policy. In his book, *The Tragedy of American Diplomacy* (43.596), Williams crystallized the thesis that "empire" was "as American as apple pie"; that is, that American foreign policy reflected the expansive interests of capitalist elites. Under the growing impact of the new social history, however, American diplomatic history declined as a vigorous field of scholarship, and only gradually did it reflect greater sensitivity to the impact of ethnoracial as well as class factors in shaping American foreign policy.

During the 1980s, historians of the United States turned increasingly toward cultural history. Studies of vaudeville, the blues, film, the dime novel, popular sports, and what some scholars have called "the spread of a therapeutic mentality in liberal religion" all received increasing attention. While intellectual historians had studied so-called high culture for decades, this era ushered in a florescence of interest in popular culture. Indeed, during the 1980s, cultural historians broadened their definition of culture to encompass much of what was heretofore described as "social" or "intellectual" history. By the early 1990s numerous scholars turned to cultural history as a way to arrest the increasing fragmentation that the emergence of social history had unleashed. Cultural historians Richard Wightman Fox and T. J. Jackson Lears advanced perhaps the most extreme statement of this tendency: "At a time of deep intellectual disarray, culture offers a provisional, nominalist version of coherence: whatever the fragmentation of knowledge, however centrifugal the spinning of the scholarly wheel, culture—which (even etymologically) conveys a sense of safe nurture, warm growth, budding or ever-present wholeness—will shelter us."

As scholars revitalized cultural history, intellectual historians deemphasized their growing connections to social history. In gravitating toward social history during the 1970s, these scholars had adopted the notion that ideas were socially determined, particularly by class and the place of thinkers in the mode of production or political economy. During the 1980s such scholars increasingly returned to the notion that ideas could be studied "in themselves," but they did not return to the old pattern of privileging the so-called "great ideas" and tracing them over time. Instead, they gravitated toward cultural anthropology, literary theory, and semiotics. These scholars now emphasized the process by which ideas were produced, transmitted, and received. The new intellectual history gained perhaps its strongest and most receptive audience among feminist scholars, who appreciated its challenge to positivist claims of objectivity and emphasized the contingent character of social categories (such as class, race, and especially gender) that once seemed immutable.

A variety of other fields also reflected the growing emphasis on sociocultural forces. The history of medicine moved from its earlier professional, institutional, and clinical emphases on the biological determinants of disease toward the various "social constructions" of disease. As medical historian Allan M. Brandt puts it, "Fundamental to the notion that disease is socially constructed is the premise that it is profoundly shaped by both biological and cultural variables." Historians of technology have also gravitated toward a focus on the "social construction" of technological innovations. These writers reject emphasis on individual inventors as the focal point of new technologies, decry technological determinism, and stress a broad range of socioeconomic, political, and cultural factors in the development of technology. Although Alfred Chandler's scholarship on the corporation has proven remarkably durable, for example, his approach is now coming under increasing scrutiny and challenge from a younger generation of scholars. Philip Scranton, one of his staunchest critics, emphasizes the shortcomings of Chandler's "internal history" of the large corporation and "the organizational forms that facilitated the managerial revolution." Scranton highlights the persistence of firms using "batch" as opposed to "bulk" production processes and suggests that the period was characterized by "complex organizational contingencies." More specifically, Scranton decries the "calculating engine model of the individual and the firm" and advocates an "open-minded inquiry" that admits the "multiple constructions of rationality."

As we approach the mid-1990s, the field of U.S. history from 1877 to 1920 is still in ferment. It seems likely that cultural history will continue to enrich our understanding, but its limitations are already on the horizon. Some cultural historians are turning away from questions of power, politics, and public life in pursuit of "webs of discourse," which are treated as if they have a life of their own. Thus, we may expect that historians will continue to wrestle with the problems of text and context, structure and agency, and power and powerlessness. The ways that we grapple with these problems will also continue to reflect not only scholarly innovations in theory and method, but ongoing socioeconomic and political transformations in our own lives as we approach the twenty-first century.

Entries are arranged under the following headings:

General Studies

Economic History
  General Studies and Historiography
  Management and Organization
  Single-Industry Studies
  Government-Business Relations
  Agriculture
  Biographies

Science, Technology, and Medicine

Labor
  General Studies
  Unions and Labor Conditions
  Management-Labor Conflict and Strikes
  Ethnic and Race Relations
  Gender
  Community Studies and Politics

Urban History
  General Studies
  Urban Development and Planning
  Social Conditions, Race, and Ethnicity
  Politics and Reform
  Suburbia

Immigration

Racial and Ethnic Minorities
  General Studies
  African Americans
  American Indians
  Asian Americans
  Latino Americans

Women
  Family and Work Force
  Feminism and Suffrage
  Biographies

Cultural History
  Visual Arts, Architecture, and Music
  Literature and Print Media
  Popular Culture
  Religion and Culture

Intellectual History

Political History
  General Studies
  Presidential and Congressional Studies
  State and Local Politics
  Political Parties
  Political Movements and Ideas
  Electoral Systems and Voting

Foreign Relations
  General Studies
  Europe and Canada
  South America and the Caribbean
  Asia and the Pacific
  Imperialism and Expansion
  World War I

[Contributors: CAM = Clyde A. Milner II, DEC = Donald E. Collins, DRJ = David R. Jardini, DUH = Daniel U. Holbrook, EDL = Eugene D. Levy, EHM = Eric H. Monkkonen, EL = Earl Lewis, JB = Jon Butler, JHH = John H. Hinshaw, JWT = Joe W. Trotter, KB = Kinley Brauer, LCP = Lewis C. Perry, LEC = Lori E. Cole, NF = Nora Faires, PAC = Patricia A. Cooper, TAM = Teresa A. Murphy, TJMcD = Terrence J. McDonald]

GENERAL STUDIES

43.1 Richard M. Abrams. *The burdens of progress, 1900–1929.* Glenview, Ill.: Scott, Foresman, 1978. ISBN 0-673-05778-X.
▸ Argues that optimistic attitudes toward industrialization overshadowed its costs. Looks at how industrialization undermined traditions. [JWT]

43.2 Edward Ayers. *The promise of the new South: life after Reconstruction.* New York: Oxford University Press, 1992. ISBN 0-19-503756-1. ▸ Detailed social history synthesis of southern life through late nineteenth century. Useful complement to Woodward 43.506. [JWT]

43.3 John Whiteclay Chambers II. *The tyranny of change: America in the Progressive Era, 1900–1917.* 2d ed. New York: St. Martin's, 1992. ISBN 0-312-03634-5 (pbk). ▸ Synthetic examination of era from political-economic perspective, integrating social, cultural, and women's history. [LEC]

43.4 Thomas C. Cochran and William Miller. *The age of enterprise: a social history of industrial America.* Rev. ed. New York: Harper, 1961. ▸ Analysis of impact of industrialism on society, 1800–1929. Stresses role of businessmen and positive results of growing union of business and government. [LEC]

43.5 John Milton Cooper, Jr. *The pivotal decades: the United States, 1900–1920.* New York: Norton, 1990. ISBN 0-393-02806-2 (cl), 0-393-95655-5 (pbk). ▸ Treatment arguing period 1900–20 set fundamental socioeconomic, political, and cultural agenda that dominated American life through late twentieth century. [JWT]

43.6 Carl N. Degler, ed. *The age of the economic revolution, 1876–1900.* 2d ed. Glenview, Ill.: Scott, Foresman, 1977. ISBN 0-673-07967-8. ▸ Study stressing transformation of American society from predominantly agricultural to industrial foundation. Maintains process shaped social, intellectual, and political life of nation. [JWT]

43.7 Arthur A. Ekrich, Jr. *Progressivism in America: a study of the era from Theodore Roosevelt to Woodrow Wilson.* New York: New Viewpoints, 1974. ISBN 0-531-05359-8 (cl), 0-531-05564-7 (pbk). ▸ Comparison of progressive goals with other reform movements in America and Europe. Concludes social movement developed unique evangelical and religious characteristics. [JWT]

43.8 John A. Garraty. *The new commonwealth, 1877–1890.* New York: Harper & Row, 1968. ▸ Study concluding central character of American civilization underwent fundamental shift from preoccupation with principles of individualism and laissez faire to emphasis on collectivity and reliance on group activity. [JWT]

43.9 Ray Ginger. *Age of excess: the United States from 1877 to 1914.* 2d ed. New York: Macmillan, 1975. ISBN 0-02-343700-6. ▸ Study organized around tremendous expansion of American productive capacity and potential for improved standard of living. Emphasizes high social and cultural costs of material progress. [JWT]

43.10 Samuel P. Hays. *The response to industrialism, 1885–1914.* 1957 ed. Chicago: University of Chicago Press, 1961. ISBN 0-226-32162-2 (pbk). ▸ Synthetic study of economic, social, and political changes; counters interpretations of progressivism as revolt of dispossessed. Topical discussions of effects on various groups. [LEC]

43.11 Howard Mumford Jones. *The age of energy: varieties of American experience, 1865–1915.* New York: Viking, 1971. ISBN 0-670-10966-5. ▸ Argues existing syntheses fail to illuminate period as a whole. Supports social "discovery and expression of energy" as alternative framework. [JWT]

43.12 Gabriel Kolko. *The triumph of conservatism: a reinterpretation of American history, 1900–1916.* 1963 ed. New York: Free Press, 1977. ISBN 0-02-916650-0 (pbk). ▸ Argues that by 1916 United States was closed rather than "progressive" society, locked into pattern of big, bureaucratic welfare state that would expand thereafter. [JWT]

43.13 Nell Irvin Painter. *Standing at armageddon: United States, 1877–1919.* 1987 ed. New York: Norton, 1989. ISBN 0-393-02405-9 (cl, 1987), 0-393-30588-0 (pbk). ‣ Exploration of Gilded Age and Progressive Era as formative periods of modern industrialism. Narrative political-labor synthesis emphasizing labor issues. [LEC]

43.14 Frederick Jackson Turner. *The significance of the frontier in American history.* 1963 ed. Harold P. Simonson, ed. New York: Continuum, 1990. ISBN 0-8044-6919-9 (pbk). ‣ Controversial, exceptionalist essay arguing that American character created from successive reenactments of contact/conflict between civilized and primitive urges on ever-shifting frontier, which determined economic, social, and political evolution of United States. Originally published in 1892. [LEC]

43.15 Walter Prescott Webb. *The Great Plains.* 1931 ed. Lincoln: University of Nebraska Press, 1981. ISBN 0-8032-9702-5 (pbk). ‣ Landmark study building on Turner's frontier thesis (43.14). Exceptionalist approach contrasting Indian versus Spanish versus American dominion; latter's successes predicated on technological/industrial advances—handguns, barbed wire, and railroads. [LEC]

43.16 Robert H. Wiebe. *The search for order, 1877–1920.* 1967 ed. Westport, Conn.: Greenwood, 1980. ISBN 0-313-22647-4. ‣ Pathbreaking reinterpretation of Progressive Era in terms of bureaucratization and professionalization, emphasizing decline of life in series of local communities. [TJMcD]

ECONOMIC HISTORY

General Studies and Historiography

43.17 Mansel Blackford. "Small business in America: a historiographical survey." *Business history review* 65 (1991) 1–26. ISSN 0007-6805. ‣ Briefly traces economic, social, and cultural role of smaller enterprises in American history. Outlines work in this area by historians, economists, political scientists, and management specialists; describes research needs. Strong bibliography. [DUH]

43.18 Hal Bridges. "The robber barons concept in American history." *Business history review* 32.1 (1958) 1–13. ISSN 0007-6805. ‣ Traces historiographical development of robber baron idea from post–Civil War era. Consensus school view of late nineteenth-century businessmen; lauds creative and moral aspects of this group, argues that idea will fall into disuse. [DUH]

43.19 Robert Higgs. *The transformation of the American economy, 1865–1914: an essay in interpretation.* New York: Wiley, 1971. ISBN 0-471-39003-8. ‣ Analysis of how informational, physical, and human capital helped bring United States economy into era of industrial capitalism. Centered on social impact of post-1865 conversion. [DEC]

43.20 Matthew Josephson. *The robber barons: the great American capitalists, 1861–1901.* 1934 ed. Norwalk, Conn.: Easton, 1987. ‣ Prosopography of prominent nineteenth-century financiers and industrialists unfavorable. Lively, well-written, but driven by presentism. Seeks origins of Great Depression in legacy of this group. [DUH]

43.21 Edward C. Kirkland. *Industry comes of age: business, labor, and public policy, 1860–1897.* 1961 ed. Chicago: Quadrangle, 1967. (Economic history of the United States, 6.) ‣ Broad survey of United States industrialization that focuses on formation of structures and institutions. Conveys generally positive appreciation of nature and ramifications of this process. [DRJ]

43.22 Glenn Porter. *The rise of big business, 1860–1910.* New York: Crowell, 1973. ISBN 0-690-70394-5. ‣ Chandlerian study (see 42.152) of underlying institutional changes that made possible rise of American big business. Focuses on changes in mar-

kets, transportation and communication, production processes, legal environment, and finance. [DRJ]

43.23 Marc A. Weiss. "Real estate history." *Business history review* 63.2 (1989) 241–82. ISSN 0007-6805. ‣ Historiographic essay that pushes field away from anecdotal, personal, and company histories toward more systematic, structural analyses of how industry's organization and management evolved in response to market forces. [DRJ]

Management and Organization

43.24 Alfred D. Chandler, Jr. *Scale and scope: the dynamics of industrial capitalism.* Cambridge, Mass.: Harvard University Press, 1990. ISBN 0-674-78994-6. ‣ Traces origins and growth of "managerial capitalism" in United States, Britain, and Germany. Concludes that industrial activities drove transformation of commercial economies into "modern" industrial economies. [JWT]

43.25 Rendigs Fels. *American business cycles, 1865–1897.* 1959 ed. Westport, Conn.: Greenwood, 1973. ISBN 0-8371-6863-5. ‣ Historical approach to explaining cyclical regularities in economic activity. Synthesizes Schumpeter, Hicks, and Gordon wave theories. Examines fit of historical events to resulting theoretical predictions. [DEC]

43.26 Louis Galambos. "The emerging organizational synthesis in modern American history." *Business history review* 44 (1970) 279–90. ISSN 0007-6805. ‣ Argues that business and economic historiographies represented solid blending of examples of bureaucratization in post-1865 United States history, as well as diverse subfields in profession. [DEC]

43.27 Samuel Haber. *Efficiency and uplift: scientific management in the Progressive Era, 1890–1920.* 1964 ed. Chicago: University of Chicago Press, 1973. ISBN 0-226-31172-4. ‣ Reform movement based on extension of Frederick Taylor's ideals from industrial into social, cultural, and political spheres. Important book on subject and era. [DUH]

43.28 John N. Ingham. *Making iron and steel: independent mills in Pittsburgh, 1820–1920.* Columbus: Ohio State University Press, 1991. ISBN 0-8142-0542-9. ‣ Challenges Chandlerian model of increasing scale and scope (see 42.152) in American business by demonstrating survival of small, specialized wrought iron producers in niche markets well into era of mass-produced steel. [DRJ]

43.29 Michael J. Piore and Charles F. Sabel. *The second industrial divide: possibilities for prosperity.* New York: Basic Books, 1984. ISBN 0-465-07562-2 (cl), 0-465-07563-0 (pbk). ‣ Argues that recent deterioration in economic performance of United States is associated with breakdown of mass-production paradigm and ascendency of "flexibly specialized" model of production based on craft production and new regulatory mechanisms. [DRJ]

43.30 Daniel Pope. *The making of modern advertising.* New York: Basic Books, 1983. ISBN 0-465-04325-9. ‣ Account of advertising as aspect of business history. Argues modern advertising emerged between 1890 and 1920 as response to mass production and national markets. [EDL]

43.31 Charles F. Sabel and Jonathan Zeitlin. "Historical alternatives to mass production." *Past and present* 108 (1985) 133–76. ISSN 0031-2746. ‣ Argues that historic prevalence of mass production during twentieth century was result of social choice from among alternative forms of production, rather than inevitable outcome of superior efficiency. [DRJ]

43.32 Philip Scranton. "Diversity in diversity: flexible production and American industrialization, 1890–1930." *Business history review* 65 (1991) 27–90. ISSN 0007-6805. ‣ Uses case studies to argue that United States economy has been characterized by bulk-and-batch producers, which correspond roughly to mass-production and flexibly-specialized models and represent contrasting management and production environments. [DRJ]

43.33 Philip Scranton. *Figured tapestry: production, markets, and power in Philadelphia textiles, 1885–1941.* Cambridge: Cambridge University Press, 1989. ISBN 0-521-34287-2. ‣ Argument for flexibly-specialized model of production in which firms combined skilled labor, versatile production methods, and rapid responsiveness to demand changes to produce highly diversified range of seasonal goods. [DRJ]

SEE ALSO
4.404 Alfred D. Chandler, Jr. *The visible hand.*
4.406 Siegfried Giedion. *Mechanization takes command.*
44.177 Alfred D. Chandler, Jr. *Strategy and structure.*

Single-Industry Studies

43.34 Lee Benson. *Merchants, farmers, and railroads: railroad regulation and New York politics, 1850–1887.* 1955 ed. New York: Russell & Russell, 1969. ‣ Economic and political history emphasizing paradox between government's attempt to control laissez faire in transportation after 1865 and its attempt to protect private enterprise. Free competition enabled protection of private businesses. [DEC]

43.35 Alfred D. Chandler, Jr., ed. and comp. *The railroads: the nation's first big business; sources and readings.* 1965 ed. New York: Arno, 1981. ISBN 0-405-13768-0. ‣ Documentary record of industry from 1830s through 1890s. Materials include railroad effects on economic development, origins of modern corporate finance and management, evolution of labor relations, and forms of competition and regulation. [DRJ]

43.36 J. Russell Doubman and John R. Whitaker. *The organization and operation of department stores.* New York: Wiley, 1927. ‣ Description of how large retail businesses were constructed and organized, how they purchased, sold, and delivered merchandise, as well as how they developed plans and competed with other chains. [DEC]

43.37 Thomas P. Hughes. *Networks of power: electrification in Western society, 1880–1930.* Baltimore: Johns Hopkins University Press, 1983. ISBN 0-8018-2873-2. ‣ Traces development of electrical power industry in United States, Germany, and England. Focuses on technology as systems which include social, political, and technological aspects. Influential development of theory of technological advance. [DUH]

43.38 Reese Jenkins. *Images and enterprise: technology and the American photographic industry, 1839 to 1925.* Baltimore: Johns Hopkins University Press, 1975. ISBN 0-8018-1588-6. ‣ Institutional economic history. Responses to and impact of innovation on market structure and price behavior. Argues that mind set of participants changed by innovation; industrial structure and practices also changed. [DUH]

43.39 Amos J. Loveday, Jr. *The rise and decline of the American cut nail industry: a study of the relationships of technology, business organization, and management techniques.* Westport, Conn.: Greenwood, 1983. ISBN 0-313-23918-5. ‣ History of cut-nail industry from its replacement of wrought-nail production in late eighteenth century to its eclipsing by wire-nail manufacture in late nineteenth century. Chandlerian analysis (see 42.152) focused on four firms in Wheeling, West Virginia. [DRJ]

43.40 Ann Markusen et al. *The rise of the gunbelt: the military remapping of industrial America.* New York: Oxford University Press, 1991. ISBN 0-19-506648-0. ‣ Argues that defense contracting created new economic map of United States. Defines five models of "military-industrial cities" and explores case studies of each. [DRJ]

43.41 Broadus Mitchell and George Sinclair Mitchell. *The industrial revolution in the South.* 1930 ed. New York: Greenwood, 1968. ‣ Compilation of over twenty articles written about development of textile manufactures below Mason-Dixon line in post–Civil War period. [DEC]

43.42 Harold C. Passer. *The electrical manufacturers, 1875–1900: a study in competition, entrepreneurship, technical change, and economic growth.* 1953 ed. New York: Arno, 1972. ISBN 0-405-04717-7. ‣ Analysis of manufacturing of electrical equipment for lighting and power. Good example of popularity and use of linear models of technological change during 1950s. [JWT]

43.43 Bernard Smith. "Market development: the case of the American corset trade, 1860–1920." *Business history review* 65 (1991) 91–129. ISSN 0007-6805. ‣ Conceptual bridge between Chandlerian big business and flexibly-specialized models of industrial development (see 42.152). Focuses on range of hybrid integrated firms that supplied specialized mass markets. [DRJ]

43.44 George David Smith. *The anatomy of a business strategy: Bell, Western Electric, and the origins of the American telephone industry.* Baltimore: Johns Hopkins University Press, 1985. ISBN 0-8018-2710-8. ‣ Chandlerian analysis (see 42.152) of Bell Telephone Company's acquisition of Western Electric Company as move to vertical integration in context of firm's external and internal environment. Traces development of integration process and practices. [DUH]

43.45 Merritt Roe Smith. *Harpers Ferry Armory and the new technology: the challenge of change.* Ithaca, N.Y.: Cornell University Press, 1977. ISBN 0-8014-0984-5. ‣ Concentrates on consequences for workers of adoption of mechanized production and interchangeable parts, and ways in which workers resisted new industrial regimen. [DRJ]

43.46 James Playsted Wood. *The story of advertising.* New York: Ronald, 1958. ‣ Well written, with broad chronological coverage of England and America. Mixes specific cases with general development of related business organizations. Less emphasis on radio and television eras. [DUH]

SEE ALSO
4.533 Robert W. Garnet. *The telephone enterprise.*

Government-Business Relations

43.47 Ari Hoogenboom and Olive Hoogenboom. *A history of the ICC: from panacea to palliative.* New York: Norton, 1976. ISBN 0-393-05565-5 (cl), 0-393-09204-6 (pbk). ‣ History of oldest of federal regulatory agencies from 1880s through 1973. Argues that this history has been one of failure to adequately address social needs in analysis, planning, and regulation. [DRJ]

43.48 Morton Keller. *Regulating a new economy: public policy and economic change in America, 1900–1933.* Cambridge, Mass.: Harvard University Press, 1990. ISBN 0-674-75362-3. ‣ Detailed survey of wide variety of regulatory activities and controversy over them; moves "affairs of state" into twentieth century. [TJMcD]

43.49 Gabriel Kolko. *Railroads and regulation, 1877–1916.* 1965 ed. Westport, Conn.: Greenwood, 1976. ISBN 0-8371-8885-7. ‣ Argues that interests of railroad industry wanted government intervention in interstate commerce and competition by end of nineteenth century. Big businesses hoped for subsequent demise of smaller companies. [DEC]

43.50 James Livingston. *Origins of the Federal Reserve System: money, class, and corporate capitalism, 1890–1913.* 1986 ed. Ithaca, N.Y.: Cornell University Press, 1989. ISBN 0-8014-1844-5 (cl), 0-8014-9703-5 (pbk). ‣ Class-based social history that argues Federal Reserve was expression of emerging capitalist ruling class and was both symptom and attempted cure for decline of competitive entrepreneurial capitalism. [DRJ]

43.51 Irwin Unger. *The greenback era: a social and political history of American finance, 1865–1879.* Princeton: Princeton University Press, 1964. ▸ Detailed study of currency issue. Concludes that debates over paper money set terms of social and political conflicts through late nineteenth century. [JWT]

43.52 Steven Usselman. "Patents purloined: railroads, inventors, and the diffusion of innovation in nineteenth-century America." *Technology and culture* 32.4 (1991) 1047–75. ISSN 0040-165x. ▸ Discussion of railroads' use of patent pools to avoid costly and technologically retarding patent suits. Concludes standard technology more important than novelty; railroad competition not technology driven. Patent system used differently by different industries. [DUH]

Agriculture

43.53 Thomas D. Isern. *Bull threshers and bindlestiffs: harvesting and threshing on the North American plains.* Lawrence: University Press of Kansas, 1990. ISBN 0-7006-0468-5. ▸ Study of individuals, not groups, 1870s to 1940s, Texas panhandle to Canadian prairies. Sees farmers as technological innovators. [CAM]

43.54 Arthur F. McEvoy. *The fisherman's problem: ecology and law in the California fisheries, 1850–1980.* Cambridge: Cambridge University Press, 1986. ISBN 0-521-32427-0 (cl), 0-521-38586-5 (pbk). ▸ Study of decline of California fisheries. Familiar but insightful tale of American Indians living in ecological harmony giving way to devastation of fisheries by unregulated private exploitation. Well-crafted arguments. [CAM]

43.55 Brian Page and Richard Walker. "From settlement to Fordism: the agro-industrial revolution in the American Midwest." *Economic geography* 67.4 (1991) 281–315. ISSN 0013-0095. ▸ Regional study emphasizing parallel development of agriculture and industry, self-contained nature of regional development, mutual reinforcement of various social activities, and distinctiveness from northeastern patterns. [DRJ]

43.56 Donald J. Pisani. *From the family farm to agribusiness: the irrigation crusade in California and the West, 1850–1931.* Berkeley: University of California Press, 1984. ISBN 0-520-05127-0. ▸ Dense analysis of water policy and its effects on agricultural society. Climate and geography helped shape institutions. Though mismanaged, irrigation was all-important to social and economic reforms of land and culture. Links California's experiences to West. [CAM]

43.57 Theodore Saloutos. "The immigrant contribution to American agriculture." *Agricultural history* 50 (1976) 45–67. ISSN 0002-1482. ▸ Early overview of patterns and regions of rural immigrant settlement. Particular attention to accomplishments and innovations in technology and crops. [LEC]

Biographies

43.58 Frederick Lewis Allen. *The great Pierpont Morgan.* 1949 ed. New York: Harper & Row, 1965. ▸ Biography of "robber baron." Shows that this banker typified American ideal of individualism and helped to transform nature of American economy. [DEC]

43.59 Robert V. Bruce. *Alexander Graham Bell and the conquest of solitude.* 1973 ed. Ithaca, N.Y.: Cornell University Press, 1990. ISBN 0-8014-9691-8. ▸ Well-documented account of telephone and its inventor before, during, and after invention. Technology well explained; human and social aspects covered. [DUH]

43.60 Julius Grodinsky. *Jay Gould: his business career, 1867–1892.* 1957 ed. New York: Arno, 1981. ISBN 0-405-13785-0. ▸ Comprehensive coverage of financier's dealings; detailed and well documented. Combines understanding of financial and personal forces. [DUH]

43.61 David Freeman Hawke. *John D.: the founding father of the Rockefellers.* New York: Harper & Row, 1980. ISBN 0-06-011813-x. ▸ Examines life and career of oil industry "baron." Argues that he not only wanted to make money, but also wanted glory for his business and his Christianity. [DEC]

43.62 Harold C. Livesay. *Andrew Carnegie and the rise of big business.* Oscar Handlin, ed. Boston: Little, Brown, 1975. ISBN 0-673-39344-5 (cl), 0-316-52870-6 (pbk). ▸ Sympathetic view: steel magnate as exemplar of American dream, moving force in development of American industrial and economic organization and management. Good overview of steel industry and contemporary business practices. [DUH]

43.63 Allan Nevins. *Study in power: John D. Rockefeller, industrialist and philanthropist.* 2 vols. New York: Scribner's, 1953. ▸ Favorable account of leading petroleum industrialist of late nineteenth and early twentieth centuries. Depicted as having engaged in many questionable activities with good motives and with generally positive outcomes. [DRJ]

43.64 Walter T. K. Nugent. *Money and American society, 1865–1880.* New York: Free Press, 1968. ▸ Analyzes socio-intellectual and international contexts in which post–Civil War currency policy was implemented in United States. Considers currency policy key to understanding society. [DEC]

43.65 Keith Sward. *The legend of Henry Ford.* 1948 ed. William Greenleaf, Preface. New York: Russell & Russell, 1968. ▸ Clinical psychologist and Congress of Industrial Organizations publicist tries to get beyond popular perception of subject. Thoughtful, perceptive and scholarly; incorporates economics and culture. [DUH]

43.66 Joseph Frazier Wall. *Andrew Carnegie.* 1970 ed. Pittsburgh: University of Pittsburgh Press, 1989. ISBN 0-8229-3828-6 (cl), 0-8229-5904-6 (pbk). ▸ Biography of nineteenth-century steel magnate; focuses on business experiences in steel, oil, railroads, bridge-building, telegraphy, and steel industries. Illustrates development of American competitive capitalism and its moral contradictions. [DRJ]

SCIENCE, TECHNOLOGY, AND MEDICINE

43.67 Garland E. Allen. "The transformation of a science: T. H. Morgan and the emergence of a new American biology." In *The organization of knowledge in modern America, 1860–1920.* Alexandra Oleson and John Voss, eds., pp. 173–210. Baltimore: Johns Hopkins University Press, 1979. ISBN 0-8018-2108-8. ▸ Late nineteenth-century naturalist-experimentalist dichotomy resolved in favor of experimentation and exact, quantitative data. Spread of approach by Morgan's students. Origins of modern biochemistry and molecular genetics. [DUH]

43.68 Wiebe Hughes Bjiker, Thomas P. Hughes, and Trevor Pinch, eds. *The social construction of technological systems: new directions in the sociology and history of technology.* Cambridge, Mass.: MIT Press, 1987. ISBN 0-262-02262-1. ▸ Foundational volume of sociology of technology, with essays by sociologists and historians; rich theoretical ground. Technologies' development incorporates social, political, and economic elements. [DUH]

43.69 James G. Burrow. *Organized medicine in the Progressive Era: the move towards monopoly.* Baltimore: Johns Hopkins University Press, 1977. ISBN 0-8018-1918-0. ▸ Examination of professionalization and politicization of doctors in American Medical Association in late nineteenth century, as well as their influence in government policy. [DEC]

43.70 Edward W. Constant II. *The origins of the turbojet revolution.* Baltimore: Johns Hopkins University Press, 1980. ISBN 0-8018-2222-x. ▸ Influential history of development of jet engine. Applies Kuhnian paradigm theory (cf. 1.516) to technological systems; also evolutionary epistemological approach to development of technologies. Focus on communities of practitioners as locus of change. [DUH]

43.71 Carolyn Cooper. "Social construction of inventions and patent management: Thomas Blanchard's woodworking machinery." *Technology and culture* 32.4 (1991) 960–98. ISSN 0040-165X. ▸ Argues that both specific nature of invention and rules by which people define "newness" are socially shaped since decision rules that define originality are formed gradually through social processes. [DRJ]

43.72 Daniel Fox. "The new historiography of American medical education." *History of education quarterly* 26 (1986) 117–26. ISSN 0018-2680. ▸ Examines recent emphasis on three themes in literature: reform, influence of health care school faculty, and subsequent growth of professionalization and hospitals since late 1800s. [DEC]

43.73 Peter Galison and Bruce Hevly, eds. *Big science: the growth of large-scale research*. Stanford, Calif.: Stanford University Press, 1992. ISBN 0-8047-1879-2. ▸ Collection of essays that seeks to understand how expansion in scale of scientific endeavor has forced scientists to confront world outside of their disciplines. Sections on big physics, sponsored research, and national security. [DRJ]

43.74 Gerald N. Grob. "The social history of medicine and disease in America: problems and possibilities." *Journal of social history* 10 (1972) 393. ISSN 0022-4529. ▸ Historiographical critique. Argues for quantitative study of health-care history "from the bottom up." [DEC]

43.75 David Hull. *Science as a process: an evolutionary account of the social and conceptual development of science*. Chicago: University of Chicago Press, 1988. ISBN 0-226-36050-4. ▸ Study of social structure of scientific communities. Evolutionary view of growth of scientific knowledge. Argues that tension between cooperation and competition drives scientific growth. [DUH]

43.76 Edwin Layton, Jr. *Revolt of the engineers: social responsibility and the American engineering profession*. 1971 ed. Baltimore: Johns Hopkins University Press, 1986. ISBN 0-8018-3286-1 (cl), 0-8018-3287-X (pbk). ▸ Excellent history of engineering professionalism, 1870s to 1940s. Examines internal debates over discipline's social responsibility, codes of ethics, issues of divided loyalties to employers, and discipline. Groundbreaking effort. [DUH]

43.77 Stuart W. Leslie. *The cold war and American science: the military-industrial-academic complex at MIT and Stanford*. New York: Columbia University Press, 1993. ISBN 0-231-07958-3. ▸ Uses case studies of M.I.T. and Stanford to argue that "golden triangle" of military, industry, and research universities created new kind of postwar science that blurred older scientific norms and owed its character to national-security state. [DRJ]

43.78 Carolyn Marvin. *When old technologies were new: thinking about electric communication in the late nineteenth century*. New York: Oxford University Press, 1988. ISBN 0-19-504468-1. ▸ Examines telephone and electric light and their effects on social relations. Shows various social groups' tactics for dealing with these innovations, study based on popular press. Important addition to history of nineteenth-century technology. [DUH]

43.79 Raymond H. Merritt. *Engineering in American society, 1850–1875*. Lexington: University Press of Kentucky, 1969. ISBN 0-8131-1189-7. ▸ Social history of engineering as a profession. Emphasizes role of engineers in technological development, growth of engineering education, emergence of scientific management, and evolution of public policy making. [DRJ]

43.80 David F. Noble. *Forces of production: a social history of industrial automation*. New York: Knopf; distributed by Random

House, 1984. ISBN 0-394-51262-6. ▸ Study of alternative machine-tool control systems. Argues that military and corporate ideology of workplace control promoted adoption of numerical control system. Leftist view of military-industrial-academic complex. [DUH]

43.81 David E. Nye. *Electrifying America: social meanings of a new technology, 1880–1949*. Cambridge, Mass.: MIT Press, 1990. ISBN 0-262-14048-9. ▸ Uses Muncie, Indiana, as case study to explore ways in which electricity functioned as "enabling technology" that affected urban forms, production technologies, arts, home life, and expectations of the future. [DRJ]

43.82 Leonard S. Reich. *The making of American industrial research: science and business at GE and Bell, 1876–1926*. New York: Cambridge University Press, 1985. ISBN 0-521-30529-2. ▸ Explores why GE and Bell began to pursue science-based research and brought to United States a type of research institution pioneered in German chemical and pharmaceutical industry decades before. [DRJ]

43.83 Charles E. Rosenberg. "Inward vision and outward balance: the shaping of the American hospital, 1880–1914." *Bulletin of the history of medicine* 53 (1979) 346–91. ISSN 0007-5140. ▸ Argues physicians' long-term outlook on professionalization and culture of social engineering led to rapid expansion of institutions in late 1800s and early twentieth century. [DEC]

43.84 Nathan Rosenberg. *Perspectives on technology*. 1976 ed. Armond, N.Y.: Sharpe, 1985. ISBN 0-87332-303-3 (pbk). ▸ Collection of essays exploring role played by technological change and diffusion in stimulating and shaping long-term economic growth. Challenges capacity of neo-classical economics to fully comprehend these phenomena. [DRJ]

43.85 David Rosner. *A once charitable enterprise: hospitals and health care in Brooklyn and New York, 1885–1915*. Cambridge: Cambridge University Press, 1982. ISBN 0-521-24217-7. ▸ Study of how larger societal changes, such as immigration, Progressive Era reforms, increasing urbanization, and political realignments affected turn-of-the-century hospitals and helped professionalize them. [DEC]

43.86 Michael L. Smith. *Pacific visions: California scientists and the environment, 1850–1915*. New Haven: Yale University Press, 1987. ISBN 0-300-03264-1. ▸ Reinterpretation of well-known California scientific controversies in late 1800s. Explains regional western science as interaction of nature, society, and intellectual life. Insightful comparisons of leading actors. [CAM]

43.87 John Staudenmaier. *Technology's storytellers: reweaving the human fabric*. Cambridge, Mass.: Society for the History of Technology and MIT Press, 1985. ISBN 0-262-19237-3. ▸ Intellectual biography of evolving discipline of history of technology. Analysis of all articles published in *Technology and Culture*; outlines themes and subthemes and shifting emphases in discipline. [DUH]

43.88 Rosemary Stevens. "Sweet charity: state aid to hospitals in Pennsylvania." *Bulletin of the history of medicine* 58 (1984) 287–314, 374–495. ISSN 0007-5140. ▸ Finds that legislature in Harrisburg, rather than individual philanthropy, increasingly involved in subsidizing emergency care institutions. Provided one-third of income by early twentieth century. [DEC]

43.89 Walter G. Vincenti. *What engineers know and how they know it: analytical studies from aeronautical history*. Baltimore: Johns Hopkins Univeristy Press, 1990. ISBN 0-8018-3974-2. ▸ Argues that engineering is distinct form of knowledge, with relationship to both science and technology. Provides variation and selective-retention model for engineering knowledge growth through case studies from aeronautical history. [DUH]

43.90 Maris A. Vinovskis. "Recent trends in American historical demography: some methodological and conceptual considerations." *Annual review of sociology* 4 (1978) 603–27. ISSN 0360-0572. ▸ Suggests some of major issues and problems in field by analyzing recent work on colonial demographic history and fertility and mortality patterns during nineteenth century. [DRJ]

43.91 Morris J. Vogel. *The invention of the modern hospital: Boston, 1870–1930.* Chicago: University of Chicago Press, 1980. ISBN 0-226-86240-2. ▸ Social analysis of impact of scientific development, urbanization, and industrialization of hospital. Evolution of hospital from voluntary organization assisting charity patients to primary supplier of health care to all social classes. [DRJ]

SEE ALSO

4.135 Daniel J. Kevles. *The physicists.*

4.408 David A. Hounshell. *From the American system to mass production, 1800–1932.*

4.418 David F. Noble. *America by design.*

4.420 Nathan Rosenberg. *Technology and American economic growth.*

4.555 David A. Hounshell and John Kenly Smith, Jr. *Science and corporate strategy.*

4.603 Daniel Hovey Calhoun. *The American civil engineer.*

4.728 Martin S. Pernick. *A calculus of suffering.*

4.786 Kenneth M. Ludmerer. *Learning to heal.*

4.787 Ronald L. Numbers, ed. *The education of American physicians.*

LABOR

General Studies

43.92 David Brody. "The old labor history and the new: in search of an American working class." *Labor history* 20 (1979) 111–26. ISSN 0023-656X. ▸ Shows how field originated with rise of labor economists of Wisconsin school. Analyzes approaches, after 1960s, inspired by E. P. Thompson (cf. 24.247). [JHH]

43.93 Mike Davis. "Why the U.S. working class is different." *New Left review* 123 (1980) 3–46. ISSN 0028-6060. ▸ Study of why socialism unsuccessful in America. Finds American working-class consciousness took depoliticized, disorganized form. Argues that, unlike Europe, American class struggle resulted in intraclass cohesion. [JHH]

43.94 Keith Dix. *What's a coal miner to do? The mechanization of coal mining.* Pittsburgh: University of Pittsburgh Press, 1988. ISBN 0-8229-3585-6. ▸ Examination of invention, development, and spread of coal-loading machine in bituminous coal industry, 1920s to 1930s. Defines technology as social process influenced by variety of factors, including workers and management. [JWT]

43.95 David Montgomery. *The fall of the house of labor: the workplace, the state, and American labor activism, 1865–1925.* Cambridge and Paris: Cambridge University Press and Éditions de la Maison des Sciences de l'Homme, 1987. ISBN 0-521-22579-5. ▸ Stellar examination of managerial-worker conflict, diverse working-class constituents, and role of militant minority of working-class activists. Synthesizes immense body of new labor scholarship. [JHH]

43.96 David Montgomery. "To study the people: the American working class." *Labor history* 21 (1980) 485–512. ISSN 0023-656X. ▸ Review of labor historiography offering order to vigorous, growing field that examines family, workplace, women, ethnicity, leisure, immigration, and politics. Calls for synthesis to integrate radical research. [JHH]

43.97 Selig Perlman. *A theory of the labor movement.* 1928 ed. New York: Kelley, 1970. ▸ Classic from Wisconsin school of labor history and economics, emphasizing division between organic goals of labor and those of radical labor intellectuals. [JHH]

43.98 Daniel T. Rodgers. *The work ethic in industrial America,*

1850–1920. Chicago: University of Chicago Press, 1978. ISBN 0-226-72351-8. ▸ Intellectual history of ideas about work, with social history insights. Shows how Protestant values that led to industrialization were undercut by practices of mature corporate capitalism. [JHH]

43.99 Philip Scranton. "None-too-porous boundaries: labor history and the history of technology." *Technology and society* 29 (1988) 722–73. ▸ Historiographical overview of labor history (including current quadripartite divisions), noting ideological sources of divergence between labor and technology historians and finding common ground through labor processes research. [LEC]

43.100 Norman J. Ware. *The labor movement in the United States, 1860–1895: a study in democracy.* 1929 ed. New York: Vintage, 1964. ▸ Study focusing on rise and decline of Knights of Labor. Argues organization's centralized government more formal than real; its failure part of general failure of democracy in America. [JWT]

43.101 Irwin Yellowitz. *Industrialization and the American labor movement, 1850–1900.* Port Washington, N.Y.: Kennikat, 1977. ISBN 0-8046-9150-9. ▸ Examination of myriad responses of workers to technologial change. Concludes trade unions varied in responses to mechanization, but their policies were compatible with system of state capitalism. [JWT]

SEE ALSO

40.254 David M. Gordon, Richard Edwards, and Michael Reich. *Segmented work, divided workers.*

40.255 James R. Green. *The world of the worker.*

Unions and Labor Conditions

43.102 Harold W. Aurand. *From the Molly Maguires to the United Mine Workers: the social ecology of an industrial union, 1869–1897.* Philadelphia: Temple University Press, 1971. ISBN 0-87722-006-9. ▸ Concludes high accident rates and low wages underlay miners' repeated attempts to overcome social fragmentation, build a union, and forge laboring class identity. [JWT]

43.103 David Bensman. *The practice of solidarity: American hat finishers in the nineteenth century.* Urbana: University of Illinois Press, 1985. ISBN 0-252-01093-0. ▸ Documents history of hatters as skilled craftsmen with own norms, values, and system of meaning. Concludes hatters organized unions for cultural as much as for material reasons. [JWT]

43.104 Harry Braverman. *Labor and monopoly capital: the degradation of work in the twentieth century.* 1974 ed. New York: Monthly Review, 1976. ISBN 0-85345-340-3 (cl, 1975), 0-85345-370-5 (pbk). ▸ Update of Marx's *Das Kapital* for twentieth-century trends. Concludes capital succeeds in deskilling and alienating labor through intensified mechanization of factory and office work. [JHH]

43.105 Ronald C. Brown. *Hard rock miners: the intermountain west, 1860–1920.* College Station: Texas A&M University Press, 1979. ISBN 0-89096-066-6. ▸ Study of workers in nonferrous mineral mines of Wyoming, Colorado, New Mexico, Arizona, Utah, and Nevada, with sections on mining towns, families, dangers, and labor structure. Social history perspective. [CAM]

43.106 Margaret Frances Byington. *Homestead: the households of a mill town.* Vol. 4 of *The Pittsburgh survey: findings in six volumes.* 1910 ed. New York: Arno, 1969. ▸ Classic survey of steel community in nonunion era, with special attention to eastern European immigration, community reorganization, and workers' standard of living. [JHH]

43.107 Robert A. Christie. *Empire in wood: a history of the carpenters' union.* Ithaca, N.Y.: Cornell University Press, 1956. ▸ Argues carpenters' union adapted to recurring changes in organization of building industry, labor markets, and tools of production, creating one of most heterogeneous unions. [JWT]

43.108 John R. Commons et al. *History of labour in the United States.* Vol. 2, pt. 6. 1918 ed. New York: Kelley, 1966. ISBN 0-678-00142-1 (set). ‣ Pioneering synthesis of labor movement, emphasizing ideology, politics, and programs of trade unions. Argues trade unions became more conservative under impact of industrialization and business consolidation. [JWT]

43.109 Melvyn Dubofsky. *Industrialism and the American worker, 1865–1920.* 2d ed. Arlington Heights, Ill.: Harlan Davidson, 1985. ISBN 0-88295-831-3 (pbk). ‣ Synthetic introduction to American labor history. Analyzes creation of deskilled, growing but diverse (in ethnicity, race, gender) blue-collar work force. Discusses community institutions as well as union and political struggles. [JHH]

43.110 Melvyn Dubofsky. *We shall be all: a history of the Industrial Workers of the World.* 2d ed. Urbana: University of Illinois Press, 1988. ISBN 0-252-01408-1. ‣ General study of important union, arguing Industrial Workers of the World appealed to society's outcasts and demonstrated that organization, i.e., self-organization, represented motive force for social change. [JWT]

43.111 Crystal Eastman. *Work-accidents and the law.* Vol. 2 of *The Pittsburgh survey: findings in six volumes.* 1910 ed. New York: Arno, 1969. ‣ In-depth analysis of work hazards and reactions to death. Concludes unregulated industrial production killed hundreds of men in one city alone; laws unsuitable to protection of workers. [JHH]

43.112 Philip S. Foner. *History of the labor movement in the United States.* Vols. 2–8. 2d ed. New York: International Publishers, 1972–. ISBN 0-7178-0092-X (v. 2, cl), 0-7178-0093-8 (v. 3, cl), 0-7178-0094-6 (v. 4, cl), 0-7178-0570-0 (v. 5, cl), 0- 7178-0602-2 (v. 6, cl), 0-7178-0638-3 (v. 7, cl), 0-7178-0653-7 (v. 8, cl), 0-7178-0388-0 (v. 2, pbk), 0-7178-0389-9 (v. 3, pbk), 0-7178-0396-1 (v. 4, pbk), 0-7178-0562-X (v. 5, pbk), 0-7178-0595-6 (v. 6, pbk), 0-7178-0627-8 (v. 7, pbk), 0-7178-0652-9 (v. 8, pbk). ‣ Multivolume study concluding that earlier emphasis on narrow job consciousness of American workers overlooked significant conflict between capital and labor. [JWT]

43.113 Ray Ginger. *The bending cross: a biography of Eugene Victor Debs.* 1949 ed. New York: Russell & Russell, 1969. ‣ Intellectual history of venerable Socialist party leader who slowly evolved from conservative railroad union leader to radical after Pullman strike. Excellent narrative history. [JHH]

43.114 David J. Goldberg. *A tale of three cities: labor organization and protest in Paterson, Passaic, and Lawrence, 1916–1921.* New Brunswick, N.J.: Rutgers University Press, 1989. ISBN 0-8135-1371-5 (cl), 0-8135-1372-3 (pbk). ‣ Documents dynamics of labor organizing in three textile-producing cities of New Jersey. Concludes efforts to organize workers during period were constrained by variety of external and internal factors. [JWT]

43.115 Gerald N. Grob. *Workers and utopia: a study of ideological conflict in the American labor movement, 1865–1900.* 1961 ed. New York: Quadrangle, 1976. ‣ Early effort to move beyond theoretical framework established by Wisconsin school of labor history. Emphasizes role of labor leadership. [JWT]

43.116 Stuart Bruce Kaufman. *Samuel Gompers and the origins of the American Federation of Labor, 1848–1896.* Westport, Conn.: Greenwood, 1973. ISBN 0-8371-6277-7. ‣ Places labor leader and movement within broader context of international labor movement. Stresses complexity of his thought and behavior. [JWT]

43.117 Michael Kazin. *Barons of labor: the San Francisco building trades and union power in the Progressive Era.* 1987 ed. Urbana: University of Illinois Press, 1989. ISBN 0-252-01345-X (cl, 1987), 0-252-06075-X (pbk). ‣ Examination of role of Building Trades

Council in economic, political, and social life of city. Argues construction tradesmen exercised influence in urban politics that belied emphasis on primacy of job consciousness. [JWT]

43.118 Paul Underwood Kellogg. *Wage-earning Pittsburgh.* Vol. 6 of *The Pittsburgh survey: findings in six volumes.* 1914 ed. New York: Arno, 1974. ISBN 0-405-05398-3. ‣ Detailed analysis of daily life, wages, working conditions, living conditions, and social institutions of workers, notably their churches and social welfare organizations. [JHH]

43.119 S. J. Kleinberg. *The shadow of the mills: working-class families in Pittsburgh, 1870–1907.* 1989 ed. Pittsburgh: University of Pittsburgh Press, 1991. ISBN 0-8229-3599-6 (cl, 1989), 0-8229-5445-1 (pbk). ‣ Documents impact of rapid industrialization and urban growth on city's manual workers. Argues industrialization intensified gendered definitions of work and family. [JWT]

43.120 Melton Alonza McLaurin. *Paternalism and protest: southern cotton mill workers and organized labor, 1875–1905.* Westport, Conn.: Greenwood, 1971. ISBN 0-8371-4662-3. ‣ Examination of union activities of millworkers. Counteracts prevailing image of millworkers as docile and tractable. [JWT]

43.121 Stephen Meyer III. *The five-dollar day: labor, management, and social control in the Ford Motor Company, 1908–1921.* Albany: State University of New York Press, 1981. ISBN 0-87395-508-0 (cl), 0-87395-509-9 (pbk). ‣ Examination of how evolution of simplified assembly line undercut craftworkers' skills; yet Ford failed to achieve control over work force, skilled and unskilled. Combines analysis of technology, labor processes, and business. [JHH]

43.122 Patrick Renshaw. *The Wobblies: the story of syndicalism in the United States.* 1967 ed. Garden City, N.Y.: Doubleday, 1968. ‣ Exploration of why Industrial Workers of the World succeeded during early twentieth century, despite its precipitous decline during and after World War I. [JWT]

43.123 Peter R. Shergold. *Working-class life: the "American standard" in comparative perspective, 1899–1913.* Pittsburgh: University of Pittsburgh Press, 1982. ISBN 0-8229-3802-2. ‣ Comparative study of Pittsburgh, Pennsylvania, and Birmingham (and, to some extent, Sheffield), England. Maintains American workers earned higher wages for their labor, but experienced lesser quality of life. [JWT]

43.124 Gibbs M. Smith. *Joe Hill.* 1969 ed. Layton, Utah: Peregrine Smith, 1984. ISBN 0-87905-154-X. ‣ Balanced account of Industrial Workers of the World legend. Although author does not reveal new primary research and refrains from pronouncing Wobbly (I.W.W.) leader murderer or martyr, loose ends are admirably tied together. [CAM]

43.125 Philip Taft. *The A. F. of L. in the time of Gompers.* 1957 ed. New York: Octagon Books, 1970. ‣ Analysis of development of American Federation of Labor as national and international organization. Argues union had little authority over its constituent bodies, but offered firm rallying center for workers in United States and Canada. [JWT]

43.126 Mark Wyman. *Hard rock epic: western miners and the industrial revolution, 1860–1910.* Berkeley: University of California Press, 1979. ISBN 0-520-03678-6. ‣ Solid labor study of underground mining of gold and silver within context of American industrial revolution. Focuses on industry's impact on miners and rise of union impulse. [CAM]

Management-Labor Conflict and Strikes

43.127 Louis Adamic. *Dynamite: the story of class violence in America.* 1934 rev. ed. New York: Chelsea House, 1983. ISBN 0-87754-214-7 (cl), 0-87754-361-5 (pbk). ‣ Nonromantic analysis of coercion and class conflict, favoring International Workers of the World method of on-the-job sabotage. Concludes American labor unions frequently resorted to force as industrialists repressed other means of expression. [JHH]

43.128 Jeremy Brecher. *Strike!* 1972 ed. Boston: South End; distributed by Two Continents, 1977. ISBN 0-8467-0364-5 (pbk). ‣ Seminal New Left critique of capitalism, trade-union, and leftist bureaucracies. Concludes mass actions by American workers, from 1877, directly and indirectly challenged capitalist organization of society, but were violently repressed. [JHH]

43.129 David Brody. *Labor in crisis: the steel strike of 1919.* 1965 ed. Urbana: University of Illinois Press, 1987. ISBN 0-252-01373-5 (pbk). ‣ Analysis of role of management, trade unions, industrial workers, government, and public in Great Steel Strike. Contends issue of radicalism undercut popular and governmental support for workers. [JWT]

43.130 David Brody. *Steelworkers in America: the nonunion era.* 1960 ed. New York: Russell & Russell, 1970. ISBN 0-06-131485-4 (pbk). ‣ Economic, business, technology, and social history. Concludes that after 1892 Homestead Strike, steel industry expanded output, mechanized industry, deskilled crafts, imported unskilled eastern European immigrants, and repressed unions. [JHH]

43.131 Wayne G. Broehl, Jr. *The Molly Maguires.* 1964 ed. Cambridge, Mass.: Harvard University Press, 1965. ‣ Analysis based on heretofore unused records of Reading Railroad and Pinkerton Detective Agency. Links activities of Irish miners to heritage of secret societies in Ireland. [JWT]

43.132 Robert V. Bruce. *1877: year of violence.* 1959 ed. Chicago: Dee, 1989. ISBN 0-929587-05-7 (pbk). ‣ Synthetic study of labor violence, class conflict, and political repression that gripped much of nation in wake of great depression of 1870s. [JWT]

43.133 Stanley Buder. *Pullman: an experiment in industrial order and community planning, 1880–1930.* 1967 ed. New York: Oxford University Press, 1972. ISBN 0-19-500838-3 (pbk). ‣ Argues sleeping-car magnate George Pullman built town to stimulate factory productivity, solve labor problems, and combine social reform with good business practice. [JWT]

43.134 Francis G. Couvares. *The remaking of Pittsburgh: class and culture in an industrializing city, 1877–1919.* New York: New York University Press, 1984. ISBN 0-87395-776-8 (cover), 0-87395-778-4 (cl), 0-87395-779-2 (pbk). ‣ Analysis of cultural changes during age of industrial capitalism, documenting destruction of craftsmen's decentralized, democratic way of life. Stresses managerial offensives against labor. [JHH]

43.135 Cletus E. Daniel. *Bitter harvest: a history of California farmworkers, 1870–1941.* 1981 ed. Berkeley: University of California Press, 1982. ISBN 0-520-04722-2 (pbk). ‣ Sympathetic, though somewhat detached, political treatment. Concludes only radical organizations sought reforms, which were undercut by conflicting goals, power of agribusiness, workers' social isolation, and unconcerned government officials. [CAM]

43.136 Philip S. Foner. *The great labor uprising of 1877.* New York: Monad for Anchor Foundation; distributed by Pathfinder, 1977. ISBN 0-913460-56-7 (cl), 0-913460-57-5 (pbk). ‣ Narrative study arguing mass action reflected emergence of labor consciousness, revolution without revolutionary intent. Follows social organization of working class. [JHH]

43.137 Jacquelyn Dowd Hall et al. *Like a family: the making of a southern cotton mill world.* Chapel Hill: University of North Carolina Press, 1987. ISBN 0-8078-1754-6 (cl), 0-8078-4196-X (pbk). ‣ Study of how rural whites were proletarianized in context of company towns of late nineteenth- and early twentieth-century Piedmont South. Uses oral histories, photographs, and traditional sources (with significant gender analysis). [LEC]

43.138 Paul Krause. *The battle for Homestead, 1880–1892: politics, culture, and steel.* Pittsburgh: University of Pittsburgh Press, 1992. ISBN 0-8229-3702-6 (cl), 0-8229-5466-4 (pbk). ‣ Demonstration of how Homestead workers advanced their own version of republicanism and challenged emerging inequalities. Links Homestead Strike of 1892 to historical development of class relations in city. [JWT]

43.139 Walter Licht. *Getting work: Philadelphia, 1840–1950.* Cambridge, Mass.: Harvard University Press, 1992. ISBN 0-674-35428-1. ‣ Analysis of how working people found employment. Emphasizes shifting relationship between structural, personal, and institutional factors. Questions usual emphasis on Taylorism or scientific management. [JWT]

43.140 Almont Lindsey. *The Pullman strike: the story of a unique experiment and of a great labor upheaval.* 1942 ed. Chicago: University of Chicago Press, 1967. ISBN 0-226-48383-5. ‣ Locates causes of strike in underlying forces of Pullman, model worker town. Argues depression of 1890s channeled mounting grievances into spirit of violent resistance against corporation. [JWT]

43.141 Priscilla Long. *Where the sun never shines: a history of America's bloody coal industry.* 1989 ed. New York: Paragon House, 1991. ISBN 1-55778-224-5 (cl, 1989), 1-55778-465-5 (pbk). ‣ Collective biography of miners' work, union struggles, and values. Accessible chronicle of 1840s to 1920s, emphasizing workplace, class conflict, and importance of coal to industrialization. [JHH]

43.142 David Montgomery. *Workers' control in America: studies in the history of work, technology, and labor struggles.* 1979 ed. Cambridge: Cambridge University Press, 1980. ISBN 0-521-22580-9 (cl, 1979), 0-521-28006-0 (pbk). ‣ Series of essays on shopfloor resistance to managerial attempts at rationalizing industrial production, i.e., scientific management. Seminal analysis of role of shopfloor culture in these class conflicts. [JHH]

43.143 Daniel Nelson. *Managers and workers: origins of the new factory system in the United States, 1880–1920.* Madison: University of Wisconsin Press, 1975. ISBN 0-299-06900-1. ‣ Discussion of shifting relationship between factory managers and industrial workers. Concludes that dominant theme of these changing social relations was increasing displacement of ad hoc decentralized controls over work force by formal centralized controls, i.e., new system of industrial administration. [JWT]

43.144 Shelton Stromquist. *A generation of boomers: the pattern of railroad labor conflict in nineteenth-century America.* Urbana: University of Illinois Press, 1987. ISBN 0-252-01302-6. ‣ Examination of strike activity, 1877–94. Uses notion of moving frontier of labor scarcity to highlight substantial regional variation in strikes and labor organizations. [JWT]

43.145 Anne Huber Tripp. *The I.W.W. and the Paterson silk strike of 1913.* Urbana: University of Illinois Press, 1987. ISBN 0-252-01382-4. ‣ Argues failure of strike reflects impact of variety of forces, including conflict between Industrial Workers of the World and Socialist Party of America that emerged in struggle in Lawrence, Massachusetts. [JWT]

43.146 Samuel Yellin. *American labor struggles.* 1936 ed. New York: Arno, 1969. ‣ Analysis of ten pivotal conflicts between capital and labor. Suggests how weapons of labor (strikes, boycotts, sabotage, etc.) and weapons of capital (lockouts, armed guards, strikebreakers, etc.) changed over time. [JWT]

Ethnic and Race Relations

43.147 Eric Arnesen. *Waterfront workers of New Orleans: race, class, and politics, 1863–1923.* New York: Oxford University Press, 1991. ISBN 0-19-505380-X. ‣ Examination of changing relationship between black and white dockworkers. Concludes dockworkers developed complex identities defying simple dichotomies of labor/race. [JWT]

43.148 Robert Asher and Charles Stephenson, eds. *Labor divided: race and ethnicity in United States labor struggles, 1835–1960.* Albany: State University of New York Press, 1990. ISBN 0-88706-970-3 (cl), 0-88706-972-X (pbk). ▸ Collection of articles on workers from white and nonwhite ethnic and racial groups. Covers variety of areas in northern and southern states as well as Hawaii. Primary focus on period 1900–45. [EL]

43.149 Dennis C. Dickerson. *Out of the crucible: black steelworkers in western Pennsylvania, 1875–1980.* Albany: State University of New York Press, 1986. ISBN 0-88706-305-5 (cl), 0-88706-306-3 (pbk). ▸ Examination of African American workers' experience. Concludes race not class determining factor. Occupational advances in nonunion period resulted in use of black strikebreakers from 1890 to 1919. Racism in community and workplace lasted generations. [JHH]

43.150 Peter J. Rachleff. *Black labor in the South: Richmond, Virginia, 1865–1890.* Philadelphia: Temple University Press, 1984. ISBN 0-87722-336-X. ▸ Analysis of how possibility of biracial unity slowly emerged in post–Civil War period, but declined in 1890s. Thick description of interplay between workplace culture and community institutions. [JHH]

SEE ALSO
40.278 Tamara K. Hareven and Randolph Langenbach. *Amoskeag.*
44.404 Mark Reisler. *By the sweat of their brow.*

Gender

43.151 Ava Baron, ed. *Work engendered: toward a new history of American labor.* Ithaca, N.Y.: Cornell University Press, 1991. ISBN 0-8014-2256-6 (cl), 0-8014-9543-1 (pbk). ▸ Essays on gender and work and meanings of masculine and feminine. Topics include cigar making, textile workers, printing, sexuality, the South, and life insurance industry. [PAC]

43.152 Elizabeth Beardsly Butler. *Women and the trades: Pittsburgh, 1907–1908.* Vol. 1 of *The Pittsburgh survey: findings in six volumes.* 1909 ed. New York: Arno, 1969. ▸ Demonstration of how female wage earners were significant part of industrial city, locked into pitiful conditions due to gender, unable to enjoy fruits of labor. [JHH]

43.153 Elizabeth Clark-Lewis. "'This work had an end': African-American domestic workers in Washington, D.C., 1910–1940." In *"To toil the livelong day": America's women at work, 1780–1980.* Carol Groneman and Mary Beth Norton, eds., pp. 196–212. Ithaca, N.Y.: Cornell University Press, 1987. ISBN 0-8014-1847-X (cl), 0-8014-9452-4 (pbk). ▸ Traces women's actions to transform live-in to day work and consequent changes in African American community organizations, including churches. Based on oral histories with African American women. [PAC]

43.154 Patricia A. Cooper. *Once a cigar maker: men, women, and work culture in American cigar factories, 1900–1919.* Urbana: University of Illinois Press, 1987. ISBN 0-252-01333-6. ▸ Analysis of work cultures of male members of Cigar Makers' International Union and largely unorganized women cigar makers. Concludes both resisted employer encroachment, but gender divided workers and inhibited collective action. [PAC]

43.155 Ruth Schwartz Cowan. *More work for mother: the ironies of household technology from the open hearth to the microwave.* New York: Basic Books, 1983. ISBN 0-465-04731-9. ▸ Study of industrialization of household work and technology. Argues changes in household work are social processes and that increased mechanization of homes created more, if different, housework than in preindustrial homes. [DUH]

43.156 Susan A. Glenn. *Daughters of the shtetl: life and labor in the immigrant generation.* Ithaca, N.Y.: Cornell University Press, 1990. ISBN 0-8014-1966-2. ▸ Study of young Jewish immigrant women garment workers, 1880s to 1920. Illustrates unique combination of ethnic, class, and gender cultures that shaped consciousness and identity. [PAC]

43.157 Maurine Weiner Greenwald. *Women, war, and work: the impact of World War I on women workers in the United States.* 1980 ed. Ithaca, N.Y.: Greenwood, 1990. ISBN 0-8014-9733-7. ▸ Examination of women's wartime employment through case studies of railroad workers, streetcar conductors, and telephone operators. Highlights jobs, unionism, gender-class relations, role of the state, reformers, and impact of war on occupational structure. [PAC]

43.158 Sharon Harley. "For the good of family and race: gender, work, and domestic roles in the black community, 1880–1930." *Signs* 15 (1990) 336–49. ISSN 0097-9740. ▸ Thorough analysis of jobs, occupational structure, and opportunities for and discrimination against African American women in District of Columbia. Unpaid home activities provided pride, status, and autonomy absent in paid work. [PAC]

43.159 David M. Katzman. *Seven days a week: women and domestic service in industrializing America.* 1978 ed. Urbana: University of Illinois Press, 1981. ISBN 0-252-00882-0 (pbk). ▸ Study of domestic workers, nature of work, employers, and efforts at reform, 1870–1920. Examines pernicious aspects of domestic work and its connection to changing economy. Particular attention to African American women. [PAC]

43.160 Alice Kessler-Harris. "Independence and virtue in the lives of wage-earning women: the United States, 1870–1930." In *Women in culture and politics: a century of change.* Judith Friedlander, Blanche Wiesen Cook, and Alice Kessler-Harris, eds., pp. 3–17. Bloomington: Indiana University Press, 1986. ISBN 0-253-31328-7 (cl), 0-253-20375-9 (pbk). ▸ Analysis of women's labor market patterns as reflection of tension and conflict between women's self-images rooted in home and motherhood and experiences of independence associated with paid work. Study of how jobs and attitudes changed by 1920. [PAC]

43.161 Alice Kessler-Harris. "Where are the organized women workers?" *Feminist studies* 3 (1975) 92–110. ISSN 0046-3663. ▸ Restates old question to transform thinking on women workers. Concludes women's potential for organization undermined by capitalist employment structures, employer hostility, union ambivalence, and consequences of some middle-class reform. [PAC]

43.162 Susan Levine. *Labor's true woman: carpet weavers, industrialization, and labor reform in the Gilded Age.* Philadelphia: Temple University Press, 1984. ISBN 0-87722-364-5. ▸ Study of women in carpet manufacture in New York and Philadelphia, examining labor communities, politics, labor protest and organization, industrial change and women's employment. Analysis of Knights of Labor and women finds internal tensions between equality and domesticity. [PAC]

Community Studies and Politics

43.163 James R. Barrett. *Work and community in the jungle: Chicago's packinghouse workers, 1894–1922.* 1987 ed. Urbana: University of Illinois Press, 1990. ISBN 0-252-01378-6 (cl, 1987), 0-252-06136-5 (pbk). ▸ Analysis of class, ethnic, and racial identities in workplace and neighborhood contexts. Concludes working-class formation shaped by managerial offenses and agency of butcher workmen. [JHH]

43.164 David Alan Corbin. *Life, work, and rebellion in the coal* *fields: the southern West Virginia miners, 1880–1922.* Urbana: University of Illinois Press, 1981. ISBN 0-252-00850-2 (cl), 0-252-00895-2 (pbk). ▸ Exploration of life in coal mining families and communities, emphasizing development of class consciousness. Moves study of miners beyond activity of United Mine Workers of America. [JWT]

43.165 John T. Cumbler. *Working-class community in industrial America: work, leisure, and struggle in two industrial cities, 1880–1930.* Westport, Conn.: Greenwood, 1979. ISBN 0-313-20615-5. ▸ Case study of how workers moved beyond simple notions of labor unionism to develop variety of formal and informal community institutions that worked to maintain class solidarity. [JWT]

43.166 Henry David. *The history of the Haymarket affair: a study in the American social-revolutionary and labor movements.* 2d ed. New York: Russell & Russell, 1958. ▸ Places this important event within broader context of origins, growth, form, and development of social-revolutionary movement in Chicago, America, and Europe. [JWT]

43.167 Leon Fink. *Workingmen's democracy: the Knights of Labor and American politics.* 1983 ed. Urbana: University of Illinois Press, 1985. ISBN 0-252-00999-1 (cl, 1983), 0-252-01256-9 (pbk). ▸ Examination of social and political impact of Knights of Labor in five cities. Concludes organization broke new ground by bringing together diverse working-class constituencies. [JWT]

43.168 Philip S. Foner, comp. *American labor songs of the nineteenth century.* 1974 ed. Urbana: University of Illinois Press, 1975. ISBN 0-252-00187-7. ▸ Compilation of song lyrics from wide range of sources, with connecting narrative and notes to provide necessary historical context. Distinctive contribution to American labor history. [EL]

43.169 Kenneth Fones-Wolf. *Trade union gospel: Christianity and labor in industrial Philadelphia, 1865–1915.* Philadelphia: Temple University Press, 1989. ISBN 0-87722-652-0. ▸ Documentation of intersection between Christianity and trade unionism. Maintains religion proved capable of supporting diverse political and class interests. [JWT]

43.170 Herbert G. Gutman. *Work, culture, and society in industrializing America: essays in American working-class and social history.* 1976 ed. New York: Vintage, 1977. ISBN 0-394-72251-5 (pbk). ▸ Seven essays spanning nineteenth century, written over fifteen-year period. Ranges from synthetic title essay to case studies. Helped usher in new labor history. [LEC]

43.171 John H. M. Laslett. *Labor and the Left: a study of socialist and radical influences in the American labor movement, 1881–1924.* New York: Basic Books, 1970. ISBN 0-465-03742-9. ▸ Analysis of rise and fall of radical influences in American labor movement. Stresses impact of political, economic, and technological changes in American society. [JWT]

43.172 Richard Jules Oestreicher. *Solidarity and fragmentation: working people and class consciousness in Detroit, 1875–1900.* 1986 ed. Urbana: University of Illinois Press, 1990. ISBN 0-252-01225-9 (cl, 1986), 0-252-06120-9 (pbk). ▸ Study challenging classical Marxist and modernization theories, arguing neither adequately explains working-class behavior and consciousness. Concludes workers experienced unity and disunity under impact of industrialization and urbanization. [JWT]

43.173 Roy Rosenzweig. *Eight hours for what we will: workers and leisure in an industrial city, 1870–1920.* 1983 ed. Cambridge: Cambridge University Press, 1985. ISBN 0-521-23916-8 (cl, 1983), 0-521-31397-X (pbk). ▸ Examines changing nature and meaning of workers' leisure as distinct from that of middle class in Worcester, Massachusetts. Emphasis on movement from ethnic to class-based consumer culture. [LEC]

URBAN HISTORY

General Studies

43.174 Paul S. Boyer. *Urban masses and moral order in America, 1820–1920.* Cambridge, Mass.: Harvard University Press, 1978. ISBN 0-674-93109-2. ▸ Examination of how ideas about proper urban social and moral order shaped middle-class response to increasing urban disorder. [EHM/TAM]

43.175 Howard Gillette, Jr. "Rethinking American urban history: new directions for the posturban era." *Social science history* 14.2 (1990) 203–08. ISSN 0145-5532. ▸ Useful survey of recent scholarship. Concludes that urban history suffers from apparent paradox: emerged out of search for solutions to urban crisis, but moved toward greater professionalization. [JWT]

43.176 Howard Gillette, Jr., and Zane L. Miller, eds. *American urbanism: a historiographical review.* New York: Greenwood, 1987. ISBN 0-313-24967-9. ▸ Bibliographic and historiographic guide, updated by Gillette's essay in *Social Science History* 14 (1990) 203–28. [EHM]

43.177 Raymond A. Mohl. *The new city: urban America in the industrial age, 1860–1920.* Arlington Heights, Ill.: Harlan Davidson, 1985. ISBN 0-88295-830-5 (pbk). ▸ Synthesis drawing upon plethora of recent studies in urban history. Documents development of American cities under impact of industrialization. [JWT]

43.178 Eric H. Monkkonen. *America becomes urban: the development of U.S. cities and towns, 1780–1980.* Berkeley: University of California Press, 1988. ISBN 0-520-06191-8 (cl), 0-520-06972-2 (pbk). ▸ Examination of transition of United States from rural to urban, focusing on social, political, geographic, and legal factors. Emphasizes impact of federal system, corporate form, and political diversity. [EHM]

43.179 Stephan Thernstrom and Richard Sennett, eds. *Nineteenth-century cities: essays in the new urban history.* New Haven: Yale University Press, 1969. ISBN 0-300-01150-4 (cl), 0-300-01151-2 (pbk). ▸ Essays from Yale conference on the nineteenth-century industrial city (1968). Provides intellectual and research program of new urban history. [EHM]

43.180 Morton White and Lucia White. *The intellectual versus the city: from Thomas Jefferson to Frank Lloyd Wright.* 1962 ed. Oxford: Oxford University Press, 1977. ISBN 0-19-519969-3. ▸ Traces antiurban sentiments of major American thinkers, showing how subtle anticity bias undercut serious efforts to conceptualize and deal with city. [EHM]

SEE ALSO
42.710 Thomas Bender. *Toward an urban vision.*

Urban Development and Planning

43.181 Gunther Barth. *Instant cities: urbanization and the rise of San Francisco and Denver.* 1975 ed. Albuquerque: University of New Mexico Press, 1988. ISBN 0-8263-1082-6 (pbk). ▸ Description of building of two western cities in very brief time span, comparing them to certain areas in Germany. [EHM]

43.182 Blaine A. Brownell. *The urban ethos in the South, 1920–1930.* Baton Rouge: Louisiana State University Press, 1975. ISBN 0-8071-0157-5. ▸ Southern city boosters used images of economic growth and progress to build their cities, but social reality of southern life meant that they could not really challenge deep inequalities and injustices. [EHM]

43.183 Clifford Edward Clark, Jr. *The American family home, 1800–1960.* Chapel Hill: University of North Carolina Press, 1986. ISBN 0-8078-1675-2 (cl), 0-8078-4151-X (pbk). ▸ Architectural and social history of housing, including builders' advertising, photographs, and floor plans. Includes detail on finance. [EHM]

43.184 Don H. Doyle. *New men, new cities, New South: Atlanta, Nashville, Charleston, Mobile, 1860–1910.* Chapel Hill: University of North Carolina Press, 1990. ISBN 0-8078-1883-6 (cl), 0-8078-4270-2 (pbk). ▸ Social and institutional history of ideology and policy of urban builders and boosters. Shows how southern thinkers pinned their hopes for economic growth on cities. [EHM]

43.185 Robert M. Fogelson. *The fragmented metropolis: Los Angeles, 1850–1930.* Cambridge, Mass.: Harvard University Press, 1967. ▸ General history of Los Angeles from village to sprawling city. Attempts to explain urbanization process in early twentieth-century West. Summarizes previous studies while adding valuable new data to arguments. [CAM]

43.186 Bessie Louise Pierce. *A history of Chicago.* 1937–57 ed. 3 vols. Chicago: University of Chicago Press, 1975. ISBN 0-226-66817-7. ▸ Model urban biography richly detailing city's social and political history. [EHM]

43.187 Harold L. Platt. *The electric city: energy and the growth of the Chicago area, 1880–1930.* Chicago: University of Chicago Press, 1991. ISBN 0-226-67075-9. ▸ Concludes centralized electric energy sources did not emerge naturally, but were result of specific business and accounting strategies that contested with dispersed electric sources. Technology, politics, and culture all played essential roles in lighting modern city. [EHM]

43.188 John W. Reps. *Views and viewmakers of urban America: lithographs of towns and cities in the United States and Canada, notes on the artists and publishers, and a union catalog of their work, 1825–1925.* Columbia: University of Missouri Press, 1984. ISBN 0-8262-0416-3. ▸ Collection of bird's-eye views, documenting their histories and creators. Establishes how accuracy of views was achieved. [EHM]

43.189 Christine Meisner Rosen. *The limits of power: great fires and the process of city growth in America.* Cambridge: Cambridge University Press, 1986. ISBN 0-521-30319-2. ▸ Study revealing how policies intended to reshape congested and ill-planned cities actually thwarted by deep economic, social, and political forces. Disastrous fires heightened consciousness on subject and showed how cities might have been built in other ways but were not. [EHM]

43.190 Peter J. Schmitt. *Back to nature: the arcadian myth in urban America.* 1969 ed. John R. Stilgoe, Foreword. Baltimore: Johns Hopkins University Press, 1990. ISBN 0-8018-4013-9 (pbk). ▸ Study of middle class's efforts from 1890s through 1920s to blend nature into modern life styles. Argues this urban response valued nature's spiritual impact more than its economic importance. [EDL]

43.191 Stanley K. Schultz. *Constructing urban culture: American cities and city planning, 1800–1920.* Philadelphia: Temple University Press, 1989. ISBN 0-87722-587-7. ▸ Cultural and intellectual history of city planning and reform ideas, locating ideas in international context and stressing culture over technological determinism. [EHM]

43.192 David Schuyler. *The new urban landscape: the redefinition of city form in nineteenth-century America.* 1986 ed. Baltimore: Johns Hopkins University Press, 1988. ISBN 0-8018-3231-4 (cl, 1986), 0-8018-3748-0 (pbk). ▸ Integrates physical planning of cities with broader themes of urban history. Urban leaders deliberately created park systems for social, political, and civic purposes. Parks were expected to avert perceived problems of European cities. [EHM]

43.193 Joel A. Tarr and Gabriel Dupuy, eds. *Technology and the rise of the networked city in Europe and America.* Philadelphia: Temple University Press, 1988. ISBN 0-87722-540-0. ▸ Product of

international conference on city and technology (1983). Comparative perspectives on urban transit, water, waste, and energy systems. [JWT]

43.194 Gwendolyn Wright. *Moralism and the model home: domestic architecture and cultural conflict in Chicago, 1873–1913.* 1980 ed. Chicago: University of Chicago Press, 1985. ISBN 0-226-90835-6 (cl), 0-226-90837-2 (pbk). ▸ Examination of how cultural vision of family shaped housing design and construction. Concludes women's movement and concept of nuclear family created new floor plans and room uses. [EHM]

Social Conditions, Race, and Ethnicity

43.195 Albert Camarillo. *Chicanos in a changing society: from Mexican pueblos to American barrios in Santa Barbara and Southern California, 1848–1930.* Cambridge, Mass.: Harvard University Press, 1979. ISBN 0-674-11395-0 (cl), 0-674-11396-9 (pbk). ▸ Study of how Mexican cities formed nucleus of United States, Anglo-dominated, Southern California cityscape. Inhabitants continued to hold political power even as economic and social power of newcomers slowly gained ascendancy. [EHM]

43.196 Michael B. Katz. *In the shadow of the poorhouse: a social history of welfare in America.* 1986 ed. New York: Basic Books, 1988. ISBN 0-465-03225-7 (cl, 1986), 0-465-03226-5 (pbk). ▸ Uses detailed records to examine social impact of poverty on lives of many kinds of poor people, from tramps to urban families. Includes descriptions of various welfare systems. [EHM]

43.197 Peter R. Knights. *Yankee destinies: the lives of ordinary nineteenth-century Bostonians.* Chapel Hill: University of North Carolina Press, 1991. ISBN 0-8078-1969-7. ▸ Examination of lives of native-born men who resided in Boston, from birthplace to final resting place; based on sample of over 2,000. Traces those who left Boston and those who stayed. [EHM]

43.198 Roger Lane. *Violent death in the city: suicide, accident, and murder in nineteenth-century Philadelphia.* Cambridge, Mass.: Harvard University Press, 1979. ISBN 0-674-93946-8. ▸ Analysis of homicide, accidental death, and suicide in Philadelphia, using court and police records. Shows homicide and accidental death both declined while suicide increased. [EHM]

43.199 Martin V. Melosi, ed. *Pollution and reform in American cities, 1870–1930.* Austin: University of Texas Press, 1980. ISBN 0-292-76459-6. ▸ Analysis capturing range of issues and research in history of urban pollution. Valuable suggestions on sources and issues. [EHM]

43.200 Joel Perlmann. *Ethnic differences: schooling and social structure among the Irish, Italians, Jews, and blacks in an American city, 1880–1935.* Cambridge: Cambridge University Press, 1988. ISBN 0-521-35093-X. ▸ Examination of Providence, Rhode Island, school attendance and performance in order to assess relationship between schooling, class, race, and ethnicity. [EHM]

43.201 Stephan Thernstrom. *The other Bostonians: poverty and progress in the American metropolis, 1880–1970.* Cambridge, Mass.: Harvard University Press, 1973. ISBN 0-674-64495-6. ▸ Study of historical social mobility. Uses different sample cohorts to trace fathers and their sons through occupational and educational careers. [EHM]

43.202 Stephan Thernstrom. *Poverty and progress: social mobility in a nineteenth-century city.* 1964 ed. Cambridge, Mass.: Harvard University Press, 1974. ISBN 0-674-09500-3 (cl), 0-674-69501-1 (pbk). ▸ Classic study of urban social history. Traces experiences of unskilled Irish laborers in Newburyport, an industrial city, examining work, family, education, and housing. [EHM]

43.203 William M. Tuttle, Jr. *Race riot: Chicago in the red summer of 1919.* 1970 ed. New York: Atheneum, 1985. ISBN 0-689-10372-7 (cl), 0-689-70287-6 (pbk). ▸ Story of black migration, white resistance, and violence played out in political environment of major United States city. [EHM]

43.204 Olivier Zunz. *The changing face of inequality: urbanization, industrial development, and immigrants in Detroit, 1880–1920.* Chicago: University of Chicago Press, 1982. ISBN 0-226-99457-0 (cl), 0-226-99458-9 (pbk). ▸ Outline of spatial, residential, and social consequences of industrial growth for multiethnic and racially differentiated city. Shows original strong influence of ethnicity altered by divisions of class and race. [EHM]

Politics and Reform

43.205 LeRoy Ashby. *Saving the waifs: reformers and dependent children, 1890–1917.* Philadelphia: Temple University Press, 1984. ISBN 0-87722-337-8. ▸ Detailed account of complex child-saving movement, including Junior Republics, which were intended to imbue children with civic cultural values. [EHM]

43.206 Robert H. Bremner. *From the depths: the discovery of poverty in the United States.* 1956 ed. New York: New York University Press, 1972. ISBN 0-8147-0055-1 (cl), 0-8147-0054-3 (pbk). ▸ Thorough discussion of poverty reformers and antipoverty organizations for both nineteenth and early twentieth centuries. [EHM]

43.207 Lawrence A. Cremin. *American education: the metropolitan experience, 1876–1980.* New York: Harper & Row, 1988. ISBN 0-06-015804-2. ▸ Description of schooling, educational reform, and reformers in American cities. Includes discussion of educational ideas and their advocates. [EHM]

43.208 Lawrence A. Cremin. *The transformation of the school: progressivism in American education, 1876–1957.* 1961 ed. New York: Vintage, 1964. ▸ Overview of schooling, focusing on institutional changes. [EHM]

43.209 Ruth Hutchinson Crocker. *Social work and social order: the settlement movement in two industrial cities, 1889–1930.* Urbana: University of Illinois Press, 1992. ISBN 0-252-01790-0. ▸ Comparison of settlement movement in two cities, showing significant African American movement. [EHM]

43.210 Allen F. Davis. *Spearheads for reform: the social settlements and the progressive movement, 1890–1914.* New Brunswick, N.J.: Rutgers University Press, 1984. ISBN 0-8135-1072-4 (cl), 0-8135-1073-2 (pbk). ▸ Although not affecting large masses of poor directly, settlement house movement educated reformers who, in turn, used them as policy laboratories for larger polity. [EHM]

43.211 Michael H. Ebner and Eugene M. Tobin, eds. *The age of urban reform: new perspectives on the Progressive Era.* Port Washington, N.Y.: Kennikat, 1977. ISBN 0-8046-9192-4 (cl), 0-8046-9204-1 (pbk). ▸ Useful collection of essays revealing variety in urban progressivism. [TJMcD]

43.212 William Issel and Robert W. Cherny. *San Francisco, 1865–1932: politics, power, and urban development.* Berkeley: University of California Press, 1986. ISBN 0-520-05263-3 (cl), 0-520-06033-4 (pbk). ▸ Study of city politics from vigilante movement bosses to reformers and labor politicians. Includes examination of pro-growth policies. [EHM]

43.213 Carl F. Kaestle and Maris A. Vinovskis. *Education and social change in nineteenth-century Massachusetts.* Cambridge: Cambridge University Press, 1980. ISBN 0-521-22191-9. ▸ Examination of schooling in its political, intellectual, and economic context. Social, political, and institutional history. [EHM]

43.214 Michael B. Katz. *Class, bureaucracy, and schools: the illusion of educational change in America.* Rev. ed. New York: Praeger, 1975. ISBN 0-275-52550-3 (cl), 0-275-85100-1 (pbk). ▸ Overview of educational changes arguing that schooling is less meritocratic

and egalitarian than Horace Mann's contemporary opinion on subject would have us believe. [EHM]

43.215 Ira Katznelson. *City trenches: urban politics and the patterning of class in the United States.* 1981 ed. Chicago: University of Chicago Press, 1982. ISBN 0-226-42673-4 (pbk). ▸ Study of how nineteenth-century Americans were organized into class politics by unions at workplace and into politics of territory and ethnicity by parties at ballot box. Concludes this split undermined possibilities for class politics. Provocative, agenda-setting work. [TJMcD]

43.216 Terrence J. McDonald. *The parameters of urban fiscal policy: socioeconomic change and political culture in San Francisco, 1860–1906.* Berkeley: University of California Press, 1986. ISBN 0-520-05494-6. ▸ Uses extensive new sources and quantitative techniques to argue both reform and machine politics had similar fiscal policies. Finds fiscal conservatism characterized all politics, showing power of underlying political culture. [EHM/TJMcD]

43.217 Eric H. Monkkonen. *Police in urban America, 1860–1920.* Cambridge: Cambridge University Press, 1981. ISBN 0-521-23454-9. ▸ Synthetic study of literature on development of United States police, emphasizing shift from class to crime control and importance to local government. [EHM]

43.218 James T. Patterson. *America's struggle against poverty, 1900–1985.* Rev. ed. Cambridge, Mass.: Harvard University Press, 1986. ISBN 0-674-03122-9 (pbk). ▸ Description of welfare programs and reform ideas at national level, including, in particular, New Deal and War on Poverty programs and debates. [EHM]

43.219 Jon C. Teaford. *The unheralded triumph: city government in America, 1870–1900.* Baltimore: Johns Hopkins University Press, 1984. ISBN 0-8018-3062-1 (cl), 0-8018-3063-X (pbk). ▸ Detailed analysis of politics and policy, demonstrating that Bryce thesis, that urban government in United States was conspicuous failure, was wrong. [EHM]

43.220 Walter I. Trattner. *From poor law to welfare state: a history of social welfare in America.* 4th ed. New York and London: Free Press and Collier Macmillan, 1989. ISBN 0-02-932711-3 (cl), 0-02-932712-1 (pbk). ▸ Legal and institutional history of social welfare and ideas about reform from colonial period to present. Includes discussions of social work and institutional reforms like settlement houses. [EHM]

43.221 Judith Ann Trolander. *Professionalism and social change: from the settlement house movement to neighborhood centers, 1886 to the present.* New York: Columbia University Press, 1987. ISBN 0-231-06472-1. ▸ Traces reform ideas and activities of settlement house movement activists as movement changed from upper-middle-class adventure in reform living to professional social work. Stresses policy and neighborhood role through twentieth century. [EHM]

43.222 David B. Tyack. *The one best system: a history of American urban education.* Cambridge, Mass.: Harvard University Press, 1974. ISBN 0-674-63780-1 (cl), 0-674-63782-8 (pbk). ▸ Locates development of American education in context of urban politics, finance, immigration, corruption, and reform. [EHM]

43.223 Laurence R. Veysey. *The emergence of the American university.* 1965 ed. Chicago: University of Chicago Press, 1970. ISBN 0-226-85455-8 (cl), 0-226-85456-6 (pbk). ▸ Examination of the American university as product of nineteenth-century political, economic, and intellectual trends. Sees contrasts between its agricultural and urban components. [EHM]

43.224 Maris A. Vinovskis. *The origins of public high schools: a reexamination of the Beverly High School controversy.* Madison: University of Wisconsin Press, 1985. ISBN 0-299-10400-1. ▸ Deals with question of economic class and public high schools. Critique of Katz thesis (43.214). [EHM]

43.225 David Ward. *Poverty, ethnicity, and the American city, 1840–1925: changing conceptions of the slum and the ghetto.* Cambridge: Cambridge University Press, 1989. ISBN 0-521-25783-2 (cl), 0-521-27711-6 (pbk). ▸ Examination of intellectual response to concentrated poverty. Discusses both reform proposals and linkage of ideas to broader cultural currents. [EHM]

43.226 Margaret Weir, Ann Shola Orloff, and Theda Skocpol, eds. *The politics of social policy in the United States.* Princeton: Princeton University Press, 1988. ISBN 0-691-09436-5 (cl), 0-691-02841-9 (pbk). ▸ Uses broad variety of both state and federal programs to analyze relationship between political system and social provision in twentieth century. [EHM]

Suburbia

43.227 Michael H. Ebner. *Creating Chicago's North Shore: a suburban history.* Chicago: University of Chicago Press, 1988. ISBN 0-226-18205-3. ▸ Photographic and social history of elite suburb, locating it in history of Chicago region. [EHM]

43.228 Robert Fishman. *Bourgeois utopias: the rise and fall of suburbia.* New York: Basic Books, 1987. ISBN 0-465-00748-1. ▸ Argues middle class took English garden suburbs as its model. By separating from urban problems, yet taking positive benefits of cities, Anglo-America did not make cities like European ones. [EHM]

43.229 Kenneth T. Jackson. *Crabgrass frontier: the suburbanization of the United States.* 1985 ed. New York: Oxford University Press, 1987. ISBN 0-19-503610-7 (cl, 1985), 0-19-504983-7 (pbk). ▸ Started "new suburban history" by treating seriously and extensively suburban cities, which began to grow as early as 1850. Much new detail on post–World War I boom, consequences of racial discrimination, and changing nature of urban community. [EHM]

43.230 Jon C. Teaford. *City and suburb: the political fragmentation of metropolitan America, 1850–1970.* Baltimore: Johns Hopkins University Press, 1979. ISBN 0-8018-2202-5 (cl), 0-8357-6838-4 (pbk). ▸ Examination of law and politics of suburban expansion, with heavy emphasis on ideals (and ultimate failure) of regional government reformers. [EHM]

43.231 Sam Bass Warner, Jr. *Streetcar suburbs: the process of growth in Boston, 1870–1900.* 2d ed. Cambridge, Mass.: Harvard University Press, 1978. ISBN 0-674-84213-8 (cl), 0-674-84211-1 (pbk). ▸ Pioneering study of suburban expansion, using building permits to discover how small entrepreneurs shaped and built early suburbs. [EHM]

IMMIGRATION

43.232 Josef J. Barton. *Peasants and strangers: Italians, Rumanians, and Slovaks in an American city, 1890–1950.* Cambridge, Mass.: Harvard University Press, 1975. ISBN 0-674-65930-9. ▸ Early comparative study of eastern and southern European immigration to Cleveland, Ohio. First half focuses on conditions within homelands; second half examines intergenerational social mobility. [LEC]

43.233 John Bodnar. *Immigration and industrialization: ethnicity in an American mill town, 1870–1940.* Pittsburgh: University of Pittsburgh Press, 1977. ISBN 0-8229-3348-9. ▸ Case study of ethnic and working-class formation in Pennsylvania steel town. Argues immigrant workers turned inward as result of hardships and discrimination they faced. [JHH]

43.234 John Bodnar, Roger Simon, and Michael P. Weber. *Lives of their own: blacks, Italians, and Poles in Pittsburgh, 1900–1960.* Urbana: University of Illinois Press, 1982. ISBN 0-252-00880-4.

▸ One of few historical studies of comparative urban ethnic and racial group experiences. [JWT]

43.235 John W. Briggs. *An Italian passage: immigrants to three American cities, 1890–1930.* New Haven: Yale University Press, 1978. ISBN 0-300-02095-3. ▸ Controversial study of Italian communities in middle-sized cities of Rochester and Utica, New York, and Kansas City, Missouri. Concludes Italians readily embraced bourgeois values, particularly apparent with respect to business and education. [LEC]

43.236 Dino Cinel. *From Italy to San Francisco: the immigration experience.* Stanford, Calif.: Stanford University Press, 1982. ISBN 0-8047-1117-8. ▸ Social history of emigrants, immigrants, and returnees from selected areas of Italy. Emphasizes major changes and continuities in immigrant experience. [JWT]

43.237 Micaela di Leonardo. *The varieties of ethnic experience: kinship, class, and gender among California Italian-Americans.* Ithaca, N.Y.: Cornell University Press, 1984. ISBN 0-8014-1632-9 (cl), 0-8014-9278-5 (pbk). ▸ Study based on in-depth interviews with second- to fourth-generation members of fifteen core families. Asserts ethnicity is constructed within specific historical, regional, economic, political, and social contexts. [LEC]

43.238 Leonard Dinnerstein, Roger L. Nichols, and David M. Reimers. *Natives and strangers: blacks, Indians, and immigrants in America.* 2d ed. New York: Oxford University Press, 1990. ISBN 0-19-505722-8. ▸ Synthetic treatment of ethnic, African American, and American Indian experience, with particular emphasis on working-class contributions to American economic growth. [LEC]

43.239 David M. Emmons. *The Butte Irish: class and ethnicity in an American mining town, 1875–1925.* 1989 ed. Urbana: University of Illinois Press, 1990. ISBN 0-252-01603-3 (cl, 1989), 0-252-06155-1 (pbk). ▸ Examination of relationship between class and ethnicity in Irish-dominated context. Sees shift from pro-union ethnic ownership to ethnically diverse work force and technological speed-ups under Standard Oil subsidiary. [LEC]

43.240 Edwin Fenton. *Immigrants and unions, a case study: Italians and American labor, 1870–1920.* New York: Arno, 1975. ISBN 0-405-06399-7. ▸ Exploration of relations between peasant immigrants and unions. Shows variety in experiences based on organization of industry, receptivity of union, and internal factors within immigrant community. [JHH]

43.241 Donna Gabaccia. *Militants and migrants: rural Sicilians become American workers.* New Brunswick, N.J.: Rutgers University Press, 1988. ISBN 0-8135-1318-9 (cl), 0-8135-1356-1 (pbk). ▸ Analysis of interconnections between international migrations of workers and growth and development of social movements in America. Notes considerable variations from place to place. [JWT]

43.242 Mario T. Garcia. *Desert immigrants: the Mexicans of El Paso, 1880–1920.* New Haven: Yale University Press, 1981. ISBN 0-300-02520-3 (cl), 0-300-02883-0 (pbk). ▸ Excellent, thought-provoking analysis of crucial role of Mexicans, who constituted cheap labor pool, in development of American West and their subsequent alienation in American society. [CAM]

43.243 Caroline Golab. *Immigrant destinations.* Philadelphia: Temple University Press, 1977. ISBN 0-87722-109-X. ▸ Study of patterns of ethnic migration to Philadelphia, 1880–1920. Explores variety of issues, including why Poles did not settle there in large numbers. [LEC]

43.244 Arthur A. Goren. *New York Jews and the quest for community: the kehillah experiment, 1908–1922.* New York: Columbia University Press, 1970. ISBN 0-231-03422-9. ▸ Treats Kehillah as dual movement designed to retain "ethnic integrity" and to achieve "social accommodation." Counteracts previous emphases on breakdown of community. [JWT]

43.245 Victor Greene. *For God and country: the rise of Polish and Lithuanian ethnic consciousness in America, 1860–1910.* Madison: State Historical Society of Wisconsin, 1975. ISBN 0-87020-155-7. ▸ Succinct, valuable account of immigrant identity. Locates development of national awareness in intragroup friction. Grassroots study delineating disputes over basis of group membership, nature of community, and religious institutions. [NF]

43.246 Oscar Handlin. *The uprooted: the epic story of the great migrations that made the American people.* 1973 2d ed. Boston: Little, Brown, 1990. ISBN 0-316-34313-7. ▸ Epic study of European immigration. Argues that massive population movement represented traumatic and socially disorganizing experience. Set framework for subsequent research. [JWT]

43.247 John Higham. *Send these to me: immigrants in urban America.* Rev. ed. Baltimore: Johns Hopkins University Press, 1984. ISBN 0-8018-2473-7 (cl), 0-8018-2438-9 (pbk). ▸ Thoughtful collection of essays on immigrant experience. Concludes that "pluralistic integration" is our best tradition. [JWT]

43.248 John Higham. *Strangers in the land: patterns of American nativism, 1860–1925.* 2d ed. New Brunswick, N.J.: Rutgers University Press, 1988. ISBN 0-8135-1317-0 (cl), 0-8135-1308-1 (pbk). ▸ Landmark study of American attitudes toward Jews, Catholics, radicals, and African Americans. Argues that attitudes toward race revealed the most intensity and change over time. [JWT]

43.249 Irving Howe. *World of our fathers.* New York: Harcourt Brace Jovanovich, 1976. ISBN 0-15-146353-0. ▸ Monumental study of eastern European Jewish migration, mainly to New York City. Concludes that Jews moved from affirmation of pariah status to one of hope for integration into modern world. [JWT]

43.250 Edward R. Kantowicz. *Polish-American politics in Chicago, 1888–1940.* 1975 ed. Chicago: University of Chicago Press, 1980. ISBN 0-226-42380-8 (cl, 1975), 0-226-42379-4 (pbk). ▸ Ethnocultural and political study of Chicago's largest white immigrant group. Group's political concerns shifted from politics of Poland to politics of *Polonja Amerykanska*, i.e., terms of assimilation, respect, and economic survival. [JHH]

43.251 Thomas Kessner. *The golden door: Italian and Jewish immigrant mobility in New York City, 1880–1915.* New York: Oxford University Press, 1977. ISBN 0-19-502116-9. ▸ Quantitative study of social mobility. Concludes that myth of upwardly mobile society squared with reality of thousands of immigrants. [JWT]

43.252 Gerd Korman. *Industrialization, immigrants, and americanizers: the view from Milwaukee, 1866–1921.* Madison: State Historical Society of Wisconsin, 1967. ▸ Examination of relationship between rationalization of production and distribution to social relations. Shows how new class of professionals established new system of welfare capitalism. [JWT]

43.253 Alan M. Kraut. *The huddled masses: the immigrant in American society, 1880–1921.* 1982 ed. Arlington Heights, Ill.: Harlan Davidson, 1986. ISBN 0-88295-810-0. ▸ Survey emphasizing individual immigrants' experiences rather than generalizing about large ethnic groups. Covers background, journey, reception, work and mobility, assimilation, and reaction to nativism. [EL]

43.254 Ewa Morawska. *For bread with butter: the life-worlds of East Central Europeans in Johnstown, Pennsylvania, 1890–1940.* Cambridge: Cambridge University Press, 1985. ISBN 0-521-30633-7. ▸ Historical and sociological study of immigration of Slavs to steel-dominated, middle-sized, central Pennsylvania city.

Emphasizes dynamic interactions of Europeans in American context. [LEC]

43.255 Gary R. Mormino. *Immigrants on the hill: Italian-Americans in St. Louis, 1882–1982.* Urbana: University of Illinois Press, 1986. ISBN 0-252-01261-5. ▸ Vigorous defense of oral history as tool for uncovering immigrant experience in major city. [JWT]

43.256 Gary R. Mormino and George Pozzetta. *The immigrant world of Ybor City: Italians and their Latin neighbors in Tampa, 1885–1985.* Urbana: University of Illinois Press, 1987. ISBN 0-252-01351-4. ▸ Unique study of immigrant life in southern city. Moves beyond comparing experiences of specific groups and emphasizes diverse group interactions and influences on each other. [JWT]

43.257 Humbert S. Nelli. *Italians in Chicago, 1880–1930: a study in ethnic mobility.* New York: Oxford University Press, 1970. ▸ Case study of immigration and assimilation. Argues growth of community institutions and neighborhoods aided creation of ethnic identity out of various regional Italian identities. [JHH]

43.258 Moses Rischin. *The promised city: New York's Jews, 1870–1914.* Rev. ed. Cambridge, Mass.: Harvard University Press, 1977. ISBN 0-674-71501-2 (pbk). ▸ Close study of Jewish life in New York City's Lower East side. Shows connection between its poverty and rise of twentieth century reform movements. [JWT]

43.259 Brinley Thomas. *Migration and economic growth: a study of Great Britain and the Atlantic economy.* 2d ed. Cambridge: Cambridge University Press, 1973. ISBN 0-521-08566-7. ▸ Seminal study of European immigration to United States, emphasizing interrelationship between migration and business cycles. [JWT]

43.260 William I. Thomas and Florian Znaniecki. *The Polish peasant in Europe and America.* Abr. ed. Eli Zaretsky, ed. Urbana: University of Illinois Press, 1984. ISBN 0-252-01090-6 (cl), 0-252-01092-2 (pbk). ▸ Classic from Chicago school of sociology that influenced social sciences and social history. Examines work, lives, social institutions, and family in Poland and United States. [JHH]

43.261 Rudolph J. Vecoli. "Contadini in Chicago: a critique of *The Uprooted.*" *Journal of American history* 51.3 (1964) 404–17. ISSN 0021-8723. ▸ Pioneering study of immigration history, emphasizing cultural tenacity of immigrants. Helped to reorient scholarship away from Handlin's social disorganization thesis (43.246). [JWT]

43.262 Virginia Yans-McLaughlin. *Family and community: Italian immigrants in Buffalo, 1880–1930.* 1977 ed. Urbana: University of Illinois Press, 1982. ISBN 0-252-00916-9 (pbk). ▸ Solid study of interplay between old and new world conditions in shaping life of Italian immigrants in industrial America. [JWT]

43.263 Virginia Yans-McLaughlin, ed. *Immigration reconsidered: history, sociology, and politics.* New York: Oxford University Press, 1990. ISBN 0-19-505510-1 (cl), 0-19-505511-X (pbk). ▸ Collection of essays on American immigration by historians and sociologists. Emphasizes global patterns and comparative methods. [EL]

43.264 Olivier Zunz. "American history and the changing meaning of assimilation." *Journal of American ethnic history* (1985) 53–72. ISSN 0278-5927. ▸ Discussion of assimilation from perspective of recent changes in American social history. Concludes questions of ethnicity—not assimilation—have engaged attention of social historians. [JWT]

SEE ALSO
    40.364 John Bodnar. *The transplanted.*

RACIAL AND ETHNIC MINORITIES

General Studies

43.265 David M. Chalmers. *Hooded Americanism: the history of the Ku Klux Klan.* 1981 3d ed. Durham, N.C.: Duke University Press, 1987. ISBN 0-8223-0730-8 (cl), 0-8223-0772-3 (pbk). ‣ Analysis of white supremacist group's northern and southern organizations and styles. Concludes Klan's political impact derived from its defense of traditional American (old stock WASP) values. [JHH]

43.266 Robert F. Heizer and Alan F. Almquist. *The other Californians: prejudice and discrimination under Spain, Mexico, and the United States to 1920.* Berkeley: University of California Press, 1971. ISBN 0-520-01735-8. ‣ Traces antiwhite prejudices in California from Gold Rush through Gilded Age. Multiracial approach; utilizes primary documents. [EL]

43.267 Ivan H. Light. *Ethnic enterprise in America: business and welfare among Chinese, Japanese, and blacks.* Berkeley: University of California Press, 1972. ISBN 0-520-01738-2. ‣ Study of credit associations, banking, church, mutual aid and insurance, Urban League, and voluntary associations, with focus on urban centers. Argues culturally derived consumer preferences and style of economic organization structured ethnic enterprise. [EL]

43.268 Stephan Thernstrom, ed. *Harvard encyclopedia of American ethnic groups.* Cambridge, Mass.: Belknap, 1980. ISBN 0-674-37512-2. ‣ Collection of lengthy (at least 8,000 words) essays covering origins, migration, and settlement patterns of each group. Useful reference for more obscure immigrant groups, e.g., Assyrians, Copts, Hutterites. Each essay includes bibliography. [EL]

SEE ALSO
44.372 Nathan Glazer and Daniel Patrick Moynihan. *Beyond the melting pot.*

African Americans

43.269 James D. Anderson. *The education of blacks in the South, 1860–1935.* Chapel Hill: University of North Carolina Press, 1988. ISBN 0-8078-1793-7 (cl), 0-8078-4221-4 (pbk). ‣ Story of African American education within broader context of American education. Emphasizes conflict between two social systems—slavery and peasantry and capitalism and free labor. [JWT]

43.270 Darrel E. Bigham. *We ask only a fair trial: a history of the black community of Evansville, Indiana.* Bloomington: Indiana University Press, 1987. ISBN 0-253-36326-8. ‣ Illuminating account of African American experience in small city during late nineteenth and early twentieth centuries. Raises important questions about interrelationship between African Americans and municipal government. [JWT]

43.271 Arna Bontemps and Jack Conroy. *Anyplace but here.* New York: Hill & Wang, 1966. ‣ Highly descriptive but useful account of African American migration to cities of North and West. Emphasizes African American population movement as quest for freedom and full citizenship rights. Revised version of *They Seek a City* (1945). [JWT]

43.272 Francis L. Broderick. *W.E.B. Du Bois: Negro leader in a time of crisis.* Stanford, Calif.: Stanford University Press, 1959. ‣ Political biography concludes Du Bois's scholarly and literary achievements were less significant than his singular and unrelenting attack on racial inequality. [JWT]

43.273 Pete Daniel. *The shadow of slavery: peonage in the South, 1901–1969.* Urbana: University of Illinois Press, 1972. ISBN 0-252-00206-7. ‣ Documents persistence of debt-peonage in early twentieth-century South. Concludes federal, state, and local governments—mainly through institutional apathy—failed to protect these workers' rights. [JWT]

43.274 Douglas Henry Daniels. *Pioneer urbanites: a social and cultural history of black San Francisco.* 1980 ed. Berkeley: University of California Press, 1991. ISBN 0-520-07399-1 (pbk). ‣ Study of African American life in urban West counteracting prevailing emphasis on ghetto as pathological phenomenon. Concludes black San Franciscans were quite prepared for life in metropolis. [JWT]

43.275 John Dittmer. *Black Georgia in the Progressive Era, 1900–1920.* Urbana: University of Illinois Press, 1977. ISBN 0-252-00306-3. ‣ Argues history of African Americans in Georgia more than merely contradiction to progressive image of era; it also represented intense struggle of African Americans against racial proscription. [JWT]

43.276 Philip Durham and Everett L. Jones. *The Negro cowboys.* 1965 ed. Lincoln: University of Nebraska Press, 1983. ISBN 0-8032-6560-3 (pbk). ‣ Descriptive but useful account of African American workers on industrializing western frontier. [JWT]

43.277 Robert Francis Engs. *Freedom's first generation: black Hampton, Virginia, 1861–1890.* Philadelphia: University of Pennsylvania Press, 1979. ISBN 0-8122-7768-6. ‣ Documentation of emergence and development of two separate visions of post–Civil War African American life. Shows how blacks pressed for full equality while whites adopted paternalistic posture that hampered black progress. [JWT]

43.278 Vincent P. Franklin. *The education of black Philadelphia: the social and educational history of a minority community, 1900–1950.* Philadelphia: University of Pennsylvania Press, 1979. ISBN 0-8122-7769-4. ‣ Places African American public education within larger social, political, and economic context of African American life in city. Concludes white vision of black education relegated them to subordinate position. [JWT]

43.279 George M. Fredrickson. *The black image in the white mind: the debate on Afro-American character and destiny, 1817–1914.* 1971 ed. Middletown, Conn.: Wesleyan University Press; distributed by Harper & Row, 1987. ISBN 0-8195-6188-6 (pbk). ‣ Analysis of intellectual underpinnings of variety of racist formulations, abolitionist to segregationist. [JHH]

43.280 Willard B. Gatewood, Jr. *Black Americans and the white man's burden, 1898–1903.* Urbana: University of Illinois Press, 1975. ISBN 0-252-00475-2. ‣ Examination of divided and racially distinct responses of African Americans to imperialism and racism. Concludes early support faded as African Americans saw their situation deteriorate at home. Many were ambivalent throughout period. [KB]

43.281 David A. Gerber. *Black Ohio and the color line, 1860–1915.* Urbana: University of Illinois Press, 1976. ISBN 0-252-00534-1. ‣ Documents interplay between shifting patterns of race relations and internal development of African American communities. Shows substantial variation from place to place. [JWT]

43.282 Peter Gottlieb. *Making their own way: southern blacks' migration to Pittsburgh, 1916–30.* Urbana: University of Illinois Press, 1987. ISBN 0-252-01354-9. ‣ Places African American migration within broader context of worldwide, rural to urban shift. Discusses mechanics of movement and patterns of adjustment and community formation in industrial context. [LEC]

43.283 James R. Grossman. *Land of hope: Chicago, black southerners, and the Great Migration.* 1989 ed. Chicago: University of Chicago Press, 1990. ISBN 0-226-30994-0 (cl, 1989), 0-226-30995-9 (pbk). ‣ Examination of meaning of Great Migration from perspective of migrants. Argues southern African Americans developed own indigenous leadership, channels of information, and decisions about movement north. [JWT]

43.284 Lawrence Grossman. *The Democratic party and the Negro: northern and national politics, 1868–92.* 1976 ed. Urbana:

University of Illinois Press, 1991. ISBN 0-252-00575-9. ‣ Argues that, despite ties to its racist southern wing, northern Democratic party developed and retained form of racial liberalism that attracted African American voters and helped to undermine Republican efforts to secure African American vote. [JWT]

43.285 William Ivy Hair. *Carnival of fury: Robert Charles and the New Orleans race riot of 1900*. Baton Rouge: Louisiana State University Press, 1976. ISBN 0-8071-0178-8. ‣ Analysis of bloody New Orleans riot and life of Robert Charles (black man who resisted mob alone) within broader context of southern, African American, and Louisiana history. [JWT]

43.286 Louis R. Harlan. *Booker T. Washington*. Vol. 1: *The making of a black leader, 1856–1901*. 1972 ed. New York: Oxford University Press, 1975. ISBN 0-19-501915-6 (pbk). ‣ Transcends polarized views of Booker T. Washington as either realistic African American philosopher during age of Jim Crow or intellectual opposite of W.E.B. Du Bois. [JWT]

43.287 Louis R. Harlan. *Booker T. Washington*. Vol. 2: *The wizard of Tuskegee, 1901–1915*. 1983 ed. New York: Oxford University Press, 1986. ISBN 0-19-504229-8 (pbk). ‣ Builds on earlier study (43.286) and documents African American leader's life to his death in 1915. Elaborates on previous argument that Washington was complex, enigmatic figure. [JWT]

43.288 Florette Henri. *Black migration: movement north, 1900–1920*. Garden City, N.Y.: Anchor, 1975. ISBN 0-385-04030-X. ‣ Synthesis of African American migration to northern cities. Anticipated recent emphases on African American migration as phenomenon rooted in choices African Americans made and actions they took. [JWT]

43.289 Evelyn Brooks Higginbotham. "African American women's history and the meta-language of race." *Signs* 17 (1992) 251–74. ISSN 0097-9740. ‣ Groundbreaking theoretical discussion of race as social construction like gender and class. Emphasizes significance of this insight for understanding experiences of African American women. [JWT]

43.290 Darlene Clark Hine. "Black migration to the urban Midwest: the gender dimension, 1915–1945." In *The Great Migration in historical perspective: new dimensions of race, class, and gender*. Joe William Trotter, Jr., ed., pp. 127–46. Bloomington: Indiana University Press, 1991. ISBN 0-253-36075-7 (cl), 0-253-20669-3 (pbk). ‣ Seminal essay arguing that African American migration studies must move beyond role of women in kinship networks and identify unique gender dimensions of African American population movement. [JWT]

43.291 Darlene Clark Hine, ed. *Black women in American history: the twentieth century*. 4 vols. Brooklyn, N.Y.: Carlson, 1990. ISBN 0-926019-15-5 (set). ‣ Rich collection of essays arranged alphabetically by author. Wide range of topics includes clubs, education, blues, segregation, tobacco workers, local and national leaders, domestic workers, religion, artists, and writers. [PAC]

43.292 David M. Katzman. *Before the ghetto: black Detroit in the nineteenth century*. Urbana: University of Illinois Press, 1973. ISBN 0-252-00279-2. ‣ Analysis using caste model to describe developments in African American urban life before rise of large central city ghettos. [JWT]

43.293 Charles Flint Kellogg. *NAACP: a history of the National Association for the Advancement of Colored People*. Baltimore: Johns Hopkins University Press, 1967. ISBN 0-317-20667-2 (pbk). ‣ Argues NAACP's formative years represented explicit effort to reestablish linkages with old abolitionist tradition that had helped to end slavery. [JWT]

43.294 Jack Temple Kirby. *Darkness at the dawning: race and reform in the progressive South*. Philadelphia: Lippincott, 1972. ISBN 0-397-47263-3 (cl), 0-397-47209-9 (pbk). ‣ Maintains that

once nation solved its sectional cleavages through disenfranchisement of blacks, white South joined nationwide reform movement to achieve progress in wide variety of areas. [JWT]

43.295 Kenneth L. Kusmer. "The black urban experience in American history." In *The state of Afro-American history: past, present, and future*. 1986 ed. Darlene Clark Hine, ed. Thomas C. Holt, Introduction., pp. 91–122. Baton Rouge: Louisiana State University Press, 1989. ISBN 0-8071-1254-2 (cl, 1986), 0-8071-1581-9 (pbk). ‣ Historiographical essay analyzing development of African American urban history as field of study and concluding with call for greater attention to interplay of external, internal, and structural factors in history of urban African Americans. [JWT]

43.296 Kenneth L. Kusmer. *A ghetto takes shape: black Cleveland, 1870–1930*. Urbana: University of Illinois Press, 1976. ISBN 0-252-00289-X (cl), 0-252-00690-0 (pbk). ‣ Relates economic, social, political, and cultural changes in African American urban life to developing ghetto. Concludes racially segregated neighborhoods in Cleveland developed later than elsewhere in urban North. [JWT]

43.297 Eugene Levy. *James Weldon Johnson: black leader, black voice*. Chicago: University of Chicago Press, 1973. ISBN 0-226-47603-0. ‣ Treats Johnson as transition figure in transformation of African American ideology and politics—from defensive posture of Booker T. Washington to aggressive civil rights activism of mid-twentieth century. [JWT]

43.298 Earl Lewis. *In their own interests: race, class, and power in twentieth-century Norfolk, Virginia*. Berkeley: University of California Press, 1991. ISBN 0-520-06644-8. ‣ Advances new conceptual framework for understanding African American urban history. Emphasizes African American quest for empowerment at work, at home (including family and community life), or in some combination of two. [JWT]

43.299 Rayford W. Logan. *Betrayal of the Negro: from Rutherford B. Hayes to Woodrow Wilson*. 1965 rev. ed. New York: Collier, 1972. ‣ Synthesis of African American history during early segregationist era. Concludes African American life reached its nadir during 1890s, symbolized by rise of Booker T. Washington following his "Atlanta Compromise" address. [JWT]

43.300 James M. McPherson. *The abolitionist legacy: from Reconstruction to the NAACP*. Princeton: Princeton University Press, 1975. ISBN 0-691-04637-9. ‣ Study maintaining that struggle of white abolitionists did not end in 1870, as many argue, but continued into early twentieth century. Proved influential in postbellum southern educational reforms, before returning to militant political action in early 1900s. [JHH]

43.301 August Meier. *Negro thought in America, 1880–1915: racial ideologies in the age of Booker T. Washington*. 1963 ed. Ann Arbor: University of Michigan Press, 1988. ISBN 0-472-64230-8 (cl), 0-472-06118-6 (pbk). ‣ Discussion of shifting African American ideologies. Relates ideological changes to major institutional developments within African American community and to major streams of thought in American society. [JWT]

43.302 August Meier and Elliott Rudwick. *Black history and the historical profession, 1915–1980*. Urbana: University of Illinois Press, 1986. ISBN 0-252-01269-0 (cl), 0-252-01274-7 (pbk). ‣ Oral history of rise and transformation of African American history as research field. [JWT]

43.303 Judy Jolley Mohraz. *The separate problem: case studies of black education in the North, 1900–1930*. Westport, Conn.: Greenwood, 1979. ISBN 0-313-20411-X. ‣ Examination of contours of black education in northern schools in Philadelphia, Chicago, and Indianapolis. As Great Migration swelled each African

American community, black children faced hardening racism and segregation as well as class-based education reforms. [JHH]

43.304 Gilbert Osofsky. *Harlem, the making of a ghetto: Negro New York, 1890–1930.* 2d ed. New York: Harper & Row, 1971. ISBN 0-06-131572-9 (pbk). ▸ Documents racial transformation of Harlem from white upper-middle-class community to predominantly African American community. Locates roots of ghetto formation in pre–World War I years. [JWT]

43.305 Nell Irvin Painter. *Exodusters: black migration to Kansas after Reconstruction.* 1976 ed. Lawrence: University Press of Kansas, 1986. ISBN 0-7006-0288-7 (pbk). ▸ Treats this early African American population movement as millennial working-class movement. Not merely demographic but political—a challenge to white supremacy. [JHH]

43.306 Howard N. Rabinowitz. *Race relations in the urban South, 1865–1890.* 1978 ed. Urbana: University of Illinois Press, 1980. ISBN 0-252-00811-1 (pbk). ▸ Examination of African American life in five capital cities—Atlanta, Montgomery, Nashville, Raleigh, and Richmond. Concludes racial segregation supplanted earlier and often more pernicious system of exclusion from full citizenship rights. [JWT]

43.307 Arnold Rampersad. *The art and imagination of W.E.B. Du Bois.* 1976 ed. New York: Schocken, 1990. ISBN 0-8052-0985-9 (pbk). ▸ Counteracts earlier studies by maintaining that Du Bois's greatest gift was poetic in nature and that his work as scholar and political activist drew its ultimate power from this source. [JWT]

43.308 Edwin S. Redkey. *Black exodus: black nationalist and back-to-Africa movements, 1890–1910.* New Haven: Yale University Press, 1969. ISBN 0-300-01138-5 (cl), 0-300-01139-3 (pbk). ▸ Study of unsuccessful African American nationalist tenant farmer movement led by Henry M. Turner and its promotion of emigration to Africa to escape racial oppression. Nationalist aspect of movement more successful than emigration effort. [KB]

43.309 Elliott Rudwick. *Race riot at East St. Louis, July 2, 1917.* 1964 ed. Urbana: University of Illinois Press, 1982. ISBN 0-252-00951-7 (pbk). ▸ Concludes East St. Louis riot more violent than others because, for first time, large numbers of northern African Americans aggressively made claims to equal rights. [JWT]

43.310 Elliott Rudwick. *W.E.B. Du Bois: a study in minority group leadership.* Philadelphia: University of Pennsylvania Press, 1960. ▸ Documents Du Bois's role as lecturer and editor who marshalled ideological arguments and symbols to combat racism. Concludes Du Bois's aloofness from masses limited his effectiveness. [JWT]

43.311 Roberta Senechal. *The sociogenesis of a race riot: Springfield, Illinois, in 1908.* Urbana: University of Illinois Press, 1990. ISBN 0-252-01694-7. ▸ Analysis of historical and social science literature on racial violence. Advances new interpretation that riot resulted from variety of factors, transcending emphases on job competition and residential segregation. [JWT]

43.312 Allan H. Spear. *Black Chicago: the making of a Negro ghetto, 1890–1920.* Chicago: University of Chicago Press, 1967. ISBN 0-226-76857-0 (pbk). ▸ Analysis of development of segregated African American community on city's south side. Specifies both internal and external forces that created ghetto and concludes ghetto was primarily product of white hostility. [JWT]

43.313 Donald Spivey. *Schooling for the new slavery: black industrial education, 1868–1915.* Westport, Conn.: Greenwood, 1978. ISBN 0-313-20051-3. ▸ Analysis of origins, goals, and impact of industrial education in American South. Views Tuskegee Institute as tool to control social reproduction of cheap, docile African American labor for northern capitalists. [JHH]

43.314 Quintard Taylor. "The emergence of black communities in the Pacific Northwest, 1865–1910." *Journal of Negro history* 64 (1979) 342–45. ISSN 0022-2992. ▸ Examination of migration of approximately 10,000 African Americans to major urban centers in states of Idaho, Montana, Oregon, and Washington. Shows how these migrants formed core of African American community life. [JWT]

43.315 Joe W. Trotter, Jr., ed. *The Great Migration in historical perspective: new dimensions of race, class, and gender.* Bloomington: Indiana University Press, 1991. ISBN 0-253-36075-7 (cl), 0-253-20669-3 (pbk). ▸ Six essays plus historiographical introduction reflecting proletarian approach to African American migration. Emphasizes migration as not merely northeastern phenomenon, citing West Virginia mines, Norfolk, Virginia, and northern California. Also discusses experience of women as distinct from men. [LEC]

43.316 Walter B. Weare. *Black business in the New South: a social history of the North Carolina Mutual Life Insurance Company.* Urbana: University of Illinois Press, 1973. ISBN 0-252-00285-7. ▸ Documents history of major African American business during late nineteenth and early twentieth centuries. Argues insurance firm more significant as illustration of ideology of racial self-help and progress than as economic venture. [JWT]

43.317 Joel Williamson. *The crucible of race: black-white relations in the American South since emancipation.* New York: Oxford University Press, 1984. ISBN 0-19-503382-5. ▸ Intellectual, cultural, and political synthesis of race relations. Shows how southern white elites increasingly separated from African Americans and realigned with white poor and working classes. [JWT]

43.318 C. Vann Woodward. "The strange career of a historical controversy." In *American counterpoint: slavery and racism in the North/South dialogue.* 1971 ed, pp. 234–60. Oxford: Oxford University Press, 1983. ISBN 0-19-503269-1 (pbk). ▸ Illuminating discussion of variety of responses to author's book, *The Strange Career of Jim Crow* (40.155), published more than two decades earlier. [JWT]

43.319 George C. Wright. *Life behind a veil: blacks in Louisville, Kentucky, 1865–1930.* Baton Rouge: Louisiana State University Press, 1985. ISBN 0-8071-1224-0. ▸ Influential study that helped initiate historical scholarship on African American life in southern cities. Concludes that, unlike vicious pattern of race relations further south, Louisville developed system of "polite" racism. [JWT]

SEE ALSO

American Indians

43.320 Christine Bolt. *American Indian policy and American reform: case studies of the campaign to assimilate the American Indians.* London: Allen & Unwin, 1987. ISBN 0-04-900037-3 (cl), 0-04-900039-X (pbk). ▸ Combination of general history and case studies. Places American Indian policy and reform within context of racial and ethnic ideologies of period. [EL]

43.321 Dee Brown. *Bury my heart at Wounded Knee: an Indian history of the American West.* 1970 ed. New York: Holt, 1991. ISBN 0-8050-1730-5. ▸ Attempt to recover Indian voices using contemporary interviews of Indians by reporters, anthropologists, and government officials. Covers period 1860–90, with focus on Indian wars and treaties with United States government. [EL]

43.322 Richard Drinnon. *Facing West: the metaphysics of Indian-hating and empire-building.* 1980 ed. New York: Schocken, 1990. ISBN 0-8052-0978-6. ▸ Outline of distinctive patterns of response to colonization. Section on imperialism includes chapters on Open Door policy, Philippines, and continued racism in America. [EL]

43.323 Frederick E. Hoxie. *A final promise: the campaign to assimilate the Indians, 1880–1920.* 1984 ed. Cambridge: Cambridge University Press, 1989. ISBN 0-521-37987-3. ▸ Exemplary ethnohistory focusing on policies of time and failures of vision. Reveals how ideals of assimilationist programs produced social and economic suffering among native peoples. [CAM]

43.324 Robert H. Keller. "Hostile language: bias in historical writing about American Indian resistance." *Journal of American culture* 9 (1986) 9–23. ISSN 0191-1813. ▸ Linguistic criticism of historical writings on American Indians with call for attention to bias. [EL]

43.325 Margaret Maier Murdock. "Putting Indians back into the central role in their own history." *Social science journal* 24 (1987) 341–42. ISSN 0362-3319. ▸ Delineation of weaknesses in current American Indian historiography by highlighting secondary role played by American Indians in telling their histories. [EL]

43.326 Francis Paul Prucha. *American Indian policy in crisis: Christian reformers and the Indian, 1865–1900.* 1975 ed. Norman: University of Oklahoma Press, 1976. ISBN 0-8061-1279-4. ▸ Detailed study of change in United States policy toward American Indians during period of pacification and establishment of reservation system. [EL]

43.327 Francis Paul Prucha. *The churches and the Indian schools, 1888–1912.* Lincoln: University of Nebraska Press, 1979. ISBN 0-8032-3657-3. ▸ Analysis of conflict between Protestants and Catholics over Indian education: both desired federal funding. Significant political and religious figures joined battle. Excellent use of public and court records. [CAM]

43.328 Robert A. Trennert, Jr. "Educating Indian girls at non-reservation boarding schools, 1878–1920." In *Unequal sisters: a multicultural reader in U.S. women's history.* Ellen Carol DuBois and Vicki L. Ruiz, eds., pp. 224–38. New York: Routledge, 1990. ISBN 0-415-90271-1 (cl), 0-415-90272-X (pbk). ▸ Details goals, plans, and failures of federal government's policy of removing Indian girls from their homes and transferring them to government schools in attempt to americanize them. [EL]

43.329 Robert A. Trennert, Jr. *The Phoenix Indian School: forced assimilation in Arizona, 1891–1935.* Norman: University of Oklahoma Press, 1988. ISBN 0-8061-2104-1. ▸ Excellent microcosmic view including important chapter on student life. Judges federally mandated policy a failure: administrators hampered by many constraints and criticized by reformers, yet many educational successes were achieved. [CAM]

SEE ALSO
36.166 Vine Deloria, Jr., and Clifford M. Lytle. *The nations within.*
36.258 Paul Stuart. *Nations within a nation.*
36.260 William R. Swagerty, ed. *Scholars and the Indian experience.*
40.399 Robert F. Berkhofer, Jr. *The white man's Indian.*

Asian Americans

43.330 Gunther Barth. *Bitter strength: a history of the Chinese in the United States, 1850–1870.* Cambridge, Mass.: Harvard University Press, 1964. ISBN 0-8737-1669-9 (pbk). ▸ Outline of emergence of anti-Chinese hostility. Contrasts Chinese immigrant experience to other groups (sojourners versus settlers). Author was student of Oscar Handlin. [EL]

43.331 Jack Chen. *The Chinese of America.* 1980 ed. San Francisco: Harper & Row, 1982. ISBN 0-06-250140-2 (cl, 1980), 0-06-250139-9 (pbk). ▸ Seven chapters covering gangsterism, Chinese community in America, and Chinese Exclusion Acts and their effects. [EL]

43.332 Roger Daniels. *The politics of prejudice: the anti-Japanese movement in California and the struggle for Japanese exclusion.* 2d ed. Berkeley: University of California Press, 1977. ISBN 0-520-03412-0 (cl), 0-520-03411-2 (pbk). ▸ Exploration of motivations for California exclusionists. Little focus on Japanese immigrants. [EL]

43.333 Yuji Ichioka. *The issei: the world of the first generation of Japanese immigrants, 1885–1924.* New York and London: Free Press and Collier Macmillan, 1988. ISBN 0-02-915370-0. ▸ Detailed study of immigration policy, social circumstances, and general social milieu of first generation of Japanese in America. [EL]

43.334 John Modell. *The economics and politics of racial accommodation: the Japanese of Los Angeles, 1900–1942.* Urbana: University of Illinois Press, 1977. ISBN 0-252-00622-4. ▸ Expands study of Japanese Americans beyond perspective of relocation camps of World War II. Concludes accommodation represented responsible strategy because opportunities were so visible. [JWT]

43.335 Mei Nakano. *Japanese American women: three generations, 1890–1990.* Berkeley and San Francisco: Mina and National Japanese American Historical Society, 1990. ISBN 0-942610-05-9 (cl), 0-942610-06-7 (pbk). ▸ Situates life experience of three generations of Japanese and Japanese American women in national and international contexts. Strives to allow women to tell their own stories whenever possible; written for broad audience. [EL]

43.336 Gary Y. Okihiro. *Cane fires: the anti-Japanese movement in Hawaii, 1865–1945.* Philadelphia: Temple University Press, 1991. ISBN 0-87722-799-3. ▸ Revelation of systematic oppression and surveillance of Asian Americans. Conceptualizes their resistance, social relations, and status through generations. Suggests comparisons with other minority groups. Substantially revises image of island as tolerant. [CAM]

43.337 Alexander Saxton. *The indispensable enemy: labor and the anti-Chinese movement in California.* Berkeley: University of California Press, 1970. ISBN 0-520-01721-8. ▸ Exploration of level of anti-Asian, especially anti-Chinese, sentiment in labor movement of late nineteenth-century California. Discusses Working Men's group in San Francisco. [EL]

43.338 Ronald T. Takaki. *Strangers from a different shore: a history of Asian Americans.* 1989 ed. New York: Penguin, 1990. ISBN 0-14-013885-4. ▸ Lyrical overview of immigrant and resident experiences of Asians and Asian Americans. [EL]

SEE ALSO
40.181 Sucheng Chan. *This bittersweet soil.*
40.370 Evelyn Nakano Glenn. *Issei, nisei, war bride.*

Latino Americans

43.339 Rodolfo Acuña. *Occupied America: a history of Chicanos.* 3d ed. New York: Harper & Row, 1988. ISBN 0-06-040163-X (pbk). ▸ Overview of immigration, labor, and political history of Chicanos. Divided into two parts—nineteenth and twentieth centuries. [EL]

43.340 Tomas Almaguer. "Ideological distortions in recent Chicano historiography: the internal model and Chicano historical interpretation." *Aztlan* 18 (1987) 7–28. ISSN 0005-2604. ▸ Part of special issue on Mexican American history. Argues recent historiography has unwittingly obscured complexities of their history. Focuses on experience in nineteenth-century California. [EL]

43.341 L. H. Gann and Peter J. Duigan. *The Hispanics in the United States: a history.* Boulder: Westview, 1986. ISBN 0-8133-0335-4. ▸ Conservative history of Spanish-speaking immigrants. Uncritical of American capitalist society and pro-assimilationist. [EL]

43.342 David G. Guitierrez. "The third generation: recent trends in Chicano/Mexican American historiography." *Mexican studies/Estudios mexicanos* 5 (1989) 281–97. ISSN 0742-9797. ▸ Concludes scholarship in field has evolved into its third generation. Current generation moving toward interdisciplinary approach emphasizing internal dynamics and stratification in Mexican American society. [JHH]

43.343 Ruth Horowitz. *Honor and the American dream: culture and social identity in a Chicano community.* New Brunswick, N.J.: Rutgers University Press, 1983. ISBN 0-8135-0966-1 (cl), 0-8135-0991-2 (pbk). ▸ Ethnography of Mexican American youth in Chicago, utilizing participant-observer methodology. [EL]

43.344 Alfredo Mirande. *The Chicano experience: an alternative perspective.* Notre Dame, Ind.: University of Notre Dame Press, 1985. ISBN 0-268-00748-9 (cl), 0-268-00749-7 (pbk). ▸ Call for development of a Mexican American sociology. Extensive bibliography and statistics. [EL]

43.345 Leonard Pitt. *The decline of the Californios: a social history of the Spanish-speaking Californians, 1846–1890.* Berkeley: University of California Press, 1966. ISBN 0-520-01637-8 (pbk). ▸ Social history of Latino immigrants in California. [EL]

43.346 Robert J. Rosenbaum. *Mexicano resistance in the Southwest: "the sacred right of self-preservation."* Austin: University of Texas Press, 1981. ISBN 0-292-77562-8. ▸ Analysis of politics in New Mexico during territorial years, focusing on Las Gorras Blancas, organization of poor Mexicans. Based on author's dissertation. [EL]

43.347 George Sanchez. "'Go after the women': americanization and the Mexican immigrant woman, 1915–1929." In *Unequal sisters: a multicultural reader in U.S. women's history.* Ellen Carol DuBois and Vicki L. Ruiz, eds., pp. 250–63. New York: Routledge, 1990. ISBN 0-415-90271-1 (cl), 0-415-90272-X (pbk). ▸ Examination of United States policy of americanizing Mexican female immigrants, including its failure. [EL]

43.348 Alex M. Saragoza. "Recent Chicano historiography: an interpretive essay." *Aztlan* 19 (1990) 1–77. ISSN 0005-2604. ▸ Lengthy review essay, with bibliography, assessing Mexican American historiography over last decade. [EL]

SEE ALSO
40.358 Richard Allen Griswold del Castillo. *La familia.*
40.362 David Montejano. *Anglos and Mexicans in the making of Texas, 1836–1986.*
40.398 Mario Barrera. *Race and class in the Southwest.*
44.320 Vicki L. Ruiz. *Cannery women, cannery lives.*
44.403 Alejandro Portes and Robert L. Bach. *Latin journey.*

WOMEN

Family and Work Force

43.349 Susan Armitage and Elizabeth Jameson, eds. *The women's west.* Norman: University of Oklahoma Press, 1987. ISBN 0-8061-2043-6 (cl), 0-8061-2067-3 (pbk). ▸ Essays on mining communities, prostitution, women's work, violence, and representations of women in West from early nineteenth through twentieth century. [PAC]

43.350 Cindy Sondik Aron. *Ladies and gentlemen of the civil service: middle-class workers in Victorian America.* New York: Oxford University Press, 1987. ISBN 0-19-504874-1. ▸ Study of expansion of women's and men's white-collar work in government offices as part of growth and transformation of middle class after Civil War. Explores complicated interconnections among class and gender identities. [PAC]

43.351 Susan Porter Benson. *Counter-cultures: saleswomen, managers, and customers in American department stores, 1890–1940.* 1986 ed. Urbana: University of Illinois Press, 1988. ISBN 0-252-01252-6 (cl, 1986), 0-252-06013-X (pbk). ▸ Analysis of saleswomen's complex relations with managers and consumers. Concludes formation and operation of workplace cultures rooted in class/gender identities and conflicts and affected by developing culture of consumption. [PAC]

43.352 Ellen Chesler. *Woman of valor: Margaret Sanger and the birth control movement in America.* New York: Simon & Schuster, 1992. ISBN 0-671-60088-5. ▸ Story of movement's controversial leader. Argues Sanger's motives for championing eugenics not racist. Challenges older interpretations that Sanger discarded her feminism. [PAC]

43.353 Margery W. Davies. *Woman's place is at the typewriter: office work and office workers, 1870–1930.* 1982 ed. Philadelphia: Temple University Press, 1984. ISBN 0-87722-368-8 (pbk). ▸ Study of creation of secretarial proletariat through transformation of clerical jobs from mobile middle-class male apprenticeship to working-class women's routinized work. Concludes managerial reorganization of work, not typewriter, feminized and degraded work. [PAC]

43.354 Sarah Deutsch. *No separate refuge: culture, class, and gender on an Anglo-Hispanic frontier in the American Southwest, 1880–1940.* 1987 ed. New York: Oxford University Press, 1989. ISBN 0-19-504421-5 (cl, 1987), 0-19-506073-3 (pbk). ▸ Study of white-Hispanic relations in Colorado and New Mexico. Stresses contested power/control and dynamic aspects of Hispanic cultures. Highlights transformation of women's work and experiences and ways gender shaped frontier communities. [PAC]

43.355 Ileen A. DeVault. *Sons and daughters of labor: class and clerical work in turn-of-the-century Pittsburgh.* Ithaca, N.Y.: Cornell University Press, 1990. ISBN 0-8014-2026-1. ▸ Analysis of location of clerical work in class hierarchy and discussion of gendered understandings of class identity, job choices, and social status. Argues line between white- and blue-collar occupations blurred; sees gender as essential for analyzing class. [PAC]

43.356 Nancy Schrom Dye. *As equals and as sisters: feminism, the labor movement, and the Women's Trade Union League of New York.* Columbia: University of Missouri Press, 1980. ISBN 0-8262-0318-3. ▸ Study of New York Women's Trade Union League alliance between working-class and upper-class women. Examines difficulties in combining class and feminist goals and resulting shift from trade unionism to reform and protective legislation. [PAC]

43.357 Sarah Eisenstein. *Give us bread but give us roses: working women's consciousness in the United States, 1890 to the First World War.* London: Routledge & Kegan Paul, 1983. ISBN 0-7100-9479-5 (pbk). ▸ Collection of essays examining women workers' identities, attitudes, and experiences, especially in contrast to middle-class ideals of womanhood. Shows how new experiences in workplace transformed working-class women's outlooks and actions. [PAC]

43.358 Elizabeth Ewen. *Immigrant women in the land of dollars: life and culture on the Lower East Side, 1890–1925.* New York: Monthly Review, 1985. ISBN 0-85345-681-X (cl), 0-85345-682-8 (pbk). ▸ Examination of lives and struggles of Italian and Jewish women immigrants in New York City, including culture, resistance, networks, values, consumption, families, and work. Concludes focus on women alters conceptions of immigrant experience, americanization, and cultural identity. [PAC]

43.359 Lisa M. Fine. *The souls of the skyscraper: female clerical workers in Chicago, 1870–1930.* Philadelphia: Temple University Press, 1990. ISBN 0-87722-674-1. ▸ Study of feminization of clerical work, stressing women's active choices and discourses on occupation's gender definition. Argues devaluation of clerical work occurred not because of deskilling, but because workers were women. Adds to debate on occupational segregation. [PAC]

43.360 Dolores Hayden. *The grand domestic revolution: a history of feminist designs for American homes, neighborhoods, and cities.* 1981 ed. Cambridge, Mass.: MIT Press, 1983. ISBN 0-262-08108-3 (cl, 1981), 0-262-58055-1 (pbk). ▸ Study of feminist proposals, including Charlotte Perkins Gilman's, for restructuring city space and women's household and childcare work. Shows how these challenged, although imperfectly, capitalism and suggested spatial revolution necessary for women's equality. [PAC]

43.361 Darlene Clark Hine. *Black women in white: racial conflict and cooperation in the nursing profession, 1890–1950.* Bloomington: Indiana University Press, 1989. ISBN 0-253-32773-3 (cl), 0-253-20529-8 (pbk). ▸ Study of African American women's fight against racism in professional nursing, efforts to aid African American community, and actions to expand women's opportunities. Broad social history. [PAC]

43.362 Darlene Clark Hine. "Rape and the inner lives of black women in the Middle West: preliminary thoughts on the culture of dissemblance." *Signs* 14 (1989) 912–20. ISSN 0097-9740. ▸ Examination of rape as noneconomic motive for migration. Concludes race, class, and gender conflict necessitated veil of secrecy regarding personal lives, but African American women's institutions created culture of autonomy and resistance. [PAC]

43.363 Yuji Ichioka. "*Amerika nadeshiko*: Japanese immigrant women in the United States, 1900–1924." *Pacific historical review* 49 (1980) 339–57. ISSN 0030-8684. ▸ Uses oral histories and documents to survey conditions for Japanese women immigrants. Examines picture bride practices, various motives for migration, and problems on arrival. Studies how women's presence changed Japanese American society. [PAC]

43.364 Dolores E. Janiewski. *Sisterhood denied: race, gender, and class in a New South community.* Philadelphia: Temple University Press, 1985. ISBN 0-87722-361-0. ▸ Study of struggles among women in Durham, North Carolina, tobacco and textile factories. Concludes failures of unionism rooted in race and gender divisions and separation from community institutions. Based on interviews with workers, manufacturers, and other residents. [PAC]

43.365 Susan Lehrer. *Origins of protective labor legislation for women, 1905–1925.* Albany: State University of New York Press, 1987. ISBN 0-88706-506-6 (cl), 0-88706-505-8 (pbk). ▸ Study of development of labor laws for women, including social forces producing them, effect on class and gender relations, and state's interest. Argues laws mediated contradiction between women's roles in family and reproduction and in capitalist production. [PAC]

43.366 Joanne J. Meyerowitz. *Women adrift: independent wage earners in Chicago, 1880–1930.* Chicago: University of Chicago Press, 1988. ISBN 0-226-52197-4. ▸ History of self-supporting women's struggles, organizations and networks, work experiences, and housing, and their portrayal by middle-class reformers. Finds women's subcultures addressed problems and created sense of community. [PAC]

43.367 Gloria Moldow. *Women doctors in Gilded Age Washington: race, gender, and professionalization.* Urbana: University of Illinois Press, 1987. ISBN 0-252-01379-4. ▸ Study of limited opportunities, professional organizations, careers, and training for women physicians. Sees important role of Howard University

and looks at why brief period of promise ended by early twentieth century. [PAC]

43.368 Elizabeth Ann Payne. *Reform, labor, and feminism: Margaret Dreier Robins and the Women's Trade Union League.* Urbana: University of Illinois Press, 1988. ISBN 0-252-01445-6. ▸ Argues that complex partnership between unionism and feminism in Progressive Era brought some victories but many obstacles. Success of longstanding female culture ironically signaled its demise in 1920s. [PAC]

43.369 Kathy Peiss. *Cheap amusements: working women and leisure in turn-of-the-century New York.* Philadelphia: Temple University Press, 1986. ISBN 0-87722-389-0 (cl), 0-87722-500-1 (pbk). ▸ Lively, descriptive analysis of development of heterosexual working women's leisure culture. Argues it both subverted and reinforced conventional gender relations and constructions. Explores dynamics of cultural change and consumerism. [PAC]

43.370 Ruth Rosen. *The lost sisterhood: prostitution in America, 1900–1918.* 1982 ed. Baltimore: Johns Hopkins University Press, 1984. ISBN 0-8018-2664-0 (cl, 1982), 0-8018-2665-9 (pbk). ▸ Study of prostitution during Progressive Era, highlighting racial and class variations among those associated with it. Treats organization of business, prostitutes as working women, and reformers' campaign against it. Stresses prostitutes' subculture and community. [PAC]

43.371 Leslie Woodcock Tentler. *Wage-earning women: industrial work and family life in the United States, 1900–1930.* 1979 ed. Oxford: Oxford University Press, 1982. ISBN 0-19-502627-6 (cl, 1979), 0-19-503211-X (pbk). ▸ Examination of lives of white women employed in factories in northeastern and midwestern cities. Argues work experience did not transform values, but reinforced traditional gender roles and identity. [PAC]

43.372 Judy Yung. "The social awakening of Chinese American women as reported in *Chung Sai Yat Po*, 1900–1911." In *Unequal sisters: a multicultural reader in U.S. women's history.* Ellen Carol DuBois and Vicki L. Ruiz, eds., pp. 195–207. New York: Routledge, 1990. ISBN 0-415-90271-1 (cl), 0-415-90272-X (pbk). ▸ Analysis of popular, progressive Chinese American newspapers' attitudes toward women's status, particularly regarding women's education, women's rights, and prohibitions against foot-binding. Argues debates more influential in China than in United States. [PAC]

SEE ALSO

4.813 Regina Markell Morantz-Sanchez. *Sympathy and science.*
40.180 Anne M. Butler. *Daughters of joy, sisters of misery.*

Feminism and Suffrage

43.373 Karen J. Blair. *The clubwoman as feminist: true womanhood redefined, 1868–1914.* Annette K. Baxter, Preface. New York: Holmes & Meier, 1980. ISBN 0-8419-5038-X (cl), 0-8419-1261-0 (pbk). ▸ Development of women's club movement including specific clubs and national federation. Argues movement expanded women's activities in public sphere, but never transcended basic belief in domestic feminism. [PAC]

43.374 Ruth Bordin. *Woman and temperance: the quest for power and liberty, 1873–1900.* 1981 ed. New Brunswick, N.J.: Rutgers University Press, 1990. ISBN 0-8135-1543-2. ▸ Analysis of Women's Christian Temperance Union as feminist reform organization that placed women in public sphere and provided mass base essential for later success of suffrage movement. [PAC/TJMcD]

43.375 Elsa Barkley Brown. "Womanist consciousness: Maggie Lena Walker and the Independent Order of Saint Luke." *Signs* 14 (1989) 610–33. ISSN 0097-9740. ▸ Study of Walker's career as banker/reformer in Richmond, Virginia, 1880s to 1920s. Argues Walker's multiple activities reflected womanist theory that interpreted gender, race, and class as simultaneous and interdependent, avoiding either/or dichotomies. [PAC]

43.376 Steven M. Buechler. *The transformation of the woman suffrage movement: the case of Illinois, 1850–1920.* New Brunswick, N.J.: Rutgers University Press, 1986. ISBN 0-8135-1131-3. ‣ Case study of suffrage movement in Illinois, including role of social class in shaping it and regional variations. Argues class factors and developing organizational processes explain transformation of movement over entire period. [PAC/TJMcD]

43.377 Mari Jo Buhle. *Women and American socialism, 1870–1920.* 1981 ed. Urbana: University of Illinois Press, 1983. ISBN 0-252-00873-1 (cl), 0-252-01045-0 (pbk). ‣ Discussion of development of socialist women's movement and its leaders. Contrasts outlooks of immigrant and native-born women and treats debates/struggles over labor, suffrage, and prostitution. Revises traditional view of American socialism. [PAC]

43.378 Blanche Wiesen Cook. "Female support networks and political activism: Lillian Wald, Crystal Eastman, Emma Goldman." *Chrysalis* 3 (1977) 43–61. ISSN 0888-9384. ‣ Critique of historians' denial of lesbian history, arguing importance of understanding power of communities of independent women who loved each other. [PAC]

43.379 Ellen Carol DuBois. "Working women, class relations, and suffrage militance: Harriot Stanton Blatch and the New York woman suffrage movement, 1894–1909." *Journal of American history* 74 (1987) 34–58. ISSN 0021-8723. ‣ Examination of tension between elite reform tradition and working-class politics within woman suffrage movement as seen through daughter of feminist Elizabeth Cady Stanton. Examines what suffrage movement suggests about nature of political change during Progressive Era. [PAC]

43.380 Ellen Fitzpatrick. *Endless crusade: women social scientists and Progressive reform.* New York: Oxford University Press, 1990. ISBN 0-19-506121-7. ‣ Study of careers of four leading reformers: Sophonisba Breckinridge, Edith Abbott, Katharine Bement Davis, and Frances Kellor. Shows how University of Chicago–trained women fused social science inquiry and social activism to shape progressive agenda. [PAC]

43.381 Noralee Frankel and Nancy Schrom Dye, eds. *Gender, class, race, and reform in the Progressive Era.* Lexington: University Press of Kentucky, 1991. ISBN 0-8131-1763-1. ‣ Twelve essays from 1988 conference. Topics include African American women's fight against segregation in Atlanta and antilynching networks, Hull House reformers, Harriot Stanton Blatch, and immigrant women and reform. [PAC]

43.382 Estelle B. Freedman. "Separatism as strategy: female institution building and American feminism, 1870–1930." *Feminist studies* 5 (1979) 519–29. ISSN 0046-3663. ‣ Concludes strengths of autonomous women's organizing in Women's Christian Temperance Union, settlement house movement, and woman suffrage explain women's success, although ultimately efforts limited by divisions of race and class. [PAC]

43.383 Estelle B. Freedman. *Their sisters' keepers: women's prison reform in America, 1830–1930.* Ann Arbor: University of Michigan Press, 1981. ISBN 0-472-10008-4 (cl), 0-472-08052-0 (pbk). ‣ Analysis of white middle-class women's concerns for women prisoners. Concludes reformers' stress on sexual difference limited achievements; later reformers questioned, but unable to overcome, this strategy. [PAC]

43.384 Sherna Berger Gluck. *From parlor to prison: five American suffragists talk about their lives.* 1976 ed. New York: Monthly Review, 1985. ISBN 0-85345-676-3 (pbk). ‣ Oral history narratives of five unheralded white middle-class women revealing grass-

roots suffrage activism, personal choices and later careers, and participation in birth control, labor, and reform causes. [PAC]

43.385 Lynn D. Gordon. *Gender and higher education in the Progressive Era.* New Haven: Yale University Press, 1990. ISBN 0-300-04550-6. ‣ Analysis of experience of second generation college-educated women through comparisons of five institutions, including University of Chicago, Sophie Newcomb, and Vassar. Examines links to progressivism and women's rights, as well as hostility from men, separatism, and equality. [PAC]

43.386 Patricia R. Hill. *The world their household: the American woman's foreign mission movement and cultural transformation, 1870–1920.* Ann Arbor: University of Michigan Press, 1985. ISBN 0-472-10055-6. ‣ Examiniation of how middle-class white female religious benevolence movement expanded participants' sphere and reflected shifting constructions of ideal womanhood. Movement included over three million in 1915, but declined as women's professional opportunities expanded. [PAC]

43.387 Robyn Muncy. *Creating a female dominion in American reform, 1890–1935.* New York: Oxford University Press, 1991. ISBN 0-19-505702-3. ‣ Study of development of white women professionals' career culture in Progressive Era and its influence over state policy on child welfare. Shows importance of Hull House and Children's Bureau and unintended but oppressive results of their efforts. [PAC/TJMcD]

43.388 Cynthia Neverdon-Morton. *Afro-American women of the South and the advancement of the race, 1895–1925.* Knoxville: University of Tennessee Press, 1989. ISBN 0-87049-583-6 (cl), 0-87049-684-0 (pbk). ‣ Study of leadership, philosophy, and activities of African American women's social service organizations, including women's role in national organizations such as National Association for the Advancement of Colored People. Concludes gender and class relations affected goals and practice. [PAC]

43.389 Rosalind Rosenberg. *Beyond separate spheres: intellectual roots of modern feminism.* New Haven: Yale University Press, 1982. ISBN 0-300-02695-1 (cl), 0-300-03092-4 (pbk). ‣ Study of female social scientists at new research universities who studied sex differences and denied Victorian views of women's nature during Progressive Era and after. Covers careers, writings, arguments, and lives of these pioneers. [PAC]

43.390 Jacqueline Anne Rouse. *Lugenia Burns Hope: black southern reformer.* Athens: University of Georgia Press, 1989. ISBN 0-8203-1082-4. ‣ Biography of leading African American reformer who organized Neighborhood Union in Atlanta and was part of network of African American women activists across South. Discusses her skills, outspokenness, perspective, and marriage to John Hope. [PAC]

43.391 Anne Firor Scott and Andrew MacKay Scott. *One half the people: the fight for woman suffrage.* 1975 ed. Urbana: University of Illinois Press, 1982. ISBN 0-252-01011-6 (cl), 0-252-01005-1 (pbk). ‣ Brief narrative history of suffrage campaign, including twenty-six documents, tables on congressional voting patterns, demographic profile of leading suffragists, list of states adopting suffrage and dates, and bibliographic essay. [PAC]

43.392 Kathryn Kish Sklar. "Hull House in the 1890s: a community of women reformers." *Signs* 10 (1985) 657–77. ISSN 0097-9740. ‣ Study of how Chicago women reformers created and sustained their own institutions free of male control. Concludes they successfully developed alliances with male reformers, but were limited by male-dominated political system. [PAC]

43.393 Rosalyn Terborg-Penn. "Discrimination against Afro-American women in the women's movement, 1830–1920." In *The Afro-American woman: struggles and images.* Sharon Harley and Rosalyn Terborg-Penn, eds., pp. 17–27. Port Washington,

N.Y.: Kennikat, 1978. ISBN 0-8046-9209-2 (cl), 0-8046-9294-7 (pbk). ‣ Analysis of African American women's suffrage movement and leaders, including Mary Church Terrell and Ida B. Wells Barnett. Argues white women's suffrage movement was racist and excluded black women, yet black women were very active in suffrage fight. [PAC]

SEE ALSO
4.324 Cynthia Eagle Russett. *Sexual science.*
40.196 Peggy Pascoe. *Relations of rescue.*

Biographies

43.394 Allen F. Davis. *American heroine: the life and legend of Jane Addams.* 1973 ed. New York: Oxford University Press, 1975. ISBN 0-19-501694-7 (cl, 1973), 0-19-501897-4 (pbk). ‣ Biography focusing on progressive reformer's personality and symbolism in American culture. Argues Addams manipulated her public image and criticizes her for consequences. [PAC]

43.395 Richard Drinnon. *Rebel in paradise: a biography of Emma Goldman.* 1961 ed. Chicago: University of Chicago Press, 1982. ISBN 0-226-16364-4 (pbk). ‣ Romantic but scholarly biography of anarchist and her relationship to American capitalism. Follows public life and passion for justice from birth through death in 1940. [PAC]

43.396 Candace Falk. *Love, anarchy, and Emma Goldman: a biography.* 1984 ed. New Brunswick, N.J.: Rutgers University Press, 1990. ISBN 0-8135-1512-2 (cl), 0-8135-1513-0 (pbk). ‣ Intimate biography based on personal correspondence joining and illuminating inner and public lives. Reveals anarchist's pain and despair as well as daring and defiance. By editor of Goldman papers. [PAC]

43.397 Mamie Garvin Fields. *Lemon Swamp and other places: a Carolina memoir.* Rev. ed. New Brunswick, N.J.: Rutgers University Press, 1990. ISBN 0-8135-1512-2 (cl), 0-8135-1513-0 (pbk). ‣ Autobiography of African American school teacher and community activist in Charleston, South Carolina, 1890s to 1940s. Vivid accounts of teaching in isolated areas, grassroots organizations and resistance, segregation, and importance of family and community history. [PAC]

43.398 Robert Booth Fowler. *Carrie Catt: feminist politician.* Boston: Northeastern University Press, 1986. ISBN 0-930350-86-3 (cl), 1-555-53005-2 (pbk). ‣ Portrait of suffrage leader, politician, and progressive reformer. Argues Catt believed political participation essential for equality and women's oppression rooted in political and economic structures, but overall had modest feminist goals. [PAC]

43.399 Evelyn Nakano Glenn. "The dialectic of wage work: Japanese-American women and domestic service, 1905–1940." *Feminist studies* 6 (1980) 432–71. ISSN 0046-3663. ‣ Uses interviews to study experience of *issei* (first generation) women domestic workers in San Francisco. Examines struggles against oppression in workplace and connections between paid work and family. Shows interrelationship of oppressive and liberating consequences of women's work. [PAC]

43.400 Ann Lane. *To "herland" and beyond: the life and work of Charlotte Perkins Gilman.* 1990 ed. New York: Meridian, 1991. ISBN 0-452-01080-2 (pbk). ‣ Study of intellectual legacy and personal life of leading feminist theorist, including Gilman's extensive writings and her personal struggle for life of autonomy and achievement. Set in context of broad trends of period. [PAC]

43.401 Ruth Barnes Moynihan. *Rebel for rights: Abigail Scott Duniway.* New Haven: Yale University Press, 1983. ISBN 0-300-02952-7. ‣ Account of life of Oregon's pioneer feminist and suffragist leader, discussing her independent personality, conflicts with new prohibitionist-suffragists and eastern leaders. Stress on

women's economic independence and proto-populist philosophy. [PAC/CAM]

CULTURAL HISTORY
Visual Arts, Architecture, and Music

43.402 Mardges Bacon. *Ernest Flagg: beaux-arts architect and urban reformer.* New York and Cambridge, Mass.: Architectural History Foundation and MIT Press, 1986. ISBN 0-262-02222-2. ‣ Study of life and work of leading American exponent of French *beaux-arts* design. Sees Flagg as progressive in tenement house reform, skyscraper design, and modular houses. [EDL]

43.403 Edward A. Berlin. *Ragtime: a musical and cultural history.* 1980 ed. Berkeley: University of California Press, 1984. ISBN 0-520-03671-9 (cl, 1980), 0-520-05219-6 (pbk). ‣ Scholarly study of turn-of-century America's most popular musical form. Analyzes musical style as well as social and cultural context, especially as ragtime relates to race and class. [EDL]

43.404 Eileen Bowser. *The transformation of cinema, 1907–1915.* New York and Toronto: Scribner's and Collier Macmillan Canada, 1990. ISBN 0-684-18414-1. ‣ Examination of filmmaking as intregal part of American social, cultural, and economic life in decade following establishment of industry and before advent of feature film. [EDL]

43.405 Carl W. Condit. *The Chicago school of architecture: a history of commercial and public building in the Chicago area, 1875–1925.* 1964 ed. Chicago: University of Chicago Press, 1973. ISBN 0-226-11455-4 (pbk). ‣ Examination of interrelationship between architecture, especially newly developed skyscraper, and social, intellectual, and economic trends in Chicago. Emphasizes work of leading architects such as Daniel Burnham and Louis Sullivan. [EDL]

43.406 Ronald L. Davis. *A history of music in American life.* Vol. 2: *The gilded years, 1865–1920.* Huntington, N.Y.: Krieger, 1980. ISBN 0-89874-003-7. ‣ Detailed survey covering, among other topics, emergence of symphony orchestras and grand opera, developments in vaudeville and musical theater, and story of ragtime and early jazz. [EDL]

43.407 William K. Everson. *American silent film.* New York: Oxford University Press, 1978. ISBN 0-19-502348-X. ‣ Wide-ranging study of American silent films, 1890s to 1920s, by leading scholar in field. Explores impact of movies on American culture. [EDL]

43.408 David Ewen. *The life and death of Tin Pan Alley: the golden age of American popular music.* New York: Funk & Wagnalls, 1964. ‣ History of popular music and of its center of publication in New York City, 1880s to 1920s. Focuses on songs, their composers, and music industry. [EDL]

43.409 John L. Fell, ed. *Film before Griffith.* Berkeley: University of California Press, 1983. ISBN 0-520-04738-9 (cl), 0-520-04758-3 (pbk). ‣ Collection of essays on films and filmmakers, production companies, audiences, distribution systems, exhibitors, and social context and significance of films through first decade of twentieth century. [EDL]

43.410 C. Jane Gover. *The positive image: women photographers in turn-of-the-century America.* Albany: State University of New York Press, 1988. ISBN 0-88706-533-3 (cl), 0-88706-535-X (pbk). ‣ Study of lives and careers of number of prominent photographers, arguing ideals of cult of true womanhood alternated with progressive expectations in iconography of women photographers. [EDL]

43.411 Adele Heller and Lois Rudnick, eds. *1915, the cultural moment: the new politics, the new woman, the new psychology, the new art, and the new theatre in America.* New Brunswick, N.J.:

Rutgers University Press, 1991. ISBN 0-8135-1720-6 (cl), 0-8135-1721-4 (pbk). ▸ Collection of essays on emergence of modernism in turn-of-century American culture. Emphasis on struggle to americanize European cultural and intellectual influences. [EDL]

43.412 Patricia Hills. *Turn-of-the-century America: paintings, graphics, photographs, 1890–1910.* New York: Whitney Museum of American Art, 1977. ISBN 0-87427-019-7. ▸ Essays on American painting, photography, popular art, etc., emphasizing social, cultural, and economic influences. Also notes importance of European models. [EDL]

43.413 Helen Lefkowitz Horowitz. *Culture and the city: cultural philanthropy in Chicago from the 1880s to 1917.* Lexington: University Press of Kentucky, 1976. ISBN 0-8131-1344-X. ▸ Study of establishment of institutions of high culture (Art Institute, University of Chicago, etc.) Covers role of business elites, professional managers, artists, and social reformers in defining culture. [EDL]

43.414 Elizabeth Johns. *Thomas Eakins: the heroism of modern life.* Princeton: Princeton University Press, 1983. ISBN 0-691-04022-2. ▸ Study of Eakins's relationship to late nineteenth-century American culture. Sees artist as naturalist showing men and women were physical creatures, subject to forces of nature beyond their control. [EDL]

43.415 H. Wayne Morgan. *New muses: art in American culture, 1865–1920.* Norman: University of Oklahoma Press, 1978. ISBN 0-8061-1479-7. ▸ Study of broad cultural context in which art was received, debated, and analyzed. Emphasizes reaction to European painting by both artists and public. [EDL]

43.416 Lewis Mumford. *The brown decades: a study of the arts in America, 1865–1895.* Rev. ed. New York: Dover, 1971. ISBN 0-486-20200-3. ▸ Examination of interrelationship of architecture, painting, and literature in late nineteenth-century America. Helped reshape study of American architectural history. [EDL]

43.417 Joseph A. Mussulman. *Music in the cultured generation: a social history of music in America, 1870–1900.* Evanston, Ill.: Northwestern University Press, 1971. ISBN 0-8101-0350-8. ▸ Uses reviews and articles in *Atlantic Monthly, Harpers Monthly, Scribners,* and *Century* to trace zeal of middle-class Americans in making classical music part of their culture. [EDL]

43.418 James F. O'Gorman. *Three American architects: Richardson, Sullivan, and Wright, 1865–1915.* Chicago: University of Chicago Press, 1991. ISBN 0-226-62071-9. ▸ Study of development of mature style of each architect and linkage between them. Emphasizes two American building types: tall office building and detached, single-family dwelling. [EDL]

43.419 William B. Rhoads. "The discovery of America's architectural past, 1874–1914." In *The architectural historian in America: a symposium in celebration of the fiftieth anniversary of the founding of the Society of Architectural Historians.* Elisabeth Blair MacDougall, ed., pp. 23–39. Washington, D.C.: National Gallery of Art; distributed by University Press of New England, 1990. (Center for Advanced Study in the Visual Arts, Symposium papers, 19.) ISBN 0-89468-139-7. ▸ Description of turn-of-century efforts, largely by architects, to document sources of American building styles. [EDL]

43.420 Thomas L. Riis. *Just before jazz: black musical theater in New York, 1890–1915.* Washington, D.C.: Smithsonian Institution Press, 1989. ISBN 0-87474-788-0. ▸ Fully documented account of contribution of black entertainers and musicians. Argues for music's influence in shaping jazz of 1920s and 1930s. [EDL]

43.421 Walter Rosenblum, Naomi Rosenblum, and Alan Trachtenberg. *America and Lewis Hine: photographs, 1904–1940.* Millerton, N.Y.: Aperture, 1977. ISBN 0-89381-008-8 (cl), 0-89381-017-7 (pbk). ▸ Selection of photographs of America's greatest photographer of industrial work and workers. Biographical notes and essay setting Hine's work in historical context. [EDL]

43.422 William J. Schafer and Johannes Riedel. *The art of ragtime: form and meaning of an original black American art.* Baton Rouge: Louisiana State University Press, 1973. ISBN 0-8071-0220-2. ▸ Examination of ragtime as key link between African American folk music and jazz. Detailed study of ragtime's form and structure and its influence on white popular music and culture. [EDL]

43.423 Gunther Schuller. *Early jazz: its roots and musical development.* 1968 ed. New York: Oxford University Press, 1986. ISBN 0-19-504043-0 (pbk). ▸ Comprehensive history of jazz to 1930s, emphasizing details of music. Analyzes African musical-social traditions, compositions, soloists, small groups, big bands, and transition to swing. [EDL]

43.424 Kevin Starr. *Inventing the dream: California through the Progressive Era.* New York: Oxford University Press, 1985. ISBN 0-19-503489-9. ▸ Second volume (with 43.440) in author's ambitious cultural history of Golden State, moving from mid-nineteenth century through initial rise of Hollywood. Provocative cultural study. [CAM]

43.425 Nicholas E. Tawa. *The coming of age of American art music: New England's classical romanticists.* New York: Greenwood, 1991. ISBN 0-313-27797-4. ▸ Study of six turn-of-century musicians who formed first significant group of American art composers. Includes biographical information, evaluation of music, and account of audiences. [EDL]

43.426 Nicholas E. Tawa. *A sound of strangers: musical culture, acculturation, and the post–Civil War ethnic American.* Metuchen, N.J.: Scarecrow, 1982. ISBN 0-8108-1504-4. ▸ Examination of music's place in immigrant cultures. Discusses music brought to America, influences of American musical styles, and importance of ethnic Americans in early twentieth-century popular music. [EDL]

43.427 Robert Twombly. *Louis Sullivan: his life and work.* 1986 ed. Chicago: University of Chicago Press, 1987. ISBN 0-226-82006-8 (pbk). ▸ Comprehensive study of one of America's greatest architects. Sets his work firmly within context of turn-of-century culture and society. [EDL]

43.428 Richard Guy Wilson, Dianne H. Pilgrim, and Richard N. Murray. *The American Renaissance, 1876–1917.* Brooklyn, N.Y.: Brooklyn Museum; distributed by Pantheon, 1979. ISBN 0-394-50807-6 (cl), 0-87273-075-1 (pbk). ▸ Fully illustrated, scholarly account of painters, architects, collectors, etc., who believed European Renaissance could provide useful sources for development of national American art. [EDL]

SEE ALSO
40.567 Lawrence W. Levine. *Highbrow/lowbrow.*

Literature and Print Media

43.429 Elizabeth Ammons. *Conflicting stories: American women writers at the turn into the twentieth century.* New York: Oxford University Press, 1991. ISBN 0-19-506030-X. ▸ Study of seventeen fiction writers in relationship to social history of period, focusing on role of gender, class, and race in shaping their writings and their lives. [EDL]

43.430 Maxwell H. Bloomfield. *Alarms and diversions: the American mind through American magazines, 1900–1914.* The Hague: Mouton, 1967. ▸ Analysis of fiction, nonfiction, and poetry in five widely circulated magazines. Argues that during period there was basic shift from individualism to sense of community. [EDL]

43.431 Charles Fanning. *Finley Peter Dunne and Mr. Dooley: the Chicago years*. Lexington: University Press of Kentucky, 1978. ISBN 0-8131-1365-2. ▸ Study of one of best-known American humorists. Emphasis on Dunne as literary realist and acute social commentator, especially of Irish American life, in 1890s. [EDL]

43.432 Arthur John. *The best years of the "Century": Richard Watson Gilder, "Scribner's Monthly," and "Century Magazine," 1870–1909*. Urbana: University of Illinois Press, 1981. ISBN 0-252-00857-X. ▸ Study of leading exponent of genteel ideals. Argues Gilder's magazine became rallying point for conservatives seeking to stabilize and guide American society in period of stress and change. [EDL]

43.433 R. Gordon Kelly. *Mother was a lady: self and society in selected American children's periodicals, 1865–1890*. Westport, Conn.: Greenwood, 1974. ISBN 0-8371-6451-6. ▸ Examination of how cultural elite socialized children to gentry ideal. Uses sociological theory to argue children's fiction served as strategy for reassurance in era of social turmoil. [EDL]

43.434 Brian Lee. *American fiction, 1865–1940*. London: Longman, 1987. ISBN 0-582-49317-X (cl), 0-582-49316-1 (pbk). ▸ Effective survey of subject concentrating on, but not limited to, major novelists of period. Sets fiction firmly within its cultural and historical context. [EDL]

43.435 Frank Luther Mott. *A history of American magazines*. Vol. 4: *1885–1905*. Cambridge, Mass.: Belknap, 1957. ISBN 0-7837-4087-5 (pbk). ▸ Comprehensive, descriptive account, treating, for example, business practices, editors, writers, illustrations, and subject areas (politics, religion, economics, etc.). Also sketches of more widely circulated magazines. [EDL]

43.436 Vernon Louis Parrington. *The beginnings of critical realism in America, 1860–1920: completed to 1900 only*. 1930 ed. David W. Levy, Foreword. Norman: University of Oklahoma Press, 1987. (Main currents in American thought: an interpretation of American literature from the beginnings to 1920, 3.) ISBN 0-8061-2079-7 (cl), 0-8061-2082-7 (pbk). ▸ Groundbreaking work emphasizing how political, social, and economic forces influenced American writers. Influential in shaping study of American literature in mid-twentieth century. [EDL]

43.437 Robert A. Rosenstone. *Romantic revolutionary: a biography of John Reed*. 1975 ed. Cambridge, Mass.: Harvard University Press, 1990. ISBN 0-674-77938-X (pbk). ▸ Scholarly interpretation of Reed (1887–1920), covering his activities in United States, Mexico, and Russia. Informative account of artistic and political radicalism in early twentieth-century America. [EDL]

43.438 Henry D. Shapiro. *Appalachia on our mind: the southern mountains and mountaineers in the American consciousness, 1870–1920*. Chapel Hill: University of North Carolina Press, 1978. ISBN 0-8078-1293-5. ▸ Study of creation by writers, both inside and outside region, of idea of Appalachia as strange land of peculiar people. Argues concept shaped region's history. [EDL]

43.439 Herbert F. Smith. *The popular American novel, 1865–1920*. Boston: Twayne, 1980. ISBN 0-8057-7310-X. ▸ Survey of widely read, minor writers treating regional novels, social satires, westerns, sentimental fiction, and political novels. Concludes study with reluctant innovators who expressed unconventional views. [EDL]

43.440 Kevin Starr. *Material dreams: southern California through the 1920s*. 1990 ed. New York: Oxford University Press, 1991. ISBN 0-19-504487-8 (cl, 1990), 0-19-507260-X (pbk). ▸ Thorough cultural history with emphasis on state's literati. Broad in scope and attentive to detail, work is nonetheless weakened by failure to interpret economic and social conditions of period. See also Starr 43.424. [CAM]

43.441 Salme Harju Steinberg. *Reformer in the marketplace:*

Edward W. Bok and "The Ladies' Home Journal." Baton Rouge: Louisiana State University Press, 1979. ISBN 0-8071-0398-5. ▸ Study of reform-minded editor during early years of mass-circulation, general-interest magazines. Significant contribution to histories of journalism and advertising. [EDL]

43.442 Cecelia Tichi. *Shifting gears: technology, literature, culture in modernist America*. Chapel Hill: University of North Carolina Press, 1987. ISBN 0-8078-1715-5 (cl), 0-8078-4167-6 (pbk). ▸ Innovative study of wide-ranging responses to gear-and-girder technology, 1890s to 1920s. Argues such technology was generally, if cautiously, welcomed. [EDL]

43.443 Alan Trachtenberg. *The incorporation of America: culture and society in the Gilded Age*. New York: Hill & Wang, 1982. ISBN 0-8090-5827-8 (cl), 0-8090-0145-4 (pbk). ▸ Topical approach to effects of corporate system on culture, values, and outlooks in Gilded Age. Innovative work in cultural analysis. [EDL]

Popular Culture

43.444 Eileen Boris. *Art and labor: Ruskin, Morris, and the craftsman ideal in America*. Philadelphia: Temple University Press, 1986. ISBN 0-87722-384-X. ▸ Study of how Americans during Progressive Era reshaped British arts and crafts movement to their own needs. Emphasizes role of class and gender. [EDL]

43.445 Michael Denning. *Mechanic accents: dime novels and working-class culture in America*. London: Verso, 1987. ISBN 0-86091-178-0 (cl), 0-86091-889-0 (pbk). ▸ Examination of place of dime novels in nineteenth-century working-class culture. Argues they can, if read historically, give valuable insight into workers' thoughts, feelings, and actions. [EDL]

43.446 James J. Flink. *America adopts the automobile, 1895–1910*. Cambridge, Mass.: MIT Press, 1970. ISBN 0-262-06036-1. ▸ Traces emerging relationship of cars and carmakers to American social and cultural environment. Short on theory; covers early associations, legal developments, good-roads movement, and technology. [DUH]

43.447 James B. Gilbert. *Perfect cities: Chicago's utopias of 1893*. Chicago: University of Chicago Press, 1991. ISBN 0-226-29317-3 (cl), 0-226-29318-1 (pbk). ▸ Analysis of struggle between elite and popular culture as seen in World's Columbian Exposition, Pullman's model city, and Dwight Moody's evangelical efforts in Chicago. Chicago's World Fair also gave urban planners and architects chance to demonstrate ideas for making cities better. [EDL/EHM]

43.448 David Glassberg. *American historical pageantry: the uses of tradition in the early twentieth century*. Chapel Hill: University of North Carolina Press, 1990. ISBN 0-8078-1916-6 (cl), 0-8078-4286-9 (pbk). ▸ Exploration of how historical pageants were used, especially in Progressive period, to forge feeling of community solidarity and collective purpose. Important attempt to marry urban politics and cultural analysis that tells much about urban progressivism. [EDL/TJMcD]

43.449 John F. Kasson. *Amusing the million: Coney Island at the turn of the century*. New York: Hill & Wang, 1978. ISBN 0-8090-2617-1 (cl), 0-8090-0133-0 (pbk). ▸ Analysis of revolt against genteel cultural standards and emergence of mass culture as seen in amusement parks of Coney Island. Innovative study in cultural history. [EDL]

43.450 Elizabeth Kendall. *Where she danced*. New York: Knopf, 1979. ISBN 0-394-40029-1. ▸ Study of development of modern dance in America in early 1900s. Traces cultural and social changes in Europe and America encouraging women to experiment with free-form dance. [EDL]

43.451 Peter Levine. *A. G. Spalding and the rise of baseball: the promise of American sport*. New York: Oxford University Press,

1985. ISBN 0-19-503552-6. ▸ Study of central figure in late nineteenth-century emergence of professional baseball as national sport. Places Spalding's activities as promoter in era's broader social and cultural context. [EDL]

43.452 Lary May. *Screening out the past: the birth of mass culture and the motion picture industry.* New York: Oxford University Press, 1980. ISBN 0-19-502762-0. ▸ Examination of American films as evidence of transition from Victorian to modern life. In-depth socio-cultural analysis of films and leading filmmakers, 1900–30. [EDL]

43.453 Benjamin McArthur. *Actors and American culture, 1880–1920.* Philadelphia: Temple University Press, 1984. ISBN 0-87722-333-5. ▸ Analysis of relationship of actors to emergence of theater as commercial, New York–centered, mass entertainment. Argues actors became a more telling reflection of cultural values than play. [EDL]

43.454 Donald J. Mrozek. *Sport and American mentality: 1880–1910.* Knoxville: University of Tennessee Press, 1983. ISBN 0-87049-394-9 (cl), 0-87049-395-7 (pbk). ▸ Study of rapid growth of organized sports in turn-of-century America. Argues elites saw various sports as providing order and stability in changing society. [EDL]

43.455 Charles Musser. *The emergence of cinema: the American screen to 1907.* New York and Toronto: Scribner's and Collier Macmillan Canada, 1990. ISBN 0-684-18413-3. ▸ Narrative history of motion pictures up to nickelodeon era. Comprehensive account of technologies, films, exhibition practices, production companies, and leading individuals. [EDL]

43.456 James D. Norris. *Advertising and the transformation of American society, 1865–1920.* New York: Greenwood, 1990. ISBN 0-313-26801-0. ▸ Analysis of broad range of consumer product advertisements. Concludes early emphasis on product qualities shifted by 1920 to selling of consumption as means to achieve social status. [EDL]

43.457 Steven A. Riess. *Touching base: professional baseball and American culture in the Progressive Era.* Westport, Conn.: Greenwood, 1980. ISBN 0-313-20671-6. ▸ Approaches baseball through its myths, realities, symbols, and rituals. Chapters on audiences, politics, social reform, and social mobility. Argues baseball's ideology fit progressivism's quest for cultural order. [EDL]

43.458 Robert W. Rydell. *All the world's a fair: visions of empire at American international expositions, 1876–1916.* Chicago: University of Chicago Press, 1984. ISBN 0-226-73239-8. ▸ Study of dozen expositions from Philadelphia (1876) to San Diego (1915–16). Emphasizes ideological implications, especially in presentation of nationalist and racist views of European-American world hegemony. [EDL]

43.459 Robert W. Snyder. *The voice of the city: vaudeville and popular culture in New York.* New York: Oxford University Press, 1989. ISBN 0-19-505285-4. ▸ Examination of growth of vaudeville from mid-nineteenth-century Bowery bawdiness to popular theater that, by 1890s, appealed to middle- and working-class audiences from many ethnic backgrounds. [EDL]

SEE ALSO
40.570 Robert C. Toll. *On with the show!*

Religion and Culture

43.460 Robert D. Cross. *The emergence of liberal Catholicism in America.* 1958 ed. Chicago: Quadrangle, 1968. ▸ Study of efforts in 1890s of liberal leaders such as Archbishop John Ireland and Cardinal James Gibbons to adjust Catholic church practices to American culture and institutions. [EDL]

43.461 Susan Curtis. *A consuming faith: the social gospel and mod-*

ern American culture. Baltimore: Johns Hopkins University Press, 1991. ISBN 0-8018-4167-4. ▸ Examination of careers of fifteen Protestant social gospel exponents. While not abandoning ideas of social justice, they contributed to reorientation of American culture that validated abundance, consumption, and self-realization. [EDL]

43.462 David B. Danbom. *"The world of hope": progressives and the struggle for an ethical public life.* Philadelphia: Temple University Press, 1987. ISBN 0-87722-453-6. ▸ Intellectual history tracing rise of Christian progressivism followed by emergence of scientific progressivism. Indicates internal and external conflicts that ended progressive idea of reforming society. [EDL]

43.463 Donald K. Gorrell. *The age of social responsibility: the social gospel in the Progressive Era, 1900–1920.* Macon, Ga.: Mercer University Press, 1988. ISBN 0-86554-316-X. ▸ Description of growing influence of social reform–minded Protestant ministers within own denominations and in society at large. Sees 1908–12 as period of greatest influence. [EDL]

43.464 Charles Howard Hopkins. *The rise of the social gospel in American Protestantism, 1865–1915.* 1940 ed. New Haven: Yale University Press, 1967. ▸ Pioneering study of social gospel as product of nineteenth-century idealism and commitment to ameliorating harshness of industrial capitalism. [EDL]

43.465 William R. Hutchison. *The modernist impulse in American Protestantism.* 1976 ed. Durham, N.C.: Duke University Press, 1992. ISBN 0-8223-1237-9 (cl), 0-8223-1248-4 (pbk). ▸ Inquiry into ideas and individuals central to liberal Protestantism, with emphasis on modernist phase during Progressive period. Landmark study in American intellectual and religious history. [EDL]

43.466 Benny Kraut. *From reform Judaism to ethical culture: the religious evolution of Felix Adler.* Cincinnati: Hebrew Union College Press, 1979. ISBN 0-87820-404-0. ▸ Study of leading late nineteenth-century Jewish intellectual who founded nondenominational, religio-ethical movement. Detailed examination of religious forces, tensions, and problems of period. [EDL]

43.467 Ralph E. Luker. *The social gospel in black and white: American racial reform, 1885–1912.* Chapel Hill: University of North Carolina Press, 1991. ISBN 0-8078-1978-6. ▸ Study of leading exponents, both black and white, of social Christianity. Argues, contrary to accepted view, that race relations were of vital concern in social gospel movement. [EDL]

43.468 George M. Marsden. *Fundamentalism and American culture: the shaping of twentieth-century evangelicalism, 1870–1925.* 1980 ed. New York: Oxford University Press, 1982. ISBN 0-19-502758-2 (cl, 1980), 0-19-503083-4 (pbk). ▸ Groundbreaking study of how those committed to typically American versions of evangelical Christianity responded to and were influenced by social, intellectual, and religious crises of time. [EDL]

43.469 Jay Martin. *Harvests of change: American literature, 1865–1914.* Englewood Cliffs, N.J.: Prentice-Hall, 1967. ▸ Wide-ranging study of literature in era of rapid social change. Interprets writers as insightful delineators of contemporary American urban-technological society. [EDL]

43.470 James R. Moore. *The post-Darwinian controversies: a study of the Protestant struggle to come to terms with Darwin in Great Britain and America, 1870–1900.* Cambridge: Cambridge University Press, 1979. ISBN 0-521-21989-2. ▸ Critical study of substance and historiography of subject. Argues there was no war between religion and Darwinism and that orthodox Protestants accepted Darwinism more readily than liberal theologians. [EDL]

43.471 Jon H. Roberts. *Darwinism and the divine in America: Protestant intellectuals and organic evolution, 1859–1900.* Madison: University of Wisconsin Press, 1988. ISBN 0-299-11590-9. ▸ Closely focused study in history of ideas. Argues intellectuals increasingly used science and especially evolutionary concepts to redefine character of Protestant theology. [EDL]

43.472 Gary Scott Smith. *The seeds of secularization: Calvinism, culture, and pluralism in America, 1870–1915.* Grand Rapids: Christian University Press, 1985. ISBN 0-8028-0058-0 (pbk). ‣ Examination of response of Calvinist theologians and laity to rapidly changing, urban-industrial culture. Treats impact of evolutionary thought, struggle over schools, and involvement in politics. [EDL]

43.473 Timothy P. Weber. *Living in the shadow of the second coming: American premillennialism, 1875–1982.* Rev. ed. Chicago: University of Chicago Press, 1987. ISBN 0-226-87732-9 (pbk). ‣ Outline of impact of premillennialism on variety of theological and secular controversies, including biblical interpretation, education, and Zionist movement. Skillful blend of social and religious history. [EDL]

SEE ALSO
40.464 Mark C. Carnes. *Secret ritual and manhood in Victorian America.*

INTELLECTUAL HISTORY

43.474 Edward Abrahams. *The lyrical Left: Randolph Bourne, Alfred Stieglitz, and the origins of cultural radicalism in America.* Charlottesville: University Press of Virginia, 1986. ISBN 0-8139-1080-3. ‣ Innovative study of leading figures among radical idealists who urged transpolitical, redemptive vision of personal freedom and social liberation in first decades of twentieth century. [EDL]

43.475 Robert C. Bannister. *Social Darwinism: science and myth in Anglo-American social thought.* 1979 ed. Philadelphia: Temple University Press, 1988. ISBN 0-87722-566-4 (pbk). ‣ Comprehensive study arguing principal legacy of *Origin of Species* is reform Darwinism: liberal reaction against idea of survival of fittest. [EDL]

43.476 Martha Banta. *Imaging American women: ideas and ideals in cultural history.* New York: Columbia University Press, 1987. ISBN 0-231-06126-9. ‣ Well-documented study of images of American women in wide range of media, 1876–1918. Uses semiotic theory to explore era's symbols of womanhood. [EDL]

43.477 Paul A. Carter. *The spiritual crisis of the Gilded Age.* DeKalb: Northern Illinois University Press, 1971. ISBN 0-87580-026-2 (cl), 0-87580-507-8 (pbk). ‣ Study of impact of scientific thought, especially Darwinism, on American culture in late nineteenth century. Argues for complex interaction of science and religion during period. [EDL/JB]

43.478 John Clendenning. *The life and thought of Josiah Royce.* Madison: University of Wisconsin Press, 1985. ISBN 0-299-10310-2. ‣ Biography of tragic figure who, with William James and Charles Sanders Peirce, shaped turn-of-century American philosophy. Explores Royce's concepts of idealism, loyalty, and community. [EDL]

43.479 Michael P. Cohen. *The pathless way: John Muir and the American wilderness.* Madison: University of Wisconsin Press, 1984. ISBN 0-299-09720-X. ‣ Detailed study of Muir's environmental ideas. Intellectual biography juxtaposing Muir's youthful vision of nature with his mature writings. [EDL]

43.480 David R. Contosta. *Henry Adams and the American experiment.* Oscar Handlin, ed. Boston: Little, Brown, 1980. ISBN 0-316-15401-6 (jacket), 0-316-15400-8 (cl). ‣ Brief, well-informed biography of late nineteenth-century American man of letters. Argues Adams saw nation losing its sense of national purpose. [EDL]

43.481 George Cotkin. *Reluctant modernism: American thought and culture, 1880–1900.* New York and Toronto: Twayne and Maxwell Macmillan Canada, 1992. ISBN 0-8057-9054-3 (cl), 0-8057-9059-4 (pbk). ‣ Survey emphasizing impact of Darwinism on wide range of American intellectuals. Shows development of new forms of popular culture. [EDL]

43.482 Neil Coughlan. *Young John Dewey: an essay in American intellectual history.* Chicago: University of Chicago Press, 1975. ISBN 0-226-11604-2. ‣ Study of philosopher's life and thought through 1894, arguing emergence of modern university and decline of nineteenth-century evangelical Protestantism shaped Dewey's version of pragmatism. [EDL]

43.483 Thomas L. Haskell. *The emergence of professional social science: the American Social Science Association and the nineteenth-century crisis of authority.* Urbana: University of Illinois Press, 1977. ISBN 0-252-00609-7. ‣ History of American Social Science Association, representing last generation of amateur social scientists. Emphasizes profound reorientation of social thought and culture of 1890s. [EDL]

43.484 Richard Hofstadter. *Social Darwinism in American thought.* 1955 rev. ed. Richard Foner, Introduction. Boston: Beacon, 1992. ISBN 0-8070-5461-5 (cl), 0-8070-5503-4 (pbk). ‣ Fundamental work arguing that rapidly expanding capitalism led Americans to see society in terms of tooth-and-claw version of natural selection. Shaped future studies. [EDL]

43.485 James T. Kloppenberg. *Uncertain victory: social democracy and progressivism in European and American thought, 1870–1920.* New York: Oxford University Press, 1986. ISBN 0-19-503749-9. ‣ Key work in comparative intellectual history, arguing for interaction of certain philosophers with political activists, 1870–1920, to create middle group between Marxists and nineteenth-century liberals. [EDL]

43.486 Bruce Kuklick. *The rise of American philosophy: Cambridge, Massachusetts, 1860–1930.* New Haven: Yale University Press, 1977. ISBN 0-300-02039-2. ‣ Intellectual and institutional history of Harvard department that dominated philosophical studies from "golden age" through triumph of academic professionalism. Seminal work in history of ideas. [EDL]

43.487 T. J. Jackson Lears. *No place of grace: antimodernism and the transformation of American culture, 1880–1920.* New York: Pantheon, 1981. ISBN 0-394-50816-5. ‣ Innovative study of those who rejected rationality and materialism dictated by late Victorian society. Argues efforts ironically led to consumption-oriented society. [EDL]

43.488 Arthur Lipow. *Authoritarian socialism in America: Edward Bellamy and the nationalist movement.* Berkeley: University of California Press, 1982. ISBN 0-520-04005-8. ‣ Study of political and social thought of Bellamy as revealed primarily in *Looking Backward.* Emphasizes Bellamy's commitment to elite control of antidemocratic, hierarchical society. [EDL]

43.489 David W. Marcell. *Progress and pragmatism: James, Dewey, Beard, and the American idea of progress.* Westport, Conn.: Greenwood, 1974. ISBN 0-8371-6387-0. ‣ Analysis of reshaping of idea of progress as result of evolutionary thought. Stresses centrality of progress in pragmatism of William James, John Dewey, and Charles Beard. [EDL]

43.490 Henry F. May. *The end of American innocence: a study of the first years of our own time, 1912–1917.* 1959 ed. Chicago: Quadrangle, 1964. ‣ Study of emergence of modernism in American culture during second decade of twentieth century rather than in 1920s. Emphasizes importance of ideas in social change. [EDL]

43.491 David W. Noble. *The progressive mind, 1890–1917.* Rev. ed. Minneapolis: Burgess, 1981. ISBN 0-8087-1441-4 (pbk). ‣ Examination of progressive thinking in variety of areas, including politics, gender, arts, and race relations. Argues progressive ideas resulted from profound cultural crisis within middle class. [EDL]

43.492 Alexandra Oleson and John Voss, eds. *The organization of knowledge in modern America, 1860–1920.* Baltimore: Johns Hopkins University Press, 1979. ISBN 0-8018-2108-8. ‣ Well-documented essays on growth of academic disciplines, universities, professional societies, libraries, and museums that served to institutionalize ideas in America. Important insights. [EDL/LCP]

43.493 G. Edward White. *The eastern establishment and the western experience: the West of Frederic Remington, Theodore Roosevelt, and Owen Wister.* 1968 ed. Austin: University of Texas Press, 1989. ISBN 0-292-72065-3 (pbk). ‣ Discussion of nineteenth-century division between East and West in United States. Cross-disciplinary use of history, sociology, biography, and psychology. Emphasis on qualitative relationships and prominent figures. [CAM]

43.494 Morton White. *Social thought in America: the revolt against formalism.* 1957 2d ed. London: Oxford University Press, 1976. ISBN 0-19-519837-9. ‣ History and critique of liberal social philosophy of John Dewey, Oliver Wendell Holmes, Jr., James Harvey Robinson, and Thorstein Veblen. Key work in American intellectual history. [EDL]

43.495 R. Jackson Wilson. *In quest of community: social philosophy in the United States, 1860–1920.* 1968 ed. London: Oxford University Press, 1970. ISBN 0-19-500807-3. ‣ Study arguing Charles Sanders Peirce, G. Stanley Hall, James Mark Baldwin, E. A. Ross, and Josiah Royce shared rejection of individualism and generation of concepts of community. [EDL]

43.496 Irvin G. Wyllie. *The self-made man in America: the myth of rags to riches.* 1954 ed. New York: Free Press, 1966. ‣ Study of myths of upward mobility in late nineteenth century, employing wide range of sources. Concludes businessmen largely rejected Darwinism to draw on Christianity and on Enlightenment thought. [EDL]

POLITICAL HISTORY

General Studies

43.497 Richard Franklin Bensel. *Sectionalism and American political development, 1880–1980.* Madison: University of Wisconsin Press, 1984. ISBN 0-299-09830-3. ‣ Study of American politics a product of sectional stress. Rigorous analysis of effects of geographical alignments in House of Representatives. Insightful, provocative look at American politics. [TJMcD]

43.498 John D. Buenker. *Urban liberalism and progressive reform.* 1973 ed. New York: Norton, 1978. ISBN 0-393-00880-0. ‣ Overview of politics of reform in Progressive Era in urban industrial states, arguing urban new-stock politicians played important role. Useful synthesis of this strand of interpretation. [TJMcD]

43.499 Alan Dawley. *Struggles for justice: social responsibility and the liberal state.* Cambridge, Mass.: Belknap, 1991. ISBN 0-674-84580-3. ‣ Examination of how activist state emerged by time of New Deal. Most recent attempt to synthesize literature on protean period, 1890–1930. Emphasizes imbalance between dynamic, expansive, urban-industrial society and existing liberal state. [TJMcD/JWT]

43.500 Samuel P. Hays. *American political history as social analysis: essays.* Knoxville: University of Tennessee Press, 1980. ISBN 0-87049-276-4. ‣ Fundamental, still important, agenda-setting essays of historian who truly reshaped field of political history in 1960s and 1970s. [TJMcD]

43.501 David M. Kennedy. *Over here: the First World War and American society.* New York: Oxford University Press, 1980. ISBN 0-19-502729-9. ‣ Traditional, cautious, but useful account of World War I as fulfillment and frustration of modernizing reform. Emphasizes shifting attitudes toward growing authority of state. [TJMcD/JWT]

43.502 Michael E. McGerr. *The decline of popular politics: the American North, 1865–1928.* New York: Oxford University Press, 1986. ISBN 0-19-503682-4. ‣ Analysis of cultural changes underlying decline in American political participation in late nineteenth and early twentieth centuries. [TJMcD]

43.503 Martin J. Sklar. *The corporate reconstruction of American capitalism, 1890–1916: the market, the law, and politics.* Cambridge: Cambridge University Press, 1988. ISBN 0-521-30921-2 (cl), 0-521-31382-1 (pbk). ‣ Analysis of political economy from Sherman Anti-Trust Act to World War I as adjustment of state to new corporate order. Dense, difficult, controversial, important. [TJMcD]

43.504 Stephen Skowronek. *Building a new American state: the expansion of national administrative capacities, 1877–1920.* Cambridge: Cambridge University Press, 1982. ISBN 0-521-23022-5 (cl), 0-521-28865-7 (pbk). ‣ Examination of formative years of transition at federal level of decentralized state of courts and parties into centralized, bureaucratic giant. Pioneering, important attempt to place history of American politics into broader framework of state-formation process. [TJMcD]

43.505 James Weinstein. *The corporate ideal in the liberal state, 1900–1918.* 1968 ed. Westport, Conn.: Greenwood, 1981. ISBN 0-313-22709-8. ‣ Collection of essays providing pioneering analysis of rise of corporate liberalism in American politics. [TJMcD]

43.506 C. Vann Woodward. *Origins of the New South, 1877–1913.* 1951 ed. Baton Rouge: Louisiana State University Press, 1971. ISBN 0-8071-0036-0 (cl), 0-8071-0039-0 (pbk). ‣ Analysis of role of redeemers and populists in making of modern South. Pathbreaking, influential political history. [TJMcD]

Presidential and Congressional Studies

43.507 John Morton Blum. *The republican Roosevelt.* 1977 2d ed. Cambridge, Mass.: Harvard University Press, 1981. ISBN 0-674-76301-7 (cl), 0-674-76302 5 (pbk). ‣ Excellent brief account of Theodore Roosevelt and his terms of office. [TJMcD]

43.508 David W. Brady. *Critical elections and congressional policy making.* Stanford, Calif.: Stanford University Press, 1988. ISBN 0-8047-1442-8. ‣ Examination of political realignments of 1850s, 1890s, and 1930s, concluding they did have policy effect by changing patterns of institutional power in House of Representatives. Rigorous, important attempt to answer question crucial to political realignment theory: what difference do realignments make? [TJMcD]

43.509 John Milton Cooper, Jr. *The warrior and the priest: Woodrow Wilson and Theodore Roosevelt.* Cambridge, Mass.: Belknap, 1983. ISBN 0-674-94750-9. ‣ Study of most famous Progressive Era presidents in stream of American political philosophy and in contrast to one another. Careful attempt to differentiate presidents often seen as too similar. [TJMcD]

43.510 Justus D. Doenecke. *The presidencies of James A. Garfield and Chester A. Arthur.* 1981 ed. Lawrence: University Press of Kansas, 1985. ISBN 0-7006-0208-9. ‣ Most recent basic history of these less-than-notable presidencies. [TJMcD]

43.511 Lewis L. Gould. *Reform and regulation: American politics from Roosevelt to Wilson.* 2d ed. New York: Knopf, 1986. ISBN 0-394-35413-3 (pbk). ‣ Brief, expert survey of national domestic politics of Progressive Era, focusing on effects of nonpartisanship and regulation. Useful bibliography. [TJMcD]

43.512 Henry F. Graff, ed. *The presidents: a reference history.*

New York: Scribner's, 1984. ISBN 0-684-17607-6. ▸ Very useful compilation of brief histories and annotated bibliographies of works on American presidents through Jimmy Carter. [TJMcD]

43.513   William H. Harbaugh. *The life and times of Theodore Roosevelt.* Rev. ed. London: Oxford University Press, 1975. ISBN 0-19-519822-0 (pbk). ▸ Still standard one-volume biography of Roosevelt. Broadly based in secondary sources. [TJMcD]

43.514   J. Rogers Hollingsworth. *The whirligig of politics: the democracy of Cleveland and Bryan.* Chicago: University of Chicago Press, 1963. ▸ Standard account of Democratic party of Grover Cleveland and William Jennings Bryan. Shows how inflexible leadership helped put Democratic party into the wilderness, 1893–1904. [TJMcD]

43.515   Arthur S. Link. *Wilson.* 5 vols. to date. Princeton: Princeton University Press, 1947–65. ▸ Monumental biography of Woodrow Wilson, whose careers in academia and politics come close to defining progressivism. [TJMcD]

43.516   William S. McFeely. *Grant: a biography.* 1981 ed. New York: Norton, 1982. ISBN 0-393-01372-3 (cl, 1981), 0-393-30046-3 (pbk). ▸ Useful, if highly critical, biography of Ulysses S. Grant, whose life tells much about his times. [TJMcD]

43.517   H. Wayne Morgan. *From Hayes to McKinley: national party politics, 1877–1896.* Syracuse, N.Y.: Syracuse University Press, 1969. ▸ Gilded Age political history from top down, revising image of period as one of political corruption and inertia. Revisionist in its time and still useful. [TJMcD]

43.518   H. Wayne Morgan. *William McKinley and his America.* 1963 ed. Syracuse, N.Y.: Syracuse University Press, 1964. ▸ Standard one-volume biography of this transitional president. [TJMcD]

43.519   William E. Nelson. *The roots of American bureaucracy, 1830–1900.* Cambridge, Mass.: Harvard University Press, 1982. ISBN 0-674-77945-2. ▸ Provocative, stimulating analysis of bureaucratic state as outcome of conflict between majoritarian and pluralistic political and legal philosophies. [TJMcD]

43.520   Allan Nevins. *Grover Cleveland: a study in courage.* 1932 ed. Freeport, N.Y.: Books for Libraries, 1973. ISBN 0-518-19064-1. ▸ Standard biography of Cleveland, although both dated and uncritical. Cleveland's impact, however, on his political generation is indisputable. [TJMcD]

43.521   David J. Rothman. *Politics and power: the United States Senate, 1869–1901.* Cambridge, Mass.: Harvard University Press, 1966. ▸ Examination of how much derided "millionaire's club" reorganized and disciplined itself to produce legislation for changing society. Well-researched attack on treason of Senate point of view. [TJMcD]

43.522   David Sarasohn. *The party of reform: Democrats in the Progressive Era.* Jackson: University of Mississippi Press, 1989. ISBN 0-87805-367-0. ▸ Study of congressional Democrats as spearheads of reform in Progressive Era. Interesting revisionist account of party of William Jennings Bryan and Woodrow Wilson. [TJMcD]

SEE ALSO
40.51 Joel H. Silbey. "Delegates fresh from the people."
44.570 Robert K. Murray. *The Harding era.*

State and Local Politics

43.523   Paula Baker. *The moral frameworks of public life: gender, politics, and the state in rural New York, 1870–1930.* New York: Oxford University Press, 1991. ISBN 0-19-506452-6. ▸ Deeply researched, wide-ranging, important look at how gender structured and was structured by politics. [TJMcD]

43.524   Geoffrey Blodgett. *The gentle reformers: Massachusetts Democrats in the Cleveland era.* Cambridge, Mass.: Harvard University Press, 1966. ▸ Examination of Irish, Yankees, and Mugwumps in making of state politics. Especially good on Mugwumps. [TJMcD]

43.525   M. Craig Brown and Charles N. Halaby. "Machine politics in America, 1870–1945." *Journal of interdisciplinary history* 17 (1987) 587–612. ISSN 0022-1953. ▸ Important revisionist analysis of prevalence and periodization of urban machine politics in America. Concludes powerful political machines both rarer and appeared later than most historians have thought. [TJMcD]

43.526   Ballard Campbell. *Representative democracy: public policy and midwestern legislatures in the late nineteenth century.* Cambridge, Mass.: Harvard University Press, 1980. ISBN 0-674-76275-4. ▸ Important revisionist roll-call analysis of state legislatures in Illinois, Wisconsin, and Iowa, 1886–95. Reveals power and complexity of legislative partisanship and responsiblity of state legislatures. [TJMcD]

43.527   Steven P. Erie. *Rainbow's end: Irish Americans and the dilemmas of urban machine politics, 1840–1985.* Berkeley: University of California Press, 1988. ISBN 0-520-06119-5. ▸ Thoughtful revisionist account of history and theory of urban machine politics in America. [TJMcD]

43.528   Linda Gordon, ed. *Women, the state, and welfare.* Madison: University of Wisconsin Press, 1990. ISBN 0-299-12660-9 (cl), 0-299-12664-1 (pbk). ▸ Useful collection of essays, many on Progressive Era, using gender analysis to probe aspects of American politics and state formation in late nineteenth and twentieth centuries. [TJMcD]

43.529   Lewis L. Gould. *Progressives and prohibitionists: Texas Democrats in the Wilson era.* Austin: University of Texas Press, 1973. ISBN 0-262-76407-3. ▸ Meticulously researched account of how rural, dry politicians seized Texas, making it reform state and allying themselves with President Wilson. Argues Democrats experienced cultural conflicts in 1910s from rural to urban, North to South, and wet to dry. [CAM]

43.530   Steven Hahn. *Roots of southern populism: yeoman farmers and the transformation of the Georgia upcountry, 1850–1890.* 1983 ed. New York: Oxford University Press, 1984. ISBN 0-19-503249-7 (cl, 1983), 0-19-503508-9 (pbk). ▸ Analysis of how changing economic relationships in rural Georgia led to agrarian radical politics. Thoughtful reconstruction of moral economy of rural area. [TJMcD]

43.531   David C. Hammack. *Power and society: Greater New York at the turn of the century.* 1982 ed. New York: Columbia University Press, 1987. ISBN 0-231-06641-4 (pbk). ▸ Analysis of four types of decision making reveals neither political bosses nor economic elites ruled New York City. Pluralist analysis at its best produces important revisionist account of New York politics. [TJMcD]

43.532   Carl V. Harris. *Political power in Birmingham, 1871–1921.* Knoxville: University of Tennessee Press, 1977. ISBN 0-87049-211-X. ▸ Careful test of pluralist and elitist theories of local power in context of local government decision making. Thoughtful presentation of theory and stimulating analysis of local government. [TJMcD]

43.533   Richard J. Jensen. *The winning of the Midwest: social and political conflict, 1888–1896.* Chicago: University of Chicago Press, 1971. ISBN 0-226-39825-0. ▸ Analysis of post–Civil War partisanship, based in ethnoreligious worldviews, and triumph of Republicans in 1890s. One of founding works of so-called ethnocultural approach to political history. [TJMcD]

43.534   Richard L. McCormick. *From realignment to reform: political change in New York state, 1893–1910.* Ithaca, N.Y.: Cornell

University Press, 1981. ISBN 0-8014-1326-5. ‣ Study of state-level progressivism as political process. Thoughtful attempt to combine social and political analyses of progressive reform. [TJMcD]

43.535 Terrence J. McDonald. "The burdens of urban history: the theory of the state in recent American social history." *Studies in American political development* 3 (1989) 3–29. ISSN 0898-588X. ‣ Broad survey of works in working-class and political history arguing conceptions of urban politics spring from pluralist theoretical origins. [TJMcD]

43.536 Zane L. Miller. *Boss Cox's Cincinnati: urban politics in the Progressive Era*. 1968 ed. Chicago: University of Chicago Press, 1980. ISBN 0-226-52598-8 (pbk). ‣ Presents urban politics in Progressive Era as conflict of center versus periphery. [TJMcD]

43.537 John F. Reynolds. *Testing democracy: electoral behavior and Progressive reform in New Jersey, 1880–1920*. Chapel Hill: University of North Carolina Press, 1988. ISBN 0-8078-1789-9. ‣ Well-researched, rigorously tested, important case study of this significant development. Concludes often noted late nineteenth-century decline in political participation occurred earlier and was result of more factors than heretofore believed. [TJMcD]

43.538 Bradley Robert Rice. *Progressive cities: the commission government movement in America, 1901–1920*. Austin: University of Texas Press, 1977. ISBN 0-292-76441-3. ‣ Standard work on rise and fall of short-lived product of Progressive Era. Well focused, informative. [TJMcD]

43.539 William L. Riordan. *Plunkitt of Tammany Hall: a series of very plain talks on very practical politics*. Terrence J. McDonald, ed. Boston: Bedford, 1993. ISBN 0-312-09666-6 (cl), 0-312-08444-7 (pbk). ‣ Account of machine politics in New York by Tammany Hall district leader. New introduction raises questions about both Plunkitt's politics and construction of account. [TJMcD]

43.540 Martin J. Schiesl. *The politics of efficiency: municipal administration and reform in America, 1880–1920*. 1977 ed. Berkeley: University of California Press, 1980. ISBN 0-520-03067-2 (cl, 1977), 0-520-04086-4 (pbk). ‣ Now standard account (from standpoint of reformers) of movement for structural reform—strong mayor, city manager, urban research bureaus, etc.—in urban America. [TJMcD]

43.541 Jon C. Teaford. "Finis for Tweed and Steffens: rewriting the history of urban rule." *Reviews in American history* 10 (1982) 143–53. ISSN 0048-7511. ‣ Useful introduction to recent historiography of urban politics. Stresses variety of urban political actors and extent of urban policy arenas that need to be considered. [TJMcD]

Political Parties

43.542 William Nisbet Chambers and Walter Dean Burnham, eds. *The American party systems: stages of political development*. 2d ed. New York: Oxford University Press, 1975. ISBN 0-19-501916-4 (cl), 0-19-501917-2 (pbk). ‣ Pioneering, enormously influential collection of essays on development of successive American political party systems. Concepts from collection still reverberate through American political history. [TJMcD]

43.543 Jerome M. Clubb, William H. Flanigan, and Nancy H. Zingale. *Partisan realignment: voters, parties, and government in American history*. 1980 ed. Boulder: Westview, 1990. ISBN 0-8133-1031-8 (pbk). ‣ Now standard work on history and theory of political realignments. Useful place to start to understand concept crucial for period 1877–1920, which saw two such purported realignments. [TJMcD]

43.544 Robert D. Marcus. *Grand Old Party: political structure in the Gilded Age, 1880–1896*. New York: Oxford University Press, 1971. ‣ Examination of struggle between centralizing and decentralized power bases in Republican party. Insightful national political history from top down. [TJMcD]

43.545 Richard L. McCormick. *The party period and public policy: American politics from the age of Jackson to the Progressive Era*. New York: Oxford University Press, 1986. ISBN 0-19-503860-6. ‣ Outstanding collection of historical and historiographical essays, indispensable for understanding trends in nineteenth-century American political historiography. [TJMcD]

43.546 Arthur M. Schlesinger, Jr., ed. *History of U.S. political parties*. 4 vols. New York: Chelsea House, 1973. ISBN 0-8352-0594-0. ‣ Useful compilation of articles and documents. Volumes 2 and 3 cover 1877–1920. [TJMcD]

43.547 C. K. Yearley. *The money machines: the breakdown and reform of governmental and party finance in the North, 1860–1920*. Albany: State University of New York Press, 1970. ISBN 0-87395-072-0. ‣ Somewhat neglected but pioneering analysis of fiscal politics in America. [TJMcD]

SEE ALSO
40.51 Joel H. Silbey. "Delegates fresh from the people."
42.21 Joel H. Silbey. *The American political nation, 1838–1893*.

Political Movements and Ideas

43.548 Robert M. Crunden. *Ministers of reform: the progressives' achievement in American civilization, 1889–1920*. 1982 ed. Urbana: University of Illinois Press, 1984. ISBN 0-252-01167-8 (pbk). ‣ Wide-ranging analysis of progressivism as moral movement and climate of creativity, focusing on lives and careers of twenty-one representatives of period. Interesting attempt to combine politics and aesthetics under same rubric. [TJMcD]

43.549 Louis Filler. *The muckrakers*. University Park: Pennsylvania State University Press, 1976. ISBN 0-271-01212-9 (cl), 0-271-01213-7 (pbk). ‣ Still useful starting point for history of muckraking, although lack of analysis demonstrates need for newer studies of phenomenon. Earlier title: *Crusaders for American Liberalism* (1939). [TJMcD]

43.550 Eric Foner. "Why is there no socialism in the United States?" *History workshop journal* 17 (1984) 57–80. ISSN 0309-2984. ‣ Best recent overview of time-worn, but still important, question. [TJMcD]

43.551 Charles Forcey. *The crossroads of liberalism: Croly, Weyl, Lippmann, and the Progressive Era, 1900–1925*. 1961 ed. New York: Oxford University Press, 1972. ‣ Still useful analysis of thought and politics of leading lights of conservative magazine, *New Republic*, in its first years. [TJMcD]

43.552 Lawrence Goodwyn. *Democratic promise: the populist moment in America*. New York: Oxford University Press, 1976. ISBN 0-19-501996-2. ‣ Examination of populism as radical, democratic movement based in economic experience of cooperatives. First comprehensive study of populist movement since 1931; direct attack on interpretation of populism in Hofstadter's *Age of Reform* (43.555). One-volume abridgement also available, titled *The Populist Moment* (1978). Rich, controversial, enormously influential. [TJMcD]

43.553 Robert W. Gordon. "Critical legal histories." *Stanford law review* 36 (1984) 57–125. ISSN 0038-9765. ‣ Exceptionally useful introduction to approaches and findings of these new works in American legal history. [TJMcD]

43.554 James R. Green. *Grass-roots socialism: radical movements in the Southwest, 1895–1943*. Baton Rouge: Louisiana State University Press, 1978. ISBN 0-8071-0367-5 (cl), 0-8071-0773-5 (pbk). ‣ Pioneering analysis of movement from populism to socialism in Oklahoma, Texas, Louisiana, Kansas, and Arkansas. Crucial for understanding socialism's rural wing. [TJMcD]

43.555 Richard Hofstadter. *The age of reform: from Bryan to F.D.R.* New York: Knopf, 1955. ‣ Brilliant attempt to provide usable past for pragmatic, New Deal–style liberalism by revealing moralism of populism and progressivism. More valuable now as document in history of American liberalism than as historical analysis of formative years of that movement. Still powerful, impressive piece of writing. [TJMcD]

43.556 Melvin G. Holli. *Reform in Detroit: Hazen S. Pingree and urban politics.* 1969 ed. Westport, Conn.: Greenwood, 1981. ISBN 0-313-22671-7. ‣ Political biography of mayor of Detroit and later governor of Michigan in 1890s that first developed dichotomy between social and structural urban reformers during Progressive Era. [TJMcD]

43.557 Ari Hoogenboom. *Outlawing the spoils: a history of the civil service reform movement, 1865–1883.* 1961 ed. Westport, Conn.: Greenwood, 1982. ISBN 0-313-22821-3. ‣ Standard history of federal civil service reform through Pendleton Act. [TJMcD]

43.558 Justin Kaplan. *Lincoln Steffens: a biography.* 1974 ed. New York: Simon & Schuster, 1988. ISBN 0-671-22035-7 (pbk). ‣ Full-scale biography of man whose life and work informed, symbolized, and personified formative years of American liberalism. Crucial for understanding Steffens's life and times. [TJMcD]

43.559 Morton Keller. *Affairs of state: public life in late nineteenth-century America.* Cambridge, Mass.: Belknap, 1977. ISBN 0-674-00721-2. ‣ Examination of late nineteenth-century public sphere as shaped by contending forces of nationalism, reform, and government intervention on one hand, and localism, laissez faire, and racism on the other. Indispensable, encyclopedic survey. [TJMcD]

43.560 J. Morgan Kousser. *The shaping of southern politics: suffrage restriction and the establishment of the one-party South, 1880–1910.* New Haven: Yale University Press, 1974. ISBN 0-300-01696-4. ‣ Thoughtful, detailed, state-by-state analysis of politics and process of suffrage restriction. Standard work with implications for history of Progressive Era suffrage reform elsewhere. [TJMcD]

43.561 Aileen S. Kraditor. *The ideas of the woman suffrage movement, 1890–1920.* 1965 ed. New York: Norton, 1981. ISBN 0-393-01449-5 (cl), 0-393-00039-7 (pbk). ‣ Charts shift in movement's arguments on behalf of suffrage from broader ground of simple justice to narrower grounds of expediency. Still standard work on ideology of this important movement. [TJMcD]

43.562 Christopher Lasch. *The new radicalism in America, 1889–1963: the intellectual as a social type.* 1965 ed. New York: Norton, 1986. ISBN 0-393-30319-5 (pbk). ‣ Provocative set of biographical and intellectual essays on relationship between American liberalism and development of self-conscious intellectuals. Especially useful essays on some Progressive Era figures, e.g., Jane Addams and Lincoln Steffens. [TJMcD]

43.563 John H. M. Laslett and Seymour Martin Lipset, eds. *Failure of a dream? Essays in the history of American socialism.* Rev. ed. Berkeley: University of California Press, 1984. ISBN 0-520-03539-9 (cl), 0-520-04452-5 (pbk). ‣ Most recent compendium of essays on American exceptionalism. Good starting point for entering debate. [TJMcD]

43.564 T. J. Jackson Lears. "The concept of cultural hegemony: problems and possibilities." *American historical review* 90 (1985) 567–93. ISSN 0002-8762. ‣ Careful attempt to explicate and advocate use of this term in historical analysis. Exemplifies use by reference to late nineteenth-century political movements. [TJMcD]

43.565 David W. Levy. *Herbert Croly of "The New Republic": the life and thought of an American Progressive.* Princeton: Princeton University Press, 1985. ISBN 0-691-04725-1. ‣ Authoritative biography of founder of *The New Republic*, author of *The Promise of American Life*, and one of most important figures of Progressive Era. [TJMcD]

43.566 Christine A. Lunardini. *From equal suffrage to equal rights: Alice Paul and the National Woman's party, 1910–1928.* New York: New York University Press, 1986. ISBN 0-8147-5022-2. ‣ Revisionist history of relations between two major groups in fight for women's suffrage, giving more credit to Alice Paul's militant Congressional Union than to mainstream National American Woman Suffrage Association. Broader scope than title implies. [TJMcD]

43.567 R. Jeffrey Lustig. *Corporate liberalism: the origins of modern American political theory, 1890–1920.* Berkeley: University of California Press, 1982. ISBN 0-520-04387-1. ‣ Examination of transition from classical to corporate liberalism in work of wide variety of Progressive Era thinkers. Provocative synthesis rather than sustained analysis of individuals or works. [TJMcD]

43.568 C. Roland Marchand. *The American peace movement and social reform, 1898–1918.* 1972 ed. Princeton: Princeton University Press, 1973. ISBN 0-691-04609-3. ‣ Excellent study arguing changes in leadership and varying purposes among elite reformers significantly affected popularity of peace movement, which was also closely related to domestic interests and involvements of leaders. [KB]

43.569 Thomas K. McCraw. *Prophets of regulation: Charles Francis Adams, Louis D. Brandeis, James M. Landis, Alfred E. Kahn.* Cambridge, Mass.: Belknap, 1984. ISBN 0-674-71607-8 (cl), 0-674-71608-6 (pbk). ‣ Dry subject of economy regulation rendered vital by biographical approach. Pulitzer Prize–winning introduction to and discussion of modern American political economy. [TJMcD]

43.570 Thomas K. McCraw, ed. *Regulation in perspective: historical essays.* 1981 ed. Cambridge, Mass.: Graduate School of Business Administration, Harvard University; distributed by Harvard University Press, 1983. ISBN 0-87584-124-4 (pbk). ‣ Important collection of essays on history and historiography of regulation. [TJMcD]

43.571 Stanley B. Parsons. *The populist context: rural versus urban power on a Great Plains frontier.* Westport, Conn.: Greenwood, 1973. ISBN 0-8371-6392-7. ‣ Study of populism as drama of agrarian life, focusing on Nebraska. Concludes industrialization caused reaction by farmers; farmers, formerly in "golden age," now sought parity with other groups. [CAM]

43.572 Stanley B. Parsons et al. "The role of cooperatives in the development of the movement culture of populism." *Journal of American history* 69 (1983) 866–85. ISSN 0021-8723. ‣ Statistical analysis questioning argument of Goodwyn 43.552 and others that dynamism and radicalism of populism based on experience of economic cooperatives. [TJMcD]

43.573 Daniel T. Rodgers. "In search of progressivism." *Reviews in American history* 10 (1982) 113–31. ISSN 0048-7511. ‣ Examination of three social languages of progressivism. Most recent historiographical analysis of period. [TJMcD]

43.574 Robert A. Rosenstone. *Romantic revolutionary: a biography of John Reed.* 1975 ed. Cambridge, Mass.: Harvard University Press, 1990. ISBN 0-674-77938-X (pbk). ‣ Rescues interpretation of famous turn-of-century radical from political battles of 1930s. Movie *Reds* based in part on book. Skip movie; all excitement, poignancy, and meaning of Reed's life are here. Informative account of artistic and political radicalism. [TJMcD/EDL]

43.575 Nick Salvatore. *Eugene V. Debs: citizen and socialist.* Urbana: University of Illinois Press, 1982. ISBN 0-252-00967-3. ‣ Bancroft Prize–winning biography of most famous oppositional figure of late nineteenth and early twentieth centuries. Reveals much by rooting him in social and cultural context from which he emerged. [TJMcD]

43.576 Theda Skocpol. *Protecting soldiers and mothers: the political origins of social policy in the United States.* Cambridge, Mass.: Belknap, 1992. ISBN 0-674-71765-1. ▸ Historical sociologist's account of politics of social policy, 1880–1920. Highlights significance of women's movement in origins of American welfare state. Detailed, clearly written, powerful. [TJMcD]

43.577 John G. Sproat. *"The best men": liberal reformers in the Gilded Age.* 1968 ed. Chicago: University of Chicago Press, 1982. ISBN 0-226-76990-9 (pbk). ▸ Study of Mugwumps from Civil War to 1884. Thoughtful exploration of their major concerns. [TJMcD]

43.578 Bruce M. Stave, ed. *Socialism and the cities.* Port Washington, N.Y.: Kennikat, 1975. ISBN 0-8046-9133-9. ▸ Useful collection exploring variety and complexity of American municipal socialism. Reveals both power of its electoral appeal and poignancy of its attempt to build socialist municipal islands in a sea of capitalism. [TJMcD]

43.579 David P. Thelen. *The new citizenship: origins of progressivism in Wisconsin, 1885–1900.* Columbia: University of Missouri Press, 1972. ISBN 0-8262-0111-3. ▸ Study of how progressivism was broad-based coalition built in response to depression of 1893–97. Interesting shift of origins of progressivism from producers to consumers. [TJMcD]

43.580 John L. Thomas. *Alternative America: Henry George, Edward Bellamy, Henry Demarest Lloyd, and the adversary tradition.* Cambridge, Mass.: Belknap, 1983. ISBN 0-674-01676-9. ▸ Insightful excavation of similar neorepublican foundations of thought of three popular radicals of late nineteenth century. [TJMcD/EDL]

43.581 James Weinstein. *The decline of socialism in America, 1912–1925.* 1967 ed. New Brunswick, N.J.: Rutgers University Press, 1984. ISBN 0-8135-1068-6 (cl), 0-8135-1069-4 (pbk). ▸ Examination of effects of wartime repression and Socialist Party of America's split from Communists (1919). Now standard interpretation of Socialist party's rise and demise. [TJMcD]

SEE ALSO
40.43 Jack P. Greene, ed. *Encyclopedia of American political history.*
40.431 Eleanor Flexner. *Century of struggle.*
44.111 Ronald Steel. *Walter Lippmann and the American century.*
44.276 Nancy F. Cott. *The grounding of modern feminism.*

Electoral Systems and Voting

43.582 Peter H. Argersinger. *Structure, process, and party: essays in American political history.* Armonk, N.Y.: Sharpe, 1992. ISBN 0-87332-798-5. ▸ Excellent set of essays on how election laws and procedures actually affected voting and representation in Gilded Age. Useful bibliograpies. [TJMcD]

43.583 Paul Kleppner. *Continuity and change in electoral politics, 1893–1928.* New York: Greenwood, 1987. ISBN 0-313-24069-8. ▸ Analysis of fate of ethnocultural politics after 1896. Thoughtful attempt to explain end of party period of American history. [TJMcD]

43.584 Paul Kleppner. *The third electoral system, 1853–1892: parties, voters, and political cultures.* Chapel Hill: University of North Carolina Press, 1979. ISBN 0-8078-1328-1. ▸ Sees nineteenth-century politics as expression of ethnocultural, not economic, social divisions. The *summa* of ethnocultural school of political analysis. Careful and thoughtful, crucial to understanding this approach. [TJMcD]

43.585 Richard Jules Oestreicher. "Urban working-class political behavior and theories of American electoral politics, 1870–1940." *Journal of American history* 74 (1988) 1257–86. ISSN 0021-8723. ▸ Thoughtful attempt to synthesize literature of new working-class and political histories. [TJMcD]

SEE ALSO
40.61 Paul Kleppner. *Who voted?*
40.62 Paul Kleppner et al. *The evolution of American electoral systems.*
44.592 Walter Dean Burnham. *Critical elections and the mainsprings of American politics.*

FOREIGN RELATIONS

General Studies

43.586 Robert L. Beisner. *From the old diplomacy to the new, 1865–1900.* 2d ed. Arlington Heights, Ill.: Harlan Davidson, 1986. ISBN 0-88295-833-X (pbk). ▸ Significantly modified traditional approach challenging continuity interpretation. Argues American foreign policy underwent paradigm change in 1880s as old system gave way to new. [KB]

43.587 Charles S. Campbell. *The transformation of American foreign relations, 1865–1900.* New York: Harper & Row, 1976. ISBN 0-06-010618-2 (cl), 0-06-090531-X (pbk). ▸ Detailed synthesis analyzing America's evolution into imperial nation. Traditional view, well balanced by addition of revisionist insights. [KB]

43.588 J.A.S. Grenville and George Berkeley Young. *Politics, strategy, and American diplomacy: studies in foreign policy, 1873–1917.* New Haven: Yale University Press, 1966. ▸ Excellent traditionalist interpretation emphasizing role of individuals and domestic political rivalry in shaping American foreign policy at expense of strategic design. [KB]

43.589 Sondra R. Herman. *Eleven against war: studies in American internationalist thought, 1898–1921.* Stanford, Calif.: Hoover Institution Press, Stanford University, 1969. ▸ Study arguing that, depending on their social backgrounds and overseas interests, internationalists supported either entry into formal international organizations or promotion of informal reformist international community. Presents Woodrow Wilson as nationalist determined to preserve American global interests. Ideological focus. [KB]

43.590 Michael J. Hogan and Thomas G. Paterson, eds. *Explaining the history of American foreign relations.* Cambridge: Cambridge University Press, 1991. ISBN 0-521-40383-9 (cl), 0-521-40736-2 (pbk). ▸ Essays on various conceptual and analytical approaches and methods in study of American foreign relations. Discusses innovative and cross-disciplinary techniques. [KB]

43.591 Ernest R. May. *American imperialism: a speculative essay.* New York: Atheneum, 1968. ▸ Methodological analysis of public opinion suggesting American adoption and rejection of imperialism at turn of century stemmed from European ideas transmitted to and through United States by cosmopolitan establishment. [KB]

43.592 Ernest R. May. *Imperial democracy: the emergence of America as a great power.* 1961 ed. New York: Harper & Row, 1973. ISBN 0-06-131694-6. ▸ Traditionalist, multiarchival study suggesting United States acquired great power status when Europe grudgingly recognized its existence. Maintains United States had empire thrust upon it chiefly by popular demand and domestic politics. [KB]

43.593 Carl P. Parrini. *Heir to empire: United States economic diplomacy, 1916–1923.* Pittsburgh: University of Pittsburgh Press, 1969. ISBN 0-8229-3178-8. ▸ Study arguing pragmatic American leaders in business and government sought commercial expansion in reorganized stable world community. Sees much continuity between Wilson and Harding administrations. [KB]

43.594 David S. Patterson. *Toward a warless world: the travail of the American peace movement, 1887–1914*. Bloomington: Indiana University Press, 1976. ISBN 0-253-36019-6. ▸ Detailed examination of assumptions, programs, and internal and external problems that led to frustration and failure of diverse, elitist, and internationalistic American peace movement. [KB]

43.595 Richard Hume Werking. *The master architects: building the United States Foreign Service, 1890–1913*. Lexington: University Press of Kentucky, 1977. ISBN 0-8131-1342-3. ▸ Examination of organization and reorganization of foreign affairs bureaucracy that laid basis for modern American foreign service. Broad study identifying relations between structural change and personal ambitions. [KB]

43.596 William Appleman Williams. *The tragedy of American diplomacy*. 1972 rev. 2d ed. New York: Norton, 1988. ISBN 0-393-30493-0 (pbk). ▸ Classic revisionist study of American informal imperialism and commercial expansion through establishment of global open door in order to preserve laissez-faire capitalism and social order and ideological system at home. [KB]

Europe and Canada

43.597 Stuart Anderson. *Race and rapprochement: Anglo-Saxonism and Anglo-American relations, 1895–1904*. Rutherford, N.J.: Fairleigh Dickinson University Press, 1981. ISBN 0-8386-3001-4. ▸ Study of role of belief in Anglo-Saxon racial superiority and common conflict with "lesser" races in promoting diplomatic rapprochement. Emphasizes intellectual, emotional, moral, and cultural bonds between Britons and Americans. [KB]

43.598 John W. Coogan. *The end of neutrality: the United States, Britain, and maritime rights, 1899–1915*. Ithaca, N.Y.: Cornell University Press, 1981. ISBN 0-8014-1407-5. ▸ Examination of international maritime law developed from Boer and Russo-Japanese wars and conferences. Wilson's toleration of British violations in World War I to avoid entanglement ended American neutrality. Hostile view of Wilson's diplomacy. [KB]

43.599 Edward P. Crapol. *America for Americans: economic nationalism and Anglophobia in the late nineteenth century*. Westport, Conn.: Greenwood, 1973. ISBN 0-8371-6273-4. ▸ Study of how economic rivalry in Western Hemisphere and Pacific fostered perceptions of Britain as rival and nemesis during period of strident American nationalism and commercial expansion. Excellent revisionist analysis. [KB]

43.600 Reinhard R. Doerries. *Imperial challenge: Ambassador Count Bernstorff and German-American relations 1908–1917*. Christa D. Shannon, trans. Chapel Hill: University of North Carolina Press, 1989. ISBN 0-8078-1820-8. ▸ Deeply researched analysis of German-American relations through diplomacy of Bernstorff, who wanted accommodation but faced opposition from Berlin, whose leaders, unlike Bernstorff, underestimated United States. Major study. [KB]

43.601 Lloyd C. Gardner. *Safe for democracy: Anglo-American response to revolution, 1913–1923*. 1984 ed. New York: Oxford University Press, 1987. ISBN 0-19-503429-5 (cl), 0-19-504155-0 (pbk). ▸ Revisionist interpretation of British and American responses to revolutions in China, Mexico, and Russia, and attempts to find liberal alternatives. Both nations recognized that industrialization made it dangerous to ignore local wars and distant revolutions. [KB]

43.602 Thomas J. Noer. *Briton, Boer, and Yankee: the United States and South Africa, 1870–1914*. Kent, Ohio: Kent State University Press, 1978. ISBN 0-89338-216-1. ▸ Exploration of role of economic, evangelistic, and racist notions in dealing with conflict between Boers and British. Americans grudgingly supported British. Liberal nonrevisionist treatment. [KB]

43.603 Bradford Perkins. *The great rapprochement: England and the United States, 1895–1914*. New York: Atheneum, 1968. ▸ Analysis of shifts in attitudes based on Anglo-Saxonism, British realism, cultural affinity, complementary policies, and common rivals. Concludes process vital but not entirely completed before outbreak of World War I. [KB]

43.604 Clara Eve Schieber. *The transformation of American sentiment toward Germany, 1870–1914*. 1923 ed. New York: Russell & Russell, 1973. ISBN 0-8462-1707-4. ▸ Broad study of American shift from support for Germany to opposition as consequence of diplomatic confrontations and commercial rivalry in Asia, Pacific, and Caribbean. [KB]

43.605 Charles Callan Tansill. *Canadian-American relations, 1875–1911*. 1943 ed. Gloucester, Mass.: Smith, 1964. ▸ Detailed examination emphasizing economic disparities and geopolitical realities that promoted tension but ended in permanent friendship. Traditional interpretation of major, understudied topic. [KB]

43.606 Charles Callan Tansill. *The foreign policy of Thomas F. Bayard, 1885–1897*. 1940 ed. New York: Kraus Reprint, 1969. ▸ Traditional interpretation demonstrating that U.S. secretary of state and ambassador to Britain paved way for rapprochement with Britain. Massively detailed, sympathetic study covering wide range of foreign problems. [KB]

43.607 Larzer Ziff. *The American 1890s: life and times of a lost generation*. 1966 ed. Lincoln: University of Nebraska Press, 1979. ISBN 0-8032-4900-4 (cl), 0-8032-9900-1 (pbk). ▸ Wide-ranging study of writers of 1890s. Sees them as precursors of modern American literature in their awareness of cultural diversity, commercialism, and sexual conflicts. [EDL]

SEE ALSO
47.418 Betty M. Unterberger. *The United States, revolutionary Russia, and the rise of Czechoslovakia.*

South America and the Caribbean

43.608 Gregg Andrews. *Shoulder to shoulder? The American Federation of Labor, the United States, and the Mexican Revolution, 1910–1924*. Berkeley: University of California Press, 1991. ISBN 0-520-07230-8. ▸ Examination of political, economic, and strategic concerns of American Federation of Labor during Mexican Revolution of 1910–24 and its effect on thought of Samuel Gompers and other A.F. of L. leaders toward domestic and international concerns. [KB]

43.609 Philip S. Foner. *The Spanish-Cuban-American war and the birth of American imperialism, 1895–1902*. Vol. 1: *1895–1898*. Vol. 2: *1898–1902*. New York: Monthly Review, 1972. ISBN 0-8357-3546-X (v. 1, pbk), 0-8357-3547-8 (v. 2, pbk). ▸ Marxist interpretation of American involvement in Cuban Revolution in which Americans seized control of Cuba and established model for subsequent neocolonialism in Latin America by American monopolies. Highly detailed, forcefully argued. [KB]

43.610 Mark T. Gilderhus. *Diplomacy and revolution: U.S.-Mexican relations under Wilson and Carranza*. Tucson: University of Arizona Press, 1977. ISBN 0-8165-0630-2 (cl), 0-8165-0561-6 (pbk). ▸ Examination of American intervention in Mexico stemming from Wilson's liberal-capitalist ideology. Argues Wilson's policy was dynamic and responsive to circumstances in this first application of his foreign policy. [KB]

43.611 Mark T. Gilderhus. *Pan American visions: Woodrow Wilson in the Western Hemisphere, 1913–1921*. Tucson: University of Arizona Press, 1986. ISBN 0-8165-0936-0. ▸ Analysis of American promotion of peace, prosperity, and strategic security through regional integration that appealed more to North Americans than Latin Americans, whose mistrust caused effort to fail. Centers on programs in Argentina, Brazil, and Chile. [KB]

43.612 David Healy. *Drive to hegemony: the United States in the Caribbean, 1898–1917.* Madison: University of Wisconsin Press, 1988. ISBN 0-299-11720-0. ▸ Study of rise of American official and unofficial dominance of independent states of Central America and Greater Antilles. Maintains Americans had mixed motives in adopting European colonial practices. Revisionist view of American failure. [KB]

43.613 David Healy. *The United States in Cuba, 1898–1902: generals, politicians, and the search for policy.* Madison: University of Wisconsin Press, 1963. ▸ Study arguing occupation of Cuba and Philippines required new policies that led Americans to develop informal empire in Cuba. Concludes domestic politics more important than racism or economic expansionism. [KB]

43.614 Friedrich Katz. *The secret war in Mexico: Europe, the United States, and the Mexican Revolution.* 1981 ed. Loren Goldner, trans. Chicago: University of Chicago Press, 1983. ISBN 0-226-42588-6 (cl), 0-226-42589-4 (pbk). ▸ Broad, detailed examination of effect of international economic, strategic, social, and ideological forces on Mexican Revolution, based on extensive multiarchival research. [KB]

43.615 David McCullough. *The path between the seas: the creation of the Panama Canal, 1870–1914.* New York: Simon & Schuster, 1977. ISBN 0-671-22563-4. ▸ Detailed, well-written, and absorbing popular study. Construction of canal presented as epochal engineering feat involving host of intriguing characters from several nations. [KB]

43.616 Dana G. Munro. *Intervention and dollar diplomacy in the Caribbean, 1900–1921.* 1964 ed. Westport, Conn.: Greenwood, 1980. ISBN 0-313-22510-9. ▸ Conservative interpretation contends United States intervened in Caribbean to promote stability and progress in order to prevent imperialist European nations from intervening and thus threaten American security. [KB]

43.617 Dexter Perkins. *The Monroe doctrine, 1867–1907.* 1937 ed. Gloucester, Mass.: Smith, 1966. ▸ Classic multiarchival examination stressing extension of doctrine, growth of no-transfer principle, and application in Caribbean. Conservative but critical study of doctrine at zenith of its authority. [KB]

43.618 Robert E. Quirk. *An affair of honor: Woodrow Wilson and the occupation of Veracruz.* 1962 ed. New York: Norton, 1967. ▸ Able, well-written account of effect of Wilson's and general American ethnocentrism and missionary zeal in causing unnecessary, counterproductive intervention in Mexican Revolution. [KB]

Asia and the Pacific

43.619 David L. Anderson. *Imperialism and idealism: American diplomats in China, 1861–1898.* Bloomington: Indiana University Press, 1985. ISBN 0-253-32918-3. ▸ Study of ambivalence and inconsistency in China policy, caused by tension between ideals and self-interest, and role of eight diplomats who established distinctive policies before Open Door policy. Biographical approach. [KB]

43.620 William Reynolds Braisted. *The United States Navy in the Pacific, 1897–1909.* 1958 ed. Austin: University of Texas Press, 1977. ISBN 0-292-78505-4. ▸ Sympathetic analysis of influence of navy leaders on formulation of American policies in China, Philippines, and Japan, and role of navy in diplomacy during Theodore Roosevelt's administration. Emphasis on strategic issues. [KB]

43.621 Kenton J. Clymer. *Protestant missionaries in the Philippines, 1898–1916: an inquiry into the American colonial mentality.* Urbana: University of Illinois Press, 1986. ISBN 0-252-01210-0. ▸ Assessment of attitudes, ideas, ideals, and effects of missionaries in Philippines as means of understanding American colonial experience and Filipino colonial mentality. Missionaries had mixed successes and failures. Careful, cautious, sympathetic interpretation. [KB]

43.622 Roy Watson Curry. *Woodrow Wilson and Far Eastern policy, 1913–1921.* 1957 ed. New York: Octagon Books, 1968. ▸ Sympathetic analysis of president's attempt to contain Japan and preserve Chinese Open Door policy after war in Europe ended Asian balance of power. Argues Wilson promoted traditional goals and moral policy during period of revolutionary change in Asia. [KB]

43.623 Raymond A. Esthus. *Theodore Roosevelt and Japan.* 1966 ed. Seattle: University of Washington Press, 1967. ▸ Sympathetic treatment contending Roosevelt and Japanese officials overcame many obstacles to preserve official friendship and establish rapprochement in 1908. President's policies based on realism, not racism. [KB]

43.624 Michael H. Hunt. *Frontier defense and the Open Door: Manchuria in Chinese-American relations, 1895–1911.* New Haven: Yale University Press, 1973. ISBN 0-300-01616-6. ▸ Masterful examination of failure of Chinese-American cooperation in Manchuria due to Chinese misunderstanding of American policy and American economic imperialism and insensitivity. Based on Chinese and American sources. [KB]

43.625 Michael H. Hunt. *The making of a special relationship: the United States and China to 1914.* New York: Columbia University Press, 1983. ISBN 0-231-05516-1. ▸ Major innovative analysis of American diplomatic, economic, and religious programs in China and Chinese policies. Also considers effect of domestic American anti-Chinese programs on Chinese-American relations. Based on Chinese as well as American materials. [KB]

43.626 Jane Hunter. *The gospel of gentility: American women missionaries in turn-of-the-century China.* New Haven: Yale University Press, 1984. ISBN 0-300-02878-4 (cl), 0-300-04603-0 (pbk). ▸ Analysis of evangelists' involvement in American imperial expansion. Argues women promoted conservative values, including limited activities for women, and adopted many colonializers' attitudes toward Chinese. [KB]

43.627 Jerry Israel. *Progressivism and the Open Door: America and China, 1905–1921.* Pittsburgh: University of Pittsburgh Press, 1971. ISBN 0-8229-3210-5. ▸ Insightful study of American penetration of China market as overseas extension of domestic conflict between advocates of unfettered capitalism and advocates of coordinated regulation. [KB]

43.628 Thomas J. McCormick. *China market: America's quest for informal empire, 1893–1901.* 1967 ed. Chicago: Dee, 1990. ISBN 0-929587-24-3. ▸ Major revisionist study depicting late nineteenth-century imperialism as consequence of economic interest, social fears, and ideology, shaped by new power elite. [KB]

43.629 Delber L. McKee. *Chinese exclusion versus the Open Door policy, 1900–1906: clashes over China policy in the Roosevelt era.* Detroit: Wayne State University Press, 1977. ISBN 0-8143-1565-8. ▸ Discussion of contradictory United States policies stemming from demands of wide variety of interest groups leading to Chinese resentment, anti-American programs, and weakening of Open Door policy. Sees Roosevelt as defensive. [KB]

43.630 Charles E. Neu. *An uncertain friendship: Theodore Roosevelt and Japan, 1906–1909.* Cambridge, Mass.: Harvard University Press, 1967. ▸ Argues that, believing Asia of secondary importance to United States and beset by American racism, president sought friendly relations with Japan while building United

States power in Pacific. Strongest on American problems and policies. [KB]

43.631 James Reed. *The missionary mind and American East Asia policy, 1911–1915*. Cambridge, Mass.: Harvard University, Council on East Asian Studies; distributed by Harvard University Press, 1983. (Harvard East Asian monographs, 104.) ISBN 0-674-57657-8. ▸ Critical examination of disastrous effect of missionary's misunderstandings of China on popular American perceptions and official policies such as nonrecognition. Focuses on images of China and official policy. [KB]

43.632 Sylvester K. Stevens. *American expansion in Hawaii, 1842–1898*. 1945 ed. New York: Russell & Russell, 1968. ▸ Treatment arguing annexation of Hawaii marked culmination of frontier expansion, neither connected to Spanish-American War nor aberration. American domination made annexation inevitable. Stresses continuity in American policy. [KB]

43.633 Paul A. Varg. *The making of a myth: the United States and China, 1897–1912*. 1968 ed. Westport, Conn.: Greenwood, 1980. ISBN 0-313-22125-1. ▸ Argues United States paternalism and sentiment confused policy, which was amalgam of genuine concern, self-righteousness, and naïveté, often irrelevant to Chinese aspirations. Conservative interpretation that nevertheless stresses economics and security questions. [KB]

43.634 Richard E. Welch, Jr. *Response to imperialism: the United States and the Philippine-American War, 1899–1902*. Chapel Hill: University of North Carolina Press, 1979. ISBN 0-8078-1348-6. ▸ Analysis of responses of various groups to imperialism and war and impact of war in terms of contemporary American social beliefs and political divisions. Notes important differences with Vietnam War. [KB]

43.635 Marilyn Blatt Young. *The rhetoric of empire: American China policy, 1895–1901*. Cambridge, Mass.: Harvard University Press, 1968. ▸ Study of rise of commercial and missionary interest generating rhetoric that determined policy largely divorced from contemporary realities. Subtle, sophisticated examination of critical formative period. [KB]

SEE ALSO
14.98 Jongsuk Chay. *Diplomacy of asymmetry*.
47.299 Akira Iriye. *Pacific estrangement*.

Imperialism and Expansion

43.636 Howard K. Beale. *Theodore Roosevelt and the rise of America to world power*. 1956 ed. Baltimore: Johns Hopkins University Press, 1984. ISBN 0-8018-3249-7 (pbk). ▸ Detailed, balanced examination of Roosevelt's understanding and manipulation of balance of power in promoting American global interests. Traditional diplomatic biography. [KB]

43.637 Robert L. Beisner. *Twelve against empire: the anti-imperialists, 1898–1900*. New York: McGraw-Hill, 1968. ISBN 0-7004-344-2. ▸ Sympathetic, liberal, but traditional interpretation of ideas, interests, and sentiments of Mugwump and dissident republican anti-imperialists critical of American expansionism. [KB]

43.638 William Reynolds Braisted. *The United States Navy in the Pacific, 1909–1922*. Austin: University of Texas Press, 1971. ISBN 0-292-70037-7. ▸ Description of expansion of navy's role in developing foreign policies on both oceans including concern about Japan, security for Panama canal, and communications linkages. Solid study stressing strategic concerns. [KB]

43.639 David H. Burton. *Theodore Roosevelt: confident imperialist*. 1968 ed. Philadelphia: University of Pennsylvania Press, 1969. ISBN 0-8122-7582-9. ▸ Intellectual biography dealing with major problem. Contends Roosevelt guided and developed American imperialism to fulfill special American mission. Based on published materials. [KB]

43.640 Richard D. Challener. *Admirals, generals, and American foreign policy, 1898–1914*. Princeton: Princeton University Press, 1973. ISBN 0-691-06916-6. ▸ Analysis of civil-military relations and military contribution to policy formation, challenging realist interpretation. Supports revisionist argument but argues policy shaped by more than economic considerations. [KB]

43.641 Kenton J. Clymer. *John Hay: the gentleman as diplomat*. Ann Arbor: University of Michigan Press, 1975. ISBN 0-472-23400-5. ▸ Sympathetic ideological portrait of thought of major secretary of state who developed his ideas in domestic context and applied them in foreign relations. Hay was amiable, genteel, conservative, elitist, racist, and thorough Anglophile. [KB]

43.642 Richard H. Collin. *Theodore Roosevelt, culture, diplomacy, and expansion: a new view of American imperialism*. Baton Rouge: Louisiana State University Press, 1985. ISBN 0-8071-1214-3. ▸ Conservative analysis arguing Roosevelt led United States into position of world cultural and diplomatic leadership. United States did not engage in any other imperialism in period clouded by legends and faulty historical interpretations. [KB]

43.643 Calvin DeArmond Davis. *The United States and the First Hague Peace Conference*. Ithaca, N.Y.: Cornell University Press for American Historical Association, 1962. ▸ Superb study of arbitrations, arms-limitation discussions, and revision of international law, which ended in failure. Argues Americans talked of peace while preparing for war with Spain and imperial ventures. [KB]

43.644 Calvin DeArmond Davis. *The United States and the Second Hague Peace Conference: American diplomacy and international organization, 1899–1914*. 1975 ed. Durham, N.C.: Duke University Press, 1976. ISBN 0-8223-0346-9. ▸ Discussion of how armaments, international law, and international court improved codification of laws of war and set basis for World Court. Examines American involvement in and uses of World Court. Reconsideration and expansion of earlier study. [KB]

43.645 Frederick C. Drake. *The empire of the seas: a biography of Rear Admiral Robert Wilson Shufeldt, U.S.N.* Honolulu: University of Hawaii Press, 1984. ISBN 0-8248-0846-0. ▸ Important biography of major naval theorist and commander, and diplomat who opened Korea and promoted commercial expansion to alleviate domestic racial and economic problems. Explores connections among diplomatic, economic, and naval policies. Revisionist interpretation. [KB]

43.646 Raymond A. Esthus. *Theodore Roosevelt and the international rivalries*. 1970 ed. New York: Regina, 1982. ISBN 0-941690-04-0 (cl), 0-941690-05-9 (pbk). ▸ Highly sympathetic study of American emergence from isolation. Treats Roosevelt as pragmatic statesman rather than crusader. Emphasizes American relations with Europe and East Asia; neglects Latin America. [KB]

43.647 James A. Field, Jr. "American imperialism: the worst chapter in almost any book." *American historical review* 83 (1978) 644–83. ISSN 0002-8762. ▸ Criticism of revisionist and whig interpretations of late nineteenth-century American imperialism. Maintains Americans sought only freedom for themselves and others. Walter LaFeber and Robert L. Beisner respond. [KB]

43.648 Kenneth J. Hagan. *American gunboat diplomacy and the old navy, 1877–1889*. Westport, Conn.: Greenwood, 1973. ISBN 0-8371-6274-2. ▸ Examination of development of naval theory and operations in support of American commercial expansion during revolutionary period caused by major technological changes, new ideas, and revival of European colonial imperialism. [KB]

43.649 David Healy. *U.S. expansionism: the imperialist urge in the*

1890s. Madison: University of Wisconsin Press, 1970. ISBN 0-299-05851-4 (cl), 0-299-05854-9 (pbk). ▸ Moderate revisionist study arguing Americans justified imperialist movement in variety of ways that merged expediency with morality. Places imperialism in global context. [KB]

43.650 Walter LaFeber. *The new empire: an interpretation of American expansion, 1860–1898*. 1963 ed. Ithaca, N.Y.: Cornell University Press for American Historical Association, 1967. ISBN 0-8014-9048-0 (pbk). ▸ Masterly, revisionist interpretation of effect of industrialization on American foreign policy. Argues American imperialism at end of century was culmination of expansionist policies pursued and justified during previous thirty years. [KB]

43.651 Frederick W. Marks III. *Velvet on iron: the diplomacy of Theodore Roosevelt*. Lincoln: University of Nebraska Press, 1979. ISBN 0-8032-3057-5 (cl), 0-8032-8115-3 (pbk). ▸ Conservative analysis of Roosevelt's diplomacy, emphasizing his restrained use of power and moral basis of his policies. Emphasizes Roosevelt in relation to his times, his strategy and techniques, and his benign international reputation. [KB]

43.652 Milton Plesur. *America's outward thrust: approaches to foreign affairs, 1865–1890*. De Kalb: Northern Illinois University Press, 1971. ISBN 0-87580-019-X. ▸ Treatment emphasizing public attitudes about United States economic, political, and cultural involvement overseas as prelude to imperialism at end of century. Sees continuity in policy. [KB]

43.653 David M. Pletcher. *The awkward years: American foreign relations under Garfield and Arthur*. Columbia: University of Missouri Press, 1962. ISBN 0-8262-0143-1. ▸ Study of evolution of expansionist policy in relation to domestic politics and economic growth in response to nationalism, economic pressures, European competition, and imperialism. Concludes isolationists frustrated attempts to secure greater prestige, markets, and security in this middle period. [KB]

43.654 Julius William Pratt. *Expansionists of 1898: the acquisition of Hawaii and the Spanish islands*. 1936 ed. Chicago: Quadrangle, 1964. ▸ Classic traditional study argues ideology, followed by commerce and strategic concerns, drove American expansionism in 1890s, which led to accidental acquisition of empire. [KB]

43.655 Robert Seager II. *Alfred Thayer Mahan: the man and his letters*. Annapolis, Md.: Naval Institute, 1977. ISBN 0-87021-359-8. ▸ Full examination of America's foremost naval theorist and propagandist, considering his personality, ideas, attitudes, and opinions. Sympathetic but critical and objective portrait. [KB]

43.656 E. Berkeley Tompkins. *Anti-imperialism in the United States: the great debate, 1890–1920*. Philadelphia: University of Pennsylvania Press, 1970. ISBN 0-8122-7595-0. ▸ Study of effects of industrialization, European imperialism, social Darwinism, racism, and massive economic growth in causing temporary shift from anti-imperialism to imperialism. Debate preceded Philippine issue. [KB]

43.657 Alice Felt Tyler. *The foreign policy of James G. Blaine*. 1927 ed. Hamden, Conn.: Archon, 1965. ▸ Highly sympathetic, detailed examination of powerful political figure who inaugurated new era in United States foreign relations. Maintains Blaine had clear purpose in seeking commercial expansion: hemispheric stability under United States hegemony. [KB]

43.658 Betty M. Unterberger. *America's Siberian expedition, 1918–1920: a study of national policy*. 1956 ed. New York: Greenwood, 1969. ISBN 0-8371-0726-1. ▸ Major interpretation arguing United States intervention in Siberia sought primarily to contain Japanese expansion and preserve Open Door policy. Policy of intervention thus traditional, but it also shaped attitudes toward Soviet Russia and marked first offensive against Japan. [KB]

43.659 Mira Wilkins. *The emergence of multinational enterprise: American business abroad from the colonial era to 1914*. Cambridge, Mass.: Harvard University Press, 1970. ISBN 0-674-24830-9. ▸ Detailed discussion of American business involvement overseas, concentrating on period after 1870 in Europe, Canada, Mexico, and rest of Latin America. Demonstrates that leading American inventors, manufacturers, and marketers were deeply interested in international business in period. [KB]

World War I

43.660 Thomas Andrew Bailey. *Wilson and the peacemakers: combining Woodrow Wilson and the lost peace and Woodrow Wilson and the great betrayal*. 2 vols. in 1. New York: Macmillan, 1947. ▸ Critical examination of blunders at Versailles and tragic defeat of peace treaty at home. Sympathetic to Wilson, whose realism and prophetic vision is praised, but discusses his mistakes and shortcomings as well. [KB]

43.661 Edward H. Buehrig. *Woodrow Wilson and the balance of power*. 1955 ed. New York: Smith, 1968. ISBN 0-8446-0522-0. ▸ Study emphasizing close, friendly Anglo-American political, economic, cultural, and strategic relations and concurrent deterioration in relations with Germany. Argues United States entered World War I when it feared that Germany would destroy British dominance of seas. [KB]

43.662 Frederick S. Calhoun. *Power and principle: armed intervention in Wilsonian foreign policy*. Kent, Ohio: Kent State University Press, 1986. ISBN 0-87338-327-3. ▸ Deeply researched study arguing president identified goals, established methods, and defined terms of using force as part of idealistic policy in interventions in Mexico, Haiti, Santo Domingo, France, and Russia. [KB]

43.663 John Milton Cooper, Jr. *The vanity of power: American isolationism and the First World War, 1914–1917*. Westport, Conn.: Greenwood, 1969. ISBN 0-8371-2342-9. ▸ Analysis of conflict between idealists and ultranationalists in isolationist movement about overseas commitments shortly before World War I. Emphasizes ideas and sentiments of isolationists. [KB]

43.664 Robert H. Ferrell. *Woodrow Wilson and World War I, 1917–1921*. New York: Harper & Row, 1985. ISBN 0-06-011229-8 (cl), 0-06-091216-2 (pbk). ▸ Superb analysis of critical period. Treats Wilson as tragic figure in this synthesis covering domestic as well as foreign, military, and diplomatic developments. [KB]

43.665 Ross Gregory. *The origins of American intervention in the First World War*. New York: Norton, 1971. ISBN 0-393-05438-1 (cl), 0-393-09980-6 (pbk). ▸ Analysis of domestic sources of American neutrality and policies developed in England and Germany that made American noninvolvement crucial element in war. Well-written synthesis with some original research. [KB]

43.666 Burton I. Kaufman. *Efficiency and expansion: foreign trade organization in the Wilson administration, 1913–1921*. Westport, Conn.: Greenwood, 1974. ISBN 0-8371-7338-8. ▸ Study arguing American loss of confidence in commercial competition with Europe led to government-business coordination along scientific management lines. Fundamental changes occurred in American commercial policy amid much tension. American fears diminished after 1917. [KB]

43.667 George F. Kennan. *Soviet-American relations, 1917–1920*. 1956–58 ed. 3 vols. Princeton: Princeton University Press, 1989–. ISBN 0-691-00847-7 (set), 0-691-00841-8 (v. 1), 0-691-00842-6 (v. 2). ▸ Detailed examination, by master diplomat-historian, of American diplomacy from Bolshevik Revolution to Treaty of Brest-Litovsk and subsequent American and Allied intervention in Russia. Emphasizes chaos and complexity. [KB]

43.668 Linda Killen. *The Russian bureau: a case study in Wilson-*

ian diplomacy. Lexington: University Press of Kentucky, 1983. ISBN 0-8131-1495-0. ▸ Discussion of assistance provided through War Trade Board of American Russian Bureau to Russian provisional government as example of public-private cooperation and expression of complex and varied motivations behind policies toward Russia. Program failed because it lacked clear goals and purposes. [KB]

43.669 Simeon Larson. *Labor and foreign policy: Gompers, the A.F.L., and the First World War, 1914–1918.* 1974 ed. Rutherford, N.J.: Fairleigh Dickinson University Press, 1975. ISBN 0-8386-1290-3. ▸ Assessment of role and impact of organized labor on development and implementation of Woodrow Wilson's foreign policy, focusing on labor leader's motivation in supporting Wilson and reaction of workers to both Gompers's and Wilson's policies. [KB]

43.670 N. Gordon Levin, Jr. *Woodrow Wilson and world politics: America's response to war and revolution.* 1968 ed. London: Oxford University Press, 1970. ISBN 0-19-500803-0. ▸ Insightful ideological interpretation of Wilson's attempt to negotiate between revolutionary socialism and reactionary imperialism and to create international liberal-capitalist order under American leadership. [KB]

43.671 Arthur S. Link. *Woodrow Wilson: revolution, war, and peace.* Arlington Heights, Ill.: Harlan Davidson, 1979. ISBN 0-88295-799-6 (cl), 0-88295-798-8 (pbk). ▸ Sympathetic overview of Wilson's ideas and diplomacy by his chief biographer and editor of his papers. Presents case for Wilson as liberal and realistic statesman with only highest motives. [KB]

43.672 Ernest R. May. *The World War and American isolation, 1914–1917.* 1959 ed. Chicago: Quadrangle, 1966. ▸ Major, multiarchival examination of political debates in Britain and Germany over American question before United States' entry on British side. Wilson wrestled with his conscience but could not stay out of war due to American interests and European decisions. [KB]

43.673 Arno J. Mayer. *Political origins of the new diplomacy, 1917–1918.* 1959 ed. New York: Fertig, 1969. ▸ Sweeping comparative view of contest between conservative parties of order and revolutionary parties of movement and between old and new diplomacy. V. I. Lenin and Woodrow Wilson emerge as champions of latter. Revisionist interpretation. [KB]

43.674 Ralph Stone. *The irreconcilables: the fight against the League of Nations.* 1970 ed. New York: Norton, 1973. ISBN 0-393-00671-9. ▸ Balanced treatment of ideas and methods of sixteen senators who would not compromise. Group was diverse, and members saw themselves as responsible, reasonable, courageous, and principled; their critics have not. [KB]

43.675 Arthur Walworth. *Wilson and his peacemakers: American diplomacy at the Paris Peace Conference, 1919.* New York: Norton, 1986. ISBN 0-393-01867-9. ▸ Massively detailed, sympathetic interpretation of Wilson as idealist with prophetic vision at Versailles, conducting, with enormous difficulty, the first major peace conference based on democratic principles. [KB]

43.676 William C. Widenor. *Henry Cabot Lodge and the search for an American foreign policy.* Berkeley: University of California Press, 1980. ISBN 0-520-03778-2 (cl), 0-520-04962-4 (pbk). ▸ Intellectual biography centering on foreign policy and relation between ideas and diplomacy and between domestic and foreign policy. Lodge, Republican Senator from Massachusetts, presented as idealist in conflict with Woodrow Wilson's different idealism. Sympathetic but critical. [KB]

SEE ALSO
47.407 Daniel M. Smith. *The great departure.*
47.425 Lloyd E. Ambrosius. *Woodrow Wilson and the American diplomatic tradition.*
47.451 Arno J. Mayer. *Politics and diplomacy of peacemaking.*
47.462 Klaus Schwabe. *Woodrow Wilson, revolutionary Germany, and peacemaking, 1918–1919.*

JAMES T. PATTERSON

United States History since 1920

Historical writing about the United States since 1920 has mushroomed in recent years. The eight hundred–odd entries in this annotated bibliography represent only a small percentage of the vast outpouring of books and articles on the social, economic, intellectual, cultural, political, military, and diplomatic history of the era. Lacking space in this essay to mention specific authors and titles, I will write instead about some major historiographical trends.

Three circumstances have presented unique opportunities to and problems for scholars and popular historians in this thriving field. The first is the closeness of these years to our own times. Historians who write about the recent past have the special advantage that comes from familiarity with the people and events they study. If written sources seem inadequate, scholars can interview historical actors or make site visits that add vividness to their prose. Oral sources, not widely used thirty years ago, have become the stock in trade of many recent historians, who have further benefited from access to a spreading institutional network of oral history journals, conferences, and archives.

But closeness to the times has other effects. Unlike historians who write about earlier eras, scholars probing the recent past do not know what will be truly important to readers in the future. They necessarily have trouble determining the periodization appropriate to their histories, and their writing is deeply influenced by the era in which they live. This has been a time of often profound generational tension, racial conflict, Cold War, and rising ethnic and gender consciousness that today emphasizes the multicultural roots of American life. These events help explain recent historians' choice of subject matter—African American, ethnic, and women's history have shown enormous growth—and approach, which has tended to be highly critical of American society and institutions.

The second circumstance is the nature of sources for this era; they are unprecedentedly numerous and varied. Historians studying the period since 1920 have access not only to traditional written records (and to oral sources) but also to film, recordings, and television. A large number of newspapers and increasingly specialized magazines print syndicated columns, features, and op-ed pieces that are the envy of historians studying other cultures or eras. The published documentary record, especially from national, state, and local governments, is vast. Archives, ranging from presidential libraries to institutions housing collections of films and television tapes, have collected masses of data. A proliferation of bibliographical aids, including such basic tools as the

New York Times Index, the *Reader's Guide to Periodical Literature*, and *America: History and Life* (1954–), exist to help researchers find their way through the maze of information. Huge compilations of references on compact disc, such as the *Expanded Academic Index* (1985–), offer further assistance to researchers comfortable with the technological world of modern libraries. If there is a strong relationship between the quantity of available data and the quality of historical scholarship, writing about the United States since 1920 should be as exciting as any ever created.

This quantity of data, however, is a mixed blessing. Scholars of recent American history, confronted by mountains of information, need special skill at selecting and discriminating. Heavy reliance on oral sources raises an obvious problem: is memory reliable? Researchers seeking truly revealing archival sources, traditionally the major quest of historians, encounter formidable obstacles. People who once committed their ideas to paper have, since 1920, been much more likely to do their thinking over the telephone, the great enemy of historical research into the recent past. (The spread of FAX, however, may prove to be a blessing for scholars in the future.)

Important documents from government, too, can be scanty. Policies mandating privacy shield census data about individuals for seventy years, while security-conscious bureaucrats have been quick to stamp "classified" on all sorts of paper dealing with foreign and military policies, especially for the years since 1960. Although a few historians have used the provisions of the Freedom of Information Act to gain access to government documents, they have frequently remained frustrated by security regulations.

The third circumstance, much harder to describe briefly, concerns the turbulent domestic history of the United States since the 1950s. This history, especially of racial, gender, and generational conflict, has encouraged considerable growth in the amount of writing about ordinary or forgotten people, especially African Americans, other racial and ethnic minorities, and women. Historians have emphasized the social, economic, and political forces that have oppressed such Americans. Most, however, have refused to describe these forgotten Americans as helpless pawns in the face of such injustice. They have accordingly stressed the agency of the powerless, the creative ways in which African Americans, women, immigrants, and other once-slighted groups have made their own history. The test for subtle historians is to strike a proper balance between the oppression and the agency.

Many historians seeking such balance have looked carefully at modern forces that shape experience. One of these forces has been the rise of the consumer culture. A flourishing, often contentious field of research has developed concerning trends in advertising and public relations, film, radio, television, journalism, sports, and other manifestations of popular culture. Although few historians have so far adopted postmodern frameworks rooted in relativistic and linguistically based cultural analysis, many have deplored the influence of advertising or television, concluding that these institutions have amassed an ill-used hegemonic power over American culture. The seductive allure of consumerism, these critics add, dampens social unrest and undermines efforts to broaden justice and equality. Other historians have questioned these interpretations, emphasizing instead the ability of ordinary people to resist or transform the blandishments of commercialization. Most of these writers have attempted to show how trends in popular culture expose changes over time in values, attitudes, styles of life, and personal and familial relationships.

A few of these social and cultural historians have led a chorus calling for the end of old-fashioned political history that focuses on the words and deeds of presidents and well-known national politicians. They have only partly succeeded in this quest: political history of this sort probably retains more vitality for the years since 1920 than it does for earlier eras of U.S. history—it was mainly in these years, after all, that the state began to matter much in the lives of ordinary American citizens.

Most leading scholars of this kind of political history write from a liberal perspective. Many have filled gaps in our understanding of the New Deal of Franklin D. Roosevelt, although without substantially changing the cautiously positive interpretation of Roosevelt advanced by W. Leuchtenburg (44.505) in 1963. The Truman administration, well received by most historians, has also attracted able scholars. McCarthyism and its political and cultural consequences have been subjects of considerable historical scholarship, much of which portrays McCarthy as a latecomer to a broader coalition of anticommunist interest groups and right-wing politicians. Critics and revisionists have vigorously debated the pros and cons of the Eisenhower administration, which is more favorably regarded in the 1990s than it used to be. Scholars have also critically evaluated the domestic policies of John F. Kennedy and Lyndon Johnson. Subsequent presidential adminstrations have received considerable attention from thoughtful journalists and command increasing interest among scholars. Judicial history and biography continue to attract their modest share of researchers, including lawyers, journalists, and political scientists.

Still, since the 1950s there has been some movement away from political history that focuses on the activities of policy-making elites. Many scholars working in this field have been less interested in political leaders than in the rise of protest movements particularly those on the Left. There are large and growing stacks of books on the struggles of African Americans and the civil rights movement, the New Left of the 1960s, and the rise of feminism. Other historians have written excellent accounts of earlier twentieth-century leftist movements, seeking especially to explain why it is that these movements have failed to gain much of a popular following.

Political historians (and other social scientists) in recent years have also looked more closely at the underlying structures and functions of politics than at the hoopla of party conventions or the claims of political rhetoric. They have accordingly given growing attention to electoral behavior, to the flaws of socioeconomic policy, to the role of lobbies and interest groups, and to the influence of television and "sound-bites." Other writers, including a few neo-Marxists, have stressed the profound structural obstacles—notably the weakness of the state—to substantial economic reform in the United States.

Other political and economic historians have rejected the dualisms of an older progressive history that highlighted struggles between liberals and conservatives or the "people" against the "interests." Some of these writers have employed modernization theory to focus on the enhanced role—in politics as well as in the economy—of large-scale organizations and of experts in American life. These organizations, it is argued, have been much more important in accounting for economic trends and political policies than the often ritualistic rhetoric of progressives or conservatives. Although critics of this organizational synthesis worry that it minimizes the role of ideas and of human agency in history, they agree that any synthesis of a society as complex as the United States since 1920 must go beyond simplistic dualisms such as rich versus poor or Right versus Left.

Satisfactory syntheses of recent American political and economic history, many historians add, must rethink previously accepted approaches to periodization. These approaches tended to periodize the era since 1920 according to what they considered to be the political culture of various decades (the conservative 1920s, the liberal 1960s) or according to presidential administrations (the age of Roosevelt, the Nixon years). Such periodizing still proves useful, especially to political and diplomatic historians, but it also encounters considerable criticism. Many historians today question the validity of the older notion that the Republican administrations of the 1920s were uniformly conservative or that the New Deal was consistently liberal. Those who study policies concerning race, ethnic, and gender relations since 1920 often see more continuity than liberal-to-conservative fluctuations in the recent American past. While many scholars accept the special importance of World War II as a watershed in the social, economic, diplomatic, and military history of the United States, there is as yet no solid consensus concerning the more detailed periodization of the American past since 1920.

Scholars writing since 1960 have generally welcomed another trend: the decline of a consensus school of historical writing, strong in the politically moderate Eisenhower years of the 1950s. This school, later critics complained, paid relatively little attention to important conflicts—racial, ethnic, regional, religious, ideological, or economic—in the American past. In fact, there was no such school in any formal sense, and historians thought to hold such views differed among themselves. But there is no doubt that historians writing during and since the turbulent 1960s have identified much more conflict than consensus in twentieth-century U.S. history. Many of these scholars have written at length about the forces—patriarchy, corporate power, racism, and American imperialism—they consider to be major sources of such conflict.

This sort of critical stance has had a noteworthy impact on the writing of military and diplomatic history. Prior to the mid-1960s, when American escalation of the war in Vietnam promoted widespread cultural and political unrest, much of this writing celebrated the eclipse of pre–World War II isolationism in America, the heroic defeat of fascism in World War II, and the praiseworthy anti-Soviet stance of American political leaders during the Cold War years. The tragedy of the Vietnam War prompted a reevaluation of such positive assumptions about U.S. foreign policy, resulting in a number of impressive studies of American foreign and military policies since the 1920s. Even America's "Good War" against Germany and Japan, some scholars wrote, deserved hard-hitting reexamination.

The critical mood following the 1960s also encouraged a flurry of revisionist scholarship, especially concerning the origins and escalation of the Cold War. Scholars in the 1980s and 1990s have now subjected this flurry to postrevisionist examinations that have qualified some of its more critical conclusions. In all these ways the fields of diplomatic and military history have revealed the impact of contemporary international developments. The collapse of communism in the Soviet Union and Eastern Europe will bring about yet another round of revisions in existing scholarship concerning foreign policies since the 1940s.

All these developments since 1960—the growth of social history, the emphasis on conflict over consensus, and the rise of more critical approaches to politics and institutions—have greatly changed the nature of American historical writing. But these historiographical trends have also made some observers uneasy. Social history, they agree, has properly broadened the scope of inquiry into the lives of previously overlooked people, often rescuing them from obscurity. But has this focus become so intense that it has contributed to the neglect of other kinds of history, including the study of institutions? Some critics think so, arguing that some areas of historical writing seem shortchanged, for the years since 1945 as well as for earlier periods. These areas include established but now rather quiet fields of inquiry such as business, rural, religious, and educational history. They include also relatively undeveloped areas such as the history of science, medicine, and technology. Labor historians have produced fine work on the years prior to 1945 but comparatively little on the postwar years. Despite some excellent studies in the field of intellectual history, this area of research, too, has not attracted very many scholars. Environmental history, while growing, is not yet a major field of research. Scholarship on regions in the twentieth century, especially the new western history, appears to be gaining in vitality, but has yet to produce a quantity of work comparable to that for earlier periods.

Some critics also complain that too many recent historians have over-imbibed the anti-institutional spirit of post-1960 culture, thereby producing highly ideological scholarship. Graduate schools in the humanities and social sciences, they add, have been dominated by left-of-center scholars who have encouraged adversarial approaches. The result, critics say, has been a spate of critical tomes that scarcely begin to convey the progressive character of the United States since 1920, notably the remarkable stability of democratic institutions and the resourceful foreign policies of American political leaders amid the topsy-turvy events of twentieth-century world history. Critics add that studies produced by adversarial writers fail to capture the considerable progress—in standards of living, in the treatment of minorities, in religious toleration, in social policies, and in scientific and technological creativity—that ought to be the grand themes of historical writing about United States history since 1920.

These critics are correct in identifying the occasionally angry tone of academic scholarship about the recent past. They are also correct in noting the academic character of much of this writing: a gulf has arisen between the critical, highly specialized, and sometimes jargon-laden scholarly histories, which few Americans read, and many happier narrative accounts, which are much more accessible to a broader general public. But these critics need also to remember that historical writing unavoidably reflects contemporary popular concerns. It is therefore not surprising that many American historians in recent years have focused on highly charged contemporary issues involving Cold War fears, racial and class tensions, multiculturalism, consumerism, and gender relations.

Finally, critics complain about what they see as the tendency of some contemporary historians to over-identify with whatever oppressed group they are studying, thereby producing romanticized accounts. A number of social histories, they add, are local, narrow monographs that fail to link the experiences of a particular group to broader economic, intellectual, and political contexts. Readers of such studies, it is alleged, end up with a highly fragmented picture that confounds any attempt to produce syntheses of the recent past.

Although this criticism has some merit when applied to historical writing about nineteenth-century America, it seems less valid concerning writing about the more recent past, which continues to attract a significant number of scholars working in areas other than social history. Moreover, historians dealing with the twentieth century have tried to synthesize segments of the period since 1920. Some identify social and ideological changes, especially as driven by the civil rights movement, as the underlying forces in American life since the 1940s. Others focus on the synthesizing power of economic and demographic trends, notably the affluence and baby boom of the 1940s and 1950s. Still others, rejecting the parochialism of specialized local studies, link the social and cultural history of ethnic groups and of women to broader political developments. Many of these efforts emphasize the role of World War II in producing what they argue is the very different recent history of the United States since 1945. While these syntheses do not satisfy every reader, they indicate that historians have not thrown up their hands in despair when confronted by the complexity of recent American life.

The criticism that social history fragments the recent past may also be countered by emphasizing again that the United States itself is fragmented. Americans between 1920 and the early 1990s lived through four major wars, bewildering oscillations of the economy, scarcely imaginable technological change, and major population movements. They experienced powerful but not always unilinear social developments, such as the growth of consumerism, feminism, and the movement for civil rights. Long gone are the days when historians, or anyone else, could chart a steady line of progress, let alone talk confidently about an identifiable American national character.

Given the continuing divisiveness of American society, and the rapidly changing nature of world politics and economics, it is hardly surprising that historians have had problems synthesizing the American experience since 1920. No simple history can do justice to the complex and contentious real world of the United States in the twentieth century.

[Contributors: AIM = Alan I. Marcus, BBY = Bernard B. Yamron, BES = Bruce E. Seely, CAM = Clyde A. Milner II, CKF = Carole K. Fink, CSH = Christopher S. Hamlin, DLC = David L. Carlton, EH-D = Evelyn Hu-DeHart, FGN = F.G. Noteholter, JGC = Jonathan G. Cederbaum, JSH = John S. Hill, JTL = John T. Landry, JTP = James T. Patterson, LGB = Lucy G. Barber, NMK = Nicholas M. Kliment, PBI = Paul B. Israel, PEC = Paul E. Ceruzzi, PFF = Phyllis F. Field, PLH = Peter L. Hahn, RJW = Richard J. Walter, RKG = Robert K. Griffith, Jr., RLM = Richard L. Miller, TCL = Theodore C. Liazos, TSR = Terry S. Reynolds, UGP = Uta G. Poiger, WMD = William M. Doyle, WWR = William W. Register, Jr.]

CULTURAL AND INTELLECTUAL HISTORY

General Studies

44.1 Charles Alexander. *Nationalism in American thought, 1930–1945*. Chicago: Rand McNally, 1969. ▸ Intellectual history; brief survey of Depression era culture, including art, literature, film, radio, science, religion, music. Finds reassertion of nationalist identity in response to economic crisis. [WWR]

44.2 Frederick Lewis Allen. *"Only yesterday" and "Since yesterday": a popular history of the 20s and 30s*. 1931–41 ed. New York: Bonanza; distributed by Crown, 1986. ISBN 0-517-60355-1. ▸ Engaging, influential narrative of 1920s by one who lived it. Contributed to era's jazzy reputation of hedonistic pleasure and moral decline. Useful as both primary and secondary resource. [WWR]

44.3 Robert Hamlett Bremner, John Braeman, and David Brody, eds. *Change and continuity in twentieth-century America: the 1920s*. Columbus: Ohio State University Press, 1968. ▸ Useful essays providing general overview of social, cultural, political, and intellectual phenomena of decade. [WWR]

44.4 John C. Burnham. *Bad habits: drinking, smoking, taking drugs, gambling, sexual misbehavior, and swearing in American history*. New York: New York University Press, 1993. ISBN 0-8147-1187-1. ▸ Bold interpretive account focusing on rise of such "bad habits," mainly since 1920s, dividing point in American cultural history. [JTP]

44.5 Norman H. Clark. *Deliver us from evil: an interpretation of American prohibition*. New York: Norton, 1976. ISBN 0-393-05584-1 (cl), 0-393-09170-8 (pbk). ▸ Sympathetic examination of ideas and values behind temperance movement through 1920s, treating crusaders as reformers grappling with problem of alcohol during time of immense social change. [WWR]

44.6 Peter Clecak. *America's quest for the ideal self: dissent and fulfillment in the 60s and 70s*. New York: Oxford University Press, 1983. ISBN 0-19-503226-8. ▸ Examination of claims to social justice, cultural space, and personal fulfillment uniting 1960s and 1970s. Treats white ethnics, religious groups, neoconservatives, New Right, taxpayers, and antiwar and feminist movements. [UGP]

44.7 Robert Crunden. *From self to society, 1919–1941*. Englewood Cliffs, N.J.: Prentice-Hall, 1972. ISBN 0-13-331421-9 (cl),

0-13-331413-8 (pbk). ▸ Valuable, concise biographies portray era when intellectuals reassessed social role, from concern with self apart from society to celebration of community. Reflected rise of collectivist political ideologies during Depression. [WWR]

44.8 Morris Dickstein. *Gates of Eden: American culture in the sixties.* 1977 ed. New York: Penguin, 1989. ISBN 0-14-011617-6. ▸ Brief, readable interpretation of 1960s cultural renewal addressing intellectual trends, hippies, United States imperialism, civil rights, rock music, and media. Combines political commentary, autobiography, and literary criticism. [UGP]

44.9 Barbara Ehrenreich, Elizabeth Hess, and Gloria Jacobs. *Remaking love: the feminization of sex.* Garden City, N.J.: Anchor and Doubleday, 1986. ISBN 0-385-18498-0. ▸ Wide-ranging, exploratory essays on origins of sexual revolution: girls in 1950s, youth cultures, 1970s sex debates, liberalization of marital sex, fundamentalism, and rise of backlash against social revolution. [UGP]

44.10 Robert H. Elias. *"Entangling alliances with none": an essay on the individual in the American twenties.* New York: Norton, 1973. ISBN 0-393-01097-X. ▸ Intelligently argued interpretation of work of psychologists, writers, and other intellectuals to portray decade as epitome of individualism—the negation of Progressive reform era. [WWR]

44.11 Todd Gitlin. *The sixties: years of hope, days of rage.* 1987 ed. New York: Bantam, 1989. ISBN 0-553-05233-0 (cl, 1987), 0-553-34601-6 (pbk). ▸ Vivid picture of culture from which New Left emerged combining autobiography with history of leftist movement. [UGP]

44.12 Joseph C. Goulden. *The best years, 1945–1950.* New York: Atheneum, 1976. ISBN 0-689-10708-0. ▸ Sympathetic yet critical recreation of life in America combining personal recollection; interviews; and analysis of politics, economy, House Un-American Activities Committee hearings, plight of veterans, afternoon soap operas, and early television. [UGP]

44.13 William Graebner. *The age of doubt: American thought and culture in the 1940s.* Boston: Twayne, 1991. ISBN 0-8057-9061-6 (cl), 0-8057-9070-5 (pbk). ▸ Stimulating examination of how anxiety and search for wholeness unified 1940s and shaped Americans' examination of consumer culture, new technologies, and political orthodoxy. Includes analyses of comic strips, movies, bebop, systems theory, and existentialism. [UGP]

44.14 Marty Jezer. *The dark ages: life in the U.S., 1945–1960.* Boston: South End Press, 1982. ISBN 0-89608-128-1 (cl), 0-89608-127-3 (pbk). ▸ Spirited critique of rise of corporate liberalism, of which acquiescence to anticommunism was defining characteristic. Discussion of how resulting problems led to 1960s domestic upheaval. [UGP]

44.15 Alfred Kazin. *On native grounds: an interpretation of modern American prose literature.* 1942 ed. San Diego, Calif.: Harcourt Brace Jovanovich, 1982. ISBN 0-15-668731-8 (pbk). ▸ Landmark literary history of twentieth-century by leading figure of New York intellectual community. [WWR]

44.16 Harvey Levenstein. *Paradox of plenty: a social history of eating in modern America.* New York: Oxford University Press, 1992. ISBN 0-19-505543-8. ▸ Scholarly, lively treatment of American eating habits since 1930. Excellent social and cultural history. [JTP]

44.17 Lary May, ed. *Recasting America: culture and politics in the age of the cold war.* Chicago: University of Chicago Press, 1989. ISBN 0-226-51175-8 (cl), 0-226-51176-6 (pbk). ▸ Fourteen brief, scholarly essays on evolution of social scientific and historical thought, anticommunism, suburbia, arts, popular culture, and gender roles; traces anxiety amid affluence. [UGP]

44.18 Roderick Nash. *The nervous generation: American thought, 1917–1930.* Chicago: Rand McNally, 1970. ▸ Brief history of 1920s that disposes of image of jazz age frivolity by stressing anxiety among intellectuals of period. Useful as survey of cultural figures. [WWR]

44.19 Richard H. Pells. *Radical visions and American dreams: culture and social thought in the Depression years.* 1973 ed. Middletown, Conn.: Wesleyan University Press, 1984. ISBN 0-8195-6122-3 (pbk). ▸ Important survey of search for alternative culture to liberal capitalism in works of leading leftist intellectuals, writers, and filmmakers. Values artistic ferment but sees underlying conservatism in ideas and their implications. [WWR]

44.20 Warren I. Susman. *Culture as history: the transformation of American society in the twentieth century.* New York: Pantheon, 1984. ISBN 0-394-53364-X (cl), 0-394-72161-6 (pbk). ▸ Influential essays on popular culture. Models for enlisting cultural artifacts to construct engaging, sometimes dense analyses unusually sympathetic to urban mass society. [WWR]

44.21 Stephen J. Whitfield. *The culture of the cold war.* Baltimore: Johns Hopkins University Press, 1991. ISBN 0-8018-4081-3 (cl), 0-8018-4082-1 (pbk). ▸ Fair-minded, well-informed study of collective reaction to fear of international communism resulting in political conservatism and search for comfort in religion, popular culture, and suburban homes. [UGP]

Advertising

44.22 Stuart Ewen. *Captains of consciousness: advertising and the social roots of the consumer culture.* New York: McGraw-Hill, 1976. ISBN 0-07-019845-4. ▸ Influential, much-disputed study of 1920s advertising as systematic effort by corporate capitalism to hoodwink American public into adopting consumer ethic. [WWR]

44.23 Stephen Fox. *The mirror makers: a history of American advertising and its creators.* New York: Morrow, 1984. ISBN 0-688-02256-1. ▸ Useful portraits of late nineteenth- and twentieth-century industry pioneers. Argues advertising's power to shape consumer behavior peaked in 1920s; declined afterward in inverse relation to its proliferation. [WWR]

44.24 Roland Marchand. *Advertising the American dream: making way for modernity, 1920–1940.* Berkeley: University of California Press, 1985. ISBN 0-520-05253-6. ▸ Important examination of strategies and images invented to sell goods as promise of and antidote to modern life—paradoxical messages that reflected ad creators' own concerns. [WWR]

44.25 Otis A. Pease. *The responsibilities of American advertising.* New Haven: Yale University Press, 1958. ▸ First major scholarly study of historical development of advertising. Treats subject as central institution in twentieth-century culture. [WWR]

44.26 Michael Schudson. *Advertising, the uneasy persuasion: its dubious impact on American society.* New York: Basic Books, 1984. ISBN 0-465-00078-9 (cl), 0-465-00079-7 (pbk). ▸ Sociologist's influential skeptical assessment of advertising's role in twentieth-century economy. Rejects perspective that assigns medium unusual power; argues it is only one of many social and cultural factors determining consumer choices. [WWR]

Art and Photography

44.27 James Agee and Walker Evans. *Let us now praise famous men: three tenant families.* 1941 rev. ed. Boston: Houghton-Mifflin, 1988. ISBN 0-395-48901-6 (cl), 0-395-48897-4 (pbk). ▸ Collaboration of reportorial prose and photography to record and celebrate ordinary life of Alabama sharecropper families in 1930s. Classic study. [WWR]

44.28 Donald J. Bush. *The streamlined decade.* New York: Braziller, 1975. ISBN 0-8076-0792-4 (cl), 0-8076-0793-2 (pbk). ▸ Surveys industrial design, 1927 through 1939 New York World's Fair. Adaptation of scientific principles and values to commodity, urban design constructed optimistic vision of efficiency and order amid Depression. Abundant illustrations. [WWR]

44.29 James M. Dennis. *Grant Wood: a study in American art and culture*. Rev. ed. Columbia: University of Missouri Press, 1986. ISBN 0-8262-0616-6 (cl), 0-8262-0480-5 (pbk). ‣ Standard biography of important Iowa-born artist and satirist linking major paintings and efforts in thirties to promote indigenous, regionally based art to larger historical and cultural developments. [WWR]

44.30 Carl Fleischhauer and Beverly W. Brannan, eds. *Documenting America, 1935–43*. Lawrence W. Levine and Alan Trachtenberg, essays. Berkeley: University of California Press and Library of Congress, 1988. ISBN 0-520-06220-5 (cl), 0-520-06221-3 (pbk). ‣ Reprints of work by twelve photographers employed in Farm Security Administration during Depression. Critical essays set historical and ideological context. [WWR]

44.31 Serge Guilbaut. *How New York stole the idea of modern art: abstract expressionism, freedom, and the cold war*. Arthur Goldhammer, trans. Chicago: University of Chicago Press, 1983. ISBN 0-226-31038-8. ‣ Success of American avant-garde explained primarily by its ideology in world of international competition (1940s to 1950s), not to formal superiority. Controversial, dense account combines intellectual and art history with analysis of broader culture and politics. [UGP]

44.32 Thomas Hine. *Populuxe*. New York: Knopf, 1986. ISBN 0-394-54593-1. ‣ Well-illustrated, well-written social history of American fashion in popular consumption of material goods, including home decor and cars in 1950s and 1960s. [UGP]

44.33 Sam Hunter. *American art of the twentieth century*. New York: Abrams, 1972. ISBN 0-8109-0030-0. ‣ Well-illustrated history of American artists, their imagery and changing role in society, post-1940 focus. Treats impressionism, surrealism, realism, abstract expressionism, pop art, and conceptual art. Analysis of movements, individual biographies, paintings, and sculptures. [UGP]

44.34 F. Jack Hurley. *Portrait of a decade: Roy Stryker and the development of documentary photography in the thirties*. 1972 ed. New York: Da Capo, 1977. ISBN 0-306-80058-6. ‣ Balanced account of division of New Deal's Farm Security Administration that accumulated landmark photographic record of Depression era agricultural poor. Includes useful reprints. [WWR]

44.35 Jerre G. Mangione. *The dream and the Deal: the Federal Writers' Project, 1935–1943*. 2d ed. Philadelphia: University of Pennsylvania Press, 1983. ISBN 0-8122-1141-3 (pbk). ‣ Spirited history of Works Progress Administration's short-lived bureaucratic writers' collective, through sardonic perceptive eyes of participants. Emphasizes contribution to future of American letters. [WWR]

44.36 William F. McDonald. *Federal Relief Administration and the arts: the origins and administrative history of the arts projects of the Works Progress Administration*. Columbus: Ohio State University Press, 1969. ‣ Encyclopedic reference source on New Deal sponsorship of art and institutional history of administration. [WWR]

44.37 Richard D. McKinzie. *The New Deal for artists*. Princeton: Princeton University Press, 1973. ISBN 0-691-04613-1. ‣ Surveys government patronage of public art and arts projects during Depression, focusing on organizations, bureaucracies, and their leaders rather than artworks. [WWR]

44.38 Jeffrey L. Meikle. *Twentieth century limited: industrial design in America, 1925–1939*. Philadelphia: Temple University Press, 1979. ISBN 0-87722-158-8. ‣ Important analysis of profession from 1925 Paris Exposition through 1939 New York World's Fair using biographies of pioneering designers. Critical of optimistic faith in alliance of technology and art to improve society. [WWR]

44.39 William Stott. *Documentary expression and thirties America*. 1973 ed. Chicago: University of Chicago Press, 1986. ISBN 0-226-77559-3 (pbk). ‣ Intelligent cultural history of social importance of genre in Depression era. Emphasizes mediating, ideological artistry, rather than objectivity, of photographers seeking to improve as well as celebrate subjects' lives. [WWR]

44.40 Robert C. Twombly. *Frank Lloyd Wright: an interpretive biography*. New York: Harper & Row, 1973. ISBN 0-06-014467-X. ‣ Useful account that ties life and ideas of architect to larger cultural history of United States. Comprehensive bibliography on architect. [WWR]

SEE ALSO
40.571 Alan Trachtenberg. *Reading American photographs*.

Automobile Travel

44.41 Warren James Belasco. *Americans on the road: from autocamp to motel, 1910–1945*. Cambridge, Mass.: MIT Press, 1979. ISBN 0-262-02123-4. ‣ Original study of commercial culture and new social roles and conflicts resulting from and reflected in automobile revolution. Chronicles channeling of Americans' longing for escape into roadside lodging industry. [WWR]

44.42 Dean MacCannell. *The tourist: a new theory of the leisure class*. 1976 ed. New York: Schocken, 1989. ISBN 0-8052-0895-X. ‣ Highly technical, but influential analysis of tourism as part of middle-class search for authentic experience and commodity of intense pleasure and vicarious cultivation. [WWR]

44.43 Earl Spencer Pomeroy. *In search of the golden West: the tourist in western America*. New York: Knopf, 1957. ‣ Wide-ranging history of tourism beyond Mississippi from nineteenth-century frontier era through automobile age of 1920s. [WWR]

Consumption and Consumer Culture

44.44 Richard Butsch, ed. *For fun and profit: the transformation of leisure into consumption*. Philadelphia: Temple University Press, 1990. ISBN 0-87722-676-8. ‣ Theoretical essays and case studies provide good introduction to evolution of commercial leisure. Disputes capitalist domination; asserts interaction between consumer and corporations in formation of new commodities and activities. [WWR]

44.45 Robert Ernst. *Weakness is a crime: the life of Bernard Macfadden*. Syracuse, N.Y.: Syracuse University Press, 1991. ISBN 0-8156-2512-X (cl), 0-8156-0252-9 (pbk). ‣ Valuable biography of one of pioneering physical-fitness gurus, founder of *Physical Culture* and *True Story* magazines and perennial presidential candidate. [WWR]

44.46 Richard Wightman Fox and T. J. Jackson Lears, eds. *The culture of consumption: critical essays in American history, 1880–1980*. New York: Pantheon, 1983. ISBN 0-394-51131-X (cl), 0-394-71611-6 (pbk). ‣ Influential essays reflect 1980s historical assessment of consumption. Condemns consumer society for promising fulfillment but delivering domination by corporate capitalism and elites who make consumption predominant way of seeing world. [WWR]

44.47 Charles R. Hearn. *The American dream in the Great Depression*. Westport, Conn.: Greenwood, 1977. ISBN 0-8371-9478-4. ‣ Comprehensive examination of advice literature, popular magazines, and art to measure effect of economic crisis on success myth. Sees shift from rags to riches, rugged individualism to personal security, and fulfillment through consumption. [WWR]

44.48 Theodore B. Peterson. *Magazines in the twentieth century*.

2d ed. Urbana: University of Illinois Press, 1964. ▸ Good general source on broad spectrum of publications, examined within context of developing market system that necessitated advertising medium to facilitate widespread distribution of consumer goods. [WWR]

SEE ALSO
40.565 Richard Wightman Fox and T. J. Jackson Lears, eds. *The power of culture.*

Education and Youth

44.49 Lawrence Arthur Cremin. *Popular education and its discontents.* New York: Harper & Row, 1990. ISBN 0-06-016270-8. ▸ Perceptive introduction to American educational policy after World War II as attempt to solve social problems. Discusses both popularization and politicization. Diversification of American education overall success. [UGP]

44.50 Paula S. Fass. *The damned and the beautiful: American youth in the 1920's.* 1977 ed. New York: Oxford University Press, 1979. ISBN 0-19-502148-7 (cl), 0-19-502492-3 (pbk). ▸ Social history of middle-class university students of 1920s, focusing on changes in attitudes, beliefs, and activities as they adjusted and conformed to new ethic of consumption. Neglected area of study. [WWR]

44.51 Patricia Albjerg Graham. *Progressive education: from Arcady to academe: a history of the Progressive Education Association, 1919–1965.* New York: Teachers College Press, 1967. ▸ Solid study of ideas and institutional development of major organization pushing for progressive education. [WWR]

44.52 Diane Ravitch. *The troubled crusade: American education, 1945–1980.* New York: Basic Books, 1983. ISBN 0-465-08756-6. ▸ Basic interpretive account of shift from intellectual emphasis to social utility in educational thought and practice. Deals with influence of social science, GI Bill, McCarthyism, Sputnik-induced changes, and reforms in 1960s and 1970s. [UGP]

44.53 Ellen W. Schrecker. *No ivory tower: McCarthyism and the universities.* New York: Oxford University Press, 1986. ISBN 0-19-503557-7. ▸ Provocative study of anticommunism among administrators, trustees, faculty, and students, drawing on House Un-American Activities Committee hearings, institutional and private papers, and interviews. Considers silencing of radical intellectuals and of opposition to cold war. [UGP]

Film, Theater, and Music

44.54 Peter Biskind. *Seeing is believing: how Hollywood taught us to stop worrying and love the fifties.* New York: Pantheon, 1983. ISBN 0-394-52729-1 (cl), 0-394-72115-2 (pbk). ▸ Documents contradictory messages in box office hits on issues like conformity, dissent, minorities, delinquency, and anticommunism. In-depth film readings highlight constructions of femininity, masculinity, and nation. [UGP]

44.55 R. Serge Denisoff. *Great day coming: folk music and the American Left.* Urbana: University of Illinois Press, 1971. ISBN 0-252-00179-6. ▸ Useful information on folk revival of 1930s and 1940s and attraction of political radicals, especially Communists, to idiom. [WWR]

44.56 Thomas Doherty. *Teenagers and teenpics: the juvenilization of American movies in the 1950s.* Boston: Unwin Hyman, 1988. ISBN 0-04-445139-3 (cl), 0-04-445140-7 (pbk). ▸ Readable study of how younger age of movie audience changed content of Hollywood productions. Examination of individual films as validations of emerging teen subculture. [UGP]

44.57 David E. James. *Allegories of cinema: American film in the sixties.* Princeton: Princeton University Press, 1989. ISBN 0-691-04755-3 (cl), 0-691-00604-0 (pbk). ▸ Suggestive synthesis explores avant-garde films and filmmakers and relationship to Hollywood. Reflects on contradictions and dilemmas of alternative culture. [UGP]

44.58 Clayton R. Koppes and Gregory D. Black. *Hollywood goes to war: how politics, profits, and propaganda shaped World War II movies.* New York: Free Press, 1987. ISBN 0-02-903550-3. ▸ Tracks systematic effort of Office of War Information to employ movies to promote wartime image of harmonious, united nation. Critical of government censorship and propaganda. Useful plot summaries. [WWR]

44.59 Gerald Mast. *A short history of the movies.* 4th ed. New York: Macmillan, 1986. ISBN 0-02-580500-2 (cl), 0-02-377060-0 (pbk). ▸ Comprehensive, highly regarded survey of films and film industry, examined within social, cultural, and economic context. Bibliography of books and movies. [WWR]

44.60 Jane De Hart Mathews. *The federal theater, 1935–1939: plays, relief, and politics.* 1967 ed. New York: Octagon Books, 1980. ▸ Useful season-by-season account of short-lived experimental Works Project Administration theater, effort to create drama relevant to social crisis of Depression, and conflicts arising from tensions between social, political, and artistic aspirations. [WWR]

44.61 Lary May. *Screening out the past: the birth of mass culture and the motion picture industry.* 1980 ed. Chicago: University of Chicago Press, 1983. ISBN 0-226-51173-1 (pbk). ▸ Examines evolution of urban life through comprehensive history of movie industry as powerful social force undermining older moral standards with new values of personal pleasure and consumption. [WWR]

44.62 Nora Sayre. *Running time: films of the cold war.* New York: Dial, 1982. ISBN 0-385-27621-4. ▸ Fair-minded essays on how 1950s political history influenced movie content and form. Seemingly escapist material reflection of fears. Examines portrayal of sexuality, antisemitism, racism, and bigotry. [UGP]

44.63 Robert Sklar. *Movie-made America: a social history of American movies.* 1975 ed. New York: Vintage, 1976. ISBN 0-394-48327-8 (cl), 0-394-72120-9 (pbk). ▸ Important survey of film, filmmakers, and movie companies, 1880–1970. Emphasizes how social and economic developments influenced movies and industry. [WWR]

44.64 Marshall W. Stearns. *The story of jazz.* 1970 ed. New York: Oxford University Press, 1977. ISBN 0-19-5911269-0. ▸ Most recent edition of major survey of jazz through first half of twentieth century. [WWR]

44.65 William R. Taylor, ed. *Inventing Times Square: commerce and culture at the crossroads of the world, 1880–1939.* New York: Russell Sage Foundation, 1991. ISBN 0-87154-843-7. ▸ Original, provocative essays on popular culture's colorful urban center. Examines rise and fall of mass marketplace for legitimate and illegitimate entertainments, exposes larger cultural conflicts and changes in United States. [WWR]

44.66 Bob Thomas. *Walt Disney: an American original.* New York: Simon & Schuster, 1976. ISBN 0-671-22332-1. ▸ Comprehensive but largely uncritical account of public life of key figure in movie industry and history of animation. [WWR]

44.67 Linda Williams. *Hard core: power, pleasure, and the frenzy of the visible.* Berkeley: University of California Press, 1989. ISBN 0-520-06652-9 (cl), 0-520-06653-7 (pbk). ▸ History of heterosexual pornographic movies and videos, focusing on 1960s to 1980s. Argues against constructions of sexuality and gender as natural. Innovative use of reader response, genre, form analysis, and feminist film theory. [UGP]

SEE ALSO
43.459 Robert W. Snyder. *The voice of the city.*

Media

44.68 Erik Barnouw. *Tube of plenty: the evolution of American television.* 2d rev. ed. New York: Oxford University Press, 1990. ISBN 0-19-506483-6 (cl), 0-19-506484-4 (pbk). ▸ Basic study of how television shaped and has been shaped by American culture; from beginnings in 1950s to decline of major networks, expansion of cable, HBO (Home Box Office), MTV (Music Television), and arrival of VCR (video cassette recorder) in 1980s. [UGP]

44.69 James L. Baughman. *The republic of mass culture: journalism, filmmaking, and broadcasting in America since 1941.* Baltimore: Johns Hopkins University Press, 1991. ISBN 0-8018-4276-X (cl), 0-8018-4277-8 (pbk). ▸ Careful survey of subject, emphasizing impact of television on other media. Addresses how television's competitors had to develop separate markets. [UGP]

44.70 William Boddy. *Fifties television: the industry and its critics.* Urbana: University of Illinois Press, 1990. ISBN 0-252-01699-8. ▸ Thorough overview of how commercial, standardized programs of networks replaced aesthetic experimentation. Combines content analysis with history of regulation and political economy. [UGP]

44.71 Richard Campbell. *60 Minutes and the news: a mythology for middle America.* Urbana: University of Illinois Press, 1991. ISBN 0-252-01777-3. ▸ Thoughtful, scholarly study of how CBS (Columbia Broadcasting System) series reflects middle-class myth of supremacy of individualism over institutions, 1970s to 1980s. [UGP]

44.72 Todd Gitlin. *The whole world is watching: mass media in the making and unmaking of the New Left.* Berkeley: University of California Press, 1980. ISBN 0-520-03889-4 (cl), 0-520-04024-4 (pbk). ▸ Lively interpretation of how media first ignored, then misrepresented radical movements as trivial and illegitimate, 1960s to 1970s. Draws on media coverage, interviews with activists and reporters, and communications theory. [UGP]

44.73 E. Ann Kaplan. *Rocking around the clock: Music Television, postmodernism, and consumer culture.* 1987 ed. New York: Routledge, 1987. ISBN 0-415-03653-4 (cl), 0-415-03005-6 (pbk). ▸ Survey of creation of new sensibility in viewers in 1980s. Analysis of aesthetics in video clips; effects on music industry. [UGP]

44.74 Lynn Spigel and Denise Mann, eds. *Private screenings: television and the female consumer.* Minneapolis: University of Minnesota Press, 1992. ISBN 0-8166-2052-0 (cl), 0-8166-2053-9 (pbk). ▸ Innovative, wide-ranging essays on how television industry has entered women's lives at home and in marketplace, 1950s to 1980s. Treatment of race, class, and gender in various genres. [UGP]

Popular Culture

44.75 Barbara Ehrenreich. *The hearts of men: American dreams and the flight from commitment.* New York: Anchor, 1983. ISBN 0-385-17614-7 (cl), 0-385-17615-5 (pbk). ▸ Iconoclastic essays; men's increasing rebellion against breadwinner role in nuclear family in 1950s as root of sexual revolution. Feminist historical analysis of popular culture. [UGP]

44.76 Simon Frith. *Sound effects: youth, leisure, and the politics of rock.* 1983 rev. ed. London: Constable, 1985. ISBN 0-09-464940-5 (cl), 0-09-464950-2 (pbk). ▸ Good introduction to development of rock, music industry, and consumption and reception in United States and Britain, 1950s to 1980s. [UGP]

44.77 Susan Jeffords. *The remasculinization of America: gender and the Vietnam War.* Bloomington: Indiana University Press, 1989. ISBN 0-253-33188-9 (cl), 0-253-20530-1 (pbk). ▸ Important investigation by literary scholar of how postmodern condition leaves gender distinctions intact. Examines representations of Vietnam experience in film, oral history, novels, and short stories. Finds reaffirmation of patriarchal values in 1970s and 1980s. [UGP]

44.78 W. T. Lhamon, Jr. *Deliberate speed: the origins of a cultural style in the American 1950s.* Washington, D.C.: Smithsonian Institution Press, 1990. ISBN 0-87474-379-6. ▸ Intriguing, thoughtful study of emergence of styles and behavior associated with 1960s. Examines film, rock music, novels, art, civil rights, Beats, and technological innovations of this watershed decade. [UGP]

44.79 George Lipsitz. *Class and culture in cold war America: rainbow at midnight.* New York: Praeger Scientific, 1981. ISBN 0-03-059207-0. ▸ Well-argued essays linking rhythm and blues and film noir to mass demonstrations and strikes of post–World War II era. [UGP]

44.80 George Lipsitz. *Time passages: collective memory and American popular culture.* Minneapolis: University of Minnesota Press, 1990. ISBN 0-8166-1805-4 (cl), 0-8166-1806-2 (pbk). ▸ Innovative study of dialectic relationship of popular culture to oppositional politics, 1950s to 1980s. Explores formation of historical consciousness through television shows, music, film, and novels written by women and minorities. Employs diverse cultural theories. [UGP]

44.81 Janice Radway. *Reading the romance: women, patriarchy, and popular literature.* Rev. ed. Chapel Hill: University of North Carolina Press, 1984. ISBN 0-8078-4349-0 (pbk). ▸ Pioneering study of how 1980s women use romances to escape temporarily roles prescribed by patriarchy. Combines reader response, anthropology, feminist psychology, and analysis of production methods. [UGP]

44.82 David H. Rosenthal. *Hard bop: jazz and black music, 1955–65.* New York: Oxford University Press, 1992. ISBN 0-19-505869-0. ▸ Accessible, entertaining account of diverse time in jazz, influences of rhythm and blues, gospel, blues, and Ravel, examining artists' milieux and success as black neighborhood music. Interpretation of music pieces. [UGP]

44.83 Nicholas E. Tawa. *A most wondrous babble: American art composers, their music, and the American scene, 1950–1985.* Westport, Conn.: Greenwood, 1987. ISBN 0-313-15692-6, ISSN 0193-9041. ▸ Detailed social history of electronic sound, serialism, atonality, ethnic sources, and mainstream music. Gulf between composers' intentions and public perception. Draws on biographical information, music reviews, and author's listening experience. [UGP]

44.84 Joseph Witek. *Comic books as history: the narrative art of Jack Jackson, Art Spiegelman, and Harvey Pekar.* Jackson: University Press of Mississippi, 1991. ISBN 0-87805-405-7 (cl), 0-87805-406-5 (pbk). ▸ Scholarly analysis of use of social and historical themes in adult comics, 1970s to 1980s, demonstrating significance of new literary medium in American popular culture. [UGP]

Radicals and Social Thought

44.85 Daniel Aaron. *Writers on the Left: episodes in American literary communism.* 1962 ed. New York: Octagon Books, 1974. ISBN 0-374-90005-1. ▸ Standard account of left-wing writers' romance with Communist party in interwar years, especially Popular Front of mid-thirties. Ties literary radicalism to American traditions of protest. Useful biographies. [WWR]

44.86 Jerold S. Auerbach. *Unequal justice: lawyers and social change in modern America.* New York: Oxford University Press, 1976. ISBN 0-19-501939-3. ▸ Highly critical history, indictment of legal practice in twentieth century. Targets racism and class bias as persistent evils undermining justice and equal treatment and functioning to preserve power and wealth of elites. [WWR]

44.87 Daniel Bell. *The end of ideology: on the exhaustion of political ideas.* Rev. ed. Cambridge, Mass.: Harvard University Press, 1988. ISBN 0-674-25229-2 (cl), 0-674-25230-6 (pbk). ▸ Influential essays by leading social critic; title essay expresses late 1950s notion of consensus. [UGP]

44.88 Terry A. Cooney. *The rise of the New York intellectuals: "Partisan Review" and its circle.* Madison: University of Wisconsin Press, 1986. ISBN 0-299-10710-8. ▸ Valuable study. Sees consistency in political, ideological fluctuations of influential literary quarterly and writers associated with it. Identified as cosmopolitan spirit of openness and striving of peculiar urban intellectual subculture. [WWR]

44.89 John Patrick Diggins. *The rise and fall of the American Left.* New York: Norton, 1992. ISBN 0-393-03075-X. ▸ Critical intellectual history of radicalism in twentieth century with emphasis on generational definition of leftist politics reflecting gradual divorce from working class. Basic, brief treatment. [WWR]

44.90 James B. Gilbert. *A cycle of outrage: America's reaction to the juvenile delinquent in the 1950s.* New York: Oxford University Press, 1986. ISBN 0-19-503721-9. ▸ Sound social history of idea of generational conflict and delinquent behavior. Addresses relationship between debates on youth's consumption of mass culture, societal regulation of cultural consumption, and cold war. [UGP]

44.91 James B. Gilbert. *Designing the industrial state: the intellectual pursuit of collectivism in America, 1880–1940.* Chicago: Quadrangle, 1972. ISBN 0-8129-0219-X. ▸ Provocative, critical assessment of six intellectuals from various fields who accepted and promoted hierarchical, efficient modern corporation as model for harmonious social life. [WWR]

44.92 James B. Gilbert. *Writers and partisans: a history of literary radicalism in America.* New York: Wiley, 1968. ▸ Valuable history of important little magazines in 1930s and 1940s, from early Marxist association and search for radical literature through disaffection and later opposition to totalitarianism and politicized art. [WWR]

44.93 William Graebner. *The engineering of consent: democracy and authority in twentieth-century America.* Madison: University of Wisconsin Press, 1987. ISBN 0-299-11170-9. ▸ Highly critical history of social engineering in interwar years. Attributes appeal to post–World War I crisis of authority resulting from scientific and psychological developments and crises of Depression and European fascism. [WWR]

44.94 J. David Hoeveler, Jr. *Watch on the Right: conservative intellectuals in the Reagan era.* Madison: University of Wisconsin Press, 1991. ISBN 0-299-12810-5. ▸ Reliable, concise examination of neoconservatives' move to the Right. Analysis of work and personal histories of eight well-known academic and nonacademic writers, 1970s to 1980s. [UGP]

44.95 David A. Hollinger. *Morris R. Cohen and the scientific ideal.* Cambridge, Mass.: MIT Press, 1975. ISBN 0-262-08084-2. ▸ Russian-born professional philosopher whose ideas and teaching influenced interwar generation of liberals looking to science to construct coherent moral community. Valuable account of interwar American philosophy. [WWR]

44.96 Neil Jumonville. *Critical crossings: the New York intellectuals in postwar America.* Berkeley: University of California Press, 1991. ISBN 0-520-06858-0. ▸ Useful study of influential strands of intellectual thought on American culture and their connections to changing political commitments. Intellectuals shared anticommunist outlook and commitment to rationalism, pluralism, and civility. [UGP]

44.97 Barry Dean Karl. *Charles E. Merriam and the study of politics.* Chicago: University of Chicago Press, 1974. ISBN 0-226-42516-9. ▸ Revealing intellectual biography of important progressive political scientist and politician, academic entrepreneur, and New Deal ideologue. Reveals connections between academia, social sciences, government, business, and philanthropy. [WWR]

44.98 Christopher Lasch. *The culture of narcissism: American life in an age of diminishing expectations.* 1978 ed. New York: Warner, 1980. ISBN 0-446-97495-1. ▸ Controversial critique of modern condition of cultural radicalism. How decay of competitive individualism and competence has led to neurotically dependent, aimless narcissism. Analyses of movies, psychoanalysis, and sports. [UGP]

44.99 Fred H. Matthews. *Quest for an American sociology: Robert E. Park and the Chicago school.* Montreal: McGill-Queen's University Press, 1977. ISBN 0-7735-0243-2 (cl), 0-7735-0263-7 (pbk). ▸ Intellectual history of leading architect of discipline, 1920s to 1930s. Attentive both to scholarly and institutional contributions and to historical context of work and career. [WWR]

44.100 Mary Sperling McAuliffe. *Crisis on the Left: cold war politics and American liberals, 1947–1954.* Amherst: University of Massachusetts Press, 1978. ISBN 0-87023-241-X. ▸ Well-researched introduction to liberals' participation in denial of civil liberties to radicals and preoccupation with national security. Focus on debates in liberal journals, organizations, and congressional politics. [UGP]

44.101 Dennis McNally. *Desolation angel: Jack Kerouac, the Beat generation, and America.* New York: Random House, 1979. ISBN 0-394-50011-3. ▸ Introductory evaluation of how art and lives of Beat writers reflect historical changes of post–World War II, and their significance in American culture. Sociohistory. [UGP]

44.102 Michael O'Brien. *The idea of the American South, 1920–1941.* Baltimore: Johns Hopkins University Press, 1979. ISBN 0-8018-2166-5. ▸ Useful critical analysis of self-consciously southern writers and intellectuals, most associated with agrarian movement of interwar years. Focuses on idea of South as intellectual construction. [WWR]

44.103 Richard H. Pells. *The liberal mind in a conservative age: American intellectuals in the 1940s and 1950s.* 2d ed. Middletown, Conn.: Wesleyan University Press, 1989. ISBN 0-8195-6225-4. ▸ Well-researched, wide-ranging study of responses to cold war, McCarthyism, nuclear race, affluence, middle-class life styles, and mass media; also rise of New Left. Disillusionment of 1940s and 1950s quiescence paved way for social explosions of 1960s. [UGP]

44.104 Edward A. Purcell, Jr. *The crisis of democratic theory: scientific naturalism and the problem of values.* Lexington: University Press of Kentucky, 1973. ISBN 0-8131-1282-6 (cl), 0-8131-0141-7 (pbk). ▸ Careful, balanced account of academic intellectuals' search, 1910–50, for philosophical basis of American democracy under assault from relativist scientific theories and European totalitarianism. [WWR]

44.105 David Riesman et al. *The lonely crowd: a study of the changing American character.* 1961 ed. New Haven: Yale University Press, 1980. ▸ Influential sociological discussion of national character, 1950. How rise of mass consumer culture increased peer pressure and conformity. Resulting shift from inner- to outer-directed personality. [UGP]

44.106 Andrew Ross. *No respect: intellectuals and popular culture.* New York: Routledge, 1989. ISBN 0-415-90036-0 (cl), 0-415-90037-9 (pbk). ▸ Provocative case studies of conflicts over cultural taste among intellectuals, from cold war debate over television to 1980s pornography debate. Critical of champions of high culture; favors cultural politics of some feminist and gay activists. [UGP]

44.107 Joan Shelley Rubin. *Constance Rourke and American culture.* Chapel Hill: University of North Carolina Press, 1980. ISBN 0-8078-1402-4 (cl), 0-8078-1402-9 (pbk). ▸ Best available biography of important anthropologist and writer whose work discovered and valorized native tradition and folk culture. [WWR]

44.108 Joan Shelley Rubin. *The making of middlebrow culture.* Chapel Hill: University of North Carolina Press, 1992. ISBN 0-8078-2010-5 (cl), 0-8078-4354-7 (pbk). ▸ Provocative description and analysis of middlebrow culture such as Book-of-the-Month Club. [JTL]

44.109 Mark Silk. *Spiritual politics: religion and America since World War II.* New York: Simon & Schuster, 1988. ISBN 0-671-43910-3. ▸ History of exclusivism and strife among various religions and entanglement of religion and anticommunism, focusing on celebrities and intellectuals. [UGP]

44.110 Martin Staniland. *American intellectuals and African nationalists, 1955–1970.* New Haven: Yale University Press, 1991. ISBN 0-300-04838-6. ▸ Stimulating review of liberal, conservative, leftist, and African American images of Africa illustrating aspects of American political and intellectual culture. Considers responses of United States to colonialism and decolonization. [UGP]

44.111 Ronald Steel. *Walter Lippmann and the American century.* Boston: Little, Brown, 1980. ISBN 0-316-81190-4. ▸ Critical biography of most important journalist from World War I through Vietnam that also serves as history of period. Emphasizes subject's attraction to power but marginal status as American Jew. [WWR]

44.112 Robert B. Westbrook. *John Dewey and American democracy.* Ithaca, N.Y.: Cornell University Press, 1991. ISBN 0-8014-2560-3. ▸ Major biography of leading philosopher and reformer of twentieth century that emphasizes radicalism of his thought. [WWR]

44.113 William Whyte. *The organization man.* 1956 ed. New York: Simon & Schuster, 1972. ISBN 0-671-21235-4. ▸ Influential critique of suburbanization and corporate conformity in post–World War II era. [UGP]

SEE ALSO
4.191 Carl N. Degler. *In search of human nature.*

Religion

44.114 Stephen Bates. *Battleground: one mother's crusade, the religious Right, and the struggle for control of our classrooms.* New York: Poseidon, 1993. ISBN 0-671-79358-6. ▸ Well-written, remarkably balanced history of struggles in Tennessee during 1980s between fundamentalist groups and others over what should be taught in schools. Includes discussion of court cases. [JTP]

44.115 Paul S. Boyer. *When time shall be no more: prophecy belief in modern American culture.* Cambridge, Mass.: Harvard University Press, 1992. ISBN 0-674-95128-x. ▸ Large, sweeping account of prophetic religious figures and groups, mainly since 1945. Thorough, thoughtful, and balanced. [JTP]

44.116 Paul A. Carter. *The decline and revival of the social gospel: social and political liberalism in American Protestant churches, 1920–1940.* 1956 ed. Hamden, Conn.: Archon, 1971. ISBN 0-208-01083-1. ▸ Standard study of decline of liberal Protestantism's optimistic social and moral vision after World War I. Discusses influence of European critical theology and social disruption of Depression decade. Sees progress in theological evolution. [WWR]

44.117 Richard Wightman Fox. *Reinhold Niebuhr: a biography.*

New York: Pantheon, 1985. ISBN 0-394-51659-1. ▸ Portrait of leading midcentury theologian and social critic. Author attentive to Niebuhr's shortcomings; praises him as cerebral preacher rather than rigorous thinker. Model intellectual biography. [WWR]

44.118 Norman F. Furniss. *The fundamentalist controversy, 1918–1931.* 1954 ed. Hamden, Conn.: Archon, 1963. ▸ Standard study of national context of religious conservativism notoriously revealed by Scopes trial. Systematic survey of anti-evolution campaigns; fundamentalist doctrines; and regional, denominational differences. [WWR]

44.119 Ray Ginger. *Six days or forever? Tennessee v. John Thomas Scopes.* 1958 ed. London: Oxford University Press, 1974. ISBN 0-19-519784-4. ▸ Colorful, detailed narrative of courtroom battle between religious fundamentalism and evolution and educational freedom as fought by William Jennings Bryan and Clarence Darrow in Dayton, Tennessee in 1925. [WWR]

44.120 Michael J. Lacey, ed. *Religion and twentieth-century American intellectual life.* Washington, D.C., and Cambridge: Woodrow Wilson International Center for Scholars and Cambridge University Press, 1989. ISBN 0-521-37560-6. ▸ Important essays by leading intellectual and cultural historians and scholars of religion on various aspects of religious thought and practice. [WWR]

44.121 Lawrence W. Levine. *Defender of the faith: William Jennings Bryan, the last decade, 1915–1925.* New York: Oxford University Press, 1965. ▸ Sympathetic account of years between resignation from Wilson cabinet through Scopes monkey trial. Restores Bryan's integrity by uncovering cultural conservatism of Progressive reformers in urban, industrial America. [WWR]

44.122 Donald B. Meyer. *The positive thinkers: popular religious psychology from Mary Baker Eddy to Norman Vincent Peale and Ronald Reagan.* Rev. ed. Middletown, Conn.: Wesleyan University Press; distributed by Harper & Row, 1988. ISBN 0-8195-5160-0 (cl), 0-8195-6166-5 (pbk). ▸ Wide-ranging, provocative study of social context of popular therapeutic psychologies and positive thinking as central aspects of twentieth-century culture. Emphasizes pioneering role of women in constructing and disseminating religion. [WWR]

44.123 Donald B. Meyer. *The Protestant search for political realism, 1919–1941.* 2d ed. Middletown, Conn.: Wesleyan University Press, 1988. ISBN 0-8195-5203-8 (cl), 0-8195-6210-6 (pbk). ▸ Critical examination of efforts of liberal Protestants to adopt tools and findings of social sciences to guide ministry in confronting social conflict. [WWR]

44.124 Robert Moats Miller. *Harry Emerson Fosdick: preacher, pastor, prophet.* New York: Oxford University Press, 1985. ISBN 0-19-503512-7. ▸ Long study of life of leading midcentury liberal Protestant minister, founder of New York City's Riverside Church, social reformer, and radio preacher. [WWR]

44.125 David J. O'Brien. *American Catholics and social reform: the New Deal years.* New York: Oxford University Press, 1968. ▸ Detailed survey of wide variety of Catholic responses to application of church's teachings to social crisis of Depression. Attentive to conflict between individuals' responses to social crisis and their identities as American Catholics. [WWR]

44.126 Leo P. Ribuffo. *The old Christian Right: the Protestant Far Right from the Great Depression to the cold war.* Philadelphia: Temple University Press, 1983. ISBN 0-87722-297-5. ▸ Stimulating examination of religious extremists Gerald L. K. Smith, William Dudley Pelley, and Gerald B. Winrod to demonstrate American nature of their respective versions of racist and antisemitic Christian nationalism. [WWR]

Science, Medicine, and Technology

44.127 Hugh G. J. Aitken. *The continuous wave: technology and American radio, 1900–1932.* Princeton: Princeton University Press, 1985. ISBN 0-691-08376-2 (cl), 0-691-02390-5 (pbk). ‣ Useful, concise examination of evolution from wireless telephone to radio broadcasting; explored within social, political, economic, and intellectual context. [WWR/PBI]

44.128 Erik Barnouw. *A history of broadcasting in the United States.* Vol. 1: *A tower of Babel, to 1933.* Vol. 2: *The golden web, 1933 to 1953.* Vol. 3: *The image of empire, from 1953.* 3 vols. New York: Oxford University Press, 1966–70. ‣ Pioneering narrative history of radio in America focusing on evolution of giant network broadcasters. Anecdotal, readable account of business side of story. [WWR]

44.129 James P. Baxter. *Scientists against time.* 1946 ed. Cambridge, Mass.: MIT Press, 1968. ‣ Readable narrative and analysis of World War II scientists and science. [JTL]

44.130 Joan Lisa Bromberg. *Fusion: science, politics, and the invention of a new energy source.* Cambridge, Mass.: MIT Press, 1982. ISBN 0-262-02180-3. ‣ Scholarly study of important area of scientific research. [JTL]

44.131 John C. Burnham. *How superstition won and science lost: popularizing science and health in the United States.* New Brunswick, N.J.: Rutgers University Press, 1987. ISBN 0-8135-1238-7 (cl), 0-8135-1265-4 (pbk). ‣ Provocative argument that increasingly specialized scientists abandoned educating public, resulting in inaccurate, fragmentary information through media, especially since 1930s. Studies of health, psychology, and natural sciences. [UGP]

44.132 Tom DeLong. *The mighty music box: the golden age of musical radio.* Los Angeles: Amber Crest, 1980. ISBN 0-86533-000-X. ‣ Major survey of broad range of music programing from early days of radio. [WWR]

44.133 Elizabeth Fee and Daniel M. Fox, eds. *AIDS: the making of a chronic disease.* Berkeley: University of California Press, 1992. ISBN 0-520-07569-2 (cl), 0-520-07778-4 (pbk). ‣ Wide-ranging essays written with historical perspective explore scientific knowledge, public representations, government policy, and affected groups. AIDS in 1990s viewed as chronic disease managed in long term. [UGP]

44.134 Daniel S. Greenberg. *The politics of pure science.* 1967 ed. New York: New American Library, 1971. ‣ Highly critical, readable exploration of nature of and funding for scientific research in postwar United States. [JTL]

44.135 Gerald N. Grob. *From asylum to community: mental health policy in modern America.* Princeton: Princeton University Press, 1991. ISBN 0-691-04790-1. ‣ Revealing study shows how World War II's traumas convinced psychiatrists to shift to treating patients in communities rather than institutions, but middle-class bias against designing centers to oversee released patients led to homelessness. [WWR]

44.136 Ruth Hubbard. *The politics of women's biology.* New Brunswick, N.J.: Rutgers University Press, 1990. ISBN 0-8135-1489-4 (cl), 0-8135-1490-8 (pbk). ‣ Examination of how fields of genetics, evolution, and sociobiology have contributed to constructions of gender. Important feminist critique reveals science as profoundly political. [UGP]

44.137 Janice M. Irvine. *Disorders of desire: sex and gender in modern American sexology.* Philadelphia: Temple University Press, 1990. ISBN 0-87722-689-X. ‣ Lively overview of difficulties of professionalization of sex research in context of shifting attitudes toward sex and gender in postwar decades. [UGP]

44.138 J. Fred MacDonald. *Don't touch that dial! Radio program-ming in American life, 1920–1960.* Chicago: Nelson-Hall, 1979. ISBN 0-88229-528-4. ‣ Critical history of golden age of radio programing. [WWR]

44.139 James T. Patterson. *The dread disease: cancer and modern American culture.* Cambridge, Mass.: Harvard University Press, 1987. ISBN 0-674-21625-3. ‣ Study of changing attitudes toward and cultural importance of cancer in twentieth century. More broadly examines history of individual and institutional responses to disease. Useful bibliography. [WWR]

44.140 Thomas A. Preston, Diana B. Dutton, and Nancy E. Pfund. *Worse than the disease: pitfalls of medical progress.* Cambridge: Cambridge University Press, 1988. ISBN 0-521-34023-3. ‣ Interdisciplinary study of uncritical faith in science, marriage of media and research interests, problems of rising costs, and risks in capitalist environment in post–World War II era. Case studies of DES (morning sickness preventative which caused birth defects), artificial hearts, swine flu vaccine, and genetic engineering. [UGP]

44.141 Don K. Price. *The scientific estate.* 1965 ed. London: Oxford University Press, 1968. ‣ Charts rise of scientific research in universities and elsewhere during and after World War II and the effect of government sponsorship. Groundbreaking, thoughtful study. [JTL]

44.142 Michael Riordan. *The hunting of the quark: a true story of modern physics.* New York: Simon & Schuster, 1987. ISBN 0-671-50466-5 (cl), 0-671-64884-5 (pbk). ‣ Examination of how high energy physicists overthrew dominant view of nuclear matter, 1964–80. Insider's story of experiments, effects on theory, and physicists' intellectual framework. [UGP]

44.143 Philip T. Rosen. *The modern stentors: radio broadcasters and the federal government, 1920–1934.* Westport, Conn.: Greenwood, 1980. ISBN 0-313-21231-7, ISSN 0084-9235. ‣ Concise history focusing on role of Commerce Department and especially first secretary, Herbert Hoover, as architects of broadcast system and industry. [WWR]

44.144 David J. Rothman. *Strangers at the bedside: a history of how law and bioethics transformed medical decision making.* New York: Basic Books, 1991. ISBN 0-465-08209-2. ‣ Well-written analysis of moral backlash after revelations of nontherapeutic experimentation on powerless persons in 1960s and 1970s, resulting in end of physicians' monopoly over medical decision making. [UGP]

44.145 Ronald C. Tobey. *The American ideology of national science, 1919–1930.* Pittsburgh: University of Pittsburgh Press, 1971. ISBN 0-8229-3227-X. ‣ Describes efforts by scientists to develop financial support for scientific research, mainly private and nongovernmental. [JTL]

44.146 Tom Wolfe. *The right stuff.* 1979 ed. New York: Bantam, 1988. ISBN 0-553-27556-9. ‣ Fast-paced, iconoclastic study of space program in context of cultural attitudes in cold war, uncovering shift from individual pioneers to bureaucratization. [UGP]

44.147 Herbert York. *The advisors: Oppenheimer, Teller, and the superbomb.* 1976 ed. Stanford, Calif.: Stanford University Press, 1989. ISBN 0-8047-1713-3 (cl), 0-8047-1714-1 (pbk). ‣ Thorough treatment of major postwar controversies over developments in atomic weaponry. [JTL]

44.148 James Harvey Young. *The medical messiahs: a social history of health quackery in twentieth-century America.* Rev. ed. Princeton: Princeton University Press, 1992. ISBN 0-691-00579-6 (pbk). ‣ Colorful, wide-ranging scholarly treatment of unorthodox medical practitioners in twentieth century. [JTP]

Sports

44.149 Allen Guttmann. *A whole new ballgame: an interpretation of American sports.* Chapel Hill: University of North Carolina Press, 1988. ISBN 0-8078-1786-4. ▸ Good overview of how American fascination with sports reflects secular, bureaucratic, and in theory democratic tradition of American culture. Development from pre-Columbian rituals to quantified, scientific present. Treats women's sports, alternative sports, and failure of racial equality. [UGP]

44.150 Benjamin G. Rader. *In its own image: how television has transformed sports.* New York: Free Press, 1984. ISBN 0-02-925700-x. ▸ Thorough, at times, angry exploration of how sports changed to fit entertainment and commercial interests of mass media, from radio to television, and resulting problems for amateur sports. Case studies of football, baseball, and boxing. [UGP]

44.151 Randy Roberts and James Stuart Olson. *Winning is the only thing: sports in America since 1945.* Baltimore: Johns Hopkins University Press, 1989. ISBN 0-8018-3830-4. ▸ Introduction to decline of amateurism before onslaught of commercialism. Attention to racial integration, cold war, mass media technology, drug abuse, corruption, fitness craze, and Olympic Games. [UGP]

SOCIAL AND ECONOMIC HISTORY

Social and Economic Trends

44.152 Carl Abbott. *The new urban America: growth and politics in sunbelt cities.* Rev. ed. Chapel Hill: University of North Carolina Press, 1987. ISBN 0-8078-4180-3 (pbk). ▸ Sunbelt prospered after 1941 but faced familiar fragmentation after 1960 when suburbanites and no-growth liberals challenged downtown boosters. Specialist study of six cities. [JTL]

44.153 Bennett M. Berger. *Working-class suburbs: a study of auto workers in suburbia.* 1960 ed. Berkeley: University of California Press, 1971. ISBN 0-520-00108-7. ▸ Ford workers who moved to suburbia lived in better material conditions but did not embrace middle-class values. Suburbia not as conformist as appears. Influential book. [JTL]

44.154 Michael A. Bernstein. *The Great Depression: delayed recovery and economic change in America, 1929–1939.* Cambridge: Cambridge University Press, 1987. ISBN 0-521-34048-9. ▸ Depression lasted unusually long because it coincided with difficult long-term shift in economy from basic heavy industry to consumer nondurables and luxury goods. Provocative emphasis on long-term. [JTL]

44.155 David P. Calleo. *The imperious economy.* Cambridge, Mass.: Harvard University Press, 1982. ISBN 0-674-44522-8. ▸ Special study of how post–World War II effort to preserve both international predominance and domestic prosperity led to debilitating inflation by 1970s. Author is suspicious of free trade and floating currency. [JTL]

44.156 John T. Cumbler. *A social history of economic decline: business, politics, and work in Trenton.* New Brunswick, N.J.: Rutgers University Press, 1989. ISBN 0-8135-1373-1 (cl), 0-8135-1374-X (pbk). ▸ Broad study of how city lost control of its economy 1900–50 due to national, centralizing industrial consolidation that made abandonment inevitable and caused heightened class conflict. [JTL]

44.157 Peter Fearon. *War, prosperity, and depression: the U.S. economy, 1917–1945.* Lawrence: University Press of Kansas, 1987. ISBN 0-7006-0348-4 (cl), 0-7006-0349-2 (pbk). ▸ Broad, balanced overview. Discusses competing explanations of Great Depression in detail. [JTL]

44.158 Robert M. Fogelson. *Big-city police.* Cambridge, Mass.: Harvard University Press, 1977. ISBN 0-674-07281-2. ▸ Waves of reform in 1890s and 1950s broke up patronage and enforced vice laws but then shut minorities out of service. Survey up to 1970. [JTL]

44.159 Milton Friedman and Anna Jacobson Schwartz. *A monetary history of the United States, 1867–1960.* 1963 ed. Princeton: Princeton University Press, 1971. (National Bureau of Economic Research, Studies in business cycles, 12.) ISBN 0-691-04147-4 (cl), 0-691-00354-8 (pbk). ▸ Classic monetarist history of cyclical changes in economic output, including influential explanation of Great Depression. Abrupt alterations in money supply, often due to mistaken political decisions, magnified normal economic downturns. [JTL]

44.160 John Kenneth Galbraith. *The great crash, 1929.* 1972 3d ed. Boston: Houghton-Mifflin, 1988. ISBN 0-395-13935-x (cl), 0-395-47805-7 (pbk). ▸ Speculative fever gripped investors, leading entrepreneurs to erect unstable pyramids that crashed when difficulties came. Lively narrative concentrating on events and irrational personalities in 1929. [JTL]

44.161 Herbert J. Gans. *The Levittowners: ways of life and politics in a new suburban community.* Rev. ed. New York: Columbia University Press, 1982. ISBN 0-231-05570-6 (cl), 0-231-05571-4 (pbk). ▸ Pioneering study of lower-middle-class suburb in New Jersey. Joys of living in largely homogeneous community that integrated painlessly. [JTL]

44.162 Robert Staughton Lynd and Helen Merrell Lynd. *Middletown: a study in American culture.* 1929 ed. New York: Harcourt Brace & World, 1982. ISBN 0-15-659550-8. ▸ Classic sociological study of Muncie, Indiana, in 1920s. Skeptical view of modern improvements that have fragmented and diminished people's participation in work and society. [JTL]

44.163 John H. Mollenkopf. *The contested city.* Princeton: Princeton University Press, 1983. ISBN 0-691-07659-6 (cl), 0-691-02220-8 (pbk). ▸ Stimulating analysis differs from economic or pluralist models by emphasizing politics as independent force with own internal logic. Concludes political entrepreneurs constructed pro-growth coalitions after 1930. [JTL]

44.164 George Henry Soule. *Prosperity decade: from war to depression, 1917–1929.* 1947 ed. Armonk, N.Y.: Sharpe, 1989. ISBN 0-87332-098-0. ▸ Still only comprehensive account of economy in 1920s. Keynesian but nondogmatic approach to explaining Great Depression. [JTL]

44.165 Jon C. Teaford. *The twentieth-century urban city: problems, promises, and reality.* Baltimore: Johns Hopkins University Press, 1986. ISBN 0-8018-3094-X (cl), 0-8018-3096-6 (pbk). ▸ Pessimistic, brief survey. Reformers seeking harmony in vice laws in 1900 or revival in urban renewal in 1950s failed because people preferred fragmentation to unified metropolis. [JTL]

44.166 Richard S. Tedlow. *New and improved: the story of mass marketing in America.* New York: Basic Books, 1990. ISBN 0-465-05023-9 (cl), 0-465-05024-7 (pbk). ▸ Clear, readable case studies of four industries showing shift from fragmented to mass and then to segmented markets, 1880 to 1960. Mass consumption as social construction, not natural. [JTL]

44.167 Peter Temin. *Lessons from the Great Depression.* 1989 ed. Cambridge, Mass.: MIT Press, 1992. ISBN 0-262-20073-2 (cl, 1989), 0-262-70044-1 (pbk). ▸ Dogged international faith in gold standard despite World War I's disruptions ultimately led to slump and to statist policies. Accessible account shows this prominent Keynesian's conversion to modified monetarist position. [JTL]

44.168 United States President's Research Committee on Social Trends. *Recent social trends in the United States.* 1933 ed. 2 vols. New York: Arno, 1979. ISBN 0-405-12107-5. ▸ Well-informed reports on dozens of topics. Comments on society's lag in adjusting to industrial change, especially in coordinating these adjustments. Perceives shift in authority from family and church to industry and government. [JTL]

44.169 Harold G. Vatter. *The U.S. economy in World War II.* New York: Columbia University Press, 1985. ISBN 0-231-05768-7. ▸ General survey of how war accelerated and provided basis for transition to mixed economy. Includes some discussion of social changes. [JTL]

SEE ALSO
40.279 Kenneth T. Jackson. *The crabgrass frontier.*

Agriculture

44.170 Willard W. Cochrane and Mary Ellen Ryan. *American farm policy, 1948–1973.* Minneapolis: University of Minnesota Press, 1976. ISBN 0-8166-1783-4. ▸ Scholarly, detailed study of excess capacity and surplus production addressed by expensive but worthwhile federal programs. Much on political process of legislation. [JTL]

44.171 Pete Daniel. *Breaking the land: the transformation of cotton, tobacco, and rice cultures since 1880.* Urbana: University of Illinois Press, 1985. ISBN 0-252-01147-3 (cl), 0-252-01391-3 (pbk). ▸ Thoughtful, readable account of how Southern mechanization encouraged by federal policy erased distinctive work patterns and folk culture; argues shift not inevitable. Explores devaluation of rural populations. [JTL]

44.172 Gilbert C. Fite. *American farmers: the new minority.* Bloomington: Indiana University Press, 1981. ISBN 0-253-30182-3. ▸ General account of how farmers' political power rose during interwar period through unity but declined thereafter, above all because technological advances decreased number of farmers. Author is skeptical about government programs. [JTL]

44.173 Grant McConnell. *The decline of agrarian democracy.* 1953 ed. New York: Atheneum, 1969. ▸ Provocative account of Farm Bureau Federation's transformation into organization after 1900 that benefited rich farmers and undermined government attempts to help poor farmers. Social inequality and compliant politicians betrayed populism's promise. [JTL]

44.174 John L. Shover. *Cornbelt rebellion: the Farmers' Holiday Association.* Urbana: University of Illinois Press, 1965. ▸ Specialist study of normally prosperous farmers' protest against middlemen and low prices by withholding produce during Great Depression. Big business won by using political power and making partial concessions. [JTL]

44.175 Donald Worster. *Dust bowl: the southern plains in the 1930s.* 1979 ed. New York: Oxford University Press, 1982. ISBN 0-19-503212-8 (pbk). ▸ Pioneering environmental history arguing that calamity due to traditional capitalist farming practices that robbed land of natural protections. Popular exploitive practices continued despite crisis. Case studies of four counties. [JTL]

Business

44.176 Josephine Young Case and Everett Needham Case. *Owen D. Young and American enterprise: a biography.* Boston: Godine, 1982. ISBN 0-87923-360-5. ▸ Mildly critical biography of prominent General Electric executive, 1912–45. Rise and demise of cooperative corporate liberal alternative to adversarial New Deal. [JTL]

44.177 Alfred D. Chandler, Jr. *Strategy and structure: chapters in the history of the American industrial enterprise.* 1962 ed. Cambridge, Mass.: MIT Press, 1969. ISBN 0-262-53009-0 (pbk). ▸ Important analysis of changes in organizational and administrative practices that enabled firms to cope with expansion. Large diversifying corporations, 1910–45, switched from traditional

unitary form to decentralized multidivisional structure prevalent now. Author's insights established framework for history of modern business. [JTL/WMD]

44.178 Neil Fligstein. *The transformation of corporate control.* Cambridge, Mass.: Harvard University Press, 1990. ISBN 0-674-90358-7. ▸ Large corporations, 1880–1980, sought control over markets using different strategies at different times. Government influenced strategies to greater extent than did technologies. Based largely on statistical correlations. Provides alternative to established view. [JTL]

44.179 James J. Flink. *The automobile age.* Cambridge, Mass.: MIT Press, 1988. ISBN 0-262-06111-2. ▸ Comprehensive history of industry and of car's influence on society and culture. Includes international developments. [JTL/BES]

44.180 Louis Galambos. *Competition and cooperation: the emergence of a national trade association.* Baltimore: Johns Hopkins University Press, 1966. ISBN 0-317-41662-6 (pbk). ▸ Thorough, specialist study of continued failure of cotton textile manufacturers to cooperate, 1870–1940, despite destructive competition and increasingly sophisticated organizing. Technology of industry rather than class ties determined whether firms could unite. Also available in photocopy from Ann Arbor: University Microfilms International, 1991. [JTL]

44.181 John Kenneth Galbraith. *The new industrial state.* 4th ed. Boston: Houghton-Mifflin, 1985. ISBN 0-395-38991-7. ▸ Rise of big business transformed economy into stable system administered jointly by business and government. Witty, influential condemnation of economics for staying with old ideas of small competitive firms. [JTL]

44.182 Bennett Harrison and Barry Bluestone. *The great U-turn: corporate restructuring and the polarizing of America.* New York: Basic Books, 1988. ISBN 0-465-02719-9. ▸ Controversial study of how profit squeeze in 1960s led corporations to reduce workers' benefits and control and to seek short-term benefits from financial dealings. Consumption binge of 1980s exacerbated increasing inequality. [JTL]

44.183 Morrell Heald. *The social responsibilities of business: company and community, 1900–1960.* 1970 ed. New Brunswick, N.J.: Transaction, 1988. ISBN 0-88738-231-2. ▸ Study of relationship between philanthropy and big business. Large corporations run by professional managers and freed from intense competition led way in institutionalizing philanthropy after World War I. Based on published writings of businessmen. [JTL]

44.184 David A. Hounshell and John Kenly Smith, Jr. *Science and corporate strategy: Du Pont R & D, 1902–1980.* Cambridge: Cambridge University Press, 1988. ISBN 0-521-32767-9. ▸ Study of role research and development played in corporate transformation. Excellent analysis of managers' struggle without resolution over strategies (pure or applied) and organization (centralized or divisional) of research and development. Detailed on executives' motivations. [JTL/TR]

44.185 Herman E. Krooss. *Executive opinion: what business leaders said and thought on economic issues.* Garden City, N.Y.: Doubleday, 1970. ▸ Ambitious study of diverse group which illustrates these executives' growing uncertainty over extent of social responsibility of business, 1920–60. Most businessmen had predictable middle-class values that changed over time to allow mixed economy and sometimes unions. [JTL]

44.186 David C. Mowery and Nathan Rosenberg. *Technology and the pursuit of economic growth.* Cambridge: Cambridge University Press, 1989. ISBN 0-521-38033-2. ▸ Wide-ranging, comparative essays arguing that innovation arose not from simple market demands but from complicated institutional forces. Government since World War II helped both directly and indirectly. [JTL]

44.187 David F. Noble. *Forces of production: a social history of industrial automation.* 1984 ed. New York: Oxford University Press, 1986. ISBN 0-19-504046-5 (pbk). ‣ Groundbreaking account of how distrust of workers, fascination with automation, and political influence made industry and government choose an apparently less efficient technology for control of metal-cutting machines. Case study in 1945–60. [JTL/PEC]

44.188 George David Smith. *From monopoly to competition: the transformation of Alcoa, 1888–1986.* Cambridge: Cambridge University Press, 1988. ISBN 0-521-35261-4. ‣ State-of-the-art corporate history of this benevolent monopoly, broken up by government, which then suffered under competition. Emphasizes persistent paternalistic corporate culture at aluminum company. [JTL/BES]

44.189 Paul A. Tiffany. *The decline of American steel: how management, labor, and government went wrong.* New York: Oxford University Press, 1988. ISBN 0-19-504382-0. ‣ Detailed, thoughtful study which focuses on delays in adopting crucial innovations, 1945–80. Rejects prevailing literature emphasizing oligopolistic smugness of steel managers; blames all three actors, along with fortuitous events. [JTL]

44.190 Mira Wilkins. *The maturing of multinational enterprise: American business abroad from 1914 to 1970.* Cambridge, Mass.: Harvard University Press, 1974. ISBN 0-674-55475-2. ‣ Prodigious research, encyclopedic coverage of important, controversial subject. American companies won global hegemony due more to internal pressures and capabilities than to governmental assistance. Multinationals as logical step in development of modern corporation. Vital reference book for expanded international history. [JTL/JSH/PLH]

Demography and Family

44.191 Richard A. Easterlin. *Birth and fortune: the impact of numbers on personal welfare.* 2d ed. Chicago: University of Chicago Press, 1987. ISBN 0-226-18032-8 (pbk). ‣ Influential analysis of nation's birthrate and its variations. Low birthrates associated with Depression increased with prosperity resulting in so-called baby boom, but children, facing competition for jobs as young adults, delayed parenthood causing baby bust. [JTL]

44.192 John D'Emilio. *Sexual politics, sexual communities: the making of a homosexual minority in the United States, 1940–1970.* Chicago: University of Chicago Press, 1983. ISBN 0-226-14265-5. ‣ Broad analysis of both organized movement and informal institutions. War began movement of solidarity: new psychology along with protests by other minorities in 1960s overcame postwar repression. [JTL]

44.193 Landon Y. Jones. *Great expectations: America and the baby boom generation.* 1980 ed. New York: Ballantine, 1981. ISBN 0-345-29750-4 (pbk). ‣ Anecdotal introduction to history of generation born 1946–64 with much on its economic and cultural influence. Sees link between hopefulness in society and high fertility. [JTL]

44.194 Christopher Lasch. *Haven in a heartless world: the family besieged.* 1977 ed. New York: Basic Books, 1979. ISBN 0-465-02883-7 (cl), 0-465-02884-5 (pbk). ‣ Psychologists and other professionals undermined family by transferring its functions to marketplace. Influential conservative critique that blames capitalism along with naive liberals. [JTL]

44.195 Elaine Tyler May. *Homeward bound: American families in the cold war era.* New York: Basic Books, 1988. ISBN 0-465-03054-8 (cl), 0-465-03055-6 (pbk). ‣ Anxiety over competition with Soviets forced men and women into rigid roles, ending independence women had gained 1930–45. Focuses on middle-class, nonethnic families in 1950s. Provocative linking of popular culture and foreign concerns. [JTL]

44.196 Arlene S. Skolnick. *Embattled paradise: the American family in an age of uncertainty.* New York: Basic Books, 1991. ISBN 0-465-01923-4. ‣ Intelligent demographic and psychological approach showing how increased choices brought by industrialization altered family. Intense domesticity of 1950s was radical and unstable departure due to preceding dislocations. [JTL]

Political Economy and Regulation

44.197 Robert M. Collins. *The business response to Keynes, 1929–1964.* New York: Columbia University Press, 1981. ISBN 0-231-04486-0. ‣ Careful, scholarly study of how big businessmen adapted government's economic responsibility to conservative ends; small businessmen continued to oppose deficit financing. Sees conservative Keynesianism as corporate liberalism reborn. [JTL]

44.198 Tony Freyer. *Regulating big business: antitrust in Great Britain and America, 1880–1990.* Cambridge: Cambridge University Press, 1992. ISBN 0-521-35207-X. ‣ Detailed, comparative analysis of why social and ideological differences made Americans oppose cartels much earlier than British, hastening shift from owner-run to more efficient managerial capitalism. Convergence after World War II. [JTL]

44.199 Louis Galambos and Joseph Pratt. *The rise of the corporate commonwealth: U.S. business and public policy in the twentieth century.* New York: Basic Books, 1988. ISBN 0-465-07029-9. ‣ Broad study of how public and private institutions successfully evolved due to flexibility of business system in adjusting to political demands. Society and firms accepted increased regulation in exchange for greater economic stability. [JTL]

44.200 Otis L. Graham. *Losing time: the industrial policy debate.* Cambridge, Mass.: Harvard University Press, 1992. ISBN 0-674-53919-2. ‣ Specialist study. Political leaders in 1980s agreed existing policy misguided and economy weak, but found no solution. Both sides misused history. [JTL]

44.201 Kim McQuaid. *Big business and presidential power: from FDR to Reagan.* New York: Morrow, 1982. ISBN 0-688-01313-9. ‣ Accessible, detailed account of how many businessmen set up councils to influence federal policy. This response to a permanent, interventionist state had much, but rarely total, success. [JTL]

44.202 David Musto. *The American disease: origins of narcotic control.* Rev. ed. New York: Oxford University Press, 1988. ISBN 0-19-505211-0 (pbk). ‣ Nativism, racism, and class bias heavily influenced government decisions to control narcotic use. Best available account. [JTL]

44.203 Hugh Rockoff. *Drastic measures: a history of wage and price controls in the United States.* Cambridge: Cambridge University Press, 1984. ISBN 0-521-24496-X. ‣ Controls prevented inflation but only when run according to proper economic theory. Specialist study, sees history as empirical test of policy, colonial period to Vietnam War. [JTL]

44.204 Alfred Runte. *National parks: the American experience.* 2d rev. ed. Lincoln: University of Nebraska Press, 1987. ISBN 0-8032-3878-9 (pbk). ‣ Standard, scholarly discussion of evolution of ideas, not parks themselves. Nineteenth-century legislators persuaded land was worthless except as scenery; then as business wanted land, wilderness and ecology came to be valued. [JTL]

44.205 Herbert Stein. *The fiscal revolution in America.* Rev. ed. Washington, D.C.: American Enterprise Institute Press; distributed by National Book Network, 1990. (American Enterprise

Institute studies, 515.) ISBN 0-8447-3737-2 (pbk). ▸ Literate economist and presidential adviser shows how World War II experience mattered more than Keynes in overcoming dogma for balanced budget; covers presidents Hoover to Johnson. [JTL]

44.206 Herbert Stein. *Presidential economics: the making of economic policy from Roosevelt to Reagan and beyond.* 2d rev. ed. Washington, D.C.: American Enterprise Institute for Public Policy Research, 1988. (American Enterprise Institute studies, 473.) ISBN 0-8447-3656-2 (pbk). ▸ Critical survey by former insider. Sympathetic to monetarist position. [JTL]

44.207 Peter Temin. *Taking your medicine: drug regulation in the United States.* Cambridge, Mass.: Harvard University Press, 1980. ISBN 0-674-86725-4. ▸ Innovative argument that government regulation was response to perceived crisis, not actual need. Evolving market favored large firms with patented products but regulation did not keep pace with product (drug) development. [JTL]

44.208 Richard H. K. Vietor. *Energy policy in America since 1945: a study of business-government relations.* Cambridge: Cambridge University Press, 1984. ISBN 0-521-26658-0. ▸ Well-researched study details changes in policy and effects on prices and supply. Regulation failed because all sides, including business, ignored market forces and decided policy on political grounds. [JTL]

44.209 David Vogel. *Fluctuating fortunes: the political power of business in America.* New York: Basic Books, 1989. ISBN 0-465-02470-X. ▸ Clear, balanced account of cycle of falling then rising power, 1960 to present. Business' influence waned in prosperity and resurged in stagnant economy. [JTL]

44.210 Lawrence J. White. *The S & L debacle: public policy lessons for bank and thrift regulation.* New York: Oxford University Press, 1991. ISBN 0-19-506733-9 (cl), 0-19-507484-X (pbk). ▸ Serious economic study concludes crisis due to unusual economic conditions of early 1980s, hasty deregulation and flawed accounting, more than rampant fraud. Contains history of thrifts from New Deal to present restructuring. [JTL]

44.211 James Whorton. *Before Silent Spring: pesticides and public health in pre-DDT America.* Princeton: Princeton University Press, 1974. ISBN 0-691-08139-5. ▸ Accessible study of public concern about toxic environmental chemicals, chiefly inorganic pesticides, from 1860s to 1940s, and evolution of and resistance to federal policy to appease consumer anxieties. Consumers' point of view. [JTL/CSH]

44.212 John F. Witte. *The politics and development of the federal income tax.* Madison: University of Wisconsin Press, 1985. ISBN 0-299-10200-9. ▸ Wars and federal deficits, not rare attempts at redistributing income, explain increases in taxes. Except in crises, people always called for lower taxes. Well organized, covering 1812–1982 with section on theory. [JTL]

Labor and Management

44.213 Loren Baritz. *The servants of power: a history of the use of social science in American industry.* 1960 ed. Westport, Conn.: Greenwood, 1974. ISBN 0-8371-7275-6. ▸ Polemical study of big business, which used social scientists after 1920 not to improve working conditions but to control workers and increase effort. [JTL]

44.214 Irving Bernstein. *The lean years: a history of the American worker, 1920–1933.* 1960 ed. New York: Da Capo, 1983. ISBN 0-306-80202-3 (pbk). ▸ Wages rose less than productivity; pro-business social climate and voluntaristic craft-oriented American Federation of Labor hindered unionization. Depression broke up unions, bringing not revolt but transience. Well-written narrative. [JTL]

44.215 Irving Bernstein. *The turbulent years: a history of the*

American worker, 1933–1941. 1969 ed. Boston: Houghton-Mifflin, 1970. ▸ Unions and collective bargaining spread due to industrial unionism and New Deal; crisis made pragmatic workers embrace the Democratic party. Well-written institutional history. [JTL]

44.216 David Brody. *Workers in industrial America: essays in the twentieth-century struggle.* New York: Oxford University Press, 1980. ISBN 0-19-502490-7 (cl), 0-19-502491-5 (pbk). ▸ Influential interpretation of rise of modern organized labor. Workers won unions and shop-floor rights in exchange for renouncing autonomy. Emphasizes inherent conflict with management but also workers' conservatism; New Deal organizing a triumph. Excellent, balanced essays. [JTL/DLC]

44.217 Lizabeth Cohen. *Making a new deal: industrial workers in Chicago, 1919–1939.* New York: Cambridge University Press, 1990. ISBN 0-521-38134-7. ▸ Depression made workers switch loyalties from ethnic elites and paternalistic employers to Democratic party and unions. Challenges institutional labor historiography by examining social and cultural dynamics. Well researched and written. [JTL]

44.218 Melvyn Dubofsky and Warren van Tine. *John L. Lewis: a biography.* New York: Quadrangle/New York Times, 1977. ISBN 0-8129-0673-X. ▸ Exhaustive biographical account of union leader's rise to and use of power. Lewis's social ambition attributed to political opportunism and lack of working-class philosophy. Lewis and Congress of Industrial Organizations distrusted government yet needed it. [JTL]

44.219 Richard C. Edwards. *Contested terrain: the transformation of the workplace in the twentieth century.* New York: Basic Books, 1979. ISBN 0-465-01412-7 (cl), 0-465-01413-5 (pbk). ▸ Provocative account of how industrial consolidation around 1900 made employers replace direct control of workers with control based on technology or later bureaucracy. Different forms of control fragmented working class, diminishing democracy. Much sociological theory. [JTL]

44.220 Steve Fraser. *Labor will rule: Sidney Hillman and the rise of American labor.* New York: Free Press, 1991. ISBN 0-02-910630-3. ▸ Lengthy study of influential leader and pragmatic head of American Clothing Workers. Won stable jobs and material gains for workers in exchange for limiting rank-and-file participation, offending traditionalists. [JTL]

44.221 Joshua Benjamin Freeman. *In transit: the Transport Workers Union in New York City, 1933–1966.* New York: Oxford University Press, 1989. ISBN 0-19-504511-4. ▸ Study of pioneering public-sector union that successfully used but then cast off ties to Communist party, while maintaining ethnic ties and building local political influence. Sophisticated approach, integrates institutional aspects with workers' culture. [JTL]

44.222 Peter Friedlander. *The emergence of a UAW local, 1936–1939: a study in class and culture.* Pittsburgh: University of Pittsburgh Press, 1975. ISBN 0-8229-3295-4. ▸ Ambitious cultural case study of United Auto Workers' local, based largely on critical use of interviews. Workers with prebourgeois culture transferred their passivity and deference from company to union, generating union bureaucracy and conservative tendencies. [JTL]

44.223 Gary Gerstle. *Working-class Americanism: the politics of labor in a textile city, 1914–60.* New York: Cambridge University Press, 1989. ISBN 0-521-36131-1. ▸ Ethnic leaders joined by Roosevelt administration dissuaded Franco-American workers from republican radicalism encouraged by union leaders. Stimulating cultural approach. [JTL]

44.224 Howell John Harris. *The right to manage: industrial relations policies of American businesses in the 1940s.* Madison: University of Wisconsin Press, 1982. ISBN 0-299-08640-2. ▸ Scholarly analysis of reaction of large corporations to Congress of Industrial Organizations. Argues most used realist model of confrontation rather than pure anti-unionism or new collaborative alternative. [JTL]

44.225 Benjamin K. Hunnicut. *Work without end: abandoning shorter hours for the right to work.* Philadelphia: Temple University Press, 1988. ISBN 0-87722-520-6. ▸ Well-researched, suggestive account of why hours of work stopped declining after 1920s: employers worried about productivity, workers adopted consumer values, and decline in workers' subculture made leisure time less enjoyable. [JTL]

44.226 Sanford M. Jacoby. *Employing bureaucracy: managers, unions, and the transformation of work in American industry, 1900–1945.* New York: Columbia University Press, 1985. ISBN 0-231-05756-3 (cl), 0-231-05757-1 (pbk). ▸ Specialist study of hiring practices. External pressures from social workers, government and unions, not competitive demands for efficiency, overcame managers' resistance to setting up personnel rules by 1930s. Based on contemporaneous studies and speeches. [JTL]

44.227 Harvey A. Levenstein. *Communism, anticommunism, and the CIO.* Westport, Conn.: Greenwood, 1981. ISBN 0-313-22072-7, ISSN 0084-9219. ▸ Positive view of Communists' role in labor movement until 1940s, when rigid Stalinism of party leaders led to unwise tactical decisions. Covers national as well as union politics. [JTL]

44.228 Nelson Lichtenstein. *Labor's war at home: the CIO in World War II.* Cambridge: Cambridge University Press, 1982. ISBN 0-521-23472-7. ▸ CIO's fateful decision to collaborate with government and business to solidify its tenuous hold rather than continue its combative strikes. Congress of Industrial Organizations flourished but at cost of union democracy. Standard book on subject. [JTL]

44.229 Bruce Nelson. *Workers on the waterfront: seamen, longshoremen, and unionism in the 1930s.* Urbana: University of Illinois Press, 1988. ISBN 0-252-01487-1. ▸ Definitive account of maritime workers and their union activism during Depression. Workers' distinct subculture fostered resistance. Concentrates on West Coast. [JTL]

44.230 Robert Ozanne. *A century of labor-management relations at McCormick and International Harvester.* Madison: University of Wisconsin Press, 1967. ▸ Innovative, specialized study of management policy at this large company. Pressure from unions crucial in improvements in wages and working conditions 1860–1960, more so than relatively constant productivity increases. [JTL]

44.231 Christopher L. Tomlins. *The state and the unions: labor relations, law, and the organized labor movement in America, 1880–1960.* Cambridge: Cambridge University Press, 1985. ISBN 0-521-25840-5 (cl), 0-521-31452-6 (pbk). ▸ Workers' move away from radicalism and ultimately toward New Deal reforms fatal since capitalist state always subordinated workers' interests to concerns for industrial stability. Much legal detail. [JTL]

44.232 Robert Zieger. *American workers, American unions, 1920–1985.* Baltimore: Johns Hopkins University Press, 1986. ISBN 0-8018-3126-1 (cl), 0-8018-3128-8 (pbk). ▸ Introductory account that emphasizes institutional development in organized labor movement but briefly explores cultural and economic issues as well. Depicts unions as remarkable success given constraints of business and government. [JTL]

Poverty and Class

44.233 Steven Brint and Jerome Karabel. *The diverted dream: community colleges and the promise of educational opportunity in America, 1900–1985.* New York: Oxford University Press, 1989. ISBN 0-19-504815-6 (cl), 0-19-504816-4 (pbk). ▸ Critical, revisionist study of role of two-year colleges. Poor students saw colleges as means of upward mobility, but educators stressed vocational training, diminishing aggregate democratizing effect. [JTL]

44.234 Sheldon H. Danziger and Daniel H. Weinberg, eds. *Fighting poverty: what works and what doesn't.* Cambridge, Mass.: Harvard University Press, 1986. ISBN 0-674-30085-8 (cl), 0-674-30086-6 (pbk). ▸ Wide-ranging essays by liberals who defend Great Society–type social policy against critics who see all programs as failures. Emphasizes lack of income, rather than lifestyle choices, in explaining poverty. [JTL]

44.235 Michael Harrington. *The other America: poverty in America.* 1969 rev. ed. New York: Penguin, 1988. ISBN 0-14-021308-2. ▸ Postwar affluence concealed and disheartened remaining and still numerous poor. Influential, angry critique helped bring about government programs to break vicious circle of poverty. [JTL]

44.236 Jacqueline Jones. *The dispossessed: America's underclasses from the Civil War to the present.* New York: Basic Books, 1992. ISBN 0-465-00127-0. ▸ Hard-hitting historical description and analysis of poverty, with focus on South and Appalachia. Critical of American policy makers. [JTP]

44.237 Michael B. Katz, ed. *The "underclass" debate: views from history.* Princeton: Princeton University Press, 1993. ISBN 0-691-04810-X (cl), 0-691-00628-8 (pbk). ▸ Thoughtful essays providing historical background for understanding of African American central city life in 1980s and 1990s. [JTP]

44.238 Frank Levy. *Dollars and dreams: the changing American income distribution.* Rev. ed. New York: Norton, 1988. ISBN 0-393-30557-0 (pbk). ▸ Balanced, readable analysis of distribution of income since 1947. Finds increased inequality since 1970s, resulting from flawed economy. [JTL]

44.239 James T. Patterson. *America's struggle with poverty, 1900–1985.* Rev. ed. Cambridge, Mass.: Harvard University Press, 1986. ISBN 0-674-03122-9 (pbk). ▸ Interpretive survey of ideas about and policies against poverty. [TCL]

44.240 Stephan Thernstrom. *The other Bostonians: poverty and progress in the American metropolis, 1880–1970.* Cambridge, Mass.: Harvard University Press, 1973. ISBN 0-674-64495-6. ▸ Influential, pioneering quantitative study using varied samples and multivariate analysis. Found small degree of upward social mobility for residents who remained in city. [JTL]

44.241 Stanley Wenocur and Michael Reisch. *From charity to enterprise: the development of American social work in a market economy.* Urbana: University of Illinois Press, 1989. ISBN 0-252-01556-8. ▸ Sensible, scholarly review of changes in philosophy of social work. Around 1900, professional aspiration of some social workers resulted in poverty explained as individual rather than social failure; not conspiracy but complex development. [JTL]

44.242 Jeffrey G. Williamson and Peter H. Lindert. *American inequality: a macroeconomic history.* New York: Academic Press, 1980. ISBN 0-12-757160-4. ▸ Specialized, often statistical analysis of income inequality between skilled and unskilled workers: increased 1774–1929, then reversed until 1950s. Concludes capital accumulation caused inequality rather than other way around. Much fragmentary evidence. [JTL]

Regions

44.243 James C. Cobb. *The selling of the South: the southern crusade for industrial development, 1936–80.* Baton Rouge: Louisiana State University Press, 1982. ISBN 0-8071-0994-0. ▸ Boosters' policy favored large companies and relied on docile labor force, so region's development did not reduce inequality. Fear of bad public relations moderated racial discrimination. Specialist study. [JTL]

44.244 Robert L. Dorman. *Revolt of the provinces: the regionalist movement in America, 1920–1945.* Chapel Hill: University of North Carolina Press, 1993. ISBN 0-8078-2101-2. ▸ Beautifully written description and analysis of various regional writers and movements, mainly 1920–40. [JTP]

44.245 James N. Gregory. *American exodus: the dust bowl migration and Okie culture in California.* New York: Oxford University Press, 1989. ISBN 0-19-504423-1. ▸ Most migrants came from cities and settled all over. Many maintained their culture and even influenced host society with conservatism and country music. Excellent mix of economic and cultural history. [JTL]

44.246 Jack Temple Kirby. *Rural worlds lost: the American South, 1920–1960.* Baton Rouge: Louisiana State University Press, 1987. ISBN 0-8071-1300-X (cl), 0-8071-1360-3 (pbk). ▸ Broad account of how modernization at different rates across region affected social structure and personal life in different ways; migrants to cities retained much of their rural culture. Many anecdotes. [JTL]

44.247 Roger W. Lotchin. *Fortress California: from warfare to welfare.* New York: Oxford University Press, 1992. ISBN 0-19-504779-6. ▸ Challenging approach to war and society identifies tripartite interplay: city boosters, military, and state. City boosters systematically encouraged and accommodated military spending, which resulted from activities of modern nation-state. [JTL/CAM]

44.248 Michael P. Malone and Richard W. Etulain. *The American West: a twentieth-century history.* Lincoln: University of Nebraska Press, 1989. ISBN 0-8032-3093-1. ▸ Survey of region's changes and rise to national leadership in urbanization, technology, and federal programs. Demographic, economic, political, and cultural coverage. Extensive bibliographic essay, not footnoted. [JTL]

44.249 Gerald D. Nash. *The American West transformed: the impact of the Second World War.* Bloomington: Indiana University Press, 1985. ISBN 0-253-30649-3. ▸ Basic study of war's crucial role in shift from colonial and parochial colony to center of growth, economic activity, and cultural change. Broad coverage of social change; emphasizes region's vitality. [JTL]

44.250 Gerald D. Nash. *World War II and the West: reshaping the economy.* Lincoln: University of Nebraska Press, 1990. ISBN 0-8032-3303-5. ▸ Thoroughly researched sequel to *The American West Transformed* (44.249), analyzing economic significance of region's transformation. Focus on heavy industry; notes impact on environment. [JTL]

44.251 Bruce J. Schulman. *From cotton belt to sunbelt: federal policy, economic development, and the transformation of the South, 1938–1980.* New York: Oxford University Press, 1991. ISBN 0-19-505703-1. ▸ Government developed region without reducing inequality or poverty. Fearful of losing congressional votes or presidential elections, left implementation of programs to state and local officials. Specialist study. [JTL]

44.252 George Brown Tindall. *Emergence of the New South, 1913–1945.* 1967 ed. Baton Rouge: Louisiana State University Press, 1970. ISBN 0-8071-0010-2 (cl), 0-8071-0020-X (pbk). ▸ Comprehensive, standard treatment emphasizing economic rise via changing labor conditions and technological advance. Sees convergence with North in values as well as techniques. [JTL]

44.253 Donald Worster. *Rivers of empire: water, aridity, and the growth of the American West.* New York: Pantheon, 1986. ISBN 0-394-51680-X. ▸ Provocative account of how need for grand water projects led to social stratification, pollution, and technocratic loss of democracy. Focus on California. [JTL]

44.254 Gavin Wright. *Old South, New South: revolutions in the southern economy since the Civil War.* New York: Basic Books, 1986. ISBN 0-465-05193-6 (cl), 0-465-05194-4 (pbk). ▸ South developed slowly due to its mostly enclosed labor market, which

New Deal wage standards broke open. Wide-ranging, influential book. [JTL]

SEE ALSO
40.186 Norris Hundley, Jr. *The great thirst.*

WOMEN'S HISTORY

General Studies

44.255 Suzanne M. Bianchi and Daphne Spain. *American women in transition.* New York: Russell Sage Foundation, 1986. ISBN 0-87154-111-4 (cl), 0-87154-112-2 (pbk). ▸ Analysis of women's rates of marriage, childbearing, educational achievement, labor force participation, and income since 1940. Sound starting point for clearly explained census data. [LGB]

44.256 Dorothy M. Brown. *Setting a course: American women in the 1920s.* Boston: Twayne, 1987. ISBN 0-8057-9906-0 (cl), 0-8057-9908-7 (pbk). ▸ Introductory survey stressing centrality of women to cultural transitions of decade. [JGC]

44.257 Ginette Castro. *American feminism: a contemporary history.* Elizabeth Loverde-Baswell, trans. New York: New York University Press, 1990. ISBN 0-8147-1435-8 (cl), 0-8147-1448-X (pbk). ▸ Intellectual history of feminist thought in United States since 1960s. Perceptive insights from French sociologist. [LGB]

44.258 William H. Chafe. *The American woman: her changing social, economic, and political role, 1920–1970.* 1972 ed. London: Oxford University Press, 1974. ISBN 0-19-501578-9 (cl), 0-19-501785-4 (pbk). ▸ Study of World War II and especially women's expanded participation in paid labor force as basis for fundamental changes in women's social position after war and for rise of women's movement. Focal point of subsequent historiographical debate. [JGC]

44.259 William H. Chafe. *The paradox of change: American women in the twentieth century.* New York: Oxford University Press, 1991. ISBN 0-19-504418-5 (cl), 0-19-504419-3 (pbk). ▸ Revision of 44.258, drawing on more recent secondary literature. Pays greater attention to diversity within female population. [JGC]

44.260 Flora Davis. *Moving the mountain: the woman's movement since 1960.* New York: Simon & Schuster, 1991. ISBN 0-671-60207-1. ▸ Readable study of various origins of feminist movement in sixties and its evolution into multicentered movement of seventies and eighties. Concludes much was accomplished because of this divided structure. [LGB]

44.261 Estelle B. Freedman. "The new woman: changing views of women in the 1920s." *Journal of American history* 61.2 (1974) 372–93. ISSN 0021-8723. ▸ Historiographical survey questioning image of 1920s as decade of political apathy, sexual liberation, and domestic fulfillment. Reprinted in Scharf and Jensen 44.268. [JGC]

44.262 Linda Gordon. *Heroes of their own lives: the politics and history of family violence.* 1988 ed. New York: Penguin, 1989. ISBN 0-14-010468-2 (pbk). ▸ Relationship between gender norms and reactions to family violence between 1880 and 1960. Important in showing how women used and shaped welfare agencies to deal with own problems. [LGB]

44.263 Susan M. Hartmann. *The home front and beyond: American women in the 1940s.* Boston: Twayne, 1982. ISBN 0-8057-9901-X (cl), 0-8057-9903-6 (pbk). ▸ Introductory survey. [JGC]

44.264 Marianne Hirsch and Evelyn Fox Keller, eds. *Conflicts in feminism.* New York: Routledge, 1990. ISBN 0-415-90177-4 (cl), 0-415-90178-2 (pbk). ▸ Essays on reproductive technology, race, class, pornography, and other divisive issues in current feminist theory. Insight into theoretical issues informing history of women. [LGB]

44.265 Jacqueline Jones. *Labor of love, labor of sorrow: black women, work, and the family from slavery to the present.* 1985 ed. New York: Vintage, 1986. ISBN 0-394-74536-1 (pbk). ▸ Excellent integration of African American labor and family history. Focuses on importance of family in decision making for African American women. [LGB]

44.266 Eugenia Kaledin. *Mothers and more: American women in the 1950s.* Boston: Twayne, 1984. ISBN 0-8057-9904-4 (cl), 0-8057-9907-9 (pbk). ▸ Survey of experiences of white middle-class women and successful women of fifties. Finds roots of feminist movement of late sixties. [LGB]

44.267 Rosalind Rosenberg. *Divided lives: American women in the twentieth century.* New York: Hill & Wang, 1992. ISBN 0-809097-84-2. ▸ Sprightly, up-to-date survey and interpretation of women. [JTP]

44.268 Lois Scharf and Joan M. Jensen, eds. *Decades of discontent: the women's movement, 1920–1940.* 1983 ed. Boston: Northeastern University Press, 1987. ISBN 1-55553-013-3 (pbk). ▸ Important anthology covering economic, cultural, and political developments during interwar years. Useful bibliographical note. [JGC]

44.269 Barbara Sicherman and Carol Hurd Green, eds. *Notable American women: the modern period, a biographical dictionary.* Vol. 4 of *Notable American women, 1607–1950.* Cambridge, Mass.: Belknap, 1980. ISBN 0-674-62732-6 (cl), 0-674-62733-4 (pbk). ▸ Essential entry point into many activities of women during twentieth century. Includes women who died 1951–75. Well-written sketches and references to further information. [LGB]

44.270 Winifred D. Wandersee. *On the move: American women in the 1970s.* Boston: Twayne, 1988. ISBN 0-8057-9909-5 (cl), 0-8057-9910-9 (pbk). ▸ Basic survey of feminist movement based on archival materials, media reports, and some interviews. How focus of movement on politics of personal issues spread to other social movements. [LGB]

44.271 Susan Ware. *Holding their own: American women in the 1930s.* Boston: Twayne, 1982. ISBN 0-8057-9900-1 (cl), 0-8057-9902-8 (pbk). ▸ Introductory survey stressing small relative gains for women in number of areas. Useful bibliographical essay. [JGC]

Politics, Reform, and Feminism

44.272 Susan D. Becker. *The origins of the Equal Rights Amendment: American feminism between the wars.* Westport, Conn.: Greenwood, 1981. ISBN 0-313-22818-3. ▸ Detailed monograph discussing efforts of National Woman's party on behalf of Equal Rights Amendment and conflicts between National Woman's party and other women's organizations. [JGC]

44.273 Mary Frances Berry. *Why ERA failed: politics, women's rights, and the amending process of the Constitution.* 1986 ed. Bloomington: Indiana University Press, 1988. ISBN 0-253-36537-6 (cl, 1986), 0-253-20459-3 (pbk). ▸ Compelling and useful comparison of struggle for Equal Rights Amendment to earlier attempts to amend Constitution. Failure to pass due to lack of state-based organization and wide debate over amendment's meaning. [LGB]

44.274 Blanche Wiesen Cook. *Eleanor Roosevelt.* Vol. 1: *1884–1933.* New York: Viking, 1992. ISBN 0-670-80486-X. ▸ Controversial feminist interpretation of Roosevelt's life, stressing independence of her political career and importance of her relationships with women. [JGC]

44.275 Lela B. Costin. *Two sisters for social justice: a biography of Grace and Edith Abbott.* Urbana: University of Illinois Press, 1983. ISBN 0-252-01013-2. ▸ Readable portrait of two leaders in profes-sionalization of social work and development of social welfare policy from Progressive Era to early New Deal. [JGC]

44.276 Nancy F. Cott. *The grounding of modern feminism.* New Haven: Yale University Press, 1987. ISBN 0-300-03892-5 (cl), 0-300-04228-0 (pbk). ▸ Influential study of extensiveness and variety of women's continued activism in 1920s and modern feminism's basic ideological dilemma: equality based on individualism, but advancement dependent on group consciousness. [JGC]

44.277 Alice Echols. *Daring to be bad: radical feminism in America, 1967–1975.* Minneapolis: University of Minnesota Press, 1989. ISBN 0-8166-1786-4 (cl), 0-8166-1787-2 (pbk). ▸ Detailed and provocative account of evolution of American feminism in late 1960s and 1970s. Highlights divisions between radical feminist thought, stressing freedom from gender norms, and cultural feminist thought, calling for gender solidarity. [LGB]

44.278 Sara M. Evans. *Personal politics: the roots of women's liberation in the civil rights movement and the New Left.* 1979 ed. New York: Vintage, 1980. ISBN 0-394-74228-1 (pbk). ▸ Contributions of women to 1960s' social movements and how participants moved into feminism. Influential interpretation emphasizes how experiences of sexual discrimination led to separatism. [LGB]

44.279 Jo Freeman. *The politics of women's liberation: a case study of an emerging social movement and its relation to the policy process.* 1975 ed. New York: Longman, 1978. ISBN 0-582-28009-5 (pbk). ▸ Insider's groundbreaking assessment of origins and course of feminist movement. Applies relative deprivation theory to attachment of white, middle-class women to movement. [LGB]

44.280 Joyce Gelb and Marian Leif Palley. *Women and public policies.* Rev. ed. Princeton: Princeton University Press, 1987. ISBN 0-691-07710-X (cl), 0-691-02251-8 (pbk). ▸ Basic review of activities of women's organizations in 1970s and early 1980s. Successful policies brought gender role equity (such as credit rights); others seemed to change roles (such as abortion rights). [LGB]

44.281 Linda Gordon, ed. *Women, the state, and welfare.* Madison: University of Wisconsin Press, 1990. ISBN 0-299-12660-9 (cl), 0-299-12664-1 (pbk). ▸ Useful anthology of historical and theoretical articles on women and gender and the shaping of American social insurance and public assistance policies, mostly from late nineteenth century to present. [JGC]

44.282 Jacquelyn Dowd Hall. *Revolt against chivalry: Jesse Daniel Ames and the women's campaign against lynching.* New York: Columbia University Press, 1979. ISBN 0-231-04040-7 (cl), 0-231-04041-5 (pbk). ▸ Brilliant use of biography of Ames and analysis of organization she founded in 1930 to get at larger issues of women's activism and sexual and racial relations in the South. Stresses links to earlier women's activism. [JGC]

44.283 Cynthia Ellen Harrison. *On account of sex: the politics of women's issues, 1945–68.* Berkeley: University of California Press, 1988. ISBN 0-520-06121-7 (cl), 0-520-06663-4 (pbk). ▸ Carefully traces policies on the Equal Rights Amendment, number of women appointed to federal office, and equal pay acts during period. Focuses on why policy emerged without powerful women's rights movement. [LGB]

44.284 Susan M. Hartmann. *From margin to mainstream: American women and politics since 1960.* New York: Knopf, 1989. ISBN 0-394-35610-1 (pbk). ▸ Basic account of how individuals and groups put women's issues on public agenda. Sees trend of achievement during period. [LGB]

44.285 Joan Hoff-Wilson and Marjorie Lightman, eds. *Without precedent: the life and career of Eleanor Roosevelt.* Bloomington: Indiana University Press, 1984. ISBN 0-253-19100-9 (cl), 0-253-20327-9 (pbk). ▸ Anthology of brief conference papers examining Roosevelt's political life and legacy. [JGC]

44.286 Joan M. Jensen. "The campaign for women's community property rights in New Mexico." In *New Mexico women: intercultural perspectives*. Joan M. Jensen and Darlis A. Miller, eds., pp. 333–35. Albuquerque: University of New Mexico Press, 1986. ISBN 0-8263-0826-0 (cl), 0-8263-0827-9 (pbk). ▸ Details network of women associated with efforts to equalize property law for married women. Explains how women working within political parties achieved limited gains during 1950s. [LGB]

44.287 Mary Fainsod Katzenstein. "Feminism within American institutions: unobtrusive mobilization in the 1980s." *Signs* 16 (Autumn 1990) 27–54. ISSN 0097-9740. ▸ Provocative case studies of Catholic church and American military to examine spread of gender consciousness. Disputes feminism declined during this period. [LGB]

44.288 Rebecca E. Klatch. *Women of the New Right*. Philadelphia: Temple University Press, 1987. ISBN 0-87722-470-6 (cl), 0-87722-590-7 (pbk). ▸ Careful analysis of two major groups of 1980s conservative women. Points to split between those concerned about laissez-faire economic policy and those desiring socially conservative policies. [LGB]

44.289 J. Stanley Lemons. *The woman citizen: social feminism in the 1920s*. 1973 ed. Urbana: University of Illinois Press, 1975. ISBN 0-252-00267-9 (cl), 0-252-00563-5 (pbk). ▸ Informative analysis of persistence of women's reform efforts after suffrage victory as link between progressivism and New Deal. [JGC]

44.290 Jane J. Mansbridge. *Why we lost the ERA*. Chicago: University of Chicago Press, 1986. ISBN 0-226-50357-7 (cl), 0-226-50358-5 (pbk). ▸ Sociological account examines campaign for Equal Rights Amendment from perspective of social movements. Identifies clearly issues such as women in combat which contributed to defeat and argues campaign was beneficial to general women's movement. [LGB]

44.291 George Martin. *Madame Secretary, Frances Perkins*. Boston: Houghton-Mifflin, 1976. ISBN 0-395-24293-2. ▸ Workmanlike biography of first female member of Cabinet, Franklin Roosevelt's secretary of labor, 1933–45, which stresses religious roots of Perkins's commitment to social reform. Written before new wave of women's political history. [JGC]

44.292 Donald G. Mathews and Jane Sherron De Hart. *Sex, gender, and the politics of the ERA: a state and the nation*. New York: Oxford University Press, 1990. ISBN 0-19-503858-4. ▸ Vivid portrait of battle for and against Equal Rights Amendment in North Carolina, 1972–82. Argues that debate quickly centered on meaning of word "sex." [LGB]

44.293 Robin Morgan, ed. *Sisterhood is powerful: an anthology of writings from the women's liberation movement*. New York: Random House, 1970. ISBN 0-394-70539-4. ▸ Remarkable collection of writings from early years of women's liberation movement. Documents historical moment and provides analysis of origins of movement. [LGB]

44.294 Elisabeth Israels Perry. *Belle Moskowitz: feminine politics and the exercise of power in the age of Alfred E. Smith*. New York: Oxford University Press, 1987. ISBN 0-19-504426-6. ▸ Well-researched biography of leading woman in New York state and national Democratic party politics during 1920s. Case study of women reformers as links between progressivism and New Deal. [JGC]

44.295 Jo Ann Gibson Robinson. *The Montgomery bus boycott and the women who started it: the memoirs of Jo Ann Gibson Robinson*. David J. Garrow, ed. Knoxville: University of Tennessee Press, 1987. ISBN 0-87049-524-0 (cl), 0-87049-527-5 (pbk). ▸ Illustrates importance of Woman's Political Caucus of Montgomery in sustaining this early civil rights protest. Unique document of role of southern African American women in movement. [LGB]

44.296 Leila J. Rupp and Verta Taylor. *Survival in the doldrums: the American women's rights movement, 1945 to the 1960s*. 1987 ed. Columbus: Ohio State University Press, 1990. ISBN 0-8142-0516-x (pbk). ▸ Innovative contribution to debate concerning feminist movement of forties and fifties. Stresses activities of National Women's party and offers case study of activist women in Ohio. [LGB]

44.297 Ingrid Winther Scobie. *Center stage: Helen Gahagan Douglas, a life*. New York: Oxford University Press, 1992. ISBN 0-19-506896-3. ▸ Biography of actress, singer, liberal Democrat, and congresswoman from California defeated by Richard Nixon for Senate in 1950. [JTP]

44.298 Anne Firor Scott. "After suffrage: southern women in the twenties." *Journal of southern history* 30.3 (1964) 298–318. ISSN 0022-4642. ▸ Classic early study of continuing efforts of women in politics and social reform amid lack of larger changes in women's social position. [JGC]

44.299 Judith Sealander. *As minority becomes majority: federal reaction to the phenomenon of women in the work force, 1920–1963*. Westport, Conn.: Greenwood, 1983. ISBN 0-313-23750-6. ▸ Detailed monograph on Women's Bureau of United States Department of Labor and women who staffed it, their relations with other women's organizations, and with rest of federal government. [JGC]

44.300 Amy Swerdlow. "Ladies' day at the Capitol: Women Strike for Peace versus HUAC." In *Unequal sisters: a multicultural reader in U.S. women's history*. Ellen Carol DuBois and Vicki L. Ruiz, eds., pp. 400–17. New York: Routledge, 1990. ISBN 0-415-90271-1 (cl), 0-415-90272-x (pbk). ▸ Stimulating and readable discussion of events leading up to December 1962 hearing on communist influences on this women's organization that worked against nuclear arms race. [LGB]

44.301 Louise A. Tilly and Patricia Gurin, eds. *Women, politics, and change*. New York: Russell Sage Foundation, 1990. ISBN 0-87154-884-4. ▸ Wide-ranging anthology of essays by historians, political scientists, and sociologists concerning women's changing political roles, 1880–1980. Excellent bibliography. [JGC]

44.302 Susan Ware. *Beyond suffrage: women in the New Deal*. Cambridge, Mass.: Harvard University Press, 1981. ISBN 0-674-06921-8 (cl), 0-674-06922-6 (pbk). ▸ Study of networks of support and influence among twenty-eight female New Deal appointees, centering on Eleanor Roosevelt, Labor Secretary Frances Perkins, and Democratic party official Molly Dewson. [JGC]

44.303 Susan Ware. *Partner and I: Molly Dewson, feminism, and New Deal politics*. New Haven: Yale University Press, 1987. ISBN 0-300-03820-8. ▸ Innovative dual biography of first head of Democratic National Committee's Women's Division (1932–37) and her lifelong companion Polly Porter. Stresses importance of women's friendships in supporting women's emergence into public life. [JGC]

44.304 Patricia G. Zelman. *Women, work, and national policy: the Kennedy-Johnson years*. Ann Arbor: UMI Research Press, 1982. ISBN 0-8357-1282-6. ▸ Detailed study of such political developments in 1960s as Presidential Commission on the Status of Women and Equal Pay Act based on extensive archival research. Also available in photocopy from Ann Arbor: University Microfilms International, 1989. [LGB]

SEE ALSO
43.387 Robyn Muncy. *Creating a female dominion in American reform, 1890–1935*.

Economics and Labor

44.305 Teresa L. Amott. "Black women and AFDC: making entitlement out of necessity." In *Women, the state, and welfare.* Linda Gordon, ed., pp. 280–98. Madison: University of Wisconsin Press, 1990. ISBN 0-299-12660-9 (cl), 0-299-12664-1 (pbk). ▸ Examination of causes of large number of single African American mothers receiving welfare. Original interpretation sees applying for welfare as political act, because African American women on welfare increased power in relations with men, families, and government. [LGB]

44.306 Eileen Boris. "Regulating industrial homework: the triumph of 'sacred motherhood.'" *Journal of American history* 71.4 (1985) 745–63. ISSN 0021-8723. ▸ Debate over New Deal era regulation of industrial homework, beginning with exclusion of homework from National Recovery Administration codes of 1934. Explores important questions of effect of public policy on women, especially tradeoff between improving working conditions and further entrenching of traditional sexual division of labor. [JGC]

44.307 Philip Sheldon Foner. *Women and the American labor movement.* Vol. 2: *From World War I to the present.* New York: Free Press, 1980. ISBN 0-02-910380-0. ▸ Detailed account of relationship of women to organized labor. Developments such as rise of women-dominated clothing unions in 1910s to formation of Coalition of Labor Union Women in 1974. [LGB]

44.308 Betty Friedan. *The feminine mystique.* 1974 ed. New York: Norton, 1983. ISBN 0-393-01775-3. ▸ Very influential study combining interviews with analysis of popular culture to identify limited nature of women's opportunities in 1950s and 1960s. [LGB]

44.309 Nancy Gabin. *Feminism in the labor movement: women and the UAW, 1935–1975.* Ithaca, N.Y.: Cornell University Press, 1990. ISBN 0-8014-2435-6 (cl), 0-8014-9725-6 (pbk). ▸ Stimulating study of women members of United Auto Workers. Argues labor women had a feminism based on workplace rather than personal politics of women's liberation movement. [LGB]

44.310 Claudia D. Goldin. *Understanding the gender gap: an economic history of American women.* New York: Oxford University Press, 1990. ISBN 0-19-505077-0 (cl), 0-19-507270-7 (pbk). ▸ Comprehensive, subtle, and often technical analysis of changes in economic lives of women. Analysis of cohorts of women explains changes in female employment rates in twentieth century. [LGB]

44.311 Jacquelyn Dowd Hall. "Disorderly women: gender and labor militancy in the Appalachian South." *Journal of American history* 73 (1986) 354–82. ISSN 0021-8723. ▸ Examination of central role of women in southern textile strikes of 1920s and 1930s. Provocative for its stress on importance of cultural tensions, particularly over women's sexuality and public presence in labor strife. [JGC]

44.312 Dolores E. Janiewski. *Sisterhood denied: race, gender, and class in a New South community.* Philadelphia: Temple University Press, 1985. ISBN 0-87722-361-0. ▸ Study of militancy among textile and tobacco workers in Durham, North Carolina, during 1930s and 1940s. Careful, groundbreaking study of racial divisions as obstacles to gender solidarity. [JGC]

44.313 Carolyn C. Jones. "Split income and separate spheres: tax law and gender roles in the 1940s." *Law and history review* 6.2 (1988) 259–310. ISSN 0147-7307. ▸ Groundbreaking analysis of implementation of joint tax returns for married couples in light of postwar changes and desire to preserve traditional gender roles. Integrates records of court cases, public commentary, and legislative debate. [LGB]

44.314 Alice Kessler-Harris. "Equal Employment Opportunity Commission vs. Sears, Roebuck and Company: a personal account." In *Unequal sisters: a multicultural reader in U.S. women's history.* Ellen Carol DuBois and Vicki L. Ruiz, eds., pp. 432–46. New York: Routledge, 1990. ISBN 0-415-90271-1 (cl), 0-415-90272-X (pbk). ▸ Chronicle of two historians of women's work on opposite sides of equal opportunity case. Careful review of difficulties in using women's labor history to support contemporary attempts to gain equal opportunity. [LGB]

44.315 Alice Kessler-Harris. "Problems of coalition building: women and trade unions in the 1920s." In *Women, work, and protest: a century of U.S. women's labor history.* Ruth Milkman, ed., pp. 110–38. Boston: Routledge & Kegan Paul, 1985. ISBN 0-7100-9940-1. ▸ Uses garment industry for revealing case study of sources of tension between male-dominated trade unions and female workers, particularly in garment industry. [JGC]

44.316 Barbara Kingsolver. *Holding the line: women in the great Arizona mine strike of 1983.* Ithaca, N.Y.: ILR Press, 1989. ISBN 0-87546-155-7 (cl), 0-87546-156-5 (pbk). ▸ Revealing study of role of women involved in prolonged labor dispute in 1980s. How women in traditional roles in home as well as women involved in nontraditional labor became involved in radical action. [LGB]

44.317 Louise Lamphere. *From working daughters to working mothers: immigrant women in a New England industrial community.* Ithaca, N.Y.: Cornell University Press, 1987. ISBN 0-8014-1945-X (cl), 0-8014-9441-9 (pbk). ▸ Provocative combination of history and anthropology compares experience of Rhode Island textile workers since late nineteenth century. [LGB]

44.318 Ruth Milkman. *Gender at work: the dynamics of job segregation by sex during World War II.* Urbana: University of Illinois Press, 1987. ISBN 0-252-01352-2 (cl), 0-252-01357-3 (pbk). ▸ Influential sociological study of shifting boundaries between men's work and women's work, particularly in automobile and electrical goods industries. Focus on World War II's lack of long-term impact on occupational patterns. [JGC]

44.319 Diana Pearce. "Welfare is not for women: why the war on poverty cannot conquer the feminization of poverty." In *Women, the state, and welfare.* Linda Gordon, ed., pp. 265–79. Madison: University of Wisconsin Press, 1990. ISBN 0-299-12660-9 (cl), 0-299-12664-1 (pbk). ▸ Careful summary of how major welfare programs are based on two types of males, breadwinner or pauper. Neither type applies to women with small children who face discrimination in labor market. [LGB]

44.320 Vicki L. Ruiz. *Cannery women, cannery lives: Mexican women, unionization, and the California food processing industry, 1930–1950.* Albuquerque: University of New Mexico Press, 1987. ISBN 0-8263-1006-0 (cl), 0-8263-0988-7 (pbk). ▸ Pioneering study of Mexican American women in union movement and their leadership roles in growth of United Cannery, Agricultural, Packing, and Allied Workers of America in southern California during heyday of industrial unionism. [JGC]

44.321 Ruth Sidel. *Women and children last: the plight of poor women in affluent America.* 1986 ed. New York: Penguin, 1987. ISBN 0-14-010013-X (pbk). ▸ Outline of creation and limits of poverty policy as it affects women, based on statistics and interviews. Argues need for more comprehensive family care system. [LGB]

44.322 Carol Stack. *All our kin: strategies for survival in a black community.* 1974 ed. New York: Harper & Row, 1975. ISBN 0-06-090424-0 (cl), 0-06-131982-1 (pbk). ▸ Influential sociological study of African American women in 1970, analyzing family and regional ties. Family networks critical to women in both urban and rural regions. [LGB]

44.323 Frank Stricker. "Cookbooks and lawbooks: the hidden history of professional women in twentieth-century America." In *A heritage of her own: toward a new social history of American* *women.* Nancy F. Cott and Elizabeth H. Pleck, eds., pp. 476–98. New York: Simon & Schuster, 1979. ISBN 0-671-25068-X (cl), 0-671-25069-8 (pbk). ▸ Clever reexamination of statistics and periodical literature challenges accepted idea of sharp decline in women's interest in professional careers during 1920s. Feminism as political movement separable from women's attachment to feminist goal of economic independence. [JGC]

44.324 Sharon Hartman Strom. "Challenging 'woman's place': feminism, the Left, and industrial unionism in the 1930s." *Feminist studies* 9.2 (1983) 359–86. ISSN 0046-3663. ▸ Feminist analysis of organizing efforts among female clerical workers and of Congress of Industrial Organizations unions' failure to organize larger numbers of women workers. Stresses structural, economic, and political factors. [JGC]

44.325 Winifred D. Wandersee. *Women's work and family values, 1920–1940.* Cambridge, Mass.: Harvard University Press, 1981. ISBN 0-674-95535-8. ▸ Revisionist study arguing for middle-class women's continuing commitment to primacy of domestic responsibilities despite married women's growing participation in labor force during 1920s and 1930s. [JGC]

44.326 Patricia Zavella. *Women's work and Chicano families: cannery workers of the Santa Clara valley.* Ithaca, N.Y.: Cornell University Press, 1987. ISBN 0-8014-9410-9 (cl), 0-8014-1730-9 (pbk). ▸ Interview-based account of Mexican American women working seasonally during 1970s. Anthropological approach gives insight into how ethnicity, gender, and family roles intersect in modern workplace. [LGB]

SEE ALSO
4.759 Barbara Melosh. *"The physician's hand."*
40.451 Margaret W. Rossiter. *Women scientists in America.*

Domestic Responsibilities

44.327 Ruth Schwartz Cowan. "The Industrial Revolution and the home: household technology in the twentieth century." *Technology and culture* 17.1 (1976) 1–23. ISSN 0040-165X. ▸ Early revisionist study challenging functionalist view of industrialization's impact on family. Post–World War I changes in household technology reshaped but did not reduce middle-class women's domestic labor. [JGC]

44.328 Ruth Schwartz Cowan. "Two washes in the morning and a bridge party at night: the American housewife between the wars." *Women's studies* 3.2 (1976) 147–72. ISSN 0049-7878. ▸ Influential study finding origins of feminine mystique—modern middle-class ideal of female fulfillment in servantless, appliance-laden domesticity—during 1920s, not after World War II. Reprinted in Friedman, Shade, and Capozzoli 40.443 and Scharf and Jensen 44.268. [JGC]

44.329 Joann Vanek. "Time spent in housework." In *A heritage of her own: toward a new social history of American women.* Nancy F. Cott and Elizabeth H. Pleck, eds., pp. 499–506. New York: Simon & Schuster, 1979. ISBN 0-671-25068-X (cl), 0-671-25069-8 (pbk). ▸ Brief overview of government surveys showing that, despite technological improvements, no decline in overall time spent in housework occurred from 1920 to 1960. [JGC]

Sexuality, Health, and Culture

44.330 Wini Breines. *Young, white, and miserable: growing up female in the fifties.* Boston: Beacon, 1992. ISBN 0-8070-7502-7. ▸ Intelligent analysis of painful contradictions of 1950s for white middle-class girls. Feminist movement of 1960s as culmination of series of smaller rebellions against conventional roles. [LGB]

44.331 Vern L. Bullough and Bonnie Bullough. "Lesbianism in the 1920s and 1930s: a newfound study." *Signs* 2.4 (1977) 895–904. ISSN 0097-9740. ▸ Unusual 1938 manuscript from Salt Lake

City, Utah, describing lives of approximately twenty-five lesbians in community. [JGC]

44.332 Madeline D. Davis and Elizabeth Lapovsky Kennedy. "Oral history and the study of sexuality in the lesbian community: Buffalo, New York, 1940–1960." In *Unequal sisters: a multicultural reader in U.S. women's history.* Ellen Carol DuBois and Vicki L. Ruiz, eds., pp. 387–99. New York: Routledge, 1990. ISBN 0-415-90271-1 (cl), 0-415-90272-X (pbk). ▸ Description of strict division of roles between "butch" and "femme" lesbians, based on oral history. Unique culture fostered group and self-satisfaction culminating in gay pride movement of late 1960s. [LGB]

44.333 Benita Eisler. *Private lives: men and women of the fifties.* New York: Watts, 1986. ISBN 0-531-15010-0. ▸ Provocative oral histories of sixteen college graduates between 1950 and 1960, analyzing their stories in terms of popular culture and media. Explores myth and reality behind relationships, sexuality, and family. [LGB]

44.334 Lillian Faderman. *Odd girls and twilight lovers: a history of lesbian life in twentieth-century America.* 1991 ed. New York: Penguin, 1992. ISBN 0-14-017122-3. ▸ Comprehensive survey of lesbian experiences in United States since 1900. [LGB]

44.335 Peter G. Filene. *Him/her/self: sex roles in modern America.* 2d ed. Baltimore: Johns Hopkins University Press, 1986. ISBN 0-8018-2893-7 (cl), 0-8018-2895-3 (pbk). ▸ During 1890–1980, middle-class expectations about men's and women's roles underwent fundamental shift from "Victorian" to "modern" after World War I. Evidence from private documents as well as popular literature. [JGC]

44.336 Molly Haskell. *From reverence to rape: the treatment of women in the movies.* 2d ed. Chicago: University of Chicago Press, 1987. ISBN 0-226-31884-2 (cl), 0-226-31885-0 (pbk). ▸ Influential analysis of changes in depiction of women in films since 1920s. Heyday for strong women in 1930s, followed by weak images in 1940s and 1950s. [LGB]

44.337 David M. Kennedy. *Birth control in America: the career of Margaret Sanger.* 1970 ed. New Haven: Yale University Press, 1971. ISBN 0-300-01202-0 (cl, 1970), 0-300-01495-3 (pbk). ▸ Critical biography of Sanger and analysis of birth control movement she spearheaded, 1914–43. Movement's shift from radical effort aimed at working class to more moderate middle-class campaign embodied in Planned Parenthood. [JGC]

44.338 Mirra Komarovsky. *Blue-collar marriage.* 2d ed. New Haven: Yale University Press, 1987. ISBN 0-300-03918-2 (cl), 0-300-03858-5 (pbk). ▸ One of earliest case studies of working-class marriages and role of housewife. Argues that wife and husband operated in very different spheres. [LGB]

44.339 Kristin Luker. *Abortion and the politics of motherhood.* 1984 ed. Berkeley: University of California Press, 1985. ISBN 0-520-04314-6 (cl, 1984), 0-520-05597-7 (pbk). ▸ Valuable comparative study of women in pro-choice and pro-life movements, based on interviews and questionnaire. Distinct life paths led women to each movement and viewpoint. [LGB]

44.340 Patricia Mellencamp. "Situation comedy, feminism, and Freud: discourse of Gracie and Lucy." In *Studies in entertainment: critical approaches to mass culture.* Tania Modleski, ed., pp. 80–95. Bloomington: Indiana University Press, 1986. ISBN 0-253-35566-4 (cl), 0-253-20395-3 (pbk). ▸ Model analysis of two of most popular television shows of 1950s which featured women comics as stars. Suggests these women used humor to offer critique of traditional femininity. [LGB]

44.341 James Reed. *The birth control movement in American society: from private vice to public virtue.* 1978 ed. Princeton: Princeton University Press, 1983. ISBN 0-691-09404-7 (cl), 0-691-02830-3 (pbk). ▸ Revisionist study arguing for diversity of motivations and strategies behind struggle for medical and social legitimation of contraception: feminism, family stability, and social conservatism. From nineteenth century to creation of "the pill" in 1950s. [JGC]

44.342 Mary P. Ryan. "The projection of a new womanhood: the movie moderns in the 1920s." In *Decades of discontent.* 1983 ed. Lois Scharf and Joan M. Jensen, eds., pp. 113–30. Boston: Northeastern University Press, 1987. ISBN 1-55553-013-3 (pbk). ▸ Useful discussion of "new woman" that shows 1920s movies helped to inculcate new ideal of femininity for young women: self-confident, sexually alluring, and able to escape tedium of clerical work via upwardly mobile marriage. [JGC]

44.343 Christina Simmons. "Companionate marriage and the lesbian threat." *Frontiers* 4.3 (1979) 54–59. ISSN 0160-9009. ▸ Early effort to explain definition of lesbianism as threatening form of sexual deviance by linking it to use of companionate marriage ideal in social science and popular advice literature of 1920s and 1930s. [JGC]

44.344 Rickie Solinger. *Wake up little Susie: single pregnancy and race before Roe v. Wade.* New York: Routledge, 1992. ISBN 0-415-90448-X. ▸ Detailed and groundbreaking study of treatment of unwed mothers, 1945–65. Argues that public opinion depicted black women as naturally able to take care of children, while unwed white mothers were psychologically suspect. [LGB]

44.345 Nancy Pottishman Weiss. "Mother, the invention of necessity: Dr. Spock's Baby and Child Care." *American quarterly* 29 (1977) 519–46. ISSN 0003-0678. ▸ Stimulating comparison of advice of early child-rearing books to 1946 classic. Observes that earlier books stressed maternal well-being while Spock's book expected mothers to focus on children's needs. [LGB]

Great Depression

44.346 Julia Kirk Blackwelder. *Women of the Depression: caste and culture in San Antonio, 1929–1939.* College Station: Texas A&M University Press, 1984. ISBN 0-89096-177-8. ▸ Monograph on differences in coping with Depression hardships among white, African American, and Mexican American women. Caste as most appropriate theoretical approach to understanding these differences. [JGC]

44.347 John Arthur Garraty. *The Great Depression: an inquiry into the causes, course, and consequences of the worldwide depression as seen by contemporaries and in the light of history.* 1986 ed. New York: Anchor and Doubleday, 1987. ISBN 0-385-24085-6 (pbk). ▸ Broad survey showing how ordinary people got by and governments responded. Much international comparison. [JTL]

44.348 Ruth Milkman. "Women's work and the economic crisis: some lessons from the Great Depression." In *A heritage of her own: toward a new social history of American women.* Nancy F. Cott and Elizabeth H. Pleck, eds., pp. 507–41. New York: Simon & Schuster, 1979. ISBN 0-671-25068-X (cl) 0-671-25069-8 (pbk). ▸ Rigidity of sexual segregation of occupations ironically afforded women some protection against unemployment during Great Depression while pushing women to increase unpaid domestic labors to compensate for lost income. Excellent starting point for Depression's impact on women. [JGC]

44.349 Lois Scharf. *To work and to wed: female employment, feminism, and the Great Depression.* Westport, Conn.: Greenwood, 1980. ISBN 0-313-21445-X (cl), 0-313-25059-6 (pbk), ISSN 0147-104X. ▸ Monograph using both census statistics and periodical literature to show Depression's damaging impact on feminist goal of combining career and marriage: intensified domestic labor, gains in paid employment confined to low-status jobs, and heightened hostility to married women in work force. [JGC]

World War II

44.350 Karen Tucker Anderson. "Last hired, first fired: black women workers during World War II." *Journal of American history* 69.1 (1982) 82–97. ISSN 0021-8723. ▸ Pioneering study of persistence during tight World War II labor market of segregation and other forms of discrimination keeping black women at bottom of job hierarchy. Evidence largely from St. Louis. [JGC]

44.351 Karen Tucker Anderson. *Wartime women: sex roles, family relations, and the status of women during World War II.* Westport, Conn.: Greenwood, 1981. ISBN 0-313-20884-0. ▸ Monograph on underlying continuity in attitudes toward women's social roles despite wartime upheavals. Uses evidence largely from government reports, popular periodicals. Focus on Seattle, Baltimore, and Detroit. [JGC]

44.352 D'Ann Campbell. *Women at war with America: private lives in a patriotic era.* Cambridge, Mass.: Harvard University Press, 1984. ISBN 0-674-95475-0. ▸ Innovative study based on private letters and documents, shows continuity of values despite women's changing employment experiences during World War II as evidenced by transition to suburban ideal of companionate, child-centered marriage of postwar decades. Women as WACs, nurses, factory workers, volunteers, and housewives. [JGC]

44.353 Leila J. Rupp. *Mobilizing women for war: German and American propaganda, 1939–1945.* Princeton: Princeton University Press, 1978. ISBN 0-691-04649-2. ▸ Careful, comparative study of government manipulation of images to increase women's paid employment while upholding traditional sex roles. [JGC]

44.354 William M. Tuttle, Jr. *"Daddy's gone to war": the Second World War in the lives of America's children.* New York: Oxford University Press, 1993. ISBN 0-19-504905-5. ▸ Interviews and other data combine to provide clear account of impact, then and later, of World War II on American children. [JTP]

ETHNIC AND RACE RELATIONS
General Studies

44.355 Reynolds Farley and Walter Allen. *The color line and the quality of life in America.* 1987 ed. New York: Oxford University Press, 1989. ISBN 0-19-506029-6. ▸ Comprehensive, balanced study of African American conditions. Emphasizes economic and demographic trends; focus on 1940s to 1980s. [NMK]

44.356 John Hope Franklin and August Meier, eds. *Black leaders of the twentieth century.* Urbana: University of Illinois Press, 1982. ISBN 0-252-00870-7 (cl), 0-252-00939-8 (pbk). ▸ Excellent scholarly essays concerning major figures in African American life. [NMK]

44.357 Paula Giddings. *When and where I enter: the impact of black women on race and sex in America.* 1984 ed. Toronto: Bantam, 1985. ISBN 0-553-34225-8 (pbk). ▸ Accessible, narrative analysis from African American women's perspective of their impact on civil rights and women's rights movements. Also, overview of role in slavery, migration, urbanization, and two world wars. [NMK]

44.358 Robert Huckfeldt and Carol Wetzel Kohfeld. *Race and the decline of class in American politics.* Urbana: University of Illinois Press, 1989. ISBN 0-252-01600-9. ▸ Survey since 1964 drawing heavily on statistics, model building, and simulation. [NMK]

44.359 Gerald David Jaynes and Robin M. Williams, Jr., eds. *A common destiny: blacks and American society.* Washington, D.C.: National Academy Press, 1989. ISBN 0-309-03998-3 (cl), 0-309-03988-6 (pbk). ▸ Massive report of Committee on the Status of Black Americans, Commission on Behavioral and Social Sciences and Education, National Research Council, on trends in black experience since World War II in tradition of Myrdal (44.362) and Kerner Commission (44.463) studies. Despite changes, significant problems remain. [NMK]

44.360 Nicholas Lemann. *The promised land: the great black migration and how it changed America.* 1991 ed. New York: Vintage, 1992. ISBN 0-679-73347-7 (pbk). ‣ Study of black sharecroppers' move to Chicago; also larger story of African American diaspora from rural South to urban North since World War II and response of Washington policy makers to ghetto poverty. Very readable. [NMK]

44.361 Manning Marable. *Race, reform, and rebellion: the second Reconstruction in black America, 1945–1990.* 2d ed. Jackson: University Press of Mississippi, 1991. ISBN 0-87805-505-3 (cl), 0-87805-493-6 (pbk). ‣ Focuses on emergence of African American working-class protest movements. Blames continued racial inequality on conservatism of African American elites, white racism, and deterioration of urban infrastructure. African American socialist perspective. [NMK]

44.362 Gunnar Myrdal. *An American dilemma: the Negro problem and modern democracy.* 1944 ed. 2 vols. New York: Pantheon, 1975. ISBN 0-394-73042-9 (v. 1, pbk), 0-394-73043-7 (v. 2, pbk). ‣ Classic, exhaustive study of race relations combining sociology and history. Challenged Americans to bring treatment of African Americans into line with accepted American ideals. [NMK]

44.363 Dorothy K. Newman, ed. *Protest, politics, and prosperity: black Americans and white institutions, 1940–1975.* New York: Pantheon, 1978. ISBN 0-394-41202-8 (cl), 0-394-73448-3 (pbk). ‣ Scholarly essays evaluating socioeconomic status of African Americans since Myrdal's assessment in 1940. Enforceable sanctions against discrimination, general economic prosperity, and militant constituency yielded substantial gains. [NMK]

44.364 Talcott Parsons and Kenneth B. Clark, eds. *The Negro American.* 1966 ed. Boston: Beacon, 1970. ISBN 0-8070-4183-1 (pbk). ‣ Essays by well-known historians, sociologists, political scientists, and others on context of plight of African Americans. Historiographically significant, among first scholarship to respond to 1960s urban race crisis. [NMK]

44.365 Alphonso Pinkney. *The myth of black progress.* Cambridge: Cambridge University Press, 1984. ISBN 0-521-25983-5 (cl), 0-521-31047-4 (pbk). ‣ Analysis of status of African Americans since 1964 Civil Rights Act. Challenges neoconservative posture that race no longer important aspect of struggle for socioeconomic equality. [NMK]

44.366 Richard Polenberg. *One nation divisible: class, race, and ethnicity in the United States since 1938.* New York: Viking, 1980. ISBN 0-670-22497-9. ‣ Well-written survey, using wide array of sources. Though precise nature and effects of racial, ethnic, and class divisions have changed, distinctions continue to shape lives of most Americans. [NMK]

SEE ALSO
40.332 Lawrence H. Fuchs. *The American kaleidoscope.*

Multiethnic Studies

44.367 Ronald H. Bayor. *Neighbors in conflict: the Irish, Germans, Jews, and Italians of New York City, 1929–1941.* 2d ed. Urbana: University of Illinois Press, 1988. ISBN 0-252-01437-5 (pbk). ‣ In-depth analysis of ethnic conflict of 1930s. Not explainable by simple prejudice; interlocking, mutual reinforcement of factors pertaining to real and perceived threats to self-interest. Foreign affairs, residential succession, and political campaigns played role. [NMK]

44.368 John Bodnar, Roger Simon, and Michael P. Weber. *Lives of their own: blacks, Italians, and Poles in Pittsburgh, 1900–1960.* Urbana: University of Illinois Press, 1982. ISBN 0-252-00880-4.

‣ Innovative and detailed comparison of differing experiences of immigrant groups to city. Urban environment neither destroyed premigration cultures, nor allowed them to persist unchanged. [NMK]

44.369 John Crewdson. *The tarnished door: the new immigrants and the transformation of America.* New York: Times Books, 1983. ISBN 0-8129-1042-7. ‣ Compelling introduction to problem of illegal immigration by Pulitzer Prize–winning journalist. Suggests aliens do not hurt United States; country that calls itself free cannot fully control borders. [NMK]

44.370 Peter K. Eisinger. *The politics of displacement: racial and ethnic transition in three American cities.* New York: Academic Press, 1980. ISBN 0-12-235560-1. ‣ Useful monograph which compares reactions of white elites to election of black mayors in Atlanta and Detroit in 1973 to the transition to Irish mayors in Boston in late nineteenth and early twentieth centuries. [NMK]

44.371 Herbert J. Gans. *The urban villagers: group and class in the life of Italian-Americans.* 2d ed. New York and London: Free Press and Collier Macmillan, 1982. ISBN 0-02-911250-8 (cl), 0-02-911240-0 (pbk). ‣ Classic participant-observer study of white working-class, ethnic community in Boston, subsequently demolished by urban renewal. Middle-class reformers imposed values on community that merely appeared dysfunctional. [NMK]

44.372 Nathan Glazer and Daniel Patrick Moynihan. *Beyond the melting pot: the Negroes, Puerto Ricans, Jews, Italians, and Irish of New York City.* 2d ed. Cambridge, Mass.: MIT Press, 1970. ISBN 0-262-07039-1 (cl), 0-262-57022-X (pbk). ‣ Influential melting pot as comforting, but neither true nor helpful, notion. Racial and ethnic identities continue from generation to generation and have transformed themselves into interest groups of varying strengths. [NMK]

44.373 Jonathan Kaufman. *Broken alliance: the turbulent times between blacks and Jews in America.* New York: Scribner's, 1988. ISBN 0-684-18699-3. ‣ Account by journalist on years since World War II, particularly within civil rights movement. Five individual and one family case study create hopeful but nuanced perspective on the relations between these groups. [NMK]

44.374 Stanley Lieberson. *A piece of the pie: blacks and white immigrants since 1880.* Berkeley: University of California Press, 1980. ISBN 0-520-04123-2. ‣ Valuable, well-researched look at wide range of factors in comparing African Americans and southern and Eastern European immigrants to explain why European immigrants fared better in United States. Emphasizes institutional discrimination. [NMK]

44.375 Michael Novak. *Rise of the unmeltable ethnics: politics and culture in the seventies.* 1972 ed. New York: Macmillan, 1975. ‣ Controversial book celebrating ethnic diversity in United States; melting pot no longer a desirable description. [NMK]

44.376 Alejandro Portes and Ruben G. Rumbaut. *Immigrant America: a portrait.* Berkeley: University of California Press, 1990. ISBN 0-520-06894-7 (cl), 0-520-07038-0 (pbk). ‣ Account of diverse adaptations of new (post-1965) immigrants. Celebrates positive effect they have had on American life and economy. [NMK]

44.377 David M. Reimers. *Still the golden door: the Third World comes to America.* 2d ed. New York: Columbia University Press, 1992. ISBN 0-231-07680-0 (cl), 0-231-07681-9 (pbk). ‣ Balanced survey of policy since Immigration Act of 1965, when bulk of newcomers no longer came from Europe. Emphasis on connection with foreign policy rather than economic factors. [NMK]

44.378 Judith E. Smith. *Family connections: a history of Italian and Jewish immigrant lives in Providence, Rhode Island, 1900–1940.* Albany: State University of New York Press, 1985. ISBN 0-87395-

964-7 (cl), 0-87395-965-5 (pbk). ▸ Detailed and innovative study of family history in larger socioeconomic context. Ethnic groups influence on each other as well as interaction with American culture and institutions. Oral and quantitative as well as traditional sources. [NMK]

44.379 Paul R. Spickard. *Mixed blood: intermarriage and ethnic identity in twentieth-century America.* Madison: University of Wisconsin Press, 1989. ISBN 0-299-12110-0. ▸ Study of African American, Japanese, and Jewish marriage practices. Comparisons with marriage patterns of other groups of European or Christian background. [NMK]

SEE ALSO
48.357 Gil Loescher and John A. Scanlan. *Calculated kindness.*

American Indians

44.380 Marjane Ambler. *Breaking the iron bonds: Indian control of energy development.* Lawrence: University Press of Kansas, 1990. ISBN 0-7006-0422-7 (cl), 0-7006-0518-5 (pbk). ▸ Generally optimistic survey of struggle for tribal control of energy resources on which their livelihood depended. Focuses on Council of Energy Resource Tribes. Contains general background on Indian history. [NMK]

44.381 Alison R. Bernstein. *American Indians and World War II: toward a new era in Indian affairs.* Norman: University of Oklahoma Press, 1991. ISBN 0-8061-2330-3. ▸ War led to developments in tribal governments and federal policies and altered conditions within tribal communities. Pathbreaking examination. [JTL]

44.382 Colin G. Calloway, ed. *New directions in American Indian history.* Norman: University of Oklahoma Press, 1988. (D'Arcy McNickle Center bibliographies in American Indian history, 1.) ISBN 0-8061-2147-5. ▸ Useful essays and bibliographies charting developments in historiography since 1983. [NMK]

44.383 Donald L. Fixico. *Termination and relocation: federal Indian policy, 1945–1960.* Albuquerque: University of New Mexico Press, 1986. ISBN 0-8263-0908-9. ▸ Discussion of three-fold federal policy under presidents Truman and Eisenhower: relocation from reservations to cities, end to tribal-federal relations, and transfer to state jurisdiction. Good introduction to post–World War II federal American Indian policy. [NMK]

44.384 Laurence M. Hauptman. *Formulating American Indian policy in New York state, 1970–1986.* Albany: State University of New York Press, 1988. ISBN 0-88706-754-9 (cl), 0-88706-755-7 (pbk). ▸ Based on report to governor of New York. Includes overview of state–American Indian relations since 1777. Critical of state's delivery of social services and misguided focus on land-rights claims. [NMK]

44.385 Harry A. Kersey, Jr. *The Florida Seminoles and the New Deal, 1933–1942.* Boca Raton: Florida Atlantic University Press, 1989. ISBN 0-8130-0928-6. ▸ Specialized study explores uneven effects of federal policies to assimilate American Indians, who developed culture of resistance. [TCL]

44.386 Sharon O'Brien. *American Indian tribal governments.* Norman: University of Oklahoma Press, 1989. ISBN 0-8061-2199-8. ▸ Survey, contemporary and historical, of American Indian self-governance and relations with whites and federal government. [NMK]

44.387 Kenneth R. Philp. *John Collier's crusade for Indian reform, 1920–1954.* Tucson: University of Arizona Press, 1977. ISBN 0-8165-0595-0 (cl), 0-8165-0472-5 (pbk). ▸ Indian policy reformer, founder of American Indian Defense Association, and commissioner of Indian Affairs, 1933–45. Architect of shift in federal policy from assimilation to cultural pluralism. Sound biography, emphasis on political context. [NMK]

Asian Americans

44.388 Nathan Caplan, John K. Whitmore, and Marcella H. Choy. *The boat people and achievement in America: a study of economic and educational success.* Ann Arbor: University of Michigan Press, 1989. ISBN 0-472-09397-5. ▸ Study of Southeast Asian immigrants who arrived in 1978. Sociological study of Asian immigrants to United States cities. Attributes relative prosperity to individual motivation. [NMK]

44.389 Roger Daniels. *Concentration camps, North America: Japanese in the United States and Canada during World War II.* Rev. ed. Malabar, Fla.: Krieger, 1981. ISBN 0-89874-025-8. ▸ Standard treatment on conception, execution, and aftermath of Japanese internment during World War II. [NMK]

44.390 Roger Daniels, Sandra C. Taylor, and Harry H. L. Kitano, eds. *Japanese Americans: from relocation to redress.* Rev. ed. Seattle: University of Washington Press, 1991. ISBN 0-295-97117-7. ▸ Varied and fascinating collection of many short essays from International Conference on Relocation and Redress of 1983, includes analysis by scholars and accounts by internees. [NMK]

44.391 Arthur W. Helweg and Usha M. Helweg. *An immigrant success story: East Indians in America.* Philadelphia: University of Pennsylvania Press, 1990. ISBN 0-8122-8228-0. ▸ Overview of immigration from India since 1790, emphasis since 1947. Generally smooth acceptance by host society; existence in United States as model minority. [NMK]

44.392 Peter H. Irons. *Justice at war.* New York: Oxford University Press, 1983. ISBN 0-19-503273-X. ▸ Informative legal history of cases upholding constitutionality of Japanese internment during World War II. Highlights racism and tortured logic and suppression of evidence by government officials. [NMK]

Hispanic Americans

44.393 Frank D. Bean and Marta Tienda. *The Hispanic population of the United States.* New York: Russell Sage Foundation, 1987. ISBN 0-87154-104-1 (cl), 0-87154-105-X (pbk). ▸ Overview of Hispanic population, based on census data, 1960, 1970, 1980, for Mexicans, Puerto Ricans, and Cubans. Covers wide range of demographic, sociological, and economic issues. [NMK]

44.394 James D. Cockcroft. *Outlaws in the promised land: Mexican immigrant workers and America's future.* New York: Grove, 1986. ISBN 0-394-54592-3 (cl), 0-394-62365-7 (pbk). ▸ Overview of role and importance of mostly undocumented Mexican workers in development of American economy and industry and of economic relationship between United States and Mexico. Argues American policy exploitive. Controversial thesis convincingly argued. [NMK/EH-D]

44.395 Suzanne Forrest. *The preservation of the village: New Mexico's Hispanics and the New Deal.* Albuquerque: University of New Mexico Press, 1989. ISBN 0-8263-1135-0 (cl), 0-8263-1147-4 (pbk). ▸ Scholarly, well-written account of how idealistic New Dealers hoped to preserve preindustrial communities from decay of modern society. Teaching of modern economic values and techniques undermined this aim. [NMK]

44.396 Mario T. Garcia. *Mexican Americans: leadership, ideology, and identity, 1930–1960.* New Haven: Yale University Press, 1989. ISBN 0-300-04246-9. ▸ Well-crafted survey of first generation born in United States, showing ideological diversity that laid groundwork for Mexican American movements of 1960s and 1970s. Challenges view that group accommodated negative judgments of whites. [NMK]

44.397 Leo Grebler et al. *Mexican-American people: the nation's second largest minority.* New York: Free Press, 1970. ▸ Encyclopedic treatment of Mexican American population in five southwestern states. Sociological treatment, but in historical context. [NMK]

44.398 Abraham Hoffman. *Unwanted Mexican Americans in the Great Depression: repatriation pressures, 1929–1939.* Tucson: University of Arizona Press, 1974. ISBN 0-8165-0366-4. ‣ Nearly one-half million people returned to Mexico. Federal and local policies, discrimination, and economic downturn pushed them back; promises of land and cultural ties pulled them back. Specialized, but readable analysis focuses on California, though national dimensions explored. [NMK]

44.399 Felix Roberto Masud-Piloto. *With open arms: Cuban migration to the United States.* Totowa, N.J.: Rowman & Littlefield, 1988. ISBN 0-8476-7566-1. ‣ Succinct, but deeply critical analysis of Open Door policy since Cuban Revolution of 1959. Challenges notion of United States' humanitarian motivation; cold war with Soviet Union explains acceptance of migrants. [NMK]

44.400 Mauricio Mazon. *The zoot suit riots: the psychology of symbolic annihilation.* Austin: University of Texas Press, 1984. ISBN 0-292-79801-6. ‣ Innovative, in-depth study of Los Angeles riots of 1943. Argues that riots were not primarily motivated by racial hatred against Mexican Americans in stylish zoot suits, but were instead opportunity for soldiers to relieve wartime anxieties through symbolic enemy. [NMK]

44.401 Matt S. Meier and Feliciano Rivera. *The Chicanos: a history of Mexican Americans.* New York: Hill & Wang, 1972. ISBN 0-8090-3416-6 (cl), 0-8090-1365-7 (pbk). ‣ Survey since Spanish contact, ends with discussion of four important Mexican American leaders of 1960s. [NMK]

44.402 Carlos Munoz, Jr. *Youth, identity, and power: the Chicano movement.* London: Verso, 1989. ISBN 0-86091-197-7 (cl), 0-86091-913-7 (pbk). ‣ Groundbreaking history recovers role of Mexican men in civil rights and radical student movements of 1960s, who rejected accommodationist view of their parents and fashioned politics based on ethnic pride and consciousness. [NMK]

44.403 Alejandro Portes and Robert L. Bach. *Latin journey: Cuban and Mexican immigrants in the United States.* Berkeley: University of California Press, 1985. ISBN 0-520-05003-7 (cl), 0-520-05004-5 (pbk). ‣ Longitudinal study over six years of legally admitted Cuban and Mexican men, mid to late 1970s. Examines issues of class, ethnicity, integration, and cultural resilience. Sociological study, using sophisticated methodology. [NMK]

44.404 Mark Reisler. *By the sweat of their brow: Mexican immigrant labor in the United States, 1900–1940.* Westport, Conn.: Greenwood, 1976. ISBN 0-8371-8894-6. ‣ Scholarly examination of development of federal policy, public reaction toward Mexican laborers' immigration to United States, reasons for migration, and life and thoughts of workers themselves. [NMK]

44.405 Virginia E. Sanchez Korrol. *From colonia to community: the history of Puerto Ricans in New York, 1917–1948.* Westport, Conn.: Greenwood, 1983. ISBN 0-313-23458-2, ISSN 0196-7088. ‣ Solid community structure based on homeland customs developed before heavy migration after World War II. Values informed political and socioeconomic interaction with host land. Sensitive account based on voices of Puerto Ricans themselves. [NMK]

African Americans: Cultural and Intellectual Trends

44.406 Jervis Anderson. *This was Harlem: a cultural portrait, 1900–1950.* New York: Farrar, Straus & Giroux, 1982. ISBN 0-374-27623-4 (cl), 0-374-51757-6 (pbk). ‣ Accessible and kaleidoscopic history follows area from primarily white origins to hey-

day as international center of African American culture, to poverty and despair. Leaders died, clubs moved downtown, churches remained. Pictures and word portraits. [NMK]

44.407 Stokely Carmichael and Charles V. Hamilton. *Black power: the politics of liberation in America.* New York: Random House, 1967. ISBN 0-394-70033-3. ‣ Description of rise and content of black power movement, mid to late 1960s, and conditions that spawned it. Controversial account by two movement's leaders. [NMK]

44.408 Harold Cruse. *The crisis of the Negro intellectual.* 1967 ed. New York: Quill, 1984. ISBN 0-688-01390-2 (cl), 0-688-03886-7 (pbk). ‣ Radical assessment of black power movement by way of review of African American intellectual history. African American nationalism without viable political philosophy ineffectual; failure most clear during Harlem renaissance. Marxist slant. [NMK]

44.409 St. Clair Drake and Horace R. Cayton. *Black metropolis: a study of Negro life in a northern city.* Rev. ed. 2 vols. New York: Harcourt Brace & World, 1970. ‣ Classic description and analysis of African American community on Chicago's South Side. [NMK]

44.410 Melvin Patrick Ely. *The adventures of Amos 'n' Andy: a social history of an American phenomenon.* New York: Free Press, 1991. ISBN 0-02-909502-6. ‣ Accessible and fascinating discussion of significance of long-running radio and television comedy; presented both unsavory and humanized stereotypes, also commonalities of lower-middle-class life. Contributed to low-level changes in racial thinking of many whites. [NMK]

44.411 Charles P. Henry. *Culture and African American politics.* Bloomington: Indiana University Press, 1990. ISBN 0-253-32754-7. ‣ Provocative survey of African American culture, argues for distinctive African American politics rooted in moral vision and international insight. [NMK]

44.412 Nathan Irvin Huggins. *The Harlem renaissance.* 1971 ed. New York: Oxford University Press, 1977. ISBN 0-19-501665-3. ‣ Critical reassessment in wider context of American culture. Except for jazz, little truly original created. Shows interdependence of white and black artistry. Important study. [NMK]

44.413 Walter A. Jackson. *Gunnar Myrdal and America's conscience: social engineering and racial liberalism, 1938–1947.* Chapel Hill: University of North Carolina Press, 1990. ISBN 0-8078-1911-5. ‣ Well-researched study of author of *An American Dilemma* (44.362). Discusses organization of work, reception, and legacy. [NMK]

44.414 Bruce Kellner, ed. *The Harlem renaissance: a historical dictionary for the era.* 1984 ed. New York and London: Methuen and Routledge & Kegan Paul, 1987. ISBN 0-416-01671-5 (pbk). ‣ Over 1,500 indexed entries on well- and lesser-known blacks and whites associated with phenomenon. Very good introduction to topic. [NMK]

44.415 David L. Lewis. *When Harlem was in vogue.* 1981 ed. New York: Oxford University Press, 1989. ISBN 0-19-505969-7 (pbk). ‣ Study of Harlem renaissance, 1905–35, concentrating on 1920s. Broader than Huggins 44.412 but less literary analysis. Clear color line between black and white; social distance between lighter-skinned talented tenth and darker hoi polloi. [NMK]

44.416 Morton Sosna. *In search of the silent South: southern liberals and the race issue.* New York: Columbia University Press, 1977. ISBN 0-231-03843-7. ‣ Thoughtful, critical studies of leading southern intellectuals, mid-twentieth century. [NMK]

44.417 Jules Tygiel. *Baseball's great experiment: Jackie Robinson and his legacy.* New York: Oxford University Press, 1983. ISBN

0-19-503300-0. ▸ Well-researched account of impact of first African American to play major league baseball. [NMK]

BLACK-WHITE RACE RELATIONS
Racism and Its Opponents

44.418 Numan V. Bartley. *The rise of massive resistance: race and politics in the South during the 1950s.* Baton Rouge: Louisiana State University Press, 1969. ISBN 0-8071-0848-0. ▸ Detailed, at times overly judicious, account of movement against desegregation in the eleven former Confederate states, primarily in realm of education. [NMK]

44.419 Dominic J. Capeci, Jr. *Race relations in wartime Detroit: the Sojourner Truth housing controversy of 1942.* Philadelphia: Temple University Press, 1984. ISBN 0-87722-339-4. ▸ Account of tensions between African and Polish Americans leading to violence over African American occupation of public housing project. Race relations watershed, prefigures 1960s riots. Sophisticated, exhaustive treatment. [NMK]

44.420 Dan T. Carter. *Scottsboro: a tragedy of the American South.* Rev. ed. Baton Rouge: Louisiana State University Press, 1979. ISBN 0-8071-0568-6 (cl), 0-8071-0498-1 (pbk). ▸ Case study of court case in early thirties. Nine African American teenagers tried, convicted, and sentenced to death for rape of two white women in rural Alabama. Powerful, detailed account reveals political and social implications. [NMK]

44.421 Richard M. Dalfiume. *Desegregation of the U.S. armed forces: fighting on two fronts, 1939–1953.* Columbia: University of Missouri Press, 1969. ISBN 0-8262-8318-7. ▸ Informative, well-researched discussion of struggle over segregation in military under presidents Franklin Roosevelt and Truman in its wider political and social context. [NMK]

44.422 Scott Ellsworth. *Death in a promised land: the Tulsa race riot of 1921.* Baton Rouge: Louisiana State University Press, 1982. ISBN 0-8071-0878-2. ▸ Whites attacked more than 1,000 black homes; twenty-two blacks, nine whites killed in ensuing riot. Fine study of one of century's most serious racial confrontations. [NMK]

44.423 Ronald P. Formisano. *Boston against busing: race, class, and ethnicity in the 1960s and 1970s.* Chapel Hill: University of North Carolina Press, 1991. ISBN 0-8078-1929-8 (cl), 0-8078-4292-3 (pbk). ▸ Analysis of city's struggle with school desegregation. Study of opposition of whites and gap between promise of democracy and ghetto poverty. Complements more pessimistic account of journalist Lukas 44.428. [NMK]

44.424 Kenneth T. Jackson. *The Ku Klux Klan in the city, 1915–1930.* New York: Oxford University Press, 1967. ▸ Study of America's largest wave of Klan activity. Not just southern and rural, also response to tensions of growing cities of the mid-Southwest. Klan members not primarily simple-minded, violent bigots but rather Americans with wide range of anxieties. [NMK]

44.425 William D. Jenkins. *Steel valley Klan: the Ku Klux Klan in Ohio's Mahoning Valley.* Kent, Ohio: Kent State University, 1990. ISBN 0-87338-415-6. ▸ Revisionist study of Klan in 1920s. Klan not extremist organization; drew from broad cross-section of white Protestant society. Racial, sectarian biases reined in and run (unsuccessfully) like conventional civic-action group. [NMK]

44.426 James H. Jones. *Bad blood: the Tuskegee syphilis experiment, a tragedy of race and medicine.* Rev. ed. New York: Free Press, 1992. ISBN 0-02-916675-6 (cl), 0-02-916676-4 (pbk). ▸ Balanced, highly readable account of study of "Untreated Syphilis in the Male Negro" in rural Alabama, 1932–72. Reveals racism of white medical establishment and complicity of African American middle-class institutions that sponsored research. [NMK]

44.427 Richard Kluger. *Simple justice: the history of Brown vs. the Board of Education and black America's struggle for equality.* 1975 ed. New York: Vintage, 1977. ISBN 0-394-47289-6 (cl, 1975), 0-394-72255-8 (pbk). ▸ Exhaustive study of legal, political, and sociological developments and personalities leading to landmark case outlawing segregation in public schools. [NMK]

44.428 J. Anthony Lukas. *Common ground: a turbulent decade in the lives of three American families.* 1985 ed. New York: Vintage, 1986. ISBN 0-394-41150-1 (cl, 1985), 0-394-74616-3 (pbk). ▸ Gripping study of three families (African American, Irish American, and Protestant) facing turmoil surrounding Boston's court-ordered school desegregation battle, late 1960s to early 1970s. Addresses complexities of race, class, and authority in urban America, emphasizing class. See also Formisano 44.423. [NMK]

44.429 Morris J. MacGregor, Jr. *Integration of the armed forces, 1940–1965.* Washington, D.C.: United States Department of the Army, Center for Military History, 1981. ▸ Basic history of racial integration of armed forces. Indicts services for failures and incomplete successes. Quest for military efficiency foremost among many causes of integration. [NMK/BBY]

44.430 J. Harvie Wilkinson III. *From Brown to Bakke: the Supreme Court and school integration, 1954–1978.* New York: Oxford University Press, 1979. ISBN 0-19-502567-9. ▸ Well-informed survey of legal history and social context of Supreme Court's landmark *Brown vs. Board of Education* case of 1954 and school desegregation cases waged in its aftermath. Some discussion of affirmative action. [NMK]

44.431 Raymond Wolters. *The burden of Brown: thirty years of school desegregation.* Knoxville: University of Tennessee Press, 1984. ISBN 0-87049-423-6. ▸ Highly critical study of five school desegregation cases, four of which failed. Concludes though desegregation proper in theory, courts wrongly assumed responsibility for social policy more appropriately left to elected officials. [NMK]

Race and Class Relations

44.432 Ken Auletta. *The underclass.* New York: Random House, 1982. ISBN 0-394-52343-1 (cl), 0-394-7138-8 (pbk). ▸ Reporter's research on New York jobs program with implications for question of urban underclass. Author has empathy for wide range of challenges and limits of poor minority participants. [NMK]

44.433 Robert D. Bullard, ed. *In search of the New South: the black urban experience in the 1970s and 1980s.* Tuscaloosa: University of Alabama Press, 1989. ISBN 0-8173-0425-8. ▸ Studies of six cities. Status of middle-class African Americans improved, but condition of ghetto blacks worsened. South will not be "new" until African Americans obtain economic parity. [NMK]

44.434 Kenneth B. Clark. *Dark ghetto: dilemmas of social power.* 1965 ed. Middletown, Conn.: Wesleyan University Press, 1989. ISBN 0-8195-6226-2. ▸ Influential but gloomy survey of inner-city African American life by leading African American psychologist. [NMK]

44.435 William H. Harris. *Keeping the faith: A. Philip Randolph, Milton P. Webster, and the Brotherhood of Sleeping Car Porters, 1925–37.* Urbana: University of Illinois Press, 1977. ISBN 0-252-00453-1. ▸ Comprehensive and sensible study of leadership activities of important African American union in years before its recognition by Pullman. [NMK]

44.436 Arnold R. Hirsch. *Making the second ghetto: race and housing in Chicago, 1940–1960.* Cambridge: Cambridge University Press, 1983. ISBN 0-521-24569-9 (cl), 0-521-31506-9 (pbk). ▸ Well-researched, scholarly study brings history of ghetto into second half of century. Public and business sectors combined with intransigent racism of white ethnics to extend Chicago's African American ghetto. [NMK]

44.437 Christopher Jencks. *Rethinking social policy: race, poverty, and the underclass*. Cambridge, Mass.: Harvard University Press, 1992. ISBN 0-674-76678-4. ‣ Thoughtful, often revisionist, chapters on education, crime, and economic status with policy suggestions. [NMK]

44.438 Christopher Jencks and Paul E. Peterson, eds. *The urban underclass*. Washington, D.C.: Brookings Institution, 1991. ISBN 0-8157-4606-7 (cl), 0-8157-4605-9 (pbk). ‣ Well-researched essays by leading social scientists. [NMK]

44.439 Robin D. G. Kelley. *Hammer and hoe: Alabama Communists during the Great Depression*. Chapel Hill: University of North Carolina Press, 1990. ISBN 0-8078-1921-2 (cl), 0-8078-4288-5 (pbk). ‣ Study of party activism of working-class African Americans, 1930s to demise in 1950s. African American members shaped Marxist agenda into tool for racial equality. [NMK]

44.440 Bart Landry. *The new black middle class*. Berkeley: University of California Press, 1987. ISBN 0-520-05942-5 (cl), 0-520-06465-8 (pbk). ‣ Useful survey of civil rights gains and expanding economy which defused somewhat white resistance to black entry into skilled jobs. Sees gaps widening between white and black middle class and between middle class and underclass. [NMK]

44.441 August Meier and Elliott M. Rudwick. *Black Detroit and the rise of the UAW*. New York: Oxford University Press, 1979. ISBN 0-19-502561-X, (cl), 0-19-502895-3 (pbk). ‣ Important study of relationship between race and class. United Automobile Workers, federal government, and African American community interactions. African American workers changed from pro-industry to pro-union. [NMK]

44.442 Joe William Trotter, Jr. *Black Milwaukee: the making of an industrial proletariat, 1915–1945*. Urbana: University of Illinois Press, 1985. ISBN 0-252-01124-4 (cl), 0-252-06035-0 (pbk). ‣ Traces formation of African American working class; important historiographical essay in appendix. Neo-Marxist view that economic, proletarianization model describes African American history better than spatial, race-contact thrust of ghetto paradigm. [NMK]

44.443 Joe William Trotter, Jr. *Coal, class, and color: blacks in southern West Virginia, 1915–1932*. Urbana: University of Illinois Press, 1990. ISBN 0-252-01707-2 (cl), 0-252-06119-5 (pbk). ‣ Scholarly study of southern rural African Americans who became coal miners within context of social and employment segregation. Close attention to class dynamics and power of miners to shape their own destinies. [NMK]

44.444 William Julius Wilson. *The declining significance of race: blacks and changing American institutions*. 2d ed. Chicago: University of Chicago Press, 1980. ISBN 0-226-90729-7 (pbk). ‣ Controversial revisionist interpretation tracing African Americans from slavery to 1950s. Civil rights movement opened opportunities, but cohort of desperate poor remained. Class status predicts quality of African American life better than nature of interactions with whites. [NMK]

44.445 William Julius Wilson. *The truly disadvantaged: the inner city, the underclass, and public policy*. Chicago: University of Chicago Press, 1987. ISBN 0-226-90130-0 (cl), 0-226-90131-9 (pbk). ‣ Landmark sociological study of origins of urban underclass. Though racial prejudice remains factor, emphasizes economic, industrial, and demographic changes since 1960. [NMK]

Struggles for Racial Justice and Civil Rights

44.446 Herman Belz. *Equality transformed: a quarter-century of affirmative action*. New Brunswick, N.J.: Transaction, 1991. ISBN 0-88738-882-5 (cl), 0-88738-393-9 (pbk). ‣ Critical, scholarly discussion of policies of preference and clash of theories of equality in national politics since 1950s with emphasis on years since Kennedy administration. Espouses conservative, equality-of-opportunity view. [NMK]

44.447 Jack M. Bloom. *Class, race, and the civil rights movement*. Bloomington: Indiana University Press, 1987. ISBN 0-253-31212-4 (cl), 0-253-20407-0 (pbk). ‣ Scholarly analysis of history of civil rights movement and structural roots of southern racism based on sociological theory. Racial attitudes embedded in class structure; decline of white elites allowed emergence of effective protest. [NMK]

44.448 Rhoda Lois Blumberg. *Civil rights: the 1960s freedom struggle*. Rev. ed. Boston: Twayne, 1991. ISBN 0-8057-3733-5 (cl), 0-8057-9734-3 (pbk). ‣ Brief, balanced, well-paced introduction to civil rights movement written from vantage point of social movement theory. [NMK]

44.449 Taylor Branch. *Parting the waters: America in the King years, 1954–63*. New York: Simon & Schuster, 1988. ISBN 0-671-46097-8 (cl), 0-671-68742-5 (pbk). ‣ Highly readable narrative of civil rights movement and its context, placing Martin Luther King, Jr., and struggle for racial equality at heart of American politics and culture. [NMK]

44.450 Albert Russell Buchanan. *Black Americans in World War II*. Santa Barbara, Calif.: Clio, 1977. ISBN 0-87436-227-6. ‣ Survey of both fighting and home fronts, including chapter on black women. War exacerbated tensions in social order; African American leaders strove to harness energy for change. [NMK]

44.451 Paul Burstein. *Discrimination, jobs, and politics: the struggle for equal employment opportunity in the United States since the New Deal*. Chicago: University of Chicago Press, 1985. ISBN 0-226-08134-6 (cl), 0-226-08135-4 (pbk). ‣ African Americans and other minorities have made employment gains, but only those sustainable by public opinion and political possibilities. Useful quantitative analysis supplements other forms of research. [NMK]

44.452 Dominic J. Capeci, Jr. *The Harlem riot of 1943*. Philadelphia: Temple University Press, 1977. ISBN 0-87722-094-8. ‣ Riot result of long-standing grievances and expectations aroused by World War II. Sets riot in context of local and national disturbances as well as Great Depression and New Deal. [NMK]

44.453 Clayborne Carson. *In struggle: SNCC and the black awakening of the 1960s*. Cambridge, Mass.: Harvard University Press, 1980. ISBN 0-674-44725-5. ‣ Sympathetic study of rise and decline of Student Non-Violent Coordinating Committee and its internal struggles; also its considerable impact on philosophy of civil rights and radical culture of 1960s. [NMK]

44.454 William H. Chafe. *Civilities and civil rights: Greensboro, North Carolina, and the black struggle for freedom*. New York: Oxford University Press, 1980. ISBN 0-19-502625-X (cl), 0-19-502919-4 (pbk). ‣ Pioneering account of race relations in Greensboro, 1940–70. Uses written and oral sources emphasizing role of ordinary citizens in civil rights movement. African Americans rejected mannerly communication insisted on by whites, called boldly for equality. [NMK]

44.455 Adam Fairclough. *To redeem the soul of America: the Southern Christian Leadership Conference and Martin Luther King, Jr*. Athens: University of Georgia Press, 1987. ISBN 0-8203-0898-6 (cl), 0-8203-0938-9 (pbk). ‣ Well-documented history of organization King lifted to prominence. Shows King to be unifying figure of institution "created for him but not by him." [NMK]

44.456 Sidney Fine. *Violence in the model city: the Cavanaugh administration, race relations, and the Detroit riot of 1967*. Ann Arbor: University of Michigan Press, 1989. ISBN 0-472-10104-8. ‣ Massive account, effects in local and national context. Disturbances not class-based or result of hoodlums. Rather, spontaneous warning directed against police and merchants, born of hope rather than despair. [NMK]

44.457   Lee Finkle. *Forum for protest: the black press during World War II.* Rutherford, N.J.: Fairleigh Dickinson University Press, 1975. ISBN 0-8386-1577-5. ▸ Standard treatment of African American press coverage and involvement in war effort. Contends African Americans more militant than African American press. [NMK]

44.458   Robert M. Fogelson. *Violence as protest: a study of riots and ghettos.* 1971 ed. Westport, Conn.: Greenwood, 1980. ISBN 0-313-22642-3. ▸ Early study of riots of 1960s, seen as understandable, self-conscious way to communicate legitimate grievances. Sociological treatment. [NMK]

44.459   David J. Garrow. *Protest at Selma: Martin Luther King, Jr., and the Voting Rights Act of 1965.* New Haven: Yale University Press, 1978. ISBN 0-300-02247-6 (cl), 0-300-02498-3 (pbk). ▸ Thorough study of proponents, opponents, and media coverage of voting rights agitation. Particular interest in movement dynamics, tactics, and role of media. [NMK]

44.460   Kenneth W. Goings. *"The NAACP comes of age": the defeat of Judge John J. Parker.* Bloomington: Indiana University Press, 1990. ISBN 0-253-32585-4. ▸ Recounts confirmation fight over Hoover nominee to Supreme Court in 1930. Argues victory heralded movement of African Americans from Republican to Democratic party and affirmed National Association for the Advancement of Colored People as leading voice of African Americans. [NMK]

44.461   David R. Goldfield. *Black, white, and southern: race relations and southern culture, 1940 to the present.* Baton Rouge: Louisiana State University Press, 1990. ISBN 0-8071-1532-0. ▸ Balanced, useful survey of southern civil rights movement. Blacks and whites shared understanding of history and belief in reconciling power of religion and region. Average white less committed to racism than usually believed. [NMK]

44.462   Herbert H. Haines. *Black radicals and the civil rights mainstream, 1954–1970.* Knoxville: University of Tennessee Press, 1988. ISBN 0-87049-563-1. ▸ Revisionist study by sociologist challenges notion that radical groups like Student Non-Violent Coordinating Committee and Black Panthers undermined support for more established civil rights groups. Rather, such groups achieved goals faster. [NMK]

44.463   Kerner Commission. *The Kerner report: the 1968 report of the National Advisory Commission on Civil Disorders.* 1968 ed. New York: Pantheon, 1988. ISBN 0-679-72078-2 (pbk). ▸ Landmark government study of 1967 riots. Complex historical, economic, and social forces, especially white racism, responsible. Argues federal programs necessary to prevent black and white societies, separate and unequal. [NMK]

44.464   Steven F. Lawson. *Black ballots: voting rights in the South, 1944–1969.* New York: Columbia University Press, 1976. ISBN 0-231-03978-6 (cl), 0-231-08352-1 (pbk). ▸ Well-written, even-handed narrative of voting rights obstacles and how they were overcome. Discussion of internal workings of rights groups. Though under real constraints, federal officials made compromises that needlessly delayed equality. [NMK]

44.465   Steven F. Lawson. *In pursuit of power: southern blacks and electoral politics, 1965–1982.* New York: Columbia University Press, 1985. ISBN 0-231-04626-X. ▸ Carries earlier study (44.464) forward to early 1980s. [NMK]

44.466   Steven F. Lawson. *Running for freedom: civil rights and black politics in America since 1941.* Philadelphia: Temple University Press, 1991. ISBN 0-87722-792-6. ▸ Well-researched study. Rather than emphasizing big leaders, institutions, or mass move-ments, highlights links between local action and national politics. Movement prepared African Americans for extensive political participation after 1965. [NMK]

44.467   Doug McAdam. *Freedom Summer.* New York: Oxford University Press, 1988. ISBN 0-19-504367-7. ▸ Compelling account based on interviews which refute idea that most Freedom Summer activists lost liberal idealism post-1964. Shows seeds of women's movement in civil rights movement. [NMK]

44.468   Doug McAdam. *Political process and the development of black insurgency, 1930–1970.* 1982 ed. Chicago: University of Chicago Press, 1985. ISBN 0-226-55551-8 (cl, 1982), 0-226-55552-6 (pbk). ▸ Growth of African American political strength result of more political opportunities and awareness of effectiveness as well as organizational possibilities. Sociological argument grounded on social strain and resource mobilization theory. [NMK]

44.469   Richard Patrick McCormick. *The black student protest movement at Rutgers.* New Brunswick, N.J.: Rutgers University Press, 1990. ISBN 0-8135-1575-0. ▸ Analysis of unrest, 1968–69, and university's response. Placed in wider context of voting and civil rights movements, Martin Luther King, Jr.'s death, and role of academia in addressing basic social tensions. [NMK]

44.470   August Meier and Elliott M. Rudwick. *CORE: a study in the civil rights movement.* 1973 ed. Urbana: University of Illinois Press, 1975. ISBN 0-252-00567-8. ▸ Encyclopedic study of rise and decline of Congress of Racial Equality, begun 1942 as small, interracial group committed to nonviolent direct action. Eventually nationwide constituency, but rejected interracial character. [NMK]

44.471   Aldon D. Morris. *The origins of the civil rights movement: black communities organizing for change.* New York: Free Press, 1984. ISBN 0-02-922120-X. ▸ Basic study of movement emphasizing economic and leadership resources of African American churches as its birthplace, 1953–63. Based on resource mobilization theory. [NMK]

44.472   Frank R. Parker. *Black votes count: political empowerment in Mississippi after 1965.* Chapel Hill: University of North Carolina Press, 1990. ISBN 0-8078-1901-8 (cl), 0-8078-4274-5 (pbk). ▸ Informed account by lawyer who led successful fight against second wave of disenfranchising policies. Refutes argument that African Americans received unfair advantages. See also Thernstrom 44.476. [NMK]

44.473   Howell Raines. *My soul is rested: movement days in the deep South remembered.* 1977 ed. Harmondsworth: Penguin, 1983. ISBN 0-14-006753-1 (pbk). ▸ Widely cited oral history of civil rights movement, Montgomery bus boycott to death of Martin Luther King, Jr. Interviews of famous and ordinary whites and blacks, both in and against movement. [NMK]

44.474   Harvard Sitkoff. "Racial militancy and interracial violence in the Second World War." *Journal of American history* 58.3 (1971) 661–81. ISSN 0021-8723. ▸ Useful article on African Americans and organizations that agitated, largely unsuccessfully, for immediate equality early in war. Government inaction led to serious rioting in 1943. [NMK]

44.475   Harvard Sitkoff. *The struggle for black equality, 1954–1992.* Rev. ed. New York: Hill & Wang, 1993. ISBN 0-374-52356-8. ▸ Well-paced survey of economic, legal, political, and social roots and effects of civil rights movement. Gains achieved by African American protest occurred in context of expanding economy, not at white expense. [NMK]

44.476   Abigail M. Thernstrom. *Whose votes count? Affirmative action and minority voting rights.* Cambridge, Mass.: Harvard University Press, 1987. ISBN 0-674-95195-6. ▸ Only area in which affirmative action has avoided controversy yet also spurred creation of minority voting districts which may undermine possibility for true racial cooperation. Important work. [NMK]

44.477 Mark V. Tushnet. *The NAACP's legal strategy against segregated education, 1925–1950.* Chapel Hill: University of North Carolina Press, 1987. ISBN 0-8078-1723-6 (cl), 0-8078-4173-0 (pbk). ‣ Detailed study of National Association for Advancement of Colored People's legal tactics in context of national politics. Battle challenging dual school system became frontal attack on segregation itself. [NMK]

44.478 Patrick S. Washburn. *A question of sedition: the federal government's investigation of the black press during World War II.* New York: Oxford University Press, 1986. ISBN 0-19-503984-X. ‣ Review of federal monitoring of African American press, 1917–43, with emphasis on 1941–43. Stresses government concern over African American papers' demands for civil rights at home while fighting racism abroad. [NMK]

44.479 Robert Weisbrot. *Freedom bound: a history of America's civil rights movement.* New York: Norton, 1990. ISBN 0-393-02704-X. ‣ Survey of movement, 1950s to 1980s, based on wide array of sources. Unity on statutory goals until 1965; liberal orthodoxy that constitutional guarantees ensured racial equality proved hollow. [NMK]

44.480 Nancy Joan Weiss. *Farewell to the party of Lincoln: black politics in the age of FDR.* Princeton: Princeton University Press, 1983. ISBN 0-691-04703-0 (cl), 0-691-10151-5 (pbk). ‣ Comprehensive account of African Americans' political activities during Franklin Roosevelt administration—issue activists, party politicians, and voters. Argues African Americans supported Roosevelt for economic reasons, despite president's poor record on racial issues. [TCL]

44.481 Stephen J. Whitfield. *A death in the Delta: the story of Emmett Till.* New York: Free Press, 1988. ISBN 0-02-935121-9. ‣ Well-written study of celebrated murder, 1955, of African American teenager in Mississippi; suspects acquitted. Emphasizes motivating effect on civil rights groups and African American community. [NMK]

44.482 Neil A. Wynn. *The Afro-American and the Second World War.* New York: Holmes & Meier, 1976. ISBN 0-8419-0231-3. ‣ Basic survey of war's effect on African American civilians and soldiers. Migration to war industry centers and military service led to rising expectations and domestic upheaval. Laid key groundwork for major gains of 1950s and 1960s. [NMK]

44.483 Robert L. Zangrando. *The NAACP crusade against lynching, 1909–1950.* Philadelphia: Temple University Press, 1980. ISBN 0-87722-174-X. ‣ Thoroughly researched account of congressional lobbying efforts, 1920s and 1930s, of National Association for the Advancement of Colored People. Campaign never produced antilynching act, though publicity surrounding effort helpful for cause of racial equality generally. [NMK]

Biographies and Autobiographies

44.484 Ralph David Abernathy. *And the walls came tumbling down: an autobiography.* New York: Harper & Row, 1989. ISBN 0-06-016192-2. ‣ Revealing, accessible autobiography of Martin Luther King, Jr.'s right-hand man and successor as head of Southern Christian Leadership Conference. Focuses on their lives together in movement and Abernathy's attempts to carry on King's legacy. [NMK]

44.485 James H. Cone. *Martin and Malcolm and America: a dream or a nightmare?* Maryknoll, N.Y.: Orbis, 1991. ISBN 0-88344-721-5. ‣ Provocative comparison and synthesis of lives and ideals of rival leaders of struggle for African American equal-

ity and their relationship to American society. Distance between them waned. [NMK]

44.486 Edmund David Cronon. *Black Moses: the story of Marcus Garvey and the Universal Negro Improvement Association.* 2d ed. Madison: University of Wisconsin Press, 1974. ISBN 0-299-01211-5 (cl), 0-299-01214-X (pbk). ‣ First full-length, even-handed biography of celebrated, controversial leader and molder of hopes and dreams of African Americans in 1920s. [NMK]

44.487 James Farmer. *Lay bare the heart: an autobiography of the civil rights movement.* 1985 ed. New York: New American Library, 1986. ISBN 0-452-25803-0 (pbk). ‣ Memoirs of civil rights leader and national director of Congress of Racial Equality, 1961–66. Honest, sometimes moving, critical assessment of self and movement. [NMK]

44.488 David J. Garrow. *Bearing the cross: Martin Luther King, Jr., and the Southern Christian Leadership Conference.* 1986 ed. New York: Vintage, 1988. ISBN 0-688-04794-7. ‣ Definitive biography, movingly chronicling King's life and role in civil rights struggle. [NMK]

44.489 Anne Moody. *Coming of age in Mississippi.* 1968 ed. New York: Dell, 1976. ISBN 0-440-31488-7 (pbk). ‣ Gripping autobiography of African American woman's experience in civil rights movement in South. [NMK]

44.490 William A. Nunnelley. *Bull Connor.* Tuscaloosa: University of Alabama Press, 1991. ISBN 0-8173-0495-9. ‣ Well-researched account of life of police commissioner primarily responsible for Birmingham's status as bastion of white supremacy during civil rights movement. Provides appropriate context. [NMK]

44.491 Bruce Perry. *Malcolm: the life of the man who changed Black America.* Barrytown, N.Y.: Station Hill Press; distributed by Talman, 1991. ISBN 0-88268-103-6. ‣ Controversial, revisionist biography. [NMK]

44.492 Paula F. Pfeffer. *A. Philip Randolph: pioneer of the civil rights movement.* Baton Rouge: Louisiana State University Press, 1990. ISBN 0-8071-1554-1. ‣ Labor organizer, insightful, long-time leader in struggle for African American equality. Paved way for militant nonviolence of 1960s. Comprehensive account places him in broad context of events of his time. [NMK]

44.493 Judith Stein. *The world of Marcus Garvey: race and class in modern society.* Baton Rouge: Louisiana State University Press, 1986. ISBN 0-8071-1236-4. ‣ Innovative and provocative analysis of Marcus Garvey and his middle-class United Negro Improvement Association. Class, rather than race, explained power and popularity. [NMK]

44.494 Denton L. Watson. *Lion in the lobby: Clarence Mitchell, Jr.'s struggle for the passage of civil rights laws.* New York: Morrow, 1990. ISBN 0-688-05097-2. ‣ Meticulously researched life of National Association for the Advancement of Colored People's Washington, D.C., bureau chief, 1950–78; important figure in mid-century civil rights movement. [NMK]

44.495 Nancy Joan Weiss. *Whitney M. Young, Jr., and the struggle for civil rights.* Princeton: Princeton University Press, 1989. ISBN 0-691-04757-X. ‣ Life and contributions of important African American leader, eventually executive director of National Urban League, 1961–71. Led normally social-service oriented African American organization more deeply into civil rights movement. [NMK]

44.496 Malcolm X and Alex Haley. *The autobiography of Malcolm X.* 1965 ed. New York: Ballantine, 1992. ISBN 0-345-37975-6 (cl), 0-345-37671-4 (pbk). ‣ Influential life story of important, radical, black Muslim leader. Malcolm X provided angry alternative to civil rights leader Martin Luther King, Jr. [NMK]

POLITICS AND PUBLIC POLICY

General Studies

44.497 Anthony Badger. *The New Deal: the Depression years, 1933–40.* New York: Farrar, Straus & Giroux, 1989. ISBN 0-374-52174-3 (pbk). ‣ Well-informed, up-to-date, detailed survey of New Deal policies. [TCL]

44.498 John Morton Blum. *V was for victory: politics and American culture during World War II.* New York: Harcourt Brace Jovanovich, 1976. ISBN 0-15-194080-0. ‣ Broadly synthetic, provocative essays. Released from Great Depression, American culture became security- and pleasure-seeking. [TCL]

44.499 John Morton Blum. *Years of discord: American politics and society, 1961–1974.* New York: Norton, 1991. ISBN 0-393-02969-7. ‣ Well-written survey stressing presidential politics and policies. [LGB]

44.500 John Braeman, Robert Hamlett Bremner, and David Brody, eds. *The New Deal. Vol. 1: The national level.* Columbus: Ohio State University Press, 1975. ISBN 0-8142-0200-4 (v. 1). ‣ Excellent starting point. Eleven essays covering African Americans, agriculture, economy, labor, lawyers, and World War II. [TCL]

44.501 Peter N. Carroll. *It seemed like nothing happened: the tragedy and promise of America in the 1970s.* 1982 ed. New Brunswick, N.J.: Rutgers University Press, 1990. ISBN 0-8135-1538-6 (pbk). ‣ Good, basic review of events of "me decade." Continuity and growth of political and social protest of 1960s. [LGB]

44.502 William H. Chafe. *The unfinished journey: America since World War II.* 2d ed. New York: Oxford University Press, 1991. ISBN 0-19-506626-X (cl), 0-19-506627-8 (pbk). ‣ Sweeping, well-informed survey of postwar history using triad of race, class, and gender to interpret period. Sees 1968 as linchpin of era. [LGB]

44.503 John Patrick Diggins. *The proud decades: America in war and peace, 1941–1960.* 1988 ed. New York: Norton, 1989. ISBN 0-393-02548-9 (cl, 1988), 0-393-95656-3 (pbk). ‣ Favorable account of years from World War II to President Kennedy's election. Emphasis on conservative expectations of government by public. [LGB]

44.504 Steve Fraser and Gary Gerstle, eds. *The rise and fall of the New Deal order, 1930–1980.* Princeton: Princeton University Press, 1989. ISBN 0-691-04761-8 (cl), 0-691-00607-5 (pbk). ‣ Wide-ranging collection of essays on various aspects of political arena. Stresses how weakening of labor movement and strength of regional and other political ties limited social reform. [LGB]

44.505 Frank B. Freidel. *Franklin D. Roosevelt: a rendezvous with destiny.* New York: Little, Brown, 1991. ISBN 0-316-29260-5. ‣ Fine biography sees Roosevelt as highly effective political figure. Distills mass of scholarship with focus on public events. [TCL]

44.506 Alonzo L. Hamby. *Liberalism and its challengers: from FDR to Bush.* 2d ed. New York: Oxford University Press, 1992. ISBN 0-19-507029-1 (cl), 0-19-507030-5 (pbk). ‣ Good introduction to leaders of this period. Uses biographical portraits to illustrate changes in liberal thought and practice since Great Depression. [LGB]

44.507 John Donald Hicks. *Republican ascendancy, 1921–1933.* New York: Harper & Row, 1960. ‣ Angry synthesis of period characterized by reactionary, business-dominated administrations and social and technological changes. [TCL]

44.508 Godfrey Hodgson. *America in our time.* 1976 ed. New York: Vintage, 1978. ISBN 0-394-72517-4. ‣ Readable, well-argued account of development of liberal consensus based on affluence during 1940s and 1950s. Consensus destroyed by Vietnam War. [LGB]

44.509 Haynes Johnson. *Sleepwalking through history: America in the Reagan years.* New York: Norton, 1991. ISBN 0-393-02937-9. ‣ Critical portrait of American politics and culture in 1980s. Concentrates on government and business scandals that author sees as representative of period. [LGB]

44.510 Barry Dean Karl. *The uneasy state: the United States from 1915–1945.* Chicago: University of Chicago Press, 1985. ISBN 0-226-42519-3 (cl, 1983), 0-226-42520-7 (pbk). ‣ Wide-ranging synthesis of period with focus on developing sense of national identity and problems of federal-state relations. [TCL]

44.511 William E. Leuchtenburg. *Franklin D. Roosevelt and the New Deal, 1932–1940.* New York: Harper & Row, 1963. ISBN 0-06-133025-6 (pbk). ‣ Comprehensive, authoritative synthesis. New Deal overcame powerful conservative opposition, helped labor and agriculture organize to compete with business for power and prestige. Failed, however, to provide for African Americans, women, and consumers. [TCL]

44.512 William E. Leuchtenburg. *The perils of prosperity, 1914–1932.* 1958 ed. Chicago: University of Chicago Press, 1973. ISBN 0-226-47369-4 (pbk). ‣ Standard account which traces demise of nineteenth-century liberal outlook and advent of modern industrial society during 1920s. Essays covering political, cultural, and social developments. [TCL]

44.513 Theodore J. Lowi. *The end of liberalism: the second republic of the United States.* 2d ed. New York: Norton, 1979. ISBN 0-393-05710-0 (cl), 0-393-09000-0 (pbk). ‣ Regulatory state created by New Deal inadequate to United States needs, producing crises of legitimacy. Liberalism's boldest ideas never fully practiced. Scholarly account rooted in political science. [TCL]

44.514 Richard Lowitt. *The New Deal and the West.* Bloomington: Indiana University Press, 1984. ISBN 0-253-34005-5. ‣ Pioneering effort at synthetic regional history. Focus on conservation policy and development. [TCL]

44.515 Allen J. Matusow. *The unraveling of America: a history of liberalism in the 1960s.* New York: Harper & Row, 1984. ISBN 0-06-015224-9 (cl), 0-06-091086-0 (pbk). ‣ Important, deeply researched interpretation of failure of attempts to solve problems of United States. Identifies weakness of policy initiatives of War on Poverty in their lack of planning and execution. [LGB]

44.516 J. Ronald Oakley. *God's country: America in the fifties.* 1986 ed. New York: Dembner; distributed by Norton, 1990. ISBN 0-934878-70-6 (cl, 1986), 0-942837-24-0 (pbk). ‣ Careful review of social and political events. Refutes notions of complacency of population. [LGB]

44.517 William O'Neill. *American high: the years of confidence, 1945–1960.* 1986 ed. New York: Free Press, 1989. ISBN 0-02-923680-0 (cl, 1986), 0-02-923679-7 (pbk). ‣ Readable, intelligent survey of life in United States in late forties and fifties. Compatibility of popular culture and Eisenhower's political style. [LGB]

44.518 Gary Orfield and Carole Ashkinaze. *The closing door: conservative policy and black opportunity.* Chicago: University of Chicago Press, 1991. ISBN 0-226-63272-5. ‣ Comprehensive case study of Atlanta in 1970s and 1980s focusing on growing economic inequality. Critical of conservative social policy, dominant since late 1960s, emphasizing market forces and self-reliance. [NMK]

44.519 Richard Polenberg. *War and society: the United States, 1941–1945.* 1972 ed. Westport, Conn.: Greenwood, 1980. ISBN 0-313-22348-3. ‣ General survey with liberal viewpoint. Main themes: expansion of state power and its limits and failures, modernization of agriculture and economy, wide-spread conviction war morally right. [TCL]

44.520 Arthur M. Schlesinger, Jr. *The coming of the New Deal.*

Vol. 2 of *The age of Roosevelt.* 1957 ed. Boston: Houghton-Mifflin, 1988. ISBN 0-395-48905-9 (pbk). ▸ First, standard liberal synthesis. Roosevelt and Americans triumphed over Depression, dangers of extremism, and reaction; created modern and beneficent liberal state, 1933–34. [TCL]

44.521 Arthur M. Schlesinger, Jr. *The crisis of the old order, 1919–1933.* Vol. 1 of *The age of Roosevelt.* 1957 ed. Boston: Houghton-Mifflin, 1988. ISBN 0-395-48903-2. ▸ First, standard liberal synthesis. Conservative politics of 1920s last gasp of nineteenth-century, business-dominated era; led to Great Depression and gave rise to 1932 Roosevelt candidacy. [TCL]

44.522 Arthur M. Schlesinger, Jr. *The politics of upheaval.* Vol. 3 of *The age of Roosevelt.* 1960 ed. Boston: Houghton-Mifflin, 1988. ISBN 0-395-48904-0. ▸ First, standard liberal synthesis. Extremists on Left and Right emerged; Roosevelt and American people charted sensible middle course, 1935–36. [TCL]

44.523 Frederick Siegel. *A troubled journey: from Pearl Harbor to Reagan.* New York: Hill & Wang, 1984. ISBN 0-8090-9443-6 (cl), 0-8090-0155-1 (pbk). ▸ Survey of postwar period exploring causes and results of expansion of federal power. [LGB]

44.524 Harvard Sitkoff. *A new deal for blacks: the emergence of civil rights as a national issue, the Depression decade.* 1978 ed. Oxford: Oxford University Press, 1981. ISBN 0-19-502418-4 (cl, 1978), 0-19-502893-7 (pbk). ▸ Standard liberal interpretation of racial politics of 1930s. Unappreciated turning point that prepared way for later, better known civil rights movement of 1950s and 1960s. [TCL/JTL]

The Courts and the United States Supreme Court

44.525 William H. Harbaugh. *Lawyer's lawyer: the life of John W. Davis.* 1973 ed. Charlottesville: University Press of Virginia, 1990. ISBN 0-8139-1267-9. ▸ Definitive biography of important legal traditionalist; placed private needs first, public second. [TCL]

44.526 Peter H. Irons. *The courage of their convictions.* New York: Free Press, 1988. ISBN 0-02-915670-X. ▸ Interesting, biographical study of sixteen plaintiffs to Supreme Court. Integrates oral and legal history to explore these civil rights cases. [LGB]

44.527 Peter H. Irons. *The New Deal lawyers.* Princeton: Princeton University Press, 1982. ISBN 0-691-04688-3. ▸ Specialized study of litigating styles in key Supreme Court cases about federal government power; focus on Agricultural Adjustment Administration, National Recovery Administration, National Labor Relations Board. Biographies of lawyers and judges; legal history of cases. [TCL]

44.528 William E. Leuchtenburg. "The Constitutional revolution of 1937." In *The Great Depression: essays and memoirs from Canada and the United States.* Victor Hoar, ed., pp. 31–83. Vancouver, B.C.: Copp Clark, 1969. ▸ Classic liberal interpretation. Dramatic reversal in court decisions allowed expansion of federal and state power, greater protection of individual's civil rights, and less protection for corporations. [TCL]

44.529 Anthony Lewis. *Gideon's trumpet.* 1964 ed. Birmingham, Ala.: Leslie B. Adams, Jr., 1991. ▸ Valuable, model case study of *Gideon v. Wainwright* (1963) which resulted in broad rights to counsel for indigent defendants. Introduction to workings of Supreme Court during 1960s in context of single case. [LGB]

44.530 Alpheus Thomas Mason. *Harlan Fiske Stone: pillar of the law.* 1956 ed. Hamden, Conn.: Archon, 1968. ▸ Standard biography of Columbia Law School dean (1910–23), attorney general (1924–25), Supreme Court justice (1925–40), and chief justice (1941–46). [TCL]

44.531 Bruce Allen Murphy. *The Brandeis/Frankfurter connec-*

tion: the secret political activities of two Supreme Court justices. New York: Oxford University Press, 1982. ISBN 0-19-503122-9. ▸ Provocative biography and legal history. Though restrained on bench, judges politically active behind scenes. [TCL]

44.532 Paul L. Murphy. *The Constitution in crisis times, 1918–69.* 1971 ed. New York: Harper & Row, 1972. ISBN 0-06-013118-7 (cl, 1971), 0-06-131617-2 (pbk). ▸ Thorough, standard treatment of major Supreme Court cases. [TCL]

44.533 David M. O'Brien. *Storm center: the Supreme Court in American politics.* 2d ed. New York: Norton, 1990. ISBN 0-393-95912-0. ▸ Introduction to function and politics of judicial branch. Focus on period since 1935 during which activist Court brought itself into center of politics. Third edition expected 1993. [LGB]

44.534 Karen Orren. *Belated feudalism: labor, the law, and liberal development in the United States.* Cambridge: Cambridge University Press, 1991. ISBN 0-521-41039-8 (cl), 0-521-42254-X (pbk). ▸ United States not liberal from start; labor law reflected feudal logic until changed by New Deal. Close reading of language in relevant legal decisions and labor and state actions. [TCL]

44.535 Michael E. Parrish. "The Hughes court, the Great Depression, and historians." *The historian* 40 (1978) 286–308. ISSN 0018-2370. ▸ Historiographic essay on major interpretations of Chief Justice Hughes's tenure, 1930–41. [TCL]

44.536 Melvin I. Urofsky. *The continuity of change: the Supreme Court and individual liberties, 1953–86.* Belmont, Calif.: Wadsworth, 1991. ISBN 0-534-12960-9. ▸ Useful summary of key rulings on civil liberties under Warren and Burger courts. Stresses dependence on precedent in both courts, rather than radical shifts in interpretation. [LGB]

44.537 Samuel Walker, Jr. *In defense of American liberties: a history of the ACLU.* New York: Oxford University Press, 1990. ISBN 0-19-504539-4. ▸ Comprehensive history of American Civil Liberties Union: internal politics, case histories. [TCL]

44.538 G. Edward White. *Earl Warren.* New York: Oxford University Press, 1982. ISBN 0-19-503121-0. ▸ Readable biography of chief justice. Insights into nature and causes of Court revolution of 1950s and 1960s. [LGB]

Presidents and the Executive Branch

44.539 Stephen E. Ambrose. *Eisenhower.* Vol. 2: *The president.* 1983 ed. New York: Simon & Schuster, 1984. ISBN 0-671-49901-4 (cl, 1983), 0-671-60565-8 (pbk). ▸ Careful account of strengths (fiscal policy, arms control) and weaknesses (civil rights, cold war) of this chief executive. Stresses his positive performance. [LGB]

44.540 Stephen E. Ambrose. *Nixon.* Vol. 1: *The education of a politician, 1913–1962.* Vol. 2: *The triumph of a politician, 1962–1972.* Vol. 3: *Ruin and recovery, 1973–90.* New York: Simon & Schuster, 1987–92. ISBN 0-671-52836-X (v. 1, cl), 0-671-52837-8 (v. 2, cl), 0-671-69188-0 (v. 3, cl), 0-671-65722-4 (v. 1, pbk), 0-671-72506-8 (v. 2, pbk). ▸ Details drive of highly successful politician of 1950s and 1960s. Puts Watergate in context of earlier Nixon misdeeds and political practices. Nixon's accomplishments and energies in foreign rather than domestic policy. [LGB]

44.541 Larry Berman, ed. *Looking back on the Reagan presidency.* Baltimore: Johns Hopkins University Press, 1990. ISBN 0-8018-3921-1 (cl), 0-8018-3922-X (pbk). ▸ Collection of essays exploring what did and did not change during Reagan presidency in terms of foreign policy, judiciary, congressional politics, and fiscal policy. [LGB]

44.542 William C. Berman. *The politics of civil rights in the Truman administration.* Columbus: Ohio State University Press,

1970. ISBN 0-8142-0142-3. ▸ Basic assessment of Truman's civil rights policy. Revises reputation as reformer by showing action motivated by fear of losing African American vote in 1948. [NMK]

44.543 John Morton Blum. *Roosevelt and Morgenthau.* 1970 ed. Boston: Houghton-Mifflin, 1972. ▸ President Franklin Roosevelt's treasury secretary was partisan of rural way of life, saw world politics as fight between good and evil. Comprehensive analysis of Morgenthau's 800-volume diary. [TCL]

44.544 Carl M. Brauer. *John F. Kennedy and the second Reconstruction.* New York: Columbia University Press, 1977. ISBN 0-231-03862-3. ▸ Sympathetic well-researched account of Kennedy's record on civil rights. Committed to racial equality on principle, not merely as expedient. [NMK]

44.545 Robert Fredrick Burk. *The Eisenhower administration and black civil rights.* Knoxville: University of Tennessee Press, 1984. ISBN 0-87049-431-7 (cl), 0-87049-493-7 (pbk). ▸ Argues that African American gains minimal under president who favored elimination of second-class treatment in some areas, but who failed to move beyond tepid support for voting rights and other constitutional guarantees. Effective synthesis of previous scholarship and primary research. [NMK]

44.546 David Burner. *Herbert Hoover, a public life.* 1978 ed. New York: Knopf, 1979. ISBN 0-394-46134-7. ▸ Comprehensive biography, from early years to death. [TCL]

44.547 David Burner. *John F. Kennedy and a new generation.* Oscar Handlin, ed. Glenview, Ill.: Scott, Foresman and Little, Brown College Division, 1988. ISBN 0-673-39810-2 (pbk). ▸ Brief overview of Kennedy's life and administration, studying his style and purpose. Attributes other changes during his presidency (student movement, détente) to Kennedy's spirit. [LGB]

44.548 James MacGregor Burns. *Roosevelt: soldier of freedom.* New York: Harcourt Brace Jovanovich, 1970. ISBN 0-15-178871-5. ▸ Stimulating analysis of President Franklin Roosevelt's wartime leadership; president deeply divided between realpolitik and idealism, with adverse policy consequences. [TCL]

44.549 James MacGregor Burns. *Roosevelt: the lion and the fox.* 1956 ed. Norwalk, Conn.: Easton, 1989. ▸ Well-researched, balanced account of President Franklin Roosevelt's acts from liberal perspective. Roosevelt's first term focused and purposeful; second, wayward and uncertain. [TCL]

44.550 Lou Cannon. *President Reagan: a role of a lifetime.* New York: Simon & Schuster, 1991. ISBN 0-671-54294-X. ▸ Thoughtful study of Reagan's career from California to White House. Stresses that this actor-politician was inadequate as administrator while highly influential as leader. [LGB]

44.551 Robert A. Caro. *The years of Lyndon Johnson.* Vol. 1: *The path to power.* Vol. 2: *Means of ascent.* New York: Knopf, 1982–91. ISBN 0-394-49973-5 (v. 1, cl), 0-394-52835-2 (v. 2, cl), 0-394-71654-X, (v. 1, pbk). ▸ First two volumes of detailed and harsh biography of this president, takes his life through 1948. Emphasizes hard drive for power, accommodation to corrupt politics, and relationship to broader trends in politics. [LGB]

44.552 Paul Keith Conkin. *Big Daddy from the Pedernales: Lyndon Baines Johnson.* Boston: Twayne, 1986. ISBN 0-8057-7762-8 (cl), 0-8057-7772-5 (pbk). ▸ Useful single-volume biography showing continuity from days as New Dealer in Texas to leadership in Washington. Certain personality traits, such as determination and impulsiveness, shaped his actions. [LGB]

44.553 Robert A. Dallek. *Lone star rising: Lyndon Johnson, 1908–1960.* New York: Oxford University Press, 1991. ISBN 0-19-505435-0. ▸ Well-researched, balanced account of pre-presidential career in context of changing political landscape. [LGB]

44.554 Robert J. Donovan. *Conflict and crisis: the presidency of Harry S. Truman, 1945–1948.* New York: Norton, 1977. ISBN 0-393-05636-8 (cl), 0-393-00924-6 (pbk). ▸ Detailed, balanced account of first term of presidency. Influence of aftermath of World War II on both foreign policy and domestic problems. [LGB]

44.555 Robert J. Donovan. *Tumultuous years: the presidency of Harry S. Truman, 1949–1953.* New York: Norton, 1982. ISBN 0-393-01619-6 (cl), 0-393-30164-8 (pbk). ▸ Second part of 44.554, with equally useful account of second term of Truman presidency. New initiatives common, but overall, term was not successful. [LGB]

44.556 James N. Giglio. *The presidency of John F. Kennedy.* Lawrence: University Press of Kansas, 1991. ISBN 0-7006-0515-0 (cl), 0-7006-0520-7 (pbk). ▸ Solid, fair-minded brief account; excellent starting place for study of Kennedy presidency. [JTP]

44.557 Doris Kearns Goodwin. *Lyndon Johnson and the American dream.* 1976 ed. New York: New American Library, 1977. ISBN 0-451-07609-5. ▸ Anecdotal, fascinating account that reveals Johnson as leader and manipulator. Places responsibility for failures of his presidency on man himself, seen as representative of good and bad in United States. [LGB]

44.558 Fred I. Greenstein. *The hidden-hand presidency: Eisenhower as leader.* New York: Basic Books, 1982. ISBN 0-465-02948-5 (cl), 0-465-02951-5 (pbk). ▸ Controversial account of Eisenhower's presidential style, emphasizing effectiveness. Argues he relied on subordinates, public support, and delegated authority to achieve most of his goals. [LGB]

44.559 Fred I. Greenstein, ed. *Leadership in the modern presidency.* Cambridge, Mass.: Harvard University Press, 1988. ISBN 0-674-51854-3 (cl), 0-674-51855-1 (pbk). ▸ Essays on each president since Franklin Roosevelt explore style and success of their leadership. Provides entry points into each administration and criteria for evaluating presidents. [LGB]

44.560 Alonzo L. Hamby. *Beyond the New Deal: Harry S. Truman and American liberalism.* New York: Columbia University Press, 1973. ISBN 0-231-03335-4. ▸ Carefully examines Truman's policies and actions to evaluate liberalism during cold war period. Reveals successes in expansion of social security and failures to achieve national health care or aid for education. Refutes New Left scholarship. [LGB]

44.561 Joan Hoff-Wilson. *Herbert Hoover: forgotten progressive.* Boston: Little, Brown, 1975. ▸ Influential revisionist interpretation. President Hoover, insightful critic of foreign policy, offered prescient critique of state growth; more active during Depression than popularly conceded. [TCL]

44.562 Kathleen Hall Jamieson. *Packaging the presidency: a history and criticism of presidential campaign advertising.* 2d ed. New York: Oxford University Press, 1992. ISBN 0-19-507298-7 (cl), 0-19-507299-5 (pbk). ▸ Detailed look at rise of television-based political campaigns. Focuses on forms, messages, and strategies behind new techniques. [LGB]

44.563 Haynes Johnson. *In the absence of power: governing America.* New York: Viking, 1980. ISBN 0-670-20548-6. ▸ Early account of Carter's presidency. Illustrates how outsider stance, used effectively by Carter during election, backfired during his presidency. [LGB]

44.564 Michael J. Lacey, ed. *The Truman presidency.* 1989 ed. Cambridge, Mass.: Woodrow Wilson International Center for Scholars and Cambridge University Press, 1991. ISBN 0-521-37559-2 (cl, 1989), 0-521-40773-7 (pbk). ▸ Collection of essays on Truman's policies and times, mostly exploring foreign policy, but including significant pieces on domestic issues. Stresses continuities between issues facing Truman and those of 1980s. [LGB]

44.565 William E. Leuchtenburg. *In the shadow of FDR: from Harry Truman to Ronald Reagan.* Rev. ed. Ithaca, N.Y.: Cornell University Press, 1989. ISBN 0-8014-2341-4 (cl), 0-8014-9559-8 (pbk). ▸ Original and readable analysis of personal and political legacy of Roosevelt on subsequent presidents. Use of Roosevelt as political symbol prevalent even if policy choices quite different. [LGB]

44.566 Donald J. Lisio. *Hoover, blacks, and lily-whites: a study of southern strategies.* Chapel Hill: University of North Carolina Press, 1985. ISBN 0-8078-1645-0. ▸ Revisionist, well-researched study of President Hoover, well-meaning but inept with regard to racial attitudes, and his effect on politics. Refutes that he was mean-spirited racist who forced African Americans out of southern Republican party leadership spots. [NMK]

44.567 Patrick J. Maney. *The Roosevelt presence: a biography of Franklin Delano Roosevelt.* New York: Twayne, 1992. ISBN 0-8057-7758-X (cl), 0-8057-7786-5 (pbk). ▸ Well-written brief study of Roosevelt as president. Useful starting place for study of subject. [JTP]

44.568 Donald R. McCoy. *Calvin Coolidge: the quiet president.* 1967 ed. Lawrence: University Press of Kansas, 1988. ISBN 0-7006-0350-6 (cl), 0-7006-0351-4 (pbk). ▸ Coolidge's inactive administration was what Americans wanted, not result of special flaw in Coolidge. Best available biography, focused on presidential years. [TCL]

44.569 Donald R. McCoy and Richard T. Reutten. *Quest and response: minority rights and the Truman administration.* Lawrence: University Press of Kansas, 1973. ISBN 0-7006-0099-X. ▸ Balanced coverage of African, Japanese, Mexican, Indian, Jewish, Catholic, and Puerto Rican Americans' struggle for equality. Asserts Truman primarily responsible for whatever rights these groups gained. [NMK]

44.570 Robert K. Murray. *The Harding era: Warren G. Harding and his administration.* Minneapolis: University of Minnesota Press, 1969. ISBN 0-8357-3333-5 (pbk). ▸ Comprehensive account of presidency. Capable president faced with difficult problems of postwar adjustment; set tone for Republican policies throughout decade. [TCL]

44.571 John Kennedy Ohl. *Hugh S. Johnson and the New Deal.* De Kalb: Northern Illinois University Press, 1985. ISBN 0-87580-110-2. ▸ Johnson's failure—personal and political—a tragedy. Familiar interpretation of National Recovery Administration head, using new source materials. [TCL]

44.572 Herbert S. Parmet. *JFK: the presidency of John F. Kennedy.* 1983 ed. Harmondsworth: Penguin, 1984. ISBN 0-14-007054-0 (pbk). ▸ Balanced account of Kennedy's term in office with focus on specific issues, such as civil rights and Bay of Pigs. Sees limitation of leadership despite popularity. [LGB]

44.573 Richard Polenberg. *Reorganizing Roosevelt's government: the controversy over executive reorganization, 1936–1939.* Cambridge, Mass.: Harvard University Press, 1966. ▸ Detailed history of President Franklin Roosevelt's failed Executive Reorganization Bill of 1937–38. Bill important in modern political science accounts as illustrative of limits of New Deal state building. [TCL]

44.574 Gerald L. Posner. *Case closed: Lee Harvey Oswald and the assassination of JFK.* New York: Random House, 1993. ISBN 0-679-41825-3. ▸ Well-documented refutation of many "conspiracy" theories about assassination. Focuses on Oswald. [JTP]

44.575 Arthur M. Schlesinger, Jr. *A thousand days: John F. Kennedy in the White House.* 1965 ed. New York: Fawcett, 1971. ISBN 0-449-30852-9 (cl), 0-449-30021-8 (pbk). ▸ Insider's account of president's term. Supportive, reveals some flaws in Kennedy's leadership style. [LGB]

44.576 T. H. Watkins. *Righteous pilgrim: the life and times of Harold Ickes, 1874–1952.* New York: Holt, 1990. ISBN 0-8050-0917-5. ▸ Exhaustive biography of New Deal secretary of interior, conservationist, and exemplar of modern liberalism who favored pluralism and government activism. [TCL]

44.577 Garry Wills. *Nixon agonistes: the crisis of the self-made man.* Rev. ed. New York: New American Library, 1979. ISBN 0-451-61750-9. ▸ Portrays Nixon as classic liberal. Interesting account of his life before Watergate. [LGB]

44.578 Betty Houchin Winfield. *FDR and the news media.* Urbana: University of Illinois Press, 1990. ISBN 0-252-01672-6. ▸ Detailed history of relations between president and press. Press resisted White House efforts to slant coverage in favor of New Deal, became less critical with onset of World War II. [TCL]

United States Congress

44.579 Charles W. Eagles. *Democracy delayed: congressional reapportionment and urban-rural conflict in the 1920s.* Athens: University of Georgia Press, 1990. ISBN 0-8203-1185-5. ▸ Traces evidence of conflict between urban and rural areas in congressional roll call votes on reapportionment. Pioneering research using quantitative and traditional historical methods. [TCL]

44.580 J. Joseph Huthmacher. *Senator Robert F. Wagner and the rise of modern liberalism.* 1968 ed. New York: Atheneum, 1971. ▸ Sympathetic survey of Wagner's role in Congress, especially in housing and labor legislation. Liberal legislation often initiated in Congress, not executive branch, during New Deal. [TCL]

44.581 Richard Lowitt. *George W. Norris: the persistence of a progressive, 1913–1933.* Urbana: University of Illinois Press, 1971. ISBN 0-252-00176-1. ▸ First part of standard biography of Nebraskan senator who was loyal agrarian progressive, often against federal trends. [TCL]

44.582 Richard Lowitt. *George W. Norris: triumph of a progressive, 1933–1944.* Urbana: University of Illinois Press, 1978. ISBN 0-252-00223-7. ▸ Norris worked closely with Franklin Roosevelt administration; sympathetic to president's ideas. Championed especially Tennessee Valley Authority project. Second part of standard biography. [TCL]

44.583 James T. Patterson. *Congressional conservatism and the New Deal: the growth of the conservative coalition in Congress, 1933–1939.* 1967 ed. Westport, Conn.: Greenwood, 1981. ISBN 0-313-22676-8. ▸ Standard study of conservative opposition to President Franklin Roosevelt's domestic policies. Provides biographies of conservative Democratic and Republican congressmen; focus on second term. [TCL]

44.584 James T. Patterson. *Mr. Republican: a biography of Robert A. Taft.* Boston: Houghton-Mifflin, 1972. ISBN 0-395-23938-4. ▸ Readable portrait of leading conservative of postwar era. Explores nature of republican conservatism and politics. [LGB]

44.585 Mark A. Peterson. *Legislating together: the White House and Capitol Hill from Eisenhower to Reagan.* Cambridge, Mass.: Harvard University Press, 1990. ISBN 0-674-52415-2. ▸ Study of relationship between presidency and Congress using both quantitative analysis of legislative success and interviews. Demonstrates high level of cooperation. [LGB]

44.586 James L. Sundquist. *The decline and resurgence of Congress.* Washington, D.C.: Brookings Institution, 1981. ISBN 0-8157-8224-1 (cl), 0-8157-8223-3 (pbk). ▸ Balanced, detailed study of relations between executive and legislative branches. Between 1921 and 1972, presidents tended to set agendas; since 1972, Congress has asserted itself through creation of independent monitoring agencies. [LGB]

44.587 Charles W. Whalen and Barbara Whalen. *The longest* *debate: a legislative history of the 1964 Civil Rights Act.* Cabin John, Md.: Seven Locks Press, 1985. ISBN 0-932020-34-8. ▸ Detailed account of passage of landmark statute using newspapers, congressional sources, personal papers, and interviews. [NMK]

Elections and Political Parties

44.588 Ellsworth Barnard. *Wendell Willkie, fighter for freedom.* Amherst: University of Massachusetts Press, 1971. ISBN 0-87023-088-3 (cl), 0-87023-095-6 (pbk). ▸ Standard biography of moderate republican presidential candidate in 1940. Led party to accept permanence of New Deal and internationalism; saved it from obsolescence. Standard biography. [TCL]

44.589 Earl Black and Merle Black. *Politics and society in the South.* Cambridge, Mass.: Harvard University Press, 1987. ISBN 0-674-68958-5 (cl), 0-674-68959-3 (pbk). ▸ Thorough examination of changes in political culture in this crucial region since 1950. Stresses political values of voters, especially their entrepreneurial individualism that shaped local and national allegiances. [LGB]

44.590 Earl Black and Merle Black. *The vital South: how presidents are elected.* Cambridge, Mass.: Harvard University Press, 1992. ISBN 0-674-94130-6. ▸ Explores dramatic shift in party allegiance from Democratic to Republican parties in South since 1960s, resulting in Republican advantage in presidential elections. [LGB]

44.591 David Burner. *The politics of provincialism: the Democratic party in transformation, 1918–1932.* 1968 ed. Cambridge, Mass.: Harvard University Press, 1986. ISBN 0-674-68940-2. ▸ Democratic party split between rural and urban interests until Depression, when President Franklin Roosevelt unified it. Broadly synthetic, influential. [TCL]

44.592 Walter Dean Burnham. *Critical elections and the mainsprings of American politics.* New York: Norton, 1970. ISBN 0-393-09962-8 (cl), 0-393-09397-2 (pbk). ▸ Seminal quantitative analysis of trends in voting and party alignment in twentieth century. Long-term weakening of Americans' allegiance to parties interrupted by New Deal; but weakening returned, signaling widespread discontent. [TCL]

44.593 Walter Dean Burnham. *The current crisis in American politics.* New York: Oxford University Press, 1982. ISBN 0-19-503219-5 (cl), 0-19-503220-9 (pbk). ▸ Influential collection of essays on decline in party support, emergence of combination of lack of faith in both political parties and presidential leadership during 1970s. [LGB]

44.594 Edwin Diamond and Stephen Bates. *The spot: the rise of political advertising on television.* 3d ed. Cambridge, Mass.: MIT Press, 1992. ISBN 0-262-04130-8 (cl), 0-262-54065-7 (pbk). ▸ Readable, balanced analysis of use and development of "polispots" since 1950s. How advertisements do and do not influence voters. [LGB]

44.595 Thomas Bryne Edsall. *The new politics of inequality.* New York: Norton, 1984. ISBN 0-393-01868-7. ▸ Integrates class and economics into readable brief history of change in support of Democratic and Republican parties since 1960s. Sees increase in poverty as result of weakness of Democrats. [LGB]

44.596 Thomas Byrne Edsall and Mary D. Edsall. *Chain reaction: the impact of race, rights, and taxes on American politics.* New York: Norton, 1991. ISBN 0-393-30903-7. ▸ Focuses on 1980s and background to 1992 campaign. Criticizes Democrats for losing working-class–based majorities in presidential politics. [JTP]

44.597 Thomas Ferguson. "Industrial conflict and the coming of the New Deal: the triumph of multinational liberalism in America." In *The rise and fall of the New Deal order, 1930–1980.* Gary Gerstle and Steve Fraser, eds., pp. 3–31. Princeton: Princeton University Press, 1989. ISBN 0-691-04761-8 (cl), 0-691-00607-5 (pbk). ▸ Provocative, neo-Marxist study of New Deal coalition-building at elite level. Labor-intensive, protectionist, industrialist elite joined by rising bloc of capital-intensive, multinational firms. Marxist history. [TCL]

44.598 Steven M. Gillon. *The Democrats' dilemma: Walter M. Mondale and the liberal legacy.* New York: Columbia University Press, 1992. ISBN 0-231-07630-4. ▸ Analysis of difficulties of liberalism, especially in 1960s, 1970s, and 1980s, with focus on Mondale. [JTP]

44.599 Paul Kleppner. *Chicago divided: the making of a black mayor.* De Kalb: Northern Illinois University Press, 1985. ISBN 0-87580-106-4 (cl), 0-87580-532-9 (pbk). ▸ Readable summary of forces leading to election of city's first African American mayor in 1983. Focus on African American organization and biracial and class coalitions. [NMK]

44.600 Everett C. Ladd, Jr. and Charles D. Hadley. *Transformation of the American party system: political coalitions from the New Deal to the 1970s.* 2d ed. New York: Norton, 1978. ISBN 0-393-05660-0 (cl), 0-393-09065-5 (pbk). ▸ Broad overview of election trends, shifts in popular support for parties after New Deal realignment. Party discipline declined, political system increasingly open and fluid. [TCL]

44.601 Allan J. Lichtman. *Prejudice and the old politics: the presidential election of 1928.* Charlotte: University of North Carolina Press, 1979. ISBN 0-8078-71358-3. ▸ Anti-Catholicism decisive to election outcome; prejudice a powerful, enduring feature of American society. Challenges more benign liberal view, especially Lubell 44.602. Quantitative political history buttressed with traditional historical sources. [TCL]

44.602 Samuel Lubell. *The future of American politics.* 1952 ed. Westport, Conn.: Greenwood, 1984. ISBN 0-313-24377-8. ▸ Strategic analysis of elections 1916–50, tracing effects of Roosevelt revolution, realignment of political parties and voters. Fast-paced analysis. [TCL]

44.603 Kevin P. Phillips. *The emerging Republican majority.* New Rochelle, N.Y.: Arlington House, 1969. ISBN 0-87000-058-6. ▸ Influential analysis of changes between 1940 and 1960s that led to virtual Republican dominance of presidential politics. Accurately predicted political shifts of 1970s and 1980s. [LGB]

44.604 Nicol C. Rae. *The decline and fall of the liberal Republicans: from 1952 to the present.* New York: Oxford University Press, 1989. ISBN 0-19-505605-1. ▸ Carefully details organizations and participants in this crucial faction. Shows how ineptitude and rise of party conservatives meant demise of this faction by 1970s. [LGB]

44.605 David W. Reinhard. *The Republican Right since 1945.* Lexington: University Press of Kentucky, 1983. ISBN 0-8131-1484-5. ▸ Influence of conservative branch of Republican party on both internal party struggles and broader politics. Focus on period 1945 to 1965 provides insight into strength of group in 1980s. [LGB]

44.606 Byron E. Shafer. *Quiet revolution: the struggle for the Democratic party and the shaping of post-reform politics.* New York: Russell Sage Foundation, 1983. ISBN 0-87154-765-1. ▸ Changes in rules regulating presidential conventions between 1968 and 1972 gave access to previously excluded groups. Reveals in detail how small changes in party policy resulted in dramatic change. [LGB]

44.607 Martin P. Wattenberg. *The decline of American political parties, 1952–1988.* Rev. ed. Cambridge, Mass.: Harvard University Press, 1990. ISBN 0-674-19432-2. ▸ Statistical analysis of causes of drop-off in partisanship in United States. Asserts that lack of partisan allegiance by members of Congress and candidate-centered politics main cause. [LGB]

44.608 Robert B. Westbrook. "Politics as consumption: managing the modern American election." In *The culture of consumption: critical essays in American history, 1880–1980*. Richard Wightman Fox and T. J. Jackson Lears, eds., pp. 143–73. New York: Pantheon, 1983. ISBN 0-394-51131-X (cl), 0-394-71611-6 (pbk). ▸ Review of development and changes in techniques of political consultant since 1930s. Deplores switch from convincing voters to choose candidate to marketing candidate to different sets of voters. [LGB]

State and Local Politics, Federalism

44.609 John M. Allswang. *The New Deal and American politics: a study in political change*. New York: Wiley, 1978. ISBN 0-471-02515-1 (cl), 0-471-02516-X (pbk). ▸ Extensive quantitative survey of local and state politics. New Deal perpetuated some urban political machines; encouraged states to start ambitious social programs, "little New Deals." [TCL]

44.610 Joseph L. Arnold. *The New Deal in the suburbs: a history of the Greenbelt town program*. Columbus: Ohio State University Press, 1971. ISBN 0-8142-0153-9. ▸ Specialist study tracing government attempt to create planned communities; finds program was confused and at odds with American political culture, abandoned as failure. [TCL]

44.611 Paul Keith Conkin. *Tomorrow a new world: the New Deal community program*. Ithaca, N.Y.: Cornell University Press for the American Historical Association, 1961. ▸ Survey of political ideas in 100 communities. [TCL]

44.612 Mark I. Gelfand. *A nation of cities: the federal government and urban America, 1933–1965*. New York: Oxford University Press, 1975. ISBN 0-19-501941-5. ▸ New Deal's relief, employment, and wartime planning policies emerged despite lack of federal commitment to cities; often undermined by local traditions and institutions. [TCL]

44.613 Thomas Kessner. *Fiorello H. LaGuardia and the making of modern New York*. 1989 ed. New York: Penguin, 1991. ISBN 0-14-014358-0 (pbk). ▸ Best biography of New York City congressman (1917–32) and mayor (1934–45). Determined politician, better executive than legislator, led New York to modernity. [TCL]

44.614 James T. Patterson. *The New Deal and the states: federalism in transition*. 1969 ed. Westport, Conn.: Greenwood, 1981. ISBN 0-313-22841-8. ▸ New Deal unable to make major changes in state politics and policies. Broadly synthetic, pioneering work on effect of New Deal on states. [TCL]

44.615 Lynn Spigel. *Make room for TV: television and the family ideal in post-war America*. Chicago: University of Chicago Press, 1992. ISBN 0-226-76966-6 (cl), 0-226-76967-4 (pbk). ▸ Accessible, fascinating account that focuses on effect of introduction of television between 1948 and 1960. Social, spatial, and cultural effect of this "window to the world." [TCL]

44.616 Bruce M. Stave. *The New Deal and the last hurrah: Pittsburgh machine politics*. 1970 ed. Pittsburgh: University of Pittsburgh Press, 1987. ISBN 0-8229-3200-8. ▸ Statistical analysis and local history. New Deal invigorated boss system by giving bosses control of federal relief funds and patronage; New Deal transfer of power from republican-democratic machines. Also available in photocopy from Ann Arbor: University Microfilms International, 1987. [TCL]

Policy and Government Agencies

44.617 James Bamford. *The puzzle palace: a report on America's most secret agency*. Rev. ed. Harmondsworth: Penguin, 1983. ISBN 0-14-006748-5 (pbk). ▸ Intellectually ambitious study of National Security Agency leadership, style, successes, and failures. Warns of growing bureaucratic efficiency in penetrating all forms of communication leading to Orwellian effect if not checked. [BBY]

44.618 William J. Barber. *From new era to New Deal: Herbert Hoover, the economists, and American economic policy, 1921–1933*. Cambridge: Cambridge University Press, 1986. ISBN 0-521-30526-8. ▸ Summary of President Hoover's economic thought, policies, and interplay with academics. Hoover closer to understanding Depression than most contemporary economists, but unwilling to act because of political philosophy. [TCL]

44.619 Edward D. Berkowitz. *America's welfare state: from Roosevelt to Reagan*. Baltimore: Johns Hopkins University Press, 1991. ISBN 0-8018-4127-5 (cl), 0-8018-4128-3 (pbk). ▸ Basic introduction to development of programs for poor, unemployed, and elderly since New Deal. [LGB]

44.620 Barton J. Bernstein. "The New Deal: the conservative achievements of liberal reform." In *Towards a new past: dissenting essays in American history*. 1968 ed. Barton J. Bernstein, ed., pp. 263–88. New York: Vintage, 1969. ▸ Pioneering New Left attack on consensus historiography. During Depression, New Deal helped stabilize capitalist order threatened by profound public discontent. [TCL]

44.621 Robert Hamlett Bremner, Gary W. Reichard, and Richard J. Hopkins, eds. *American choices: social dilemmas and public policy since 1960*. Columbus: Ohio State University Press, 1986. ISBN 0-8142-0368-X. ▸ Excellent starting point for histories of recent domestic social policies on poverty, civil rights, nuclear policy, and women's rights. Stress on influence of history on government action. [LGB]

44.622 Alan Brinkley. "The New Deal and the idea of the state." In *The rise and fall of the New Deal order, 1930–1980*. Gary Gerstle and Steve Fraser, eds., pp. 85–121. Princeton: Princeton University Press, 1989. ISBN 0-691-04761-8 (cl), 0-691-00607-5 (pbk). ▸ End of World War II marks American acceptance of large corporations and government. Fiscal stimulus, not regulation, central mission of government. [TCL]

44.623 Christiana Campbell. *The Farm Bureau Federation and the New Deal: a study of the making of national farm policy, 1933–1940*. 1962 ed. Urbana: University of Illinois Press, 1981. ISBN 0-8357-9676-0. ▸ American Farm Bureau Federation's favored policies (e.g., parity) conservative and unimaginative. Farmer and labor interests difficult to reconcile, complicated by sectional rivalries. Also available in photocopy from Ann Arbor: University Microfilms International. [TCL]

44.624 Thomas R. Dunlap. *DDT: scientists, citizens, and public policy*. Princeton: Princeton University Press, 1981. ISBN 0-691-04680-8. ▸ Account of ways in which dangers of pesticide were recognized. Interesting case study of how consciousness of environmental concerns developed in public and government. [LGB/AIM]

44.625 Richard A. Gabriel. *Military incompetence: why the American military doesn't win*. New York: Hill & Wang, 1985. ISBN 0-8090-6928-8 (cl), 0-8090-0166-7 (pbk). ▸ Ineffectiveness of bloated military establishment attributed to inadequate training, values, planning, procurement, logistical capacities, and flawed officer corps. Despite huge defense budgets, military incapable of success. Controversial study. [BBY]

44.626 David J. Garrow. *The FBI and Martin Luther King, Jr.: from "Solo" to Memphis*. New York: Norton, 1981. ISBN 0-393-01509-2. ▸ Comprehensive study reveals shocking institutional vendetta against King, fueled by racism, hatred of communism, and deep fear of cultural and political change for which King fought. [NMK]

44.627 Michael Goldfield. "Worker insurgency, radical organization, and New Deal labor legislation." *American political science* *review* 83 (1989) 1257–82. ISSN 0003-0554. ▸ Marxist analysis asserts that worker insurgency and radical organizations decisive in passage of labor legislation and growth of labor movement. Challenge to state-centered theories of Depression politics, especially Skocpol 44.670. [TCL]

44.628 William Graebner. *A history of retirement: the meaning and function of an American institution, 1885–1978.* 1980 ed. New Haven: Yale University Press, 1984. ISBN 0-300-02356-1 (cl, 1980), 0-300-03300-1 (pbk). ▸ Revisionist, administrative history concluding policies governing retirement derive not from needs of elderly but rather perceived political and economic needs. [TCL]

44.629 Hugh Davis Graham. *The civil rights era: origins and development of national policy.* New York: Oxford University Press, 1990. ISBN 0-19-504531-9. ▸ Detailed survey and interpretation of actions of Washington, D.C., elites, particularly Equal Employment Opportunity Commission, during 1960s and early 1970s. [NMK]

44.630 Hugh Davis Graham. *The uncertain triumph: federal education policy in the Kennedy and Johnson years.* Chapel Hill: University of North Carolina Press, 1984. ISBN 0-8078-1599-3. ▸ Thoughtful, brief analysis and interpretation of policies, 1961–68. Often critical. [JTL]

44.631 Nancy L. Grant. *TVA and black Americans: planning for the status quo.* Philadelphia: Temple University Press, 1990. ISBN 0-87722-626-1. ▸ Challenge to liberal historiography. Critical of New Deal's failure to bring greater racial equality to South. Cites limits of New Deal administrators; explores magnitude and kinds of opposition to change. [TCL]

44.632 Laurence M. Hauptman. *The Iroquois and the New Deal.* 1981 ed. Syracuse, N.Y.: Syracuse University Press, 1988. ISBN 0-8156-2247-3 (cl, 1981), 0-8156-2439-5 (pbk). ▸ Well-researched study identifies some beneficial consequences of New Deal for American Indians despite serious flaws. [TCL]

44.633 Robert H. Haveman. *Poverty policy and poverty research: the Great Society and the social sciences.* Madison: University of Wisconsin Press, 1987. ISBN 0-299-11150-4. ▸ Scholarly study of relationship between academic research and government as welfare policy developed during 1960s. Argues that policy stimulated research on poverty more than research influenced policy. [LGB]

44.634 Ellis Hawley. "Herbert Hoover, the commerce secretariat, and the vision of the 'associative state,' 1921–1928." *Journal of American history* 61 (1974) 116–40. ISSN 0021-8723. ▸ Influential interpretation of Hoover's political thought. As head of Commerce Department, ambitious Hoover sought ways to reconcile American individualism and scientific rationalism in modern economy. [TCL]

44.635 Ellis Hawley. *The New Deal and the problem of monopoly: a study in economic ambivalence.* 1966 ed. Princeton: Princeton University Press, 1974. ISBN 0-691-00564-8 (pbk). ▸ Foremost pluralist analysis of political-economic system that emerged from Depression. Not planned, rather array of interests competed for state favors. Planning for common good and long-term nearly impossible. Also available in photocopy from Ann Arbor, Mich.: University Microfilms International, 1980. [TCL]

44.636 Samuel P. Hays and Barbara D. Hays. *Beauty, health, and permanence: environmental politics in the United States, 1955–1985.* 1987 ed. Cambridge: Cambridge University Press, 1989. ISBN 0-521-32428-9 (cl, 1987), 0-521-38928-3 (pbk). ▸ Comprehensive and accessible account of modern conservation movement with focus on leading environmental groups and policymakers. Stresses ways that field is both highly politicized and not as effective as many wish. [LGB]

44.637 James A. Hodges. *New Deal labor policy and the southern cotton textile industry, 1933–1941.* Knoxville: University of Tennessee Press, 1986. ISBN 0-87049-496-1. ▸ Detailed study confirms accepted view that New Deal did little to improve condition of southern workers. Administrative and labor history. [TCL]

44.638 Jeanne Holm. *Women in the military: an unfinished revolution.* Rev. ed. Novato, Calif.: Presidio, 1992. ISBN 0-89141-450-9. ▸ Account of utilization of women in armed forces. Surveys changing values and organizational answers to military employment of women showing prejudice, irrationality, and inequality of past service policies. [BBY]

44.639 Dennis S. Ippolito. *Uncertain legacies: federal budget policy from Roosevelt through Reagan.* Charlottesville: University Press of Virginia, 1990. ISBN 0-8139-1287-3. ▸ Scholarly review of continuities and changes in size and cause of federal deficit since 1930s. Sees indexing of entitlements as major influence on deficit in recent years. [LGB]

44.640 Kenneth T. Jackson. "The spatial dimensions of social control: race, ethnicity, and government housing policy in the United States, 1918–1968." In *Modern industrial cities: history, policy, and survival.* Bruce M. Stave, ed., pp. 79–128. Beverly Hills, Calif.: Sage, 1981. ISBN 0-8039-1760-0 (cl), 0-8039-1761-9 (pbk). ▸ Federal housing policy, in accordance with preferences of majority of American citizens, helped move middle-class families to suburbs; had effect of putting seal of approval on ethnic and race discrimination. [NMK]

44.641 Don E. Kash and Robert W. Rycrofts. *U.S. energy policy: crisis and complacency.* Norman: University of Oklahoma Press, 1984. ISBN 0-8061-1869-5. ▸ Balanced, well-researched account of controversial area since 1973 oil crisis. Favors program of active government intervention similar to President Carter's. [LGB]

44.642 Lawrence C. Kelly. *The assault on assimilation: John Collier and the origins of Indian policy reform.* Albuquerque: University of New Mexico Press, 1983. ISBN 0-8263-0657-8. ▸ Traces Collier's career through 1928 intragovernmental debates. Argues Collier engineered major turning point in federal Indian policy—from assimilation to rudimentary pluralism—in mid-1920s. Also available in photocopy from Ann Arbor: University Microfilms International. [TCL]

44.643 Richard Stewart Kirkendall. *Social scientists and farm politics in the age of Roosevelt.* Columbia: University of Missouri Press, 1966. ▸ Department of Agriculture's early development of administrative, research, and lobbying apparatus anomalous in American state. Influential among political scientists making arguments about state capacity. [TCL]

44.644 Paul A. C. Koistinen. *The military-industrial complex: a historical perspective.* New York: Praeger, 1980. ISBN 0-03-055766-6. ▸ Thorough study traces evolution of military-industrial complex. Partnership of government with business destructive for armed forces, undermining professional military ethic and injuring capacity of Defense Department to deter or wage war. [BBY]

44.645 Michael J. Lacey, ed. *Government and environmental policies: essays on historical developments since World War II.* Washington, D.C.: Wilson Center Press; distributed by University Press of America, 1989. ISBN 0-943875-16-1 (cl), 0-943875-15-3 (pbk). ▸ Collection of informed essays exploring diverse subjects such as policy developments in nuclear power, rise of environmental lobbyists, and case studies of agencies such as National Park Service. [LGB]

44.646 Walter Laqueur. *A world of secrets: the uses and limits of intelligence.* New York: Basic Books, 1985. ISBN 0-465-09237-3. ▸ Comparative study of intelligence agencies. Focus on intelligence doctrine; failures; influence on policy, process, secrecy, and democratic accountability since World War II. [BBY]

44.647 Mark Hugh Leff. *The limits of symbolic reform: the New Deal and taxation, 1933–1939.* Cambridge: Cambridge University Press, 1984. ISBN 0-521-26268-2. ▸ President Franklin Roosevelt not interested in tax reform or redistribution of wealth. New Deal created two-part tax system: regressive provided most revenue, progressive provided opportunity for rhetoric. Survey of tax law and Washington politics. [TCL]

44.648 Robert Lekachman. *The age of Keynes.* 1966 ed. New York: McGraw-Hill, 1975. ISBN 0-07-037154-7. ▸ Summary of Keynes's general theory and applications by American policy makers. Written from committed pro-Keynesian viewpoint. [TCL]

44.649 Ray Lubove. *The struggle for social security, 1900–1935.* 2d ed. Pittsburgh: University of Pittsburgh Press, 1986. ISBN 0-8229-5379-X (pbk). ▸ Philosophy of voluntarism limited United States income maintenance programs. Close attention to political debates involved in numerous programs. [TCL]

44.650 Thomas K. McCraw. *Prophets of regulation: Charles Francis Adams, Louis D. Brandeis, James M. Landis, Alfred E. Kahn.* Cambridge, Mass.: Belknap, 1984. ISBN 0-674-71607-8 (cl), 0-674-71608-6 (pbk). ▸ Development of regulation related through thoughtful biographies of major figures. Stresses importance of individuals to process, suggests rules for successful regulation. [TCL]

44.651 Thomas K. McCraw. *TVA and the power fight: 1933–1939.* New York: Lippincott, 1971. ▸ Finds clash between American tradition of private power and New Deal's call for public regulation. Attention both to individual agendas and social milieu. [TCL]

44.652 Walter A. McDougall. . . . *the heavens and the earth: a political history of the space age.* New York: Basic Books, 1985. ISBN 0-465-02887-X (cl), 0-465-02888-8 (pbk). ▸ Study of decision to explore space interwoven with comparison of United States and Soviet Union's approach to this challenge and in context of cold war. Stress on developmental period of 1957 to 1964. Richly detailed pioneering work. [LGB]

44.653 Charles Murray. *Losing ground: American social policy, 1950–1980.* New York: Basic Books, 1984. ISBN 0-465-04231-7 (cl), 0-465-04232-5 (pbk). ▸ Sweeping interpretation attacks failure of 1960s Great Society programs to help poor. Framed by belief that poverty programs must create independence. Influential conservative interpretation. [LGB]

44.654 James Stuart Olson. *Saving capitalism: the Reconstruction Finance Corporation and the New Deal, 1933–40.* Princeton: Princeton University Press, 1988. ISBN 0-691-04749-9. ▸ Biography of Reconstruction Finance Corporation chair; detailed account of Corporation's philosophy and actions. Government's refinancing of credit institutions and homeowner mortgages averted total economic collapse. [TCL]

44.655 Keith W. Olson. *The GI Bill, the veterans, and the colleges.* Lexington: University Press of Kentucky, 1974. ISBN 0-8131-1288-5. ▸ Survey of how this popular post–World War II legislation affected colleges, veterans, and government. [LGB]

44.656 Kenneth O'Reilly. *"Racial matters": the FBI's secret file on black America, 1960–1972.* 1989 ed. New York: Free Press, 1991. ISBN 0-02-923681-9 (cl, 1989), 0-02-923682-7 (pbk). ▸ Readable, indignant documentation of FBI surveillance and harassment, presided over by Director J. Edgar Hoover, with knowledge, sometimes help, of president and other executive agencies. Chronicles agency's growing conservatism and white backlash. [NMK]

44.657 David Osborne. *Laboratories of democracies.* Rev. ed. Boston: Harvard Business School Press, 1990. ISBN 0-87584-233-X (pbk). ▸ Detailed case studies of policy initiatives at state level. By showing effectiveness of such programs, argues for increased funds for state programs. [LGB]

44.658 Benjamin I. Page and Robert Y. Shapiro. *The rational public: fifty years of trends in American's policy preferences.* Chicago: University of Chicago Press, 1992. ISBN 0-226-64477-4 (cl), 0-226-64478-2 (pbk). ▸ Chapters on specific policies, including economic, foreign, and social policy, provide details on changes in public opinion since 1940s. Careful attention to differences across race, gender, and age. [LGB]

44.659 Michael E. Parrish. *Securities regulation and the New Deal.* New Haven: Yale University Press, 1970. ISBN 0-300-01215-2. ▸ Specialist analysis of major policies and opinions of reformers and business community. Reform strengthened stability and prerogative of existing securities firms. [TCL]

44.660 David Plotke. "The Wagner Act, again: politics and labor, 1935–37." *Studies in American political development* 3 (1989) 105–56. ISSN 0898-588X. ▸ Sophisticated, multicausal analysis of New Deal labor policy. Progressive reformers, empowered by political conditions, determined shape of Wagner Act and subsequent regime of labor-management relations. [TCL]

44.661 John Ranelagh. *The agency: the rise and decline of the CIA.* Rev. ed. New York: Simon & Schuster, 1987. ISBN 0-671-63994-3 (pbk). ▸ Thoroughly documents evolution of agency from defensive organization to interventionist service utilized to prevent trouble as cold war intensified. Agency eventually became distrusted mature bureaucracy, excluded from policy making. [BBY]

44.662 A. James Reichley. *Conservatives in an age of change: the Nixon and Ford administrations.* Washington, D.C.: Brookings Institution, 1981. ISBN 0-8157-7380-3 (cl), 0-8157-7379-X (pbk). ▸ Careful review of most aspects of federal policy during these presidents' terms. Assesses extent and form of conservative ideology that informed these policies. [LGB]

44.663 Mark H. Rose. *Interstate: express highway politics, 1939–1989.* Rev. ed. Knoxville: University of Tennessee Press, 1990. ISBN 0-87049-671-9 (pbk). ▸ Scholarly analysis of various political forces that shaped modern highway system. Case study of kind of coalitions necessary for major government initiatives. [LGB]

44.664 Louis Ruchames. *Race, jobs, and politics: the story of FEPC.* 1953 ed. Westport, Conn.: Negro Universities Press, 1971. ISBN 0-8371-5948-2. ▸ Best available history of Fair Employment Practices Commission, 1941–46. Commission's policies, accomplishments, and demise due to lack of presidential support. [TCL]

44.665 John A. Salmond. *The Civilian Conservation Corps, 1933–42: a New Deal case study.* 1967 ed. Durham: North Carolina University Press, 1990. ▸ Detailed, well-researched history of Civilian Conservation Corps; failure to challenge segregation in South biggest shortcoming. Administrative history with close attention to administrator goals, agency problems, and accomplishments. Also available in photocopy from Ann Arbor: University Microfilms International. [TCL]

44.666 Theodore Saloutos. *The American farmer and the New Deal.* Ames: Iowa State University Press, 1982. ISBN 0-8138-1076-0. ▸ Standard liberal history which synthesizes social and political history. New Deal helped all farmers; limits to improvements understandable given longstanding bars to change. [TCL]

44.667 Robert D. Schulzinger. *The wise men of foreign affairs: the history of the Council on Foreign Relations.* New York: Columbia University Press, 1984. ISBN 0-231-05528-5. ▸ Readable specialist study argues council was effort to mold moderate bipartisanship in elitist tradition of Wilsonian internationalism. Highly placed businessmen mixed with professional diplomats to influence policy and public opinion. [BBY]

44.668 Bonnie Fox Schwartz. *The Civil Works Administration, 1933–34: the business of emergency employment in the New Deal.* Princeton: Princeton University Press, 1984. ISBN 0-691-04718-9. ▸ Balanced, thorough monograph of New Deal agency based on archival sources. [TCL]

44.669 C. Brant Short. *Ronald Reagan and the public lands: America's conservation debate, 1979–1984.* College Station: Texas A&M University Press, 1989. ISBN 0-89096-382-7 (cl), 0-89096-411-4 (pbk). ▸ Balanced study of significant opposition to federal environmental policy in New Right movement. Conflict between two views, one advocating free market for environment and other supporting federal management. [LGB]

44.670 Theda Skocpol. "Political response to capitalist crisis: neo-Marxist theories of the state and the case of the New Deal." *Politics and society* 10.2 (1980) 155–201. ISSN 0032-3292. ▸ Important exposition of state capacity theory: political motives and state capacities, not popular protest or business desires, decisive in shaping New Deal. [TCL]

44.671 Joel H. Spring. *The sorting machine revisited: national educational policy since 1945.* Rev. ed. New York: Longman, 1989. ISBN 0-8013-0279-x. ▸ Highly critical review of federal involvement in education. Stresses connection between education policy and other areas of government's agenda: foreign policy, poverty program, job training, and national unity. [LGB]

44.672 James L. Sundquist. *Politics and policy: the Eisenhower, Kennedy, and Johnson years.* Washington, D.C.: Brookings Institution, 1968. ISBN 0-8157-8222-5. ▸ Comprehensive account of domestic policy initiatives in 1950s and 1960s. Emphasis on unemployment, conservation, education, and civil rights. [LGB]

44.673 Donald C. Swain. *Federal conservation policy, 1921–33.* Berkeley: University of California Press, 1963. ▸ Useful discussion of relevant bureaucracy heads, agencies, and policies. Significant advances made in federal conservation policy in 1920s, extending work of progressives and presaging New Deal reforms. [TCL]

44.674 Hanes Walton, Jr. *When the marching stopped: the politics of civil rights regulatory agencies.* Albany: State University of New York Press, 1988. ISBN 0-88706-687-9 (cl), 0-88706-688-7 (pbk). ▸ Thorough, administrative history of implementation of Title VI of Civil Rights Act of 1964, which prohibited federal funding for programs practicing racial discrimination. Impact undercut by weak enforcement. [NMK]

44.675 Margaret Weir, Ann Shola Orloff, and Theda Skocpol, eds. *The politics of social policy in the United States.* Princeton: Princeton University Press, 1988. ISBN 0-691-09436-5 (cl), 0-691-02841-9 (pbk). ▸ Collection of essays on late development of welfare state in America and need for state interaction. Examines bureaucratic structures, federal-state system, and party influence. [LGB/PFF]

44.676 Allan M. Winkler. *The politics of propaganda: the Office of War Information 1942–5.* New Haven: Yale University Press, 1978. ISBN 0-300-02148-8. ▸ Brief account of leadership attitudes and policy development. Emphasis on politics, not content of propaganda. [TCL]

Political Movements and Popular Opinion

44.677 Brian Balogh. "Reorganizing the organizational synthesis: federal-professional relations in modern America." *Studies in American political development* 5 (Spring 1991) 119–72. ISSN 0898-588x. ▸ Significant revision of organizational synthesis. Close alliance between policy professionals and government bureaucrats, characteristic of modern politics, slow to form, never certain. [TCL]

44.678 David T. Beito. *Taxpayers in revolt: tax resistance during the Great Depression.* Charlotte: University of North Carolina Press, 1989. ISBN 0-8078-1836-4. ▸ Case study of 1929–33 Chicago taxpayers' strike. Valuable account of little-studied dynamic: popular resistance to local taxes and authorities' response. [TCL]

44.679 Wini Breines. *Community and organization in the New Left, 1962–1968: the great refusal.* 2d ed. New Brunswick, N.J.: Rutgers University Press, 1989. ISBN 0-8135-1402-9 (cl), 0-8135-1403-7 (pbk). ▸ Detailed study of actions of Students for a Democratic Society's Economic Research and Action Program and its direct community intervention. Though conscious of limits of movement, sympathetic to serious and critical reform program that motivated student activists. [LGB]

44.680 William W. Bremer. *Depression winters: New York social workers and the New Deal.* Philadelphia: Temple University Press, 1984. ISBN 0-87722-350-5. ▸ Brief monograph examines how New York state social work community shaped President Franklin Roosevelt's early thought on welfare, but became increasingly radical, displeased with New Deal by 1934–35. [TCL]

44.681 Alan Brinkley. *Voices of protest: Huey Long, Father Coughlin, and the Great Depression.* 1982 ed. New York: Vintage, 1983. ISBN 0-394-71628-0 (pbk). ▸ Stimulating synthesis of biography with political and cultural history. Long and Coughlin appealed to many Americans' fear of rising modern, impersonal society. [TCL]

44.682 William H. Chafe. *Never stop running: Allard Lowenstein and the struggle to save American liberalism.* New York: Basic Books, 1993. ISBN 0-465-00103-3. ▸ Well-researched biography of leading mobilizer of student and anti–Vietnam War sentiment. Study of liberalism as well as of Lowenstein. [JTP]

44.683 Clarke A. Chambers. *Seedtime of reform: American social service and social action.* 1963 ed. Westport, Conn.: Greenwood, 1980. ISBN 0-313-22666-0. ▸ Groundbreaking account of social welfare movement between 1919 and 1932. Private welfare agencies not quiescent; increasingly sophisticated, adopted professional methods and scholarly disciplines. Made important preparations for New Deal reforms. [TCL]

44.684 Allan Crawford. *Thunder on the Right: the "New Right" and the politics of resentment.* New York: Pantheon, 1980. ISBN 0-394-50663-4. ▸ Clear, but critical study of nature of, support for, policies of, and divisions in conservative movement of 1970s and 1980s. Though divided between fiscal and family conservatives, share common enemy in liberals. [LGB]

44.685 Roger Daniels. *The Bonus March.* Westport, Conn.: Greenwood, 1971. ISBN 0-8371-5174-0. ▸ Standard account outlining and overturning myths about Bonus March, including origins and government response at federal and city levels. Builds to argument about treatment of veterans and protestors. [TCL]

44.686 Barbara Epstein. *Political protest and cultural revolution: nonviolent direct action in the 1970s and 1980s.* Berkeley: University of California Press, 1991. ISBN 0-520-07010-0. ▸ Original and provocative discussion of rise of antinuclear, environmental, and other social movements in 1970s and their use of tactics like blockades, purposeful arrests, and sabotage in context of feminism, 1960s, and new anarchy. [LGB]

44.687 David R. Farber. *Chicago '68.* Chicago: University of Chicago Press, 1988. ISBN 0-226-23800-8. ▸ Events at Democratic party convention in 1968 from standpoints of Yippies, Chicago city government, and police. Compelling account that relates different political views to nature of disorder. [LGB]

44.688 Steven M. Gillon. *Politics and vision: the ADA and modern liberalism, 1947–1985.* New York: Oxford University Press, 1987. ISBN 0-19-504973-x. ▸ Well-researched study of vision and politics of Americans for Democratic Action. Outlines conflict between idealism and practical politics that troubled this and other public interest groups. [LGB]

44.689 Felice Gordon. *After winning: the legacy of the New Jersey suffragettes, 1920–1947.* New Brunswick, N.J.: Rutgers University Press, 1986. ISBN 0-8135-1137-2 (pbk). ▸ Scholarly monograph examines tactical, ideological split between party-affiliated and issue-oriented feminists in interwar years. [TCL]

44.690 David G. Green. *The new conservatism: the counterrevolution in political, economic, and social thought.* New York: St. Martin's, 1987. ISBN 0-312-00477-X. ▸ Useful review of thought on neo-Conservatives in both United States and Britain by a conservative thinker. Emphasis on variety of thinking as well as transnational similarities. [LGB]

44.691 John A. Hudson and George Wolfskill. *All but the people: Franklin D. Roosevelt and his critics, 1933–1939.* New York: Macmillan, 1969. ▸ Lengthy catalog of source material; brief, spirited defense of Roosevelt. Attacks on president, in letters and print, bordered on irrational. [TCL]

44.692 Maurice Isserman. *If I had a hammer. . .: the death of the Old Left and the birth of the New Left.* New York: Basic Books, 1987. ISBN 0-465-03197-8. ▸ Sympathetic account of American radicalism after World War II. Sees continuity between small movements of 1950s and rise of student Left in 1960s. [LGB]

44.693 Glen Jeansonne. *Gerald L. K. Smith: minister of hate.* New Haven: Yale University Press, 1988. ISBN 0-300-04148-9. ▸ Career of prominent Far Right spokesman and publicist with America First, Union party, and pro-Nazi affiliations. [TCL]

44.694 Jim Miller. *"Democracy is in the streets": from Port Huron to the siege of Chicago.* New York: Simon & Schuster, 1987. ISBN 0-671-53056-9 (cl), 0-671-66235-X (pbk). ▸ Detailed discussion of development and personnel of Students for a Democratic Society, best known of 1960s student groups. Critical of organizational shortcomings that interfered with group's hopes for revitalized democracy. [LGB]

44.695 George H. Nash. *The conservative intellectual movement in America since 1945.* 1976 ed. New York: Basic Books, 1979. ISBN 0-465-01401-1 (cl, 1976). ▸ Comprehensive survey of major thinkers and trends in conservative intellectual movement of postwar era. [LGB]

44.696 Frances Fox Piven and Richard A. Cloward. *Poor people's movements: why they succeed, how they fail.* 1977 ed. New York: Vintage, 1979. ISBN 0-394-72697-9 (pbk). ▸ Controversial examination of workers' organizations during 1930s, civil rights movement of 1960s, and welfare rights groups of 1970s. Imposition of bureaucratic structure on insurgent groups reduced impact of protest. [LGB]

44.697 Frances Fox Piven and Richard A. Cloward. *Regulating the poor: the functions of public welfare.* 1971 ed. New York: Vintage, 1972. ISBN 0-394-71743-0. ▸ Influential, controversial study of relation between relief policies and social protest. Argues civil disorder resulted in more access to relief, which was later tightened to encourage return to work force. [LGB]

44.698 Kirkpatrick Sale. *SDS.* New York: Vintage, 1973. ISBN 0-394-47889-4. ▸ Sympathetic, well-researched history of Students for a Democratic Society. Addresses aspirations of this well-known 1960s student group and causes of its collapse. [LGB]

44.699 Peter Steinfels. *The neo-conservatives: the men who are changing America's politics.* New York: Simon & Schuster, 1979. ISBN 0-671-22665-7. ▸ Balanced, considered account of the thought and politics of conservatives who emerged from 1960s. Case studies of three major figures—Irving Kristol, Senator Daniel Patrick Moynihan, and Daniel Bell—illustrate variations and consistencies. [LGB]

44.700 George Wolfskill. *Revolt of the conservatives: a history of the American Liberty League, 1934–40.* New York: Houghton-Mifflin, 1962. ▸ Standard history of conservative, business-led political organization opposed to Franklin Roosevelt. [TCL]

Communism and Socialism

44.701 Theodore Draper. *American communism and Soviet Russia: the formative period.* 1960 ed. New York: Vintage, 1986. ISBN 0-394-74308-3 (pbk). ▸ Thorough coverage of party documents. Communist party of the United States of America followed Soviet directives to the letter during years 1923–29. [TCL]

44.702 Theodore Draper. *The roots of American communism.* 1957 ed. New York: Octagon Books, 1977. ISBN 0-374-92342-6. ▸ Groundbreaking account of United States Communist party formation, 1919–22, based on extensive use of primary sources. Highly critical of relations between United States party and Moscow. [TCL]

44.703 Irving Howe and Lewis Coser. *The American Communist party: a critical history.* 1962 ed. New York: Da Capo, 1974. ISBN 0-306-70636-9. ▸ Excellent party history covering period 1919–57. Details party's devotion to Stalinism; how Soviet Union corrupted American radicalism. [TCL]

44.704 Harvey Klehr. *The heyday of American communism: the Depression decade.* New York: Basic Books, 1984. ISBN 0-465-02945-0. ▸ Standard account, similar to Draper 44.701, 44.702. At height of its influence in United States, American Communist party closely followed Soviet Union's demands. [TCL]

44.705 Earl Latham. *The communist controversy in Washington: from the New Deal to McCarthy.* 1966 ed. Cambridge, Mass.: Harvard University Press, 1991. ▸ Comprehensive account of Communist party policy and governmental response to perceived threat. Concludes Communist party members had almost no influence in federal government. [TCL]

44.706 David Allen Shannon. *The Socialist party of America.* 1955 ed. Chicago: Quadrangle, 1967. ▸ Balanced study of party's efforts and effects. American exceptionalism—unusual mobility, political culture, and diverse ethnicities—reason for demise of America's socialist political party. [TCL/PFF]

Anticommunism

44.707 Richard M. Fried. *Nightmare in red: the McCarthy era in perspective.* 1990 ed. New York: Oxford University Press, 1991. ISBN 0-19-504360-X (cl, 1990), 0-19-504361-8 (pbk). ▸ Balanced account of anticommunist impulse in and relationship to other political and cultural trends of time. [LGB]

44.708 Robert Griffith. *Politics of fear: Joseph R. McCarthy and the Senate.* 2d ed. Amherst: University of Massachusetts Press, 1987. ISBN 0-87023-554-0 (cl), 0-87023-555-9 (pbk). ▸ Detailed, influential account of anticommunist senator's activities. Stresses ways in which he used structure and weaknesses of Senate to further his accusations. [LGB]

44.709 Stanley I. Kutler. *The American inquisition: justice and injustice in the cold war.* New York: Hill & Wang, 1982. ISBN 0-8090-2475-6 (cl), 0-8090-0157-8 (pbk). ▸ Angrily details widespread violation of civil liberties during McCarthy era. Integrates role of bureaucracy with that of Supreme Court and executive branch. [LGB]

44.710 Kenneth O'Reilly. *Hoover and the Un-Americans: the FBI, HUAC, and the Red Menace.* Philadelphia: Temple University Press, 1983. ISBN 0-87722-301-7. ▸ Scholarly study of relations between Federal Bureau of Investigation and House Un-American Activities Committee during 1950s. Shows how Bureau complemented public activities of Committee by leaking materials. [LGB]

44.711 David M. Oshinsky. *A conspiracy so immense: the world of Joe McCarthy.* New York: Free Press, 1983. ISBN 0-02-923490-5 (cl), 0-02-923760-2 (pbk). ▸ Well-written biography of anticommunist senator revealing his internal conflicts and placing him in broader context of period. [LGB]

44.712 Thomas C. Reeves. *The life and times of Joe McCarthy: a biography.* 1982 ed. New York: Stein & Day, 1983. ISBN 0-8128-2337-0 (cl, 1982), 0-8128-6200-7 (pbk). ▸ Gives essential details and background on how and why this anticommunist crusader emerged. Clearly sees McCarthy as part of broader, longer-lasting trend. [LGB]

44.713 Athan G. Theoharis and John Stuart Cox. *The boss: J. Edgar Hoover and the great American inquisition.* 1988 ed. New York: Bantam, 1990. ISBN 0-553-28539-4 (pbk). ▸ Readable, detailed account of life of powerful director of FBI. Very revealing and critical of interference with political organizations. [LGB]

44.714 Allen Weinstein. *Perjury: the Hiss-Chambers Case.* 1978 ed. New York: Vintage, 1979. ISBN 0-394-72830-0. ▸ Detectivelike account of this famous trial of suspected Communist in 1949. Provides context and evaluates evidence. [LGB]

INTERWAR FOREIGN AFFAIRS

General Studies

44.715 John Patrick Diggins. *Mussolini and fascism: the view from America.* Princeton: Princeton University Press, 1972. ISBN 0-691-04604-2. ▸ Wide-ranging interpretation of American responses to rise of fascism in 1920s. Worship of industrial efficiency led many to believe Mussolini's programs worthwhile. [RKG]

44.716 Robert K. Griffith, Jr. *Men wanted for the U.S. army: America's experience with an all-volunteer army between the world wars.* Westport, Conn.: Greenwood, 1982. ISBN 0-313-22546-X, ISSN 0084-9251. ▸ Specialized study of enlisted army from demobilization following World War I to enactment of first peacetime draft in 1940. Examines impact of Depression and growing war threat on peacetime regular army. [RKG]

44.717 Frederick S. Harrod. *Manning the new navy: the development of a modern naval enlisted force, 1899–1940.* Westport, Conn.: Greenwood, 1978. ISBN 0-8371-9759-7, ISSN 0084-9219. ▸ Detailed account of transformation of navy to ocean-going armored force with emphasis on administrative changes. New recruiting, training, and socialization practices required new relationship between sailors and officers by 1941. [RKG]

44.718 D. Clayton James. *The years of MacArthur.* Vol. 1: *1880–1941.* Boston: Houghton-Mifflin, 1970. ▸ Analysis of general's rise between world wars. Evaluates political skills in battles to preserve size of army during Depression; questions judgment in planning Philippines defense. Detailed, standard work. [RKG]

44.719 Robert Gordon Kaufman. *Arms control during the prenuclear era: the United States and naval limitation between the two world wars.* New York: Columbia University Press, 1990. ISBN 0-231-07136-1. ▸ Provocative, wide-ranging analysis of major naval limitation treaties negotiated between 1921 and 1936; treaties based on erroneous assumptions. Focus on impact on navy in Pacific in face of expansionist Japan. [RKG]

44.720 Robert James Maddox. *William E. Borah and American foreign policy.* 1969 ed. Baton Rouge: Louisiana State University Press, 1970. ISBN 0-8071-0907-X. ▸ Stimulating revisionist view of leading opponent of League of Nations and champion of isolationism as naive idealist. Portrays Borah as unshakable fatalist who employed whatever tactics necessary to serve his ends. [RKG]

44.721 Arnold A. Offner. *The origins of the Second World War: American foreign policy and world politics, 1917–1941.* New York: Praeger, 1975. ISBN 0-275-50270-8 (cl), 0-275-84750-0 (pbk). ▸ Synthesis of United States world role between wars from multinational perspective; emphasizes continuity from presidents Harding to Hoover. Portrays Franklin Roosevelt as irresolute and indecisive through 1939. [RKG]

44.722 Forrest C. Pogue. *George C. Marshall.* Vol. 1: *Education of a general, 1880–1939.* New York: Viking, 1963. ▸ Detailed narrative analysis traces Marshall through beginning of World War II in Europe and his appointment as army chief of staff. Insightful on Marshall's role in shaping prewar plans and mobilization effort. [RKG]

44.723 David F. Schmitz. *The United States and fascist Italy, 1922–1940.* Chapel Hill: University of North Carolina Press, 1988. ISBN 0-8078-1766-X. ▸ Controversial account argues that economic motives and Open Door policy meant United States turned blind eye to true nature of fascism in Italy. Response to rise of Mussolini carried over to early response to Nazis. [RKG]

44.724 Mark S. Watson. *Chief of staff: prewar plans and preparations.* Washington, D.C.: United States Department of the Army, Historical Division, 1950. ▸ Very detailed, highly critical examination of army between wars, especially from 1936 forward; draws extensively from War Department and army staff files on mobilization, training, and procurement plans. [RKG]

Foreign and Military Policy, 1920–1932

44.725 Thomas H. Buckley. *The United States and the Washington conference, 1921–1922.* 1970 ed. Knoxville: University of Tennessee Press, 1978. ISBN 0-87049-108-3. ▸ Scholarly examination of origins, goals, methods, and results of post–World War I naval arms limitation conference held at United States invitation. Analyzes ingredients that led to successful negotiation of three treaties. [RKG]

44.726 Lewis Ethan Ellis. *Republican foreign policy, 1921–1933.* New Brunswick, N.J.: Rutgers University Press, 1968. ▸ Standard review of policies of period in context of events as protagonists perceived them. American leaders applied lessons of World War I to serve their generation; public desired stability, order, and noninvolvement. [RKG]

44.727 Robert H. Ferrell. *American diplomacy in the Great Depression: Hoover-Stimson foreign policy, 1929–1933.* 1957 ed. New York: Norton, 1970. ISBN 0-393-00511-9. ▸ Standard treatment of foreign policy of Hoover's presidency in terms of overriding goal of preservation of peace. Argues United States diplomacy relied excessively on legalistic solutions that witnessed triumph of events over intelligence. [RKG]

44.728 Peter G. Filene. *Americans and the Soviet experiment, 1917–1933.* Cambridge, Mass.: Harvard University Press, 1967. ▸ Stimulating reconstruction of American attitudes and popular responses to Russian Revolution and rise of Soviet Union through end of United States nonrecognition policy. Ideological and economic analysis. [RKG]

44.729 Betty Glad. *Charles Evans Hughes and the illusion of innocence: a study in American diplomacy.* Urbana: University of Illinois Press, 1966. ▸ Intellectual biography of President Harding's secretary of state who played major role in defining foreign policy to World War II. Nineteenth-century assumptions and attitudes persisted in face of evidence that era of foreign involvement had begun. [RKG]

44.730 Joan Hoff-Wilson. *Ideology and economics: U.S. relations with the Soviet Union, 1918–1933.* Columbia: University of Missouri Press, 1974. ISBN 0-8262-0157-1. ▸ Provocative analysis of nonrecognition policy driven more by bureaucrats in Commerce and State departments than by business interests; ideologically based policy originated with President Hoover. President Franklin Roosevelt's recognition in 1933 changed little. [RKG]

44.731 Alfred F. Hurley. *Billy Mitchell: crusader for air power.* New ed. Bloomington: Indiana University Press, 1975. ISBN 0-253-31203-5 (cl), 0-253-20180-2 (pbk). ▸ Specialized study of pioneering advocate of air power who borrowed ideas from international community of military aviators. Flamboyant actions and defiance of opponents calculated to demonstrate potential of air power and win public pressure for independent air force. [RKG]

44.732 Akira Iriye. *After imperialism: the search for a new order in the Far East, 1921–1931.* 1965 ed. Chicago: Imprint, 1990. ISBN 1-879176-00-9 (pbk). ▸ Balanced analysis of United States Asian policy from World War I to Manchurian crisis of 1931. Delineates three phases: Soviet, Japanese, and Nationalist Chinese initiatives failed to create new order. [RKG]

Foreign and Military Policy, 1933–1938

44.733 Robert A. Divine. *The illusion of neutrality.* Chicago: University of Chicago Press, 1962. ▸ Well-researched, balanced study of neutrality legislation of 1930s from intellectual origins in 1920s through major reforms of 1939. Focuses on isolationists seeking to prevent involvement in future wars. [RKG]

44.734 George Q. Flynn. *Roosevelt and Romanism: Catholics and American diplomacy, 1937–1945.* Westport, Conn.: Greenwood, 1976. ISBN 0-8371-8581-5. ▸ Sophisticated study of how American Catholic church foreign policy between world wars swayed between isolationism and interventionism. Opinion moved from opposition to support of involvement contributing to nationalization of church. [RKG]

44.735 Lloyd C. Gardner. *Economic aspects of New Deal diplomacy.* 1964 ed. Boston: Beacon, 1971. ISBN 0-8070-5435-6. ▸ Broadly conceived analysis of President Franklin Roosevelt's foreign policy ambitions, effort to create open world economy from trading blocs of Depression. Except for brief period in 1933–34, consistent with mainstream economic concepts. Essential for American diplomatic historians. [RKG]

44.736 Bryce Wood. *The making of the Good Neighbor policy.* New York: Columbia University Press, 1961. ▸ Scholarly analysis of origins and implementation of President Franklin Roosevelt's new approach to Latin America from 1933 to 1945. United States abandoned right to intervene and expropriate by force. [RKG]

SEE ALSO
48.159 Irwin F. Gellman. *Good Neighbor diplomacy.*
48.165 Dorothy Borg. *The United States and the Far Eastern crisis of 1933–1938.*
48.197 Robert Dallek. *Franklin D. Roosevelt and American foreign policy, 1932–1945.*

WORLD WAR II

United States Entry into World War II

44.737 Charles A. Beard. *President Roosevelt and the coming of the war, 1941.* 1948 ed. Hamden, Conn.: Archon, 1968. ISBN 0-208-00265-0. ▸ Highly provocative indictment of Franklin Roosevelt by leading prewar isolationist. Notes discrepancies between official statements and conduct of foreign and military affairs in 1941; results of war did not justify entry. [RKG]

44.738 Mark Lincoln Chadwin. *The hawks of World War II.* Chapel Hill: University of North Carolina Press, 1968. ▸ Standard account of makeup, motives, methods, and accomplishments of Century Group and Fight for Freedom. Concludes establishment cabal did not lead America into war; enjoyed little influence but countered isolationists. [RKG]

44.739 J. Garry Clifford and Samuel R. Spencer, Jr. *The first*

peacetime draft. Lawrence: University Press of Kansas, 1986. ISBN 0-7006-0305-0. ▸ Well-written monograph on great debate of 1940 between isolationists, internationalists, and interventionists, responding to German *Blitzkrieg* of Europe and leading to enactment of first peacetime draft. [RKG]

44.740 Wayne S. Cole. *Charles A. Lindbergh and the battle against American intervention in World War II.* New York: Harcourt Brace Jovanovich, 1974. ISBN 0-15-118168-3. ▸ Sympathetic, well-researched account of Lindbergh's stance which emphasized limits of power, argued United States could but should not try to remake world in its own image, and warned against excessive executive power. [RKG]

44.741 Wayne S. Cole. *Roosevelt and the isolationists, 1932–1945.* Lincoln: University of Nebraska Press, 1983. ISBN 0-8032-1410-3. ▸ Excellent scholarly study of transition from traditional isolationism in United States to multilateral involvement. Assigns key role to President Franklin Roosevelt who orchestrated it. [RKG]

44.742 Waldo Heinrichs. *Threshold of war: Franklin D. Roosevelt and American entry into World War II.* New York: Oxford University Press, 1988. ISBN 0-19-504424-X (cl), 0-19-506168-3 (pbk). ▸ Excellent brief interpretation, placing in global context deepening involvement of United States in war against Hitler and diplomatic slide in Far East. Integrates military, foreign, and domestic policy with public opinion. No substitute for Feis 48.166 or Langer and Gleason 44.745. [RKG/CKF/JSH]

44.743 Warren F. Kimball. *The most unsordid act: Lend-Lease, 1939–1941.* Baltimore: Johns Hopkins University Press, 1969. ISBN 0-8018-1017-5. ▸ More than any other action short of war declaration, passage of Lend-Lease signaled United States participation on side of Allies. Basic work details genesis of act, congressional debate, and behind scenes maneuvering. [RKG]

44.744 William L. Langer and S. Everett Gleason. *The challenge to isolation: the world crisis of 1937–1940 and American foreign policy.* 1952 ed. 2 vols. Gloucester, Mass.: Smith, 1970. ▸ Groundbreaking internationalist perspective on conduct of United States foreign policy leading to United States intervention. President Franklin Roosevelt aroused country to dangers of world situation but temporized when it came to action. [RKG]

44.745 William L. Langer and S. Everett Gleason. *The undeclared war, 1940–1941.* 1953 ed. Gloucester, Mass.: Smith, 1968. ▸ Comprehensive analysis of foreign and military policy and actions from fall of France in May 1940 to attack on Pearl Harbor. Supportive but not uncritical of President Franklin Roosevelt and internationalists. [RKG]

44.746 Callum A. MacDonald. *The United States, Britain, and appeasement, 1936–1939.* New York: St. Martin's, 1980. ISBN 0-312-83313-X. ▸ Detailed study of American foreign policy, 1936–39, focusing on impact of American policy on British foreign relations at height of appeasement. United States economic goals initially promoted appeasement. [RKG]

44.747 Keith D. McFarland. *Harry H. Woodring: a political biography of FDR's controversial secretary of war.* Lawrence: University Press of Kansas, 1975. ISBN 0-7006-0130-9. ▸ Specialized study of role of secretary of war in Roosevelt administration during time of army's lowest strength and readiness between world wars. Isolationist Woodring resigned over aid to Allies in 1940. [RKG]

44.748 Forrest C. Pogue. *George C. Marshall.* Vol. 2: *Ordeal and hope, 1939–1942.* 1966 ed. New York: Viking, 1986. ISBN 0-670-33686-6. ▸ Detailed study of general's efforts to prepare army for war during period between beginning of World War II in Europe and Pearl Harbor when United States was deeply divided between isolation and intervention. [RKG]

44.749 David L. Porter. *The Seventy-sixth Congress and World War II, 1939–1940.* Columbia: University of Missouri Press,

1979. ISBN 0-8262-0281-0. ▸ Well-researched monograph on Congress during transition from isolationism to intervention. Congress more independent and dynamic than accepted; played significant role in shaping United States response to world events. [RKG]

44.750 Gordon W. Prange. *Pearl Harbor: the verdict of history.* New York: McGraw-Hill, 1986. ISBN 0-07-050668-x. ▸ Comprehensive examination of responsibility for surprise attack. All levels of society, from public and Congress through White House, diplomatic corps, and Washington and Hawaiian military commands doubted attack possible. [RKG]

44.751 David Reynolds. *The creation of the Anglo-American alliance, 1937–1941.* 1981 ed. Chapel Hill: University of North Carolina Press, 1982. ISBN 0-8078-1507-1 (cl), 0-8078-4229-x (pbk). ▸ Impressive analysis of formative years of special relationship between Britain and United States from Munich to Pearl Harbor. Places movement toward diplomatic and military cooperation in cultural perspective. [RKG]

44.752 Bruce M. Russett. *No clear and present danger: a skeptical view of U.S. entry into World War II.* New York: Harper & Row, 1972. ISBN 0-06-131649-0. ▸ Very stimulating, brief study questioning basic assumptions about entry into war against both Japan and Germany; challenges Good War orthodoxy. Concludes United States entry into war against Germany unnecessary; options existed to avoid conflict with Japan. [RKG]

44.753 Michael Schaller. *The U.S. crusade in China, 1938–1945.* New York: Columbia University Press, 1979. ISBN 0-231-04454-2. ▸ Lively, provocative analysis of the decision to support regime of nationalist Chiang Kai-Shek after Japanese aggression. Hostility to communist rivals doomed postwar plans. [RKG]

44.754 Charles Callan Tansill. *Back door to war: the Roosevelt foreign policy, 1933–1941.* 1952 ed. Westport, Conn.: Greenwood, 1975. ISBN 0-8371-7990-4. ▸ Classic isolationist statement purports to show how internationalist cabal conditioned public to idea that United States would again have to intervene in Europe and maneuvered Japan into firing first shot to assure entry. [RKG]

44.755 Lawrence S. Wittner. *Rebels against war: the American peace movement, 1933–1983.* Rev. ed. Philadelphia: Temple University Press, 1984. ISBN 0-87722-346-7 (cl), 0-87722-342-4 (pbk). ▸ Sympathetic study of peace movement prior to World War II, its collapse in face of total war, and reemergence in cold war based on new attitudes, assumptions, and approaches. [RKG]

44.756 Roberta Wohlstetter. *Pearl Harbor: warning and decision.* Stanford, Calif.: Stanford University Press, 1962. ▸ Classic account analyzing why, with so many signals of impending attack, United States forces in Hawaii caught by surprise. Concludes that many signs of attack submerged in excess of intelligence information. [RKG]

SEE ALSO
48.166 Herbert Feis. *The road to Pearl Harbor.*

Fighting World War II

44.757 Stephen E. Ambrose. *Eisenhower and Berlin, 1945: the decision to halt at the Elbe.* Rev. ed. New York: Norton, 1986. ISBN 0-393-09730-7 (pbk). ▸ Brief, well-argued analysis of Allied failure to capture Berlin ahead of Soviet forces. Rejects as myth that Eisenhower thereby could have avoided division of Germany; decision based on military considerations. [RKG]

44.758 Stephen E. Ambrose. *Rise to globalism: American foreign policy since 1938.* 5th rev. ed. New York: Penguin, 1988. ISBN 0-14-022826-8 (pbk). ▸ Widely used interpretive account of transformation of policy from isolationist through crusading interventionist to unlimited containment. Examines assumptions of each stage and of role of World War II in change. [RKG]

44.759 Stephen E. Ambrose. *The supreme commander: the war years of General Dwight D. Eisenhower.* 1969 ed. London: Cassell, 1971. ISBN 0-304-93818-1. ▸ Basic narrative biography of Eisenhower from his appointment as chief, War Plans Division, in December 1941 to German surrender. [RKG]

44.760 Allan Berube. *Coming out under fire: the history of gay men and women in World War Two.* New York: Free Press, 1990. ISBN 0-02-903100-1. ▸ Pioneering study arguing wartime military service major impetus in recognition by gay men and lesbians of common interests; contributed to emergence of overt gay community. [RKG]

44.761 Martin Blumenson. *Patton: the man behind the legend, 1885–1945.* New York: Morrow, 1985. ISBN 0-688-06082-x. ▸ Critical biography by editor of Patton papers. Examines turbulent career of controversial American World War II field commander. Contrasts sensitive caring private person with flamboyant bombastic public figure. [RKG]

44.762 Thomas M. Coffey. *HAP: the story of the U.S. Air Force and the man who built it, general Henry H. "HAP" Arnold.* New York: Viking, 1982. ISBN 0-670-36069-4. ▸ Life-and-times analysis of aviator who received flight training from Wright brothers, rose to command Army Air Forces in World War II, and became first chief of staff of independent air force. [RKG]

44.763 George Q. Flynn. *Lewis B. Hershey: Mr. Selective Service.* Chapel Hill: University of North Carolina Press, 1985. ISBN 0-8078-1621-3. ▸ Stimulating, accessible biography of controversial director of selective service system from World War II to Vietnam. Examines origins of draft in America and explains why peacetime draft possible in 1940. [RKG]

44.764 Paul Fussell. *Wartime: understanding and behavior in the Second World War.* New York: Oxford University Press, 1989. ISBN 0-19-503797-9 (cl), 0-19-506577-8 (pbk). ▸ Controversial analysis of psychological and emotional response of Americans and Britains to war; public knowledge and understanding contrasted with that of combatants. Questions Good War thesis. [RKG]

44.765 Jack Goodman, ed. *While you were gone: a report on wartime life in the United States.* 1946 ed. New York: Da Capo, 1974. ISBN 0-306-70605-9. ▸ Collection of interpretive essays by prominent authors of day on aspects of homefront in World War II. Covers attitudes about war, youth and minorities, government and politics, work and leisure, and popular culture. [RKG]

44.766 J. Glenn Gray. *The warriors: reflections on men in battle.* 1959 ed. New York: Harper & Row, 1970. ISBN 0-06-090580-3 (cl), 0-06-090580-8 (pbk). ▸ Thoughtful essays by veteran of World War II on war experience in terms of emotions of battle, love-hate relationships of soldiers in war, survivor guilt, and enduring fascination with war as human institution. [RKG]

44.767 Anne Bosanko Green. *One woman's war: letters home from the Women's Army Corps, 1944–1946.* St. Paul: Minnesota Historical Society Press, 1989. ISBN 0-87351-246-4. ▸ Edited letters of Minnesota girl who enlisted in Women's Army Corps and served as medical assistant. Stimulating insight into women's life in man's war. Introduction provides overview of women in war. [RKG]

44.768 Kent Roberts Greenfield. *American strategy in World War II: a reconsideration.* 1963 ed. Westport, Conn.: Greenwood, 1979. ISBN 0-313-21175-2. ▸ Well-crafted brief essays focus on four major topics: nature of coalition warfare, United States–British relations, President Franklin Roosevelt as commander in chief, and role of air power, by chief historian of United States Army from 1946 to 1958. [RKG]

44.769 Kent Roberts Greenfield, ed. *Command decisions.* Washington, D.C.: United States Department of the Army, Office of the Chief of Military History, 1960. ▸ Classic essays by army historians analyzing key decisions of World War II, including decision to fight Germany first, Japan's decision for war, Japanese internment, North African invasion, halt at Elbe, and use of atomic bomb. [RKG]

44.770 Godfrey Hodgson. *The colonel: Henry Stimson's life and wars, 1867–1952.* New York: Knopf; distributed by Random House, 1990. ISBN 0-394-57441-9. ▸ Critical biography of President Hoover's secretary of state and President Franklin Roosevelt's wartime secretary of war. Stimson's perspective provides insight into transition to and conduct of war. [RKG]

44.771 Akira Iriye. *Power and culture: the Japanese American war, 1941–1945.* Cambridge, Mass.: Harvard University Press, 1981. ISBN 0-674-69580-1. ▸ Thoroughly documented revisionist examination of how both United States and Japan defined their war objectives and followed those definitions in mobilizing and fighting one another. Sees war as part of Japanese and American search for new international order, not power projection. [RKG/FGN]

44.772 D. Clayton James. *The years of MacArthur.* Vol. 2: *1941–1945.* Boston: Houghton-Mifflin, 1975. ▸ Detailed examination of General Douglas MacArthur from unsuccessful defense of Philippines to acceptance of Japanese surrender. Analyzes jockeying with President Franklin Roosevelt, General George C. Marshall, and Admiral Chester Nimitz for political and military preeminence. [RKG]

44.773 Robert Jungk. *Brighter than a thousand suns: a personal history of the atomic scientists.* 1958 ed. James Cleugh, trans. Harmondsworth: Penguin, 1982. ISBN 0-14-020667-1 (pbk). ▸ Readable memoir of Manhattan Project member. Traces evolution of nuclear science and weapons program through early 1950s, addressing conflicts between scientists and policy makers over use of weapon and sharing of secrets. [RKG]

44.774 Kathryn Kane. *Visions of war: Hollywood combat films of World War II.* Ann Arbor: UMI Research Press, 1982. ISBN 0-8357-1286-9. ▸ Scholarly analysis of films with combat themes produced 1941–45. Early films redundant in reinforcing justification of America in war; by 1945 shift to themes of futility and suffering. [RKG]

44.775 Ulysses Lee. *The employment of Negro troops.* Washington, D.C.: United States Department of the Army, Office of the Chief of Military History, 1966. ▸ Definitive word on African American military participation. Special attention to development of policies, morale of troops, and contribution to war efforts. [NMK]

44.776 Charles B. MacDonald. *The mighty endeavor: the American war in Europe.* Rev. ed. New York: Quill, 1986. ISBN 0-688-06074-9 (pbk). ▸ Synthesis of official histories of United States Army operations in Europe. Largely devoted to operations and combat; addresses major military decisions and disputes between Allies. [RKG]

44.777 Bill Mauldin. *Up front: text and pictures.* 1945 ed. New York: Norton, 1968. ▸ Classic cartoons and commentary by combat artist syndicated in Stars and Stripes newspaper. Insight into soldiers' war in Europe and challenges of combat news gathering and reporting. [RKG]

44.778 Lee G. Miller. *The story of Ernie Pyle.* New York: Viking, 1950. ▸ Biography of widely read war correspondent of World War II. Addresses issues of freedom of press in wartime, challenges faced by front-line correspondents, and relations with military and political command structures. [RKG]

44.779 Samuel Eliot Morison. *The two-ocean war: a short history of the United States Navy in the Second World War.* Boston: Little, Brown, 1963. ▸ Synthesis of author's classic fifteen-volume history of naval operations in war with extended analysis of navy

between world wars, detailing most important campaigns and actions. [RKG]

44.780 Louis Morton. *The fall of the Philippines.* Washington, D.C.: United States Department of the Army, Office of the Chief of Military History, 1953. ▸ Critical analysis from official records of United States and Japanese forces from origins of prewar plans for defense through response to initial attacks; also withdrawal to and sieges and surrender of Bataan and Corregidor. [RKG]

44.781 Alan M. Osur. *Blacks in the Army Air Forces during World War II: the problem of race relations.* 1977 ed. New York: Arno, 1980. ISBN 0-405-12199-7. ▸ Well-researched monograph details how semi-autonomous air force totally excluded African Americans until 1943 when political pressures forced creation of African American units. Performance of air groups had positive impact on air force attitudes toward African Americans. [RKG]

44.782 Brendan Phibbs. *The other side of time: a combat surgeon in World War II.* Boston: Little, Brown, 1987. ISBN 0-316-70510-1. ▸ Eloquent, revealing memoir of army surgeon assigned to armored combat unit in Europe from Normandy landing to liberation of concentration camps. Insight into combat medicine and reaction of ordinary soldiers to battle. [RKG]

44.783 Forrest C. Pogue. *George C. Marshall.* Vol. 3: *Organizer of victory, 1943–1945.* New York: Viking, 1973. ISBN 0-670-33694-7 (v. 3). ▸ Influential analysis of Marshall as wartime army chief of staff, evolution of relationships with President Franklin Roosevelt and Prime Minister Churchill, and insistence on separation of political aspects of war from military decisions and operational conduct. [RKG]

44.784 Richard Rhodes. *The making of the atomic bomb.* New York: Simon & Schuster, 1986. ISBN 0-671-44133-7 (cl), 0-671-65719-4 (pbk). ▸ Comprehensive narrative analysis of melding of science, technology, and policy to design, build, and use nuclear weapon in World War II. Examines motives, debates, decisions, and personalities involved. Important work. [RKG]

44.785 Ronald Schaffer. *Wings of judgment: American bombing in World War II.* New York: Oxford University Press, 1985. ISBN 0-19-503629-8. ▸ Provocative collective biography of American civilian, military, scientific, and technical air-war leaders; all questioned moral implications of their work. Includes discussion of origins of United States strategic bombing doctrine and bombing of civilians. [RKG]

44.786 Michael S. Sherry. *The rise of American air power: the creation of Armageddon.* New Haven: Yale University Press, 1987. ISBN 0-300-03600-0. ▸ Innovative analysis of cultural, political, and military considerations in use of bombs, including atomic ones. Contemporaries had difficulty comprehending air war as it evolved; effects of strategic bombing campaigns conditioned intellectual environment. [RKG]

44.787 Mulford Q. Sibley and Philip E. Jacob. *Conscription of conscience: the American state and the conscientious objector, 1940–1947.* 1952 ed. New York: Johnson Reprint, 1965. ▸ Detailed, specialized study shows American tolerance for conscientious objectors limited in World War II. Analyzes programs for alternative service and treatment of outright resisters; 50,000 objectors drafted or jailed. [RKG]

44.788 Ronald H. Spector. *Eagle against the sun: the American war against Japan.* New York: Free Press, 1985. ISBN 0-02-930360-5. ▸ Critical single-volume synthesis of official histories of war; combines Allied and Japanese accounts. Updates existing work based on availability of new sources and provides fresh perspective. Presents opposing views of key issues. [RKG/FGN]

44.789 Henry L. Stimson and McGeorge Bundy. *On active service in peace and war.* 1947 ed. New York: Octagon Books, 1971. ISBN 0-374-97627-9. ▸ Detailed coverage of Stimson's tenure as President Hoover's secretary of state and President Franklin

Roosevelt's secretary of war from 1940 to 1945. Written from Stimson's diary, official records, and interviews. [RKG]

44.790 Studs Terkel. *"The Good War": an oral history of World War Two.* New York: Pantheon, 1984. ISBN 0-394-53103-5. ▸ Classic compendium of interviews with those who served, high and low, in and out of uniform. Interviews with participants on both sides of major events such as Pearl Harbor attack, Normandy invasion, and Hiroshima bombing. [RKG]

44.791 Mattie E. Tredwell. *The Women's Army Corps.* Washington, D.C.: United States Department of the Army, Office of the Chief of Military History, 1954. ▸ Standard, administrative history of evolution and organization of Women's Army Corps and expanding role of women in army. Analyzes integration of women into nontraditional roles, recruiting, training, and employment worldwide. [RKG]

44.792 Russell F. Weigley. *Eisenhower's lieutenants: the campaign of France and Germany, 1944–1945.* Bloomington: Indiana University Press, 1981. ISBN 0-253-13333-5. ▸ Comprehensive narrative analysis of United States Army's greatest campaign from perspective of its commanders. Campaign represented culmination of army's transformation from American Indian–fighting constabulary to world-class military force. [RKG]

SEE ALSO
48.227 John W. Dower. *War without mercy.*

Diplomacy

44.793 Robert A. Divine. *Roosevelt and World War II.* 1970 ed. New York: Penguin, 1975. ISBN 0-14-021191-8. ▸ Graceful essays rehabilitate President Franklin Roosevelt's role as wartime president. Credits Roosevelt for uniting country against fascist challenge; concedes he failed to turn Grand Alliance into true postwar order for preserving international peace. [RKG]

44.794 Herbert Feis. *The atomic bomb and the end of World War II.* Rev. ed. Princeton: Princeton University Press, 1966. ISBN 0-691-05601-3. ▸ Controversial revisionist examination of Allied demands for unconditional Japanese surrender at Potsdam Conference and timing of use of atomic bomb to compel surrender. Earlier title: *Japan Subdued.* [RKG/FGN]

44.795 George C. Herring, Jr. *Aid to Russia, 1941–1946: strategy, diplomacy, the origins of the cold war.* New York: Columbia University Press, 1973. ISBN 0-231-03336-2 (cl), 0-231-08348-3 (pbk). ▸ Influential analysis of development and implementation of aid policy, impact on American-Soviet relations, significance to Soviet war effort, and perceptions by both of each other. [RKG]

44.796 Gabriel Kolko. *The politics of war: the world and United States foreign policy, 1943–1945.* Rev. ed. New York: Pantheon, 1990. ISBN 0-679-72757-4. ▸ Highly critical, detailed, revisionist study. Defines foreign policy in World War II as driven by three overriding concerns: question of the Left; problem of Soviet Union; and problem of Britain. [RKG]

44.797 Gaddis Smith. *American diplomacy during the Second World War, 1941–1945.* 2d ed. New York: Knopf, 1985. ISBN 0-394-34202-X. ▸ Analysis of diplomatic events in context of time. Assesses major objectives of wartime alliance against defined nature of alliance diplomacy; avoids retrospective judgment of cold war perspective. Useful short survey. [RKG]

SEE ALSO
21.280 David Wyman. *The abandonment of the Jews.*
48.254 Diane Shaver Clemens. *Yalta.*

POST–WORLD WAR II FOREIGN AFFAIRS
General Studies

44.798 Richard J. Barnet. *Intervention and revolution: the United States in the Third World.* Rev. ed. New York: New American Library, 1980. ISBN 0-452-00610-4. ▸ Wide-ranging study of American reaction to revolution, from Greece to Vietnam. Ambiguity of revolution promoted global campaign to channel development into acceptable paths, often involving military force. [BBY]

44.799 David P. Calleo. *Beyond American hegemony: the future of the Western alliance.* New York: Basic Books, 1987. ISBN 0-465-00655-8. ▸ Provocative interpretation sees American monetary strategies since 1945 designed to exploit international economy. As other nations revived, United States became hegemon in decay due to military overextension resulting from agreements with Western allies. [BBY]

44.800 Clark Clifford. *Counsel to the president: a memoir.* New York: Random House, 1991. ISBN 0-394-56995-4. ▸ Insightful reflections of adviser to Democratic leaders from presidents Truman through Johnson. Coverage of the Republican era (Nixon to Reagan) yields insights on both foreign and domestic policies. [BBY]

44.801 Robert A. Dallek. *The American style in foreign policy: cultural politics and foreign affairs.* New York: Knopf; distributed by Random House, 1983. ISBN 0-394-51360-6. ▸ Symbolic meaning of foreign affairs utilized to express unresolved domestic tensions. Quest for individualism and social harmony transposed onto international arena where domestic strife caused belligerent policy. Pioneering study of "new" diplomatic history. [BBY/PLH]

44.802 George Q. Flynn. *The draft, 1940–1945.* Lawrence: University Press of Kansas, 1993. ISBN 0-7006-0568-X. ▸ Narrative, analytical history of major force in American life and culture. [JTP]

44.803 Paul Hollander. *Anti-Americanism: critiques at home and abroad, 1965–1990.* New York: Oxford University Press, 1992. ISBN 0-19-503824-X (cl), 0-19-503097-4 (pbk). ▸ Introductory study. Documents hostility to United States, including anti-American activities and terrorism abroad. United States foreign policy often cause of hatred rather than reaction to it. [BBY]

44.804 Ernest R. May. *"Lessons" of the past: the use and misuse of history in American foreign policy.* 1973 ed. New York: Oxford University Press, 1975. ISBN 0-19-501890-7 (pbk). ▸ Stimulating interpretation contends preoccupation with events in recent past shaped American policies. Selective historical perceptions prevented leaders from making best use of historical knowledge, particularly in cold war, Korea, and Vietnam. [BBY]

44.805 Thomas J. McCormick. *America's half-century: United States foreign policy in the cold war.* Baltimore: Johns Hopkins University Press, 1989. ISBN 0-8018-3876-2 (cl), 0-8018-3877-0 (pbk). ▸ Comprehensive survey documents efforts to exploit power and manage unified world system dedicated to free market principles and American prosperity and security. Soviet resistance caused cold war and limited new world order achievements. [BBY]

SEE ALSO
40.674 Michael H. Hunt. *Ideology and U. S. foreign policy.*
48.354 John Lewis Gaddis. *Strategies of containment.*

Cold War

44.806 Hugh DeSantis. *Diplomacy of silence: the American foreign service, the Soviet Union, and the cold war, 1933–1947.* 1980 ed. Chicago: University of Chicago Press, 1983. ISBN 0-226-14337-6 (cl, 1980), 0-226-14338-4 (pbk). ▸ Well-researched study defines four images of Soviet Union formed by American diplomats. After 1946 all agreed on realistic confrontation, encouraging cold war. Reveals impact of people, not abstract forces, on policy. [BBY]

44.807 John Lewis Gaddis. *The United States and the origins of the cold war, 1941–1947.* New York: Columbia University Press,

1972. ISBN 0-231-03289-7 (cl), 0-231-08302-5 (pbk). ▸ Classic interpretation argues cold war resulted from impact of domestic political system on American foreign policy. United States freedom of action limited after World War II. Important postrevisionist synthesis counters New Left indictment of capitalism. [BBY]

44.808 Walter Isaacson and Evan Thomas. *The wise men, six friends and the world they made: Acheson, Bohlen, Harriman, Kennan, Lovett, McCloy*. New York: Simon & Schuster, 1986. ISBN 0-671-50465-7. ▸ Study of containment strategy developed by elite American foreign policy establishment. Readable biographical approach reveals shortcomings of statesmen and linkage of business and government policy. Public oversimplification of containment yielded misguided decisions. [BBY]

44.809 Robert A. Pollard. *Economic security and the origins of the cold war, 1945–1950*. New York: Columbia University Press, 1985. ISBN 0-231-05830-6 (cl) 0-231-05831-4 (pbk). ▸ Influential postrevisionist economic interpretation argues American leaders designed new world order to provide economic interdependence, prosperity, and security. Soviet rebuffs forced modifications, cold war, and economic expansion in West. [BBY]

SEE ALSO
48.373 Bruce R. Kuniholm. *The origins of the cold war in the Near East.*
48.374 Melvyn P. Leffler. *A preponderance of power.*
48.380 Daniel Yergin. *Shattered peace.*
48.387 Michael J. Hogan. *The Marshall Plan.*
48.389 Alan S. Milward. *The reconstruction of Western Europe, 1945–51.*
48.430 Lawrence S. Kaplan. *NATO and the United States.*

Asia

44.810 H. W. Brands. *India and the United States: the cold peace*. Boston: Twayne, 1990. ISBN 0-8057-7915-9 (cl), 0-8057-9207-4 (pbk). ▸ Readable introductory survey. Efforts to bring India into communist containment network unsuccessful. India felt it was model to be imitated by other nations, resisted American pressures. Tension yielded uncertain peace. [BBY]

44.811 Theodore Cohen. *Remaking Japan: the American occupation as New Deal*. Herbert Passin, ed. New York: Free Press, 1987. ISBN 0-02-906050-8. ▸ Intellectually stimulating chronicle of United States social and economic planning, anticommunist crusade, and creation of Japanese consumerism. American mission to impose democracy with reforms inspired by New Deal ideas. [BBY]

44.812 Burton Ira Kaufman. *The Korean War: challenges in crisis, credibility, and command*. Philadelphia: Temple University Press, 1986. ISBN 0-87722-418-8. ▸ Basic survey explores ill-fated United States involvement in superpower struggle superimposed on Korean civil war. North Korea acted independently of Soviet Union and China, drawing United States into wrong war in wrong place. [BBY]

44.813 Lewis McCarroll Purifoy. *Harry Truman's China policy: McCarthyism and the diplomacy of hysteria, 1947–1951*. New York: New Viewpoints, 1976. ISBN 0-531-05386-5 (cl), 0-531-05593-0 (pbk). ▸ Groundbreaking examination of policy shift from ignoring Asian mainland to containment of China. Concludes McCarthyite attacks on government for softness on communism led to engagement in Asia. [BBY]

44.814 Michael Schaller. *The United States and China in the twentieth century*. 2d ed. New York: Oxford University Press, 1990. ISBN 0-19-505865-8 (cl), 0-19-505866-6 (pbk). ▸ United States military-diplomatic efforts to reshape Asian political relations often ill-advised and misinformed. Despite mistakes, by

1980s United States achieved balance sought since 1900. Best available survey. [BBY]

44.815 William Whitney Stueck. *The road to confrontation: American policy toward China and Korea, 1947–1950*. Chapel Hill: University of North Carolina Press, 1981. ISBN 0-8078-1445-8 (cl), 0-8078-4080-7 (pbk). ▸ Provocative interpretation argues that, while ideology, bureaucracy, and domestic politics influenced decision to respond militarily in Korea, concern for American credibility with allies and enemies explains initial intervention and subsequent invasion beyond 38th Parallel. [BBY]

SEE ALSO
14.130 Bruce Cumings. *The origins of the Korean War.*
48.526 Gordon H. Chang. *Friends and enemies.*
48.529 Rosemary Foot. *The wrong war.*
48.543 Michael Schaller. *The American occupation of Japan.*

Nuclear Weapons and Disarmament

44.816 Paul S. Boyer. *By the bomb's early light: American thought and culture at the dawn of the atomic age*. New York: Pantheon, 1985. ISBN 0-394-52878-6. ▸ Pioneering, detailed study of significance of bomb in popular mythology, 1945–50, considering scientific implications, debates among African Americans, religious communities, pacifist movement, and portrayal or fictionalization in books and movies. [UGP/PEC]

44.817 Robert A. Divine. *Blowing on the wind: the Nuclear Test Ban debate, 1954–1960*. New York: Oxford University Press, 1978. ISBN 0-19-502390-0. ▸ Specialist study chronicles debate over nuclear testing both inside and outside government. Test ban represented irrational escape from coming to grips with possibility of nuclear destruction. [BBY]

44.818 Gregg Herken. *Counsels of war*. Rev. ed. New York: Oxford University Press, 1987. ISBN 0-19-504986-1 (pbk). ▸ Critical, ambitious study of civilian defense intellectuals who shaped nuclear strategy. Think tanks of RAND Corporation, Harvard University, and MIT isolated from political, economic, and social realities developed secret, often dangerous, military strategies for bomb use. [BBY]

44.819 Strobe Talbott. *Endgame: the inside story of SALT II*. 1979 ed. New York: Harper & Row, 1980. ISBN 0-06-014213-8 (cl, 1979), 0-06-131977-5 (pbk). ▸ Best available guide to Carter administration techniques of handling strategic arms limitation talks. Internal division among policy makers complicated negotiations with Soviets and contributed to failed ratification efforts. [BBY]

44.820 Allan M. Winkler. *Life under a cloud: American anxiety about the atom*. New York: Oxford University Press, 1993. ISBN 0-19-507821-7. ▸ Useful brief history of American ideas and emotions concerning atom bombs and atomic energy, 1930s through 1980s. [JTP]

SEE ALSO
48.278 Martin J. Sherwin. *A world destroyed.*
48.297 Gregg Herken. *The winning weapon.*

Eisenhower Era

44.821 Townsend Hoopes. *The devil and John Foster Dulles*. Boston: Little, Brown, 1973. ISBN 0-316-37235-8. ▸ Traditional interpretation views Secretary of State Dulles's vigilant anticommunist crusade central to 1950s foreign policy which confused revolutionary feelings with nationalist movements. Dangerously combatted all challenges with stiff rhetoric and nuclear threats. [BBY]

44.822 Richard H. Immerman, ed. *John Foster Dulles and the diplomacy of the cold war*. 1989 ed. Princeton: Princeton University Press, 1990. ISBN 0-691-04765-0. ▸ Influential revisionist study demonstrates Dulles's subtle understanding of international relations. Despite bomb-rattling rhetoric secretary of state realized reliance on nuclear weapons ill-fitted United States problems around world; gave much thought to policy decisions. [BBY]

SEE ALSO
48.404 Robert A. Divine. *Eisenhower and the cold war.*
48.406 Burton Ira Kaufman. *Trade and aid.*

Kennedy Era

44.823 Michael R. Beschloss. *The crisis years: Kennedy and Khrushchev, 1960–1963.* New York: Burlingame, 1991. ISBN 0-06-016454-9. ▸ Very detailed exploration of crises (Bay of Pigs, Vienna Conference, Berlin, and Cuban Missile) through prism of superpower leaders acting out personal passions and calculations. [BBY]

44.824 Raymond L. Garthoff. *Reflections on the Cuban Missile Crisis.* Rev. ed. Washington, D.C.: Brookings Institution, 1989. ISBN 0-8157-3053-5 (pbk). ▸ Explores events bearing on both United States and Soviet Union. Concludes that once crisis began, actions not well planned or controlled, merely result of leaders attempting to stand firm but avoid nuclear war. [BBY]

44.825 Thomas G. Paterson, ed. *Kennedy's quest for victory: American foreign policy, 1961–1963.* New York: Oxford University Press, 1989. ISBN 0-19-504585-8 (cl), 0-19-504584-X (pbk). ▸ Provocative essays by experienced scholars demythologizing Kennedy. President suffered from cold war, ethnocentric perspective of his generation, aggravated by personality and style. Inflexible foreign policy produced few positive results, many negative legacies. Valuable starting point. [BBY/CKF/JSH]

SEE ALSO
48.405 Trumbull Higgins. *The perfect failure.*

Détente

44.826 Seymour M. Hersh. *The price of power: Kissinger in the Nixon White House.* New York: Summit, 1983. ISBN 0-671-44760-2 (cl), 0-671-50688-9 (pbk). ▸ Provocative study depicting Kissinger's early years as national security adviser. Explains foreign policy of Nixon years as result of Kissinger's obsession with power at any cost. [BBY]

44.827 William G. Hyland. *Mortal rivals: superpower relations from Nixon to Reagan.* New York: Random House, 1987. ISBN 0-394-55768-9. ▸ Comprehensive survey contends United States made proper decisions over time despite basic distrust of Soviet Union within Ford administration, infighting of Carter administration, and contradictions of Reagan's simultaneous belief in Soviet weakness and expansionism. [BBY]

44.828 Henry A. Kissinger. *White House years.* Boston: Little, Brown, 1979. ISBN 0-316-49661-8. ▸ Lengthy and self-serving memoir chronicling Vietnam War, détente with Soviet Union, reopening of ties with China, Middle East shuttle diplomacy, troubled relations with European allies, and other episodes through January 1973. [BBY]

44.829 Robert D. Schulzinger. *Henry Kissinger: doctor of diplomacy.* New York: Columbia University Press, 1989. ISBN 0-231-06952-9. ▸ Influential analysis of Kissinger diplomacy. Achieved success through reprehensible, unethical, unscrupulous methods; changed nature of cold war by acknowledging limits of power and advising Americans to accept reality. [BBY]

SEE ALSO
48.414 Raymond L. Garthoff. *Détente and confrontation.*

Vietnam War

44.830 Loren Baritz. *Backfire: a history of how American culture led us into Vietnam and made us fight the way we did.* New York: Morrow, 1985. ISBN 0-688-04185-X. ▸ Intellectually stimulating interpretation argues United States stood for revolutionary ideals: liberty, justice, and freedom. Previous success, combined with technology, created hubris that led to failure in Southeast Asia. [BBY]

44.831 Lawrence M. Baskir and William A. Straus. *Chance and circumstance: the draft, the war, and the Vietnam generation.* New York: Knopf, 1978. ISBN 0-394-41275-3. ▸ Groundbreaking study of selective service as instrument of Darwinian policy. Rich, educated escaped war, others fought. Enforcement of law inconsistent due to local variations of granting deferments and prosecuting violators. [BBY]

44.832 Larry Berman. *Lyndon Johnson's war: the road to stalemate in Vietnam.* New York: Norton, 1989. ISBN 0-393-02636-1. ▸ Study of president as tragic hero, deceiver of public, and chief architect of failure to win war. Intent on presenting favorable image of war effort, Johnson encouraged wishful thinking and made flawed policy decisions. Based on archival sources. [BBY]

44.833 Peter Braestrup. *Big story: how the American press and television reported and interpreted the crisis of Tet 1968 in Vietnam and Washington.* 2 vols. Boulder: Westview, 1977. ISBN 0-89158-012-3. ▸ Important study of media. Hostile relations between press and President Johnson and reporters' inability to cope with ambiguous events caused distortion, transforming North Vietnamese military setback into United States defeat. [BBY]

44.834 Phillip B. Davidson. *Vietnam at war: the history, 1946–1975.* Novato, Calif.: Presidio, 1988. ISBN 0-89141-306-5. ▸ Comprehensive military history. Explains how and why war fought as it was. Documents how mistakes, successes, and failures misinterpreted by media and other observers. [BBY]

44.835 Charles DeBenedetti and Charles Chatfield. *An American ordeal: the antiwar movement of the Vietnam era.* Syracuse, N.Y.: Syracuse University Press, 1990. ISBN 0-8156-0244-8 (cl), 0-8156-0245-6 (pbk). ▸ Encyclopedic record of peace movement that emerged from liberal pacifist-disarmament organizations of late 1940s and 1950s. Critics of war sought to correct perceived moral deafness and prevent devolution into institutionalized insanity. [BBY]

44.836 Frances FitzGerald. *Fire in the lake: the Vietnamese and the Americans in Vietnam.* 1972 ed. New York: Vintage, 1989. ISBN 0-679-72394-3 (pbk). ▸ Despite encounters with Vietnamese society, American leaders unaware of popular support for revolutionary forces. Hatred and misunderstanding of peasant culture generated misguided policies and hopeless cause. Influential early critique. [BBY]

44.837 James Gibson. *The perfect war: technowar in Vietnam.* Boston: Atlantic Monthly Press, 1986. ISBN 0-87113-063-7. ▸ Specialized study contends American reliance on technology led military officers to become business managers, not combat leaders, resulting in mismanagement, falsification of reports, and slaughter of civilians. Disillusionment yielded defeat. [BBY]

44.838 David Halberstam. *The best and the brightest.* 1969 ed. New York: Random House, 1992. ISBN 0-679-41062-7. ▸ Decision makers in Washington suffered from 1950s anticommunist excesses. Vietnam policy weak since Far East specialists driven out of government, leaving successors demoralized and intimidated. Biographically organized, classic study critical of United States. [BBY]

44.839 George C. Herring, Jr. *America's longest war: the United States and Vietnam, 1950–1975.* 2d ed. Philadelphia: Temple University Press, 1986. ISBN 0-87722-419-6. ▸ Basic study and essential starting point. Excellent, balanced synthesis of immense secondary literature. Documents failed global containment policy, culminating in military defeat. America's inability to recognize marginal importance of Vietnam to its interests produced continual escalation without victory. [BBY/JSH]

44.840 Gary R. Hess. *The United States emergence as a Southeast Asian power, 1940–1950.* New York: Columbia University Press, 1987. ISBN 0-231-06190-0. ‣ Comprehensive introduction shows American policy in region often grew out of perceived needs in Europe and Japan. Ultimate goal was to protect interests by preventing revolution in emerging nations. [BBY]

44.841 Stanley Karnow. *Vietnam: a history.* Rev. ed. New York: Penguin, 1991. ISBN 0-14-014533-8. ‣ Comprehensive, readable general history of Vietnam and American involvement in extended Southeast Asian struggle that began centuries before American intervention. [BBY]

44.842 Andrew Krepinevich, Jr. *The army and Vietnam.* Baltimore: Johns Hopkins University Press, 1986. ISBN 0-8018-2863-5. ‣ Controversial interpretation argues United States mission in Southeast Asia foredoomed. Army relied on inappropriate World War II techniques, could have succeeded with greater attention to counterinsurgency warfare and concern for Vietnamese population. [BBY]

44.843 Guenter Lewy. *America in Vietnam.* 1978 ed. Oxford: Oxford University Press, 1980. ISBN 0-19-502391-9 (cl), 0-19-502732-9 (pbk). ‣ Provocative study counters charges of officially condoned illegal-immoral conduct by Americans in Vietnam. Concludes war was just cause and guilt created by war in minds of many Americans unwarranted. [BBY]

44.844 John M. Newman. *JFK and Vietnam: deception, intrigue, and the struggle for power.* New York: Warner, 1992. ISBN 0-446-51678-3. ‣ Provocative, debated interpretation. While publicly proclaiming continued commitment and modest withdrawal, Kennedy secretly planned to withdraw completely from Indochina after his reelection. [BBY]

44.845 D. Michael Shafer, ed. *The legacy: the Vietnam War in the American imagination.* Boston: Beacon, 1990. ISBN 0-8070-5400-3. ‣ Groundbreaking study explores United States involvement in Indochina and war's place in popular culture. Emphasis on race, gender, class, and role of media demonstrates how different memories of war appear in film, drama, and fiction. [BBY]

44.846 William Shawcross. *Sideshow: Kissinger, Nixon, and the destruction of Cambodia.* Rev. ed. New York: Simon & Schuster, 1987. ISBN 0-671-64103-4. ‣ In-depth study of decision to conduct military operations in Cambodia. Foreign affairs equivalent of Watergate ensured eventual takeover by Khmer Rouge. [BBY]

44.847 Neil Sheehan. *A bright shining lie: John Paul Vann and America in Vietnam.* 1988 ed. New York: Vintage, 1989. ISBN 0-679-72414-1 (pbk). ‣ Moving account of Vann's life as military adviser, strategist, and lobbyist for American efforts in Vietnam. Vann's views of war mirrored America's, from commitment to disillusionment with strategy and tactics. [BBY]

44.848 Wallace Terry, ed. *Bloods: an oral history of the Vietnam war by black veterans.* New York: Random House, 1984. ISBN 0-394-53028-4. ‣ Necessary combat troop cooperation overrode racial animosities. African Americans forced to appear patriotic to avoid condemnation of American troops and all African Americans in United States. Methodologically unique study. [BBY]

UNITED STATES POLICY

Middle East

44.849 Zvi Ganin. *Truman, American Jewry, and Israel, 1945–1948.* New York: Holmes & Meier, 1979. ISBN 0-8419-0401-4

(cl), 0-8419-0497-9 (pbk). ‣ Controversial account argues president hesitant to support creation of Israel in light of State Department opposition. Infighting among Jewish organizations added to Truman's confusion. Final decision based on national interests not politics. [BBY]

44.850 William R. Polk. *The Arab world today.* 5th ed. Cambridge, Mass.: Harvard University Press, 1991. ISBN 0-674-04319-7 (cl), 0-674-04320-0 (pbk). ‣ United States policies in crisis-haunted Middle East since 1948 suggest America was ignorant of crises and paid little attention to area, limiting options open to Arabs, Israelis, and Americans. Comprehensive survey. [BBY]

44.851 Barry M. Rubin. *Paved with good intentions: the American experience in Iran.* 1980 ed. Harmondsworth: Penguin, 1981. ISBN 0-14-005964-4 (pbk). ‣ Detailed narrative documents inconsistent policy based on mutual misunderstanding and distrust; covers period 1905–80. American status in Persian Gulf region tarnished by intervention in Iranian Revolution (1979–80). [BBY]

SEE ALSO
40.655 Daniel Yergin. *The prize.*
48.516 William B. Quandt. *Decade of decisions.*
48.517 William B. Quandt. *Camp David.*

Western Hemisphere

44.852 Robert Jackson Alexander. *The tragedy of Chile.* Westport, Conn.: Greenwood, 1978. ISBN 0-313-20034-3, ISSN 0147-1066. ‣ Military rule and authoritarian and totalitarian governments Chilean tragedies. United States intervention, capitalism, and Central Intelligence Agency did not deter socialism's development since Salvador Allende had no mandate to achieve socialism. Basic introductory survey. [BBY]

44.853 Thomas H. Carothers. *In the name of democracy: United States policy toward Latin America in the Reagan years.* Berkeley: University of California Press, 1991. ISBN 0-520-07319-3. ‣ Survey of United States diplomacy in Western Hemisphere. As in Eastern Europe, United States ardently battled communism but did not contribute substantially to resurgence of democracy in Latin American nations. Clear, objective analysis by one involved in process. [BBY/RJW]

44.854 Theodore Draper. *A very thin line: the Iran-Contra affair.* New York: Hill & Wang, 1991. ISBN 0-8090-9613-7. ‣ Detailed, well-researched indictment of Reagan's national security staff which diverted money from illegal arms sales to Iran to Nicaraguan Contras. Unchecked executive authority indicated dangerous disorder in body politic. [BBY]

44.855 Roy Gutman. *Banana diplomacy: the making of American policy in Nicaragua, 1981–1987.* New York: Simon & Schuster, 1988. ISBN 0-671-60626-3. ‣ Controversial, highly critical account of Reagan administration policies by veteran reporter. United States policy toward Nicaragua came from bottom up, inspired by uncontrolled, anticommunist right wing determined to roll back Sandinistas. Lacking direction from above, administration drifted toward commitment to Contras. [BBY/RLM]

44.856 Richard H. Immerman. *The CIA in Guatemala: the foreign policy of intervention.* Austin: University of Texas Press, 1982. ISBN 0-292-78045-1 (cl), 0-292-71083-6 (pbk). ‣ Thorough monograph arguing United Fruit Company not sole ingredient in complex United States actions. Propaganda and fear, not military force, key causes of successful coup. Experience affected future United States decisions in region. [BBY]

44.857 Robert A. Pastor. *Condemned to repetition: the United States and Nicaragua.* Rev. ed. Princeton: Princeton University Press, 1988. ISBN 0-691-02291-7 (pbk). ‣ Detailed study based on extensive research by member of National Security Council staff.

Demonstrates limits on American power, challenges hegemonic assumption that United States controls internal affairs of other nations. Explains why United States repeated mistakes of Cuban relationship despite desire to avoid similar outcome. [BBY/RLM]

44.858 Gordon T. Stewart. "'A special contiguous country economic regime': an overview of America's Canadian policy." *Diplomatic history* 6.4 (1982) 339–57. ISSN 0145-2096. ▸ Despite Canada's role as important market, field of foreign investment and military ally, has received low priority in United States policy. Nature and geography allow uniquely exploitive American imperialism. Controversial interpretation. [BBY]

SEE ALSO
   48.492 Walter LaFeber. *Inevitable revolutions.*
   48.495 Morris Morley. *Imperial state and revolution.*

Africa

44.859 Richard E. Bissell. *South Africa and the United States: the erosion of an influence relationship.* New York: Praeger, 1982. ISBN 0-03-047026-9 (cl), 0-03-047021-8 (pbk). ▸ Best-available treatment examines changes in United States–South African relations due to ever-increasing perceptions of political, economic, military, and social threats. South African government outmaneuvered United States when confronted on core values. [BBY]

44.860 Michael G. Schatzberg. *Mobutu or chaos? The United States and Zaire, 1960–1990.* Lanham, Md.: University Press of America, 1991. ISBN 0-8191-8130-7 (cl), 0-8191-8131-5 (pbk). ▸ Relations with authoritarian Mobutu justified in 1960 as means to noble goal. Human rights violations by Mobutu government made rationalization of United States support difficult and bedeviled policy makers. Well-researched survey. [BBY]

44.861 Stephen R. Weissman. *American foreign policy in the Congo, 1960–1964.* Ithaca, N.Y.: Cornell University Press, 1974. ISBN 0-8014-0812-1. ▸ Clouded understanding of nationalism led policy makers to overlook complexities of Congo politics, defer to Belgian officials, and intervene on basis of anticommunism. Policy failure for presidents Eisenhower, Kennedy, and Johnson. [BBY]

SEE ALSO
   48.481 Thomas J. Noer. *Cold war and black liberation.*

Foreign Policy since Nixon

44.862 Joseph S. Nye, Jr. *Bound to lead: the changing nature of American power.* New York: Basic Books, 1990. ISBN 0-465-00177-7. ▸ Important study refuting claims of United States decline. America still predominant in all arsenals of power: territory, population, military might, economic vitality, technology, culture, and multinational influence. Poised to lead new world order. [BBY]

44.863 Strobe Talbott. *The Russians and Reagan.* New York: Vintage, 1984. ISBN 0-394-72035-9 (pbk). ▸ Provocative chronicle traces deterioration of East-West relations before Gorbachev. Criticizes Reagan administration's record on arms control and Soviet relations, arguing that intellect necessary to deal with complicated Moscow relationship was lacking. [BBY]

SEE ALSO
   48.420 Gaddis Smith. *Morality, reason, and power.*

Section 45

JOHN M. BUMSTED

Canada

At the outset, it is perhaps important to point out that Canadian history is quite different from American history, intersecting and overlapping at many points but with its own dynamic and perspective. A large portion of what is now Canada began as part of the French colonial empire, and a number of provinces remained part of the British empire after American independence, confederating as an autonomous nation in 1867. This Dominion of Canada brought vast sections of the West and North under its sovereignty after 1867; the province of Newfoundland joined the confederation in 1949. Unlike the United States, Canada is officially a bilingual and bicultural country. It has experienced no revolution or civil war in its national formation. Although it is a nation populated by immigration, the percentage of native peoples within its population is far greater than that in the United States. Canadian historiography has usually been exceptionalistic in its approach and interpretation, assuming as a given that Canadian development is unique and distinctive.

Until the end of the nineteenth century, the writing of the history of Canada was done chiefly by nonacademics. Before 1867 there was no Canadian nation to chronicle; historical work concentrated on the various provinces and regions. Much history was written by firsthand participants, its purpose often to publicize or celebrate. Confederation encouraged the conscious creation of a national historiography; indeed, the creation and development of the Canadian nation served as the basis of the mainstream paradigm of historical writing from 1867 to around 1970. Countering this national story, often seen as coterminous with that of central Canada, is regional history, particularly of those regions (basically all except Ontario) that felt ill served by the national purpose. Since the late nineteenth century, if not earlier, French Canada had its own historiographical tradition focusing on the survival of traditional French and Roman Catholic values in the midst of Anglophone Protestantism. Much of Canadian historiography is and has been defined by these two visions of Canada.

Before 1914 most Canadian history was written within the context of the British empire, but the quest for full autonomy gradually became part of the story. By the start of World War I, departments of history had been created at most Canadian universities, and Canadian historical writing increasingly took on a professional and academic edge, especially after the establishment of the *Canadian Historical Review* in 1920 and the Canadian Historical Association in 1922. Canadian historians between 1920 and 1970 were often among the leading nationalist intellectuals of their generation. At the outset, academics and nonacademics, both Anglophone and Francophone, cooperated in the association, but gradually the association became controlled by academic historians from Anglophone Canada, especially after the expansion of the Canadian universities in the 1960s. The result was a further affirmation of the sense of division between Quebec's historians and those in the remainder of Canada.

Between 1920 and the mid-1960s Canadian academic history was dominated by a few graduate schools, mainly in Canada, although some Canadians went to the United States, the United Kingdom, or France for graduate training. In English-speaking Canada, the dominant departments were all at the University of Toronto, which held a virtual monopoly on doctoral work and controlled both the major academic publisher, the University of Toronto Press, and the *Canadian Historical Review*. History at the University of Toronto was not confined to the history department; the influential economic historian, Harold Innis, was a member of the political economy department. Most history at Toronto was unabashedly national in scope and nationalistic in spirit, largely under the spell of the Laurentian school of H. Innis and D. Creighton, which saw the St. Lawrence River system as providing an east-west transportation and communication base around which the nation could and did develop.

Canadian history as taught at Toronto concentrated on political and economic developments, paying full attention to related military and imperial constitutional activity. Before confederation, the focus had been on the creation of responsible government providing an autonomy within the British empire and on a continental economy, both of which ultimately led to national unification. After confederation, the perspective shifted to Ottawa and to the building of the new nation, which gradually achieved full independence from Great Britain. From this perspective, there was an inevitable and inexorable coincidence between the needs of central Canada and those of the nation as a whole. Regional specialist W. L. Morton caused quite a stir at the Canadian Historical Association in 1946 when he challenged this assumption by arguing that "western history" should be added to "French survival" and the "dominance of Ontario" as a major theme of Canadian history. In Quebec, academic departments of history were not established at Laval and Montreal until after World War II, despite the appointment in 1915 of Abbé Lionel Groulx to the chair of Canadian history at the Montreal campus of Laval University (subsequently the University of Montreal); graduate training did not begin in earnest until the 1960s. There were two major currents of French Canadian history writing before the 1950s: one, symbolized by Groulx, synthesized an ardent French Canadian nationalism with an equally passionate Roman Catholicism; the other, represented by T. Chapais, concentrated on the distinctively French period of Quebec's history before 1763. French Canadian historians have always focused heavily on New France, and many historiographical debates with important modern resonances have been conducted over seemingly obscure developments in the seventeenth and eighteenth centuries. Since the 1950s, French Canadian historians have increasingly concentrated on the recent past.

While there was often little overlap between French Canadian and English Canadian historiographical traditions, there was considerable similarity in the demographic profiles of the historians themselves. Before the 1960s the historical profession in Canada was a cozy male preserve composed almost exclusively of representatives of the dominant cultural groups within what novelist Hugh MacLennan once called "the two solitudes." Women, native peoples, and minority ethnic groups, particularly from fairly recent immigrant communities, were seriously underrepresented. Many members of the profession spent much of the summer together researching at the Public Archives of Canada in Ottawa, where most of the documents for the preferred history were housed. It was then possible to read everything written in Canadian history, specialization was uncommon, and everyone knew everyone else in the "old boy's network." This world began falling apart in the 1960s, fueled by the vast university expansion of that decade. Expansion briefly provided jobs for a new generation of graduate students, as well as graduate education within Canada. Graduate departments turned out large numbers of Ph.D.s only as the job market began to collapse. Nevertheless, the total number of graduate students in Canadian history more than tripled in the decade after 1966. Many of Canada's younger scholars still do not have regular academic employment.

Other developments of the 1960s also affected the profession. Among the most important was the institution of an extensive system of grants, mainly from the Canadian federal government, to finance both scholarly research and publication. The extent and prevalence of research grants for Canadian academics became the envy of the Western world. Publication grants were regarded as essential in Canada to compensate for the small market for works in either official language and for the extent of foreign competition—less than 10 percent of books sold in Canada were published there. Along with research grants came the introduction of wide-scale photocopying and inexpensive intercontinental and international travel via jet airliner. The result was the opportunity to conduct research on an international scale outside the national archives and libraries whose holdings had previously controlled what could readily be studied. Research topics expanded both horizontally and vertically, with new subjects being explored with a thoroughness of documentation previously impossible. Publication grants helped disguise the extent to which these new studies were losing contact with a wider reading public.

The development of the new Canadian historiography spawned by these changes in many ways paralleled the changes in Canada itself, both in political-constitutional and cultural terms. As the old political consensus reflected in the traditional historiography was undermined by a whole new set of issues never before examined, more international and socially concerned approaches to the study of history became increasingly compelling.

Younger historians of Canada began asking new questions about race, class, ethnicity, and gender that emerged out of the political turmoil of the late 1960s and about the glaring neglect in traditional histories of native peoples, women, the working class, and racial minorities. Much of this revisionism was international in scope, but Canadian scholars gave it a particular, distinctive cast, derived from a national experience different from other nations. Scholars in Quebec may have been influenced by the Annales school of French historical analysis, for example, but they harnessed this and other European historical styles to Quebec's own political and socioeconomic aspirations. Requiring new methodologies and theories, the new research and writing in Canadian social and economic history asked implicitly whether the old paradigm of nation-building was flexible enough to provide a framework for new discoveries; by 1970 it was becoming increasingly clear that it was not. Mainstream Canadian historians, however, had no idea how to resolve the dilemma, merely adding new material as additional chapters to textbooks that continued to focus on the nation and the problems of nation-building. Those holding to a concept of national history did not easily surrender their ground.

By the early 1970s the writing of Canadian history, particularly within the academy, had altered as substantially as had the milieu in which it was being written. Academic history became more specialized and concentrated moving away from the biographical and narrative approach, which it abandoned to an increasingly successful group of popular historians. Young historians were indifferent to such large and nebulous topics as the national character, preferring instead to study various niches of history from a particular perspective, to examine regional history, or to explore subjects in specific fields such as labor, business, or medicine. Like the nation itself, which was dividing into squabbling regions and provinces split ideologically, Canadian history had experienced both fissure and diffusion. Not surprisingly, the topics most frequently explored were also those with the greatest public resonance, so that Canadian history, although isolated by the walls of the academy from popular opinion, was at the same time receptive and responsive to current events.

In yet another sense, the writing of Canadian history in recent years has responded to the profession's perception of public demand for "relevance." There has been a distinct shift away from the earlier formative periods of Canadian development (usually labeled "preconfederation" in the national paradigm) in the direction of more modern and contemporary periods, particularly the twentieth century. Modern history poses all sorts of difficulties for the historian. Obtaining a perspective on what is truly significant is only one of them. Equally serious is the problem of the sources, often too voluminous in the public arena and too sketchy in the private. Perhaps most important of all, researchers of modern history in Canada are confronted by freedom-of-information and privacy legislation that protects the rights of the living from the intrusion of historians and journalists.

Canadian historians' interaction with and influence on the Canadian reading public has changed as much as the discipline. In the years after World War II, biography was frequently employed to make national history accessible to a wider audience. The earlier nationalist school of Canadian historiography provided positive role models and an uplifting view of the past. In recent years, however, the public has been exposed less and less to formal history in the educational system at the same time as the profession has moved away from the heroic and progressive view of the past. Recent historical writing, particularly but not only that focused on women and minorities, instead documents a past of exploitation and disadvantage bordering on the conspiratorial. All Canadian history, but especially modern history, is often at odds with living historical participants who often dispute the interpretations given by historians to the events in which they were involved. Canadian history in the academy has become alienated from the larger audience, partly because of its critical view of the past and partly because of modern nonnarrative techniques of presentation. While the public laments the loss of its heroes and familiar narratives, historians themselves lament the loss of their influence.

As we approach the twenty-first century, probably the most apparent trends in Canadian historiography are, first, the deepening division between historians of Quebec and those of the remainder of the nation, and, second, the continuing diffusion of the historical enterprise in both linguistic solitudes. The division between Anglophone and Francophone historians is not simply a matter of language and perspective, although the differences in both are profound. There are also considerable differences in philosophy, theory, and personal style. Historians in English Canada tend to be far more empirical, descriptive, and deductive than their French Canadian counterparts, who rely far more heavily on abstract theoretical constructs. Perhaps even more important is the matter of personal style. French Canadian historians are far more politically active and involved in the affairs of Quebec society—in French, they are *engagé*—than are most English-speaking historians in their societies.

The diffusion of the historical enterprise has been less geographical than disciplinary, although regional history obviously flourishes in the regions and Quebec history in Quebec. As the acceptable topics for historical research have broadened and the social sciences in Canada both expanded and adopted historical dimensions, far fewer Canadian historians are to be found in traditional history departments than in those of other disciplines. Geography, sociology, anthropology, and archaeology, among others, all have important historical wings. Specialized historians—such as those of law, medicine, sport, or education—flourish in their respective faculties, often having precious little contact with the history department per se. Historians of women and those concentrating on native peoples are frequently found in interdisciplinary units. The long-range impact of this diffusion is uncertain, but clearly it is reshaping the pre-1970 profession, as well as the discipline.

[Contributors: AED = Angela E. Davis, AGL = Allan G. Levine, DJL = Debra J. Lindsay, GNE = George N. Emery, JMB = John M. Bumsted, JR = Jacques Rouillard, MBT = M. Brook Taylor, RF = Renée Fossett]

REFERENCE WORKS

45.1 Marianne Gosztonyi Ainley, ed. *Despite the odds: essays on Canadian women and science*. Montreal: Vehicule; distributed by University of Toronto Press, 1990. ISBN 0-919890-96-2 (pbk). ▸ Groundbreaking essays on history of women in science. Includes studies of individual scientists, surveys of women in various scientific fields, and discussions of contemporary issues of education and acceptance within profession. [AED]

45.2 Donald Harron Akenson, ed. *Canadian papers in rural history*. Gananoque, Ont.: Langdale, 1978–. ISBN 0-9690772-0-3 (v. 1). ▸ Ongoing series of collections of essays and papers dealing with all aspects of rural Canada and agriculture, including rural conditions from which Canadians originated. Stimulating and essential. [JMB]

45.3 Paul Aubin and Louis-Marie Cote, ed. *Bibliographie de l'histoire du Québec et du Canada*. Vols. 1–2: *1946–1965*. Vols. 3–4: *1966–1975*. Vols. 5–6: *1976–1980*. Vols. 7–8: *1981–1985*. 8 vols. Quebec: Institut Québécois de Recherche sur la Culture; distributed by Diffusion Prologue, 1981–90. ISBN 2-89224-098-0 (v. 1–2), 2-89224-003-4 (v. 3–4), 2-89224-055-7 (v. 5–6), 2-89224-142-1 (v. 7–8). ▸ Exhaustive inventory of books, articles, and theses relating to history and social sciences in context of Quebec and its relationship with Canada. Entries organized chronologically, by subject and by author. [JR]

45.4 Joanna Dean and David Fraser, comps. *Women's archives guide: manuscript sources for the history of women*. Ottawa, Ont.: National Archives of Canada, 1991. ISBN 0-662-58074-5 (pbk). ▸ Guide to manuscript sources about women in various repositories of National Archives of Canada. Listings in both French and English. [JMB]

45.5 Frances G. Halpenny, ed. *Dictionary of Canadian biography*. 12 vols. to date. Toronto: University of Toronto Press, 1966–. ISBN 0-8020-3142-0 (v. 1), 0-8020-3240-0 (v. 2), 0-8020-3314-8 (v. 3), 0-8020-3351-2 (v. 4), 0-8020-3398-9 (v. 5), 0-8020-3436-5 (v. 6), 0-8020-3452-7 (v. 7), 0-8020-3422-5 (v. 8), 0-8020-3319-9 (v. 9), 0-8020-3287-7 (v. 10), 0-8020-3367-9 (v. 11), 0-8020-3460-8 (v. 12). ▸ Well-researched biographical sketches of prominent (and occasionally less prominent) Canadians, ranging from a few hundred to 10,000 words; tends to elitism. Volumes organized by date of death, presently to 1900. Also in French. [JMB]

45.6 Richard Colebrook Harris, ed. *Historical atlas of Canada*. Vol. 1: *From the beginning to 1800*. Geoffrey J. Matthews, Cartographer. Toronto: University of Toronto Press, 1987. ISBN 0-8020-2495-5. ▸ Much acclaimed record of Canada's early development, exploring relationship between land and people through maps, charts, and other visual aids. Much attention to everyday life. [JMB]

45.7 Donald Kerr and Deryck Holsworth, eds. *Historical atlas of Canada*. Vol. 3: *Addressing the twentieth century, 1891–1961*. Geoffrey J. Matthews, Cartographer. Toronto: University of Toronto Press, 1990. ISBN 0-8020-3448-9. ▸ Highly acclaimed record of Canadian development relating land to people through use of maps, charts, plates, and other visual aids. Much emphasis on ordinary people. [JMB]

45.8 F. H. Leacy, ed. *Historical statistics of Canada*. 2d ed. Ottawa, Ont.: Statistics Canada and Social Science Federation of Canada, 1983. ISBN 0-660-11259-0. ▸ Wide-ranging collection of historical statistics relating to Canada, from population to industrial output to immigration data to criminal material to politics. [JMB]

45.9 Beth Light and Veronica Strong-Boag, comps. *True daughters of the North: Canadian women's history, an annotated bibliography*. Toronto: Ontario Institute for Studies in Education Press, 1980. (Ontario Institute for Studies in Education bibliography series, 5.) ISBN 0-7744-0185-0 (pbk). ▸ Somewhat dated, annotated bibliography of history of Canadian women, organized chronologically. [JMB]

45.10 James H. Marsh, ed. *The Canadian encyclopedia*. 2d ed. 4 vols. Edmonton: Hurtig, 1988. ISBN 0-88830-326-2 (set), 0-88830-327-0 (v. 1), 0-88830-328-9 (v. 2), 0-88830-329-7 (v. 3), 0-88830-330-0 (v. 4). ▸ Multivolume encyclopedia of information past and present relating exclusively to Canada. Basic, essential reference work. [JMB]

45.11 Jacques Rouillard, ed. *Guide d'histoire du Québec, du régime français à nos jours: bibliographie commentée*. Montreal: Meridien, 1991. ISBN 2-89415-052-0. ▸ Selection of best works in French and English on Quebec history by group of well-known historians. Most works chosen include short summary and sometimes critical comment. [JR]

GENERAL STUDIES

Canada

45.12 Alfred Goldsworthy Bailey. *Culture and nationality: essays*. Toronto: McClelland & Stewart, 1972. ▸ Collection of essays by Canada's pioneer historical anthropologist, treating his lifelong concerns, including cultural conflict between native peoples and Europeans; cultural renaissance in maritime Canada, New

Brunswick, and confederation; and origins of Canadian nationalism. [JMB]

45.13 Gerald A. Beaudoin. *La constitution du Canada: institutions, partage des pouvoirs, droits et libertés.* Montreal: Wilson & Lafleur, 1990. ISBN 2-89127-149-1. ▸ Analysis of Canadian constitution, its nature, evolution, distribution of powers, and court judgments by one of best constitutional experts actively involved in constitutional reform. Essential reading. [JR]

45.14 Carl Berger. *The writing of Canadian history: aspects of English-Canadian historical writing since 1900.* 2d ed. Toronto: University of Toronto Press, 1986. ISBN 0-8020-2546-3 (cl), 0-8020-6568-6 (pbk). ▸ Essential study of Canadian historiography in twentieth century with particular reference to national school of history centered at University of Toronto and dominant until 1960s. [JMB]

45.15 Michael Bliss. *Northern enterprise: five centuries of Canadian business.* Toronto: McClelland & Stewart, 1987. ISBN 0-7710-1577-1. ▸ General history of Canadian business from first European arrival to 1980s, tracing development from natural resource extraction to multinational corporations. Generally sympathetic to capitalism and entrepreneurialism. [JMB]

45.16 Jean R. Burnet and Howard Palmer. *"Coming Canadians": an introduction to a history of Canadian peoples.* Toronto: McClelland & Stewart with Multiculturalism Directorate, 1988. (Generations: a history of Canada's peoples.) ISBN 0-7710-1783-9 (pbk). ▸ Introductory volume to *Generations* series of histories of Canada's ethnic groups. Treats "other Canadians" both as immigrants to Canada and as members of ethnic groups. Focuses on common experiences and distinctive histories. Provocative synthesis. [JMB]

45.17 J.M.S. Careless. *Careless at work: selected Canadian historical studies.* Toronto: Dundurn, 1990. ISBN 1-55002-067-6. ▸ Collection of important essays by one of Canada's most influential and innovative historians. Includes his seminal articles: "Frontierism and Metropolitanism" and "Limited Identities." [JMB]

45.18 Wayne Fraser. *The domination of women: the personal and the political in Canadian women's literature.* New York: Greenwood, 1991. ISBN 0-313-26749-9. ▸ Revisionist attempt, successful on its own terms, to write history of women's literature in Canada, emphasizing close interconnection for women between personal and political statement. Provocative and groundbreaking. [JMB]

45.19 Alan Gowans. *Building Canada: an architectural history of Canadian life.* Rev. ed. Toronto: Oxford University Press, 1966. ▸ General survey of architecture and building in Canada, colonial times to 1960s. Argues explicitly and implicitly against concept of Canadian architecture as totally derivative. Best on domestic architecture. Earlier title: *Looking at Architecture in Canada.* [JMB]

45.20 J. L. Granatstein and Norman Hillmer. *For better or for worse: Canada and the United States to the 1990s.* Toronto: Copp Clark Pitman, 1991. ISBN 0-7730-5177-5 (cl), 0-7730-5166-X (pbk). ▸ Study of Canadian-American relations since 1860 with special focus on period since Great War and particularly since 1945. Convincing demonstration of Canada's continuing subordinate position in relationship. [JMB]

45.21 Dennis Guest. *The emergence of social security in Canada.* 2d ed. Vancouver: University of British Columbia Press, 1985. ISBN 0-7748-0226-X (pbk). ▸ General history of development of public welfare and social security in Canada, colonial period to 1970s. Emphasizes twentieth century; focuses on politics and administration. [JMB]

45.22 J. Russell Harper. *Painting in Canada: a history.* 2d ed. Toronto: University of Toronto Press, 1977. ISBN 0-8020-2271-5 (cl), 0-8020-6307-1 (pbk). ▸ Survey of European-influenced Canadian painting, 1665–1950. Records emerging nationhood as well as history of art. Contains 173 black-and-white reproductions and selected bibliography. [AED]

45.23 Robin Sutton Harris. *A history of higher education in Canada, 1663–1960.* 1976 ed. Toronto: University of Toronto Press, 1977. ISBN 0-8020-3336-9. ▸ General survey of historical development of higher education in Canada, 1604 to 1970s. Concentrates on institutional matters. [JMB]

45.24 Helmut Kallmann. *A history of music in Canada, 1534–1914.* Rev. ed. Toronto: University of Toronto Press, 1987. ISBN 0-8020-6102-8 (pbk). ▸ Survey of music as part of Canadian life from amateur to professional music making. Considers influences of religion, social activities, and work and folk song. [AED]

45.25 Carl F. Klinck et al., eds. *Literary history of Canada: Canadian literature in English.* 2d ed. 4 vols. Toronto: University of Toronto Press, 1976–90. ISBN 0-8020-2211-1 (v. 1, cl), 0-8020-2213-8 (v. 2, cl), 0-8020-2214-6 (v. 3, cl), 0-8020-6276-8 (v. 1, pbk), 0-8020-6277-6 (v. 2, pbk), 0-8020-6278-4 (v. 3, pbk). ▸ Multivolume collection of essays on Canadian literature in English from sixteenth century to 1970s. Discusses interaction between literature and other aspects of development. Essential reference work. See 45.29 for volume 4. [AED]

45.26 Don Morrow et al. *A concise history of sport in Canada.* Toronto: Oxford University Press, 1989. ISBN 0-19-540693-1 (pbk). ▸ General survey. Emphasizes Canadian developments and contributions, especially in organized competitive sports. [JMB]

45.27 Desmond Morton. *A military history of Canada.* Edmonton: Hurtig, 1985. ISBN 0-88830-276-2. ▸ Survey of military history of Canada from first conflict with native peoples to cold war. Insists wars made modern Canada possible; helped shape divided national identity. [JMB]

45.28 R. Tom Naylor. *Canada in the European age, 1453–1919.* Vancouver, B.C.: New Star, 1987. ISBN 0-919573-70-3 (cl), 0-919573-69-X (pbk). ▸ General survey of economic history of Canada in international context to end of Great War. Controversial neo-Marxist approach. [JMB]

45.29 William H. New, ed. *Literary history of Canada: Canadian literature in English.* Vol. 4. Toronto: University of Toronto Press, 1990. ISBN 0-8020-5685-7 (cl), 0-8020-6610-0 (pbk). ▸ Collection of essays on Canadian writing, 1972–84, exploring new approaches in areas of methodology, critical theory, and context. New disciplines include film, television, and translation. See 45.25 for volumes 1–3. [AED]

45.30 Kenneth Harold Norrie and Douglas Owram. *A history of the Canadian economy.* Toronto: Harcourt Brace Jovanovich, 1991. ISBN 0-7747-3087-0 (pbk). ▸ General survey of Canada's economic history from earliest colonial period to present, chronologically organized. Written in Canadian political economy tradition. [JMB]

45.31 Bryan D. Palmer. *Working-class experience: the rise and reconstitution of Canadian labour, 1800–1991.* 2d ed. Boston: Butterworth, 1991. ISBN 0-7710-6945-6. ▸ General survey of history of Canadian labor to 1991 from neo-Marxist perspective. Discusses class antagonism, rise of working-class culture, and post–World War II labor militancy and legitimation. [JMB]

45.32 Joy Parr, ed. *Childhood and family in Canadian history.* Toronto: McClelland & Stewart, 1982. ISBN 0-7710-6938-3 (pbk). ▸ Collection of eight essays on Canadian childhood experience, fur trade period to 1940. Covers labor practices, poverty, children in institutions, and theories of child rearing. Best introduction available. [AED]

45.33 Alison Prentice et al. *Canadian women: a history.* Toronto:

Harcourt Brace Jovanovich, 1988. ISBN 0-7747-3112-5 (pbk). ‣ Major survey of Canadian women's history, pre-European period through French and British occupations to contemporary social, political, economic, and cultural issues. [AED]

45.34 Dennis Reid. *A concise history of Canadian painting.* 2d ed. Toronto: Oxford University Press, 1988. ISBN 0-19-540664-8 (cl), 0-19-540663-x (pbk). ‣ Useful guide to Canadian painting by French and English artists. Concentrates on individual painters, 1665 to 1980. Color plates and black-and-white reproductions. [AED]

45.35 E. E. Rich. *The fur trade and the Northwest to 1857.* Toronto: McClelland & Stewart, 1967. (Canadian centenary series, 11.) ‣ History of preconfederation Canadian West, emphasizing role of fur trade and especially North West Company and Hudson's Bay Company. Important synthesis, somewhat dated. [DJL]

45.36 S.E.D. Shortt, ed. *Medicine in Canadian society: historical perspectives.* Montreal: McGill-Queen's University Press, 1981. ISBN 0-7735-0356-0 (cl), 0-7735-0369-2 (pbk). ‣ Revisionist collection of essays in social history of Canadian medicine, eighteenth to twentieth century. Provocative introductory collection. [JMB]

45.37 Richard Simeon and Ian Robinson. *State, society, and the development of Canadian federalism.* Toronto: University of Toronto Press with Royal Commission on the Economic Union and Development Prospects for Canada and Government Publishing Centre, 1990. (Collected research studies, 71.) ISBN 0-8020-7319-0, ISSN 0829-2396. ‣ Study of federal-provincial relations in Canada from confederation period to late 1980s, chronologically organized. Traces development of classic federalism through World War II and development of modern federalism since 1945. Influential introduction. [JMB]

45.38 Gilbert A. Stelter and Alan F. J. Artibise, eds. *The Canadian city: essays in urban and social history.* Rev. ed. Ottawa, Ont.: Carleton University Press; distributed by Oxford University Press, 1984. ISBN 0-88629-018-x (pbk). ‣ Major collection of essays in Canadian urban history from colonial period to 1980s. Concentrates on metropolitan growth, physical environment, urban society, and urban reform and government. Weak on suburbanization. [JMB]

45.39 Edgar Wickberg, ed. *From China to Canada: a history of the Chinese communities in Canada.* Toronto: McClelland & Stewart with Multiculturalism Directorate, 1982. (Generations: a history of Canada's peoples.) ISBN 0-7710-2241-7 (pbk). ‣ Survey of Chinese community in Canada, 1858 to 1970s, partly from Chinese perspective using viewpoints derived from Chinese sources. [JMB]

45.40 J. Donald Wilson, Robert M. Stamp, and Louis-Philippe Audet, eds. *Canadian education: a history.* Scarborough, Ont.: Prentice-Hall, 1970. ISBN 0-13-113050-1. ‣ General survey of development of education in Canada to end of 1960s. Good coverage of formal institutions. [JMB]

45.41 Robin W. Winks. *The blacks in Canada: a history.* New Haven: Yale University Press, 1971. ISBN 0-300-01361-2. ‣ General study of blacks in Canada to 1970, based on considerable archival research. Good chapters on slavery, black loyalists, Underground Railroad, and modern developments. Includes appendix on numbers of immigrants. [JMB]

Atlantic Provinces

45.42 David G. Alexander. *Atlantic Canada and confederation: essays in Canadian political economy.* Eric W. Sager, Lewis R. Fisher, and Stuart O. Pierson, comps. Toronto: University of Toronto Press with Memorial University of Newfoundland,

1983. ISBN 0-8020-2487-4 (cl), 0-8020-6512-0 (pbk). ‣ Posthumous collection of articles focusing on regional political economy. Analyses confirm integrity and viability of small societies within national and global blocs. [MBT]

45.43 James P. Bickerton. *Nova Scotia, Ottawa, and the politics of regional development.* Toronto: University of Toronto Press, 1990. ISBN 0-8020-2711-3 (cl), 0-8020-6745-X (pbk). ‣ Provincial case study of federal response to regional inequalities. Center-periphery approached as political issue and policy field, informed by class analysis. Provocative and controversial. [MBT]

45.44 Andrew Hill Clark. *Three centuries and the island: a historical geography of settlement and agriculture in Prince Edward Island, Canada.* Toronto: University of Toronto Press, 1959. ‣ Pioneering historical geography of Canada's smallest province, focusing on settlement and agriculture. Many useful maps and charts. Based entirely on published sources. [JMB]

45.45 Jean Daigle, ed. *The Acadians of the Maritimes: thematic studies.* Moncton, N.B.: Centre d'Études Acadiennes, 1982. ISBN 0-916910-21. ‣ General study of Acadians from colonial times to present. Particularly insightful on Acadian renaissance of twentieth century. [JMB]

45.46 Philip Girard and Jim Phillips, eds. *The Nova Scotia experience.* Toronto: University of Toronto Press for Osgoode Society, 1990. (Essays in the history of Canadian law, 3.) ISBN 0-8020-5863-9. ‣ Revisionist collection of essays on history of law in Nova Scotia Includes studies of divorce, law reform, child custody, and criminal law. Opens new field. [JMB]

45.47 John G. Reid. *Six crucial decades: times of change in the history of the Maritimes.* Halifax, N.S.: Nimbus, 1987. ISBN 0-920852-84-X (pbk). ‣ Survey of history of maritime provinces focusing on change in six selected decades, seen as exemplifying turning points in development of region. [JMB]

Prairie Provinces

45.48 John H. Archer. *Saskatchewan: a history.* Saskatoon, Sask.: Western Producer Prairie, 1981. ISBN 0-88833-062-6. ‣ General history of province of Saskatchewan from earliest inhabitants to 1980. Essential regional survey. [JMB]

45.49 Gerald Friesen. *The Canadian prairies: a history.* Lincoln and Toronto: University of Nebraska Press and University of Toronto Press, 1984. ISBN 0-8032-1972-5, 0-8020-2513-7. ‣ Award-winning regional history of prairie provinces from first inhabitants to 1980s. General survey often focused around historiographical controversies. [JMB]

45.50 W. L. Morton. *Manitoba: a history.* 1967 2d ed. Toronto: University of Toronto Press, 1970. ISBN 0-8020-1711-8 (cl), 0-8020-6070-6 (pbk). ‣ General history of province of Manitoba from earliest inhabitants to 1960s. Strongest on period before Canadian confederation in 1870. After 1870, concentrates on political affairs. [JMB]

45.51 Howard Palmer and Tamara Palmer. *Alberta: a new history.* Edmonton: Hurtig, 1990. ISBN 0-88830-340-8. ‣ General history of province of Alberta from aboriginal nomadic life to contemporary economic, political, and social issues. Includes maps, photographs, and annotated bibliography. Important regional history. [AED]

British Columbia

45.52 Jean Barman. *The West beyond the West: a history of British Columbia.* Toronto: University of Toronto Press, 1991. ISBN 0-8020-2739-3. ‣ General history of province of British Columbia from earliest inhabitants to 1990. [JMB]

45.53 Margaret A. Ormsby. *British Columbia: a history.* 1958 ed.

Toronto: Macmillan, 1971. ▸ General survey of history of province of British Columbia from first explorers to 1960s. Concentrates on political developments; weak on economics and native peoples. [JMB]

Quebec

45.54 Micheline Dumont-Johnson and Collectif Clio. *L'histoire des femmes au Québec depuis quatre siècles.* Rev. ed. Montreal: Le Jour, 1992. ISBN 2-89044-440-6. ▸ Groundbreaking overview of history of women in Quebec from women's perspective, from New France to 1990. English translation of first edition available under title *Quebec Women: A History.* [JR]

45.55 Serge Gagnon. *Quebec and its historians, 1840–1920.* 1982 ed. Jane Brierley, trans. Montreal: Harvest House, 1982. ISBN 0-88772-026-9 (cl), 0-88772-213-X (pbk). ▸ Assessment of major historians who, before 1920, shaped French-Canadian view of past. Emphasizes historical interpretation, values, and ideology. Essential reading. [JR]

45.56 Jacques Rouillard. *Histoire du syndicalisme Québeçois.* Montreal: Boréal Express, 1989. ISBN 2-89052-243-1. ▸ Standard examination of Quebec trade union movement from nineteenth century to 1980 with emphasis on recent period. Shows relationship to and differences with North American labor movement in cultural and religious terms. [JR]

45.57 Ronald Rudin. *The forgotten Quebecers: a history of English-speaking Quebec, 1759–1980.* Quebec: Institut Québeçois de Recherche sur la Culture; distributed by Diffusion Prologue, 1985. ISBN 2-89224-068-9 (pbk). ▸ Pioneering account of important Quebec minority, particularly crucial in economic development of Montreal. Examines ethnic origins, religious diversity, regional distribution, and political role. [JR]

45.58 Gerard Tougas. *History of French Canadian literature.* 1966 2d ed. Alta Lind Cook, trans. Westport, Conn.: Greenwood, 1976. ISBN 0-8371-8858-X. ▸ Useful translation of older survey of French Canadian literature establishing its main tendencies. Updated French version published in 1974. [JR]

45.59 Susan Mann Trofimenkoff. *The dream of nation: a social and intellectual history of Quebec.* 1982 ed. Toronto: Gage, 1983. ISBN 0-7715-5691-8. ▸ Interpretive synthesis tracing development of Quebec from colonial beginnings to 1980. Well documented, particularly good on nationalism, social developments, and women's history. [JR]

DISCOVERY AND SETTLEMENT TO 1763

North America

45.60 John Bartlet Brebner. *The explorers of North America, 1492–1806.* 1933 ed. Cleveland: World, 1966. ▸ Classic survey of North American exploration from Canadian perspective. Also available in photocopy from Ann Arbor: University Microfilms International, 1981. [DJL]

45.61 Tryggvi J. Oleson. *Early voyages and northern approaches, 1000–1632.* Toronto: McClelland & Stewart, 1963. (Canadian centenary series, 1.) ▸ Controversial survey of early exploration focusing on northern rather than southern approaches. Debatable thesis on origins of Thule, Eskimos who replaced Dorset Paleoeskimos. [DJL]

45.62 David B. Quinn. *North America from earliest discovery to first settlements: the Norse voyages to 1612.* New York: Harper & Row, 1977. ISBN 0-06-013458-5. ▸ Survey of early European discovery and exploration of North America to 1610. Focuses on European activity rather than cultural contact and conflict, although American Indian context not ignored. [JMB]

45.63 Robert-Lionel Séguin. *La civilisation traditionnelle de*

l'habitant aux dix-neuvième et dix-huitième siècles. 2d ed. Montreal: Fides, 1973. ▸ Old but still useful compendium of ethnographic information on how peoples in New France lived and adapted to their physical environment. [JR]

Atlantic Region

45.64 John Bartlet Brebner. *New England's outpost: Acadia before the conquest of Canada.* 1927 ed. New York: Franklin, 1973. ISBN 0-8337-5107-7. ▸ Classic study examining peculiar problems of Acadians in international conflict between French and English, culminating in their expulsion from Nova Scotia in 1755. [DJL]

45.65 Gillian T. Cell. *English enterprise in Newfoundland, 1577–1660.* Toronto: University of Toronto Press, 1969. ISBN 0-8020-5232-0. ▸ Study of organization of Newfoundland fishery and attempts at colonization, 1610–60. Concludes settlement not necessary to make fishery profitable. Still essential reading. [JMB]

45.66 Naomi E. S. Griffiths. *The contexts of Acadian history, 1686–1784.* Montreal: McGill-Queen's University Press, 1992. ISBN 0-7735-0883-X (cl), 0-7735-0886-4 (pbk). ▸ Series of lectures summarizing lifetime of work on early Acadia. Covers period of settlement, establishment of Acadian identity, and notorious expulsions, ending with triumph over exile. Provocative summary. [JMB]

45.67 W. Gordon Handcock. *Soe longe as there comes noe women: origins of English settlement in Newfoundland.* St. John's, Nfld.: Breakwater, 1989. ISBN 0-920911-80-3 (cl), 0-920911-55-2 (pbk). ▸ Important study of English migration to and settlement of Newfoundland from beginning of sixteenth century to 1830, focusing particularly on English origins in West Country districts. [JMB]

45.68 C. Grant Head. *Eighteenth-century Newfoundland: a geographer's perspective.* Toronto: McClelland & Stewart, 1976. ISBN 0-7710-9799-9. ▸ Regional history examining transformation of migratory fishing camps into permanent settlements. Refutes idea that land was occupied illegally. Groundbreaking, not yet superceded. [DJL]

45.69 Christopher Moore. *Louisbourg portraits: life in an eighteenth-century garrison town.* 1982 ed. Toronto: Macmillan, 1983. ISBN 0-7715-9712-6 (cl, 1982), 0-7715-9755-X (pbk). ▸ Prize-winning social history consisting of series of vignettes describing lives of common people, based on variety of manuscript sources. Earlier title: *Louisbourg Portraits: Five Dramatic, True Tales of People Who Lived in an Eighteenth-Century Garrison Town.* [DJL]

45.70 John G. Reid. *Acadia, Maine, and New Scotland: marginal colonies in the seventeenth century.* Toronto: University of Toronto Press with Huronia Historical Parks and Ontario Ministry of Culture and Recreation, 1981. ISBN 0-8020-5508-7. ▸ Important comparative study of three marginal North American colonies, showing how and why colonization process could and did fail. [DJL]

New France

45.71 Hubert Charbonneau et al. *Naissance d'une population: les Français établis au Canada au seizième.* Paris and Montreal: Institut National d'Études Demographiques and Presses de l'Université de Montréal, 1987. (Institut National d'Études Demographiques: travaux et documents, 118.) ISBN 2-7332-0118-2, 2-7606-0806-9, ISSN 0071-8823. ▸ Demographic analysis of French immigration to St. Lawrence Valley before 1680. Studies migration policy, marriage rates, fecundity, and mortality. Basic work. [JR]

45.72 Louise Dechene. *Habitants and merchants in Montreal in the seventeenth century.* Montreal: McGill-Queen's University Press, 1992. ISBN 0-7735-0658-6. ▸ Groundbreaking, influential study of population, commerce, agriculture, and social structure during first seventy years of French settlement of Montreal.

Demonstrates fur trade and peasant agriculture largely unconnected, especially in personnel. [JR]

45.73 William John Eccles. *Canada under Louis XIV, 1663–1701.* New York and Toronto: Oxford University Press and McClelland & Stewart, 1964. (Canadian centenary series, 3.) ▸ Useful, if somewhat dated, general account of New France during period of intensive growth and establishment of institutions. Stresses institutional and political evolution as well as economic and social development. [JR]

45.74 William John Eccles. *France in America.* Rev. ed. East Lansing: Michigan State University Press, 1990. ISBN 0-87013-284-9. ▸ Survey of history of New France and other French colonies in America until 1783. Especially illuminating on relationship of Canadian history with early history of United States. [JR]

45.75 Guy Fregault. *Canada: the war of the conquest.* Margaret M. Cameron, trans. Toronto: Oxford University Press, 1969. ▸ Study of Seven Years' War from French-Canadian viewpoint. Stresses horrors of war, military occupation, and lack of support from metropolis. Provocative at time of publication. [JR]

45.76 R. Cole Harris. *The seigneurial system in early Canada: a geographical study.* 1966 ed. Kingston, Ont.: McGill-Queen's University Press, 1984. ISBN 0-7735-0431-1 (cl), 0-7735-0434-6 (pbk). ▸ Analysis of land-use and distribution system in New France. Refutes claims that seigneurial system was most important factor in settlement of colony. Useful introduction. [DJL]

45.77 Jacques Mathieu. *La Nouvelle-France: les Français en Amérique du Nord, XVIe–XVIIIe siècle.* Laval, Que.: Les Presses de l'Université Laval, 1991. ISBN 2-7637-7250-1. ▸ Short introduction to history of New France based on most recent research. Not only discusses institutions and economic growth, but also history of population, family, and life cycles. [JR]

45.78 C. P. Stacey. *Quebec 1759: the siege and the battle.* 1959 ed. Toronto: Macmillan, 1984. ISBN 0-7715-9868-8 (pbk). ▸ Classic work by military historian. Detailed account of military events that ended French presence in North America. [JR]

45.79 George F. G. Stanley. *New France: the last phase, 1744–1760.* Toronto: McClelland & Stewart, 1968. (Canadian centenary series, 5.) ▸ Balanced overview of last decades of French period in North America. Stresses military history and imperial policy. [JR]

45.80 Marcel Trudel. *The beginnings of New France, 1526–1663.* Patricia Claxton, trans. Toronto: McClelland & Stewart, 1973. (Canadian centenary series, 2.) ISBN 0-7710-8610-5. ▸ Overview by leading specialist of period. Well documented and political in approach. Views period as series of setbacks for French settlement. [JR]

45.81 Marcel Trudel. *Histoire de la Nouvelle-France.* Vol. 3: *La seigneurie des Cents-Associés, 1627–1663.* Vol. 3.1: *Les événements.* Vol. 3.2: *La société.* Montreal: Fides, 1963–83. ISBN 2-7621-0788-1 (v. 3.1), 2-7621-1215-X (v. 3.2). ▸ Best, very detailed account of this early period. Careful examination of fact, some stress on role of individuals. [JR]

Canadian West

45.82 Arthur J. Ray and Donald B. Freeman. *"Give us good measure": an economic analysis of relations between the Indians and the Hudson's Bay Company before 1763.* Toronto: University of Toronto Press, 1978. ISBN 0-8020-5418-8 (cl), 0-8020-6334-9 (pbk). ▸ Reconstruction of trading system adopted by Hudson's Bay Company, focusing on relationship with and role of native peoples. Quantitative methodology employed to good effect. [DJL]

COLONIAL PERIOD, 1760–1870

British North America

45.83 Constance Backhouse. *Petticoats and prejudice: women and law in nineteenth-century Canada.* Toronto: Women's Press for Osgoode Society, 1991. ISBN 0-88961-161-0 (pbk). ▸ Groundbreaking, provocative study of legal status of women in nineteenth-century British North America. Examines experience of individuals in relation to law, including marriage, rape, and abortion; also labor rights. [AED]

45.84 Wallace Brown and Hereward Senior. *Victorious in defeat: the loyalists in Canada.* New York: Facts on File, 1984. ISBN 0-87196-957-2. ▸ General study of loyalists, beginning with treatment in United States and migration to British North America. Includes sections on African blacks and Indians. [JMB]

45.85 Phillip A. Buckner. *The transition to responsible government: British policy in British North America, 1815–1850.* Westport, Conn.: Greenwood, 1985. ISBN 0-313-24630-0, ISSN 0163-3813. ▸ Revisionist study of British colonial policy and colonial politics in British North America. Particularly detailed on colonial system and development of responsible government. Useful introduction. [JMB]

45.86 John M. Bumsted. *The people's clearance: highland emigration to British North America, 1770–1815.* 1967 ed. Edinburgh: Edinburgh University Press, 1982. ISBN 0-85224-419-3. ▸ Controversial study of highland emigration to British North America, 1770–1815. Sees notorious clearances evicting tenants as less important factors in emigration than voluntary decisions of population to seek better opportunity. [JMB]

45.87 Helen I. Cowan. *British emigration to British North America: the first hundred years.* Rev. ed. Toronto: University of Toronto Press, 1961. ISBN 0-8020-7062-0. ▸ Classic study of overall patterns of immigration before confederation. Includes statistical appendixes. Also available in photocopy from Ann Arbor: University Microfilms International, 1981. [JMB]

45.88 Donald Grant Creighton. *The empire of the St. Lawrence.* 1937 ed. Toronto: Macmillan, 1956. ▸ Classic study; first to propose influential nationalist thesis that St. Lawrence River was basis of transcontinental East-West system which eventually produced nation. Earlier title: *Commercial Empire of the St. Lawrence, 1760–1850.* [JMB]

45.89 Donald Grant Creighton. *The road to confederation: the emergence of Canada, 1863–1867.* 1964 ed. Westport, Conn.: Greenwood, 1976. ISBN 0-8371-8435-5. ▸ Classic study of political unification of Canada in 1860s. Whiggish, progressive, and nationalistic in approach. [JMB]

45.90 Bruce S. Elliott. *Irish migrants in the Canadas: a new approach.* Kingston, Ont. and Belfast: McGill-Queen's University Press and Institute of Irish Studies, Queens University of Belfast, 1988. ISBN 0-7735-0607-1. ▸ Important study of migration from northern Ireland to British North America in nineteenth century. Emphasizes chain migration, by which immigrants followed one another across the Atlantic, using genealogical information to link migrants. [JMB]

45.91 Judith Fingard. *Jack in port: sailortowns of eastern Canada.* Toronto: University of Toronto Press, 1982. ISBN 0-8020-2458-0 (cl), 0-8020-6467-1 (pbk). ▸ Fascinating exploration of life and problems of merchant seaman on shore in Halifax, St. John, and Quebec. Includes chapters on labor market and labor rights. [JMB]

45.92 Jakob Johann Benjamin Forster. *A conjunction of interests: business, politics, and tariffs, 1825–1879.* Toronto: University of Toronto Press, 1986. ISBN 0-8020-5680-6 (cl), 0-8020-6612-7 (pbk). ▸ Study of politics of protectionism in British North America and Canada, 1825–79. Discusses reciprocity, confederation, and development of national policy. Important introduction. [JMB]

45.93 John Garner. *The franchise and politics in British North America, 1755–1867.* Toronto: University of Toronto Press, 1969. ISBN 0-8020-3219-2. ▸ Definitive study of relationship of voting franchise and politics in British North America, including religious and other disqualifications (such as gender). Wider in scope than title suggests. [JMB]

45.94 Gerald S. Graham. *Sea power and British North America, 1783–1820: a study in British colonial policy.* 1941 ed. New York: Greenwood, 1968. ▸ Classic study of mercantile and naval relations of North Atlantic in period after American Revolution, focusing on breakdown of self-contained empire and American challenge. [JMB]

45.95 J. Mackay Hitsman. *The incredible War of 1812: a military history.* Toronto: University of Toronto Press, 1965. ▸ Standard study of War of 1812 from Canadian perspective, including both military and diplomatic aspects. [JMB]

45.96 Cecil J. Houston and William J. Smyth. *Irish emigration and Canadian settlement: patterns, links, and letters.* Toronto and Belfast: University of Toronto Press and Ulster Historical Foundation, 1990. ISBN 0-8020-5829-9, 0-901905-45-3. ▸ Revisionist study of process of emigration from Ireland to British North America. Particularly good on Ulster and its migrants. Includes three collections of immigrant letters. [JMB]

45.97 Arthur R. M. Lower. *Great Britain's woodyard: British America and the timber trade, 1763–1867.* Montreal: McGill-Queen's University Press, 1973. ISBN 0-7735-0096-0. ▸ Study of timber trade in British North America, one of major resource industries of colonies. Particularly good on British tariff policy and trade. [JMB]

45.98 Ged Martin, ed. *The causes of Canadian confederation.* Fredericton, N.B.: Acadiensis Press, 1990. ISBN 0-919107-25-7. ▸ Collection of papers from conference at Edinburgh in 1988. Excellent papers on anticonfederates, as well as on maritime provinces and confederation. Revisionist. [JMB]

45.99 Donald C. Masters. *The Reciprocity Treaty of 1854: its history, its relation to British colonial and foreign policy and to the development of Canadian fiscal autonomy.* 1937 ed. Toronto: McClelland & Stewart, 1963. ▸ Classic study of first Canadian-American treaty to encourage free trade. Argues specific provisions of treaty less important for British North America than its commercial orientation. [JMB]

45.100 Alan Metcalfe. *Canada learns to play: the emergence of organized sport, 1807–1914.* Toronto: McClelland & Stewart, 1987. ISBN 0-7710-5870-5. ▸ Groundbreaking survey of origins of organized sport in Canada, 1807–1914. Concentrates on sporting clubs, organized team sport, and development of both amateurism and professionalism. [JMB]

45.101 George F. G. Stanley. *Canada invaded, 1775–1776.* 1973 ed. Toronto: Stevens, 1977. (Canadian War Museum historical publications, 8.) ISBN 0-88866-537-7 (cl), 0-88866-578-4 (pbk). ▸ Account of first effort to incorporate Canada into continental union, stressing military strategy of American invasion and repulse of invaders at Quebec. [JR]

45.102 Gordon T. Stewart. *The origins of Canadian politics: a comparative approach.* Vancouver: University of British Columbia Press, 1986. ISBN 0-7748-0260-X (pbk). ▸ Revisionist survey of Canadian politics, emphasizing origins in England and United States. Sees period of instability, 1828–64, followed by stability, 1864–1914. [JMB]

45.103 Martin Brook Taylor. *Promoters, patriots, and partisans:*

historiography in nineteenth-century Canada. Toronto: University of Toronto Press, 1989. ISBN 0-8020-2683-4 (cl), 0-8020-6716-6 (pbk). ▸ Study of growth of Canadian historical writing prior to establishment of academic discipline. From colonial advocacy through emphasis on national growth to conflicts between nation and region. Essential survey of early historiography. [AED]

45.104 Gilbert Norman Tucker. *The Canadian commercial revolution, 1845–1851.* 1936 ed. Hamden, Conn.: Archon, 1971. ISBN 0-208-01026-2. ▸ Classic study of ending of British Navigation Laws in 1840s and subsequent commercial shift of Canada from transatlantic empire to intercontinentalism. [JMB]

45.105 Peter B. Waite. *The life and times of confederation, 1864–1867: politics, newspapers, and the union of British North America.* 2d ed. Toronto: University of Toronto Press, 1967. ▸ Classic study of debate over Canadian confederation in various provinces of British North America, relying on newspapers as main source material. [JMB]

45.106 W. Peter Ward. *Courtship, love, and marriage in nineteenth-century English Canada.* Montreal: McGill-Queen's University Press, 1990. ISBN 0-7735-0749-3. ▸ Pioneering study of courtship, love, and marriage, relying heavily on literary sources. Emphasizes increased presence of romantic love over century. [JMB]

45.107 Carol Wilton, ed. *Beyond the law: lawyers and business in Canada, 1830 to 1930.* Toronto: Butterworth for the Osgoode Society, 1991. (Essays in the history of Canadian law, 4.) ISBN 0-409-89777-9. ▸ Pioneering collection of essays treating interaction between lawyers and business, in century prior to 1930, in facilitating commercial law, in establishing framework of business transactions, and as advisers to business, as well as businessmen themselves. [JMB]

45.108 Suzanne Elizabeth Zeller. *Inventing Canada: early Victorian science and the idea of a transcontinental nation.* Toronto: University of Toronto Press, 1987. ISBN 0-8020-2644-3 (cl), 0-8020-6606-2 (pbk). ▸ Groundbreaking, provocative study of early development of scientific empiricism in Canada and its harnessing to nationalist and expansionist impulse. [DJL]

Upper and Lower Canada

45.109 Donald Harron Akenson. *The Irish in Ontario: a study in rural history.* Kingston, Ont.: McGill-Queen's University Press, 1984. ISBN 0-7735-0430-3. ▸ Controversial study of settlement of Irish in rural Upper Canada. Emphasizes Irish settlement problems more connected with time of arrival than with their cultural past. [JMB]

45.110 J.M.S. Careless. *Brown of "The Globe."* Vol. 1: *The voice of Upper Canada, 1818–1859.* 1959 ed. Toronto: Dundurn, 1989. ISBN 1-55002-050-1. ▸ Classic biography of one of leading Canadian newspaper editors and politicians, mid-nineteenth century, head of True Grit party and principal father of confederation. [JMB]

45.111 J.M.S. Careless. *Brown of "The Globe."* Vol. 2: *Statesman of confederation, 1860–1880.* 1963 ed. Toronto: Dundurn, 1989. ISBN 1-55002-051-X. ▸ Classic biography of major Canadian newspaper publisher and politician. [JMB]

45.112 J.M.S. Careless, ed. *The pre-confederation premiers: Ontario government leaders, 1841–1867.* Toronto: University of Toronto Press, 1980. ISBN 0-8020-3363-6. ▸ Study of political life of province of Canada from perspective of five Upper Canadian premiers, each one sketched by leading Canadian historian. [JMB]

45.113 Marjorie Griffin Cohen. *Women's work, markets, and economic development in nineteenth-century Ontario.* Toronto: University of Toronto Press, 1988. ISBN 0-8020-2651-6 (cl), 0-8020-6677-1 (pbk). ▸ Assessment of women's productive contribution in household and industrial economy. Revises traditional view of **Canadian** economic development, making British model inapplicable to Ontario. Groundbreaking study. [AED]

45.114 Gerald M. Craig. *Upper Canada: the formative years, 1784–1841.* New York and Toronto: Oxford University Press and McClelland & Stewart, 1963. (Canadian centenary series, 7.) ‣ Survey of Upper Canada from its founding to union with Lower Canada in 1841. Best on political and constitutional matters; traditional discussion of economic and social matters. [JMB]

45.115 Donald Grant Creighton. *John A. Macdonald.* Vol. 1: *The young politician.* 1952 ed. Toronto: Macmillan, 1966. ‣ Classic biography of formative years of Canada's first prime minister. Admired for its literary style. [JMB]

45.116 Jane Errington. *The lion, the eagle, and Upper Canada: a developing colonial ideology.* Toronto: McGill-Queen's University Press, 1987. ISBN 0-7735-0603-9. ‣ Provocative, revisionist study of early ideological conflict focusing on press in Upper Canada. Details struggle between British and American values and triumph of British principles during and after War of 1812. [JMB]

45.117 David Gagan. *Hopeful travellers: families, land, and social change in mid-Victorian Peel County, Canada West.* Toronto: University of Toronto Press, 1981. ISBN 0-8020-2435-1. ‣ Pioneering computer-based study, partly quantitative, of families and land in one county of Upper Canada–Ontario in mid-nineteenth century. Major themes are mobility and persistence. [JMB]

45.118 James Keith Johnson. *Becoming prominent: regional leadership in Upper Canada, 1791–1841.* Kingston, Ont.: McGill-Queen's University Press, 1989. ISBN 0-7735-0641-1. ‣ Controversial study of regional elites of Upper Canada, 1791–1841, concluding elites made a living in multiple ways. Finds complicated relationship between becoming and staying prominent. [JMB]

45.119 Michael B. Katz. *The people of Hamilton, Canada West: family and class in a mid-nineteeenth-century city.* Cambridge, Mass.: Harvard University Press, 1975. ISBN 0-674-66125-7. ‣ Pioneering study of mid-nineteenth-century Canadian city based on quantitative techniques. Explores social structure, mobility, entrepreneurialism, and family structure. [JMB]

45.120 John McCallum. *Unequal beginnings: agriculture and economic development in Quebec and Ontario until 1870.* Toronto: University of Toronto Press, 1980. ISBN 0-8020-5455-2 (cl), 0-8020-6362-4 (pbk). ‣ Comparative study of agriculture and economic development in Quebec and Ontario, arguing former unable to use grain cultivation for economic development while latter based growth on wheat. Important thesis, well presented. [JMB]

45.121 Marianne McLean. *The people of Glengarry: highlanders in transition, 1745–1820.* Montreal: McGill-Queen's University Press, 1991. ISBN 0-7735-0814-7. ‣ Provocative, stimulating, revisionist study of relationship between economic change in highlands and migration to early Canada, insisting that clearances evicting tenants played major role in process. [JMB]

45.122 David Mills. *The idea of loyalty in Upper Canada, 1784–1850.* Kingston, Ont.: McGill-Queen's University Press, 1988. ISBN 0-7735-0660-8. ‣ Useful, revisionist study of ideology of loyalty in Upper Canada and its political uses. Argues loyalty one of principal party issues in Upper Canada before 1850. [JMB]

45.123 Sidney John Roderick Noel. *Patrons, clients, brokers: Ontario society and politics, 1791–1896.* Toronto: University of Toronto Press, 1990. ISBN 0-8020-5858-2 (cl), 0-8020-6774-3 (pbk). ‣ Revisionist study of politics in Upper Canada, later Ontario, focusing on relationships among patrons, clients, and political brokers. Sees province's political culture as modified American one, with loyalists as key element. [JMB]

45.124 Paul Romney. *Mr. Attorney: the attorney general for Ontario in court, cabinet, and legislature, 1791–1899.* Toronto: University of Toronto Press for Osgoode Society, 1986. ISBN 0-8020-3431-4. ‣ Pioneering study of role of attorney general in political and judicial administration of Upper Canada–Ontario. Important to new legal history. [JMB]

45.125 William Westfall. *Two worlds: the Protestant culture of nineteenth-century Ontario.* Kingston, Ont.: McGill-Queen's University Press, 1989. ISBN 0-7735-0669-1. ‣ Controversial study of interrelationship of religious and secular ideals and resulting impact on social and cultural attitudes of period, creating distinct Ontario culture. [AED]

45.126 Bruce G. Wilson. *The enterprises of Robert Hamilton: a study of wealth and influence in early Upper Canada, 1776–1812.* Ottawa, Ont.: Carleton University Press; distributed by Oxford University Press, 1983. ISBN 0-88629-010-4 (cl), 0-88629-009-0 (pbk). ‣ Detailed study of early development of Niagara peninsula of Ontario, emphasizing networks of trade and commerce that came together in person of merchant Robert Hamilton. [JMB]

Province of Canada

45.127 J.M.S. Careless. *The union of the Canadas: the growth of Canadian institutions, 1841–1857.* Toronto: McClelland & Stewart, 1967. (Canadian centenary series, 10.) ‣ Study of province of united Canada from its creation in 1840 to 1857. Best on politics, but also considers economic, social, and cultural developments. [JMB]

45.128 Douglas McCalla. *The Upper Canada trade, 1834–1872: a study of the Buchanan's business.* Toronto: University of Toronto Press, 1979. ISBN 0-8020-5444-0. ‣ Stimulating study of major family merchant firm active in Upper Canada in Toronto and Hamilton, founding to collapse. Demonstrates strengths and weaknesses of family enterprise. [JMB]

45.129 Jacques Monet. *The last cannon shot: a study of French-Canadian nationalism, 1837–1850.* Toronto: University of Toronto Press, 1969. ISBN 0-8020-5211-8. ‣ Study of orientations and strategies of French Canadian politicians at crucial historical point, examining debate on union, campaign for responsible government, and crises over American annexation. [JR]

Canada

45.130 Harold A. Innis. *The fur trade in Canada: an introduction to Canadian economic history.* 1956 rev. ed. Toronto: University of Toronto Press, 1977. ISBN 0-8020-4029-2 (cl), 0-8020-6001-3 (pbk). ‣ Classic economic history based on theory of centrality of certain staple resources for Canadian economic development, in this case fur trade. Serious discusson of native peoples. [DJL]

45.131 W. L. Morton. *The critical years: the union of British North America, 1857–1873.* 1964 ed. Toronto: McClelland & Stewart, 1977. (Canadian centenary series, 12.) ISBN 0-7710-6561-2. ‣ Classic study of confederation of provinces of British North America from first discussion to inclusion of Prince Edward Island in 1873. [JMB]

Atlantic Provinces

45.132 Thomas William Acheson. *Saint John: the making of a colonial urban community.* Toronto: University of Toronto Press, 1985. ISBN 0-8020-2586-2. ‣ Study of early development of Canadian city, founded by loyalists and noted for its shipbuilding. Includes chapters on economy, social order, temperance, education, political reform, and policing. Important urban study. [JMB]

45.133 J. Murray Beck. *Joseph Howe.* Vol. 1: *Conservative reformer, 1804–1848.* 1982 ed. Kingston, Ont.: McGill-Queen's

University Press, 1984. ISBN 0-7735-0387-0 (cl, 1982), 0-7735-0445-1 (pbk). ▸ First volume of detailed biography (with 45.134) of leading newspaperman and political reformer in British North America. [JMB]

45.134 J. Murray Beck. *Joseph Howe.* Vol. 2: *The Briton becomes Canadian, 1848–1873.* 1983 ed. Kingston, Ont.: McGill-Queen's University Press, 1984. ISBN 0-7735-0388-9 (cl, 1983), 0-7735-0447-8 (pbk). ▸ Full-scale biography (with 45.133) of Joseph Howe, newspaper editor, reform politician, premier of Nova Scotia, and opponent of confederation. [JMB]

45.135 Winthrop Pickard Bell. *The "foreign Protestants" and the settlement of Nova Scotia: the history of a piece of arrested colonial policy in the eighteenth century.* 1961 ed. Fredericton, N.B.: Acadiensis Press, 1990. ISBN 0-919107-28-1. ▸ Classic study of recruitment and settlement in Nova Scotia of Protestants from France, Germany, and Switzerland in 1760s. Reprints many documents. [JMB]

45.136 John Bartlet Brebner. *The neutral Yankees of Nova Scotia: a marginal colony during the revolutionary years.* 1937 ed. New York: Russell & Russell, 1970. ▸ Pioneering, classic study. Argues that Nova Scotia's Yankee population adopted position of neutrality because of its isolation, poverty, military weakness, and dependence on Britain. [DJL]

45.137 John M. Bumsted. *Land, settlement, and politics on eighteenth-century Prince Edward Island.* Kingston, Ont.: McGill-Queen's University Press, 1987. ISBN 0-7735-0566-0. ▸ Prize-winning study of early development of island of St. John (Prince Edward Island after 1799). Emphasizes British colonial policy, complex land question, arrival of Loyalists, and escheat movement. [JMB]

45.138 Ann Gorman Condon. *The loyalist dream for New Brunswick: the envy of the American states.* Fredericton, N.B.: New Ireland Press, 1984. ISBN 0-920483-01-1 (pbk). ▸ Provocative study of migration of loyalist elite to New Brunswick, focusing particularly on twenty leading figures in larger context of disbanded soldiers and ordinary refugees. [JMB]

45.139 Gertrude E. Gunn. *The political history of Newfoundland, 1832–1864.* Toronto: University of Toronto Press, 1966. ▸ Classic study of political development of Newfoundland from granting of representative assembly to Quebec Conference of 1864. [JMB]

45.140 Stephen J. Hornsby. *Nineteenth-century Cape Breton: a historical geography.* Montreal: McGill-Queen's University Press, 1992. ISBN 0-7735-0889-9. ▸ Case study arguing expansion of European capital and labor into North America created two broad patterns of development: agricultural settlement and staples exploitation. Important new regional history. [MBT]

45.141 Neil MacKinnon. *This unfriendly soil: the loyalist experience in Nova Scotia, 1783–1791.* Kingston, Ont.: McGill-Queen's University Press, 1986. ISBN 0-7735-0596-2. ▸ Study of loyalist settlement of Nova Scotia, emphasizing varied origins and many tribulations. Argues many eventually returned to United States. Useful survey. [JMB]

45.142 William Stewart MacNutt. *The Atlantic provinces: the emergence of colonial society, 1712–1857.* Toronto: McClelland & Stewart, 1965. (Canadian centenary series, 9.) ▸ Pioneering regional study of early history of Atlantic provinces; better on politics than on social and cultural developments. Still not superceded. [JMB]

45.143 William Stewart MacNutt. *New Brunswick: a history.* 1963 ed. Toronto: Macmillan, 1984. ISBN 0-7715-9818-1. ▸ Classic study of history of New Brunswick from founding to confederation. Particularly informative on politics. [JMB]

45.144 Shannon Ryan. *Fish out of water: the Newfoundland salt-fish trade, 1814–1914.* St. John's, Nfld.: Breakwater, 1986. ISBN 0-919519-47-4 (cl), 0-919519-90-3 (pbk). ▸ Analysis of classic staple-based single-export economy. Concludes political independence incompatible with commercial reality of declining markets. Important new regional study. [MBT]

45.145 Eric W. Sager. *Maritime capital: the shipping industry in Atlantic Canada, 1820–1914.* Montreal: McGill-Queen's University Press, 1990. ISBN 0-7735-0764-7. ▸ Rise and fall of regional shipbuilding and shipowning. Revisionist and controversial account suggesting landward focus of merchant capital within Canadian confederation produced decline. [MBT]

45.146 Eric W. Sager. *Seafaring labour: the merchant marine of Atlantic Canada, 1820–1914.* Kingston, Ont.: McGill-Queen's University Press, 1989. ISBN 0-7735-0670-5. ▸ Study of merchant seaman in Atlantic Canada, based on files of Atlantic shipping project at Memorial University of Newfoundland. Documents transition from preindustrial to industrial workplace. Significant quantitative study. [JMB]

45.147 Gordon T. Stewart and George Rawlyk. *A people highly favoured of God: the Nova Scotia Yankees and the American Revolution.* Hamden, Conn.: Archon, 1972. ISBN 0-208-01283-4. ▸ Provocative study of New Englanders in Nova Scotia in years before American Revolution and response to it, particularly emergence of religious revival led by Henry Alline. [JMB]

45.148 Peter Thomas. *Strangers from a secret land: the voyages of the brig Albion and the founding of the first Welsh settlements in Canada.* Toronto: University of Toronto Press, 1986. ISBN 0-8020-5694-6 (cl), 0-8020-6620-8 (pbk). ▸ Study of Welsh origins and subsequent establishment of first Welsh settlements in Nova Scotia and New Brunswick. Heavily based on Welsh-language newspapers. Imaginatively researched monograph. [JMB]

45.149 Leslie F. S. Upton. *Micmacs and colonists: Indian-white relations in the Maritimes, 1713–1867.* Vancouver: University of British Columbia Press, 1979. ISBN 0-7748-0114-X. ▸ Study of relationship between Micmacs and European intruders. Argues British conquest led to dispossession and irrelevancy to British governments. Essential if dated survey. [DJL]

45.150 James W. St. G. Walker. *The black loyalists: the search for a promised land in Nova Scotia and Sierra Leone, 1783–1870.* 1976 ed. Toronto: University of Toronto Press, 1992. ISBN 0-8020-7402-2. ▸ Groundbreaking study of blacks in American war of independence, departure for Nova Scotia as loyalists, and exodus in 1792 to Sierra Leone. [JMB]

45.151 Graeme Wynn. *Timber colony: a historical geography of early nineteenth-century New Brunswick.* Toronto: University of Toronto Press, 1981. ISBN 0-8020-5515-3 (cl), 0-8020-6407-8 (pbk). ▸ Key regional study of lumber trade of New Brunswick in first half of nineteenth century. Focuses on rise of sawmilling, entrepreneurialism, and regulation, environmental exploitation. [JMB]

Quebec

45.152 Michel Brunet. *Les Canadiens après la conquête, 1759–1775.* Montreal: Fides, 1969. ▸ Study of impact of conquest on French Canadian society. Nationalist interpretation; sees defeat in subordination of French, loss of collective freedom, and abnormal development. Highly controversial. [JR]

45.153 Serge Courville. *Entre ville et campagne: l'essor du village dans les seigneuries du Bas-Canada.* Quebec: Presses de l'Université Laval, 1990. ISBN 2-7637-7232-3. ▸ Study of rise of villages in Lower Canada between 1815 and 1851 by geographer. Explains important development in terms of population growth and expansion of rural industry. Important regional study. [JR]

45.154 Jean-Marie Fecteau. *Un nouvel ordre de choses: la pauvreté, le crime, l'état au Québec de la fin du dix-huitième siècle à 1840.* Outremont and Ville Saint Laurent, Que.: VLB Editeur and Diffusion Dimedia, 1989. ISBN 2-89005-359-8. ▸ Study of state management of crime and poverty in period of transition from feudal-like society to commercial and capitalist economy. Sees social institutions as means of social regulation. [JR]

45.155 Allan Greer. *Peasant, lord, and merchant: rural society in three Quebec parishes, 1740–1840.* Toronto: University of Toronto Press, 1985. ISBN 0-8020-2559-5 (cl), 0-8020-6578-3 (pbk). ▸ Influential case study of three parishes in Richelieu Valley, examining roles of seigneurialism and merchant capitalism in development of French Canada. [DJL]

45.156 Helen Taft Manning. *The revolt of French Canada, 1800–1835: a chapter in the history of the British Commonwealth.* New York: St. Martin's, 1962. ▸ Classic assessment of development of French Canadian nationalism, political conflicts in Lower Canada, and especially effects on policies of British government. [JR]

45.157 Fernand Ouellet. *Economic and social history of Quebec, 1760–1850: structures and conjunctures.* Toronto: Gage with Carleton University, Institute of Canadian Studies, 1980. ISBN 0-7715-5660-8. ▸ Major study influenced by Annales school. Socioeconomic approach based on cycles of economic change and influence on social class combined with cultural conflict. [JR]

45.158 Fernand Ouellet. *Lower Canada, 1791–1840: social change and nationalism.* Patricia Claxton, trans. Toronto: McClelland & Stewart, 1980. (Canadian centenary series, 8.) ISBN 0-7710-6921-9 (cl), 0-7710-6922-7 (pbk). ▸ Important survey influenced by Annales school. Focuses on cyclical economic change and cultural conflict as well as emergence of Quebec nationalism. [JR]

45.159 Gilles Paquet and Jean-Pierre Wallot. *Lower Canada at the turn of the nineteenth century: restructuring and modernization.* Ottawa, Ont.: Canadian Historical Association, 1988. ISBN 0-88798-135-6 (pbk). ▸ Short English-language summary of research of two authors published extensively in French. Based on Annales school, interprets conflict as between two bourgeoisies, one continental and one regional. [JR]

45.160 Gerald J. J. Tulchinsky. *The river barons: Montreal businessmen and the growth of industry and transportation.* Toronto: University of Toronto Press, 1977. ISBN 0-8020-5339-4. ▸ Examination of development of business community in Montreal at beginnings of industrialization, focusing on objectives and aspirations. Important monograph. [JR]

45.161 Jean-Pierre Wallot. *Un Québec qui bougeait: trame sociopolitique du Québec au tournant du dix-neuvième siècle.* Montreal: Boréal Express; distributed by Fides, 1973. ▸ Collection of articles with neonationalist perspective mainly on political and religious topics. Demonstrates Quebec was part of forward-moving society in Atlantic world. Highly controversial. [JR]

45.162 Brian Young. *George-Etienne Cartier: Montreal bourgeois.* Kingston, Ont.: McGill-Queen's University Press, 1981. ISBN 0-7735-0370-6 (cl), 0-7735-0371-4 (pbk). ▸ Key biography of one of fathers of Canadian confederation, main Federalist among French Canadians. Analyses his life as "grand bourgeois" of Montreal. [JR]

Canadian West

45.163 Jennifer S. H. Brown. *Strangers in blood: fur trade company families in Indian country.* Vancouver: University of British Columbia Press, 1980. ISBN 0-7748-0125-5 (cl), 0-7748-0251-5 (pbk). ▸ Study contrasting domestic lives of Hudson's Bay Company traders and North West Company traders in eighteenth- and nineteenth-century Canadian West. Emphasizes differences and lasting impact on family structure and identity. Discusses assimilation of mixed-blood descendants and emergence of *métis*. Groundbreaking combination of anthropology and history. [AED/RF]

45.164 Thomas Flanagan. *Louis "David" Riel: prophet of the New World.* 1979 ed. Halifax, N.S.: Formac, 1983. ISBN 0-88780-118-8. ▸ Biography of famous *métis* leader. Argues Riel was not mentally unstable but spiritually possessed. [DJL]

45.165 John S. Galbraith. *The Hudson's Bay Company as an imperial factor, 1821–69.* Berkeley: University of California Press, 1957. ▸ Classic analysis of business policies of Hudson's Bay Company after its merger with North West Company. Argues while company stifled competition, it also played important imperial role. [DJL]

45.166 Alvin C. Gluek, Jr. *Minnesota and the manifest destiny of the Canadian Northwest: a study in Canadian-American relations.* Toronto: University of Toronto Press, 1965. ▸ Study of relationship between Minnesota and Red River settlement in mid-nineteenth century, period when annexation to United States appeared possible. Useful summary. [JMB]

45.167 Margaret Arnett MacLeod and W. L. Morton. *Cuthbert Grant of Grantown: warden of the plains of Red River.* 1963 ed. Toronto: McClelland & Stewart, 1974. ISBN 0-7710-9771-9 (pbk). ▸ Biography of early mixed-blood leader of Red River, best known for role in Seven Oaks incident of 1816, in which European settlers were killed by *métis*, and later founder of community on Assiniboine River. Important introduction to period. [JMB]

45.168 W. L. Morton, ed. *Alexander Begg's Red River journal and other papers relative to the Red River resistance of 1869–1870.* 1956 ed. New York: Greenwood, 1969. ▸ Edition of lengthy journal of Riel uprising against transfer of territory to Canada by English-speaking observer. Contains substantial editorial introduction discussing class structure of Red River at length. [JMB]

45.169 Michael Payne. *The most respectable place in the territory: everyday life in the Hudson's Bay Company service, York Factory, 1788 to 1870.* Ottawa, Ont.: Canadian Parks Service, Environment Canada, National Historic Parks and Sites, 1988. ISBN 0-660-12940-X, ISSN 0821-1027. ▸ Social history of everyday routine at York factory. Reconstructs work, leisure, and education. [DJL]

45.170 Richard I. Ruggles. *A country so interesting: the Hudson's Bay Company and two centuries of mapping, 1670–1870.* Montreal: McGill-Queen's University Press, 1991. (Rupert's Land Record Society series, 2.) ISBN 0-7735-0678-0, 0-921206-06-2. ▸ Hudson's Bay Company as seen over two centuries through maps. Also covers much of early history of mapping in Canada. Profusely illustrated. [AED]

45.171 Sylvia Van Kirk. *"Many tender ties": women in fur-trade society, 1670–1870.* 1980 ed. Norman: University of Oklahoma Press, 1983. ISBN 0-8061-1842-3 (cl), 0-8061-1847-4 (pbk). ▸ Study explores marriages (within and without church) between native women and fur trade employees of Hudson's Bay and North West companies. Emphasizes women's role in developing western Canada. [AED]

DOMINION OF CANADA, 1870–1921

Canada

45.172 Richard Allen. *The social passion: religion and social reform in Canada, 1914–28.* 1971 ed. Toronto: University of Toronto Press, 1973. ISBN 0-8020-5252-5 (cl), 0-8020-6199-0 (pbk). ▸ Study of rise of Social Gospel in Canada. Discusses Social Gospel's relationship to political reform, labor, church union, prohibition, and pacifism over early decades of twentieth century. Important summary. [JMB]

45.173 Christopher Armstrong. *The politics of federalism: Ontario's relations with the federal government, 1867–1942.* Toronto: University of Toronto Press, 1981. ISBN 0-8020-2434-3 (cl), 0-8020-3374-1 (pbk). ▸ Struggle between two jurisdictions led to gains for provincial government. Private interests played one government off against the other. Occasionally repetitive in thematic organization. [GNE]

45.174 Christopher Armstrong and H. V. Nelles. *Monopoly's moment: the organization and regulation of Canadian utilities, 1830–1930.* Philadelphia: Temple University Press, 1986. ISBN 0-87722-404-8. ▸ Important study of development of Canadian utilities, emphasizing technological transfer, civic populism, trend to monopoly, and spectrum of regulation. [JMB]

45.175 Donald Avery. *"Dangerous foreigners": European immigrant workers and labour radicalism in Canada, 1896–1932.* Toronto: McClelland & Stewart, 1979. ISBN 0-7710-0826-0. ▸ Study refuting traditional view that immigrants came to Canadian West as farmers. Discusses working conditions, labor legislation, and xenophobia. [DJL]

45.176 Robert H. Babcock. *Gompers in Canada: a study in American continentalism before the First World War.* Toronto: University of Toronto Press, 1974. ISBN 0-8020-2142-5 (cl), 0-8020-6242-3 (pbk). ▸ Useful introduction to development in Canada of American Federation of Labor under Samuel Gompers. Discusses many problems created by labor continentalism and American insensitivity. [JMB]

45.177 Carol Lee Bacchi. *Liberation deferred? The ideas of English-Canadian suffragists, 1877–1918.* Toronto: University of Toronto Press, 1983. ISBN 0-8020-2455-6 (cl), 0-8020-6466-3 (pbk). ▸ Controversial analysis of suffrage movement and middle-class "maternal" feminism. Argues members of Anglo-Saxon professional elite promoted moral and social reform at expense of feminist reform. [AED]

45.178 Carl Berger. *Science, God, and nature in Victorian Canada: the Joanne Goodman Lectures, 1982.* Toronto: University of Toronto Press, 1983. ISBN 0-8020-2501-3 (cl), 0-8020-6523-6 (pbk). ▸ One of few efforts to produce overview of development of Canadian science in nineteenth century, in this case, for general audience. [JMB]

45.179 Carl Berger. *The sense of power: studies in the ideas of Canadian imperialism, 1867–1914.* 1970 ed. Toronto: University of Toronto Press, 1971. ISBN 0-8020-1669-3 (cl, 1970), 0-8020-6113-3 (pbk). ▸ Pioneering intellectual history of Canada, analyzing ideas and beliefs of leaders of imperialist movement in nineteenth-century Canada. Insists imperialism and nationalism were compatible. [DJL]

45.180 Pierre Berton. *The last spike: the great railway, 1881–1885.* Toronto: McClelland & Stewart, 1971. ISBN 0-7710-1327-2. ▸ Second volume of two-volume history, by Canada's leading nonacademic historian, covering construction of Canadian Pacific Railway. Distinguished by strong narrative line and telling anecdotal material. [JMB]

45.181 Michael Bliss. *A Canadian millionaire: the life and business times of Sir Joseph Flavelle, Bart., 1858–1939.* 1978 ed. Toronto: University of Toronto Press, 1992. ISBN 0-8020-7351-4. ▸ Biography of one of Canada's leading capitalists who headed nation's wartime production board during Great War. Very sympathetic treatment of much-hated figure. [JMB]

45.182 Michael Bliss. *A living profit: studies in the social history of Canadian business, 1883–1911.* Toronto: McClelland & Stewart, 1974. ISBN 0-7710-1572-0. ▸ One of few studies of ideological assumptions of Canadian businessmen. Analyzes attitude toward competition, labor unions, protectionism, and nationalism. [JMB]

45.183 Robert Craig Brown. *Robert Laird Borden: a biography.*

Vol. 2: *1914–1937.* Toronto: Macmillan, 1980. ISBN 0-7705-1854-0. ▸ Second volume of standard biography of Robert Laird Borden, Canadian prime minister during Great War. Covers wartime period. [JMB]

45.184 Robert Craig Brown and Ramsay Cook. *Canada, 1896–1921: a nation transformed.* Toronto: McClelland & Stewart, 1974. (Canadian centenary series, 14.) ISBN 0-7710-2268-9. ▸ Survey of development of Canada, 1896–1921. One of best volumes of distinguished series. [JMB]

45.185 Catherine L. Cleverdon. *The woman suffrage movement in Canada.* 2d ed. Ramsay Cook, Introduction. Toronto: University of Toronto Press, 1974. ISBN 0-8020-2108-5 (cl), 0-8020-6218-0 (pbk). ▸ Standard history of political emancipation of Canadian women published originally in 1950. Emphasis on local organizations and individual activists. [AED]

45.186 Ramsay Cook. *The regenerators: social criticism in late Victorian English Canada.* Toronto: University of Toronto Press, 1985. ISBN 0-8020-5670-9 (cl), 0-8020-6609-7 (pbk). ▸ Series of essays on various aspects of social criticism in Victorian Canada, as traditional religion shattered into variety of nostrums and beliefs and ultimately produced secular vision. Important new perspective. [JMB]

45.187 Paul Craven. *"An impartial umpire": industrial relations and the Canadian state, 1900–1911.* Toronto: University of Toronto Press, 1980. ISBN 0-8020-5505-2 (cl), 0-8020-6401-9 (pbk). ▸ Basic study of critical period in development of industrial relations in Canada. Focuses on growth of mediation and conciliation as techniques for resolving problems. [JMB]

45.188 Donald Grant Creighton. *John A. Macdonald.* Vol. 2: *The old chieftain.* 1955 ed. Toronto: Macmillan, 1973. ▸ Classic, standard biography of father of confederation most responsible for achievement of union. Follows career as Canada's first and third prime minister. [JMB]

45.189 J. H. Dales. *The protective tariff in Canada's development: eight essays on trade and tariffs when factors move, with special reference to Canadian protectionism, 1870–1955.* Toronto: University of Toronto Press, 1966. ▸ Influential collection of essays on Canadian tariffs and protectionism, analyzing comparative advantage of protectionism as national policy. [JMB]

45.190 John English. *The decline of politics: the Conservatives and the party system, 1901–20.* Toronto: University of Toronto Press, 1977. ISBN 0-8020-5386-6. ▸ Revisionist study of Conservative party of Canada in early years of twentieth century, from opposition to power to wartime coalition. Views coalition as logical consequence of conservative ideology. [JMB]

45.191 Roger Graham. *Arthur Meighen.* Vol. 1: *The door of opportunity.* 1960 ed. Toronto: Clarke, Irwin, 1968. ▸ First volume of standard biography of wartime cabinet minister, leader of Conservative party, and prime minister of Canada, covering period to 1920. [JMB]

45.192 J. L. Granatstein and J. Mackay Hitsman. *Broken promises: a history of conscription in Canada.* Toronto: Oxford University Press, 1977. ISBN 0-19-540258-8. ▸ Standard study of problem for Canadian government of conscription in two world wars and cold war. [JMB]

45.193 Harold Kaplan. *Reform, planning, and city politics: Montreal, Winnipeg, Toronto.* Toronto: University of Toronto Press, 1982. ISBN 0-8020-5543-5. ▸ Study of complex relationships among reform, city planning, and municipal politics in three major Canadian cities. Focuses on development of metropolitan areas in Toronto and Winnipeg. Groundbreaking comparative analysis. [JMB]

45.194 Graham S. Lowe. *Women in the administrative revolution:*

the feminization of clerical work. Toronto: University of Toronto Press, 1987. ISBN 0-8020-2757-5 (cl), 08020-6686-0 (pbk). ‣ Controversial study of impact of industrialization and managerial rationalization on clerical work force in twentieth century. Gender and class in relation to labor and scientific management. [AED]

45.195 Michele Martin. *"Hello Central?" Gender, technology, and culture in the formation of telephone systems.* Montreal: McGill-Queen's University Press, 1991. ISBN 0-7735-0830-9. ‣ Groundbreaking, revisionist study of development of telephone in Canada in context of gender differentiation. Argues women played key role, chiefly through their emerging dominance as telephone operators and users. [JMB]

45.196 Wendy Mitchinson. *The nature of their bodies: women and their doctors in Victorian Canada.* Toronto: University of Toronto Press, 1991. ISBN 0-8020-5901-5 (cl), 0-8020-6840-5 (pbk). ‣ Revisionist analysis arguing Victorian social and cultural perceptions of women defined medical attitudes toward female natural functions as well as toward illness. Doctors saw women as deviating from male norm. Important monograph. [AED]

45.197 Desmond Morton and J. L. Granatstein. *Marching to Armageddon: Canadians and the Great War, 1914–1919.* Toronto: Lester & Orpen Dennys, 1989. ISBN 0-88619-209-9 (cl), 0-88619-211-0 (pbk). ‣ Survey of Canadian participation in Great War, treating fighting in Europe, home front, political difficulties, and effects of war, as well as demobilization and reconstruction. [JMB]

45.198 H. Blair Neatby. *Laurier and a liberal Quebec.* Toronto: McClelland & Stewart, 1973. ‣ Standard study of Laurier's fifteen years as prime minister of Canada. Argues success based on electoral support of Quebec and illustrates how support for Liberal party achieved. [JR]

45.199 G.W.L. Nicholson. *Canadian Expeditionary Force, 1914–1919: official history of the Canadian Army in the First World War.* 1962 ed. Ottawa, Ont.: Duhamel, Queen's Printer and Controller of Stationery, 1964. ‣ Official history of Canadian Expeditionary Force in Europe, 1914–19, treating recruiting and equipping, as well as leadership, participation in campaigns, and battles. [JMB]

45.200 Bryan D. Palmer. *A culture in conflict: skilled workers and industrial capitalism in Hamilton, Ontario, 1860–1914.* Montreal: McGill-Queen's University Press, 1979. ISBN 0-7735-0346-3 (cl), 0-7735-0347-1 (pbk). ‣ Controversial study of culture of industrialism in Hamilton, Ontario, in street, field, hall, and workplace. Argues popular culture of industrialism more complex than previously realized. [JMB]

45.201 Joy Parr. *The gender of breadwinners: women, men, and change in two industrial towns, 1880–1950.* Toronto: University of Toronto Press, 1990. ISBN 0-8020-5833-1 (cl), 0-8020-6760-3 (pbk). ‣ Pioneering study of sexual division of labor in two Ontario towns (Paris and Hanover) through period of industrialization. [JMB]

45.202 Joy Parr. *Labouring children: British immigrant apprentices to Canada, 1869–1924.* Montreal: McGill-Queen's University Press, 1980. ISBN 0-7735-0517-2. ‣ Persuasive account of experience of British immigrant children in Victorian Canada. As agricultural laborers or domestic servants, children's lives did not benefit from supposed improvement in conditions. [AED]

45.203 Dennis Reid. *"Our own country Canada": being an account of the national aspirations of the principal landscape artists in Montreal and Toronto, 1860–1890.* Ottawa, Ont.: National Gallery of Canada, 1979. ISBN 0-88884-360-7. ‣ Survey of ideas and work of landscape painters and photographers during period of high Victorian romanticism. Impact on popular concepts of Canadian nationhood. Black-and-white reproductions. [AED]

45.204 Paul Rutherford. *A Victorian authority: the daily press in late nineteenth-century Canada.* Toronto: University of Toronto Press, 1982. ISBN 0-8020-5588-5 (cl), 0-8020-6459-0 (pbk). ‣ Detailed study of growth of daily press and modern mass communications. Urban expansion, literacy, and business affected rise of publishing and printing within context of Victorian moral and economic values. [AED]

45.205 A. E. Safarian. *Foreign ownership of Canadian industry: a study of company policies and performance.* 2d ed. Toronto: University of Toronto Press, 1973. ISBN 0-8020-6126-4 (pbk). ‣ Pioneering study of effect of foreign ownership on Canadian economy. Dated and simplistic in its assumptions and methodologies. [AGL]

45.206 S.E.D. Shortt. *The search for an ideal: six Canadian intellectuals and their convictions in an age of transition, 1890–1930.* Toronto: University of Toronto Press, 1976. ISBN 0-8020-5350-5 (cl), 0-8020-6285-7 (pbk). ‣ Pioneering study of intellectual debate in Canada between idealism and empiricism as reflected in ideas of six representative Canadian thinkers of late Victorian era. [JMB]

45.207 C. P. Stacey. *Canada and the age of conflict: a history of Canadian external policies.* Vol. 1: *1867–1921.* 1977 ed. Toronto: University of Toronto Press, 1984. ISBN 0-8020-6560-0. ‣ Well-regarded survey of Canadian foreign relations and foreign policy from confederation to League of Nations. Emphasizes growth of independent Canadian presence, process completed by World War I. [JMB]

45.208 Neil Sutherland. *Children in English-Canadian society: framing the twentieth-century consensus.* Toronto: University of Toronto Press, 1976. ISBN 0-8020-5340-8. ‣ Revisionist study of development of changing attitudes to children in English-speaking Canada, particularly in public health, education, and criminal prevention. Important introduction. [JMB]

45.209 Peter B. Waite. *Canada, 1874–1896: arduous destiny.* Toronto: McClelland & Stewart, 1971. (Canadian centenary series, 13.) ISBN 0-7710-8800-0. ‣ Survey of development of Canada over last decades of nineteenth century. Emphasis on political and constitutional matters, but includes economic, social, and cultural issues. [JMB]

Atlantic Provinces

45.210 Phillip A. Buckner and David Frank, eds. *Atlantic Canada after confederation.* 2d ed. 2 vols. Fredericton, N.B.: Acadiensis Press, 1988–90. ISBN 0-919107-29-X (v. 1), 0-919107-18-4 (v. 2, cl), 0-919107-16-8 (v. 2, pbk). ‣ Collection of selected articles from regional journal. Primary focus on social, economic, and political consequences of industrialization and urbanization; causes and consequences of regional disparities. Basic reading. [MBT]

45.211 Judith Fingard. *The dark side of life in Victorian Halifax.* Porters Lake, N.S.: Pottersfield, 1989. ISBN 0-919001-58-0 (pbk). ‣ Case studies of ninety-two recidivists, 1864–73. Life stories as vehicles for analysis of underclass and middle-class reaction to recidivism. Provocative and entertaining. [MBT]

Ontario

45.212 Ian M. Drummond. *Progress without planning: the economic history of Ontario from confederation to the Second World War.* Toronto: University of Toronto Press, 1987. ISBN 0-8020-2614-1 (cl), 0-8020-6661-5 (pbk). ‣ General survey of economic development, organized both topically and chronologically. Although critical of traditional staples and emergent neo-Marxist interpretations, preoccupied more with detail than general interpretation. [GNE]

45.213 Chad Gaffield. *Language, schooling, and cultural conflict: the origins of French-language controversy in Ontario.* Kingston,

Ont.: McGill-Queen's University Press, 1987. ISBN 0-7735-0602-0. ‣ Revisionist study of origins and development of French-language problem in Ontario education. Broader than title suggests; deals with history of French-speaking population in Ontario in nineteenth century. Important summary. [JMB]

45.214 Gregory S. Kealey. *Toronto workers respond to industrial capitalism, 1867–1892.* 1980 ed. Toronto: University of Toronto Press, 1991. ISBN 0-8020-6883-9. ‣ Cultural adaptation of workers to change in nature of work and community with emphasis on shop-floor and political struggle. New working-class history in tradition of E. P. Thompson (cf. 24.247). Provocative. [GNE]

45.215 H. V. Nelles. *The politics of development: forests, mines, and hydro-electric power in Ontario, 1849–1941.* Hamden, Conn.: Archon, 1974. ISBN 0-208-01450-0. ‣ Influential study argues politics of staple development reduced state to client of business community. Treats business-state relations, problems of continental economic integration, and captains of industry. [GNE]

45.216 Michael Piva. *The condition of the working class in Toronto, 1900–1921.* Ottawa, Ont.: University of Ottawa Press, 1979. ISBN 2-7603-5009-6. ‣ Controversial study of declining real wages, unemployment, poverty, housing and living conditions, absence of state regulation, and declining trade unionism. Focuses on individual male workers rather than families. [GNE]

Quebec

45.217 Michael Bliss. *Plague: a story of smallpox in Montreal.* Toronto: HarperCollins, 1991. ISBN 0-00-215693-8 (cl), 0-00-637890-0 (pbk). ‣ Fascinating, provocative study of Montreal smallpox epidemic of 1885. Analysis of why 6,000 casualties concentrated in poorer French Canadian parts of city. [DJL]

45.218 Jean de Bonville. *La presse Québécoise de 1884 à 1914: genèse d'un media de masse.* Quebec: Les Presses de l'Université Laval, 1988. ISBN 2-7637-7136-X. ‣ Study of some Quebec daily and weekly newspapers that became part of mass media. Examines transformation in terms of technology, finances, editorial content, circulation, publicity, and readership. [JR]

45.219 Terry Copp. *The anatomy of poverty: the condition of the working class in Montreal, 1897–1929.* Toronto: McClelland & Stewart, 1974. ISBN 0-7710-2252-2 (pbk). ‣ Highly regarded description of various aspects of workers' lives, including income, families, education, housing, public health, welfare, and strikes. Concludes conditions improved only slightly in this prosperous period. [JR]

45.220 Marta Danylewycz. *Taking the veil: an alternative to marriage, motherhood, and spinsterhood in Quebec, 1840–1920.* Paul-Andre Linteau, Alison Prentice, and William Westfall, eds. Toronto: McClelland & Stewart, 1987. ISBN 0-7710-2550-5 (pbk). ‣ Study of two religious communities in Quebec, demonstrating choices women made in religious careers. Rejection of women's procreative role in male world offered social and educational advantages to many women. [AED]

45.221 Nadia Fahmy-Eid and Micheline Dumont-Johnson. *Maitresses de maison, maitresses d'école: femmes, familles, et education dans l'histoire du Quebec.* Montreal: Boréal Express, 1983. ISBN 2-89052-070-6. ‣ Collection of articles on history of women, focusing on family and school. Useful historiographical introduction. [JR]

45.222 Jean Hamelin and Nicole Gagnon. *Histoire du Catholicisme Québéçois: le vingtième siècle.* Vol. 3.1: *1898–1940.* Montreal: Boréal Express, 1984. ISBN 2-89052-099-4 (v. 3.1, pbk). ‣ Part of grand synthesis of history of Roman Catholic church in Quebec, institution closely linked to French Canadian society. In this period church put structures in place to keep its hold on urbanizing society. [JR]

45.223 Jean Hamelin and Yves Roby. *Histoire économique du Québec, 1851–1896.* Montreal: Fides, 1971. ‣ Overview of economic development during province's economic "take-off." Studies transportation, agricultural mutations, mineral and manufacturing industries, and commercial activity. [JR]

45.224 Marie Lavigne and Yolande Pinard, eds. *Travailleuses et féministes: les femmes dans la société québeçoise.* 1977 ed. Montreal: Boréal Express, 1983. ISBN 2-89052-071-4. ‣ Collection of articles on women's history since nineteenth century. Focuses on women at work and women's movements. Includes historiographical discussions. Earlier title: *Les femmes dans la société québeçoise.* [JR]

45.225 Paul-Andre Linteau. *Histoire de Montréal depuis la confederation.* Montreal: Boréal Express, 1992. ISBN 2-89052-441-8. ‣ Useful study of main industrial and commercial center of Canada for a century. Examines economy, population, social structure, conditions of life, culture, municipal politics. [JR]

45.226 Paul-Andre Linteau, Rene Durocher, and Jean-Claude Robert. *Quebec: a history, 1867–1929.* Robert Chandos, trans. Toronto: Lorimer, 1983. ISBN 0-88862-605-3 (cl), 0-88862-604-5 (pbk). ‣ Reliable synthesis organized thematically around population, economy, society, politics, and ideology. Revisionist interpretation stressing province's complexity and diversity in North American context. [JR]

45.227 Normand Séguin. *Agriculture et colonisation au Québec: aspects historiques.* Montreal: Boréal Express, 1980. ISBN 2-89052-011-0. ‣ Studies in history of agriculture and colonization from 1850. Reviews of historical writings and historiography. Useful probes. [JR]

45.228 A. I. Silver. *The French-Canadian idea of confederation, 1864–1900.* Toronto: University of Toronto Press, 1982. ISBN 0-8020-5557-5 (cl), 0-8020-6441-8 (pbk). ‣ Study of French Canadian views of Canada before and after confederation, based on periodical press. Argues for evolution from commitment to Quebec as homeland to concern for equality in new dominion. Important analysis. [JR]

Northern Canada

45.229 Morris Zaslow. *The opening of the Canadian North, 1870–1914.* 1971 ed. Toronto: McClelland & Stewart, 1981. (Canadian centenary series, 16.) ISBN 0-7710-9072-2 (cl, 1971), 0-7710-9080-3 (pbk). ‣ Useful summary of extension of Canada into north, focusing on nonnative initiatives, especially from government. [DJL]

Western Canada

45.230 Alan F. J. Artibise. *Winnipeg: a social history of urban growth, 1874–1914.* Montreal: McGill-Queen's University Press, 1975. ISBN 0-7735-0202-5. ‣ Innovative study of development of Winnipeg as first city of western Canada. Emphasizes leadership of commercial elite, construction of urban community, and immigrant problem. [JMB]

45.231 David Jay Bercuson. *Confrontation at Winnipeg: labour, industrial relations, and the General Strike.* Rev. ed. Montreal: McGill-Queen's University Press, 1990. ISBN 0-7735-0794-9. ‣ Study of Winnipeg General Strike in 1919, which was defeated through federal government intervention, setting back Canadian labor movement. Important if controversial summary of key event. [JMB]

45.232 David H. Breen. *The Canadian prairie West and the ranching frontier, 1874–1924.* Toronto: University of Toronto Press, 1983. ISBN 0-8020-5548-6. ‣ Study of cattle industry in western Canada, from open range to regulation of public domain. Sees more gradual retreat before settlement than other scholars. Important regional analysis. [JMB]

45.233 John A. Eagle. *The Canadian Pacific Railway and the development of western Canada, 1896–1914*. Kingston, Ont.: McGill-Queen's University Press, 1989. ISBN 0-7735-0674-8. ‣ Balanced study of developmental importance of railway to western Canada. Discusses freight rates, competition with Grant Trunk and Canadian Northern railways, as well as land and settlement policies. [JMB]

45.234 Thomas Flanagan. *Métis lands in Manitoba*. Calgary, Alta.: University of Calgary Press, 1991. ISBN 0-919813-87-9 (cl), 0-919813-98-4 (pbk). ‣ Controversial piece of advocacy history, intended to support government case in native peoples land trial. Argues *métis* in Manitoba after 1870 were treated well and fairly by federal government, which honored its promises. [JMB]

45.235 Vernon C. Fowke. *The national policy and the wheat economy*. 1957 ed. Toronto: University of Toronto Press, 1973. (Social credit in Alberta, its background and development, 7.) ISBN 0-8020-6224-5. ‣ Examination of federal government's attempt to reorient postconfederation Canadian economy through wheat cultivation, formulating policy for benefit of eastern Canada at western expense. Classic analysis. [DJL]

45.236 A. Ross McCormack. *Reformers, rebels, and revolutionaries: the western Canadian radical movement, 1899–1919*. Toronto: University of Toronto Press, 1977. ISBN 0-8020-5385-8 (cl), 0-8020-6316-6 (pbk). ‣ Careful study of growth of political radicalism in western Canada through World War I. Concentrates on emergence of socialism, labor radicalism, and militant industrial unionism. [JMB]

45.237 Douglas Owram. *Promise of Eden: the Canadian expansionist movement and the idea of the West, 1856–1900*. 1980 ed. Toronto: University of Toronto Press, 1992. ISBN 0-8020-7390-5. ‣ Imaginative analysis of nineteenth-century literature on Canadian West, assessing relationship of perceived reality and material reality, which was adjusted to suit nationalistic purpose. [DJL]

45.238 Patricia E. Roy. *A white man's province: British Columbia politicians and Chinese and Japanese immigrants, 1858–1914*. Vancouver: University of British Columbia Press, 1989. ISBN 0-7748-0330-4. ‣ Balanced study treating racial hostility in British Columbia as political problem. Emphasizes concerns over public health, immigration restriction, and fears of economic competition. [JMB]

45.239 George F. G. Stanley. *The birth of western Canada: a history of the Riel rebellions*. Rev. ed. Toronto: University of Toronto Press, 1992. ISBN 0-8020-6931-2. ‣ Classic study employing now outdated terminology. Analysis of rebellions as clash of cultures remains influential, demonstrating also how rebellions disrupted English-French relations in eastern Canada. [DJL]

45.240 John Herd Thompson. *The harvests of war: the prairie West, 1914–1918*. Toronto: McClelland & Stewart, 1978. ISBN 0-7710-8560-5. ‣ Well-constructed analysis of social, economic, and political ramifications of World War I on prairie West. Overplanting and triumph of reform (prohibition, women's suffrage) are some of results discussed. [DJL]

45.241 Paul Leonard Voisey. *Vulcan: the making of a prairie community*. Toronto: University of Toronto Press, 1988. ISBN 0-8020-2642-7 (cl), 0-8020-6676-3 (pbk). ‣ Inventive study of Alberta community founded at turn of century. Set comparatively in North American context of community studies. Finds ethnicity and religion far less influential factors than elsewhere. [JMB]

45.242 W. Peter Ward. *White Canada forever: popular attitudes and public policy toward Orientals in British Columbia*. 2d ed. Montreal: McGill-Queen's University Press, 1990. ISBN 0-7735-0824-4. ‣ Controversial study of origins and practice of Sinopho-

bia in British Columbia, including attitudes toward Chinese, East Indians, and Japanese. [JMB]

SEE ALSO
36.32 D. N. Sprague. *Canada and the métis, 1869–1885*.
36.39 Douglas Cole. *Captured heritage*.

CANADA SINCE 1920

Canada

45.243 Irving Abella and Harold Troper. *None is too many: Canada and the Jews of Europe, 1933–1948*. 3d ed. Toronto: Lester, 1991. ISBN 1-895555-06-X. ‣ Canada's pathetic record of refusing to admit Jewish European refugees during Nazi era. How antisemitism and political expediency shaped Canadian immigration policy in thirties. Essential reading. [AGL]

45.244 Nancy Adamson et al. *Feminists organizing for change: the contemporary women's movement in Canada*. Toronto: Oxford University Press, 1988. ISBN 0-19-540658-3 (pbk). ‣ Treats women's movement as part of 1960s belief in change and egalitarianism, founded in grassroots activity and local organizations. Insists knowledge of history essential for further progress. Groundbreaking. [AED]

45.245 Gregory Baum. *Catholics and Canadian socialism: political thought in the thirties and forties*. Toronto: Lorimer, 1980. ISBN 0-88862-295-3 (cl), 0-88862-294-5 (pbk). ‣ Revisionist analysis of reaction of Roman Catholic church to socialism in Canada. Focuses on vocal dissident minority that made contribution to social thought of Left. Important monograph. [AGL]

45.246 Michael Bliss. *The discovery of insulin*. Chicago: University of Chicago Press, 1982. ISBN 0-226-05897-2 (cl), 0-226-05898-0 (pbk). ‣ Best-selling study, based on new documentary evidence, of discovery of insulin by three Canadian scientists. [DJL]

45.247 Robert Bothwell, Ian M. Drummond, and John English. *Canada since 1945: power, politics, and provincialism*. Rev. ed. Toronto: University of Toronto Press, 1989. ISBN 0-8020-2647-8 (cl), 0-8020-6672-0 (pbk). ‣ Sweeping study of Canada after World War II, intended as university textbook. Analyzes foreign investment and American cultural influences, as well as Canada's national politics. [AGL]

45.248 G. Bruce Doern and Brian W. Tomlin. *Faith and fear: the free trade story*. Toronto: Stoddart, 1991. ISBN 0-7737-2534-2. ‣ Balanced study examining negotiations of Canada–United States trade agreement of 1987. Focuses on federal government's political calculations. Argues free trade agreement was watershed in Canadian history. [AGL]

45.249 James George Eayrs. *In defence of Canada*. Vol. 4: *Growing up allied*. Toronto: University of Toronto Press, 1980. ISBN 0-8020-2345-2. ‣ Final volume of highly regarded multivolume series dealing with development of Canadian foreign and military relations. Focuses on creation of North Atlantic Treaty Alliance and subsequent nuclear policy. [JMB]

45.250 John English. *Shadow of heaven: the life of Lester Pearson*. Vol. 1: *1897–1948*. Toronto: Lester & Orpen Dennys, 1989. ISBN 0-88619-165-3 (cl), 0-88619-169-6 (pbk). ‣ First installment of detailed biography of Canada's fourteenth prime minister examining his rise as chief external affairs bureaucrat in Ottawa. Success came through hard work and self-promotion. [AGL]

45.251 Gary Evans. *John Grierson and the National Film Board: the politics of wartime propaganda*. 1984 ed. Toronto: University of Toronto Press, 1985. ISBN 0-8020-2519-6 (cl, 1984), 0-8020-6613-5 (pbk). ‣ Controversial study of documentary film in pretelevision era as focus for propaganda, using government support and technology to influence wartime attitudes. Grierson sought to raise national awareness of democracy. [AED]

45.252 Alvin Finkel. *Business and social reform in the thirties.* Toronto: Lorimer, 1979. ISBN 0-88862-236-8 (cl), 0-88862-235-x (pbk). ▸ Important analysis of reaction of Canadian government and business to problems of Great Depression. Revisionist argument that big business led way in supporting state interventionism. [JMB]

45.253 J. L. Granatstein. *Canada's war: the politics of the Mackenzie King government, 1939–1945.* 1975 ed. Toronto: University of Toronto Press, 1990. ISBN 0-8020-6797-2. ▸ Scholarly but sympathetic study of how Prime Minister King and his administration dealt with issues of World War II. Argues war experience shaped Canadian nationalism and consolidated strength of Liberals. [AGL]

45.254 J. L. Granatstein. *The Ottawa men: the civil service mandarins, 1935–1957.* Toronto: Oxford University Press, 1982. ISBN 0-19-540386-X (cl), 0-19-540387-8 (pbk). ▸ Contentious analysis of bureaucrats who transformed Canadian state by creating government structure and foreign policy. Exaggerates influence of these men while ignoring their political masters. [AGL]

45.255 J. L. Granatstein and Robert Bothwell. *Pirouette: Pierre Trudeau and Canadian foreign policy.* Toronto: University of Toronto Press, 1990. ISBN 0-8020-5780-2. ▸ Influential analysis of Prime Minister Trudeau's approach to international affairs, 1968–1984, based on restricted external affairs documents. Argues that contrary to common belief, Trudeau made few changes in policy. [AGL]

45.256 J. L. Granatstein and Desmond Morton. *A nation forged in fire: Canadians and the Second World War, 1939–1945.* Toronto: Lester & Orpen Dennys, 1989. ISBN 0-88619-213-7 (cl), 0-88619-215-3 (pbk). ▸ Popular illustrated narrative of Canadian war against Nazi Germany. Synthetic study, arguing political and military developments fostered Canadian nationalism. [AGL]

45.257 Freda Hawkins. *Canada and immigration: public policy and public concern.* 2d ed. Kingston, Ont.: McGill-Queen's University Press, 1988. ISBN 0-7735-0632-2 (cl), 0-7735-0633-0 (pbk). ▸ Critical study of Canadian immigration policy since 1945 in context of international migration. Considers four historic periods and offers critique of current practice. Useful analysis and critique. [JMB]

45.258 John W. Holmes. *The shaping of peace: Canada and the search for world order, 1943–1957.* 2 vols. Toronto: University of Toronto Press, 1979. ISBN 0-8020-5461-7 (v. 1), 0-8020-5541-9 (v. 2). ▸ Study of Canadian contribution to postwar peacemaking process and role in United Nations, written by former foreign service officer and policy maker. Based on diligent research. Reluctantly accepts Canadian subservience to United States. [AGL]

45.259 Michiel Horn. *The League for Social Reconstruction: intellectual origins of the democratic Left in Canada, 1930–1942.* Toronto: University of Toronto Press, 1980. ISBN 0-8020-5487-0. ▸ History of group inspired by British Fabianism that laid intellectual foundations of Co-operative Commonwealth Federation. Exaggerates British influence in history of Canadian socialism. [AGL]

45.260 Linda Kealey and Joan Sangster, eds. *Beyond the vote: Canadian women and politics.* Toronto: University of Toronto Press, 1989. ISBN 0-8020-2677-X (cl), 0-8020-6650-X (pbk). ▸ Collection of thirteen essays exploring variety of women's political experiences in Canada in twentieth century. Emphasizes value of women's organizations and alternative approaches. Important introductions to topic. [AED]

45.261 Mary Kinnear. *Margaret McWilliams: an interwar femi-*

nist. Montreal: McGill-Queen's University Press, 1991. ISBN 0-7735-0857-0. ▸ Useful biography of one of Canada's leading feminists, founder and first president of Canadian Federation of University Women and advocate of married women's activity outside home. [JMB]

45.262 Paul Litt. *The muses, the masses, and the Massey Commission.* Toronto: University of Toronto Press, 1992. ISBN 0-8020-5003-4 (cl), 0-8020-6932-0 (pbk). ▸ Revisionist analysis of work of Royal Commission on National Development in the Arts, Letters, and Sciences (1950–51), which set agenda for much of Canada's high cultural policy for period 1950 to 1975. Key work of cultural history. [JMB]

45.263 Kenneth McNaught. *A prophet in politics: a biography of J. S. Woodsworth.* 1959 ed. Toronto: University of Toronto Press, 1975. ISBN 0-8020-6018-8. ▸ Classic, often reprinted biography of Methodist minister who became active in urban missions in Winnipeg, Winnipeg General Strike, and eventually leader of Co-operative Commonwealth Federation (CCF). [JMB]

45.264 David Milne. *Tug of war: Ottawa and the provinces under Trudeau and Mulroney.* Toronto: Lorimer, 1986. ISBN 0-88862-978-8 (cl), 0-88862-977-X (pbk). ▸ Useful survey of recent political history concentrating on constitution, energy, economic policy, and financing postsecondary education and health. Prime Minister Trudeau's centrist approach provoked provincialist response of Mulroney era. [AGL]

45.265 Marc Milner. *North Atlantic run: the Royal Canadian Navy and the battle for the convoys.* Toronto: University of Toronto Press, 1985. ISBN 0-8020-2544-7. ▸ Balanced history of Royal Canadian Navy's role in convoy protection during World War II, emphasizing both struggle at sea with Germans and behind scenes with British. [JMB]

45.266 David J. Mitchell. *W.A.C. Bennett and the rise of British Columbia.* Vancouver, B.C.: Douglas & McIntyre, 1983. ISBN 0-88894-395-4. ▸ Life-and-times study of political career of man who headed British Columbia Social Credit party and government of British Columbia through unprecedented period (1952–72) of resource exploitation. [JMB]

45.267 W. L. Morton. *The Progressive party in Canada.* Corrected 1950 ed. Toronto: University of Toronto Press, 1967. (Social credit in Alberta, its background and development, 1.) ▸ Account of rise and fall of western agrarian third party. Sets Progressive party in metropolitan-hinterland relationship and East-West economic system. Classic study never superceded. [AGL]

45.268 H. Blair Neatby. *William Lyon Mackenzie King.* Vol. 3: *The prism of unity, 1932–1939.* Toronto: University of Toronto Press, 1976. ISBN 0-8020-5381-5. ▸ Third volume of official biography, explaining prime minister's caution as resulting from desire for national unity. Utilizes his diary to explore briefly his curious private life, but generally magisterial in tone. [AGL]

45.269 Peter C. Newman. *Renegade in power: the Diefenbaker years.* 1963 ed. Toronto: McClelland & Stewart, 1989. ISBN 0-7710-6747-x (pbk). ▸ Critical, controversial study of Prime Minister Diefenbaker's administration, 1957–63. Pioneering work of historical journalism employing investigative techniques of American reporters. [AGL]

45.270 Douglas Owram. *The government generation: Canadian intellectuals and the state, 1900–1945.* Toronto: University of Toronto Press, 1986. ISBN 0-8020-2581-1 (cl), 0-8020-6604-6 (pbk). ▸ Important, provocative, revisionist study of middle-class university-trained social scientists, especially in new disciplines of sociology and political economy, who shaped Canadian civil service and its agenda. [AGL]

45.271 Graeme H. Patterson. *History and communications: Har-*

old Innis, Marshall McLuhan, the interpretation of history. Toronto: University of Toronto Press, 1990. ISBN 0-8020-2764-4 (cl), 0-8020-6810-3 (pbk). ▸ Provocative study of theories of Canadian communications thinkers Harold A. Innis and Marshall McLuhan, set in context of larger historiographical patterns. [JMB]

45.272 Murray Peden. *A thousand shall fall.* 2d ed. Stittsville, Ont.: Canada's Wings, 1981. ISBN 0-920002-07-2. ▸ Insightful historical account of Canadian unit of Royal Air Force (Great Britain), Squadron 214. Treats aerial operations and narratives of its personnel during World War II. [JMB]

45.273 Frank W. Peers. *The politics of Canadian broadcasting, 1920–1951.* Toronto: University of Toronto Press, 1969. ISBN 0-8020-5214-2. ▸ Magisterial overview of development of broadcasting prior to era of television by participant in process. Contrasts Canadian system with American; emphasizes nation building and problems of government control. [AED]

45.274 Ruth Roach Pierson. *"They're still women after all": the Second World War and Canadian womanhood.* Toronto: McClelland & Stewart, 1986. ISBN 0-7710-6958-8 (pbk). ▸ Study emphasizing that recruitment into male-defined work force did not give women equal recognition during or after war. Women's work seen as temporary; postwar return to domesticity expected. [AED]

45.275 John Porter. *The vertical mosaic: an analysis of social class and power in Canada.* 1965 ed. Toronto: University of Toronto Press, 1971. ISBN 0-8020-1357-0 (cl), 0-8020-6055-2 (pbk). ▸ Classic study of power in contemporary Canada, emphasizing it remained in hands of elites that overrepresented groups of British origin. [JMB]

45.276 Douglas A. Ross. *In the interests of peace: Canada and Vietnam, 1954–1973.* Toronto: University of Toronto Press, 1984. ISBN 0-8020-5632-6. ▸ Balanced study of Canadian involvement on International Commission for Supervision and Control of Indochina. Argues that Canada played significant autonomous role in conflict. [AGL]

45.277 Jean-Louis Roy. *Le choix d'un pays: le débat constitutionnel, Québec-Canada, 1960–1976.* Montreal: Lemeac, 1978. ISBN 0-7761-5026-X. ▸ Useful introduction to evolution of Quebec's constitutional position, 1960–76. Tries to explain why Quebec since Quiet Revolution (peaceable modernization of Quebec in 1960s) has sought fundamental constitutional reform. [JR]

45.278 Paul Rutherford. *When television was young: primetime Canada, 1952–1967.* Toronto: University of Toronto Press, 1990. ISBN 0-8020-5830-2 (cl), 0-8020-6647-X (pbk). ▸ Important revisionist study of growth of national television in Canada. Discusses issues of public versus private programing, Canadian productions, American competition, and influence of medium on audiences. [AED]

45.279 A. E. Safarian. *The Canadian economy in the Great Depression.* 1959 ed. Toronto: McClelland & Stewart, 1970. ▸ Comprehensive examination of Canadian economic response to Great Depression. Finds government policies inadequate. [AGL]

45.280 Joan Sangster. *Dreams of equality: women on the Canadian Left, 1920–1950.* Toronto: McClelland & Stewart, 1989. ISBN 0-7710-7946-X (pbk). ▸ Contentious study of separation of women from general ideologies of socialist parties. Argues women created autonomous socialist feminist agenda distinct from earlier reform movements. [AED]

45.281 Donald J. Savoie. *Regional economic development: Canada's search for solutions.* 2d ed. Toronto: University of Toronto Press, 1992. ISBN 0-8020-2781-4. ▸ Controversial assessment of regional economic policies by evaluation of various federal pro-grams. Concludes alleviation of regional disparities an unrealistic goal. [AGL]

45.282 Marlene Shore. *The science of social redemption: McGill, the Chicago school, and the origins of social research in Canada.* Toronto: University of Toronto Press, 1987. ISBN 0-8020-5733-0 (cl), 0-8020-6645-3 (pbk). ▸ Development of sociology in Canada from foundation in Christian social and moral values to academic discipline. New theories of social science raised difficulties for academic freedom and academic politics. Key cultural study. [AED]

45.283 Jeffrey Simpson. *Discipline of power: the conservative interlude and the liberal restoration.* Toronto: Macmillan, 1984. ISBN 0-7715-9875-0. ▸ Journalistic study of how progressive-conservative government of Joe Clark squandered 1979 electoral victory and allowed Pierre Trudeau and Liberals to regain power in 1980. Good narrative account. [AGL]

45.284 C. P. Stacey. *Arms, men, and governments: the war policies of Canada, 1939–1945.* Ottawa, Ont.: Queen's Printer, 1970. ▸ Authorized history of Canadian government and its policies during World War II. Considers conscription, wartime industrial buildup, and military policy. [JMB]

45.285 Denis Stairs. *The diplomacy of constraint: Canada, the Korean War, and the United States.* Toronto: University of Toronto Press, 1974. ISBN 0-8020-5282-7. ▸ Standard study of Canada's reluctant involvement in Korean conflict and its several attempts to extricate itself honorably. [JMB]

45.286 Veronica Strong-Boag. *The new day recalled: lives of girls and women in English Canada, 1919–1939.* Toronto: Copp Clark Pitman and Penguin, 1988. ISBN 0-7730-4741-7 (cl), 0-14-010838-6 (pbk). ▸ Revisionist study of lives of Canadian women after gaining vote. Emphasizes that little change occurred in childhood, work experience, marriage, domestic expectations, and marriage. Significant monograph. [AED]

45.287 James Struthers. *No fault of their own: unemployment and the Canadian welfare state, 1914–1941.* Toronto: University of Toronto Press, 1983. ISBN 0-8020-2480-7 (cl), 0-8020-6502-3 (pbk). ▸ Provocative study of Canada's procrastination in introduction of workable unemployment insurance scheme and national employment service. Revisionist interpretation blames federal government rather than provinces. [AGL]

45.288 Ann Gomer Sunahara. *The politics of racism: the uprooting of Japanese Canadians during the Second World War.* Toronto: Lorimer, 1981. ISBN 0-88862-414-X (cl), 0-88862-413-1 (pbk). ▸ Critical study of decision to evacuate Japanese Canadians from coastal areas in 1941 and its aftermath. Deals with problems of evacuees in exile and in seeking postwar compensation. [JMB]

45.289 Malcolm G. Taylor. *Health insurance and Canadian public policy: the seven decisions that created the Canadian Health Insurance System and their outcomes.* 2d ed. Toronto: Institute of Public Administration of Canada and McGill-Queen's University Press, 1987. (Canadian public administration series, 10.) ISBN 0-7735-0628-4 (cl), 0-7735-0629-2 (pbk). ▸ Detailed scholarly analysis of key decisions in development of Canada's universal health insurance. [AGL]

45.290 John Herd Thompson. *Canada, 1922–1939: decades of discord.* 1985 ed. Toronto: McClelland & Stewart, 1986. (Canadian centenary series, 15.) ISBN 0-7710-8564-8 (cl, 1985), 0-7710-8553-3 (pbk). ▸ Comprehensive survey of Canada, 1922–39. Mainly concerned with politics, but lengthy discussions of economic, social, and cultural affairs. [AGL]

45.291 Dale C. Thomson. *Louis St. Laurent: Canadian.* 1967 ed. New York: St. Martin's, 1968. ▸ Standard narrative biography of Canada's twelfth prime minister, in office 1948–57. Attempts to separate him from arrogant and partisan policies of his administration. [AGL]

45.292 Maria Tippett. *Emily Carr: a biography.* 1979 ed. Markham, Ont.: Penguin, 1985. ISBN 0-14-006457-5 (pbk). ‣ Prize-winning biography of one of Canada's major artists. Carr inspired by forests and native peoples of British Columbia. Spirituality of landscape major theme of her painting. [AED]

45.293 Maria Tippett. *Making culture: English-Canadian institutions and the arts before the Massey Commission.* Toronto: University of Toronto Press, 1990. ISBN 0-8020-2743-1 (cl), 0-8020-6784-0 (pbk). ‣ Provocative revisionist study of English Canadian cultural development from late nineteenth century to 1950. Emphasizes early cultural activity among amateurs, slow growth of professionalism and public patronage. [AED]

45.294 Tom Traves. *The state and enterprise: Canadian manufacturers and the federal government, 1917–1931.* Toronto: University of Toronto Press, 1979. ISBN 0-8020-5445-5 (cl), 0-8020-6353-5 (pbk). ‣ History of relationship between Canadian government and business after World War I with particular emphasis on reconstruction and regulation. Important monograph. [JMB]

45.295 Pierre Elliott Trudeau. *Federalism and the French Canadians.* New York: St. Martin's, 1968. ‣ Collection of writings of Prime Minister Trudeau before he entered politics, mainly from Quebec journal *Cité Libre.* Demonstrates Trudeau's policies in office based on longstanding positions. Key document in modern constitutional history. [AGL]

45.296 Brian Loring Villa. *Unauthorized action: Mountbatten and the Dieppe raid.* Toronto: Oxford University Press, 1989. ISBN 0-19-540679-6. ‣ Highly controversial assessment of Canadian and British commando raid on port of Dieppe (19 August 1942); reads like detective story. Concludes raid foolhardy and never properly authorized, but carried through because both Canadian military and government wanted it. [JMB]

45.297 T. Kue Young. *Health care and cultural change: the Indian experience in the central subarctic.* Toronto: University of Toronto Press, 1988. ISBN 0-8020-5784-5 (cl), 0-8020-6697-6 (pbk). ‣ Revisionist study of changing patterns of health care in Canada, focused on northern native peoples. Concludes medical care now has achieved acceptable levels; continuing problems of health require new approaches. Provocative analysis. [JMB]

45.298 Walter D. Young. *The National CCF, 1932–1961: the anatomy of a party.* 1969 ed. Toronto: University of Toronto Press, 1991. ISBN 0-8020-5221-5 (cl), 0-8020-6117-6 (pbk). ‣ Standard study of rise and fall of socialist Co-operative Commonwealth Federation, distinguishing success of nonpartisan movement from failure of political party. Also available in photocopy from Ann Arbor: University Microfilms International, 1991. [AGL]

Atlantic Provinces

45.299 Ernest R. Forbes. *Challenging the regional stereotype: essays on the twentieth-century Maritimes.* Fredericton, N.B.: Acadiensis Press, 1989. ISBN 0-919107-22-2. ‣ Analyses of regional disparities and progressive movements. Suggests cause of first and failure of second due not to people's inherent conservatism but to lack of national economic and political power. Controversial. [MBT]

45.300 Ernest R. Forbes. *The maritime rights movement, 1919–1927: a study in Canadian regionalism.* Montreal: McGill-Queen's University Press, 1979. ISBN 0-7735-0321-8 (cl), 0-7735-0330-7 (pbk). ‣ Standard study of rise and fall of organized regional protest against economic underdevelopment and political marginalization. Revisionist study emphasizes vigorous progressivism transcending political party. [MBT]

45.301 Peter Neary. *Newfoundland in the North Atlantic world, 1929–1949.* Kingston, Ont.: McGill-Queen's University Press, 1988. ISBN 0-7735-0668-3. ‣ Sets Newfoundland history in international context to explain entry into Canadian confederation. Argues experience of Depression and World War II crucial in final decision. Good analysis. [MBT]

Ontario

45.302 Paul Axelrod. *Scholars and dollars: politics, economics, and the universities of Ontario.* Toronto: University of Toronto Press, 1982. ISBN 0-8020-5609-1 (cl), 0-8020-6492-2 (pbk). ‣ Controversial study of tremendous expansion of Ontario's universities in post–World War II period. Documents how politicians and particularly businessmen exercised control over higher education to serve capitalism. [AGL]

45.303 K. J. Rea. *The prosperous years: the economic history of Ontario, 1939–1975.* Toronto: University of Toronto Press, 1985. ISBN 0-8020-2576-5 (cl), 0-8020-6592-9 (pbk). ‣ General survey of economic development and change, organized thematically. More coverage of public policy than of private sector. [GNE]

Quebec

45.304 Michael D. Behiels. *Prelude to Quebec's Quiet Revolution: liberalism versus neo-nationalism, 1945–1960.* Kingston, Ont.: McGill-Queen's University Press, 1985. ISBN 0-7735-0423-0 (cl), 0-7735-0424-9 (pbk). ‣ Important study describes intellectual origins of Quebec's Quiet Revolution, peaceable modernization of Quebec in 1960s. Locates two groups fighting tradition of French Canadian nationalism, one liberal, democratic, and federalistic; the other secular neonationalist. [JR]

45.305 Conrad Black. *Duplessis.* Toronto: McClelland & Stewart, 1977. ISBN 0-7710-1530-5. ‣ Biography of Maurice Duplessis, premier (or prime minister) of Quebec 1936–39, 1944–59, dominant official of period. Well documented but uncritical in approach. [JR]

45.306 William D. Coleman. *The independence movement in Quebec, 1945–1980.* Toronto: University of Toronto Press, 1984. ISBN 0-8020-2529-3 (cl), 0-8020-6542-2 (pbk). ‣ Study with misleading title, since most of work deals with economic, social, and political changes that induced aspirations for more political autonomy rather than independence. Stresses Quiet Revolution (peaceable modernization of Quebec in 1960s) and class conflict. Useful summary. [JR]

45.307 Jean Hamelin. *Histoire du Catholicisme Québeçois.* Vol. 3.2: *Le vingtième siècle: de 1940 à nos jours.* Montreal: Boréal Express, 1984. ISBN 2-89052-100-1 (v. 3.2, pbk). ‣ Standard overview of this central institution in French Canadian society. Explains why church quickly lost control over Quebec society after 1960s. [JR]

45.308 Richard Handler. *Nationalism and the politics of culture in Quebec.* Madison: University of Wisconsin Press, 1988. ISBN 0-299-11510-0 (cl), 0-299-11514-3 (pbk). ‣ Insightful study of Quebec nationalism by cultural anthropologist, focusing on phenomena such as folklore revivals, language legislation, and politics of culture, 1976–84. Concludes nationalism defined by cultural units is futile. [JR]

45.309 Andrée Lévesque. *Virage à gauche interdit: les communistes, les socialistes, et leurs ennemis au Québec, 1929–1939.* Montreal: Boréal Express, 1984. ISBN 2-89052-111-7. ‣ Study of Communist and Co-operative Commonwealth Federation parties and their opposition in Quebec of 1930s. Explains why they failed to enlist significant membership in period favorable to political protest. [JR]

45.310 Paul-Andre Linteau et al. *Quebec since 1930*. Robert Chandos and Ellen Garmaise, trans. Toronto: Lorimer, 1991. ISBN 1-55028-298-0 (cl), 1-55028-296-4 (pbk). ▸ Excellent survey integrating current research on Quebec history. Thematic organization. Revisionist interpretation roots modernization of Quebec prior to World War II or to Quiet Revolution. [JR]

45.311 Kenneth McRoberts. *Quebec: social change and political crisis*. 3d ed. Toronto: McClelland & Stewart, 1988. ISBN 0-7710-5515-3. ▸ Balanced analysis of developments in Quebec, 1945 to 1980s, stressing political life and rise of neonationalism. Deals with Quebec referendum, constitutional revision, and Meech Lake. Carefully documented. [JR]

45.312 Edward McWhinney. *Quebec and the constitution, 1960–1978*. Toronto: University of Toronto Press, 1979. ISBN 0-8020-5456-0 (cl), 0-8020-6364-0 (pbk). ▸ Important examination of two decades of constitutional development by constitutional adviser to Canadian and Quebec governments. Looks at Quebec demands for social, economic, linguistic, and political self-determination. [JR]

45.313 Maurice Pinard. *The rise of a third party: a study in crisis politics*. Rev. ed. Montreal: McGill-Queen's University Press, 1975. ISBN 0-7735-0231-9. ▸ Examination by political scientist of unanticipated rise of Social Credit party in Quebec in 1962 federal election. Studies origins and development of party in context of factors underlying voter change. Standard study. [JR]

45.314 Susan Mann Trofimenkoff. *Action Française: French-Canadian nationalism in the twenties*. Toronto: University of Toronto Press, 1975. ISBN 0-8030-5320-3. ▸ Study of *Action Française*, review directed by priest-historian Lionel Groulx and guided by traditional French Canadian nationalism; conservative, clerical, culturally protective. Concludes journal had slight impact. [JR]

Western Canada

45.315 Alvin Finkel. *The Social Credit phenomenon in Alberta*. Toronto: University of Toronto Press, 1989. ISBN 0-8020-5821-3 (cl), 0-8020-6731-X (pbk). ▸ Revisionist study of Social Credit movement in Alberta from appearance in 1930s to disappearance in early 1980s; much attention to post-Aberhart party. Useful summary. [JMB]

45.316 James H. Gray. *The winter years: the Depression on the prairies*. 1966 ed. Toronto: Macmillan, 1990. ISBN 0-7715-9957-9 (pbk). ▸ Highly regarded autobiographical memoir of 1930s Depression in western Canada, emphasizing individuals and personal experience of author. Regards Depression as catalyst for change. [AED]

STUART MACINTYRE

Australasia and Oceania

When the last edition of the *Guide* appeared, Australian history was set fair on a course of professional growth and disciplinary consolidation. Up to the World War II the country's six universities had employed no more than a score of historians, and their limited opportunities for research and publication circumscribed the possibility of teaching Australian history. The creation of the journal *Historical Studies: Australia and New Zealand* (now *Australian Historical Studies*) in 1940 was an early indication of vernal renewal. After the war came the rapid growth in the size and number of the universities, a new level of provision for research, and a concomitant expansion of the opportunities for postgraduate research (the first doctoral thesis in history was submitted in 1948). The establishment of a research school in the Australian National University provided the base for such essential tools as the *Australian Dictionary of Biography* (46.7).

The increased attention to the study of Australian history spoke to altered national circumstances. The war in the Pacific convinced Australians that they could no longer rely on their membership in the British empire. The ambitious program of postwar reconstruction affirmed aspirations to national self-fulfillment, and the program of large-scale immigration called for clarification of national identity. In the growing literature generated by the academic discipline of Australian history, there was an attempt to mark out the growth and development from inauspicious origins of a prosperous, dynamic nation. This literature paid particular attention to the processes of political, economic, and social maturation. It was strongly influenced by the radical nationalist school of writers who discerned within the Australian experience a distinctive national ethos—self-reliant, disrespectful of authority, and egalitarian. The radical nationalist interpretation found its clearest expression in R. Ward's *The Australian Legend* (46.176), though its pervasive effects are apparent in a wide range of writings that includes C.E.W. Bean's official war history (46.44).

These trends continued for another decade. Further growth created an academic profession of more than four hundred university-based historians by the early 1970s. This in turn fostered increased specialization in the various subdisciplines that generated their own associations, periodicals, and literature, which in turn resulted in a growing tension between the study of history in the service of a national culture and historical research for professional prestige, advancement, and participation in the international scholarly community. At the same time the discipline was subjected to far-reaching internal criticism by a new generation of younger scholars caught up in the radical movements of that era. The meliorist interpretation of Australian history was challenged by work on class, gender, and race. As was the case elsewhere, the new social history paradigm became extremely influential in the 1970s and 1980s and has generated a substantial literature in which women's and Aboriginal history are increasingly prominent. The old monocultural historiography has definitely yielded to a decentered historiography. Associated with these developments is an increased interest in the theoretical basis of historical knowledge that turned during the 1980s from social theory to literary theory with discernible effects on the emphases and interpretations offered by students of these and other fields. The earlier concentration on political, institutional, and economic history and the history of public affairs has yielded to the study of difference, subjectivity, and forms of representation.

The disciplinary confidence that was so apparent in 1960 has diminished sharply. Within the universities there has been a shift of resource allocation toward vocational training and commercial research; the diminished support of the humanities and social sciences has also shifted from history to the interdisciplinary studies that speak more directly to social concerns. Beyond the universities it is no longer possible for academic historians to assume they possess the authority to interpret the past. The more recent publications that are listed here demonstrate the need to identify, perhaps even construct, new audiences and to speak to them with new modes of historical interpretation.

In contrast to the history of Australia, the history of New Zealand had made little progress when the last edition of the *Guide* appeared. Although history was widely taught in New Zealand schools and universities, little New Zealand history featured in the curriculum at either level. The few courses at university level dealt with New Zealand history in its larger Pacific or imperial context as a colony of British settlement. The situation was being transformed at that time, however, as a new generation of historians decided that the study of New Zealand history was worthy of their talents and sufficiently challenging to engage them. A considerable number of monographs appeared during the 1950s and 1960s that called in question the older imperial paradigm and brought a fresh revisionist perspective to bear on many of New Zealand's major historical myths. Much of the more interesting work appeared either in *Historical Studies: Australia and New Zealand* or the journals of other disciplines, such as *Political Science* and *Landfall*. In 1967, thanks largely to the energy of Professor Keith Sinclair, the first meeting of the New Zealand Historical Association took place in Palmerston North and on its behalf the History Department at the University of Auckland undertook to publish the *New Zealand Journal of History*. The existence of that journal played a decisive role in transforming the nature and status of New Zealand history. Within twenty years the profession was booming. Most university departments have at least two faculty members engaged in teaching New Zealand history and supervising research, and many others, while not teaching the subject, undertake research and supervision also. When the government agreed to finance the *Dictionary of New Zealand Biography* (46.189), a new edition of the *New Zealand Atlas* (46.193), and adopted an expansive approach towards the History Branch of the Department of Internal Affairs, the profession finally attained a central position in relation to New Zealand society.

The interests of the profession across this period have changed in much the same way as the profession in the world generally. For various reasons New Zealanders and New Zealand historians have long had a strong interest in Maori history and the history of relations between Maoris and Europeans; this interest developed in vigorous and interesting ways. The new social history also transformed the nature of the subject and generated a large agenda for graduate students. Because the size of the profession in New Zealand has meant that most of the subspecialities that have flourished in the last twenty years number only one or two practitioners, historians have of necessity forged close associations with historians in other areas; this and the new social history have stimulated significant reinterpretation of the development of New Zealand society and the centrality of social developments in understanding politics and culture. Other associations have also proliferated. Archivists and oral historians have organized; the country boasts a dense network of regional historical societies (many of which publish their own journals); and the *Turnbull Library Record* (first published in 1967) also provides an avenue for dealing with issues at the interface of archives and history. The Turnbull Library's *National Register of Archives and Manuscripts in New Zealand* (three volumes) has provided an indispensable bibliographic tool for historical research. The National Library's ongoing series of subject bibliographies is also an invaluable contribution.

Pacific Island history, too, was in its infancy in 1960, although it did have an institutional base—a research department at the Australian National University. Jim Davidson, who founded that department, came from New Zealand where scholars already studied Maori history, Polynesian ethnography, and European explorers; and he had taught British colonial history in Cambridge, where he was influenced by the nationalist (especially Africanist) reaction against empire. His advocacy of Island-centered history was one dimension of a commitment to decolonization and cultural autonomy for Islanders. Scholars had addressed indigenous topics as early as the 1930s in New Zealand and Hawaii, but by 1962 their re-creations of defunct monarchies seemed as antiquarian as the editing of explorers' journals. Davidson encouraged participant-observers and academic colleagues to analyze more topical and political questions. Empiricism was the method, activism the mode, and positivism the implicit theory that animated the program.

Since 1960 new methods and perspectives have flooded in, mainly through anthropology, which saw in the Pacific Islands a classic field for social theory. Before 1960, functionalist anthropology had little use for history, so at first it was useful mainly for ethnographic detail. While functionalism was in the ascendancy, historians addressed colonial administrative and mission topics, albeit sensitive to the corrosive effects of colonial power, intransigent evangelism, and plantation production. Only in the 1960s did historians and anthropologists engage more directly in epistemological debate.

There were always some anthropologists—such as P. Lawrence (46.370)—whose historical interests transcended the profession's orthodoxy. Douglas L. Oliver's historical ethnographies (e.g., 46.293), unfashionable but meticulous, attracted historians' attention, especially for Polynesian topics. A newer source of inspiration is M. D. Sahlins (46.308), less for his Polynesian ethnography than for his bold historical speculation and analyses of the interaction of past and present. Many of his and Oliver's perceptions reached Australia and New Zealand through the teaching and writing of G. Dening (e.g., 46.301), who studies both history and anthropology and has become the most lucid analyst of topics where the disciplines overlap. More recently, N. Thomas (46.313) has channeled postmodern and poststructuralist insights into the agenda of historical writing.

This account might suggest a simple antipodean empiricism modified only by North American theory. A truer account must acknowledge the lively tradition of empirical history and historical ethnography fostered by the Bishop Museum and the University of Hawaii, Pacific outliers of the North American intellectual world; conversely, anthropological theory evolved vigorously in Canberra, Sydney, and Auckland. Further to confuse the mapping of intellectual streams, Thomas and K. Neumann (46.336) have recently linked both disciplines to west European philosophy. That connection is new: most Pacific historians have been able to proceed directly from non-Marxist to post-Marxian positions, without inscribing Marxism in Oceania. More influential is the bracing feminist critique, a trend so new that it is poorly represented in this bibliography. That challenge is timely: female subjects of biography—still a popular genre—are as rare as they are underrepresented in every other field of historical writing.

Oceania has been dominated by anthropology and its sibling, geography, rather than economics or sociology. Equally unusual, North America, New Zealand, and Australia have provided most of the scholars and institutional bases. Indigenous scholars are now achieving the critical mass to make their collective voices heard more regularly, and another—trenchant but valid—postcolonial critique is mounting against the cultural Eurocentrism lurking within most historians' commitment to political autonomy.

A final feature of the historical scholarship of Australasia and Oceania is its geographically fragmented character. The former term was once a common appellation for the British settler societies in the southwest Pacific but has little currency in New Zealand because of its hegemonic implications; the latter term usually marks off the indigenous island societies from Australia and New Zealand. The historical experience of the entire region over the past two centuries has been shaped by European and especially British influences, yet the replacement of imperial by national institutions encouraged histories that erased the common experience. Australian history makes little reference to New Zealand history; the activities of Australians and New Zealanders in the Pacific Island are studied in isolation from their domestic histories. Only now, as indigenous mobilizations call the Australian and New Zealand nations into question, is a regional perspective reopening.

ACKNOWLEDGMENTS   *This essay was written by Stuart Macintyre (Australia), Erik N. Olsen (New Zealand), and Donald Denoon and Norah Foster (Oceania).*

[Contributors: DD = Donald Denoon, ENO = Erik N. Olssen, HCF = Honore C. Forster, SM = Stuart Macintyre]

AUSTRALIA

Reference Works

46.1 *Australian national bibliography, 1901–1950.* 4 vols. Canberra: National Library of Australia, 1988. ISBN 0-642-10445-X (set), 0-642-10446-8 (v. 1), 0-642-10447-6 (v. 2), 0-642-10449-2 (v. 3), 0-642-10450-6 (v. 4). ▸ Continuation of Ferguson's bibliography of Australian publications (46.4) with author, title, and subject indexes. [SM]

46.2 Victor Crittenden et al., comps. *Index to journal articles on Australian history.* 6 vols. Kensington: History Project (Australian Reference Publications); Australia 1788–1988 a Bicentennial History, 1981–87. (Historical bibliography monographs, 2, 5, 6, 10, 15, 16.) ISBN 0-949776-01-7 (v. 2), 0-949776-03-3 (v. 5), 0-949776-06-8 (v. 6), 0-949776-15-7 (v. 10), 0-9587876-0-3 (v. 15), 0-9587876-3-8 (v. 17). ▸ Continuation of index to journal articles begun by Hogan 46.5; covers years 1974–83. Continues under same title but different publisher. [SM]

46.3 Frank K. Crowley et al., eds. *Australians: a historical library.* 11 vols. Broadway, Australia: Fairfax, Syme & Weldon, 1987. ISBN 0-949288-09-8 (set). ▸ Ambitious collaborative work divided

into two series: reference and narrative. Five volumes (unnumbered) of reference series consisting of historical atlas, historical dictionary, chronology and gazetteer, statistics, and sources (see 46.22 for narrative series). [SM]

46.4 John Alexander Ferguson, comp. *Bibliography of Australia.* 7 vols. Sydney: Angus & Robertson, 1941–69. ISBN 0-642-99043-3. ▸ Standard bibliography of Australian titles published through 1900; coverage incomplete. Reissued with one volume of addenda by National Library of Australia, 1975–77. [SM]

46.5 Terry Hogan, A. T. Yarwood, and Russel Ward, comps. *Index to journal articles on Australian history.* Adelaide, Australia: University Press of New England, 1976. ISBN 0-85834-137-9. ▸ List of journal articles on Australian history up to 1973; continued by Crittenden 46.2. [SM]

46.6 James Jupp, ed. *The Australian people: an encyclopedia of the nation, its people, and their origins.* North Ryde, Australia: Angus & Robertson, 1988. ISBN 0-207-15427-9. ▸ Large reference work on ethnic components of Australian nation. Multicultural in presentation and sympathy. [SM]

46.7 Douglas Henry Pike et al., eds. *Australian dictionary of biography.* 12 vols. with index. Melbourne: Melbourne University Press, 1966–91. ISBN 0-522-84236-4. ▸ Standard reference containing over 10,000 biographical entries with short bibliographies. [SM]

46.8 W. S. Ramson, ed. *The Australian national dictionary: a dictionary of Australianisms on historical principles.* Melbourne: Oxford University Press, 1988. ISBN 0-19-554736-5. ▸ Voluminous repository of Australian usage, rich in historical leads. [SM]

Historiography

46.9 C.M.H. Clark. *Occasional writings and speeches.* Sydney: Fontana/Collins, 1980. ISBN 0-00-635723-7 (pbk). ▸ Essays marking progress of author's understanding of Australian history with important contributions to cultural history. [SM]

46.10 R. M. Crawford, C.M.H. Clark, and Geoffrey Blainey. *Making history.* Fitzroy, Australia: McPhee-Gribble and Penguin, 1985. ISBN 0-14-007982-3 (pbk). ▸ Based on lectures by three eminent historians about their intellectual formation. [SM]

46.11 John Anthony Moses. *Historical disciplines and culture in Australasia: an assessment.* St. Lucia: University of Queensland Press; distributed by Prentice-Hall, 1979. ISBN 0-7022-1295-4. ▸ Collection of articles on various aspects of Australian historiography. [SM]

46.12 Rob Pascoe. *The manufacture of Australian history.* Melbourne: Oxford University Press, 1979. ISBN 0-19-550569-7 (cl), 0-19-550579-4 (pbk). ▸ Early attempt to discern patterns in Australian historiography drawing on categories of Hayden White (1.334). [SM]

General and Comparative Studies

46.13 John C. Beaglehole. *The life of Captain James Cook.* Stanford, Calif.: Stanford University Press, 1974. ISBN 0-8047-0848-7. ▸ Still standard biography of English navigatior who charted New Zealand and eastern coast of Australia. See also 46.357. [SM]

46.14 Geoffrey C. Bolton. *1942–1988: the middle way.* Vol. 5 of *Oxford history of Australia.* Melbourne: Oxford University Press, 1990. ISBN 0-19-554613-X. ▸ Most recent and comprehensive general history of modern era; as title suggests, eschews extremes in favor of temperate meliorism. [SM]

46.15 Verity Burgmann and Jenny Lee, eds. *A people's history of Australia since 1788.* 4 vols. Fitzroy, Australia: McPhee-Gribble and Penguin, 1988. ISBN 0-14-011055-0 (v. 1), 0-14-011056-9 (v. 2), 0-14-011057-7 (v. 3), 0-14-011058-5 (v. 4). ▸ Survey of Australian history from radical viewpoint. Sixty-six thematic essays, organized in four volumes, covering settlement and international relations, social and intellectual life, and culture and popular movements. [SM]

46.16   Paul Carter. *The road to Botany Bay: an essay in spatial history*. London: Faber & Faber, 1987. ISBN 0-571-14551-5. ▸ Discursive reading of exploration and settlement as epistemological process. [SM]

46.17   C.M.H. Clark. *A history of Australia*. 6 vols. Carlton: Melbourne University Press, 1962–87. ISBN 0-522-84008-6 (v. 1), 0-522-84166-X (v. 2), 0-522-84054-X (v. 3, cl), 0-522-84147-3 (v. 4, cl), 0-522-84223-2 (v. 5, cl), 0-522-84154-6 (v. 3, pbk), 0-522-84144-9 (v. 4, pbk), 0-522-84224-0 (v. 5, pbk), 0-522-84352-2 (v. 6). ▸ Massive idiosyncratic general history by Australia's most influential postwar historian. Grand narrative animated by author's prophetic vision. [SM]

46.18   R. M. Crawford. *An Australian perspective*. Madison: University of Wisconsin Press, 1960. ▸ Influential essay on interplay of aristocratic and democratic values in maturation of Australia from colony to independent nation. Based on 1958 Knaplund lectures at Wisconsin. [SM]

46.19   Frank K. Crowley, ed. *A new history of Australia*. Melbourne: Heinemann, 1974. ISBN 0-85561-035-2. ▸ General history organized in twelve chronological periods. Dated but not superseded. [SM]

46.20   Donald Denoon. *Settler capitalism: the dynamics of dependent development in the Southern Hemisphere*. Oxford: Clarendon, 1983. ISBN 0-19-828291-5. ▸ Major comparative study of settler societies of Southern Hemisphere; emphasis on economic, social, and political trajectories. [SM]

46.21   Alan Frost. *Convicts and empire: a naval question, 1776–1811*. Melbourne: Oxford University Press, 1980. ISBN 0-19-554255-X. ▸ Influential reinterpretation of British settlement of Australia, emphasizing strategic rather than penal motives. [SM]

46.22   Alan D. Gilbert and K. S. Inglis, eds. *Australians: a historical library*. 5 vols. of unnumbered ten-volume series. Sydney: Fairfax, Syme & Weldon, 1987. ISBN 0-949288-09-8 (set), 0-949288-18-7 (set, deluxe), 0-949288-31-4 (guide & index), 0-949288-32-2 (guide & index, deluxe). ▸ Ambitious collaborative work divided into two series, narrative and reference: first volume on Aboriginal Australia, succeeding volumes organized in fifty-year segments (see 46.3 for reference series). [SM]

46.23   William Keith Hancock. *Australia*. 1930 ed. New York: Scribner's, 1931. ▸ Frequently reissued, seminal interpretation. Main themes concerning utilitarian character of Australian politics have become axioms of Australian historiography. [SM]

46.24   Beverley Kingston. *1860–1900: glad, confident morning*. Vol. 3 of *Oxford history of Australia*. Melbourne: Oxford University Press, 1988. ISBN 0-19-554611-3. ▸ General history with strong thematic emphasis on social history. [SM]

46.25   Stuart Macintyre. *1901–1942: the succeeding age*. Vol. 4 of *Oxford history of Australia*. Melbourne: Oxford University Press, 1986. ISBN 0-19-554612-1. ▸ General history of Australia from Federation to World War II with social and political emphases. [SM]

46.26   David Mackay. *A place of exile: the European settlement of New South Wales*. Melbourne: Oxford University Press, 1985. ISBN 0-19-554632-6. ▸ Discussion of reasons for British settlement of Australia, arguing against Frost 46.21 that disposal of convicts was crucial consideration. [SM]

46.27   Ged Martin, ed. *The founding of Australia: the argument about Australia's origins*. Rev. ed. Sydney: Hale & Iremonger, 1981. ISBN 0-908094-08-6 (cl), 0-908094-00-0 (pbk). ▸ Collection

of articles debating motives for British settlement of Australia. Now dated but sets out principal positions. [SM]

46.28   Derek John Mulvaney. *The prehistory of Australia*. Rev. ed. Ringwood, Australia: Penguin, 1975. ISBN 0-14-021773-8. ▸ Authoritative general account by eminent archaeologist. [SM]

46.29   E. M. Webster. *Whirlwinds in the plain: Ludwig Leichardt, friends, foes, and history*. Carlton: Melbourne University Press, 1980. ISBN 0-522-84181-3. ▸ Lost explorer and cultural icon is subject of this critical exercise in popular genre of exploration history. [SM]

46.30   Glyndwr Williams and Alan Frost, eds. *Terra Australis to Australia*. Melbourne: Oxford University Press with Australian Academy of the Humanities, 1988. ISBN 0-19-554908-2. ▸ Collection of articles on exploration and early settlement of Australia, commemorative in tone with emphasis on cognitive aspects. [SM]

Aboriginal History

46.31   Jeremy R. Beckett, ed. *Past and present: the construction of Aboriginality*. Canberra: Australian Institute of Aboriginal Studies, 1988. ISBN 0-85575-190-8. ▸ Stimulating collection of interdisciplinary essays concerned with ways in which Aboriginal identity has been constructed. [SM]

46.32   Diane Bell. *Daughters of the dreaming*. North Sydney: Allen & Unwin, 1983. ISBN 0-86861-464-5 (cl), 0-86861-472-6 (pbk). ▸ Influential ethnographic study of women's sacred and secular spheres, contesting anthropological orthodoxy that women occupied subordinate position in Aboriginal society. [SM]

46.33   Geoffrey Blainey. *Triumph of the nomads: a history of ancient Australia*. Rev. ed. South Melbourne: Macmillan, 1982. ISBN 0-333-33837-5. ▸ Popular history of Aboriginal material culture before white contact. First published in 1975 and influential in revaluing adequacy of hunter-gatherer living standards. [SM]

46.34   N. G. Butlin. *Our original aggression: Aboriginal populations of southeastern Australia, 1788–1850*. North Sydney: Allen & Unwin, 1983. ISBN 0-86861-223-5 (pbk). ▸ Revises earlier estimates of Aboriginal population upwards and explores traumatic demographic effects of European settlement using statistical models. [SM]

46.35   Luise Hercus and Peter Sutton, eds. *This is what happened: historical narratives by Aborigines*. Canberra: Australian Institute of Aboriginal Studies, 1986. ISBN 0-85575-144-4. ▸ Important collection of Aboriginal narratives. [SM]

46.36   Kenneth Maddock. *The Australian Aborigines: a portrait of their society*. 2d ed. Ringwood, Australia: Penguin, 1982. ISBN 0-14-022396-7. ▸ Lucid overview of Aboriginal society before advent of Europeans by anthropologist with strong historical interests. [SM]

46.37   Ann McGrath. *"Born in the cattle": Aborigines in the cattle country*. North Sydney: Allen & Unwin, 1987. ISBN 0-04-150084-9. ▸ Significant contribution to recent Aboriginal history, emphasizing agency of Aboriginal women employed in North Australian pastoral industry. [SM]

46.38   Henry Reynolds. *The law of the land*. New York: Viking Penguin, 1987. ISBN 0-14-010586-7 (pbk). ▸ Provocative reconsideration of colonial policy toward Aborigines, taking issue with doctrine of *terra nullius*. [SM]

46.39   Henry Reynolds. *The other side of the frontier: an interpretation of the Aboriginal response to the invasion and settlement of Australia*. Townsville: James Cook University of North Queensland for the History Department, 1981. ISBN 0-86443-024-8 (pbk). ▸ Pathbreaking study of creative Aboriginal responses to European invasion. Interpretive concept of frontier has been challenged, but study opened new area of historical scholarship. [SM]

46.40 Deborah Bird Rose. *Hidden histories: black stories from Victoria River Downs, Humbert River, and Wave Hill Stations.* Canberra: Aboriginal Studies Press, 1991. ISBN 0-85575-224-6. ▸ Sophisticated use of Aboriginal narratives to explore Aboriginal responses to pastoral settlement of Northern Territory. [SM]

46.41 Lyndall Ryan. *The Aboriginal Tasmanians.* Vancouver: University of British Columbia Press, 1981. ISBN 0-7748-0146-8. ▸ Draws on recent archaeology to combine examination of Tasmanian Aborigines before European occupation of island with account of bloody impact of settlers. Now standard account. [SM]

46.42 Bruce Shaw. *Countrymen: the life histories of four Aboriginal men as told to Bruce Shaw.* Canberra: Australian Institute of Aboriginal Studies, 1986. ISBN 0-85575-169-x. ▸ Sophisticated oral history of Aboriginal pastoral workers. [SM]

46.43 W.E.H. Stanner. *White man got no dreaming: essays, 1938–1973.* Canberra: Australian National University Press; distributed by Books Australia, 1979. ISBN 0-7081-1802-x. ▸ Essays by distinguished anthropologist and government adviser interpreting Aboriginal religion and other issues. [SM]

Foreign Relations and Military History

46.44 C.E.W. Bean, ed. *Official history of Australia in the war of 1914–1918.* 1921–42 ed. 12 vols. St. Lucia: University of Queensland Press with Australian War Memorial, 1981. ISBN 0-7022-1585-6 (v. 1, cl), 0-7022-1603-8 (v. 2, cl), 0-7022-1586-4 (v. 1, pbk), 0-7022-1604-6 (v. 2, pbk). ▸ Large-scale war history. Bean, official war correspondent, wrote six volumes; celebration of fighting qualities of volunteer force influential in nationalist historiography. [SM]

46.45 Raymond Evans. *Loyalty and disloyalty: social conflict on the Queensland homefront, 1914–1918.* North Sydney: Allen & Unwin, 1987. ISBN 0-04-994006-6. ▸ Most sophisticated of regional studies of domestic impact of Great War; emphasis on racial and class conflict. [SM]

46.46 Bill Gammage. *The broken years: Australian soldiers in the Great War.* 1974 ed. New York: Penguin, 1975. ISBN 0-14-003383-1. ▸ Social history using letters, diaries, and other literary sources to reconstruct experience of Australian soldiers in Great War. Stimulated revival of interest. [SM]

46.47 Gavin Long, ed. *Australia in the war of 1939–1945.* 22 vols. Canberra: Australian War Memorial, 1952–77. ISBN 0-642-99366-1 (set). ▸ Official history, organized in five series: army, navy, air, civil (including political and economic volumes), and medical. [SM]

46.48 Michael McKernan. *The Australian people and the Great War.* Melbourne: Nelson, 1980. ISBN 0-17-005765-8. ▸ Synthetic history of domestic impact of Australian participation in World War I. [SM]

46.49 Neville K. Meaney. *Australia and the world: a documentary history from the 1870s to the 1970s.* Melbourne: Longman Cheshire, 1985. ISBN 0-582-71124-x. ▸ Large-scale documentary history of external relations with extensive commentary. [SM]

46.50 T. B. Millar. *Australia in peace and war: external relations since 1788.* 2d ed. Sydney: Australian National University Press and Macmillan, 1991. ISBN 0-02-946820-5. ▸ Survey history of Australian foreign policy. [SM]

46.51 John Robertson. *Australia at war, 1939–45.* Melbourne: Heinemann, 1981. ISBN 0-85561-046-8. ▸ Best general account of Australian participation in World War II, covering European and Pacific theaters. [SM]

46.52 L. L. Robson. *The first A.I.F.: a study of its recruitment, 1914–18.* 1970 ed. Carlton: Melbourne University Press, 1982. ISBN 0-522-84237-2. ▸ Statistical analysis of composition of volunteer force in Great War; significant implications for its place in nationalist historiography. [SM]

46.53 Geoffrey Serle. *John Monash: a biography.* Melbourne: Melbourne University Press with Monash University; distributed by International Scholarly Book Services, 1982. ISBN 0-522-84239-9. ▸ Distinguished biography of engineer who was Australia's most distinguished military commander in Great War. [SM]

46.54 Gavin Souter. *Lion and kangaroo: the initiation of Australia, 1901–1919.* Rev. ed. Sydney: Sun, 1992. ISBN 0-7251-0696-4. ▸ Imaginative treatment of early commonwealth period with emphasis on imperial relations and Australian involvement in Great War. [SM]

State, Regional, Local, and Urban History

46.55 Alan Atkinson. *Camden.* Melbourne: Oxford University Press, 1988. ISBN 0-19-554951-1. ▸ Rich local study applying ethnographic methods to early white settlement in New South Wales. [SM]

46.56 Weston Bate. *Lucky city: the first generation at Ballarat, 1851–1901.* Carlton: Melbourne University Press; distributed by International Scholarly Book Services, 1978. ISBN 0-522-84157-0. ▸ Distinguished history of largest of inland urban centers created by 1850s gold rush, showing transition from squalor and impermanence to settled community. [SM]

46.57 Graeme Davison. *The rise and fall of marvellous Melbourne.* Carlton: Melbourne University Press; distributed by International Scholarly Book Services, 1978. ISBN 0-522-84135-x (cl), 0-522-84191-0 (pbk). ▸ Study of spectacular urban growth of Australia's largest city in 1880s and its collapse in 1890s, with particular attention to economic and social structures. Most accomplished Australian contribution to urban history. [SM]

46.58 Ross Fitzgerald. *A history of Queensland: from the dreaming to 1915.* 1982 ed. St. Lucia: University of Queensland Press, 1986. ISBN 0-7022-1634-8 (cl, 1982), 0-7022-2028-0 (pbk). ▸ Fullest history of state of Queensland with strong emphasis on destructive consequences of cupidity. See also 46.59. Earlier title: *From the Dreaming to 1915: A History of Queensland.* [SM]

46.59 Ross Fitzgerald. *A history of Queensland: from 1915 to the early 1980s.* 1984 ed. St. Lucia: University of Queensland Press; distributed by Technical Impex, 1985. ISBN 0-7022-1734-4 (cl), 0-7022-1957-6 (pbk). ▸ Sequel to 46.58; continues same approach with particular attention to failure of political system to restrain exploitation and oppression. Earlier title: *From 1915 to the Early 1980s: A History of Queensland.* [SM]

46.60 Bill Gammage. *Narrandera Shire.* Narrandera, Australia: Narrandera Shire Council, 1986. ISBN 1-86252-522-8. ▸ Distinguished history of rural locality. [SM]

46.61 Donald S. Garden. *Victoria, a history.* Melbourne: Nelson, 1984. ISBN 0-17-005873-5. ▸ Fullest history of state of Victoria with particular attention to political history. [SM]

46.62 J. B. Hirst. *Adelaide and the country, 1870–1917: their social and political relationship.* Carlton: Melbourne University Press, 1973. ISBN 0-522-84045-0. ▸ Innovative study of colonial city and its hinterland; cuts across urban and regional history. [SM]

46.63 Margaret Kiddle. *Men of yesterday: a social history of the western district of Victoria.* 1961 ed. Melbourne: Melbourne University Press, 1967. ISBN 0-522-84208-9. ▸ Rich social history of woolgrowers of region and their distinctive mode of life in second half of nineteenth century. Most distinguished of regional studies. [SM]

46.64 Janet McCalman. *Struggletown: public and private life in Richmond, 1900–1965.* 1984 ed. Carlton: Melbourne University Press; distributed by International Scholarly Book Services, 1985. ISBN 0-522-84246-1 (cl), 0-522-84303-4 (pbk). ▸ Richly rewarding application of local history to study of working-class suburb. [SM]

46.65 J. W. McCarty and C. B. Schedvin, eds. *Australian capital cities: historical essays.* Sydney: Sydney University Press; distributed by International Scholarly Book Services, 1978. ISBN 0-424-00048-2. ▸ Articles on each state capital of Australia. Strong comparative dimension. [SM]

46.66 Douglas Henry Pike. *Paradise of dissent: South Australia, 1829–1857.* 2d ed. Melbourne: Melbourne University Press, 1967. ▸ Important account of nonpenal colony planned on theories of British reformer Edward Gibbon Wakefield. [SM]

46.67 Eric Richards, ed. *The Flinders history of South Australia.* Vol. 1: *Social history.* Netley, Australia: Wakefield, 1986. ISBN 1-86254-003-9 (set, cl), 1-86254-002-0 (set, pbk), 1-86254-004-7 (set, deluxe). ▸ Large-scale general social history. [SM]

46.68 L. L. Robson. *A history of Tasmania.* 2 vols. Melbourne: Oxford University Press, 1983–91. ISBN 0-19-554434-X (set), 0-19-554364-5 (v. 1), 0-19-553031-4 (v. 2). ▸ Large-scale narrative history with particular emphasis on follies and gothic horrors of early colonial era. [SM]

46.69 Geoffrey Serle. *The golden age: a history of the colony of Victoria, 1851–1861.* Rev. ed. Melbourne: Melbourne University Press, 1968. ▸ Deals with 1850s gold rush and its effects; impressive range. [SM]

46.70 C. T. Stannage. *The people of Perth: a social history of Western Australia's capital city.* Perth: Carroll's for Perth City Council, 1979. ISBN 0-909994-85-4 (limited ed.), 0-909994-86-2 (cl), 0-909994-87-0 (pbk). ▸ Closely researched urban history with strong social dimension, emphasizing diverse circumstances and experiences of inhabitants. [SM]

46.71 C. T. Stannage, ed. *A new history of Western Australia.* Nedlands: University of Western Australia Press, 1981. ISBN 0-85564-170-3 (cl), 0-85564-181-9 (pbk). ▸ Large-scale history with strong social history emphasis. [SM]

46.72 D. B. Waterson. *Squatter, selector, and storekeeper: a history of the Darling Downs, 1859–93.* Sydney: Sydney University Press, 1968. ISBN 0-424-05740-9. ▸ Perhaps most evocative and incisive of regional studies of agricultural settlement. [SM]

Political, Legal, and Administrative History

46.73 Alex C. Castles. *An Australian legal history.* Sydney: Law Book, 1982. ISBN 0-455-19609-5 (pbk). ▸ Comprehensive formal account of development of Australian legal system. [SM]

46.74 Francis G. Castles. *Australian public policy and economic vulnerability: a comparative and historical perspective.* North Sydney: Allen & Unwin, 1988. ISBN 0-04-335058-5 (cl), 0-04-324021-6 (pbk). ▸ Provocative interpretation locating distinctive features of Australian political economy in international comparison with particular emphasis on government policies. [SM]

46.75 L. F. Crisp. *Ben Chifley: a political biography.* 1961 ed. London: Angus & Robertson, 1977. ISBN 0-207-13453-7 (pbk). ▸ Biography of Labor party prime minister who led Australia during post–World War II reconstruction. Still important account of period. [SM]

46.76 L. F. Fitzhardinge. *William Morris Hughes: a political biography.* 2 vols. Sydney: Angus & Robertson, 1963–79. ISBN 0-207-

13245-3. ▸ Detailed biography of prime minister during Great War who broke with Labor party on issue of military conscription and formed Nationalist party. [SM]

46.77 Brian H. Fletcher. *Ralph Darling: a governor maligned.* Melbourne: Oxford University Press, 1984. ISBN 0-19-554564-8. ▸ Major study of early governor of New South Wales and his administration. [SM]

46.78 Leonie Foster. *High hopes: the men and motives of the Australian Round Table.* Carlton: Melbourne University Press with Australian Institute of International Affairs; distributed by International Specialized Book Services, 1986. ISBN 0-522-84325-5. ▸ Detailed study identifying members and describing changing activities of influential political pressure group. [SM]

46.79 Brian Galligan. *Politics of the High Court: a study of the judicial branch of government in Australia.* St. Lucia: University of Queensland Press, 1987. ISBN 0-7022-2006-X (pbk). ▸ Best available history of role of High Court in interpreting Commonwealth Constitution with particular attention to composition of Court, judges' attitudes, and impact of their decisions. [SM]

46.80 James A. Gillespie. *The price of health: Australian governments and medical policy, 1910–60.* Cambridge: Cambridge University Press, 1991. ISBN 0-521-38183-5. ▸ Painstaking analysis of interaction of government health policy and professional association of medical profession. [SM]

46.81 B. D. Graham. *The formation of the Australian country parties.* Canberra: Australian National University Press, 1966. ▸ Still the essential examination of origins and early history of important rural political movement. [SM]

46.82 Cameron Hazlehurst, ed. *Australian conservatism: essays in twentieth-century political history.* Canberra: Australian National University Press, 1979. ISBN 0-7081-1359-1. ▸ Diverse essays on aspects of nonlabor politics; neglected subject. [SM]

46.83 J. B. Hirst. *Convict society and its enemies: a history of early New South Wales.* North Sydney: Allen & Unwin, 1983. ISBN 0-86861-341-X (cl), 0-86861-349-5 (pbk). ▸ Important reinterpretation of early colonial period, arguing that penal regime contained seeds of free society. [SM]

46.84 J. B. Hirst. *The strange birth of colonial democracy: New South Wales, 1848–1884.* North Sydney: Allen & Unwin, 1988. ISBN 0-04-327100-6. ▸ Provocative treatment of advent of democracy and flawed outcomes of colonial liberalism. [SM]

46.85 W. J. Hudson. *Casey.* Melbourne: Oxford University Press, 1986. ISBN 0-19-554730-6. ▸ Biography of Australian diplomat who entered national politics and served as minister for external relations before appointment as governor-general. [SM]

46.86 Roger Joyce. *Samuel Walker Griffith.* St. Lucia: University of Queensland Press, 1984. ISBN 0-7022-1688-7. ▸ Major study of colonial lawyer and politician who played leading role in Australian federation and was first chief justice of High Court. [SM]

46.87 T. H. Kewley. *Social security in Australia, 1900–72.* Sydney: Sydney University Press, 1973. ISBN 0-424-05020-X. ▸ Detailed institutional study of public welfare in twentieth century. Restricted analysis but essential reference. [SM]

46.88 John Andrew La Nauze. *Alfred Deakin: a biography.* 2 vols. New York: Cambridge University Press, 1965. ▸ Distinguished biography of Victorian politician and later Australian prime minister who guided federal movement and shaped early commonwealth. [SM]

46.89 John Andrew La Nauze. *The making of the Australian constitution.* Melbourne: Melbourne University Press, 1972. ISBN 0-522-84016-7. ▸ Authoritative account of deliberations that resulted in Australian federation in 1901 with particular attention to drafting of Commonwealth Constitution. [SM]

46.90 Peter Loveday, A. W. Martin, and R. S. Parker, eds. *The emergence of the Australian party system.* Sydney: Hale & Iremonger, 1977. ISBN 0-908094-11-6 (cl), 0-908094-03-5 (pbk). ▸ Comparative study employing quantitative analysis to examine early party system in federal and state politics. Stronger on institutional than ideological aspects. [SM]

46.91 Stuart Macintyre. *Winners and losers: the pursuit of social justice in Australian history.* 1985 ed. North Sydney: Allen & Unwin, 1986. ISBN 0-86861-470-X (cl, 1985), 0-86861-462-9 (pbk). ▸ Synthetic overview assessing changing meanings attached to social justice as force in Australian history. [SM]

46.92 David Marr. *Barwick.* 2d ed. North Sydney: Allen & Unwin, 1992. ISBN 1-86373-269-1. ▸ Distinguished biography of influential conservative politician and judge who, as chief justice of High Court from 1964 to 1981, exercised strong influence on constitutional law. [SM]

46.93 A. W. Martin. *Henry Parkes: a biography.* Carlton: Melbourne University Press; distributed by International Scholarly Book Services, 1980. ISBN 0-522-84174-0. ▸ Authoritative biography of dominant figure in New South Wales colonial politics. [SM]

46.94 David Neal. *The Rule of Law in a penal colony: law and power in early New South Wales.* Melbourne: Cambridge University Press, 1991. ISBN 0-521-37264-X. ▸ Response to Hirst (46.84) and other revisionist historians of convict experience. Emphasizes disabilities of convicts. Rule of Law provided basis for subsequent achievement of free institutions. [SM]

46.95 Warren G. Osmond. *Frederic Eggleston: an intellectual in Australian politics.* North Sydney: Allen & Unwin, 1985. ISBN 0-86861-445-9. ▸ Illuminating biography of lawyer, politician, and public intellectual who led liberal tradition across fifty years of activity. [SM]

46.96 John David Rickard. *Class and politics: New South Wales, Victoria, and the early commonwealth, 1890–1910.* Canberra: Australian National University Press, 1976. ISBN 0-7081-0643-9. ▸ Adventurous blend of political and social history. Considers institutional responses to class mobilization of late colonial and early commonwealth years. [SM]

46.97 John David Rickard. *H. B. Higgins: the rebel as judge.* North Sydney: Allen & Unwin, 1984. ISBN 0-86861-681-8. ▸ Study of lawyer, politician, and president of Commonwealth Arbitration Court who fashioned Australian industrial jurisdiction. Close attention to emotional life. [SM]

46.98 John Douglas Ritchie. *Lachlan Macquarie: a biography.* Carlton: Melbourne University Press; distributed by International Specialized Book Services, 1986. ISBN 0-522-84321-2. ▸ Study of governor of New South Wales who played central role in transition from penal settlement. [SM]

46.99 Michael Roe. *Quest for authority in eastern Australia, 1835–1851.* Parkville: Melbourne University Press with Australian National Library, 1965. ▸ Trenchant analysis of debates on eve of self-government about alternative forms of political, social, and religious order. [SM]

46.100 Tim Rowse. *Australian liberalism and national character.* Melbourne, Australia: Kibble, 1978. ISBN 0-908150-02-4. ▸ Forceful, critical examination of variants of liberalism as hegemonic ideology of twentieth-century Australian public life. [SM]

46.101 A.G.L. Shaw. *Convicts and the colonies: a study of penal transportation from Great Britain and Ireland to Australia and other parts of the British empire.* 1966 ed. Carlton: Melbourne University

Press, 1977. ISBN 0-522-84114-7. ▸ Most comprehensive account of system of penal transportation. [SM]

46.102 Gavin Souter. *Acts of Parliament: a narrative history of the Senate and House of Representatives, Commonwealth of Australia.* Carlton: Melbourne University Press; distributed by International Specialized Book Services, 1988. ISBN 0-522-84367-0. ▸ Rich narrative of federal parliamentary politics. [SM]

Women, Gender, and Family

46.103 Ann Curthoys, Susan Eade, and Peter Spearritt, eds. *Women at work.* Canberra: Australian Society for the Study of Labour History, 1975. ISBN 0-909944-01-6. ▸ Early collection of essays on women in work force and labor movement that opened up field of research. [SM]

46.104 Kay Daniels, ed. *So much hard work: women and prostitution in Australian history.* Sydney: Fontana/Collins, 1984. ISBN 0-00-636557-4 (pbk). ▸ Collection of articles on prostitution in nineteenth and twentieth centuries. Interprets prostitution, not always convincingly, as form of women's work. [SM]

46.105 Desley Deacon. *Managing gender: the state, the new middle class, and women workers, 1830–1930.* Melbourne: Oxford University Press, 1989. ISBN 0-19-554817-5. ▸ Important study of interaction between state formation, labor movement, and gender boundaries. [SM]

46.106 Miriam Dixson. *The real Matilda: woman and identity in Australia, 1788 to 1975.* Rev. ed. Ringwood, Australia: Penguin, 1984. ISBN 0-14-022559-5. ▸ Influential, controversial (see Grimshaw 45.107) early feminist history arguing that women occupied subordinate place in Australian society for reasons associated with historical development of national character. [SM]

46.107 Patricia Grimshaw. "Women and the family in Australian history: a reply to *The Real Matilda.*" *Historical studies* 18.72 (1979) 412–21. ISSN 1031-461X. ▸ Important article reevaluating experience of women in colonial Australia. Argues against Dixson 46.106 that women's role was augmented in colonial circumstances. Argument had major impact on subsequent research. [SM]

46.108 Patricia Grimshaw, Chris McConville, and Ellen McEwen, eds. *Families in colonial Australia.* North Sydney: Allen & Unwin, 1985. ISBN 0-86861-513-7 (cl), 0-86861-521-8 (pbk). ▸ Important collection of articles on history of family in nineteenth-century Australia with strong demographic content. [SM]

46.109 Neville D. Hicks. *"This sin and scandal": Australia's population debate, 1891–1911.* Canberra: Australian National University Press, 1978. ISBN 0-7081-1344-3 (cl), 0-7081-1347-8 (pbk). ▸ Analysis of pronatalist forces in early commonwealth period. Based, rather narrowly, on Royal Commission into Birth-Rate. [SM]

46.110 Beverley Kingston. *My wife, my daughter, and poor Mary Ann: women and work in Australia.* Melbourne: Nelson, 1975. ISBN 0-17-001992-6. ▸ Pioneering account of modes of women's work in late nineteenth century. Good coverage of domestic service. [SM]

46.111 Jill Julius Matthews. *Good and mad women: the historical construction of femininity in twentieth-century Australia.* North Sydney: Allen & Unwin, 1984. ISBN 0-86861-657-5 (cl), 0-86861-665-6 (pbk). ▸ Considers historical construction of femininity and correlations of successful and failed femininity with normality and madness. [SM]

46.112 Kerreen Reiger. *The disenchantment of the home: modernizing the Australian family, 1880–1940.* Melbourne: Oxford University Press, 1985. ISBN 0-19-554594-X (cl), 0-19-554593-1 (pbk). ▸ Ambitious work of historical sociology, tracing application of applied science and instrumental reason to roles of wives and mothers. [SM]

46.113 Portia Robinson. *The hatch and brood of time: a study of the first generation of native-born white Australians, 1788–1828.* Melbourne: Oxford University Press, 1985. ISBN 0-19-554569-9 (set), 0-19-554497-8 (v. 1). ▸ Detailed reevaluation of individual fortunes of penal colony residents of New South Wales, advancing somewhat triumphalist account of social regeneration. [SM]

46.114 Edna Ryan and Anne Conlon. *Gentle invaders: Australian women at work.* Rev. ed. Ringwood, Australia: Penguin, 1989. ISBN 0-14-011722-9. ▸ Spirited critical examination of women in paid workforce and patterns of gender inequality institutionalized in early commonwealth; first published 1975. [SM]

Labor

46.115 Ken D. Buckley. *The Amalgamated Engineers in Australia, 1852–1920.* Canberra: Australian National University Press for the Department of Economic History, Research School of the Social Sciences, 1970. ISBN 0-7081-0083-X. ▸ Influential study of leading trade union of craft workers formed as branch of parent British union. Continued by Sheridan 46.127. [SM]

46.116 Verity Burgmann. *"In our time": socialism and the rise of labor, 1885–1905.* North Sydney: Allen & Unwin, 1985. ISBN 0-86861-529-3 (cl), 0-86861-537-4 (pbk). ▸ Historical survey of Australian socialists with particular attention to doctrine. Argues for importance of socialism in early history of Australian labor. [SM]

46.117 R. W. Connell and T. H. Irving. *Class structure in Australian history: poverty and progress.* Melbourne: Longman Cheshire, 1992. ISBN 0-582-71190-8. ▸ Ambitious interpretation of class formation and class relations with documentary extracts and extensive references. [SM]

46.118 Ann Curthoys and Andrew Markus, eds. *Who are our enemies? Racism and the Australian working class.* Neutral Bay: Hale & Iremonger with Australian Society for the Study of Labour History, 1978. ISBN 0-908094-34-5 (cl), 0-908094-35-3 (pbk). ▸ Special issue of journal, *Labour History*, marking new awareness of issue of race and race relations. [SM]

46.119 Robin Gollan. *Radical and working-class politics: a study of eastern Australia, 1850–1910.* 1960 ed. Carlton: Melbourne University Press with Australian National University Press, 1976. ISBN 0-522-83998-3. ▸ Pioneering study of emergence of industrial and political labor movement. [SM]

46.120 Jim Hagan. *The history of the A.C.T.U.* Melbourne: Longman Cheshire, 1981. ISBN 0-582-71117-7 (cl), 0-582-71115-0 (pbk). ▸ Substantial analytical study of principal organization of Australian labor movement, Australian Congress of Trade Unions. [SM]

46.121 Peter Love. *Labour and the money power: Australian labour populism, 1890–1950.* Carlton: Melbourne University Press, 1984. ISBN 0-522-84266-6 (pbk). ▸ Study of populist ideas about money and credit and their influence on Australian Labor party. [SM]

46.122 Ross McMullin. *The light on the hill: the Australian Labor party, 1891–1991.* Oxford: Oxford University Press, 1991. ISBN 0-19-554966-X. ▸ Major work commissioned for centenary of Australian Labor party. Narrative with strong emphasis on parliamentary leadership. [SM]

46.123 Humphrey McQueen. *A new Britannia: an argument concerning the social origins of Australian radicalism and nationalism.* 3d ed. Ringwood, Australia: Penguin, 1986. ISBN 0-14-010126-8 (pbk). ▸ First published 1970, signaled beginning of New Left

revision of labor history. Strongly critical of labor movement. [SM]

46.124 John Merritt. *The making of the AWU.* Melbourne: Oxford University Press, 1986. ISBN 0-19-554667-9. ▸ Superb panoramic study of how workforce of pastoral industry, the shearers, were organized into Australia's largest trade union, Australian Workers Union. [SM]

46.125 Bede Nairn. *Civilising capitalism: beginnings of the Australian Labor party.* Rev. ed. Carlton: Melbourne University Press, 1989. ▸ Interprets early history of labor movement as reformist and doggedly eschews class analysis. [SM]

46.126 Thomas Sheridan. *Division of labour: industrial relations in the Chifley years, 1945–1949.* Melbourne: Oxford University Press, 1989. ISBN 0-19-554961-9. ▸ Careful examination of postwar conflict between labor government and unions. Refutes orthodox interpretation of communist intransigence. [SM]

46.127 Thomas Sheridan. *Mindful militants: the Amalgamated Engineering Union in Australia, 1920–72.* Cambridge: Cambridge University Press, 1975. ISBN 0-521-20680-4. ▸ Sequel to Buckley's history (46.115) of same key union. Traces its transformation from a restrictive craft union to pacesetter in Australian industrial relations with perceptive observations on wider labor movement. [SM]

46.128 Ian Turner. *Industrial labour and politics: the dynamics of the labour movement in eastern Australia, 1900–1921.* 1965 ed. Sydney: Hale & Iremonger, 1979. ISBN 0-908094-44-2 (cl), 0-908094-33-7 (pbk). ▸ Spirited account of mobilization of labor movement and its turn to syndicalism. [SM]

Economic History

46.129 John Bach. *A maritime history of Australia.* Melbourne: Nelson, 1976. ISBN 0-17-005087-4. ▸ General history of Australian seaborne transport and communication. [SM]

46.130 Geoffrey Blainey. *The rush that never ended: a history of Australian mining.* 3d ed. Carlton: Melbourne University Press; distributed by International Specialized Book Services, 1978. ISBN 0-522-84145-7. ▸ General history of mining in Australia from 1840s, drawing on author's previous local studies with emphasis on changing technology and entrepreneurial dynamic. [SM]

46.131 Geoffrey Blainey. *The tyranny of distance: how distance shaped Australia's history.* Rev. ed. South Melbourne: Macmillan, 1982. ISBN 0-333-33836-7. ▸ Original, influential interpretation of theme of distance in Australian settlement and development. Also contested penal explanation for British settlement of Australia (see Martin, ed. 46.27). First published 1966. [SM]

46.132 N. G. Butlin. *Australian domestic product, investment, and foreign borrowing, 1861–1938/39.* Cambridge: Cambridge University Press, 1962. ▸ Estimates of private and public capital formation, capital inflow, and economic output; of profound significance for all subsequent work on Australian economic history. [SM]

46.133 N. G. Butlin. *Investment in Australian economic development, 1861–1900.* Cambridge: Cambridge University Press, 1964. ▸ Reinterpretation of dynamics of Australian economic growth based on detailed statistical analysis. Exerted major influence on Australian economic history and shifted emphasis from external to domestic dynamics of colonial economy. [SM]

46.134 N. G. Butlin, A. Barnard, and Jonathan J. Pincus. *Government and capitalism: public and private choice in twentieth-century Australia.* North Sydney: Allen & Unwin, 1982. ISBN 0-86861-187-5. ▸ Uneven but important historical study of interaction between public and private decision making in investment, enterprise, social welfare, and economic policy. [SM]

46.135 T. A. Coghlan. *Labour and industry in Australia: from the first settlement in 1788 to the establishment of the commonwealth in 1901.* 1918 ed. 4 vols. Melbourne: Macmillan, 1969. ‣ Compendium of economic and social progress by former official statistician of New South Wales. Valuable for information on wages and working conditions. [SM]

46.136 B. R. Davidson. *European farming in Australia: an economic history of Australian farming.* Amsterdam: Elsevier; distributed by Elsevier North-Holland, 1981. ISBN 0-444-41993-4. ‣ Comprehensive account of Australian agriculture with particular emphasis on changing economic conditions. [SM]

46.137 Brian Fitzpatrick. *The British empire in Australia: an economic history, 1834–1939.* Rev. 2d ed. Melbourne: Macmillan, 1969. ‣ Critical interpretation of Australia's relations with Britain. First published in 1941, had major impact on subsequent radical nationalist historiography. [SM]

46.138 G.J.R. Linge. *Industrial awakening: a geography of Australian manufacturing, 1788–1890.* Canberra: Australian National University Press; distributed by Books Australia, 1979. ISBN 0-7081-0419-3. ‣ Detailed historical geography of early Australian industry. [SM]

46.139 Rodney Maddock and Ian W. McLean, eds. *The Australian economy in the long run.* Cambridge: Cambridge University Press, 1987. ISBN 0-521-32674-5 (cl), 0-521-33933-2 (pbk). ‣ Best available comprehensive account of twentieth-century economy. [SM]

46.140 Ann Moyal. *Clear across Australia: a history of telecommunications.* Melbourne: Nelson, 1984. ISBN 0-17-006266-X. ‣ Clear general history of development of telecommunications, firmly contextualized. [SM]

46.141 Stephen Nicholas, ed. *Convict workers: reinterpreting Australia's past.* Cambridge: Cambridge University Press, 1988. ISBN 0-521-36126-5. ‣ Ambitious, if polemically excessive, reconsideration of contribution of convicts to early Australian work force. [SM]

46.142 C. B. Schedvin. *Australia and the Great Depression: a study of economic development and policy in the 1920s and 1930s.* Sydney: Sydney University Press, 1970. ISBN 0-424-06050-7. ‣ Fullest history of economic crisis of 1930s with particular emphasis on analysis of public policy. [SM]

Social History

46.143 Geoffrey C. Bolton. *A fine country to starve in.* Nedlands: University of Western Australia Press, 1972. ISBN 0-85564-061-8. ‣ Regional study of 1930s depression with emphasis on social cohesion anchored in staunch localism. [SM]

46.144 Ray Broomhill. *Unemployed workers: a social history of the Great Depression in Adelaide.* St. Lucia: University of Queensland Press, 1978. ISBN 0-7022-1235-0. ‣ Regional study of 1930s depression; pays particular attention to experience of unemployed and draws on classic study of Marienthal by Jahoda (1933) to emphasize social-psychological aspects. [SM]

46.145 Graeme Davison, David Dunstan, and Chris McConville, eds. *The outcasts of Melbourne: essays in social history.* North Sydney: Allen & Unwin, 1985. ISBN 0-86861-454-8 (cl), 0-86861-446-7 (pbk). ‣ Important collection of essays exploring poverty and low life in late nineteenth-century colonial city. [SM]

46.146 Paul De Serville. *Port Phillip gentlemen and good society in Melbourne before the gold rushes.* Melbourne: Oxford University Press, 1980. ISBN 0-19-554212-6. ‣ Engaging, if somewhat mannered, reconstruction of genteel society in Victoria in first half of nineteenth century with significant implications for colonial social structure. [SM]

46.147 David Denholm. *The colonial Australians.* Ringwood, Australia: Penguin, 1979. ISBN 0-14-070081-1. ‣ Original, provocative but uneven exploration of material culture of nineteenth-century Australia. [SM]

46.148 Shirley Fitzgerald. *Rising damp: Sydney, 1870–90.* Melbourne: Oxford University Press, 1987. ISBN 0-19-554750-0. ‣ Careful analysis of working-class conditions in colonial city with particular attention to circumstances of women. [SM]

46.149 Stephen Garton. *Medicine and madness: a social history of insanity in New South Wales, 1880–1940.* Kensington: New South Wales University Press, 1988. ISBN 0-86840-306-7. ‣ Study of construction of mental illness and its institutional treatment. Important application of new approach to social policy. [SM]

46.150 Robert Hughes. *The fatal shore.* 1986 ed. New York: Knopf; distributed by Random House, 1987. ISBN 0-394-50668-5. ‣ Major literary history of convict system of Australia, taking issue with revisionists Hirst (46.83) and Robinson (46.113) and restating harsh view of penal discipline. [SM]

46.151 K. S. Inglis. *The Australian colonists: an exploration of Australian social history, 1788–1870.* Carlton: Melbourne University Press, 1974. ISBN 0-522-84072-8. ‣ Stylish and perceptive; emphasizes leisure, ceremony, and ritual to pursue emergence of distinctive colonial identity. [SM]

46.152 Marilyn Lake. *Limits of hope: soldier settlement in Victoria, 1915–1938.* Melbourne: Oxford University Press, 1987. ISBN 0-19-554666-0. ‣ Highly critical examination of experience of rural settlement after Great War with particular emphasis on gender relations. [SM]

46.153 Judy Mackinolty. *The wasted years? Australia's Great Depression.* North Sydney: Allen & Unwin, 1981. ISBN 0-86861-123-9 (cl), 0-86861-131-X (pbk). ‣ Collection of articles on depression of 1930s, its social impact, and response of unemployed. [SM]

46.154 John McQuilton. *The Kelly outbreak, 1878–1880: the geographical dimension of social banditry.* 1979 ed. Carlton: Melbourne University Press, 1987. ISBN 0-522-84108-5 (1979), 0-522-84189-5 (1979), 0-522-84332-8 (1987). ‣ Accomplished study of legendary bushranger, Ned Kelly, as social bandit, contextualized in rural society of northern Victoria. [SM]

46.155 Anne O'Brien. *Poverty's prison: the poor in New South Wales, 1880–1918.* Carlton: Melbourne University Press, 1988. ISBN 0-522-84343-3. ‣ Strongly critical analysis of structural features of poverty in city with special emphasis on the family. [SM]

46.156 Patrick O'Farrell. *The Irish in Australia.* 1986 ed. Notre Dame, Ind.: University of Notre Dame Press, 1987. ISBN 0-268-01164-8. ‣ Powerfully written history of Irish immigration and incorporation into Australia. Argues Irish played crucial role in defining Australian nationalism. [SM]

46.157 L. L. Robson. *The convict settlers of Australia: an enquiry into the origins and characteristics of the convicts transported to New South Wales and Van Diemen's Land, 1787–1852.* 1965 ed. Carlton: Melbourne University Press, 1970. ‣ Basic to its field, analyzes origins and treatment of convicts transported to eastern Australia on basis of statistical study of convict indentures (official documents recording details of convicts). [SM]

Cultural and Educational History

46.158 Leigh Astbury. *City bushmen: the Heidelberg school and the rural mythology.* Melbourne: Oxford University Press, 1985. ISBN 0-19-554501-X. ‣ Ambitious exercise in art history. Considers influential Heidelberg school of artists in context of historical debates over Australian nationalism and rural-urban divide. [SM]

46.159 Alan Barcan. *A history of Australian education.* Mel-

bourne: Oxford University Press, 1980. ISBN 0-19-554251-7.
‣ Survey history of Australian education with particular emphasis on institutions and curriculum. [SM]

46.160   Robert Dixon. *The course of empire: neo-classical culture in New South Wales, 1788–1860.* Melbourne: Oxford University Press, 1986. ISBN 0-19-554663-6. ‣ Elegant application of Enlightenment and neoclassical cultural scholarship to literature, art, and thought of colonial New South Wales. [SM]

46.161   H. M. Green. *A history of Australian literature.* Rev. ed. 2 vols. Dorothy Green, ed. London: Angus & Robertson, 1984–85. ISBN 0-207-14335-8 (set). ‣ Extended, descriptive survey of fictional and nonfictional literature to 1950. First published 1961; dated but not replaced. [SM]

46.162   Richard Haese. *Rebels and precursors: the revolutionary years of Australian art.* 2d ed. Ringwood, Australia: Penguin, 1988. ISBN 0-14-010634-0. ‣ Provocative study of modernist art movement in Australia from Great Depression to cold war. [SM]

46.163   Laurie Hergenhan, ed. *The Penguin new literary history of Australia.* Ringwood, Australia: Penguin, 1988. ISBN 0-14-007514-3. ‣ Draws on recent literary history to assemble diverse, largely decanonized account of Australian writing. [SM]

46.164   K. S. Inglis. *This is the ABC: the Australian Broadcasting Commission, 1932–1983.* Carlton: Melbourne University Press, 1983. ISBN 0-522-84258-5. ‣ Authoritative account of government-funded broadcasting service and Australian communications policy. [SM]

46.165   Lesley Johnson. *The unseen voice: a cultural study of early Australian radio.* London: Routledge, 1988. ISBN 0-415-02763-2 (cl), 0-416-03892-1 (pbk). ‣ Theoretically fluent examination of early history of radio in Australia with particular attention to its role in defining domesticity. [SM]

46.166   Terence Lane and Jessie Serle. *Australians at home: a documentary history of Australian domestic interiors from 1788 to 1914.* Melbourne: Oxford University Press, 1990. ISBN 0-19-553128-0. ‣ Lavishly illustrated history of domestic architecture with preponderance of grand homes but an eye for full range of habitation. [SM]

46.167   Sylvia Lawson. *The Archibald paradox: a strange case of authorship.* Ringwood, Australia: Lane, 1983. ISBN 0-7139-014-54. ‣ Innovative study of J. F. Archibald, editor of weekly magazine, the *Bulletin*, usually treated as vehicle for demotic nationalism but here seen as complex and innovative hybrid. [SM]

46.168   Marguerite Mahood. *The loaded line: Australian political caricature, 1788–1901.* Carlton: Melbourne University Press, 1973. ISBN 0-522-84041-8. ‣ Definitive study of colonial political caricature with firm grasp of historical and artistic context. [SM]

46.169   Brian Matthews. *Louisa.* Melbourne: McPhee-Gribble, 1987. ISBN 0-86914-038-8. ‣ Innovative, multivocal biography of late nineteenth-century feminist and publisher, Louisa Lawson. [SM]

46.170   Drusilla Modjeska. *Exiles at home: Australian women writers, 1925–1945.* London: Sirius, 1981. ISBN 0-207-14616-0. ‣ Powerfully sustained study of group of women writers of major significance in interwar reorientation of Australian literature. [SM]

46.171   R.J.W. Selleck. *Frank Tate: a biography.* Carlton: Melbourne University Press; distributed by International Specialized Book Services, 1982. ISBN 0-522-84229-1. ‣ Lucid biography of leading educational administrator who shaped government school system in early twentieth century. [SM]

46.172   Geoffrey Serle. *The creative spirit in Australia: a cultural history.* Melbourne: Heinemann, 1987. ISBN 0-85561-104-9. ‣ Survey history of literature, art, architecture, music, and other cultural forms; emphasis on growth of national maturity. Earlier title: *From Deserts the Prophets Come.* [SM]

46.173   Bernard Smith. *European vision and the South Pacific.* 2d ed. New Haven: Yale University Press, 1985. ISBN 0-300-02815-6 (cl), 0-300-04479-8 (pbk). ‣ Landmark of historical scholarship, first published 1960, exploring aesthetic and intellectual response of Europeans to region. [SM/DD/HCF]

46.174   Terry Smith and Bernard Smith. *Australian painting, 1788–1990.* 3d ed. Melbourne: Oxford University Press, 1991. ISBN 0-19-554901-5. ‣ General treatment by doyens of Australian art historians. First published 1971. [SM]

46.175   David Walker. *Dream and disillusion: a search for Australian cultural identity.* Canberra: Australian National University Press; distributed by Baker & Taylor, 1976. ISBN 0-7081-0825-3. ‣ Innovative exercise in cultural history. Examines attempt of group of writers and progressive intellectuals to establish national literary tradition. [SM]

46.176   Russel Ward. *The Australian legend.* 3d ed. Melbourne: Oxford University Press, 1978. ISBN 0-19-550551-4. ‣ Crucial statement of leftist nationalist interpretation of Australian history seeing genesis of distinctive mores and attitudes in nineteenth-century experience. [SM]

Science and Environment

46.177   William Keith Hancock. *Discovering Monaro: a study of man's impact on his environment.* Cambridge: Cambridge University Press, 1972. ISBN 0-521-08439-3. ‣ Social and environmental history of mountain region of southeastern Australia. Pathbreaking work notable for early appreciation of Aboriginal ecology by doyen of Australian historians. [SM]

46.178   Rod W. Home, ed. *Australian science in the making.* 1988 ed. Cambridge: Cambridge University Press with Australian Academy of Science, 1990. ISBN 0-521-39640-9. ‣ Solid collection of articles on history of Australian science. [SM]

46.179   Ann Moyal. *"A bright and savage land": scientists in colonial Australia.* Sydney: Collins, 1986. ISBN 0-00-217555-X. ‣ Authoritative study of scientific activity in nineteenth century. [SM]

46.180   J. M. Powell. *An historical geography of modern Australia: the restive fringe.* Cambridge: Cambridge University Press, 1988. ISBN 0-521-25619-4. ‣ Authoritative introduction to Australian historical geography. [SM]

46.181   C. B. Schedvin. *Shaping science and industry: a history of Australia's Council for Scientific and Industrial Research, 1926–49.* North Sydney: Allen & Unwin, 1987. ISBN 0-04-909036-4. ‣ Distinguished commissioned history of first quarter-century of government scientific organization. [SM]

46.182   Richard White. *Inventing Australia.* North Sydney: Allen & Unwin, 1981. ISBN 0-86861-027-5 (cl), 0-86861-035-6 (pbk). ‣ Lively survey of changing representations of Australia. [SM]

Religion

46.183   D.W.A. Baker. *Days of wrath: a life of John Dunmore Lang.* Carlton: Melbourne University Press; distributed by International Specialized Book Services, 1985. ISBN 0-522-84297-6. ‣ Detailed study of Presbyterian minister whose turbulent career embraced education, sectarian agitation, radical politics, and writing of history. [SM]

46.184   Hugh R. Jackson. *Churches and people in Australia and New Zealand, 1860–1930.* Wellington: Allen & Unwin, 1987. ISBN 0-86861-714-8 (cl), 0-86861-698-2 (pbk). ‣ Brief but effective comparative study of place of organized religion in Australia and New Zealand. [SM/ENO]

46.185 Patrick O'Farrell. *The Catholic church and community in Australian history.* Rev. ed. Kensington: New South Wales University Press, 1985. ISBN 0-86840-225-7. ‣ Critical, engaged account of history of Catholic church in Australia and its role in religious and public life. [SM]

46.186 Walter Phillips. *Defending a "Christian country": churchmen and society in New South Wales in the 1880s and after.* St. Lucia: University of Queensland Press, 1981. ISBN 0-7022-1539-2. ‣ Regional study of role of religion in public life at time of evangelical fervor. [SM]

46.187 Jillian Roe. *Beyond belief: theosophy in Australia, 1879–1939.* Kensington: New South Wales University Press, 1986. ISBN 0-86840-042-4 (pbk). ‣ Reveals significance of theosophy on small but influential group of Australians. [SM]

NEW ZEALAND
Reference Works

46.188 Austin G. Bagnall, ed. *New Zealand national bibliography to the year 1960.* Vol. 1: To 1889. Vols. 2–4: 1890–1960. Vol. 5: *Supplement and index.* Wellington: A.R. Shearer, Government Printer, 1970–85. ISBN 0-477-01088-1 (set), 0-477-01087-3 (v. 1). ‣ Despite errors and omissions, invaluable work. Still suffers from lack of an adequate subject index. [ENO]

46.189 *The dictionary of New Zealand biography.* Wellington: Allen & Unwin with Historical Publications Branch, Department of Internal Affairs, 1990. ISBN 0-0-4641052-X (v. 1). ‣ First of four volumes containing some 500 entries on many Maori, women, and ordinary persons, plus prominent politicians, generals, businessmen, et al. [ENO]

46.190 Charlotte Macdonald, Merimeri Penfold, and Bridget Williams, eds. *The book of New Zealand women=Ko kui ma te kaupapa.* Wellington: Bridget Williams Books, 1991. ISBN 0-908912-04-8. ‣ Stimulating brief biographies of humble and powerful, Pakeha and Maori, infamous and famous. [ENO]

46.191 Alexander H. McLintock, ed. *An encyclopedia of New Zealand.* 3 vols. Wellington: R.E. Owen, Government Printer, 1966. ‣ Essays on historical topics and people, natural history, geography, and such topics as New Zealand coat-of-arms. Explores and documents diversity and variety of liberal-democratic society. [ENO]

46.192 Robert McNab, ed. *Historical records of New Zealand.* 1908–14 ed. 2 vols. Wellington: A.R. Shearer, Government Printer, 1973. ‣ Well-edited Rankean compilation including documents relating to British involvement with New Zealand, private and official, based on thorough research in newspapers, government archives, and private manuscripts. [ENO]

46.193 Ian Wards, ed. *New Zealand atlas.* Wellington: A.R. Shearer, Government Printer, 1976. ISBN 0-477-01000-8. ‣ Best available historical atlas with useful introductory essays on such subjects as land forms, transport, and government. [ENO]

Historiography

46.194 W. H. Oliver. "A destiny at home." *New Zealand journal of history* 21 (1987) 9–15. ISSN 0028-8322. ‣ Critical but sympathetic assessment of Sir Keith Sinclair as historian. [ENO]

46.195 Erik N. Olssen. "Where to from here?" *New Zealand journal of history* 26 (1992) 54–77. ISSN 0028-8322. ‣ Analysis of major themes and preoccupations of post-1945 scholarship. [ENO]

46.196 Keith Sinclair. "History in New Zealand." In *Historical disciplines and culture in Australasia: an assessment.* John Anthony Moses, ed., pp. 228–38. St. Lucia: University of Queensland

Press, 1979. ISBN 0-7022-1295-4. ‣ Doyen of profession sketches discipline's development. [ENO]

46.197 Keith Sinclair. "New Zealand." In *The historiography of the British empire-commonwealth: trends, interpretations, and resources.* Robin Winks, ed., pp. 174–96. Durham, N.C.: Duke University Press, 1966. ‣ Incisive introduction followed by dense bibliographical essay. [ENO]

General Studies

46.198 Peter H. Buck. *Vikings of the sunrise.* 1954 ed. Westport, Conn.: Greenwood, 1985. ISBN 0-313-24522-3. ‣ Classic study of Polynesian colonization of New Zealand. [ENO]

46.199 John B. Condliffe. *New Zealand in the making: a study of economic and social development.* 2d rev. ed. London: Allen & Unwin, 1959. ‣ Classic study, culminates in family farm as basis of economic democracy. First published in 1930. [ENO]

46.200 William J. Gardner, ed. *General history, 1854–76, and cultural aspects, 1850–1950.* Vol. 2 of *A history of Canterbury.* Christchurch, New Zealand: Whitcombe & Tombs for the Canterbury Centennial Historical and Literary Committee, 1957–71. ‣ Only full cultural history of community; old fashioned but comprehensive. [ENO]

46.201 R. Knox, ed. *New Zealand's heritage: the making of a nation.* 7 vols. Auckland: Hamlyn, 1979. ‣ Impressive for range of illustrative material and attempt to focus on ordinary people and minority ethnic groups. Work originally appeared in weekly installments. [ENO]

46.202 W. H. Oliver. *The story of New Zealand.* 2d ed. London: Faber & Faber, 1963. ‣ Based largely on secondary sources and centered on country's main post-1945 problems; emphasizes importance of British heritage. [ENO]

46.203 William P. Reeves and Angus J. Harrop. *The long white cloud: Ao tea roa.* 4th rev. ed. Auckland: Viking, 1987. ISBN 0-670-82003-2. ‣ Classic, first published 1898, stresses South Island themes such as Wakefield, gold rushes, and land reform in creating democratic society. [ENO]

46.204 Geoffrey Rice, ed. *The Oxford history of New Zealand.* 2d ed. W. H. Oliver and B. R. Williams, (1st edition) eds. Auckland: Oxford University Press, 1992. ISBN 0-19-558257-8. ‣ Highly integrated collection of essays attempting to provide full history. Innovative chapters on Maori and social history. [ENO]

46.205 Keith Sinclair. *A history of New Zealand.* 4th rev. ed. Auckland: Penguin, 1991. ISBN 0-14-015430-2. ‣ Classic, first published 1959, stresses North Island themes such as Maori wars, frontier, and equality. [ENO]

Contact Period

46.206 John Boultbee. *Journal of a rambler: the journal of John Boultbee.* June Starke, ed. Auckland: Oxford University Press, 1986. ISBN 0-19-558120-2. ‣ Fascinating account of Maori society in 1820s. [ENO]

46.207 Harry Morton. *The whale's wake.* Honolulu: University of Hawaii Press, 1982. ISBN 0-8248-0830-4. ‣ Comprehensive analysis of whaling industry from 1790s to 1840s, organized topically. [ENO]

46.208 Eric Ramsden. *Busby of Waitangi: H.M.'s resident at New Zealand, 1833–40.* Sydney: Angus & Robertson, 1942. ‣ Still useful biography of first British official appointed to establish law and order in Far North. [ENO]

46.209 Anne Salmond. *Two worlds: first meetings between Maori and Europeans, 1642–1772.* Honolulu: University of Hawaii Press, 1991. ISBN 0-8248-1467-3. ‣ Ambitious attempt to understand

Maori and European interpretations of contact before 1772. [ENO]

46.210 William B. Williams. *The Turanga journals, 1840–1850: letters and journals of William and Jane Williams, missionaries to Poverty Bay.* Frances Porter, ed. Wellington: Price Milburn for Victoria University Press, 1974. ISBN 0-507-70372-0. ‣ Influential missionary family's observations and account of their relations with East Coast tribes. [ENO]

46.211 Harrison M. Wright. *New Zealand, 1769–1840: early years of Western contact.* Cambridge, Mass.: Harvard University Press, 1959. ‣ Provocative and still invaluable; exaggerates collapse of Maori culture in explaining Maori conversion to Christianity. [ENO]

Maori, 1870–1950

46.212 Judith Binney, Gillian Chaplin, and Craig Wallace. *Mihaia: the prophet Rua Kenana and his community at Maungapohatu.* Wellington: Oxford University Press, 1979. ISBN 0-19-558042-7 (cl), 0-19-558052-4 (pbk). ‣ Well-illustrated study of important Maori prophet and conflict with government. [ENO]

46.213 John B. Condliffe. *Te Rangi Hiroa: the life of Sir Peter Buck.* Christchurch, New Zealand: Whitcombe & Tombs, 1971. ISBN 0-7233-0316-9. ‣ Useful, if Eurocentric, biography of great New Zealander and anthropologist. [ENO]

46.214 Michael King. *Moriori: a people rediscovered.* Auckland: Viking, 1989. ISBN 0-670-82655-3. ‣ Prize-winning history of inhabitants of Chatham Islands and their response to Maori and European invasions. [ENO]

46.215 Michael King. *Te Puea.* 1977 ed. Auckland: Sceptre, 1987. ISBN 0-340-42096-0 (pbk). ‣ Sympathetic biography of one of most important Maori leaders and her Waikato people. [ENO]

46.216 Michael King. *Whina: a biography of Whina Cooper.* 1983 ed. Auckland: Penguin, 1991. ISBN 0-14-014722-5. ‣ Based largely on interviews with important leader of Maori renaissance. [ENO]

46.217 Piritihana Mikaere. *Te Maiharoa and the promised land.* Auckland: Heinemann, 1988. ISBN 0-86863-585-5. ‣ Moving study of influential Ngai Tahu prophet. [ENO]

46.218 Apirana Ngata. *Na to hoa aroha, from your dear friend: the correspondence between Sir Apirana Ngata and Sir Peter Buck, 1925–1950.* 3 vols. M. P. K. Sorrenson, ed. Auckland: Auckland University Press and Oxford University Press with Alexander Turnbull Library Endowment Trust and Maori Purposes Fund Board; distributed by Oxford University Press, 1986–88. ISBN 0-19-648035-3 (v. 1), 1-86940-011-9 (v. 2) 1-86940-019-4 (v. 3). ‣ Excellent edition of correspondence between two major intellectual and political figures; excellent introduction. [ENO]

46.219 John Adrian Williams. *Politics of the New Zealand Maori: protest and cooperation, 1891–1909.* Seattle: University of Washington Press, 1969. ‣ Careful introductory study of Maori politics (and race relations) from attempt to form Maori Parliament to Young Maori party. [ENO]

Colonization, 1840–1890

46.220 Rollo Arnold. *The farthest promised land: English villagers, New Zealand immigrants of the 1870s.* Wellington: Victoria University Press with Price Milburn, 1981. ISBN 0-7055-0696-7. ‣ Gold mine of detail on 1870s immigrants. [ENO]

46.221 Patricia Burns. *Fatal success: a history of the New Zealand Company.* Henry Richardson, ed. Auckland: Heinemann Reed, 1989. ISBN 0-7900-0011-3. ‣ Full study of six Wakefield settlements reflecting revisionist work of last forty years. [ENO]

46.222 Alfred W. Crosby, Jr. *Ecological imperialism: the biological expansion of Europe, 900–1900.* Cambridge: Cambridge University Press, 1986. ISBN 0-521-32009-7 (cl), 0-521-33613-9 (pbk). ‣ Excellent chapter on impact of Europeans, their plants and animals. [ENO]

46.223 Charlotte Macdonald. *A woman of good character: single women as immigrant settlers in nineteenth-century New Zealand.* Wellington: Allen & Unwin with Historical Publications Branch, Department of Internal Affairs, 1990. ISBN 0-04-658258-4. ‣ Sound analysis of single women immigrants of 1860s and transplantation of double standard. [ENO]

46.224 J. S. Marais. *The colonisation of New Zealand.* 1927 ed. New York: AMS Press, 1971. ISBN 0-404-04184-1. ‣ Classic study of systematic colonization of New Zealand in 1840s. [ENO]

46.225 Philip R. May. *The West Coast gold rushes.* 2d rev. ed. Christchurch, New Zealand: Pegasus, 1967. ‣ Lengthy but loving story of one of colony's largest gold rushes. [ENO]

46.226 John Owen Miller. *Early Victorian New Zealand: a study of racial tension and social attitudes, 1839–1852.* 1958 ed. Westport, Conn.: Greenwood, 1986. ISBN 0-313-25283-1. ‣ Witty, influential analysis of racial attitudes of settlers in first Wakefield settlements. [ENO]

46.227 Angus Ross. *New Zealand aspirations in the Pacific in the nineteenth century.* Oxford: Clarendon, 1964. ‣ Full analysis of New Zealand imperialism in South Pacific and construction of an imperial identity. [ENO]

Provincial History

46.228 Austin G. Bagnall. *Wairarapa: an historical excursion.* Masterton, New Zealand: Hedley's Bookshop for Masterton Trust Lands Trust, 1976. ‣ Thoroughly researched study of fertile region in lower North Island. [ENO]

46.229 James Hight and Carl R. Staubel, eds. *A history of Canterbury.* Vol. 1: *To 1854.* Christchurch, New Zealand: Whitcombe & Tombs for Canterbury Centennial Historical and Literary Committee, 1957–71. ‣ Although somewhat disorganized, contains some excellent chapters and very useful narrative history of province. [ENO]

46.230 Alexander H. McLintock. *The history of Otago: the origins and growth of a Wakefield class settlement.* 1949 ed. Christchurch, New Zealand: Capper, 1975. ‣ Subtitle misleading, work focuses on settlement and debates over land policy and politics. [ENO]

46.231 Erik N. Olssen. *A history of Otago.* Dunedin, New Zealand: McIndoe, 1984. ISBN 0-86868-058-3. ‣ Study of rise and fall of country's wealthiest and most populous province, its identity, and impact of economic decline. [ENO]

46.232 William H. Scotter, ed. *A history of Canterbury.* Vol. 3: *1876–1950.* Christchurch, New Zealand: Whitcombe & Tombs for Canterbury Centennial Historical and Literary Committee, 1957–71. ‣ Thorough account providing useful check on larger generalizations. [ENO]

British Sovereignty and Authority, 1840–1870

46.233 Peter Adams. *Fatal necessity: British intervention in New Zealand, 1830–1847.* Auckland: Auckland University Press and Oxford University Press, 1977. ISBN 0-19-647950-9. ‣ Judicious account, focusing on New Zealand and London and analyzing contradictions in official policy. [ENO]

46.234 James Belich. *The Victorian interpretation of racial conflict: the Maori, the British, and the New Zealand wars.* 1986 ed. Montreal: McGill-Queen's University Press, 1989. ISBN 0-7735-0750-7 (cl), 0-7735-0739-6 (pbk). ‣ Outstanding, prize-winning analysis of Victorian interpretation of Maori military successes. [ENO]

46.235 James Cowan. *The New Zealand wars: a history of the Maori campaigns and the pioneering period.* 1922 ed. 2 vols. New York: AMS Press, 1969. ISBN 0-404-00600-0. ▸ Classic study of wars, based on documentary and oral research, arguing wars created mutual respect. [ENO]

46.236 Alexander H. McLintock. *Crown colony government in New Zealand.* Wellington: R.E. Owen, Government Printer, 1958. ▸ Full account of Crown colony government and settlers' campaign for self-government. [ENO]

46.237 William P. Morrell. *British colonial policy in the age of Peel and Russell.* 1930 ed. New York: Barnes & Noble, 1966. ▸ Classic, comparative analysis of imperial policy toward New Zealand. [ENO]

46.238 Claudia Orange. *The Treaty of Waitangi.* Wellington: Allen & Unwin and Port Nicholson Press with Historical Publications Branch, Department of Internal Affairs, 1987. ISBN 0-86861-634-6 (cl), 0-86861-427-0 (pbk). ▸ Skillful synthesis of origins, meaning, and changing significance of treaty since 1840. [ENO]

46.239 James Rutherford. *Sir George Grey, K.C.B., 1812–1898: a study in colonial government.* London: Cassell, 1961. ▸ Best, if excessively sympathetic, portrait of governor who became prime minister. [ENO]

46.240 Keith Sinclair. *The origins of the Maori wars.* 1961 2d ed. Wellington: Auckland University Press and Oxford University Press, 1976. ISBN 0-19-647912-6. ▸ Classic analysis of background of Maori wars, showing how they were transformed into land wars. [ENO]

46.241 Alan D. Ward. *A show of justice: racial "amalgamation" in nineteenth-century New Zealand.* 1973 ed. Auckland: Auckland University Press and Oxford University Press, 1978. ISBN 0-19-647974-6. ▸ Detailed analysis of development of official policy toward Maori. [ENO]

Nineteenth-Century Politics and Society, 1854–1890

46.242 Raewyn M. Dalziel. "The colonial helpmeet: women's role and the vote in nineteenth-century New Zealand." *New Zealand journal of history* 11.2 (1977) 112–23. ISSN 0028-8322. ▸ Argues consensus about women's domestic role explains early adoption of women's suffrage. [ENO]

46.243 Raewyn M. Dalziel. *Julius Vogel: business politician.* Auckland: Auckland University Press and Oxford University Press, 1986. ISBN 0-19-648047-7. ▸ Thorough study of colony's most important nineteenth-century politician and politics of development. [ENO]

46.244 Miles H. Fairburn. *The ideal society and its enemies: the foundations of modern New Zealand society, 1850–1900.* Auckland: Auckland University Press; distributed by Oxford University Press, 1989. ISBN 1-86940-028-3 (pbk). ▸ Controversial analysis of colony's animating ideal and bondless or atomized society. [ENO]

46.245 Ross A. Galbreath. *Walter Buller: the reluctant conservationist.* Wellington: G.P. Books, 1989. ISBN 0-477-01416-X. ▸ Careful study of cantankerous but influential natural historian. [ENO]

46.246 Frances Porter. *Born to New Zealand: a biography of Jane Maria Atkinson.* Wellington: Allen & Unwin and Port Nicholson Press, 1989. ISBN 0-04-614008-5. ▸ Prize-winning biography of colonial housewife and mother who was related to many prominent men. [ENO]

46.247 Russell C. J. Stone. *Makers of fortune: a colonial business community and its fall.* Auckland: Auckland University Press and Oxford University Press, 1973. ISBN 0-19-647713-1. ▸ Collective biography of Auckland business elite. [ENO]

46.248 Russell C. J. Stone. *Young Logan Campbell.* Auckland: Auckland University Press and Oxford University Press, 1982. ISBN 0-19-648019-1. ▸ First of two-volume study of father of Auckland. [ENO]

46.249 Peter Allan Stuart. *Edward Gibbon Wakefield in New Zealand: his political career, 1853–4.* Wellington: Price Milburn for Victoria University, 1971. ISBN 0-7055-0334-8. ▸ Careful analysis revealing British reformer's opportunism and role in winning self-government for settlers. [ENO]

Liberals

46.250 Peter J. Coleman. *Progressivism and the world of reform: New Zealand and the origins of the American welfare state.* Lawrence: University Press of Kansas, 1987. ISBN 0-7006-0321-2. ▸ Careful analysis of what American visitors wrote about New Zealand's land and labor laws. [ENO]

46.251 Patricia Grimshaw. *Women's suffrage in New Zealand.* 1972 rev. ed. Auckland: Auckland University Press, 1987. ISBN 1-86940-026-7 (cl), 1-86940-021-6 (pbk). ▸ Careful analysis of women's role and political coalitions involved in enacting reform in 1893. [ENO]

46.252 David A. Hamer. *The New Zealand Liberals: the years of power, 1891–1912.* Auckland: Auckland University Press; distributed by Oxford University Press, 1988. ISBN 1-86940-014-3. ▸ Detailed analysis of origins and achievements of Liberals. Largely ignores labor policies. [ENO]

46.253 James Holt. *Compulsory arbitration in New Zealand: the first forty years.* Auckland: Auckland University Press, 1986. ISBN 1-86940-006-2. ▸ Lucid study of origins of reform and development of arbitration system. [ENO]

46.254 Kerry R. Howe. *Singer in a songless land: a life of Edward Tregear, 1846–1931.* Auckland: Auckland University Press, 1991. ISBN 1-86940-058-5. ▸ Biography of first head of Department of Labour and important intellectual. [ENO]

46.255 W. H. Oliver. "Reeves, Sinclair, and the social pattern." In *The feel of truth: essays in New Zealand and Pacific history.* P. Munz, ed. Wellington: A.H. & A.W. Reed for Victoria University, 1969. ▸ Incisive, influential critique of view that Liberals represented politics of class or that class helps explain New Zealand history. [ENO]

46.256 Keith Sinclair. *William Pember Reeves: New Zealand Fabian.* Oxford: Clarendon, 1965. ▸ Biography of architect of liberal labor reforms, by whose fall party's retreat from radicalism is measured. [ENO]

War

46.257 Paul J. Baker. *King and country call: New Zealanders, conscription, and the Great War.* Auckland: Auckland University Press; distributed by Oxford University Press, 1988. ISBN 1-86940-034-8 (pbk). ▸ Careful analysis of debate over and political impact of conscription. [ENO]

46.258 Dan Davin. *Crete.* Wellington: Department of Internal Affairs, War History Branch, 1953. ▸ Skillful account of New Zealand Division's major defeat in World War II. [ENO]

46.259 Christopher Pugsley. *Gallipoli: the New Zealand story.* 1984 ed. London: Hodder & Stoughton, 1985. ISBN 0-340-33877-6. ▸ Densely detailed account of battle that many see as formative national experience. [ENO]

46.260 Christopher Pugsley. *On the fringe of hell: New Zealanders and military discipline in the First World War.* Auckland: Hodder

& Stoughton, 1991. ISBN 0-340-53321-8 (pbk). ► Careful analysis, based on disciplinary archives, of New Zealand Division's reputation. [ENO]

46.261 Nancy M. Taylor. *The home front: the New Zealand people at war.* 2 vols. Wellington: V. R. Ward, Government Printer for Department of Internal Affairs, Historical Publications Branch, 1986. ISBN 0-477-01360-0 (set), 0-477-01259-0 (v. 1), 0-477-01260-4 (v. 2). ► Full study of every aspect of World War II's impact on New Zealand. [ENO]

46.262 Frederick L. W. Wood. *The New Zealand people at war: political and external affairs.* 1958 ed. Wellington: Department of Internal Affairs, Historical Publications Branch with A. H. & A. W. Reed, 1971. ISBN 0-589-00634-7. ► Elegant narrative of strategic, military, and political events. [ENO]

Labor, 1905–1940

46.263 Francis G. Castles. *The working class and welfare: reflections on the political development of the welfare state in Australia and New Zealand, 1890–1980.* Wellington: Allen & Unwin with Port Nicholson Press, 1985. ISBN 0-86861-669-9 (cl), 0-86861-661-3 (pbk). ► Comparative analysis of development of wage worker's welfare state. [ENO]

46.264 John B. Condliffe. *The welfare state in New Zealand.* 1959 ed. Westport, Conn.: Greenwood, 1975. ISBN 0-8371-7298-5. ► Classic account of economics of insulation and welfare. [ENO]

46.265 Barry S. Gustafson. *From the cradle to the grave: a biography of Michael Joseph Savage.* 1986 ed. Auckland: Penguin, 1988. ISBN 0-14-010223-X. ► Moving biography of Labour party's first prime minister. [ENO]

46.266 Barry S. Gustafson. *Labour's path to political independence: the origins and establishment of the New Zealand Labour party, 1900–19.* Auckland: Auckland University Press and Oxford University Press, 1980. ISBN 0-19-647986-X. ► Well-illustrated analysis of formation and early years of Labour party. [ENO]

46.267 Patrick O'Farrell. *Harry Holland: militant socialist.* Canberra: Australian National University Press, 1964. ► Sympathetic biography of socialist Left's major leader who became leader of party. [ENO]

46.268 Patrick O'Farrell. *Vanished kingdoms, Irish in Australia and New Zealand: a personal excursion.* Kensington: New South Wales University Press; distributed by International Specialized Book Services, 1990. ISBN 0-86840-148-X. ► Outstanding historian uses family memoir to explore Irish impact on Labour and left-wing dreams. [ENO]

46.269 Erik N. Olssen. *John A. Lee.* Dunedin, New Zealand: University of Otago Press, 1977. ISBN 0-908569-04-1. ► Biography of major figure in left-wing rebellion against Labour government. [ENO]

46.270 Erik N. Olssen. *The red feds: revolutionary industrial unionism and the New Zealand Federation of Labour, 1908–14.* Auckland: Oxford University Press, 1988. ISBN 0-19-558122-9. ► Full analysis of origins of revolutionary industrial unionism and prewar industrial unrest. [ENO]

46.271 Tony Simpson. *The sugarbag years: an oral history of the 1930s depression in New Zealand.* 2d ed. Auckland: Hodder & Stoughton, 1984. ISBN 0-340-35822-X. ► Skillful account of Great Depression's impact, based on oral and written sources. [ENO]

46.272 Keith Sinclair. *Walter Nash.* New York: Oxford University Press, 1976. ISBN 0-19-647949-5. ► Full biography of major figure in first Labour government and prime minister in second. [ENO]

Social History, 1890–1940

46.273 John C. Beaglehole. *Victoria University College: an essay towards a history.* Wellington: New Zealand University Press, 1949. ► Lively analysis of changing values of university students and their clashes with authority. [ENO]

46.274 Herbert Guthrie-Smith. *Tutira: the story of a New Zealand sheep station.* 4th ed. Wellington: Reed, 1969. ► Classic study of New Zealand history in microcosm, author's sheep station in Hawke's Bay. [ENO]

46.275 Jock Phillips. *A man's country? The image of the Pakeha male, a history.* Auckland: Penguin, 1987. ISBN 0-14-009334-6. ► Innovative interpretive exploration of construction of New Zealand male identity. [ENO]

46.276 Keith Sinclair. *A destiny apart: New Zealand's search for national identity.* Wellington: Allen & Unwin with Port Nicholson Press, 1986. ISBN 0-86861-690-7 (cl), 0-86861-682-6 (pbk). ► Wide-ranging history of formation of New Zealand's national identity. [ENO]

46.277 Hugh C. D. Somerset. *Littledene, patterns of change.* Rev. ed. Wellington: New Zealand Council for Educational Research, 1974. (Educational research series, 51.) ► Sociological classic, in tradition of the Lynds' *Middletown* (44.162), based on rural town. Contains Somerset's original *Littledene, a New Zealand Rural Community,* 1938, and incomplete sequel, *Littledene Revisited.* [ENO]

46.278 William B. Sutch. *The quest for security in New Zealand, 1840–1966.* Wellington: Oxford University Press, 1966. ► Lively, if vulgar, Marxist work emphasizing continuing significance of poverty, unemployment, and social class. [ENO]

46.279 Brian Sutton-Smith. *The games of New Zealand children.* Berkeley: University of California Press, 1959. ► Innovative social history of children's games, illuminating wider processes of social change. [ENO]

Art and Literature

46.280 Gil Docking. *Two hundred years of New Zealand painting.* Rev. 2d ed. Auckland: Bateman, 1990. ISBN 1-86953-045-4. ► Despite errors, comprehensive and lavishly illustrated survey. [ENO]

46.281 Eric H. McCormick. *New Zealand literature: a survey.* London: Oxford University Press, 1959. ► Classic analysis first published for the centennial and still valuable. [ENO]

46.282 Frank M. McKay. *The life of James K. Baxter.* Auckland: Oxford University Press, 1990. ISBN 0-19-558134-2. ► Prize-winning study of major poet and symbol of countercultural values. [ENO]

46.283 Terry Sturm, ed. *The Oxford history of New Zealand literature in English.* Auckland: Oxford University Press, 1991. ISBN 0-19-558211-X. ► Comprehensive essays on traditional genres and others such as popular fiction and nonfiction. [ENO]

46.284 John M. Thomson. *A distant music: the life and times of Alfred Hill, 1870–1960.* Auckland: Oxford University Press, 1980. ISBN 0-19-554347-5 (cl), 0-19-558051-6 (pbk). ► Sympathetic study of country's first major composer and musical scene before Hill moved to Australia. [ENO]

46.285 Denys Trussell. *Fairburn.* Auckland: Auckland University Press and Oxford University Press, 1984. ISBN 0-19-648028-0. ► Full biography of country's first self-conscious Bohemian and poet. [ENO]

OCEANIA

Reference Works

46.286 Alan Butler, comp. *A New Guinea bibliography*. 5 vols. Waigani: University of Papua New Guinea Press, 1984–90. ▸ Comprehensive listing of published work in natural and social sciences. [DD/HCF]

46.287 Robert D. Craig and Frank P. King. *Historical dictionary of Oceania*. Westport, Conn.: Greenwood, 1981. ISBN 0-313-21060-8. ▸ Covers individuals, topics, and key events with chronologies. Despite some important omissions, very useful reference tool. [DD/HCF]

46.288 Ronald G. Crocombe. *The South Pacific: an introduction*. 4th rev. ed. Christchurch, New Zealand: University of the South Pacific, 1989. ISBN 0-582-71813-9. ▸ Survey of important trends affecting island communities of South Pacific, conscientiously updated. Earlier editions entitled *The New South Pacific* and *The South Pacific*. [DD/HCF]

46.289 Norman Douglas and Ngaire Douglas. *Pacific Islands year book*. 16th ed. North Ryde, Australia: Angus & Robertson with Nationwide News, 1989. ISBN 0-207-16114-3, ISSN 0078-7523. ▸ Basic information on all island groups, including history, current political and economic developments, maps, list of obsolete and modern place names, statistical tables of population change, government finances, and education, and index. [DD/HCF]

46.290 Sally Elridge, comp. *Solomon Islands bibliography to 1980*. Suva, Fiji: University of the South Pacific, Institute of Pacific Studies; Alexander Turnbull Library; Solomon Islands National Library, 1985. ISBN 0-908702-03-5. ▸ Best available listing of published work. [DD/HCF]

46.291 Honore Forster, comp. *The South Sea whaler: an annotated bibliography of published historical, literary, and art material relating to whaling in the Pacific Ocean in the nineteenth century*. Sharon and Fairhaven, Mass.: Kendall Whaling Museum and Edward J. Lefkowicz, 1985. ISBN 0-937854-22-0. ▸ Comprehensive guide to published, nonscientific literature relating to whaling in Pacific. Supplement, *More South Sea Whaling* (1991), includes author indexes for both volumes. [DD/HCF]

46.292 Gerald W. Fry and Rufino Mauricio, comps. *Pacific basin and Oceania*. Oxford: ABC-Clio, 1987. ISBN 1-85109-015-0. ▸ Comprehensive, multidisciplinary, fully annotated listing of 1,178 items, mainly in English with author, title, and subject indexes. [DD/HCF]

46.293 Douglas L. Oliver. *The Pacific Islands*. 3d ed. Honolulu: University of Hawaii Press, 1989. ISBN 0-8428-1233-6. ▸ Justifiably most widely used reference work for ethnographers and ethnographic historians, although much particular analysis superseded. [DD/HCF]

46.294 Peter Ryan, ed. *Encyclopaedia of Papua and New Guinea*. 3 vols. Melbourne: Melbourne University Press with University of Papua and New Guinea, 1972. ISBN 0-522-84025-6. ▸ Fuller treatment of physical sciences than social sciences and of administrative and ethnographic forces than political forces. [DD/HCF]

46.295 Philip A. Snow, comp. *A bibliography of Fiji, Tonga, and Rotuma*. Preliminary working ed. Canberra: Australian National University Press, 1969. ▸ Only bibliography of these islands. 10,000 numbered entries listed by subject under author's name or by title, for three regions together and also separately for Fiji, Tonga, and Rotuma. Indexed. Comprehensive to date of publication. [DD/HCF]

General Studies

46.296 Harold C. Brookfield. *Colonialism, development, and independence: the case of the Melanesian Islands in the South Pacific*. Cambridge: Cambridge University Press, 1972. ISBN 0-521-08590-x. ▸ Island economies and societies distorted by colonial administration and forms of economic development. Author's geographical expertise lends authority, breadth, and texture to otherwise orthodox argument. [DD/HCF]

46.297 Ken D. Buckley and Kris Klugman. *The Australian presence in the Pacific: Burns Philp, 1914–46*. North Sydney: Allen & Unwin, 1983. ISBN 0-86861-007-0. ▸ Thorough research throwing baleful light on company that became dominant in South Pacific and represented Australian diplomatic interest there. Continues 46.298. [DD/HCF]

46.298 Ken D. Buckley and Kris Klugman. *The history of Burns Philp: the Australian Company in the South Pacific*. Sydney: Burns Philp, 1981. ▸ Thorough research throwing baleful light on company that became dominant in South Pacific and represented Australian diplomatic interests there. Continued in 46.297. [DD/HCF]

46.299 James Wightman Davidson. "Problems in Pacific history." *Journal of Pacific history* 1 (1966) 5–21. ISSN 0022-3344. ▸ Argues for island-centered research and writing about Pacific Islands. Telling critique of colonial focus of research in 1960s; argument remains cogent because advice has proved difficult to implement. [DD/HCF]

46.300 Gavan Daws. "Looking at Islanders: European ways of thinking about Polynesians in the eighteenth and nineteenth centuries." *Topics in culture learning* 2 (1974) 51–56. ISSN 0190-6488. ▸ Europeans brought many of their own images to bear on Pacific Islands, thus their writings tell us more about authors than about their subjects. Introduces techniques and ideas of psychohistory to understanding culture contact, bringing new sophistication to writing of biographies. Preface to *A Dream of Islands* (46.376). [DD/HCF]

46.301 Greg Dening. *History's anthropology: the death of William Gooch*. Lanham, Md.: University Press of America, 1988. ISBN 0-8191-7032-1 (cl), 0-8191-7033-x (pbk). ▸ Historians and their use of images can be analyzed just as thoroughly as tribal society. Witty, perceptive, and disconcerting. [DD/HCF]

46.302 Greg Dening. *Islands and beaches: discourses on a silent land, Marquesas, 1774–1880*. Carlton: Melbourne University Press, 1980. ISBN 0-522-84196-1. ▸ Fertile source of ideas and metaphors in evolution of reflexive and ethnographic history. Inspired excellent monographs which apply anthropological concept of liminality to first encounters between representatives of radically different cultural traditions. [DD/HCF]

46.303 T. Scarlett Epstein. *Capitalism primitive and modern: some aspects of Tolai economic growth*. East Lansing: Michigan State University Press, 1968. ▸ Analyzes impact of colonial economic policies and practices on already vigorous system of production and exchange. Widely read and applied. [DD/HCF]

46.304 Kerry R. Howe. *Where the waves fall: a new South Sea Islands history from first settlement to colonial rule*. Honolulu: University of Hawaii Press, 1984. ISBN 0-8248-0921-1 (cl), 0-8248-0921-1 (pbk). ▸ Synthesis of precolonial island history. First and best, although ends abruptly with establishment of colonial rule. [DD/HCF]

46.305 Margaret Jolly and Martha Macintyre, eds. *Family and gender in the Pacific: domestic contradictions and the colonial impact*. Cambridge: Cambridge University Press, 1989. ISBN 0-521-34667-3. ▸ Uneven but provocative essays on influence of colonial administration and mission teachings on gender and domestic relations. [DD/HCF]

46.306 Alan Moorehead. *The fatal impact: the invasion of the South Pacific, 1767–1840*. New York: Harper & Row, 1987. ISBN 0-06-015800-x. ▸ Immediately, profoundly influential argument that continues to influence popular discourse although its vision of catastrophe not endorsed by scholars. [DD/HCF]

46.307 Caroline Ralston. *Grass huts and warehouses: Pacific beach communities of the nineteenth century.* 1977 ed. Honolulu: University of Hawaii Press, 1978. ISBN 0-8248-0597-6. ▸ Description of influence of beachcomber on political and economic life in islands. Suggests numbers of people involved, manner in which powerholders used beachcombers' skills in pursuit of indigenous ambitions, and attendant risks to both patrons and clients. [DD/HCF]

46.308 Marshall Sahlins. *Islands of history.* Chicago: University of Chicago Press, 1985. ISBN 0-226-73357-2 (cl), 0-226-73358-0 (pbk). ▸ Most fruitful, illuminating, and often cited analysis of interaction of past and present. [DD/HCF]

46.309 Marshall Sahlins. *Stone Age economics.* Chicago: Aldine-Atherton, 1972. ISBN 0-202-01098-8. ▸ Economic transactions in precapitalist societies so embedded in social relations that conventional economic analysis cannot be applied. Foundation stone of economic history as well as economic anthropology. [DD/HCF]

46.310 Richard F. Salisbury. *From stone to steel: economic consequences of a technical change in New Guinea.* Melbourne: Melbourne University Press for Australian National University, 1962. ▸ Analysis of societies' adjustments to introduction of labor-saving (and wealth-creating) technology. Much cited for its empirical precision. [DD/HCF]

46.311 Deryck Scarr. *The history of the Pacific Islands: kingdoms and reefs.* South Melbourne: Macmillan, 1990. ISBN 0-7329-0210-x (cl), 0-7329-0209-6 (pbk). ▸ Synthesis of history of all island communities. Well-researched but densely written. [DD/HCF]

46.312 Dorothy Shineberg. *They came for sandalwood: a study of the sandalwood trade in the South-West Pacific, 1830–1865.* Melbourne: Melbourne University Press, 1967. ▸ Trade required unprecedented numbers of Islanders and sailors to interact. Demonstrates hitherto neglected importance of this trade in introducing new economic needs, habits, and social relations. [DD/HCF]

46.313 Nicholas Thomas. *Out of time: history and evolution in anthropological discourse.* Cambridge: Cambridge University Press, 1989. ISBN 0-521-36667-4. ▸ Brilliant deconstruction of ethnographic method. Concludes classic anthropologists allowed and disallowed certain forms of evidence. [DD/HCF]

46.314 Geoffrey M. White and Lamont Lindstrom, eds. *The Pacific theater: island representation of World War II.* Honolulu: University of Hawaii Press, 1989. ISBN 0-8248-1146-1. ▸ Narratives told to and analyzed by anthropologists forty years after events described. Adds necessary dimension to history of Pacific War. [DD/HCF]

Colonial Powers

46.315 Robert Aldrich. *The French presence in the South Pacific, 1842–1940.* Honolulu: University of Hawaii Press, 1990. ISBN 0-8248-1268-9. ▸ Survey of French ambitions, practices, and mixed fortunes. Vague about Islander responses. [DD/HCF]

46.316 Donald Denoon. "Capitalism in Papua New Guinea." *Journal of Pacific history* 20.3 (1985) 119–34. ISSN 0022-3344. ▸ Description of attempts by Australian colonial administration to promote capitalist economy in absence of adequate private capital. Australians more concerned about preserving social order than generating economic activity. [DD/HCF]

46.317 Stewart G. Firth. *Nuclear playground.* North Sydney: Allen & Unwin, 1987. ISBN 0-04-172010-5 (cl), 0-04-172009-1 (pbk). ▸ Scholarly, reader-friendly study of ruthless use of Pacific Islands by France and United States as testing grounds for

nuclear weaponry with scant regard for social consequences. [DD/HCF]

46.318 Peter J. Hempenstall. *Pacific Islanders under German rule: a study in the meaning of colonial resistance.* Canberra: Australian National University Press, 1978. ISBN 0-7081-1350-8. ▸ Application of African analytic model to anticolonial militancy in Samoa, New Guinea, and Pohnpei. Made possible subsequent, more nuanced analysis of resistance. [DD/HCF]

46.319 Stephen Henningham. *France and the South Pacific: a contemporary history.* Honolulu: University of Hawaii Press, 1992. ISBN 0-8248-1305-7. ▸ Political history of New Caledonia, Vanuatu, and French Polynesia. Illuminates evolving and elusive French policy. [DD/HCF]

46.320 Mark R. Peattie. *Nan'yō: the rise and fall of the Japanese in Micronesia, 1885–1945.* Honolulu: University of Hawaii Press for the Center for Pacific Islands Studies Program, School of Hawaiian, Asian, and Pacific Studies, 1988. ISBN 0-8248-1087-2. ▸ Thorough and revealing analysis of Japanese strategy, colonial policies, and programs in the islands mandated to them. [DD/HCF]

46.321 Nicholas Thomas. "Partial texts: representation, colonialism, and agency in Pacific history." *Journal of Pacific history* 25.2 (1990) 139–58. ISSN 0022-3344. ▸ Fair assessment that historians have concentrated excessively on first contact period, glossing over colonial era and overstating power of Islanders to influence colonial administration. [DD/HCF]

Island History and Topical Studies

46.322 Azeem Amarshi, Kenneth Good, and Rex Mortimer. *Development and dependency: the political economy of Papua New Guinea.* Melbourne: Oxford University Press, 1979. ISBN 0-19-550582-4 (cl), 0-19-550583-2 (pbk). ▸ Argument that peripheral capitalism under colonial conditions generated enduring dependency even after political independence. Some sloppy research reduced impact of this first full-scale radical analysis. [DD/HCF]

46.323 Judith A. Bennett. *Wealth of the Solomons: a history of a Pacific archipelago, 1800–1978.* Honolulu: University of Hawaii Press for the Pacific Islands Studies Program, Center for Asian and Pacific Studies, 1987. ISBN 0-8248-1078-3. ▸ Economic and social history of Solomon Islands. Rare professionalism applied to island group largely neglected by historians. [DD/HCF]

46.324 James Wightman Davidson. *Samoa mo Samoa: the emergence of the independent state of Western Samoa.* Melbourne: Oxford University Press, 1967. ▸ Participant account of politics and constitutional negotiations leading to independence. Quintessential Davidson blend of politics and scholarship, activism and commentary. [DD/HCF]

46.325 Gavan Daws. *Shoal of time: a history of the Hawaiian Islands.* 1968 ed. Honolulu: University of Hawaii Press, 1982. ISBN 0-8248-0324-8 (pbk). ▸ Deservedly popular because of its narrative flair and vignettes of event and personality; more serious and scholarly work than at first appears. [DD/HCF]

46.326 Stewart G. Firth. *New Guinea under the Germans.* Carlton: Melbourne University Press; distributed by International Specialized Book Services, 1983. ISBN 0-522-84220-8. ▸ Archive-based account of colonization, administration, evangelization, and economic exploitation. Elegantly explains colonial administration whose incompetence was often fatal to Islanders and colonists. [DD/HCF]

46.327 Richard P. Gilson. *The Cook Islands, 1820–1950.* Ronald G. Crocombe, ed. Wellington: Victoria University Press with University of the South Pacific, Institute of Pacific Studies, 1980. ISBN 0-7055-0735-1 (pbk). ▸ Well-researched analysis of precolonial conditions and colonial experience. [DD/HCF]

46.328 James Griffin, Hank Nelson, and Stewart G. Firth. *Papua New Guinea: a political history.* Richmond, Australia: Heinemann, 1979. ISBN 0-85859-197-9. ‣ Overview of vexed constitutional and political history of country until its 1975 independence. Three distinct authorial styles ornament judicious and straightforward analysis. [DD/HCF]

46.329 David Hanlon. *Upon a stone altar: a history of the island of Pohnpei to 1890.* Honolulu: University of Hawaii Press, 1988. ISBN 0-8248-1124-0. ‣ Exploration of long and fragmented history, using scant documentary and rich but perplexing oral evidence. Exemplary narrative history enriched by careful cultural sensitivity. [DD/HCF]

46.330 Francis X. Hezel. *The first taint of civilization: a history of the Caroline and Marshall Islands in pre-colonial days, 1521–1885.* Honolulu: University of Hawaii Press for the Pacific Islands Studies Program, Center for Asian and Pacific Studies, 1983. (Pacific Islands monograph series, 1.) ISBN 0-8248-0840-1. ‣ Narrative of Spanish carelessness and incaution and appalling consequences for Islanders. Written with care and controlled passion. [DD/HCF]

46.331 Bruce Knapman. *Fiji's economic history, 1874–1939: studies of capitalist colonial development.* Canberra: Australian National University, Research School of Pacific Studies, National Centre for Development Studies, 1987. (Pacific research monograph, 15.) ISBN 0-86784-977-0, ISSN 0155-9060. ‣ Study of Fiji's colonial experience. Economic innovation more ruthless than in most islands, but generated new forms of production and modern economic institutions. Balanced and precise. [DD/HCF]

46.332 Ralph S. Kuykendall. *The Hawaiian kingdom.* Vol. 1: *1778–1854, foundation and transformation.* Vol. 2: *1854–74, twenty critical years.* Vol. 3: *1874–93, the Kalakaua dynasty.* 1938 ed. Honolulu: University of Hawaii Press, 1966. ‣ Monumental, pioneering work on Hawaiian history until annexation; now mainly used (frequently) for reference. [DD/HCF]

46.333 Grant McCall. *Rapanui: tradition and survival on Easter Island.* 1980 ed. Honolulu: University of Hawaii Press, 1981. ISBN 0-8248-0746-4. ‣ Ethnographic and historical reconstruction of small population inured to surviving ecological and political disaster. Eloquent tribute to Islanders' survival despite appalling privations. [DD/HCF]

46.334 Barrie Macdonald. *Cinderellas of the empire: towards a history of Kiribati and Tuvalu.* Canberra: Australian National University Press, 1982. ISBN 0-7081-1616-7 (pbk). ‣ Administrative history written with cultural sensitivity. Effective use of documentary and oral evidence. [DD/HCF]

46.335 Malama Meleisea. *The making of modern Samoa: traditional authority and colonial administration in the history of Western Samoa.* Suva, Fiji: University of the South Pacific, Institute of Pacific Studies, 1987. ISBN 982-02-0031-8. ‣ Constructs and analyzes formation of colonial state by German authorities, despite best divisive efforts of Samoan powerholders. Effective use of colonial archives, court records, and oral tradition. [DD/HCF]

46.336 Klaus Neumann. *Not the way it really was: constructing the Tolai past.* Honolulu: University of Hawaii Press, 1992. ISBN 0-8248-1333-2. ‣ Contrasts narratives of colonial authorities and Tolai of Papua New Guinea to challenge positivism of conventional historical research and writing. Demands readers find value in indigenous narratives even when they run counter to form and content of colonial accounts. [DD/HCF]

46.337 Colin Walter Newbury. *Tahiti nui: change and survival in French Polynesia, 1767–1945.* Honolulu: University of Hawaii Press, 1980. ISBN 0-8248-0630-1. ‣ Narrative social history of Tahiti and Tahitians. Creates conventional and accessible his-

torical narrative from travelers' accounts, colonial administrative evidence, and ethnographic analyses. [DD/HCF]

46.338 Douglas L. Oliver. *Ancient Tahitian society.* Vol. 1: *Ethnography.* Vol. 2: *Social relations.* Vol. 3: *Rise of the Pomares.* Honolulu: University of Hawaii Press, 1974. ISBN 0-8248-9267-5. ‣ Ethnography and historical reconstruction in positivist mode. Now contested by poststructuralists, but hightly valued by historical researchers. [DD/HCF]

46.339 Richard J. Parmentier. *The sacred remains: myth, history, and polity in Belau.* Chicago: University of Chicago Press, 1987. ISBN 0-226-64695-5 (cl), 0-226-64696-3 (pbk). ‣ Analyzes interaction of historical events, creation of legend and myth, and present-day life. [DD/HCF]

46.340 Charles D. Rowley. *The New Guinea villager: a retrospect from 1964.* 2d ed. Melbourne: Cheshire, 1972. ISBN 0-7015-1226-1. ‣ Lucid, sympathetic, and well-rounded analysis of effect of Australian colonial administration on rural Papua New Guineans. [DD/HCF]

46.341 Deryck Scarr. *Fiji: a short history.* Laie, Hawaii: Brigham Young University, Institute for Polynesian Studies, 1984. ISBN 0-939154-36-6. ‣ Centered on narrative account of colonial administrative history. Criticized for favoring some administrators and quasi-traditional chiefly structure; nonetheless cited as authoritative. [DD/HCF]

46.342 Michael Spencer, Alan Ward, and John Connell, eds. *New Caledonia: essays in nationalism and dependency.* St. Lucia: University of Queensland Press, 1988. ISBN 0-7022-2126-0 (pbk). ‣ Collected essays reviewing origins and nature of Melanesian nationalism in New Caledonia. Up to date but disconnected. Reference work; lacks index. [DD/HCF]

46.343 Nicholas Thomas. *Marquesan societies: inequality and political transformation in eastern Polynesia.* Oxford: Clarendon, 1990. ISBN 0-19-827748-2. ‣ Analyzes impact of colonial forces on established patterns of hierarchy and social relations. Excellent, self-aware ethnographic reconstruction. [DD/HCF]

46.344 Nancy Viviani. *Nauru: phosphate and political progress.* Canberra: Australian National University Press, 1970. ISBN 0-7081-0765-6. ‣ Narrative of appalling history of phosphate extraction; foresees political difficulties in achieving and sustaining independence. Essential background reading for continuing international litigation for compensation arising from mining operations. [DD/HCF]

Population Studies

46.345 Donald Denoon, Kathy Dugan, and Lesley Marshall. *Public health in Papua New Guinea: medical possibility and social constraint, 1884–1984.* Cambridge: Cambridge University Press, 1989. ISBN 0-521-36030-7. ‣ Explains enthusiasms and strategies of doctors who developed public health policies during and after colonial period; some attention to gender and racial politics. [DD/HCF]

46.346 Norma McArthur. *Island populations of the Pacific.* Canberra: Australian National University Press, 1967. ‣ First serious demographic study, yet to be surpassed. [DD/HCF]

46.347 Jean-Louis Rallu. *Les populations océaniennes aux XIX et XX siècles.* Paris: Presses Universitaires de France, Institut Nationale d'Études Démographiques, 1990. (Travaux et documents cahier, 128.) ISBN 2-7332-0128-X. ‣ Standard reference for historical demography of French dependencies. Complements McArthur 46.346 by employing later evidence and French colonial sources. [DD/HCF]

46.348 Ralph Shlomowitz. "Mortality and the Pacific labour trade." *Journal of Pacific history* 22.1 (1987) 34–55. ISSN 0022-

3344. ▸ Comprehensive and thorough documentation of demographic consequences of nineteenth- and twentieth-century labor migration. Each new wave of migrant laborers suffered early and massive morbidity and mortality, but health conditions became less appalling over time. [DD/HCF]

46.349 Alan Thorne and Robert Raymond. *Man on the rim: the peopling of the Pacific.* North Ryde, Australia: Angus & Robertson, 1989. ISBN 0-207-16246-8. ▸ Illustrated text of popular and illuminating television series; also available in video recording (four cassettes), Sydney Australian Broadcasting Corporation, 1988. Far-reaching vision complemented by comprehensive archaeological research. [DD/HCF]

Labor

46.350 Peter Corris. *Passage, port, and plantation: a history of Solomon Islands labour migration, 1870–1914.* Carlton: Melbourne University Press, 1973. ISBN 0-522-04050-7. ▸ Narrative labor history, carefully researched. Offers glimpses of narrative skills that made Corris best-selling crime writer. [DD/HCF]

46.351 Michael Hess. *Unions under economic development: private sector unions in Papua New Guinea.* Melbourne: Oxford University Press, 1992. ISBN 0-19-553266-X. ▸ In curious conditions of colonialism, trade unions (rather than employers) became allies of state in modernizing work patterns. Includes British and Australian background material for Papua New Guinea readers; locally based chapters are well researched and lucidly written. [DD/HCF]

46.352 Brij V. Lal. *Girmitiyas: the origins of the Fiji Indians.* Canberra: Journal of Pacific History, 1983. ISBN 0-9595477-3-8 (pbk). ▸ Social history of Indians brought to Fiji as indentured workers. Thoroughly researched and clearly narrated; reliable source. [DD/HCF]

46.353 Harry E. Maude. *Slavers in paradise: the Peruvian labour trade in Polynesia, 1862–1864.* Stanford, Calif.: Stanford University Press, 1981. ISBN 0-8047-1106-2. ▸ Lucid reconstruction of brief but disgraceful episode. Peruvians demonstrated how not to recruit, transport, employ, and repatriate Islanders. [DD/HCF]

46.354 Clive Moore, Jacqueline Leckie, and Doug Munro, eds. *Labour in the South Pacific.* Townsville, Australia: James Cook University of North Queensland, 1990. ISBN 0-86443-382-4. ▸ Twenty-six studies of recruitment, labor conditions, and labor politics. Uneven quality and accessibility but fine reference work. [DD/HCF]

46.355 Hank N. Nelson. *Black, white, and gold: goldmining in Papua New Guinea, 1878–1930.* Canberra: Australian National University Press, 1976. ISBN 0-7081-0487-8 (cl), 0-7081-0488-6 (pbk). ▸ Definitive social and economic account of small-scale prospecting and mining. [DD/HCF]

Discovery and Exploration

46.356 John C. Beaglehole. *The exploration of the Pacific.* 1966 3d ed. Stanford, Calif.: Stanford University Press, 1968. ISBN 0-8047-0311-6 (pbk). ▸ Completely revised edition of work first published in 1934; authoritative and reliable. [DD/HCF]

46.357 John C. Beaglehole, ed. *The journals of Captain James Cook on his voyages of discovery.* Vol. 1: *The voyage of the Endeavour, 1768–1771.* Vol. 2: *The voyage of the Resolution and Adventure, 1772–1775.* Vol. 3: *The voyage of the Resolution and Discovery, 1776–1780.* 4 vols. Cambridge: Cambridge University Press for the Hakluyt Society, 1955–74. (Works issued by the Hakluyt Society, Extra series, 34–37.) ▸ Definitive and scholarly edition of records of most famous voyager and cartographer of region. Volume 4 cited at 46.13. [DD/HCF]

46.358 Jules-Sebastien-Cesar Dumont d'Urville. *An account in*

two volumes of two voyages to the South Seas...to Australia, New Zealand, Oceania, 1826–29, in the corvette Astrolabe and to the Straits of Magellan, Chile, Oceania, South East Asia, Australia, Antartica, New Zealand, and Torres Strait, 1837–40, in the corvettes Astrolabe and Zélée. Vol. 1: *Astrolabe, 1826–29.* Vol. 2: *Astrolabe and Zélée, 1837–40.* Helen Rosenman, ed. and trans. Carlton: Melbourne University Press, 1987. ISBN 0-522-84338-7 (set), 0-522-84348-4 (v. 1), 0-522-84349-2 (v. 2). ▸ Significant texts of important voyages, admirably edited. [DD/HCF]

46.359 Ben R. Finney. *Hokule'a: the way to Tahiti.* New York: Dodd Mead, 1979. ISBN 0-396-07719-6. ▸ Polynesian navigation techniques demonstrated to have been highly reliable, suggesting deliberate voyaging within (and perhaps beyond) Polynesian triangle of Hawaii, Tahiti, and New Zealand. Clarifies and helps resolve protracted argument on mechanisms of Polynesian colonization of region. [DD/HCF]

46.360 Rüdiger Joppien and Bernard Smith. *The art of Captain Cook's voyages.* Vol. 1: *The voyage of the Endeavor, 1768–71.* Vol. 2: *The voyage of the Resolution and Adventure, 1771–75.* Vol. 3: *The voyage of the Resolution and Discovery, 1776–80.* 3 vols. in 4. New Haven: Yale University Press for the Paul Mellon Centre for Studies in British Art, 1985–88. ISBN 0-300-03450-4 (v. 1), 0-300-03451-2 (v. 2), 0-300-04105-5 (v. 3). ▸ Collector's item for art (and other) historians. [DD/HCF]

46.361 David Lewis. *Voyaging stars: secrets of the Pacific Island navigators.* Sydney: Collins, 1978. ISBN 0-00-216404-3. ▸ Description and analysis of navigation techniques of Islanders. Analysis informed by practical experience. Illuminates navigation technology that enabled Islanders to determine their location at sea and make landfall safely. [DD/HCF]

46.362 Andrew Sharp. *The discovery of the Pacific Islands.* Oxford: Clarendon, 1960. ▸ Exhaustive account of which navigators charted which islands. Admirable reference work. [DD/HCF]

46.363 O.H.K. Spate. *The Pacific since Magellan.* Vol. 1: *The Spanish lake.* Vol. 2: *Monopolists and freebooters.* Vol. 3: *Paradise found and lost.* 3 vols. Minneapolis: University of Minnesota Press, 1979–89. ISBN 0-8166-0882-2 (v. 1), 0-8166-1121-0 (v. 2, cl), 0-8166-1121-1 (v. 2, pbk), 0-8166-1715-5 (v. 3). ▸ Narrative history, placing European exploration in technical, political, and diplomatic context. Magisterial, authoritative, well illustrated, and superbly literate. [DD/HCF]

46.364 Étienne Taillemite, ed. *Bouganville et ses compagnons autour du monde, 1766–1769: journaux de navigation.* 2 vols. Paris: Nationale, 1977. ISBN 2-11-080710-5. ▸ First publication of full text of journal kept by Bougainville on Boudeuse. Also journals and narratives by other members of expeditions and contemporary testimony. Extensive introduction and annotations by editor. Work of major significance. [DD/HCF]

SEE ALSO
2.65 Peter S. Bellwood. *Man's conquest of the Pacific.*

Religion, Including Missions

46.365 James A. Boutilier, Daniel T. Hughes, and Shannon W. Tiffany, eds. *Mission, church, and sect in Oceania.* Ann Arbor: University of Michigan Press; distributed by University Microfilms International, 1978. ISBN 0-87991-364-9. ▸ Anthropological analyses of many instances of conversion to Christianity in plethora of places and circumstances. Disconnected essays arising from symposium. [DD/HCF]

46.366 John Garrett. *To live among the stars: Christian origins in Oceania.* Geneva: University of the South Pacific, World Council of Churches with Institute of Pacific Studies, 1982. ISBN 2-8254-

0692-9. ‣ Reliable reference work with few analytic pretensions. [DD/HCF]

46.367 Niel Gunson. *Messengers of grace: evangelical missionaries in the South Seas, 1797–1860.* Melbourne: Oxford University Press, 1978. ISBN 0-19-550517-4. ‣ First Protestant missionaries in Pacific and setters of precedents both inspiring and dismaying. Lavishly reconstructed with more care and affection than missionaries themselves usually displayed toward peoples they encountered. [DD/HCF]

46.368 Diane L. Langmore. *Missionary lives: Papua, 1874–1914.* Honolulu: University of Hawaii Press, 1989. ISBN 0-8248-1163-1. ‣ Group biography, leading to social and theological analysis of all recorded missionaries and their spouses in Papua. Different missions recruited from distinct social backgrounds and created radically different career paths (from short-term contracts through lifetime service) in mission fields. [DD/HCF]

46.369 Sione Lātūkefu. *Church and state in Tonga: the Wesleyan Methodist missionaries and political development, 1822–1875.* Canberra: Australian National University Press, 1974. ISBN 0-7081-0402-9. ‣ Missionary advice and Christian ideology matched personal ambition of founder of present dynasty. Cautiously and convincingly understated. [DD/HCF]

46.370 Peter Lawrence. *Road belong cargo: a study of the cargo movement in the Southern Madang district, New Guinea.* Rev. ed. Prospect Heights, Ill.: Waveland, 1989. ISBN 0-88133-458-8. ‣ Anthropological fieldwork carefully recorded and illuminated by analogy to European millennarian episodes. Concludes cargo cultism can be device for rewriting folk history to understand otherwise baffling world. [DD/HCF]

46.371 Ralph M. Wiltgen. *The founding of the Roman Catholic church in Oceania, 1825–1850.* Canberra: Australian National University Press, 1979. ISBN 0-7081-0835-0. ‣ Careful reconstruction of earliest heroic, and mainly unsuccessful, phase of Catholic evangelicalism. [DD/HCF]

46.372 Peter Worsley. *The trumpet shall sound: a study of "cargo" cults in Melanesia.* 2d ed. London: Paladin, 1970. ISBN 0-586-08029-5. ‣ Uses library material to construct argument that cargo cults were form of incipient anticolonial nationalism. Richly satisfying vengeance on colonial authorities who denied Worsley research permit. [DD/HCF]

Biography

46.373 James Clifford. *Person and myth: Maurice Leenhardt in the Melanesian world.* Berkeley: University of California Press, 1982. ISBN 0-520-04247-6. ‣ Leenhardt was missionary, ethnographer, and anticolonial activist and writer in New Caledonia. Important figure cautiously delineated. [DD/HCF]

46.374 James Wightman Davidson. *Peter Dillon of Vanikoro: chevalier of the South Seas.* O.H.K. Spate, ed. Melbourne: Oxford University Press, 1975. ISBN 0-19-550457-7. ‣ Dillon's

obscure career an imperfect platform on which two great scholars explore issues that transcend his biography. [DD/HCF]

46.375 Tom Davis (Pa Tuterangi Ariki). *Island boy: an autobiography.* Suva, Fiji: University of the South Pacific, Institute of Pacific Studies, 1992. ISBN 982-02-0071-7. ‣ Davis left islands to become doctor, worked for NASA, returned to islands, and became prime minister. His account describes career and suggests how (and how far) Davis succeeded. [DD/HCF]

46.376 Gavan Daws. *A dream of islands: voyages of self-discovery in the South Seas: John Williams, Herman Melville, Walter Murray Gibson, Robert Louis Stevenson, Paul Gauguin.* New York: Norton, 1980. ISBN 0-393-01293-X. ‣ Five riveting and economical narratives, combining psychoanalytic skill with documentary research. [DD/HCF]

46.377 Gavan Daws. *Holy man: Father Damien of Molokai.* 1973 ed. Honolulu: University of Hawaii Press, 1984. ISBN 0-8248-0920-3. ‣ Sympathetic and readable account translated into many European languages. Damien expected to be beatified. [DD/HCF]

46.378 Albert Maori Kiki. *Kiki: ten thousand years in a lifetime, a New Guinea autobiography.* New York: Praeger, 1968. ‣ First full-scale Papua New Guinean autobiography, revealing much about man and his career in government and politics. [DD/HCF]

46.379 Eric H. McCormick. *Omai: Pacific envoy.* Auckland: Auckland University Press and Oxford University Press, 1977. ISBN 0-19-647952-5. ‣ First Tahitian to discover Europe, Omai achieved eminence in Europe but disappointment when he returned to Tahiti. Omai's career raises wider questions than are treated here. [DD/HCF]

46.380 *Ongka: a self account by a New Guinea big-man.* Andrew Strathern, trans. New York: St. Martin's, 1979. ISBN 0-312-58566-7. ‣ Transcribed and translated oral autobiography. Exceptional in presenting Ongka's memories and narratives in indigenous forms and idioms. [DD/HCF]

46.381 Daniel J. Peacock. *Lee Boo of Belau: a prince in London.* Honolulu: University of Hawaii Press for the Pacific Islands Studies Program, Center for Asian and Pacific Studies, 1987. ISBN 0-8248-1086-4. ‣ Rather romantic account of first Palauan to discover Europe. [DD/HCF]

46.382 Francis James West. *Hubert Murray: the Australian proconsul.* Melbourne: Oxford University Press, 1968. ‣ Thoroughly researched biography mainly from Murray's rich correspondence and official archives. Tends to endorse Murray's worldview. [DD/HCF]

46.383 A. H. Wood and Elizabeth Wood Ellem. "Queen Sālote Tupou III." In *Friendly islands: a history of Tonga.* Noel Rutherford, ed. Melbourne: Oxford University Press, 1977. ISBN 0-19-550519-0. ‣ Sālote left school in New Zealand to become queen and survived political, dynastic, and sectarian challenges to become respected and much-loved leader. Authors' scholarship, religious background, and friendship with Sālote inform and illumine political biography. [DD/HCF]

PAUL W. SCHROEDER

International Relations, 1815–1920

Charles S. Maier's controversial judgment a decade ago that recent American historiography of international relations was "marking time" (in M. Kammen, ed., *The Past Before Us*, 1.9, pp. 355–87) might apply to certain parts of the general historiography of nineteenth-century international relations, but certainly not to the whole. There is no doubt (or reason to regret) that the prominence the field once enjoyed in the nineteenth and early twentieth centuries is irretrievably lost. Even the controversies that raged decades ago over the primacy of foreign or domestic policy or the relative importance of socioeconomic, political, and cultural-ideological factors in foreign policy decision making seem either to have died out or to be simmering, without any resolution or prospect of one. At the same time, the sort of offhand dismissal of diplomatic history as an inferior, superficial kind of history dealing with ephemeral events rather than deep structures, frequently encountered a generation ago, is less fashionable now. For one thing, the importance of international politics in history and current affairs is too obvious; for another, recent developments in the study of international relations among social and behavioral sciences have been little short of spectacular, and the work of historians is plainly indispensable for this. But above all, the verdict simply does not fit much of the international history now being written.

This is not because diplomatic history has been reformed and transformed by integrating it, along with politics in general, into some allegedly deeper kind of structural history. Many schemes for this integration have been proposed, for example, the total history of the Annales school, various Marxist and semi-Marxist approaches, and *Gesellschaftsgeschichte*; few have worked or generally taken hold. Most international historians have found that the models either do not accommodate their evidence or, where they do, are too broad and general to answer the questions or analyze the crucial developments they see as most important. Yet the practice of international history has not remained unchanged. Everyone now concedes or insists that foreign and domestic developments are inextricably related, and it is standard practice to try to interweave them. Attempts to study foreign policy decision making by analyzing elites, institutions, and class interests are common if not universal; the importance of analyzing underlying assumptions, collective mentalities, and ideologies is widely recognized. The impact of the burgeoning social science literature on international relations, with the many competing theoretical approaches it offers (behavioral and traditional, political economy, regime, hegemony, cognitive theory, etc.), is harder to assess. Although too many diplomatic historians still tend to ignore theory and concentrate on "the facts," awareness of and respect for the potential contribution of political science is growing among historians (1.482–488). Yet just as political scientists often acknowledge the indispensable value of international history for their work, though treat it as raw data for their manipulations, so international historians have tended to pick and choose among social science theories ad hoc, using whatever the occasion seems to demand.

Thus the recent historiography of international relations shows an evolution rather than a revolution from diplomatic history of the past. More important, work on nineteenth-century international relations of, by and large, good quality has continued to emerge—a rivulet on the early decades of the century, a steady stream on the middle decades, a strong current dealing with the turn of the century, and a flood covering the decade before, during, and after World War I. Three major problem areas of historiography, moreover, have been permanently changed in the past thirty years or so: the politics of World War I and the peace settlement; the origins of the war (and/or the breakdown of the nineteenth-century system); and the so-called New Imperialism of the late nineteenth and early twentieth centuries.

Scholarly interest has thus concentrated disproportionately on the last half of the period, and it is not hard to understand why. The international events of the period were undoubtedly more dramatic and seemed intrinsically more significant. They were connected with revolutions in imperial Russia, Germany, eastern Europe, China, and much of the Third World that, at least until very recently, seemed not only to have effected great changes in the world but even to have controlled the fate of the greater part of it. Nineteenth-century imperialism, World War I, and the failed or sabotaged peace settlement were without question the foundation for even greater changes and worse conflicts later in the twentieth century and still have much to teach us now at its end. The resemblance, for example, between some aspects of Balkan politics in the 1990s and those of the pre-1914 era is almost uncanny. Professional reasons also help explain the scholarly emphasis on the last half of the century—the flood of documentary material opened up for international historians to exploit and the fact that historians, like other scholars, like to join a crowd, jump into the fray, be on the cutting edge, and sell books.

In all three problem areas enumerated above, old controversies continue but with their terms considerably altered. All that can be done here is to indicate some points of apparent consensus or persistent dispute. The most heated, prolonged, and influential debate, on the so-called Fischer thesis, has also been in some respects the most misleading. The main thrust of F. Fischer's first book (47.375) was not that Germany was guilty of provoking the war. This charge, laid incidentally in the first, became the central theme of Fischer's succeeding works (especially 47.338). His main gravamen was Germany's pursuit of imperialist war aims, as a fundamentally imperialist state and society. The charge tied into an old German debate, though one long suppressed or ignored by orthodox German historiography, and on this score Fischer seems to have won. Even his opponents, including G. Ritter (47.403), accept the main facts about German imperialist ambitions during World War I, though not necessarily Fischer's explanation of them or his almost exclusive concentration on them. (For an important exception, see 47.408.)

While heated debate centered on Germany's wartime policy, a great deal of less controversial work has been devoted to the war aims and policies of the other major powers, above all Great Britain, and those of lesser powers, especially the Balkan states and the Ottoman empire. Except for certain issues (such as the American entry into the war, Allied intervention in Russia, or British Middle Eastern policy and the origins of Arab-Israeli conflict, especially the Balfour Declaration), neither major controversies nor clear consensus has emerged; in fact, certain divergences of view may have been underplayed. (For example, a serious debate over Allied, and especially British, wartime policy toward Austria-Hungary and East Central Europe is possible and needed.) Newer literature gives the overall impression that expansionist, aggressive aims prevailed almost everywhere, even where states were waging a fundamentally defensive war and were dominated by fear and desire for security, as were France, Belgium, and Austria-Hungary. This suggests that imperialist policies in World War I, however much they were promoted and exploited for domestic-political, class, or economic reasons, derived structurally from a fundamental security dilemma—the breakdown of the existing international system, the impossibility of restoring it, and the sheer unavailability of security save in victory and superiority for oneself and permanent insecurity for one's present and future foes.

On the peace settlement, most attention is still given, perhaps unwisely, to the Versailles treaty and Allied relations with Germany as the key to success or failure in the settlement as a whole. Yet the discussion has at least advanced well beyond both the wholesale condemnation of the treaty nourished by the German nationalism and Western guilt of the 1920s and early 1930s and the claim common during and after World War II that the only thing really wrong with Versailles was that it was not enforced. What appears instead to be emerging is a recognition of the inherent fragility and unenforceability of the whole peace settlement, not just Versailles, even where it was reasonably just and morally defensible. Important factors include the facts that vast areas (Russia, eastern and southeastern Europe, and the Middle East) were wholly or largely beyond the control of the victors; that the prewar conflict between new anti-imperialist and old imperialist forces was greatly intensified by the war; and that a terrible burden of military, political, and economic chaos and insecurity weighed on almost everyone, even the victors, with no consensus on how to alleviate it. Certain themes remain highly controversial; for example, the roles of Woodrow Wilson and the reparations question at the Peace Conference, but here too at least old categories of praise and blame have been transcended or abandoned.

As for the origins of the war, the revived German war-guilt thesis launched early in the 1960s remains alive and influential to this day, although the controversy is dying down. Almost all scholars recognize the restless, aggressive character of German policy as one important contributing factor in the outbreak of war; many see it as decisive. Dissent persists, however, over whether this restless and aggressive policy was mainly internally generated or a reaction to Germany's steadily worsening international position and over whether it represented the main cause of systemic breakdown and war in 1914. For example, two recent books on Austro-Hungarian policy by F. R. Bridge (47.29) and S. R. Williamson (47.360) implicitly deny the German war-guilt thesis in insisting that Vienna's decisions in 1914 were its own and not the product of German pressure. But, as in the literature on wartime diplomacy, the majority of newer studies on the origins of the war, although often presenting clear theses, is not part of any particular debate. Major contributions include new studies of the policies of various great powers and of crucial smaller states, especially in the Balkans; a masterly overall synthesis by J. Joll (47.344); many works tying the origins of the war to the wider European imperialist rivalry and cooperation; and further close investigation of Anglo-German rivalry (especially Kennedy, 47.184).

The clearest instance of continuity between old and new controversies is found in the literature on new imperialism, much of which sets out to refute, revise, or rehabilitate the old Hobson–Hilferding–Kautsky–Luxemburg–Lenin thesis on the capitalist roots of imperialism. Joseph Schumpeter, M. Weber, W. L. Langer, and other earlier theorists also receive more than passing attention. At the same time, new perspectives and fuel for the flames have been added by I. Wallerstein and his followers, H.-U.

Wehler and the German *Gesellschaftsgeschichte* school, and various dependency theorists. Much of the resultant work, to be sure, deals little with international relations in the ordinary sense, concentrating instead on the economic, social, cultural-intellectual, and domestic-political factors and structures promoting imperialism both in the metropolis and in the periphery. Yet some of the best and most important work on new imperialism largely views and explains imperialism in terms of international politics and as an integral part of it. The Robinson-Gallagher thesis, for example, stresses the political-strategic motives of British imperialism in Africa (see 47.241 and 47.249); a critic like D.C.M. Platt (47.218) responds by offering an essentially different version of British foreign policy; G. N. Sanderson (47.250, 47.251), as well as many others, emphasizes the interplay of European and extra-European political maneuvers; most of the major work on French imperialism stresses its political motives, both domestic and foreign; newer middle-range explanatory theories (e.g., "turbulent frontier" and "man on the spot") emphasize political action and political control. Indeed, it seems increasingly recognized that whatever factors may have inspired or motivated imperialism, at its heart the process involved international politics, the imposition of direct or indirect political control over foreign peoples and territories.

Less work has focused on the evolution or devolution of the European international system in the Bismarckian and immediate post-Bismarckian era, but it is important nonetheless. Here, without seeing new conceptual breakthroughs, one notes the emergence of a more critical stand toward Bismarck's policy generally and a sense that his system was never as sound or stable as it has often been painted (in A. Hillgruber's phrase [47.182], a "labile half-hegemony"). This trend clearly is connected with the wider criticism of the Second Reich by revisionist historians and the overall rejection of the old Little German model of German unification as necessary and good either for Germany or for Europe as a whole (see, for example, Gruner 47.22).

Still less historiographical activity characterizes two periods, the Restoration and pre-March eras (1815–1848) and the wars of national unification (1848–1870). "Marking time" might not be an unfair capsule judgment for these eras, and again the reason is clear. The field, once overworked, now may appear pretty well exhausted. To illustrate, the era of the French Revolution, just prior to the period covered by this section and fundamentally important for it, received an enormous amount of scholarly attention and reappraisal in connection with its recent bicentenary; but among the flood of publications, works on the international politics of the Revolution were conspicuous by their rarity. While everyone recognizes the Congress of Vienna as a crucial turning point in international relations, international events after 1815 seem less dramatic and crises less profound and dangerous than in other eras; often they seem downright tedious and insignificant. In contrast, the wars and crises after 1848 were important and dramatic, but, like those of the French Revolution and Napoleon, done to death by earlier nationalist historiography. In addition, international politics and the states system were highly Eurocentric during these periods—a tendency in Western historiography many historians and the wider public dislike and would like to escape. Finally, in this period, at least for Anglo-American historiography, a conventional British-whig balance-of-power paradigm for international relations still holds almost unchallenged sway.

It would be wrong, however, to ignore some fairly important debates, in particular over the Crimean War, the process of German reunification, and Bismarck's wars, and still more mistaken to overlook contributions to our knowledge and understanding made by many works which have not provoked much controversy. A good example is recent work on Metternich and the Metternich system. When H. Ritter von Srbik published his Metternich biography in the 1920s, it generated a great deal of dispute.

Work on Metternich by recent scholars, especially that of G. de Bertier de Sauvigny (47.38 and 47.56) has had no such dramatic effect; indeed, Bertier's writing is notably detached and serene in tone. Yet what he and others have done constitutes a major revision and advance in the reigning picture all the same. There are also encouraging signs of change in several prevailing assumptions—recognition, for example, that the Vienna system was not a restoration but something genuinely new in international politics, and challenges to the realist balance-of-power paradigm as applied to the first half of the nineteenth century.

Thus the history of nineteenth-century international relations overall represents neither a burgeoning field in historiography nor an exhausted volcano, and it may yet display unsuspected and interesting new possibilities. The dramatic events of the 1980s and 1990s may finally convince international historians that explaining cooperation and peace is as interesting and important as explaining conflict and war and that more things are possible in international politics than was dreamt of in their philosophy. If so, the early nineteenth century, which represented a first great breakthrough toward international peace and cooperation, could become a lively topic once again.

Entries are arranged under the following headings:

[Contributors: APS = Ann Pottinger Saab, AS = Antonio Santosuosso, BJCM = Brian J. C. McKercher, CKF = Carole K. Fink, CSA = Celia S. Applegate, DHK = David H. Kaiser, DSC = Donald Stephen Cloyd, DW = Douglas Wheeler, EM = Ezra Mendelsohn, EWM = E. William Monter, FGN = F. G. Notehelfer, GRG = Gene R. Garthwaite, GS = Gale Stokes, HLA = Hugh L. Agnew, JKS = John K. Smith, JML = Jennifer M. Lloyd, JSH = John S. Hill, JWB = John W. Boyer, JWC = John W. Cell, KAH = Keith A. Hitchins, LLC = Linda L. Clark, MMF = Margorie M. Farrar, NR = Norman Rich, PWS = Paul W. Schroeder, RC = Richard Clogg, RFW = Richard F. Wetzell, RJW = Richard J. Walter, RRM = Ralph R. Menning, RS = Reeva Simon, SBV = Steven Béla Várdy, SLH = Steven L. Hoch, SM = Sally Marks, WAF = Willard Allen Fletcher, WLB = William Lee Blackwood]

GENERAL STUDIES

Broad Surveys and Introductory Works

47.1 F. R. Bridge and Roger Bullen. *The great powers and the European states system, 1815–1914.* London: Longman, 1980. ISBN 0-582-49134-7 (cl), 0-582-49135-5 (pbk). ▸ Compact survey, mainly narrative with useful bibliography. First half to 1871 less satisfactory in clarity, factual accuracy, and interpretation than latter. [PWS]

47.2 Ludwig Dehio. *The precarious balance: four centuries of the European power struggle.* 1962 ed. Charles Fullman, trans. New York: Vintage, 1965. ▸ Interpretation of European history since sixteenth century as one of repeated renewal of balance of power after frustrated attempts at hegemony. More influential than scholarly. Translation of 1948 work, *Gleichgewicht oder Hegemonie.* [PWS]

47.3 Paul M. Kennedy. *The rise and fall of the great powers: economic change and military conflict from 1500 to 2000.* 1987 ed. New York: Vintage, 1989. ISBN 0-679-72019-7 (pbk). ▸ Massive review of international politics over four centuries, concentrating on

nineteenth to twentieth centuries. Argues for centrality of economic developments as basis for power struggles and ultimate outcomes. Impressive scholarship, influential but challengeable argument. [PWS/CKF]

47.4 Alan W. Palmer. *The chancelleries of Europe.* London: Allen & Unwin, 1983. ISBN 0-04-490071-1. ▸ Based on wide reading though not original research. Well-written, generally reliable narrative of European high politics, seldom profound but always well informed and sensible. [PWS]

47.5 Pierre Renouvin. *Le dix-neuvième siècle.* Vol. 1: *De 1815 à 1871: l'Europe des nationalités et l'éveil de nouveaux mondes.* Vol. 2: *De 1871 à 1914: l'apogée de l'Europe.* 1954–55 ed. 2 vols. Paris: Hachette, 1965–67. ▸ Master work by master craftsman; better for integrating foreign policy developments into broad political, social, and economic forces and developments than explaining diplomatic events or foreign policy as such. Mostly moderate, irenic interpretations. [PWS]

47.6 Norman Rich. *Great power diplomacy, 1814–1914.* New York: McGraw-Hill, 1992. ISBN 0-07-052254-5. ▸ Masterly survey in classical diplomatic history style; Europe-centered with attention to extra-European policies, actors, and theaters including New World. Mainly factual narrative, but takes stand on contested issues. [PWS]

47.7 A.J.P. Taylor. *The struggle for mastery in Europe, 1848–1918.* 1954 ed. Oxford: Clarendon, 1987. ISBN 0-19-881270-1. ▸ Classic work, always interesting, alternately enlightening and provoking in its insights, aphorisms, and controversial judgments. Interprets era as characterized by consistent concern for balance of power. [PWS]

Nineteenth-Century International Relations

47.8 Richard B. Elrod. "The Concert of Europe: a fresh look at an international system." *World politics* 28.2 (1976) 159–74. ISSN 0043-8871. ▸ Argues for Concert of Europe as new system rather than variant on traditional power politics; analyzes its rules and presuppositions. Widely cited in political science literature. [PWS]

47.9 F. H. Hinsley. *Power and the pursuit of peace: theory and practice in the history of international relations between states.* 1963 ed. London: Cambridge University Press, 1967. ISBN 0-521-09448-8. ▸ Wide-ranging, provocative discussion of theories and action evidencing search for order within international anarchy. Too reliant on English-language sources, but stimulating in ideas and interpretations. [PWS]

47.10 Carsten Holbraad. *The Concert of Europe: a study in German and British international theory, 1815–1914.* 1970 ed. New York: Barnes & Noble, 1971. ISBN 0-389-04110-6. ▸ Careful analysis of ideas of nineteenth-century theorists and statesmen on Concert. Posits Austro-Prussian conservative outlook degenerating into *Machtpolitik* and imperialism and British progressive view tending toward humanitarian internationalism. [PWS]

47.11 Jack S. Levy. *War in the modern great power system, 1495–1975.* Lexington: University Press of Kentucky, 1983. ISBN 0-8131-1497-7. ▸ One of many political science efforts to quantify incidence and violence of wars. Perhaps most useful for historians are massive statistical compilations and correlations without excessive extrapolation. [PWS]

47.12 Pierre Renouvin and Jean-Baptiste Duroselle. *Introduction to the history of international relations.* Mary Ilford, trans. New York: Praeger, 1967. ▸ Moderate and sensible if not profound attempt to analyze motive forces behind international politics—societal, economic, demographic, ideological, diplomatic, etc. Draws mainly on nineteenth- and twentieth-century European history. [PWS]

47.13 Paul W. Schroeder. "The nineteenth-century international system: changes in the structure." *World politics* 39.1 (1986) 1–26. ISSN 0043-8871. ▸ Challenges "realist" views, arguing peaceful character of nineteenth-century European politics resulted from structural systemic change derived from treaty guarantees, Concert rules, intermediary bodies, and devices shielding Europe from extra-European conflict. [PWS]

47.14 Daniel H. Thomas and Lynn M. Case, eds. *The new guide to the diplomatic archives of Western Europe.* Rev. ed. Philadelphia: University of Pennsylvania Press, 1975. ISBN 0-8122-7697-3. ▸ Essays by experts with comprehensive coverage of many archives; helpful information on history, holdings, access, classifications, regulations, etc. Useful survey of archives of European states and United Nations, but not European Community. [PWS/JML]

47.15 R. J. Vincent and Moorhead Wright, eds. "Special issue on the balance of power." *Review of international studies* 15.2 (1989). ISSN 0260-2105. ▸ Collection of original essays, both theoretical and historical, by historians and social scientists. Includes diverse views; challenges meaning and usability of balance of power as concept and practical tool. [PWS]

Themes and Problems

47.16 Matthew S. Anderson. *The Eastern question, 1774–1923: a study in international relations.* New York: St. Martin's, 1966. ▸ Excellent scholarly survey; lucid exposition, wide range of sources, objective and fair to all parties, including Ottoman Turks. Somewhat stronger on eighteenth and nineteenth centuries than on twentieth century. [PWS/GS]

47.17 Raymond F. Betts. *The false dawn: European imperialism in the nineteenth century.* Minneapolis: University of Minnesota Press, 1976. ISBN 0-8166-0762-1. ▸ Readable, helpful overview; successfully compresses vast, complex story. Moderate and eclectic explanations, but emphasis on political nature of process. Centered on Europe rather than periphery, especially Britain and France. [PWS]

47.18 Ernst Birke. *Frankreich und Ostmitteleuropa im neunzehnten Jahrhundert: Beiträge zur Politik und Geistesgeschichte.* Cologne: Böhlau, 1960. ▸ Analysis of France's repeated but sporadic and unsuccessful attempts to recover its lost eighteenth-century position and construct new barriers against Russia and Germany; probably overemphasizes continuity on policy. [PWS]

47.19 Henry Blumenthal. *France and the United States: their diplomatic relations, 1789–1914.* Chapel Hill: University of North Carolina Press, 1970. ISBN 0-8078-1126-2. ▸ Readable, well-informed survey of relationship mostly indirect, sporadic, and tangential, yet sometimes important (Civil War, Mexico). Depicts French policy as more complex and uncertain than American. [PWS]

47.20 Kenneth Bourne. *Britain and the balance of power in North America, 1815–1908.* Berkeley: University of California Press, 1967. ▸ Interesting portrait of British efforts, gradually abandoned after 1890, to preserve naval and territorial balance against United States by means of Canadian and British seapower based at Halifax. [PWS]

47.21 Friederich Engel-Janosi. *Österreich und der Vatikan, 1846–1918.* 2 vols. Graz: Verlag Styria, 1958–60. ▸ Thorough, scholarly treatment of neglected theme important well beyond Austro-papal history. Links Habsburg monarchy and papal state as representatives of international idea in an age of nationalism. [PWS]

47.22 Wolf D. Gruner. *Die deutsche Frage: ein Problem der europäischen Geschichte seit 1800.* Munich: Beck, 1985. ISBN 3-406-08467-2. ▸ Almost too compressed and structured for readability, but effectively argues important thesis: main issue in nineteenth-

and twentieth-century German question was always what kind of Germany would be compatible with working European system. [PWS]

47.23 Barbara Jelavich. *Russia's Balkan entanglements, 1806–1914.* Cambridge: Cambridge University Press, 1991. ISBN 0-521-40126-7. ▸ Compact, fact-filled survey of Russia's involvement in various Near Eastern crises. Sober, moderate thesis, depicting Russia as more dragged-in than expansionist; game never worth the candle. [PWS]

47.24 Horst Lademacher. *Die belgische Neutralität als Problem der europäischen Politik, 1830–1914.* Bonn: Rohrscheid, 1971. ▸ Valuable complement to Belgian and Anglo-French–centered works. Treats Belgian neutrality from standpoint of general European politics, especially policies of continental powers. [PWS]

47.25 Heinrich Lutz and Helmut Rumpler, eds. *Österreich und die deutsche Frage im neunzehnten und zwanzigsten Jahrhundert: Probleme der politisch-staatlichen und soziokulturellen Differenzierung im deutschen Mitteleuropa.* Munich: Oldenbourg, 1982. ISBN 3-486-51231-5. ▸ Essays by leading scholars attempting, usually successfully, to break through old *kleindeutsch*, *grossdeutsch*, and *gesamtdeutsch* categories in understanding Austria's role in German and Central European questions. [PWS]

47.26 Raymond Poidevin and Jacques Bariéty. *Les relations franco-allemandes, 1815–1975.* 2d rev. ed. Paris: Colin, 1977. ▸ Well-balanced, impartial survey by leading French scholars (Bariéty for nineteenth century). Stresses economics and sociocultural links along with politics, integration, and conflict. [PWS]

47.27 Daniel H. Thomas. *The guarantee of Belgian independence and neutrality in European diplomacy, 1830's–1930's.* Kingston, R.I.: Thomas, 1983. ▸ Detailed discussion of guarantee's legal-political aspects and Belgian and foreign attitudes and actions in various controversies and crises. Argues guarantee worked well and should have been retained after 1914. Based on exhaustive research. [PWS/WAF]

Policies of Individual States

47.28 Kenneth Bourne. *The foreign policy of Victorian England, 1830–1902.* Oxford: Clarendon, 1970. ISBN 0-19-873007-1. ▸ Lengthy historical essay embodying standard assumptions of British policy and European system. Judicious selection of representative documents. [PWS]

47.29 F. R. Bridge. *The Habsburg monarchy among the great powers, 1815–1918.* New York: Berg; distributed by St. Martin's, 1990. ISBN 0-85496-307-3. ▸ Revision and chronological expansion of 47.285. Accurate, sound synthesis based on Austrian archives; especially strong on Austro-German-Russian relations. Minimizes impact of domestic political influences in conduct of foreign policy, while emphasizing gap between reality and appearance of Austria-Hungary's status as great power. [PWS/JWB]

47.30 Jonathan E. Helmreich. *Belgium and Europe: a study in small power diplomacy.* The Hague: Mouton, 1976. ISBN 90-2797-561-2. ▸ Valuable survey of Belgian foreign policy, readable and reliable, concentrating on Belgium's efforts to preserve and exploit its neutral position. [PWS]

47.31 Christopher H. D. Howard. *Britain and the casus belli, 1822–1902: a study of Britain's international position from Canning to Salisbury.* London: Athlone; distributed by Humanities Press, 1974. ISBN 0-485-11149-7. ▸ Analysis of extent to which Britain accepted treaty obligations involving possible commitment to war or forceful action. Demonstrates (unsurprisingly) strong British reluctance to do so. [PWS]

47.32 Taras Hunczak, ed. *Russian imperialism from Ivan the*

Great to the Revolution. New Brunswick, N.J.: Rutgers University Press, 1974. ISBN 0-8135-0737-5. ‣ Collection of essays of diverse value, mainly on nineteenth century. Tendency to overstress continuity and purposiveness of Russian imperialism, but valuable in demonstrating historical roots and interwoven European-Asian aspects. [PWS]

47.33 Ronald Hyam. *Britain's imperial century, 1815–1914: a study of empire and expansion.* 2d ed. Basingstoke, England: Macmillan, 1992. ISBN 0-333-48946-2. ‣ Excellent single-volume treatment, topically organized. Covers many aspects, but especially good on international politics, imperial strategy, search for stability against imperial decline, and American challenge. Seeks to reconcile theses of Robinson and Gallagher (47.249) and Platt (47.218). [PWS/RRM]

47.34 Barbara Jelavich. *St. Petersburg and Moscow: tsarist and Russian foreign policy, 1814–1974.* Bloomington: Indiana University Press, 1974. ISBN 0-253-35050-6 (cl), 0-253-35051-4 (pbk). ‣ Good popular narrative survey, mainly nineteenth century, highly organized by reigns. Better on European than Asiatic side and on high policy than domestic motivations. [PWS]

47.35 C. J. Lowe and F. Marzari. *Italian foreign policy, 1870–1940.* London: Routledge & Kegan Paul, 1975. ISBN 0-7100-7987-7. ‣ Balanced, reliable synthesis of Italian goals, achievements, and failures in foreign policy. Much in need of updating. [AS/CKF/JSH]

47.36 Adam Wandruszka and Peter Urbanitsch, eds. *Die Habsburgermonarchie im System der internationalen Beziehungen.* Vienna: Verlag der Österreichischen Akademie der Wissenschaften, 1989. (Die Habsburgermonarchie, 1848–1918, 6.1.) ISBN 3-7001-1682-9. ‣ Massive, scholarly collection of essays, including narrative survey by F. Roy Bridge, discussions of commercial policy, internal organization, and other topics, though not international system itself. [PWS]

1815–1848

General Studies

47.37 C. J. Bartlett. *Great Britain and sea power, 1815–1853.* Oxford: Clarendon, 1963. ‣ Survey and analysis of British efforts to maintain naval supremacy, preserve and expand empire, repress slave trade, and police seas despite budgetary restrictions and friction with rivals. [PWS]

47.38 Guillaume de Bertier de Sauvigny. *Metternich.* Paris: Fayard, 1986. ISBN 2-213-01796-4. ‣ Best modern biography of Austrian diplomat; thorough and penetrating on Metternich's diplomacy, especially 1809–30. Emphasizes uncertainties, flexibility, and improvisation beneath Metternich's system and dogmas. [PWS]

47.39 Muriel E. Chamberlain. *Lord Aberdeen: a political biography.* London: Longman, 1983. ISBN 0-582-50462-7. ‣ Important light on Aberdeen's often underrated role in and influence on foreign policy from 1813 to Crimean War, including European and American issues. Shows importance of his conservative Christian semipacifist outlook. [PWS]

47.40 Georges Lacour-Gayet. *Talleyrand.* 1928 ed. 4 vols. in 1. Paris: Payot, 1991. ‣ Despite flaws (purely French sources, moralistic tone, French nationalist viewpoint) important for French statesman's diplomacy, especially in two restorations, Vienna Congress, and Belgian question. Sees Talleyrand as better at executing others' policies than fashioning his own. [PWS]

47.41 Alan W. Palmer. *Alexander I: tsar of war and peace.* New York: Harper & Row, 1974. ISBN 0-06-013264-7. ‣ Political biography stressing foreign policy. Accepts Alexander's idealism and emphasizes his desire to shine on world stage. Based on wide

reading; seldom profound but usually accurate and interesting. [PWS]

47.42 Alan W. Palmer. *Metternich.* New York: Harper & Row, 1972. ISBN 0-06-013261-7. ‣ Best biography in English of Austrian statesman, using some Austrian archival sources. Sound portrayal of Metternich's personality and diplomatic style; factually accurate on European politics; conventional view of European system. [PWS]

47.43 Alan Sked, ed. *Europe's balance of power, 1815–1848.* New York: Barnes & Noble, 1979. ISBN 0-06-496323-3. ‣ Collection of essays by British historians on various aspects of Vienna settlement and Vienna system. Standard balance-of-power framework and assumptions, but some unconventional arguments and conclusions. [PWS]

47.44 Lawrence Sondhaus. *The Habsburg empire and the sea: Austrian naval policy, 1797–1866.* West Lafayette, Ind.: Purdue University Press, 1989. ISBN 0-911198-97-0. ‣ Original study shedding considerable light not only on Austria's lethargic maritime and commercial development in Adriatic, but also on international policy that lay behind it. [PWS]

47.45 Paul R. Sweet. *Friederich von Gentz, defender of the old order.* 1941 ed. Westport, Conn.: Greenwood, 1970. ‣ Excellent study of this erratic and venal, but original and influential, publicist and secretary of Europe. Portrays Gentz's close collaboration with Metternich and gradual break with Metternichean conservatism after 1830. [PWS]

Congress of Vienna and the Peace Settlement

47.46 Ulrike Eich. *Russland und Europa: Studien zur russischen Deutschlandpolitik in der Zeit des Wiener Kongresses.* Cologne: Böhlau, 1986. ISBN 3-412-04985-9. ‣ Thorough, somewhat pedantic analysis covering 1805–20, centered on Vienna Congress and relations with South German states. Stresses continuity of Russian principles and interests, primacy of Poland, and defensive stabilizing policy in Germany. [PWS]

47.47 Karl Griewank. *Der Wiener Kongress und die europäische Restauration, 1814/15.* 2d ed. Leipzig: Koehler & Amelang, 1954. ‣ Overall still best detailed study of Congress, especially on Polish-Saxon and German questions. Edition largely free of "great German" bias of 1942 original. [PWS]

47.48 Edward Vose Gulick. *Europe's classical balance of power: a case history of the theory and practice of one of the great concepts of European statecraft.* 1955 ed. New York: Norton, 1967. ‣ Detailed study of Polish-Saxon question at Congress of Vienna in support of interpretation of 1815 balance of power as embodying cooperative Concert principles. [PWS]

47.49 Henry A. Kissinger. *A world restored: Metternich, Castlereagh, and the problems of peace, 1812–22.* 1957 ed. Boston: Houghton-Mifflin, 1973. ISBN 0-395-17229-2. ‣ Stresses interplay between Metternich's search for stable social-international order and Castlereagh's quest for working balance of power mechanism. Sometimes inaccurate or inadequate on facts, but contains important and influential insights. Account influenced by Austrian historian Heinrich Ritter von Srbik. [PWS/DSC]

47.50 Enno E. Kraehe. *Metternich's German policy.* Vol. 1: *The contest with Napoleon, 1799–1814.* Vol. 2: *The Congress of Vienna, 1814–1815.* Princeton: Princeton University Press, 1963–83. ISBN 0-691-05186-0 (v. 2, cl), 0-691-10133-7 (v. 2, pbk). ‣ Important both for Metternich's policy and general evolution of settlement. Both volumes portray Metternich's contest as more with Russia than Napoleon. Second volume depicts in detail his flexible shifts and improvisations in search of harmonious, independent European center. Shows Metternich more midwife to than creator of German confederation. [PWS]

47.51 Bradford Perkins. *Castlereagh and Adams: England and the United States, 1812–1823.* Berkeley: University of California Press, 1964. ▸ Completes author's series of books on the War of 1812 (see also 41.254). Sympathetic treatment of both men, showing how their realistic pragmatism overcame mutual antipathy, turning Anglo-American relations and world politics in different direction. [PWS]

47.52 Alan J. Reinerman. *Austria and the papacy in the age of Metternich.* Vol.1: *Between conflict and cooperation, 1809–1830.* Washington, D.C.: Catholic University of America Press, 1979. ISBN 0-8132-0548-4. ▸ Exhaustive research in Austrian and Italian sources, vital for Austro-papal and Italian questions; sympathetic to Metternich's program of conciliation and "reform," Cardinal Consalvi's attempt to strengthen papal sovereignty. [PWS]

47.53 G. J. Renier. *Great Britain and the establishment of the kingdom of the Netherlands, 1813–1815: a study in British foreign policy.* London: Allen & Unwin, 1930. ▸ Based on published sources; despite age, useful study of British policy. Needs supplementing from Dutch side; see van der Sas 47.91. [PWS]

47.54 C. K. Webster. *The foreign policy of Castlereagh, 1812–1815: Britain and the reconstruction of Europe.* London: Bell, 1931. ▸ Classic and still indispensable on final coalition and peace settlement; solid research in British and Austrian archives. View of Castlereagh as main architect of coalition unity and peace largely justified. [PWS]

SEE ALSO
28.245 R. John Rath. *The fall of the Napoleonic kingdom of Italy, 1814.*
28.246 R. John Rath. *The provisional Austrian regime in Lombardy-Venetia, 1814–1815.*

Congress Era and the Greek Question, 1815–1830

47.55 Russell H. Bartley. *Imperial Russia and the struggle for Latin American independence, 1808–1828.* Austin: University of Texas Press, Institute of Latin American studies, 1978. (Latin American monographs, 43.) ISBN 0-292-73811-0 (cl), 0-292-73812-9 (pbk). ▸ Wide-ranging research, focusing on diplomatic maneuvering 1808–18. Portrays Russia's attempts to maintain its territorial footholds to compete with Britain and United States, and to expand its commerce and political influence. May overemphasize importance of policy; demonstrates its decline and failure. Complements Whitaker 38.74. [PWS/RJW]

47.56 Guillaume de Bertier de Sauvigny. *Metternich et la France après le Congrès de Vienne.* Vol. 1: *De Napoléon à decazes, 1815–1820.* Vol. 2: *Les grands Congrès, 1820–1824.* Vol. 3: *Au temps de Charles X, 1824–1830.* Paris: Hachette and Presses Continentales, 1968–71. ▸ Excellent research in French and Austrian archives, urbane style; indispensable for whole period. Stresses Franco-Austrian competition and distrust despite ideological kinship, especially in Italy; internal rifts and political instability in France; Metternich's devious flexibility; Austria's essential rigidity of position and France's search for lost prestige. [PWS]

47.57 Maurice Bourquin. *Histoire de la Sainte Alliance, avec un autographe inédit du prince de Metternich.* Geneva: Georg, 1954. ▸ Sound, perceptive account of European international developments, 1815–22. Especially good on revolutions and congresses and in balancing ideological and practical aspects of system. [PWS]

47.58 Peter Burg. *Der deutsche Trias in Idee und Wirklichkeit: vom alten Reich zum deutschen Zollverein.* Stuttgart: Steiner, 1989. (Veröffentlichungen des Instituts für Europäische Geschichte, Mainz, 136, Abteilung Universalgeschichte.) ISBN 3-515-04914-2. ▸ Analysis of middle states' genuine desire, but feeble and ineffective efforts, to unite Third Germany against Austro-Prussian domination. Important also for history of German Confedera-

tion, the *Zollverein* (Customs Union), and Austro-Prussian relations. [PWS]

47.59 Henry Contamine. *Diplomatie et diplomates sous la Restauration, 1814–1830.* Paris: Hachette, 1970. ▸ Sympathetic analysis of French policies and personalities and Restoration struggle to repair foreign policy damage done by Revolution, Napoleon, Hundred Days, and domestic instability and lack of realism. [PWS]

47.60 Loyal Cowles. "The failure to restrain Russia: Canning, Nesselrode, and the Greek question, 1825–1827." *International history review* 12.4 (1990) 688–720. ISSN 0707-5332. ▸ Advancing earlier revisionist work, argues that Canning had no real Greek policy; Russia skillfully exploited this to lead Britain and emancipate Russia from European control in Near East. [PWS]

47.61 Douglas Dakin. *The Greek struggle for independence, 1821–1833.* Berkeley: University of California Press, 1973. ISBN 0-520-02342-0. ▸ Solid research focusing more on Greek politics, British and French policy, and formation of Greek state than on Russian-Turkish War and broader international complications. [PWS]

47.62 Nikiforos P. Diamandouros et al., eds. *Hellenism and the First Greek War of Liberation (1821–1830): continuity and change.* Thessalonike: Institute for Balkan Studies, 1976. ▸ Collection of essays by Greek experts, valuable especially for showing character of revolution and war as rising out of military class, explaining its dimensions as international issue. [PWS]

47.63 William W. Kaufmann. *British policy and the independence of Latin America, 1804–1828.* 1951 ed. Hamden, Conn.: Archon, 1967. ▸ With Webster 47.68 most useful account of Britain's key role in struggle for Latin American independence. [PWS]

47.64 William Spence Robertson. *France and Latin-American independence.* Baltimore: Johns Hopkins University Press, 1939. ▸ Sensible survey and analysis of French policy as essentially moderate, mediating, and progressive. Useful corrective to anti-French views (e.g., Temperley 47.66). [PWS]

47.65 Paul W. Schroeder. *Metternich's diplomacy at its zenith, 1820–1823.* 1962 ed. New York: Greenwood, 1967. ISBN 0-8371-2471-9. ▸ Analysis of congresses of Troppau, Laibach, and Verona from Austrian sources. Controversial thesis; praises Metternich's skill in preserving peace and promoting Austrian interests, but downgrades any deeper European purpose or principles in his policy. [PWS]

47.66 Harold W. V. Temperley. *The foreign policy of Canning, 1822–1827: England, the neo-Holy Alliance, and the New World.* 2d ed. Hamden, Conn.: Archon, 1966. ▸ Influential as classic liberal exposition and defense of Canning's policy, especially in Latin America, Spain, and Greece. Engaging style but serious problems in evidence and interpretation. [PWS]

47.67 C. K. Webster. *The foreign policy of Castlereagh, 1815–1822: Britain and the European Alliance.* 1934 2d ed. London: Bell, 1963. ▸ Like 47.54, indispensable study, showing solid research and thorough command of facts. Whig viewpoint evident; underestimates Metternich's contributions, but sound analysis of Castlereagh's achievements. [PWS]

47.68 C. K. Webster, ed. *Britain and the independence of Latin America, 1812–1830: select documents from the Foreign Office archives.* 2 vols. London: Oxford University Press, 1938. ▸ Broad, judicious selection of documents. Long introductory essay analyzing evolution of British policy and backing thesis that Britain, not United States, contributed most to Latin American independence. [PWS]

The 1830 Revolutions: Belgium, Poland, Germany, and Italy

47.69 Lawrence J. Baack. *Christian Bernstorff and Prussia: diplomacy and reform conservatism, 1818–1832.* New Brunswick, N.J.: Rutgers University Press, 1980. ISBN 0-8135-0884-3. ▸ Convincing rehabilitation of Bernstorff as attempting middle path of progressive conservatism between Metternichian standstill and liberalism. Important especially on *Zollverein* (Customs Union) and German politics in revolutions of 1830–32. [PWS]

47.70 J. A. Betley. *Belgium and Poland in international relations, 1830–1831.* The Hague: Mouton, 1960. ▸ Overemphasizes Russian desire to intervene in Belgium and possibilities for Anglo-French intervention in Poland; underestimates risks, but provides valuable information. Based on British and Belgian sources. [PWS]

47.71 Robert D. Billinger, Jr. *Metternich and the German question: states' rights and federal duties, 1820–1834.* Cranbury, N.J.: University of Delaware Press, 1991. ISBN 0-87413-407-2. ▸ Sound analysis of Metternich's tactics in defeating South German and Prussian challenges; more dubious thesis that he espoused alternative form of German nationalism. Useful counterpart to Burg 47.58 and Baack 47.69. [PWS/JWB]

47.72 J. S. Fishman. *Diplomacy and revolution: the London conference of 1830 and the Belgian revolt.* Amsterdam: Uitgevery Chev, 1988. ISBN 90-5068-003-8. ▸ Useful account based on French, Austrian, and British sources; complements Lannoy 47.75. Recognizes conference's achievements in overcoming obstacles (e.g., Belgian irredentism) slighted in other accounts. [PWS]

47.73 Wolf D. Gruner. "Die belgisch-luxemburgische Frage im Spannungsfeld europäischer Politik, 1830–1839." *Francia* 5 (1977) 299–328. ISSN 0251-3609. ▸ Important both for Belgian question as whole and central, oft-neglected struggle over Luxembourg. Demonstrates how German Confederation, though vitally involved, was shunted aside by great powers. [PWS]

47.74 Hans-Werner Hahn. *Geschichte des deutschen Zollvereins.* Göttingen: Vandenhoeck & Ruprecht, 1984. ISBN 3-525-33500-8. ▸ Excellent narrative of developments and analysis of motives and benefits of Customs Union for Prussia and smaller states. Praises Prussia's shrewd initiative and leadership; appraises political and economic results as important but open ended. [PWS]

47.75 Fleury de Lannoy. *Histoire diplomatique de l'indépendence belge.* Brussels: Albert DeWit, 1930. ▸ Belgian nationalist viewpoint, somewhat narrowly focused, yet valuable as fullest account of diplomatic struggle over Belgium, especially at London. [PWS]

47.76 R. F. Leslie. *Polish politics and the revolution of November 1830.* 1956 ed. Westport, Conn.: Greenwood, 1969. ISBN 0-8371-2416-6. ▸ Little on diplomacy, but shows both deep roots and contingent, accidental development of revolt and Russo-Polish War. Explains revolt's international impact and importance for Polish nationalism. [PWS]

47.77 Alan J. Reinerman. *Revolution and reaction, 1830–1838.* Vol. 2 of *Austria and the papacy in the age of Metternich.* Washington, D.C.: Catholic University of America Press, 1989. ISBN 0-8132-0669-3. ▸ Exhaustive, authoritative treatment of Roman revolts and Austrian, French, and European interventions in 1830–32. Sees Roman conference as theoretical advance, but practical failure; blames French policy and papal reactionaries. [PWS]

SEE ALSO

33.309 Christopher M. Woodhouse. *The Greek War of Independence.*

33.484 Marian Kukiel. *Czartoryski and European unity, 1770–1861.*

Imperial Conflict, Near Eastern Crises, and European Tensions, 1832–1848

47.78 Roger Bullen. *Palmerston, Guizot, and the collapse of the Entente Cordiale.* London: Athlone, 1974. ISBN 0-485-13136-6. ▸ Convincing analysis of Anglo-French alienation in 1840s, centered on competition in Spain. Critical of both English and French ministers, minimizes long-range impact of quarrel. Based on French and British archival sources. [PWS]

47.79 William Carr. *Schleswig-Holstein, 1815–48: a study in national conflict.* Manchester: Manchester University Press, 1963. ▸ Explains origins of this major national and international issue in 1848 revolutions. Nationality and international conflict rise from local patriotisms and cultural competition between dominant Germans and awakening Danes. [PWS]

47.80 John F. Coverdale. *The Basque phase of Spain's First Carlist War.* Princeton: Princeton University Press, 1984. ISBN 0-691-05411-8. ▸ Important for Spanish side of international politics in 1830s, showing how and why Carlist wars became internationally and ideologically significant and why Basque forces could sustain struggle for so long. [PWS]

47.81 Henry-Thierry Deschamps. *La Belgique devant la France de Juillet: l'opinion et l'attitude françaises de 1839 à 1848.* Paris: Belles Lettres, 1956. (Bibliothèque de la Faculte de philosophie et lettres de l'Université de Liège, 137.) ▸ Good analysis of impact of French and Belgian public and official opinion on Franco-Belgian relations, especially abortive projects for customs union in 1840s. [PWS]

47.82 Hermann von der Dunk. *Der deutsche Vormärz und Belgien, 1830/1848.* Wiesbaden: Steiner, 1966. (Veröffentlichungen des Instituts für europäische Geschichte Mainz, 41, Abteilung Universalgeschichte.) ▸ Illuminates important, neglected aspect of Belgian question and prerevolutionary era: growing political and economic connections linking Belgium and Germany, especially Prussia, and attendant rise of liberalism. [PWS]

47.83 Gerald S. Graham. *The China station: war and diplomacy, 1830–60.* New York: Oxford University Press, 1979. ISBN 0-19-822472-9. ▸ Important for Britain's diplomacy, protection of commerce, war and expansion in the Far East, especially origins of two Anglo-Chinese wars. [PWS]

47.84 Robert A. Huttenback. *British relations with Sind, 1799–1843: an anatomy of imperialism.* Berkeley: University of California Press, 1962. ▸ Brief, scholarly analysis of shifts in British policy from indifference to annexation, based on interests of commerce, security, strategy, and prestige. Emphasizes role of men on the spot. [PWS]

47.85 Harold N. Ingle. *Nesselrode and the Russian rapprochement with Britain, 1836–1844.* Berkeley: University of California Press, 1976. ISBN 0-520-02795-7. ▸ Convincing rehabilitation of neglected, underrated diplomat. Depicts efforts at partnership with Britain in Europe, Near East, and Central Asia and Palmerston's confrontational response. Policies avoided war but did not achieve larger goals. [PWS/SLH]

47.86 Edward Ingram. *The beginning of the great game in Asia, 1828–1834.* New York: Oxford University Press, 1979. ISBN 0-19-822470-2. ▸ Challenging reinterpretation of British imperial policy. Argues that possession of India made Britain conservative land power like Austria. Preservation of Persia and the Ottoman empire as buffers for India a prime goal. [PWS]

47.87 Edward Ingram. *In defence of British India: Great Britain in the Middle East, 1775–1842.* London: Cass, 1984. ISBN 0-7146-3246-5. ▸ Essays on various aspects of British Middle Eastern policy, especially involving Persia. Bold, controversial, similar in thesis to 47.86. [PWS]

47.88 Salvo Mastellone. *La politica estera del Guizot (1840 a 1847), l'unione doganale, la lega borbonica*. Florence: Nuova Italia, 1957. ▸ Analysis of Guizot's continental policy, important for showing its Mediterranean and Italian focus and anti-Austrian rather than anti-British aims. [PWS]

47.89 E. Jones Parry. *The Spanish marriages, 1841–1846: a study of the influence of dynastic ambition upon foreign policy*. London: Macmillan, 1936. (London School of Economics and Political Science, Studies in international history and relations, 1.) ▸ Somewhat narrow diplomatic study, but still important for disentangling complex, half-absurd affair that alienated Britain and France in mid-1840s and weakened Orleans monarchy. [PWS]

47.90 Raymond Poidevin and Heinz-Otto Sieburg, eds. *Aspects des relations Franco-Allemandes, 1830–1848 (Actes du Colloque d'Otzenhausen, 3–5 Octobre 1977)*. Metz, France: Centre de Recherches Relations Internationales, Université de Metz, 1978. (Publications du Centre de Recherches Relations Internationales de l'Université de Metz, 9.) ISBN 2-85730-009-3. ▸ Important collection of essays on various aspects of Franco-German relations, including 1840 crisis, German Confederation, France and South Germany, economic relations, and *Zollverein* (Customs Union). [PWS]

47.91 N.C.F. van der Sas. *Onze natuurlijkste bondgenoot: Nederland, England, en Europa, 1813–1831*. Groningen: Wolters, 1985. ISBN 906-24305-03. ▸ Important revisionist study of Anglo-Dutch relationship based on archives. Emphasizes tensions caused by King William I's European ambitions and commercial and colonial rivalry. Illuminates background of 1830–31 developments. [PWS]

47.92 Nicholas Tarling. *British policy in the Malay Peninsula and Archipelago, 1824–1871*. 1957 ed. Kuala Lumpur, Malaysia: Oxford University Press, 1969. ▸ Important not only for expansion and development of British and Dutch empires, but for evidence of how imperial rivalry in early nineteenth century could be conducted without destroying political relations in Europe. [PWS]

47.93 Irmline Veit-Brause. "Die deutsch-französische Krise von 1840: Studien zur deutschen Einheitsbewegung." Ph.D. dissertation. Cologne: University of Cologne, 1967. ▸ Useful study of neglected crisis, important for origins of German nationalism and Franco-German rivalry. Thorough, balanced, but somewhat pedantic. [PWS]

47.94 C. K. Webster. *The foreign policy of Palmerston, 1830–1841: Britain, the liberal movement, and the Eastern question*. 2 vols. London: Bell, 1951. ▸ Thorough research and detailed factual exposition, indispensable for Palmerston's policy and history of Belgian, Iberian, and Near Eastern questions. Whig viewpoint, defense of Palmerston, anti-French and anti-Holy Alliance tendencies prominent. [PWS]

47.95 M. E. Yapp. *Strategies of British India: Britain, Iran, and Afghanistan, 1798–1850*. New York: Oxford University Press, 1980. ISBN 0-19-822481-8. ▸ Massive, scholarly account of British defense of Northwest frontier. Stresses improvisations in policy, crucial roles of men on the spot, and priority of internal over external security of India. [PWS]

SEE ALSO

  16.136 Nicholas Tarling. *Anglo-Dutch rivalry in the Malay world, 1780–1824*.

  18.321 Afaf Lutfi al-Sayyid-Marsot. *Egypt in the reign of Muhammad Ali*.

  24.373 Kenneth Bourne. *Palmerston*.

  26.110 Douglas W. J. Johnson. *Guizot*.

  33.295 John A. Petropoulos. *Politics and statecraft in the kingdom of Greece, 1833–1843*.

1848–1871

The 1848 Revolutions

47.96 James Chastain. *The liberation of sovereign peoples: the French foreign policy of 1848*. Athens: Ohio University Press, 1988. ISBN 0-8214-0888-7. ▸ Details Alphonse de Lamartine's and Jules Bastide's secret initiatives on behalf of suppressed nationalities and describes blueprints for remaking European map; contra Jennings 47.99. Probably overrates significance of such activities. [APS/LLC]

47.97 Anselm Doering-Manteuffel. *Vom Wiener Kongress zur Pariser Konferenz: England, die deutsche Frage, und das Mächtesystem, 1815–1856*. Göttingen: Vandenhoeck & Ruprecht, 1991. (Veröffentlichungen des Deutschen Historischen Instituts, London, 28.) ISBN 3-525-36313-3. ▸ Detailed archive-based analysis of Britain's German policy, 1848–56, centered on Prussia and South Germany. Argues convincingly that Britain abandoned former support of confederation and European solidarity in essentially anti-Austrian stand. [PWS]

47.98 Brison D. Gooch. *Belgium and the February Revolution*. The Hague: Nijhoff, 1963. ▸ Description of Belgian reactions to threats of French invasion or pro-French domestic upheaval. Argues Belgium saved by its liberal government elected in 1847. Based on diplomatic accounts. [APS]

47.99 Lawrence C. Jennings. *France and Europe in 1848*. Oxford: Clarendon, 1973. ISBN 0-19-822514-8. ▸ Argues revolutionary government adopted fundamentally conservative policies, fearing war might bring radical control and recognizing dangers from Italian and German national ambitions. Utilizes extensive archival research and General Louis Eugène Cavaignac's papers. [APS]

47.100 A.J.P. Taylor. *The Italian problem in European diplomacy, 1847–1849*. 1934 ed. New York: Barnes & Noble, 1970. ISBN 0-7190-0399-7. ▸ Classic early account finds 1848–49 war changed Austrian despotism of diplomacy into despotism of force. Stimulating, judgmental look at British, French, and Austrian archival materials and memoirs. [APS]

47.101 Günter Wollstein. *Das "Grossdeutschland" der Paulskirche: nationale Ziele in der bürgerlichen Revolution, 1848/49*. Düsseldorf: Droste, 1977. ISBN 3-7700-0474-4. ▸ Important analysis of dangerously expansionist goals of Frankfort Parliament in Poland, Schleswig-Holstein, and elsewhere, resulting from German nationalism, internal politics, and bourgeois liberal fear of social revolution. [PWS]

Crimean War

47.102 Winfried Baumgart. *The peace of Paris, 1856: studies in war, diplomacy, and peacemaking*. Ann Pottinger Saab, trans. Santa Barbara: ABC-Clio, 1981. ISBN 0-87436-309-8. ▸ Argues, especially given Palmerston's radicalism, war might have evolved into World War I; credits Austria's foreign minister Buol-Schauenstein with preventing this. Uses Austrian archives and enormous array of secondary works. [APS]

47.103 J. B. Conacher. *The Aberdeen coalition, 1852–1855: a study in mid-nineteenth-century party politics*. Cambridge: Cambridge University Press, 1968. ▸ Considers Cabinet forward-looking association of Peelites and Whigs which anticipated later Liberal party, but came to grief through unreformed army's deficiencies. High political treatment mines private papers. [APS]

47.104 J. B. Conacher. *Britain and the Crimea, 1855–56: problems of war and peace*. New York: St. Martin's, 1987. ISBN 0-312-01242-X. ▸ High political sequel to 47.103. Argument more narrowly based and weaker: Palmerston ministry pursued war more uncompromisingly, but was better able to sell moderate peace to parliament and public. [APS]

47.105 John Shelton Curtiss. *Russia's Crimean War*. Durham, N.C.: Duke University Press, 1979. ISBN 0-8223-0374-4. ▸ Treats genesis, diplomacy, campaigns, peacemaking, and significant results. Argues Russia's defeat was constructive, because it led to reform. One of first Americans to use Russian archival materials; judges Russia's Near Eastern policy to be largely defensive. [APS/SLH]

47.106 Brison D. Gooch. "A century of historiography on the origins of the Crimean War." *American historical review* 62 (1956) 33–58. ISSN 0002-8762. ▸ Excellent summary and critique of scholarship that tends to refute Alexander Kinglake's condemnation of Napoleon III and lessen blame of Nicholas I, but confirms suspicions of British policy while emphasizing dispersion of responsibility. [APS]

47.107 Waltraud Heindl. *Graf Buol-Schauenstein in St. Petersburg und London, 1848–52*. Vienna: Böhlau, 1970. ISBN 3-205-08578-7. ▸ One of first to reevaluate foreign minister, arguing that his pro-Western policy originated while he represented Austria abroad; policy continued Ambassador Felix Schwarzenberg's ideas. Close analysis of Buol-Schauenstein's dispatches and private papers. [APS]

47.108 Gavin Burns Henderson. *Crimean War diplomacy, and other historical essays*. 1947 ed. New York: Russell & Russell, 1975. ISBN 0-8462-1734-1. ▸ Classic account of allied policy judging Foreign Minister Buol-Schauenstein harshly. Highly readable, occasionally repetitious collection of essays based on extensive research in British archives, supplemented chiefly by work in Vienna. [APS]

47.109 Andrew D. Lambert. *The Crimean War: British grand strategy, 1853–56*. Manchester: Manchester University Press; distributed by St. Martin's, 1990. ISBN 0-7190-2978-3 (cl), 0-7190-3564-3 (pbk). ▸ Useful for integrating Baltic and Crimean campaigns; assumes British aim was curtailment of Russian power. Argues enhanced naval strategy decided Russian surrender. Relies on British sources. [APS]

47.110 Stanley Lane-Poole. *The life of the right honourable Stratford Canning, viscount Stratford de Redcliffe: from his memoirs and private and offical papers*. 1888 ed. 2 vols. New York: AMS Press, 1976. ISBN 0-404-07387-5. ▸ Hero-worshiping account of life and fifty-year Eastern career of the Great Elchi, exaggerating his role in Ottoman reform and hotly defending him against suspicions he might have written his own instructions, especially in 1853. Based primarily on fragmentary autobiography, subsequently lost, and on Stratford Canning's voluminous and self-justifying dispatches. [APS]

47.111 Kingsley Martin. *The triumph of Lord Palmerston: a study of public opinion in England before the Crimean War*. Rev. ed. London: Hutchinson, 1963. ▸ Argues that British public, outraged by official failure to support 1848 revolutionaries, enthusiastically followed Palmerstonian propaganda into war against "despotic" tsar. Pioneering study of public opinion. [APS]

47.112 Luc Monnier. *Étude sur les origines de la guerre de Crimée*. Geneva: Librairie Droz, 1977. ▸ Interesting argument that Napoleon at first wanted to win allies and fight Russia; then backed down but was forced to continue belligerent policy by England. Uses French documents including Napoleon's brief correspondence with his cousin. [APS]

47.113 Vernon John Puryear. *England, Russia, and the Straits question, 1844–56*. 1931 ed. Hamden, Conn.: Archon, 1965. ▸ Natural Anglo-Russian political and commercial rivalry, artificially suppressed by 1844 Convention, rebounded in 1853 with Stratford Canning's help. Juxtaposes trade statistics and diplomatic documents to explain Crimean War; critical of Stratford Canning's role. [APS]

47.114 Vernon John Puryear. *International economics and diplomacy in the Near East: a study of British commercial policy in the Levant, 1834–1853*. 1935 ed. Hamden, Conn.: Archon, 1969. ISBN 0-208-00699-0. ▸ Dry but useful description of rise of British economic imperialism after Ottoman Empire become virtual free-trade region in 1838. Analyzes trade patterns and related strategic considerations as background to Anglo-Russian conflict. [APS]

47.115 Norman Rich. *Why the Crimean War? A cautionary tale*. Hanover, N.H.: University Press of New England for Brown University, 1985. ISBN 0-87451-328-6. ▸ Study of attempts to deal peacefully with containment of Russia. Asserts that no power gained: France won a useless victory, Russia continued as threat, while Austrian policy (following traditional judgment) led directly to World War I. Synthesis of recent scholarly literature. [APS/SLH]

47.116 Ann Pottinger Saab. *Origins of the Crimean alliance*. Charlottesville: University Press of Virginia, 1977. ISBN 0-8139-0699-7. ▸ Rare study of war origins from Ottoman viewpoint. Claims conflict was about what shape modernization should assume and which European powers should gain. Uses Ottoman archival materials. [APS]

47.117 Ann Pottinger Saab, John M. Knapp and Françoise de Bourqueney Knapp. "A reassessment of French foreign policy based on the papers of Adolphe de Bourqueney." *French historical studies* 14 (1986) 467–96. ISSN 0016-1071. ▸ Helpful in showing importance of close relations with Austria to French foreign policy establishment during Crimean War. Demonstrates disarray and divergence between private views and official statements within establishment. [APS]

47.118 Paul W. Schroeder. *Austria, Great Britain, and the Crimean War: the destruction of the European Concert*. Ithaca, N.Y.: Cornell University Press, 1972. ISBN 0-8014-0742-7. ▸ Revisionist argument based mainly on British and Austrian archival materials, arguing Austrian Foreign Minister Buol-Schauenstein diligently tried to uphold Concert of Europe, but was frustrated by mischievous British policy leading to international anarchy and ultimately World War I. [APS]

47.119 Harold W. V. Temperley. *England and the Near East: the Crimea*. 1936 ed. Hamden, Conn.: Archon, 1964. ▸ Chronicles Ottoman reform as seen by Europeans, 1808–54. Defends Stratford Canning, blames Crimean War on Turkish indolence and hypocrisy and Lord Aberdeen's cabinet, especially Aberdeen himself. Brilliant style, dubious use of evidence. [APS]

47.120 Bernhard Unckel. *Österreich und der Krimkrieg: Studien zur Politik der Donaumonarchie in den Jahren 1852–1856*. Lübeck: Matthiesen, 1969. ▸ Using Austrian military, financial, and diplomatic materials, argues Emperor Franz Joseph mainly determined Austria's tilt toward West, against most military advice and for reasons of domestic political integration. Good research, challengeable thesis. [APS]

47.121 David Wetzel. *The Crimean War: a diplomatic history*. Boulder: East European Monographs; distributed by Columbia University Press, 1985. ISBN 0-88033-086-4. ▸ Describes and understands war in terms of consequences for Central Europe and national unification movements, developing theories of Taylor (47.7). Trenchantly written synthesis, heavily dependent on earlier secondary treatments. [APS]

After the Crimean War: General Studies

47.122 Roy A. Austensen. "Count Buol and the Metternich tradition." *Austrian history yearbook* 9/10 (1973–74) 173–93. ISSN 0067-2378. ▸ Revisionist view placing Foreign Minister Buol-Schauenstein squarely in European-focused, Metternichian camp; argues his policies, especially during Crimean War, represented sound choices among bad alternatives for Austria, but were outpaced by events. [APS]

47.123 Nancy Nichols Barker. *Distaff diplomacy: the Empress Eugenie and the foreign policy of the Second Empire.* Austin: University of Texas Press, 1967. ▸ Analysis of Eugenie's influence particularly relative to Italian and German questions. Demonstrates incoherence of French policy making. Based on extensive archival research including Eugenie's papers. [APS]

47.124 Nancy Nichols Barker. *The French experience in Mexico, 1821–1861: a history of constant misunderstanding.* Chapel Hill: University of North Carolina Press, 1979. ISBN 0-8078-1339-7. ▸ Traces relations from Mexico's achievement of independence. Interesting argument that, in contemporary context, French intervention was normal operation supported by much conventional wisdom. Uses French, Austrian, and Mexican sources. [APS]

47.125 Stanislaw Bobr-Tylingo. *Napoleon III, l'Europe, et la Pologne en 1863–4.* Rome: Polish Historical Institute of Rome, 1963. (*Antemurale* [1963], 7–8.) ▸ Pro-Polish argument contending that Napoleon missed opportunity to cement hegemony by failing to intervene militarily in Poland, dissuaded by lack of support from England and especially Austria and by machinations of French financiers. [APS]

47.126 Lynn M. Case. *Edouard Thouvenel et la diplomatie du Second Empire.* Guillaume de Bertier de Sauvigny, trans. Paris: Pedone, 1976. ISBN 2-233-00025-0. ▸ Isolates Thouvenel's leadership particularly in Crimean and Italian questions; praises him as competent professional, lawyer, realist, moderate nationalist, and man of peace. Especial use of Thouvenel's and others' private papers. [APS]

47.127 Lynn M. Case. *French opinion on war and diplomacy during the Second Empire.* 1954 ed. New York: Octagon Books, 1972. ISBN 0-374-91302-1. ▸ Analysis of popular opinion on international issues throughout Napoleon's reign. Revisionist account based on innovative use of prefectural reports demonstrates Napoleon's sensitivity to public's views. [APS]

47.128 Lynn M. Case and Warren F. Spencer. *The United States and France: Civil War diplomacy.* Philadelphia: University of Pennsylvania Press, 1970. ISBN 0-8122-7604-3. ▸ Description of French government as originally favoring union, becoming more secessionist through economic distress and Napoleon's belief South had become a nation. Exhaustive treatment uses French and American public and private papers. [APS]

47.129 Domna N. Dontas. *Greece and the great powers, 1863–1875.* Thessalonike: Institute for Balkan Studies, 1966. (Hetaireia Makedonikon Spoudon. Hidryma Meleton Chersonesou tou Haimou, Ekdoseis, 87.) ▸ Discussion of development of Eastern question, focusing on Greek irredentism and Cretan crisis. Uses Greek archival materials as well as British, French, and Austrian documents. Interesting for its interpretation of motives. [APS/KAH]

47.130 W. G. East. *The union of Moldavia and Wallachia, 1859: an episode in diplomatic history.* 1929 ed. New York: Octagon Books, 1973. ISBN 0-374-92450-3. ▸ Napoleon III favored union as case study in nationalism, but was checked by the powers; union came from direct action in principalities. Narrowly diplomatic, based primarily on British documents. [APS]

47.131 William E. Echard. *Napoleon III and the Concert of Europe.* Baton Rouge: Louisiana State University Press, 1983. ISBN 0-8071-1056-6. ▸ Revisionist account emphasizing Napoleon's sympathy for foreign nationalism. Argues that Napoleon sought, throughout his reign, to destroy 1815 settlement by redrawing map of Europe at general congress. [APS/LLC]

47.132 Ann G. Imlah. *Britain and Switzerland, 1845–60: a study*

of Anglo-Swiss relations during some critical years for Swiss neutrality. Hamden, Conn.: Archon, 1966. ▸ Conventional narrative of mid-nineteenth-century Anglo-Swiss diplomacy. Traces process by which Swiss neutrality became accepted, relating it to need for central buffer despite anomaly of liberal sanctuary. British support, evidenced in British documents and private papers, vital. [APS/WAF/EWM]

47.133 Enno E. Kraehe. "Austria and the problem of reform in the German confederation, 1851–1863." *American historical review* 56 (1951) 276–94. ISSN 0002-8762. ▸ Relates effectiveness of Austrian leadership to progress of internal imperial restructuring after 1848 revolutions; suggests timely opportunity missed in 1850s. Illuminating analysis uses published German documents. [APS]

47.134 Beatrice Marinescu. *Romanian-British political relations, 1848–1877.* Liliana Teodoreanu, trans. Bucharest: Academy of the Socialist Republic of Romania, 1983. (Bibliotheca historica Romaniae, 66.) ▸ Explains complex economic but especially political reasons for British foot-dragging toward Romanian nationalism and details Romanian efforts to influence British public. Uses Romanian sources and British consular reports. [APS]

47.135 Werner E. Mosse. *The rise and fall of the Crimean system, 1855–1871: the story of a peace settlement.* New York: St. Martin's, 1963. ▸ Documentary synthesis of Triple Treaty (England, France, Austria) designed to contain Russia. Strained by concurrent Franco-Russian rapprochement and by Austria's conservatism; collapsed when Russia won repudiation of Black Sea neutralization. [APS]

47.136 Bernard Porter. *The refugee question in mid-Victorian politics.* Cambridge: Cambridge University Press, 1979. ISBN 0-521-22638-4. ▸ Description of all aspects of situation of foreign political dissidents, especially in 1850s. Fascinating study at intersection of social, political, constitutional, and diplomatic history. [APS]

47.137 Thad W. Riker. *The making of Roumania.* 1931 ed. New York: Arno Press, 1971. ISBN 0-405-02772-9. ▸ Sets achievement of nationhood into context of great powers' often irrelevant interests and quarrels. Pro-Romanian account based on wide array of foreign diplomatic and consular materials plus published Romanian sources. [APS]

47.138 Maureen M. Robson. "Lord Clarendon and the Cretan question, 1868–9." *Historical journal* 3.1 (1960) 38–55. ISSN 0018-246X. ▸ Examines use of mediation, as stipulated by protocol 23 of Peace of Paris, in peace-keeping attempt moving beyond informal procedures of Concert toward twentieth-century international law. Uses British documents. [APS]

47.139 Kenneth W. Rock. "Felix Schwarzenberg, military diplomat." *Austrian history yearbook* 11 (1975) 85–100. ISSN 0067-2378. ▸ Contends Schwarzenberg's plan for empire of seventy million was genuine *Realpolitik* foreshadowing that of Camillo Cavour in Italy and Otto von Bismarck in Germany, but frustrated by his premature death. See Austensen 47.148 for contrasting view. [APS]

47.140 Martin Senner. *Die Donaufürstentumer als Tauschobjekt für die österreichischen Besitzungen in Italien (1853–1866).* Stuttgart: Steiner, 1988. ISBN 3-515-04906-1. ▸ Exhaustive collection of all Napoleon III's overtures, suggesting seriousness of plan, conspiratorial nature of regime, and reasons why Austria objected. Based on wide reading in archival sources. [APS]

47.141 F. A. Wellesley, ed. *Secrets of the Second Empire: private letters from the Paris embassy; selections from the papers of Henry Richard Charles Wellesley, first earl Cowley, ambassador at Paris, 1852–1867.* 1928 ed. New York: Harper, 1929. ▸ Acerbic but insightful portrait of Napoleon III and his government emphasizing its incoherent and conspiratorial nature. Firsthand account by legendary British diplomat presented by his son. Earlier title: *The Paris Embassy during the Second Empire.* [APS]

Unification of Italy

47.142 Derek E. D. Beales. *England and Italy, 1859–1860.* London: Nelson, 1961. ▸ Well-documented and researched examination of British policy toward Italian unification in context of public opinion, parliamentary maneuvering, cabinet in-fighting, and relations with sovereign and with France. Concludes pro-Italian ministers succeeded beyond intentions. [APS/AS]

47.143 Arnold Blumberg. *A carefully planned accident: the Italian war of 1859.* Selinsgrove, Pa.: Susquehanna University Press, 1990. ISBN 0-945636-07-5. ▸ Good analysis of contrasting aims of Sardinian premier Cavour and French emperor Napoleon III. Napoleon, conspiratorial mastermind, outclassed by Cavour; unable to prevent emergence of Italy more powerful than he wished. Based on French and British archives, published Italian documents. [APS/AS]

47.144 John W. Bush. *Venetia redeemed: Franco-Italian relations, 1864–1866.* Syracuse, N.Y.: Syracuse University Press, 1967. ▸ Suggests Napoleon III's priorities, driven by obligation to win Venetia for Italy, stopped short of complete national self-realization for Italy or Germany. Thorough examination of Italian and other relevant documents. [APS]

47.145 Lynn M. Case. *Franco-Italian relations, 1860–1865: the Roman question and the Convention of September.* 1932 ed. New York: AMS Press, 1970. ISBN 0-404-01405-4. ▸ Detailed study of long-drawn-out negotiation over Rome. Concludes willing Napoleon III frustrated primarily by Italian instability; friendship saved by transfer of capital to Florence. Based on French, British, and published Italian documents. [APS]

47.146 Richard B. Elrod. "Austria and the Venetian question, 1860–1866." *Central European history* 4 (1971) 149–70. ISSN 0008-9389. ▸ Detailed analysis of many schemes to persuade Austria to relinquish Venetia. Concludes Vienna, faced with impossibility of buying off nationalism, rightly refused. Based on wide reading in published documents. [APS]

47.147 S. William Halperin. *Diplomat under stress: Visconti-Venosta and the Crisis of July, 1870.* Chicago: University of Chicago Press, 1963. ▸ Careful documentary study of minor, though potentially important theater. Visconti-Venosta, though pro-French and convinced France would win, wisely kept Italy neutral, opposing schemes to use crisis explicitly to gain Rome. [APS/AS]

Unification of Germany and the Franco-Prussian War

47.148 Roy A. Austensen. "Austria and the 'struggle for supremacy in Germany,' 1848–64." *Journal of modern history* 52 (1980) 195–225. ISSN 0022-2801. ▸ Good review of literature supplemented by work in Austrian archives. Argues Austria rightly continued Metternich's devotion to legality, emphasis on Europe, and optimistic cooperation with Prussia. Controversial critique of previous historiographical assumptions. [APS/JWB]

47.149 G. Bonnin, ed. *Bismarck and the Hohenzollern candidature for the Spanish throne.* London: Chatto & Windus, 1957. ▸ Reveals extent of German chancellor's role through publication of previously secret Prussian documents captured in World War II. Brief editorial introduction emphasizes history of papers. [APS]

47.150 Chester Wells Clark. *Franz Joseph and Bismarck: the diplomacy of Austria before the war of 1866.* Cambridge, Mass.: Harvard University Press, 1934. ▸ Considers Emperor Franz Joseph primarily responsible for policy; faults his overambitious

and poorly executed attempt to preserve Austrian power both in Germany and Italy. Extensive documentation from Austrian, Prussian, British archives. [APS]

47.151 Willard Allen Fletcher. *The mission of Viscount Benedetti to Berlin, 1864–1870.* The Hague: Nijhoff, 1965. ▸ Thorough treatment largely exonerating Ambassador Benedetti from his role in instigating Franco-Prussian War. Instead blames secrecy, internal divisions, and poor judgment of Napoleon III and his ministers in Paris for disaster in 1870. Careful examination of archival materials. [APS]

47.152 Heinrich Friedjung. *The struggle for supremacy in Germany, 1859–1866.* 1935 ed. A.J.P. Taylor and W. L. McElwee, trans. New York: Russell & Russell, 1966. ▸ Considers Austro-Prussian contest inevitable, though brilliantly manipulated by Bismarck; also inevitable, given backward-looking policies, was Austria's defeat. Hope for Austrian Germans was reunification. Abridged, annotated translation of 1897 classic. [APS]

47.153 Herbert Geuss. *Bismarck und Napoleon III: ein Beitrag zur Geschichte der preussisch-französosischen Beziehungen, 1851–1871.* Cologne: Böhlau, 1959. ▸ Careful study of Chancellor Bismarck's attitudes and plans. Sound argument that he wished to work with, not against, Napoleon and more dubious argument that he intended Hohenzollern candidature to avert war. [PWS]

47.154 Robert I. Giesberg. *The Treaty of Frankfurt: a study in diplomatic history, September 1870–September 1873.* Philadelphia: University of Pennsylvania Press, 1966. ▸ French inability to grasp Germany's new supremacy sabotaged early peace-making efforts and made German terms harsher, leading to French revenge. Detailed analysis of French, German, and British archival materials. [APS]

47.155 Charles W. Hallberg. *Franz Joseph and Napoleon III, 1852–1864: a study of Austro-French relations.* 1955 ed. New York: Octagon Books, 1973. ISBN 0-374-93380-4. ▸ While admitting complicating factors, attributes tension between Austria and France primarily to profound ideological differences, rendering Napoleon Austria's nemesis. Painstaking examination of French and Austrian archives. [APS]

47.156 Eberhard Kolb. *Der Kriegsausbruch 1870: politische Entscheidungsprozesse und Verantwortlichkeiten in der Julikrise 1870.* Göttingen: Vandenhoeck & Ruprecht, 1970. ▸ Compact, scholarly account of immediate origins of war, concentrating on motives and presuppositions of various actors. Downgrades economic and domestic-political factors, largely exonerates Bismarck, criticizes French for provoking crisis and demanding privileged role in system. [PWS]

47.157 Eberhard Kolb. *Der Weg aus dem Krieg: Bismarcks Politik im Krieg und die Friedensanbahnung, 1870/71.* Munich: Oldenbourg, 1989. ISBN 3-486-54641-4. ▸ Probing study of pressures faced by chancellor and alternatives developed by him in translating Prussia's military victory into viable peace settlement. [RRM]

47.158 Robert Howard Lord. *The origins of the war of 1870: new documents from the German archives.* 1924 ed. New York: Russell & Russell, 1966. ▸ Brief but trenchant introduction to documentary collection drawn from open Prussian files giving moment-by-moment analysis. Looks behind facile French enthusiasm for war to expose Chancellor Bismarck's deliberate entrapment. [APS]

47.159 Richard Millman. *British foreign policy and the coming of the Franco-Prussian War.* Oxford: Clarendon, 1965. ▸ Britain played minor role because of military weakness and general preference for Prussia, linked to distrust of French designs on Belgium. Monograph based on extensive archival research. [APS]

47.160 Allan Mitchell. *Bismarck and the French nation, 1848–*

1890. New York: Pegasus, 1971. ▸ Brief introduction to Franco-Prussian diplomacy against background of other reciprocal influences. Cautions against thesis that Bismarck copied Bonapartist themes. Useful bibliographic essay. [RRM]

47.161 Werner E. Mosse. *The European powers and the German question, 1848–71, with special reference to England and Russia.* 1958 ed. New York: Octagon Books, 1969. ▸ Comprehensive diplomatic history examining context of German unification. Concludes that Bismarck, no superman, was favored by the powers' diverse interests precluding combination against him. Based on British and Austrian documents. [APS/DSC]

47.162 Hermann Oncken. *Napoleon III and the Rhine: the origin of the war of 1870–1871.* 1928 ed. Edwin H. Zeydel, trans. New York: Russell & Russell, 1967. ▸ Napoleon III, in French tradition, schemed to create friendly Rhenish buffer state and, after Prussia's unexpected 1866 victory, plotted war of revenge. Originally published as introduction to extensive documentary collection. [APS]

47.163 Ann E. Pottinger. *Napoleon III and the German crisis, 1865–1866.* Cambridge, Mass.: Harvard University Press, 1966. ▸ Retells story of Napoleon III's policy in Austro-Prussian War from presupposition that Napoleon favored German unification—on the right terms. Useful but mechanistic survey of competing hypotheses. [APS]

47.164 Theodor Schieder and Ernst Deuerlein, eds. *Reichsgründung, 1870/71: Tatsachen, Kontroversen, Interpretationen.* Stuttgart: Busse & Seewald, 1970. ▸ Essays by leading scholars on background, circumstances, and consequences of German unification, covering constitutional, economic, cultural, diplomatic, and historiographic aspects. [RRM]

47.165 Hans A. Schmitt. "Count Beust and Germany, 1866–1870: reconquest, realignment, or resignation?" *Central European history* 1 (1968) 20–34. ISSN 0008-9389. ▸ Praises Imperial Chancellor Beust for rebuilding Austria by eschewing risky revenge while encouraging German particularism. Concludes this potentially successful policy was torpedoed in 1870 by French bellicosity. Thorough reconstruction from Austrian documents. [APS]

47.166 Paul W. Schroeder. "The lost intermediaries: the impact of 1870 on the European system." *International history review* 6 (1984) 1–27. ISSN 0707-5332. ▸ Analysis of role of Franco-German War in evolution of the state system, synthesizing important secondary sources. Argues its main effect was to destroy South German states which had balanced European system. [APS]

47.167 Heinrich Ritter von Srbik. *Deutsche Einheit: Idee und Wirklichkeit vom heiligen Reich bis Königgratz.* 4 vols. Munich: Bruckmann, 1935–63. ▸ Classic pan-German account justifying Austria's twentieth-century reintegration into Germany. Puts Metternich in German as well as European tradition arguing his successors wrongly changed to policy of confrontation with Prussia, leading inexorably to defeat and Austria's exclusion from her true, historical place in German nationality. [APS]

47.168 Lawrence D. Steefel. *Bismarck, the Hohenzollern candidacy, and the origins of the Franco-German War of 1870.* Cambridge, Mass.: Harvard University Press, 1962. ▸ Partial explanation of French fears, concluding that, in divided French government, excitable Foreign Minister Gramont unwisely seized initiative against Prussia. Introduces published Spanish sources. [APS]

47.169 Lawrence D. Steefel. *The Schleswig-Holstein question.* Cambridge, Mass.: Harvard University Press, 1932. ▸ Multifaceted, balanced account, beginning in 1850s, concentrates on 1863–64. Shows Bismarck as canniest player, not controlling genius. Incorporates material from all relevant archives, including Danish. [APS]

1871–1890

47.170 Nicolas der Bagdaserian. *The Austro-German rapprochement, 1870–1879: from the Battle of Sedan to the Dual Alliance.* Rutherford, N.J.: Fairleigh Dickinson University Press, 1976. ISBN 0-8386-1527-9. ▸ Standard examination of origins of Dual Alliance stressing conflicting aims of signatories. Nadir of bilateral relations (1875) overcome during Balkan crisis. Good on abrogation of Schleswig provisions of Treaty of Prague. [RRM]

47.171 David J. Bederman. "The 1871 London Declaration, *rebus sic stantibus,* and a primitivist view of the law of nations." *American journal of international law* 82.1 (1988) 1–40. ISSN 0002-9300. ▸ Survey of secondary literature on principle, written into treaty law in 1871, that multilateral treaties can only be modified with consent of all signatories and *rebus sic stantibus* exception to this rule. [RRM]

47.172 E. Malcolm Carroll. *French public opinion and foreign affairs, 1870–1914.* 1931 ed. Hamden, Conn.: Archon, 1964. ▸ Excerpts from large selection of French editorial opinion on international politics. Summarizes Russian subsidies to French press in 1890s and after 1912. [RRM]

47.173 E. Malcolm Carroll. *Germany and the great powers, 1866–1914: a study in public opinion and foreign policy.* New York: Prentice-Hall, 1938. ▸ Wide coverage of German newspapers. Government cultivated press to enlist public support for foreign policy. Editorials often believed by outside observers to be indicative of official aims. Centrist, progressive, and socialist, press largely immune from government interference. [RRM]

47.174 Lamar Cecil. *The German diplomatic service, 1871–1914.* Princeton: Princeton University Press, 1976. ISBN 0-691-05235-2. ▸ Profile of German diplomats, their background and careers; valuable discussion of soldier-diplomats with emphasis on 1880s and 1890s. Utilizes vast range of German archival sources. [RRM]

47.175 Egon Caesar Conti Corti. *Alexander von Battenberg.* E. M. Hodgeson, trans. London: Cassell, 1954. ▸ Biography of ill-fated prince of Bulgaria with emphasis on Bismarck's opposition to his marriage plans. Based on Battenberg-Hartenau archive. Indispensable for diplomatic ramifications of Bulgarian problem of 1880s. [RRM]

47.176 Helga Deininger. *Frankreich—Russland—Deutschland, 1871–1891: die Interdependenz von Aussenpolitik, Wirtschaftsinteressen, und Kulturbeziehungen im Vorfeld des russisch-französischen Bündnisses.* Munich: Oldenbourg, 1983. ISBN 3-486-51031-2. ▸ Detailed archive-based analysis of Franco-Russian relations, 1885–90, stressing economic and financial ties; argues, not surprisingly, that Russia's fiscal dependence paved the way for alliance in 1891–94, without determining it. Stronger on France and Germany than Russia. [PWS]

47.177 István Diószegi. *Die Aussenpolitik der österreichisch-ungarischen Monarchie, 1871–1877.* Johanna Till, trans. Vienna: Böhlau, 1985. ISBN 3-205-00553-8. ▸ Hungarian Prime Minister Andrássy's resistance to military's and emperor's expansionist zeal in Balkans overcome by crisis of 1875–77. Habsburg foreign policy determined by Vienna court, not by interests of favored nationalities. Utilizes Austrian, Hungarian, Russian archives. [RRM]

47.178 Fritz T. Epstein. "Der Komplex 'Die russische Gefahr' und sein Einfluss auf die deutsch-russischen Beziehungen im neunzehten Jahrhundert." In *Deutschland in der Weltpolitik des neunzehnten und zwanzigsten Jahrhunderts.* Imanuel Geiss and Bernd Jürgen Wendt, eds., pp. 143–59. Düsseldorf: Bertelsmann Universitätsverlag, 1974. ISBN 3-571-09199-x. ▸ Discussion of origins of German nineteenth-century fear of Russia, often promoted by pamphleteers and academics of German Baltic descent. Emphasizes consistency in Bismarck's aversion to preventive war against Russia. [RRM]

47.179 Imanuel Geiss. *German foreign policy, 1871–1914*. London: Routledge & Kegan Paul, 1976. ISBN 0-7100-8303-3. ‣ Objective of German foreign policy was to serve antidemocratic instincts of elites. One such manifestation, World Policy, after 1897 made world war almost inevitable. Lacks balance, nuance, and comparative dimension. Later version, *Der lange Weg in die Katastrophe: die Vorgeschichte des ersten Welkrieges 1815–1914* (1990), adds little new information. [RRM]

47.180 Klaus Hildebrand. *Deutsche Aussenpolitik, 1871–1918*. Munich: Oldenbourg, 1989. ISBN 3-486-55321-6 (cl), 3-486-55311-9 (pbk). ‣ Historiographical survey of German foreign policy with emphasis on major scholarly debates on Bismarckian legacy, Wilhelmine World Policy, and Germany's role in origins of World War I. Extensive bibliography. [RRM]

47.181 Klaus Hildebrand. *German foreign policy from Bismarck to Adenauer: the limits of statecraft*. Louise Willmot, trans. London: Unwin Hyman, 1989. ISBN 0-04-445070-2. ‣ Three of ten essays on European state system, 1870s to 1960s, focus on Anglo-German relations in 1870s. Important counterpoint to Kennedy 47.184. [RRM]

47.182 Andreas Hillgruber. *Bismarcks Aussenpolitik*. 2d ed. Freiburg: Rombach, 1981. ISBN 3-7930-0966-1. ‣ Interpretive essay arguing against primacy of domestic politics in making of Bismarck's foreign policy. Domestic motives and systemic pressures were intertwined. [RRM]

47.183 Barbara Jelavich. *The Ottoman empire, the great powers, and the Straits question, 1870–1887*. Bloomington: Indiana University Press, 1973. ISBN 0-253-34276-7. ‣ Valuable study of London Black Sea conference of 1871, fate of settlement, and its interpretations at Congress of Berlin and by 1887 Mediterranean agreements. Postscript on Straits question in Bosnian crisis of 1908–1909. Based on Turkish, British, and Austrian archives. [RRM]

47.184 Paul M. Kennedy. *The rise of the Anglo-German antagonism, 1860–1914*. London: Allen & Unwin, 1980. ISBN 0-04-940060-6 (cl), 0-04-940064-9 (pbk). ‣ Thorough, often elegant, but deterministic examination of institutional, popular, and economic forces that shaped Anglo-German relationship with emphasis on pivotal years, 1880–1903. Critical of Bismarckian legacy while largely charitable to British policy makers. See also Berghahn 47.333. [RRM/DSC]

47.185 Sigrid Kumpf-Korfes. *Bismarcks "Draht nach Russland": zum Problem der sozial-ökonomischen Hintergründe der russisch-deutschen Entfremdung im Zeitraum von 1878 bis 1891*. Berlin [East]: Akademie, 1968. ‣ Marxist interpretation ascribing deterioration in Russo-German relations between Bismarck's tariffs of 1879 and lapse of Reinsurance Treaty in 1890 to economic motivations and class interests. Good on pro- and anti-German sentiment among Russian officials. [RRM]

47.186 William L. Langer. *European alliances and alignments, 1871–1890*. 1931 ed. Westport, Conn.: Greenwood, 1977. ISBN 0-8371-9518-7. ‣ Reissue, with updated bibliographies, of masterful 1931 study. Focuses on European states system and Bismarck's role within it. Indispensable starting point and guide to older monograph literature. Also available in microfilm from New Haven: Yale University Library, 1990. [RRM]

47.187 Ulrich Lappenküper. *Die Mission Radowitz: Untersuchungen zur Russlandpolitik Otto von Bismarcks, 1871–1875*. Göttingen: Vandenhoeck & Ruprecht, 1990. ISBN 3-525-35941-1. ‣ Exhaustive analysis of Russo-German relations after unification

of Germany in context of general diplomatic problems of day, from Spain to Schleswig to Montenegro. By 1875, Germany threatened by possibility of hostile Austro-French-Russian or Kaunitz coalition. [RRM]

47.188 W. N. Medlicott. *Bismarck, Gladstone, and the Concert of Europe*. London: Athlone, 1956. ‣ Views diplomacy in Near East and Mediterranean between 1880 and 1881 in context of conflicting German and English programs. Attributes to Prime Minister Gladstone desire to reestablish European Concert, while "Bismarck was singularly unconvincing as the great architect of peace." Corrective in Schroeder 47.198. [RRM]

47.189 W. N. Medlicott. *The Congress of Berlin and after: a diplomatic history of the Near Eastern settlement, 1878–1880*. 2d ed. Hamden, Conn.: Archon, 1963. ‣ Great power tensions over implementation of Berlin settlement further fanned by risings of Balkan Muslims: Bosnians opposing Austrian occupation, Pomaks against Russian armies in Bulgaria, and Albanians objecting to Ottoman territorial cessions to Greece and Montenegro. [RRM]

47.190 Ralph Melville and Hans-Jürgen Schröder, eds. *Der Berliner Kongress von 1878: die Politik der Grossmächte und die Probleme der Modernisierung in Südosteuropa in der zweiten Hälfte des neunzehten Jahrhunderts*. Wiesbaden: Steiner, 1982. ISBN 3-515-02939-1. ‣ Essays in English, German, and French on policies of great powers in Balkan crisis of 1875–78, on responses of local actors, and on economic and ethnographic complexities largely side-stepped by Congress of Berlin. [RRM]

47.191 Richard Millman. *Britain and the Eastern question, 1875–1878*. New York: Oxford University Press, 1979. ISBN 0-19-822379-x. ‣ Revision of Seton-Watson's judgment (47.199) on perspicacity of Prime Minister Gladstone's Near Eastern policy, takes more pro-Disraeli stance. Good on deadlock over policy between Disraeli and his foreign secretary Derby. [RRM]

47.192 Allan Mitchell. *The German influence in France after 1870: the formation of the French Republic*. Chapel Hill: University of North Carolina Press, 1979. ISBN 0-8078-1357-5 (cl), 0-8078-1374-5 (pbk). ‣ Able study of how fear of Germany and German manipulation shaped party politics, constitutional disputes, finance, and tariffs. [RRM]

47.193 Horst Müller-Link. *Industrialisierung und Aussenpolitik: Preussen-Deutschland und das Zarenreich von 1860 bis 1890*. Göttingen: Vandenhoeck & Ruprecht, 1977. ISBN 3-525-35977-2. ‣ Great Depression of mid-1870s unmasked structural antagonisms in Russo-German relationship. Bismarck's subsequent diplomacy characterized by desire to deter Russia. Prose marred by pseudo-scientific jargon. [RRM]

47.194 Norman Rich. *Friedrich von Holstein: politics and diplomacy in the era of Bismarck and Wilhelm II*. 2 vols. Cambridge: Cambridge University Press, 1965. ‣ Detailed examination of German foreign policy, 1880s to 1906, from perspective of secretive official in German foreign ministry who became scapegoat for failures of his superiors. Superb study of Germany's place in European states system and sources of political power in Bismarckian and Wilhelmine Germany. [RRM]

47.195 Norman Rich and M. H. Fisher, eds. *The Holstein papers*. 4 vols. Cambridge: Cambridge University Press, 1955–63. ‣ Scholarly edition of manuscript fragments, diaries, and correspondence of highly placed official in German foreign ministry. Indispensable for understanding of German foreign policy, 1880s to 1906, and relationship between Wilhelm II and his chancellors. [RRM]

47.196 Ann Pottinger Saab. *Reluctant icon: Gladstone, Bulgaria, and the working classes, 1856–1878*. Cambridge, Mass.: Harvard University Press, 1991. ISBN 0-674-75965-6. ‣ Uses collective-behavior model to explain how social groups not part of political process could sometimes affect official planning; Bulgarian agitation reshaped relationship between Gladstone and Liberals. Valuable for British perceptions of Ottoman empire since Crimean War and for later phases of Bulgarian agitation. [RRM]

47.197 Gregor Schöllgen. *Imperialismus und Gleichgewicht: Deutschland, England, und die orientalische Frage, 1871–1914.* Munich: Oldenbourg, 1984. ISBN 3-486-52001-6. ▸ British distrust of Bismarck's policy on Eastern question changed to overt hostility with growth of German political influence in Ottoman empire under Bismarck's successors. After 1911, German leadership used economic position in Ottoman empire as bargaining chip for general improvement in relations with Britain. [RRM]

47.198 Paul W. Schroeder. "Gladstone as Bismarck." *Canadian journal of history* 15.2 (1980) 163–95. ISSN 0008-4107. ▸ Critical analysis of Gladstone's foreign policy, 1880–85. Argues, while proclaiming moral principles, Gladstone pursued British interests at Austrian and German expense and at expense of general European stability. [PWS]

47.199 R. W. Seton-Watson. *Disraeli, Gladstone, and the Eastern question: a study in diplomacy and party politics.* 1935 ed. New York: Norton, 1972. ISBN 0-393-00594-1. ▸ Well-written, influential early study of Balkan crisis of 1875–78, its interaction with British party politics, and effect of both on Prime Minister Disraeli's foreign policy. Based on private papers and British and Austrian archives. [RRM]

47.200 Wolfgang Steglich. "Bismarcks englische Bündnissondierungen und Bündnisvorschläge, 1887–89." In *Historia Integra: Festschrift für Erich Hassinger zum siebzigsten Geburtstag.* Hans Fenske, Wolfgang Reinhard, and Ernst Schulin, eds., pp. 283–348. Berlin: Duncker & Humblot, 1977. ISBN 3-428-03972-6. ▸ Summary of historiographical debate on Bismarck's sincerity in offering alliance to England. Concludes Bismarck's initiative must be understood in context of revanchist nationalist threat in France. [RRM]

47.201 B. H. Sumner. *Russia and the Balkans, 1870–1880.* 1937 ed. Hamden, Conn.: Archon, 1962. ▸ Pioneering study of domestic roots of Russian foreign policy. Excellent portraits of Russian diplomats as well as pan-Slavists within and outside of government. [RRM/GS]

47.202 Bruce Waller. *Bismarck at the crossroads: the reorientation of German foreign policy after the Congress of Berlin, 1878–1880.* London: Athlone; distributed by Humanities Press, 1974. ISBN 0-485-13135-8. ▸ Detailed examination of Russo-German estrangement after 1878 and of Bismarck's motivations, mainly tactical, for Austro-German alliance. Stresses importance of animosity between chancellor and Russian foreign minister Gorchakov. Still great diplomatic history of subject. [RRM/GS]

SEE ALSO
33.734 Charles Jelavich. *Tsarist Russia and Balkan nationalism.*
33.738 David MacKenzie. *The Serbs and Russian pan-Slavism, 1875–1878.*

IMPERIALISM

General Studies

47.203 Klaus J. Bade. *Friedrich Fabri und der Imperialismus in der Bismarckzeit: Revolution, Depression, Expansion.* Freiburg: Atlantis, 1975. ISBN 3-7611-0476-6. ▸ Biography of Rhenish missionary turned social imperialist, who advocated overseas expansion to cure ills brought on by economic downturn of mid-1870s. Points to socioeconomic pressures behind German colonial drive. [RRM]

47.204 Winfried Baumgart. *Imperialism: the idea and reality of British and French colonial expansion, 1880–1914.* Rev. ed. New York: Oxford University Press, 1982. ISBN 0-19-873041-1 (cl), 0-19-873040-3 (pbk). ▸ Identifies diplomatic system and metropolitan state as driving forces behind imperialism, but discusses other explanations: national and social-psychological; economic; and social-imperialist. Useful comparisons among British, French, and German colonial empires. [RRM]

47.205 Henri Brunschwig. *French colonialism, 1871–1914: myths and realities.* Rev. ed. William G. Brown, trans. New York: Praeger, 1966. ▸ Pioneering synthesis, focusing on expansion into Asia and Africa (founded on prestige, not profits or protectionism), response to local crisis (loss of Franco-Prussian War), and Anglo-French rivalry. Colonial movement phenomenon of 1890s spurred by British successes. [RRM/LLC]

47.206 P. J. Cain and Antony G. Hopkins. "The political economy of British expansion overseas, 1750–1914." *Economic history review* 33.4 (1980) 463–90. ISSN 0013-0117. ▸ Survey of monograph literature. Concludes causes of overseas expansion varied with sectoral interests. Distinguishes between imperialism of high finance and that of manufacturing. [RRM]

47.207 Phillip Darby. *Three faces of imperialism: British and American approaches to Asia and Africa, 1870–1970.* New Haven: Yale University Press, 1987. ISBN 0-300-03748-1. ▸ Examination of motives for imperialism: power politics, moral reponsibility, economic interest. Comparative treatment of British pre-1939 policies and United States post-1939 policies. [NR]

47.208 Clarence B. Davis and Kenneth E. Wilburn, eds. *Railway imperialism.* Westport, Conn.: Greenwood, 1991. ISBN 0-313-25966-6. ▸ Useful collection of essays on politics and financing of railroads in Canada, Mexico, Argentina, South and Central Africa, Hyderabad, Thailand, China, plus article on Chinese Eastern Railway. Despite regional variations, railroad concessions were vanguards of informal empire. [RRM]

47.209 Lance Edwin Davis, Robert A. Huttenback, and Susan Gray Davis. *Mammon and the pursuit of empire: the economics of British imperialism.* Cambridge: Cambridge University Press, 1986. ISBN 0-521-23611-8. ▸ Massively researched assessment of balance sheet of all British colonies, trading companies, and foreign investment. Indicates certain economic interests and sectors gained, but British taxpayer lost. [NR]

47.210 Michael Edelstein. *Overseas investment in the age of high imperialism: the United Kingdom, 1850–1914.* New York: Columbia University Press, 1982. ISBN 0-231-04438-0 (cl), 0-231-04439-9 (pbk). ▸ Dry but valuable econometric analysis of British capital flows to United States, Canada, and Australia. Investments stimulated by higher rates of return overseas (1877–86, 1897–1909) and declining growth rates of United Kingdom economy. [RRM]

47.211 C. C. Eldridge. *England's mission: the imperial idea in the age of Gladstone and Disraeli, 1868–1880.* London: Macmillan, 1973. ISBN 0-333-14797-9. ▸ Mid-Victorian imperialism suffered crisis of opinion. Prime ministers Gladstone and Disraeli accepted conventional empire but neither was imperial enthusiast. [RRM]

47.212 Byron Farwell. *Queen Victoria's little wars.* 1972 ed. New York: Norton, 1985. ISBN 0-393-30235-0 (pbk). ▸ Popular history of British military campaigns in Asia and Africa from Opium to Boer wars. Victorian era featured continuous small-scale warfare overseas. [RRM]

47.213 Herbert Feis. *Europe, the world's banker, 1870–1914: an account of European foreign investment and the connection of world finance with diplomacy before World War I.* 1930 ed. New York: Norton, 1965. ▸ Pioneering study of British, French, and German capital flowing to Russia, Italy, Portugal, Balkan states, Ottoman empire, Persia, China, and Japan. Thesis now revised in details, but still good introduction to older literature and to specifics of financial imperialism. [RRM/DSC]

47.214 Heinz Gollwitzer. *Zeitalter des Imperialismus und der Weltkriege.* Vol. 2 of *Geschichte des weltpolitischen Denkens.* Göttingen: Vandenhoeck & Ruprecht, 1982. ISBN 3-525-36148-3. ▸ Surveys ideas about, debates on, and critics of desirability of empire, 1870–1945. Good sketches of leading thinkers (e.g., John Robert Seeley, Alfred Thayer Mahan, Jan Christiaan Smuts, Karl Haushofer et al.). [RRM]

47.215 Daniel R. Headrick. *The tools of empire: technology and European imperialism in the nineteenth century.* New York: Oxford University Press, 1981. ISBN 0-19-502831-7 (cl), 0-19-502832-5 (pbk). ▸ Excellent analysis of importance of technological factor in imperialist enterprise. New technologies unleashed great force at minimal cost, allowing Europeans to colonize Asia and Africa. [NR/JKS]

47.216 Paul Gordon Lauren. *Power and prejudice: the politics and diplomacy of racial discrimination.* Boulder: Westview, 1988. ISBN 0-8133-0678-7 (cl), 0-8133-0679-5 (pbk). ▸ Examination of race as factor propelling empire and twentieth-century efforts to secure racial equality. Excellent discussion of Japanese attempt to introduce racial equality clause into League Covenant. Detailed footnotes and documentation. [RRM]

47.217 Wolfgang J. Mommsen. *Theories of imperialism.* 1980 ed. P. S. Falla, trans. Chicago: University of Chicago Press, 1982. ISBN 0-226-53396-4 (pbk). ▸ Superb survey, from classic, Eurocentric view—still important perspective—of origins of imperialism to more recent recognition of role of periphery. Includes debates on social imperialism, imperialism of free trade, role of local factors, and connection between neocolonialism and underdevelopment. [RRM/DSC]

47.218 D.C.M. Platt. *Finance, trade, and politics in British foreign policy, 1815–1914.* Oxford: Clarendon, 1968. ISBN 0-19-821377-8. ▸ Analyzing "official mind" and policy of Foreign Office, disputes Robinson-Gallagher thesis (47.249). Until 1880s, Britain intervened overseas only to open markets, uphold international law, and secure fair, equal treatment for British interests. Impressive research. [RRM]

47.219 Gregor Schöllgen. *Das Zeitalter des Imperialismus.* Munich: Oldenbourg, 1986. ISBN 3-486-48901-1 (cl), 3-486-49781-2 (pbk). ▸ Historiographical summary of European overseas expansion against background of overall diplomatic, political, economic, and social developments. Ultimate responsibility for imperialism rested with states and official policy makers. Extensive bibliography. [RRM]

47.220 Woodruff D. Smith. *European imperialism in the nineteenth and twentieth centuries.* Chicago: Nelson-Hall, 1982. ISBN 0-88229-706-6 (cl), 0-88229-812-7 (pbk). ▸ Brief overview of major issues, theories, definitions, and motives for new imperialism; scramble for Asia, Africa, Middle East, Latin America; impact of colonial rule in these areas; and process of decolonization. [NR]

47.221 Woodruff D. Smith. *The German colonial empire.* Chapel Hill: University of North Carolina Press, 1978. ISBN 0-8078-1322-2. ▸ Sound study of German imperialism and colonial rule. [NR]

SEE ALSO
24.456 Bernard Porter. *The lion's share.*
24.463 C. C. Eldridge, ed. *British imperialism in the nineteenth century.*

Africa

47.222 Eric Axelson. *Portugal and the scramble for Africa, 1875–1891.* Johannesburg: Witwatersrand University Press for the Ernest Oppenheimer Institute of Portugese Studies, 1967. ▸ Dis-

cussion of Britain's thwarting of Portuguese ambition to construct transcontinental empire from Angola to Mozambique, culminating in British ultimatum of 1890. Good also on Portuguese position in Congo question. [RRM]

47.223 Darrell Bates. *The Fashoda incident of 1898: encounter on the Nile.* Oxford: Oxford University Press, 1984. ISBN 0-19-211771-8. ▸ Colorful narrative of race to Upper Nile and resulting Anglo-French crisis that proved preliminary to 1904 Entente Cordiale, an aftermath treated only briefly. [NR]

47.224 Norman Robert Bennett. *Arab versus European: diplomacy and war in nineteenth-century East Central Africa.* New York: Africana, 1986. ISBN 0-8419-0861-3. ▸ Analysis of destruction of Zanzibar sultanate and its system, stretching from Indian Ocean to Burundi and Lake Tanganyika, at hands of British and Germans. [RRM]

47.225 Robert O. Collins. *King Leopold, England, and the Upper Nile, 1899–1909.* New Haven, Conn.: Yale University Press, 1968. ▸ Analysis of unsuccessful attempts by Belgian king to retain Lado enclave, giving Congo Free State access to White Nile. [RRM]

47.226 James J. Cooke. *New French imperialism, 1880–1910: the Third Republic and colonial expansion.* Hamden, Conn.: Archon, 1973. ISBN 0-208-01320-2. ▸ Focus on French expansion in Africa, examining relationship among French governments, colonial officials, colonial lobby, and diplomatic constraints. Colonialism promoted revitalization of France after 1870 defeat. [RRM]

47.227 S. E. Crowe. *The Berlin West African Conference, 1884–1885.* 1942 ed. Westport, Conn.: Negro Universities Press, 1970. ISBN 0-8371-3287-8. ▸ Straightforward account of shortcomings of conference; real victors Britain and Leopold II. Anglo-German disputes at conference without foundation; obscured by English and French rivalry. [RRM]

47.228 D. A. Farnie. *East and west of Suez: the Suez Canal in history, 1854–1956.* Oxford: Clarendon, 1969. ISBN 0-19-822322-6. ▸ Massively detailed but diffuse survey culled from secondary and memoir literature. Emphasis on economic implications of Suez Canal; good discussion of its legal status. [RRM]

47.229 Stig Förster, Wolfgang J. Mommsen, and Ronald E. Robinson, eds. *Bismarck, Europe, and Africa: the Berlin West Africa Conference, 1884–1885, and the onset of partition.* Oxford: Oxford University Press, 1988. ISBN 0-19-920500-0. ▸ Essays on great powers (and Spain, Portugal, United States, and Association Internationale du Congo), African responses, the place of conference in international law, role of trade, missionaries, and European press. [RRM]

47.230 Lewis H. Gann and Peter Duignan, eds. *The history and politics of colonialism, 1870–1914.* Vol. 1 of *Colonialism in Africa, 1870–1960.* Cambridge: Cambridge University Press, 1969. ISBN 0-521-07373-1. ▸ Articles examining colonialism by region, from point of view of imperial powers, and advancing various explanations for causes of scramble for Africa. Editors, more sympathetic to colonialism than most, promote pluralistic explanation. Concluding essay critiques Eurocentric approach. [RRM]

47.231 Prosser Gifford and Wm. Roger Louis, eds. *Britain and Germany in Africa: imperial rivalry and colonial rule.* New Haven: Yale University Press, 1967. ▸ Important collection of essays examining pivotal moments and issues in Anglo-German relations in Africa, 1884–1939, comparative colonial rule, and administration of former German colonies under mandate. [RRM]

47.232 Prosser Gifford and Wm. Roger Louis, eds. *France and Britain in Africa: imperial rivalry and colonial rule.* New Haven: Yale University Press, 1971. ISBN 0-300-01289-6. ▸ Similar to 47.231; essays focus on imperial rivalry in Nile valley and North and West Africa. Collection includes articles by Francophone scholars: Guillen (Morocco), Ganiage (Tunis), Stengers (Congo). [RRM]

47.233 Clement Francis Goodfellow. *Great Britain and South African confederation, 1870–1881.* Cape Town: Oxford University Press, 1966. ▸ British schemes for confederation driven by contradictory fears for security of empire and desire to curtail expenditure. Middle period, 1874–78, reflected initiative of dominant personalities, colonial secretary Carnarvon and colonial administrator Frere. [RRM]

47.234 Pierre Guillen. *L'Allemagne et le Maroc de 1870 à 1905.* Paris: Presses Universitaires de France, 1967. ▸ Massively detailed thesis that Morocco played important role in calculations of German diplomats and business interests long before 1905 crisis. Yet concludes Germany's Morocco policy determined by considerations of international politics. [NR]

47.235 R. J. Hammond. *Portugal and Africa, 1815–1910: a study in uneconomic imperialism.* Stanford, Calif.: Stanford University Press, 1966. ISBN 0-8047-0296-9. ▸ Focus on Portuguese failure, 1880–90, to translate territorial claims into effective control along Zambezi River. Later chapters deal with Portugal as object of Anglo-German diplomacy. Based on British archives but takes Portuguese point of view. [RRM/DW]

47.236 John D. Hargreaves. *The elephants and the grass.* Vol. 2 of *West Africa partitioned.* Madison: University of Wisconsin Press, 1985. ISBN 0-299-09990-3. ▸ Synthetic study of West Africa as object of great power rivalry, 1889–95, as European powers translated ambiguous principles of 1884 Berlin conference into effective control. [RRM]

47.237 John D. Hargreaves. *The loaded pause, 1885–1889.* Vol. 1 of *West Africa partitioned.* Madison: University of Wisconsin Press, 1974. ISBN 0-299-06720-3. ▸ British, French, German penetration of West African societies, from Senegambia to Cameroons, resulted not from master plan hatched in foreign ministries but local interaction. [RRM]

47.238 John D. Hargreaves. *Prelude to the partition of West Africa.* New York: St. Martin's, 1963. ▸ Focus on period 1860 to Berlin West Africa Conference (1884). Local European interests frustrated schemes of English and French metropolitan bureaucracies to reapportion their spheres in West Africa. [RRM]

47.239 Claire Hirshfield. *The diplomacy of partition: Britain, France, and the creation of Nigeria, 1890–1898.* The Hague: Nijhoff; distributed by Kluwer, 1979. ISBN 90-247-2099-0. ▸ Background of present configuration of Nigeria. Detailed analysis of acrimonious Anglo-French disputes. [NR]

47.240 A. S. Kanya-Forstner. *The conquest of the western Sudan: a study in French military imperialism.* London: Cambridge University Press, 1969. ISBN 0-521-07378-2. ▸ Focuses on aims and administrative methods of military commanders on the spot and their conflicts with civilian authorities in Paris. Convincing emphasis on military careerism as major motive behind imperialism. [RRM]

47.241 Wm. Roger Louis, ed. *Imperialism: the Robinson and Gallagher controversy.* New York: New Viewpoints, 1976. ISBN 0-531-05375-X (cl), 0-531-05582-5 (pbk). ▸ Selection of seminal and controversial essays on Robinson and Gallagher hypothesis (47.249) and its implications. Introduction, with notes, offers valuable guide to full range of literature (up to mid-1970s) on motives for European partition of Africa. [RRM]

47.242 J. S. Marais. *The fall of Kruger's republic.* Oxford: Clarendon, 1961. ▸ Most thorough study, from Boer viewpoint, of developments between 1895 and 1899. [NR]

47.243 Arthur Marsden. *British diplomacy and Tunis, 1875–*

1902: a case study in Mediterranean policy. 1971 ed. New York: Africana, 1972. ISBN 0-8419-0110-4. ▸ Study of British reactions to establishment of French protectorate in 1881. Tunis, in British view, object to be bartered for compensations elsewhere. [RRM]

47.244 Colin Walter Newbury. *The western slave coast and its rulers: European trade and administration among the Yoruba and Adja-speaking peoples of south-western Nigeria, southern Dahomey, and Togo.* 1961 ed. Oxford: Clarendon, 1966. ▸ Analysis of relationship of trade to establishment of protectorates and outright colonial administration. Based on British, French, and German archival sources. [RRM]

47.245 Colin Walter Newbury and A. S. Kanya-Forstner. "French policy and the origins of the scramble for Africa." *Journal of African history* 10.2 (1969) 253–76. ISSN 0021-8537. ▸ Decision to expand in West Africa served French national interest, came as early as 1879–80, and was most vigorously promoted by French premier Freycinet and minister of marine, General Jauréguiberry. [RRM]

47.246 Thomas Pakenham. *The Boer War.* New York: Random House, 1979. ISBN 0-394-42742-4. ▸ Well-written, authoritative account not only of war itself but also its origins, critical role of Rand economic interests, and important part played by black Africans. [NR]

47.247 Thomas Pakenham. *The scramble for Africa, 1876–1912.* New York: Random House, 1991. ISBN 0-394-51576-5. ▸ Explanation of reasons for scramble less satisfactory than superb narrative of how it took place throughout all of Africa. Seen almost exclusively from viewpoint of participants. [NR]

47.248 Frederick V. Parsons. *The origins of the Morocco question, 1880–1900.* London: Duckworth, 1976. ISBN 0-7156-0926-2. ▸ Minutely detailed examination of rivalry among great powers (plus Spain), covering every gyration of Moroccan question in 1880s. Extensive commentary on archival and secondary sources. [RRM]

47.249 Ronald E. Robinson and John Gallagher. *Africa and the Victorians: the official mind of imperialism.* 2d ed. London: Macmillan, 1981. ISBN 0-333-31006-3 (pbk). ▸ Essential work, landmark in debate on nature of imperialism. Replaces simplistic, Eurocentric, mainly Leninist interpretation with narrative taking account of non-European politics and crises. Strategic concerns transformed mid-nineteenth-century imperialism of free trade into formal empire. [RRM/DSC/JWC]

47.250 G. N. Sanderson. *England, Europe, and the Upper Nile, 1882–1899: a study in the partition of Africa.* Edinburgh: Edinburgh University Press, 1965. ▸ British success in securing Nile due to men on the spot, not dithering metropolitan bureaucracies. With Fashoda campaign, French aimed to keep open Egyptian question. Excellent on subsidiary players, documents entente between Mahdists and Ethiopian emperor Menelik II from archival sources in Sudan. [RRM]

47.251 G. N. Sanderson. "The European partition of Africa: coincidence or conjuncture?" In *European imperialism and the partition of Africa.* E. F. Penrose, ed., pp. 1–54. London: Cass; distributed by International Scholarly Book Services, 1975. ISBN 0-7146-3058-6. ▸ Important survey of existing secondary literature. Argues, contra Robinson and Gallagher 47.249, partition set in motion by French in West Africa, Belgian king's Congo venture, and British bungling of Bismarck's Angra Pequena diplomacy. By 1890s, scramble acquired militaristic and social Darwinist dimension. [RRM]

47.252 Gustav Schmidt. *Der europäische Imperialismus.* Munich: Oldenbourg, 1985. ISBN 3-486-52401-1. ▸ Compressed but valuable survey of events, analysis of research problems and trends, and critical bibliographical essay. Broad in scope, but concentrates on interweaving of international politics and economic developments and of foreign and domestic policies; strongest on Germany. [PWS]

47.253 D. M. Schreuder. *Gladstone and Kruger: liberal government and colonial "Home Rule," 1880–85.* London: Routledge & Kegan Paul, 1969. ISBN 0-7100-3157-2. ‣ Convincing account of failure of Gladstonian policy of conciliation in South Africa, prompted by other pressures—Ireland, Egypt, Afghanistan, and German bid for colonies. On local level, British feared sympathy of Cape Dutch for Boer republics. [RRM]

47.254 D. M. Schreuder. *The scramble for southern Africa, 1877–1895: the politics of partition reappraised.* Cambridge: Cambridge University Press, 1980. ISBN 0-521-20279-5. ‣ Cautions against monocausal explanations, but identifies subimperial pressure, not metropolitan authority, as driving force behind scramble. Local crisis elicited British response before new imperialism; Germany contributed to ongoing process of local partition; last strategic frontier closed by 1895. [RRM]

47.255 Ruth Slade. *King Leopold's Congo: aspects of the development of race relations in the Congo independent state.* 1962 ed. Westport, Conn.: Greenwood, 1974. ISBN 0-8371-5953-9. ‣ History of Congo Free State, 1885–1908, with emphasis on triangular relationship among Europeans, Africans, and Arabs; incorporation of Katanga; and international campaign to remove Free State from Leopold's control. [RRM]

47.256 Henry S. Wilson. *The imperial experience in sub-Saharan Africa since 1870.* Minneapolis: University of Minnesota Press, 1977. ISBN 0-8166-0797-4. ‣ Useful introduction to scramble for Africa and development of colonial regimes. Based on synthesis of secondary sources. [RRM]

Asia and the Pacific

47.257 David J. Dallin. *The rise of Russia in Asia.* 1949 ed. Hamden, Conn.: Archon, 1971. ISBN 0-208-00995-7. ‣ Despite age, valuable survey of motives and course of Russian imperialism in Asia and its place in global affairs. [NR]

47.258 E. W. Edwards. *British diplomacy and finance in China, 1895–1914.* New York: Oxford University Press, 1987. ISBN 0-19-822916-x. ‣ Japan's victory in 1895 opened gates to new international competition; British government reluctantly emulated foreign governments in providing support for British economic interests. [NR]

47.259 Grace Fox. *Britain and Japan, 1858–1883.* Oxford: Clarendon, 1969. ‣ Analysis of British-Japanese interaction, based on British, American, and Japanese archival sources. Emphasis on Anglo-Japanese diplomacy, including British efforts to mediate Sino-Japanese crisis (1871–74) and Britain's role in modernization of Japan. Discusses British influence on trade, finance, currency, newspapers, and medicine. [RRM]

47.260 David Gillard. *The struggle for Asia, 1828–1914: a study in British and Russian imperialism.* London: Methuen, 1977. ISBN 0-416-13250-2. ‣ Compact survey of British policy in guarding routes to India and resultant rivalry with Russia. No startling thesis, but much useful information and reasonable interpretation. Contrasts British and Russian governments, societies, and similarities of their policies to contest view that foreign policy governed by institutions and historical development. [NR/PWS]

47.261 Michael H. Hunt. *Frontier defense and the Open Door: Manchuria in Chinese-American relations, 1895–1911.* New Haven: Yale University Press, 1973. ISBN 0-300-01616-6. ‣ Critical analysis of American failure to understand either China or own interests in Manchuria. Draws on Chinese as well as American sources. [NR]

47.262 Paul M. Kennedy. *The Samoan tangle: a study in Anglo-*

American-German relations, 1878–1900. New York: Barnes & Noble, 1974. ISBN 0-06-493635-x. ‣ Study of breakdown of tridominium for Samoa and division of islands between Germany and United States. Shows importance of Samoa as mirror for shift in German aspirations, from Chancellor Bismarck to Prince Bülow, and for deterioration of overall Anglo-German relationship. [RRM]

47.263 George Alexander Lensen. *Balance of intrigue: international rivalry in Korea and Manchuria, 1884–1899.* 2 vols. Tallahassee: University Presses of Florida, 1982. ISBN 0-8130-0722-4. ‣ Important revisionist account of East Asian crises of 1894–98, based on Russian, Japanese, and Korean archives. Russia's policy restrained and dictated by prudence and infrastructural weaknesses; its objectives in state of flux. [RRM]

47.264 George Alexander Lensen. *The Russian push toward Japan: Russo-Japanese relations, 1697–1875.* 1959 ed. New York: Octagon Books, 1971. ISBN 0-374-94936-0. ‣ Survey of Russo-Japanese relations from self-isolation of shogunate to 1875 treaty assigning Sakhalin to Russia and Kuriles to Japan. Russian policy restrained, probably because of small volume of Russian trade. [RRM]

47.265 Andrew Malozemoff. *Russian Far Eastern policy, 1881–1904, with special emphasis on the causes of the Russo-Japanese War.* 1958 ed. New York: Octagon Books, 1977. ISBN 0-374-95262-0. ‣ Detailed survey from Russian point of view with emphasis on developments following Sino-Japanese War, 1894–95. [NR]

47.266 Gerald Morgan. *Anglo-Russian rivalry in Central Asia, 1810–1895.* London: Cass, 1981. ISBN 0-7146-3179-5. ‣ Convincing argument that Britain consistently overestimated Russian military and economic resources; Russia never had will or ability to invade India or Afghanistan and Britain never gave adequate consideration to strategic factors or logistics. [NR]

47.267 John Anthony Moses and Paul M. Kennedy, eds. *Germany in the Pacific and Far East, 1870–1914.* St. Lucia: University of Queensland Press, 1977. ISBN 0-7022-1330-6. ‣ Useful essays on German acquisition of Pacific island empire with emphasis on diplomatic context, 1884–99. Treats German commercial interests, colonial rule, missionaries, and native resistance. Bibliographies. [RRM]

47.268 Ian H. Nish. *The Anglo-Japanese alliance: the diplomacy of two island empires, 1894–1907.* 2d ed. London: Athlone, 1985. (University of London historical studies, 18.) ISBN 0-485-13139-0. ‣ Persuasive argument that alliance marked recognition of Japan as great power, but not prelude to Japanese war with Russia. Initiative came from Britain to shore up interests in Asia. [NR]

47.269 Rosemary K. I. Quested. *The Russo-Chinese Bank: a multi-national financial base of tsarism in China.* Birmingham: University of Birmingham, Department of Russian Language and Literature, 1977. ISBN 0-7044-0266-1. ‣ Authoritative study of key factor of Russian influence and international intrigue. [NR]

47.270 B. H. Sumner. *Tsardom and imperialism in the Far East and Middle East, 1880–1914.* 1942 ed. Hamden, Conn.: Archon, 1968. ‣ Good introduction, based on documents published by Soviets. Interbureaucratic rivalries over Manchurian policy affected by depression of 1900. Men on the spot set pace in Persia. From 1940 lecture. [RRM]

47.271 Harmon Tupper. *To the great ocean: Siberia and the Trans-Siberian Railway.* Boston: Little, Brown, 1965. ‣ Good popular narrative. Concentrates on building of railway itself; only brief treatment of international implications. [NR]

47.272 L. K. Young. *British policy in China, 1895–1902.* Oxford: Oxford University Press, 1970. ISBN 0-19-822316-1. ‣ Sees British role in scramble for China as essentially defensive, concerned with protection of treaty rights and maintenance of dominant commercial position. Interesting for Britain's failed efforts at Russian and German partnerships before turning to Japan. [NR]

SEE ALSO
9.312 Seymour Becker. *Russia's protectorates in Central Asia.*

Middle East

47.273 Briton Cooper Busch. *Britain and the Persian Gulf, 1894–1914.* Berkeley: University of California Press, 1967. ▸ Valuable discussion of policy of various offices concerned with this strategic area and their reaction to policies of interlopers. Focuses on forms of British control and strategies for warding off foreign challenges. [NR]

47.274 Maybelle Rebecca (Kennedy) Chapman. "Great Britain and the Bagdad Railway, 1888–1914." Ph.D. dissertation. Northampton, Mass., 1948. (Smith College studies in history, 31.) ▸ Analysis of British misconceptions of German plans and motives and their political and financial efforts to prevent railway's construction. Written before availability of documents covering final Anglo-German agreement. [NR]

47.275 Isaiah Friedman. *Germany, Turkey, and Zionism, 1897–1918.* Oxford: Clarendon, 1977. ISBN 0-19-822528-8. ▸ Excellent study of Germany's Palestine policy and its European implications. Concludes that without German intervention on their behalf, there would have been no Jews in Palestine to give rise to Balfour Declaration. [SM/EM]

47.276 Rose L. Greaves. *Persia and the defence of India, 1884–1892: a study in the foreign policy of the third marquis of Salisbury.* London: Athlone with University of London, 1959. ▸ Salisbury's policy dominated by fear of Russian expansion; worked for maintenance of tier of buffer states in which Persia played key role. [NR]

47.277 Joseph Heller. *British policy towards the Ottoman empire, 1908–1914.* London: Cass, 1983. ISBN 0-7146-3127-2. ▸ Fundamental British consideration was preservation of agreements with France and Russia; both threatened by Young Turks, hence British abandoned defense of Ottoman empire. [NR]

47.278 J. C. Hurewitz, ed. and trans. *European expansion, 1535–1914.* Vol. 1 of *The Middle East and North Africa in world politics: a documentary record.* 2d ed. New Haven: Yale University Press, 1975. ISBN 0-300-01294-2. ▸ Selection of treaties, agreements, and conventions between European powers and Ottoman empire, Persia, Afghanistan, Gulf emirates, Tunis, Algiers, and Morocco. Scholarly introductions contextualize documents and survey secondary literature. [RRM]

47.279 Firuz Kazemzadeh. *Russia and Britain in Persia, 1864–1914: a study in imperialism.* New Haven: Yale University Press, 1968. ▸ Contends diplomacy was principal instrument of both states, though military power loomed in background. Economic competition never played decisive role, largely by-product of political conflict. Focus on 1907 Convention. Extensive use of Russian and Persian sources. [NR/GRG]

47.280 Jacques Thobie. *Intérêts et impérialisme français dans l'empire Ottoman, 1895–1914.* Paris: Imprimerie Nationale, 1977. ISBN 2-11-080700-8. ▸ Massively detailed study with important material on great power competition in financing of public works (e.g., railways, harbors). [NR]

47.281 Keith M. Wilson, ed. *Imperialism and nationalism in the Middle East: the Anglo-Egyptian experience, 1882–1982.* London: Mansell; distributed by Wilson, 1983. ISBN 0-7201-1682-1. ▸ Essays examining pivotal role of Suez Canal for British strategy and for Anglo-Egyptian relationship. [RRM]

47.282 John B. Wolf. *The diplomatic history of the Bagdad Railroad.* 1936 ed. New York: Octagon Books, 1973. ISBN 0-374-

98709-2. ▸ Published before availability of British documents covering final negotiations, but still valuable for period before final settlement. [NR]

1890–1910

47.283 Christopher M. Andrew. *Théophile Delcassé and the making of the Entente Cordiale: a reappraisal of French foreign policy, 1898–1905.* New York: St. Martin's, 1968. ▸ Revealing study of ardent nationalist foe of Germany, and engineer of remarkable turnabout in Anglo-French relations from Fashoda crisis to Entente Cordiale. Based largely on French sources. [NR]

47.284 Michael Behnen. *Rüstung, Bündnis, Sicherheit: Dreibund und informeller Imperialismus, 1900–1908.* Tübingen: Niemeyer, 1985. (Bibliothek des Deutschen Historischen Instituts in Rom, 60.) ISBN 3-484-82060-8, ISSN 0070-4156. ▸ Analysis of transformation of Triple Alliance emphasizing finance as diplomatic tool, Austrian-Italian-Romanian relations, and imperialism factor. Provides much new information, but poorly organized and buried in detail. [NR]

47.285 F. R. Bridge. *From Sadowa to Sarajevo: the foreign policy of Austria-Hungary, 1866–1914.* London: Routledge & Kegan Paul, 1972. ISBN 0-7100-7269-4. ▸ Admirable survey, sympathetic to Austria. Emphasizes difficulties stemming from foreign support for irredentist movements within empire, loss of British support, and mounting Austrian desperation. [NR]

47.286 F. R. Bridge. "Izvolsky, Aehrenthal, and the end of the Austro-Russian entente, 1906–8." *Mitteilungen des österreichischen Staatsarchivs* 29 (1976) 315–62. ▸ Analysis of eleven documents (reprinted in translation) from Charykov-Izvolsky correspondence, making clear that Russian foreign minister anticipated imminent Austrian annexation of Bosnia-Herzegovina in September 1908. [RRM]

47.287 Wilhelm Mauritz Carlgren. *Iswolsky und Aehrenthal vor der bosnischen Annexionskrise: Russische und österreichisch-ungarische Balkan Politik, 1906–1908.* Uppsala: Almqvist & Wiksell, 1955. ▸ Background of crisis from Austro-Russian entente, 1897. Hopes of both ministers to improve relations through bargain over Bosnia and Straits frustrated by Young Turks' Revolution forcing Austrian foreign minister to annex Bosnia prematurely. [NR]

47.288 Jost Dülffer. *Regeln gegen den Krieg? Die Haager Friedenskonferenzen von 1899 und 1907 in der internationalen Politik.* Frankfort: Ullstein, 1981. ISBN 3-550-07942-7. ▸ Thorough, scholarly analysis of conferences as failed, flawed, but important efforts at change in international system. Primarily blames Germany à la Fischer 47.338, 47.375 for substituting *Weltpolitik* for reforms; sees negotiations of 1907 as aspect of first American bid for world leadership. [PWS]

47.289 Gerhard Ebel, ed. *Botschafter Paul Graf von Hatzfeldt: nachgelassene Papiere, 1838–1901.* 2 vols. Boppard am Rhein: Boldt, 1976. ▸ Edited papers, mostly correspondence, of German ambassador to Madrid (1874–78), Constantinople (1879–82), and London (1885–1901). Particularly informative on German tactics and aims in Anglo-German frictions of 1890s. [RRM]

47.290 Raymond A. Esthus. *Double eagle and rising sun: the Russians and Japanese at Portsmouth in 1905.* Durham, N.C.: Duke University Press, 1988. ISBN 0-8223-0778-2. ▸ Straightforward account of pivotal event in East Asian history. Neglects critical impact on relations between European powers. [NR]

47.291 Keith Eubank. *Paul Cambon: master diplomatist.* Norman: University of Oklahoma Press, 1960. ▸ Somewhat narrow study of Cambon's role in undermining Bismarck's alliances and building up those of France. Calls for renewed appreciation of secret diplomacy and of able diplomats. [NR]

47.292 Aaron L. Friedberg. *The weary titan: Britain and the experience of relative decline, 1895–1905*. Princeton: Princeton University Press, 1988. ISBN 0-691-05532-7. ▸ Fine scholarship by political scientist, assessing factors that make for state's power. Argues British leadership could have done more to shore up British power, but feared public backlash against spending. Neglects public willingness to pay for naval increases. See also Kennedy 24.346. [NR/BJCM]

47.293 Michael G. Fry. *Lloyd George and foreign policy, 1890–1916*. Montreal: McGill-Queen's University Press, 1977. ISBN 0-7735-0274-2. ▸ Excellent detailed analysis concentrating on changing attitude toward Germany, from desire for improved relations to suspicion and hostility. [NR]

47.294 René Girault. *Emprunts russes et investissements français en Russie, 1887–1914: recherches sur l'investissement international*. Paris: Colin, 1973. (Publications de la Sorbonne, n.s., 3.) ▸ Chronicles placement, by 1914, of about 5 percent of French private wealth in Russia; purchase of 1890s bonds driven by high interest and 1906 loan by political considerations (Morocco). Good research but leaves open fundamental question on precise interplay of finance and politics in Franco-Russian alliance. [RRM]

47.295 J.A.S. Grenville. *Lord Salisbury and foreign policy: the close of the nineteenth century*. 1964 ed. London: Athlone, 1970. ISBN 0-485-12014-3. ▸ Survey of transition from Prime Minister Salisbury's pragmatism and avoidance of long-term commitments to Foreign Secretary Lansdowne's entry into such commitments in response to Russian expansionism and perception of German menace. Older study but still unsurpassed in depth and breadth of treatment of foreign policy at peak of British power. [NR/BJCM]

47.296 Oron James Hale. *Publicity and diplomacy with special reference to England and Germany, 1890–1914*. 1940 ed. Gloucester, Mass.: Smith, 1964. ▸ Pioneering examination of influence of press on foreign policy. Important example of pre–World War II viewpoint. [NR]

47.297 Oswald Hauser. *Deutschland und der englisch-russische Gegensatz, 1900–1914*. Göttingen: Musterschmidt, 1958. ▸ Older but still valuable analysis, emphasizing failure of Anglo-German efforts to exploit British differences with Russia and to bridge own differences. [NR]

47.298 Christopher H. D. Howard. *Splendid isolation: a study of ideas concerning Britain's international position and foreign policy during the later years of the third marquis of Salisbury*. New York: St. Martin's, 1967. ▸ Brief analysis of entire concept of isolationism and whether British policy was in fact isolationist. Concludes all domestic differences on subject ended with entry into alliance with Japan in 1902. [NR]

47.299 Akira Iriye. *Pacific estrangement: Japanese and American expansion, 1897–1911*. Cambridge, Mass.: Harvard University Press, 1972. ISBN 0-674-65075-1. ▸ Wide-ranging examination of Japanese-American interaction, influence of American example on Japanese policies, and American and European reactions to Japanese imperialism. Focus on problems that arose as result of physical and cultural-intellectual encounters. [NR/FGN]

47.300 Peter Jakobs. *Das Werden des französisch-russischen Zweibundes, 1890–1894*. Wiesbaden: Harrassowitz, 1968. ▸ Concentrates on role of Russia and search for security after breakoff of Reinsurance Treaty with Germany. Contains detailed character sketches of Alexander III, Foreign Minister Giers, and chief of staff, General Obruchev. Particularly valuable analysis of military considerations. [NR]

47.301 George F. Kennan. *The decline of Bismarck's European order: Franco-Russian relations, 1875–1890*. Princeton: Princeton University Press, 1979. ISBN 0-691-05282-4. ▸ First volume of author's exploration into entanglements leading to World War I. Misguided, bungling Russian foreign policy led to disadvantageous rupture with Germany and potentially costly and irrational alliance with France. Designed to defend European order and status quo, it could not withstand fundamental forces of social change. [NR/DHK/DSC]

47.302 George F. Kennan. *The fateful alliance: France, Russia, and the coming of the First World War*. New York: Pantheon, 1984. ISBN 0-394-53494-8. ▸ Good narrative history; regards alliance as tragic mistake. French and Russians failed to recognize implications of treaty provision requiring full mobilization in response to any mobilization by member of Triple Alliance, ensuring escalation of 1914 crisis. [NR/DSC]

47.303 Rainer Lahme. *Deutsche Aussenpolitik, 1890–1894: von der Gleichgewichtspolitik Bismarcks zur Allianzstrategie Caprivis*. Göttingen: Vandenhoeck & Ruprecht, 1990. (Schriftenreihe der Historischen Kommission bei der Bayerischen Akademie der Wissenschaften, 39.) ISBN 3-525-35940-3. ▸ Overly detailed but valuable analysis, stressing Germany's narrow options, progressive and peaceful goals of Caprivi's tariff reforms, tension between "English option" (Holstein-Hatzfeldt) and "free hand" (Kiderlen-Marschall) in German policy. [PWS]

47.304 Ivo Nikolai Lambi. *The navy and German power politics, 1862–1914*. London: Allen & Unwin, 1984. ISBN 0-04-943035-1. ▸ Author purposely ignores domestic factors to concentrate on disastrous effect on Germany's international position and lack of coordination between agencies of German government. [NR]

47.305 William L. Langer. *The diplomacy of imperialism, 1890–1902*. 1935 ed. New York: Knopf, 1951. ▸ Coverage of great power relations and imperial rivalries, 1890 to conclusion of Anglo-Japanese Alliance. Remains supreme work in field; overpoweringly detailed. [NR]

47.306 Richard Langhorne. *The collapse of the Concert of Europe: international politics, 1890–1914*. New York: St. Martin's, 1981. ISBN 0-312-14723-6. ▸ Useful survey; ascribes collapse to impossibility of maintaining international status quo the system was designed to defend, technological changes, and domestic pressures resulting from changes in structures of societies and governments. [NR]

47.307 Paul Gordon Lauren. *Diplomats and bureaucrats: the first institutional responses to twentieth-century diplomacy in France and Germany*. Stanford, Calif.: Hoover Institution Press, 1976. (Hoover Institution publications, 153.) ISBN 0-8179-6531-9. ▸ Analysis of reform and reorganization of French and German foreign ministries, demonstrating ability to respond creatively to increasingly diffuse problems of twentieth century. [NR]

47.308 Folke A. Lindberg. *Scandinavia in great power politics, 1905–1908*. Stockholm: Almqvist & Wiksell, 1958. (Acta Universitatis Stockholmiensis, Stockholm studies in history, 1.) ▸ Coverage of neglected subjects of dissolution of Swedish-Norwegian union (1905) and negotiations leading to international treaties of 1907 and 1908, designed to protect territorial integrity of states bordering North and Baltic seas. [NR]

47.309 C. J. Lowe. *The reluctant imperialists: British foreign policy, 1878–1902*. 1967 ed. New York: Macmillan, 1969. ▸ Expert overview and analysis. Emphasizes role of trade, religion, and naval superiority, yet sees foreign policy as largely determined by relations with other great powers. [NR]

47.310 C. J. Lowe. *Salisbury and the Mediterranean, 1886–1896*. London: Routledge & Kegan Paul, 1965. ▸ Able defense of prime minister's policy, concluding he clung to defense of Straits in concert with Triple Alliance until forced by changes in German policy to abandon traditional course, including agreements with Austria. [NR]

47.311 Gordon Martel. *Imperial diplomacy: Rosebery and the failure of foreign policy.* Kingston, Ont.: McGill-Queen's University Press, 1986. ISBN 0-7735-0442-7. ▸ Broad picture from Lord Rosebery's perspective. Prime minister primarily concerned with balance of power, not with imperial interests; policy dedicated to defending what Britain already had, not with taking more. [NR/BJCM]

47.312 Robert K. Massie. *Dreadnought: Britain, Germany, and the coming of the Great War.* New York: Random House, 1991. ISBN 0-394-52833-6. ▸ Popular history on background of war built around First Sea Lord Fisher's reforms of British navy. Flavorful narrative and biographical sketches marred by uncritical use of sources. [NR]

47.313 George W. Monger. *The end of isolation: British foreign policy, 1900–1907.* 1963 ed. Westport, Conn.: Greenwood, 1976. ISBN 0-8371-8628-5. ▸ Study of transformation of British foreign policy from splendid isolation (never so isolationist as author implies) to alliances and ententes with Japan, France, and Russia. [NR]

47.314 Charles E. Neu. *The troubled encounter: the United States and Japan.* New York: Wiley, 1975. ISBN 0-471-63190-6 (cl), 0-471-63191-4 (pbk). ▸ Synthesis work explaining why two nations that have interacted so continuously on cultural, economic, and diplomatic levels should have understood each other so poorly. [NR]

47.315 Ian H. Nish. *Japanese foreign policy, 1869–1942: Kasumigaseki to Miyakezaka.* London: Routledge & Kegan Paul, 1977. ISBN 0-7100-8421-8. ▸ Best available survey concentrating on role of foreign ministers, thus bypassing many critical factors in making of Japanese foreign policy. Also strong on interwar period. Includes translated documents. [NR/JSH]

47.316 Ian H. Nish. *The origins of the Russo-Japanese War.* London: Longman, 1985. ISBN 0-582-49114-2 (pbk). ▸ Good synthesis arguing war came to be regarded as necessary by statesmen of both governments to maintain and extend influence in East Asia. Stresses decisive factor of human influence and responsibility. [NR]

47.317 B. E. Nol'de. *L'alliance franco-russe: les origines du système diplomatique d'avant-guerre.* Paris: Droz, 1936. (Collection historique de l'Institute d'Études Slaves, 7.) ▸ Massively detailed study dealing almost exclusively with diplomatic and military exchanges. [NR]

47.318 Shumpei Okamoto. *The Japanese oligarchy and the Russo-Japanese War.* New York: Columbia University Press, 1970. ISBN 0-231-03404-0 (cl). ▸ Important supplement to diplomatic studies of origins of war; analyses divisions and decisions within Japanese government and role of public pressure. [NR]

47.319 Peter Padfield. *The great naval race: the Anglo-German naval rivalry, 1900–1914.* New York: McKay, 1974. ISBN 0-679-50472-9. ▸ Popular history, justifiably critical of German leadership. [NR]

47.320 Raymond Poidevin. *Les relations économiques et financières entre la France et l'Allemagne de 1898 à 1914.* Paris: Colin, 1969. ▸ Authoritative survey of vital factor in Franco-German relations. [NR]

47.321 John C. G. Röhl, ed. *Philipp Eulenburgs politische Korrespondenz.* 3 vols. Boppard am Rhein: Boldt, 1976–83. (Deutsche Geschichtsquellen des neunzehten und zwanzigsten Jahrhunderts, 52.) ISBN 3-7646-1642-3 (v. 1). ▸ Thorough, abundantly footnoted edition of correspondence of intimate of Wilhelm II. Essential to understanding of German policy of 1890s, domestic or foreign. Eulenburg's influence decisive in high-level appointments, dismissal of Chancellor Caprivi, and advancement of Count Bülow to chancellorship. [RRM]

47.322 P.J.V. Rolo. *Entente Cordiale: the origins and negotiation of the Anglo-French agreements of 8 April 1904.* New York: St. Martin's, 1970. ISBN 0-312-25690-6. ▸ Based on published sources; sees Entente as shattering German assumption that Britain could never settle differences with France. Leaves open question of Entente's contribution to World War I. [NR]

47.323 Jonathan Steinberg. *Yesterday's deterrent: Tirpitz and the birth of the German battle fleet.* 1965 ed. New York: Macmillan, 1966. ▸ Uses captured German documents to explore fateful problem of naval buildup and consequences for Germany's international position. Somewhat overtaken by later scholarship. [NR]

47.324 Zara S. Steiner. *The Foreign Office and foreign policy, 1898–1914.* 1969 ed. London: Ashfield, 1986. ISBN 0-09-486600-7 (pbk). ▸ Fascinating study of personalities and attitudes within small elite fashioning British policy. Account of 1905 reforms giving foreign office new power to make and execute foreign policy before 1914. Describes generational shift in anti-German direction with Foreign Secretary Grey's coming to power. [PWS/BJCM]

47.325 Barbara Vogel. *Deutsche Russlandpolitik: das Scheitern der deutschen Weltpolitik unter Bülow, 1900–1906.* Düsseldorf: Bertelsmann Universitätsverlag, 1973. ▸ Despite increasing German economic influence in Russia, Chancellor Bülow failed to achieve alliance with Russia largely because of inept German and skillful French policies. More critical of Bülow than Winzen 47.330. [NR]

47.326 Donald Cameron Watt. *Succeeding John Bull, America in Britain's place, 1900–75: a study of the Anglo-American relationship and world politics in the context of British and American foreign-policy-making in the twentieth century.* Cambridge: Cambridge University Press, 1984. ISBN 0-521-25022-6. ▸ Concentrates on how process was perceived and understood (or misconceived and misunderstood) by British and American policy makers. Acute criticism of many accepted attitudes, including revisionists, on this complex subject. [NR]

47.327 John Albert White. *The diplomacy of the Russo-Japanese war.* Princeton: Princeton University Press, 1964. ▸ Valuable analysis of peace negotiations and subsequent efforts to achieve new balance of power in East Asia. Concludes war result of conviction on both sides of need to defend national interests. [NR]

47.328 Keith M. Wilson. *Empire and continent: studies in British foreign policy from the 1880s to the First World War.* London: Mansell, 1987. ISBN 0-7201-1859-X. ▸ Contribution to debates on British foreign policy, diplomatic strategy, role of Foreign Office in policy formulation, and relationship between foreign and domestic politics. Similar in revisionist emphasis to 47.329. [NR]

47.329 Keith M. Wilson. *The policy of the Entente: essays on the determinants of British foreign policy, 1904–1914.* Cambridge: Cambridge University Press, 1985. ISBN 0-521-30195-5. ▸ Controversial essays. Britain saw themselves less threatened by Germany than by Russia, hence maintenance of good relations with Russia principal objective. [NR]

47.330 Peter Winzen. *Bülows Weltmachtkonzept: Untersuchungen zur Frühphase seiner Aussenpolitik, 1897–1901.* Boppard am Rhein: Boldt, 1977. ISBN 3-764-61643-1. ▸ Foreign Secretary Bülow driven by long-term strategy, not opportunism. Establishment of Germany as world power necessitated construction of large fleet and diplomacy of free hand. Opposed feelers for alliance with England, inclined toward Russia. [RRM]

47.331 Edward H. Zabriskie. *American-Russian rivalry in the Far East: a study in diplomacy and power politics, 1895–1914.* 1946 ed. Westport, Conn.: Greenwood, 1973. ISBN 0-8371-6666-7. ▸ Useful description of deterioration of traditional Russo-American friendship into rivalry over China, temporary success of President Theodore Roosevelt's policy of balanced Russo-Japanese antagonism, and failure of President Taft's dollar diplomacy against anti-American Russo-Japanese front. [PWS]

SEE ALSO
33.714 Fikret Adanir. *Die makedonische Frage, ihre Entstehung und Entwicklung bis 1908*.

WORLD WAR I

Causes

47.332 Jean-Claude Allain. *Agadir 1911: une crise imperialiste en Europe pour la conquête du Maroc*. Paris: Université de Paris, Panthéon-Sorbonne, Institute d'Histoire des Relations Internationales Contemporaines, 1976. ISBN 2-859-44004-6. ▸ Heavily archival, strikingly revisionist study of background (Cherifian decay, French economic and military penetration) and course of crisis. Stresses French military and political adventurism, sees German response as essentially pacific. [PWS]

47.333 Volker R. Berghahn. *Germany and the approach of war in 1914*. New York: St. Martin's, 1973. ▸ Revisionist survey of course and causes of German diplomacy, including armaments policy and political perceptions. Following Fischer 47.338, 47.375, assigns primary responsibility to Germany and paralysis of its political elites. [SM/CSA]

47.334 Richard J. B. Bosworth. *Italy and the approach of the First World War*. New York: St. Martin's, 1983. ISBN 0-312-43924-5. ▸ Competent introductory survey of Italian policy, 1900–15. Concludes Italy's role in war's origins was marginal; blames Italy's muddled entry on Foreign Minister Sonnino and domestic politics. [SM]

47.335 Richard J. B. Bosworth. *Italy, the least of the great powers: Italian foreign policy before the First World War*. Cambridge: Cambridge University Press, 1979. ISBN 0-521-22360-0. ▸ Standard survey of Italian foreign relations in domestic context, 1870–1914, especially roles of Foreign Minister San Guiliano and Premier Giolitti. Sees liberal diplomacy as less bellicose precursor of fascist policy, both lacking power. [SM]

47.336 F. R. Bridge. *Great Britain and Austria-Hungary, 1906–1914: a diplomatic history*. London: Weidenfeld & Nicolson, 1972. ISBN 0-297-99512-0. ▸ Austro-British relations deteriorated despite Foreign Minister Aehrenthal's efforts. Attributes this to cabinet policies and balance of power. Rehabilitates Aehrenthal's reputation. [SM]

47.337 Richard J. Crampton. *The hollow detente: Anglo-German relations in the Balkans, 1911–1914*. Atlantic Highlands, N.J.: Humanities Press, 1979. ISBN 0-391-02159-1. ▸ Scholarly study of Anglo-German detente in Balkan crises. Argues Germany's goal was British neutrality in continental war, but agreement only peripheral. [SM]

47.338 Fritz Fischer. *War of illusions: German policies from 1911 to 1914*. Marion Jackson, trans. New York: Norton, 1975. ISBN 0-393-05480-2. ▸ Important but difficult specialist study of relations between German domestic and foreign policy in war's origins. Argues Germany sought war for hegemony; imperialist foreign policy would buttress position of ruling classes. [SM]

47.339 Fritz Fischer. *World power or decline: the controversy over Germany's aims in the First World War*. L. Farrar Lancelot, Jr., Robert Kimber, and Rita Kember, trans. New York: Norton, 1974. ISBN 0-393-05451-3 (cl), 0-393-09413-8 (pbk). ▸ Brief restatement in response to critics of his views on Germany's responsibility for and aims in World War I. Includes essay on historiography of controversy. [SM]

47.340 Imanuel Geiss, ed. *July 1914, the outbreak of the First World War: selected documents*. 1967 ed. New York: Norton, 1974. ISBN 0-393-00722-7. ▸ Useful collection of diplomatic documents and narrative account of July crisis detailing maneuvers that led to outbreak of war; by student of Fischer. With Fischer 47.338, 47.375, argues German policy decisive and determined primarily by domestic considerations and assorted complexes. Abridged and revised translation of 1963–64 work. [SM/RFW/DSC]

47.341 Georges Haupt. *Socialism and the Great War: the collapse of the Second International*. Oxford: Clarendon, 1972. ISBN 0-19-827184-0. ▸ Careful, specialized examination of sudden 1914 disintegration of rhetorical internationalism. Attributes this to fatalism, powerlessness, and integration of moderate socialists into ordered society. Argues war delayed revolution. [SM]

47.342 Cameron Hazlehurst. *Politicians at war, July 1914 to May 1915: a prologue to the triumph of Lloyd George*. New York: Knopf, 1971. ISBN 0-394-44122-2. ▸ Scholarly study of cabinet decision making about coming and conduct of war in Asquith precoalition premiership. Defends Churchill and Lloyd George; British interests, not Belgium, mandated British entry into war. [SM]

47.343 F. H. Hinsley, ed. *British foreign policy under Sir Edward Grey*. Cambridge: Cambridge University Press, 1977. ISBN 0-521-12347-9. ▸ Essays of varying quality carefully examining adjustment to changing international situation, 1905–14, and subordination of traditional diplomacy to needs of war policy, 1914–16. Based on archival research. [SM/BJCM]

47.344 James Joll. *The origins of the First World War*. 2d ed. London: Longman, 1992. ISBN 0-582-08920-4. ▸ Thoughtful, superbly written synthesis stressing factors, not countries and crises. Examines alliances, militarism, domestic politics, economics, imperialism, and prevailing mood without choosing a single causative factor. Classic work for students and scholars alike. [SM/DSC]

47.345 John F. V. Keiger. *France and the origins of the First World War*. New York: St. Martin's, 1983. ISBN 0-312-30292-4. ▸ Introductory survey sketching French policy after 1870, dwelling on President Poincaré's diplomacy, Franco-Prussian alliance, and French decision making. Concludes sensibly that his policy led to rigidification of alliances but otherwise France followed, not led, events. [SM/MMF]

47.346 Paul M. Kennedy, ed. *The war plans of the great powers, 1880–1914*. London: Allen & Unwin, 1979. ISBN 0-04-940056-8. ▸ Uneven essays on aspects of strategic planning by and among powers. Stresses lack of realism, coherence, and coordination and decisive importance of Schlieffen plan. For more extensive works see Ritter 47.403, Showalter 31.204, and Williamson 47.361. [SM/DSC]

47.347 Laurence Lafore. *The long fuse: an interpretation of the origins of World War I*. Philadelphia: Lippincott, 1965. ▸ Clear, well-written survey based on secondary literature and focusing on southeastern Europe, especially Austria and Serbia. Rejects Fischer thesis (47.338, 47.375) and downplays German responsibility. [SM]

47.348 John W. Langdon. *July 1914: the long debate, 1918–1990*. New York: Berg; distributed by St. Martin's, 1991. ISBN 0-85496-880-3. ▸ Well-written, compact analysis of controversy over origins of war down to 1990. Though not comprehensive, discusses viewpoints and contributions dispassionately, arguing that debate, while owing much to Fischer (47.338, 47.375), has gone beyond him. [PWS/DSC]

47.349 Dwight E. Lee. *Europe's crucial years: the diplomatic background of World War I, 1902–1914*. Hanover, N.H.: University Press of New England for Clark University Press, 1974. ISBN 0-87451-094-5. ▸ Readable general synthesis of diplomatic revolution. Points to Franco-German territorial and Anglo-German naval tension in West, Austro-Russian Balkan rivalry in East. [SM]

47.350 D.C.B. Lieven. *Russia and the origins of the First World War*. New York: St. Martin's, 1983. ISBN 0-312-69608-6 (cl), 0-312-69611-6 (pbk). ▸ Introductory survey of Russian policy and groups influencing it. Refutes Turner 47.359 concerning Russian mobilization, stresses Russia's reluctance, sensibly assigning primary responsibility to Germany. [SM]

47.351 Arthur J. Marder. *The road to war, 1904–1914*. Vol. 1 of *From the Dreadnought to Scapa Flow: the Royal Navy in the Fisher era, 1904–1919*. London: Oxford University Press, 1961. ▸ Scholarly study of British aspects of Anglo-German naval rivalry. Concludes Britain viewed German seapower as aimed at world hegemony, thus threat and key factor poisoning Anglo-German relations. [SM]

47.352 Steven E. Miller, Sean M. Lynn-Jones, and Stephen Van Evera, eds. *Military strategy and the origins of the First World War*. Rev. ed. Princeton: Princeton University Press, 1991. ISBN 0-691-02349-2 (pbk). ▸ Uneven collection of essays examining various theses, including "cult of the offensive" and theory of inadvertence. Contains various challenges to standard viewpoints on role of military plans and doctrines. [SM]

47.353 John Anthony Moses. *The politics of illusion: the Fischer controversy in German historiography*. New York: Barnes & Noble, 1975. ISBN 0-06-495000-X. ▸ Examination of German debate over Fischer revolution in German historiography and also relationship between historiography and politics. Sympathetic to Fischer who, he argues, destroyed German statist tradition and orthodoxy. [SM]

47.354 Joachim Remak. *The origins of World War I, 1871–1914*. New York: Holt, Rinehart & Winston, 1967. ▸ Brief, erratic entry-level survey of key factors and crises. Rejects Fischer thesis (47.338, 47.375), placing primary responsibility on Austria and Serbia and secondary emphasis on Russia and Germany, noting alliances, militarism, and lack of imagination. [SM]

47.355 Andrew Rossos. *Russia and the Balkans: inter-Balkan rivalries and Russian foreign policy, 1908–1914*. Toronto: University of Toronto Press, 1981. ISBN 0-8020-5516-8. ▸ Specialized examination of Russian policy and that of Balkan states, especially on Macedonian question. Argues new Russian dominance, blocking Austria, evaporated owing to weak policy in Second Balkan War. Most recent in distinguished line of books on Balkan wars; good bibliography. [SM/NR/GS]

47.356 Bernd F. Schulte. *Vor dem Kriegsausbruch, 1914: Deutschland, die Türkei, und der Balkan*. Düsseldorf: Droste, 1980. ISBN 3-7700-0574-0. ▸ Argues that Turkish defeat in Balkan wars forced German reassessment, delaying showdown with France and Russia. Sees more effective civil-military cooperation in Germany than other authors. [SM]

47.357 Zara S. Steiner. *Britain and the origins of the First World War*. New York: St. Martin's, 1977. ISBN 0-312-09818-9 (cl), 0-312-09819-7 (pbk). ▸ Introductory examination of domestic politics, diplomats, and Britain's relations with other powers. Argues Britain passive and bore little responsibility for war, but responded to perceived German threat. [SM]

47.358 Edward C. Thaden. *Russia and the Balkan alliance of 1912*. University Park: Pennsylvania State University Press, 1965. ▸ Specialized study of Russia's role in anti-Turkish alliance. Concludes Russian policy was cautious, realistic, limited, and more anti-Austrian than anti-Turkish. [SM]

47.359 L.C.F. Turner. *Origins of the First World War*. New York: Norton, 1970. ISBN 0-393-09947-4 (pbk). ▸ Acerbic, controversial survey of 1909–14, stressing tragedy of miscalculations. Rejects Fischer 47.338, 47.375, assigning primary responsibility to Russia's growing military power and decision to mobilize its army. [SM]

47.360 Samuel R. Williamson, Jr. *Austria-Hungary and the origins of the First World War*. New York: St. Martin's, 1991. ISBN 0-312-05239-1 (cl), 0-312-05283-9 (pbk). ▸ Able study of Austrian policy formulation and diplomacy in July crisis. Assigns larger role to Austria than others do, but blames Russia for enlarging war, and concludes Austria acted to end perceived Serbian threat. [SM/JWB]

47.361 Samuel R. Williamson, Jr. *The politics of grand strategy: Britain and France prepare for war, 1910–1914*. 1969 ed. London: Ashfield, 1990. ISBN 0-948660-13-9 (pbk). ▸ Careful study of strategic-political interplay in development, consolidation, and war preparations of Entente. Concludes this diplomatic revolution benefited both Britain and France and shaped British prewar policy in favor of France and postwar policy against France. [SM]

SEE ALSO
33.684 Vladimir Dedijer. *The road to Sarajevo*.
33.748 John D. Treadway. *The falcon and the eagle*.

War Aims and Diplomacy

47.362 Bernd Bonwetsch. *Kriegsallianz und Wirtschaftsinteressen: Russland in den Wirtschaftsplänen Englands und Frankreichs, 1914–1917*. Dusseldorf: Bertelsmann Universitätsverlag, 1973. ISBN 3-571-09070-3. ▸ Scholarly monograph tracing Anglo-French efforts to supplant Germany as Russia's major supplier. Attributes failure to tsarist resistance and progressive Anglo-French economic deterioration. [SM]

47.363 Robert E. Bunselmeyer. *The cost of the war, 1914–1919: British economic war aims and the origin of reparations*. Hamden, Conn.: Archon, 1975. ISBN 0-208-01551-5. ▸ Careful examination of wartime origins of British reparations policy and economic aims in political, Allied, and dominion contexts. Argues Article 231 expressed moral outrage and economic anxiety. [SM]

47.364 Kathleen Burk. *Britain, America, and the sinews of war, 1914–1918*. Boston: Allen & Unwin, 1985. ISBN 0-04-940076-2. ▸ Scholarly examination of transformation wrought by British economic and financial dependence on United States. Concludes consequently postwar America had power but lacked responsibility, whereas inverse true for Britain. [SM]

47.365 Briton Cooper Busch. *Britain, India, and the Arabs, 1914–1921*. Berkeley: University of California Press, 1971. ISBN 0-520-01821-4. ▸ Exploration of (British) Indian and Cairene factors in Britain's Middle Eastern policy. Argues government of India impeded development of unified coherent policy. Also examines World War I Mesopotamian campaign and postwar policy in Iraq. [SM/RS]

47.366 Kenneth J. Calder. *Britain and the origins of the new Europe, 1914–1918*. Cambridge: Cambridge University Press, 1976. ISBN 0-521-20897-1. ▸ Scholarly examination of British conduct toward Polish, Czech, and Yugoslavian movements. Argues policy of secondary importance to Britain, evolved in response to military situation. [SM]

47.367 Madeleine Chi. *China diplomacy, 1914–1918*. Cambridge, Mass.: Harvard University, East Asian Research Center; distributed by Harvard University Press, 1970. (Harvard East Asian monographs, 31.) ISBN 0-674-11825-1. ▸ Pioneering study tracing China's struggle against wartime encroachments. Attributes failure to disorganization, Anglo-American ignorance and lack of cooperation, and Allied need for Japanese aid. [SM]

47.368 Alexander Dallin et al. *Russian diplomacy and Eastern Europe, 1914–1917*. New York: King's Crown, 1963. ▸ Essays of varying quality on Russian policy toward borderlands. Describes tsarist diplomacy as confused and contradictory with much subordinated to ambiguous Straits policy. [SM]

47.369 Richard K. Debo. *Revolution and survival: the foreign pol-*

icy of Soviet Russia, 1917–18. Toronto: University of Toronto Press, 1979. ISBN 0-8020-5411-0. ‣ Substantial scholarly examination of first year of bolshevik policy in its wartime and revolutionary setting. Attributes bolshevik survival to Lenin's primacy, realism, adaptability, and genius (despite utopian errors). [SM]

47.370 Charles Howard Ellis. *The British "intervention" in Transcaspia, 1918–1919.* Berkeley: University of California Press, 1963. ‣ Specialist exploration of ramifications of British military interventions in Caucasus and Transcaspia. Argues Britain acted against a Turko-German threat to India and Afghanistan, not primarily against bolshevism. [SM]

47.371 L. L. Farrar, Jr. *Divide and conquer: German efforts to conclude a separate peace, 1914–1918.* Boulder: East European Quarterly; distributed by Columbia University Press, 1978. ISBN 0-914710-38-9. ‣ Summary recapitulation of Germany's efforts to reduce number of its enemies and related issues. Argues dividing Entente was major German goal en route to European hegemony and world power. [SM]

47.372 L. L. Farrar, Jr. *The short-war illusion: German policy, strategy, and domestic affairs, August-December 1914.* Santa Barbara: ABC-Clio, 1973. ISBN 0-87436-118-4 (cl), 0-87436-119-2 (pbk). ‣ Survey of policy and power within German and European contexts. Says German policies and balance of power rendered short war unlikely, but long war made peace improbable, causing efforts to split Entente. [SM]

47.373 Oleh S. Fedyshyn. *Germany's drive to the East and the Ukrainian Revolution, 1917–1918.* New Brunswick, N.J.: Rutgers University Press, 1971. ISBN 0-8135-0677-8. ‣ Best available analysis of German plans for and occupation policy in Ukraine and Crimea. Concludes venture was confused, improvised, and largely failed despite Ukraine's satellite status. [SM]

47.374 Wilfried Fest. *Peace or partition; the Habsburg monarchy and British policy, 1914–1918.* New York: St. Martin's, 1978. ISBN 0-312-59935-8. ‣ Detailed study of British efforts toward separate Austrian peace and role of pressure groups and military crises in shift toward dismemberment. Though latter was second choice, Britain played substantial role in its realization. Much useful information, but lacks both strong thesis and systematic conclusions. [SM/JWB]

47.375 Fritz Fischer. *Germany's aims in the First World War.* New York: Norton, 1967. ISBN 0-393-05347-4 (cl), 0-393-09798-6 (pbk). ‣ Abridged translation of seminal, controversial work (*Griff nach der Weltmacht*) dominating twentieth-century German historiography. Controversy following publication focused on introductory chapters which argued Chancellor Bethmann Hollweg deliberately risked war and bears much responsibility for its outbreak. [SM/RFW]

47.376 W. B. Fowler. *British-American relations, 1917–1918: the role of Sir William Wiseman.* Princeton: Princeton University Press, 1969. ISBN 0-691-04594-1. ‣ Careful study addressing diplomacy of co-belligerency, focusing on link between two powers. Concludes President Wilson's policies, well elaborated by British ambassador Wiseman to Whitehall, were flexible and realistic. [SM]

47.377 David French. *British strategy and war aims, 1914–1916.* London: Allen & Unwin, 1986. ISBN 0-04-942197-2. ‣ Provocative, persuasive study of link between military policy and war aims of Asquith's cabinets. Argues Britain meant to act as financier and supplier to allies with new mass army reserved for use after military exhaustion of allies and enemies. Britain sought security against its allies but exhausted its assets, becoming dependent upon America. [SM]

47.378 Isaiah Friedman. *The question of Palestine: British-Jewish-*Arab relations, 1914–1918.* 2d ed. New Brunswick, N.J.: Transaction, 1992. ISBN 0-88738-214-2. ‣ Important study of British policy culminating in Balfour Declaration. Pro-British and pro-Zionist, defends Sykes-Picot, declares Liberal aims not annexationist, British hands clean, and Britain's policy directed against Germany and Turkey. [SM]

47.379 Wolfgang-Uwe Friedrich. *Bulgarien und die Mächte, 1913–1915: ein Beitrag zur Weltkriegs und Imperialismusgeschichte.* Stuttgart: Steiner, 1985. ISBN 3-515-04050-1. ‣ Thorough, scholarly, somewhat pedantic account of intense prewar and wartime competition for Bulgaria. Final outcome result of Bulgarian irredentism, Serbian intransigence, Turkish compromise, and German military and political skill. [PWS]

47.380 David Fromkin. *A peace to end all peace: creating the modern Middle East, 1914–1922.* New York: Holt, 1989. ISBN 0-8050-0857-8. ‣ Detailed survey of Turkish war and peace focused on Churchill (secretary of state for war and air) and European decision making. Argues *de facto* 1922 settlement based on nineteenth-century thinking derived from Sykes's plan and obsolete before it took effect. [SM]

47.381 Paul Guinn. *British strategy and politics, 1914 to 1918.* Oxford: Clarendon, 1965. ‣ Well-written analysis of British grand strategy in relation to war aims, domestic politics, and tactical situations. Vigorous determination gained victory but not Britain's aims. [SM]

47.382 Harry Hanak. *Great Britain and Austria-Hungary during the First World War: a study in the formation of public opinion.* London: Oxford University Press, 1962. ‣ Sophisticated study of propaganda of British intellectuals and Czechoslovak and Yugoslav emigrés toward breakup of Austria-Hungary. Argues their efforts helped bring divided British cabinet to accept dismemberment. [SM]

47.383 Stephan M. Horak. *The first treaty of World War I: Ukraine's treaty with the central powers of February 9, 1918.* Boulder: East European Monographs; distributed by Columbia University Press, 1988. ISBN 0-88033-133-X. ‣ Best available study of establishment of Ukrainian state and treaty of Brest-Litovsk. Attributes failure of treaty to German domination, Allied nonrecognition, Soviet hostility, Polish attack, Russian civil war, and weak leadership. [SM]

47.384 Kalervo Hovi. *Cordon sanitaire or barrière de l'est: the emergence of the new French Eastern European alliance policy, 1917–1919.* Turku: Turun Yliopisto; distributed by Akateeminen Kirjakauppa, 1975. ISBN 951-641-245-9. ‣ Specialist examination of development of French policy after Bolshevik Revolution in balance-of-power terms. Argues French alliances primarily against Germany, not Russia. [SM]

47.385 Barry Hunt and Adrian Preston, eds. *War aims and strategic policy in the Great War, 1914–1918.* Totowa, N.J.: Rowman & Littlefield, 1977. ISBN 0-87471-872-4. ‣ Collection of essays of varying quality examining extent to which aims guided strategy of major powers. Good synthesis of Fischer's argument on this issue (47.338, 47.375). [SM]

47.386 Karl-Heinz Janssen. *Der Kanzler und der General: der Führungskrise um Bethmann Hollweg und Falkenhayn, 1914–1916.* Göttingen: Musterschmidt, 1967. ‣ Scholarly examination of conflict between strategy and diplomacy in pursuit of German aims and separate peace. Concludes dismissal of Falkenhayn as chief of staff led to that of Bethmann Hollweg and to defeat. [SM]

47.387 Karl-Heinz Janssen. *Macht und Verblendung: Kriegsziel-politik der deutschen Bundesstaaten, 1914/18.* Göttingen: Musterschmidt, 1963. ‣ Controversial discussion of role of larger German states in shaping war aims. Disputes Fischer 47.338, 47.375, defends Bethmann Hollweg, and maintains federal character of *Reich* rendered war of conquest impossible. [SM]

47.388 André Kaspi. *Le temps des Americains: le concours americain à la France en 1917–1918*. Paris: Publications de la Sorbonne, 1976. ISBN 2-85944-000-3. ▸ Detailed study of American entry into war and impact on France. Concludes that United States pursued own interests, was militarily decisive, and had peace program which only French Socialists endorsed. [SM]

47.389 Elie Kedourie. *In the Anglo-Arab labyrinth: the McMahon-Husayn correspondence and its interpretations, 1914–1939*. Cambridge: Cambridge University Press, 1976. ISBN 0-521-20826-2. ▸ Highly specialized, chronological study of origins, text, effects, and interpretations of 1915–16 British commitment to Arab independence. Argues ambiguous British Middle Eastern promises did not conflict, despite later guilt feelings affecting policy. [SM]

47.390 Marian Kent, ed. *The great powers and the end of the Ottoman empire*. London: Allen & Unwin, 1984. ISBN 0-04-956013-1. ▸ Useful essays covering 1900–23 and organized by European powers. Consensus that responsibility for empire's collapse should be shared by great powers and Ottomans. [SM]

47.391 Michael Kettle. *The Allies and the Russian collapse, March 1917–March 1918*. Vol. 1 of *Russia and the Allies, 1917–1920*. Minneapolis: University of Minnesota Press, 1981. ISBN 0-8166-0981-0. ▸ Account of British efforts to cope with Russian revolutions and keep Russia in war. Concludes Brest-Litovsk Treaty signaled Allied failure. [SM]

47.392 George B. Leon (Leontaritis). *Greece and the great powers, 1914–1917*. Thessalonike: Institute for Balkan Studies, 1974. ▸ Massive, balanced, and heavily researched pioneering account of diplomatic maneuverings during Greece's supposed neutrality. Concludes no power behaved honorably and documents Constantine's German ties. [SM]

47.393 George B. Leon (Leontaritis). *Greece and the First World War: from neutrality to intervention, 1917–1918*. Boulder: East European Monographs; distributed by Columbia University Press, 1990. ISBN 0-88033-181-X. ▸ Scholarly study of domestic and international factors affecting Greece's role. Critical of Venizelos's policy as overly ambitious and dependent on Allies. [SM]

47.394 Horst Günther Linke. *Das zarische Russland und der erste Weltkrieg: Diplomatie und Kriegsziele, 1914–1917*. Munich: Fink, 1982. ISBN 3-7705-2051-3. ▸ General survey of tsarist wartime diplomacy. Argues that political, administrative, economic, and financial constraints inhibited pursuit of hegemonic goals in central and southeastern Europe. [SM]

47.395 Peter Lowe. *Great Britain and Japan, 1911–15: a study of British Far Eastern policy*. New York: St. Martin's, 1969. ▸ Scholarly study of role of Anglo-Japanese alliance in Britain's Asian policy. Stresses growing disharmony as Japan became stronger, Britain weaker, and revolutionary China became an issue. [SM]

47.396 Arthur J. May. *The passing of the Habsburg monarchy*. 2 vols. Philadelphia: University of Pennsylvania Press, 1966. ▸ Massive examination of death throes of great power. Attributes dissolution to nationalism; Magyar intransigence; weak leaders; Russian revolutions; Allied diplomacy, war aims, and propaganda; and especially lost war. Based on wide reading and control of sources, but sometimes dated and questionable in interpretation. Especially useful for survey of press opinion during war. [SM/JWB]

47.397 Alexander S. Mitrakos. *France in Greece during World War I: a study in the politics of power*. Boulder: East European Monographs; distributed by Columbia University Press, 1982. (East European monographs, 101.) ISBN 0-914710-95-8. ▸ Narrow study of goals and conduct of French diplomacy, 1915–17, based on French archives. Revisionist assessment of Constantine

and Venizelos. Argues France opposed alliance with Greece, preferring docile neutrality, but even coercion failed to yield control. [SM]

47.398 Keith Neilson. *Strategy and supply: the Anglo-Russian alliance, 1914–17*. London: Allen & Unwin, 1984. ISBN 0-04-940072-X. ▸ Competent analysis of British wartime policy formulation toward pre-Soviet Russia. Defends lords Grey and Kitchener, attacks Lloyd George, and argues that Britain's Russian policy dictated by military necessity. [SM]

47.399 William J. Olson. *Anglo-Iranian relations during World War I*. London: Cass, 1984. ISBN 0-7146-3178-7. ▸ Addresses Britain's reluctant involvement in Persian realities. Argues resultant frustration arose from sweeping victory and Persian resistance but British interests survived ineffectual policy. [SM]

47.400 Melvin E. Page, ed. *Africa and the First World War*. London: Macmillan, 1987. ISBN 0-333-40619-2. ▸ Essays addressing African responses to white man's war and implications for imperial future. Concludes war generally led more to collaboration than to rebellion. Uneven but best available work. [SM]

47.401 Richard Georg Plaschka and Karlheinz Mack, eds. *Die Auflösung des Habsburgreiches: Zusammenbruch und Neuorientierung im Donauraum*. Vienna: Geschichte und Politik, 1970. (Schriftenreihe der Österreichischen Ost und Sudosteuropa-Instituts, 3.) ▸ Symposium on collapse of Habsburg monarchy and emergence of successor states. Reinforces standard view of interaction between internal and external factors. [SM]

47.402 Olav Riste. *The neutral ally: Norway's relations with belligerent powers in the First World War*. Oslo: Universitets Forlaget, 1965. ▸ Pioneering study tracing prosperous neutrality, 1914–16, and its eclipse, 1916–18, owing to British blockade. Criticizes Norwegian diplomacy, asserting only Wilson's insistence rendered neutrality precariously feasible. [SM]

47.403 Gerhard Ritter. *The tragedy of statesmanship: Bethmann Hollweg as war chancellor, 1914–1917*. Vol. 3 of *The sword and the scepter: the problem of militarism in Germany*. Heinz Norden, trans. Coral Gables, Fla.: University of Miami Press, 1972. ISBN 0-87024-182-6. ▸ Massive study of relationship between politics and war in Second Reich. Classic German nationalist rebuttal to Fischer 47.338, 47.375 regarding German war aims. [SM]

47.404 Victor Rothwell. *British war aims and peace diplomacy, 1914–1918*. Oxford: Clarendon, 1971. ISBN 0-19-822349-8. ▸ Somewhat disorganized study of why British leaders thought Germany's defeat necessary and how they tried to detach its allies. Argues latter effort was chimerical, but Britain achieved its limited aims, securing Britain and its empire. [SM]

47.405 Hugh Seton-Watson and Christopher Seton-Watson. *The making of a new Europe: R.W. Seton-Watson and the last years of Austria-Hungary*. Seattle: University of Washington Press, 1981. ISBN 0-295-95792-1. ▸ Narrowly specialized study of role of propaganda and influence in shaping policy and creating Czechoslovakia, Yugoslavia, and greater Romania. Attributes Austrian collapse to war, Italian factor, and Seton-Watson's indirect influence. [SM]

47.406 Gerard E. Silberstein. *The troubled alliance: German-Austrian relations, 1914 to 1917*. Lexington: University Press of Kentucky, 1970. ISBN 0-8131-1196-X. ▸ Systematic examination of Austro-German policies regarding Balkan coalition. Argues Austrian thinking more subtle while German more realistic and usually dominant. [SM]

47.407 Daniel M. Smith. *The great departure: the United States and World War I, 1914–1920*. New York: Wiley, 1965. ISBN 0-471-80006-6. ▸ Clear, entry-level survey of America's debut as great power. Focuses on dealings with Allies. Concludes 1920 represented only temporary setback to Wilsonian internationalism. [SM]

47.408 Georges-Henri Soutou. *L'or et le sang: les buts de guerre économiques de la première guerre mondiale.* Paris: Fayard, 1989. ISBN 2-213-02215-1. ▸ Pathbreaking, fascinating analysis of economic war aims of Germany, France, Britain, and United States. Many important revisionist theses (e.g., that Germany never really abandoned liberal economics for autarchy, that Allies aimed at draconian economic peace throughout war) backed by massive research. [PWS]

47.409 Wolfgang Steglich. *Die Friedenspolitik der Mittelmächte, 1917/18.* Wiesbaden: Steiner, 1964. ▸ Detailed, factual analysis of Austro-German offers of negotiated peace, December 1916 to March 1918. Disputes Fischer 47.338, 47.375, arguing Germany had security and then peace policy, not war aims policy. [SM]

47.410 Leonard Stein. *The Balfour Declaration.* New York: Simon & Schuster, 1961. ▸ Detailed study of Palestine question, 1914–20, chiefly in British terms. Argues British rivalry with France and then first Russian Revolution aided Zionist cause. [SM]

47.411 David Stevenson. *The First World War and international politics.* Oxford: Oxford University Press, 1988. ISBN 0-19-873049-7. ▸ General factual survey of wartime diplomacy and brief discussion of peace settlement. Studies dynamics of coalition diplomacy, concluding war was product of international system and accomplished little good. [SM]

47.412 David Stevenson. *French war aims against Germany, 1914–1919.* Oxford: Clarendon, 1982. ISBN 0-19-822574-1. ▸ Important, detailed study of elaboration of France's goals by civilian leaders, especially Premier Clemenceau. Concludes cost was high and results meager because French concern for security encountered dominant Anglo-American preference for stabilization. [SM/MMF]

47.413 Wiktor Sukiennicki. *East Central Europe during World War I: from foreign domination to national independence.* 2 vols. Maciej Siekierski, ed. Boulder: East European Monographs; distributed by Columbia University Press, 1984. (East European monographs, 119.) ISBN 0-88033-012-0 (set). ▸ Massive, dispassionate, pioneering study by Lithuanian of all wartime schemes for eastern borderlands. Concludes November 1918 power vacuum nullified plans of victors and losers alike. [SM]

47.414 Jan Karl Tanenbaum. *France and the Arab Middle East, 1914–1920.* Philadelphia: American Philosophical Society, 1978. (Transactions of the American Philosophical Society, 68.7.) ISBN 0-87169-687-8, ISSN 0065-9746. ▸ Delineates France's Middle Eastern policies to explain how it gained Syria and Lebanon. Concludes France did so by military force only after policies of Britain, France, and Faisal had failed. [SM]

47.415 David F. Trask. *The United States in the Supreme War Council: American war aims and inter-Allied strategy, 1917–1918.* 1961 ed. Westport, Conn.: Greenwood, 1978. ISBN 0-313-20009-8. ▸ Careful consideration of American diplomatic and military policy vis-à-vis Allies. Maintains Wilson successfully pursued coherent policy toward victory and retained diplomatic independence. [SM]

47.416 Ulrich Trumpener. *Germany and the Ottoman empire, 1914–1918.* Princeton: Princeton University Press, 1968. ▸ Scholarly examination of nature and results of Germany's wartime Turkish policies. Germany was less than dominant before and during war owing to Turkish resistance; alliance was improvised, not planned. Contra Fischer 47.338, 47.375. [SM]

47.417 Richard H. Ullman. *Intervention and the war.* Vol. 1 of *Anglo-Soviet relations, 1917–1921.* Princeton: Princeton University Press, 1961. ▸ Specialized examination of British policy

toward Bolsheviks from March Revolution to Armistice. Argues British domination of Allied policy produced halfhearted attempt to solve political problem by military means. [SM]

47.418 Betty M. Unterberger. *The United States, revolutionary Russia, and the rise of Czechoslovakia.* Chapel Hill: University of North Carolina Press, 1989. ISBN 0-8078-1853-4. ▸ Study of American intervention in Siberia to rescue Czech Legion in broad European and Asian contexts. Attributes reluctant Wilsonian intervention to Czech plight and potential Japanese imperialism. [SM/HLA]

47.419 Leo Valiani. *The end of Austria-Hungary.* Eric Mosbacher, trans. New York: Knopf; distributed by Random House, 1973. ISBN 0-394-46641-1. ▸ Discussion of diplomacy of nationalist movements within wartime Austria-Hungary, especially role of Hungary and Italy. Acute analysis of empire's collapse with special attention to role of Italy and Italians in ethnic conflicts that paralleled war. Excellent endnotes. Attributes disintegration to democracy, demography, defeat, and Austro-Hungarian passivity, internally and externally. [SM/JWB]

47.420 Rex A. Wade. *The Russian search for peace, February–October 1917.* Stanford, Calif.: Stanford University Press, 1969. ISBN 0-8047-0707-3. ▸ Highly specialized analysis of efforts of moderate Socialists to save their revolution through diplomacy. Allied resistance to negotiated peace and Russian halfheartedness were crucial to bolshevik victory. [SM]

47.421 Arthur Walworth. *America's moment, 1918: American diplomacy at the end of World War I.* New York: Norton, 1977. ISBN 0-393-05591-4. ▸ Well-written study of peak of American influence, sympathetic to Colonel House. Attributes decline to Allied resistance, waning popular enthusiasm, American disorganization and inexperience, and Wilson's political difficulties and wartime oratory. [SM]

47.422 Frank G. Weber. *Eagles on the crescent: Germany, Austria, and the diplomacy of the Turkish alliance, 1914–1918.* Ithaca, N.Y.: Cornell University Press, 1970. ISBN 0-8014-0566-1. ▸ Careful study of alliance, portraying it as reluctant German expedient advocated by Austria and Turkey, which caused Austro-German dissension and was self-defeating at best. [SM]

47.423 Z.A.B. Zeman. *The break-up of the Habsburg empire, a study in national and social revolution.* 1961 ed. New York: Octagon Books, 1977. ISBN 0-374-98847-1. ▸ Careful, impartial examination of internal and external pressures leading to collapse. Argues nationalist movements, exile organizations, and Habsburg irresolution were more decisive than early 1918 Allied encouragement. [SM]

47.424 Z.A.B. Zeman. *The gentlemen negotiators: a diplomatic history of World War I.* New York: Macmillan, 1971. ▸ Well-written general history of wartime diplomacy, moving from capital to capital and sketching strategic-diplomatic interplay. Depicts collapse of Europe's "old diplomacy" under pressures of war and Wilson. [SM]

Peace Settlement

47.425 Lloyd E. Ambrosius. *Woodrow Wilson and the American diplomatic tradition: the treaty fight in perspective.* Cambridge: Cambridge University Press, 1987. ISBN 0-521-33453-5. ▸ Synthetic analysis of Wilson's engagement with League of Nations question, 1916–20. Redefines internationalist-isolationist debate as interdependence-pluralism. Argues that despite dualism and intellectual fallacies, Wilson's legacy had lasting influence. [SM]

47.426 Christopher M. Andrew and A. S. Kanya-Forstner. *The climax of French imperial expansion, 1914–1924.* Stanford, Calif.: Stanford University Press, 1981. ISBN 0-8047-1101-1. ▸ Penetrating analysis of expansion of French empire despite clear lack of interest by most Frenchmen. Argues primacy of continental over colonial concerns both helped and hindered imperial cause while both fostered tension with Britain. [SM/JSH]

47.427 J.F.N. Bradley. *Allied intervention in Russia, 1917–1920.* 1968 ed. Lanham, Md.: University Press of America, 1984. ISBN 0-8191-3849-5 (pbk). ▸ Compact general survey of Entente policy against Bolsheviks. Attributes failure to lateness, poor planning, attachment to losing causes, military weakness, diverse aims, and Allied rivalries. [SM]

47.428 George A. Brinkley. *The volunteer army and Allied intervention in South Russia: a study in the politics and diplomacy of the Russian civil war.* Notre Dame, Ind.: University of Notre Dame Press, 1966. ▸ Analysis of relationship between Russian domestic upheaval and context of foreign involvement. Concludes intervention failed from inadequacy, muddle, Allied division, and weakness of general who led anti-bolshevik forces. [SM]

47.429 Briton Cooper Busch. *Mudros to Lausanne: Britain's frontier in West Asia, 1918–1923.* Albany: State University of New York Press, 1976. ISBN 0-87395-265-0. ▸ Model study of British security dilemmas along lifeline to India, post–World War I. Helpful in understanding fears of decision makers. Argues Britain failed to impose its desires on Turkey, 1915–22, and reduced its dominance to Arab areas in Armenia, Persia, and Kurdistan. Good command of archival sources; clearly written. [SM/JSH]

47.430 John Darwin. *Britain, Egypt, and the Middle East: imperial policy in the aftermath of war, 1918–1922.* New York: St. Martin's, 1981. ISBN 0-312-09736-0. ▸ Using British sources, traces start of Britain's imperial decline more a withdrawal from advanced wartime positions than retreat before nationalism. Lloyd George's government applied traditional policies and assumptions regardless of altered circumstances. [SM/JSH]

47.431 Roger Dingman. *Power in the Pacific: the origins of naval arms limitation, 1914–1922.* Chicago: University of Chicago Press, 1976. ISBN 0-226-15331-2. ▸ Ambitious, thoughtful analysis of role of British, Japanese, and American diplomacy and domestic politics in achieving arms limitation. Domestic considerations were decisive in each capital. Valuable complement to Buckley 48.83. [SM]

47.432 Michael L. Dockrill and J. Douglas Goold. *Peace without promise: Britain and the peace conferences, 1919–23.* Hamden, Conn.: Archon, 1981. ISBN 0-208-01909-X. ▸ General survey of formulation of high policy by principal leaders regarding entire settlement, including Lausanne Treaty. Concludes British goals traditional and largely unachieved. [SM]

47.433 George W. Egerton. *Great Britain and the creation of the League of Nations: strategy, politics, and international organization, 1914–1919.* Chapel Hill: University of North Carolina Press, 1978. ISBN 0-8078-1320-6. ▸ Excellent, specialized examination of Britain's wartime strategic debate about international organization and role in its realization. Argues Prime Minister Lloyd George tolerated Wilson's scheme provided the president cooperated elsewhere, but disliked resultant League. [SM]

47.434 Howard Elcock. *Portrait of a decision: the Council of Four and the Treaty of Versailles.* London: Methuen, 1972. ISBN 0-413-28370-4. ▸ Chronological account of Paris Peace Conference, November 1918 to June 1919. Defends Versailles treaty as compromise solution and thus not responsible for all ills of next decade. [SM]

47.435 Inga Floto. *Colonel House in Paris: a study of American policy at the Paris Peace Conference, 1919.* 1973 ed. Princeton: Princeton University Press, 1980. ISBN 0-691-04662-X. ▸ Detailed examination of Wilson's adviser, Edward M. House, within broader context of American policy. Sees House as diplomati-

cally inept, duped by Premier Clemenceau, and disloyal to President Wilson. [SM]

47.436 Paul C. Helmreich. *From Paris to Sevres: the partition of the Ottoman empire at the peace conference of 1919–1920.* Columbus: Ohio State University Press, 1974. ISBN 0-8142-0170-9. ▸ Best available study of Sèvres Treaty. Traces Allied diplomacy toward Turkey, 1915–20, using Western sources. Argues nineteenth-century imperial treaty to consolidate victory was stillborn owing to twentieth-century nationalism. [SM]

47.437 Harry N. Howard. *The King-Crane Commission: an American inquiry in the Middle East.* Beirut: Khayat, 1963. ▸ Pioneering, detailed examination of 1919 investigation of local wishes in Ottoman territories regarding Allies' mandatories. Concludes generally wise methods and recommendations came too late and were tragically overtaken by events. Also available in microfilm from Washington, D.C.: Library of Congress Photoduplication Service, 1986. [SM]

47.438 Lorna S. Jaffe. *The decision to disarm Germany: British policy toward postwar German disarmament, 1914–1919.* Boston: Allen & Unwin, 1985. ISBN 0-04-943034-3. ▸ Careful analysis of emergence of German disarmament as British goal and Lloyd George's pursuit of it. Argues domestic politics, strategic considerations, and war's impact were factors, as was search for lasting peace. [SM]

47.439 Dimitri Kitsikis. *Propagande et pressions en politique internationale: la Grèce et ses revendications à la conférence de la paix (1919–1920).* Paris: Presses Universitaires de France, 1963. (Publications de la Faculté des Lettres et Sciences Humaines de Paris, 9. Recherches: Travaux de l'Institut d'Histoire des Relations Internationales, 3.) ▸ Systematic study of propaganda campaign orchestrated by Prime Minister Venizelos in support of Greek claims. Treaty of Sèvres largely realized his dream of Greater Greece. Useful discussion of role of propaganda in diplomacy. [SM]

47.440 Dimitri Kitsikis. *La role des experts à la conférence de la paix de 1919: gestation d'une technocratie en politique internationale.* Ottawa, Ont.: Éditions de l'Université d'Ottawa, 1972. ▸ Valuable study of use and misuse of experts, especially British and American, at Paris conference. Concludes experts should not formulate policy as they are not politically responsible. [SM]

47.441 Peter Krüger. *Deutschland und die Reparationen, 1918/19: die Genesis des Reparationsproblems in Deutschland zwischen Waffenstillstand und Versailler Friedensschluss.* Stuttgart: Deusche Verlags-Anstalt, 1973. ▸ Specialized study of domestic origins of German reparations policy, including roles of industrial and financial circles and bureaucrats. Sees link between war guilt and reparations, self-delusion, and "continuity of error" in German outlook. [SM]

47.442 Warren F. Kuehl. *Seeking world order: the United States and international organization to 1920.* Nashville: Vanderbilt University Press, 1969. ISBN 0-8265-1137-6. ▸ Study of twentieth-century movement for international organization. Attributes American rejection to President Wilson's errors, especially including Article X, and Covenant's divergence from prevailing internationalist thought. [SM]

47.443 Ivo J. Lederer. *Yugoslavia at the Paris Peace Conference: a study in frontiermaking.* New Haven: Yale University Press, 1963. ▸ Authoritative, scholarly monograph, focusing on territorial problems in Yugoslavia's creation, 1918–20. Maintains great power failure to resolve matters forced Yugoslavia to accept Italian terms. [SM]

47.444 Antony Lentin. *Lloyd George, Woodrow Wilson, and the guilt of Germany: an essay in the pre-history of appeasement.* Baton Rouge: Louisiana State University Press, 1984. ISBN 0-8071-

1231-3. ▸ Study from British liberal viewpoint, tracing evolution of Wilsonian peace into Carthaginian peace, focusing on war-guilt clause. Clause evoked British sense of guilt, laying basis for appeasement. [SM]

47.445 N. Gordon Levin, Jr. *Woodrow Wilson and world politics: America's response to war and revolution.* 1968 ed. New York: Oxford University Press, 1970. ISBN 0-19-500803-0. ▸ Interpretive analysis of theory and practice of Wilsonian policy, 1917–19, chiefly regarding Leninist Russia and Weimar Germany. Concludes Wilson launched trend to anti-imperial, antisocialist liberal globalism. [SM]

47.446 Wm. Roger Louis. *Great Britain and Germany's lost colonies, 1914–1919.* Oxford: Clarendon, 1967. ▸ Analysis of Britain's conquest and acquisition of most of Germany's Asian and African colonies. Maintains Britain achieved primary war aims, ending German threat to empire and securing its future. [SM]

47.447 Alfred D. Low. *The Anschluss movement, 1918–1919, and the Paris Peace Conference.* Philadelphia: American Philosophical Society, 1974. (Memoirs of the American Philosophical Society, 103.) ISBN 0-87169-103-5, ISSN 0065-9738. ▸ Solid study based on extensive archival and secondary research. Addresses Anschluss question in terms of Austria, Germany, and peace conference. Argues earlier notification by Allies of prohibition of merger would have prevented or reduced controversy generated in 1919, and although Allies unanimously, but weakly, denied self-determination for strategic reasons, Anschluss would not have satisfied Germany. [SM/JWB]

47.448 C. J. Lowe and Michael L. Dockrill. *The mirage of power.* 3 vols. London: Routledge & Kegan Paul, 1972. ISBN 0-7100-7092-6 (v. 1), 0-7100-7093-4 (v. 2), 0-7100-7094-2 (v. 3). ▸ Massive, global study (with documents) of British policy before, during, and after World War I. Concludes it was fundamentally defensive, resulting in little profit and great loss especially of peace. [SM/NR]

47.449 Kay Lundgreen-Nielson. *The Polish problem at the Paris Peace Conference: a study of the policies of the great powers and the Poles, 1918–1919.* Alison Borch-Johansen, trans. Odense: Odense University Press, 1979. ISBN 87-7492-261-0. ▸ Excellent, authoritative, exhaustive multinational, multifaceted study. Argues Polish disunity and ties to France generated Anglo-American distrust. These, plus Allied lack of force in Eastern Europe, were determining. Excellent source for understanding Poland's position in interwar Europe. [SM/WLB]

47.450 Sally Marks. *Innocent abroad: Belgium at the Paris Peace Conference of 1919.* Chapel Hill: University of North Carolina Press, 1981. ISBN 0-8078-1451-2. ▸ Sympathetic account, narrowly focused on problem and role of Belgium before, during, and after conference. Argues Belgium was prisoner of British indifference, French imperialism, and own past, but became hinge of Anglo-French Entente. Impressive documentation on formulation of objectives, priorities, and conflicts of interest. [SM/WAF]

47.451 Arno J. Mayer. *Politics and diplomacy of peacemaking: containment and counterrevolution at Versailles, 1918–1919.* New York: Knopf, 1967. ▸ Massively researched study of impact of bolshevism, domestic politics, and Wilson-Lenin rivalry on peacemaking. Sympathetic to Lenin, hostile to President Wilson, and critical of settlement and counterrevolution. Questionable thesis. [SM/DSC]

47.452 Harold I. Nelson. *Land and power: British and Allied policy on Germany's frontiers, 1916–19.* 1963 ed. Newton Abbot, England: David & Charles, 1971. ISBN 0-7153-5243-1 (pbk). ▸ Able, specialized study addressing Britain's role in German territorial settlement. Contradictory British policy sought stronger France, stable borders, maintenance of Anglo-French-American unity, and politically acceptable settlement. [SM]

47.453 Ian H. Nish. *Alliance in decline: a study in Anglo-Japanese relations, 1908–23.* London: Athlone; distributed by Oxford University Press, 1972. ISBN 0-485-13133-1. ▸ Best available study of alliance's final decade. Attributes end to differences over China, British dissatisfaction at Japanese expansionism, danger to relations with Australia, Canada, and United States, and American intervention. [SM/NR]

47.454 Peter Pastor. *Hungary between Wilson and Lenin: the Hungarian Revolution of 1918–1919 and the Big Three.* Boulder: East European Quarterly; distributed by Columbia University Press, 1976. ISBN 0-914710-13-3. ▸ Account of Karolyi regime's relations with Big Three. Admires Karolyi and blames failure on Anglo-American aloofness. [SM/SBV]

47.455 D. S. Perman. *The shaping of the Czechoslovak state: diplomatic history of the boundaries of Czechoslovakia, 1914–1920.* Leiden: Brill, 1962. ▸ Authoritative study of diplomatic origins of Czechoslovakia and Czech-Allied relations at peace conference. Argues Czech territorial success arose from extraneous factors. Detailed history of process through which decisions were made. [SM/HLA]

47.456 N. Petsalis-Diomidis. *Greece at the Paris Peace Conference, 1919.* Thessalonike: Institute for Balkan Studies, 1978. ▸ Heavily researched examination of Greek efforts to eliminate and replace Ottoman empire. Argues Prime Minister Venizelos was Britain's cat's-paw until support for Greece, outgunned by Turkey, became too costly. [SM/RC]

47.457 Harry J. Psomiades. *The Eastern question, the last phase: a study in Greek-Turkish diplomacy.* Thessalonike: Institute for Balkan Studies, 1968. ▸ Study of Greek role in politics of struggle for Ottoman succession, 1919–23, especially Lausanne settlement. Oddly organized but balanced, well researched, and clear. Argues Lausanne was final, eliminating Greater Greece policy, and led to Greco-Turk governmental détente. [SM]

47.458 Pierre Renouvin. *L'armistice de Réthondes, 11 Novembre 1918.* Paris: Gallimard, 1968. ▸ Detailed study of negotiation and operation of armistice, July 1918 to June 1919, based on archival sources. Balanced analysis and defense of actions of both sides in view of circumstances and existing knowledge. [SM]

47.459 Pierre Renouvin. *Le Traité de Versailles.* Paris: Flammarian, 1969. ▸ Brief basic survey of context and settlement with documents and debates. Concludes rigorous clauses with few enforcement instruments meant resentful Germany with sufficient power against divided victors. [SM]

47.460 Keith Robbins. *The abolition of war: the "peace movement" in Britain, 1914–1919.* Cardiff: University of Wales Press, 1976. ISBN 0-7083-0622-5. ▸ Detailed authoritative examination of wartime transformation of British pacifism, its war aims, and support of League of Nations. Criticizes movement for intolerance, fragmentation, and lack of wisdom. [SM]

47.461 Gerhard Schulz. *Revolutions and peace treaties, 1917–1920.* 1972 ed. Marion Jackson, trans. London: Methuen; distributed by Harper & Row, 1974. ISBN 0-416-81320-8 (pbk). ▸ Highly compact, synthetic examination of nexus of war, revolutions, and peace settlement. Suggests failure to establish equilibrium arose primarily from factors beyond control of peacemakers. [SM]

47.462 Klaus Schwabe. *Woodrow Wilson, revolutionary Germany, and peacemaking, 1918–1919: missionary diplomacy and the realities of power.* Robert Kimber and Rita Kimber, trans. Chapel Hill: University of North Carolina Press, 1985. ISBN 0-8087-1618-3. ▸ Massively researched analysis of Wilsonian and Weimar peace policies in relation to bolshevism. Rejects theories of antibolshevik conspiracy and argues weakening American support for Germany resulted from disengagement, not betrayal. [SM]

47.463 Alan Sharp. *The Versailles settlement: peacemaking in Paris, 1919.* New York: St. Martin's, 1991. ISBN 0-312-06049-1 (cl), 0-312-05579-X (pbk). ‣ Useable, introductory, general survey of major aspects of entire Paris settlement. Distributes blame evenhandedly and concludes peacemakers were victims of both their virtues and their vices. [SM]

47.464 Michael Llewellyn Smith. *Ionian vision: Greece in Asia Minor, 1919–1922.* New York: St. Martin's, 1973. ‣ Well-written description of "Greater Greece" Anatolian venture and its collapse, using British and Greek archives. Attributes Greek ambition to longstanding dream and British encouragement. [SM]

47.465 Sherman David Spector. *Rumania at the Paris Peace Conference: a study of the diplomacy of Ioan I.C. Bratianu.* New York: Bookman, 1962. ‣ Best available account of Romania's wartime role and peace conference policy from Romanian viewpoint. Attributes emergence of Greater Romania to Premier Bratianu's *Realpolitik* and Russia's absence. [SM]

47.466 John M. Thompson. *Russia, bolshevism, and the Versailles peace.* Princeton: Princeton University Press, 1966. ‣ Standard analysis of Russian problem at Peace Conference. Stresses Allied confusion, frustration, and failure owing to ideology, indecision, disagreement, domestic factors, and lack of information and power in Eastern Europe. [SM]

47.467 Seth P. Tillman. *Anglo-American relations at the Paris Peace Conference of 1919.* Princeton: Princeton University Press, 1961. ‣ Authoritative examination of patterns of Anglo-American cooperation and conflict. Sees community of enlightened interest but not common strategy, especially on League of Nations and conflict on naval, colonial, and economic issues. [SM]

47.468 Richard H. Ullman. *Britain and the Russian Civil War, November 1919–February 1920.* Vol. 2 of *Anglo-Soviet relations, 1917–1921.* Princeton: Princeton University Press for Princeton University, Center for International Studies, 1968. ‣ Heavily researched analysis of British efforts to unseat Bolsheviks. Attributes intervention's failure to Allied disunity, anti-bolshevik ineptitude, inadequate forces, and British opinion. [SM]

47.469 Arthur Walworth. *Wilson and his peacemakers: American diplomacy at the Paris Peace Conference, 1919.* New York: Norton, 1986. ISBN 0-393-01867-9. ‣ Massive but uneven study of America's 1919 diplomacy. Generally sympathetic to Colonel Edward M. House and critical of President Wilson, especially for ignoring advisers and exceeding what electorates would accept. [SM]

47.470 Dragan R. Zivojinovic. *America, Italy, and the birth of Yugoslavia (1917–1919).* Boulder: East European Quarterly; distributed by Columbia University Press, 1972. (East European Monographs, 2.) ‣ Well-researched study of clash between Italian imperialism and American commitment to self-determination. Hostile to Italy, argues President Wilson was flexible, reluctant to use financial weapons, and little involved in policy formulation. [SM]

SEE ALSO

33.615 Piotr S. Wandycz. *Soviet-Polish relations, 1917–1921.*

International Relations since 1920

The end of the Soviet empire and of the Cold War has presented twentieth-century international historians with the challenge of vast, untapped archival materials as well as new interpretive vistas and perspectives. The bipolar world of almost a half century, structured by the ubiquitous rivalry between ideological and nuclear superpowers, has suddenly been replaced by a tumultuous international environment; along with the ravages of communism and the proliferation of weapons of mass destruction, long dormant problems have resurfaced everywhere. This section addresses the challenge of dealing historically with recent events and also examines the longstanding great power rivalries and fundamental economic, social, political, military, cultural, and scientific components of twentieth-century international history.

The choice of titles for this section of the *Guide* is based on a very broad conception of international history and includes topics not formerly contained under the rubric of diplomatic history. Indeed, it gives heavy weight to the international political economy, because domestic and global distributive contests provided much of the substance for interstate strife and cooperation throughout this century. In addition, there has been an emphasis on the most recent scholarship and an attempt to provide equal coverage to both halves of the twentieth century. Entries in the earlier editions of the *Guide* will continue to be helpful. Later editions of the *Guide* will certainly contain more non-Western authors and titles as well as a more informed and reflective literature on recent events. The guiding principles of this compilation have been to achieve coverage and balance in terms of chronology and geography and to identify themes of general importance useful to historians and to scholars in other fields.

Where do we stand? For the years between the end of World War I and the end of World War II, we are now the beneficiaries of more than four decades of archive-based research and of new syntheses that have expanded and modified earlier views. Three major points have emerged. The first deals with structure. In the aftermath of World War I, four huge empires disappeared and no durable organization emerged to maintain international order; the Paris Peace settlement divided states into victors and vanquished; the latter unreconciled and revisionist, the former timid and divided. The result was a second devastating struggle for European and world hegemony that ultimately destroyed the Axis powers and gave victory to the Grand Alliance, but also unleashed the United States–Soviet rivalry over the new arrangement of the European and global peace settlement.

Europe's demotion from its pre-1914 economic power and leadership is a second important point. Crippled by the war's short- and long-term costs and by continuing internal division over the allocation of shrinking resources, Europe lost its preponderance to the emerging United States. The eruption of nationalist movements in the Middle East, Asia, and North Africa indicated an irreversible trend toward decolonization and new forms of international economic relations.

There was a strong ideological dimension in the diplomacy of the first half of the twentieth century. Classical European conservatism, liberalism, and socialism were transformed by the mass mobilization and centralized control of World War I; they were further altered by the powerful messages of Lenin, Wilson, Mussolini, and Hitler. As politicians increasingly appealed to popular emotion and support, international relations became heavily infused with the rhetoric and rituals of class, democracy, and international solidarity as well as with nationalism, racism, and antisemitism.

There are still lacunae, however, such as the history of the Comintern, particular aspects of Stalin's diplomacy, and specific policies of East European governments, that may be filled when the records in the former Soviet Union and in Eastern Europe are completely opened. There are issues to be explored further, such as the overall development of civilian and military intelligence services up to 1945. And there are syntheses still to be formulated, such as the activities and efficacy of the League of Nations and of other fledgling international organizations. Within the next decade we may anticipate comprehensive histories of the Paris Peace Conference, the reparations diplomacy of the twenties, the Great Depression and the march toward a second global war during the thirties, and World War II itself.

The post–World War II period is the frontier of current research in international history, and promises to remain so in the foreseeable period. Several interrelated issues have captured scholars' attention. First, there is the establishment of a Cold War balance-of-power system that paradoxically produced more stability and even more prosperity than existed earlier in this century. The prolonged commitment by the United States and the Soviet Union to maintaining high levels of military might, while avoiding head-on confrontation and exerting dominance and control over their clients, gave the world a respite, despite a few tense moments, from a third world war (see J. L. Gaddis 48.353; G. Lundestad 48.43). Even before the documents have been released, contemporary historians have investigated many of the chief components of the Cold War framework: the military alliance systems, the development of space and technology, and the culture and belief systems that underlay the clash of leaders and interests between 1945 and 1989.

A second theme is the pursuit of economic growth, which ultimately transcended the bipolar rivalry of the Cold War. In the immediate postwar period, fortuitous conditions and Keynesian policies in the West, and even the heavily managed economies in the East, generated wealth in an unprecedentedly large area of the globe; but beginning with the oil shocks of the 1970s, the world increasingly divided into haves and have-nots (so-called North-South), producing a new set of conflicts among states. Indeed the primacy of economic over political, ideological, and military power became a guiding theme of diplomacy and scholarship in the 1980s, even engendering some nostalgia for a simpler, more idealistic age.

Many scholars have traced the centrality of the populous, resource-rich, unevenly developing Third World to the United States–Soviet rivalry. For forty years, numerous advisers and vast amounts of military, economic, and humanitarian aid have flowed to strategically located lands. Bloody, often uncontained civil and interstate wars have been fought directly or through surrogates in Asia, Africa, the Middle East, and Central America. With the receding of the Cold War, the world's poorest states now confront the danger of neglect by the powerful and the unending threats of famine and epidemics, the ravaging of their environment, and the subjugation, expulsion, or annihilation of their minorities. There is a considerable amount of past history still to be explored: the myths and realities of decolonization; the process of self-organization pursued by the newly liberated states; international borrowing and investment policies and practices; and the North-South dialogue that began in the sixties.

It is evident that all three areas of post–World War II history—the global structure, the rival forms of economic growth in the core states, and developments in the regions producing raw materials—are deeply interrelated. Indeed, the best research has tried to link these topics, as international historians have begun to trace the outlines of a tumultuous, but remarkably coherent, postwar era (e.g., A. J. Rotter 48.542; R.W.D. Boyce 48.132).

What problems do we face in the future? First, historians suffer from both too many and too few primary sources. Thanks to the explosion of twentieth-century bureaucracies, we are inundated by documents that promise to grow exponentially. We will need a massive number of finding aids and guides, readily available, in order to define and conceive our work. At the same time, we lack adequate sources for many subjects, such as the growth of national and international businesses whose records are often closed to scholars. Many key private papers have been closely guarded, subject to legal restrictions, lost, or destroyed. The increasing use of the telephone and electronic communication and of technology such as tape-erasers and paper-shredders has impeded research; the proliferation of nonwritten materials (from airbrushed Soviet photographs to old aerial photographs of Palestine) has made new demands on our expertise.

The official documentary record itself will likely remain problematic. In the West, there are still restrictions on sensitive files. In Eastern Europe and the former Soviet Union, there may be crucial gaps, and in parts of the Third World a continuing ban on access by foreigners. The official publication of various governments' documents has proceeded selectively and slowly; it may now be further reduced and delayed by shrinking budgets.

The increase of independent nations from 1918 to 1992 has greatly complicated the scholar's task, and not only in regard to obtaining access to new archives that may or may not be constituted and maintained in a traditional manner. We have the task of integrating a growing number of peoples and states into the study of international history. We can no longer study subjects such as decolonization by searching a single Western archive, or even several Western repositories, and neglect the records and perspectives of non-Western actors (P. Gifford and W. R. Louis 48.311, 48.312). It is also desirable to think afresh about the process of creation and dissolution of nation-states and empires in this century.

It is to be hoped that scholars of international history will produce more comparative studies and interdisciplinary work incorporating insights from the behavioral and social sciences as well as from social and cultural history. American diplomatic historians already have included gender, bureaucracy, dependency, corporatism, and world systems theory in their studies of foreign relations (M. Hogan and T. Patterson, eds. 40.603; C. S. Maier in M. Kammen, ed. 1.29). There are many fruitful areas for cooperation between historians and political scientists (see S. E. Miller, S. M. Lynn-Jones, and S. van Evera, eds. 47.352).

What sort of interpretive framework will be established for the twentieth century, where history undoubtedly has not "ended" (F. Fukuyama 1.143)? Most historians will continue to search the archives, produce accounts of the behavior of individual and groups of nation-states, analyze structural components, and dissect their political, economic, and ideological character. Others may stress specific themes, such as this century's progress toward international order: the attenuation of national sovereignty through the creation of regional, continental, and international organizations. Still others, taking the *longue durée* approach, may interpret the eight decades since World

War I in the context of the extended North-South conflict and treat the great power rivalries as episodes in a larger historical development (see P. Dukes 48.352).

Whichever framework is chosen, the student of international history will face a burgeoning literature in many languages; a host of problems, topics, and interpretations; and probably more limited personal and institutional resources than in the past. A possible device, heralded as early as 1929 in the *Annales d'histoire économique et sociale* by Marc Bloch and Lucien Febvre, is to organize international collaborative projects according to a coordinated research design (see A. R. Millet and W. Murray 48.45; C. K. Fink et al. 48.106).

The great challenges remain: to examine state power in all its manifestations as it extends into the international arena; to grasp the central and dynamic issues of the world economy and world politics; to discern the elements of continuity and discontinuity, of comparison and uniqueness; and everywhere to recognize the human hand and the ideals and ambitions that have shaped twentieth-century international history.

ACKNOWLEDGMENTS   *The editor gratefully acknowledges the immense and indispensable contribution of the principal contributor to this section, John S. Hill.*

[Contributors: AF = Andrea Feldman, AS = Antonio Santosuosso, BBY = Bernard B. Yamron, BJCM = Brian J. C. McKercher, BMG = Bertram M. Gordon, CKF = Carole K. Fink, CVF = Carter Vaughn Findley, DSC = Donald Stephen Cloyd, FGN = F. G. Notehelfer, GRG = Gene R. Garthwaite, GS = Gale Stokes, IB = Ivo Banac, JBD = John B. Duncan, JHC = James H. Cole, JSH = John S. Hill, JWB = John W. Boyer, JWC = John W. Cell, LLC = Linda L. Clark, MMF = Marjorie M. Farrar, NDC = Noel D. Cary, NMK = Nicholas M. Kliment, PH = Peter Hayes, PM = Philip Mattar, RJC = Richard J. Crampton, RJY = Robert J. Young, RKG = Robert K. Griffith, Jr., RLM = Richard L. Millett, RML = Robert M. Levine, RJW = Richard J. Walter, SBV = Steven Béla Várdy, WLB = William Lee Blackwood]

REFERENCE WORKS

Bibliographies and Guides

48.1 Mark R. Amstutz. *Economics and foreign policy: a guide to information sources*. Detroit: Gale Research, 1977. (International relations information guide series, 7.) ISBN 0-8103-1321-9. ▸ Well-constructed, annotated bibliography of about 750 titles on international political economy published before 1976. Subject, title, and author indexes facilitate use. Unfortunately excludes documentary sources. [JSH]

48.2 Sadao Asada, ed. *Japan and the world, 1853–1952: a bibliographic guide to Japanese scholarship in foreign relations*. New York: Columbia University Press, 1989. ISBN 0-231-06690-2. ▸ Bibliographical essays by period and substantial chapter on guides to documents, archives, and reference works. Excellent. [JSH]

48.3 Sidney Aster, ed. and comp. *British foreign policy, 1918–1945: a guide to research and research materials*. Rev. ed. Wilmington, Del.: Scholarly Resources, 1991. ISBN 0-8420-2310-0. ▸ Discussion of research facilities and aids, published sources, and 1,950 monographs and other titles. Wide ranging in conception; probably most useful single volume in series. [JSH]

48.4 Alexine L. Atherton. *International organizations: a guide to information sources*. Detroit: Gale Research, 1976. (International relations information guide series, 1.) ISBN 0-8103-1324-3. ▸ Annotated bibliogaphy of approximately 1,500 English-language sources on global, rather than regional, international organizations such as League of Nations and United Nations. Valuable aid for all scholars. [JSH]

48.5 George W. Baer, ed. and comp. *International organizations, 1918–1945: a guide to research and research materials*. Rev. 2d ed. Wilmington, Del.: Scholarly Resources, 1991. ISBN 0-8420-2309-7. ▸ Valuable guide to many organizations associated with League of Nations. [JSH]

48.6 Paul W. Blackstock and Frank L. Schaf. *Intelligence, espionage, counterespionage, and covert operations: a guide to information sources*. Detroit: Gale Research, 1978. (International relations information guide series, 2.) ISBN 0-8103-1323-5. ▸ Annotated bibliography of about 800 books and articles, mostly in English. Excellent foundation for all levels of research. [JSH]

48.7 Richard Dean Burns, ed. *Guide to American foreign relations since 1700*. Santa Barbara, Calif.: ABC-Clio for Society of Historians of American Foreign Relations, 1983. ISBN 0-87436-323-3. ▸ Chapters 20–37 cover events since 1920; chapters 38–40 deal with thematic issues. Author and subject indexes. Outstanding work. [CKF/JSH]

48.8 Alan Cassels. *Italian foreign policy, 1918–1945: a guide to research and research materials*. 2d ed. Wilmington, Del.: Scholarly Resources, 1991. ISBN 0-8420-2307-0. ▸ Superb research aid for fascist period, both for those working in Italian archives and for those using published sources. [JSH]

48.9 J. Bryan Collester. *The European communities: a guide to information sources*. Detroit: Gale Research, 1979. (International relations information guide series, 9.) ISBN 0-8103-1322-7. ‣ Separate chapters cover political science and historical literature, institutions, security, relations among European Community members and with nonmembers, primary sources, and periodicals. Excellent starting point for further investigations. [JSH]

48.10 Chris Cook and Geoff Pugh. *Diplomacy and international affairs*. Vol. 2 of *Sources in European political history*. New York: Facts on File, 1989. ISBN 0-8160-1756-5 (v. 2). ‣ Descriptive list of personal papers of one thousand figures involved in European diplomacy, 1870–1945. [JSH]

48.11 John J. Finan and John Child, eds. *Latin America: international relations, a guide to information sources*. Detroit: Gale Research, 1981. (International relations information guide series, 11.) ISBN 0-8013-1325-1. ‣ Substantial (1,400 titles), well-organized, annotated bibliography covering foreign policies of various states and of the United States in relation to Latin America. Addresses culture, science, and technology; strategy and security; economics; and Organization of American States. [JSH]

48.12 Helga Hernes. *The multinational corporation: a guide to information sources*. Detroit: Gale Research, 1977. (International relations information guide series, 4.) ISBN 0-8103-1327-8. ‣ Disappointing contribution to this series of bibliographies. Entries are dated and weighted toward journals rather than monographs. Sections on international business operations and on relations between multinational corporations and nation-states. [CKF/JSH]

48.13 Robert H. Johnston, ed. and comp. *Soviet foreign policy, 1918–1945: a guide to research and research materials*. Wilmington, Del.: Scholarly Resources, 1991. ISBN 0-8420-2312-7. ‣ Annotated bibliography of 900 titles; very valuable, brief history of Narkomindel and Comintern; Guide to Soviet, German, French, British, and American archives and libraries with sources on Soviet diplomacy. [JSH]

48.14 Christoph M. Kimmich, ed. and comp. *German foreign policy, 1918–1945: a guide to research and research materials*. Rev. ed. Wilmington, Del.: Scholarly Resources, 1991. ISBN 0-8420-2311-9. ‣ Well-prepared guide to archival holdings on German diplomatic history and helpful bibliography of immense secondary literature. [JSH]

48.15 Richard J. Kozicki, ed. *The international relations of South Asia, 1947–80: a guide to information sources*. Detroit: Gale Research, 1981. (International relations information guide series, 10.) ISBN 0-8013-1329-4. ‣ Annotated bibliography. Dominated by India's bilateral relations but substantial attention devoted to Pakistan, and appropriate attention to Bangladesh, Sri Lanka, Bhutan, Nepal, and Afghanistan. [JSH]

48.16 Robert L. Pfaltzgraff, Jr. *The study of international relations: a guide to information sources*. Detroit: Gale Research, 1977. (International relations information guide series, 5.) ISBN 0-8103-1331-6. ‣ Brief essays introduce topical bibliographies on main issues in contemporary international relations. Contains much useful information on primary sources, scholarly journals, and analytical problems. Author-title-subject index. [JSH]

48.17 Ann Schlutz. *International and regional politics in the Middle East and North Africa: a guide to information sources*. Detroit: Gale Research, 1977. (International relations information guide series, 6.) ISBN 0-8013-1326-X. ‣ Excellent, if somewhat dated, annotated bibliography covering regional issues; foreign policies of fifteen states from Morocco to Afghanistan; policies of foreign powers actively involved in regional affairs; Arab-Israeli conflict; and oil. Additional useful sections on reference materials and periodicals. [JSH]

48.18 W.A.E. Skurnik. *Sub-Saharan Africa: a guide to information sources*. Detroit: Gale Research, 1977. (International relations information guide series, 3.) ISBN 0-8013-1391-X. ‣ Annotated bibliography dealing with pan-Africanism; Africa's relations with foreign powers; African liberation movements; and reference works. Useful essays introduce each section. Underdeveloped state of scholarship in this area in mid-seventies indicated by the approximately 300 titles. [JSH]

48.19 United States. Department of Public Information. *Yearbook of the United Nations*. New York: United Nations, 1946–. ‣ Thick, annual report on activities of international organizations with references to voluminous documentation produced each year. [JSH]

48.20 Robert J. Young, ed. *French foreign policy, 1918–1945: a guide to research and research materials*. 2d ed. Wilmington, Del.: Scholarly Resources, 1991. ISBN 0-8420-2308-9. ‣ All who work in French archives owe great debt to Young for this clear and helpful display of knowledge. [JSH]

Atlases

48.21 Gérard Chaliand and Jean-Pierre Rageau. *A strategic atlas: comparative geopolitics of the world's powers*. 3d ed. Tony Berrett, trans. New York: Harper & Row, 1992. ISBN 0-06-271554-2 (cl), 0-06-273153-X (pbk). ‣ Frequently revised volume contains maps and charts displaying relationships in terms of wealth, military power, financial resources, and many other factors. Interesting and valuable. [JSH]

48.22 Michael L. Dockrill. *The Collins atlas of twentieth-century world history*. Glasgow: HarperCollins, 1991. ISBN 0-00-435061-8. ‣ Combination of multicolor maps, graphic representations, chronological tables, photographs, and narrative text. Bibliography lists other atlases for more detailed information. Good source for general background maps. [JSH]

48.23 Martin Gilbert. *The Macmillan atlas of the Holocaust*. New York: Macmillan, 1982. ISBN 0-02-543380-6. ‣ Over three hundred black-and-white maps and many photographs. Introductory essay and explanatory text; extensive bibliography and list of sources. [JSH]

48.24 John Keegan, ed. *The Times atlas of the Second World War*. New York: Harper & Row, 1989. ISBN 0-06-016178-7. ‣ Over four hundred multicolor maps and charts, divided by theaters of operation and chronology. Photographs, chronology, glossary, bibliography, and index. Lavish. [JSH]

48.25 John Keegan and Andrew Wheatcroft. *Zones of conflict: an atlas of future wars*. New York: Simon & Schuster, 1986. ISBN 0-671-60115-6 (cl), 0-671-62411-3 (pbk). ‣ Chapters illustrate territorial conflicts and military constraints in Europe, Middle East, South and Southeast Asia, Far East, Africa, and the Americas. Of continuing interest as new world order emerges. [JSH]

General Studies

48.26 Christopher Andrew and David Dilks, eds. *The missing dimension: governments and intelligence communities in the twentieth century*. Champaign: University of Illinois Press, 1984. ISBN 0-252-01157-0. ‣ Anglocentric group of scholarly essays on problems of gathering and utilizing intelligence. Useful introduction to this still ill-defined but important aspect of history of international relations. [JSH]

48.27 David Armstrong. *The rise of the international organisation: a short history*. New York: St. Martin's, 1982. ISBN 0-312-68427-4. ‣ Brief, reliable introductory survey of cooperation between states as focus of concern shifted from national security to social security. [JSH]

48.28 Raymond F. Betts. *Uncertain dimensions: Western overseas empires in the twentieth century*. Minneapolis: University of Minnesota Press, 1985. ISBN 0-8166-1308-7 (cl), 0-8166-1309-5 (pbk). ‣ Changes within empires and metropoles rapidly eroded formal political links, but left many other connections. Excellent introductory work in comparative framework and equipped with good bibliography. [JSH]

48.29 James L. Brierly. *The law of nations: an introduction to the international law of peace.* 6th ed. Humphrey Waldock, ed. New York: Oxford University Press, 1978. ISBN 0-19-825105-X. ▸ Much revised version of longstanding classic introduction to international law. [JSH]

48.30 Hedley Bull and Adam Watson, eds. *The expansion of international society.* Oxford: Clarendon, 1984. ISBN 0-19-821942-3. ▸ Episodic but entertaining review of outward thrust of European international system since eighteenth century. Traditional introductions to many issues, but slights non-Western world. [CKF/JSH]

48.31 Peter Calvocoressi. *Independent Africa and the world.* London: Longman, 1985. ISBN 0-582-29654-4 (pbk). ▸ Competent survey by very knowledgeable observer of international politics with wide-ranging interests. Sympathetic, yet maintains a certain distance. [JSH]

48.32 Peter Calvocoressi. *World politics since 1945.* 6th ed. New York: Longman, 1991. ISBN 0-582-07379-0 (pbk). ▸ Relations among great powers, followed by region-by-region survey. Densely packed summary of developments uncluttered by elaborate interpretive scheme. Expanded more than revised edition. Useful as reference or introduction. [JSH]

48.33 Alvin D. Coox and Hilary Conroy, eds. *China and Japan: search for balance since World War I.* Santa Barbara, Calif.: ABC-Clio, 1978. ISBN 0-8743-6275-X. ▸ Uneven collection of original and previously published work on selected aspects of Sino-Japanese relations. Most useful as orientation to still underdeveloped field. [CKF/JSH]

48.34 Harold Eugene Davis et al. *Latin American diplomatic history: an introduction.* Baton Rouge: Louisiana State University Press, 1977. ISBN 0-8071-0260-1 (cl), 0-8071-0286-5 (pbk). ▸ Basic introduction escaping from North American–centered approach. Latin American states move from targets of other's diplomacy to actors in their own right. [CKF/JSH]

48.35 Rebecca Grant and Kathleen Newland, eds. *Gender and international relations.* Bloomington: Indiana University Press, 1991. ISBN 0-253-32613-3 (cl), 0-253-21265-0 (pbk). ▸ Brief collection of essays outlining innovative perspectives. [JSH]

48.36 Michael I. Handel. *The diplomacy of surprise: Hitler, Nixon, Sadat.* Cambridge, Mass.: Harvard University, Center for International Affairs, 1981. (Harvard studies in international affairs, 44.) ISBN 0-8767-4048-4 (cl), 0-8767-4049-2 (pbk). ▸ Fascinating study of startling diplomatic initiatives. Hitler's remilitarization of Rhineland and Nazi-Soviet Pact, Sadat's visit to Jerusalem, and Nixon's opening to China provide case studies. [JSH]

48.37 C. Wilfred Jenks. *The prospects of international relations: the law of international institutions.* Dobb's Ferry, N.Y.: Oceana, 1964. ▸ Thoughtful examination of one approach to the peaceful settlement of disputes. [JSH]

48.38 David Kahn. *The codebreakers: the story of secret writing.* New York: Macmillan, 1967. ▸ Standard history of cryptography and cryptanalysis from earliest times to mid-twentieth century. Massive in detail and documentation; not introductory work. [JSH]

48.39 Paul M. Kennedy. *The rise and fall of the great powers: economic change and military conflict from 1500 to 2000.* 1987 ed. New York: Vintage, 1989. ISBN 0-679-72019-7 (pbk). ▸ Reliable history of shift in balance of power over five centuries. Traces convergence and divergence of economic and military factors. [CKF]

48.40 William R. Keylor. *The twentieth-century world: an international history.* 2d ed. New York: Oxford University Press, 1992. ISBN 0-19-503369-8 (cl), 0-19-503370-1 (pbk). ▸ Valuable for discerning broad patterns in evolving international system. Excellent on international political economy; weaker on ideology and military affairs. Best available textbook. [JSH]

48.41 Donald F. Lach and Edmund S. Wehrle. *International politics in East Asia since World War II.* Rev. ed. New York: Praeger, 1975. ISBN 0-275-05420-9. ▸ Study of foreign policies of Peoples' Republic of China and Japan with one chapter on wars in Vietnam, 1945–73. No discussion of other states. [JSH]

48.42 George Lenczowski. *The Middle East in world affairs.* 4th ed. Ithaca, N.Y.: Cornell University Press, 1980. ISBN 0-8014-1273-0 (cl), 0-8014-9872-4 (pbk). ▸ Encyclopedic in coverage, highly reliable for readers seeking introduction to particular topics or as reference work. [JSH]

48.43 Geir Lundestad. *East, West, North, South: major developments in international politics, 1945–1986.* 1986 rev. ed. Gail Adams Kvam, trans. Oslo: Norwegian University Press, 1991. ISBN 8-2002-1319-6. ▸ Excellent, balanced introduction to whole range of international relations since World War II. [JSH]

48.44 Michael R. Marrus. *The unwanted: European refugees in the twentieth century.* New York: Oxford University Press, 1985. ISBN 0-19-503615-8. ▸ Encyclopedic coverage of refugee movements entwined with intelligent account of international institutional responses. Indispensable for general and advanced readers for particular events and larger patterns. [CKF/JSH]

48.45 Allan R. Millett and Williamson Murray, eds. *Military effectiveness.* 3 vols. Boston: Allen & Unwin, 1988. ISBN 0-04-44503-2 (v. 1), 0-04-445054-0 (v. 2), 0-04-0445055-9 (v. 3). ▸ Performance of military organizations of Britain, Germany, United States, Italy, France, Japan, and Russia/Soviet Union between 1914 and 1945. Highly structured comparative history by knowledgeable scholars with instructive summary chapters for each volume. Chapter notes offer valuable guide for students of military affairs. [JSH]

48.46 Hans Morgenthau and Kenneth Thompson. *Politics among nations: the struggle for power and peace.* 6th ed. New York: McGraw-Hill, 1985. ISBN 0-07-554469-5. ▸ Realistic appraisal in form of durable textbook. [JSH]

48.47 David G. Scanlon and James J. Shields. *Problems and prospects in international education.* New York: Teachers College Press, 1968. ISBN 0-685-23632-3 (cl), 0-685-202606-3 (pbk). ▸ Collection of previously published articles on international exchange of students and teachers, technical education, cultural relations, and politico-economic background. Bibliography well organized, but now somewhat dated. [JSH]

48.48 Hansjakob Stehle. *Eastern politics of the Vatican, 1917–1979.* Sandra Smith, trans. Athens: Ohio University Press, 1981. ISBN 0-8214-0367-2 (cl), 0-8214-0564-0 (pbk). ▸ Generally excellent, although somewhat partisan, explanation of papacy's alternation between conciliation of and confrontation with communist regimes. [CKF/JSH]

48.49 Hugh Tinker. *Race, conflict, and the international order: from empire to United Nations.* London: Macmillan, 1977. ISBN 0-333-19664-3 (cl), 0-333-19665-1 (pbk). ▸ Trim, sprightly introduction to role of race relations in international affairs during twentieth century. Revolt against racism was also revolt of poor and non-Western against rich West. Usefully points the way to a subject still in need of much study. [JSH]

National Foreign Policies

48.50 Warren I. Cohen. *America's response to China: a history of Sino-American relations.* New York: Columbia University Press,

1990. ISBN 0-231-06804-2 (cl), 0-231-06805-0 (pbk). ‣ Reliable introductory text. American diplomacy defended Chinese integrity against feared partition that would have excluded American traders, but defense was more talk than action. [JSH]

48.51 Robert H. Ferrell. *American diplomacy: a history.* 3d ed. New York: Norton, 1975. ISBN 0-393-09309-3. ‣ Detailed, balanced, reliable, and often charming textbook with good annotated bibliography. [JSH]

48.52 Alfred Grosser. *Affaires extérieures: la politique de la France, 1944–1989.* 1984 ed. Paris: Flammarion, 1989. ISBN 2-08-081209-2. ‣ Fine survey of French foreign policy when power not equal to international responsibilities by journalist-scholar who has closely observed events for three decades. Intelligent, stimulating, and informative, if episodic. Excellent bibliography of secondary literature in three languages. [JSH/BMG]

48.53 George Frost Kennan. *Russia and the West under Lenin and Stalin.* 1961 ed. New York: New America Library, 1962. ‣ Interpretation rather than history of significant episodes and larger patterns by life-long student and maker of foreign policy. Still stimulating on Soviet and other topics. [JSH]

48.54 C. J. Lowe and F. Marzari. *Italian foreign policy, 1870–1940.* London: Routledge & Kegan Paul, 1975. ISBN 0-7100-7987-7. ‣ Continuous tension between cautiousness and adventurism over seven decades. Best synthesis available, but much in need of updating. [CKF/JSH]

48.55 Jacques Neré. *The foreign policy of France from 1914 to 1945.* London: Routledge & Kegan Paul, 1975. ISBN 0-7100-7968-0. ‣ Good introduction to main features of French policy with shrewd judgments and collection of important documents appended. [CKF/JSH]

48.56 Ian H. Nish. *Japanese foreign policy, 1869–1942: Kasumigaseki to Miyakezaka.* Boston: Routledge & Kegan Paul, 1977. ISBN 0-7100-8421-8. ‣ Best available survey, with translated documents appended. Focuses on foreign ministry; particularly strong on interwar period. [JSH]

48.57 David Reynolds. *Britannia overruled: British policy and world power in the twentieth century.* London: Longman, 1991. ISBN 0-582-08427-X (cl, cased), 0-582-55276-1 (pbk). ‣ Stimulating, up-to-date survey by student of Anglo-American relationship. Perceptive assessment of Britain's decline from great power status; shows decline not inevitable. [JSH/BJCM]

48.58 Adam B. Ulam. *Dangerous relations: the Soviet Union in world politics, 1970–1982.* New York: Oxford University Press, 1983. ISBN 0-19-503237-3 (cl), 0-19-503424-4 (pbk). ‣ Intelligent, accessible study arguing domestic preoccupations of American leaders inhibited understanding that Soviet Union was in crisis. [JSH]

48.59 Adam B. Ulam. *Expansion and coexistence: Soviet foreign policy, 1917–73.* 2d ed. New York: Praeger, 1974. ISBN 0-275-33270-5 (cl), 0-275-88630-1 (pbk). ‣ Best available survey and starting point although more recent scholarship revises some points. Quest for security and power under bolshevik and Stalinist systems. [JSH]

SEE ALSO
22.317 David P. Calleo. *The German problem reconsidered.*
47.30 Jonathan E. Helmreich. *Belgium and Europe.*

Documentary Collections

48.60 Académie Royale des Sciences, des Lettres, et des Beaux-Arts de Belgique, Commission royale d'histoire. *Documents diplomatiques belges, 1920–1940.* 5 vols. Charles de Visscher and Fernand Van Langehove, eds. Brussels: Palais des Académies,

1964–66. ‣ Somewhat thin selection of sources, but facilitates study of small-power diplomacy between two world wars. [JSH]

48.61 Australia. Department of Foreign Affairs. *Documents on Australian foreign policy, 1937–1949.* 9 vols. to date. R. G. Neale et al., eds. Canberra: Australian Government Publishing Service, 1975–. ISBN 0-642-00994-5 (v. 1). ‣ Ongoing series of enlightening documents. Volumes 1–7 cover 1938–44, foreign policy of increasingly restive dominion. [JSH]

48.62 Kenneth Bourne and Donald Cameron Watt, eds. *British documents on foreign affairs: reports and papers from the Foreign Office Confidential Print.* 44 vols. to date. Frederick, Md.: University Publications of America, 1984–91. ISBN 0-89093-601-3 (series A, set), 0-89093-603-X (series B, set), 0-89093-605-6 (series C, set), 0-89093-607-2 (series D, set), 0-89093-612-9 (series E, set), 0-89093-613-7 (series F, set), 0-89093-608-0 (series H, set), 0-89093-609-9 (series I, set), 0-89093-614-5 (series J, set). ‣ Massive publication of telegrams and papers. Part 2: series A = Soviet Union, 1917–39; series B = Turkey, Iran, and Middle East; series C = North America, 1919–39; series D = Latin America, 1914–39; series E = Asia, 1914–39; series F = Europe, 1919–39; series H = First World War, 1914–19; series I = Paris Peace Conference of 1919; series J = League of Nations, 1918–41. Subsections group sources by region. Rich representation of archives, better than volumes of *Documents on British Policy Overseas* (48.64). [JSH]

48.63 Bundesarchiv and Institut für Zeitgeschichte. *Akten zur Vorgeschichte der Bundesrepublik Deutschland, 1945–1949.* 5 vols. Munich: Oldenbourg, 1976–83. ‣ Useful collection of documents on post–World War II formation of Germany. American and British collections, however, tell real story. [JSH]

48.64 Rohan Butler et al., eds. *Documents on British policy overseas.* 6 vols. to date. London: Her Majesty's Stationery Office, 1984–. ISBN 0-11-591682-2 (series 1, v. 1). ‣ Ongoing series publishing important documents in two series: series 1, 1945–50; series 2, 1950–55. Less satisfactory than series on interwar period (48.80) but still very welcome. [JSH]

48.65 Canada. Department of External Affairs. *Documents on Canadian external relations.* 12 vols. to date. Ottawa: Queen's Printer, 1967–. ‣ Ongoing series publishing important documents. Volumes 2–10 cover years 1919–45, later volumes beginning to explore postwar years. Useful for transit from British to American orbit. [JSH]

48.66 Commission Nationale pour la Publication des Documents Diplomatiques Suisses. *Documents diplomatiques suisses, 1848–1945.* 13 vols to date. Bern: Benteli, 1979–. ‣ Continuing series publishing significant Swiss diplomatic documents. Volumes 7–10 cover November 1918 to December 1933. Clarifies foreign policy of alert and important neutral state. [JSH]

48.67 Jane Degras, ed. *Soviet documents on foreign policy.* 3 vols. London: Oxford University Press for Royal Institute of International Affairs, 1951–53. ‣ Three-volume selection of translated published Soviet documents. Helps delineate Soviet official positions. [JSH]

48.68 France. Commission de Publication des Documents Relatifs aux Origines de la Guerre. *Documents diplomatiques français, 1932–1939.* 31 vols. Paris: Imprimerie Nationale, 1963–86. ‣ Multivolume set of published documents from French Ministry of Foreign Affairs. Series 1: thirteen volumes, 1 July 1932–31 December 1935; Series 2: eighteen volumes, 1 January 1935–25 August 1939. Good source on French response to rising German danger. [JSH]

48.69 France. Ministère des Affaires Étrangères, Commission de Publication des Documents Français. *Documents diplomatiques français, 1954–.* Paris: Imprimerie Nationale, 1987–. ‣ Ongoing series publishing important documents. Beginning after Geneva Convention, very little on decision making within Foreign Ministry or government but still useful. [JSH]

48.70 Germany. Auswärtiges Amt. *Akten zur deutschen auswärtigen Politik, 1918–1945.* Baden-Baden: Imprimerie Nationale, 1950–. ▸ Ongoing series publishing documents on German foreign policy. Series A, 1918–November 1925; Series B, December 1925–January 1933; Series C, January 1933–August 1937; Series D, September 1937–December 1941; December 1941–1945. English translations of Series C and D are available. Foreign policy of major actor in international affairs before 1945. [JSH]

48.71 Edvard Hambro. *The case law of the International Court: a repertoire of judgements, advisory opinions, and orders of the Permanent Court of International Justice of the International Court of Justice.* Leiden: Sijthoff, 1952–. ▸ Valuable, ongoing collection of judgments of International Court, classified according to whether they deal with sources of international law, persons, pacific settlement of disputes, or international conflicts. [JSH]

48.72 Israeli State Archives. *Documents on the foreign policy of Israel.* Yehoshua Freudlich et al. Jerusalem: Government Printer, 1979. ISBN 9-652-79002-8 (v. 2), 9-652-79000-1 (v. 3). ▸ Publication of diplomatic documents and cabinet discussions; in Hebrew. Preliminary volume covers December 1947–May 1948; Volumes 1–3 cover 15 May 1948–July 1949. Companion volumes contain summaries of documents in English and full translations of front matter. Valuable for Middle Eastern diplomacy. [JSH]

48.73 Italy. Commissione per la Pubblicazione dei Documenti Diplomatici. *I documenti diplomatici italiani, 1861–1943.* Rome: Libreria dello Stato, 1952–. ▸ Ongoing series publishing important documents in nine series: Series 6, 1918–22; Series 7, 1922–35; Series 8, 1935–39; Series 9, 1939–43. [JSH]

48.74 Nicholas Mansergh and Penderel Moon, eds. *The transfer of power, 1942–7.* 12 vols. London: Her Majesty's Stationery Office, 1970–83. ▸ Large collection of documents on dismantling of British empire in India and emergence of new states. Very well done. [JSH]

48.75 Minsterstvo Inostrannikh del SSSR. *Dokumenty vneshnei politiki SSSR* (Documents on the Foreign policy of the USSR). 21 vols. A. A. Gromyko et al. Moscow: State Publishing House, 1955–77. ▸ Publication of important documents from Soviet Union. Covers 1917–38. [JSH]

48.76 J. Murray and S. R. Ashton, eds. *British documents on the end of empire.* 8 vols. to date. London: Her Majesty's Stationary Office for the Institute of Commonwealth Relations, 1992–. ▸ Series A, three volumes, treats whole range of issues involved in dismantling of empire, 1924–57. Series B, five volumes, on Ghana, Sri Lanka, Malaya, Egypt, and Sudan. Series C contains guides to British archival sources. Superb editing. [JSH]

48.77 Netherlands. Departement van Buitenlandse Zaken. *Documenten betreffende de buitenlandse politiek van Nederland, 1919–1945.* 14 vols. to date. The Hague: Nijhoff, 1976–. (Rijks geschiedkundige publicatie, 156–57, 160, 162, 172–73, 181, 188, 191–92, 199, 203, 212, 220.) ▸ Ongoing series publishing important documents. In three series: series A, 1919–30; series B, 1931–40; series C, 1940–45. [JSH]

48.78 Hans-Peter Schwartz, ed. *Akten zur auswärtigen Politik der Bundesrepublik Deutschland.* 2 vols. to date. Munich: Oldenbourg, 1989–. ▸ Useful volumes treating relations between Chancellor Adenauer and Allied High Commission. [JSH]

48.79 United States. Department of State. *Papers relating to the foreign relations of the United States.* Washington, D.C.: Superintendent of Documents, United States Government Printing Office, 1861–. ISBN 1048-6445. ▸ Ongoing series publishing important documents. Multivolume topical coverage for each

year through 1951, triannual editions thereafter. Fundamental source for understanding twentieth-century international affairs. Also available on microfiche from Washington, D.C.: U.S. Government Printing Office. [JSH]

48.80 E. L. Woodward et al., eds. *Documents on British foreign policy, 1919–1939.* 62 vols. to date. London: Her Majesty's Stationery Office, 1946–. ISBN 0-11-591517-6 (series 1, v. 17). ▸ Ongoing series publishing important documents of interwar period. Series 1, 1919–29 complete in twenty-seven volumes; Series 1A, 1925–29, complete in seven volumes; Series 2, 1930–38, in progress; Series 3, March 1938–2 September 1939, complete in ten volumes. Fine collection on all aspects of British diplomacy between the wars. [JSH]

THE NEW DIPLOMACY

International Institutions

48.81 Antony Alcock. *A history of the International Labor Organization.* New York: Octagon Books, 1971. ISBN 0-374-90127-9. ▸ Capable if bland institutional history based on organization's archives. Useful to specialists working on international organization generally; of less value in understanding groups that used organization as forum. [CKF/JSH]

48.82 Franz Borkenau. *World communism: a history of the Communist International.* 1938 ed. Raymond Aron, Introduction. Ann Arbor: University of Michigan Press, 1962. ▸ Authoritative older study by former official of Communist International. [JSH]

48.83 David P. Forsythe. *Humanitarian politics: the International Committee of the Red Cross.* Baltimore: Johns Hopkins University Press, 1977. ISBN 0-8018-1983-0. ▸ Reliable account by close observer, explaining functions and organization of committee with several case studies. Useful reference and introduction, but far from definitive. [JSH]

48.84 Hsi-Huey Liang. *The rise of modern police and the European state system from Metternich to the Second World War.* Cambridge: Cambridge University Press, 1992. ISBN 0-521-43022-4. ▸ Detailed study of international police cooperation, little noticed aspect of national responses to transnational problems. [JSH]

48.85 Kermit E. McKenzie. *Comintern and world revolution, 1928–1943: the shaping of doctrine.* 1964 ed. New York: Columbia University Press, 1966. ▸ Discussion of Stalinization of foreign communist movements in interest of Soviet foreign policy. Mechanical sifting of Comintern publications and statements. [JSH]

48.86 F. S. Northedge. *The League of Nations: its life and times, 1920–1946.* New York: Holmes & Meier, 1986. ISBN 0-8419-1065-0. ▸ Standard if somewhat narrowly conceived history of League. Ready reference on many aspects of institutional activities but there is still room for interpretation of place of international organizations in system of competitive states. [JSH]

48.87 Michla Pomerance. *The advisory function of the International Court in the League and U.N. eras.* Baltimore: Johns Hopkins University Press, 1973. ISBN 0-8018-1291-7. ▸ Clear, full analysis of development before World War II and curtailing after war of Court's involvement in pacific settlement of disputes among states. [CKF/JSH]

48.88 United Nations Library, Graduate Institute of International Studies. *The League of Nations in retrospect: proceedings of the symposium, organized by the United Nations Library and the Graduate Institute of International Studies, Geneva, 6–9 November 1980.* Berlin: de Gruyter, 1983. (United Nations Library, Geneva. Series E, Guides and studies, 3.) ISBN 3-1100-8733-2. ▸ Selective coverage of League activities, emphasizing nonpolitical achievements. Valuable to specialists as complement to standard treatments and for concise versions of several monographs. [JSH]

Public Opinion and Pacifism

48.89   Donald S. Birn. *The League of Nations Union, 1918–1945.* New York: Clarendon, 1981. ISBN 0-19-822650-0. ▸ Definitive study of organization that became focus of British liberal hopes in twenties, only to wither as it became clear that sovereign states still ruled the field. [JSH]

48.90   Martin Ceadel. *Pacifism in Britain, 1914–1945: the defining of a faith.* Oxford: Clarendon, 1980. ISBN 0-19-821882-6. ▸ Stimulating, enlightening study of pacifism; particularly valuable on interwar period, but omits as full a consideration of impact on British foreign policy as one might wish. [JSH]

48.91   Paul Hollander. *Political pilgrims: travels of Western intellectuals to the Soviet Union, China, and Cuba, 1928–1978.* 1981 ed. Lanham, Md.: University Press of America, 1989. ISBN 0-8191-7384-3 (pbk). ▸ Well-written, carefully documented study of intellectual background to criticism of statesmen in democratic countries during periods of international strife. [JSH]

48.92   Norman Ingram. *The politics of dissent: pacifism in France, 1919–1939.* Oxford: Oxford University Press, 1991. ISBN 0-19-822295-5. ▸ Social and intellectual history, but neglects movement's great impact on France's international behavior. Nevertheless, can be usefully mined as source for pacifism's effect on others. [JSH]

48.93   Solomon Wank, ed. *Doves and diplomats: foreign offices and peace movements in Europe and America in the twentieth century.* Westport, Conn.: Greenwood, 1978. ISBN 0-313-20027-0. ▸ Only four of twelve essays discuss movements after 1920. Of some use to specialists in peace history but skips comparative evaluation and analysis of interwar Germany and France. [JSH]

EUROPEAN RECONSTRUCTION

General Studies

48.94   Magda Ádam. *Richtung Selbstvernichtung: die kleine Entente, 1920–1938.* Vienna: Österreichischer Bundesverlag, 1988. ISBN 3-215-06381-6. ▸ Critique of Czechoslovak-Yugoslav-Romanian alliance which ignored multiethnic character of successor states and in author's opinion destabilized interwar Europe. Extensive archival research. Occasionally partisan analysis. [CKF]

48.95   Michael J. Hogan. *Informal entente: the private structure of cooperation in Anglo-American economic diplomacy, 1918–1928.* 1977 ed. Chicago: Imprint, 1991. ISBN 1-879176-02-5. ▸ Pioneering effort to discern elements of cooperation on both governmental and private levels of relationship normally characterized as rivalry. Profits from use of British archives. [CKF/JSH]

48.96   C. A. Macartney. *National states and national minorities.* 1934 ed. New York: Russell & Russell, 1968. ▸ Invaluable reference for students of minorities problem in interwar eastern Europe, but also of considerable interest to those concerned with new nations since 1945 and after collapse of Soviet empire. [JSH]

48.97   Sally Marks. *The illusion of peace: international relations in Europe, 1918–1933.* New York: St. Martin's, 1976. ISBN 0-312-40635-5 (pbk). ▸ First-rate introduction to main elements of European international affairs from peace treaty to Hitler. Needs updating to incorporate decade of publications. [CKF/JSH]

48.98   Keith Nelson. *Victors divided: America and the Allies in Germany, 1918–1923.* Berkeley: University of California Press, 1975. ISBN 0-520-02315-3. ▸ Exhaustive research on American occupation policy in Germany. Finds Republican leaders gave as

much thought to resolving German problem as to other international issues. Excellent bibliography. [JSH]

48.99   Stephen Roskill. *Naval policy between the wars.* 2 vols. New York: Walker, 1968–76. ISBN 0-87021-848-4 (v. 2). ▸ Interwar defense problems viewed from British Admiralty. Remains foundation for research on subject, despite much new work of high quality. [JSH]

48.100   Joseph Rothschild. *East Central Europe between the two world wars.* Seattle: University of Washington Press, 1974. ISBN 0-295-95350-0 (cl), 0-295-95337-8 (pbk). ▸ Able compressed histories of lands between German-speaking Europe and Soviet Union. Emphasizes common features and problems. Valuable introduction and overview. [CKF/JSH]

48.101   Peter M. R. Stirk, ed. *European unity in context: the interwar period.* London: Pinter, 1989. ISBN 0-86187-987-2. ▸ Conference volume. Uneven but contains interesting contributions by Stirk on continuities, Boyce on British business, and Krüger on Weimar. [JSH]

48.102   Arnold Wolfers. *Britain and France between two wars: conflicting strategies of peace from Versailles to World War II.* 1940 ed. New York: Norton, 1968. ▸ Examines debate over strategies of coercion and conciliation for containing German aggression and maintaining peace in pre–World War II Europe. Classic still worth reading. [JSH]

SEE ALSO
3.236 Charles S. Maier. *Recasting bourgeois Europe.*

Conference Diplomacy

48.103   Thomas H. Buckley. *The United States and the Washington Conference, 1921–1922.* Knoxville: University of Tennessee Press, 1970. ISBN 0-87049-108-3. ▸ Best available, but not quite definitive, study of multinational negotiations dominated by quest of Britain, Japan, and United States for political settlement of their disputes. [JSH]

48.104   Robert H. Ferrell. *Peace in their time: the origins of the Kellogg-Briand Pact.* 1952 ed. New York: Norton, 1969. ▸ Study of State Department maneuvering against both French efforts to obtain security guarantee and domestic pacifist pressures. Still essential reading. [JSH]

48.105   Carole K. Fink. *The Genoa Conference: European diplomacy, 1921–1922.* 1984 ed. Syracuse: Syracuse University Press, 1993. ISBN 0-8156-2603-7. ▸ First scholarly account of multinational conference on European reconstruction. Balanced presentation of complex and enduring problems of diplomacy in twenties. [JSH]

48.106   Carole K. Fink, Axel Frohn, and Jürgen Heideking, eds. *Genoa, Rapallo, and European reconstruction in 1922.* New York: Cambridge University Press, 1991. ISBN 0-521-41167-X. ▸ Collaborative work by thirteen scholars based on current archival research, providing new perspectives on attempt to revise economic and political settlement. Highly useful charts, maps, bibliography. [JSH]

48.107   Jürgen Heideking. *Aeropag der Diplomaten: die Pariser Botschafterkonferenz der alliierten Hauptmächte und die Probleme der europäischen Politik, 1920–1931.* Husum, Germany: Matthiesen, 1979. ISBN 3-7868-1436-8. ▸ First-rate study of effort to preserve victory over Germany in 1918 by creating institution to oversee implementation of peace terms. [JSH]

48.108   Jon Jacobson. *Locarno diplomacy: Germany and the West, 1925–1929.* Princeton: Princeton University Press, 1972. ISBN 0-691-05190-9. ▸ Standard work emphasizing Locarno agreements did not initiate new era in European diplomacy because British, French, and German statesmen continued to pursue conflicting national interests. Based on wide research in British and German archives. [JSH]

National Policies

48.109 Jacques Bariéty. *Les relations franco-allemandes après la première guerre mondiale: 10 novembre 1918–10 janvier 1925, de l'exécution à la négociation.* Paris: Pedone, 1977. (Publications de la Sorbonne, Série internationale, 8.) ISBN 2-233-00034-X. ▸ Franco-German relations from armistice to Locarno. Supported by immense research and learning. One of key monographs in international history of twenties. [JSH]

48.110 Alan Cassels. *Mussolini's early diplomacy.* Princeton: Princeton University Press, 1970. ISBN 0-691-05179-8. ▸ Mussolini's foreign policy, 1922–27, contained all elements characteristic of his adventurism in thirties: supported revisionism and spokesman for aggressive nationalism. Exemplary monograph of interest to all students of interwar European diplomacy. [JSH/AS]

48.111 Frank Costigliola. *Awkward dominion: American political, economic, and cultural relations with Europe, 1919–1933.* Ithaca, N.Y.: Cornell University Press, 1984. ISBN 0-8014-1679-5 (cl), 0-8014-9505-9 (pbk). ▸ Intellectually ambitious exploration of America's multifarious influences on exhausted Continent. Standard introduction to American interpretation of story. Requires European complement. [JSH]

48.112 John Robert Ferris. *Men, money, and diplomacy: the evolution of British strategic policy, 1919–1926.* Ithaca, N.Y.: Cornell University Press, 1989. ISBN 0-8014-2236-1. ▸ Provocative revisionist study based on wide research. Argues Britain continued to support large military budgets until domestic social conflicts forced redirection of spending in late twenties. [JSH/BJCM]

48.113 John Hiden. *The Baltic states and Weimar Ostpolitik.* New York: Cambridge University Press, 1987. ISBN 0-521-32037-2. ▸ Well-researched, strong presentation of German statesman Gustav Stresemann's strategy to promote Germany's revival as major power through his efforts to penetrate Baltic area. [CKF/JSH]

48.114 Joan Hoff-Wilson. *Ideology and economics: U.S. relations with the Soviet Union, 1918–1933.* Columbia: University of Missouri Press, 1974. ISBN 0-8262-0157-1. ▸ Stimulating examination of debates over recognizing Soviet Union. Minority of businessmen favored selling Bolsheviks rope with which to hang themselves, while ideological diplomats resisted. [JSH]

48.115 Michael Howard. *The continental commitment.* 1972 ed. London: Ashfield, 1989. ISBN 0-948660-07-4. ▸ Discussion of problems of British imperial defense planning, 1900–42, under awareness of weakness. Extremely lucid, intelligent exposition of basic issues by fine historian. Valuable work for all readers. [JSH]

48.116 Peter Krüger. *Die Aussenpolitik der Republik von Weimar.* Darmstadt: Wissenschaftliche Buchgesellschaft, 1985. ISBN 3-534-07250-2. ▸ Changes in foreign policy reflected larger evolution of Weimar republic as conservatives first recoiled from harsh terms, then sought reconciliation, then revived their grievances. Masterful scholarship, definitive interpretation. [CKF/JSH]

48.117 Anne Orde. *British policy and European reconstruction after the First World War.* Cambridge: Cambridge University Press, 1990. ISBN 0-521-37150-3. ▸ Informative study based on substantial archival research; lacks systematic analysis. British policy for reviving European prosperity through granting credits for production and helping to restore public finances. [CKF/JSH]

48.118 Neal Pease. *Poland, the United States, and the stabilization of Europe, 1919–1933.* New York: Oxford University Press, 1986. ISBN 0-19-504050-3. ▸ Well-executed case study based on extensive research in American archives and existing literature on

twenties. Emphasizes American policies rather than larger international context. [CKF/JSH]

48.119 Harald von Riekhoff. *German-Polish relations, 1918–1933.* Baltimore: Johns Hopkins University Press, 1971. ISBN 0-8018-1310-7. ▸ Heavy dependence on German documents makes this more a study of German policy toward Poland, particularly under Foreign Minister Gustav Stresemann. Reliable source for important element of Weimar diplomacy. [JSH]

48.120 Teddy J. Uldricks. *Diplomacy and ideology: the origins of Soviet foreign relations, 1917–1930.* London: Sage, 1979. ISBN 0-8039-9848-1 (cl), 0-8039-9849-X (pbk). ▸ Valuable examination of nuts and bolts of Soviet foreign policy machinery as hopes for immediate world revolution gave way to defense of Soviet state. Detailed and reliable. [JSH]

48.121 Richard Ullman. *Anglo-Soviet relations, 1917–1921.* Vol. 3: *The Anglo-Soviet accord.* Princeton: Princeton University Press for Center of International Studies, 1972. ISBN 0-691-05616-1. ▸ Masterly study of Anglo-Soviet relations interpreting British opening to bolshevik regime as one reflection of sense of weakness which required appeasement of conflicts. [JSH]

48.122 Piotr S. Wandycz. *France and her eastern allies, 1919–1925: French-Czechoslovak-Polish relations from the Paris Peace Conference to Locarno.* Minneapolis: University of Minnesota Press, 1962. ▸ Important, although not exhaustive, study of French efforts to construct new alliance system in eastern Europe to shore up Versailles settlement. [JSH]

48.123 Piotr S. Wandycz. *The twilight of French eastern alliances, 1926–1936: French-Czechoslovak-Polish relations from Locarno to the remilitarization of the Rhineland.* Princeton: Princeton University Press, 1988. ISBN 0-691-05528-9. ▸ Model monograph based on thorough command of sources and mature understanding of issues. Finds Locarno agreements and Depression converged to ruin French alliance system. [JSH]

INTERNATIONAL ECONOMIC RELATIONS
General Studies

48.124 Derek H. Aldcroft. *From Versailles to Wall Street, 1919–1929.* Berkeley: University of California Press, 1977. ISBN 0-520-03336-1 (pbk). ▸ Accomplished review of economic trends with clear discussions of many academic controversies, focused mainly in Europe. Essential reference but slights theme of international distributive contests. [CKF/JSH/DSC]

48.125 Josef Becker and Klaus Hildebrand, eds. *Internationale Beziehungen in der Weltwirtschaftskrise, 1929–1933.* Munich: Vogel, 1980. (Schriften der Philosophische Fakultäten der Universität Augsburg, 18.) ISBN 3-920896-62-9. ▸ Important essays by leading international scholars on foreign policies of major powers in the midst of economic catastrophe; struggle over disarmament; links between German economic policy and international relations; and painful situation of Southeast European states. Valiant effort to grapple with complex question of Depression's impact on international structures. [JSH]

48.126 Alice Teichova and P. L. Cottrell, eds. *International business and Central Europe, 1918–1939.* New York: St. Martin's, 1983. ISBN 0-312-41982-1. ▸ Excellent conference volume examining rush by West European corporations into Habsburg successor states. Essential for understanding these states' economic development and subsequent international competition. [JSH]

SEE ALSO
31.372 Carl-Ludwig Holtfrerich. *The German inflation, 1914–1923.*
44.190 Mira Wilkins. *The maturing of multinational enterprise.*

War Debts and Reparation

48.127 Denise Artaud. *La question des dettes interalliées et la reconstruction de l'Europe, 1917–1929.* 2 vols. Lille, France: Université de Lille Atelier National de Reproduction des Thèses, 1978. ISBN 2-7295-0037-5. ▸ Indictment of American policy for using financial leverage and war debts to shape European choices. Copious documentation of exciting argument. [JSH]

48.128 Bruce Kent. *The spoils of war: the politics, economics, and diplomacy of reparations, 1918–1932.* Oxford: Oxford University Press, 1989. ISBN 0-19-822738-8. ▸ Unique perspective based on much research and thought. Creditor governments understood Germany could not pay, but prolonged agony to stave off challenge from below. [JSH]

48.129 Stephen A. Schuker. *American "reparations" to Germany, 1919–33: implications for the Third World debt crisis.* Princeton: Princeton University, Department of Economics, International Finance Section, 1988. (Princeton studies in international finance, 61.) ISBN 0-88165-233-4. ▸ Compares interwar German national bankruptcy and contemporary debt crisis in some developing countries: both viewed as devices for capturing foreign resources. Scintillating study. [JSH]

48.130 Stephen A. Schuker. *The end of French predominance in Europe: the financial crisis of 1924 and the adoption of the Dawes Plan.* Chapel Hill: University of North Carolina Press, 1976. ISBN 0-8078-1253-6. ▸ Masterful multinational study of decisive turning point in interwar history, based on exhaustive archival research and perceptive analysis. [CKF/JSH]

48.131 Marc Trachtenberg. *Reparation in world politics: France and European economic diplomacy, 1916–1923.* New York: Columbia University Press, 1980. ISBN 0-231-04786-X. ▸ Important study argues that French efforts to use reparations claims to shift costs of war and reconstruction to other countries were repeatedly rebuffed by other major powers. [CKF/JSH]

Diplomacy of Trade and Payments

48.132 Robert W. D. Boyce. *British capitalism at the crossroads, 1919–1932: a study in politics, economics, and international relations.* Cambridge: Cambridge University Press, 1987. ISBN 0-5213-2535-8. ▸ Essential reading for historians of Britain and diplomacy. Discusses British efforts to resist shift in power in world economy and heavy costs incurred by that effort. [JSH]

48.133 Stephen V. O. Clarke. *Central bank cooperation, 1924–1931.* New York: Federal Reserve Bank of New York, 1967. ▸ Expert discussion of quiet international financial diplomacy of twenties. Personal goodwill could not override forces of economic nationalism. For all specialists in field. [JSH]

48.134 Ian M. Drummond. *Imperial economic policy, 1917–1939: studies in expansion and protection.* London: Allen & Unwin, 1974. ISBN 0-04-330243-2 (cl), 0-04-330244-0 (pbk). ▸ Analysis of frustrations of British efforts to negotiate favorable relations with dominions. Source to be mined by specialists. [CKF/JSH]

48.135 Barry Eichengreen. *Elusive stability: essays in the history of international finance, 1919–1939.* Cambridge: Cambridge University Press, 1990. ISBN 0-521-36538-4. ▸ Important, demanding essays. France, Britain, and America predominate, while Germany scarcely appears. Best if readers have some quantitative skills. [JSH]

48.136 William C. McNeil. *American money and the Weimar republic: economics and politics on the eve of the Great Depression.* New York: Columbia University Press, 1986. ISBN 0-231-06236-2. ▸ German elites sought to transfer costs of lost war to victors to avoid domestic distributive contests that might challenge their position. Well written but not for beginners. [JSH]

48.137 D. E. Moggridge. *British monetary policy, 1924–1931: the Norman conquest of $4.86.* Cambridge: Cambridge University Press, 1972. (University of Cambridge, Department of Applied Economics, Monographs, 1.) ISBN 0-521-08225-0. ▸ Britain's fight to retain world financial leadership without possessing means had harmful effect on domestic industries. Very good on leaders' woolly thinking but ultimately not persuasive. [JSH]

48.138 Melchior Palyi. *The twilight of gold, 1914–1936: myths and realities.* Chicago: Regnery, 1972. ▸ Violent denunciation of managed currencies and autarkic trade blocs by close observer of events in Germany and former adviser to Reichsbank. Informative but approach with caution. [JSH]

48.139 Carl P. Parrini. *Heir to empire: United States economic diplomacy, 1916–1923.* Pittsburgh: University of Pittsburgh Press, 1969. ISBN 0-8229-3178-8. ▸ Valuable, durable, pathbreaking study of continuity in American foreign policy. Americans sought to open closed economic spheres using tariffs, banking, and foreign direct investment as levers. [JSH]

48.140 Benjamin M. Rowland, ed. *Balance of power or hegemony: the interwar monetary system.* New York: New York University Press, 1976. ISBN 0-8147-7368-0. ▸ Interesting attempt to apply historical knowledge to contemporary public policy issues. Essays on system, its historiography, and on British, French, and American policies; Germany sadly absent. [JSH]

48.141 Clemens A. Wurm. *Business, politics, and international relations: steel, cotton, and international cartels in British politics, 1924–1939.* New York: Cambridge University Press, 1993. ISBN 0-521-40520-3. ▸ Important study of British response to international challenge to staple industries which provided foundation for British power. Also useful for its contemporary implications. [JSH]

International Economic Crisis

48.142 Edward W. Bennett. *Germany and the diplomacy of the financial crisis, 1931.* Cambridge, Mass.: Harvard University Press, 1962. ▸ Thorough research and coverage of German chancellor Heinrich Brüning's pursuit of foreign policy victory for domestic purposes. Few Western leaders emerge from this important work with reputations intact. [JSH]

48.143 Charles P. Kindleberger. *The world in depression, 1929–1939.* Rev. ed. Berkeley: University of California Press, 1986. ISBN 0-520-05591-8 (cl), 0-520-05592-6 (pbk). ▸ Economic history of Depression lucidly presented with perhaps excessively engaging interpretation. Much on origins, but little on consequences. Required reading for every historian of twentieth century. [JSH]

48.144 Kenneth Mouré. *Managing the franc Poincaré: economic understanding and political constraint in French monetary policy, 1928–1936.* Cambridge: Cambridge University Press, 1991. ISBN 0-521-39458-9. ▸ Superb study giving careful attention to one important aspect of French policy with profound effects on national psychology, social cohesion, political stability, and military power. [JSH]

48.145 R. J. Overy. *The Nazi economic recovery, 1932–1938.* London: Macmillan for Economic History Society, 1982. ISBN 0-333-31119-1 (pbk). ▸ Brief essay summarizing research and controversy on much debated issue. Very good work intended as introduction for general readers. Clear exposition of controversies; extensive bibliography. [CKF/JSH]

MIDDLE EAST, 1920–1945

48.146 George Antonius. *The Arab awakening: the story of the Arab national movement.* 1938 ed. New York: Capricorn, 1965. ▸ Clear, balanced, and well-informed survey of growth of Arab nationalism from mid-nineteenth to mid-twentieth century. Still valuable as introduction and as contemporary history. [JSH]

48.147 Briton Cooper Busch. *Mudros to Lausanne: Britain's frontier in West Asia, 1918–1923*. Albany: State University of New York Press, 1976. ISBN 0-87395-265-0. ▸ Model study of British security dilemmas along lifeline to India immediately after World War I. Helpful in understanding fears of decision makers. Good command of archival sources and clearly written. [JSH]

48.148 John Darwin. *Britain, Egypt, and the Middle East: imperial policy in the aftermath of war, 1918–1922*. New York: St. Martin's, 1981. ISBN 0-312-09736-0. ▸ Britain's rapid reduction in direct control was more voluntary withdrawal from advanced positions taken during war than coerced retreat before aroused local nationalism. Important contribution. [JSH]

48.149 Ahmed M. Gomaa. *The foundation of the League of Arab States: wartime diplomacy and inter-Arab politics, 1941 to 1945*. London: Longman, 1977. ISBN 0-582-78073-X. ▸ Interesting attempt to offer complex explanation of permissive and propulsive forces leading to creation of Arab League. Based on British archives and private papers with some Arab League documents. [JSH]

48.150 Philip S. Khoury. *Syria and the French mandate: the politics of Arab nationalism, 1920–1945*. Princeton: Princeton University Press, 1987. ISBN 0-691-05486-X. ▸ Finely crafted study of struggle by Damascus elites to retain their power by hoisting nationalist banner, a device which intensified rivalries among Syrian nationalism, pan-Arabism, and Zionism. [JSH]

48.151 Aaron S. Klieman. *Foundations of British policy in the Arab world: the Cairo Conference of 1921*. Baltimore: Johns Hopkins University Press, 1970. ISBN 0-8018-1125-2. ▸ Survey of British efforts to maintain war gains in Middle East in face of Arab nationalism and scarce resources, 1918–21. Excellent overview of imperial concerns. [JSH]

48.152 Yehoshua Porath. *In search of Arab unity, 1930–1945*. London: Cass, 1986. ISBN 0-7146-3264-3 (cl), 0-7146-4051-4 (pbk). ▸ Analysis of failed quest for unity, especially on Palestine issue, and British response. Informative for Middle Eastern specialists but prose and organization difficult for others. Draws on British and Zionist archival sources and Arabic memoir literature. [CKF/JSH/CVF]

48.153 Bernard Wasserstein. *The British in Palestine: the mandatory government and the Arab-Jewish conflict, 1917–1929*. 2d ed. Oxford: Blackwell, 1991. ISBN 0-631-17574-1. ▸ Sound study of how British officials in Palestine sought to deal with consequences of Balfour Declaration, which most came to regard as mistake. Valuable work for specialists. [JSH]

SEE ALSO
18.511 Ann Mosely Lesch. *Arab politics in Palestine, 1917–1939*.
18.522 Yehoshua Porath. *The emergence of the Palestinian-Arab national movement, 1918–1929* (vol. 1). *The Palestinian-Arab national movement, 1929–1939* (vol. 2).
28.330 Claudio G. Segré. *Fourth shore*.
47.426 Christopher M. Andrew and A. S. Kanya-Forstner. *The climax of French imperial expansion, 1914–1924*.

FAR EAST, 1920–1945

48.154 John E. Dreifort. *Myopic grandeur: the ambivalence of French foreign policy toward the Far East, 1919–1945*. Kent, Ohio: Kent State University Press, 1991. ISBN 0-87338-441-5. ▸ Rich display of research offering another perspective on interwar developments in Far East. Inadequate military resources and lack of support from United States and Britain explain French passivity in twenties and thirties. [CKF/JSH/RJY]

48.155 Roger Dingman. *Power in the Pacific: the origins of naval arms limitation, 1914–1922*. Chicago: University of Chicago Press, 1976. ISBN 0-226-15331-2. ▸ Ambitious, thoughtful emphasis on role of domestic political and economic concerns in promoting Washington treaties. Uses Japanese, British, and American archival sources. Valuable complement to Buckley 48.103. [JSH]

48.156 Edmund S. K. Fung. *The diplomacy of imperial retreat: Britain's South China policy, 1924–1931*. New York: Oxford University Press, 1991. ISBN 0-19-585284-2. ▸ Careful tracing of skillful British adaptation to Chinese nationalism in era of Washington Conference treaty system that established a balance of power in Far East. Useful supplement to Iriye 48.157. [CKF/JSH]

48.157 Akira Iriye. *After imperialism: the search for a new order in the Far East, 1921–1931*. 1965 ed. Chicago: Imprint, 1990. ISBN 1-879176-00-9 (pbk). ▸ Analysis of great power strategies for exploiting or containing growth of Asian nationalism from Washington Conference to Japanese seizure of Manchuria (1931). Fundamental work on interwar diplomacy. [JSH]

48.158 Ramon H. Myers and Mark R. Peattie, eds. *The Japanese colonial empire, 1895–1945*. Princeton: Princeton University Press, 1984. ISBN 0-691-05398-7 (cl), 0-691-10222-8 (pbk). ▸ Unusually well-crafted conference volume with sections on origins, administration, economics, and legacy of empire. Long introductory essay helps pull pieces together. Invaluable bibliographical essay; detailed index. [JSH/FGN]

INTER-AMERICAN RELATIONS, 1920–1945

48.159 Irwin F. Gellman. *Good Neighbor diplomacy: United States policies in Latin America, 1933–1945*. Baltimore: Johns Hopkins University Press, 1979. ISBN 0-8018-2250-5. ▸ Narrative overview, buttressed by extensive research in papers of policy makers. Where public opinion allowed, Franklin Roosevelt expanded international activity of United States, creating broader base for American world power in process. Stimulating work on a central event. Read with Wood 38.77. [CKF/JSH/RJW/RKG]

48.160 Stanley E. Hilton. *Brazil and the great powers, 1930–1939: the politics of trade rivalry*. Austin: University of Texas Press for Institute of Latin American Studies, 1975. (Latin American monographs, 38.) ISBN 0-292-70713-4. ▸ Controversial, well-researched study. Description of tug of war between Allied and Axis powers on Brazilian trade and, ultimately, participation in war. Brazilian government, especially military, responded with strategy for economic development and authoritarian efficiency. [JSH/RLML]

48.161 Frank D. McCann, Jr. *The Brazilian-American alliance, 1937–1945*. Princeton: Princeton University Press, 1973. ISBN 0-691-05655-2. ▸ Important work on inter-American relations. History of Brazilian Expeditionary Force, its combat role in Europe and return to Brazil. United States displaced Britain as leading foreign power in Brazil and built relations with state whose future importance is always promised. [JSH/RLML]

48.162 J. Lloyd Mecham. *The United States and inter-American security, 1889–1960*. Austin: University of Texas Press, 1961. ▸ Military, political, and economic relations between United States and Latin America during period of former's rise to superpower status. Clear, comprehensive introduction in need of revision. [JSH/RJW]

48.163 Bryce Wood. *The United States and Latin American wars, 1932–1942*. New York: Columbia University Press, 1966. ▸ Reliable account by leading scholar. Particularly valuable for treatment of conflicts within continent often slighted by diplomatic historians. [JSH]

FAR EASTERN CRISES, 1931–1939

48.164 Michael A. Barnhart. *Japan prepares for total war: the search for economic security, 1919–1941.* Ithaca, N.Y.: Cornell University Press, 1987. ISBN 0-8014-1915-8 (cl), 0-8014-9529-6 (pbk). ▸ Discussion of economic roots of Japanese expansionism in quest for secure resource base. Fine partial explanation of origins of Pacific War. [JSH]

48.165 Dorothy Borg. *The United States and the Far Eastern crisis of 1933–1938: from the Manchurian Incident through the initial stage of the undeclared Sino-Japanese War.* Cambridge, Mass.: Harvard University Press, 1964. ▸ Detailed explanation of conflict between Japan and United States. Focus on feeble response of Franklin Roosevelt administration to Japanese aggression in China before outbreak of Second World War. Highly regarded at publication and still useful. [JSH/RKG]

48.166 Herbert Feis. *The road to Pearl Harbor: the coming of the war between the United States and Japan.* 1950 ed. Princeton: Princeton University Press, 1971. ISBN 0-691-05632-3 (cl), 0-691-01061-7 (pbk). ▸ Often reprinted, older classic tracing deepening alienation between two states, 1937–41, which moved in stages toward war as diplomacy failed to resolve fundamental disagreements. [JSH/RKG]

48.167 John P. Fox. *Germany and the Far Eastern crisis, 1931–1938: a study in diplomacy and ideology.* Oxford: Clarendon for London School of Economics and Political Science, 1982. ISBN 0-19-822573-3. ▸ Effective contribution to debate on Hitler's diplomacy based on wide research in British and German archives. Argues that Hitler imposed ideological goals on exponents of traditional alliances and economic interests. [CKF/JSH]

48.168 Bradford A. Lee. *Britain and the Sino-Japanese War, 1937–1939: a study in the dilemmas of British decline.* Stanford, Calif.: Stanford University Press, 1973. ISBN 0-8047-0799-5. ▸ Well-constructed examination of Britain's policy toward Far East; particularly rewarding for insights into reasonable, although mistaken, assumptions of British leaders at height of appeasement. [CKF/JSH]

48.169 James W. Morley, ed. *Japan erupts: the London Naval Conference and the Manchurian Incident, 1928–1932; selected translations from Taiheiyo senso e no michi, kaisen qaiko shi.* Vol. 1 of *Japan's road to the Pacific War.* New York: Columbia University Press, 1984. ISBN 0-231-05782-2. ▸ Valuable collection of translated articles making research in Japanese primary sources available. Illuminates difficulty in controlling military. Essential reading for students of prewar Far East. [JSH]

48.170 James W. Morley, ed. *The China quagmire: Japan's expansion on the Asian continent, 1933–1941; selected translations from Taiheiyo senso e no michi, kaisen qaiko shi.* Vol. 2 of *Japan's road to the Pacific War.* New York: Columbia University Press, 1983. ISBN 0-231-05522-6. ▸ Three long, translated studies treating Kwantung Army, Marco Polo Bridge Incident, and relations with Western powers. Highly useful accounts of Japanese military aggression in China based on Japanese records. [JSH]

48.171 James W. Morley, ed. *Deterrent diplomacy: Japan, Germany, and the USSR, 1935–1940; selected translations from Taiheiyo senso e no michi, kaisen qaiko shi.* Vol. 3 of *Japan's road to the Pacific War.* New York: Columbia University Press, 1976. ISBN 0-231-08969-4. ▸ Translations of Japanese scholarship on Anti-Comintern Pact, Japanese-Soviet relations, and Tripartite Pact between Germany, Italy, and Japan. Invaluable source on interwar politics and diplomacy for those who do not read Japanese. Incorporates most important Japanese scholarship on topic. [JSH]

48.172 James W. Morley, ed. *The fateful choice: Japan's advance into Southeast Asia, 1939–1941; selected translations from Taiheiyo*

senso e no michi, kaisen qaiko shi. Vol. 4 of *Japan's road to the Pacific War.* New York: Columbia University Press, 1980. ISBN 0-231-04804-1. ▸ Translations of five substantial essays by Japanese historians on neutrality agreement with Soviet Union, relations with Western colonial possessions to South, and Japanese naval politics. Fundamental work. [CKF/JSH]

48.173 James Neidpath. *The Singapore naval base and the defense of Britain's Far Eastern empire, 1919–1941.* Oxford: Clarendon, 1981. ISBN 0-19-822474-5. ▸ One of several good works treating Singapore base. Comprehensive archival research supports stimulating exposition of failed British efforts to match inadequate resources to vast commitments. [JSH]

48.174 Ian H. Nish. *Japan's struggle with internationalism: Japan, China, and the League of Nations, 1931–1933.* New York: Routledge, 1993. ▸ Expert deploys his forces in examination of domestic and international aspects of Japan's policy in China at critical moment when Japan renewed its campaign of territorial expansion. [JSH]

48.175 Christopher Thorne. *The limits of foreign policy: the West, the League, and the Far Eastern crisis of 1931–1933.* New York: Putnam, 1972. ISBN 0-399-11124-7. ▸ Classic work in international history. Reexamination of British and United States policies toward Japanese expansion into Manchuria (1931). Punctures myths that Western powers could have effectively opposed Japan and that Japanese aggression opened door to aggressors in Europe. [JSH/FGN]

48.176 Ann Trotter. *Britain and East Asia, 1933–1937.* London: Cambridge University Press for London School of Economics and Political Science, Centre for International Studies, 1975. ISBN 0-521-20475-5. ▸ Study of British officials' fruitless debate on best means to maintain sound relations in Far East. Pioneering work in British archives; best read with Lee 48.168. [JSH]

ORIGINS OF WORLD WAR II IN EUROPE

Collapse of the Peace in Europe

48.177 P.M.H. Bell. *The origins of the Second World War in Europe.* London: Longman, 1986. ISBN 0-582-49112-6 (pbk). ▸ Excellent introduction to debate on origins of war; examines debates, ideologies, economic crises, and strategic situation in 1930s. Notes and bibliography provide good access to English-language literature. [JSH/DSC]

48.178 Eberhard Jäckel. *Hitler's world view: a blueprint for power.* Herbert Arnold, trans. Cambridge, Mass.: Harvard University Press, 1981. ISBN 0-674-40425-4. ▸ Concise, well-documented, and persuasively argued work of interest to all diplomatic historians. Argues Hitler sought territorial empire by conquest in Eastern Europe and destruction of Jews. [JSH]

48.179 David E. Kaiser. *Economic diplomacy and the origins of the Second World War: Germany, Britain, France, and Eastern Europe, 1930–1939.* Princeton: Princeton University Press, 1980. ISBN 0-691-05312-X (cl), 0-691-10101-9 (pbk). ▸ Ambitious, provocative, but not entirely successful attempt to explore German economic expansion. Argues British and French failure to coordinate economic policies with political goals allowed Germany to exploit Eastern Europe to pay for rearmament. [CKF/JSH/DSC]

48.180 Gordon Martel, ed. *The "Origins of the Second World War" reconsidered: the A.J.P. Taylor debate after twenty-five years.* Boston: Allen & Unwin, 1986. ISBN 0-04-940084-3 (cl), 0-04-940085-1 (pbk). ▸ Diverse collection of essays summarizing two decades of research on interwar period. Generally castigates Taylor 48.186 but admits he stimulated debate. Valuable contributions by Marks, Schuker, Kennedy, and Uldricks. [CKF/JSH/DSC]

48.181 Wolfgang J. Mommsen and Lothar Kettenacker, eds. *The fascist challenge and the policy of appeasement.* London: Allen

& Unwin for German Historical Institute, 1983. ISBN 0-04-940068-1. ▸ Richly documented introduction to recent scholarship on foreign policies of major Western states in 1930s. Regrettable absence of contributions on other states. [JSH/DSC]

48.182 Williamson Murray. *The change in the European balance of power, 1938–1939: the path to ruin.* Princeton: Princeton University Press, 1984. ISBN 0-691-05413-4 (cl), 0-691-10161-2 (pbk). ▸ Close assessment of distribution of material resources suggesting balance of power did not shift until after Western statesmen allowed Hitler's advance in 1938. Challenges other interpretations. Best study of strategic consequences of appeasement. [JSH/DSC]

48.183 Barry R. Posen. *The sources of military doctrine: France, Britain, and Germany between the world wars.* Ithaca, N.Y.: Cornell University Press, 1984. ISBN 0-8014-1633-7. ▸ Suggestive application of organizational theory and other political science concepts to explain adoption of military doctrines by Britain, France, and Germany which had their outcome in battles of 1940. [JSH]

48.184 Gaines Post, Jr. *Dilemmas of appeasement: British deterrence and defense, 1934–1937.* Ithaca, N.Y.: Cornell University Press, 1993. ISBN 0-8014-2748-7. ▸ Rational assessment of dangers and resources by British decision makers for period between first tremors of German reassertion and arrival of Neville Chamberlain in power. Engrossing reading based on thorough examination of archives. [JSH]

48.185 Stephen A. Schuker. "France and the remilitarization of the Rhineland, 1936." *French historical studies* 14.3 (1986) 299–328. ▸ Wide-ranging archival research provides basis for persuasive reinterpretation of failed French response to one important violation of German commitments. [JSH]

48.186 A.J.P. Taylor. *The origins of the Second World War.* 1961 ed. New York: Atheneum, 1983. ISBN 0-689-70658-8 (pbk). ▸ Brilliant if flawed revisionist study concludes Allied policy must bear considerable responsibility for Second World War. New essay, "Second Thoughts," replies to his critics. [CKF/JSH/DSC]

48.187 Christopher Thorne. *The approach of war, 1938–1939.* 1967 ed. London: Macmillan, 1973. ▸ Best brief survey of prewar diplomacy as Hitler began rapid territorial advance. Discusses crises over Austria, Czechoslovakia, and Poland. Able introduction with excellent references for scholars. [JSH]

48.188 Mario Toscano. *The origins of the Pact of Steel.* 1967 ed. Baltimore: Johns Hopkins University Press, 1968. ▸ Important, durable work based chiefly on Italian documentation. Discusses Mussolini's mismanaged effort to profit from international instability by entangling Hitler in Italian alliance. [JSH]

48.189 Donald Cameron Watt. *Too serious a business: European armed forces and the approach to the Second World War.* Berkeley: University of California Press, 1975. ISBN 0-520-02829-5. ▸ Stimulating effort portraying World War II as military conflict powerfully shaped by larger social and intellectual forces. Important book for readers at many levels. [JSH]

Failure of Disarmament

48.190 Edward W. Bennett. *German rearmament and the West, 1932–1933.* Princeton: Princeton University Press, 1979. ISBN 0-691-05269-7. ▸ Analysis of German plans for rearmament, Western understanding of those plans, and diplomatic response. Exemplary work of great value to students of modern Germany and of diplomacy. [JSH]

48.191 Michael Geyer. *Aufrüstung oder Sicherheit: die Reichswehr in der Krise der Machtpolitik, 1924–1936.* Wiesbaden: Steiner, 1980. ISBN 3-5150-2812-9. ▸ Examination of German military's loss of realistic perspective under impact of Hitler's ambitions.

Breaks conceptual boundaries of conventional military history; model of how to proceed on several scores. [JSH]

48.192 Stephen E. Pelz. *Race to Pearl Harbor: the failure of the Second London Naval Conference and the onset of World War II.* Cambridge, Mass: Harvard University Press, 1974. ISBN 0-674-74575-2. ▸ Thorough account, particularly valuable for use of Japanese sources. Argues incompatible political ambitions first blocked agreement on arms limitation between Britain, America, and Japan, then fueled arms race. [JSH]

48.193 Maurice Vaïsse. *Sécurité d'abord: la politique française en matière de désarmement, 9 décembre 1930–17 avril 1934.* Paris: Pedone, 1981. (Publications de la Sorbonne, Série Internationale, 18.) ISBN 2-233-00099-4. ▸ First-rate study, based on prodigious research, of wide interest to historians for exposition of how highly charged political environment obstructed coherent technical agreements. [JSH]

National Policies

48.194 Anthony Adamthwaite. *France and the coming of the Second World War, 1936–1939.* London: Cass, 1977. ISBN 0-7146-3035-7. ▸ Analysis of policy makers' reluctance to defend Czechoslovakia. France initially sought accommodation with Germany by jettisoning its Central European obligations, acting with greater confidence as its strength recovered. Provocative, thoroughly researched, and important study of key issues. [CKF/JSH/LLC]

48.195 Berenice A. Carroll. *Design for total war: arms and economics in the Third Reich.* The Hague: Mouton, 1968. ISBN 90-2790-299-2. ▸ Standard account of German economy before and during World War II. [JSH]

48.196 Maurice Cowling. *The impact of Hitler: British politics and British policy, 1933–1940.* 1975 ed. Chicago: University of Chicago Press, 1977. ISBN 0-226-11660-3. ▸ Important contribution to literature on 1930s. Conservative foreign policy, both appeasement and resistance, shaped by desire to defend domestic social order. For specialists. [JSH]

48.197 Robert A. Dallek. *Franklin D. Roosevelt and American foreign policy, 1932–1945.* 1979 ed. Oxford: Oxford University Press, 1981. ISBN 0-19-502457-5 (cl), 0-19-502894-5 (pbk). ▸ Lucid, comprehensive summation of existing scholarship on Roosevelt's diplomacy and starting point for any further inquiry. Roosevelt took active role in setting policy, imposing personal views and interpretations at critical points. [JSH/RKG]

48.198 Jean-Baptiste Duroselle. *Politique étrangère de la France: la décadence, 1932–1939.* Paris: Imprimerie Nationale, 1979. (Collection points, Série histoire, H63.) ISBN 2-11-080723-7. ▸ Magnificent example of historical scholarship, both in sophistication of analysis and mastery of complicated source materials. Traces paralysis of French initiative under Hitler's lengthening shadow. [JSH/MMF]

48.199 Robert Frankenstein. *Le prix du réarmement français, 1935–1939.* Paris: Publications de la Sorbonne, 1982. (France dix-neuvième-vingtième siècles, 13.) ISBN 2-85944-050-X. ▸ Stimulating revisionist study of French defense spending under Popular Front and Daladier regimes. Provides helpful reconsideration of late Third Republic. [JSH]

48.200 Jonathan Haslam. *Soviet foreign policy, 1930–1933: the impact of the Depression.* New York: St. Martin's, 1983. ISBN 0-312-74838-8. ▸ Concise, valuable study for advanced students of interwar diplomacy. Domestic preoccupations suggested cautious foreign policy that ill-suited dangerous environment created by Hitler's rise to power in Germany. [JSH]

48.201 Jonathan Haslam. *The Soviet Union and the struggle for collective security in Europe, 1933–1939.* New York: St. Martin's,

1984. ISBN 0-312-74908-2. ▸ Stimulating interpretation using published primary sources. Traces Soviet policy of attempting to create alliances to contain Hitler and Western response. Read with Hochman 48.202. [JSH]

48.202 Jiri Hochman. *The Soviet Union and the failure of collective security, 1934–1938.* Ithaca, N.Y.: Cornell University Press, 1984. ISBN 0-8014-1655-8. ▸ Extensively researched argument, including Eastern European sources, that Soviet Union must bear much of blame for failure to contain Germany. Sharp contrast to Haslam 48.201. [JSH]

48.203 Nicole Jordan. *The Popular Front and Central Europe: the dilemmas of French impotence, 1918–1940.* Cambridge: Cambridge University Press, 1992. ISBN 0-521-41077-0. ▸ Focuses on French and especially on French premier Leon Blum's relations with military and diplomats. Useful as sequel to works by Wandycz 48.122, 48.123. Broad context and excellent bibliography. [JSH]

48.204 William L. Langer and S. Everett Gleason. *The world crisis and American foreign policy.* 1952–53 ed. 2 vols. New York: Harper, 1964–68. ▸ Old, semi-official history of American diplomacy in shadow of new world war. Intelligent reconstruction of policy in wide context. [JSH]

48.205 Callum A. MacDonald. *The United States, Britain, and appeasement, 1936–1939.* New York: St. Martin's, 1981. ISBN 0-312-83313-X. ▸ Exhaustive research in British and American archives demonstrating how deep mutual distrust poisoned Anglo-American relations when cooperation might have aided resistance to Hitler. [JSH]

48.206 Keith Middlemas. *The strategy of appeasement: the British government and Germany, 1937–1939.* Chicago: Quadrangle, 1972. ISBN 0-8129-0241-6. ▸ Analysis of Chamberlain's effort to guide British policy through Munich and afterward, based on wide array of British sources. Much information and stimulating conclusions, despite murky prose. [JSH]

48.207 Arnold A. Offner. *American appeasement: United States foreign policy and Germany, 1933–1938.* Cambridge, Mass.: Belknap, 1969. ▸ Wide-ranging inquiry into lack of vigorous American response to Hitler by Roosevelt administration. Important example of revisionism in American diplomatic history, although less satisfactory on motives. [JSH]

48.208 G. C. Peden. *British rearmament and the treasury, 1932–1939.* Edinburgh: Scottish Academic Press, 1979. ISBN 0-7073-0229-3. ▸ Study of treasury efforts to balance rearmament against limited resources available to economy in midst of reconstruction. Useful specialist contribution to new history of appeasement. [JSH]

48.209 Hans-Jürgen Schröder. *Deutschland und die Vereinigten Staaten von Amerika, 1933–1939: Wirtschaft und Politik in der Entwicklung des deutsch-amerikanischen Gegensatzes.* Wiesbaden: Steiner, 1970. ▸ German Autarky versus American Open Door policy as German efforts to seal off protected sphere in Eastern Europe and invade American markets in Latin America led American officials to perceive Germany as economic as well as military peril. [JSH]

48.210 William I. Shorrock. *From ally to enemy: the enigma of fascist Italy in French foreign policy, 1920–1940.* Kent, Ohio: Kent State University Press, 1988. ISBN 0-87338-350-8. ▸ Valuable, well-documented account of deterioration of Franco-Italian relations, based on French archives. Both countries suffered from grievous blunders of Mussolini and Popular Front. [CKF/JSH]

48.211 Wesley K. Wark. *The ultimate enemy: British intelligence and Nazi Germany, 1933–1939.* Ithaca, N.Y.: Cornell University Press, 1985. ISBN 0-8014-1821-6. ▸ British assessment of German capabilities and intentions. Essential reading on appeasement; also valuable for understanding role of perceptions, decision

making, and several sorts of intelligence failures in international affairs. [JSH]

48.212 Gerhard L. Weinberg. *The foreign policy of Hitler's Germany.* 2 vols. Chicago: University of Chicago Press, 1970–80. ISBN 0-226-88509-7 (v. 1, cl), 0-226-88511-9 (v. 2, cl), 0-226-88513-5 (v. 1, pbk). ▸ How Hitler toppled established order between 1933 and 1936, then launched Europe toward war, 1936–39. Superb example of traditional diplomatic history. [JSH]

48.213 Robert J. Young. *In command of France: French foreign policy and military planning, 1933–1940.* Cambridge, Mass.: Harvard University Press, 1978. ISBN 0-674-44536-8. ▸ Competent and useful but not definitive study of links between foreign policy and armed forces and responses to problem of interwar security against Germany. Emphasizes political, economic, and strategic factors. More favorable to French leaders than was once common. [JSH/RJY]

SEE ALSO
44.735 Lloyd C. Gardner. *Economic aspects of New Deal diplomacy.*

Outbreak of War in Europe

48.214 Anna M. Cienciała. *Poland and the Western powers, 1938–1939: a study in the interdependence of Eastern and Western Europe.* London: Routledge & Kegan Paul, 1968. ISBN 0-7100-5021-6. ▸ Trenchant examination of Poland's position in prewar European order. Useful for presentation of Polish material, but out of date in assessment of Western diplomacy. [JSH/WLB]

48.215 James Thomas Emmerson. *The Rhineland crisis, 7 March 1936: a study in multilateral diplomacy.* Ames: Iowa State University Press, 1977. ISBN 0-8138-1865-6. ▸ Britain's weak response to German aggression paralyzed effective Western response. Good account of events. Read with Post 48.184. [CKF/JSH]

48.216 Eva H. Haraszti. *Treaty-breakers or "Realpolitiker"? The Anglo-German Naval Agreement of June 1935.* Sandor Simon, trans. Boppard, Germany: Boldt, 1974. ISBN 3-7646-1578-8. ▸ Workmanlike study with broader than usual base of sources. [JSH]

48.217 Konrad H. Jarausch. *The Four Power Pact, 1933.* Madison: State Historical Society of Wisconsin for University of Wisconsin, Department of History, 1965. ▸ Careful delineation of minor incident; still useful to specialists. Anglo-Italian efforts to introduce certain order into great power relations soon after Hitler's arrival in power. [JSH]

48.218 Maya Latynski, ed. *Reappraising the Munich Pact: continental perspectives.* Washington, D.C.: Woodrow Wilson Center Press, 1992. ISBN 0-943875-38-2 (cl), 0-943875-39-0 9 (pbk). ▸ Slim collection of conference papers attempting to escape Anglocentric orientation of literature. Chiefly of interest for summaries of Czech and Polish historiography formerly hard to obtain. [JSH]

48.219 Alfred D. Low. *The Anschluss movement, 1931–1938, and the great powers.* Boulder: East European Monographs; distributed by Columbia University Press, 1985. (East European monographs, 185.) ISBN 0-88033-078-3. ▸ Useful study for specialists. Defenders of Austrian independence at home or abroad always few and disappeared almost entirely as likelihood of war increased in later thirties. Sequel to 47.447. [JSH/JWB]

48.220 Anthony Read and David Fisher. *The deadly embrace: Hitler, Stalin, and the Nazi-Soviet Pact, 1939–1941.* New York: Norton, 1988. ISBN 0-393-02528-4. ▸ Lengthy exposition of competing strategies of British, Germans, and Soviets before and during period of Soviet Union's benevolent neutrality toward Germany. [JSH]

48.221 Esmonde M. Robertson. *Mussolini as empire-builder: Europe and Africa, 1932–1936.* New York: St. Martin's, 1977. ISBN 0-312-55589-X. ▸ Useful for patching together history of Italian dictator's diplomacy. Pushed out of Central Europe by Germany, Mussolini was driven back into Hitler's arms by Western resistance to his colonial ambitions. [JSH]

48.222 Telford Taylor. *Munich: the price of peace.* Garden City, N.Y.: Doubleday, 1979. ISBN 0-385-02053-8. ▸ Balanced examination of diplomacy of appeasement and its apogee at Munich. Reasserts received wisdom on possibility of taking strong line against dictators before 1939. Standard work on appeasement. [CKF/JSH/DSC]

48.223 Donald Cameron Watt. *How war came: the immediate origins of the Second World War, 1938–1939.* New York: Pantheon, 1989. ISBN 0-394-57916-X. ▸ Detailed account of European diplomacy between Munich conference and German invasion of Poland. Fascinating on war origins and valuable as reference. [JSH]

SEE ALSO
29.288 Hugh Thomas. *The Spanish Civil War.*

WORLD WAR II

General Studies

48.224 James Butler, ed. *History of the Second World War: United Kingdom military series.* 1952– ed. 30 vols. to date. London: Her Majesty's Stationery Office, 1956–. ▸ Three volumes on war in Western Europe, five on war against Japan, six on Mediterranean, three on naval war, four on air war. Related volumes in Hancock, ed. 48.231. [JSH]

48.225 Peter Calvocoressi, Guy Wint, and John Pritchard. *Total war: causes and courses of the Second World War.* 2d ed. 2 vols. New York: Pantheon, 1990. ISBN 0-679-73091-5 (v. 1), 0-679-73099-0 (v. 2). ▸ Excellent overview of global war, although better on Europe than on Asia. Richer in detail than Wright 22.576 but less analytical. Rewarding for general reader. [JSH]

48.226 Winston Churchill. *The Second World War.* 1948–53 ed. 6 vols. Boston: Houghton-Mifflin, 1985–86. ISBN 0-395-07541-6 (cl, set), 0-395-41685-X (pbk, set). ▸ Part memoir, part history, wonderful reading. Suitable monument to scholar-statesman; now requires supplementary reading. Also available in abridged edition (1990). [CKF/JSH]

48.227 John W. Dower. *War without mercy: race and power in the Pacific War.* New York: Pantheon, 1986. ISBN 0-394-50030-X (cl), 0-304-75172-8 (pbk). ▸ Stimulating, controversial study examines link between racism and war, attributing barbarism to mutually racist attitudes springing from different sources. Important both for argument and for methodology. [JSH/FGN/RKG]

48.228 Jean-Baptiste Duroselle. *Politique étrangère de la France.* Vol. 2: *L'abîme, 1939–1945.* Paris: Imprimerie Nationale, 1982. ISBN 2-1108-0786-5. ▸ Meticulous account of French wartime diplomacy. [CKF/JSH]

48.229 John Erickson. *Stalin's war with Germany.* 1975 ed. 2 vols. Boulder: Westview, 1983–84. ISBN 0-86531-774-5 (v. 1), 0-89158-795-0 (v. 2). ▸ Superb military history of Eastern Front from Russian perspective by master of sources. Volume 1 ends in Stalingrad, volume 2, in Berlin. [CKF/JSH]

48.230 Germany. Militärgeschichtliches Forschungsamt. *Germany and the Second World War.* 10 vols. P. S. Falla, trans. Oxford: Clarendon, 1990–. ISBN 0-19-822866-X (v. 1), 0-19-822885-6 (v. 2). ▸ Ten-volume German official history; two volumes translated thus far. Very broad conception and magnificent execution make volumes essential reading for serious students of war's origins and course. [JSH]

48.231 W. Keith Hancock, ed. *History of the Second World War: United Kingdom civil series.* 25 vols. London: Her Majesty's Stationery Office, 1948–71. ▸ Many of the volumes deal with international aspects of British war effort, such as allocation of raw materials and shipping, procurement of weapons in United States, and war finance. Very fine series of official histories. [JSH]

48.232 F. P. King. *The new internationalism: Allied policy and the European peace, 1939–1945.* Hamden, Conn.: Archon, 1973. ISBN 0-208-01399-7. ▸ Pedestrian treatment of negotiation with defeated states during World War II, but contains much information on subjects often slighted in other accounts. [JSH]

48.233 B. H. Liddell Hart. *History of the Second World War.* 1970 ed. New York: Perigee, 1982. ISBN 0-399-50445-1. ▸ Highly regarded, comprehensive military history with incisive analysis of fighting. Leading historian, controversialist, and military thinker engages many debates. [JSH]

48.234 Alan S. Milward. *War, economy, and society, 1939–1945.* Berkeley: University of California Press, 1977. ISBN 0-520-03338-8 (cl), 0-520-03942-4 (pbk). ▸ Richly detailed investigation, vital for understanding course and impact of Second World War. Comparative economic history surveying production efforts, technology, agriculture organization, war-driven changes, and economic warfare. Concentrates on Europe, but also compares Japan and United States. [CKF/JSH/DSC]

48.235 Norman Rich. *Hitler's war aims.* 2 vols. New York: Norton, 1973–74. ISBN 0-393-05454-3 (v. 1), 0-393-05509-4 (v. 2). ▸ Essential reading for interpretation and valuable source for further studies. Ideology drove Hitler to pursue conquests and then to impose new order on conquered peoples. [JSH]

48.236 Leon V. Sigal. *Fighting to a finish: the politics of war termination in the United States and Japan, 1945.* Ithaca, N.Y.: Cornell University Press, 1988. ISBN 0-8014-2086-5. ▸ Shrewd application of social science models to understanding obstacles to ending war whose outcome had been decided. Emphasizes internal factional struggles and difficulty in arresting bureaucratic inertia. [JSH]

48.237 John Snell. *Illusion and necessity: the diplomacy of global war, 1939–1945.* Boston: Houghton-Mifflin, 1963. ▸ Compact traditional interpretation stressing links between managing coordinated war effort and victory or defeat for rival coalitions. [JSH]

48.238 Gerhard L. Weinberg. *World in the balance: behind the scenes of World War II.* Hanover, N.H.: University Press of New England for Brandeis University Press, 1981. (Studies of the Tauber Institute, 1.) ISBN 0-87451-216-6 (cl), 0-87451-217-4 (pbk). ▸ Two lectures on grand strategy of World War II, filled out with four previously published articles. Stimulating prefiguring of forthcoming history of war. Good bibliography. [JSH]

48.239 Llewellyn Woodward. *British foreign policy in the Second World War.* 5 vols. London: Her Majesty's Stationery Office, 1971–76. ISBN 0-11-630052-3 (v. 1), 0-11-630068-X (v. 2), 0-11-630054-X (v. 3), 0-11-630055-8 (v. 4), 0-11-630191-0 (v. 5). ▸ Somewhat narrowly conceived high quality official history. Essential starting point for studies of wartime alliance diplomacy. [CKF/JSH]

SEE ALSO
22.576 Gordon Wright. *The ordeal of total war, 1939–1945.*

Axis Triumphant, 1939–1941

48.240 P.M.H. Bell. *A certain eventuality: Britain and the fall of France.* London: Saxon House, 1974. ISBN 0-347-00010-X. ▸ Careful examination of British official attitudes and policies toward France during and immediately after defeat in summer 1940. Useful to specialists on Anglo-French relations. [JSH]

48.241 Dorothy Borg and Shumpei Okamoto, eds. *Pearl Harbor as history: Japanese-American relations, 1931–1941*. New York: Columbia University Press, 1973. ISBN 0-231-03734-1 (cl), 0-231-03890-9 (pbk). ▸ First-rate collection of conference papers by twenty-six Japanese and American scholars, exploring formative influences on Japanese-American relations in broad perspective. Offers many useful topical and methodological starting points. [JSH/FGN]

48.242 William Carr. *Poland to Pearl Harbor: the making of the Second World War*. London: Arnold, 1985. ISBN 0-7131-6438-7 (pbk). ▸ Thoughtful survey of expansion of European war into world war, concentrating on Germany, Japan, and United States. Rewarding for all levels of readers. [JSH]

48.243 Saul Friedländer. *Prelude to downfall: Hitler and the United States, 1939–1941*. Aline B. Werth and Alexander Werth, trans. New York: Knopf, 1967. ▸ German policy toward United States between outbreak of war and Pearl Harbor. Competent summation of traditional views, based on German, American, and British archives. [JSH]

48.244 Gabriel Gorodetsky. *Stafford Cripps' mission to Moscow, 1940–1942*. Cambridge: Cambridge University Press, 1984. ISBN 0-521-23866-8. ▸ Contribution to debate over Soviet-Western relations in early years of World War II, arguing real opportunities for reconciliation existed. Much research on restricted topic. [CKF/JSH]

48.245 MacGregor Knox. *Mussolini unleashed, 1939–1941: politics and strategy in fascist Italy's last war*. Cambridge: Cambridge University Press, 1982. ISBN 0-521-23917-6. ▸ Well-researched, controversial thesis: Italian dictator's pursuit of "parallel war" showed him to be as fundamentally violent and aggressive as his German ally. Excellent contribution to debate over character of fascism. See also volume 23 of *Storia d'Italia* (28.3). [JSH/AS]

48.246 Steven Merritt Miner. *Between Churchill and Stalin: the Soviet Union, Great Britain, and the origins of the Grand Alliance*. Chapel Hill: University of North Carolina Press, 1988. ISBN 0-8078-1796-1. ▸ Judicious discussion of Anglo-Soviet relations during first three years of World War II. Provocative interpretation on several points; based on thorough examination of British archives. [CKF/JSH]

48.247 R. T. Thomas. *Britain and Vichy: the dilemma of Anglo-French relations, 1940–1942*. New York: St. Martin's, 1979. ISBN 0-312-09822-7. ▸ British policy toward Vichy government, General de Gaulle, and United States from fall of France to occupation of North Africa. Excellent introduction to tangled political issues from London's perspective. [JSH]

SEE ALSO
44.742 Waldo Heinrichs. *Threshold of war*.

Axis Policies, 1942–1945

48.248 Alexander Dallin. *German rule in Russia, 1941–1945: a study of occupation policies*. 2d ed. Boulder: Westview, 1981. ISBN 0-86531-102-1. ▸ Pioneering work, updated by additional research, on what Germans did with empire they conquered and with captives they retained while retreating. Essential reading on war aims. [CKF/JSH]

48.249 F.W.D. Deakin. *The brutal friendship: Mussolini, Hitler, and the fall of Italian fascism*. New York: Harper & Row, 1962. ▸ Immensely detailed study of German-Italian relations, 1943–45. Definitive study, filled with extended quotations from documents, but not easy reading. Very useful to specialists on wartime diplomacy. [CKF//JSH]

48.250 Stanley E. Hilton. *Hitler's secret war in South America, 1939–1945: German military espionage and Allied counterespionage in Brazil*. Baton Rouge: Louisiana State University Press, 1981.

ISBN 0-8071-0751-4. ▸ Accurate, archive-based account of struggle of limited significance except as barometer of United States interest in its Latin American resource base and Nazi Germany's narrow reach. [JSH]

48.251 Bernd Martin. *Deutschland und Japan im Zweiten Weltkrieg: vom Angriff auf Pearl Harbor bis zur deutschen Kapitulation*. Göttingen: Musterschmidt, 1969. ▸ Germany and Japan failed to coordinate war efforts against very powerful common foes on opposite sides of globe. Valuable for comparing grand strategies of opposing coalitions. [CKF/JSH]

48.252 Johanna Menzel Meskill. *Hitler and Japan: the hollow alliance*. New York: Atherton, 1966. ▸ Germany and Japan distrusted one another, pursued incompatible goals, and failed to coordinate strategies against powerful foes. Best available study, of interest to all students of World War II. [JSH]

Diplomacy of the Grand Alliance, 1942–1945

48.253 Elisabeth Barker. *British policy in South-East Europe in the Second World War*. New York: Macmillan, 1976. ISBN 0-333-15994-2. ▸ Sophisticated, detailed study. Britain entered Balkans to thwart occupying Germans, then bargained with advancing Soviets in 1944 for spheres of influence. Balanced explanation of British support for Tito. [JSH/AF/IB]

48.254 Diane Shaver Clemens. *Yalta*. New York: Oxford University Press, 1970. ▸ Systematic analysis of decision making at wartime Allied conference, defending its outcome and faulting United States for abandoning Yalta agreements. [CKF/JSH/RKG]

48.255 Robert Conquest. *The nation killers: the Soviet deportation of nationalities*. Rev. ed. New York: Macmillan, 1970. ▸ Discussion of Stalin's wartime forced deportation of subject nationalities whom he distrusted. Valuable reference and model for scholars attempting to penetrate barriers to inquiry raised by closed society. Earlier title: *The Soviet Deportation of Nationalities*. [JSH]

48.256 Herbert Feis. *Between war and peace: the Potsdam Conference*. 1960 ed. Westport, Conn.: Greenwood, 1983. ISBN 0-313-24219-4. ▸ Study of tense tripartite negotiations after common goal of defeating Hitler had been accomplished but war in Pacific continued. Standard account; rewarding for specialists. [JSH]

48.257 Herbert Feis. *Churchill, Roosevelt, Stalin: the war they waged and the peace they sought*. 2d ed. Princeton: Princeton University Press, 1967. ISBN 0-691-05607-2 (cl), 0-691-01050-1 (pbk). ▸ Balanced, thorough presentation of coalition diplomacy at peak, 1940 through defeat of Germany. Careful scholarship and familiarity with issues; required reading. [JSH]

48.258 John W. Garver. *Chinese-Soviet relations, 1937–1945: the diplomacy of Chinese nationalism*. New York: Oxford University Press, 1988. ISBN 0-19-505432-6. ▸ Important contribution on underappreciated alliance between Chiang Kai-shek's government and Soviet Union during Sino-Japanese War. Both Nationalists and Communists defended independence from Soviet Union even while fighting each other and Japanese. [JSH/JHC]

48.259 Warren F. Kimball. *The juggler: Franklin Roosevelt as wartime statesman*. Princeton: Princeton University Press, 1991. ISBN 0-691-04787-1. ▸ Valuable collection of essays arguing Roosevelt sought realistic version of Wilsonianism as foundation of postwar international order. [CKF/JSH]

48.260 Martin Kitchen. *British policy towards the Soviet Union during the Second World War*. New York: St. Martin's, 1986. ISBN 0-312-10422-7. ▸ Study of official attitudes toward hostile neutral, important ally, and potential threat, based on Foreign Office archives, military records, and private papers. Will benefit informed specialists. [JSH]

48.261 Wm. Roger Louis. *Imperialism at bay: the United States* *and the decolonization of the British empire, 1941–1945.* New York: Oxford University Press, 1978. ISBN 0-19-821125-2. ‣ Outstanding study of American pressure on wartime ally to dismantle empire for which, in part, British fought. Model of historian's craft and essential reading for international historians. [JSH/JWC]

48.262 Vojtěch Mastný. *Russia's road to the cold war: diplomacy, warfare, and the politics of communism, 1941–1945.* New York: Columbia University Press, 1979. ISBN 0-231-04360-0. ‣ Best available study of Stalin's wartime foreign policy. Argues Stalin's ambitions expanded to fill whatever vacuum presented itself. Of great interest to students of twentieth-century Europe. [CKF/JSH]

48.263 William H. McNeill. *America, Britain, and Russia: their co-operation and conflict, 1941–1946.* 1953 ed. New York: Johnson Reprint, 1970. ‣ Old but perceptive and detailed account of alliance of necessity among powers with very different goals and assumptions. Necessary reading for students of hot and cold wars. [JSH]

48.264 Raymond O'Connor. *Diplomacy for victory: FDR and unconditional surrender.* New York: Norton, 1971. ISBN 0-393-05441-1 (cl), 0-393-09765-x (pbk). ‣ Brief, authoritative study of origins of Casablanca policy demanding unconditional surrender by Germany, Italy, and Japan. Emphasizes Roosevelt's concern with need to hold coalition together and learn lessons of 1918. Good bibliographical essay. [JSH]

48.265 Walter R. Roberts. *Tito, Mihailović, and the Allies, 1941–1945.* 1973 ed. Durham, N.C.: Duke University Press, 1987. ISBN 0-8223-0773-1 (pbk). ‣ Careful presentation and perceptive analysis of tensions between civil war and war against Germans within Yugoslavia and between short- and long-term interests of Western powers. [JSH]

48.266 Keith Sainsbury. *The turning point: Roosevelt, Stalin, Churchill, and Chiang Kai-shek, 1943; the Moscow, Cairo, and Teheran conferences.* Oxford: Oxford University Press, 1985. ISBN 0-19-215858-9. ‣ Analysis of shifting balance of forces within Grand Alliance during 1943 and resulting strains and consequences. Largely based on British documents; invaluable for students of wartime diplomacy. [JSH]

48.267 Mark A. Stoler. *The politics of the second front: American military planning and diplomacy in coalition warfare, 1941–1943.* Westport, Conn.: Greenwood, 1977. ISBN 0-8371-9438-5. ‣ American military favored invading northwestern Europe to support national interests that conflicted with those of Russia and Britain. Valuable to specialists as summary of fundamental controversies. [JSH]

48.268 Christopher Thorne. *Allies of a kind: the United States, Britain, and the war against Japan, 1941–1945.* Oxford: Oxford University Press, 1978. ISBN 0-19-520173-6. ‣ Essential study of Allied misunderstanding, mistrust, and missed opportunities in struggle against Japan and each other for future of Asia. [JSH/FGN]

48.269 Randall Bennett Woods. *A changing of the guard: Anglo-American relations, 1941–1946.* Chapel Hill: University of North Carolina Press, 1990. ISBN 0-8078-1877-1. ‣ Lucid examination of Anglo-American economic relations in wartime, based on thorough research. Supplants all earlier studies. [JSH]

The Intelligence War

48.270 R. V. Jones. *The wizard war: British scientific intelligence, 1939–1945.* New York: Coward, McCann & Geoghegan, 1978. ISBN 0-698-10896-5. ‣ Wartime struggles of British intelligence to penetrate and counter German efforts to turn scientific knowledge into military power. Fascinating account, readily accessible to nonspecialists, and important to understanding war. [JSH]

48.271 David Kahn. *Hitler's spies: German military intelligence in*

World War II. New York: Macmillan, 1978. ISBN 0-02-560610-7. ‣ Massive, meticulous, lively study of German intelligence operations by leading student of cryptography. Wider import for understanding Nazi regime and policy making. [JSH]

48.272 Ronald Lewin. *The American magic: codes, ciphers, and the defeat of Japan.* New York: Farrar, Straus & Giroux, 1982. ISBN 0-374-10417-4. ‣ Excellent complement to British official histories of intelligence operations. Shows rapid development of American decrypting ability under pressure of war. [JSH]

SEE ALSO
24.393 F. H. Hinsley et al. *British intelligence in the Second World War.*

The Holocaust

48.273 Martin Gilbert. *Auschwitz and the Allies.* New York: Holt, Rinehart & Winston, 1981. ISBN 0-03-059284-4. ‣ Brilliant display of evidence showing how human failings of heart and mind led Western Allies to miss or neglect opportunities to help persecuted Jews. [JSH]

48.274 Walter Laqueur. *The terrible secret: an investigation into the suppression of information about Hitler's "Final Solution."* London: Weidenfeld & Nicolson, 1980. ISBN 0-316-51474-8. ‣ By mid to late 1942 British government knew that Nazis were engaged in mass murder; statesmen then had to decide what to do. Careful reconstruction of evidence. [JSH]

48.275 Monty Noam Penkower. *The Jews were expendable: free world diplomacy and the Holocaust.* Urbana: University of Illinois Press, 1983. ISBN 0-252-00747-6. ‣ Nine fervent, well-documented essays on representative cases of diplomacy of moral abdication by states battling Nazi Germany. Final essay suggests broad and troubling implications for diplomacy. [JSH]

48.276 Bernard Wasserstein. *Britain and the Jews of Europe, 1939–1945.* 1979 ed. London: Institute of Jewish Affairs and Oxford University Press, 1988. ISBN 0-19-282185-7. ‣ Britain's strategic needs in Middle East explain exclusion of Jewish refugees from Palestine in 1939; hard hearts and small minds explain it thereafter. Of interest to all students of World War II. [JSH]

SEE ALSO
21.295 Raul Hilberg. *The destruction of the European Jews.*

Atomic Weapons

48.277 Margaret Gowing. *Britain and atomic energy, 1939–1945.* Kenneth Jay, Introduction. New York: St. Martin's, 1964. ‣ Very full official history of British contribution to atomic bomb. Covers negotiations with French and Americans. Reference work for specialists. Read with Pierre 48.301. [CKF/JSH]

48.278 Martin J. Sherwin. *A world destroyed: the atomic bomb and the Grand Alliance.* 1975 ed. New York: Vintage, 1977. ISBN 0-394-72148-9. ‣ Important, deeply researched, and forcefully presented analysis of role of Anglo-American ambitions for atomic monopoly in bringing on cold war. Debatable argument, but much information. [JSH]

48.279 Mark Walker. *German national socialism and the quest for nuclear power, 1939–1949.* Cambridge: Cambridge University Press, 1990. ISBN 0-521-36413-2. ‣ Account of failed German effort to master nuclear energy for war. Meticulous scholarship and important findings for students of World War II and of science in service of national power. [JSH]

European Resistance Movements

48.280 M.R.D. Foot. *SOE in France: an account of the work of the British Special Operations Executive in France, 1940–1944.* 1966 ed. Frederick, Md.: University Publications of America, 1984.

ISBN 0-89093-594-7. ‣ Outstanding study of British efforts to foster and support resistance, sabotage, and espionage in German-occupied Europe by participant-scholar successful in both career paths. [JSH]

48.281 Callum A. MacDonald. *The killing of SS Obergruppenführer Reinhard Heydrich, 27 May 1942.* New York: Free Press, 1989. ISBN 0-02-919561-6. ‣ Exemplary study of origins, execution, and consequences of one special operation in German-occupied Europe. [JSH]

SEE ALSO
33.791 Milovan Djilas. *Wartime.*

POST–WORLD WAR II

New International Structures

48.282 Maureen R. Berman and Joseph E. Johnson, eds. *Unofficial diplomats.* New York: Columbia University Press, 1977. ISBN 0-231-04396-1 (cl), 0-231-04397-X (pbk). ‣ Survey of diplomacy by private citizens and organizations, tolerated because it is hard to police and sometimes helpful. Sketchy but useful demonstration that topic requires more study. [JSH]

48.283 April Carter. *Peace movements: international protest and world politics since 1945.* New York: Longman, 1992. ISBN 0-582-02774-8 (cl), 0-582-02773-X (pbk). ‣ Balanced, comprehensive account of peace organizations, activities, and beliefs within framework of cold war international relations. [CKF]

48.284 Werner J. Feld. *Nongovernmental forces and world politics: a study of business, labor, and political groups.* New York: Praeger, 1972. ‣ Discussion of how proliferation of organizations operating across national borders altered international system. Sound introduction to issues without excessive theorizing. [JSH]

48.285 Blanche Finley. *The structure of the United Nations General Assembly: an organizational approach to its work, 1974–1980s.* 2 vols. White Plains, N.Y.: UNIPUB and Kraus, 1988. ISBN 0-527-91618-8 (set). ‣ Helpful reference to United Nations committees and conferences on human rights, disarmament, international law, and many other subjects. Chapter references offer excellent guide to United Nations documentation for scholars. [JSH]

48.286 Leland M. Goodrich. *The United Nations in a changing world.* New York: Columbia University Press, 1974. ISBN 0-231-03824-0. ‣ Reliable introduction to history of first quarter-century of United Nations, although analysis tends toward optimistic and favors United Nations. Good starting place. [JSH]

48.287 Ernst B. Haas, Mary Pat Williams, and Don Babai. *Scientists and world order: the uses of technical knowledge in international organizations.* Berkeley: University of California Press, 1977. ISBN 0-520-03341-8. ‣ Examination of scientists' attitudes toward own contributions to more rational world order. Modest claims and narrow sampling mask intelligent questions of growing importance. [JSH]

48.288 Robert C. Hilderbrand. *Dumbarton Oaks: the origins of the United Nations and the search for postwar security.* Chapel Hill: University of North Carolina Press, 1990. ISBN 0-8078-1894-1. ‣ Competent and authoritative study. Concludes Big Three created United Nations to preserve commanding voice in international affairs, rather than as new parliament of man. [JSH]

48.289 Harold K. Jacobson. *Networks of interdependence: international organizations and the global political system.* 2d ed. New York: Knopf, 1984. ISBN 0-394-33164-8. ‣ Clear, wide-ranging discussion of scholarly and policy issues; no bibliography, but notes and suggested readings follow chapters. Considers historical context, security, economics, welfare, and human rights. [JSH]

48.290 Robert O. Keohane and Joseph S. Nye, Jr., eds. *Transnational relations and world politics.* Cambridge, Mass.: Harvard University Press, 1972. ISBN 0-674-90481-8 (cl), 0-674-90482-6 (pbk). ‣ Immensely stimulating conference volume, papers argue for importance of international relations beyond those between states. Wide topical coverage and high-quality analysis. Fundamental work. [JSH]

48.291 Indar Jit Rikhye, Michael Harbottle, and Bjorn Egge. *The thin blue line: international peacekeeping and its future.* New Haven: Yale University Press, 1974. ISBN 0-300-01782-0. ‣ Three former United Nations peacekeepers collaborate in well-crafted manual on limits and possibilities of international intervention. Fascinating deflation of excessive claims with good deal of factual data. [JSH]

Nuclear Weapons and the Space Age

48.292 Robert A. Divine. *Blowing on the wind: the Nuclear Test Ban debate, 1954–1960.* New York: Oxford University Press, 1978. ISBN 0-19-502390-0. ‣ Careful analysis of many issues central to postwar conceptions of national security. Stimulating reading for those trying to understand nuclear revolution and its impact on government. [JSH]

48.293 Robert A. Divine. *The Sputnik challenge: Eisenhower's response to the Soviet satellite.* New York: Oxford University Press, 1993. ISBN 0-19-505008-8. ‣ Clear presentation of early space race, first spy satellites, and founding of National Aeronautics Space Administration, with excellent detail and firm conclusions. [CKF]

48.294 Lawrence Freedman. *The evolution of nuclear strategy.* 2d ed. New York: St. Martin's, 1989. ISBN 0-312-02817-2 (cl), 0-312-02843-1 (pbk). ‣ Discusses how ideas about strategic use of nuclear weapons have changed since 1945. Powerful statement of importance of central political issues in strategy and diplomacy of cold war. Richly rewarding for all readers. [JSH]

48.295 David C. Gompert et al. *Nuclear weapons and world politics: alternatives for the future.* New York: McGraw-Hill, 1977. ISBN 0-07-023713-1 (cl), 0-07-023714-X (pbk). ‣ Careful, detailed reasoning on four possible developments for nuclear weaponry. Grim, but thought provoking. Very helpful appendix outlines basic issues in nuclear weapons for beginners. [CKF/JSH]

48.296 Jonathan E. Helmreich. *Gathering rare ores: the diplomacy of uranium acquisition, 1943–1954.* Princeton: Princeton University Press, 1986. ISBN 0-691-04738-3. ‣ Important case study of resource diplomacy. Evanescent fear that uranium would prove in short supply helped Belgium, Netherlands, and Brazil stockpile dollar holdings as Americans scrambled for control. [CKF/JSH]

48.297 Gregg Herken. *The winning weapon: the atomic bomb in the cold war, 1945–1950; with a new preface.* 1980 ed. Princeton: Princeton University Press, 1988. ISBN 0-691-02286-0 (pbk). ‣ Provocative interpretation of America's atomic diplomacy of rashly brandishing its temporary monopoly of nuclear weapons in a way that intensified Soviet suspicions. [JSH/BBY]

48.298 David Holloway. *The Soviet Union and the arms race.* 2d ed. New Haven: Yale University Press, 1984. ISBN 0-300-03280-3 (cl), 0-300-03281-1 (pbk). ‣ Best available study of dramatic buildup of Soviet nuclear forces in institutional and political setting. Clear, well-documented work by leading student of Soviet military. [JSH]

48.299 Robert Jervis. *The meaning of the nuclear revolution: statecraft and the prospect of Armageddon.* Ithaca, N.Y.: Cornell University Press, 1989. ISBN 0-8014-2304-X (cl), 0-8014-9565-2 (pbk). ‣ Analysis of impact of nuclear weapons on international affairs with reflections on strategy and ethical issues. Convenient, intelligent survey of developments combined with searching analysis of implications for war. [JSH]

48.300 George Frost Kennan. *The nuclear delusion: Soviet-American relations in the atomic age.* 2d ed. New York: Pantheon, 1983. ISBN 0-394-71318-4 (pbk). ‣ Collection of essays published over past thirty years on dangers posed by nuclear weapons to both human survival and rational thought about international relations. Stimulating reading. [JSH]

48.301 Andrew Pierre. *Nuclear politics: the British experience with an independent strategic force, 1939–1970.* Oxford: Oxford University Press, 1972. ISBN 0-19-212955-4. ‣ Britain's pursuit of nuclear weapons as product of domestic political competition as much as of clear strategic thinking. Sound introduction based on published sources. [JSH]

48.302 Ronald E. Powaski. *March to Armageddon: the United States and the nuclear arms race, 1939 to the present.* New York: Oxford University Press, 1987. ISBN 0-19-503878-9. ‣ Comprehensive, comprehensible summary of knowledge on America's role in arms race. Innovative analysis, useful to all levels of scholars. [JSH]

48.303 Thomas R. Rochon. *Mobilizing for peace: the antinuclear movements in Western Europe.* Princeton: Princeton University Press, 1988. ISBN 0-691-05671-4. ‣ Comparative analysis of peace movements in Britain, France, West Germany, and Holland during 1980s. Examines roots and growth. Best study to date. [JSH]

48.304 Paul B. Stares. *The militarization of space: U.S. policy, 1945–1984.* Ithaca, N.Y.: Cornell University Press, 1985. ISBN 0-8014-1810-0. ‣ Technological advances have made space a part of American military frontier since 1945. Rich source of information for specialists but short on analytical framework. Read with McDougall 44.652. [JSH]

48.305 Richard Taylor. *Against the bomb: the British peace movement, 1958–1965.* Oxford: Clarendon, 1988. ISBN 0-19-827537-4. ‣ Erosion of cold war political consensus became apparent in campaign against nuclear weapons in Britain. Not strictly chronological account. [JSH]

48.306 Marc Trachtenberg. *History and strategy.* Princeton: Princeton University Press, 1991. ISBN 0-691-07881-5 (cl), 0-691-02343-3 (pbk). ‣ Essays on American nuclear strategy, 1949–66, alliance relationships; Cuban missile crisis; Berlin crisis; and parallels between contemporary international system and one destroyed in 1914. Much research, penetrating analysis. [JSH]

48.307 Leon Wieseltier. *Nuclear war, nuclear peace.* New York: Holt, Rinehart & Winston, 1983. ISBN 0-03-064082-2 (cl), 0-03-064029-6 (pbk). ‣ Study of fundamental role of nuclear deterrence in preserving hard and bitter peace. Provocative but uneven introduction for general readers. [JSH]

48.308 Lawrence S. Wittner. *The struggle against the bomb.* Vol. 1: *One world or none: a history of the world nuclear disarmament movement through 1953.* Stanford, Calif.: Stanford University Press, 1993. ISBN 0-8047-2141-6. ‣ Global history of activism against nuclear weaponry during early, critical years of cold war. Meticulously researched and intensely written. [CKF]

SEE ALSO
44.652 Walter A. McDougall. . . . *the heavens and the earth.*

Transformation of Colonial Empires

48.309 Raymond F. Betts. *France and decolonization.* New York: St. Martin's, 1991. ISBN 0-312-06050-5. ‣ Concise, intelligent introduction by master of colonial history. Concludes with thoughtful essay on significance of empire for cultures involved. Short bibliography. [JSH]

48.310 John Darwin. *Britain and decolonization: the retreat from empire in the postwar world.* New York: St. Martin's, 1988. ISBN 0-312-02464-9. ‣ First acquired empire to increase power, then dismantled it to defend international position under different conditions. Stimulating introduction to subject now much studied. [JSH]

48.311 Prosser Gifford and Wm. Roger Louis, eds. *Decolonization and African independence: the transfers of power, 1960–1980.* New Haven: Yale University Press, 1988. ISBN 0-300-04070-9 (cl), 0-300-04388-0 (pbk). ‣ Twenty-one essays discussing implementation of independence as former colonial rulers struggled to preserve strategic, political, and economic advantages while ruthlessly scaling back obligations. Rich bibliography. [JSH]

48.312 Prosser Gifford and Wm. Roger Louis, eds. *The transfer of power in Africa: decolonization, 1940–1960.* New Haven: Yale University Press, 1982. ISBN 0-300-02568-8. ‣ Nineteen substantial essays, several comparative and several historiographical, plus bibliographical essay. Valuable work for all interested in postwar international relations. [JSH]

48.313 R. F. Holland. *European decolonization, 1918–1981: an introductory survey.* New York: St. Martin's, 1985. ISBN 0-312-27060-7. ‣ Creative, although Anglocentric, study of European abandonment of empires as they realized that they could obtain benefits without costs. Best current assessment of scholarship. [JSH]

48.314 Alistair Horne. *A savage war of peace: Algeria, 1954–1962.* Rev. ed. New York: Penguin, 1987. ISBN 0-14-010191-8 (pbk). ‣ High cost of holding on to empire for both France and Algerians. Best account available in English, but no work in any language is yet definitive. [JSH]

48.315 Wm. Roger Louis. *The British empire in the Middle East, 1945–1951: Arab nationalism, the United States, and postwar imperialism.* Rev. ed. New York: Penguin, 1987. ISBN 0-14-010191-8. ‣ Analysis of Labor government's vain effort to preserve Britain's position in Middle East as gauge of great power status. Excellent scholarship. [JSH]

48.316 W. David McIntyre. *The commonwealth of nations: origins and impact, 1869–1971.* Minneapolis: University of Minnesota Press, 1977. ISBN 0-8166-0792-3. ‣ Currently, best introduction to growth of new nations within existing multinational organization. British better at disseminating ideas, institutions, and ambitions than at understanding consequences. [JSH]

48.317 Edward E. Rice. *Wars of the third kind: conflict in underdeveloped countries.* Berkeley: University of California Press, 1988. ISBN 0-520-06236-1. ‣ Comparative analysis of how insurgencies develop and what countermeasures are most effective. Intriguing examination of some twentieth-century conflicts; useful for both general and advanced readers. [JSH]

48.318 Peter Willetts. *The non-aligned movement: the origins of a Third World alliance.* New York: Nichols, 1978. ISBN 0-89397-044-1. ‣ Analysis of United Nations voting patterns of Third World countries on defining issues. Concludes real alliance exists behind verbosity. Welcome addition but much work remains to be done. [JSH]

International Political Economy

48.319 Gunnar Adler-Karlsson. *Western economic warfare, 1947–1967: a case study in foreign economic policy.* Stockholm: Almqvist & Wiksell, 1968. ‣ Searching examination of Western embargo of communist countries. Emphasizes disputes within alliance and institutions created to implement blockade. Attempts to quantify costs to both sides. [CKF/JSH]

48.320 William R. Cline. *International monetary reform and the developing countries.* Washington, D.C.: Brookings Institution, 1976. ISBN 0-8157-1476-9 (cl), 0-8157-1475-0 (pbk). ‣ Brief study of response of developing countries to new monetary measures devised to replace deteriorating international monetary system originally devised at 1945 Bretton Woods Conference. Important work for specialists on neglected topic. [JSH]

48.321 Alfred E. Eckes, Jr. *A search for solvency: Bretton Woods and the international monetary system, 1941–1971*. Austin: University of Texas Press, 1975. ISBN 0-292-70712-6. ▸ First-rate study of Bretton Woods Conference on international monetary relations; American officials sought to reconstruct open world economy for benefit of all peoples. Sketchy on postwar developments. [CKF/JSH]

48.322 Lawrence Franko. *The European multinationals: a renewed challenge to American and British big business*. Stamford, Conn.: Greylock, 1976. ISBN 0-89223-036-3. ▸ Discerns important strategic differences in continental multinationals setting them apart from Anglo-Saxon corporations. Valuable reference source and aid in understanding competition within West. Of interest to specialists. [JSH]

48.323 Theodore Geiger. *The future of the international system: the United States and the world political economy*. Boston: Allen & Unwin, 1988. ISBN 0-04-445094-X (cl), 0-04-445100-8 (pbk). ▸ Description of decay of international economic cooperation since seventies, analyzing causes and proposing solutions. Identifies failure of American leadership as main culprit. Sound, opinionated introduction. [JSH]

48.324 Robert Gilpin. *The political economy of international relations*. Princeton: Princeton University Press, 1987. ISBN 0-691-07732-0 (cl), 0-691-02262-3 (pbk). ▸ Survey of chief features in contemporary international political economy. Fundamental work by leading scholar. [JSH]

48.325 Robert Gilpin. *U.S. power and the multinational corporation: the political economy of foreign direct investment*. New York: Basic Books, 1975. ISBN 0-465-08951-8. ▸ Examination of impact on America's international standing of its postwar foreign direct investment strategies. Essential reading for students of international political economy and American foreign relations. [JSH]

48.326 Lincoln Gordon. *Growth policies and the international order*. New York: McGraw-Hill, 1979. ISBN 0-07-023812-X (cl), 0-07-023813-8 (pbk). ▸ Quest for wealth has become central function of states and will become subject of increasingly close international cooperation. Concise introduction to issues; unfortunately slim bibliography. [JSH]

48.327 Robert J. Gordon and Jacques Pelkmans. *Challenges to interdependent economies: the industrial West in the coming decade*. New York: McGraw-Hill, 1979. ISBN 0-07-023810-3 (cl), 0-07-023811-1 (pbk). ▸ One essay discussing management of American economy, another dealing with successes and failures of international cooperation on management of national economies. Set in historical context and very accessible. [JSH]

48.328 Joseph Grunwald and Kenneth Flamm. *The global factory: foreign assembly in international trade*. Washington, D.C.: Brookings Institution, 1985. ISBN 0-8157-3304-6 (cl), 0-8157-3303-8 (pbk). ▸ Discussion of shift of goods and resources between developing and developed economies. Dry, detailed analysis of process too little understood but central to international patterns of change. [JSH]

48.329 Fred Hirsch et al. *Alternatives to monetary disorder*. New York: McGraw-Hill, 1977. ISBN 0-07-029046-6 (cl), 0-07-029047-4 (pbk). ▸ Two extended essays proposing ways to reconstruct international monetary system to better accord with growing politicization of national strategies. Clearly defines alternative courses. Important statement of issues. [JSH]

48.330 Franklyn D. Holzman. *International trade under communism: politics and economics*. New York: Basic Books, 1976. ISBN

0-465-03381-4. ▸ Superb introduction to international economic relations of communist countries and to their domestic economies. Clear explication of complicated issues. Valuable aid to understanding impact of *Ostpolitik*. [JSH]

48.331 Raymond F. Hopkins and Donald Puchala. *Global food interdependence: challenge to American foreign policy*. New York: Columbia University Press, 1980. ISBN 0-2310-4858-0 (cl), 0-2310-4859-9 (pbk). ▸ Reliable presentation of main issues in recurring international problem. Discusses world trade in food, role of international agencies, and strategies of nation-states. [JSH]

48.332 Miles Kahler, ed. *The politics of international debt*. Ithaca, N.Y.: Cornell University Press, 1986. ISBN 0-8014-1911-5 (cl), 0-8014-9385-4 (pbk). ▸ Eight essays by economists and political scientists on contemporary problems of international indebtedness. Very useful introduction to problem. Articles by Fishlow, Haggard, and Lipson provide historical context. [JSH]

48.333 Peter J. Katzenstein, ed. *Between power and plenty: foreign economic policies of advanced industrial states*. Madison: University of Wisconsin Press, 1978. ISBN 0-299-07560-5 (cl), 0-299-07564-8 (pbk). ▸ Discussion of how domestic political and economic structures interact with foreign economic policies. Although narratives somewhat dated, conceptual devices continue to dominate analysis of international political economy. [JSH]

48.334 Robert O. Keohane. *After hegemony: cooperation and discord in the world political economy*. Princeton: Princeton University Press, 1984. ISBN 0-691-07676-6 (cl), 0-691-02228-3 (pbk). ▸ Reliable capsule histories of international cooperation on money, oil, and trade since 1945, framed by chapters of elaborate theorizing. Historical overviews useful, theories worth considering. [CKF/JSH]

48.335 Klaus Knorr. *The power of nations: the political economy of international relations*. New York: Basic Books, 1975. ISBN 0-465-06142-7 (cl), 0-465-06143-5 (pbk). ▸ Best single introduction to political economy. Stress on economic needs and resources shaping policy should be compared to Spero's insistence on primacy of politics (48.343). [JSH]

48.336 Melvyn B. Krauss. *The new protectionism: the welfare state and international trade*. New York: New York University Press for the International Center for Economic Policy Studies, 1978. ISBN 0-8147-4570-9 (cl), 0-8147-4571-7 (pbk). ▸ Controversial, opinionated tract arguing for burden on adaptation to changing conditions imposed by heavy domestic spending. Brief, stimulating introduction to issue central to past and present concerns. [JSH]

48.337 Charles Lipson. *Standing guard: protecting foreign capital in the nineteenth and twentieth centuries*. Berkeley: University of California Press, 1985. ISBN 0-520-03468-6 (cl), 0-520-05327-3 (pbk). ▸ Invigorating specialist work on international contentions surrounding foreign direct and portfolio investment. Special attention given to American policy since 1945. Weak political science, but interesting history. [JSH]

48.338 Edward S. Mason and Robert E. Asher. *The World Bank since Bretton Woods: the origins, policies, operations, and impact of the International Bank for Reconstruction and Development and the other members of the World Bank group, the International Finance Corporation, the International Development Association and the International Centre for Settlement of Investment Disputes*. Washington, D.C.: Brookings Institution, 1973. ISBN 0-8157-5492-2. ▸ Massive official history of International Bank for Reconstruction and Development during its first quarter-century of lending for economic development. Reference for specialists; favorable rather than celebratory. [JSH]

48.339 Carmine Nappi. *Commodity market controls: a historical*

review. Lexington, Mass.: Lexington Books, 1979. ISBN 0-669-02812-6. ▸ Standard, reliable, bland discussion of efforts to regulate highly unstable markets. Particularly valuable for understanding inability of other developing economies to replicate success of Organization of Petroleum Exporting Countries. [JSH]

48.340 Peter R. Odell. *Oil and world power*. 8th ed. New York: Penguin, 1986. ISBN 0-14-022731-8 (pbk). ▸ Clear discussion of energy industry; Soviet, American, Japanese, and Western European positions; place of developing nations; and role in international relations. Essential starting point; helpful bibliographical essay. [JSH]

48.341 Ernest H. Preeg. *Traders and diplomats: an analysis of the Kennedy round of negotiations under the General Agreement on Tariffs and Trade*. Washington, D.C.: Brookings Institution, 1970. ISBN 0-8157-7176-2. ▸ Analysis of multilateral negotiations on tariff reduction and economic development in 1960s. Valuable source on economic diplomacy by member of American delegation. [JSH]

48.342 Andrew Schonfield, ed. *International economic relations of the Western world, 1959–1971*. 2 vols. New York: Oxford University Press for Royal Institute of International Affairs, 1976. ISBN 0-19-218314-1 (v. 1), 0-19-218317-6 (v. 2). ▸ Interaction of politics and economics in shaping of international monetary and trade policies during 1960s. Indispensable work for understanding last two tumultuous decades. [JSH]

48.343 Joan Edelman Spero. *The politics of international economic relations*. 4th ed. New York: St. Martin's, 1990. ISBN 0-312-04063-6 (cl), 0-312-00497-4 (pbk). ▸ First-rate synthesis of huge literature. Excellent as introduction or as reference work. Can be read as debate with Knorr 48.335 on primacy of politics or economics. [JSH]

48.344 Angela Stent. *From embargo to Ostpolitik: the political economy of West German–Soviet relations, 1955–1980*. Cambridge: Cambridge University Press, 1982. ISBN 0-521-23667-3. ▸ Economic relations lie at center of this well-researched study. Emphasizes role of trade in *Ostpolitik* and place of *Ostpolitik* in larger process of détente. Read with Garton Ash 48.451. [JSH]

48.345 Brian Tew. *The evolution of the international monetary system, 1945–1988*. 4th ed. London: Hutchinson, 1988. ISBN 0-09-175671-5 (cl), 0-09-173140-2 (pbk). ▸ Often updated, introductory text. Simple, clear discussion of nuts and bolts of monetary relations with competent history of system's evolution. Good starting place for novice. [JSH]

48.346 Fiona Venn. *Oil diplomacy in the twentieth century*. New York: St. Martin's, 1986. ISBN 0-312-58307-9 (pbk). ▸ Compact introduction to subject about which there has been explosion of literature since 1973. Much reading and research condensed into easily managed units. [JSH]

48.347 David Wall. *The charity of nations: the political economy of foreign aid*. New York: Basic Books, 1973. ISBN 0-465-00964-6. ▸ Concise, accessible introduction to main issues in foreign aid in all their variety. Also summarizes where knowledge stood in aftermath of "development decade," 1960s. [JSH]

48.348 Herman van der Wee. *Prosperity and upheaval: the world economy, 1945–1980*. Robin Hogg and Max R. Hall, trans. Berkeley: University of California Press, 1986. ISBN 0-520-05709-0 (cl), 0-520-05819-4 (pbk). ▸ World economic history emphasizing institutional factors and experience of Western industrial states. Rich in data and analysis. Vital reading for all historians of postwar world. [JSH]

48.349 John Williamson. *The failure of world monetary reform, 1971–1974*. New York: New York University Press, 1977. ISBN 0-8147-9173-5 (cl), 0-8147-9174-3 (pbk). ▸ Informed account of international negotiations to replace failing Bretton Woods system with new monetary mechanism. Clear presentation of complicated, important material. Valuable for readers at all levels. [JSH]

COLD WAR

General Studies

48.350 Stephen R. Ashton. *In search of detente: the politics of East-West relations since 1945*. London: Macmillan, 1989. ISBN 0-333-34387-5 (cl), 0-333-34388-3 (pbk). ▸ Ambitious, clear, brief introduction for beginners; effort to incorporate developments within Europe and non-European world in framework of Soviet-American confrontation. Brief but well-chosen bibliography. [JSH]

48.351 Vernon V. Aspaturian, comp. *Process and power in Soviet foreign policy*. Boston: Little, Brown, 1971. ▸ Scholarly analysis of policy-making process in Soviet Union with special attention to domestic politics as factor in formation of foreign policy. [JSH]

48.352 Paul Dukes. *The last great game: U.S.A. versus U.S.S.R., events, conjunctures, structures*. New York: St. Martin's, 1989. ISBN 0-312-03228-5. ▸ Curious but interesting application of Braudelian analysis to fundamental international relationship. [JSH]

48.353 John Lewis Gaddis. "The long peace: elements of stability in the postwar international system." In *The long peace: inquiries into the history of the cold war*, pp. 215–45. New York: Oxford University Press, 1987. ISBN 0-19-504336-7 (cl), 0-19-504335-9 (pbk). ▸ Important essay sketching one of chief pillars of postwar international order. [JSH]

48.354 John Lewis Gaddis. *Strategies of containment: a critical appraisal of postwar American national security policy*. New York: Oxford University Press, 1982. ISBN 0-19-502944-5 (cl), 0-19-503097-4 (pbk). ▸ Fundamental work on cold war international relations. American strategy alternated between defense of key areas and resistance to communist challenge wherever it appeared. Stimulating analysis. [JSH/BBY]

48.355 Bennett Kovrig. *Of walls and bridges: the United States and Eastern Europe*. New York: New York University Press, 1991. ISBN 0-8147-4612-8 (cl), 0-8147-4613-6 (pbk). ▸ Informative, well-organized study of shift of American policy toward slow disintegration of Soviet empire through détente. Good demonstration of Soviet Union's sensitivity to threats to its position in Eastern Europe. [JSH/GS]

48.356 Walter LaFeber. *America, Russia, and the cold war, 1945–1992*. 6th ed. New York: McGraw-Hill, 1991. ISBN 0-07-557557-4. ▸ Reliable textbook introduction to Soviet-American aspects of conflict. Much updated from earlier editions. Theme of costs of empire to American democracy often present. [JSH]

48.357 Gil Loescher and John A. Scanlan. *Calculated kindness: refugees and America's half-open door, 1945 to the present*. New York: Free Press, 1986. ISBN 0-02-927340-4. ▸ Study of selective admission of refugees as weapon in cold war. Useful exploration of one aspect of total diplomacy practiced by ideological rivals throughout history. [JSH/NMK]

48.358 Alfred D. Low. *Sino-Soviet confrontation since Mao Zedong: dispute, detente, or conflict*. Boulder: East European Monographs; distributed by Columbia University Press, 1987. ISBN 0-88033-958-6. ▸ Employs selections from Soviet and Chinese press as they appeared in translation to analyze fluctuating relationship between leading communist states. Useful continuation of 48.359. [JSH]

48.359 Alfred D. Low. *The Sino-Soviet dispute: an analysis of the polemics*. Rutherford, N.J.: Fairleigh Dickinson University Press, 1976. ISBN 0-8386-1479-5. ▸ Propaganda and vilification substituted for military violence since neither state wanted quarrels to turn into war. Highly specialized study but not full treatment of conflict. [CKF/JSH]

48.360 Richard Mayne. *The recovery of Europe, 1945–1973.* Rev. ed. Garden City, N.Y.: Anchor, 1973. ISBN 0-385-07251-1. ‣ Older optimistic survey of movement for European integration by proponent. Balanced in interpretation, richly informative on many important issues. Engrossing reading, if now increasingly dated. [JSH]

48.361 Rajan Menon. *Soviet power and the Third World.* New Haven: Yale University Press, 1986. ISBN 0-300-03500-4. ‣ Analysis of Soviet military and economic power as instruments of power projection in troubled Third World in early 1980s. Uneven treatment of issues, most useful for advanced studies. [JSH]

48.362 Nicola Miller. *Soviet relations with Latin America, 1959–1987.* New York: Cambridge University Press, 1989. ISBN 0-521-35193-6 (cl), 0-521-35979-1 (pbk). ‣ Soviet reluctance to make serious commitment to Latin American regimes due to cautious regard for predominance of United States. Superior scholarship for specialists. [JSH]

48.363 Alvin Z. Rubinstein. *Soviet foreign policy since World War II: imperial and global.* 4th ed. New York: HarperCollins, 1992. ISBN 0-673-52163-X (cl), 0-673-39893-5 (pbk). ‣ Topical coverage of Soviet policy in Europe, the Americas, Far East, and Middle East. Distinctly conservative interpretation emphasizing aggressive Soviet Union. Introductory survey for nonspecialists. [JSH]

48.364 Sarah Meiklejohn Terry, ed. *Soviet policy in Eastern Europe.* New Haven: Yale University Press, 1984. ISBN 0-300-03131-9. ‣ Collection of excellent essays by leading authorities on Soviet policy toward regional problems and individual nations in early 1980s. Valuable for advanced students, but will need updating. [CKF/JSH]

48.365 Adam B. Ulam. *The rivals: America and Russia since World War II.* New York: Viking, 1971. ISBN 0-670-59959-X. ‣ Lively introduction to first two decades of cold war. America's moral superiority over Soviets went hand in hand with uninformed rigidity, making compromise difficult. [CKF/JSH]

48.366 John W. Young. *Cold war Europe, 1945–1989: a political history.* London: Arnold, 1991. ISBN 0-340-55142-9 (cl), 0-340-55324-3 (pbk). ‣ Clear, balanced history of postwar Europe. Emphasizes political, economic, and diplomatic aspects. Particularly strong on ambiguous character of movements toward integration when national loyalties remained powerful. [JSH]

Origins of the Cold War

48.367 Terry H. Anderson. *The United States, Great Britain, and the cold war, 1944–1947.* Columbia: University of Missouri Press, 1981. ISBN 0-8262-0328-0. ‣ Useful introduction to European contribution to coming of cold war. British officials sought to awaken Americans to danger posed by Soviet Union. [JSH]

48.368 Lynn Etheridge Davis. *The cold war begins: Soviet-American conflict over Eastern Europe.* Princeton: Princeton University Press, 1974. ISBN 0-691-05217-4. ‣ Yalta marked watershed for American diplomats as they shifted from postponing decisions to haplessly resisting Soviet domination of Eastern Europe. Important study of one theater of conflict. [JSH]

48.369 Anne Deighton, ed. *Britain and the first cold war.* New York: St. Martin's, 1990. ISBN 0-312-04020-2. ‣ Conference presentations by younger British scholars on British diplomacy, military strategy, and relationships with Middle and Far Eastern states in postwar decade. Prefigures many forthcoming monographs. [JSH]

48.370 Herbert Feis. *From trust to terror: the onset of the cold war,* *1945–1950.* New York: Norton, 1970. ISBN 0-393-05425-X. ‣ Rapid deterioration of Soviet-American relations after end of enforced wartime cooperation. Less well-documented than earlier works but major statement of traditional interpretation. [JSH]

48.371 James L. Gormly. *The collapse of the Grand Alliance, 1945–1948.* Baton Rouge: Louisiana State University Press, 1987. ISBN 0-8071-1320-4. ‣ Valuable synthesis of literature; argues 1946 marked watershed between decay of wartime alliance and crystalization of new hostile blocs. [JSH]

48.372 Fraser J. Harbutt. *The Iron Curtain: Churchill, America, and the origins of the cold war.* New York: Oxford University Press, 1986. ISBN 0-19-503817-7 (cl), 0-19-505422-9 (pbk). ‣ Examines early cold war as extension of wartime rivalries within Grand Alliance into postwar period when defeat of Hitler removed any incentive to continued cooperation. [JSH]

48.373 Bruce R. Kuniholm. *The origins of the cold war in the Near East: great power conflict and diplomacy in Iran, Turkey, and Greece.* Princeton: Princeton University Press, 1980. ISBN 0-691-04665-4 (cl), 0-691-10083-7 (pbk). ‣ Soviet pressure and American counterpressure in Near East must be added to causes of cold war. Best available study, based on meticulous scholarship. [JSH/BBY]

48.374 Melvyn P. Leffler. *A preponderance of power: national security, the Truman administration, and the cold war.* Stanford, Calif.: Stanford University Press, 1992. ISBN 0-8047-1924-1. ‣ Study of American quest for security from World War II to cold war. Critical of United States; definitive on American perceptions and aims, but international history of period remains to be written. [JSH/BBY]

48.375 Wilfred Loth. *The division of the world, 1941–1955.* New York: St. Martin's, 1988. ISBN 0-312-02045-7. ‣ New look at early struggle between two different societies by European historian using conventional sources. Suggests emergence of blocs helped Soviet system survive. [JSH]

48.376 Leon Martel. *Lend-Lease, loans, and the coming of the cold war: a study of the implementation of foreign policy.* Boulder: Westview, 1979. ISBN 0-89158-453-6. ‣ International tensions and painful choices resulted from replacement of Lend-Lease by loans at end of World War II. Useful complement to works on strategy and politics. [JSH]

48.377 Frank A. Ninkovich. *The diplomacy of ideas: U.S. foreign policy and cultural relations, 1938–1950.* Cambridge: Cambridge University Press, 1981. ISBN 0-521-23241-8. ‣ Pioneering study of foreign policy as product of cultural forces. Employs interdisciplinary approach. Stimulating work in both approach and findings. [JSH]

48.378 William Taubman. *Stalin's American policy: from entente to detente to cold war.* New York: Norton, 1982. ISBN 0-393-01406-1 (cl), 0-393-30130-3 (pbk). ‣ Analysis of Stalin's approach to United States during decade of international conflict. Fresh, refreshing examination of much debated subject. [JSH]

48.379 John W. Wheeler-Bennett and Anthony Nicholls. *The semblance of peace: the political settlement after the Second World War.* New York and London: St. Martin's and Macmillan, 1972. ISBN 0-333-04302-2. ‣ Powerful restatement of traditional interpretation of cold war origins. Detailed coverage of European diplomatic developments in aftermath of defeat of Germany. [CKF/JSH]

48.380 Daniel Yergin. *Shattered peace: the origins of the cold war.* 1977 ed. New York: Penguin, 1990. ISBN 0-14-012177-3. ‣ Important example of revisionist interpretation. Hardline anti-Soviets gained control of policy debate in Washington after death of Roosevelt, resulting in cold war. [JSH/BBY]

SEE ALSO
40.674 Michael H. Hunt. *Ideology and U.S. foreign policy.*

Communist Seizure of Power in Eastern Europe

48.381 Michael M. Boll. *The cold war in the Balkans: American foreign policy and the emergence of communist Bulgaria, 1943–1947.* Lexington: University Press of Kentucky, 1984. ISBN 0-8131-1527-2. ▸ Case study of Soviet-American confrontation based on American, Soviet, and Bulgarian sources. Concludes United States had clearer political objectives in Bulgaria than Soviet Union. [CKF/JSH/RJC]

48.382 Krystyna Kersten. *The establishment of communist rule in Poland, 1943–1948.* John Micgiel and Michael H. Bernhard, trans. Berkeley: University of California Press, 1991. ISBN 0-520-06219-1. ▸ Stimulating examination of details of communist manipulation of individuals and of social groups during conversion of Poland into a dictatorship. Contains much information from Polish sources which became available during Solidarity period. [JSH]

48.383 Martin McCauley, ed. *Communist power in Europe, 1944–1949.* New York: Barnes & Noble, University of London, School of Slavonic and East European Studies, 1977. ISBN 0-06-494680-0. ▸ Dozen essays on problems and strengths of communist parties and Soviet Union in early cold war. Reliable summation of scholarly knowledge, not pathbreaking; omits Yugoslavia. [JSH]

48.384 Joseph Rothschild. *A return to diversity: a political history of East Central Europe since World War II.* New York: Oxford University Press, 1988. ISBN 0-19-504574-2 (cl), 0-19-504574-2 (pbk). ▸ Survey of seven countries, but not German Democratic Republic. First-rate introduction for general readers. [CKF/JSH]

48.385 Wayne S. Vucinich, ed. *At the brink of war and peace: the Tito-Stalin split in a historic perspective.* New York: Social Science Monographs, Brooklyn College Press, 1982. (East European monographs, v. 124. Brooklyn College Studies on society in change, v. 19. War and society in East Central Europe, 10.) ISBN 0-914710-98-2. ▸ Impressive conference volume examining consequences of Tito-Stalin split, largely from Yugoslav perspective. [CKF/JSH]

SEE ALSO
33.10 Zbigniew K. Brzezinski. *The Soviet Bloc.*

American "Empire by Invitation"

48.386 John Gimbel. *The origins of the Marshall Plan.* Stanford, Calif.: Stanford University Press, 1976. ISBN 0-8047-0903-3. ▸ Marshall Plan created to resolve bureaucratic and interallied struggles, rather than from fear of Soviets or drive for markets. Important partial explanation. [JSH]

48.387 Michael J. Hogan. *The Marshall Plan: America, Britain, and the reconstruction of Western Europe, 1947–1952.* New York: Cambridge University Press, 1987. ISBN 0-521-25140-0 (cl), 0-521-37840-0 (pbk). ▸ Best available work on Marshall Plan. Important contribution to understanding Anglo-American relations since World War II. [JSH]

48.388 James Edward Miller. *The United States and Italy, 1940–1950: the politics and diplomacy of stabilization.* Chapel Hill: University of North Carolina Press, 1986. ISBN 0-8078-1673-6. ▸ Excellent study based on thorough research in American archives. United States sought to foster centrist-reformist postwar social order as solution to interwar political polarization. [JSH]

48.389 Alan S. Milward. *The reconstruction of Western Europe, 1945–1951.* Berkeley: University of California Press, 1984. ISBN 0-520-06035-0. ▸ Important, controversial approach to understanding origins of great economic surge of postwar decades. Interesting for its argument, useful for its substantial narrative. Required reading. [JSH]

48.390 Frederico Romero. *The United States and the European trade union movement, 1944–1951.* Harvey Fergusson, trans. Chapel Hill: University of North Carolina Press, 1992. ISBN 0-8078-2065-2. ▸ Able discussion of unsuccessful effort to introduce American social pluralism into postwar Europe. [CKF]

48.391 Irwin M. Wall. *The United States and the making of postwar France, 1945–1954.* New York: Cambridge University Press, 1991. ISBN 0-521-40217-4. ▸ United States held hostage to survival of its weak client, unable to impose its own agenda. Sound analysis based on French and American archives. [JSH]

48.392 Lawrence S. Wittner. *American intervention in Greece, 1943–1949.* New York: Columbia University Press, 1982. ISBN 0-231-04196-9. ▸ Sees source of many subsequent problems in illusions of American leaders about complicated Greek situation and its outcome. Important revisionist account based on extensive research. [JSH]

The German Problem

48.393 John H. Backer. *Priming the German economy: American occupation policies, 1945–1948.* Durham, N.C.: Duke University Press, 1971. ISBN 0-8223-0243-8. ▸ Skillful introduction to complicated efforts to deal with postwar German economy through relief, reparations, and reform. Essential study of German revival and cold war origins. [JSH]

48.394 Anne Deighton. *The impossible peace: Britain, the division of Germany, and the origins of the cold war.* Oxford: Clarendon, 1990. ISBN 0-19-827332-0. ▸ Fine example of emerging trend in scholarship on European contribution to cold war. British suspicion of Soviets led them to promote partition of Germany and to win American support. [JSH]

48.395 Ludolf Herbst, Werner Bührer, and Hanno Sowade, eds. *Vom Marshallplan zur EWG: die Eingliederung der Bundesrepublik Deutschland in der westliche Welt.* Munich: Oldenbourg, 1990. (Quellen und Darstellungen zur Zeitgeschichte herausgegeben vom Institut für Zeitgeschichte, 30.) ISBN 3-486-55601-0. ▸ Cutting-edge research on many aspects of West Germany's integration into Atlantic and European communities after World War II. Discusses German policy; diversion of German energies into quest for prosperity rather than power; Germany's contribution to political, economic, and military integration of Europe; and attitudes of other Western powers. Superb bibliography. [JSH]

48.396 Bruce Kuklick. *American policy and the division of Germany: the clash with Russia over reparations.* Ithaca, N.Y.: Cornell University Press, 1972. ISBN 0-8014-0710-9. ▸ Reliable study for specialists. American determination to integrate Germany into open world economy helped disrupt Grand Alliance after war. [JSH]

48.397 Robert McGeehan. *The German rearmament question: American diplomacy and European defense after World War II.* Urbana: University of Illinois Press, 1971. ISBN 0-252-00160-5. ▸ Changing content of America's policy of promoting West German armament from Pleven Plan to West Germany's entry into North Atlantic Treaty Organization. Detailed, solid introduction based on published sources. [JSH]

48.398 Thomas Alan Schwartz. *America's Germany: John J. McCloy and the Federal Republic of Germany.* Cambridge, Mass.: Harvard University Press, 1991. ISBN 0-674-03115-6. ▸ Well-crafted book has importance far greater than title would suggest. American High Commissioner's actions allowed thorough discussion of enduring issues in Atlantic alliance. Sees McCloy as representative of best and worst elements of American policy making in this era. [JSH/PH]

48.399 Avi Shlaim. *The United States and the Berlin blockade, 1948–1949: a study in crisis decision-making.* 1983 ed. Berkeley: University of California Press, 1989. ISBN 0-520-06619-7. ▸ Best available analysis of American response to Soviet blockade of overland routes to Berlin. Based on wide research in British and American archives. [JSH]

48.400 Robert M. Slusser. *The Berlin crisis of 1961: Soviet-American relations and the struggle for power in the Kremlin, June–November 1961.* Baltimore: Johns Hopkins University Press, 1973. ISBN 0-8018-1404-9. ▸ Analysis of perils of collective foreign policy leadership in contested environment. Richly informative on both events and on reading of Soviet sources. [JSH]

48.401 Rolf Steininger. *The German question: the Stalin note of 1952 and the problem of reunification.* Mark Cioc, ed. Jane T. Hedges, trans. New York: Columbia University Press, 1990. ISBN 0-231-07216-3. ▸ Brief, narrowly focused revision of orthodox interpretation that Chancellor Adenauer's attitude toward German reunification and cold war rejected no real chances for German reunification. Based on British and American archives. [JSH]

U.S. Containment Policies, 1952–1968

48.402 H. W. Brands. *Cold warriors: Eisenhower's generation and American foreign policy.* New York: Columbia University Press, 1988. ISBN 0-231-06526-4. ▸ Sensitive reading of policies of figures from Eisenhower administration by historian who has worked widely in primary sources. Stresses lessons of World War II. [JSH]

48.403 Herbert S. Dinerstein. *The making of a missile crisis: October 1962.* Baltimore: Johns Hopkins University Press, 1976. ISBN 0-8018-1788-9. ▸ Broad historical account of deterioration of Cuban-American relations set in context of cold war's shift toward developing nations. Dated on details but still useful overview. [JSH]

48.404 Robert A. Divine. *Eisenhower and the cold war.* New York: Oxford University Press, 1981. ISBN 0-19-502823-6 (cl), 0-19-502824-4 (pbk). ▸ Thoughtful example of early Eisenhower revisionism. Depicts Eisenhower as consummate politician who avoided war and defused crises. Still effective as introduction. [CKF/JSH/BBY]

48.405 Trumbull Higgins. *The perfect failure: Kennedy, Eisenhower, and the CIA at the Bay of Pigs.* 1987 ed. New York: Norton, 1989. ISBN 0-393-02473-3 (cl, 1987), 0-393-30563-5 (pbk). ▸ Fullest account so far of disastrous attempt to topple Castro. Inadequate scholarly apparatus and awkward prose, but much information brought to light. [CKF/JSH/BBY]

48.406 Burton Ira Kaufman. *Trade and aid: Eisenhower's foreign economic policy, 1953–1961.* Baltimore: Johns Hopkins University Press, 1982. ISBN 0-8018-2623-3. ▸ Eisenhower's original commitment to trade expansion yielded to foreign aid as cold war spread to Third World. Well-researched, balanced monograph joins ranks of Eisenhower revisionists. [CKF/JSH/BBY]

SEE ALSO
44.825 Thomas G. Paterson, ed. *Kennedy's quest for victory.*

Détente

48.407 Coit D. Blacker. *Reluctant warriors: the United States, the Soviet Union, and arms control.* New York: Freeman, 1987. ISBN 0-7167-1861-8 (cl), 0-7167-1862-6 (pbk). ▸ Account and analysis of Soviet-American arms control negotiations. Brief, clear, unbiased introduction to subject central to cold war but easily mired in polemics and technicalities. [JSH]

48.408 Adam Bromke and Derry Novak, eds. *The communist states in the era of detente, 1971–1977.* Oakville, Ontario: Mosaic, 1978. ISBN 0-88962-095-4. ▸ Well-coordinated conference volume offers specialists even-handed assessments of impact of détente on both domestic and international relations of Eastern Bloc states. [JSH]

48.409 Lawrence Y. Caldwell and William Diebold, Jr., eds. *Soviet-American relations in the 1980s: superpower politics and East-West trade.* New York: McGraw-Hill, 1981. ISBN 0-07-009615-5 (cl), 0-07-009616-3 (pbk). ▸ Now dated but instructive attempt to predict Soviet policy in crisis environment. Hypothesized future Soviet-American relations and place of former Soviet Bloc economies. [CKF/JSH]

48.410 Alexander Dallin. *Black box: KAL 007 and the superpowers.* Berkeley: University of California Press, 1985. ISBN 0-520-05515-2 (cl), 0-520-05516-0 (pbk). ▸ Meticulous examination of evidence and testing of theories about tragedy. Finds disturbing implications for crisis management. Extensive endnotes offer much food for thought. [JSH]

48.411 Robin Edmonds. *Soviet foreign policy: the Brezhnev years.* New York: Oxford University Press, 1983. ISBN 0-19-215878-3 (cl), 0-19-285125-x (pbk). ▸ Survey by leading British diplomat who favored return to détente. Very knowledgeable about Soviet Union without pretending to penetrate all mysteries. Read after Ulam 48.59. [JSH]

48.412 Richard Eichenberg. *Public opinion and national security in Western Europe.* Ithaca, N.Y.: Cornell University Press, 1989. ISBN 0-8014-2237-X. ▸ Analysis of what public opinion polls can tell scholars and statesmen about attitudes of Europeans toward foreign policy. Careful scholarship and many insights on neglected policy issues. [CKF/JSH]

48.413 Paolo Filo della Torre, Edward Mortimer, and Jonathan Story, eds. *Eurocommunism: myth or reality?* Harmondsworth: Penguin, 1979. ISBN 0-1402-2077-1. ▸ Collection of judgments by well-informed contemporary observers forms a useful complement to Tokes 48.423. [JSH]

48.414 Raymond L. Garthoff. *Detente and confrontation: American-Soviet relations from Nixon to Reagan.* Washington, D.C.: Brookings Institution, 1985. ISBN 0-8157-3044-6 (cl), 0-8157-3043-8 (pbk). ▸ Comprehensive, highly critical assessment of détente and of America's role in its collapse. Although not entirely persuasive, massive tome is standard reference work. [JSH/BBY]

48.415 Jeffrey Herf. *War by other means: Soviet Power, West German resistance, and the battle of the euromissiles.* New York: Free Press, 1991. ISBN 0-02-915030-2. ▸ Absorbing account of Soviet influence on anti-nuclear Left and struggle between West German elites and popular forces during last years of cold war. [JSH/NDC]

48.416 Bruce W. Jentleson. *Pipeline politics: the complex political economy of East-West energy trade.* Ithaca, N.Y.: Cornell University Press, 1986. ISBN 0-8014-1923-9. ▸ Significant case study with wide implications. Relative decline of America's economic power undermined ability to use economic levers to coerce or reward Soviet behavior. [CKF/JSH]

48.417 Diana Johnstone. *The politics of euromissiles: Europe's role in America's world.* London: Verso; distributed by Schocken, 1984. ISBN 0-86091-082-2 (cl), 0-86091-787-8 (pbk). ▸ Stimulating, but not even-handed, study of impact of missile-force modernization on relations among European North Atlantic Treaty Organization states and their domestic politics. Engaged journalistic account emphasizing West Germany and France. [JSH]

48.418 Walter Laqueur. *The age of terrorism.* Boston: Little, Brown, 1987. ISBN 0-316-51478-0. ▸ Terrorism, umbrella concept for wide variety of nonstate violence: ideological, international, ethnic, and criminal. Single best volume on subject plagued by presentism. [JSH]

48.419 Paul H. Nitze et al. *Securing the seas: the Soviet naval challenge and Western alliance options; an Atlantic Council policy study.* Boulder: Westview, 1979. ISBN 0-8915-8359-9 (cl), 0-8915-8360-2 (pbk). ▸ Thorough assessment of balance of naval power in seventies with analysis of strategic implications. Still important for specialists in second cold war. [CKF/JSH]

48.420 Gaddis Smith. *Morality, reason, and power: American diplomacy in the Carter years.* New York: Hill & Wang, 1986. ISBN 0-8090-70170-0. ▸ Sets United States president in context broader than American expectations of foreign policy. Policies crippled by infighting, public opinion shifts, congressional resistance, and world events. Best available account but relies excessively on memoirs. [JSH/BBY]

48.421 Stephen L. Spiegel, Mark A. Heller, and Jacob Goldberg, eds. *The Soviet-American competition in the Middle East.* Lexington, Mass.: Lexington Books, 1988. ISBN 0-669-15357-5 (cl), 0-669-16891-2 (pbk). ▸ Collection of essays examining dangers to superpowers from rivalry in region and shared difficulty in managing clients. Informative work for regional specialists. [JSH]

48.422 Richard W. Stevenson. *The rise and fall of detente: relaxations of tensions in US-Soviet relations, 1953–84.* Champaign: University of Illinois Press, 1985. ISBN 0-252-01215-1. ▸ Alternating fear and complacency explain why Soviet-American relations passed through cycles of tension and relaxation. Suggestive formulations by political scientist; need to be tested against documents. [CKF/JSH]

48.423 Rudolf L. Tokes. *Eurocommunism and detente.* New York: New York University Press for Council on Foreign Relations, 1978. ISBN 0-8247-8161-6 (cl), 0-8147-8162-4 (pbk). ▸ Nine chapters by historically minded political scientists on domestic and international consequences of major movement of 1970s. Well worth reading. [JSH]

48.424 Donald S. Zagoria, ed. *Soviet policy in East Asia.* New Haven: Yale University Press, 1982. ISBN 0-300-02738-9. ▸ Wide-ranging essays arguing Soviet policy in Far East arose from sense of weakness. Valuable for advanced students. [CKF/JSH]

Military and Economic Pacts

48.425 Paul Buteux. *The politics of nuclear consultation in NATO, 1965–1980.* New York: Cambridge University Press, 1983. ISBN 0-521-24798-5. ▸ Study of Nuclear Planning Group that emerged from European pressure for greater voice in organization's nuclear weapons policy. Model example of contemporary history in absence of archives. [JSH]

48.426 Robert W. Clawson and Lawrence S. Kaplan, eds. *The Warsaw Pact: political purpose and military means.* Wilmington, Del.: Scholarly Resources, 1982. ISBN 0-8420-2198-1 (cl), 0-8420-2199-X (pbk). ▸ Fourteen essays, nine on military forces, doctrines, and weapons. Others offer quick survey of pact's dynamics and relations with North Atlantic Treaty Organization. Introductory work. [CKF/JSH]

48.427 Audrey Kurth Cronin. *Great power politics and the struggle over Austria, 1945–1955.* Ithaca, N.Y.: Cornell University Press, 1986. ISBN 0-8014-1854-2. ▸ Competent but not definitive survey based chiefly on English-language sources. Khrushchev's desire for détente finally made it possible to reach agreement on Austrian neutralization. [JSH/JWB]

48.428 Alfred Grosser. *The Western alliance: European-American relations since 1945.* 1980 ed. Michael Shaw, trans. New York: Vintage, 1982. ISBN 0-394-70815-6. ▸ Superb history of European politics in alliance; particularly good on anti-Americanism. Finds European "pillar" of alliance too weak to balance Americans. Somewhat dated and episodic but contains observations of well-informed and shrewd European political scientist–historian. [JSH/DSC]

48.429 Francis H. Heller and John R. Gillingham, eds. *NATO: the founding of the Atlantic alliance and the integration of Europe.* New York: St. Martin's, 1992. ISBN 0-312-06585-X. ▸ Thick collection of papers containing original research on evolution of Atlantic alliance during fifties. Many riches to be mined from papers and their documentation. [JSH]

48.430 Lawrence S. Kaplan. *NATO and the United States: the enduring alliance.* Boston: Twayne, 1988. ISBN 0-8057-7906-X (cl), 0-8057-9200-7 (pbk). ▸ Most important scholar of North Atlantic Treaty Organization summarizes knowledge and views in readily accessible volume. Documents value of alliance as token of common purposes of Western democracies, containing communism and integrating capitalist economies and activities of West. [JSH/BBY]

48.431 Michael Charles Kaser and E. A. Radice, eds. *The economic history of Eastern Europe, 1919–1975.* 3 vols. to date. Oxford: Clarendon, 1985–. ISBN 0-19-828444-6 (v. 1), 0-19-828445-4 (v. 2), 0-19-828446-2 (v. 3). ▸ Volume 2 contains three chapters on postwar reconstruction; volume 3 deals with institutional changes within planned economy 1950–75, and foreign trade; volumes 4 and 5 will treat domestic performance and external trade relations. [JSH]

48.432 Chester J. Pach, Jr. *Arming the free world: the origins of the United States military assistance program, 1945–1950.* Chapel Hill: University of North Carolina Press, 1991. ISBN 0-8078-1943-3. ▸ Able study of important element in postwar international relations. Chiefly of interest to specialists. [JSH]

48.433 Rolf Tamnes. *The United States and the cold war in the high north.* Brookfield, Vt.: Gower, 1991. ISBN 1-85521-223-4. ▸ Comprehensive study of United States and NATO's offensive and defensive strategy concerning crucial Northern Flank, especially Norway. [CKF]

WESTERN EUROPE SINCE 1945

Integration

48.434 Josef Becker and Franz Knipping, eds. *Power in Europe? Great Britain, France, Germany, and Italy in a postwar world, 1945–1950.* New York: de Gruyter, 1986. ISBN 0-89925-261-3. ▸ Exciting collection produced by international conference of scholars assessing economic, political, diplomatic, and cultural situation of four West European states in immediate aftermath of war. More than a score of excellent reports. [JSH]

48.435 Ennio Di Nolfo, ed. *Power in Europe.* Vol. 2: *Great Britain, France, Germany, Italy, and the origins of EEC, 1952–1957.* Berlin: de Gruyter, 1992. ISBN 0-89925-816-6. ▸ Continuation of Becker and Knipping 48.434. Twenty-six papers on extension of effort at economic integration and on political conditions giving rise to that effort. Important guide to current scholarship and substantial bibliography. [JSH]

48.436 Edward Fursdon. *The European defense community: a history.* New York: St. Martin's, 1980. ISBN 0-312-26927-7. ▸ Workmanlike study by British soldier-scholar. Advantage of more sources and distance than earlier studies, but neglects passion aroused by European Defense Community. [JSH]

48.437 John Gillingham. *Coal, steel, and the rebirth of Europe, 1945–1955: the Germans and French from Ruhr conflict to economic community.* New York: Cambridge University Press, 1991. ISBN 0-521-40059-7. ▸ Elegantly written, provocative, well-researched study. Implementation of Schuman Plan helped overcome longstanding antagonism in core relationship of postwar settlement.

Essential reading on postwar reconstruction and cold war. [CKF/JSH/DSC/NDC]

48.438 Toivo Miljan. *The reluctant Europeans: the attitudes of the Nordic countries towards European integration.* Montreal: McGill-Queen's University Press, 1977. ISBN 0-7735-0293-9. ‣ Examination of Scandinavian reluctance to be drawn into integrative process. Valuable for its Scandinavian sources and cogent narrative, but thin on analysis. [JSH]

48.439 Alan S. Milward, George Brennan, and Frederico Romero. *The European rescue of the nation-state.* Berkeley: University of California Press, 1992. ISBN 0-520-08137-4. ‣ Detailed history of origins of European community. Sequel and companion to Milward 48.389. [CKF]

48.440 Roger Morgan and Caroline Bray, eds. *Partners and rivals in Western Europe: Britain, France, and Germany.* Aldershot: Gower, 1986. ISBN 0-566-00983-8. ‣ Useful collection of essays by political scientists on continuing international competition within movement toward supranational integration. Very helpful for understanding difficulties facing further integration. [JSH]

48.441 Raymond Poidevin. *Robert Schuman: homme d'état, 1886–1963.* Paris: Imprimerie Nationale, 1986. ISBN 2-11-080886-1 (cl), 2-11-080885-3 (pbk). ‣ Biography of key French leader illuminates progress and problems of Franco-German reconciliation in twentieth century. Valuable reference thanks to mastery of sources and full discussion. [JSH]

48.442 Raymond Poidevin, ed. *Histoire des débuts de la construction européenne, mars 1948–mai 1950/Origins of the European integration, March 1948–May 1950.* Brussels: Bruylant, 1986. ISBN 3-7890-1270-X. ‣ Fine conference volume reporting early archival findings of historians on contribution of United States to European integration, hesitations of British government, and first steps toward political cooperation. Valuable orientation to important issues. [JSH]

48.443 Paula Scalingi. *The European Parliament: the three-decade search for a united Europe.* Westport, Conn.: Greenwood, 1980. ISBN 0-313-21493-X. ‣ Useful study, but narrowly focused on one aspect of integration process. Competing national interests and rivalry between federal and confederal approaches to integration have balanced against external dangers. [JSH]

48.444 Klaus Schwabe, ed. *Die Anfänge des Schuman-Plans, 1950/51: Beiträge des Kolloquiums in Aachen, 28.–30. Mai 1986/The beginnings of the Schuman Plan, 1950–51: contributions to the Symposium in Aachen, May 28–30, 1986.* Baden-Baden: Nomos, 1988. ISBN 3-7890-1543-1. ‣ Close examination of origin, negotiation, and implementation of Schuman Plan for European Coal and Steel Community as device for pacification of Franco-German conflicts. Leading scholars examine negotiations; roles of Robert Schuman, Jean Monnet, and Konrad Adenauer; economic conditions; role of domestic politics; and stance of Anglo-Americans. Important source; successor volume in press on foundation of European Economic Community (Enrico Serra, editor). [JSH]

48.445 Haig Simonian. *The privileged partnership: Franco-German relations in the European community, 1969–1984.* Oxford: Clarendon, 1985. ISBN 0-19-821959-8. ‣ Informative discussion of some features of European integration. Finds French and German statesmen have fostered close relationship despite important disputes over agricultural and monetary policy. [CKF/JSH]

48.446 Derek W. Urwin. *The community of Europe: a history of European integration since 1945.* New York: Longman, 1991. ISBN 0-582-04530-4 (cl), 0-582-04531-2 (pbk). ‣ Chiefly devoted to evolution of European community after 1957 with adequate discussion of postwar decade. Many shrewd judgments on politics, economics, and ideas; best existing introduction. [JSH]

48.447 F. Roy Willis. *Italy chooses Europe.* New York: Oxford University Press, 1971. ISBN 0-19-501383-2. ‣ Italian policy toward European integration as product of complicated domestic forces. First-rate investigation of neglected topic in history of postwar Europe. [JSH]

48.448 John W. Young. *Britain, France, and the unity of Europe, 1945–1951.* Leicester: Leicester University Press, 1984. ISBN 0-7185-1246-4. ‣ Anglo-French hopes for collaboration strained by British preoccupation with America and French preoccupation with Germany. Dense compression of research in British archives; best study currently available. [JSH]

National Foreign Policies

48.449 Alan Bullock. *Ernest Bevin: foreign secretary, 1945–1951.* New York: Norton, 1983. ISBN 0-393-01825-3. ‣ Discussion of British foreign, defense, and imperial policy during crucial postwar period. Important contribution to understanding retreat from empire and advance toward cold war. [JSH]

48.450 A. W. DePorte. *Europe between the superpowers: the enduring balance.* 2d ed. New Haven: Yale University Press, 1986. ISBN 0-300-02229-8 (cl), 0-300-03758-9 (pbk). ‣ Optimistic assessment of durability of balance of power and division in Europe. Despite recent events remains intelligent examination of relationship among postwar Western European states. [JSH/DSC]

48.451 Timothy Garton Ash. *In Europe's name: Germany and the divided continent.* New York: Random House, 1993. ISBN 0-394-55711-5. ‣ Masterly analysis of how Yalta division of Europe was overcome by decades of West German *Ostpolitik*, which paralleled but also diverged from United States policy of détente. [CKF]

48.452 Misha Glenny. *The fall of Yugoslavia: the Third Balkan War.* New York: Viking Penguin, 1992. ISBN 0-14-017288-2. ‣ Incisive, fairly objective account by journalist of Balkan tragedy. [CKF]

48.453 William E. Griffith. *The Ostpolitik of the Federal Republic of Germany.* Cambridge, Mass.: MIT Press, 1978. ISBN 0-262-07072-3. ‣ Willy Brandt's *Ostpolitik* of seventies set against very detailed background portrait of German domestic and foreign policy in twentieth century. Systematic, dense narrative of events; weak on interpretation. Read with Garton Ash 48.451. [JSH/NDC]

48.454 Michael H. Haltzel and Joseph Kruzel. *Between the blocs: problems and prospects for Europe's neutral and nonaligned states.* Cambridge: Cambridge University Press, 1989. ISBN 0-521-37558-4. ‣ Substantial papers with commentary offering interesting approach to postwar foreign policy. Discussion of contrasting forms and conceptions of neutrality, impact of growing interdependence, and security problems of neutral states. [JSH]

48.455 Wolfram F. Hanrieder. *Germany, America, Europe: forty years of German foreign policy.* New Haven: Yale University Press, 1989. ISBN 0-300-04022-9. ‣ Prosperity and steady loyalty to North Atlantic Treaty Organization brought recovery of Germany's international influence and encouraged convergence of views among political parties. Analysis remains best introduction. [CKF/JSH]

48.456 Michael M. Harrison. *The reluctant ally: France and Atlantic security.* Baltimore: Johns Hopkins University Press, 1981. ISBN 0-8018-2474-5. ‣ Analysis of de Gaulle's policy toward North Atlantic Treaty Organization; despite withdrawal from military command, still supported alliance. Fourth and Fifth Republics both pursued security, status, and material benefits. Not yet supplanted by more recent work. [JSH/BMG]

48.457 Wm. Roger Louis and Hedley Bull, eds. *The "special relationship": Anglo-American relations since 1945.* Oxford: Clarendon, 1986. ISBN 0-19-822925-9 (cl), 0-19-820183-4 (pbk). ▸ Current state of knowledge on bilateral relationship that stands at center of so much contemporary international historiography. Important starting point for work on many topics. [JSH]

48.458 John Palmer. *Europe without America? The crisis in Atlantic relations.* Oxford: Oxford University Press, 1988. ISBN 0-19-215894-5. ▸ Neutralist journalist asserts Atlanticism and alliance have endured long beyond actual benefits. Stimulating challenge to conventional academic positions. [CKF/JSH]

48.459 Yaacov Ro'i. *The struggle for Soviet Jewish emigration, 1948–1967.* New York: Cambridge University Press, 1991. ISBN 0-521-39084-2. ▸ Meticulous analysis of awakening of Soviet Jewry and initial international efforts to secure their release, foreshadowing the more extensive campaign of 1970s and 1980s. [CKF]

48.460 Sergiu Verona. *Military occupation and diplomacy: Soviet troops in Romania, 1944–1958.* Durham, N.C.: Duke University Press, 1992. ISBN 0-8223-1171-2. ▸ Based on United States and British archival material and lacking Soviet and Romanian sources, nevertheless provides useful case study of bilateral realtions inside Warsaw Pact at height of cold war. [CKF]

48.461 John W. Young. *France, the cold war, and the Western alliance, 1944–1949: French foreign policy and post-war Europe.* New York: St. Martin's, 1990. ISBN 0-312-04193-4. ▸ Large ambitions and lack of resources drew France into anti-Soviet bloc. Reliable account, well grounded in French and British archives and unlikely to be supplanted soon. [CKF/JSH]

EASTERN BLOC SINCE 1945

48.462 Seweryn Bialer. *The Soviet paradox: external expansion and internal decline.* New York: Knopf, 1986. ISBN 0-394-54095-6. ▸ Study of connections between Soviet domestic and foreign policies in early 1980s. Extremely informative and stimulating; good bibliographical essay on Soviet politics and diplomacy. [JSH]

48.463 Seweryn Bialer and Michael Mandelbaum, eds. *Gorbachev's Russia and American foreign policy.* Boulder: Westview, 1988. ISBN 0-8133-0748-1 (cl), 0-8133-0751-1 (pbk). ▸ Impact of Gorbachev reforms on international relations. Ambitious effort at comprehensive assessment by leading scholars. [JSH]

48.464 Coit D. Blacker. *Hostage to revolution: Gorbachev and Soviet security policy, 1985–1991.* New York: Council on Foreign Relations Press, 1993. ISBN 0-87609-143-5. ▸ Careful assessment by experienced observer of Soviet security policy of reorientation of Soviet positions in light of domestic upheaval. [JSH]

48.465 Aurel Braun. *Romanian foreign policy since 1965: the political and military limits of autonomy.* New York: Praeger, 1978. ISBN 0-03-043471-8. ▸ Best available explanation of how Romanian leader Ceauşescu managed to pursue foreign policy that often annoyed Soviets. Although chiefly for specialists, illuminates workings of Soviet empire. [JSH]

48.466 Aurel Braun, ed. *The Soviet–East European relationship in the Gorbachev era: the prospects for adaptation.* Boulder: Westview, 1990. ISBN 0-8133-7799-4. ▸ Collection of essays by noted experts on Soviet military, economic, and political interests in Eastern Europe and East European responses. Superior concluding essay by editor. [CKF/JSH]

48.467 Charles Gati. *The bloc that failed: Soviet–East European relations in transition.* Bloomington: University of Indiana Press with Center for Strategic and International Studies, 1990. ISBN 0-253-32531-5 (cl), 0-253-20561-1 (pbk). ▸ Capsule account of developments, 1953–88, concentrating on military, economic, and political aspects by experienced student of Warsaw Pact countries. Devotes bulk of text to recent upheavals. Excellent brief bibliographical essay; good for classroom use. [JSH/GS]

48.468 Charles Gati. *Hungary and the Soviet Bloc.* Durham, N.C.: Duke University Press, 1986. ISBN 0-8223-0684-0 (cl), 0-8223-0747-2 (pbk). ▸ Collection of insightful essays on various aspects of Hungarian politics and relations with Soviet Union and other members of Soviet Bloc since World War II. [JSH/SBV]

48.469 Robert L. Hutchings. *Soviet–East European relations: consolidation and conflict, 1968–1980.* 1983 ed. Madison: University of Wisconsin Press, 1987. ISBN 0-299-09310-7. ▸ Soviet strategy of drowning dissent in material goods, acquired through ties with West, boomeranged when rising oil prices slowed world economy. Important and useful interpretation. [JSH]

48.470 Marie Lavigne, ed. *The Soviet Union and Eastern Europe in the global economy.* Cambridge: Cambridge University Press, 1992. ISBN 0-521-41417-2. ▸ Collection of recent studies useful for understanding region's difficulties in making transformation from command to market economies. [JSH]

48.471 Avril Pittman. *From Ostpolitik to reunification: West German–Soviet political relations since 1974.* New York: Cambridge University Press, 1992. ISBN 0-521-40166-6. ▸ Account of how *Ostpolitik* weathered storm of deterioration of détente in 1980s. Useful sequel to works by Griffith 48.453 and Stent 48.344; greatly supplemented by Garton Ash 48.451. [JSH]

48.472 Jiri Valenta. *Soviet intervention in Czechoslovakia, 1968: anatomy of a decision.* Rev. ed. Baltimore: Johns Hopkins University Press, 1991. ISBN 0-8018-4297-2 (cl), 0-8018-4117-8 (pbk). ▸ Lack of effective, consistent policy from post-Stalinist collective leadership produced numerous blunders. Useful source on Czech and Soviet developments, but more complex explanation required. [JSH]

48.473 Gerhard Wettig. *Community and conflict in the socialist camp: the Soviet Union, East Germany, and the German problem, 1965–1972.* Edwina Moreton and Hannes Adomeit, trans. New York: St. Martin's, 1975. ▸ Brief, serviceable sketch of debate on German problem in Eastern Europe during Brandt era (1962–72). Useful summary of complex negotiations by well-informed observer. [JSH]

48.474 Z.A.B. Zeman. *The making and breaking of communist Europe.* Rev. ed. Oxford: Blackwell, 1991. ISBN 0-631-17836-8. ▸ Controversial interpretation emphasizing distinctiveness of East European development during this century, regardless of which nation held overlordship. More interpretive essay than monograph. Earlier title: *Pursued by the Bear.* [CKF/JSH]

SEE ALSO
33.21 Timothy Garton Ash. *The magic lantern.*
33.455 Paul E. Zinner. *Revolution in Hungary.*

AFRICA SINCE 1945

48.475 Julius A. Amin. *The Peace Corps in Cameroon.* Kent, Ohio: Kent State University Press, 1992. ISBN 0-87338-450-4. ▸ Useful case study of imaginative cold war program between 1962 and 1966. Lacks adequate historical background for colonial period. [CKF]

48.476 James Barber and John Barratt. *South Africa's foreign policy: the search for status and security, 1945–1988.* New York: Cambridge University Press, 1990. ISBN 0-521-37313-1 (cl), 0-521-38876-1 (pbk). ▸ South Africa's response to internal and external dangers threatening apartheid regime. Thorough, balanced assessment, important for understanding regional developments. Best book available. [JSH]

48.477 Thomas Borstelmann. *Apartheid's reluctant uncle: the United States and southern Africa in the early cold war.* New York: Oxford University Press, 1993. ISBN 0-19-507942-6. ▸ Examination of dilemmas of Truman administration as decision makers in Washington had to choose apparent lesser of two evils in area peripheral to main American concerns. [JSH]

48.478 P. Olisanwuche Esedebe. *Pan-Africanism: the idea and the movement, 1776–1963.* Washington, D.C.: Howard University Press, 1982. ISBN 0-88258-124-4 (cl), 0-88258-125-2 (pbk). ‣ Reexamination by Nigerian scholar from documents of its exponents instead of records of imperial states. Not entirely dispassionate. [CKF/JSH]

48.479 Paul B. Henze. *The horn of Africa: from war to peace.* New York: St. Martin's, 1991. ISBN 0-312-06138-2. ‣ Concise explanation of origins of regional disputes, subsequent superpower involvement, and rapid deterioration of local situation by former American diplomat with deep affection for region. [JSH]

48.480 Colin Legum et al. *Africa in the 1980s: a continent in crisis.* Catherine Gwin, Introduction. New York: McGraw-Hill, 1979. ISBN 0-07-037081-8 (cl), 0-07-037082-6 (pbk). ‣ Sound general introduction to African problems. Essays consider dangers of coups and foreign intervention arising from instability rooted in asymmetric resource distribution and relations with developed economies. [JSH]

48.481 Thomas J. Noer. *Cold war and black liberation: the United States and white rule in Africa, 1948–1968.* Columbia: University of Missouri Press, 1985. ISBN 0-8262-0458-9. ‣ American policy subordinated Africa to global concerns and in so doing tended to support white rule in South Africa, Rhodesia, Angola, and Mozambique. Important pioneering work. [JSH/BBY]

48.482 Olatunde J.C.B. Ojo et al. *African international relations.* New York: Longman, 1985. ISBN 0-582-64394-5 (cl), 0-582-64393-7 (pbk). ‣ Ten essays grouped into useful primer. No bibliography but each chapter concludes with list of helpful sources. [JSH]

48.483 Ralph I. Onwuka and Olajide Aluko, eds. *The future of Africa and the new international economic order.* New York: St. Martin's, 1986. ISBN 0-312-31412-4. ‣ Group of African scholars assess rejection by industrial states of calls for new international economic order and impact on Africa. [JSH]

48.484 Ronald W. Walters. *Pan-Africanism in the African diaspora: an analysis of modern Afrocentric political movements.* Detroit: Wayne State University Press, 1993. ISBN 0-8143-2184-4. ‣ Detailed comparative analysis of connections between United States, Britain, Caribbean, Brazil, and South Africa. Very useful as example of nongovernmental transnational movements. [JSH]

48.485 Stephen Wright and Janice N. Brownfoot, eds. *Africa in world politics: changing perspectives.* Basingstoke, England: Macmillan, 1987. ISBN 0-333-39630-8. ‣ Collection of papers deserving wide audience. Finds political fragmentation inhibits cooperation necessary to obtain help from uncaring world. [CKF/JSH]

48.486 I. William Zartman. *Ripe for resolution: conflict and intervention in Africa.* Rev. ed. New York: Oxford University Press, 1989. ISBN 0-19-505931-X (pbk). ‣ Leading American Africanist assigns blame for unrest in Africa to local conflicts, rather than to commonly denounced machinations of outsiders. Chapters deal with specific regions; useful chapter references. [JSH]

LATIN AMERICA SINCE 1945

48.487 Cole Blasier. *The hovering giant: U.S. responses to revolutionary change in Latin America, 1910–1985.* Rev. ed. Pittsburgh: University of Pittsburgh Press, 1985. ISBN 0-8229-3521-X (cl), 0-8229-5372-2 (pbk). ‣ Sure-footed examination by political scientist sensitive to historical issues of various stages in evolution of United States policy toward revolutions in Mexico, Bolivia, Guatemala, and Cuba. Concludes threats to local interests balanced against threats to general security. Useful starting point. [JSH/RJW]

48.488 Jack Child. *Geopolitics and conflict in South America: quarrels among neighbors.* New York: Praeger, 1985. ISBN 0-0300-1453-0. ‣ Concise introduction showing relationship between geopolit-ical strategies and development of national security state in 1960s and 1970s. Concludes decline of American hegemony in region and still prominent role of military will provoke quarrels among states over resources. Provocative, pioneering linkage of domestic and international orders. [JSH/RJW]

48.489 Elizabeth G. Ferris and Jennie K. Lincoln, eds. *Latin American foreign policies: global and regional dimensions.* Boulder: Westview, 1981. ISBN 0-8653-1258-3. ‣ Essays on growing range of international contacts by Latin American states as they seek more diverse patrons. Treats both global and regional relations. For advanced students. [JSH]

48.490 Max Hastings and Simon Jenkins. *The battle for the Falklands.* Rev. ed. London: Joseph, 1992. ISBN 0-7181-2578-9 (cl). ‣ British view of war by military historian turned correspondent and well-placed political journalist. Even-handed judgments, sharp criticism, and clear analysis make excellent introduction. [JSH]

48.491 Pedro-Pablo Kuczynski. *Latin American debt.* Baltimore: Johns Hopkins University Press, 1988. ISBN 0-8018-3659-X (cl), 0-8018-3660-3 (pbk). ‣ Historically grounded account of debt crisis by banker and government official who has seen problem from both sides. Emphasizes grim implications for international stability. [JSH]

48.492 Walter LaFeber. *Inevitable revolutions: the United States in Central America.* Rev. ed. New York: Norton, 1984. ISBN 0-393-01787-7 (cl, 1983), 0-393-30212-1 (pbk). ‣ Critical analysis of American policy of fostering dependency among Central American states, then lashing out with armed force when inevitable resentment turned to revolution. Not entirely balanced; hampered by lack of Spanish-language sources but most comprehensive study available. [JSH/BBY/RLM]

48.493 Walter LaFeber. *The Panama Canal: the crisis in historical perspective.* Rev. ed. New York: Oxford University Press, 1989. ISBN 0-19-505930-1. ‣ Wide-ranging, lucid background study; useful both on specific topic and on larger issues of relations between United States and other American republics. Relies heavily on United States materials. [JSH/RLM]

48.494 Lester P. Langley. *The United States and the Caribbean in the twentieth century.* 4th ed. Athens: University of Georgia Press, 1989. ISBN 0-8203-1153-7 (cl), 0-8203-1154-5 (pbk). ‣ Sound, balanced synthesis, concluding United States has sought to promote political stability, prosperity, and honest government by range of devices. [JSH]

48.495 Morris Morley. *Imperial state and revolution: the United States and Cuba, 1952–1986.* Cambridge: Cambridge University Press, 1987. ISBN 0-521-30988-3 (cl), 0-521-35762-4 (pbk). ‣ American policy toward Cuban revolution as example of its policy toward all revolutions. Useful for detailed accounts and interpretive perspective. [CKF/JSH/BBY]

48.496 Heraldo Muñoz and Joseph S. Tulchin, eds. *Latin American nations in world politics.* Boulder: Westview, 1984. ISBN 0-86531-688-0 (cl), 0-86531-689-9 (pbk). ‣ Sixteen brief essays covering selected aspects of contemporary Latin American diplomacy. Short bibliography reflects urgent need for more work in this area. [JSH]

48.497 Stephen G. Rabe. *Eisenhower and Latin America: the foreign policy of anticommunism.* Chapel Hill: University of North Carolina Press, 1988. ISBN 0-8078-1761-9 (cl), 0-8078-4204-4 (pbk). ‣ Concise, well-written overview. Signs of unrest caused Eisenhower administration to shift from support for local strongmen to interventionist policy of encouraging democracy and prosperity. Best point of entry to subject. [JSH/RJW]

48.498 Lars Schoultz. *Human rights and United States policy toward Latin America.* Princeton: Princeton University Press, 1981. ISBN 0-691-07630-8 (cl), 0-691-02204-6 (pbk). ‣ Comprehensive examination of emergence during seventies of human rights as important theme in American foreign policy and its uneven implementation. Detailed case study based on extensive interviews and research in government documents. Particularly interesting for specialists. [JSH/RJW]

48.499 Wayne S. Smith, ed. *Toward resolution? The Falklands/ Malvinas dispute.* Boulder: Reinner, 1991. ISBN 1-555-87265-4. ▸ Brief, informed presentation of international dialogue on conflicting claims and possible paths to solution of problem that led to war. No bibliography or notes. [JSH]

MIDDLE EAST SINCE 1945

48.500 Mohammed E. Ahrari. *OPEC: the falling giant.* Lexington: University Press of Kentucky, 1986. ISBN 0-8131-1552-3. ▸ Discussion of disintegration of powerful cartel under pressure of market forces. Based on scrupulous examination of published sources; extremely useful as reference, but slights political analysis. [JSH]

48.501 James A. Bill. *The eagle and the lion: the tragedy of American-Iranian relations.* New Haven: Yale University Press, 1988. ISBN 0-300-04097-0 (cl), 0-300-04412-7 (pbk). ▸ Superb history covering several decades. Sharply critical of United States government's willful ignorance of Iran and incompetence, from 1953 to Iran-Contra scandal. Employs Farsi as well as American sources. Best account available. [JSH/GRKG]

48.502 William J. Burns. *Economic aid and American policy toward Egypt, 1955–1981.* Albany: State University of New York Press, 1985. ISBN 0-8739-58683 (cl), 0-8739-5869-1 (pbk). ▸ Study of efforts to use aid as lever. Helpful to specialists for its detail, interesting to all for careful examination of effectiveness of economism. [JSH]

48.503 Shahram Chubin and Charles Tripp. *Iran and Iraq at war.* Boulder: Westview, 1988. ISBN 0-8133-0734-1. ▸ Political, diplomatic, social, and economic aspects of conflict, rather than military history. Valuable for all students of Middle Eastern affairs, but stimulating for students of international conflict. [JSH]

48.504 Michael J. Cohen. *Palestine and the great powers.* Princeton: Princeton University Press, 1982. ISBN 0-691-05371-5. ▸ Comprehensive, balanced, and deeply researched work for regional specialists. Relative unity of Zionists gave them advantage over Arabs, British, and Americans, who all suffered from factionalism. [JSH]

48.505 Anthony Cordesman. *After the storm: the changing military balance in the Middle East.* Boulder: Westview, 1993. ISBN 0-8133-1692-8. ▸ Very detailed quantitative and qualitative assessment of fighting power of all states in wake of Gulf War by able student of military issues. [JSH]

48.506 Peter L. Hahn. *The United States, Great Britain, and Egypt, 1945–1956: strategy and diplomacy in the early cold war.* Chapel Hill: University of North Carolina Press, 1991. ISBN 0-8078-1942-5. ▸ Good study of Anglo-American relationship in a third country. Concludes that when Britain and United States found interests at odds with ideals in Egypt, they subordinated their ideals. [JSH]

48.507 P. Edward Haley. *Qaddafi and the United States since 1969.* New York: Praeger, 1984. ISBN 0-03-070587-8. ▸ Exhaustive account, mostly based on press accounts, of downward spiral in relations between superpower tormented by impotence and its *bête noire*. Rich in information but little analysis. [JSH]

48.508 Dilip Hiro. *Holy wars: the rise of Islamic fundamentalism.* New York: Routledge, 1989. ISBN 0-415-90207-X (cl), 0-415-90208-8 (pbk). ▸ Forceful discussion of fundamentalism with chapters examining Egypt, Syria, Saudi Arabia, Iran, and

Afghanistan. Well-written but shaped by author's sympathies; weak on analysis. Best for informed specialists. [JSH]

48.509 Malcolm H. Kerr. *The Arab cold war: Gamal 'Abd al-Nasir and his rivals, 1958–1970.* 3d ed. New York: Oxford University Press for Royal Institute of International Affairs, 1971. ISBN 0-19-501475-8. ▸ Interpretive essay on ideology and tactics making strong argument for Arab politics as autonomous of Western policies. Written by Western observer with long experience of Arab world. Earlier title: *The Arab Cold War, 1958–1965.* [JSH]

48.510 Bruce R. Kuniholm. *The Persian Gulf and United States policy: a guide to issues and references.* Claremont, Calif.: Regina, 1984. ISBN 0-941690-12-1 (cl), 0-941690-11-3 (pbk). ▸ Extended essay on American interests and problems likely to arise in defending them. Rich, well-organized bibliography with wide coverage. Excellent introduction. [JSH]

48.511 Diane B. Kunz. *The economic diplomacy of the Suez crisis.* Chapel Hill: University of North Carolina Press, 1991. ISBN 0-8078-1967-0. ▸ Britain's crumbling economic and financial foundations first contributed to trouble with Nasser, then forced humiliating retreat. Masterful exploration of wide interest to all British and diplomatic historians. [JSH]

48.512 Wm. Roger Louis and Roger Owen, eds. *Suez, 1956: the crisis and its consequences.* Oxford: Clarendon, 1989. ISBN 0-19-820141-9 (cl), 0-19-820241-5 (pbk). ▸ Collection presents full range of scholarship on great power relations and Middle Eastern problems. Essential starting point. [JSH]

48.513 Benny Morris. *The birth of the Palestinian refugee problem, 1947–1949.* Cambridge: Cambridge University Press, 1987. ISBN 0-521-33028-9. ▸ Best available study. Concludes Arab flights were inspired by lack of leadership and by fear, but Israelis obstructed return in order to increase security of their state. [CKF/ JSH]

48.514 Henry Munson, Jr. *Islam and revolution in the Middle East.* New Haven: Yale University Press, 1988. ISBN 0-300-04127-6 (cl), 0-300-04604-9 (pbk). ▸ Introduction to Sunnī-Shīī differences with background on Iran, Saudi Arabia, Syria, and Egypt and discussion of why revolution in Iran was unique. Useful at introductory level. [JSH]

48.515 Ritchie Ovendale. *The origins of the Arab-Israeli wars.* 2d ed. New York: Longman, 1992. ISBN 0-582-06369-8. ▸ Concise introductory history of Arab-Israeli relations, 1894-1973, set against backdrop of great power rivalries. Bibliography provides short list of books and Anglo-American archival sources. [JSH]

48.516 William B. Quandt. *Camp David: peacemaking and politics.* Washington, D.C.: Brookings Institution, 1986. ISBN 0-8157-7290-4 (cl), 0-8157-7289-0 (pbk). ▸ Careful examination of important conference by scholar and member of National Security Council. Reveals much about nature of Middle Eastern affairs and American diplomacy. Excellent case study for all levels. [JSH/BBY]

48.517 William B. Quandt. *Decade of decisions: American policy toward the Arab-Israeli conflict, 1967–1976.* Berkeley: University of California Press, 1977. ISBN 0-520-03469-4 (cl), 0-520-03536-4 (pbk). ▸ Key book presenting detailed, balanced analysis. Growing dependence on foreign oil and fear of Soviet adventurism engaged United States ever more deeply in Middle Eastern affairs. National interest, domestic politics, bureaucracy, and executive power blended to form American Middle East policy. [JSH/BBY/PM]

48.518 Itamar Rabinovich. *The road not taken: early Arab-Israeli negotiations.* New York: Oxford University Press, 1991. ISBN 0-19-506066-0. ▸ Archive-based study explaining why peace could not be negotiated before ideologically driven soldiers took command in Arab capitals. Strenuous engagement with historiographical debates. Stimulating discussion. [JSH]

48.519 Nadav Safran. *Israel: the embattled ally; with a new preface and postscript.* 1978 ed. Cambridge, Mass.: Belknap, 1981. ISBN 0-674-46881-3 (cl, 1978), 0-674-46882-1 (pbk). ▸ Discussion of Israeli-American "special relationship," from foundations of Israel to 1973 War. Lucid explanation of how United States became involved in region. Essentially pro-Israeli viewpoint. [JSH]

48.520 Tom Segev. *The seventh million: the Israelis and the Holocaust.* Haim Watzman, trans. New York: Hill & Wang, 1993. ISBN 0-8090-8563-1. ▸ Passionate work by journalist depicting institutionalization of memory in Israel's domestic politics and foreign relations. [CKF]

48.521 Yitzhak Shichor. *The Middle East in China's foreign policy, 1949–1977.* New York: Cambridge University Press, 1979. ISBN 0-521-22214-1. ▸ Analysis of People's Republic of China's movement from unconditional support of national liberation in Middle East to containment of Soviet influence there. Important contribution to understanding evolution of China's foreign policy and especially of Sino-Soviet relations. [JSH]

48.522 Mark Urban. *War in Afghanistan.* 2d ed. New York: St. Martin's, 1990. ISBN 0-312-04255-8. ▸ Soviet Union's Vietnam, a remote war which has yielded few scholarly studies. [CKF/JSH]

48.523 John Waterbury and Ragaei El Mallakh. *The Middle East in the coming decade: from wellhead to well-being?* Catherine Gwin, Introduction. New York: McGraw-Hill, 1978. ISBN 0-07-068445-6 (cl), 0-07-068446-4 (pbk). ▸ Two essays on possibilities of transforming Middle East from object of contests among local and foreign powers into area using its enormous wealth for general benefit. [JSH]

48.524 Samuel F. Wells, Jr., and Mark A. Bruzonsky, eds. *Security in the Middle East: regional change and great power strategies.* Boulder: Westview, 1987. ISBN 0-8133-0121-1 (cl), 0-8133-0122-x (pbk). ▸ Sixteen essays on diverse aspects of Middle Eastern security problems with special attention to Palestinians and Soviets. Essays overtaken by events. [CKF/JSH]

48.525 Mary C. Wilson. *King Abdullah, Britain, and the making of Jordan.* Cambridge: Cambridge University Press, 1987. ISBN 0-521-32421-1 (cl), 0-521-39987-4 (pbk). ▸ Zionists and Jordanian dynasty found common profit in defeating Palestinian nationalism at time of partition. Important work for students of Middle Eastern politics and diplomacy. [JSH]

SEE ALSO

ASIA SINCE 1945

48.526 Gordon H. Chang. *Friends and enemies: the United States, China, and the Soviet Union, 1948–1972.* Stanford, Calif.: Stanford University Press, 1990. ISBN 0-8047-1565-3. ▸ Excellent study of American official opinion. American policy sought to drive Soviets and Chinese apart by first driving them together, until Nixon reversed course. [JSH/BBY]

48.527 Bruce Cumings. *The origins of the Korean War.* Vol. 1: *Liberation and the emergence of separate regimes, 1945–1947.* Vol. 2: *The Roaring of the Cataract, 1947–1950.* 2 vols. Princeton: Princeton University Press, 1981–90. ISBN 0-691-09383-0 (v. 1, cl), 0-691-07843-2 (v. 2, cl), 0-691-10113-2 (v. 1, pbk), 0-691-02538-x (v. 2, pbk). ▸ Sharply revisionist account based on massive study of documents. Important contribution. [JSH/JBD]

48.528 Herbert J. Ellison, ed. *Japan and the Pacific quadrille: the major powers in East Asia.* Boulder: Westview, 1987. ISBN 0-8133-7314-X (pbk). ▸ Very recent assessments of Japan's relations with People's Republic of China, Soviet Union, and United States set in larger thematic framework. Reliable rather than pathbreaking. [JSH]

48.529 Rosemary Foot. *The wrong war: American policy and the dimensions of the Korean conflict, 1950–1953.* Ithaca, N.Y.: Cornell University Press, 1985. ISBN 0-8014-1800-3. ▸ Well-researched, important study of turning point for Asian diplomacy. Military, congressional, and public pressures to expand war to include China offset by influence of United Nations and North Atlantic Treaty Organization urging caution and restraint. American leaders decided not to expand war and agreed to oppose any future Korean expansionism. [JSH/BBY]

48.530 Leslie H. Gelb and Richard K. Betts. *The irony of Vietnam: the system worked.* Washington, D.C.: Brookings Institution, 1979. ISBN 0-8157-3072-1 (cl), 0-8157-3071-3 (pbk). ▸ Controversial study of decision making; essential reading. Concludes broad national consensus in support of containment led inevitably to American involvement in Vietnam. [JSH]

48.531 Akira Iriye. *The cold war in Asia: a historical introduction.* Englewood Cliffs, N.J.: Prentice-Hall, 1974. ISBN 0-13-139659-5 (cl), 0-13-139642-0 (pbk). ▸ Systemic analysis of international relations, 1945–50, arguing collapse of nationalist Chinese regime drew two superpowers into undesired conflict in Far East. Interesting methodology. [JSH]

48.532 Yuen Foong Khong. *Analogies at war: Korea, Munich, Dien Bien Phu, and the Vietnamese decisions of 1965.* Princeton: Princeton University Press, 1992. ISBN 0-691-07846-7 (cl), 0-691-02535-5 (pbk). ▸ Shrewd analysis based on extensive research demonstrating how historical analogies misled United States policy makers during cold war. [CKF]

48.533 Ilpyong J. Kim. *The strategic triangle: China, the United States, and the Soviet Union.* New York: Paragon House, 1987. ISBN 0-943852-20-X (cl), 0-943852-21-8 (pbk). ▸ Collection of scholarly articles assessing relationship of three powers in Far East during mid-eighties. Stimulating observations provide supplementary reading for those grappling with Asian politics. [JSH]

48.534 Staffan Burenstam Linder. *The Pacific century: economic and political consequences of Asian-Pacific dynamism.* Stanford, Calif.: Stanford University Press, 1986. ISBN 0-8047-1294-8 (cl), 0-8047-1305-7 (pbk). ▸ Brief, highly stimulating introduction to major current of development with implications for future. Accessible to economic novice and suitable as introduction to competition within Pacific basin. [JSH]

48.535 Neville Maxwell. *India's China war.* New York: Pantheon, 1970. ISBN 0-2246-1887-3. ▸ Intelligent, balanced journalistic account covering origins of war as well as fighting. Sino-Indian conflicts over undefined border illustrate travails of postimperial diplomacy. [CKF/JSH]

48.536 Robert J. McMahon. *Colonialism and cold war: the United States and the struggle for Indonesian independence, 1945–49.* Ithaca, N.Y.: Cornell University Press, 1981. ISBN 0-8014-1388-5. ▸ Model case study based on British, American, and United Nations archives. American opposition to European empires was not undermined by greater fear of communism under exceptional circumstances prevailing in Indonesia. [JSH]

48.537 Robert S. Ozaki and Walter Arnold, eds. *Japan's foreign relations: a global search for economic security.* Boulder: Westview, 1985. ISBN 0-86531-778-X (cl), 0-86531-779-8 (pbk). ▸ Collection of essays on policy of postwar years from perspective of Japanese decision to seek economic security through diversification. Updates Scalapino 13.365 to mid-eighties as Japanese policies began to arouse widespread alarm. Topic lacks good overview by single author. [JSH/FGN]

48.538 Bruce Palmer, Jr. *The twenty-five-year war: America's military role in Vietnam.* Lexington: University Press of Kentucky, 1984. ISBN 0-8131-1513-2. ‣ Important statement of chief lessons learned by American military in Vietnam by one close to peak of decision making. [CKF/JSH]

48.539 B. N. Pandey. *South and South-East Asia, 1945–1979: problems and policies.* London: Macmillan, 1980. ISBN 0-333-01259-3 (cl), 0-333-04978-0 (pbk). ‣ Fine, brief introduction to range of domestic and international problems facing India, Pakistan, Burma, Malaya, Indochina, Indonesia, and Philippines after collapse of European empires. Bibliography displays full range of issues in nation-building but ends in mid-1970s. [JSH]

48.540 Guy J. Pauker et al. *Diversity and development in Southeast Asia: the coming decade.* New York: McGraw-Hill, 1977. ISBN 0-07-048917-3 (cl), 0-07-048918-1 (pbk). ‣ Three essays summarizing basic political-military power relationships, economic strategies, and ethnic divisions. Concise, reliable presentations of information in historical context. Annotated chapter bibliographies assist further reading. [JSH]

48.541 Michael C. Pugh. *The ANZUS crisis, nuclear visiting, and deterrence.* Cambridge: Cambridge University Press, 1989. ISBN 0-521-34355-0. ‣ Origins and development of Australia–New Zealand–United States alliance (ANZUS) as background for recent disputes. Useful historical survey but account of disputes should be approached with caution. [JSH]

48.542 Andrew J. Rotter. *The path to Vietnam: origins of the American commitment to Southeast Asia.* Ithaca, N.Y.: Cornell University Press, 1987. ISBN 0-8014-1958-1. ‣ Excellent work demonstrating American leaders, recognizing importance of Southeast Asia for stabilizing Japan and Western Europe, committed United States to Asian containment. [JSH]

48.543 Michael Schaller. *The American occupation of Japan: the origins of the cold war in Asia.* New York: Oxford University Press, 1985. ISBN 0-19-503626-3. ‣ Study of American effort to make Japan a bastion in struggle against communism in Far East. Focus on interagency rivalry in Washington, animosity between superpowers, and Soviet excuse for domination in Eastern Europe. Better on formation of American policies than impact on Japan. [JSH/BBY]

48.544 Robert R. Simmons. *The strained alliance: Peking, P'yongyang, Moscow, and the politics of the Korean civil war.* New York: Free Press, 1975. ISBN 0-02-928880-0. ‣ Pioneering work showing what can and cannot be accomplished with available sources. Sino-Soviet conflicts existed from beginning and North Koreans had to acquiesce. [JSH]

48.545 Nancy Bernkopf Tucker. *Patterns in the dust: Chinese-American relations and the recognition controversy, 1949–50.* New York: Columbia University Press, 1983. ISBN 0-231-05362-2 (cl), 0-231-05363-0 (pbk). ‣ Korean War and Chinese intervention wrecked sensible American policy of allowing tempers to cool before extending recognition to People's Republic of China. Highly readable classic; massive research. [JSH]

48.546 Wang Gungwu. *China and the world since 1949: the impact of independence, modernity, and revolution.* New York: St. Martin's, 1977. ISBN 0-312-13352-9 (cl), 0-312-13353-7 (pbk). ‣ Extended interpretive essay on goals and determinants of Chinese foreign policy during Maoist period with due attention to impact of domestic upheaval. Competent and balanced; brief bibliography. [JSH]

48.547 Odd Arne Westad. *Cold war and revolution: Soviet-American rivalry and the origins of the Chinese Civil War.* New York: Columbia University Press, 1993. ISBN 0-231-07984-2. ‣ Exam-

ines interaction between international and domestic conflicts in early post-1945 phase of Chinese Civil War. [JSH]

48.548 Allen S. Whiting and Robert F. Dernberger. *China's future: foreign policy and economic development in the post-Mao era.* Bayless Manning, Introduction. New York: McGraw-Hill, 1977. ISBN 0-07-069958-5 (cl), 0-07-069959-3 (pbk). ‣ Informative, thoughtful analysis of fundamental international and economic factors shaping Chinese policies, regardless of ruling personalities. Well worth reading and consideration by all interested in contemporary Asian affairs. [JSH]

48.549 Stanley Wolpert. *Roots of confrontation in South Asia: Afghanistan, Pakistan, India, and the superpowers.* New York: Oxford University Press, 1982. ISBN 0-19-502994-1. ‣ Broad-ranging survey of origins of great power conflict in region brought to crisis by Soviet invasion of Afghanistan. Very useful introduction to American policy. [JSH]

SEE ALSO
13.390 Robert A. Scalapino, ed. *The foreign policy of modern Japan.*
44.839 George C. Herring, Jr. *America's longest war.*

APPEALS FOR A NEW INTERNATIONAL ECONOMIC ORDER

48.550 Robert L. Ayres. *Banking on the poor: the World Bank and world poverty.* Cambridge, Mass.: MIT Press, 1983. ISBN 0-262-01070-4 (cl), 0-262-51028-6 (pbk). ‣ Study of bank's shift during seventies from infrastructure investment to raising living standards as growth strategy. Essential reading on postwar international political economy and North-South (rich versus poor nations) debate. [CKF/JSH]

48.551 Paul Bairoch. *The economic development of the Third World since 1900.* 1975 ed. Cynthia Postan, trans. Berkeley: University of California Press, 1977. ISBN 0-520-03554-2 (pbk). ‣ Remarkable learning clearly displayed on demography, agriculture, industry, trade, and social issues. Essential starting place before turning to polemics. Senior scholars also will find much that is useful. [JSH]

48.552 Bela Balassa. *Change and challenge in the world economy.* New York: St. Martin's, 1985. ISBN 0-312-12854-1. ‣ Opinionated essays by development economist offer useful way to track intellectual debate associated with struggle between rich and poor nations for last two decades. [JSH]

48.553 P. T. Bauer. *Dissent on development.* Rev. ed. Cambridge, Mass.: Harvard University Press, 1976. ISBN 0-674-212812-7. ‣ Collection of theoretical essays, specific case studies, and review articles on Third World economic development. Intentionally controversial, very stimulating. Many debates remain open; still essential reading. [JSH]

48.554 Arghiri Emmanuel. *Unequal exchange: a study of the imperialism of trade.* Brian Pearce, trans. Charles Bettelheim, Comments. New York: Monthly Review Press, 1972. ISBN 0-85345-188-5. ‣ International trade relations between developed and developing economies force poverty on latter. Classic statement of case against export-led development. Provocative analysis with considerable impact on policy. [JSH]

48.555 Albert Fishlow et al. *Rich and poor nations in the world economy.* New York: McGraw-Hill, 1978. ISBN 0-07-021114-0 (cl), 0-07-021115-9 (pbk). ‣ Four essays debating, first, desirable degree of openness of developing economies and, second, allocation of any redistribution of world resources. Essential introduction to issues. [JSH]

48.556 Enzo R. Grilli. *The European community and the developing countries.* Cambridge: Cambridge University Press, 1992. ISBN 0-521-38511-3. ‣ Most recent contribution to studies considering unbalanced economic relationships between former imperial states and former colonies. Development assistance also figures in bargaining between Europeans. [JSH]

48.557 Paul Hallwood and Stuart W. Sinclair. *Oil, debt, and development: OPEC in the Third World.* London: Allen & Unwin, 1981. ISBN 0-04-382027-1. ▸ Careful examination of postwar political economy. Concludes transfer of wealth from oil consumers to oil producers struck both developed and developing nations very hard. [JSH]

48.558 Stephen D. Krasner. *Structural conflict: the Third World against global liberalism.* Berkeley: University of California Press, 1985. ISBN 0-520-05400-8 (cl), 0-520-05478-4 (pbk). ▸ Study of struggle during seventies over allocating resources and rewards between developed and developing economies with latter opposing market forces without avail. Intelligent account will serve until history is written. [JSH]

48.559 Robert L. Rothstein. *Global bargaining: UNCTAD and the quest for a new international economic order.* Princeton: Princeton University Press, 1979. ISBN 0-691-07610-3 (cl), 0-691-02190-2 (pbk). ▸ Account of failure of negotiations between developing nations and developed nations (United Nations Conference on Trade and Development) to produce new international economic order. Clear-sighted analysis of major problem in postwar economic diplomacy. [JSH]

A NEW INTERNATIONAL AGENDA

48.560 Richard Elliott Benedick. *Ozone diplomacy: new directions in safeguarding the planet.* Cambridge, Mass.: Harvard University Press with World Wildlife Fund, Conservation Foundation, and Georgetown University, Institute for the Study of Diplomacy, 1991. ISBN 0-674-65000-X (cl), 0-674-65001-8 (pbk). ▸ Better than most polemics flooding bookstores. [JSH]

48.561 William Diebold, Jr. *Industrial policy as an international issue.* New York: McGraw-Hill, 1980. ISBN 0-07-016809-1 (cl), 0-07-016810-5 (pbk). ▸ Discussion of national strategies for adapting to industrial change in competitive environment. Clear review of past experience as guide to future conduct by experienced student of international economic cooperation. [JSH]

48.562 Jack Donnelly. *Universal human rights in theory and practice.* Ithaca, N.Y.: Cornell University Press, 1989. ISBN 0-8014-2316-3 (cl), 0-8014-9570-9 (pbk). ▸ Detailed discussion of theory of universal human rights, bolstered by much factual data on actual practices in developing nations. Best single work on subject. [JSH]

48.563 Stephen Green. *International disaster relief: toward a responsive system.* New York: McGraw-Hill, 1977. ISBN 0-07-024287-9 (cl), 0-07-024288-7 (pbk). ▸ Brief but very informative on this aspect of North-South relations. Concludes proliferation of natural and man-made disasters in developing nations requires clearly thought out system of response. [JSH]

48.564 Ted Greenwood et al. *Nuclear proliferation: motivations, capabilities, and strategies for control.* David C. Gompert, Introduction. New York: McGraw-Hill, 1977. ISBN 0-07-024344-1 (cl), 0-07-024345-X (pbk). ▸ Politics predominates over technology in these essays on main issues of growing international problem. Clear overview suitable as introduction to problem. [JSH]

48.565 Andrew Hurrell and Benedict Kingsbury, eds. *The international politics of the environment: actors, interests, and institutions.* New York: Oxford University Press, 1992. ISBN 0-19-827365-7 (cl), 0-19-827778-4 (pbk). ▸ Collection of twenty papers; skillful mix of theory, case studies, and solid common sense. Good bibliography. [JSH]

48.566 Robert O. Keohane, Joseph S. Nye, and Stanley Hoffmann, eds. *After the cold war: international institutions and state strategies in Europe, 1989–1991.* Cambridge, Mass.: Harvard University Press, 1993. ISBN 0-674-00863-4. ▸ Collection combining work of junior and senior scholars. Explores impact of end of cold war on trade, international finance, foreign direct investment, environmental protection, and military security. [CKF]

48.567 Leo Kuper. *Genocide: its political use in the twentieth century.* New Haven: Yale University Press, 1981. ISBN 0-300-02795-8. ▸ Informative study showing that many states in developed and developing worlds have resorted to mass murder of minority social or ethnic groups. International agreements have done nothing to dissuade them. [JSH]

48.568 Daniel Patrick Moynihan. *Pandaemonium: ethnicity in international politics.* New York: Oxford University Press, 1993. ISBN 0-19-827787-3. ▸ Sweeping but informed discussion of ethnic unrest and its political and international ramifications. [CKF]

48.569 Barry R. Posen. *Inadvertent escalation: conventional war and nuclear risks.* Ithaca, N.Y.: Cornell University Press, 1991. ISBN 0-8014-2563-8. ▸ Disturbing, intelligent book in age of nuclear proliferation. Doubts firebreak between conventional and nuclear weapons can be preserved in war when both parties possess both types of weapons. [JSH]

48.570 Paul B. Stares, ed. *The new Germany and the new Europe.* Washington, D.C.: Brookings Institution, 1992. ISBN 0-8157-8138-5 (cl), 0-8157-8137-7 (pbk). ▸ Forward-looking essays assess impact of German unification on international political economy, security of Eastern Europe, and politics of European states. First-rate collection by experts; richly informative. [JSH]

48.571 Georges Tapinos and Phyllis T. Piotrow. *Six billion people: demographic dilemmas and world politics.* Edward L. Morse, Introduction. New York: McGraw-Hill, 1978. ISBN 0-07-062876-9 (cl), 0-07-062877-7 (pbk). ▸ Impact of population on international system. Examines different growth projections and role of international aid. Much useful information clearly presented. Strongly recommended. [JSH]

48.572 Paul A. Volker and Toyoo Gyohten. *Changing fortunes: the world's money and the threat to American leadership.* New York: Times Books, 1992. ISBN 0-81-292018-X. ▸ International monetary management over three decades as seen by two of most influential managers. Combines institutional history with contemporary policy analysis, salted with personal anecdotes. Essential reading. [JSH]

48.573 W. Howard Wriggins and Gunnar Adler-Karlsson. *Reducing global inequities.* Catherine Gwin, Introduction. New York: McGraw-Hill, 1978. ISBN 0-07-071925-X (cl), 0-07-071926-8 (pbk). ▸ Two long essays stressing real possibilities for action by developing nations. Much food for thought on bargaining between developed and developing economies and prospects for elimination of starvation, disease, and ignorance. [JSH]

LIST OF JOURNALS

Theory and Practice of History

Clio ISSN 0884-2043
Historical methods ISSN 0161-5440
History and memory ISSN 0935-560X
History and theory ISSN 0018-2656
Storia della storiografia/History of historiography ISSN 0392-8926

Prehistory

Advances in archaeological method and theory ISSN 0162-8003
Advances in world archaeology ISSN 0733-5121
African archaeological review ISSN 0263-0338
American antiquity ISSN 0002-7316
Anatolian studies ISSN 0066-1546
Annual review of anthropology ISSN 0084-6570
Antiquity ISSN 0003-598X
Archaeological method and theory ISSN 1043-1691
Archaeology ISSN 0003-8113
Archaeology in Oceania ISSN 0003-8121
Archaeometry ISSN 0003-813X
Berytus ISSN 0067-6195
Current anthropology ISSN 0011-3204
Journal of archaeological science ISSN 0305-4403
Journal of field archaeology ISSN 0093-4690
Journal of world prehistory ISSN 0892-7537
Kölner Jahrbuch für Vor- und Frühgeschichte ISSN 0075-6512
Latin American antiquity: a journal of the Society for American Archaeology ISSN 1045-6635
Norwegian archaeological review ISSN 0029-3652
Paléorient ISSN 0153-9345
Prähistorische Zeitschrift
Radiocarbon ISSN 0033-8222
World archaeology ISSN 0043-8243

World History

American historical review ISSN 0002-8762
Comparative studies in society and history ISSN 0010-4175
Journal of economic history ISSN 0022-0507
Journal of interdisciplinary history ISSN 0022-1953
Journal of social history ISSN 0022-4529
Journal of world history (Honolulu) ISSN 1045-6007
Journal of world history (Paris) ISSN 0022-5436
Journal of world prehistory ISSN 0892-7537
Past and present ISSN 0031-2746
Review (Fernand Braudel Center) ISSN 0147-9032

Science, Technology, and Medicine

Agricultural history ISSN 0002-1482
American heritage of invention and technology ISSN 8756-7296
Annals of science ISSN 0003-3790

British journal for the history of science ISSN 0007-0874
Bulletin of the history of medicine ISSN 0007-5140
Clio medica ISSN 0045-7183
Historical studies in the physical and biological sciences ISSN 0890-9997
History of science ISSN 0073-2753
History of technology ISSN 0307-5451
ISIS ISSN 0021-1753
Journal of the history of medicine and allied sciences ISSN 0022-5045
Medical history ISSN 0025-7273
Minerva ISSN 0026-4695
Osiris: a research journal devoted to the history of science and its cultural influences ISSN 0369-7827
Perspectives on science: historical, philosophical, social ISSN 1063-6145
Science in context ISSN 0269-8897
Science, technology, and human values ISSN 0162-2439
Social history of medicine ISSN 0307-6792
Social studies of science ISSN 0306-3127
Studies in history and philosophy of science ISSN 0039-3681
Technology and culture: the international quarterly of the Society for the History of Technology ISSN 0040-165X
Technology in society: an international journal ISSN 0160-791X
Transactions and studies of the College of Physicians of Philadelphia: medicine and history ISSN 0010-1087

Ancient Near East

Acta Sumerologica ISSN 0387-8082
Aegyptus ISSN 0001-9046
Altorientalische Forschungen ISSN 0232-8461
Anatolian studies ISSN 0066-1546
Annales du Service des Antiquités de l'Égypte
Archaeologia antiqua
Archaeologia Iranica et Orientalis
Archäologische Mitteilungen aus Iran
Archäologischer Anzeiger ISSN 0003-8105
Archiv für Orientforschung ISSN 0066-6440
Archiv Orientálni ISSN 0044-8699
Assur ISSN 0145-6334
Aula Orientalis ISSN 0212-5730
Biblica ISSN 0006-0887
Biblical archaeologist ISSN 0006-0895
Biblioteca Orientalis ISSN 0291-0054
Bulletin de l'Institut Français d'Archéologie Orientale
Bulletin of the American Schools of Oriental Research ISSN 0003-097X
Bulletin of the Egyptological Seminar ISSN 0041-977X
Bulletin of the School of Oriental and African Studies ISSN 0041-977X
Cahiers de la Délégation Archéologique Française en Iran ISSN 0765-104X

Catholic biblical quarterly ISSN 0008-7912

*Chronique d'Égypte: bulletin periodique de la Fondation
Égyptologique Reine Elisabeth* ISSN 0009-6067

Göttinger Miszellen ISSN 0344-385X

Hethitica

Iran ISSN 0578-6967

Iranica antiqua ISSN 0021-0870

Iraq ISSN 0021-0889

Israel exploration journal ISSN 0021-2059

Journal of cuneiform studies ISSN 0022-0256

Journal of Egyptian archaeology ISSN 0075-4234

Journal of Near Eastern studies ISSN 0022-2968

Journal of Semitic studies ISSN 0022-4480

Journal of the American Oriental Society ISSN 0003-0279

Journal of the American Research Center in Egypt ISSN 0065-9991

Journal of the British Institute of Persian Studies

Journal of the economic and social history of the Orient ISSN 0022-4995

Kemi ISSN 0355-1628

Kush: journal of the Sudan Antiquities Service ISSN 0454-6989

Mitteilungen des Deutschen Archäologischen Instituts, Abteilung Kairo

N. A.B.U.

Newsletter for Anatolian studies ISSN 8755-0997

Orientalia ISSN 0030-5367

Paléorient ISSN 0153-9345

Revue biblique ISSN 0035-0907

Revue d'assyriologie et d'archéologie orientale ISSN 0373-6032

Revue d'égyptologie ISSN 0035-1849

Revue hittite et asianique ISSN 0080-2603

The SSEA [Society for the Study of Egyptian Art] journal ISSN 0383-9753

State archives of Assyria bulletin ISSN 1120-4699

Studia Iranica ISSN 0221-5004

Studien zur altägyptischen Kultur ISSN 0340-2215

Sumer: a journal of archaeology and history in Iraq ISSN 0081-9271

Syria: revue d'art oriental et d'archéologie ISSN 0039-7946

Ugaritica

Vetus Testamentum ISSN 0042-4935

Zeitschrift für ägyptische Sprache und Altertumskunde ISSN 0044-216X

Zeitschrift für Assyriologie und vorderasiatische Archäologie ISSN 0084-5299

Zeitschrift für die alttestamentliche Wissenschaft ISSN 0044-2526

Die Welt des Orients: wissenschaftliche Beiträge zur Kunde des Morgenlandes ISSN 0043-2547

Classical Greece and Rome

Acta antiqua Academiae Scientiarum Hungaricae ISSN 0044-5975

Acta archaeologica (Copenhagen) ISSN 0065-101X

Acta archaeologica Academiae Scientiarum Hungaricae ISSN 0001-5210

Acta classica ISSN 0065-1141

Africa ISSN 0091-9909

American journal of ancient history ISSN 0362-8914

American journal of archaeology ISSN 0002-9114

American journal of numismatics ISSN 1053-8356

American journal of philology ISSN 0002-9475

Ancient history: resources for teachers ISSN 0310-5814

Ancient history bulletin ISSN 0835-3638

Ancient society ISSN 0066-1619

The ancient world ISSN 0160-9645

Annales: économies, sociétés, civilisations ISSN 0395-2649

L'année épigraphique

L'année philologique

The annual of the American Schools of Oriental Research ISSN 0066-0035

Annual of the British School at Athens ISSN 0068-2454

Annual of the Department of Antiquities (Jordan) ISSN 0449-1564

Antichthon ISSN 0066-4774

Antike Welt ISSN 0003-570X

Antiquaries journal ISSN 0003-5815

L'antiquité classique ISSN 077-2817

Antiquités africaines ISSN 0066-4871

Anzeiger für die Altertumswissenschaft ISSN 0003-6393

Aquileia nostra

Archäologischer Anzeiger ISSN 0003-8105

Archäologisches Korrespondenzblatt ISSN 0342-734X

Archeologické rozhledy ISSN 0323-1267

Archiv für Papyrusforschung und verwandte Gebiete ISSN 0066-6459

Archivo español de arqueología ISSN 0066-6742

Arethusa ISSN 0004-0975

Arion ISSN 0095-5809

Atene e Roma

Athenaeum ISSN 0004-6574

'Atiqot ISSN 0066-488X

Atti della Pontificia Accademia Romana di Archeologia ISSN 8502-0090

Bayerische Vorgeschichtsblätter ISSN 0341-3918

Bericht der Römisch-Germanischen Kommission ISSN 0341-9312

Bonner Jahrbücher des Rheinischen Landesmuseum in Bonn und des Vereins von Altertumsfreunden im Rheinlande

Britannia ISSN 0068-113X

Bulletin. Museum of Mediterranean and Near Eastern Antiquities ISSN 0585-3214

Bulletin. Museums of Art and Archaeology. University of Michigan ISSN 0076-8391

Bulletin archéologique. Comité des Travaux Historiques et Scientifiques ISSN 0997-5322

Bulletin d'archéologie algérienne ISSN 0525-1133

Bulletin de correspondance hellénique

Bulletin of the American Schools of Oriental Research ISSN 0003-097X

Bulletin of the Institute of Classical Studies ISSN 0076-0730

Bulletin of the School of Oriental and African Studies ISSN 0041-977X

Caesarodunum: bulletin de l'Institute d'Études Latines de la Faculté des Lettres et Sciences Humaine d'Orléans-Tours ISSN 0245-5196

Cahiers des études anciennes ISSN 0317-5065

Cahiers de Tunisie ISSN 0008-0012

Centre d'études et de documentation archéologique de la conservation de Carthage, Bulletin

Chiron ISSN 0069-3715

Classica et mediaevalia ISSN 0106-5815

Classical antiquity ISSN 0278-6656

Classical journal ISSN 0009-8353

Classical philology ISSN 0009-837X

Classical quarterly ISSN 0009-8388

Classical review ISSN 0009-840X

Classical world ISSN 0009-8418

List of Journals

Comparative studies in society and history ISSN 0010-4175
*Comptes rendus des séances de l'anneé de l'Académie des
   Inscriptions et Belles-Lettres* ISSN 0065-0536
Échos du monde classique/Classical views ISSN 0012-9356
Eirene: studia graeca et latina
Epigraphica Anatolica
Eranos: acta philologica suecana ISSN 0013-9947
Études celtiques ISSN 0373-1928
Études classiques
Florilegium ISSN 0709-5201
Francia ISSN 0251-3609
*Gallia: fouilles et monuments archéologiques en France
   métropolitaine* ISSN 0016-4119
Germania ISSN 0016-8874
Gnomon ISSN 0017-1417
Greece and Rome ISSN 0017-3835
Greek, Roman, and Byzantine studies ISSN 0017-3916
Gymnasium ISSN 0342-5231
Harvard studies in classical philology ISSN 0073-0688
Helvetia archaeologica ISSN 0018-0173
Hermathena ISSN 0018-0750
Hermes. Zeitschrift für klassische Philologie ISSN 0018-0777
*Hesperia: journal of the American School of Classical Studies at
   Athens* ISSN 0018-098X
Hispania antiqua ISSN 1130-0515
Historia: Zeitschrift für alte Geschichte ISSN 0018-2311
Israel exploration journal ISSN 0021-2059
Jahrbuch für Antike und Christentum ISSN 0075-2541
Jahrbuch. Römisch-Germanischen Zentralmuseums
*Jahrbuch der Schweizerischen Gesellschaft für Ur- und
   Frühgeschichte* ISSN 0252-1881
Jahrbuch für Numismatik und Geldgeschichte ISSN 0075-2711
Jahreshefte des Österreichischen Archäologischen Instituts
Journal of ecclesiastical history ISSN 0022-0469
Journal of Egyptian archaeology
Journal of field archaeology ISSN 0093-4690
Journal of glass studies ISSN 0075-4250
Journal of Hellenic studies ISSN 0075-4269
Journal of Roman archaeology ISSN 1047-7594
Journal of Roman studies ISSN 0075-4358
Journal of theological studies ISSN 0022-5185
Karthago: revue d'archéologie africaine ISSN 0453-3429
Klio ISSN 0075-6334
Kölner Jahrbuch für Vor- und Frühgeschichte ISSN 0075-6512
Latomus ISSN 0023-8856
Libyan studies: annual report of the Society for Libyan Studies
Liverpool classical monthly ISSN 0309-3700
Lustrum ISSN 0024-7421
Mediterranean archaeology ISSN 1030-8482
Mélanges de l'École Française de Rome. Antiquité ISSN 0223-5102
*Mitteilungen des Deutschen Archäologischen Instituts, Römische
   Abteilung* ISSN 0342-1287
Mnemosyne ISSN 0026-7074
Museum Helveticum ISSN 0024-4054
Notizie degli scavi di antichità
Numismatic chronicle ISSN 0078-2696
Numismatische Zeitschrift
*Opus: rivista internazionale per la storia economica e sociale
   dell'antichità* ISSN 0392-4645
*Oudheidkundige mededelingen uit het Rijksmuseum van Oudheiden
   te Leiden*
Papers of the British School at Rome ISSN 0068-2462

Parola del passato ISSN 0031-2355
Past and present ISSN 0031-2746
Philologus: Zeitschrift für Klassische Philologie ISSN 0031-7985
Phoenix: the journal of the Classical Association of Canada ISSN
   0031-8299
Pro Aventico
Pro Vindonissa
Proceedings of the Cambridge Philological Society ISSN 0068-6735
Proceedings of the Prehistoric Society ISSN 0079-497X
Quaderni di archeologia della Libia ISSN 0079-8258
Rei Cretariae Romanae Fautorum Acta
Revue archéologique de l'Est et du Centre-Est ISSN 0035-0745
Revue belge d'archéologie et d'histoire de l'art ISSN 0035-077X
Revue belge de numismatique et de sigillographie
Revue belge de philologie et d'histoire ISSN 0035-0818
Revue de philologie, de littérature, et d'histoire anciennes ISSN
   0035-1652
Revue des études anciennes ISSN 0035-2004
Revue des études grecques ISSN 0035-2039
Revue des études latines
Revue numismatique ISSN 0484-8942
Rheinisches Museum für Philologie ISSN 0035-449X
Rivista di filologia e di istruzione classica ISSN 0035-6220
Rivista di studi fenici
Rivista storica dell'antichità
Saalburg-Jahrbuch
Saeculum ISSN 0080-5319
Scholia
Scripta classica Israelica ISSN 0334-4509
Studi etruschi ISSN 0391-7762
Studi italiani di filologia classica ISSN 0039-2987
Supplementum epigraphicum Graecum ISSN 0920-8399
Symbolae Osloenses ISSN 0039-7679
Syria: revue d'art oriental et d'archéologie ISSN 0039-7946
*Talanta: proceedings of the Dutch Archaeological and Historical
   Society*
Transactions of the American Philological Association ISSN 0065-
   9711
*Trierer Zeitschrift für Geschichte und Kunst des Trierer Landes
   und seiner Nachbargebiete* ISSN 0041-2953
Tyche
Wiener Studien ISSN 0085-005X
Yale classical studies ISSN 0084-330X
*Zeitschrift der Savigny-Stiftung für Rechtsgeschichte. Romanistische
   Abteilung*
Zeitschrift für Papyrologie und Epigraphik ISSN 0084-5388
Ziva Antika ISSN 0514-7727

Byzantium

Byzantina ISSN 1105-0772
Byzantine and modern Greek studies ISSN 0307-0131
Byzantine studies/Études byzantines ISSN 0095-4608; continued
   by *Revue des études byzantines*
Byzantinische Zeitschrift ISSN 0007-7704
Byzantinoslavica ISSN 0007-7712
Byzantion ISSN 0378-2506
*Congrès international des études byzantines/International
   Byzantine Congress/Internazionaler Byzantinen- Kongress/
   Congresso internazionale di studi bizantini/Actes/Papers/Atti/
   Berichte*
Dumbarton Oaks papers ISSN 0070-7546

Epeteris hetaireias byzantinon spoudon

Études byzantines

Jahrbuch der Österreichischen Byzantinischen Gesellschaft ISSN 0075-2355

Jahrbuch der Österreichischen Byzantinistik ISSN 0378-8660

Koinonia ISSN 0393-2230

Revue des études byzantines ISSN 0373-5729; continues *Byzantine studies*

Rivista di studi bizantini e neoellenici ISSN 0557-1367

Rivista di studi bizantini e slavi

Travaux et mémoires ISSN 0577-1471

Trudy sovetskich učenych k XIII, XIV, XV, XVI, XVIII meždunarodnomu kongressu vizantinistov

Typika

Vizantiiskie očerki

Vizantiiskii vremennik ISSN 0132-3776

Zbornik radova Vizantošoskog Instituta ISSN 0584-9888

Central, East, South, and Southeast Asia

Acta Orientalia Acadamiae Scientiarum Hungaricae ISSN 0001-6446

Archivum Eurasiae medii aevi ISSN 0724-8822

Asia major ISSN 0004-4482

Asian studies newsletter ISSN 0362-4811

Asian survey ISSN 0363-2717

Australian journal of Chinese affairs ISSN 0156-7365

Bijdragen tot de Taal-, Land-, en Volkenkunde ISSN 0006-2294

Bulletin de l'École Française d'Extrême-Orient ISSN 0336-1519

Bulletin of Concerned Asian Scholars ISSN 0007-4810

Bulletin of Sung-Yüan studies; see Journal of Sung-Yüan studies

CCP [Chinese Communist Party] research newsletter ISSN 1044-7075

CEAL [Committee on East Asian Libraries] bulletin ISSN 0148-6225

Central Asiatic journal ISSN 0008-9182

China quarterly ISSN 0305-7410, ISSN 0009-4439

Chinese business history

Chinese historians: the journal of Chinese historians in the United States ISSN 1043-643X

Chinese studies in history: a journal of translations ISSN 0009-4633

Christianity in China: historical studies

Comparative studies in society and history in the United States ISSN 0010-4175

Contributions to Indian sociology ISSN 0069-9659

Current contents of foreign periodicals in Chinese studies

Early China ISSN 0362-5028

Economic and political weekly ISSN 0012-9976

Études chinoises: bulletin de l'Association Française d'études chinoises ISSN 0755-5857

Eurasian studies yearbook ISSN 0042-0786; continues *Ural-Altaische Jahrbücher: Fortsetzung der "Ungarischen Jahrbücher"*

Folia Orientalia ISSN 0015-5675

Harvard journal of Asiatic studies ISSN 0073-0548

Indian economic and social history review ISSN 0019-4646

Indian historical review ISSN 0376-9836

Indo-Iranian journal ISSN 0024-8215

Indonesia

Japan interpreter ISSN 0021-4450

Japan quarterly ISSN 0021-4590

Journal of American–East Asian relations ISSN 1058-3947

Journal of arts and ideas ISSN 0970-5309

Journal of Asian and African studies ISSN 0021-9096

Journal of Asian history ISSN 0021-910X

Journal of Asian studies ISSN 0021-9118

Journal of Chinese philosophy ISSN 0301-8121

Journal of Chinese religions ISSN 0737-769X

Journal of contemporary Asia ISSN 0047-2336

Journal of imperial and commonwealth history ISSN 0308-6534

Journal of Indian history ISSN 0022-1775

Journal of Japanese studies ISSN 0095-6848

Journal of Korean studies ISSN 0731-1613

Journal of Oriental studies ISSN 0022-331X

Journal of peasant studies ISSN 0306-6150

Journal of social sciences and humanities ISSN 0023-4044

Journal of Southeast Asian history ISSN 0022-4634

Journal of Sung-Yüan studies ISSN 1059-3152; continues *Bulletin of Sung-Yüan studies* ISSN 0275-4118

Journal of the American Oriental Society ISSN 0003-0279

Journal of the Burma Research Society

Journal of the Malaysian Branch, Royal Asiatic Society ISSN 0126-7353

Journal of the Pakistan Historical Society ISSN 0030-9796

Journal of the Royal Asiatic Society ISSN 0035-869X

Journal of the Siam Society ISSN 0857-7099

Korea journal ISSN 0023-3900

Korean repository

Korean studies ISSN 0145-840X

Late imperial China ISSN 0884-3236; continues *Ch'ing-shih wen-t'i*

Law in Japan: an annual ISSN 0458-8584

Ming studies ISSN 0147-037X

Modern Asian studies ISSN 0026-749X

Modern China ISSN 0097-7004

Mongolian studies ISSN 0190-3667

Monumenta Nipponica: studies in Japanese culture ISSN 0027-0741

Monumenta serica/cura Universitatas Catholicae Pekini edita ISSN 0077-149X

Pacific affairs ISSN 0030-851X

Past and present ISSN 0031-2746

Philippine studies ISSN 0031-7837

Philosophy East and West ISSN 0031-8221

Proceedings of the Indian History Congress

Republican China; continues Chinese republican studies newsletter

Revue bibliographique de sinologie ISSN 0080-2484

Rocznik Orientalistyszny ISSN 0080-3545

Seoul journal of Korean studies

Sino-Japanese studies ISSN 1041-8830; continues *Sino-Japanese newsletter*

Sino-Western cultural relations journal ISSN 1041-875X ; continues *China mission studies (1550-1800) bulletin*

Social sciences in China ISSN 0252-9203

Social scientist ISSN 0970-0293

South Asia ISSN 0085-6401

South Asia bulletin ISSN 0732-3867

South Asia research ISSN 0262-7280

Studies in history ISSN 0258-1698

T'ang studies ISSN 0737-5034

T'oung pao ISSN 0082-5433

Taiwan studies newsletter ISSN 1048-2342

Transactions of the Asiatic Society of Japan

Transactions of the Royal Asiatic Society (Korea Branch) ISSN 0035-869X

Ural-Altaische Jahrbücher: Fortsetzung der "Ungarischen Jahrbücher" ISSN 0174-0652; continued by *Eurasian Studies Yearbook*

Middle East and North Africa

Arab studies quarterly ISSN 0271-3519.

Asian and African studies: journal of the Israel Oriental Society ISSN 0066-8281.

British journal of Middle Eastern studies ISSN 0305-6139; continues *British Society for Middle Eastern Studies. Bulletin*

Cahiers de Tunisie ISSN 0008-0012

Hespéris-tamuda ISSN 0018-1005

Institut des Belles Lettres Arabes ISSN 0018-862X

International journal of Middle East studies ISSN 0020-7438

International journal of Turkish studies ISSN 0272-7919

Iranian studies ISSN 0021-0862

Der Islam ISSN 0021-1818

Journal of Arab affairs ISSN 0275-3588

Journal of Palestine studies ISSN 0377-919X

Journal of South Asian and Middle Eastern studies ISSN 0149-1784

The Kurdish times ISSN 0885-386X

Maghreb-Machrek ISSN 0336-6324

The Middle East ISSN 0305-0734

Middle East economic digest (MEED) ISSN 0047-7230

Middle East international ISSN 0047-7249

The Middle East journal ISSN 0026-3141

Middle East policy ISSN 0731-6763

Middle East report ISSN 0888-0328

Middle Eastern studies ISSN 0026-3206

Orient ISSN 0030-5227

Revue d'histoire maghrébine

Revue du monde musulman et de la Méditerranée ISSN 0997-1327

Turcica ISSN 0082-6847

Africa

Africa ISSN 0001-9720

African affairs ISSN 0001-9909

African archaeological review ISSN 0263-0338

African economic history ISSN 0145-2258

Cahiers d'études africaines ISSN 0008-0055

Canadian journal of African studies ISSN 0008-3968

International journal of African historical studies ISSN 0361-7882

Journal of African history ISSN 0021-8537 [18]

Journal of southern African studies ISSN 0305-7070

Review of African political economy ISSN 0305-6244

Medieval Europe

Anglo-Norman studies ISSN 0261-9857

Anglo-Saxon England ISSN 0263-6751

Archéologie médiévale ISSN 0153-9337

Archives d'histoire doctrinale et littéraire du moyen âge ISSN 0373-5478

Bulletin of medieval canon law ISSN 0146-2989

Bulletin de théologie ancienne et médiévale ISSN 0007-442X

Centro italiano di studi sull'alto medioevo ISSN 0528-5666

Church history ISSN 0009-6407

Franciscan studies ISSN 0080-5452

Journal of ecclesiastical history ISSN 0022-0469

Journal of medieval history ISSN 0304-4181

Journal of theological studies ISSN 0022-5185

Journées internationales d'histoire

Mediaeval studies ISSN 0076-5872

Medieval archaeology ISSN 0076-6097

Le moyen âge ISSN 0027-2841

Revue d'histoire ecclésiastique ISSN 0035-2381

Revue des sciences philosophiques et théologiques ISSN 0035-2209

Speculum ISSN 0038-7134

Studia Gratiana

Studies in medieval and Renaissance history ISSN 0081-8224

Traditio ISSN 0362-1529

Viator ISSN 0083-5897

Vivarium ISSN 0042-7543

Zeitschrift der Savigny-Stiftung für Rechtsgeschichte, Canonistische Abteilung ISSN 0323-4142

Zeitschrift für Archäologie des Mittelalters ISSN 0340-0824

Jewish History

AJS review: the journal of the Association for Jewish Studies ISSN 0364-0094

American Jewish archives ISSN 0002-905X

American Jewish history ISSN 0164-0178

American Jewish yearbook ISSN 0065-8987

Cathedra: for the history of Eretz Israel and its yishuv

Da'at: a journal of Jewish philosophy and kabbalah ISSN 0334-2336

Hebrew Union College annual ISSN 360-9049

Italia, studi e ricerche sulla storia, la cultura, e la letteratura: degli ebrei d'Italia ISSN 0334-360X

Jerusalem studies in Jewish thought ISSN 0333-7081

Jewish history ISSN 0334-701X

Jewish quarterly review ISSN 0021-6682

Jewish social studies ISSN 0021-6704

Journal of Jewish studies ISSN 0022-2097

Mikhael (Tel Aviv) ISSN 0334-4150

Modern Judaism ISSN 0276-1114

Pe'amim, studies in Oriental Jewry ISSN 0334-4088

Polin: a journal of Polish-Jewish studies ISSN 0268-1056

Proceedings. American Academy for Jewish Research ISSN 0065-6798

La rassegna mensile di Israel ISSN 0033-9792

Revue des études juives

Sefarad ISSN 0037-0894

Sefunot ISSN 0582-3943

Shalem: studies in the history of the Jews in Eretz Yisrael

Tarbiz: a quarterly journal for Jewish studies ISSN 0334-3650

Western states Jewish history ISSN 0043-4221

Yad Vashem studies ISSN 0084-3296

Yearbook of the Leo Baeck Institute

Yivo annual of Jewish social science ISSN 0084-4209

Zion: a quarterly for research in Jewish history ISSN 0044-4758

Early Modern and Modern Europe

Agricultural historical review ISSN 0002-1482

American historical review ISSN 0002-8762

Annales: économies, sociétés, civilisations ISSN 0395-2649

Bibliothèque de l'humanisme et Renaissance: travaux et documents ISSN 0006-1999

Bulletin of the John Rylands University Library of Manchester ISSN 0301-102X

Cambridge historical journal
Canadian journal of history ISSN 0008-4107
Church history ISSN 0009-6407
Comparative studies in society and history ISSN 0010-4175
Consortium on Revolutionary Europe, Proceedings, 1750–1850 ISSN 0093-2574
Continuity and change ISSN 0268-4160
Economic history review ISSN 0013-0117
Eighteenth-century studies ISSN 0013-2586
English historical review ISSN 0013-8266
Explorations in economic history ISSN 0014-4983
Fides et historia: official publication of the Conference on Faith and History ISSN 0884-5379
Gender and history ISSN 0953-5233
Geographical journal ISSN 0016-7398
The historian: a journal of history ISSN 0018-2370
Historical journal ISSN 0018-246X
Historical reflections/Réflexions historiques
Historische Zeitschrift ISSN 0018-2613
History ISSN 0018-2648
History of education ISSN 0046-760X
History of European ideas ISSN 0191-6599
History of political economy ISSN 0018-2702
History of political thought ISSN 0143-7816
International labor and working-class history ISSN 0147-5479
International review of social history ISSN 0020-8590
A journal of church and state ISSN 0021-969X
Journal of contemporary history ISSN 0022-0094
Journal of ecclesiastical history ISSN 0022-0469
Journal of economic history ISSN 0022-0507
Journal of ecumenical studies ISSN 0022-0558
Journal of European economic history ISSN 0391-5115
Journal of European studies ISSN 0047-2441
Journal of family history ISSN 0363-1990
Journal of historical geography ISSN 0305-7488
Journal of historical sociology ISSN 0952-1909
Journal of interdisciplinary history ISSN 0022-1953
Journal of medieval and Renaissance studies ISSN 0047-2573
Journal of modern history ISSN 0022-2801
Journal of political economy ISSN 0022-3808
Journal of social history ISSN 0022-4529
Journal of the history of ideas ISSN 0022-5037
Journal of the history of philosophy ISSN 0022-5053
Journal of the history of sexuality ISSN 1043-4070
Journal of the Warburg and Courtauld Institutes ISSN 0075-4390
Journal of women's studies ISSN 0707-1981
Lituanus ISSN 0024-5089
Le mouvement social ISSN 0027-2671
Parliaments, estates, and representation ISSN 0260-6755
Past and present ISSN 0031-2746
Politic science ISSN 0030-8269; continued by *PS, political science and politics*
Political science quarterly ISSN 0032-3195
Political theory ISSN 0090-5917
PS, political science and politics ISSN 1049-0965; continues *Politic science*
Renaissance drama ISSN 0486-3739
Renaissance quarterly ISSN 0034-4338
Revue d'histoire moderne et contemporaine ISSN 0048-8003
Revue historique ISSN 0035-3264
Revue internationale d'histoire militaire ISSN 0254-8186
Rivista storica Italiana ISSN 0035-7073
Shigaku zasshi (Journal of historical science) ISSN 0018-2478

Signs ISSN 0097-9740
Sixteenth century journal ISSN 0361-0160
Social history ISSN 0307-1022
Transactions of the Royal Historical Society ISSN 0080-4401
Vierteljahrsschrift für Sozial- und Wirtschaftsgeschichte ISSN 0340-8728
War and society ISSN 0729-2473
Western economic journal ISSN 0715-4577

BRITISH ISLES

Albion ISSN 0095-1390
Enlightenment and Dissent ISSN 0262-7617; continues *Price-Priestley newsletter*
Historical research ISSN 0041-9761; continues *Bulletin of the Institute of Historical Research*
History today ISSN 0018-2753
History workshop: a journal of socialist history ISSN 0309-2984
Ireland-Eire
Irish historical studies ISSN 0021-1214
Journal of British studies ISSN 0021-9371
Journal of imperial and commonwealth history ISSN 0308-6534
London journal ISSN 0305-8034
Midland history ISSN 048-729X; continues *University of Birmingham historical journal*
Northern history ISSN 0078-172X
Parliamentary history ISSN 0264-2824
Past and present ISSN 0031-2746
Price-Priestly newsletter ISSN 0140-8537; continued by *Enlightment and dissent*
Scottish historical review
Scottish studies ISSN 0036-9411
Social history ISSN 0307-1022
Southern history ISSN 0142-4688
Utilitas ISSN 0953-8208
Victorian periodicals newsletter ISSN 0049-6189; continued by *Victorian periodicals review*
Victorian periodicals review ISSN 0709-4698; continues *Victorian periodicals newsletter*
Victorian studies ISSN 0042-5222
Welsh history review ISSN 0043-2431

FRANCE

Actes de la recherche en sciences sociales ISSN 0335-5322
Annales de Bourgogne ISSN 0003-3901
Annales du Midi ISSN 0003-4398
Annales historiques de la Révolution française ISSN 0003-4436
Bibliothèque de l'École des Chartes ISSN 0343-6237
Bulletin de la Société de l'Histoire du Protestantisme Français ISSN 0037-9050
Bulletin de la Société de la Révolution de 1848 et des Révolutions du XIXe siècle
Bulletin du Centre d'Histoire de la France Contemporaine ISSN 0249-3624
Cahiers d'histoire ISSN 0008-008X
Contemporary French civilization ISSN 0147-9156
Dix-septième siècle ISSN 0012-4273
French historical studies ISSN 0016-1071
French history ISSN 0269-1191
French politics and society ISSN 0082-1267
Histoire de l'éducation ISSN 0221-6280
Information historique
Modern and contemporary France ISSN 0267-761X
Nineteenth-century French studies ISSN 0146-7891

List of Journals

Proceedings. French Colonial Historical Society

Proceedings of the annual meeting of the Western Society for French History ISSN 0099-0329

Recherches contemporaines

Revue d'histoire de l'Église de France ISSN 0300-9505

Revue d'histoire de la Restauration et de la monarchie constitutionnelle

Revue d'histoire littéraire de la France ISSN 0035-2411

Revue d'histoire moderne et contemporaine ISSN 0048-8003

Revue du Nord ISSN 0035-2624

Revue française de science politique ISSN 0035-2950

Revue française de sociologie ISSN 0035-2969

The Tocqueville review

Yale French studies ISSN 0044-0078

LOW COUNTRIES

Acta historiae Neerlandicae ISSN 0065-129X

Archief voor de geschiedenis van de Katholieke kerk in Holland ISSN 0003-8326

Bevolking en Gezin=Population et famille ISSN 0523-1159

Bijdragen en Mededelingen betreffende de Geschiedenis der Nederlanden ISSN 0165-0505

Hémecht: Zeitschrift für luxemburger Geschichte ISSN 0018-0270

The Netherlands' journal of social sciences: a publication of The Netherlands' Sociological and Anthropological Society ISSN 0038-0172; continues *Netherlands journal of sociology*

Netherlands journal of sociology; continued by *The Netherlands' journal of social sciences*

Population et famille=Bevolking en Gezin ISSN 0523-1159

Revue belge de philologie et d'histoire ISSN 0035-0818

Revue belge d'histoire contemporaine

Revue belge d'histoire militaire

Revue générale belge ISSN 0035-3078; continues *Revue belge* and *Revue générale*

Studia Rosenthalania: Tijdschrift voor Joodse wetenchap en geschiedenis in Nederland ISSN 0039-3347

Tijdschrift voor Geschiedenis ISSN 0040-7518

Tijdschrift voor sociale geschiedenis

ITALY

Catholic historical review ISSN 0008-8080

Rinascimento ISSN 0080-3037

Rivista storica Italiana ISSN 0035-7073

Studi storici ISSN 0039-3037

Studi Veneziani ISSN 0081-6264

Studies in medieval and Renaissance history ISSN 0081-8224

SPAIN AND PORTUGAL

L'avenc ISSN 0210-0150

Ayer

Analise social ISSN 0003-2573

Boletín de la Real Academia de Historia ISSN 0034-0626

Bulletin of Hispanic studies ISSN 0007-490X

Hispania: revista española de historia ISSN 0018-2141

Historia 16 ISSN 0210-6353

Historia social ISSN 0214-2570

Pedralbes ISSN 0211-9587

Recerques ISSN 0210-380X

Studia historica: historica contemporanea ISSN 0213-2087

GERMAN STATES, HABSBURG EMPIRE, AND GERMANY

Archiv für Kulturgeschichte ISSN 0003-9233

Archiv für Sozialgeschichte ISSN 0066-6506

Archiv für Reformationsgeschichte ISSN 0003-9381

Austrian history yearbook ISSN 0067-2378

Blätter für deutsche Landesgeschichte; continued by *Korrespondenzblatt*

Central European history ISSN 0008-9389

Deutschland-Archiv

German history: journal of the German Historical Society ISSN 0266-3554

German studies review ISSN 0149-7952

Geschichte und Gesellschaft ISSN 0340-613X

Geschichte in Wissenschaft und Unterricht ISSN 0016-9056

Historisches Jahrbuch ISSN 0018-2621

Historisches Zeitschrift

Jahrbuch für die Geschichte Mittel- und Ostdeutschlands ISSN 0075-2614

Jahrbuch für Geschichte ISSN 0448-1526

Jahrbuch für Wirtschaftsgeschichte ISSN 0075-2800

Korrespondenzblatt; continues *Blätter für deutsche Landesgeschichte*

Mennonite historical review

Mennonitische Geschichtsblätter ISSN 0342-1171

Vierteljahrshefte für Zeitgeschichte ISSN 0042-5702

Zeitschrift für bayerische Landesgeschichte

Zeitschrift für die Geschichte des Oberrheins ISSN 0044-2607

Zeitschrift für historische Forschung ISSN 0340-0174

SCANDINAVIA AND THE BALTIC STATES

Fortid og nutid ISSN 0106-4797

Heimen ISSN 0017-9841

Historiallinen aikakauskirja ISSN 0018-2362

Historie: Jyske samlinger ISSN 0107-4725

Historisk tidsskrift (Denmark) ISSN 0106-4991

Historisk tidsskrift (Norway) ISSN 0018-263X

Historisk tidsskrift (Sweden) ISSN 0345-469X

Historisk tidskrift för Finland ISSN 0046-7596

Journal of Baltic studies ISSN 0162-9778

Norwegian-American studies ISSN 0078-1983

Scandia ISSN 0036-5483

Scandinavian economic history review ISSN 0358-5522

Scandinavian journal of history ISSN 0346-8755

Scandinavian studies ISSN 0036-5637

Scandinavica ISSN 0036-5653

Swedish-American historical quarterly ISSN 0730-028X

Eastern Europe, Russia, and the Soviet Union

Cahiers du monde russe et soviétique ISSN 0008-0160

Canadian Slavonic papers ISSN 0008-5006

Canadian-American Slavic studies ISSN 0090-8290

East European quarterly ISSN 0012-8449

Eastern European politics and societies ISSN 0888-3254

The eighteenth century ISSN 0161-0996

Europa Archiv

Europe-Asia studies ISSN 0038-5859; continues *Soviet studies*

Harvard Ukrainian studies ISSN 0363-5570

Historische Veröffentlichungen: Forshungen zur osteuropäischen Geschichte

Istoriia SSSR; continued by *Otechestvennaia Istoria*

Izvestiia ISSN 0235-7097

Jahrbücher für Geschichte Osteuropas ISSN 0021-4019

Osteuropa ISSN 0030-6428

Otechestvennaia Istoria ISSN 0131-3150; continues *Istoriia SSSR*

Oxford Slavonic papers ISSN 0078-7256

Post-Soviet affairs ISSN 0882-6994; continues *Soviet economy*
Problems of communism ISSN 0032-941X
Russian review ISSN 0036-0341
Russian history ISSN 0094-288X
Russian studies in history ISSN 0038-5867; continues *Soviet studies in history*
Slavic review ISSN 0037-6779
Slavonic and East European review ISSN 0037-6795
Soviet economy; continued by *Post-Soviet affairs*
Soviet history
Soviet studies; continued by *Europe-Asia studies*
Soviet studies in history; continued by *Russian studies in history*
The Soviet Union ISSN 0163-6057
Studies in comparative communism ISSN 0588-8174
Südosteuropäische Arbeiten: Südost-Institut München
Südostforschungen ISSN 0081-9077
Survey: a journal of East and West studies ISSN 0039-6192
Voprosy istorii (Problems of history) ISSN 0042-8779
Voprosy istorii KPSS (Problems of history of the Communist party of the USSR) ISSN 0320-8907

Native Peoples of the Americas

America indigena ISSN 0185-1179
American Indian culture and research journal ISSN 0161-6463
American Indian quarterly ISSN 0095-182X
Bulletin de l'Institut Français d'Études Andines
Ethnohistory ISSN 0014-1801
Historia y cultura ISSN 0258-2104/0073-2486
Journal de la Société des Américanistes ISSN 0037-9174
Journal of anthropological research ISSN 0091-7710
Ñawpa Pacha ISSN 0077-6287

Latin America

The Americas: a quarterly review
Anuario de estudios americanos ISSN 0210-5810
Colonial Latin American historical review ISSN 1063-5769
Colonial Latin American review ISSN 1060-9164
Bibliography: Seminar on the Acquisition of Latin American Library Materials ISSN 0250-6262
Ethnohistory ISSN 0014-1801
Handbook of Latin American studies ISSN 0072-9833
Hispanic American historical review ISSN 0018-2168
Historia mexicana ISSN 0185-0172
Inter-American economic affairs ISSN 0020-4943
Jahrbuch für Geschichte von Staat, Wirtschaft, und Gesellschaft Lateinamerikas ISSN 0075-2673
Journal of interamerican studies and world affairs ISSN 0022-1937
Journal of Latin American studies ISSN 0022-216X
Latin American perspectives ISSN 0094-582X
Latin American research review ISSN 0023-8791
Latin American weekly report
Luso-Brazilian review ISSN 0024-7413
Proceedings of the Rocky Mountain Council for Latin American Studies
Revista interamericana de bibliografía/Review of inter-American bibliography ISSN 0020-4994
Statistical abstract of Latin America ISSN 0081-4687

North America

Acadiensis ISSN 0044-5851
Agricultural history ISSN 0002-1482
Amerasia journal ISSN 0044-7471
American historical review ISSN 0002-8762
American journal of legal history ISSN 0002-9319
American journal of sociology ISSN 0002-9602
American literary history ISSN 0896-7148
American political science review ISSN 0003-0554
American quarterly ISSN 0003-0678
American sociological review ISSN 0003-1224
American studies ISSN 0026-3079
Architectural forum ISSN 0003-8539
Archivaria ISSN 0318-6954
Arts magazine ISSN 0004-4059
The beaver ISSN 0005-7517
BC studies ISSN 0005-2949
Bulletin of the history of medicine ISSN 0007-5140
Business history review ISSN 0007-6805
Canadian historical review ISSN 0008-3755
Comparative studies in society and history ISSN 0010-4175
Demography ISSN 0070-6805
Diplomatic history ISSN 0145-2096
Ethnohistory ISSN 0014-1801
Feminist studies: FS ISSN 0046-3663
Film culture ISSN 0015-1211
Foreign affairs ISSN 0015-1211
Gender and history ISSN 0953-5233
Great Plains quarterly ISSN 0275-7664
Harvard law review ISSN 0017-811X
Histoire sociale/Social history ISSN 0018-2257
History of education quarterly ISSN 0018-2680
The history teacher ISSN 0018-2745
International labor and working-class history ISSN 0147-5479
ISIS ISSN 0021-1753
Journal of American ethnic history ISSN 0278-5927
Journal of American history ISSN 0021-8723
Journal of Canadian studies ISSN 0021-9495
Journal of economic history ISSN 0022-0507
Journal of family history ISSN 0363-1990
Journal of interdisciplinary studies ISSN 0890-0132
Journal of Negro history ISSN 0022-2992
Journal of policy history ISSN 0898-0306
Journal of social history ISSN 0022-4529
Journal of southern history ISSN 0022-4642
Journal of the early republic ISSN 0275-1275
Journal of the history of ideas ISSN 0022-5037
Journal of the history of medicine and allied sciences ISSN 0022-5045
Journal of urban history ISSN 0096-1442
Journal of women's history ISSN 1042-7961
Labor history ISSN 0023-656X
Labour/Le travailleur ISSN 0700-3862
New England quarterly ISSN 0028-4866
Ontario history ISSN 0030-2953
Pacific historical review ISSN 0030-8684
Past and present ISSN 0031-2746
Political science quarterly ISSN 0032-3195
Politics and society ISSN 0032-3292
Prairie forum ISSN 0317-6282
Prologue: the journal of the National Archives ISSN 0033-1031

Prospects: an annual of American cultural studies ISSN 0361-2333
The public historian ISSN 0272-3433
Radical America ISSN 0033-7617
Radical history review ISSN 0163-6545
Reviews in American history ISSN 0048-7511
Revue d'histoire de l'Amérique française ISSN 0035-2357
Sage ISSN 0741-8639
Science and society ISSN 0036-8237
Signs ISSN 0097-9740
Slavery and abolition ISSN 0144-039X
Social forces ISSN 0037-7732
Social science history ISSN 0145-5532
Southwestern historical quarterly ISSN 0038-478X
Studies in American political development ISSN 0898-588X
Western historical quarterly ISSN 0043-3810
William and Mary quarterly ISSN 0043-5597

Australasia and Oceania

Aboriginal history ISSN 0314-8769
Australian cultural history ISSN 0728-8433
Australian economic history review ISSN 0004-8992
Australian feminist studies ISSN 0816-4649
Australian historical studies ISSN 0018-2559; continues *Historical studies*
Australian journal of politics and history ISSN 0004-9522
The contemporary Pacific ISSN 1043-898X
Historical records of Australian science; ISSN 0067-155X continues *Records of the Australian Academy of Science*
Historical studies: Australia and New Zealand
History of education review ISSN 0819-8691; continues *Journal of the Australian and New Zealand History of Education Society*
Journal de la Société des Oceanistes ISSN 0300-953X
Journal of Pacific history ISSN 0022-3344
Journal of religious history ISSN 0022-4227
Journal of the Australian and New Zealand History of Education Society; continued by *History of Education Review*
Journal of the Polynesian Society ISSN 0032-4000
Journal of the Royal Australian Historical Society ISSN 0035-8762
Labour history ISSN 0023-6942
Landfall ISSN 0023-7930
National register of archives and manuscripts in New Zealand ISSN 0110-7178
New Zealand journal of history ISSN 0028-8322
Oceania ISSN 0029-8077
Pacific studies ISSN 0275-3596
Political science ISSN 0032-3187
Records of the Australian Academy of Science; continued by *Historical records of Australian Science*
Turnbull Library record

International Relations

American political science review ISSN 0003-0554
Aussenpolitik ISSN 0587-3835
Australian journal of politics and history ISSN 0004-9522
British journal of politics and history
China quarterly ISSN 0305-7410, ISSN 0009-4439
Contemporary European history ISSN 0960-7773
Current history ISSN 0011-3530
Department of State Bulletin ISSN 0041-7610
Diplomacy and statecraft ISSN 0959-2296
Diplomatic history ISSN 0145-2096
East European quarterly ISSN 0012-8449
European studies review ISSN 0014-3111
Foreign affairs ISSN 0015-7120
Foreign policy ISSN 0015-7228
Francia ISSN 0251-3609
Guerres mondiales et conflits contemporains
International affairs ISSN 0020-5850
The international history review ISSN 0707-5332
International organization ISSN 0020-8183
International security ISSN 0162-2889
Jerusalem quarterly ISSN 0334-4800
Journal of Central European affairs ISSN 0885-2472
Journal of Common Market studies ISSN 0021-9886
Journal of conflict resolution ISSN 0022-0027
Journal of contemporary history ISSN 0022-0094
Journal of military history ISSN 0899-3718
Journal of modern history ISSN 0022-2801
Journal of strategic studies ISSN 0140-2390
Militärgeschichtliche Mitteilungen ISSN 0026-3826
Millennium ISSN 0305-8289
Orbis ISSN 0030-4387
Pacific historical review ISSN 0030-8684
Parameters ISSN 0031-1723
Peace and change ISSN 0149-0508
Relations internationales
Review of international studies ISSN 0260-2105
Revue d'histoire de la Deuxieme Guerre Mondiale et des conflits contemporains ISSN 0755-1584
Revue d'histoire diplomatique ISSN 0035-2365
Revue d'histoire moderne et contemporaine ISSN 0048-8003
The Russian review ISSN 0036-0341
Slavic review ISSN 0037-6779
Storia contemporanea ISSN 0039-1875
Storia e politica
Strategic survey ISSN 0459-7230
Survival ISSN 0039-6338
Transactions of the Royal Historical Society ISSN 0080-4401
World politics ISSN 0043-8871
The world today ISSN 0043-9134

AUTHOR INDEX

Ahmad, Zahiruddin 9.306
Ahmann, Rolf 32.409
Ahmat, Sharom 16.259–60
Ahmed, Akbar S. 15.828–29, 18.79
Ahmed, Leila 18.121
Ahmed, Rafiuddin 15.659
Ahrari, Mohammed E. 48.500
Ahroni, Reuben 21.212
Ahrweiler, Hélène 8.6–7, 8.245, 8.314
Ahsan, M. Manazir 17.305
Ahvenainen, Jorma 32.66
Aidoo, Agnes 19.845
Aikens, C. Melvin 2.53, 12.26
Ainley, Marianne Gosztonyi 45.1
Ainslie, Douglas 1.305
Ainsworth, Peter F. 20.307
Aitken, Hugh G. J. 4.40, 44.127, 4.527–28
Aiyar, K. G. Sesha 15.194
Ajami, Fouad 18.39
Ajayi, Jacob F. Ade 19.7, 19.139, 19.141, 19.145, 19.194–95, 19.888
Akagi, Roy H. 39.78
Akaha, Tsuneo 13.377
Akai, Tatsurō 12.226
Akamatsu, Paul 13.75
Akazawa Takeru 12.26
Akenson, Donald Harron 45.2, 45.109
Akers, Charles W. 39.654, 41.335, 41.506
Akhavi, Shahrough 18.559
Akhinzhanov, Serzhan Musataevich 9.196
Akhmedov, Buri 9.284
Akhromeev, S. F. 35.346
Akin Rabibhadana, M. R. 16.159
Akiner, Shirin 9.1
Akinjogbin, I. A. 19.146
Akintoye, Stephen Adebanji 19.196
Akita, George 13.112
Akkerman, Phyllis 17.501
Aksenov, Arthur 34.441
Akurgal, Ekrem 5.370, 5.399–400
Alagoa, E. J. 19.147
Alam, Muzaffar 15.405
Alapuro, Risto 32.258
Alatorre, Antonio 29.54, 29.194
Alatri, Paolo 28.421
Alazard, Jean 25.5
Albanese, Catherine L. 40.503–4, 41.178
Albenda, Pauline 5.190
Albers, Patricia 36.207
Albert, Bill 38.78
Albert, Peter J. 41.107, 41.172–73, 41.248, 41.368, 41.512
Albert, Phyllis Cohen 21.131
Alberti, Iohannes Baptista 6.74
Albertini, Luigi 28.359
Albertini, Rudolf von 3.213
Alberts, Robert 41.521
Alberts, Wybe Jappe 27.1
Albion, Robert Greenhalgh 4.497, 42.150
Albisetti, James C. 31.257
Albrecht-Carrié, René 28.401

Albrektson, B. 5.230
Albright, William Foxwell 3.105, 5.13, 5.201, 5.231, 5.290, 5.574
Alcalá Galve, Angel 29.49
Alchon, Suzanne Austin 37.201
Alcock, Antony 48.81
Alcock, Leslie 20.110
Alcock, Rutherford 13.245
Aldcroft, Derek H. 22.1, 24.155, 48.124
Alden, Dauril 19.926, 36.441, 37.70, 37.399, 37.456–57
Alden, John R. 39.139, 39.161, 39.198, 41.1, 41.117, 41.307, 41.365, 41.522–24
Alderman, Geoffrey 24.206
Aldgate, Anthony 29.248
Aldred, Cyril 5.524, 5.575–76
Aldrich, Robert 26.207, 46.315
Aldridge, A. Owen 29.160, 41.141
Alef, Gustave 34.62, 34.111
Alekseev, N. A. 9.47
Alexander, Adele Logan 40.417
Alexander, Boyd 29.339
Alexander, Charles 44.1
Alexander, Christine 7.513
Alexander, David G. 45.42
Alexander, Dorothy 30.265
Alexander, Edward P. 4.328
Alexander, George M. 33.237
Alexander, John K. 41.184, 41.372
Alexander, John T. 34.78, 34.86, 34.153, 34.444
Alexander, Martin S. 29.249
Alexander, Paul J. 8.83, 8.148
Alexander, R. S. 26.101
Alexander, Robert Jackson 38.79–81, 38.470–71, 38.675, 44.852
Alexander, Robert L. 5.401–3
Alexander, Roberta Sue 42.820
Alexander, Stella 33.758–59
Alexander, Thomas B. 42.99
Alexandre, Pierre 20.21
Alexandris, Alexis 33.238
Al-Faruqi, Isma'il Ragi 3.1, 17.81
Al-Faruqi, Lamya 18.122
Al-Fasi, Allal 18.349
Alföldi, Andreas 7.160
Alföldy, Géza 7.432
Alford, B.W.E. 24.137
Algar, Hamid 18.560
Al-Hassan, Ahmad Y. 4.379
Ali, Imran 15.691
Ali, Mahmud 15.690
Ali, Muhammad 17.104
Âli, Mustafa 18.169
Ali al-Haji Riau, Raja 16.90
Alisky, Marvin 38.82
Alitto, Guy S. 11.502
Alkim, U. Bahadir 5.370, 5.404
Allain, Jean-Claude 47.332
Allan, Sarah 10.165–66
Allchin, Bridget 2.38, 15.62
Allchin, F. Raymond 2.38–39

Allen, Barbara 1.109, 40.127
Allen, Bruce 31.531
Allen, Calvin H., Jr. 18.533
Allen, Charles 15.459
Allen, D. F. 7.1
Allen, David Elliston 24.348
Allen, David Grayson 39.79, 39.93
Allen, Frederick Lewis 43.58, 44.2
Allen, G. C. 13.32
Allen, Garland E. 4.204–5, 43.67
Allen, Harry C. 40.612
Allen, J. W. 22.153
Allen, James Smith 26.235
Allen, Jelisaveta Stanojevich 8.32
Allen, Jim 2.64
Allen, John Scott 4.484
Allen, Michael 41.308
Allen, P. S. 22.154
Allen, R. E. 6.252
Allen, Richard 45.172
Allen, Richard C. 14.129
Allen, Richard E. 33.366
Allen, Robert C. 23.133
Allen, Walter 44.355
Allen, William Sheridan 31.413
Allinson, Gary D. 13.214, 13.349
Allis, Frederick S., Jr. 39.773
Allison, Henry E. 30.321
Allison, Roy 32.259
Allmand, Christopher 20.483–84
Allmendinger, David F., Jr. 42.622
Allon, Dafna 35.347
Allouche, Adel 18.220
Alloula, Malek 18.123
Allsen, Thomas T. 9.209, 9.230, 9.239, 9.242
Allshouse, Robert H. 34.42
Allswang, John M. 44.609
Allum, Percy A. 28.451
Allwood, John 4.329
Allworth, Edward A. 9.285, 9.309–10
Almaguer, Tomas 43.340
Almana, Mohammed 18.534
Almeida, Fortunato de 29.335
Almog, Shmuel 18.456
Almquist, Alan F. 43.266
Al-Naqar, Umar 19.197
Alon, Gedalia 5.202, 7.453
Alpers, Edward A. 19.846, 19.889
Alpers, Svetlana 1.438
Alphandéry, Paul 20.317
Al-Qazzaz, Ayad 18.124
Alster, Bendt 5.94
Alt, Albrecht 5.247
Altekar, Anant Sadashiv 15.138, 15.155, 15.215
Alter, George 42.265
Alter, Robert 5.232–33
Althoff, Gerd 20.245, 20.653
Althusser, Louis 1.131
Altman, Ida 29.50, 37.115, 37.237, 39.348
Altmann, Alexander 21.132

Baker, Donald L. 14.78–80
Baker, Donald N. 26.287
Baker, Frank 41.336
Baker, Houston A. 42.516
Baker, Hugh D. R. 11.174, 11.747
Baker, J.N.L. 22.55
Baker, Jean H. 42.2
Baker, John H. 20.503, 23.272
Baker, Keith Michael 25.90–91, 25.231
Baker, Leonard 41.527
Baker, Maurice E. 40.176
Baker, Paul J. 46.257
Baker, Paula 40.54, 43.523
Baker, Richard A. 40.34
Baker, M. N. 4.582
Bakewell, Peter J. 37.238–41
Bakhash, Shaul 18.563
Bakhtin, Mikhail M. 25.40
Bakhuizen, S. C. 6.433
Bakir, Abd el-Mohsen 5.526
Bakirtzis, Charalampos N. 8.206
Bakken, Gordon Morris 42.401
Baklanoff, Eric N. 38.84
Bakó, Elemér 33.317–18
Bakvis, Herman 27.230
Baladhuri, Ahmad ibn Yahya 17.109
Baladié, Raoul 6.398
Balakrishnan Nayar, T. 15.83
Balandier, Georges 19.583
Balard, Michel 20.14, 20.837
Balassa, Bela 48.552
Balasubrahmanyam, S. R. 15.234
Balazs, Étienne 10.209, 10.353
Balázs, K. 33.320
Balcer, Jack Martin 5.438
Balderston, Theo 31.372
Baldick, Robert 22.234
Baldwin, Frank 14.142
Baldwin, John W. 20.485, 20.576
Baldwin, Marshall W. 17.229, 17.233,
  17.244, 17.246, 17.251, 17.260, 17.336,
  20.326, 20.1085
Baldwin, Peter 22.620, 31.358, 31.462,
  32.217
Bales, Maria 33.368
Balfour, Neil 33.765
Balfour, Sebastian 29.294
Balibar, Étienne 1.131, 3.457
Balinky, Alexander 41.528
Bálint, Csanád 9.20
Baljon, J.M.S. 15.406
Ball, Alan M. 35.90
Ball, M. Margaret 38.44
Ball, V. 3.303
Ball, Warwick 15.65
Ballard, Martin 1.522
Ballesteros Beretta, Antonio 20.908
Ballhatchet, Kenneth 15.460
Balmer, Randall H. 39.655
Balmori, Diana 38.85
Balogh, Barna 9.205
Balogh, Brian 4.560, 44.677
Baloyra, Enrique A. 38.308

Balsdon, J.P.V.D. 7.128, 7.378
Balsvik, Randi R. 19.326
Balteau, J. 25.2, 26.1
Balthasar, Hans U. von 8.357
Baltzell, E. Digby 40.292
Bamba, Nobuya 13.179, 13.247
Bambrough, Renford 6.592
Bamford, James 44.617
Bamford, P. W. 25.365
Bamforth, Douglas B. 36.71
Ban, Sung Hwan 14.150
Banac, Ivo 33.2, 33.690, 33.766–67
Banani, Amin 18.564
Bandarage, Asoka 15.745
Banerjee, N. R. 15.66
Banerjee, Sumanta 15.623, 15.787
Bang, Willy 9.201
Banga, Indu 15.391, 15.561–62
Banister, Judith 11.630
Bank, Mirra 40.419
Banker, James R. 20.1442
Banks, Arthur S. 3.2
Banks, J. A. 24.125–26
Bankwitz, Philip C. F. 26.134
Bann, Stephen 1.339
Banner, James M., Jr. 41.294
Banner, Lois W. 40.420, 42.617, 42.620
Banning, Lance 41.265
Bannister, Robert C. 43.475
Banno, Masataka 11.78
Bannon, John Francis 37.567–68
Banta, Martha 43.476
Banuazizi, Ali 18.5
Bar Hebraeus, Gregory 17.234
Barager, Joseph R. 38.25
Barahona, Renato 29.214
Baram, Amatzia 18.432
Baránski, Zygmunt G. 28.452
Barany, George 33.319
Baratier, Edouard 20.44
Barber, Benjamin R. 27.273
Barber, James 48.476
Barber, John 35.124–25, 35.252
Barber, Karin 19.123
Barber, Malcolm 20.1189
Barber, William J. 40.548, 44.618
Barbier, Jacques A. 29.161–63, 37.23,
  37.42, 37.476–78
Barbir, Karl K. 18.173
Barbour, Hugh 40.507
Barbour, Philip L. 39.141
Barbour, Ruth 8.58
Barbour, Violet 27.81
Barbu, Zevedei 1.459
Barcan, Alan 46.159
Bárcenas, J. Roberto 36.467
Barchatova, Y. 34.38
Barclay, George W. 11.707
Bardley, Ritamary 20.1481
Barea, Ilsa 31.300
Bareau, André 15.123
Barfield, Thomas 9.118, 9.85
Barghoorn, Frederick C. 35.374

Bariéty, Jacques 47.26, 48.109
Baring, Arnulf 31.510, 31.532
Baritz, Loren 39.583, 40.293, 44.213,
  44.830
Bark, Dennis L. 31.488
Barkai, Avraham 31.437, 31.456
Barkan, Ömer Lutfi 18.174
Barker, Charles Albro 40.483, 41.373
Barker, Elisabeth 33.768, 48.253
Barker, Ernest 6.97, 6.593, 22.19, 22.181
Barker, Francis 1.347
Barker, Graeme 2.83, 7.150, 7.363
Barker, John W. 8.126, 8.188
Barker, Nancy Nichols 25.196, 47.123–24
Barker, Thomas M. 33.752
Barker-Benfield, G. J. 40.421
Barkin, Kenneth D. 31.224, 31.237
Barkindo, Bawuro Mubi 19.148
Barley, M. W. 20.293
Barlow, Frank 20.202, 20.504, 20.1117–18,
  20.1443
Barman, Jean 36.48, 45.52
Barman, Roderick J. 38.500
Barnadas, Josep M. 36.389
Barnard, A. 46.134
Barnard, Ellsworth 44.588
Barnard, F. M. 1.279, 1.150, 30.322
Barnard, T. C. 23.414
Barnavi, Elie 25.141, 25.152
Barnes, Gilbert Hobbs 42.512
Barnes, Gina Lee 2.54, 2.62, 12.28, 14.24
Barnes, Jennifer 5.34, 5.429
Barnes, Jonathan 6.594
Barnes, Sandra T. 19.848
Barnes, Thomas C. 37.1
Barnes, Timothy David 7.407, 7.530–31,
  7.585
Barnet, Richard J. 3.224, 40.670, 44.798
Barnett, A. Doak 11.368, 11.577
Barnett, Marguerite Ross 15.698
Barnett, Richard B. 15.407
Barnett, Richard D. 5.192, 5.315
Barnett, Robert W. 13.396
Barnett-Robisheaux, Thomas see
  Robisheaux, Thomas
Barnhart, Michael A. 13.248, 48.164
Barnhart, Richard M. 11.361
Barnish, S.J.B. 7.578
Barnouw, Erik 15.625, 44.68, 44.128
Barnwell, P. S. 20.138
Baron, Ava 42.258, 43.151
Baron, Beth 18.129
Baron, Hans 28.10–11
Baron, Jeanette Meisel 21.243
Baron, Margaret E. 4.111
Baron, Salo Wittmayer 17.388, 21.1,
  21.134–35, 21.245, 21.175, 21.243,
  22.237
Baron, Samuel H. 34.64, 34.261–62
Barraclough, Geoffrey 1.16, 3.3–4, 3.225–
  26, 20.610–11, 20.966, 20.1086, 22.77
Barral i Altet, Xavier 20.893
Barratt, Glynn 34.183

Burrell, David B. 20.1354
Burrow, J. A. 20.1418
Burrow, James G. 43.69
Burrow, John W. 24.333
Burrow, T. 5.516
Burrowes, Robert D. 18.538
Burrus, Ernest J. 37.588
Bursian, Conrad 6.5
Bursill-Hall, G. L. 20.1263–64, 20.1271
Burstein, Paul 44.451
Burstein, Stanley M. 6.133, 6.478
Burston, W. H. 1.525
Burton, David H. 40.737, 43.639
Burton, Isabel 3.277
Burton, Orville Vernon 42.306
Burton, Richard F. 3.277
Burton, Robert M. 4.113
Burton, Stojana Čulić 6.424
Burtt, Edwin Arthur 4.81, 22.161
Bury, John B. 8.129, 8.256, 22.162
Bury, J.P.T. 22.316
Busch, Briton Cooper 47.273, 47.365, 47.429, 48.147
Büsch, Otto 31.18
Bush, Donald J. 44.28
Bush, John W. 47.144
Bush, M. L. 22.239
Bush, Richard C. 11.489
Bush, Richard C., Jr. 11.660
Bush, Susan 10.306
Bushkovitch, Paul 34.263, 34.424
Bushman, Richard L. 1.461, 39.85, 39.208, 39.620
Bushnell, Amy 37.569
Bushnell, David 38.28, 38.96, 38.409, 38.602
Bushnell, John 34.193, 35.430
Busolt, Georg 6.162, 6.450
Busse, Heribert 17.178–79
Bustin, Edouard 19.587
Buswell, Geoffrey 5.295
Buswell, Robert E., Jr. 10.105, 14.42–43
Buteux, Paul 48.425
Butland, Gilbert J. 37.7
Butler, Alan 46.286
Butler, Alfred J. 17.110
Butler, Anne M. 40.180, 42.461
Butler, David 24.47
Butler, Elizabeth Beardsly 43.152
Butler, James 48.224
Butler, Jeffrey 19.734
Butler, Jon 39.561, 39.662, 40.723
Butler, Lee A. 12.190
Butler, Marilyn 24.312
Butler, Martin 23.336
Butler, Pierce 22.163
Butler, Rohan 48.64
Butler, Thomas 33.729
Butlin, N. G. 46.34, 46.132–34
Butow, Robert J. C. 13.291–92
Butsch, Richard 44.44

Butterfield, Herbert 1.20–21, 1.215, 22.164
Butterfield, L. H. 34.184
Butters, Humfrey C. 28.94
Butterworth, Douglas S. 38.97
Buttery, Alan 5.105
Buttigieg, Joseph A. 28.218
Buttinger, Joseph 16.200–201
Butwell, Richard A. 16.139
Butzer, Karl W. 3.92, 5.528–29
Buve, R. 38.200
Buytaert, Eligius M. 20.1368
Buzzetti, Sandro 20.1457
Byars, Robert S. 38.5
Byas, Hugh 13.293
Byatt, I.C.R. 24.138
Byers, Edward 39.364, 41.375
Byington, Margaret Frances 43.106
Bynum, Caroline Walker 20.1500–1502
Bynum, Victoria E. 42.307
Bynum, William F. 4.1, 4.709
Byock, Jesse L. 20.661
Byrn, John D., Jr. 24.387
Byrnes, Robert F. 33.12
Byron, John 11.373
Byron, Robert 3.278

Caballero, Manuel 38.98
Cabral, Adolfo 29.381
Cabral, Manuel Villaverde 29.393
Cachia, Pierre 17.232, 20.181
Cadogan, Gerald 6.38
Cadoux, T. J. 6.286
Cady, John F. 16.126, 16.140–41, 16.202
Cadzow, John F 33.391
Caenegem, R. C. van 20.3, 20.30
Cafagna, Luciano 28.336
Cagnat, R. 7.46
Cahan, David 31.258
Cahen, Claude 17.14, 17.260–61, 17.276, 17.299, 17.310, 17.359
Cahill, James Francis 10.43, 11.327
Cail, Robert E. 36.36
Caillat, Colette 15.125
Caille, Jacqueline 20.895
Cain, P. J. 47.206
Cairns, Craig 23.374
Calabria, Antonio 28.121
Calam, John 39.741
Caldarola, Carlo 13.527
Calder, Angus 39.23
Calder, Bruce J. 38.369
Calder, Kenneth J. 47.366
Calder, William M., III 6.148–50
Calderón de la Barca, Frances Erskine Inglis 38.201
Caldwell, John 23.337
Caldwell, Lawrence Y. 48.409
Caldwell, Patricia 39.756
Caldwell, Ronald J. 22.8–9
Calhoon, Robert M. 41.123–24, 41.340

Calhoun, Arthur W. 40.310
Calhoun, Daniel Hovey 4.603, 42.667
Calhoun, Frederick S. 43.662
Călinescu, George 33.630
Calinescu, Matei 33.639
Calinger, Ronald 4.114
Callahan, William J. 28.198, 29.167–69, 29.215
Callard, Keith B. 15.832
Callari, Antonio 28.218
Calleo, David P. 22.317, 31.19, 44.155, 44.799
Callesen, Gerd 32.1
Callow, Alexander B. 40.274
Calloway, Colin G. 36.127, 36.210, 44.382
Calmann, Marianne 21.89
Calmes, Albert 27.199, 27.204
Calmes, Christian 27.199, 27.204
Calmette, Joseph 20.918
Calvert, Monte A. 42.203
Calvert, Peter 38.603
Calvert, Robert A. 40.175
Calvert, Susan 38.603
Calvet, Y. 5.522
Calvi, Giulia 4.689
Calvin, John 22.124
Calvocoressi, Peter 48.31–32, 48.225
Camarillo, Albert 40.356, 43.195
Cameron, Alan 7.560, 8.247, 8.391, 8.453
Cameron, Averil 5.159, 5.163, 7.260, 7.533, 8.130, 8.257, 8.392
Cameron, Euan 22.125
Cameron, George G. 5.444–45, 5.479
Cameron, Iain A. 25.370
Cameron, Margaret M. 45.75
Cameron, Meribeth E. 11.82
Cameron, Nigel 11.735
Camiller, Patrick 3.407
Camilleri, Joseph 11.580
Cammell, Diarmid 18.373
Cammett, John M. 28.402
Camões, Luis Vaz de 29.347
Camp, John M. 6.278
Camp, Roderic Ai 38.202–3
Camp, Wesley D. 25.236
Campbell, Alec 19.809
Campbell, Alexander E. 40.737
Campbell, Ballard 43.526
Campbell, Bernard G. 3.68
Campbell, Bruce M. S. 20.351
Campbell, Charles S. 40.616, 43.587
Campbell, Christiana 44.623
Campbell, D'Ann 44.352
Campbell, David A. 6.215
Campbell, F. Gregory 33.152
Campbell, G. L. 20.35
Campbell, Gwyn 19.676–77, 19.891–92
Campbell, J. B. 7.312
Campbell, James 20.204–5
Campbell, John C. 33.774–75
Campbell, John Creighton 13.354

Castañeda, Carmen 37.401
Castberg, A. Didrick 13.472
Castedo, Leopoldo 37.402
Castillo, Arcadio del 7.3
Castles, Alex C. 46.73
Castles, Francis G. 46.74, 46.263
Castles, Lance 16.116
Castro, Américo 20.919
Castro, Ferrira de 36.453
Castro, Ginette 44.257
Castro y Velazquez, Jan 36.436
Catanach, I. J. 15.502
Cathcart, Kevin J. 5.19
Cattell, David T. 29.258
Catto, J. I. 20.1316
Catton, Bruce 42.755
Catz, Rebecca D. 3.295
Caute, David 3.228
Cauwenberghe, Eddy van 27.116
Cavallo, Guglielmo 8.59–60, 8.108
Caven, Brian 7.208
Caviedes, Cesar 38.684
Cawelti, John G. 40.29, 42.384, 42.695
Cawkwell, George 6.87, 6.226
Cayleff, Susan 42.612
Cayton, Andrew R. L. 40.166, 41.310
Cayton, Horace R. 44.409
Cayton, Mary Kupiec 40.2
Cazden, Elizabeth 42.583
Cazelles, Raymond 20.398, 20.595–96
Cazin, Paul 33.457
Ceadel, Martin 48.90
Cebik, L. B. 1.237, 1.318
Cecil, Lamar 31.225–26, 47.174
Cekalska, Krystyna 33.472
Cell, Gillian T. 45.65
Cell, John W. 19.736, 24.470
Censer, Jack R. 25.94–95, 26.45–46
Censer, Jane Turner 42.309
Centlivres, Pierre 15.851
Ceplair, Larry 42.513
Cerny, Gerald 27.123
Černý, Jaroslav 5.580–81
Certeau, Michel de 1.341
Cesarani, David 21.284
Céspedes del Castillo, Guillermo 37.74
Chabod, Federico 28.71, 28.322, 28.379
Chadwick, Henry 20.1040–41
Chadwick, John 6.151, 6.173–74, 6.192–93
Chadwick, Owen 3.499, 22.126, 22.385, 24.285–87, 28.199
Chadwick, Whitney 22.22
Chadwin, Mark Lincoln 44.738
Chafe, William H. 40.425, 44.258–59, 44.454, 44.502, 44.682
Chaffee, John W. 10.140, 10.307
Chai, Ch'u 10.205
Chai, Winberg 10.205
Chai-anan, Samudavanija 16.173
Chaklador, Haran Chandra 15.85
Chakrabarti, Dilip K. 15.67–68
Chakrabarty, Dipesh 15.538

Chakravarti, Adhir 16.36
Chalandon, Ferdinand 8.177
Chaliand, Gérard 3.7, 3.459, 48.21
Challener, Richard D. 43.640
Challinor, Joan R. 40.323
Challis, C. E. 23.137
Challoner, W. H. 22.455
Chalmers, David M. 43.265
Chaloner, W. H. 27.91, 31.105
Chamberlain, Basil Hall 13.102
Chamberlain, Dennis 3.130
Chamberlain, Greg 38.14
Chamberlain, Muriel E. 47.39
Chamberlin, William Henry 35.19, 35.58
Chambers, Clarke A. 44.683
Chambers, David 28.110
Chambers, Frances 25.6
Chambers, J. D. 24.131
Chambers, John Whiteclay, II 43.3
Chambers, Mortimer 6.94, 6.100–101, 6.152, 6.303
Chambers, William Nisbet 40.55, 41.227, 43.542
Chambers-Schiller, Lee Virginia 42.624
Champion, Timothy C. 2.85–86
Champlin, Edward 7.130, 7.408
Chan, Albert 10.354
Chan, Anita 11.633
Chan, David B. 10.355
Chan, F. Gilbert 11.374
Chan, Hok-lam 10.150, 10.325–26
Chan, Ming K. 11.178, 11.506
Chan, Sin-wai 11.291
Chan, Sucheng 40.181
Chan, Wai Kwan 11.748
Chan, Wellington K. K. 11.234
Chan, Wing-tsit 10.49–50, 10.134–36, 10.138, 10.158
Chan Lau, Kit-ching 11.736
Chanana, Dev Raj 15.140
Chance, John K. 37.341–42, 37.492, 38.97
Chandaman, C. D. 23.8
Chandler, Alfred D., Jr. 4.403–4, 40.230, 42.152, 43.24, 43.35, 44.177
Chandler, Billy Jaynes 38.509
Chandler, D. S. 37.6, 37.155, 37.493
Chandler, David G. 26.85–86
Chandler, David L. 37.220
Chandler, David P. 16.12, 16.227–28
Chandler, Lester V. 40.212
Chandler, Ralph Clark 40.37
Chandler, Richard E. 29.4
Chandler, Tertius 3.306
Chandler, William U. 4.512
Chandos, Robert 45.226, 45.310
Chandra, Bipan 15.25, 15.665, 15.723
Chandra, Moti 15.141
Chandra, Satish 15.317, 15.332
Chandra, Sudhir 15.628
Chandra, Vipan 14.97
Chandran, Jeshurun 16.165
Chaney, Elsa M. 38.100

Chang, Arnold 11.661
Chang, Chih-i 11.491
Chang, Chung-li 11.179, 11.235
Chang, Chun-ming 11.396
Chang, Chun-shu 10.304
Chang, Gordon H. 48.526
Chang, Hao 11.292–93
Chang, Hsin-pao 11.83
Chang, K'ang-i Sun 10.370
Chang, Kwang-chih 3.93, 10.35, 10.167–69, 10.179, 10.194, 10.214
Chang, Maria Hsia 11.375
Chang, Sidney H. 11.294
Chang, Tŭk-chin 14.1
Channell, David F. 4.604
Channing, Steven A. 42.748
Chanock, Martin 19.588
Chao, Ju-kua 10.293
Chao, Kang 10.36, 11.236–37
Chapelot, Jean 20.65
Chapin, Elizabeth 20.399
Chaplin, Gillian 46.212
Chaplin, Joyce E. 39.406, 41.424
Chapman, Anne 36.492
Chapman, Herrick 26.350
Chapman, Maybelle Rebecca (Kennedy) 47.274
Chapman, Stanley 24.153
Chapsal, Jacques 26.209
Charaire, Veronique 33.67
Charanis, Peter 8.9–10, 8.132
Charbonneau, Hubert 45.71
Chardin, John 3.281
Charle, Christophe 26.242, 26.337
Charles, Joseph 41.228
Charles, Lindsey 23.287
Charlesworth, M. P. 3.249
Charlesworth, Neil 15.503, 15.539
Charlot, Jean 26.210, 38.206
Charney, Paul 37.343
Charnvit Kasetsiri 16.74
Charpin, Dominique 5.62
Chartier, Roger 1.419, 25.26–28, 25.36, 26.47, 26.243
Chartres, J. A. 23.138
Charvát, Petr 5.46–47
Charvat, William 42.668
Charvet, P. E. 25.20
Chary, Frederick B. 33.96
Chase, Colin 20.206
Chase, Gilbert 40.539
Chase, Malcolm 24.229
Chase, William J. 35.254–55
Chase-Dunn, Christopher 3.411
Chasin, Barbara H. 3.325
Chassin, Lionel Max 11.376
Chastain, James 26.118, 47.96
Châtellier, Louis 30.59
Chatfield, Charles 44.835
Chatterjee, Asim Kumar 15.126
Chatterjee, Partha 15.666, 15.702, 15.724
Chatthip Nartsupha 16.166

Churchill, Bernadita Reyes 16.328
Churchill, Irene Josephine 20.1128
Churchill, Winston 48.226
Chuvin, Pierre 7.94
Cid, Rafael del 38.322
Ciechanowski, Jan M. 33.532–33, 33.604
Cienciała, Anna M. 33.534–35, 48.214
Cinel, Dino 43.236
Cingari, Gaetano 28.238
Cintas, Pierre 7.26
Cioc, Mark 31.513, 48.401
Cioranescu, Alexandre 25.7–9
Cipolla, Carlo M. 3.307, 3.542, 4.449,
    4.618, 20.31, 20.295, 22.23, 22.240,
    22.447–50, 27.92, 27.283, 28.336, 29.208,
    29.299, 32.81
Ciria, Alberto 38.604
Cissoko, S. M. 19.125, 19.153
Claeys, Gregory 24.331
Clagett, Marshall 4.25, 4.33, 4.45, 20.1282,
    20.1388–89
Claman, Elizabeth 1.125
Clanchy, M. T. 20.512–13, 20.1317
Clapham, Christopher 19.330–31
Clapham, J. H. 22.24, 22.451, 24.110
Clarence-Smith, W. G. 19.589, 19.827,
    19.893
Clarfield, Gerard H. 41.536
Clark, Alice 22.241, 23.289
Clark, Andrew Hill 39.332, 45.44
Clark, Anne B. 11.27
Clark, Bruce A. 36.50
Clark, C.M.H. 46.9, 46.10, 46.17
Clark, Carolyn M. 19.434
Clark, Charles E. 39.86, 39.850, 41.377
Clark, Chester Wells 47.150
Clark, Christopher 41.376, 42.153
Clark, Clifford Edward, Jr. 42.641, 43.183
Clark, Donald N. 14.54, 14.95
Clark, Dora Mae 39.38
Clark, Frances Ida 26.395
Clark, G. Kitson 1.5
Clark, G. N. 22.19, 22.62, 24.76, 27.18,
    27.57
Clark, J.C.D. 23.10
Clark, J. Desmond 2.12, 3.69
Clark, James M. 20.1472
Clark, Jeannine 3.152
Clark, John 22.539
Clark, John G. 25.374, 40.652
Clark, Katerina 35.394
Clark, Kenneth B. 44.364, 44.434
Clark, Linda L. 26.244, 26.288
Clark, Martin 28.298
Clark, Nancy 19.737
Clark, Norman H. 44.5
Clark, Paul 11.665
Clark, Peter 23.230, 29.67
Clark, Priscilla Parkhurst 26.245
Clark, Robert P. 29.297, 29.324
Clark, Samuel 24.416
Clark, Terry Nichols 26.246

Clark, Timothy J. 26.247
Clark, Victor S. 40.243
Clarke, Aidan 23.422
Clarke, Alice L. 32.106
Clarke, Desmond 39.210
Clarke, Edwin 4.168
Clarke, Grahame 3.70
Clarke, H. B. 20.1018
Clarke, Helen 20.232, 20.352
Clarke, Hermann Frederick 39.87
Clarke, Howard B. 20.120
Clarke, James F. 33.97–98
Clarke, John 24.375
Clarke, John R. 7.478, 7.514
Clarke, M. L. 7.271
Clarke, Mary Patterson 39.211
Clarke, P. F. 24.49
Clarke, Peter 24.332
Clarke, Prescott 11.68
Clarke, Roger A. 35.99
Clarke, Stephen V. O. 48.133
Clark-Lewis, Elizabeth 43.153
Clarkson, L. A. 23.140, 24.412
Clarkson, Paul S. 41.537
Clasen, Claus-Peter 30.19
Classen, E. 2.45
Claudin, Fernando 3.460
Clausen, C. A. 32.324
Clausen, W. V. 7.63
Clausewitz, Carl von 31.104
Clauss, Manfred 6.6
Clavijo, Ruy Gonzalez de 9.251
Clawson, Mary Ann 40.466
Clawson, Robert W. 48.426
Claxton, Patricia 45.80, 45.158
Claxton, Robert H. 38.102
Clay, C.G.A. 23.141
Clayton, Anthony 19.472, 19.828
Clayton, Lawrence A. 37.249, 37.306,
    37.326
Cleary, M. C. 26.276
Cleaves, Francis Woodman 9.222
Cleaves, Peter S. 38.685
Clecak, Peter 44.6
Cleere, Henry 7.2, 20.65
Clegg, H. A. 24.230
Clemens, Clay 31.503
Clemens, Diane Shaver 48.254
Clemens, Paul G. E. 39.408
Clemens, Walter C., Jr. 32.410
Clement, Besse Alberta 17.210, 37.445
Clementi, Dione 20.879
Clements, Barbara Evans 34.280, 35.21–
    22, 35.302
Clemmensen, Niels 32.235
Clendenen, Clarence C. 40.653
Clendenning, John 43.478
Clendenning, Philip 34.13
Clendinnen, Inga 36.271, 36.282
Clerke, Agnes M. 4.142
Clermont, E. 28.317
Cleugh, James 7.567, 44.773

Cleverdon, Catherine L. 45.185
Clifford, Clark 44.800
Clifford, J. Garry 40.606, 44.739
Clifford, James 46.373
Clifford, Nicholas R. 11.382
Clifton, James A. 36.211
Climo, T. A. 1.238
Cline, Cheryl 22.10
Cline, Howard Francis 36.317, 38.6,
    38.207
Cline, S. L. 36.283
Cline, William R. 48.320
Clinton, Catherine 40.421, 42.310, 42.564
Clinton, Robert Lowry 41.269
Clissold, Stephen 33.776–78, 38.686
Clist, Bernard 2.19
Clive, John 1.22, 1.39
Cloché, Paul 6.415
Cloet, Michel 27.144
Clogg, Mary Jo 33.245
Clogg, Richard 33.101, 33.245–51, 33.763
Clokey, Richard M. 42.417
Close, Angela E. 2.13
Clough, Ralph N. 11.693
Clough, Shepard B. 28.211
Clout, Hugh D. 26.277
Clover, Carol J. 20.233
Clover, Frank M. 7.580
Cloward, Richard A. 44.696–97
Clowes, Edith W. 34.264
Clowse, Converse D. 39.409
Clubb, Jerome M. 40.56, 43.543
Clulee, Nicholas H. 4.64, 23.318
Clymer, Kenton J. 43.621, 43.641
Cmiel, Kenneth 40.564, 42.500
Coakley, John 3.461
Coaldrake, William H. 12.210
Coale, Ansley J. 22.452
Coates, Austin 11.737
Coates, John F. 4.503, 6.392
Coates, Kenneth S. 36.38, 36.51
Coates, Peter A. 4.595
Coatsworth, John H. 37.76, 38.208
Cobb, James C. 40.136, 44.243
Cobb, Richard 26.48
Cobban, Alan B. 20.972, 20.1318
Cobban, Alfred 26.19, 26.49
Cobban, Helena 18.497
Cobbing, Julian 19.678–80
Cobble, Dorothy Sue 40.19
Cobet, Justus 6.149
Coble, Parks M. 11.383–84
Coblin, Weldon South 10.44
Cochran, Sherman 11.239, 11.470
Cochran, Terry 29.112
Cochran, Thomas C. 40.158, 42.133,
    42.204, 43.4
Cochrane, Charles Norris 20.1042
Cochrane, Eric W. 28.184, 28.200
Cochrane, Lydia G. 1.419, 25.26–27,
    25.139, 26.47, 28.148
Cochrane, Willard W. 44.170

Connell, R. W. 46.117

Connell-Smith, Gordon 38.45

Connelly, Owen 26.3, 26.89

Conner, Albert Z. 35.352

Conner, Paul W. 39.212

Conners, Jane Frances 3.510

Conniff, Michael L. 37.386, 38.105, 38.333–34, 38.512–13

Connolly, Harold X. 40.337

Connolly, Sean J. 23.423, 24.410–11

Connor, W. Robert 6.79, 6.304, 6.579

Connor, Walker 35.185

Connors, Lesley 13.152

Conover, Helen F. 19.15

Conquest, Robert 35.104, 35.143, 35.186, 35.217, 48.255

Conrad, Alfred H. 42.295

Conrad, David C. 19.126–27

Conrad, Geoffrey W. 3.133, 36.360

Conrad, Lawrence I. 17.484–85, 18.49

Conrad, Robert Edgar 38.514–16, 38.570

Conrad, Susan P. 42.684

Conradt, David P. 31.490

Conroy, Hilary 13.58, 13.253, 14.100, 48.33

Conroy, Jack 43.271

Constable, Archibald 3.275

Constable, Giles 8.118, 20.319–20, 20.973, 20.1155–56, 20.1280

Constable, Pamela 38.688

Constant, Edward W., II 4.570, 43.70

Constant, Stephen 33.99

Constantelos, Demetrios J. 8.359

Constantine VII Porphyrogenitus 8.395

Constantino, Letizia R. 16.329

Constantino, Renato 16.13, 16.329, 16.361

Constas, Dimitri 33.252

Contamine, Henry 47.59

Contamine, Philippe 20.32, 20.309, 20.442, 20.597, 25.150

Contenau, Georges 5.115

Contosta, David R. 43.480

Contreni, John J. 20.128, 20.272, 20.1066

Contreras, Jaime 29.69

Conway, J. S. 31.386, 31.447

Conway, John 5.439

Conze, Edward 15.128

Conze, Werner 1.65, 31.3, 31.105

Conzen, Kathleen Neils 42.233–34

Coogan, John W. 43.598

Cook, Alexandra Parma 37.344

Cook, Alice H. 13.439

Cook, Alta Lind 45.58

Cook, Blanche Wiesen 43.160, 43.378, 44.274

Cook, Chris 48.10

Cook, Edward M., Jr. 39.88

Cook, George A. 39.316

Cook, Harold F. 14.101

Cook, Harold J. 4.690

Cook, J. M. 5.447

Cook, Jeannine 3.152

Cook, Michael A. 17.78, 17.337, 17.379, 17.419

Cook, Noble David 36.391, 36.418, 37.205, 37.344

Cook, R. M. 6.626

Cook, Ramsay 45.184–86

Cook, Sherburne F. 37.202–3, 37.206–8, 37.244, 37.571

Cook, Warren L. 37.572

Cooke, Dorian 33.802

Cooke, Jacob E. 41.539–40

Cooke, James J. 47.226

Cooke, Miriam 18.128

Cook-Radmore, D. 27.158

Coolhaas, W. Ph. 16.3

Coomaraswamy, Ethel M. 15.206

Coomaraswamy, Radhika 15.841

Coombs, Douglas 23.111

Cooney, Terry A. 44.88

Coons, Lorraine 26.352

Coontz, Stephanie 40.312

Coope, A. E. 16.123

Cooper, Adrienne 15.640

Cooper, Carolyn 43.71

Cooper, Donald B. 37.403

Cooper, Eve Marie 20.1160

Cooper, Frederick 19.81, 19.436, 19.474–75, 19.894–95

Cooper, J. P. 22.63, 34.70

Cooper, Jerrold S. 5.38, 5.48

Cooper, John Milton, Jr. 43.5, 43.509, 43.663

Cooper, Julian 35.271, 35.278, 35.293

Cooper, Malcolm 24.388

Cooper, Michael 12.170–71, 12.181

Cooper, Patricia A. 43.154

Cooper, Richard S. 17.333

Cooper, William J., Jr. 40.137, 42.103

Cooperman, Bernard Dov 21.92

Coopersmith, Jonathan 35.459

Coox, Alvin D. 13.294, 35.353, 48.33

Copeland, William R. 32.261

Copenhaver, Brian P. 28.64

Copleston, Frederick C. 20.974, 22.387

Copp, Terry 45.219

Coppa, Frank J. 28.206, 28.212, 28.267–68, 28.278–79, 28.353

Copper, John F. 11.36

Coquery-Vidrovitch, Catherine 19.12, 19.590–91, 19.829

Coquillette, Daniel R. 39.288

Corbett, Percy Ellwood 7.70

Corbin, Alain 26.248, 26.396

Corbin, David Alan 43.164

Corbin, Henry 17.473

Corcos, David 18.359

Cordeiro, Daniel Raposo 37.32

Cordell, Dennis D. 19.53–54, 19.264, 19.546, 19.896, 19.940

Cordell, Linda S. 36.75

Cordesman, Anthony 48.505

Cordier, Henri 3.304

Córdoba de la Llave, Ricardo 20.810

Cordy-Collins, Alana 2.105

Corfield, Penelope J. 15.596, 23.145, 23.231

Corish, Patrick J. 23.424

Corke, Bettina 38.8

Corkran, David H. 39.542–43

Corley, T.A.B. 26.124

Cormack, Robin 8.435

Corn, Joseph J. 4.571

Cornelius, Janet Duitsman 42.327

Cornelius, Wayne A. 38.106, 38.211–12

Cornell, Laurel L. 12.268–70

Cornell, Richard 32.236

Cornell, Stephen 36.164

Cornell, Vincent J. 17.198, 17.439

Corner, Paul 28.410

Cornet, Joseph 19.634

Corni, Gustavo 31.438

Cornish, Dudley T. 42.756

Cornish, W. R. 24.76

Corns, Thomas N. 23.339

Cornwall, Mark 31.339

Coronel, Gustavo 38.475

Corput, Jeannette C. van de 13.259

Corrigan, Eileen 36.289

Corrigan, John 39.664, 41.341

Corris, Peter 46.350

Corrsin, Stephen D. 21.177

Corsa, Leslie, Jr. 22.444

Corsi, Pietro 4.2

Corsi, Susan 28.205

Cortada, James W 4.541, 29.5, 29.203, 29.261, 40.618

Cortazzi, Hugh 13.103, 13.108

Cortés, Hernán 36.285, 37.117

Cortés Conde, Roberto 38.9, 38.107

Cortesao, Armando 16.67

Corti, Egon Caesar Conti 47.175

Corvisier, André 22.242

Corwin, Arthur F. 38.30

Corwin, Edward Samuel 40.38

Cosenza, Mario Emilio 13.258, 28.7

Coser, Lewis A. 1.121, 44.703

Cosgrove, Art 20.514

Cosío Villegas, Daniel 38.213

Costa, Emilia Viotti da 38.517

Costa Gomes, Rita 20.920

Costelloe, M. Joseph 20.1010

Costeloe, Michael P. 29.217

Costerveen,Karla 42.651

Costigliola, Frank 48.111

Costin, Lela B. 44.275

Cote, Louis-Marie 45.3

Cotkin, George 43.481

Cotler, Julio 38.46

Cott, Nancy F. 41.509, 42.566, 42.625, 44.276, 44.323, 44.329, 44.348

Cottam, Richard 18.572

Cottereau, Alain 26.353

Cotterell, Brian 4.380

Cottrell, Alvin J. 18.539

Dolan, Claire 25.155
Dolan, Jay P. 40.511, 42.480
Dolan, John T. 20.1095, 22.406
Dölger, Franz 8.1, 8.69–70, 8.258
Dolkart, Ronald H. 38.608
Dollar, Charles M. 1.102
Dolley, Michael 20.517
Dollimore, Jonathan 23.342
Dollinger, Philippe 20.634, 20.640
Dols, Michael W. 17.486–87
Dolukhanov, Paul M. 2.75
Domandi, Mario 22.165, 28.228
Domar, Evsey 34.232
Domenico, Roy Palmer 28.453
Domergue-Cloarec, Danielle 19.934,
Domes, Jürgen 11.33, 11.584–85
Dominguez, Jorge I. 1.488, 38.31, 38.353
Domínguez Ortiz, Antonio 29.6, 29.71–
  73, 29.171–72
Domonkos, L. S. 33.382
Dömötör, Tekla 33.334
Donagan, Alan 1.52, 1.240, 1.281
Donagan, Barbara L. 1.52
Donaghy, Peter J. 29.325
Donahue, Charles, Jr. 20.1221
Donald, David 42.31, 42.828
Donald, P. J. 8.37
Donaldson, Gordon 23.377
Donegan, Jane 42.613–14
Donham, Donald L. 19.339–40
Donia, Robert J. 33.685
Donkin, R. A. 20.375
Donnan, Elizabeth 22.249
Donnelly, Alton S. 9.276
Donnelly, Jack 48.562
Donnelly, Marian Card 39.820
Donner, Fred M. 17.54, 17.68, 17.79–80,
  17.115
Donovan, Peter Williams 11.388
Donovan, Robert J. 44.554–55
Dontas, Domna N. 47.129
Donzelot, Jacques 22.457
Doolin, Dennis J. 11.288, 11.586
Doornbos, Martin R. 19.477
Dopsch, Heinz 20.641
Doran, Susan 23.176
Dore, Elizabeth 38.452
Doré, Henry 11.307
Dore, Ronald P. 12.217, 12.290, 13.60,
  13.218, 13.235, 13.333, 13.413–14
Dorey, T. A. 7.259
Dorfman, Joseph 40.552
Dorigo, Wladimiro 7.567
Dorman, Robert L. 44.244
Dorn, Walter Louis 22.64, 30.110
Dorner, Peter 38.112
Dorpalen, Andreas 31.26, 31.259, 31.361
Dorson, Richard M. 40.592–94
Dorwart, Reinhold August 30.111–12
Dossal, Mariam 15.567
Dostert, Paul 27.206
Dothan, Trude 5.306

Dotzauer, Winfried 31.6
Doubman, J. Russell 43.36
Doucet, Roger 25.156
Doughtie, Edward 23.343
Doughty, Paul L. 36.412, 37.78
Douglas, Ann 40.429, 42.567
Douglas, David C. 20.490–91, 20.518
Douglas, Mary 1.120
Douglas, Ngaire 46.289
Douglas, Norman 46.289
Douglas, Richard M. 28.164
Douglas, Susan J. 4.532
Douglass, Elisha P. 41.150
Douglass, Frederick 42.516
Douglass, Jane Dempsey 22.131
Douglass, William A. 28.343, 29.291
Douie, Decima L. 20.1192
Doukas 8.397
Doumani, Beshara B. 18.498
Doumas, Christos G. 6.176
Dover, K. J. 6.71, 6.567
Dow, F. D. 23.378
Dow, Sterling 6.328
Dowd, Gregory Evans 36.94
Dowe, Dieter 22.541
Dower, John W. 12.2, 12.199, 13.9,
  13.114, 13.297, 13.334, 48.227
Downey, Glanville 7.456, 8.133
Downing, Antoinette F. 39.821
Downs, A.H.C. 20.1477
Dowson, John 15.208
Doyle, Don H. 43.184
Doyle, William 22.65, 25.235, 25.373,
  26.50–51
Dozier, Craig L. 38.325
Dozier, Edward P. 36.218
Dozon, Auguste 9.294
Drabble, John H. 16.241
Drachkovitch, Milorad M. 22.323
Drachmann, A. G. 4.374
Dragnich, Alex N. 33.732, 33.793
Drake, Fred W. 11.308
Drake, Frederick C. 43.645
Drake, Michael 32.93
Drake, Paul W. 38.113, 38.114, 38.690
Drake, Richard 28.365
Drake, St. Clair 44.409
Drake, Stillman 4.87
Draper, Theodore 44.701–2, 44.854
Dray, William H. 1.53, 1.241–42, 1.269,
  1.282, 1.359
Drège, Jean-Pierre 11.241
Dreifort, John E. 48.154
Dreisziger, Nándor F. 33.393, 33.414
Drekmeier, Charles 15.156
Drescher, Seymour 24.447
Dresden, Arnold 4.44
Drew, Philip 13.571
Drewes, G.W.J. 16.99
Drews, Robert 6.177, 6.197, 6.480
Drexel, John 3.12
Drexhage, Hans-Joachim 6.7

Dreyer, Edward L. 10.356
Dreyer, June Teufel 11.637
Dreze, Jean 19.883
Drifte, Reinhard 13.378, 13.398
Drijvers, H.J.W. 7.113
Drijvers, Jan Wilhelm 5.434
Drinkwater, John F. 7.436, 7.607–8,
  20.140
Drinnon, Richard 43.322, 43.395
Driver, J. E. Stapleton 9.83
Dronke, Peter 20.977, 20.1284, 20.1419–
  21
Drouot, Henri 25.157
Drower, Margaret S. 5.553, 5.583
Droysen, Johann Gustav 1.344
Drucker, Philip 36.219
Drukier, Bolesław 33.591
Drummond, Gordon D. 31.504
Drummond, Helga 9.229, 17.282
Drummond, Ian M. 45.212, 45.247,
  48.134
Drummond, Richard Henry 13.529
Drummond, Stuart 9.229, 17.282
Drury, John 26.367, 38.565
Dryer, Ronald 1.489
Drysdale, Alasdair 18.48
Du Bois, W.E.B. 3.204, 42.829
Du Boulay, F.R.H. 20.615, 20.642
Duara, Prasenjit 11.90
Dubar, Claude 18.397
Dubbert, Joe L. 40.468
Dübeck, Inger 32.132
Duben, Alan 18.268
Duberman, Martin 42.517
Dublin, Thomas 4.627, 40.456, 42.601–2
Dubofsky, Melvyn 40.252, 43.109–10,
  44.218
DuBois, Ellen Carol 42.585, 42.596,
  43.328, 43.347, 43.372, 43.379, 44.300,
  44.314, 44.332
Dubow, Saul 19.748
Dubs, Homer H. 10.238
Duby, Georges 7.397, 20.66–67, 20.98,
  20.100, 20.107, 20.120, 20.279, 20.353–
  54, 20.445–48, 25.39, 25.329–30, 26.380,
  26.385
Duchen, Claire 26.398
Duchesne-Guillemin, Jacques 5.484
Ducker, James H. 42.422
Duckett, Eleanor Shipley 20.1005,
  20.1067
Dudden, Arthur Power 40.621
Dudden, Faye E. 42.603
Duddington, Natalie 34.71
Duden, Barbara 30.155
Due, John F. 4.468
Due-Nielsen, Carsten 32.238
Duff, Wilson 36.54
Duff Gordon, Lucie 18.141
Duffin, Lorna 23.287
Duffy, John 4.657, 4.692, 4.772, 8.89,
  8.379, 39.800

Echols, Alice 44.277
Echols, Anne 20.19
Eck, Alexandre 34.200
Eckenstein, Lina 20.1504
Eckert, Carter J. 14.7, 14.121
Eckes, Alfred E., Jr. 48.321
Eckhardt, Celia Morris 42.586
Eckhoff, Frederic C. 28.170
Eckstein, Arthur M. 7.226
Ecsedy, Hilda 9.127
Edbury, Peter W. 20.329, 20.840–41
Eddie, Scott M. 31.303
Edel, Elmar 5.391
Edel, Leon 1.462
Edelberg, Cynthia Dubin 41.126
Edelman, Robert 34.140, 34.270
Edelstein, Joel C. 38.101
Edelstein, Michael 47.210
Eder, W. 7.163
Edgar, C. C. 6.136
Edgerton, William F. 5.584
Edgren, Lars 32.17, 32.365
Edinger, Lewis J. 31.514
Edmonds, Richard Louis 11.5
Edmonds, Robin 48.411
Edmondson, C. Earl 31.395
Edmondson, Linda H. 34.138, 34.281
Edmonson, Munro S. 37.404
Edmunds, R. David 36.95, 36.131, 41.311,
    42.447
Edsall, Mary D. 44.596
Edsall, Thomas Byrne 44.595–96
Edwards, E. W. 47.258
Edwards, G. Thomas 40.184
Edwards, George W. 40.215
Edwards, I.E.S. 5.2, 5.315, 5.326–27,
    5.350–52, 5.528, 5.536, 5.547–48, 5.553,
    5.558, 5.566, 5.571–72, 5.574, 5.576,
    5.581, 5.583, 5.586, 5.589, 5.610
Edwards, Jill 29.263
Edwards, John 21.93, 29.33
Edwards, Kathleen 20.1133
Edwards, Lovett F. 33.1, 33.740
Edwards, Mark U., Jr. 30.21, 30.33
Edwards, Nancy 20.225
Edwards, Paul 1.66, 19.160, 33.483, 41.484
Edwards, R. Randle 11.88
Edwards, Richard C. 40.254, 44.219
Edwards, Robert W. 8.234
Edwards, Ruth Dudley 24.418
Edwards, Stewart 26.145
Edwards, Walter 12.27
Edzard, Dietz Otto 5.49, 5.147
Eeghen, I. H. van 27.124
Effenterre, Henri van 6.178, 6.437
Effra, Helmut von 41.444
Egan, Clifford L. 41.298
Egan, Ronald C. 10.201, 10.312
Egbert, Virginia Wylie 20.402
Egerbladh, Inez 32.94
Egerton, George W. 47.433
Eggan, Fred 36.220

Egge, Bjorn 48.291
Eggermont, P.H.L. 15.170
Egnal, Marc 41.60
Egret, Jean 25.236
Eguchi, Paul Kazuhisa 10.330
Ehalt, Hubert Ch. 31.304
Ehlers, Eckart 17.5
Ehmer, Josef 31.141
Ehrenberg, Margaret R. 2.90
Ehrenberg, Richard 22.250
Ehrenberg, Victor 6.213, 6.366, 6.451
Ehrenkreutz, Andrew S. 17.241
Ehrenreich, Barbara 44.9, 44.75
Ehret, Christopher 19.56, 19.388
Ehrhard, Albert 8.380
Ehrich, Robert W. 15.78, 15.80
Ehrlich, Cyril 24.211, 24.313
Ehrlich, Paul R. 3.311
Ehrlich, Richard 42.605
Ehrman, John 24.14
Eich, Ulrike 47.46
Eichelberg, M. 21.34, 21.228
Eichenberg, Richard 48.412
Eichengreen, Barry 48.135
Eichler, Barry L. 5.168
Eickelman, Dale F. 3.285, 17.69
Eidelberg, Philip Gabriel 33.636
Eidlin, Fred H. 33.156
Einarsson, Ingimar 32.311
Einhorn, Eric S. 32.239
Eire, Carlos M. N. 30.276
Eisenberg, Peter L. 38.529
Eisenhower, John S. D. 42.69
Eisenstadt, S. N. 3.109, 3.187, 3.435,
    18.465
Eisenstein, Elizabeth L. 22.172, 28.239
Eisenstein, Sarah 43.357
Eisinger, Peter K. 44.370
Eisler, Benita 44.333
Ekejiuba, Felicia 19.159
Ekholm, Kajsa 19.547
Ekirch, A. Roger 39.217, 39.454
Eklof, Ben 34.233, 34.352
Ekrich, Arthur A., Jr. 43.7
Eksteins, Modris 22.528, 31.362
El Saadawi, Nawal 18.134
Elat, Moshe 5.284
Elazar, Daniel 40.107
Elbaum, Bernard 24.113
Elbert, Sarah 42.719
Elcock, Howard 47.434
Eldredge, Elizabeth A. 19.686–89
Eldridge, C. C. 24.463, 47.211
Eley, Geoff 1.406, 31.174, 31.208, 31.227,
    31.241
Elfasi, M. 19.128, 19.132
El-Hibri, Tayyeb 17.146
Eliade, Mircea 1.195, 3.488, 9.51, 15.129
Elias, Ney 9.255
Elias, Norbert 22.251, 30.277
Elias, Peter Douglas 36.20

Elias, Robert H. 44.10
Eliot, Charles 13.514
Elison, George 12.155–57, 12.160, 12.167,
    12.174, 12.182–83
Elisséeff, Nikita 17.242
Elkin, Judith Laikin 38.116
Elkins, Sharon K. 20.1505
Elkins, Stanley 40.121, 42.279
Elkiss, T. H. 19.646
Elleinstein, Jean 3.464
Ellem, Elizabeth Wood 46.383
Ellenson, David H. 21.138
Elliott, Bruce S. 45.90
Elliott, Emory 39.668, 40.532
Elliott, H. M. 15.208
Elliott, John H. 3.157, 22.67–68, 29.7–8,
    29.62, 29.74–77, 37.79–80, 37.117
Elliott, Marianne 26.48
Ellis, Charles Howard 47.370
Ellis, David Maldwyn 40.159
Ellis, Harold A. 25.103
Ellis, Ieuan 24.280
Ellis, J. R. 6.227
Ellis, Jack D. 26.146
Ellis, John Tracy 39.669
Ellis, Joseph J. 39.588, 41.445, 41.544
Ellis, Lewis Ethan 44.726
Ellis, Maria de J. 5.63, 5.121, 5.133, 5.143
Ellis, Richard E. 41.274, 42.79
Ellis, Stephen 19.690
Ellis, Steven G. 23.426–27
Ellison, Herbert J. 48.528
Ellner, Steve 38.477
Ellsworth, Scott 44.422
Ellwood, Robert S. 13.505
Ellwood, Sheelagh M. 29.264, 29.298
Elman, Benjamin A. 11.310–11
Elon, Amos 18.466
Elphick, Richard 19.647–48, 19.734
Elphinstone, Mountstuart 15.771
Elridge, Sally 46.290
Elrod, Richard B. 47.8, 47.146
Elson, R. E. 16.290–91
Elson, Ruth 42.672
Elteto, Louis J. 33.391
Eltis, David 19.899, 22.252
Elton, Arthur 4.635
Elton, Geoffrey R. 1.8, 1.490, 22.69,
    23.17–19
Elton, Hugh 7.608, 20.140
Elvin, Mark 10.6, 10.37, 10.298, 10.350,
    11.186
Elwitt, Sanford 26.147
Elwood, Ralph Carter 35.144
Ely, Melvin Patrick 44.410
Embree, Ainslie T. 13.1, 15.49, 15.464,
    15.667
Embree, John F. 13.233
Emden, A. B. 20.1336
Emerson, Donald E. 28.240, 31.126
Emery, Walter Bryan 5.549
Emmanuel, Arghiri 48.554

Geiger, Wilhelm 15.206, 15.249
Geikie, Roderick 27.75
Geisberg, Max 30.282
Geison, Gerald L. 4.174, 4.207, 24.355, 26.339
Geiss, Imanuel 3.466, 47.178–79, 47.340
Geist, Christopher D. 40.566
Gelas, Louis 11.376
Gelb, Ignace J. 5.4, 5.65, 5.117–18, 5.134, 5.146–47, 5.151
Gelb, Joyce 44.280
Gelb, Leslie H. 48.530
Gelbart, Nina Rattner 25.108
Gelber, Carol 19.243
Gelder, H. A. Enno van 27.58
Gelderen, Martin van 27.23, 27.33
Gelfand, Mark I. 44.612
Gelfand, Toby 4.781
Gélis, Jacques 4.809
Gellately, Robert 31.245, 31.460
Gelling, Margaret 20.211
Gellman, Irwin F. 48.159
Gellner, Ernest 3.42, 17.55, 18.365–66, 22.389, 29.243
Gelzer, Matthias 7.188, 7.272
Gemery, Henry A. 19.903
Gemzell, Carl-Axel 32.20
Gendzier, Irene L. 18.134
Genet, Jean-Philippe 20.282, 20.310
Genicot, Léopold 20.6, 20.72, 27.4, 27.12
Genière, Juliette de la 8.242
Genovese, Eugene D. 40.139, 42.281–82, 42.299, 42.333–34
Gentleman, Judith 38.212
Gentles, Ian 23.114
George, Agnes 15.475
George, Alexander L. 35.170
George, M. Dorothy 23.237
George, Peter 40.234
George, Wilma 4.48
Georgescu, Vlad 33.638–39
Georgevitch [Djordjević], Tihomir R. 33.718
Gerard, David 25.30
Gerardi, Pamela 5.77, 5.108
Gerber, David A. 40.411, 42.238, 42.255, 42.268, 43.281
Gerber, Haim 18.50, 18.139, 18.183
Gerber, Jane S. 21.226
Gerber, Margy 31.534
Gerberding, Richard A. 20.187
Gerbet, Marie-Claude 20.815
Gerbi, Antonello 3.160, 37.406
Gerevich, László 33.339
Gerger, Torvald 32.386
Gerhard, Dietrich 3.372, 30.118
Gerhard, Peter 37.10–12, 37.329
Gerhart, Gail M. 19.753
Gerlach, Don R. 41.554, 41.562
Gerlach, Larry R. 41.387
Germino, Dante L. 28.423

Gernet, Jacques 10.23, 10.109, 10.303, 11.313
Gernet, Louis 6.371, 6.454, 6.552
Gernsheim, Alison 22.501
Gernsheim, Helmut 22.501
Gero, Joan M. 2.4
Gero, Stephen 8.152–53
Gerrard, Timothy 19.214
Gerrity, Michael 18.527
Gerschenkron, Alexander 3.416, 28.338, 31.76, 33.107
Gersh, Stephen 20.1046–47
Gershevitch, Ilya 5.425, 5.427, 5.480, 5.612, 6.239, 9.105
Gershoni, Israel 18.311
Gershoy, Leo 22.73
Gerstle, C. Andrew 12.297
Gerstle, Gary 44.223, 44.504, 44.597, 44.622
Gerstner, Jonathan Neil 19.649
Gerteis, Klaus 30.256
Gerth, Hans H. 1.376, 5.300, 10.66
Gertzel, Cherry 19.481
Gerulaitis, Leonardas Vytautas 28.57
Gervais, Raymond 19.940
Gervers, Michael 17.391, 20.328
Gesick, Lorraine 16.15
Getty, Ian A. L. 36.55
Getty, J. Arch 35.108–9, 35.335
Getzler, Israel 35.65
Geuss, Herbert 47.153
Gevitz, Norman 4.716
Gewehr, Wesley M. 39.675, 41.344
Geyer, Dietrich 34.186
Geyer, Michael 48.191
Geyl, Pieter 1.146, 26.92, 27.15, 27.34, 27.59–60
Ghalioungui, Paul 4.666, 5.533
Ghazzali, Abu Hamid al- 17.412
Ghellinck, Joseph de 20.1291
Ghirshman, Roman 5.428, 5.518, 9.90
Ghisalberti, Alberto M. 28.1, 28.280
Ghosh, Arun 2.40, 15.507
Ghoshal, U. N. 15.90, 15.142, 15.157
Ghosheh, Zaki R. 18.17
Ghurye, G. S. 15.91, 15.196
Giardina, A. 7.235
Gibb, Hamilton A. R. 9.159, 17.20, 17.27, 17.117–18, 17.156, 17.235, 17.243–46, 17.381, 17.464, 18.90
Gibbens, Byrd 42.415
Gibbon, Edward 8.111
Gibbs, Donald A. 11.7
Gibbs, Donald L. 37.178
Gibbs, Graham C. 27.127–28
Giblin, James L. 19.441, 19.939
Gibney, Frank 13.39
Gibson, Charles 36.98, 36.287, 37.34, 37.82, 37.121
Gibson, James R. 39.335
Gibson, James W. 44.837

Gibson, Margaret T. 20.1048, 20.1070, 20.1292
Gibson, McGuire 5.5, 8.268
Gibson, Ralph 26.326
Giddings, Paula 40.341, 44.357
Giddy, Lisa 5.534
Gidwani, N. N. 15.3
Giedion, Siegfried 4.406, 4.634
Gienapp, William E. 42.10
Gierke, Otto 22.181
Giesberg, Robert I. 47.154
Giesey, Ralph E. 20.816, 25.133, 25.160–61, 25.164
Gieysztor, Aleksander 33.472
Giffard, Ann 32.264
Gifford, Prosser 19.278, 47.231–32, 48.311–12
Giglio, James N. 44.556
Gijswijt-Hofstra, Marijke 27.94
Gil, Federico G. 38.693–94
Gil, Moshe 17.184, 21.29
Giladi, Avner 17.313
Gilbar, G. G. 18.577–78
Gilberg, Trond 33.640–41
Gilbert, Alan D. 24.288, 46.22
Gilbert, Arthur N. 1.491
Gilbert, Basil 22.597
Gilbert, Bentley B. 24.53, 24.217
Gilbert, Creighton 22.285
Gilbert, Dennis L. 38.454
Gilbert, Felix 1.24, 1.26, 28.73–74, 31.23, 41.257
Gilbert, G. Nigel 1.512
Gilbert, James B. 43.447, 44.90–92
Gilbert, Joan 17.421
Gilbert, John 37.112
Gilbert, Martin 3.230, 18.13, 24.54, 28.297, 34.50, 48.23, 48.273
Gilbert, Neal W. 20.1371
Gilbert, Stuart 8.438, 26.80
Gilby, Thomas 20.1406
Gilchrist, John T. 20.329, 20.1225
Gildea, Robert 22.327, 26.291
Gilderhus, Mark T. 38.50, 43.610–11
Gildrie, Richard P. 39.369
Giles, H. A. 3.286
Giliomee, Hermann 19.648
Gilje, Paul A. 41.388
Gill, Graeme 35.27, 35.110
Gill, Joseph 8.363, 20.1093, 28.155
Gillard, David 18.51, 47.260
Gille, Bertrand 4.392
Gillespie, Charles Guy 38.739
Gillespie, James A. 46.80
Gillespie, Michael Allen 41.196
Gillespie, Raymond 23.418, 23.430
Gillespie, Richard 29.305, 38.614
Gillett, M. C. 15.772
Gillett, Paula 24.305
Gillette, Howard, Jr. 43.175–76
Gilliam, Harriet 1.307

Hallett, Judith P. 7.136
Hallett, Robin 19.152
Halleux, Robert 4.67
Hallewell, L. 38.544
Halliday, Jon 13.158
Hallman, Barbara McClung 28.166
Hallmark, R. E. 25.23
Hallo, William W. 5.7, 5.50, 5.67, 5.160, 5.173, 5.274
Hallock, R. T. 5.480
Hallwood, Paul 48.557
Halpenny, Frances G. 45.5
Halperin, Charles J. 9.212, 34.171–72, 34.282
Halperin, S. William 28.318, 47.147
Halperín-Donghi, Tulio 38.129, 38.618
Halpern, Baruch 5.251
Halpern, Ben 18.471
Halphen, Louis 22.28
Halsband, Robert 18.154
Halsberghe, Gaston H. 7.98
Halsey, Frank D. 20.303
Halttunen, Karen 42.712
Haltzel, Michael H. 29.407, 32.403, 48.454
Halveti, Tosun Bayrak al-Jerrahi al- 17.435
Halvorsen, Solveig 32.218
Hamabata, Matthews Masayuki 13.416
Hamalainen, Pekka Kalevi 32.266
Hamann, Brigitte 31.294
Hambis, Louis 9.226
Hambly, Gavin 9.76, 15.334, 18.562
Hambrick-Stowe, Charles E. 39.683
Hambro, Edvard 48.71
Hamburg, Gary M. 34.135, 34.143, 34.163
Hamburger, Joseph 24.335
Hamby, Alonzo L. 44.506, 44.560
Hamed bin Muhammed 19.443
Hamel, Bernard 20.737
Hamelin, Jean 45.222–23, 45.307
Hameln, Glückel of 21.95
Hamer, David A. 46.252
Hamerly, Michael T. 37.509
Hamerow, Theodore S. 22.331, 31.128, 31.196–97
Hames, Peter 33.162
Hamill, Hugh M., Jr. 38.228
Hamilton, Alistair 29.86
Hamilton, Annie 20.158
Hamilton, Bernard 8.324, 20.842, 20.1162
Hamilton, Carolyn Anne 19.694
Hamilton, Charles D. 6.216
Hamilton, Charles V. 44.407
Hamilton, Earl J. 29.87–88, 29.176
Hamilton, George Heard 22.502, 22.590, 34.409
Hamilton, Holman 42.114
Hamilton, J. R. 3.112, 6.233, 6.247
Hamilton, James Russell 9.133
Hamilton, John D. B. 6.552

Hamilton, Kerry 22.485
Hamilton, Michael P. 40.692
Hamilton, Nora 38.229–30
Hamlin, Christopher 4.776
Hamm, Charles 40.541
Hamm, Michael F. 34.253
Hammack, David C. 43.531
Hammarneh, Saleh K. 17.119
Hammel, Eugene A. 1.402
Hammen, Oscar J. 31.163
Hammer, Ellen J. 16.194
Hammer-Purgstall, J. 9.278
Hammond, Bray 42.217
Hammond, Mason 3.97
Hammond, Michael 1.246
Hammond, N.G.L. 6.21, 6.32, 6.165, 6.248, 6.430–31
Hammond, Norman 2.39
Hammond, Peter 33.263
Hammond, Philip C. 5.209
Hammond, R. J. 47.235
Hammond, Thomas 33.24
Hamnett, Brian R. 37.510, 38.231
Hamon, Hervé 26.212
Hamori, Andras 17.382
Hamori, Ruth 17.382
Hamouda, O. F. 1.394
Hampe, Karl 20.692
Hampson, Norman 22.185, 26.55
Hampsten, Elizabeth 42.415
Hamrin, Carol Lee 11.672
Hamscher, Albert N. 25.206–7
Han, Fei Tzu 10.86
Han, Sungjoo 14.132
Han, Woo-keun 14.9
Han, Yu-shan 10.17
Hanagan, Michael 26.357, 31.250, 40.753
Hanak, Harry 47.382
Hanák, Péter 20.59, 33.340
Hanawalt, Barbara A. 4.630, 20.376–77, 22.257
Hanbury-Tenison, Sarah 20.34, 31.65
Hancock, Ian 33.14
Hancock, William Keith 19.761, 24.450, 28.282, 46.23, 46.177, 48.231
Handcock, W. Gordon 45.67
Handel, Michael I. 48.36
Handelman, Howard 38.457
Handelsman, Marceli 33.474
Handler, Andrew 17.224, 33.341
Handler, Jerome S. 39.516–17
Handler, Richard 45.308
Handlin, Joanna F. 10.154
Handlin, Mary Flug 42.156
Handlin, Oscar 21.254, 39.104, 39.160, 39.697, 40.160, 40.372, 41.352, 42.156, 42.241, 43.62, 43.246, 43.480, 44.547
Hands, A. R. 6.554
Handy, Jim 38.316
Hane, Mikiso 12.13, 12.314, 13.41, 13.65, 13.236, 13.305, 13.441
Haneda, Masashi 18.226

Hanfmann, George, M. A. 5.409
Hanham, H. J. 24.18, 24.434
Hanisch, Ernst 31.406
Hanke, Lewis 36.103, 36.330, 37.15, 37.143–44, 37.158–59, 37.333, 37.349
Hankins, James 28.39, 28.65
Hankins, Thomas L. 4.15
Hanks, Lucien M. 16.177
Hanley, Sarah 25.134, 25.357
Hanley, Susan B. 12.225, 12.237, 12.271, 13.30
Hanlon, David 46.329
Hanlon, Joseph 19.600
Hann, John H. 37.580
Hanna, William S. 39.224
Hannah, Leslie 24.116
Hannaway, Owen 4.158
Hanneman, Robert A. 4.799
Hannestad, Niels 7.300
Hanrieder, Wolfram F. 48.455
Hans, Nicholas Adolph 34.353
Hansel, Alfred von 22.49
Hansen, Bent 18.52
Hansen, Chad 10.80
Hansen, Chadwick 39.684
Hansen, Edward C. 29.308
Hansen, Erik 27.232, 27.259
Hansen, Esther V. 6.262
Hansen, Holger Bernt 19.483
Hansen, James R. 4.573
Hansen, Karen Tranberg 19.859
Hansen, Marcus Lee 40.373, 42.251
Hansen, Mogens Herman 6.330–31, 6.374–75
Hansen, Per H. 32.241
Hansen, Roger D. 38.232
Hansen, Valerie 10.122
Hansman, John 5.453, 18.249
Hanson, Alice M. 31.150
Hanson, Carl A. 29.359
Hanson, Harlan P. 31.348
Hanson, Laurence 23.30
Hanson, Victor Davis 6.519–20
Hansson, Carola 35.307–8
Hao, Yen-p'ing 11.245–46
Haque, Ziaul 17.335
Harada, Kumao 13.301
Harada, Minoru 13.573
Haraguchi, Torao 12.219
Haran, Menahem 5.278, 5.293
Haraszti, Eva H. 48.216
Haraway, Donna 4.208
Harbaugh, William H. 43.513, 44.525
Harbert, Earl N. 41.264
Harbeson, John W. 19.344
Harbison, E. Harris 22.186
Harbison, Mark A. 13.412
Harbison, Winfred A. 40.78
Harbottle, Michael 48.291
Harbsmeier, Christoph 11.522
Harbutt, Fraser J. 48.372
Harcourt, Freda 3.233

Inden, Ronald B. 15.20, 15.259
Inder Singh, Anita 15.733
Ingham, John N. 43.28
Ingle, Harold N. 47.85
Ingleson, John 16.297
Inglis, G. Douglas 37.522
Inglis, K. S. 24.275, 46.22, 46.151, 46.164
Ingram, Edward 47.86–87
Ingram, James C. 16.171
Ingram, Martin 23.300
Ingram, Norman 48.92
Ingrao, Charles W. 30.121–23
Inikori, J. E. 19.904–5
Inkster, Ian 4.620
Innes, Jocasta 27.272
Innes, Stephen 39.457–58, 39.506, 41.430
Innis, Harold A. 45.130
Inoguchi, Takashi 13.202
Inoue, Kyoko 13.339
Inscoe, John C. 42.286
Insler, S. 5.488
Ionescu, Ghiţa 33.650
Ionescu-Pârâu, Adriana 33.633
Iongh, R. C. de 16.107
Ip, David Fu-keung 11.9
Ippolito, Dennis S. 44.639
Iram, Yaacov 32.431
Irby, Adelina Paulina 33.720
Irie, Hiroshi 12.256
Iriye, Akira 1.495, 13.261–63, 13.308,
    40.631, 40.675, 40.743, 44.732, 44.771,
    47.299, 48.157, 48.531
Irokawa, Daikichi 13.133
Irons, Peter H. 44.392, 44.526–27
Irschick, Eugene F. 15.710
Irvine, Janice M. 44.137
Irvine, Keith 36.499
Irvine, William 15.417
Irvine, William D. 26.157–58
Irving, Robert Grant 15.468
Irving, T. H. 46.117
Irwin, George J. 1.50
Irwin, Graham W. 3.21, 16.245
Irwin, Joyce L. 22.135
Irwin, Paul 19.65
Irwin, Robert 17.293
Irwin, Terence 6.610
Isaac, Benjamin 6.182, 6.485, 7.318
Isaac, Rhys 39.149
Isaacman, Allen F. 19.66, 19.696, 19.765–
    66
Isaacman, Barbara 19.765–66
Isaacson, Walter 44.808
Isacson, Maths 32.78
Isager, Signe 6.375
Isbell, Billie Jean 36.414
Isern, Thomas D. 43.53
Isherwood, Robert M. 25.70, 25.114
Ishida, Takeshi 13.360, 13.417
Ishida, Tomoo 5.253, 5.287, 5.305
Ishii, Ryōsuke 12.106, 12.274
Ishii, Susumu 12.75

Ishii, Yoneo 16.172
Ishimoto, Shidzue 13.443
Ishino, Iwao 13.216
Isichei, Elizabeth 24.290
Isidore of Charax 3.257
Islam, M. Mufakharul 15.513
Islam, Sirajul 15.514
Islami, A. Reza S. 18.543
Ismael, Tareq Y. 18.61
Ismail Hussain, D. 16.123
Isocrates 6.92
Israel, Jerry 43.627
Israel, John 11.410–11
Israel, Jonathan I. 3.190, 21.97, 21.101,
    23.119, 27.63, 27.64, 27.97, 37.267,
    37.350
Israel, Paul 4.519, 4.534
Issawi, Charles P. 18.62–63, 18.275,
    18.404, 18.581
Issel, William 40.188, 43.212
Isser, Natalie 26.125
Isserman, Maurice 44.692
Isusov, Mito 33.113
Iswolsky, Helene 25.40
Itaska, Gen 13.3
Ito, Hirobumi 13.116
Ito, Miyoji 13.116
Itoh, Hiroshi 13.481
Itzkowitz, Norman 18.194, 18.217, 18.295
Ivanov, P. P. 9.291
Ivanov, Viascheslav V. 9.31
Iverson, Margaret 1.347
Iverson, Peter 36.177
Ives, E. W. 23.42, 23.279
Ives, John W. 36.1
Ivie, Robert L. 41.299
Iwao, Seichi 12.172
Iwata, Masakazu 13.94
Iyad, Abu 18.505
Iyer, Raghavan 15.469
Izenberg, Gerald N. 22.405, 22.612

Jaarsveld, Floris A. van 19.813
Jabs, Wolfgang 22.597
Jachimczyk, Maciej 21.172
Jack Simmons 19.438
Jäckel, Eberhard 31.422, 48.178
Jackson, David 17.249
Jackson, Donald 36.125, 42.370, 42.378
Jackson, Erika 20.660
Jackson, Gabriel 29.268
Jackson, George 34.4
Jackson, Gordon 4.513
Jackson, Guida M. 3.516
Jackson, Harvey H. 39.164, 41.599
Jackson, Henry F. 18.370
Jackson, Hugh R. 46.184
Jackson, Jack 37.582
Jackson, Julian 26.159–60
Jackson, Kenneth T. 40.6, 40.279, 40.280,
    43.229, 44.424, 44.640
Jackson, Luther P. 42.360

Jackson, Marion 47.338, 47.461
Jackson, Marvin R. 33.36
Jackson, Peter 3.300, 9.213, 9.260–61,
    18.229, 20.332
Jackson, Ralph 4.669
Jackson, Richard A. 25.136
Jackson, W.T.H. 20.660, 20.978
Jackson, Walter A. 44.413
Jacob, Ernest F. 20.557, 20.1324
Jacob, Margaret C. 23.324, 27.130–31
Jacob, Philip E. 44.787
Jacobitti, Edmund E. 28.367
Jacobs, Auke Pieter 37.140
Jacobs, Charles M. 22.141
Jacobs, Dan N. 11.529
Jacobs, Gloria 44.9
Jacobs, Harriet A. 42.336
Jacobs, J. Bruce 11.10, 11.697
Jacobs, Louis 21.186
Jacobs, Noah Jonathan 21.167
Jacobs, Travis Beal 32.271
Jacobs, Wilbur R. 36.105, 39.548
Jacobsen, Gertrude A. 39.45
Jacobsen, Lis Rubin 20.18
Jacobsen, Nils 37.512, 38.147
Jacobsen, Thorkild 5.51–53, 5.119, 5.135,
    5.144, 5.166, 5.169, 5.174, 5.184
Jacobsohn, Annette 35.10
Jacobsohn, Peter 35.10
Jacobson, Harold K. 48.289
Jacobson, Jon 48.108
Jacobson, Max 32.272
Jacobsthal, Paul 7.13
Jacoby, David 8.16, 8.324, 20.843–44
Jacoby, Felix 6.68, 6.110, 6.143, 6.281
Jacoby, Sanford M. 44.226
Jacquart, J. 25.330
Jacques, T. Carlos 1.323
Jacquot, Jean 25.48
Jacyna, L. S. 4.168
Jaeger, C. Stephen 20.671, 20.1423
Jaeger, Hans 1.206
Jaenen, Cornelius J. 36.11, 39.688
Jaffa, Harry V. 42.117
Jaffar, S. M. 15.302
Jaffe, Irma B. 41.450
Jaffe, Lorna S. 47.438
Jafri, S.H.M. 17.451
Jagchid, Sechin 9.9, 9.87, 9.143, 9.144
Jägerskiöld, Stig 32.273
Jago, Charles 29.92
Jahan, Rounaq 15.835
Jahiz, Amr ibn Bahr 17.322
Jahn, K. 17.374
Jaiswal, Suvira 15.134
Jaki, Stanley L. 4.149
Jakobs, Peter 47.300
Jaksic, Ivan 38.695
Jalal, Ayesha 15.734
Jalland, Pat 24.201
Jamaspasa, K. M. 5.484
James, Bruno S. 20.1168

Leonard, Karen Isaksen 15.583
Leonard, Thomas M. 38.293
Leonard, V. W. 38.624
Leone, Alfonso 20.760
León-Portilla, Charles E. 36.304
León-Portilla, Miguel 3.166, 36.295–96,
  36.304
Leopold, John A. 31.365
Lepak, Keith John 33.572
Lepelley, Claude 7.611
Lepenies, Wolf 22.415
Lepovitz, Helen Waddy 31.155
Lepper, Frank A. 5.457, 7.321
Leppert, Richard 23.354
Lepre, Aurelio 28.225, 28.243
Lequin, Yves 26.25, 26.361
Lerman, Katharine Anne 31.231
Lerner, Daniel 3.438, 5.20, 5.43
Lerner, Gerda 1.479, 3.521, 40.445–46,
  42.521, 42.571, 42.593
Lerner, Max 40.732
Lerner, Ralph 41.34
Lerner, Robert E. 20.1199
Leroy, Béatrice 20.934–35
Lery, Jean de 3.167
Lesch, Ann Mosely 18.511
Lesch, John E. 4.722
Lesko, Barbara S. 5.10
Lesky, Erna 4.784
Leslie, Donald D. 10.18, 10.55, 11.69
Leslie, R. F. 33.486–88, 47.76
Leslie, Stuart W. 43.77
Lesnick, Daniel R. 20.1456
Lessa, Almerindo 11.754
Lettrich, Jozef 33.184
Leuchtenburg, William E. 44.511–12,
  44.528, 44.565
Leung, Chi-keung 11.9
Leung, Edwin Pak-wah 11.32
Leung, Yuen-sang 11.118
Leupp, Gary P. 12.258
Leur, J. C. van 16.22
Leuschner, Joachim 20.698
Lev, Yaacov 17.211–12
Levack, Brian P. 22.201
Levenson, Jay A. 29.39
Levenson, Joseph R. 3.138, 11.326
Levenstein, Harvey A. 44.16, 44.227
Leventhal, Herbert 41.471
Leverenz, David 39.764, 42.723
Lévesque, Andrée 45.309
Levey, Michael 22.292–93
Levi, Anthony H. T. 25.52, 25.73
Levi, Darrell E. 38.378, 38.555
Levi, Gershon 7.453
Levich, Marvin 1.251
Levick, Barbara 7.428–29
Levij, I. S. 4.784
Levin, Alfred 34.147–48
Levin, Arthur 21.193, 34.220
Levin, Claora S. 34.220
Levin, David 39.597

Levin, Elena 34.184
Levin, Eve 34.283
Levin, M. G. 9.27
Levin, Miriam R. 4.636
Levin, N. Gordon, Jr. 43.670, 47.445
Levin, Saul 20.1260
Levine, Baruch A. 5.216
Levine, Bruce 40.258, 42.266
Levine, Daniel H. 38.142, 38.485
Levine, David 23.244–45, 23.270, 24.127
Levine, Herbert S. 35.273
Levine, I. H. 21.75
Levine, Joseph M. 23.213
Levine, Lawrence W. 40.346, 40.567,
  44.30, 44.121
Levine, Lee I. 5.310
Levine, Louis D. 5.85
Levine, Peter 43.451
Levine, Robert M. 38.143, 38.556–58
Levine, Solomon B. 13.196, 13.225
Levine, Steven I. 11.409, 11.424
Levine, Susan 43.162
Levi-Provençal, Évariste 17.228
Levison, Wilhelm 20.1075
Levitats, Isaac 21.191
Levitt, James H. 39.425
Levitt, Marcus C. 34.341
Levkov, Ilya I. 31.515
Levtzion, Nehemia 15.301, 18.99, 19.79,
  19.104, 19.131, 19.133, 19.174
Levy, Barry 39.481
Levy, Darline Gay 25.242, 27.231
Levy, David W. 43.436, 43.565
Levy, Eugene 43.297
Levy, Frank 44.238
Levy, Howard S. 10.254–55
Levy, Jack S. 47.11
Levy, Leonard W. 39.306, 41.200–202,
  41.566, 42.65
Levy, Reuben 17.158, 17.254, 17.315,
  17.463, 17.467
Levy, Marion J., Jr. 3.439
Levy, Richard S. 31.210
Lévy-Leboyer, Maurice 26.281
Lewalski, Barbara Kiefer 23.355
Lewandowski, Susan 15.571
Lewchuck, Wayne 24.144
Lewin, Leif 32.377
Lewin, Linda 38.559
Lewin, Moshe 35.232–33
Lewin, Roger 3.80
Lewin, Ronald 48.272
Lewin, Zofia 33.519
Lewinstein, Keith 17.126
Lewis, Andrew W. 20.587
Lewis, Anthony 22.294, 44.529
Lewis, Archibald R. 3.139, 3.354, 20.114,
  20.177, 20.190, 20.898
Lewis, Bernard 1.126, 3.193, 9.60, 17.25–
  26, 17.32–33, 17.60, 17.316, 17.453–54,
  18.56, 18.69, 18.176, 18.281, 21.36,
  21.217

Lewis, C. S. 20.986
Lewis, Cathleen S. 4.578
Lewis, Charlton M. 11.119
Lewis, Colin M. 38.625
Lewis, David 46.361
Lewis, David L. 44.415
Lewis, David M. 5.458, 6.123, 6.212,
  6.282, 6.296, 6.390, 6.487
Lewis, Earl 43.298
Lewis, Gavin 19.774
Lewis, Gordon K. 38.342–43, 38.386,
  39.598
Lewis, Gwynne 25.393
Lewis, Ioan M. 19.357
Lewis, Jan 39.482, 41.516
Lewis, Jane 23.289, 24.202
Lewis, Jill 31.401
Lewis, John Wilson 11.606, 11.640
Lewis, Michael 13.161
Lewis, Milton 4.724
Lewis, Naphtali 6.265, 7.52, 7.460
Lewis, Norman N. 18.409
Lewis, P. S. 20.605, 25.172
Lewis, Paul H. 38.626, 38.725–27
Lewis, Richard 35.288
Lewis, Ronald L. 39.521, 40.347
Lewis, Thomas T. 1.252
Lewisohn, Leonard 17.440
Lewit, Tamara 7.368
Lewitova, Iris 2.80
Lewitter, L. R. 34.342, 34.356
Lewy, Guenter 44.843
Ley, Charles David 29.111
Leyburn, James Graham 39.568
Leyda, Jay 11.539, 35.423
Leyden, Wolfgang von 1.208, 1.289
Leys, Colin 19.498
Leyser, Henrietta 20.1176
Leyser, Karl J. 8.168, 20.250, 20.627
Lhamon, W. T., Jr. 44.78
Lhotsky, Alphons 20.628
L'Huillier, Fernand 22.346
Li, Chi 2.50
Li, Chih-Chang 10.338
Li, Chu-tsing 11.327
Li, K. T. 11.724
Li, Lillian M. 11.254, 11.265
Li, Lincoln 11.425
Li, Peter 11.73
Li, Victor H. 11.607
Li, Xueqin 10.194
Li, Yun-chen 11.7
Li, Yu-ning 11.328
Liang, Ch'i-ch'ao 11.329
Liang, Fang-chung 10.352
Liang, Hsi-Huey 48.84
Liao, Kuang-sheng 11.120
Lias, Godfrey 33.143
Liashchenko, Peter I. 34.199
Liberles, Robert 21.154
Liberty, Margot 36.184, 36.198, 36.269
Libo, Kenneth 21.259

Lloyd, Janet 6.66, 6.503, 6.516, 11.313, 11.465, 22.509, 26.115–16, 26.194, 26.234
Lloyd, John 7.363
Lloyd, John Edward 20.51
Lloyd, Peter 19.227
Lloyd, Seton 5.184, 5.196
Lloyd, Simon 20.458, 20.589
Lloyd, T. H. 20.411
Lo, Ch'in-shu 10.156
Lo, Irving Yucheng 10.318
Lo, Jeannie 13.423
Lo, Jung-pang 11.331
Lo, Winston W. 10.145, 10.287
Lo Curto, Vito 28.263
Loach, Jennifer 23.77
Loades, David M. 23.51, 23.68
Lobban, Michael 24.78
Lobban, Richard A. 18.332
Lobel, M. D. 20.412
Lock, Margaret M. 13.500–1
Lockard, Craig Alan 3.440, 16.249
Lockhart, Audrey 39.356
Lockhart, James 36.278, 36.293, 36.297–98, 37.44, 37.89, 37.136–37, 37.237, 37.275, 37.360
Lockhart, Laurence 9.260–61, 15.420, 18.229, 18.232–33
Lockhart, Paul D. 32.249
Lockie, D. McN. 25.228
Lockman, Zachary 18.301
Lockridge, Kenneth A. 32.105, 39.12, 39.371, 39.376, 39.483, 39.635, 39.746
Lockwood, William W. 13.197–98
Lockyer, Roger 23.52
Lodder, Christina 35.404
Lodge, Tom 19.80, 19.775
Loeber, Dietrich Ander 32.415
Loescher, Gil 48.357
Loewe, Michael A. N. 9.115, 10.25, 10.101, 10.211, 10.213, 10.220–21
Loewe, Raphael 21.98
Loewen, Royden 42.229
Loewenberg, Gerhard 1.499
Loewenberg, Peter 1.466
Lofchie, Michael F. 19.500
Löfgren, Orvar 32.369
Lofstrom, William Lee 38.395
Lofton, John 42.340
Logan, F. Donald 20.1233
Logan, John F. 1.351
Logan, Marie-Rose 1.351
Logan, Oliver 28.51
Logan, Rayford W. 43.299
Logio, George Clenton 33.120
Logoreci, Anton 33.80
Logsdon, John M. 4.576
Logue, Larry M. 42.406
Logue, William 26.256
Loh, Pichon P. Y. 11.332, 11.427
Lohmann Villena, Guillermo 37.161–62
Lohrmann, Dietrich 20.261
Loit, Aleksander 32.414

Løkkegaard, Frede 17.341
Lokken, Roy N. 39.233
Lomask, Milton 41.567
Lomax, Derek W. 20.936–37
Lomax, William 33.421–22
Lombard, Denys 16.100
Lombard, Maurice 20.270
Lombardi, Cathryn L. 37.17
Lombardi, John V. 37.17, 37.45, 37.526, 38.486–87
London, Kurt 35.384
Lonergan, Bernard J. 20.1354
Long, A. A. 6.615–16
Long, Clarence D. 42.158
Long, Gavin 46.47
Long, J. Anthony 36.43
Long, Pamela O. 4.393
Long, Priscilla 43.141
Longley, Lawrence D. 40.48
Longmore, Paul K. 41.568
Longrigg, Stephen Hemsley 18.410, 18.445–46
Longworth, Philip 34.73, 34.315
Lonie, Ian M. 4.702
Lonn, Ella 39.56, 42.762
Lönnroth, Erik 20.714
Lonsdale, John M. 19.80, 19.469, 19.501
Loomis, Noel M. 37.589
Loomis, W. T. 6.353
Lopach, James J. 36.185
Lopes Sierra, João 37.163
López, Adalberto 37.447
López Austin, Alfredo 36.275
Lopez, Robert S. 8.95, 17.229, 20.90–91, 20.300, 20.786–87
López de Gómara, Francisco 36.299, 37.124
López Morillas, Frances A. 29.30, 29.37, 37.334
Lora, Guillermo 38.396
L'Orange, Hans Peter 7.568
Lord, Robert Howard 33.489, 47.158
Lordkipanidse, Otar 2.34
Lorimer, Edith O. 20.697
Lorton, David 5.539
Lortz, Joseph 30.30
Lorwin, Val R. 37.58
Lory, Bernard 33.121
Lory, Hillis 13.311
Losee, John 4.300
Losman, Arne 32.172
Lot, Ferdinand 3.140, 20.52
Lotchin, Roger W. 44.247
Loth, Wilfred 48.375
Lothrop, Samuel K. 36.501–2
Lottin, Alain 27.148
Lottinville, Savoie 1.13
Lottman, Herbert R. 26.257
Lotveit, Trygve 11.428
Lotze, Barbara 33.414
Loubère, Leo A. 26.168, 26.282
Louch, A. R. 1.325
Loud, G. A. 20.819

Loud, John F. 33.683
Loudon, Irvine 4.785
Lougee, Carolyn C. 25.74
Lough, John 25.34
Louie, Kam 11.678
Louis, Pierre 8.417
Louis, Wm. Roger 18.315, 18.512, 18.570, 19.278, 19.502, 19.612, 22.348, 24.374, 24.464, 47.231–32, 47.241, 47.446, 48.261, 48.311–12, 48.315, 48.457, 48.512
Loulis, John C. 33.284
Lounsbury, Ralph Greenlee 39.426
Lourie, Elena 20.938
Lourie, Richard 21.182, 21.288, 35.472
Love, Edgar F. 37.361
Love, Janet 20.1103
Love, Joseph L. 38.5, 38.147, 38.560–61
Love, Peter 46.121
Loveday, Amos J., Jr. 43.39
Loveday, Peter 46.90
Lovejoy, Arthur O. 1.434, 22.202
Lovejoy, David S. 39.57, 39.693, 41.396
Lovejoy, Paul E. 19.81, 19.202, 19.228–29, 19.436, 19.829, 19.908–9, 37.224
Lovelace, Richard F. 39.694
Lovell, W. George 36.335, 37.205, 37.362
Loveman, Brian 38.148, 38.699–700
Loverde-Baswell, Elizabeth 44.257
Lovett, A. W. 29.17, 29.107–8
Lovett, Clara M. 28.256–58, 28.448
Lovett, Gabriel H. 29.221
Low, Alfred D. 31.402, 47.447, 48.219, 48.358–59
Low, Bobbi S. 32.106
Low, Donald Anthony 15.4, 15.675–77, 15.686, 19.449, 19.503–5, 24.465
Low, Marilyn 20.86
Lowance, Mason I., Jr. 39.695, 39.765
Lowe, C. J. 47.35, 47.309–10, 47.448, 48.54
Lowe, Eileen M. 12.69
Lowe, Graham S. 45.194
Lowe, H. Y. 11.481
Löwe, Heinz 20.228
Lowe, Peter 47.395
Lowe, Richard G. 42.300, 42.806
Lowell, B. Lindsay 32.340
Lowens, Irving 39.778
Lowenstein, Steven M. 21.267
Lowenthal, Abraham F. 38.62–63, 38.149
Lowenthal, Richard 35.178
Lowenthal, Rudolf 9.301
Lower, Arthur R. M. 45.97
Lowi, Theodore J. 44.513
Lowie, Robert H. 36.239
Löwith, Karl 1.198, 22.418
Lowitt, Richard 40.205, 44.514, 44.581–82
Lowndes, Susan 29.1
Lowrie, Ernest Benson 39.599
Lowry, Glenn D. 9.258
Lowry, Martin 28.54–55
Lowy, Michael 35.197
Loy, Jane M. 37.527

Macek, Josef 33.186
Macey, David 1.156
Macey, David A. J. 34.160
Macey, Samuel L. 4.452
Macfarlane, Alan 23.246, 23.303–4
Macfarlane, Leslie J. 23.393
MacFarquhar, Roderick 11.54–55, 11.610–11
MacGaffey, Wyatt 19.613
MacGregor, Arthur 30.290
Macgregor, D. C. 6.506
Macgregor, Gordon 36.186
MacGregor, Morris J., Jr. 44.429
Machetzki, Rudiger 11.584
Machin, G.I.T. 24.269
Machinist, Peter 5.42, 5.70, 5.214
Machlowitz Klein, Jenny 21.194
Macías, Anna 38.246
Macinnes, Allan I. 23.394
Macinnes, Lesley 7.309
Macintyre, Martha 46.305
Macintyre, Stuart 24.338, 46.25, 46.91
Mack, Karlheinz 47.401
Mack, Pamela E. 4.577
Mack Smith, Denis 28.214, 28.284–85, 28.292–93, 28.302, 28.311, 28.392
MacKay, Angus 20.940
Mackay, David 46.26
MacKay, P. A. 17.269
Mackay, Sally 33.765
MacKendrick, Paul 6.290
MacKenzie, David 33.736–38, 35.7
MacKenzie, Donald 4.490
MacKenzie, John M. 19.841, 24.453
Mackenzie [Sebright], Georgina Mary Muir 33.720
Mackerras, Colin 9.134, 10.18, 11.29, 11.69, 11.204, 11.335, 11.688
Mackesy, Piers 41.108
MacKinnon, Neil 45.141
MacKinnon, Stephen R. 11.125
Mackinolty, Judy 46.153
Maclachlan, Colin M. 36.441, 37.90–91, 37.448, 37.464
Maclagan, Michael 8.250
Maclean, Derryl N. 15.304
Maclean, Fitzroy 33.810–11
Maclean, Ian 22.203, 25.75
MacLeod, Anne Scott 42.724
MacLeod, Christine 23.154
MacLeod, D. Peter 36.25
Macleod, Duncan J. 41.491
MacLeod, Margaret Arnett 45.167
MacLeod, Murdo J. 36.318, 37.276
MacLeod, Roy M. 4.724, 24.88–89, 24.95, 24.361
MacMaster, Neil 29.271
Macmillan, Harold 33.517
MacMillan, Margaret 15.470
MacMillan, William M. 19.700–1
MacMullen, Ramsay 7.102, 7.119, 7.301, 7.385–86, 7.535, 7.540, 7.575, 7.600
MacNicol, Fred 33.376

MacNutt, William Stewart 45.142–43
Macqueen, J. G. 5.368
MacQueen, John 23.214
Macrides, Ruth J. 8.273–74
Macro, Eric 18.250
Macy, Gary 20.1525
Maday, Béla C. 33.402
Madden, Edward H. 42.687
Maddern, Philippa C. 20.459
Maddex, Jack P., Jr. 42.807
Maddicott, J. R. 20.460, 20.560
Maddison, Angus 3.422
Maddison, Francis 23.325
Maddock, Kenneth 46.36
Maddock, Rodney 46.139
Maddox, J. R. 4.129
Maddox, Robert James 44.720
Madej, Victor 33.624
Madelung, Wilferd 9.62, 17.187–89, 17.404, 17.455
Madison, James H. 40.170
Madsen, Richard 11.633, 11.679
Maeda, Daisaku 13.425
Maehler, H. 8.60
Maenchen-Helfen, Otto 9.175
Maertz, Joseph 27.211
Maestro, Marcello 28.203
Magalhães, José Calvet de 29.21
Magdalino, Paul 8.184, 8.455
Magdol, Edward 42.790
Magie, David 7.227
Magie, William Francis 4.137
Magner, Lois N. 4.659
Magnou-Nortier, Elisabeth 20.899
Magnússon, Finnur 32.314
Magnusson, Lars 32.29, 32.78, 32.173–74, 32.382
Magnússon, Magnús S. 32.315
Magocsi, Paul R. 33.187, 34.51
Magoulias, Harry J. 8.393, 8.397, 8.456
Magrath, C. Peter 41.281
Maguire, G. Andrew 19.506
Maguire, Henry 8.335, 8.388, 8.443
Maguire, Robert A. 35.401
Mahalingam, T. V. 15.198, 15.359
Mahdi, Muhsin 1.157, 17.61
Mahler, Raphael 21.194
Mahoney, Edward P. 20.1375
Mahood, Marguerite 46.168
Maienschein, Jane 4.206, 4.219
Maier, Anneliese 4.57, 20.1394
Maier, Charles S. 1.500, 3.236, 22.522, 22.625, 31.464
Maier, Hendrik M. J. 16.250
Maier, Joseph 38.151
Maier, Lothar 33.659
Maier, Pauline 41.73–74
Maimonides, Obadiah ben Abraham ben Moses 21.37
Main, Gloria L. 39.154
Main, Jackson Turner 39.100, 41.158–60, 41.203, 41.434
Mainardi, Patricia 26.258

Mainga, Mutumba 19.557
Maingot, A. P. 38.348
Mair, Victor H. 10.84, 10.111
Mairet, Philip 25.285
Maisel, David 21.19, 21.105, 26.183
Maisels, Charles Keith 3.99
Maitland, Frederic William 20.217
Maître, Jean 26.8
Maity, Sachindra Kumar 15.145, 15.189
Maizlish, Stephen E. 42.120
Majerus, Pierre 27.201–2
Majeska, George P. 8.19
Majno, Guido 4.670
Major, J. Russell 25.174–77
Major, R. H. 3.291
Majul, Cesar Adib 16.341–42
Majumdar, R. C. 15.32, 15.120, 15.146, 16.53
Makdisi, George 17.270, 17.369, 17.405, 17.423–25
Makey, Walter 23.395
Maki, John M. 13.482
Makk, Ferenc 8.336
Makler, Harry M. 29.396
Makriyiannes, Ionnes 33.285
Maksay, F. 20.675
Maksimović, Ljubomir 8.275
Malafeev, A. N. 35.289
Malaga Medina, Alejandro 36.394
Malalgoda, Kitsiri 15.751
Malamat, Abraham 5.254–57, 5.279–80
Malamut, Elisabeth 8.219
Malandra, William H. 5.489
Malbran-Labat, Florence 5.109
Malcolm, John 18.587
Malcolmson, Robert 23.247
Male, D. J. 35.234
Mâle, Emile 22.295
Malefakis, Edward A. 29.272
Malet, Michael 35.75
Maley, William 15.857
Malgeri, Francesco 28.328
Malherbe, V. C. 19.655
Malia, Martin Edward 34.373, 35.9
Malik, Charles 18.100
Malik, S. C. 15.121
Malik, Zahir Uddin 15.421
Malin, James C. 42.429
Malina, Jaroslav 1.89, 2.76
Malino, Frances 21.155
Malinowski, B. 19.492
Malinowski, Władysław 33.482
Malka, Salomon 21.143
Mallakh, Ragaei El 48.523
Malle, Silvana 35.76
Mallett, Michael E. 28.83–84, 28.127
Mallon, Florencia E. 38.460
Mallory, J. P. 2.77, 5.520, 9.32
Mallory, Nina A. 29.109
Malloy, James M. 38.152, 38.397–98
Mally, Lynn 35.77
Malm, William P. 13.587
Malone, Ann Patton 42.341

McDowell, Andrea Griet 5.601
McDowell, Gary L. 40.79
McElderry, Andrea Lee 11.257
McElroy, John Harmon 40.727
McElwee, W. L. 31.193, 47.152
McEvedy, Colin 3.19
McEvoy, Arthur F. 40.194, 43.54
McEvoy, James 20.1357
McEwan, J. R. 12.316
McEwen, Ellen 46.108
McFarland, H. Neill 13.537
McFarland, Keith D. 44.747
McFarlane, Anthony 37.501
McFarlane, I. D. 25.20
McFarlane, K. B. 20.461, 20.1200
McFeely, William S. 42.522, 42.763, 42.834, 43.516
McGann, Thomas Francis 38.628–29, 38.644–45
McGaw, Judith A. 4.415
McGee Deutsch, Sandra 38.630
McGeehan, Robert 48.397
McGerr, Michael E. 40.728, 43.502
McGill, William J. 30.131
McGinn, Bernard 20.987, 20.992
McGovern, James R. 13.12
McGowan, Bruce 18.207
McGrade, Arthur Stephen 20.1407
McGrath, Alisdair E. 30.31–32
McGrath, Ann 46.37
McGrath, William J. 22.421, 31.313–14
McGreal, L. F. 11.307
McGreevey, William Paul 38.35, 38.417
McGregor, J. F. 23.186
McGregor, Malcolm Francis 6.37, 6.313
McGrew, Roderick E. 34.448
McGuire, Gregory R. 4.263
McGuire, Martin Rawson Patrick 20.988
McHale, Vincent E. 32.416
McHugh, John 5.283
McIlwain, Charles Howard 20.1408, 41.38
McIntire, C. T. 1.160, 1.199, 1.257
McIntosh, James T. 42.42
McIntosh, Malcolm 13.401
McIntosh, Marjorie Keniston 23.249
McIntosh, Roderick James 2.20, 19.113–14, 19.136
McIntosh, Susan Keech 2.20, 19.112–14, 19.136
McIntyre, Sylvia 20.413
McIntyre, W. David 24.466, 48.316
McKay, Alwyn 4.565
McKay, Angus 20.924
McKay, C. G. 32.384
McKay, Derek 30.132
McKay, Frank M. 46.282
McKay, John P. 34.216
McKean, Margaret A. 13.488
McKean, Robert B. 34.274
McKechnie, Paul R. 6.95, 6.560
McKee, Delber L. 43.629

McKee, Sharon 35.407
McKeithan, James E. 9.193
McKellar, Marian 3.135
McKelvey, John J., Jr. 19.945
McKendrick, Malveena 29.117
McKendrick, Neil 23.250
McKenzie, Frederick A. 14.109–10
McKenzie, Kermit E. 48.85
McKenzie, R. T. 24.26, 24.62
McKeon, Michael 23.358
McKercher, B.J.C. 24.380
McKernan, Michael 46.48
McKibbin, Ross 24.176, 24.236
McKinley, P. Michael 37.531
McKinnon-Evans, Stuart 30.224, 31.75
McKinzie, Richard D. 44.37
McKisack, May 20.562
McKitrick, Eric L. 40.121, 42.835
McKitterick, Rosamond 20.1008, 20.1077–78
McKivigan, John R. 42.523
McKnight, Brian 10.162, 10.288
McKnight, Stephen A. 1.161
McLachlan, Jean O. 29.188
McLane, John R. 15.680
McLaren, Angus 23.307, 24.128, 26.314
McLaren, Walter Wallace 13.118–19
McLaughlin, Andrew Cunningham 41.209
McLaughlin, Kathleen 1.329
McLaughlin, Mary Martin 22.215
McLaurin, Melton Alonza 42.342, 43.120
McLean, Don G. 36.26
McLean, Ian W. 46.139
McLean, Marianne 45.121
McLellan, Joyce 20.9
McLennan, Gregor 1.162
McLeod, W. H. 15.260
McLintock, Alexander H. 46.191, 46.230, 46.236
McLintock, David 30.73
McLoughlin, William G. 36.143, 39.697–98, 40.520–21, 41.63, 41.352
McMahon, A. Michael 4.612
McMahon, Gregory 5.339
McMahon, Robert J. 48.536
McManamon, John M. 28.20–21
McManis, Douglas R. 39.338
McManners, John 3.497, 25.314, 26.331–32
McManus, Edgar J. 39.308, 39.524–25
McMillan, James F. 26.409
McMinn, Joseph 23.359
McMullen, David 10.102
McMullin, I. J. 12.317
McMullin, Neil 12.165
McMullin, Ross 46.122
McMurry, Dean S. 31.427–28
McMurtrie, Douglas C. 39.855
McNab, Bruce 20.650
McNab, Robert 46.192
McNair, Philip Murray Jourdan 28.180

McNally, Dennis 44.101
McNally, Raymond T. 34.374
McNamara, Brooks 39.837, 40.572
McNamara, Dennis L. 14.124
McNamara, Jo Ann 20.198
McNamara, Martin 20.1061
McNaught, Kenneth 45.263
McNeal, Robert H. 34.316, 35.313
McNeil, David O. 25.53
McNeil, Maureen 4.628
McNeil, William C. 48.136
McNeill, John Robert 37.449
McNeill, John T. 20.1009, 22.124, 22.143
McNeill, William H. 1.42, 3.44–48, 3.195, 3.332–33, 3.386–87, 4.492, 33.1, 33.39–40, 33.288, 37.148, 48.263
McNellie, William 38.196
McNickle, D'Arcy 36.241
McPhail, Helen 26.175, 26.365
McPherson, James M. 42.123, 42.738–39, 42.791, 43.300
McQuaid, Kim 44.201
McQueen, Humphrey 46.123
McQuilton, John 46.154
McRae, John R. 10.112
McReynolds, Louise 34.324
McRoberts, Kenneth 45.311
McVeigh, Joseph 40.643
McVey, Ruth T. 16.131, 16.283, 16.302
McWhiney, Grady 42.764
McWhinney, Edward 45.312
McWilliams, Carey 40.195, 40.360
McWilliams, John P., Jr. 41.453
McWilliams, Tennant S. 40.677
Meacham, Standish 24.257
Mead, Margaret 33.12
Mead, Sidney E. 41.353–54
Mead, W. R. 32.57
Meade, E. Grant 14.140
Meaker, Gerald H. 29.238
Meaney, Neville K. 46.49
Means, Gardiner C. 40.229
Mecham, J. Lloyd 38.155, 40.635, 48.162
Mechoulan, Henry 21.99
Medhurst, Kenneth N. 38.418
Medicine, Beatrice 36.207
Medick, Hans 30.163, 30.175, 30.209, 30.240
Medlicott, W. N. 47.188–89
Medvedev, Igor' P. 8.75
Medvedev, Roy 35.113–14
Medvedev, V. E. 9.145
Medvedev, Zhores A. 35.236
Meech-Pekarik, Julia 13.579
Meehan-Waters, Brenda 34.120
Meek, Christine 28.104
Meeks, Wayne A. 7.120
Meer, Fatima 19.783
Meere, J.M.M. 27.247
Megaro, Gaudens 28.231, 28.393
Megaw, Arthur H. S. 8.220
Megaw, J.V.S. 2.86

Moote, A. Lloyd 25.217–18
Mora, Carl J. 38.251
Mora, Enrique Ayala 38.436
Moraes Farias, P. F. de 19.123, 19.130
Morais, Herbert M. 39.701
Morales Carrión, Arturo 38.387
Morales, O.F.M., Francisco 37.187
Morales Padrón, F. 20.785
Moran, Daniel 31.104, 31.122
Moran, E. E. 11.30
Moran, Gerald F. 39.484
Moran, Gerard T. 27.24
Moran, Jo Ann Hoeppner 20.1331
Moran, Theodore H. 38.704
Moran, William L. 5.51–53, 5.119, 5.135, 5.169, 5.217
Morantz, Toby 36.7
Morantz-[Sanchez], Regina Markell 4.813, 42.617–18
Moravcsik, Gyula 8.340–41, 8.395, 9.172, 9.180
Moraw, Peter 20.629
Morawska, Ewa 43.254
Moreen, Vera B. 9.266, 21.38
Moreland, W. H. 15.283, 15.342
Morell, David 16.173
Morelli, Emilia 28.222
Moreno, Dario 38.294
Moreno Cebrián, Alfredo 37.534
Moreno Fraginals, Manuel 38.345
Moreta Velayos, Salustiano 20.824
Moreton, Edwina 48.473
Moretti, Luigi 6.51
Morey, Adrian 23.187
Morey, Nancy 36.464
Morey, Robert V. 36.443, 36.464
Morga, Antonio de 16.106
Morgan, Charles Hill 8.52
Morgan, David O. 3.300, 9.214, 17.35, 17.277–78
Morgan, David W. 31.336
Morgan, Edmund S. 39.104, 39.155, 39.319, 39.485–86, 39.608, 39.702, 41.14–15, 41.40, 41.76–77, 41.356
Morgan, Frederick 3.554
Morgan, Gerald 47.266
Morgan, Gwenda 39.378
Morgan, H. Wayne 43.415, 43.517–18
Morgan, Helen M. 41.77
Morgan, Kenneth O. 22.551, 24.64, 24.442–43
Morgan, Philip D. 39.145, 39.324, 39.505, 41.480–81
Morgan, Robert J. 41.210
Morgan, Robert P. 22.592
Morgan, Robin 44.293
Morgan, Roger 48.440
Morgan, William N. 36.83
Morgen, Sandra 3.525
Morgenthau, Hans 48.46
Moriarty, Michael 25.79
Moriceau, Jean-Marc 25.338

Morimoto, Kosei 17.342
Morin, Claude 37.535
Morineau, Michel 25.347, 25.390, 37.314
Morishima, Akio 13.475
Morishima, Michio 13.201
Morison, David L. 3.253
Morison, Elting E. 4.502
Morison, John S. 4.503
Morison, Mary 22.383
Morison, Samuel Eliot 3.172–75, 37.107, 39.609, 39.749–50, 44.779
Moriya, Takeshi 12.261
Morkot, R. 5.602
Morley, James W. 13.15, 13.29, 13.167, 13.271–72, 48.169–72
Morley, John F. 22.583
Morley, Morris 48.495
Morley, Samuel A. 38.567
Mormino, Gary R. 43.255–56
Mörner, Magnus 32.388, 37.48, 37.94, 37.188, 37.367–69, 38.156
Morony, Michael G. 17.127
Morrall, John B. 20.1410
Morrell, Jack 24.362
Morrell, William P. 46.237
Morrill, James R. 41.398
Morrill, John S. 23.56–57
Morris, A.E.J. 20.92
Morris, Aldon D. 44.471
Morris, Benny 18.517, 48.513
Morris, Clarence 11.80
Morris, Colin 20.1104, 20.1301
Morris, Craig 36.370
Morris, Dana R. 12.36
Morris, H. F. 19.510
Morris, Ian 6.204
Morris, Ivan J. 12.58, 13.162
Morris, J. 8.73
Morris, James 24.455
Morris, James A. 38.320
Morris, John 7.42
Morris, Margaret 33.366
Morris, Mary 22.392
Morris, Morris David 15.548–49
Morris, Nancy 38.677
Morris, Peter 26.2
Morris, R. J. 24.177, 24.194
Morris, Richard B. 3.21, 39.268, 39.309, 39.462, 39.525, 41.162, 41.175, 41.211
Morris, Rosemary 4.809, 8.169
Morris, V. Dixon 12.133, 12.174, 14.28
Morrison, Barrie M. 15.223
Morrison, George 17.468
Morrison, Hugh 39.838
Morrison, J. S. 6.392, 6.528
Morrison, Karl F. 20.701, 20.1033–35
Morrison, Kenneth M. 36.112
Morrison, M. A. 5.112
Morrison, R. Bruce 36.62
Morriss, Roger 24.395
Morrissey, Robert J. 25.125
Morrisson, Cécile 8.42, 8.289

Morrow, Don 45.26
Morrow, Glenn R. 6.598
Morrow, Ian F. D. 31.340
Morse, Edward L. 48.571
Morse, Edward S. 13.107
Morse, Hosea Ballou 11.133
Morse, Richard M 38.568–69
Morsey, Rudolf 31.357, 31.389
Mortel, Richard T. 17.343, 17.457
Mortensen, Peder 2.29
Mortimer, Edward 48.413
Mortimer, Rex 16.303, 46.322
Mortimer, Richard 20.623
Mortimore, Doretha E. 14.117
Morton, Desmond 45.27, 45.197, 45.256
Morton, F.W.O. 37.468
Morton, Fred 19.450
Morton, Harry 46.207
Morton, Louis 39.430, 44.780
Morton, W. L. 45.50, 45.131, 45.167–68, 45.267
Morton, William Fitch 13.273
Mosbacher, Eric 22.286, 47.419
Moscati, Sabatino 7.15, 7.34
Moseley, Michael E. 2.104–5
Mosely, Philip E. 35.20
Moser, Charles A. 33.130
Moser, Hans Joachim 30.345
Moses, Claire Goldberg 26.410
Moses, John Anthony 46.11, 46.196, 47.267, 47.353
Moses, L. G. 36.188
Mosher, J. Randolph 29.239
Mosk, Carl 12.278
Moskoff, William 35.241
Moskos, Charles C. 33.290
Mosley, D. J. 6.467
Moss, Alfred A., Jr. 40.340
Moss, Bernard 26.364
Moss, David 28.455
Moss, Henry St. L. B. 8.103
Moss, J. R. 7.541
Mossé, Claude 6.224, 6.322
Mosse, George L. 21.308, 21.316, 22.82, 22.584, 31.61, 31.269, 31.451
Mosse, Werner E. 21.160, 22.351, 47.135, 47.161
Mossek, Moshe 18.479
Mossuz-Lavau, Janine 26.411–12
Mostyn, Trevor 18.26
Mote, Frederick W. 10.54, 10.340, 10.365
Motley, John L. 27.39–40
Motley, Mark 25.80
Mott, Frank Luther 41.457, 43.435
Mottahedeh, Roy P. 17.159, 17.191–92, 18.588
Motyl, Alexander J. 35.202
Motz, Lloyd 4.125
Moule, A. C. 9.227
Moulin, Anne Marie 4.727
Moulton, Gary E. 42.375
Mounsey, Augustus H. 13.87

Northcutt, Wayne 26.10
Northedge, F. S. 48.86
Northrup, David 19.621, 19.918
Norton, Anne 42.677
Norton, Augustus Richard 18.415
Norton, Mary Beth 40.30, 40.434, 40.450, 41.132, 41.517, 42.331, 42.611, 42.636, 43.153
Norton, Thomas Elliot 39.432
Norwich, John Julius 20.883–84
Norwood, Frederick A. 40.525
Norwood, Susan 36.350
Nosco, Peter 12.296, 12.323–24, 12.326
Nossiter, T. J. 15.813–14
Notehelfer, F. G. 13.105, 13.138–39
Noth, Martin 5.218–19
Nottingham, John 19.521
Notton, Camille 16.82
Novák, Arne 33.199
Novak, Barbara 42.727
Novak, Bogdan C. 33.816
Novak, Derry 48.408
Novak, Grga 33.704
Novak, Michael 44.375
Novak, Steven J. 41.473
Novak, Viktor 33.817
Novak-Deker, Nikolai K. 35.318
Novarr, David 1.469
Nove, Alec 35.239, 35.290
Nove, Irene 35.233
Novick, Peter 1.369
Novosel'tsev, Anatolii Petrovich 9.190
Novotny, Fritz 22.512
Nowak, Jan 33.584
Nowell, Charles E. 13.29
Nowell-Smith, Geoffrey 25.30
Noyé, Ghislaine 20.77
Noyen, René A. van 6.182
Noyes, George Rapall 33.741
Noyes, John Humphrey 42.553
Noyes, P. H. 31.168
Nugent, Donald 25.281
Nugent, Walter T. K. 42.660, 43.64
Numbers, Ronald L. 4.307, 4.660, 4.720, 4.787, 4.803, 37.425, 42.319, 42.491
Nummela, Ilkka 32.290
Nunes Leal, Victor 38.572
Núñez, Benjamín 38.17
Nunn, Charles F. 37.451
Nunn, Frederick M. 38.158, 38.705
Nunn, G. Raymond 13.16
Nunnelley, William A. 44.490
Nurse, Derek 19.86, 19.405
Nuseibeh, Hazem Zaki 18.349
Nussbaum, Frederick L. 22.92
Nussdorfer, Laurie 28.190
Nuttall, Geoffrey F. 23.188
Nutter, G. Warren 35.295
Nutton, Vivian 4.671
Nyakatura, John W. 19.406
Nybakken, Elizabeth I. 40.319
Nye, David E. 4.523, 43.81
Nye, Joseph S., Jr. 44.862, 48.290, 48.566

Nye, Mary Jo 26.299
Nye, Robert A. 26.260
Nye, Russel Blaine 40.110, 42.678
Nyeko, Balam 19.747
Nygren, Ingemar 32.389
Nylander, Carl 5.507
Nyman, Kristina 32.5

Ó Corráin, Donnchadh 20.533
O Gráda, Cormac 24.413
Oakes, Guy 1.276
Oakes, James 42.288
Oakeshott, Michael Joseph 1.292
Oakley, Francis C. 20.1105, 20.1237, 20.1381, 20.1411–12
Oakley, J. Ronald 44.516
Oakley, Stewart P. 32.6, 32.12, 32.59, 32.126
Oates, David 5.25
Oates, Joan 5.26, 5.90
Oates, John F. 6.130
Oates, Stephen B. 42.343, 42.524, 42.741
O'Barr, Jean F. 3.526, 22.33
Obayemi, Ade 19.139
Obelkevich, James 24.277
Obenaus, Herbert 31.131
Ober, Josiah 6.334
Oberem, Udo 36.397, 36.424
Oberholzer, Emil, Jr. 39.705
Oberlé, Philippe 19.369
Oberman, Heiko A. 20.1382, 20.1462, 21.107, 30.34–35
Oberoi, Harjot 15.617
Oberschall, Anthony 4.266
Obeyesekere, Gananath 15.750
Obolensky, Chloe 34.41
Obolensky, Dimitri 8.343, 20.981, 34.24, 34.175
Obradović, Dositej 33.741
Obrerg, Barbara 41.455
O'Brian, Patrick 26.215
O'Brien, Anne 46.155
O'Brien, C. Bickford 34.74
O'Brien, David J. 44.125
O'Brien, David M. 44.533
O'Brien, George Dennis 1.165
O'Brien, James A. 13.563
O'Brien, Kevin J. 11.614
O'Brien, Michael 40.147, 44.102
O'Brien, Patricia 26.227
O'Brien, Patrick 24.121
O'Brien, Philip 38.709
O'Brien, Sharon 44.386
O'Brien, Thomas F., Jr. 37.387, 38.706
O'Callaghan, Joseph F. 20.55, 20.946, 20.1181
Ochieng', William Robert 19.407
Ochmanski, Jerzy 32.207
Ochsenwald, William L. 18.546–47
Ocko, Jonathan K. 11.135
O'Connell, James F. 2.73
O'Connell, Marvin 22.93
O'Connell, Robert L. 4.494

O'Connnell, Matthew 20.976
O'Connor, Colin 7.503
O'Connor, David 5.615
O'Connor, John E. 1.447
O'Connor, Raymond 48.264
O'Cróinín, David 20.1060
O'Crouley, Pedro Alonso 37.536
O'Day, Alan 24.204
O'Day, Rosemary 23.189–90, 23.252
Oddie, Geoffrey A. 15.618–19
Oded, Arye 19.452
Oded, Bustenay 5.124
Odell, Peter R. 48.340
Odendaal, Andre 19.791
Odling-Smee, J. C. 24.120
Odložilík, Otakar 33.200–1
Odom, William E. 35.341
O'Donnell, Guillermo A. 38.634
O'Donnell, James J. 20.1055
O'Donnell, John M. 4.267
O'Dowd, Mary 23.306, 23.438
Odum, Howard W. 40.130
Oertzen, Eleonore von 36.342
Oestreich, Brigitta 30.73
Oestreich, Gerhard 30.72–73
Oestreicher, Richard Jules 43.172, 43.585
O'Fahey, R. S. 18.107, 19.367–68
O'Farrell, Patrick 46.156, 46.185, 46.267–68
Offen, Karen M. 3.527, 22.445, 26.173, 26.397, 26.413–14
Offer, Avner 24.31
Offler, H. S. 27.268
Offner, Arnold A. 44.721, 48.207
Offner, Jerome A. 36.276
Offord, Derek 34.381
O'Flaherty, James C. 30.347
O'Flaherty, Wendy Doniger 15.111
O'Flynn, John Michael 7.537
Ofosu-Appiah, L. H. 19.36
Ogata, Sadako N. 13.313
Ogden, Dennis 34.201
Ogelsby, J.C.M. 37.452
Ogg, David 22.94
Ogilvie, R. M. 7.167
O'Gorman, Edmundo 37.149
O'Gorman, Frank 24.32
O'Gorman, James F. 43.418
Ogot, Bethwell A. 19.408–10, 19.433, 19.453, 19.516, 19.524
O'Grady, Colm 20.1061
Ogura, Takekazu 13.240
Oh, John Kie-chiang 14.143
Ohadike, Don C. 19.236
O'Hanlon, Rosalind 15.588
Ohkawa, Kazushi 13.205–6
Ohl, John Kennedy 44.571
Ohland, Klaudine 36.348
Ohlin, Göran 32.53
Ohlsson, Rolf 32.91
Ohnuki-Tierney, Emiko 13.502
Ohsson, Constantin d' 9.215
Oi, Jean C. 11.615

Outhwaite, R. Brian 23.157
Outhwaite, William 1.293
Outram, Dorinda 4.181, 4.317
Ouweneel, Arij 37.212, 37.537
Ou-yang, Hsiu 10.254–55, 10.259
Ovchinnikova, L. P. 35.315
Ovendale, Ritchie 48.515
Overfield, James H. 30.301
Overmier, Judith 4.182
Overmyer, Daniel L. 11.338, 11.728
Overy, R. J. 22.574, 31.431, 48.145
Oviedo y Baños, José de 37.138
Ovitt, George, Jr. 4.385
Owen, D. I. 5.112
Owen, David 24.95
Owen, John B. 23.58
Owen, Norman G. 16.347–48
Owen, Roger 3.423, 18.70, 18.105, 18.315, 18.317, 18.519, 48.512
Owen, Stephen 10.263–64
Owen, Thomas C. 34.217, 34.266
Owens, Leslie Howard 42.345
Owings, Donnell MacClure 39.238
Owram, Douglas 45.30, 45.237, 45.270
Owsley, Frank Lawrence, Jr. 41.320, 42.742
Owsley, Harriet Chappell 42.93
Owst, Gerald R. 20.1459
Oxley, Robert M. 38.574
Oxnam, Robert B. 11.136
Ōyama Kyōhei 12.89
Ozaki, Robert S. 48.537
Ozanne, Robert 44.230
Özbudun, Ergun 18.286
Özgüç, Tahsin 5.377
Ozment, Steven E. 22.16, 22.95, 30.36–37, 30.166–67, 30.302
Ozouf, Jacques 25.32, 26.290, 26.300
Ozouf, Mona 26.5, 26.67, 26.300

Paasivirta, Juhani 32.291–92
Paavonen, Tapani 32.293
Pacey, Arnold 3.553, 4.355–56
Pach, Chester J., Jr. 48.432
Pachai, Bridglal 19.412
Pacheco Pereira, Duarte 19.177
Pachmuss, Temira 32.212
Pachter, Henry M. 1.264
Pack, Robert 11.373
Packard, George R., III 13.363
Packard, Randall M. 19.455, 19.871, 19.946–47
Packe, Michael St. John 28.286
Packman, Brenda 19.269
Păcurariu, Mircea 33.663
Paczynska, Maria 33.464
Padden, Robert C. 36.478, 37.125, 37.334
Padfield, Peter 47.319
Padgug, Robert A. 40.477
Pagden, Anthony 22.207, 36.285, 37.117, 37.141, 37.150, 37.427
Page, Benjamin I. 44.658

Page, Brian 43.55
Page, D. L. 6.136, 6.183
Page, David 15.738
Page, Joseph A. 38.635
Page, Melvin E. 47.400
Page, Stanley W. 32.418
Pagel, Walter 4.698
Pahl, Jon 39.320
Paik, Lak-Geoon George 14.115
Paine, Robert Treat 13.581
Painter, Kenneth 7.525
Painter, Nell Irvin 43.13, 43.305
Pakenham, Thomas 47.246–47
Paksoy, Hasan B. 9.349
Pal, Pratapaditya 15.476
Palacios, Marco 38.420
Palacios Martín, Bonifacio 20.947
Palais, James B. 14.40–41, 14.61, 14.74, 14.112
Palermo, Miguel Angel 36.479
Palladino, Grace 42.779
Palley, Marian Leif 44.280
Palli, Heldur 32.102
Palliser, D. M. 20.420
Pallot, Judith 34.48
Pallottino, Massimo 7.154–56
Palmade, Guy 26.284
Palmai, Eva 33.5–6, 33.368, 33.375
Palmer, Alan W. 47.4, 47.41–42
Palmer, Anne-Marie 7.563
Palmer, Beverly Wilson 42.43
Palmer, Bruce, Jr. 48.538
Palmer, Bryan D. 45.31, 45.200
Palmer, Colin A. 37.226–27
Palmer, David Scott 38.462
Palmer, Gabrielle G. 37.428
Palmer, Howard 45.16, 45.51
Palmer, J.J.N. 20.464
Palmer, John 48.458
Palmer, Michael A. 40.637
Palmer, R. R. 22.353, 25.244, 25.316, 26.62, 26.68, 26.84, 26.301, 41.16–17
Palmer, Robert C. 20.535
Palmer, Robin 19.793, 19.887
Palmer, Stanley 3.403
Palmer, Stephen E., Jr. 33.818
Palmer, Tamara 45.51
Palmer, William 34.429
Palmore, Erdman B. 13.425
Palóczi Horváth, András 9.202
Palombini, Barbara von 18.236
Paludan, Helge 20.677
Paludan, Phillip S. 42.766, 42.780
Paluden, Ann 10.375
Palyi, Melchior 48.138
Pámlenyi, Ervin 33.366
Pamuk, Şevket 18.287
Pan, Ku 10.103, 10.225, 10.237–38
Pandey, B. N. 15.454, 48.539
Pandey, Gyanendra 15.684, 15.711–12, 15.739–40
Pandey, Kanti Chandra 15.263

Pang, Eul-Soo 38.573
Panikkar, K. M. 3.245, 15.57, 15.322, 15.361
Panikkar, K. N. 15.653
Pannekoek, A. 4.151
Pano, Nicholas C. 33.82
Panofsky, Erwin 20.1438, 22.297–98, 30.303–4
Pantelidis, Veronica S. 18.28
Pantin, W. A. 20.1139
Panzac, Daniel 18.288–89
Papacosma, S. Victor 33.292
Papadopoullos, Theodoros H. 33.293
Papadopulos, Aberkios T. 8.78
Papastratis, Procopis 33.294
Papenfuse, Edward C. 39.152, 41.404
Paperno, Irina 34.397
Papmehl, K. A. 34.328
Pappworth, Joanna 1.114
Paquet, Gilles 45.159
Paquet, Jacques 20.1323
Paradis, James G. 4.201
Paredes, J. Anthony 36.191
Paredi, Angelo 20.1010
Parent, David J. 1.380
Parente, James A., Jr. 30.305–6
Pares, Richard 23.122, 24.34, 39.180, 39.270, 39.433–34
Paret, Peter 22.354, 30.134, 31.104, 31.107, 31.109–10
Parfitt, Tudor 18.480
Parias, Louis Henri 26.302
Parish, Richard 25.302
Parish, William L. 11.641, 11.648
Park, James William 38.421
Park, Katharine 4.684
Park, Mungo 19.178
Park, Rebecca 35.312
Park, Seong-Rae 14.33, 14.62
Parke, H. W. 6.389
Parker, A. J. 7.352
Parker, David 25.220–21
Parker, Dorothy R. 36.192
Parker, Frank R. 44.472
Parker, Geoffrey 22.96, 22.97, 22.277, 23.121, 27.43–45, 29.114, 29.124–27
Parker, Harold T. 1.11, 28.375
Parker, John 41.18
Parker, Kenneth L. 23.191
Parker, R. S. 46.90
Parker, Richard A. 4.31
Parker, Robert 6.590
Parker, Rozsika 22.34
Parker, S. Thomas 7.327
Parker, William N. 4.460, 40.231, 42.140
Parkerson, Donald H. 42.661
Parkes, James William 21.71
Parkman, Patricia 38.312
Parks, Joseph H. 42.743
Parman, Donald L. 36.193
Parmentier, Richard J. 46.339
Parmet, Herbert S. 44.572

Pomeroy, Earl Spencer 40.199, 44.43
Pomeroy, Sarah B. 6.571–72
Pomfret, John E. 39.128–30
Pompa, Leon 1.168, 1.269
Pomper, Philip 1.470, 34.398–400
Pond, Elizabeth 31.543
Pond, Kathleen 20.1187
Ponomarev, B. N. 35.173
Ponteil, Felix 22.357
Pool, Ithiel de Sola 4.536
Poole, Stafford 37.147, 37.191–93
Poos, L. R. 20.387
Pope, Arthur Upham 5.508, 17.501
Pope, Daniel 43.30
Pope, Deborah 22.33
Pope, Robert G. 39.710
Popkin, Jeremy D. 25.95, 25.245
Popkin, Richard Henry 21.99, 22.212,
    25.247
Popkin, Samuel L. 16.220
Popovic, Alexandre 9.254
Poppe, Andrzej 34.421
Poppe, Nikolai Nikolaevich 9.34
Popper, Karl Raimund 1.169, 6.602
Popper, William 17.292
Poppino, Rollie E. 38.163, 38.502
Porada, Edith 5.509
Poralla, Paul 6.408
Porath, Yehoshua 18.71, 18.522, 48.152
Porch, Douglas 26.40, 26.174, 29.408
Porchnev, Boris 25.361
Porras Barrenechea, Raul 36.399
Porten, Bezalel 5.281
Porter, Bernard 24.456, 47.136
Porter, Catherine 35.442
Porter, Dale H. 1.328
Porter, David L. 44.749
Porter, Dorothy 4.729, 4.731
Porter, Frances 46.210, 46.246
Porter, Glenn 40.240, 40.246, 40.249,
    42.161, 43.22
Porter, H. C. 39.551
Porter, James I. 21.107
Porter, John A. 45.275
Porter, Jonathan 11.140
Porter, Roy 4.1, 4.237, 4.709, 4.729–31,
    4.765, 23.253, 23.328, 26.248
Porter, Susan L. 41.456
Porter, Theodore M. 4.121
Portes, Alejandro 44.376, 44.403
Posas, Mario 38.322
Posel, Deborah 19.797
Posen, Barry R. 48.183, 48.569
Posener, G. 5.460
Posnansky, Merrick 19.56
Posner, Donald 22.287
Posner, Gerald L. 44.574
Pospielovsky, Dimitry 35.454
Possehl, Gregory L. 2.42, 3.101, 15.76–78
Post, Gaines 20.1239, 20.1282, 20.1335
Post, Gaines, Jr. 48.184
Post, R. R. 20.1483

Post, Robert C. 4.358, 42.160
Postan, Cynthia 20.66, 20.445, 48.551
Postan, Michael Moissey 1.311, 7.549–50,
    20.39–40, 20.388, 22.465, 22.473, 22.628,
    34.204
Postel-Vinay, Gilles 25.338
Poster, Mark 26.262
Postgate, J. N. 5.29, 5.107, 5.125
Postgate, Raymond 3.65
Posthumus Meyjes, G.H.M. 27.134
Posthumus, N. W. 27.105
Potapov, L. P. 9.27
Potash, Robert A. 38.36, 38.636–37
Potichnyj, Peter J. 33.495
Potter, David 25.180
Potter, David M. 40.149, 40.699, 42.124,
    42.751
Potter, G. R. 22.103, 27.268, 27.294
Potter, Jack M. 11.755
Potter, Janice 41.134
Potter, M. W. 33.140
Potter, T. W. 7.371, 7.445, 20.78
Pottinger, Ann E. 47.163
Potts, Daniel T. 5.623–26
Potts, Denys 25.297, 27.132
Potts, Louis W. 41.587
Poucet, Jacques 7.168
Pouchepadass, Jacques 15.525
Poullada, Leon B. 15.776
Poulton, Hugh 33.45
Pounds, Norman John Greville 4.460,
    22.48
Pouthas, Charles H. 22.358
Pouwels, Randall L. 19.414
Powaski, Ronald E. 48.302
Powell, Edward 20.565
Powell, G. Bingham, Jr. 31.483
Powell, Irena 13.564
Powell, J. C. 22.214
Powell, J. E. 6.63
Powell, J. M. 46.180
Powell, James M. 20.10, 20.335
Powell, John Duncan 38.491
Powell, Lawrence N. 42.842
Powell, Marvin A. 5.148–49, 5.554, 5.585
Powell, Peter J. 36.150
Powell, Philip Wayne 37.126, 37.331
Powell, R. B. 27.69
Powell, Ralph L. 11.141
Powell, Sumner Chilton 39.383
Powell, T.G.E. 7.17, 38.253
Powell, Victoria A. 5.149
Powell, William S. 39.165
Power, Eileen 20.1512
Power, Richard Lyle 40.172
Powers, Elizabeth 13.445
Powers, James F. 20.795–96
Powers, Marla N. 36.251
Powesland, Pamela 3.237
Powicke, F. M. 20.1336
Powicke, Maurice 20.536
Poyo, Gerald E. 37.596

Pozzetta, George E. 40.383–84, 43.256
Pradhan, Kumar 15.758
Prakash, Gyan 15.526–27, 15.648
Prakash, Om 15.384
Prange, Gordon W. 13.316–19, 44.750
Prasad, Akhowri Braj Ballav 15.225
Prasad, Pushpa 15.287
Prasert na Nagara 16.83
Pratt, Harold L. 4.525
Pratt, Joseph 44.199
Pratt, Julius William 43.654
Pratt, R. Cranford 19.504, 19.518
Prawer, Joshua 17.250, 20.854–855
Prayon, Friedhelm von 5.416
Prazmowska, Anita 33.592
Préaux, Claire 6.270, 6.510
Prebble, John 39.182
Pred, Allan R. 32.391, 42.192–93
Preeg, Ernest H. 48.341
Prelinger, Catherine M. 31.156
Prendergast, Christopher 26.248
Prentice, Alison 45.33, 45.220
Presbyter, Theophilus 4.386
Prescott, William H. 29.48, 37.127
Presler, Franklin A. 15.620
Presniakov, Alexander Evgen'evich
    34.79, 34.80
Presser, J. 27.237
Presser, Stephen B. 41.286
Prest, John 24.96
Prest, Wilfrid R. 23.254, 23.282
Prestage, Edgar 29.370
Preston, Adrian 47.385
Preston, Paul 29.277–79, 29.316–18,
    29.331–32
Preston, Samuel H. 12.276
Preston, Thomas A. 44.140
Prestwich, Menna 22.145, 25.257, 30.60
Prestwich, Michael 20.537, 20.566–67
Preucel, Robert W. 2.6
Preuss, E. 6.8
Preuss, Hans 30.308
Preuss, Peter 1.202
Prevenier, Walter 27.29
Prevost, Gary 29.329
Preziosi, Donald 1.448
Pribitchevitch, Svetozar 33.823
Pribram, Karl 22.428
Price, A. Grenfell 3.393–95
Price, B. B. 1.394, 20.1276
Price, Barbara J. 3.102
Price, Charles 33.296
Price, Curtis 23.363
Price, David 30.309
Price, David C. 23.364
Price, Derek de Solla 3.556
Price, Don C. 11.142
Price, Don K. 44.141
Price, Jacob M. 37.58, 39.437–39
Price, Jane L. 11.435, 23.123, 27.137
Price, Martin Jessop 6.236
Price, Nancy T. 2.47

Rafael, Vicente L. 16.113
Rafeq, Abdul-Karim 18.210
Raffan, John 6.576
Rafiqi, Abdul Qaiyum 15.311
Raftis, J. A. 20.389–90
Ragan, Bryant T., Jr. 4.689
Rageau, Jean-Pierre 3.7, 48.21
Raghavan, V. 15.264
Ragsdale, Hugh 34.97
Rahbek Schmidt, Knud 20.244
Rahman, Fazlur 17.73, 17.385, 18.109
Rahman, Hannah 17.87
Raimo, Tuomela 1.255
Raina, Peter K. 33.596–97
Rainbolt, John C. 39.440
Raines, Howell 44.473
Rainey, Anson F. 5.199, 5.301
Rainey, Lawrence Scott 29.89
Rainger, Ronald 4.206, 4.218–19
Raitt, Jill 20.992
Rajak, Tessa 7.118, 7.414
Rakob, F. 7.37
Rakove, Jack N. 41.167
Raleigh, Donald J. 35.17, 35.42, 35.54, 35.101
Rallu, Jean-Louis 46.347
Ralston, Caroline 46.307
Ralston, David B. 26.176
Ram, Rajendra 15.265
Ramachandra Dikshitar, V. R. 15.179, 15.191
Ramachandran, R. 15.58
Ramage, Andrew 7.472
Ramage, Nancy H. 7.472
Ramanujan, A. K. 15.266
Ramaswamy, Viyaya 15.242
Ramazani, Rouhollah K. 18.590–91
Rambaud, Jacqueline 20.985
Ramelli, Agostino 4.396
Ramet, Pedro see Ramet, Sabrina Petra
Ramet, Sabrina Petra 33.46–47, 33.824–25
Ramirez, Susan E. 36.481, 37.139, 37.281
Ramm, Agatha 31.188
Ramos, Donald 37.228–29, 37.469
Ramos, Joseph 38.164
Rampersad, Arnold 43.307
Ramsay, G. D. 27.106
Ramsay, Nigel 20.83
Ramsay, William Mitchell 6.41, 8.22
Ramsden, Eric 46.208
Ramsden, H. 29.241
Ramsden, John 24.41
Ramsey, Matthew 4.789
Ramsey, Robert W. 39.384
Ramsey, S. Robert 10.46
Ramson, W. S. 46.8
Ramstad, Jan 32.343
Ramusack, Barbara N. 15.491
Ranajit Guha 15.494
Rancière, Jacques 26.367
Rand, Edward Kennard 20.1056
Randall, John Herman, Jr. 20.1383, 22.167

Randall, Laura 38.638
Randall, Robert 36.376
Randall, Stephen J. 38.423
Randsborg, Klavs 20.130, 20.241
Ranelagh, John 44.661
Ranger, Terence O. 1.122, 19.39, 19.519, 19.626, 19.627, 19.709, 19.799
Ranis, Gustave 11.724
Ränk, Gustav 20.631
Ranke, Leopold von 22.105, 22.146, 29.137, 30.38, 33.744
Ránki, György 33.5–6, 33.48, 33.322, 33.370
Rankin, Charles E. 42.372
Rankin, Hugh F. 39.782, 41.112
Rankin, Mary Backus 11.143–44, 11.188
Ranlet, Philip 41.135
Ranney, Austin 40.65
Ransel, David L. 34.126, 34.286–87
Ransom, Roger L. 42.792
Ranum, Orest A. 25.81, 25.222–24, 25.252, 25.333–34
Ranum, Patricia M. 20.1455, 25.252, 25.333–34
Rao, M.S.A. 15.798
Rao, Velcheru Narayana 15.362
Raper, Horace W. 42.811
Raphael, Marc Lee 21.272
Rapp, F. 30.39
Rapp, George R., Jr. 6.181
Rapp, Rayna 1.399
Rapp, Richard Tilden 28.192
Rappaport, Steve 23.255
Rappard, William E. 27.280
Ras, J. J. 16.114
Raschke, Manfred G. 3.261, 7.355
Rashdall, Hastings 20.1336
Rashid al-Din, Fadlallah 17.273
Rashid al-Din, Tabib 9.228
Rasidondug, S. 9.340
Rasmussen, R. Kent 19.31, 19.710
Rasmussen, Randall 37.24
Rasmussen, Tom 7.477
Rasnake, Roger Neil 36.427
Ratanapañña Thera 16.84
Ratchnevsky, Paul 9.235, 10.341
Ratcliff, Richard Earl 38.722
Rath, R. John 28.244–46, 31.169
Rathbone, Dominic 7.372
Rathbone, Richard 19.779, 19.837, 19.867
Rathkolb, Oliver 31.478
Ratnagar, Shereen 3.262, 15.79
Rau, Wilhelm 15.98
Rauch, Georg von 32.38, 32.419, 35.10
Raun, Toivo U. 32.61, 32.213–15, 32.425, 35.205
Rausch, Jane M. 37.543
Rausch, Wilhelm 20.648
Rautkallio, Hannu 32.298
Rautsi, Inari 18.441
Raven, Charles E. 4.97
Raven, J. E. 6.612
Raven, Susan 7.446

Ravicz, Marilyn Ekdahl 37.431
Ravid, Benjamin C. I. 21.91, 21.111
Ravitch, Diane 44.52
Ravitch, Norman 25.258
Rawick, George 42.346
Rawley, James A. 22.270
Rawlinson, H. G. 3.126
Rawlinson, John L. 11.145
Rawlyk, George A. 39.191, 45.147
Rawski, Evelyn Sakakida 11.57, 11.212–13, 11.264, 11.320, 11.363
Rawski, Thomas G. 11.265, 11.493
Rawson, Beryl 7.139, 7.140
Rawson, Elizabeth 7.228, 7.255, 7.279
Rawson, I. M. 28.260
Rawson, Jessica 10.176
Rawson, Marion 6.171
Ray, Arthur J. 36.31, 36.44, 45.82
Ray, Benjamin C. 19.456
Ray, Dorothy Jean 36.196
Ray, Himanshu Prabha 15.201
Ray, Niharranjan 15.180
Ray, Rajat Kanta 15.553–54, 15.713–14
Ray, Ratnalekha 15.528
Rayback, Joseph G. 42.125
Raychaudhuri, Tapan 15.324, 15.344, 15.386, 15.638
Raymond, André 18.72, 18.211, 18.419
Raymond, Irving W. 20.91
Raymond, Robert 46.349
Razi, Zvi 20.391
Rea, K. J. 45.303
Read, Albert 37.188, 38.741
Read, Anthony 48.220
Read, Christopher 35.83
Read, Herbert Harold 4.238
Read, James 31.239
Read, James S. 19.510
Reade, Julian 5.95
Reader, Ian 13.511
Reader, W. J. 24.195
Reardon, Bernard M. G. 22.429
Reardon-Anderson, James 11.343
Rearick, Charles 26.263
Reay, Barry 23.186, 23.192, 23.256
Rebas, Hain 32.39
Rebel, Herman 30.212
Reber, Vera Blinn 38.639
Rebérioux, Madeleine 26.170
Redcliff, M. R. 38.438
Reddaway, William F. 33.496
Reddy, William M. 22.487, 26.368
Redesdale, Algernon Bertram Freeman-Mitford 13.108
Redford, Donald B. 5.542–43, 5.604–5
Rediker, Marcus 39.463
Redkey, Edwin S. 43.308
Redlich, Fritz 40.224
Redlich, Josef 31.290, 31.342
Redman, Charles L. 2.28, 20.164
Redmond, Kent C. 4.544
Redmond, Walter Bernard 37.49
Reece, Jack E. 26.382

SUBJECT INDEX

Guadalajara (Mexico) 37.274, 37.357, 37.401, 37.508
Guahibo 36.443, 36.464
Guaman Poma de Ayala, Felipe 36.387–88, 37.131, 37.409
Guarantee clause (U.S. Constitution) 41.219
Guatemala
  art and architecture 37.422
  biographies 38.315
  conquest 37.362
  cultural history 36.318, 37.372, 37.418
  demography 36.344, 37.362
  economic history 37.565, 38.318
  foreign relations 38.314–15, 38.317, 44.856
  geography 37.362
  intellectual history 37.415
  local and regional history 36.356, 37.362, 37.372, 37.398, 37.422, 37.455
  medicine 37.426, 37.434
  military history 36.347, 37.455
  politics and government 36.357, 38.314–15, 38.317
  religion 37.200
  social history 36.335, 36.347, 37.362, 37.455, 38.318
  sources and documents 36.343
  surveys 38.316
Guatemalan Revolution 38.314
Guayaquil (Ecuador) 37.249, 37.386, 37.509
Guaycurua 36.473, 36.481, 37.546
Guaymi 36.351
Gudea 5.55
Guernica (Spain) 29.287
Guerrilla warfare
  Angola 19.616
  Bolivia 38.390
Guerzoni, Giuseppe 28.291
Guesdism 26.189
Guest workers (West Germany) 31.520
Guevara, Che 38.390
Guiana 36.439
Guicciardini, Francesco 28.74, 28.78
Guilds
  Byzantine empire 8.186, 8.260, 8.296, 8.302
  China 11.215
  Florence 28.106
  German states 30.181, 30.183, 30.262
  Iran 18.575
  Japan 12.138
  Mexico 37.316
  Ottoman empire 18.172
  Portugal 29.343
  Safavid empire 18.230
  Sweden 32.365
Guilt (concept) 22.171, 25.250
Guinea Coast 19.177, 19.181, 19.188
Guinea region 19.129, 19.150, 19.215; see also Ivory coast; Gold coast; Slave coast

Guinefort, saint 20.1460
Guizot, François 22.373, 26.110, 47.78, 47.88
Gujarat (India) 15.496, 15.501, 15.707
Gujarat sultanate 15.282, 15.314, 15.382
Gukansho 12.65
Gulag system 35.116
Gulf War (1991) 48.505
Gullah 41.482, 42.338–39
Gun War (Lesotho, 1880–1881) 19.675
Gunfighters see Crime
Gunkimono 12.59
Gunpowder 3.554, 4.500, 4.624
Guntur (India) 15.448
Gupta empire
  art and architecture 15.193
  biographies 15.188
  decline 15.216
  essay collections 15.192
  politics and government 15.188, 15.191
  surveys 15.189–90, 19.407
Gurjara Pratihara dynasty 15.225
Gusii 19.407
Gustavus II, Adolphus (Sweden, r. 1611–32) 32.159, 32.186–87
Gustavus III (Sweden, r. 1771–92) 32.200
Guyenne (France) 25.370
Guzmán, Nuño de 37.116, 37.130
Gwynedd (Wales) 20.896
Gynecology 4.693, 32.253; see also Medicine
Gypsies 31.459, 33.14

Habiru 5.208
Habits, bad see Vices and virtues
Habsburg empire see also German states; Holy Roman Empire
  art and architecture 22.303, 30.267, 30.292, 30.337
  bibliographies 31.11
  biographies 1.49, 30.9, 30.15, 30.25, 30.101–2, 30.128, 30.131–32, 30.351, 31.133, 31.292, 31.294, 47.38, 47.42, 47.45, 47.56, 47.139
  Bohemia 21.152, 30.147, 33.177
  Bosnia-Hercegovina 33.684–85, 33.688–89
  Croatia 33.709; biographies 33.694, 33.711; cultural history 33.699; literature 33.323; military history 30.136–37; politics and government 33.691, 33.694–95, 33.706–8; religion 33.711; social history 33.699, 33.708
  cultural history 30.28, 30.279, 30.330, 30.351, 31.150, 31.306, 31.309, 31.311, 31.314, 31.316
  Czech lands 33.150; biographies 33.206, 33.234–35; historiography 33.210–11; intellectual history 33.150, 33.225; politics and government

Habsburg empire, cont.
  33.160, 33.173, 33.187, 33.189, 33.203–4, 33.206, 33.212, 33.225, 33.230; social history 33.153, 33.178, 33.204; sources and documents 33.189
  Czechoslovakia 33.144
  demography 27.93, 30.201, 33.352
  economic history 27.93, 30.100, 30.109, 30.142, 30.201, 30.232, 31.76–77, 31.85, 31.139, 31.141, 31.285, 31.303, 31.307, 33.352
  encyclopedias 30.261
  essay collections 30.2, 31.287
  foreign relations 31.34, 47.29, 47.36, 47.107, 47.118, 47.122, 47.139, 47.148, 47.152, 47.177, 47.285, 47.360; Bohemia 33.155; Central Europe 47.25; Europe 30.122, 31.297; France 31.102, 31.108, 47.56, 47.140, 47.155; German states 31.193, 31.282, 47.71; Germany 31.343, 33.232, 47.50, 47.170, 47.406; Great Britain 47.336; Montenegro 33.748; North Africa 18.190; Ottoman empire 18.190, 30.23, 47.422; papacy 28.247, 47.21, 47.52; Poland 33.478, 33.489; Prussia 47.150; Russian empire 47.50, 47.108, 47.286–87; Serbia 33.749; Venetia 47.146; Venice 28.194
  historiography 1.49, 31.282
  Hungary 30.130, 33.353, 33.383, 33.401, 33.405; bibliographies 33.379; biographies 33.314, 33.319, 33.325–26, 33.450; economic history 33.329, 33.368, 33.400; foreign relations 33.332, 33.359; historiography 33.381; literature 33.323; local and regional history 33.358; military history 33.330; politics and government 33.319, 33.325, 33.331, 33.333, 33.341, 33.344, 33.349, 33.355, 33.364, 33.375, 33.434, 33.450; religion 33.359; social history 33.355, 33.364
  intellectual history 30.25, 30.279, 30.339, 31.309, 31.311–15, 31.318, 33.405
  Italy see individual states
  Jewish history 21.157, 21.162, 21.170–71, 31.289, 31.301
  legal history 30.103, 30.141, 31.281
  literature 31.317–18
  local and regional history 27.93, 30.14, 30.29, 30.125, 30.254, 30.330, 31.141, 31.150, 31.169, 31.284, 31.298–301, 31.304–5, 31.308, 31.310, 31.313, 31.315, 31.317, 31.344
  military history 18.245, 18.271, 28.194, 30.132, 31.50, 31.63, 31.171, 31.190, 31.339–40, 31.342, 47.120, 47.374, 47.396, 47.409
  Netherlands 27.155; art and